EMPLOYMENT, HOURS, AND EARNINGS

STATES AND AREAS

Seventh Edition
2012

EMPLOYMENT, HOURS, AND EARNINGS

STATES AND AREAS

Seventh Edition
2012

Edited by Gwenavere W. Dunn

Bernan Press

Lanham, MD

Published in the United States of America
by Bernan Press, a wholly owned subsidiary of
The Rowman & Littlefield Publishing Group, Inc.
4501 Forbes Boulevard, Suite 200
Lanham, Maryland 20706

Bernan Press
800-865-3457
info@bernan.com
www.bernan.com

ISBN-13: 978-1-59888-530-9
e-ISBN-13: 978-1-59888-531-6

∞™ The paper used in this publication meets the minimum requirements of American National Standard
for Information Sciences—Permanence of Paper for Printed Library Materials, ANSI/NISO Z39.48-1992.
Manufactured in the United States of America.

CONTENTS

PART A: STATE DATA

PART A: STATE DATA—*Continued*

PART B: METROPOLITAN STATISTICAL AREA (MSA) DATA

PART B: METROPOLITAN STATISTICAL AREA DATA—_Continued_

Bernan Press is proud to present the seventh edition of *Employment, Hours, and Earnings: States and Areas, 2012.* This reference is a special edition of Bernan Press's *Handbook of U.S. Labor Statistics: Employment, Earnings, Prices, Productivity, and Other Labor Data.* A consolidated wealth of employment data compiled by the Bureau of Labor Statistics (BLS), this edition of *Employment, Hours, and Earnings* provides monthly and annual data covering the years 2000 through 2011.

This edition includes:

- Nearly 300 tables with data on employment for each state, the District of Columbia, and the nation's 75 largest metropolitan statistical areas (MSAs)

- Detailed, non-seasonally adjusted, industry data organized by month and year

- Hours and earnings data for each state, by industry, where available

- An introduction for each state and the District of Columbia that denotes salient data and noteworthy trends, including changes in population and the civilian labor force, industry increases and declines, employment and unemployment statistics, and a chart detailing employment percentages, by industry

- Ranking of the 75 largest MSAs, including 2011 Census population estimates, unemployment rates for 2010 and 2011, and the percent change in total nonfarm employment from 2000 through 2011

- Concise technical notes that explain pertinent facts about the data, including sources, definitions, and significant changes, and provide references for further guidance

- A comprehensive appendix that details the geographical components of the MSAs

The employment, hours, and earnings data in this publication provide a detailed and timely picture of the 50 states, the District of Columbia, and the nation's 75 largest MSAs. These data can be used to analyze key factors affecting state and local economies and to compare national cyclical trends to local-level economic activity.

This reference is an excellent source of information for analysts in both the public and private sectors. Readers who are involved in public policy can use the data to determine the health of the economy, to clearly identify which sectors are growing and which are declining, and to determine the need for federal assistance. State and local jurisdictions can use the data to determine the need for services, including training and unemployment assistance, and for planning and budgetary purposes. In addition, the data can be used to forecast tax revenue. In private industry, the data can be used by business owners to compare their business to the economy as a whole, and to identify suitable areas when making decisions about plant locations, wholesale and retail trade outlets, and for locating a particular sector base.

Gwenavere W. Dunn is a research editor with Bernan Press. She holds a Master of Science degree in Human Resource Management from Trinity Washington University and is a former senior editor with the Board of Governors of the Federal Reserve System and former managing editor of the *Federal Reserve Bulletin.* She has also served as assistant editor of *The Who, What, and Where of America*, and editor of *Crime in the United States*, also published by Bernan Press.

TECHNICAL NOTES

OVERVIEW

In this seventh edition, *Employment, Hours, and Earnings: States and Areas* presents monthly and annual average data on employment for each state, the District of Columbia, and the nation's 75 largest metropolitan statistical areas (MSAs). In addition, hours and earnings data are provided, where available, for each state. The industry data are based on the North American Industry Classification System (NAICS), which is discussed in greater detail later in these notes. The employment data are presented on a monthly and annual basis for 2000 through 2011. The hours and earnings data are available from 2007 through 2011.

The Bureau of Labor Statistics (BLS), the statistical agency within the U.S. Department of Labor, conducts the Current Employment Statistics (CES) survey to provide industry data on the employment, hours, and earnings of workers on nonfarm payrolls. The unemployment data and the civilian labor force estimates in this publication were obtained from the Local Area Unemployment Statistics (LAUS) program, which provides monthly employment and unemployment data for approximately 7,300 geographic areas, including Census regions and divisions, states, counties, metropolitan areas, and many cities and towns.

The data from both the CES and LAUS are derived from federal-state cooperative collection efforts in which state employment security agencies prepare data using concepts, definitions, and technical procedures prescribed by the BLS. Although the estimation of the two data sets are based on differing methodologies (described in more detail later in this section), their inclusion together in this reference is intended to provide a broad overview of state and local labor market conditions.

THE CURRENT EMPLOYMENT STATISTICS (CES) SURVEY—EMPLOYMENT, HOURS, AND EARNINGS DATA

The CES survey is a monthly survey commonly referred to as the establishment or payroll survey that provides estimates of employment, hours, and earnings data by industry. Its estimates are derived from a sample of about 141,000 private nonfarm businesses and federal, state, and local government entities, which cover approximately 486,000 individual worksites in all 50 states, the District of Columbia, Puerto Rico, the U.S. Virgin Islands, and more than 350 metropolitan areas and divisions. These establishments are classified on the basis of their primary activity by major industry groupings in accordance with NAICS. For an establishment engaging in more than one activity, the entire establishment is included under the industry indicated as the principal activity.

All establishments with 1,000 employees or more are asked to participate in the survey, along with a representative sample of smaller businesses. The BLS Regional Data Collection Centers gather the data every month. Each firm is initially enrolled by telephone and the data is then collected for several months by a process called Computer Assisted Telephone Interviewing (CATI). Whenever possible, respondents are transferred to a self-reporting mode such as Touchtone Data Entry (TDE), fax, or Internet collection. Gathering data via the Internet is one of the fastest growing forms of data collection, but still remains a relatively small percentage of the total data collected each month. Electronic Data Interchange (EDI), in which each firm provides the BLS with an electronic file in a prescribed format, remains the most popular method for collecting data.

State estimation procedures are designed to produce accurate data for each individual state. The BLS independently develops the national series and does not force state estimates to sum to the national total. Because each state series is subject to larger sampling and nonsampling errors than the national series, summing them cumulates individual state level errors and can cause significant distortions at an aggregate level. As a result of these statistical limitations, the BLS does not compile a "sum of states" employment series, and cautions users that doing so may result in a series with a relatively large and volatile error structure.

More information on the exact methodology used to obtain data for employment, hours, and earnings was originally detailed in the *BLS Handbook of Methods*. The *Handbook* was updated in 2003 and can be found online at www.bls.gov/opub/hom. Information on the CES survey can also be found on the BLS Web site at www.bls.gov/sae.

CONCEPTS

Employment is the total number of persons employed either full- or part-time in nonfarm business establishments during a specific payroll period. Temporary employees are included as well as civilian government employees. Unpaid family members working in a family-owned business, domestic workers in private homes, farm employees, and self-employed persons are excluded from the CES, as well as military personnel and employees of the Central Intelligence Agency, the National Security Agency, the National Imagery and Mapping Agency, and the Defense Intelligence Agency. In addition, employees on layoff, on leave without pay, on strike for the entire pay period, or who had been hired but did not start work during the pay period are also excluded.

The reference period includes all persons who worked during or received pay for any part of the pay period that includes the 12th of the month, a standard for all federal agencies collecting employment data from business establishments. Workers who are on paid sick leave (when pay is received directly from the employer) or paid holiday or vacation, or who worked during only part of the specified pay period (because of unemployment or strike during the rest of the pay period) are counted as employed. Employees on the payroll of more than one establishment during the pay period are counted in each establishment that reports them, whether the duplication is due to turnover or dual jobholding.

Nonfarm employment includes employment in all goods-producing and service-providing industries. The goods-producing sector includes mining and logging, construction, and manufacturing, the last of which is made up of durable and nondurable goods (these breakdowns are not provided in this publication). The service-providing sector includes both private service-providing and government employment. Private service sector employment includes trade, transportation, and utilities (which is comprised of wholesale trade, retail trade, and transportation and utilities); information; financial activities; professional and business services; educational and health services; leisure and hospitality; and other services. Government employment encompasses federal-, state-, and local-level civilian employees. Subcategories of these industries are available on the BLS Web site at www.bls.gov/sae.

Unemployment consists of those who were not employed during the reference week but were available for work, except for temporary illness, and had made specific efforts to find employment some time during the 4-week period ending with the reference week. Persons who were waiting to be recalled to a job from which they had been laid off are classified as unemployed even if they have not been looking for another job.

The *unemployment rate* is the number of unemployed persons as a percent of the civilian labor force.

The *civilian labor force* consists of all persons classified as employed or unemployed as described above.

Hours and earnings data for each state are based on reports from industry payrolls and the corresponding hours paid for construction workers, production workers, and nonsupervisory workers. The data include workers who received pay for any part of the pay period that includes the 12th day of the month. Because not all sample respondents report production worker hours and earnings data, insufficient sample sizes preclude hours and earnings data from many sectors in many states. Therefore, the data available, and thus published, vary from state to state.

The payroll for these workers is reported before deductions of any kind, including Social Security, unemployment insurance, group health insurance, withholding taxes, retirement plans, or union dues.

Included in the payroll report of earnings is pay for all hours worked, including overtime, shift premiums, vacations, holiday, and sick-leave pay. Bonuses and commissions are excluded unless they are earned and paid regularly

each pay period. Benefits, such as health insurance and contribution to a retirement fund, are also excluded.

Hours include all hours worked (including overtime hours) and hours paid for holidays, vacations, and sick leave during the pay period that includes the 12th day of the month. Average weekly hours differ from the concept of scheduled hours worked because of factors such as unpaid absenteeism, labor turnover, part-time work, and strikes, as well as fluctuations in work schedules. Average weekly hours are typically lower than scheduled hours of work.

Average hourly earnings are derived by dividing gross payrolls by total hours, reflecting the actual earnings of workers (including premium pay). They differ from wage rates, which are the amounts stipulated for a given unit of work or time. Average hourly earnings do not represent total labor costs per hour because they exclude retroactive payments and irregular bonuses, employee benefits, and the employer's share of payroll taxes. Earnings for employees not included in the production worker or nonsupervisory categories are not reflected in the estimates in this publication.

Average weekly earnings are derived by multiplying average weekly hours by average hourly earnings.

Users should note that in the context of historical data, long-term trends in hours and earnings data also reflect structural changes, such as the changing mixes of full-time and part-time employees and highly paid and lower-wage workers within businesses and across industries.

METROPOLITAN STATISTICAL AREAS (MSAs) AND NEW ENGLAND CITY AND TOWN AREAS (NECTAs)

A metropolitan statistical area (MSA) is a core area with a large population nucleus, combined with adjacent communities that have high degrees of economic and social integration with the core area. The standard definition of an MSA is determined by the Office of Management and Budget (OMB), which updates the definition based on the decennial census and updated information provided by the Census Bureau between the censuses. Each MSA must have at least one urbanized area of 50,000 inhabitants or more.

New England city and town areas (NECTAs) are similar to MSAs, but are defined using cities and towns instead of counties in the six New England states. The BLS only provides employment data on NECTAs in the New England region. Employment and Unemployment data are provided for the following NECTAs in this publication: Boston–Cambridge–Quincy, MA; Bridgeport–Stamford–Norwalk, CT; Hartford–West Hartford–East Hartford, CT; New Haven, CT; Providence–Fall River–Warwick, RI; and Worcester, MA. All other areas are MSAs.

The appendix that follows the tables details the geographic components for each MSA and NECTA.

REVISIONS TO THE DATA

North American Industry Classification System (NAICS)

The most far-reaching revision of the CES data occurred when the industrial classification system was changed from the 60-year-old Standard Industrial Classification (SIC) system to the North American Industry Classification System (NAICS) in January 2003. The revision changed the way establishments were classified into industries to more accurately reflect the current composition of U.S. businesses. In March 2008, the CES state and area nonfarm payroll series was converted to the 2007 NAICS series. This resulted in relatively minor changes. NAICS was adopted as the standard measure of industry classification by statistical agencies in the United States, Canada, and Mexico to enhance the comparability of economic data across the North American Free Trade Association (NAFTA) trade area. Comparisons between the NAICS and the old SIC are limited; however, the historical industry series from April 1995 through 2001 are available on both SIC and NAICS bases. The BLS has not updated the SIC data nor (for the most part) linked the historical SIC data with the current NAICS data.

Every five years the NAICS is updated to reflect changes in the U.S. economy, recognize new and emerging industries, and strive for international compatibility.

Benchmark Revisions

Employment estimates are adjusted annually to a complete count of jobs—called benchmarks—which are primarily derived from tax reports submitted by employers covered by state unemployment laws (which cover most establishments). In this re-anchoring of sample-based employment estimates to full population counts, the original sample-based estimates are replaced with the benchmark data from the previous year. The benchmark information is used to adjust monthly estimates between the new benchmark and the preceding benchmark, thereby preserving the continuity of the series and establishing the level of employment for the new benchmark month.

Seasonal Adjustment

Over the course of a year, the size of a state's employment level undergoes sharp fluctuations because of changes in the weather, reduced or expanded production, harvests, major holidays, and the like. Because these seasonal events follow a more or less regular pattern each year, adjusting the data on a month-to-month basis may eliminate their influence on data trends. These adjustments make it easier for users to observe the cyclical and other nonseasonal movements in the data series, but it must be noted that the seasonally adjusted series are only an approximation based on past experience. The seasonally adjusted data have a broader margin of error than the unadjusted data because they are subject to both sampling and other errors in the seasonal adjustment process. The data presented in this publication are not seasonally adjusted; therefore, the month-to-month variations in the data contain seasonal variations that may distort month-to-month comparisons. Data for the MSAs are also not seasonally adjusted, as the sample sizes do not allow for reliable estimates for seasonal adjustment factors.

THE LOCAL AREA UNEMPLOYMENT STATISTICS (LAUS) PROGRAM

The Local Area Unemployment Statistics (LAUS) program provides monthly and annual estimates on several labor force concepts, including employment, unemployment, labor force totals, and the employment-population ratio. The unemployment data as well as the civilian labor force estimates presented in this publication are from the LAUS program. For each state the unemployment rate in 2000, 2010, and 2011 is shown along with the rank. The rankings are from lowest to highest. In 2011, unemployment ranged from a low of 3.5 percent in North Dakota to 13.5 percent in Nevada. Therefore, North Dakota is ranked first and Nevada is ranked 51st. Unemployment data are not available by industry.

The concepts and definitions underlying the LAUS program come from the Current Population Survey (CPS), the household survey conducted by the Census Bureau for the BLS. The LAUS models combine current and historical data from the CPS, Current Employment Statistics (CES), and the State Unemployment Insurance (UI) Systems. Numerous conceptual and technical differences exist between the household and establishment surveys, and estimates of monthly employment changes from these two surveys usually do not match in size or even direction. As a result, the unemployment data and the civilian labor force estimates on each state header page presented in this edition are not directly comparable to the employment data. However, this publication includes this information to provide complementary information on labor market conditions in each state and the District of Columbia. Monthly and annual data are available from the BLS on their Web site at www.bls.gov/lau. More information on the differences between the surveys, as well as guidance on the complex methods used to obtain the LAUS data, is provided on the BLS Web site at www.bls.gov/lau/laufaq.htm.

PART A

STATE DATA

ALABAMA
At a Glance

Population:
  2000 census: 4,447,100
  2010 census: 4,779,736
  2011 estimate: 4,802,740

Percent change in population:
  2000–2010: 7.5%
  2010–2011: 0.5%

Percent change in total nonfarm employment:
  2000–2010: -3.1
  2010–2011: -0.2%

Industry with the largest growth in employment, 2000–2011 (thousands):
  Education and Health Services, 40.5

Industry with the largest decline or smallest growth in employment, 2000–2011 (thousands):
  Manufacturing, -114.1

Civilian labor force:
  2000: 2,154,545
  2010: 2,179,163
  2011: 2,190,519

Unemployment rate and rank among states (lowest to highest):
  2000: 4.1%, 32nd
  2010: 9.5%, 32nd
  2011: 9.0%, 33rd

Over-the-year change in unemployment rates:
  2010–2011: -0.5%

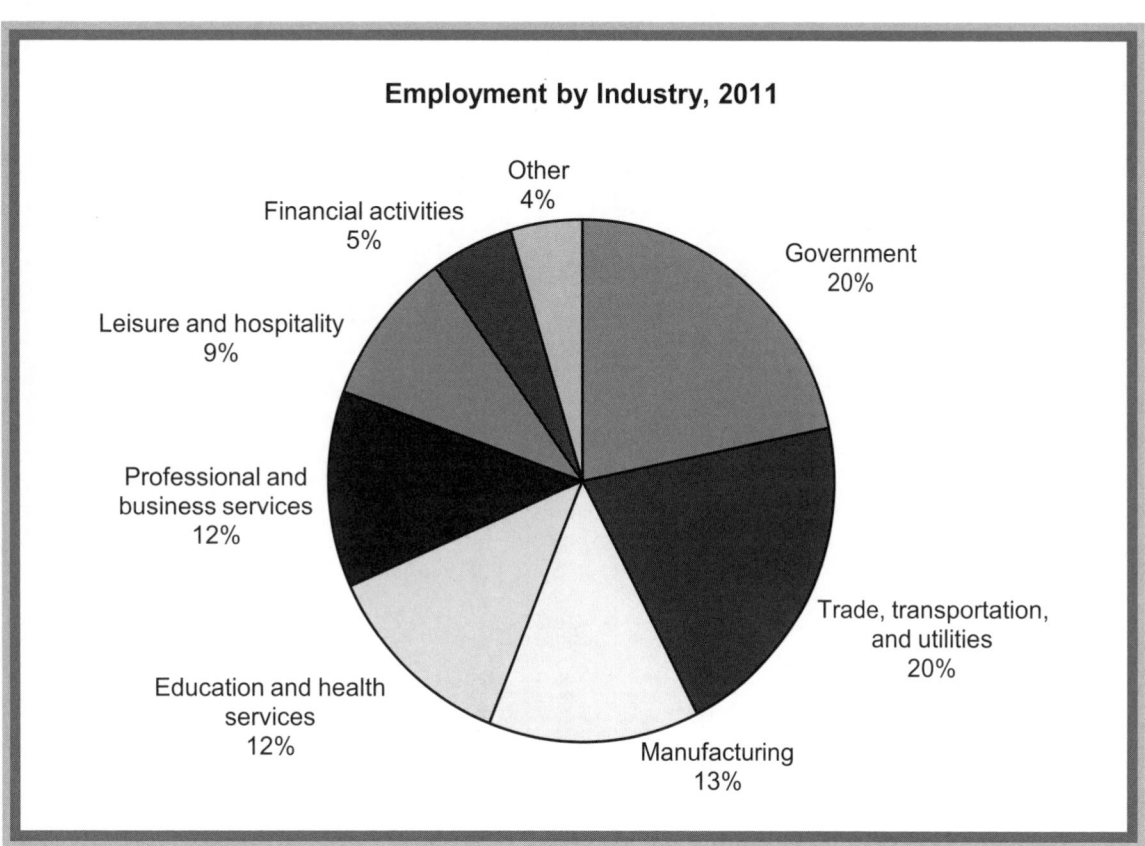

Employment by Industry, 2011

Other 4%
Financial activities 5%
Leisure and hospitality 9%
Professional and business services 12%
Education and health services 12%
Manufacturing 13%
Government 20%
Trade, transportation, and utilities 20%

1. Employment by Industry: Alabama, Selected Years, 2000–2011

(Numbers in thousands, not seasonally adjusted)

Industry and year	January	February	March	April	May	June	July	August	September	October	November	December	Annual average
Total Nonfarm													
2000	1,903.3	1,910.4	1,929.1	1,931.3	1,945.0	1,941.0	1,922.4	1,928.7	1,941.2	1,936.3	1,941.9	1,943.7	1,931.2
2001	1,894.4	1,903.9	1,914.8	1,919.6	1,921.2	1,918.6	1,897.5	1,905.2	1,910.2	1,903.5	1,908.1	1,907.9	1,908.7
2002	1,859.7	1,868.4	1,882.6	1,888.3	1,891.6	1,886.1	1,872.4	1,879.8	1,888.3	1,889.9	1,897.0	1,894.8	1,883.2
2003	1,857.0	1,864.0	1,875.0	1,879.1	1,882.2	1,875.8	1,862.1	1,869.3	1,877.1	1,883.7	1,889.6	1,891.8	1,875.6
2004	1,862.6	1,872.4	1,886.5	1,899.3	1,903.8	1,908.8	1,900.9	1,903.9	1,908.4	1,915.6	1,926.2	1,932.4	1,901.7
2005	1,899.8	1,910.5	1,925.1	1,943.1	1,948.2	1,951.4	1,939.6	1,947.9	1,958.2	1,961.9	1,974.2	1,979.2	1,944.9
2006	1,944.9	1,956.1	1,974.5	1,978.5	1,984.2	1,994.6	1,972.0	1,981.0	1,990.4	1,984.2	1,994.6	2,000.1	1,979.6
2007	1,974.9	1,987.3	2,004.4	2,000.9	2,009.4	2,018.4	1,994.0	2,004.4	2,013.3	2,012.4	2,022.0	2,026.7	2,005.7
2008	1,986.0	1,994.5	2,002.7	2,008.7	2,012.5	2,012.1	1,989.0	1,991.1	1,992.2	1,981.3	1,970.9	1,964.4	1,992.1
2009	1,905.6	1,899.9	1,900.1	1,900.1	1,899.7	1,895.5	1,873.5	1,870.8	1,872.6	1,868.4	1,875.8	1,876.0	1,886.5
2010	1,840.1	1,844.6	1,860.7	1,872.1	1,888.2	1,889.3	1,870.4	1,868.7	1,872.3	1,877.1	1,883.4	1,882.4	1,870.8
2011	1,839.4	1,853.3	1,865.6	1,874.2	1,876.6	1,875.4	1,863.7	1,859.3	1,866.9	1,874.2	1,878.6	1,871.2	1,866.5
Total Private													
2000	1,551.7	1,556.0	1,570.8	1,574.7	1,580.3	1,592.6	1,583.9	1,592.0	1,590.8	1,583.0	1,588.0	1,589.8	1,579.5
2001	1,542.9	1,548.5	1,559.6	1,564.4	1,566.0	1,570.1	1,557.7	1,563.8	1,557.7	1,547.8	1,551.5	1,551.3	1,556.8
2002	1,507.2	1,512.5	1,526.0	1,530.0	1,534.1	1,534.8	1,531.1	1,537.2	1,532.0	1,529.7	1,535.4	1,533.4	1,528.6
2003	1,498.7	1,502.0	1,512.1	1,515.7	1,518.9	1,521.4	1,517.7	1,522.9	1,517.7	1,521.1	1,526.5	1,530.3	1,517.1
2004	1,503.9	1,510.7	1,524.6	1,536.5	1,541.9	1,550.0	1,552.1	1,553.3	1,548.4	1,553.9	1,563.1	1,569.2	1,542.3
2005	1,539.7	1,547.5	1,561.6	1,578.3	1,582.7	1,587.2	1,587.2	1,592.8	1,595.3	1,594.5	1,606.1	1,611.4	1,582.0
2006	1,578.2	1,587.1	1,603.9	1,606.4	1,611.2	1,622.4	1,612.0	1,618.4	1,618.8	1,610.3	1,619.8	1,624.8	1,609.4
2007	1,600.7	1,610.7	1,626.5	1,622.5	1,630.1	1,639.3	1,629.4	1,635.8	1,635.5	1,632.0	1,640.1	1,644.9	1,629.0
2008	1,605.7	1,610.4	1,617.4	1,622.1	1,624.4	1,624.2	1,616.8	1,616.1	1,609.1	1,593.7	1,583.7	1,576.6	1,608.4
2009	1,522.5	1,514.7	1,514.0	1,511.6	1,510.9	1,507.9	1,502.3	1,497.6	1,490.6	1,481.6	1,488.5	1,488.0	1,502.5
2010	1,456.0	1,458.0	1,471.1	1,480.9	1,487.9	1,494.7	1,494.2	1,492.6	1,488.4	1,490.1	1,495.2	1,494.3	1,483.6
2011	1,455.2	1,466.6	1,477.8	1,487.3	1,490.3	1,492.8	1,494.5	1,490.7	1,489.6	1,494.8	1,499.2	1,495.0	1,486.2
Goods Producing													
2000	469.5	469.5	472.3	472.2	472.5	476.7	471.9	475.0	473.3	467.6	465.7	464.6	470.9
2001	448.8	448.8	451.4	450.3	449.4	447.6	441.8	443.9	443.0	436.6	434.4	431.7	444.0
2002	420.1	419.9	422.5	422.3	423.5	422.2	418.9	421.9	421.4	420.1	418.3	415.7	420.6
2003	408.4	408.2	409.7	407.8	407.6	406.4	402.6	404.7	404.1	405.6	403.9	404.3	406.1
2004	398.3	400.1	402.7	404.5	405.9	407.0	409.0	408.3	409.2	412.1	412.1	412.4	406.8
2005	405.6	406.8	411.0	416.8	417.5	417.5	418.0	419.6	421.3	422.2	424.6	425.4	417.2
2006	421.6	423.7	427.6	427.9	428.0	430.5	427.7	427.2	426.6	423.3	422.3	422.6	425.8
2007	420.1	421.6	423.9	420.9	421.3	423.9	421.0	421.8	423.2	423.0	421.0	420.6	421.9
2008	413.2	412.5	412.1	411.1	411.2	411.1	409.0	406.0	404.6	397.1	389.8	386.1	405.3
2009	369.7	363.7	360.9	356.0	352.9	348.9	347.3	344.3	342.3	339.5	339.2	339.1	350.3
2010	332.1	331.5	334.3	336.6	338.3	339.4	338.6	337.4	336.8	335.3	333.9	331.9	335.5
2011	322.5	326.3	329.0	330.1	331.6	332.2	332.0	328.9	329.7	328.1	325.5	326.3	328.5
Mining and Logging													
2000	14.6	14.4	14.4	13.8	13.7	13.8	13.7	13.7	13.7	13.7	13.7	13.6	13.9
2001	13.4	13.5	13.5	13.6	13.5	13.5	13.5	13.5	13.5	13.4	13.3	13.3	13.5
2002	13.2	13.1	13.2	13.0	13.0	13.0	12.9	12.9	13.0	12.9	12.6	12.5	12.9
2003	12.5	12.4	12.5	12.5	12.5	12.5	12.4	12.5	12.6	12.5	12.5	12.5	12.5
2004	12.2	12.2	12.2	12.2	12.3	12.4	12.4	12.5	12.6	12.7	12.6	12.7	12.4
2005	12.7	12.7	12.7	12.8	13.0	13.0	13.1	13.0	13.2	13.0	13.1	13.1	13.0
2006	13.0	13.1	13.1	13.0	13.0	13.2	13.1	13.1	13.2	12.9	13.0	13.1	13.1
2007	12.9	13.0	13.1	12.8	12.9	12.9	12.8	12.9	12.8	12.8	12.7	12.8	12.9
2008	12.5	12.6	12.6	12.6	12.4	12.5	12.6	12.6	12.7	12.6	12.5	12.5	12.6
2009	12.2	12.2	11.9	11.8	11.7	11.8	11.8	11.6	11.7	11.7	11.7	11.6	11.8
2010	11.7	11.7	11.7	11.9	12.0	12.0	12.1	12.2	12.1	12.3	12.2	12.2	12.0
2011	12.1	12.1	12.1	12.3	12.3	12.4	12.4	12.5	12.5	12.5	12.5	12.5	12.4
Construction													
2000	101.1	101.7	103.6	104.6	105.0	106.8	107.3	108.3	109.4	107.2	106.6	105.9	105.6
2001	101.6	102.7	104.8	106.6	107.7	107.9	106.3	106.2	105.8	104.7	104.4	102.1	105.1
2002	96.8	98.3	100.5	99.7	100.9	100.0	100.3	101.4	102.1	102.7	101.1	99.2	100.3
2003	97.3	97.6	99.3	98.4	98.8	98.9	99.0	100.1	100.7	103.2	102.4	101.7	99.8
2004	99.6	101.2	103.0	102.4	102.6	102.6	104.1	103.1	103.2	104.9	104.0	103.3	102.8
2005	100.6	101.6	104.2	106.2	105.4	105.2	105.2	106.2	107.0	108.6	108.6	107.5	105.5
2006	105.1	106.2	109.5	110.2	110.2	111.1	110.4	111.0	111.7	111.1	111.0	110.2	109.8
2007	109.4	110.7	113.2	112.0	112.3	113.1	112.0	113.2	114.7	114.9	113.6	113.1	112.7
2008	109.5	110.0	110.4	110.3	110.9	110.7	110.1	109.0	108.8	105.9	103.8	102.3	108.5
2009	94.8	93.6	94.3	92.9	93.3	92.9	92.0	90.5	89.7	88.5	89.0	89.3	91.7
2010	85.4	85.4	87.4	88.2	89.1	90.2	89.3	88.2	87.8	86.8	85.1	83.5	87.2
2011	77.2	79.2	81.1	80.7	82.1	81.9	81.0	78.3	78.7	77.5	74.2	74.7	78.9
Manufacturing													
2000	353.8	353.4	354.3	353.8	353.8	356.1	350.9	353.0	350.2	346.7	345.4	345.1	351.4
2001	333.8	332.6	333.1	330.1	328.2	326.2	322.0	324.2	323.7	318.5	316.7	316.3	325.5
2002	310.1	308.5	308.8	309.6	309.6	309.2	305.7	307.5	306.4	304.8	304.7	304.0	307.4
2003	298.6	298.2	297.9	296.9	296.3	295.0	291.2	292.1	290.8	289.9	289.0	290.1	293.8
2004	286.5	286.7	287.5	289.9	291.0	292.0	292.5	292.7	293.4	294.5	295.5	296.4	291.6
2005	292.3	292.5	294.1	297.8	299.1	299.3	299.7	300.4	301.1	300.6	302.9	304.8	298.7
2006	303.5	304.4	305.0	304.7	304.8	306.2	304.2	303.1	301.7	299.3	298.3	299.3	302.9
2007	297.8	297.9	297.6	296.1	296.1	297.9	296.2	295.7	295.7	295.3	294.7	294.7	296.3
2008	291.2	289.9	289.1	288.2	287.9	287.9	286.3	284.4	283.1	278.6	273.5	271.3	284.3
2009	262.7	257.9	254.7	251.3	247.9	244.2	243.5	242.2	240.9	239.3	238.5	238.2	246.8
2010	235.0	234.4	235.2	236.5	237.2	237.2	237.2	237.0	236.9	236.2	236.6	236.2	236.3
2011	233.2	235.0	235.8	237.1	237.2	237.9	238.6	238.1	238.5	238.1	238.8	239.1	237.3

1. Employment by Industry: Alabama, Selected Years, 2000–2011—*Continued*

(Numbers in thousands, not seasonally adjusted)

Industry and year	January	February	March	April	May	June	July	August	September	October	November	December	Annual average
Service-Providing													
2000	1,433.8	1,440.9	1,456.8	1,459.1	1,472.5	1,464.3	1,450.5	1,453.7	1,467.9	1,468.7	1,476.2	1,479.1	1,460.3
2001	1,445.6	1,455.1	1,463.4	1,469.3	1,471.8	1,471.0	1,455.7	1,461.3	1,467.2	1,466.9	1,473.7	1,476.2	1,464.8
2002	1,439.6	1,448.5	1,460.1	1,466.0	1,468.1	1,463.9	1,453.5	1,457.9	1,466.9	1,469.8	1,478.7	1,479.1	1,462.7
2003	1,448.6	1,455.8	1,465.3	1,471.3	1,474.6	1,469.4	1,459.5	1,464.6	1,473.0	1,478.1	1,485.7	1,487.5	1,469.5
2004	1,464.3	1,472.3	1,483.8	1,494.8	1,497.9	1,501.8	1,491.9	1,495.6	1,499.2	1,503.5	1,514.1	1,520.0	1,494.9
2005	1,494.2	1,503.7	1,514.1	1,526.3	1,530.7	1,533.9	1,521.6	1,528.3	1,536.9	1,539.7	1,549.6	1,553.8	1,527.7
2006	1,523.3	1,532.4	1,546.9	1,550.6	1,556.2	1,564.1	1,544.3	1,553.8	1,563.8	1,560.9	1,572.3	1,577.5	1,553.8
2007	1,554.8	1,565.7	1,580.5	1,580.0	1,588.1	1,594.5	1,573.0	1,582.6	1,590.1	1,589.4	1,601.0	1,606.1	1,583.8
2008	1,572.8	1,582.0	1,590.6	1,597.6	1,601.3	1,601.0	1,580.0	1,585.1	1,587.6	1,584.2	1,581.1	1,578.3	1,586.8
2009	1,535.9	1,536.2	1,539.2	1,544.1	1,546.8	1,546.6	1,526.2	1,526.5	1,530.3	1,528.9	1,536.6	1,536.9	1,536.2
2010	1,508.0	1,513.1	1,526.4	1,535.5	1,549.9	1,549.9	1,531.8	1,531.3	1,535.5	1,541.8	1,549.5	1,550.5	1,535.3
2011	1,516.9	1,527.0	1,536.6	1,544.1	1,545.0	1,543.2	1,531.7	1,530.4	1,537.2	1,546.1	1,553.1	1,544.9	1,538.0
Trade, Transportation, and Utilities													
2000	381.6	379.9	382.0	380.9	384.4	386.4	383.4	384.5	385.2	386.4	393.0	396.6	385.4
2001	379.9	377.7	379.9	379.4	380.8	382.3	378.5	379.0	377.3	378.3	384.8	387.6	380.5
2002	371.1	369.3	372.0	370.1	371.0	370.5	371.0	370.0	368.6	370.2	377.0	380.9	371.8
2003	366.0	364.2	367.1	368.1	369.2	370.7	372.2	372.9	371.9	374.4	379.5	383.5	371.6
2004	371.3	370.8	374.5	375.0	375.9	377.0	376.4	376.0	374.4	377.3	384.1	389.6	376.9
2005	376.6	376.0	378.3	380.5	381.6	382.9	382.4	382.8	382.5	383.3	391.2	396.3	382.9
2006	382.6	381.5	385.4	384.1	385.2	387.4	386.3	387.3	388.1	388.9	396.8	401.7	387.9
2007	387.8	387.5	391.8	390.8	394.4	396.2	395.2	394.8	395.1	394.9	402.6	406.0	394.8
2008	390.7	388.8	391.1	389.6	390.2	390.4	389.6	389.8	388.4	385.9	389.0	390.2	389.5
2009	371.3	367.5	366.8	364.9	366.0	366.0	364.4	363.2	363.0	361.1	366.8	368.7	365.8
2010	356.7	355.7	358.6	359.1	360.7	361.2	360.7	360.8	359.9	363.1	368.8	372.0	361.4
2011	358.8	358.8	360.7	361.9	362.5	364.0	366.6	364.4	362.7	368.1	372.4	370.5	364.3
Wholesale Trade													
2000	83.4	83.6	84.1	83.6	84.1	84.5	84.3	84.6	84.6	84.7	84.9	85.1	84.3
2001	84.1	84.4	84.2	84.0	83.9	83.8	83.3	83.2	82.8	82.4	81.8	81.7	83.3
2002	79.9	79.5	79.5	78.7	78.6	78.6	78.5	78.5	78.4	78.0	78.2	78.4	78.7
2003	76.8	76.8	77.0	76.6	77.1	77.2	77.3	77.3	77.4	77.9	77.9	78.1	77.3
2004	76.9	77.0	77.6	78.1	78.3	78.6	78.7	78.7	78.5	79.0	78.8	79.1	78.3
2005	78.1	78.4	78.8	79.3	79.3	79.5	79.8	79.7	80.0	79.9	80.0	80.5	79.4
2006	79.9	80.3	81.0	81.0	81.5	81.9	81.9	82.0	82.1	81.9	82.1	82.5	81.5
2007	81.3	81.6	82.1	81.9	82.3	82.8	82.2	82.2	82.4	82.5	82.3	82.4	82.2
2008	80.8	80.8	81.0	81.0	81.3	81.3	80.9	80.8	80.7	80.4	79.5	79.1	80.6
2009	77.0	76.3	75.9	75.0	74.8	74.4	73.6	73.6	73.3	73.3	73.2	72.9	74.4
2010	71.7	71.5	71.5	71.8	72.1	71.9	72.0	71.9	71.6	72.1	71.9	71.8	71.8
2011	70.9	71.3	71.5	71.6	71.8	71.8	72.7	72.4	71.9	73.1	71.7	70.5	71.8
Retail Trade													
2000	231.1	229.0	230.6	230.4	232.6	233.8	231.2	231.9	232.9	234.0	240.3	243.8	233.5
2001	229.2	226.0	227.9	227.4	228.6	229.7	227.0	227.4	226.5	228.1	235.5	238.2	229.3
2002	226.4	225.0	227.3	225.5	225.8	225.2	225.3	224.1	223.0	225.3	231.9	235.7	226.7
2003	223.5	222.2	224.8	226.6	226.6	227.7	228.7	229.6	228.7	230.7	236.0	239.7	228.7
2004	229.5	228.8	231.0	231.2	231.5	231.8	231.1	230.7	229.6	231.9	238.7	243.4	232.4
2005	232.7	231.5	233.1	234.3	234.9	235.4	234.6	235.2	234.3	234.7	242.4	246.3	235.8
2006	234.2	232.7	235.2	233.6	233.9	234.9	234.0	234.6	234.9	236.2	243.5	247.1	236.2
2007	236.4	235.7	238.9	238.5	240.8	241.7	241.5	241.0	240.7	240.7	248.0	250.5	241.2
2008	239.1	237.5	239.7	237.7	237.8	238.2	237.2	237.2	236.0	234.6	239.0	240.6	237.9
2009	227.5	224.7	224.7	224.0	224.8	225.1	224.4	223.0	223.2	221.8	227.5	229.0	225.0
2010	220.0	219.2	221.9	221.5	222.4	222.9	222.0	222.1	221.2	224.1	229.8	232.3	223.3
2011	221.5	220.7	222.1	223.4	223.5	224.8	225.8	225.6	225.3	228.5	234.3	233.2	225.7
Transportation and Utilities													
2000	67.1	67.3	67.3	66.9	67.7	68.1	67.9	68.0	67.7	67.7	67.8	67.7	67.6
2001	66.6	67.3	67.8	68.0	68.3	68.8	68.2	68.4	68.0	67.8	67.5	67.7	67.9
2002	64.8	64.8	65.2	65.9	66.6	66.7	67.2	67.4	67.2	66.9	66.9	66.8	66.4
2003	65.7	65.2	65.3	64.9	65.5	65.8	66.2	66.0	65.8	65.8	65.6	65.7	65.6
2004	64.9	65.0	65.9	65.7	66.1	66.6	66.6	66.6	66.3	66.4	66.6	67.1	66.2
2005	65.8	66.1	66.4	66.9	67.4	68.0	68.0	67.9	68.2	68.7	68.8	69.5	67.6
2006	68.5	68.5	69.2	69.5	69.8	70.6	70.4	70.7	71.1	70.8	71.2	72.1	70.2
2007	70.1	70.2	70.8	70.4	71.3	71.7	71.5	71.6	72.0	71.7	72.3	73.1	71.4
2008	70.8	70.5	70.4	70.9	71.1	70.9	71.5	71.8	71.7	70.9	70.5	70.5	71.0
2009	66.8	66.5	66.2	65.9	66.4	66.5	66.4	66.6	66.5	66.0	66.1	66.8	66.4
2010	65.0	65.0	65.2	65.8	66.2	66.4	66.7	66.8	67.1	66.9	67.1	67.9	66.3
2011	66.4	66.8	67.1	66.9	67.2	67.4	68.1	66.4	65.5	66.5	66.4	66.8	66.8
Information													
2000	32.4	32.5	33.0	32.9	33.2	33.7	34.2	34.5	34.4	34.6	34.8	35.2	33.8
2001	35.0	34.9	35.0	34.5	34.6	34.5	34.0	33.8	33.3	33.1	33.2	33.2	34.1
2002	32.9	32.6	32.8	32.5	32.4	32.4	32.3	31.9	31.4	31.4	31.4	31.3	32.1
2003	30.7	30.8	30.8	29.8	29.9	30.0	30.0	29.7	29.3	29.5	29.8	29.9	30.0
2004	29.5	29.4	29.5	29.6	29.6	29.7	29.7	29.5	29.3	29.3	29.5	29.6	29.5
2005	29.3	29.3	29.3	29.4	29.3	29.3	29.3	29.3	29.0	28.9	29.0	29.1	29.2
2006	28.7	28.7	28.8	28.7	28.8	28.8	28.5	28.4	28.2	28.1	28.2	28.3	28.5
2007	27.9	28.1	28.2	28.2	28.4	28.4	28.0	27.9	27.7	27.7	27.9	27.9	28.0
2008	27.4	27.3	27.3	27.3	27.3	27.1	26.9	26.8	26.4	26.2	26.2	26.3	26.9
2009	25.8	25.6	25.5	25.3	25.3	25.4	24.9	24.8	24.7	24.6	24.7	24.8	25.1
2010	24.5	24.4	24.3	24.1	24.2	24.2	24.0	23.9	23.7	23.7	23.7	23.6	24.0
2011	23.5	23.4	23.2	23.1	23.3	23.3	23.2	23.2	23.6	23.8	23.1	23.1	23.3

1. Employment by Industry: Alabama, Selected Years, 2000–2011—*Continued*

(Numbers in thousands, not seasonally adjusted)

Industry and year	January	February	March	April	May	June	July	August	September	October	November	December	Annual average
Financial Activities													
2000	97.3	97.3	98.0	98.5	98.7	99.3	100.0	100.0	99.4	99.4	99.4	99.8	98.9
2001	96.9	97.0	97.4	97.9	98.3	99.0	99.0	98.9	98.3	97.7	97.5	98.0	98.0
2002	96.8	96.4	96.7	97.3	97.6	97.8	97.9	97.8	97.0	97.0	96.8	97.2	97.2
2003	95.9	95.5	95.7	96.0	96.2	96.8	97.3	97.2	96.4	96.3	96.4	96.7	96.4
2004	95.6	95.9	96.2	96.5	96.8	97.7	97.7	97.8	97.2	97.7	97.7	97.9	97.1
2005	96.2	96.8	97.3	97.6	97.6	98.2	98.4	98.1	98.5	101.2	99.9	100.1	98.3
2006	97.1	98.3	98.5	98.4	98.8	99.4	99.1	99.1	98.9	98.8	99.1	99.7	98.8
2007	99.0	99.1	99.7	99.2	99.7	100.6	100.3	100.2	100.1	99.8	100.0	100.2	99.8
2008	98.8	99.2	99.2	99.2	99.2	99.6	99.8	99.7	99.2	99.0	98.4	98.2	99.1
2009	96.9	96.6	96.6	96.6	96.9	96.9	96.4	95.8	95.0	94.3	93.7	93.6	95.8
2010	92.1	92.0	92.4	92.3	92.5	92.7	92.2	91.8	91.2	91.7	91.7	91.9	92.0
2011	91.1	91.5	91.6	92.4	93.8	93.0	93.0	92.4	92.4	92.8	92.8	93.3	92.5
Professional and Business Services													
2000	177.9	180.0	183.0	184.9	183.6	186.2	185.6	188.2	189.2	188.5	187.9	187.2	185.2
2001	183.2	185.3	187.7	187.7	186.6	188.3	187.5	190.0	189.0	187.4	185.4	184.8	186.9
2002	178.9	180.6	184.6	185.9	185.6	187.2	187.5	190.6	189.8	190.1	189.1	187.7	186.5
2003	184.1	185.8	187.4	188.2	188.2	188.7	187.9	189.5	189.3	189.5	190.3	190.3	188.3
2004	188.9	190.2	192.7	196.5	197.6	200.0	201.0	202.5	201.3	202.1	201.4	202.4	198.1
2005	200.1	202.9	204.2	206.8	206.3	207.8	209.7	212.0	213.5	214.7	215.4	214.9	209.0
2006	208.8	211.4	213.5	213.7	213.7	216.7	214.2	217.1	217.8	216.7	217.0	217.1	214.8
2007	215.4	218.1	221.1	219.8	219.9	221.7	218.8	221.8	222.4	222.2	223.7	224.8	220.8
2008	220.1	221.5	222.2	223.8	222.1	222.1	220.0	220.5	220.1	219.7	216.8	214.1	220.3
2009	205.6	205.3	204.7	205.5	203.4	205.0	205.0	205.0	202.9	202.6	203.8	203.3	204.3
2010	200.3	201.5	203.4	206.1	207.0	210.9	212.9	212.0	212.2	212.8	213.8	213.9	208.9
2011	208.2	211.1	211.9	212.6	211.6	211.9	210.9	213.0	213.0	215.6	216.6	215.8	212.7
Education and Health Services													
2000	172.1	173.4	174.1	175.1	175.0	175.0	175.3	175.9	177.4	177.3	178.6	178.1	175.6
2001	171.8	174.8	174.9	176.9	176.3	175.8	175.9	176.8	179.1	179.8	182.5	182.4	177.3
2002	177.1	180.9	181.2	183.2	182.5	182.2	181.0	182.7	185.0	185.9	188.3	187.1	183.1
2003	184.4	186.2	186.5	187.7	187.4	185.7	185.6	185.8	186.6	188.1	190.0	189.3	186.9
2004	188.0	189.4	190.0	192.3	191.7	191.7	191.9	192.9	194.3	195.1	197.7	197.7	192.7
2005	196.0	197.3	198.2	199.4	200.1	199.1	199.2	200.3	202.6	200.7	202.2	201.8	199.7
2006	199.6	200.4	202.1	203.2	203.8	203.1	202.0	203.9	205.3	205.5	207.5	206.5	203.6
2007	204.8	206.6	207.5	207.8	208.3	207.8	207.3	209.8	210.1	210.5	211.4	212.1	208.7
2008	208.2	210.1	210.7	211.1	211.8	210.4	210.0	211.6	212.3	212.8	212.3	211.8	211.1
2009	209.2	209.8	209.9	210.7	211.3	209.3	209.7	211.0	211.7	212.3	214.1	212.7	211.0
2010	210.9	212.4	212.4	213.4	213.7	212.5	214.0	215.4	216.1	216.7	217.3	216.2	214.3
2011	213.2	214.3	215.7	216.0	215.9	214.2	213.9	213.7	218.5	218.3	220.2	219.7	216.1
Leisure and Hospitality													
2000	141.8	143.5	147.3	149.1	151.7	153.6	151.8	152.4	150.5	147.8	147.3	146.7	148.6
2001	143.1	145.3	148.8	152.6	154.8	157.1	155.4	155.5	152.2	149.8	148.9	149.0	151.0
2002	144.3	146.2	149.2	151.9	154.6	155.9	156.3	156.2	153.5	150.3	150.1	149.6	151.5
2003	146.1	148.0	151.5	154.5	156.4	158.6	158.3	159.3	157.1	154.9	154.4	154.3	154.5
2004	151.2	153.5	157.2	160.2	162.2	164.1	164.1	164.2	161.3	159.1	159.4	158.4	159.6
2005	155.1	157.5	162.0	166.4	168.5	170.4	168.7	169.6	167.2	163.6	163.9	163.6	164.7
2006	160.3	163.3	167.6	170.1	172.6	174.9	173.5	174.8	173.4	169.0	168.8	168.7	169.8
2007	165.8	169.2	172.9	174.6	176.7	178.9	177.6	178.5	176.1	172.9	172.3	171.9	174.0
2008	166.3	169.2	172.7	177.8	180.3	181.2	179.3	179.9	176.6	171.8	170.3	169.3	174.6
2009	163.8	166.0	169.2	172.3	174.6	175.7	174.0	173.4	171.5	167.5	166.9	166.4	170.1
2010	160.3	161.0	165.9	169.5	171.4	173.0	170.9	171.0	168.8	166.5	166.5	165.5	167.5
2011	159.5	162.3	166.5	171.5	171.8	173.9	174.3	175.0	169.7	167.7	167.5	165.8	168.8
Other Services													
2000	79.1	79.9	81.1	81.1	81.2	81.7	81.7	81.5	81.4	81.4	81.3	81.6	81.1
2001	84.2	84.7	84.5	85.1	85.2	85.5	85.6	85.9	85.5	85.1	84.8	84.6	85.1
2002	86.0	86.6	87.0	86.8	86.9	86.6	86.2	86.1	85.3	84.7	84.4	83.9	85.9
2003	83.1	83.3	83.4	83.6	84.0	84.5	83.8	83.8	83.0	82.8	82.2	82.0	83.3
2004	81.1	81.4	81.8	81.9	82.2	82.8	82.3	82.1	81.4	81.2	81.2	81.2	81.7
2005	80.8	80.9	81.3	81.4	81.8	82.0	81.5	81.1	80.7	79.9	79.9	80.2	81.0
2006	79.5	79.8	80.4	80.3	80.3	81.6	80.7	80.6	80.5	80.0	80.1	80.2	80.3
2007	79.9	80.5	81.4	81.2	81.4	81.8	81.2	81.0	80.8	81.0	81.2	81.4	81.1
2008	81.0	81.8	82.1	82.2	82.3	82.3	82.2	81.8	81.5	81.2	80.9	80.6	81.7
2009	80.2	80.2	80.4	80.3	80.5	80.7	80.6	80.1	79.5	79.7	79.3	79.4	80.1
2010	79.1	79.5	79.8	79.8	80.1	80.8	80.9	80.3	79.7	80.3	79.5	79.3	79.9
2011	78.4	78.9	79.2	79.7	79.8	80.3	80.6	80.1	80.0	80.4	81.1	80.5	79.9
Government													
2000	351.6	354.4	358.3	356.6	364.7	348.4	338.5	336.7	350.4	353.3	353.9	353.9	351.7
2001	351.5	355.4	355.2	355.2	355.2	348.5	339.8	341.4	352.5	355.7	356.6	356.6	352.0
2002	352.5	355.9	356.6	358.3	357.5	351.3	341.3	342.6	356.3	360.2	361.6	361.4	354.6
2003	358.3	362.0	362.9	363.4	363.3	354.4	344.4	346.4	359.4	362.6	363.1	361.5	358.5
2004	358.7	361.7	361.9	362.8	361.9	358.8	348.8	350.6	360.0	361.7	363.1	363.2	359.4
2005	360.1	363.0	363.5	364.8	365.5	364.2	352.4	355.1	362.9	367.4	368.1	367.8	362.9
2006	366.7	369.0	370.6	372.1	373.0	372.2	360.0	362.6	371.6	373.9	374.8	375.3	370.2
2007	374.2	376.6	377.9	378.4	379.3	379.1	364.6	368.6	377.8	380.4	381.9	381.8	376.7
2008	380.3	384.1	385.3	386.6	388.1	387.9	372.2	375.0	383.1	387.6	387.2	387.8	383.8
2009	383.1	385.2	386.1	388.5	388.8	387.6	371.2	373.2	382.0	386.8	387.3	388.0	384.0
2010	384.1	386.6	389.6	391.2	400.3	394.6	376.2	376.1	383.9	387.0	388.2	388.1	387.2
2011	384.2	386.7	387.8	386.9	386.3	382.6	369.2	368.6	377.3	379.4	379.4	376.2	380.4

2. Average Weekly Hours by Selected Industry: Alabama, 2007–2011

(Not seasonally adjusted)

Industry and year	January	February	March	April	May	June	July	August	September	October	November	December	Annual average
Total Private													
2007	36.2	36.2	36.6	36.9	36.8	36.7	36.7	36.7	36.8	36.5	36.6	36.8	36.6
2008	36.0	36.1	36.3	36.1	36.2	36.6	36.0	36.1	36.2	35.6	35.7	35.3	36.0
2009	34.8	35.2	35.1	34.8	34.7	35.0	34.6	35.1	34.6	34.6	34.9	34.7	34.8
2010	34.6	34.8	34.8	35.0	35.5	35.2	35.4	35.5	35.0	35.2	35.3	35.1	35.1
2011	34.8	35.0	35.0	34.9	35.2	35.0	35.2	35.6	35.7	35.7	35.3	35.7	35.3
Goods-Producing													
2007	41.1	40.4	41.3	41.3	41.5	41.4	41.1	41.7	41.7	41.4	41.6	41.9	41.4
2008	41.1	41.0	41.5	41.4	40.9	41.5	40.6	40.6	40.9	40.4	40.1	39.1	40.8
2009	38.4	39.0	39.1	38.9	38.8	39.2	38.7	39.3	38.6	38.9	39.2	39.3	38.9
2010	39.4	39.5	39.4	39.6	40.4	40.1	40.4	40.4	40.2	40.6	40.7	40.5	40.1
2011	39.9	40.1	40.2	39.7	40.5	40.4	39.8	41.2	41.8	41.0	41.0	41.5	40.6
Construction													
2007	41.7	41.6	41.7	41.6	41.6	41.8	41.8	41.7	41.7	41.8	41.7	41.6	41.7
2008	41.5	41.6	41.7	41.8	41.6	41.8	41.7	41.6	41.6	41.4	41.3	41.3	41.6
2009	41.2	41.4	41.2	41.1	41.0	41.1	41.0	41.1	41.0	40.9	40.8	40.8	41.1
2010	41.2	41.6	41.9	42.3	42.4	42.3	42.2	42.4	42.3	42.5	42.4	42.5	42.2
2011	42.3	42.4	42.2	41.6	42.7	42.5	42.8	43.3	43.4	42.3	41.4	42.0	42.4
Manufacturing													
2007	41.8	41.8	41.8	41.9	41.8	41.9	41.9	41.9	41.8	41.7	41.7	41.8	41.8
2008	41.7	41.6	41.7	41.8	41.6	41.7	41.6	41.6	41.5	41.4	41.3	41.4	41.6
2009	41.3	41.4	41.3	41.3	41.2	41.1	41.1	41.2	41.0	41.1	41.2	41.3	41.2
2010	41.3	41.2	41.3	41.2	41.3	41.1	41.3	41.2	41.1	41.2	41.3	41.2	41.2
2011	41.0	41.2	41.2	40.4	40.8	40.6	40.3	41.2	41.5	40.6	40.7	41.2	40.9
Trade, Transportation, and Utilities													
2007	36.0	36.0	36.1	36.1	36.0	36.0	36.1	35.9	36.1	36.0	36.0	36.1	36.0
2008	36.0	36.1	36.1	36.0	36.2	36.3	36.1	36.3	36.1	36.2	36.1	36.3	36.1
2009	36.1	36.3	36.4	36.2	36.3	36.5	36.3	36.5	36.3	36.2	36.2	36.4	36.3
2010	36.3	36.4	36.3	36.6	36.9	36.7	36.5	36.6	36.5	36.6	36.5	36.7	36.5
2011	36.5	36.6	36.5	36.5	36.1	35.5	36.2	35.9	35.7	35.6	35.3	35.8	36.0
Financial Activities													
2007	38.4	38.3	38.2	38.9	38.2	38.4	38.5	38.6	38.9	38.2	38.3	38.6	38.5
2008	37.2	37.2	37.8	37.7	37.5	37.9	37.4	37.2	37.5	37.1	37.3	36.5	37.4
2009	36.8	36.6	36.6	36.4	37.4	36.9	36.1	36.8	36.7	36.5	37.1	36.6	36.7
2010	36.6	36.6	36.9	36.8	37.0	36.6	36.4	36.7	36.4	36.4	36.0	36.2	36.6
2011	36.4	36.3	35.9	36.0	37.2	36.2	36.4	36.8	36.4	37.8	37.2	37.1	36.6
Professional and Business Services													
2007	35.1	35.0	35.4	35.4	35.3	35.4	35.5	35.6	35.6	35.4	35.3	35.4	35.4
2008	35.3	35.5	35.7	35.5	35.6	35.7	35.5	35.7	35.8	35.6	35.8	35.7	35.6
2009	35.8	35.9	36.0	36.2	36.1	36.3	36.1	36.2	36.0	36.0	36.1	36.0	36.1
2010	35.9	36.0	36.1	36.3	36.5	36.4	36.6	36.8	36.7	36.8	36.8	36.8	36.5
2011	36.6	36.7	36.9	37.3	37.5	36.8	36.8	37.1	37.1	37.5	36.3	36.8	37.0
Education and Health Services													
2007	36.7	37.0	36.5	36.7	36.3	36.2	36.1	36.0	36.1	35.9	36.2	36.4	36.3
2008	35.6	35.7	35.7	35.7	35.6	35.8	35.7	35.8	35.7	35.3	35.5	35.5	35.6
2009	35.3	35.5	35.0	34.7	34.4	34.3	34.4	34.8	34.4	34.5	34.8	34.5	34.7
2010	34.6	34.5	34.7	34.5	35.0	34.6	34.8	35.0	35.0	34.8	35.0	34.8	34.8
2011	35.1	35.3	34.9	34.4	35.1	34.7	35.1	35.0	35.3	35.1	34.5	34.7	34.9
Leisure and Hospitality													
2007	26.2	26.0	26.0	26.2	26.4	26.7	26.5	27.0	26.8	27.0	26.9	26.9	26.6
2008	25.9	26.0	26.1	26.2	26.2	26.5	26.3	25.7	25.9	25.6	25.8	25.7	26.0
2009	25.3	25.5	25.5	25.6	25.8	26.7	26.2	26.4	26.0	26.3	26.5	26.3	26.0
2010	26.5	27.0	27.0	27.2	27.3	27.1	27.3	26.8	26.5	26.7	26.5	26.6	26.9
2011	26.4	26.5	26.5	26.5	26.4	27.1	27.1	27.1	26.7	27.4	27.0	27.5	26.9
Other Services													
2007	31.4	31.8	31.4	31.7	31.6	31.9	31.7	32.6	32.8	32.4	32.4	32.5	32.0
2008	31.3	31.3	31.1	31.2	31.1	31.4	31.0	31.4	30.5	30.5	30.8	30.6	31.0
2009	30.0	30.3	30.7	30.9	31.7	30.9	31.0	31.3	30.2	30.4	30.3	29.9	30.6
2010	30.0	30.0	29.7	29.8	30.1	30.2	30.3	30.5	30.2	30.1	30.2	30.4	30.1
2011	30.4	30.4	30.5	30.9	31.7	31.6	31.9	32.5	32.1	32.6	31.4	31.2	31.4

3. Average Hourly Earnings by Selected Industry: Alabama, 2007–2011

(Dollars, not seasonally adjusted)

Industry and year	January	February	March	April	May	June	July	August	September	October	November	December	Annual average
Total Private													
2007	19.25	19.29	19.40	19.53	19.42	19.36	19.35	19.29	19.37	19.25	19.34	19.56	19.37
2008	19.27	19.37	19.39	19.29	19.49	19.53	19.47	19.60	19.67	19.83	20.00	19.87	19.56
2009	19.82	19.87	19.57	19.69	19.64	19.41	19.44	19.58	19.66	19.70	19.86	19.87	19.68
2010	19.95	19.94	19.95	19.94	19.90	19.79	19.70	19.68	19.83	19.81	19.87	19.95	19.86
2011	19.97	19.95	19.85	20.04	20.24	20.20	20.19	20.19	20.34	20.43	20.19	20.07	20.14
Goods-Producing													
2007	19.59	19.56	19.83	19.87	19.81	19.88	19.63	19.75	19.84	19.80	19.88	20.14	19.80
2008	19.85	19.77	19.82	19.86	20.15	19.94	20.00	20.28	20.36	20.55	20.75	20.88	20.17
2009	20.84	21.01	20.94	21.07	20.87	20.91	21.09	20.92	21.20	21.20	21.32	21.22	21.05
2010	21.25	21.36	21.32	21.24	21.18	21.26	21.40	21.33	21.51	21.45	21.47	21.70	21.37
2011	21.77	21.54	21.53	21.36	21.56	21.66	22.18	21.93	22.13	22.08	21.87	21.57	21.77
Construction													
2007	18.05	18.08	18.04	18.03	18.05	18.12	18.16	18.04	18.08	18.11	18.03	18.00	18.07
2008	17.97	18.02	18.10	18.29	18.16	18.23	18.20	18.16	18.20	18.06	18.04	18.06	18.13
2009	17.97	18.20	18.13	18.04	17.94	18.04	18.04	18.07	18.03	18.08	18.05	18.00	18.05
2010	17.96	18.16	18.19	18.16	18.22	18.38	18.36	18.49	18.46	18.55	18.50	18.53	18.33
2011	18.41	18.50	18.69	18.38	19.46	19.59	19.68	19.46	19.60	19.68	19.85	19.07	19.20
Manufacturing													
2007	20.54	20.56	20.52	20.56	20.52	20.66	20.61	20.55	20.55	20.50	20.56	20.60	20.56
2008	20.52	20.49	20.52	20.55	20.50	20.59	20.55	20.50	20.46	20.40	20.38	20.40	20.49
2009	20.35	20.40	20.38	20.44	20.37	20.32	20.37	20.43	20.34	20.38	20.41	20.45	20.39
2010	20.47	20.43	20.46	20.52	20.53	20.51	20.61	20.58	20.56	20.63	20.66	20.62	20.55
2011	20.51	20.62	20.52	20.67	20.56	20.83	21.06	20.97	21.00	21.28	20.97	20.96	20.83
Trade, Transportation, and Utilities													
2007	16.65	16.58	16.68	16.67	16.62	16.60	16.64	16.58	16.61	16.55	16.61	16.65	16.62
2008	16.59	16.65	16.68	16.64	16.78	16.84	16.79	16.86	16.73	16.84	16.72	16.95	16.76
2009	16.80	16.93	16.97	16.86	16.96	17.12	17.03	17.14	17.05	17.00	17.06	17.12	17.00
2010	17.11	17.12	17.10	17.12	17.27	17.33	17.27	17.31	17.29	17.31	17.25	17.34	17.24
2011	17.25	17.31	17.34	17.66	18.71	18.48	18.54	18.62	18.87	18.93	18.41	18.44	18.21
Financial Activities													
2007	19.96	20.12	19.81	20.39	20.23	20.67	20.74	20.96	21.15	20.55	20.66	20.63	20.49
2008	20.11	20.02	20.24	20.26	20.32	20.34	20.27	20.32	20.41	20.36	20.31	20.34	20.28
2009	20.33	20.47	20.48	20.54	20.22	20.49	20.70	20.68	20.76	20.79	20.72	20.76	20.58
2010	20.83	20.97	20.90	20.84	20.75	20.63	20.75	20.68	20.63	20.64	20.89	20.73	20.77
2011	20.57	20.54	20.76	21.23	21.53	21.19	20.98	20.95	21.12	21.54	20.59	20.58	20.97
Professional and Business Services													
2007	23.11	23.18	23.28	23.34	23.24	23.29	23.32	23.36	23.42	23.36	23.34	23.38	23.30
2008	23.33	23.40	23.46	23.38	23.49	23.51	23.43	23.51	23.55	24.26	24.48	24.44	23.68
2009	24.48	24.52	24.55	24.67	24.56	24.65	24.54	24.59	24.50	24.51	24.59	24.53	24.56
2010	24.50	24.56	24.60	24.43	24.32	24.27	24.31	24.39	24.34	24.34	24.36	24.41	24.40
2011	24.34	24.40	24.38	24.39	24.25	23.89	23.75	23.45	23.43	23.31	23.04	22.65	23.77
Education and Health Services													
2007	20.02	20.28	20.21	20.20	20.18	20.19	20.14	19.94	20.02	20.03	20.16	20.18	20.13
2008	19.67	19.83	19.89	19.83	19.66	19.86	19.76	19.69	19.69	19.70	19.68	19.52	19.74
2009	19.40	19.42	19.26	19.39	19.60	19.52	19.51	19.79	19.80	19.82	19.81	19.85	19.60
2010	19.74	19.74	19.74	20.04	19.78	19.94	19.83	19.75	19.70	19.88	19.84	19.91	19.82
2011	19.70	19.71	19.52	20.11	19.69	20.26	20.22	20.40	20.38	20.73	20.65	20.70	20.17
Leisure and Hospitality													
2007	9.75	9.72	9.88	9.80	9.74	9.48	9.61	9.80	9.70	9.73	9.80	9.89	9.74
2008	9.91	9.97	10.04	10.04	9.97	10.03	10.08	10.03	10.04	10.12	10.05	10.10	10.03
2009	9.95	10.06	10.05	10.08	10.17	10.17	10.15	10.23	10.28	10.30	10.25	10.24	10.16
2010	10.29	10.32	10.30	10.34	10.34	10.30	10.37	10.41	10.41	10.44	10.59	10.64	10.40
2011	10.74	10.70	10.62	10.67	10.71	10.57	10.53	10.62	10.53	10.58	10.65	10.90	10.65
Other Services													
2007	17.29	17.67	17.76	17.86	17.86	17.86	17.19	17.30	17.40	17.29	17.29	17.24	17.50
2008	16.46	16.52	16.41	16.43	16.40	16.53	16.41	16.39	16.25	16.23	16.79	16.44	16.44
2009	16.20	16.28	16.09	16.09	15.58	15.40	15.65	15.58	15.77	15.77	15.89	15.84	15.84
2010	15.92	15.96	16.10	16.19	16.14	15.88	16.11	16.22	16.34	16.34	16.22	16.03	16.12
2011	16.10	16.19	16.32	16.78	17.41	17.75	17.45	17.51	17.17	17.34	18.19	18.87	17.27

4. Average Weekly Earnings by Selected Industry: Alabama, 2007–2011

(Dollars, not seasonally adjusted)

Industry and year	January	February	March	April	May	June	July	August	September	October	November	December	Annual average
Total Private													
2007	696.85	698.30	710.04	720.66	714.66	710.51	710.15	707.94	712.82	702.63	707.84	719.81	709.45
2008	693.72	699.26	703.86	696.37	705.54	714.80	700.92	707.56	712.05	705.95	714.00	701.41	704.70
2009	689.74	699.42	686.91	685.21	681.51	679.35	672.62	687.26	680.24	681.62	693.11	689.49	685.64
2010	690.27	693.91	694.26	697.90	706.45	696.61	697.38	698.64	694.05	697.31	701.41	700.25	697.58
2011	694.96	698.25	694.75	699.40	712.45	707.00	710.69	718.76	726.14	729.35	712.71	716.50	710.08
Goods-Producing													
2007	805.15	790.22	818.98	820.63	822.12	823.03	806.79	823.58	827.33	819.72	827.01	843.87	819.04
2008	815.84	810.57	822.53	822.20	824.14	827.51	812.00	823.37	832.72	830.22	832.08	816.41	822.42
2009	800.26	819.39	818.75	819.62	809.76	819.67	816.18	822.16	818.32	824.68	835.74	833.95	819.70
2010	837.25	843.72	840.01	841.10	855.67	852.53	864.56	861.73	864.70	870.87	873.83	878.85	857.17
2011	868.62	863.75	865.51	847.99	873.18	875.06	882.76	903.52	925.03	905.28	896.67	895.16	883.55
Construction													
2007	752.69	752.13	752.27	750.05	750.88	757.42	759.09	752.27	753.94	757.00	751.85	748.80	753.20
2008	745.76	749.63	754.77	764.52	755.46	762.01	758.94	755.46	757.12	747.68	745.05	745.88	753.63
2009	740.36	753.48	746.96	741.44	735.54	741.44	739.64	742.68	739.23	741.28	738.25	734.40	741.13
2010	739.95	755.46	762.16	768.17	772.53	777.47	774.79	783.98	780.86	788.38	784.40	787.53	773.28
2011	778.74	784.40	788.72	764.61	830.94	832.58	842.30	842.62	850.64	832.46	821.79	800.94	814.19
Manufacturing													
2007	858.57	859.41	857.74	861.46	857.74	865.65	863.56	861.05	858.99	854.85	857.35	861.08	859.79
2008	855.68	852.38	855.68	858.99	852.80	858.60	854.88	852.80	849.09	844.56	841.69	844.56	851.92
2009	840.46	844.56	841.69	844.17	839.24	835.15	837.21	841.72	833.94	837.62	840.89	844.59	840.21
2010	845.41	841.72	845.00	845.42	847.89	842.96	851.19	847.90	845.02	849.96	853.26	849.54	847.10
2011	840.91	849.54	845.42	835.07	838.85	845.70	848.72	863.96	871.50	863.97	853.48	863.55	851.78
Trade, Transportation, and Utilities													
2007	599.40	596.88	602.15	601.79	598.32	597.60	600.70	595.22	599.62	595.80	597.96	601.07	598.88
2008	597.24	601.07	602.15	599.04	607.44	611.29	606.12	612.02	603.95	609.61	603.59	615.29	605.73
2009	606.48	614.56	617.71	610.33	615.65	624.88	618.19	625.61	618.92	615.40	617.57	623.17	617.38
2010	621.09	623.17	620.73	626.59	637.26	636.01	630.36	633.55	631.09	633.55	629.63	636.38	629.94
2011	629.63	633.55	632.91	644.59	675.43	656.04	671.15	668.46	673.66	673.91	649.87	660.15	655.84
Financial Activities													
2007	766.46	770.60	756.74	793.17	772.79	793.73	798.49	809.06	822.74	785.01	791.28	796.32	788.08
2008	748.09	744.74	765.07	763.80	762.00	770.89	758.10	755.90	765.38	755.36	757.56	742.41	757.46
2009	748.14	749.20	749.57	747.66	756.23	756.08	747.27	761.02	761.89	758.84	768.71	759.82	755.10
2010	762.38	767.50	771.21	766.91	767.75	755.06	755.30	758.96	750.93	751.30	752.04	750.43	759.30
2011	748.75	745.60	745.28	764.28	800.92	767.08	763.67	770.96	768.77	814.21	765.95	763.52	768.28
Professional and Business Services													
2007	811.16	811.30	824.11	826.24	820.37	824.47	827.86	831.62	833.75	826.94	823.90	827.65	824.17
2008	823.55	830.70	837.52	829.99	836.24	839.31	831.77	839.31	843.09	863.66	876.38	872.51	843.52
2009	876.38	880.27	883.80	893.05	886.62	894.80	885.89	890.16	882.00	882.36	887.70	883.08	885.55
2010	879.55	884.16	888.06	886.81	887.68	883.43	889.75	897.55	893.28	895.71	896.45	898.29	890.15
2011	890.84	895.48	899.62	909.75	909.38	879.15	874.00	870.00	869.25	874.13	836.35	833.52	878.33
Education and Health Services													
2007	734.73	750.36	737.67	741.34	732.53	730.88	727.05	717.84	722.72	719.08	729.79	734.55	731.50
2008	700.25	707.93	710.07	707.93	699.90	710.99	705.43	704.90	705.43	695.41	698.64	692.96	703.31
2009	684.82	689.41	674.10	672.83	674.24	669.54	671.14	688.69	681.12	683.79	689.39	684.83	680.34
2010	683.00	681.03	684.98	691.38	692.30	689.92	690.08	691.25	689.50	691.82	694.40	692.87	689.22
2011	691.47	695.76	681.25	691.78	691.12	703.02	709.72	714.00	719.41	727.62	712.43	718.29	704.80
Leisure and Hospitality													
2007	255.45	252.72	256.88	256.76	257.14	253.12	254.67	264.60	259.96	262.71	263.62	266.04	258.64
2008	256.67	259.22	262.04	263.05	261.21	265.80	265.10	257.77	260.04	259.07	259.29	259.57	260.79
2009	251.74	256.53	256.28	258.05	262.39	271.54	265.93	270.07	267.28	270.89	271.63	269.31	264.32
2010	272.69	278.64	278.10	281.25	282.28	279.13	283.10	278.99	275.87	278.75	280.64	283.02	279.38
2011	283.54	283.55	281.43	282.76	282.74	286.45	285.36	287.80	281.15	289.89	287.55	299.75	286.01
Other Services													
2007	542.91	561.91	557.66	566.16	564.38	569.73	544.92	563.98	570.72	560.20	560.20	560.30	560.28
2008	515.20	517.08	510.35	512.62	510.04	519.04	508.71	514.65	495.63	495.02	517.13	503.06	509.89
2009	486.00	493.28	493.96	497.18	493.89	475.86	485.15	487.65	476.25	479.41	481.47	473.62	485.33
2010	477.60	478.80	478.17	482.46	485.81	479.58	488.13	494.71	493.47	491.83	489.84	487.31	485.61
2011	489.44	492.18	497.76	518.50	551.90	560.90	556.66	569.08	551.16	565.28	571.17	588.74	543.17

ALASKA
At a Glance

Population:
2000 census: 626,932
2010 census: 710,231
2011 estimate: 722,718

Percent change in population:
2000–2010: 13.3%
2010–2011: 1.8%

Percent change in total nonfarm employment:
2000–2010: 14.6%
2010–2011: 1.1%

Industry with the largest growth in employment, 2000–2011 (thousands):
Education and Health Services, 18.3

Industry with the largest decline or smallest growth in employment, 2000–2011 (thousands):
Other Services, -1.2

Civilian labor force:
2000: 319,002
2010: 363,949
2011: 367,042

Unemployment rate and rank among states (lowest to highest):
2000: 6.2%, 51st
2010: 8.0%, 18th
2011: 7.6%, 22nd

Over-the-year change in unemployment rates:
2010–2011: -0.4%

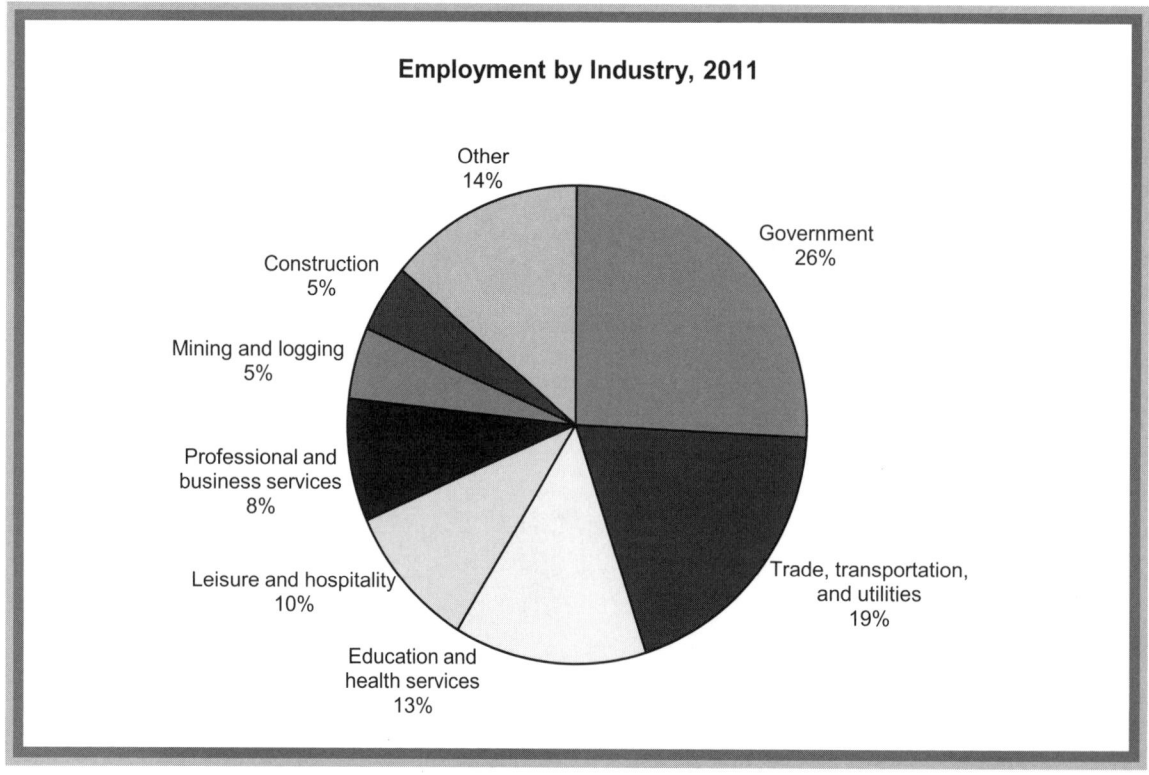

Employment by Industry, 2011

Other 14%
Government 26%
Construction 5%
Mining and logging 5%
Professional and business services 8%
Leisure and hospitality 10%
Education and health services 13%
Trade, transportation, and utilities 19%

1. Employment by Industry: Alaska, Selected Years, 2000–2011

(Numbers in thousands, not seasonally adjusted)

Industry and year	January	February	March	April	May	June	July	August	September	October	November	December	Annual average
Total Nonfarm													
2000	260.9	268.2	271.7	276.0	288.5	298.5	305.4	304.8	297.5	284.3	275.7	274.4	283.8
2001	264.8	274.2	276.8	281.9	293.4	303.8	311.7	312.4	305.1	290.4	280.3	277.3	289.3
2002	271.1	280.3	283.5	287.0	297.7	308.5	315.1	315.8	309.8	297.3	287.9	286.0	295.0
2003	278.2	284.5	287.5	290.2	303.8	314.7	319.9	320.5	314.7	299.6	290.5	288.5	299.4
2004	283.3	286.8	291.2	295.2	306.3	318.9	327.1	325.9	320.6	305.6	296.0	294.3	304.3
2005	288.6	293.0	296.3	301.3	313.5	325.4	333.4	333.1	325.5	308.7	301.2	297.1	309.8
2006	291.4	298.0	302.4	307.3	319.8	336.9	337.8	337.6	330.3	311.4	305.0	301.8	315.0
2007	296.3	303.0	305.8	309.9	322.1	336.6	339.8	340.4	332.2	315.5	308.2	304.9	317.9
2008	300.4	306.1	308.5	313.0	327.2	341.0	346.3	345.5	337.3	319.1	311.7	309.1	322.1
2009	302.7	307.8	308.9	313.7	323.1	338.2	344.0	342.6	334.2	317.5	310.4	307.3	320.9
2010	302.9	307.2	309.5	315.7	325.9	344.0	349.8	348.2	341.4	324.7	317.5	314.4	325.1
2011	308.8	314.4	316.8	321.4	330.3	348.5	354.4	351.3	342.0	325.7	318.3	313.2	328.8
Total Private													
2000	188.5	194.0	196.1	200.3	211.2	225.3	234.3	233.7	223.4	209.0	200.6	199.2	209.6
2001	189.4	196.2	197.9	201.9	212.4	226.0	236.4	236.7	225.4	209.8	200.1	197.5	210.8
2002	193.8	200.2	202.6	205.3	216.0	228.6	239.7	238.8	228.2	215.5	206.1	203.3	214.8
2003	198.6	202.8	204.9	207.3	220.4	233.4	243.4	243.1	232.4	217.3	208.6	206.5	218.2
2004	202.8	205.4	208.6	212.5	224.0	238.9	250.8	249.0	239.4	223.4	214.1	212.0	223.4
2005	208.7	211.4	214.2	218.4	230.6	245.5	257.6	256.3	244.2	226.5	219.1	215.4	229.0
2006	212.8	216.3	220.0	224.1	236.5	254.9	261.9	260.4	248.3	229.3	223.2	220.2	234.0
2007	217.4	221.1	223.2	226.8	239.0	256.1	264.1	263.5	250.2	232.3	225.5	222.4	236.8
2008	220.0	223.7	225.8	229.0	244.3	258.9	269.0	266.8	253.8	235.1	227.9	225.8	240.0
2009	221.1	224.2	225.3	228.0	239.7	253.9	264.6	262.3	249.3	231.5	224.9	221.8	237.2
2010	219.8	222.0	223.8	228.6	240.1	257.2	268.7	266.2	254.1	237.3	230.7	227.7	239.7
2011	224.6	228.6	231.3	234.8	245.6	262.9	274.6	271.2	255.8	239.0	232.4	227.3	244.0
Goods-Producing													
2000	28.5	32.1	32.5	34.2	36.5	41.4	49.0	48.2	43.4	37.7	32.5	30.2	37.2
2001	29.9	35.0	35.5	35.6	37.2	41.7	49.9	49.4	44.6	38.4	32.4	29.8	38.3
2002	30.9	35.0	35.3	34.5	36.2	40.9	48.9	47.9	43.6	39.2	33.8	31.0	38.1
2003	31.1	34.7	35.3	33.8	37.2	43.3	50.9	49.5	44.7	39.8	34.0	31.0	38.8
2004	33.7	35.0	35.6	35.6	38.3	44.8	53.2	50.8	46.0	40.6	35.2	32.3	40.1
2005	35.3	36.6	37.6	37.7	39.8	46.1	54.7	53.5	47.9	42.1	37.4	34.1	41.9
2006	36.3	38.2	39.3	40.0	41.7	50.6	56.6	54.9	49.3	43.6	39.2	35.8	43.8
2007	38.0	39.7	40.0	40.6	42.1	50.0	57.3	56.2	50.5	45.0	40.2	37.0	44.7
2008	38.6	40.7	41.2	41.1	43.8	51.2	58.5	57.1	51.3	45.1	40.1	37.7	45.5
2009	38.8	40.7	41.0	41.1	42.7	50.2	58.2	55.6	48.2	41.9	38.0	35.0	44.3
2010	37.2	38.5	39.4	39.9	41.9	50.0	58.8	56.3	50.0	43.6	39.3	36.2	44.3
2011	37.6	40.0	40.9	41.1	42.6	51.3	59.3	56.6	48.0	42.0	38.3	33.5	44.3
Mining and Logging													
2000	8.9	10.1	10.3	10.4	10.9	11.2	11.7	12.1	12.8	11.8	11.4	11.5	11.1
2001	10.5	11.5	11.6	11.8	12.0	12.3	12.2	12.1	12.0	11.8	11.2	10.7	11.6
2002	10.5	10.7	10.8	11.1	10.9	11.1	11.6	11.5	11.2	11.1	10.8	10.5	11.0
2003	10.0	10.2	10.3	10.2	10.4	10.3	10.4	10.4	10.3	10.0	9.8	9.7	10.2
2004	9.4	9.7	9.9	10.2	10.3	10.4	10.5	10.6	10.3	10.1	10.0	10.1	10.1
2005	9.9	10.3	10.5	10.4	10.5	10.8	11.1	11.2	11.2	11.3	11.3	11.3	10.8
2006	11.0	11.4	11.5	12.1	12.4	12.8	12.7	12.9	12.9	12.8	12.8	12.9	12.4
2007	12.9	13.2	13.3	13.5	13.6	14.1	14.3	14.5	14.5	14.5	14.2	14.3	13.9
2008	14.2	14.5	14.7	14.8	15.1	15.5	15.7	16.0	16.0	15.9	15.7	16.1	15.4
2009	15.4	15.6	15.5	15.4	15.5	15.8	15.3	15.4	15.1	14.5	14.4	14.3	15.2
2010	14.0	14.2	14.5	14.8	15.3	16.0	16.4	16.5	16.3	15.9	15.6	15.6	15.4
2011	14.8	15.2	15.3	15.5	15.8	16.4	16.6	16.7	16.5	16.2	15.9	15.9	15.9
Construction													
2000	11.1	11.5	11.8	12.5	14.3	16.6	17.0	17.7	16.6	15.8	13.3	12.5	14.2
2001	10.9	11.5	12.1	13.3	14.9	17.2	18.2	19.0	18.1	16.8	14.1	13.1	14.9
2002	12.2	12.4	12.8	13.4	15.8	18.1	19.0	19.6	18.9	17.7	15.5	14.3	15.8
2003	12.5	12.7	13.1	14.6	17.4	19.3	20.4	21.0	20.5	19.2	16.8	15.5	16.9
2004	13.7	13.8	14.1	15.3	17.7	20.1	21.4	21.7	21.0	19.6	17.5	16.2	17.7
2005	14.6	14.7	15.3	17.1	19.0	21.1	22.3	22.8	21.7	20.2	17.6	16.3	18.6
2006	14.5	14.7	15.3	16.6	18.8	21.0	21.4	21.5	21.0	19.8	17.4	16.1	18.2
2007	14.3	14.8	14.9	16.1	18.0	20.2	20.8	21.2	20.3	19.1	16.7	15.5	17.7
2008	13.7	14.1	14.5	15.7	17.8	19.9	20.7	21.2	20.1	18.7	15.7	14.7	17.2
2009	12.9	13.3	13.6	14.4	16.8	18.7	19.6	19.8	18.7	17.6	15.4	14.4	16.3
2010	12.8	12.7	12.9	14.1	16.3	18.6	19.6	19.8	19.0	17.9	15.2	14.1	16.1
2011	12.3	12.5	12.8	14.1	16.0	18.1	18.2	18.1	17.7	16.5	13.7	12.4	15.2
Manufacturing													
2000	8.5	10.5	10.4	11.3	11.3	13.6	20.3	18.4	14.0	10.1	7.8	6.2	11.9
2001	8.5	12.0	11.8	10.5	10.3	12.2	19.5	18.3	14.5	9.8	7.1	6.0	11.7
2002	8.2	11.9	11.7	10.0	9.5	11.7	18.3	16.8	13.5	10.4	7.5	6.2	11.3
2003	8.6	11.8	11.9	9.0	9.4	13.7	20.1	18.1	13.9	10.6	7.4	5.8	11.7
2004	10.6	11.5	11.6	10.1	10.3	14.3	21.3	18.5	14.7	10.9	7.7	6.0	12.3
2005	10.8	11.6	11.8	10.2	10.3	14.2	21.3	19.5	15.0	10.6	8.5	6.5	12.5
2006	10.8	12.1	12.5	11.3	10.5	16.8	22.5	20.5	15.4	11.0	9.0	6.8	13.3
2007	10.8	11.7	11.8	11.0	10.5	15.7	22.2	20.5	15.7	11.4	9.3	7.2	13.2
2008	10.7	12.1	12.0	10.6	10.9	15.8	22.1	19.9	15.2	10.5	8.7	6.9	13.0
2009	10.5	11.8	11.9	11.3	10.4	15.7	23.3	20.4	14.4	9.8	8.2	6.3	12.8
2010	10.4	11.6	12.0	11.0	10.3	15.4	22.8	20.0	14.7	9.8	8.5	6.5	12.8
2011	10.5	12.3	12.8	11.5	10.8	16.8	24.5	21.8	13.8	9.3	8.7	5.2	13.2

1. Employment by Industry: Alaska, Selected Years, 2000–2011—*Continued*

(Numbers in thousands, not seasonally adjusted)

Industry and year	January	February	March	April	May	June	July	August	September	October	November	December	Annual average
Service-Providing													
2000	232.4	236.1	239.2	241.8	252.0	257.1	256.4	256.6	254.1	246.6	243.2	244.2	246.6
2001	234.9	239.2	241.3	246.3	256.2	262.1	261.8	263.0	260.5	252.0	247.9	247.5	251.1
2002	240.2	245.3	248.2	252.5	261.5	267.6	266.2	267.9	266.2	258.1	254.1	255.0	256.9
2003	247.1	249.8	252.2	256.4	266.6	271.4	269.0	271.0	270.0	259.8	256.5	257.5	260.6
2004	249.6	251.8	255.6	259.6	268.0	274.1	273.9	275.1	274.6	265.0	260.8	262.0	264.2
2005	253.3	256.4	258.7	263.6	273.7	279.3	278.7	279.6	277.6	266.6	263.8	263.0	267.9
2006	255.1	259.8	263.1	267.3	278.1	286.3	281.2	282.7	281.0	267.8	265.8	266.0	271.2
2007	258.3	263.3	265.8	269.3	280.0	286.6	282.5	284.2	281.7	270.5	268.0	267.9	273.2
2008	261.8	265.4	267.3	271.9	283.4	289.8	287.8	288.4	286.0	274.0	271.6	271.4	276.6
2009	263.9	267.1	267.9	272.6	280.4	288.0	285.8	287.0	286.0	275.6	272.4	272.3	276.6
2010	265.7	268.7	270.1	275.8	284.0	294.0	291.0	291.9	291.4	281.1	278.2	278.2	280.8
2011	271.2	274.4	275.9	280.3	287.7	297.2	295.1	294.7	294.0	283.7	280.0	279.7	284.5
Trade, Transportation, and Utilities													
2000	56.5	56.6	57.1	57.8	61.3	63.9	64.7	65.2	63.3	60.1	59.0	59.1	60.4
2001	55.6	55.3	55.7	57.8	61.2	64.0	65.6	65.5	63.4	60.5	58.8	58.7	60.2
2002	56.6	57.0	57.9	58.8	62.4	64.9	66.3	66.4	64.1	61.2	59.4	59.3	61.2
2003	57.1	56.8	57.2	58.5	62.2	64.4	65.3	65.6	63.8	60.0	59.2	59.6	60.8
2004	57.0	57.0	58.0	59.5	63.6	65.8	67.5	67.4	65.7	62.0	60.7	60.7	62.1
2005	58.3	58.4	59.0	60.7	64.8	66.9	68.5	68.5	66.3	62.6	61.4	61.0	63.0
2006	59.4	58.9	60.0	61.6	65.8	68.6	69.0	69.0	66.5	62.2	61.8	61.9	63.7
2007	59.9	59.8	60.4	61.8	65.9	68.7	69.5	69.5	67.0	63.0	62.1	62.4	64.2
2008	60.8	60.6	61.3	62.5	66.9	69.0	69.8	69.5	67.2	63.0	62.3	62.5	64.6
2009	60.0	59.5	60.0	61.4	64.9	66.8	67.7	68.0	66.0	61.7	61.3	61.1	63.2
2010	58.9	58.6	59.0	60.6	64.2	66.9	67.7	67.8	65.2	61.7	61.0	61.3	62.7
2011	58.9	58.9	59.8	61.0	64.9	67.3	68.7	68.9	66.0	62.2	61.6	61.6	63.3
Wholesale Trade													
2000	6.0	6.1	6.2	6.1	6.2	6.4	6.8	6.8	6.5	6.1	6.0	6.0	6.3
2001	5.9	5.9	5.9	6.0	6.2	6.4	7.0	6.9	6.4	6.0	5.9	5.9	6.2
2002	5.7	5.7	5.8	6.1	6.2	6.5	7.0	6.9	6.4	6.0	5.9	5.9	6.2
2003	5.9	5.8	5.8	5.9	6.1	6.4	6.5	6.5	6.4	6.1	6.0	6.0	6.1
2004	5.9	6.0	6.1	6.1	6.2	6.4	6.6	6.6	6.4	6.2	6.0	6.1	6.2
2005	5.9	6.0	6.0	6.1	6.4	6.5	6.8	6.7	6.5	6.3	6.2	6.2	6.3
2006	6.2	6.2	6.3	6.3	6.6	6.8	7.0	7.0	6.8	6.5	6.3	6.4	6.5
2007	6.3	6.3	6.4	6.5	6.6	6.9	6.9	7.0	6.7	6.5	6.4	6.4	6.6
2008	6.3	6.3	6.3	6.4	6.6	6.8	7.0	6.9	6.6	6.3	6.2	6.2	6.5
2009	6.2	6.1	6.2	6.2	6.4	6.6	6.7	6.6	6.4	6.0	6.0	6.0	6.3
2010	5.9	5.9	6.0	6.1	6.3	6.5	6.8	6.8	6.4	6.2	6.1	6.2	6.3
2011	6.0	6.1	6.1	6.1	6.3	6.5	6.7	6.7	6.2	6.0	6.0	6.0	6.2
Retail Trade													
2000	32.1	31.7	32.0	32.4	33.9	35.1	35.2	35.1	34.4	33.5	33.6	33.8	33.6
2001	31.5	31.0	31.1	32.0	33.4	34.9	35.1	35.1	34.3	33.5	33.4	33.4	33.2
2002	32.0	31.9	32.2	32.6	34.2	35.4	35.8	35.6	34.9	34.3	34.0	34.2	33.9
2003	32.3	32.1	32.2	32.8	34.3	35.6	35.8	35.7	35.1	34.1	33.9	34.3	34.0
2004	32.4	32.2	32.8	33.7	35.4	36.9	37.3	37.2	36.3	35.3	35.4	35.5	35.0
2005	33.8	33.7	33.9	34.8	36.3	37.7	38.0	37.9	37.0	35.8	35.7	35.8	35.9
2006	34.3	33.6	34.0	34.9	36.5	37.9	37.8	37.5	36.5	35.4	35.5	35.7	35.8
2007	34.3	33.8	34.2	34.9	36.5	37.8	38.2	37.9	36.8	35.7	35.8	36.2	36.0
2008	35.0	34.3	34.6	35.3	36.7	37.9	38.1	37.6	36.8	36.0	35.9	36.0	36.2
2009	34.2	33.6	33.8	34.7	36.1	37.0	37.3	37.3	36.6	35.4	35.6	35.5	35.6
2010	34.0	33.7	33.7	34.7	35.9	37.2	37.4	37.1	36.0	35.2	35.4	35.5	35.5
2011	34.0	33.6	33.9	34.6	36.0	37.2	37.5	37.4	36.4	35.4	35.3	35.1	35.5
Transportation and Utilities													
2000	18.4	18.8	18.9	19.3	21.2	22.4	22.7	23.3	22.4	20.5	19.4	19.3	20.6
2001	18.2	18.4	18.7	19.8	21.6	22.7	23.5	23.5	22.7	21.0	19.5	19.4	20.8
2002	18.9	19.4	19.9	20.1	22.0	23.0	23.5	23.9	22.8	20.9	19.5	19.2	21.1
2003	18.9	18.9	19.2	19.8	21.8	22.4	23.0	23.4	22.3	19.8	19.3	19.3	20.7
2004	18.7	18.8	19.1	19.7	22.0	22.5	23.6	23.6	23.0	20.5	19.3	19.1	20.8
2005	18.6	18.7	19.1	19.8	22.1	22.7	23.7	23.9	22.8	20.5	19.5	19.0	20.9
2006	18.9	19.1	19.7	20.4	22.7	23.9	24.2	24.5	23.2	20.3	20.0	19.8	21.4
2007	19.3	19.7	19.8	20.4	22.8	24.0	24.2	24.6	23.5	20.8	19.9	19.8	21.6
2008	19.5	20.0	20.4	20.8	23.6	24.3	24.7	25.0	23.8	20.7	20.2	20.3	21.9
2009	19.6	19.8	20.0	20.5	22.4	23.2	23.7	24.1	23.0	20.3	19.7	19.6	21.3
2010	19.0	19.0	19.3	19.8	22.0	23.2	23.5	23.9	22.8	20.3	19.5	19.6	21.0
2011	18.9	19.2	19.8	20.3	22.6	23.6	24.5	24.8	23.4	20.8	20.3	20.5	21.6
Information													
2000	7.5	7.5	7.5	7.5	7.5	7.7	7.7	7.6	7.5	7.4	7.4	7.5	7.5
2001	7.3	7.4	7.4	7.2	7.4	7.5	7.5	7.5	7.3	7.3	7.3	7.2	7.4
2002	6.9	6.8	6.9	7.1	7.1	7.2	7.4	7.2	7.2	7.1	7.0	7.1	7.1
2003	6.8	6.8	6.8	6.9	7.0	7.1	7.1	7.0	7.0	6.9	6.9	6.9	6.9
2004	6.8	6.8	6.8	6.8	6.9	6.9	6.9	6.9	6.9	6.9	6.9	7.0	6.9
2005	6.8	6.9	6.9	6.9	7.0	7.0	7.0	7.0	7.0	6.9	7.0	7.0	7.0
2006	6.9	7.0	7.0	6.9	7.0	7.1	7.0	7.1	7.0	7.0	7.0	7.0	7.0
2007	6.9	6.9	6.9	6.8	6.9	7.0	7.0	7.0	7.0	6.9	6.9	6.9	6.9
2008	6.8	6.9	6.9	6.9	7.1	7.1	7.1	7.1	7.1	7.0	7.0	7.0	7.0
2009	6.7	6.8	6.7	6.6	6.5	6.6	6.6	6.5	6.55	6.5	6.4	6.4	6.6
2010	6.3	6.3	6.3	6.3	6.3	6.5	6.6	6.5	6.7	7.0	6.9	6.6	6.5
2011	6.3	6.3	6.4	6.4	6.3	6.4	6.5	6.4	6.4	6.4	6.4	6.4	6.4

1. Employment by Industry: Alaska, Selected Years, 2000–2011—*Continued*

(Numbers in thousands, not seasonally adjusted)

Industry and year	January	February	March	April	May	June	July	August	September	October	November	December	Annual average
Financial Activities													
2000	13.5	13.5	13.6	13.6	13.8	14.5	14.5	14.6	14.2	14.0	13.7	13.8	13.9
2001	13.4	13.4	13.4	13.6	14.0	14.5	14.3	14.5	14.0	13.7	13.5	13.5	13.8
2002	13.2	13.1	13.4	13.3	13.7	14.2	14.3	14.4	14.2	14.0	13.9	13.8	13.8
2003	13.6	13.6	13.9	14.0	14.4	14.8	15.0	15.1	14.8	14.6	14.3	14.4	14.4
2004	13.9	14.0	14.1	14.5	14.6	15.0	15.0	15.2	14.9	14.7	14.6	14.7	14.6
2005	14.3	14.2	14.2	14.4	14.7	15.1	15.3	15.3	15.2	15.1	14.9	14.8	14.8
2006	14.5	14.5	14.6	14.7	15.0	15.4	15.5	15.6	15.2	14.8	14.7	14.7	14.9
2007	14.4	14.6	14.7	14.8	15.2	15.6	15.5	15.7	15.2	15.0	14.8	14.8	15.0
2008	14.4	14.5	14.6	14.6	15.0	15.2	15.3	15.3	15.0	14.6	14.5	14.5	14.8
2009	14.3	14.3	14.2	14.4	14.6	15.0	15.3	15.3	14.9	14.8	14.7	14.7	14.7
2010	14.6	14.5	14.3	14.6	14.9	15.4	15.5	15.5	15.1	14.9	14.8	14.6	14.9
2011	14.4	14.4	14.5	14.6	14.7	15.1	15.2	15.2	14.9	15.2	15.1	14.8	14.8
Professional and Business Services													
2000	22.2	22.7	23.0	23.6	24.6	26.1	26.1	26.0	25.3	24.7	23.8	24.0	24.3
2001	21.2	21.8	22.0	22.2	23.1	24.2	24.5	24.7	23.6	22.4	21.7	21.7	22.8
2002	21.2	21.8	22.0	22.2	23.1	24.0	23.9	24.2	23.2	22.6	22.0	21.9	22.7
2003	21.7	21.7	21.9	22.5	23.9	24.7	24.5	24.9	23.8	22.7	22.2	22.3	23.1
2004	21.7	21.9	22.4	22.6	23.2	24.4	24.9	25.0	24.7	23.4	22.8	22.9	23.3
2005	21.9	22.4	22.3	23.0	24.2	25.6	25.7	25.9	25.0	23.4	23.1	23.0	23.8
2006	22.2	22.9	23.3	23.8	25.0	26.1	25.9	25.9	25.6	24.1	23.6	23.8	24.4
2007	23.2	23.7	23.9	24.4	25.7	26.7	26.5	26.6	26.2	24.8	24.6	24.4	25.1
2008	24.1	24.6	24.7	25.6	27.0	27.9	28.2	28.1	27.5	26.3	25.8	25.9	26.3
2009	25.2	25.5	25.6	25.5	26.7	27.5	27.5	27.4	27.0	25.8	25.1	25.1	26.2
2010	24.7	25.1	25.2	25.4	26.4	27.7	27.7	27.9	27.6	26.5	25.8	25.6	26.3
2011	25.4	26.0	25.9	26.5	27.4	28.6	29.2	29.2	29.0	27.4	26.8	26.6	27.3
Education and Health Services													
2000	25.5	26.1	26.1	26.0	26.3	26.3	25.9	26.1	26.3	26.3	26.4	26.7	26.2
2001	26.8	27.3	27.5	27.7	28.0	28.3	28.4	28.7	28.7	28.9	29.3	29.4	28.3
2002	29.4	29.8	30.1	30.5	30.9	31.2	31.2	31.4	31.2	31.6	31.9	32.3	31.0
2003	31.6	32.4	32.6	33.2	33.5	33.6	33.7	33.9	33.8	34.0	34.2	34.6	33.4
2004	34.2	34.6	34.9	35.2	35.4	35.3	35.0	34.8	35.1	35.3	35.5	35.9	35.1
2005	35.5	35.8	36.3	36.2	36.5	36.8	36.4	36.5	36.5	36.6	36.8	37.1	36.4
2006	36.8	37.3	37.4	37.6	37.9	38.0	37.7	37.7	37.6	37.2	37.4	37.5	37.5
2007	37.1	37.7	37.9	37.9	37.9	37.7	37.3	37.5	37.1	37.3	37.4	37.6	37.5
2008	37.4	37.9	38.1	38.1	38.3	38.1	38.3	38.3	38.1	38.4	38.6	38.9	38.2
2009	38.5	39.0	39.1	39.5	39.6	39.7	39.9	40.0	40.0	40.6	40.5	40.9	39.8
2010	40.8	41.2	41.3	41.9	42.1	42.2	42.4	42.3	42.6	43.1	43.2	43.5	42.2
2011	43.5	43.9	44.0	44.3	44.5	44.4	44.1	44.3	44.7	45.4	45.2	45.1	44.5
Leisure and Hospitality													
2000	23.1	23.6	24.2	25.5	28.9	32.9	34.1	33.9	31.2	26.6	25.5	25.5	27.9
2001	23.8	24.5	24.7	26.0	29.3	33.5	34.1	34.2	31.7	26.7	25.3	25.4	28.3
2002	24.0	24.9	25.0	26.9	30.5	34.3	35.7	35.4	33.0	28.3	26.7	26.6	29.3
2003	25.7	25.7	26.0	27.1	30.8	34.1	35.6	35.8	33.4	28.1	26.7	26.6	29.6
2004	24.9	25.3	25.9	27.1	30.5	35.0	37.1	37.5	34.8	29.2	27.2	27.4	30.2
2005	25.8	26.1	26.8	28.3	32.4	36.7	38.6	38.3	35.1	28.6	27.3	27.3	30.9
2006	25.8	26.5	27.2	28.5	32.9	37.9	38.8	38.9	35.7	29.0	28.1	28.2	31.5
2007	26.8	27.3	27.9	29.3	33.8	39.0	39.8	39.6	35.9	29.1	28.3	28.1	32.1
2008	27.0	27.4	27.8	29.0	34.8	38.9	40.3	39.9	36.2	29.2	28.3	28.1	32.2
2009	26.5	27.1	27.5	28.1	33.1	36.5	37.7	37.8	35.1	29.0	27.7	27.5	31.1
2010	26.4	26.9	27.2	28.6	32.9	36.9	38.4	38.4	35.5	29.2	28.5	28.8	31.5
2011	27.5	28.0	28.6	29.6	33.8	38.2	40.4	39.9	36.2	29.7	28.6	28.5	32.4
Other Services													
2000	11.7	11.9	12.1	12.1	12.3	12.5	12.3	12.1	12.2	12.2	12.3	12.4	12.2
2001	11.4	11.5	11.7	11.8	12.2	12.3	12.1	12.2	12.1	11.9	11.8	11.8	11.9
2002	11.6	11.8	12.0	12.0	12.1	11.9	12.0	11.9	11.7	11.5	11.4	11.3	11.8
2003	11.0	11.1	11.2	11.3	11.4	11.4	11.3	11.3	11.1	11.2	11.1	11.1	11.2
2004	10.6	10.8	10.9	11.2	11.5	11.7	11.2	11.4	11.3	11.3	11.2	11.1	11.2
2005	10.8	11.0	11.1	11.2	11.2	11.3	11.4	11.3	11.2	11.2	11.2	11.1	11.2
2006	10.9	11.0	11.2	11.0	11.2	11.2	11.4	11.3	11.4	11.4	11.4	11.3	11.2
2007	11.1	11.4	11.5	11.2	11.5	11.4	11.4	11.4	11.3	11.2	11.2	11.2	11.3
2008	10.9	11.1	11.2	11.2	11.4	11.5	11.5	11.5	11.4	11.5	11.3	11.2	11.3
2009	11.1	11.3	11.2	11.4	11.6	11.6	11.7	11.7	11.6	11.2	11.2	11.1	11.4
2010	10.9	10.9	11.1	11.3	11.4	11.6	11.6	11.5	11.4	11.3	11.2	11.1	11.3
2011	11.0	11.1	11.2	11.3	11.4	11.6	11.2	10.7	10.6	10.7	10.4	10.8	11.0
Government													
2000	72.4	74.2	75.6	75.7	77.3	73.2	71.1	71.1	74.1	75.3	75.1	75.2	74.2
2001	75.4	78.0	78.9	80.0	81.0	77.8	75.3	75.7	79.7	80.6	80.2	79.8	78.5
2002	77.3	80.1	80.9	81.7	81.7	79.9	75.4	77.0	81.6	81.8	81.8	82.7	80.2
2003	79.6	81.7	82.6	82.9	83.4	81.3	76.5	77.4	82.3	82.3	81.9	82.0	81.2
2004	80.5	81.4	82.6	82.7	82.3	80.0	76.3	76.9	81.2	82.2	81.9	82.3	80.9
2005	79.9	81.6	82.1	82.9	82.9	79.9	75.8	76.8	81.3	82.2	82.1	81.7	80.8
2006	78.6	81.7	82.4	83.2	83.3	82.0	75.9	77.2	82.0	82.1	81.8	81.6	81.0
2007	78.9	81.9	82.6	83.1	83.1	80.5	75.7	76.9	82.0	83.2	82.7	82.5	81.1
2008	80.4	82.4	82.7	84.0	82.9	82.1	77.3	78.7	83.5	84.0	83.8	83.3	82.1
2009	81.6	83.6	83.6	85.7	83.4	84.3	79.4	80.3	84.9	86.0	85.5	85.5	83.7
2010	83.1	85.2	85.7	87.1	85.8	86.8	81.1	82.0	87.3	87.4	86.8	86.7	85.4
2011	84.2	85.8	85.5	86.6	84.7	85.6	79.8	80.1	86.2	86.7	85.9	85.9	84.8

2. Average Weekly Hours by Selected Industry: Alaska, 2007–2011

(Not seasonally adjusted)

Industry and year	January	February	March	April	May	June	July	August	September	October	November	December	Annual average
Total Private													
2007	34.4	35.7	35.9	35.8	34.1	35.8	37.1	36.9	36.3	35.0	34.1	34.2	35.5
2008	33.8	35.3	35.7	34.4	34.8	36.2	36.4	36.8	35.7	34.8	34.9	34.2	35.3
2009	33.2	34.5	35.3	33.9	34.0	35.1	36.0	37.3	35.4	35.1	34.8	34.4	35.0
2010	34.1	34.6	34.7	34.3	37.1	36.1	36.8	36.8	34.2	34.4	34.6	35.5	35.3
2011	36.5	36.4	35.8	34.9	35.5	36.1	36.8	36.3	35.6	36.1	34.5	34.2	35.7
Goods-Producing													
2007	40.0	46.5	47.6	45.4	40.7	44.9	47.0	48.5	47.2	44.2	40.8	40.9	44.8
2008	39.2	47.3	46.5	42.3	42.5	45.1	47.7	48.8	45.5	43.4	43.0	42.6	44.8
2009	39.2	42.8	47.3	41.3	41.1	42.9	45.4	47.9	43.9	44.5	41.3	43.2	43.6
2010	42.2	42.9	42.6	39.9	40.4	38.7	39.2	39.5	30.9	31.0	31.5	31.3	37.5
2011	42.6	42.3	42.7	38.0	38.7	40.6	44.1	42.5	40.7	42.4	38.0	37.5	41.0
Construction													
2007	37.6	36.7	38.1	38.9	39.6	43.3	45.1	46.8	47.9	46.2	40.3	39.2	42.1
2008	38.7	39.3	40.8	40.2	40.9	43.2	41.9	44.7	42.1	40.7	38.4	39.1	41.1
2009	38.7	40.4	41.0	41.8	40.7	42.9	44.3	44.5	41.1	41.4	37.7	40.5	41.4
2010	39.8	40.7	39.7	41.4	38.3	39.0	38.6	38.3	37.2	35.2	33.2	34.1	37.9
2011	35.5	36.7	37.1	38.3	39.0	40.1	40.6	41.4	41.4	40.6	36.2	34.2	38.8
Manufacturing													
2007	34.8	55.5	56.8	51.3	42.1	48.5	49.8	51.7	46.0	40.4	40.1	36.3	47.2
2008	30.0	51.9	48.0	37.0	37.3	40.9	51.0	50.8	45.4	41.9	46.2	45.3	44.7
2009	35.5	40.5	52.1	31.5	31.5	36.6	41.3	49.5	42.6	44.1	41.4	42.1	41.2
2010	42.3	49.2	48.5	40.6	43.7	42.6	47.5	52.0	29.0	28.0	28.9	25.7	41.7
2011	40.0	47.3	47.7	41.0	40.4	44.7	52.2	47.0	40.3	45.6	38.7	40.7	44.9
Trade, Transportation, and Utilities													
2007	35.0	34.4	34.9	35.0	32.2	33.2	34.5	32.9	32.2	31.6	32.3	32.1	33.3
2008	31.7	31.9	32.9	31.8	32.6	33.6	32.5	33.2	32.8	31.9	32.9	31.4	32.5
2009	31.1	32.8	32.6	31.9	33.0	33.0	33.9	35.7	35.2	34.1	34.6	33.6	33.5
2010	33.3	33.8	33.5	33.6	34.6	34.1	34.5	35.0	33.5	33.6	34.6	37.4	34.3
2011	36.5	36.1	34.9	34.8	35.5	36.0	35.9	35.3	34.7	35.4	34.6	34.2	35.3
Professional and Business Services													
2007	35.7	38.5	38.3	38.8	37.4	38.3	38.7	39.5	38.4	37.5	35.4	35.8	37.7
2008	35.9	35.0	35.6	35.2	36.0	37.2	35.8	36.2	36.1	34.7	35.3	36.6	35.8
2009	34.8	35.0	35.2	35.7	35.2	37.0	36.2	38.4	36.0	36.8	37.0	36.1	36.1
2010	35.7	36.4	37.0	37.2	39.1	36.1	38.7	39.1	38.5	38.7	38.1	39.2	37.8
2011	40.2	39.3	38.6	38.1	38.3	38.8	38.3	38.6	38.3	38.6	37.0	37.0	38.4
Leisure and Hospitality													
2007	24.6	25.2	24.5	26.1	27.5	30.5	30.7	30.2	27.3	25.7	25.1	26.0	27.3
2008	26.2	26.4	27.7	26.7	26.1	28.9	29.6	28.9	27.9	27.4	26.9	27.2	27.6
2009	25.9	26.4	26.5	25.7	26.2	27.5	27.5	28.0	26.3	25.5	25.2	24.9	26.4
2010	24.1	25.2	26.0	25.4	25.0	25.1	27.1	24.3	21.5	22.6	23.6	23.6	24.5
2011	23.6	23.5	23.0	23.5	24.8	25.0	25.9	26.3	25.2	25.4	24.8	24.4	24.7

3. Average Hourly Earnings by Selected Industry: Alaska, 2007–2011

(Dollars, not seasonally adjusted)

Industry and year	January	February	March	April	May	June	July	August	September	October	November	December	Annual average
Total Private													
2007	25.27	24.51	24.73	24.87	25.89	24.37	23.90	23.60	24.71	25.01	24.86	25.12	24.70
2008	24.74	24.10	24.68	25.27	25.22	25.35	24.77	24.97	25.60	25.21	25.16	24.86	25.00
2009	24.80	24.64	24.38	25.21	25.02	24.41	24.25	24.36	24.97	25.40	25.02	25.29	24.79
2010	25.31	24.84	24.89	25.35	24.23	23.96	23.49	23.56	24.36	22.36	22.49	22.20	23.89
2011	23.60	23.54	23.81	24.67	24.45	24.23	24.17	24.26	25.20	25.12	25.05	25.19	24.43
Goods-Producing													
2007	31.79	27.38	28.75	28.52	32.45	29.26	27.96	27.80	29.90	30.76	31.18	31.75	29.57
2008	30.43	26.87	28.73	31.86	33.65	31.68	28.80	29.56	31.37	30.05	29.43	30.12	30.16
2009	29.60	27.63	25.70	30.21	31.00	29.19	27.63	27.04	30.73	31.37	30.64	32.13	29.20
2010	31.68	29.52	29.66	32.08	34.03	32.81	30.74	29.20	33.88	33.33	33.55	35.74	31.92
2011	32.83	31.94	31.59	35.93	35.36	34.10	30.82	31.33	34.91	33.94	35.24	35.63	33.39
Construction													
2007	29.42	30.07	31.37	29.50	32.17	31.45	31.76	31.76	32.21	32.33	31.78	30.41	31.35
2008	29.18	30.06	31.76	32.38	34.07	34.95	34.22	34.78	34.41	32.78	32.05	31.45	33.00
2009	31.54	32.21	32.40	33.74	33.58	35.38	35.11	35.30	36.12	35.24	33.80	33.83	34.25
2010	34.61	34.40	34.62	33.47	36.07	37.96	39.55	38.02	37.74	34.69	34.78	34.44	36.14
2011	35.38	36.10	35.73	36.49	35.51	36.98	36.94	36.47	37.25	35.61	34.46	35.79	36.16
Manufacturing													
2007	23.38	19.47	19.02	22.24	22.75	18.35	16.93	16.88	17.89	19.35	22.96	24.69	19.37
2008	22.02	18.07	18.52	22.69	24.33	19.94	17.33	17.41	19.24	18.32	19.59	21.34	19.24
2009	17.89	16.26	14.54	17.88	21.77	17.41	15.30	14.64	18.59	20.66	20.79	24.12	17.35
2010	21.10	18.06	19.15	22.48	23.30	19.81	17.30	16.15	19.70	21.67	22.75	25.98	19.44
2011	20.80	17.57	17.56	22.47	22.90	19.28	16.42	16.77	19.44	19.32	23.75	24.31	19.02
Trade, Transportation, and Utilities													
2007	21.93	22.27	21.66	22.07	22.86	17.91	18.17	17.77	19.05	18.98	18.65	19.29	20.01
2008	19.28	19.50	19.74	19.63	19.40	18.56	18.81	18.87	19.62	19.98	20.45	19.82	19.45
2009	20.16	20.42	20.84	20.38	20.02	19.64	20.03	21.12	20.64	21.29	20.99	20.83	20.53
2010	20.58	20.87	21.04	21.18	21.31	20.53	20.04	20.79	21.17	21.01	20.88	19.17	20.70
2011	20.71	20.68	20.49	20.75	20.55	19.78	20.08	19.97	20.34	20.66	20.64	20.60	20.42
Professional and Business Services													
2007	29.98	28.73	28.56	30.45	28.17	30.60	28.32	28.13	28.65	29.28	29.86	33.35	29.46
2008	30.85	31.09	30.71	30.82	29.89	29.91	30.09	30.18	30.68	31.09	33.53	32.23	30.89
2009	32.13	32.69	32.77	32.30	31.89	30.41	29.51	29.93	29.81	31.05	32.19	31.55	31.30
2010	31.84	31.55	31.21	31.36	31.63	31.24	30.70	30.97	31.25	31.88	32.79	33.01	31.61
2011	33.79	34.48	34.05	34.19	33.27	32.71	32.69	32.62	33.14	33.32	33.05	33.34	33.37
Leisure and Hospitality													
2007	13.58	13.89	13.68	13.64	12.99	12.98	13.16	13.28	13.48	13.76	13.55	13.77	13.42
2008	13.43	13.50	13.64	13.36	13.50	13.41	13.51	13.52	13.57	13.47	13.31	13.45	13.48
2009	13.06	13.20	13.37	13.37	12.83	12.96	12.95	13.16	13.12	13.40	13.45	13.75	13.19
2010	13.88	13.73	13.66	13.64	13.61	13.97	12.65	13.78	13.37	13.49	13.14	13.85	13.54
2011	13.84	14.03	14.29	14.21	13.96	13.60	13.90	13.69	14.18	14.13	14.02	14.17	13.98

4. Average Weekly Earnings by Selected Industry: Alaska, 2007–2011

(Dollars, not seasonally adjusted)

Industry and year	January	February	March	April	May	June	July	August	September	October	November	December	Annual average
Total Private													
2007	869.29	875.01	887.81	890.35	882.85	872.45	886.69	870.84	896.97	875.35	847.73	859.10	876.08
2008	836.21	850.73	881.08	869.29	877.66	917.67	901.63	918.90	913.92	877.31	878.08	850.21	882.50
2009	823.36	850.08	860.61	854.62	850.68	856.79	873.00	908.63	883.94	891.54	870.70	869.98	867.09
2010	863.07	859.46	863.68	869.51	898.93	864.96	864.43	867.01	833.11	769.18	778.15	788.10	843.74
2011	861.40	856.86	852.40	860.98	867.98	874.70	889.46	880.64	897.12	906.83	864.23	861.50	873.39
Goods-Producing													
2007	1,271.60	1,273.17	1,368.50	1,294.81	1,320.72	1,313.77	1,314.12	1,348.30	1,411.28	1,359.59	1,272.14	1,298.58	1,323.48
2008	1,192.86	1,270.95	1,335.95	1,347.68	1,430.13	1,428.77	1,373.76	1,442.53	1,427.34	1,304.17	1,265.49	1,283.11	1,350.45
2009	1,160.32	1,182.56	1,215.61	1,247.67	1,274.10	1,252.25	1,254.40	1,295.22	1,349.05	1,395.97	1,265.43	1,388.02	1,273.02
2010	1,336.90	1,266.41	1,263.52	1,279.99	1,374.81	1,269.75	1,205.01	1,153.40	1,046.89	1,033.23	1,056.83	1,118.66	1,196.91
2011	1,398.56	1,351.06	1,348.89	1,365.34	1,368.43	1,384.46	1,359.16	1,331.53	1,420.84	1,439.06	1,339.12	1,336.13	1,370.19
Construction													
2007	1,106.19	1,103.57	1,195.20	1,147.55	1,273.93	1,361.79	1,432.38	1,486.37	1,542.86	1,493.65	1,280.73	1,192.07	1,320.87
2008	1,129.27	1,181.36	1,295.81	1,301.68	1,393.46	1,509.84	1,433.82	1,554.67	1,448.66	1,334.15	1,230.72	1,229.70	1,355.45
2009	1,220.60	1,301.28	1,328.40	1,410.33	1,366.71	1,517.80	1,555.37	1,570.85	1,484.53	1,458.94	1,274.26	1,370.12	1,419.43
2010	1,377.48	1,400.08	1,374.41	1,385.66	1,381.48	1,480.44	1,526.63	1,456.17	1,403.93	1,221.09	1,154.70	1,174.40	1,369.21
2011	1,255.99	1,324.87	1,325.58	1,397.57	1,384.89	1,482.90	1,499.76	1,509.86	1,542.15	1,445.77	1,247.45	1,224.02	1,402.76
Manufacturing													
2007	813.62	1,080.59	1,080.34	1,140.91	957.78	889.98	843.11	872.70	822.94	781.74	920.70	896.25	913.89
2008	660.60	937.83	888.96	839.53	907.51	815.55	883.83	884.43	873.50	905.06	966.70	860.84	
2009	635.10	658.53	757.53	563.22	685.76	637.21	631.89	724.68	791.93	911.11	860.71	1,015.45	715.79
2010	892.53	888.55	928.78	912.69	1,018.21	843.91	821.75	839.80	571.30	606.76	657.48	667.69	810.42
2011	832.00	831.06	837.61	921.27	925.16	861.82	857.12	788.19	783.43	880.99	919.13	989.42	854.73
Trade, Transportation, and Utilities													
2007	767.55	766.09	755.93	772.45	736.09	594.61	626.87	584.63	613.41	599.77	602.40	619.21	667.12
2008	611.18	622.05	649.45	624.23	632.44	623.62	611.33	626.48	643.54	637.36	672.81	622.35	631.22
2009	626.98	669.78	679.38	650.12	660.66	648.12	679.02	753.98	726.53	725.99	726.25	699.89	687.89
2010	685.31	705.41	704.84	711.65	737.33	700.07	691.38	727.65	709.20	705.94	722.45	716.96	709.79
2011	755.92	746.55	715.10	722.10	729.53	712.08	720.87	704.94	705.80	731.36	714.14	704.52	721.46
Professional and Business Services													
2007	1,070.29	1,106.11	1,093.85	1,181.46	1,053.56	1,171.98	1,095.98	1,111.14	1,100.16	1,098.00	1,057.04	1,193.93	1,111.32
2008	1,107.52	1,088.15	1,093.28	1,084.86	1,076.04	1,112.65	1,077.22	1,092.52	1,107.55	1,078.82	1,183.61	1,179.62	1,106.52
2009	1,118.12	1,144.15	1,153.50	1,153.11	1,122.53	1,125.17	1,068.26	1,149.31	1,073.16	1,142.64	1,191.03	1,138.96	1,131.14
2010	1,136.69	1,148.42	1,154.77	1,166.59	1,236.73	1,127.76	1,188.09	1,210.93	1,203.13	1,233.76	1,249.30	1,293.99	1,196.11
2011	1,358.36	1,355.06	1,314.33	1,302.64	1,274.24	1,269.15	1,252.03	1,259.13	1,269.26	1,286.15	1,222.85	1,233.58	1,280.65
Leisure and Hospitality													
2007	334.07	350.03	335.16	356.00	357.23	395.89	404.01	401.06	368.00	353.63	340.11	358.02	366.21
2008	351.87	356.40	377.83	356.71	352.35	387.55	399.90	390.73	378.60	369.08	358.04	365.84	372.32
2009	338.25	356.40	354.31	343.61	336.15	356.40	356.13	368.48	345.06	341.70	338.94	342.38	348.35
2010	334.51	346.00	355.16	346.46	340.25	350.65	342.82	334.85	287.46	304.87	310.10	326.86	331.32
2011	326.62	329.71	328.67	333.94	346.21	340.00	360.01	360.05	357.34	358.90	347.70	345.75	345.83

ARIZONA
At a Glance

Population:
  2000 census: 5,130,247
  2010 census: 6,392,017
  2011 estimate: 6,482,505

Percent change in population:
  2000–2010: 24.6%
  2010–2011: 1.4%

Percent change in total nonfarm employment:
  2000–2010: 6.2%
  2010–2011: 1.0%

Industry with the largest growth in employment, 2000–2011 (thousands):
  Education and Health Services, 142.7

Industry with the largest decline or smallest growth in employment, 2000–2011 (thousands):
  Manufacturing, -60.2

Civilian labor force:
  2000: 2,505,306
  2010: 3,100,253
  2011: 3,034,262

Unemployment rate and rank among states (lowest to highest):
  2000: 4.0%, 28th
  2010: 10.5%, 41st
  2011: 9.5%, 38th

Over-the-year change in unemployment rates:
  2010–2011: -1.0%

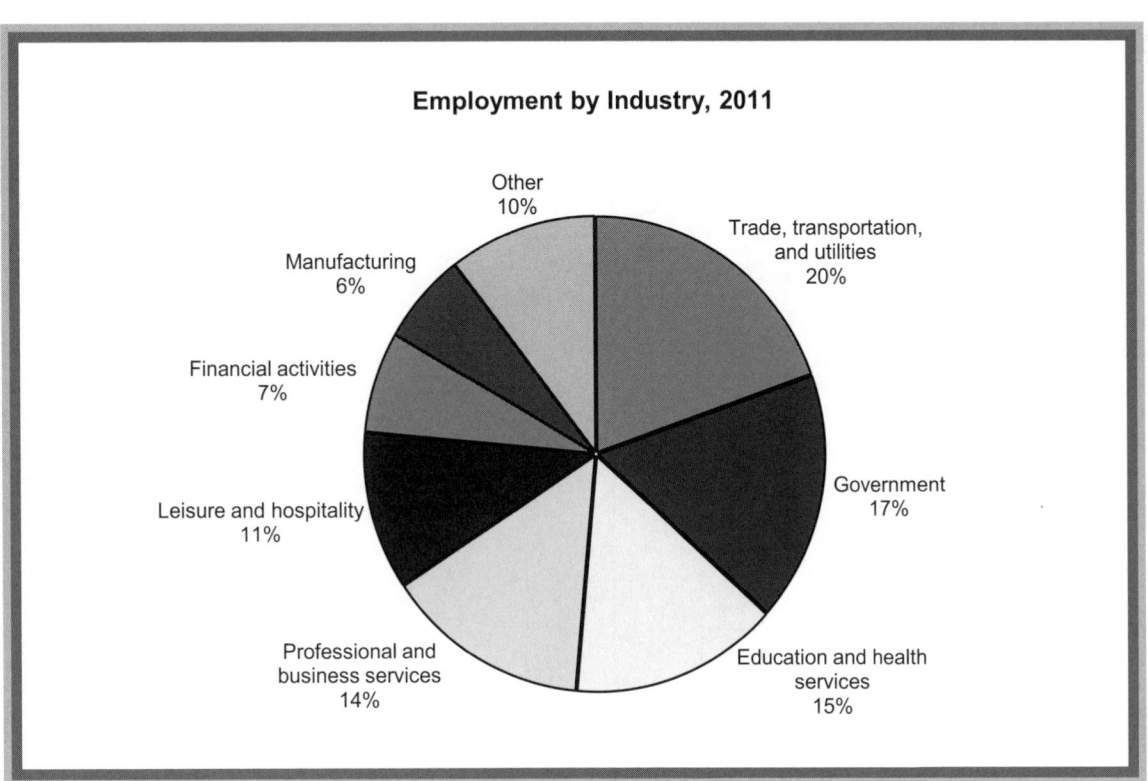

Employment by Industry, 2011

- Other 10%
- Trade, transportation, and utilities 20%
- Manufacturing 6%
- Financial activities 7%
- Government 17%
- Leisure and hospitality 11%
- Professional and business services 14%
- Education and health services 15%

1. Employment by Industry: Arizona, Selected Years, 2000–2011

(Numbers in thousands, not seasonally adjusted)

Industry and year	January	February	March	April	May	June	July	August	September	October	November	December	Annual average
Total Nonfarm													
2000	2,184.1	2,220.3	2,239.7	2,240.3	2,253.5	2,224.9	2,192.9	2,218.5	2,259.3	2,274.6	2,293.1	2,311.5	2,242.7
2001	2,239.4	2,275.4	2,291.5	2,287.0	2,279.8	2,251.8	2,216.2	2,243.8	2,267.8	2,270.9	2,278.0	2,282.7	2,265.4
2002	2,229.4	2,253.0	2,269.5	2,281.2	2,277.4	2,252.3	2,211.2	2,247.2	2,267.7	2,283.8	2,312.5	2,313.5	2,266.6
2003	2,254.4	2,280.8	2,293.7	2,299.1	2,301.4	2,272.8	2,241.0	2,281.2	2,304.6	2,332.5	2,348.9	2,365.0	2,298.0
2004	2,310.1	2,340.8	2,359.5	2,377.5	2,379.0	2,354.6	2,333.5	2,370.1	2,398.6	2,437.7	2,457.5	2,477.5	2,383.0
2005	2,414.9	2,456.4	2,475.5	2,507.9	2,509.7	2,483.1	2,470.0	2,509.3	2,547.7	2,560.0	2,587.4	2,606.5	2,510.7
2006	2,564.0	2,608.4	2,631.2	2,636.8	2,645.8	2,618.4	2,590.1	2,627.3	2,658.9	2,671.7	2,689.9	2,701.2	2,637.0
2007	2,633.8	2,671.7	2,689.5	2,679.5	2,684.5	2,653.0	2,626.7	2,665.4	2,686.0	2,698.5	2,715.6	2,716.9	2,676.8
2008	2,647.6	2,670.3	2,669.4	2,659.0	2,652.0	2,602.6	2,560.5	2,598.6	2,604.4	2,597.4	2,593.9	2,578.8	2,619.5
2009	2,495.6	2,490.5	2,481.7	2,464.2	2,448.5	2,388.1	2,360.0	2,384.1	2,397.2	2,403.8	2,418.1	2,418.3	2,429.2
2010	2,362.5	2,381.3	2,392.9	2,403.1	2,409.9	2,347.5	2,322.4	2,353.1	2,369.6	2,397.8	2,418.6	2,425.3	2,382.0
2011	2,376.1	2,398.5	2,411.4	2,422.3	2,419.3	2,360.5	2,337.8	2,388.9	2,417.5	2,437.6	2,447.5	2,448.2	2,405.5
Total Private													
2000	1,825.5	1,848.7	1,863.0	1,862.1	1,870.4	1,880.7	1,860.5	1,876.2	1,886.5	1,895.6	1,913.0	1,930.5	1,876.1
2001	1,873.9	1,891.5	1,906.4	1,900.3	1,896.2	1,898.2	1,875.5	1,882.9	1,880.4	1,877.3	1,881.3	1,887.2	1,887.6
2002	1,847.1	1,857.7	1,872.8	1,880.7	1,882.7	1,881.1	1,860.7	1,873.2	1,871.0	1,878.8	1,900.1	1,907.8	1,876.1
2003	1,865.6	1,876.8	1,889.9	1,895.8	1,899.5	1,898.1	1,888.4	1,903.1	1,907.7	1,926.6	1,943.2	1,958.7	1,904.5
2004	1,919.7	1,934.7	1,952.8	1,969.4	1,973.2	1,977.6	1,976.5	1,985.7	1,989.8	2,021.9	2,041.8	2,060.8	1,983.7
2005	2,019.3	2,041.8	2,063.6	2,095.4	2,099.9	2,104.5	2,104.6	2,120.3	2,136.6	2,145.1	2,171.0	2,191.2	2,107.8
2006	2,163.6	2,192.1	2,214.9	2,220.6	2,228.1	2,235.9	2,219.6	2,233.2	2,242.2	2,246.8	2,264.4	2,280.1	2,228.5
2007	2,224.0	2,246.1	2,262.6	2,253.0	2,258.6	2,261.4	2,241.6	2,253.4	2,252.9	2,261.7	2,275.7	2,277.7	2,255.7
2008	2,217.7	2,227.7	2,227.8	2,216.2	2,210.1	2,196.2	2,169.4	2,176.4	2,165.6	2,154.7	2,148.7	2,136.2	2,187.2
2009	2,065.5	2,050.9	2,043.8	2,024.0	2,014.8	1,996.3	1,978.1	1,979.1	1,970.2	1,973.2	1,986.8	1,991.1	2,006.2
2010	1,944.1	1,951.7	1,964.8	1,971.6	1,969.4	1,960.1	1,946.4	1,954.3	1,950.4	1,976.1	1,994.1	2,005.5	1,965.7
2011	1,964.3	1,975.8	1,989.4	1,998.8	1,997.9	1,987.9	1,979.4	1,989.0	1,995.8	2,013.7	2,020.7	2,028.6	1,995.1
Goods-Producing													
2000	375.6	378.6	380.7	382.1	384.5	391.2	390.5	393.6	394.4	393.7	393.6	395.5	387.8
2001	384.7	386.4	389.8	387.9	388.6	390.5	389.3	389.6	384.9	379.8	375.1	371.4	384.8
2002	363.5	363.5	365.1	364.8	365.6	367.4	367.0	368.4	365.1	362.7	361.2	359.4	364.5
2003	353.9	353.2	354.5	356.0	358.1	360.8	360.7	362.9	362.5	363.6	363.8	365.1	359.6
2004	360.6	363.7	366.6	368.9	371.6	377.1	380.5	381.7	383.2	388.4	389.9	393.1	377.1
2005	386.4	391.6	396.7	403.2	406.3	413.0	415.5	418.0	419.7	420.5	423.9	428.2	410.3
2006	423.7	430.4	435.0	437.9	440.4	445.0	443.5	442.6	439.8	434.6	430.1	428.5	436.0
2007	418.8	421.9	422.7	419.1	420.3	425.2	423.1	423.7	418.8	414.0	408.1	402.2	418.2
2008	391.5	388.9	386.8	383.1	381.6	380.2	376.2	373.5	367.1	357.8	347.3	338.6	372.7
2009	322.2	312.0	306.6	298.8	295.6	294.5	291.1	287.7	283.3	280.2	277.2	274.5	293.6
2010	267.7	267.8	268.7	271.0	271.2	272.7	273.0	272.3	270.6	272.5	271.9	271.3	270.9
2011	266.3	266.2	268.1	269.7	271.3	273.9	274.5	275.8	277.9	282.1	275.9	273.4	272.9
Mining and Logging													
2000	9.6	9.7	9.7	9.7	9.8	10.0	9.9	9.9	9.8	9.7	9.6	9.7	9.8
2001	9.6	9.6	9.6	9.6	9.7	9.7	9.6	9.6	9.5	9.5	9.4	9.2	9.6
2002	8.9	8.9	8.9	9.0	8.8	8.9	8.7	8.7	8.7	8.6	8.4	8.4	8.7
2003	8.2	8.0	7.9	8.0	8.0	8.1	8.1	8.1	8.0	8.0	8.0	8.0	8.0
2004	7.8	7.9	7.9	8.1	8.3	8.4	8.4	8.5	8.5	8.7	8.7	8.7	8.3
2005	8.6	8.7	8.8	9.0	9.1	9.3	8.1	8.0	8.0	8.0	8.4	9.0	8.6
2006	9.0	9.1	9.2	9.5	9.7	10.1	10.2	10.3	10.4	10.4	10.5	10.5	9.9
2007	10.5	10.5	10.7	10.7	10.9	11.2	11.8	12.1	12.1	12.3	12.4	12.5	11.5
2008	12.7	12.7	12.9	13.0	13.3	13.7	14.0	14.2	14.4	14.0	13.8	13.8	13.5
2009	12.6	12.1	12.1	10.9	10.6	10.7	10.7	10.8	10.7	10.8	10.8	10.8	11.1
2010	10.8	10.9	10.8	10.9	11.0	11.0	10.8	10.8	10.7	11.0	11.1	11.2	10.9
2011	11.3	11.4	11.5	11.2	11.4	11.6	11.7	11.7	11.6	11.7	11.7	11.8	11.6
Construction													
2000	159.6	161.2	162.9	164.3	166.7	170.3	169.9	171.9	172.5	172.9	172.1	173.4	168.1
2001	166.5	168.8	172.4	172.1	173.6	176.7	177.5	179.6	177.3	174.9	172.9	170.4	173.6
2002	167.0	167.4	169.7	170.1	172.0	174.0	174.1	176.6	174.8	174.3	173.9	172.4	172.2
2003	168.7	169.0	170.5	172.0	174.7	177.1	177.7	179.8	180.1	181.6	181.5	181.7	176.2
2004	178.3	180.6	183.0	185.8	187.9	191.4	194.3	195.7	197.1	201.0	201.8	203.8	191.7
2005	199.2	203.3	207.9	213.7	215.9	220.8	224.1	226.0	228.2	228.8	231.6	233.3	219.4
2006	229.7	234.4	238.7	241.1	244.0	247.5	246.1	245.6	243.8	240.0	237.8	235.4	240.3
2007	226.7	227.6	228.5	226.4	227.6	231.7	228.7	229.1	225.9	221.4	215.7	210.0	224.9
2008	200.7	198.8	198.2	195.1	193.6	192.0	188.6	186.3	181.1	173.9	165.8	158.8	186.1
2009	147.3	140.4	137.4	132.7	131.0	130.8	128.2	125.3	122.0	119.3	116.5	114.0	128.7
2010	109.0	109.0	109.9	111.8	111.6	113.0	113.3	113.0	111.8	113.1	112.0	110.7	111.5
2011	106.6	106.4	107.9	109.6	110.1	112.4	112.9	114.2	116.4	118.9	113.2	112.1	111.7
Manufacturing													
2000	206.4	207.7	208.1	208.1	208.0	210.9	210.7	211.8	212.1	211.1	211.9	212.4	209.9
2001	208.6	208.0	207.8	206.2	205.3	204.1	202.2	200.4	198.1	195.4	192.8	191.8	201.7
2002	187.6	187.2	186.5	185.7	184.8	184.5	184.2	183.1	181.6	179.8	178.9	178.6	183.5
2003	177.0	176.2	176.1	176.0	175.4	175.6	174.9	175.0	174.4	174.0	174.3	175.4	175.4
2004	174.5	175.2	175.7	175.0	175.4	177.3	177.8	177.5	177.6	178.7	179.4	180.6	177.1
2005	178.6	179.6	180.0	180.5	181.3	182.9	183.3	184.0	183.5	183.7	183.9	185.9	182.3
2006	185.0	186.9	187.1	187.3	186.7	187.4	187.2	186.7	185.6	184.2	181.8	182.6	185.7
2007	181.6	183.8	183.5	182.0	181.8	182.3	182.6	182.5	180.8	180.3	180.0	179.7	181.7
2008	178.1	177.4	175.7	175.0	174.7	174.5	173.6	173.0	171.6	169.9	167.7	166.0	173.1
2009	162.3	159.5	157.1	155.2	154.0	153.0	152.2	151.6	150.6	150.1	149.9	149.7	153.8
2010	147.9	147.9	148.0	148.3	148.6	148.7	148.9	148.5	148.1	148.4	148.8	149.4	148.5
2011	148.4	148.4	148.7	148.9	149.8	149.9	149.9	149.9	149.9	151.5	151.0	149.5	149.7

1. Employment by Industry: Arizona, Selected Years, 2000–2011—*Continued*

(Numbers in thousands, not seasonally adjusted)

Industry and year	January	February	March	April	May	June	July	August	September	October	November	December	Annual average
Service-Providing													
2000	1,808.5	1,841.7	1,859.0	1,858.2	1,869.0	1,833.7	1,802.4	1,824.9	1,864.9	1,880.9	1,899.5	1,916.0	1,854.9
2001	1,854.7	1,889.0	1,901.7	1,899.1	1,891.2	1,861.3	1,826.9	1,854.2	1,882.9	1,891.1	1,902.9	1,911.3	1,880.5
2002	1,865.9	1,889.5	1,904.4	1,916.4	1,911.8	1,884.9	1,844.2	1,878.8	1,902.6	1,921.1	1,951.3	1,954.1	1,902.1
2003	1,900.5	1,927.6	1,939.2	1,943.1	1,943.3	1,912.0	1,880.3	1,918.3	1,942.1	1,968.9	1,985.1	1,999.9	1,938.4
2004	1,949.5	1,977.1	1,992.9	2,008.6	2,007.4	1,977.5	1,953.0	1,988.4	2,015.4	2,049.3	2,067.6	2,084.4	2,005.9
2005	2,028.5	2,064.8	2,078.8	2,104.7	2,103.4	2,070.1	2,054.5	2,091.3	2,128.0	2,139.5	2,163.5	2,178.3	2,100.5
2006	2,140.3	2,178.0	2,196.2	2,198.9	2,205.4	2,173.4	2,146.6	2,184.7	2,219.1	2,237.1	2,259.8	2,272.7	2,201.0
2007	2,215.0	2,249.8	2,266.8	2,260.4	2,264.2	2,227.8	2,203.6	2,241.7	2,267.2	2,284.5	2,307.5	2,314.7	2,258.6
2008	2,256.1	2,281.4	2,282.6	2,275.9	2,270.4	2,222.4	2,184.3	2,225.1	2,237.3	2,239.6	2,246.6	2,240.2	2,246.8
2009	2,173.4	2,178.5	2,175.1	2,165.4	2,152.9	2,093.6	2,068.9	2,096.4	2,113.9	2,123.6	2,140.9	2,143.8	2,135.5
2010	2,094.8	2,113.5	2,124.2	2,132.1	2,138.7	2,074.8	2,049.4	2,080.8	2,099.0	2,125.3	2,146.7	2,154.0	2,111.1
2011	2,109.8	2,132.3	2,143.3	2,152.6	2,148.0	2,086.6	2,063.3	2,113.1	2,139.6	2,155.5	2,171.6	2,174.8	2,132.5
Trade, Transportation, and Utilities													
2000	432.5	433.1	432.2	429.5	430.5	433.6	430.6	433.7	436.4	442.2	455.7	464.0	437.8
2001	444.1	441.9	440.9	439.7	438.4	438.5	434.8	434.9	434.7	439.1	447.2	452.5	440.6
2002	437.2	434.0	436.7	437.4	439.1	439.9	435.3	436.8	438.1	442.1	452.9	460.9	440.9
2003	442.6	441.7	442.7	440.7	441.1	440.5	439.5	441.4	441.9	450.3	461.3	469.0	446.1
2004	453.6	453.1	455.0	456.8	458.4	458.8	459.1	460.5	459.0	468.4	481.0	488.8	462.7
2005	476.8	477.8	479.9	481.8	482.3	482.3	485.8	487.2	490.1	494.4	507.7	516.8	488.6
2006	502.1	501.6	505.9	505.7	506.4	506.4	507.8	509.8	510.9	517.9	531.3	540.4	512.2
2007	522.0	520.8	523.2	522.7	524.0	523.8	524.2	525.2	526.0	528.8	542.4	549.2	527.7
2008	527.9	525.2	524.2	518.7	519.2	517.8	510.4	511.4	507.5	508.6	514.8	515.3	516.8
2009	495.5	487.2	484.8	479.3	478.0	474.4	471.7	471.1	469.1	468.8	478.2	483.0	478.4
2010	467.9	466.7	467.2	467.6	467.7	465.6	463.1	463.0	459.9	465.6	476.6	482.8	467.8
2011	468.0	467.5	468.9	471.3	471.7	471.1	468.4	468.8	470.0	473.8	484.9	487.1	472.6
Wholesale Trade													
2000	94.4	95.3	95.8	93.6	93.7	94.3	93.9	93.9	94.4	95.4	97.1	98.7	95.0
2001	97.6	98.3	98.5	97.3	96.3	95.8	94.8	94.6	94.0	94.0	94.3	95.2	95.9
2002	94.2	94.4	95.0	93.5	94.3	94.0	93.4	93.4	93.3	94.0	94.6	95.4	94.1
2003	94.3	94.6	94.4	93.2	93.3	92.9	91.8	91.7	91.6	91.9	92.7	94.1	93.0
2004	94.3	94.5	94.8	94.5	94.9	95.3	95.8	95.8	94.5	96.4	97.0	98.5	95.5
2005	97.6	98.6	99.2	99.3	99.3	99.6	100.0	99.9	100.2	100.9	102.2	104.1	100.1
2006	103.5	104.3	104.8	104.6	104.7	105.3	105.6	105.8	106.2	106.8	107.9	109.4	105.7
2007	107.7	108.3	108.9	108.1	108.2	108.9	108.9	108.7	108.5	108.9	110.0	110.9	108.8
2008	109.3	109.7	109.6	108.3	108.4	107.9	107.0	107.1	106.9	107.2	107.1	106.8	107.9
2009	104.5	103.4	102.2	100.5	99.5	98.5	98.0	97.6	96.7	97.0	97.0	97.3	99.4
2010	95.8	96.1	96.3	96.2	96.1	95.8	95.3	94.7	93.9	94.8	95.6	95.9	95.5
2011	95.0	95.7	95.7	96.2	96.3	96.6	96.2	96.0	95.7	95.2	95.7	97.0	95.9
Retail Trade													
2000	264.3	264.2	263.5	263.2	263.9	265.7	262.8	265.2	267.1	271.4	282.3	288.4	268.5
2001	270.0	266.8	265.7	265.6	264.7	265.1	262.9	263.3	264.2	269.0	277.4	282.4	268.1
2002	268.9	265.6	267.0	268.6	269.2	269.4	265.8	266.8	268.4	270.6	280.7	287.8	270.7
2003	271.5	270.3	271.4	270.9	271.2	271.3	271.7	273.5	273.9	281.1	291.2	297.0	276.3
2004	282.4	281.8	282.7	284.5	285.5	285.5	285.1	286.4	286.6	292.0	303.9	309.9	288.9
2005	299.5	299.1	300.6	302.7	302.3	302.0	305.0	305.8	307.8	311.5	322.4	328.1	307.2
2006	316.0	314.8	318.2	317.8	318.2	317.6	318.2	319.2	319.1	325.7	337.4	343.1	322.1
2007	328.5	326.6	328.5	328.4	329.0	327.7	328.6	329.3	330.0	332.8	344.7	348.4	331.9
2008	331.9	328.4	327.7	323.7	324.0	323.3	317.5	318.0	314.8	315.9	321.4	321.3	322.3
2009	306.3	299.8	298.8	296.8	296.5	294.3	292.6	292.2	291.6	291.6	301.0	304.0	297.1
2010	292.5	291.0	291.4	291.7	291.7	289.7	288.0	287.9	285.5	289.6	299.2	302.5	291.7
2011	291.2	289.7	290.8	292.5	292.4	291.2	289.0	290.6	291.9	295.5	306.6	306.7	294.0
Transportation and Utilities													
2000	73.8	73.6	72.9	72.7	72.9	73.6	73.9	74.6	74.9	75.4	76.3	76.9	74.3
2001	76.5	76.8	76.7	76.8	77.4	77.6	77.1	77.0	76.5	76.1	75.5	74.9	76.6
2002	74.1	74.0	74.7	75.3	75.6	76.5	76.1	76.6	76.4	77.5	77.6	77.7	76.0
2003	76.8	76.8	76.9	76.6	76.6	76.3	76.0	76.2	76.4	77.3	77.4	77.9	76.8
2004	76.9	76.8	77.5	77.8	78.0	78.0	78.2	78.3	77.9	80.0	80.1	80.4	78.3
2005	79.7	80.1	80.1	79.8	80.7	80.7	80.8	81.5	82.1	82.0	83.1	84.6	81.3
2006	82.6	82.5	82.9	83.3	83.5	83.5	84.0	84.8	85.6	85.4	86.0	87.9	84.3
2007	85.8	85.9	85.8	86.2	86.8	87.2	86.7	87.2	87.5	87.1	87.7	89.9	87.0
2008	86.7	87.1	86.9	86.7	86.8	86.6	85.9	86.3	85.8	85.5	86.3	87.2	86.5
2009	84.7	84.0	83.8	82.0	82.0	81.6	81.1	81.3	80.8	80.2	80.2	81.7	82.0
2010	79.6	79.6	79.5	79.7	79.9	80.1	79.8	80.4	80.5	81.2	81.8	84.4	80.5
2011	81.8	82.1	82.4	82.6	83.0	83.3	83.2	82.2	82.4	83.1	82.6	83.4	82.7
Information													
2000	51.1	52.1	54.3	54.6	55.1	55.1	54.7	54.7	54.1	53.1	53.6	54.1	53.9
2001	53.3	54.5	54.0	54.0	53.4	53.8	53.3	53.4	52.8	52.6	53.6	52.8	53.5
2002	52.8	52.7	52.2	52.2	51.8	51.2	51.1	50.9	50.1	49.4	50.2	50.3	51.2
2003	49.0	49.3	49.5	49.5	49.4	49.5	48.9	48.7	48.0	48.1	49.1	48.9	49.0
2004	47.9	47.9	48.2	48.1	47.4	47.1	46.2	45.3	44.0	44.2	44.7	44.3	46.3
2005	43.6	44.2	44.5	45.3	45.5	45.1	44.7	44.5	44.0	44.3	44.9	45.5	44.7
2006	44.8	44.9	44.9	43.9	44.0	43.9	43.1	43.0	42.1	41.7	42.3	42.4	43.4
2007	40.6	41.5	41.4	41.7	42.3	42.1	41.8	41.5	41.1	40.8	41.7	41.3	41.5
2008	40.6	41.5	41.9	41.0	42.1	41.7	40.5	40.2	40.6	39.7	40.2	40.4	40.9
2009	39.1	39.4	38.8	38.8	39.1	38.3	37.9	37.6	37.0	36.4	36.9	36.8	38.0
2010	36.4	36.6	36.8	36.8	36.8	37.1	36.2	36.1	35.8	35.6	36.1	36.6	36.4
2011	36.2	36.3	36.4	36.5	36.6	36.7	36.7	36.8	36.4	36.4	36.8	37.7	36.6

1. Employment by Industry: Arizona, Selected Years, 2000–2011—*Continued*

(Numbers in thousands, not seasonally adjusted)

Industry and year	January	February	March	April	May	June	July	August	September	October	November	December	Annual average
Financial Activities													
2000	147.2	149.9	149.9	149.2	150.1	151.6	150.5	151.4	152.0	152.7	153.0	154.4	151.0
2001	149.2	150.8	152.3	152.4	152.8	153.5	154.4	154.6	154.7	154.6	155.3	156.3	153.4
2002	153.2	154.7	154.2	155.2	154.6	154.5	154.2	154.4	154.5	155.7	157.7	158.6	155.1
2003	156.5	157.4	158.9	158.7	159.5	160.0	160.8	162.0	161.3	161.2	161.5	162.4	160.0
2004	160.3	161.2	162.2	164.3	164.0	164.2	165.1	165.5	165.2	167.4	168.0	169.2	164.7
2005	167.3	168.8	169.4	172.1	172.5	173.5	174.9	176.6	177.6	179.0	179.8	181.2	174.4
2006	178.5	179.9	180.9	181.4	182.2	182.7	182.8	183.5	184.0	185.1	185.3	187.2	182.8
2007	184.3	185.9	186.5	186.5	186.3	185.9	185.2	182.9	181.8	180.5	180.3	181.0	183.9
2008	176.4	177.7	177.6	177.1	177.0	176.5	175.1	174.8	174.0	173.3	172.2	172.1	175.3
2009	168.4	168.3	168.0	167.5	167.7	167.0	166.6	166.6	165.3	165.0	164.7	165.6	166.7
2010	163.0	163.5	164.0	162.6	162.8	162.8	163.2	163.6	162.8	165.1	165.6	167.0	163.8
2011	164.4	165.2	165.9	166.1	165.7	166.3	166.3	165.9	164.9	165.7	166.6	169.2	166.0
Professional and Business Services													
2000	310.0	316.6	322.4	325.1	328.7	329.7	325.8	330.2	331.0	332.1	333.0	335.7	326.7
2001	319.5	324.9	329.1	326.8	324.5	325.1	318.5	318.8	317.7	314.9	311.0	312.6	320.3
2002	304.0	308.2	313.6	317.4	316.4	317.2	314.2	317.7	316.0	315.3	317.7	317.7	314.6
2003	309.4	313.8	317.9	320.3	321.2	322.2	318.8	321.7	323.3	326.6	326.9	329.7	321.0
2004	319.6	323.3	328.1	335.8	335.7	338.9	341.0	342.3	344.5	351.9	353.2	356.7	339.3
2005	346.6	352.1	356.7	364.2	363.8	367.1	368.3	372.0	375.4	374.8	377.8	380.3	366.6
2006	374.6	383.3	387.2	390.2	392.5	397.2	395.4	399.6	403.1	404.3	405.7	408.1	395.1
2007	395.4	400.2	404.8	402.7	402.9	405.5	402.8	406.4	405.1	408.5	409.8	407.6	404.3
2008	395.1	398.1	396.1	393.9	390.5	387.3	383.7	385.8	382.5	380.8	376.9	374.0	387.1
2009	359.2	356.1	353.2	349.3	345.1	342.4	340.7	338.5	337.3	341.7	344.6	345.0	346.1
2010	334.5	335.8	339.5	341.9	339.8	338.6	336.4	337.1	336.0	343.5	344.8	349.5	339.8
2011	340.1	343.4	345.3	346.3	343.1	342.3	338.6	339.9	340.3	344.2	346.8	350.7	343.4
Education and Health Services													
2000	208.7	211.4	212.1	211.1	211.3	210.6	208.1	211.2	213.7	214.8	215.8	217.7	212.2
2001	214.5	216.8	218.6	218.5	218.2	218.5	215.3	220.1	223.0	224.7	226.5	228.8	220.3
2002	228.5	230.6	231.9	231.3	233.0	232.4	228.6	233.8	235.7	239.1	241.5	242.3	234.1
2003	241.2	243.9	244.5	247.1	247.6	246.6	244.8	249.6	252.0	253.1	254.6	256.0	248.4
2004	255.2	256.9	258.2	260.5	261.2	260.5	257.9	262.7	265.1	269.0	270.3	272.1	262.5
2005	268.0	270.2	273.2	277.5	278.6	275.7	273.4	278.9	281.6	282.9	284.8	286.2	277.6
2006	284.5	288.2	290.9	291.4	292.6	291.5	289.8	295.6	298.2	299.8	301.9	305.0	294.1
2007	299.7	304.3	306.0	304.2	305.7	305.2	302.5	308.0	310.7	315.5	316.4	318.2	308.0
2008	314.0	318.6	320.1	322.2	323.5	321.0	319.6	325.2	327.9	329.9	332.0	333.8	324.0
2009	328.1	330.5	331.2	331.4	332.3	329.5	327.9	334.0	335.9	339.7	342.3	343.9	333.9
2010	339.5	341.0	342.5	342.3	343.3	340.0	338.2	345.0	346.7	352.2	353.7	353.6	344.8
2011	349.3	351.7	352.6	354.3	355.2	348.7	349.1	354.3	358.0	361.6	361.6	362.0	354.9
Leisure and Hospitality													
2000	224.1	229.3	233.2	233.2	232.4	230.1	222.6	224.1	227.6	229.4	230.3	230.6	228.9
2001	226.7	232.8	236.9	236.9	235.4	231.7	224.4	225.6	226.5	227.4	227.9	228.0	230.0
2002	223.0	228.4	232.5	235.7	235.2	230.8	224.3	225.1	225.3	228.3	232.6	232.2	229.5
2003	228.0	232.2	235.8	238.0	236.8	232.4	227.5	228.5	230.2	234.6	236.4	237.7	233.2
2004	234.7	239.5	244.9	246.2	246.0	241.8	237.2	238.1	239.4	242.4	244.5	246.0	241.7
2005	242.5	248.1	252.9	259.9	259.0	255.7	250.6	251.8	256.1	256.6	258.8	259.4	254.3
2006	258.1	264.2	268.9	271.6	270.1	267.6	261.3	262.6	266.6	267.5	271.0	271.1	266.7
2007	266.8	272.9	278.4	278.1	277.9	273.0	264.0	267.7	269.9	273.9	276.2	276.9	273.0
2008	272.0	276.3	279.1	279.2	275.1	270.3	263.2	265.3	266.0	265.6	266.2	263.8	270.2
2009	257.5	261.2	264.9	264.6	262.7	255.9	249.1	250.9	250.2	250.6	252.2	251.8	256.0
2010	247.3	251.7	257.1	261.2	259.1	254.2	248.3	249.8	251.4	253.8	257.1	256.2	253.9
2011	252.1	256.5	263.0	265.1	264.3	258.7	253.8	257.2	258.8	260.2	258.8	260.5	259.1
Other Services													
2000	76.3	77.7	78.2	77.3	77.8	78.8	77.7	77.3	77.3	77.6	78.0	78.5	77.7
2001	81.9	83.4	84.8	84.1	84.9	86.6	85.5	85.9	86.1	84.2	84.7	84.8	84.7
2002	84.9	85.6	86.6	86.7	87.0	87.7	86.0	86.1	86.2	86.2	86.3	86.4	86.3
2003	85.0	85.3	86.1	85.5	85.8	86.1	87.4	88.3	88.5	89.1	89.6	89.7	87.2
2004	87.8	89.1	89.6	88.8	88.9	89.2	89.5	89.6	89.4	90.2	90.2	90.6	89.4
2005	88.1	89.0	90.3	91.4	91.9	92.1	91.4	91.3	92.1	92.6	93.3	93.6	91.4
2006	97.3	99.6	101.2	98.5	99.9	101.6	95.9	96.5	97.5	95.9	96.8	97.4	98.2
2007	96.4	98.6	99.6	98.0	99.2	100.7	98.0	98.0	99.5	99.7	100.8	101.3	99.2
2008	100.2	101.4	102.0	101.0	101.1	101.4	100.7	100.2	100.0	99.0	99.1	98.2	100.4
2009	95.5	96.2	96.3	94.3	94.3	94.3	93.1	92.7	92.1	90.8	90.7	90.5	93.4
2010	87.8	88.6	89.0	88.2	88.7	89.1	88.0	87.4	87.2	87.8	88.3	88.5	88.2
2011	87.9	89.0	89.2	89.5	90.0	90.2	92.0	90.3	89.5	89.7	89.3	88.0	89.6
Government													
2000	358.6	371.6	376.7	378.2	383.1	344.2	332.4	342.3	372.8	379.0	380.1	381.0	366.7
2001	365.5	383.9	385.1	386.7	383.6	353.6	340.7	360.9	387.4	393.6	396.7	395.5	377.8
2002	382.3	395.3	396.7	400.5	394.7	371.2	350.5	374.0	396.7	405.0	412.4	405.7	390.4
2003	388.8	404.0	403.8	403.3	401.9	374.7	352.6	378.1	396.9	405.9	405.7	406.3	393.5
2004	390.4	406.1	406.7	408.1	405.8	377.0	357.0	384.4	408.8	415.8	415.7	416.7	399.4
2005	395.6	414.6	411.9	412.5	409.8	378.6	365.4	389.0	411.1	414.9	416.4	415.3	402.9
2006	400.4	416.3	416.3	416.2	417.7	382.5	370.5	394.1	416.7	424.9	425.5	421.1	408.5
2007	409.8	425.6	426.9	426.5	425.9	391.6	385.1	412.0	433.1	436.8	439.9	439.2	421.0
2008	429.9	442.6	441.6	442.8	441.9	406.4	391.1	422.2	438.8	447.2	445.2	442.6	432.3
2009	430.1	439.6	437.9	440.2	433.7	391.8	381.9	405.0	427.0	430.6	431.3	427.2	423.0
2010	418.4	429.6	428.1	431.5	440.5	387.4	376.0	398.8	419.2	421.7	424.5	419.8	416.3
2011	411.8	422.7	422.0	423.5	421.4	372.6	358.4	399.9	421.7	423.9	426.8	419.6	410.4

2. Average Weekly Hours by Selected Industry: Arizona, 2007–2011

(Not seasonally adjusted)

Industry and year	January	February	March	April	May	June	July	August	September	October	November	December	Annual average
Total Private													
2007	35.4	35.5	35.5	35.7	35.2	35.4	35.5	35.2	35.0	34.7	34.6	35.1	35.2
2008	34.1	34.3	34.8	34.5	34.5	35.4	34.8	35.1	34.9	35.2	35.5	34.9	34.8
2009	34.8	35.0	35.1	34.5	34.5	34.5	34.6	35.1	34.6	34.8	35.3	34.7	34.8
2010	34.5	35.3	35.0	34.9	35.5	35.4	35.4	35.8	35.1	35.2	35.4	35.0	35.2
2011	35.2	35.0	35.1	35.1	35.1	35.0	34.9	35.0	34.9	35.4	34.8	34.7	35.0
Goods-Producing													
2007	38.9	38.8	38.7	38.6	38.8	38.6	38.3	38.4	38.3	38.4	38.2	37.7	38.5
2008	36.6	36.7	37.1	36.9	37.5	38.2	37.6	38.3	38.2	38.0	37.8	38.2	37.6
2009	37.6	36.5	37.1	36.4	36.5	37.4	37.2	37.8	37.1	37.6	37.8	37.3	37.2
2010	37.3	37.3	36.9	37.7	38.0	37.9	38.3	38.4	37.9	38.6	38.4	38.3	37.9
2011	38.1	38.1	38.0	38.3	37.8	38.9	37.4	38.5	38.3	38.1	38.2	37.4	38.1
Construction													
2007	38.9	38.7	38.6	38.0	38.5	38.3	37.9	38.2	37.7	37.9	37.7	37.1	38.1
2008	36.0	35.8	35.9	35.5	36.4	37.2	36.4	37.4	37.3	37.1	36.7	36.9	36.5
2009	36.5	35.5	36.2	35.7	36.0	37.0	36.8	37.1	36.4	37.0	36.9	35.9	36.4
2010	36.1	36.3	35.4	36.4	36.5	37.3	37.0	37.3	36.5	37.8	36.7	36.4	36.6
2011	36.7	36.8	36.3	36.5	35.7	37.4	35.8	37.1	36.8	36.6	36.2	34.6	36.4
Manufacturing													
2007	38.8	38.9	38.6	39.1	38.9	38.7	38.5	38.4	39.0	39.0	38.8	38.5	38.8
2008	37.6	38.0	38.6	38.6	38.5	39.0	38.7	38.3	38.3	38.3	38.4	39.1	38.4
2009	38.4	37.4	38.0	37.0	36.9	37.7	37.7	38.5	37.7	38.1	38.6	38.5	37.9
2010	38.3	38.1	38.5	38.6	39.3	38.3	38.6	38.6	38.5	38.7	39.6	39.8	38.7
2011	39.2	39.2	39.5	39.9	39.8	40.4	39.1	39.9	40.0	39.7	40.4	40.9	39.8
Trade, Transportation, and Utilities													
2007	35.7	36.1	36.2	36.2	35.9	36.4	36.1	36.1	36.5	35.5	35.4	36.4	36.0
2008	35.3	35.6	36.2	35.9	36.0	37.0	36.5	36.6	36.7	36.9	37.3	36.5	36.4
2009	36.1	36.3	36.0	35.5	35.6	35.6	35.2	35.6	35.5	35.1	35.9	35.2	35.6
2010	34.7	35.2	34.9	35.0	35.9	35.4	35.5	36.1	35.4	35.6	35.9	36.1	35.5
2011	36.3	35.9	35.9	36.1	36.1	36.0	36.2	36.1	35.8	36.4	35.5	35.8	36.0
Financial Activities													
2007	37.3	37.1	37.1	37.5	36.1	36.4	36.8	36.6	36.3	36.5	35.7	36.7	36.7
2008	36.4	36.1	36.7	36.5	36.3	37.3	36.8	36.5	36.3	37.0	37.5	37.0	36.7
2009	37.2	37.3	37.4	37.0	35.9	36.2	37.1	37.6	37.2	37.5	38.4	37.7	37.2
2010	37.5	38.3	38.3	38.3	39.2	38.7	38.8	38.8	38.2	38.2	38.7	38.6	38.5
2011	39.5	38.9	38.7	38.8	39.5	39.2	39.7	39.0	39.5	39.9	39.2	38.6	39.2
Professional and Business Services													
2007	35.8	36.0	36.1	36.3	35.7	36.3	36.5	35.8	35.7	35.5	35.5	35.9	35.9
2008	35.9	35.9	36.8	36.2	35.5	36.2	35.4	35.7	35.3	35.9	36.1	35.2	35.8
2009	35.7	35.5	35.7	35.4	35.5	34.7	34.3	35.3	34.5	35.1	35.4	34.6	35.1
2010	34.8	35.0	34.4	34.7	35.6	34.8	35.0	36.0	35.2	35.5	35.7	34.8	35.1
2011	34.6	34.6	34.7	34.8	35.3	34.9	35.1	35.3	34.8	35.8	35.3	36.0	35.1
Education and Health Services													
2007	35.0	34.7	34.7	34.8	34.5	34.7	34.8	34.6	34.7	34.1	34.1	34.0	34.6
2008	33.6	34.2	34.5	34.4	34.5	34.6	34.5	34.8	34.6	34.7	35.0	34.9	34.5
2009	35.0	35.5	35.5	35.0	35.1	35.0	35.6	35.6	35.2	35.1	35.5	35.6	35.3
2010	35.1	35.4	35.2	34.8	34.8	34.7	34.3	34.4	33.8	34.2	34.1	34.3	34.6
2011	34.7	33.7	34.1	33.9	34.0	33.6	33.4	33.4	33.4	33.9	33.3	33.2	33.7
Leisure and Hospitality													
2007	28.4	28.6	29.0	29.3	28.7	28.6	28.5	27.8	27.8	27.9	28.3	28.4	28.4
2008	27.7	28.3	28.7	28.1	28.0	28.0	27.2	27.6	27.4	28.0	27.8	27.0	27.8
2009	26.7	27.5	27.7	27.1	26.9	26.5	26.5	26.7	26.8	26.4	27.1	26.4	26.9
2010	26.7	27.1	27.0	27.0	27.4	27.6	27.0	27.6	27.0	26.9	27.2	26.6	27.1
2011	27.1	27.5	27.1	27.1	26.6	26.0	25.9	26.0	26.6	27.0	26.6	26.2	26.6
Other Services													
2007	34.3	34.9	35.1	35.8	35.6	34.8	34.7	35.7	35.1	35.3	34.6	34.3	35.0
2008	33.4	32.4	32.5	32.8	32.6	32.3	31.7	32.5	31.6	32.3	33.0	32.0	32.4
2009	31.7	31.7	32.6	31.9	32.1	32.5	32.8	33.1	32.2	32.8	33.2	34.0	32.5
2010	34.3	34.1	34.6	34.2	34.4	34.3	33.6	33.7	33.3	33.1	33.1	33.0	33.8
2011	33.4	34.2	34.2	33.6	34.1	32.8	32.7	32.6	32.6	32.4	31.4	31.6	33.0

3. Average Hourly Earnings by Selected Industry: Arizona, 2007–2011

(Dollars, not seasonally adjusted)

Industry and year	January	February	March	April	May	June	July	August	September	October	November	December	Annual average
Total Private													
2007	19.98	20.03	19.93	20.05	19.97	19.98	19.61	19.58	19.86	19.61	19.51	19.91	19.84
2008	19.83	19.98	20.42	20.34	20.42	20.59	20.80	20.88	21.05	21.04	21.44	21.53	20.69
2009	21.71	21.93	21.78	21.86	21.90	21.87	22.13	22.08	22.17	22.27	22.20	22.55	22.03
2010	22.57	22.22	22.53	22.39	22.11	21.91	22.05	22.00	22.05	21.95	21.81	22.40	22.16
2011	22.57	22.59	22.59	22.75	22.73	22.40	22.61	22.40	22.53	22.61	22.42	22.54	22.56
Goods-Producing													
2007	20.68	20.66	20.59	20.95	20.79	20.74	21.00	20.60	20.71	21.19	20.97	21.52	20.86
2008	21.73	21.90	21.76	21.63	21.99	22.09	22.10	22.75	22.09	22.08	22.55	22.61	22.10
2009	22.61	22.92	23.01	23.13	23.11	23.16	23.21	22.92	23.27	23.24	23.29	23.69	23.12
2010	23.23	23.23	23.13	23.01	22.89	22.66	22.44	22.25	22.11	22.09	21.96	22.56	22.62
2011	22.43	22.84	23.20	23.24	23.24	22.88	23.06	23.03	23.12	23.29	23.42	24.08	23.15
Construction													
2007	19.61	19.44	19.37	19.87	19.53	19.53	19.68	19.57	19.84	19.85	20.37	20.86	19.78
2008	21.20	21.50	21.43	21.38	21.67	21.97	21.71	21.65	21.91	22.11	22.26	22.64	21.76
2009	22.23	22.46	22.20	22.38	22.41	22.63	22.53	22.40	23.00	22.86	22.91	23.25	22.59
2010	22.74	22.87	23.13	23.03	22.79	22.47	22.47	22.07	21.91	21.66	21.79	22.41	22.44
2011	22.25	22.57	22.89	22.52	22.08	21.66	21.53	21.91	21.87	21.85	21.79	22.39	22.10
Manufacturing													
2007	21.83	22.03	22.05	22.21	22.35	22.30	22.72	22.03	21.94	22.59	21.91	22.56	22.21
2008	22.63	22.49	22.33	22.05	22.45	22.28	22.64	23.31	22.61	22.31	22.97	22.67	22.56
2009	23.10	23.41	23.78	23.84	23.69	23.64	23.85	23.41	23.54	23.60	23.65	24.13	23.63
2010	23.71	23.55	23.09	22.91	22.95	22.80	22.31	22.38	22.28	22.45	22.06	22.58	22.75
2011	22.56	23.09	23.41	23.89	24.37	24.17	24.78	24.28	24.56	24.85	24.83	25.56	24.21
Trade, Transportation, and Utilities													
2007	19.15	18.98	19.37	19.39	19.31	19.25	18.36	18.58	18.85	18.33	18.52	18.09	18.84
2008	18.59	18.80	19.11	19.16	19.44	19.06	19.28	19.25	19.65	19.43	19.81	20.04	19.30
2009	20.64	20.86	20.33	20.32	20.28	20.60	21.06	20.55	20.61	20.88	20.69	20.64	20.62
2010	21.03	19.86	20.29	20.50	20.04	20.42	20.21	20.26	20.25	20.32	19.99	19.91	20.25
2011	20.14	20.15	20.15	20.25	20.25	19.96	20.29	19.90	20.37	20.80	20.56	20.51	20.28
Financial Activities													
2007	23.00	23.44	23.01	22.76	22.55	22.84	22.19	21.92	22.56	21.88	22.33	22.99	22.63
2008	22.36	22.56	23.22	22.60	22.60	22.11	21.97	21.95	22.24	22.34	22.90	22.49	22.45
2009	22.65	23.02	23.02	23.08	23.46	23.16	23.85	24.52	24.46	24.35	24.19	24.11	23.66
2010	24.02	24.49	23.89	24.00	23.82	23.28	23.50	23.57	23.21	23.01	22.76	23.03	23.54
2011	23.23	23.04	23.13	23.62	23.24	23.15	23.61	23.73	23.78	23.66	23.71	23.79	23.48
Professional and Business Services													
2007	21.46	21.83	21.28	21.60	21.80	21.94	22.23	22.28	22.94	22.25	22.11	22.66	22.03
2008	22.66	23.19	23.55	24.24	23.98	24.69	24.78	24.68	24.85	25.18	25.57	25.67	24.40
2009	25.59	26.04	26.49	26.52	26.50	26.47	26.94	26.71	26.42	26.26	26.70	26.43	26.42
2010	26.46	26.48	27.17	27.48	27.02	26.88	27.36	26.69	27.21	26.60	26.83	27.52	26.98
2011	28.02	28.16	27.93	28.11	27.82	27.31	27.26	26.99	27.15	26.90	26.40	25.94	27.32
Education and Health Services													
2007	21.66	21.65	21.81	21.91	22.09	21.61	21.38	21.45	22.01	22.20	22.18	22.84	21.90
2008	22.84	22.78	22.97	22.78	22.70	22.43	23.10	22.83	23.27	23.10	23.39	23.60	22.99
2009	23.53	23.50	23.56	23.60	23.63	23.37	23.31	23.45	23.60	23.77	23.51	23.43	23.52
2010	23.65	23.53	23.56	23.68	23.35	23.31	23.61	23.43	23.86	23.90	23.49	23.60	23.58
2011	23.53	23.88	23.89	23.85	23.92	23.46	23.65	23.53	23.56	23.17	23.29	23.56	23.61
Leisure and Hospitality													
2007	12.06	12.09	12.03	11.94	11.92	11.96	11.77	12.12	12.00	12.17	12.07	12.43	12.05
2008	12.06	12.30	12.51	12.76	12.63	12.54	12.64	12.62	12.99	12.85	13.09	13.28	12.68
2009	13.10	13.07	13.17	13.23	12.98	13.08	12.83	12.93	13.19	13.25	13.29	13.28	13.12
2010	13.22	13.31	13.28	13.44	13.49	13.22	12.97	13.02	12.93	13.06	13.21	13.41	13.22
2011	13.26	13.24	13.16	13.54	13.99	13.67	13.73	13.46	13.53	13.71	13.89	13.83	13.58
Other Services													
2007	16.92	16.73	16.81	16.88	16.45	16.40	16.73	16.23	16.14	15.66	16.12	16.60	16.47
2008	16.53	16.03	16.51	16.12	15.78	16.25	16.49	16.21	16.39	16.34	16.34	16.49	16.29
2009	16.42	16.61	16.19	16.54	16.20	16.13	16.05	16.24	16.49	16.13	16.16	15.85	16.25
2010	15.44	15.78	15.88	15.79	15.96	15.56	15.85	16.23	16.03	15.65	15.98	16.40	15.88
2011	16.12	16.29	16.49	16.89	16.83	16.71	17.15	16.88	16.92	16.89	17.3	17.4	16.82

4. Average Weekly Earnings by Selected Industry: Arizona, 2007–2011

(Dollars, not seasonally adjusted)

Industry and year	January	February	March	April	May	June	July	August	September	October	November	December	Annual average
Total Private													
2007	707.29	711.07	707.52	715.79	702.94	707.29	696.16	689.22	695.10	680.47	675.05	698.84	698.92
2008	676.20	685.31	710.62	701.73	704.49	728.89	723.84	732.89	734.65	740.61	761.12	751.40	720.48
2009	755.51	767.55	764.48	754.17	755.55	754.52	765.70	775.01	767.08	775.00	783.66	782.49	766.66
2010	778.67	784.37	788.55	781.41	784.91	775.61	780.57	787.60	773.96	772.64	772.07	784.00	780.54
2011	794.46	790.65	792.91	798.53	797.82	784.00	789.09	784.00	786.30	800.39	780.22	782.14	790.24
Goods-Producing													
2007	804.45	801.61	796.83	808.67	806.65	800.56	804.30	791.04	793.19	813.70	801.05	811.30	802.73
2008	795.32	803.73	807.30	798.15	824.63	843.84	830.96	871.33	843.84	839.04	852.39	863.70	830.39
2009	850.14	836.58	853.67	841.93	843.52	866.18	863.41	866.38	863.32	873.82	880.36	883.64	859.75
2010	866.48	866.48	853.50	867.48	869.82	858.81	859.45	854.40	837.97	852.67	843.26	864.05	857.84
2011	854.58	870.20	881.60	890.09	878.47	890.03	862.44	886.66	885.50	887.35	894.64	900.59	881.87
Construction													
2007	762.83	752.33	747.68	755.06	751.91	748.00	745.87	747.57	747.97	752.32	767.95	773.91	754.25
2008	763.20	769.70	769.34	758.99	788.79	817.28	790.24	809.71	817.24	820.28	816.94	835.42	794.94
2009	811.40	797.33	803.64	798.97	806.76	837.31	829.10	831.04	837.20	845.82	845.38	834.68	822.17
2010	820.91	830.18	818.80	838.29	831.84	838.13	831.39	823.21	799.72	818.75	799.69	815.72	822.13
2011	816.58	830.58	830.91	821.98	788.26	810.08	770.77	812.86	804.82	799.71	788.80	774.69	803.84
Manufacturing													
2007	847.00	856.97	851.13	868.41	869.42	863.01	874.72	845.95	855.66	881.01	850.11	868.56	860.98
2008	850.89	854.62	861.94	851.13	864.33	868.92	876.17	892.77	865.96	854.47	882.05	886.40	867.30
2009	887.04	875.53	903.64	882.08	874.16	891.23	899.15	901.29	887.46	899.16	912.89	929.01	895.08
2010	908.09	897.26	888.97	884.33	901.94	873.24	861.17	863.87	857.78	868.82	873.58	898.68	881.49
2011	884.35	905.13	924.70	953.21	969.93	976.47	968.90	968.77	982.40	986.55	1003.13	1045.40	964.15
Trade, Transportation, and Utilities													
2007	683.66	685.18	701.19	701.92	693.23	700.70	662.80	670.74	688.03	650.72	655.61	658.48	679.17
2008	656.23	669.28	691.78	687.84	699.84	705.22	703.72	704.55	721.16	716.97	738.91	731.46	702.03
2009	745.10	757.22	731.88	721.36	721.97	733.36	741.31	731.58	731.66	732.89	742.77	726.53	734.85
2010	729.74	699.07	708.12	717.50	719.44	722.87	717.46	731.39	716.85	723.39	717.64	718.75	718.58
2011	731.08	723.39	723.39	731.03	731.03	718.56	734.50	718.39	729.25	757.12	729.88	734.26	730.19
Financial Activities													
2007	857.90	869.62	853.67	853.50	814.06	831.38	816.59	802.27	818.93	798.62	797.18	843.73	829.97
2008	813.90	814.42	852.17	824.90	820.38	824.70	808.50	801.18	807.31	826.58	858.75	832.13	823.71
2009	842.58	858.65	860.95	853.96	842.21	838.39	884.84	921.95	909.91	913.13	928.90	908.95	880.06
2010	900.75	937.97	914.99	919.20	933.74	900.94	911.80	914.52	886.62	878.98	880.81	888.96	905.65
2011	917.59	896.26	895.13	916.46	917.98	907.48	937.32	925.47	939.31	944.03	929.43	918.29	920.39
Professional and Business Services													
2007	768.27	785.88	768.21	784.08	778.26	796.42	811.40	797.62	818.96	789.88	784.91	813.49	791.51
2008	813.49	832.52	866.64	877.49	851.29	893.78	877.21	881.08	877.21	903.96	923.08	903.58	874.64
2009	913.56	924.42	945.69	938.81	940.75	918.51	924.04	942.86	911.49	921.73	945.18	914.48	928.40
2010	920.81	926.80	934.65	953.56	961.91	935.42	957.60	960.84	957.79	944.30	957.83	957.70	947.44
2011	969.49	974.34	969.17	978.23	982.05	953.12	956.83	952.75	944.82	963.02	931.92	933.84	959.08
Education and Health Services													
2007	758.10	751.26	756.81	762.47	762.11	749.87	744.02	742.17	763.75	757.02	756.34	776.56	756.78
2008	767.42	779.08	792.47	783.63	783.15	776.08	796.95	794.48	805.14	801.57	818.65	823.64	793.78
2009	823.55	834.25	836.38	826.00	829.41	817.95	829.84	834.82	830.72	834.33	834.61	834.11	830.53
2010	830.12	832.96	829.31	824.06	812.58	808.86	809.82	805.99	806.47	817.38	801.01	809.48	815.62
2011	816.49	804.76	814.65	808.52	813.28	788.26	789.91	785.90	786.90	785.46	775.56	782.19	795.82
Leisure and Hospitality													
2007	342.50	345.77	348.87	349.84	342.10	342.06	335.45	336.94	333.60	339.54	341.58	353.01	342.67
2008	334.06	348.09	359.04	358.56	353.64	351.12	343.81	348.31	355.93	359.80	363.90	358.56	352.90
2009	349.74	359.43	364.81	358.53	349.16	346.62	340.00	345.23	353.49	349.80	360.16	350.59	352.42
2010	352.97	360.70	358.56	362.88	369.63	364.87	350.19	359.35	349.11	351.31	359.31	356.71	358.03
2011	359.35	364.10	356.64	366.93	372.13	355.42	355.61	349.96	359.90	370.17	369.47	362.35	361.89
Other Services													
2007	580.36	583.88	590.03	604.30	585.62	570.72	580.53	579.41	566.51	552.80	557.75	569.38	576.67
2008	552.10	519.37	536.58	528.74	514.43	524.88	522.73	526.83	517.92	527.78	539.22	527.68	528.17
2009	520.51	526.54	527.79	527.63	520.02	524.23	526.44	537.54	530.98	529.06	536.51	538.90	528.85
2010	529.59	538.10	549.45	540.02	549.02	533.71	532.56	546.95	533.80	518.02	528.94	541.20	536.82
2011	538.41	557.12	563.96	567.50	573.90	548.09	560.81	550.29	551.59	547.24	543.22	549.84	554.37

ARKANSAS
At a Glance

Population:
    2000 census: 2,673,293
    2010 census: 2,915,918
    2011 estimate: 2,937,979

Percent change in population:
    2000–2010: 9.1%
    2010–2011: 0.8%

Percent change in total nonfarm employment:
    2000–2010: 0.2%
    2010–2011: 0.8%

Industry with the largest growth in employment, 2000–2011 (thousands):
    Education and Health Services, 39.5

Industry with the largest decline or smallest growth in employment, 2000–2011 (thousands):
    Manufacturing, -82.1

Civilian labor force:
    2000: 1,260,256
    2010: 1,356,625
    2011: 1,369,853

Unemployment rate and rank among states (lowest to highest):
    2000: 4.2%, 33rd
    2010: 7.9%, 16th
    2011: 8.0%, 25th

Over-the-year change in unemployment rates:
    2010–2011: 0.1%

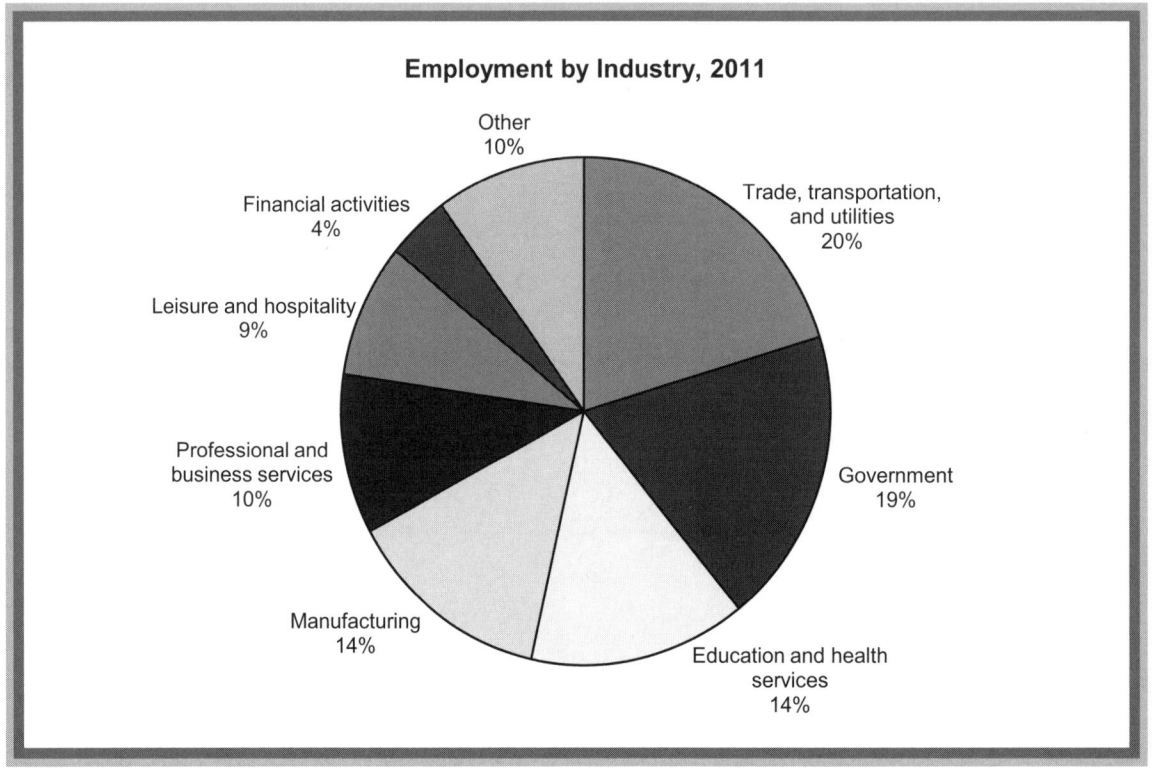

Employment by Industry, 2011

Other 10%

Trade, transportation, and utilities 20%

Financial activities 4%

Leisure and hospitality 9%

Professional and business services 10%

Government 19%

Manufacturing 14%

Education and health services 14%

1. Employment by Industry: Arkansas, Selected Years, 2000–2011

(Numbers in thousands, not seasonally adjusted)

Industry and year	January	February	March	April	May	June	July	August	September	October	November	December	Annual average
Total Nonfarm													
2000	1,135.6	1,143.8	1,158.4	1,158.7	1,166.5	1,168.3	1,148.2	1,156.6	1,168.4	1,168.1	1,167.4	1,163.1	1,158.6
2001	1,139.8	1,147.3	1,157.0	1,160.8	1,162.8	1,161.3	1,143.9	1,151.5	1,159.6	1,155.5	1,154.2	1,151.0	1,153.7
2002	1,125.3	1,132.8	1,144.1	1,148.4	1,155.3	1,155.0	1,138.2	1,143.2	1,157.2	1,151.7	1,151.8	1,152.4	1,146.3
2003	1,128.7	1,133.1	1,140.4	1,142.6	1,149.2	1,146.0	1,131.1	1,141.2	1,155.5	1,159.1	1,156.3	1,158.4	1,145.1
2004	1,135.2	1,142.5	1,152.9	1,157.7	1,162.2	1,161.1	1,146.8	1,155.4	1,169.0	1,168.7	1,172.0	1,173.6	1,158.1
2005	1,151.0	1,162.1	1,173.0	1,178.4	1,182.2	1,180.9	1,165.3	1,172.0	1,192.7	1,189.1	1,193.1	1,194.7	1,177.9
2006	1,178.2	1,186.6	1,198.5	1,203.8	1,206.7	1,205.3	1,184.1	1,193.2	1,208.6	1,205.5	1,205.7	1,207.3	1,198.6
2007	1,184.9	1,193.3	1,207.8	1,207.4	1,211.2	1,209.7	1,188.1	1,200.1	1,213.2	1,211.2	1,213.0	1,214.2	1,204.5
2008	1,190.8	1,200.0	1,207.9	1,207.9	1,212.6	1,208.4	1,189.8	1,198.4	1,211.8	1,205.4	1,200.8	1,195.9	1,202.5
2009	1,166.3	1,169.2	1,174.2	1,174.9	1,171.0	1,164.0	1,150.7	1,153.2	1,165.2	1,162.0	1,163.8	1,162.5	1,164.8
2010	1,134.1	1,137.6	1,154.0	1,162.7	1,173.5	1,175.7	1,156.5	1,160.9	1,170.7	1,169.6	1,170.2	1,171.2	1,161.4
2011	1,144.3	1,146.5	1,160.6	1,176.6	1,170.5	1,164.9	1,146.9	1,151.8	1,161.2	1,164.9	1,167.7	1,164.1	1,160.0
Total Private													
2000	947.1	952.0	964.0	965.3	969.2	977.9	971.9	975.2	977.1	973.6	972.2	968.7	967.9
2001	948.5	951.8	960.5	963.7	966.4	970.3	965.1	969.1	963.8	956.5	954.0	951.2	960.1
2002	930.4	933.8	944.1	949.6	956.8	962.1	957.7	959.7	961.0	952.6	951.3	952.1	950.9
2003	932.0	932.8	939.0	941.7	948.7	950.3	945.8	952.7	954.7	955.4	951.8	954.6	946.6
2004	935.7	939.3	948.9	954.8	959.7	964.4	962.5	964.6	966.1	963.4	965.2	968.0	957.7
2005	950.1	956.1	966.6	970.5	975.6	979.5	976.9	979.4	985.2	980.2	983.7	986.3	974.2
2006	972.6	976.6	987.3	992.0	996.1	1,001.2	992.3	996.2	997.8	993.2	992.1	995.0	991.0
2007	976.8	979.7	993.2	992.9	998.0	1,001.1	994.4	1,000.0	999.3	995.3	996.0	998.1	993.7
2008	979.8	983.6	990.6	990.5	995.0	996.6	992.3	996.0	995.3	986.8	981.4	977.3	988.8
2009	952.1	949.8	953.7	953.4	950.6	949.2	948.1	946.9	948.1	940.2	941.2	940.2	947.8
2010	919.8	919.5	933.0	940.6	946.0	954.8	950.2	953.0	952.5	949.0	948.9	950.5	943.2
2011	929.2	927	939.4	954.8	948.3	948	944.6	942.3	939.1	939.2	941.4	939.5	941.1
Goods-Producing													
2000	297.2	297.7	301.0	300.0	301.3	303.5	302.5	302.4	302.1	299.8	298.1	297.0	300.2
2001	291.1	288.9	290.7	290.0	289.9	290.7	289.0	289.8	287.3	283.7	280.4	279.0	287.5
2002	273.3	273.4	274.6	274.9	276.7	278.9	277.8	277.3	276.7	273.1	270.9	270.1	274.8
2003	265.2	263.5	263.9	263.1	264.0	264.5	263.4	264.6	264.8	264.3	261.3	262.0	263.7
2004	257.8	257.7	259.8	262.3	263.8	265.3	264.7	265.0	264.8	262.5	261.5	260.8	262.2
2005	258.7	259.2	261.3	261.9	264.0	265.2	264.4	265.4	266.7	265.2	265.5	265.6	263.6
2006	262.8	263.7	263.6	265.4	266.3	268.7	266.1	266.9	265.9	262.5	259.2	259.9	264.3
2007	256.2	255.1	258.1	257.5	258.2	258.5	257.1	257.1	256.4	254.6	253.1	253.5	256.3
2008	249.7	249.5	251.2	251.0	252.2	253.2	253.1	253.4	253.1	250.5	246.4	243.8	250.6
2009	235.9	232.5	230.3	227.0	224.9	224.0	224.5	225.2	224.6	220.1	219.1	218.3	225.5
2010	213.5	212.4	216.6	219.0	220.8	224.8	223.5	223.4	222.1	220.2	219.3	219.3	219.6
2011	214.0	213.9	216.5	218.7	217.9	217.5	218	216.9	217.4	215.1	214	212.8	216.1
Mining and Logging													
2000	6.7	6.6	6.6	6.5	6.7	6.9	6.9	7.0	7.0	6.9	6.7	6.8	6.8
2001	6.5	6.6	6.7	6.9	7.1	7.2	7.3	7.3	7.2	7.1	7.0	6.8	7.0
2002	6.5	6.5	6.6	6.6	6.8	6.9	6.9	7.0	7.0	6.9	6.9	6.8	6.8
2003	6.5	6.6	6.6	6.8	7.0	7.1	7.0	7.2	7.2	7.2	7.2	7.2	7.0
2004	7.0	6.9	6.9	6.9	7.0	7.0	7.0	7.2	7.2	7.0	6.8	6.8	7.0
2005	6.5	6.6	6.7	6.9	7.0	7.2	7.2	7.3	7.3	7.2	7.2	7.3	7.0
2006	6.8	6.8	6.9	7.4	7.6	7.8	7.7	7.8	8.1	8.0	8.1	8.2	7.6
2007	8.4	8.7	9.0	9.0	9.3	9.6	9.6	9.9	10.0	9.8	9.8	9.9	9.4
2008	9.9	9.8	10.0	10.2	10.6	10.8	11.0	11.0	11.1	11.3	11.4	11.2	10.7
2009	10.6	10.5	10.5	10.3	10.1	10.2	10.4	10.4	10.3	9.9	10.0	10.0	10.3
2010	9.9	9.8	10.2	10.6	10.8	11.0	10.8	10.9	10.9	10.9	10.9	11.0	10.6
2011	10.6	10.6	10.7	11.0	10.8	11.0	11.0	11.0	11.1	11.0	10.9	10.9	10.9
Construction													
2000	50.3	50.7	53.0	52.5	53.4	54.5	54.1	54.5	55.0	53.9	52.8	52.0	53.1
2001	49.6	49.9	52.2	52.9	54.4	55.3	56.1	56.6	55.7	54.4	53.9	53.3	53.7
2002	51.3	51.7	53.2	54.0	55.2	56.6	57.1	57.1	56.0	54.2	53.0	52.2	54.3
2003	49.3	48.7	49.5	50.1	51.3	51.7	51.9	52.4	52.2	51.9	50.5	50.2	50.8
2004	47.8	47.8	49.7	51.3	52.4	53.3	53.3	53.4	53.3	52.1	51.6	51.2	51.4
2005	50.3	50.9	52.5	53.8	55.3	55.7	56.0	56.5	56.8	55.9	55.9	56.2	54.7
2006	54.0	55.0	54.8	56.6	57.9	58.9	57.8	58.4	59.0	57.3	56.1	56.4	56.9
2007	53.9	53.6	56.4	56.7	57.4	58.0	57.1	57.5	57.2	56.3	56.0	55.5	56.3
2008	53.4	53.8	55.1	55.7	56.6	57.3	57.8	58.5	58.2	57.4	56.0	55.0	56.2
2009	52.1	51.9	51.6	51.0	50.7	51.7	53.2	53.6	53.3	50.5	49.9	49.2	51.6
2010	46.0	45.0	47.3	48.8	49.7	51.3	51.1	50.8	50.0	48.9	47.8	47.5	48.7
2011	43.6	43.6	45.5	47.1	46.8	47.8	49.5	48.4	49.7	48.3	46.8	45.8	46.9
Manufacturing													
2000	240.2	240.4	241.4	241.0	241.2	242.1	241.5	240.9	240.1	239.0	238.6	238.2	240.4
2001	235.0	232.4	231.8	230.2	228.4	228.2	225.6	225.9	224.4	222.2	219.5	218.9	226.9
2002	215.5	215.2	214.8	214.3	214.7	215.4	213.8	213.2	213.7	212.0	211.0	211.1	213.7
2003	209.4	208.2	207.8	206.2	205.7	205.7	204.5	205.0	205.4	205.2	203.6	204.6	205.9
2004	203.0	203.0	203.2	204.1	204.4	205.0	204.4	204.4	204.3	203.4	203.1	202.8	203.8
2005	201.9	201.7	202.1	201.2	201.7	202.3	201.2	201.6	202.6	202.1	202.4	202.1	201.9
2006	202.0	201.9	201.9	201.4	200.8	202.0	200.6	200.7	198.8	197.2	195.0	195.3	199.8
2007	193.9	192.8	192.7	191.8	191.5	190.9	190.4	189.7	189.2	188.5	187.3	188.1	190.6
2008	186.4	185.9	186.1	185.1	185.0	185.1	184.3	183.9	183.8	181.8	179.0	177.6	183.7
2009	173.2	170.1	168.2	165.7	164.1	162.1	160.9	161.2	161.0	159.7	159.2	159.1	163.7
2010	157.6	157.6	159.1	159.6	160.3	162.5	161.6	161.7	161.2	160.4	160.6	160.8	160.3
2011	159.8	159.7	160.3	160.6	160.3	158.7	157.5	157.5	156.6	155.8	156.3	156.1	158.3

1. Employment by Industry: Arkansas, Selected Years, 2000–2011—*Continued*

(Numbers in thousands, not seasonally adjusted)

Industry and year	January	February	March	April	May	June	July	August	September	October	November	December	Annual average
Service-Providing													
2000	838.4	846.1	857.4	858.7	865.2	864.8	845.7	854.2	866.3	868.3	869.3	866.1	858.4
2001	848.7	858.4	866.3	870.8	872.9	870.6	854.9	861.7	872.3	871.8	873.8	872.0	866.2
2002	852.0	859.4	869.5	873.5	878.6	876.1	860.4	865.9	880.5	878.6	880.9	882.3	871.5
2003	863.5	869.6	876.5	879.5	885.2	881.5	867.7	876.6	890.7	894.8	895.0	896.4	881.4
2004	877.4	884.8	893.1	895.4	898.4	895.8	882.1	890.4	904.2	906.2	910.5	912.8	895.9
2005	892.3	902.9	911.7	916.5	918.2	915.7	900.9	906.6	926.0	923.9	927.6	929.1	914.3
2006	915.4	922.9	934.9	938.4	940.4	936.6	918.0	926.3	942.7	943.0	946.5	947.4	934.4
2007	928.7	938.2	949.7	949.9	953.0	951.2	931.0	943.0	956.8	956.6	959.9	960.7	948.2
2008	941.1	950.5	956.7	956.9	960.4	955.2	936.7	945.0	958.7	954.9	954.4	952.1	951.9
2009	930.4	936.7	943.9	947.9	946.1	940.0	926.2	928.0	940.6	941.9	944.7	944.2	939.2
2010	920.6	925.2	937.4	943.7	952.7	950.9	933.0	937.5	948.6	949.4	950.9	951.9	941.8
2011	930.3	932.6	944.1	957.9	952.6	947.4	928.9	934.9	943.8	949.8	953.7	951.3	943.9
Trade, Transportation, and Utilities													
2000	237.8	237.8	239.9	240.5	241.3	243.1	241.3	242.2	242.6	243.5	245.8	247.6	242.0
2001	238.6	237.5	240.4	241.5	242.5	243.2	241.4	241.7	240.9	241.2	243.7	244.6	241.4
2002	236.9	236.9	239.8	240.4	242.0	242.5	241.6	241.4	241.8	240.4	243.0	244.4	240.9
2003	236.2	235.3	236.7	237.3	238.2	238.7	238.5	239.7	240.9	242.4	244.1	246.3	239.5
2004	237.6	237.6	239.3	240.1	241.4	242.2	242.1	242.4	243.2	243.2	245.8	248.7	242.0
2005	241.1	240.6	242.7	244.2	244.9	246.0	245.7	245.4	247.2	246.4	249.7	252.0	245.5
2006	244.8	244.4	247.8	247.3	248.8	248.8	247.7	248.3	249.2	249.6	252.5	254.6	248.7
2007	246.2	245.9	250.3	248.2	250.2	250.8	249.7	250.4	250.4	249.8	253.5	255.2	250.1
2008	247.2	246.4	248.2	247.2	248.3	248.7	247.1	247.2	246.4	244.2	245.9	246.3	246.9
2009	237.3	235.2	236.8	236.3	235.9	235.3	235.4	234.0	234.2	233.3	235.9	237.0	235.6
2010	229.7	228.7	231.6	231.9	233.6	235.7	235.6	236.1	234.8	236.6	239.6	241.4	234.6
2011	233.7	231.3	233.9	238.0	236.2	237.0	235.4	235.4	232.8	232.2	235.4	240.7	235.2
Wholesale Trade													
2000	44.6	44.9	45.6	45.6	45.9	46.7	46.4	46.2	46.2	45.9	45.6	45.6	45.8
2001	45.1	45.3	45.8	45.8	45.9	46.3	46.1	45.9	45.5	45.3	45.0	44.9	45.6
2002	44.2	44.2	44.8	44.9	45.1	45.6	45.3	45.2	45.3	44.9	44.6	44.6	44.9
2003	43.9	44.1	44.4	44.4	44.9	45.4	45.1	45.2	45.4	45.3	45.1	45.2	44.9
2004	44.6	44.8	45.4	46.0	46.5	46.8	46.9	46.5	46.6	46.5	46.6	47.1	46.2
2005	46.5	46.8	47.3	47.5	47.8	48.0	47.8	47.6	47.6	47.2	47.1	47.5	47.4
2006	46.9	47.1	47.5	47.9	48.2	48.5	48.1	48.1	48.2	47.9	47.9	48.2	47.9
2007	47.2	47.4	48.0	48.1	48.3	48.6	48.2	48.1	47.9	48.0	48.0	48.3	48.0
2008	47.8	48.1	48.4	48.6	48.9	49.0	48.9	48.8	48.8	48.4	48.2	48.1	48.5
2009	47.0	47.0	47.2	47.2	47.3	47.2	47.0	46.7	46.3	46.2	46.1	46.1	46.8
2010	45.3	45.4	46.0	46.4	46.6	47.0	46.6	46.4	46.0	46.5	46.3	46.3	46.2
2011	45.5	45.4	45.8	46.8	46.3	46.4	45.6	46.2	45.5	45.8	45.7	45	45.8
Retail Trade													
2000	130.2	130.2	131.2	131.6	132.3	132.9	131.7	132.6	132.5	133.1	135.9	137.4	132.6
2001	130.5	129.0	130.9	131.5	132.4	132.5	130.9	130.8	130.3	130.3	133.5	134.6	131.4
2002	128.6	127.5	129.1	129.7	130.8	130.7	130.1	129.5	129.4	128.8	131.8	133.5	130.0
2003	127.1	126.0	126.8	127.3	127.8	127.9	127.9	128.7	129.3	130.2	132.4	134.6	128.8
2004	128.5	128.1	129.4	129.8	130.5	130.7	130.3	130.6	130.6	131.1	134.0	135.6	130.8
2005	129.9	128.8	130.2	131.3	131.5	132.1	131.6	131.4	131.9	132.2	135.5	136.9	131.9
2006	131.8	130.9	133.5	132.6	133.6	132.9	132.2	132.7	132.6	133.2	136.0	137.5	133.3
2007	132.3	131.4	134.6	132.9	134.2	134.3	134.0	134.1	134.3	133.9	137.7	139.4	134.4
2008	133.7	132.6	133.9	132.8	133.6	134.2	133.4	133.7	132.9	131.6	133.9	135.1	133.5
2009	129.2	128.0	129.6	129.6	130.0	129.7	129.2	129.2	129.3	129.0	131.6	132.7	129.8
2010	126.7	125.6	127.5	127.7	128.9	130.1	129.8	130.1	128.9	130.4	133.5	134.8	129.5
2011	129.4	127.4	129.1	131.4	130.2	130.5	130	129.5	127.1	127.5	131	135.1	129.9
Transportation and Utilities													
2000	63.0	62.7	63.1	63.3	63.1	63.5	63.2	63.4	63.9	64.5	64.3	64.6	63.6
2001	63.0	63.2	63.7	64.2	64.2	64.4	64.4	65.0	65.1	65.6	65.2	65.1	64.4
2002	64.1	65.2	65.9	65.8	66.1	66.2	66.2	66.7	67.1	66.7	66.6	66.3	66.1
2003	65.2	65.2	65.5	65.6	65.5	65.4	65.5	65.8	66.2	66.9	66.6	66.5	65.8
2004	64.5	64.7	64.5	64.3	64.4	64.7	64.9	65.3	66.0	65.6	65.2	66.0	65.0
2005	64.7	65.0	65.2	65.4	65.6	65.9	66.3	66.4	67.7	67.0	67.1	67.6	66.2
2006	66.1	66.4	66.8	66.8	67.0	67.4	67.4	67.5	68.4	68.5	68.6	68.9	67.5
2007	66.7	67.1	67.7	67.2	67.7	67.9	67.5	68.2	68.2	67.9	67.8	67.5	67.6
2008	65.7	65.7	65.9	65.8	65.8	65.5	64.8	64.7	64.7	64.2	63.8	63.1	65.0
2009	61.1	60.2	60.0	59.5	58.6	58.4	59.2	58.1	58.6	58.1	58.2	58.2	59.0
2010	57.7	57.7	58.1	57.8	58.1	58.6	59.2	59.6	59.9	59.7	59.8	60.3	58.9
2011	58.8	58.5	59	59.8	59.7	60.1	59.8	59.7	60.2	58.9	58.7	60.6	59.5
Information													
2000	19.9	19.9	20.1	19.8	20.1	20.4	20.6	21.0	21.1	21.2	21.4	21.5	20.6
2001	21.2	21.2	21.0	20.8	20.8	20.9	21.1	21.1	21.0	20.8	20.9	20.8	21.0
2002	20.8	20.5	20.2	20.2	20.2	20.5	20.4	20.3	20.2	20.2	20.4	20.3	20.4
2003	20.1	20.1	20.1	19.9	20.0	20.2	20.4	20.3	20.1	20.2	20.3	20.3	20.2
2004	20.1	20.0	20.0	19.8	19.8	19.9	19.7	19.7	19.6	19.5	19.7	19.7	19.8
2005	19.6	19.8	19.7	19.4	19.4	19.3	19.2	19.3	19.0	19.0	19.0	19.0	19.3
2006	18.8	18.8	18.8	18.8	18.7	18.6	18.6	18.7	18.6	18.3	18.3	18.3	18.6
2007	18.4	18.4	18.4	18.4	18.4	18.2	18.1	18.1	18.0	17.8	17.8	17.8	18.2
2008	17.6	17.7	17.6	17.8	17.5	17.6	17.5	17.5	17.2	17.0	16.9	16.9	17.4
2009	16.5	16.4	16.4	16.4	16.4	16.5	16.4	16.2	16.0	15.8	15.7	15.7	16.2
2010	15.3	15.4	15.5	15.4	15.5	15.8	15.3	15.2	15.2	15.1	15.1	15.1	15.3
2011	15.0	15.0	14.9	14.9	14.8	14.8	14.6	14.5	14.3	14.3	14.4	14.2	14.6

1. Employment by Industry: Arkansas, Selected Years, 2000–2011—*Continued*

(Numbers in thousands, not seasonally adjusted)

Industry and year	January	February	March	April	May	June	July	August	September	October	November	December	Annual average
Financial Activities													
2000	49.1	49.1	49.4	49.6	49.5	50.1	49.6	49.4	49.2	49.1	49.1	49.4	49.4
2001	48.7	48.9	49.0	49.1	49.4	49.8	49.8	49.7	49.6	49.2	49.4	49.9	49.4
2002	49.4	49.2	49.5	49.5	49.7	50.0	50.0	49.9	49.8	49.3	49.4	49.8	49.6
2003	49.4	49.4	49.6	49.9	50.2	50.7	50.9	50.9	50.7	50.6	50.8	51.3	50.4
2004	50.2	50.3	50.5	50.7	50.9	51.3	51.2	51.1	51.1	50.8	50.9	51.4	50.9
2005	50.8	50.7	50.9	50.7	51.0	51.6	51.8	51.8	51.7	51.8	52.5	51.4
2006	51.8	51.8	52.0	52.2	52.5	52.9	52.9	53.1	53.0	52.7	52.9	53.2	52.6
2007	52.4	52.4	52.6	53.1	53.3	53.7	53.7	53.6	53.4	53.2	53.1	53.3	53.2
2008	52.6	52.6	52.7	52.5	52.7	52.7	52.5	52.5	52.3	51.6	51.5	52.0	52.4
2009	51.0	50.7	50.8	50.8	50.9	51.0	50.5	50.3	50.1	49.7	49.6	49.8	50.4
2010	48.7	48.6	48.5	48.8	48.7	49.1	48.9	48.9	48.7	48.8	48.8	49.1	48.8
2011	48.2	48.0	48.2	48.7	48.3	48.5	47.9	47.3	47.7	48.0	48.1	48.2	48.1
Professional and Business Services													
2000	98.3	99.4	101.4	100.2	100.9	102.4	101.9	103.9	104.2	103.2	102.6	100.5	101.6
2001	100.9	102.4	102.6	102.1	102.4	103.0	102.3	104.0	102.7	100.7	99.6	98.3	101.8
2002	96.4	96.9	99.1	100.4	101.2	102.4	102.3	103.3	104.5	103.7	102.6	102.9	101.3
2003	101.0	101.5	102.0	103.0	104.2	104.4	102.6	105.5	105.7	107.2	105.8	105.3	104.0
2004	105.2	105.2	106.5	107.1	107.1	107.9	109.0	109.7	109.3	110.4	110.7	110.7	108.2
2005	107.1	108.8	110.5	110.6	110.7	111.5	111.8	112.8	113.2	113.1	113.1	113.3	111.4
2006	111.5	112.9	115.1	114.5	114.9	115.6	114.0	114.6	115.6	115.1	114.7	114.6	114.4
2007	114.0	115.1	116.6	116.5	116.8	117.4	116.2	118.8	119.2	118.5	117.8	117.7	117.1
2008	115.0	117.2	117.3	117.0	117.8	117.2	116.4	117.9	118.1	117.9	116.3	115.5	117.0
2009	112.7	113.3	113.5	113.5	112.2	111.7	112.1	112.9	113.2	113.7	114.6	115.1	113.2
2010	113.3	114.0	116.2	117.4	117.1	117.9	117.8	118.4	118.6	118.0	117.3	117.8	117.0
2011	116.2	116.9	118.7	120.9	119.1	119.8	117.9	117.7	116.7	118	116.5	116.1	117.9
Education and Health Services													
2000	125.5	126.9	127.7	127.7	127.0	126.0	124.9	125.4	128.9	129.3	129.6	129.1	127.3
2001	127.8	130.0	130.4	131.0	130.5	129.6	129.3	130.8	132.9	134.0	134.4	134.5	131.3
2002	133.0	133.8	135.0	135.4	135.3	134.1	133.2	134.9	137.4	137.9	138.6	138.7	135.6
2003	137.3	138.6	139.6	139.8	140.0	137.9	136.7	138.4	141.4	142.2	142.0	142.4	139.7
2004	140.1	141.4	142.3	142.7	142.3	141.2	140.2	141.1	143.9	144.9	145.3	145.2	142.6
2005	144.1	145.4	145.8	146.0	146.0	144.1	143.6	144.9	148.1	149.1	148.9	148.6	146.2
2006	148.4	149.7	150.7	151.2	150.9	150.0	148.2	149.8	152.5	152.7	152.8	153.0	150.8
2007	150.8	153.0	153.9	154.2	154.4	153.6	152.2	154.3	156.0	156.3	156.7	157.0	154.4
2008	156.8	157.7	158.5	157.5	157.6	156.3	155.3	156.9	159.3	160.0	160.0	159.7	158.0
2009	158.1	160.2	161.6	163.4	162.6	162.1	161.0	161.6	165.1	165.7	166.0	166.0	162.7
2010	163.7	164.5	165.2	165.3	165.6	164.5	163.6	165.3	168.2	168.2	168.4	168.5	165.9
2011	165.5	165.3	166.7	168.0	166.9	164.4	163.8	164.8	167.6	169.0	170.8	169.2	166.8
Leisure and Hospitality													
2000	78.9	80.6	83.5	86.5	87.8	90.4	89.4	89.4	87.8	86.5	84.8	82.9	85.7
2001	79.7	82.3	85.3	88.3	89.8	91.3	90.7	90.6	88.5	86.4	85.2	83.7	86.8
2002	80.5	82.8	85.2	88.0	90.6	92.0	91.0	91.3	89.6	87.5	85.9	85.3	87.5
2003	82.6	84.3	86.6	88.0	91.0	92.2	92.0	92.1	90.2	87.7	86.7	86.1	88.3
2004	84.2	86.4	89.5	90.8	92.9	94.4	93.8	94.1	92.9	91.1	90.1	90.0	90.9
2005	87.5	90.1	93.5	94.9	96.6	98.3	97.1	96.8	96.2	93.4	93.3	92.7	94.2
2006	92.0	92.7	96.2	99.0	99.8	101.7	99.8	99.7	98.0	97.5	96.7	96.1	97.4
2007	94.0	94.9	97.8	99.7	101.3	102.8	101.8	102.1	100.6	99.9	98.8	98.2	99.3
2008	95.9	97.3	99.5	101.7	102.9	104.4	104.0	104.3	102.7	99.9	99.0	97.5	100.8
2009	95.6	96.5	99.1	100.9	102.6	104.1	103.1	102.1	100.7	98.3	97.0	95.2	99.6
2010	93.0	93.5	96.6	99.7	101.4	103.0	101.9	102.3	101.6	99.0	97.4	96.5	98.8
2011	93.8	94.0	97.3	101.6	101.9	102.3	103.3	101.8	99.0	99.1	98.3	95.4	99.0
Other Services													
2000	40.4	40.6	41.0	41.0	41.3	42.0	41.7	41.5	41.2	41.0	40.8	40.7	41.1
2001	40.5	40.6	41.1	40.9	41.1	41.8	41.5	41.4	40.9	40.5	40.4	40.4	40.9
2002	40.1	40.3	40.7	40.8	41.1	41.7	41.4	41.3	41.0	40.5	40.5	40.6	40.8
2003	40.2	40.1	40.5	40.7	41.1	41.7	41.3	41.2	40.9	40.8	40.8	40.9	40.9
2004	40.5	40.7	41.0	41.3	41.5	42.2	41.8	41.5	41.3	41.0	41.2	41.5	41.3
2005	41.2	41.5	42.2	42.8	43.0	43.5	43.3	43.0	43.0	42.3	42.4	42.6	42.6
2006	42.5	42.6	43.1	43.6	44.2	44.9	45.0	45.1	45.0	44.8	45.0	45.3	44.3
2007	44.8	44.9	45.5	45.3	45.4	46.1	45.6	45.6	45.3	45.2	45.2	45.4	45.4
2008	45.0	45.2	45.6	45.8	46.0	46.5	46.4	46.3	46.2	45.7	45.4	45.6	45.8
2009	45.0	45.0	45.2	45.1	45.0	45.4	45.1	44.6	44.2	43.6	43.3	43.1	44.6
2010	42.6	42.4	42.8	43.1	43.3	44.0	43.6	43.4	43.3	43.1	43.0	42.8	43.1
2011	42.8	42.6	43.2	44.0	43.2	43.7	43.7	43.9	43.6	43.5	43.9	42.9	43.4
Government													
2000	188.5	191.8	194.4	193.4	197.3	190.4	176.3	181.4	191.3	194.5	195.2	194.4	190.7
2001	191.3	195.5	196.5	197.1	196.4	191.0	178.8	182.4	195.8	199.0	200.2	199.8	193.7
2002	194.9	199.0	200.0	198.8	198.5	192.9	180.5	183.5	196.2	199.1	200.5	200.3	195.4
2003	196.7	200.3	201.4	200.9	200.5	195.7	185.3	188.5	200.8	203.7	204.5	203.8	198.5
2004	199.5	203.2	204.0	202.9	202.5	196.7	184.3	190.8	202.9	205.3	206.8	205.6	200.4
2005	200.9	206.0	206.4	207.9	206.6	201.4	188.4	192.6	207.5	208.9	209.4	208.4	203.7
2006	205.6	210.0	211.2	211.8	210.6	204.1	191.8	197.0	210.8	212.3	213.6	212.3	207.6
2007	208.1	213.6	214.6	214.5	213.2	208.6	193.7	200.1	213.9	215.9	217.0	216.1	210.8
2008	211.0	216.4	217.3	217.4	217.6	211.8	197.5	202.4	216.5	218.6	219.4	218.6	213.7
2009	214.2	219.4	220.5	221.5	220.4	214.8	202.6	206.3	217.1	221.8	222.6	222.3	217.0
2010	214.3	218.1	221.0	222.1	227.5	220.9	206.3	207.9	218.2	220.6	221.3	220.7	218.2
2011	215.1	219.5	221.2	221.8	222.2	216.9	202.3	209.5	222.1	225.7	226.3	224.6	218.9

2. Average Weekly Hours by Selected Industry: Arkansas, 2007–2011

(Not seasonally adjusted)

Industry and year	January	February	March	April	May	June	July	August	September	October	November	December	Annual average
Total Private													
2007	33.7	34.2	34.2	35.4	35.5	36.3	35.5	35.3	35.3	34.9	34.9	35.5	35.1
2008	34.8	34.8	35.7	34.8	34.6	36.1	35.0	35.4	35.3	35.1	35.3	34.9	35.2
2009	34.6	35.3	34.0	33.8	34.3	34.7	34.4	35.3	34.3	34.6	35.1	34.8	34.6
2010	34.3	33.6	34.7	34.9	35.2	35.4	35.0	35.5	34.8	35.0	34.7	35.1	34.9
2011	34.1	33.1	35.0	35.0	35.5	35.4	35.3	35.1	35.3	36.0	35.2	35.3	35.0
Goods-Producing													
2007	37.3	39.0	39.5	39.6	40.0	40.8	39.8	40.2	40.7	40.5	39.9	40.8	39.8
2008	38.7	38.3	39.7	38.6	38.9	39.4	38.3	39.3	39.0	39.0	38.4	38.7	38.9
2009	37.6	37.9	36.4	36.1	37.7	38.2	37.3	39.2	37.3	38.4	39.6	39.2	37.9
2010	39.4	37.0	39.6	39.7	39.6	39.9	39.3	39.3	38.8	39.5	39.2	39.4	39.2
2011	36.2	35.3	39.2	38.4	39.0	39.3	39.7	39.4	40.5	40.9	39.8	41.1	39.1
Construction													
2007	36.5	35.5	37.8	37.4	39.2	40.7	37.8	40.2	38.3	39.1	39.0	36.6	38.2
2008	37.6	37.2	38.8	37.5	37.4	38.2	37.9	38.2	38.5	38.5	36.4	36.7	37.8
2009	37.9	36.6	34.7	36.5	36.7	38.5	37.0	38.7	36.9	36.5	38.4	36.5	37.1
2010	38.3	36.3	38.3	39.2	37.2	38.8	37.7	38.0	36.2	37.0	36.2	36.7	37.5
2011	31.0	32.0	37.6	36.0	36.9	38.1	38.0	37.6	38.7	38.4	37.6	38.0	36.7
Manufacturing													
2007	37.3	39.8	39.9	40.1	40.2	40.8	40.3	40.1	41.4	40.6	40.1	42.0	40.2
2008	38.6	38.3	39.6	38.6	39.1	39.5	38.0	39.6	39.0	39.0	38.9	39.2	38.9
2009	37.4	37.8	37.3	35.9	37.5	37.0	36.4	38.3	37.6	39.4	39.2	39.9	37.8
2010	39.3	37.9	39.1	39.0	39.7	39.3	38.8	38.7	38.9	39.1	39.1	39.3	39.0
2011	38.3	36.9	39.4	39.3	39.7	39.7	40.3	40.3	41.1	41.8	40.7	41.9	39.9
Trade, Transportation, and Utilities													
2007	37.4	36.3	36.2	37.0	36.2	37.2	37.1	36.8	37.1	36.6	36.5	37.2	36.8
2008	36.5	36.7	37.3	36.7	35.9	37.2	36.0	35.7	35.8	35.0	36.0	34.5	36.1
2009	35.0	36.4	35.0	35.7	35.5	36.5	36.1	36.6	36.6	36.1	36.1	35.6	35.9
2010	35.7	35.5	36.1	36.5	36.8	37.0	37.2	37.5	36.9	36.8	36.3	37.3	36.6
2011	36.3	35.3	36.6	37.0	37.3	37.5	37.2	36.7	36.3	37.1	35.6	35.1	36.5
Financial Activities													
2007	37.3	36.9	36.7	37.7	37.6	38.7	38.6	37.1	38.8	37.1	37.3	38.9	37.7
2008	38.5	38.6	39.7	37.4	36.8	39.4	37.2	38.0	38.1	38.0	37.9	37.3	38.1
2009	37.9	37.4	37.2	36.8	37.1	37.1	37.0	38.0	37.4	37.8	38.2	37.1	37.4
2010	37.2	37.1	37.4	37.2	38.4	38.2	37.6	37.6	37.3	37.5	37.3	37.2	37.5
2011	38.0	36.4	38.0	37.2	38.0	37.5	37.6	37.8	37.2	38.7	37.4	37.5	37.6
Professional and Business Services													
2007	32.8	37.3	36.9	37.2	36.7	35.4	36.2	36.4	36.2	35.7	35.2	35.2	35.9
2008	34.3	34.8	34.9	35.2	35.2	36.2	35.8	35.6	36.1	35.7	36.6	35.9	35.5
2009	34.9	35.9	34.5	33.7	33.0	33.5	33.0	34.4	32.6	32.0	33.7	34.5	33.8
2010	33.3	33.2	34.2	34.5	34.9	34.1	33.4	35.1	33.2	32.8	33.1	32.7	33.7
2011	32.2	32.3	33.8	34.6	35.9	34.6	34.8	34.9	35.3	35.9	35.6	35.3	34.6
Education and Health Services													
2007	30.0	29.2	29.0	32.6	32.6	33.6	31.4	31.3	31.3	31.2	31.5	31.7	31.3
2008	31.8	31.5	31.9	32.6	32.5	32.5	32.7	31.8	31.4	31.6	32.4	32.0	32.1
2009	32.1	32.7	32.2	32.0	32.3	32.6	32.8	33.0	32.8	32.7	33.0	32.8	32.6
2010	32.2	31.5	32.3	32.5	33.1	33.3	32.5	33.1	32.7	32.4	32.3	32.1	32.5
2011	32.2	31.2	32.4	32.6	32.7	32.6	32.5	32.4	32.2	32.9	32.5	32.6	32.4
Leisure and Hospitality													
2007	24.7	25.4	25.8	26.9	28.6	30.1	29.3	29.1	28.6	28.1	27.3	27.1	27.6
2008	26.2	26.6	26.6	26.7	26.7	28.7	27.4	27.7	26.4	27.0	26.4	26.5	26.9
2009	26.3	27.1	26.5	26.5	27.1	27.3	27.8	27.7	26.2	27.1	25.7	25.7	26.8
2010	24.9	25.9	26.2	26.0	26.7	27.2	27.7	27.3	26.5	26.7	26.3	26.6	26.5
2011	25.7	25.0	26.1	25.6	25.9	26.2	25.9	25.9	25.9	26.3	25.6	25.5	25.8

3. Average Hourly Earnings by Selected Industry: Arkansas, 2007–2011

(Dollars, not seasonally adjusted)

Industry and year	January	February	March	April	May	June	July	August	September	October	November	December	Annual average
Total Private													
2007	15.89	15.96	15.91	16.19	15.94	15.88	16.40	16.31	16.52	16.68	16.62	16.93	16.27
2008	16.88	16.97	17.15	17.01	17.05	17.13	17.29	17.19	17.35	17.38	17.58	17.51	17.21
2009	17.73	17.85	17.91	18.01	18.05	17.82	17.79	17.90	17.99	18.10	18.27	18.28	17.97
2010	18.31	18.43	17.95	18.00	17.93	17.89	18.19	18.02	17.99	17.93	18.16	18.15	18.07
2011	18.58	18.62	18.26	18.21	18.38	18.12	18.16	18.13	18.42	18.54	18.40	18.52	18.36
Goods-Producing													
2007	16.24	15.98	15.92	16.03	16.19	16.47	16.31	16.43	16.85	17.22	17.17	17.12	16.50
2008	17.30	17.29	17.21	17.04	17.11	16.97	17.24	17.25	17.20	17.42	17.48	17.63	17.26
2009	17.47	17.74	17.69	17.54	17.38	17.16	17.10	17.08	17.15	17.15	17.15	17.39	17.33
2010	17.32	17.90	17.30	17.33	17.11	17.21	17.73	17.12	17.26	17.15	17.32	17.59	17.36
2011	18.26	18.39	18.02	18.03	18.28	17.93	17.91	18.09	18.21	18.25	18.29	18.62	18.19
Construction													
2007	16.67	16.55	16.58	16.99	17.04	16.58	17.07	16.77	17.56	17.50	17.72	17.68	17.06
2008	17.89	17.71	17.56	17.63	17.52	17.87	17.93	18.20	18.60	18.44	19.43	19.33	18.17
2009	18.90	19.08	19.20	19.18	19.06	18.32	18.15	18.00	18.11	18.40	18.03	19.01	18.61
2010	18.67	19.17	18.69	18.65	18.34	18.52	20.52	18.31	18.45	18.51	18.81	18.45	18.76
2011	19.30	19.01	18.23	18.08	18.15	17.58	17.69	17.87	18.08	18.56	18.33	18.33	18.23
Manufacturing													
2007	16.08	15.78	15.66	15.66	15.85	16.38	15.92	16.15	16.53	17.11	16.93	16.96	16.25
2008	17.12	17.13	17.08	16.83	16.92	16.59	16.95	16.88	16.56	16.91	16.71	16.86	16.88
2009	16.69	16.71	15.87	15.70	15.77	15.81	15.87	15.99	16.12	16.05	16.39	16.44	16.13
2010	16.45	16.64	16.38	16.43	16.37	16.52	16.67	16.70	16.85	16.65	16.82	16.94	16.62
2011	17.06	17.26	17.14	17.30	17.70	17.55	17.50	17.68	17.78	17.78	17.96	18.44	17.60
Trade, Transportation, and Utilities													
2007	15.35	15.05	15.21	15.60	15.51	15.28	16.52	15.70	16.26	15.65	15.66	16.35	15.68
2008	16.21	16.47	16.60	16.40	15.88	16.20	16.11	16.41	16.83	16.67	16.86	16.70	16.44
2009	16.99	16.98	17.10	17.15	17.20	17.03	17.17	17.44	17.29	17.32	17.59	17.65	17.24
2010	17.81	17.92	17.88	18.19	18.23	18.24	18.56	18.38	18.76	18.79	19.00	18.97	18.40
2011	18.87	18.94	18.79	19.08	19.15	18.83	19.05	18.43	18.83	18.70	18.31	18.66	18.81
Financial Activities													
2007	21.58	21.93	21.66	21.73	20.80	21.18	21.45	21.28	21.13	21.06	20.78	20.79	21.28
2008	21.23	20.95	21.43	21.13	21.00	21.14	21.11	20.43	20.32	20.73	21.46	21.30	21.02
2009	21.67	23.26	22.42	22.73	23.62	23.11	23.06	23.68	23.61	24.32	24.43	23.94	23.32
2010	23.75	23.99	23.68	23.33	23.72	23.66	23.37	23.80	23.40	23.31	23.34	23.45	23.57
2011	23.53	23.26	22.71	22.48	22.19	21.65	21.45	21.59	21.59	23.37	22.60	22.54	22.42
Professional and Business Services													
2007	16.16	16.52	17.53	18.85	18.23	17.96	19.22	18.70	18.99	18.77	19.39	20.31	18.40
2008	19.54	19.19	20.09	19.55	20.99	20.58	20.58	20.56	20.42	20.48	20.86	20.48	20.28
2009	20.23	20.16	20.23	20.28	20.32	20.75	20.65	20.49	20.46	20.27	20.65	20.41	20.41
2010	20.63	20.39	19.92	20.16	20.09	19.98	20.22	19.80	20.03	20.14	19.99	20.32	20.13
2011	20.65	20.78	20.04	19.96	20.72	20.49	20.83	20.80	21.22	21.45	21.95	21.61	20.88
Education and Health Services													
2007	15.61	16.16	15.75	15.84	15.57	15.20	15.96	15.83	15.99	16.10	16.08	16.44	15.87
2008	16.44	16.59	16.26	16.16	16.00	15.97	15.96	15.96	16.17	16.14	16.21	16.25	16.17
2009	16.31	16.16	16.40	16.32	16.44	16.39	16.51	16.66	16.83	17.10	16.91	16.95	16.59
2010	16.92	16.98	16.81	16.68	16.55	16.70	16.64	16.76	16.60	16.61	16.64	16.63	16.71
2011	16.52	16.87	16.88	16.69	16.80	16.99	17.22	17.30	17.40	17.58	17.45	17.51	17.10
Leisure and Hospitality													
2007	9.38	9.59	9.48	9.65	9.56	9.48	9.41	9.35	9.32	9.39	9.25	9.43	9.44
2008	9.26	9.43	9.67	9.49	9.36	9.19	9.31	9.36	9.57	9.79	9.84	9.81	9.50
2009	9.72	9.86	9.87	9.98	10.17	9.86	9.88	10.05	10.05	10.42	10.28	10.37	10.04
2010	10.48	10.51	10.33	10.28	10.19	10.08	10.06	10.21	10.10	10.30	10.21	10.18	10.24
2011	10.33	10.49	10.41	10.32	10.44	10.31	10.28	10.34	10.34	10.65	10.74	10.77	10.45

4. Average Weekly Earnings by Selected Industry: Arkansas, 2007–2011

(Dollars, not seasonally adjusted)

Industry and year	January	February	March	April	May	June	July	August	September	October	November	December	Annual average
Total Private													
2007	535.49	545.83	544.12	573.13	565.87	576.44	582.20	575.74	583.16	582.13	580.04	601.02	570.46
2008	587.42	590.56	612.26	591.95	589.93	618.39	605.15	608.53	612.46	610.04	620.57	611.10	604.90
2009	613.46	630.11	608.94	608.74	619.12	618.35	611.98	631.87	617.06	626.26	641.28	636.14	621.81
2010	628.03	619.25	622.87	628.20	631.14	633.31	636.65	639.71	626.05	627.55	630.15	637.07	630.17
2011	633.58	616.32	639.10	637.35	652.49	641.45	641.05	636.36	650.23	667.44	647.68	653.76	643.21
Goods-Producing													
2007	605.75	623.22	628.84	634.79	647.60	671.98	649.14	660.49	685.80	697.41	685.08	698.50	657.29
2008	669.51	662.21	683.24	657.74	665.58	668.62	660.29	677.93	670.80	679.38	671.23	682.28	670.70
2009	656.87	672.35	643.92	633.19	655.23	655.51	637.83	669.54	639.70	658.56	679.14	681.69	656.87
2010	682.41	662.30	685.08	688.00	677.56	686.68	696.79	672.82	669.69	677.43	678.94	693.05	680.96
2011	661.01	649.17	706.38	692.35	712.92	704.65	711.03	712.75	737.51	746.43	727.94	765.28	710.70
Construction													
2007	608.46	587.53	626.72	635.43	667.97	674.81	645.25	674.15	672.55	684.25	691.08	647.09	651.80
2008	672.66	658.81	681.33	661.13	655.25	682.63	679.55	695.24	716.10	709.94	707.25	709.41	686.03
2009	716.31	698.33	666.24	700.07	699.50	705.32	671.55	696.60	668.26	671.60	692.35	693.87	689.93
2010	715.06	695.87	715.83	731.08	682.25	718.58	773.60	695.78	667.89	684.87	680.92	677.12	703.44
2011	598.30	608.32	685.45	650.88	669.74	669.80	672.22	671.91	699.70	712.70	689.21	696.54	669.76
Manufacturing													
2007	599.78	628.04	624.83	627.97	637.17	668.30	641.58	647.62	684.34	694.67	678.89	712.32	653.49
2008	660.83	656.08	676.37	649.64	661.57	655.31	644.10	668.45	645.84	659.49	650.02	660.91	657.40
2009	624.21	631.64	591.95	563.63	591.38	584.97	577.67	612.42	606.11	632.37	642.49	655.96	609.48
2010	646.49	630.66	640.46	640.77	649.89	649.24	646.80	646.29	655.47	651.02	657.66	665.74	648.48
2011	653.40	636.89	675.32	679.89	702.69	696.74	705.25	712.50	730.76	743.20	730.97	772.64	703.03
Trade, Transportation, and Utilities													
2007	574.09	546.32	550.60	577.20	561.46	568.42	612.89	577.76	603.25	572.79	571.59	608.22	577.14
2008	591.67	604.45	619.18	601.88	570.09	602.64	579.96	585.84	602.51	583.45	606.96	576.15	593.74
2009	594.65	618.07	598.50	612.26	610.60	621.60	619.84	638.30	632.81	625.25	635.00	628.34	619.51
2010	635.82	636.16	645.47	663.94	670.86	674.88	690.43	689.25	692.24	691.47	689.70	707.58	674.38
2011	684.98	668.58	687.71	705.96	714.30	706.13	708.66	676.38	683.53	693.77	651.84	654.97	686.40
Financial Activities													
2007	804.93	809.22	794.92	819.22	782.08	819.67	827.97	789.49	819.84	781.33	775.09	808.73	802.73
2008	817.36	808.67	850.77	790.26	772.80	832.92	785.29	776.34	774.19	787.74	813.33	794.49	800.38
2009	821.29	869.92	834.02	836.46	876.30	857.38	853.22	899.84	883.01	919.30	933.23	888.17	872.24
2010	883.50	890.03	885.63	867.88	910.85	903.81	878.71	894.88	872.82	874.13	870.58	872.34	883.53
2011	894.14	846.66	862.98	836.26	843.22	811.88	806.52	816.10	803.15	904.42	845.24	845.25	843.26
Professional and Business Services													
2007	530.05	616.20	646.86	701.22	669.04	635.78	695.76	680.68	687.44	670.09	682.53	714.91	661.30
2008	670.22	667.81	701.14	688.16	738.85	745.00	736.76	731.94	737.16	731.14	763.48	735.23	720.63
2009	706.03	723.74	697.94	683.44	670.56	695.13	681.45	704.86	667.00	648.64	695.91	704.15	689.90
2010	686.98	676.95	681.26	695.52	701.14	681.32	675.35	694.98	665.00	660.59	661.67	664.46	678.76
2011	664.93	671.19	677.35	690.62	743.85	708.95	724.88	725.92	749.07	770.06	781.42	762.83	722.55
Education and Health Services													
2007	468.30	471.87	456.75	516.38	507.58	510.72	501.14	495.48	500.49	502.32	506.52	521.15	496.69
2008	522.79	522.59	518.69	526.82	520.00	519.03	521.89	507.53	507.74	510.02	525.20	520.00	518.51
2009	523.55	528.43	528.08	522.24	531.01	534.31	541.53	549.78	552.02	559.17	558.03	555.96	540.51
2010	544.82	534.87	542.96	542.10	547.81	556.11	540.80	554.76	542.82	538.16	537.47	533.82	543.04
2011	531.94	526.34	546.91	544.09	549.36	553.87	559.65	560.52	560.28	578.38	567.13	570.83	554.20
Leisure and Hospitality													
2007	231.69	243.59	244.58	259.59	273.42	285.35	275.71	272.09	266.55	263.86	252.53	255.55	260.75
2008	242.61	250.84	257.22	253.38	249.91	263.75	255.09	259.27	252.65	264.33	259.78	259.97	255.79
2009	255.64	267.21	261.56	264.47	275.61	269.18	274.66	278.39	263.31	282.38	264.20	266.51	268.67
2010	260.95	272.21	270.65	267.28	272.07	274.18	278.66	278.73	267.65	275.01	268.52	270.79	271.48
2011	265.48	262.25	271.70	264.19	270.40	270.12	266.25	267.81	267.81	280.10	274.94	274.64	269.63

CALIFORNIA
At a Glance

Population:
  2000 census: 33,871,653
  2010 census: 37,253,956
  2011 estimate: 37,691,912

Percent change in population:
  2000–2010: 10.0%
  2010–2011: 1.2%

Percent change in total nonfarm employment:
  2000–2010: -3.8%
  2010–2011: 0.9%

Industry with the largest growth in employment, 2000–2011 (thousands):
  Education and Health Services, 426.7

Industry with the largest decline or smallest growth in employment, 2000–2011 (thousands):
  Manufacturing, -609.7

Civilian labor force:
  2000: 16,857,578
  2010: 18,316,411
  2011: 18,384,886

Unemployment rate and rank among states (lowest to highest):
  2000: 4.9%, 43rd
  2010: 12.4%, 49th
  2011: 11.7%, 50th

Over-the-year change in unemployment rates:
  2010–2011: -0.7%

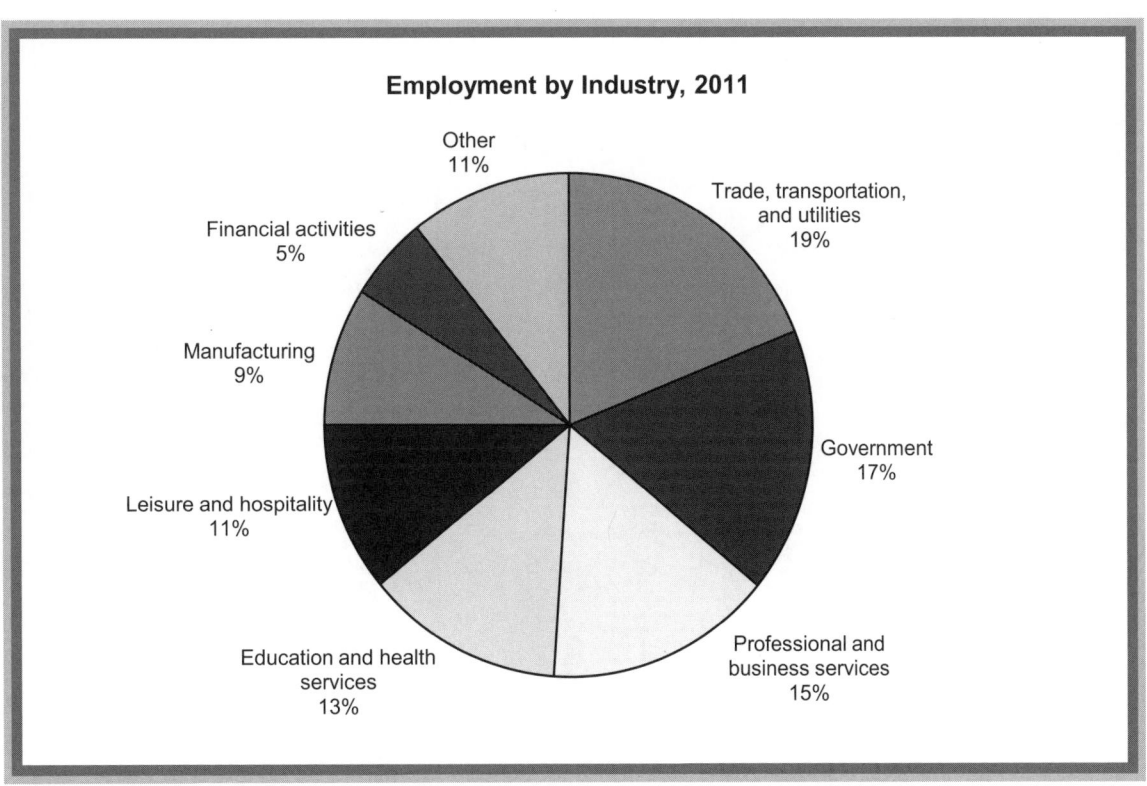

Employment by Industry, 2011

Other 11%
Financial activities 5%
Manufacturing 9%
Leisure and hospitality 11%
Education and health services 13%
Professional and business services 15%
Government 17%
Trade, transportation, and utilities 19%

1. Employment by Industry: California, Selected Years, 2000–2011

(Numbers in thousands, not seasonally adjusted)

Industry and year	January	February	March	April	May	June	July	August	September	October	November	December	Annual average
Total Nonfarm													
2000	14,031.2	14,170.7	14,323.9	14,354.6	14,494.1	14,600.4	14,450.6	14,522.5	14,645.5	14,650.4	14,761.4	14,859.8	14,488.8
2001	14,514.0	14,598.7	14,713.7	14,650.6	14,698.1	14,752.8	14,495.4	14,535.4	14,552.4	14,550.2	14,569.8	14,599.5	14,602.6
2002	14,238.3	14,328.7	14,459.8	14,449.4	14,531.8	14,582.4	14,353.6	14,405.1	14,466.6	14,506.2	14,575.8	14,604.7	14,458.5
2003	14,240.8	14,302.9	14,381.0	14,380.0	14,439.7	14,494.5	14,283.5	14,329.5	14,387.5	14,453.3	14,489.0	14,540.4	14,393.5
2004	14,233.4	14,329.3	14,442.5	14,463.0	14,545.6	14,606.3	14,498.6	14,505.2	14,576.0	14,671.1	14,745.4	14,784.2	14,533.4
2005	14,456.0	14,572.4	14,675.3	14,730.1	14,784.7	14,852.8	14,738.7	14,795.3	14,907.0	14,953.3	15,044.0	15,115.6	14,802.1
2006	14,761.1	14,887.2	14,971.7	14,974.7	15,086.2	15,174.5	15,004.5	15,057.4	15,144.8	15,180.1	15,244.9	15,289.0	15,064.7
2007	14,946.7	15,056.4	15,161.3	15,112.3	15,203.1	15,276.2	15,147.3	15,157.0	15,216.4	15,254.2	15,320.6	15,362.1	15,184.5
2008	14,955.3	15,046.6	15,098.1	15,106.4	15,138.7	15,161.1	14,947.2	14,930.5	14,954.7	14,923.4	14,860.4	14,817.7	14,995.0
2009	14,358.3	14,289.5	14,263.2	14,193.5	14,197.7	14,163.0	13,870.0	13,847.9	13,865.4	13,998.0	14,020.6	14,030.8	14,091.5
2010	13,697.8	13,739.9	13,810.1	13,946.8	14,037.8	14,048.1	13,837.1	13,859.3	13,917.3	14,068.3	14,122.0	14,155.6	13,936.7
2011	13,861.9	13,947.0	14,008.5	14,064.9	14,105.0	14,119.4	13,916.8	13,934.0	14,057.7	14,182.7	14,250.0	14,277.8	14,060.5
Total Private													
2000	11,748.9	11,859.6	11,982.5	12,005.0	12,094.6	12,240.2	12,224.6	12,313.3	12,366.1	12,314.2	12,399.4	12,500.1	12,170.7
2001	12,171.1	12,232.2	12,329.9	12,242.9	12,280.0	12,333.4	12,202.0	12,250.4	12,193.3	12,129.4	12,122.7	12,158.6	12,220.5
2002	11,815.7	11,878.9	11,980.6	11,958.9	12,034.8	12,090.3	11,994.6	12,063.0	12,058.6	12,039.3	12,092.6	12,130.0	12,011.4
2003	11,789.9	11,840.0	11,900.9	11,905.3	11,966.0	12,024.2	11,938.0	12,013.4	12,016.6	12,034.4	12,056.0	12,124.6	11,967.4
2004	11,836.1	11,917.0	12,012.3	12,027.5	12,107.5	12,167.8	12,185.5	12,216.3	12,220.1	12,259.2	12,314.1	12,364.7	12,135.7
2005	12,052.3	12,142.6	12,229.2	12,278.2	12,325.4	12,399.1	12,406.8	12,468.5	12,516.5	12,513.5	12,584.9	12,666.2	12,381.9
2006	12,329.9	12,430.3	12,498.3	12,497.8	12,600.6	12,690.4	12,637.0	12,703.7	12,723.0	12,698.8	12,742.7	12,796.6	12,612.4
2007	12,471.6	12,557.6	12,640.1	12,587.4	12,667.7	12,741.7	12,740.0	12,763.9	12,754.5	12,739.8	12,783.9	12,830.6	12,689.9
2008	12,444.1	12,509.4	12,543.8	12,544.2	12,566.9	12,587.7	12,522.6	12,516.7	12,479.8	12,394.0	12,317.4	12,286.6	12,476.1
2009	11,844.3	11,756.6	11,712.0	11,630.2	11,639.9	11,620.0	11,512.6	11,508.9	11,484.9	11,525.0	11,540.2	11,568.2	11,611.9
2010	11,253.7	11,279.9	11,329.9	11,420.5	11,465.7	11,516.7	11,506.9	11,548.8	11,546.8	11,620.6	11,656.8	11,712.9	11,488.3
2011	11,437.5	11,501.4	11,539.3	11,595.1	11,640.3	11,668.0	11,666.5	11,693.9	11,730.7	11,773.4	11,822.9	11,872.5	11,661.8
Goods-Producing													
2000	2,513.7	2,528.4	2,555.5	2,566.4	2,590.6	2,638.6	2,649.7	2,674.9	2,682.0	2,658.0	2,658.3	2,668.8	2,615.4
2001	2,603.1	2,611.2	2,631.8	2,608.2	2,615.7	2,628.5	2,604.9	2,618.0	2,588.1	2,544.4	2,505.3	2,481.9	2,586.8
2002	2,402.2	2,412.0	2,429.4	2,422.8	2,441.3	2,459.4	2,443.3	2,469.1	2,459.7	2,432.7	2,410.8	2,393.7	2,431.4
2003	2,334.6	2,332.0	2,345.2	2,340.0	2,357.6	2,379.7	2,370.9	2,400.8	2,399.8	2,378.1	2,362.0	2,361.3	2,363.5
2004	2,318.4	2,331.3	2,353.2	2,371.9	2,392.2	2,418.2	2,442.0	2,453.0	2,449.8	2,427.5	2,405.0	2,397.1	2,396.6
2005	2,336.3	2,363.4	2,384.6	2,403.5	2,419.6	2,448.9	2,472.7	2,490.6	2,493.5	2,473.2	2,460.3	2,456.6	2,433.6
2006	2,404.9	2,427.4	2,430.7	2,417.3	2,456.7	2,483.9	2,479.6	2,496.2	2,494.2	2,457.4	2,428.8	2,409.8	2,448.9
2007	2,356.3	2,368.2	2,385.2	2,371.9	2,390.0	2,418.0	2,424.7	2,428.9	2,410.2	2,376.6	2,347.5	2,325.7	2,383.6
2008	2,261.2	2,265.7	2,264.8	2,256.8	2,265.7	2,274.1	2,274.2	2,276.4	2,257.7	2,213.9	2,163.5	2,127.4	2,241.8
2009	2,042.2	1,993.7	1,977.7	1,945.8	1,944.8	1,940.9	1,921.4	1,919.8	1,902.4	1,882.0	1,862.9	1,839.7	1,931.1
2010	1,802.4	1,794.1	1,805.2	1,808.9	1,824.9	1,839.6	1,849.7	1,861.8	1,851.4	1,846.5	1,830.6	1,816.5	1,827.6
2011	1,787.4	1,794.3	1,797.0	1,809.7	1,824.1	1,840.0	1,856.1	1,866.8	1,860.9	1,849.4	1,830.9	1,819.7	1,828.0
Mining and Logging													
2000	24.2	24.0	24.0	25.1	26.7	27.5	27.9	28.3	28.1	27.7	27.3	26.7	26.5
2001	24.6	24.1	24.2	25.1	26.4	26.8	26.4	26.7	26.6	26.2	25.6	24.2	25.6
2002	22.5	22.4	22.1	22.1	23.0	23.6	23.6	23.9	23.9	23.8	23.6	22.7	23.1
2003	20.8	21.0	21.0	21.0	21.8	22.7	23.2	23.2	22.9	23.5	23.0	22.7	22.2
2004	21.5	21.6	21.7	22.2	23.0	23.4	23.4	23.5	23.5	23.8	23.3	22.9	22.8
2005	21.7	21.9	22.0	22.4	23.0	23.8	24.5	24.7	24.8	24.9	24.6	24.3	23.6
2006	23.0	23.4	23.3	23.4	24.8	25.7	26.2	26.6	26.7	26.4	25.9	25.2	25.1
2007	24.6	24.8	24.6	25.3	26.3	27.0	27.7	28.0	28.0	28.2	28.0	27.5	26.7
2008	26.6	27.0	27.0	27.9	28.6	29.2	29.9	30.0	29.9	30.2	29.5	28.7	28.7
2009	27.1	26.5	26.0	25.4	25.5	26.1	26.4	26.3	26.2	26.3	25.8	25.2	26.1
2010	25.0	24.6	25.1	25.4	27.0	27.5	28.1	28.2	28.2	28.1	27.7	27.0	26.8
2011	26.7	27.0	26.9	27.7	28.3	28.9	29.5	29.7	29.7	29.7	29.2	28.3	28.5
Construction													
2000	678.1	678.9	691.4	705.8	721.7	745.2	750.1	762.9	769.8	764.6	765.1	767.5	733.4
2001	738.7	742.9	760.1	766.7	783.0	798.1	800.2	814.7	804.7	797.1	785.0	773.4	780.4
2002	736.1	742.5	753.0	756.6	770.8	783.3	783.4	801.8	798.1	795.9	790.3	780.9	774.4
2003	755.0	752.3	764.9	770.1	788.6	805.9	810.9	827.0	826.6	825.4	819.3	815.7	796.8
2004	792.8	798.3	811.6	830.0	842.5	861.3	875.2	884.1	886.9	884.1	871.5	866.4	850.4
2005	823.8	844.8	862.3	880.4	895.0	915.7	931.5	942.8	947.4	944.2	940.1	935.6	905.3
2006	903.9	916.0	914.6	908.8	940.9	959.0	957.9	966.3	962.7	941.3	923.8	908.8	933.7
2007	874.6	879.9	894.0	890.6	903.5	917.8	918.7	919.8	905.3	886.9	868.9	850.8	892.6
2008	803.3	804.8	803.7	800.3	803.6	805.9	803.2	802.4	788.4	769.6	744.2	723.5	787.7
2009	674.4	647.7	644.1	630.4	632.2	632.3	621.7	619.6	607.6	600.2	594.2	576.2	623.1
2010	550.6	542.7	549.3	553.9	562.2	568.8	572.4	574.8	566.9	566.5	560.4	549.6	559.8
2011	532.7	535.1	534.3	543.8	551.9	560.0	567.3	568.8	568.2	566.5	561.8	554.5	553.7
Manufacturing													
2000	1,811.4	1,825.5	1,840.1	1,835.5	1,842.2	1,865.9	1,871.7	1,883.7	1,884.1	1,865.7	1,865.9	1,874.6	1,855.5
2001	1,839.8	1,844.2	1,847.5	1,816.4	1,806.3	1,803.6	1,778.3	1,776.6	1,756.8	1,721.1	1,694.7	1,684.3	1,780.8
2002	1,643.6	1,647.1	1,654.3	1,644.1	1,647.5	1,652.5	1,636.3	1,643.4	1,637.7	1,613.0	1,596.9	1,590.1	1,633.9
2003	1,558.8	1,558.7	1,559.3	1,548.9	1,547.2	1,551.1	1,536.8	1,550.6	1,550.3	1,529.2	1,519.7	1,522.9	1,544.5
2004	1,504.1	1,511.4	1,519.9	1,519.7	1,526.7	1,533.5	1,543.4	1,545.4	1,539.4	1,519.6	1,510.2	1,507.8	1,523.4
2005	1,490.8	1,496.7	1,500.3	1,500.7	1,501.6	1,509.4	1,516.7	1,523.1	1,521.3	1,504.1	1,495.6	1,496.7	1,504.8
2006	1,478.0	1,488.0	1,492.8	1,485.1	1,491.0	1,499.2	1,495.5	1,503.3	1,504.8	1,489.7	1,479.1	1,475.8	1,490.2
2007	1,457.1	1,463.5	1,466.6	1,456.0	1,460.2	1,473.2	1,478.3	1,481.1	1,476.9	1,461.5	1,450.6	1,447.4	1,464.4
2008	1,431.3	1,433.9	1,434.1	1,428.6	1,433.5	1,439.0	1,441.1	1,444.0	1,439.4	1,414.1	1,389.8	1,375.2	1,425.3
2009	1,340.7	1,322.5	1,307.6	1,290.0	1,287.1	1,282.5	1,273.3	1,273.9	1,268.6	1,255.5	1,242.9	1,238.3	1,281.9
2010	1,226.8	1,226.8	1,230.8	1,229.6	1,235.7	1,243.3	1,249.2	1,258.8	1,256.3	1,251.9	1,242.5	1,239.9	1,241.0
2011	1,228.0	1,232.2	1,235.8	1,238.2	1,243.9	1,251.1	1,259.3	1,268.3	1,263.0	1,253.2	1,239.9	1,236.9	1,245.8

1. Employment by Industry: California, Selected Years, 2000–2011—*Continued*

(Numbers in thousands, not seasonally adjusted)

Industry and year	January	February	March	April	May	June	July	August	September	October	November	December	Annual average
Service-Providing													
2000	11,517.5	11,642.3	11,768.4	11,788.2	11,903.5	11,961.8	11,800.9	11,847.6	11,963.5	11,992.4	12,103.1	12,191.0	11,873.4
2001	11,910.9	11,987.5	12,081.9	12,042.4	12,082.4	12,124.3	11,890.5	11,917.4	11,964.3	12,005.8	12,064.5	12,117.6	12,015.8
2002	11,836.1	11,916.7	12,030.4	12,026.6	12,090.5	12,123.0	11,910.3	11,936.0	12,006.9	12,073.5	12,165.0	12,211.0	12,027.2
2003	11,906.2	11,970.9	12,035.8	12,040.0	12,082.1	12,114.8	11,912.6	11,928.7	11,987.7	12,075.2	12,127.0	12,179.1	12,030.0
2004	11,915.0	11,998.0	12,089.3	12,091.1	12,153.4	12,188.1	12,056.6	12,052.2	12,126.2	12,243.6	12,340.4	12,387.1	12,136.8
2005	12,119.7	12,209.0	12,290.7	12,326.6	12,365.1	12,403.9	12,266.0	12,304.7	12,413.5	12,480.1	12,583.7	12,659.0	12,368.5
2006	12,356.2	12,459.8	12,541.0	12,557.4	12,629.5	12,690.6	12,524.9	12,561.2	12,650.6	12,722.7	12,816.1	12,879.2	12,615.8
2007	12,590.4	12,688.2	12,776.1	12,740.4	12,813.1	12,858.2	12,722.6	12,728.1	12,806.2	12,877.6	12,973.1	13,036.4	12,800.9
2008	12,694.1	12,780.9	12,833.3	12,849.6	12,873.0	12,887.0	12,673.0	12,654.1	12,697.0	12,709.5	12,696.9	12,690.3	12,753.2
2009	12,316.1	12,295.8	12,285.5	12,247.7	12,252.9	12,222.1	11,948.6	11,928.1	11,963.0	12,116.0	12,157.7	12,191.1	12,160.4
2010	11,895.4	11,945.8	12,004.9	12,137.9	12,212.9	12,208.5	11,987.4	11,997.5	12,065.9	12,221.8	12,291.4	12,339.1	12,109.0
2011	12,074.5	12,152.7	12,211.5	12,255.2	12,280.9	12,279.4	12,060.7	12,067.2	12,196.8	12,333.3	12,419.1	12,458.1	12,232.5
Trade, Transportation, and Utilities													
2000	2,671.8	2,665.4	2,676.9	2,672.0	2,690.0	2,717.3	2,719.1	2,730.5	2,737.9	2,746.7	2,807.5	2,866.0	2,725.1
2001	2,753.9	2,732.3	2,743.2	2,727.5	2,733.5	2,752.3	2,733.7	2,736.5	2,736.7	2,732.8	2,770.4	2,807.2	2,746.7
2002	2,695.9	2,678.4	2,692.8	2,689.4	2,705.2	2,724.7	2,710.5	2,717.9	2,726.0	2,728.7	2,780.2	2,828.4	2,723.2
2003	2,698.1	2,681.1	2,684.9	2,679.1	2,692.1	2,708.4	2,693.5	2,702.1	2,712.0	2,746.7	2,776.0	2,821.8	2,716.3
2004	2,700.5	2,690.4	2,705.2	2,707.9	2,727.1	2,746.7	2,744.8	2,749.6	2,755.9	2,786.6	2,846.1	2,881.4	2,753.5
2005	2,776.8	2,759.9	2,766.9	2,768.0	2,782.9	2,796.9	2,807.9	2,820.8	2,835.4	2,849.9	2,909.7	2,964.3	2,820.0
2006	2,830.3	2,815.3	2,828.8	2,828.9	2,849.1	2,869.6	2,870.0	2,884.2	2,893.3	2,905.1	2,970.7	3,013.4	2,879.9
2007	2,902.8	2,878.9	2,886.3	2,872.8	2,890.4	2,901.7	2,917.3	2,921.9	2,923.8	2,935.0	2,999.5	3,044.2	2,922.9
2008	2,907.8	2,881.6	2,877.7	2,862.2	2,865.4	2,866.6	2,855.5	2,848.1	2,839.1	2,829.2	2,847.7	2,859.8	2,861.7
2009	2,722.2	2,677.9	2,655.7	2,629.1	2,636.1	2,631.8	2,609.9	2,608.7	2,614.9	2,625.9	2,669.3	2,699.4	2,648.4
2010	2,599.5	2,578.6	2,577.0	2,589.1	2,602.2	2,609.7	2,611.4	2,621.7	2,620.0	2,643.0	2,697.7	2,732.5	2,623.5
2011	2,632.6	2,615.8	2,614.3	2,627.7	2,641.4	2,647.5	2,656.1	2,665.6	2,673.9	2,679.9	2,736.6	2,763.0	2,662.9
Wholesale Trade													
2000	627.7	633.5	637.9	637.7	641.1	647.6	646.0	648.2	649.8	647.8	648.9	654.4	643.4
2001	654.0	659.9	663.0	659.4	659.0	663.4	657.1	656.4	654.5	653.3	650.1	650.3	656.7
2002	641.9	645.3	649.4	649.3	651.7	654.3	650.6	652.7	652.9	649.8	650.3	651.8	650.0
2003	642.4	644.5	647.7	648.7	650.6	653.1	647.1	648.9	648.7	645.8	644.3	646.9	647.4
2004	639.5	643.0	646.3	648.4	651.9	657.2	655.9	656.0	655.9	659.7	660.8	661.6	653.0
2005	658.0	660.6	664.3	669.7	673.0	675.7	676.5	677.8	679.5	681.5	682.2	684.7	673.6
2006	681.4	688.0	692.2	695.0	699.1	704.9	704.2	705.7	708.3	706.6	707.4	710.2	700.3
2007	702.5	706.9	711.5	710.5	714.1	716.9	719.7	718.8	719.0	720.8	720.2	722.4	715.3
2008	710.6	711.8	713.7	710.4	710.0	709.1	705.4	703.1	699.5	696.0	688.9	684.0	703.5
2009	665.6	660.5	654.6	649.3	648.1	646.9	640.7	637.3	634.8	637.1	634.9	634.2	645.3
2010	629.8	631.1	632.8	641.8	645.3	647.2	648.4	649.1	648.6	650.8	651.1	651.9	644.0
2011	645.7	648.7	649.2	655.8	658.8	659.8	663.4	665.2	664.9	665.1	665.4	665.4	659
Retail Trade													
2000	1,534.4	1,522.4	1,527.5	1,520.4	1,533.0	1,549.4	1,551.9	1,560.1	1,565.8	1,577.1	1,635.8	1,683.5	1,563.4
2001	1,582.5	1,558.7	1,562.8	1,550.7	1,556.8	1,570.1	1,560.5	1,564.0	1,566.9	1,566.0	1,616.3	1,655.7	1,575.9
2002	1,568.2	1,545.6	1,558.0	1,551.9	1,561.8	1,575.8	1,567.1	1,570.8	1,579.3	1,585.7	1,637.9	1,684.2	1,582.2
2003	1,577.0	1,558.5	1,558.7	1,553.4	1,561.7	1,572.3	1,566.8	1,573.7	1,579.7	1,615.9	1,648.8	1,693.7	1,588.4
2004	1,589.5	1,575.6	1,584.0	1,584.3	1,597.1	1,607.9	1,604.7	1,609.3	1,611.3	1,631.1	1,689.9	1,728.3	1,617.8
2005	1,638.6	1,618.0	1,622.0	1,615.6	1,624.5	1,634.8	1,643.5	1,654.7	1,664.1	1,676.5	1,735.0	1,783.8	1,659.3
2006	1,664.1	1,641.7	1,648.1	1,646.5	1,656.8	1,666.7	1,670.0	1,680.3	1,681.8	1,696.0	1,758.5	1,792.4	1,683.6
2007	1,702.5	1,673.6	1,677.8	1,662.4	1,672.2	1,677.7	1,686.7	1,693.0	1,689.4	1,699.7	1,763.7	1,800.0	1,699.9
2008	1,695.6	1,663.1	1,661.3	1,649.1	1,646.5	1,648.6	1,645.4	1,639.4	1,631.2	1,629.5	1,657.7	1,672.2	1,653.3
2009	1,571.4	1,537.1	1,522.8	1,506.4	1,512.8	1,510.3	1,500.1	1,502.2	1,507.3	1,516.8	1,564.3	1,591.6	1,528.6
2010	1,509.2	1,487.6	1,485.1	1,488.2	1,493.8	1,496.9	1,497.3	1,504.4	1,501.2	1,520.2	1,573.8	1,601.8	1,513.3
2011	1,523.0	1,503.1	1,500.0	1,504.6	1,511.0	1,515.7	1,521.1	1,527.3	1,533.3	1,538.0	1,592.4	1,614.4	1,532.0
Transportation and Utilities													
2000	509.7	509.5	511.5	513.9	515.9	520.3	521.2	522.2	522.3	521.8	522.8	528.1	518.3
2001	517.4	513.7	517.4	517.4	517.7	518.8	516.1	516.1	515.3	513.5	504.0	501.2	514.1
2002	485.8	487.5	485.4	488.2	491.7	494.6	492.8	494.4	493.8	493.2	492.0	492.4	491.0
2003	478.7	478.1	478.5	477.0	479.8	483.0	479.6	479.5	483.6	485.0	482.9	481.2	480.6
2004	471.5	471.8	474.9	475.2	478.1	481.6	484.2	484.3	488.7	495.8	495.4	491.5	482.8
2005	480.2	481.3	480.6	482.7	485.4	486.4	487.9	488.3	491.8	491.9	492.5	495.8	487.1
2006	484.8	485.6	488.5	487.4	493.2	498.0	495.8	498.2	503.2	502.5	504.8	510.8	496.1
2007	497.8	498.4	497.0	499.9	504.1	507.1	510.9	510.1	515.4	514.5	515.6	521.8	507.7
2008	501.6	506.7	502.7	502.7	508.9	508.9	504.7	505.6	508.4	503.7	501.1	503.6	504.9
2009	485.2	480.3	478.3	473.4	475.2	474.6	469.1	469.2	472.8	472.0	470.1	473.6	474.5
2010	460.5	459.9	459.1	459.1	463.1	465.6	465.7	468.2	470.2	472.0	472.8	478.8	466.3
2011	463.9	464.0	465.1	467.3	471.6	472.0	471.6	473.1	475.7	476.8	478.8	483.2	471.9
Information													
2000	537.8	550.5	560.5	562.9	572.8	580.2	580.3	590.4	588.2	592.7	603.0	601.0	576.7
2001	587.3	588.8	590.2	571.4	557.8	554.8	537.6	534.7	529.4	524.2	523.7	522.8	551.9
2002	510.2	511.4	519.9	502.6	502.3	501.6	484.6	490.5	481.4	487.8	495.8	479.4	497.3
2003	480.3	487.1	481.7	470.7	475.2	467.9	467.1	478.4	466.3	476.9	483.7	477.8	476.1
2004	485.6	490.7	487.8	477.6	483.5	474.0	478.8	479.4	470.6	483.4	492.5	484.3	482.4
2005	473.1	477.0	480.7	470.3	469.9	470.3	466.9	473.2	472.5	471.4	480.2	477.9	473.6
2006	468.2	476.3	475.5	467.7	468.6	470.7	464.8	464.9	459.4	456.0	456.5	463.4	466.0
2007	463.3	471.2	473.5	464.6	470.1	473.5	471.4	475.7	474.4	464.1	470.3	477.9	470.8
2008	459.2	469.4	477.7	477.1	482.2	485.8	478.3	479.2	481.0	474.0	470.8	471.5	475.5
2009	450.2	451.3	453.5	442.0	440.0	442.0	437.1	436.6	437.0	427.8	430.3	437.1	440.4
2010	424.5	424.6	427.6	419.6	421.2	427.8	428.2	432.5	432.3	426.5	430.6	437.5	427.7
2011	429.4	429.7	431.1	428.2	428.1	430.0	431.1	432.7	430.7	432.4	437.8	447.1	432.4

1. Employment by Industry: California, Selected Years, 2000–2011—*Continued*

(Numbers in thousands, not seasonally adjusted)

Industry and year	January	February	March	April	May	June	July	August	September	October	November	December	Annual average
Financial Activities													
2000	790.9	796.4	800.4	794.4	797.7	804.7	799.0	803.6	802.9	802.4	803.7	813.4	800.8
2001	812.2	820.2	827.8	825.4	828.5	834.8	828.4	832.1	830.8	834.7	837.6	844.3	829.7
2002	828.8	834.4	837.7	838.7	842.4	847.4	846.2	851.5	851.8	853.9	860.2	867.6	846.7
2003	859.1	864.3	869.3	874.6	880.5	884.9	883.3	887.5	886.0	883.8	883.9	888.3	878.8
2004	879.9	883.5	887.9	889.4	892.0	895.1	900.3	901.7	900.2	900.7	903.2	908.2	895.2
2005	901.7	905.8	910.7	911.8	915.2	919.1	923.6	927.0	927.9	930.6	931.4	938.3	920.3
2006	926.9	929.7	932.8	931.9	935.7	934.9	928.3	927.9	925.2	920.4	918.7	921.1	927.8
2007	906.4	912.6	914.3	905.5	904.6	904.0	899.5	895.9	886.6	879.7	875.5	874.7	896.6
2008	856.5	857.5	855.9	849.2	847.6	845.8	843.4	840.0	832.8	828.1	822.9	822.2	841.8
2009	805.8	802.1	798.9	791.3	786.7	784.9	778.5	774.3	766.8	770.4	767.6	768.6	783.0
2010	756.6	757.7	759.3	758.8	758.7	761.1	760.9	760.8	758.9	762.7	761.1	765.3	760.2
2011	758.2	760.1	761.0	758.5	759.4	761.4	761.7	758.9	759.4	765.4	764.6	768.8	761.5
Professional and Business Services													
2000	2,110.2	2,140.8	2,172.1	2,194.4	2,204.2	2,241.4	2,238.1	2,265.1	2,273.0	2,264.8	2,274.5	2,292.1	2,222.6
2001	2,203.8	2,217.0	2,234.6	2,203.7	2,207.2	2,213.3	2,178.8	2,184.5	2,168.4	2,150.3	2,139.4	2,145.4	2,187.2
2002	2,096.1	2,109.3	2,132.2	2,114.9	2,117.7	2,125.5	2,112.2	2,127.5	2,123.7	2,120.8	2,127.8	2,130.8	2,119.9
2003	2,065.3	2,078.8	2,096.6	2,091.5	2,089.7	2,097.0	2,075.4	2,090.0	2,085.9	2,080.6	2,082.4	2,090.8	2,085.3
2004	2,033.8	2,055.6	2,079.0	2,079.0	2,086.7	2,102.6	2,102.8	2,116.0	2,112.9	2,126.4	2,133.8	2,145.8	2,097.9
2005	2,095.9	2,122.6	2,138.1	2,143.8	2,140.5	2,157.5	2,162.9	2,179.5	2,189.8	2,188.1	2,198.1	2,211.0	2,160.7
2006	2,165.5	2,193.2	2,210.1	2,216.2	2,226.2	2,251.8	2,248.8	2,268.0	2,273.7	2,280.9	2,284.7	2,290.5	2,242.5
2007	2,213.6	2,241.3	2,257.0	2,244.7	2,252.1	2,270.3	2,267.5	2,277.6	2,277.1	2,292.4	2,293.9	2,297.7	2,265.4
2008	2,226.4	2,248.1	2,253.9	2,256.5	2,248.0	2,254.6	2,246.3	2,251.7	2,243.2	2,230.7	2,207.9	2,193.6	2,238.4
2009	2,111.4	2,095.3	2,079.2	2,058.5	2,048.0	2,045.1	2,032.0	2,037.8	2,027.8	2,059.3	2,064.1	2,064.8	2,060.3
2010	2,003.3	2,024.6	2,034.2	2,057.7	2,058.0	2,076.7	2,080.3	2,093.2	2,089.0	2,125.0	2,124.2	2,126.3	2,074.4
2011	2,072.1	2,095.9	2,104.1	2,109.7	2,111.0	2,120.9	2,117.0	2,127.5	2,148.0	2,163.3	2,161.9	2,183.8	2,126.3
Education and Health Services													
2000	1,384.1	1,409.1	1,419.0	1,408.1	1,410.5	1,401.0	1,380.9	1,383.0	1,420.4	1,420.3	1,427.1	1,419.4	1,406.9
2001	1,412.7	1,437.0	1,450.8	1,448.0	1,457.1	1,447.8	1,420.6	1,441.0	1,460.4	1,480.4	1,493.1	1,498.3	1,453.9
2002	1,471.7	1,497.9	1,509.2	1,502.3	1,510.5	1,497.3	1,480.4	1,483.1	1,506.3	1,524.8	1,537.1	1,538.8	1,505.0
2003	1,509.0	1,530.8	1,541.2	1,554.2	1,557.3	1,547.0	1,520.5	1,519.6	1,543.5	1,557.3	1,564.4	1,571.1	1,543.0
2004	1,542.6	1,565.1	1,576.5	1,572.0	1,571.8	1,561.6	1,539.4	1,538.5	1,562.9	1,586.2	1,592.3	1,593.6	1,566.9
2005	1,564.2	1,587.0	1,594.9	1,602.9	1,603.9	1,590.5	1,563.0	1,563.8	1,593.5	1,612.7	1,621.5	1,621.2	1,593.3
2006	1,590.1	1,616.3	1,626.1	1,625.4	1,627.5	1,616.7	1,590.1	1,594.5	1,624.6	1,641.9	1,649.7	1,652.4	1,621.3
2007	1,633.9	1,665.5	1,679.8	1,672.6	1,679.9	1,666.9	1,651.7	1,653.6	1,685.1	1,707.4	1,718.0	1,721.9	1,678.0
2008	1,697.6	1,730.2	1,735.7	1,747.5	1,746.4	1,730.5	1,697.9	1,702.4	1,730.2	1,750.4	1,758.0	1,768.2	1,732.9
2009	1,735.1	1,756.8	1,764.0	1,767.5	1,769.2	1,753.1	1,723.4	1,726.5	1,750.9	1,783.3	1,787.5	1,796.9	1,759.5
2010	1,751.4	1,772.2	1,782.4	1,804.9	1,803.0	1,784.6	1,754.4	1,757.4	1,786.1	1,811.1	1,820.1	1,832.5	1,788.3
2011	1,800.9	1,829.2	1,838.7	1,843.7	1,841.1	1,820.2	1,798.4	1,799.4	1,827.5	1,857.9	1,873.5	1,873.1	1,833.6
Leisure and Hospitality													
2000	1,267.1	1,289.6	1,311.7	1,320.3	1,339.6	1,361.6	1,368.3	1,375.2	1,368.3	1,340.9	1,336.4	1,347.6	1,335.6
2001	1,313.8	1,333.9	1,352.8	1,360.7	1,378.0	1,394.5	1,396.9	1,401.4	1,377.3	1,361.3	1,352.7	1,358.1	1,365.1
2002	1,318.3	1,335.5	1,355.6	1,382.3	1,403.3	1,419.2	1,410.0	1,417.2	1,402.9	1,384.1	1,375.0	1,385.6	1,382.4
2003	1,345.9	1,362.7	1,376.5	1,388.7	1,404.4	1,425.8	1,425.3	1,432.5	1,418.7	1,406.9	1,401.8	1,411.7	1,400.1
2004	1,380.9	1,400.7	1,418.0	1,425.4	1,447.2	1,460.7	1,471.1	1,474.1	1,461.4	1,443.3	1,438.5	1,450.5	1,439.4
2005	1,408.5	1,424.5	1,446.1	1,468.6	1,483.0	1,502.3	1,504.9	1,509.6	1,497.4	1,483.1	1,480.9	1,492.9	1,475.2
2006	1,451.1	1,472.8	1,491.8	1,506.5	1,526.6	1,548.3	1,548.4	1,556.2	1,540.4	1,526.8	1,523.6	1,535.9	1,519.0
2007	1,496.8	1,514.2	1,534.7	1,548.1	1,569.4	1,590.5	1,593.5	1,595.5	1,580.0	1,567.2	1,562.8	1,571.7	1,560.4
2008	1,529.7	1,545.4	1,563.1	1,578.5	1,593.0	1,609.9	1,611.7	1,607.5	1,585.8	1,559.2	1,543.7	1,544.1	1,572.6
2009	1,489.9	1,491.5	1,494.2	1,504.2	1,522.3	1,529.4	1,526.5	1,522.7	1,504.9	1,491.8	1,476.9	1,482.3	1,503.1
2010	1,440.8	1,450.0	1,462.9	1,497.1	1,510.0	1,526.9	1,533.9	1,536.0	1,523.2	1,515.8	1,505.0	1,517.1	1,501.6
2011	1,476.9	1,491.1	1,506.6	1,526.6	1,541.8	1,554.7	1,557.7	1,559.3	1,545.0	1,537.0	1,532.2	1,534.2	1,530.3
Other Services													
2000	473.3	479.4	486.4	486.5	489.2	495.4	489.2	490.6	493.4	488.4	488.9	491.8	487.7
2001	484.3	491.8	498.7	498.0	502.2	507.4	501.1	502.2	502.2	501.3	500.5	500.6	499.2
2002	492.5	500.0	503.8	505.9	512.1	515.2	507.4	506.2	506.8	506.5	505.7	505.7	505.7
2003	497.6	503.2	505.5	506.5	509.2	513.5	502.0	502.5	504.4	504.1	501.8	501.8	504.3
2004	494.4	499.7	504.7	504.3	507.0	508.9	506.3	504.0	506.4	504.1	502.7	503.8	503.9
2005	495.8	502.4	507.2	509.3	510.4	513.6	504.9	504.0	506.5	504.5	502.8	504.0	505.5
2006	492.9	499.3	502.5	503.9	510.2	514.5	507.0	511.8	512.2	510.3	510.0	510.1	507.1
2007	498.5	505.7	509.3	507.2	511.2	516.8	514.4	514.8	517.3	517.4	516.4	516.8	512.2
2008	505.7	511.5	515.0	516.4	518.6	520.4	515.3	511.4	510.0	508.5	502.9	499.8	511.3
2009	487.5	488.0	488.8	491.8	492.8	492.8	483.8	482.5	480.2	484.5	481.6	479.4	486.1
2010	475.2	478.1	481.3	484.4	487.7	490.3	488.1	485.4	485.9	490.0	487.5	485.2	484.9
2011	480.0	485.3	486.5	491.0	493.4	493.3	488.4	483.7	485.3	488.1	485.4	482.8	486.9
Government													
2000	2,282.3	2,311.1	2,341.4	2,349.6	2,399.5	2,360.2	2,226.0	2,209.2	2,279.4	2,336.2	2,362.0	2,359.7	2,318.1
2001	2,342.9	2,366.5	2,383.8	2,407.7	2,418.1	2,419.4	2,293.4	2,285.0	2,359.1	2,420.8	2,447.1	2,440.9	2,382.1
2002	2,422.6	2,449.8	2,479.2	2,490.5	2,497.0	2,492.1	2,359.0	2,342.1	2,408.0	2,466.9	2,483.2	2,474.7	2,447.1
2003	2,450.9	2,462.9	2,480.1	2,474.7	2,473.7	2,470.3	2,345.5	2,316.1	2,370.9	2,418.9	2,433.0	2,415.8	2,426.1
2004	2,397.3	2,412.3	2,430.2	2,435.5	2,438.1	2,438.5	2,313.1	2,288.9	2,355.9	2,411.9	2,431.3	2,419.5	2,397.7
2005	2,403.7	2,429.8	2,446.1	2,451.9	2,459.3	2,453.7	2,331.9	2,326.8	2,390.5	2,439.8	2,459.1	2,449.4	2,420.2
2006	2,431.2	2,456.9	2,473.4	2,476.9	2,485.6	2,484.1	2,367.5	2,353.7	2,421.8	2,481.3	2,502.2	2,492.4	2,452.3
2007	2,475.1	2,498.8	2,521.2	2,524.9	2,535.4	2,534.5	2,407.3	2,393.1	2,461.9	2,514.4	2,536.7	2,531.5	2,494.6
2008	2,511.2	2,537.2	2,554.3	2,562.2	2,571.8	2,573.4	2,424.6	2,413.8	2,474.9	2,529.4	2,543.0	2,531.1	2,518.9
2009	2,514.0	2,532.9	2,551.2	2,563.3	2,557.8	2,543.0	2,357.4	2,339.0	2,380.5	2,473.0	2,480.4	2,462.6	2,479.6
2010	2,444.1	2,460.0	2,480.2	2,526.3	2,572.1	2,531.4	2,330.2	2,310.5	2,370.5	2,447.7	2,465.2	2,442.7	2,448.4
2011	2,424.4	2,445.6	2,469.2	2,469.8	2,464.7	2,451.4	2,250.3	2,240.1	2,327.0	2,409.3	2,427.1	2,405.3	2,398.7

2. Average Weekly Hours by Selected Industry: California, 2007–2011

(Not seasonally adjusted)

Industry and year	January	February	March	April	May	June	July	August	September	October	November	December	Annual average
Total Private													
2007	33.9	34.1	34.3	34.7	34.4	34.6	35.2	34.8	35.2	34.3	34.2	34.7	34.5
2008	33.4	33.7	34.5	33.9	34.1	34.9	34.1	34.4	34.3	34.3	34.8	34.1	34.2
2009	33.8	34.2	34.2	33.7	33.7	33.5	33.6	34.1	33.3	33.8	34.3	33.6	33.8
2010	33.5	33.6	33.6	33.7	34.6	33.9	34.0	34.9	33.9	34.1	33.9	34.2	34.0
2011	34.6	34.1	34.1	34.1	34.9	34.1	34.3	34.5	34.3	35.1	34.2	34.3	34.4
Goods-Producing													
2007	36.8	37.0	37.9	37.9	38.4	37.9	37.8	37.9	38.1	37.6	37.3	37.0	37.6
2008	35.9	36.6	37.4	37.4	37.3	37.8	37.5	37.8	38.0	37.9	37.7	38.0	37.4
2009	37.2	36.2	36.9	36.5	37.1	37.4	37.5	37.4	36.4	36.8	37.5	37.6	37.0
2010	37.1	37.2	37.7	37.7	38.2	37.9	37.9	38.7	37.5	38.5	38.8	39.0	38.0
2011	39.0	38.6	38.5	38.5	39.1	38.9	38.7	39.0	38.8	39.1	38.4	38.4	38.8
Construction													
2007	34.6	35.1	35.9	35.9	37.0	35.4	35.3	35.3	35.5	35.1	34.8	34.5	35.4
2008	33.1	33.8	35.2	35.4	35.5	36.0	35.7	36.2	35.8	35.7	34.7	35.9	35.2
2009	35.5	33.3	35.5	34.2	35.2	35.6	36.1	36.1	34.6	35.0	35.6	35.2	35.2
2010	35.3	34.1	35.4	33.9	34.9	35.3	35.8	36.4	34.6	35.4	34.7	35.0	35.1
2011	34.7	34.6	34.5	35.1	35.7	35.6	35.5	35.9	35.4	35.8	34.6	35.1	35.2
Manufacturing													
2007	38.2	38.3	39.2	39.3	39.4	39.6	39.4	39.5	39.7	39.2	38.9	39.0	39.1
2008	37.9	38.6	39.0	38.8	38.6	39.0	38.7	38.8	39.2	39.0	39.2	39.0	38.8
2009	38.0	37.6	37.5	37.5	37.9	38.2	37.0	37.8	37.4	37.8	38.5	39.0	37.8
2010	38.2	38.2	38.4	38.5	38.9	38.6	38.4	39.4	38.5	39.4	39.4	39.7	38.8
2011	39.7	39.2	39.2	39.1	39.7	39.5	38.8	39.1	39.1	39.5	39.2	39.1	39.3
Trade, Transportation, and Utilities													
2007	35.1	35.1	35.3	35.8	35.3	35.7	36.3	35.9	36.3	35.3	35.0	36.0	35.6
2008	34.6	34.5	35.3	34.6	35.4	36.0	35.3	35.6	35.3	35.2	35.3	34.9	35.2
2009	34.6	34.9	34.9	34.7	34.8	34.1	34.3	33.4	33.4	35.1	33.8	33.7	34.3
2010	33.3	33.3	33.4	33.6	34.4	34.0	34.1	34.9	34.3	34.3	34.0	34.7	34.0
2011	34.5	34.0	34.5	34.8	35.3	34.8	34.9	35.1	35.0	35.6	34.6	35.1	34.9
Information													
2007	33.8	34.2	34.5	35.5	34.0	35.3	36.7	36.2	36.5	36.3	36.2	35.5	35.4
2008	34.3	34.3	35.9	35.3	35.2	35.8	35.3	35.4	35.6	35.8	36.1	36.1	35.4
2009	35.2	36.4	35.4	34.9	35.0	35.6	35.6	36.3	35.7	36.1	36.7	35.8	35.7
2010	35.5	35.5	35.6	36.0	36.5	36.6	36.9	37.0	36.4	36.8	36.8	37.2	36.4
2011	37.0	36.5	36.9	36.8	37.8	36.3	36.7	36.6	37.1	38.6	37.4	37.4	37.1
Financial Activities													
2007	35.9	36.0	35.7	37.2	36.2	37.2	38.5	37.4	38.3	36.9	36.8	38.0	37.0
2008	36.4	36.5	37.9	36.5	36.4	37.9	36.4	36.9	36.3	36.6	37.9	36.1	36.8
2009	36.1	37.4	37.2	36.2	36.1	36.3	36.7	37.9	36.6	36.7	38.0	36.5	36.8
2010	36.6	36.9	36.2	36.4	38.1	36.6	36.2	37.9	36.1	36.4	36.2	36.3	36.7
2011	37.2	36.0	35.7	36.0	37.1	36.5	36.7	36.3	36.8	38.1	36.7	36.5	36.6
Professional and Business Services													
2007	35.7	36.4	36.3	36.3	36.0	36.3	36.9	36.4	37.0	35.9	35.9	36.0	36.3
2008	34.6	35.1	36.1	35.3	35.3	36.2	35.2	35.7	35.7	36.0	36.9	35.7	35.6
2009	35.4	36.2	36.0	35.5	35.2	34.3	33.8	35.2	34.6	34.7	36.1	34.9	35.2
2010	35.1	35.2	35.4	35.5	36.5	35.5	35.5	36.6	35.2	35.7	35.3	35.6	35.6
2011	36.4	35.7	35.6	36.0	36.9	36.1	35.9	36.2	36.1	37.0	36.0	35.8	36.1
Education and Health Services													
2007	32.1	32.1	32.1	32.9	32.5	32.3	33.4	32.9	33.5	32.7	32.8	33.8	32.8
2008	32.5	32.7	33.4	32.7	32.9	33.6	33.1	33.0	33.1	33.1	34.0	33.2	33.1
2009	33.2	34.0	34.0	33.3	33.4	33.3	33.4	34.1	33.1	33.2	34.2	33.9	33.6
2010	33.8	33.6	33.4	33.5	34.3	33.4	33.3	34.1	33.6	33.4	33.3	33.5	33.6
2011	34.0	33.6	33.5	32.4	33.3	31.5	32.9	32.7	32.9	33.5	33.0	33.2	33.0
Leisure and Hospitality													
2007	26.1	26.2	26.2	27.0	26.4	26.7	27.5	26.8	27.1	26.2	26.2	27.0	26.6
2008	25.8	26.2	27.0	26.3	26.3	27.3	26.4	26.7	26.2	26.2	26.6	25.7	26.4
2009	25.5	26.3	26.1	25.6	25.5	25.8	26.0	27.5	26.2	26.1	27.0	25.9	26.1
2010	25.6	26.2	26.0	26.1	27.0	26.2	26.5	27.4	26.1	26.1	25.9	25.9	26.3
2011	26.6	26.6	26.4	26.5	27.2	26.5	26.6	26.7	26.0	26.9	26.0	26.1	26.5
Other Services													
2007	30.9	30.5	30.9	31.5	30.5	31.0	31.6	30.8	31.5	31.2	30.0	31.0	31.0
2008	29.7	29.9	30.9	30.6	30.4	31.9	30.5	31.1	31.0	30.8	31.3	30.2	30.7
2009	30.6	30.6	31.0	30.9	30.6	30.7	31.2	31.7	30.3	29.7	30.5	29.3	30.6
2010	30.7	30.6	30.5	30.5	31.9	31.1	31.4	32.2	31.2	31.0	30.8	30.3	31.0
2011	32.5	31.5	31.4	31.7	32.2	32.3	32.3	32.5	31.7	32.6	31.1	31.3	31.9

3. Average Hourly Earnings by Selected Industry: California, 2007–2011

(Dollars, not seasonally adjusted)

Industry and year	January	February	March	April	May	June	July	August	September	October	November	December	Annual average
Total Private													
2007	25.02	24.74	24.83	24.92	24.67	24.64	24.78	24.45	24.70	24.42	24.50	24.44	24.68
2008	24.19	24.16	24.48	24.60	24.55	24.64	24.66	24.62	24.79	24.87	25.22	25.54	24.69
2009	25.40	25.40	25.59	25.42	25.18	25.28	25.20	25.47	25.52	25.68	25.76	25.68	25.47
2010	26.43	26.27	26.24	26.40	26.41	26.21	26.30	26.35	26.30	26.37	26.54	26.69	26.38
2011	26.88	27.08	27.16	27.02	27.17	26.67	26.88	26.63	26.80	27.01	26.88	26.84	26.92
Goods-Producing													
2007	25.23	24.68	24.67	24.98	24.95	25.09	25.28	25.29	25.54	25.58	25.71	25.50	25.21
2008	25.03	24.65	24.99	25.12	25.40	25.79	26.05	26.19	26.45	26.64	27.33	28.64	26.02
2009	27.87	27.70	28.32	28.03	27.88	28.04	27.56	28.03	27.77	27.83	28.03	28.25	27.94
2010	27.90	27.03	27.41	28.19	28.58	28.35	28.47	28.60	28.69	28.65	28.71	28.91	28.30
2011	28.52	28.16	28.30	28.44	28.25	28.03	28.41	28.39	28.45	28.54	28.59	28.92	28.42
Construction													
2007	26.73	25.07	24.94	25.07	24.98	25.72	26.07	26.35	26.77	27.13	27.40	27.00	26.08
2008	24.83	25.01	25.21	25.40	25.70	26.44	26.07	26.67	26.20	26.75	28.26	30.25	26.37
2009	26.95	25.28	26.67	26.42	26.62	27.15	27.52	28.03	28.68	28.82	28.70	29.12	27.47
2010	28.77	26.61	26.94	26.82	26.90	27.42	27.92	28.27	28.46	28.61	29.00	29.40	27.94
2011	27.59	26.21	26.69	26.80	26.90	27.33	27.68	28.30	28.63	28.67	28.88	29.73	27.80
Manufacturing													
2007	24.32	24.38	24.43	24.85	24.85	24.66	24.76	24.64	24.75	24.65	24.72	24.75	24.65
2008	24.85	24.80	25.12	25.02	25.20	25.38	25.23	25.13	25.25	25.40	25.84	26.23	25.28
2009	26.97	26.70	27.08	26.71	26.72	26.55	26.68	26.64	26.68	26.76	27.16	27.37	26.84
2010	27.03	26.49	26.60	26.62	27.10	26.88	26.90	27.03	27.28	27.26	27.31	27.47	27.00
2011	27.07	26.72	26.96	27.28	27.14	26.80	27.02	26.92	27.03	27.27	27.40	27.56	27.10
Trade, Transportation, and Utilities													
2007	20.41	20.08	20.24	20.37	20.51	20.27	20.43	20.13	20.35	20.11	19.98	20.15	20.25
2008	20.05	20.17	20.60	20.46	20.31	20.40	20.24	20.29	20.40	20.58	20.70	20.49	20.39
2009	20.84	21.15	20.90	20.91	20.77	20.72	20.79	21.04	21.21	22.08	21.97	21.48	21.15
2010	24.27	24.39	24.08	23.97	24.07	23.66	23.55	23.32	23.19	23.23	23.15	22.99	23.64
2011	23.10	23.20	24.23	23.97	23.65	23.22	23.09	22.65	22.63	22.69	22.46	22.02	23.07
Information													
2007	35.64	34.63	35.63	35.38	34.19	34.25	35.08	34.52	35.34	34.75	35.36	35.45	35.02
2008	35.30	35.45	35.23	34.77	34.95	34.75	34.59	34.82	34.94	33.79	34.22	34.46	34.77
2009	34.40	33.38	33.38	34.04	34.54	34.37	33.77	33.37	33.75	34.04	32.80	33.27	33.75
2010	35.00	35.49	35.89	35.79	36.40	36.42	36.40	36.70	36.65	36.55	36.98	37.16	36.30
2011	39.05	40.09	39.73	39.80	40.34	39.64	40.23	40.49	40.33	40.58	42.02	40.95	40.28
Financial Activities													
2007	38.75	37.85	37.58	37.50	35.59	34.99	34.69	33.87	33.42	31.92	32.49	32.50	35.09
2008	31.87	32.03	31.50	31.51	30.98	31.12	30.86	30.30	30.22	30.16	29.88	29.93	30.87
2009	31.02	30.84	30.44	30.14	30.21	29.80	30.53	30.94	31.13	30.75	30.93	30.94	30.64
2010	31.13	29.89	30.08	30.09	30.82	30.26	30.86	30.46	30.15	30.14	30.22	30.58	30.39
2011	31.14	31.17	30.59	30.25	30.66	29.78	29.71	30.04	30.16	30.37	30.12	29.89	30.32
Professional and Business Services													
2007	30.19	30.06	30.38	30.41	30.21	30.31	30.40	29.59	30.14	29.76	29.54	29.50	30.04
2008	28.84	28.74	29.80	30.63	30.62	30.66	30.76	30.12	30.49	30.56	31.31	31.67	30.35
2009	30.95	31.00	32.19	31.67	30.79	31.46	31.78	32.00	31.91	31.66	31.83	31.62	31.57
2010	32.18	32.34	32.14	32.47	32.22	32.10	32.39	32.69	32.41	32.47	32.89	33.16	32.46
2011	33.86	34.81	34.35	34.23	34.86	34.07	34.36	33.80	33.93	34.42	33.80	33.90	34.20
Education and Health Services													
2007	24.53	24.54	24.55	24.44	24.31	24.52	24.76	24.63	24.73	24.68	25.01	25.02	24.65
2008	25.05	25.09	25.02	24.90	24.96	24.95	25.04	25.49	25.44	25.38	25.53	25.65	25.21
2009	25.60	25.65	25.35	25.46	25.28	25.35	25.08	25.30	25.49	25.53	25.47	25.39	25.41
2010	25.19	25.38	25.26	25.51	25.12	25.15	25.29	25.37	25.60	25.62	25.93	26.25	25.47
2011	26.03	26.22	26.14	25.85	26.32	25.82	26.56	26.05	26.41	26.71	26.87	27.26	26.36
Leisure and Hospitality													
2007	13.80	13.65	13.59	13.97	13.90	13.80	13.78	13.74	13.84	13.72	13.83	13.99	13.80
2008	14.15	14.05	14.11	14.31	14.20	14.09	14.08	14.08	14.06	14.16	14.28	14.57	14.18
2009	14.48	14.35	14.27	14.22	14.30	14.28	14.24	14.19	14.23	14.29	14.47	14.74	14.34
2010	14.83	14.81	14.75	14.64	14.68	14.51	14.42	14.46	14.63	14.60	14.81	14.97	14.67
2011	14.90	15.00	14.91	14.76	14.89	14.72	14.71	14.71	14.79	14.76	14.61	14.65	14.78
Other Services													
2007	18.23	18.41	18.53	18.89	18.73	18.55	19.06	18.78	19.07	19.02	19.35	19.20	18.82
2008	19.20	19.11	19.05	18.94	18.83	19.18	19.29	19.24	19.33	19.60	20.01	20.36	19.34
2009	20.36	20.64	20.89	20.94	20.90	20.87	20.50	20.84	20.86	21.16	21.41	22.07	20.95
2010	21.42	21.32	20.98	20.79	19.99	19.76	19.81	20.21	19.90	20.19	20.44	20.66	20.45
2011	21.20	21.04	20.95	21.10	21.44	20.85	20.79	20.83	21.11	21.23	20.96	20.84	21.03

4. Average Weekly Earnings by Selected Industry: California, 2007–2011

(Dollars, not seasonally adjusted)

Industry and year	January	February	March	April	May	June	July	August	September	October	November	December	Annual average
Total Private													
2007	848.18	843.63	851.67	864.72	848.65	852.54	872.26	850.86	869.44	837.61	837.90	848.07	851.88
2008	807.95	814.19	844.56	833.94	837.16	859.94	840.91	846.93	850.30	853.04	877.66	870.91	844.71
2009	858.52	868.68	875.18	856.65	848.57	846.88	846.72	868.53	849.82	867.98	883.57	862.85	861.05
2010	885.41	882.67	881.66	889.68	913.79	888.52	894.20	919.62	891.57	899.22	899.71	912.80	896.82
2011	930.05	923.43	926.16	921.38	948.23	909.45	921.98	918.74	919.24	948.05	919.30	920.61	925.86
Goods-Producing													
2007	928.46	913.16	934.99	946.74	958.08	950.91	955.58	958.49	973.07	961.81	958.98	943.50	948.73
2008	898.58	902.19	934.63	939.49	947.42	974.86	976.88	989.98	1,005.10	1,009.66	1,030.34	1,088.32	973.95
2009	1,036.76	1,002.74	1,045.01	1,023.10	1,034.35	1,048.70	1,033.50	1,048.32	1,010.83	1,024.14	1,051.13	1,062.20	1,034.91
2010	1,035.09	1,005.52	1,033.36	1,062.76	1,091.76	1,074.47	1,079.01	1,106.82	1,075.88	1,103.03	1,113.95	1,127.49	1,076.00
2011	1,112.28	1,086.98	1,089.55	1,094.94	1,104.58	1,090.37	1,099.47	1,107.21	1,103.86	1,115.91	1,097.86	1,110.53	1,101.15
Construction													
2007	924.86	879.96	895.35	900.01	924.26	910.49	920.27	930.16	950.34	952.26	953.52	931.50	922.70
2008	821.87	845.34	887.39	899.16	912.35	951.84	930.70	965.45	937.96	954.98	980.62	1,085.98	929.42
2009	956.73	841.82	946.79	903.56	937.02	966.54	993.47	1,011.88	992.33	1,008.70	1,021.72	1,025.02	965.75
2010	1,015.58	907.40	953.68	909.20	938.81	967.93	999.54	1,029.03	984.72	1,012.79	1,006.30	1,029.00	979.77
2011	957.37	906.87	920.81	940.68	960.33	972.95	982.64	1,015.97	1,013.50	1,026.39	999.25	1,043.52	979.14
Manufacturing													
2007	929.02	933.75	957.66	976.61	979.09	976.54	975.54	973.28	982.58	966.28	961.61	965.25	964.81
2008	941.82	957.28	979.68	970.78	972.72	989.82	976.40	975.04	989.80	990.60	1,012.93	1,022.97	981.43
2009	1,024.86	1,003.92	1,015.50	1,001.63	1,012.69	1,014.21	987.16	1,006.99	997.83	1,011.53	1,045.66	1,067.43	1,015.61
2010	1,032.55	1,011.92	1,021.44	1,024.87	1,054.19	1,037.57	1,032.96	1,064.98	1,050.28	1,074.04	1,076.01	1,090.56	1,047.72
2011	1,074.68	1,047.42	1,056.83	1,066.65	1,077.46	1,058.60	1,048.38	1,052.57	1,056.87	1,077.17	1,074.08	1,077.60	1,063.97
Trade, Transportation, and Utilities													
2007	716.39	704.81	714.47	729.25	724.00	723.64	741.61	722.67	738.71	709.88	699.30	725.40	720.82
2008	693.73	695.87	727.18	707.92	718.97	734.40	714.47	722.32	720.12	724.42	730.71	715.10	717.04
2009	721.06	738.14	729.41	725.58	722.80	706.55	713.10	702.74	708.41	775.01	742.59	723.88	725.83
2010	808.19	812.19	804.27	805.39	828.01	804.44	803.06	813.87	795.42	796.79	787.10	797.75	804.60
2011	796.95	788.80	835.94	834.16	834.85	808.06	805.84	795.02	792.05	807.76	777.12	772.90	803.88
Information													
2007	1,204.63	1,184.35	1,229.24	1,255.99	1,162.46	1,209.03	1,287.44	1,249.62	1,289.91	1,261.43	1,280.03	1,258.48	1,239.44
2008	1,210.79	1,215.94	1,264.76	1,227.38	1,230.24	1,244.05	1,221.03	1,232.63	1,243.86	1,209.68	1,235.34	1,244.01	1,231.75
2009	1,210.88	1,215.03	1,181.65	1,188.00	1,208.90	1,223.57	1,202.21	1,211.33	1,204.88	1,228.84	1,203.76	1,191.07	1,205.79
2010	1,242.50	1,259.90	1,277.68	1,288.44	1,328.60	1,332.97	1,343.16	1,357.90	1,334.06	1,345.04	1,360.86	1,382.35	1,321.47
2011	1,444.85	1,463.29	1,466.04	1,464.64	1,524.85	1,438.93	1,476.44	1,481.93	1,496.24	1,566.39	1,571.55	1,531.53	1,494.14
Financial Activities													
2007	1,391.13	1,362.60	1,341.61	1,395.00	1,288.36	1,301.63	1,335.57	1,266.74	1,279.99	1,177.85	1,195.63	1,235.00	1,298.47
2008	1,160.07	1,169.10	1,193.85	1,150.12	1,127.67	1,179.45	1,123.30	1,118.07	1,096.99	1,103.86	1,132.45	1,080.47	1,136.67
2009	1,119.82	1,153.42	1,132.37	1,091.07	1,090.58	1,081.74	1,120.45	1,172.63	1,139.36	1,128.53	1,175.34	1,129.31	1,127.74
2010	1,139.36	1,102.94	1,088.90	1,095.28	1,174.24	1,107.52	1,117.13	1,154.43	1,088.42	1,097.10	1,093.96	1,110.05	1,114.12
2011	1,158.41	1,122.12	1,092.06	1,089.00	1,137.49	1,086.97	1,090.36	1,090.45	1,109.89	1,157.10	1,105.40	1,090.99	1,110.86
Professional and Business Services													
2007	1,077.78	1,094.18	1,102.79	1,103.88	1,087.56	1,100.25	1,121.76	1,077.08	1,115.18	1,068.38	1,060.49	1,062.00	1,089.21
2008	997.86	1,008.77	1,075.78	1,081.24	1,080.89	1,109.89	1,082.75	1,075.28	1,088.49	1,100.16	1,155.34	1,130.62	1,082.11
2009	1,095.63	1,122.20	1,158.84	1,124.29	1,083.81	1,079.08	1,074.16	1,126.40	1,104.09	1,098.60	1,149.06	1,103.54	1,110.06
2010	1,129.52	1,138.37	1,137.76	1,152.69	1,176.03	1,139.55	1,149.85	1,196.45	1,140.83	1,159.18	1,161.02	1,180.50	1,155.35
2011	1,232.50	1,242.72	1,222.86	1,232.28	1,286.33	1,229.93	1,233.52	1,223.56	1,224.87	1,273.54	1,216.80	1,213.62	1,236.00
Education and Health Services													
2007	787.41	787.73	788.06	804.08	790.08	792.00	826.98	810.33	828.46	807.04	820.33	845.68	807.49
2008	814.13	820.44	835.67	814.23	821.18	838.32	828.82	841.17	842.06	840.08	868.02	851.58	834.73
2009	849.92	872.10	861.90	847.82	844.35	844.16	837.67	862.73	843.72	847.60	871.07	860.72	853.70
2010	851.42	852.77	843.68	854.59	861.62	840.01	842.16	865.12	860.16	855.71	863.47	879.38	855.93
2011	885.02	880.99	875.69	837.54	876.46	813.33	873.82	851.84	868.89	894.79	886.71	905.03	870.97
Leisure and Hospitality													
2007	360.18	357.63	356.06	377.19	366.96	368.46	378.95	368.23	375.06	359.46	362.35	377.73	367.45
2008	365.01	368.11	380.97	376.35	373.46	384.66	371.71	375.94	368.37	370.99	379.85	374.45	374.19
2009	369.24	377.41	372.45	364.03	364.65	368.42	370.24	390.23	372.83	372.97	390.69	381.77	374.53
2010	379.65	388.02	383.50	382.10	396.36	380.16	382.13	396.20	381.84	381.06	383.58	387.72	385.21
2011	396.34	399.00	393.62	391.14	405.01	390.08	391.29	392.76	384.54	397.04	379.86	382.37	391.88
Other Services													
2007	563.31	561.51	572.58	595.04	571.27	575.05	602.30	578.42	600.71	593.42	580.50	595.20	582.53
2008	570.24	571.39	588.65	579.56	572.43	611.84	588.35	598.36	599.23	603.68	626.31	614.87	593.66
2009	623.02	631.58	647.59	647.05	639.54	640.71	639.60	660.63	632.06	628.45	653.01	646.65	640.85
2010	657.59	652.39	639.89	634.10	637.68	614.54	622.03	650.76	620.88	625.89	629.55	626.00	634.19
2011	689.00	662.76	657.83	668.87	690.37	673.46	671.52	676.98	669.19	692.10	651.86	652.29	671.41

COLORADO
At a Glance

Population:
  2000 census: 4,302,086
  2010 census: 5,029,196
  2011 estimate: 5,116,796

Percent change in population:
  2000–2010: 16.9%
  2010–2011: 1.7%

Percent change in total nonfarm employment:
  2000–2010: 0.4%
  2010–2011: 1.5%

Industry with the largest growth in employment, 2000–2011 (thousands):
  Education and Health Services, 80.1

Industry with the largest decline or smallest growth in employment, 2000–2011 (thousands):
  Manufacturing, -59.9

Civilian labor force:
  2000: 2,364,990
  2010: 2,725,202
  2011: 2,723,027

Unemployment rate and rank among states (lowest to highest):
  2000: 2.7%, 3rd
  2010: 8.9%, 29th
  2011: 8.3%, 28th

Over-the-year change in unemployment rates:
  2010–2011: -0.6%

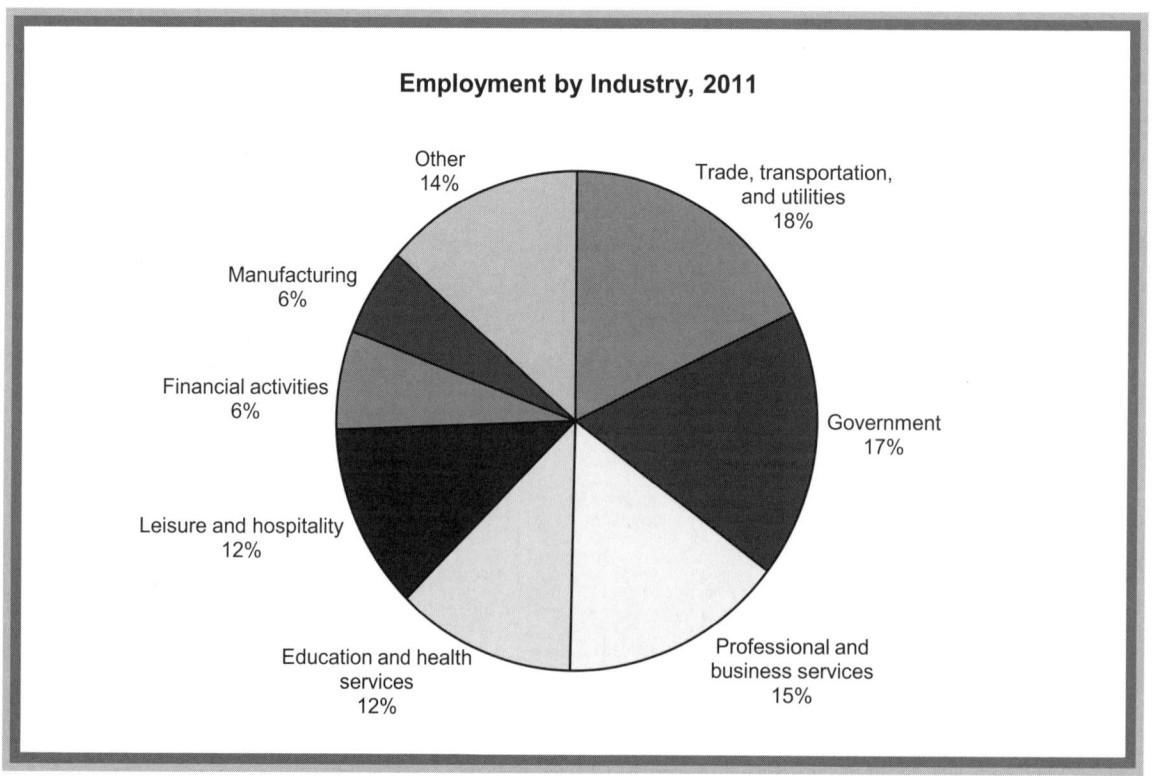

Employment by Industry, 2011

Other 14%
Trade, transportation, and utilities 18%
Manufacturing 6%
Financial activities 6%
Leisure and hospitality 12%
Education and health services 12%
Professional and business services 15%
Government 17%

1. Employment by Industry: Colorado, Selected Years, 2000–2011

(Numbers in thousands, not seasonally adjusted)

Industry and year	January	February	March	April	May	June	July	August	September	October	November	December	Annual average
Total Nonfarm													
2000	2,134.4	2,156.2	2,181.4	2,188.0	2,202.3	2,234.0	2,227.4	2,239.1	2,239.6	2,237.5	2,251.4	2,274.6	2,213.8
2001	2,210.5	2,222.7	2,236.5	2,230.5	2,232.1	2,261.9	2,240.1	2,240.2	2,225.5	2,206.4	2,203.7	2,212.1	2,226.9
2002	2,148.8	2,159.6	2,172.9	2,181.8	2,191.1	2,214.2	2,193.6	2,199.7	2,189.0	2,178.8	2,183.0	2,197.7	2,184.2
2003	2,131.3	2,135.4	2,139.3	2,138.4	2,147.2	2,169.2	2,156.1	2,163.8	2,158.1	2,159.4	2,158.0	2,177.4	2,152.8
2004	2,123.5	2,132.9	2,151.7	2,168.0	2,174.1	2,201.8	2,190.0	2,196.3	2,197.2	2,195.9	2,199.6	2,224.4	2,179.6
2005	2,163.5	2,181.9	2,199.1	2,207.3	2,215.8	2,244.7	2,238.4	2,241.5	2,247.8	2,244.0	2,251.3	2,276.6	2,226.0
2006	2,220.1	2,235.1	2,254.9	2,259.9	2,274.4	2,307.5	2,286.3	2,294.1	2,295.1	2,293.2	2,302.9	2,325.8	2,279.1
2007	2,262.6	2,280.5	2,306.3	2,313.1	2,327.7	2,358.3	2,342.0	2,350.4	2,352.2	2,350.5	2,359.1	2,372.9	2,331.3
2008	2,314.6	2,331.0	2,343.6	2,349.0	2,359.8	2,379.0	2,363.3	2,369.4	2,361.0	2,351.9	2,341.0	2,340.5	2,350.3
2009	2,271.2	2,261.8	2,257.9	2,248.1	2,250.8	2,258.7	2,238.1	2,235.4	2,232.0	2,231.3	2,227.1	2,234.8	2,245.6
2010	2,174.8	2,188.6	2,201.2	2,211.7	2,225.6	2,241.0	2,231.6	2,234.2	2,228.7	2,236.6	2,238.4	2,254.7	2,222.3
2011	2,202.9	2,213.4	2,229.1	2,246.6	2,251.3	2,273.4	2,264.1	2,272.3	2,272.6	2,276.4	2,276.6	2,285.1	2,255.3
Total Private													
2000	1,810.6	1,820.8	1,840.7	1,846.5	1,853.2	1,896.4	1,906.2	1,916.5	1,901.8	1,893.6	1,906.1	1,929.3	1,876.8
2001	1,878.4	1,878.6	1,891.5	1,885.2	1,883.5	1,917.8	1,911.9	1,910.0	1,878.0	1,853.0	1,847.9	1,857.0	1,882.7
2002	1,804.7	1,804.7	1,814.7	1,823.6	1,828.8	1,858.5	1,854.9	1,859.2	1,832.5	1,814.0	1,817.1	1,833.0	1,828.8
2003	1,780.8	1,774.9	1,776.8	1,778.0	1,781.0	1,813.4	1,818.1	1,825.1	1,801.9	1,797.0	1,795.7	1,816.8	1,796.6
2004	1,773.9	1,773.5	1,789.5	1,804.4	1,807.8	1,842.7	1,851.4	1,855.0	1,836.8	1,828.9	1,831.8	1,857.9	1,821.1
2005	1,810.7	1,817.2	1,833.2	1,839.8	1,845.1	1,881.7	1,893.2	1,896.4	1,882.8	1,873.1	1,880.6	1,906.9	1,863.4
2006	1,863.3	1,866.7	1,883.3	1,889.1	1,899.9	1,939.4	1,937.5	1,942.7	1,925.3	1,918.0	1,926.9	1,950.5	1,911.9
2007	1,902.3	1,905.8	1,928.3	1,934.6	1,945.7	1,983.7	1,986.5	1,991.1	1,972.7	1,966.4	1,973.5	1,988.9	1,956.6
2008	1,943.9	1,947.7	1,957.3	1,962.1	1,967.2	1,997.0	1,998.7	1,999.5	1,972.5	1,956.4	1,945.0	1,947.2	1,966.2
2009	1,888.7	1,869.7	1,863.2	1,851.5	1,849.3	1,868.8	1,869.0	1,864.4	1,839.5	1,831.2	1,827.9	1,837.9	1,855.1
2010	1,792.4	1,792.6	1,801.4	1,811.6	1,814.0	1,846.5	1,857.1	1,860.2	1,835.8	1,836.3	1,837.0	1,856.2	1,828.4
2011	1,819.5	1,817.5	1,830.7	1,846.2	1,848.0	1,881.1	1,892.6	1,900.0	1,877.6	1,875.4	1,875.3	1,886.8	1,862.6
Goods-Producing													
2000	345.8	349.0	354.8	357.0	363.6	372.0	373.6	374.9	373.2	372.8	369.9	369.5	364.7
2001	356.8	356.6	360.4	360.7	365.0	370.5	369.2	367.9	362.6	356.7	350.5	344.1	360.1
2002	330.2	329.3	332.8	336.5	342.3	346.7	346.0	345.8	340.0	336.8	331.9	327.1	337.1
2003	314.4	311.6	311.0	313.1	317.8	323.3	323.2	323.0	319.2	319.4	315.4	312.6	317.0
2004	303.3	302.2	306.8	312.8	316.8	323.9	326.3	326.5	324.5	324.9	322.0	319.7	317.5
2005	309.5	312.1	316.4	319.4	324.2	332.6	337.4	338.7	337.0	335.9	335.0	333.3	327.6
2006	325.1	326.2	330.7	333.4	339.3	347.0	346.1	346.4	343.9	342.1	338.7	336.6	338.0
2007	323.1	323.6	330.5	334.2	341.5	349.2	350.2	350.2	346.3	347.0	344.4	338.8	339.9
2008	328.0	327.8	330.2	332.5	338.4	344.1	343.5	343.2	338.4	335.9	329.7	320.4	334.3
2009	302.6	295.5	291.6	286.5	286.7	288.6	287.1	284.4	280.2	277.6	273.6	267.2	285.1
2010	256.4	254.9	256.3	260.6	264.1	269.9	272.0	271.4	269.5	270.5	268.2	266.3	265.0
2011	256.1	254.9	258.8	264.9	267.4	273.7	275.2	278.7	277.5	275.7	273.2	270.6	268.9
Mining and Logging													
2000	11.9	11.9	12.0	12.0	12.2	12.3	12.5	12.5	12.5	12.3	12.2	12.2	12.2
2001	11.9	12.1	12.4	12.5	12.8	13.2	13.5	13.4	13.4	13.3	13.4	13.3	12.9
2002	12.9	12.8	12.9	12.8	12.9	13.1	13.2	13.1	13.1	13.0	12.8	12.7	12.9
2003	12.5	12.6	12.7	12.8	13.1	13.3	13.4	13.5	13.4	13.6	13.6	13.5	13.2
2004	13.2	13.4	13.6	13.9	14.2	14.5	14.9	15.1	15.0	15.0	15.2	15.3	14.4
2005	15.4	15.8	16.1	16.2	16.5	17.2	17.7	18.1	18.1	18.2	18.5	18.7	17.2
2006	18.7	19.1	19.6	19.7	20.3	21.1	21.6	22.2	22.2	22.7	22.8	23.3	21.1
2007	23.1	23.6	23.9	24.5	25.2	25.9	25.9	26.2	25.8	25.9	26.2	26.2	25.2
2008	26.4	26.7	26.8	27.5	28.0	28.6	28.9	29.2	29.2	30.0	30.2	29.9	28.5
2009	28.4	27.0	26.0	24.2	23.9	23.6	23.1	23.0	22.9	22.8	22.7	22.8	24.2
2010	22.5	22.8	23.0	23.5	23.9	24.4	25.0	25.2	25.1	25.4	25.5	26.0	24.4
2011	25.7	25.9	26.3	26.7	27.2	27.9	28.1	27.8	27.9	28.1	28.1	28.1	27.3
Construction													
2000	146.5	149.6	154.8	157.7	163.9	170.4	171.5	172.8	171.2	170.6	167.7	165.9	163.6
2001	159.1	159.4	163.1	165.3	169.7	175.2	175.7	176.1	172.9	169.6	165.4	160.3	167.7
2002	150.5	151.3	154.5	158.8	164.3	168.4	168.5	168.8	164.5	162.2	158.5	154.3	160.4
2003	145.2	143.1	143.4	145.6	150.3	155.3	156.1	155.9	153.4	153.7	149.8	147.2	149.9
2004	140.1	138.7	142.7	147.7	151.1	156.3	158.3	158.2	157.0	157.4	154.8	152.7	151.3
2005	144.7	146.3	150.1	153.3	157.7	164.6	168.1	169.3	168.3	167.2	166.0	164.2	160.0
2006	157.7	158.3	161.9	164.7	169.7	175.7	174.6	174.4	172.6	170.7	167.6	165.3	167.8
2007	154.0	154.4	160.5	164.1	169.8	175.7	176.9	176.7	173.1	173.1	170.1	164.7	167.8
2008	155.4	155.6	157.9	160.0	165.0	169.6	169.5	169.2	166.0	163.4	158.5	151.3	161.8
2009	138.4	134.8	133.3	131.4	132.7	135.5	135.0	133.2	130.0	127.9	124.6	118.9	131.3
2010	110.3	108.6	109.6	112.9	115.3	119.3	120.6	119.6	118.2	118.3	115.8	113.1	115.1
2011	104.3	102.7	105.3	110.1	111.6	116.0	115.7	119.5	118.8	118.2	116.1	112.6	112.6
Manufacturing													
2000	187.4	187.5	188.0	187.3	187.5	189.3	189.6	189.6	189.5	189.9	190.0	191.4	188.9
2001	185.8	185.1	184.9	182.9	182.5	182.1	180.0	178.4	176.3	173.8	171.7	170.5	179.5
2002	166.8	165.2	165.4	164.9	165.1	165.2	164.3	163.9	162.4	161.6	160.6	160.1	163.8
2003	156.7	155.9	154.9	154.7	154.4	154.7	153.7	153.6	152.4	152.1	152.0	151.9	153.9
2004	150.0	150.1	150.5	151.2	151.5	153.1	153.1	153.2	152.5	152.5	152.0	151.7	151.8
2005	149.4	150.0	150.2	149.9	150.0	150.8	151.6	151.3	150.6	150.5	150.5	150.4	150.4
2006	148.7	148.8	149.2	149.0	149.3	150.2	149.9	149.8	149.1	148.7	148.3	148.0	149.1
2007	146.0	145.6	146.1	145.6	146.5	147.6	147.4	147.3	147.4	148.0	148.1	147.9	147.0
2008	146.2	145.5	145.5	145.0	145.4	145.9	145.1	144.8	143.2	142.5	141.0	139.2	144.1
2009	135.8	133.7	132.3	130.9	130.1	129.5	129.0	128.2	127.3	126.9	126.3	125.5	129.6
2010	123.6	123.5	123.7	124.2	124.9	126.2	126.4	126.6	126.2	126.8	126.9	127.2	125.5
2011	126.1	126.3	127.2	128.1	128.6	129.8	131.4	131.4	130.8	129.4	129.0	129.9	129.0

1. Employment by Industry: Colorado, Selected Years, 2000–2011—*Continued*

(Numbers in thousands, not seasonally adjusted)

Industry and year	January	February	March	April	May	June	July	August	September	October	November	December	Annual average
Service-Providing													
2000	1,788.6	1,807.2	1,826.6	1,831.0	1,838.7	1,862.0	1,853.8	1,864.2	1,866.4	1,864.7	1,881.5	1,905.1	1,849.2
2001	1,853.7	1,866.1	1,876.1	1,869.8	1,867.1	1,891.4	1,870.9	1,872.3	1,862.9	1,849.7	1,853.2	1,868.0	1,866.8
2002	1,818.6	1,830.3	1,840.1	1,845.3	1,848.8	1,867.5	1,847.6	1,853.9	1,849.0	1,842.0	1,851.1	1,870.6	1,847.1
2003	1,816.9	1,823.8	1,828.3	1,825.3	1,829.4	1,845.9	1,832.9	1,840.8	1,838.9	1,840.0	1,842.6	1,864.8	1,835.8
2004	1,820.2	1,830.7	1,844.9	1,855.2	1,857.3	1,877.9	1,863.7	1,869.8	1,872.7	1,871.0	1,877.6	1,904.7	1,862.1
2005	1,854.0	1,869.8	1,882.7	1,887.9	1,891.6	1,912.1	1,901.0	1,902.8	1,910.8	1,908.1	1,916.3	1,943.3	1,898.4
2006	1,895.0	1,908.9	1,924.2	1,926.5	1,935.1	1,960.5	1,940.2	1,947.7	1,951.2	1,951.1	1,964.2	1,989.2	1,941.2
2007	1,939.5	1,956.9	1,975.8	1,978.9	1,986.2	2,009.1	1,991.8	2,000.2	2,005.9	2,003.5	2,014.7	2,034.1	1,991.4
2008	1,986.6	2,003.2	2,013.4	2,016.5	2,021.4	2,034.9	2,019.8	2,026.2	2,022.6	2,016.0	2,011.3	2,020.1	2,016.0
2009	1,968.6	1,966.3	1,966.3	1,961.6	1,964.1	1,970.1	1,951.0	1,951.0	1,951.8	1,953.7	1,953.5	1,967.6	1,960.5
2010	1,918.4	1,933.7	1,944.9	1,951.1	1,961.5	1,971.1	1,959.6	1,962.8	1,959.2	1,966.1	1,970.2	1,988.4	1,957.3
2011	1,946.8	1,958.5	1,970.3	1,981.7	1,983.9	1,999.7	1,988.9	1,993.6	1,995.1	2,000.7	2,003.4	2,014.5	1,986.4
Trade, Transportation, and Utilities													
2000	410.1	409.1	409.3	411.2	412.1	416.8	416.5	420.6	419.7	423.7	435.1	443.0	418.9
2001	425.2	420.3	421.4	420.2	420.7	425.2	423.8	423.6	420.7	419.8	425.4	429.3	423.0
2002	409.0	405.3	406.4	408.1	410.3	415.0	413.7	413.6	410.6	409.8	418.3	424.6	412.1
2003	405.6	401.6	400.8	399.2	399.3	402.0	402.5	404.1	402.6	405.4	412.2	418.3	404.5
2004	401.7	397.7	399.3	401.5	403.2	406.9	407.9	408.6	406.3	408.2	415.6	422.8	406.6
2005	405.8	403.7	406.1	405.9	407.4	411.7	413.7	413.3	414.3	416.7	425.1	431.8	413.0
2006	414.2	409.5	411.9	413.3	414.8	419.6	418.9	419.6	418.7	421.9	431.2	438.3	419.3
2007	424.2	419.7	422.3	422.7	424.4	428.9	430.5	430.8	429.7	431.6	440.1	445.3	429.2
2008	430.9	426.6	428.2	427.7	427.8	431.5	431.8	431.7	427.8	426.1	428.8	432.1	429.3
2009	413.4	406.4	403.2	400.7	401.5	404.0	402.7	402.1	399.4	399.9	404.2	408.4	403.8
2010	393.0	391.0	391.6	392.7	394.6	398.6	400.0	400.4	396.5	398.8	404.5	409.6	397.6
2011	395.1	392.6	393.8	397.2	399.1	402.9	402.9	403.6	402.0	403.8	406.4	411.4	400.9
Wholesale Trade													
2000	96.9	97.5	98.4	98.9	99.8	100.6	99.3	99.6	99.4	100.2	100.5	101.1	99.4
2001	100.0	100.8	101.0	100.5	100.4	100.7	100.1	100.0	99.2	98.5	98.1	98.0	99.8
2002	95.7	95.7	95.7	95.6	95.7	95.8	95.6	95.1	94.5	93.9	93.7	94.0	95.1
2003	92.8	92.3	92.4	92.2	92.2	92.5	92.2	91.9	91.5	91.9	91.5	91.8	92.1
2004	90.6	90.7	91.2	91.6	91.8	92.5	92.3	92.4	92.3	92.4	92.6	92.8	91.9
2005	91.7	92.1	92.6	92.9	93.2	93.7	94.2	94.4	94.4	94.2	94.3	94.7	93.5
2006	93.9	94.3	94.9	95.4	96.1	97.2	97.0	97.4	97.2	97.5	97.9	98.5	96.4
2007	97.2	97.7	98.4	98.7	99.2	100.0	99.9	100.0	99.6	100.2	100.3	100.5	99.3
2008	99.5	99.8	100.1	100.4	100.7	101.0	101.0	100.7	100.2	99.7	99.0	98.8	100.1
2009	96.7	95.7	94.7	93.8	93.6	93.4	92.8	92.4	91.7	91.7	91.3	91.4	93.3
2010	90.1	89.9	90.0	90.4	90.6	91.1	91.3	91.3	90.9	91.3	91.2	91.4	90.8
2011	90.5	90.6	91.0	91.7	92.1	92.6	93.1	92.8	91.6	91.9	91.2	92.9	91.8
Retail Trade													
2000	240.5	238.6	238.1	238.6	239.1	242.6	242.7	246.1	245.6	248.5	257.9	264.6	245.2
2001	247.0	242.0	242.8	242.3	243.1	246.7	245.6	244.9	243.6	244.0	250.9	255.3	245.7
2002	240.2	236.4	237.6	239.1	240.8	244.9	243.5	243.5	241.3	241.3	249.1	254.5	242.7
2003	238.7	235.4	234.6	234.5	235.5	238.0	238.3	239.9	239.0	240.9	247.2	252.2	239.5
2004	238.8	234.7	235.6	236.9	238.3	240.7	241.4	242.2	240.4	242.4	249.5	254.7	241.3
2005	240.9	238.3	240.3	240.1	241.9	244.8	245.7	245.1	246.2	248.4	256.4	261.0	245.8
2006	246.3	241.4	243.0	244.2	245.0	247.4	247.3	247.5	246.8	250.0	258.4	262.5	248.3
2007	251.1	246.7	248.4	248.3	249.6	252.6	254.3	254.4	253.8	254.7	262.2	265.4	253.5
2008	254.0	250.3	251.4	250.7	250.6	253.5	253.7	254.1	251.7	251.3	254.3	256.1	252.6
2009	242.9	237.9	236.3	234.3	236.0	238.2	237.8	237.6	236.2	236.7	241.6	244.0	238.3
2010	232.9	230.8	231.5	233.1	234.8	237.9	239.3	239.4	236.2	237.6	243.0	245.9	236.9
2011	235.0	233.0	233.7	236.4	237.9	240.6	240.1	240.4	239.8	241.9	244.9	247.0	239.2
Transportation and Utilities													
2000	72.7	73.0	72.8	73.7	73.2	73.6	74.5	74.9	74.7	75.0	76.7	77.3	74.3
2001	78.2	77.5	77.6	77.4	77.2	77.8	78.1	78.7	77.9	77.3	76.4	76.0	77.5
2002	73.1	73.2	73.1	73.4	73.8	74.3	74.6	75.0	74.8	74.6	75.5	76.1	74.3
2003	74.1	73.9	73.8	72.5	71.6	71.5	72.0	72.3	72.1	72.6	73.5	74.3	72.9
2004	72.3	72.3	72.5	73.0	73.1	73.7	74.2	74.0	73.6	73.4	73.5	75.3	73.4
2005	73.2	73.3	73.2	72.9	72.3	73.2	73.8	73.8	73.7	74.1	74.4	76.1	73.7
2006	74.0	73.8	74.0	73.7	73.7	75.0	74.6	74.7	74.7	74.4	74.9	77.3	74.6
2007	75.9	75.3	75.5	75.7	75.6	76.3	76.3	76.4	76.3	76.7	77.6	79.4	76.4
2008	77.4	76.5	76.7	76.6	76.5	77.0	77.1	76.9	75.9	75.1	75.5	77.2	76.5
2009	73.8	72.8	72.2	72.6	71.9	72.4	72.1	72.1	71.5	71.5	71.3	73.0	72.3
2010	70.0	70.3	70.1	69.2	69.2	69.6	69.4	69.7	69.4	69.9	70.3	72.3	70.0
2011	69.6	69.0	69.1	69.1	69.1	69.7	69.7	70.4	70.6	70.0	70.3	71.5	69.8
Information													
2000	102.1	103.7	105.0	106.0	107.1	108.8	110.3	111.0	111.2	111.3	112.0	112.8	108.4
2001	113.2	112.8	112.0	110.3	109.3	109.3	106.6	105.5	103.8	102.2	101.7	100.5	107.3
2002	98.1	97.0	96.2	95.2	94.1	93.7	91.7	91.0	89.9	89.3	89.4	88.6	92.9
2003	86.5	86.1	85.7	84.9	84.8	84.8	84.5	84.2	83.3	83.1	83.6	83.7	84.6
2004	82.7	82.8	82.6	81.9	81.9	81.9	81.2	80.9	79.5	79.3	79.6	79.6	81.2
2005	78.3	77.9	77.8	77.1	77.1	77.1	76.8	76.4	76.0	75.8	76.0	76.2	76.9
2006	75.8	75.6	75.8	75.4	75.7	75.7	75.3	75.2	74.7	75.0	75.4	75.5	75.4
2007	74.9	75.0	75.0	75.8	76.2	77.0	76.7	76.8	76.3	77.3	77.6	77.9	76.4
2008	77.4	77.6	77.4	77.2	77.0	77.2	77.0	76.8	76.3	76.1	76.0	76.1	76.8
2009	76.7	76.2	76.0	75.4	75.0	74.8	74.5	73.9	73.5	73.5	73.6	72.9	74.7
2010	72.2	71.9	72.0	71.7	71.8	72.3	71.8	72.0	71.5	71.9	72.5	72.5	72.0
2011	72.3	72.2	71.8	71.9	71.9	72.0	71.6	71.1	70.3	70.9	71.5	71.0	71.5

1. Employment by Industry: Colorado, Selected Years, 2000–2011—*Continued*

(Numbers in thousands, not seasonally adjusted)

Industry and year	January	February	March	April	May	June	July	August	September	October	November	December	Annual average
Financial Activities													
2000	146.3	147.1	147.7	146.5	145.8	147.3	147.1	147.3	146.3	146.2	147.0	149.6	147.0
2001	147.0	147.7	149.0	148.7	148.1	149.7	149.4	148.9	147.4	147.3	147.5	149.2	148.3
2002	147.7	148.3	148.7	147.8	147.6	149.0	149.3	150.2	149.6	150.3	151.8	154.1	149.5
2003	152.4	152.8	153.2	153.3	153.2	154.6	155.5	156.0	154.6	154.2	153.8	155.9	154.1
2004	153.5	153.8	154.2	154.0	153.3	154.7	155.2	155.2	154.6	154.6	154.8	157.1	154.6
2005	155.2	156.0	157.0	157.2	157.1	158.7	159.6	160.0	159.9	159.3	159.9	162.4	158.5
2006	159.3	159.8	160.2	160.0	160.0	161.3	161.0	161.1	160.3	159.8	160.1	162.3	160.4
2007	159.6	160.1	160.4	159.9	159.2	160.5	160.3	160.0	158.7	157.8	157.9	159.2	159.5
2008	157.0	157.4	157.7	156.9	156.0	156.6	156.6	155.7	154.0	153.2	152.5	153.7	155.6
2009	150.5	149.8	149.1	148.7	147.9	148.3	147.9	147.7	146.1	146.1	145.9	147.4	148.0
2010	144.9	144.6	144.7	144.2	143.2	144.2	144.7	144.7	143.6	143.7	143.6	145.7	144.3
2011	143.6	143.4	143.5	143.2	142.6	143.9	144.1	143.2	143.6	143.8	143.8	144.3	143.6
Professional and Business Services													
2000	302.2	303.1	308.2	313.1	316.6	322.8	325.9	328.2	327.9	326.6	325.1	325.8	318.8
2001	311.3	313.1	315.4	316.6	317.4	320.1	318.1	317.1	310.6	306.3	301.2	300.4	312.3
2002	288.6	291.0	292.8	297.4	300.0	301.7	299.6	302.7	298.7	295.8	293.4	293.0	296.2
2003	282.6	283.7	284.4	288.4	290.7	295.7	296.2	299.0	295.8	297.0	294.0	296.2	292.0
2004	287.2	289.8	293.7	301.9	303.8	309.2	311.7	312.5	310.4	310.0	308.2	310.9	304.1
2005	302.6	303.7	306.4	314.1	315.9	320.7	322.9	324.1	322.9	322.5	321.6	324.6	316.8
2006	314.7	318.4	321.6	327.4	331.9	338.6	337.8	340.0	338.1	337.5	337.0	339.1	331.8
2007	332.0	334.0	338.8	344.2	348.9	355.1	354.7	356.6	355.3	353.4	350.9	351.4	347.9
2008	342.5	345.3	346.6	352.9	354.4	358.6	358.1	359.5	355.8	354.0	348.8	346.5	351.9
2009	334.1	330.2	329.2	330.1	330.9	332.6	331.9	330.8	327.9	328.7	328.1	327.5	330.2
2010	318.0	319.8	322.4	327.9	330.1	334.3	335.9	336.1	331.5	333.6	332.2	331.2	329.4
2011	327.2	328.6	329.5	337.1	339.5	342.6	346.8	347.9	344.2	346.0	345.2	343.2	339.8
Education and Health Services													
2000	187.4	189.3	190.1	191.3	191.8	193.0	192.1	193.4	194.6	195.2	196.9	198.0	192.8
2001	196.1	198.0	198.7	199.1	200.0	200.5	199.7	201.5	201.3	203.8	204.9	206.2	200.8
2002	204.2	205.7	206.4	208.0	208.7	208.4	207.7	209.1	209.7	210.2	211.4	212.0	208.5
2003	209.8	211.1	211.7	212.4	212.9	213.1	212.3	213.1	213.5	214.5	215.2	216.1	213.0
2004	214.7	216.0	217.1	217.6	218.2	218.3	217.0	218.1	219.5	220.5	221.6	223.1	218.5
2005	220.3	223.0	223.5	224.0	225.0	225.3	223.6	224.6	225.2	225.5	226.9	228.0	224.6
2006	225.9	228.5	229.3	230.0	231.1	231.2	229.4	230.8	232.1	233.9	235.3	236.5	231.2
2007	233.7	236.8	238.4	238.8	239.9	240.1	238.7	240.5	241.7	243.8	245.7	247.1	240.4
2008	244.5	247.6	248.0	248.8	250.2	249.3	248.9	250.6	251.6	254.2	256.1	256.1	250.5
2009	254.1	255.8	256.0	256.5	257.2	256.4	256.1	256.8	256.9	259.5	260.4	261.2	257.2
2010	258.9	261.3	262.1	263.5	264.4	263.8	263.6	265.0	265.3	268.6	269.3	270.3	264.7
2011	268.0	270.0	271.4	272.3	272.9	272.3	271.9	274.4	274.0	275.4	276.5	275.2	272.9
Leisure and Hospitality													
2000	237.5	240.5	245.6	242.3	236.6	254.0	258.9	259.5	248.5	238.0	240.5	250.1	246.0
2001	246.2	247.4	251.2	246.3	239.4	257.0	259.9	260.3	247.9	233.8	233.7	243.6	247.2
2002	242.2	243.4	246.1	245.2	240.3	256.9	259.6	260.0	248.7	237.2	236.0	248.5	247.0
2003	243.8	242.8	244.8	241.2	236.6	252.5	256.6	258.8	247.6	238.2	236.1	247.9	245.6
2004	244.8	245.5	249.7	248.2	244.0	259.6	263.5	264.5	253.9	243.3	242.2	256.1	251.3
2005	250.8	252.7	257.5	253.7	250.0	266.0	269.7	270.0	259.1	249.5	248.6	262.5	257.5
2006	258.5	259.0	263.3	259.2	256.5	273.7	277.2	277.9	266.7	257.4	258.7	271.0	264.9
2007	263.4	264.7	270.0	266.5	263.0	278.6	281.9	282.6	271.7	262.5	264.1	275.7	270.4
2008	269.7	271.1	274.5	271.7	268.7	283.7	286.4	285.9	273.3	262.3	259.1	268.7	272.9
2009	262.2	261.3	263.5	260.2	256.6	269.4	274.5	274.7	262.6	253.3	250.0	260.7	262.4
2010	256.7	257.0	259.9	259.3	253.7	270.1	275.7	277.2	265.6	257.4	255.0	268.6	263.0
2011	265.4	264.1	269.4	266.9	261.6	279.5	286.1	286.3	272.0	264.8	264.2	277.6	271.5
Other Services													
2000	79.2	79.0	80.0	79.1	79.6	81.7	81.8	81.6	80.4	79.8	79.6	80.5	80.2
2001	82.6	82.7	83.4	83.3	83.6	85.5	85.2	85.2	83.7	83.1	83.0	83.7	83.8
2002	84.7	84.7	85.3	85.4	85.5	87.1	87.3	86.8	85.3	84.6	84.9	85.1	85.6
2003	85.7	85.2	85.2	85.5	85.7	87.4	87.3	86.9	85.3	85.2	85.4	86.1	85.9
2004	86.0	85.7	86.1	86.5	86.6	88.2	88.6	88.7	88.1	88.1	87.8	88.6	87.4
2005	88.2	88.1	88.5	88.4	88.4	89.6	89.5	89.3	88.4	87.9	87.5	88.1	88.5
2006	89.8	89.7	90.5	90.4	90.6	92.3	91.8	91.7	90.8	90.4	90.5	91.2	90.8
2007	91.4	91.9	92.9	92.5	92.6	94.3	93.5	93.6	93.0	93.0	92.8	93.5	92.9
2008	93.9	94.3	94.7	94.4	94.7	96.0	96.4	96.1	95.3	94.6	94.0	93.6	94.8
2009	95.1	94.5	94.6	93.4	93.5	94.7	94.3	94.0	92.9	92.6	92.1	92.6	93.7
2010	92.3	92.1	92.4	91.7	92.1	93.3	93.4	93.4	92.3	91.8	91.7	92.0	92.4
2011	91.8	91.7	92.5	92.7	93.0	94.2	94.0	94.8	94.0	95.0	94.5	93.5	93.5
Government													
2000	323.8	335.4	340.7	341.5	349.1	337.6	321.2	322.6	337.8	343.9	345.3	345.3	337.0
2001	332.1	344.1	345.0	345.3	348.6	344.1	328.2	330.2	347.5	353.4	355.8	355.1	344.1
2002	344.1	354.9	358.2	358.2	362.3	355.7	338.7	340.5	356.5	364.8	365.9	364.7	355.4
2003	350.5	360.5	362.5	360.4	366.2	355.8	338.0	338.7	356.2	362.4	362.3	360.6	356.2
2004	349.6	359.4	362.2	363.6	366.3	359.1	338.6	341.3	360.4	367.0	367.8	366.5	358.5
2005	352.8	364.7	365.9	367.5	370.7	363.0	345.2	345.1	365.0	370.9	370.7	369.7	362.6
2006	356.8	368.4	371.6	370.8	374.5	368.1	348.8	351.4	369.8	375.2	376.0	375.3	367.2
2007	360.3	374.7	378.0	378.5	382.0	374.6	355.5	359.3	379.5	384.1	385.6	384.0	374.7
2008	370.7	383.3	386.3	386.9	392.6	382.0	364.6	369.9	388.5	395.5	396.0	393.3	384.1
2009	382.5	392.1	394.7	396.6	401.5	389.9	369.1	371.0	392.5	400.1	399.2	396.9	390.5
2010	382.4	396.0	399.8	400.1	411.6	394.5	374.5	374.0	392.9	400.3	401.4	398.5	393.8
2011	383.4	395.9	398.4	400.4	403.3	392.3	371.5	372.3	395.0	401.0	401.3	398.3	392.8

2. Average Weekly Hours by Selected Industry: Colorado, 2007–2011

(Not seasonally adjusted)

Industry and year	January	February	March	April	May	June	July	August	September	October	November	December	Annual average
Total Private													
2007	34.2	34.3	34.5	34.8	34.6	35.2	35.6	35.0	35.4	35.0	35.0	35.0	34.9
2008	34.3	34.4	35.0	34.5	34.7	35.6	35.1	34.9	34.7	35.3	35.3	34.1	34.8
2009	33.9	34.6	34.8	34.2	34.4	34.5	34.6	34.8	34.2	34.1	34.5	33.4	34.3
2010	33.6	33.6	33.5	33.8	34.8	34.6	34.7	35.0	34.4	34.4	34.6	34.2	34.3
2011	34.3	33.9	33.9	34.2	35.1	34.5	34.7	34.5	34.6	35.4	34.7	34.6	34.5
Goods-Producing													
2007	37.7	37.9	38.3	38.2	38.8	39.2	38.5	38.0	38.0	38.6	39.2	38.0	38.4
2008	37.2	37.6	38.0	37.6	37.9	39.7	38.8	38.9	38.8	38.9	39.6	37.9	38.4
2009	37.6	37.6	38.2	36.7	37.8	38.1	38.0	38.2	37.4	37.9	38.2	36.6	37.7
2010	37.5	37.3	37.2	37.5	38.1	38.4	38.5	38.8	37.9	38.4	38.3	38.1	38.0
2011	36.5	37.0	37.5	38.5	39.1	38.9	39.2	38.9	39.4	39.5	39.2	38.7	38.6
Construction													
2007	37.0	36.5	37.9	37.4	38.6	38.6	38.0	37.4	37.3	38.2	39.2	37.2	37.8
2008	36.6	37.4	38.2	37.4	38.7	40.4	39.4	39.3	38.9	38.8	38.9	37.0	38.5
2009	36.4	36.5	37.5	37.4	38.5	38.9	39.4	39.4	37.3	38.1	38.5	36.3	37.8
2010	38.0	37.2	36.8	37.5	37.8	39.3	39.6	39.7	38.3	39.0	38.8	38.5	38.4
2011	35.3	35.8	36.6	37.6	38.2	38.0	38.7	38.4	38.2	38.4	37.4	36.8	37.5
Manufacturing													
2007	37.7	38.5	38.2	38.6	38.5	39.0	38.5	38.1	38.3	38.7	38.7	38.5	38.4
2008	37.6	37.8	37.8	37.7	37.6	39.7	38.7	39.0	38.9	39.3	40.3	38.9	38.6
2009	38.7	38.4	38.5	37.8	38.1	38.2	38.0	38.3	37.6	37.8	38.4	36.7	38.1
2010	36.6	37.1	37.5	37.5	38.5	38.1	38.1	38.5	37.8	38.0	38.2	38.6	37.9
2011	37.9	38.2	38.5	39.2	39.6	39.5	39.5	39.1	39.8	40.0	39.9	40.2	39.3
Trade, Transportation, and Utilities													
2007	34.1	34.2	34.3	34.0	34.4	35.2	35.8	35.2	36.2	35.5	35.6	36.1	35.1
2008	34.7	35.0	35.4	34.6	34.9	35.8	35.4	35.1	35.0	34.7	35.5	34.8	35.1
2009	34.2	35.0	35.0	34.8	34.9	35.1	35.3	35.5	35.1	34.8	34.8	34.0	34.9
2010	34.1	34.3	34.4	34.4	35.0	35.0	34.8	35.4	34.9	34.9	35.8	35.9	34.9
2011	35.7	35.0	35.0	35.2	36.0	35.8	36.2	36.0	36.3	36.8	36.2	36.3	35.9
Financial Activities													
2007	36.3	35.8	35.6	36.3	34.9	35.7	36.8	35.4	35.8	35.6	35.0	37.2	35.9
2008	36.4	36.1	36.8	35.5	35.5	37.1	35.8	35.4	35.4	35.5	35.0	34.6	35.8
2009	34.9	35.4	35.7	35.4	35.3	35.3	35.2	35.2	34.6	34.8	36.1	35.3	35.3
2010	35.7	35.6	35.7	34.6	35.9	35.7	36.1	36.4	35.9	35.5	36.2	36.2	35.8
2011	37.1	36.6	36.7	36.9	38.4	36.4	36.9	36.8	37.0	37.8	36.8	36.3	37.0
Professional and Business Services													
2007	35.2	35.5	35.4	36.4	35.5	36.4	37.3	36.7	37.6	36.4	36.2	36.6	36.3
2008	35.7	35.8	36.1	36.1	36.0	36.7	36.1	36.3	36.2	36.5	37.2	35.8	36.2
2009	35.9	36.6	36.4	36.4	36.2	36.7	36.6	36.9	36.3	36.5	37.3	35.6	36.4
2010	35.9	35.7	36.0	36.5	36.8	36.9	37.1	37.5	37.0	36.8	37.1	36.8	36.7
2011	36.9	36.7	36.2	36.6	37.2	36.6	36.5	36.3	36.2	37.3	36.5	36.7	36.6
Education and Health Services													
2007	34.0	34.1	34.2	34.4	33.9	34.4	34.9	34.5	34.9	34.5	35.4	35.0	34.5
2008	34.5	34.7	35.1	34.7	34.4	34.5	34.8	34.6	34.5	34.5	34.5	35.0	34.6
2009	34.7	35.1	35.0	34.5	34.4	34.1	34.1	34.4	34.1	34.0	34.0	33.6	34.3
2010	33.8	33.7	32.9	33.2	33.4	33.0	33.0	33.5	33.1	32.9	33.1	32.8	33.2
2011	33.5	33.5	33.0	33.3	33.4	33.0	33.0	32.7	33.0	34.1	33.2	33.4	33.3
Leisure and Hospitality													
2007	24.6	24.6	25.3	25.1	24.9	25.7	26.0	25.7	24.8	23.9	23.0	23.3	24.8
2008	23.5	23.8	24.5	23.7	24.4	25.6	25.6	25.3	24.9	24.1	23.8	23.5	24.4
2009	23.9	24.3	24.7	24.3	24.6	25.2	25.5	26.3	25.1	24.3	24.1	24.0	24.7
2010	24.7	25.4	25.1	24.9	26.0	26.2	26.5	27.4	26.1	25.9	25.3	24.8	25.7
2011	25.4	25.4	26.3	25.7	26.8	26.9	27.1	26.8	26.3	27.1	26.2	26.2	26.4
Other Services													
2007	33.5	35.2	35.2	34.9	34.0	34.7	34.3	33.8	33.9	33.7	34.8	33.3	34.3
2008	33.3	33.3	33.8	33.5	32.8	33.8	33.8	33.7	33.5	33.5	34.8	32.9	33.6
2009	33.0	33.1	33.0	32.7	33.4	33.4	32.8	33.8	33.4	33.2	34.2	32.6	33.2
2010	32.7	30.9	31.3	31.2	31.8	32.0	32.9	33.3	32.8	32.2	32.6	33.1	32.2
2011	33.3	31.6	31.1	31.0	33.2	32.6	32.1	32.4	32.6	34.0	32.6	33.3	32.5

3. Average Hourly Earnings by Selected Industry: Colorado, 2007–2011

(Dollars, not seasonally adjusted)

Industry and year	January	February	March	April	May	June	July	August	September	October	November	December	Annual average
Total Private													
2007	22.67	22.97	23.06	23.23	22.83	22.91	23.26	23.06	23.34	23.22	23.33	23.62	23.13
2008	23.68	23.92	24.07	23.84	23.59	23.46	23.61	23.57	23.71	23.74	24.18	24.23	23.80
2009	24.13	24.16	24.18	23.75	23.66	23.42	23.60	23.66	23.52	23.63	23.76	23.90	23.78
2010	23.71	23.69	23.76	23.87	23.97	23.63	23.70	23.78	23.62	23.83	23.86	24.10	23.79
2011	24.11	24.09	23.87	24.02	23.90	23.53	23.75	23.66	23.87	24.31	24.11	24.20	23.95
Goods-Producing													
2007	24.99	24.41	24.40	24.74	24.29	24.21	24.87	24.56	24.99	25.21	25.71	26.05	24.87
2008	26.16	26.12	25.98	26.23	26.07	25.53	26.06	25.84	25.59	25.47	26.06	26.35	25.95
2009	26.45	26.71	26.76	27.14	26.35	25.64	25.65	25.67	25.58	25.55	25.54	25.90	26.09
2010	25.98	25.77	25.74	26.15	25.98	25.64	25.82	25.74	25.67	25.61	25.95	26.18	25.85
2011	26.39	26.19	25.97	26.08	25.63	25.70	25.30	25.20	25.53	25.40	25.27	25.70	25.68
Construction													
2007	22.77	22.98	23.05	23.26	23.04	22.99	23.72	23.32	23.18	24.21	24.50	24.69	23.49
2008	24.78	24.67	24.53	24.54	24.61	24.09	24.20	24.18	24.23	24.23	24.76	24.88	24.46
2009	24.82	24.51	24.55	24.63	24.31	23.76	23.53	23.54	23.41	24.04	24.02	24.14	24.10
2010	24.04	23.78	23.60	23.78	24.05	23.48	23.44	23.45	23.52	23.53	23.98	23.94	23.71
2011	23.89	24.02	24.07	24.58	24.08	23.97	23.58	23.55	23.52	23.57	23.77	23.95	23.87
Manufacturing													
2007	26.59	25.19	25.22	25.69	25.06	24.88	25.61	25.61	26.68	25.96	26.92	27.12	25.88
2008	27.31	27.42	27.41	27.95	27.82	27.27	28.05	27.42	26.95	26.83	27.31	27.91	27.47
2009	27.69	27.75	27.77	27.72	27.59	27.39	27.20	27.09	27.06	27.29	27.23	27.33	27.43
2010	27.27	27.06	27.34	27.59	27.38	27.21	27.49	27.16	27.02	27.07	27.39	27.43	27.28
2011	27.51	27.26	27.01	26.87	26.57	26.67	26.20	26.18	26.91	26.57	26.10	26.29	26.67
Trade, Transportation, and Utilities													
2007	18.85	19.48	19.70	19.25	19.38	19.13	19.42	19.33	19.52	19.39	18.92	18.95	19.27
2008	19.50	19.20	19.53	19.21	19.20	19.26	19.20	19.24	19.45	19.41	19.57	19.27	19.34
2009	19.52	19.47	19.60	19.59	19.50	19.47	19.56	19.57	19.31	19.33	19.47	19.41	19.48
2010	19.12	19.16	19.26	19.37	19.37	19.48	19.27	19.41	19.42	19.40	19.68	19.51	19.40
2011	19.77	19.69	19.39	19.46	19.96	19.67	20.04	20.12	20.58	21.05	21.22	21.11	20.19
Financial Activities													
2007	23.09	22.69	22.27	22.94	22.76	23.81	23.88	22.97	23.74	22.64	22.62	22.10	22.96
2008	21.92	22.58	22.30	22.64	22.74	22.40	22.56	22.33	22.63	23.05	23.18	21.86	22.51
2009	21.88	21.91	21.96	21.76	22.21	22.27	22.20	22.04	21.75	21.82	22.07	21.90	21.98
2010	22.07	22.38	21.46	21.19	21.77	21.37	21.47	21.56	21.76	22.04	22.30	22.58	21.83
2011	22.57	22.52	22.64	23.17	23.94	23.61	24.06	23.95	23.88	24.97	24.32	24.35	23.67
Professional and Business Services													
2007	27.20	27.79	28.21	28.95	27.50	28.03	28.65	28.02	28.43	28.17	29.36	30.34	28.40
2008	30.39	30.79	31.00	30.27	28.95	28.86	29.05	29.18	29.53	29.53	30.34	30.76	29.87
2009	30.04	29.89	30.12	29.43	29.33	29.11	29.07	29.19	29.10	29.26	29.54	30.10	29.51
2010	30.11	29.83	29.71	29.41	29.46	29.12	29.00	29.09	28.97	29.16	29.57	29.74	29.42
2011	30.21	29.92	29.71	29.84	29.63	29.06	29.52	29.26	29.27	30.42	29.64	29.94	29.70
Education and Health Services													
2007	20.57	22.17	22.39	20.83	20.81	20.95	21.09	22.26	21.53	21.45	21.25	21.55	21.41
2008	21.31	22.11	22.25	21.72	21.75	22.04	22.18	22.17	22.00	22.14	22.46	23.03	22.10
2009	22.79	22.91	23.05	22.35	22.66	22.57	22.62	22.78	22.86	22.97	23.20	23.29	22.84
2010	22.90	23.26	24.01	24.13	24.17	24.16	24.17	24.09	23.85	23.95	23.86	23.90	23.87
2011	23.86	24.20	24.23	24.33	24.40	24.37	24.30	24.51	24.39	24.42	24.65	24.49	24.35
Leisure and Hospitality													
2007	12.70	13.02	13.22	12.89	12.98	13.42	13.55	13.27	13.32	13.19	13.14	13.54	13.19
2008	13.49	13.47	13.66	13.31	13.51	13.37	13.53	13.53	13.76	14.02	14.13	14.30	13.66
2009	14.31	14.44	14.49	14.32	14.09	13.99	14.11	14.20	14.13	14.13	14.07	14.26	14.21
2010	14.22	14.11	14.39	14.21	13.87	13.84	14.12	14.08	13.99	13.96	13.97	14.18	14.08
2011	14.27	14.51	14.51	14.43	14.24	13.94	14.14	14.08	14.34	14.34	14.45	14.36	14.30
Other Services													
2007	20.97	21.44	20.45	21.94	21.78	20.62	20.37	20.34	21.01	21.47	20.34	20.76	20.96
2008	20.87	20.72	20.67	20.86	21.32	20.95	20.87	20.68	20.58	20.48	21.02	20.50	20.79
2009	20.57	20.83	20.80	20.73	20.71	20.80	20.81	20.69	20.52	20.62	20.58	20.24	20.66
2010	20.17	20.42	20.53	20.73	21.20	21.08	20.72	20.83	20.68	20.88	21.22	21.04	20.79
2011	20.95	21.01	21.07	21.10	21.30	20.94	21.88	21.13	21.60	21.24	21.35	21.60	21.27

4. Average Weekly Earnings by Selected Industry: Colorado, 2007–2011

(Dollars, not seasonally adjusted)

Industry and year	January	February	March	April	May	June	July	August	September	October	November	December	Annual average
Total Private													
2007	775.31	787.87	795.57	808.40	789.92	806.43	828.06	807.10	826.24	812.70	816.55	826.70	807.24
2008	812.22	822.85	842.45	822.48	818.57	835.18	828.71	822.59	822.74	838.02	853.55	826.24	828.64
2009	818.01	835.94	841.46	812.25	813.90	807.99	816.56	823.37	804.38	805.78	819.72	798.26	816.36
2010	796.66	795.98	795.96	806.81	834.16	817.60	822.39	832.30	812.53	819.75	825.56	824.22	815.64
2011	826.97	816.65	809.19	821.48	838.89	811.79	824.13	816.27	825.90	860.57	836.62	837.32	827.03
Goods-Producing													
2007	942.12	925.14	934.52	945.07	942.45	949.03	957.50	933.28	949.62	973.11	1,007.83	989.90	954.37
2008	973.15	982.11	987.24	986.25	988.05	1,013.54	1,011.13	1,005.18	992.89	990.78	1,031.98	998.67	996.85
2009	994.52	1,004.30	1,022.23	996.04	996.03	976.88	974.70	980.59	956.69	968.35	975.63	947.94	983.22
2010	974.25	961.22	957.53	980.63	989.84	984.58	994.07	998.71	972.89	983.42	993.89	997.46	982.72
2011	963.24	969.03	973.88	1,004.08	1,002.13	999.73	991.76	980.28	1,005.88	1,003.30	990.58	994.59	990.04
Construction													
2007	842.49	838.77	873.60	869.92	889.34	887.41	901.36	872.17	864.61	924.82	960.40	918.47	887.73
2008	906.95	922.66	937.05	917.80	952.41	973.24	953.48	950.27	942.55	940.12	963.16	920.56	940.53
2009	903.45	894.62	920.63	921.16	935.94	924.26	927.08	927.48	873.19	915.92	924.77	876.28	912.15
2010	913.52	884.62	868.48	891.75	909.09	922.76	928.22	930.97	900.82	917.67	930.42	921.69	910.55
2011	843.32	859.92	880.96	924.21	919.86	910.86	912.55	904.32	898.46	905.09	889.00	881.36	894.74
Manufacturing													
2007	1,002.44	969.82	963.40	991.63	964.81	970.32	985.99	975.74	1,021.84	1,004.65	1,041.80	1,044.12	994.81
2008	1,026.86	1,036.48	1,036.10	1,053.72	1,046.03	1,082.62	1,085.54	1,069.38	1,048.36	1,054.42	1,100.59	1,085.70	1,060.30
2009	1,071.60	1,065.60	1,069.15	1,047.82	1,051.18	1,046.30	1,033.60	1,037.55	1,017.46	1,031.56	1,045.63	1,003.01	1,043.84
2010	998.08	1,003.93	1,025.25	1,034.63	1,054.13	1,036.70	1,047.37	1,045.66	1,021.36	1,028.66	1,046.30	1,058.80	1,033.66
2011	1,042.63	1,041.33	1,039.89	1,053.30	1,052.17	1,053.47	1,034.90	1,023.64	1,071.02	1,062.80	1,041.39	1,056.86	1,047.70
Trade, Transportation, and Utilities													
2007	642.79	666.22	675.71	654.50	666.67	673.38	695.24	680.42	706.62	688.35	673.55	684.10	675.75
2008	676.65	672.00	691.36	664.67	670.08	689.51	679.68	675.32	680.75	673.53	694.74	670.60	678.25
2009	667.58	681.45	686.00	681.73	680.55	683.40	690.47	694.74	677.78	672.68	677.56	659.94	679.41
2010	651.99	657.19	662.54	666.33	681.80	674.45	675.47	687.47	677.06	686.83	698.46	704.36	677.16
2011	705.79	689.15	678.65	684.99	718.56	704.19	725.45	724.32	747.05	774.64	768.16	766.29	724.33
Financial Activities													
2007	838.17	812.30	792.81	832.72	794.32	850.02	878.78	813.14	849.89	805.98	791.70	822.12	823.55
2008	797.89	815.14	820.64	803.72	807.27	831.04	807.65	790.48	801.10	818.28	811.30	756.36	805.13
2009	763.61	775.61	783.97	770.30	784.01	786.13	781.44	775.81	752.55	759.34	796.73	773.07	775.19
2010	787.90	796.73	766.12	733.17	781.54	762.91	775.07	784.78	781.18	782.42	807.26	817.40	781.44
2011	837.35	824.23	830.89	854.97	919.30	859.40	887.81	881.36	883.56	943.87	894.98	883.91	875.33
Professional and Business Services													
2007	957.44	986.55	998.63	1,053.78	976.25	1,020.29	1,068.65	1,028.33	1,068.97	1,025.39	1,062.83	1,110.44	1,030.45
2008	1,084.92	1,102.28	1,119.10	1,092.75	1,042.20	1,059.16	1,048.71	1,059.23	1,068.99	1,077.85	1,128.65	1,101.21	1,081.78
2009	1,078.44	1,093.97	1,096.37	1,071.25	1,061.75	1,068.34	1,063.96	1,077.11	1,056.33	1,067.99	1,101.84	1,071.56	1,075.67
2010	1,080.95	1,064.93	1,069.56	1,073.47	1,084.13	1,074.53	1,075.90	1,090.88	1,071.89	1,073.09	1,097.05	1,094.43	1,079.26
2011	1,114.75	1,098.06	1,075.50	1,092.14	1,102.24	1,063.60	1,077.48	1,062.14	1,059.57	1,134.67	1,081.86	1,098.80	1,088.29
Education and Health Services													
2007	699.38	756.00	765.74	716.55	705.46	720.68	736.04	767.97	751.40	740.03	752.25	754.25	738.95
2008	735.20	767.22	780.98	753.68	748.20	760.38	771.86	767.08	759.00	763.83	774.87	806.05	765.84
2009	790.81	804.14	806.75	771.08	779.50	769.64	771.34	783.63	779.53	780.98	788.80	782.54	784.09
2010	774.02	783.86	789.93	801.12	807.28	797.28	797.61	807.02	789.44	787.96	789.77	783.92	792.53
2011	799.31	810.70	799.59	810.19	814.96	804.21	801.90	801.48	804.87	832.72	818.38	817.97	809.72
Leisure and Hospitality													
2007	312.42	320.29	334.47	323.54	323.20	344.89	352.30	341.04	330.34	315.24	302.22	315.48	326.59
2008	317.02	320.59	334.67	315.45	329.64	342.27	346.37	342.31	342.62	337.88	336.29	336.05	333.55
2009	342.01	350.89	357.90	347.98	346.61	352.55	359.81	373.46	354.66	343.36	339.09	342.24	351.07
2010	351.23	358.39	361.19	353.83	360.62	362.61	374.18	385.79	365.14	361.56	353.44	351.66	361.86
2011	362.46	368.55	381.61	370.85	381.63	374.99	383.19	377.34	377.14	388.61	378.59	376.23	376.78
Other Services													
2007	702.50	754.69	719.84	765.71	740.52	715.51	698.69	687.49	712.24	723.54	707.83	691.31	718.24
2008	694.97	689.98	698.65	698.81	699.30	708.11	705.41	696.92	689.43	686.08	731.50	674.45	697.82
2009	678.81	689.47	686.40	677.87	691.71	694.72	682.57	699.32	685.37	684.58	703.84	659.82	686.31
2010	659.56	630.98	642.59	646.78	674.16	674.56	681.69	693.64	678.30	672.34	691.77	696.42	670.21
2011	697.64	663.92	655.28	654.10	707.16	682.64	702.35	684.61	704.16	722.16	696.01	719.28	690.97

CONNECTICUT
At a Glance

Population:
    2000 census: 3,405,650
    2010 census: 3,574,097
    2011 estimate: 3,580,709

Percent change in population:
    2000–2010: 4.9%
    2010–2011: 0.2%

Percent change in total nonfarm employment:
    2000–2010: -5.0%
    2010–2011: 1.0%

Industry with the largest growth in employment, 2000–2011 (thousands):
    Education and Health Services, 69.3

Industry with the largest decline or smallest growth in employment, 2000–2011 (thousands):
    Manufacturing, -69.3

Civilian labor force:
    2000: 1,736,831
    2010: 1,916,596
    2011: 1,918,127

Unemployment rate and rank among states (lowest to highest):
    2000: 2.3%, 1st
    2010: 9.3%, 30th
    2011: 8.8%, 32nd

Over-the-year change in unemployment rates:
    2010–2011: -0.5%

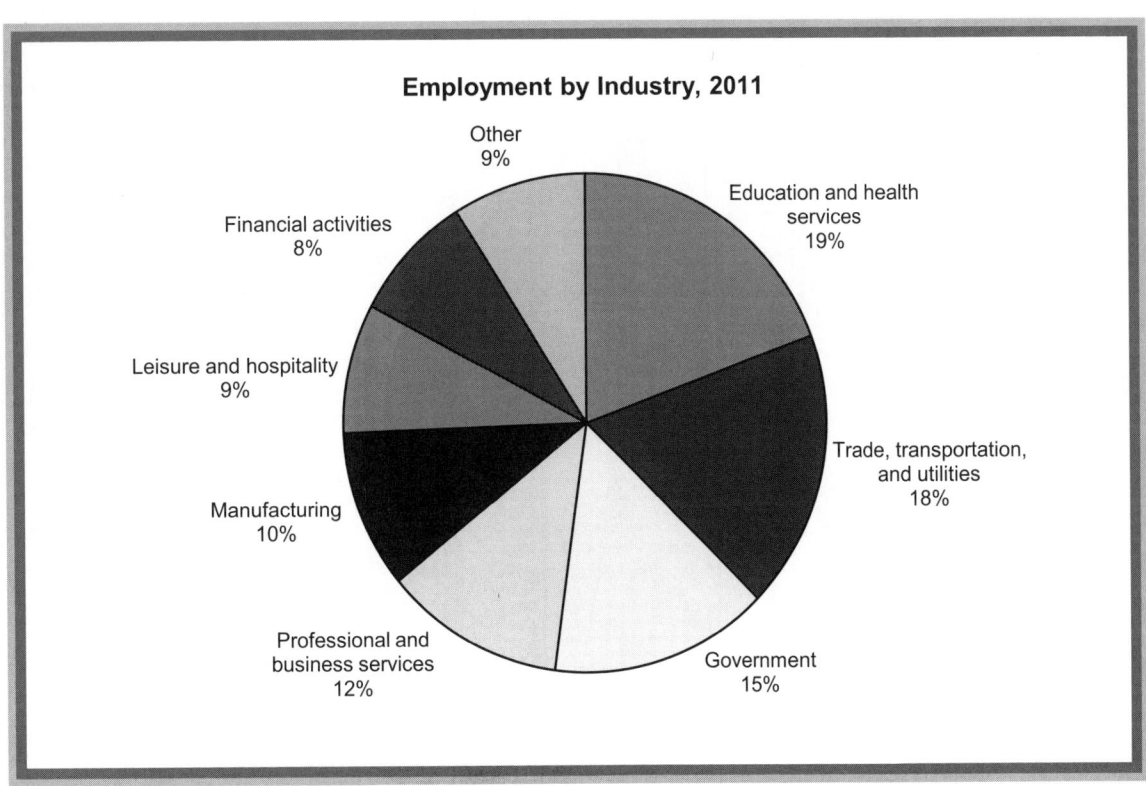

Employment by Industry, 2011

Other 9%
Education and health services 19%
Financial activities 8%
Trade, transportation, and utilities 18%
Leisure and hospitality 9%
Manufacturing 10%
Government 15%
Professional and business services 12%

1. Employment by Industry: Connecticut, Selected Years, 2000–2011

(Numbers in thousands, not seasonally adjusted)

Industry and year	January	February	March	April	May	June	July	August	September	October	November	December	Annual average
Total Nonfarm													
2000	1,655.0	1,661.4	1,675.9	1,687.0	1,700.9	1,713.0	1,695.6	1,685.8	1,703.4	1,704.2	1,712.1	1,723.9	1,693.2
2001	1,665.2	1,661.0	1,667.3	1,677.0	1,690.4	1,699.4	1,676.5	1,669.7	1,683.4	1,687.9	1,694.2	1,701.2	1,681.1
2002	1,648.1	1,648.7	1,657.5	1,670.2	1,679.9	1,687.0	1,655.0	1,652.0	1,663.3	1,665.2	1,673.1	1,678.2	1,664.9
2003	1,630.9	1,626.0	1,630.8	1,641.6	1,653.8	1,659.7	1,633.2	1,630.5	1,642.6	1,655.7	1,663.3	1,665.7	1,644.5
2004	1,616.6	1,618.6	1,627.7	1,646.3	1,658.3	1,667.0	1,644.2	1,642.0	1,655.7	1,664.6	1,675.4	1,681.3	1,649.8
2005	1,630.3	1,636.0	1,639.6	1,663.5	1,670.4	1,681.7	1,653.9	1,651.0	1,668.0	1,673.3	1,683.9	1,692.8	1,662.0
2006	1,648.5	1,650.7	1,656.0	1,678.4	1,687.3	1,698.5	1,672.5	1,673.7	1,685.3	1,694.5	1,704.9	1,716.6	1,680.6
2007	1,666.5	1,668.4	1,671.9	1,689.8	1,705.6	1,720.4	1,691.4	1,690.4	1,704.3	1,714.2	1,724.2	1,730.9	1,698.2
2008	1,685.3	1,687.8	1,692.5	1,705.6	1,717.7	1,724.5	1,690.4	1,686.7	1,697.2	1,700.9	1,701.4	1,698.0	1,699.0
2009	1,639.2	1,634.8	1,626.8	1,627.0	1,639.7	1,640.7	1,608.5	1,602.5	1,617.4	1,623.1	1,628.3	1,631.1	1,626.6
2010	1,569.1	1,571.9	1,575.2	1,600.4	1,622.4	1,625.0	1,607.3	1,604.2	1,616.7	1,629.1	1,635.5	1,639.3	1,608.0
2011	1,591.4	1,597.9	1,600.4	1,628.2	1,634.5	1,637.4	1,620.6	1,615.0	1,626.8	1,641.4	1,644.3	1,644.5	1,623.5
Total Private													
2000	1,417.6	1,417.1	1,428.6	1,439.8	1,450.2	1,470.4	1,466.5	1,460.6	1,463.3	1,459.3	1,465.5	1,477.2	1,451.3
2001	1,423.4	1,414.3	1,420.0	1,429.8	1,443.3	1,456.8	1,449.0	1,443.1	1,438.9	1,436.7	1,438.7	1,446.0	1,436.7
2002	1,399.4	1,393.8	1,401.7	1,415.6	1,425.7	1,436.9	1,423.9	1,418.1	1,416.5	1,413.6	1,417.8	1,423.7	1,415.6
2003	1,380.6	1,373.4	1,377.6	1,390.1	1,402.6	1,413.6	1,405.0	1,400.4	1,400.4	1,408.2	1,413.0	1,417.0	1,398.5
2004	1,374.3	1,371.2	1,378.9	1,398.2	1,411.4	1,425.0	1,419.2	1,413.7	1,416.3	1,417.5	1,425.3	1,432.6	1,407.0
2005	1,388.8	1,389.1	1,393.2	1,414.9	1,422.6	1,437.1	1,428.8	1,422.6	1,424.8	1,424.1	1,432.1	1,440.9	1,418.3
2006	1,402.9	1,401.3	1,406.8	1,428.2	1,437.5	1,453.7	1,444.4	1,440.9	1,441.4	1,444.3	1,451.8	1,463.1	1,434.7
2007	1,419.0	1,416.0	1,420.1	1,437.5	1,453.6	1,471.9	1,460.5	1,456.2	1,456.1	1,458.2	1,465.5	1,472.9	1,449.0
2008	1,432.7	1,430.1	1,435.8	1,448.6	1,460.1	1,472.2	1,456.6	1,450.4	1,447.1	1,443.4	1,441.6	1,439.9	1,446.5
2009	1,387.5	1,379.1	1,371.8	1,372.2	1,384.7	1,392.4	1,379.4	1,372.3	1,373.3	1,372.9	1,375.2	1,379.4	1,378.4
2010	1,323.3	1,322.1	1,327.3	1,353.0	1,368.4	1,381.1	1,379.4	1,375.1	1,376.3	1,381.7	1,386.6	1,391.4	1,363.8
2011	1,350.4	1,352.8	1,355.3	1,380.8	1,389.6	1,401.7	1,400.0	1,393.0	1,391.5	1,400.0	1,400.2	1,401.6	1,384.7
Goods-Producing													
2000	293.9	292.7	295.6	298.8	300.7	304.4	304.0	304.9	306.2	304.1	303.8	303.4	301.0
2001	293.5	291.3	292.5	295.4	296.7	298.5	295.1	294.7	292.8	289.6	287.3	285.8	292.8
2002	277.2	274.5	275.5	277.7	278.8	280.2	276.3	276.6	275.2	272.7	270.9	268.5	275.3
2003	261.0	257.3	257.9	261.5	264.1	266.2	264.3	265.1	264.4	264.2	264.0	262.4	262.7
2004	255.1	253.4	256.5	262.2	264.8	268.1	267.6	268.2	267.8	267.2	266.8	265.5	263.6
2005	258.0	255.9	257.1	261.7	263.8	267.0	265.6	265.2	263.6	262.4	261.9	260.2	261.9
2006	255.4	254.8	253.5	261.0	262.8	266.5	265.8	265.7	263.9	262.9	262.3	261.7	261.4
2007	255.1	253.0	254.8	258.4	261.0	265.1	264.2	264.5	262.7	261.8	261.4	259.3	260.1
2008	252.5	250.4	251.4	254.9	256.9	259.0	257.2	256.9	254.8	252.4	249.0	244.7	253.3
2009	233.9	229.3	227.5	227.4	228.4	229.8	226.8	225.7	225.0	222.7	221.2	219.3	226.4
2010	209.2	207.1	208.2	214.0	216.8	220.0	220.5	220.5	220.3	219.7	219.4	218.0	216.1
2011	211.4	211.2	212.3	216.4	218.9	222.2	224.2	223.2	220.4	221.5	219.7	216.6	218.2
Mining and Logging													
2000	0.7	0.6	0.7	0.8	0.8	0.8	0.9	0.8	0.8	0.8	0.8	0.8	0.8
2001	0.7	0.6	0.7	0.7	0.8	0.8	0.8	0.8	0.8	0.7	0.7	0.7	0.7
2002	0.7	0.6	0.7	0.7	0.8	0.8	0.8	0.8	0.8	0.8	0.8	0.8	0.7
2003	0.7	0.6	0.6	0.7	0.8	0.8	0.8	0.8	0.8	0.8	0.8	0.7	0.7
2004	0.6	0.6	0.7	0.7	0.8	0.8	0.8	0.8	0.8	0.8	0.8	0.7	0.7
2005	0.7	0.6	0.6	0.7	0.8	0.8	0.8	0.8	0.8	0.8	0.8	0.7	0.7
2006	0.7	0.7	0.7	0.8	0.8	0.8	0.8	0.8	0.8	0.8	0.8	0.7	0.8
2007	0.7	0.6	0.6	0.7	0.7	0.8	0.8	0.8	0.8	0.8	0.8	0.7	0.7
2008	0.7	0.6	0.7	0.7	0.8	0.8	0.8	0.8	0.8	0.8	0.8	0.7	0.8
2009	0.6	0.6	0.6	0.6	0.7	0.7	0.7	0.7	0.7	0.6	0.6	0.6	0.6
2010	0.5	0.5	0.5	0.6	0.6	0.6	0.6	0.6	0.6	0.6	0.6	0.6	0.6
2011	0.5	0.5	0.5	0.5	0.6	0.6	0.6	0.6	0.6	0.6	0.6	0.5	0.6
Construction													
2000	58.1	57.1	59.9	62.9	65.0	67.0	68.0	68.5	68.0	67.3	67.1	66.0	64.6
2001	59.1	58.3	59.6	64.2	66.7	68.5	69.8	70.0	68.8	67.6	66.6	65.1	65.4
2002	59.4	58.5	59.9	63.3	65.0	66.4	66.8	66.7	65.5	64.5	63.7	61.3	63.4
2003	56.2	54.3	55.2	59.1	62.4	64.0	65.9	66.4	65.6	65.5	65.3	63.3	61.9
2004	57.5	56.4	58.6	64.3	66.9	68.7	69.9	70.5	69.9	69.5	68.8	67.1	65.7
2005	60.9	59.6	60.5	65.2	67.1	69.0	70.0	70.1	68.9	67.7	67.2	65.1	65.9
2006	60.9	60.4	61.9	66.0	67.8	69.8	70.9	71.3	70.2	69.8	68.9	67.6	67.1
2007	62.6	60.7	62.4	67.1	69.7	71.9	72.7	72.9	71.9	71.7	71.0	68.8	68.6
2008	63.0	61.9	62.9	66.2	67.5	68.4	68.6	68.4	67.1	65.8	63.5	60.5	65.3
2009	53.8	52.0	51.8	53.7	55.5	56.7	56.8	56.6	56.1	55.2	54.2	52.2	54.6
2010	44.3	42.9	43.6	49.1	50.9	52.3	53.3	53.7	53.1	52.9	52.6	50.9	50.0
2011	45.6	45.3	46.0	50.1	52.0	53.7	55.5	55.3	53.2	54.6	52.4	50.6	51.2
Manufacturing													
2000	235.1	235.0	235.0	235.1	234.9	236.6	235.1	235.6	237.4	236.0	235.9	236.6	235.7
2001	233.7	232.4	232.2	230.5	229.2	229.2	224.5	223.9	223.2	221.3	220.0	220.0	226.7
2002	217.1	215.4	214.9	213.7	213.0	213.0	208.7	209.1	208.9	207.4	206.4	206.4	211.2
2003	204.1	202.4	202.1	201.7	200.9	201.4	197.6	197.9	198.0	197.9	197.9	198.4	200.0
2004	197.0	196.4	197.2	197.2	197.1	198.6	196.9	196.9	197.1	196.9	197.2	197.7	197.2
2005	196.4	195.7	196.0	195.8	195.9	197.2	194.8	194.3	193.9	193.9	193.9	194.4	195.2
2006	193.8	193.7	190.9	194.2	194.2	195.9	194.1	193.6	192.9	192.3	192.6	193.4	193.5
2007	191.8	191.7	191.8	190.6	190.6	192.4	190.7	190.8	190.0	189.3	189.6	189.8	190.8
2008	188.8	187.9	187.8	188.0	188.6	189.8	187.8	187.7	186.9	185.8	184.7	183.5	187.3
2009	179.5	176.7	175.1	173.1	172.2	172.4	169.3	168.4	168.2	166.9	166.4	166.5	171.2
2010	164.4	163.7	164.1	164.3	165.3	167.1	166.6	166.2	166.6	166.2	166.2	166.5	165.6
2011	165.3	165.4	165.8	165.8	166.3	167.9	168.1	167.3	166.6	166.3	166.7	165.5	166.4

1. Employment by Industry: Connecticut, Selected Years, 2000–2011—*Continued*

(Numbers in thousands, not seasonally adjusted)

Industry and year	January	February	March	April	May	June	July	August	September	October	November	December	Annual average
Service-Providing													
2000	1,361.1	1,368.7	1,380.3	1,388.2	1,400.2	1,408.6	1,391.6	1,380.9	1,397.2	1,400.1	1,408.3	1,420.5	1,392.1
2001	1,371.7	1,369.7	1,374.8	1,381.6	1,393.7	1,400.9	1,381.4	1,375.0	1,390.6	1,398.3	1,406.9	1,415.4	1,388.3
2002	1,370.9	1,374.2	1,382.0	1,392.5	1,401.1	1,406.8	1,378.7	1,375.4	1,388.1	1,392.5	1,402.2	1,409.7	1,389.5
2003	1,369.9	1,368.7	1,372.9	1,380.1	1,389.7	1,393.5	1,368.9	1,365.4	1,378.2	1,391.5	1,399.3	1,403.3	1,381.8
2004	1,361.5	1,365.2	1,371.2	1,384.1	1,393.5	1,398.9	1,376.6	1,373.8	1,387.9	1,397.4	1,408.6	1,415.8	1,386.2
2005	1,372.3	1,380.1	1,382.5	1,401.8	1,406.6	1,414.7	1,388.3	1,385.8	1,404.4	1,410.9	1,422.0	1,432.6	1,400.2
2006	1,393.1	1,395.9	1,402.5	1,417.4	1,424.5	1,432.0	1,406.7	1,408.0	1,421.4	1,431.6	1,442.6	1,454.9	1,419.2
2007	1,411.4	1,415.4	1,417.1	1,431.4	1,444.6	1,455.3	1,427.2	1,425.9	1,441.6	1,452.4	1,462.8	1,471.6	1,438.1
2008	1,432.8	1,437.4	1,441.1	1,450.7	1,460.8	1,465.5	1,433.2	1,429.8	1,442.4	1,448.5	1,452.4	1,453.3	1,445.7
2009	1,405.3	1,405.5	1,399.3	1,399.6	1,411.3	1,410.9	1,381.7	1,376.8	1,392.4	1,400.4	1,407.1	1,411.8	1,400.2
2010	1,359.9	1,364.8	1,367.0	1,386.4	1,405.6	1,405.0	1,386.8	1,383.7	1,396.4	1,409.4	1,416.1	1,421.3	1,391.9
2011	1,380.0	1,386.7	1,388.1	1,411.8	1,415.6	1,415.2	1,396.4	1,391.8	1,406.4	1,419.9	1,424.6	1,427.9	1,405.4
Trade, Transportation, and Utilities													
2000	314.8	311.6	313.0	314.5	316.1	318.4	313.1	312.2	316.9	319.5	326.7	333.2	317.5
2001	314.2	306.4	307.0	308.8	311.5	313.6	309.5	307.8	310.0	313.6	318.9	324.7	312.2
2002	309.4	303.8	305.4	307.7	309.7	312.7	305.9	304.3	308.6	308.2	314.3	320.4	309.2
2003	306.3	300.9	302.5	301.4	304.0	306.9	300.5	299.4	303.9	308.5	313.6	318.1	305.5
2004	304.9	301.0	302.3	303.7	306.4	309.3	304.4	302.6	307.2	310.5	318.3	324.2	307.9
2005	310.2	306.3	306.6	308.4	310.0	312.4	306.2	304.9	309.2	310.2	317.5	324.5	310.5
2006	311.7	305.4	307.3	308.6	310.3	313.2	306.2	305.0	308.4	311.2	318.8	325.1	310.9
2007	311.2	305.3	306.6	306.3	311.4	314.9	308.2	306.7	310.4	312.7	320.3	327.0	311.8
2008	314.7	308.1	308.9	308.2	310.9	313.1	306.2	304.7	307.6	307.9	312.4	316.4	309.9
2009	300.4	294.3	292.3	287.8	293.1	295.5	288.0	286.9	290.2	291.9	297.3	301.8	293.3
2010	287.2	282.2	283.0	283.1	289.2	293.0	288.0	287.2	288.9	292.4	298.6	304.3	289.8
2011	290.4	287.0	287.2	291.5	293.5	296.4	292.0	291.0	293.7	295.9	299.9	306.4	293.7
Wholesale Trade													
2000	66.9	67.0	67.3	68.1	68.5	68.7	68.4	68.2	68.5	68.4	68.9	69.3	68.2
2001	67.0	67.1	67.3	67.9	68.1	68.2	67.7	67.2	66.9	67.2	66.8	67.2	67.4
2002	65.9	65.5	65.7	66.1	66.3	66.4	66.3	66.2	66.0	65.8	65.8	66.2	66.0
2003	65.3	65.0	65.4	65.4	65.5	66.0	65.5	65.4	65.2	65.5	65.6	65.7	65.5
2004	64.8	64.9	65.4	65.9	66.2	66.7	66.0	66.0	65.8	65.4	65.8	66.2	65.8
2005	65.7	65.4	65.6	65.9	66.3	66.7	66.8	66.8	66.9	66.9	67.1	67.5	66.5
2006	66.9	66.8	67.1	67.5	67.7	68.1	67.7	67.6	67.3	67.7	67.7	67.9	67.5
2007	67.5	67.5	67.5	67.7	67.9	68.6	68.5	68.6	68.7	68.7	68.7	69.5	68.3
2008	69.2	69.1	69.5	69.4	69.8	70.0	69.4	69.1	68.9	68.7	68.6	68.4	69.2
2009	67.2	66.5	65.9	65.2	65.1	65.1	64.6	64.4	64.2	63.7	63.4	63.6	64.9
2010	61.9	61.6	61.9	62.3	62.7	63.3	63.1	63.2	62.8	62.7	63.1	63.4	62.7
2011	62.2	62.3	62.4	63.3	63.6	64.2	63.9	64.4	65.5	65.0	64.9	64.9	63.9
Retail Trade													
2000	196.4	192.9	194.4	194.5	195.7	197.8	194.8	195.0	195.7	197.3	204.2	210.6	197.4
2001	195.6	188.6	189.4	190.0	192.3	194.6	193.6	193.8	193.0	195.3	201.4	206.8	194.5
2002	194.9	189.5	191.1	192.0	193.7	196.5	193.2	192.9	192.8	192.0	198.2	204.0	194.2
2003	192.1	187.3	188.2	187.5	189.6	191.6	189.3	189.3	189.3	192.2	197.3	201.7	191.3
2004	191.1	187.2	188.0	188.0	189.9	191.9	191.4	190.4	190.3	192.2	199.2	204.6	192.0
2005	193.0	189.3	189.1	190.1	191.0	192.4	190.2	189.8	189.2	190.4	196.7	202.2	192.0
2006	192.3	186.4	187.8	188.7	189.8	191.9	189.6	189.4	188.4	190.5	197.8	202.4	191.3
2007	191.1	185.5	186.7	186.4	190.6	192.9	190.4	190.0	188.7	190.7	198.0	202.7	191.1
2008	192.9	186.5	186.8	185.8	187.9	189.5	186.7	186.8	185.1	185.6	190.1	193.3	188.1
2009	181.2	176.3	175.2	173.9	177.1	179.5	176.5	176.8	175.9	178.0	183.7	186.9	178.4
2010	176.6	172.0	172.5	173.6	177.0	179.8	178.7	178.3	176.2	179.6	184.9	188.9	178.2
2011	179.1	175.4	175.3	178.1	179.4	181.2	179.5	178.8	176.3	179.3	183.1	188.1	179.5
Transportation and Utilities													
2000	51.5	51.7	51.3	51.9	51.9	51.9	49.9	49.0	52.7	53.8	53.6	53.3	51.9
2001	51.6	50.7	50.3	50.9	51.1	50.8	48.2	46.8	50.1	51.1	50.7	50.7	50.3
2002	48.6	48.8	48.6	49.6	49.7	49.8	46.4	45.2	49.8	50.4	50.3	50.2	49.0
2003	48.9	48.6	48.9	48.5	48.9	49.3	45.7	44.7	49.4	50.8	50.7	50.7	48.8
2004	49.0	48.9	48.9	49.8	50.3	50.7	47.0	46.2	51.1	52.9	53.3	53.4	50.1
2005	51.5	51.6	51.9	52.4	52.7	53.3	49.2	48.3	53.1	52.9	53.7	54.8	52.1
2006	52.5	52.2	52.4	52.4	52.8	53.2	48.9	48.0	52.7	53.0	53.3	54.8	52.2
2007	52.6	52.3	52.4	52.2	52.9	53.4	49.3	48.1	53.0	53.3	53.6	54.8	52.3
2008	52.6	52.5	52.6	53.0	53.2	53.6	50.1	48.8	53.6	53.6	53.7	54.7	52.7
2009	52.0	51.5	51.2	48.7	50.9	50.9	46.9	45.7	50.1	50.2	50.2	51.3	50.0
2010	48.7	48.6	48.6	47.2	49.5	49.9	46.2	45.7	49.9	50.1	50.6	52.0	48.9
2011	49.1	49.3	49.5	50.1	50.5	51.0	48.6	47.8	51.9	51.6	51.9	53.4	50.4
Information													
2000	45.2	45.4	45.7	45.5	45.8	46.5	46.9	47.0	47.0	47.1	47.4	47.6	46.4
2001	46.3	46.4	46.0	45.3	45.1	45.1	44.2	44.2	43.6	43.2	43.3	43.3	44.7
2002	42.1	41.9	41.8	41.5	41.4	41.5	41.0	40.7	40.2	40.0	39.9	40.0	41.0
2003	40.1	39.9	39.8	39.6	39.5	39.8	39.6	39.5	39.1	39.2	39.4	39.5	39.6
2004	39.2	38.8	38.9	38.9	39.0	39.4	39.3	39.3	38.8	38.6	38.9	38.8	39.0
2005	38.5	38.6	38.3	38.2	38.2	38.5	38.2	38.0	37.6	37.5	37.7	37.8	38.1
2006	37.9	37.9	37.9	37.7	37.8	37.9	38.0	38.0	37.7	37.8	38.1	38.3	37.9
2007	37.5	37.9	37.7	38.0	39.0	38.6	38.8	38.9	39.2	39.0	38.1	38.2	38.4
2008	37.9	38.2	37.9	38.5	38.6	38.6	37.9	38.1	37.1	36.9	36.9	37.0	37.8
2009	36.4	36.3	35.5	35.1	34.6	34.5	34.3	34.0	33.3	32.7	32.8	32.3	34.3
2010	31.8	31.7	31.6	31.5	31.7	31.6	31.6	32.0	31.8	31.6	31.7	31.8	31.7
2011	31.5	31.5	31.5	31.4	31.3	31.4	31.8	31.5	31.2	31.5	31.6	31.8	31.5

1. Employment by Industry: Connecticut, Selected Years, 2000–2011—*Continued*

(Numbers in thousands, not seasonally adjusted)

Industry and year	January	February	March	April	May	June	July	August	September	October	November	December	Annual average
Financial Activities													
2000	141.2	141.2	141.8	141.5	142.1	144.2	145.1	145.3	143.9	143.0	143.0	144.1	143.0
2001	142.1	141.8	142.1	142.0	142.5	144.1	144.8	144.9	143.1	142.3	142.4	143.2	142.9
2002	142.8	142.1	142.1	141.4	142.1	143.4	143.9	143.8	142.5	141.8	142.5	143.1	142.6
2003	142.4	141.7	141.7	142.6	143.3	144.7	144.3	144.0	142.4	141.5	141.4	142.0	142.7
2004	140.1	139.6	139.8	139.7	140.1	141.6	142.0	142.1	140.7	140.3	140.7	141.1	140.7
2005	140.5	140.5	140.5	141.6	141.5	143.4	144.2	144.0	142.7	142.4	142.6	143.5	142.3
2006	143.0	142.7	142.9	142.9	143.4	145.1	145.6	145.8	144.5	144.6	145.1	145.6	144.3
2007	144.9	144.4	144.1	144.1	144.4	146.3	146.2	145.7	144.0	143.6	143.5	144.1	144.6
2008	143.0	143.3	144.0	143.2	143.5	145.3	144.8	144.9	142.8	142.0	142.1	142.0	143.4
2009	139.8	139.4	139.3	137.7	137.5	138.5	138.2	137.6	135.8	135.9	135.8	135.8	137.6
2010	134.1	134.1	134.4	134.0	134.3	136.1	136.7	137.0	135.1	135.1	135.6	135.9	135.2
2011	135.4	135.2	135.3	134.9	135.0	135.6	136.1	135.0	134.6	134.2	133.8	133.1	134.9
Professional and Business Services													
2000	207.7	208.9	211.6	214.4	216.1	220.9	219.7	219.5	219.4	217.6	217.2	218.0	215.9
2001	207.3	204.7	206.6	209.6	214.4	215.2	212.4	212.1	211.7	209.3	207.8	207.4	209.9
2002	197.7	197.7	200.7	203.2	203.9	206.2	203.3	204.1	203.4	201.6	201.2	201.0	202.0
2003	193.5	193.4	194.4	196.9	197.1	198.5	196.6	197.7	197.8	198.1	198.7	198.3	196.8
2004	191.2	191.3	193.4	196.7	197.7	200.7	199.3	199.6	199.4	197.2	198.5	199.6	197.1
2005	191.9	193.2	195.3	199.1	199.2	203.1	202.4	202.3	203.3	202.2	203.1	204.0	199.9
2006	196.0	198.5	200.8	204.6	204.7	208.8	205.0	206.2	206.8	205.7	206.3	208.3	204.3
2007	199.4	200.4	201.6	206.1	207.7	211.4	207.4	208.2	207.8	208.2	208.7	210.4	206.4
2008	203.6	203.3	205.0	207.9	207.6	210.2	206.9	206.2	204.8	202.6	200.9	199.8	204.9
2009	192.3	189.7	188.6	190.5	189.8	190.7	187.8	188.3	187.8	188.6	188.9	189.9	189.4
2010	179.5	181.7	182.8	190.9	191.2	193.7	193.1	192.8	192.5	193.7	193.3	193.7	189.9
2011	188.0	189.8	189.6	196.4	196.1	198.1	196.7	196.4	195.6	198.3	197.7	197.3	195.0
Education and Health Services													
2000	243.4	245.6	246.7	246.3	245.7	244.5	244.2	240.6	244.6	245.7	247.0	248.8	245.3
2001	248.3	252.0	252.0	251.7	248.5	249.8	249.4	247.5	254.7	257.5	259.6	260.8	252.7
2002	255.1	258.9	258.9	260.3	259.6	257.1	255.9	253.7	259.4	264.4	266.5	266.9	259.7
2003	261.1	264.3	263.0	265.1	264.6	261.4	260.0	257.0	262.4	268.5	270.0	270.3	264.0
2004	264.4	268.2	267.0	270.3	270.3	266.6	264.3	261.3	268.3	274.0	275.0	274.8	268.7
2005	269.0	273.4	271.8	275.6	274.0	270.1	268.6	265.9	273.1	278.3	279.7	279.8	273.3
2006	274.7	278.4	277.2	280.9	279.5	276.1	275.8	273.7	280.6	284.8	286.4	287.2	279.6
2007	282.1	286.6	285.2	289.3	287.5	285.9	283.8	281.3	288.5	293.0	294.7	295.4	287.8
2008	290.7	295.8	295.3	297.9	296.2	294.4	292.2	289.8	296.8	302.2	304.6	304.7	296.7
2009	299.1	304.3	301.6	302.8	301.9	299.0	298.4	296.3	302.3	306.7	307.5	308.4	302.4
2010	301.8	304.9	304.4	308.8	307.3	304.1	302.9	300.6	308.0	312.8	313.9	313.8	306.9
2011	310.1	313.0	312.7	316.2	314.6	311.3	310.3	309.0	316.0	320.5	320.9	320.1	314.6
Leisure and Hospitality													
2000	111.9	112.1	114.2	118.2	122.9	129.6	130.9	129.3	124.1	120.9	119.0	120.3	121.1
2001	111.0	111.0	112.7	115.8	122.9	127.7	129.7	128.6	121.2	118.9	116.9	118.0	119.5
2002	112.9	113.0	115.0	120.8	126.4	131.4	133.5	131.6	125.2	122.9	120.2	121.0	122.8
2003	114.7	114.6	116.4	121.3	127.8	132.9	136.1	134.7	128.7	126.2	123.9	124.1	125.1
2004	117.9	117.5	119.2	124.4	130.5	136.0	138.3	137.0	131.8	127.5	124.8	126.0	127.6
2005	119.1	119.5	121.5	127.6	133.0	138.5	139.5	138.8	132.8	128.6	126.9	127.7	129.5
2006	122.1	121.8	124.8	129.3	135.2	141.6	142.8	141.7	135.7	133.1	130.6	132.3	132.6
2007	125.4	125.2	126.5	131.4	138.5	144.4	146.4	146.0	139.5	136.1	135.0	134.5	135.7
2008	127.5	128.3	130.3	134.8	142.7	147.1	147.4	146.1	140.7	136.8	133.3	133.0	137.3
2009	124.2	124.9	125.9	129.9	138.1	142.2	143.8	141.9	137.8	133.7	131.0	130.9	133.7
2010	120.3	121.3	123.3	130.8	137.4	141.0	144.4	143.1	139.1	135.8	133.6	133.3	133.6
2011	124.3	125.7	127.2	133.7	139.7	144.9	147.2	145.5	139.4	137.9	136.2	135.8	136.5
Other Services													
2000	59.5	59.6	60.0	60.6	60.8	61.9	62.6	61.8	61.2	61.4	61.4	61.8	61.1
2001	60.7	60.7	61.1	61.2	61.7	62.8	63.9	63.3	61.8	62.3	62.5	62.8	62.1
2002	62.1	61.9	62.3	63.0	63.8	64.4	64.1	63.3	62.0	62.0	62.3	62.8	62.8
2003	61.5	61.3	61.9	61.7	62.2	63.2	63.6	63.0	61.7	62.0	62.0	62.3	62.2
2004	61.5	61.4	61.8	62.3	62.6	63.3	64.0	63.6	62.3	62.2	62.3	62.6	62.5
2005	61.6	61.7	62.1	62.7	62.9	64.1	64.1	63.5	62.5	62.5	62.7	63.4	62.8
2006	62.1	61.8	62.4	63.2	63.8	64.5	65.2	64.8	63.8	64.2	64.2	64.6	63.7
2007	63.4	63.2	63.6	63.9	64.1	65.3	65.5	64.9	64.0	63.8	63.8	64.0	64.1
2008	62.8	62.7	63.0	63.2	63.7	64.5	64.0	63.7	62.5	62.6	62.4	62.3	63.1
2009	61.4	60.9	61.1	61.0	61.3	62.2	62.1	61.6	61.1	60.7	60.7	61.0	61.3
2010	59.4	59.1	59.6	59.9	60.5	61.6	62.2	61.9	60.6	60.6	60.5	60.6	60.5
2011	59.3	59.4	59.5	60.3	60.5	61.8	61.7	61.4	60.6	60.2	60.4	60.5	60.5
Government													
2000	237.4	244.3	247.3	247.2	250.7	242.6	229.1	225.2	240.1	244.9	246.6	246.7	241.8
2001	241.8	246.7	247.3	247.2	247.1	242.6	227.5	226.6	244.5	251.2	255.5	255.2	244.4
2002	248.7	254.9	255.8	254.6	254.2	250.1	231.1	233.9	246.8	251.6	255.3	254.5	249.3
2003	250.3	252.6	253.2	251.5	251.2	246.1	228.2	230.1	242.2	247.5	250.3	248.7	246.0
2004	242.3	247.4	248.8	248.1	246.9	242.0	225.0	228.3	239.4	247.1	250.1	248.7	242.8
2005	241.5	246.9	246.4	248.6	247.8	244.6	225.1	228.4	243.2	249.2	251.8	251.9	243.8
2006	245.6	249.4	249.2	250.2	249.8	244.8	228.1	232.8	243.9	250.2	253.1	253.5	245.9
2007	247.5	252.4	251.8	252.3	252.0	248.5	230.9	234.2	248.2	256.0	258.7	258.0	249.2
2008	252.6	257.7	256.7	257.0	257.6	252.3	233.8	236.3	250.1	257.5	259.8	258.1	252.5
2009	251.7	255.7	255.0	254.8	255.0	248.3	229.1	230.2	244.1	250.2	253.1	251.7	248.2
2010	245.8	249.8	247.9	247.4	254.0	243.9	227.9	229.1	240.4	247.4	248.9	247.9	244.2
2011	241.0	245.1	245.1	247.4	244.9	235.7	220.6	222.0	235.3	241.4	244.1	242.9	238.8

2. Average Weekly Hours by Selected Industry: Connecticut, 2007–2011

(Not seasonally adjusted)

Industry and year	January	February	March	April	May	June	July	August	September	October	November	December	Annual average
Total Private													
2007	34.0	33.6	33.9	34.3	34.5	34.6	34.6	34.6	34.5	34.3	34.5	34.2	34.3
2008	34.2	33.9	34.3	34.1	34.1	34.3	33.9	34.0	34.0	33.7	33.6	33.3	34.0
2009	33.3	33.4	33.1	32.7	33.1	32.9	33.0	33.1	33.0	32.4	33.0	32.7	33.0
2010	33.0	32.5	33.1	33.3	33.5	33.3	33.3	33.6	33.4	33.6	33.5	33.8	33.3
2011	33.2	33.6	33.7	33.7	34.1	33.8	33.9	34.1	34.1	34.4	34.1	34.2	33.9
Goods-Producing													
2007	39.4	39.2	40.0	40.3	40.8	40.0	40.6	41.0	41.1	41.1	41.1	40.5	40.4
2008	41.2	40.3	41.0	40.9	40.8	40.8	40.6	40.7	40.3	40.2	38.6	38.4	40.3
2009	38.0	37.7	37.8	37.0	37.9	38.0	38.6	38.3	38.4	38.3	38.8	38.5	38.1
2010	38.5	37.6	38.7	38.9	38.9	39.0	39.1	38.9	39.0	38.6	38.9	38.9	38.8
2011	36.8	38.1	38.5	38.5	38.6	38.7	38.8	39.1	39.0	39.0	39.2	39.4	38.6
Construction													
2007	35.8	35.0	35.3	36.4	38.4	37.5	39.2	39.3	38.9	39.5	38.7	37.6	37.7
2008	38.2	37.8	38.0	38.0	37.8	37.9	38.2	38.6	37.7	37.1	36.5	35.5	37.6
2009	34.3	35.0	35.5	35.4	36.6	36.5	37.2	37.4	36.4	36.8	36.5	35.5	36.1
2010	35.4	34.6	35.7	36.5	36.8	37.4	37.4	37.8	37.5	37.3	37.1	36.8	36.8
2011	34.0	35.4	35.9	35.9	36.5	36.8	36.9	37.8	37.2	36.6	36.3	37.1	36.4
Manufacturing													
2007	40.4	40.4	41.4	41.6	41.7	40.9	41.2	41.7	42.0	41.7	41.9	41.4	41.4
2008	41.5	40.5	41.5	41.6	41.6	41.6	41.2	41.3	41.0	41.2	40.2	40.1	41.1
2009	40.0	39.2	39.1	38.2	38.7	38.8	39.3	38.9	39.3	39.2	39.9	39.9	39.2
2010	39.9	39.1	39.9	39.8	39.8	39.6	39.7	39.4	39.7	39.3	39.7	40.1	39.7
2011	38.2	39.3	39.5	39.5	39.5	39.6	39.7	39.8	39.9	40.1	40.4	40.4	39.7
Trade, Transportation, and Utilities													
2007	34.0	33.5	33.7	34.5	34.6	35.3	35.2	34.9	34.8	34.3	34.3	33.8	34.4
2008	33.5	33.5	34.0	33.9	34.1	34.7	34.0	34.0	34.1	33.2	33.8	33.7	33.9
2009	33.7	33.4	33.4	33.0	33.5	33.3	33.2	33.3	33.6	33.0	33.3	33.8	33.4
2010	33.2	32.7	33.0	33.1	33.7	33.7	33.3	33.5	33.6	33.8	33.7	34.2	33.5
2011	33.9	34.5	34.4	34.5	34.7	34.3	34.2	34.4	34.8	35.1	35.0	35.3	34.6
Financial Activities													
2007	34.1	34.1	34.5	34.8	34.4	34.6	35.6	35.2	35.5	35.1	35.3	36.1	34.9
2008	35.4	35.7	36.5	35.6	35.7	36.0	35.3	35.2	35.1	34.7	35.8	35.6	35.6
2009	35.8	35.8	35.9	35.4	35.5	35.7	35.2	36.0	35.5	35.7	37.1	36.0	35.8
2010	36.0	36.1	36.5	36.2	37.2	36.7	36.9	37.2	36.6	36.8	37.1	37.3	36.7
2011	37.3	37.0	37.1	36.8	37.4	36.8	36.8	36.8	37.0	37.7	37.0	37.0	37.1
Professional and Business Services													
2007	34.0	33.4	34.1	34.6	34.8	35.1	34.4	34.5	34.1	33.8	33.7	34.1	34.2
2008	34.2	33.5	34.0	34.9	35.1	35.5	34.3	34.5	34.6	34.7	34.7	34.1	34.5
2009	33.0	33.6	33.2	33.2	33.5	33.1	33.1	33.5	32.7	33.2	34.1	33.0	33.3
2010	33.4	32.8	33.6	34.0	34.4	33.8	33.3	34.0	33.3	33.4	33.5	33.7	33.6
2011	33.7	33.8	34.0	34.0	35.2	35.1	35.0	34.8	35.0	34.9	34.4	34.4	34.5
Education and Health Services													
2007	32.3	31.5	31.5	31.8	31.5	31.8	31.1	31.3	31.1	30.9	31.6	31.0	31.4
2008	31.1	30.9	30.9	30.8	30.7	30.8	30.7	31.0	30.9	30.8	30.9	30.5	30.8
2009	30.7	31.0	30.5	30.0	30.1	30.1	30.3	30.3	30.8	30.7	30.5	30.6	30.5
2010	30.7	30.0	30.3	30.4	30.6	30.6	30.9	31.1	30.6	30.5	30.3	30.6	30.5
2011	30.2	30.6	30.7	30.9	30.9	30.8	31.0	31.2	31.0	31.1	30.9	31.3	30.9
Leisure and Hospitality													
2007	25.6	26.3	26.4	26.5	27.9	28.0	28.2	28.4	28.2	28.3	28.6	27.9	27.6
2008	27.4	27.8	28.0	26.2	26.5	26.0	27.1	26.2	26.3	26.4	26.3	26.1	26.7
2009	25.6	27.0	26.0	26.5	26.5	25.9	26.5	26.5	26.2	26.8	26.7	25.9	26.3
2010	25.0	25.1	25.1	26.5	26.3	25.9	26.7	26.8	26.5	26.8	26.7	26.3	26.2
2011	25.0	26.4	26.2	26.4	26.6	26.7	27.0	26.8	26.7	27.0	27.1	26.9	26.6
Other Services													
2007	33.4	32.6	32.7	33.3	32.4	32.6	32.3	31.5	31.9	31.8	32.9	31.7	32.4
2008	31.1	31.7	31.0	30.6	30.3	30.1	30.3	29.7	30.2	30.7	30.3	29.1	30.4
2009	29.2	28.8	28.8	28.7	29.5	29.7	29.6	29.7	29.5	29.8	29.7	29.2	29.3
2010	29.0	28.8	29.0	28.7	29.1	28.9	30.2	30.2	29.7	30.3	30.1	30.1	29.5
2011	29.4	29.9	29.2	29.9	30.8	30.5	31.8	32.0	31.0	32.1	31.1	31.2	30.8

3. Average Hourly Earnings by Selected Industry: Connecticut, 2007–2011

(Dollars, not seasonally adjusted)

Industry and year	January	February	March	April	May	June	July	August	September	October	November	December	Annual average
Total Private													
2007	25.86	26.27	25.99	26.38	26.79	26.84	26.80	26.44	26.74	26.81	26.80	27.34	26.59
2008	27.36	27.45	27.66	27.79	27.51	27.97	27.74	27.43	27.73	27.89	27.95	28.09	27.71
2009	27.96	28.17	28.33	27.98	27.57	27.43	27.64	27.82	27.43	27.56	27.93	27.95	27.81
2010	27.75	28.22	28.04	28.43	28.43	27.83	27.78	28.12	28.12	28.01	28.09	28.15	28.08
2011	28.39	28.35	28.29	28.21	28.24	27.88	28.15	28.07	28.14	28.47	28.37	28.32	28.24
Goods-Producing													
2007	28.00	28.39	27.65	28.16	27.92	28.76	27.92	27.74	28.12	28.09	28.43	28.71	28.16
2008	28.42	28.81	28.78	28.89	28.92	29.05	29.26	29.08	29.19	29.11	29.08	29.80	29.03
2009	29.89	29.53	29.64	29.93	29.72	29.68	29.33	29.52	29.15	29.36	29.11	29.85	29.56
2010	29.72	29.92	29.76	29.55	29.83	29.74	29.72	29.79	30.06	29.87	29.78	30.17	29.83
2011	30.44	30.32	30.43	30.26	29.85	30.27	30.13	30.22	30.26	30.41	30.15	30.75	30.29
Construction													
2007	28.07	28.89	28.49	28.46	28.82	28.75	28.29	28.69	28.64	28.26	27.92	27.88	28.43
2008	28.80	29.17	29.49	29.11	28.79	28.85	28.89	28.72	28.60	28.91	28.82	28.86	28.91
2009	29.20	29.16	28.86	28.75	28.53	28.29	28.29	28.61	28.70	29.27	29.23	29.63	28.86
2010	29.65	30.22	30.42	29.11	29.05	28.63	29.01	28.98	29.35	28.87	28.79	29.14	29.22
2011	29.64	29.54	29.69	28.92	28.35	28.50	29.14	28.79	29.08	29.12	29.33	29.15	29.08
Manufacturing													
2007	28.02	28.30	27.46	28.11	27.70	28.83	27.85	27.44	27.96	28.03	28.57	28.92	28.10
2008	28.39	28.76	28.61	28.84	28.97	29.13	29.38	29.19	29.37	29.19	29.21	29.94	29.08
2009	29.93	29.31	29.55	30.02	29.85	29.90	29.57	29.76	29.19	29.20	28.90	29.77	29.58
2010	29.75	29.87	29.58	29.60	30.02	29.93	29.82	29.91	30.15	30.22	30.12	30.42	29.95
2011	30.60	30.47	30.58	30.61	30.29	30.80	30.42	30.47	30.41	30.64	30.26	31.02	30.55
Trade, Transportation, and Utilities													
2007	21.58	21.84	21.86	21.85	21.98	21.69	21.80	21.54	21.92	21.80	22.41	21.95	21.85
2008	22.24	22.58	22.22	23.00	22.65	22.55	22.37	22.30	22.60	22.22	21.95	21.71	22.37
2009	22.55	22.62	22.59	23.16	22.39	22.37	21.46	21.47	21.61	21.16	21.10	21.00	21.95
2010	21.47	22.11	21.50	22.39	22.84	22.54	22.99	22.80	23.17	23.25	23.61	23.83	22.73
2011	24.25	24.73	24.46	24.89	25.38	25.06	25.49	25.18	25.74	25.69	26.06	25.11	25.18
Financial Activities													
2007	38.70	40.40	38.23	40.59	40.75	41.84	40.96	40.13	39.70	41.03	40.29	42.66	40.45
2008	43.19	42.14	42.63	41.95	41.47	43.77	41.73	40.98	41.13	44.55	43.41	42.39	42.44
2009	40.42	42.19	43.26	41.48	41.41	40.49	40.92	41.82	39.72	41.15	41.98	41.57	41.37
2010	40.01	40.11	40.68	41.69	42.21	40.86	41.23	42.14	41.10	41.69	42.03	42.46	41.36
2011	43.10	42.87	42.82	42.75	43.56	42.39	42.18	42.58	40.61	42.77	41.54	41.60	42.40
Professional and Business Services													
2007	28.37	28.39	27.98	28.41	28.94	28.78	29.29	28.65	29.41	29.54	29.36	29.89	28.92
2008	30.28	31.20	31.53	30.99	30.62	31.63	31.81	30.97	30.96	30.38	30.89	31.78	31.09
2009	32.18	32.06	32.07	30.70	30.37	29.92	29.67	29.99	30.07	29.38	29.64	30.21	30.52
2010	30.48	30.40	30.26	29.51	29.81	29.39	29.70	30.08	29.97	30.39	30.18	30.30	30.03
2011	31.44	30.97	30.68	30.55	30.12	29.45	29.99	29.99	30.11	30.39	30.35	30.48	30.36
Education and Health Services													
2007	22.77	23.20	23.67	23.35	23.26	23.13	23.61	23.39	23.47	23.86	23.49	23.82	23.42
2008	24.00	23.93	24.56	24.65	24.45	24.23	24.66	24.37	24.61	24.63	25.28	25.86	24.61
2009	25.92	25.74	26.03	26.09	26.15	26.09	26.14	25.98	25.79	25.83	25.89	25.70	25.94
2010	25.76	25.98	26.01	25.91	26.09	26.10	26.09	26.06	26.04	26.40	26.42	26.54	26.12
2011	26.95	26.27	26.17	26.19	26.18	26.27	26.78	26.34	26.41	26.47	26.56	26.59	26.43
Leisure and Hospitality													
2007	14.85	14.68	15.13	15.15	15.23	14.89	15.14	15.24	15.47	15.57	15.63	16.37	15.29
2008	15.58	15.48	15.30	15.69	15.62	15.84	15.35	15.29	15.67	15.35	15.58	15.65	15.53
2009	15.55	15.40	15.17	15.16	15.02	15.40	15.26	15.53	15.71	15.34	15.22	15.45	15.35
2010	15.37	15.29	15.01	15.16	15.25	15.26	14.91	15.23	15.54	15.45	15.35	15.65	15.29
2011	15.55	15.46	15.49	15.42	15.38	14.96	15.02	14.90	15.21	15.03	15.11	15.17	15.21
Other Services													
2007	20.48	19.79	20.16	21.22	21.04	21.73	21.41	21.53	21.34	20.92	21.12	21.77	21.04
2008	21.58	22.03	22.36	22.58	22.24	22.72	22.98	22.72	23.78	23.08	23.03	22.98	22.67
2009	22.67	22.38	22.19	22.71	21.95	21.82	21.67	21.71	21.95	21.93	22.08	22.35	22.11
2010	22.36	22.05	22.14	22.10	21.86	21.83	21.76	21.81	21.95	21.80	21.77	22.35	21.98
2011	22.60	21.56	21.22	21.03	20.83	20.57	19.61	19.25	19.88	19.30	19.38	19.12	20.32

4. Average Weekly Earnings by Selected Industry: Connecticut, 2007–2011

(Dollars, not seasonally adjusted)

Industry and year	January	February	March	April	May	June	July	August	September	October	November	December	Annual average
Total Private													
2007	879.24	882.67	881.06	904.83	924.26	928.66	927.28	914.82	922.53	919.58	924.60	935.03	912.61
2008	935.71	930.56	948.74	947.64	938.09	959.37	940.39	932.62	942.82	939.89	939.12	935.40	941.16
2009	931.07	940.88	937.72	914.95	912.57	902.45	912.12	920.84	905.19	892.94	921.69	913.97	917.58
2010	915.75	917.15	928.12	946.72	952.41	926.74	925.07	944.83	939.21	941.14	941.02	951.47	935.66
2011	942.55	952.56	953.37	950.68	962.98	942.34	954.29	957.19	959.57	979.37	967.42	968.54	957.43
Goods-Producing													
2007	1,103.20	1,112.89	1,106.00	1,134.85	1,139.14	1,150.40	1,133.55	1,137.34	1,155.73	1,154.50	1,168.47	1,162.76	1,138.45
2008	1,170.90	1,161.04	1,179.98	1,181.60	1,179.94	1,185.24	1,187.96	1,183.56	1,176.36	1,170.22	1,122.49	1,144.32	1,170.53
2009	1,135.82	1,113.28	1,120.39	1,107.41	1,126.39	1,127.84	1,132.14	1,130.62	1,119.36	1,124.49	1,129.47	1,149.23	1,126.37
2010	1,144.22	1,124.99	1,151.71	1,149.50	1,160.39	1,159.86	1,162.05	1,158.83	1,172.34	1,152.98	1,158.44	1,173.61	1,155.84
2011	1,120.19	1,155.19	1,171.56	1,165.01	1,152.21	1,171.45	1,169.04	1,181.60	1,180.14	1,185.99	1,181.88	1,211.55	1,170.50
Construction													
2007	1,004.91	1,011.15	1,005.70	1,035.94	1,106.69	1,078.13	1,108.97	1,127.52	1,114.10	1,116.27	1,080.50	1,048.29	1,072.38
2008	1,100.16	1,102.63	1,120.62	1,106.18	1,088.26	1,093.42	1,103.60	1,108.59	1,078.22	1,072.56	1,051.93	1,024.53	1,087.99
2009	1,001.56	1,020.60	1,024.53	1,017.75	1,044.20	1,032.59	1,052.39	1,070.01	1,044.68	1,077.14	1,066.90	1,051.87	1,042.47
2010	1,049.61	1,045.61	1,085.99	1,062.52	1,069.04	1,070.76	1,084.97	1,095.44	1,100.63	1,076.85	1,068.11	1,072.35	1,073.97
2011	1,007.76	1,045.72	1,065.87	1,038.23	1,034.78	1,048.80	1,075.27	1,088.26	1,081.78	1,065.79	1,064.68	1,081.47	1,058.76
Manufacturing													
2007	1,132.01	1,143.32	1,136.84	1,169.38	1,155.09	1,179.15	1,147.42	1,144.25	1,174.32	1,168.85	1,197.08	1,197.29	1,162.02
2008	1,178.19	1,164.78	1,187.32	1,199.74	1,205.15	1,211.81	1,210.46	1,205.55	1,204.17	1,202.63	1,174.24	1,200.59	1,195.40
2009	1,197.20	1,148.95	1,155.41	1,146.76	1,155.20	1,160.12	1,162.10	1,157.66	1,147.17	1,144.64	1,153.11	1,187.82	1,159.83
2010	1,187.03	1,167.92	1,180.24	1,178.08	1,194.80	1,185.23	1,183.85	1,178.45	1,196.96	1,187.65	1,195.76	1,219.84	1,187.95
2011	1,168.92	1,197.47	1,207.91	1,209.10	1,196.46	1,219.68	1,207.67	1,212.71	1,213.36	1,228.66	1,222.50	1,253.21	1,211.46
Trade, Transportation, and Utilities													
2007	733.72	731.64	736.68	753.83	760.51	765.66	767.36	751.75	762.82	747.74	768.66	741.91	751.90
2008	745.04	756.43	755.48	779.70	772.37	782.49	760.58	758.20	770.66	737.70	741.91	731.63	757.62
2009	759.94	755.51	754.51	764.28	750.07	744.92	712.47	714.95	726.10	698.28	702.63	709.80	732.79
2010	712.80	723.00	709.50	741.11	769.71	759.60	765.57	763.80	778.51	785.85	795.66	814.99	760.54
2011	822.08	853.19	841.42	858.71	880.69	859.56	871.76	866.19	895.75	901.72	912.10	886.38	871.09
Financial Activities													
2007	1,319.67	1,377.64	1,318.94	1,412.53	1,401.80	1,447.66	1,458.18	1,412.58	1,409.35	1,440.15	1,422.24	1,540.03	1,413.43
2008	1,528.93	1,504.40	1,556.00	1,493.42	1,480.48	1,575.72	1,473.07	1,442.50	1,443.66	1,545.89	1,554.08	1,509.08	1,508.89
2009	1,447.04	1,510.40	1,553.03	1,468.39	1,470.06	1,445.49	1,440.38	1,505.52	1,410.06	1,469.06	1,557.46	1,496.52	1,481.11
2010	1,440.36	1,447.97	1,484.82	1,509.18	1,570.21	1,499.56	1,521.39	1,567.61	1,504.26	1,534.19	1,559.31	1,583.76	1,519.01
2011	1,607.63	1,586.19	1,588.62	1,573.20	1,629.14	1,559.95	1,552.22	1,566.94	1,502.57	1,612.43	1,536.98	1,539.20	1,571.17
Professional and Business Services													
2007	964.58	948.23	954.12	982.99	1,007.11	1,010.18	1,007.58	988.43	1,002.88	998.45	989.43	1,019.25	989.79
2008	1,035.58	1,045.20	1,072.02	1,081.55	1,074.76	1,122.87	1,091.08	1,068.47	1,071.22	1,054.19	1,071.88	1,083.70	1,072.88
2009	1,061.94	1,077.22	1,064.72	1,019.24	1,017.40	990.35	982.08	1,004.67	983.29	975.42	1,010.72	996.93	1,015.50
2010	1,018.03	997.12	1,016.74	1,003.34	1,025.46	993.38	989.01	1,022.72	998.00	1,015.03	1,011.03	1,021.11	1,009.23
2011	1,059.53	1,046.79	1,043.12	1,038.70	1,060.22	1,033.70	1,049.65	1,043.65	1,053.85	1,060.61	1,044.04	1,048.51	1,048.47
Education and Health Services													
2007	735.47	730.80	745.61	742.53	732.69	735.53	734.27	732.11	729.92	737.27	742.28	738.42	736.44
2008	746.40	739.44	758.90	759.22	750.62	746.28	757.06	755.47	760.45	758.60	781.15	788.73	758.69
2009	795.74	797.94	793.92	782.70	787.12	785.31	792.04	787.19	794.33	792.98	794.82	783.85	790.68
2010	790.83	779.40	788.10	787.66	798.35	798.66	806.18	810.47	796.82	805.20	800.53	812.12	797.83
2011	813.89	803.86	803.42	809.27	808.96	809.12	830.18	821.81	818.71	823.22	820.70	832.27	816.31
Leisure and Hospitality													
2007	380.16	386.08	399.43	401.48	424.92	416.92	426.95	432.82	436.25	440.63	447.02	456.72	421.54
2008	426.89	430.34	428.40	411.08	413.93	411.84	415.99	400.60	412.12	405.24	409.75	408.47	414.28
2009	398.08	415.80	394.42	401.74	398.03	398.86	404.39	411.55	411.60	411.11	406.37	400.16	404.40
2010	384.25	383.78	376.75	401.74	401.08	395.23	398.10	408.16	411.81	414.06	409.85	411.60	400.19
2011	388.75	408.14	405.84	407.09	409.11	399.43	405.54	399.32	406.11	405.81	409.48	408.07	404.50
Other Services													
2007	684.03	645.15	659.23	706.63	681.70	708.40	691.54	678.20	680.75	665.26	694.85	690.11	682.26
2008	671.14	698.35	693.16	690.95	673.87	683.87	696.29	674.78	718.16	708.56	697.81	668.72	689.59
2009	661.96	644.54	639.07	651.78	647.53	648.05	641.43	644.79	647.53	653.51	655.78	652.62	648.89
2010	648.44	635.04	642.06	634.27	636.13	630.89	657.15	658.66	651.92	660.54	655.28	672.74	648.45
2011	664.44	644.64	619.62	628.80	641.56	627.39	623.60	616.00	616.28	619.53	602.72	596.54	625.01

DELAWARE
At a Glance

Population:
  2000 census: 783,559
  2010 census: 897,934
  2011 estimate: 907,135

Percent change in population:
  2000–2010: 14.6%
  2010–2011: 1.0%

Percent change in total nonfarm employment:
  2000–2010: -1.6%
  2010–2011: 0.8%

Industry with the largest growth in employment, 2000–2011 (thousands):
  Education and Health Services, 20.6

Industry with the largest decline or smallest growth in employment, 2000–2011 (thousands):
  Manufacturing, -15.8

Civilian labor force:
  2000: 416,503
  2010: 436,822
  2011: 439,181

Unemployment rate and rank among states (lowest to highest):
  2000: 3.3%, 14th
  2010: 8.0%, 18th
  2011: 7.3%, 16th

Over-the-year change in unemployment rates:
  2010–2011: -0.7%

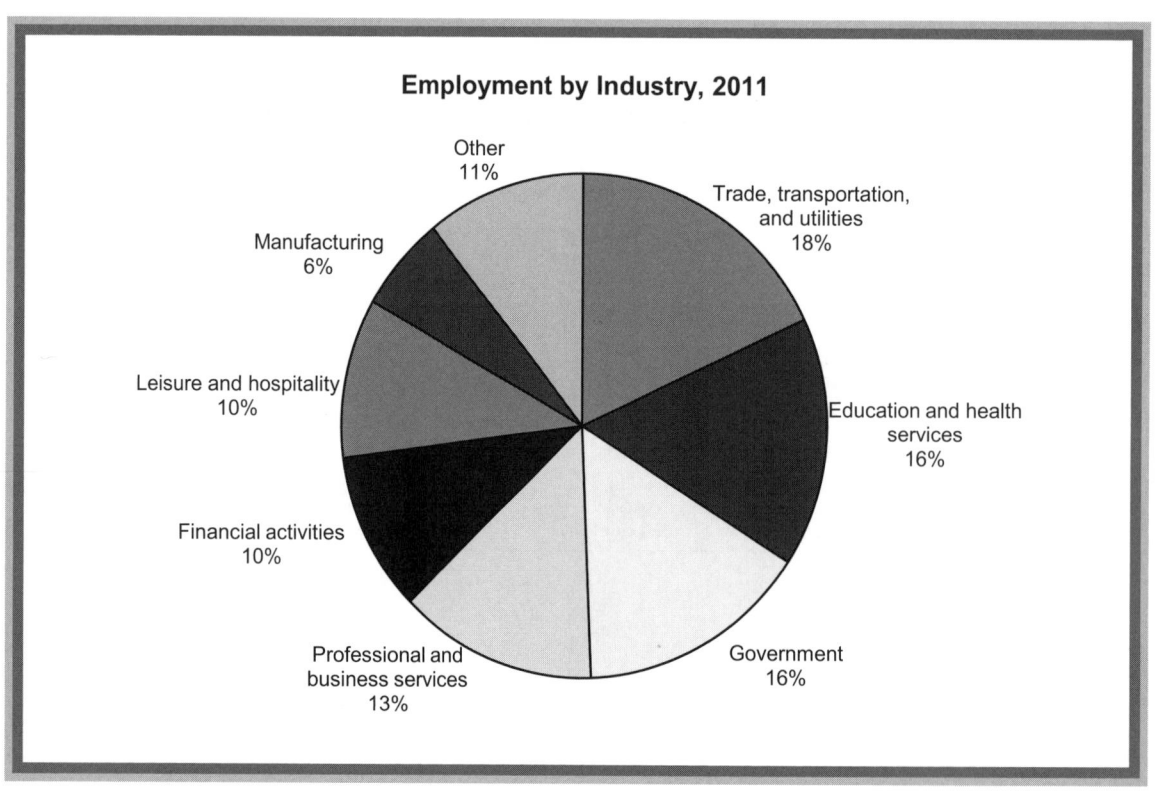

Employment by Industry, 2011

Other 11%
Trade, transportation, and utilities 18%
Manufacturing 6%
Leisure and hospitality 10%
Education and health services 16%
Financial activities 10%
Professional and business services 13%
Government 16%

1. Employment by Industry: Delaware, Selected Years, 2000–2011

(Numbers in thousands, not seasonally adjusted)

Industry and year	January	February	March	April	May	June	July	August	September	October	November	December	Annual average
Total Nonfarm													
2000	407.4	409.3	415.6	418.2	421.7	427.1	426.3	424.0	422.9	422.4	424.7	426.5	420.5
2001	411.5	412.9	420.3	420.5	423.6	427.9	423.6	422.2	418.7	418.6	420.7	420.6	420.1
2002	404.3	405.9	408.8	412.5	418.2	420.2	419.5	418.9	420.5	416.8	419.3	419.9	415.4
2003	404.1	401.5	405.7	411.0	417.2	422.5	419.2	419.2	420.2	420.9	422.4	424.1	415.7
2004	412.0	413.9	418.7	419.4	425.9	431.3	428.3	427.9	428.6	430.2	432.5	432.3	425.1
2005	418.6	419.5	424.4	430.6	434.9	436.3	436.0	436.2	437.4	437.6	442.5	441.3	432.9
2006	427.5	428.0	432.5	436.3	441.6	444.3	439.6	439.2	439.9	441.0	442.9	444.8	438.1
2007	428.7	427.6	432.8	436.7	442.3	445.8	441.6	441.1	440.2	440.5	444.3	445.7	438.9
2008	430.7	431.8	434.9	439.7	441.8	443.7	439.7	438.2	436.3	435.4	435.9	433.4	436.8
2009	415.7	414.2	415.0	416.9	422.0	421.5	416.7	415.6	415.0	416.1	415.7	414.8	416.6
2010	399.9	397.2	403.9	411.5	417.2	419.8	420.2	418.9	419.3	418.0	419.2	420.4	413.8
2011	406.8	407.9	411.8	418.6	420.7	423.0	422.9	419.0	418.7	419.7	418.9	419.4	417.3
Total Private													
2000	353.1	353.6	358.1	360.4	363.4	369.9	369.4	369.3	367.7	365.9	367.0	368.7	363.9
2001	355.3	355.9	362.1	362.0	365.5	371.0	367.1	367.5	364.0	362.0	363.2	362.9	363.2
2002	348.6	348.9	351.1	354.6	360.5	364.0	364.7	365.5	363.0	358.2	360.0	360.9	358.3
2003	347.4	344.2	348.0	352.8	358.6	365.3	364.3	365.4	363.0	362.5	364.1	365.6	358.4
2004	354.9	356.1	359.9	361.3	367.3	374.0	373.1	373.2	370.4	371.7	373.8	373.5	367.4
2005	360.6	360.6	364.3	370.0	374.1	378.2	378.5	379.8	377.5	375.9	380.6	379.7	373.3
2006	367.6	366.9	370.1	373.8	378.3	384.7	381.2	382.1	379.5	378.8	380.3	382.3	377.1
2007	368.1	365.9	369.9	373.5	378.8	385.1	382.1	382.5	378.7	376.9	380.4	382.0	377.0
2008	368.6	369.0	370.9	375.2	377.2	382.2	379.4	378.6	373.6	371.2	371.9	369.6	374.0
2009	353.6	350.6	349.9	351.7	356.9	359.6	357.2	356.3	352.4	350.8	350.4	350.1	353.3
2010	337.9	334.2	339.2	346.2	350.8	356.4	358.7	358.6	355.6	353.2	353.8	355.2	350.0
2011	344.1	344.2	346.9	353.3	355.5	359.2	361.1	358.1	354.3	354.5	353.3	353.9	353.2
Goods-Producing													
2000	64.3	64.8	66.1	66.3	67.0	68.3	66.5	66.7	66.4	66.8	65.8	65.4	66.2
2001	60.9	61.3	64.1	64.4	64.8	66.1	64.8	64.8	64.5	63.7	63.8	63.3	63.9
2002	60.5	61.1	61.2	59.7	61.8	62.2	62.3	62.2	61.9	61.1	60.8	60.8	61.3
2003	57.5	57.1	57.9	58.7	60.2	61.8	60.5	61.2	61.4	62.0	61.8	60.5	60.1
2004	58.7	59.1	60.1	60.8	61.2	62.2	62.2	62.1	61.2	61.7	61.6	61.0	61.0
2005	58.1	59.0	60.0	61.2	61.9	61.1	61.1	62.4	62.3	61.9	64.2	61.2	61.2
2006	61.7	61.3	62.0	62.7	63.1	64.1	63.0	63.7	63.8	63.7	63.2	62.8	62.9
2007	60.3	59.0	60.1	60.6	61.5	61.9	60.9	61.4	60.5	59.9	61.0	60.4	60.6
2008	57.3	58.1	58.0	58.6	57.6	58.6	56.9	56.8	55.5	54.7	55.4	53.9	56.8
2009	50.5	48.9	48.3	48.2	48.5	48.5	47.8	47.7	46.9	47.2	46.8	46.1	48.0
2010	44.4	42.9	43.9	45.4	45.5	46.3	45.9	46.1	45.8	45.8	45.6	45.5	45.3
2011	44.0	43.9	44.7	45.8	46.0	45.8	45.7	44.9	45.2	46.2	45.4	44.8	45.2
Mining, Logging, and Construction													
2000	24.1	23.2	24.5	24.9	24.8	25.5	25.1	25.1	24.9	25.5	24.5	24.2	24.7
2001	23.0	23.1	23.6	23.9	24.4	25.4	24.8	25.2	25.1	25.0	25.5	24.9	24.5
2002	23.4	23.1	23.2	24.0	24.4	24.9	25.3	25.1	24.6	24.1	24.0	24.2	24.2
2003	23.0	21.6	22.2	23.4	24.3	24.9	25.5	25.5	25.2	25.7	25.8	25.6	24.4
2004	24.4	24.1	25.1	25.8	26.1	27.0	27.4	27.5	27.3	27.7	27.6	26.8	26.4
2005	25.9	25.5	26.3	27.5	27.9	28.5	28.7	28.5	28.4	29.6	30.4	28.9	28.0
2006	28.0	27.8	28.3	29.3	29.6	30.5	30.1	30.2	30.1	30.1	29.5	29.1	29.4
2007	27.2	26.0	26.8	27.4	28.0	28.2	28.1	28.0	28.0	27.3	27.5	26.9	27.5
2008	25.7	25.1	25.3	26.3	26.1	26.1	25.8	25.6	24.7	23.8	23.6	22.7	25.1
2009	20.7	19.9	20.1	20.0	20.4	20.6	20.4	20.3	19.6	19.8	19.5	19.1	20.0
2010	18.0	17.1	18.0	19.3	19.6	20.1	19.9	20.1	19.8	20.0	20.0	19.9	19.3
2011	18.7	18.6	19.3	20.2	20.1	20.0	19.9	19.2	19.4	20.3	19.6	19.3	19.6
Manufacturing													
2000	40.2	41.6	41.6	41.4	42.2	42.8	41.4	41.6	41.5	41.3	41.3	41.2	41.5
2001	37.9	38.2	40.5	40.5	40.4	40.7	40.0	39.6	39.4	38.7	38.3	38.4	39.4
2002	37.1	38.0	38.0	35.7	37.4	37.3	37.0	37.1	37.3	37.0	36.8	36.6	37.1
2003	34.5	35.5	35.7	35.3	35.9	36.9	35.0	35.7	36.2	36.3	36.0	34.9	35.7
2004	34.3	35.0	35.0	35.0	35.1	35.2	34.8	34.6	33.9	34.0	34.0	34.2	34.6
2005	32.2	33.5	33.7	33.7	34.0	32.6	32.4	33.9	33.9	32.3	33.8	32.3	33.2
2006	33.7	33.5	33.7	33.4	33.5	33.6	32.9	33.5	33.7	33.6	33.7	33.7	33.5
2007	33.1	33.0	33.3	33.2	33.5	33.7	32.8	33.4	32.5	32.6	33.5	33.5	33.2
2008	31.6	33.0	32.7	32.3	31.5	32.5	31.1	31.2	30.8	30.9	31.8	31.2	31.7
2009	29.8	29.0	28.2	28.2	28.1	27.9	27.4	27.4	27.3	27.4	27.3	27.0	27.9
2010	26.4	25.8	25.9	26.1	25.9	26.2	26.0	26.0	26.0	25.8	25.6	25.6	25.9
2011	25.3	25.3	25.4	25.6	25.9	25.8	25.8	25.7	25.8	25.9	25.8	25.5	25.7
Service-Providing													
2000	343.1	344.5	349.5	351.9	354.7	358.8	359.8	357.3	356.5	355.6	358.9	361.1	354.3
2001	350.6	351.6	356.2	356.1	358.8	361.8	358.8	357.4	354.2	354.9	356.9	357.3	356.2
2002	343.8	344.8	347.6	352.8	356.4	358.0	357.2	356.7	358.6	355.7	358.5	359.1	354.1
2003	346.6	344.4	347.8	352.3	357.0	360.7	358.7	358.0	358.8	358.9	360.6	363.6	355.6
2004	353.3	354.8	358.6	358.6	364.7	369.1	366.1	365.8	367.4	368.5	370.9	371.3	364.1
2005	360.5	360.5	364.4	369.4	373.0	375.2	374.9	373.8	375.1	375.7	378.3	380.1	371.7
2006	365.8	366.7	370.5	373.6	378.5	380.2	376.6	375.5	376.1	377.3	379.7	382.0	375.2
2007	368.4	368.6	372.7	376.1	380.8	383.9	380.7	379.7	379.7	380.6	383.3	385.3	378.3
2008	373.4	373.7	376.9	381.1	384.2	385.1	382.8	381.4	380.8	380.7	380.5	379.5	380.0
2009	365.2	365.3	366.7	368.7	373.5	373.0	368.9	367.9	368.1	368.9	368.9	368.7	368.7
2010	355.5	354.3	360.0	366.1	371.7	373.5	374.3	372.8	373.5	372.2	373.6	374.9	368.5
2011	362.8	364.0	367.1	372.8	374.7	377.2	377.2	374.1	373.5	373.5	373.5	374.6	372.1

1. Employment by Industry: Delaware, Selected Years, 2000–2011—*Continued*

(Numbers in thousands, not seasonally adjusted)

Industry and year	January	February	March	April	May	June	July	August	September	October	November	December	Annual average
Trade, Transportation, and Utilities													
2000	77.4	76.6	76.7	77.9	78.5	79.7	79.6	79.4	79.5	79.4	80.9	83.0	79.1
2001	76.7	76.0	76.6	75.3	75.7	77.0	76.3	76.2	76.1	77.2	78.3	79.4	76.7
2002	74.9	74.2	75.1	75.4	76.9	77.8	77.8	77.7	77.9	77.3	79.0	80.4	77.0
2003	76.1	75.1	76.2	77.0	78.3	79.4	78.9	79.4	79.1	79.8	81.3	83.3	78.7
2004	78.6	78.1	78.7	79.4	80.2	81.8	81.3	81.0	80.8	81.5	83.6	84.5	80.8
2005	79.9	78.9	79.8	80.3	81.1	81.8	82.1	82.1	81.7	82.5	84.5	86.1	81.7
2006	81.1	80.1	80.9	81.7	82.8	83.5	83.0	82.4	81.9	82.5	84.7	85.6	82.5
2007	81.9	80.6	81.1	81.3	82.9	83.9	83.8	83.7	83.2	82.8	85.2	86.1	83.0
2008	81.5	80.4	80.9	80.4	81.3	81.9	81.3	80.9	80.3	80.7	81.7	82.6	81.2
2009	76.3	74.9	74.7	74.3	75.1	75.5	75.0	74.9	74.9	74.8	76.3	76.8	75.3
2010	72.6	71.2	72.2	73.2	74.5	75.2	75.0	74.8	74.8	75.1	77.1	78.0	74.5
2011	74.0	73.4	73.7	75.1	75.3	76.0	75.9	75.2	75.1	74.9	76.3	77.2	75.2
Wholesale Trade													
2000	12.7	12.8	12.9	13.3	13.2	13.3	13.4	13.5	13.5	13.6	13.6	13.7	13.3
2001	13.4	13.5	13.6	13.3	13.3	13.4	13.3	13.3	13.3	13.4	13.3	13.4	13.4
2002	13.3	13.2	13.6	13.5	13.7	13.8	13.8	13.9	13.8	13.7	13.6	13.7	13.6
2003	13.6	13.6	13.9	14.0	14.3	14.2	14.4	14.5	14.4	14.3	14.3	14.4	14.2
2004	14.3	14.3	14.4	14.7	14.8	14.9	15.0	14.9	14.8	15.0	14.9	14.9	14.7
2005	14.8	14.8	14.9	14.9	14.9	14.8	14.8	14.9	14.8	15.0	15.1	15.3	14.9
2006	14.9	15.0	15.0	15.2	15.3	15.3	15.3	15.2	15.1	15.0	14.9	15.2	15.1
2007	14.8	14.7	14.7	14.9	15.0	15.1	15.2	15.2	15.0	14.8	14.9	14.9	14.9
2008	14.7	14.7	14.8	14.6	14.8	14.7	14.7	14.5	14.4	14.5	14.4	14.2	14.6
2009	13.7	13.6	13.5	13.5	13.4	13.2	13.2	13.1	12.9	12.9	12.8	12.7	13.2
2010	12.4	12.5	12.5	12.6	12.6	12.5	12.6	12.5	12.6	12.4	12.4	12.4	12.5
2011	12.5	12.6	12.5	12.6	12.5	12.6	12.5	12.3	12.5	12.3	12.3	12.1	12.4
Retail Trade													
2000	50.3	49.4	49.4	50.2	50.9	52.2	52.2	51.9	51.7	51.5	53.1	55.0	51.5
2001	50.4	49.7	50.1	49.1	49.6	50.7	50.4	50.6	50.2	50.7	52.1	53.3	50.6
2002	49.6	48.7	49.3	49.7	50.7	51.7	51.9	51.9	51.6	51.0	52.8	54.2	51.1
2003	50.0	49.0	49.8	50.5	51.3	52.4	52.4	52.8	51.8	52.4	53.8	55.1	51.8
2004	51.0	50.3	50.7	51.1	51.9	53.2	53.1	53.2	52.4	52.8	54.9	55.7	52.5
2005	52.0	51.1	51.6	52.3	53.1	53.8	54.4	54.4	53.4	53.7	55.6	57.0	53.5
2006	52.9	51.7	52.4	52.9	53.6	54.2	54.3	53.9	52.8	53.2	55.7	56.1	53.6
2007	53.1	52.1	52.7	52.8	53.9	54.9	55.1	54.9	54.2	54.1	56.5	57.2	54.3
2008	53.4	52.2	52.5	52.2	52.8	53.6	53.2	53.1	52.2	52.4	53.5	54.3	53.0
2009	49.9	48.6	48.6	48.4	49.2	49.9	50.2	50.1	49.5	49.4	51.0	51.6	49.7
2010	48.0	46.7	47.6	48.5	49.6	50.5	50.9	50.8	49.9	50.3	52.3	53.0	49.8
2011	49.2	48.5	48.9	50.1	50.3	51.1	50.9	50.5	49.5	49.5	50.9	51.5	50.1
Transportation and Utilities													
2000	14.4	14.4	14.4	14.4	14.4	14.2	14.0	14.0	14.3	14.3	14.2	14.3	14.3
2001	12.9	12.8	12.9	12.9	12.8	12.9	12.6	12.3	12.6	13.1	12.9	12.7	12.8
2002	12.0	12.3	12.2	12.2	12.5	12.3	12.1	11.9	12.5	12.6	12.6	12.5	12.3
2003	12.5	12.5	12.5	12.5	12.7	12.8	12.1	12.1	12.9	13.1	13.2	13.8	12.7
2004	13.3	13.5	13.6	13.6	13.5	13.7	13.2	12.9	13.6	13.7	13.8	13.9	13.5
2005	13.1	13.0	13.3	13.1	13.1	13.2	12.9	12.8	13.5	13.8	13.8	13.8	13.3
2006	13.3	13.4	13.5	13.6	13.9	14.0	13.4	13.3	14.0	14.3	14.1	14.3	13.8
2007	14.0	13.8	13.7	13.6	14.0	13.9	13.5	13.6	14.0	13.9	13.8	14.0	13.8
2008	13.4	13.5	13.6	13.6	13.7	13.6	13.4	13.3	13.7	13.8	13.8	14.1	13.6
2009	12.7	12.7	12.6	12.4	12.5	12.4	11.6	11.7	12.5	12.5	12.5	12.5	12.3
2010	12.2	12.0	12.1	12.1	12.3	12.2	11.5	11.5	12.3	12.4	12.4	12.6	12.1
2011	12.3	12.3	12.3	12.4	12.5	12.3	12.5	12.4	13.1	13.1	13.1	13.6	12.7
Information													
2000	8.1	8.3	8.4	8.0	8.1	8.1	8.3	7.6	8.3	8.1	8.2	8.2	8.1
2001	8.0	8.0	8.1	8.1	8.1	8.2	8.2	8.2	8.1	7.9	8.0	8.0	8.1
2002	7.8	7.8	7.8	7.7	7.7	7.8	7.8	7.9	7.7	7.6	7.7	7.6	7.7
2003	7.5	7.5	7.5	7.4	7.4	7.4	7.4	7.4	7.3	7.1	7.2	7.2	7.4
2004	7.3	7.2	7.3	7.0	7.0	7.0	7.0	7.0	6.9	7.0	7.0	7.0	7.1
2005	6.4	6.4	6.5	6.7	6.8	6.8	6.8	6.7	6.7	6.8	6.8	6.8	6.7
2006	6.7	6.7	6.6	6.6	6.6	6.7	6.7	6.8	6.7	6.7	6.8	6.8	6.7
2007	6.8	6.8	6.8	6.8	6.8	6.9	7.0	7.0	7.0	7.1	7.1	7.1	6.9
2008	7.0	7.1	7.1	7.1	7.1	7.2	7.0	7.1	7.0	7.0	6.9	6.8	7.0
2009	6.8	6.7	6.7	6.6	6.6	6.5	6.5	6.4	6.3	6.4	6.2	6.1	6.5
2010	5.9	5.9	6.0	6.1	6.0	6.0	6.0	5.9	6.0	5.9	5.9	5.8	6.0
2011	5.8	5.8	5.8	5.8	5.6	5.8	5.9	5.3	5.8	5.8	5.8	5.7	5.7
Financial Activities													
2000	46.2	46.4	46.3	46.0	46.1	46.6	46.7	46.9	46.4	46.2	46.5	46.8	46.4
2001	46.6	46.7	46.9	47.0	47.1	47.3	47.3	47.2	46.8	46.3	46.0	45.8	46.8
2002	46.7	46.6	46.6	46.3	46.5	46.7	47.1	46.9	46.2	45.8	45.8	45.8	46.4
2003	45.5	45.3	45.2	45.6	45.6	45.7	46.5	46.0	45.3	44.2	44.2	44.2	45.3
2004	44.1	44.1	44.3	44.3	44.6	45.0	45.6	45.7	45.0	44.4	44.6	44.5	44.7
2005	45.1	45.1	44.9	44.8	45.0	45.3	45.9	45.8	45.3	45.1	45.2	45.2	45.2
2006	44.5	44.4	44.2	44.5	44.4	44.6	44.7	45.3	45.0	44.9	45.0	45.2	44.7
2007	44.8	44.9	44.9	45.1	45.3	45.8	45.8	45.6	45.2	45.3	45.2	45.2	45.3
2008	45.0	45.0	45.2	45.5	45.7	46.3	46.5	46.5	45.5	45.3	45.0	44.6	45.5
2009	44.3	44.0	43.9	43.9	44.2	44.5	44.6	44.2	43.9	43.3	43.1	43.0	43.9
2010	42.4	42.4	42.6	42.5	42.5	43.1	43.4	43.4	43.0	42.3	42.2	42.8	42.7
2011	42.3	42.4	42.3	42.3	42.3	42.8	42.9	42.7	42.9	42.9	42.8	43.2	42.7

1. Employment by Industry: Delaware, Selected Years, 2000–2011—*Continued*

(Numbers in thousands, not seasonally adjusted)

Industry and year	January	February	March	April	May	June	July	August	September	October	November	December	Annual average
Professional and Business Services													
2000	64.9	64.8	65.9	65.6	65.2	66.2	66.7	67.0	67.0	66.7	67.2	67.3	66.2
2001	66.6	66.6	67.3	66.2	66.3	66.5	65.3	66.0	65.1	64.7	65.6	65.2	66.0
2002	61.0	60.6	60.3	61.2	61.0	60.1	60.5	60.9	60.9	60.5	60.8	61.3	60.8
2003	59.1	57.9	58.2	58.3	58.7	58.9	58.5	58.5	58.8	59.6	59.8	60.8	58.9
2004	59.8	61.2	61.8	60.1	61.5	62.2	61.4	61.7	61.5	62.4	63.0	63.5	61.7
2005	60.8	60.7	61.2	62.6	62.7	63.1	62.7	62.7	62.7	62.7	63.3	64.3	62.5
2006	60.8	61.0	61.5	61.3	61.4	61.2	60.7	61.0	60.7	60.7	60.9	62.6	61.2
2007	58.3	58.5	59.4	60.2	60.5	61.0	60.3	60.3	60.2	60.6	61.5	62.7	60.3
2008	59.6	59.4	59.4	60.3	59.9	60.0	59.6	59.4	59.0	59.0	59.5	59.5	59.6
2009	56.0	55.9	55.7	55.8	56.2	56.1	55.1	54.9	54.5	55.0	55.3	56.2	55.6
2010	53.2	53.3	53.5	54.1	54.7	55.0	55.7	55.5	55.2	55.7	55.5	56.8	54.9
2011	54.0	54.4	54.3	56.2	55.6	55.8	56.4	56.5	55.6	55.9	56.0	56.0	55.6
Education and Health Services													
2000	44.9	45.3	45.7	45.8	45.7	45.8	45.9	46.1	46.6	46.6	47.0	47.2	46.1
2001	47.0	47.5	47.9	48.0	48.1	48.1	47.4	47.7	48.4	49.1	49.1	49.1	48.1
2002	48.4	48.8	49.1	49.5	49.7	49.5	49.0	49.7	50.2	50.3	50.6	50.7	49.6
2003	50.7	50.7	51.1	51.3	51.4	51.4	50.8	51.1	51.9	52.3	52.6	52.9	51.5
2004	52.3	52.4	52.7	52.9	53.2	53.2	52.6	52.7	53.6	54.9	54.8	55.1	53.4
2005	54.7	54.9	55.3	55.6	55.8	55.9	55.0	55.1	55.9	56.1	56.4	56.6	55.6
2006	56.5	56.7	57.0	57.4	57.7	57.9	58.0	57.9	58.3	58.6	59.1	59.2	57.9
2007	58.9	59.0	59.3	59.6	59.9	59.8	59.5	59.6	60.5	60.8	61.0	61.4	59.9
2008	61.4	62.0	61.9	62.6	62.8	62.7	62.1	62.4	62.9	63.0	63.4	63.4	62.6
2009	63.3	63.4	63.4	63.6	63.8	63.5	63.3	63.4	63.5	64.1	64.3	64.2	63.7
2010	63.7	63.6	64.2	64.8	64.9	64.5	65.1	65.4	65.2	65.3	65.5	65.5	64.8
2011	65.4	65.6	66.2	66.3	66.4	66.1	66.5	66.6	66.9	67.7	68.0	68.1	66.7
Leisure and Hospitality													
2000	31.8	31.9	33.3	35.0	37.0	39.1	39.7	39.5	37.6	35.6	34.9	34.4	35.8
2001	32.4	32.7	33.9	35.8	38.1	39.9	40.4	40.0	37.8	35.8	35.1	34.7	36.4
2002	32.4	32.6	33.7	37.0	38.9	41.5	42.0	42.0	40.4	37.3	37.1	36.0	37.6
2003	33.3	33.0	34.2	36.6	38.9	42.1	43.1	43.1	40.8	38.9	38.4	37.9	38.4
2004	35.5	35.3	36.1	38.2	40.9	43.6	44.1	44.1	42.7	40.6	40.0	38.7	40.0
2005	36.3	36.3	37.2	39.2	41.2	44.4	45.0	45.0	43.1	40.7	40.0	39.2	40.6
2006	36.3	36.6	37.6	39.3	42.0	46.1	44.6	44.7	43.1	41.3	40.1	39.3	40.9
2007	36.8	37.0	38.0	39.7	41.7	45.3	44.6	44.9	42.2	40.3	39.3	38.9	40.7
2008	36.8	36.9	38.3	40.3	42.4	44.8	45.4	45.3	43.2	41.3	39.9	38.7	41.1
2009	36.6	37.0	37.5	39.6	42.5	44.7	44.9	44.9	42.8	40.6	39.0	38.3	40.7
2010	36.4	35.9	37.4	40.5	43.0	46.1	47.7	47.5	45.9	43.4	42.4	41.2	42.3
2011	39.1	39.2	40.4	42.2	44.5	46.9	47.8	47.3	43.7	41.9	40.1	39.7	42.7
Other Services													
2000	15.5	15.5	15.7	15.8	15.8	16.1	16.0	16.1	15.9	16.5	16.5	16.4	16.0
2001	17.1	17.1	17.3	17.2	17.3	17.9	17.4	17.4	17.2	17.3	17.3	17.4	17.3
2002	16.9	17.2	17.3	17.8	18.0	18.4	18.2	18.2	17.8	18.3	18.2	18.3	17.9
2003	17.7	17.6	17.7	17.9	18.1	18.6	18.6	18.7	18.4	18.6	18.8	18.8	18.3
2004	18.6	18.7	18.9	18.6	18.7	19.0	18.9	18.9	18.7	19.2	19.2	19.2	18.9
2005	19.3	19.3	19.4	19.6	19.6	19.8	19.9	20.0	19.8	20.1	20.2	20.3	19.8
2006	20.0	20.1	20.3	20.3	20.3	20.6	20.5	20.3	20.0	20.4	20.5	20.8	20.3
2007	20.3	20.1	20.3	20.2	20.2	20.5	20.2	20.0	19.9	20.1	20.1	20.2	20.2
2008	20.0	20.1	20.1	20.4	20.4	20.7	20.6	20.5	20.2	20.2	20.1	20.1	20.3
2009	19.8	19.8	19.7	19.7	20.0	20.3	20.0	19.9	19.6	19.4	19.4	19.4	19.8
2010	19.3	19.0	19.4	19.6	19.7	20.2	19.9	20.0	19.7	19.7	19.6	19.6	19.6
2011	19.5	19.5	19.5	19.6	19.8	20.0	20.0	19.6	19.1	19.2	18.9	19.2	19.5
Government													
2000	54.3	55.7	57.5	57.8	58.3	57.2	56.9	54.7	55.2	56.5	57.7	57.8	56.6
2001	56.2	57.0	58.2	58.5	58.1	56.9	56.5	54.7	54.7	56.6	57.5	57.7	56.9
2002	55.7	57.0	57.7	57.9	57.7	56.2	54.8	53.4	57.5	58.6	59.3	59.0	57.1
2003	56.7	57.3	57.7	58.2	58.6	57.2	54.9	53.8	57.2	58.4	58.3	58.5	57.2
2004	57.1	57.8	58.8	58.1	58.6	57.3	55.2	54.7	58.2	58.5	58.7	58.8	57.7
2005	58.0	58.9	60.1	60.6	60.8	58.1	57.5	56.4	59.9	61.7	61.9	61.6	59.6
2006	59.9	61.1	62.4	62.5	63.3	59.6	58.4	57.1	60.4	62.2	62.6	62.5	61.0
2007	60.6	61.7	62.9	63.2	63.5	60.7	59.5	58.6	61.5	63.6	63.9	63.7	62.0
2008	62.1	62.8	64.0	64.5	64.6	61.5	60.3	59.6	62.7	64.2	64.0	63.8	62.8
2009	62.1	63.6	65.1	65.2	65.1	61.9	59.5	59.3	62.6	65.3	65.3	64.7	63.3
2010	62.0	63.0	64.7	65.3	66.4	63.4	61.5	60.3	63.7	64.8	65.4	65.2	63.8
2011	62.7	63.7	64.9	65.3	65.2	63.8	61.8	60.9	64.4	65.2	65.6	65.5	64.1

2. Average Weekly Hours by Selected Industry: Delaware, 2007–2011

(Not seasonally adjusted)

Industry and year	January	February	March	April	May	June	July	August	September	October	November	December	Annual average
Total Private													
2007	33.5	33.6	33.5	33.9	33.9	34.2	34.5	34.6	34.8	34.7	35.5	34.6	34.3
2008	34.0	34.0	34.6	34.3	33.7	34.4	34.1	33.9	33.4	33.3	33.1	33.0	33.8
2009	32.6	32.7	32.8	32.6	32.8	32.8	32.8	33.3	32.7	32.4	32.4	32.4	32.7
2010	32.4	31.6	32.8	32.7	33.0	32.5	32.5	32.7	32.0	32.2	32.2	32.7	32.4
2011	32.8	32.8	32.6	32.8	33.2	33.0	33.3	33.3	33.3	33.6	33.1	33.3	33.1
Goods-Producing													
2007	38.4	36.9	37.9	38.8	39.3	39.5	38.4	39.7	39.2	38.8	38.4	37.7	38.6
2008	37.0	36.3	37.5	37.7	36.6	37.8	37.4	37.6	37.8	37.0	35.9	37.8	37.2
2009	36.0	36.0	36.2	36.4	37.1	37.3	37.6	37.5	36.9	37.5	36.9	37.9	36.9
2010	37.4	36.4	37.2	36.6	36.8	37.2	36.9	36.9	36.5	37.7	37.5	38.1	37.1
2011	36.9	37.3	37.1	37.3	38.7	38.3	39.0	38.8	39.6	38.6	38.5	39.5	38.3
Mining, Logging, and Construction													
2007	37.6	35.1	36.6	37.4	39.1	38.7	38.7	38.4	38.0	37.4	37.1	36.1	37.5
2008	35.8	34.8	37.0	36.0	35.2	37.6	38.4	37.9	37.8	37.4	36.2	35.7	36.7
2009	35.7	36.2	36.1	34.9	36.0	35.5	36.3	36.2	35.4	35.8	35.8	36.6	35.9
2010	35.2	34.6	34.8	34.7	34.4	35.2	34.5	34.9	34.2	35.2	35.9	36.4	35.0
2011	35.2	35.7	35.4	36.1	36.6	37.1	37.7	37.6	39.1	36.9	38.0	38.0	37.0
Manufacturing													
2007	39.0	38.3	38.9	39.9	39.4	40.1	38.2	40.7	40.3	40.0	39.4	38.9	39.4
2008	37.9	37.4	37.9	39.1	37.8	37.9	36.6	37.4	37.8	36.7	35.6	39.3	37.6
2009	36.2	35.7	36.2	37.5	37.9	38.7	38.6	38.4	38.0	38.7	37.8	38.8	37.7
2010	38.8	37.6	38.8	38.1	38.6	38.8	38.8	38.5	38.3	39.5	38.7	39.4	38.6
2011	38.3	38.5	38.5	38.3	40.4	39.2	40.0	39.7	40.0	40.0	38.8	40.6	39.3
Trade, Transportation, and Utilities													
2007	32.7	32.1	33.0	33.0	33.4	33.8	33.3	33.9	33.9	35.1	38.2	36.6	34.1
2008	34.9	34.6	35.8	35.5	34.6	34.2	33.7	33.2	33.2	33.0	33.1	33.2	34.1
2009	32.8	33.0	33.0	32.9	33.5	33.1	33.1	33.1	33.5	32.7	32.5	33.0	33.0
2010	33.0	31.7	32.5	33.5	33.9	33.2	32.5	33.0	32.5	32.8	32.8	33.2	32.9
2011	33.3	33.0	33.2	33.0	33.8	33.4	33.7	33.4	33.5	33.4	33.4	33.1	33.4
Financial Activities													
2007	38.1	38.4	38.4	38.5	38.3	38.0	39.2	38.8	39.5	39.1	39.4	39.6	38.8
2008	39.2	39.5	39.6	39.2	38.8	39.2	38.5	38.3	37.9	38.5	38.7	38.2	38.8
2009	38.2	37.5	37.5	37.0	36.9	36.8	36.1	35.8	35.3	35.2	34.6	35.0	36.3
2010	35.4	36.0	36.7	36.1	36.7	36.1	36.2	36.5	36.2	36.3	36.5	36.9	36.3
2011	37.2	37.1	37.3	37.3	38.0	37.9	38.3	37.9	38.1	38.9	37.8	37.1	37.7
Professional and Business Services													
2007	33.7	33.1	33.0	33.8	33.3	33.9	35.4	34.5	35.1	33.3	33.5	34.3	33.9
2008	33.3	33.1	33.8	33.9	33.7	34.6	33.7	33.9	33.3	33.3	33.4	33.2	33.6
2009	33.1	33.9	33.7	33.6	32.9	32.7	32.6	33.3	32.9	33.2	33.6	32.7	33.2
2010	32.6	31.5	32.2	32.8	33.5	34.0	33.2	34.1	33.1	33.1	33.3	33.7	33.1
2011	33.9	33.7	33.1	33.8	34.5	33.8	33.3	34.4	34.3	35.6	34.0	34.7	34.1
Education and Health Services													
2007	31.2	31.3	31.3	31.4	31.2	31.1	31.3	30.7	32.1	31.4	31.8	32.3	31.4
2008	32.2	32.2	33.1	32.4	32.0	33.0	33.3	32.5	32.3	33.1	32.7	31.9	32.6
2009	32.0	32.6	33.2	33.2	33.6	33.8	34.3	34.5	34.6	33.9	34.1	33.6	33.6
2010	34.2	33.6	33.5	33.7	34.3	33.9	34.0	33.7	33.7	33.2	32.9	33.5	33.7
2011	33.7	33.3	33.4	33.5	33.8	33.5	33.7	33.2	33.4	33.3	33.1	33.5	33.4
Leisure and Hospitality													
2007	24.9	24.4	24.4	25.7	25.9	27.4	28.1	27.8	26.7	25.9	25.9	25.9	26.2
2008	24.6	25.0	25.3	25.2	25.7	25.7	26.1	25.8	24.6	24.6	24.3	24.2	25.1
2009	23.9	24.6	24.3	24.5	24.3	25.2	25.7	25.9	24.5	23.8	23.6	23.8	24.6
2010	23.1	22.6	23.1	23.8	23.4	23.9	24.6	24.7	23.7	23.7	23.6	23.3	23.7
2011	23.7	24.0	24.0	24.6	24.2	24.7	25.6	25.9	24.4	24.8	24.4	24.5	24.6

3. Average Hourly Earnings by Selected Industry: Delaware, 2007–2011

(Dollars, not seasonally adjusted)

Industry and year	January	February	March	April	May	June	July	August	September	October	November	December	Annual average
Total Private													
2007	22.05	22.24	22.10	22.57	21.58	21.38	21.79	21.70	22.21	21.79	21.72	22.64	21.98
2008	21.74	23.13	22.55	22.41	22.40	23.18	23.13	22.87	22.92	22.84	23.07	22.50	22.73
2009	22.49	22.53	22.43	22.04	21.69	21.46	22.04	22.63	22.64	22.57	22.71	22.41	22.30
2010	22.76	23.21	22.59	22.91	22.84	22.66	22.42	22.63	22.51	22.74	22.51	22.84	22.72
2011	22.85	22.58	22.40	22.46	22.25	21.87	21.82	22.01	22.40	22.43	22.27	22.55	22.32
Goods-Producing													
2007	22.25	22.71	22.47	22.42	23.25	22.88	23.34	23.55	23.69	23.64	23.35	24.35	23.16
2008	23.74	24.80	24.93	24.80	23.96	24.24	23.28	23.72	23.79	23.79	23.05	23.47	23.98
2009	22.60	22.87	22.96	22.68	22.53	22.36	22.56	22.86	23.12	22.59	23.03	22.91	22.75
2010	22.81	23.71	23.64	23.23	23.63	23.68	23.57	23.78	23.67	23.36	23.93	23.61	23.55
2011	24.12	24.13	23.98	23.99	23.44	23.66	23.48	23.39	23.77	23.58	23.67	23.65	23.73
Mining, Logging, and Construction													
2007	22.95	23.74	23.51	23.04	23.97	23.64	23.89	25.14	24.94	23.54	23.72	24.44	23.88
2008	25.63	26.25	25.80	25.94	26.29	25.78	25.58	26.25	26.29	26.09	25.78	26.56	26.01
2009	26.46	26.64	26.21	25.85	25.13	25.54	25.03	25.50	26.09	25.24	25.62	26.19	25.79
2010	25.80	26.77	27.23	26.77	27.80	28.08	28.10	28.47	28.36	27.61	28.21	27.51	27.59
2011	28.35	28.20	27.79	27.51	27.24	27.37	27.15	27.24	27.86	27.59	27.63	27.40	27.60
Manufacturing													
2007	21.70	21.97	21.69	21.94	22.65	22.27	22.87	22.30	22.68	23.72	23.07	24.28	22.59
2008	22.28	23.77	24.27	23.95	22.17	23.01	21.28	21.62	21.79	21.98	20.99	21.42	22.41
2009	19.94	20.25	20.65	20.59	20.73	20.21	20.83	21.01	21.14	20.83	21.28	20.73	20.68
2010	20.97	21.85	21.40	20.84	20.81	20.62	20.48	20.49	20.47	20.43	20.83	20.82	20.83
2011	21.25	21.34	21.30	21.37	20.76	20.96	20.81	20.66	20.76	20.68	20.72	21.00	20.96
Trade, Transportation, and Utilities													
2007	17.99	18.36	18.27	18.15	15.24	15.29	15.58	16.41	16.11	16.34	16.59	16.35	16.69
2008	16.77	17.11	16.97	17.43	16.94	16.94	17.35	17.38	17.20	17.54	18.21	17.88	17.30
2009	18.48	18.41	18.45	18.34	18.16	18.06	18.15	18.19	17.94	18.02	18.02	17.85	18.17
2010	18.40	18.73	18.40	18.59	18.40	18.79	18.84	19.12	19.22	18.91	18.88	19.11	18.79
2011	19.41	19.09	19.23	19.68	19.57	19.29	19.32	19.40	19.35	19.47	19.25	19.66	19.39
Financial Activities													
2007	28.08	28.34	27.89	29.63	28.21	28.12	29.07	27.93	29.67	27.95	27.55	29.49	28.50
2008	27.57	28.11	29.53	28.57	28.54	29.98	30.63	28.95	28.59	28.37	27.45	27.53	28.66
2009	27.16	27.62	27.71	27.15	26.13	25.91	26.65	26.30	26.31	26.80	26.74	26.32	26.74
2010	27.00	27.21	27.14	27.15	26.81	26.94	26.88	27.26	27.09	27.55	26.92	27.35	27.11
2011	28.21	27.38	27.40	27.79	27.32	26.21	25.92	26.58	26.68	27.35	25.99	26.12	26.91
Professional and Business Services													
2007	25.37	24.86	25.73	25.22	24.65	25.18	26.52	26.51	27.04	26.73	27.54	30.14	26.32
2008	27.97	27.90	28.68	28.58	28.88	29.02	29.23	29.24	29.33	29.35	30.00	29.18	28.95
2009	29.23	29.45	29.32	28.28	28.05	27.64	27.81	27.80	27.62	27.44	28.04	27.31	28.17
2010	27.36	28.18	27.19	26.76	27.08	27.14	27.09	27.21	27.13	27.73	27.73	27.76	27.36
2011	27.82	27.28	26.96	26.68	26.88	26.10	26.01	26.51	26.48	26.50	26.81	26.90	26.74
Education and Health Services													
2007	20.43	20.45	20.60	21.33	20.93	21.50	21.87	21.38	21.13	21.15	21.46	21.62	21.16
2008	20.72	22.02	20.52	20.37	20.65	20.58	20.96	20.89	21.41	21.16	23.15	21.20	21.14
2009	21.65	21.60	21.40	21.26	21.07	21.21	20.87	20.25	20.63	20.96	21.31	21.23	21.11
2010	21.18	21.18	21.13	21.45	21.47	21.76	21.79	22.31	22.06	22.33	21.87	22.47	21.75
2011	21.69	21.84	21.70	22.02	21.83	22.13	22.43	22.06	22.67	22.61	22.53	23.09	22.22
Leisure and Hospitality													
2007	12.96	13.19	12.90	13.16	13.70	12.95	11.47	11.93	12.19	12.38	12.06	12.12	12.55
2008	12.27	12.20	12.01	12.28	12.27	12.38	12.44	12.70	12.73	12.93	12.65	12.82	12.48
2009	12.83	12.87	12.86	12.61	12.77	12.63	12.36	12.39	12.79	12.88	12.94	12.97	12.73
2010	13.26	13.51	13.20	12.75	13.01	12.84	13.14	13.39	13.33	13.44	13.03	13.31	13.18
2011	13.40	13.23	13.34	12.87	12.93	12.73	12.85	12.82	13.25	13.33	13.47	13.74	13.14

4. Average Weekly Earnings by Selected Industry: Delaware, 2007–2011

(Dollars, not seasonally adjusted)

Industry and year	January	February	March	April	May	June	July	August	September	October	November	December	Annual average
Total Private													
2007	738.68	747.26	740.35	765.12	731.56	731.20	751.76	750.82	772.91	756.11	771.06	783.34	753.48
2008	739.16	786.42	780.23	768.66	754.88	797.39	788.73	775.29	765.53	760.57	763.62	742.50	768.72
2009	733.17	736.73	735.70	718.50	711.43	703.89	722.91	753.58	740.33	731.27	735.80	726.08	728.90
2010	737.42	733.44	740.95	749.16	753.72	736.45	728.65	740.00	720.32	732.23	724.82	746.87	736.75
2011	749.48	740.62	730.24	736.69	738.70	721.71	726.61	732.93	745.92	753.65	737.14	750.92	738.50
Goods-Producing													
2007	854.40	838.00	851.61	869.90	913.73	903.76	896.26	934.94	928.65	917.23	896.64	918.00	893.46
2008	878.38	900.24	934.88	934.96	876.94	916.27	870.67	891.87	899.26	880.23	827.50	887.17	891.78
2009	813.60	823.32	831.15	825.55	835.86	834.03	848.26	857.25	853.13	847.13	849.81	868.29	840.47
2010	853.09	863.04	879.41	850.22	869.58	880.90	869.73	877.48	863.96	880.67	897.38	899.54	873.75
2011	890.03	900.05	889.66	894.83	907.13	906.18	915.72	907.53	941.29	910.19	911.30	934.18	909.06
Mining, Logging, and Construction													
2007	862.92	833.27	860.47	861.70	937.23	914.87	924.54	965.38	947.72	880.40	880.01	882.28	896.67
2008	917.55	913.50	954.60	933.84	925.41	969.33	982.27	994.88	993.76	975.77	933.24	948.19	953.47
2009	944.62	964.37	946.18	902.17	904.68	906.67	908.59	923.10	923.59	903.59	917.20	958.55	925.11
2010	908.16	926.24	947.60	928.92	956.32	988.42	969.45	993.60	969.91	971.87	1,012.74	1,001.36	966.10
2011	997.92	1,006.74	983.77	993.11	996.98	1,015.43	1,023.56	1,024.22	1,089.33	1,018.07	1,049.94	1,041.20	1,019.80
Manufacturing													
2007	846.30	841.45	843.74	875.41	892.41	893.03	873.63	907.61	914.00	948.80	908.96	944.49	890.80
2008	844.41	889.00	919.83	936.45	838.03	872.08	778.85	808.59	823.66	806.67	747.24	841.81	843.03
2009	721.83	722.93	747.53	772.13	785.67	782.13	804.04	806.78	803.32	806.12	804.38	804.32	779.74
2010	813.64	821.56	830.32	794.00	803.27	800.06	794.62	788.87	784.00	806.99	806.12	820.31	804.98
2011	813.88	821.59	820.05	818.47	838.70	821.63	832.40	820.20	830.40	827.20	803.94	852.60	824.65
Trade, Transportation, and Utilities													
2007	588.27	589.36	602.91	598.95	509.02	516.80	518.81	556.30	546.13	573.53	633.74	598.41	569.30
2008	585.27	592.01	607.53	618.77	586.12	579.35	584.70	577.02	571.04	578.82	602.75	593.62	589.75
2009	606.14	607.53	608.85	603.39	608.36	597.79	600.77	602.09	600.99	589.25	585.65	589.05	599.88
2010	607.20	593.74	598.00	622.77	623.76	623.83	612.30	630.96	624.65	620.25	619.26	634.45	617.66
2011	646.35	629.97	638.44	649.44	661.47	644.29	651.08	647.96	648.23	650.30	642.95	650.75	646.90
Financial Activities													
2007	1,069.85	1,088.26	1,070.98	1,140.76	1,080.44	1,068.56	1,139.54	1,083.68	1,171.97	1,092.85	1,085.47	1,167.80	1,105.04
2008	1,080.74	1,110.35	1,169.39	1,119.94	1,107.35	1,175.22	1,179.26	1,108.79	1,083.56	1,092.25	1,062.32	1,051.65	1,112.09
2009	1,037.51	1,035.75	1,039.13	1,004.55	964.20	953.49	962.07	941.54	928.74	943.36	925.20	921.20	971.29
2010	955.80	979.56	996.04	980.12	983.93	972.53	973.06	994.99	980.66	1,000.07	982.58	1,009.22	984.29
2011	1,049.41	1,015.80	1,022.02	1,036.57	1,038.16	993.36	992.74	1,007.38	1,016.51	1,063.92	982.42	969.05	1,015.61
Professional and Business Services													
2007	854.97	822.87	849.09	852.44	820.85	853.60	938.81	914.60	949.10	890.11	922.59	1,033.80	892.69
2008	931.40	923.49	969.38	968.86	973.26	1,004.09	985.05	991.24	976.69	977.36	1,002.00	968.78	972.65
2009	967.51	998.36	988.08	950.21	922.85	903.83	906.61	925.74	908.70	911.01	942.14	893.04	934.98
2010	891.94	887.67	875.52	877.73	907.18	922.76	899.39	927.86	898.00	917.86	923.41	935.51	905.43
2011	943.10	919.34	892.38	901.78	927.36	882.18	866.13	911.94	908.26	943.40	911.54	933.43	911.57
Education and Health Services													
2007	637.42	640.09	644.78	669.76	653.02	668.65	684.53	656.37	678.27	664.11	682.43	698.33	664.99
2008	667.18	709.04	679.21	659.99	660.80	679.14	697.97	678.93	691.54	700.40	757.01	676.28	688.20
2009	692.80	704.16	710.48	705.83	707.95	716.90	715.84	698.63	713.80	710.54	726.67	713.33	709.57
2010	724.36	711.65	707.86	722.87	736.42	737.66	740.86	751.85	743.42	741.36	719.52	752.75	732.68
2011	730.95	727.27	724.78	737.67	737.85	741.36	755.89	732.39	757.18	752.91	745.74	773.52	743.20
Leisure and Hospitality													
2007	322.70	321.84	314.76	338.21	354.83	354.83	322.31	331.65	325.47	320.64	312.35	313.91	328.32
2008	301.84	305.00	303.85	309.46	315.34	318.17	324.68	327.66	313.16	318.08	307.40	310.24	313.43
2009	306.64	316.60	312.50	308.95	310.31	318.28	317.65	320.90	313.36	306.54	305.38	308.69	312.46
2010	306.31	305.33	304.92	303.45	304.43	306.88	323.24	330.73	315.92	318.53	307.51	310.12	312.01
2011	317.58	317.52	320.16	316.60	312.91	314.43	328.96	332.04	323.30	330.58	328.67	336.63	323.41

DISTRICT OF COLUMBIA
At a Glance

Population:
    2000 census: 572,086
    2010 census: 601,723
    2011 estimate: 617,996

Percent change in population:
    2000–2010: 5.2%
    2010–2011: 2.7%

Percent change in total nonfarm employment:
    2000–2010: 9.5%
    2010–2011: 2.2%

Industry with the largest growth in employment, 2000–2011 (thousands):
    Education and Health Services, 27.8

Industry with the largest decline or smallest growth in employment, 2000–2011 (thousands):
    Information, -6.9

Civilian labor force:
    2000: 309,421
    2010: 343,379
    2011: 344,333

Unemployment rate and rank among states (lowest to highest):
    2000: 5.7%, 49th
    2010: 10.7%, 37th
    2011: 10.2%, 43rd

Over-the-year change in unemployment rates:
    2010–2011: 0.1%

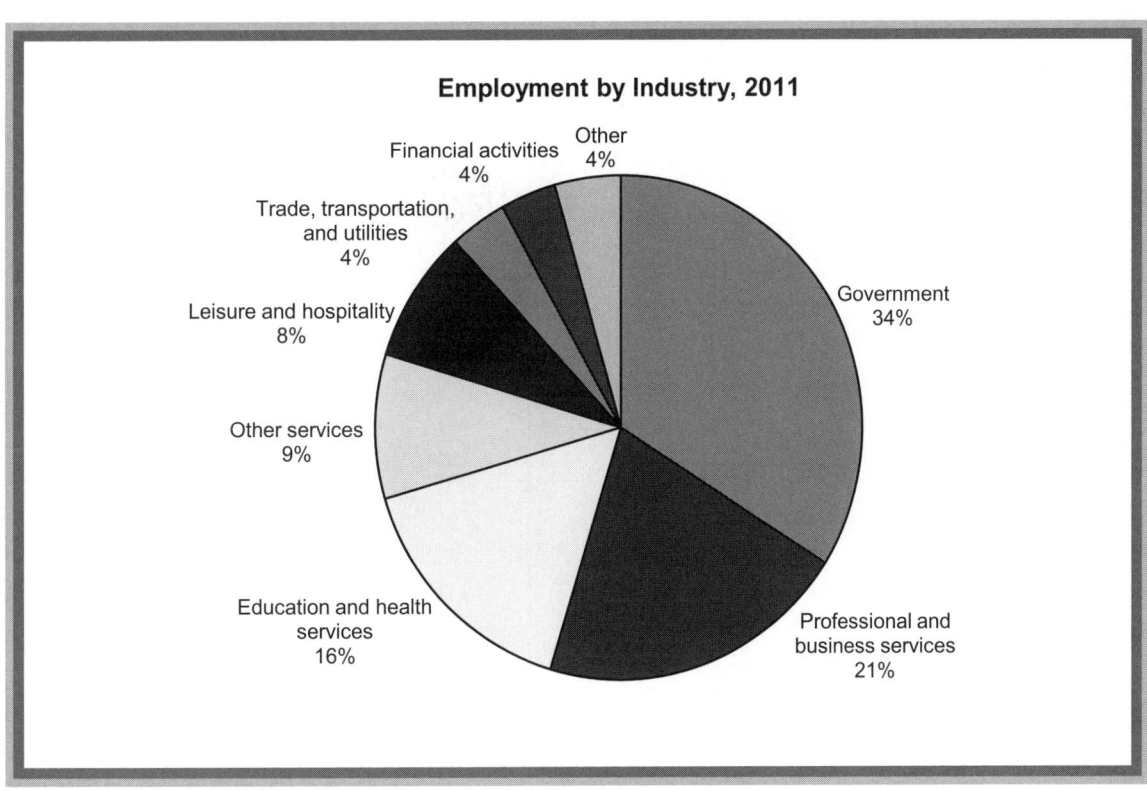

Employment by Industry, 2011

- Other 4%
- Financial activities 4%
- Trade, transportation, and utilities 4%
- Leisure and hospitality 8%
- Other services 9%
- Education and health services 16%
- Government 34%
- Professional and business services 21%

1. Employment by Industry: District of Columbia, Selected Years, 2000–2011

(Numbers in thousands, not seasonally adjusted)

Industry and year	January	February	March	April	May	June	July	August	September	October	November	December	Annual average
Total Nonfarm													
2000	628.8	634.5	638.9	643.9	644.0	652.1	661.5	656.6	654.0	659.0	662.9	667.2	650.3
2001	640.7	641.9	647.1	647.2	649.9	654.6	662.6	662.9	656.7	661.1	659.3	659.8	653.7
2002	648.3	653.3	660.3	662.6	660.9	664.8	674.4	669.9	666.9	667.4	670.9	671.1	664.2
2003	656.9	659.0	665.2	666.3	665.7	666.5	672.6	663.7	665.8	667.0	668.0	669.5	665.5
2004	657.9	665.1	670.7	673.8	673.9	676.6	680.0	679.0	675.0	678.8	680.8	678.6	674.2
2005	670.3	676.0	679.3	681.9	681.6	683.3	688.1	684.8	679.7	684.2	688.5	688.7	682.2
2006	675.4	681.8	686.2	685.3	684.6	689.4	695.5	689.8	685.3	691.4	693.6	693.4	687.6
2007	680.7	689.2	692.0	692.1	689.6	691.3	701.4	695.5	690.3	700.0	701.1	701.8	693.8
2008	689.0	693.6	698.2	701.2	702.7	704.1	720.0	715.9	705.1	705.9	706.0	704.5	703.9
2009	697.8	697.4	697.2	696.5	697.3	698.1	718.1	706.6	694.2	703.8	706.8	705.6	701.6
2010	698.2	695.5	703.4	713.6	715.4	715.4	731.9	707.4	710.7	716.8	717.9	716.8	711.9
2011	713.3	716.2	720.6	725.4	725.5	729.3	739.9	725.5	728.4	734.2	739.7	735.8	727.8
Total Private													
2000	407.1	413.1	417.4	422.3	420.1	426.3	428.8	427.3	430.6	438.2	441.2	443.5	426.3
2001	419.7	423.3	427.2	427.2	428.6	428.8	427.8	428.1	427.4	431.4	430.8	429.9	427.5
2002	418.0	424.2	430.5	433.8	431.4	432.3	434.3	432.3	435.0	438.2	440.5	439.9	432.5
2003	427.3	429.4	434.2	435.9	435.2	434.3	435.5	432.2	435.6	438.1	439.8	441.0	434.9
2004	429.0	436.5	441.3	444.5	445.4	445.7	443.8	441.4	445.0	447.8	448.6	446.0	442.9
2005	438.6	444.8	448.1	450.1	449.7	448.6	446.1	443.4	448.8	452.0	455.5	456.1	448.5
2006	443.6	450.4	454.8	455.3	453.9	455.9	452.7	449.4	454.6	460.2	462.4	462.0	454.6
2007	453.8	461.4	464.9	465.2	462.3	461.3	459.8	456.9	461.6	467.3	469.0	469.5	462.8
2008	458.1	463.0	467.1	471.4	471.8	470.1	471.5	469.5	472.6	471.7	471.7	469.6	469.0
2009	463.7	463.4	463.3	462.0	462.0	459.3	458.3	454.4	455.9	463.3	465.5	465.2	461.4
2010	456.9	454.8	462.5	471.5	470.6	467.9	464.0	461.1	464.7	468.0	468.9	469.0	465.0
2011	466.4	469.8	473.8	479.3	479.0	480.6	478.9	477.9	482.0	488.9	494.6	490.7	480.2
Goods-Producing													
2000	13.8	13.7	14.5	14.6	14.8	15.0	15.3	15.5	15.5	15.4	15.7	15.8	15.0
2001	14.9	14.7	14.8	15.0	15.4	15.6	15.2	15.4	15.0	14.8	14.6	14.4	15.0
2002	14.3	14.4	14.6	14.4	14.9	15.3	15.9	16.2	16.3	16.5	16.4	16.3	15.5
2003	15.6	15.4	15.8	15.4	15.2	15.4	15.7	15.7	15.7	15.4	15.2	14.9	15.5
2004	14.3	14.4	14.7	14.9	15.1	14.7	15.0	14.8	14.8	15.0	15.0	14.8	14.8
2005	14.5	14.8	14.8	15.1	15.2	15.2	14.8	14.9	14.5	14.3	14.4	14.4	14.7
2006	13.7	14.0	14.2	14.1	14.3	14.5	14.7	14.8	14.6	14.2	14.0	13.8	14.2
2007	13.9	13.7	13.8	13.9	14.3	14.5	14.6	15.0	14.9	14.8	14.7	14.2	14.4
2008	14.4	14.5	14.5	14.1	14.5	14.6	14.6	15.0	14.5	14.6	14.5	14.2	14.5
2009	14.0	14.0	13.5	13.4	13.4	13.3	12.8	12.7	12.4	11.9	11.7	11.6	12.9
2010	11.3	10.4	11.2	11.8	11.8	11.8	12.2	12.0	11.8	12.1	12.0	12.0	11.7
2011	12.1	12.1	12.3	12.6	12.9	13.1	13.7	13.6	13.2	13.3	13.8	13.2	13.0
Mining, Logging, and Construction													
2000	10.1	10.1	10.8	10.9	11.1	11.3	11.6	11.8	11.8	11.7	12.0	12.0	11.3
2001	11.4	11.2	11.2	11.5	11.9	12.1	11.8	12.0	11.7	11.6	11.4	11.3	11.6
2002	11.1	11.3	11.4	11.5	12.0	12.4	12.8	13.1	13.2	13.4	13.3	13.3	12.4
2003	13.0	12.8	13.2	12.8	12.7	12.9	13.2	13.2	13.2	12.9	12.7	12.4	12.9
2004	11.9	11.9	12.2	12.5	12.7	12.3	12.5	12.3	12.3	12.6	12.6	12.5	12.4
2005	12.3	12.6	12.6	12.9	13.0	13.0	12.7	12.8	12.5	12.4	12.5	12.4	12.6
2006	11.9	12.2	12.4	12.3	12.5	12.7	13.0	13.1	12.9	12.5	12.3	12.1	12.5
2007	12.2	12.0	12.1	12.2	12.6	12.8	12.9	13.4	13.2	13.1	13.0	12.5	12.7
2008	12.7	12.8	12.8	12.6	12.9	13.0	13.1	13.5	13.1	13.2	13.1	12.8	13.0
2009	12.6	12.6	12.2	12.1	12.1	12.0	11.5	11.4	11.2	10.7	10.5	10.4	11.6
2010	10.1	9.2	10.1	10.7	10.7	10.7	11.1	11.0	10.7	11.0	11.0	11.0	10.6
2011	11.0	11.1	11.2	11.6	11.9	12.0	12.6	12.5	12.2	12.3	12.8	12.2	12.0
Manufacturing													
2000	3.7	3.6	3.7	3.7	3.7	3.7	3.7	3.7	3.7	3.7	3.7	3.8	3.7
2001	3.5	3.5	3.6	3.5	3.5	3.5	3.4	3.4	3.3	3.2	3.2	3.1	3.4
2002	3.2	3.1	3.2	2.9	2.9	2.9	3.1	3.1	3.1	3.1	3.1	3.0	3.1
2003	2.6	2.6	2.6	2.6	2.5	2.5	2.5	2.5	2.5	2.5	2.5	2.5	2.5
2004	2.4	2.5	2.5	2.4	2.4	2.4	2.5	2.5	2.5	2.4	2.4	2.3	2.4
2005	2.2	2.2	2.2	2.2	2.2	2.2	2.1	2.1	2.0	1.9	1.9	2.0	2.1
2006	1.8	1.8	1.8	1.8	1.8	1.8	1.7	1.7	1.7	1.7	1.7	1.7	1.8
2007	1.7	1.7	1.7	1.7	1.7	1.7	1.7	1.6	1.7	1.7	1.7	1.7	1.7
2008	1.7	1.7	1.7	1.5	1.6	1.6	1.5	1.5	1.4	1.4	1.4	1.4	1.5
2009	1.4	1.4	1.3	1.3	1.3	1.3	1.3	1.3	1.2	1.2	1.2	1.2	1.3
2010	1.2	1.2	1.1	1.1	1.1	1.1	1.1	1.0	1.1	1.1	1.0	1.0	1.1
2011	1.1	1.0	1.1	1.0	1.0	1.1	1.1	1.1	1.0	1.0	1.0	1.0	1.0
Service-Providing													
2000	615.0	620.8	624.4	629.3	629.2	637.1	646.2	641.1	638.5	643.6	647.2	651.4	635.3
2001	625.8	627.2	632.3	632.2	634.5	639.0	647.4	647.5	641.7	646.3	644.7	645.4	638.7
2002	634.0	638.9	645.7	648.2	646.0	649.5	658.5	653.7	650.6	650.9	654.5	654.8	648.8
2003	641.3	643.6	649.4	650.9	650.5	651.1	656.9	648.0	650.1	651.6	652.8	654.6	650.1
2004	643.6	650.7	656.0	658.9	658.8	661.9	665.0	664.2	660.2	663.8	665.8	663.8	659.4
2005	655.8	661.2	664.5	666.8	666.4	668.1	673.3	669.9	665.2	669.9	674.1	674.3	667.5
2006	661.7	667.8	672.0	671.2	670.3	674.9	680.8	675.0	670.7	677.2	679.6	679.6	673.4
2007	666.8	675.5	678.2	678.2	675.3	676.8	686.8	680.5	675.4	685.2	686.4	687.6	679.4
2008	674.6	679.1	683.7	687.1	688.2	689.5	705.4	700.9	690.6	691.3	691.5	690.3	689.4
2009	683.8	683.4	683.7	683.1	683.9	684.8	705.3	693.9	681.8	691.9	695.1	694.0	688.7
2010	686.9	685.1	692.2	701.8	703.6	703.6	719.7	695.4	698.9	704.7	705.9	704.8	700.2
2011	701.2	704.1	708.3	712.8	712.6	716.2	726.2	711.9	715.2	720.9	725.9	722.6	714.8

1. Employment by Industry: District of Columbia, Selected Years, 2000–2011—*Continued*

(Numbers in thousands, not seasonally adjusted)

Industry and year	January	February	March	April	May	June	July	August	September	October	November	December	Annual average
Trade, Transportation, and Utilities													
2000	29.3	29.4	29.4	29.2	29.2	29.8	29.1	29.0	29.4	29.7	30.5	31.3	29.6
2001	28.2	27.8	28.0	27.7	27.9	28.3	27.7	28.0	28.1	28.3	28.5	28.8	28.1
2002	27.5	27.7	27.4	27.6	27.7	28.0	27.9	27.6	27.7	27.9	28.4	29.0	27.9
2003	27.5	27.3	27.7	27.5	27.6	28.1	27.9	27.9	27.9	28.3	28.7	29.2	28.0
2004	27.8	27.7	28.1	27.9	28.1	28.3	27.8	27.4	27.6	27.6	28.0	28.4	27.9
2005	27.3	27.1	27.6	27.4	27.5	27.6	27.8	27.5	27.6	28.2	28.4	29.3	27.8
2006	28.1	27.9	27.8	27.5	27.6	27.9	27.7	27.6	27.8	27.9	28.2	28.6	27.9
2007	27.5	27.2	27.4	27.8	27.9	27.9	27.7	27.5	27.6	27.6	28.1	28.4	27.7
2008	27.4	27.5	27.4	27.9	27.9	28.2	28.3	27.9	28.0	27.6	28.3	28.5	27.9
2009	27.3	26.8	26.7	26.8	26.6	26.5	26.5	26.4	26.5	27.0	27.5	27.5	26.8
2010	26.9	26.1	26.9	27.4	27.4	27.6	27.4	27.2	27.2	27.6	28.1	28.2	27.3
2011	27.3	27.1	27.1	27.5	27.3	27.4	26.8	26.5	26.7	27.0	27.8	28.0	27.2
Wholesale Trade													
2000	4.5	4.5	4.5	4.4	4.4	4.4	4.3	4.3	4.3	4.4	4.4	4.5	4.4
2001	4.3	4.3	4.3	4.3	4.3	4.4	4.5	4.5	4.5	4.4	4.3	4.4	4.4
2002	4.1	4.2	4.2	4.2	4.2	4.3	4.5	4.4	4.5	4.5	4.5	4.6	4.4
2003	4.5	4.5	4.5	4.4	4.5	4.5	4.6	4.5	4.5	4.6	4.6	4.6	4.5
2004	4.5	4.6	4.5	4.6	4.6	4.6	4.6	4.5	4.6	4.5	4.6	4.6	4.6
2005	4.6	4.6	4.6	4.6	4.6	4.7	4.6	4.6	4.6	4.6	4.5	4.6	4.6
2006	4.7	4.7	4.6	4.6	4.6	4.6	4.7	4.7	4.7	4.7	4.7	4.8	4.7
2007	4.8	4.8	4.8	4.8	4.8	4.8	4.8	4.8	4.8	4.8	4.8	4.8	4.8
2008	4.7	4.8	4.7	4.7	4.7	4.9	5.0	4.9	4.8	4.8	4.7	4.7	4.8
2009	4.7	4.6	4.6	4.6	4.6	4.6	4.6	4.5	4.5	4.6	4.6	4.6	4.6
2010	4.6	4.6	4.6	4.7	4.7	4.8	4.7	4.6	4.6	4.7	4.7	4.7	4.7
2011	4.6	4.6	4.6	4.6	4.6	4.6	4.5	4.5	4.5	4.5	4.6	4.6	4.6
Retail Trade													
2000	17.1	17.0	17.2	16.9	17.0	17.4	17.1	17.1	17.6	17.8	18.5	18.9	17.5
2001	17.3	17.0	17.1	16.7	16.9	17.0	16.6	16.9	17.0	17.5	17.9	18.1	17.2
2002	17.3	17.2	17.0	17.0	17.1	17.2	17.0	16.8	16.9	17.0	17.5	18.0	17.2
2003	16.7	16.6	16.7	16.8	16.8	17.3	17.0	17.1	17.2	17.5	17.9	18.5	17.2
2004	17.2	17.1	17.3	17.4	17.6	17.9	17.6	17.4	17.5	17.6	17.9	18.4	17.6
2005	17.4	17.1	17.5	17.3	17.4	17.4	17.6	17.4	17.5	17.9	18.2	18.9	17.6
2006	18.0	17.9	17.8	17.5	17.5	17.9	17.8	17.7	18.0	18.2	18.5	18.8	18.0
2007	18.0	17.8	17.8	18.2	18.2	18.3	18.1	17.9	18.0	18.2	18.6	18.9	18.2
2008	18.1	18.2	18.2	18.6	18.5	18.6	18.5	18.3	18.5	18.1	18.9	19.0	18.5
2009	18.0	17.6	17.5	17.5	17.3	17.3	17.3	17.4	17.6	18.1	18.7	18.8	17.8
2010	18.3	17.5	18.1	18.4	18.4	18.5	18.4	18.3	18.3	18.6	19.1	19.3	18.4
2011	18.6	18.4	18.3	18.6	18.5	18.5	18.2	17.9	18.1	18.5	19.1	19.3	18.5
Transportation and Utilities													
2000	7.7	7.9	7.7	7.9	7.8	8.0	7.7	7.6	7.5	7.5	7.6	7.9	7.7
2001	6.6	6.5	6.6	6.7	6.7	6.9	6.6	6.6	6.6	6.4	6.3	6.3	6.6
2002	6.1	6.3	6.2	6.4	6.4	6.5	6.4	6.4	6.3	6.4	6.4	6.4	6.4
2003	6.3	6.2	6.5	6.3	6.3	6.3	6.3	6.3	6.2	6.2	6.2	6.1	6.3
2004	6.1	6.0	6.3	5.9	5.9	5.8	5.6	5.5	5.5	5.5	5.5	5.4	5.8
2005	5.3	5.4	5.5	5.5	5.5	5.5	5.6	5.5	5.5	5.7	5.7	5.8	5.5
2006	5.4	5.3	5.4	5.4	5.5	5.4	5.2	5.2	5.1	5.0	5.0	5.0	5.2
2007	4.7	4.6	4.8	4.8	4.9	4.8	4.8	4.8	4.8	4.6	4.7	4.7	4.8
2008	4.6	4.5	4.5	4.6	4.7	4.7	4.8	4.7	4.7	4.7	4.7	4.8	4.7
2009	4.6	4.6	4.6	4.7	4.7	4.6	4.6	4.5	4.4	4.3	4.2	4.1	4.5
2010	4.0	4.0	4.2	4.3	4.3	4.3	4.3	4.3	4.3	4.3	4.3	4.2	4.2
2011	4.1	4.1	4.2	4.3	4.2	4.3	4.1	4.1	4.1	4.0	4.1	4.1	4.1
Information													
2000	24.3	24.5	24.7	24.8	24.7	25.6	25.9	26.1	26.2	26.0	26.2	26.5	25.5
2001	25.3	25.5	25.5	25.8	25.8	25.8	25.5	26.3	26.0	26.0	26.0	26.1	25.8
2002	25.7	25.6	26.0	25.7	25.7	25.8	25.3	25.3	25.1	24.6	24.7	24.7	25.4
2003	25.0	25.3	25.4	24.5	24.6	24.4	24.5	24.4	24.4	23.9	24.0	23.8	24.5
2004	24.3	24.1	24.2	24.0	24.1	24.1	24.4	24.4	24.0	22.9	22.8	22.7	23.8
2005	22.8	23.0	22.8	22.6	22.4	22.6	22.7	22.5	22.4	22.2	22.3	22.3	22.6
2006	22.0	21.9	22.2	22.1	22.1	22.4	22.4	22.2	22.3	22.0	22.1	22.1	22.2
2007	22.4	22.5	22.4	21.8	21.8	22.2	22.5	22.3	21.4	21.3	21.3	21.3	21.9
2008	21.1	21.2	21.3	20.9	21.0	20.9	21.0	21.0	20.8	20.6	20.6	20.4	20.9
2009	19.8	19.7	19.0	19.4	19.3	19.4	19.1	18.8	18.6	18.6	18.5	18.5	19.1
2010	18.5	18.4	18.5	18.7	18.6	18.9	19.0	18.7	18.8	18.7	18.5	18.7	18.7
2011	18.3	18.5	18.6	18.7	18.5	18.9	18.8	18.7	18.6	18.6	18.5	18.5	18.6
Financial Activities													
2000	29.4	29.6	29.9	29.5	29.2	29.6	30.1	30.3	30.3	30.5	30.7	31.4	30.0
2001	30.4	30.4	30.5	31.0	31.0	31.1	31.5	31.5	31.2	31.3	31.2	31.5	31.1
2002	30.4	30.6	30.9	30.3	30.3	30.6	31.0	31.2	31.0	31.2	31.3	31.3	30.8
2003	30.8	30.8	30.8	30.9	31.0	31.0	31.1	30.9	30.7	30.4	30.3	30.5	30.8
2004	30.0	30.1	30.2	30.8	31.0	31.2	30.6	30.5	30.5	30.6	30.7	30.7	30.6
2005	29.9	30.1	29.8	30.6	30.7	30.5	30.3	30.2	30.3	30.1	30.0	30.4	30.2
2006	29.5	29.7	29.9	29.2	29.3	29.4	29.6	29.6	29.5	29.3	29.1	29.2	29.4
2007	29.5	29.7	29.7	29.3	29.0	29.1	29.3	29.1	28.9	28.9	29.0	28.9	29.2
2008	28.3	28.4	28.3	28.4	28.3	28.4	28.2	28.2	28.2	27.8	27.8	27.6	28.2
2009	27.2	26.9	26.8	26.6	26.6	26.9	26.8	26.8	26.9	27.0	27.1	27.2	26.9
2010	26.8	26.7	27.0	27.1	27.0	27.2	26.4	26.3	25.8	26.7	26.8	26.8	26.7
2011	26.6	26.5	26.6	26.9	26.8	26.7	26.7	27.0	27.2	27.0	27.2	26.9	26.8

1. Employment by Industry: District of Columbia, Selected Years, 2000–2011—*Continued*

(Numbers in thousands, not seasonally adjusted)

Industry and year	January	February	March	April	May	June	July	August	September	October	November	December	Annual average
Professional and Business Services													
2000	126.4	128.5	128.8	130.5	131.0	133.9	135.6	134.8	135.1	139.3	140.1	141.4	133.8
2001	135.9	137.3	138.4	137.6	138.0	140.8	140.2	139.5	137.4	139.9	139.9	140.1	138.8
2002	135.2	136.2	137.5	139.3	139.1	141.1	141.2	140.2	139.5	139.6	140.0	140.5	139.1
2003	137.7	137.9	138.8	142.3	143.0	144.2	143.4	142.4	142.3	142.2	142.3	143.3	141.7
2004	137.7	139.5	140.9	142.9	144.0	146.8	146.2	145.5	145.1	146.0	145.5	146.1	143.9
2005	144.2	145.5	147.0	147.4	147.8	150.3	150.3	149.5	149.4	149.5	149.6	150.1	148.4
2006	147.4	149.2	150.5	151.4	152.1	155.8	153.7	152.5	152.3	153.4	153.5	153.5	152.1
2007	150.7	152.3	152.8	152.6	153.5	155.4	153.1	152.7	151.7	152.3	152.9	153.3	152.8
2008	150.5	152.0	153.3	153.6	153.6	155.0	153.6	152.9	151.9	151.8	150.6	150.1	152.4
2009	149.2	148.9	148.5	146.1	146.4	148.4	148.7	147.1	145.4	147.1	147.7	148.0	147.6
2010	145.8	145.8	147.3	148.7	148.6	150.0	149.1	148.2	146.8	147.2	147.2	147.4	147.7
2011	146.7	147.4	148.4	149.9	149.9	151.2	150.0	150.3	150.4	151.7	152.9	152.8	150.1
Education and Health Services													
2000	84.2	86.0	86.7	87.9	85.3	85.5	86.6	86.7	87.6	89.9	91.0	90.8	87.4
2001	84.5	85.5	86.2	86.6	86.1	81.5	83.0	83.3	86.3	87.7	86.8	85.7	85.3
2002	86.9	89.7	92.1	92.1	88.5	85.6	86.3	86.5	89.5	92.2	93.5	92.4	89.6
2003	88.3	89.7	90.7	89.1	86.8	84.1	86.4	85.5	88.8	90.8	91.8	91.4	88.6
2004	89.7	94.2	94.9	94.7	92.2	89.0	88.8	88.2	92.1	94.5	95.1	93.5	92.2
2005	91.6	94.7	94.6	93.8	91.5	87.4	86.5	86.0	91.3	94.6	97.4	96.4	92.2
2006	92.6	96.0	96.4	96.6	93.1	88.8	88.3	87.5	92.6	97.1	99.4	98.8	93.9
2007	97.3	101.6	102.4	101.3	96.9	92.1	92.3	91.5	97.5	102.9	103.0	103.2	98.5
2008	99.4	100.8	101.5	102.6	102.2	97.8	99.7	99.7	103.8	104.8	105.9	106.2	102.0
2009	104.9	106.0	106.6	106.8	105.3	100.3	100.9	100.2	103.4	107.9	109.1	108.9	105.0
2010	107.4	107.2	108.4	111.3	110.4	104.7	103.1	103.5	109.6	109.1	109.9	109.9	107.9
2011	112.7	113.6	114.1	113.5	113.6	112.6	112.4	111.1	116.8	120.2	122.2	119.6	115.2
Leisure and Hospitality													
2000	43.5	44.7	46.2	48.4	48.7	49.3	48.6	47.7	49.0	50.2	50.6	50.3	48.1
2001	45.9	47.6	48.6	48.0	48.6	49.1	48.9	48.3	47.7	46.7	47.0	46.2	47.7
2002	43.4	44.9	46.7	48.3	49.2	49.5	49.6	48.5	49.3	49.9	49.9	49.3	48.2
2003	47.4	47.7	49.2	50.3	50.8	50.5	49.6	48.9	49.4	50.5	50.6	50.4	49.6
2004	48.0	49.0	50.3	50.9	52.1	52.1	51.3	51.0	51.6	52.1	51.9	51.0	50.9
2005	50.5	51.5	52.8	54.2	55.4	55.1	54.1	53.4	54.4	54.4	54.3	53.8	53.7
2006	51.7	52.7	54.3	54.6	55.3	55.8	54.5	53.9	54.5	54.9	54.3	53.6	54.2
2007	51.5	52.8	54.5	56.3	56.3	56.4	56.4	55.7	56.5	56.4	56.6	56.3	55.5
2008	53.9	55.2	56.4	59.1	59.2	59.0	59.1	58.6	59.4	58.9	58.1	56.6	57.8
2009	56.0	56.0	57.4	58.4	59.8	59.1	58.5	57.8	58.6	59.2	59.1	58.4	58.2
2010	56.1	56.1	58.6	61.7	61.4	61.4	60.5	59.6	59.6	60.9	60.4	59.7	59.7
2011	57.2	58.5	60.1	63.5	63.1	63.0	62.1	62.1	61.8	63.2	63.6	63.0	61.8
Other Services													
2000	56.2	56.7	57.2	57.4	57.2	57.6	57.6	57.2	57.5	57.2	56.4	56.0	57.0
2001	54.6	54.5	55.2	55.5	55.8	56.6	55.8	55.8	55.7	56.7	56.8	57.1	55.8
2002	54.6	55.1	55.3	56.1	56.0	56.4	57.1	56.8	56.6	56.3	56.3	56.4	56.1
2003	55.0	55.3	55.8	55.9	56.2	56.6	56.9	56.5	56.4	56.6	56.9	57.5	56.3
2004	57.2	57.5	58.0	58.4	58.8	59.5	59.7	59.6	59.3	59.1	59.6	58.8	58.8
2005	57.8	58.1	58.7	59.0	59.2	59.9	59.6	59.4	58.9	58.7	59.1	59.4	59.0
2006	58.6	59.0	59.5	59.8	60.1	61.3	61.8	61.3	61.0	61.4	61.8	62.4	60.7
2007	61.0	61.6	61.9	62.2	62.6	63.7	63.9	63.1	63.1	63.1	63.4	63.9	62.8
2008	63.1	63.4	64.4	64.8	65.1	66.2	67.0	66.2	66.0	65.6	65.9	66.0	65.3
2009	65.3	65.1	64.8	64.5	64.6	65.4	65.0	64.6	64.1	64.6	64.8	65.1	64.8
2010	64.1	64.1	64.6	64.8	65.4	66.3	66.3	65.6	65.1	65.7	66.0	66.3	65.4
2011	65.5	66.1	66.6	66.7	66.9	67.7	68.4	68.6	67.3	67.9	68.6	68.7	67.4
Government													
2000	221.7	221.4	221.5	221.6	223.9	225.8	232.7	229.3	223.4	220.8	221.7	223.7	224.0
2001	221.0	218.6	219.9	220.0	221.3	225.8	234.8	234.8	229.3	229.7	228.5	229.9	226.1
2002	230.3	229.1	229.8	228.8	229.5	232.5	240.1	237.6	231.9	229.2	230.4	231.2	231.7
2003	229.6	229.6	231.0	230.4	230.5	232.2	237.1	231.5	230.2	228.9	228.2	228.5	230.6
2004	228.9	228.6	229.4	229.3	228.5	230.9	236.2	237.6	230.0	231.0	232.2	232.6	231.3
2005	231.7	231.2	231.2	231.8	231.9	234.7	242.0	241.4	230.9	232.2	233.0	232.6	233.7
2006	231.8	231.4	231.4	230.0	230.7	233.5	242.8	240.4	230.7	231.2	231.2	231.4	233.0
2007	226.9	227.8	227.1	226.9	227.3	230.0	241.6	238.6	228.7	232.7	232.1	232.3	231.0
2008	230.9	230.6	231.1	229.8	230.9	234.0	248.5	246.4	232.5	234.2	234.3	234.9	234.8
2009	234.1	234.0	233.9	234.5	235.3	238.8	259.8	252.2	238.3	240.5	241.3	240.4	240.3
2010	241.3	240.7	240.9	242.1	244.8	247.5	267.9	246.3	246.0	248.8	249.0	247.8	246.9
2011	246.9	246.4	246.8	246.1	246.5	248.7	261.0	247.6	246.4	245.3	245.1	245.1	247.7

2. Average Weekly Hours by Selected Industry: District of Columbia, 2007–2011

(Not seasonally adjusted)

Industry and year	January	February	March	April	May	June	July	August	September	October	November	December	Annual average
Total Private													
2007	35.7	35.5	36.1	37.4	36.7	36.5	36.9	36.1	36.6	36.1	35.9	36.4	36.3
2008	35.2	35.4	36.1	35.5	35.2	36.3	36.0	36.1	35.7	36.0	36.1	35.8	35.8
2009	36.7	36.8	36.5	36.2	35.9	36.1	36.0	36.6	36.2	36.0	36.4	35.6	36.2
2010	35.8	34.6	34.8	35.1	35.4	34.8	34.1	35.2	35.1	35.6	35.6	35.8	35.2
2011	36.3	35.7	35.0	35.3	35.9	35.3	35.3	35.3	35.2	36.1	35.1	35.0	35.5
Goods-Producing													
2007	32.1	31.5	32.4	32.9	32.4	31.9	30.7	30.5	30.2	29.3	30.1	31.3	31.2
2008	31.0	31.2	32.1	32.3	32.9	32.7	32.3	32.7	33.1	31.8	32.1	31.7	32.2
2009	32.1	32.4	32.6	32.4	32.7	32.8	33.0	33.0	32.7	33.0	32.5	32.6	32.6
2010	32.7	32.9	32.7	33.3	33.6	34.1	36.2	34.8	35.1	35.1	35.7	33.7	34.2
2011	34.5	35.7	36.7	36.3	37.0	38.2	36.7	37.6	38.7	38.1	36.4	36.3	36.9
Trade, Transportation, and Utilities													
2007	35.8	37.1	37.8	37.9	37.1	36.5	37.3	37.1	37.0	36.8	37.9	37.5	37.2
2008	37.2	37.0	37.1	37.0	36.2	36.7	36.3	36.4	36.6	37.0	36.5	36.4	36.7
2009	37.0	36.7	36.8	36.6	36.1	36.4	36.6	36.9	36.7	36.3	35.8	35.3	36.4
2010	35.6	33.3	34.0	34.5	35.6	35.5	35.9	36.4	35.2	35.5	35.2	35.3	35.2
2011	35.3	35.3	35.3	35.3	34.8	35.3	35.9	36.3	35.7	36.8	36.2	36.5	35.7
Professional and Business Services													
2007	38.1	37.9	37.5	38.9	37.8	37.7	38.8	37.7	38.1	37.4	37.6	38.0	38.0
2008	37.6	37.8	38.1	37.6	37.0	38.3	37.9	38.0	37.3	37.1	37.2	36.8	37.6
2009	37.1	37.3	37.0	36.7	36.4	36.8	36.8	37.7	37.1	36.6	37.5	36.2	36.9
2010	36.3	35.2	34.6	34.7	34.6	33.6	32.3	34.0	33.2	33.6	33.6	33.9	34.1
2011	34.5	33.7	32.9	33.8	34.6	33.9	33.6	34.2	34.3	35.6	34.7	34.6	34.2
Leisure and Hospitality													
2007	29.7	28.8	30.9	31.4	31.5	30.9	30.1	30.0	30.9	31.6	30.9	30.4	30.6
2008	29.1	30.3	31.7	32.0	31.6	32.9	32.4	31.7	32.4	33.1	32.8	33.1	32.0
2009	32.9	32.8	32.9	32.9	33.1	33.6	33.5	33.2	33.1	33.0	32.7	32.1	33.0
2010	32.7	31.2	33.6	34.1	34.2	33.6	33.2	33.9	32.6	32.7	32.4	31.6	33.0
2011	30.3	31.6	32.3	32.6	32.5	31.6	31.6	30.6	31.2	30.5	30.2	29.4	31.2
Other Services													
2007	34.0	33.3	33.6	34.4	33.7	34.1	34.2	34.4	34.6	35.0	34.6	34.4	34.2
2008	33.5	34.1	34.6	34.1	34.5	35.3	34.9	35.5	34.9	34.9	35.3	35.0	34.7
2009	35.1	35.3	35.8	35.7	35.8	35.7	36.0	36.3	35.9	36.1	36.3	35.9	35.8
2010	35.8	36.0	36.2	36.2	36.4	36.1	36.1	36.5	36.2	36.1	36.3	36.4	36.2
2011	36.7	35.8	35.3	35.1	35.9	35.3	35.6	35.2	34.7	35.5	34.7	34.9	35.4

3. Average Hourly Earnings by Selected Industry: District of Columbia, 2007–2011

(Dollars, not seasonally adjusted)

Industry and year	January	February	March	April	May	June	July	August	September	October	November	December	Annual average
Total Private													
2007	32.94	33.83	33.38	34.03	33.69	33.93	33.84	33.34	33.57	33.26	33.19	33.41	33.54
2008	33.21	33.24	33.19	32.65	33.09	32.34	32.25	31.78	32.18	31.48	31.67	31.40	32.37
2009	30.89	31.50	31.38	31.17	30.94	31.07	30.70	31.43	31.11	31.45	32.33	32.40	31.37
2010	32.74	33.68	33.85	34.29	34.61	33.52	34.22	34.54	34.25	34.49	34.64	35.24	34.18
2011	35.63	34.72	35.24	35.12	35.58	34.86	35.19	34.98	35.60	36.24	35.68	36.47	35.45
Goods-Producing													
2007	34.90	35.89	36.17	36.80	37.16	36.90	37.73	36.44	35.46	35.41	34.76	33.71	35.96
2008	34.22	33.81	34.55	33.90	33.79	34.05	33.90	34.12	33.03	33.96	34.10	35.05	34.03
2009	32.91	32.97	33.23	33.09	33.62	33.92	33.52	33.41	33.58	33.63	34.04	34.30	33.50
2010	34.38	35.29	33.32	32.42	32.23	32.32	30.63	29.79	29.17	29.39	29.15	30.93	31.46
2011	30.76	30.33	29.21	29.21	29.01	28.91	29.00	29.30	28.96	28.40	29.14	31.09	29.41
Trade, Transportation, and Utilities													
2007	25.34	24.43	23.90	23.14	22.69	22.58	22.09	21.80	21.20	21.75	20.95	21.55	22.60
2008	21.81	21.56	21.55	21.54	22.24	22.55	22.63	23.04	23.15	23.41	24.00	23.75	22.61
2009	23.39	23.55	23.61	23.89	23.68	23.71	23.60	23.84	23.24	23.72	24.55	24.18	23.75
2010	24.39	25.09	24.32	24.03	23.52	24.06	24.75	23.93	23.61	23.03	23.85	23.28	23.98
2011	23.55	23.19	22.82	22.98	23.12	22.53	22.66	23.37	24.20	25.26	24.43	23.47	23.47
Professional and Business Services													
2007	37.62	38.39	37.77	38.05	38.63	38.79	38.00	37.50	38.05	38.01	37.99	38.50	38.11
2008	37.80	38.59	38.44	38.22	39.30	38.25	38.27	37.45	38.60	37.80	38.00	37.70	38.20
2009	37.00	37.96	38.33	38.23	37.59	37.95	37.33	37.71	37.25	37.57	38.00	38.22	37.76
2010	38.69	39.79	39.25	39.47	40.14	38.10	38.52	39.64	38.60	38.33	38.85	39.48	39.08
2011	39.51	38.52	39.23	39.46	40.49	40.05	40.84	40.00	41.16	42.30	41.77	43.18	40.57
Leisure and Hospitality													
2007	19.95	19.15	17.90	17.94	18.30	18.67	18.51	18.15	18.40	18.00	18.55	18.33	18.47
2008	18.10	17.83	17.28	17.48	17.41	16.75	16.73	16.98	17.20	17.13	17.06	17.25	17.25
2009	16.82	16.70	16.63	16.66	16.53	16.41	16.28	16.39	16.50	16.77	17.35	17.57	16.71
2010	17.25	17.96	17.63	18.06	17.31	17.02	16.66	16.80	17.25	17.42	17.61	18.05	17.41
2011	17.82	17.83	18.17	18.18	18.46	17.95	17.57	17.24	17.86	18.10	17.76	18.09	17.92
Other Services													
2007	37.69	37.92	38.50	37.37	37.28	37.80	38.20	39.35	39.60	39.85	39.50	39.28	38.54
2008	38.94	38.34	39.20	38.75	38.34	38.52	38.60	38.83	39.00	38.69	39.20	39.13	38.80
2009	38.88	39.08	38.75	38.71	38.44	38.77	38.81	39.12	39.35	39.14	39.33	39.06	38.95
2010	39.54	39.23	38.49	39.13	39.23	38.15	39.11	39.97	39.98	40.22	40.59	40.81	39.54
2011	41.60	40.23	41.61	40.62	40.67	39.61	39.36	39.60	40.68	40.00	39.88	40.36	40.35

4. Average Weekly Earnings by Selected Industry: District of Columbia, 2007–2011

(Dollars, not seasonally adjusted)

Industry and year	January	February	March	April	May	June	July	August	September	October	November	December	Annual average
Total Private													
2007	1,175.96	1,200.97	1,205.02	1,272.72	1,236.42	1,238.45	1,248.70	1,203.57	1,228.66	1,200.69	1,191.52	1,216.12	1,218.07
2008	1,168.99	1,176.70	1,198.16	1,159.08	1,164.77	1,173.94	1,161.00	1,147.26	1,148.83	1,133.28	1,143.29	1,124.12	1,157.71
2009	1,133.66	1,159.20	1,145.37	1,128.35	1,110.75	1,121.63	1,105.20	1,150.34	1,126.18	1,132.20	1,176.81	1,153.44	1,137.03
2010	1,172.09	1,165.33	1,177.98	1,203.58	1,225.19	1,166.50	1,166.90	1,215.81	1,202.18	1,227.84	1,233.18	1,261.59	1,201.91
2011	1,293.37	1,239.50	1,233.40	1,239.74	1,277.32	1,230.56	1,242.21	1,234.79	1,253.12	1,308.26	1,252.37	1,276.45	1,257.15
Goods-Producing													
2007	1,120.29	1,130.54	1,171.91	1,210.72	1,203.98	1,177.11	1,158.31	1,111.42	1,070.89	1,037.51	1,046.28	1,055.12	1,122.94
2008	1,060.82	1,054.87	1,109.06	1,094.97	1,111.69	1,113.44	1,094.97	1,115.72	1,093.29	1,079.93	1,094.61	1,111.09	1,095.33
2009	1,056.41	1,068.23	1,083.30	1,072.12	1,099.37	1,112.58	1,106.16	1,102.53	1,098.07	1,109.79	1,106.30	1,118.18	1,092.19
2010	1,124.23	1,161.04	1,089.56	1,079.59	1,082.93	1,102.11	1,108.81	1,036.69	1,023.87	1,031.59	1,040.66	1,042.34	1,075.67
2011	1,061.22	1,082.78	1,072.01	1,060.32	1,073.37	1,104.36	1,064.30	1,101.68	1,120.75	1,082.04	1,060.70	1,128.57	1,085.02
Trade, Transportation, and Utilities													
2007	907.17	906.35	903.42	877.01	841.80	824.17	823.96	808.78	784.40	800.40	794.01	808.13	839.70
2008	811.33	797.72	799.51	796.98	805.09	827.59	821.47	838.66	847.29	866.17	876.00	864.50	829.55
2009	865.43	864.29	868.85	874.37	854.85	863.04	863.76	879.70	852.91	861.04	878.89	853.55	864.44
2010	868.28	835.50	826.88	829.04	837.31	854.13	888.53	871.05	831.07	817.57	839.52	821.78	843.17
2011	831.32	818.61	805.55	811.19	804.58	795.31	813.49	848.33	863.94	929.57	884.37	856.66	838.26
Professional and Business Services													
2007	1,433.32	1,454.98	1,416.38	1,480.15	1,460.21	1,462.38	1,474.40	1,413.75	1,449.71	1,421.57	1,428.42	1,463.00	1,446.57
2008	1,421.28	1,458.70	1,464.56	1,437.07	1,454.10	1,464.98	1,450.43	1,423.10	1,439.78	1,402.38	1,413.60	1,387.36	1,434.96
2009	1,372.70	1,415.91	1,418.21	1,403.04	1,368.28	1,396.56	1,373.74	1,421.67	1,381.98	1,375.06	1,425.00	1,383.56	1,394.54
2010	1,404.45	1,400.61	1,358.05	1,369.61	1,388.84	1,280.16	1,244.20	1,347.76	1,281.52	1,287.89	1,305.36	1,338.37	1,333.64
2011	1,363.10	1,298.12	1,290.67	1,333.75	1,400.95	1,357.70	1,372.22	1,368.00	1,411.79	1,505.88	1,449.42	1,494.03	1,387.73
Leisure and Hospitality													
2007	592.52	551.52	553.11	563.32	576.45	576.90	557.15	544.50	568.56	568.80	573.20	557.23	565.20
2008	526.71	540.25	547.78	559.36	550.16	551.08	542.05	538.27	557.28	567.00	559.57	570.98	551.05
2009	553.38	547.76	547.13	548.11	547.14	551.38	545.38	544.15	546.15	553.41	567.35	564.00	551.31
2010	564.08	560.35	592.37	615.85	592.00	571.87	553.11	569.52	562.35	569.63	570.56	570.38	574.48
2011	539.95	563.43	586.89	592.67	599.95	567.22	555.21	527.54	557.23	552.05	536.35	531.85	559.15
Other Services													
2007	1,281.46	1,262.74	1,293.60	1,285.53	1,256.34	1,288.98	1,306.44	1,353.64	1,370.16	1,394.75	1,366.70	1,351.23	1,317.98
2008	1,304.49	1,307.39	1,356.32	1,321.38	1,322.73	1,359.76	1,347.14	1,378.47	1,361.10	1,350.28	1,383.76	1,369.55	1,347.20
2009	1,364.69	1,379.52	1,387.25	1,381.95	1,376.15	1,384.09	1,397.16	1,420.06	1,412.67	1,412.95	1,427.68	1,402.25	1,395.45
2010	1,415.53	1,412.28	1,393.34	1,416.51	1,427.97	1,377.22	1,411.87	1,458.91	1,447.28	1,451.94	1,473.42	1,485.48	1,431.41
2011	1,526.72	1,440.23	1,468.83	1,425.76	1,460.05	1,398.23	1,401.22	1,393.92	1,411.60	1,420.00	1,383.84	1,408.56	1,427.78

FLORIDA
At a Glance

Population:
    2000 census: 15,982,571
    2010 census: 18,801,310
    2011 estimate: 19,057,542

Percent change in population:
    2000–2010: 17.6%
    2010–2011: 1.4%

Percent change in total nonfarm employment:
    2000–2010: 1.8%
    2010–2011: 1.1%

Industry with the largest growth in employment, 2000–2011 (thousands):
    Education and Health Services, 264.8

Industry with the largest decline or smallest growth in employment, 2000–2011 (thousands):
    Manufacturing, -166.1

Civilian labor force:
    2000: 7,869,690
    2010: 9,132,470
    2011: 9,248,503

Unemployment rate and rank among states (lowest to highest):
    2000: 3.8%, 25th
    2010: 11.3%, 47th
    2011: 10.5%, 46th

Over-the-year change in unemployment rates:
    2010–2011: -0.8%

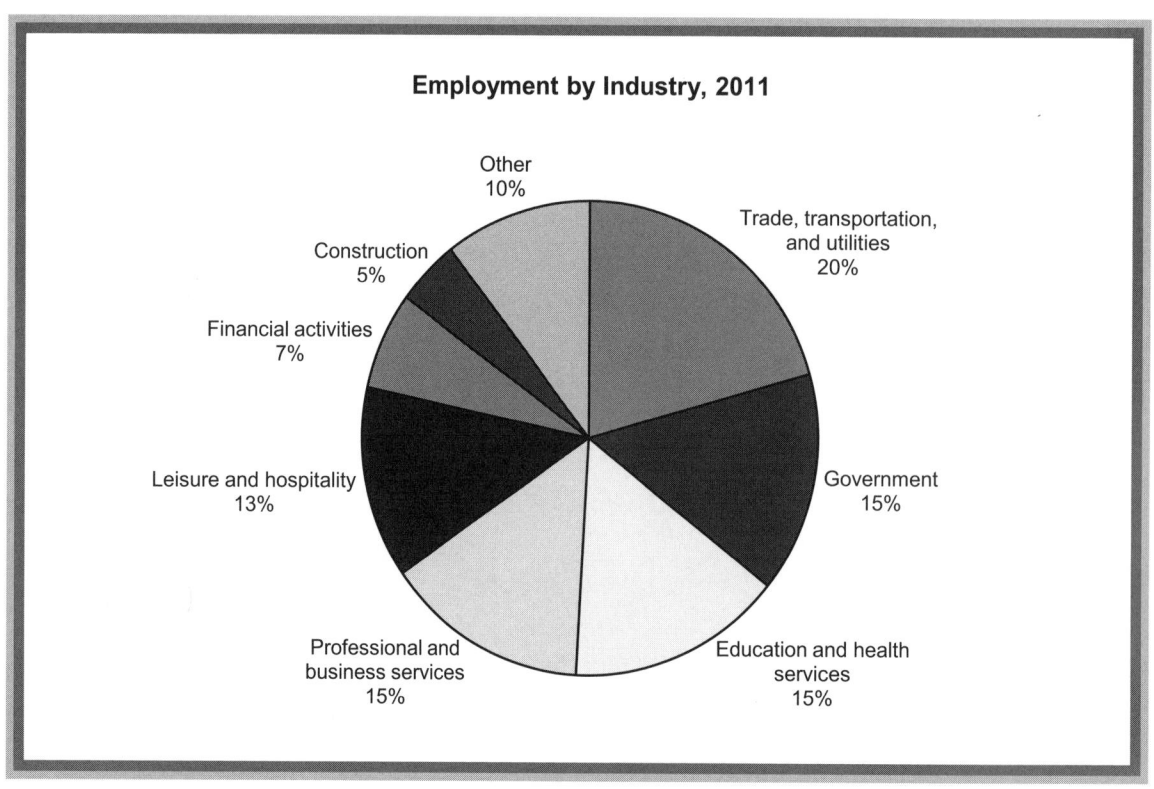

Employment by Industry, 2011

- Other 10%
- Trade, transportation, and utilities 20%
- Construction 5%
- Financial activities 7%
- Government 15%
- Leisure and hospitality 13%
- Professional and business services 15%
- Education and health services 15%

1. Employment by Industry: Florida, Selected Years, 2000–2011

(Numbers in thousands, not seasonally adjusted)

Industry and year	January	February	March	April	May	June	July	August	September	October	November	December	Annual average
Total Nonfarm													
2000	6,919.5	6,981.9	7,061.4	7,045.6	7,079.3	7,029.7	6,963.8	7,069.9	7,104.9	7,118.3	7,197.1	7,262.5	7,069.5
2001	7,096.7	7,167.7	7,229.5	7,194.7	7,198.5	7,135.1	7,046.0	7,147.1	7,147.8	7,138.8	7,187.0	7,228.0	7,159.7
2002	7,089.1	7,144.9	7,206.4	7,186.4	7,198.3	7,116.4	7,037.0	7,143.5	7,154.3	7,184.2	7,253.2	7,310.5	7,168.7
2003	7,176.8	7,232.3	7,287.6	7,262.3	7,266.8	7,184.5	7,116.9	7,217.7	7,238.0	7,283.2	7,331.2	7,403.3	7,250.1
2004	7,332.7	7,404.7	7,470.8	7,507.1	7,511.6	7,444.1	7,405.6	7,493.2	7,471.0	7,555.0	7,657.0	7,736.5	7,499.1
2005	7,621.9	7,704.9	7,751.6	7,794.2	7,812.4	7,718.4	7,698.1	7,815.0	7,860.0	7,866.8	7,941.2	8,014.6	7,799.9
2006	7,882.6	7,957.3	8,037.8	8,018.1	8,035.9	7,951.3	7,878.1	7,994.8	8,011.0	8,012.8	8,096.3	8,153.2	8,002.4
2007	8,011.9	8,078.5	8,142.9	8,094.9	8,089.6	7,981.0	7,872.1	7,971.5	7,958.2	7,947.3	8,020.1	8,053.2	8,018.4
2008	7,871.8	7,927.8	7,949.4	7,865.8	7,834.3	7,693.3	7,583.2	7,657.8	7,629.2	7,600.6	7,607.9	7,607.2	7,735.7
2009	7,398.8	7,398.3	7,393.7	7,345.7	7,305.7	7,173.6	7,085.2	7,152.8	7,147.2	7,172.5	7,226.3	7,245.7	7,253.8
2010	7,116.9	7,167.4	7,214.5	7,235.1	7,258.4	7,137.1	7,079.9	7,165.8	7,155.5	7,219.1	7,280.4	7,309.3	7,195.0
2011	7,196.1	7,246.4	7,293.4	7,337.1	7,313.6	7,199.5	7,153.6	7,224.4	7,250.1	7,299.2	7,352.6	7,392.2	7,271.5
Total Private													
2000	5,927.9	5,980.4	6,051.7	6,031.0	6,045.2	6,081.4	6,031.1	6,064.2	6,095.0	6,100.1	6,171.7	6,233.4	6,067.8
2001	6,082.0	6,139.5	6,195.2	6,159.5	6,161.9	6,166.3	6,093.1	6,113.9	6,108.6	6,097.1	6,139.2	6,178.8	6,136.3
2002	6,055.2	6,100.7	6,157.6	6,137.1	6,144.6	6,138.5	6,073.0	6,095.3	6,097.7	6,122.2	6,188.4	6,243.0	6,129.4
2003	6,124.1	6,168.8	6,220.5	6,196.7	6,194.8	6,190.6	6,135.9	6,160.7	6,175.1	6,212.2	6,257.4	6,327.6	6,197.0
2004	6,268.1	6,326.9	6,390.2	6,427.6	6,432.1	6,440.6	6,413.4	6,421.7	6,394.9	6,471.1	6,565.1	6,643.2	6,432.9
2005	6,540.8	6,611.4	6,655.8	6,698.7	6,713.7	6,719.2	6,697.4	6,731.9	6,762.1	6,758.7	6,830.3	6,905.0	6,718.8
2006	6,782.3	6,846.4	6,923.1	6,906.7	6,928.0	6,937.2	6,863.3	6,891.9	6,895.9	6,883.9	6,959.6	7,019.8	6,903.2
2007	6,888.1	6,943.4	7,002.3	6,955.7	6,954.0	6,940.0	6,831.0	6,841.4	6,820.0	6,801.7	6,868.8	6,903.8	6,895.9
2008	6,731.5	6,776.0	6,800.2	6,718.9	6,693.4	6,648.6	6,539.4	6,524.7	6,487.0	6,454.7	6,463.1	6,467.7	6,608.8
2009	6,265.7	6,259.1	6,256.8	6,203.1	6,175.2	6,138.2	6,051.0	6,039.1	6,023.3	6,043.9	6,094.5	6,120.4	6,139.2
2010	5,995.0	6,039.4	6,086.1	6,101.0	6,096.7	6,089.1	6,046.6	6,053.7	6,040.2	6,096.8	6,155.0	6,192.3	6,082.7
2011	6,081.5	6,122.1	6,170.7	6,213.9	6,201.7	6,178.9	6,138.6	6,137.6	6,154.7	6,187.5	6,240.4	6,284.6	6,176.0
Goods-Producing													
2000	951.2	958.8	967.1	960.6	965.6	975.3	971.8	975.1	980.7	974.4	976.4	979.1	969.7
2001	964.7	966.8	969.6	962.3	963.3	967.4	959.4	962.3	959.3	957.4	956.6	956.2	962.1
2002	937.5	938.5	941.6	936.9	939.5	941.0	932.3	939.3	938.7	942.5	945.6	946.4	940.0
2003	932.4	936.0	939.2	931.7	937.2	941.9	935.9	942.0	944.9	946.8	947.5	955.3	940.9
2004	953.1	962.7	974.2	980.2	984.7	992.7	995.6	998.6	997.9	1,007.5	1,015.6	1,024.4	990.6
2005	1,013.8	1,024.5	1,032.5	1,043.4	1,052.2	1,061.6	1,066.1	1,072.9	1,081.5	1,082.6	1,089.7	1,098.8	1,060.0
2006	1,085.7	1,099.2	1,111.6	1,110.2	1,117.3	1,123.6	1,110.2	1,112.0	1,109.5	1,098.3	1,093.7	1,091.4	1,105.2
2007	1,063.3	1,064.8	1,068.6	1,048.1	1,047.2	1,048.8	1,022.7	1,019.2	1,009.5	990.8	983.6	977.1	1,028.6
2008	945.2	944.0	938.8	915.5	911.9	908.8	886.6	880.1	872.7	852.8	838.1	823.5	893.2
2009	784.9	771.5	762.4	741.3	734.7	730.6	714.5	708.3	701.9	693.2	687.4	683.2	726.2
2010	660.6	662.1	664.5	668.6	669.1	672.4	673.1	670.7	666.2	661.3	658.4	657.0	665.3
2011	643.0	645.6	648.4	651.1	652.1	653.8	649.0	645.2	646.6	641.1	642.8	644.2	646.9
Mining and Logging													
2002	7.3	7.4	7.3	7.3	7.3	7.3	7.2	7.2	7.1	7.0	7.0	7.0	7.2
2003	7.1	7.0	7.0	6.9	7.1	7.1	7.1	7.2	7.2	7.2	7.2	7.2	7.1
2004	7.2	7.2	7.2	7.2	7.1	7.1	7.1	7.1	7.1	7.0	7.1	7.1	7.1
2005	7.1	7.1	7.1	7.2	7.2	7.2	7.2	7.2	7.0	6.8	6.8	6.9	7.1
2006	6.6	6.6	6.7	6.7	6.7	6.8	6.6	6.4	6.5	6.5	6.6	6.6	6.6
2007	6.7	6.8	6.7	6.8	6.8	6.9	6.6	6.7	6.6	6.6	6.7	6.7	6.7
2008	6.6	6.6	6.5	6.4	6.3	6.2	6.1	6.1	6.0	5.9	5.8	5.8	6.2
2009	5.7	5.6	5.5	5.5	5.5	5.5	5.4	5.4	5.4	5.4	5.4	5.4	5.5
2010	5.3	5.3	5.2	5.3	5.3	5.4	5.4	5.5	5.6	5.6	5.7	5.7	5.4
2011	5.7	5.7	5.7	5.7	5.7	5.7	5.6	5.6	5.6	5.6	5.6	5.6	5.7
Construction													
2000	469.2	473.7	479.3	474.8	478.6	485.7	485.1	488.3	493.0	490.2	491.9	493.8	483.6
2001	488.5	491.3	494.7	492.0	494.7	500.8	500.8	504.5	504.5	506.7	507.6	507.0	499.4
2002	495.9	497.0	499.8	498.5	502.0	503.7	500.3	506.9	507.6	513.5	516.1	516.8	504.8
2003	507.6	512.0	515.4	513.3	519.1	524.2	524.0	529.2	531.5	534.2	535.6	541.5	524.0
2004	540.7	548.2	557.1	561.9	565.2	572.4	576.9	579.6	580.4	590.5	597.1	603.7	572.8
2005	597.3	605.8	612.3	621.9	629.1	636.9	643.2	649.1	656.8	659.0	665.7	672.3	637.5
2006	661.7	673.4	684.3	685.1	690.9	696.1	687.9	690.0	688.1	680.4	676.3	672.6	682.2
2007	650.0	651.0	655.1	637.3	636.9	639.0	619.0	616.2	608.6	593.2	587.2	581.2	622.9
2008	554.4	553.6	550.6	531.1	528.8	527.1	511.1	506.0	501.0	486.4	475.4	465.3	515.9
2009	434.1	426.2	421.4	407.0	402.8	400.6	390.8	386.0	381.6	374.7	368.9	365.4	396.6
2010	347.5	349.2	351.5	355.1	353.8	356.1	357.8	355.7	351.6	347.3	343.3	340.4	350.8
2011	328.5	330.3	332.6	334.1	334.3	335.1	332.5	330.0	330.5	323.5	324.7	324.6	330.1
Manufacturing													
2000	473.2	476.3	478.9	477.2	478.3	480.8	478.1	478.2	479.0	475.4	475.9	476.7	477.3
2001	467.9	467.2	466.6	462.1	460.3	458.4	450.5	449.9	446.9	443.0	441.4	441.6	454.7
2002	434.3	434.1	434.5	431.1	430.2	430.0	424.8	425.2	424.0	422.0	422.5	422.6	427.9
2003	417.7	417.0	416.8	411.5	411.0	410.6	404.8	405.6	406.2	405.4	404.7	406.6	409.8
2004	405.2	407.3	409.9	411.1	412.4	413.2	411.6	411.9	410.4	410.0	411.4	413.6	410.7
2005	409.4	411.6	413.1	414.3	415.9	417.5	415.7	416.6	417.7	416.8	417.2	419.6	415.5
2006	417.4	419.2	420.6	418.4	419.7	420.7	415.7	415.6	414.9	411.4	410.8	412.2	416.4
2007	406.6	407.0	406.8	404.0	403.5	402.9	397.1	396.3	394.3	391.0	389.7	389.2	399.0
2008	384.2	383.8	381.7	378.0	376.8	375.5	369.4	368.0	365.7	360.5	356.9	352.4	371.1
2009	345.1	339.7	335.5	328.8	326.4	324.5	318.3	316.9	314.9	313.1	313.1	312.4	324.1
2010	307.8	307.6	307.8	308.2	310.0	310.9	309.9	309.5	309.0	308.4	309.4	310.9	309.1
2011	308.8	309.6	310.1	311.3	312.1	313.0	310.9	309.6	310.5	312.0	312.5	314.0	311.2

1. Employment by Industry: Florida, Selected Years, 2000–2011—*Continued*

(Numbers in thousands, not seasonally adjusted)

Industry and year	January	February	March	April	May	June	July	August	September	October	November	December	Annual average
Service-Providing													
2000	5,968.3	6,023.1	6,094.3	6,085.0	6,113.7	6,054.4	5,992.0	6,094.8	6,124.2	6,143.9	6,220.7	6,283.4	6,099.8
2001	6,132.0	6,200.9	6,259.9	6,232.4	6,235.2	6,167.7	6,086.6	6,184.8	6,188.5	6,181.4	6,230.4	6,271.8	6,197.6
2002	6,151.6	6,206.4	6,264.8	6,249.5	6,258.8	6,175.4	6,104.7	6,204.2	6,215.6	6,241.7	6,307.6	6,364.1	6,228.7
2003	6,244.4	6,296.3	6,348.4	6,330.6	6,329.6	6,242.6	6,181.0	6,275.7	6,293.1	6,336.4	6,383.7	6,448.0	6,309.2
2004	6,379.6	6,442.0	6,496.6	6,526.9	6,526.9	6,451.4	6,410.0	6,494.6	6,473.1	6,547.5	6,641.4	6,712.1	6,508.5
2005	6,608.1	6,680.4	6,719.1	6,750.8	6,760.2	6,656.8	6,632.0	6,742.1	6,778.5	6,784.2	6,851.5	6,915.8	6,740.0
2006	6,796.9	6,858.1	6,926.2	6,907.9	6,918.6	6,827.7	6,767.9	6,882.8	6,901.5	6,914.5	7,002.6	7,061.8	6,897.2
2007	6,948.6	7,013.7	7,074.3	7,046.8	7,042.4	6,932.2	6,849.4	6,952.3	6,948.7	6,956.5	7,036.5	7,076.1	6,989.8
2008	6,926.6	6,983.8	7,010.6	6,950.3	6,922.4	6,784.5	6,696.6	6,777.7	6,756.5	6,747.8	6,769.8	6,783.7	6,842.5
2009	6,613.9	6,626.8	6,631.3	6,604.4	6,571.0	6,443.0	6,370.7	6,444.5	6,445.3	6,479.3	6,538.9	6,562.5	6,527.6
2010	6,456.3	6,505.3	6,550.0	6,566.5	6,589.3	6,464.7	6,406.8	6,495.1	6,489.3	6,557.8	6,622.0	6,652.3	6,529.6
2011	6,553.1	6,600.8	6,645.0	6,686.0	6,661.5	6,545.7	6,504.6	6,579.2	6,603.5	6,658.1	6,709.8	6,748.0	6,624.6
Trade, Transportation, and Utilities													
2000	1,508.0	1,506.9	1,515.1	1,507.3	1,512.0	1,519.0	1,503.4	1,514.1	1,518.4	1,524.0	1,561.3	1,592.4	1,523.5
2001	1,521.9	1,517.5	1,527.4	1,516.7	1,514.2	1,510.4	1,497.9	1,502.9	1,502.7	1,505.3	1,531.9	1,554.7	1,517.0
2002	1,502.5	1,493.4	1,500.6	1,493.3	1,494.4	1,488.9	1,477.3	1,483.6	1,484.5	1,491.5	1,518.5	1,547.4	1,498.0
2003	1,488.2	1,480.6	1,483.1	1,478.5	1,479.0	1,474.7	1,470.3	1,475.9	1,480.2	1,493.9	1,520.9	1,551.2	1,489.7
2004	1,508.4	1,506.2	1,513.0	1,517.6	1,520.5	1,518.8	1,517.4	1,519.1	1,513.3	1,535.4	1,575.5	1,607.7	1,529.3
2005	1,558.5	1,561.7	1,568.5	1,579.1	1,584.3	1,582.9	1,583.5	1,589.2	1,593.1	1,600.6	1,629.3	1,660.8	1,591.0
2006	1,611.0	1,610.2	1,621.5	1,617.7	1,620.6	1,618.5	1,607.7	1,612.2	1,611.8	1,619.0	1,656.0	1,685.6	1,624.3
2007	1,632.4	1,629.1	1,638.1	1,632.2	1,636.9	1,631.7	1,615.8	1,617.5	1,617.5	1,620.7	1,660.7	1,681.5	1,634.5
2008	1,625.3	1,620.6	1,621.5	1,602.7	1,599.3	1,587.7	1,569.6	1,567.3	1,558.3	1,555.5	1,572.5	1,586.9	1,588.9
2009	1,520.3	1,507.1	1,498.5	1,482.3	1,479.2	1,470.6	1,454.0	1,452.7	1,449.7	1,455.4	1,485.2	1,503.5	1,479.9
2010	1,457.2	1,455.7	1,460.4	1,461.7	1,463.4	1,461.6	1,450.7	1,454.2	1,449.3	1,466.8	1,501.2	1,523.8	1,467.2
2011	1,477.3	1,475.2	1,480.1	1,489.3	1,488.9	1,486.5	1,485.0	1,489.5	1,487.1	1,498.8	1,530.7	1,551.4	1,495.0
Wholesale Trade													
2000	311.5	312.7	315.8	314.6	316.2	318.1	316.6	317.7	320.0	319.1	320.4	323.0	317.1
2001	315.5	317.3	319.1	318.2	318.2	317.2	314.5	314.9	315.1	314.8	314.9	316.4	316.3
2002	313.9	315.2	316.0	314.0	315.5	315.1	313.7	314.6	315.3	316.4	318.3	320.2	315.7
2003	315.4	316.3	316.8	316.3	316.4	316.1	315.8	316.6	317.6	318.1	319.6	322.7	317.3
2004	321.4	323.8	325.5	326.3	327.8	328.4	327.3	327.9	327.3	330.5	333.6	336.0	328.0
2005	333.7	336.0	336.8	339.9	341.9	341.9	341.6	342.4	343.6	343.9	345.5	349.1	341.4
2006	344.8	347.5	349.5	350.4	352.1	352.6	350.7	351.6	352.1	352.9	354.5	357.3	351.3
2007	355.7	358.2	359.3	357.9	358.8	358.6	354.7	354.6	354.4	354.9	355.9	357.5	356.7
2008	351.9	353.5	353.0	349.2	349.5	347.8	343.4	342.4	341.5	339.7	338.2	338.0	345.7
2009	329.0	327.8	324.8	321.2	320.3	317.7	313.4	312.5	311.0	311.7	312.4	313.8	318.0
2010	307.3	308.3	308.9	308.9	310.5	309.3	306.9	307.2	306.6	308.7	309.8	312.1	308.7
2011	305.3	306.7	307.5	309.1	309.2	308.4	308.6	307.9	307.1	309.6	310.7	314.2	308.7
Retail Trade													
2000	947.1	944.5	948.7	942.4	945.4	950.5	936.8	945.9	946.6	953.7	987.3	1,009.8	954.9
2001	957.5	951.2	958.3	947.7	946.2	943.9	934.5	938.8	938.7	943.0	970.0	986.7	951.4
2002	946.0	936.0	940.6	935.5	936.0	931.9	922.1	927.7	928.5	934.7	958.8	982.2	940.0
2003	935.5	928.1	930.0	925.7	927.6	925.7	922.4	926.6	929.9	942.8	967.7	990.7	937.7
2004	952.6	947.3	951.5	954.4	956.8	955.4	954.0	953.1	948.1	964.0	997.9	1,021.3	963.0
2005	981.8	981.6	986.4	992.4	994.6	995.1	996.1	1,000.6	1,001.9	1,009.3	1,033.0	1,055.4	1,002.4
2006	1,016.7	1,013.0	1,020.7	1,016.4	1,017.4	1,015.8	1,009.6	1,011.2	1,009.5	1,016.8	1,049.7	1,068.9	1,022.1
2007	1,027.1	1,021.7	1,028.3	1,022.5	1,027.0	1,022.5	1,012.7	1,014.0	1,013.5	1,015.7	1,051.1	1,065.1	1,026.8
2008	1,023.3	1,016.4	1,017.4	1,004.7	1,001.7	994.8	983.8	982.4	976.2	974.9	992.2	1,001.0	997.4
2009	953.1	943.4	939.2	929.5	928.6	924.4	915.0	915.4	914.7	919.6	947.3	958.8	932.4
2010	926.3	922.9	926.4	928.2	928.8	928.8	921.3	924.5	920.8	934.2	964.6	978.8	933.8
2011	943.6	939.2	941.9	948.7	948.6	947.0	947.9	952.6	949.4	958.6	986.4	995.1	954.9
Transportation and Utilities													
2000	249.4	249.7	250.6	250.3	250.4	250.4	250.0	250.5	251.8	251.2	253.6	259.6	251.5
2001	248.9	249.0	250.0	250.8	249.8	249.3	248.9	249.2	248.9	247.5	247.0	251.6	249.2
2002	242.6	242.2	244.0	243.8	242.9	241.9	241.5	241.3	240.7	240.4	241.4	245.0	242.3
2003	237.3	236.2	236.3	236.5	235.0	232.9	232.1	232.7	232.7	233.0	233.6	237.8	234.7
2004	234.4	235.1	236.0	236.9	235.9	235.0	236.1	238.1	237.9	240.9	244.0	249.4	238.3
2005	243.0	244.1	245.3	246.8	247.8	245.9	245.8	246.2	247.6	247.4	250.8	256.3	247.3
2006	249.5	249.7	251.3	250.9	251.1	250.1	247.4	249.4	250.2	249.3	251.8	259.4	250.8
2007	249.6	249.2	250.5	251.8	251.1	250.6	248.4	248.9	249.6	250.1	253.7	258.9	251.0
2008	250.1	250.7	251.1	248.8	248.1	245.1	242.4	242.5	240.6	240.9	242.1	247.9	245.9
2009	238.2	235.9	234.5	231.6	230.3	228.5	225.6	224.8	224.0	224.1	225.5	230.9	229.5
2010	223.6	224.5	225.1	224.6	224.1	223.5	222.5	222.5	221.9	223.9	226.8	232.9	224.7
2011	228.4	229.3	230.7	231.5	231.1	231.1	228.5	229.0	230.6	230.6	233.6	242.1	231.4
Information													
2000	175.9	177.1	180.5	177.3	178.9	182.4	184.0	185.5	187.2	187.0	188.6	190.5	182.9
2001	186.1	187.1	187.7	185.9	185.8	185.5	183.3	182.2	180.3	178.4	178.4	179.1	183.3
2002	176.1	175.6	175.8	173.6	173.9	173.4	171.9	171.3	170.4	169.8	170.4	171.0	172.8
2003	167.3	167.6	168.0	165.7	166.7	166.3	166.1	166.1	165.1	164.9	165.6	166.3	166.3
2004	163.1	162.5	163.6	162.4	163.1	163.5	162.4	162.5	161.3	162.3	163.6	164.2	162.9
2005	161.9	162.7	162.9	162.1	163.8	163.9	163.5	163.5	164.0	162.6	163.6	164.0	163.2
2006	160.5	161.3	161.5	161.2	162.3	163.0	162.7	162.0	161.0	160.8	161.8	162.6	161.7
2007	160.2	161.2	161.8	162.4	163.1	163.4	161.7	161.4	160.0	159.8	159.8	160.3	161.3
2008	158.7	159.2	159.0	157.7	157.9	157.4	156.5	155.2	152.9	152.4	152.0	151.0	155.8
2009	147.9	147.5	146.5	144.9	144.1	143.7	141.5	140.3	138.4	137.9	137.8	137.9	142.4
2010	136.3	136.0	136.8	135.8	135.6	135.7	135.4	135.5	134.6	135.2	135.7	135.3	135.7
2011	134.8	134.9	134.8	134.8	134.9	134.7	133.1	133.4	132.9	133.8	134.3	135.0	134.3

1. Employment by Industry: Florida, Selected Years, 2000–2011—*Continued*

(Numbers in thousands, not seasonally adjusted)

Industry and year	January	February	March	April	May	June	July	August	September	October	November	December	Annual average
Financial Activities													
2000	462.3	464.0	468.4	467.9	470.1	476.2	472.0	473.2	473.9	473.7	475.2	478.4	471.3
2001	468.4	471.7	475.5	477.1	477.8	481.2	479.7	481.0	479.5	478.9	479.6	481.4	477.7
2002	477.8	480.0	481.6	480.1	481.0	483.2	483.8	485.1	483.8	484.8	487.6	490.0	483.2
2003	484.2	486.0	488.0	490.0	491.9	494.6	495.9	498.2	497.7	498.6	498.6	503.2	493.9
2004	498.8	501.8	505.2	509.5	510.8	512.8	515.1	515.9	514.1	518.9	520.9	525.9	512.5
2005	520.4	524.3	526.2	531.7	534.4	538.3	540.7	542.4	543.6	546.6	550.1	556.3	537.9
2006	546.4	550.6	554.1	554.8	556.8	558.3	555.0	555.7	553.7	555.0	556.0	560.4	554.7
2007	548.8	552.4	554.4	552.1	552.6	553.8	550.3	548.6	545.4	543.2	544.1	545.8	549.3
2008	535.5	536.3	536.3	530.6	529.9	527.8	523.0	520.5	516.0	512.0	509.7	510.2	524.0
2009	495.8	493.8	492.0	489.4	488.7	488.1	483.8	481.8	477.4	477.7	478.1	479.3	485.5
2010	471.2	472.4	474.1	473.7	475.0	476.8	476.6	476.8	474.0	478.5	480.5	483.6	476.1
2011	477.0	478.8	481.4	482.7	483.0	483.7	482.7	483.1	481.6	482.2	487.6	490.6	482.9
Professional and Business Services													
2000	886.7	901.2	920.5	916.2	920.6	928.6	919.2	931.6	942.9	939.0	948.9	957.0	926.0
2001	937.1	960.8	973.1	963.8	964.1	965.8	950.5	956.0	954.5	951.2	952.7	953.3	956.9
2002	930.9	952.3	966.5	967.5	968.6	966.1	955.0	950.4	951.8	956.3	968.3	975.2	959.1
2003	957.0	975.3	992.1	989.5	980.2	976.7	957.9	960.8	960.9	978.9	979.6	985.4	974.5
2004	979.7	999.3	1,015.8	1,035.2	1,033.4	1,038.7	1,032.2	1,033.3	1,029.4	1,052.9	1,069.5	1,086.3	1,033.8
2005	1,069.2	1,090.6	1,097.4	1,107.0	1,106.9	1,108.4	1,106.1	1,116.0	1,125.3	1,117.7	1,131.6	1,142.1	1,109.9
2006	1,121.5	1,136.6	1,156.7	1,153.3	1,159.7	1,166.4	1,153.2	1,162.9	1,168.2	1,160.1	1,173.1	1,184.3	1,158.0
2007	1,165.5	1,180.9	1,192.0	1,180.3	1,176.3	1,174.1	1,153.5	1,157.1	1,150.4	1,149.7	1,155.1	1,158.9	1,166.2
2008	1,112.2	1,127.3	1,131.4	1,114.1	1,105.9	1,098.7	1,077.6	1,076.5	1,073.5	1,069.7	1,063.6	1,062.5	1,092.8
2009	1,019.1	1,019.9	1,017.2	1,008.6	1,003.4	1,001.5	987.1	987.6	988.3	997.5	1,006.2	1,009.1	1,003.8
2010	987.9	1,000.0	1,008.0	1,010.5	1,010.5	1,015.2	1,011.7	1,017.4	1,017.7	1,032.5	1,037.3	1,043.9	1,016.1
2011	1,024.9	1,038.6	1,045.9	1,058.5	1,053.7	1,052.2	1,041.4	1,044.4	1,052.7	1,063.9	1,070.7	1,072.4	1,051.6
Education and Health Services													
2000	821.5	829.2	836.1	832.8	835.0	835.8	831.3	838.1	847.5	850.8	856.1	861.3	839.6
2001	844.4	853.1	858.1	859.2	862.5	864.7	855.2	862.9	871.5	876.5	881.2	887.3	864.7
2002	870.5	878.3	885.9	882.8	886.1	884.8	874.9	884.3	892.6	898.9	905.0	909.3	887.8
2003	900.8	911.1	916.9	915.8	919.2	917.3	910.3	919.1	929.0	931.7	934.3	939.7	920.4
2004	933.2	941.3	945.5	948.4	951.1	947.1	939.1	944.5	945.9	953.3	959.2	962.2	947.6
2005	953.2	962.0	965.1	969.8	971.2	965.8	961.2	970.3	978.0	979.9	983.3	988.8	970.7
2006	977.5	985.9	992.5	992.7	996.6	994.0	985.0	995.8	1,003.2	1,005.1	1,011.7	1,017.5	996.5
2007	1,007.4	1,018.4	1,023.7	1,025.7	1,028.1	1,026.0	1,012.8	1,024.5	1,032.4	1,035.7	1,042.2	1,047.0	1,027.0
2008	1,037.2	1,046.8	1,051.3	1,049.0	1,051.7	1,044.8	1,033.2	1,041.0	1,047.3	1,053.4	1,060.4	1,064.9	1,048.4
2009	1,047.9	1,054.7	1,058.8	1,058.6	1,061.6	1,055.3	1,046.7	1,053.6	1,061.6	1,075.3	1,081.8	1,084.2	1,061.7
2010	1,069.8	1,077.2	1,082.0	1,083.3	1,084.7	1,077.0	1,067.7	1,071.8	1,077.4	1,091.5	1,097.1	1,096.7	1,081.4
2011	1,087.9	1,095.6	1,098.0	1,105.9	1,106.4	1,095.4	1,088.0	1,093.8	1,108.2	1,116.4	1,127.8	1,128.8	1,104.4
Leisure and Hospitality													
2000	830.5	849.0	866.6	871.4	863.8	862.7	849.4	847.5	843.9	849.3	863.3	871.9	855.8
2001	860.4	881.0	899.6	891.8	889.9	883.9	862.5	861.6	855.5	844.7	852.0	858.2	870.1
2002	850.6	870.7	890.0	890.4	887.1	885.4	864.1	866.5	860.8	860.4	872.6	882.1	873.4
2003	873.6	888.6	906.6	900.0	894.8	892.5	878.8	879.5	877.4	878.7	892.2	905.2	889.0
2004	907.9	926.7	945.3	945.2	938.1	933.5	920.9	917.8	903.6	912.4	929.2	941.7	926.9
2005	931.7	951.2	967.6	969.0	963.7	961.0	941.5	943.6	940.7	936.3	949.2	959.3	951.2
2006	949.1	968.4	987.6	980.4	976.1	971.9	952.9	954.3	949.7	946.4	965.5	974.2	964.7
2007	966.8	989.2	1,011.8	1,006.9	1,001.6	993.2	972.1	971.5	963.4	959.9	978.8	986.3	983.5
2008	973.9	995.7	1,013.7	1,005.5	993.9	982.5	959.0	951.8	938.8	934.5	945.1	949.0	970.3
2009	933.9	948.5	964.4	961.4	947.7	934.1	913.3	905.7	897.8	897.4	908.1	912.8	927.1
2010	904.2	926.1	948.7	955.0	946.8	939.1	923.0	920.1	914.9	922.2	935.4	942.6	931.5
2011	931.5	946.5	973.0	980.4	971.5	962.8	952.2	945.0	940.6	946.1	943.1	955.6	954.0
Other Services													
2000	291.8	294.2	297.4	297.5	299.2	301.4	300.0	299.1	300.5	301.9	301.9	302.8	299.0
2001	299.0	301.5	304.2	302.7	304.3	307.4	304.6	305.0	305.3	304.7	306.8	308.6	304.5
2002	309.3	311.9	315.6	312.5	314.0	315.7	313.7	314.8	315.1	318.0	320.4	321.6	315.2
2003	320.6	323.6	326.6	325.5	325.8	326.6	320.7	319.1	319.9	318.7	318.7	321.3	322.3
2004	323.9	326.4	327.6	329.1	330.4	333.5	330.7	330.0	329.4	328.4	331.6	331.8	329.4
2005	332.1	334.4	335.6	336.6	337.2	337.3	334.8	334.0	335.9	332.4	333.5	334.9	334.9
2006	330.6	334.2	337.6	336.4	338.6	341.5	336.6	337.0	338.8	339.2	341.8	343.8	338.0
2007	343.7	347.4	351.9	348.0	348.2	349.0	342.1	341.6	341.4	341.9	344.5	346.9	345.6
2008	343.5	346.1	348.2	343.8	342.9	340.9	333.9	332.3	327.5	324.4	321.7	319.7	335.4
2009	315.9	316.1	317.0	316.6	315.8	314.3	310.1	309.1	308.2	309.5	309.9	310.4	312.7
2010	307.8	309.9	311.6	312.4	311.6	311.3	308.4	307.2	306.1	308.8	309.4	309.4	309.5
2011	305.1	306.9	309.1	311.2	311.2	309.8	307.2	303.2	305.0	305.2	303.4	306.6	307.0
Government													
2000	991.6	1,001.5	1,009.7	1,014.6	1,034.1	948.3	932.7	1,005.7	1,009.9	1,018.2	1,025.4	1,029.1	1,001.7
2001	1,014.7	1,028.2	1,034.3	1,035.2	1,036.6	968.8	952.9	1,033.2	1,039.2	1,041.7	1,047.8	1,049.2	1,023.5
2002	1,033.9	1,044.2	1,048.8	1,049.3	1,053.7	977.9	964.0	1,048.2	1,056.6	1,062.0	1,064.8	1,067.5	1,039.2
2003	1,052.7	1,063.5	1,067.1	1,065.6	1,072.0	993.9	981.0	1,057.0	1,062.9	1,071.0	1,073.8	1,075.7	1,053.0
2004	1,064.6	1,077.8	1,080.6	1,079.5	1,079.5	1,003.5	992.2	1,071.5	1,076.1	1,083.9	1,091.9	1,093.3	1,066.2
2005	1,081.1	1,093.5	1,095.8	1,095.5	1,098.7	999.2	1,000.7	1,083.1	1,097.9	1,108.1	1,110.9	1,109.6	1,081.2
2006	1,100.3	1,110.9	1,114.7	1,111.4	1,107.9	1,014.1	1,014.8	1,102.9	1,115.1	1,128.9	1,136.7	1,133.4	1,099.3
2007	1,123.8	1,135.1	1,140.6	1,139.2	1,135.6	1,041.0	1,041.1	1,130.1	1,138.2	1,145.6	1,151.3	1,149.4	1,122.6
2008	1,140.3	1,151.8	1,149.2	1,146.9	1,140.9	1,044.7	1,043.8	1,133.1	1,142.2	1,145.9	1,144.8	1,139.5	1,126.9
2009	1,133.1	1,139.2	1,136.9	1,142.6	1,130.5	1,035.4	1,034.2	1,113.7	1,123.9	1,128.6	1,131.8	1,125.3	1,114.6
2010	1,121.9	1,128.0	1,128.4	1,134.1	1,161.7	1,048.0	1,033.3	1,112.1	1,115.3	1,122.3	1,125.4	1,117.0	1,112.3
2011	1,114.6	1,124.3	1,122.7	1,123.2	1,111.9	1,020.6	1,015.0	1,086.8	1,095.4	1,111.7	1,112.2	1,107.6	1,095.5

2. Average Weekly Hours by Selected Industry: Florida, 2007–2011

(Not seasonally adjusted)

Industry and year	January	February	March	April	May	June	July	August	September	October	November	December	Annual average
Total Private													
2007	35.2	35.8	35.3	35.9	35.1	35.4	35.6	35.2	35.4	35.0	35.2	35.7	35.4
2008	35.7	35.2	35.3	35.0	35.0	36.2	35.4	35.1	34.9	35.1	35.2	34.8	35.2
2009	34.7	35.0	34.9	34.8	34.7	34.8	35.0	35.2	35.1	34.9	35.4	35.4	35.0
2010	35.4	35.6	35.5	35.8	36.0	35.6	35.4	35.6	34.9	35.2	35.2	35.2	35.5
2011	35.4	35.2	35.1	35.2	35.0	34.7	34.7	34.5	34.4	34.7	34.5	34.6	34.8
Goods-Producing													
2007	40.9	40.5	40.9	41.3	40.3	39.5	40.2	39.9	39.9	39.6	40.5	41.9	40.5
2008	39.9	39.8	40.1	38.9	39.8	39.7	39.5	39.8	40.6	39.9	38.8	38.6	39.6
2009	37.8	38.7	38.5	38.0	38.1	38.4	38.9	39.1	40.2	41.0	41.7	41.8	39.3
2010	41.4	40.3	40.1	40.6	40.9	40.8	39.8	39.8	39.0	39.7	39.8	39.5	40.1
2011	39.4	39.2	39.5	40.1	40.0	40.2	39.8	39.6	40.2	40.1	40.2	40.4	39.9
Construction													
2007	39.5	39.2	40.3	40.9	39.1	37.8	38.8	38.6	38.6	38.2	39.8	40.1	39.2
2008	38.8	39.3	39.6	38.1	38.8	38.8	39.1	39.7	41.0	40.2	39.3	39.1	39.3
2009	38.3	39.4	39.1	38.3	38.4	38.8	38.4	38.4	38.9	41.0	41.0	40.9	39.2
2010	40.0	39.4	39.1	40.3	40.7	40.7	40.0	39.8	39.0	39.6	39.8	39.6	39.8
2011	39.5	39.1	39.5	40.4	40.3	40.7	40.2	40.0	40.4	40.7	40.6	40.4	40.1
Manufacturing													
2007	42.9	42.3	41.9	41.8	41.8	41.8	42.1	41.7	41.7	41.5	41.4	44.3	42.1
2008	41.1	40.3	40.6	39.7	40.8	40.7	39.7	39.7	40.1	39.7	38.3	38.0	39.9
2009	37.3	37.8	38.0	37.5	37.5	37.7	37.3	38.0	37.8	37.4	38.2	39.0	37.8
2010	40.1	38.8	38.9	38.9	39.1	39.1	38.3	38.6	38.0	38.5	39.6	39.6	39.0
2011	38.9	39.0	39.0	39.3	39.3	39.2	38.9	38.8	39.7	39.2	39.5	40.2	39.3
Trade, Transportation, and Utilities													
2007	34.2	34.7	33.5	33.8	34.0	34.1	34.4	34.3	34.4	33.7	33.5	34.6	34.1
2008	33.9	34.3	34.7	34.3	34.1	34.7	34.5	34.1	34.1	34.3	35.1	34.6	34.4
2009	34.6	35.1	35.0	34.8	34.9	34.7	34.8	35.0	34.7	34.6	35.0	35.1	34.9
2010	35.3	35.7	35.6	36.9	36.8	36.1	35.9	36.0	35.2	35.7	35.7	36.0	35.9
2011	35.3	35.7	35.5	35.4	35.0	34.6	34.6	34.1	33.9	33.8	33.7	34.1	34.6
Financial Activities													
2007	36.1	36.9	36.3	38.5	36.1	36.7	37.5	37.1	38.0	37.0	36.1	37.2	37.0
2008	36.4	36.5	36.9	36.4	36.2	37.0	36.6	37.0	37.0	37.0	37.4	37.5	36.8
2009	37.6	37.3	37.2	37.6	37.5	37.6	37.5	37.8	37.3	37.1	37.8	38.1	37.5
2010	37.7	38.1	38.3	37.8	38.9	38.1	37.9	38.8	38.1	37.8	37.7	37.4	38.0
2011	37.5	37.1	36.9	37.0	37.5	36.9	37.7	36.5	37.2	37.9	37.0	37.0	37.2
Professional and Business Services													
2007	34.9	36.5	36.2	37.4	37.5	37.8	37.9	37.8	38.2	37.8	37.6	37.9	37.3
2008	42.3	37.1	37.2	36.7	36.7	37.4	36.7	36.4	36.4	36.8	36.7	36.1	37.2
2009	35.7	36.3	36.1	36.3	36.2	36.9	36.9	37.1	37.2	36.8	37.2	36.6	36.6
2010	36.0	36.7	36.1	36.4	36.5	35.9	35.9	36.5	35.6	36.1	36.3	36.4	36.2
2011	36.7	36.8	36.6	36.9	37.1	36.7	36.3	36.5	36.3	37.0	36.6	36.7	36.7
Education and Health Services													
2007	35.3	36.0	35.8	36.1	34.8	36.0	35.7	34.8	35.3	34.9	36.1	35.1	35.5
2008	34.4	34.7	34.4	35.3	34.8	34.5	35.2	34.7	34.8	34.8	35.2	35.2	34.8
2009	35.4	35.7	35.7	35.7	35.7	35.3	35.6	35.2	35.2	35.1	35.3	35.3	35.4
2010	35.6	35.3	35.3	35.2	35.4	35.0	35.1	35.2	34.8	35.1	35.0	34.9	35.2
2011	35.3	35.0	34.8	34.8	34.5	34.1	34.2	34.1	34.1	34.5	34.0	34.1	34.5
Leisure and Hospitality													
2007	29.1	29.6	29.0	29.9	27.9	28.7	28.7	28.2	27.3	28.0	28.1	28.3	28.6
2008	26.9	29.1	29.4	29.1	29.2	28.9	28.8	28.4	27.4	28.4	28.6	27.9	28.5
2009	28.0	28.4	28.2	28.4	27.9	27.7	28.2	28.5	28.4	28.2	28.6	29.6	28.3
2010	29.8	30.4	30.5	29.7	29.7	30.1	29.5	29.4	28.3	27.7	27.8	27.9	29.2
2011	28.6	28.8	29.0	28.5	27.8	27.4	27.7	27.6	26.5	27.5	27.7	27.2	27.9
Other Services													
2007	34.3	34.4	34.0	34.0	34.0	33.6	33.7	33.8	34.4	33.4	34.4	35.3	34.1
2008	34.2	34.1	34.2	34.7	34.2	35.3	34.4	34.8	34.9	34.4	34.5	34.5	34.5
2009	34.0	33.8	34.2	33.8	33.9	33.8	33.6	34.0	34.3	34.4	34.9	34.7	34.1
2010	35.1	35.0	34.9	34.8	35.3	34.0	34.6	35.6	34.5	35.1	34.8	34.9	34.9
2011	35.4	34.9	34.7	34.7	35.2	33.9	34.2	34.5	34.1	34.4	33.7	33.4	34.4

3. Average Hourly Earnings by Selected Industry: Florida, 2007–2011

(Dollars, not seasonally adjusted)

Industry and year	January	February	March	April	May	June	July	August	September	October	November	December	Annual average
Total Private													
2007	20.21	20.21	20.17	20.05	20.35	20.54	20.82	20.81	20.94	20.64	20.74	21.45	20.57
2008	20.64	20.72	21.53	20.94	20.99	20.84	20.75	20.94	20.94	21.07	21.27	21.42	21.00
2009	21.52	21.68	21.60	21.37	21.60	21.38	21.63	21.80	21.62	21.66	21.79	21.65	21.61
2010	21.39	21.56	21.48	21.50	21.27	21.20	21.31	21.27	21.51	21.68	21.55	21.59	21.44
2011	21.66	21.62	21.43	21.46	21.50	21.35	21.34	21.26	21.46	21.59	21.42	21.41	21.46
Goods-Producing													
2007	20.29	20.35	20.41	20.07	20.11	20.07	20.16	20.84	20.47	20.47	20.88	20.77	20.40
2008	20.92	20.53	21.61	20.91	20.90	20.96	21.27	21.80	21.26	21.55	21.57	22.50	21.30
2009	22.94	22.72	23.24	22.69	22.89	22.52	22.99	23.12	22.56	22.72	22.61	23.47	22.87
2010	22.33	22.28	22.76	22.12	22.15	22.05	22.13	21.89	22.04	22.07	22.07	22.29	22.18
2011	22.48	22.67	22.53	22.54	22.54	22.39	22.33	22.54	22.42	22.54	22.31	22.37	22.47
Construction													
2007	20.13	19.92	20.39	19.91	19.91	19.67	19.72	19.86	19.84	19.98	20.11	20.54	20.00
2008	20.25	19.70	19.68	19.70	19.41	19.40	20.31	21.29	20.54	20.51	20.48	21.87	20.24
2009	21.99	21.58	21.82	21.85	21.76	21.73	22.34	22.44	22.42	22.21	21.48	21.98	21.96
2010	21.59	21.77	21.81	21.62	21.53	21.51	21.42	21.18	21.12	21.41	21.66	21.75	21.53
2011	22.16	22.19	22.20	22.21	21.92	21.74	21.46	21.62	21.31	21.27	21.09	21.10	21.69
Manufacturing													
2007	20.50	20.95	20.48	20.25	20.33	20.51	20.71	22.08	21.23	21.06	21.91	21.11	20.92
2008	21.77	21.59	22.33	22.15	21.96	22.20	22.49	22.49	21.82	22.06	22.57	22.96	22.19
2009	23.87	23.93	24.67	24.17	24.20	24.05	24.35	24.52	24.40	24.99	25.58	25.23	24.49
2010	24.69	24.24	24.98	24.65	24.56	24.15	24.24	23.85	24.11	23.83	23.39	23.55	24.19
2011	23.13	23.45	23.15	23.13	23.45	23.34	23.56	23.79	23.83	24.16	23.87	23.90	23.57
Trade, Transportation, and Utilities													
2007	18.48	18.95	19.13	19.14	19.30	19.47	19.51	19.09	19.56	19.16	19.19	18.81	19.15
2008	18.78	18.72	18.75	18.56	18.60	19.00	18.89	18.65	18.73	18.97	19.02	19.10	18.81
2009	19.02	19.08	19.18	18.73	18.87	18.67	18.99	19.22	19.31	19.16	19.55	19.23	19.08
2010	19.30	19.30	19.20	19.05	18.49	18.12	18.32	18.40	18.98	18.92	18.73	18.80	18.80
2011	18.74	18.86	18.41	18.46	18.30	18.06	17.78	17.65	18.06	18.10	18.03	18.18	18.22
Financial Activities													
2007	23.33	23.69	23.48	22.57	23.19	23.81	22.96	22.19	22.54	22.28	22.73	23.88	23.05
2008	22.79	22.76	23.59	23.05	22.95	23.78	23.22	23.32	23.39	23.43	24.44	24.89	23.47
2009	25.30	26.76	26.73	27.00	27.07	26.80	27.20	27.88	27.26	27.30	27.57	26.62	26.95
2010	26.23	26.98	26.25	26.42	26.24	26.07	26.10	25.97	25.36	25.76	25.60	26.03	26.08
2011	25.82	25.59	25.74	25.66	26.16	25.81	25.22	25.06	24.90	25.46	25.40	25.10	25.49
Professional and Business Services													
2007	21.91	21.84	21.84	22.72	22.43	23.02	23.66	23.71	23.99	23.27	23.82	24.31	23.05
2008	23.71	23.89	24.09	24.25	24.25	22.78	23.87	23.55	23.14	23.23	23.34	22.70	23.58
2009	23.20	23.44	23.52	23.50	23.55	23.54	23.85	23.93	23.57	23.61	23.54	23.64	23.57
2010	23.11	22.95	23.22	23.83	23.90	24.10	24.40	24.00	24.57	24.79	24.62	24.99	24.05
2011	25.26	24.75	24.61	24.73	24.88	24.78	25.08	25.01	25.16	25.45	25.16	25.46	25.03
Education and Health Services													
2007	21.92	21.63	21.65	21.58	22.26	22.40	22.95	23.00	22.76	22.73	22.37	22.37	22.30
2008	18.61	22.80	23.21	21.77	22.89	23.06	22.86	22.70	22.79	23.32	23.33	23.86	22.61
2009	22.79	22.75	22.97	22.88	22.93	23.51	23.42	23.54	23.39	23.28	23.23	23.23	23.16
2010	23.28	23.48	23.46	23.68	23.35	23.45	23.27	23.42	23.52	23.51	23.34	23.53	23.44
2011	23.56	23.14	23.20	23.25	23.26	23.39	23.57	23.45	23.74	23.77	23.79	23.79	23.49
Leisure and Hospitality													
2007	13.37	13.71	13.76	13.31	13.99	13.72	14.31	14.15	14.15	13.74	13.49	13.80	13.79
2008	14.06	13.61	13.78	14.35	14.44	14.17	14.04	14.23	14.28	13.85	13.90	13.81	14.04
2009	13.81	13.81	13.98	14.52	14.53	14.17	14.10	13.94	13.91	14.14	14.38	14.18	14.12
2010	14.19	14.42	14.51	14.22	14.13	14.09	14.01	13.93	13.86	13.86	13.76	13.71	14.07
2011	13.75	13.89	13.88	13.78	13.68	13.29	13.29	13.12	13.46	13.44	13.41	13.38	13.54
Other Services													
2007	18.63	18.53	16.97	17.27	17.42	17.42	17.59	18.07	18.55	19.17	19.24	20.66	18.30
2008	20.93	20.75	21.45	22.09	21.77	21.77	20.73	20.79	20.50	20.06	19.79	20.11	20.91
2009	20.62	20.61	20.85	20.80	20.74	20.68	20.68	20.36	20.51	20.78	20.92	20.98	20.71
2010	20.43	20.45	20.28	20.18	20.05	19.82	19.60	19.33	19.27	18.89	19.07	19.13	19.71
2011	19.35	19.13	19.07	18.69	18.99	19.06	18.85	18.80	18.48	18.40	18.70	18.49	18.84

4. Average Weekly Earnings by Selected Industry: Florida, 2007–2011

(Dollars, not seasonally adjusted)

Industry and year	January	February	March	April	May	June	July	August	September	October	November	December	Annual average
Total Private													
2007	711.39	723.52	712.00	719.80	714.29	727.12	741.19	732.51	741.28	722.40	730.05	765.77	728.52
2008	736.85	729.34	760.01	732.90	734.65	754.41	734.55	734.99	730.81	739.56	748.70	745.42	740.13
2009	746.74	758.80	753.84	743.68	749.52	744.02	757.05	767.36	758.86	755.93	771.37	766.41	756.03
2010	757.21	767.54	762.54	769.70	765.72	754.72	754.37	757.21	750.70	763.14	758.56	759.97	760.18
2011	766.76	761.02	752.19	755.39	752.50	740.85	740.50	733.47	738.22	749.17	738.99	740.79	747.10
Goods-Producing													
2007	829.86	824.18	834.77	828.89	810.43	792.77	810.43	831.52	816.75	810.61	845.64	870.26	825.28
2008	834.71	817.09	866.56	813.40	831.82	832.11	840.17	867.64	863.16	859.85	836.92	868.50	843.90
2009	867.13	879.26	894.74	862.22	872.11	864.77	894.31	903.99	906.91	931.52	942.84	981.05	898.87
2010	924.46	897.88	912.68	898.07	905.94	899.64	880.77	871.22	859.56	876.18	878.39	880.46	890.46
2011	885.71	888.66	889.94	903.85	901.60	900.08	888.73	892.58	901.28	903.85	896.86	903.75	896.41
Construction													
2007	795.14	780.86	821.72	814.32	778.48	743.53	765.14	766.60	765.82	763.24	800.38	823.65	784.90
2008	785.70	774.21	779.33	750.57	753.11	752.72	794.12	845.21	842.14	824.50	804.86	855.12	795.36
2009	842.22	850.25	853.16	836.86	835.58	843.12	857.86	861.70	872.14	910.61	880.68	898.98	860.95
2010	863.60	857.74	852.77	871.29	876.27	875.46	856.80	842.96	823.68	847.84	862.07	861.30	857.69
2011	875.32	867.63	876.90	897.28	883.38	884.82	862.69	864.80	860.92	865.69	856.25	852.44	870.77
Manufacturing													
2007	879.45	886.19	858.11	846.45	849.79	857.32	871.89	920.74	885.29	873.99	907.07	935.17	880.67
2008	894.75	870.08	906.60	879.36	895.97	903.54	892.85	892.85	874.98	875.78	864.43	872.48	885.51
2009	890.35	904.55	937.46	906.38	907.50	906.69	908.26	931.76	922.32	934.63	977.16	983.97	925.30
2010	990.07	940.51	971.72	958.89	960.30	944.27	928.39	920.61	916.18	917.46	926.24	932.58	942.24
2011	899.76	914.55	902.85	909.01	921.59	914.93	916.48	923.05	946.05	947.07	942.87	960.78	924.96
Trade, Transportation, and Utilities													
2007	632.02	657.57	640.86	646.93	656.20	663.93	671.14	654.79	672.86	645.69	642.87	650.83	652.92
2008	636.64	642.10	650.63	636.61	634.26	659.30	651.71	635.97	638.69	650.67	667.60	660.86	647.04
2009	658.09	669.71	671.30	651.80	658.56	647.85	660.85	672.70	670.06	662.94	684.25	674.97	665.28
2010	681.29	689.01	683.52	702.95	680.43	654.13	657.69	662.40	668.10	675.44	668.66	676.80	675.04
2011	661.52	673.30	653.56	653.48	640.50	624.88	615.19	601.87	612.23	611.78	607.61	619.94	631.15
Financial Activities													
2007	842.21	874.16	852.32	868.95	837.16	873.83	861.00	823.25	856.52	824.36	820.55	888.34	851.95
2008	829.56	830.74	870.47	839.02	830.79	879.86	849.85	862.84	865.43	866.91	914.06	933.38	863.97
2009	951.28	998.15	994.36	1,015.20	1,015.13	1,007.68	1,020.00	1,053.86	1,016.80	1,012.83	1,042.15	1,014.22	1,011.57
2010	988.87	1,027.94	1,005.38	998.68	1,020.74	993.27	989.19	1,007.64	966.22	973.73	965.12	973.52	992.46
2011	968.25	949.39	949.81	949.42	981.00	952.39	950.79	914.69	926.28	964.93	939.80	928.70	947.93
Professional and Business Services													
2007	764.66	797.16	790.61	849.73	841.13	870.16	896.71	896.24	916.42	879.61	895.63	921.35	859.54
2008	1,002.93	886.32	896.15	889.98	889.98	851.97	876.03	857.22	842.30	854.86	856.58	819.47	877.57
2009	828.24	850.87	849.07	853.05	852.51	868.63	880.07	887.80	876.80	868.85	875.69	865.22	862.89
2010	831.96	842.27	838.24	867.41	872.35	865.19	875.96	876.00	874.69	894.92	893.71	909.64	870.53
2011	927.04	910.80	900.73	912.54	923.05	909.43	910.40	912.87	913.31	941.65	920.86	934.38	918.14
Education and Health Services													
2007	773.78	778.68	775.07	779.04	774.65	806.40	819.32	800.40	803.43	793.28	807.56	785.19	791.42
2008	640.18	791.16	798.42	768.48	796.57	795.57	804.67	787.69	793.09	811.54	821.22	839.87	787.59
2009	806.77	812.18	820.03	816.82	818.60	829.90	833.75	828.61	823.33	817.13	820.02	820.02	820.61
2010	828.77	828.84	828.14	833.54	826.59	820.75	816.78	824.38	818.50	825.20	816.90	821.20	824.13
2011	831.67	809.90	807.36	809.10	802.47	797.60	806.09	799.65	809.53	820.07	808.86	811.24	809.46
Leisure and Hospitality													
2007	389.07	405.82	399.04	397.97	390.32	393.76	410.70	399.03	386.30	384.72	379.07	390.54	393.90
2008	378.21	396.05	405.13	417.59	421.65	409.51	404.35	404.13	391.27	393.34	397.54	385.30	400.52
2009	386.68	392.20	394.24	412.37	405.39	392.51	397.62	397.29	395.04	398.75	411.27	419.73	400.24
2010	422.86	438.37	442.56	422.33	419.66	424.11	413.30	409.54	392.24	383.92	382.53	382.51	411.21
2011	393.25	400.03	402.52	392.73	380.30	364.15	368.13	362.11	356.69	369.60	371.46	363.94	377.15
Other Services													
2007	639.01	637.43	576.98	587.18	592.28	585.31	592.78	610.77	638.12	640.28	661.86	729.30	624.16
2008	715.81	707.58	733.59	766.52	744.53	768.48	713.11	723.49	715.45	690.06	682.76	693.80	721.80
2009	701.08	696.62	713.07	703.04	703.09	698.98	694.85	692.24	703.49	714.83	730.11	728.01	706.54
2010	717.09	715.75	707.77	702.26	707.77	673.88	678.16	688.15	664.82	663.04	663.64	667.64	687.47
2011	684.99	667.64	661.73	648.54	668.45	646.13	644.67	648.60	630.17	632.96	630.19	617.57	648.55

GEORGIA
At a Glance

Population:
    2000 census: 8,186,653
    2010 census: 9,687,653
    2011 estimate: 9,815,210

Percent change in population:
    2000–2010: 18.3%
    2010–2011: 1.3%

Percent change in total nonfarm employment:
    2000–2010: -2.7%
    2010–2011: 1.0%

Industry with the largest growth in employment, 2000–2011 (thousands):
    Education and Health Services, 146.4

Industry with the largest decline or smallest growth in employment, 2000–2011 (thousands):
    Manufacturing, -188.0

Civilian labor force:
    2000: 4,242,889
    2010: 4,694,930
    2011: 4,725,104

Unemployment rate and rank among states (lowest to highest):
    2000: 3.5%, 19th
    2010: 10.2%, 39th
    2011: 9.8%, 41st

Over-the-year change in unemployment rates:
    2010–2011: -0.4%

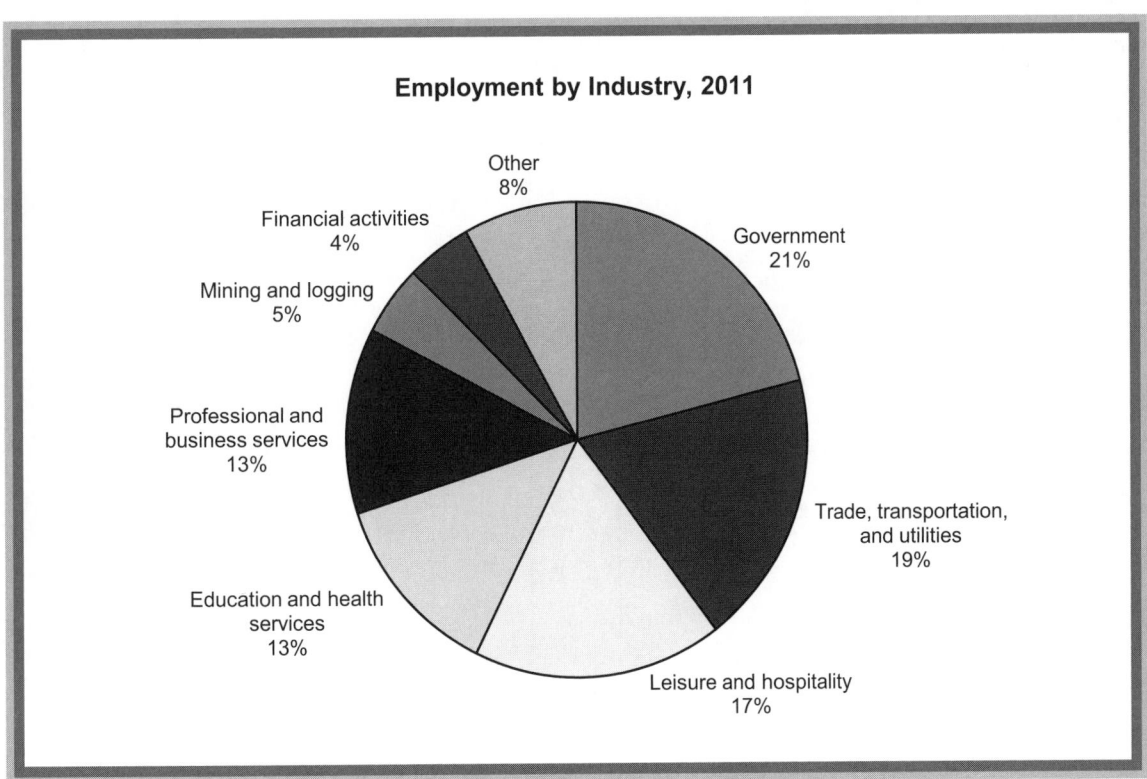

Employment by Industry, 2011

Other 8%
Financial activities 4%
Mining and logging 5%
Professional and business services 13%
Education and health services 13%
Leisure and hospitality 17%
Trade, transportation, and utilities 19%
Government 21%

1. Employment by Industry: Georgia, Selected Years, 2000–2011

(Numbers in thousands, not seasonally adjusted)

Industry and year	January	February	March	April	May	June	July	August	September	October	November	December	Annual average
Total Nonfarm													
2000	3,851.6	3,880.3	3,922.2	3,925.5	3,958.5	3,971.6	3,944.4	3,970.5	3,978.7	3,982.0	3,994.0	4,012.1	3,949.3
2001	3,931.3	3,945.2	3,971.8	3,951.6	3,958.4	3,962.4	3,915.3	3,947.1	3,939.0	3,929.7	3,933.0	3,934.7	3,943.3
2002	3,816.4	3,833.3	3,860.3	3,870.6	3,885.1	3,895.4	3,841.1	3,875.6	3,874.5	3,881.7	3,896.8	3,903.3	3,869.5
2003	3,797.4	3,809.7	3,832.0	3,836.4	3,847.1	3,842.0	3,819.9	3,858.1	3,863.3	3,861.1	3,878.0	3,892.1	3,844.9
2004	3,816.2	3,836.1	3,864.9	3,888.9	3,898.9	3,892.0	3,883.7	3,920.8	3,907.9	3,943.5	3,961.9	3,967.3	3,898.5
2005	3,908.8	3,929.5	3,937.0	3,993.3	4,011.1	3,996.2	3,982.7	4,032.3	4,031.3	4,044.6	4,071.8	4,076.0	4,001.2
2006	4,016.0	4,037.5	4,056.5	4,082.6	4,098.5	4,091.0	4,057.9	4,099.9	4,096.7	4,128.1	4,150.7	4,153.6	4,089.1
2007	4,094.3	4,114.8	4,130.9	4,140.2	4,158.8	4,147.3	4,115.8	4,160.0	4,154.3	4,164.0	4,184.8	4,181.1	4,145.5
2008	4,110.8	4,130.7	4,131.8	4,137.5	4,148.4	4,120.4	4,079.7	4,107.4	4,084.3	4,074.6	4,061.7	4,039.3	4,102.2
2009	3,934.8	3,924.7	3,910.2	3,912.6	3,911.4	3,878.4	3,839.2	3,851.2	3,841.3	3,850.3	3,863.3	3,853.6	3,880.9
2010	3,775.9	3,789.0	3,809.3	3,842.1	3,874.0	3,849.1	3,833.9	3,850.3	3,842.3	3,876.2	3,889.3	3,879.9	3,842.7
2011	3,786.6	3,838.6	3,859.3	3,904.4	3,910.9	3,888.1	3,863.4	3,889.5	3,877.6	3,903.7	3,922.1	3,915.6	3,880.0
Total Private													
2000	3,259.3	3,283.4	3,321.2	3,324.5	3,346.3	3,374.5	3,367.3	3,385.5	3,384.2	3,381.8	3,391.6	3,408.3	3,352.3
2001	3,331.1	3,339.2	3,363.0	3,342.7	3,347.5	3,356.2	3,329.9	3,340.8	3,323.7	3,308.9	3,309.2	3,312.3	3,333.7
2002	3,200.3	3,214.7	3,235.8	3,245.1	3,258.1	3,277.3	3,243.6	3,255.3	3,242.5	3,248.2	3,260.8	3,270.4	3,246.0
2003	3,166.0	3,173.4	3,194.2	3,199.4	3,212.5	3,220.4	3,217.1	3,237.0	3,233.4	3,224.1	3,239.6	3,255.1	3,214.4
2004	3,188.6	3,201.5	3,229.1	3,246.9	3,259.8	3,267.9	3,277.8	3,289.1	3,266.5	3,299.7	3,314.7	3,323.6	3,263.8
2005	3,269.0	3,282.3	3,288.4	3,344.6	3,362.8	3,360.8	3,366.3	3,385.1	3,377.6	3,387.6	3,412.6	3,417.7	3,354.6
2006	3,362.9	3,376.8	3,393.7	3,421.8	3,438.1	3,439.4	3,430.7	3,444.8	3,431.4	3,457.7	3,476.5	3,480.3	3,429.5
2007	3,427.5	3,439.1	3,453.6	3,464.9	3,483.6	3,483.6	3,476.6	3,494.4	3,478.5	3,480.8	3,498.1	3,495.4	3,473.0
2008	3,426.5	3,436.4	3,435.9	3,443.2	3,453.6	3,437.8	3,418.7	3,422.2	3,394.5	3,374.7	3,357.0	3,337.9	3,411.5
2009	3,239.1	3,223.1	3,208.1	3,210.7	3,213.6	3,195.9	3,181.5	3,177.6	3,154.0	3,163.2	3,175.2	3,168.2	3,192.5
2010	3,094.6	3,103.1	3,120.9	3,153.7	3,172.1	3,166.1	3,175.7	3,184.3	3,172.6	3,201.3	3,212.2	3,205.9	3,163.6
2011	3,118.4	3,163.7	3,182.4	3,230.4	3,238.6	3,227.1	3,222.5	3,226.5	3,205.9	3,228.2	3,245.6	3,240.0	3,210.8
Goods-Producing													
2000	752.0	755.8	762.8	761.5	764.2	769.3	762.0	764.7	762.5	755.7	751.8	752.4	759.6
2001	741.9	742.8	743.2	735.7	733.5	733.9	722.9	723.6	717.8	707.3	700.4	699.3	725.2
2002	678.4	684.1	686.8	685.7	686.3	687.6	684.3	684.0	680.5	675.5	672.7	670.2	681.3
2003	658.4	661.6	661.2	658.9	661.0	661.6	656.5	658.8	659.4	658.3	656.6	658.9	659.3
2004	648.2	651.5	655.3	656.1	656.7	661.5	664.8	666.3	662.7	667.2	666.5	666.7	660.3
2005	657.2	659.5	658.8	668.0	672.1	673.5	673.9	678.3	678.0	674.2	678.1	677.2	670.7
2006	672.0	674.8	676.1	679.0	681.9	685.0	681.7	684.7	682.0	678.8	674.4	671.7	678.5
2007	667.6	668.5	667.8	667.3	669.0	669.2	666.2	667.2	662.3	657.7	657.3	654.0	664.5
2008	643.8	642.3	638.7	634.4	633.7	631.0	626.0	623.5	617.0	608.9	596.9	586.9	623.6
2009	567.3	558.6	551.9	544.0	540.9	534.0	525.7	522.5	518.4	514.6	512.1	508.3	533.2
2010	500.0	499.1	500.1	501.9	505.4	505.1	507.6	507.9	506.6	506.3	505.5	502.2	504.0
2011	491.2	500.4	503.7	507.9	509.0	509.4	509.8	512.2	506.0	502.2	500.5	503.3	504.6
Mining and Logging													
2000	14.0	14.2	14.2	13.8	13.9	13.9	14.0	14.0	13.9	13.8	13.8	13.8	13.9
2001	13.6	13.5	13.5	13.2	13.2	13.2	13.1	13.2	13.0	12.9	12.9	12.8	13.2
2002	12.7	12.7	12.8	12.6	12.6	12.6	12.1	12.3	12.2	11.9	11.8	12.0	12.4
2003	12.1	12.1	12.1	12.2	12.4	12.4	12.3	12.4	12.4	12.3	12.4	12.4	12.3
2004	12.3	12.2	12.2	12.1	12.1	12.2	12.3	12.3	12.2	12.1	12.1	12.2	12.2
2005	11.8	11.9	11.9	12.1	12.2	12.2	12.3	12.3	12.2	12.1	12.1	12.1	12.1
2006	12.4	12.1	12.1	12.3	12.3	12.3	12.3	12.3	12.1	12.2	12.1	12.1	12.2
2007	12.1	12.1	12.1	12.0	12.0	11.9	11.9	11.9	11.8	11.7	11.6	11.4	11.9
2008	10.8	10.6	10.5	10.5	10.4	10.3	10.3	10.3	10.3	10.3	10.2	10.1	10.4
2009	9.7	9.5	9.3	9.4	9.4	9.4	9.3	9.4	9.2	9.3	9.3	9.2	9.4
2010	9.3	9.2	9.2	9.2	9.2	9.2	9.3	9.3	9.3	9.3	9.3	9.1	9.2
2011	9.0	9.1	9.0	9.1	9.0	9.0	8.9	9.0	8.9	8.9	8.9	8.7	9.0
Construction													
2000	198.1	200.6	205.8	205.5	207.5	211.8	211.2	211.4	211.4	209.9	207.6	207.9	207.4
2001	201.9	203.6	205.3	207.1	209.1	211.3	211.0	211.0	208.7	207.3	204.9	203.7	207.1
2002	195.2	197.8	199.1	198.3	199.0	200.0	199.3	199.5	198.2	196.5	195.8	194.3	197.8
2003	188.5	190.0	191.7	191.2	193.1	194.7	196.9	197.9	198.9	199.0	198.6	199.1	195.0
2004	193.7	193.3	196.0	196.8	197.2	200.4	203.7	203.6	200.9	204.4	204.0	203.7	199.8
2005	199.8	200.6	200.0	206.3	209.1	210.0	212.2	213.9	213.4	213.4	214.6	212.7	208.8
2006	209.2	211.0	212.5	215.4	217.9	220.6	223.0	224.5	223.7	223.6	222.9	221.4	218.8
2007	218.6	220.2	221.3	221.7	223.2	224.1	223.0	224.1	221.7	220.7	219.5	216.6	221.2
2008	211.1	211.4	209.9	208.7	209.5	208.1	206.9	204.5	201.2	197.4	193.0	187.7	204.1
2009	177.8	175.9	172.9	170.4	170.1	167.9	164.5	162.0	159.3	158.3	157.0	153.9	165.8
2010	148.1	148.4	148.9	150.1	151.0	150.6	152.0	151.6	150.7	150.3	149.5	145.6	149.7
2011	137.9	143.6	146.3	148.1	147.8	148.0	147.9	151.8	145.7	143.6	142.0	143.6	145.5
Manufacturing													
2000	539.9	541.0	542.8	542.2	542.8	543.6	536.8	539.3	537.2	532.0	530.4	530.7	538.2
2001	526.4	525.7	524.5	515.4	511.2	509.4	498.8	499.4	496.1	487.1	482.6	482.8	505.0
2002	470.5	473.6	474.9	474.8	474.7	475.0	472.9	472.2	470.1	467.1	465.1	463.9	471.2
2003	457.8	459.5	457.4	455.5	455.5	454.5	447.3	448.5	448.1	447.0	445.6	447.4	452.0
2004	442.2	446.0	447.1	447.2	447.4	448.9	448.8	450.4	449.6	450.7	450.4	450.8	448.3
2005	445.6	447.0	446.9	449.6	450.8	451.3	449.4	452.1	452.4	448.7	451.4	452.4	449.8
2006	450.4	451.7	451.5	451.3	451.7	452.1	446.4	447.9	446.2	443.0	439.4	438.2	447.5
2007	436.9	436.2	434.4	433.6	433.8	433.2	431.3	431.2	428.8	425.3	426.2	426.0	431.4
2008	421.9	420.3	418.3	415.2	413.8	412.6	408.8	408.7	405.5	401.2	393.7	389.1	409.1
2009	379.8	373.2	369.7	364.2	361.4	356.7	351.9	351.1	349.9	347.0	345.8	345.2	358.0
2010	342.6	341.5	342.0	342.6	345.2	345.3	346.3	347.0	346.6	346.7	346.7	347.5	345.0
2011	344.3	347.7	348.4	350.7	352.2	352.4	353.0	351.4	351.4	349.7	349.6	351.0	350.2

1. Employment by Industry: Georgia, Selected Years, 2000–2011—*Continued*

(Numbers in thousands, not seasonally adjusted)

Industry and year	January	February	March	April	May	June	July	August	September	October	November	December	Annual average
Service-Providing													
2000	3,099.6	3,124.5	3,159.4	3,164.0	3,194.3	3,202.3	3,182.4	3,205.8	3,216.2	3,226.3	3,242.2	3,259.7	3,189.7
2001	3,189.4	3,202.4	3,228.5	3,215.9	3,224.9	3,228.5	3,192.4	3,223.5	3,221.2	3,222.4	3,232.6	3,235.4	3,218.1
2002	3,138.0	3,149.2	3,173.5	3,184.9	3,198.8	3,207.8	3,156.8	3,191.6	3,194.0	3,206.2	3,224.1	3,233.1	3,188.2
2003	3,139.0	3,148.1	3,170.8	3,177.5	3,186.1	3,180.4	3,163.4	3,199.3	3,205.9	3,202.8	3,221.4	3,233.2	3,185.7
2004	3,168.0	3,184.6	3,209.6	3,232.8	3,242.2	3,230.5	3,218.9	3,254.5	3,245.2	3,276.3	3,295.4	3,300.6	3,238.2
2005	3,251.6	3,270.0	3,278.2	3,325.3	3,339.0	3,322.7	3,308.8	3,354.0	3,353.3	3,370.4	3,393.7	3,398.8	3,330.5
2006	3,344.0	3,362.7	3,380.4	3,403.6	3,416.6	3,406.0	3,376.2	3,415.2	3,414.7	3,449.3	3,476.3	3,481.9	3,410.6
2007	3,426.7	3,446.3	3,463.1	3,472.9	3,489.8	3,478.1	3,449.6	3,492.8	3,492.0	3,506.3	3,527.5	3,527.1	3,481.0
2008	3,467.0	3,488.4	3,493.1	3,503.1	3,514.7	3,489.4	3,453.7	3,483.9	3,467.3	3,465.7	3,464.8	3,452.4	3,478.6
2009	3,367.5	3,366.1	3,358.3	3,368.6	3,370.5	3,344.4	3,313.5	3,328.7	3,322.9	3,335.7	3,351.2	3,345.3	3,347.7
2010	3,275.9	3,289.9	3,309.2	3,340.2	3,368.6	3,344.0	3,326.3	3,342.4	3,335.7	3,369.9	3,383.8	3,377.7	3,338.7
2011	3,295.4	3,338.2	3,355.6	3,396.5	3,401.9	3,378.7	3,353.6	3,377.3	3,371.6	3,401.5	3,421.6	3,412.3	3,375.4
Trade, Transportation, and Utilities													
2000	851.3	853.1	861.6	863.1	867.0	870.9	865.2	871.2	871.2	877.6	890.8	902.6	870.5
2001	872.0	866.0	870.9	856.1	857.7	858.9	858.5	859.1	858.1	857.0	867.5	873.7	863.0
2002	835.2	830.5	834.0	833.7	837.1	840.6	832.8	834.0	833.4	844.4	858.4	871.0	840.4
2003	819.0	814.2	818.2	814.4	818.6	819.5	820.2	823.9	824.7	828.5	842.1	851.4	824.6
2004	817.4	813.9	820.0	820.9	825.7	826.3	829.5	830.8	826.6	837.8	852.4	860.6	830.2
2005	832.8	831.4	833.1	846.2	850.1	848.4	856.3	855.2	853.3	861.4	878.8	887.7	852.9
2006	856.2	853.2	857.4	865.0	870.4	869.0	865.2	867.3	866.9	880.1	898.6	906.2	871.3
2007	880.7	874.8	877.1	878.5	884.2	884.7	885.1	885.7	884.9	889.9	906.6	910.2	886.9
2008	883.5	879.3	880.2	876.6	877.7	874.0	873.1	872.3	867.6	864.4	868.6	869.6	873.9
2009	834.9	824.0	819.8	816.6	818.9	815.2	814.0	813.7	808.9	811.5	823.5	826.8	819.0
2010	799.6	797.2	798.9	803.5	808.2	807.5	809.7	810.8	806.6	819.6	831.0	835.7	810.7
2011	805.0	809.8	812.4	819.3	823.4	821.8	819.7	816.2	813.9	826.8	839.4	843.9	821.0
Wholesale Trade													
2000	209.2	210.7	212.4	213.1	214.1	215.4	214.3	215.1	214.8	215.5	214.8	215.1	213.7
2001	215.5	215.7	216.4	212.4	212.3	213.1	214.4	213.7	212.8	211.7	210.2	209.1	213.1
2002	206.1	206.1	207.4	207.2	207.2	207.8	206.3	205.8	205.0	207.5	206.7	206.7	206.7
2003	204.0	204.3	205.3	204.6	205.1	205.0	205.3	205.3	205.4	204.9	205.4	206.2	205.1
2004	202.8	202.9	204.2	205.7	206.8	207.2	207.7	208.3	207.2	209.1	209.2	209.6	206.7
2005	207.9	209.0	209.1	211.5	211.8	211.8	212.7	213.4	213.6	213.5	213.7	214.2	211.9
2006	211.8	212.6	213.0	214.2	215.8	215.4	216.2	216.3	216.5	219.2	218.2	218.4	215.6
2007	216.7	217.4	217.5	218.8	219.1	218.8	219.4	219.5	219.0	219.8	220.0	219.6	218.8
2008	218.0	218.8	218.2	219.0	219.0	218.0	217.7	217.9	217.0	216.2	213.8	211.6	217.1
2009	206.8	204.8	202.1	201.2	200.2	198.4	198.2	197.5	195.9	197.1	197.1	196.2	199.6
2010	194.2	194.5	194.4	195.7	196.4	195.8	196.4	196.4	195.0	197.1	197.0	195.8	195.7
2011	194.2	195.5	195.2	197.3	198.4	197.7	197.5	195.5	194.8	196.4	196.6	197.3	196.4
Retail Trade													
2000	462.1	462.5	467.9	466.3	469.2	471.3	466.9	470.9	470.9	474.0	488.2	499.6	472.5
2001	473.0	467.3	471.6	461.4	462.7	463.0	459.7	461.4	462.0	460.4	475.0	482.3	466.7
2002	453.9	449.3	452.2	449.9	452.4	453.9	449.9	451.3	452.6	453.4	467.3	467.8	455.4
2003	440.7	436.1	438.6	437.6	440.5	441.1	440.8	443.7	443.9	446.9	459.2	470.9	444.7
2004	439.8	436.3	440.1	439.1	441.8	442.3	443.4	443.6	441.2	449.2	462.7	470.9	445.9
2005	447.5	443.6	444.8	454.9	457.7	456.6	460.8	459.5	456.4	464.3	479.3	486.1	459.3
2006	464.3	460.3	462.9	468.0	470.6	468.6	464.0	465.4	463.6	474.1	492.9	497.5	471.0
2007	479.3	472.3	474.0	473.4	476.5	474.7	475.9	475.2	473.9	477.9	494.2	496.3	478.6
2008	474.5	469.2	470.3	466.7	467.0	464.0	464.0	463.5	459.9	459.0	466.0	467.5	466.0
2009	443.3	436.3	435.2	435.4	438.1	436.0	435.3	436.2	433.3	434.3	446.0	448.7	438.2
2010	428.6	425.9	427.3	430.0	432.7	432.0	433.2	433.8	430.3	439.0	450.1	453.4	434.7
2011	431.3	432.7	434.4	439.5	441.3	439.8	438.8	437.5	436.4	445.9	458.0	460.7	441.4
Transportation and Utilities													
2000	180.0	179.9	181.3	183.7	183.7	184.2	184.0	185.2	185.5	188.1	187.8	187.9	184.3
2001	183.5	183.0	182.9	182.3	182.7	182.8	184.4	184.0	183.3	184.9	182.3	182.3	183.2
2002	175.2	175.1	174.4	176.6	177.5	178.9	176.6	176.9	175.8	183.5	184.4	185.3	178.4
2003	174.3	173.8	174.3	172.2	173.0	173.4	174.1	174.9	175.4	176.7	177.5	177.4	174.8
2004	174.8	174.7	175.7	176.1	177.1	176.8	178.4	178.9	178.2	179.5	180.5	180.1	177.6
2005	177.4	178.8	179.2	179.8	180.6	180.0	182.8	182.3	183.3	183.6	185.8	187.4	181.8
2006	180.1	180.3	181.5	182.8	184.0	185.0	185.0	185.6	186.8	186.8	187.5	190.3	184.6
2007	184.7	185.1	185.6	186.3	188.6	191.2	189.8	191.0	192.0	192.2	192.4	194.3	189.4
2008	191.0	191.3	191.7	190.9	191.7	192.0	191.4	190.9	190.7	189.2	188.8	190.5	190.8
2009	184.8	182.9	182.5	180.0	180.6	180.8	180.5	180.0	179.7	180.1	180.4	181.9	181.2
2010	176.8	176.8	177.2	177.8	179.1	179.7	180.1	180.6	181.3	183.5	183.9	186.5	180.3
2011	179.5	181.6	182.8	182.5	183.7	184.3	183.4	183.2	182.7	184.5	184.8	185.9	183.2
Information													
2000	138.7	139.1	138.8	137.8	139.0	141.6	142.0	143.3	143.2	144.4	145.3	146.7	141.7
2001	143.4	144.1	144.7	142.9	142.9	143.5	141.5	140.8	139.7	139.2	139.7	139.4	141.8
2002	132.5	132.3	130.9	130.2	129.9	129.4	129.0	128.5	127.2	128.2	126.2	126.2	129.2
2003	126.4	125.4	123.3	121.3	120.2	119.7	118.0	117.4	115.0	114.7	115.6	115.4	119.4
2004	114.3	113.9	114.2	115.3	115.0	115.5	114.8	114.3	113.4	112.1	113.0	112.9	114.1
2005	111.9	112.2	112.6	112.5	111.7	113.1	112.5	111.1	111.2	111.7	111.7	113.1	112.2
2006	111.5	111.8	112.5	111.5	112.0	111.6	110.1	110.2	110.2	110.8	111.8	112.3	111.4
2007	112.8	112.5	112.5	111.0	111.6	111.7	111.3	111.4	111.3	110.4	111.0	111.0	111.5
2008	108.7	109.6	109.7	109.5	110.0	110.4	109.3	109.1	108.4	107.3	107.8	107.8	109.0
2009	106.9	106.7	106.1	105.7	105.5	105.3	104.1	103.8	103.3	102.2	102.3	103.0	104.6
2010	100.9	100.7	100.9	100.9	101.3	100.8	99.6	99.4	99.1	97.4	98.0	98.4	99.8
2011	97.4	98.1	98.0	98.6	98.5	97.9	98.0	96.9	96.3	96.2	95.8	95.4	97.3

1. Employment by Industry: Georgia, Selected Years, 2000–2011—*Continued*

(Numbers in thousands, not seasonally adjusted)

Industry and year	January	February	March	April	May	June	July	August	September	October	November	December	Annual average
Financial Activities													
2000	208.9	209.6	210.3	213.1	213.8	215.6	213.9	213.9	212.3	211.7	211.9	213.5	212.4
2001	210.5	210.8	211.8	213.3	213.5	214.2	216.7	217.1	215.8	215.5	215.5	215.9	214.2
2002	214.4	213.7	213.5	213.6	214.4	215.2	214.8	215.5	214.1	215.8	216.0	217.3	214.9
2003	213.1	213.0	214.6	214.8	216.3	217.7	218.8	219.6	219.3	216.3	216.4	217.2	216.4
2004	214.9	215.9	216.4	217.7	218.0	218.0	219.5	219.7	218.5	221.9	221.8	222.7	218.8
2005	222.3	223.3	223.0	223.9	225.1	225.3	224.7	225.7	225.3	228.0	228.2	229.6	225.4
2006	226.0	227.4	227.8	229.6	230.7	230.6	231.2	232.3	231.7	233.5	233.5	234.1	230.7
2007	230.5	232.1	232.0	231.6	231.7	231.6	232.1	232.0	230.2	230.5	230.4	230.0	231.2
2008	226.3	227.1	226.1	226.3	226.6	225.5	225.6	224.5	222.0	222.5	219.8	219.0	224.3
2009	216.1	215.1	213.5	213.1	213.2	212.5	212.0	210.9	208.8	208.7	208.2	208.1	211.7
2010	204.6	204.3	204.3	204.6	205.9	206.1	206.2	207.1	206.4	208.5	209.3	209.8	206.4
2011	207.1	207.8	207.9	209.4	210.0	209.6	209.6	208.7	208.0	208.7	209.9	209.0	208.8
Professional and Business Services													
2000	513.1	519.7	526.4	518.8	522.4	530.5	529.0	533.4	535.1	530.2	529.4	531.5	526.6
2001	517.7	519.3	522.5	517.9	516.4	517.0	515.3	520.3	515.9	513.7	509.4	509.5	516.2
2002	491.0	496.7	499.4	503.8	505.2	506.7	506.5	510.6	507.7	506.5	506.9	505.2	503.9
2003	482.5	487.2	490.0	491.3	489.4	492.2	495.7	501.1	500.6	499.5	500.2	502.6	494.4
2004	495.3	500.5	507.0	509.4	509.7	510.8	516.0	517.8	513.7	523.8	523.1	523.3	512.5
2005	519.1	524.2	524.5	531.0	532.4	533.7	536.4	544.5	545.7	547.5	548.3	546.4	536.1
2006	539.8	543.5	546.2	551.3	550.0	553.3	553.9	556.8	553.8	556.0	556.3	557.5	551.5
2007	549.9	555.1	560.6	558.9	561.8	563.6	562.4	569.7	567.7	569.2	569.7	574.7	563.6
2008	559.0	562.0	559.7	565.8	565.1	565.9	556.2	558.1	553.3	550.1	544.8	540.9	556.7
2009	516.2	514.3	509.6	508.3	505.7	508.2	508.0	507.0	504.9	515.9	518.9	519.4	511.3
2010	504.8	509.5	514.5	523.3	524.6	526.7	529.9	531.3	531.2	540.2	540.7	539.7	526.4
2011	518.7	531.7	535.5	549.3	547.2	547.4	546.1	551.8	554.7	559.1	563.4	559.7	547.1
Education and Health Services													
2000	341.7	346.0	347.8	349.9	350.9	350.9	349.9	353.2	356.9	360.8	361.9	361.4	352.6
2001	356.2	359.4	362.6	362.2	362.7	363.4	360.6	364.9	368.7	371.5	373.1	373.4	364.9
2002	366.7	370.5	374.7	375.0	376.0	375.3	373.2	378.5	380.5	382.7	384.8	384.8	376.9
2003	385.1	387.4	392.1	396.0	398.3	396.5	394.4	399.6	401.7	401.9	403.9	405.0	396.8
2004	403.0	406.3	407.7	409.3	410.5	406.6	408.4	413.3	412.5	420.1	421.5	421.0	411.7
2005	418.5	420.5	417.6	426.3	427.8	422.5	424.6	429.1	430.5	434.7	436.1	435.5	427.0
2006	436.3	439.1	438.5	440.8	442.0	436.2	437.6	441.7	442.1	452.9	453.9	453.0	442.8
2007	449.7	453.8	453.0	457.3	458.1	453.4	453.8	460.7	463.0	467.1	468.5	465.9	458.7
2008	462.4	468.0	467.3	468.9	470.6	462.7	463.6	470.4	470.4	475.3	476.5	475.5	469.3
2009	473.3	475.9	473.6	476.4	478.5	470.2	471.0	476.7	475.3	482.1	483.7	482.2	476.6
2010	478.6	482.7	484.0	486.6	488.9	481.7	483.8	490.4	491.1	498.9	499.1	496.8	488.5
2011	489.6	497.1	496.9	502.1	501.1	492.7	493.0	499.3	498.5	504.5	507.5	505.6	499.0
Leisure and Hospitality													
2000	319.6	323.1	333.2	336.0	341.4	344.9	348.4	347.9	343.1	338.9	337.1	334.3	337.3
2001	323.5	328.0	335.3	342.2	347.6	350.9	345.1	346.3	340.4	338.4	337.4	335.3	339.2
2002	321.3	325.5	334.4	343.0	348.4	361.0	346.8	347.7	343.0	338.5	338.3	339.1	340.6
2003	328.5	331.4	340.3	348.4	353.1	356.2	356.6	359.6	356.0	349.2	348.9	348.9	348.1
2004	340.6	344.6	352.0	361.2	366.9	370.7	366.9	369.5	363.6	361.8	361.2	361.6	360.1
2005	352.3	355.4	362.9	378.5	384.4	384.9	377.6	380.0	374.6	371.9	371.9	369.9	372.0
2006	364.2	369.6	377.7	385.3	390.6	392.6	389.7	391.3	385.6	386.3	388.5	387.0	384.0
2007	378.2	383.7	391.6	399.7	405.6	406.9	403.2	405.4	398.6	395.2	394.1	390.6	396.1
2008	383.3	387.2	393.4	400.2	407.2	405.1	402.4	402.3	395.4	386.6	383.3	379.9	393.9
2009	367.4	370.9	376.7	388.7	392.3	391.9	388.0	386.1	379.2	373.7	372.3	367.6	379.6
2010	355.2	358.1	366.4	379.2	382.9	383.6	383.0	382.8	377.9	375.9	374.1	370.7	374.2
2011	358.7	366.0	375.2	388.8	393.4	391.8	390.0	386.2	375.6	379.1	377.9	372.9	379.6
Other Services													
2000	134.0	137.0	140.3	144.3	147.6	150.8	156.9	157.9	159.9	162.5	163.4	165.9	151.7
2001	165.9	168.8	171.9	172.4	173.2	174.4	169.3	168.7	167.3	166.3	166.2	165.8	169.2
2002	160.8	161.4	162.1	160.1	160.8	161.5	156.2	156.5	156.1	156.6	157.5	156.6	158.9
2003	153.0	153.2	154.5	154.3	155.6	157.0	156.9	157.0	156.7	155.7	155.9	155.7	155.5
2004	154.9	154.9	156.5	157.0	157.3	158.5	157.9	157.4	155.5	155.0	155.2	154.8	156.2
2005	154.9	155.8	155.9	158.2	159.2	159.4	160.3	161.2	159.0	158.2	158.6	158.3	158.3
2006	156.9	157.4	157.5	159.3	160.5	161.1	161.3	160.5	159.1	159.3	159.5	158.5	159.2
2007	158.1	158.6	159.0	160.6	161.6	162.5	162.5	162.3	160.5	160.8	160.5	159.0	160.5
2008	159.5	160.9	160.8	161.5	162.7	163.2	162.5	162.0	160.4	159.6	159.3	158.3	160.9
2009	157.0	157.6	156.9	157.9	158.6	158.6	158.7	156.9	155.2	154.5	154.2	152.8	156.6
2010	150.9	151.5	151.8	153.7	154.9	154.6	155.9	154.6	153.7	154.5	154.5	152.6	153.6
2011	150.7	152.8	152.8	155.0	156.0	156.5	156.3	155.2	152.9	151.6	151.2	150.2	153.4
Government													
2000	592.3	596.9	601.0	601.0	612.2	597.1	577.1	585.0	594.5	600.2	602.4	603.8	597.0
2001	600.2	606.0	608.8	608.9	610.9	606.2	585.4	606.3	615.3	620.8	623.8	622.4	609.6
2002	616.1	618.6	624.5	625.5	627.0	618.1	597.5	620.3	632.0	633.5	636.0	632.9	623.5
2003	631.4	636.3	637.8	637.0	634.6	621.6	602.8	621.1	631.9	637.0	638.4	637.0	630.6
2004	627.6	634.6	635.8	642.0	639.1	624.1	605.9	631.7	641.4	643.8	647.2	643.7	634.7
2005	639.8	647.2	648.6	648.7	648.3	635.4	616.4	647.2	653.7	657.0	659.2	658.3	646.7
2006	653.1	660.7	662.8	660.8	660.4	651.6	627.2	655.1	665.3	670.4	674.2	673.3	659.6
2007	666.8	675.7	677.3	675.3	675.2	663.7	639.2	665.6	675.8	683.2	686.7	685.7	672.5
2008	684.3	694.3	695.9	694.3	694.8	682.6	661.0	685.2	689.8	699.9	704.7	701.4	690.7
2009	695.7	701.6	702.1	701.9	697.8	682.5	657.7	673.6	687.3	687.1	688.1	685.4	688.4
2010	681.3	685.9	688.4	688.4	701.9	683.0	658.2	666.0	669.7	674.9	677.1	674.0	679.1
2011	668.2	674.9	676.9	674.0	672.3	661.0	640.9	663.0	671.7	675.5	676.5	675.6	669.2

2. Average Weekly Hours by Selected Industry: Georgia, 2007–2011

(Not seasonally adjusted)

Industry and year	January	February	March	April	May	June	July	August	September	October	November	December	Annual average
Total Private													
2007	35.0	34.9	34.8	35.7	35.4	35.7	36.0	35.6	36.4	35.8	35.8	35.9	35.6
2008	35.0	35.2	35.6	35.3	35.4	35.9	35.2	35.6	35.0	34.9	35.5	34.9	35.3
2009	34.6	35.1	35.1	34.4	34.6	34.3	34.6	34.7	34.1	34.3	35.0	34.6	34.6
2010	34.3	34.2	34.4	34.9	35.2	34.9	34.7	35.1	34.7	34.9	34.8	34.8	34.7
2011	33.5	34.6	34.7	34.7	35.1	34.7	34.8	34.7	34.6	35.1	34.8	34.9	34.7
Goods-Producing													
2007	39.8	39.2	39.7	39.8	39.8	39.8	39.6	41.0	40.2	39.7	40.1	40.3	39.9
2008	39.1	39.3	39.2	39.5	39.6	39.8	39.2	39.0	38.6	38.1	38.0	37.4	38.9
2009	36.9	37.2	37.5	36.9	37.8	37.4	38.1	37.6	37.4	37.9	38.4	38.5	37.6
2010	38.4	37.5	38.2	39.0	39.3	39.0	39.0	38.7	38.2	38.9	38.7	39.1	38.7
2011	35.9	39.1	39.2	39.4	39.6	39.2	39.5	39.9	39.7	39.7	40.1	40.4	39.3
Construction													
2007	38.8	37.6	38.5	38.5	39.6	39.7	39.0	40.5	39.9	40.0	39.8	39.6	39.3
2008	38.1	37.9	37.6	38.6	38.8	39.3	38.1	38.2	37.6	37.0	36.8	35.6	37.8
2009	36.2	36.4	36.9	35.6	36.5	35.8	36.5	36.3	37.0	37.4	38.0	37.6	36.7
2010	36.9	35.9	36.0	36.6	37.0	37.3	37.5	38.0	37.7	38.8	38.7	38.3	37.4
2011	34.0	38.7	37.9	39.3	39.7	39.3	39.1	39.3	39.5	38.7	39.1	38.5	38.6
Manufacturing													
2007	40.4	40.8	41.0	41.1	40.3	39.8	40.0	41.2	40.3	41.0	41.7	40.9	40.7
2008	39.9	39.6	39.8	39.6	39.8	39.9	39.7	39.5	39.1	38.8	38.7	38.6	39.4
2009	37.3	37.0	37.3	37.3	37.9	37.8	38.7	38.5	37.7	38.4	39.0	39.4	38.0
2010	39.6	38.7	39.4	40.0	39.8	39.4	39.4	38.7	38.2	38.7	39.3	39.5	39.2
2011	36.8	39.3	39.9	39.4	39.5	39.3	39.9	40.4	40.0	40.2	40.6	41.5	39.7
Trade, Transportation, and Utilities													
2007	34.6	34.1	34.5	35.4	34.9	35.5	35.3	33.9	35.8	35.2	35.8	35.7	35.1
2008	35.2	35.2	35.9	35.7	35.5	35.8	35.1	35.3	35.2	34.8	35.8	35.3	35.4
2009	34.3	35.0	35.2	34.8	35.2	34.8	34.6	34.9	34.3	34.8	34.9	34.7	34.8
2010	34.2	34.2	34.0	34.6	35.1	34.9	34.8	35.5	34.9	34.9	34.9	35.0	34.8
2011	33.7	34.6	34.7	34.6	35.0	34.7	34.8	34.5	34.7	35.0	34.7	35.0	34.7
Financial Activities													
2007	36.4	36.1	35.6	36.3	35.4	36.5	35.9	34.5	35.7	35.1	35.0	35.6	35.7
2008	34.3	34.7	36.0	35.3	35.4	36.7	35.9	35.8	35.7	36.5	37.8	37.0	35.9
2009	36.2	36.6	36.2	35.1	34.8	34.6	35.1	36.2	36.0	36.2	36.1	34.6	35.6
2010	35.1	35.2	35.7	35.2	34.9	34.4	34.5	35.3	34.8	34.4	34.8	35.0	34.9
2011	36.3	35.0	35.5	35.1	36.5	35.6	35.9	35.4	35.6	37.2	35.9	35.8	35.8
Professional and Business Services													
2007	33.4	34.4	34.0	35.0	34.9	34.5	35.0	34.6	36.5	35.3	35.0	34.9	34.8
2008	33.4	34.3	35.1	34.5	34.8	35.6	34.6	35.5	34.0	34.4	35.4	34.3	34.7
2009	34.3	35.4	35.0	34.7	35.0	34.6	34.9	35.3	34.5	34.5	35.6	35.1	34.9
2010	34.1	34.8	35.0	35.4	35.2	34.9	35.1	35.4	35.0	35.0	34.9	35.1	35.0
2011	34.2	35.2	35.1	35.5	36.1	36.3	35.9	35.6	35.5	36.6	35.9	35.9	35.7
Education and Health Services													
2007	37.5	37.7	36.9	38.6	38.5	39.2	39.3	38.0	38.2	37.9	38.1	38.2	38.2
2008	37.2	38.0	38.1	37.4	37.2	37.3	36.8	37.5	36.3	36.3	36.4	36.0	37.0
2009	37.1	35.8	36.1	35.5	35.7	35.4	35.5	35.5	35.0	34.9	35.6	35.1	35.6
2010	34.8	34.7	34.9	35.0	35.5	35.2	35.1	35.3	35.3	35.1	35.3	35.1	35.1
2011	34.9	35.4	35.5	35.5	35.6	35.3	35.3	35.1	35.2	35.5	35.1	34.9	35.3
Leisure and Hospitality													
2007	27.7	27.7	26.8	27.9	28.5	28.4	29.2	29.0	28.7	28.1	27.8	27.5	28.1
2008	26.9	27.5	28.0	27.9	27.7	28.5	27.9	27.7	27.2	27.1	27.3	27.6	27.6
2009	28.1	29.0	29.0	28.4	28.5	27.7	28.1	27.8	27.2	27.6	27.5	27.7	28.1
2010	27.0	26.9	27.1	27.3	27.4	27.5	27.2	27.2	26.8	27.0	26.9	26.9	27.1
2011	25.3	26.9	27.0	27.0	27.2	26.7	26.9	26.8	26.2	26.5	26.3	26.3	26.6
Other Services													
2007	30.5	30.3	30.4	31.9	33.0	32.7	32.0	32.8	33.0	32.3	32.0	32.1	31.9
2008	31.8	32.6	32.8	32.5	33.1	32.8	30.7	31.4	32.2	32.0	32.1	31.7	32.1
2009	31.6	32.2	31.8	31.2	30.9	31.9	31.2	31.1	31.0	30.9	31.7	31.9	31.4
2010	31.7	32.2	32.3	32.9	33.3	32.9	33.2	33.5	33.7	33.3	33.5	33.6	33.0
2011	31.8	33.3	32.8	32.9	32.7	32.3	31.6	31.8	31.1	31.5	31.3	29.9	31.9

3. Average Hourly Earnings by Selected Industry: Georgia, 2007–2011

(Dollars, not seasonally adjusted)

Industry and year	January	February	March	April	May	June	July	August	September	October	November	December	Annual average
Total Private													
2007	20.07	20.13	20.83	20.05	19.79	21.03	20.34	20.96	20.58	20.74	20.62	20.08	20.44
2008	20.19	20.43	20.46	20.34	20.41	20.67	20.97	20.90	20.91	20.96	21.50	21.53	20.77
2009	21.10	21.49	21.32	21.07	20.53	20.70	20.82	21.05	21.00	20.99	21.46	21.37	21.08
2010	21.20	21.30	21.40	21.53	21.49	21.42	21.61	21.85	21.56	21.80	21.81	21.87	21.57
2011	22.40	21.77	21.61	21.83	21.77	21.72	21.78	21.75	21.80	21.98	21.83	21.78	21.83
Goods-Producing													
2007	18.47	18.37	18.57	18.21	18.02	18.75	18.50	18.52	19.45	19.78	19.89	19.02	18.79
2008	18.78	18.67	18.84	18.55	18.85	19.07	19.25	19.49	19.19	19.07	19.87	20.37	19.15
2009	20.31	20.06	20.10	20.30	20.05	20.69	20.54	20.80	21.03	21.05	21.53	21.36	20.64
2010	21.21	21.27	21.03	20.72	20.77	20.83	20.99	21.31	21.00	21.10	21.54	21.61	21.11
2011	21.84	21.21	20.99	21.31	21.47	21.94	21.82	21.63	21.87	22.10	21.88	22.14	21.68
Construction													
2007	18.61	16.99	17.68	17.61	17.10	17.27	17.83	18.11	18.81	18.37	18.57	18.75	17.98
2008	18.69	18.36	18.94	18.54	19.06	18.90	19.74	19.26	19.54	20.10	21.36	21.11	19.42
2009	20.90	20.58	20.71	20.53	20.39	21.08	21.28	21.62	21.94	21.98	21.75	21.61	21.18
2010	21.65	21.61	21.41	21.57	21.45	21.16	21.17	21.45	21.10	21.25	21.45	21.31	21.38
2011	22.29	21.18	21.02	21.39	21.39	21.66	21.48	21.53	21.78	22.17	21.93	22.34	21.67
Manufacturing													
2007	20.19	19.64	19.48	18.90	18.93	20.08	19.16	18.96	18.56	18.71	18.74	19.43	19.23
2008	19.03	19.05	18.95	18.66	18.80	19.25	19.00	19.66	18.99	18.35	18.83	19.89	19.04
2009	19.79	19.47	19.50	20.08	19.60	20.25	19.81	20.03	19.88	19.95	20.08	19.91	19.86
2010	19.86	20.12	19.98	19.73	19.93	20.26	20.48	20.76	20.44	20.56	20.39	20.80	20.28
2011	20.79	20.51	20.33	20.69	21.00	21.73	21.60	21.37	21.60	21.96	21.74	21.94	21.28
Trade, Transportation, and Utilities													
2007	19.31	19.77	20.05	19.11	18.76	19.52	19.37	19.07	19.34	19.64	19.00	18.81	19.31
2008	19.02	19.94	19.49	19.31	19.59	19.67	20.10	20.11	19.90	19.99	20.14	20.49	19.81
2009	19.94	20.25	20.26	20.11	19.70	19.73	19.75	19.96	19.69	19.16	19.63	19.44	19.80
2010	19.13	19.37	19.69	19.60	19.51	19.84	19.99	20.13	19.91	19.73	19.75	19.88	19.71
2011	20.19	20.04	20.11	20.16	20.20	20.08	20.22	20.21	20.16	20.26	19.92	20.07	20.13
Financial Activities													
2007	25.47	25.03	26.14	24.97	24.88	23.72	23.79	22.91	24.59	24.30	23.21	24.09	24.43
2008	23.76	24.01	24.83	25.00	25.11	25.49	25.30	24.98	25.02	24.52	25.57	25.73	24.95
2009	25.34	26.12	26.09	25.35	25.84	25.75	26.16	25.89	25.37	25.13	25.07	24.78	25.58
2010	24.69	25.08	24.81	25.55	25.65	25.20	25.50	25.66	25.24	24.80	24.46	24.59	25.10
2011	24.71	24.50	24.36	24.64	24.81	24.29	24.71	24.43	24.46	24.68	24.45	24.20	24.52
Professional and Business Services													
2007	25.98	25.69	25.62	25.69	25.17	26.38	24.88	24.61	25.66	25.09	24.86	25.60	25.43
2008	26.13	25.24	25.91	25.93	25.76	25.99	26.07	26.02	26.41	26.72	27.50	26.91	26.21
2009	27.20	27.32	27.16	26.35	26.11	26.15	25.74	26.15	26.31	26.39	27.00	27.00	26.58
2010	26.90	27.12	26.50	26.85	26.61	26.22	26.22	26.86	26.55	26.41	26.60	26.30	26.59
2011	27.57	26.41	26.35	26.56	26.60	26.70	26.81	26.81	26.84	27.02	27.20	27.23	26.84
Education and Health Services													
2007	20.14	20.29	20.72	20.34	19.97	19.41	19.75	19.72	20.52	20.41	20.77	20.18	20.18
2008	20.35	20.19	20.33	20.08	20.30	20.75	21.10	20.91	21.29	21.47	22.10	21.94	20.90
2009	21.28	21.88	21.74	22.10	21.65	21.89	22.02	21.97	21.85	22.40	22.49	22.16	21.95
2010	22.12	22.36	22.20	22.50	22.41	22.21	22.32	22.14	21.76	22.54	22.30	22.24	22.26
2011	22.60	22.11	21.87	22.19	21.83	21.86	22.25	21.94	21.91	22.22	22.24	22.01	22.08
Leisure and Hospitality													
2007	11.92	11.81	12.25	12.31	13.22	12.12	12.54	11.48	12.11	12.29	11.98	12.23	12.19
2008	12.43	12.22	12.14	12.27	12.14	11.90	11.90	11.78	11.91	11.87	11.92	11.83	12.02
2009	11.59	11.57	11.39	11.29	11.23	11.24	11.35	11.57	11.75	11.69	11.67	11.86	11.51
2010	11.70	11.80	11.83	11.87	11.90	11.72	11.77	12.00	12.02	12.02	12.12	12.07	11.90
2011	12.40	12.15	12.04	12.22	12.25	12.05	12.04	12.12	12.29	12.46	12.37	12.46	12.23
Other Services													
2007	16.06	15.88	16.21	15.66	14.73	14.95	14.79	14.53	14.40	14.29	15.18	16.01	15.20
2008	14.59	14.61	15.22	14.79	14.70	15.50	15.55	15.82	15.70	15.98	16.44	16.59	15.45
2009	16.67	16.91	17.01	16.93	16.74	16.89	16.91	17.19	17.40	17.69	17.63	17.90	17.15
2010	18.15	18.34	18.15	18.12	18.35	18.24	18.05	18.30	18.16	17.95	17.74	18.01	18.13
2011	18.74	18.12	17.77	18.12	17.81	17.72	17.74	17.39	17.66	17.89	17.55	18.02	17.88

4. Average Weekly Earnings by Selected Industry: Georgia, 2007–2011

(Dollars, not seasonally adjusted)

Industry and year	January	February	March	April	May	June	July	August	September	October	November	December	Annual average
Total Private													
2007	702.45	702.54	724.88	715.79	700.57	750.77	732.24	746.18	749.11	742.49	738.20	720.87	727.20
2008	706.65	719.14	728.38	718.00	722.51	742.05	738.14	744.04	731.85	731.50	763.25	751.40	732.70
2009	730.06	754.30	748.33	724.81	710.34	710.01	720.37	730.44	716.10	719.96	751.10	739.40	729.62
2010	727.16	728.46	736.16	751.40	756.45	747.56	749.87	766.94	748.13	760.82	758.99	761.08	749.47
2011	750.40	753.24	749.87	757.50	764.13	753.68	757.94	754.73	754.28	771.50	759.68	760.12	757.45
Goods-Producing													
2007	735.11	720.10	737.23	724.76	717.20	746.25	732.60	759.32	781.89	785.27	797.59	766.51	750.16
2008	734.30	733.73	738.53	732.73	746.46	758.99	754.60	760.11	740.73	726.57	755.06	761.84	745.16
2009	749.44	746.23	753.75	749.07	757.89	773.81	782.57	782.08	786.52	797.80	826.75	822.36	776.54
2010	814.46	797.63	803.35	808.08	816.26	812.37	818.61	824.70	802.20	820.79	833.60	844.95	816.44
2011	784.06	829.31	822.81	839.61	850.21	860.05	861.89	863.04	868.24	877.37	877.39	894.46	852.53
Construction													
2007	722.07	638.82	680.68	677.99	677.16	685.62	695.37	733.46	750.52	734.80	739.09	742.50	706.41
2008	712.09	695.84	712.14	715.64	739.53	742.77	752.09	735.73	734.70	743.70	786.05	751.52	734.56
2009	756.58	749.11	764.20	730.87	744.24	754.66	776.72	784.81	811.78	822.05	826.50	812.54	776.64
2010	798.89	775.80	770.76	789.46	793.65	789.27	793.88	815.10	795.47	824.50	830.12	816.17	799.43
2011	757.86	819.67	796.66	840.63	849.18	851.24	839.87	846.13	860.31	857.98	857.46	860.09	836.74
Manufacturing													
2007	815.68	801.31	798.68	776.79	762.88	799.18	766.40	781.15	747.97	767.11	781.46	794.69	782.86
2008	759.30	754.38	754.21	738.94	748.24	768.08	754.30	776.57	742.51	711.98	728.72	767.75	750.51
2009	738.17	720.39	727.35	748.98	742.84	765.45	766.65	771.16	749.48	766.08	783.12	784.45	754.82
2010	786.46	778.64	787.21	789.20	793.21	798.24	806.91	803.41	780.81	795.67	801.33	821.60	795.27
2011	765.07	806.04	811.17	815.19	829.50	853.99	861.84	863.35	864.00	882.79	882.64	910.51	845.69
Trade, Transportation, and Utilities													
2007	668.13	674.16	691.73	676.49	654.72	692.96	683.76	646.47	692.37	691.33	680.20	671.52	676.98
2008	669.50	701.89	699.69	689.37	695.45	704.19	705.51	709.88	700.48	695.65	721.01	723.30	701.28
2009	683.94	708.75	713.15	699.83	693.44	686.60	683.35	696.60	675.37	666.77	685.09	674.57	688.97
2010	654.25	662.45	669.46	678.16	684.80	692.42	695.65	714.62	694.86	688.58	689.28	695.80	685.18
2011	680.40	693.38	697.82	697.54	707.00	696.78	703.66	697.25	699.55	709.10	691.22	702.45	698.04
Financial Activities													
2007	927.11	903.58	930.58	906.41	880.75	865.78	854.06	790.40	877.86	852.93	812.35	857.60	871.63
2008	814.97	833.15	893.88	882.50	888.89	935.48	908.27	894.28	893.21	894.98	966.55	952.01	896.17
2009	917.31	955.99	944.46	889.79	899.23	890.95	918.22	937.22	913.32	909.71	905.03	857.39	911.74
2010	866.62	882.82	885.72	899.36	895.19	866.88	879.75	905.80	878.35	853.12	851.21	860.65	877.06
2011	896.97	857.50	864.78	864.86	905.57	864.72	887.09	864.82	870.78	918.10	877.76	866.36	878.28
Professional and Business Services													
2007	867.73	883.74	871.08	899.15	878.43	910.11	870.80	851.51	936.59	885.68	870.10	893.44	884.90
2008	872.74	865.73	909.44	894.59	896.45	925.24	902.02	923.71	897.94	919.17	973.50	923.01	908.42
2009	932.96	967.13	950.60	914.35	913.85	904.79	898.33	923.10	907.70	910.46	961.20	947.70	927.78
2010	917.29	943.78	927.50	950.49	936.67	915.08	920.32	950.84	929.25	924.35	928.34	923.13	930.59
2011	942.89	929.63	924.89	942.88	960.26	969.21	962.48	954.44	952.82	988.93	976.48	977.56	957.18
Education and Health Services													
2007	755.25	764.93	764.57	785.12	768.85	760.87	776.18	749.36	783.86	773.54	791.34	770.88	770.48
2008	757.02	767.22	774.57	750.99	755.16	773.98	776.48	784.13	772.83	779.36	804.44	789.84	773.92
2009	789.49	783.30	784.81	784.55	772.91	774.91	781.71	779.94	764.75	781.76	800.64	777.82	781.41
2010	769.78	775.89	774.78	787.50	795.56	781.79	783.43	781.54	768.13	791.15	787.19	780.62	781.45
2011	788.74	782.69	776.39	787.75	777.15	771.66	785.43	770.09	771.23	788.81	780.62	768.15	779.07
Leisure and Hospitality													
2007	330.18	327.14	328.30	343.45	376.77	344.21	366.17	332.92	347.56	345.35	333.04	336.33	342.82
2008	334.37	336.05	339.92	342.33	336.28	339.15	332.01	326.31	323.95	321.68	325.42	326.51	332.06
2009	325.68	335.53	330.31	320.64	320.06	311.35	318.94	321.65	319.60	322.64	320.93	328.52	322.88
2010	315.90	317.42	320.59	324.05	326.06	322.30	320.14	326.40	322.14	324.54	326.03	324.68	322.59
2011	313.72	326.84	325.08	329.94	333.20	321.74	323.88	324.82	322.00	330.19	325.33	327.70	325.45
Other Services													
2007	489.83	481.16	492.78	499.55	486.09	488.87	473.28	476.58	475.20	461.57	485.76	513.92	485.33
2008	463.94	476.29	499.22	480.68	486.57	508.40	477.39	496.75	505.54	511.36	527.72	525.90	496.58
2009	526.77	544.50	540.92	528.22	517.27	538.79	527.59	534.61	539.40	546.62	558.87	571.01	539.33
2010	575.36	590.55	586.25	596.15	611.06	600.10	599.26	613.05	611.99	597.74	594.29	605.14	598.47
2011	595.93	603.40	582.86	596.15	582.39	572.36	560.58	553.00	549.23	563.54	549.32	538.80	570.66

HAWAII
At a Glance

Population:
　2000 census: 1,211,497
　2010 census: 1,360,301
　2011 estimate: 1,374,810

Percent change in population:
　2000–2010: 12.3%
　2010–2011: 1.1%

Percent change in total nonfarm employment:
　2000–2010: 6.4%
　2010–2011: 0.9%

Industry with the largest growth in employment, 2000–2011 (thousands):
　Education and Health Services, 15.6

Industry with the largest decline or smallest growth in employment, 2000–2011 (thousands):
　Information, -4.1

Civilian labor force:
　2000: 609,018
　2010: 649,158
　2011: 660,694

Unemployment rate and rank among states (lowest to highest):
　2000: 4.0%, 28th
　2010: 6.9%, 7th
　2011: 6.7%, 11th

Over-the-year change in unemployment rates:
　2010–2011: -0.2%

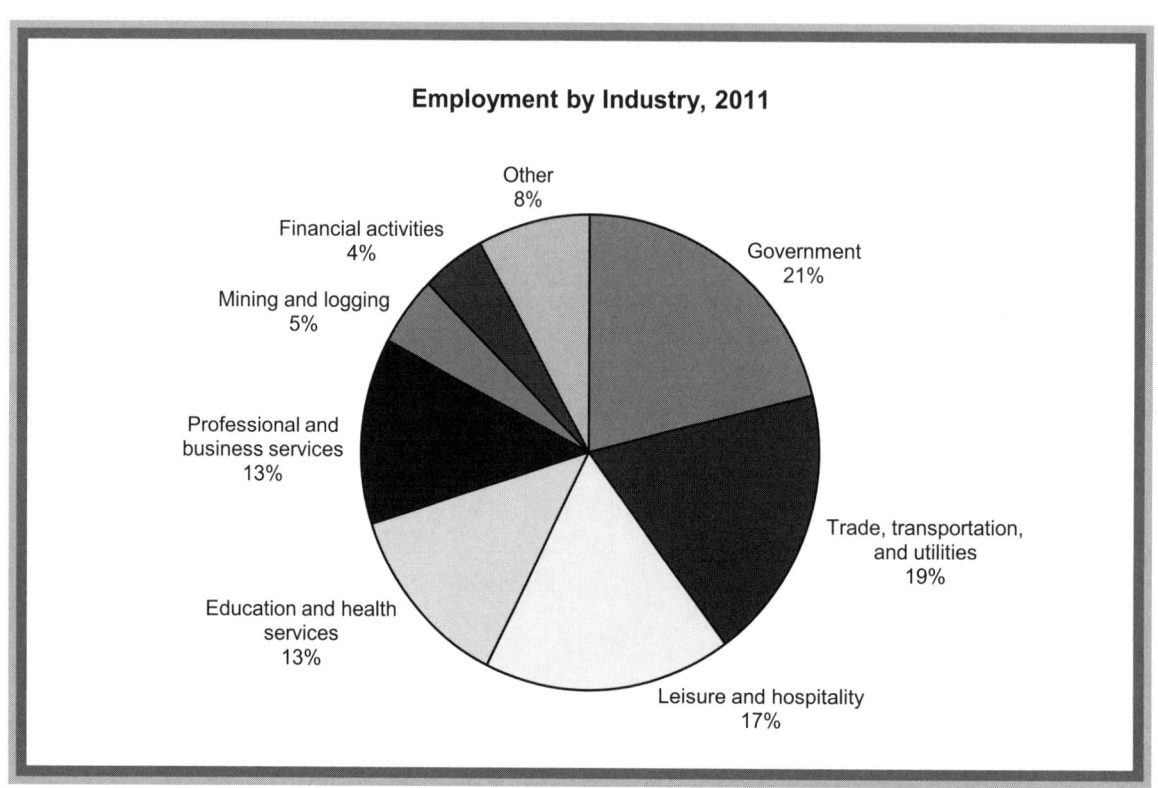

Employment by Industry, 2011

Other 8%
Financial activities 4%
Mining and logging 5%
Professional and business services 13%
Education and health services 13%
Leisure and hospitality 17%
Government 21%
Trade, transportation, and utilities 19%

1. Employment by Industry: Hawaii, Selected Years, 2000–2011

(Numbers in thousands, not seasonally adjusted)

Industry and year	January	February	March	April	May	June	July	August	September	October	November	December	Annual average
Total Nonfarm													
2000	535.1	542.9	548.8	548.3	552.2	556.3	547.6	548.2	552.3	555.3	561.9	567.4	551.4
2001	546.9	557.4	561.2	556.1	557.5	562.9	552.5	554.6	555.5	548.1	551.9	555.4	555.0
2002	542.0	549.4	554.0	547.9	558.1	564.6	553.2	554.2	557.3	560.7	566.8	573.3	556.8
2003	559.6	564.5	567.8	562.7	568.2	568.9	562.3	563.4	566.1	570.0	576.2	581.9	567.6
2004	568.9	574.5	578.0	578.6	582.4	584.2	578.9	580.5	584.1	589.8	599.2	601.8	583.4
2005	585.0	593.1	597.4	598.5	602.0	604.4	597.3	601.3	604.2	605.8	611.8	618.9	601.6
2006	600.2	611.0	615.2	612.5	617.9	621.0	610.6	615.7	620.4	618.2	630.3	632.3	617.1
2007	615.0	622.9	626.5	618.5	627.1	630.5	618.0	619.7	624.6	626.4	632.3	637.0	624.9
2008	619.9	626.6	629.4	620.5	626.6	624.4	612.6	613.4	613.0	611.5	618.1	614.8	619.2
2009	597.6	599.3	600.6	594.8	595.0	594.3	583.0	580.8	584.3	587.1	588.6	592.5	591.5
2010	578.9	583.9	587.6	586.7	589.9	586.2	581.1	577.7	584.8	589.6	597.3	599.2	586.9
2011	583.8	592.2	595.9	592.0	592.8	591.0	587.6	581.8	589.8	595.8	599.7	602.5	592.1
Total Private													
2000	424.5	427.8	431.4	431.2	432.6	438.6	437.9	439.1	442.0	441.2	445.3	449.3	436.7
2001	438.8	441.3	444.1	440.9	442.7	445.6	443.7	444.8	443.5	432.6	432.8	435.4	440.5
2002	427.4	430.3	433.4	433.4	436.6	440.6	441.2	441.9	443.0	441.9	445.9	450.8	438.9
2003	440.7	442.9	445.4	443.7	445.8	447.8	448.4	450.3	451.8	450.3	454.9	460.0	448.5
2004	450.5	453.6	455.5	456.9	459.2	463.3	464.7	465.9	467.4	469.4	474.6	478.9	463.3
2005	468.8	472.1	475.2	477.1	479.3	482.9	483.3	485.6	487.7	485.7	490.0	496.3	482.0
2006	484.5	489.1	492.3	490.3	494.0	498.7	496.1	499.7	500.4	495.9	502.1	507.0	495.8
2007	495.1	498.7	501.6	498.6	501.8	507.0	502.6	504.3	503.7	502.7	506.8	510.4	502.8
2008	498.5	501.4	502.4	498.7	498.7	498.5	494.2	493.1	489.7	484.5	485.1	485.9	494.2
2009	472.5	472.2	471.6	465.8	464.8	466.3	462.8	462.0	461.9	461.7	462.4	465.5	465.8
2010	456.6	458.5	460.0	459.1	460.1	460.1	460.1	461.2	462.5	464.3	466.6	471.6	461.7
2011	460.5	465.3	468.2	464.8	464.7	465.5	468.1	466.5	467.3	470.2	472.4	474.6	467.3
Goods-Producing													
2000	39.1	39.1	39.9	40.2	40.6	41.3	42.0	42.5	42.7	42.3	42.3	42.6	41.2
2001	41.4	41.3	41.4	40.9	41.2	41.2	41.3	41.6	41.5	40.5	40.6	40.7	41.1
2002	40.0	39.9	40.6	40.2	40.6	41.6	41.8	42.1	41.7	41.8	42.1	42.2	41.2
2003	41.4	41.5	41.8	42.4	42.8	43.1	43.4	43.7	43.8	43.9	43.9	43.8	43.0
2004	42.9	43.3	42.7	43.8	44.3	45.1	45.4	45.5	45.8	45.9	46.3	46.7	44.8
2005	45.9	46.3	47.0	47.5	48.1	48.7	49.1	49.7	50.2	49.9	50.1	50.6	48.6
2006	49.5	49.8	50.1	50.1	50.9	51.7	52.0	52.8	53.5	53.1	53.9	54.6	51.8
2007	52.8	53.2	53.4	53.5	54.0	54.9	54.7	55.1	55.3	55.1	55.3	55.2	54.4
2008	53.9	54.1	54.0	53.7	53.2	53.3	53.0	52.9	52.4	51.4	50.8	50.1	52.7
2009	48.0	47.1	46.6	45.5	45.4	45.3	44.9	44.3	44.1	43.6	43.2	43.1	45.1
2010	42.2	41.9	42.0	41.7	41.7	41.5	41.7	41.6	41.7	42.1	42.2	42.4	41.9
2011	40.6	41.2	41.3	41.5	41.3	41.9	41.9	41.8	41.5	42.2	41.1	41.4	41.5
Mining, Logging, and Construction													
2000	23.0	23.1	23.7	24.0	24.4	24.8	25.5	25.8	26.0	25.6	25.6	25.9	24.8
2001	24.8	24.7	24.8	24.4	24.6	24.6	24.8	25.0	25.0	24.5	24.6	24.7	24.7
2002	24.4	24.3	24.9	25.1	25.4	26.2	26.6	27.0	26.8	26.9	27.1	27.2	26.0
2003	26.7	26.8	27.1	27.5	27.9	28.1	28.4	28.7	28.7	28.6	28.5	28.3	27.9
2004	27.6	27.9	27.4	28.4	28.9	29.5	30.0	30.1	30.4	30.6	30.9	31.3	29.4
2005	30.8	31.1	31.8	32.4	33.0	33.6	34.0	34.4	34.9	34.7	34.9	35.3	33.4
2006	34.5	34.7	34.9	35.0	35.7	36.4	36.7	37.3	37.9	37.8	38.4	39.0	36.5
2007	37.5	37.9	38.1	38.3	38.7	39.5	39.5	39.8	40.0	40.0	40.1	39.9	39.1
2008	38.9	39.0	38.9	38.6	38.1	38.2	38.1	37.9	37.7	37.0	36.3	35.6	37.9
2009	33.9	33.2	32.7	31.8	31.7	31.7	31.4	30.7	30.4	30.1	29.7	29.6	31.4
2010	29.0	28.8	28.9	28.8	28.8	28.7	28.9	28.7	28.8	29.1	29.1	29.2	28.9
2011	27.6	28.0	28.1	28.3	28.2	28.8	28.7	28.5	28.2	29.0	27.7	28.1	28.3
Manufacturing													
2000	16.1	16.0	16.2	16.2	16.2	16.5	16.5	16.7	16.7	16.7	16.7	16.7	16.4
2001	16.6	16.6	16.6	16.5	16.6	16.6	16.5	16.6	16.5	16.0	16.0	16.0	16.4
2002	15.6	15.6	15.7	15.1	15.2	15.4	15.2	15.1	14.9	14.9	15.0	15.0	15.2
2003	14.7	14.7	14.7	14.9	14.9	15.0	15.0	15.0	15.1	15.3	15.4	15.5	15.0
2004	15.3	15.4	15.3	15.4	15.4	15.6	15.4	15.4	15.4	15.3	15.4	15.4	15.4
2005	15.1	15.2	15.2	15.1	15.1	15.1	15.1	15.3	15.3	15.2	15.2	15.3	15.2
2006	15.0	15.1	15.2	15.1	15.2	15.3	15.3	15.5	15.6	15.3	15.5	15.6	15.3
2007	15.3	15.3	15.3	15.2	15.3	15.4	15.2	15.3	15.3	15.1	15.2	15.3	15.3
2008	15.0	15.1	15.1	15.1	15.1	15.1	14.9	15.0	14.7	14.4	14.5	14.5	14.9
2009	14.1	13.9	13.9	13.7	13.7	13.6	13.5	13.6	13.7	13.5	13.5	13.5	13.7
2010	13.2	13.1	13.1	12.9	12.9	12.8	12.8	12.9	12.9	13.0	13.1	13.2	13.0
2011	13.0	13.2	13.2	13.2	13.1	13.1	13.2	13.3	13.3	13.2	13.4	13.3	13.2
Service-Providing													
2000	496.0	503.8	508.9	508.1	511.6	515.0	505.6	505.7	509.6	513.0	519.6	524.8	510.1
2001	505.5	516.1	519.8	515.2	516.3	521.7	511.2	513.0	514.0	507.6	511.3	514.7	513.9
2002	502.0	509.5	513.4	507.7	517.5	523.0	511.4	512.1	515.6	518.9	524.7	531.1	515.6
2003	518.2	523.0	526.0	520.3	525.4	525.8	518.9	519.7	522.3	526.1	532.3	538.1	524.7
2004	526.0	531.2	535.3	534.8	538.1	539.1	533.5	535.0	538.3	543.9	552.9	555.1	538.6
2005	539.1	546.8	550.4	551.0	553.9	555.7	548.2	551.6	554.0	555.9	561.7	568.3	553.1
2006	550.7	561.2	565.1	562.4	567.0	569.3	558.6	562.9	566.9	565.1	576.4	577.7	565.3
2007	562.2	569.7	573.1	565.0	573.1	575.6	563.3	564.6	569.3	571.3	577.0	581.8	570.5
2008	566.0	572.5	575.4	566.8	573.4	571.1	559.6	560.5	560.6	560.1	567.3	564.7	566.5
2009	549.6	552.2	554.0	549.3	549.6	549.0	538.1	536.5	540.2	543.5	545.4	549.4	546.4
2010	536.7	542.0	545.6	545.0	548.2	544.7	539.4	536.1	543.1	547.5	555.1	556.8	545.0
2011	543.2	551.0	554.6	550.5	551.5	549.1	545.7	540.0	548.3	553.6	558.6	561.1	550.6

1. Employment by Industry: Hawaii, Selected Years, 2000–2011—*Continued*

(Numbers in thousands, not seasonally adjusted)

Industry and year	January	February	March	April	May	June	July	August	September	October	November	December	Annual average
Trade, Transportation, and Utilities													
2000	109.5	109.3	109.3	108.6	108.9	110.4	110.4	110.9	111.4	111.6	114.1	115.4	110.8
2001	112.3	111.7	111.9	111.2	111.5	112.2	111.8	112.0	111.6	108.9	107.6	109.2	111.0
2002	105.5	104.8	104.9	105.0	105.5	106.5	107.0	107.3	107.1	107.5	109.0	111.0	106.8
2003	107.4	107.0	106.8	106.2	106.4	106.9	107.6	107.9	108.0	108.2	110.1	112.2	107.9
2004	109.3	108.8	109.1	110.1	110.8	111.9	112.1	112.6	113.0	114.5	116.8	118.4	112.3
2005	114.9	114.9	115.2	115.5	116.4	117.3	118.2	118.7	119.1	118.9	120.7	122.9	117.7
2006	119.2	118.9	119.8	119.5	120.0	121.3	120.7	121.7	121.7	120.6	123.2	125.0	121.0
2007	121.6	120.3	121.4	120.3	120.8	121.6	121.3	121.4	121.2	121.5	124.5	126.4	121.9
2008	122.1	120.7	120.9	118.9	118.6	118.2	117.2	117.1	116.1	115.0	115.8	116.5	118.1
2009	113.4	112.3	111.7	110.3	110.0	110.5	110.2	109.8	110.1	110.0	111.4	112.8	111.0
2010	109.7	109.1	109.0	109.2	108.9	109.3	109.7	110.2	109.8	110.4	112.1	114.0	110.1
2011	110.8	110.3	110.5	109.9	110.1	110.4	111.2	110.7	110.6	111.2	112.2	113.5	111.0
Wholesale Trade													
2000	16.0	16.0	16.1	16.0	16.0	16.3	16.3	16.4	16.4	16.4	16.5	16.5	16.2
2001	16.4	16.4	16.4	16.4	16.5	16.6	16.5	16.6	16.5	16.3	16.2	16.4	16.4
2002	16.1	16.1	16.2	16.2	16.3	16.4	16.5	16.5	16.5	16.6	16.7	16.9	16.4
2003	16.5	16.5	16.6	16.6	16.7	16.7	16.8	16.8	16.8	16.8	16.8	16.9	16.7
2004	16.7	16.8	16.8	16.9	17.0	17.1	17.1	17.1	17.1	17.2	17.3	17.4	17.0
2005	17.1	17.3	17.4	17.4	17.5	17.6	17.7	17.8	17.9	17.9	17.9	18.1	17.6
2006	17.7	17.7	17.7	17.8	17.9	18.1	18.0	18.2	18.2	18.2	18.4	18.5	18.0
2007	18.2	18.2	18.4	18.3	18.4	18.6	18.6	18.7	18.8	18.8	19.0	19.1	18.6
2008	18.7	18.8	18.9	18.8	18.9	18.9	18.9	18.8	18.8	18.7	18.6	18.6	18.8
2009	18.2	18.1	18.0	17.9	17.8	17.8	17.8	17.7	17.8	17.7	17.7	17.8	17.9
2010	17.5	17.5	17.6	17.6	17.6	17.6	17.7	17.7	17.6	17.7	17.7	17.8	17.6
2011	17.4	17.3	17.3	17.3	17.4	17.4	17.7	17.6	17.3	17.1	17.1	17.2	17.3
Retail Trade													
2000	66.0	65.5	65.3	64.7	65.0	65.7	65.9	66.3	66.4	66.7	68.8	70.0	66.4
2001	67.2	66.5	66.5	65.9	65.9	66.3	66.1	66.3	66.0	64.9	65.3	66.7	66.1
2002	63.8	63.0	62.9	62.8	63.0	63.7	64.1	64.1	63.9	64.1	65.3	67.1	64.0
2003	64.0	63.4	63.1	62.8	63.0	63.7	64.3	64.4	64.3	64.6	66.4	68.4	64.4
2004	65.8	65.1	65.2	65.1	65.6	66.3	66.6	66.9	67.0	68.1	70.1	71.8	67.0
2005	68.5	68.1	68.2	67.8	68.0	68.3	69.1	69.3	69.3	69.7	71.3	73.3	69.2
2006	70.0	69.5	69.8	69.1	69.2	69.8	69.4	69.7	69.4	69.5	71.7	73.1	70.0
2007	70.4	69.4	70.1	69.3	69.6	70.1	69.9	69.8	69.6	69.8	72.4	73.8	70.4
2008	70.6	69.9	70.7	69.7	69.6	70.1	70.0	69.8	69.2	68.5	69.5	70.3	69.8
2009	67.9	67.0	66.6	65.6	65.3	65.8	65.7	65.5	65.9	66.0	67.5	68.6	66.5
2010	66.0	65.4	65.3	65.3	65.0	65.5	65.7	65.8	65.5	65.8	67.5	68.9	66.0
2011	66.6	66.0	66.2	65.8	65.9	66.2	66.7	66.5	66.3	66.7	67.9	68.7	66.6
Transportation and Utilities													
2000	27.5	27.8	27.9	27.9	27.9	28.4	28.2	28.2	28.6	28.5	28.8	28.9	28.2
2001	28.7	28.8	29.0	28.9	29.1	29.3	29.2	29.1	29.1	27.7	26.1	26.1	28.4
2002	25.6	25.7	25.8	26.0	26.2	26.4	26.4	26.7	26.7	26.8	27.0	27.0	26.4
2003	26.9	27.1	27.1	26.8	26.7	26.5	26.5	26.7	26.9	26.8	26.9	26.9	26.8
2004	26.8	26.9	27.1	28.1	28.2	28.5	28.4	28.6	28.9	29.2	29.4	29.2	28.3
2005	29.3	29.5	29.6	30.3	30.9	31.4	31.4	31.6	31.9	31.3	31.5	31.5	30.9
2006	31.5	31.7	32.3	32.6	32.9	33.4	33.3	33.8	34.1	32.9	33.1	33.4	32.9
2007	33.0	32.7	32.9	32.7	32.8	32.9	32.8	32.9	32.8	32.9	33.1	33.5	32.9
2008	32.8	32.0	31.3	30.4	30.1	29.2	28.3	28.5	28.1	27.8	27.7	27.6	29.5
2009	27.3	27.2	27.1	26.8	26.9	26.9	26.7	26.6	26.4	26.3	26.2	26.4	26.7
2010	26.2	26.2	26.1	26.3	26.3	26.2	26.3	26.7	26.7	26.9	26.9	27.3	26.5
2011	26.8	27.0	27.0	26.8	26.8	26.8	26.8	26.6	27.0	27.4	27.2	27.6	27.0
Information													
2000	11.5	11.5	11.7	12.4	12.3	12.7	12.0	12.5	13.3	12.9	12.4	12.1	12.3
2001	12.1	12.1	12.4	11.8	12.1	11.9	11.7	11.9	11.5	11.5	11.7	11.6	11.9
2002	11.7	11.7	11.6	11.5	11.5	11.3	11.2	11.3	12.0	11.1	11.1	11.7	11.5
2003	10.8	10.9	10.9	10.5	11.1	10.9	10.1	10.0	9.9	9.9	10.0	10.1	10.4
2004	10.2	10.1	10.4	10.2	10.5	10.6	11.1	11.0	11.1	11.1	11.6	11.5	10.8
2005	10.4	10.6	10.4	10.7	10.9	10.5	10.5	10.9	11.0	10.9	11.1	11.6	10.8
2006	10.8	11.1	10.9	10.2	11.0	10.8	10.3	10.5	11.0	10.3	10.8	10.9	10.7
2007	10.4	11.0	10.9	10.5	11.1	11.1	10.3	10.8	10.4	10.2	10.3	10.4	10.6
2008	9.6	10.1	10.4	10.4	10.7	11.1	9.9	9.6	9.6	9.4	9.8	10.0	10.1
2009	9.1	9.6	9.4	9.4	9.1	9.1	8.7	8.8	9.0	9.2	9.0	9.0	9.1
2010	8.9	9.7	9.9	9.5	10.7	10.0	8.8	9.4	11.1	9.8	9.4	10.3	9.8
2011	8.5	9.4	10.2	8.1	7.9	7.8	7.6	7.7	7.7	7.7	7.7	8.1	8.2
Financial Activities													
2000	28.4	28.6	28.6	28.4	28.4	28.6	28.7	28.7	28.5	28.5	28.4	28.9	28.6
2001	28.1	28.2	28.4	28.2	28.2	28.3	28.1	28.1	28.0	27.6	27.6	27.7	28.0
2002	27.2	27.3	27.6	27.4	27.6	27.8	27.8	27.8	27.8	27.9	28.1	28.4	27.7
2003	27.7	27.9	28.1	28.0	28.2	28.5	28.6	28.8	28.6	28.6	28.5	28.8	28.4
2004	28.5	28.5	28.6	28.7	28.7	28.9	28.9	28.8	28.7	29.0	29.1	29.3	28.8
2005	28.7	29.0	29.0	28.9	29.1	29.2	29.4	29.5	29.5	29.5	29.7	29.9	29.3
2006	29.5	29.6	29.9	29.9	30.0	30.2	30.1	30.2	30.0	29.9	30.1	30.3	30.0
2007	29.9	30.0	30.2	29.9	30.0	30.2	30.2	30.1	29.9	30.0	29.9	30.1	30.0
2008	29.4	29.7	29.6	29.7	29.8	29.7	29.6	29.5	29.2	28.7	28.9	28.8	29.4
2009	27.9	27.9	27.8	27.8	27.8	27.8	27.6	27.6	27.5	27.5	27.4	27.5	27.7
2010	27.1	27.0	27.1	26.9	26.9	26.8	27.0	26.9	26.8	26.9	26.9	26.9	26.9
2011	26.5	26.6	26.7	26.5	26.5	26.6	27.1	27.1	27.1	27.4	27.7	27.5	26.9

1. Employment by Industry: Hawaii, Selected Years, 2000–2011—*Continued*

(Numbers in thousands, not seasonally adjusted)

Industry and year	January	February	March	April	May	June	July	August	September	October	November	December	Annual average
Professional and Business Services													
2000	59.3	59.8	60.6	60.7	60.7	61.4	61.6	61.7	62.4	62.5	63.0	63.7	61.5
2001	62.3	63.1	63.9	63.3	63.8	64.7	64.4	64.9	64.8	63.5	64.1	64.4	63.9
2002	63.5	64.9	65.4	65.9	66.5	67.5	67.8	68.6	68.8	68.8	68.6	70.6	67.2
2003	69.0	68.6	69.2	68.9	68.8	69.6	69.4	70.3	70.8	69.6	70.6	71.1	69.7
2004	69.4	70.1	70.6	70.2	69.5	70.2	70.6	71.4	71.2	71.3	71.7	72.7	70.7
2005	71.9	72.5	73.1	73.6	73.0	74.0	74.2	74.9	74.8	75.1	76.1	77.3	74.2
2006	75.3	76.8	77.2	76.7	76.6	77.6	77.5	77.7	77.2	75.6	76.1	77.2	76.8
2007	75.1	75.7	76.0	75.0	75.3	77.1	76.4	76.6	76.8	77.1	77.2	78.1	76.4
2008	75.8	76.1	76.3	76.1	75.8	75.5	75.4	75.6	75.1	74.7	74.5	75.4	75.5
2009	73.1	72.9	72.9	71.5	71.0	71.1	70.5	70.4	70.0	71.2	70.8	71.6	71.4
2010	70.2	70.6	70.9	70.9	70.8	71.2	71.9	71.8	71.9	72.5	72.8	73.5	71.6
2011	73.2	74.3	75.0	75.0	74.5	74.9	74.5	75.0	75.0	75.1	75.5	75.1	74.8
Education and Health Services													
2000	58.2	59.4	59.9	59.4	59.7	60.7	60.0	59.1	60.0	60.0	60.9	61.5	59.9
2001	59.9	61.0	61.4	61.4	61.8	62.2	62.1	61.5	62.0	62.0	63.0	63.1	61.8
2002	61.6	62.6	62.9	63.0	63.5	63.4	63.5	62.5	63.7	63.8	64.9	64.3	63.3
2003	63.1	64.6	65.1	65.0	65.2	64.9	65.2	64.7	66.0	66.0	66.8	67.2	65.3
2004	65.5	66.6	67.1	66.9	67.7	67.7	67.4	67.0	68.3	68.5	69.4	69.9	67.7
2005	68.7	69.5	69.9	69.9	70.2	70.3	69.5	69.0	70.2	69.9	70.4	70.8	69.9
2006	68.9	70.1	70.7	70.7	71.4	71.8	70.6	71.2	71.7	71.8	72.6	73.0	71.2
2007	71.1	72.7	72.9	72.9	73.4	73.8	72.6	72.4	73.2	73.3	73.6	73.8	73.0
2008	72.5	73.7	73.9	73.8	74.2	74.7	74.0	73.8	74.4	74.7	75.2	75.5	74.2
2009	73.8	74.8	75.0	74.5	74.6	75.1	74.1	73.7	74.3	74.5	75.0	75.4	74.6
2010	74.5	75.2	75.6	75.2	75.6	75.3	74.9	74.6	74.6	75.9	75.9	76.3	75.3
2011	73.9	75.8	75.9	75.7	75.9	75.1	75.9	74.8	74.8	75.4	76.5	76.7	75.5
Leisure and Hospitality													
2000	96.7	97.7	98.8	98.8	99.2	100.5	100.3	100.6	100.7	100.2	100.6	101.5	99.6
2001	99.5	100.5	101.0	100.4	100.5	101.1	100.4	101.1	100.4	95.3	94.9	95.3	99.2
2002	94.7	95.8	96.8	96.8	97.7	98.7	98.3	98.5	98.0	97.2	98.2	98.6	97.4
2003	97.8	98.5	99.5	98.5	99.0	99.5	99.9	100.6	100.4	99.9	100.5	102.2	99.7
2004	100.9	102.1	102.6	102.7	103.1	104.2	104.7	105.1	104.9	104.4	105.0	105.5	103.8
2005	103.8	104.7	105.9	105.9	106.2	107.5	107.2	107.5	107.4	106.1	106.4	107.4	106.3
2006	105.9	107.1	107.8	107.3	107.9	109.1	108.9	109.3	109.0	108.2	108.9	109.5	108.2
2007	108.4	109.6	110.4	110.2	110.7	111.7	110.5	111.1	110.0	108.5	108.9	109.4	110.0
2008	108.5	109.7	109.8	108.6	108.7	108.7	108.1	107.5	105.8	103.6	103.1	102.7	107.1
2009	101.2	101.4	101.8	100.9	101.0	101.5	101.0	101.5	100.8	99.7	99.6	100.2	100.9
2010	98.8	99.4	99.8	99.7	99.4	100.0	100.2	100.8	100.7	100.7	101.4	102.3	100.3
2011	101.5	101.9	102.9	102.3	102.6	102.9	104.0	103.7	104.9	105.4	105.7	106.1	103.7
Other Services													
2000	21.8	22.4	22.6	22.7	22.8	23.0	22.9	23.1	23.0	23.2	23.6	23.6	22.9
2001	23.2	23.4	23.7	23.7	23.6	24.0	23.9	23.7	23.7	23.3	23.3	23.4	23.6
2002	23.2	23.3	23.6	23.6	23.7	23.8	23.8	23.8	23.9	23.8	23.9	24.0	23.7
2003	23.5	23.9	24.0	24.2	24.3	24.4	24.2	24.3	24.3	24.2	24.5	24.6	24.2
2004	23.8	24.1	24.4	24.3	24.6	24.7	24.5	24.5	24.4	24.7	24.7	24.9	24.5
2005	24.5	24.6	24.7	25.1	25.4	25.4	25.2	25.4	25.5	25.4	25.5	25.8	25.2
2006	25.4	25.7	25.9	25.9	26.2	26.2	26.0	26.3	26.3	26.4	26.5	26.5	26.1
2007	25.8	26.2	26.4	26.3	26.5	26.6	26.6	26.8	26.9	27.0	27.1	27.0	26.6
2008	26.7	27.3	27.5	27.5	27.7	27.3	27.0	27.1	27.1	27.0	27.0	26.9	27.2
2009	26.0	26.2	26.4	25.9	25.9	25.9	25.8	25.9	26.1	26.0	26.0	25.9	26.0
2010	25.2	25.6	25.7	26.0	26.1	26.0	25.9	25.9	25.9	26.0	25.9	25.9	25.8
2011	25.5	25.8	25.7	25.8	25.9	25.9	25.9	25.7	25.7	25.8	26.0	26.2	25.8
Government													
2000	110.6	115.1	117.4	117.1	119.6	117.7	109.7	109.1	110.3	114.1	116.6	118.1	114.6
2001	108.1	116.1	117.1	115.2	114.8	117.3	108.8	109.8	112.0	115.5	119.1	120.0	114.5
2002	114.6	119.1	120.6	114.5	121.5	124.0	112.0	112.3	114.3	118.8	120.9	122.5	117.9
2003	118.9	121.6	122.4	119.0	122.4	121.1	113.9	113.1	114.3	119.7	121.3	121.9	119.1
2004	118.4	120.9	122.5	121.7	123.2	120.9	114.2	114.6	116.7	120.4	124.6	122.9	120.1
2005	116.2	121.0	122.2	121.4	122.7	121.5	114.0	115.7	116.5	120.1	121.8	122.6	119.6
2006	115.7	121.9	122.9	122.2	123.9	122.3	114.5	116.0	120.0	122.3	128.2	125.3	121.3
2007	119.9	124.2	124.9	119.9	125.3	123.5	115.4	115.4	120.9	123.7	125.5	126.6	122.1
2008	121.4	125.2	127.0	121.8	127.9	125.9	118.4	120.3	123.3	127.0	133.0	128.9	125.0
2009	125.1	127.1	129.0	129.0	130.2	128.0	120.2	118.8	122.4	125.4	126.2	127.0	125.7
2010	122.3	125.4	127.6	127.6	129.8	126.1	121.0	116.5	122.3	125.3	130.7	127.6	125.2
2011	123.3	126.9	127.7	127.2	128.1	125.5	119.5	115.3	122.5	125.6	127.3	127.9	124.7

2. Average Weekly Hours by Selected Industry: Hawaii, 2007–2011

(Not seasonally adjusted)

Industry and year	January	February	March	April	May	June	July	August	September	October	November	December	Annual average
Total Private													
2007	32.5	32.5	32.0	33.2	32.0	32.4	33.4	32.6	33.4	32.1	32.2	32.9	32.6
2008	32.7	32.7	33.2	32.7	32.3	33.1	32.5	32.6	32.3	32.2	33.0	31.9	32.6
2009	32.3	33.4	33.0	32.5	32.3	32.5	32.3	32.6	32.0	32.2	32.7	32.2	32.5
2010	32.3	32.3	32.2	32.4	33.4	32.6	32.8	33.8	32.6	32.8	32.9	33.4	32.8
2011	34.1	33.3	33.0	33.4	34.1	33.4	33.1	33.1	33.1	34.0	32.7	32.6	33.3
Goods-Producing													
2007	36.0	36.1	35.4	36.1	35.6	33.4	34.3	33.4	34.9	33.6	34.2	34.7	34.8
2008	35.3	37.3	37.5	36.4	36.4	35.8	36.4	36.8	36.8	36.0	35.1	35.3	36.3
2009	36.1	36.6	37.0	36.5	36.4	35.4	36.2	35.5	34.3	34.3	34.7	36.1	35.8
2010	36.3	35.7	35.7	36.4	36.9	36.1	37.9	38.5	37.5	36.4	36.1	37.9	36.8
2011	36.3	37.7	36.6	37.7	37.2	36.8	36.7	36.3	36.5	35.0	33.7	35.7	36.4
Mining, Logging, and Construction													
2007	36.6	36.6	36.3	37.0	35.6	33.1	34.1	33.0	35.0	33.4	33.9	34.5	34.9
2008	35.5	37.9	37.8	36.6	36.9	35.3	36.6	36.4	36.4	35.5	34.0	35.5	36.2
2009	36.5	37.0	37.5	36.9	37.1	35.8	36.8	35.7	34.4	34.5	34.4	36.5	36.1
2010	37.1	36.0	35.8	36.8	37.4	36.2	38.5	38.9	37.9	36.2	36.2	37.8	37.0
2011	36.3	38.7	37.4	38.9	37.3	36.9	37.1	37.3	37.3	34.8	34.1	36.4	36.9
Manufacturing													
2007	34.7	34.9	33.2	33.8	35.6	34.3	34.9	34.4	34.7	34.3	35.1	35.2	34.6
2008	34.7	35.7	36.8	35.8	35.0	36.9	35.8	37.7	37.9	37.4	37.9	34.8	36.4
2009	35.2	35.7	35.7	35.4	35.1	34.4	34.7	35.1	34.2	34.1	35.2	35.3	35.0
2010	34.8	35.1	35.6	35.4	36.0	35.9	36.8	37.7	36.4	37.0	36.1	38.0	36.2
2011	36.3	35.8	34.9	35.5	36.8	36.6	35.9	34.2	35.0	35.5	32.9	34.1	35.3
Trade, Transportation, and Utilities													
2007	32.8	33.5	32.7	34.3	33.2	34.0	35.0	34.1	35.2	33.7	34.0	34.2	33.9
2008	33.7	33.5	34.1	34.0	32.8	34.1	32.5	32.9	32.8	32.1	32.5	31.6	33.1
2009	32.7	33.3	33.3	33.0	32.5	33.5	32.8	33.5	33.9	33.9	32.8	33.3	33.3
2010	32.7	33.5	32.9	33.4	34.5	34.5	34.0	34.1	33.6	33.8	34.2	35.0	33.9
2011	35.1	34.1	34.0	34.1	35.3	34.4	34.4	34.2	34.4	35.1	34.0	34.1	34.4
Professional and Business Services													
2007	33.2	32.9	31.3	33.1	31.5	31.4	32.7	31.8	32.4	31.2	30.7	31.6	32.0
2008	31.9	31.1	32.1	31.7	31.6	32.2	31.0	31.3	31.8	31.9	32.9	32.2	31.8
2009	31.8	33.0	33.0	32.6	32.4	32.7	32.3	32.6	32.1	32.6	33.3	33.0	32.6
2010	32.8	33.1	33.6	33.1	34.1	33.5	33.1	34.2	33.4	34.4	34.3	34.4	33.7
2011	35.1	35.6	35.2	35.9	34.8	34.6	33.8	33.2	33.0	34.6	33.9	34.5	34.5
Education and Health Services													
2007	32.0	31.6	31.1	32.4	31.0	32.8	33.2	32.8	32.9	32.1	32.3	33.5	32.3
2008	32.9	33.0	33.0	32.5	32.4	33.1	32.8	32.7	32.1	32.2	33.2	31.2	32.6
2009	30.8	32.5	31.7	30.9	30.8	30.2	30.9	31.2	30.8	30.2	31.0	30.7	31.0
2010	29.9	30.0	29.8	30.4	30.9	30.0	30.3	30.7	30.6	30.0	30.1	30.8	30.3
2011	32.4	31.7	31.2	31.3	32.8	31.5	31.2	31.6	31.8	33.2	32.0	31.8	31.9
Leisure and Hospitality													
2007	30.1	29.9	29.7	30.8	29.4	30.2	31.4	30.0	30.6	29.3	29.5	30.3	30.1
2008	30.2	29.7	30.3	29.9	29.8	30.8	30.9	30.7	29.7	29.9	30.7	29.3	30.2
2009	29.9	31.0	30.4	29.6	29.3	29.9	29.5	30.2	29.4	29.2	29.8	29.2	29.8
2010	29.6	29.2	29.4	28.9	29.9	29.0	29.4	30.9	28.8	29.3	29.6	29.4	29.4
2011	30.4	29.5	28.9	29.1	30.0	29.0	29.7	29.6	29.2	30.0	28.9	28.4	29.4

3. Average Hourly Earnings by Selected Industry: Hawaii, 2007–2011

(Dollars, not seasonally adjusted)

Industry and year	January	February	March	April	May	June	July	August	September	October	November	December	Annual average
Total Private													
2007	20.63	20.38	20.62	20.65	20.65	20.62	20.64	20.61	20.78	20.66	20.67	21.17	20.68
2008	20.41	20.51	20.48	20.75	20.74	20.71	20.78	20.92	20.99	21.12	21.06	21.17	20.80
2009	21.01	21.12	21.12	20.94	20.84	20.93	21.04	21.10	21.30	21.18	21.37	21.46	21.11
2010	21.39	21.38	21.38	21.33	21.36	21.35	21.65	21.90	22.02	21.97	21.82	22.20	21.65
2011	22.46	22.23	22.16	22.12	22.23	22.14	22.14	22.04	22.00	22.08	21.97	22.20	22.15
Goods-Producing													
2007	27.13	28.07	27.92	27.87	28.32	28.43	28.16	28.33	28.50	27.83	28.90	29.63	28.26
2008	29.14	29.56	29.25	29.65	30.02	29.50	29.89	29.69	29.40	29.82	29.48	30.21	29.63
2009	29.60	29.62	29.82	30.07	29.85	29.93	29.86	29.71	30.07	29.92	29.96	30.09	29.87
2010	30.15	29.76	29.84	30.25	30.22	30.26	30.42	30.17	30.63	30.20	30.15	30.66	30.23
2011	30.21	30.22	30.55	30.51	30.41	30.22	30.47	30.31	30.31	29.88	29.56	29.83	30.21
Mining, Logging, and Construction													
2007	30.61	31.50	31.18	31.22	31.99	32.15	31.83	32.23	32.06	31.28	32.70	33.35	31.84
2008	32.50	32.91	32.66	33.31	33.73	33.17	33.43	33.35	32.87	33.49	33.07	33.34	33.15
2009	32.76	32.77	33.10	33.40	33.03	33.22	33.27	33.40	33.82	33.73	33.97	33.81	33.33
2010	33.95	33.40	33.70	33.98	33.97	34.13	34.22	34.00	34.57	34.41	34.07	34.79	34.10
2011	34.50	34.32	34.80	34.69	34.81	34.67	34.98	34.54	34.81	34.56	33.93	34.07	34.56
Manufacturing													
2007	18.13	19.16	19.06	18.62	19.05	19.23	18.85	18.60	19.11	18.93	19.23	20.13	19.01
2008	20.21	20.36	20.21	20.08	20.14	20.61	20.64	20.76	20.87	20.86	21.42	22.38	20.71
2009	21.72	21.86	21.74	22.01	22.07	21.96	21.42	21.21	21.65	21.31	21.34	21.67	21.67
2010	21.24	21.50	21.25	21.61	21.55	21.54	21.40	21.34	21.53	21.00	21.46	21.59	21.42
2011	21.10	20.82	20.93	20.66	20.81	20.32	20.33	20.41	20.13	19.81	20.19	20.26	20.48
Trade, Transportation, and Utilities													
2007	18.35	17.61	18.17	17.83	17.71	17.92	17.78	17.52	17.82	17.39	17.17	18.22	17.79
2008	17.75	17.57	17.67	17.52	17.65	17.88	17.96	18.43	18.21	18.55	18.25	18.34	17.97
2009	18.20	18.40	18.35	18.57	18.56	18.54	18.70	18.83	18.96	18.67	19.00	18.94	18.64
2010	19.22	19.16	19.29	19.40	19.21	19.23	19.74	20.09	19.63	19.49	19.38	19.58	19.45
2011	20.24	19.66	19.48	19.53	19.61	19.29	20.12	19.49	19.54	19.73	19.98	20.28	19.75
Professional and Business Services													
2007	18.35	17.61	18.17	17.83	17.71	17.92	17.78	17.52	17.82	17.39	17.17	18.22	17.79
2008	17.75	17.57	17.67	17.52	17.65	17.88	17.96	18.43	18.21	18.55	18.25	18.34	17.97
2009	18.20	18.40	18.35	18.57	18.56	18.54	18.70	18.83	18.96	18.67	19.00	18.94	18.64
2010	19.22	19.16	19.29	19.40	19.21	19.23	19.74	20.09	19.63	19.49	19.38	19.58	19.45
2011	20.24	19.66	19.48	19.53	19.61	19.29	20.12	19.49	19.54	19.73	19.98	20.28	19.75
Education and Health Services													
2007	22.96	22.82	23.24	23.06	23.19	22.63	22.77	22.66	22.79	23.12	23.05	23.29	22.96
2008	23.42	22.79	22.97	23.22	23.19	23.08	23.35	22.99	23.56	23.41	24.17	23.53	23.31
2009	22.76	22.71	23.05	22.86	22.56	22.40	22.13	21.98	22.01	22.17	22.19	22.05	22.41
2010	22.09	21.87	21.74	21.60	21.37	21.54	21.33	21.66	21.89	22.11	22.13	22.42	21.81
2011	22.54	22.40	22.73	22.83	23.07	22.83	23.39	23.38	23.65	23.92	24.35	24.64	23.32
Leisure and Hospitality													
2007	17.26	17.07	16.96	17.26	17.07	17.35	17.35	17.44	17.43	17.60	17.62	17.83	17.35
2008	17.51	17.89	17.72	17.71	17.37	17.16	17.16	17.35	17.29	17.48	17.08	17.07	17.40
2009	17.16	17.11	16.93	17.04	16.71	17.17	17.04	16.86	17.20	16.76	17.08	17.32	17.03
2010	16.92	16.89	16.50	16.30	16.29	16.59	16.49	16.51	16.69	16.46	16.47	16.56	16.55
2011	16.49	16.56	16.76	16.81	16.62	16.72	16.82	16.89	16.85	16.72	16.01	16.03	16.61

4. Average Weekly Earnings by Selected Industry: Hawaii, 2007–2011

(Dollars, not seasonally adjusted)

Industry and year	January	February	March	April	May	June	July	August	September	October	November	December	Annual average
Total Private													
2007	670.48	662.35	659.84	685.58	660.80	668.09	689.38	671.89	694.05	663.19	665.57	696.49	674.38
2008	667.41	670.68	679.94	678.53	669.90	685.50	675.35	681.99	677.98	680.06	694.98	675.32	678.14
2009	678.62	705.41	695.31	680.55	673.13	680.23	679.59	687.86	681.60	682.00	698.80	691.01	686.33
2010	690.90	690.57	688.44	691.09	713.42	696.01	710.12	740.22	717.85	720.62	717.88	741.48	709.93
2011	765.89	740.26	731.28	738.81	758.04	739.48	732.83	729.52	728.20	750.72	718.42	723.72	738.31
Goods-Producing													
2007	976.68	1,013.33	988.37	1,006.11	1,008.19	949.56	965.89	946.22	994.65	935.09	988.38	1,028.16	983.75
2008	1,028.64	1,102.59	1,096.88	1,079.26	1,092.73	1,056.10	1,088.00	1,092.59	1,081.92	1,073.52	1,034.75	1,066.41	1,074.29
2009	1,068.56	1,084.09	1,103.34	1,097.56	1,086.54	1,059.52	1,080.93	1,054.71	1,031.40	1,026.26	1,039.61	1,086.25	1,068.81
2010	1,094.45	1,062.43	1,065.29	1,101.10	1,115.12	1,092.39	1,152.92	1,161.55	1,148.63	1,099.28	1,088.42	1,162.01	1,111.92
2011	1,096.62	1,139.29	1,118.13	1,150.23	1,131.25	1,112.10	1,118.25	1,100.25	1,106.32	1,045.80	996.17	1,064.93	1,098.36
Mining, Logging, and Construction													
2007	1,120.33	1,152.90	1,131.83	1,155.14	1,138.84	1,064.17	1,085.40	1,063.59	1,122.10	1,044.75	1,108.53	1,150.58	1,111.05
2008	1,153.75	1,247.29	1,234.55	1,219.15	1,244.64	1,170.90	1,223.54	1,213.94	1,196.47	1,188.90	1,124.38	1,183.57	1,200.59
2009	1,195.74	1,212.49	1,241.25	1,232.46	1,225.41	1,189.28	1,224.34	1,192.38	1,163.41	1,163.69	1,168.57	1,234.07	1,204.21
2010	1,259.55	1,202.40	1,206.46	1,250.46	1,270.48	1,235.51	1,317.47	1,322.60	1,310.20	1,245.64	1,233.33	1,315.06	1,263.09
2011	1,252.35	1,328.18	1,301.52	1,349.44	1,298.41	1,279.32	1,297.76	1,288.34	1,298.41	1,202.69	1,157.01	1,240.15	1,274.10
Manufacturing													
2007	629.11	668.68	632.79	629.36	678.18	659.59	657.87	639.84	663.12	649.30	674.97	708.58	657.63
2008	701.29	726.85	743.73	718.86	704.90	760.51	738.91	782.65	790.97	780.16	811.82	778.82	752.85
2009	764.54	780.40	776.12	779.15	774.66	755.42	743.27	744.47	740.43	726.67	751.17	764.95	758.02
2010	739.15	754.65	756.50	764.99	775.80	773.29	787.52	804.52	783.69	777.00	774.71	820.42	775.66
2011	765.93	745.36	730.46	733.43	765.81	743.71	729.85	698.02	704.55	703.26	664.25	690.87	722.26
Trade, Transportation, and Utilities													
2007	601.88	589.94	594.16	611.57	587.97	609.28	622.30	597.43	627.26	586.04	583.78	623.12	602.93
2008	598.18	588.60	602.55	595.68	578.92	609.71	583.70	606.35	597.29	595.46	593.13	579.54	594.11
2009	595.14	612.72	611.06	612.81	603.20	621.09	613.36	630.81	642.74	632.91	644.10	621.23	619.96
2010	628.49	641.86	634.64	647.96	662.75	663.44	671.16	685.07	659.57	658.76	662.80	685.30	658.53
2011	710.42	670.41	662.32	665.97	692.23	663.58	692.13	666.56	672.18	692.52	679.32	691.55	680.05
Professional and Business Services													
2007	757.62	734.99	718.96	762.62	739.94	726.60	766.49	724.72	738.07	706.68	691.06	715.42	731.75
2008	722.22	696.02	723.86	698.99	691.72	709.69	682.31	682.97	697.06	694.14	730.38	709.69	703.25
2009	700.55	737.55	721.38	702.86	694.66	705.99	696.71	709.05	696.89	702.53	719.95	707.52	707.92
2010	713.07	721.58	744.58	733.50	779.19	761.12	763.62	799.60	786.57	805.30	806.39	796.02	767.76
2011	839.24	846.57	836.35	840.06	858.86	832.13	804.78	799.46	798.60	839.05	818.69	828.35	828.09
Education and Health Services													
2007	734.72	721.11	722.76	747.14	718.89	742.26	755.96	743.25	749.79	742.15	744.52	780.22	741.94
2008	770.52	752.07	758.01	754.65	751.36	763.95	765.88	751.77	756.28	753.80	802.44	734.14	759.57
2009	701.01	738.08	730.69	706.37	694.85	676.48	683.82	685.78	677.91	669.53	687.89	676.94	694.17
2010	660.49	656.10	647.85	656.64	660.33	646.20	646.30	664.96	669.83	663.30	666.11	690.54	660.63
2011	730.30	710.08	709.18	714.58	756.70	719.15	729.77	738.81	752.07	794.14	779.20	783.55	743.35
Leisure and Hospitality													
2007	519.53	510.39	503.71	531.61	501.86	523.97	544.79	523.20	533.36	515.68	519.79	540.25	522.35
2008	528.80	531.33	536.92	529.53	517.63	528.53	530.24	532.65	513.51	522.65	524.36	500.15	524.85
2009	513.08	530.41	514.67	504.38	489.60	513.38	502.68	509.17	505.68	489.39	508.98	505.74	507.31
2010	500.83	493.19	485.10	471.07	487.07	481.11	484.81	510.16	480.67	482.28	487.51	486.86	487.53
2011	501.30	488.52	484.36	489.17	498.60	484.88	499.55	499.94	492.02	501.60	462.69	455.25	488.02

IDAHO
At a Glance

Population:
    2000 census: 1,293,953
    2010 census: 1,567,582
    2011 estimate: 1,584,985

Percent change in population:
    2000–2010: 21.1%
    2010–2011: 1.1%

Percent change in total nonfarm employment:
    2000–2010: 7.9%
    2010–2011: 0.5%

Industry with the largest growth in employment, 2000–2011 (thousands):
    Education and Health Services, 33.9

Industry with the largest decline or smallest growth in employment, 2000–2011 (thousands):
    Manufacturing, -15.3

Civilian labor force:
    2000: 662,958
    2010: 763,498
    2011: 770,639

Unemployment rate and rank among states (lowest to highest):
    2000: 4.6%, 41st
    2010: 8.8%, 28th
    2011: 8.7%, 31st

Over-the-year change in unemployment rates:
2010–2011: -0.1%

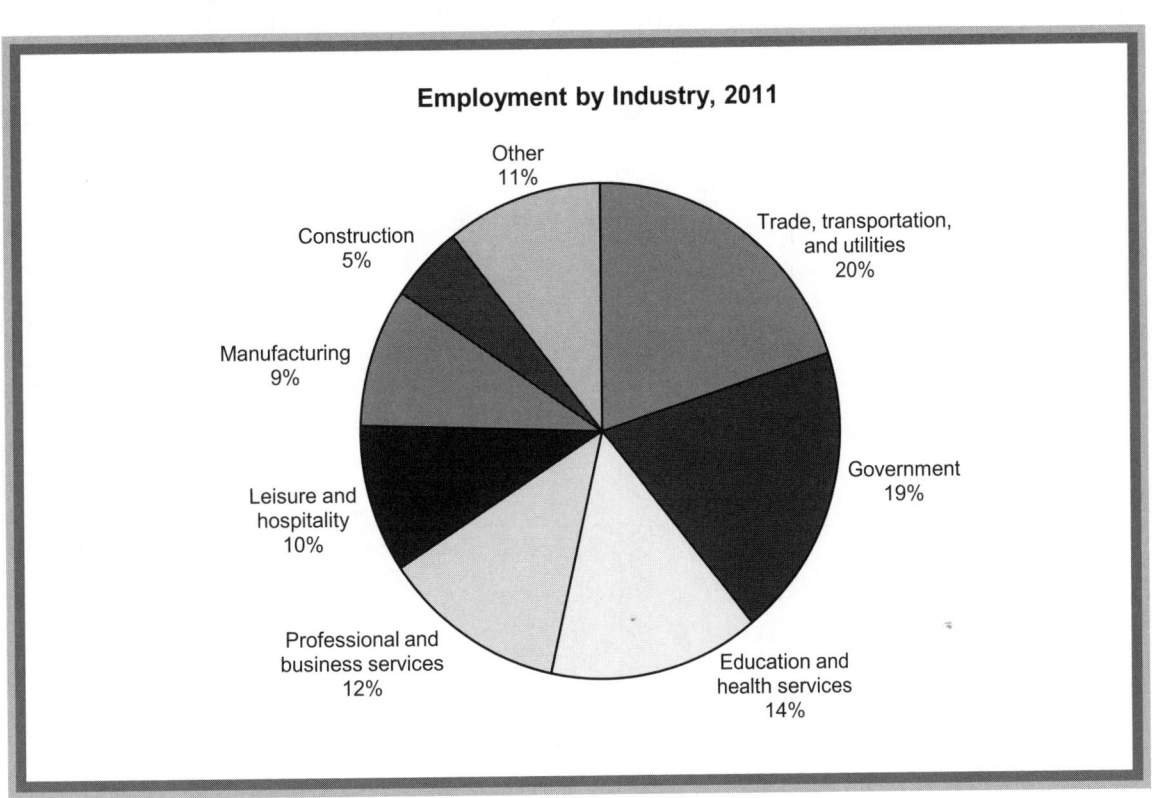

Employment by Industry, 2011

- Other 11%
- Trade, transportation, and utilities 20%
- Construction 5%
- Government 19%
- Manufacturing 9%
- Leisure and hospitality 10%
- Education and health services 14%
- Professional and business services 12%

1. Employment by Industry: Idaho, Selected Years, 2000–2011

(Numbers in thousands, not seasonally adjusted)

Industry and year	January	February	March	April	May	June	July	August	September	October	November	December	Annual average
Total Nonfarm													
2000	533.0	537.1	543.9	552.9	562.0	569.2	564.6	569.0	574.0	570.2	570.7	568.5	559.6
2001	549.3	553.7	561.0	565.2	571.1	578.9	572.3	576.3	578.0	572.5	568.7	565.6	567.7
2002	545.8	548.2	553.8	562.1	569.4	578.4	574.2	575.9	579.7	579.1	577.2	575.0	568.2
2003	555.3	556.5	561.2	564.8	571.5	580.4	574.9	578.2	583.1	581.0	578.6	578.2	572.0
2004	558.3	564.1	571.9	581.7	589.1	597.5	594.6	596.9	601.3	600.2	599.8	598.9	587.9
2005	581.5	588.5	594.4	603.2	609.5	617.9	617.5	621.1	628.4	624.0	624.6	625.0	611.3
2006	607.9	615.0	622.6	631.7	640.4	649.7	645.7	649.2	654.0	649.0	648.6	647.4	638.4
2007	628.2	635.5	642.3	649.8	659.6	668.7	661.6	665.3	666.9	661.6	661.3	658.3	654.9
2008	633.3	639.4	643.6	649.3	657.7	663.0	659.6	659.4	659.0	648.7	639.1	633.6	648.8
2009	606.7	605.5	604.1	607.8	612.8	618.1	610.9	611.0	614.2	612.9	608.7	605.5	609.9
2010	581.6	587.3	591.9	600.6	610.1	610.5	608.8	610.1	612.7	613.5	610.1	606.1	603.6
2011	585.9	592.5	595.2	604.6	609.9	612.7	611.4	611.5	616.3	616.9	612.9	611.4	606.8
Total Private													
2000	428.0	429.3	435.2	441.8	447.0	458.3	460.5	465.8	465.8	459.4	460.1	458.6	450.8
2001	443.7	444.0	450.2	453.9	458.6	468.2	467.1	471.8	466.8	458.6	455.3	453.0	457.6
2002	436.4	436.2	440.6	448.8	454.9	464.1	467.4	470.3	467.7	464.6	462.5	461.1	456.2
2003	444.7	443.9	447.1	451.5	456.0	465.3	467.1	471.4	469.2	465.1	463.2	463.6	459.0
2004	447.9	450.0	457.0	465.6	472.3	482.9	485.7	488.3	485.8	482.8	482.6	483.0	473.7
2005	469.4	472.6	477.8	486.4	492.1	501.8	508.4	512.3	511.7	505.9	506.8	508.5	496.1
2006	493.9	497.6	504.8	513.1	521.1	532.4	535.7	539.6	537.6	530.6	530.8	530.9	522.3
2007	515.1	518.7	525.1	531.6	540.4	550.8	551.0	553.5	547.8	542.1	542.3	539.6	538.2
2008	517.9	519.9	523.5	528.9	536.0	542.8	545.8	545.2	538.4	527.2	517.6	512.5	529.6
2009	489.0	485.9	483.0	484.3	489.9	496.2	498.4	498.1	495.6	491.5	487.7	485.0	490.4
2010	466.7	467.6	471.2	478.5	484.5	490.3	496.4	497.6	494.5	493.8	491.4	487.5	485.0
2011	472.8	473.8	476.0	483.9	488.7	495.3	501.1	502.5	500.5	498.5	495.7	495.2	490.3
Goods-Producing													
2000	105.0	104.8	106.0	107.9	110.5	114.5	115.3	116.3	115.8	114.4	114.0	111.7	111.4
2001	107.7	107.2	108.6	109.5	112.0	115.6	115.7	116.6	114.5	111.6	108.0	104.8	111.0
2002	100.0	98.8	99.6	101.8	105.5	108.8	110.5	111.0	110.0	109.2	107.8	105.7	105.7
2003	99.6	98.6	98.0	99.5	101.8	104.9	105.7	106.4	106.0	106.2	104.0	102.1	102.7
2004	97.9	97.9	99.8	103.1	105.5	108.8	110.4	111.4	110.4	110.6	109.1	107.7	106.1
2005	103.1	103.7	105.7	108.5	110.9	114.5	116.9	118.3	118.5	118.2	117.2	116.9	112.7
2006	112.4	113.5	115.9	118.8	122.4	127.1	128.1	128.4	127.8	126.0	124.5	122.6	122.3
2007	117.3	118.0	119.4	121.4	124.7	127.7	128.1	127.6	125.4	122.9	121.2	118.5	122.7
2008	111.6	110.2	110.7	112.0	114.6	116.7	117.2	116.5	114.8	111.8	106.5	102.9	112.1
2009	94.1	90.9	89.7	89.8	91.8	94.0	95.1	95.1	94.4	93.8	91.1	88.1	92.3
2010	83.3	82.6	83.4	85.4	87.6	89.9	91.3	92.2	91.6	91.6	89.7	86.2	87.9
2011	82.3	82.5	83.3	85.1	87.5	89.9	91.5	92.6	93.1	94.0	92.7	90.0	88.7
Mining and Logging													
2000	4.6	4.5	3.9	3.7	4.2	4.9	5.2	5.2	5.2	5.0	4.8	4.6	4.7
2001	4.2	4.1	3.6	3.1	3.4	4.2	4.6	4.7	4.6	4.4	4.1	3.9	4.1
2002	3.7	3.6	3.2	2.7	3.1	4.0	4.3	4.3	4.3	4.2	4.0	3.7	3.8
2003	3.5	3.2	2.9	2.7	3.1	3.7	4.1	4.2	4.2	4.1	3.9	3.6	3.6
2004	3.6	3.5	3.2	3.1	3.7	4.2	4.5	4.5	4.6	4.4	4.2	4.0	4.0
2005	3.8	3.6	3.5	3.4	3.8	4.3	4.5	4.7	4.7	4.6	4.3	4.2	4.1
2006	3.8	3.7	3.7	3.5	4.0	4.6	4.7	4.7	4.8	4.5	4.3	4.3	4.2
2007	4.0	4.0	3.8	3.6	4.3	4.8	4.9	5.0	4.9	4.7	4.6	4.4	4.4
2008	4.1	4.1	3.7	3.5	4.0	4.5	4.8	4.8	4.6	4.4	4.1	3.9	4.2
2009	3.4	3.2	2.7	2.5	2.7	3.2	3.6	3.7	3.7	3.6	3.4	3.2	3.2
2010	3.0	2.9	2.8	2.8	3.2	3.7	3.9	4.1	4.1	4.1	3.8	3.5	3.5
2011	3.4	3.4	3.3	3.0	3.2	3.8	4.1	4.2	4.2	4.1	3.9	3.7	3.7
Construction													
2000	31.4	31.2	32.6	34.9	36.5	38.7	39.3	40.1	39.7	38.5	37.6	36.0	36.4
2001	33.2	32.8	34.6	36.8	38.9	41.0	41.5	42.3	41.1	39.6	37.8	35.2	37.9
2002	31.5	31.0	31.9	34.4	37.3	38.6	40.0	40.1	39.4	39.0	38.0	36.8	36.5
2003	32.3	32.0	32.7	34.5	36.7	38.4	39.6	40.2	39.8	39.6	38.4	37.1	36.8
2004	33.6	33.5	35.4	38.3	40.1	41.8	43.0	43.7	43.0	42.8	42.1	41.1	39.9
2005	37.7	38.2	40.0	42.8	44.3	46.9	48.4	49.1	49.0	48.3	48.5	47.2	45.0
2006	44.4	45.4	47.4	50.1	52.8	55.9	56.2	56.5	55.6	54.3	53.5	51.4	52.0
2007	47.4	47.8	49.4	51.4	53.6	55.6	55.8	56.1	54.4	52.5	51.0	48.9	52.0
2008	43.3	42.1	43.2	44.8	46.9	48.2	48.5	48.2	47.1	45.0	42.2	39.8	44.9
2009	33.7	31.9	31.8	32.8	34.6	36.0	36.8	36.9	36.3	35.5	33.9	31.7	34.3
2010	28.1	27.6	28.6	30.2	31.8	32.9	33.9	34.2	33.7	32.9	31.8	29.4	31.3
2011	25.7	25.6	26.2	28.0	29.8	31.4	32.3	32.9	32.8	33.2	32.8	30.1	30.1
Manufacturing													
2000	69.0	69.1	69.5	69.3	69.8	70.9	70.8	71.0	70.9	70.9	71.6	71.1	70.3
2001	70.3	70.3	70.4	69.6	69.7	70.4	69.6	69.6	68.8	67.6	66.1	65.7	69.0
2002	64.8	64.2	64.5	64.7	65.1	66.2	66.2	66.6	66.3	66.0	65.8	65.2	65.5
2003	63.8	63.4	62.4	62.3	62.0	62.8	62.0	62.0	62.0	62.5	61.7	61.4	62.4
2004	60.7	60.9	61.2	61.7	61.7	62.8	62.9	63.2	62.8	63.4	62.8	62.6	62.2
2005	61.6	61.9	62.2	62.3	62.8	63.3	64.0	64.5	64.8	65.3	64.4	65.5	63.6
2006	64.2	64.4	64.8	65.2	65.6	66.6	67.2	67.2	67.4	67.2	66.7	66.9	66.1
2007	65.9	66.2	66.2	66.4	66.8	67.3	67.4	66.5	66.1	65.7	65.6	65.2	66.3
2008	64.2	64.0	63.8	63.7	63.7	64.0	63.9	63.5	63.1	62.4	60.2	59.2	63.0
2009	57.0	55.8	55.2	54.5	54.5	54.8	54.7	54.5	54.4	54.7	53.8	53.2	54.8
2010	52.2	52.1	52.0	52.4	52.6	53.3	53.5	53.9	53.8	53.8	54.6	54.1	53.3	53.2
2011	53.2	53.5	53.8	54.1	54.5	54.7	55.1	55.5	56.1	56.7	56.0	56.2	55.0

1. Employment by Industry: Idaho, Selected Years, 2000–2011—*Continued*

(Numbers in thousands, not seasonally adjusted)

Industry and year	January	February	March	April	May	June	July	August	September	October	November	December	Annual average
Service-Providing													
2000	428.0	432.3	437.9	445.0	451.5	454.7	449.3	452.7	458.2	455.8	456.7	456.8	448.2
2001	441.6	446.5	452.4	455.7	459.1	463.3	456.6	459.7	463.5	460.9	460.7	460.8	456.7
2002	445.8	449.4	454.2	460.3	463.9	469.6	463.7	464.9	469.7	469.9	469.4	469.3	462.5
2003	455.7	457.9	463.2	465.3	469.7	475.5	469.2	471.8	477.1	474.8	474.6	476.1	469.2
2004	460.4	466.2	472.1	478.6	483.6	488.7	484.2	485.5	490.9	489.6	490.7	491.2	481.8
2005	478.4	484.8	488.7	494.7	498.6	503.4	500.6	502.8	509.9	505.8	507.4	508.1	498.6
2006	495.5	501.5	506.7	512.9	518.0	522.6	517.6	520.8	526.2	523.0	524.1	524.8	516.1
2007	510.9	517.5	522.9	528.4	534.9	541.0	533.5	537.7	541.5	538.7	540.1	539.8	532.2
2008	521.7	529.2	532.9	537.3	543.1	546.3	542.4	542.9	544.2	536.9	532.6	530.7	536.7
2009	512.6	514.6	514.4	518.0	521.0	524.1	515.8	515.9	519.8	519.1	517.6	517.4	517.5
2010	498.3	504.7	508.5	515.2	522.5	520.6	517.5	517.9	521.1	521.9	520.4	519.9	515.7
2011	503.6	510.0	511.9	519.5	522.4	522.8	519.9	518.9	523.2	522.9	520.2	521.4	518.1
Trade, Transportation, and Utilities													
2000	117.0	116.3	117.5	119.1	120.4	122.2	122.6	124.5	124.5	124.2	125.5	125.3	121.6
2001	116.2	115.3	116.1	116.4	117.4	118.3	116.6	117.0	117.2	116.7	118.0	118.4	117.0
2002	113.7	112.8	113.5	114.8	116.0	116.8	116.6	117.1	117.2	116.9	118.6	119.1	116.1
2003	114.0	113.2	114.1	114.5	115.2	116.3	116.4	117.2	117.2	116.9	118.7	119.5	116.1
2004	114.1	113.7	114.9	116.6	118.1	119.1	119.5	119.5	119.3	119.9	121.8	122.9	118.3
2005	118.4	118.4	119.6	121.0	122.0	123.4	124.5	125.2	125.5	125.2	127.4	128.5	123.3
2006	123.6	123.3	124.4	126.0	127.3	129.0	128.8	129.8	130.2	130.3	132.6	133.6	128.2
2007	129.5	129.3	130.8	131.4	132.4	133.6	133.7	134.2	133.8	134.2	136.6	136.9	133.0
2008	131.4	130.6	131.1	131.6	132.6	133.3	133.9	133.7	132.3	131.6	132.0	131.8	132.2
2009	124.1	122.6	122.2	122.0	123.0	123.1	123.0	123.1	122.8	122.5	123.6	123.3	122.9
2010	119.0	117.9	118.5	119.9	121.1	121.7	122.3	123.3	122.1	122.8	124.0	124.1	121.4
2011	119.0	118.3	118.9	120.5	121.4	121.7	121.8	122.6	122.1	123.6	125.0	125.9	121.7
Wholesale Trade													
2000	24.7	24.7	25.0	25.3	25.4	25.6	25.5	25.4	25.7	25.4	25.4	25.4	25.3
2001	24.8	24.8	25.1	25.1	25.2	25.2	24.6	24.3	24.6	24.6	24.6	24.4	24.8
2002	23.9	24.1	24.3	24.5	24.7	24.8	24.6	24.4	24.7	24.5	24.7	24.4	24.5
2003	23.8	23.9	23.9	24.4	24.5	24.5	24.6	24.4	24.6	24.0	24.2	24.3	24.3
2004	23.8	24.0	24.4	24.7	24.9	25.1	25.4	25.4	25.5	25.4	25.5	25.4	25.0
2005	25.7	25.9	26.4	26.6	26.6	26.6	26.8	26.7	27.0	26.7	26.8	26.8	26.6
2006	26.1	26.4	26.7	27.0	27.1	27.3	27.1	27.1	27.3	27.1	27.4	27.4	27.0
2007	27.2	27.5	27.7	27.8	28.0	28.3	28.3	28.3	28.4	28.1	28.1	28.1	28.0
2008	27.6	27.7	27.9	27.8	28.0	28.1	28.3	28.0	28.1	27.8	27.5	27.3	27.8
2009	26.4	26.3	26.3	26.1	26.1	26.1	26.2	25.7	25.9	25.7	25.6	25.4	26.0
2010	25.1	25.1	25.4	25.8	26.0	26.1	26.3	26.3	26.1	26.3	26.0	25.9	25.9
2011	25.4	25.4	25.7	26.1	26.2	26.2	26.3	26.6	26.7	27.3	27.0	27.8	26.4
Retail Trade													
2000	73.4	72.7	73.7	74.9	76.1	77.1	77.6	79.1	78.9	78.8	80.3	79.6	76.9
2001	71.8	71.1	71.5	71.8	72.6	73.3	72.4	72.8	72.6	72.3	73.8	74.5	72.5
2002	70.9	69.7	70.3	71.3	72.2	72.7	72.9	73.1	72.8	72.5	74.2	75.0	72.3
2003	70.8	70.1	70.9	71.2	71.8	72.6	72.5	73.2	72.9	73.1	74.8	75.4	72.4
2004	71.0	70.5	71.1	72.5	73.7	74.2	74.4	74.4	74.0	74.6	76.4	77.4	73.7
2005	73.4	73.0	73.8	74.9	75.9	76.9	77.5	78.1	78.0	77.9	80.0	80.8	76.7
2006	77.3	76.6	77.5	78.5	79.7	80.7	80.9	81.6	81.7	82.0	83.9	84.5	80.4
2007	81.1	80.6	82.1	82.4	83.1	83.7	84.0	84.1	83.5	83.9	86.3	86.5	83.4
2008	82.4	81.5	82.0	82.4	83.1	83.4	83.8	83.6	82.2	81.7	82.6	82.4	82.6
2009	76.5	75.4	75.5	75.5	76.5	76.8	76.8	76.8	76.0	75.6	76.9	76.9	76.3
2010	73.4	72.4	73.1	74.0	74.9	75.2	75.5	76.0	74.9	75.3	76.7	76.6	74.8
2011	72.8	72.1	72.4	73.5	74.5	74.9	74.6	74.6	73.9	74.7	76.5	76.6	74.3
Transportation and Utilities													
2000	18.9	18.9	18.8	18.9	18.9	19.5	19.5	20.0	19.9	20.0	19.8	20.3	19.5
2001	19.6	19.4	19.5	19.5	19.6	19.8	19.6	19.9	20.0	19.8	19.6	19.5	19.7
2002	18.9	19.0	18.9	19.0	19.1	19.3	19.1	19.6	19.7	19.9	19.7	19.7	19.3
2003	19.4	19.2	19.3	18.9	18.9	19.2	19.3	19.6	19.7	19.8	19.7	19.8	19.4
2004	19.3	19.2	19.4	19.4	19.5	19.8	19.7	19.7	19.8	19.9	19.9	20.1	19.6
2005	19.3	19.5	19.4	19.5	19.5	19.9	20.2	20.4	20.5	20.6	20.6	20.9	20.0
2006	20.2	20.3	20.2	20.5	20.5	21.0	20.8	21.1	21.2	21.2	21.3	21.7	20.8
2007	21.2	21.2	21.0	21.2	21.3	21.6	21.4	21.8	21.9	22.2	22.2	22.3	21.6
2008	21.4	21.4	21.2	21.4	21.5	21.8	21.8	22.1	22.0	22.1	21.9	22.1	21.7
2009	21.2	20.9	20.4	20.4	20.4	20.2	20.0	20.6	20.9	21.2	21.1	21.0	20.7
2010	20.5	20.4	20.0	20.1	20.2	20.4	20.5	21.0	21.1	21.2	21.3	21.6	20.7
2011	20.8	20.8	20.8	20.9	20.7	20.6	20.9	21.4	21.5	21.6	21.5	21.5	21.1
Information													
2000	9.3	9.4	9.7	9.4	9.6	9.8	9.8	9.8	9.8	9.7	9.7	9.8	9.7
2001	9.6	9.7	9.7	9.6	9.6	9.8	9.7	9.8	9.5	9.4	9.4	9.4	9.6
2002	9.2	9.1	9.1	9.2	9.3	9.3	9.1	9.1	9.1	9.1	9.3	9.3	9.2
2003	9.1	9.1	9.1	9.2	9.2	9.2	9.1	9.1	9.1	9.1	9.3	9.3	9.2
2004	9.2	9.2	9.3	9.4	9.7	10.0	10.0	10.1	9.9	9.9	9.9	9.9	9.7
2005	10.0	10.1	10.1	10.3	10.4	10.4	10.5	10.3	10.3	10.5	10.4	10.6	10.3
2006	10.3	10.3	10.3	10.5	10.6	10.8	10.8	10.8	10.7	10.6	10.7	10.8	10.6
2007	10.6	10.6	10.7	10.8	10.9	11.0	10.9	11.0	10.8	10.9	11.0	11.0	10.9
2008	11.0	11.1	11.3	10.9	11.1	11.1	11.2	11.5	11.1	10.7	10.7	10.6	11.0
2009	10.4	10.5	10.3	10.0	10.0	10.1	10.0	9.8	9.7	9.7	9.8	9.8	10.0
2010	9.8	9.7	9.7	9.6	9.7	9.7	9.7	9.7	9.5	9.4	9.5	9.5	9.6
2011	9.4	9.3	9.3	9.5	9.5	9.5	9.5	9.5	9.3	9.2	9.3	9.3	9.4

1. Employment by Industry: Idaho, Selected Years, 2000–2011—*Continued*

(Numbers in thousands, not seasonally adjusted)

Industry and year	January	February	March	April	May	June	July	August	September	October	November	December	Annual average
Financial Activities													
2000	24.9	24.9	24.9	25.1	25.2	25.4	25.3	25.4	25.4	25.1	25.2	25.1	25.2
2001	24.2	24.2	24.5	24.8	24.9	25.2	25.4	25.7	25.2	25.1	25.1	25.4	25.0
2002	25.1	25.2	25.3	25.3	25.7	25.8	26.3	26.3	26.1	26.1	26.2	26.4	25.8
2003	26.1	26.1	26.3	26.5	26.8	27.2	27.5	27.6	27.4	27.4	27.3	27.6	27.0
2004	26.9	27.0	27.4	27.6	27.7	28.0	28.3	28.3	28.4	28.5	28.5	28.8	28.0
2005	28.3	28.5	28.4	28.8	29.1	29.6	30.2	30.4	30.5	30.5	30.7	30.8	29.7
2006	30.5	30.7	31.1	31.4	31.6	31.9	32.2	32.4	32.3	32.0	32.0	32.3	31.7
2007	31.8	31.9	32.0	32.3	32.7	32.7	33.0	32.8	32.4	32.3	32.5	32.4	32.4
2008	31.6	31.6	31.6	31.8	31.9	32.1	32.2	32.0	31.8	31.3	30.9	31.1	31.7
2009	30.1	30.0	29.8	29.8	29.7	29.7	29.7	29.5	29.2	29.3	29.2	29.4	29.6
2010	28.7	28.6	28.7	28.9	29.1	29.2	29.7	29.5	29.2	29.4	29.4	29.6	29.2
2011	29.2	29.2	29.2	29.4	29.5	29.5	29.4	29.6	29.5	29.5	29.2	29.2	29.4
Professional and Business Services													
2000	54.9	55.5	57.2	58.2	59.6	61.4	61.0	62.0	62.7	62.4	62.7	61.9	60.0
2001	63.3	63.2	65.1	66.0	67.5	68.7	68.4	70.4	68.9	67.8	67.4	66.4	66.9
2002	63.0	63.8	64.8	67.8	68.4	70.1	70.1	71.2	70.5	71.0	70.1	69.2	68.3
2003	65.5	66.3	67.5	68.6	69.2	70.8	70.0	71.4	71.2	70.2	69.8	69.6	69.2
2004	66.4	67.4	69.1	71.3	72.8	74.7	74.6	75.4	75.0	74.4	74.2	74.1	72.5
2005	70.8	72.6	73.8	76.3	77.3	78.4	79.1	80.0	79.9	78.2	78.6	78.1	76.9
2006	75.3	76.6	78.1	80.2	81.9	83.2	82.6	83.6	83.1	81.2	81.2	80.3	80.6
2007	76.8	78.1	79.5	82.2	83.5	85.3	84.5	85.7	85.1	83.9	83.2	82.4	82.5
2008	76.4	78.0	78.8	81.7	82.7	83.3	83.3	84.0	82.5	80.4	78.3	77.3	80.6
2009	73.8	73.5	72.8	73.7	74.5	75.3	75.4	75.9	76.0	75.5	74.9	74.6	74.7
2010	70.0	70.5	71.5	73.4	74.2	74.4	75.7	76.3	75.6	76.2	76.0	75.2	74.1
2011	72.4	72.5	72.9	74.1	74.6	75.4	76.9	77.4	76.1	75.8	74.5	74.9	74.8
Education and Health Services													
2000	51.3	51.9	52.2	52.3	51.4	51.8	51.7	52.3	53.9	54.3	54.7	55.3	52.8
2001	54.9	55.8	56.2	57.0	55.7	56.1	56.0	56.6	58.1	58.5	59.1	59.6	57.0
2002	58.6	58.9	59.4	59.8	58.9	59.1	59.0	59.1	60.4	60.8	61.3	61.6	59.7
2003	61.3	61.4	61.7	62.3	61.6	61.8	61.6	61.8	63.2	63.4	64.0	64.1	62.4
2004	63.2	64.0	64.6	65.2	64.4	65.0	64.4	64.6	66.3	67.0	67.6	67.3	65.3
2005	66.9	67.5	67.4	67.8	67.0	67.1	66.6	67.1	68.4	68.3	68.6	68.6	67.6
2006	67.8	68.5	69.2	69.2	68.8	68.8	69.9	70.4	71.8	72.1	72.7	72.7	70.2
2007	71.7	72.5	72.8	72.9	73.3	73.8	73.3	73.8	74.4	75.8	76.7	76.7	74.0
2008	75.9	77.0	77.5	77.5	77.3	77.5	77.6	76.3	78.0	79.2	79.3	79.6	77.7
2009	78.7	80.2	80.2	80.7	80.6	80.8	80.5	79.6	81.6	82.8	83.0	83.2	81.0
2010	80.9	83.0	83.5	83.8	84.0	83.6	83.6	81.9	84.3	85.7	85.9	85.7	83.8
2011	85.4	86.2	86.2	86.5	86.7	86.7	86.7	85.1	87.1	87.7	87.6	88.5	86.7
Leisure and Hospitality													
2000	48.5	49.2	50.2	52.1	52.2	55.1	56.7	57.3	55.8	51.6	50.6	51.4	52.6
2001	50.0	50.6	51.7	52.3	53.2	55.9	56.8	57.2	55.3	51.7	50.6	51.3	53.1
2002	49.5	50.0	50.8	52.1	53.1	56.0	57.2	57.8	56.3	53.4	51.2	51.9	53.3
2003	51.4	51.4	52.4	52.8	54.1	56.8	58.3	59.2	56.9	53.9	52.1	53.4	54.4
2004	52.5	53.0	53.8	54.0	55.7	58.7	59.6	60.1	58.2	54.4	53.4	54.2	55.6
2005	54.0	53.7	54.7	55.4	57.0	59.8	61.5	62.0	60.1	56.5	55.4	56.6	57.2
2006	55.7	56.2	57.2	58.2	59.6	62.3	63.6	64.5	62.5	59.4	58.2	59.6	59.8
2007	58.7	59.4	60.7	61.3	63.4	66.9	67.6	68.3	66.3	62.7	61.8	62.3	63.3
2008	60.5	61.3	61.9	62.1	64.3	66.8	68.2	68.9	66.1	61.2	59.1	58.4	63.2
2009	56.7	56.9	56.8	57.1	58.9	61.5	63.0	63.3	60.8	57.3	55.6	56.1	58.7
2010	54.2	54.3	54.9	56.6	57.8	60.6	62.3	63.2	61.2	57.8	56.1	56.5	58.0
2011	54.6	55.2	55.7	57.9	58.5	61.4	63.7	64.4	62.1	57.7	56.3	56.5	58.7
Other Services													
2000	17.1	17.3	17.5	17.7	18.1	18.1	18.1	18.2	17.9	17.7	17.7	18.1	17.8
2001	17.8	18.0	18.3	18.3	18.3	18.6	18.5	18.5	18.1	17.8	17.7	17.7	18.1
2002	17.3	17.6	18.1	18.0	18.0	18.2	18.6	18.7	18.1	18.1	17.9	18.1
2003	17.7	17.8	18.0	18.1	18.1	18.3	18.5	18.7	18.2	18.0	18.0	17.9	18.1
2004	17.7	17.8	18.1	18.4	18.4	18.6	18.9	18.9	18.3	18.1	18.1	18.1	18.3
2005	17.9	18.1	18.1	18.3	18.4	18.6	19.1	19.0	18.5	18.5	18.5	18.4	18.5
2006	18.3	18.5	18.6	18.8	18.9	19.3	19.7	19.7	19.2	19.0	18.9	19.0	19.0
2007	18.7	18.9	19.2	19.3	19.5	19.8	19.9	20.1	19.6	19.4	19.3	19.4	19.4
2008	19.5	20.1	20.6	21.3	21.5	22.0	22.2	22.3	21.8	21.0	20.8	20.8	21.2
2009	21.1	21.3	21.2	21.2	21.4	21.7	21.7	21.8	21.1	20.6	20.5	20.5	21.2
2010	20.8	21.0	21.0	20.9	21.0	21.2	21.8	21.5	21.0	20.9	20.8	20.7	21.1
2011	20.5	20.6	20.5	20.9	21.0	21.2	21.6	21.3	21.2	21.0	21.1	20.9	21.0
Government													
2000	105.0	107.8	108.7	111.1	115.0	110.9	104.1	103.2	108.2	110.8	110.6	109.9	108.8
2001	105.6	109.7	110.8	111.3	112.5	110.7	105.2	104.5	111.2	113.9	113.4	112.6	110.1
2002	109.4	112.0	113.2	113.3	114.5	114.3	106.8	105.6	112.0	114.5	114.7	113.9	112.0
2003	110.6	112.6	114.1	113.3	115.5	115.1	107.8	106.8	113.9	115.9	115.4	114.6	113.0
2004	110.4	114.1	114.9	116.1	116.8	114.6	108.9	108.6	115.5	117.4	117.2	115.9	114.2
2005	112.1	115.9	116.6	116.8	117.4	116.1	109.1	108.8	116.7	118.1	117.8	116.5	115.2
2006	114.0	117.4	117.8	118.6	119.3	117.3	110.0	109.6	116.4	118.4	117.8	116.5	116.1
2007	113.1	116.8	117.2	118.2	119.2	117.9	110.6	111.8	119.1	119.5	119.0	118.7	116.8
2008	115.4	119.5	120.1	120.4	121.7	120.2	113.8	114.2	120.6	121.5	121.5	121.1	119.2
2009	117.7	119.6	121.1	123.5	122.9	121.9	112.5	112.9	118.6	121.4	121.0	120.5	119.5
2010	114.9	119.7	120.7	122.1	125.6	120.2	112.4	112.5	118.2	119.7	118.7	118.6	118.6
2011	113.1	118.7	119.2	120.7	121.2	117.4	110.3	109.0	115.8	118.4	117.2	116.2	116.4

2. Average Weekly Hours by Selected Industry: Idaho, 2007–2011

(Not seasonally adjusted)

Industry and year	January	February	March	April	May	June	July	August	September	October	November	December	Annual average
Total Private													
2007	33.9	33.8	33.7	34.8	34.4	34.4	34.5	34.7	35.0	34.3	33.9	34.2	34.3
2008	33.5	33.5	34.0	33.6	33.7	34.9	34.5	34.3	34.4	33.7	33.4	33.0	33.9
2009	32.7	33.3	33.3	33.1	33.4	33.3	33.9	35.0	33.7	33.9	34.2	33.2	33.6
2010	33.2	33.1	33.0	33.3	33.4	33.2	33.6	34.4	33.6	33.6	33.5	33.6	33.5
2011	34.1	33.3	33.0	33.7	34.2	34.1	34.0	33.9	33.7	34.6	33.9	33.8	33.9
Goods-Producing													
2007	36.5	36.7	36.9	37.0	37.6	37.6	36.6	37.7	38.1	37.5	37.1	37.2	37.2
2008	35.9	36.3	36.1	36.4	36.8	37.4	36.9	36.9	38.0	37.2	34.9	35.3	36.5
2009	34.4	35.2	35.3	35.0	36.1	36.2	37.1	38.2	36.9	38.0	37.7	35.7	36.3
2010	35.3	36.1	36.7	36.0	36.3	36.3	36.7	37.0	38.5	38.3	38.2	38.4	39.8	37.3
2011	40.9	40.0	39.8	40.3	40.4	40.3	39.6	40.1	39.8	40.4	39.2	39.7	40.0
Construction													
2007	33.2	34.4	35.1	36.7	38.1	38.0	36.8	37.6	38.4	37.5	37.2	36.2	36.7
2008	34.0	35.0	32.3	33.7	35.4	36.4	36.0	34.9	36.1	34.3	32.7	32.1	34.5
2009	29.9	30.7	31.4	31.3	33.4	33.7	35.1	37.1	33.6	34.7	33.4	33.9	33.3
2010	31.9	33.0	35.4	34.5	33.2	34.8	35.7	36.8	36.4	36.5	36.9	35.0	35.0
2011	34.4	34.0	33.9	36.0	35.2	36.7	35.6	37.5	36.9	38.3	35.3	35.9	35.9
Manufacturing													
2007	37.7	37.4	37.5	36.8	37.0	37.0	35.9	37.1	37.4	37.0	37.1	37.3	37.1
2008	36.4	36.5	37.5	37.3	37.2	37.6	37.1	37.7	38.8	38.5	35.8	36.7	37.3
2009	36.3	37.3	37.0	36.7	37.0	37.2	37.6	38.1	38.0	39.1	39.7	38.2	37.7
2010	38.3	38.3	38.9	39.0	39.3	38.4	38.6	40.0	39.9	39.5	39.4	38.8	39.1
2011	40.6	39.5	39.6	39.9	40.6	40.0	39.4	39.3	39.4	40.0	39.4	40.0	39.8
Trade, Transportation, and Utilities													
2007	35.1	34.8	34.3	35.5	35.1	35.2	35.5	35.8	35.9	35.1	35.1	35.0	35.2
2008	34.2	34.2	34.9	34.6	34.7	35.5	35.7	36.0	35.2	34.5	34.5	34.6	34.9
2009	34.1	34.4	34.0	34.2	34.4	34.8	34.8	35.1	33.6	33.5	34.4	33.1	34.2
2010	32.9	32.7	31.7	32.7	33.6	33.5	33.9	34.8	34.0	33.9	33.9	34.0	33.5
2011	34.0	33.2	33.4	34.5	34.6	35.1	34.9	34.6	34.5	35.1	34.6	34.7	34.4
Financial Activities													
2007	37.3	35.8	35.6	37.5	35.1	34.8	37.1	34.7	36.2	35.4	35.7	37.5	36.1
2008	36.5	36.9	37.4	36.5	36.3	37.3	36.6	36.7	36.1	35.8	37.4	36.3	36.6
2009	37.2	37.4	37.2	36.5	36.1	35.9	36.7	38.1	37.0	37.0	38.0	36.5	36.9
2010	37.8	36.9	36.2	35.7	36.6	35.9	35.9	37.4	36.1	35.4	35.7	35.3	36.2
2011	36.5	36.3	35.7	36.2	37.1	36.3	36.4	36.5	36.5	37.6	36.1	35.9	36.4
Professional and Business Services													
2007	35.1	34.2	34.7	36.4	35.0	35.3	35.5	35.5	35.8	34.4	34.3	34.6	35.1
2008	34.0	33.9	34.6	34.7	34.5	36.0	35.7	35.0	35.7	34.4	34.3	33.6	34.7
2009	33.5	34.3	34.4	34.3	34.7	34.5	34.5	34.6	34.4	33.3	34.3	33.3	34.2
2010	33.8	33.3	34.0	34.6	33.3	33.1	33.7	34.4	33.9	33.8	34.0	33.7	33.8
2011	33.3	33.8	33.5	34.6	35.0	35.1	34.7	34.4	34.7	35.2	34.4	34.0	34.4
Education and Health Services													
2007	29.8	31.1	29.9	31.5	31.1	30.6	30.5	29.6	30.4	30.8	30.6	30.3	30.5
2008	29.9	30.0	30.8	30.0	30.4	31.6	31.3	31.1	31.4	31.4	32.4	30.6	30.9
2009	31.1	31.4	31.6	31.4	31.7	31.3	33.3	33.5	32.0	33.0	33.4	33.9	32.3
2010	34.3	33.4	33.0	33.2	33.3	32.9	32.4	32.5	31.9	32.6	32.2	32.0	32.8
2011	32.8	32.0	31.5	32.0	32.5	32.1	32.0	31.4	31.3	32.3	32.1	32.0	32.0
Leisure and Hospitality													
2007	23.9	24.0	24.7	26.4	26.2	26.6	27.7	27.4	27.5	26.0	25.9	26.5	26.1
2008	25.7	26.0	27.5	26.0	26.2	28.4	28.9	29.1	26.9	26.3	25.5	24.4	26.8
2009	23.8	25.7	25.6	24.2	25.2	23.9	24.5	25.4	23.2	22.8	21.5	21.5	24.0
2010	21.3	22.1	21.8	21.8	23.7	22.9	23.6	25.1	22.7	22.5	21.8	21.5	22.6
2011	22.1	21.6	21.0	21.2	22.4	21.8	23.1	23.0	22.0	23.6	22.3	21.9	22.2

3. Average Hourly Earnings by Selected Industry: Idaho, 2007–2011

(Dollars, not seasonally adjusted)

Industry and year	January	February	March	April	May	June	July	August	September	October	November	December	Annual average
Total Private													
2007	15.93	15.94	16.05	16.05	16.10	16.35	16.36	16.42	17.19	17.22	17.25	17.22	16.51
2008	17.08	16.98	17.12	17.26	17.41	17.53	17.81	17.65	17.98	17.75	17.74	18.00	17.53
2009	18.38	18.88	19.04	19.02	19.03	19.07	19.23	19.26	19.52	19.70	19.95	19.96	19.26
2010	20.38	20.68	20.99	20.92	20.98	20.76	22.05	21.09	20.97	21.07	21.17	21.26	21.03
2011	21.09	21.16	21.03	20.78	20.64	20.43	20.79	20.50	20.82	20.82	20.71	20.77	20.79
Goods-Producing													
2007	19.43	19.70	19.62	19.80	19.94	20.02	20.50	20.79	20.82	20.97	21.03	21.08	20.32
2008	20.90	20.54	20.66	20.67	20.78	20.81	21.01	20.98	21.29	21.29	21.37	22.06	21.02
2009	22.34	22.65	22.90	23.07	22.44	22.29	22.59	22.54	22.88	22.75	22.90	22.98	22.69
2010	23.47	24.14	24.28	24.12	24.10	23.87	24.20	24.05	24.14	24.38	24.30	23.82	24.08
2011	23.48	23.64	23.74	23.53	23.16	23.14	23.15	23.28	23.54	23.42	23.43	23.78	23.44
Construction													
2007	16.09	16.42	16.39	16.64	16.87	17.06	16.80	16.95	17.71	17.87	17.83	17.87	17.07
2008	17.54	17.22	17.46	17.29	17.45	17.40	17.60	17.65	17.92	18.15	18.05	18.16	17.65
2009	18.36	19.13	19.56	19.25	18.47	18.64	18.68	19.08	19.28	19.46	19.44	19.81	19.09
2010	19.12	20.20	20.61	20.87	21.17	21.08	21.18	21.50	21.97	21.53	21.47	22.05	21.12
2011	21.64	21.46	21.55	21.82	20.96	21.22	20.92	21.29	21.45	21.28	20.76	21.85	21.33
Manufacturing													
2007	21.68	21.87	21.74	21.97	22.11	22.33	22.56	22.81	22.67	22.55	22.61	22.72	22.30
2008	22.48	22.06	22.25	22.41	22.46	22.45	22.64	22.50	22.70	22.73	22.81	22.94	22.53
2009	23.20	23.58	23.62	24.10	24.07	23.85	24.31	24.17	24.43	23.99	24.24	24.20	23.98
2010	24.89	25.26	25.17	24.99	25.11	24.93	25.60	25.21	25.22	25.21	25.15	25.66	25.20
2011	25.16	25.13	25.19	24.91	24.50	24.42	24.64	24.65	24.89	24.71	24.79	24.79	24.81
Trade, Transportation, and Utilities													
2007	14.72	14.85	14.97	14.84	14.93	15.16	15.04	15.16	16.07	15.76	15.76	15.87	15.27
2008	15.91	15.84	15.52	16.08	15.88	15.94	16.00	16.12	16.34	16.32	16.39	16.47	16.07
2009	17.05	17.25	17.44	17.03	17.40	17.34	17.50	17.55	17.70	17.58	17.61	17.53	17.41
2010	17.76	18.20	17.81	17.69	17.75	17.70	17.71	17.81	17.61	17.70	17.52	17.45	17.72
2011	17.65	17.61	17.64	17.63	17.48	17.18	17.67	17.19	17.38	17.60	17.20	17.23	17.45
Financial Activities													
2007	19.61	19.52	19.67	19.78	19.78	19.69	19.74	19.05	19.44	19.44	19.41	19.37	19.54
2008	20.02	19.84	19.77	19.99	20.12	19.80	20.09	19.87	19.84	20.15	20.24	20.26	20.00
2009	20.41	20.28	20.30	20.85	20.56	20.81	21.56	21.97	21.06	21.41	21.01	21.01	20.94
2010	21.58	21.56	21.95	21.46	21.89	21.28	21.47	21.76	21.41	21.23	21.68	22.30	21.63
2011	20.78	20.31	20.60	20.41	20.84	20.39	20.73	20.26	20.77	20.87	20.78	20.62	20.61
Professional and Business Services													
2007	19.07	19.22	19.90	19.85	20.22	20.62	20.68	21.75	22.12	23.11	23.07	23.01	21.08
2008	22.96	22.89	23.10	23.25	23.34	23.39	22.59	22.26	22.50	21.31	21.41	21.52	22.56
2009	22.10	22.93	23.32	23.64	23.77	24.22	24.40	25.19	25.28	25.85	26.48	26.53	24.48
2010	27.09	27.21	28.15	28.23	28.31	27.80	32.07	27.93	27.21	27.23	27.32	27.58	28.02
2011	28.12	28.33	27.77	27.11	26.74	26.43	27.10	27.18	28.18	27.80	27.97	27.54	27.51
Education and Health Services													
2007	15.49	15.42	15.68	15.73	15.77	15.99	16.06	16.30	16.35	16.44	16.54	16.54	16.03
2008	16.51	16.42	16.52	16.71	16.83	16.83	17.04	17.21	17.40	17.50	17.65	17.76	17.04
2009	17.48	18.45	18.58	18.62	18.39	17.67	17.15	16.48	17.10	17.36	17.94	17.78	17.74
2010	18.44	18.22	18.44	18.57	19.55	19.37	19.45	20.31	20.47	20.28	20.61	20.73	19.53
2011	20.38	20.72	20.31	19.83	19.86	19.98	20.26	19.48	19.94	19.83	19.88	20.22	20.06
Leisure and Hospitality													
2007	9.57	9.56	9.67	9.61	9.69	9.87	9.86	9.89	9.82	9.75	9.82	9.94	9.76
2008	9.86	9.89	10.01	10.06	10.25	10.49	9.98	9.89	10.05	10.02	10.07	10.12	10.06
2009	10.11	10.38	10.36	10.39	10.65	10.42	10.23	10.33	10.18	10.53	10.69	10.66	10.40
2010	10.72	10.54	10.71	10.80	11.00	10.91	11.03	11.50	11.38	11.18	11.55	11.52	11.08
2011	11.37	11.41	11.47	11.38	11.46	11.07	11.48	11.43	11.44	11.53	11.61	11.77	11.45

4. Average Weekly Earnings by Selected Industry: Idaho, 2007–2011

(Dollars, not seasonally adjusted)

Industry and year	January	February	March	April	May	June	July	August	September	October	November	December	Annual average
Total Private													
2007	540.03	538.77	540.89	558.54	553.84	562.44	564.42	569.77	601.65	590.65	584.78	588.92	566.64
2008	572.18	568.83	582.08	579.94	586.72	611.80	614.45	605.40	618.51	598.18	592.52	594.00	593.97
2009	601.03	628.70	634.03	629.56	635.60	635.03	651.90	674.10	657.82	667.83	682.29	662.67	646.85
2010	676.62	684.51	692.67	696.64	700.73	689.23	740.88	725.50	704.59	707.95	709.20	714.34	703.81
2011	719.17	704.63	693.99	700.29	705.89	696.66	706.86	694.95	701.63	720.37	702.07	702.03	703.99
Goods-Producing													
2007	709.20	722.99	723.98	732.60	749.74	752.75	750.30	783.78	793.24	786.38	780.21	784.18	756.17
2008	750.31	745.60	745.83	752.39	764.70	778.29	775.27	774.16	809.02	791.99	745.81	778.72	767.91
2009	768.50	797.28	808.37	807.45	810.08	806.90	838.09	861.03	844.27	864.50	863.33	820.39	824.53
2010	828.49	871.45	891.08	868.32	874.83	876.03	895.40	925.93	924.56	931.32	933.12	948.04	897.87
2011	960.33	945.60	944.85	948.26	935.66	932.54	916.74	933.53	936.89	946.17	918.46	944.07	938.24
Construction													
2007	534.19	564.85	575.29	610.69	642.75	648.28	618.24	637.32	680.06	670.13	663.28	646.89	625.92
2008	596.36	602.70	563.96	582.67	617.73	633.36	633.60	615.99	646.91	622.55	590.24	582.94	608.52
2009	548.96	587.29	614.18	602.53	616.90	628.17	655.67	707.87	647.81	675.26	649.30	671.56	634.83
2010	609.93	666.60	729.59	720.02	702.84	733.58	756.13	791.20	799.71	785.85	792.24	771.75	739.87
2011	744.42	729.64	730.55	785.52	737.79	778.77	744.75	798.38	791.51	815.02	732.83	784.42	765.47
Manufacturing													
2007	817.34	817.94	815.25	808.50	818.07	826.21	809.90	846.25	847.86	834.35	838.83	847.46	827.26
2008	818.27	805.19	834.38	835.89	835.51	844.12	839.94	848.25	880.76	875.11	816.60	841.90	839.63
2009	842.16	879.53	873.94	884.47	890.59	887.22	914.06	920.88	928.34	938.01	962.33	924.44	903.51
2010	953.29	967.46	979.11	974.61	986.82	957.31	988.16	1,008.40	1,006.28	995.80	990.91	995.61	984.33
2011	1,021.50	992.64	997.52	993.91	994.70	976.80	970.82	968.75	980.67	988.40	976.73	991.60	987.68
Trade, Transportation, and Utilities													
2007	516.67	516.78	513.47	526.82	524.04	533.63	533.92	542.73	576.91	553.18	553.18	555.45	537.49
2008	544.12	541.73	541.65	556.37	551.04	565.87	571.20	580.32	575.17	563.04	565.46	569.86	560.56
2009	581.41	593.40	592.96	582.43	598.56	603.43	609.00	616.01	594.72	588.93	605.78	580.24	595.66
2010	584.30	595.14	564.58	578.46	596.40	592.95	600.37	619.79	598.74	600.03	593.93	593.30	593.31
2011	600.10	584.65	589.18	608.24	604.81	603.02	616.68	594.77	599.61	617.76	595.12	597.88	601.07
Financial Activities													
2007	731.45	698.82	700.25	741.75	694.28	685.21	732.35	661.04	703.73	688.18	692.94	726.38	704.63
2008	730.73	732.10	739.40	729.64	730.36	738.54	735.29	729.23	716.22	721.37	756.98	735.44	732.90
2009	759.25	758.47	755.16	761.03	742.22	747.08	791.25	837.06	779.22	792.17	798.38	766.87	773.05
2010	815.72	795.56	794.59	766.12	801.17	763.95	770.77	813.82	772.90	751.54	773.98	787.19	783.87
2011	758.47	737.25	735.42	738.84	773.16	740.16	754.57	739.49	758.11	784.71	750.16	740.26	750.84
Professional and Business Services													
2007	669.36	657.32	690.53	722.54	707.70	727.89	734.14	772.13	791.90	794.98	791.30	796.15	739.19
2008	780.64	775.97	799.26	806.78	805.23	842.04	806.46	779.10	803.25	733.06	734.36	723.07	783.10
2009	740.35	786.50	802.21	810.85	824.82	835.59	841.80	871.57	869.63	860.81	908.26	883.45	836.66
2010	915.64	906.09	957.10	976.76	942.72	920.18	1,080.76	960.79	922.42	920.37	928.88	929.45	946.92
2011	936.40	957.55	930.30	938.01	935.90	927.69	940.37	934.99	977.85	978.56	962.17	936.36	946.63
Education and Health Services													
2007	461.60	479.56	468.83	495.50	490.45	489.29	489.83	482.48	497.04	506.35	506.12	501.16	489.25
2008	493.65	492.60	508.82	501.30	511.63	531.83	533.35	535.23	546.36	549.50	571.86	543.46	526.88
2009	543.63	579.33	587.13	584.67	582.96	553.07	571.10	552.08	547.20	572.88	599.20	602.74	573.20
2010	632.49	608.55	608.52	616.52	651.02	637.27	630.18	660.08	652.99	661.13	663.64	663.36	640.72
2011	668.46	663.04	639.77	634.56	645.45	641.36	648.32	611.67	624.12	640.51	638.15	647.04	641.78
Leisure and Hospitality													
2007	228.72	229.44	238.85	253.70	253.88	262.54	273.12	270.99	270.05	253.50	254.34	263.41	255.02
2008	253.40	257.14	275.28	261.56	268.55	297.92	288.42	287.80	270.35	263.53	256.79	246.93	269.69
2009	240.62	266.77	265.22	251.44	268.38	249.04	250.64	262.38	236.18	240.08	229.84	229.19	249.35
2010	228.34	232.93	233.48	235.44	260.70	249.84	260.31	288.65	258.33	251.55	251.79	247.68	250.64
2011	251.28	246.46	240.87	241.26	256.70	241.33	265.19	262.89	251.68	272.11	258.90	257.76	253.88

ILLINOIS
At a Glance

Population:
    2000 census: 12,419,927
    2010 census: 12,830,632
    2011 estimate: 12,869,257

Percent change in population:
    2000–2010: 3.3%
    2010–2011: 0.3%

Percent change in total nonfarm employment:
    2000–2010: -7.1%
    2010–2011: 0.9%

Industry with the largest growth in employment, 2000–2011 (thousands):
    Education and Health Services, 168.6

Industry with the largest decline or smallest growth in employment, 2000–2011 (thousands):
    Manufacturing, -296.6

Civilian labor force:
    2000: 6,467,692
    2010: 6,602,659
    2011: 6,565,504

Unemployment rate and rank among states (lowest to highest):
    2000: 4.5%, 38th
    2010: 10.5%, 41st
    2011: 9.8%, 41st

Over-the-year change in unemployment rates:
    2010–2011: -0.7%

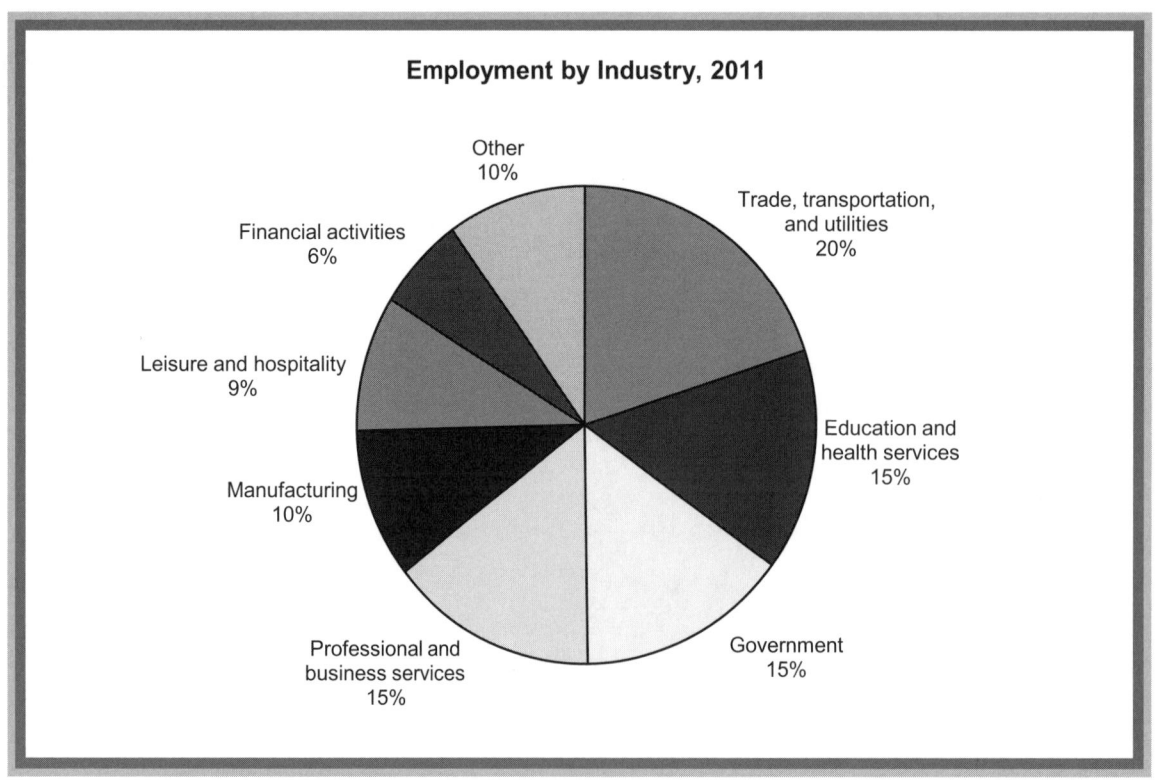

Employment by Industry, 2011

Other 10%

Financial activities 6%

Leisure and hospitality 9%

Manufacturing 10%

Professional and business services 15%

Trade, transportation, and utilities 20%

Education and health services 15%

Government 15%

1. Employment by Industry: Illinois, Selected Years, 2000–2011

(Numbers in thousands, not seasonally adjusted)

Industry and year	January	February	March	April	May	June	July	August	September	October	November	December	Annual average
Total Nonfarm													
2000	5,874.4	5,906.8	5,973.3	6,025.9	6,078.8	6,124.8	6,061.6	6,080.5	6,095.3	6,092.5	6,115.2	6,108.5	6,044.8
2001	5,906.2	5,930.3	5,977.0	6,016.0	6,060.4	6,093.1	6,013.3	6,012.8	6,006.1	5,976.1	5,977.2	5,974.4	5,995.2
2002	5,778.6	5,781.4	5,819.3	5,875.3	5,921.8	5,948.7	5,897.0	5,910.8	5,914.5	5,914.1	5,926.8	5,918.3	5,883.9
2003	5,713.0	5,712.1	5,742.5	5,797.6	5,843.1	5,869.6	5,829.7	5,839.2	5,843.1	5,845.7	5,842.4	5,851.7	5,810.8
2004	5,666.8	5,673.3	5,723.9	5,789.2	5,842.7	5,877.9	5,855.2	5,855.0	5,854.9	5,872.1	5,882.2	5,897.6	5,815.9
2005	5,700.8	5,716.3	5,756.8	5,844.9	5,886.3	5,904.9	5,905.1	5,907.1	5,921.3	5,922.6	5,938.7	5,938.4	5,861.9
2006	5,774.8	5,798.4	5,845.0	5,904.9	5,953.7	6,003.7	5,966.3	5,972.5	5,982.5	5,987.1	6,002.3	6,001.7	5,932.7
2007	5,843.2	5,845.5	5,903.2	5,958.4	6,017.5	6,049.1	6,009.7	6,011.7	6,020.6	6,024.2	6,044.4	6,036.5	5,980.3
2008	5,869.4	5,874.8	5,903.8	5,962.1	6,011.8	6,023.1	5,984.9	5,982.4	5,972.9	5,967.4	5,940.3	5,899.7	5,949.4
2009	5,679.2	5,659.0	5,653.0	5,671.0	5,699.2	5,693.6	5,641.7	5,626.6	5,640.3	5,647.6	5,648.4	5,629.2	5,657.4
2010	5,462.4	5,482.7	5,515.5	5,595.9	5,655.8	5,663.2	5,612.7	5,636.0	5,654.2	5,687.1	5,698.0	5,688.3	5,612.7
2011	5,527.2	5,545.6	5,589.8	5,664.5	5,702.5	5,723.7	5,684.5	5,675.3	5,685.7	5,728.8	5,727.0	5,703.0	5,663.1
Total Private													
2000	5,057.8	5,065.8	5,123.3	5,178.3	5,216.7	5,278.9	5,251.7	5,274.2	5,261.9	5,243.1	5,258.7	5,251.9	5,205.2
2001	5,079.7	5,077.5	5,120.1	5,159.7	5,196.0	5,242.0	5,188.1	5,194.2	5,158.0	5,111.7	5,108.2	5,103.3	5,144.9
2002	4,932.8	4,915.3	4,946.8	4,999.5	5,040.3	5,083.5	5,069.0	5,088.1	5,064.3	5,042.3	5,049.9	5,043.0	5,022.9
2003	4,865.9	4,846.5	4,874.2	4,927.0	4,972.7	5,013.4	5,001.6	5,019.4	5,002.8	4,988.6	4,983.8	4,995.5	4,957.6
2004	4,829.6	4,821.1	4,867.3	4,934.3	4,988.1	5,036.6	5,034.4	5,039.2	5,021.2	5,016.1	5,022.6	5,044.8	4,971.3
2005	4,867.8	4,865.2	4,900.7	4,990.7	5,029.1	5,067.8	5,078.7	5,085.9	5,076.4	5,067.1	5,079.2	5,084.0	5,016.1
2006	4,942.5	4,945.0	4,988.3	5,050.2	5,095.7	5,158.7	5,146.2	5,157.4	5,136.8	5,133.3	5,144.4	5,148.9	5,087.3
2007	5,008.2	4,988.7	5,043.8	5,096.4	5,154.0	5,204.2	5,190.2	5,197.1	5,169.5	5,163.2	5,179.6	5,177.9	5,131.1
2008	5,027.8	5,010.5	5,038.8	5,094.4	5,140.6	5,172.4	5,158.7	5,163.8	5,117.8	5,097.4	5,070.0	5,033.2	5,093.8
2009	4,834.8	4,794.5	4,787.1	4,794.8	4,822.9	4,840.5	4,813.2	4,810.9	4,781.6	4,777.1	4,775.9	4,764.2	4,799.8
2010	4,618.2	4,616.3	4,649.4	4,724.1	4,769.8	4,809.0	4,794.4	4,818.6	4,804.6	4,828.6	4,838.2	4,835.6	4,758.9
2011	4,698.0	4,695.4	4,738.7	4,811.3	4,848.5	4,891.6	4,876.3	4,877.7	4,854.3	4,884.1	4,880.0	4,861.4	4,826.4
Goods-Producing													
2000	1,112.9	1,115.9	1,132.6	1,150.3	1,160.8	1,174.3	1,169.7	1,170.9	1,166.6	1,159.9	1,154.2	1,134.0	1,150.2
2001	1,091.1	1,093.2	1,102.0	1,113.9	1,122.0	1,131.3	1,114.4	1,114.7	1,106.3	1,092.0	1,082.5	1,068.2	1,102.7
2002	1,020.9	1,015.9	1,023.0	1,037.9	1,047.3	1,060.2	1,055.9	1,059.7	1,055.8	1,048.5	1,041.8	1,026.8	1,041.1
2003	982.6	975.7	982.6	999.2	1,009.1	1,018.3	1,013.7	1,016.3	1,010.5	999.8	990.7	981.5	998.3
2004	939.1	934.1	948.0	967.5	982.5	996.7	996.6	997.1	996.3	992.4	987.8	980.7	976.6
2005	931.9	931.2	940.0	963.7	974.0	984.9	984.1	985.2	984.0	980.1	976.5	963.5	966.6
2006	935.7	935.2	942.7	964.8	973.9	991.2	987.9	988.5	985.5	981.3	975.7	964.0	968.9
2007	931.2	918.6	936.6	953.0	967.3	980.6	975.6	975.8	970.8	963.8	961.1	947.5	956.8
2008	913.1	904.6	912.8	927.3	939.1	948.0	947.2	947.2	939.8	929.0	912.5	884.5	925.4
2009	831.9	818.0	813.3	807.3	805.8	808.8	804.7	804.6	800.9	793.8	783.3	766.9	803.3
2010	731.1	729.6	739.9	761.0	770.9	782.7	778.7	789.9	787.9	791.4	786.1	771.3	768.4
2011	743.6	742.6	755.1	773.0	783.7	796.2	798.1	798.8	794.2	795.4	789.2	775.0	778.7
Mining and Logging													
2000	9.7	9.5	9.7	9.8	9.8	9.9	10.0	10.0	10.0	10.1	10.1	9.9	9.9
2001	9.4	9.4	9.8	10.0	10.1	10.2	10.4	10.2	10.2	10.1	10.1	10.0	10.0
2002	9.6	9.5	9.7	9.6	9.6	9.8	9.8	9.7	9.7	9.7	9.8	9.7	9.7
2003	9.1	9.1	9.3	9.6	9.6	9.8	9.4	9.5	9.5	9.5	9.5	9.3	9.4
2004	8.6	8.6	9.0	9.3	9.5	9.7	9.7	9.7	9.8	9.5	9.6	9.5	9.4
2005	8.8	8.9	9.2	9.6	9.8	10.1	10.2	10.2	10.3	10.4	10.4	10.4	9.9
2006	10.0	9.9	10.0	10.1	10.4	10.6	10.5	10.3	10.3	10.4	10.3	10.2	10.3
2007	9.7	9.7	10.0	10.2	10.5	10.7	10.5	10.3	10.0	10.1	10.1	9.7	10.1
2008	9.3	9.3	9.6	9.5	9.9	9.9	9.9	10.1	10.0	10.0	9.9	9.8	9.8
2009	9.2	9.3	9.4	9.6	9.5	9.7	9.5	9.3	9.4	9.1	9.1	8.9	9.3
2010	8.4	8.4	8.5	9.0	9.1	9.3	9.5	9.4	9.6	9.6	9.5	9.4	9.1
2011	9.0	8.8	9.0	9.3	9.5	9.7	9.7	9.7	9.7	9.9	9.9	9.8	9.5
Construction													
2000	234.8	234.6	248.2	266.1	276.3	285.2	287.1	289.7	286.6	284.7	279.6	263.8	269.7
2001	239.0	241.5	252.3	272.0	284.5	293.0	295.5	297.6	292.8	291.1	289.4	278.9	277.3
2002	246.4	244.1	251.4	268.3	278.9	289.5	295.2	298.3	296.4	295.4	289.9	276.9	277.6
2003	246.8	240.8	248.2	268.1	280.1	289.4	295.1	297.7	294.0	287.4	280.1	270.1	274.8
2004	238.8	233.7	245.1	263.4	274.8	283.7	287.7	287.4	286.0	285.6	281.2	273.4	270.1
2005	236.7	235.7	243.1	263.5	273.8	281.6	285.0	285.8	285.6	284.8	280.5	266.4	268.5
2006	245.2	244.7	252.9	272.5	281.8	292.3	292.1	293.6	289.9	287.9	281.7	269.0	275.3
2007	244.5	233.6	249.8	266.5	279.8	288.9	289.4	290.1	287.2	284.3	278.9	263.8	271.4
2008	236.3	231.2	239.2	255.3	266.9	273.2	277.3	278.8	274.7	269.7	257.8	239.1	258.3
2009	205.8	201.9	206.1	214.1	221.8	227.7	231.2	231.0	227.8	224.2	215.3	199.7	217.2
2010	172.5	169.9	178.9	196.6	203.5	210.9	206.6	215.1	213.4	213.9	207.1	190.6	198.3
2011	168.9	167.7	177.2	192.2	201.4	209.2	210.4	212.8	208.4	208.3	201.4	185.3	195.3
Manufacturing													
2000	868.4	871.8	874.7	874.4	874.7	879.2	872.6	871.2	870.0	865.1	864.5	860.3	870.6
2001	842.7	842.3	839.9	831.9	827.4	828.1	808.5	806.9	803.3	791.0	783.0	779.3	815.4
2002	764.9	762.3	761.9	760.0	758.8	760.9	751.0	751.7	749.7	743.3	742.2	740.2	753.9
2003	726.7	725.8	725.1	721.5	719.4	719.1	709.2	709.1	707.0	702.9	701.1	702.1	714.1
2004	691.7	691.8	693.9	694.8	698.2	703.3	699.2	700.0	700.5	697.3	697.0	697.8	697.1
2005	686.4	686.6	687.7	690.6	690.4	693.2	688.9	689.2	688.1	684.9	685.6	686.7	688.2
2006	680.5	680.6	679.8	682.2	681.7	688.3	685.3	684.6	685.3	683.0	683.7	684.8	683.3
2007	677.0	675.3	676.8	676.3	677.0	681.0	675.7	675.4	673.6	669.4	672.1	674.0	675.3
2008	667.5	664.1	664.0	662.5	662.3	664.9	660.0	658.3	655.1	649.3	644.8	635.6	657.4
2009	616.9	606.8	597.8	583.6	574.5	571.4	564.0	564.3	563.7	560.5	558.9	558.3	576.7
2010	550.2	551.3	552.5	555.4	558.3	562.5	562.6	565.4	564.9	567.9	569.5	571.3	561.0
2011	565.7	566.1	568.9	571.5	572.8	577.3	578.0	576.3	576.1	577.2	577.9	579.9	574.0

1. Employment by Industry: Illinois, Selected Years, 2000–2011—*Continued*

(Numbers in thousands, not seasonally adjusted)

Industry and year	January	February	March	April	May	June	July	August	September	October	November	December	Annual average
Service-Providing													
2000	4,761.5	4,790.9	4,840.7	4,875.6	4,918.0	4,950.5	4,891.9	4,909.6	4,928.7	4,932.6	4,961.0	4,974.5	4,894.6
2001	4,815.1	4,837.1	4,875.0	4,902.1	4,938.4	4,961.8	4,898.9	4,898.1	4,899.8	4,883.9	4,894.7	4,906.2	4,892.6
2002	4,757.7	4,765.5	4,796.3	4,837.4	4,874.5	4,888.5	4,841.1	4,851.1	4,858.7	4,865.6	4,885.0	4,891.5	4,842.7
2003	4,730.4	4,736.4	4,759.9	4,798.4	4,834.0	4,851.3	4,816.0	4,822.9	4,832.6	4,845.9	4,851.7	4,870.2	4,812.5
2004	4,727.7	4,739.2	4,775.9	4,821.7	4,860.2	4,881.2	4,858.6	4,857.9	4,858.6	4,879.7	4,894.4	4,916.9	4,839.3
2005	4,768.9	4,785.1	4,816.8	4,881.2	4,912.3	4,920.0	4,921.0	4,921.9	4,937.3	4,942.5	4,962.2	4,974.9	4,895.3
2006	4,839.1	4,863.2	4,902.3	4,940.1	4,979.8	5,012.5	4,978.4	4,984.0	4,997.0	5,005.8	5,026.6	5,037.7	4,963.9
2007	4,912.0	4,926.9	4,966.6	5,005.4	5,050.2	5,068.5	5,034.1	5,035.9	5,049.8	5,060.4	5,083.3	5,089.0	5,023.5
2008	4,956.3	4,970.2	4,991.0	5,034.8	5,072.7	5,075.1	5,037.7	5,035.2	5,033.1	5,038.4	5,027.8	5,015.2	5,024.0
2009	4,847.3	4,841.0	4,839.7	4,863.7	4,893.4	4,884.8	4,837.0	4,822.0	4,839.4	4,853.8	4,865.1	4,862.3	4,854.1
2010	4,731.3	4,753.1	4,775.6	4,834.9	4,884.9	4,880.5	4,834.0	4,846.1	4,866.3	4,895.7	4,911.9	4,917.0	4,844.3
2011	4,783.6	4,803.0	4,834.7	4,891.5	4,918.8	4,927.5	4,886.4	4,876.5	4,891.5	4,933.4	4,937.8	4,928.0	4,884.4
Trade, Transportation, and Utilities													
2000	1,232.7	1,220.7	1,226.6	1,231.2	1,238.7	1,246.8	1,242.8	1,249.5	1,249.3	1,256.9	1,280.0	1,295.7	1,247.6
2001	1,241.9	1,225.7	1,230.2	1,233.2	1,236.7	1,242.1	1,225.1	1,224.0	1,221.6	1,217.0	1,234.9	1,246.2	1,231.6
2002	1,194.2	1,176.7	1,182.1	1,186.3	1,193.8	1,198.7	1,192.2	1,195.6	1,196.6	1,200.7	1,221.0	1,235.1	1,197.8
2003	1,180.2	1,168.0	1,171.1	1,173.2	1,181.7	1,186.2	1,173.0	1,177.0	1,178.7	1,185.8	1,201.8	1,217.3	1,182.8
2004	1,164.7	1,153.2	1,159.7	1,167.1	1,179.1	1,184.7	1,176.7	1,178.6	1,180.0	1,188.3	1,206.5	1,222.3	1,180.1
2005	1,170.9	1,159.2	1,166.4	1,176.0	1,184.5	1,188.6	1,184.2	1,187.0	1,188.4	1,193.0	1,213.1	1,230.2	1,186.8
2006	1,182.0	1,171.7	1,179.7	1,185.1	1,195.2	1,203.4	1,195.6	1,197.5	1,197.8	1,203.0	1,226.4	1,242.2	1,198.3
2007	1,201.3	1,185.7	1,196.3	1,195.8	1,209.8	1,217.5	1,210.4	1,210.1	1,211.1	1,214.5	1,240.7	1,254.6	1,212.3
2008	1,210.4	1,194.0	1,199.0	1,200.1	1,209.1	1,212.2	1,203.4	1,203.1	1,198.4	1,200.2	1,210.9	1,216.9	1,204.8
2009	1,161.9	1,143.9	1,138.2	1,134.0	1,140.7	1,141.7	1,128.8	1,129.4	1,127.1	1,129.9	1,145.2	1,153.2	1,139.5
2010													
2011	1,109.4	1,099.7	1,104.1	1,113.9	1,123.5	1,128.7	1,124.1	1,127.9	1,124.7	1,133.9	1,151.9	1,165.4	1,125.6
Wholesale Trade													
2000	315.9	316.3	318.2	319.5	321.0	323.6	322.9	322.5	321.9	322.6	322.2	323.2	320.8
2001	316.8	316.5	317.6	319.8	319.8	320.7	318.2	317.4	315.9	312.7	312.1	311.8	316.6
2002	305.7	305.0	305.9	307.0	307.9	310.4	308.1	307.8	307.3	307.3	307.7	307.7	307.3
2003	303.6	303.2	304.2	304.2	305.0	305.6	303.9	302.4	301.2	300.8	300.8	301.0	303.0
2004	296.0	295.4	297.1	298.9	301.0	302.6	301.6	301.0	300.3	301.5	301.6	302.4	300.0
2005	296.7	296.9	299.5	302.0	303.1	305.2	305.2	304.7	304.7	304.7	305.4	306.6	302.9
2006	303.2	303.3	305.2	306.7	308.4	311.2	309.7	308.9	308.3	308.8	308.8	310.0	307.7
2007	305.9	305.5	307.6	308.8	310.7	313.8	312.8	312.1	311.7	312.9	312.9	313.8	310.7
2008	309.0	308.2	309.5	310.7	312.8	314.1	312.3	311.4	309.7	309.9	308.8	307.4	310.3
2009	299.2	296.7	295.6	293.8	293.2	293.2	290.4	289.1	287.1	287.9	287.6	287.5	291.8
2010	281.8	280.9	282.7	285.1	286.6	288.2	287.7	287.6	286.5	287.4	287.0	287.2	285.7
2011	284.3	284.3	285.9	288.7	289.9	292.3	290.9	290.6	291.1	292.0	291.3	289.2	289.2
Retail Trade													
2000	644.4	632.8	636.2	637.2	642.2	648.6	645.7	650.4	648.3	654.0	676.8	690.7	650.6
2001	650.5	636.2	638.6	638.1	640.9	647.5	637.0	637.4	633.9	634.2	655.4	669.4	643.3
2002	630.4	615.4	620.3	620.9	626.9	632.2	628.2	629.8	628.2	630.9	651.4	665.7	631.7
2003	621.0	611.1	613.4	614.7	621.0	626.4	620.3	623.5	622.1	627.5	643.7	658.8	625.3
2004	618.1	608.0	611.4	614.5	622.3	628.9	622.4	624.2	621.8	626.0	644.5	659.5	625.1
2005	619.9	608.1	611.4	617.0	623.2	626.6	625.8	627.4	624.1	627.3	645.4	659.3	626.3
2006	622.6	611.8	615.8	618.2	624.2	630.8	627.3	628.5	622.8	628.5	650.8	661.7	628.6
2007	632.8	618.0	624.5	623.3	632.6	638.2	635.6	634.1	630.3	632.4	657.1	667.1	635.5
2008	635.6	620.4	623.0	623.4	628.0	632.2	628.8	626.7	620.4	621.9	633.7	639.1	627.8
2009	604.1	590.7	587.6	588.6	594.8	597.9	593.2	592.9	588.5	590.4	605.6	611.4	595.5
2010	580.8	572.0	574.4	579.1	585.6	591.1	589.9	590.2	583.5	590.2	607.1	617.1	588.4
2011	587.0	577.5	580.2	586.9	591.5	596.8	592.8	590.8	583.7	588.4	603.5	613.3	591.0
Transportation and Utilities													
2000	272.4	271.6	272.2	274.5	275.5	274.6	274.2	276.6	279.1	280.3	281.0	281.8	276.2
2001	274.6	273.0	274.0	275.3	276.0	273.9	269.9	269.2	271.8	270.1	267.4	265.0	271.7
2002	258.1	256.3	255.9	258.4	259.0	256.1	255.9	258.0	261.1	262.5	261.9	261.7	258.7
2003	255.6	253.7	253.5	254.3	255.7	254.2	248.8	251.1	255.4	257.5	257.3	257.5	254.6
2004	250.6	249.8	251.2	253.7	255.8	253.2	252.7	253.4	257.9	260.8	260.4	260.4	255.0
2005	254.3	254.2	255.5	257.0	258.2	256.8	253.2	254.9	259.6	261.0	262.3	264.3	257.6
2006	256.2	256.6	258.7	260.2	262.6	261.4	258.6	260.1	266.7	265.7	266.8	270.5	262.0
2007	262.6	262.2	264.2	263.7	266.5	265.5	262.0	263.9	269.1	269.2	270.7	273.7	266.1
2008	265.8	265.4	266.5	266.0	268.3	265.9	262.3	265.0	268.3	268.4	268.4	270.4	266.7
2009	258.6	256.5	255.0	251.6	252.7	250.6	245.2	247.4	251.5	251.6	252.0	254.3	252.3
2010	246.8	246.8	247.0	249.7	251.3	249.4	246.5	250.1	254.7	256.3	257.8	261.1	251.5
2011	254.7	255.0	256.1	258.3	259.9	258.5	253.3	253.2	262.9	265.2	266.7	267.1	259.2
Information													
2000	143.9	144.4	145.8	145.8	147.0	148.5	148.9	149.5	147.8	148.7	150.0	150.8	147.6
2001	148.0	148.4	148.8	148.6	149.0	150.4	148.3	147.8	145.7	143.7	143.9	144.4	147.3
2002	141.3	140.6	140.4	140.3	140.0	139.6	136.7	136.2	133.5	133.0	132.5	132.0	137.2
2003	129.0	128.9	127.8	128.0	128.1	128.4	128.1	127.4	126.3	126.0	126.1	126.2	127.5
2004	122.2	122.1	121.8	121.6	121.7	121.8	121.1	120.4	118.9	119.2	119.3	120.0	120.8
2005	118.8	118.3	118.4	119.0	119.0	119.4	119.3	118.4	117.3	116.6	116.7	117.0	118.2
2006	116.4	116.0	116.2	116.9	117.1	117.4	117.1	116.3	115.1	115.3	115.3	115.9	116.3
2007	115.3	115.7	115.7	115.7	116.2	116.9	116.9	116.8	115.6	115.5	115.7	116.0	116.0
2008	115.4	115.4	115.9	115.6	115.9	115.8	115.5	115.5	115.0	113.0	112.1	111.7	114.4
2009	109.9	108.9	108.2	107.4	107.0	106.7	105.7	105.4	104.5	104.2	103.8	104.8	106.4
2010	103.3	102.3	102.3	102.1	102.1	102.4	101.8	101.9	101.9	100.6	100.9	101.1	101.8
2011	100.6	99.9	100.1	100.3	100.6	100.9	100.8	100.7	98.8	100.7	100.4	100.6	100.4

1. Employment by Industry: Illinois, Selected Years, 2000–2011—*Continued*

(Numbers in thousands, not seasonally adjusted)

Industry and year	January	February	March	April	May	June	July	August	September	October	November	December	Annual average
Financial Activities													
2000	403.0	402.8	402.6	402.1	402.7	407.4	406.2	406.8	402.1	402.8	403.1	407.6	404.1
2001	400.4	401.1	403.5	402.9	404.3	408.7	407.6	406.7	402.0	400.7	401.8	403.7	403.6
2002	398.7	398.3	399.1	398.2	399.4	403.3	402.7	402.9	400.1	400.2	401.3	403.7	400.7
2003	398.9	398.1	399.3	400.1	402.1	406.3	406.1	406.5	403.0	399.4	399.7	401.7	401.8
2004	396.7	396.2	398.0	397.0	398.6	402.5	403.0	403.0	399.1	398.7	398.8	401.7	399.4
2005	396.2	395.9	396.6	399.6	400.9	403.9	406.4	406.3	403.8	403.7	403.6	406.2	401.9
2006	401.0	401.1	402.4	403.2	404.5	408.1	408.6	408.7	405.6	406.0	405.7	407.3	405.2
2007	403.3	402.8	402.8	403.3	404.3	407.2	406.5	404.9	400.4	399.5	398.9	399.5	402.8
2008	393.6	393.5	393.7	393.4	394.1	396.0	394.3	393.7	388.6	387.6	385.7	385.7	391.7
2009	378.4	376.3	374.7	373.8	373.7	374.7	372.9	371.7	367.7	366.7	366.1	366.7	372.0
2010	361.3	360.7	360.8	362.3	363.2	365.9	365.6	365.9	362.8	364.7	364.7	366.0	363.7
2011	360.9	360.7	360.5	361.3	361.8	364.5	364.7	363.1	359.7	361.6	361.3	362.6	361.9
Professional and Business Services													
2000	799.5	807.1	822.3	839.0	843.5	859.3	855.3	865.2	863.3	856.3	853.7	848.0	842.7
2001	812.2	810.9	816.3	823.7	828.2	837.2	828.8	832.7	824.4	818.0	807.9	804.0	820.4
2002	771.2	769.7	773.2	789.7	792.8	799.3	802.8	810.9	806.4	799.3	795.5	786.8	791.5
2003	754.9	753.7	757.2	769.9	774.7	779.2	781.8	789.9	793.4	795.3	789.2	789.2	777.4
2004	758.5	762.3	771.0	791.9	798.3	810.7	813.5	817.1	815.8	815.5	811.8	817.8	798.7
2005	786.6	790.8	797.8	820.0	821.6	832.1	838.5	843.2	845.1	850.4	848.7	844.4	826.6
2006	815.2	819.1	830.0	847.3	852.4	866.4	866.5	873.1	870.6	874.9	870.2	865.2	854.2
2007	835.2	837.5	847.2	866.4	872.5	882.9	884.9	889.7	884.6	886.3	882.2	878.8	870.7
2008	846.7	848.9	850.5	866.0	869.7	874.0	872.5	875.0	865.0	860.9	850.6	838.8	859.9
2009	797.3	788.0	780.1	785.5	787.7	789.9	787.7	788.8	783.1	789.3	790.2	786.0	787.8
2010	762.0	766.1	768.9	795.3	799.8	809.6	813.0	818.6	815.6	825.1	825.1	823.2	801.9
2011	794.9	798.4	804.5	826.1	826.0	837.6	838.2	843.7	842.6	854.8	848.0	839.6	829.5
Education and Health Services													
2000	671.6	676.6	680.0	681.5	682.9	684.2	673.8	675.4	683.8	684.3	689.0	690.4	681.1
2001	682.2	688.5	694.9	696.8	698.0	697.7	692.0	695.5	702.4	703.2	706.7	707.9	697.2
2002	699.8	706.1	709.9	711.1	713.9	710.3	703.0	705.0	712.8	716.0	719.4	720.5	710.7
2003	709.0	712.2	716.0	715.6	717.9	716.7	712.7	715.1	720.5	724.8	727.2	728.7	718.0
2004	719.7	723.9	727.3	729.7	730.9	727.4	723.6	724.7	731.3	736.9	740.0	743.5	729.9
2005	734.6	738.3	740.1	745.5	746.9	741.7	740.8	740.8	748.8	752.4	755.1	757.2	745.2
2006	748.0	755.2	758.7	759.3	762.0	760.5	756.2	759.3	767.5	770.6	774.6	775.2	762.3
2007	765.9	773.8	777.4	777.6	779.2	777.3	772.7	774.1	782.4	788.6	793.0	795.2	779.8
2008	785.8	791.9	793.5	798.6	801.1	798.6	795.6	799.1	806.9	811.8	815.9	817.1	801.3
2009	806.5	812.4	816.1	815.3	817.6	814.7	810.3	809.7	816.2	823.0	826.4	828.0	816.4
2010	817.9	823.7	827.9	831.1	834.4	831.3	826.2	826.9	836.0	844.0	848.2	849.7	833.1
2011	838.4	844.0	848.9	848.3	849.7	846.8	842.2	843.0	848.2	861.5	863.4	861.6	849.7
Leisure and Hospitality													
2000	454.1	457.1	469.7	483.6	496.1	509.4	506.9	508.6	501.5	489.5	483.5	479.5	486.6
2001	459.6	463.5	475.1	490.5	506.3	518.3	514.4	516.1	504.0	488.0	480.2	477.9	491.2
2002	459.7	460.6	469.9	486.1	502.6	515.0	515.6	517.6	508.1	494.9	488.0	486.7	492.1
2003	464.7	463.5	471.5	492.3	509.2	522.0	520.8	521.7	513.7	501.0	493.6	494.0	497.3
2004	473.9	473.3	483.5	501.5	518.3	528.8	531.4	531.4	522.4	507.8	501.5	499.5	506.1
2005	476.4	478.5	487.0	511.0	525.4	534.8	537.8	537.7	530.9	514.3	508.4	506.4	512.4
2006	487.5	491.0	500.7	517.9	533.4	548.1	547.9	547.4	537.1	524.3	518.6	518.9	522.7
2007	500.7	499.2	509.4	526.6	544.6	555.9	553.7	556.0	544.6	534.9	527.6	524.7	531.5
2008	504.7	503.5	513.1	532.8	548.8	559.7	556.7	557.6	543.9	533.3	521.1	517.0	532.7
2009	493.4	491.4	499.5	515.1	532.4	541.3	538.0	537.1	527.9	514.9	506.0	502.7	516.6
2010	482.1	483.2	492.6	511.5	527.8	538.5	536.4	538.9	530.0	520.2	513.1	509.9	515.4
2011	488.4	487.5	500.0	519.5	534.2	544.5	542.0	542.2	527.3	519.8	512.7	507.7	518.8
Other Services													
2000	240.1	241.2	243.7	244.8	245.0	249.0	248.1	248.3	247.5	244.7	245.2	245.9	245.3
2001	244.3	246.2	249.3	250.1	251.5	256.3	257.5	256.7	251.6	248.9	250.3	251.0	251.1
2002	247.0	247.4	249.2	249.9	250.5	257.1	260.1	260.2	251.0	249.7	250.4	251.4	252.0
2003	246.6	246.4	248.7	248.7	249.9	256.3	265.4	265.5	256.7	256.5	255.5	256.9	254.4
2004	254.8	256.0	258.0	258.0	258.7	264.0	268.5	266.9	257.4	257.3	256.9	259.3	259.7
2005	252.4	253.0	254.4	255.9	256.8	262.4	267.6	267.3	258.1	256.6	257.1	259.1	258.4
2006	256.7	255.7	257.9	255.7	257.2	263.6	266.4	266.6	257.6	257.9	257.9	260.2	259.5
2007	255.3	255.4	258.4	258.0	260.1	265.9	269.5	269.7	260.0	260.1	260.4	261.6	261.2
2008	258.1	258.7	260.3	260.6	262.8	268.1	273.5	273.1	262.2	262.5	261.6	261.6	263.6
2009	255.5	255.6	257.0	256.4	258.0	262.7	265.1	264.2	254.2	255.3	254.9	255.9	257.9
2010	251.1	251.0	252.9	246.9	248.1	249.9	248.6	248.6	247.0	248.4	248.2	249.0	249.1
2011	245.2	245.5	247.4	248.9	251.2	253.5	253.3	251.6	245.8	244.7	243.5	244.7	247.9
Government													
2000	816.6	841.0	850.0	847.6	862.1	845.9	809.9	806.3	833.4	849.4	856.5	856.6	839.6
2001	826.5	852.8	856.9	856.3	864.4	851.1	825.2	818.6	848.1	864.4	869.0	871.1	850.4
2002	845.8	866.1	872.5	875.8	881.5	865.2	828.0	822.7	850.2	871.8	876.9	875.3	861.0
2003	847.1	865.6	868.3	870.6	870.4	856.2	828.1	819.8	840.3	857.1	858.6	856.2	853.2
2004	837.2	852.2	856.6	854.9	854.6	841.3	820.8	815.8	833.7	856.0	859.6	852.8	844.6
2005	833.0	851.1	856.1	854.2	857.2	837.1	826.4	821.2	844.9	855.5	859.5	854.4	845.9
2006	832.3	853.4	856.7	854.7	858.0	845.0	820.1	815.1	845.7	853.8	857.9	852.8	845.5
2007	835.0	856.8	859.4	862.0	863.5	844.9	819.5	814.6	851.1	861.0	864.8	858.6	849.3
2008	841.6	864.3	865.0	867.7	871.2	850.7	826.2	818.6	855.1	870.0	870.3	866.5	855.6
2009	844.4	864.5	865.9	876.2	876.3	853.1	828.5	815.7	858.7	870.5	872.5	865.0	857.6
2010	844.2	866.4	866.1	871.8	886.0	854.2	818.3	817.4	849.6	858.5	859.8	852.7	853.8
2011	829.2	850.2	851.1	853.2	854.0	832.1	808.2	797.6	831.4	844.7	847.0	841.6	836.7

2. Average Weekly Hours by Selected Industry: Illinois, 2007–2011

(Not seasonally adjusted)

Industry and year	January	February	March	April	May	June	July	August	September	October	November	December	Annual average
Total Private													
2007	33.9	33.9	34.3	34.4	34.3	34.5	34.7	34.3	35.0	34.3	34.2	34.7	34.4
2008	33.7	33.9	34.5	34.2	34.3	34.5	34.3	34.5	34.5	34.4	34.5	34.3	34.3
2009	34.1	34.5	34.5	34.4	34.4	34.4	34.4	34.5	34.5	34.4	34.5	34.5	34.4
2010	34.4	34.3	34.3	34.4	34.4	34.3	34.3	34.3	34.4	34.5	34.4	34.3	34.4
2011	34.3	34.3	34.4	34.5	34.7	34.5	34.5	34.5	34.6	35.0	34.6	34.7	34.6
Goods-Producing													
2007	39.0	38.8	39.7	39.3	40.0	40.1	39.3	39.7	40.3	39.8	39.6	39.6	39.6
2008	39.1	38.8	39.1	38.9	39.5	39.1	39.1	39.2	39.1	39.1	38.9	38.8	39.1
2009	38.8	38.8	39.2	39.1	39.3	39.4	39.3	39.5	39.4	39.6	39.7	39.6	39.3
2010	39.6	39.4	39.3	39.4	39.3	39.2	39.3	39.3	39.3	39.3	39.3	39.4	39.3
2011	39.3	39.2	39.5	39.5	40.1	39.6	39.2	39.9	39.8	40.0	39.5	39.9	39.6
Construction													
2007	36.0	34.0	36.9	36.3	38.3	38.7	37.7	37.8	38.5	38.3	37.3	36.1	37.2
2008	36.4	36.4	36.3	35.8	36.1	36.2	36.3	36.5	36.4	36.5	36.5	36.4	36.3
2009	36.3	37.5	37.6	37.6	37.7	37.9	37.8	38.0	37.9	38.1	38.1	38.2	37.7
2010	38.4	38.0	38.0	38.1	38.2	38.1	38.3	38.4	38.4	38.2	38.1	37.4	38.1
2011	37.4	37.3	37.6	37.9	38.6	38.3	39.4	39.6	39.2	39.0	37.5	37.8	38.4
Manufacturing													
2007	40.1	40.4	40.7	40.4	40.6	40.5	39.8	40.4	40.9	40.4	40.5	41.0	40.5
2008	40.2	39.9	40.2	39.9	40.1	39.7	39.6	39.7	39.6	39.5	39.5	39.4	39.8
2009	39.3	39.4	39.6	39.5	39.6	39.7	39.8	39.9	39.8	40.0	40.2	40.0	39.7
2010	40.2	40.1	40.3	40.4	40.5	40.3	40.2	40.2	40.2	40.4	40.5	40.9	40.4
2011	40.8	40.7	40.9	40.8	41.1	40.7	39.7	40.6	40.6	41.0	40.8	41.1	40.7
Trade, Transportation, and Utilities													
2007	33.6	33.7	34.0	34.3	34.3	34.6	34.6	34.2	35.2	34.5	34.3	34.9	34.4
2008	33.5	33.9	34.3	34.1	34.3	34.7	34.6	34.8	34.8	34.7	34.9	34.7	34.4
2009	33.6	33.9	33.9	33.9	33.9	33.7	33.8	33.9	33.9	33.8	34.0	34.2	33.9
2010	34.1	34.2	34.2	34.2	34.3	34.2	34.2	34.2	34.3	34.5	34.4	34.6	34.3
2011	34.6	34.5	34.5	34.7	35.0	35.0	35.1	35.0	35.2	35.5	35.2	35.2	35.0
Information													
2007	35.3	36.0	35.6	35.7	35.2	35.1	36.3	36.5	38.3	37.9	37.6	38.1	36.5
2008	36.8	36.9	37.7	37.4	37.0	37.3	37.0	37.3	37.3	37.4	37.5	37.3	37.2
2009	37.2	39.5	39.6	39.3	39.2	39.2	39.3	39.4	39.3	39.3	39.4	39.5	39.2
2010	39.3	39.1	39.0	39.1	39.2	39.1	39.2	39.2	39.1	39.0	38.9	38.5	39.1
2011	38.4	38.4	37.0	36.5	36.9	36.9	36.4	36.3	36.4	37.8	37.4	37.7	37.2
Financial Activities													
2007	37.4	37.8	37.0	37.9	36.4	36.6	37.9	36.7	37.4	35.9	36.0	36.6	37.0
2008	36.0	36.3	36.8	36.2	35.9	36.2	36.0	36.1	36.0	36.1	36.2	36.3	36.2
2009	36.4	37.0	37.0	36.9	36.8	36.8	37.0	37.1	37.0	36.8	36.8	36.7	36.9
2010	36.8	36.7	36.9	36.7	36.8	36.7	36.6	36.8	36.7	36.5	36.6	36.3	36.7
2011	36.4	36.6	36.6	36.6	36.7	36.3	36.6	36.3	36.6	37.8	37.7	37.3	36.8
Professional and Business Services													
2007	34.3	34.6	34.9	35.2	35.5	35.5	35.8	35.3	36.1	35.4	35.0	36.0	35.3
2008	34.9	35.1	36.4	35.8	36.0	36.3	36.1	36.3	36.2	36.3	36.3	36.3	36.0
2009	36.2	37.2	37.1	36.9	37.0	36.8	36.7	36.8	36.7	36.7	36.9	36.7	36.8
2010	36.5	36.4	36.4	36.5	36.6	36.5	36.4	36.5	36.4	36.5	36.4	35.9	36.4
2011	36.0	36.1	36.1	36.3	36.7	36.1	35.8	35.8	35.9	36.4	35.7	35.6	36.0
Education and Health Services													
2007	32.5	32.2	32.5	32.6	32.2	32.5	32.9	32.5	33.2	31.8	32.2	32.4	32.5
2008	32.1	32.1	32.4	32.2	31.9	32.2	32.0	32.2	32.3	32.3	32.4	32.3	32.2
2009	32.4	32.4	32.4	32.3	32.3	32.4	32.5	32.7	32.7	32.7	32.6	32.4	32.5
2010	32.4	32.3	32.1	32.2	32.3	32.2	32.1	32.4	32.6	32.8	32.7	32.8	32.4
2011	32.9	32.8	32.9	33.0	33.2	32.9	33.4	33.1	33.2	33.5	33.2	33.1	33.1
Leisure and Hospitality													
2007	25.3	25.4	25.8	25.5	25.4	25.7	25.8	25.5	25.4	25.3	25.0	25.4	25.5
2008	24.2	24.7	25.1	25.0	25.2	25.5	25.4	25.3	25.2	25.1	25.2	25.1	25.1
2009	25.0	26.1	26.1	26.0	26.1	26.2	26.0	25.8	25.7	25.5	25.7	25.6	25.8
2010	25.4	25.6	25.7	25.8	25.9	25.8	25.6	25.5	25.4	25.5	25.4	24.7	25.5
2011	24.6	24.5	25.2	25.2	25.0	25.3	25.2	25.2	25.1	25.4	25.2	25.5	25.1
Other Services													
2007	30.7	30.2	31.1	31.1	31.1	31.8	32.1	31.3	31.7	31.7	31.4	31.9	31.3
2008	31.0	32.2	32.5	32.7	32.7	32.9	32.7	32.8	32.7	32.3	32.7	31.8	32.4
2009	32.0	32.1	32.2	32.1	32.3	32.2	32.4	32.6	32.6	32.4	32.3	32.1	32.3
2010	32.1	32.3	32.2	32.4	32.3	32.3	32.2	32.2	32.1	32.3	32.2	32.2	32.2
2011	32.3	32.2	32.0	32.2	32.6	32.3	32.9	32.5	32.5	32.9	31.9	32.1	32.4

3. Average Hourly Earnings by Selected Industry: Illinois, 2007–2011

(Dollars, not seasonally adjusted)

Industry and year	January	February	March	April	May	June	July	August	September	October	November	December	Annual average
Total Private													
2007	22.61	22.91	22.71	23.36	23.12	23.02	23.34	23.02	23.34	22.49	22.50	22.80	22.94
2008	22.81	22.50	22.63	22.63	22.54	22.63	22.66	22.67	22.74	22.75	22.74	22.77	22.67
2009	22.81	23.04	23.11	23.07	22.97	22.99	23.07	23.12	23.12	23.10	23.13	23.12	23.05
2010	23.12	23.09	23.05	23.06	23.07	23.06	23.10	23.14	23.17	23.23	23.22	23.44	23.15
2011	23.45	23.37	23.15	23.36	23.55	23.38	23.60	23.54	23.71	24.00	23.84	23.96	23.58
Goods-Producing													
2007	23.48	23.12	23.40	23.96	23.87	24.03	24.53	24.30	24.48	24.04	23.95	24.05	23.94
2008	23.63	23.73	24.04	24.21	24.19	24.49	24.63	24.72	24.74	24.83	24.71	24.77	24.39
2009	24.62	24.74	24.99	25.04	24.89	24.81	24.97	25.04	25.06	25.00	25.14	25.00	24.94
2010	24.85	24.82	24.85	24.94	25.00	24.99	24.95	24.95	24.94	25.13	25.11	25.28	24.99
2011	25.31	25.24	25.23	25.50	25.67	25.62	26.04	25.94	25.91	26.29	26.13	26.17	25.76
Construction													
2007	30.78	30.85	30.68	30.93	30.90	31.10	31.42	31.45	31.71	30.72	30.61	31.66	31.08
2008	30.22	30.90	31.17	31.32	31.46	31.59	31.59	31.58	31.48	31.45	31.32	31.53	31.32
2009	31.52	32.18	32.29	32.23	32.16	32.03	32.15	32.20	32.22	32.20	32.29	32.48	32.16
2010	32.29	32.32	32.48	32.45	32.34	32.51	32.40	32.32	32.32	32.31	32.32	33.25	32.44
2011	33.22	33.24	32.91	33.15	33.18	33.23	33.20	33.32	32.98	33.50	33.66	33.89	33.29
Manufacturing													
2007	22.54	22.25	22.13	22.57	22.06	22.05	22.52	22.15	22.20	21.54	21.67	21.76	22.12
2008	21.65	21.44	21.55	21.70	21.46	21.56	21.64	21.69	21.76	21.86	21.89	21.93	21.67
2009	21.92	22.05	22.13	22.12	22.08	22.14	22.05	22.11	22.13	22.00	22.20	22.22	22.09
2010	22.12	22.19	22.15	22.32	22.47	22.38	23.33	23.38	23.39	23.48	23.67	23.94	22.91
2011	23.90	23.99	23.89	23.93	24.08	23.89	24.16	23.93	24.02	24.23	24.05	24.29	24.03
Trade, Transportation, and Utilities													
2007	19.03	19.29	19.36	19.71	19.78	19.67	19.87	19.77	20.22	19.73	19.66	19.60	19.65
2008	19.95	19.43	19.32	19.29	19.27	19.42	19.50	19.42	19.56	19.43	19.54	19.46	19.47
2009	19.51	19.69	19.85	19.74	19.67	19.83	19.75	19.80	19.80	19.70	19.72	20.00	19.76
2010	20.05	19.82	19.76	19.86	20.00	20.19	20.34	20.32	20.44	20.47	20.47	20.79	20.21
2011	20.69	20.55	20.21	20.70	20.95	20.73	21.19	20.88	21.26	21.59	21.40	21.50	20.98
Information													
2007	26.97	26.80	26.60	26.60	27.32	26.63	27.21	27.70	27.70	26.20	26.05	26.90	26.89
2008	27.29	26.17	26.47	26.06	26.16	26.29	26.02	26.07	26.09	26.01	26.13	26.20	26.25
2009	26.30	26.19	26.22	26.39	26.39	26.47	26.62	26.74	26.76	26.77	26.61	26.57	26.50
2010	26.57	26.45	26.62	26.76	26.62	26.56	26.53	26.56	26.53	26.53	26.68	26.86	26.61
2011	26.83	26.82	27.21	27.29	27.21	26.63	27.19	27.00	27.77	26.91	27.26	26.15	27.02
Financial Activities													
2007	28.17	30.76	29.68	29.76	29.69	29.55	29.95	29.33	29.92	27.64	27.58	27.69	29.16
2008	27.41	27.70	27.81	28.11	27.77	27.89	27.69	27.80	27.71	27.80	27.78	27.87	27.78
2009	27.97	29.04	29.04	28.95	29.05	28.93	28.94	29.05	29.03	29.13	29.05	29.00	28.93
2010	28.80	28.96	28.89	28.83	28.78	27.83	27.87	27.72	27.75	27.62	27.48	28.14	28.22
2011	28.22	28.29	28.10	28.53	29.00	28.28	28.22	28.61	28.65	29.28	29.13	29.36	28.64
Professional and Business Services													
2007	29.06	29.23	28.82	29.36	28.11	28.16	28.49	27.68	28.18	26.65	26.90	28.30	28.23
2008	28.33	27.45	27.95	27.76	27.45	27.65	27.63	27.58	27.66	27.50	27.65	27.68	27.69
2009	27.78	28.15	28.19	28.09	28.00	28.08	28.24	28.16	28.15	28.00	28.17	28.00	28.08
2010	28.07	28.04	28.04	28.02	28.02	28.00	28.12	28.22	28.26	28.37	28.38	28.15	28.14
2011	28.26	28.22	27.80	27.71	28.07	27.92	28.06	27.86	27.69	28.10	27.83	28.15	27.97
Education and Health Services													
2007	21.12	21.00	21.05	21.57	21.20	21.11	21.22	20.91	21.04	21.72	21.79	21.94	21.31
2008	21.83	21.58	21.34	21.67	21.78	21.65	21.66	21.68	21.75	21.80	21.77	21.85	21.70
2009	21.90	22.07	22.11	22.19	22.07	22.10	22.19	22.17	22.19	22.26	22.24	22.30	22.15
2010	22.35	22.51	22.46	22.33	22.33	22.43	22.29	22.42	22.38	22.21	22.15	22.52	22.36
2011	22.47	22.47	22.34	22.45	22.64	22.85	22.89	23.03	23.22	23.42	23.30	23.41	22.88
Leisure and Hospitality													
2007	12.84	12.95	12.60	15.29	16.01	15.38	15.44	15.16	15.05	12.47	12.54	12.34	14.05
2008	12.27	12.44	12.39	12.29	12.27	12.23	12.33	12.37	12.48	12.48	12.37	12.53	12.37
2009	12.41	12.62	12.58	12.57	12.57	12.55	12.60	12.80	12.80	12.67	12.48	12.40	12.59
2010	12.29	12.39	12.29	12.24	12.26	12.39	12.43	12.49	12.53	12.75	12.78	13.16	12.50
2011	13.16	13.23	13.12	13.29	12.65	12.47	12.48	12.65	12.96	12.40	12.59	12.80	12.81
Other Services													
2007	21.10	21.79	20.87	21.67	21.49	21.27	21.65	21.76	22.20	21.26	21.38	21.74	21.52
2008	21.85	21.62	21.88	21.49	21.63	21.48	21.31	21.27	21.24	21.89	21.64	21.93	21.60
2009	21.99	21.53	21.59	21.64	21.76	21.81	21.99	22.04	22.02	22.13	22.18	22.04	21.89
2010	22.21	22.00	22.16	22.08	22.10	22.07	22.08	22.07	22.00	22.01	22.03	22.39	22.10
2011	22.21	21.21	21.31	21.27	21.68	21.72	21.49	21.45	21.88	21.97	21.78	22.31	21.69

4. Average Weekly Earnings by Selected Industry: Illinois, 2007–2011

(Dollars, not seasonally adjusted)

Industry and year	January	February	March	April	May	June	July	August	September	October	November	December	Annual average
Total Private													
2007	766.48	776.65	778.95	803.58	793.02	794.19	809.90	789.59	816.90	771.41	769.50	791.16	788.70
2008	768.70	762.75	780.74	773.95	773.12	780.74	777.24	782.12	784.53	782.60	784.53	781.01	777.78
2009	777.82	794.88	797.30	793.61	790.17	790.86	793.61	797.64	797.64	794.64	797.99	797.64	793.55
2010	795.33	791.99	790.62	793.26	793.61	790.96	792.33	793.70	797.05	801.44	798.77	803.99	795.37
2011	804.34	801.59	796.36	805.92	817.19	806.61	814.20	812.13	820.37	840.00	824.86	831.41	815.01
Goods-Producing													
2007	915.72	897.06	928.98	941.63	954.80	963.60	964.03	964.71	986.54	956.79	948.42	952.38	948.31
2008	923.93	920.72	939.96	941.77	955.51	957.56	963.03	969.02	967.33	970.85	961.22	961.08	952.82
2009	955.26	959.91	979.61	979.06	978.18	977.51	981.32	989.08	987.36	990.00	998.06	990.00	980.25
2010	984.06	977.91	976.61	982.64	982.50	979.61	980.54	980.54	980.14	987.61	986.82	996.03	982.94
2011	994.68	989.41	996.59	1,007.25	1,029.37	1,014.55	1,020.77	1,035.01	1,031.22	1,051.60	1,032.14	1,044.18	1,020.91
Construction													
2007	1,108.08	1,048.90	1,132.09	1,122.76	1,183.47	1,203.57	1,184.53	1,188.81	1,220.84	1,176.58	1,141.75	1,142.93	1,157.44
2008	1,100.01	1,124.76	1,131.47	1,121.26	1,135.71	1,143.56	1,146.72	1,152.67	1,145.87	1,147.93	1,143.18	1,147.69	1,137.36
2009	1,144.18	1,206.75	1,214.10	1,211.85	1,212.43	1,213.94	1,215.27	1,223.60	1,221.14	1,226.82	1,230.25	1,240.74	1,213.81
2010	1,239.94	1,228.16	1,234.24	1,236.35	1,235.39	1,238.63	1,240.92	1,241.09	1,241.09	1,234.24	1,231.39	1,243.55	1,237.12
2011	1,242.43	1,239.85	1,237.42	1,256.39	1,280.75	1,272.71	1,308.08	1,319.47	1,292.82	1,306.50	1,262.25	1,281.04	1,276.83
Manufacturing													
2007	903.85	898.90	900.69	911.83	895.64	893.03	896.30	894.86	907.98	870.22	877.64	892.16	895.28
2008	870.33	855.46	866.31	865.83	860.55	855.93	856.94	861.09	861.70	863.47	864.66	864.04	862.18
2009	861.46	868.77	876.35	873.74	874.37	878.96	877.59	882.19	880.77	880.00	892.44	888.80	877.68
2010	889.22	889.82	892.65	901.73	910.04	901.91	937.87	939.88	940.28	948.59	958.64	979.15	924.48
2011	975.12	976.39	977.10	976.34	989.69	972.32	959.15	971.56	975.21	993.43	981.24	998.32	978.82
Trade, Transportation, and Utilities													
2007	639.41	650.07	658.24	676.05	678.45	680.58	687.50	676.13	711.74	680.69	674.34	684.04	674.88
2008	668.33	658.68	662.68	657.79	660.96	673.87	674.70	675.82	680.69	674.22	681.95	675.26	670.43
2009	655.54	667.49	672.92	669.19	666.81	668.27	667.55	671.22	671.22	665.86	670.48	684.00	669.22
2010	683.71	677.84	675.79	679.21	686.00	690.50	695.63	694.94	701.09	706.22	704.17	719.33	693.06
2011	715.87	708.98	697.25	718.29	733.25	725.55	743.77	730.80	748.35	766.45	753.28	756.80	733.42
Information													
2007	952.04	964.80	946.96	949.62	961.66	934.71	987.72	1,011.05	1,060.91	992.98	979.48	1,024.89	980.56
2008	1,004.27	965.67	997.92	974.64	967.92	980.62	962.74	972.41	973.16	972.77	979.88	977.26	977.46
2009	978.36	1,034.51	1,038.31	1,037.13	1,034.49	1,037.62	1,046.17	1,053.56	1,051.67	1,052.06	1,048.43	1,049.52	1,038.14
2010	1,044.20	1,034.20	1,038.18	1,046.32	1,043.50	1,038.50	1,039.98	1,041.15	1,037.32	1,034.67	1,037.85	1,034.11	1,039.24
2011	1,030.27	1,029.89	1,006.77	996.09	1,004.05	982.65	989.72	980.10	1,010.83	1,017.20	1,019.52	985.86	1,004.39
Financial Activities													
2007	1,053.56	1,162.73	1,098.16	1,127.90	1,080.72	1,081.53	1,135.11	1,076.41	1,119.01	992.28	992.88	1,013.45	1,078.01
2008	986.76	1,005.51	1,023.41	1,017.58	996.94	1,009.62	996.84	1,003.58	997.56	1,003.58	1,005.64	1,011.68	1,004.89
2009	1,018.11	1,074.48	1,074.48	1,068.26	1,069.04	1,064.62	1,070.78	1,077.76	1,074.11	1,071.98	1,069.04	1,064.30	1,066.38
2010	1,059.84	1,062.83	1,066.04	1,058.06	1,059.10	1,021.36	1,020.04	1,020.10	1,018.43	1,008.13	1,005.77	1,021.48	1,034.97
2011	1,027.21	1,035.41	1,028.46	1,044.20	1,064.30	1,026.56	1,032.85	1,038.54	1,048.59	1,106.78	1,098.20	1,095.13	1,053.87
Professional and Business Services													
2007	996.76	1,011.36	1,005.82	1,033.47	997.91	999.68	1,019.94	977.10	1,017.30	943.41	941.50	1,018.80	996.74
2008	988.72	963.50	1,017.38	993.81	988.20	1,003.70	997.44	1,001.15	1,001.29	998.25	1,003.70	1,004.78	996.84
2009	1,005.64	1,047.18	1,045.85	1,036.52	1,036.00	1,033.34	1,036.41	1,036.29	1,033.11	1,027.60	1,039.47	1,027.60	1,033.60
2010	1,024.56	1,020.66	1,020.66	1,022.73	1,025.53	1,022.00	1,023.57	1,030.03	1,028.66	1,035.51	1,033.03	1,010.59	1,024.85
2011	1,017.36	1,018.74	1,003.58	1,005.87	1,030.17	1,007.91	1,004.55	997.39	994.07	1,022.84	993.53	1,002.14	1,008.08
Education and Health Services													
2007	686.40	676.20	684.13	703.18	682.64	686.08	698.14	679.58	698.53	690.70	701.64	710.86	691.57
2008	700.74	692.72	691.42	697.77	694.78	697.13	693.12	698.10	702.53	704.14	705.35	705.76	698.67
2009	709.56	715.07	716.36	716.74	712.86	716.04	721.18	724.96	725.61	727.90	725.02	722.52	719.52
2010	724.14	727.07	720.97	719.03	721.26	722.25	715.51	726.41	729.59	728.49	724.31	738.66	724.83
2011	739.26	737.02	734.99	740.85	751.65	751.77	764.53	762.29	770.90	784.57	773.56	774.87	757.29
Leisure and Hospitality													
2007	324.85	328.93	325.08	389.90	406.65	395.27	398.35	386.58	382.27	315.49	313.50	313.44	357.68
2008	296.93	307.27	310.99	307.25	309.20	311.87	313.18	312.96	314.50	313.25	311.72	314.50	310.39
2009	310.25	329.38	328.34	326.82	328.08	328.81	327.60	330.24	328.96	323.09	320.74	317.44	325.09
2010	312.17	317.18	315.85	315.79	317.53	319.66	318.21	318.50	318.26	325.13	324.61	325.05	319.04
2011	323.74	324.14	330.62	334.91	316.25	315.49	314.50	318.78	325.30	314.96	317.27	326.40	321.72
Other Services													
2007	647.77	658.06	649.06	673.94	668.34	676.39	694.97	681.09	703.74	673.94	671.33	693.51	674.52
2008	677.35	696.16	711.10	702.72	707.30	706.69	696.84	697.66	694.55	707.05	707.63	697.37	700.22
2009	703.68	691.11	695.20	694.64	702.85	702.28	712.48	718.50	717.85	717.01	716.41	707.48	706.55
2010	712.94	710.60	713.55	715.39	713.83	712.86	710.98	710.65	706.20	710.92	709.37	720.96	712.37
2011	717.38	682.96	681.92	684.89	706.77	701.56	707.02	697.13	711.10	722.81	694.78	716.15	701.98

INDIANA
At a Glance

Population:
2000 census: 6,080,827
2010 census: 6,483,802
2011 estimate: 6,516,922

Percent change in population:
2000–2010: 6.6%
2010–2011: 0.5%

Percent change in total nonfarm employment:
2000–2010: -6.8%
2010–2011: 1.2%

Industry with the largest growth in employment, 2000–2011 (thousands):
Education and Health Services, 95.5

Industry with the largest decline or smallest growth in employment, 2000–2011 (thousands):
Manufacturing, -200.3

Civilian labor force:
2000: 3,144,379
2010: 3,176,657
2011: 3,188,260

Unemployment rate and rank among states (lowest to highest):
2000: 2.9%, 10th
2010: 10.1%, 37th
2011: 9.0%, 33rd

Over-the-year change in unemployment rates:
2010–2011: -1.1%

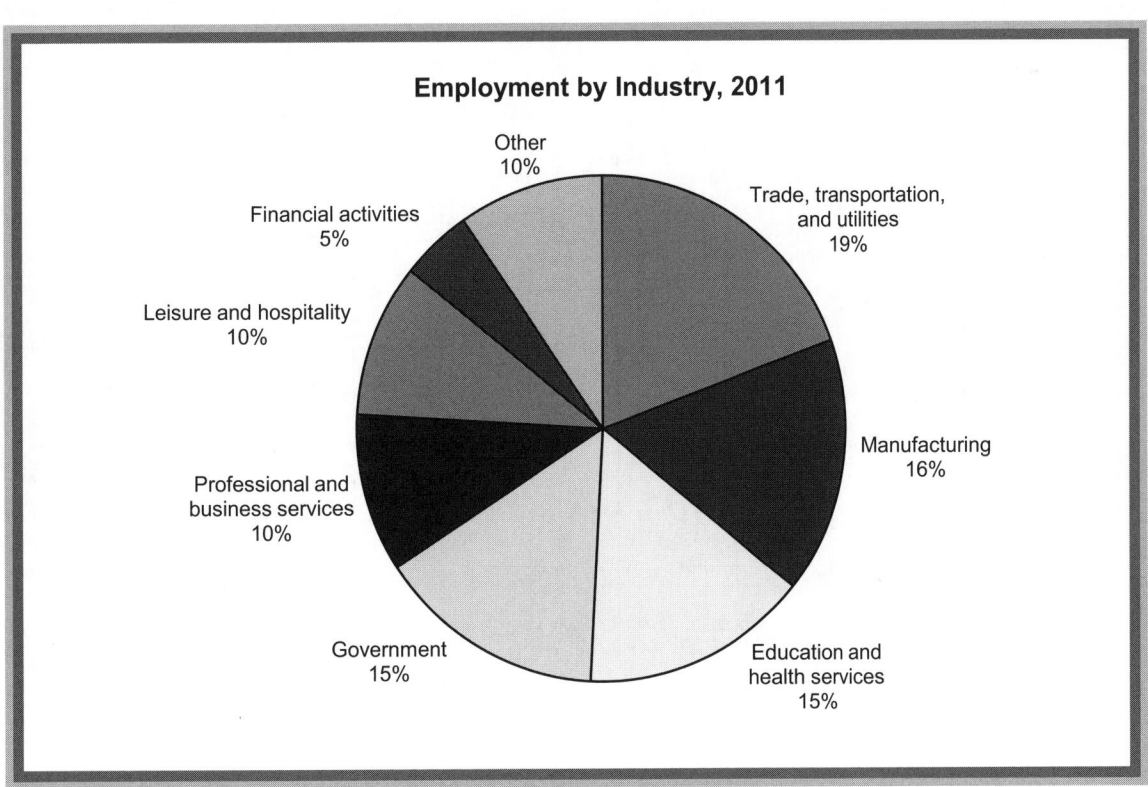

Employment by Industry, 2011

Other 10%
Financial activities 5%
Leisure and hospitality 10%
Professional and business services 10%
Government 15%
Education and health services 15%
Manufacturing 16%
Trade, transportation, and utilities 19%

1. Employment by Industry: Indiana, Selected Years, 2000–2011

(Numbers in thousands, not seasonally adjusted)

Industry and year	January	February	March	April	May	June	July	August	September	October	November	December	Annual average
Total Nonfarm													
2000	2,947.2	2,957.5	2,989.7	3,016.3	3,046.3	3,024.0	2,971.9	2,986.0	3,030.8	3,014.3	3,011.7	3,005.0	3,000.1
2001	2,901.7	2,915.7	2,937.1	2,959.2	2,969.7	2,949.5	2,892.6	2,918.5	2,953.7	2,938.8	2,935.3	2,928.8	2,933.4
2002	2,833.3	2,847.0	2,865.1	2,893.0	2,921.6	2,907.8	2,885.3	2,912.7	2,940.0	2,932.8	2,938.9	2,933.2	2,900.9
2003	2,846.3	2,849.6	2,868.9	2,894.4	2,919.4	2,896.1	2,854.0	2,887.2	2,922.5	2,936.4	2,935.7	2,933.2	2,895.3
2004	2,851.2	2,857.3	2,891.0	2,934.1	2,951.5	2,935.8	2,910.0	2,923.1	2,971.4	2,974.5	2,979.0	2,967.9	2,928.9
2005	2,882.2	2,900.6	2,923.1	2,963.7	2,974.5	2,956.2	2,925.3	2,940.6	2,997.9	3,000.0	3,003.7	2,994.0	2,955.2
2006	2,911.1	2,927.8	2,957.9	2,979.2	2,993.2	2,984.2	2,934.0	2,958.2	3,006.1	3,009.4	3,012.3	3,011.3	2,973.7
2007	2,921.6	2,924.6	2,965.4	2,989.3	3,010.6	3,000.7	2,949.7	2,984.7	3,018.3	3,021.9	3,026.6	3,015.7	2,985.8
2008	2,925.3	2,936.2	2,950.0	2,975.7	3,004.3	2,980.6	2,924.5	2,961.6	2,980.4	2,972.3	2,950.1	2,918.8	2,956.7
2009	2,793.8	2,785.8	2,791.7	2,799.1	2,809.5	2,778.9	2,720.2	2,754.7	2,797.9	2,806.3	2,806.4	2,797.7	2,786.8
2010	2,715.1	2,723.2	2,755.0	2,803.3	2,829.8	2,807.4	2,777.7	2,805.1	2,827.3	2,838.5	2,837.3	2,829.8	2,795.8
2011	2,761.9	2,771.6	2,807.1	2,842.6	2,856.5	2,834.9	2,797.7	2,821.4	2,863.9	2,871.4	2,870.3	2,864.4	2,830.3
Total Private													
2000	2,540.9	2,544.1	2,572.8	2,598.0	2,620.9	2,633.1	2,606.8	2,618.1	2,613.4	2,602.1	2,598.9	2,593.9	2,595.3
2001	2,492.4	2,492.9	2,511.4	2,534.7	2,549.6	2,559.3	2,532.2	2,543.9	2,534.1	2,514.2	2,510.6	2,505.3	2,523.4
2002	2,423.8	2,423.0	2,441.2	2,466.4	2,496.5	2,514.7	2,508.5	2,521.3	2,512.2	2,498.3	2,503.0	2,498.0	2,483.9
2003	2,427.7	2,418.6	2,435.1	2,462.9	2,486.4	2,493.0	2,475.3	2,495.2	2,490.8	2,497.4	2,496.8	2,493.7	2,472.7
2004	2,424.5	2,422.7	2,452.7	2,496.9	2,516.5	2,530.5	2,527.5	2,533.8	2,534.2	2,532.9	2,537.7	2,530.9	2,503.4
2005	2,453.4	2,461.4	2,484.1	2,524.7	2,538.5	2,553.3	2,545.3	2,553.8	2,558.8	2,557.1	2,562.9	2,556.3	2,529.1
2006	2,485.4	2,490.3	2,519.3	2,542.1	2,557.1	2,580.0	2,558.0	2,567.5	2,567.6	2,566.7	2,568.7	2,567.4	2,547.5
2007	2,493.6	2,484.0	2,521.4	2,548.1	2,572.9	2,590.7	2,569.8	2,576.3	2,575.1	2,575.2	2,579.4	2,569.1	2,554.6
2008	2,490.5	2,487.2	2,498.5	2,525.8	2,552.4	2,557.8	2,529.9	2,538.6	2,531.7	2,518.1	2,495.8	2,468.0	2,516.2
2009	2,354.2	2,338.0	2,340.2	2,348.6	2,355.1	2,360.7	2,341.6	2,347.2	2,350.8	2,348.6	2,353.7	2,345.9	2,348.7
2010	2,275.1	2,274.0	2,305.8	2,349.8	2,369.4	2,382.9	2,385.0	2,393.6	2,387.5	2,394.7	2,394.3	2,391.7	2,358.7
2011	2,332.4	2,334.4	2,368.2	2,403.9	2,423.4	2,433.6	2,421.7	2,424.7	2,429.8	2,433.2	2,431.7	2,430.3	2,405.6
Goods-Producing													
2000	810.7	811.4	818.8	825.7	831.5	838.2	831.8	834.3	827.6	817.1	809.6	800.3	821.4
2001	770.4	770.9	773.1	779.1	783.4	786.6	777.0	778.7	770.7	759.6	753.7	746.6	770.8
2002	723.6	724.0	729.0	735.7	744.1	754.3	753.2	757.8	752.9	745.6	742.7	734.6	741.5
2003	716.2	712.4	715.9	720.9	728.5	732.8	724.3	736.2	729.8	729.7	724.9	721.0	724.4
2004	703.2	701.6	710.5	723.6	732.6	740.0	735.2	741.7	738.8	734.2	730.4	726.6	726.5
2005	707.5	707.2	713.2	725.7	729.8	736.0	731.4	737.1	735.3	733.3	730.9	726.8	726.2
2006	710.2	707.8	715.8	723.6	728.1	738.2	729.9	734.1	727.9	724.3	718.9	716.1	722.9
2007	695.2	688.2	700.4	706.5	714.9	722.3	718.5	719.5	715.3	710.5	707.8	701.0	708.3
2008	679.2	676.7	675.7	681.2	689.2	692.8	676.7	682.0	673.0	663.1	649.0	628.8	672.3
2009	589.0	578.7	571.7	570.5	562.9	563.1	562.7	568.6	567.2	565.0	564.1	559.2	568.6
2010	540.6	538.7	548.8	564.7	572.1	579.1	585.1	586.2	582.4	583.3	578.0	574.8	569.5
2011	562.5	562.4	572.8	584.4	591.4	599.6	601.1	602.5	607.6	608.1	602.8	602.3	591.5
Mining and Logging													
2000	6.5	6.5	6.6	6.8	6.9	6.9	6.9	6.9	6.9	6.8	6.8	6.7	6.8
2001	6.4	6.5	6.7	7.1	7.2	7.3	7.4	7.4	7.4	7.4	7.3	7.1	7.1
2002	6.8	6.9	7.0	7.2	7.2	7.3	7.2	7.2	7.2	7.1	7.0	7.0	7.1
2003	6.6	6.7	6.7	7.0	7.0	7.1	7.1	7.1	7.2	7.1	7.1	7.0	7.0
2004	6.8	6.7	7.0	7.3	7.4	7.4	7.3	7.3	7.2	6.9	6.9	6.8	7.1
2005	6.7	6.7	6.8	7.0	7.0	7.1	7.0	7.0	6.9	6.9	6.9	6.8	6.9
2006	6.5	6.5	6.6	7.0	7.1	7.2	7.2	7.1	7.1	7.1	7.0	7.0	7.0
2007	6.8	6.7	6.9	7.0	7.1	7.1	7.1	7.1	7.1	7.0	6.9	6.8	7.0
2008	6.4	6.4	6.5	6.7	6.8	6.9	6.8	6.9	6.9	6.9	6.8	6.7	6.7
2009	6.3	6.3	6.5	6.6	6.7	6.8	6.8	6.8	6.8	6.7	6.7	6.5	6.6
2010	6.2	6.2	6.4	6.6	6.6	6.6	6.7	6.7	6.8	6.7	6.7	6.6	6.6
2011	6.3	6.4	6.6	6.7	6.8	6.9	6.9	6.9	6.9	6.9	6.8	6.7	6.7
Construction													
2000	138.0	136.8	144.3	151.1	155.3	159.1	159.2	159.3	156.4	151.7	148.5	142.7	150.2
2001	130.6	132.1	138.2	146.3	152.2	156.7	157.3	158.5	154.8	153.0	152.4	147.5	148.3
2002	134.4	133.5	137.0	142.9	147.9	152.3	155.2	155.1	152.6	149.5	148.1	143.6	146.0
2003	131.7	128.5	133.0	141.8	148.0	149.9	153.0	154.2	151.3	152.4	148.6	144.7	144.8
2004	131.4	129.6	136.5	146.7	152.6	155.6	158.9	156.8	155.0	153.5	151.1	146.5	147.9
2005	132.4	132.1	136.8	147.7	150.2	154.1	156.6	156.8	155.5	155.1	153.2	148.2	148.2
2006	136.9	136.1	140.9	148.0	153.4	157.1	157.3	157.8	156.2	156.4	154.3	152.0	150.5
2007	138.9	132.4	142.1	149.0	155.6	159.2	159.4	159.5	157.6	156.9	155.7	149.1	151.3
2008	135.5	133.2	137.6	143.6	148.7	151.8	153.2	152.0	150.0	149.2	143.3	133.7	144.3
2009	115.9	113.2	116.6	120.2	123.5	125.6	125.9	124.7	122.9	122.4	120.0	113.5	120.4
2010	100.3	98.3	104.5	115.0	118.3	121.1	126.1	124.7	121.9	123.0	120.9	114.0	115.7
2011	104.2	102.2	108.0	116.1	121.6	124.9	126.3	127.5	131.0	130.9	129.5	124.0	120.5
Manufacturing													
2000	666.2	668.1	667.9	667.8	669.3	672.2	665.7	668.1	664.3	658.6	654.3	650.9	664.5
2001	633.4	632.3	628.2	625.7	624.0	622.6	612.3	612.8	608.5	599.2	594.0	592.0	615.4
2002	582.4	583.6	585.0	585.6	589.0	594.7	590.8	595.5	593.1	589.0	587.6	584.0	588.4
2003	577.9	577.2	576.2	572.1	573.5	575.8	564.2	574.9	571.3	570.2	569.2	569.3	572.7
2004	565.0	565.3	567.0	569.6	572.6	577.0	569.0	577.6	576.6	573.8	572.4	573.3	571.6
2005	568.4	568.4	569.6	571.0	572.6	574.8	567.8	573.3	572.9	571.3	570.8	571.8	571.1
2006	566.8	565.2	568.3	568.6	567.6	573.9	565.4	569.2	564.6	560.8	557.6	557.1	565.4
2007	549.5	549.1	551.4	550.5	552.2	556.0	552.0	552.9	550.6	546.6	545.2	545.1	550.1
2008	537.3	537.1	531.6	530.9	533.7	534.1	516.7	523.1	516.1	507.0	498.9	488.4	521.2
2009	466.8	459.2	448.6	443.7	432.7	430.7	430.0	437.1	437.5	435.9	437.4	439.2	441.6
2010	434.1	434.2	437.9	443.1	447.2	451.4	452.3	454.8	453.7	453.6	450.4	454.2	447.2
2011	452.0	453.8	458.2	461.6	463.0	467.8	467.9	468.1	469.7	470.3	466.5	471.6	464.2

1. Employment by Industry: Indiana, Selected Years, 2000–2011—*Continued*

(Numbers in thousands, not seasonally adjusted)

Industry and year	January	February	March	April	May	June	July	August	September	October	November	December	Annual average
Service-Providing													
2000	2,136.5	2,146.1	2,170.9	2,190.6	2,214.8	2,185.8	2,140.1	2,151.7	2,203.2	2,197.2	2,202.1	2,204.7	2,178.6
2001	2,131.3	2,144.8	2,164.0	2,180.1	2,186.3	2,162.9	2,115.6	2,139.8	2,183.0	2,179.2	2,181.6	2,182.2	2,162.6
2002	2,109.7	2,123.0	2,136.1	2,157.3	2,177.5	2,153.5	2,132.1	2,154.9	2,187.1	2,187.2	2,196.2	2,198.6	2,159.4
2003	2,130.1	2,137.2	2,153.0	2,173.5	2,190.9	2,163.3	2,129.7	2,151.0	2,192.7	2,206.7	2,210.8	2,212.2	2,170.9
2004	2,148.0	2,155.7	2,180.5	2,210.5	2,218.9	2,195.8	2,174.8	2,181.4	2,232.6	2,240.3	2,248.6	2,241.3	2,202.4
2005	2,174.7	2,193.4	2,209.9	2,238.0	2,244.7	2,220.2	2,193.9	2,203.5	2,262.6	2,266.7	2,272.8	2,267.2	2,229.0
2006	2,200.9	2,220.0	2,242.1	2,255.6	2,265.1	2,246.0	2,204.1	2,224.1	2,278.2	2,285.1	2,293.4	2,295.2	2,250.8
2007	2,226.4	2,236.4	2,265.0	2,282.8	2,295.7	2,278.4	2,231.2	2,265.2	2,303.0	2,311.4	2,318.8	2,314.7	2,277.4
2008	2,246.1	2,259.5	2,274.3	2,294.5	2,315.1	2,287.8	2,247.8	2,279.6	2,307.4	2,309.2	2,301.1	2,290.0	2,284.4
2009	2,204.8	2,207.1	2,220.0	2,228.6	2,246.6	2,215.8	2,157.5	2,186.1	2,230.7	2,241.3	2,242.3	2,238.5	2,218.3
2010	2,174.5	2,184.5	2,206.2	2,238.6	2,257.7	2,228.3	2,192.6	2,218.9	2,244.9	2,255.2	2,259.3	2,255.0	2,226.3
2011	2,199.4	2,209.2	2,234.3	2,258.2	2,265.1	2,235.3	2,196.6	2,218.9	2,256.3	2,263.3	2,267.5	2,262.1	2,238.9
Trade, Transportation, and Utilities													
2000	607.2	602.1	607.9	611.1	615.8	617.9	616.0	617.0	615.3	622.2	632.1	639.5	617.0
2001	602.0	594.3	596.1	599.2	602.4	604.6	599.0	599.4	596.2	595.6	604.0	608.0	600.1
2002	579.0	572.6	574.5	575.9	581.1	584.0	582.7	583.2	580.7	579.3	590.8	595.6	581.6
2003	568.8	561.7	564.6	570.2	573.7	575.1	572.5	574.0	572.7	576.9	586.4	591.1	574.0
2004	566.6	561.1	565.9	572.2	576.9	579.4	579.9	580.5	576.5	581.4	591.2	596.1	577.3
2005	570.1	567.6	571.7	578.4	583.6	584.0	585.2	585.4	585.0	588.0	597.7	600.9	583.1
2006	576.9	572.6	577.4	579.2	584.4	587.0	584.8	585.7	584.5	587.8	598.6	602.8	585.1
2007	578.8	572.5	579.9	582.0	588.3	592.1	588.3	587.1	585.4	587.4	599.6	602.7	587.0
2008	576.4	571.9	574.4	577.2	583.9	584.9	582.0	583.0	578.9	578.6	582.0	582.4	579.6
2009	553.1	545.7	544.5	545.6	550.3	551.6	547.9	547.1	544.6	545.9	552.8	554.4	548.6
2010	532.3	527.1	532.3	537.6	542.5	544.9	545.5	545.3	542.1	547.9	555.9	558.4	542.7
2011	539.3	536.2	539.5	546.3	551.7	553.6	550.0	550.4	545.8	549.8	555.6	559.9	548.2
Wholesale Trade													
2000	123.8	124.2	125.5	125.7	126.4	127.2	126.9	126.8	126.2	126.2	126.0	125.8	125.9
2001	123.7	123.6	124.1	123.8	124.1	124.5	123.8	123.4	122.8	122.4	121.8	121.7	123.3
2002	119.7	119.3	119.3	120.0	120.6	121.1	120.5	119.9	119.2	118.5	118.3	118.3	119.6
2003	117.6	117.3	117.4	117.6	118.1	118.5	118.0	117.5	116.8	116.9	116.9	117.1	117.5
2004	116.1	116.3	117.5	118.9	119.8	120.6	121.2	120.8	119.8	120.5	120.5	120.6	119.4
2005	119.0	119.2	119.8	121.1	121.8	122.5	122.9	122.5	121.8	122.0	122.1	122.3	121.4
2006	121.1	121.2	122.0	122.8	123.8	125.0	124.4	123.8	123.4	123.6	123.5	123.9	123.2
2007	122.8	122.9	124.0	124.7	125.5	126.5	127.4	126.2	125.4	125.5	125.8	125.8	125.2
2008	124.0	124.1	124.6	125.3	126.2	126.4	125.9	125.2	124.2	123.7	122.6	121.7	124.5
2009	117.9	116.8	116.2	115.4	115.7	115.5	115.4	114.1	113.1	113.3	112.9	112.8	114.9
2010	111.3	111.1	112.1	113.1	113.5	113.8	114.5	113.6	113.0	113.2	112.7	112.4	112.9
2011	112.3	112.5	113.3	114.5	115.5	116.2	115.6	116.1	115.0	115.7	115.6	115.7	114.8
Retail Trade													
2000	354.0	348.6	352.1	353.9	357.8	358.9	355.7	356.2	355.5	360.2	372.6	379.4	358.7
2001	351.8	344.9	345.4	346.5	349.4	350.8	346.0	345.8	344.6	346.1	355.7	358.8	348.8
2002	338.8	333.7	335.8	336.3	340.5	342.8	340.7	340.6	339.1	337.7	348.4	353.8	340.7
2003	331.1	325.4	327.8	331.0	334.3	335.8	333.0	334.4	333.4	335.2	345.0	349.5	334.7
2004	329.7	323.8	326.1	328.3	332.0	333.8	332.0	332.3	329.3	332.3	341.9	346.3	332.3
2005	325.4	321.8	324.5	328.1	332.0	331.5	332.5	331.9	331.3	333.7	342.4	345.7	331.7
2006	326.9	322.0	325.0	325.9	329.0	329.8	328.5	329.3	327.6	330.5	340.3	343.4	329.9
2007	325.6	319.5	324.0	324.7	329.1	330.7	327.7	326.9	325.4	327.1	338.0	340.5	328.3
2008	321.3	316.8	317.9	319.0	323.7	324.3	323.4	323.5	321.2	321.6	326.4	327.8	322.2
2009	308.4	303.0	303.1	305.6	309.4	311.0	308.4	307.8	305.8	306.3	313.5	315.4	308.1
2010	299.7	294.9	297.8	300.9	304.4	305.9	305.6	305.3	302.0	306.8	314.5	316.9	304.6
2011	302.2	298.1	300.4	304.7	308.0	308.8	307.6	306.1	303.0	305.4	310.1	311.9	305.5
Transportation and Utilities													
2000	129.4	129.3	130.3	131.5	131.6	131.8	133.4	134.0	133.6	135.8	133.5	134.3	132.4
2001	126.5	125.8	126.6	128.9	128.9	129.3	129.2	130.2	128.8	127.1	126.5	127.5	127.9
2002	120.5	119.6	119.4	119.6	120.0	120.1	121.5	122.7	122.4	123.1	124.1	123.5	121.4
2003	120.1	119.0	119.4	121.6	121.3	120.8	121.5	122.1	122.5	124.8	124.5	124.5	121.8
2004	120.8	121.0	122.3	125.0	125.1	125.0	126.7	127.4	127.4	128.6	128.8	129.2	125.6
2005	125.7	126.6	127.4	129.2	129.8	130.0	129.8	131.0	131.9	132.3	133.2	132.9	130.0
2006	128.9	129.4	130.4	130.5	131.6	132.2	131.9	132.6	133.5	133.7	134.8	135.5	132.1
2007	130.4	130.1	131.9	132.6	133.7	134.9	133.2	134.0	134.6	134.8	135.8	136.4	133.5
2008	131.1	131.0	131.9	132.9	134.0	134.2	132.7	134.3	133.5	133.3	133.0	132.9	132.9
2009	126.8	125.9	125.2	124.6	125.2	125.1	124.1	125.2	125.7	126.3	126.4	126.2	125.6
2010	121.3	121.1	122.4	123.6	124.6	125.2	125.4	126.4	127.1	127.9	128.7	129.1	125.2
2011	124.8	125.6	125.8	127.1	128.2	128.6	126.8	128.2	127.8	128.7	129.9	132.3	127.8
Information													
2000	45.7	45.9	46.4	45.4	46.0	46.7	46.1	46.4	46.1	45.7	46.2	46.3	46.1
2001	45.5	45.3	45.6	45.0	45.2	45.3	45.0	44.6	44.0	43.6	43.8	43.9	44.7
2002	42.9	42.6	42.9	42.5	42.8	43.1	42.8	42.8	42.1	41.7	41.9	41.8	42.5
2003	41.0	40.7	41.1	40.8	41.4	42.0	41.9	42.1	41.4	41.0	41.2	41.3	41.3
2004	40.8	40.4	40.9	40.8	41.3	41.8	41.4	41.1	40.3	40.5	40.6	40.8	40.9
2005	40.0	40.1	40.1	40.2	40.7	41.0	40.8	40.7	40.0	39.7	40.0	40.4	40.3
2006	39.5	39.8	39.8	39.9	40.2	40.6	40.3	40.1	39.5	39.3	39.6	39.8	39.9
2007	39.5	39.6	39.5	39.6	40.1	40.6	40.6	40.5	39.9	39.6	39.9	40.0	40.0
2008	39.6	39.6	39.7	39.8	40.3	40.5	40.4	40.2	39.5	39.1	39.1	39.3	39.8
2009	38.6	38.4	38.1	37.8	38.1	38.4	37.8	37.6	36.8	36.4	36.5	36.7	37.6
2010	35.9	35.7	35.7	35.7	36.1	36.4	35.8	35.6	35.0	34.9	34.9	34.9	35.6
2011	34.4	34.2	34.4	34.2	34.6	34.6	34.8	34.5	33.9	33.4	33.7	34.1	34.2

1. Employment by Industry: Indiana, Selected Years, 2000–2011—*Continued*

(Numbers in thousands, not seasonally adjusted)

Industry and year	January	February	March	April	May	June	July	August	September	October	November	December	Annual average
Financial Activities													
2000	144.4	144.1	144.5	144.7	145.7	147.1	146.3	146.0	144.7	143.9	143.9	144.9	145.0
2001	142.0	142.2	142.8	143.6	144.3	146.0	144.6	144.0	141.8	140.8	140.8	141.5	142.9
2002	139.2	138.9	138.9	138.8	139.8	141.1	141.5	141.6	140.3	139.8	140.1	140.8	140.1
2003	139.5	139.5	140.2	140.5	141.9	143.1	143.2	143.3	141.8	141.0	140.4	140.9	141.3
2004	138.6	138.6	138.9	139.2	140.3	141.6	141.7	141.6	139.8	139.5	139.3	140.0	139.9
2005	137.2	137.2	137.2	138.0	138.7	139.9	140.4	140.7	139.6	139.0	138.8	139.4	138.8
2006	138.4	138.6	138.8	139.1	139.9	141.2	140.6	140.5	139.2	138.8	138.5	139.3	139.4
2007	137.5	137.8	138.1	138.4	139.1	140.3	140.1	139.6	138.5	138.2	137.7	138.0	138.6
2008	135.6	135.8	136.0	136.1	136.6	137.6	137.8	137.1	135.5	134.9	134.0	134.0	135.9
2009	132.3	131.7	131.6	131.5	132.0	132.4	132.3	131.8	130.4	130.0	129.5	129.9	131.3
2010	129.9	129.4	129.7	129.7	130.4	131.7	132.3	132.2	130.9	131.6	131.3	131.7	130.9
2011	130.9	130.9	131.3	131.3	132.2	132.9	133.0	132.8	131.6	130.3	129.3	129.9	131.4
Professional and Business Services													
2000	249.1	250.4	255.3	261.0	263.4	266.1	261.5	263.8	264.5	260.9	259.4	256.4	259.3
2001	241.6	242.2	246.1	250.3	251.7	253.8	252.1	256.2	252.7	251.9	249.6	247.6	249.7
2002	239.4	240.8	244.8	251.4	255.8	258.2	259.1	261.7	260.2	258.9	257.9	256.3	253.7
2003	246.5	246.5	248.2	251.2	254.4	255.4	254.4	257.8	257.8	259.7	260.1	257.4	254.1
2004	248.9	251.7	256.7	264.8	266.9	269.7	272.2	274.3	273.1	273.7	274.1	270.6	266.4
2005	260.5	264.1	266.8	273.1	274.2	276.2	276.2	279.8	280.4	281.2	280.5	278.2	274.3
2006	266.5	269.5	274.7	280.0	282.6	285.5	282.8	288.9	288.2	286.5	285.8	285.0	281.3
2007	275.8	276.8	283.5	289.6	292.3	294.0	290.1	295.7	295.5	295.1	293.7	292.0	289.5
2008	280.1	279.4	282.2	287.7	287.9	289.3	286.4	290.2	289.6	288.8	282.9	276.6	285.1
2009	259.4	257.7	258.3	259.1	257.9	259.1	255.8	260.8	263.1	267.7	271.1	269.2	261.6
2010	256.9	258.4	263.0	272.7	274.5	277.3	278.5	283.1	281.9	284.4	285.1	285.8	275.1
2011	275.3	276.2	282.2	288.2	287.2	287.2	283.0	287.1	292.7	294.9	293.9	292.2	286.7
Education and Health Services													
2000	327.0	330.6	332.4	333.6	333.7	326.9	321.5	324.1	332.9	334.8	335.5	336.4	330.8
2001	335.6	338.4	340.0	341.8	337.0	330.0	327.7	330.2	346.3	346.7	348.3	349.1	339.3
2002	345.2	347.3	348.4	349.4	348.6	344.1	342.7	344.5	353.5	355.7	357.2	357.8	349.5
2003	357.5	359.6	360.8	362.7	359.2	351.5	350.3	349.0	362.0	367.7	367.6	367.8	359.6
2004	365.3	367.3	369.5	372.7	365.0	359.0	360.3	356.3	373.7	378.1	379.7	376.8	368.6
2005	371.6	375.7	377.5	380.6	373.1	371.3	369.8	366.6	382.9	388.5	390.1	387.0	377.9
2006	381.7	386.7	389.5	389.8	382.4	380.8	377.6	374.0	390.5	396.7	397.2	394.5	386.8
2007	389.2	391.4	393.6	396.5	392.2	389.8	387.3	385.5	400.2	407.5	408.7	406.5	395.7
2008	401.1	404.2	405.4	407.2	405.7	400.7	397.6	394.4	410.2	416.3	417.6	419.0	406.6
2009	409.6	412.9	416.4	416.8	416.9	415.7	408.8	405.3	419.7	422.5	423.6	423.0	415.9
2010	417.2	421.1	425.6	428.1	424.7	419.3	415.2	416.5	427.1	429.4	430.3	428.9	423.6
2011	423.2	425.9	430.2	432.3	429.6	425.1	418.7	418.0	424.9	428.8	429.7	428.8	426.3
Leisure and Hospitality													
2000	250.0	251.9	258.4	266.8	274.6	279.2	274.2	276.9	273.0	269.1	264.0	261.7	266.7
2001	249.0	252.5	259.5	267.1	276.0	282.0	277.6	281.9	275.2	269.7	264.2	262.2	268.1
2002	250.5	252.1	257.1	266.2	276.3	280.9	278.7	282.1	276.1	271.2	266.5	265.0	268.6
2003	253.9	253.2	258.4	270.0	279.6	284.1	280.2	284.3	277.5	273.8	269.0	266.5	270.9
2004	255.0	255.3	262.5	274.4	283.6	287.7	285.6	287.2	281.8	275.1	272.4	269.9	274.2
2005	257.5	260.0	266.9	277.2	286.2	292.0	289.2	291.4	284.4	276.8	274.6	273.0	277.4
2006	263.2	266.0	272.6	279.2	287.2	293.3	289.8	292.2	286.4	282.5	279.9	279.1	281.0
2007	268.1	268.1	275.1	283.4	292.8	297.4	291.8	296.0	288.7	285.3	280.9	277.6	283.8
2008	267.9	268.8	273.8	284.0	294.9	297.8	295.5	298.8	293.2	285.3	280.1	277.2	284.8
2009	263.6	264.5	270.4	278.2	287.5	290.1	286.8	287.6	281.8	273.8	269.2	266.5	276.7
2010	256.3	257.7	263.5	273.4	280.9	284.8	283.1	285.9	279.8	274.8	270.5	269.1	273.3
2011	259.7	261.1	268.7	277.8	286.8	289.7	290.6	289.3	284.0	278.8	277.7	273.8	278.2
Other Services													
2000	106.8	107.7	109.1	109.7	110.2	111.0	109.4	109.6	109.3	108.4	108.2	108.4	109.0
2001	106.3	107.1	108.2	108.6	109.6	111.0	109.2	108.9	107.2	106.3	106.2	106.4	107.9
2002	104.0	104.7	105.6	106.5	108.0	109.0	107.8	107.6	106.4	106.1	105.9	106.1	106.5
2003	104.3	105.0	105.9	106.6	107.7	109.0	108.5	108.5	107.8	107.6	107.2	107.7	107.2
2004	106.1	106.7	107.8	109.2	109.9	111.3	111.2	111.1	110.2	110.4	110.0	110.1	109.5
2005	109.0	109.5	110.7	111.5	112.2	112.9	112.3	112.1	111.2	110.6	110.3	110.6	111.1
2006	109.0	109.3	110.7	111.3	112.3	113.4	112.2	112.0	111.4	110.8	110.2	110.8	111.1
2007	109.5	109.6	111.3	112.1	113.2	114.2	113.1	112.4	111.6	111.6	111.1	111.3	111.8
2008	110.6	110.8	111.3	112.6	113.9	114.2	113.5	112.9	111.8	112.0	111.1	110.7	112.1
2009	108.6	108.4	109.2	109.1	109.5	110.3	109.5	108.4	107.2	107.3	106.9	107.0	108.5
2010	106.0	105.9	107.2	107.9	108.2	109.4	109.5	108.8	108.3	108.4	108.3	108.1	108.0
2011	107.1	107.5	109.1	109.4	109.9	110.9	110.5	110.1	109.3	109.1	109.0	109.3	109.3
Government													
2000	406.3	413.4	416.9	418.3	425.4	390.9	365.1	367.9	417.4	412.2	412.8	411.1	404.8
2001	409.3	422.8	425.7	424.5	420.1	390.2	360.4	374.6	419.6	424.6	424.7	423.5	410.0
2002	409.5	424.0	423.9	426.6	425.1	393.1	376.8	391.4	427.8	434.5	435.9	435.2	417.0
2003	418.6	431.0	433.8	431.5	433.0	403.1	378.7	392.0	431.7	439.0	438.9	439.5	422.6
2004	426.7	434.6	438.3	437.2	435.0	405.3	382.5	389.3	437.2	441.6	441.3	437.0	425.5
2005	428.8	439.2	439.0	439.0	436.0	402.9	380.0	386.8	439.1	442.9	440.8	437.7	426.0
2006	425.7	437.5	438.6	437.1	436.1	404.2	376.0	390.7	438.5	442.7	443.6	443.9	426.2
2007	428.0	440.6	444.0	441.2	437.7	410.0	379.9	408.4	443.2	446.7	447.2	446.6	431.1
2008	434.8	449.0	451.5	449.9	451.9	422.8	394.6	423.0	448.7	454.2	454.3	450.8	440.5
2009	439.6	447.8	451.5	450.5	454.4	418.2	378.6	407.5	447.1	457.7	452.7	451.8	438.1
2010	440.0	449.2	449.2	453.5	460.4	424.5	392.7	411.5	439.8	443.8	443.0	438.1	437.1
2011	429.5	437.2	438.9	438.7	433.1	401.3	376.0	396.7	434.1	438.2	438.6	434.1	424.7

2. Average Weekly Hours by Selected Industry: Indiana, 2007–2011

(Not seasonally adjusted)

Industry and year	January	February	March	April	May	June	July	August	September	October	November	December	Annual average
Total Private													
2007	35.3	34.3	35.5	35.7	36.0	35.8	35.6	35.6	35.9	35.4	35.4	35.7	35.5
2008	35.1	35.0	35.4	34.9	35.0	35.3	34.6	35.0	34.7	34.7	34.9	34.9	35.0
2009	34.4	34.9	34.7	34.1	34.1	34.3	34.7	35.0	34.4	34.5	35.2	35.1	34.6
2010	34.8	34.5	35.0	35.0	35.1	35.1	35.1	35.4	35.2	35.2	35.5	35.1	35.1
2011	35.0	34.9	35.0	34.9	35.2	35.0	34.8	35.1	35.1	35.3	34.8	34.7	35.0
Goods-Producing													
2007	40.5	38.3	40.7	40.4	40.3	40.6	40.2	40.7	41.5	40.5	40.8	41.0	40.5
2008	40.2	39.8	40.6	39.7	40.0	40.5	39.1	40.6	39.9	39.8	39.8	39.8	40.0
2009	37.9	38.7	38.6	38.0	38.3	39.2	39.2	39.9	39.3	39.7	41.0	41.0	39.2
2010	40.5	39.8	40.6	40.6	40.7	41.0	40.8	41.1	41.0	41.5	41.6	41.5	40.9
2011	41.3	41.1	41.3	40.9	41.2	40.7	40.1	41.3	41.3	41.6	40.8	41.0	41.0
Construction													
2007	38.7	34.6	38.6	37.7	39.8	39.7	39.7	39.2	39.4	39.5	38.6	38.7	38.7
2008	37.3	37.1	37.6	36.5	37.1	37.9	38.1	39.9	38.6	38.9	38.5	37.7	38.0
2009	36.4	37.7	38.3	37.3	38.2	38.3	40.1	40.6	38.6	38.3	40.2	37.8	38.5
2010	38.5	36.6	38.7	39.6	38.1	39.4	40.7	40.6	38.4	40.2	39.3	38.1	39.1
2011	37.4	36.5	37.4	37.7	39.7	38.4	38.8	39.7	38.8	39.1	37.7	38.0	38.3
Manufacturing													
2007	40.7	39.9	41.7	41.1	42.0	41.9	41.2	41.8	42.7	41.3	41.8	42.0	41.5
2008	41.2	40.7	41.2	40.4	40.3	40.5	39.6	40.1	40.0	39.9	40.3	39.3	40.3
2009	37.2	37.7	37.7	37.3	37.6	38.7	38.2	39.0	38.8	39.4	40.7	41.4	38.6
2010	40.8	40.5	40.2	40.1	40.9	40.9	40.7	41.1	41.1	41.3	41.8	41.8	40.9
2011	41.8	41.8	42.0	41.6	41.4	41.1	40.3	41.5	41.5	41.9	41.3	41.5	41.5
Trade, Transportation, and Utilities													
2007	36.5	36.4	36.6	37.5	38.2	37.7	37.6	37.5	37.4	37.3	37.0	37.3	37.3
2008	36.5	36.6	36.8	36.6	36.9	37.4	36.6	36.9	36.8	36.7	36.6	36.2	36.7
2009	36.1	36.1	35.7	35.5	35.7	35.9	36.4	36.3	36.1	36.1	36.4	36.1	36.0
2010	35.8	36.0	36.1	36.5	36.7	36.5	36.6	36.8	36.6	36.6	36.5	36.3	36.4
2011	35.0	34.6	35.0	35.2	35.3	35.7	35.3	35.2	35.1	35.2	34.3	34.3	35.0
Financial Activities													
2007	35.8	35.5	37.6	37.4	37.2	36.7	36.9	36.2	37.0	36.8	36.6	36.6	36.7
2008	36.3	37.1	36.7	36.7	37.3	36.9	36.6	36.6	36.8	36.7	37.0	36.8	36.8
2009	36.3	36.6	36.1	35.3	36.2	35.6	35.5	36.6	36.3	36.8	37.8	38.0	36.4
2010	37.2	37.0	37.0	37.2	37.4	37.3	37.6	37.4	36.6	37.1	37.3	35.8	37.1
2011	36.8	36.4	36.3	36.8	37.5	36.9	37.1	36.3	36.5	36.9	36.4	36.6	36.7
Professional and Business Services													
2007	33.7	32.7	33.7	34.4	35.0	34.4	34.3	34.4	34.9	34.8	34.8	34.9	34.3
2008	34.2	33.9	34.1	34.3	33.6	34.8	34.1	34.1	34.4	34.3	34.7	34.8	34.3
2009	34.9	35.5	35.7	35.2	34.4	34.9	35.3	35.7	34.7	34.5	35.0	35.1	35.1
2010	35.6	35.3	35.2	35.2	35.6	35.3	35.2	37.1	35.5	35.8	36.6	36.1	35.7
2011	36.0	35.8	35.5	35.5	36.2	36.0	35.1	35.4	35.7	36.1	35.4	34.9	35.6
Education and Health Services													
2007	32.7	32.4	32.9	33.2	33.5	32.7	32.8	32.7	32.9	32.3	32.8	32.9	32.8
2008	32.5	32.3	32.6	32.1	32.4	33.0	32.7	32.5	32.5	32.8	33.3	32.6	32.6
2009	33.0	33.0	33.0	32.8	32.7	32.5	33.5	33.6	32.5	32.1	33.0	32.7	32.9
2010	32.4	32.1	32.2	32.3	32.6	32.4	32.2	32.4	32.3	31.9	32.4	32.4	32.3
2011	32.1	32.1	32.4	32.3	32.6	32.4	32.5	32.5	32.6	32.7	32.7	32.7	32.5
Leisure and Hospitality													
2007	25.8	24.8	25.6	25.5	25.7	26.4	26.0	25.8	25.5	25.1	24.5	24.5	25.4
2008	24.1	24.5	24.6	24.1	24.6	25.2	25.4	25.1	24.7	24.6	24.9	24.4	24.7
2009	24.4	25.7	25.5	24.8	25.3	25.6	25.9	26.3	25.4	25.3	25.5	25.2	25.4
2010	24.9	25.5	26.1	25.7	25.8	25.9	26.4	26.5	26.5	26.3	26.5	26.0	26.0
2011	25.8	26.3	26.4	26.3	26.4	26.3	26.3	26.2	25.8	26.0	26.0	25.6	26.1
Other Services													
2007	28.2	27.8	29.4	28.4	28.6	29.2	29.0	28.5	28.0	27.5	28.4	28.8	28.5
2008	29.1	28.7	29.9	29.2	28.6	29.2	28.5	29.5	29.3	29.7	29.9	29.1	29.2
2009	29.1	29.3	29.7	28.8	28.5	30.0	29.7	29.6	29.7	29.5	31.0	30.1	29.6
2010	29.7	29.4	29.9	28.7	29.3	29.9	30.1	29.8	30.2	30.1	30.0	28.9	29.7
2011	29.1	28.7	29.1	28.8	28.0	28.6	28.6	28.6	28.7	29.2	28.7	28.4	28.7

3. Average Hourly Earnings by Selected Industry: Indiana, 2007–2011

(Dollars, not seasonally adjusted)

Industry and year	January	February	March	April	May	June	July	August	September	October	November	December	Annual average
Total Private													
2007	19.76	20.01	19.83	19.97	19.61	19.71	19.93	19.96	20.17	19.86	20.06	20.37	19.94
2008	20.05	20.29	20.40	20.43	20.15	20.38	20.25	20.34	20.42	20.31	20.36	20.23	20.30
2009	20.50	21.00	20.74	20.67	20.55	20.52	20.41	20.36	20.51	20.34	20.52	20.60	20.56
2010	20.59	20.64	20.58	20.54	20.57	20.44	20.53	20.39	20.55	20.72	20.58	20.74	20.57
2011	20.79	20.55	20.43	20.30	20.44	20.32	20.61	20.63	20.72	21.01	20.88	21.14	20.65
Goods-Producing													
2007	22.22	22.69	22.64	23.06	22.68	22.65	23.23	23.31	23.32	22.90	23.10	23.45	22.94
2008	22.85	23.46	23.84	23.74	23.44	23.71	23.38	23.36	23.85	23.53	23.74	23.73	23.55
2009	23.54	24.18	23.87	24.00	23.86	23.71	23.83	23.45	23.66	23.51	23.92	23.30	23.73
2010	23.24	23.28	23.21	23.43	23.56	23.29	23.50	23.20	23.18	23.65	23.26	23.28	23.34
2011	23.32	22.91	23.12	23.00	23.27	23.18	23.51	23.57	23.64	24.11	23.99	24.43	23.51
Construction													
2007	23.06	23.65	23.45	22.72	22.85	22.63	22.96	22.71	23.34	23.05	23.42	23.62	23.10
2008	23.33	23.44	23.70	23.45	23.00	23.04	23.35	23.13	23.17	23.22	23.50	23.85	23.34
2009	23.83	24.04	24.30	24.59	24.31	24.49	24.56	24.47	24.60	24.38	24.40	24.56	24.39
2010	24.74	25.45	25.20	25.75	25.66	26.05	26.81	26.03	25.66	26.61	26.43	27.22	26.01
2011	26.65	26.33	26.45	26.09	26.62	26.14	26.07	26.21	26.33	26.05	26.68	26.94	26.37
Manufacturing													
2007	22.05	22.52	22.48	23.16	22.69	22.72	23.29	22.98	22.91	22.49	22.69	22.87	22.74
2008	22.25	23.01	22.70	22.76	22.59	22.68	22.44	22.46	22.53	22.40	22.77	22.79	22.61
2009	22.64	23.38	23.01	22.91	22.62	22.51	22.71	22.33	22.70	22.54	23.08	22.38	22.73
2010	22.27	22.30	22.22	22.32	22.60	22.19	22.26	22.27	22.43	22.73	22.31	22.26	22.35
2011	22.49	22.13	22.33	22.20	22.33	22.32	22.70	22.71	22.81	23.38	23.08	23.64	22.68
Trade, Transportation, and Utilities													
2007	17.68	17.79	17.51	17.32	16.99	17.29	17.37	17.20	17.51	17.02	17.15	17.33	17.34
2008	17.47	17.21	17.50	17.63	17.17	17.61	17.32	17.49	17.78	17.66	17.92	18.01	17.56
2009	18.31	18.34	18.53	18.24	18.20	18.60	18.30	18.66	18.78	18.65	18.80	19.07	18.54
2010	19.36	19.28	19.24	19.36	19.27	19.58	19.49	19.33	19.75	19.62	19.70	19.57	19.46
2011	20.04	19.59	19.31	19.23	19.35	19.12	19.30	19.27	19.36	19.54	19.49	19.30	19.41
Financial Activities													
2007	23.23	24.43	23.31	24.20	23.29	23.62	23.26	22.94	22.66	21.98	22.55	22.30	23.15
2008	21.69	21.91	21.99	22.01	21.24	21.48	21.45	21.46	21.86	21.77	21.62	21.90	21.70
2009	21.88	22.29	23.71	24.17	22.85	23.25	22.76	21.69	21.96	23.81	23.79	23.95	23.01
2010	24.45	24.17	24.40	23.36	23.81	23.94	23.57	23.99	24.09	23.43	22.87	24.17	23.85
2011	24.38	23.42	23.11	22.90	22.72	22.72	22.85	23.02	22.72	23.08	22.68	21.94	22.96
Professional and Business Services													
2007	19.23	19.94	19.66	19.65	19.14	19.37	19.36	19.64	19.64	19.36	19.30	19.64	19.49
2008	19.47	19.75	19.82	19.44	19.44	19.57	19.64	19.53	19.78	19.65	19.71	19.61	19.62
2009	21.21	21.64	21.05	20.83	21.31	21.22	21.19	21.05	20.83	19.22	19.48	19.65	20.71
2010	19.46	19.79	19.44	19.10	19.58	19.52	19.66	19.59	19.78	20.10	20.38	20.58	19.76
2011	20.86	20.67	20.67	20.49	20.94	20.78	21.37	21.28	21.18	21.27	21.63	21.83	21.08
Education and Health Services													
2007	21.24	20.80	20.81	20.96	21.23	21.40	21.54	21.30	21.53	21.81	22.01	21.96	21.39
2008	21.69	21.68	21.77	21.76	21.67	21.60	21.98	21.84	22.13	21.88	21.97	22.08	21.84
2009	21.64	21.56	21.50	21.50	21.62	21.58	21.56	21.40	21.54	21.48	21.42	21.85	21.55
2010	21.50	21.65	21.71	21.56	21.51	21.30	21.77	21.41	21.63	21.76	21.51	21.66	21.58
2011	21.54	21.72	21.59	21.43	21.59	21.84	22.23	22.13	22.07	22.27	21.95	22.42	21.90
Leisure and Hospitality													
2007	11.32	11.74	11.61	11.52	10.89	10.75	10.77	10.94	11.04	11.39	11.48	11.56	11.24
2008	11.15	11.27	11.13	11.18	11.19	11.28	11.19	11.49	11.53	11.64	11.61	11.95	11.38
2009	12.07	11.93	11.51	11.91	11.68	11.45	11.61	11.76	12.09	12.19	12.14	12.56	11.90
2010	12.80	12.88	12.72	12.29	12.25	12.31	12.29	12.15	12.34	12.27	12.25	12.85	12.44
2011	12.83	12.82	12.66	12.44	12.35	12.24	12.26	12.22	12.51	12.30	12.46	12.80	12.48
Other Services													
2007	17.07	17.22	16.24	17.23	16.16	16.48	16.69	16.44	16.54	16.09	16.40	16.85	16.61
2008	16.50	17.25	16.50	17.00	16.92	16.81	17.00	17.67	17.16	16.65	16.45	16.71	16.88
2009	17.95	18.32	18.14	17.89	18.14	17.11	17.44	18.23	18.41	18.75	19.00	19.23	18.22
2010	18.97	19.25	18.80	19.08	18.75	17.73	17.80	18.58	18.77	19.30	19.06	19.24	18.77
2011	18.96	18.85	18.62	18.31	18.13	17.59	16.99	16.73	16.57	16.60	16.49	16.94	17.56

4. Average Weekly Earnings by Selected Industry: Indiana, 2007–2011

(Dollars, not seasonally adjusted)

Industry and year	January	February	March	April	May	June	July	August	September	October	November	December	Annual average
Total Private													
2007	697.53	686.34	703.97	712.93	705.96	705.62	709.51	710.58	724.10	703.04	710.12	727.21	707.97
2008	703.76	710.15	722.16	713.01	705.25	719.41	700.65	711.90	708.57	704.76	710.56	706.03	709.83
2009	705.20	732.90	719.68	704.85	700.76	703.84	708.23	712.60	705.54	701.73	722.30	723.06	711.76
2010	716.53	712.08	720.30	718.90	722.01	717.44	720.60	721.81	723.36	729.34	730.59	727.97	721.69
2011	727.65	717.20	715.05	708.47	719.49	711.20	717.23	724.11	727.27	741.65	726.62	733.56	722.28
Goods-Producing													
2007	899.91	869.03	921.45	931.62	914.00	919.59	933.85	948.72	967.78	927.45	942.48	961.45	928.31
2008	918.57	933.71	967.90	942.48	937.60	960.26	914.16	948.42	951.62	936.49	944.85	944.45	941.71
2009	892.17	935.77	921.38	912.00	913.84	929.43	934.14	935.66	929.84	933.35	980.72	955.30	930.95
2010	941.22	926.54	942.33	951.26	958.89	954.89	958.80	953.52	950.38	981.48	967.62	966.12	954.77
2011	963.12	941.60	954.86	940.70	958.72	943.43	942.75	973.44	976.33	1,002.98	978.79	1,001.63	965.14
Construction													
2007	892.42	818.29	905.17	856.54	909.43	898.41	911.51	890.23	919.60	910.48	904.01	914.09	895.23
2008	870.21	869.62	891.12	855.93	853.30	873.22	889.64	922.89	894.36	903.26	904.75	899.15	885.83
2009	867.41	906.31	930.69	917.21	928.64	937.97	984.86	993.48	949.56	933.75	980.88	928.37	938.90
2010	952.49	931.47	975.24	1,019.70	977.65	1,026.37	1,091.17	1,056.82	985.34	1,069.72	1,038.70	1,037.08	1,016.76
2011	996.71	961.05	989.23	983.59	1,056.81	1,003.78	1,011.52	1,040.54	1,021.60	1,018.56	1,005.84	1,023.72	1,010.70
Manufacturing													
2007	897.44	898.55	937.42	951.88	952.98	951.97	959.55	960.56	978.26	928.84	948.44	960.54	943.89
2008	916.70	936.51	935.24	919.50	910.38	918.54	888.62	900.65	901.20	893.76	917.63	895.65	911.46
2009	842.21	881.43	867.48	854.54	850.51	871.14	867.52	870.87	880.76	888.08	939.36	926.53	878.24
2010	908.62	903.15	893.24	895.03	924.34	907.57	905.98	915.30	921.87	938.75	932.56	930.47	914.93
2011	940.08	925.03	937.86	923.52	924.46	917.35	914.81	942.47	946.62	979.62	953.20	981.06	940.64
Trade, Transportation, and Utilities													
2007	645.32	647.56	640.87	649.50	649.02	651.83	653.11	645.00	654.87	634.85	634.55	646.41	646.06
2008	637.66	629.89	644.00	645.26	633.57	658.61	633.91	645.38	654.30	648.12	655.87	651.96	644.90
2009	660.99	662.07	661.52	647.52	649.74	667.74	666.12	677.36	677.96	673.27	684.32	688.43	668.09
2010	693.09	694.08	694.56	706.64	707.21	714.67	713.33	711.34	722.85	718.09	719.05	710.39	708.89
2011	701.40	677.81	675.85	676.90	683.06	682.58	681.29	678.30	679.54	687.81	668.51	661.99	679.54
Financial Activities													
2007	831.63	867.27	876.46	905.08	866.39	866.85	858.29	830.43	838.42	808.86	825.33	816.18	849.31
2008	787.35	812.86	807.03	807.77	792.25	792.61	785.07	785.44	804.45	798.96	799.94	805.92	798.26
2009	794.24	815.81	855.93	853.20	827.17	827.70	807.98	793.85	797.15	876.21	899.26	910.10	838.00
2010	909.54	894.29	902.80	868.99	890.49	892.96	886.23	897.23	881.69	869.25	853.05	865.29	884.30
2011	897.18	852.49	838.89	842.72	852.00	838.37	847.74	835.63	829.28	851.65	825.55	803.00	842.85
Professional and Business Services													
2007	648.05	652.04	662.54	675.96	669.90	666.33	664.05	675.62	685.44	673.73	671.64	685.44	669.44
2008	665.87	669.53	675.86	666.79	653.18	681.04	669.72	665.97	680.43	674.00	683.94	682.43	672.37
2009	740.23	768.22	751.49	733.22	733.06	740.58	748.01	751.49	722.80	663.09	681.80	689.72	726.41
2010	692.78	698.59	684.29	672.32	697.05	689.06	692.03	726.79	702.19	719.58	745.91	742.94	705.80
2011	750.96	739.99	733.79	727.40	758.03	748.08	750.09	753.31	756.13	767.85	765.70	761.87	751.25
Education and Health Services													
2007	694.55	673.92	684.65	695.87	711.21	699.78	706.51	696.51	708.34	704.46	721.93	722.48	701.84
2008	704.93	700.26	709.70	698.50	702.11	712.80	718.75	709.80	719.23	717.66	731.60	719.81	712.18
2009	714.12	711.48	709.50	705.20	706.97	701.35	722.26	719.04	700.05	689.51	706.86	714.50	708.32
2010	696.60	694.97	699.06	696.39	701.23	690.12	700.99	693.68	698.65	694.14	696.92	701.78	697.05
2011	691.43	697.21	699.52	692.19	703.83	707.62	722.48	719.23	719.48	728.23	717.77	733.13	710.98
Leisure and Hospitality													
2007	292.06	291.15	297.22	293.76	279.87	283.80	280.02	282.25	281.52	285.89	281.26	283.22	285.87
2008	268.72	276.12	273.80	269.44	275.27	284.26	284.23	288.40	284.79	286.34	289.09	291.58	281.12
2009	294.51	306.60	293.51	295.37	295.50	293.12	300.70	309.29	307.09	308.41	309.57	316.51	302.45
2010	318.72	328.44	331.99	315.85	316.05	318.83	324.46	321.98	327.01	322.70	324.63	334.10	323.64
2011	331.01	337.17	334.22	327.17	326.04	321.91	322.44	320.16	322.76	319.80	323.96	327.68	326.02
Other Services													
2007	481.37	478.72	477.46	489.33	462.18	481.22	484.01	468.54	463.12	442.48	465.76	485.28	473.28
2008	480.15	495.08	493.35	496.40	483.91	490.85	484.50	521.27	502.79	494.51	491.86	486.26	493.42
2009	522.35	536.78	538.76	515.23	516.99	513.30	517.97	539.61	546.78	553.13	589.00	578.82	538.89
2010	563.41	565.95	562.12	547.60	549.38	530.13	535.78	553.68	566.85	580.93	571.80	556.04	556.90
2011	551.74	541.00	541.84	527.33	507.64	503.07	485.91	478.48	475.56	484.72	473.26	481.10	504.14

IOWA
At a Glance

Population:
    2000 census: 2,926,538
    2010 census: 3,046,355
    2011 estimate: 3,062,309

Percent change in population:
    2000–2010: 4.1%
    2010–2011: 0.5%

Percent change in total nonfarm employment:
    2000–2010: -0.6%
    2010–2011: 0.6%

Industry with the largest growth in employment, 2000–2011 (thousands):
    Education and Health Services, 34.0

Industry with the largest decline or smallest growth in employment, 2000–2011 (thousands):
    Manufacturing, -44.1

Civilian labor force:
    2000: 1,601,920
    2010: 1,669,841
    2011: 1,663,592

Unemployment rate and rank among states (lowest to highest):
    2000: 2.8%, 8th
    2010: 6.3%, 5th
    2011: 5.9%, 6th

Over-the-year change in unemployment rates:
    2010–2011: -0.4%

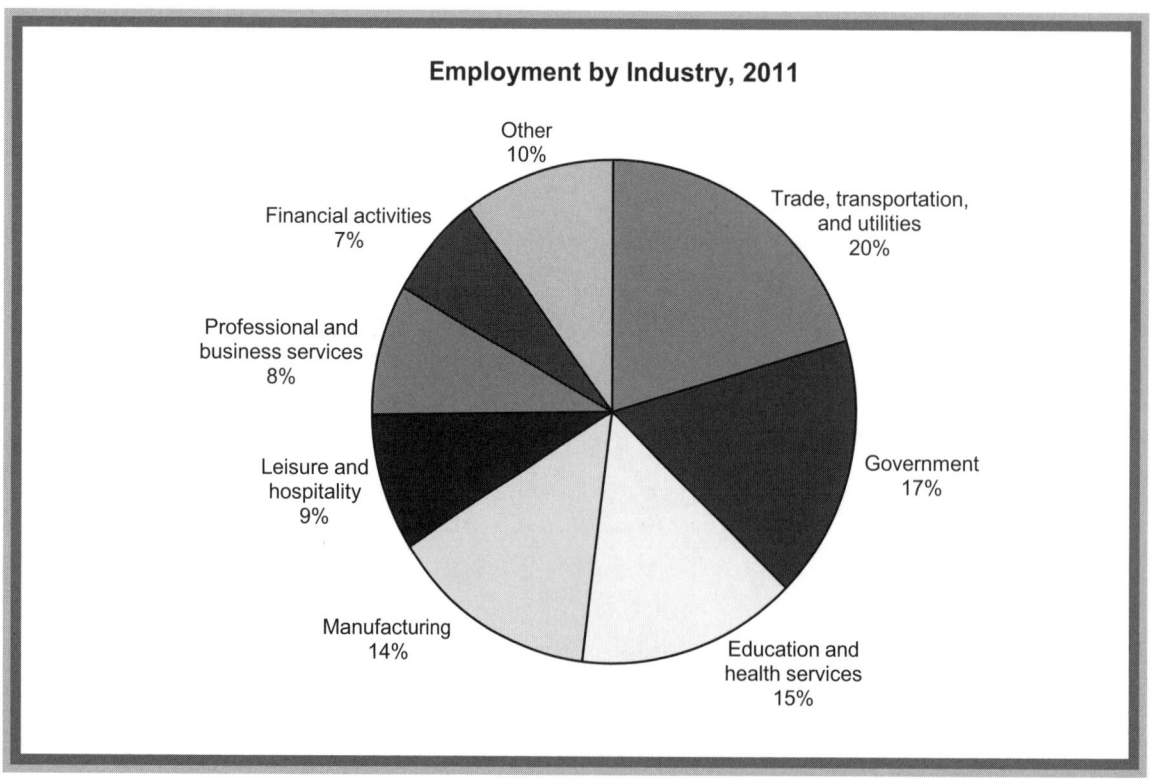

Employment by Industry, 2011

Other 10%
Trade, transportation, and utilities 20%
Financial activities 7%
Professional and business services 8%
Leisure and hospitality 9%
Manufacturing 14%
Government 17%
Education and health services 15%

1. Employment by Industry: Iowa, Selected Years, 2000–2011

(Numbers in thousands, not seasonally adjusted)

Industry and year	January	February	March	April	May	June	July	August	September	October	November	December	Annual average
Total Nonfarm													
2000	1,443.6	1,446.8	1,465.5	1,479.2	1,493.0	1,495.9	1,474.0	1,473.8	1,487.2	1,494.5	1,497.3	1,490.7	1,478.5
2001	1,446.7	1,444.5	1,455.0	1,475.3	1,488.0	1,490.3	1,457.6	1,458.1	1,469.9	1,468.0	1,468.7	1,464.8	1,465.6
2002	1,422.6	1,420.8	1,429.7	1,453.1	1,466.4	1,469.6	1,437.7	1,435.6	1,454.4	1,457.5	1,462.0	1,458.6	1,447.3
2003	1,411.9	1,411.4	1,420.5	1,440.2	1,453.7	1,455.2	1,427.0	1,430.3	1,450.8	1,460.6	1,462.4	1,461.3	1,440.4
2004	1,417.8	1,419.7	1,433.0	1,460.0	1,469.2	1,476.6	1,450.7	1,449.9	1,467.6	1,477.3	1,482.5	1,482.7	1,457.3
2005	1,434.2	1,442.3	1,459.1	1,483.4	1,494.3	1,499.3	1,473.1	1,472.6	1,496.0	1,501.7	1,505.7	1,504.3	1,480.5
2006	1,462.9	1,471.0	1,484.8	1,506.6	1,519.6	1,527.0	1,492.6	1,492.5	1,515.6	1,523.4	1,527.6	1,527.2	1,504.2
2007	1,482.6	1,485.7	1,496.4	1,517.8	1,534.1	1,542.2	1,508.5	1,508.8	1,529.3	1,538.6	1,545.9	1,538.9	1,519.1
2008	1,496.1	1,499.9	1,509.6	1,529.6	1,546.6	1,544.7	1,515.3	1,514.8	1,534.4	1,540.8	1,535.6	1,525.3	1,524.4
2009	1,471.7	1,472.0	1,473.0	1,488.5	1,497.8	1,493.6	1,460.6	1,461.3	1,479.2	1,487.2	1,486.8	1,476.9	1,479.1
2010	1,432.2	1,437.4	1,449.8	1,477.0	1,489.1	1,486.4	1,457.3	1,455.7	1,474.3	1,490.6	1,493.9	1,487.7	1,469.3
2011	1,443.9	1,449.9	1,460.8	1,485.4	1,496.0	1,488.8	1,469.1	1,467.6	1,481.3	1,499.6	1,502.0	1,489.5	1,477.8
Total Private													
2000	1,202.1	1,201.1	1,217.5	1,230.7	1,240.2	1,249.6	1,248.4	1,249.6	1,245.9	1,246.7	1,248.1	1,241.6	1,235.1
2001	1,202.1	1,196.3	1,205.9	1,225.1	1,236.7	1,241.8	1,230.7	1,232.9	1,225.4	1,217.6	1,216.4	1,214.1	1,220.4
2002	1,177.4	1,172.5	1,180.5	1,203.4	1,214.7	1,221.6	1,214.3	1,214.0	1,212.7	1,209.2	1,211.7	1,208.3	1,203.4
2003	1,168.9	1,162.7	1,170.7	1,190.1	1,201.7	1,207.5	1,203.1	1,207.5	1,206.7	1,209.8	1,210.1	1,208.4	1,195.6
2004	1,174.5	1,171.3	1,184.0	1,209.4	1,217.7	1,226.9	1,227.1	1,226.8	1,224.3	1,227.1	1,230.7	1,232.0	1,212.7
2005	1,191.8	1,194.3	1,209.7	1,233.2	1,241.8	1,250.8	1,248.9	1,248.2	1,250.5	1,249.9	1,252.6	1,251.9	1,235.3
2006	1,219.1	1,220.3	1,233.5	1,254.8	1,265.9	1,275.4	1,266.9	1,266.9	1,267.8	1,269.9	1,272.7	1,272.8	1,257.2
2007	1,235.0	1,232.0	1,242.8	1,263.8	1,277.6	1,288.7	1,279.9	1,280.3	1,279.0	1,281.7	1,287.8	1,281.8	1,269.2
2008	1,246.2	1,244.0	1,252.6	1,272.4	1,286.1	1,288.6	1,284.0	1,283.8	1,279.7	1,280.5	1,274.3	1,265.2	1,271.5
2009	1,218.6	1,213.3	1,213.3	1,227.4	1,234.7	1,235.8	1,226.3	1,227.1	1,224.8	1,226.5	1,225.4	1,217.7	1,224.2
2010	1,181.9	1,181.5	1,191.5	1,218.6	1,225.7	1,228.7	1,224.5	1,223.7	1,223.0	1,232.5	1,233.5	1,229.0	1,216.2
2011	1,194.3	1,194.4	1,204.3	1,228.3	1,238.1	1,241.4	1,240.4	1,238.7	1,232.8	1,244.3	1,245.8	1,235.6	1,228.2
Goods-Producing													
2000	304.9	303.4	310.2	316.1	321.0	327.2	327.9	326.7	322.8	320.9	318.0	311.3	317.5
2001	300.6	298.7	300.7	307.8	312.8	317.1	316.0	314.9	309.7	302.6	299.9	296.7	306.5
2002	284.3	281.7	284.2	293.4	298.8	303.3	302.3	300.8	297.3	295.2	293.9	289.1	293.7
2003	277.2	273.3	275.7	283.0	288.2	292.9	292.7	294.3	292.5	293.4	292.1	288.6	287.0
2004	277.9	275.7	280.8	291.4	295.3	302.0	303.8	301.4	300.5	300.4	301.1	297.9	293.9
2005	285.5	284.9	290.8	300.0	304.3	311.0	312.6	312.0	309.7	308.6	307.9	303.6	302.6
2006	295.7	295.0	298.8	306.2	310.4	316.3	316.1	315.6	313.0	310.8	309.0	305.5	307.7
2007	293.6	289.3	292.9	299.5	305.2	311.5	313.1	313.3	310.8	310.2	309.9	304.7	304.5
2008	293.9	290.9	293.0	301.0	307.7	311.0	312.8	312.5	308.7	305.5	300.8	292.3	302.5
2009	274.3	268.5	266.4	270.3	272.2	274.2	272.3	273.4	271.6	268.4	266.9	260.8	269.9
2010	250.0	248.5	252.1	263.7	266.4	270.5	272.3	272.1	270.7	270.7	269.6	263.8	264.2
2011	254.0	253.4	257.5	266.9	272.3	277.3	281.8	281.6	279.8	281.8	281.4	275.6	272.0
Mining and Logging													
2000	1.8	1.8	2.0	2.1	2.2	2.3	2.3	2.3	2.3	2.3	2.2	1.9	2.1
2001	1.6	1.7	1.8	2.1	2.2	2.2	2.2	2.2	2.1	2.0	2.0	2.0	2.0
2002	1.7	1.7	1.9	2.0	2.1	2.1	1.9	2.1	2.0	2.0	2.0	1.9	2.0
2003	1.5	1.5	1.6	1.9	2.0	2.1	2.0	2.2	2.2	2.1	2.1	2.0	1.9
2004	1.6	1.6	1.9	2.2	2.3	2.3	2.2	2.2	2.2	2.2	2.1	2.0	2.1
2005	1.7	1.7	2.0	2.1	2.2	2.3	2.3	2.3	2.2	2.2	2.2	2.0	2.1
2006	1.8	1.8	1.9	2.2	2.3	2.4	2.4	2.4	2.3	2.2	2.2	2.1	2.2
2007	1.8	1.7	2.0	2.1	2.2	2.3	2.3	2.3	2.3	2.3	2.3	2.1	2.1
2008	1.7	1.8	1.9	2.2	2.3	2.3	2.3	2.4	2.3	2.3	2.3	2.1	2.2
2009	1.6	1.8	2.0	2.3	2.4	2.4	2.4	2.5	2.4	2.3	2.3	2.1	2.2
2010	1.6	1.7	1.8	2.3	2.3	2.3	2.3	2.3	2.3	2.4	2.3	2.1	2.1
2011	1.7	1.8	1.8	2.2	2.3	2.4	2.4	2.4	2.4	2.4	2.4	2.2	2.2
Construction													
2000	54.5	53.4	58.2	62.8	66.4	69.9	70.9	70.8	68.2	67.0	65.0	60.0	63.9
2001	53.4	52.6	54.1	61.0	66.6	70.4	71.5	71.9	69.4	68.5	67.4	63.7	64.2
2002	54.8	53.1	55.4	62.9	67.1	70.2	71.2	70.9	68.6	68.2	67.1	63.4	64.4
2003	55.2	52.5	54.6	62.0	66.9	69.8	71.2	72.2	70.7	70.9	69.2	66.0	65.1
2004	57.5	55.6	59.7	67.9	70.8	74.3	75.4	75.2	73.5	72.3	71.7	69.2	68.6
2005	59.0	58.4	62.3	69.9	72.7	76.6	78.5	78.8	77.0	76.4	75.9	71.3	71.4
2006	64.9	64.6	67.1	72.8	76.3	79.7	80.8	80.7	79.7	77.8	76.2	72.4	74.4
2007	64.0	60.7	63.4	69.5	74.6	78.4	79.0	79.4	77.9	77.7	76.6	71.4	72.7
2008	63.1	60.5	62.4	70.0	75.9	78.4	81.6	81.5	79.4	78.0	75.0	69.8	73.0
2009	58.7	57.2	58.2	64.5	67.5	69.5	70.7	70.2	68.9	68.0	66.0	60.1	65.0
2010	51.6	50.3	52.3	62.2	64.7	67.2	68.1	67.2	66.1	66.0	64.5	58.8	61.6
2011	50.6	49.6	52.1	60.7	64.4	67.2	69.6	69.2	67.4	68.4	66.9	61.6	62.3
Manufacturing													
2000	248.6	248.2	250.0	251.2	252.4	255.0	254.7	253.6	252.3	251.6	250.8	249.4	251.5
2001	245.6	244.4	244.8	244.7	244.0	244.5	242.3	240.8	238.2	232.1	230.5	231.0	240.2
2002	227.8	226.9	226.9	228.5	229.6	231.0	229.2	227.8	226.7	225.0	224.8	223.8	227.3
2003	220.5	219.3	219.5	219.1	219.3	221.0	219.5	219.9	219.6	220.4	220.8	220.6	220.0
2004	218.8	218.5	219.2	221.3	222.2	225.4	226.2	224.0	224.8	225.9	226.3	226.7	223.3
2005	224.8	224.8	226.5	228.0	229.4	232.1	231.8	230.9	230.5	230.0	229.8	230.3	229.1
2006	229.0	228.6	229.8	231.2	231.8	234.2	232.9	232.5	231.0	230.8	230.6	231.0	231.1
2007	227.8	226.9	227.5	227.9	228.4	230.8	231.8	231.6	230.6	230.2	231.0	231.2	229.6
2008	229.1	228.6	228.7	228.8	229.5	230.3	228.9	228.6	227.0	225.2	223.5	220.4	227.4
2009	214.0	209.5	206.2	203.5	202.3	202.3	199.2	200.7	200.3	198.1	198.6	198.6	202.8
2010	196.8	196.5	198.0	199.2	199.4	201.0	201.9	202.6	202.3	202.3	202.8	202.9	200.5
2011	201.7	202.0	203.6	204.0	205.6	207.7	209.8	210.0	210.0	211.0	212.1	211.8	207.4

1. Employment by Industry: Iowa, Selected Years, 2000–2011—*Continued*

(Numbers in thousands, not seasonally adjusted)

Industry and year	January	February	March	April	May	June	July	August	September	October	November	December	Annual average
Service-Providing													
2000	1,138.7	1,143.4	1,155.3	1,163.1	1,172.0	1,168.7	1,146.1	1,147.1	1,164.4	1,173.6	1,179.3	1,179.4	1,160.9
2001	1,146.1	1,145.8	1,154.3	1,167.5	1,175.2	1,173.2	1,141.6	1,143.2	1,160.2	1,165.4	1,168.8	1,168.1	1,159.1
2002	1,138.3	1,139.1	1,145.5	1,159.7	1,167.6	1,166.3	1,135.4	1,134.8	1,157.1	1,162.3	1,168.1	1,169.5	1,153.6
2003	1,134.7	1,138.1	1,144.8	1,157.2	1,165.5	1,162.3	1,134.3	1,136.0	1,158.3	1,167.2	1,170.3	1,172.7	1,153.5
2004	1,139.9	1,144.0	1,152.2	1,168.6	1,173.9	1,174.6	1,146.9	1,148.5	1,167.1	1,176.9	1,182.4	1,184.8	1,163.3
2005	1,148.7	1,157.4	1,168.3	1,183.4	1,190.0	1,188.3	1,160.5	1,160.6	1,186.3	1,193.1	1,197.8	1,200.7	1,177.9
2006	1,167.2	1,176.0	1,186.0	1,200.4	1,209.2	1,210.7	1,176.5	1,176.9	1,202.6	1,212.6	1,218.6	1,221.7	1,196.5
2007	1,189.0	1,196.4	1,203.5	1,218.3	1,228.9	1,230.7	1,195.4	1,195.5	1,218.5	1,228.4	1,236.0	1,234.2	1,214.6
2008	1,202.2	1,209.0	1,216.6	1,228.6	1,238.9	1,233.7	1,202.5	1,202.3	1,225.7	1,235.3	1,234.8	1,233.0	1,221.9
2009	1,197.4	1,203.5	1,206.6	1,218.2	1,225.6	1,219.4	1,188.3	1,187.9	1,207.6	1,218.8	1,219.9	1,216.1	1,209.1
2010	1,182.2	1,188.9	1,197.7	1,213.3	1,222.7	1,215.9	1,185.0	1,183.6	1,203.6	1,219.9	1,224.3	1,223.9	1,205.1
2011	1,189.9	1,196.5	1,203.3	1,218.5	1,223.7	1,211.5	1,187.3	1,186.0	1,201.5	1,217.8	1,220.6	1,213.9	1,205.9
Trade, Transportation, and Utilities													
2000	310.4	308.4	310.6	313.7	315.1	317.0	317.0	316.9	315.9	317.9	322.6	324.2	315.8
2001	310.8	306.3	306.9	310.3	312.6	313.2	311.9	312.8	310.5	309.7	314.7	315.4	311.3
2002	303.6	299.1	300.3	304.2	305.6	307.9	307.2	307.4	306.0	306.4	310.9	312.3	305.9
2003	299.5	295.7	297.6	301.1	304.0	304.1	304.6	304.5	303.1	304.9	308.8	310.0	303.2
2004	299.5	296.8	298.6	302.7	304.0	305.4	307.1	307.1	304.8	306.0	310.7	313.0	304.6
2005	300.1	298.2	301.1	305.4	306.9	307.8	308.3	307.5	306.7	307.5	312.3	314.9	306.4
2006	303.8	301.5	303.6	308.0	309.9	311.1	309.3	308.6	307.6	309.5	314.3	316.5	308.6
2007	305.5	302.5	304.1	306.9	310.6	312.2	310.1	308.8	307.7	309.0	314.7	315.9	309.0
2008	306.6	304.1	306.0	307.5	310.6	311.2	310.6	310.5	308.7	310.4	313.2	314.3	309.5
2009	301.9	299.3	299.7	301.8	304.2	305.0	303.8	303.3	300.4	300.8	304.8	304.7	302.5
2010	294.7	291.9	293.8	298.5	300.5	302.1	301.0	300.6	297.9	301.2	305.0	306.8	299.5
2011	295.9	294.2	296.3	300.7	303.9	305.1	302.6	300.5	299.3	302.3	307.1	308.1	301.3
Wholesale Trade													
2000	66.4	66.3	67.5	68.8	68.7	69.2	70.6	69.2	68.8	68.5	67.7	67.4	68.3
2001	66.7	66.3	67.0	68.4	68.9	69.0	70.2	70.1	69.4	68.1	67.6	67.0	68.2
2002	65.8	65.4	65.5	66.9	66.8	67.3	68.8	68.0	67.3	67.0	66.5	66.0	66.8
2003	64.1	63.7	64.2	65.4	65.7	65.9	67.0	66.6	65.7	65.7	65.2	64.7	65.3
2004	63.9	63.7	64.4	66.2	66.1	66.6	67.8	67.4	66.6	67.0	67.0	66.8	66.1
2005	65.3	65.3	66.2	67.8	67.9	68.1	68.7	68.1	67.9	68.1	67.7	67.3	67.4
2006	66.6	66.3	66.8	68.0	68.1	68.3	68.4	67.9	67.7	67.5	67.7	67.1	67.5
2007	66.2	65.9	66.5	67.8	68.4	68.6	68.8	68.2	68.3	68.9	69.0	68.4	67.9
2008	67.3	67.2	67.8	68.7	69.8	69.6	69.8	69.2	68.5	69.4	68.7	68.2	68.7
2009	66.1	66.1	66.2	67.6	67.6	67.5	67.6	66.7	66.0	66.9	66.8	66.4	66.8
2010	64.7	64.4	64.9	67.1	66.8	66.8	66.6	66.0	65.8	66.7	66.7	66.0	66.0
2011	65.0	64.8	65.5	66.9	67.4	67.6	66.6	65.0	64.9	66.7	68.5	66.5	66.3
Retail Trade													
2000	187.2	185.3	185.7	187.0	188.5	189.8	188.6	189.4	189.1	191.0	196.5	198.7	189.7
2001	187.7	183.6	183.3	185.1	186.6	186.8	185.0	185.6	184.4	184.8	190.1	191.5	186.2
2002	182.4	178.5	179.2	181.2	182.3	183.6	181.1	181.5	181.2	181.3	185.9	187.7	182.2
2003	179.0	175.8	176.6	178.7	180.8	181.0	180.1	180.0	179.7	180.9	185.3	186.9	180.4
2004	178.5	176.1	176.6	178.2	179.5	180.3	180.7	181.0	179.6	180.2	185.3	187.9	180.3
2005	177.6	175.6	176.8	179.0	180.2	180.8	180.4	180.1	179.1	179.5	184.3	186.7	180.0
2006	177.8	176.0	176.9	179.4	180.7	181.2	179.8	178.9	177.8	179.5	183.9	186.1	179.8
2007	178.0	175.3	175.7	177.1	179.6	180.6	179.4	178.3	177.0	177.6	182.7	184.3	178.8
2008	177.4	175.2	176.3	177.1	178.2	179.1	178.5	178.4	177.1	177.9	181.3	182.5	178.3
2009	174.7	172.5	172.8	173.8	175.9	177.3	176.3	176.3	174.0	173.8	177.6	177.6	175.2
2010	171.4	169.1	170.0	171.6	173.6	174.6	173.7	173.3	170.7	172.6	176.0	177.5	172.8
2011	170.8	169.1	170.1	172.5	174.6	175.4	173.7	173.3	172.4	173.4	175.9	177.5	173.2
Transportation and Utilities													
2000	56.8	56.8	57.4	57.9	57.9	58.0	57.8	58.3	58.0	58.4	58.4	58.1	57.8
2001	56.4	56.4	56.6	56.8	57.1	57.4	56.7	57.1	56.7	56.8	57.0	56.9	56.8
2002	55.4	55.2	55.6	56.1	56.5	57.0	57.3	57.9	57.5	58.1	58.5	58.6	57.0
2003	56.4	56.2	56.8	57.0	57.5	57.2	57.5	57.9	57.7	58.3	58.3	58.4	57.4
2004	57.1	57.0	57.6	58.3	58.4	58.5	58.6	58.7	58.6	58.8	58.4	58.3	58.2
2005	57.2	57.3	58.1	58.6	58.8	58.9	59.2	59.3	59.7	59.9	60.3	60.9	59.0
2006	59.4	59.2	59.9	60.6	61.1	61.6	61.1	61.8	62.1	62.5	62.7	63.3	61.3
2007	61.3	61.3	61.9	62.0	62.6	63.0	61.9	62.3	62.4	62.5	63.0	63.2	62.3
2008	61.9	61.7	61.9	61.7	62.6	62.5	62.3	62.9	63.1	63.1	63.2	63.6	62.5
2009	61.1	60.7	60.7	60.4	60.7	60.2	59.9	60.3	60.4	60.1	60.4	60.7	60.5
2010	58.6	58.4	58.9	59.8	60.1	60.7	60.7	61.3	61.4	61.9	62.3	63.3	60.6
2011	60.1	60.3	60.7	61.3	61.9	62.1	62.3	62.2	62.0	62.2	62.7	64.1	61.8
Information													
2000	39.8	39.7	40.2	40.6	40.8	41.3	40.5	40.0	39.7	39.9	40.6	41.2	40.4
2001	38.5	38.5	39.0	38.1	37.8	37.8	37.7	36.8	36.5	36.5	36.3	36.0	37.5
2002	35.6	35.6	35.4	35.5	35.6	35.6	34.8	34.7	34.4	34.4	34.7	34.5	35.1
2003	33.6	33.9	33.7	33.4	33.6	33.7	33.9	33.5	33.5	33.5	33.6	33.7	33.6
2004	33.3	33.3	33.4	33.6	33.6	33.7	34.0	34.0	33.7	33.7	33.9	34.0	33.7
2005	33.4	33.3	33.5	33.3	33.2	33.1	33.1	32.6	32.5	32.4	32.5	32.7	33.0
2006	32.2	32.4	32.6	32.9	33.0	33.2	33.1	33.0	33.0	33.1	33.4	33.7	33.0
2007	33.0	33.5	33.7	34.1	34.3	34.4	33.6	33.3	33.2	33.1	33.4	33.4	33.6
2008	33.2	33.5	33.5	33.8	33.9	33.6	32.6	32.6	32.3	32.3	31.9	31.7	32.9
2009	31.3	31.4	31.4	31.0	31.1	30.6	30.0	29.5	29.2	29.3	29.3	29.4	30.3
2010	29.0	29.2	29.0	29.1	29.2	28.8	28.6	28.3	27.7	28.2	28.4	28.7	28.7
2011	28.2	28.4	28.3	28.4	28.5	28.2	27.9	27.6	27.3	27.3	27.4	27.4	27.9

1. Employment by Industry: Iowa, Selected Years, 2000–2011—*Continued*

(Numbers in thousands, not seasonally adjusted)

Industry and year	January	February	March	April	May	June	July	August	September	October	November	December	Annual average
Financial Activities													
2000	88.8	88.7	88.5	89.1	89.5	90.6	90.5	90.7	90.0	89.6	89.8	90.3	89.7
2001	90.0	89.8	90.4	90.8	91.5	93.0	93.2	93.1	92.6	92.6	93.1	94.1	92.0
2002	93.0	93.0	93.3	93.7	93.7	94.7	95.0	94.7	93.8	93.8	93.7	94.2	93.9
2003	94.2	94.2	94.2	94.4	95.0	95.8	95.9	96.0	95.4	95.4	95.6	95.9	95.2
2004	95.3	95.4	95.4	96.3	96.7	97.6	98.1	98.3	97.3	97.3	97.3	98.1	96.9
2005	97.3	97.4	97.5	97.6	98.0	98.9	99.0	99.0	98.6	98.4	98.5	99.4	98.3
2006	98.8	99.0	99.7	99.8	100.4	101.6	101.5	101.3	101.2	101.1	100.9	101.8	100.6
2007	101.1	101.2	101.6	101.9	102.4	103.8	103.8	103.4	102.8	103.0	103.2	103.5	102.6
2008	102.6	102.7	102.8	102.6	102.8	103.6	103.6	103.2	102.0	101.8	101.9	102.4	102.7
2009	101.7	101.4	101.5	101.8	102.2	102.9	102.8	102.7	101.6	101.6	101.6	102.3	102.0
2010	101.1	100.9	101.1	100.8	101.2	101.9	101.7	101.6	100.8	101.1	101.0	101.7	101.2
2011	100.8	100.4	100.3	100.3	100.5	100.7	101.0	100.7	99.9	99.7	100.2	100.6	100.4
Professional and Business Services													
2000	103.9	103.9	106.4	107.3	107.1	108.6	109.1	109.2	108.5	109.7	109.2	108.7	107.6
2001	107.3	106.2	106.7	108.8	109.1	109.1	106.9	108.3	106.8	107.4	105.6	105.4	107.3
2002	102.4	102.6	103.7	105.5	105.5	107.5	107.4	107.0	107.0	106.1	106.9	106.1	105.6
2003	102.3	102.2	102.5	105.6	104.8	106.2	106.6	107.9	107.2	107.8	107.0	107.1	105.6
2004	104.1	104.3	105.3	108.8	108.3	109.2	110.0	110.2	108.7	110.9	110.8	110.7	108.4
2005	107.0	108.4	109.8	112.6	112.5	113.9	114.6	115.1	116.1	116.7	116.3	116.2	113.3
2006	111.7	112.6	114.3	116.8	117.2	118.7	118.5	118.8	118.7	120.0	120.4	119.4	117.3
2007	116.1	117.1	117.7	121.4	120.9	123.2	123.1	124.0	122.9	123.6	123.9	123.2	121.4
2008	119.6	119.9	120.4	123.5	123.6	124.8	126.2	125.7	124.5	125.2	122.4	121.3	123.1
2009	117.1	117.3	116.0	117.3	116.8	117.6	117.2	118.0	117.2	119.0	118.5	118.0	117.5
2010	115.7	116.7	117.7	121.6	121.2	122.0	123.5	124.1	123.1	125.3	125.1	124.5	121.7
2011	121.5	121.7	121.5	124.9	123.8	124.4	124.8	125.8	123.8	125.5	124.3	121.5	123.6
Education and Health Services													
2000	180.3	182.2	184.0	183.6	182.5	177.9	173.3	174.4	181.5	187.0	187.9	187.7	181.9
2001	183.8	185.5	187.9	188.9	187.3	182.0	176.4	177.5	184.9	190.0	190.4	190.7	185.4
2002	187.0	188.7	189.6	190.4	189.5	183.6	178.7	179.4	187.9	192.6	193.8	194.3	188.0
2003	189.9	191.9	193.1	191.9	190.4	185.3	180.3	180.6	188.7	193.7	194.6	194.5	189.6
2004	191.2	193.0	194.3	194.1	192.7	187.6	182.5	182.6	190.5	195.5	196.5	197.2	191.5
2005	193.1	195.5	196.7	197.2	196.0	191.1	186.7	186.8	195.5	199.9	200.9	201.5	195.1
2006	197.5	199.8	201.0	201.6	200.3	195.2	190.4	190.6	198.6	203.5	204.8	205.3	199.1
2007	201.2	204.1	205.5	205.7	204.1	199.2	193.7	194.7	203.1	208.2	210.1	209.8	203.3
2008	206.1	208.4	209.7	210.1	208.4	202.4	197.5	197.8	206.6	213.1	214.8	214.8	207.5
2009	210.5	212.9	213.9	214.6	212.5	206.4	201.6	202.1	211.1	218.4	219.2	219.3	211.9
2010	214.2	216.3	217.8	217.6	215.0	208.4	203.0	202.7	212.4	219.7	220.6	221.0	214.1
2011	215.6	218.0	219.1	219.6	216.9	210.1	205.0	206.1	214.5	221.4	222.1	222.0	215.9
Leisure and Hospitality													
2000	118.0	118.7	121.2	123.7	127.4	129.6	132.6	134.5	130.7	124.9	123.0	121.5	125.5
2001	115.3	115.5	118.1	123.9	129.0	132.2	131.7	132.8	128.4	122.7	120.4	119.6	124.1
2002	115.7	115.9	117.7	123.9	129.1	131.6	131.7	132.9	129.8	124.0	121.2	121.5	124.6
2003	116.6	116.0	118.0	124.4	129.4	132.8	132.6	134.2	130.1	124.8	122.3	122.2	125.3
2004	117.3	117.3	120.3	126.2	130.7	134.3	134.5	136.5	132.4	126.8	125.1	124.7	127.2
2005	120.1	121.1	124.3	130.7	134.6	137.7	137.6	138.6	135.2	130.3	128.1	127.3	130.5
2006	123.5	124.3	127.3	132.9	137.8	141.5	140.6	141.9	138.9	135.1	132.9	133.3	134.2
2007	127.9	127.9	130.2	136.7	142.1	145.3	144.2	144.9	140.9	136.8	134.8	133.4	137.1
2008	127.1	127.7	130.0	136.2	140.9	143.3	141.9	143.4	139.1	134.0	131.2	130.4	135.4
2009	124.6	125.2	127.0	132.9	137.8	140.6	140.3	140.7	136.6	131.9	128.2	126.2	132.7
2010	120.9	121.7	123.2	130.0	134.8	137.3	137.1	137.4	133.9	129.3	127.1	125.8	129.9
2011	122.1	122.2	124.9	131.1	135.6	138.6	140.4	139.6	132.3	129.7	126.4	124.0	130.6
Other Services													
2000	56.0	56.1	56.4	56.6	56.8	57.4	57.5	57.2	56.8	56.8	57.0	56.7	56.8
2001	55.8	55.8	56.2	56.5	56.6	57.4	56.9	56.7	56.0	56.1	56.0	56.2	56.4
2002	55.8	55.9	56.3	56.8	56.9	57.4	57.2	57.1	56.5	56.7	56.6	56.3	56.6
2003	55.6	55.5	55.9	56.3	56.3	56.7	56.5	56.5	56.2	56.3	56.1	56.4	56.2
2004	55.9	55.5	55.9	56.3	56.4	57.1	57.1	56.7	56.4	56.5	56.3	56.4	56.4
2005	55.3	55.5	56.0	56.4	56.3	57.3	57.0	56.6	56.2	56.1	56.1	56.3	56.3
2006	55.9	55.7	56.2	56.6	56.9	57.8	57.4	57.1	56.8	56.8	57.0	57.3	56.8
2007	56.6	56.4	57.1	57.6	58.0	59.1	58.3	57.9	57.6	57.8	57.8	57.9	57.7
2008	57.1	56.8	57.2	57.7	58.2	58.7	58.4	58.1	57.8	58.2	58.1	58.0	57.9
2009	57.2	57.3	57.4	57.7	57.9	58.5	58.3	57.4	57.1	57.1	56.9	57.0	57.5
2010	56.3	56.3	56.8	57.3	57.4	57.7	57.3	56.9	56.5	57.0	56.7	56.7	56.9
2011	56.2	56.1	56.4	56.4	56.6	57.0	56.9	56.8	55.9	56.6	56.9	56.4	56.5
Government													
2000	241.5	245.7	248.0	248.5	252.8	246.3	225.6	224.2	241.3	247.8	249.2	249.1	243.3
2001	244.6	248.2	249.1	250.2	251.3	248.5	226.9	225.2	244.5	250.4	252.3	250.7	245.2
2002	245.2	248.3	249.2	249.7	251.7	248.0	223.4	221.6	241.7	248.3	250.3	250.3	244.0
2003	243.0	248.7	249.8	250.1	252.0	247.7	223.9	222.8	244.1	250.8	252.3	252.9	244.8
2004	243.3	248.4	249.0	250.6	251.5	249.7	223.6	223.1	243.3	250.2	251.8	250.7	244.6
2005	242.4	248.0	249.4	250.2	252.5	248.5	224.2	224.4	245.5	251.8	253.1	252.4	247.0
2006	243.8	250.7	251.3	251.8	253.7	251.6	225.7	225.6	247.8	253.5	254.9	254.4	247.1
2007	247.6	253.7	253.6	254.0	256.5	253.5	228.6	228.5	250.3	256.9	258.1	257.1	249.9
2008	249.9	255.9	257.0	257.2	260.5	256.1	231.3	231.0	254.7	260.3	261.3	260.1	252.9
2009	253.1	258.7	259.7	261.1	263.1	257.8	234.3	234.2	254.4	260.7	261.4	259.2	254.8
2010	250.3	255.9	258.3	258.4	263.4	257.7	232.8	232.0	251.3	258.1	260.4	258.7	253.1
2011	249.6	255.5	256.5	257.1	257.9	247.4	228.7	228.9	248.5	255.3	256.2	253.9	249.6

2. Average Weekly Hours by Selected Industry: Iowa, 2007–2011

(Not seasonally adjusted)

Industry and year	January	February	March	April	May	June	July	August	September	October	November	December	Annual average
Total Private													
2007	33.6	33.8	33.9	34.0	34.3	34.7	34.6	34.3	34.6	34.2	34.3	34.2	34.2
2008	33.4	33.1	33.9	33.5	34.1	34.3	34.2	34.3	34.0	33.9	33.8	33.1	33.8
2009	32.8	33.3	32.8	32.8	32.8	33.1	33.4	34.0	33.8	33.9	34.1	33.3	33.3
2010	33.5	33.7	33.8	34.6	34.2	34.1	34.2	34.3	34.2	34.4	34.1	33.9	34.1
2011	33.8	33.2	33.5	33.8	34.1	34.0	33.9	34.1	34.1	34.7	34.2	34.2	34.0
Goods-Producing													
2007	39.4	38.9	39.6	39.2	40.8	41.0	40.8	40.9	41.3	41.2	41.5	40.3	40.4
2008	39.9	39.2	40.0	39.3	40.9	40.4	40.7	40.9	40.5	40.3	39.4	38.0	40.0
2009	36.8	37.3	36.7	36.5	37.2	38.2	38.1	39.0	39.7	40.2	40.0	38.0	38.1
2010	38.4	38.6	39.1	40.2	39.4	39.6	40.3	39.7	40.4	41.0	40.3	40.6	39.8
2011	39.8	38.6	39.3	39.5	40.3	40.1	40.0	40.7	40.4	41.0	40.4	40.5	40.1
Construction													
2007	37.5	37.4	38.7	37.9	41.0	42.2	42.0	40.9	40.8	41.3	41.4	40.6	40.3
2008	40.0	37.8	39.2	37.6	40.7	40.0	41.2	42.0	39.2	40.5	38.8	38.1	39.7
2009	37.1	38.0	37.4	38.5	38.1	41.8	42.4	42.2	42.0	41.6	41.5	38.5	40.1
2010	39.1	38.9	39.4	41.6	41.0	40.7	41.5	40.2	40.6	41.7	40.8	40.2	40.5
2011	39.0	37.9	38.8	39.5	41.2	41.7	40.7	41.9	41.3	41.3	39.5	38.8	40.3
Manufacturing													
2007	40.1	39.5	40.0	39.8	40.8	40.6	40.4	40.9	41.5	41.2	41.5	40.9	40.6
2008	40.5	40.2	40.7	40.3	40.6	40.2	40.2	40.2	40.8	40.1	39.6	38.0	40.1
2009	36.7	37.1	36.4	35.9	37.0	37.9	37.3	38.6	39.6	40.4	40.1	39.2	38.0
2010	39.2	39.4	39.8	40.5	40.3	40.5	40.6	40.3	41.0	41.7	41.7	41.0	40.5
2011	40.4	39.9	40.5	40.4	40.6	40.0	40.4	40.8	40.8	41.6	41.4	41.7	40.7
Trade, Transportation, and Utilities													
2007	31.8	32.0	31.9	31.6	31.7	32.2	32.0	31.7	31.6	31.7	32.1	32.2	31.9
2008	31.0	31.0	31.4	31.3	32.3	32.3	32.0	32.2	31.5	31.9	31.7	31.5	31.7
2009	31.3	31.6	31.8	32.1	31.6	31.7	32.1	32.4	32.3	32.3	33.1	31.5	32.0
2010	31.7	32.0	32.2	33.1	32.6	32.8	33.1	33.3	33.2	33.7	32.6	32.6	32.7
2011	32.3	31.9	31.8	32.6	32.9	32.7	32.7	33.0	32.9	33.0	33.0	32.7	32.6
Financial Activities													
2007	36.9	36.9	36.4	37.4	36.1	36.4	37.1	36.1	36.9	36.2	36.1	37.1	36.6
2008	35.3	34.7	35.8	35.2	35.2	36.5	35.3	35.9	35.5	35.4	36.5	35.5	35.6
2009	36.1	36.5	35.9	35.7	35.9	36.0	36.7	37.3	36.9	37.0	37.8	36.9	36.6
2010	37.5	38.1	37.6	37.7	38.3	37.9	37.8	38.8	37.9	37.9	38.5	37.8	38.0
2011	38.4	37.6	37.6	37.4	38.3	37.7	37.8	37.6	37.9	38.6	38.1	37.9	37.9
Professional and Business Services													
2007	33.1	33.7	34.3	35.2	34.8	34.8	34.7	33.9	34.6	34.0	33.3	33.5	34.2
2008	32.2	33.1	33.7	33.8	33.2	33.2	33.1	32.7	32.0	32.8	33.0	33.0	33.0
2009	32.6	33.8	32.5	32.3	32.2	32.9	33.5	33.4	32.6	33.4	33.8	33.2	33.0
2010	33.6	33.8	34.3	35.0	35.1	34.3	34.6	34.8	34.1	34.3	34.0	33.4	34.3
2011	33.3	32.8	33.7	34.3	34.7	34.7	34.2	33.8	34.3	34.9	34.5	34.0	34.1
Education and Health Services													
2007	31.7	32.5	32.1	32.6	32.3	33.2	32.8	32.3	32.9	32.5	32.7	32.9	32.5
2008	32.7	32.5	33.4	33.1	33.0	33.2	33.1	33.0	33.2	32.4	32.7	31.8	32.8
2009	32.6	32.7	31.4	31.7	31.3	31.2	31.7	32.1	31.4	31.2	31.5	31.0	31.6
2010	31.3	31.1	31.0	31.8	31.5	31.6	30.9	31.0	30.8	30.4	30.9	30.8	31.1
2011	31.2	30.8	30.9	31.2	31.3	31.3	31.1	31.1	31.1	31.4	31.2	31.4	31.2
Leisure and Hospitality													
2007	23.6	24.2	24.3	24.9	24.9	25.9	25.4	25.3	25.1	24.7	25.0	24.4	24.8
2008	23.9	23.2	24.3	23.6	24.0	24.9	25.1	25.1	24.8	24.7	24.6	23.3	24.3
2009	23.6	24.3	24.6	24.4	24.7	25.2	25.7	25.6	24.6	24.5	24.9	23.8	24.7
2010	23.5	23.8	23.9	24.4	23.8	24.6	24.3	24.4	24.3	24.1	24.3	24.0	24.1
2011	24.4	24.4	23.9	23.9	23.7	24.0	23.7	24.1	24.0	24.4	23.8	23.6	24.0
Other Services													
2007	26.3	27.6	26.6	27.6	27.8	27.9	28.3	28.2	28.2	27.0	26.6	26.2	27.4
2008	26.5	27.0	27.7	27.3	28.3	27.4	28.9	28.9	29.5	29.0	28.4	27.4	28.0
2009	27.2	27.9	27.9	27.8	27.8	28.4	27.8	29.1	28.2	28.1	27.7	27.1	27.9
2010	27.9	27.9	28.3	28.9	28.3	28.5	29.2	29.3	28.8	29.3	28.3	28.3	28.6
2011	28.5	28.3	29.1	29.1	29.4	30.1	29.6	29.0	29.0	29.7	28.3	28.3	29.0

3. Average Hourly Earnings by Selected Industry: Iowa, 2007–2011

(Dollars, not seasonally adjusted)

Industry and year	January	February	March	April	May	June	July	August	September	October	November	December	Annual average
Total Private													
2007	18.15	18.39	18.09	17.84	17.61	17.86	17.98	17.89	18.22	18.10	17.97	18.11	18.01
2008	17.61	17.77	17.87	18.07	18.15	18.28	18.14	18.64	18.65	18.65	18.90	19.50	18.35
2009	19.78	19.94	19.77	19.77	19.93	19.86	20.05	20.04	19.94	20.09	20.30	20.61	20.01
2010	20.27	20.80	20.44	20.46	20.33	20.18	20.10	20.23	20.46	20.51	20.26	20.49	20.38
2011	20.23	20.37	20.12	20.19	20.14	19.97	20.17	20.08	20.29	20.42	20.25	20.45	20.22
Goods-Producing													
2007	19.13	19.92	19.18	19.57	19.18	19.40	19.55	19.28	19.77	19.44	19.47	19.61	19.46
2008	17.86	18.52	18.35	18.24	18.87	19.21	19.01	19.32	19.02	19.37	19.74	20.37	18.99
2009	20.39	20.55	20.90	20.36	20.45	20.73	20.61	20.92	20.63	20.55	20.88	21.03	20.67
2010	21.07	20.97	21.02	20.77	20.88	20.71	20.68	20.79	20.73	21.04	20.83	20.85	20.86
2011	20.38	20.53	20.16	20.20	20.30	20.04	20.07	20.04	20.40	20.57	20.45	20.90	20.34
Construction													
2007	20.00	20.40	20.96	20.69	20.62	20.58	20.46	20.61	21.03	20.74	21.03	21.19	20.70
2008	19.75	20.30	20.56	20.43	21.18	21.45	21.16	21.87	20.71	21.21	21.03	21.86	21.01
2009	22.01	21.72	21.85	21.85	21.77	22.49	22.30	22.36	22.27	22.38	22.54	22.48	22.19
2010	22.82	22.72	23.11	22.43	22.51	22.52	22.20	22.26	22.54	22.76	22.35	22.89	22.57
2011	22.57	22.71	22.64	22.49	22.49	22.18	22.05	22.08	22.75	22.31	22.12	22.68	22.40
Manufacturing													
2007	18.84	19.77	18.58	19.17	18.59	18.86	19.12	18.72	19.26	18.90	18.85	18.98	18.97
2008	17.15	17.90	17.62	17.53	17.97	18.36	18.13	18.30	18.37	18.66	19.27	19.84	18.24
2009	19.77	20.04	20.46	19.68	19.83	19.92	20.22	20.61	20.23	20.07	20.44	20.75	20.17
2010	20.69	20.60	20.50	20.28	20.36	20.12	20.14	20.28	20.09	20.41	20.33	20.83	20.38
2011	20.28	20.40	19.87	19.83	19.83	19.51	19.59	19.50	19.70	20.11	20.00	20.43	19.92
Trade, Transportation, and Utilities													
2007	16.15	16.39	16.26	16.22	15.70	15.58	15.75	15.90	15.94	16.02	15.77	15.97	15.97
2008	16.27	16.12	16.25	16.37	16.37	16.10	15.96	16.04	16.58	16.39	16.43	17.49	16.36
2009	18.12	18.42	18.21	18.55	18.16	17.90	18.02	17.95	17.12	17.24	17.18	16.44	17.77
2010	16.45	16.73	16.49	16.74	16.90	17.14	16.89	17.29	17.54	16.85	16.88	16.95	16.91
2011	17.33	17.57	17.49	17.55	17.47	17.38	17.54	17.39	17.61	17.64	17.52	17.39	17.49
Financial Activities													
2007	23.69	23.77	23.62	23.35	23.71	24.46	24.58	24.37	24.40	23.76	24.12	23.93	23.98
2008	23.96	23.92	24.28	25.17	25.09	24.88	25.11	25.31	25.49	25.46	25.38	25.35	24.95
2009	25.31	25.66	25.90	25.42	25.95	25.84	26.01	25.89	25.55	25.66	25.73	25.69	25.72
2010	25.48	25.64	25.43	25.78	25.59	25.63	25.52	25.41	25.54	25.49	25.18	25.38	25.51
2011	25.52	25.96	25.61	25.87	26.03	25.96	25.90	25.95	25.90	26.05	25.99	26.05	25.90
Professional and Business Services													
2007	21.49	21.19	20.93	20.84	20.36	21.72	20.29	20.13	20.15	20.04	19.52	20.04	20.55
2008	19.81	19.77	20.22	20.75	20.40	21.62	20.34	23.30	21.71	21.47	22.88	22.43	21.23
2009	23.48	23.71	21.73	21.23	22.49	21.72	21.72	22.07	21.67	21.42	21.45	21.62	22.02
2010	21.32	21.13	20.47	21.20	21.52	21.12	21.06	21.35	21.64	22.13	21.83	22.22	21.42
2011	22.16	22.20	21.74	21.26	21.41	20.81	21.26	21.02	21.00	21.39	20.83	21.06	21.34
Education and Health Services													
2007	15.98	15.98	15.54	15.87	15.70	15.77	16.31	16.13	16.57	16.64	16.93	16.98	16.21
2008	16.34	16.37	16.45	16.81	16.60	16.67	16.60	17.11	17.35	17.17	17.56	18.27	16.94
2009	18.37	18.25	18.21	19.48	18.73	18.97	19.10	19.01	19.37	20.27	19.26	20.21	19.10
2010	19.46	19.39	19.39	19.84	19.26	19.17	19.51	19.53	19.92	20.40	19.70	20.65	19.69
2011	20.43	20.62	20.51	20.97	20.65	20.75	21.28	21.03	21.32	21.38	21.19	21.42	20.96
Leisure and Hospitality													
2007	10.75	11.05	11.01	10.94	10.73	10.53	10.91	10.71	11.07	11.26	11.12	11.33	10.94
2008	11.44	11.45	11.31	11.19	11.13	10.92	11.07	11.23	11.40	11.47	11.49	11.84	11.32
2009	11.83	11.82	11.78	11.84	11.73	11.58	11.57	11.73	11.94	11.93	11.95	12.25	11.82
2010	12.34	12.24	12.03	11.91	11.88	11.57	11.68	11.63	11.66	11.57	11.55	11.70	11.80
2011	11.69	11.76	11.74	11.79	11.77	11.55	11.80	11.59	11.69	11.64	11.78	11.93	11.72
Other Services													
2007	15.97	14.52	14.61	14.47	14.00	14.31	14.05	14.27	14.63	14.65	14.31	14.32	14.50
2008	14.46	14.12	14.05	14.11	13.91	14.22	15.40	15.05	15.28	15.60	15.52	15.37	14.77
2009	15.61	15.66	15.80	15.67	15.85	15.53	15.48	15.56	16.27	15.98	16.39	16.56	15.86
2010	16.45	16.31	16.82	16.29	16.75	16.66	16.35	16.77	16.90	17.34	17.59	17.27	16.79
2011	17.43	17.38	17.19	17.45	17.57	17.92	18.25	19.04	19.05	19.14	19.31	18.76	18.21

4. Average Weekly Earnings by Selected Industry: Iowa, 2007–2011

(Dollars, not seasonally adjusted)

Industry and year	January	February	March	April	May	June	July	August	September	October	November	December	Annual average
Total Private													
2007	609.84	621.58	613.25	606.56	604.02	619.74	622.11	613.63	630.41	619.02	616.37	619.36	616.33
2008	588.17	588.19	605.79	605.35	618.92	627.00	620.39	639.35	634.10	632.24	638.82	645.45	620.68
2009	648.78	664.00	648.46	648.46	653.70	657.37	669.67	681.36	673.97	681.05	692.23	686.31	667.25
2010	679.05	700.96	690.87	707.92	695.29	688.14	687.42	693.89	699.73	705.54	690.87	694.61	694.75
2011	683.77	676.28	674.02	682.42	686.77	678.98	683.76	684.73	691.89	708.57	692.55	699.39	687.10
Goods-Producing													
2007	753.72	774.89	759.53	767.14	782.54	795.40	797.64	788.55	816.50	800.93	808.01	790.28	786.67
2008	712.61	725.98	734.00	716.83	771.78	776.08	773.71	790.19	770.31	780.61	777.76	774.06	759.13
2009	750.35	766.52	767.03	743.14	760.74	791.89	785.24	815.88	819.01	826.11	835.20	799.14	788.23
2010	809.09	809.44	821.88	834.95	822.67	820.12	833.40	825.36	837.49	862.64	839.45	846.51	830.55
2011	811.12	792.46	792.29	797.90	818.09	803.60	802.80	815.63	824.16	843.37	826.18	846.45	814.86
Construction													
2007	750.00	762.96	811.15	784.15	845.42	868.48	859.32	842.95	858.02	856.56	870.64	860.31	833.97
2008	790.00	767.34	805.95	768.17	862.03	858.00	871.79	918.54	811.83	859.01	815.96	832.87	833.51
2009	816.57	825.36	817.19	841.23	829.44	940.08	945.52	943.59	935.34	931.01	935.41	865.48	889.04
2010	892.26	883.81	910.53	933.09	922.91	916.56	921.30	894.85	915.12	949.09	911.88	920.18	915.19
2011	880.23	860.71	878.43	888.36	926.59	924.91	897.44	925.15	939.58	921.40	873.74	879.98	901.91
Manufacturing													
2007	755.48	780.92	743.20	762.97	758.47	765.72	772.45	765.65	799.29	778.68	782.28	776.28	770.16
2008	694.58	719.58	717.13	706.46	729.58	738.07	728.83	735.66	749.50	748.27	763.09	753.92	731.89
2009	725.56	743.48	744.74	706.51	733.71	754.97	754.21	795.55	801.11	810.83	819.64	813.40	766.30
2010	811.05	811.64	815.90	821.34	820.51	814.86	817.68	817.28	823.69	851.10	847.76	854.03	825.68
2011	819.31	813.96	804.74	801.13	805.10	780.40	791.44	795.60	803.76	836.58	828.00	851.93	811.06
Trade, Transportation, and Utilities													
2007	513.57	524.48	518.69	512.55	497.69	501.68	504.00	504.03	503.70	507.83	506.22	514.23	509.01
2008	504.37	499.72	510.25	512.38	528.75	520.03	510.72	516.49	522.27	522.84	520.83	550.94	518.39
2009	567.16	582.07	579.08	595.46	573.86	567.43	578.44	581.58	552.98	556.85	568.66	517.86	568.37
2010	521.47	535.36	530.98	554.09	550.94	562.19	559.06	575.76	582.33	567.85	550.29	552.57	553.69
2011	559.76	560.48	556.18	572.13	574.76	568.33	573.56	573.87	579.37	582.12	578.16	568.65	570.66
Financial Activities													
2007	874.16	877.11	859.77	873.29	855.93	890.34	911.92	879.76	900.36	860.11	870.73	887.80	878.51
2008	845.79	830.02	869.22	885.98	883.17	908.12	886.38	908.63	904.90	901.28	926.37	899.93	887.46
2009	913.69	936.59	929.81	907.49	931.61	930.24	954.57	965.70	942.80	949.42	972.59	947.96	940.13
2010	955.50	976.88	956.17	971.91	980.10	971.38	964.66	985.91	967.97	966.07	969.43	959.36	968.84
2011	979.97	976.10	962.94	967.54	996.95	978.69	979.02	975.72	981.61	1,005.53	990.22	987.30	981.79
Professional and Business Services													
2007	711.32	714.10	717.90	733.57	708.53	755.86	704.06	682.41	697.19	681.36	650.02	671.34	702.06
2008	637.88	654.39	681.41	701.35	677.28	717.78	673.25	761.91	694.72	704.22	755.04	740.19	700.22
2009	765.45	801.40	706.23	685.73	724.18	711.30	727.62	737.14	706.44	715.43	725.01	717.78	727.03
2010	716.35	714.19	702.12	742.00	755.35	724.42	728.68	742.98	737.92	759.06	742.22	742.15	734.18
2011	737.93	728.16	732.64	729.22	742.93	722.11	727.09	710.48	720.30	746.51	718.64	716.04	727.68
Education and Health Services													
2007	506.57	519.35	498.83	517.36	507.11	523.56	534.97	521.00	545.15	540.80	553.61	558.64	527.40
2008	534.32	532.03	549.43	556.41	547.80	553.44	549.46	564.63	576.02	556.31	574.21	580.99	556.37
2009	598.86	596.78	571.79	617.52	586.25	591.86	605.47	610.22	608.22	632.42	606.69	626.51	604.56
2010	609.10	603.03	601.09	630.91	606.69	605.77	602.86	605.43	613.54	620.16	608.73	636.02	612.07
2011	637.42	635.10	633.76	654.26	646.35	649.48	661.81	654.03	663.05	671.33	661.13	672.59	653.40
Leisure and Hospitality													
2007	253.70	267.41	267.54	272.41	267.18	272.73	277.11	270.96	277.86	278.12	278.00	276.45	271.77
2008	273.42	265.64	274.83	264.08	267.12	271.91	277.86	281.87	282.72	283.31	282.65	275.87	275.15
2009	279.19	287.23	289.79	288.90	289.73	291.82	297.35	300.29	293.72	292.29	297.56	291.55	291.76
2010	289.99	291.31	287.52	290.60	282.74	284.62	283.82	283.77	283.34	278.84	280.67	280.80	284.73
2011	285.24	286.94	280.59	281.78	278.95	277.20	279.66	279.32	280.56	284.02	280.36	281.55	281.27
Other Services													
2007	420.01	400.75	388.63	399.37	389.20	399.25	397.62	402.41	412.57	395.55	380.65	375.18	396.72
2008	383.19	381.24	389.19	385.20	393.65	389.63	445.06	434.95	450.76	452.40	440.77	421.14	414.06
2009	424.59	436.91	440.82	435.63	440.63	441.05	430.34	452.80	458.81	449.04	454.00	448.78	442.69
2010	458.96	455.05	476.01	470.78	474.03	474.81	477.42	491.36	486.72	508.06	497.80	488.74	480.02
2011	496.76	491.85	500.23	507.80	516.56	539.39	540.20	552.16	552.45	568.46	546.47	530.91	528.63

KANSAS
At a Glance

Population:
  2000 census: 2,688,925
  2010 census: 2,853,118
  2011 estimate: 2,871,238

Percent change in population:
  2000–2010: 6.1%
  2010–2011: 0.6%

Percent change in total nonfarm employment:
  2000–2010: -1.4%
  2010–2011: 0.7%

Industry with the largest growth in employment, 2000–2011 (thousands):
  Education and Health Services, 35.9

Industry with the largest decline or smallest growth in employment, 2000–2011 (thousands):
  Manufacturing, -39.6

Civilian labor force:
  2000: 1,405,104
  2010: 1,504,883
  2011: 1,505,043

Unemployment rate and rank among states (lowest to highest):
  2000: 3.8%, 25th
  2010: 7.2%, 12th
  2011: 6.7%, 11th

Over-the-year change in unemployment rates:
  2010–2011: -0.5%

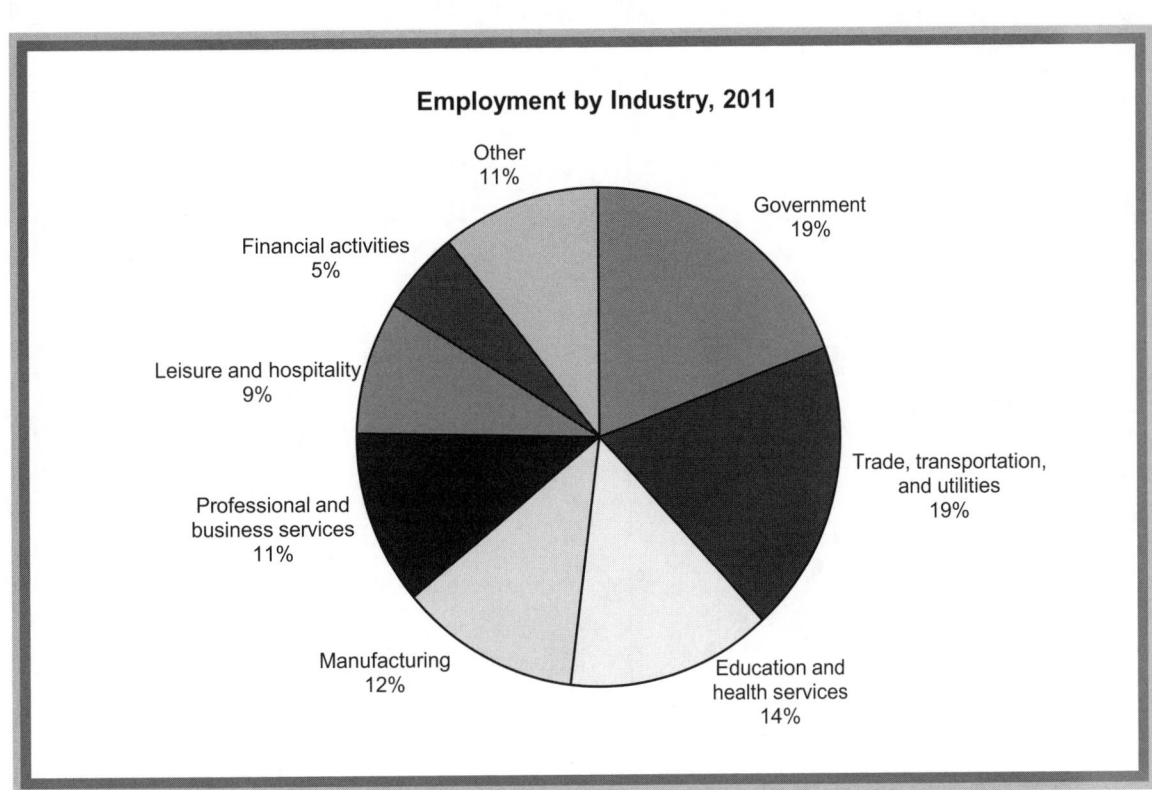

Employment by Industry, 2011

- Other 11%
- Government 19%
- Financial activities 5%
- Trade, transportation, and utilities 19%
- Leisure and hospitality 9%
- Professional and business services 11%
- Manufacturing 12%
- Education and health services 14%

1. Employment by Industry: Kansas, Selected Years, 2000–2011

(Numbers in thousands, not seasonally adjusted)

Industry and year	January	February	March	April	May	June	July	August	September	October	November	December	Annual average
Total Nonfarm													
2000	1,317.3	1,320.0	1,334.4	1,350.7	1,360.1	1,365.4	1,333.8	1,332.6	1,351.0	1,359.4	1,364.7	1,363.7	1,346.1
2001	1,330.0	1,333.1	1,347.0	1,356.7	1,363.1	1,365.5	1,337.9	1,333.7	1,351.5	1,355.2	1,356.1	1,356.2	1,348.8
2002	1,320.9	1,319.8	1,331.7	1,345.4	1,352.0	1,354.6	1,325.9	1,324.7	1,339.7	1,335.9	1,341.7	1,340.6	1,336.1
2003	1,301.0	1,302.0	1,307.9	1,316.3	1,325.4	1,324.7	1,297.5	1,295.8	1,315.6	1,320.7	1,324.9	1,326.3	1,313.2
2004	1,290.3	1,291.1	1,308.0	1,327.9	1,336.2	1,339.9	1,316.0	1,312.8	1,339.6	1,342.2	1,346.2	1,349.3	1,325.0
2005	1,302.6	1,315.3	1,329.3	1,338.2	1,344.3	1,349.4	1,311.8	1,312.2	1,341.4	1,344.7	1,352.3	1,355.9	1,333.1
2006	1,317.9	1,333.2	1,345.9	1,351.5	1,361.3	1,369.7	1,330.3	1,335.8	1,369.9	1,371.8	1,374.5	1,384.0	1,353.8
2007	1,341.2	1,351.9	1,372.9	1,377.7	1,387.1	1,397.5	1,369.4	1,368.1	1,391.2	1,396.8	1,404.6	1,402.1	1,380.0
2008	1,366.0	1,377.0	1,389.2	1,399.4	1,405.8	1,404.9	1,375.1	1,370.0	1,395.3	1,403.4	1,402.2	1,398.7	1,390.6
2009	1,357.7	1,355.3	1,355.7	1,356.0	1,358.9	1,349.1	1,317.7	1,312.7	1,332.9	1,338.3	1,341.2	1,337.0	1,342.7
2010	1,299.7	1,303.3	1,314.0	1,332.4	1,344.7	1,340.4	1,316.3	1,316.7	1,330.7	1,345.6	1,343.3	1,343.3	1,327.5
2011	1,313.2	1,315.0	1,324.6	1,346.1	1,353.4	1,339.0	1,319.8	1,322.9	1,340.4	1,350.2	1,356.2	1,347.1	1,337.0
Total Private													
2000	1,078.0	1,077.4	1,086.7	1,098.7	1,103.8	1,113.8	1,107.7	1,109.2	1,110.6	1,108.2	1,110.6	1,110.1	1,101.2
2001	1,084.9	1,084.3	1,094.3	1,102.6	1,108.2	1,117.4	1,108.9	1,108.4	1,103.7	1,099.4	1,098.7	1,098.6	1,100.8
2002	1,070.4	1,067.7	1,075.7	1,088.8	1,093.1	1,098.9	1,093.3	1,093.9	1,090.7	1,081.6	1,085.3	1,084.1	1,085.3
2003	1,050.4	1,049.4	1,052.2	1,060.6	1,066.9	1,069.6	1,066.0	1,067.7	1,068.1	1,066.1	1,068.1	1,068.6	1,062.8
2004	1,040.9	1,039.1	1,053.0	1,070.1	1,076.5	1,083.0	1,085.9	1,085.4	1,087.9	1,085.4	1,087.7	1,090.1	1,073.8
2005	1,057.2	1,061.1	1,071.3	1,079.5	1,084.7	1,092.5	1,089.7	1,089.7	1,089.8	1,086.2	1,091.9	1,094.7	1,082.4
2006	1,069.8	1,075.0	1,084.7	1,091.7	1,097.8	1,109.2	1,104.6	1,108.3	1,112.4	1,109.1	1,110.4	1,118.8	1,099.3
2007	1,090.0	1,091.8	1,109.5	1,115.0	1,121.9	1,131.4	1,132.8	1,133.1	1,131.4	1,131.8	1,137.7	1,135.3	1,121.8
2008	1,111.7	1,114.3	1,122.6	1,133.3	1,135.6	1,144.3	1,140.2	1,134.6	1,134.6	1,135.4	1,132.3	1,128.2	1,130.6
2009	1,095.5	1,089.1	1,087.8	1,086.9	1,085.2	1,087.1	1,082.3	1,078.8	1,072.8	1,070.8	1,072.2	1,068.1	1,081.4
2010	1,039.8	1,039.8	1,046.4	1,063.5	1,068.6	1,073.7	1,074.5	1,073.4	1,067.8	1,079.0	1,079.0	1,078.4	1,065.3
2011	1,051.6	1,051.6	1,059.4	1,079.0	1,084.7	1,083.7	1,084.4	1,086.6	1,083.8	1,087.5	1,092.9	1,087.7	1,079.1
Goods-Producing													
2000	267.6	267.5	269.8	273.1	274.6	278.7	277.1	276.2	275.5	273.8	271.8	268.1	272.8
2001	262.0	260.4	264.4	268.3	269.6	272.5	271.5	270.9	268.0	265.8	264.3	260.5	266.5
2002	251.6	250.1	251.8	254.0	255.6	258.4	257.0	258.0	255.9	251.3	249.9	248.1	253.5
2003	239.9	241.2	242.2	242.5	245.6	245.2	245.9	246.5	245.5	245.2	244.1	242.3	243.8
2004	237.0	235.0	240.5	245.4	246.9	249.4	253.2	252.2	251.7	251.8	250.5	250.2	247.0
2005	240.4	241.7	245.9	248.5	251.0	254.8	255.7	255.3	253.2	252.6	252.6	251.5	250.3
2006	247.0	248.8	251.1	252.7	254.7	259.9	260.5	260.6	259.2	257.8	256.4	257.1	255.5
2007	251.9	250.2	256.2	256.7	258.7	263.5	265.5	265.8	264.8	263.9	264.7	262.5	260.4
2008	257.1	256.7	260.1	262.2	261.5	267.3	267.9	261.7	264.5	262.4	259.5	256.4	261.4
2009	245.6	241.9	239.7	236.5	232.8	233.6	232.3	231.1	227.8	226.6	224.5	220.6	232.8
2010	214.1	213.6	215.7	221.4	222.8	225.9	227.9	227.7	226.4	226.9	224.9	222.9	222.5
2011	214.4	213.8	217.7	221.6	223.0	224.7	226.6	226.9	225.6	226.4	226.6	224.8	222.7
Mining and Logging													
2000	6.2	6.2	6.4	6.6	6.6	6.8	6.6	6.7	6.7	6.9	7.0	6.9	6.6
2001	6.6	6.6	6.7	6.8	7.0	7.1	7.1	7.3	7.3	7.1	7.0	7.0	7.0
2002	6.6	6.5	6.5	6.6	6.6	6.7	6.6	6.5	6.5	6.4	6.4	6.4	6.5
2003	6.2	6.2	6.3	6.4	6.5	6.6	6.6	6.7	6.7	6.7	6.8	6.8	6.5
2004	6.6	6.5	6.7	6.8	6.9	7.0	7.3	7.5	7.6	7.4	7.3	7.3	7.1
2005	7.2	7.3	7.3	7.4	7.5	7.6	7.6	7.7	7.7	7.9	7.9	8.0	7.6
2006	8.0	8.2	8.4	8.3	8.5	8.7	8.8	8.9	8.9	8.9	9.0	9.1	8.6
2007	8.9	8.9	9.0	9.2	9.1	9.1	9.3	9.3	9.2	9.3	9.3	9.4	9.2
2008	9.4	9.4	9.5	9.6	9.6	9.7	10.0	10.2	10.1	10.0	9.9	9.8	9.8
2009	8.7	8.3	8.1	7.8	7.7	7.8	8.0	8.0	8.0	8.1	8.0	8.1	8.1
2010	7.8	7.9	8.0	8.3	8.3	8.4	8.5	8.5	8.5	8.8	8.6	8.6	8.4
2011	8.4	8.3	8.5	8.7	8.6	8.8	8.9	8.9	8.9	9.0	9.0	9.0	8.8
Construction													
2000	60.5	60.3	62.2	65.8	67.1	69.7	69.8	69.8	68.8	67.0	64.5	61.4	65.6
2001	57.8	57.5	60.8	64.9	66.7	68.9	68.3	68.0	65.8	65.1	64.5	62.2	64.2
2002	58.2	57.7	59.5	62.3	64.1	66.3	67.1	66.7	65.2	64.3	63.5	62.3	63.1
2003	58.0	58.2	59.7	62.3	63.9	65.6	65.8	65.8	64.8	64.3	63.1	60.8	62.7
2004	57.4	54.7	59.0	63.3	64.1	66.5	67.6	66.8	65.8	65.4	64.1	63.0	63.1
2005	55.1	56.0	59.3	61.7	63.3	65.6	66.7	66.6	65.3	64.5	63.6	61.6	62.4
2006	59.2	59.8	61.7	63.2	64.4	67.2	67.7	67.4	66.3	64.6	63.9	63.6	64.1
2007	60.6	57.8	62.5	63.6	64.8	67.8	68.5	68.6	67.8	67.3	67.0	64.4	65.1
2008	59.9	59.0	61.8	64.5	66.3	68.2	68.5	67.9	66.3	65.1	63.8	62.2	64.5
2009	56.1	55.5	56.2	57.3	58.9	60.3	61.4	60.0	58.4	57.0	55.9	53.1	57.5
2010	47.2	46.7	49.2	53.8	54.7	56.9	58.6	58.4	57.4	57.6	55.5	53.2	54.1
2011	47.1	46.8	49.9	52.6	53.8	55.1	57.3	57.2	54.5	54.9	54.2	52.2	53.0
Manufacturing													
2000	200.9	201.0	201.2	200.7	200.9	202.2	200.7	199.7	200.0	199.9	200.3	199.8	200.6
2001	197.6	196.3	196.9	196.6	195.9	196.5	196.1	195.6	194.9	193.6	192.8	191.3	195.3
2002	186.8	185.9	185.8	185.1	184.9	185.4	183.3	184.8	184.2	180.6	180.0	179.4	183.9
2003	175.7	176.8	176.2	173.8	175.2	173.0	173.5	174.0	174.0	174.2	174.2	174.7	174.6
2004	173.0	173.8	174.8	175.3	175.9	175.9	178.3	177.9	178.3	179.0	179.1	179.9	176.8
2005	178.1	178.4	179.3	179.4	180.2	181.6	181.4	181.0	180.2	180.2	181.1	181.9	180.2
2006	179.8	180.8	181.0	181.2	181.8	184.0	184.0	184.3	184.0	184.3	183.5	184.4	182.8
2007	182.4	183.5	184.7	183.9	184.8	186.6	187.7	187.9	187.8	187.3	188.4	188.7	186.1
2008	187.8	188.3	188.8	188.1	185.6	189.4	189.4	183.6	188.1	187.3	185.8	184.4	187.2
2009	180.8	178.1	175.4	171.4	166.2	165.5	162.9	163.1	161.4	161.5	160.6	159.4	167.2
2010	159.1	159.0	158.5	159.3	159.8	160.6	160.8	160.8	160.5	160.5	160.8	161.1	160.1
2011	158.9	158.7	159.3	160.3	160.6	160.8	160.4	160.8	162.2	162.5	163.4	163.6	161.0

1. Employment by Industry: Kansas, Selected Years, 2000–2011—*Continued*

(Numbers in thousands, not seasonally adjusted)

Industry and year	January	February	March	April	May	June	July	August	September	October	November	December	Annual average
Service-Providing													
2000	1,049.7	1,052.5	1,064.6	1,077.6	1,085.5	1,086.7	1,056.7	1,056.4	1,075.5	1,085.6	1,092.9	1,095.6	1,073.3
2001	1,068.0	1,072.7	1,082.6	1,088.4	1,093.5	1,093.0	1,066.4	1,062.8	1,083.5	1,089.4	1,091.8	1,095.7	1,082.3
2002	1,069.3	1,069.7	1,079.9	1,091.4	1,096.4	1,096.2	1,068.9	1,066.7	1,083.8	1,084.6	1,091.8	1,092.5	1,082.6
2003	1,061.1	1,060.8	1,065.7	1,073.8	1,079.8	1,079.5	1,051.6	1,049.3	1,070.1	1,075.5	1,080.8	1,084.0	1,069.3
2004	1,053.3	1,056.1	1,067.5	1,082.5	1,089.3	1,090.5	1,062.8	1,060.6	1,087.9	1,090.4	1,095.7	1,099.1	1,078.0
2005	1,062.2	1,073.6	1,083.4	1,089.7	1,093.3	1,094.6	1,056.1	1,056.9	1,088.2	1,092.1	1,099.7	1,104.4	1,082.9
2006	1,070.9	1,084.4	1,094.8	1,098.8	1,106.6	1,109.8	1,069.8	1,075.2	1,110.7	1,114.0	1,118.1	1,126.9	1,098.3
2007	1,089.3	1,101.7	1,116.7	1,121.0	1,128.4	1,134.0	1,103.9	1,102.3	1,126.4	1,132.9	1,139.9	1,139.6	1,119.7
2008	1,108.9	1,120.3	1,129.1	1,137.2	1,144.3	1,137.6	1,107.2	1,108.3	1,130.8	1,141.0	1,142.7	1,142.3	1,129.1
2009	1,112.1	1,113.4	1,116.0	1,119.5	1,126.1	1,115.5	1,085.4	1,081.6	1,105.1	1,111.7	1,116.7	1,116.4	1,110.0
2010	1,085.6	1,089.7	1,098.3	1,111.0	1,121.9	1,114.5	1,088.4	1,089.0	1,104.3	1,118.7	1,118.4	1,120.4	1,105.0
2011	1,098.8	1,101.2	1,106.9	1,124.5	1,130.4	1,114.3	1,093.2	1,096.0	1,114.8	1,123.8	1,129.6	1,122.3	1,114.4
Trade, Transportation, and Utilities													
2000	273.6	271.4	272.3	273.8	274.5	276.8	273.8	274.8	274.7	275.8	280.5	282.6	275.4
2001	272.5	269.2	269.2	270.4	271.9	272.5	271.3	271.8	270.5	271.6	274.1	276.5	271.8
2002	266.6	262.8	263.1	266.4	267.4	268.7	266.0	266.0	265.6	265.9	269.4	271.0	266.6
2003	260.2	258.0	258.3	260.0	261.2	261.3	260.9	261.8	262.5	263.0	266.5	268.7	261.9
2004	258.7	256.6	257.6	260.3	262.5	263.7	261.8	261.7	263.6	263.2	267.2	268.7	262.1
2005	258.6	257.5	258.5	259.7	261.0	261.7	260.4	260.8	260.4	260.4	264.8	267.4	260.9
2006	257.3	256.1	257.7	258.0	259.1	260.4	258.8	260.2	260.9	260.6	264.2	267.9	260.1
2007	258.9	257.7	261.5	261.2	262.8	263.9	263.4	263.5	262.9	264.1	268.5	269.7	263.2
2008	261.4	260.0	260.9	261.4	262.4	263.6	264.2	263.1	261.7	263.2	265.9	266.8	262.9
2009	258.1	255.9	255.6	254.6	254.9	255.7	254.2	253.2	252.2	252.9	256.0	256.8	255.0
2010	248.3	246.9	248.1	251.0	252.5	253.8	253.4	253.0	251.6	255.0	258.2	259.7	252.6
2011	251.7	250.5	249.8	253.1	254.5	253.7	254.1	253.5	252.1	251.8	256.0	257.7	253.2
Wholesale Trade													
2000	61.6	61.6	61.9	61.6	61.9	63.2	62.6	62.0	61.7	61.6	61.3	61.4	61.9
2001	61.4	61.2	61.3	61.5	61.9	62.8	62.5	61.7	61.1	61.3	60.9	61.1	61.6
2002	60.6	60.5	60.7	61.2	61.1	61.9	61.9	61.3	60.8	60.3	60.1	60.1	60.9
2003	58.8	58.6	58.6	58.5	58.7	59.6	59.7	59.2	58.7	58.7	58.7	59.0	58.9
2004	57.5	57.5	57.9	58.3	58.8	60.1	60.2	59.7	59.3	59.3	59.2	59.0	58.9
2005	58.5	58.6	58.9	59.7	59.9	61.2	60.8	60.4	60.1	59.2	59.3	59.6	59.7
2006	58.9	59.1	59.3	58.3	58.7	60.2	60.1	59.8	59.7	59.3	59.2	59.8	59.4
2007	59.3	59.3	60.0	59.7	59.9	61.2	61.3	60.6	60.3	61.0	61.0	60.9	60.4
2008	61.1	60.9	60.8	61.1	61.4	62.3	63.0	62.0	61.5	61.7	61.6	61.3	61.6
2009	61.4	61.2	61.2	59.7	59.5	60.3	60.4	59.4	59.1	59.0	58.8	58.4	59.9
2010	57.6	57.6	57.9	59.4	59.4	60.3	60.2	59.5	58.9	59.3	58.8	58.7	59.0
2011	58.5	58.6	58.9	59.5	59.8	60.4	60.8	61.2	60.0	59.6	59.8	59.6	59.7
Retail Trade													
2000	157.9	155.9	156.4	156.7	157.3	158.5	156.6	157.8	157.8	158.2	163.5	165.5	158.5
2001	156.7	154.0	154.1	155.0	156.0	156.6	155.8	156.3	155.4	155.7	159.2	161.8	156.4
2002	153.9	150.7	150.9	152.6	153.5	154.1	152.1	152.2	152.2	152.6	156.3	158.0	153.3
2003	149.5	147.5	147.9	148.8	149.7	150.0	149.7	150.7	151.0	151.4	155.0	157.0	150.7
2004	150.3	148.2	149.0	150.1	151.5	151.5	149.6	149.2	151.3	150.4	154.5	156.3	151.0
2005	148.1	146.8	147.3	147.9	148.9	148.8	147.7	147.3	147.1	148.2	152.1	153.7	148.7
2006	146.3	145.0	146.3	147.0	147.8	147.7	146.8	147.2	147.6	147.7	151.2	153.3	147.8
2007	146.3	145.3	147.8	147.3	148.5	148.1	148.2	148.1	147.4	148.3	152.3	153.3	148.4
2008	146.7	145.3	146.5	146.5	147.2	147.5	147.5	147.0	146.0	145.9	148.6	149.4	147.0
2009	142.2	140.5	140.7	141.6	142.4	142.4	141.5	141.3	141.1	141.7	144.5	145.4	142.1
2010	139.4	138.0	138.7	139.9	141.1	141.2	140.7	140.4	139.2	141.2	144.5	145.5	140.8
2011	139.2	138.0	139.0	141.3	142.2	142.1	142.2	140.9	139.8	140.5	143.9	144.6	141.1
Transportation and Utilities													
2000	54.1	53.9	54.0	55.5	55.3	55.1	54.6	55.0	55.2	56.0	55.7	55.7	55.0
2001	54.4	54.0	53.8	53.9	54.0	53.1	53.0	53.8	54.0	54.6	54.0	53.6	53.9
2002	52.1	51.6	51.5	52.6	52.8	52.7	52.0	52.5	52.6	53.0	53.0	52.9	52.4
2003	51.9	51.9	51.8	52.7	52.8	51.7	51.5	51.9	52.8	52.9	52.8	52.7	52.3
2004	50.9	50.9	50.7	51.9	52.2	52.1	52.0	52.8	53.0	53.5	53.5	53.4	52.2
2005	52.0	52.1	52.3	52.1	52.2	51.7	51.9	53.1	53.2	53.0	53.4	54.1	52.6
2006	52.1	52.0	52.1	52.7	52.6	52.5	51.9	53.2	53.6	53.6	53.8	54.8	52.9
2007	53.3	53.1	53.7	54.2	54.4	54.6	53.9	54.8	55.2	54.8	55.2	55.5	54.4
2008	53.6	53.8	53.6	53.8	53.8	53.8	53.7	54.1	54.2	55.6	55.7	56.1	54.3
2009	54.5	54.2	53.7	53.3	53.0	53.0	52.3	52.5	52.0	52.2	52.7	53.0	53.0
2010	51.3	51.3	51.5	51.7	52.0	52.3	52.5	53.1	53.5	54.5	54.9	55.5	52.8
2011	54.0	53.9	51.9	52.3	52.5	51.2	51.1	51.4	52.3	51.7	52.3	53.5	52.3
Information													
2000	44.7	44.7	45.1	46.8	46.9	47.6	48.5	48.5	48.8	47.8	48.7	48.9	47.3
2001	51.0	51.3	51.4	50.9	50.5	51.4	50.7	50.7	50.2	49.5	49.7	50.0	50.6
2002	50.0	49.8	49.9	50.0	49.5	49.3	48.9	48.4	47.6	46.8	47.2	47.2	48.7
2003	46.7	46.0	45.7	45.1	44.7	44.9	44.3	43.6	43.3	42.9	42.9	42.9	44.4
2004	42.9	42.7	42.5	42.5	42.6	42.6	42.3	41.8	41.2	40.0	40.1	40.5	41.8
2005	40.2	40.3	40.0	40.3	40.2	40.1	40.0	39.4	39.2	38.2	38.6	38.9	39.6
2006	38.6	38.6	39.0	40.1	40.1	40.5	40.4	40.2	40.1	40.5	40.7	40.9	40.0
2007	41.2	41.2	41.3	41.3	41.3	41.3	41.3	40.9	40.3	40.0	40.0	40.0	40.8
2008	39.8	39.8	39.7	39.7	39.2	39.2	39.1	38.6	37.8	38.0	37.4	37.3	38.8
2009	36.6	36.4	36.3	36.6	36.1	35.6	35.2	34.6	33.8	31.9	31.8	31.8	34.7
2010	31.2	31.1	30.9	30.9	30.7	30.4	30.0	29.6	29.2	29.0	29.0	29.1	30.1
2011	28.8	28.7	28.7	28.3	28.2	28.1	27.8	27.4	26.5	26.7	26.7	27.2	27.8

1. Employment by Industry: Kansas, Selected Years, 2000–2011—*Continued*

(Numbers in thousands, not seasonally adjusted)

Industry and year	January	February	March	April	May	June	July	August	September	October	November	December	Annual average
Financial Activities													
2000	64.7	64.7	64.5	65.0	65.5	66.1	66.3	66.4	65.9	65.8	65.6	66.6	65.6
2001	66.0	66.0	66.3	66.5	67.0	67.8	68.4	68.3	67.6	67.7	67.9	68.4	67.3
2002	68.2	68.4	68.8	68.4	68.7	69.0	69.5	69.3	68.8	69.0	69.3	69.6	68.9
2003	68.5	68.5	69.0	69.5	69.6	70.0	70.1	70.5	69.7	69.6	69.4	69.7	69.5
2004	68.8	69.0	69.6	69.9	70.0	70.6	71.0	70.8	70.0	69.8	69.7	70.3	70.0
2005	69.3	69.4	69.6	70.0	70.1	70.7	71.1	71.0	70.8	71.0	71.1	71.8	70.5
2006	70.9	70.8	71.0	71.6	72.1	72.5	73.3	73.2	73.0	72.9	73.3	74.2	72.4
2007	73.2	73.3	73.9	73.7	74.1	74.7	75.1	74.9	74.5	74.1	74.1	74.5	74.2
2008	73.0	73.1	72.9	73.3	73.4	73.7	73.6	73.5	72.7	72.9	72.7	73.0	73.2
2009	71.6	71.6	71.5	70.9	70.9	71.4	72.1	72.2	71.3	71.7	71.8	71.9	71.6
2010	70.8	70.8	70.6	71.0	71.4	71.4	71.6	71.6	70.9	71.8	71.7	72.0	71.3
2011	70.9	70.9	71.0	73.1	74.0	74.2	74.5	73.8	73.4	73.0	72.9	71.9	72.8
Professional and Business Services													
2000	128.3	127.5	130.7	130.9	131.2	133.1	130.5	131.5	131.4	132.3	132.2	132.5	131.0
2001	128.8	130.3	132.3	131.2	131.2	133.6	131.1	130.6	130.7	129.1	127.6	127.5	130.3
2002	124.5	125.4	127.4	130.2	129.5	130.7	131.2	130.8	130.2	127.2	128.0	127.7	128.6
2003	123.5	123.1	122.9	126.0	125.5	127.7	124.9	125.3	124.6	124.6	124.7	126.2	124.9
2004	121.0	122.1	125.1	127.8	127.8	129.7	130.1	131.6	132.0	131.6	131.9	132.7	128.6
2005	127.8	128.7	130.5	131.8	131.3	133.0	133.9	135.2	135.3	135.8	136.8	137.7	133.2
2006	133.5	135.5	137.5	138.0	137.2	139.2	138.0	138.6	140.2	140.5	140.5	142.0	138.4
2007	138.1	139.5	141.3	143.5	144.0	145.0	146.6	147.7	148.0	147.8	149.2	148.4	144.9
2008	143.9	145.1	147.0	149.1	148.8	150.3	149.4	149.9	149.5	150.2	149.6	148.1	148.4
2009	142.8	141.2	140.8	141.6	140.9	140.9	140.5	139.8	138.8	140.0	141.1	141.2	140.8
2010	137.7	137.6	139.2	144.7	143.8	144.4	146.5	146.3	144.3	147.6	147.2	147.5	143.9
2011	143.7	144.5	146.0	149.8	149.0	148.0	148.4	151.4	150.8	153.7	156.0	154.3	151.0
Education and Health Services													
2000	144.8	145.5	146.2	146.9	147.3	146.4	147.3	147.8	150.4	150.6	151.3	151.7	148.0
2001	150.0	151.6	152.3	153.4	153.8	153.4	151.7	152.2	154.3	153.3	154.2	155.4	153.0
2002	154.2	155.1	155.9	157.8	158.4	157.1	155.8	156.3	158.7	159.0	159.5	159.6	157.3
2003	156.0	156.2	155.9	158.2	157.8	155.6	155.4	155.7	158.2	158.5	158.8	158.8	157.1
2004	157.4	158.2	159.3	160.4	160.6	159.6	160.4	160.5	162.9	164.2	164.6	164.2	161.0
2005	163.3	163.9	164.2	165.1	165.1	164.4	161.7	161.8	164.6	163.8	164.4	165.0	163.9
2006	163.1	164.3	165.1	165.6	166.3	166.3	164.3	164.9	168.5	169.0	169.1	169.9	166.4
2007	167.6	168.8	170.1	170.7	171.0	171.3	170.0	170.4	173.0	174.3	174.5	174.8	171.4
2008	173.4	174.9	175.6	177.0	177.2	176.6	174.2	175.5	177.6	178.6	179.2	179.2	176.6
2009	178.2	179.0	179.1	179.9	180.3	179.7	178.5	178.9	180.5	181.9	182.2	182.4	180.1
2010	179.1	180.0	179.9	179.2	179.8	179.0	177.7	177.9	179.2	181.8	182.4	182.6	179.9
2011	182.8	183.2	183.2	184.8	185.0	183.0	183.4	182.3	183.5	184.5	186.1	185.5	183.9
Leisure and Hospitality													
2000	103.1	104.5	106.4	110.8	112.1	113.3	112.2	112.0	111.6	109.8	108.4	107.5	109.3
2001	102.9	103.7	106.1	109.5	111.7	113.5	111.6	111.6	110.0	109.4	108.2	107.3	108.8
2002	103.0	103.7	106.0	108.9	110.9	111.8	111.8	112.3	110.6	109.5	109.2	108.0	108.8
2003	103.4	103.9	105.5	106.9	109.4	111.7	111.5	111.5	111.3	109.4	108.7	106.8	108.3
2004	103.0	103.2	105.7	110.2	112.8	113.9	114.0	113.9	113.1	111.6	110.6	110.3	110.2
2005	105.5	106.8	109.2	111.3	113.3	115.2	114.8	114.5	113.9	111.7	111.1	110.3	111.5
2006	107.6	108.7	110.7	114.1	116.4	118.4	117.9	118.9	118.2	116.2	114.7	114.9	114.7
2007	108.3	109.8	113.0	115.4	117.7	119.3	118.8	117.6	115.6	114.4	113.7	112.6	114.7
2008	110.7	111.5	113.0	116.9	119.2	120.3	118.3	118.9	117.5	116.5	114.6	114.4	116.0
2009	109.9	110.1	112.0	114.1	116.6	117.8	117.4	117.2	116.3	113.5	112.5	111.4	114.1
2010	107.1	108.2	110.3	113.4	115.8	117.4	116.3	116.2	114.9	114.2	113.4	112.5	113.3
2011	108.3	108.5	111.4	115.4	118.2	119.6	117.8	119.2	119.0	118.3	115.7	113.7	115.4
Other Services													
2000	51.2	51.6	51.7	51.4	51.7	51.8	52.0	52.0	52.3	52.3	52.1	52.2	51.9
2001	51.7	51.8	52.3	52.4	52.5	52.7	52.6	52.3	52.4	53.0	52.7	53.0	52.5
2002	52.3	52.4	52.8	53.1	53.1	53.9	53.1	52.8	53.3	52.9	52.8	52.9	53.0
2003	52.2	52.5	52.7	52.4	53.1	53.2	53.0	52.8	53.0	52.9	53.0	53.2	52.8
2004	52.1	52.3	52.7	53.6	53.3	53.5	53.1	52.9	53.4	53.2	53.1	53.2	53.0
2005	52.1	52.8	53.4	52.8	52.7	52.6	52.1	51.7	52.4	52.7	52.5	52.1	52.5
2006	51.8	52.2	52.6	51.6	51.9	52.0	51.4	51.7	52.3	51.6	51.5	51.9	51.9
2007	50.8	51.3	52.2	52.5	52.3	52.4	52.1	52.3	52.3	53.2	53.0	52.8	52.3
2008	52.4	53.2	53.4	53.7	53.9	53.3	53.5	53.4	53.3	53.6	53.4	53.0	53.3
2009	52.7	53.0	52.8	52.7	52.7	52.4	52.1	51.8	52.1	52.3	52.3	52.0	52.4
2010	51.5	51.6	51.7	51.9	51.8	51.4	51.1	51.1	51.3	52.7	52.2	52.1	51.7
2011	51.0	51.5	51.6	52.9	52.8	52.4	51.8	52.1	52.9	53.1	52.9	52.6	52.3
Government													
2000	239.3	242.6	247.7	252.0	256.3	251.6	226.1	223.4	240.4	251.2	254.1	253.6	244.9
2001	245.1	248.8	252.7	254.1	254.9	248.1	229.0	225.3	247.8	255.8	257.4	257.6	248.1
2002	250.5	252.1	256.0	256.6	258.9	255.7	232.6	230.8	249.0	254.3	256.4	256.5	250.8
2003	250.6	252.6	255.7	255.7	258.5	255.1	231.5	228.1	247.5	254.6	256.8	257.7	250.4
2004	249.4	252.0	255.0	257.8	259.7	256.9	230.1	227.4	251.7	256.8	258.5	259.2	251.2
2005	245.4	254.2	258.0	258.7	259.6	256.9	222.1	222.5	251.6	258.5	260.4	261.2	250.8
2006	248.1	258.2	261.2	259.8	263.5	260.5	225.7	227.5	257.5	262.7	264.1	265.2	254.5
2007	251.2	260.1	263.4	262.7	265.2	266.1	236.6	235.0	259.8	265.0	266.9	266.8	258.2
2008	254.3	262.7	266.6	266.1	270.2	260.6	234.9	235.4	260.7	268.0	269.9	270.5	260.0
2009	262.2	266.2	267.9	269.1	273.7	262.0	235.4	233.9	260.1	267.5	269.0	268.9	261.3
2010	259.9	263.5	267.6	268.9	276.1	266.7	241.8	243.3	262.9	266.6	264.3	264.9	262.2
2011	261.6	263.4	265.2	267.1	268.7	255.3	235.4	236.3	256.6	262.7	263.3	259.4	257.9

2. Average Weekly Hours by Selected Industry: Kansas, 2007–2011

(Not seasonally adjusted)

Industry and year	January	February	March	April	May	June	July	August	September	October	November	December	Annual average
Total Private													
2007	33.4	33.8	34.1	34.3	34.4	35.5	35.8	35.2	35.5	34.7	34.7	34.9	34.7
2008	34.5	34.6	34.9	34.4	34.8	35.7	35.0	35.1	34.6	34.7	34.9	34.1	34.8
2009	33.8	34.2	34.1	33.5	33.4	34.1	34.2	35.4	34.3	34.2	34.9	33.8	34.2
2010	33.6	33.6	33.5	34.0	34.4	34.5	34.3	34.7	33.9	34.2	34.1	34.4	34.1
2011	33.9	33.8	34.1	34.4	34.8	34.7	34.7	34.5	34.5	35.2	34.5	34.6	34.5
Goods-Producing													
2007	37.9	38.3	39.3	38.5	39.3	40.0	40.4	39.9	40.6	40.0	39.9	40.4	39.6
2008	40.5	40.5	40.7	39.9	41.5	42.9	41.9	42.6	40.9	40.5	40.6	39.7	41.0
2009	39.0	39.1	39.6	38.7	39.1	39.6	39.7	43.9	42.1	43.0	43.7	41.9	40.7
2010	42.1	41.2	41.6	42.6	42.7	42.8	41.8	41.9	40.5	41.5	41.1	41.9	41.8
2011	39.6	40.6	41.5	41.7	42.1	42.2	41.7	41.5	42.0	42.2	41.5	40.9	41.5
Construction													
2007	34.6	33.0	37.5	35.1	38.4	38.5	39.4	38.9	38.0	37.3	38.5	33.1	36.9
2008	35.2	35.8	37.5	35.1	41.3	39.8	40.1	41.3	37.3	37.4	38.7	35.9	38.0
2009	35.6	36.5	37.3	36.2	38.5	37.8	39.9	41.2	36.3	39.2	40.5	36.6	38.0
2010	39.0	36.8	37.7	41.1	40.0	41.9	43.2	43.4	39.8	41.7	39.0	40.7	40.5
2011	36.0	36.2	38.4	39.8	41.0	40.9	40.8	39.5	41.1	40.4	38.3	38.7	39.4
Manufacturing													
2007	39.5	40.6	40.3	40.2	40.0	41.0	41.1	40.6	41.6	41.1	40.4	42.7	40.8
2008	42.2	42.0	41.7	41.5	41.4	44.1	42.3	42.8	41.9	41.2	40.9	40.6	41.9
2009	39.8	39.5	40.0	39.1	38.8	39.9	39.3	44.6	43.7	44.2	44.6	43.7	41.4
2010	43.0	42.6	42.8	42.8	43.6	43.0	42.1	42.0	41.6	41.9	42.4	42.5	42.5
2011	41.4	41.4	42.0	41.8	41.9	42.1	41.5	41.9	41.8	42.4	42.4	41.6	41.9
Trade, Transportation, and Utilities													
2007	33.9	34.2	34.9	35.0	35.0	35.3	35.9	35.5	35.3	34.7	34.8	35.5	35.0
2008	34.4	34.3	34.6	34.6	34.7	35.4	35.1	34.7	34.4	34.8	34.8	34.3	34.7
2009	34.1	34.4	34.3	33.8	34.0	34.5	35.0	35.3	34.3	34.0	34.4	34.4	34.4
2010	33.9	33.5	32.5	34.0	33.7	34.1	34.0	34.2	33.4	33.4	32.6	32.7	33.5
2011	32.5	32.1	33.0	33.5	34.0	33.9	34.1	34.0	33.7	34.2	33.8	34.7	33.6
Financial Activities													
2007	33.0	33.3	32.8	33.8	32.7	33.8	34.2	34.2	34.9	34.1	34.3	34.6	33.8
2008	34.0	34.2	35.1	33.7	34.4	35.4	35.2	34.6	34.4	34.9	36.6	35.2	34.8
2009	36.5	37.7	37.1	36.4	36.2	36.4	36.6	37.9	36.7	36.8	38.1	36.3	36.9
2010	36.2	36.4	36.3	36.5	37.0	36.8	36.9	37.9	36.9	37.3	36.8	37.1	36.8
2011	38.1	37.4	37.2	37.1	37.6	37.1	37.2	37.0	37.0	38.4	37.5	37.5	37.4
Professional and Business Services													
2007	32.5	33.2	33.7	33.7	33.1	34.3	34.4	33.4	34.5	33.4	34.1	33.3	33.6
2008	33.0	33.3	34.2	33.5	33.7	34.1	33.0	33.1	33.8	34.2	34.3	33.4	33.6
2009	32.9	34.1	34.2	32.7	33.0	33.4	33.0	33.0	32.4	32.4	33.5	31.9	33.0
2010	31.0	32.1	32.4	32.5	32.7	33.0	33.2	34.4	33.8	34.5	34.4	34.1	33.2
2011	34.9	35.2	35.0	35.6	35.7	35.8	35.7	35.4	35.3	36.3	35.6	35.4	35.5
Education and Health Services													
2007	32.1	32.3	32.1	32.7	33.1	36.0	35.8	34.8	34.9	33.9	34.0	34.2	33.8
2008	33.6	33.7	33.9	33.6	32.9	33.8	32.9	33.1	33.2	32.7	32.8	32.3	33.2
2009	32.1	31.5	31.5	32.6	31.0	33.1	33.1	33.2	32.7	31.2	32.2	31.3	32.1
2010	31.4	31.2	31.3	31.2	32.2	31.4	31.7	32.2	31.7	31.8	31.6	31.7	31.6
2011	32.3	31.8	31.3	31.6	32.3	32.1	32.2	31.9	32.0	32.3	31.5	31.7	31.9
Leisure and Hospitality													
2007	23.4	24.1	24.0	24.5	24.7	25.1	25.5	24.7	24.9	24.8	24.3	23.6	24.5
2008	23.1	23.4	23.6	23.5	23.3	24.3	24.2	24.7	24.0	24.2	24.4	23.4	23.8
2009	23.0	24.0	23.6	23.4	23.9	24.4	24.2	24.5	23.6	23.5	24.0	22.9	23.8
2010	22.6	23.1	23.3	23.4	23.8	24.3	24.2	24.7	24.0	24.2	23.7	24.3	23.8
2011	24.1	24.1	24.6	24.7	24.6	24.8	24.6	25.3	24.9	25.9	25.2	25.0	24.8
Other Services													
2007	30.9	31.1	32.6	33.2	34.3	35.2	34.9	34.6	33.3	30.6	30.0	33.2	32.8
2008	33.5	33.8	33.7	33.6	35.4	35.8	33.8	34.2	31.8	31.9	32.7	31.1	33.4
2009	31.4	32.8	32.0	31.3	30.0	29.6	31.5	32.8	30.0	30.4	31.2	30.1	31.1
2010	30.1	31.1	30.7	30.5	30.2	31.7	32.0	32.1	30.7	30.4	30.0	30.4	30.8
2011	30.9	30.1	30.6	30.8	30.7	32.3	31.9	31.1	30.0	31.1	30.6	30.8	30.9

3. Average Hourly Earnings by Selected Industry: Kansas, 2007–2011

(Dollars, not seasonally adjusted)

Industry and year	January	February	March	April	May	June	July	August	September	October	November	December	Annual average
Total Private													
2007	19.56	19.82	19.13	19.76	19.69	19.57	19.42	19.33	19.50	19.63	19.78	20.48	19.64
2008	20.13	20.00	20.06	20.16	19.91	19.96	19.92	20.02	20.01	20.03	20.44	20.92	20.13
2009	20.40	20.54	20.40	20.27	20.46	20.07	20.22	19.57	19.82	20.12	20.13	20.16	20.18
2010	20.07	20.19	19.97	20.04	20.22	19.79	20.03	20.13	20.40	20.18	19.86	20.06	20.08
2011	20.58	20.65	20.34	20.45	20.47	20.36	20.47	20.44	20.42	20.63	20.67(C)	20.63	20.51
Goods-Producing													
2007	21.12	21.11	21.11	21.26	22.49	21.01	20.84	21.09	21.27	21.07	21.24	23.01	21.39
2008	22.40	22.06	21.99	21.89	21.83	22.24	22.08	22.31	22.10	21.99	22.33	24.27	22.28
2009	22.56	22.28	22.38	22.64	22.80	22.34	22.34	20.03	20.60	21.26	21.31	22.68	21.91
2010	21.55	21.84	21.42	21.46	21.61	20.81	21.04	21.10	21.61	21.63	20.92	21.17	21.34
2011	21.58	21.87	21.88	21.82	21.75	21.73	21.70	21.86	21.91	22.06	22.07	22.24	21.87
Construction													
2007	17.51	17.99	18.00	18.09	19.80	18.91	19.13	19.25	20.17	19.79	19.65	21.74	19.20
2008	20.42	20.30	20.47	20.62	20.34	20.29	20.67	20.80	21.19	21.32	21.52	21.57	20.79
2009	21.82	21.46	21.99	22.43	22.65	22.04	21.89	21.70	22.38	22.59	23.09	23.66	22.30
2010	23.05	23.55	22.72	22.41	22.43	22.07	21.21	20.90	21.22	21.45	21.39	21.71	21.93
2011	21.76	21.63	21.12	21.18	21.68	21.58	21.36	21.82	22.09	22.17	22.66	22.49	21.80
Manufacturing													
2007	22.48	22.34	22.29	22.42	23.55	21.82	21.51	21.84	21.75	21.58	21.85	23.53	22.25
2008	23.05	22.65	22.40	22.26	22.23	22.84	22.50	22.76	22.33	22.25	22.61	25.19	22.75
2009	22.76	22.39	22.26	22.52	22.70	22.41	22.52	19.47	20.09	20.81	20.69	22.59	21.74
2010	21.12	21.35	21.05	21.24	21.48	21.09	20.99	21.20	21.80	21.78	20.79	21.06	21.24
2011	21.66	22.09	22.25	22.12	21.92	21.76	21.81	21.87	21.80	22.00	21.78	22.17	21.94
Trade, Transportation, and Utilities													
2007	18.37	18.16	17.67	18.19	17.88	17.79	17.83	17.95	18.21	17.62	17.83	18.10	17.96
2008	17.96	17.74	17.78	17.97	17.72	17.34	17.47	17.66	17.67	17.66	18.02	17.85	17.74
2009	17.99	18.10	18.31	18.02	18.08	17.77	17.95	18.28	18.34	18.70	18.66	17.95	18.18
2010	17.88	17.97	18.17	18.28	18.26	18.10	18.07	18.23	18.38	18.11	18.09	18.18	18.14
2011	18.37	18.44	18.27	18.67	18.69	18.68	18.71	18.64	18.82	19.34	19.25	18.96	18.74
Financial Activities													
2007	23.46	23.59	22.63	23.84	22.76	26.01	22.52	21.68	22.17	21.46	21.36	22.10	22.79
2008	21.83	21.94	22.24	21.84	21.45	22.03	20.61	20.85	20.79	21.17	22.26	21.67	21.56
2009	21.43	22.48	23.14	21.68	22.51	21.94	22.22	22.76	22.32	22.56	23.56	22.86	22.46
2010	23.27	23.23	22.69	23.10	23.46	23.17	23.88	23.91	23.81	23.89	23.91	23.88	23.52
2011	23.86	23.40	23.10	23.48	23.85	23.46	23.65	23.33	23.40	23.45	23.16	22.73	23.41
Professional and Business Services													
2007	22.46	25.77	22.09	24.13	22.59	21.59	22.70	22.77	23.22	23.94	24.89	25.02	23.43
2008	24.77	25.15	25.09	25.32	25.26	24.99	25.00	25.06	24.66	25.50	25.61	26.11	25.21
2009	26.23	26.27	25.52	25.53	25.86	25.46	25.92	25.59	25.24	25.35	24.60	25.55
2010	25.03	24.44	24.21	23.99	24.23	23.77	23.71	23.94	25.01	24.59	24.86	25.65	24.46
2011	26.07	25.45	25.16	24.99	25.29	25.00	25.40	25.12	24.52	24.75	24.56	24.91	25.09
Education and Health Services													
2007	16.85	16.66	16.55	17.13	17.33	17.44	18.17	17.41	16.94	18.91	18.64	18.90	17.60
2008	18.03	17.80	17.81	18.65	17.62	17.53	18.14	18.02	18.46	17.79	18.75	18.78	18.11
2009	17.90	18.35	17.76	18.08	18.40	18.14	18.40	17.77	17.90	18.34	17.43	17.90	18.03
2010	18.26	18.90	18.40	18.42	18.98	18.93	19.23	18.72	18.89	18.83	19.08	19.65	18.86
2011	20.02	20.39	19.55	19.48	19.21	19.34	19.36	19.34	19.41	19.47	19.57	19.41	19.54
Leisure and Hospitality													
2007	9.19	9.28	9.32	9.37	9.68	9.23	9.47	9.72	9.79	9.87	9.99	10.17	9.59
2008	10.52	10.56	10.56	10.51	10.79	10.69	10.71	10.65	10.74	10.82	10.75	10.76	10.67
2009	11.04	10.88	10.66	10.74	10.81	10.71	10.71	10.70	10.83	10.97	10.97	11.04	10.83
2010	11.04	11.04	10.90	11.17	10.96	10.73	10.67	10.70	10.74	10.90	10.97	10.75	10.88
2011	10.89	11.20	11.10	11.07	11.00	10.98	11.12	11.53	11.52	11.46	11.43	11.42	11.23
Other Services													
2007	18.11	17.45	17.05	16.56	16.14	16.22	17.76	17.69	17.40	17.82	17.73	18.38	17.34
2008	17.85	18.06	19.08	18.31	17.52	18.52	19.30	19.70	19.46	19.10	19.22	19.07	18.75
2009	20.32	20.45	20.68	20.85	21.05	21.31	21.56	21.34	21.09	21.02	21.27	20.87	20.98
2010	20.82	20.55	20.52	20.63	20.31	19.80	19.99	19.95	19.51	19.21	18.89	18.84	19.92
2011	19.42	19.71	19.39	19.69	19.65	19.29	19.17	19.36	19.11	19.34	19.29	19.32	19.39

4. Average Weekly Earnings by Selected Industry: Kansas, 2007–2011

(Dollars, not seasonally adjusted)

Industry and year	January	February	March	April	May	June	July	August	September	October	November	December	Annual average
Total Private													
2007	653.30	669.92	652.33	677.77	677.34	694.74	695.24	680.42	692.25	681.16	686.37	714.75	681.24
2008	694.49	692.00	700.09	693.50	692.87	712.57	697.20	702.70	692.35	695.04	713.36	713.37	699.89
2009	689.52	702.47	695.64	679.05	683.36	684.39	691.52	692.78	679.83	688.10	702.54	681.41	689.25
2010	674.35	678.38	669.00	681.36	695.57	682.76	687.03	698.51	691.56	690.16	677.23	690.06	684.83
2011	697.66	697.97	693.59	703.48	712.36	706.49	710.31	705.18	704.49	726.18	713.12	713.80	706.99
Goods-Producing													
2007	800.45	808.51	829.62	818.51	883.86	840.40	841.94	841.49	863.56	842.80	847.48	929.60	846.02
2008	907.20	893.43	894.99	873.41	905.95	954.10	925.15	950.41	903.89	890.60	906.60	963.52	914.15
2009	879.84	871.15	886.25	876.17	891.48	884.66	886.90	879.32	867.26	914.18	931.25	950.29	892.74
2010	907.26	899.81	891.07	914.20	922.75	890.67	879.47	884.09	875.21	897.65	859.81	887.02	892.16
2011	854.57	887.92	908.02	909.89	915.68	917.01	904.89	907.19	920.22	930.93	915.91	909.62	907.15
Construction													
2007	605.85	593.67	675.00	634.96	760.32	728.04	753.72	748.83	766.46	738.17	756.53	719.59	709.49
2008	718.78	726.74	767.63	723.76	840.04	807.54	828.87	859.04	790.39	797.37	832.82	774.36	790.62
2009	776.79	783.29	820.23	811.97	872.03	833.11	873.41	894.04	812.39	885.53	935.15	865.96	847.32
2010	898.95	866.64	856.54	921.05	897.20	924.73	916.27	907.06	844.56	894.47	834.21	883.60	887.44
2011	783.36	783.01	811.01	842.96	888.88	882.62	871.49	861.89	907.90	895.67	867.88	870.36	857.82
Manufacturing													
2007	887.96	907.00	898.29	901.28	942.00	894.62	884.06	886.70	904.80	886.94	882.74	1,004.73	906.82
2008	972.71	951.30	934.08	923.79	920.32	1,007.24	951.75	974.13	935.63	916.70	924.75	1,022.71	952.87
2009	905.85	884.41	890.40	880.53	880.76	894.16	885.04	868.36	877.93	919.80	922.77	987.18	899.37
2010	908.16	909.51	900.94	909.07	936.53	906.87	883.68	890.40	906.88	912.58	881.50	895.05	903.33
2011	896.72	914.53	934.50	924.62	918.45	916.10	905.12	916.35	911.24	932.80	923.47	922.27	918.08
Trade, Transportation, and Utilities													
2007	622.74	621.07	616.68	636.65	625.80	627.99	640.10	637.23	642.81	611.41	620.48	642.55	628.83
2008	617.82	608.48	615.19	621.76	614.88	613.84	613.20	612.80	607.85	614.57	627.10	612.26	614.99
2009	613.46	622.64	628.03	609.08	614.72	613.07	628.25	645.28	629.06	635.80	641.90	617.48	624.90
2010	606.13	602.00	590.53	621.52	615.36	617.21	614.38	623.47	613.89	604.87	589.73	594.49	607.75
2011	597.03	591.92	602.91	625.45	635.46	633.25	638.01	633.76	634.23	661.43	650.65	657.91	630.27
Financial Activities													
2007	774.18	785.55	742.26	805.79	744.25	879.14	770.18	741.46	773.73	731.79	732.65	764.66	770.49
2008	742.22	750.35	780.62	736.01	737.88	779.86	725.47	721.41	715.18	738.83	814.72	762.78	750.41
2009	782.20	847.50	858.49	789.15	814.86	798.62	813.25	862.60	819.14	830.21	897.64	829.82	828.85
2010	842.37	845.57	823.65	843.15	868.02	852.66	881.17	906.19	878.59	891.10	879.89	885.95	866.65
2011	909.07	875.16	859.32	871.11	896.76	870.37	879.78	863.21	865.80	900.48	868.50	852.38	875.92
Professional and Business Services													
2007	729.95	855.56	744.43	813.18	747.73	740.54	780.88	760.52	801.09	799.60	848.75	833.17	788.29
2008	817.41	837.50	858.08	848.22	851.26	852.16	825.00	829.49	833.51	872.10	878.42	872.07	848.03
2009	862.97	895.81	872.78	834.83	853.38	850.36	855.36	822.69	829.12	817.78	849.23	784.74	844.10
2010	775.93	784.52	784.40	779.68	792.32	784.41	787.17	823.54	845.34	848.36	855.18	874.67	811.82
2011	909.84	895.84	880.60	889.64	902.85	895.00	906.78	889.25	865.56	898.43	874.34	881.81	890.54
Education and Health Services													
2007	540.89	538.12	531.26	560.15	573.62	627.84	650.49	605.87	591.21	641.05	633.76	646.38	595.44
2008	605.81	599.86	603.76	626.64	579.70	592.51	596.81	596.46	612.87	581.73	615.00	606.59	601.49
2009	574.59	578.03	559.44	589.41	570.40	600.43	609.04	589.96	585.33	572.21	561.25	560.27	579.13
2010	573.36	589.68	575.92	574.70	611.16	594.40	609.59	602.78	598.81	598.79	602.93	622.91	596.23
2011	646.65	648.40	611.92	615.57	620.48	620.81	623.39	616.95	621.12	628.88	616.46	615.30	623.75
Leisure and Hospitality													
2007	215.05	223.65	223.68	229.57	239.10	231.67	241.49	240.08	243.77	244.78	242.76	240.01	234.80
2008	243.01	247.10	249.22	246.99	251.41	259.77	259.18	263.06	257.76	261.84	262.30	251.78	254.56
2009	253.92	261.12	251.58	251.32	258.36	261.32	259.18	262.15	255.59	257.80	263.28	252.82	257.42
2010	249.50	255.02	253.97	261.38	260.85	260.74	258.21	264.29	257.76	263.78	259.99	261.23	259.01
2011	262.45	269.92	273.06	273.43	270.60	272.30	273.55	291.71	286.85	296.81	288.04	285.50	278.86
Other Services													
2007	559.60	542.70	555.83	549.79	553.60	570.94	619.82	612.07	579.42	545.29	531.90	610.22	569.27
2008	597.98	610.43	643.00	615.22	620.21	663.02	652.34	673.74	618.83	609.29	628.49	593.08	627.19
2009	638.05	670.76	661.76	652.61	631.50	630.78	679.14	699.95	632.70	639.01	663.62	628.19	652.25
2010	626.68	639.11	629.96	629.22	613.36	627.66	639.68	640.40	598.96	583.98	566.70	572.74	613.88
2011	600.08	593.27	593.33	606.45	603.26	623.07	611.52	602.10	573.30	601.47	590.27	595.06	599.41

KENTUCKY
At a Glance

Population:
    2000 census: 4,042,193
    2010 census: 4,339,367
    2011 estimate: 4,369,356

Percent change in population:
    2000–2010: 7.4%
    2010–2011: 0.7%

Percent change in total nonfarm employment:
    2000–2010: -4.3%
    2010–2011: 1.1%

Industry with the largest growth in employment, 2000–2011 (thousands):
    Professional and Business Services, 27.4

Industry with the largest decline or smallest growth in employment, 2000–2011 (thousands):
    Manufacturing, -97.8

Civilian labor force:
    2000: 1,949,013
    2010: 2,060,180
    2011: 2,067,527

Unemployment rate and rank among states (lowest to highest):
    2000: 4.2%, 33rd
    2010: 10.2%, 39th
    2011: 9.5%, 38th

Over-the-year change in unemployment rates:
    2010–2011: -0.7%

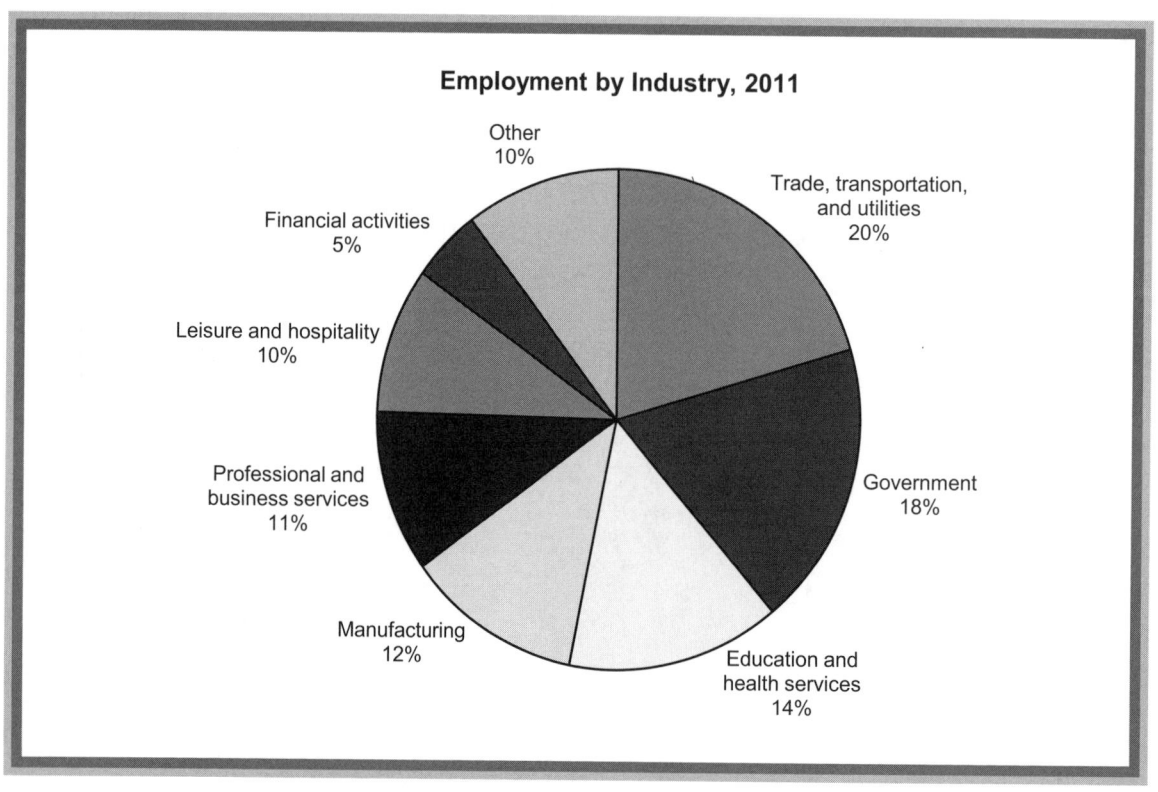

Employment by Industry, 2011

- Other 10%
- Trade, transportation, and utilities 20%
- Financial activities 5%
- Government 18%
- Leisure and hospitality 10%
- Education and health services 14%
- Professional and business services 11%
- Manufacturing 12%

1. Employment by Industry: Kentucky, Selected Years, 2000–2011

(Numbers in thousands, not seasonally adjusted)

Industry and year	January	February	March	April	May	June	July	August	September	October	November	December	Annual average
Total Nonfarm													
2000	1,803.8	1,815.8	1,839.5	1,850.1	1,865.5	1,862.9	1,844.2	1,853.1	1,860.6	1,865.5	1,867.4	1,867.8	1,849.7
2001	1,791.5	1,796.6	1,800.6	1,813.4	1,821.5	1,824.7	1,800.3	1,807.0	1,803.6	1,801.4	1,804.6	1,799.8	1,805.4
2002	1,759.5	1,762.0	1,774.7	1,787.6	1,800.6	1,801.8	1,783.5	1,790.8	1,796.1	1,799.6	1,806.6	1,803.0	1,788.8
2003	1,754.8	1,752.5	1,767.8	1,780.4	1,793.8	1,793.0	1,770.4	1,785.0	1,794.8	1,798.5	1,802.5	1,806.6	1,783.3
2004	1,760.8	1,763.1	1,779.0	1,796.9	1,803.7	1,808.8	1,789.1	1,803.3	1,811.9	1,817.1	1,824.1	1,825.4	1,798.6
2005	1,778.9	1,787.2	1,801.4	1,822.9	1,833.2	1,838.3	1,818.2	1,834.8	1,841.5	1,840.1	1,849.5	1,848.2	1,824.5
2006	1,810.2	1,814.1	1,836.0	1,845.6	1,857.1	1,859.5	1,833.9	1,850.7	1,856.4	1,855.4	1,865.8	1,876.7	1,846.8
2007	1,830.8	1,830.9	1,849.8	1,865.0	1,881.9	1,886.6	1,860.5	1,869.7	1,874.7	1,875.2	1,887.6	1,887.4	1,866.7
2008	1,839.1	1,839.8	1,848.2	1,861.9	1,878.4	1,872.2	1,849.6	1,859.5	1,847.8	1,844.6	1,844.3	1,835.5	1,851.7
2009	1,765.1	1,756.4	1,762.1	1,773.7	1,778.8	1,775.7	1,759.6	1,764.2	1,767.7	1,771.9	1,779.2	1,777.6	1,769.3
2010	1,725.9	1,719.3	1,743.4	1,769.5	1,785.3	1,787.5	1,766.9	1,772.3	1,782.2	1,791.5	1,797.9	1,803.2	1,770.4
2011	1,749.5	1,754.2	1,771.6	1,793.7	1,798.2	1,803.6	1,784.3	1,795.1	1,796.2	1,807.2	1,813.1	1,818.6	1,790.4
Total Private													
2000	1,506.4	1,507.2	1,526.1	1,535.9	1,548.1	1,553.5	1,548.9	1,556.1	1,555.1	1,555.4	1,555.8	1,556.3	1,542.1
2001	1,482.9	1,483.4	1,486.5	1,499.0	1,505.4	1,511.6	1,498.9	1,503.1	1,489.9	1,486.2	1,488.4	1,484.1	1,493.3
2002	1,447.2	1,445.6	1,456.5	1,468.2	1,480.9	1,486.9	1,480.8	1,489.3	1,480.3	1,481.2	1,486.9	1,485.0	1,474.1
2003	1,442.1	1,435.4	1,450.0	1,461.9	1,473.5	1,479.7	1,471.2	1,484.1	1,482.7	1,485.5	1,489.0	1,495.0	1,470.8
2004	1,451.5	1,450.4	1,464.7	1,481.3	1,489.9	1,499.7	1,490.7	1,504.1	1,501.4	1,504.8	1,510.8	1,513.8	1,488.6
2005	1,469.3	1,473.3	1,486.2	1,505.6	1,514.9	1,525.0	1,515.3	1,526.8	1,525.9	1,522.5	1,530.7	1,530.5	1,510.5
2006	1,496.3	1,496.0	1,516.4	1,524.1	1,534.5	1,544.3	1,527.2	1,538.0	1,535.9	1,533.1	1,542.5	1,553.9	1,528.5
2007	1,513.0	1,508.9	1,526.2	1,538.5	1,553.7	1,563.3	1,546.6	1,551.5	1,549.6	1,549.7	1,560.4	1,559.7	1,543.4
2008	1,516.5	1,513.7	1,521.0	1,535.2	1,550.5	1,550.3	1,538.8	1,544.1	1,528.0	1,519.3	1,518.3	1,510.2	1,528.8
2009	1,447.3	1,436.6	1,439.4	1,445.6	1,449.6	1,451.1	1,445.2	1,445.3	1,441.6	1,441.1	1,448.0	1,447.5	1,444.9
2010	1,401.2	1,391.3	1,412.4	1,435.2	1,443.7	1,452.2	1,447.9	1,452.7	1,451.1	1,457.4	1,462.8	1,469.2	1,439.8
2011	1,421.0	1,421.1	1,436.9	1,459.0	1,463.6	1,473.6	1,466.4	1,472.9	1,467.4	1,475.9	1,481.0	1,487.6	1,460.5
Goods-Producing													
2000	411.3	409.9	415.3	417.6	420.3	421.3	418.7	420.6	420.6	418.8	417.1	417.4	417.4
2001	400.6	401.1	400.1	404.0	405.4	407.3	401.1	402.0	398.8	395.1	393.5	390.2	399.9
2002	378.6	377.0	378.2	379.3	380.2	382.0	378.1	381.3	379.0	378.9	377.2	375.0	378.7
2003	364.4	360.6	363.4	365.1	367.5	369.1	367.7	370.3	370.7	371.1	369.4	370.4	367.5
2004	361.0	358.9	361.4	365.0	368.0	370.2	363.4	371.5	371.3	370.1	370.1	369.3	366.7
2005	358.9	359.1	362.2	366.8	369.4	372.3	365.4	372.0	372.3	371.8	372.5	370.6	367.8
2006	364.3	362.6	365.6	366.7	368.6	371.3	364.4	371.1	369.8	364.1	363.8	367.7	366.7
2007	358.7	356.1	358.5	363.5	366.1	369.8	362.7	364.6	367.2	362.6	365.9	361.8	363.1
2008	353.9	352.5	353.6	355.6	362.1	360.1	354.4	357.6	353.6	349.5	348.4	340.0	353.4
2009	321.4	317.5	314.6	313.5	311.4	310.3	307.4	308.0	307.7	306.0	305.1	303.0	310.5
2010	292.1	286.1	293.2	297.9	299.3	300.8	299.7	303.6	304.6	305.0	303.4	301.8	299.0
2011	292.5	293.1	296.7	301.7	302.9	307.2	304.2	308.0	307.2	309.0	305.0	305.5	302.8
Mining and Logging													
2000	20.1	19.8	20.2	19.5	19.5	19.6	19.2	19.2	19.2	18.8	18.8	18.6	19.4
2001	18.7	19.0	19.2	19.8	20.2	20.6	20.8	21.2	21.3	21.5	21.8	21.8	20.5
2002	21.2	21.0	20.8	20.4	20.4	20.5	20.2	20.2	20.2	19.8	19.8	19.7	20.4
2003	19.4	19.3	19.3	18.7	18.6	18.8	18.7	18.9	19.1	19.0	19.0	19.5	19.0
2004	19.1	18.9	19.2	19.6	19.6	19.6	19.8	19.7	19.8	19.7	20.1	20.3	19.7
2005	20.1	20.1	20.5	20.9	21.2	21.5	21.6	21.8	22.2	22.3	22.6	22.7	21.5
2006	22.3	22.3	22.7	22.9	23.0	23.2	23.2	23.1	23.1	22.9	22.9	22.9	22.9
2007	22.2	22.2	22.4	22.1	22.0	22.2	22.0	22.1	22.1	22.1	22.1	22.2	22.1
2008	22.2	22.1	22.3	22.8	23.4	23.7	24.0	24.6	24.8	25.4	25.5	25.6	23.9
2009	25.1	25.0	25.2	24.9	24.3	24.0	23.0	22.7	22.8	22.1	22.1	22.0	23.6
2010	21.3	21.3	21.5	21.8	21.9	22.3	22.2	22.4	22.5	22.4	22.5	22.7	22.1
2011	22.0	22.1	22.3	22.8	22.9	23.2	22.9	22.9	22.8	22.6	22.3	22.0	22.6
Construction													
2000	81.8	81.8	86.1	87.3	88.9	89.9	90.1	89.2	89.3	89.8	88.8	88.6	87.6
2001	79.9	81.4	82.3	87.9	89.8	92.2	92.5	92.0	90.8	89.2	88.4	85.4	87.7
2002	77.9	78.2	79.7	82.0	83.4	85.1	85.7	86.7	86.2	86.1	85.3	83.3	83.3
2003	76.6	74.2	78.4	82.4	84.4	85.5	86.5	86.3	86.0	87.1	85.4	83.8	83.1
2004	77.5	76.5	78.8	82.6	84.5	86.0	87.5	86.9	86.7	85.8	85.2	83.7	83.5
2005	76.2	77.4	79.5	83.2	85.6	87.6	89.1	88.0	87.2	87.0	86.0	84.0	84.2
2006	78.8	78.2	80.2	82.1	84.3	85.5	85.8	86.0	85.2	84.4	84.0	83.1	83.1
2007	77.4	75.5	80.9	84.3	86.5	88.3	88.7	89.1	88.9	89.3	88.4	85.8	85.3
2008	79.1	77.8	79.6	84.0	87.8	88.4	88.8	88.7	87.7	86.4	83.9	81.0	84.4
2009	72.7	71.1	71.9	73.3	74.4	75.4	76.1	75.5	75.1	75.3	74.1	71.9	73.9
2010	63.6	61.5	64.7	68.2	68.7	69.2	71.1	70.6	70.1	70.6	69.3	66.7	67.9
2011	60.4	60.7	63.7	67.3	68.9	71.1	71.4	71.8	70.2	70.5	67.9	67.6	67.6
Manufacturing													
2000	309.4	308.3	309.0	310.8	311.9	311.8	309.4	312.2	312.1	310.2	309.5	310.2	310.4
2001	302.0	300.7	298.6	296.3	295.4	294.5	287.8	288.8	286.7	284.4	283.3	283.0	291.8
2002	279.5	277.8	277.7	276.9	276.4	276.4	272.2	274.4	272.6	273.0	272.1	272.0	275.1
2003	268.4	267.1	265.7	264.0	264.5	264.8	262.5	265.1	265.6	265.0	265.0	267.1	265.4
2004	264.4	263.5	263.4	262.8	263.9	264.4	256.2	264.8	264.9	264.2	264.8	265.3	263.6
2005	262.6	261.6	262.2	262.7	262.6	263.2	254.7	262.2	262.9	262.5	263.9	263.9	262.1
2006	263.2	262.1	262.7	261.7	261.3	262.6	255.4	262.0	261.5	256.8	256.9	261.7	260.7
2007	259.1	258.4	255.2	257.1	257.6	259.3	252.0	253.4	256.2	251.2	255.4	253.8	255.7
2008	252.6	252.6	251.7	248.8	250.9	248.0	241.6	244.3	241.1	237.7	239.0	233.4	245.1
2009	223.6	221.4	217.5	215.3	212.7	210.9	208.3	209.8	209.8	208.6	208.9	209.1	213.0
2010	207.2	203.3	207.0	207.9	208.7	209.3	206.4	210.6	212.0	212.0	211.6	212.4	209.0
2011	210.1	210.3	210.7	211.6	211.1	212.9	209.9	213.3	214.2	215.9	214.8	215.9	212.6

1. Employment by Industry: Kentucky, Selected Years, 2000–2011—*Continued*

(Numbers in thousands, not seasonally adjusted)

Industry and year	January	February	March	April	May	June	July	August	September	October	November	December	Annual average
Service-Providing													
2000	1,392.5	1,405.9	1,424.2	1,432.5	1,445.2	1,441.6	1,425.5	1,432.5	1,440.0	1,446.7	1,450.3	1,450.4	1,432.3
2001	1,390.9	1,395.5	1,400.5	1,409.4	1,416.1	1,417.4	1,399.2	1,405.0	1,404.8	1,406.3	1,411.1	1,409.6	1,405.5
2002	1,380.9	1,385.0	1,396.5	1,408.3	1,420.4	1,419.8	1,405.4	1,409.5	1,417.1	1,420.7	1,429.4	1,428.0	1,410.1
2003	1,390.4	1,391.9	1,404.4	1,415.3	1,426.3	1,423.9	1,402.7	1,414.7	1,424.1	1,427.4	1,433.1	1,436.2	1,415.9
2004	1,399.8	1,404.2	1,417.6	1,431.9	1,435.7	1,438.6	1,425.7	1,431.8	1,440.6	1,447.0	1,454.0	1,456.1	1,431.9
2005	1,420.0	1,428.1	1,439.2	1,456.1	1,463.8	1,466.0	1,452.8	1,462.8	1,469.2	1,468.3	1,477.0	1,477.6	1,456.7
2006	1,445.9	1,451.5	1,470.4	1,478.9	1,488.5	1,488.2	1,469.5	1,479.6	1,486.6	1,491.3	1,502.0	1,509.0	1,480.1
2007	1,472.1	1,474.8	1,491.3	1,501.5	1,515.8	1,516.8	1,497.8	1,505.1	1,507.5	1,512.6	1,521.7	1,525.6	1,503.6
2008	1,485.2	1,487.3	1,494.6	1,506.3	1,516.3	1,512.1	1,495.2	1,501.9	1,494.2	1,495.1	1,495.9	1,495.5	1,498.3
2009	1,443.7	1,438.9	1,447.5	1,460.2	1,467.4	1,465.4	1,452.2	1,456.2	1,460.0	1,465.9	1,474.1	1,474.6	1,458.8
2010	1,433.8	1,433.2	1,450.2	1,471.6	1,486.0	1,486.7	1,467.2	1,468.7	1,477.6	1,486.5	1,494.5	1,501.4	1,471.5
2011	1,457.0	1,461.1	1,474.9	1,492.0	1,495.3	1,496.4	1,480.1	1,487.1	1,489.0	1,498.2	1,508.1	1,513.1	1,487.7
Trade, Transportation, and Utilities													
2000	383.6	381.0	384.7	387.3	390.3	391.4	392.0	392.9	392.3	394.6	400.0	402.1	391.0
2001	383.0	379.4	378.9	379.5	379.8	380.0	377.9	378.2	375.8	378.2	383.2	384.3	379.9
2002	370.1	367.1	369.5	369.1	371.7	372.1	371.7	372.3	370.6	372.1	378.9	382.8	372.3
2003	366.0	362.9	365.9	366.8	369.7	370.2	369.0	372.2	371.5	373.9	379.2	383.5	370.9
2004	367.9	365.3	368.1	370.0	372.2	373.6	371.7	373.5	373.5	377.0	383.1	386.5	373.5
2005	372.4	370.1	372.7	375.1	377.5	378.5	378.3	379.0	377.8	377.9	385.5	388.7	377.8
2006	374.7	371.6	376.5	377.1	380.2	381.9	378.5	379.4	379.1	381.9	389.2	394.2	380.4
2007	381.1	378.2	383.2	382.9	386.4	388.3	384.9	384.9	385.2	387.6	394.4	396.6	386.1
2008	381.1	377.7	378.8	380.4	383.1	383.4	381.2	382.1	378.0	377.5	383.0	386.2	381.0
2009	366.0	360.0	360.2	360.6	362.8	363.4	361.2	360.9	360.4	360.9	367.3	370.5	362.9
2010	354.7	352.0	355.1	357.4	359.9	361.2	360.4	361.2	359.8	363.9	370.2	375.2	360.9
2011	358.7	356.9	360.0	362.4	363.9	365.9	363.6	363.9	362.8	365.0	370.6	374.3	364.0
Wholesale Trade													
2000	72.7	72.6	73.1	73.3	73.5	73.5	73.0	73.1	73.1	74.5	75.3	75.1	73.6
2001	73.7	73.5	73.3	72.9	73.1	73.3	72.8	72.8	72.1	72.4	72.5	72.8	72.9
2002	72.2	72.1	71.5	71.8	72.3	72.2	71.9	72.1	71.8	72.3	72.8	73.2	72.2
2003	72.8	72.6	72.4	72.7	73.2	73.4	73.0	73.5	73.3	73.2	73.7	74.3	73.2
2004	73.7	73.5	73.6	73.9	73.9	74.1	74.3	74.2	73.9	74.2	74.8	75.2	74.1
2005	74.3	74.0	74.1	74.4	74.6	74.6	74.5	74.6	74.5	74.5	74.8	75.2	74.5
2006	74.7	74.7	75.4	75.8	76.2	76.5	75.9	76.0	75.9	76.5	76.7	77.3	76.0
2007	76.6	76.6	77.2	77.2	77.2	77.6	77.0	76.9	77.0	76.8	76.9	77.2	77.0
2008	76.5	76.6	76.6	76.4	76.6	76.9	76.5	76.4	75.8	75.9	75.9	75.7	76.3
2009	73.9	72.9	72.6	72.4	72.5	72.3	72.1	71.8	71.7	71.7	72.2	72.6	72.4
2010	71.4	71.1	71.4	71.2	71.6	71.9	72.0	71.8	71.7	72.0	72.1	72.2	71.7
2011	71.0	71.4	71.7	71.4	71.8	72.1	69.7	69.9	69.4	69.8	70.1	70.2	70.7
Retail Trade													
2000	220.6	218.6	221.1	221.1	223.8	225.1	224.8	226.0	225.8	224.6	229.7	232.1	224.4
2001	217.0	214.1	214.6	214.8	216.4	216.6	213.5	214.1	213.0	214.0	219.3	220.6	215.7
2002	209.6	207.5	210.6	211.4	213.3	213.8	211.2	211.4	210.8	210.9	217.3	220.6	212.4
2003	207.3	204.3	206.4	207.5	209.8	210.2	209.7	211.3	211.2	212.3	217.6	221.0	210.7
2004	208.4	206.1	208.1	209.2	210.8	211.6	209.4	210.6	211.0	212.4	218.0	220.8	211.4
2005	210.0	207.7	209.5	210.6	212.5	212.7	212.2	212.0	210.9	211.1	217.5	220.3	212.3
2006	209.8	207.4	210.5	210.5	212.3	212.2	210.2	210.5	209.2	211.2	217.4	220.0	211.8
2007	211.0	208.5	212.3	212.0	214.8	214.8	213.6	212.8	212.2	212.7	219.0	220.4	213.7
2008	210.4	208.1	209.8	210.1	211.5	211.8	210.9	211.2	208.7	208.3	212.6	214.0	210.6
2009	202.2	198.4	199.0	200.8	202.5	203.0	201.7	200.8	200.3	200.7	205.5	206.8	201.8
2010	197.0	195.2	197.6	199.5	201.1	200.7	200.5	200.7	198.8	201.7	205.9	207.6	200.5
2011	198.3	196.2	198.3	200.7	201.4	201.6	202.5	202.1	200.8	202.6	206.1	207.7	201.5
Transportation and Utilities													
2000	90.3	89.8	90.5	92.9	93.0	92.8	94.2	93.8	93.4	95.5	95.0	94.9	93.0
2001	92.3	91.8	91.0	91.8	90.3	90.1	91.6	91.3	90.7	91.8	91.4	90.9	91.3
2002	88.3	87.5	87.4	85.9	86.1	86.1	88.6	88.8	88.0	88.9	88.8	89.0	87.8
2003	85.9	86.0	87.1	86.6	86.7	86.6	86.3	87.4	87.0	88.4	87.9	88.2	87.0
2004	85.8	85.7	86.4	86.9	87.5	87.9	88.0	88.7	88.6	90.4	90.3	90.5	88.1
2005	88.1	88.4	89.1	90.1	90.4	91.2	91.6	92.4	92.4	92.3	93.2	93.2	91.0
2006	90.2	89.5	90.6	90.8	91.7	93.2	92.4	92.9	94.0	94.2	95.1	96.9	92.6
2007	93.5	93.1	93.7	93.7	94.4	95.9	94.3	95.2	96.0	98.1	98.5	99.0	95.5
2008	94.2	93.0	92.4	93.9	95.0	94.7	93.8	94.5	93.5	93.3	94.5	96.5	94.1
2009	89.9	88.7	88.6	87.4	87.8	88.1	87.4	88.3	88.4	88.5	89.6	91.1	88.7
2010	86.3	85.7	86.1	86.7	87.2	88.6	87.9	88.7	89.3	90.2	92.2	95.4	88.7
2011	89.4	89.3	90.0	90.3	90.7	92.2	91.4	91.9	92.6	92.6	94.4	96.4	91.8
Information													
2000	31.9	32.2	32.8	32.8	33.2	33.4	33.5	33.7	33.7	33.4	33.4	33.5	33.1
2001	33.3	33.4	33.6	33.3	33.4	33.4	33.0	32.7	32.2	31.9	31.8	31.9	32.8
2002	32.3	32.2	32.2	31.6	31.5	31.6	31.3	31.2	30.9	30.5	30.7	30.8	31.4
2003	30.5	30.6	30.8	30.1	30.2	29.9	29.5	29.3	28.8	29.0	29.0	29.1	29.7
2004	28.9	29.0	29.0	29.0	29.1	29.4	29.3	29.1	28.7	28.9	29.1	29.4	29.1
2005	28.6	28.7	29.0	29.0	29.4	29.6	29.6	29.6	29.3	29.2	29.5	29.7	29.3
2006	29.4	29.5	29.5	29.4	29.6	29.7	29.5	29.4	29.2	29.5	29.6	29.7	29.5
2007	29.6	29.5	29.6	29.9	30.3	30.5	30.3	30.2	30.1	29.9	30.2	30.3	30.0
2008	29.8	29.7	29.7	29.6	29.8	30.1	29.7	29.6	29.1	28.5	28.6	28.3	29.4
2009	27.9	27.7	27.5	27.3	27.3	27.2	27.0	26.9	26.5	26.5	26.6	26.7	27.1
2010	26.2	26.1	26.2	26.2	26.4	26.5	26.1	26.2	26.1	26.2	26.7	27.4	26.4
2011	27.1	26.9	26.8	26.7	26.8	26.8	26.6	26.6	26.4	26.7	26.7	26.7	26.7

1. Employment by Industry: Kentucky, Selected Years, 2000–2011—*Continued*

(Numbers in thousands, not seasonally adjusted)

Industry and year	January	February	March	April	May	June	July	August	September	October	November	December	Annual average
Financial Activities													
2000	82.6	82.7	82.3	82.1	82.6	83.6	80.9	81.0	80.5	80.7	80.9	80.8	81.7
2001	81.2	81.0	81.4	82.0	82.4	83.2	83.0	83.2	82.5	81.9	82.1	82.8	82.2
2002	81.5	81.8	82.0	82.4	83.0	83.5	83.2	83.3	82.8	82.7	82.9	83.3	82.7
2003	82.7	82.6	83.1	83.7	84.3	85.0	84.9	85.7	85.3	85.3	85.4	85.8	84.5
2004	84.4	84.4	84.9	85.2	85.3	85.4	85.3	85.5	84.7	84.4	84.5	85.1	84.9
2005	84.3	84.4	84.5	85.2	85.4	86.3	86.1	86.3	86.1	86.3	86.5	87.1	85.7
2006	86.9	87.2	88.0	88.3	88.9	89.5	89.0	89.2	89.5	89.8	90.2	91.0	89.0
2007	90.2	90.2	90.3	90.8	91.1	91.8	91.9	91.8	91.2	91.4	91.5	92.1	91.2
2008	91.6	92.3	92.3	92.0	92.3	92.0	92.2	92.0	91.0	90.6	90.9	90.9	91.7
2009	89.5	88.9	88.7	88.8	89.0	88.8	88.7	88.2	87.5	87.5	87.1	87.4	88.3
2010	86.3	85.8	85.9	86.1	86.1	86.3	86.1	85.6	84.9	84.9	84.8	85.4	85.7
2011	84.2	84.4	84.6	84.7	84.8	85.4	84.7	84.0	83.8	83.5	83.6	83.5	84.3
Professional and Business Services													
2000	154.5	154.9	158.7	157.7	158.5	159.3	160.9	163.0	163.9	164.9	165.1	163.9	160.4
2001	158.4	158.5	159.2	158.6	158.2	159.3	157.0	158.9	157.5	156.5	155.9	155.1	157.8
2002	151.3	151.3	153.2	154.8	156.7	158.4	157.9	161.6	160.2	160.1	160.8	159.6	157.2
2003	153.1	151.8	153.7	155.6	156.5	156.3	155.2	158.5	158.9	162.2	163.5	164.8	157.5
2004	155.8	156.9	158.6	161.4	162.0	163.4	164.9	167.7	169.0	171.8	172.8	173.2	164.8
2005	166.2	167.8	169.6	172.1	172.0	173.8	172.5	175.8	177.8	179.5	181.1	181.1	174.1
2006	174.2	174.5	179.1	179.2	179.5	181.7	180.1	183.0	183.5	184.7	187.1	189.5	181.3
2007	179.1	179.1	181.7	182.5	184.0	184.7	182.5	184.4	184.0	187.2	189.3	191.8	184.2
2008	182.4	181.7	182.2	184.3	184.4	185.9	183.5	184.1	182.3	181.3	179.9	180.1	182.7
2009	169.5	168.6	167.6	167.8	166.7	167.5	169.0	170.9	171.2	174.6	178.8	180.4	171.1
2010	172.6	170.5	173.0	178.3	178.6	181.4	180.9	181.3	182.0	182.9	184.8	189.6	179.7
2011	179.6	178.8	181.0	184.6	183.5	185.3	187.9	190.6	191.3	193.8	197.2	199.5	187.8
Education and Health Services													
2000	227.0	229.2	230.2	230.4	231.0	230.8	230.5	232.3	232.7	233.2	233.3	233.2	231.2
2001	209.1	210.4	211.2	211.8	212.1	212.4	213.3	214.2	214.7	216.6	217.1	217.2	213.3
2002	217.3	218.2	218.7	221.5	222.0	222.2	222.3	223.4	224.6	226.1	227.3	227.5	222.6
2003	225.8	226.6	227.5	227.2	227.8	227.6	224.9	226.4	229.0	229.5	229.4	229.4	227.6
2004	227.7	229.2	230.1	230.3	230.1	230.2	230.4	231.2	232.0	233.4	234.0	234.3	231.1
2005	231.4	233.7	233.5	234.7	235.5	235.2	235.4	236.0	237.0	236.6	236.2	236.9	235.2
2006	235.1	236.3	237.3	237.7	237.6	238.1	236.7	236.8	238.0	239.3	239.3	240.1	237.7
2007	238.8	239.5	240.5	239.7	240.7	241.2	240.3	240.7	241.0	242.5	242.5	243.0	240.9
2008	241.1	241.4	242.3	242.2	244.6	244.0	243.8	244.9	245.2	246.9	247.0	247.1	244.4
2009	244.3	244.3	245.4	246.3	246.7	246.7	245.9	246.9	247.6	249.2	249.4	249.7	246.9
2010	247.1	247.9	249.6	250.1	251.0	251.0	251.3	251.5	252.5	254.2	254.5	254.8	251.3
2011	252.3	252.7	253.4	255.3	255.4	255.0	253.4	254.3	255.6	257.7	259.6	259.7	255.4
Leisure and Hospitality													
2000	140.9	142.1	146.5	152.3	156.1	157.3	157.6	157.7	156.7	155.2	151.1	150.3	152.0
2001	143.2	145.2	147.4	155.0	159.0	160.0	159.0	159.3	154.6	152.3	151.1	148.3	152.9
2002	141.8	143.5	147.8	153.7	159.7	160.2	160.2	160.3	156.7	155.0	153.1	150.0	153.5
2003	144.1	144.7	149.4	156.7	160.3	163.6	162.6	163.7	160.8	156.7	155.6	154.2	156.0
2004	149.0	149.7	155.0	161.8	164.5	168.1	168.0	167.9	164.8	162.6	160.8	159.3	161.0
2005	152.1	153.6	158.4	166.5	169.1	172.6	171.9	172.0	169.6	165.4	163.5	160.4	164.6
2006	156.6	158.8	163.9	169.8	174.0	175.5	173.3	173.9	171.7	168.8	168.4	166.4	168.4
2007	160.9	161.7	166.9	173.5	178.8	180.2	178.3	179.1	175.2	172.8	171.1	168.5	172.3
2008	162.1	163.7	166.9	174.0	178.6	179.2	179.7	179.7	175.5	171.4	167.4	165.1	171.9
2009	158.3	158.9	164.4	170.8	175.2	176.1	175.4	173.1	170.9	167.0	164.7	160.9	168.0
2010	154.2	155.2	160.5	169.7	172.7	175.0	173.4	173.4	171.6	170.0	168.3	164.9	167.4
2011	157.3	158.8	164.2	172.8	175.4	176.8	175.8	174.7	170.3	170.1	168.6	168.3	169.4
Other Services													
2000	74.6	75.2	75.6	75.7	76.1	76.4	74.8	74.9	74.7	74.6	74.9	75.1	75.2
2001	74.1	74.4	74.7	74.8	75.1	76.0	74.6	74.6	73.8	73.7	73.7	74.3	74.5
2002	74.3	74.5	74.9	75.8	76.1	76.9	76.1	75.9	75.5	75.8	76.0	76.0	75.7
2003	75.5	75.6	76.2	76.7	77.2	78.0	77.4	78.0	77.7	77.8	77.5	77.8	77.1
2004	76.8	77.0	77.6	78.6	78.7	79.4	77.7	77.7	77.4	76.6	76.4	76.7	77.6
2005	75.4	75.9	76.3	76.2	76.6	76.7	76.1	76.1	76.0	75.8	75.9	76.0	76.1
2006	75.1	75.5	76.5	75.9	76.1	76.6	75.7	75.2	75.1	75.0	74.9	75.3	75.6
2007	74.6	74.6	75.5	75.7	76.3	76.8	75.7	75.8	75.7	75.7	75.5	75.6	75.6
2008	74.5	74.7	75.2	75.1	75.6	75.6	74.3	74.1	73.3	73.6	73.1	72.5	74.3
2009	70.4	70.7	71.0	70.5	70.5	71.1	70.6	70.4	69.8	69.4	69.0	68.9	70.2
2010	68.0	67.7	68.9	69.5	69.7	70.0	70.0	69.9	69.6	70.3	70.1	70.1	69.5
2011	69.3	69.5	70.2	70.8	70.9	71.2	70.2	70.8	70.0	70.1	69.7	70.1	70.2
Government													
2000	297.4	308.6	313.4	314.2	317.4	309.4	295.3	297.0	305.5	310.1	311.6	311.5	307.6
2001	308.6	313.2	314.1	314.4	316.1	313.1	301.4	303.9	313.7	315.2	316.2	315.7	312.1
2002	312.3	316.4	318.2	319.4	319.7	314.9	302.7	301.5	315.8	318.4	319.7	318.0	314.8
2003	312.7	317.1	317.8	318.5	320.3	313.3	299.2	300.9	312.1	313.0	313.5	311.6	312.5
2004	309.3	312.7	314.3	315.6	313.8	309.1	298.4	299.2	310.5	312.3	313.3	311.6	310.0
2005	309.6	313.9	315.2	317.3	318.3	313.3	302.9	308.0	315.6	317.6	318.8	317.7	314.0
2006	313.9	318.1	319.6	321.5	322.6	315.2	306.7	312.7	320.5	322.3	323.3	322.8	318.3
2007	317.8	322.0	323.6	326.5	328.2	323.3	313.9	318.2	325.1	325.5	327.2	327.7	323.3
2008	322.6	326.1	327.2	326.7	327.9	321.9	310.8	315.4	319.8	325.3	326.0	325.3	322.9
2009	317.8	319.8	322.7	328.1	329.2	324.6	314.4	318.9	326.1	330.8	331.2	330.1	324.5
2010	324.7	328.0	331.0	334.3	341.6	335.3	319.0	319.6	331.1	334.1	335.1	334.0	330.7
2011	328.5	333.1	334.7	334.7	334.6	330.0	317.9	322.2	328.8	331.3	332.1	331.0	329.9

2. Average Weekly Hours by Selected Industry: Kentucky, 2007–2011

(Not seasonally adjusted)

Industry and year	January	February	March	April	May	June	July	August	September	October	November	December	Annual average
Total Private													
2007	36.8	36.8	37.0	37.1	36.9	37.1	37.3	37.0	36.9	36.3	36.5	36.6	36.9
2008	36.4	36.1	36.6	36.3	36.3	36.7	36.2	36.1	36.0	35.9	36.1	35.8	36.2
2009	35.6	35.9	35.7	35.2	35.2	35.3	35.2	35.5	35.1	35.1	35.7	35.4	35.4
2010	35.1	34.7	35.3	35.4	35.6	35.6	35.4	35.7	35.2	35.4	35.2	34.8	35.3
2011	34.6	34.6	34.8	34.9	35.2	35.2	35.1	35.2	35.0	35.4	34.8	34.8	35.0
Goods-Producing													
2007	39.4	39.2	39.6	39.8	39.7	40.4	40.7	40.5	40.6	40.4	41.2	40.4	40.2
2008	40.2	39.6	40.6	40.2	40.4	40.8	40.5	40.6	40.3	40.2	40.0	40.0	40.3
2009	40.1	40.2	39.8	39.3	39.4	39.5	38.9	39.5	39.3	39.7	41.0	40.9	39.8
2010	40.6	39.4	40.2	40.3	40.3	40.2	39.6	40.4	40.2	40.4	40.3	40.0	40.2
2011	39.6	40.0	40.8	40.3	40.5	40.8	40.5	41.7	40.7	41.1	40.0	40.2	40.5
Construction													
2007	36.7	36.2	37.4	37.8	37.9	38.7	39.4	39.7	39.6	39.3	40.2	37.5	38.4
2008	37.6	36.7	37.6	38.0	38.2	39.0	38.9	38.9	39.1	39.3	39.0	38.8	38.5
2009	38.8	40.0	39.5	39.1	39.1	40.3	40.8	40.8	39.7	38.3	41.9	38.5	39.7
2010	37.6	35.4	37.0	37.7	36.8	37.4	37.5	38.4	37.2	38.8	38.3	36.5	37.4
2011	36.2	36.1	37.8	37.3	39.6	39.8	38.9	40.8	38.4	39.2	39.1	37.7	38.5
Manufacturing													
2007	40.0	39.9	40.2	40.3	40.0	40.0	39.9	39.5	39.8	39.6	39.8	40.0	39.9
2008	39.7	39.2	40.2	39.5	39.4	39.8	39.6	39.7	39.2	39.0	38.9	38.8	39.4
2009	38.6	38.6	38.6	38.3	38.3	38.5	37.6	38.5	38.7	39.4	40.0	40.8	38.8
2010	40.3	39.2	40.1	40.1	40.3	40.2	40.0	40.4	40.4	40.3	40.7	40.9	40.2
2011	40.5	40.8	41.4	40.8	40.3	40.4	40.3	41.5	41.0	41.2	40.0	40.6	40.7
Trade, Transportation, and Utilities													
2007	35.7	35.6	35.7	35.5	35.7	36.0	35.7	35.8	35.9	35.1	35.0	35.6	35.6
2008	35.2	35.0	35.5	35.4	35.3	35.6	35.1	35.2	35.1	34.4	34.9	34.7	35.1
2009	34.6	34.9	34.6	34.1	34.2	34.7	34.6	34.3	34.6	34.4	34.4	34.5	34.5
2010	33.5	33.2	33.9	34.2	34.2	34.9	34.7	34.5	34.4	34.6	34.7	34.6	34.3
2011	34.0	33.9	34.0	34.5	34.8	35.2	35.2	34.9	35.0	35.4	35.0	35.0	34.7
Financial Activities													
2007	37.7	37.2	37.3	38.1	36.6	37.0	37.5	36.6	37.6	36.7	37.2	38.3	37.3
2008	37.8	38.2	38.7	38.3	37.5	38.4	37.3	37.7	37.3	37.8	38.7	38.0	38.0
2009	38.5	39.1	38.9	37.9	37.1	37.4	37.6	37.6	36.3	35.8	37.9	36.3	37.5
2010	37.2	36.9	37.6	36.7	38.8	37.5	37.9	39.7	37.5	38.1	38.5	37.4	37.8
2011	39.4	37.7	38.5	37.8	39.2	37.8	37.9	37.5	37.2	37.7	37.0	36.6	37.9
Professional and Business Services													
2007	35.8	35.6	35.6	36.1	36.1	35.7	36.2	35.6	35.9	35.5	35.6	35.5	35.8
2008	35.6	35.6	36.1	36.1	36.3	36.4	35.5	35.7	35.5	35.5	36.1	35.4	35.8
2009	35.0	35.3	35.4	35.5	35.6	35.4	35.9	36.4	36.0	36.5	36.6	36.7	35.9
2010	36.1	36.9	37.0	37.0	37.1	36.9	36.9	37.5	37.0	37.4	37.1	36.1	36.9
2011	35.2	35.2	35.4	35.9	35.9	35.6	35.5	36.2	35.4	36.2	35.2	35.1	35.6
Education and Health Services													
2007	35.6	35.4	36.0	36.0	36.2	36.7	37.4	36.9	36.6	36.0	35.8	36.1	36.2
2008	36.0	36.0	36.3	35.9	36.3	36.7	36.5	36.3	36.4	36.6	36.8	36.6	36.4
2009	36.1	36.2	36.1	35.6	35.7	35.8	35.7	36.0	35.4	35.5	36.0	35.7	35.8
2010	35.3	35.0	35.1	34.9	35.3	35.1	34.7	35.2	34.5	34.4	34.4	34.4	34.9
2011	34.7	34.8	34.6	34.7	35.2	35.2	35.1	34.9	34.9	34.9	34.6	34.6	34.9
Leisure and Hospitality													
2007	26.2	26.3	26.1	26.6	26.6	27.0	27.1	27.1	27.0	26.8	26.3	26.4	26.6
2008	26.0	26.1	26.5	26.7	27.4	27.9	27.9	27.5	27.3	27.6	27.6	26.9	27.1
2009	26.5	27.4	27.1	27.0	27.2	27.0	27.1	26.8	26.4	25.8	26.0	25.8	26.7
2010	25.0	25.3	25.8	26.2	26.7	27.2	27.2	26.9	26.5	26.4	25.4	24.9	26.2
2011	24.0	24.8	25.0	24.8	25.5	25.5	25.6	25.0	25.1	25.5	25.1	25.2	25.1

3. Average Hourly Earnings by Selected Industry: Kentucky, 2007–2011

(Dollars, not seasonally adjusted)

Industry and year	January	February	March	April	May	June	July	August	September	October	November	December	Annual average
Total Private													
2007	17.73	17.91	17.68	17.73	17.50	17.54	17.87	17.70	17.92	17.82	17.64	17.72	17.73
2008	17.76	17.91	17.94	18.05	17.95	18.00	17.98	18.06	18.23	18.20	18.35	18.44	18.07
2009	18.63	18.77	18.62	18.50	18.75	18.66	18.69	18.71	18.95	19.05	19.25	19.27	18.82
2010	19.52	19.40	19.17	19.21	19.29	19.04	19.42	19.61	19.50	19.45	19.45	19.69	19.40
2011	19.98	20.19	19.81	19.82	19.85	19.62	19.73	19.72	19.68	19.81	19.68	19.79	19.80
Goods-Producing													
2007	18.78	18.82	18.64	18.70	18.78	19.05	19.24	19.26	19.36	19.31	19.34	19.64	19.08
2008	19.44	19.76	19.79	20.05	19.97	19.91	19.98	20.04	20.27	20.52	20.64	20.78	20.09
2009	21.01	21.13	21.15	21.18	21.35	21.45	21.24	21.22	21.73	22.01	22.18	22.54	21.51
2010	22.43	21.98	21.81	21.88	21.92	21.63	21.82	21.68	21.99	21.76	21.52	21.67	21.84
2011	21.58	21.52	21.37	21.10	21.24	21.02	21.41	21.14	21.09	20.94	20.66	20.84	21.15
Construction													
2007	19.15	19.07	19.01	19.34	19.25	19.77	20.64	20.04	20.00	20.37	20.34	20.92	19.86
2008	20.57	20.83	20.60	20.65	20.89	20.45	20.60	20.40	20.44	20.84	20.66	20.57	20.62
2009	20.11	20.43	20.12	20.15	20.37	20.80	20.93	21.01	21.14	21.91	21.54	22.03	20.88
2010	22.55	22.01	22.73	22.65	22.73	21.74	21.90	22.20	22.14	22.52	22.02	22.04	22.27
2011	22.08	22.44	21.96	21.90	21.84	21.86	22.02	22.32	21.95	22.01	21.94	22.21	22.04
Manufacturing													
2007	18.49	18.57	18.51	18.40	18.53	18.51	18.36	18.52	18.72	18.56	18.65	18.93	18.56
2008	18.74	19.20	19.30	19.59	19.46	19.50	19.50	19.66	19.88	20.06	20.16	20.17	19.59
2009	20.60	20.86	21.00	20.85	21.10	21.14	21.53	21.51	22.21	22.18	22.53	22.80	21.52
2010	22.45	22.01	21.47	21.60	21.76	21.75	21.91	21.68	21.89	21.42	21.33	21.49	21.73
2011	21.34	21.19	20.96	20.57	20.81	20.42	20.90	20.34	20.49	20.30	19.90	20.11	20.61
Trade, Transportation, and Utilities													
2007	15.38	15.57	15.43	15.44	15.12	15.39	15.70	15.54	15.70	15.67	15.26	15.25	15.45
2008	15.38	15.59	15.58	15.79	15.61	15.82	15.90	15.88	15.98	16.03	16.13	16.03	15.81
2009	16.35	16.35	16.36	16.37	16.50	16.09	16.36	16.44	16.64	16.37	16.64	16.44	16.41
2010	16.87	16.76	16.64	16.50	16.82	16.72	17.36	17.57	17.57	17.89	17.98	18.04	17.24
2011	18.23	18.21	18.04	17.91	17.83	17.65	17.70	17.64	17.29	17.50	17.43	17.51	17.74
Financial Activities													
2007	19.61	20.08	19.74	19.65	19.65	19.63	20.28	20.21	20.44	20.60	20.50	21.02	20.12
2008	20.88	21.20	21.06	21.17	21.46	21.79	21.78	21.85	21.76	21.40	21.69	21.68	21.47
2009	21.44	21.73	21.92	21.41	21.15	21.45	21.24	21.43	21.42	21.93	22.25	21.56	21.58
2010	20.76	21.20	20.89	21.73	21.62	21.49	22.11	22.59	21.44	21.59	21.43	21.43	21.53
2011	21.57	21.84	20.81	20.89	20.72	20.57	20.22	20.84	20.30	21.06	21.09	20.97	20.91
Professional and Business Services													
2007	19.95	20.09	20.11	20.17	19.95	19.51	19.98	19.30	19.51	18.95	18.66	18.53	19.55
2008	18.87	19.24	19.31	19.49	19.44	19.36	19.32	19.46	19.52	19.68	19.71	19.90	19.44
2009	20.27	20.48	20.13	20.01	20.31	20.21	19.80	20.09	20.29	20.60	21.02	20.84	20.35
2010	21.20	21.53	21.21	21.04	21.25	20.95	21.20	21.99	21.92	22.18	22.24	22.00	21.57
2011	22.16	21.88	21.64	21.25	21.43	21.31	21.51	21.18	20.96	21.21	20.73	20.63	21.31
Education and Health Services													
2007	18.30	18.58	18.14	18.18	18.26	18.21	18.21	18.40	19.13	19.19	19.11	18.96	18.56
2008	19.16	19.37	19.08	19.05	19.25	19.33	19.56	19.66	19.97	19.51	19.84	20.17	19.50
2009	20.44	20.28	19.55	19.80	19.81	19.72	19.76	19.62	19.55	19.64	19.62	20.22	19.83
2010	20.66	20.25	19.92	20.04	20.26	20.10	20.62	20.93	20.66	20.95	20.91	21.05	20.53
2011	21.79	22.31	21.63	22.09	22.68	22.68	22.77	22.95	23.18	23.45	23.58	23.76	22.74
Leisure and Hospitality													
2007	10.19	10.08	10.01	10.10	10.14	9.94	10.01	9.96	10.07	10.01	10.06	10.09	10.05
2008	10.11	10.14	10.03	9.97	10.14	10.11	9.99	10.07	9.99	10.15	10.04	10.28	10.08
2009	10.34	10.38	10.26	10.29	10.63	10.61	10.78	10.70	10.71	10.67	10.77	10.70	10.57
2010	10.68	10.63	10.58	10.65	10.63	10.54	10.40	10.34	10.33	10.53	10.66	10.69	10.55
2011	10.77	10.83	10.74	10.74	10.60	10.66	10.54	10.72	10.65	10.77	10.82	10.87	10.72

4. Average Weekly Earnings by Selected Industry: Kentucky, 2007–2011

(Dollars, not seasonally adjusted)

Industry and year	January	February	March	April	May	June	July	August	September	October	November	December	Annual average
Total Private													
2007	652.46	659.09	654.16	657.78	645.75	650.73	666.55	654.90	661.25	646.87	643.86	648.55	653.35
2008	646.46	646.55	656.60	655.22	651.59	660.60	650.88	651.97	656.28	653.38	662.44	660.15	654.46
2009	663.23	673.84	664.73	651.20	660.00	658.70	657.89	664.21	665.15	668.66	687.23	682.16	666.55
2010	685.15	673.18	676.70	680.03	686.72	677.82	687.47	700.08	686.40	688.53	684.64	685.21	684.71
2011	691.31	698.57	689.39	691.72	698.72	690.62	692.52	694.14	688.80	701.27	684.86	688.69	692.58
Goods-Producing													
2007	739.93	737.74	738.14	744.26	745.57	769.62	783.07	780.03	786.02	780.12	796.81	793.46	766.35
2008	781.49	782.50	803.47	806.01	806.79	812.33	809.19	813.62	816.88	824.90	825.60	831.20	809.40
2009	842.50	849.43	841.77	832.37	841.19	847.28	826.24	838.19	853.99	873.80	909.38	921.89	856.25
2010	910.66	866.01	876.76	881.76	883.38	869.53	864.07	875.87	884.00	879.10	867.26	866.80	877.03
2011	854.57	860.80	871.90	850.33	860.22	857.62	867.11	881.54	858.36	860.63	826.40	837.77	857.25
Construction													
2007	702.81	690.33	710.97	731.05	729.58	765.10	813.22	795.59	792.00	800.54	817.67	784.50	763.21
2008	773.43	764.46	774.56	784.70	798.00	797.55	801.34	793.56	799.20	819.01	805.74	798.12	792.97
2009	780.27	817.20	794.74	787.87	796.47	838.24	853.94	857.21	839.26	839.15	902.53	848.16	829.88
2010	847.88	779.15	841.01	853.91	836.46	813.08	821.25	852.48	823.61	873.78	843.37	804.46	832.76
2011	799.30	810.08	830.09	816.87	864.86	870.03	856.58	910.66	842.88	862.79	857.85	837.32	847.90
Manufacturing													
2007	739.60	740.94	744.10	741.52	741.20	740.40	732.56	731.54	745.06	734.98	742.27	757.20	740.96
2008	743.98	752.64	775.86	773.81	766.72	776.10	772.20	780.50	779.30	782.34	784.22	782.60	772.30
2009	795.16	805.20	810.60	798.56	808.13	813.89	809.53	828.14	859.53	873.89	901.20	930.24	835.61
2010	904.74	862.79	860.95	866.16	876.93	874.35	876.40	875.87	884.36	863.23	868.13	878.94	874.47
2011	864.27	864.55	867.74	839.26	838.64	824.97	842.27	844.11	840.09	836.36	796.00	816.47	839.46
Trade, Transportation, and Utilities													
2007	549.07	554.29	550.85	548.12	539.78	554.04	560.49	556.33	563.63	550.02	534.10	542.90	550.25
2008	541.38	545.65	553.09	558.97	551.03	563.19	558.09	558.98	560.90	551.43	562.94	556.24	555.17
2009	565.71	570.62	566.06	558.22	564.30	558.32	566.06	563.89	575.74	563.13	572.42	567.18	566.00
2010	565.15	556.43	564.10	564.30	575.24	583.53	602.39	606.17	604.41	618.99	623.91	624.18	591.08
2011	619.82	617.32	613.36	617.90	620.48	621.28	623.04	615.64	605.15	619.50	610.05	612.85	616.37
Financial Activities													
2007	739.30	746.98	736.30	748.67	719.19	726.31	760.50	739.69	768.54	756.02	762.60	805.07	750.83
2008	789.26	809.84	815.02	810.81	804.75	836.74	812.39	823.75	811.65	808.92	839.40	823.84	815.52
2009	825.44	849.64	852.69	811.44	784.67	802.23	798.62	805.77	777.55	785.09	843.28	782.63	809.87
2010	772.27	782.28	785.46	797.49	838.86	805.88	837.97	896.82	804.00	822.58	825.06	801.48	814.13
2011	849.86	823.37	801.19	789.64	812.22	777.55	766.34	781.50	755.16	793.96	780.33	767.50	791.66
Professional and Business Services													
2007	714.21	715.20	715.92	728.14	720.20	696.51	723.28	687.08	700.41	672.73	664.30	657.82	699.25
2008	671.77	684.94	697.09	703.59	705.67	704.70	685.86	694.72	692.96	698.64	711.53	704.46	696.33
2009	709.45	722.94	712.60	710.36	723.04	715.43	710.82	731.28	730.44	751.90	769.33	764.83	729.83
2010	765.32	794.46	784.77	778.48	788.38	773.06	782.28	824.63	811.04	829.53	825.10	794.20	796.23
2011	780.03	770.18	766.06	762.88	769.34	758.64	763.61	766.72	741.98	767.80	729.70	724.11	757.92
Education and Health Services													
2007	651.48	657.73	653.04	654.48	661.01	668.31	681.05	678.96	700.16	690.84	684.14	684.46	672.20
2008	689.76	697.32	692.60	683.90	698.78	709.41	713.94	713.66	726.91	714.07	730.11	738.22	709.16
2009	737.88	734.14	705.76	704.88	707.22	705.98	705.43	706.32	692.07	697.22	706.32	721.85	710.39
2010	729.30	708.75	699.19	699.40	715.18	705.51	715.51	736.74	712.77	720.68	719.30	724.12	715.57
2011	756.11	776.39	748.40	766.52	798.34	798.34	799.23	800.96	808.98	818.41	815.87	822.10	792.67
Leisure and Hospitality													
2007	266.98	265.10	261.26	268.66	269.72	268.38	271.27	269.92	271.89	268.27	264.58	266.38	267.77
2008	262.86	264.65	265.80	266.20	277.84	282.07	278.72	276.93	272.73	280.14	277.10	276.53	273.62
2009	274.01	284.41	278.05	277.83	289.14	286.47	292.14	286.76	282.74	275.29	280.02	276.06	282.04
2010	267.00	268.94	272.96	279.03	283.82	286.69	282.88	278.15	273.75	277.99	270.76	266.18	275.89
2011	258.48	268.58	268.50	266.35	270.30	271.83	269.82	268.00	267.32	274.64	271.58	273.92	269.20

LOUISIANA
At a Glance

Population:
   2000 census: 4,469,035
   2010 census: 4,533,372
   2011 estimate: 4,574,836

Percent change in population:
   2000–2010: 1.4%
   2010–2011: 0.9%

Percent change in total nonfarm employment:
   2000–2010: -1.8%
   2010–2011: 1.1%

Industry with the largest growth in employment, 2000–2011 (thousands):
   Professional and Business Services, 57.6

Industry with the largest decline or smallest growth in employment, 2000–2011 (thousands):
   Manufacturing, -37.9

Civilian labor force:
   2000: 2,031,292
   2010: 2,070,068
   2011: 2,060,635

Unemployment rate and rank among states (lowest to highest):
   2000: 5.0%, 44th
   2010: 7.5%, 14th
   2011: 7.3%, 16th

Over-the-year change in unemployment rates:
   2010–2011: -0.2%

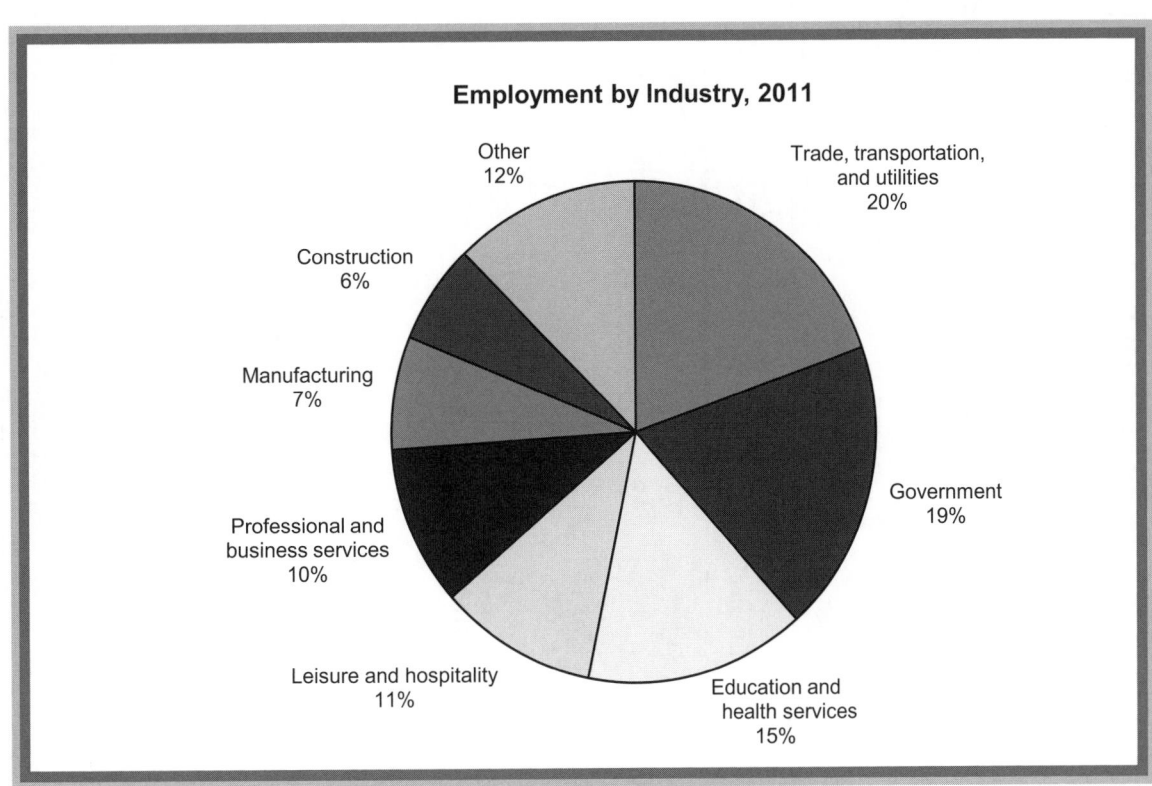

Employment by Industry, 2011

Other 12%
Trade, transportation, and utilities 20%
Construction 6%
Manufacturing 7%
Professional and business services 10%
Leisure and hospitality 11%
Education and health services 15%
Government 19%

1. Employment by Industry: Louisiana, Selected Years, 2000–2011

(Numbers in thousands, not seasonally adjusted)

Industry and year	January	February	March	April	May	June	July	August	September	October	November	December	Annual average
Total Nonfarm													
2000	1,887.8	1,901.7	1,916.5	1,922.1	1,938.3	1,929.5	1,904.4	1,907.6	1,922.4	1,921.7	1,925.8	1,935.0	1,917.7
2001	1,897.3	1,908.9	1,923.1	1,924.4	1,930.8	1,930.7	1,900.6	1,906.5	1,918.5	1,911.7	1,915.8	1,916.1	1,915.4
2002	1,872.2	1,880.1	1,890.9	1,903.1	1,907.1	1,907.5	1,883.9	1,888.2	1,899.8	1,897.6	1,908.7	1,908.4	1,895.6
2003	1,882.8	1,893.1	1,899.4	1,906.4	1,913.2	1,911.5	1,890.8	1,895.0	1,908.7	1,916.9	1,923.4	1,925.2	1,905.5
2004	1,891.4	1,902.7	1,919.7	1,924.7	1,923.0	1,924.5	1,905.9	1,908.5	1,913.3	1,922.0	1,935.8	1,939.0	1,917.5
2005	1,904.9	1,913.9	1,930.8	1,948.5	1,951.8	1,953.3	1,937.6	1,941.1	1,823.8	1,776.0	1,801.9	1,817.6	1,891.8
2006	1,789.8	1,813.1	1,839.8	1,841.5	1,854.3	1,859.4	1,835.0	1,852.4	1,874.9	1,880.5	1,892.9	1,904.6	1,853.2
2007	1,876.5	1,895.4	1,915.5	1,904.5	1,911.6	1,917.7	1,894.0	1,911.3	1,922.0	1,936.5	1,947.1	1,953.5	1,915.5
2008	1,910.6	1,928.5	1,937.6	1,939.9	1,945.5	1,940.8	1,919.8	1,938.0	1,922.5	1,950.4	1,957.5	1,958.8	1,937.5
2009	1,910.3	1,917.9	1,918.1	1,909.4	1,911.9	1,896.8	1,880.9	1,885.7	1,890.6	1,894.0	1,901.1	1,895.0	1,901.0
2010	1,855.3	1,863.7	1,880.6	1,889.2	1,897.1	1,895.0	1,872.4	1,875.4	1,884.9	1,894.8	1,899.7	1,901.4	1,884.1
2011	1,870.6	1,884.8	1,896.7	1,907.0	1,909.4	1,899.6	1,891.5	1,895.1	1,913.4	1,928.4	1,934.7	1,937.9	1,905.7
Total Private													
2000	1,517.2	1,525.1	1,537.0	1,542.9	1,553.3	1,555.6	1,539.6	1,547.9	1,550.8	1,547.9	1,552.1	1,562.0	1,544.3
2001	1,525.2	1,530.8	1,544.0	1,547.0	1,553.8	1,556.2	1,537.9	1,545.8	1,545.5	1,535.7	1,538.2	1,539.1	1,541.6
2002	1,502.2	1,504.6	1,513.8	1,525.6	1,529.5	1,531.1	1,517.2	1,523.7	1,524.7	1,518.9	1,527.5	1,529.5	1,520.7
2003	1,508.3	1,511.4	1,516.3	1,523.4	1,531.1	1,531.3	1,519.4	1,527.5	1,529.5	1,534.3	1,539.0	1,543.8	1,526.3
2004	1,514.1	1,518.6	1,533.8	1,539.3	1,539.2	1,542.6	1,532.2	1,536.7	1,530.3	1,535.9	1,548.9	1,553.4	1,535.4
2005	1,528.4	1,530.6	1,547.7	1,564.3	1,569.6	1,573.6	1,567.8	1,570.9	1,445.7	1,415.8	1,441.1	1,458.7	1,517.9
2006	1,446.8	1,463.6	1,488.7	1,492.2	1,504.4	1,517.8	1,501.0	1,513.2	1,522.0	1,526.8	1,536.9	1,549.0	1,505.2
2007	1,527.8	1,538.2	1,556.0	1,550.7	1,558.0	1,566.3	1,553.8	1,565.0	1,561.8	1,573.2	1,581.2	1,588.2	1,560.0
2008	1,553.4	1,563.4	1,573.2	1,573.2	1,578.7	1,579.8	1,566.5	1,578.6	1,557.5	1,579.3	1,583.9	1,587.9	1,573.0
2009	1,545.6	1,546.2	1,546.6	1,536.0	1,539.8	1,531.5	1,525.6	1,528.6	1,521.0	1,517.6	1,523.4	1,519.7	1,531.8
2010	1,488.7	1,492.4	1,507.0	1,516.1	1,519.1	1,524.8	1,519.9	1,522.1	1,523.9	1,529.7	1,533.3	1,536.8	1,517.8
2011	1,513.0	1,523.0	1,534.9	1,544.5	1,547.8	1,543.4	1,544.8	1,546.1	1,552.0	1,561.3	1,566.3	1,571.6	1,545.7
Goods-Producing													
2000	348.8	349.9	353.1	354.8	359.0	360.0	353.3	355.6	354.0	352.6	349.8	349.4	353.4
2001	343.7	345.5	350.7	350.2	354.6	355.6	351.2	352.4	350.0	345.2	341.3	337.2	348.1
2002	328.4	326.6	327.4	328.7	330.6	330.4	327.2	329.0	328.0	329.4	326.4	324.3	328.0
2003	321.1	320.1	320.4	319.3	324.8	325.6	321.6	322.8	322.9	324.5	320.9	319.1	321.9
2004	313.2	312.9	317.2	315.7	314.3	315.8	314.7	312.6	312.3	314.5	315.1	314.9	314.4
2005	308.9	310.5	314.4	319.9	321.9	323.5	321.6	323.0	307.5	311.6	315.1	317.7	316.3
2006	320.4	322.8	327.9	329.7	331.9	336.2	328.0	332.4	336.5	338.0	338.1	341.0	331.9
2007	332.2	335.5	338.7	340.2	342.7	344.9	342.3	344.3	343.6	345.9	345.2	344.0	341.6
2008	337.0	338.4	339.2	340.4	343.3	345.0	343.2	344.8	341.2	346.9	345.1	344.3	342.4
2009	335.5	332.6	330.4	326.0	326.6	324.2	322.5	320.7	317.6	316.7	314.9	310.9	323.2
2010	305.1	304.7	308.1	309.0	309.9	313.3	313.4	313.2	312.5	313.7	310.9	310.6	310.4
2011	305.8	308.8	312.0	314.3	314.3	313.2	315.2	315.9	319.4	320.4	317.7	316.4	314.5
Mining and Logging													
2000	44.9	45.0	44.8	46.0	46.8	47.8	48.0	48.6	49.0	48.4	48.4	49.1	47.2
2001	50.0	51.1	51.9	52.1	52.9	53.7	53.0	53.4	53.1	51.8	50.2	50.2	52.0
2002	49.5	48.8	48.5	48.2	48.6	48.9	48.7	48.8	48.7	47.5	47.4	47.4	48.4
2003	47.3	47.3	47.4	47.2	47.4	48.2	47.3	47.5	47.0	46.8	46.5	45.8	47.1
2004	44.9	44.9	45.4	45.2	44.7	45.0	44.3	44.4	43.9	44.6	44.5	44.5	44.7
2005	44.0	44.2	44.8	45.2	45.5	46.0	45.8	46.0	45.7	45.4	45.1	45.3	45.3
2006	46.4	46.9	47.3	47.2	47.6	48.6	49.1	49.7	50.5	50.1	49.9	50.1	48.6
2007	49.6	49.8	50.0	51.2	51.7	52.1	52.0	53.0	52.4	52.6	53.0	52.9	51.7
2008	53.9	53.7	54.0	54.1	54.4	55.0	55.4	55.5	54.9	56.3	55.9	55.6	54.9
2009	55.0	54.1	53.3	51.2	51.4	51.3	50.1	50.0	49.5	49.6	49.7	50.2	51.3
2010	49.4	50.6	51.1	51.5	52.1	52.6	52.0	52.2	51.8	52.2	51.9	52.0	51.6
2011	51.5	52.0	52.2	52.5	52.3	52.6	53.5	53.5	54.3	55.0	55.0	55.6	53.3
Construction													
2000	126.8	128.8	131.9	132.1	133.9	134.1	128.3	129.5	127.8	126.1	124.3	123.2	128.9
2001	118.9	120.5	124.5	124.6	127.3	127.2	126.4	127.6	126.5	125.3	124.4	121.7	124.6
2002	119.2	117.8	118.4	119.9	120.8	119.1	118.3	119.4	118.9	120.8	118.6	116.9	119.0
2003	117.2	117.3	117.0	118.1	120.9	120.3	119.6	119.9	120.1	121.5	118.7	117.6	119.0
2004	116.8	116.6	120.1	117.9	116.4	116.3	116.7	114.2	114.1	115.7	116.6	115.7	116.4
2005	112.2	113.9	116.2	120.7	121.4	121.6	120.9	121.2	114.5	118.5	121.8	122.8	118.8
2006	125.7	127.3	130.8	132.4	133.3	134.9	127.3	129.0	130.3	131.8	131.6	133.3	130.6
2007	129.1	130.5	132.7	132.2	133.8	134.3	132.3	133.8	133.5	134.7	133.6	132.8	132.8
2008	129.3	131.0	132.0	133.7	135.3	136.1	134.8	136.4	135.3	138.0	137.7	137.1	134.7
2009	132.7	132.9	132.6	130.7	131.8	130.9	131.4	130.1	128.0	127.6	126.6	123.1	129.9
2010	119.1	118.3	120.1	119.0	119.1	121.9	123.3	122.9	122.7	122.8	121.0	120.3	120.9
2011	117.5	119.5	121.9	123.4	122.7	121.5	122.0	123.5	125.1	123.8	122.0	119.3	121.9
Manufacturing													
2000	177.1	176.1	176.4	176.7	178.3	178.1	177.0	177.5	177.2	178.1	177.1	177.1	177.2
2001	174.8	173.9	174.3	173.5	174.4	174.7	171.8	171.4	170.4	168.1	166.7	165.3	171.6
2002	159.7	160.0	160.5	160.6	161.2	162.4	160.2	160.8	160.4	161.1	160.4	160.0	160.6
2003	156.6	155.5	156.0	154.0	156.5	157.1	154.7	155.4	155.8	156.2	155.7	155.7	155.8
2004	151.5	151.4	151.7	152.6	153.2	154.5	153.7	154.0	154.3	154.2	154.0	154.7	153.3
2005	152.7	152.4	153.4	154.0	155.0	155.9	154.9	155.8	147.3	147.7	148.2	149.6	152.2
2006	148.3	148.6	149.8	150.1	151.0	152.7	151.6	153.7	155.7	156.1	156.6	157.6	152.7
2007	153.5	155.2	156.0	156.8	157.2	158.5	158.0	157.5	157.7	158.6	158.6	158.3	157.2
2008	153.8	153.7	153.2	152.6	153.6	153.9	153.0	152.9	151.0	152.6	151.5	151.6	152.8
2009	147.8	145.6	144.5	144.1	143.4	142.0	141.0	140.6	140.1	139.5	138.6	137.6	142.1
2010	136.6	135.8	136.9	138.5	138.7	138.8	138.1	138.1	138.0	138.7	138.0	138.3	137.9
2011	136.8	137.3	137.9	138.4	139.3	139.1	139.7	138.9	140.0	141.6	140.7	141.5	139.3

1. Employment by Industry: Louisiana, Selected Years, 2000–2011—*Continued*

(Numbers in thousands, not seasonally adjusted)

Industry and year	January	February	March	April	May	June	July	August	September	October	November	December	Annual average
Service-Providing													
2000	1,539.0	1,551.8	1,563.4	1,567.3	1,579.3	1,569.5	1,551.1	1,552.0	1,568.4	1,569.1	1,576.0	1,585.6	1,564.4
2001	1,553.6	1,563.4	1,572.4	1,574.2	1,576.2	1,575.1	1,549.4	1,554.1	1,568.5	1,566.5	1,574.5	1,578.9	1,567.2
2002	1,543.8	1,553.5	1,563.5	1,574.4	1,576.5	1,577.1	1,556.7	1,559.2	1,571.8	1,568.2	1,582.3	1,584.1	1,567.6
2003	1,561.7	1,573.0	1,579.0	1,587.1	1,588.4	1,585.9	1,569.2	1,572.2	1,585.8	1,592.4	1,602.5	1,606.1	1,583.6
2004	1,578.2	1,589.8	1,602.5	1,609.0	1,608.7	1,608.7	1,591.2	1,595.9	1,601.0	1,607.5	1,620.7	1,624.1	1,603.1
2005	1,596.0	1,603.4	1,616.4	1,628.6	1,629.9	1,629.8	1,616.0	1,618.1	1,516.3	1,464.4	1,486.8	1,499.9	1,575.5
2006	1,469.4	1,490.3	1,511.9	1,511.8	1,522.4	1,523.2	1,507.0	1,520.0	1,538.4	1,542.5	1,554.8	1,563.6	1,521.3
2007	1,544.3	1,559.9	1,576.8	1,564.3	1,568.9	1,572.8	1,551.7	1,567.0	1,578.4	1,590.6	1,601.9	1,609.5	1,573.8
2008	1,573.6	1,590.1	1,598.4	1,599.5	1,602.2	1,595.8	1,576.6	1,593.2	1,581.3	1,603.5	1,612.4	1,614.5	1,595.1
2009	1,574.8	1,585.3	1,587.7	1,583.4	1,585.3	1,572.6	1,558.4	1,565.0	1,573.0	1,577.3	1,586.2	1,584.1	1,577.8
2010	1,550.2	1,559.0	1,572.5	1,580.2	1,587.2	1,581.7	1,559.0	1,562.2	1,572.4	1,581.1	1,588.8	1,590.8	1,573.7
2011	1,564.8	1,576.0	1,584.7	1,592.7	1,595.1	1,586.4	1,576.3	1,579.2	1,594.0	1,608.0	1,617.0	1,621.5	1,591.3
Trade, Transportation, and Utilities													
2000	384.1	385.3	388.3	387.2	390.1	391.8	387.7	390.8	391.6	390.3	396.5	402.5	390.5
2001	386.0	384.9	387.9	387.8	388.3	389.8	386.8	389.2	388.2	386.5	391.9	395.3	388.6
2002	379.9	378.4	381.6	383.6	384.8	386.6	383.8	384.3	383.8	381.8	388.2	393.0	384.2
2003	379.1	377.9	379.4	379.5	379.8	380.8	378.0	379.6	378.9	380.7	386.1	390.2	380.8
2004	376.6	376.0	379.1	379.6	380.7	381.3	377.8	377.9	376.0	378.7	383.6	388.5	379.7
2005	375.8	375.1	378.2	381.3	382.9	384.2	385.1	385.1	353.2	348.5	361.8	369.9	373.4
2006	361.1	362.9	369.6	368.9	371.4	374.4	373.2	374.6	375.2	377.0	382.4	388.6	373.3
2007	378.9	377.9	382.4	378.8	380.3	381.3	380.6	382.3	382.7	385.8	391.9	396.2	383.3
2008	383.5	381.9	384.7	382.9	384.0	383.8	381.9	383.8	378.1	382.2	386.9	390.5	383.7
2009	375.5	373.0	373.0	369.2	369.2	369.7	369.5	368.8	367.7	365.2	370.1	371.2	370.2
2010	359.6	358.6	361.7	364.2	365.6	366.4	365.9	366.6	366.1	370.5	376.3	379.9	366.8
2011	369.8	368.9	370.7	373.0	373.9	372.9	372.3	372.5	370.8	372.6	377.6	382.6	373.1
Wholesale Trade													
2000	76.2	76.4	77.2	77.8	78.4	78.6	78.4	78.6	78.4	77.3	77.3	77.8	77.7
2001	76.7	77.0	77.5	78.0	78.1	78.9	77.7	78.0	78.0	77.6	77.6	77.9	77.8
2002	76.5	76.6	76.9	77.6	78.0	78.2	77.4	77.4	77.2	76.6	76.7	76.7	77.2
2003	76.2	76.1	76.3	75.5	75.7	76.1	75.5	75.6	75.5	75.4	75.3	74.9	75.7
2004	75.1	75.1	75.6	75.9	75.9	75.7	75.3	75.4	75.3	74.3	74.4	74.4	75.2
2005	73.6	73.8	74.1	75.0	75.3	75.4	76.3	76.3	71.6	71.0	71.4	71.8	73.8
2006	70.5	71.1	71.8	72.1	72.7	73.5	73.2	73.5	73.5	73.4	73.7	74.1	72.8
2007	74.9	75.2	75.8	74.9	75.3	75.9	76.4	76.8	76.3	76.6	76.6	76.9	76.0
2008	75.6	75.9	76.3	75.9	76.1	76.1	75.8	76.0	75.5	75.4	75.0	75.2	75.7
2009	73.3	73.2	72.8	72.1	72.0	71.7	71.5	71.3	71.0	70.9	70.8	70.4	71.8
2010	69.2	69.4	69.9	70.2	70.5	70.6	70.6	70.8	70.6	71.3	71.2	71.2	70.5
2011	71.6	71.8	72.1	71.5	72.0	72.0	73.2	73.7	72.9	73.8	74.8	75.4	72.9
Retail Trade													
2000	229.1	229.3	231.6	230.1	232.0	232.8	228.9	230.7	231.4	231.3	237.5	242.3	232.3
2001	228.6	226.3	228.2	226.8	227.2	227.3	226.1	227.7	226.7	224.9	231.4	234.5	228.0
2002	223.0	221.6	224.3	225.0	225.1	226.5	224.0	224.2	223.7	221.8	227.9	232.4	225.0
2003	221.6	220.5	222.2	222.1	221.9	222.5	221.0	222.3	221.9	223.4	228.3	232.7	223.4
2004	222.1	221.2	223.1	223.8	224.3	225.0	222.5	222.2	220.6	223.3	228.2	232.2	224.0
2005	222.1	220.9	223.1	224.9	225.8	226.7	226.5	226.6	204.2	201.7	213.4	219.6	219.6
2006	213.8	214.7	219.2	218.1	219.3	220.4	219.3	219.9	219.8	222.1	226.7	230.3	220.3
2007	222.3	221.2	224.8	222.6	223.6	223.6	223.2	223.4	224.3	226.6	232.6	236.1	225.4
2008	226.6	224.5	226.6	224.6	224.9	224.9	224.0	225.0	220.6	223.5	228.5	231.4	225.4
2009	220.7	219.7	220.3	219.8	220.3	221.1	221.3	220.6	220.1	217.7	222.7	223.7	220.7
2010	215.1	214.1	216.2	216.7	217.2	217.2	216.2	216.0	215.6	218.4	224.5	226.8	217.8
2011	218.7	217.7	219.2	221.5	221.7	220.8	218.5	217.8	216.4	216.7	221.7	224.8	219.6
Transportation and Utilities													
2000	78.8	79.6	79.5	79.3	79.7	80.4	80.4	81.5	81.8	81.7	81.7	82.4	80.6
2001	80.7	81.6	82.2	83.0	83.0	83.6	83.0	83.5	83.5	84.0	82.9	82.9	82.8
2002	80.4	80.2	80.4	81.0	81.7	81.9	82.4	82.7	82.9	83.4	83.6	83.9	82.0
2003	81.3	81.3	80.9	81.9	82.2	82.2	81.5	81.7	81.5	81.9	82.5	82.6	81.8
2004	79.4	79.7	80.4	79.9	80.5	80.6	80.0	80.3	80.1	81.1	81.0	81.9	80.4
2005	80.1	80.4	81.0	81.4	81.8	82.1	82.3	82.2	77.4	75.8	77.0	78.5	80.0
2006	76.8	77.1	78.6	78.7	79.4	80.5	80.7	81.2	81.9	81.5	82.0	84.2	80.2
2007	81.7	81.5	81.8	81.3	81.4	81.8	81.0	82.1	82.1	82.6	82.7	83.2	81.9
2008	81.3	81.5	81.8	82.4	83.0	82.8	82.1	82.8	82.0	83.3	83.4	83.9	82.5
2009	81.5	80.1	79.9	77.3	76.9	76.9	76.7	76.9	76.6	76.6	76.6	77.1	77.8
2010	75.3	75.1	75.6	77.3	77.9	78.6	79.1	79.8	79.9	80.8	80.6	81.9	78.5
2011	79.5	79.4	79.4	80.0	80.2	80.1	80.6	81.0	81.5	82.1	81.1	82.4	80.6
Information													
2000	28.9	28.5	28.8	29.1	29.2	29.9	30.7	30.9	30.5	30.3	30.5	31.0	29.9
2001	30.0	30.2	30.4	30.2	30.6	30.6	30.3	30.1	29.7	30.0	30.1	29.8	30.2
2002	29.3	29.3	29.5	29.0	28.9	29.3	29.0	29.0	28.9	28.5	28.8	28.9	29.0
2003	29.2	28.9	29.1	29.0	29.4	29.8	28.4	28.9	28.8	28.7	28.9	29.0	29.0
2004	29.1	29.4	29.3	30.3	30.0	30.7	29.6	31.1	29.9	30.9	33.0	31.5	30.4
2005	31.2	30.3	30.3	29.5	29.3	29.6	30.0	30.4	28.6	26.4	26.9	27.0	29.1
2006	27.2	27.3	29.2	28.2	28.3	27.6	25.9	25.8	25.7	25.8	26.4	26.6	27.0
2007	26.5	27.5	29.6	28.7	28.5	29.0	27.9	27.4	26.2	27.0	26.7	27.1	27.7
2008	26.7	28.5	30.2	30.1	30.8	31.7	26.6	28.0	27.9	26.2	27.1	27.8	28.5
2009	24.9	25.2	25.2	24.5	24.8	24.9	24.5	24.1	23.9	24.2	25.4	24.8	24.7
2010	24.4	24.8	24.5	25.3	25.8	26.4	23.4	23.5	25.6	23.6	24.0	24.7	24.7
2011	23.4	23.5	25.1	23.7	24.5	24.0	23.9	23.5	23.1	23.2	23.4	23.6	23.7

1. Employment by Industry: Louisiana, Selected Years, 2000–2011—*Continued*

(Numbers in thousands, not seasonally adjusted)

Industry and year	January	February	March	April	May	June	July	August	September	October	November	December	Annual average
Financial Activities													
2000	97.2	97.4	97.7	96.8	97.6	97.6	97.7	97.8	97.7	97.3	97.5	98.3	97.6
2001	96.6	97.2	97.0	97.1	97.0	97.6	97.7	97.8	97.1	96.8	96.8	96.9	97.1
2002	96.7	96.6	96.8	97.8	97.9	98.0	97.8	98.1	97.7	98.0	98.4	98.7	97.7
2003	98.6	98.8	98.6	98.8	98.9	99.2	99.5	99.8	99.5	99.8	99.5	100.2	99.3
2004	99.5	99.6	100.0	100.3	100.2	100.6	100.8	100.8	100.1	100.1	99.9	100.4	100.2
2005	98.6	98.9	99.1	98.8	98.9	99.6	100.5	100.7	95.3	96.2	96.8	97.0	98.4
2006	95.2	95.2	95.4	94.8	95.1	95.4	94.8	95.1	95.1	95.6	95.6	96.2	95.3
2007	97.7	98.0	97.1	96.3	96.2	96.4	96.3	96.0	95.4	95.7	95.7	95.8	96.4
2008	94.4	94.8	95.2	94.7	94.7	95.0	94.5	94.2	93.4	95.2	94.3	94.2	94.6
2009	92.1	91.9	92.1	92.8	92.8	93.0	92.8	92.5	92.0	91.4	91.9	92.4	92.3
2010	91.4	91.6	92.2	92.2	92.5	93.3	93.8	93.7	93.4	93.8	93.7	94.1	93.0
2011	93.6	94.0	94.0	93.8	94.2	94.1	93.3	94.9	94.9	96.7	97.6	97.3	94.9
Professional and Business Services													
2000	178.4	179.3	181.1	184.7	184.1	183.4	182.5	184.1	185.3	184.6	185.1	186.6	183.3
2001	183.7	183.5	183.6	183.4	183.1	184.1	181.1	182.2	182.8	182.0	182.3	183.9	183.0
2002	181.7	182.1	183.3	183.7	182.0	182.3	179.3	180.2	179.3	177.7	177.4	177.3	180.5
2003	177.8	178.8	179.7	181.5	180.3	180.2	179.4	180.9	180.4	182.2	183.5	185.3	180.8
2004	181.8	182.9	185.0	186.5	184.8	185.9	183.2	184.2	182.9	184.1	186.1	187.1	184.5
2005	187.0	187.4	189.8	194.1	192.1	191.6	191.8	192.7	175.7	181.0	185.8	188.2	188.1
2006	185.7	188.5	191.4	192.4	193.8	195.6	193.3	195.5	196.8	197.1	197.1	198.1	193.8
2007	197.8	199.7	201.7	200.4	200.9	202.2	199.4	201.6	201.6	205.3	205.8	206.8	201.9
2008	201.7	204.2	204.1	204.5	204.8	204.1	202.6	204.7	203.6	205.9	206.5	206.3	204.4
2009	198.4	198.9	197.8	194.5	194.3	192.7	191.0	191.2	189.4	191.0	191.3	191.3	193.5
2010	187.6	189.2	191.0	193.0	193.6	195.6	196.8	196.0	194.6	195.3	194.7	194.5	193.5
2011	192.2	194.7	194.8	196.5	196.5	196.0	195.5	194.8	198.3	198.5	199.1	199.2	196.3
Education and Health Services													
2000	220.6	223.4	223.9	224.6	223.6	220.6	219.5	220.0	224.4	227.9	227.9	228.4	223.7
2001	225.9	227.8	228.3	229.6	229.2	226.6	223.0	225.4	230.9	231.9	234.2	234.4	228.9
2002	230.1	232.5	232.8	235.5	234.8	232.3	230.7	233.8	240.1	240.5	243.5	242.6	235.8
2003	242.2	243.2	242.7	244.7	244.9	241.0	240.2	242.2	247.7	249.2	251.8	250.7	245.0
2004	248.7	249.8	250.5	252.3	251.7	247.6	247.9	251.4	252.7	253.0	254.7	253.5	251.2
2005	254.9	254.9	256.2	258.1	257.1	254.9	252.3	252.6	239.8	222.7	223.3	223.2	245.8
2006	225.1	226.8	228.8	232.0	233.6	233.0	232.2	234.9	238.4	240.0	242.1	241.2	234.0
2007	241.2	243.1	244.6	246.0	245.6	245.6	243.8	248.2	249.2	251.7	253.0	253.9	247.2
2008	251.2	254.2	255.2	255.9	254.9	253.8	254.4	259.1	257.3	260.7	261.8	262.1	256.7
2009	261.0	263.4	264.1	264.9	265.5	261.0	262.3	266.4	267.3	270.2	271.0	270.8	265.7
2010	267.8	268.8	270.4	272.2	270.2	267.7	268.4	270.3	272.8	274.7	275.1	275.1	271.1
2011	272.5	274.7	275.7	277.8	277.0	275.4	280.1	282.6	288.4	290.4	290.9	290.3	281.3
Leisure and Hospitality													
2000	189.3	191.0	193.2	195.0	198.6	201.0	197.4	197.3	195.9	194.1	194.5	195.3	195.2
2001	190.4	192.5	196.3	197.4	199.4	200.1	197.1	197.6	195.7	192.7	191.3	191.6	195.2
2002	186.8	189.4	192.1	196.2	198.9	200.3	198.4	198.2	195.7	192.1	193.6	193.1	194.6
2003	190.0	193.3	195.5	199.5	201.5	202.9	202.1	203.0	200.9	198.3	197.6	198.6	198.6
2004	195.1	197.6	201.7	203.5	206.1	208.9	206.7	207.3	205.2	204.0	205.9	206.8	204.1
2005	202.0	203.3	208.3	211.0	215.6	218.0	214.3	214.3	180.4	167.3	169.8	171.9	198.0
2006	169.7	176.6	181.8	181.6	184.8	189.5	188.0	189.0	187.6	186.5	188.2	189.9	184.4
2007	186.4	188.7	193.2	192.5	195.5	198.2	195.3	196.2	193.7	192.3	193.4	194.7	193.3
2008	191.1	193.4	196.0	198.9	200.0	200.3	198.2	198.7	191.4	194.2	194.2	194.7	195.9
2009	190.7	193.4	196.1	196.3	198.5	198.2	195.2	196.0	194.0	191.3	191.2	190.6	194.3
2010	187.9	189.6	193.6	195.9	197.1	197.7	194.8	195.3	195.7	194.5	195.3	194.7	194.3
2011	192.6	195.0	198.9	201.5	203.7	203.7	201.4	198.6	194.9	197.5	198.0	199.9	198.8
Other Services													
2000	69.9	70.3	70.9	70.7	71.1	71.3	70.8	71.4	71.4	70.8	70.3	70.5	70.8
2001	68.9	69.2	69.8	71.3	71.6	71.8	70.7	71.1	71.1	70.6	70.3	70.0	70.5
2002	69.3	69.7	70.3	71.1	71.6	71.9	71.0	71.1	71.2	70.9	71.2	71.6	70.9
2003	70.3	70.4	70.9	71.1	71.5	71.8	70.2	70.3	70.4	70.9	70.7	70.7	70.8
2004	70.1	70.4	71.0	71.1	71.4	71.8	71.5	71.4	71.2	70.6	70.6	70.7	71.0
2005	70.0	70.2	71.4	71.6	71.8	72.2	72.2	72.1	65.2	62.1	62.6	63.8	68.8
2006	62.4	63.5	64.6	64.6	65.5	66.1	65.6	65.9	66.7	66.8	67.0	67.4	65.5
2007	67.1	67.8	68.7	67.8	68.3	68.7	68.2	69.0	69.4	69.5	69.5	69.7	68.6
2008	67.8	68.0	68.6	65.8	66.2	66.1	65.1	65.3	64.6	68.0	68.0	68.0	66.8
2009	67.5	67.8	67.9	67.8	68.1	67.8	67.8	68.9	69.1	67.6	67.6	67.7	68.0
2010	64.9	65.1	65.5	64.3	64.4	64.4	63.4	63.5	63.2	63.6	63.3	63.2	64.1
2011	63.1	63.4	63.7	63.9	63.7	64.1	63.1	63.3	62.2	62.0	62.0	62.3	63.1
Government													
2000	370.6	376.6	379.5	379.2	385.0	373.9	364.8	359.7	371.6	373.8	373.7	373.0	373.5
2001	372.1	378.1	379.1	377.4	377.0	374.5	362.7	360.7	373.0	376.0	377.6	377.0	373.8
2002	370.0	375.5	377.1	377.5	377.6	376.4	366.7	364.5	375.1	378.7	381.2	378.9	374.9
2003	374.5	381.7	383.1	383.0	382.1	380.2	371.4	367.5	379.2	382.6	384.4	381.4	379.3
2004	377.3	384.1	385.9	385.4	383.8	381.9	373.7	371.8	383.0	386.1	386.9	385.6	382.1
2005	376.5	383.3	383.1	384.2	382.2	379.7	369.8	370.2	378.1	360.2	360.8	358.9	373.9
2006	343.0	349.5	351.1	349.3	349.9	341.6	334.0	339.2	352.9	353.7	356.0	355.6	348.0
2007	348.7	357.2	359.5	353.8	353.6	351.4	340.2	346.3	360.2	363.3	365.9	365.3	355.5
2008	357.2	365.1	364.4	366.7	366.8	361.0	353.3	359.4	365.0	371.1	373.6	370.9	364.5
2009	364.7	371.7	371.5	373.4	372.1	365.3	355.3	357.1	369.6	376.4	377.7	375.3	369.2
2010	366.6	371.3	373.6	373.1	378.0	370.2	352.5	353.3	361.0	365.1	366.4	364.6	366.3
2011	357.6	361.8	361.8	362.5	361.6	356.2	346.7	349.0	361.4	367.1	368.4	366.3	360.0

2. Average Weekly Hours by Selected Industry: Louisiana, 2007–2011

(Not seasonally adjusted)

Industry and year	January	February	March	April	May	June	July	August	September	October	November	December	Annual average
Total Private													
2007	34.5	35.3	35.1	35.7	35.8	35.9	36.1	36.0	36.3	35.8	36.1	36.5	35.8
2008	35.9	35.9	36.3	36.2	36.4	36.9	36.8	36.8	36.0	37.1	37.5	36.4	36.5
2009	36.2	36.6	36.5	35.7	36.1	36.2	35.9	36.6	35.1	35.7	36.6	35.7	36.1
2010	35.9	35.5	36.1	36.5	37.1	36.8	36.8	37.1	36.4	36.6	36.3	36.6	. . .
2011	36.5	36.2	35.9	36.3	36.7	36.3	36.3	36.2	36.0	36.8	36.1	36.1	. . .
Goods-Producing													
2007	37.6	39.4	39.0	39.3	41.1	40.5	39.7	39.7	39.3	39.5	40.8	40.2	39.7
2008	39.9	40.2	39.8	40.0	40.6	41.3	42.2	41.8	39.7	43.2	43.2	42.0	41.2
2009	41.1	40.8	40.3	39.3	40.9	41.5	40.4	41.1	39.7	41.3	43.3	41.7	40.9
2010	41.8	40.3	42.9	43.4	43.3	42.9	42.3	41.9	41.3	42.3	42.0	42.8	42.3
2011	41.8	41.4	40.9	42.0	42.3	42.0	41.6	42.1	41.6	43.0	42.5	41.9	41.9
Construction													
2007	38.2	40.7	41.5	41.6	43.3	40.8	39.5	39.3	38.1	40.0	41.3	41.9	40.5
2008	40.7	41.4	41.0	41.4	40.5	42.2	42.0	43.1	39.8	44.4	43.4	41.9	41.8
2009	43.4	42.4	41.7	39.7	40.6	40.4	39.5	40.6	38.0	40.8	41.9	40.9	40.8
2010	40.9	40.4	43.6	42.7	43.6	42.0	42.3	41.2	40.5	41.0	41.8	42.7	41.9
2011	42.0	40.8	40.2	41.9	42.4	41.9	40.7	41.8	41.6	41.8	41.3	40.6	41.4
Manufacturing													
2007	39.0	39.6	39.5	40.1	41.0	41.5	40.7	41.5	40.8	40.6	41.6	41.3	40.6
2008	39.4	40.9	40.7	40.5	41.9	42.0	43.5	42.0	41.0	43.3	43.3	42.8	41.8
2009	40.8	40.3	40.1	38.9	40.6	41.7	40.8	41.5	40.9	41.8	43.1	42.2	41.0
2010	41.9	39.9	41.4	42.4	42.2	42.7	41.6	41.9	41.4	41.9	41.0	41.2	41.6
2011	40.8	40.8	40.6	41.0	41.1	41.2	41.2	41.1	40.2	42.8	42.2	41.8	41.2
Trade, Transportation, and Utilities													
2007	34.2	35.0	35.5	36.2	36.7	36.7	37.1	36.9	36.6	36.0	36.0	36.1	36.1
2008	35.4	35.6	35.8	36.0	36.3	36.8	37.7	38.0	35.7	37.3	37.7	36.9	36.6
2009	37.2	37.6	37.6	36.9	37.8	37.6	37.1	37.8	36.2	36.8	37.6	36.7	37.2
2010	36.3	36.3	36.7	37.0	37.4	37.6	37.3	37.9	37.0	37.1	37.2	37.5	37.1
2011	37.0	36.7	36.8	36.8	37.8	37.5	37.5	36.7	36.6	37.0	36.2	36.2	36.9
Financial Activities													
2007	36.1	35.9	35.0	36.7	35.5	35.9	36.3	35.9	37.3	36.2	36.9	36.9	36.2
2008	36.0	35.5	36.6	36.1	37.6	37.9	35.9	36.5	35.5	35.4	37.1	35.8	36.3
2009	36.1	37.4	37.7	36.3	36.5	36.5	36.6	37.1	35.8	36.1	37.5	35.9	36.6
2010	36.5	35.1	35.1	35.9	37.5	36.0	36.5	37.7	36.3	36.7	35.9	35.4	36.2
2011	37.0	36.6	36.7	36.7	38.8	37.4	37.4	37.0	37.8	39.0	37.3	37.3	37.4
Professional and Business Services													
2007	36.6	37.0	36.0	37.5	36.5	37.0	37.0	37.3	37.9	37.5	37.6	38.2	37.2
2008	36.7	36.5	37.7	36.8	36.7	38.0	36.9	37.3	36.2	38.2	38.4	37.3	37.2
2009	37.7	38.8	39.3	37.9	38.0	37.6	37.3	38.7	36.9	37.7	39.0	38.0	38.1
2010	38.1	38.5	38.8	39.0	39.4	39.0	40.1	40.8	40.3	41.1	40.6	40.9	39.7
2011	41.0	39.8	39.3	39.8	39.6	39.0	38.8	38.6	38.1	39.4	38.5	38.7	39.2
Education and Health Services													
2007	32.1	32.5	32.2	32.9	32.5	33.0	33.6	33.2	33.7	32.9	32.8	33.9	32.9
2008	33.7	33.2	33.6	33.2	33.1	33.8	33.6	33.5	34.2	35.2	34.2	33.6	33.7
2009	33.2	33.4	33.3	33.1	32.3	32.3	32.4	32.6	32.0	31.6	32.5	32.3	32.6
2010	32.6	32.0	32.4	32.6	33.0	32.7	32.6	33.0	32.5	32.6	32.8	33.0	. . .
2011	33.5	33.1	32.8	33.4	33.2	32.9	33.2	33.0	33.0	33.3	33.3	33.3	. . .
Leisure and Hospitality													
2007	28.2	28.1	28.4	28.1	28.5	28.5	28.2	28.0	28.1	28.1	27.8	28.3	28.2
2008	27.9	27.8	28.3	28.2	27.8	28.0	27.9	27.6	27.2	27.5	28.4	27.8	27.9
2009	27.0	27.3	27.2	26.7	26.7	27.2	27.1	27.5	26.6	26.5	26.9	26.5	26.9
2010	26.6	27.4	27.3	26.9	27.8	27.6	27.8	27.4	26.7	26.6	26.4	26.5	27.1
2011	25.9	26.8	26.8	26.5	26.7	26.5	26.4	26.6	26.2	26.7	26.4	26.8	26.5

3. Average Hourly Earnings by Selected Industry: Louisiana, 2007–2011

(Dollars, not seasonally adjusted)

Industry and year	January	February	March	April	May	June	July	August	September	October	November	December	Annual average
Total Private													
2007	18.01	17.93	18.30	18.76	18.56	18.60	18.66	19.08	19.34	19.14	19.08	19.24	18.73
2008	19.06	19.40	18.93	19.04	19.19	19.15	19.22	19.13	19.15	19.32	19.60	19.44	19.22
2009	19.45	19.57	19.42	19.44	19.44	19.42	19.33	19.44	19.53	19.38	19.49	19.57	19.46
2010	19.52	19.58	19.50	19.51	19.13	19.17	19.39	19.66	19.81	19.72	19.76	19.73	. . .
2011	20.07	20.08	20.04	20.34	20.42	20.41	20.72	20.74	21.07	21.21	21.23	21.10	. . .
Goods-Producing													
2007	22.05	21.95	22.42	22.13	21.82	22.25	22.70	22.84	23.10	22.83	23.01	22.99	22.51
2008	22.30	22.85	22.56	22.69	23.31	22.97	23.05	22.83	22.95	22.84	23.25	23.10	22.90
2009	22.89	22.94	22.84	22.81	22.82	22.33	22.45	23.02	23.21	23.04	22.96	23.27	22.88
2010	23.34	23.39	23.14	22.93	22.85	22.89	23.07	23.33	23.98	23.27	23.33	23.47	23.25
2011	23.69	23.81	23.94	24.12	24.09	24.13	24.55	24.10	24.71	24.58	24.50	24.46	24.23
Construction													
2007	20.38	20.66	20.31	20.98	20.38	20.87	20.52	20.19	20.87	20.18	20.52	20.71	20.55
2008	20.00	21.48	20.94	20.95	20.96	20.79	21.88	21.16	21.02	21.49	22.57	21.98	21.29
2009	21.54	21.08	21.31	21.46	21.32	20.63	19.97	20.59	20.70	21.08	21.09	21.17	21.00
2010	21.26	21.52	20.99	20.74	20.52	20.68	20.76	21.25	21.92	21.60	21.69	21.76	21.22
2011	21.66	21.93	22.03	22.10	22.14	22.01	22.17	22.10	22.47	22.74	22.68	22.82	22.24
Manufacturing													
2007	22.67	22.50	22.98	22.15	22.02	22.44	23.18	23.63	23.85	23.79	23.95	23.94	23.10
2008	23.32	23.63	23.88	24.05	24.18	23.71	23.28	23.33	23.60	23.20	23.28	23.21	23.55
2009	23.41	23.66	23.53	23.47	23.49	23.03	23.73	23.52	23.83	23.47	23.26	23.70	23.51
2010	23.98	23.85	23.78	23.64	23.80	23.62	23.80	23.84	24.62	23.60	23.61	23.51	23.80
2011	24.10	24.32	24.60	25.00	24.82	24.90	25.44	25.02	25.84	25.24	25.14	24.90	24.95
Trade, Transportation, and Utilities													
2007	15.52	15.60	16.05	16.13	16.18	16.05	15.88	15.88	15.80	15.66	15.28	15.27	15.77
2008	15.38	15.12	15.02	15.03	15.35	15.31	15.16	15.53	15.68	15.68	16.05	16.35	15.48
2009	16.36	16.68	16.77	16.62	16.89	16.85	16.74	17.01	16.64	16.50	16.96	16.74	16.73
2010	16.90	17.04	16.91	17.37	17.61	17.47	17.54	18.04	17.77	17.84	18.05	17.68	17.53
2011	18.01	17.56	17.80	18.41	18.62	18.34	19.19	19.16	19.27	19.66	20.16	19.77	18.83
Financial Activities													
2007	19.78	19.60	20.72	21.36	20.69	20.62	20.18	20.72	21.00	20.93	20.20	20.22	20.50
2008	19.80	19.50	19.76	19.96	19.14	18.82	18.91	19.06	18.37	19.48	20.46	19.12	19.37
2009	19.63	20.47	20.10	19.88	20.61	20.19	19.63	19.66	19.65	19.36	19.30	19.29	19.82
2010	19.17	19.63	19.73	19.67	19.10	18.95	19.19	19.11	19.16	19.62	19.34	18.23	19.24
2011	19.59	19.80	18.03	19.16	19.10	20.07	19.43	19.40	19.40	19.85	19.71	18.78	19.36
Professional and Business Services													
2007	22.47	22.40	22.41	23.53	22.86	23.03	23.29	23.11	23.60	22.97	23.05	23.08	22.99
2008	23.22	23.53	23.61	23.55	23.58	23.85	23.99	23.70	23.78	24.11	24.09	24.23	23.77
2009	23.86	23.72	23.84	23.80	23.20	23.43	23.55	22.90	23.52	23.24	23.28	23.67	23.50
2010	23.64	23.76	23.43	23.03	23.72	23.65	23.53	24.19	23.97	24.30	24.36	24.38	23.84
2011	24.39	24.54	24.81	24.34	24.93	24.63	24.54	24.65	25.18	25.33	25.01	25.20	24.80
Education and Health Services													
2007	15.50	15.57	15.73	15.53	15.72	15.58	15.60	15.33	15.34	15.45	15.61	15.51	15.54
2008	15.95	15.57	15.29	15.89	16.19	16.40	16.79	16.51	16.52	15.92	16.64	16.60	16.19
2009	16.84	16.71	16.69	17.14	17.17	17.23	17.40	17.48	17.68	17.45	17.31	17.15	17.19
2010	17.15	17.37	17.78	17.64	16.73	16.69	16.92	17.27	17.11	16.94	16.89	17.09	. . .
2011	17.31	17.68	17.76	18.24	18.30	18.52	18.71	19.00	19.39	19.52	19.63	20.00	. . .
Leisure and Hospitality													
2007	11.77	11.90	12.03	12.25	12.47	12.23	12.22	12.10	12.23	12.02	12.08	12.08	12.12
2008	12.19	12.01	11.88	11.90	11.70	11.67	11.67	11.70	12.01	12.14	11.74	11.58	11.85
2009	11.80	11.93	11.65	11.65	11.72	11.69	11.58	11.62	12.06	11.97	12.10	12.10	11.82
2010	12.18	11.92	11.92	11.92	11.94	11.89	11.82	11.96	12.21	12.24	12.28	12.30	12.05
2011	12.63	12.24	12.34	12.28	12.32	11.89	11.85	11.86	11.89	12.13	12.12	12.14	12.14

4. Average Weekly Earnings by Selected Industry: Louisiana, 2007–2011

(Dollars, not seasonally adjusted)

Industry and year	January	February	March	April	May	June	July	August	September	October	November	December	Annual average
Total Private													
2007	621.35	632.93	642.33	669.73	664.45	667.74	673.63	686.88	702.04	685.21	688.79	702.26	670.11
2008	684.25	696.46	687.16	689.25	698.52	706.64	707.30	703.98	689.40	716.77	735.00	707.62	701.93
2009	704.09	716.26	708.83	694.01	701.78	703.00	693.95	711.50	685.50	691.87	713.33	698.65	702.12
2010	700.77	695.09	703.95	712.12	709.72	705.46	713.55	729.39	721.08	721.75	717.29	722.12	. . .
2011	732.56	726.90	719.44	738.34	749.41	740.88	752.14	750.79	758.52	780.53	766.40	761.71	. . .
Goods-Producing													
2007	829.08	864.83	874.38	869.71	896.80	901.13	901.19	906.75	907.83	901.79	938.81	924.20	893.34
2008	889.77	918.57	897.89	907.60	946.39	948.66	972.71	954.29	911.12	986.69	1,004.40	970.20	942.63
2009	940.78	935.95	920.45	896.43	933.34	926.70	906.98	946.12	921.44	951.55	994.17	970.36	936.82
2010	975.61	942.62	992.71	995.16	989.41	981.98	975.86	977.53	990.37	984.32	979.86	1,004.52	982.61
2011	990.24	985.73	979.15	1,013.04	1,019.01	1,013.46	1,021.28	1,014.61	1,027.94	1,056.94	1,041.25	1,024.87	1,015.71
Construction													
2007	778.52	840.86	842.87	872.77	882.45	851.50	810.54	793.47	795.15	807.20	847.48	867.75	832.64
2008	814.00	889.27	858.54	867.33	848.88	877.34	918.96	912.00	836.60	954.16	979.54	920.96	890.44
2009	934.84	893.79	888.63	851.96	865.59	833.45	788.82	835.95	786.60	860.06	883.67	865.85	857.84
2010	869.53	869.41	915.16	885.60	894.67	868.56	878.15	875.50	887.76	885.60	906.64	929.15	888.93
2011	909.72	894.74	885.61	925.99	938.74	922.22	902.32	923.78	934.75	950.53	936.68	926.49	920.88
Manufacturing													
2007	884.13	891.00	907.71	888.22	902.82	931.26	943.43	980.65	973.08	965.87	996.32	988.72	938.06
2008	918.81	966.47	971.92	974.03	1,013.14	995.82	1,012.68	979.86	967.60	1,004.56	1,008.02	993.39	983.83
2009	955.13	953.50	943.55	912.98	953.69	960.35	968.18	976.08	974.65	981.05	1,002.51	1,000.14	964.73
2010	1,004.76	951.62	984.49	1,002.34	1,004.36	1,008.57	990.08	998.90	1,019.27	988.84	968.01	968.61	990.92
2011	983.28	992.26	998.76	1,025.00	1,020.10	1,025.88	1,048.13	1,028.32	1,038.77	1,080.27	1,060.91	1,040.82	1,028.79
Trade, Transportation, and Utilities													
2007	530.78	546.00	569.78	583.91	593.81	589.04	589.15	585.97	578.28	563.76	550.08	551.25	569.24
2008	544.45	538.27	537.72	541.08	557.21	563.41	571.53	590.14	559.78	584.86	605.09	603.32	566.50
2009	608.59	627.17	630.55	613.28	638.44	633.56	621.05	642.98	602.37	607.20	637.70	614.36	623.10
2010	613.47	618.55	620.60	642.69	658.61	656.87	654.24	683.72	657.49	661.86	671.46	663.00	650.45
2011	666.37	644.45	655.04	677.49	703.84	687.75	719.63	703.17	705.28	727.42	729.79	715.67	694.81
Financial Activities													
2007	714.06	703.64	725.20	783.91	734.50	740.26	732.53	743.85	783.30	757.67	745.38	746.12	742.39
2008	712.80	692.25	723.22	720.56	719.66	713.28	678.87	695.69	652.14	689.59	759.07	684.50	703.52
2009	708.64	765.58	757.77	721.64	752.27	736.94	718.46	729.39	703.47	698.90	723.75	692.51	725.77
2010	699.71	689.01	692.52	706.15	716.25	682.20	700.44	720.45	695.51	720.05	694.31	645.34	696.69
2011	724.83	724.68	661.70	703.17	741.08	750.62	726.68	717.80	733.32	774.15	735.18	700.49	724.51
Professional and Business Services													
2007	822.40	828.80	806.76	882.38	834.39	852.11	861.73	862.00	894.44	861.38	866.68	881.66	854.70
2008	852.17	858.85	890.10	866.64	865.39	906.30	885.23	884.01	860.84	921.00	925.06	903.78	885.06
2009	899.52	920.34	936.91	902.02	881.60	880.97	878.42	886.23	867.89	876.15	907.92	899.46	895.03
2010	900.68	914.76	909.08	898.17	934.57	922.35	943.55	986.95	965.99	998.73	989.02	997.14	947.00
2011	999.99	976.69	975.03	968.73	987.23	960.57	952.15	951.49	959.36	998.00	962.89	975.24	972.28
Education and Health Services													
2007	497.55	506.03	506.51	510.94	510.90	514.14	524.16	508.96	516.96	508.31	512.01	525.79	511.91
2008	537.52	516.92	513.74	527.55	535.89	554.32	564.14	553.09	564.98	560.38	569.09	557.76	546.41
2009	559.09	558.11	555.78	567.33	554.59	556.53	563.76	569.85	565.76	551.42	562.58	553.95	559.87
2010	559.09	555.84	576.07	575.06	552.09	545.76	551.59	569.91	556.08	552.24	553.99	563.97	. . .
2011	579.89	585.21	582.53	609.22	607.56	609.31	621.17	627.00	639.87	650.02	653.68	666.00	. . .
Leisure and Hospitality													
2007	331.91	334.39	341.65	344.23	355.40	348.56	344.60	338.80	343.66	337.76	335.82	341.86	341.62
2008	340.10	333.88	336.20	335.58	325.26	326.76	325.59	322.92	326.67	333.85	333.42	321.92	330.14
2009	318.60	325.69	316.88	311.06	312.92	317.97	313.82	319.55	320.80	317.21	325.49	320.65	318.39
2010	323.99	326.61	325.42	320.65	331.93	328.16	328.60	327.70	326.01	325.58	324.19	325.95	326.26
2011	327.12	328.03	330.71	325.42	328.94	315.09	312.84	315.48	311.52	323.87	319.97	325.35	322.02

MAINE

At a Glance

Population:
2000 census: 1,274,779
2010 census: 1,328,361
2011 estimate: 1,328,188

Percent change in population:
2000–2010: 4.2%
2010–2011: 0.0%

Percent change in total nonfarm employment:
2000–2010: -1.7%
2010–2011: 0.1%

Industry with the largest growth in employment, 2000–2011 (thousands):
Education and Health Services, 22.7

Industry with the largest decline or smallest growth in employment, 2000–2011 (thousands):
Manufacturing, -29.1

Civilian labor force:
2000: 672,440
2010: 700,568
2011: 704,078

Unemployment rate and rank among states (lowest to highest):
2000: 3.3%, 14th
2010: 8.2%, 21st
2011: 7.5%, 20th

Over-the-year change in unemployment rates:
2010–2011: -0.7%

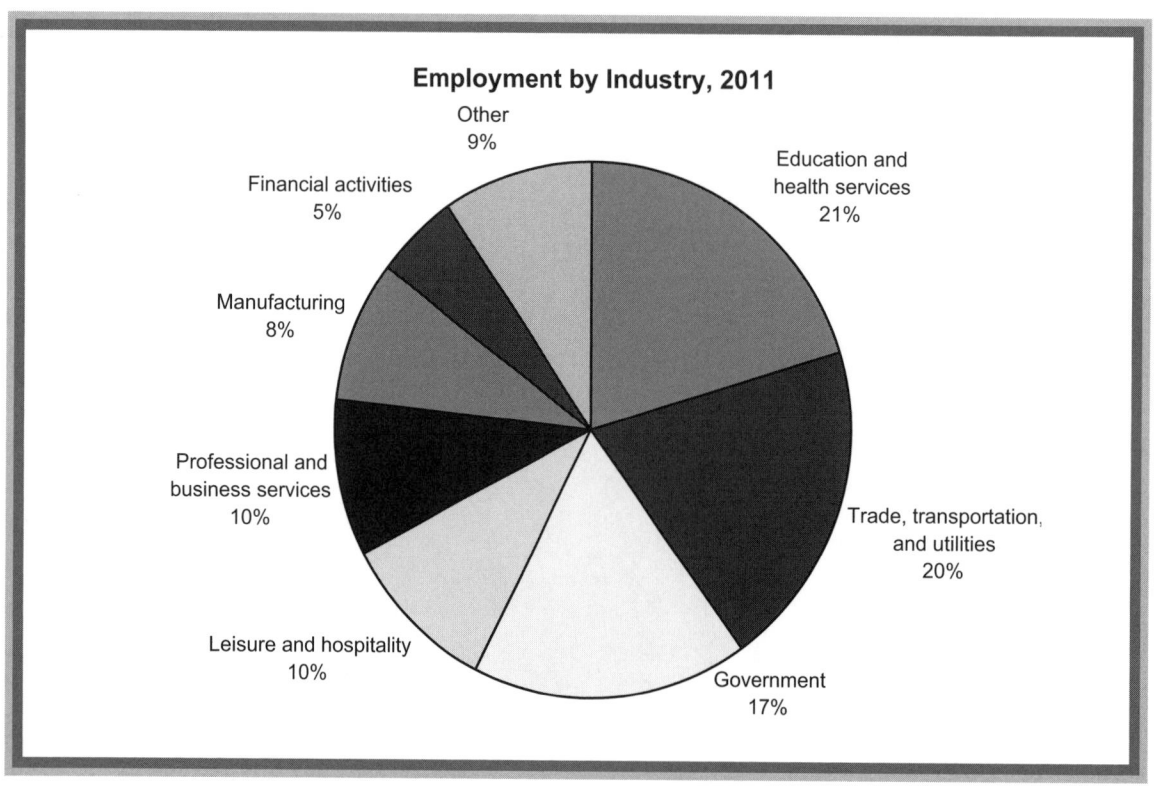

Employment by Industry, 2011

Other 9%
Financial activities 5%
Manufacturing 8%
Professional and business services 10%
Leisure and hospitality 10%
Government 17%
Trade, transportation, and utilities 20%
Education and health services 21%

1. Employment by Industry: Maine, Selected Years, 2000–2011

(Numbers in thousands, not seasonally adjusted)

Industry and year	January	February	March	April	May	June	July	August	September	October	November	December	Annual average
Total Nonfarm													
2000	576.1	580.2	586.0	593.8	606.9	617.8	615.8	614.4	614.7	611.5	612.8	611.7	603.5
2001	588.5	590.3	592.6	601.5	613.1	625.2	618.0	618.4	618.0	614.6	610.4	607.1	608.1
2002	583.7	585.5	588.9	598.3	610.4	622.3	618.5	618.2	617.1	614.2	610.5	609.9	606.5
2003	584.0	585.2	587.8	595.2	608.2	618.7	617.3	619.2	618.8	617.5	615.5	614.0	606.8
2004	588.4	591.6	594.0	601.9	614.0	625.4	622.8	623.5	622.8	620.0	619.6	616.7	611.7
2005	589.5	591.3	592.1	603.0	614.6	625.6	623.2	623.2	623.1	619.2	618.2	617.8	611.7
2006	592.1	592.6	596.1	606.5	617.4	629.9	624.1	626.6	625.1	622.9	621.1	621.4	614.7
2007	596.1	596.2	599.1	604.4	618.2	632.4	629.0	629.0	628.6	627.8	626.6	625.2	617.7
2008	599.7	600.1	601.8	609.6	623.0	633.6	630.0	628.1	625.8	625.0	617.6	612.6	617.2
2009	584.0	582.6	580.0	588.3	601.7	607.5	603.8	604.0	605.2	603.8	598.6	595.8	596.3
2010	571.9	572.9	574.8	583.7	599.1	604.6	602.7	602.6	604.4	603.8	598.7	596.2	593.0
2011	572.4	574.2	575.4	583.5	595.1	606.9	604.2	605.1	605.9	603.5	599.0	595.1	593.4
Total Private													
2000	478.7	479.0	482.2	491.5	502.7	517.0	528.3	528.4	515.0	508.7	508.4	507.0	503.9
2001	488.0	486.4	488.3	496.8	508.0	522.1	528.1	528.7	515.5	508.4	503.5	499.4	506.1
2002	481.8	480.3	482.7	492.8	504.1	517.6	526.8	527.6	514.5	508.1	502.7	501.9	503.4
2003	481.1	478.7	480.8	488.5	501.5	514.2	525.6	527.8	515.5	510.4	507.1	505.3	503.0
2004	484.8	484.3	486.2	494.0	506.3	519.6	529.7	531.0	518.3	511.9	510.2	507.6	507.0
2005	485.5	483.7	484.5	495.4	506.7	519.3	530.2	530.6	518.0	511.5	509.2	508.9	507.0
2006	487.8	485.9	488.8	499.3	509.7	525.3	532.1	533.4	520.7	514.8	512.2	512.7	510.2
2007	492.4	489.9	492.1	497.9	510.5	527.3	536.8	537.6	523.9	519.5	517.8	516.5	513.5
2008	495.8	493.6	494.4	501.9	515.1	528.4	537.9	535.8	521.4	516.8	508.8	504.1	512.8
2009	480.5	476.3	473.3	480.9	494.2	502.9	513.1	513.1	501.4	496.7	490.8	488.3	492.6
2010	468.3	466.6	467.0	476.1	489.1	499.8	510.9	511.7	501.4	496.9	491.3	489.0	489.0
2011	469.4	468.9	469.8	478.2	490.0	504.2	515.1	517.3	505.8	499.9	494.2	491.9	492.1
Goods-Producing													
2000	108.3	108.4	108.8	110.9	113.0	114.5	114.4	116.2	109.9	109.3	112.6	111.1	111.5
2001	106.7	105.3	105.8	106.2	108.7	110.9	109.1	110.1	108.3	106.0	105.4	102.8	107.1
2002	98.0	96.5	96.3	98.5	100.5	102.7	101.5	103.3	101.8	101.3	101.2	99.3	100.1
2003	93.9	92.1	92.6	94.0	97.2	99.2	99.2	100.9	99.8	99.4	99.5	97.6	97.1
2004	93.1	91.7	92.3	93.4	96.4	98.6	99.0	100.2	98.9	97.8	98.3	96.5	96.4
2005	91.3	90.5	90.5	92.8	95.0	97.2	97.6	98.1	96.6	95.6	96.3	94.8	94.7
2006	90.7	89.8	90.3	92.3	94.7	96.8	97.1	97.8	96.1	95.1	94.5	93.3	94.0
2007	89.3	87.7	88.5	89.7	92.3	95.7	96.1	96.5	95.1	95.2	95.2	93.5	92.9
2008	89.1	87.9	87.7	88.8	91.7	94.0	94.2	93.9	92.1	91.8	90.3	87.1	90.7
2009	80.9	78.6	76.8	77.6	80.1	81.3	81.9	82.0	80.9	80.8	80.0	77.6	79.9
2010	73.9	72.9	73.2	74.8	78.0	79.4	80.0	80.9	80.3	80.3	80.0	78.1	77.7
2011	74.7	73.8	74.1	75.3	77.8	80.4	80.6	80.0	79.2	80.0	79.3	77.6	77.7
Mining, Logging, and Construction													
2000	2.9	3.0	2.8	1.9	1.9	2.5	2.8	2.9	2.9	2.9	2.9	3.0	2.7
2001	2.9	2.9	2.8	2.0	1.9	2.5	2.8	2.8	2.9	2.8	2.8	2.8	2.7
2002	2.8	2.8	2.7	2.0	1.9	2.4	2.7	2.8	2.8	2.8	2.8	2.8	2.6
2003	2.7	2.7	2.6	2.0	1.8	2.4	2.7	2.8	2.7	2.7	2.7	2.7	2.5
2004	2.7	2.7	2.7	2.1	2.0	2.4	2.6	2.7	2.7	2.8	2.9	2.9	2.6
2005	2.9	2.9	2.8	2.2	2.0	2.5	2.8	2.8	2.8	2.8	2.9	2.9	2.7
2006	2.9	2.9	2.8	2.1	2.1	2.6	2.9	2.9	2.9	3.0	2.8	2.9	2.7
2007	2.9	2.9	2.9	2.0	1.8	2.5	2.8	2.8	2.8	2.8	2.9	2.8	2.7
2008	2.8	2.8	2.8	2.1	1.8	2.3	2.6	2.6	2.6	2.8	2.8	2.8	2.6
2009	2.8	2.8	2.6	1.5	1.5	1.9	2.4	2.6	2.6	2.7	2.8	2.7	2.4
2010	2.7	2.7	2.6	1.9	2.1	2.5	2.7	2.7	2.7	2.7	2.6	2.6	2.5
2011	2.6	2.6	2.6	1.9	1.8	2.4	2.7	2.8	2.9	2.9	2.9	2.9	2.6
Construction													
2000	25.7	25.4	25.8	28.4	30.2	30.8	31.7	31.7	31.2	31.0	29.9	28.8	29.2
2001	26.6	26.1	26.7	28.3	30.8	32.0	32.5	32.2	31.7	31.3	30.6	29.0	29.8
2002	26.4	25.5	25.6	28.0	30.1	31.2	31.7	31.8	31.3	31.4	30.8	29.5	29.4
2003	27.0	26.0	26.5	28.5	31.3	32.5	33.2	33.2	32.8	32.8	31.8	30.3	30.5
2004	28.0	27.5	28.3	29.4	31.7	32.6	33.3	33.0	32.3	31.9	31.2	29.9	30.8
2005	27.0	26.5	26.7	29.2	31.4	32.8	33.6	33.2	32.7	32.4	31.9	30.4	30.7
2006	28.3	27.5	28.0	30.3	32.3	33.7	33.9	33.9	33.1	32.6	31.6	30.6	31.3
2007	28.1	26.9	27.4	29.1	31.4	33.0	33.2	33.3	32.8	32.7	31.9	30.3	30.8
2008	27.6	26.7	26.6	28.0	30.6	31.8	31.8	31.5	30.8	30.9	29.3	27.1	29.4
2009	24.0	22.8	22.3	23.8	26.0	26.8	27.1	27.0	26.5	26.6	25.2	23.7	25.2
2010	21.3	20.6	20.6	22.8	25.0	25.7	26.2	26.5	26.6	26.6	25.9	24.4	24.4
2011	22.0	21.3	21.4	23.2	25.2	26.8	26.7	27.0	26.4	26.9	25.8	24.2	24.7
Manufacturing													
2000	79.7	80.0	80.2	80.6	80.9	81.2	79.9	81.6	75.8	75.4	79.8	79.3	79.5
2001	77.2	76.3	76.3	75.9	76.0	76.4	73.8	75.1	73.7	71.9	72.0	71.0	74.6
2002	68.8	68.2	68.0	68.5	68.5	69.1	67.1	68.7	67.7	67.1	67.6	67.0	68.0
2003	64.2	63.4	63.5	63.5	64.1	64.3	63.3	64.9	64.3	63.9	65.0	64.6	64.1
2004	62.4	61.5	61.3	61.9	62.7	63.6	63.1	64.5	63.9	63.1	64.2	63.7	63.0
2005	61.4	61.1	61.0	61.4	61.6	61.9	61.2	62.1	61.1	60.4	61.5	61.5	61.4
2006	59.5	59.4	59.5	59.9	60.3	60.5	60.3	61.0	60.1	59.5	60.1	59.8	60.0
2007	58.3	57.9	58.2	58.6	59.1	60.2	60.1	60.4	59.5	59.7	60.4	60.4	59.4
2008	58.7	58.4	58.3	58.7	59.3	59.9	59.8	59.8	58.7	58.1	58.2	57.2	58.8
2009	54.1	53.0	51.9	52.3	52.6	52.6	52.4	52.4	51.8	51.5	52.0	51.2	52.3
2010	49.9	49.6	50.0	50.1	50.9	51.2	51.1	51.7	51.0	51.0	51.5	51.1	50.8
2011	50.1	49.9	50.1	50.2	50.8	51.2	51.2	50.2	49.9	50.2	50.6	50.5	50.4

1. Employment by Industry: Maine, Selected Years, 2000–2011—*Continued*

(Numbers in thousands, not seasonally adjusted)

Industry and year	January	February	March	April	May	June	July	August	September	October	November	December	Annual average
Service-Providing													
2000	467.8	471.8	477.2	482.9	493.9	503.3	501.4	498.2	504.8	502.2	500.2	500.6	492.0
2001	481.8	485.0	486.8	495.3	504.4	514.3	508.9	508.3	509.7	508.6	505.0	504.3	501.0
2002	485.7	489.0	492.6	499.8	509.9	519.6	517.0	514.9	515.3	512.9	509.3	510.6	506.4
2003	490.1	493.1	495.2	501.2	511.0	519.5	518.1	518.3	519.0	518.1	516.0	516.4	509.7
2004	495.3	499.9	501.7	508.5	517.6	526.8	523.8	523.3	523.9	522.2	521.3	520.2	515.4
2005	498.2	500.8	501.6	510.2	519.6	528.4	525.6	525.1	526.5	523.6	521.9	523.0	517.0
2006	501.4	502.8	505.8	514.2	522.7	533.1	527.0	528.8	529.0	527.8	526.6	528.1	520.6
2007	506.8	508.5	510.6	514.7	525.9	536.7	532.9	532.5	533.5	532.6	531.4	531.7	524.8
2008	510.6	512.2	514.1	520.8	531.3	539.6	535.8	534.2	533.7	533.2	527.3	525.5	526.5
2009	503.1	504.0	503.2	510.7	521.6	526.2	521.9	522.0	524.3	523.0	518.6	518.2	516.4
2010	498.0	500.0	501.6	508.9	521.1	525.2	522.7	521.7	524.1	523.5	518.7	518.1	515.3
2011	497.7	500.4	501.3	508.2	517.3	526.5	523.6	525.1	526.7	523.5	519.7	517.5	515.6
Trade, Transportation, and Utilities													
2000	118.4	116.1	116.3	117.4	119.4	123.8	126.1	126.1	125.2	126.1	128.8	128.7	122.7
2001	120.9	118.2	117.7	119.3	121.8	125.4	126.7	126.6	124.7	126.0	127.9	128.1	123.6
2002	120.3	118.1	118.1	119.6	121.7	125.2	127.1	127.0	124.5	124.0	125.7	127.4	123.2
2003	119.5	116.9	116.8	118.1	120.9	124.2	126.2	127.0	124.7	125.7	128.6	129.4	123.2
2004	121.3	119.8	119.7	120.8	123.4	126.4	128.2	128.3	126.0	127.2	130.0	131.5	125.2
2005	123.1	120.7	119.8	121.3	123.0	126.1	127.7	127.9	126.1	126.4	129.4	130.8	125.2
2006	123.4	119.9	120.3	121.7	123.3	126.7	127.7	128.0	126.2	127.2	131.1	132.2	125.6
2007	123.9	120.7	121.1	121.0	123.8	127.2	129.1	129.2	126.5	127.4	131.1	132.0	126.1
2008	124.7	121.1	120.8	121.7	123.9	126.4	127.7	127.6	124.8	125.3	126.9	127.0	124.8
2009	118.8	115.4	114.3	114.9	117.6	119.6	120.9	121.3	119.3	119.4	121.6	122.4	118.8
2010	114.7	112.2	111.6	112.6	115.1	118.1	119.6	120.1	117.2	118.7	120.2	121.5	116.8
2011	114.5	112.3	111.5	112.8	114.7	117.8	119.8	121.1	120.4	119.9	122.6	123.6	117.6
Wholesale Trade													
2000	18.9	18.8	18.9	19.2	19.3	19.6	19.9	20.0	19.9	20.0	19.9	20.0	19.5
2001	20.0	19.8	19.8	20.1	20.1	20.5	20.7	20.6	20.3	20.4	20.2	20.3	20.2
2002	19.8	19.7	19.7	20.0	20.1	20.4	20.9	20.9	20.8	20.8	20.8	20.8	20.4
2003	20.4	20.2	20.3	20.6	20.9	21.3	21.5	21.6	21.5	21.4	21.5	21.5	21.1
2004	20.9	20.9	21.0	21.2	21.4	21.6	21.6	21.9	21.5	21.5	21.3	21.3	21.4
2005	20.9	20.9	20.9	21.1	21.4	21.7	21.9	21.9	21.7	21.6	21.5	21.6	21.4
2006	21.1	21.0	21.1	21.4	21.5	22.0	22.0	21.9	21.6	21.5	21.3	21.3	21.5
2007	20.8	20.7	20.9	20.9	21.2	21.4	21.6	21.5	21.2	21.1	20.9	21.0	21.1
2008	20.7	20.5	20.5	20.5	20.8	21.1	21.3	21.2	20.9	20.8	20.5	20.5	20.8
2009	19.7	19.4	19.3	19.3	19.5	19.6	19.9	19.8	19.5	19.3	19.2	19.2	19.5
2010	18.5	18.4	18.5	18.6	18.9	19.2	19.4	19.5	19.2	19.2	19.1	19.1	19.0
2011	18.7	18.6	18.5	18.7	18.8	19.3	19.5	19.4	19.5	18.8	18.5	18.5	18.9
Retail Trade													
2000	80.8	79.0	79.1	80.1	81.6	84.7	86.3	86.7	85.7	86.2	88.3	88.8	83.9
2001	82.3	80.2	79.8	81.3	83.6	86.0	87.0	86.9	85.3	85.9	88.1	88.1	84.5
2002	82.4	80.5	80.7	81.8	83.5	86.3	87.5	87.4	84.9	84.4	86.2	87.4	84.4
2003	81.2	79.4	79.4	80.6	82.7	85.0	86.5	87.0	84.7	85.4	87.8	88.3	84.0
2004	82.5	81.5	81.4	82.3	84.3	86.4	87.8	87.7	85.9	86.5	88.7	89.7	85.4
2005	83.6	81.7	81.3	82.8	84.0	86.1	87.2	87.3	85.6	85.5	88.0	89.0	85.2
2006	83.8	80.9	81.4	82.7	83.9	86.1	87.0	87.5	85.8	86.4	89.6	90.2	85.4
2007	84.3	81.6	82.0	82.2	84.5	87.0	88.5	88.4	85.8	86.4	89.7	90.2	85.9
2008	85.4	82.5	82.3	83.4	85.1	86.9	87.9	87.9	85.4	85.8	87.2	87.1	85.6
2009	81.3	79.0	78.2	78.8	81.1	82.9	83.9	84.4	82.7	82.9	84.4	84.8	82.0
2010	79.7	77.6	77.1	77.9	79.8	82.0	83.2	83.7	81.1	82.3	83.8	84.5	81.1
2011	79.4	77.6	77.0	78.0	79.7	81.8	83.2	84.2	83.3	83.3	85.8	86.5	81.7
Transportation and Utilities													
2000	18.7	18.3	18.3	18.1	18.5	19.5	19.9	19.4	19.6	19.9	20.6	19.9	19.2
2001	18.6	18.2	18.1	17.9	18.1	18.9	19.0	19.1	19.1	19.7	19.6	19.7	18.8
2002	18.1	17.9	17.7	17.8	18.1	18.5	18.7	18.7	18.8	18.8	18.7	19.2	18.4
2003	17.9	17.3	17.1	16.9	17.3	17.9	18.2	18.4	18.5	18.9	19.3	19.6	18.1
2004	17.9	17.4	17.3	17.3	17.7	18.4	18.5	18.7	18.6	19.2	20.0	20.5	18.5
2005	18.6	18.1	17.6	17.4	17.6	18.3	18.6	18.7	18.8	19.3	19.9	20.2	18.6
2006	18.5	18.0	17.8	17.6	17.9	18.6	18.7	18.6	18.8	19.3	20.2	20.7	18.7
2007	18.8	18.4	18.2	17.9	18.1	18.8	19.0	19.3	19.5	19.9	20.5	20.8	19.1
2008	18.6	18.1	18.0	17.8	18.0	18.4	18.5	18.5	18.5	18.7	19.2	19.4	18.5
2009	17.8	17.0	16.8	16.8	17.0	17.1	17.1	17.1	17.1	17.2	18.0	18.4	17.3
2010	16.5	16.2	16.0	16.1	16.4	16.9	17.0	16.9	16.9	17.2	17.3	17.9	16.8
2011	16.4	16.1	16.0	16.1	16.2	16.7	17.1	17.5	17.6	17.8	18.3	18.6	17.0
Information													
2000	12.1	12.1	12.2	12.3	12.3	12.2	12.3	11.0	12.2	12.2	12.3	12.3	12.1
2001	12.3	12.4	12.3	12.3	12.3	12.3	12.2	12.1	12.0	11.8	11.9	11.9	12.2
2002	11.8	11.7	11.6	11.6	11.7	11.7	11.6	11.5	11.4	11.3	11.5	11.6	11.6
2003	11.3	11.4	11.3	11.3	11.2	11.3	11.3	11.3	11.2	11.5	11.5	11.6	11.4
2004	11.6	11.4	11.4	11.0	10.9	11.1	11.3	11.2	11.0	11.1	11.3	11.3	11.2
2005	11.2	11.1	11.2	11.1	11.2	11.1	11.2	11.2	11.1	11.1	11.1	11.3	11.2
2006	11.2	11.2	11.1	11.1	11.1	11.3	11.3	11.3	11.1	11.3	11.3	11.4	11.2
2007	11.2	11.4	11.4	11.4	11.3	11.3	11.3	11.2	11.0	11.1	11.1	11.1	11.2
2008	10.9	10.9	10.8	10.7	10.6	10.7	10.6	10.4	10.1	10.2	10.0	9.9	10.5
2009	9.4	9.2	9.0	9.1	9.2	9.1	9.0	8.9	8.8	8.8	8.8	8.7	9.0
2010	8.7	8.8	8.7	8.7	8.8	8.8	8.8	8.7	8.6	8.6	8.6	8.5	8.7
2011	8.4	8.3	8.3	8.3	8.3	8.4	8.3	8.2	8.1	8.0	8.0	8.0	8.2

1. Employment by Industry: Maine, Selected Years, 2000–2011—*Continued*

(Numbers in thousands, not seasonally adjusted)

Industry and year	January	February	March	April	May	June	July	August	September	October	November	December	Annual average
Financial Activities													
2000	33.4	33.3	33.5	33.7	33.8	34.3	34.9	34.9	34.4	34.2	34.1	34.6	34.1
2001	34.2	34.5	34.7	35.0	35.0	35.4	35.9	35.9	35.2	35.1	35.1	35.4	35.1
2002	34.6	34.6	34.8	34.7	34.9	35.5	35.7	35.6	35.2	35.2	35.2	35.4	35.1
2003	34.8	34.8	34.9	35.0	35.0	35.2	35.7	35.5	35.0	34.9	34.9	35.3	35.1
2004	34.9	35.0	34.9	34.8	35.0	35.3	35.5	35.4	34.6	34.5	34.3	34.4	34.9
2005	34.0	33.9	34.0	33.9	34.1	34.3	34.8	34.6	34.0	34.2	34.0	34.1	34.2
2006	33.7	33.6	33.5	33.5	33.5	34.1	34.0	34.1	33.4	33.5	33.2	33.5	33.6
2007	33.0	33.0	33.0	33.1	33.3	33.7	33.9	33.7	33.1	32.8	32.7	32.8	33.2
2008	32.4	32.5	32.5	32.7	33.0	33.3	33.5	33.5	32.6	32.4	32.3	32.1	32.7
2009	31.8	31.8	31.8	31.8	32.2	32.7	32.7	32.6	32.0	31.9	31.7	31.7	32.1
2010	31.2	31.3	31.4	31.5	31.7	32.1	32.1	32.2	31.8	31.6	31.4	31.6	31.7
2011	31.2	31.2	31.3	31.2	31.4	31.8	32.4	32.5	31.8	31.7	31.8	31.8	31.7
Professional and Business Services													
2000	49.0	49.1	49.8	51.2	52.0	53.3	53.7	53.7	53.1	52.4	52.0	52.6	51.8
2001	50.8	51.0	51.4	52.7	53.2	53.8	52.8	52.5	51.4	51.1	50.6	50.4	51.8
2002	49.4	49.4	50.0	51.4	52.0	53.1	52.9	52.8	51.7	51.7	51.3	50.8	51.4
2003	49.2	49.1	49.3	50.1	50.5	51.1	51.4	51.8	51.1	50.5	49.9	49.5	50.3
2004	47.8	48.2	48.4	49.5	50.2	50.7	50.7	50.7	49.7	49.7	49.9	49.3	49.6
2005	47.8	47.8	48.2	49.7	50.6	51.2	51.9	52.1	51.3	51.2	50.9	51.0	50.3
2006	48.9	49.4	49.7	52.3	53.0	54.0	53.5	53.6	52.8	52.3	52.4	52.6	52.0
2007	51.1	51.0	51.3	53.0	54.0	55.4	55.5	55.7	54.8	55.1	55.3	55.2	54.0
2008	54.2	54.5	55.0	56.3	57.1	58.1	58.1	58.1	57.1	57.2	56.4	56.0	56.5
2009	54.2	53.9	53.6	54.7	55.9	56.1	56.2	56.3	55.5	55.9	55.9	55.5	55.3
2010	54.1	53.8	54.0	55.4	56.2	56.6	57.2	57.2	56.6	56.6	56.8	56.2	55.9
2011	54.9	55.2	55.3	56.7	57.4	58.4	58.7	59.2	58.2	57.7	57.3	55.7	57.1
Education and Health Services													
2000	94.2	96.5	96.9	97.2	97.2	95.8	96.8	96.7	98.8	99.5	100.0	100.0	97.5
2001	97.7	100.1	100.5	100.5	100.5	99.7	99.7	99.9	101.3	102.8	102.9	103.2	100.7
2002	101.9	104.2	104.8	105.5	105.3	104.0	104.4	104.0	105.2	106.4	106.8	106.6	104.9
2003	104.3	106.3	107.0	107.2	106.9	106.0	106.7	106.3	108.0	109.5	109.6	109.9	107.3
2004	108.4	110.3	111.0	111.4	110.9	109.9	110.1	110.0	111.2	112.5	113.1	112.1	110.9
2005	110.0	111.6	111.9	112.7	112.8	111.5	111.5	111.3	112.3	113.6	114.1	113.5	112.2
2006	111.6	113.6	114.2	114.4	114.1	113.0	112.9	113.3	114.4	115.5	115.9	115.9	114.1
2007	114.2	116.5	116.6	116.4	116.2	115.1	114.7	115.0	115.9	117.1	117.5	117.7	116.1
2008	115.3	117.4	117.7	117.7	117.8	116.6	116.5	116.2	117.4	119.1	119.3	119.1	117.5
2009	117.2	119.0	119.1	119.6	119.4	117.4	117.4	117.2	117.9	119.7	119.8	119.8	118.6
2010	117.5	119.3	119.3	119.8	119.6	117.5	117.2	117.0	119.3	120.3	120.3	120.2	118.9
2011	117.1	119.3	119.6	120.6	120.5	118.8	119.3	118.9	120.9	122.0	122.4	123.4	120.2
Leisure and Hospitality													
2000	45.5	45.7	46.8	50.6	56.6	64.4	71.1	70.9	62.9	56.7	50.4	49.4	55.9
2001	46.7	46.2	47.0	51.9	57.4	65.2	71.9	72.1	63.5	56.6	50.7	48.7	56.5
2002	46.7	46.7	47.9	51.9	58.2	65.4	73.0	72.8	64.6	58.5	51.3	51.1	57.3
2003	48.0	48.0	48.7	52.5	59.3	66.4	74.3	74.4	65.5	59.0	53.3	52.2	58.5
2004	48.1	48.3	48.9	53.2	59.4	67.4	74.2	74.5	66.6	59.1	53.4	52.6	58.8
2005	48.6	48.6	49.2	53.9	59.8	67.6	74.9	75.0	66.4	59.5	53.6	53.5	59.2
2006	48.9	49.0	50.2	54.5	60.3	69.4	75.3	75.2	67.1	60.2	54.1	54.0	59.9
2007	50.3	50.3	50.8	53.6	59.6	68.7	75.6	75.8	67.4	61.0	55.2	54.5	60.2
2008	49.8	49.8	50.3	54.3	61.0	69.0	76.8	76.0	67.5	60.8	53.7	53.1	60.2
2009	48.8	49.0	49.5	53.7	60.0	66.7	74.7	74.5	67.2	60.4	53.3	52.9	59.2
2010	48.9	49.0	49.5	53.8	60.0	67.4	75.6	75.5	67.7	61.1	54.3	53.4	59.7
2011	49.3	49.5	50.3	53.6	59.8	68.3	75.3	76.3	66.9	60.4	52.5	51.7	59.5
Other Services													
2000	17.8	17.8	17.9	18.2	18.4	18.7	19.0	18.9	18.5	18.3	18.2	18.3	18.3
2001	18.7	18.7	18.9	18.9	19.1	19.4	19.8	19.5	19.1	19.0	19.0	18.9	19.1
2002	19.1	19.1	19.2	19.6	19.8	20.0	20.6	20.6	20.1	19.7	19.7	19.7	19.8
2003	20.1	20.1	20.2	20.3	20.5	20.8	20.8	20.6	20.2	19.9	19.8	19.8	20.3
2004	19.6	19.6	19.6	19.9	20.1	20.2	20.7	20.7	20.3	20.0	19.9	19.9	20.0
2005	19.5	19.5	19.7	20.0	20.2	20.3	20.6	20.4	20.2	19.9	19.8	19.9	20.0
2006	19.4	19.4	19.5	19.5	19.7	20.0	20.3	20.1	19.6	19.7	19.7	19.8	19.7
2007	19.4	19.3	19.4	19.7	20.0	20.2	20.6	20.5	20.1	19.8	19.7	19.7	19.9
2008	19.4	19.5	19.6	19.7	20.0	20.3	20.5	20.1	19.8	20.0	19.9	19.8	19.9
2009	19.4	19.4	19.2	19.5	19.8	20.0	20.3	20.3	19.8	19.8	19.7	19.7	19.7
2010	19.3	19.3	19.3	19.5	19.7	19.9	20.4	20.1	19.9	19.7	19.7	19.5	19.7
2011	19.3	19.3	19.4	19.7	20.1	20.3	20.7	21.1	20.3	20.2	20.3	20.1	20.1
Government													
2000	97.4	101.2	103.8	102.3	104.2	100.8	87.5	86.0	99.7	102.8	104.4	104.7	99.6
2001	100.5	103.9	104.3	104.7	105.1	103.1	89.9	89.7	102.5	106.2	106.9	107.7	102.0
2002	101.9	105.2	106.2	105.5	106.3	104.7	91.7	90.6	102.6	106.1	107.8	108.0	103.1
2003	102.9	106.5	107.0	106.7	106.7	104.5	91.7	91.4	103.3	107.1	108.4	108.7	103.7
2004	103.6	107.3	107.8	107.9	107.7	105.8	93.1	92.5	104.5	108.1	109.4	109.1	104.7
2005	104.0	107.6	107.6	107.6	107.9	106.3	93.0	92.6	105.1	107.7	109.0	108.9	104.8
2006	104.3	106.7	107.3	107.2	107.7	104.6	92.0	93.2	104.4	108.1	108.9	108.7	104.4
2007	103.7	106.3	107.0	106.5	107.7	105.1	92.2	91.4	104.7	108.3	108.8	108.7	104.2
2008	103.9	106.5	107.4	107.7	107.9	105.2	92.1	92.3	104.4	108.2	108.8	108.5	104.4
2009	103.5	106.3	106.7	107.4	107.5	104.6	90.7	90.9	103.8	107.1	107.8	107.5	103.7
2010	103.6	106.3	107.8	107.6	110.0	104.8	91.8	90.9	103.0	106.9	107.4	107.2	103.9
2011	103.0	105.3	105.6	105.3	105.1	102.7	89.1	87.8	100.1	103.6	104.8	103.2	101.3

2. Average Weekly Hours by Selected Industry: Maine, 2007–2011

(Not seasonally adjusted)

Industry and year	January	February	March	April	May	June	July	August	September	October	November	December	Annual average
Total Private													
2007	33.6	33.6	34.0	33.9	34.2	34.4	34.7	34.6	34.8	34.4	34.1	34.3	34.2
2008	34.0	34.5	34.4	34.4	34.5	34.7	34.8	34.8	34.4	34.1	33.5	33.2	34.3
2009	33.1	33.3	33.0	33.3	33.0	33.0	33.7	33.8	33.3	33.7	33.4	33.4	33.3
2010	33.0	33.3	33.2	33.4	33.6	33.8	34.1	34.4	34.1	34.4	33.8	34.3	33.8
2011	33.7	33.9	33.7	33.7	33.8	33.9	34.3	34.4	34.0	34.2	33.9	34.2	34.0
Goods-Producing													
2007	38.6	37.8	38.9	39.1	39.5	40.0	40.3	40.1	40.4	39.7	40.2	39.9	39.6
2008	40.5	39.5	40.2	40.5	41.8	42.1	41.5	41.3	41.4	40.9	39.9	39.0	40.7
2009	39.0	39.1	38.8	38.6	39.1	38.8	38.7	39.7	39.5	40.7	40.4	39.5	39.3
2010	39.4	38.9	39.3	39.7	40.2	39.5	39.8	40.0	40.3	41.4	40.2	39.5	39.9
2011	39.2	39.6	38.9	38.8	39.1	40.1	40.0	39.7	40.2	40.1	39.4	39.4	39.5
Construction													
2007	36.8	35.2	37.8	38.0	39.8	40.3	40.0	39.8	39.6	38.8	39.2	39.5	38.8
2008	40.0	37.3	39.9	40.3	41.7	41.2	41.0	40.2	40.7	40.2	38.2	36.6	39.8
2009	37.1	38.3	37.6	38.8	38.1	37.6	38.5	40.0	38.5	40.0	39.2	38.0	38.5
2010	37.7	38.0	38.1	38.9	40.0	39.2	39.8	40.1	40.0	40.2	39.1	37.7	39.1
2011	36.7	37.4	37.3	37.6	38.5	39.1	39.7	39.0	40.3	39.5	40.2	38.8	38.8
Manufacturing													
2007	39.4	38.7	39.3	39.7	39.2	39.5	40.1	39.9	40.7	40.0	40.7	40.4	39.8
2008	41.1	40.6	40.4	40.6	40.1	40.7	40.1	40.2	40.3	40.1	39.7	39.1	40.3
2009	39.5	39.0	39.0	38.2	39.0	38.7	38.3	39.1	39.5	40.3	41.0	40.3	39.3
2010	40.1	39.2	39.8	40.3	40.6	39.9	40.0	40.1	40.3	41.8	40.6	40.4	40.3
2011	40.2	40.2	39.5	39.5	39.6	40.6	40.1	39.9	40.0	40.3	38.8	38.8	39.8
Trade, Transportation, and Utilities													
2007	32.6	32.8	33.2	32.8	33.5	33.6	33.9	33.8	33.6	33.2	31.8	32.8	33.1
2008	31.6	33.2	32.7	32.8	32.4	33.2	33.5	33.5	32.7	32.3	31.1	32.1	32.6
2009	30.8	32.0	31.3	31.4	30.4	31.1	32.4	32.8	32.0	31.5	30.8	32.3	31.6
2010	31.1	31.9	32.0	31.9	32.7	32.8	33.4	33.6	32.7	33.5	31.6	33.8	32.6
2011	31.5	32.5	32.4	32.3	32.2	32.8	33.4	33.2	32.3	32.2	31.8	33.5	32.5
Professional and Business Services													
2007	36.1	36.9	36.9	36.8	37.2	37.0	37.0	36.8	36.5	36.2	36.1	35.9	36.6
2008	35.6	36.3	36.2	36.1	35.8	35.8	35.9	36.1	36.2	36.0	36.2	35.5	36.0
2009	36.4	36.2	36.1	35.6	35.5	35.3	35.4	35.4	34.7	35.3	35.0	34.9	35.5
2010	34.1	34.6	34.5	34.9	34.8	35.3	35.5	35.4	34.7	35.4	35.1	35.5	35.0
2011	35.0	34.8	35.1	35.0	34.8	34.8	34.6	34.8	34.8	34.6	34.4	34.3	34.7
Education and Health Services													
2007	31.9	31.9	31.8	31.6	31.6	31.9	32.0	31.9	31.9	31.9	32.5	32.1	31.9
2008	32.3	32.4	32.5	32.6	32.5	32.5	32.5	32.4	32.4	32.1	32.2	31.7	32.3
2009	31.8	31.9	31.7	32.0	31.9	32.0	32.0	31.9	32.1	32.5	32.7	32.6	32.1
2010	32.6	32.5	32.2	32.3	32.4	33.1	32.9	33.4	33.5	33.5	33.5	33.7	33.0
2011	33.9	33.3	33.1	33.3	33.8	33.8	33.7	33.7	33.8	33.9	34.0	33.9	33.7
Leisure and Hospitality													
2007	23.0	23.0	23.2	23.6	23.6	24.2	26.0	26.7	24.5	24.4	23.3	23.0	24.2
2008	23.0	23.8	23.2	23.2	24.3	24.6	26.5	27.1	24.5	24.2	23.2	21.9	24.3
2009	22.1	22.9	23.5	23.4	23.8	23.6	27.3	27.2	25.6	25.8	24.2	23.1	24.6
2010	23.3	24.0	23.7	23.6	23.9	24.5	26.0	26.8	26.1	26.0	25.2	24.5	24.9
2011	24.0	25.0	24.6	25.0	25.2	25.4	28.0	28.8	26.5	26.5	25.9	25.1	26.0

3. Average Hourly Earnings by Selected Industry: Maine, 2007–2011

(Dollars, not seasonally adjusted)

Industry and year	January	February	March	April	May	June	July	August	September	October	November	December	Annual average
Total Private													
2007	18.81	18.83	18.91	19.13	18.90	18.64	18.56	18.45	18.74	18.64	18.69	18.63	18.74
2008	18.79	18.86	18.80	18.95	18.77	18.87	18.78	18.88	19.12	19.10	19.26	19.35	18.96
2009	19.30	19.39	19.27	19.25	19.09	19.00	18.76	18.96	19.23	19.05	19.38	19.24	19.16
2010	19.37	19.46	19.57	19.46	19.40	19.25	19.20	19.29	19.49	19.61	19.66	19.67	19.45
2011	19.95	19.78	19.91	20.01	19.88	19.67	19.57	19.56	20.02	20.28	20.32	20.48	19.95
Goods-Producing													
2007	20.58	20.65	20.56	20.87	20.66	20.40	20.45	20.51	20.63	20.49	20.70	20.54	20.58
2008	20.60	20.51	20.56	20.57	20.32	20.58	20.56	20.62	20.67	20.69	20.73	21.06	20.62
2009	20.90	21.13	21.05	21.07	21.15	21.26	21.14	21.27	21.63	21.11	21.33	21.45	21.21
2010	21.43	21.49	21.53	21.56	21.45	21.37	21.38	21.57	21.98	22.11	21.50	21.93	21.61
2011	22.29	22.33	22.43	22.33	22.26	21.92	21.77	22.07	22.34	22.51	22.92	22.72	22.32
Construction													
2007	18.85	19.06	19.33	19.38	19.26	18.95	18.79	18.71	18.74	18.68	18.77	18.93	18.94
2008	18.67	18.87	19.08	19.28	19.12	19.03	18.97	18.92	19.13	19.35	19.28	19.74	19.11
2009	19.71	19.94	19.72	19.95	19.79	19.83	19.71	19.98	19.99	19.82	19.89	19.92	19.86
2010	19.90	20.11	19.87	19.78	19.71	19.55	19.53	19.82	20.14	20.29	20.16	20.46	19.94
2011	20.93	20.98	20.93	20.90	20.81	20.71	20.41	20.87	21.47	21.87	21.68	22.54	21.18
Manufacturing													
2007	21.65	21.67	21.41	21.69	21.50	21.40	21.61	21.72	21.92	21.67	21.86	21.66	21.65
2008	21.81	21.51	21.52	21.48	21.29	21.61	21.66	21.84	21.81	21.68	21.74	21.95	21.66
2009	22.00	22.12	22.02	22.00	22.18	22.38	22.32	22.41	22.79	22.31	22.55	22.59	22.31
2010	22.69	22.50	22.79	22.81	22.79	22.78	22.83	22.85	23.31	23.38	22.52	22.77	22.84
2011	23.08	23.14	23.25	22.90	22.89	22.47	22.51	22.89	23.07	23.16	23.80	23.64	23.06
Trade, Transportation, and Utilities													
2007	16.78	17.15	17.27	17.23	16.97	16.71	16.77	16.69	16.85	16.60	16.52	16.41	16.82
2008	16.77	17.16	16.92	17.40	17.11	17.17	17.00	17.25	17.35	17.24	17.56	17.27	17.18
2009	17.72	17.95	17.77	17.62	17.59	17.30	17.25	17.54	17.65	17.71	17.89	17.37	17.61
2010	17.34	17.44	17.69	17.78	17.82	17.65	17.47	17.59	17.52	17.68	17.67	17.11	17.56
2011	17.45	17.47	17.58	17.87	18.16	17.55	17.62	17.29	17.44	17.58	17.62	17.48	17.59
Professional and Business Services													
2007	21.10	20.92	21.34	21.61	21.23	21.48	21.71	21.94	22.24	22.38	22.41	22.59	21.75
2008	22.53	22.86	22.57	22.48	22.44	22.46	22.59	22.57	22.69	22.48	22.36	22.57	22.55
2009	22.09	22.29	22.55	22.54	22.31	22.12	22.19	22.01	21.75	21.66	21.89	22.19	22.13
2010	22.15	22.11	22.15	22.16	22.62	22.10	22.03	22.28	22.40	22.44	22.90	22.62	22.33
2011	22.94	22.65	22.41	22.31	22.46	22.35	22.16	21.93	21.83	21.94	21.81	22.08	22.23
Education and Health Services													
2007	19.25	19.28	19.29	19.21	19.41	19.19	19.32	19.05	19.18	19.11	19.10	18.85	19.19
2008	19.17	18.93	18.98	18.70	18.90	19.15	19.40	19.29	19.50	19.40	19.31	19.57	19.19
2009	19.17	19.26	19.32	19.54	19.23	19.46	19.40	19.49	19.70	19.55	19.47	19.38	19.41
2010	19.79	19.56	19.78	19.65	19.46	19.64	19.85	19.70	19.97	20.29	20.35	20.36	19.87
2011	20.57	20.23	20.49	20.85	20.19	20.59	20.83	20.94	21.61	21.89	21.78	22.19	21.02
Leisure and Hospitality													
2007	11.91	11.92	12.06	12.17	11.89	11.57	11.37	11.53	12.01	12.17	12.19	12.28	11.88
2008	12.14	12.24	12.30	12.22	12.04	11.85	11.71	12.21	12.34	12.49	12.67	12.89	12.22
2009	12.61	12.87	12.73	12.62	12.45	12.36	11.74	12.05	12.41	12.45	12.56	12.87	12.41
2010	12.51	12.82	12.55	12.85	12.49	12.15	12.17	12.40	12.65	12.56	12.74	12.88	12.54
2011	12.70	12.88	12.75	12.78	12.71	12.54	12.64	12.82	12.89	12.94	12.86	13.01	12.79

4. Average Weekly Earnings by Selected Industry: Maine, 2007–2011

(Dollars, not seasonally adjusted)

Industry and year	January	February	March	April	May	June	July	August	September	October	November	December	Annual average
Total Private													
2007	632.02	632.69	642.94	648.51	646.38	641.22	644.03	638.37	652.15	641.22	637.33	639.01	641.22
2008	638.86	650.67	646.72	651.88	647.57	654.79	653.54	657.02	657.73	651.31	645.21	642.42	649.78
2009	638.83	645.69	635.91	641.03	629.97	627.00	632.21	640.85	640.36	641.99	647.29	642.62	638.68
2010	639.21	648.02	649.72	649.96	651.84	650.65	654.72	663.58	664.61	674.58	664.51	674.68	657.34
2011	672.32	670.54	670.97	674.34	671.94	666.81	671.25	672.86	680.68	693.58	688.85	700.42	678.01
Goods-Producing													
2007	794.39	780.57	799.78	816.02	816.07	816.00	824.14	822.45	833.45	813.45	832.14	819.55	814.41
2008	834.30	810.15	826.51	833.09	849.38	866.42	853.24	851.61	855.74	846.22	827.13	821.34	839.99
2009	815.10	826.18	816.74	813.30	826.97	824.89	818.12	844.42	854.39	859.18	861.73	847.28	834.37
2010	844.34	835.96	846.13	855.93	862.29	844.12	850.92	862.80	885.79	915.35	864.30	866.24	861.49
2011	873.77	884.27	872.53	866.40	870.37	878.99	870.80	876.18	898.07	902.65	903.05	895.17	882.72
Construction													
2007	693.68	670.91	730.67	736.44	766.55	763.69	751.60	744.66	742.10	724.78	735.78	747.74	735.43
2008	746.80	703.85	761.29	776.98	797.30	784.04	777.77	760.58	778.59	777.87	736.50	722.48	761.57
2009	731.24	763.70	741.47	774.06	754.00	745.61	758.84	799.20	769.62	792.80	779.69	756.96	764.81
2010	750.23	764.18	757.05	769.44	788.40	766.36	777.29	794.78	805.60	815.66	788.26	771.34	780.20
2011	768.13	784.65	780.69	785.84	801.19	809.76	810.28	813.93	865.24	863.87	871.54	874.55	821.14
Manufacturing													
2007	853.01	838.63	841.41	861.09	842.80	845.30	866.56	866.63	892.14	866.80	889.70	875.06	861.76
2008	896.39	873.31	869.41	872.09	853.73	879.53	868.57	877.97	878.94	869.37	863.08	858.25	871.76
2009	869.00	862.68	858.78	840.40	865.02	866.11	854.86	876.23	900.21	899.09	924.55	910.38	877.25
2010	909.87	882.00	907.04	919.24	925.27	908.92	913.20	916.29	939.39	977.28	914.31	919.91	919.33
2011	927.82	930.23	918.38	904.55	906.44	912.28	902.65	913.31	922.80	933.35	923.44	917.23	917.43
Trade, Transportation, and Utilities													
2007	547.03	562.52	573.36	565.14	568.50	561.46	568.50	564.12	566.16	551.12	525.34	538.25	557.38
2008	529.93	569.71	553.28	570.72	554.36	570.04	569.50	577.88	567.35	556.85	546.12	554.37	560.02
2009	545.78	574.40	556.20	553.27	534.74	538.03	558.90	575.31	564.80	557.87	551.01	561.05	555.96
2010	539.27	556.34	566.08	567.18	582.71	578.92	583.50	591.02	572.90	592.28	558.37	578.32	572.66
2011	549.68	567.78	569.59	577.20	584.75	575.64	588.51	574.03	563.31	566.08	560.32	585.58	571.98
Professional and Business Services													
2007	761.71	771.95	787.45	795.25	789.76	794.76	803.27	807.39	811.76	810.16	809.00	810.98	796.56
2008	802.07	829.82	817.03	811.53	803.35	804.07	810.98	814.78	821.38	809.28	809.43	801.24	811.21
2009	804.08	806.90	814.06	802.42	792.01	780.84	785.53	779.15	754.73	764.60	766.15	774.43	785.14
2010	755.32	765.01	764.18	773.38	787.18	780.13	782.07	788.71	777.28	794.38	803.79	803.01	781.23
2011	802.90	788.22	786.59	780.85	781.61	777.78	766.74	763.16	759.68	759.12	750.26	757.34	772.61
Education and Health Services													
2007	614.08	615.03	613.42	607.04	613.36	612.16	618.24	607.70	611.84	609.61	620.75	605.09	612.35
2008	619.19	613.33	616.85	609.62	614.25	622.38	630.50	625.00	631.80	622.74	621.78	620.37	620.64
2009	609.61	614.39	612.44	625.28	613.44	622.72	620.80	621.73	632.37	635.38	636.67	631.79	623.18
2010	645.15	635.70	636.92	634.70	630.50	650.08	653.07	657.98	669.00	679.72	681.73	686.13	655.18
2011	697.32	673.66	678.22	694.31	682.42	695.94	701.97	705.68	730.42	742.07	740.52	752.24	708.18
Leisure and Hospitality													
2007	273.93	274.16	279.79	287.21	280.60	279.99	295.62	307.85	294.25	296.95	284.03	282.44	287.55
2008	279.22	291.31	285.36	283.50	292.57	291.51	310.32	330.89	302.33	302.26	293.94	282.29	297.27
2009	278.68	294.72	299.16	295.31	296.31	291.70	320.50	327.76	317.70	321.21	303.95	297.30	305.36
2010	291.48	307.68	297.44	303.26	298.51	297.68	316.42	332.32	330.17	326.56	321.05	315.56	312.64
2011	304.80	322.00	313.65	319.50	320.29	318.52	353.92	369.22	341.59	342.91	333.07	326.55	332.68

MARYLAND
At a Glance

Population:
 2000 census: 5,296,647
 2010 census: 5,773,552
 2011 estimate: 5,828,289

Percent change in population:
 2000–2010: 9.0%
 2010–2011: 0.9%

Percent change in total nonfarm employment:
 2000–2010: 2.6%
 2010–2011: 1.2%

Industry with the largest growth in employment, 2000–2011 (thousands):
 Education and Health Services, 101.0

Industry with the largest decline or smallest growth in employment, 2000–2011 (thousands):
 Manufacturing, -59.1

Civilian labor force:
 2000: 2,811,657
 2010: 3,057,271
 2011: 3,072,246

Unemployment rate and rank among states (lowest to highest):
 2000: 3.6%, 20th
 2010: 7.8%, 15th
 2011: 7.0%, 15th

Over-the-year change in unemployment rates:
 2010–2011: -0.8%

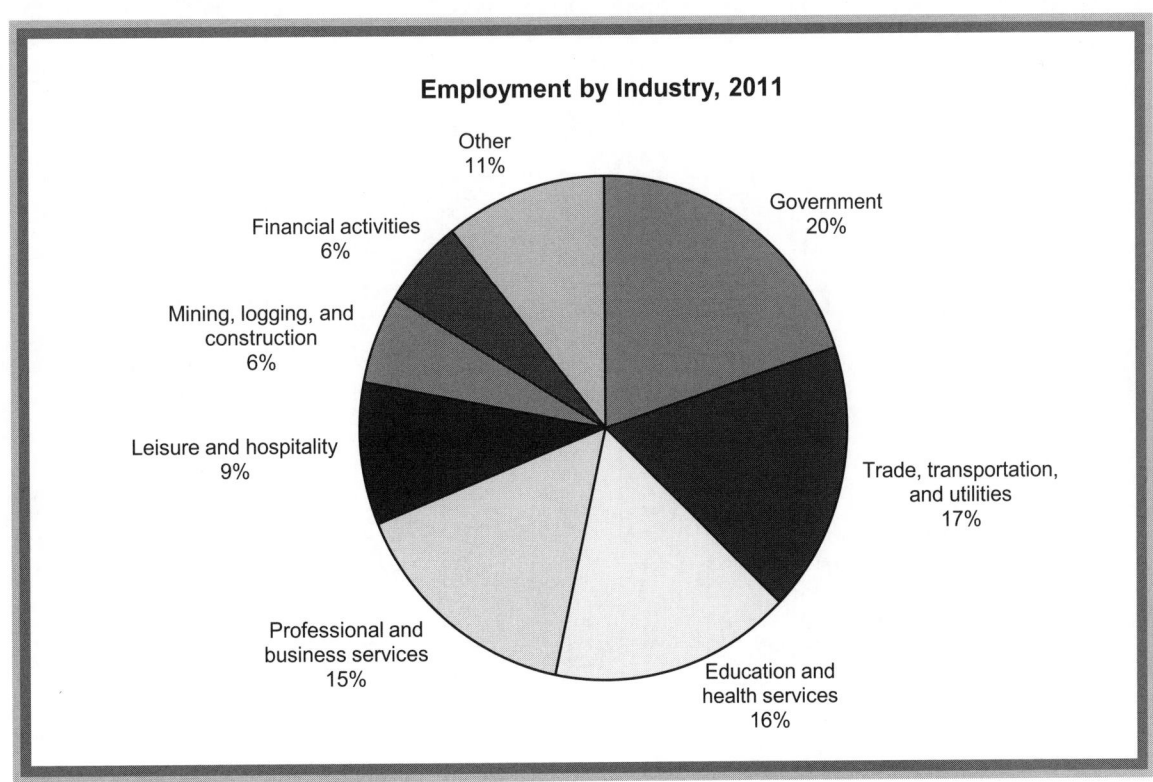

Employment by Industry, 2011

Other 11%
Government 20%
Financial activities 6%
Mining, logging, and construction 6%
Leisure and hospitality 9%
Trade, transportation, and utilities 17%
Professional and business services 15%
Education and health services 16%

1. Employment by Industry: Maryland, Selected Years, 2000–2011

(Numbers in thousands, not seasonally adjusted)

Industry and year	January	February	March	April	May	June	July	August	September	October	November	December	Annual average
Total Nonfarm													
2000	2,369.7	2,378.0	2,419.2	2,439.9	2,456.9	2,485.9	2,472.4	2,468.9	2,481.1	2,483.8	2,495.9	2,509.9	2,455.1
2001	2,415.0	2,429.2	2,450.9	2,462.7	2,482.8	2,506.2	2,481.0	2,481.4	2,474.8	2,481.9	2,493.2	2,500.7	2,471.7
2002	2,421.1	2,436.6	2,462.2	2,472.8	2,494.5	2,513.4	2,491.1	2,490.3	2,490.9	2,490.0	2,499.6	2,501.6	2,480.3
2003	2,429.3	2,426.9	2,452.7	2,477.4	2,499.9	2,519.4	2,498.8	2,495.6	2,504.0	2,505.8	2,513.3	2,519.8	2,486.9
2004	2,448.7	2,451.5	2,485.1	2,501.8	2,525.6	2,547.2	2,533.0	2,532.3	2,532.1	2,543.7	2,551.4	2,560.6	2,517.8
2005	2,482.0	2,494.1	2,513.8	2,544.2	2,565.7	2,581.1	2,572.0	2,571.0	2,580.7	2,577.4	2,589.4	2,597.1	2,555.7
2006	2,523.7	2,535.9	2,568.2	2,583.6	2,602.4	2,619.4	2,598.4	2,596.4	2,600.5	2,604.4	2,613.9	2,626.2	2,589.4
2007	2,551.5	2,553.4	2,587.1	2,599.4	2,623.3	2,637.4	2,621.9	2,620.2	2,618.5	2,620.4	2,629.5	2,637.5	2,608.3
2008	2,560.1	2,569.4	2,588.9	2,609.9	2,626.2	2,629.6	2,614.7	2,608.9	2,600.3	2,602.6	2,596.8	2,592.0	2,600.0
2009	2,499.8	2,499.0	2,512.5	2,529.4	2,545.7	2,554.4	2,529.4	2,520.2	2,517.4	2,524.8	2,526.6	2,525.1	2,523.7
2010	2,447.6	2,424.5	2,480.7	2,520.4	2,543.9	2,556.2	2,536.4	2,531.4	2,530.9	2,543.7	2,546.9	2,551.0	2,517.8
2011	2,474.1	2,488.2	2,514.7	2,542.5	2,555.3	2,568.7	2,564.9	2,551.9	2,562.7	2,580.4	2,588.4	2,584.6	2,548.0
Total Private													
2000	1,927.8	1,931.2	1,962.7	1,984.5	2,001.6	2,035.0	2,035.8	2,036.5	2,033.5	2,027.0	2,036.6	2,050.3	2,005.2
2001	1,966.8	1,971.6	1,990.1	2,000.9	2,021.6	2,051.9	2,041.2	2,042.2	2,020.0	2,017.1	2,024.2	2,031.7	2,014.9
2002	1,963.7	1,969.2	1,990.3	2,004.4	2,025.2	2,049.6	2,043.3	2,043.2	2,027.4	2,017.5	2,025.6	2,028.9	2,015.7
2003	1,970.1	1,958.5	1,981.3	2,007.1	2,029.8	2,056.6	2,054.2	2,057.7	2,043.1	2,038.5	2,045.1	2,052.4	2,024.5
2004	1,989.5	1,986.9	2,015.8	2,033.9	2,055.5	2,086.8	2,089.5	2,089.2	2,075.6	2,073.3	2,078.1	2,089.1	2,055.3
2005	2,024.8	2,027.9	2,045.8	2,074.5	2,093.1	2,119.8	2,122.6	2,122.0	2,115.0	2,102.2	2,109.7	2,119.2	2,089.7
2006	2,063.8	2,064.0	2,091.5	2,106.0	2,123.8	2,153.3	2,144.7	2,144.2	2,131.2	2,123.5	2,130.7	2,142.4	2,118.3
2007	2,084.1	2,074.9	2,102.9	2,116.3	2,137.4	2,163.8	2,160.0	2,158.8	2,143.5	2,133.2	2,137.9	2,146.2	2,129.9
2008	2,084.3	2,080.5	2,096.0	2,116.2	2,132.0	2,147.0	2,141.7	2,136.6	2,116.8	2,105.9	2,096.8	2,092.7	2,112.2
2009	2,018.5	2,005.1	2,013.3	2,027.1	2,043.4	2,064.1	2,050.4	2,044.6	2,029.8	2,020.2	2,020.0	2,019.9	2,029.7
2010	1,960.5	1,926.6	1,974.8	2,011.4	2,027.9	2,052.2	2,049.1	2,046.4	2,034.3	2,035.8	2,034.4	2,041.2	2,016.2
2011	1,980.8	1,980.0	2,000.6	2,028.3	2,042.2	2,065.2	2,073.4	2,066.9	2,057.7	2,060.1	2,068.3	2,064.1	2,040.6
Goods-Producing													
2000	320.4	318.4	326.6	329.7	332.3	338.1	339.4	340.4	339.8	338.3	336.9	336.1	333.0
2001	324.0	326.0	330.4	332.8	334.7	339.7	338.6	338.9	335.7	333.1	331.1	329.7	332.9
2002	316.6	317.4	320.9	323.2	325.1	328.6	326.4	326.9	324.1	320.2	319.6	316.8	322.2
2003	309.1	305.8	309.5	312.3	315.7	318.8	318.5	319.7	317.8	317.0	316.5	315.5	314.7
2004	306.5	305.1	311.3	315.9	319.2	323.7	325.9	326.3	324.9	323.6	322.7	323.2	319.0
2005	314.6	312.7	315.7	322.4	325.1	328.9	329.7	331.0	330.6	327.2	328.4	327.9	324.5
2006	318.6	317.9	323.1	325.0	326.5	331.2	330.9	331.0	329.2	326.5	325.2	324.9	325.8
2007	316.1	312.0	318.1	320.9	323.8	328.3	328.4	328.4	325.8	323.1	320.7	318.5	322.0
2008	310.3	308.7	310.1	310.9	311.1	313.5	313.1	312.5	309.3	304.8	300.0	294.5	308.2
2009	281.0	277.1	276.0	275.3	275.4	277.3	276.7	274.5	271.8	269.3	266.8	264.3	273.8
2010	253.8	244.3	252.7	259.7	261.7	264.6	265.6	265.1	263.0	261.0	259.9	257.7	259.1
2011	250.7	249.8	252.5	257.1	258.5	261.8	264.4	266.3	265.3	263.8	263.1	258.1	259.3
Mining and Logging													
2000	150.1	148.0	154.9	157.9	160.1	164.0	166.1	167.6	166.9	165.7	165.2	164.0	160.9
2001	155.5	157.2	161.7	164.7	167.6	171.6	171.6	172.7	170.4	169.5	168.6	167.3	166.5
2002	159.2	160.2	163.8	166.2	168.3	171.4	171.9	172.5	170.5	169.0	168.8	166.4	167.4
2003	160.8	158.3	161.7	165.1	168.8	171.7	173.8	175.5	174.5	174.5	174.0	173.3	169.3
2004	166.1	164.8	170.6	174.7	177.7	181.5	183.4	184.1	183.5	182.4	181.7	181.8	177.7
2005	174.7	173.0	175.8	182.5	185.4	189.0	190.5	191.5	191.7	189.4	190.3	189.7	185.3
2006	183.1	182.6	187.3	189.5	191.2	195.0	195.0	195.2	194.3	192.4	191.4	190.9	190.7
2007	183.9	180.2	186.0	188.9	191.5	195.2	195.6	195.9	194.0	191.5	189.4	187.0	189.9
2008	180.4	178.9	180.7	182.1	182.4	184.3	184.2	183.7	181.6	178.5	174.6	170.0	180.1
2009	158.8	156.3	155.8	156.1	156.5	158.2	158.3	156.5	154.2	151.9	149.6	147.4	155.0
2010	138.4	130.9	138.1	144.4	146.4	148.8	149.9	150.1	149.1	147.9	147.5	145.5	144.8
2011	138.0	137.2	139.5	143.7	145.1	147.8	150.3	151.8	152.3	150.8	151.3	146.9	146.2
Manufacturing													
2000	170.3	170.4	171.7	171.8	172.2	174.1	173.3	172.8	172.9	172.6	171.7	172.1	172.2
2001	168.5	168.8	168.7	168.1	167.1	168.1	167.0	166.2	165.3	163.6	162.5	162.4	166.4
2002	157.4	157.2	157.1	157.0	156.8	157.2	154.5	154.4	153.6	151.2	150.8	150.4	154.8
2003	148.3	147.5	147.8	147.2	146.9	147.1	144.7	144.2	143.3	142.5	142.5	142.2	145.4
2004	140.4	140.3	140.7	141.2	141.5	142.2	142.5	142.2	141.4	141.2	141.0	141.4	141.3
2005	139.9	139.7	139.9	139.9	139.7	139.9	139.2	139.5	138.9	137.8	138.1	138.2	139.2
2006	135.5	135.3	135.8	135.5	135.3	136.2	135.9	135.8	134.9	134.1	133.8	134.0	135.2
2007	132.2	131.8	132.1	132.0	132.3	133.1	132.8	132.7	131.8	131.6	131.3	131.5	132.1
2008	129.9	129.8	129.4	128.8	128.7	129.2	128.9	128.8	127.7	126.3	125.4	124.5	128.1
2009	122.2	120.8	120.2	119.2	118.9	119.1	118.4	118.0	117.6	117.4	117.2	116.9	118.8
2010	115.4	113.4	114.6	115.3	115.3	115.8	115.7	115.0	113.9	113.1	112.4	112.2	114.3
2011	112.7	112.6	113.0	113.4	113.4	114.0	114.1	114.5	113.0	113.0	111.8	111.2	113.1
Service-Providing													
2000	2,049.3	2,059.6	2,092.6	2,110.2	2,124.6	2,147.8	2,133.0	2,128.5	2,141.3	2,145.5	2,159.0	2,173.8	2,122.1
2001	2,091.0	2,103.2	2,120.5	2,129.9	2,148.1	2,166.5	2,142.4	2,142.5	2,139.1	2,148.8	2,162.1	2,171.0	2,138.8
2002	2,104.5	2,119.2	2,141.3	2,149.6	2,169.4	2,184.8	2,164.7	2,163.4	2,166.8	2,169.8	2,180.0	2,184.8	2,158.2
2003	2,120.2	2,121.1	2,143.2	2,165.1	2,184.2	2,200.6	2,180.3	2,175.9	2,186.2	2,188.8	2,196.8	2,204.3	2,172.2
2004	2,142.2	2,146.4	2,173.8	2,185.9	2,206.4	2,223.5	2,207.1	2,206.0	2,207.2	2,220.1	2,228.7	2,237.4	2,198.7
2005	2,167.4	2,181.4	2,198.1	2,221.8	2,240.6	2,252.2	2,242.3	2,240.0	2,250.1	2,250.2	2,261.0	2,269.2	2,231.2
2006	2,205.1	2,218.0	2,245.1	2,258.6	2,275.9	2,288.2	2,267.5	2,265.4	2,271.3	2,277.9	2,288.7	2,301.3	2,263.6
2007	2,235.4	2,241.4	2,269.0	2,278.5	2,299.5	2,309.1	2,293.5	2,291.6	2,292.7	2,297.3	2,308.8	2,319.0	2,286.3
2008	2,249.8	2,260.7	2,278.8	2,299.0	2,315.1	2,316.1	2,301.6	2,296.4	2,291.0	2,297.8	2,296.8	2,297.5	2,291.7
2009	2,218.8	2,221.9	2,236.5	2,254.1	2,270.3	2,277.1	2,252.7	2,245.7	2,245.6	2,255.5	2,259.8	2,260.8	2,249.9
2010	2,193.8	2,180.2	2,228.0	2,260.7	2,282.2	2,291.6	2,270.8	2,266.3	2,267.9	2,282.7	2,287.0	2,293.3	2,258.7
2011	2,223.4	2,238.4	2,262.2	2,285.4	2,296.8	2,306.9	2,300.5	2,285.6	2,297.4	2,316.6	2,325.3	2,326.5	2,288.8

1. Employment by Industry: Maryland, Selected Years, 2000–2011—*Continued*

(Numbers in thousands, not seasonally adjusted)

Industry and year	January	February	March	April	May	June	July	August	September	October	November	December	Annual average
Trade, Transportation, and Utilities													
2000	460.1	456.7	460.3	463.1	466.4	472.0	469.3	471.8	472.7	477.1	488.2	498.6	471.4
2001	469.0	462.0	463.3	461.9	465.6	469.2	464.4	465.2	465.6	467.7	476.5	483.3	467.8
2002	460.5	455.0	459.4	460.4	463.9	468.6	463.7	463.1	463.4	465.3	472.7	480.0	464.7
2003	455.3	449.4	452.7	454.9	459.2	463.7	460.4	462.4	463.0	466.0	475.9	482.9	462.2
2004	459.8	455.2	459.0	460.4	464.4	471.6	466.4	466.6	466.8	470.6	479.4	487.6	467.3
2005	462.1	459.4	461.7	464.0	467.9	471.8	472.6	472.0	471.8	473.4	482.0	491.8	470.9
2006	470.6	465.1	468.9	469.8	473.5	477.6	473.9	473.7	472.6	476.4	487.5	496.0	475.5
2007	474.8	467.3	471.8	470.2	475.4	479.0	476.2	474.4	473.1	474.6	484.5	493.2	476.2
2008	469.3	462.5	464.2	463.0	465.4	468.6	465.0	464.3	461.5	461.2	465.4	470.0	465.0
2009	445.5	437.6	436.6	436.1	438.9	441.8	436.5	436.4	436.6	436.8	445.6	449.9	439.9
2010	429.5	418.8	427.8	434.4	437.9	441.5	438.8	439.1	437.2	442.5	450.7	457.5	438.0
2011	436.8	432.1	434.9	438.5	441.3	444.2	442.9	441.9	439.1	443.5	451.6	455.8	441.9
Wholesale Trade													
2000	89.8	90.6	91.8	91.9	92.3	93.4	93.5	94.0	93.6	94.1	94.3	94.9	92.9
2001	93.3	93.6	94.4	94.8	94.9	94.9	94.4	94.4	94.2	94.1	94.1	94.2	94.3
2002	93.3	93.2	93.5	93.0	93.2	93.5	93.1	93.2	92.7	92.9	92.9	92.9	93.1
2003	91.1	90.7	91.3	91.0	91.5	91.8	91.4	91.4	91.2	91.1	91.3	91.4	91.3
2004	89.9	90.2	90.9	91.6	91.9	92.9	93.2	93.0	92.9	93.2	93.4	93.6	92.2
2005	92.6	92.9	93.1	93.8	94.4	95.0	95.2	95.1	94.6	94.4	94.4	95.0	94.2
2006	93.7	94.1	94.6	95.3	95.6	96.2	95.7	95.6	95.2	95.3	95.1	95.6	95.2
2007	94.0	94.3	94.7	95.1	95.4	95.7	95.3	95.2	94.9	94.3	94.3	94.7	94.8
2008	93.1	93.1	93.9	93.8	94.0	94.4	93.6	93.4	92.8	92.2	91.4	90.9	93.1
2009	89.2	88.7	88.2	88.2	88.0	87.9	87.2	87.2	86.7	86.3	86.0	85.8	87.5
2010	84.2	83.7	84.6	85.5	86.1	86.3	86.0	86.0	85.1	85.8	85.8	86.0	85.4
2011	84.8	84.8	85.3	85.9	86.6	86.8	86.3	86.5	86.5	88.7	87.2	86.0	86.3
Retail Trade													
2000	291.8	288.0	290.0	292.4	295.3	299.2	297.7	299.0	298.7	300.7	312.0	321.2	298.8
2001	297.9	291.1	291.8	289.4	292.5	296.0	293.9	294.7	294.1	295.0	304.3	311.0	296.0
2002	292.0	287.0	290.8	290.2	292.6	297.1	295.0	294.2	294.0	294.5	302.4	309.6	295.0
2003	289.7	284.5	286.3	288.9	291.7	295.3	293.9	295.5	294.5	295.8	305.4	311.6	294.4
2004	292.2	287.5	289.9	290.3	293.3	298.5	295.6	296.3	295.0	298.5	307.0	313.8	296.5
2005	291.9	288.5	289.9	292.6	295.2	297.7	299.7	299.3	297.7	299.2	307.2	314.4	297.8
2006	298.2	291.8	294.5	294.8	297.5	300.1	298.8	298.5	296.2	299.9	310.7	316.2	299.8
2007	300.2	292.5	295.9	295.2	299.1	301.5	301.0	299.7	297.5	299.6	309.4	315.3	300.6
2008	297.6	290.7	292.1	291.3	292.9	294.9	293.5	292.8	289.7	289.9	294.1	297.2	293.1
2009	279.4	273.0	272.7	272.7	275.4	277.7	275.5	275.5	274.1	275.2	283.1	286.7	276.8
2010	271.7	262.7	269.3	272.7	275.7	278.4	278.0	278.4	275.6	279.6	287.2	291.8	276.8
2011	276.4	272.2	274.1	276.8	278.5	280.7	282.9	281.7	276.8	279.1	287.9	291.5	279.9
Transportation and Utilities													
2000	78.5	78.1	78.5	78.8	78.8	79.4	78.1	78.8	80.4	82.3	81.9	82.5	79.7
2001	77.8	77.3	77.1	77.7	78.2	78.3	76.1	76.1	77.3	78.6	78.1	78.1	77.6
2002	75.2	74.8	75.1	77.2	78.1	78.0	75.6	75.7	76.7	77.9	77.4	77.5	76.6
2003	74.5	74.2	75.1	75.0	76.0	76.6	75.1	75.5	77.3	79.1	79.2	79.9	76.5
2004	77.7	77.5	78.2	78.5	79.2	80.2	77.6	77.3	78.9	78.9	79.0	80.2	78.6
2005	77.6	78.0	78.7	77.6	78.3	79.1	77.7	77.6	79.5	79.8	80.4	82.4	78.9
2006	78.7	79.2	79.8	79.7	80.4	81.3	79.4	79.6	81.2	81.2	81.7	84.2	80.5
2007	80.6	80.5	81.2	79.9	80.9	81.8	79.9	79.5	80.7	80.7	80.8	83.2	80.8
2008	78.6	78.7	78.2	77.9	78.5	79.3	77.9	78.1	79.0	79.1	79.9	81.9	78.9
2009	76.9	75.9	75.7	75.2	75.5	76.2	73.8	73.7	75.8	75.3	76.5	77.4	75.7
2010	73.6	72.4	73.9	76.2	76.1	76.8	74.8	74.7	76.5	77.1	77.7	79.7	75.8
2011	75.6	75.1	75.5	75.8	76.2	76.7	73.7	73.7	75.8	75.7	76.5	78.3	75.7
Information													
2000	56.3	56.6	57.3	57.7	58.2	59.1	59.4	54.2	60.0	60.3	60.8	62.1	58.5
2001	59.7	60.1	60.1	59.3	59.4	59.5	58.4	58.1	57.0	56.8	56.7	56.6	58.5
2002	55.2	54.9	54.8	54.4	54.4	54.0	53.3	53.0	52.2	50.7	51.4	51.1	53.3
2003	50.4	50.5	50.6	51.1	51.7	51.6	51.4	51.1	50.7	50.7	51.4	51.5	51.1
2004	50.3	49.6	50.5	50.2	50.6	51.1	49.9	50.1	49.5	49.3	49.6	49.6	50.0
2005	48.8	49.0	49.1	49.3	49.8	50.1	51.3	51.7	51.6	51.9	51.8	51.9	50.5
2006	50.5	50.8	51.2	50.6	50.9	50.9	50.2	50.2	49.9	49.6	50.2	50.5	50.5
2007	49.3	49.7	50.5	50.5	51.0	51.8	51.4	52.1	51.5	50.0	50.8	51.4	50.8
2008	50.0	50.3	50.6	50.6	50.7	50.1	49.8	49.5	49.3	48.1	49.0	48.8	49.7
2009	46.4	46.6	47.5	46.3	46.0	46.7	45.4	45.7	44.6	43.7	44.0	44.0	45.6
2010	43.2	43.6	45.0	44.8	44.7	45.5	44.1	43.1	43.9	43.4	42.3	44.2	44.0
2011	41.3	41.9	42.1	42.9	41.4	42.7	43.6	39.1	42.9	43.0	43.5	43.0	42.3
Financial Activities													
2000	144.0	144.2	145.2	145.4	146.1	148.4	148.7	148.7	147.8	147.1	147.9	149.2	146.9
2001	145.1	146.0	147.0	147.2	148.0	150.0	150.3	150.5	149.2	149.0	149.7	150.5	148.5
2002	148.7	149.2	149.3	149.8	150.6	152.2	152.5	152.8	152.1	152.0	152.6	153.7	151.3
2003	153.1	153.2	154.2	154.7	156.0	157.6	158.5	158.7	157.5	155.5	155.9	156.3	155.9
2004	153.6	153.7	154.7	154.8	155.4	156.1	157.4	157.7	156.4	157.2	157.1	157.8	156.0
2005	156.2	156.6	156.6	157.7	158.2	160.0	160.8	160.9	160.4	159.3	159.3	160.0	158.8
2006	158.5	159.0	159.6	159.6	159.9	161.6	161.2	161.0	159.8	159.1	159.1	160.1	159.9
2007	157.9	158.0	158.3	157.9	158.5	159.5	159.4	158.8	157.3	156.4	155.9	156.4	157.9
2008	153.5	153.9	154.1	153.8	153.9	154.6	154.1	153.6	151.8	151.5	150.4	150.2	153.0
2009	147.5	146.9	146.3	146.7	146.8	147.6	146.9	146.5	145.3	145.1	144.9	145.2	146.3
2010	142.4	141.8	142.5	142.8	143.3	144.9	145.0	144.8	143.9	144.3	144.2	145.1	143.8
2011	142.0	142.0	142.2	142.4	142.6	143.5	144.8	143.4	141.5	142.0	142.7	142.8	142.7

1. Employment by Industry: Maryland, Selected Years, 2000–2011—*Continued*

(Numbers in thousands, not seasonally adjusted)

Industry and year	January	February	March	April	May	June	July	August	September	October	November	December	Annual average
Professional and Business Services													
2000	352.8	357.4	365.4	367.5	369.5	374.6	373.9	377.9	375.4	372.8	373.0	373.1	369.4
2001	363.1	365.5	369.2	372.1	374.6	376.9	376.9	377.9	371.8	370.6	371.7	371.7	371.8
2002	357.3	360.1	364.2	367.2	370.0	372.5	371.9	374.4	371.0	369.4	369.9	369.8	368.1
2003	358.4	356.6	361.6	368.5	370.8	374.5	373.1	375.5	373.7	375.3	374.4	375.8	369.9
2004	364.5	366.6	373.7	375.2	378.4	382.7	383.8	384.3	382.5	384.4	383.3	384.8	378.7
2005	373.9	377.0	382.6	388.4	390.6	393.9	393.5	394.6	394.3	392.8	391.6	391.4	388.7
2006	383.4	386.3	392.7	396.3	397.4	400.9	400.2	400.9	398.5	396.7	395.5	396.1	395.4
2007	385.5	386.9	392.6	396.9	398.2	402.0	401.3	402.9	400.8	400.6	400.5	401.1	397.4
2008	390.3	391.1	394.3	400.4	400.7	402.2	402.6	403.2	399.9	398.2	395.2	392.6	397.6
2009	380.5	378.3	380.6	384.8	384.7	388.5	386.5	387.1	383.7	384.6	383.3	382.5	383.8
2010	372.7	369.4	378.7	387.2	387.3	393.0	392.8	393.1	390.9	394.7	392.2	393.4	387.1
2011	383.4	384.3	388.7	395.3	395.2	400.3	400.4	402.5	401.2	403.1	401.6	398.8	396.2
Education and Health Services													
2000	299.1	302.0	303.9	308.5	308.2	308.2	308.7	308.0	311.9	313.9	315.8	317.6	308.8
2001	310.8	314.4	316.4	318.0	319.1	321.2	317.5	316.7	319.4	323.6	326.3	328.3	319.3
2002	324.1	329.0	330.0	328.9	330.0	329.5	327.9	326.8	329.6	334.2	337.0	337.6	330.4
2003	333.4	335.0	337.3	338.8	339.7	340.5	340.0	340.3	340.5	342.2	343.8	344.6	339.7
2004	342.9	343.4	345.5	345.4	346.5	347.6	349.6	348.2	347.8	350.2	351.9	352.1	347.6
2005	347.5	350.2	351.4	353.5	353.9	353.0	352.0	351.1	354.7	358.8	360.3	361.4	354.0
2006	356.7	359.5	362.4	362.7	363.8	363.7	360.9	360.2	364.5	368.1	370.0	371.7	363.7
2007	367.6	370.1	372.8	372.8	373.6	373.4	371.4	370.6	374.1	376.7	378.2	379.5	373.4
2008	376.1	378.8	380.7	382.8	383.9	382.9	382.2	381.5	385.7	389.9	391.4	392.9	384.1
2009	388.8	391.3	392.8	394.8	395.1	395.0	391.8	390.2	393.6	397.2	398.7	399.6	394.1
2010	396.2	391.8	398.9	401.1	401.2	399.8	398.9	397.0	400.2	403.6	405.0	405.3	399.9
2011	401.7	404.9	406.3	407.9	408.0	405.8	405.2	404.0	411.9	419.8	420.8	421.5	409.8
Leisure and Hospitality													
2000	184.8	184.7	191.0	198.7	206.1	217.9	220.7	219.9	210.5	202.8	199.2	198.2	202.9
2001	186.2	187.6	192.8	199.3	208.3	221.3	221.9	222.1	210.7	205.6	201.5	200.1	204.8
2002	191.4	192.5	199.1	207.1	216.9	228.0	230.1	230.1	220.6	211.8	208.2	205.1	211.7
2003	197.5	194.7	200.3	210.7	220.1	230.9	233.2	233.1	224.6	216.8	212.7	210.5	215.4
2004	200.5	201.0	207.8	215.7	224.2	236.1	238.4	238.9	231.0	222.0	218.0	217.4	220.9
2005	206.8	207.3	212.1	222.6	230.6	244.0	245.5	243.8	235.4	223.6	220.7	218.8	225.9
2006	210.7	210.2	217.4	225.3	234.6	248.8	249.2	249.3	239.5	230.5	226.4	225.6	230.6
2007	216.7	214.7	221.4	229.5	238.6	249.9	252.0	252.5	242.5	233.5	228.7	227.3	233.9
2008	218.2	218.2	224.5	236.2	247.3	254.9	255.2	253.4	241.3	234.8	228.1	225.8	236.5
2009	213.3	212.5	218.1	227.4	240.1	249.5	249.6	248.1	238.7	228.3	221.4	218.6	230.5
2010	209.2	205.0	214.8	226.8	236.6	246.8	248.1	248.8	240.7	231.9	225.6	223.5	229.8
2011	211.8	212.1	220.4	230.1	240.6	250.9	253.7	252.7	240.0	229.5	227.0	226.1	232.9
Other Services													
2000	110.3	111.2	113.0	113.9	114.8	116.7	115.7	115.6	115.4	114.7	114.8	115.4	114.3
2001	108.9	110.0	110.9	110.3	111.9	114.1	113.2	112.8	110.6	110.7	110.7	111.5	111.3
2002	109.9	111.1	112.6	113.4	114.3	116.2	117.5	116.1	114.4	113.9	114.2	114.8	114.0
2003	112.9	113.3	115.1	116.1	116.6	119.0	119.1	116.9	115.3	115.0	114.5	115.3	115.8
2004	111.4	112.3	113.3	116.3	116.8	117.9	118.1	117.1	116.7	116.0	116.1	116.6	115.7
2005	114.9	115.7	116.6	116.6	117.0	118.1	117.2	116.9	116.2	115.2	115.6	116.0	116.3
2006	114.8	115.2	116.2	116.7	117.2	118.6	118.2	117.9	117.2	116.6	116.8	117.5	116.9
2007	116.2	116.2	117.4	117.6	118.3	119.9	119.9	118.9	118.4	118.3	118.6	118.8	118.2
2008	116.6	117.0	117.5	118.5	119.0	120.2	119.7	118.6	118.0	117.4	117.3	117.4	118.1
2009	115.5	114.8	115.4	115.7	116.4	117.7	117.0	116.1	115.5	115.2	115.3	115.8	115.9
2010	113.5	111.9	114.4	114.6	115.2	116.1	115.8	115.4	114.5	114.4	114.5	114.5	114.6
2011	113.1	112.9	113.5	114.1	114.6	116.0	118.4	117.0	115.8	115.4	118.0	118.0	115.6
Government													
2000	441.9	446.8	456.5	455.4	455.3	450.9	436.6	432.4	447.6	456.8	459.3	459.6	449.9
2001	448.2	457.6	460.8	461.8	461.2	454.3	439.8	439.2	454.8	464.8	469.0	469.0	456.7
2002	457.4	467.4	471.9	468.4	469.3	463.8	447.8	447.1	463.5	472.5	474.0	472.7	464.7
2003	459.2	468.4	471.4	470.3	470.1	462.8	444.6	437.9	460.9	467.3	468.2	467.4	462.4
2004	459.2	464.6	469.3	467.9	470.1	460.4	443.5	443.1	456.5	470.4	473.3	471.5	462.5
2005	457.2	466.2	468.0	469.7	472.6	461.3	449.4	449.0	465.7	475.2	479.7	477.9	466.0
2006	459.9	471.9	476.7	477.6	478.6	466.1	453.7	452.2	469.3	480.9	483.2	483.8	471.2
2007	467.4	478.5	484.2	483.1	485.9	473.6	461.9	461.4	475.0	487.2	491.6	491.3	478.4
2008	475.8	488.9	492.9	493.7	494.2	482.6	473.0	472.3	483.5	496.7	500.0	499.3	487.7
2009	481.3	493.9	499.2	502.3	502.3	490.3	479.0	475.6	487.6	504.6	506.6	505.2	494.0
2010	487.1	497.9	505.9	509.0	516.0	504.0	487.3	485.0	496.6	507.9	512.5	509.8	501.6
2011	493.3	508.2	514.1	514.2	513.1	503.5	491.5	485.0	505.0	520.3	520.1	520.5	507.4

2. Average Weekly Hours by Selected Industry: Maryland, 2007–2011

(Not seasonally adjusted)

Industry and year	January	February	March	April	May	June	July	August	September	October	November	December	Annual average
Total Private													
2007	34.4	34.0	34.5	34.9	34.8	34.8	35.0	34.9	35.1	35.0	35.0	35.3	34.8
2008	34.8	34.7	35.0	34.8	34.7	34.9	34.7	34.6	34.6	34.7	34.5	34.1	34.7
2009	34.3	34.5	34.4	34.1	34.3	34.4	34.6	35.0	34.7	34.4	34.6	34.3	34.5
2010	34.6	33.2	34.4	34.5	33.8	33.9	33.9	34.3	34.0	34.0	34.1	34.1	34.1
2011	34.3	34.2	34.3	34.4	34.8	34.6	34.7	34.3	34.3	34.7	34.0	33.9	34.4
Goods-Producing													
2007	38.8	37.3	39.1	39.2	40.1	39.8	39.4	39.6	39.4	39.5	39.1	39.6	39.2
2008	39.2	38.7	39.7	39.7	39.3	39.5	39.3	39.5	39.1	39.3	39.0	38.5	39.2
2009	38.4	38.6	38.6	38.0	38.2	38.0	38.4	38.5	37.6	38.0	37.5	38.0	38.2
2010	37.9	34.8	37.7	38.6	38.8	38.9	38.3	38.8	38.7	38.3	38.5	38.6	38.2
2011	38.5	38.4	38.8	38.9	39.4	39.5	39.1	39.1	38.0	38.8	39.1	39.4	38.9
Mining, Logging, and Construction													
2007	38.9	37.0	39.4	39.9	41.0	40.4	40.1	40.2	39.7	40.2	39.4	40.0	39.7
2008	39.7	38.7	40.0	40.2	39.7	40.1	39.7	39.8	39.3	39.8	38.8	38.0	39.5
2009	37.9	38.0	38.1	37.6	37.8	37.3	37.5	38.0	36.1	36.6	36.1	36.6	37.3
2010	36.5	33.1	36.0	37.8	37.8	38.2	37.3	38.0	37.9	37.3	37.6	37.3	37.1
2011	36.6	37.0	37.2	37.4	38.3	38.9	38.5	38.4	36.7	37.5	38.5	38.6	37.8
Manufacturing													
2007	38.7	37.7	38.6	38.2	38.7	38.9	38.4	38.6	39.0	38.6	38.7	39.0	38.6
2008	38.5	38.7	39.2	39.0	38.8	38.7	38.7	39.0	38.9	38.6	39.2	39.1	38.9
2009	39.1	39.4	39.2	38.6	38.7	39.0	39.7	39.2	39.6	39.8	39.4	39.8	39.3
2010	39.5	36.8	39.8	39.6	40.0	39.9	39.7	39.8	39.7	39.6	39.6	40.3	39.5
2011	40.8	40.2	40.9	40.8	40.8	40.2	40.0	40.0	39.8	40.6	40.0	40.4	40.4
Trade, Transportation, and Utilities													
2007	33.9	33.4	33.7	34.1	34.3	34.3	34.4	34.5	34.3	34.9	34.9	35.3	34.3
2008	34.3	34.1	34.2	34.1	34.1	34.5	34.1	34.0	33.7	33.6	33.8	33.9	34.0
2009	33.4	33.4	33.7	33.5	33.8	33.8	34.2	34.3	35.2	34.6	34.5	33.9	34.0
2010	33.8	31.9	34.2	34.4	34.7	34.9	34.8	34.9	34.3	34.0	33.4	33.9	34.1
2011	33.2	33.0	33.2	33.5	33.9	33.7	33.8	33.3	33.7	33.5	33.7	33.7	33.5
Financial Activities													
2007	36.6	36.4	36.0	36.8	36.4	35.9	36.5	35.9	36.6	36.3	36.0	36.6	36.3
2008	36.2	35.9	36.1	35.9	35.9	36.1	36.0	36.0	36.0	36.3	36.4	35.9	36.1
2009	36.1	36.3	36.0	35.5	35.8	35.8	36.3	36.6	36.4	36.6	36.9	36.2	36.2
2010	36.8	36.1	36.7	36.4	36.6	36.5	36.0	36.5	36.3	36.9	37.2	37.5	36.6
2011	38.4	38.0	38.3	38.4	38.2	38.3	37.8	37.9	39.0	39.7	39.2	39.1	38.5
Professional and Business Services													
2007	36.3	36.2	36.8	37.6	37.2	37.4	37.7	37.4	37.6	36.8	37.1	37.6	37.1
2008	37.0	37.3	37.9	37.4	37.2	37.3	36.7	36.7	36.9	37.2	36.4	36.0	37.0
2009	35.9	36.2	36.0	36.4	36.4	36.8	36.9	37.4	36.4	36.5	36.8	36.4	36.5
2010	36.7	35.6	37.0	36.7	36.4	36.1	35.8	36.5	36.1	36.5	37.0	37.0	36.5
2011	37.8	37.5	37.4	37.5	38.0	37.9	37.8	37.3	37.5	38.2	37.9	37.5	37.7
Education and Health Services													
2007	32.7	32.4	32.9	32.7	32.3	32.7	33.1	32.7	33.1	32.9	33.1	33.3	32.8
2008	33.1	32.8	33.0	33.0	33.2	32.9	33.4	33.3	33.4	33.5	33.6	33.2	33.2
2009	33.5	33.2	33.2	32.8	32.8	33.1	33.1	33.3	33.3	33.3	33.8	33.3	33.2
2010	33.6	33.5	33.2	33.0	33.3	33.2	33.5	33.7	33.2	33.0	33.3	32.9	33.3
2011	32.9	32.7	32.8	32.9	33.1	32.9	33.0	33.0	32.9	33.1	32.8	32.6	32.9
Leisure and Hospitality													
2007	27.0	27.2	27.5	27.6	27.8	27.6	27.8	28.3	28.0	28.0	27.5	27.3	27.6
2008	26.7	27.4	27.3	27.2	26.9	27.2	27.3	27.0	26.9	26.5	25.8	25.7	26.8
2009	25.3	26.1	26.2	25.8	26.7	27.2	27.4	27.5	26.0	25.4	25.7	25.2	26.2
2010	25.4	24.5	26.2	26.7	26.8	27.3	27.9	28.1	27.4	27.0	27.0	26.3	26.8
2011	26.5	27.0	27.1	27.0	27.4	27.3	27.7	27.4	26.3	26.9	26.3	26.2	26.9
Other Services													
2007	30.7	30.1	30.4	31.3	31.3	31.7	31.7	31.4	31.9	31.3	31.2	31.2	31.2
2008	30.6	31.1	31.4	30.7	30.5	30.5	30.5	30.7	30.4	30.7	31.1	30.7	30.7
2009	30.0	30.7	30.9	30.5	30.4	30.9	30.3	31.7	31.9	31.3	31.4	31.3	30.9
2010	31.4	30.6	32.3	33.2	33.9	34.2	33.6	33.5	34.4	34.6	34.1	34.0	33.3
2011	32.9	33.1	33.6	33.4	33.2	34.3	33.8	33.1	33.9	34.0	34.4	34.4	33.7

3. Average Hourly Earnings by Selected Industry: Maryland, 2007–2011

(Dollars, not seasonally adjusted)

Industry and year	January	February	March	April	May	June	July	August	September	October	November	December	Annual average
Total Private													
2007	24.00	24.31	24.14	24.12	23.79	23.76	23.89	23.68	24.09	24.18	24.14	24.45	24.04
2008	24.56	24.65	24.51	24.14	24.13	24.20	24.20	24.35	24.68	24.85	25.09	25.44	24.56
2009	25.23	25.82	25.24	25.32	24.83	25.00	24.99	25.46	25.49	25.57	25.99	26.06	25.42
2010	26.15	26.99	26.22	26.06	26.08	26.08	26.20	26.39	25.96	25.84	25.97	26.23	26.18
2011	26.55	26.43	25.91	25.78	25.79	25.41	25.47	25.35	25.49	25.80	25.75	25.99	25.80
Goods-Producing													
2007	24.27	24.17	23.75	23.95	23.91	23.75	23.74	23.42	23.80	23.74	23.80	24.06	23.86
2008	23.94	24.25	23.89	23.49	23.62	23.71	24.02	23.78	23.96	24.29	24.63	24.83	24.03
2009	24.51	24.27	24.32	24.26	23.98	24.04	23.89	24.21	24.39	24.67	24.81	24.74	24.34
2010	24.93	26.32	25.35	25.32	25.47	25.05	25.30	25.19	25.13	25.34	25.37	25.83	25.37
2011	25.79	25.67	25.34	25.53	25.54	25.40	25.76	25.58	25.70	25.53	25.36	25.76	25.58
Mining, Logging, and Construction													
2007	25.13	25.16	24.02	24.25	24.41	24.17	24.01	23.60	23.99	24.09	24.33	24.28	24.27
2008	24.29	24.96	24.49	24.01	24.12	24.22	24.62	24.31	24.66	24.77	25.19	25.84	24.61
2009	25.48	25.25	25.04	24.94	24.57	24.74	24.49	24.59	24.83	25.39	25.88	26.12	25.10
2010	26.04	27.62	26.72	26.29	26.07	25.92	26.33	26.02	26.13	26.37	26.49	27.35	26.42
2011	27.83	27.71	27.34	27.43	27.51	27.09	27.54	27.25	27.40	27.30	27.18	27.39	27.41
Manufacturing													
2007	23.07	22.85	23.36	23.50	23.14	23.10	23.32	23.14	23.52	23.22	23.01	23.73	23.25
2008	23.45	23.28	23.03	22.74	22.89	22.95	23.15	23.01	22.96	23.60	23.85	23.48	23.20
2009	23.30	23.04	23.41	23.40	23.22	23.16	23.13	23.72	23.86	23.81	23.55	23.14	23.39
2010	23.70	24.97	23.85	24.16	24.76	23.98	24.04	24.16	23.89	24.07	23.97	24.00	24.12
2011	23.55	23.38	23.10	23.33	23.18	23.29	23.50	23.45	23.58	23.35	23.00	23.70	23.37
Trade, Transportation, and Utilities													
2007	18.26	18.24	18.37	18.57	18.32	18.19	18.14	17.99	18.13	18.49	18.19	18.12	18.25
2008	18.41	18.72	18.47	18.31	18.15	17.99	17.97	18.16	18.45	18.57	18.52	18.94	18.39
2009	18.93	18.90	18.97	18.97	19.08	18.98	19.36	19.34	19.45	19.63	20.17	19.82	19.31
2010	20.31	20.96	20.32	20.34	20.09	19.61	19.94	20.19	20.10	19.62	19.55	19.44	20.03
2011	19.58	19.65	19.38	19.36	19.83	19.52	19.63	19.44	19.69	19.80	19.70	19.81	19.62
Financial Activities													
2007	30.61	30.94	30.25	29.80	29.52	29.66	29.25	29.03	29.71	29.23	29.22	29.89	29.76
2008	28.81	28.65	28.80	28.24	27.92	27.78	27.28	26.78	26.98	26.71	29.85	30.24	28.17
2009	28.97	29.12	28.68	28.03	28.12	27.57	28.69	30.10	29.02	28.86	29.52	28.83	28.80
2010	28.23	28.34	28.48	28.05	28.08	27.16	27.39	28.25	26.74	26.68	27.46	27.21	27.67
2011	26.61	26.72	26.28	25.52	26.04	26.15	25.94	26.30	25.40	26.12	25.88	27.09	26.17
Professional and Business Services													
2007	29.10	29.90	29.44	29.25	29.09	29.50	29.70	29.68	30.26	29.66	29.98	30.49	29.67
2008	30.61	30.83	30.59	30.11	30.52	31.02	31.03	31.38	31.94	32.13	32.27	33.00	31.28
2009	32.44	32.72	32.98	32.82	32.78	33.09	32.84	33.81	33.62	33.16	33.98	33.69	33.16
2010	33.43	34.78	33.54	33.68	34.44	33.77	33.71	34.30	33.97	33.82	34.46	35.06	34.08
2011	35.46	34.94	34.39	34.13	33.96	33.51	33.74	33.26	33.39	34.13	33.48	34.00	34.02
Education and Health Services													
2007	25.35	25.53	25.57	25.31	24.94	25.16	25.49	25.18	25.05	25.91	25.55	25.93	25.42
2008	26.14	25.84	25.84	25.63	25.33	25.74	25.93	26.35	26.54	26.36	26.18	26.57	26.04
2009	26.27	26.12	25.91	25.90	25.69	26.08	26.03	26.03	26.11	26.15	25.78	25.76	25.99
2010	25.73	25.81	25.75	25.89	25.73	25.84	26.09	25.46	25.37	25.54	25.22	25.87	25.69
2011	25.87	26.02	25.87	26.20	26.34	26.46	26.58	26.45	26.62	26.80	26.71	26.90	26.41
Leisure and Hospitality													
2007	17.13	17.53	17.44	17.53	17.19	16.89	16.87	16.73	17.33	17.41	17.62	17.61	17.26
2008	17.29	16.99	16.74	16.31	16.73	16.14	15.83	15.53	15.56	15.45	15.24	14.98	16.06
2009	14.62	14.71	14.43	14.95	14.49	14.10	14.22	13.96	14.34	14.66	14.98	15.37	14.54
2010	15.22	15.69	15.16	14.88	14.69	14.27	13.96	13.87	14.45	14.88	15.11	15.70	14.77
2011	15.55	15.63	15.33	15.14	14.94	14.57	14.28	14.18	14.43	14.55	15.10	14.99	14.86
Other Services													
2007	20.56	21.36	21.52	21.42	21.21	20.94	20.74	20.69	20.96	20.54	20.96	21.36	21.02
2008	20.76	20.35	20.05	20.17	19.84	19.89	19.80	20.25	20.20	20.43	20.73	21.00	20.30
2009	20.50	20.44	20.62	21.13	21.55	21.11	21.68	21.69	22.50	22.44	22.76	22.72	21.60
2010	22.39	22.62	22.55	21.70	21.73	21.60	22.06	21.44	21.29	21.40	22.14	22.47	21.94
2011	22.70	22.23	22.11	21.90	21.82	20.83	20.82	21.03	20.91	20.99	19.94	20.20	21.27

4. Average Weekly Earnings by Selected Industry: Maryland, 2007–2011

(Dollars, not seasonally adjusted)

Industry and year	January	February	March	April	May	June	July	August	September	October	November	December	Annual average
Total Private													
2007	825.60	826.54	832.83	841.79	827.89	826.85	836.15	826.43	845.56	846.30	844.90	863.09	837.14
2008	854.69	855.36	857.85	840.07	837.31	844.58	839.74	842.51	853.93	862.30	865.61	867.50	851.61
2009	865.39	890.79	868.26	863.41	851.67	860.00	864.65	891.10	884.50	879.61	899.25	893.86	875.84
2010	904.79	896.07	901.97	899.07	881.50	884.11	888.18	905.18	882.64	878.56	885.58	894.44	891.99
2011	910.67	903.91	888.71	886.83	897.49	879.19	883.81	869.51	874.31	895.26	875.50	881.06	887.11
Goods-Producing													
2007	941.68	901.54	928.63	938.84	958.79	945.25	935.36	927.43	937.72	937.73	930.58	952.78	936.35
2008	938.45	938.48	948.43	932.55	928.27	936.55	943.99	939.31	936.84	954.60	960.57	955.96	942.62
2009	941.18	936.82	938.75	921.88	916.04	913.52	917.38	932.09	917.06	937.46	930.38	940.12	928.95
2010	944.85	915.94	955.70	977.35	988.24	974.45	968.99	977.37	972.53	970.52	976.75	997.04	968.57
2011	992.92	985.73	983.19	993.12	1,006.28	1,003.30	1,007.22	1,000.18	976.60	990.56	991.58	1,014.94	995.79
Mining, Logging, and Construction													
2007	977.56	930.92	946.39	967.58	1,000.81	976.47	962.80	948.72	952.40	968.42	958.60	971.20	963.61
2008	964.31	965.95	979.60	965.20	957.56	971.22	977.41	967.54	969.14	985.85	977.37	981.92	971.84
2009	965.69	959.50	954.02	937.74	928.75	922.80	918.38	934.42	896.36	929.27	934.27	955.99	936.39
2010	950.46	914.22	961.92	993.76	985.45	990.14	982.11	988.76	990.33	983.60	996.02	1,020.16	980.52
2011	1,018.58	1,025.27	1,017.05	1,025.88	1,053.63	1,053.80	1,060.29	1,046.40	1,005.58	1,023.75	1,046.43	1,057.25	1,036.32
Manufacturing													
2007	892.81	861.45	901.70	897.70	895.52	898.59	895.49	893.20	917.28	896.29	890.49	925.47	897.16
2008	902.83	900.94	902.78	886.86	888.13	888.17	895.91	897.39	893.14	910.96	934.92	918.07	901.54
2009	911.03	907.78	917.67	903.24	898.61	903.24	918.26	929.82	944.86	947.64	927.87	920.97	919.24
2010	936.15	918.90	949.23	956.74	990.40	956.80	954.39	961.57	948.43	953.17	949.21	967.20	953.44
2011	960.84	939.88	944.79	951.86	945.74	936.26	940.00	938.00	938.48	948.01	920.00	957.48	943.38
Trade, Transportation, and Utilities													
2007	619.01	609.22	619.07	633.24	628.38	623.92	624.02	620.66	621.86	645.30	634.83	639.64	626.67
2008	631.46	638.35	631.67	624.37	618.92	620.66	612.78	617.44	621.77	623.95	625.98	642.07	625.80
2009	632.26	631.26	639.29	635.50	644.90	641.52	662.11	663.36	684.64	679.20	695.87	671.90	656.85
2010	686.48	668.62	694.94	699.70	697.12	684.39	693.91	704.63	689.43	667.08	652.97	659.02	683.04
2011	650.06	648.45	643.42	648.56	672.24	657.82	663.49	647.35	663.55	663.30	663.89	667.60	657.57
Financial Activities													
2007	1,120.33	1,126.22	1,089.00	1,096.64	1,074.53	1,064.79	1,067.63	1,042.18	1,087.39	1,061.05	1,051.92	1,093.97	1,081.30
2008	1,042.92	1,028.54	1,039.68	1,013.82	1,002.33	1,002.86	982.08	971.28	964.08	969.57	1,086.54	1,085.62	1,015.63
2009	1,045.82	1,057.06	1,032.48	995.07	1,006.70	987.01	1,041.45	1,101.66	1,056.33	1,056.28	1,089.29	1,043.65	1,042.58
2010	1,038.86	1,023.07	1,045.22	1,021.02	1,027.73	991.34	986.04	1,031.13	970.66	984.49	1,021.51	1,020.38	1,013.43
2011	1,021.82	1,015.36	1,006.52	979.97	994.73	1,001.55	980.53	996.77	990.60	1,036.96	1,014.50	1,059.22	1,008.23
Professional and Business Services													
2007	1,056.33	1,082.38	1,083.39	1,099.80	1,082.15	1,103.30	1,119.69	1,110.03	1,137.78	1,091.49	1,112.26	1,146.42	1,102.34
2008	1,132.57	1,149.96	1,159.36	1,126.11	1,135.34	1,157.05	1,138.80	1,151.65	1,178.59	1,195.24	1,174.63	1,188.00	1,157.24
2009	1,164.60	1,184.46	1,187.28	1,194.65	1,203.03	1,217.71	1,211.80	1,264.49	1,223.77	1,210.34	1,250.46	1,226.32	1,211.72
2010	1,226.88	1,238.17	1,240.98	1,236.06	1,253.62	1,219.10	1,206.82	1,251.95	1,226.32	1,234.43	1,275.02	1,297.22	1,242.37
2011	1,340.39	1,310.25	1,286.19	1,279.88	1,290.48	1,270.03	1,275.37	1,240.60	1,252.13	1,303.77	1,268.89	1,275.00	1,282.39
Education and Health Services													
2007	828.95	827.17	841.25	827.64	805.56	822.73	843.72	823.39	829.16	852.44	845.71	863.47	834.34
2008	865.23	847.55	852.72	845.79	840.96	846.85	866.06	877.46	886.44	883.06	879.65	882.12	864.61
2009	880.05	867.18	860.21	849.52	842.63	863.25	861.59	866.80	869.46	870.80	871.36	857.81	863.28
2010	864.53	864.64	854.90	854.37	856.81	857.89	874.02	858.00	842.28	842.82	839.83	851.12	854.94
2011	851.12	850.85	848.54	861.98	871.85	870.53	877.14	872.85	875.80	887.08	876.09	876.94	868.52
Leisure and Hospitality													
2007	462.51	476.82	479.60	483.83	477.88	466.16	468.99	473.46	485.24	487.48	484.55	480.75	477.21
2008	461.64	465.53	457.00	443.63	450.04	439.01	432.16	419.31	418.56	409.43	393.19	384.99	431.02
2009	369.89	383.93	378.07	385.71	386.88	383.52	389.63	383.90	372.84	372.36	384.99	387.32	381.67
2010	386.59	384.41	397.19	397.30	393.69	389.57	389.48	389.75	395.93	401.76	407.97	412.91	395.53
2011	412.08	422.01	415.44	408.78	409.36	397.76	395.56	388.53	379.51	391.40	397.13	392.74	400.41
Other Services													
2007	631.19	642.94	654.21	670.45	663.87	663.80	657.46	649.67	668.62	642.90	653.95	666.43	655.52
2008	635.26	632.89	629.57	619.22	605.12	606.65	603.90	621.68	618.03	627.20	644.70	644.70	623.97
2009	615.00	627.51	637.16	644.47	655.12	652.30	656.90	687.57	717.75	702.37	714.66	711.14	668.34
2010	703.05	692.17	728.37	720.44	736.65	738.72	741.22	718.24	732.38	740.44	754.97	763.98	731.02
2011	746.83	735.81	742.90	731.46	724.42	714.47	703.72	696.09	708.85	713.66	685.94	694.88	716.27

MASSACHUSETTS
At a Glance

Population:
    2000 census: 6,349,364
    2010 census: 6,547,629
    2011 estimate: 6,587,536

Percent change in population:
    2000–2010: 3.1%
    2010–2011: 0.6%

Percent change in total nonfarm employment:
    2000–2010: -4.2%
    2010–2011: 0.6%

Industry with the largest growth in employment, 2000–2011 (thousands):
    Education and Health Services, 124.0

Industry with the largest decline or smallest growth in employment, 2000–2011 (thousands):
    Manufacturing, -148.9

Civilian labor force:
    2000: 3,365,573
    2010: 3,469,270
    2011: 3,456,442

Unemployment rate and rank among states (lowest to highest):
    2000: 2.7%, 3rd
    2010: 8.5%, 23rd
    2011: 7.4%, 18th

Over-the-year change in unemployment rates:
    2010–2011: -0.9%

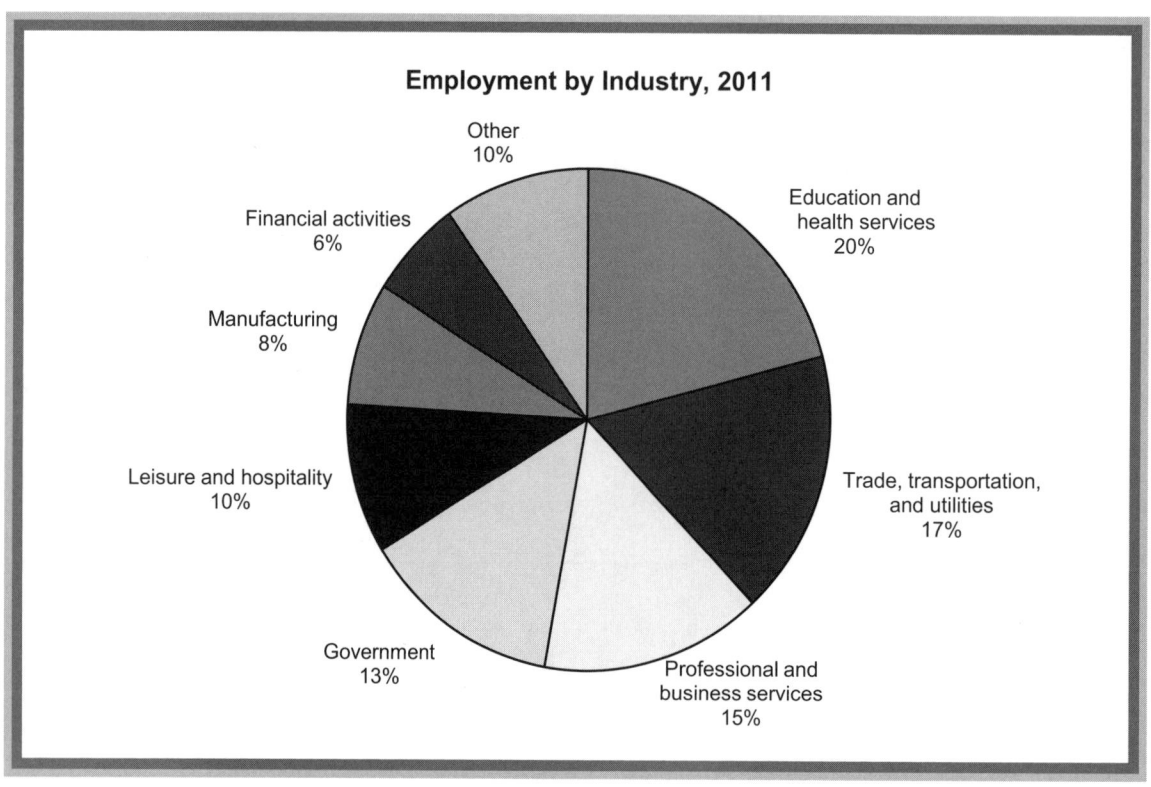

Employment by Industry, 2011

1. Employment by Industry: Massachusetts, Selected Years, 2000–2011

(Numbers in thousands, not seasonally adjusted)

Industry and year	January	February	March	April	May	June	July	August	September	October	November	December	Annual average
Total Nonfarm													
2000	3,221.4	3,240.7	3,263.5	3,308.1	3,332.3	3,362.9	3,334.5	3,325.1	3,365.2	3,385.2	3,398.3	3,413.9	3,329.3
2001	3,317.0	3,326.5	3,335.4	3,356.2	3,373.9	3,390.0	3,330.3	3,322.3	3,335.7	3,331.8	3,325.8	3,326.2	3,339.3
2002	3,217.6	3,216.2	3,235.5	3,261.5	3,284.1	3,298.0	3,258.0	3,249.2	3,272.3	3,272.6	3,274.2	3,272.1	3,259.3
2003	3,158.8	3,148.5	3,161.2	3,195.7	3,222.1	3,233.5	3,198.0	3,188.4	3,218.1	3,219.2	3,221.2	3,215.9	3,198.4
2004	3,113.0	3,123.0	3,145.8	3,188.7	3,212.0	3,232.6	3,207.8	3,194.9	3,222.4	3,230.3	3,233.0	3,235.8	3,194.9
2005	3,125.8	3,142.6	3,150.7	3,204.9	3,227.3	3,248.4	3,224.3	3,214.9	3,243.0	3,243.9	3,254.6	3,258.3	3,211.6
2006	3,158.0	3,169.0	3,189.5	3,233.2	3,256.1	3,286.0	3,258.0	3,249.7	3,274.1	3,285.3	3,290.8	3,295.8	3,245.5
2007	3,198.5	3,206.1	3,221.1	3,262.9	3,297.1	3,327.3	3,294.5	3,287.5	3,305.6	3,318.4	3,325.0	3,322.3	3,280.5
2008	3,226.2	3,238.7	3,254.1	3,293.4	3,320.2	3,336.5	3,308.0	3,296.0	3,308.4	3,317.8	3,298.5	3,282.4	3,290.0
2009	3,158.7	3,157.7	3,154.4	3,186.1	3,202.1	3,208.8	3,176.8	3,161.3	3,183.4	3,199.0	3,192.5	3,194.9	3,181.3
2010	3,115.1	3,117.8	3,130.4	3,183.7	3,218.5	3,220.8	3,204.5	3,189.2	3,207.4	3,235.7	3,233.0	3,233.3	3,190.8
2011	3,135.2	3,149.0	3,164.3	3,215.0	3,234.2	3,247.8	3,234.2	3,216.6	3,220.2	3,245.4	3,241.2	3,224.5	3,210.6
Total Private													
2000	2,789.9	2,799.9	2,823.0	2,863.3	2,879.6	2,923.9	2,927.7	2,925.9	2,929.1	2,942.6	2,952.7	2,969.4	2,893.9
2001	2,877.9	2,878.5	2,886.9	2,906.5	2,922.3	2,949.1	2,921.4	2,917.8	2,893.2	2,883.0	2,875.7	2,875.3	2,899.0
2002	2,776.2	2,767.3	2,785.9	2,814.2	2,836.3	2,860.5	2,851.1	2,847.4	2,834.7	2,835.9	2,834.4	2,834.2	2,823.2
2003	2,729.1	2,712.0	2,724.6	2,759.1	2,785.1	2,805.4	2,800.8	2,797.3	2,787.8	2,790.6	2,791.7	2,786.9	2,772.5
2004	2,693.9	2,694.0	2,715.6	2,756.9	2,779.9	2,808.4	2,816.8	2,811.1	2,798.1	2,800.9	2,801.1	2,804.8	2,773.5
2005	2,704.5	2,709.2	2,717.4	2,770.4	2,791.3	2,821.4	2,829.3	2,827.1	2,817.0	2,809.9	2,817.9	2,823.6	2,786.6
2006	2,732.9	2,733.2	2,752.6	2,795.2	2,816.2	2,853.7	2,858.4	2,857.9	2,844.1	2,847.3	2,850.0	2,856.6	2,816.5
2007	2,768.6	2,766.4	2,780.3	2,820.9	2,852.4	2,891.4	2,893.0	2,892.6	2,871.9	2,876.6	2,881.0	2,879.1	2,847.9
2008	2,792.9	2,793.8	2,808.5	2,846.1	2,871.5	2,897.8	2,901.6	2,896.5	2,870.8	2,870.7	2,850.3	2,835.6	2,853.0
2009	2,722.9	2,709.5	2,706.8	2,733.1	2,751.9	2,769.8	2,771.3	2,763.7	2,748.8	2,751.7	2,745.5	2,745.3	2,743.4
2010	2,676.5	2,671.6	2,683.1	2,732.3	2,758.3	2,778.7	2,798.7	2,791.6	2,770.7	2,788.8	2,782.4	2,784.0	2,751.4
2011	2,702.2	2,703.7	2,718.6	2,769.2	2,786.3	2,811.5	2,831.0	2,821.3	2,787.5	2,802.3	2,797.2	2,781.6	2,776.0
Goods-Producing													
2000	512.6	510.6	517.4	527.6	532.5	543.0	541.1	545.4	541.3	544.8	545.0	543.7	533.8
2001	533.6	531.0	530.4	536.1	539.5	542.3	530.5	531.8	527.2	522.2	515.3	509.7	529.1
2002	490.0	483.7	485.9	491.6	497.4	501.2	494.2	496.1	493.4	491.5	488.7	481.3	491.3
2003	462.9	453.4	454.4	463.5	469.5	472.7	467.0	468.6	465.4	462.5	461.1	454.1	462.9
2004	436.7	433.5	439.5	450.5	457.8	464.3	462.6	465.0	461.9	457.9	456.7	452.4	453.2
2005	433.9	430.1	430.6	443.3	450.4	456.4	456.0	457.1	455.4	451.2	450.7	446.7	446.8
2006	431.1	428.3	430.8	441.4	446.1	452.5	451.1	451.9	449.0	445.9	442.7	439.8	442.6
2007	425.0	419.4	421.0	428.2	437.3	445.0	443.3	444.6	441.6	437.9	435.8	430.1	434.1
2008	414.3	410.0	412.4	420.0	426.3	431.1	430.7	430.6	425.8	421.6	414.6	405.1	420.2
2009	380.8	372.0	368.2	372.1	374.1	377.4	376.2	374.3	370.9	368.8	366.3	362.2	371.9
2010	348.9	344.0	346.6	356.2	362.9	369.0	372.6	371.8	369.3	369.6	367.9	363.7	361.9
2011	349.5	345.8	348.4	359.5	365.8	372.5	373.4	374.0	369.5	370.7	367.2	361.5	363.2
Mining and Logging													
2000	1.2	1.2	1.3	1.5	1.5	1.5	1.5	1.5	1.5	1.5	1.5	1.4	1.4
2001	1.3	1.3	1.3	1.5	1.6	1.6	1.6	1.6	1.6	1.6	1.6	1.6	1.5
2002	1.3	1.3	1.4	1.6	1.7	1.7	1.7	1.7	1.8	1.8	1.8	1.7	1.6
2003	1.5	1.5	1.5	1.7	1.8	1.9	1.9	1.9	2.0	2.0	2.0	1.9	1.8
2004	1.7	1.6	1.6	1.9	2.0	2.0	2.1	2.1	2.0	2.0	2.0	2.0	1.9
2005	1.8	1.7	1.7	2.0	2.1	2.1	2.1	2.1	2.1	2.0	2.0	1.8	2.0
2006	1.6	1.6	1.7	1.8	1.9	1.9	2.0	1.9	1.9	1.9	1.9	1.7	1.8
2007	1.4	1.3	1.4	1.5	1.7	1.8	1.7	1.7	1.7	1.6	1.6	1.5	1.6
2008	1.2	1.2	1.2	1.4	1.5	1.5	1.5	1.4	1.4	1.4	1.4	1.3	1.4
2009	1.1	1.1	1.1	1.3	1.4	1.4	1.4	1.4	1.4	1.4	1.4	1.3	1.3
2010	1.0	1.0	1.0	1.2	1.3	1.3	1.2	1.2	1.2	1.1	1.1	1.1	1.1
2011	0.9	0.9	0.9	1.1	1.2	1.2	1.2	1.2	1.2	1.1	1.1	1.1	1.1
Construction													
2000	112.5	110.1	115.6	124.5	129.0	134.6	138.3	139.4	137.7	137.6	136.9	134.0	129.2
2001	124.5	123.3	125.4	135.6	142.1	146.4	147.9	148.4	146.1	145.5	143.5	139.9	139.1
2002	128.4	125.8	128.8	137.8	144.3	147.0	148.6	149.4	146.6	147.5	145.9	139.3	140.8
2003	126.9	120.6	122.7	133.2	140.5	143.5	145.5	146.0	143.7	142.2	141.0	135.8	136.8
2004	122.5	120.1	124.8	134.6	141.8	146.3	148.6	148.8	146.5	144.6	143.4	139.2	138.4
2005	124.5	120.7	122.3	135.3	141.9	146.4	150.3	150.7	149.3	145.8	145.8	141.4	139.5
2006	129.2	126.6	129.3	140.1	144.4	148.3	150.2	150.4	147.7	145.4	142.5	138.7	141.1
2007	126.7	121.5	123.8	131.8	140.2	145.4	147.5	147.6	145.7	143.9	141.8	135.9	137.7
2008	123.4	120.4	123.1	130.7	136.7	139.9	142.4	141.6	138.7	136.1	131.7	124.8	132.5
2009	109.0	104.3	103.6	110.1	114.0	116.8	118.1	117.2	114.6	113.1	110.4	106.0	111.4
2010	96.1	92.3	94.5	103.3	108.7	112.8	116.3	115.5	114.0	113.2	111.5	107.3	107.1
2011	96.8	94.0	95.8	105.3	111.0	115.7	117.1	117.0	113.2	113.8	110.8	104.2	107.9
Manufacturing													
2000	398.9	399.3	400.5	401.6	402.0	406.9	401.3	404.5	402.1	405.7	406.6	408.3	403.1
2001	407.8	406.4	403.7	399.0	395.8	394.3	381.0	381.8	379.5	375.1	370.2	368.2	388.6
2002	360.3	356.6	355.7	352.2	351.4	352.5	343.9	345.0	345.0	342.2	341.0	340.3	348.8
2003	334.5	331.3	330.2	328.6	327.2	327.3	319.6	320.7	319.7	318.3	318.1	316.4	324.3
2004	312.5	311.8	313.1	314.0	314.0	316.0	311.9	314.1	313.4	311.3	311.3	311.2	312.9
2005	307.6	307.7	306.6	306.0	306.4	307.9	303.6	304.3	304.0	303.4	302.9	303.5	305.3
2006	300.3	300.1	299.8	299.5	299.8	302.3	298.9	299.6	299.4	298.6	298.3	299.4	299.7
2007	296.9	296.6	295.8	294.9	295.4	297.8	294.1	295.3	294.2	292.4	292.4	292.7	294.9
2008	289.7	288.4	288.1	287.9	288.1	289.7	286.8	287.6	285.7	284.1	281.5	279.0	286.4
2009	270.7	266.6	263.5	260.7	258.7	259.2	256.7	255.7	254.9	254.3	254.5	254.9	259.2
2010	251.8	250.7	251.1	251.7	252.9	254.9	255.1	255.1	254.1	255.3	255.3	255.3	253.6
2011	251.8	250.9	251.7	253.1	253.6	255.6	255.1	255.8	255.1	255.8	255.3	256.2	254.2

1. Employment by Industry: Massachusetts, Selected Years, 2000–2011—*Continued*

(Numbers in thousands, not seasonally adjusted)

Industry and year	January	February	March	April	May	June	July	August	September	October	November	December	Annual average
Service-Providing													
2000	2,708.8	2,730.1	2,746.1	2,780.5	2,799.8	2,819.9	2,793.4	2,779.7	2,823.9	2,840.4	2,853.3	2,870.2	2,795.5
2001	2,783.4	2,795.5	2,805.0	2,820.1	2,834.4	2,847.7	2,799.8	2,790.5	2,808.5	2,809.6	2,810.5	2,816.5	2,810.1
2002	2,727.6	2,732.5	2,749.6	2,769.9	2,786.7	2,796.8	2,763.8	2,753.1	2,778.9	2,781.1	2,785.5	2,790.8	2,768.0
2003	2,695.9	2,695.1	2,706.8	2,732.2	2,752.6	2,760.8	2,731.0	2,719.8	2,752.7	2,756.7	2,760.1	2,761.8	2,735.5
2004	2,676.3	2,689.5	2,706.3	2,738.2	2,754.2	2,768.3	2,745.2	2,729.9	2,760.5	2,772.4	2,776.3	2,783.4	2,741.7
2005	2,691.9	2,712.5	2,720.1	2,761.6	2,776.9	2,792.0	2,768.3	2,757.8	2,787.6	2,792.7	2,803.9	2,811.6	2,764.7
2006	2,726.9	2,740.7	2,758.7	2,791.8	2,810.0	2,833.5	2,806.9	2,797.8	2,825.1	2,839.4	2,848.1	2,856.0	2,802.9
2007	2,773.5	2,786.7	2,800.1	2,834.7	2,859.8	2,882.3	2,851.2	2,842.9	2,864.0	2,880.5	2,889.2	2,892.2	2,846.4
2008	2,811.9	2,828.7	2,841.7	2,873.4	2,893.9	2,905.4	2,877.3	2,865.4	2,882.6	2,896.2	2,883.9	2,877.3	2,869.8
2009	2,777.9	2,785.7	2,786.2	2,814.0	2,828.0	2,831.4	2,800.6	2,787.0	2,812.5	2,830.2	2,826.2	2,832.7	2,809.4
2010	2,766.2	2,773.8	2,783.8	2,827.5	2,855.6	2,851.8	2,831.9	2,817.4	2,838.1	2,866.1	2,865.1	2,869.6	2,828.9
2011	2,785.7	2,803.2	2,815.9	2,855.5	2,868.4	2,875.3	2,860.8	2,842.6	2,850.7	2,874.7	2,874.0	2,863.0	2,847.5
Trade, Transportation, and Utilities													
2000	591.3	584.4	585.5	587.1	590.5	599.2	592.1	592.1	595.6	602.0	613.9	627.6	596.8
2001	595.1	584.9	585.4	587.4	591.1	600.3	589.7	588.3	588.2	589.7	599.9	607.0	592.3
2002	577.4	567.4	569.5	572.3	577.4	586.5	580.5	578.1	579.6	581.0	589.3	598.8	579.8
2003	568.8	560.2	562.2	566.2	571.6	579.6	572.6	571.7	574.2	578.2	587.2	593.5	573.8
2004	568.2	561.4	563.0	564.4	569.4	577.2	571.4	569.1	568.7	575.6	584.2	593.0	572.1
2005	565.2	559.8	559.0	563.7	568.2	575.4	569.6	569.4	568.5	570.9	579.9	590.5	570.0
2006	566.5	555.3	558.0	562.6	566.8	575.1	569.4	569.8	570.4	573.9	584.1	593.3	570.4
2007	567.3	557.2	558.8	560.7	568.5	577.5	571.1	569.3	568.9	574.1	585.7	592.2	570.9
2008	570.9	558.9	560.2	563.1	568.8	576.1	570.2	569.2	566.8	568.6	571.7	576.7	568.4
2009	547.4	536.7	533.1	533.1	539.3	547.4	539.8	538.6	539.7	544.0	550.8	556.9	542.2
2010	537.5	528.5	529.2	535.7	542.2	549.1	546.0	545.7	542.2	549.2	556.1	565.6	543.9
2011	542.3	535.3	535.3	541.3	545.7	552.7	551.0	553.3	548.2	554.0	560.5	568.4	549.0
Wholesale Trade													
2000	137.1	137.1	137.9	138.4	138.9	140.7	139.6	139.6	139.7	140.7	141.3	143.0	139.5
2001	141.5	141.6	142.0	142.5	142.3	143.3	142.4	142.0	140.8	140.1	139.8	139.9	141.5
2002	136.4	135.7	136.2	136.0	136.5	137.7	136.9	136.6	135.8	135.4	135.5	136.3	136.3
2003	135.0	134.5	134.6	134.6	134.9	135.7	135.8	135.5	134.6	134.7	135.3	135.8	135.1
2004	133.6	133.6	134.7	134.3	134.1	135.0	134.4	133.9	132.7	132.6	132.5	132.7	133.7
2005	131.4	131.2	131.1	132.1	133.1	134.2	134.6	135.0	134.6	135.3	136.1	136.8	133.8
2006	134.9	134.5	135.0	136.2	136.6	138.1	138.3	138.7	137.9	138.1	138.2	138.8	137.1
2007	136.7	136.4	136.9	136.9	137.5	139.1	139.1	138.9	137.8	138.4	138.3	138.5	137.9
2008	137.0	135.9	136.3	136.8	137.1	138.1	137.6	136.8	135.6	134.9	134.0	133.6	136.1
2009	130.0	128.5	127.7	127.2	127.0	127.5	126.6	125.8	124.4	124.2	123.5	123.2	126.3
2010	121.4	120.9	121.1	121.6	122.6	123.5	123.9	123.7	122.4	123.3	123.1	123.1	122.6
2011	121.5	121.4	121.2	122.4	122.8	123.4	124.4	125.3	123.6	123.5	123.5	123.8	123.1
Retail Trade													
2000	361.8	354.9	355.4	354.0	356.4	362.3	360.0	360.2	359.7	364.2	376.4	387.9	362.8
2001	360.9	350.7	351.0	351.7	354.9	361.9	357.2	357.2	354.1	357.2	369.7	378.0	358.7
2002	354.8	346.0	347.8	349.5	353.2	360.1	359.3	358.0	355.5	356.6	365.9	375.4	356.8
2003	348.4	341.1	342.7	346.5	350.7	357.3	354.9	355.1	353.3	357.4	366.2	372.4	353.8
2004	352.2	345.8	346.1	346.7	350.9	357.1	356.2	355.4	352.2	357.7	367.1	376.1	355.3
2005	352.3	347.2	346.5	349.5	352.2	357.3	355.1	355.4	351.0	353.4	361.7	370.3	354.3
2006	351.1	340.5	342.3	344.9	347.4	352.5	350.4	350.6	346.5	350.4	360.8	368.1	350.5
2007	347.3	338.1	338.8	340.3	346.2	352.0	350.2	350.2	349.3	349.5	361.7	366.8	348.8
2008	349.8	339.5	340.0	341.8	345.8	351.1	350.4	351.1	344.7	348.0	353.0	357.3	347.7
2009	335.7	327.3	324.6	325.1	330.4	336.9	334.7	335.4	332.1	336.5	344.2	348.9	334.3
2010	334.6	326.6	327.1	331.8	335.9	340.8	341.8	342.8	336.1	341.8	349.2	356.2	338.7
2011	338.7	332.0	331.9	336.0	338.9	343.7	344.2	344.8	338.7	344.2	351.6	357.2	341.8
Transportation and Utilities													
2000	92.4	92.4	92.2	94.7	95.2	96.2	92.5	92.3	96.2	97.1	96.2	96.7	94.5
2001	92.7	92.6	92.4	93.2	93.9	95.1	90.1	89.1	93.3	92.4	90.4	89.1	92.0
2002	86.2	85.7	85.5	86.8	87.7	88.7	84.3	83.5	88.3	89.0	87.9	87.1	86.7
2003	85.4	84.6	84.9	85.1	86.0	86.6	81.9	81.1	86.3	86.1	85.7	85.3	84.9
2004	82.4	82.0	82.2	83.4	84.4	85.1	80.8	79.8	83.8	85.3	84.6	84.2	83.2
2005	81.5	81.4	81.4	82.1	82.9	83.9	79.9	79.0	82.9	82.2	82.1	83.4	81.9
2006	80.5	80.3	80.7	81.5	82.8	84.5	80.7	80.5	86.0	85.4	85.1	86.4	82.9
2007	83.3	82.7	83.1	83.5	84.8	86.4	81.8	81.1	86.3	86.2	85.7	86.9	84.3
2008	84.1	83.5	83.9	84.5	85.9	86.9	82.2	81.3	86.5	85.7	84.7	85.8	84.6
2009	81.7	80.9	80.8	80.8	81.9	83.0	78.5	77.4	83.2	83.3	83.1	84.8	81.6
2010	81.5	81.0	81.0	82.3	83.7	84.8	80.3	79.2	83.7	84.1	83.8	86.3	82.6
2011	82.1	81.9	82.2	82.9	84.0	85.6	82.4	83.2	85.9	86.3	85.4	87.4	84.1
Information													
2000	104.1	105.2	106.8	108.6	110.4	112.7	115.4	107.3	115.1	115.0	115.9	116.7	111.1
2001	116.4	116.2	115.8	115.0	113.8	113.4	111.6	110.5	108.0	106.1	105.4	104.7	111.4
2002	103.5	102.7	102.5	100.4	100.0	99.9	99.5	98.8	96.9	96.9	96.7	96.9	99.6
2003	93.7	93.1	93.0	91.9	91.7	92.4	91.0	90.9	89.7	89.3	89.2	89.2	91.3
2004	87.4	86.8	87.5	86.8	87.2	87.8	87.8	87.7	86.9	87.0	87.6	87.7	87.4
2005	86.5	86.7	86.7	86.4	86.6	87.3	88.0	87.6	86.9	86.2	86.6	87.1	86.9
2006	86.5	86.5	86.5	85.9	86.4	87.3	87.1	87.5	86.5	87.0	87.4	88.0	86.9
2007	86.4	86.7	87.6	88.2	87.9	88.9	89.8	89.9	89.9	88.8	88.8	89.4	88.5
2008	87.7	88.7	89.4	90.7	90.6	90.5	89.7	89.5	88.8	87.7	87.6	87.8	89.1
2009	86.8	85.4	85.5	85.2	85.1	85.8	85.2	86.0	87.0	86.0	86.1	85.9	85.8
2010	84.8	84.8	85.0	85.2	85.7	86.7	85.8	85.4	84.7	83.6	83.8	84.3	85.0
2011	83.3	83.4	83.8	83.5	83.9	85.0	84.6	78.3	83.3	82.3	82.4	81.9	83.0

1. Employment by Industry: Massachusetts, Selected Years, 2000–2011—*Continued*

(Numbers in thousands, not seasonally adjusted)

Industry and year	January	February	March	April	May	June	July	August	September	October	November	December	Annual average
Financial Activities													
2000	224.7	224.0	224.6	225.7	226.0	230.0	230.3	230.6	229.0	229.5	230.0	232.4	228.1
2001	228.4	228.7	229.9	229.7	229.7	233.1	234.1	233.7	230.5	229.4	229.7	230.6	230.6
2002	230.2	228.9	228.3	226.8	227.2	229.7	230.8	230.3	226.9	226.4	225.6	226.4	228.1
2003	224.7	223.2	223.5	223.5	224.0	226.2	226.5	226.4	222.5	221.1	221.0	221.6	223.7
2004	218.8	218.6	218.9	219.3	219.6	222.2	223.3	222.6	219.8	217.9	217.4	218.5	219.7
2005	217.5	217.1	217.6	218.2	219.6	222.9	225.6	225.9	223.7	222.0	222.7	224.4	221.4
2006	220.6	220.4	220.8	221.5	222.8	225.8	227.9	227.4	225.0	224.2	224.3	225.9	223.9
2007	223.9	223.8	223.8	223.9	224.6	227.3	227.9	227.6	223.7	222.4	221.8	222.6	224.4
2008	220.5	220.2	220.5	220.7	221.2	223.7	224.8	224.3	221.1	220.2	219.2	219.3	221.3
2009	216.4	215.0	214.4	213.6	213.7	215.2	215.2	214.4	211.0	209.9	209.6	210.1	213.2
2010	207.4	206.8	206.5	206.6	207.6	209.3	210.6	210.3	207.4	207.1	206.6	207.6	207.8
2011	205.0	204.6	204.6	205.2	205.7	207.6	209.8	208.6	205.6	205.7	203.2	203.9	205.8
Professional and Business Services													
2000	464.8	468.5	475.2	485.3	487.0	499.4	504.1	508.0	505.5	504.3	506.0	507.8	493.0
2001	494.3	492.1	493.3	493.1	493.4	496.5	487.0	485.9	479.5	472.3	468.0	466.6	485.2
2002	448.6	445.3	448.4	455.8	456.9	460.7	458.5	455.0	453.5	452.2	449.8	453.6	453.6
2003	433.5	428.3	429.5	438.9	441.0	444.8	446.3	446.0	443.4	444.6	445.5	445.4	440.6
2004	431.7	431.6	435.6	448.4	450.8	457.7	460.4	461.2	459.3	458.5	458.7	459.3	451.1
2005	443.1	443.3	445.4	459.5	460.8	467.9	468.8	469.5	468.3	466.5	468.5	467.8	460.8
2006	453.0	454.7	458.4	469.1	471.8	480.4	479.3	481.0	477.5	478.2	479.0	478.2	471.7
2007	461.9	463.8	467.2	480.2	484.7	492.4	490.4	492.5	487.5	488.3	489.8	489.5	482.4
2008	475.7	477.0	478.6	488.4	491.6	497.6	496.9	496.0	491.7	490.3	485.4	480.0	487.4
2009	461.5	457.1	455.1	461.1	460.1	462.8	461.6	460.5	456.8	457.0	456.0	455.4	458.8
2010	447.4	447.3	449.2	461.9	463.7	468.5	472.8	471.9	466.3	471.6	470.1	468.7	463.3
2011	459.1	459.9	459.9	474.5	474.3	480.0	480.6	482.6	480.6	484.9	484.6	477.7	474.9
Education and Health Services													
2000	537.9	549.8	551.0	552.4	544.5	532.1	530.0	529.6	543.4	555.2	560.0	560.8	545.6
2001	543.4	556.3	557.2	560.0	553.5	541.5	541.6	541.5	553.0	566.9	571.1	572.5	554.9
2002	558.0	569.3	573.1	575.3	568.5	555.9	553.2	551.6	566.6	578.5	584.9	585.7	568.4
2003	568.3	578.1	581.5	583.3	575.5	561.9	560.8	558.1	573.9	585.3	589.9	589.4	575.5
2004	573.5	584.8	588.0	589.4	581.4	562.6	569.1	566.1	580.4	592.4	596.5	596.2	582.2
2005	578.9	591.7	593.4	596.8	589.2	576.4	576.8	574.6	588.8	601.5	606.9	606.7	590.1
2006	591.8	604.6	609.0	610.3	604.0	593.3	593.2	590.5	605.8	618.0	622.6	623.0	605.5
2007	612.0	623.1	624.7	630.3	623.8	610.7	612.9	611.1	623.9	637.8	641.7	642.4	624.5
2008	627.0	640.4	644.2	646.9	638.9	625.9	628.6	626.4	638.5	652.5	656.2	656.6	640.2
2009	641.3	653.3	656.8	659.6	651.7	637.0	641.0	639.1	651.6	663.5	667.9	668.6	652.6
2010	656.4	667.7	670.7	670.2	663.7	645.9	648.8	646.6	661.2	674.3	678.4	678.4	663.5
2011	663.5	676.1	680.4	681.1	673.5	656.1	658.9	653.7	661.5	676.0	678.8	675.7	669.6
Leisure and Hospitality													
2000	246.9	249.0	253.4	266.8	277.8	294.8	301.1	299.6	287.6	280.1	270.1	267.8	274.6
2001	254.3	256.3	260.9	271.0	285.8	303.4	306.3	305.7	291.0	280.6	270.4	267.7	279.5
2002	254.1	255.4	262.0	275.6	291.3	306.8	312.4	312.7	299.5	291.1	279.9	278.0	284.9
2003	262.2	260.9	264.5	275.6	294.4	308.3	315.6	315.8	302.1	293.6	281.4	277.2	287.6
2004	263.4	262.8	267.5	282.2	296.8	311.6	321.4	319.1	305.1	295.4	283.9	280.9	290.8
2005	265.2	265.9	269.2	285.3	298.8	314.1	322.0	321.3	307.2	294.6	285.3	282.2	292.6
2006	267.6	267.9	272.1	286.7	299.7	317.2	326.8	326.6	311.3	302.0	292.1	289.9	296.7
2007	276.2	276.0	279.8	291.1	305.6	325.4	331.7	332.2	315.6	307.4	297.1	292.4	302.5
2008	279.5	280.7	284.5	297.1	313.8	329.0	334.6	335.2	318.1	310.2	296.4	291.2	305.9
2009	272.9	274.2	276.9	290.5	308.6	321.2	327.9	327.1	313.8	304.7	291.5	288.6	299.8
2010	278.7	277.4	279.9	298.8	313.4	327.6	336.7	335.7	321.2	315.7	302.1	298.2	307.1
2011	284.1	282.8	288.7	305.2	317.6	334.5	344.3	342.5	316.5	306.4	298.5	291.4	309.4
Other Services													
2000	107.6	108.4	109.1	109.8	110.9	112.7	113.6	113.3	111.6	111.7	111.8	112.6	111.1
2001	112.4	113.0	114.0	114.2	115.5	118.6	120.6	120.4	115.8	115.8	115.9	116.5	116.1
2002	114.4	114.6	116.2	116.4	117.6	119.8	121.6	121.3	116.8	117.0	117.1	117.3	117.5
2003	115.0	114.8	116.0	116.2	117.4	119.5	121.0	119.8	116.6	116.0	116.4	116.5	117.1
2004	114.2	114.5	115.6	115.9	116.9	119.0	120.8	120.3	116.0	116.2	116.1	116.8	116.9
2005	114.2	114.6	115.5	117.2	117.7	121.0	122.5	121.7	118.2	117.0	117.3	118.2	117.9
2006	115.8	115.5	117.0	117.7	118.6	122.1	123.6	123.2	118.6	118.1	117.8	118.5	118.9
2007	115.9	116.4	117.4	118.3	120.0	124.2	125.9	125.4	120.8	119.9	120.3	120.5	120.4
2008	117.3	117.9	118.7	119.2	120.3	123.9	126.1	125.3	120.0	119.6	119.2	118.9	120.5
2009	115.8	115.8	116.8	117.9	119.3	123.0	124.4	123.7	118.0	117.8	117.3	117.6	119.0
2010	115.4	115.1	116.0	117.7	119.1	122.6	125.4	124.2	118.4	117.7	117.4	117.5	118.9
2011	115.4	115.8	117.5	118.9	119.8	123.1	128.4	128.3	122.3	122.3	122.0	121.1	121.2
Government													
2000	431.5	440.8	440.5	444.8	452.7	439.0	406.8	399.2	436.1	442.6	445.6	444.5	435.3
2001	439.1	448.0	448.5	449.7	451.6	440.9	408.9	404.5	442.5	448.8	450.1	450.9	440.3
2002	441.4	448.9	449.6	447.3	447.8	437.5	406.9	401.8	437.6	436.7	439.8	437.9	436.1
2003	429.7	436.5	436.6	436.6	437.0	428.1	397.2	391.1	430.3	428.6	429.5	429.0	425.9
2004	419.1	429.0	430.2	431.8	432.1	424.2	391.0	383.8	424.3	429.4	431.9	431.0	421.5
2005	421.3	433.4	433.3	434.5	436.0	427.0	395.0	387.8	426.0	434.0	436.7	434.7	425.0
2006	425.1	435.8	436.9	438.0	439.9	432.3	399.6	391.8	430.0	438.0	440.8	439.2	429.0
2007	429.9	439.7	440.8	442.0	444.7	435.9	401.5	394.9	433.7	441.8	444.0	443.2	432.7
2008	433.3	444.9	445.6	447.3	448.7	438.7	406.4	399.5	437.6	447.1	448.2	446.8	437.0
2009	435.8	448.2	447.6	453.0	450.2	439.0	405.5	397.6	434.6	447.3	447.0	449.6	438.0
2010	438.6	446.2	447.3	451.4	460.2	442.1	405.8	397.6	436.7	446.9	450.6	449.3	439.4
2011	433.0	445.3	445.7	445.8	447.9	436.3	403.2	395.3	432.7	443.1	444.0	442.9	434.6

2. Average Weekly Hours by Selected Industry: Massachusetts, 2007–2011

(Not seasonally adjusted)

Industry and year	January	February	March	April	May	June	July	August	September	October	November	December	Annual average
Total Private													
2007	32.8	33.2	33.2	33.6	33.5	33.8	33.8	33.9	33.9	33.5	33.6	33.8	33.5
2008	33.5	33.4	33.8	33.6	33.5	33.8	33.7	33.9	33.7	33.6	33.7	33.5	33.6
2009	33.5	33.6	33.6	33.4	33.4	33.4	33.6	33.7	33.5	33.4	33.8	33.7	33.6
2010	33.6	33.5	33.7	33.8	33.9	33.8	33.8	34.0	33.6	33.4	33.3	33.4	33.6
2011	32.9	32.9	33.0	33.1	33.2	33.1	33.2	33.2	33.2	33.1	33.1	33.1	33.1
Goods-Producing													
2007	38.6	38.8	39.2	39.0	39.2	40.4	38.6	38.5	38.9	38.3	38.7	38.9	38.9
2008	38.8	38.8	39.2	38.7	39.1	39.1	38.7	38.8	39.1	38.4	38.7	38.5	38.8
2009	38.8	38.7	38.8	38.7	38.5	39.1	38.5	39.0	38.4	39.1	40.0	40.0	39.0
2010	40.0	39.3	39.8	40.0	40.3	40.3	39.8	40.0	39.8	39.6	39.5	40.2	39.9
2011	38.7	39.6	40.1	39.8	40.0	40.2	39.7	39.8	39.9	39.2	39.6	40.0	39.7
Construction													
2007	36.4	36.1	36.4	36.8	37.7	37.7	37.1	36.2	36.3	35.2	35.9	36.6	36.5
2008	37.0	36.9	37.3	36.9	37.6	37.7	37.9	37.6	38.2	37.8	37.5	37.2	37.5
2009	37.6	37.3	37.0	38.0	38.4	38.2	38.8	39.1	37.7	36.8	37.5	37.6	37.9
2010	38.1	37.2	37.5	38.0	38.5	38.2	38.4	38.6	37.8	36.9	36.4	36.1	37.7
2011	34.0	33.2	34.1	34.6	35.7	36.0	36.3	36.4	36.8	35.4	36.7	37.3	35.6
Manufacturing													
2007	39.4	39.8	40.2	39.9	39.9	41.8	39.4	39.8	40.3	39.9	40.1	40.0	40.0
2008	39.7	39.7	40.2	39.6	39.8	39.7	39.0	39.3	39.5	38.7	39.4	39.2	39.5
2009	39.4	39.1	39.4	38.8	38.4	39.4	38.2	38.4	38.1	39.5	40.5	40.5	39.1
2010	40.2	40.0	40.4	40.2	40.4	40.3	39.9	40.2	40.0	40.1	40.2	40.5	40.2
2011	39.9	39.9	40.2	39.9	39.7	40.1	39.4	39.8	39.9	39.7	39.9	40.3	39.9
Trade, Transportation, and Utilities													
2007	31.7	32.2	32.5	32.5	32.7	32.8	33.3	33.5	33.6	32.8	32.7	33.3	32.8
2008	32.6	32.5	33.0	32.9	32.6	33.2	33.2	33.6	33.4	33.3	32.8	33.2	33.0
2009	32.6	32.9	33.1	32.8	33.0	33.0	33.2	33.0	33.1	32.7	33.2	33.4	33.0
2010	32.7	32.9	33.3	33.2	33.4	33.3	33.3	33.6	33.2	32.8	32.7	33.2	33.1
2011	31.6	32.1	32.5	32.5	32.3	32.3	32.4	32.6	33.0	32.4	33.1	33.0	32.5
Information													
2007	34.7	35.4	35.1	37.0	35.9	35.9	37.3	35.0	35.8	34.8	34.5	34.9	35.5
2008	35.2	35.0	35.8	34.1	33.5	35.0	35.2	35.1	35.1	34.9	35.8	36.5	35.1
2009	35.7	36.6	35.6	35.5	34.6	34.1	34.8	35.0	34.6	34.5	35.4	34.0	35.0
2010	34.9	35.9	36.0	36.3	36.0	35.6	36.1	36.4	36.3	36.3	36.7	36.3	36.1
2011	36.2	35.4	35.3	34.9	35.0	34.2	34.9	35.2	35.1	36.2	35.5	35.8	35.3
Financial Activities													
2007	35.2	35.7	35.5	35.6	35.0	35.6	36.4	36.3	36.1	35.5	36.2	37.2	35.9
2008	37.7	37.1	37.5	37.3	37.0	37.0	36.5	37.0	36.8	36.4	37.6	36.9	37.1
2009	37.3	37.0	37.1	36.7	35.8	36.6	36.8	37.6	37.4	36.8	37.4	37.0	37.0
2010	36.8	36.5	36.5	36.3	36.6	36.7	36.4	36.8	35.9	35.8	35.5	36.5	36.4
2011	36.6	35.7	35.6	35.8	36.6	36.0	35.4	35.6	36.0	36.3	35.8	35.6	35.9
Professional and Business Services													
2007	35.3	35.6	35.5	36.0	36.1	36.2	36.2	36.6	36.7	36.1	36.1	36.5	36.1
2008	35.9	35.8	36.8	36.6	36.2	36.8	35.8	35.8	35.5	35.6	36.0	35.4	36.0
2009	35.5	35.9	35.9	35.6	36.0	35.8	35.7	35.8	35.6	35.8	36.2	35.5	35.8
2010	35.8	35.7	35.9	36.0	36.3	35.9	35.8	36.1	35.9	35.5	34.9	34.8	35.7
2011	35.5	34.6	34.9	35.3	35.8	35.4	35.5	35.8	35.7	36.2	35.8	36.0	35.5
Education and Health Services													
2007	29.8	29.8	29.5	30.1	29.5	29.8	30.0	30.4	30.3	30.7	30.8	30.8	30.1
2008	30.7	30.7	30.7	30.6	30.6	31.0	31.4	31.5	31.2	31.4	31.5	31.2	31.0
2009	31.3	31.5	31.5	31.6	31.6	31.6	31.9	32.0	31.9	31.7	31.8	31.8	31.7
2010	31.9	31.8	31.8	31.9	31.8	31.7	31.9	31.9	31.5	31.7	31.7	31.4	31.7
2011	31.4	31.0	31.0	31.1	31.0	31.0	31.2	30.9	30.7	30.5	30.3	30.0	30.8
Leisure and Hospitality													
2007	26.9	27.9	28.1	29.2	29.6	29.4	30.0	29.8	29.1	28.7	28.3	27.5	28.8
2008	27.0	26.5	26.8	27.4	27.3	26.9	27.6	27.8	27.5	27.5	26.7	26.6	27.2
2009	25.8	25.4	25.5	25.5	26.0	26.0	26.7	26.9	26.6	26.2	25.9	25.8	26.1
2010	25.4	25.5	25.4	26.2	26.5	26.5	27.0	26.9	26.0	26.0	25.6	25.6	26.1
2011	24.8	25.7	25.6	26.0	26.1	25.9	26.6	26.6	26.2	26.1	25.8	25.8	26.0
Other Services													
2007	31.4	32.0	31.5	31.6	31.1	30.9	31.2	31.7	31.8	31.3	31.2	31.7	31.4
2008	31.3	31.7	32.1	31.5	32.1	31.7	32.3	32.8	31.8	31.5	32.0	31.8	31.9
2009	32.9	33.3	33.0	33.2	32.7	32.3	32.6	33.0	32.0	32.0	32.2	32.2	32.6
2010	32.1	32.5	32.3	32.5	33.0	32.6	32.9	33.4	32.4	32.4	32.8	32.5	32.6
2011	31.7	31.6	31.2	31.2	31.1	30.8	31.5	31.4	30.7	30.7	30.3	30.6	31.1

3. Average Hourly Earnings by Selected Industry: Massachusetts, 2007–2011

(Dollars, not seasonally adjusted)

Industry and year	January	February	March	April	May	June	July	August	September	October	November	December	Annual average
Total Private													
2007	25.90	26.13	25.88	26.44	26.10	25.70	25.95	25.81	26.18	26.28	26.14	26.33	26.07
2008	26.17	26.31	26.41	26.27	26.16	26.16	26.06	26.25	26.55	26.54	26.85	26.78	26.38
2009	26.83	27.16	27.15	27.00	26.67	26.51	26.47	26.60	26.78	26.69	27.05	27.19	26.84
2010	27.12	27.28	27.32	27.07	27.01	26.87	27.01	27.06	27.09	27.13	27.22	27.38	27.13
2011	27.79	27.50	27.37	27.46	27.52	27.24	27.39	27.17	27.68	28.11	27.99	28.09	27.61
Goods-Producing													
2007	28.00	28.21	28.23	27.63	27.45	27.14	27.66	27.63	27.98	28.07	28.02	28.49	27.87
2008	28.11	28.20	28.22	28.22	28.13	27.84	28.26	28.39	28.52	28.67	28.79	28.84	28.35
2009	28.71	29.12	28.99	28.97	28.53	28.81	28.89	29.54	29.78	29.48	29.68	30.34	29.24
2010	30.47	30.76	31.38	30.25	30.04	29.63	29.76	29.87	29.61	29.41	29.23	29.50	29.98
2011	29.68	29.50	29.24	29.24	29.16	28.76	29.25	29.35	29.38	29.65	29.60	29.74	29.38
Construction													
2007	29.31	30.00	30.17	29.69	29.41	29.23	29.20	29.25	29.59	29.83	30.34	30.86	29.72
2008	30.46	30.88	30.86	30.57	29.89	29.64	30.10	30.82	31.06	31.21	31.51	31.76	30.72
2009	31.99	32.21	32.43	31.97	31.44	31.45	31.27	32.61	31.84	31.97	32.38	33.55	32.07
2010	33.50	34.15	34.11	33.38	32.93	32.79	33.00	33.16	33.12	33.52	33.64	33.98	33.41
2011	33.81	33.77	33.42	33.13	32.98	32.80	33.03	33.03	33.46	33.18	33.33	33.86	33.29
Manufacturing													
2007	27.58	27.65	27.61	26.82	26.57	26.20	26.89	26.82	27.21	27.29	26.90	27.38	27.07
2008	27.03	27.01	27.06	27.00	27.21	26.85	27.19	26.95	27.04	27.25	27.37	27.40	27.11
2009	27.19	27.19	26.89	27.05	26.65	27.10	27.25	27.61	28.39	28.02	28.18	28.66	27.51
2010	28.76	28.76	28.52	28.70	28.63	28.06	28.27	28.00	27.86	27.95	27.95	27.97	28.28
2011	28.17	28.06	27.81	27.78	27.59	27.06	27.64	27.79	27.67	28.31	28.10	28.10	27.84
Trade, Transportation, and Utilities													
2007	23.27	23.38	22.76	23.29	23.49	22.63	23.22	23.07	23.06	23.64	22.88	23.07	23.14
2008	23.35	23.94	23.91	23.51	23.44	23.31	23.52	23.66	23.39	23.25	22.93	22.55	23.39
2009	23.23	23.19	23.13	23.03	22.98	22.53	22.88	22.83	22.68	22.22	22.48	22.49	22.80
2010	22.75	22.82	22.65	22.65	22.70	22.62	23.12	23.13	22.94	22.65	22.72	22.58	22.78
2011	22.77	22.42	22.46	22.50	22.50	22.39	22.43	22.26	22.44	22.47	22.38	21.65	22.38
Information													
2007	38.06	37.04	37.20	36.89	35.78	36.68	37.03	37.14	37.56	37.20	36.80	37.03	37.03
2008	36.43	35.88	36.18	35.70	35.78	35.86	35.58	35.42	35.84	35.26	35.82	35.42	35.76
2009	34.71	35.22	35.06	34.53	34.74	34.63	34.18	34.68	34.22	33.94	34.57	35.41	34.66
2010	35.41	35.91	36.05	35.57	35.68	35.87	35.65	35.71	35.93	35.56	35.74	35.76	35.74
2011	35.58	36.06	36.27	36.05	37.43	36.48	37.21	37.81	39.02	39.85	41.44	40.32	37.79
Financial Activities													
2007	29.33	30.37	28.07	31.33	30.46	28.88	29.86	29.57	30.50	31.63	30.43	29.17	29.96
2008	28.41	28.88	29.14	28.91	28.93	29.45	28.71	29.44	29.71	30.27	30.75	30.54	29.42
2009	30.74	31.28	31.22	31.39	31.32	31.45	31.21	31.29	30.93	31.44	31.92	31.80	31.33
2010	31.78	31.87	31.79	31.77	31.74	31.76	32.39	31.90	32.11	31.81	32.26	32.85	32.00
2011	33.89	33.20	33.21	33.01	32.76	33.11	33.30	33.21	33.76	34.31	34.45	35.00	33.60
Professional and Business Services													
2007	31.94	32.44	32.55	33.83	32.92	32.32	32.40	32.12	32.49	31.87	32.12	32.97	32.50
2008	32.31	32.26	32.51	32.51	32.32	32.32	32.34	32.69	33.36	33.17	34.07	34.17	32.83
2009	34.21	34.75	35.17	34.83	34.35	33.87	33.93	33.96	34.42	34.11	34.73	34.87	34.43
2010	34.35	34.68	34.62	34.39	34.50	34.54	34.75	34.83	34.37	34.86	35.20	35.22	34.69
2011	35.85	35.20	35.08	34.99	34.94	34.47	34.87	34.18	34.80	35.32	35.06	35.76	35.04
Education and Health Services													
2007	22.84	22.94	23.16	23.61	23.44	24.12	24.11	23.83	24.01	24.05	24.25	24.24	23.72
2008	24.43	24.34	24.31	24.41	24.43	24.63	24.53	24.76	24.97	24.89	25.09	25.03	24.66
2009	24.68	25.20	25.19	25.16	24.75	24.84	24.80	24.76	24.96	24.99	25.19	25.32	24.99
2010	24.90	25.07	25.03	25.23	25.12	25.06	25.05	25.24	25.55	25.84	25.83	26.23	25.35
2011	26.22	26.59	26.28	26.85	27.10	27.10	27.38	27.06	27.40	27.92	27.60	27.96	27.12
Leisure and Hospitality													
2007	15.59	15.72	15.90	15.64	15.37	15.16	15.02	15.28	15.80	15.92	15.99	15.37	15.55
2008	15.32	15.53	15.59	15.75	15.59	15.36	15.15	15.25	15.53	15.57	15.70	16.31	15.54
2009	15.74	15.76	15.67	15.47	15.72	15.54	15.39	15.40	15.68	15.62	15.80	15.94	15.64
2010	15.60	15.53	15.48	15.25	15.33	15.12	15.12	15.18	15.17	15.45	15.44	15.41	15.33
2011	15.34	15.02	15.08	15.05	15.09	14.88	14.83	14.85	15.11	15.29	15.17	15.25	15.07
Other Services													
2007	21.37	21.65	21.45	21.69	22.56	21.32	21.09	21.16	21.11	21.14	21.09	21.54	21.43
2008	21.22	20.89	21.11	20.91	21.02	21.25	20.93	20.54	21.56	21.87	21.80	22.03	21.25
2009	21.71	21.80	21.66	21.63	21.44	21.07	20.94	21.00	21.99	22.35	22.20	22.34	21.67
2010	22.30	22.41	22.36	22.31	22.27	22.26	22.07	21.87	22.51	22.09	21.85	22.23	22.21
2011	22.51	22.09	22.12	22.34	22.61	22.03	21.27	21.13	22.09	22.09	22.05	22.24	22.03

4. Average Weekly Earnings by Selected Industry: Massachusetts, 2007–2011

(Dollars, not seasonally adjusted)

Industry and year	January	February	March	April	May	June	July	August	September	October	November	December	Annual average
Total Private													
2007	849.52	867.52	859.22	888.38	874.35	868.66	877.11	874.96	887.50	880.38	878.30	889.95	874.51
2008	876.70	878.75	892.66	882.67	876.36	884.21	878.22	889.88	894.74	891.74	904.85	897.13	887.45
2009	898.81	912.58	912.24	901.80	890.78	885.43	889.39	896.42	897.13	891.45	914.29	916.30	900.62
2010	911.23	913.88	920.68	914.97	915.64	908.21	912.94	920.04	910.22	906.14	906.43	914.49	912.80
2011	914.29	904.75	903.21	908.93	913.66	901.64	909.35	902.04	918.98	930.44	926.47	929.78	914.07
Goods-Producing													
2007	1,080.80	1,094.55	1,106.62	1,077.57	1,076.04	1,096.46	1,067.68	1,063.76	1,088.42	1,075.08	1,084.37	1,108.26	1,084.83
2008	1,090.67	1,094.16	1,106.22	1,092.11	1,099.88	1,088.54	1,093.66	1,101.53	1,115.13	1,100.93	1,114.17	1,110.34	1,100.56
2009	1,113.95	1,126.94	1,124.81	1,121.14	1,098.41	1,126.47	1,112.27	1,152.06	1,143.55	1,152.67	1,187.20	1,213.60	1,139.04
2010	1,218.80	1,208.87	1,248.92	1,210.00	1,210.61	1,194.09	1,184.45	1,194.80	1,178.48	1,164.64	1,154.59	1,185.90	1,195.62
2011	1,148.62	1,168.20	1,172.52	1,163.75	1,166.40	1,156.15	1,161.23	1,168.13	1,172.26	1,162.28	1,172.16	1,189.60	1,166.69
Construction													
2007	1,066.88	1,083.00	1,098.19	1,092.59	1,108.76	1,101.97	1,083.32	1,058.85	1,074.12	1,050.02	1,089.21	1,129.48	1,086.09
2008	1,127.02	1,139.47	1,151.08	1,128.03	1,123.86	1,117.43	1,140.79	1,158.83	1,186.49	1,179.74	1,181.63	1,181.47	1,151.36
2009	1,202.82	1,201.43	1,199.91	1,214.86	1,207.30	1,201.39	1,213.28	1,275.05	1,200.37	1,176.50	1,214.25	1,261.48	1,214.03
2010	1,276.35	1,270.38	1,279.13	1,268.44	1,267.81	1,252.58	1,267.20	1,279.98	1,251.94	1,236.89	1,224.50	1,226.68	1,257.88
2011	1,149.54	1,121.16	1,139.62	1,146.30	1,177.39	1,180.80	1,198.99	1,202.29	1,231.33	1,174.57	1,223.21	1,262.98	1,185.57
Manufacturing													
2007	1,086.65	1,100.47	1,109.92	1,070.12	1,060.14	1,095.16	1,059.47	1,067.44	1,096.56	1,088.87	1,078.69	1,095.20	1,084.07
2008	1,073.09	1,072.30	1,087.81	1,069.20	1,082.96	1,065.95	1,060.41	1,059.14	1,068.08	1,054.58	1,078.38	1,074.08	1,070.50
2009	1,071.29	1,063.13	1,059.47	1,049.54	1,023.36	1,067.74	1,040.95	1,060.22	1,081.66	1,106.79	1,141.29	1,160.73	1,076.89
2010	1,156.15	1,150.40	1,152.21	1,153.74	1,156.65	1,130.82	1,127.97	1,125.60	1,114.40	1,120.80	1,123.59	1,132.79	1,136.99
2011	1,123.98	1,119.59	1,117.96	1,108.42	1,095.32	1,085.11	1,089.02	1,106.04	1,104.03	1,123.91	1,121.19	1,132.43	1,110.56
Trade, Transportation, and Utilities													
2007	737.66	752.84	739.70	756.93	768.12	742.26	773.23	772.85	774.82	775.39	748.18	768.23	759.23
2008	761.21	778.05	789.03	773.48	764.14	773.89	780.86	794.98	781.23	774.23	752.10	748.66	772.59
2009	757.30	762.95	765.60	755.38	758.34	743.49	759.62	753.39	750.71	726.59	746.34	751.17	752.50
2010	743.93	750.78	754.25	751.98	758.18	753.25	769.90	777.17	761.61	742.92	742.94	749.66	754.70
2011	719.53	719.68	729.95	731.25	726.75	723.20	726.73	725.68	740.52	728.03	740.78	714.45	727.22
Information													
2007	1,320.68	1,311.22	1,305.72	1,364.93	1,284.50	1,316.81	1,381.22	1,299.90	1,344.65	1,294.56	1,269.60	1,292.35	1,315.58
2008	1,282.34	1,255.80	1,295.24	1,217.37	1,198.63	1,255.10	1,252.42	1,243.24	1,257.98	1,230.57	1,282.36	1,292.83	1,255.10
2009	1,239.15	1,289.05	1,248.14	1,225.82	1,202.00	1,180.88	1,189.46	1,213.80	1,184.01	1,170.93	1,223.78	1,203.94	1,214.15
2010	1,235.81	1,289.17	1,297.80	1,291.19	1,284.48	1,276.97	1,286.97	1,299.84	1,304.26	1,290.83	1,311.66	1,298.09	1,289.04
2011	1,288.00	1,276.52	1,280.33	1,258.15	1,310.05	1,247.62	1,298.63	1,330.91	1,369.60	1,442.57	1,471.12	1,443.46	1,334.31
Financial Activities													
2007	1,032.42	1,084.21	996.49	1,115.35	1,066.10	1,028.13	1,086.90	1,073.39	1,101.05	1,122.87	1,101.57	1,085.12	1,074.37
2008	1,071.06	1,071.45	1,092.75	1,078.34	1,070.41	1,089.65	1,047.92	1,089.28	1,093.33	1,101.83	1,156.20	1,126.93	1,090.64
2009	1,146.60	1,157.36	1,158.26	1,152.01	1,121.26	1,151.07	1,148.53	1,176.50	1,156.78	1,156.99	1,193.81	1,176.60	1,157.84
2010	1,169.50	1,163.26	1,160.34	1,153.25	1,161.68	1,165.59	1,179.00	1,173.92	1,152.75	1,138.80	1,145.23	1,199.03	1,163.47
2011	1,240.37	1,185.24	1,182.28	1,181.76	1,199.02	1,191.96	1,178.82	1,182.28	1,215.36	1,245.45	1,233.31	1,246.00	1,206.67
Professional and Business Services													
2007	1,127.48	1,154.86	1,155.53	1,217.88	1,188.41	1,169.98	1,172.88	1,175.59	1,192.38	1,150.51	1,159.53	1,203.41	1,172.64
2008	1,159.93	1,154.91	1,196.37	1,189.87	1,169.98	1,189.38	1,157.77	1,170.30	1,184.28	1,180.85	1,226.52	1,209.62	1,182.45
2009	1,214.46	1,247.53	1,262.60	1,239.95	1,236.60	1,212.55	1,211.30	1,215.77	1,225.35	1,221.14	1,257.23	1,237.89	1,231.82
2010	1,229.73	1,238.08	1,242.86	1,238.04	1,252.35	1,239.99	1,244.05	1,257.36	1,233.88	1,237.53	1,228.48	1,225.66	1,239.04
2011	1,272.68	1,217.92	1,224.29	1,235.15	1,250.85	1,220.24	1,237.89	1,223.64	1,242.36	1,278.58	1,255.15	1,287.36	1,245.59
Education and Health Services													
2007	680.63	683.61	683.22	710.66	691.48	718.78	723.30	724.43	727.50	738.34	746.90	746.59	714.83
2008	750.00	747.24	746.32	746.95	747.56	763.53	770.24	779.94	779.06	781.55	790.34	780.94	765.39
2009	772.48	793.80	793.49	795.06	782.10	784.94	791.12	792.32	796.22	792.18	801.04	805.18	791.71
2010	794.31	797.23	795.95	804.84	798.82	794.40	799.10	805.16	804.83	819.13	818.81	823.62	804.82
2011	823.31	824.29	814.68	835.04	840.10	840.10	854.26	836.15	841.18	851.56	836.28	838.80	836.22
Leisure and Hospitality													
2007	419.37	438.59	446.79	456.69	454.95	445.70	450.60	455.34	459.78	456.90	452.52	422.68	447.11
2008	413.64	411.55	417.81	431.55	425.61	413.18	418.14	423.95	427.08	428.18	419.19	433.85	422.03
2009	406.09	400.30	399.59	394.49	408.72	404.04	410.91	414.26	417.09	409.24	409.22	411.25	407.33
2010	396.24	396.02	393.19	399.55	406.25	400.68	408.24	408.34	394.42	401.70	395.26	394.50	399.78
2011	380.43	386.01	386.05	391.30	393.85	385.39	394.48	395.01	395.88	399.07	391.39	393.45	391.20
Other Services													
2007	671.02	692.80	675.68	685.40	701.62	658.79	658.01	670.77	671.30	661.68	658.01	682.82	673.81
2008	664.19	662.21	677.63	658.67	674.74	673.63	676.04	673.71	685.61	688.91	697.60	700.55	677.78
2009	714.26	725.94	714.78	718.12	701.09	680.56	682.64	693.00	703.68	715.20	714.84	719.35	706.56
2010	715.83	728.33	722.23	725.08	734.91	725.68	726.10	730.46	729.32	715.72	716.68	722.48	724.65
2011	713.57	698.04	690.14	697.01	703.17	678.52	670.01	663.48	678.16	678.16	668.12	680.54	684.48

MICHIGAN
At a Glance

Population:
    2000 census: 9,938,823
    2010 census: 9,883,640
    2011 estimate: 9,876,187

Percent change in population:
    2000–2010: -0.6%
    2010–2011: -0.1%

Percent change in total nonfarm employment:
    2000–2010: -17.4%
    2010–2011: 1.9%

Industry with the largest growth in employment, 2000–2011 (thousands):
    Education and Health Services, 118.4

Industry with the largest decline or smallest growth in employment, 2000–2011 (thousands):
    Manufacturing, -391.0

Civilian labor force:
    2000: 5,143,916
    2010: 4,747,128
    2011: 4,658,108

Unemployment rate and rank among states (lowest to highest):
    2000: 3.7%, 22nd
    2010: 12.7%, 50th
    2011: 10.3%, 44th

Over-the-year change in unemployment rates:
    2010–2011: -2.4%

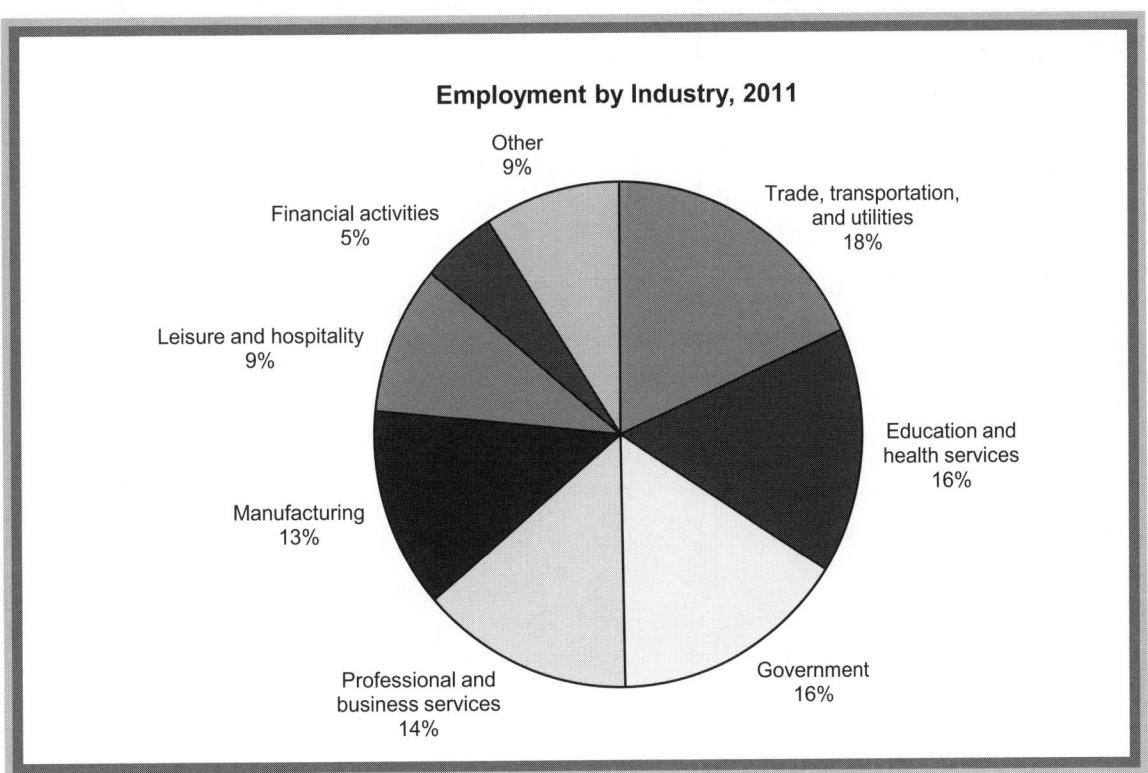

Employment by Industry, 2011

Other 9%

Financial activities 5%

Leisure and hospitality 9%

Manufacturing 13%

Professional and business services 14%

Government 16%

Education and health services 16%

Trade, transportation, and utilities 18%

1. Employment by Industry: Michigan, Selected Years, 2000–2011

(Numbers in thousands, not seasonally adjusted)

Industry and year	January	February	March	April	May	June	July	August	September	October	November	December	Annual average
Total Nonfarm													
2000	4,561.5	4,584.6	4,621.6	4,672.7	4,729.6	4,745.0	4,640.7	4,668.0	4,710.5	4,729.1	4,730.0	4,723.4	4,676.4
2001	4,511.3	4,535.2	4,557.7	4,584.1	4,629.1	4,640.7	4,519.0	4,548.3	4,572.8	4,561.7	4,555.1	4,549.3	4,563.7
2002	4,388.5	4,409.4	4,436.1	4,469.1	4,532.5	4,547.3	4,446.2	4,484.6	4,526.9	4,536.5	4,538.6	4,527.1	4,486.9
2003	4,353.0	4,356.3	4,369.8	4,395.6	4,468.6	4,475.7	4,339.8	4,392.9	4,444.8	4,467.8	4,465.2	4,461.7	4,415.9
2004	4,302.8	4,312.9	4,338.9	4,397.4	4,451.1	4,449.7	4,325.1	4,382.1	4,448.2	4,459.6	4,463.3	4,456.5	4,399.0
2005	4,289.3	4,323.0	4,339.1	4,397.8	4,448.9	4,440.3	4,325.0	4,366.0	4,444.0	4,433.2	4,443.1	4,426.7	4,389.7
2006	4,265.5	4,279.9	4,303.2	4,341.0	4,385.3	4,394.1	4,249.3	4,294.8	4,361.7	4,344.5	4,354.0	4,345.1	4,326.5
2007	4,185.6	4,212.3	4,233.0	4,261.7	4,325.4	4,330.0	4,214.2	4,256.3	4,302.3	4,293.9	4,305.7	4,292.8	4,267.8
2008	4,145.6	4,158.7	4,159.1	4,172.9	4,225.7	4,243.8	4,112.5	4,147.6	4,180.2	4,168.6	4,139.2	4,092.2	4,162.2
2009	3,863.6	3,881.9	3,872.1	3,895.8	3,910.9	3,882.6	3,793.7	3,818.3	3,876.4	3,896.0	3,886.4	3,869.0	3,870.6
2010	3,751.8	3,768.3	3,781.0	3,838.7	3,895.8	3,907.8	3,845.9	3,851.3	3,913.5	3,941.5	3,942.3	3,922.4	3,863.4
2011	3,831.6	3,846.5	3,874.2	3,923.2	3,970.9	3,982.9	3,914.8	3,930.7	3,969.4	4,002.7	3,999.0	3,982.0	3,935.7
Total Private													
2000	3,889.1	3,889.2	3,916.8	3,972.5	4,029.5	4,072.2	4,021.9	4,056.0	4,029.6	4,025.7	4,020.0	4,017.7	3,995.0
2001	3,829.7	3,834.6	3,850.5	3,880.3	3,929.5	3,959.9	3,896.2	3,927.6	3,892.8	3,856.6	3,844.8	3,842.1	3,878.7
2002	3,699.7	3,703.6	3,726.9	3,772.0	3,837.9	3,872.5	3,827.4	3,864.9	3,842.0	3,821.7	3,820.7	3,814.4	3,800.3
2003	3,662.9	3,647.1	3,661.6	3,691.5	3,767.8	3,802.2	3,725.8	3,782.3	3,767.7	3,752.9	3,751.3	3,753.2	3,730.5
2004	3,616.6	3,611.7	3,634.8	3,696.2	3,755.0	3,781.1	3,719.5	3,778.8	3,769.4	3,756.3	3,756.6	3,755.0	3,719.3
2005	3,611.8	3,625.6	3,640.2	3,700.2	3,757.0	3,777.0	3,727.6	3,767.0	3,766.2	3,737.9	3,743.1	3,733.8	3,715.6
2006	3,593.8	3,589.5	3,607.9	3,653.3	3,704.7	3,740.2	3,655.9	3,704.9	3,696.8	3,659.6	3,665.3	3,662.7	3,661.2
2007	3,525.4	3,534.4	3,550.3	3,587.4	3,652.0	3,683.2	3,622.9	3,662.2	3,647.5	3,622.6	3,633.0	3,624.4	3,612.1
2008	3,496.4	3,493.2	3,492.2	3,504.7	3,567.7	3,601.9	3,519.5	3,549.0	3,525.4	3,497.9	3,467.5	3,430.2	3,512.1
2009	3,210.9	3,216.9	3,206.1	3,226.5	3,251.0	3,243.5	3,204.1	3,228.8	3,230.7	3,232.1	3,222.0	3,212.9	3,223.8
2010	3,110.1	3,112.9	3,125.1	3,180.2	3,238.6	3,274.1	3,261.2	3,275.3	3,283.5	3,295.5	3,294.1	3,282.4	3,227.8
2011	3,206.6	3,210.3	3,235.9	3,284.7	3,345.7	3,370.6	3,346.8	3,365.5	3,350.9	3,368.7	3,364.9	3,355.5	3,317.2
Goods-Producing													
2000	1,084.2	1,084.4	1,091.5	1,116.6	1,133.4	1,147.1	1,124.0	1,139.9	1,127.5	1,126.7	1,116.2	1,104.6	1,116.3
2001	1,036.5	1,041.9	1,042.6	1,046.6	1,056.4	1,062.6	1,034.6	1,048.2	1,040.9	1,022.8	1,010.7	1,004.8	1,037.4
2002	948.3	955.0	957.3	964.2	980.9	992.5	974.1	990.3	981.8	975.7	969.0	957.8	970.6
2003	911.2	901.1	902.9	905.6	929.8	943.1	896.4	935.5	929.2	921.8	919.4	913.1	917.4
2004	875.3	870.1	878.1	896.2	911.4	918.2	876.7	921.3	919.0	913.3	909.9	901.9	899.3
2005	853.8	861.0	859.8	872.8	890.7	896.2	862.7	889.2	890.8	886.5	884.8	870.5	876.6
2006	829.6	825.3	827.8	844.8	855.4	864.1	815.2	849.1	844.0	829.8	828.4	817.9	836.0
2007	773.1	781.4	784.1	791.2	805.4	815.8	786.9	812.4	805.8	788.7	791.9	780.7	793.1
2008	746.2	743.7	732.6	730.7	744.7	770.0	724.3	748.4	741.0	728.7	716.2	692.2	734.9
2009	599.2	610.0	604.6	603.5	593.4	588.3	586.7	604.9	606.3	607.0	598.1	589.8	599.3
2010	569.0	566.1	569.1	587.2	602.8	615.4	618.4	619.0	629.0	632.1	627.7	618.1	604.5
2011	603.2	603.7	609.0	623.8	641.7	655.4	649.1	660.2	656.9	658.8	652.3	644.1	638.2
Mining and Logging													
2000	8.8	8.6	8.7	9.2	9.4	9.7	10.1	10.1	9.8	10.1	10.0	9.6	9.5
2001	8.8	8.9	9.1	9.2	9.6	9.7	9.6	9.6	9.5	9.5	9.3	9.1	9.3
2002	8.0	8.0	8.1	8.4	8.9	9.0	9.0	8.8	8.9	8.9	8.8	8.5	8.6
2003	7.6	7.6	7.6	7.9	8.6	8.9	8.3	8.3	8.3	8.4	8.2	7.9	8.1
2004	7.4	7.4	7.6	8.0	8.4	8.4	8.6	8.7	8.7	8.5	8.3	7.9	8.2
2005	7.7	7.7	7.7	8.4	8.8	9.0	9.0	8.9	8.6	8.6	8.4	8.0	8.4
2006	7.4	7.5	7.5	7.9	8.2	8.5	8.5	8.5	8.3	8.3	8.1	7.6	8.0
2007	7.2	7.2	7.0	7.3	7.8	8.2	8.2	8.1	8.0	7.9	7.7	7.4	7.7
2008	7.1	7.1	7.1	7.5	8.0	8.2	8.4	8.4	8.3	8.2	8.1	7.8	7.9
2009	6.7	6.9	6.3	6.5	6.8	7.1	7.2	7.2	7.2	7.2	7.0	6.8	6.9
2010	6.6	6.5	6.2	6.8	7.2	7.5	7.6	7.6	7.5	7.5	7.3	7.0	7.1
2011	6.7	6.7	6.7	7.0	7.4	7.8	7.9	7.8	7.7	7.8	7.6	7.1	7.4
Construction													
2000	182.4	180.5	188.5	205.8	216.8	225.0	227.9	227.3	224.4	220.8	214.1	203.4	209.7
2001	182.7	181.0	185.8	198.5	212.0	218.9	222.8	223.3	219.4	215.9	210.9	204.1	206.3
2002	182.5	178.0	180.6	192.5	207.1	213.2	216.2	216.0	210.9	207.8	201.7	190.8	199.8
2003	169.1	163.3	164.8	178.9	196.7	204.8	208.8	208.3	204.8	203.1	197.8	190.5	190.9
2004	167.1	163.7	167.7	183.5	196.0	204.2	208.9	208.1	205.5	204.2	200.8	191.5	191.8
2005	168.3	164.9	167.7	183.4	195.5	203.5	207.0	205.2	201.8	199.1	194.3	182.8	189.5
2006	162.9	159.1	162.1	174.9	185.8	192.9	192.9	191.6	188.1	183.9	177.4	169.1	178.4
2007	151.1	145.6	150.1	158.4	172.0	179.3	180.8	180.8	178.2	174.7	169.1	160.0	166.7
2008	143.2	138.2	139.7	146.8	160.5	166.4	166.6	166.6	163.7	159.8	151.1	138.9	153.5
2009	119.6	116.6	115.8	124.1	133.5	136.8	137.5	136.3	133.0	132.3	127.2	118.5	127.6
2010	102.8	100.0	103.4	114.5	123.7	129.1	133.6	134.5	133.8	134.5	129.4	120.4	121.6
2011	108.0	104.9	107.4	116.3	128.2	135.7	138.7	140.3	136.1	135.0	129.3	117.0	124.7
Manufacturing													
2000	893.0	895.3	894.3	901.6	907.2	912.4	886.0	902.5	893.3	895.8	892.1	891.6	897.1
2001	845.0	852.0	847.7	838.9	834.8	834.0	802.2	815.3	812.0	797.4	790.5	791.6	821.8
2002	757.8	769.0	768.6	763.3	764.9	770.3	748.9	765.5	762.0	759.0	758.5	758.5	762.2
2003	734.5	730.2	730.5	718.8	724.5	729.4	679.3	718.9	716.1	710.3	713.4	714.7	718.4
2004	700.8	699.0	702.8	704.7	707.0	705.6	659.2	704.5	704.8	700.6	700.8	702.5	699.4
2005	677.8	688.4	684.4	681.0	686.4	683.7	646.7	675.1	680.4	678.8	682.1	679.7	678.7
2006	659.3	658.7	658.2	662.0	661.4	662.7	613.8	649.0	647.6	637.6	642.9	641.2	649.5
2007	614.8	628.6	627.0	625.5	625.6	628.3	597.9	623.5	619.6	606.1	615.1	613.3	618.8
2008	595.9	598.4	585.8	576.4	576.2	595.4	549.3	573.4	569.0	560.7	557.0	545.5	573.6
2009	472.9	486.5	482.5	472.9	453.1	444.4	442.0	461.4	466.1	467.5	463.9	464.5	464.8
2010	459.6	459.6	459.5	465.9	471.9	478.8	477.2	476.9	487.7	490.1	491.0	490.7	475.7
2011	488.5	492.1	494.9	500.5	506.1	511.9	502.5	512.1	513.1	516.0	515.4	520.0	506.1

1. Employment by Industry: Michigan, Selected Years, 2000–2011—*Continued*

(Numbers in thousands, not seasonally adjusted)

Industry and year	January	February	March	April	May	June	July	August	September	October	November	December	Annual average
Service-Providing													
2000	3,477.3	3,500.2	3,530.1	3,556.1	3,596.2	3,597.9	3,516.7	3,528.1	3,583.0	3,602.4	3,613.8	3,618.8	3,560.1
2001	3,474.8	3,493.3	3,515.1	3,537.5	3,572.7	3,578.1	3,484.4	3,500.1	3,531.9	3,538.9	3,544.4	3,544.5	3,526.3
2002	3,440.2	3,454.4	3,478.8	3,504.9	3,551.6	3,554.8	3,472.1	3,494.3	3,545.1	3,560.8	3,569.6	3,569.3	3,516.3
2003	3,441.8	3,455.2	3,466.9	3,490.0	3,538.8	3,532.6	3,443.4	3,457.4	3,515.6	3,546.0	3,545.8	3,548.6	3,498.5
2004	3,427.5	3,442.8	3,460.8	3,501.2	3,539.7	3,531.5	3,448.4	3,460.8	3,529.2	3,546.3	3,553.4	3,554.6	3,499.7
2005	3,435.5	3,462.0	3,479.3	3,525.0	3,558.2	3,544.1	3,462.3	3,476.8	3,553.2	3,546.7	3,558.3	3,556.2	3,513.1
2006	3,435.9	3,454.6	3,475.4	3,496.2	3,529.9	3,530.0	3,434.1	3,445.7	3,517.7	3,514.7	3,525.6	3,527.2	3,490.6
2007	3,412.5	3,430.9	3,449.2	3,470.5	3,520.0	3,514.2	3,427.3	3,443.9	3,496.5	3,505.2	3,513.8	3,512.1	3,474.7
2008	3,399.4	3,415.0	3,426.5	3,442.2	3,481.0	3,473.8	3,388.2	3,399.2	3,439.2	3,439.9	3,423.0	3,400.0	3,427.3
2009	3,264.4	3,271.9	3,267.5	3,292.3	3,317.5	3,294.3	3,207.0	3,213.4	3,270.1	3,289.0	3,288.3	3,279.2	3,271.2
2010	3,182.8	3,202.2	3,211.9	3,251.5	3,293.0	3,292.4	3,227.5	3,232.3	3,284.5	3,309.4	3,314.6	3,304.3	3,258.9
2011	3,228.4	3,242.8	3,265.2	3,299.4	3,329.2	3,327.5	3,265.7	3,270.5	3,312.5	3,343.9	3,346.7	3,337.9	3,297.5
Trade, Transportation, and Utilities													
2000	866.5	858.9	864.7	869.5	881.2	886.7	874.0	879.9	878.4	889.3	905.2	919.7	881.2
2001	865.3	854.8	855.5	859.5	867.4	870.6	857.1	860.2	853.7	853.6	865.3	871.7	861.2
2002	826.1	814.9	820.4	825.6	838.6	843.5	834.7	838.3	836.8	832.8	845.8	854.0	834.3
2003	807.8	798.8	800.7	803.8	816.9	822.8	814.9	820.3	819.5	823.8	833.4	841.8	817.0
2004	796.9	789.9	792.0	800.7	812.7	817.1	811.5	814.1	808.1	813.7	826.4	834.3	809.8
2005	791.0	785.3	788.1	796.9	807.8	811.9	811.0	811.7	806.8	806.1	818.8	825.7	805.1
2006	784.5	776.1	780.3	787.3	797.5	803.6	796.8	798.8	795.0	795.4	809.1	816.0	795.0
2007	779.2	770.1	772.1	777.1	789.4	794.4	789.6	791.1	787.3	787.0	800.6	806.5	787.0
2008	771.9	763.7	765.8	764.6	776.1	780.6	774.1	774.1	769.4	765.2	769.2	769.2	770.3
2009	723.6	714.0	709.8	711.6	720.4	722.6	714.3	717.3	713.0	713.1	721.3	725.4	717.2
2010	695.0	687.9	690.8	699.4	710.3	716.6	717.1	716.8	711.6	719.0	729.6	733.6	710.6
2011	704.7	698.7	700.6	711.0	722.4	728.5	725.2	726.2	720.8	723.6	736.0	740.5	719.9
Wholesale Trade													
2000	184.0	184.8	185.8	185.8	187.1	188.0	187.0	186.7	185.2	185.8	185.3	186.4	186.0
2001	180.3	180.8	181.2	183.2	183.4	183.0	181.1	180.7	178.9	177.9	176.9	177.1	180.4
2002	173.0	173.0	173.6	175.0	177.1	177.8	176.5	176.7	175.4	175.3	175.5	175.9	175.4
2003	171.7	171.7	172.2	172.6	173.5	174.1	173.1	173.2	172.3	172.4	171.8	172.1	172.6
2004	167.2	167.4	168.8	170.2	171.6	172.6	172.3	172.0	171.0	171.1	171.0	171.3	170.5
2005	167.8	168.2	169.1	170.3	172.0	172.5	172.4	172.2	171.1	171.2	170.9	171.2	170.7
2006	167.9	168.1	169.0	171.1	172.2	173.7	172.8	172.0	170.7	170.0	169.5	169.8	170.6
2007	167.2	166.8	167.2	169.0	170.4	171.4	170.5	170.1	169.0	169.1	168.6	169.0	169.0
2008	167.0	167.1	167.7	168.5	170.0	170.6	169.1	169.0	168.1	166.9	165.3	163.8	167.8
2009	158.0	156.4	155.0	154.9	154.9	153.2	150.9	151.3	150.5	150.1	149.8	150.0	152.9
2010	146.8	147.1	147.9	149.8	151.4	152.0	152.0	152.5	151.4	152.2	152.5	152.2	150.7
2011	150.8	151.1	152.1	154.6	156.6	157.8	157.9	158.9	157.7	158.7	158.6	159.6	156.2
Retail Trade													
2000	550.0	541.8	546.3	549.1	558.5	562.1	552.8	557.5	557.9	564.6	581.7	595.5	559.8
2001	553.8	544.2	544.9	544.2	550.8	553.0	543.8	546.0	542.5	542.4	556.8	563.5	548.8
2002	526.7	515.8	519.5	522.8	531.8	534.9	530.1	532.2	532.6	528.2	542.1	551.1	530.7
2003	511.0	503.1	503.9	505.8	516.4	521.0	517.0	520.8	521.2	524.5	535.6	543.7	518.7
2004	507.6	500.1	500.9	506.2	515.6	518.0	513.7	515.4	510.5	513.5	526.9	534.5	513.6
2005	499.0	492.2	493.5	500.1	507.5	509.7	510.5	508.8	505.5	504.9	517.4	523.3	506.0
2006	490.1	481.9	484.6	488.8	496.1	499.4	497.4	497.2	494.9	496.7	510.5	514.8	496.0
2007	486.6	476.7	478.6	481.1	490.0	492.4	492.3	490.9	488.5	489.3	503.2	507.1	489.7
2008	481.0	472.2	473.5	472.4	480.5	482.3	480.7	480.0	476.3	474.8	481.1	482.3	478.1
2009	452.6	443.3	441.4	444.7	453.2	457.1	452.0	453.5	449.3	449.9	458.8	461.2	451.4
2010	437.7	431.1	432.3	438.6	446.5	450.5	451.6	450.2	445.4	450.6	460.4	463.5	446.5
2011	439.4	433.6	434.1	441.0	448.3	451.6	448.5	447.6	444.9	446.1	457.9	459.9	446.1
Transportation and Utilities													
2000	132.5	132.3	132.6	134.6	135.6	136.6	134.2	135.7	135.3	138.9	138.2	137.8	135.4
2001	131.2	129.8	129.4	132.1	133.2	134.6	132.2	133.5	132.3	133.3	131.6	131.1	132.0
2002	126.4	126.1	127.3	127.8	129.7	130.8	128.1	129.4	128.8	129.3	128.2	127.0	128.2
2003	125.1	124.0	124.6	125.4	127.0	127.7	124.8	126.3	126.0	126.9	126.0	126.0	125.8
2004	122.1	122.4	122.3	124.3	125.5	126.5	125.5	126.7	126.6	129.1	128.5	128.5	125.7
2005	124.2	124.9	125.5	126.5	128.3	129.7	128.1	130.7	130.2	130.0	130.5	131.2	128.3
2006	126.5	126.1	126.7	127.4	129.2	130.5	126.6	129.6	129.4	128.7	129.1	131.4	128.4
2007	125.4	126.6	126.3	127.0	129.0	130.6	126.8	130.1	129.8	128.6	128.8	130.4	128.3
2008	123.9	124.4	124.6	123.7	125.6	127.7	124.3	125.1	125.0	123.5	122.8	123.1	124.5
2009	113.0	114.3	113.4	112.0	112.3	112.3	111.4	112.5	113.2	113.1	112.7	114.2	112.9
2010	110.5	109.7	110.6	111.0	112.4	114.1	113.5	114.1	114.8	116.2	116.7	117.9	113.5
2011	114.5	114.0	114.4	115.4	117.5	119.1	118.8	119.7	118.2	118.8	119.5	121.0	117.6
Information													
2000	72.3	72.0	72.7	71.9	72.6	73.0	72.9	73.0	73.7	71.8	72.6	73.3	72.7
2001	71.6	71.8	72.2	71.6	72.3	72.6	72.3	72.2	71.7	71.7	72.8	72.7	72.1
2002	72.5	72.3	72.2	70.8	71.3	71.3	69.9	69.5	68.5	68.5	69.1	69.4	70.4
2003	67.8	67.6	67.9	67.7	67.9	67.9	66.8	66.7	66.0	65.9	66.4	66.8	67.1
2004	65.7	65.3	65.5	65.4	65.8	66.2	66.2	66.0	65.2	65.4	65.9	66.3	65.7
2005	65.5	64.9	65.0	65.0	65.4	65.6	65.3	65.0	64.2	63.9	64.6	64.8	64.9
2006	64.4	64.5	64.1	64.2	64.7	65.1	63.8	63.6	62.8	62.9	63.2	63.3	63.9
2007	63.4	63.4	63.1	63.4	64.1	64.0	63.2	62.9	62.0	61.8	62.0	62.0	62.9
2008	61.2	61.2	60.5	60.0	60.6	60.9	59.9	60.2	60.2	59.0	59.5	59.1	60.2
2009	57.8	57.7	56.7	56.8	57.0	57.0	56.2	55.6	55.0	55.0	55.6	55.7	56.3
2010	54.3	54.2	53.9	54.2	54.8	55.3	54.8	57.0	56.5	54.0	54.0	54.2	54.8
2011	53.8	53.5	53.4	52.6	53.1	53.3	53.0	53.5	53.1	53.6	53.9	54.0	53.4

1. Employment by Industry: Michigan, Selected Years, 2000–2011—*Continued*

(Numbers in thousands, not seasonally adjusted)

Industry and year	January	February	March	April	May	June	July	August	September	October	November	December	Annual average
Financial Activities													
2000	205.5	205.2	205.2	207.5	208.7	211.0	210.9	210.1	208.0	208.0	208.0	209.6	208.1
2001	203.8	204.8	206.0	207.4	210.7	212.9	211.7	212.0	209.1	209.0	209.3	211.0	209.0
2002	210.6	210.7	210.7	212.2	214.1	215.1	215.3	216.1	213.7	213.3	213.8	214.9	213.4
2003	213.1	213.1	213.4	216.4	218.7	220.5	220.4	220.6	217.5	215.9	214.9	215.7	216.7
2004	212.8	212.3	213.4	215.4	217.0	218.7	219.0	218.4	216.1	214.4	214.6	216.0	215.7
2005	214.5	214.5	214.5	215.5	216.9	218.8	218.4	218.4	216.2	215.0	215.0	215.2	216.1
2006	213.4	213.3	213.0	213.5	215.2	217.3	216.0	215.9	213.2	211.6	211.2	212.0	213.8
2007	209.1	209.0	208.8	209.9	211.5	213.2	213.1	211.5	208.0	207.0	206.1	206.5	209.5
2008	204.4	204.4	203.6	203.0	205.0	205.3	203.7	203.0	199.8	198.2	196.8	196.5	202.0
2009	193.1	192.6	191.4	192.4	193.5	194.3	193.2	192.6	189.8	188.4	187.8	187.5	191.4
2010	186.2	185.8	185.0	184.7	186.7	188.9	190.0	190.7	189.2	189.3	189.6	190.7	188.1
2011	190.4	190.9	191.5	191.1	192.5	194.3	195.3	194.5	194.3	194.8	193.6	195.4	193.2
Professional and Business Services													
2000	627.6	625.5	632.1	640.5	647.8	654.4	644.5	655.2	650.5	642.8	638.5	634.6	641.2
2001	607.7	608.0	609.9	616.0	618.9	623.4	610.5	620.3	613.4	602.6	596.6	592.7	610.0
2002	578.0	579.0	582.3	593.9	603.4	608.9	602.0	614.7	610.3	607.9	606.7	604.3	599.3
2003	578.6	577.0	579.2	589.3	597.6	600.6	585.4	596.0	592.4	587.9	588.6	585.9	588.2
2004	565.0	564.9	566.8	583.0	590.4	595.8	587.9	598.8	597.3	597.2	595.3	592.9	586.3
2005	573.7	574.7	576.2	592.1	596.8	599.7	594.7	604.4	606.8	601.1	600.1	597.2	593.1
2006	575.3	572.6	572.9	581.8	587.1	595.4	583.8	594.8	594.6	591.5	592.5	591.4	586.1
2007	565.0	567.7	568.1	577.5	584.5	588.3	575.5	586.3	585.8	589.8	592.1	588.4	580.8
2008	564.6	566.4	567.5	571.3	577.7	574.1	557.9	561.3	558.5	562.6	554.6	545.5	563.5
2009	510.1	509.4	505.2	506.5	506.3	495.2	480.6	484.9	497.1	507.1	509.2	506.5	501.5
2010	490.1	496.1	496.5	508.0	515.7	519.3	509.0	516.6	528.3	538.6	539.7	533.2	515.9
2011	528.2	533.4	540.0	551.4	559.8	553.6	540.8	546.2	549.7	564.1	565.2	559.8	549.4
Education and Health Services													
2000	492.6	499.1	500.1	501.4	501.5	502.0	498.0	499.1	504.0	507.0	511.0	509.3	502.1
2001	504.0	509.1	512.2	516.0	518.0	520.3	515.1	516.6	520.2	524.7	528.9	529.0	517.8
2002	522.4	528.0	531.0	536.4	538.1	538.0	528.9	530.2	536.2	541.7	546.0	544.3	535.1
2003	538.5	544.1	544.8	544.7	546.5	544.7	540.0	540.8	547.9	554.2	558.3	558.2	546.9
2004	548.8	555.2	558.5	562.0	562.1	556.6	553.2	553.4	564.1	569.6	574.0	573.3	560.9
2005	564.1	572.8	576.0	576.1	577.1	570.1	566.4	566.9	579.7	583.8	588.6	588.1	575.8
2006	575.2	580.6	585.4	583.0	586.0	580.6	573.7	573.6	587.6	588.4	592.6	593.2	583.3
2007	584.9	591.3	594.2	596.0	598.4	594.8	588.6	589.3	599.4	605.2	608.6	609.2	596.7
2008	600.0	605.4	607.2	607.2	610.3	606.1	600.1	600.1	607.8	613.8	616.0	614.6	607.4
2009	602.6	609.9	611.4	611.2	613.0	609.5	600.7	600.7	605.8	614.5	616.8	614.6	609.2
2010	603.6	609.4	610.9	611.9	613.8	609.6	605.3	605.6	610.3	618.9	621.8	620.8	611.8
2011	610.8	615.1	618.0	619.4	619.1	615.1	611.5	613.9	624.3	631.9	634.1	632.3	620.5
Leisure and Hospitality													
2000	369.7	371.5	376.2	389.7	408.4	420.6	420.5	421.4	411.8	404.7	393.1	390.7	398.2
2001	368.0	369.5	375.5	386.2	407.1	417.0	416.9	419.3	407.6	396.5	384.7	382.8	394.3
2002	367.2	367.8	375.6	390.1	411.0	421.1	421.3	424.0	414.3	402.1	391.1	389.3	397.9
2003	369.0	368.0	373.5	387.1	412.2	423.6	421.4	421.3	415.3	403.7	390.9	391.0	398.1
2004	375.3	375.9	381.3	395.1	415.5	426.7	424.8	426.3	419.1	402.6	391.3	390.5	402.0
2005	373.1	375.4	382.1	401.6	420.6	431.0	427.8	430.6	422.0	403.1	393.0	393.1	404.5
2006	376.6	381.2	386.9	401.1	419.8	433.0	428.2	430.3	421.7	403.8	392.2	391.9	405.6
2007	377.9	377.8	384.6	396.7	421.0	432.5	428.1	430.4	421.9	406.5	395.6	394.0	405.6
2008	374.8	374.2	379.8	391.9	415.2	425.3	422.0	424.5	412.6	395.5	382.5	381.2	398.3
2009	357.1	355.5	359.4	375.2	396.4	404.3	402.5	403.4	395.3	379.2	366.1	365.3	380.0
2010	348.1	348.9	353.6	369.4	387.8	400.2	398.2	401.4	392.1	377.4	365.9	365.7	375.7
2011	351.6	350.7	357.9	369.8	389.8	401.1	402.0	401.1	385.7	373.1	361.7	361.0	375.5
Other Services													
2000	170.7	172.6	174.3	175.4	175.9	177.4	177.1	177.4	175.7	175.4	175.4	175.9	175.3
2001	172.8	174.7	176.6	177.0	178.7	180.5	178.0	178.8	176.2	175.7	176.5	177.4	176.9
2002	174.6	175.9	177.4	178.8	180.5	182.1	181.2	181.8	180.4	179.7	179.2	180.4	179.3
2003	176.9	177.4	179.2	176.9	178.2	179.0	180.5	181.1	179.9	179.7	179.4	180.7	179.1
2004	176.8	178.1	179.2	178.4	180.1	181.8	180.2	180.5	180.5	180.1	179.2	179.8	179.6
2005	176.1	177.0	178.5	180.2	181.7	183.7	181.3	180.8	179.7	178.4	178.2	179.2	179.6
2006	174.8	175.9	177.5	177.6	179.0	181.1	178.4	178.8	177.9	176.2	176.1	177.0	177.5
2007	172.8	173.7	175.3	175.6	177.7	180.2	177.9	178.3	177.3	176.6	176.1	177.1	176.6
2008	173.3	174.2	175.2	176.0	178.1	179.6	177.5	177.4	176.1	174.9	172.7	171.9	175.6
2009	167.4	167.8	167.6	169.3	171.0	172.3	169.9	169.4	168.4	167.8	167.1	168.1	168.8
2010	163.8	164.5	165.3	165.4	166.7	168.8	168.4	168.2	166.5	166.2	165.8	166.1	166.3
2011	163.9	164.3	165.5	165.6	167.3	169.3	169.9	169.9	166.1	168.8	168.1	168.4	167.3
Government													
2000	672.4	695.4	704.8	700.2	700.1	672.8	618.8	612.0	680.9	703.4	710.0	705.7	681.4
2001	681.6	700.6	707.2	703.8	699.6	680.8	622.8	620.7	680.0	705.1	710.3	707.2	685.0
2002	688.8	705.8	709.2	697.1	694.6	674.8	618.8	619.7	684.9	714.8	717.9	712.7	686.6
2003	690.1	709.2	708.2	704.1	700.8	673.5	614.0	610.6	677.1	714.9	713.9	708.5	685.4
2004	686.2	701.2	704.1	701.2	696.1	668.6	605.6	603.3	678.8	703.3	706.7	701.5	679.7
2005	677.5	697.4	698.9	697.6	691.9	663.3	597.4	599.0	677.8	695.3	700.0	692.9	674.1
2006	671.7	690.4	695.3	687.7	680.6	653.9	593.4	589.9	664.9	684.9	688.7	682.4	665.3
2007	660.2	677.9	683.0	674.3	673.4	646.8	591.3	594.1	654.8	671.3	672.7	668.4	655.7
2008	649.2	665.5	666.9	668.2	658.0	641.9	593.0	598.6	654.8	670.7	671.7	662.0	650.0
2009	652.7	665.0	666.0	669.3	659.9	639.1	589.6	589.5	645.7	663.9	664.4	656.1	646.8
2010	641.7	655.4	655.9	658.5	657.2	633.7	584.7	576.0	630.0	646.0	648.2	640.0	635.6
2011	625.0	636.2	638.3	638.5	625.2	612.3	568.0	565.2	618.5	634.0	634.1	626.5	618.5

2. Average Weekly Hours by Selected Industry: Michigan, 2007–2011

(Not seasonally adjusted)

Industry and year	January	February	March	April	May	June	July	August	September	October	November	December	Annual average
Total Private													
2007	34.6	34.6	34.7	34.8	34.8	35.1	35.0	35.3	35.3	34.9	34.7	35.1	34.9
2008	34.3	34.3	34.5	34.3	34.4	34.6	34.2	34.4	34.3	34.1	33.8	33.5	34.2
2009	32.6	33.5	33.4	33.0	33.1	33.4	33.5	34.0	33.3	33.4	33.5	33.3	33.3
2010	33.0	33.0	33.2	33.4	33.8	33.9	34.0	34.3	33.9	34.1	34.1	34.0	33.7
2011	34.0	33.8	33.8	34.0	34.5	34.2	34.2	34.4	34.3	34.6	34.3	34.2	34.2
Goods-Producing													
2007	40.4	39.8	40.3	40.5	40.6	40.8	39.8	41.2	41.4	41.1	40.1	41.5	40.6
2008	40.4	40.5	40.9	40.6	40.7	41.3	40.2	40.7	40.9	40.7	39.1	39.2	40.4
2009	36.3	38.1	38.3	38.0	37.5	39.2	39.2	40.0	38.3	39.3	39.0	40.0	38.6
2010	39.3	39.2	39.7	40.1	40.6	41.1	40.7	41.4	40.8	40.9	41.0	41.0	40.5
2011	41.3	41.1	41.3	41.1	41.7	41.2	40.5	41.6	41.7	41.6	41.5	41.3	41.3
Construction													
2007	38.0	36.5	37.4	37.4	38.4	39.1	39.1	38.5	38.7	39.0	37.1	38.1	38.2
2008	37.6	37.1	38.1	38.2	38.7	38.9	38.6	38.5	38.3	38.0	37.4	37.1	38.1
2009	36.1	36.8	35.8	35.7	37.5	36.9	38.1	38.4	36.3	38.5	37.4	37.2	37.1
2010	37.0	36.5	36.9	37.7	37.9	38.5	38.2	38.7	38.0	39.5	39.0	38.4	38.1
2011	37.8	37.7	37.7	38.3	39.4	39.5	40.2	40.5	40.8	40.4	39.6	38.7	39.3
Manufacturing													
2007	40.7	40.3	40.7	40.9	40.8	41.0	39.7	41.7	41.9	41.5	40.6	41.8	41.0
2008	41.1	41.3	41.5	41.2	41.2	42.6	41.0	41.6	41.9	41.4	40.0	40.3	41.3
2009	36.8	38.9	39.4	39.1	37.9	40.3	39.9	40.7	39.0	39.6	39.5	40.7	39.3
2010	39.8	39.9	40.5	40.6	41.0	41.3	41.0	41.6	41.3	41.1	41.3	41.5	40.9
2011	41.6	41.4	41.6	41.3	41.8	41.3	40.2	41.3	41.4	41.4	41.5	41.5	41.4
Trade, Transportation, and Utilities													
2007	33.5	33.6	33.4	33.5	33.7	34.3	34.7	34.8	34.6	34.2	34.4	34.6	34.1
2008	33.7	33.5	33.7	33.6	33.6	34.0	33.8	34.0	33.8	33.3	32.8	32.4	33.5
2009	32.2	32.5	32.3	32.1	32.7	32.6	33.0	33.1	33.1	32.6	32.7	32.4	32.6
2010	32.0	32.2	32.2	32.2	32.8	32.9	33.1	33.4	33.0	33.1	32.9	33.2	32.8
2011	32.8	32.9	32.7	33.2	33.4	33.3	33.6	33.5	33.5	33.7	33.1	33.4	33.3
Information													
2007	35.2	35.8	35.7	35.9	35.1	35.6	35.5	35.0	35.6	35.2	35.2	35.7	35.5
2008	34.8	35.9	35.9	35.4	35.6	35.9	35.3	35.3	34.9	34.8	35.9	36.4	35.5
2009	35.8	36.6	36.4	35.8	37.3	36.1	35.4	36.4	36.3	35.5	36.3	35.6	36.1
2010	35.3	34.9	34.9	34.3	34.5	34.9	35.2	35.5	35.2	34.5	34.9	35.2	34.9
2011	35.6	34.7	35.2	34.9	36.5	35.7	36.0	35.8	35.7	36.3	36.0	36.1	35.7
Financial Activities													
2007	35.6	35.4	35.3	35.6	35.4	35.9	36.3	35.8	36.0	35.8	35.9	36.4	35.8
2008	35.9	35.9	36.3	36.0	36.1	36.1	36.1	36.2	36.5	36.5	36.6	36.1	36.2
2009	35.3	36.0	36.1	36.2	36.0	36.0	36.2	36.6	35.8	36.0	36.7	36.2	36.1
2010	36.3	36.1	36.7	36.4	37.2	36.9	36.6	36.9	36.7	36.4	36.2	36.3	36.6
2011	36.2	35.8	35.8	35.6	36.5	36.3	36.5	36.7	36.4	36.8	36.7	37.1	36.4
Professional and Business Services													
2007	33.7	33.9	33.9	34.4	34.6	34.8	34.9	34.4	34.8	34.6	34.4	34.8	34.4
2008	33.8	33.9	34.5	34.3	34.5	34.7	34.1	34.1	33.8	34.0	34.5	34.2	34.2
2009	33.9	34.8	34.9	34.0	34.6	34.6	34.6	35.7	34.6	34.7	35.2	34.4	34.7
2010	34.7	34.3	34.5	35.0	35.6	35.4	35.1	35.9	35.1	36.0	35.9	35.7	35.3
2011	35.7	35.2	35.5	35.8	36.5	35.7	35.7	35.9	35.6	36.5	36.0	35.7	35.8
Education and Health Services													
2007	37.2	37.6	37.8	37.4	37.4	37.0	37.0	37.2	37.3	36.5	36.6	36.4	37.1
2008	35.7	35.6	35.6	35.2	35.3	34.9	34.8	34.5	34.7	34.1	34.4	34.0	34.9
2009	33.7	34.4	34.1	33.7	33.6	33.4	33.4	33.4	33.0	33.0	32.9	32.5	33.4
2010	32.2	32.0	32.0	32.1	32.1	32.1	32.4	32.5	32.5	32.7	32.7	32.3	32.3
2011	32.5	32.1	32.1	32.1	32.3	32.2	32.3	32.0	32.0	32.2	32.0	31.9	32.1
Leisure and Hospitality													
2007	23.2	23.3	23.4	23.4	23.7	24.4	24.8	24.8	23.9	23.2	23.0	23.0	23.7
2008	22.5	22.5	22.9	23.1	23.5	23.7	24.2	24.5	23.6	23.5	22.9	23.0	23.4
2009	22.3	22.9	22.8	22.7	23.5	23.9	24.5	24.7	23.9	23.7	23.4	23.4	23.5
2010	23.0	23.4	23.6	23.8	24.0	24.7	25.4	25.3	24.5	24.4	24.0	24.0	24.2
2011	23.9	23.8	23.9	23.9	24.8	24.8	25.3	25.3	24.7	24.7	24.4	24.3	24.5
Other Services													
2007	31.3	31.2	31.2	31.4	31.8	31.7	31.8	31.9	32.2	32.1	31.4	31.3	31.6
2008	31.1	31.0	30.9	30.7	30.3	31.0	31.6	31.6	31.0	31.2	31.6	31.3	31.1
2009	31.7	31.8	31.5	31.8	31.6	31.2	31.6	32.0	31.0	30.9	31.2	30.7	31.4
2010	30.7	30.8	31.6	31.8	32.3	31.6	31.8	31.9	31.4	31.3	31.9	31.7	31.6
2011	31.8	32.0	31.2	31.8	32.0	32.0	31.9	31.7	31.7	31.8	31.6	31.4	31.7

3. Average Hourly Earnings by Selected Industry: Michigan, 2007–2011

(Dollars, not seasonally adjusted)

Industry and year	January	February	March	April	May	June	July	August	September	October	November	December	Annual average
Total Private													
2007	21.57	21.50	21.65	21.78	21.51	21.32	21.38	21.26	21.67	21.43	21.65	21.93	21.55
2008	21.93	21.90	21.97	21.73	21.30	21.43	21.09	21.17	21.45	21.54	22.00	21.93	21.62
2009	22.01	22.17	22.17	22.03	21.81	21.74	21.71	21.37	21.60	21.91	22.06	22.13	21.89
2010	22.12	22.14	22.15	22.17	22.18	21.97	22.07	22.25	22.36	22.41	22.50	22.80	22.26
2011	22.85	22.67	22.36	22.43	22.52	22.04	22.20	21.97	22.11	22.45	22.27	22.35	22.35
Goods-Producing													
2007	25.79	25.57	25.70	25.63	25.76	25.53	25.51	25.35	25.63	25.38	25.38	26.18	25.62
2008	25.64	25.64	25.78	25.34	24.99	25.07	24.50	24.40	24.76	24.71	25.16	25.37	25.11
2009	25.50	25.70	25.51	25.58	25.20	25.29	25.45	24.11	24.71	25.04	25.06	25.51	25.22
2010	25.06	25.08	25.15	25.10	25.17	25.11	25.33	25.38	25.50	25.30	25.45	25.86	25.30
2011	25.48	25.44	25.40	25.04	25.04	24.59	24.74	24.29	24.45	24.57	24.43	24.57	24.82
Construction													
2007	22.84	23.06	23.44	23.74	23.71	23.96	24.71	24.69	25.09	25.22	25.57	25.60	24.35
2008	26.29	26.45	26.50	26.76	25.96	25.84	26.17	26.11	26.54	26.05	26.22	27.06	26.31
2009	27.08	26.74	26.74	26.65	26.25	26.05	26.02	26.07	26.03	26.02	25.95	26.78	26.34
2010	26.34	26.37	26.35	26.42	26.40	26.29	26.24	26.23	26.25	26.31	26.11	26.72	26.33
2011	26.52	26.71	26.34	26.06	25.30	25.03	25.15	25.03	25.14	25.01	25.38	25.84	25.55
Manufacturing													
2007	23.12	23.14	23.79	23.97	24.07	23.94	23.93	23.92	24.34	24.15	24.20	25.11	23.98
2008	25.51	25.52	25.75	25.10	24.84	24.95	25.00	24.81	25.09	25.07	25.53	25.57	25.23
2009	25.70	24.80	24.66	24.82	24.52	24.72	24.97	23.15	24.09	24.48	24.56	24.73	24.59
2010	24.39	24.46	24.58	24.67	24.66	24.76	24.82	24.88	25.05	24.82	25.11	25.26	24.80
2011	25.43	25.35	25.37	24.95	25.09	24.58	24.75	24.16	24.35	24.55	24.29	24.51	24.77
Trade, Transportation, and Utilities													
2007	19.97	19.89	19.29	19.62	19.50	19.05	19.09	18.91	18.97	18.63	18.90	18.63	19.19
2008	19.21	19.15	18.96	19.05	18.67	18.85	18.85	18.69	18.50	18.54	18.95	18.39	18.82
2009	18.84	18.80	18.76	18.84	18.62	18.66	18.56	18.94	18.85	18.95	19.17	19.03	18.84
2010	19.50	19.23	19.21	19.46	19.46	19.55	19.46	19.65	19.64	19.67	19.78	19.98	19.55
2011	20.17	20.08	19.33	19.44	19.40	19.26	19.22	19.08	19.12	19.40	19.29	19.26	19.41
Information													
2007	22.09	21.79	21.99	22.24	22.69	22.24	22.64	22.15	22.98	22.34	22.16	22.42	22.31
2008	22.72	22.30	22.61	22.84	22.92	23.13	23.04	23.05	23.36	23.25	23.70	24.20	23.09
2009	24.78	25.27	25.29	25.27	26.12	26.25	27.51	27.18	27.11	27.83	28.74	29.16	26.69
2010	28.68	28.79	30.03	30.42	31.10	31.42	32.09	31.07	30.59	31.22	31.45	31.62	30.71
2011	32.35	31.88	31.75	32.43	32.36	31.32	31.02	30.90	30.59	31.41	31.00	30.82	31.48
Financial Activities													
2007	21.97	22.08	22.40	22.84	22.36	22.12	22.32	22.76	23.57	23.31	23.41	24.23	22.78
2008	23.60	23.27	23.69	24.08	23.45	23.97	23.59	23.39	23.21	23.20	23.80	22.90	23.51
2009	23.24	22.77	22.97	23.20	24.08	23.11	23.56	24.24	24.07	24.21	24.49	24.27	23.68
2010	24.51	24.68	24.62	25.19	24.90	24.28	24.71	24.68	24.51	24.69	24.71	25.00	24.71
2011	24.91	24.61	23.97	24.79	24.18	23.46	24.10	23.72	23.76	24.19	24.11	23.89	24.14
Professional and Business Services													
2007	24.92	25.21	25.64	25.80	25.29	25.22	25.48	25.22	25.86	24.96	25.81	26.08	25.46
2008	25.92	26.14	26.65	25.51	24.78	25.08	24.93	25.67	26.32	26.60	27.55	28.08	26.09
2009	28.08	28.99	29.03	28.44	28.13	27.80	27.66	25.96	25.98	26.21	27.05	27.01	27.53
2010	26.81	27.34	27.25	26.76	26.86	26.16	26.57	27.06	26.89	26.91	27.13	27.93	26.97
2011	28.41	27.85	27.41	27.54	28.57	27.32	27.96	27.45	27.48	28.03	27.50	27.96	27.79
Education and Health Services													
2007	18.97	18.86	19.69	19.67	19.08	19.26	19.65	19.30	19.73	19.75	19.84	20.06	19.49
2008	20.62	20.26	20.32	20.64	20.30	20.15	20.12	20.04	20.25	20.35	20.34	20.38	20.32
2009	20.59	20.45	20.51	20.53	20.54	20.80	20.86	21.08	21.49	21.86	21.24	21.27	20.93
2010	21.07	21.07	21.08	21.18	21.18	21.04	21.10	21.14	21.49	21.46	21.30	21.35	21.21
2011	21.13	21.13	20.98	21.26	21.25	21.32	21.69	21.61	21.66	21.75	21.63	21.72	21.43
Leisure and Hospitality													
2007	11.21	11.19	11.27	11.37	11.21	11.01	11.10	10.96	11.46	11.57	11.73	11.87	11.32
2008	11.56	11.53	11.60	11.48	11.45	11.28	11.23	11.20	11.50	11.38	11.55	11.60	11.44
2009	11.50	11.41	11.51	11.50	11.32	11.29	11.21	11.31	11.52	11.52	11.70	11.74	11.45
2010	11.66	11.69	11.70	11.74	11.72	11.69	11.69	11.73	11.77	11.91	11.89	11.94	11.76
2011	11.83	11.83	11.69	11.75	11.65	11.51	11.42	11.36	11.42	11.57	11.47	11.56	11.58
Other Services													
2007	19.54	19.22	19.37	19.44	19.16	19.29	19.31	19.11	19.04	19.65	19.74	19.03	19.32
2008	18.96	19.59	18.99	18.77	18.70	18.98	18.43	18.99	19.51	19.69	20.51	20.38	19.29
2009	20.42	20.02	20.32	19.64	19.64	19.44	19.06	18.78	19.05	19.20	19.03	19.43	19.50
2010	19.83	19.69	19.68	19.49	19.60	19.42	19.39	19.65	19.87	20.01	19.77	20.02	19.70
2011	20.14	19.55	19.61	19.70	19.62	19.31	19.21	19.13	19.39	19.76	19.69	19.58	19.56

4. Average Weekly Earnings by Selected Industry: Michigan, 2007–2011

(Dollars, not seasonally adjusted)

Industry and year	January	February	March	April	May	June	July	August	September	October	November	December	Annual average
Total Private													
2007	746.32	743.90	751.26	757.94	748.55	748.33	748.30	750.48	764.95	747.91	751.26	769.74	752.68
2008	752.20	751.17	757.97	745.34	732.72	741.48	721.28	728.25	735.74	734.51	743.60	734.66	739.92
2009	717.53	742.70	740.48	726.99	721.91	726.12	727.29	726.58	719.28	731.79	739.01	736.93	729.65
2010	729.96	730.62	735.38	740.48	749.68	744.78	750.38	763.18	758.00	764.18	767.25	775.20	750.94
2011	776.90	766.25	755.77	762.62	776.94	753.77	759.24	755.77	758.37	776.77	763.86	764.37	763.91
Goods-Producing													
2007	1,041.92	1,017.69	1,035.71	1,038.02	1,045.86	1,041.62	1,015.30	1,044.42	1,061.08	1,043.12	1,017.74	1,086.47	1,040.78
2008	1,035.86	1,038.42	1,054.40	1,028.80	1,017.09	1,035.39	984.90	993.08	1,012.68	1,005.70	983.76	994.50	1,015.67
2009	925.65	979.17	977.03	972.04	945.00	991.37	997.64	964.40	946.39	984.07	977.34	1,020.40	973.26
2010	984.86	983.14	998.46	1,006.51	1,021.90	1,032.02	1,030.93	1,050.73	1,040.40	1,034.77	1,043.45	1,060.26	1,024.83
2011	1,052.32	1,045.58	1,049.02	1,029.14	1,044.17	1,013.11	1,001.97	1,010.46	1,019.57	1,022.11	1,013.85	1,014.74	1,025.85
Construction													
2007	867.92	841.69	876.66	887.88	910.46	936.84	966.16	950.57	970.98	983.58	948.65	975.36	929.14
2008	988.50	981.30	1,009.65	1,022.23	1,004.65	1,005.18	1,010.16	1,005.24	1,016.48	989.90	980.63	1,003.93	1,001.77
2009	977.59	984.03	957.29	951.41	984.38	961.25	991.36	1,001.09	944.89	1,001.77	970.53	996.22	976.93
2010	974.58	962.51	972.32	996.03	1,000.56	1,012.17	1,002.37	1,015.10	997.50	1,039.25	1,018.29	1,026.05	1,003.34
2011	1,002.46	1,006.97	993.02	998.10	996.82	988.69	1,011.03	1,013.72	1,025.71	1,010.40	1,005.05	1,000.01	1,004.53
Manufacturing													
2007	940.98	932.54	968.25	980.37	982.06	981.54	950.02	997.46	1,019.85	1,002.23	982.52	1,049.60	982.24
2008	1,048.46	1,053.98	1,068.63	1,034.12	1,023.41	1,062.87	1,025.00	1,032.10	1,051.27	1,037.90	1,021.20	1,030.47	1,041.11
2009	945.76	964.72	971.60	970.46	929.31	996.22	996.30	942.21	939.51	969.41	970.12	1,006.51	966.69
2010	970.72	975.95	995.49	1,001.60	1,011.06	1,022.59	1,017.62	1,035.01	1,034.57	1,020.10	1,037.04	1,048.29	1,014.68
2011	1,057.89	1,049.49	1,055.39	1,030.44	1,048.76	1,015.15	994.95	997.81	1,008.09	1,016.37	1,008.04	1,017.17	1,024.66
Trade, Transportation, and Utilities													
2007	669.00	668.30	644.29	657.27	657.15	653.42	662.42	658.07	656.36	637.15	650.16	644.60	654.80
2008	647.38	641.53	638.95	640.08	627.31	640.90	637.13	635.46	625.30	617.38	621.56	595.84	630.75
2009	606.65	611.00	605.95	604.76	608.87	608.32	612.48	626.91	623.94	617.77	626.86	616.57	614.18
2010	624.00	619.21	618.56	626.61	638.29	643.20	644.13	656.31	648.12	651.08	650.76	663.34	640.58
2011	661.58	660.63	632.09	645.41	647.96	641.36	645.79	639.18	640.52	653.78	638.50	643.28	645.76
Information													
2007	777.57	780.08	785.04	798.42	796.42	791.74	803.72	775.25	818.09	786.37	780.03	800.39	791.07
2008	790.66	800.57	811.70	808.54	815.95	830.37	813.31	813.67	815.26	809.10	850.83	880.88	819.91
2009	887.12	924.88	920.56	904.67	974.28	947.63	973.85	989.35	984.09	987.97	1,043.26	1,038.10	964.24
2010	1,012.40	1,004.77	1,048.05	1,043.41	1,072.95	1,096.56	1,129.57	1,102.99	1,076.77	1,077.09	1,097.61	1,113.02	1,073.07
2011	1,151.66	1,106.24	1,117.60	1,131.81	1,181.14	1,118.12	1,116.72	1,106.22	1,092.06	1,140.18	1,116.00	1,112.60	1,124.20
Financial Activities													
2007	782.13	781.63	790.72	813.10	791.54	794.11	810.22	814.81	848.52	834.50	840.42	881.97	815.11
2008	847.24	835.39	859.95	866.88	846.55	865.32	851.60	846.72	847.17	846.80	871.08	826.69	850.98
2009	820.37	819.72	829.22	839.84	866.88	831.96	852.87	887.18	861.71	871.56	898.78	878.57	854.76
2010	889.71	890.95	903.55	916.92	926.28	895.93	904.39	910.69	899.52	898.72	894.50	907.50	903.30
2011	901.74	881.04	858.13	882.52	882.57	851.60	879.65	870.52	864.86	890.19	884.84	886.32	877.81
Professional and Business Services													
2007	839.80	854.62	869.20	887.52	875.03	877.66	889.25	867.57	899.93	863.62	887.86	907.58	876.81
2008	876.10	886.15	919.43	874.99	854.91	870.28	850.11	875.35	889.62	904.40	950.48	960.34	892.34
2009	951.91	1,008.85	1,013.15	966.96	973.30	961.88	957.04	926.77	898.91	909.49	952.16	929.14	954.31
2010	930.31	937.76	940.13	936.60	956.22	926.06	932.61	971.45	943.84	968.76	973.97	997.10	951.70
2011	1,014.24	980.32	973.06	985.93	1,042.81	975.32	998.17	985.46	978.29	1,023.10	990.00	998.17	995.54
Education and Health Services													
2007	705.68	709.14	744.28	735.66	713.59	712.62	727.05	717.96	735.93	720.88	726.14	730.18	723.31
2008	736.13	721.26	723.39	726.53	716.59	703.24	700.18	691.38	702.68	693.94	699.70	692.92	708.95
2009	693.88	703.48	699.39	691.86	690.14	694.72	696.72	704.07	709.17	721.38	698.80	691.28	699.58
2010	678.45	674.24	674.56	679.88	679.88	675.38	683.64	687.05	698.43	701.74	696.51	689.61	684.99
2011	686.73	678.27	673.46	682.45	686.38	686.50	700.59	691.52	693.12	700.35	692.16	692.87	688.70
Leisure and Hospitality													
2007	260.07	260.73	263.72	266.06	265.68	268.64	275.28	271.81	273.89	268.42	269.79	273.01	268.25
2008	260.10	259.43	265.64	265.19	269.08	267.34	271.77	274.40	271.40	267.43	264.50	266.80	267.10
2009	256.45	261.29	262.43	261.05	266.02	269.83	274.65	279.36	275.33	273.02	273.78	274.72	269.19
2010	268.18	273.55	276.12	279.41	281.28	288.74	296.93	296.77	288.37	290.60	285.36	286.56	284.68
2011	282.74	281.55	279.39	280.83	288.92	285.45	288.93	287.41	282.07	285.78	279.87	280.91	283.81
Other Services													
2007	611.60	599.66	604.34	610.42	609.29	611.49	614.06	609.61	613.09	630.77	619.84	595.64	610.83
2008	589.66	607.29	586.79	576.24	566.61	588.38	582.39	600.08	604.81	614.33	648.12	637.89	600.01
2009	647.31	636.64	640.08	624.55	620.62	606.53	602.30	600.96	590.55	593.28	593.74	596.50	612.72
2010	608.78	606.45	621.89	619.78	633.08	613.67	616.60	626.84	623.92	626.31	630.66	634.63	621.88
2011	640.45	625.60	611.83	626.46	627.84	617.92	612.80	606.42	614.66	628.37	622.20	614.81	620.70

MINNESOTA
At a Glance

Population:
    2000 census: 4,919,631
    2010 census: 5,303,925
    2011 estimate: 5,344,861

Percent change in population:
    2000–2010: 7.8%
    2010–2011: 0.8%

Percent change in total nonfarm employment:
    2000–2010: -1.6%
    2010–2011: 1.3%

Industry with the largest growth in employment, 2000–2011 (thousands):
    Education and Health Services, 143.7

Industry with the largest decline or smallest growth in employment, 2000–2011 (thousands):
    Manufacturing, -95.9

Civilian labor force:
    2000: 2,807,668
    2010: 2,958,686
    2011: 2,977,919

Unemployment rate and rank among states (lowest to highest):
    2000: 3.1%, 12th
    2010: 7.3%, 13th
    2011: 6.4%, 10th

Over-the-year change in unemployment rates:
    2010–2011: -0.9%

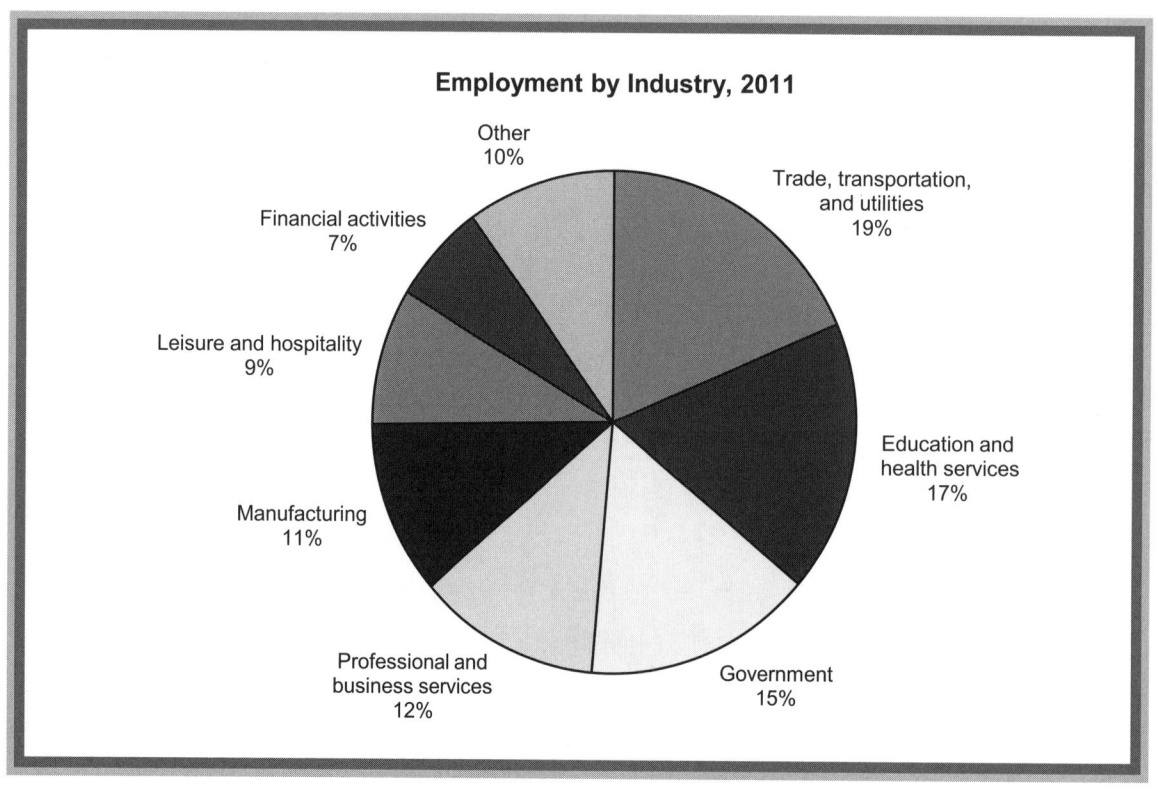

Employment by Industry, 2011

Other 10%
Trade, transportation, and utilities 19%
Financial activities 7%
Education and health services 17%
Leisure and hospitality 9%
Manufacturing 11%
Government 15%
Professional and business services 12%

1. Employment by Industry: Minnesota, Selected Years, 2000–2011

(Numbers in thousands, not seasonally adjusted)

Industry and year	January	February	March	April	May	June	July	August	September	October	November	December	Annual average
Total Nonfarm													
2000	2,600.1	2,613.2	2,633.4	2,665.8	2,700.3	2,727.8	2,690.8	2,698.9	2,713.0	2,723.5	2,727.4	2,725.0	2,684.9
2001	2,648.8	2,654.2	2,664.9	2,681.6	2,716.0	2,735.7	2,690.0	2,688.6	2,699.3	2,704.0	2,700.8	2,689.5	2,689.5
2002	2,612.2	2,610.2	2,617.1	2,641.5	2,681.6	2,706.2	2,673.8	2,673.3	2,690.0	2,690.2	2,693.5	2,684.0	2,664.5
2003	2,605.4	2,607.4	2,613.4	2,646.1	2,685.6	2,703.0	2,663.6	2,671.3	2,681.5	2,686.9	2,680.3	2,679.1	2,660.3
2004	2,598.2	2,601.3	2,612.8	2,668.0	2,705.2	2,727.4	2,690.3	2,693.1	2,707.5	2,724.7	2,720.9	2,722.9	2,681.0
2005	2,629.3	2,634.4	2,648.3	2,705.1	2,746.5	2,768.3	2,737.9	2,743.8	2,757.5	2,769.6	2,769.8	2,768.9	2,723.3
2006	2,701.9	2,700.9	2,715.7	2,737.9	2,775.2	2,810.0	2,766.1	2,767.7	2,775.9	2,781.5	2,783.9	2,781.2	2,758.2
2007	2,711.5	2,711.9	2,722.2	2,746.1	2,793.9	2,823.4	2,784.3	2,786.4	2,788.4	2,798.9	2,799.7	2,789.1	2,771.3
2008	2,719.1	2,721.8	2,729.4	2,747.2	2,792.1	2,814.6	2,775.1	2,779.1	2,777.4	2,787.8	2,768.4	2,744.1	2,763.0
2009	2,654.2	2,640.5	2,632.0	2,653.1	2,683.2	2,690.4	2,650.4	2,646.8	2,639.4	2,665.8	2,658.1	2,647.1	2,655.1
2010	2,570.3	2,571.7	2,581.3	2,628.8	2,663.1	2,683.0	2,649.6	2,654.7	2,656.9	2,685.5	2,681.6	2,667.9	2,641.2
2011	2,607.3	2,614.5	2,623.9	2,670.7	2,705.5	2,723.5	2,673.9	2,704.7	2,697.1	2,711.2	2,694.8	2,681.8	2,675.7
Total Private													
2000	2,198.8	2,201.6	2,218.7	2,246.8	2,276.2	2,312.7	2,311.0	2,322.7	2,312.5	2,311.1	2,308.3	2,307.3	2,277.3
2001	2,243.9	2,237.8	2,247.7	2,263.6	2,295.9	2,318.8	2,308.5	2,314.8	2,295.1	2,286.9	2,280.4	2,268.2	2,280.1
2002	2,197.9	2,189.8	2,197.1	2,223.3	2,261.5	2,285.3	2,282.4	2,293.5	2,279.6	2,270.3	2,266.1	2,259.0	2,250.5
2003	2,192.6	2,185.8	2,192.0	2,223.5	2,263.4	2,285.0	2,278.8	2,288.5	2,277.0	2,269.5	2,260.6	2,257.4	2,247.8
2004	2,186.6	2,182.4	2,193.9	2,247.5	2,282.8	2,312.6	2,306.6	2,313.9	2,300.4	2,305.5	2,297.5	2,298.0	2,269.0
2005	2,212.9	2,212.3	2,225.4	2,280.5	2,321.6	2,348.3	2,346.8	2,359.1	2,348.8	2,349.0	2,349.6	2,346.7	2,308.4
2006	2,286.7	2,279.4	2,293.2	2,314.9	2,351.7	2,388.3	2,374.9	2,381.3	2,365.0	2,359.1	2,358.1	2,354.2	2,342.2
2007	2,297.3	2,291.4	2,302.6	2,325.9	2,369.9	2,401.3	2,394.8	2,402.4	2,380.8	2,376.4	2,373.8	2,364.1	2,356.7
2008	2,302.0	2,297.9	2,305.0	2,323.3	2,363.9	2,388.1	2,383.0	2,390.5	2,363.5	2,360.5	2,337.8	2,314.1	2,344.1
2009	2,236.8	2,215.5	2,206.8	2,226.4	2,254.7	2,264.7	2,257.3	2,261.5	2,235.3	2,242.1	2,231.6	2,221.0	2,237.8
2010	2,153.6	2,148.2	2,155.9	2,202.5	2,232.5	2,257.2	2,260.3	2,271.5	2,252.1	2,263.2	2,255.8	2,243.1	2,224.7
2011	2,193.7	2,193.2	2,202.9	2,247.9	2,284.3	2,304.6	2,313.4	2,328.7	2,296.4	2,297.5	2,279.7	2,269.4	2,267.6
Goods-Producing													
2000	496.0	495.2	501.1	513.6	525.5	540.1	542.8	547.2	540.4	534.5	526.9	519.2	523.5
2001	500.5	496.7	497.3	501.3	511.8	520.9	523.2	524.8	519.5	511.1	502.3	490.7	508.3
2002	470.1	464.8	466.9	474.5	489.1	501.5	503.6	508.2	501.7	494.4	486.5	474.4	486.3
2003	455.7	450.3	451.6	461.9	477.3	489.6	491.1	494.8	489.1	485.2	477.3	467.4	474.3
2004	446.5	443.6	446.4	465.0	477.9	492.1	496.4	500.1	496.0	495.6	487.4	479.5	477.2
2005	454.7	452.5	455.7	470.7	487.2	499.4	502.9	506.4	500.7	494.2	488.6	477.6	482.6
2006	461.5	457.6	460.7	469.3	482.6	497.6	496.8	498.5	492.1	487.4	477.0	467.7	479.1
2007	452.0	446.6	449.4	454.9	471.9	485.5	485.0	486.9	479.0	474.8	468.0	456.5	467.5
2008	440.4	436.6	437.5	442.2	458.9	470.0	471.1	472.3	463.7	459.9	445.9	429.5	452.3
2009	406.2	395.5	389.5	391.1	399.1	406.7	407.8	407.9	402.8	400.3	392.6	381.3	398.4
2010	362.9	358.3	359.7	375.3	386.4	397.5	404.3	405.8	402.5	402.0	395.1	385.0	386.2
2011	372.9	371.2	373.6	385.8	399.0	410.8	417.7	423.7	415.4	412.5	404.5	391.3	398.2
Mining and Logging													
2000	7.8	7.7	7.7	7.8	8.2	8.3	8.5	8.5	8.4	8.4	8.1	7.8	8.1
2001	7.5	6.9	6.6	6.3	6.7	6.9	6.3	7.0	6.9	6.9	6.3	6.2	6.7
2002	6.2	5.6	6.2	6.1	6.4	6.7	6.7	6.8	6.7	6.7	6.6	6.3	6.4
2003	6.1	6.0	6.0	5.9	6.3	6.4	6.5	6.1	5.9	6.0	5.8	5.6	6.1
2004	5.6	5.6	5.6	5.8	6.1	6.3	6.4	6.5	6.4	6.2	6.1	6.0	6.1
2005	5.6	5.7	5.7	5.8	6.1	6.3	6.3	6.3	6.2	6.1	6.0	5.7	6.0
2006	5.7	5.8	5.8	5.8	5.9	6.3	6.4	6.4	6.2	6.2	6.0	5.8	6.0
2007	5.6	5.6	5.6	5.6	5.9	6.1	6.3	6.4	6.2	6.2	6.2	6.0	6.0
2008	5.9	5.9	5.9	5.9	6.3	6.4	6.7	6.7	6.5	6.5	6.3	6.0	6.3
2009	5.8	5.6	5.3	5.1	4.6	4.4	5.3	5.0	4.6	5.7	5.4	5.0	5.2
2010	5.3	5.4	5.4	5.7	6.0	5.6	6.5	6.5	6.4	6.5	6.3	6.0	6.0
2011	6.0	6.2	6.1	6.1	6.5	6.8	7.0	7.1	6.9	7.0	6.8	6.5	6.6
Construction													
2000	97.3	97.0	101.2	112.4	122.6	130.7	132.7	134.2	131.1	129.0	122.9	115.1	118.9
2001	104.0	102.6	104.9	112.5	123.9	134.0	138.1	139.3	135.0	133.6	129.2	120.0	123.1
2002	106.1	103.2	104.1	113.0	126.5	134.5	139.6	141.2	138.1	134.5	128.6	119.3	124.1
2003	106.0	102.6	103.6	113.3	127.2	136.1	140.2	141.9	138.9	137.1	130.7	121.4	124.9
2004	105.5	103.5	105.8	120.3	131.4	138.7	143.3	144.0	141.5	140.7	136.5	127.3	128.2
2005	108.3	106.5	108.5	120.6	132.7	140.9	145.5	146.1	143.2	139.0	135.1	126.4	129.4
2006	114.6	112.8	114.2	120.8	131.6	139.7	139.7	139.3	136.7	133.7	127.7	118.8	127.5
2007	108.0	104.0	106.5	110.3	124.9	132.6	132.7	133.4	129.2	126.7	121.6	111.3	120.1
2008	100.3	97.4	98.4	102.3	115.7	122.6	123.8	123.9	119.5	116.6	107.9	97.4	110.5
2009	82.1	79.6	79.6	86.5	97.7	102.4	103.9	103.8	102.3	100.0	95.2	87.3	93.4
2010	73.3	69.5	70.2	81.9	89.4	95.6	99.2	99.8	98.0	97.9	92.8	83.4	87.6
2011	74.2	72.7	74.5	83.0	93.1	100.6	102.8	105.9	102.6	102.2	95.5	83.4	90.9
Manufacturing													
2000	390.9	390.5	392.2	393.4	394.7	401.1	401.6	404.5	400.9	397.1	395.9	396.3	396.6
2001	389.0	387.2	385.8	382.5	381.2	380.0	378.8	378.5	377.6	370.6	366.8	364.5	378.5
2002	357.8	356.0	356.6	355.4	356.2	360.3	357.3	360.2	356.9	353.2	351.3	348.8	355.8
2003	343.6	341.7	342.0	342.7	343.8	347.1	344.4	346.8	344.3	342.1	340.8	340.4	343.3
2004	335.4	334.5	335.0	338.9	340.4	347.1	346.7	349.6	348.1	348.7	344.8	346.2	343.0
2005	340.8	340.3	341.5	344.3	348.4	352.2	351.1	354.0	351.3	349.1	347.5	345.5	347.2
2006	341.2	339.0	340.7	342.7	345.1	351.6	350.7	352.8	349.2	347.5	343.3	343.1	345.6
2007	338.4	337.0	337.3	339.0	341.1	346.8	346.0	347.1	343.6	341.9	340.2	339.2	341.5
2008	334.2	333.3	333.2	334.0	336.9	341.0	340.6	341.7	337.7	336.8	331.7	326.1	335.6
2009	318.3	310.3	304.6	299.5	296.8	299.9	298.6	299.1	295.9	294.6	292.0	289.0	299.9
2010	284.3	283.4	284.1	287.7	291.0	296.3	298.6	299.5	298.1	297.6	296.0	295.6	292.7
2011	292.7	292.3	293.0	296.7	299.4	303.4	307.9	310.7	305.9	303.3	302.2	301.4	300.7

1. Employment by Industry: Minnesota, Selected Years, 2000–2011—*Continued*

(Numbers in thousands, not seasonally adjusted)

Industry and year	January	February	March	April	May	June	July	August	September	October	November	December	Annual average
Service-Providing													
2000	2,104.1	2,118.0	2,132.3	2,152.2	2,174.8	2,187.7	2,148.0	2,151.7	2,172.6	2,189.0	2,200.5	2,205.8	2,161.4
2001	2,148.3	2,157.5	2,167.6	2,180.3	2,204.2	2,214.8	2,166.8	2,163.8	2,179.8	2,192.9	2,198.5	2,198.8	2,181.1
2002	2,142.1	2,145.4	2,150.2	2,167.0	2,192.5	2,204.7	2,170.2	2,165.1	2,188.3	2,195.8	2,207.0	2,209.6	2,178.2
2003	2,149.7	2,157.1	2,161.8	2,184.2	2,208.3	2,213.4	2,172.5	2,176.5	2,192.4	2,201.7	2,203.0	2,211.7	2,186.0
2004	2,151.7	2,157.7	2,166.4	2,203.0	2,227.3	2,235.3	2,193.9	2,193.0	2,211.5	2,229.1	2,233.5	2,243.4	2,203.8
2005	2,174.6	2,181.9	2,192.6	2,234.4	2,259.3	2,268.9	2,235.0	2,237.4	2,256.8	2,275.4	2,281.2	2,291.3	2,240.7
2006	2,240.4	2,243.3	2,255.0	2,268.6	2,292.6	2,312.4	2,269.3	2,269.2	2,283.8	2,294.1	2,306.9	2,313.5	2,279.1
2007	2,259.5	2,265.3	2,272.8	2,291.2	2,322.0	2,337.9	2,299.3	2,299.5	2,309.4	2,324.1	2,331.7	2,332.6	2,303.8
2008	2,278.7	2,285.2	2,291.9	2,305.0	2,333.2	2,344.6	2,304.0	2,306.8	2,313.7	2,327.9	2,322.5	2,314.6	2,310.7
2009	2,248.0	2,245.0	2,242.5	2,262.0	2,284.1	2,283.7	2,242.6	2,238.9	2,236.6	2,265.5	2,265.5	2,265.8	2,256.7
2010	2,207.4	2,213.4	2,221.6	2,253.5	2,276.7	2,285.5	2,245.3	2,248.9	2,254.4	2,283.5	2,286.5	2,282.9	2,255.0
2011	2,234.4	2,243.3	2,250.3	2,284.9	2,306.5	2,312.7	2,256.2	2,281.0	2,281.7	2,298.7	2,290.3	2,290.5	2,277.5
Trade, Transportation, and Utilities													
2000	532.2	527.9	529.0	531.8	536.8	541.1	538.3	540.0	539.1	544.9	553.9	559.9	539.6
2001	540.6	533.4	534.3	536.0	542.4	544.2	540.1	539.3	534.9	538.4	544.9	547.1	539.6
2002	525.2	516.0	516.8	521.8	527.7	529.1	523.4	523.1	521.7	524.5	534.3	538.9	525.2
2003	518.6	511.2	511.4	517.4	523.9	524.8	518.4	520.2	518.9	522.9	528.9	532.2	520.7
2004	511.5	506.0	507.0	517.3	524.6	528.9	525.4	526.0	524.6	530.0	537.8	542.6	523.5
2005	517.6	512.7	514.4	522.6	528.3	531.1	527.6	528.7	526.9	531.9	540.0	545.0	527.2
2006	525.7	519.4	520.5	523.7	529.4	534.1	527.1	527.0	526.2	527.8	538.3	541.1	528.4
2007	523.7	518.8	519.3	523.2	530.7	534.4	529.4	529.8	528.2	531.7	539.6	543.0	529.3
2008	523.6	516.8	518.2	519.9	526.7	527.2	522.4	522.2	519.0	520.7	524.1	523.7	522.0
2009	502.9	495.2	492.5	494.1	500.0	501.2	494.7	494.5	490.6	493.0	499.6	500.5	496.6
2010	482.3	476.6	477.5	486.4	491.6	496.1	491.6	491.5	489.5	494.1	500.7	503.1	490.1
2011	484.7	480.9	482.3	491.7	498.2	499.9	501.3	505.0	497.2	499.0	505.0	506.1	495.9
Wholesale Trade													
2000	126.6	126.5	127.3	128.2	129.0	131.2	130.0	130.5	129.0	129.6	130.0	130.4	129.0
2001	130.3	129.8	130.3	131.1	131.9	132.1	132.0	131.2	129.6	129.3	129.0	128.6	130.4
2002	126.6	126.4	126.2	127.4	128.1	128.6	128.7	128.1	126.5	127.0	126.6	126.3	127.2
2003	126.6	126.7	126.7	128.1	128.8	129.6	129.6	129.2	127.8	127.8	127.2	127.1	127.9
2004	125.0	125.0	125.5	129.1	130.0	131.3	131.3	131.1	129.3	129.8	129.8	129.9	128.9
2005	127.3	127.4	127.5	131.1	131.4	133.3	132.8	133.1	132.0	132.2	132.3	132.4	131.1
2006	131.3	131.4	132.2	133.1	134.0	135.1	134.6	134.5	133.1	133.0	133.0	132.7	133.2
2007	131.1	131.0	131.6	132.9	134.5	135.5	135.2	135.2	133.2	133.6	133.7	133.6	133.4
2008	131.7	131.5	132.1	132.8	134.3	134.9	135.0	134.9	132.9	132.6	132.1	131.2	133.0
2009	128.2	127.0	126.1	127.3	127.5	127.6	127.2	126.5	124.0	123.9	124.0	123.5	126.1
2010	120.8	120.4	120.8	123.0	123.6	124.9	125.1	124.8	123.0	124.3	124.2	123.6	123.2
2011	122.1	122.3	122.8	125.0	126.5	126.9	127.2	130.3	126.7	126.3	125.5	125.9	125.6
Retail Trade													
2000	303.8	299.5	299.4	300.7	304.2	306.9	306.0	307.2	305.3	309.7	318.8	324.5	307.2
2001	307.6	301.6	301.6	301.7	306.5	309.0	306.8	307.7	303.2	307.4	316.2	319.9	307.4
2002	302.5	294.6	295.8	298.4	302.6	304.8	302.7	303.4	300.7	301.4	311.7	317.5	303.0
2003	299.0	292.2	292.5	296.7	302.1	303.7	299.5	302.0	299.2	301.4	308.4	312.3	300.8
2004	296.1	290.7	291.1	295.8	301.1	304.5	302.4	303.0	299.5	302.0	309.8	314.5	300.9
2005	296.0	290.7	291.9	296.0	300.7	303.2	300.3	301.8	299.8	303.8	311.9	316.5	301.1
2006	300.3	294.7	294.8	297.4	301.4	305.2	301.5	302.2	298.5	300.0	309.0	312.5	301.5
2007	299.2	293.7	294.4	296.3	301.5	304.9	302.3	302.7	299.2	301.2	309.2	311.6	301.4
2008	297.2	290.2	290.9	292.1	296.4	297.5	295.4	295.5	290.7	291.7	296.1	296.1	294.2
2009	282.8	276.8	274.8	275.9	281.3	283.6	280.4	281.6	276.1	278.0	284.1	285.3	280.1
2010	272.8	267.9	268.2	273.7	277.8	281.2	279.3	280.5	276.2	278.0	283.9	286.1	277.1
2011	272.6	268.4	269.0	275.1	279.6	282.3	284.1	284.3	279.2	282.0	287.6	288.3	279.4
Transportation and Utilities													
2000	101.8	101.9	102.3	102.9	103.6	103.0	102.3	102.3	104.8	105.6	105.1	105.0	103.4
2001	102.7	102.0	102.4	103.2	104.0	103.1	101.3	100.4	102.1	101.7	99.7	98.6	101.8
2002	96.1	95.0	94.8	96.0	97.0	95.7	92.0	91.6	94.5	96.1	96.0	95.1	95.0
2003	93.0	92.3	92.2	92.6	93.0	91.5	89.3	89.0	91.9	93.7	93.3	92.8	92.1
2004	90.4	90.3	90.4	92.4	93.5	93.1	91.7	91.9	95.8	98.2	98.2	98.2	93.7
2005	94.3	94.6	95.0	95.5	96.2	94.6	94.5	93.8	95.1	95.9	95.8	96.1	95.1
2006	94.1	93.3	93.5	93.2	94.0	93.8	91.0	90.3	94.6	94.8	96.3	95.9	93.7
2007	93.4	94.1	93.3	94.0	94.7	94.0	91.9	91.9	95.8	96.9	96.7	97.8	94.5
2008	94.7	95.1	95.2	95.0	96.0	94.8	92.0	91.8	95.4	96.4	95.9	96.4	94.9
2009	91.9	91.4	91.6	90.9	91.2	90.0	87.1	86.4	90.5	91.1	91.5	91.7	90.4
2010	88.7	88.3	88.5	89.7	90.2	90.0	87.2	86.2	90.3	91.8	92.6	93.4	89.7
2011	90.0	90.2	90.5	91.6	92.1	90.7	90.0	90.4	91.3	90.7	91.9	91.9	90.9
Information													
2000	66.7	67.3	67.5	68.2	68.7	70.3	70.7	70.8	69.8	70.0	70.5	70.6	69.3
2001	70.6	70.6	70.6	69.8	70.6	71.5	70.3	69.7	68.5	68.9	69.1	69.0	69.9
2002	67.5	67.2	67.2	67.4	67.3	67.7	67.2	66.1	64.9	64.4	64.5	64.3	66.3
2003	62.5	62.3	62.3	62.7	62.9	62.6	62.0	61.7	60.8	60.6	61.1	61.4	61.9
2004	60.6	60.5	60.7	61.1	61.3	61.0	60.1	59.5	58.8	58.6	59.2	59.2	60.1
2005	58.7	58.6	58.7	59.7	59.8	60.0	59.6	59.0	58.5	58.4	58.7	59.0	59.1
2006	58.3	58.1	58.4	57.8	58.3	58.7	58.2	58.3	57.5	57.3	57.7	57.8	58.0
2007	57.9	57.9	58.2	58.2	58.3	58.6	58.2	58.2	57.6	57.3	57.4	57.8	58.0
2008	57.6	57.4	57.6	57.8	57.7	57.9	58.0	58.0	57.0	57.0	57.1	56.4	57.5
2009	56.1	55.9	55.7	55.1	55.2	55.3	55.6	55.5	54.9	54.7	55.0	54.8	55.3
2010	54.4	54.4	54.3	54.1	54.0	54.2	54.4	54.4	53.7	53.8	53.9	53.7	54.1
2011	53.7	53.3	53.1	53.6	53.6	53.7	52.7	52.1	51.6	52.2	52.2	52.3	52.8

1. Employment by Industry: Minnesota, Selected Years, 2000–2011—*Continued*

(Numbers in thousands, not seasonally adjusted)

Industry and year	January	February	March	April	May	June	July	August	September	October	November	December	Annual average
Financial Activities													
2000	162.0	161.9	162.5	163.1	163.6	166.0	166.4	166.7	165.6	166.3	166.3	167.7	164.8
2001	166.2	166.9	167.6	168.0	168.7	170.7	170.6	170.7	168.8	168.2	168.7	169.4	168.7
2002	168.3	168.6	168.6	169.6	170.4	171.5	173.3	173.9	173.1	173.0	173.8	174.8	171.6
2003	172.0	172.6	173.2	174.9	176.1	178.1	178.3	178.7	177.3	175.3	175.1	175.9	175.6
2004	174.9	174.6	174.6	176.6	177.0	178.8	177.7	177.9	176.4	176.4	176.5	177.3	176.6
2005	175.2	175.1	175.7	179.9	180.6	182.5	181.5	182.1	180.8	180.0	180.2	181.2	179.6
2006	179.8	179.7	180.2	179.5	180.7	182.4	181.7	181.5	180.0	179.8	180.1	181.0	180.5
2007	178.6	179.2	179.3	178.9	178.9	181.1	180.8	180.6	178.9	178.8	178.9	179.4	179.5
2008	176.7	176.8	177.0	176.6	177.0	178.4	178.8	178.5	176.4	176.0	175.6	176.4	177.0
2009	173.7	173.2	172.6	172.5	173.1	174.1	174.4	173.7	172.5	172.7	172.5	173.1	173.2
2010	170.7	170.4	170.3	170.8	171.4	173.2	173.6	173.9	172.7	174.1	174.0	175.1	172.5
2011	172.8	172.9	172.9	173.5	174.1	175.0	175.7	176.0	176.1	174.8	173.4	173.9	174.3
Professional and Business Services													
2000	308.6	307.9	311.6	316.3	317.8	325.0	323.6	325.5	323.7	325.0	324.0	322.1	319.3
2001	312.2	309.5	310.4	314.0	314.4	317.5	313.2	312.6	309.6	307.9	305.0	302.6	310.7
2002	290.1	289.8	290.4	292.7	295.5	299.7	301.3	304.4	302.2	302.9	300.3	297.7	297.3
2003	287.8	288.1	288.9	292.3	294.5	298.0	298.1	299.8	299.4	301.2	299.7	300.6	295.7
2004	288.7	290.6	292.8	299.7	302.2	306.6	306.2	307.3	304.7	306.9	305.4	304.1	301.3
2005	291.1	292.0	294.8	304.1	307.3	311.6	310.5	314.5	315.1	319.5	319.2	319.0	308.2
2006	313.2	313.6	315.3	319.8	322.9	329.0	327.0	329.5	328.1	329.6	329.5	328.6	323.8
2007	319.9	321.1	323.2	326.1	329.5	333.8	334.4	337.9	334.0	334.1	333.3	331.9	329.9
2008	322.7	323.5	323.3	326.3	329.5	332.9	333.8	336.2	332.5	332.7	328.3	324.3	328.8
2009	308.3	304.0	301.7	305.3	306.9	307.8	307.3	310.9	305.7	311.7	311.2	311.4	307.7
2010	300.1	301.0	300.9	309.7	312.0	315.9	319.5	323.6	318.2	322.7	323.1	321.4	314.0
2011	314.4	315.1	316.9	324.3	326.1	328.9	330.1	335.5	329.7	338.2	335.4	340.0	327.9
Education and Health Services													
2000	315.7	321.3	323.5	324.6	324.7	320.4	318.5	317.4	325.8	332.3	334.5	335.6	324.5
2001	328.1	332.9	335.8	337.5	339.4	334.3	332.0	332.7	339.5	348.1	350.4	350.6	338.4
2002	346.3	353.1	355.2	357.1	359.4	352.9	349.9	351.0	356.7	363.2	365.5	365.9	356.4
2003	361.7	368.3	369.8	370.1	371.5	365.7	364.0	363.3	369.0	373.3	374.8	374.0	368.8
2004	369.6	374.1	375.7	377.9	379.0	374.4	372.3	371.8	375.6	381.9	383.3	385.7	376.8
2005	377.6	384.1	385.9	388.3	392.1	387.1	388.8	389.8	394.8	399.8	402.2	403.8	391.2
2006	399.2	402.1	404.4	407.0	408.3	406.3	407.7	407.9	411.4	415.2	419.0	420.6	409.1
2007	418.0	421.1	422.9	426.1	428.1	426.3	425.6	426.0	429.4	435.1	438.4	437.6	427.9
2008	433.0	437.8	439.8	442.9	442.4	439.6	438.6	439.8	443.2	450.5	452.7	452.9	442.8
2009	448.2	452.1	453.8	458.1	457.5	450.3	448.6	448.6	448.1	458.0	458.5	458.8	453.4
2010	451.3	456.4	458.3	460.4	460.7	456.4	451.5	454.1	457.3	464.0	466.2	464.5	458.4
2011	461.7	466.4	466.7	471.5	471.9	466.0	462.9	464.3	466.9	472.4	474.2	473.1	468.2
Leisure and Hospitality													
2000	204.8	206.4	208.8	215.1	225.1	235.0	236.6	240.4	234.0	222.1	216.3	215.3	221.7
2001	209.7	211.5	214.2	219.2	230.4	241.0	242.4	248.0	237.9	226.5	220.5	220.0	226.8
2002	213.8	213.6	215.0	222.3	233.9	243.6	244.2	246.9	240.1	228.7	221.7	222.8	228.9
2003	216.6	215.1	216.4	225.8	238.5	246.5	246.4	249.4	242.4	232.0	224.6	226.1	231.7
2004	217.8	216.9	219.4	231.0	242.2	251.0	250.5	252.6	246.5	238.1	230.3	231.2	235.6
2005	223.0	222.3	224.6	237.0	247.3	256.9	256.8	259.0	252.7	246.0	241.7	241.3	242.4
2006	233.5	233.5	236.4	239.8	250.9	260.3	257.7	259.8	251.4	243.4	237.7	238.1	245.2
2007	232.1	231.9	234.0	241.6	254.8	263.3	263.6	265.1	257.0	248.1	241.3	240.5	247.8
2008	232.9	232.4	234.9	239.5	253.2	261.9	260.9	263.8	253.2	245.2	236.4	234.6	245.7
2009	226.7	224.9	225.8	234.2	246.5	252.1	252.4	254.0	245.3	237.2	228.3	227.0	237.9
2010	219.5	218.5	221.3	232.1	242.3	248.5	250.2	252.6	244.5	237.7	228.8	226.4	235.2
2011	220.8	220.4	223.8	232.8	246.3	254.1	256.6	255.1	241.9	231.7	219.2	216.5	234.9
Other Services													
2000	112.8	113.7	114.7	114.1	114.0	114.8	114.1	114.7	114.1	116.0	115.9	116.9	114.7
2001	116.0	116.3	117.5	117.8	118.2	118.7	116.7	117.0	116.4	117.8	119.5	118.8	117.6
2002	116.6	116.7	117.0	117.9	118.2	119.3	119.5	119.9	119.2	119.2	119.5	120.2	118.6
2003	117.7	117.9	118.4	118.4	118.7	119.7	120.5	120.6	120.1	119.0	119.1	119.8	119.2
2004	117.0	116.1	117.3	118.9	118.6	119.8	118.0	118.7	117.8	118.0	117.6	118.4	118.0
2005	115.0	115.0	115.6	118.2	119.0	119.7	119.1	119.6	119.3	119.3	119.0	119.8	118.2
2006	115.5	115.4	117.3	118.0	118.6	119.9	118.7	118.8	118.3	118.6	118.8	119.3	118.1
2007	115.1	114.8	116.3	116.9	117.7	118.3	117.8	117.9	116.7	116.5	116.9	117.4	116.9
2008	115.1	116.6	116.7	118.1	118.5	120.2	119.4	119.7	117.9	118.5	117.7	116.3	117.9
2009	114.7	114.7	115.2	116.0	116.4	117.2	116.5	116.4	115.4	114.5	113.9	114.1	115.4
2010	112.4	112.6	113.6	113.7	114.1	115.4	115.2	115.6	113.7	114.8	114.0	113.9	114.1
2011	112.7	113.0	113.6	114.7	115.1	116.2	116.4	117.0	117.6	116.7	115.8	116.2	115.4
Government													
2000	401.3	411.6	414.7	419.0	424.1	415.1	379.8	376.2	400.5	412.4	419.1	417.7	407.6
2001	404.9	416.4	417.2	418.0	420.1	416.9	381.5	373.8	404.2	417.1	420.4	421.3	409.3
2002	414.3	420.4	420.0	418.2	420.1	420.9	391.4	379.8	410.4	419.9	427.4	425.0	414.0
2003	412.8	421.6	421.4	422.6	422.2	418.0	384.8	382.8	404.5	417.4	419.7	421.7	412.5
2004	411.6	418.9	418.9	420.5	422.4	414.8	383.7	379.2	407.1	419.2	423.4	424.9	412.1
2005	416.4	422.1	422.9	424.6	424.9	420.0	391.1	384.7	408.7	420.6	420.2	422.2	414.9
2006	415.2	421.5	422.5	423.0	423.5	421.7	391.2	386.4	410.9	422.4	425.8	427.0	415.9
2007	414.2	420.5	419.6	420.2	424.0	422.1	389.5	384.0	407.6	422.5	425.9	425.0	414.6
2008	417.1	423.9	424.4	423.9	428.2	426.5	392.1	388.6	413.9	427.3	430.6	430.0	418.9
2009	417.4	425.0	425.2	426.7	428.5	425.7	393.1	385.3	404.1	423.7	426.5	426.1	417.3
2010	416.7	423.5	425.4	426.3	430.6	425.8	389.3	383.2	404.8	422.3	425.8	424.8	416.5
2011	413.6	421.3	421.0	422.8	421.2	418.9	360.5	376.0	400.7	413.7	415.1	412.4	408.1

2. Average Weekly Hours by Selected Industry: Minnesota, 2007–2011

(Not seasonally adjusted)

Industry and year	January	February	March	April	May	June	July	August	September	October	November	December	Annual average
Total Private													
2007	33.5	33.6	33.6	33.9	33.5	33.9	33.9	34.0	34.1	33.6	33.5	33.9	33.7
2008	33.2	33.5	33.7	33.0	33.3	33.9	33.4	33.9	33.7	33.5	33.5	32.7	33.4
2009	32.5	32.8	32.7	32.7	32.3	32.3	32.5	33.1	32.2	32.6	33.1	32.6	32.6
2010	32.7	32.7	32.7	32.7	33.1	32.8	33.0	33.5	33.1	33.2	33.0	33.0	33.0
2011	33.3	32.9	32.9	33.1	33.4	33.1	33.2	33.3	33.5	33.8	33.3	33.5	33.3
Goods-Producing													
2007	39.4	39.5	39.7	39.9	40.1	41.2	39.7	41.3	41.1	40.6	40.9	40.9	40.4
2008	39.9	41.0	40.2	39.9	40.2	40.6	40.1	40.7	40.7	40.4	39.7	38.5	40.2
2009	37.6	38.0	37.8	37.7	38.7	38.1	38.3	38.8	37.7	38.0	38.2	38.0	38.1
2010	38.1	38.0	38.1	38.8	38.8	38.1	38.8	39.2	38.8	39.4	38.6	38.6	38.6
2011	38.0	37.9	38.3	38.7	38.8	38.9	38.8	40.0	40.8	40.4	39.4	40.0	39.2
Construction													
2007	35.9	35.8	36.0	36.5	37.4	40.8	39.8	39.5	39.7	38.4	38.5	37.9	38.2
2008	37.5	36.1	37.4	36.9	38.4	38.7	38.6	39.3	39.6	39.8	38.8	35.5	38.2
2009	33.3	34.9	34.2	36.1	38.1	37.8	38.3	38.4	35.5	35.8	36.2	33.0	36.1
2010	34.7	32.7	33.0	33.9	33.9	33.3	36.4	36.7	35.4	37.8	35.6	35.9	35.1
2011	35.6	34.6	35.6	36.6	37.4	37.3	37.5	41.1	41.5	40.3	38.5	37.8	38.1
Manufacturing													
2007	40.8	41.0	41.2	41.3	41.3	41.6	39.8	39.8	39.5	39.5	40.0	40.3	40.5
2008	39.2	41.3	39.9	39.8	39.7	40.3	39.8	40.4	40.2	39.7	39.4	39.0	39.9
2009	38.6	38.8	38.8	38.2	38.5	37.9	37.8	38.2	37.9	38.4	38.4	38.8	38.4
2010	38.8	39.3	39.3	40.0	40.1	39.5	39.4	39.8	39.6	39.8	39.6	39.5	39.6
2011	39.0	39.0	39.2	39.5	39.4	39.5	39.3	40.0	40.4	40.3	39.5	40.3	39.6
Trade, Transportation, and Utilities													
2007	32.4	33.4	32.9	32.8	33.5	33.3	33.2	33.4	33.5	33.1	33.3	33.7	33.2
2008	32.1	32.6	32.7	32.0	32.5	32.6	32.8	32.9	32.5	32.1	32.0	31.7	32.4
2009	31.0	31.4	31.5	31.3	31.2	31.2	31.4	32.1	31.5	31.8	32.5	32.2	31.6
2010	31.5	31.7	31.7	31.6	32.0	31.9	32.5	33.1	32.7	32.1	31.4	31.6	32.0
2011	31.5	31.4	31.4	31.5	32.3	32.0	32.2	31.9	32.7	33.0	32.5	32.9	32.1
Financial Activities													
2007	37.1	36.4	36.2	37.1	35.8	36.4	37.3	36.2	36.9	36.1	35.3	36.8	36.5
2008	36.6	36.1	37.2	36.2	36.3	37.3	36.0	36.0	35.9	35.9	36.7	35.7	36.3
2009	37.1	36.7	36.4	35.9	35.7	35.4	35.7	36.6	35.5	35.9	37.0	36.0	36.2
2010	37.7	36.5	36.3	36.4	37.7	36.4	36.2	37.6	37.0	36.9	37.4	37.4	37.0
2011	39.2	38.0	37.6	37.5	38.4	37.3	37.5	37.8	37.7	39.0	38.3	38.2	38.0
Professional and Business Services													
2007	34.5	34.9	35.0	35.8	34.3	34.9	35.2	34.4	35.3	35.1	35.4	35.5	35.0
2008	35.1	35.0	35.8	34.7	36.0	37.1	36.3	36.8	36.6	36.4	36.5	35.1	36.0
2009	35.2	36.2	36.4	36.1	35.9	36.2	35.7	36.6	35.4	35.6	36.2	35.3	35.9
2010	34.8	35.2	35.5	35.7	36.4	35.7	36.0	36.5	35.9	36.2	36.0	35.9	35.8
2011	36.6	36.1	35.9	35.9	36.7	36.0	35.9	35.7	35.2	36.0	34.7	35.3	35.8
Education and Health Services													
2007	32.7	32.4	32.1	32.4	32.2	32.4	32.9	32.9	32.2	31.9	31.7	32.0	32.3
2008	31.8	31.5	31.7	32.3	32.4	32.5	32.4	32.4	32.2	31.8	32.0	32.4	32.1
2009	32.2	31.9	31.5	31.2	31.2	31.2	31.2	31.5	30.7	30.8	31.1	30.8	31.3
2010	30.8	30.6	30.7	30.7	30.7	30.7	30.8	31.0	30.6	30.7	30.8	30.7	30.7
2011	30.9	30.7	30.7	30.6	30.7	30.6	30.8	30.7	30.7	31.0	31.0	30.9	30.8
Leisure and Hospitality													
2007	23.3	23.5	23.8	23.3	23.3	23.7	24.4	24.0	23.6	23.2	22.6	23.2	23.5
2008	22.5	23.4	23.8	22.6	22.4	23.0	22.3	23.5	23.3	23.3	23.1	22.4	23.0
2009	22.0	22.9	22.8	22.2	22.2	22.5	23.0	23.3	22.3	22.0	22.1	21.7	22.4
2010	21.8	22.4	22.2	21.7	22.0	22.1	22.2	22.9	21.7	21.8	21.6	21.3	22.0
2011	22.1	22.1	22.1	21.9	22.0	22.4	22.7	22.9	22.3	22.8	22.4	22.7	22.4
Other Services													
2007	23.0	23.8	23.7	24.1	23.9	24.4	24.7	25.5	26.1	25.5	25.0	25.7	24.6
2008	25.5	25.7	25.9	25.9	25.6	26.6	26.2	26.9	27.0	26.0	26.6	26.8	26.2
2009	26.4	27.5	26.2	25.8	26.9	27.5	27.8	28.5	27.3	27.9	28.4	27.2	27.3
2010	28.3	27.9	27.8	27.2	27.8	28.0	27.7	28.4	27.9	27.6	27.7	27.2	27.8
2011	27.8	27.2	27.3	28.0	29.1	29.1	29.1	28.4	28.8	29.5	29.3	29.7	28.6

3. Average Hourly Earnings by Selected Industry: Minnesota, 2007–2011

(Dollars, not seasonally adjusted)

Industry and year	January	February	March	April	May	June	July	August	September	October	November	December	Annual average
Total Private													
2007	23.63	23.76	23.25	23.81	23.01	22.97	22.64	22.34	22.86	22.90	23.01	23.47	23.13
2008	22.89	23.20	23.27	23.46	23.27	22.97	23.13	22.88	23.08	23.44	23.55	23.66	23.23
2009	23.70	23.83	23.57	23.23	23.67	23.36	23.75	22.69	22.95	23.19	23.43	23.51	23.41
2010	23.64	24.02	23.70	23.67	23.71	23.23	23.63	23.65	23.88	24.19	24.28	24.61	23.85
2011	24.45	24.33	24.55	24.58	24.59	24.17	24.31	24.31	24.62	24.90	24.74	24.89	24.54
Goods-Producing													
2007	23.05	23.47	22.43	22.76	22.56	22.47	22.66	22.45	22.64	22.79	22.87	22.97	22.75
2008	23.03	22.82	23.01	22.94	22.77	22.92	23.15	23.09	23.64	23.85	24.19	23.82	23.26
2009	24.48	23.04	23.28	23.62	24.31	24.27	24.40	24.34	24.25	24.36	24.78	24.93	24.17
2010	25.04	24.81	24.55	24.82	24.72	24.58	25.13	24.68	24.97	25.67	25.58	25.70	25.03
2011	26.09	25.61	25.75	25.79	25.58	25.36	25.42	25.45	25.81	25.79	25.76	26.17	25.71
Construction													
2007	25.59	25.86	25.46	25.54	25.50	25.79	25.91	25.88	25.89	26.55	25.69	26.15	25.83
2008	26.18	26.23	26.86	26.75	26.63	26.36	27.16	26.94	27.12	27.06	27.09	25.46	26.69
2009	25.72	25.59	25.12	25.24	26.49	26.11	25.59	26.17	26.14	26.48	26.30	26.81	26.01
2010	26.37	26.98	27.43	27.53	27.38	27.24	28.10	27.63	27.46	28.11	27.59	28.21	27.55
2011	28.49	28.19	28.64	28.56	28.02	27.49	27.24	27.86	29.00	27.93	28.05	28.57	28.14
Manufacturing													
2007	22.24	22.72	21.46	21.80	21.48	21.12	21.27	21.07	21.29	21.39	21.81	22.27	21.66
2008	22.35	22.13	22.17	22.10	21.81	22.04	22.03	21.99	22.61	22.95	23.48	23.71	22.44
2009	24.47	24.24	24.00	24.18	24.30	24.02	24.47	24.60	24.34	24.57	25.16	25.09	24.45
2010	25.48	25.01	24.65	24.80	24.59	24.26	24.26	24.06	24.26	24.86	25.01	24.98	24.68
2011	25.40	24.90	24.89	24.92	24.72	24.51	24.68	24.38	24.48	24.80	24.85	25.37	24.82
Trade, Transportation, and Utilities													
2007	19.31	19.68	19.68	20.22	19.51	20.33	20.61	20.12	20.52	20.20	19.84	19.88	19.99
2008	20.44	20.74	20.24	20.78	20.77	20.40	20.06	19.67	20.05	19.96	19.86	20.06	20.25
2009	20.04	21.02	21.04	20.25	20.27	20.25	20.76	20.83	20.95	20.76	21.19	20.87	20.69
2010	21.07	21.77	20.98	21.44	21.41	20.94	21.01	21.04	22.66	21.51	21.52	21.61	21.41
2011	22.12	21.75	21.88	21.95	21.82	21.28	21.30	21.08	21.44	21.80	21.27	21.07	21.56
Financial Activities													
2007	28.23	28.64	27.71	27.85	27.89	27.48	27.94	27.67	27.92	27.22	27.62	27.83	27.83
2008	26.46	27.15	26.84	27.38	27.46	26.59	26.66	26.84	26.83	27.35	26.86	26.97	26.95
2009	26.71	28.45	27.01	26.61	27.07	25.93	26.26	27.35	26.94	27.27	27.60	27.74	27.08
2010	26.52	27.43	26.37	26.08	26.49	26.47	27.06	27.52	26.37	27.10	27.73	27.49	26.89
2011	26.51	26.96	28.65	28.36	28.66	28.61	28.55	29.02	28.86	29.55	30.20	29.90	28.65
Professional and Business Services													
2007	28.94	27.90	28.19	27.75	27.23	26.48	27.06	26.53	27.01	27.39	27.27	27.82	27.45
2008	26.99	27.64	28.26	27.90	27.51	27.30	27.63	27.39	27.41	27.74	28.45	29.49	27.80
2009	28.90	29.54	29.53	29.83	29.95	28.98	29.27	30.03	30.07	30.23	30.85	29.78
2010	30.20	30.18	30.38	30.23	30.35	29.78	30.04	29.90	29.51	29.64	29.69	30.30	30.01
2011	31.08	30.65	30.72	30.86	31.44	30.84	31.15	30.83	30.79	30.90	30.18	30.49	30.83
Education and Health Services													
2007	23.97	23.83	24.16	24.40	24.02	23.96	24.34	23.94	24.28	24.53	24.65	25.09	24.27
2008	24.11	24.40	24.58	24.93	24.54	24.05	24.57	24.41	24.74	25.04	24.90	24.46	24.56
2009	23.79	23.82	23.59	23.58	23.32	23.59	24.23	23.93	24.50	24.54	24.18	23.77	23.90
2010	23.81	23.88	23.90	23.63	23.83	22.90	23.06	23.41	24.06	23.99	23.88	24.22	23.72
2011	23.93	24.30	24.35	24.57	24.44	24.02	24.37	24.39	24.69	25.01	24.83	25.05	24.50
Leisure and Hospitality													
2007	12.03	12.11	11.95	11.93	11.84	11.75	11.68	11.74	12.04	12.25	12.27	12.54	12.00
2008	12.46	12.54	12.60	12.79	12.63	12.30	12.90	12.42	12.67	12.77	12.90	13.27	12.68
2009	13.41	13.27	13.26	13.03	12.97	12.68	12.33	12.77	13.12	13.38	13.50	13.58	13.09
2010	13.70	13.64	13.53	14.13	13.97	13.53	13.59	13.57	13.80	13.99	14.04	14.21	13.80
2011	13.97	13.95	13.69	13.69	13.47	12.98	12.95	12.81	13.01	12.99	13.25	13.20	13.31
Other Services													
2007	15.28	15.09	15.03	15.58	15.23	15.56	15.44	15.27	14.40	14.42	14.52	15.01	15.06
2008	15.28	15.66	15.61	15.18	15.24	15.66	15.83	15.96	15.53	15.58	16.10	16.50	15.68
2009	17.36	16.80	17.04	17.54	16.79	16.62	17.47	17.18	17.20	17.05	17.49	17.73	17.19
2010	18.53	18.58	18.33	18.39	18.14	18.36	18.78	18.50	18.89	19.02	18.80	19.07	18.61
2011	19.00	19.18	19.91	19.71	19.97	20.11	20.07	20.23	19.81	19.89	19.71	20.26	19.83

4. Average Weekly Earnings by Selected Industry: Minnesota, 2007–2011

(Dollars, not seasonally adjusted)

Industry and year	January	February	March	April	May	June	July	August	September	October	November	December	Annual average
Total Private													
2007	791.61	798.34	781.20	807.16	770.84	778.68	767.50	759.56	779.53	769.44	770.84	795.63	780.56
2008	759.95	777.20	784.20	774.18	774.89	778.68	772.54	775.63	777.80	785.24	788.93	773.68	776.97
2009	770.25	781.62	770.74	759.62	764.54	754.53	771.88	751.04	738.99	755.99	775.53	766.43	763.37
2010	773.03	785.45	774.99	774.01	784.80	761.94	779.79	792.28	790.43	803.11	801.24	812.13	785.94
2011	814.19	800.46	807.70	813.60	821.31	800.03	807.09	809.52	824.77	841.62	823.84	833.82	816.88
Goods-Producing													
2007	908.17	927.07	890.47	908.12	904.66	925.76	899.60	927.19	930.50	925.27	935.38	939.47	918.56
2008	918.90	935.62	925.00	915.31	915.35	930.55	928.32	939.76	962.15	963.54	960.34	917.07	934.52
2009	920.45	875.52	879.98	890.47	940.80	924.69	934.52	944.39	914.23	925.68	946.60	947.34	920.54
2010	954.02	942.78	935.36	963.02	959.14	936.50	975.04	967.46	968.84	1,011.40	987.39	992.02	966.71
2011	991.42	970.62	986.23	998.07	992.50	986.50	986.30	1,018.00	1,053.05	1,041.92	1,014.94	1,046.80	1,007.74
Construction													
2007	918.68	925.79	916.56	932.21	953.70	1,052.23	1,031.22	1,022.26	1,027.83	1,019.52	989.07	991.09	985.52
2008	981.75	946.90	1,004.56	987.08	1,022.59	1,020.13	1,048.38	1,058.74	1,073.95	1,076.99	1,051.09	903.83	1,018.43
2009	856.48	893.09	859.10	911.16	1,009.27	986.96	980.10	1,004.93	927.97	947.98	952.06	884.73	939.12
2010	915.04	882.25	905.19	933.27	928.18	907.09	1,022.84	1,014.02	972.08	1,062.56	982.20	1,012.74	966.68
2011	1,014.24	975.37	1,019.58	1,045.30	1,047.95	1,025.38	1,021.50	1,145.05	1,203.50	1,125.58	1,079.93	1,079.95	1,070.90
Manufacturing													
2007	907.39	931.52	884.15	900.34	887.12	878.59	846.55	838.59	840.96	844.91	872.40	897.48	877.28
2008	876.12	913.97	884.58	879.58	865.86	888.21	876.79	888.40	908.92	911.12	925.11	924.69	895.15
2009	944.54	940.51	931.20	923.68	935.55	910.36	924.97	939.72	922.49	943.49	966.14	973.49	937.90
2010	988.62	982.89	968.75	992.00	986.06	958.27	955.84	957.59	960.70	989.43	990.40	986.71	976.30
2011	990.60	971.10	975.69	984.34	973.97	968.15	969.92	975.20	988.99	999.44	981.58	1,022.41	983.40
Trade, Transportation, and Utilities													
2007	625.64	657.31	647.47	663.22	653.59	676.99	684.25	672.01	687.42	668.62	660.67	669.96	664.01
2008	656.12	676.12	661.85	664.96	675.03	665.04	657.97	647.14	651.63	640.72	635.52	635.90	655.66
2009	621.24	660.03	662.76	633.83	632.42	631.80	651.86	668.64	659.93	660.17	688.68	672.01	653.57
2010	663.71	690.11	665.07	677.50	685.12	667.99	682.83	696.42	740.98	690.47	675.73	682.88	684.90
2011	696.78	682.95	687.03	691.43	704.79	680.96	685.86	672.45	701.09	719.40	691.28	693.20	692.26
Financial Activities													
2007	1,047.33	1,042.50	1,003.10	1,033.24	998.46	1,000.27	1,042.16	1,001.65	1,030.25	982.64	974.99	1,024.14	1,015.06
2008	968.44	980.12	998.45	991.16	996.80	991.81	959.76	966.24	963.20	981.87	985.76	962.83	978.85
2009	990.94	1,044.12	983.16	955.30	966.40	917.92	937.48	1,001.01	956.37	978.99	1,021.20	998.64	979.10
2010	999.80	1,001.20	957.23	949.31	998.67	963.51	979.57	1,034.75	975.69	999.99	1,037.10	1,028.13	993.91
2011	1,039.19	1,024.48	1,077.24	1,063.50	1,100.54	1,067.15	1,070.63	1,096.96	1,088.02	1,152.45	1,156.66	1,142.18	1,089.99
Professional and Business Services													
2007	998.43	973.71	986.65	993.45	933.99	924.15	952.51	912.63	953.45	961.39	965.36	987.61	961.62
2008	947.35	967.40	1,011.71	968.13	990.36	1,012.83	1,002.97	1,007.95	1,003.21	1,009.74	1,038.43	1,035.10	999.72
2009	1,017.28	1,069.35	1,074.89	1,076.86	1,075.21	1,049.08	1,044.94	1,099.10	1,064.48	1,074.05	1,094.33	1,089.01	1,069.11
2010	1,050.96	1,062.34	1,078.49	1,079.21	1,104.74	1,063.15	1,081.44	1,091.35	1,059.41	1,072.97	1,068.84	1,087.77	1,075.31
2011	1,137.53	1,106.47	1,102.85	1,107.87	1,153.85	1,110.24	1,118.29	1,100.63	1,083.81	1,112.40	1,047.25	1,076.30	1,104.46
Education and Health Services													
2007	783.82	772.09	775.54	790.56	773.44	776.30	800.79	787.63	781.82	782.51	781.41	802.88	784.11
2008	766.70	768.60	779.19	805.24	795.10	781.63	796.07	790.88	796.63	796.27	796.80	792.50	788.90
2009	766.04	759.86	743.09	735.70	727.58	736.01	755.98	753.80	752.15	755.83	752.00	732.12	747.46
2010	733.35	730.73	733.73	725.44	731.58	703.03	710.25	725.71	736.24	736.49	735.50	743.55	728.81
2011	739.44	746.01	747.55	751.84	750.31	735.01	750.60	748.77	757.98	775.31	769.73	774.05	753.96
Leisure and Hospitality													
2007	280.30	284.59	284.41	277.97	275.87	278.48	284.99	281.76	284.14	284.20	277.30	290.93	282.05
2008	280.35	293.44	299.88	289.05	282.91	282.90	287.67	291.87	295.21	297.54	297.99	297.25	291.23
2009	295.02	303.88	302.33	289.27	287.93	285.30	283.59	297.54	292.58	294.36	298.35	294.69	293.50
2010	298.66	305.54	300.37	306.62	307.34	299.01	301.70	310.75	299.46	304.98	303.26	302.67	303.40
2011	308.74	308.30	302.55	299.81	296.34	290.75	293.97	293.35	290.12	296.17	296.80	299.64	297.76
Other Services													
2007	351.44	359.14	356.21	375.48	364.00	379.66	381.37	389.39	375.84	367.71	363.00	385.76	370.83
2008	389.64	402.46	404.30	393.16	390.14	416.56	414.75	429.32	419.31	405.08	428.26	442.20	411.31
2009	458.30	462.00	446.45	452.53	451.65	457.05	485.67	489.63	469.56	475.70	496.72	482.26	468.87
2010	524.40	518.38	509.57	500.21	504.29	514.08	520.21	525.40	527.03	524.95	520.76	518.70	517.33
2011	528.20	521.70	543.54	551.88	581.13	585.20	584.04	574.53	570.53	586.76	577.50	601.72	567.51

MISSISSIPPI
At a Glance

Population:
2000 census: 2,844,754
2010 census: 2,967,297
2011 estimate: 2,978,512

Percent change in population:
2000–2010: 4.3%
2010–2011: 0.4%

Percent change in total nonfarm employment:
2000–2010: -5.4%
2010–2011: -0.1%

Industry with the largest growth in employment, 2000–2011 (thousands):
Education and Health Services, 30.0

Industry with the largest decline or smallest growth in employment, 2000–2011 (thousands):
Manufacturing, -88.1

Civilian labor force:
2000: 1,314,154
2010: 1,317,216
2011: 1,343,846

Unemployment rate and rank among states (lowest to highest):
2000: 5.7%, 49th
2010: 10.5%, 41st
2011: 10.7%, 48th

Over-the-year change in unemployment rates:
2010–2011: 0.2%

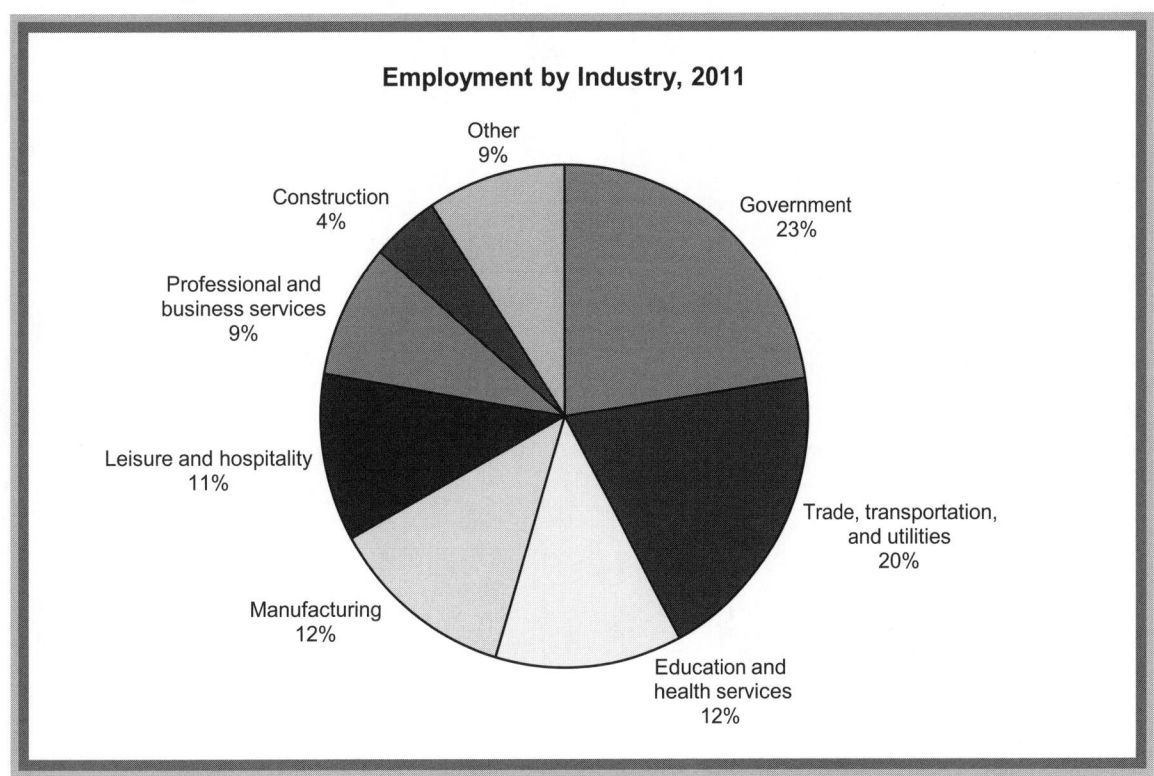

Employment by Industry, 2011

Other 9%
Construction 4%
Professional and business services 9%
Leisure and hospitality 11%
Manufacturing 12%
Education and health services 12%
Government 23%
Trade, transportation, and utilities 20%

1. Employment by Industry: Mississippi, Selected Years, 2000–2011

(Numbers in thousands, not seasonally adjusted)

Industry and year	January	February	March	April	May	June	July	August	September	October	November	December	Annual average
Total Nonfarm													
2000	1,144.3	1,145.2	1,153.9	1,158.5	1,166.9	1,164.2	1,147.4	1,157.2	1,155.5	1,150.0	1,150.9	1,150.9	1,153.7
2001	1,129.0	1,129.0	1,131.3	1,136.5	1,138.4	1,135.3	1,121.0	1,131.9	1,131.1	1,125.0	1,126.8	1,126.3	1,130.1
2002	1,111.1	1,114.0	1,120.4	1,128.0	1,131.8	1,133.4	1,119.8	1,128.5	1,130.8	1,122.3	1,121.7	1,123.4	1,123.8
2003	1,107.4	1,108.9	1,112.4	1,116.6	1,116.8	1,111.0	1,104.6	1,111.9	1,119.6	1,123.3	1,124.9	1,123.4	1,115.1
2004	1,108.5	1,113.5	1,121.1	1,130.0	1,129.6	1,125.8	1,115.2	1,124.6	1,132.5	1,130.5	1,133.1	1,133.3	1,124.8
2005	1,118.6	1,126.4	1,134.4	1,139.2	1,138.9	1,133.8	1,123.7	1,134.5	1,120.4	1,125.2	1,138.0	1,132.3	1,130.5
2006	1,116.4	1,126.3	1,137.4	1,141.3	1,145.1	1,144.2	1,125.5	1,144.0	1,153.2	1,150.2	1,156.1	1,156.3	1,141.3
2007	1,138.6	1,144.8	1,148.5	1,154.0	1,156.4	1,153.1	1,137.4	1,154.0	1,161.4	1,158.5	1,164.4	1,164.5	1,153.0
2008	1,147.5	1,153.7	1,157.8	1,161.8	1,161.2	1,152.8	1,129.8	1,144.0	1,147.4	1,143.7	1,141.4	1,131.9	1,147.8
2009	1,106.8	1,106.3	1,105.5	1,103.9	1,104.6	1,097.0	1,080.0	1,087.6	1,093.9	1,089.3	1,092.4	1,089.2	1,096.4
2010	1,071.1	1,076.4	1,086.4	1,096.4	1,103.7	1,099.7	1,082.8	1,088.6	1,096.8	1,098.4	1,097.9	1,097.2	1,091.3
2011	1,077.2	1,082.4	1,092.9	1,096.8	1,095.7	1,090.7	1,078.5	1,083.7	1,093.4	1,096.6	1,099.0	1,092.7	1,090.0
Total Private													
2000	914.1	914.0	920.4	924.1	927.7	931.8	920.3	924.5	920.4	914.2	914.0	913.8	919.9
2001	891.8	890.7	892.8	897.4	899.2	899.0	890.6	895.7	892.5	886.0	888.0	887.5	892.6
2002	872.9	874.7	880.8	887.3	890.7	893.9	886.2	889.6	888.6	879.6	878.9	880.6	883.7
2003	866.1	866.7	869.3	873.2	875.5	873.9	872.1	876.1	876.5	879.0	880.5	882.6	874.3
2004	867.8	869.9	876.1	884.2	885.7	886.1	883.3	886.8	888.0	885.0	887.5	891.9	882.7
2005	878.2	882.2	889.8	894.6	895.4	893.8	891.9	897.0	879.1	883.8	895.9	894.2	889.7
2006	878.5	885.3	896.3	900.3	905.2	906.6	898.1	907.4	909.9	907.1	912.3	916.0	901.9
2007	897.8	900.2	903.7	908.0	911.1	911.1	904.4	912.8	914.2	909.9	915.8	919.0	909.0
2008	901.7	904.3	908.0	911.0	911.8	907.3	894.9	899.8	897.2	891.6	888.9	882.5	899.9
2009	853.3	855.0	854.0	851.3	851.8	848.0	840.7	842.7	842.1	836.4	840.1	839.9	846.7
2010	822.8	824.7	832.9	844.1	848.2	848.9	844.2	846.8	849.0	847.9	848.5	848.9	842.2
2011	832.0	834.9	844.6	849.1	850.5	847.8	842.1	841.6	844.5	845.7	848.7	845.3	843.9
Goods-Producing													
2000	289.9	289.2	290.3	290.2	290.7	291.2	286.8	286.0	283.4	282.2	279.3	277.3	286.4
2001	269.0	266.8	264.3	265.9	265.0	264.9	260.1	260.9	259.8	258.3	257.6	255.1	262.3
2002	252.8	253.2	254.0	253.0	253.7	255.0	251.5	251.2	250.3	246.6	244.3	243.1	250.7
2003	239.8	239.6	239.3	239.2	239.1	238.2	236.6	236.4	237.2	238.6	237.9	237.5	238.3
2004	233.7	233.9	235.6	238.1	238.3	240.1	237.6	239.1	238.9	238.2	238.7	238.7	237.6
2005	235.9	235.8	238.0	239.7	240.2	240.7	239.4	239.8	236.0	239.8	241.9	243.7	239.2
2006	239.5	239.5	241.7	242.8	244.6	247.1	244.0	244.0	242.8	242.3	243.0	243.1	242.9
2007	239.0	238.2	235.0	239.3	238.9	238.7	236.5	237.5	238.0	236.5	236.9	237.8	237.7
2008	234.3	233.9	234.1	236.1	236.4	235.1	228.5	227.7	225.7	224.4	221.2	217.1	229.5
2009	209.3	206.5	204.8	202.8	202.8	202.2	199.9	198.6	197.4	194.3	194.3	193.9	200.6
2010	190.1	189.5	192.0	196.5	197.0	196.7	195.8	195.5	194.8	194.6	193.8	193.4	194.1
2011	190.0	190.3	193.4	193.7	195.2	195.5	192.5	192.2	191.1	191.8	191.0	190.8	192.3
Mining and Logging													
2000	9.2	9.3	9.4	9.2	9.3	9.4	9.4	9.3	9.4	9.6	9.5	9.5	9.4
2001	9.3	9.3	9.6	9.7	9.6	9.7	9.7	9.8	9.8	9.6	9.6	9.6	9.6
2002	8.9	8.9	9.0	8.9	9.0	9.0	9.0	9.0	9.0	8.8	8.7	8.5	8.9
2003	8.3	8.3	8.5	8.7	8.8	8.8	8.9	9.0	9.1	8.9	8.9	8.9	8.8
2004	8.6	8.5	8.8	8.7	8.8	8.9	9.0	9.0	8.8	8.9	9.0	8.9	8.8
2005	8.5	8.4	8.6	8.8	8.8	8.8	8.8	8.9	8.8	8.9	8.9	8.9	8.8
2006	8.9	9.0	9.2	9.6	9.6	9.5	9.5	9.7	9.6	9.7	9.8	9.6	9.5
2007	9.2	9.3	9.4	9.6	9.7	9.5	9.5	9.6	9.6	9.5	9.7	9.6	9.5
2008	9.4	9.1	9.2	9.4	9.5	9.5	9.4	9.5	9.5	10.0	10.0	9.8	9.5
2009	9.2	9.0	8.8	8.5	8.4	8.3	8.3	8.2	8.2	8.1	8.1	8.1	8.4
2010	8.1	8.1	8.4	8.8	8.9	8.9	8.9	9.0	9.0	9.0	8.9	8.8	8.7
2011	8.8	8.8	9.0	9.0	9.0	9.1	9.2	9.2	9.3	9.3	9.3	9.2	9.1
Construction													
2000	53.4	54.1	55.0	54.5	55.3	56.4	55.9	55.6	54.4	53.9	52.9	52.3	54.5
2001	48.6	49.6	49.9	51.3	51.7	52.4	52.2	53.2	53.0	53.4	54.2	53.7	51.9
2002	53.3	53.2	53.9	53.6	54.3	55.7	54.8	54.9	54.7	53.3	52.7	52.4	53.9
2003	51.0	51.1	50.8	51.1	50.9	50.9	50.6	50.6	50.7	50.4	49.6	49.2	50.6
2004	47.2	47.0	47.7	48.9	49.2	50.1	50.0	50.3	50.6	49.8	49.7	49.0	49.1
2005	47.4	47.5	49.0	50.5	51.5	52.1	52.3	52.6	54.5	55.6	56.4	57.3	52.2
2006	54.7	54.3	55.6	56.8	58.6	60.7	58.9	59.1	58.9	58.3	58.3	58.3	57.7
2007	56.9	56.6	58.4	58.0	58.2	58.7	58.5	59.0	59.4	59.5	60.2	61.2	58.7
2008	59.7	60.0	61.0	63.5	64.5	63.9	60.8	59.4	59.1	59.3	57.3	55.8	60.4
2009	52.5	52.1	52.1	52.0	53.1	53.9	52.3	51.3	49.8	48.4	48.3	47.4	51.1
2010	45.6	45.7	47.6	50.6	50.8	50.7	50.5	50.7	50.8	50.6	50.3	49.5	49.5
2011	46.9	47.2	49.1	49.3	50.3	50.5	50.2	50.2	48.6	48.3	47.9	47.2	48.8
Manufacturing													
2000	227.3	225.8	225.9	226.5	226.1	225.4	221.5	221.1	219.6	218.7	216.9	215.5	222.5
2001	211.1	207.9	204.8	204.9	203.7	202.8	198.2	197.9	197.0	195.3	193.8	191.8	200.8
2002	190.6	191.1	191.1	190.5	190.4	190.3	187.7	187.3	186.6	184.5	182.9	182.2	187.9
2003	180.5	180.2	180.0	179.4	179.4	178.5	177.1	176.8	177.4	179.3	179.4	179.4	179.0
2004	177.9	178.4	179.1	180.5	180.3	181.1	178.6	179.8	179.5	179.5	180.0	180.8	179.6
2005	180.0	179.9	180.4	180.4	179.9	179.8	178.3	178.3	172.7	175.3	176.6	177.5	178.3
2006	175.9	176.2	176.9	176.4	176.4	176.9	175.6	175.2	174.3	174.3	174.9	175.2	175.7
2007	172.9	172.3	167.2	171.7	171.0	170.5	168.5	168.9	169.0	167.5	167.0	167.0	169.5
2008	165.2	164.8	163.9	163.2	162.4	161.7	158.3	158.8	157.1	155.1	153.9	151.5	159.7
2009	147.6	145.4	143.9	142.3	141.3	140.0	139.3	139.1	139.4	137.8	137.9	138.4	141.0
2010	136.4	135.7	136.0	137.1	137.3	137.1	136.4	135.8	135.0	135.0	134.6	135.1	136.0
2011	134.3	134.3	135.3	135.4	135.9	135.9	133.1	132.8	133.2	134.2	133.8	134.4	134.4

1. Employment by Industry: Mississippi, Selected Years, 2000–2011—*Continued*

(Numbers in thousands, not seasonally adjusted)

Industry and year	January	February	March	April	May	June	July	August	September	October	November	December	Annual average
Service-Providing													
2000	854.4	856.0	863.6	868.3	876.2	873.0	860.6	871.2	872.1	867.8	871.6	873.6	867.4
2001	860.0	862.2	867.0	870.6	873.4	870.4	860.9	871.0	871.3	866.7	869.2	871.2	867.8
2002	858.3	860.8	866.4	875.0	878.1	878.4	868.3	877.3	880.5	875.7	877.4	880.3	873.0
2003	867.6	869.3	873.1	877.4	877.7	872.8	868.0	875.5	882.4	884.7	887.0	885.9	876.8
2004	874.8	879.6	885.5	891.9	891.3	885.7	877.6	885.5	893.6	892.3	894.4	894.6	887.2
2005	882.7	890.6	896.4	899.5	898.7	893.1	884.3	894.7	884.4	885.4	896.1	888.6	891.2
2006	876.9	886.8	895.7	898.5	900.5	897.1	881.5	900.0	910.4	907.9	913.1	913.2	898.5
2007	899.6	906.6	913.5	914.7	917.5	914.4	900.9	916.5	923.4	922.0	927.5	926.7	915.3
2008	913.2	919.8	923.7	925.7	924.8	917.7	901.3	916.3	921.7	919.3	920.2	914.8	918.2
2009	897.5	899.8	900.7	901.1	901.8	894.8	880.1	889.0	896.5	895.0	898.1	895.3	895.8
2010	881.0	886.9	894.4	899.9	906.7	903.0	887.0	893.1	902.0	903.8	904.1	903.8	897.1
2011	887.2	892.1	899.5	903.1	900.5	895.2	886.0	891.5	902.3	904.8	908.0	901.9	897.7
Trade, Transportation, and Utilities													
2000	225.1	224.5	225.7	226.1	227.8	228.5	226.1	227.4	227.3	226.5	229.1	231.4	227.1
2001	223.2	221.4	223.0	222.7	223.5	224.1	221.2	222.2	221.7	222.1	225.2	226.8	223.1
2002	217.9	217.1	218.1	219.7	220.9	222.6	221.2	221.6	221.7	220.6	223.1	225.6	220.8
2003	217.3	216.7	216.5	216.3	217.8	218.3	218.1	218.9	218.8	220.0	222.6	224.7	218.8
2004	217.2	216.4	218.0	218.7	219.9	220.2	219.2	219.7	219.4	220.6	223.1	226.4	219.9
2005	218.1	217.3	219.4	220.1	220.3	220.5	220.8	222.4	217.1	218.3	224.0	228.2	220.5
2006	221.3	221.5	224.7	224.7	225.8	226.1	224.8	226.1	226.2	225.7	228.7	231.8	225.6
2007	224.2	223.3	226.1	225.7	227.2	227.7	225.6	226.7	227.0	226.9	230.6	232.4	227.0
2008	225.1	224.4	226.1	224.5	224.4	224.0	222.9	224.2	223.2	221.7	224.1	225.3	224.2
2009	216.9	215.3	214.8	213.9	214.7	214.6	213.5	213.2	213.7	213.4	216.2	217.0	214.8
2010	210.3	209.6	211.3	212.9	213.8	213.5	212.7	213.3	212.8	214.3	217.3	219.8	213.5
2011	212.5	212.2	214.2	215.1	215.3	214.6	214.3	212.2	212.8	213.7	216.6	217.4	214.2
Wholesale Trade													
2000	36.9	37.0	37.0	36.9	36.9	37.2	37.0	37.4	37.2	36.7	36.5	36.6	36.9
2001	35.9	35.4	35.5	35.2	35.1	35.4	35.4	35.7	35.5	35.0	34.8	35.2	35.3
2002	34.9	34.9	34.9	34.9	34.8	35.1	35.1	35.5	35.4	35.0	34.8	35.1	35.0
2003	34.7	34.6	34.5	34.6	34.8	35.2	34.9	35.1	35.0	34.9	34.9	35.1	34.9
2004	34.8	34.7	34.7	34.9	34.8	35.0	35.1	35.2	35.1	34.9	34.9	35.2	34.9
2005	34.6	34.7	34.9	35.2	35.4	35.5	35.6	35.9	35.3	35.2	35.3	35.8	35.3
2006	35.7	35.9	36.1	35.9	36.2	36.5	36.4	37.0	36.7	36.6	36.6	37.1	36.4
2007	36.6	36.6	36.6	36.6	36.7	36.8	36.8	37.2	37.0	36.7	36.5	37.2	36.8
2008	36.8	36.7	36.6	36.5	36.5	36.6	36.3	36.4	36.0	36.1	35.7	36.0	36.4
2009	35.5	35.4	35.1	34.8	34.7	34.7	34.6	34.7	34.4	34.3	34.1	34.5	34.7
2010	34.0	34.0	33.9	34.2	34.2	34.3	34.2	34.6	34.2	34.3	34.1	34.7	34.2
2011	34.2	34.3	34.2	34.1	34.2	33.9	33.6	33.8	33.5	33.9	33.5	33.1	33.9
Retail Trade													
2000	143.7	142.9	144.0	144.2	145.5	145.8	143.9	144.6	144.7	144.6	147.6	150.0	145.1
2001	141.9	140.7	142.1	141.6	142.3	142.7	140.1	140.6	140.4	141.0	144.6	145.9	142.0
2002	138.3	137.5	138.7	139.8	140.4	141.5	140.3	139.7	139.9	139.0	141.8	144.3	140.1
2003	137.1	136.4	136.7	136.2	137.2	137.2	137.4	138.0	137.9	139.1	141.6	143.7	138.2
2004	136.8	136.0	137.2	137.5	138.2	138.3	137.6	137.4	137.2	138.3	140.9	143.3	138.2
2005	137.0	136.1	137.4	137.8	137.8	137.9	138.1	138.9	134.8	136.4	141.7	144.9	138.2
2006	139.1	138.8	141.5	141.5	142.0	142.0	141.2	141.4	141.3	141.0	143.9	145.9	141.6
2007	139.9	139.2	141.5	141.0	142.0	142.5	140.5	140.7	141.0	141.2	144.8	146.1	141.7
2008	140.2	139.5	141.2	140.0	139.7	139.1	138.3	138.7	138.1	137.0	139.6	140.8	139.4
2009	133.8	132.6	132.8	132.7	133.5	133.6	132.6	131.7	132.3	132.2	135.1	135.7	133.2
2010	130.3	129.7	131.3	132.1	133.0	132.6	131.9	131.7	131.2	132.2	135.4	136.9	132.4
2011	131.2	130.8	132.4	133.4	133.5	133.2	132.7	130.4	131.3	131.8	134.5	135.3	132.5
Transportation and Utilities													
2000	44.5	44.6	44.7	45.0	45.4	45.5	45.2	45.4	45.4	45.2	45.0	44.8	45.1
2001	45.4	45.3	45.4	45.9	46.1	46.0	45.7	45.9	45.8	46.1	45.8	45.7	45.8
2002	44.7	44.7	44.5	45.0	45.7	46.0	45.8	46.4	46.4	46.6	46.5	46.2	45.7
2003	45.5	45.7	45.3	45.5	45.8	45.9	45.8	45.8	45.9	46.0	46.1	45.9	45.8
2004	45.6	45.7	46.1	46.3	46.9	46.9	46.5	47.1	47.1	47.4	47.3	47.9	46.7
2005	46.5	46.5	47.1	47.1	47.1	47.1	47.1	47.6	47.0	46.7	47.0	47.5	47.0
2006	46.5	46.8	47.1	47.3	47.6	47.6	47.2	47.7	48.2	48.1	48.2	48.8	47.6
2007	47.7	47.5	48.0	48.1	48.5	48.4	48.3	48.8	49.0	49.0	49.3	49.1	48.5
2008	48.1	48.2	48.3	48.0	48.2	48.3	48.3	49.1	49.1	48.6	48.8	48.5	48.5
2009	47.6	47.3	46.9	46.4	46.5	46.3	46.3	46.8	47.0	46.9	47.0	46.8	46.8
2010	46.0	45.9	46.1	46.6	46.6	46.6	46.6	47.0	47.4	47.8	47.8	48.2	46.9
2011	47.1	47.1	47.6	47.6	47.6	47.5	48.0	48.0	48.0	48.0	48.6	49.0	47.8
Information													
2000	16.8	16.8	17.0	16.9	17.1	17.5	17.7	17.7	17.6	17.6	17.8	17.9	17.4
2001	17.6	17.5	17.4	17.1	17.1	17.3	17.0	16.7	16.5	16.4	16.5	16.5	17.0
2002	16.5	16.4	16.3	16.3	16.3	16.2	16.1	16.0	15.8	15.7	15.8	15.7	16.1
2003	15.5	15.3	15.3	15.1	15.1	15.0	15.0	15.0	15.0	14.9	14.9	15.0	15.1
2004	14.9	14.8	14.8	14.6	14.6	14.7	14.6	14.5	14.4	14.3	14.5	14.5	14.6
2005	14.5	14.5	14.5	14.4	14.4	14.6	14.3	14.3	14.0	14.0	14.1	14.1	14.3
2006	14.0	13.9	13.9	13.8	13.8	13.9	13.7	13.6	13.4	13.3	13.3	13.4	13.7
2007	13.2	13.3	13.3	13.3	13.3	13.5	13.6	13.5	13.4	13.3	13.5	13.5	13.4
2008	13.4	13.5	13.5	13.5	13.5	13.6	13.6	13.5	13.4	13.2	13.4	13.4	13.5
2009	13.3	13.2	13.1	13.0	12.9	12.9	12.6	12.6	12.6	12.4	12.4	12.3	12.8
2010	12.2	12.2	12.3	12.1	12.2	12.3	12.3	12.3	12.6	12.7	12.3	12.2	12.3
2011	12.0	12.0	12.0	11.9	11.9	11.9	12.0	11.8	11.8	11.8	11.9	11.8	11.9

1. Employment by Industry: Mississippi, Selected Years, 2000–2011—*Continued*

(Numbers in thousands, not seasonally adjusted)

Industry and year	January	February	March	April	May	June	July	August	September	October	November	December	Annual average
Financial Activities													
2000	45.8	45.8	45.9	45.9	46.0	46.5	46.1	45.9	46.0	45.6	45.7	46.0	45.9
2001	45.3	45.5	45.5	45.6	45.8	46.2	46.1	46.3	46.0	45.8	45.8	46.1	45.8
2002	45.6	45.4	45.5	45.7	45.7	46.1	45.8	45.8	45.6	45.7	46.0	46.0	45.7
2003	45.8	45.7	45.8	45.7	46.0	46.1	46.2	46.1	46.0	45.7	45.7	46.0	45.9
2004	45.5	45.4	45.6	45.9	45.9	46.3	46.3	46.3	46.1	46.1	46.1	46.5	46.0
2005	45.9	45.9	46.1	46.0	46.2	46.3	46.7	46.6	45.8	46.6	46.8	46.9	46.3
2006	45.6	46.3	46.3	46.2	46.3	46.7	46.8	46.8	46.7	46.5	46.8	47.1	46.5
2007	46.5	46.7	46.8	46.9	47.1	47.3	47.1	47.3	47.0	47.2	47.2	47.4	47.0
2008	47.0	47.0	47.2	47.0	47.1	47.1	47.0	46.9	46.7	47.0	46.8	47.0	47.0
2009	46.5	46.2	46.0	45.8	46.1	45.8	45.5	45.5	45.3	45.2	45.3	45.5	45.7
2010	45.0	44.9	44.9	45.0	45.1	45.2	45.2	45.0	44.8	44.7	44.7	44.9	45.0
2011	44.4	44.4	44.5	44.6	44.6	44.8	45.0	45.1	44.9	45.1	44.5	45.2	44.8
Professional and Business Services													
2000	78.5	78.7	79.4	79.9	80.0	80.5	79.0	80.6	80.3	78.3	78.7	78.2	79.3
2001	76.2	77.1	76.9	77.2	76.9	76.8	77.1	77.7	77.2	76.1	76.0	76.6	76.8
2002	76.0	76.7	77.3	78.7	78.2	79.3	78.6	79.7	78.9	77.5	76.8	77.4	77.9
2003	77.3	77.5	77.4	79.1	78.7	78.8	79.0	79.9	80.2	81.0	81.1	81.8	79.3
2004	80.7	81.4	81.9	83.4	82.8	83.1	83.2	83.0	83.6	82.9	82.9	84.4	82.8
2005	84.6	86.7	87.0	87.1	85.7	85.8	86.2	87.1	87.5	89.9	91.6	91.3	87.5
2006	90.1	92.0	93.7	94.2	94.4	93.6	91.5	92.8	92.7	92.0	92.8	92.5	92.7
2007	91.0	92.3	93.4	92.4	92.2	92.3	91.9	93.2	93.9	94.0	95.0	95.8	93.1
2008	94.5	95.4	95.5	96.3	96.1	95.7	94.1	94.6	95.2	94.6	94.1	92.2	94.9
2009	89.8	89.5	89.0	87.8	87.0	86.7	85.3	86.2	85.9	86.3	87.0	87.3	87.3
2010	85.7	87.3	87.9	90.2	92.4	95.8	95.3	93.7	95.1	94.2	93.6	93.6	92.1
2011	91.9	92.8	94.2	94.8	94.2	93.2	92.6	93.0	95.2	95.8	96.0	93.5	93.9
Education and Health Services													
2000	104.0	104.3	104.8	105.1	105.3	103.1	102.6	104.3	106.2	106.8	107.1	107.5	105.1
2001	108.0	108.7	109.3	109.8	110.2	107.6	107.6	110.0	111.4	111.8	112.2	112.6	109.9
2002	111.6	111.9	112.6	113.5	113.6	110.6	109.9	111.8	114.2	114.6	114.9	115.2	112.9
2003	114.3	114.7	115.2	116.1	116.2	113.6	112.9	115.2	116.7	118.0	118.4	118.3	115.8
2004	118.3	119.0	119.3	119.7	119.6	116.2	116.5	118.0	121.2	121.2	121.7	121.9	119.4
2005	121.3	122.0	122.3	122.6	122.4	118.9	118.6	120.9	122.1	122.0	122.3	123.1	121.5
2006	121.9	122.9	123.8	124.0	124.4	120.6	120.4	123.5	126.4	126.4	127.1	127.5	124.1
2007	126.5	127.2	127.9	127.9	128.3	125.5	124.5	128.5	129.9	129.9	129.9	129.9	128.0
2008	128.0	128.7	128.6	128.6	127.8	125.6	124.7	128.1	130.0	130.5	130.4	130.5	128.5
2009	129.1	129.4	129.7	130.0	129.5	126.9	127.1	129.9	132.1	132.6	133.0	133.1	130.2
2010	131.7	132.0	132.5	132.8	132.2	129.2	128.3	131.3	134.3	134.9	135.1	134.8	132.4
2011	133.8	134.2	134.4	134.7	133.4	131.2	130.3	134.0	137.8	138.8	139.4	139.0	135.1
Leisure and Hospitality													
2000	119.1	119.5	121.7	124.3	125.0	128.1	126.0	126.8	123.8	121.8	120.9	120.0	123.1
2001	116.4	117.5	120.0	122.5	123.8	124.6	124.3	124.7	122.7	118.6	117.8	116.8	120.8
2002	115.7	117.1	119.7	122.9	124.7	126.1	125.6	126.2	124.8	121.8	120.9	120.5	122.2
2003	118.9	119.9	121.8	123.8	124.8	125.9	126.4	127.0	125.1	123.4	122.6	121.9	123.5
2004	120.0	121.2	123.2	125.8	126.7	127.4	128.3	128.8	127.0	124.6	123.5	122.5	124.9
2005	120.9	122.4	125.0	126.9	128.4	129.2	128.5	128.6	120.1	116.8	118.8	110.4	123.0
2006	109.8	112.2	115.2	117.6	118.9	121.1	119.7	123.5	124.8	124.3	124.1	124.1	119.6
2007	120.6	122.1	123.8	125.4	126.9	128.6	127.9	128.9	127.8	125.3	125.8	125.3	125.7
2008	122.6	124.2	125.5	127.5	128.7	128.6	126.9	127.7	125.8	123.4	122.6	121.0	125.4
2009	118.0	119.6	121.2	122.4	123.3	123.3	121.3	121.6	119.9	117.5	117.3	116.3	120.1
2010	113.4	114.8	117.3	119.5	120.4	121.2	119.7	121.0	119.7	117.8	117.4	116.2	118.2
2011	113.8	115.4	118.1	120.3	121.6	122.1	121.1	118.6	116.9	115.1	115.3	113.4	117.6
Other Services													
2000	34.9	35.2	35.6	35.7	35.8	36.4	36.0	35.8	35.8	35.4	35.4	35.5	35.6
2001	36.1	36.2	36.4	36.6	36.9	37.5	37.2	37.2	37.2	36.9	36.9	37.0	36.8
2002	36.8	36.9	37.3	37.5	37.6	38.0	37.5	37.3	37.3	37.1	37.1	37.1	37.3
2003	37.2	37.3	38.0	37.9	37.8	38.0	37.9	37.6	37.5	37.4	37.3	37.4	37.6
2004	37.5	37.8	37.7	38.0	37.9	38.1	37.6	37.4	37.4	37.1	37.0	37.0	37.5
2005	37.0	37.6	37.5	37.8	37.8	37.8	37.8	37.3	36.5	36.4	36.5	36.5	37.2
2006	36.3	37.0	37.0	37.0	37.0	37.5	37.2	37.1	36.9	36.6	36.5	36.5	36.9
2007	36.8	37.1	37.4	37.1	37.2	37.5	37.3	37.2	37.2	36.8	36.9	36.9	37.1
2008	36.8	37.2	37.5	37.5	37.8	37.6	37.2	37.1	37.2	36.8	36.3	36.0	37.1
2009	35.4	35.3	35.4	35.6	35.5	35.6	35.5	35.1	35.2	34.7	34.6	34.5	35.2
2010	34.4	34.4	34.7	35.1	35.1	35.0	34.9	34.7	34.9	34.7	34.3	34.0	34.7
2011	33.6	33.6	33.8	34.0	34.3	34.5	34.3	34.7	34.0	33.6	34.0	34.2	34.1
Government													
2000	230.2	231.2	233.5	234.4	239.2	232.4	227.1	232.7	235.1	235.8	236.9	237.1	233.8
2001	237.2	238.3	238.5	239.1	239.2	236.3	230.4	236.2	238.6	239.0	238.8	238.8	237.5
2002	238.2	239.3	239.6	240.7	241.1	239.5	233.6	238.9	242.2	242.7	242.8	242.8	240.1
2003	241.3	242.2	243.1	243.4	241.3	237.1	232.5	235.8	243.1	244.3	244.4	240.8	240.8
2004	240.7	243.6	245.0	245.8	243.9	239.7	231.9	237.8	244.5	245.5	245.6	241.4	242.1
2005	240.4	244.2	244.6	244.6	243.5	240.0	231.8	237.5	241.3	241.4	242.1	238.1	240.8
2006	237.9	241.0	241.1	241.0	239.9	237.6	227.4	236.6	243.3	243.1	243.8	240.3	239.4
2007	240.8	244.6	244.8	246.0	245.3	242.0	233.0	241.2	247.2	248.6	248.6	245.5	244.0
2008	245.8	249.4	249.8	250.8	249.4	245.5	234.9	244.2	250.2	252.1	252.5	249.4	247.8
2009	248.5	251.3	251.5	252.6	252.8	249.0	239.3	244.9	251.8	252.9	252.3	249.3	249.7
2010	248.3	251.7	253.5	252.3	255.5	250.8	238.6	241.8	247.8	250.5	249.4	248.3	249.0
2011	245.2	247.5	248.3	247.7	245.2	242.9	236.4	242.1	248.9	250.9	250.3	247.4	246.1

2. Average Weekly Hours by Selected Industry: Mississippi, 2007–2011

(Not seasonally adjusted)

Industry and year	January	February	March	April	May	June	July	August	September	October	November	December	Annual average
Total Private													
2007	35.6	35.5	35.6	35.6	35.5	35.9	36.2	35.5	35.8	35.5	35.6	36.3	35.7
2008	35.7	35.7	35.8	35.5	35.3	36.1	35.6	35.6	35.6	35.5	35.8	35.4	35.6
2009	35.6	35.6	35.5	35.0	35.2	35.7	35.8	36.0	34.9	34.9	35.7	35.5	35.4
2010	35.4	34.8	35.5	36.2	36.2	36.1	36.1	36.3	35.9	35.9	36.0	36.1	35.9
2011	35.5	35.5	35.7	36.1	36.6	36.0	36.2	36.1	36.0	36.3	35.7	35.9	36.0
Goods-Producing													
2007	39.6	40.1	40.3	39.9	40.4	40.8	40.4	40.9	40.8	40.2	40.4	41.3	40.4
2008	39.5	39.2	39.7	39.4	39.5	40.4	40.9	40.2	40.8	40.2	40.1	39.9	40.0
2009	40.7	40.2	39.8	39.8	40.1	41.4	41.7	41.3	39.6	39.8	40.5	40.3	40.4
2010	40.4	38.6	41.0	42.1	41.6	41.5	41.8	40.9	40.8	40.5	41.1	40.8	40.9
2011	39.0	39.2	39.9	40.5	41.0	40.5	40.7	41.3	41.3	41.4	40.6	41.4	40.6
Construction													
2007	40.0	39.4	40.9	40.1	40.7	40.7	39.3	41.6	39.3	40.8	40.7	40.6	40.3
2008	37.9	38.9	39.9	39.8	39.4	40.7	39.6	39.0	41.4	39.7	38.6	36.9	39.3
2009	38.8	38.3	37.8	38.1	38.3	39.7	38.8	39.9	36.4	35.2	38.3	35.3	37.9
2010	37.7	35.1	38.1	42.1	41.4	41.4	42.0	40.5	40.7	40.5	40.7	39.8	40.1
2011	38.7	39.1	39.4	40.8	41.5	41.2	41.2	41.2	39.5	39.3	37.9	38.5	39.9
Manufacturing													
2007	39.7	40.2	39.9	39.5	40.0	40.5	40.4	40.5	41.1	40.0	40.3	41.6	40.3
2008	40.5	39.6	39.8	39.5	39.6	40.2	41.4	40.4	40.2	40.1	40.1	40.5	40.2
2009	40.8	40.4	40.1	39.1	39.3	40.6	40.4	40.4	39.8	40.3	40.5	40.9	40.2
2010	40.2	38.7	41.1	41.1	40.6	40.5	40.7	40.7	40.5	40.0	40.7	40.9	40.5
2011	39.1	39.2	40.0	40.4	40.9	40.2	40.5	41.1	41.5	41.6	41.1	42.0	40.6
Trade, Transportation, and Utilities													
2007	34.9	33.8	34.3	33.8	33.9	34.8	35.2	33.9	34.4	33.3	33.8	35.0	34.3
2008	35.2	35.7	35.8	35.6	35.7	36.3	35.6	35.8	35.1	35.0	35.0	35.1	35.5
2009	34.7	35.0	34.9	34.5	34.5	34.7	34.2	34.9	34.1	34.0	34.0	34.6	34.5
2010	34.9	34.7	35.0	35.3	35.7	35.6	35.8	36.1	36.3	35.9	36.2	36.4	35.7
2011	35.8	35.9	35.7	36.4	37.0	36.5	36.4	36.3	36.4	36.3	36.1	36.3	36.3
Financial Activities													
2007	35.7	36.5	35.7	38.4	35.9	36.0	39.2	36.8	38.6	37.0	36.7	38.3	37.1
2008	36.7	36.3	38.5	37.7	37.2	38.7	36.8	37.5	37.2	36.5	38.9	36.9	37.4
2009	37.9	39.2	38.9	37.5	37.1	37.7	36.2	38.8	35.8	35.8	37.8	35.4	37.3
2010	35.2	35.4	35.3	36.1	37.8	36.0	35.9	37.5	36.5	36.6	36.6	36.5	36.3
2011	37.4	37.2	37.2	37.0	38.8	37.4	38.0	37.4	37.4	38.8	37.0	37.2	37.6
Professional and Business Services													
2007	35.0	35.5	35.6	35.6	36.5	36.6	36.5	35.6	35.9	37.4	36.8	37.0	36.2
2008	36.5	35.8	36.7	37.1	35.7	36.6	35.4	36.5	36.1	36.3	36.0	34.9	36.1
2009	35.3	35.0	35.4	34.9	35.6	35.5	34.6	36.1	34.0	34.4	35.9	35.8	35.2
2010	35.5	35.3	35.4	35.9	35.4	35.9	35.3	36.0	34.8	34.9	34.9	35.0	35.4
2011	35.0	34.7	35.8	36.2	36.5	35.9	35.8	36.1	35.1	36.3	35.2	35.5	35.7
Education and Health Services													
2007	35.4	35.2	35.1	35.2	34.2	34.5	34.5	34.3	34.3	34.1	34.4	34.5	34.6
2008	33.9	34.8	33.6	34.0	33.4	34.1	34.0	33.5	33.8	33.7	34.1	34.0	33.9
2009	33.8	33.2	33.8	33.9	34.1	34.3	34.2	34.3	34.5	34.5	34.9	34.7	34.2
2010	34.7	34.3	34.1	34.7	34.8	34.6	34.4	34.7	34.5	34.0	34.3	34.2	34.4
2011	34.3	33.5	33.2	33.8	34.2	33.7	34.0	33.8	33.8	33.9	33.8	33.5	33.8
Leisure and Hospitality													
2007	26.5	25.8	25.9	26.3	26.2	26.0	26.7	25.3	26.1	26.7	26.5	26.7	26.2
2008	27.0	27.4	27.4	26.7	27.1	28.0	27.2	27.5	27.7	28.4	28.9	28.9	27.7
2009	28.7	29.3	29.0	28.7	29.3	29.7	32.3	31.9	30.8	30.8	31.4	30.8	30.2
2010	30.4	30.3	30.5	30.5	30.4	30.6	30.4	30.0	28.8	29.3	28.7	29.0	29.9
2011	29.0	29.4	29.3	28.8	28.8	28.9	29.1	28.5	28.0	28.7	28.1	27.5	28.7

3. Average Hourly Earnings by Selected Industry: Mississippi, 2007–2011

(Dollars, not seasonally adjusted)

Industry and year	January	February	March	April	May	June	July	August	September	October	November	December	Annual average
Total Private													
2007	16.47	16.51	16.58	16.62	16.37	16.28	16.46	16.47	16.48	16.38	16.41	16.47	16.46
2008	16.53	16.78	16.81	16.75	16.69	16.85	16.92	17.04	17.04	17.10	17.22	16.99	16.89
2009	17.06	17.42	17.64	17.62	17.78	17.78	17.94	18.13	18.24	18.19	18.39	18.25	17.87
2010	18.29	18.25	18.19	17.98	18.14	17.93	17.95	17.95	17.92	17.98	17.96	18.08	18.05
2011	18.31	18.19	18.12	18.06	18.06	17.94	17.91	17.98	18.07	18.36	18.14	18.43	18.13
Goods-Producing													
2007	16.24	16.07	16.11	16.36	16.24	16.29	16.45	16.40	16.37	16.49	16.59	16.69	16.36
2008	16.76	17.15	17.19	17.10	17.14	17.25	17.32	17.33	17.29	17.36	17.57	17.03	17.21
2009	17.10	17.51	18.07	18.07	18.40	18.64	18.87	18.84	18.61	18.47	18.59	18.63	18.31
2010	18.65	18.55	18.60	18.40	18.57	18.49	18.68	18.23	18.26	18.17	18.22	18.22	18.42
2011	18.26	18.18	18.39	18.46	18.39	18.27	18.38	18.42	18.38	18.32	18.38	19.24	18.42
Construction													
2007	17.03	16.48	16.44	16.55	16.32	16.58	16.64	16.52	16.65	16.78	16.87	17.15	16.67
2008	17.30	17.89	17.81	17.79	17.95	17.67	17.93	17.98	18.04	18.10	18.29	18.06	17.90
2009	18.37	18.60	18.86	18.71	18.75	18.73	18.60	18.66	17.59	17.89	17.68	18.45	18.43
2010	18.84	18.97	18.69	18.46	18.37	18.52	18.76	18.69	18.84	18.70	18.79	18.77	18.69
2011	18.88	18.83	19.30	19.21	19.31	18.79	18.80	19.11	18.70	18.68	18.64	20.25	19.04
Manufacturing													
2007	15.99	15.92	15.89	16.23	16.17	16.14	16.33	16.32	16.20	16.26	16.39	16.36	16.18
2008	16.42	16.74	16.71	16.60	16.63	16.83	16.86	16.96	16.71	16.73	16.97	16.28	16.70
2009	16.32	16.83	17.37	17.26	17.46	17.65	17.49	17.57	17.69	17.48	17.78	17.62	17.37
2010	17.48	17.36	17.53	17.33	17.55	17.48	17.44	17.18	17.27	17.32	17.44	17.49	17.41
2011	17.37	17.38	17.51	17.66	17.53	17.59	17.74	17.75	17.90	17.82	17.95	17.96	17.68
Trade, Transportation, and Utilities													
2007	14.76	15.26	15.45	15.22	15.11	14.87	14.74	14.84	15.05	14.62	14.72	14.72	14.94
2008	14.92	14.87	14.88	15.01	14.92	14.84	14.58	15.78	15.73	15.48	15.30	14.81	15.09
2009	14.90	15.46	15.18	15.25	15.29	15.01	14.95	15.02	15.28	15.42	15.58	15.41	15.23
2010	15.52	15.48	15.39	15.58	15.83	15.93	15.90	16.03	16.12	16.15	16.25	16.22	15.87
2011	16.15	16.28	16.12	16.37	16.35	16.02	15.94	16.18	16.33	16.53	16.19	16.30	16.23
Financial Activities													
2007	19.12	18.88	20.06	18.69	17.14	17.60	18.07	18.57	18.04	17.97	18.57	18.45	18.42
2008	18.36	19.31	20.43	19.85	19.86	20.05	19.83	19.25	19.10	19.22	19.14	19.03	19.46
2009	19.06	18.99	19.14	19.29	19.23	19.39	19.56	19.60	19.58	19.64	19.82	20.06	19.44
2010	20.03	20.02	19.87	19.71	19.92	19.64	19.67	19.90	19.87	19.73	19.86	20.17	19.87
2011	20.30	20.23	20.31	20.40	20.61	20.40	20.28	20.26	20.46	20.89	20.53	20.72	20.45
Professional and Business Services													
2007	19.63	19.05	19.09	19.09	18.71	18.14	18.60	18.82	18.72	18.66	18.48	18.43	18.78
2008	18.63	18.03	18.13	17.94	17.74	17.89	18.27	18.13	18.39	18.97	18.79	18.98	18.32
2009	18.81	19.68	19.84	19.90	19.86	19.99	19.98	19.87	19.97	20.45	20.66	20.72	19.97
2010	20.68	20.58	20.48	20.29	20.31	19.72	19.56	19.69	19.79	19.81	19.77	19.42	20.00
2011	19.58	19.52	19.42	18.96	19.47	19.56	19.77	19.62	19.70	20.12	19.61	19.95	19.61
Education and Health Services													
2007	17.45	17.49	17.50	17.61	17.67	17.86	18.14	17.89	17.80	17.81	17.61	17.92	17.73
2008	18.00	18.40	18.43	18.45	18.36	18.54	19.02	19.02	18.80	18.69	18.60	18.84	18.60
2009	18.82	19.04	19.02	19.15	19.27	19.27	19.47	19.63	19.82	19.75	19.96	19.75	19.42
2010	19.79	19.84	19.83	19.64	19.54	19.54	19.72	19.74	19.58	19.62	19.47	19.40	19.64
2011	19.44	19.33	19.22	19.21	19.00	19.33	19.18	19.17	19.26	19.59	19.34	19.33	19.28
Leisure and Hospitality													
2007	10.26	10.23	10.20	10.38	10.26	10.02	10.07	10.23	10.45	10.12	10.42	10.79	10.29
2008	10.79	11.34	11.00	10.85	10.82	10.67	10.79	10.69	10.69	10.81	11.20	11.19	10.90
2009	11.23	11.75	11.59	11.57	11.50	11.42	11.42	11.56	11.69	11.70	11.74	11.96	11.59
2010	12.06	12.19	12.10	12.14	12.03	11.94	12.01	12.24	12.22	12.31	12.39	12.28	12.16
2011	12.39	12.42	12.27	12.27	12.31	12.19	12.22	12.36	12.37	12.47	12.47	12.48	12.35

4. Average Weekly Earnings by Selected Industry: Mississippi, 2007–2011

(Dollars, not seasonally adjusted)

Industry and year	January	February	March	April	May	June	July	August	September	October	November	December	Annual average
Total Private													
2007	586.33	586.11	590.25	591.67	581.14	584.45	595.85	584.69	589.98	581.49	584.20	597.86	587.88
2008	590.12	599.05	601.80	594.63	589.16	608.29	602.35	606.62	606.62	607.05	616.48	601.45	602.04
2009	607.34	620.15	626.22	616.70	625.86	634.75	642.25	652.68	636.58	634.83	656.52	647.88	632.95
2010	647.47	635.10	645.75	650.88	656.67	647.27	648.00	651.59	643.33	645.48	646.56	652.69	647.54
2011	650.01	645.75	646.88	651.97	661.00	645.84	648.34	649.08	650.52	666.47	647.60	661.64	652.10
Goods-Producing													
2007	643.10	644.41	649.23	652.76	656.10	664.63	664.58	670.76	667.90	662.90	670.24	689.30	661.32
2008	662.02	672.28	682.44	673.74	677.03	696.90	708.39	696.67	705.43	697.87	704.56	679.50	687.88
2009	695.97	703.90	719.19	719.19	737.84	771.70	786.88	778.09	736.96	735.11	752.90	750.79	740.31
2010	753.46	716.03	762.60	774.64	772.51	767.34	780.82	745.61	745.01	735.89	748.84	743.38	753.95
2011	712.14	712.66	733.76	747.63	753.99	739.94	748.07	760.75	759.09	758.45	746.23	796.54	747.45
Construction													
2007	681.20	649.31	672.40	663.66	664.22	674.81	653.95	687.23	654.35	684.62	686.61	696.29	672.57
2008	655.67	695.92	710.62	708.04	707.23	719.17	710.03	701.22	746.86	718.57	705.99	666.41	704.11
2009	712.76	712.38	712.91	712.85	718.13	743.58	721.68	744.53	640.28	629.73	677.14	651.29	699.20
2010	710.27	665.85	712.09	777.17	760.52	766.73	787.92	756.95	766.79	757.35	764.75	747.05	748.91
2011	730.66	736.25	760.42	783.77	801.37	774.15	774.56	787.33	738.65	734.12	706.46	779.63	759.39
Manufacturing													
2007	634.80	639.98	634.01	641.09	646.80	653.67	659.73	660.96	665.82	650.40	660.52	680.58	652.27
2008	665.01	662.90	665.06	655.70	658.55	676.57	698.00	685.18	671.74	670.87	680.50	659.34	670.69
2009	665.86	679.93	696.54	674.87	686.18	716.59	706.60	709.83	704.06	704.44	720.09	720.66	698.51
2010	702.70	671.83	720.48	712.26	712.53	707.94	709.81	699.23	699.44	692.80	709.81	715.34	704.53
2011	679.17	681.30	700.40	713.46	716.98	707.12	718.47	729.53	742.85	741.31	737.75	754.32	718.46
Trade, Transportation, and Utilities													
2007	515.12	515.79	529.94	514.44	512.23	517.48	518.85	503.08	517.72	486.85	497.54	515.20	511.99
2008	525.18	530.86	532.70	534.36	532.64	538.69	519.05	564.92	552.12	541.80	535.50	519.83	535.62
2009	517.03	541.10	529.78	526.13	527.51	520.85	511.29	524.20	521.05	524.28	529.72	533.19	525.52
2010	541.65	537.16	538.65	549.97	565.13	567.11	569.22	578.68	585.16	579.79	588.25	590.41	566.13
2011	578.17	584.45	575.48	595.87	604.95	584.73	580.22	587.33	594.41	600.04	584.46	591.69	588.53
Financial Activities													
2007	682.58	689.12	716.14	717.70	615.33	633.60	708.34	683.38	696.34	664.89	681.52	706.64	682.92
2008	673.81	700.95	786.56	748.35	738.79	775.94	729.74	721.88	710.52	701.53	744.55	702.21	727.94
2009	722.37	744.41	744.55	723.38	713.43	731.00	708.07	760.48	700.96	703.11	749.20	710.12	725.90
2010	705.06	708.71	701.41	711.53	752.98	707.04	706.15	746.25	725.26	722.12	726.88	736.21	720.69
2011	759.22	752.56	755.53	754.80	799.67	762.96	770.64	757.72	765.20	810.53	759.61	770.78	768.12
Professional and Business Services													
2007	687.05	676.28	679.60	679.60	682.92	663.92	678.90	669.99	672.05	697.88	680.06	681.91	679.19
2008	680.00	645.47	665.37	665.57	633.32	654.77	646.76	661.75	663.88	688.61	676.44	662.40	661.98
2009	663.99	688.80	702.34	694.51	707.02	709.65	691.31	717.31	678.98	703.48	741.69	741.78	703.48
2010	734.14	726.47	724.99	728.41	718.97	707.95	690.47	708.84	688.69	691.37	689.97	679.70	707.11
2011	685.30	677.34	695.24	686.35	710.66	702.20	707.77	708.28	691.47	730.36	690.27	708.23	699.54
Education and Health Services													
2007	617.73	615.65	614.25	619.87	604.31	616.17	625.83	613.63	610.54	607.32	605.78	618.24	614.06
2008	610.20	640.32	619.25	627.30	613.22	632.21	646.68	637.17	635.44	629.85	634.26	640.56	630.53
2009	636.12	632.13	642.88	649.19	657.11	660.96	665.87	673.31	683.79	681.38	696.60	685.33	663.95
2010	686.71	680.51	676.20	681.51	679.99	676.08	678.37	684.98	675.51	667.08	667.82	663.48	676.40
2011	666.79	647.56	638.10	649.30	649.80	651.42	652.12	647.95	650.99	664.10	653.69	647.56	651.63
Leisure and Hospitality													
2007	271.89	263.93	264.18	272.99	268.81	260.52	268.87	258.82	272.75	270.20	276.13	288.09	269.81
2008	291.33	310.72	301.40	289.70	293.22	298.76	293.49	293.98	296.11	307.00	323.68	323.39	301.77
2009	322.30	344.28	336.11	332.06	336.95	339.17	368.87	368.76	360.05	360.36	368.64	368.37	350.41
2010	366.62	369.36	369.05	370.27	365.71	365.36	365.10	367.20	351.94	360.68	355.59	356.12	363.62
2011	359.31	365.15	359.51	353.38	354.53	352.29	355.60	352.26	346.36	357.89	350.41	343.20	354.14

MISSOURI
At a Glance

Population:
  2000 census: 5,596,564
  2010 census: 5,988,927
  2011 estimate: 6,010,688

Percent change in population:
  2000–2010: 7.0%
  2010–2011: 0.4%

Percent change in total nonfarm employment:
  2000–2010: -3.6%
  2010–2011: 0.0%

Industry with the largest growth in employment, 2000–2011 (thousands):
  Education and Health Services, 81.8

Industry with the largest decline or smallest growth in employment, 2000–2011 (thousands):
  Manufacturing, -117.5

Civilian labor force:
  2000: 2,973,092
  2010: 3,052,847
  2011: 3,046,302

Unemployment rate and rank among states (lowest to highest):
  2000: 3.3%, 14th
  2010: 9.4%, 31st
  2011: 8.6%, 29th

Over-the-year change in unemployment rates:
  2010–2011: -0.8%

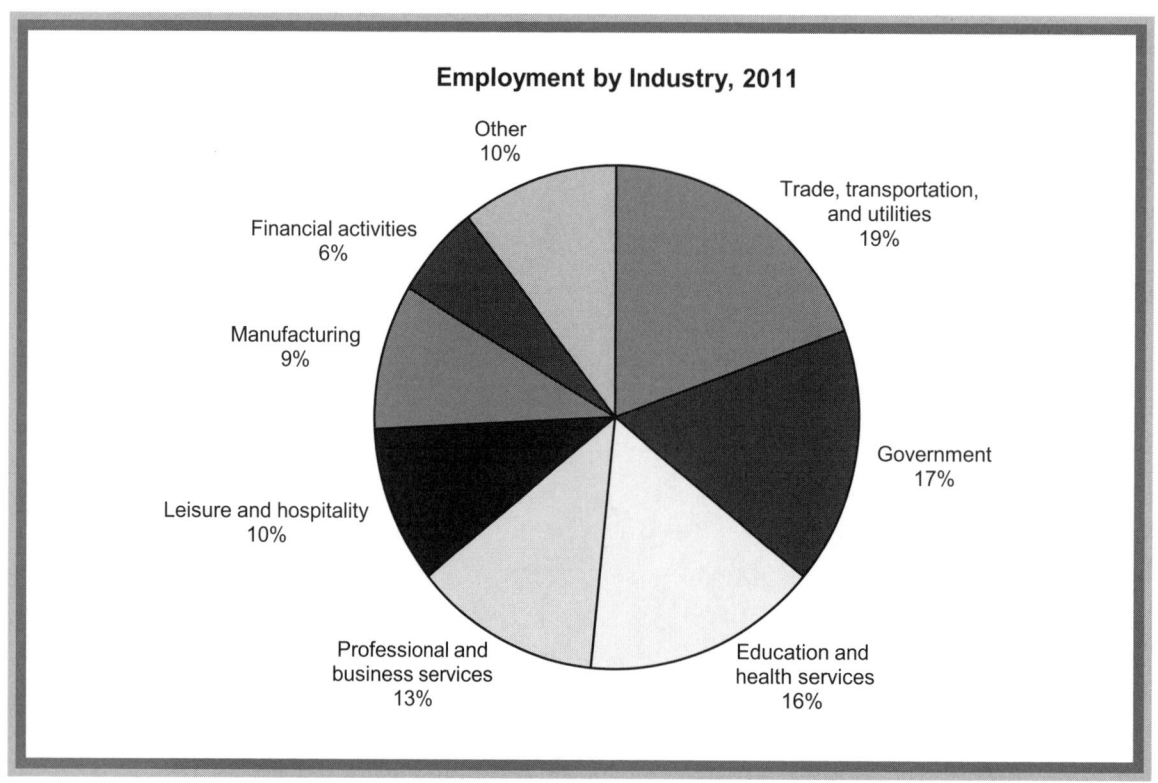

Employment by Industry, 2011

Other 10%
Financial activities 6%
Manufacturing 9%
Leisure and hospitality 10%
Professional and business services 13%
Education and health services 16%
Government 17%
Trade, transportation, and utilities 19%

1. Employment by Industry: Missouri, Selected Years, 2000–2011

(Numbers in thousands, not seasonally adjusted)

Industry and year	January	February	March	April	May	June	July	August	September	October	November	December	Annual average
Total Nonfarm													
2000	2,691.1	2,701.2	2,735.0	2,758.5	2,774.3	2,786.1	2,729.9	2,733.5	2,763.2	2,771.8	2,774.5	2,766.2	2,748.8
2001	2,688.3	2,700.8	2,727.1	2,751.7	2,765.9	2,775.1	2,708.4	2,717.0	2,738.2	2,730.3	2,731.9	2,730.4	2,730.4
2002	2,660.5	2,667.2	2,690.7	2,705.7	2,720.2	2,727.9	2,661.0	2,677.5	2,719.1	2,716.1	2,720.5	2,720.0	2,698.9
2003	2,640.4	2,643.1	2,664.8	2,690.0	2,703.5	2,709.6	2,654.6	2,662.6	2,695.0	2,704.2	2,699.1	2,698.5	2,680.5
2004	2,629.6	2,630.8	2,666.9	2,702.5	2,713.1	2,724.1	2,673.1	2,684.3	2,717.9	2,730.2	2,730.2	2,730.9	2,694.5
2005	2,656.0	2,671.5	2,703.3	2,749.3	2,758.2	2,764.0	2,721.5	2,735.7	2,761.0	2,763.2	2,768.9	2,771.5	2,735.3
2006	2,706.5	2,722.9	2,755.6	2,784.7	2,798.2	2,804.6	2,751.6	2,760.9	2,793.4	2,797.3	2,805.4	2,809.4	2,774.2
2007	2,729.0	2,741.7	2,785.3	2,803.5	2,824.4	2,825.6	2,768.0	2,785.8	2,815.1	2,815.3	2,822.4	2,818.7	2,794.6
2008	2,747.8	2,761.1	2,782.3	2,809.9	2,828.8	2,828.5	2,768.7	2,780.1	2,803.2	2,800.7	2,786.8	2,771.7	2,789.1
2009	2,681.2	2,679.1	2,692.8	2,709.0	2,716.2	2,709.1	2,649.9	2,658.0	2,681.4	2,680.8	2,677.5	2,671.6	2,683.9
2010	2,590.2	2,602.1	2,632.4	2,665.2	2,683.7	2,673.5	2,623.1	2,650.3	2,667.6	2,675.1	2,674.0	2,668.2	2,650.5
2011	2,597.5	2,602.8	2,636.9	2,675.4	2,687.8	2,678.9	2,639.2	2,636.9	2,663.5	2,668.8	2,668.4	2,648.0	2,650.3
Total Private													
2000	2,265.6	2,267.5	2,294.5	2,325.0	2,336.2	2,355.6	2,336.3	2,340.2	2,338.7	2,342.4	2,338.6	2,330.9	2,322.6
2001	2,260.2	2,265.4	2,290.2	2,314.3	2,327.4	2,341.0	2,317.3	2,324.5	2,305.8	2,293.7	2,292.5	2,287.9	2,301.7
2002	2,224.6	2,228.1	2,250.0	2,264.7	2,277.2	2,294.2	2,271.1	2,286.9	2,287.6	2,275.9	2,277.3	2,275.9	2,267.8
2003	2,203.0	2,200.5	2,221.4	2,242.8	2,255.0	2,269.0	2,265.0	2,273.0	2,263.0	2,266.2	2,260.2	2,260.4	2,248.3
2004	2,198.3	2,193.4	2,226.1	2,260.4	2,273.6	2,294.8	2,282.5	2,291.6	2,285.8	2,292.4	2,289.9	2,292.0	2,265.1
2005	2,228.2	2,235.0	2,264.3	2,309.0	2,318.9	2,335.1	2,324.9	2,335.0	2,331.5	2,327.3	2,329.7	2,331.9	2,305.9
2006	2,274.8	2,281.4	2,311.0	2,339.8	2,352.2	2,373.7	2,356.0	2,361.9	2,357.4	2,353.9	2,358.8	2,363.2	2,340.3
2007	2,292.4	2,295.3	2,336.2	2,353.0	2,372.0	2,387.5	2,370.7	2,381.6	2,372.2	2,363.4	2,367.7	2,365.3	2,354.8
2008	2,306.3	2,307.9	2,327.8	2,352.9	2,370.2	2,381.6	2,365.8	2,367.9	2,354.3	2,341.5	2,326.1	2,311.7	2,342.8
2009	2,232.3	2,221.5	2,232.9	2,242.4	2,249.7	2,255.9	2,240.7	2,242.7	2,225.2	2,216.9	2,214.0	2,209.5	2,232.0
2010	2,140.3	2,142.8	2,169.9	2,202.2	2,212.7	2,226.9	2,224.9	2,230.2	2,219.6	2,223.7	2,221.5	2,218.2	2,202.7
2011	2,154.9	2,155.0	2,186.8	2,222.0	2,233.7	2,244.2	2,246.4	2,237.7	2,225.8	2,224.2	2,221.9	2,202.6	2,212.9
Goods-Producing													
2000	501.8	500.9	505.3	509.6	513.7	520.5	510.0	511.4	508.3	512.7	509.6	503.9	509.0
2001	488.3	489.9	494.7	499.1	500.8	502.8	488.5	495.2	489.2	481.0	480.7	477.2	490.6
2002	461.9	462.5	465.8	464.5	465.6	470.8	458.1	471.2	469.8	465.5	462.9	461.2	465.0
2003	447.8	444.8	448.9	451.1	454.5	458.6	452.4	459.3	456.3	457.9	454.8	452.1	453.2
2004	439.9	435.9	445.7	453.2	456.0	462.4	453.6	462.8	460.3	458.0	455.6	454.4	453.2
2005	440.0	441.4	448.6	457.5	461.4	465.6	456.0	466.0	464.0	463.6	462.2	460.5	457.2
2006	449.7	451.0	457.6	462.0	463.4	470.3	464.1	465.4	462.5	459.8	458.8	457.4	460.2
2007	443.4	440.4	451.7	453.6	458.4	462.6	456.2	460.8	458.2	453.7	451.9	447.3	453.2
2008	433.9	432.5	434.5	438.4	443.3	446.3	441.8	439.9	437.0	431.0	422.9	413.6	434.6
2009	391.7	386.2	386.4	382.8	379.7	381.3	379.5	375.4	371.4	366.4	362.6	356.2	376.6
2010	340.7	338.6	345.8	352.2	353.4	359.2	358.7	360.5	358.6	359.5	356.9	353.9	353.2
2011	338.9	337.8	345.9	352.8	356.0	361.0	365.9	363.0	361.4	359.6	355.9	349.9	354.0
Mining and Logging													
2000	5.5	5.5	5.6	6.0	6.0	6.0	5.5	5.5	5.4	5.4	5.3	5.1	5.6
2001	4.8	4.9	5.0	5.2	5.1	5.2	5.1	5.2	5.0	4.8	4.7	4.6	5.0
2002	4.5	4.5	4.5	4.5	4.6	4.7	4.7	4.7	4.7	4.6	4.6	4.5	4.6
2003	4.4	4.4	4.4	4.5	4.6	4.7	4.6	4.7	4.6	4.6	4.5	4.5	4.5
2004	4.6	4.5	4.6	4.8	4.8	4.9	5.0	5.0	5.0	4.9	4.8	4.7	4.8
2005	4.9	4.9	5.1	5.3	5.4	5.5	5.5	5.5	5.4	5.4	5.4	5.4	5.3
2006	5.3	5.3	5.4	5.4	5.5	5.6	5.6	5.5	5.5	5.4	5.3	5.2	5.4
2007	5.1	5.0	5.2	5.2	5.2	5.4	5.7	6.2	6.1	6.0	6.0	5.7	5.6
2008	5.4	5.2	5.1	5.0	4.9	5.0	5.1	5.3	5.4	5.4	4.9	4.7	5.1
2009	4.4	4.3	4.3	4.3	4.2	4.3	4.3	4.4	4.3	4.3	4.2	4.1	4.3
2010	3.8	3.9	4.1	4.3	4.3	4.4	4.4	4.4	4.3	4.3	4.3	4.2	4.2
2011	3.9	3.8	4.2	4.3	4.3	4.4	4.4	4.4	4.4	4.4	4.4	4.3	4.3
Construction													
2000	129.0	128.6	133.0	136.8	139.7	144.2	143.7	144.9	144.1	142.9	140.1	135.1	138.5
2001	128.2	129.2	134.8	140.6	144.0	149.0	148.1	148.1	144.7	143.0	141.1	138.3	140.8
2002	129.8	129.0	132.1	131.8	134.0	138.9	141.7	141.0	138.8	137.4	135.1	133.8	135.3
2003	125.3	123.1	126.4	131.7	134.9	138.5	141.2	141.0	139.1	139.4	136.6	133.3	134.2
2004	126.2	122.3	130.3	136.5	139.0	142.7	145.2	144.2	142.3	141.3	139.1	137.7	137.2
2005	126.5	127.6	133.9	142.0	145.6	148.6	150.9	151.1	149.9	148.8	147.0	144.8	143.1
2006	139.1	139.5	143.6	147.8	149.2	153.9	153.6	153.4	151.1	149.3	146.9	145.1	147.7
2007	138.2	133.1	143.4	146.4	150.7	155.2	154.7	154.9	152.0	150.2	147.7	143.0	147.5
2008	136.0	132.5	137.4	140.4	144.3	146.6	147.3	147.2	143.9	141.0	136.8	130.7	140.3
2009	117.9	116.7	119.0	119.7	121.6	123.4	124.4	121.8	119.3	116.2	114.2	108.9	118.6
2010	97.7	95.6	101.0	106.7	106.8	110.7	112.1	111.4	110.2	109.9	107.6	104.1	106.2
2011	91.6	90.5	96.9	102.8	105.2	108.2	112.0	109.4	107.9	105.0	101.6	96.8	102.3
Manufacturing													
2000	367.3	366.8	366.7	366.8	368.0	370.3	360.8	361.0	358.8	364.4	364.2	363.7	364.9
2001	355.3	355.8	354.9	353.3	351.7	348.6	335.3	341.9	339.5	333.2	334.9	334.3	344.9
2002	327.6	329.0	329.2	328.2	327.0	327.2	311.7	325.5	326.3	323.5	323.2	322.9	325.1
2003	318.1	317.3	318.1	314.9	315.0	315.4	306.6	313.6	312.6	313.9	313.7	314.3	314.5
2004	309.1	309.1	310.8	311.9	312.2	314.8	303.4	313.6	313.0	311.8	311.7	312.0	311.1
2005	308.6	308.9	309.6	310.2	310.4	311.5	299.6	309.4	308.7	309.4	309.8	310.3	308.9
2006	305.3	306.2	308.6	308.8	308.7	310.8	304.9	306.5	305.9	305.1	306.6	307.1	307.0
2007	300.1	302.3	303.1	302.0	302.5	302.0	295.8	299.7	300.1	297.5	298.2	298.6	300.2
2008	292.5	294.8	292.0	293.0	294.1	294.7	289.4	287.4	287.7	284.6	281.2	278.2	289.1
2009	269.4	265.2	263.1	258.8	253.9	253.6	250.8	249.2	247.8	245.9	244.2	243.2	253.8
2010	239.2	239.1	240.7	241.2	242.3	244.1	242.2	244.7	244.1	245.3	245.0	245.6	242.8
2011	243.4	243.5	244.8	245.7	246.5	248.4	249.5	249.2	249.1	250.2	249.9	248.8	247.4

1. Employment by Industry: Missouri, Selected Years, 2000–2011—*Continued*

(Numbers in thousands, not seasonally adjusted)

Industry and year	January	February	March	April	May	June	July	August	September	October	November	December	Annual average
Service-Providing													
2000	2,189.3	2,200.3	2,229.7	2,248.9	2,260.6	2,265.6	2,219.9	2,222.1	2,254.9	2,259.1	2,264.9	2,262.3	2,239.8
2001	2,200.0	2,210.9	2,232.4	2,252.6	2,265.1	2,272.3	2,219.9	2,221.8	2,249.0	2,249.3	2,251.2	2,253.2	2,239.8
2002	2,198.6	2,204.7	2,224.9	2,241.2	2,254.6	2,257.1	2,202.9	2,206.3	2,249.3	2,250.6	2,257.6	2,258.8	2,233.9
2003	2,192.6	2,198.3	2,215.9	2,238.9	2,249.0	2,251.0	2,202.2	2,203.3	2,238.7	2,246.3	2,244.3	2,246.4	2,227.2
2004	2,189.7	2,194.9	2,221.2	2,249.3	2,257.1	2,261.7	2,219.5	2,221.5	2,257.6	2,272.2	2,274.6	2,276.5	2,241.3
2005	2,216.0	2,230.1	2,254.7	2,291.8	2,296.8	2,298.4	2,265.5	2,269.7	2,297.0	2,299.6	2,306.7	2,311.0	2,278.1
2006	2,256.8	2,271.9	2,298.0	2,322.7	2,334.8	2,334.3	2,287.5	2,295.5	2,330.9	2,337.5	2,346.6	2,352.0	2,314.0
2007	2,285.6	2,301.3	2,333.6	2,349.9	2,366.0	2,363.0	2,311.8	2,325.0	2,356.9	2,361.6	2,370.5	2,371.4	2,341.4
2008	2,313.9	2,328.6	2,347.8	2,371.5	2,385.5	2,382.2	2,326.9	2,340.2	2,366.2	2,369.7	2,363.9	2,358.1	2,354.5
2009	2,289.5	2,292.9	2,306.4	2,326.2	2,336.5	2,327.8	2,270.4	2,282.6	2,310.0	2,314.4	2,314.9	2,315.4	2,307.3
2010	2,249.5	2,263.5	2,286.6	2,313.0	2,330.3	2,314.3	2,264.4	2,289.8	2,309.0	2,315.6	2,317.1	2,314.3	2,297.3
2011	2,258.6	2,265.0	2,291.0	2,322.6	2,331.8	2,317.9	2,273.3	2,273.9	2,302.1	2,309.2	2,312.5	2,298.1	2,296.3
Trade, Transportation, and Utilities													
2000	550.9	548.1	552.9	555.0	557.1	556.3	553.8	553.5	559.0	561.6	571.0	576.8	558.0
2001	544.1	538.8	541.3	542.4	544.6	545.7	541.8	541.5	542.7	544.8	553.4	556.2	544.8
2002	535.9	530.9	535.1	533.6	537.9	539.1	537.5	537.0	542.3	540.7	549.8	554.0	539.5
2003	529.4	524.8	527.6	528.8	530.7	530.4	529.1	530.1	530.4	538.0	543.8	547.3	532.5
2004	525.1	519.7	524.7	527.6	531.6	533.2	530.0	530.1	532.2	537.2	545.8	551.0	532.4
2005	530.4	526.0	531.2	538.0	540.8	541.5	540.4	541.2	541.0	542.8	551.9	556.3	540.1
2006	538.3	534.1	538.8	541.2	544.4	545.7	541.3	543.3	544.7	547.1	555.6	561.0	544.6
2007	542.1	538.4	546.0	546.5	550.2	549.9	545.7	546.0	547.3	548.8	559.4	562.1	548.5
2008	542.4	537.1	540.4	542.7	545.7	546.0	542.0	542.1	540.9	540.2	544.2	545.1	542.4
2009	522.7	516.9	516.8	517.9	520.1	519.8	515.8	517.0	516.7	517.3	523.5	525.2	519.1
2010	506.4	502.2	506.8	510.6	514.4	515.2	512.6	514.3	511.9	514.0	521.5	524.9	512.9
2011	506.9	503.5	507.9	515.6	517.9	518.1	516.0	512.6	509.9	509.5	516.4	516.6	512.6
Wholesale Trade													
2000	120.5	121.2	122.1	121.6	121.6	122.3	121.7	121.4	122.2	122.1	122.6	123.2	121.9
2001	120.8	121.0	121.2	121.1	121.1	121.6	121.1	120.6	120.3	119.6	118.9	119.2	120.5
2002	119.3	119.2	119.8	119.4	119.5	120.1	120.3	119.3	119.4	118.8	118.8	118.7	119.4
2003	117.8	117.9	118.1	118.4	118.6	118.9	119.1	119.2	118.2	118.3	118.4	118.6	118.5
2004	117.7	117.6	118.6	119.6	119.8	121.2	120.9	120.1	121.0	120.4	120.4	121.1	119.9
2005	121.7	120.9	121.5	121.6	121.7	122.6	122.5	122.4	121.3	120.9	121.3	121.8	121.7
2006	120.7	120.5	121.5	122.3	123.0	124.0	123.1	123.4	123.3	123.5	123.8	124.8	122.8
2007	123.0	123.7	124.8	124.6	124.9	125.9	125.5	125.5	125.2	125.3	125.6	126.1	125.0
2008	124.7	124.6	125.2	125.6	125.7	126.3	125.9	125.7	125.0	124.5	123.6	123.4	125.0
2009	120.6	119.8	119.2	118.9	118.5	118.6	118.0	117.4	116.6	117.1	116.7	117.1	118.2
2010	115.2	115.0	116.0	116.4	116.7	117.0	116.7	116.0	115.5	115.9	115.7	116.1	116.0
2011	114.2	114.3	115.1	116.6	116.7	117.3	117.6	116.4	115.9	116.5	117.6	115.8	116.2
Retail Trade													
2000	310.1	306.1	309.1	311.0	312.5	312.7	311.1	311.0	312.8	314.9	324.2	329.8	313.8
2001	310.6	305.1	306.7	308.0	310.0	311.9	308.9	308.4	309.3	312.3	321.5	325.0	311.5
2002	308.6	304.1	307.3	306.0	309.2	310.7	308.3	308.6	312.8	311.5	320.9	326.4	311.2
2003	305.3	300.7	303.7	305.3	307.3	308.0	307.2	308.6	309.1	315.8	322.6	326.1	310.0
2004	306.7	301.4	304.6	305.8	309.1	310.7	308.9	308.8	308.9	313.6	322.0	326.1	310.6
2005	309.2	305.7	309.5	313.8	316.0	316.3	316.8	316.4	315.3	317.5	325.8	328.7	315.9
2006	313.3	309.3	312.7	314.1	316.0	316.7	314.5	314.6	314.4	316.8	324.8	328.0	316.3
2007	312.9	308.6	314.0	315.4	317.9	318.2	315.4	314.4	314.3	315.9	325.5	327.2	316.6
2008	312.7	307.3	309.6	311.2	313.5	314.7	311.8	311.3	309.6	310.1	315.2	316.4	312.0
2009	300.5	296.3	297.4	298.6	301.1	302.6	300.3	300.9	300.6	301.1	307.8	309.3	301.4
2010	294.9	291.5	294.5	296.1	299.1	301.0	299.9	300.2	297.6	299.4	306.8	309.2	299.2
2011	295.9	292.3	295.4	300.1	302.1	303.0	300.6	298.9	295.9	295.9	301.5	302.7	298.7
Transportation and Utilities													
2000	120.3	120.8	121.7	122.4	123.0	121.3	121.0	121.1	124.0	124.6	124.2	123.8	122.4
2001	112.7	112.7	113.4	113.3	113.5	112.2	111.8	112.5	113.1	112.9	113.0	112.0	112.8
2002	108.0	107.6	108.0	108.2	109.2	108.3	108.9	109.1	110.1	110.4	110.1	108.9	108.9
2003	106.3	106.2	105.8	105.1	104.8	103.5	102.8	102.3	103.1	103.9	102.6	102.6	104.1
2004	100.7	100.7	101.5	102.2	102.7	101.3	100.2	101.2	102.3	103.2	103.4	103.8	101.9
2005	99.5	99.4	100.2	102.6	103.1	102.6	101.1	102.4	104.4	104.4	104.8	105.8	102.5
2006	104.3	104.3	104.6	104.8	105.4	105.0	103.7	105.3	107.0	106.8	107.0	108.2	105.5
2007	106.2	106.1	107.2	106.5	107.4	105.8	104.8	106.1	107.8	107.6	108.3	108.8	106.9
2008	105.0	105.2	105.6	105.9	106.5	105.0	104.3	105.1	106.3	105.6	105.4	105.3	105.4
2009	101.6	100.8	100.2	100.4	100.5	98.6	97.5	98.7	99.5	99.1	99.0	98.8	99.6
2010	96.3	95.7	96.3	98.1	98.6	97.2	96.0	98.1	98.8	98.7	99.0	99.6	97.7
2011	96.8	96.9	97.4	98.9	99.1	97.8	97.8	97.3	98.1	97.1	97.3	98.1	97.7
Information													
2000	77.0	76.9	76.8	76.8	76.6	76.6	76.3	76.2	76.0	75.9	75.9	75.7	76.4
2001	74.8	75.3	75.6	75.1	74.9	75.4	74.9	74.6	74.1	73.1	73.1	71.9	74.4
2002	72.8	72.8	72.4	70.9	71.1	71.1	69.2	69.1	68.7	66.9	67.4	67.6	70.0
2003	68.0	68.5	68.6	67.1	66.6	67.0	66.0	65.5	65.0	64.5	64.6	65.0	66.4
2004	65.1	65.2	65.3	64.8	64.6	64.7	63.9	63.2	62.8	63.6	64.1	63.6	64.2
2005	62.8	62.9	63.2	64.2	64.3	64.5	64.4	64.0	63.8	63.9	63.9	64.0	63.8
2006	63.0	63.0	63.2	62.9	63.0	63.4	62.9	62.8	62.8	62.7	63.1	63.5	63.0
2007	62.2	62.4	62.9	62.6	63.1	63.7	63.4	63.6	63.7	64.0	64.4	64.6	63.4
2008	64.3	64.0	64.2	63.8	64.4	64.9	64.6	64.5	64.1	64.2	64.0	64.5	64.3
2009	64.0	64.0	63.7	64.4	64.5	64.9	63.6	63.6	63.2	61.1	61.0	61.4	63.3
2010	58.9	58.6	58.8	61.3	61.0	61.4	60.5	60.5	60.3	60.2	60.1	60.0	60.1
2011	58.5	58.3	58.2	58.5	58.7	58.9	58.5	58.5	58.6	57.9	57.6	58.2	58.4

1. Employment by Industry: Missouri, Selected Years, 2000–2011—*Continued*

(Numbers in thousands, not seasonally adjusted)

Industry and year	January	February	March	April	May	June	July	August	September	October	November	December	Annual average
Financial Activities													
2000	155.3	155.6	156.4	157.8	158.0	159.9	160.2	159.8	158.8	159.3	159.7	160.6	158.5
2001	158.2	158.3	159.0	159.8	161.0	162.4	162.4	162.3	160.6	159.6	159.7	160.2	160.3
2002	158.5	158.4	160.7	160.3	160.8	161.5	161.3	161.6	160.8	160.8	161.1	162.0	160.7
2003	160.5	160.4	160.8	161.8	162.5	163.9	165.4	165.7	164.1	163.4	162.7	162.9	162.8
2004	160.1	159.8	160.4	161.8	162.2	164.1	164.5	164.8	163.1	163.2	162.7	163.1	162.5
2005	160.8	161.6	162.2	162.7	162.7	164.1	165.4	165.0	164.3	163.9	163.9	164.3	163.4
2006	162.1	162.5	163.3	164.5	165.6	167.0	166.9	167.2	166.4	165.1	165.0	165.6	165.1
2007	164.5	164.9	165.6	165.3	166.2	167.6	167.8	167.6	166.2	166.2	165.6	166.0	166.1
2008	165.3	165.6	165.3	165.3	166.2	166.8	167.3	167.3	165.8	165.7	165.3	165.1	165.9
2009	163.8	163.4	163.8	163.9	164.2	164.9	163.9	163.6	161.7	162.4	161.7	161.6	163.2
2010	160.9	160.8	161.1	162.1	162.6	163.6	163.7	162.9	161.9	162.5	162.5	162.3	162.2
2011	159.8	160.1	160.3	160.4	160.8	161.1	160.0	160.4	158.2	157.8	156.8	156.3	159.3
Professional and Business Services													
2000	307.9	309.1	313.8	319.6	317.6	323.7	320.5	321.6	320.5	318.3	317.3	315.0	317.1
2001	312.8	314.8	318.3	318.9	317.1	318.7	313.7	315.1	311.8	310.1	307.8	308.7	314.0
2002	299.4	302.5	304.7	306.3	304.8	305.9	303.7	305.2	305.5	307.0	307.5	306.7	304.9
2003	296.5	297.0	299.7	301.2	299.9	302.4	301.4	303.2	303.2	303.2	301.4	302.8	301.0
2004	296.5	296.8	302.4	306.5	305.3	310.5	310.0	311.7	310.8	312.3	311.8	313.6	307.4
2005	309.4	311.9	316.0	321.8	319.2	322.8	323.2	323.1	324.7	323.5	324.1	325.4	320.4
2006	318.7	322.2	327.2	331.6	330.5	335.4	332.7	334.4	334.2	336.6	336.8	339.1	331.6
2007	327.6	328.9	334.8	337.4	337.2	340.8	339.9	342.0	340.2	339.7	340.0	341.1	337.5
2008	335.1	337.3	341.0	347.1	344.0	345.7	343.8	344.4	342.3	339.1	335.4	332.8	340.7
2009	321.6	319.9	319.3	319.2	316.8	317.6	315.3	316.2	313.5	314.5	315.4	316.9	317.2
2010	309.9	312.8	315.9	322.1	320.2	322.5	324.9	326.2	324.3	326.6	325.8	326.8	321.5
2011	321.3	322.9	327.7	334.7	333.1	334.5	335.0	332.7	330.9	334.3	335.8	333.0	331.3
Education and Health Services													
2000	328.5	331.4	332.7	335.2	333.7	332.5	332.1	332.1	336.0	337.2	338.2	338.0	334.0
2001	336.4	339.1	340.8	342.8	342.9	342.7	342.8	343.0	345.2	346.7	348.3	348.4	343.3
2002	345.6	348.4	348.8	349.7	350.5	349.8	348.1	348.7	353.4	352.8	354.1	354.4	350.4
2003	349.7	352.0	353.1	353.2	352.3	351.3	352.2	352.1	354.8	355.5	356.1	356.7	353.3
2004	352.2	355.9	356.9	358.1	358.0	357.2	357.4	357.1	360.4	363.5	363.8	364.2	358.7
2005	359.6	363.1	364.4	368.7	368.1	367.2	367.2	367.4	371.7	374.6	375.4	376.2	368.6
2006	369.6	374.0	375.3	377.2	377.0	375.5	373.9	374.1	379.6	382.1	384.9	384.1	377.3
2007	376.3	381.2	383.2	384.5	384.4	382.7	382.4	383.4	387.5	389.3	390.6	391.5	384.8
2008	384.8	389.8	390.0	392.3	391.8	390.7	390.6	391.7	395.2	399.7	400.9	401.5	393.3
2009	395.1	398.2	399.0	399.8	399.9	397.6	397.8	399.4	402.7	406.3	407.5	408.4	401.0
2010	400.2	404.2	405.2	407.3	407.3	404.8	404.2	404.8	409.3	413.8	415.1	415.0	407.6
2011	410.0	413.4	414.6	415.7	414.5	411.3	412.7	413.3	419.3	423.1	422.4	418.7	415.8
Leisure and Hospitality													
2000	231.3	232.1	242.1	256.0	264.1	270.1	267.8	269.7	263.9	261.0	250.6	244.2	254.4
2001	230.2	233.3	243.0	258.0	267.0	272.8	273.7	273.3	264.0	260.8	251.8	247.5	256.3
2002	234.9	236.5	245.6	261.8	268.6	276.8	274.9	276.0	269.4	264.6	257.2	252.7	259.9
2003	235.5	237.0	245.8	262.1	270.6	276.4	277.6	276.7	270.4	265.0	258.5	255.0	260.9
2004	242.6	243.0	252.5	268.7	276.1	281.7	282.1	281.3	276.0	274.2	266.3	262.6	267.3
2005	247.2	249.7	259.9	276.2	282.6	288.3	287.6	288.0	282.5	276.0	269.8	266.2	272.8
2006	254.3	256.5	266.6	280.2	288.0	294.6	292.9	293.8	286.9	280.4	274.4	272.2	278.4
2007	257.7	260.1	271.7	282.6	291.3	298.3	293.9	297.2	288.9	281.8	276.0	272.9	281.0
2008	260.5	261.3	271.4	282.1	293.0	298.5	293.3	295.8	287.4	280.0	273.2	269.6	280.5
2009	255.2	254.6	265.1	275.6	285.4	290.1	285.4	288.9	278.4	271.6	265.3	262.8	273.2
2010	248.2	250.3	260.5	274.4	281.3	286.9	286.9	287.9	281.2	274.5	267.3	263.2	271.9
2011	248.7	248.2	260.1	271.1	279.2	285.2	284.4	283.1	275.2	270.6	266.5	258.9	269.3
Other Services													
2000	112.9	113.4	114.5	115.0	115.4	116.0	115.6	115.9	116.2	116.4	116.3	116.7	115.4
2001	115.4	115.9	117.5	118.2	119.1	120.5	119.5	119.5	118.2	117.6	117.7	117.8	118.1
2002	115.6	116.1	116.9	117.6	117.9	119.2	118.3	118.1	117.7	117.6	117.3	117.3	117.5
2003	115.6	116.0	116.9	117.5	117.9	119.0	120.9	120.4	118.8	118.7	118.3	118.6	118.2
2004	116.8	117.1	118.2	119.7	119.8	121.0	121.0	120.6	120.2	120.4	119.8	119.5	119.5
2005	118.0	118.4	118.8	119.9	119.8	121.1	120.7	120.3	119.5	119.0	118.5	119.0	119.4
2006	119.1	118.1	119.0	120.2	120.3	121.8	121.3	120.9	120.3	120.1	120.2	120.3	120.1
2007	118.6	119.0	120.3	120.5	121.2	121.9	121.4	121.0	120.2	119.9	119.8	119.8	120.3
2008	120.0	120.3	121.0	121.2	121.8	122.7	122.4	122.2	121.6	121.6	120.2	119.5	121.2
2009	118.2	118.3	118.8	118.8	119.1	119.7	119.4	118.6	117.6	117.3	117.0	117.0	118.3
2010	115.1	115.3	115.8	112.2	112.5	113.3	113.4	113.1	112.1	112.6	112.3	112.1	113.3
2011	110.8	110.8	112.1	113.2	113.5	114.1	113.9	114.1	112.3	111.4	110.5	111.0	112.3
Government													
2000	425.5	433.7	440.5	433.5	438.1	430.5	393.6	393.3	424.5	429.4	435.9	435.3	426.2
2001	428.1	435.4	436.9	437.4	438.5	434.1	391.1	392.5	432.4	436.6	439.4	442.5	428.7
2002	435.9	439.1	440.7	441.0	443.0	433.7	389.6	390.6	431.5	440.2	443.2	444.1	431.1
2003	437.4	442.6	443.4	447.2	448.5	440.6	389.6	389.6	432.0	438.0	438.9	438.1	432.2
2004	431.3	437.4	440.8	442.1	439.5	429.3	390.6	392.7	432.1	437.8	440.3	438.9	429.4
2005	427.8	436.5	439.0	440.3	439.3	428.9	396.6	400.7	429.5	435.9	439.2	439.6	429.4
2006	431.7	441.5	444.6	444.9	446.0	430.9	395.6	399.0	436.0	443.4	446.6	446.2	433.9
2007	436.6	446.4	449.1	450.5	452.4	438.1	397.3	404.2	442.9	451.9	454.7	453.4	439.8
2008	441.5	453.2	454.5	457.0	458.6	446.9	402.9	412.2	448.9	459.2	460.7	460.0	446.3
2009	448.9	457.6	459.9	466.6	466.5	453.2	409.2	415.3	456.2	463.9	463.5	462.1	451.9
2010	449.9	459.3	462.5	463.0	471.0	446.6	398.2	420.1	448.0	451.4	452.5	450.0	447.7
2011	442.6	447.8	450.1	453.4	454.1	434.7	392.8	399.2	437.7	444.6	446.5	445.4	437.4

2. Average Weekly Hours by Selected Industry: Missouri, 2007–2011

(Not seasonally adjusted)

Industry and year	January	February	March	April	May	June	July	August	September	October	November	December	Annual average
Total Private													
2007	33.9	33.8	34.4	34.6	34.1	34.6	34.9	34.4	34.9	34.5	34.1	34.6	34.4
2008	34.2	34.0	34.8	34.3	34.4	35.1	34.6	34.7	34.5	34.8	34.6	33.9	34.5
2009	33.7	34.4	33.9	33.4	33.6	33.3	33.8	34.4	33.9	33.7	34.5	33.8	33.9
2010	33.7	33.9	33.8	33.9	34.1	33.8	33.7	34.3	33.7	33.8	33.9	34.1	33.9
2011	34.6	34.3	34.5	34.6	35.0	34.9	34.8	34.7	34.9	35.3	34.5	34.5	34.7
Goods-Producing													
2007	37.5	37.0	38.8	38.8	38.6	39.5	39.4	39.4	39.5	39.4	38.8	38.7	38.8
2008	38.4	37.9	38.5	38.0	38.1	38.4	39.4	40.0	39.2	39.3	37.9	37.4	38.5
2009	36.7	37.7	37.5	36.9	37.9	37.9	38.9	39.7	38.7	38.8	39.4	38.7	38.2
2010	38.4	38.9	38.8	39.4	38.7	39.3	38.7	39.2	38.7	39.2	38.4	38.4	38.8
2011	37.6	38.4	38.0	38.3	38.7	39.1	39.4	39.2	39.7	39.7	38.5	38.9	38.8
Construction													
2007	36.0	34.9	37.7	35.2	37.0	38.2	38.5	38.4	38.1	38.1	37.7	37.1	37.3
2008	37.4	36.7	37.3	36.6	36.6	36.0	37.0	37.2	36.0	37.9	35.8	35.3	36.7
2009	35.6	35.8	35.3	35.2	37.0	37.9	39.0	38.5	36.5	37.1	37.1	35.3	36.7
2010	34.3	34.6	35.7	36.5	34.6	36.2	36.0	37.0	36.2	37.0	35.0	35.6	35.8
2011	34.7	35.3	35.0	35.2	36.3	36.8	37.0	37.3	37.5	37.7	35.6	36.0	36.3
Manufacturing													
2007	38.2	38.7	39.1	40.2	39.1	39.8	39.6	39.7	39.9	39.8	39.4	39.5	39.4
2008	39.0	39.0	39.7	39.2	39.3	39.8	40.2	40.4	40.5	39.8	38.8	38.3	39.5
2009	37.4	38.0	37.8	37.2	37.9	37.4	38.2	38.9	38.5	38.5	39.4	39.4	38.2
2010	39.4	40.0	39.5	40.0	39.9	40.1	39.5	39.8	39.7	39.5	39.5	39.2	39.7
2011	38.4	39.3	39.0	39.4	39.6	39.9	40.4	40.0	40.7	40.6	40.1	40.7	39.8
Trade, Transportation, and Utilities													
2007	33.3	33.4	34.1	33.9	34.3	34.1	34.5	33.9	34.5	34.1	33.8	34.3	34.0
2008	33.7	33.9	34.9	34.4	34.8	35.3	34.9	34.6	34.6	34.7	35.1	34.7	34.6
2009	33.7	34.8	34.4	34.4	34.9	34.0	34.6	34.8	34.7	34.1	34.5	33.9	34.4
2010	33.2	33.6	33.9	34.2	34.2	33.8	34.3	34.4	34.7	34.3	34.1	34.5	34.1
2011	33.8	33.9	34.3	34.7	35.3	35.3	35.2	35.4	35.6	35.7	35.0	35.6	35.0
Financial Activities													
2007	36.9	36.9	36.3	37.7	36.5	38.7	38.1	37.9	38.1	37.3	36.8	37.4	37.4
2008	36.5	36.1	37.7	36.9	36.3	38.1	36.2	36.8	36.5	36.8	38.1	36.6	36.9
2009	37.4	37.9	37.9	36.9	36.5	36.8	36.7	38.1	37.6	37.3	38.8	37.5	37.4
2010	37.9	37.6	37.3	37.3	38.2	37.2	37.2	37.9	37.5	38.3	38.0	37.2	37.6
2011	37.6	37.1	37.5	37.5	37.7	37.3	37.2	36.9	37.4	38.3	37.3	37.1	37.4
Professional and Business Services													
2007	34.7	35.6	35.7	35.9	34.3	34.8	35.9	35.6	36.5	35.6	35.5	36.1	35.5
2008	35.2	35.0	36.4	36.0	36.0	37.0	35.8	35.8	35.5	37.0	35.8	34.3	35.8
2009	34.7	35.4	35.1	34.8	34.5	34.2	34.4	35.7	34.3	35.0	35.9	34.9	34.9
2010	35.0	35.6	35.4	35.7	35.5	34.7	34.5	35.3	34.9	35.4	35.3	35.4	35.2
2011	35.8	35.0	35.2	35.4	35.9	35.6	35.1	35.1	35.1	35.8	34.7	34.7	35.3
Education and Health Services													
2007	33.3	32.9	33.2	33.7	33.0	33.2	33.7	32.9	33.3	32.7	32.4	32.9	33.1
2008	33.0	32.6	33.0	32.6	32.2	32.8	32.8	32.8	32.8	32.8	33.0	32.0	32.7
2009	32.3	32.7	32.4	32.0	31.9	32.3	32.2	32.2	32.3	31.8	32.5	31.9	32.2
2010	31.9	31.8	31.9	31.9	32.1	32.3	31.7	32.4	32.5	32.1	32.6	32.9	32.2
2011	33.8	33.1	33.5	33.4	34.1	34.1	33.9	33.9	33.8	34.3	33.8	33.7	33.8
Leisure and Hospitality													
2007	26.1	26.5	26.9	26.5	26.2	27.4	27.7	27.2	26.8	26.6	26.2	26.3	26.7
2008	25.8	26.1	26.0	25.7	26.4	27.2	26.2	25.6	24.9	25.1	25.1	24.6	25.7
2009	23.5	24.1	24.1	23.8	24.4	24.4	25.5	25.0	24.4	24.4	24.4	24.6	24.4
2010	23.8	24.1	24.3	24.1	24.5	24.8	24.9	24.9	24.4	24.5	25.2	25.3	24.6
2011	25.7	25.6	26.4	26.0	26.2	26.5	26.4	26.0	25.7	26.6	25.8	25.6	26.0

3. Average Hourly Earnings by Selected Industry: Missouri, 2007–2011

(Dollars, not seasonally adjusted)

Industry and year	January	February	March	April	May	June	July	August	September	October	November	December	Annual average
Total Private													
2007	19.71	20.04	19.77	19.80	19.71	19.58	19.55	19.51	19.97	19.75	19.77	20.29	19.79
2008	19.84	20.38	20.47	20.29	20.46	20.34	20.33	20.61	20.58	20.90	21.32	21.28	20.57
2009	21.17	21.06	21.00	20.76	20.93	20.91	20.77	20.95	20.86	20.80	21.05	20.97	20.94
2010	21.04	21.15	21.12	21.02	21.33	21.01	21.25	21.03	21.24	21.31	21.37	21.42	21.19
2011	20.78	20.86	20.62	20.79	20.83	20.54	20.78	20.66	20.69	20.93	20.95	21.05	20.79
Goods-Producing													
2007	21.49	21.73	22.05	22.07	22.13	21.74	21.80	21.99	22.75	22.55	22.67	23.23	22.19
2008	22.87	23.09	23.48	23.59	23.99	23.46	23.84	24.19	23.72	24.20	24.60	25.27	23.85
2009	24.95	25.92	25.61	25.40	25.52	25.47	25.25	24.92	24.92	24.94	25.28	24.66	25.24
2010	24.44	23.88	24.40	24.27	24.15	24.08	24.40	24.51	24.68	24.77	24.71	24.81	24.43
2011	24.59	24.01	23.95	23.77	23.65	22.99	23.14	22.90	22.83	22.88	23.13	22.83	23.37
Construction													
2007	22.90	23.67	23.63	23.96	23.82	23.55	23.55	23.63	23.88	24.19	24.30	24.17	23.78
2008	24.57	25.14	25.11	25.26	26.16	24.96	25.96	26.38	26.06	26.63	26.86	27.30	25.86
2009	27.11	27.84	26.01	26.34	26.84	26.25	26.49	26.68	27.10	27.70	28.33	27.34	26.99
2010	28.09	27.48	27.11	26.84	26.60	26.59	26.78	26.63	26.92	27.26	27.04	27.28	27.03
2011	27.99	27.45	27.43	27.19	27.06	26.63	26.83	26.98	27.29	26.86	28.31	28.48	27.34
Manufacturing													
2007	20.93	21.09	21.42	21.37	21.41	20.92	21.01	21.26	22.32	21.91	22.12	22.96	21.56
2008	22.23	22.30	22.78	22.87	22.96	23.31	22.70	23.02	23.14	23.47	23.98	24.74	23.11
2009	24.30	25.05	25.48	24.99	24.80	25.04	24.63	24.46	24.36	24.11	24.41	24.05	24.64
2010	23.54	22.91	23.62	23.47	23.39	23.26	23.59	23.78	23.76	23.69	23.75	23.83	23.55
2011	23.40	22.83	22.62	22.37	22.14	21.71	21.80	21.36	21.11	21.36	20.98	20.57	21.83
Trade, Transportation, and Utilities													
2007	16.98	17.25	16.72	17.12	16.99	16.73	16.84	16.79	17.01	16.69	16.72	17.42	16.94
2008	16.90	17.91	17.64	17.61	17.80	17.71	17.47	17.75	17.94	17.97	18.37	18.81	17.83
2009	18.65	18.38	18.28	18.13	17.94	18.10	18.46	18.40	18.40	18.19	18.19	18.01	18.26
2010	18.91	18.74	18.94	19.08	19.30	18.96	18.90	19.22	19.37	18.96	18.98	18.94	19.03
2011	19.05	18.74	18.56	18.94	18.82	18.64	19.10	18.67	18.57	19.14	18.93	18.89	18.84
Financial Activities													
2007	23.01	24.92	24.06	24.24	23.03	24.10	23.24	22.83	22.51	22.30	22.17	23.18	23.30
2008	22.39	23.72	23.32	22.88	23.05	22.88	23.15	23.04	22.92	23.64	23.50	23.14	23.14
2009	22.91	23.15	22.20	21.92	22.56	22.08	22.21	22.21	22.58	22.26	22.17	22.38	22.37	22.40
2010	21.57	22.28	22.11	22.08	22.62	21.75	22.25	22.49	22.70	22.69	22.69	22.19	22.29
2011	22.40	23.31	22.16	22.20	21.89	21.16	21.60	21.63	21.65	21.90	21.89	21.93	21.98
Professional and Business Services													
2007	28.09	27.86	27.18	27.59	27.32	27.32	27.34	27.05	27.41	27.02	26.45	26.71	27.27
2008	26.63	26.54	27.16	26.26	26.67	26.45	26.14	26.37	25.92	26.43	27.11	26.04	26.48
2009	25.61	26.06	25.71	25.50	26.29	26.77	26.35	26.42	26.31	25.96	26.23	26.51	26.14
2010	25.94	25.93	25.17	24.30	25.09	24.65	24.84	24.80	24.77	24.60	24.88	25.58	25.04
2011	25.67	26.08	25.90	25.44	25.48	25.24	25.50	25.83	26.13	26.28	26.48	26.69	25.89
Education and Health Services													
2007	18.10	17.90	18.59	17.41	18.30	18.38	18.46	18.59	19.16	18.80	19.08	19.32	18.51
2008	19.15	19.55	19.69	19.73	19.60	19.80	19.20	19.59	19.66	19.68	20.38	20.05	19.68
2009	20.17	19.82	20.34	20.07	20.67	20.47	20.01	20.07	19.54	19.68	19.94	19.73	20.04
2010	20.25	20.85	20.52	21.23	21.46	21.43	21.42	21.27	21.40	21.56	21.53	21.51	21.21
2011	21.50	21.38	21.01	21.32	21.22	21.43	21.43	21.02	20.94	21.02	20.69	21.06	21.17
Leisure and Hospitality													
2007	11.55	11.58	11.31	11.43	11.40	11.31	11.51	11.47	11.56	11.62	11.68	12.11	11.54
2008	12.12	12.25	12.22	12.15	12.09	12.10	12.11	11.91	12.22	12.01	12.32	12.78	12.18
2009	12.92	12.82	12.86	12.47	12.53	12.59	12.59	12.51	12.64	12.57	12.76	13.05	12.69
2010	12.90	12.76	12.53	12.21	12.21	12.13	12.13	12.34	12.28	12.30	12.60	12.36
2011	11.76	11.91	11.74	11.74	11.57	11.57	11.70	11.73	11.99	11.83	12.07	12.26	11.82

4. Average Weekly Earnings by Selected Industry: Missouri, 2007–2011

(Dollars, not seasonally adjusted)

Industry and year	January	February	March	April	May	June	July	August	September	October	November	December	Annual average
Total Private													
2007	668.17	677.35	680.09	685.08	672.11	677.47	682.30	671.14	696.95	681.38	674.16	702.03	680.71
2008	678.53	692.92	712.36	695.95	703.82	713.93	703.42	715.17	710.01	727.32	737.67	721.39	709.10
2009	713.43	724.46	711.90	693.38	703.25	696.30	702.03	720.68	707.15	700.96	726.23	708.79	709.04
2010	709.05	716.99	713.86	712.58	727.35	710.14	716.13	721.33	715.79	720.28	724.44	730.42	718.62
2011	718.99	715.50	711.39	719.33	729.05	716.85	723.14	716.90	722.08	738.83	722.78	726.23	721.73
Goods-Producing													
2007	805.88	804.01	855.54	856.32	854.22	858.73	858.92	866.41	898.63	888.47	879.60	899.00	860.70
2008	878.21	875.11	903.98	896.42	914.02	900.86	939.30	967.60	929.82	951.06	932.34	945.10	919.37
2009	915.67	977.18	960.38	937.26	967.21	965.31	982.23	989.32	964.40	967.67	996.03	954.34	964.47
2010	938.50	928.93	946.72	956.24	934.61	946.34	944.28	960.79	955.12	970.98	948.86	952.70	948.87
2011	924.58	921.98	910.10	910.39	915.26	898.91	911.72	897.68	906.35	908.34	890.51	888.09	906.91
Construction													
2007	824.40	826.08	890.85	843.39	881.34	899.61	906.68	907.39	909.83	921.64	916.11	896.71	886.48
2008	918.92	922.64	936.60	924.52	957.46	898.56	960.52	981.34	938.16	1,009.28	961.59	963.69	947.89
2009	965.12	996.67	918.15	927.17	993.08	994.88	1,033.11	1,027.18	989.15	1,027.67	1,051.04	965.10	990.75
2010	963.49	950.81	967.83	979.66	920.36	962.56	964.08	985.31	974.50	1,008.62	946.40	971.17	966.54
2011	971.25	968.99	960.05	957.09	982.28	979.98	992.71	1,006.35	1,023.38	1,012.62	1,007.84	1,025.28	991.30
Manufacturing													
2007	799.53	816.18	837.52	859.07	837.13	832.62	832.00	844.02	890.57	872.02	871.53	906.92	849.85
2008	866.97	869.70	904.37	896.50	902.33	927.74	912.54	930.01	937.17	934.11	930.42	947.54	912.96
2009	908.82	951.90	963.14	929.63	939.92	936.50	940.87	951.49	937.86	928.24	961.75	947.57	941.31
2010	927.48	916.40	932.99	938.80	933.26	932.73	931.81	946.44	943.27	935.76	938.13	934.14	934.30
2011	898.56	897.22	882.18	881.38	876.74	866.23	880.72	854.40	859.18	867.22	841.30	837.20	870.07
Trade, Transportation, and Utilities													
2007	565.43	576.15	570.15	580.37	582.76	570.49	580.98	569.18	586.85	569.13	565.14	597.51	576.21
2008	569.53	607.15	615.64	605.78	619.44	625.16	609.70	614.15	620.72	623.56	644.79	652.71	617.39
2009	628.51	639.62	628.83	623.67	626.11	615.40	638.72	640.32	638.48	620.28	627.56	610.54	628.15
2010	627.81	629.66	642.07	652.54	660.06	640.85	648.27	661.17	672.14	650.33	647.22	653.43	648.84
2011	643.89	635.29	636.61	657.22	664.35	657.99	672.32	660.92	661.09	683.30	662.55	672.48	659.05
Financial Activities													
2007	849.07	919.55	873.38	913.85	840.60	932.67	885.44	865.26	857.63	831.79	815.86	866.93	871.04
2008	817.24	856.29	879.16	844.27	836.72	871.73	838.03	847.87	836.58	869.95	895.35	846.92	853.33
2009	856.83	877.39	841.38	808.85	823.44	812.54	815.11	860.30	836.98	826.94	868.34	838.88	838.82
2010	817.50	837.73	824.70	823.58	864.08	809.10	827.70	852.37	851.25	869.03	862.22	825.47	838.64
2011	842.24	864.80	831.00	832.50	825.25	789.27	803.52	798.15	809.71	838.77	816.50	813.60	822.22
Professional and Business Services													
2007	974.72	991.82	970.33	990.48	937.08	950.74	981.51	962.98	1,000.47	961.91	938.98	964.23	968.69
2008	937.38	928.90	988.62	945.36	960.12	978.65	935.81	944.05	920.16	977.91	970.54	893.17	948.51
2009	888.67	922.52	902.42	887.40	907.01	915.53	906.44	943.19	902.43	908.60	941.66	925.20	912.59
2010	907.90	923.11	891.02	867.51	890.70	855.36	856.98	875.44	864.47	870.84	878.26	905.53	882.01
2011	918.99	912.80	911.68	900.58	914.73	898.54	895.05	906.63	917.16	940.82	918.86	926.14	913.45
Education and Health Services													
2007	602.73	588.91	617.19	586.72	603.90	610.22	622.10	611.61	638.03	614.76	618.19	635.63	612.59
2008	631.95	637.33	649.77	643.20	631.12	649.44	629.76	642.55	644.85	645.50	672.54	641.60	643.38
2009	651.49	648.11	659.02	642.24	659.37	661.18	644.32	646.25	631.14	625.82	648.05	629.39	645.47
2010	645.98	663.03	654.59	677.24	688.87	692.19	679.01	689.15	695.50	692.08	701.88	707.68	682.47
2011	726.70	707.68	703.84	712.09	723.60	730.76	726.48	712.58	707.77	720.99	699.32	709.72	715.08
Leisure and Hospitality													
2007	301.46	306.87	304.24	302.90	298.68	309.89	318.83	311.98	309.81	309.09	306.02	318.49	308.27
2008	312.70	319.73	317.72	312.26	319.18	329.12	317.28	304.90	304.28	301.45	309.23	314.39	313.54
2009	303.62	308.96	309.93	296.79	305.73	307.20	321.05	312.75	308.42	306.71	311.34	321.03	309.48
2010	307.02	307.52	304.48	294.26	299.15	300.82	302.04	302.04	301.10	300.86	309.96	318.78	303.84
2011	302.23	304.90	309.94	305.24	303.13	306.61	308.88	304.98	308.14	314.68	311.41	313.86	307.81

MONTANA
At a Glance

Population:
  2000 census: 902,200
  2010 census: 989,415
  2011 estimate: 998,199

Percent change in population:
  2000–2010: 9.7%
  2010–2011: 0.9%

Percent change in total nonfarm employment:
  2000–2010: 9.4%
  2010–2011: -0.1%

Industry with the largest growth in employment, 2000–2011 (thousands):
  Education and Health Services, 15.2

Industry with the largest decline or smallest growth in employment, 2000–2011 (thousands):
  Manufacturing, -5.7

Civilian labor force:
  2000: 468,865
  2010: 500,078
  2011: 504,410

Unemployment rate and rank among states (lowest to highest):
  2000: 4.8%, 42nd
  2010: 6.9%, 7th
  2011: 6.8%, 14th

Over-the-year change in unemployment rates:
  2010–2011: -0.1%

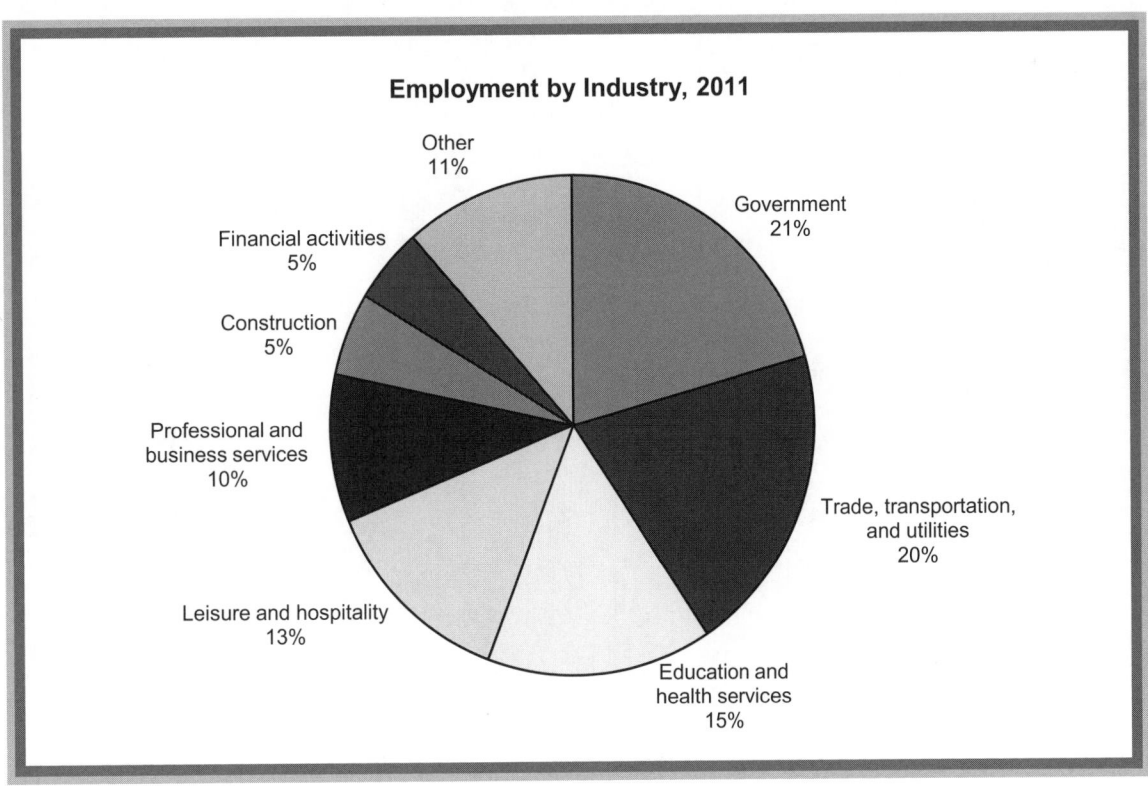

Employment by Industry, 2011

Other 11%
Government 21%
Financial activities 5%
Construction 5%
Professional and business services 10%
Trade, transportation, and utilities 20%
Leisure and hospitality 13%
Education and health services 15%

1. Employment by Industry: Montana, Selected Years, 2000–2011

(Numbers in thousands, not seasonally adjusted)

Industry and year	January	February	March	April	May	June	July	August	September	October	November	December	Annual average
Total Nonfarm													
2000	376.4	378.3	385.4	387.3	396.1	398.6	395.5	398.1	399.7	395.0	393.4	390.3	391.2
2001	379.6	380.9	384.9	387.8	395.9	400.3	395.0	397.0	397.1	395.0	392.4	390.8	391.4
2002	381.4	383.0	385.3	390.4	398.6	404.4	400.0	401.6	403.7	401.1	399.3	399.3	395.7
2003	386.0	388.3	390.0	396.7	403.7	406.7	404.0	407.2	407.8	406.6	403.1	403.4	400.3
2004	390.0	393.8	398.9	408.6	413.9	420.8	418.5	417.8	418.6	417.1	415.6	416.0	410.8
2005	400.1	405.3	410.0	414.1	420.7	427.8	427.6	427.8	429.0	428.1	426.9	426.1	420.3
2006	413.9	418.4	423.2	429.0	436.9	446.5	445.9	442.3	439.8	438.4	436.9	438.4	434.1
2007	426.2	429.3	435.7	439.1	446.9	453.4	452.1	452.9	449.4	449.6	447.1	447.1	444.1
2008	432.7	435.5	439.2	441.4	449.8	454.0	452.4	453.3	450.3	447.1	442.5	439.8	444.8
2009	420.1	420.0	419.7	425.4	431.6	438.2	435.5	435.6	433.6	432.0	428.7	426.8	428.9
2010	413.3	414.0	418.6	423.8	432.2	437.4	436.7	437.5	435.6	433.0	428.0	427.4	428.1
2011	413.7	415.7	419.7	426.0	430.8	437.8	435.1	434.9	432.7	430.7	425.8	424.0	427.7
Total Private													
2000	293.9	294.2	298.7	301.4	307.9	316.6	317.8	319.2	314.7	308.3	306.9	305.3	307.1
2001	295.5	295.6	298.9	302.1	308.4	316.2	317.0	318.7	313.2	309.2	307.0	305.9	307.3
2002	297.8	297.9	299.6	304.6	311.0	319.3	320.7	322.5	318.2	314.8	311.9	311.6	310.8
2003	302.9	302.6	304.0	308.6	314.6	322.0	323.8	325.8	320.7	318.2	314.9	315.4	314.5
2004	305.9	306.8	311.3	320.0	324.5	333.1	336.5	336.7	331.6	328.5	326.2	327.4	324.0
2005	315.3	318.1	322.4	326.5	332.4	341.6	346.3	347.6	342.9	339.8	337.9	337.7	334.0
2006	329.1	330.8	334.8	340.2	346.6	357.4	357.6	359.0	353.3	349.6	347.2	349.9	346.3
2007	340.5	341.3	346.7	351.0	357.6	366.3	368.6	370.0	363.8	359.5	357.5	358.4	356.8
2008	347.3	347.6	350.7	353.3	359.0	365.9	368.7	369.3	362.3	355.9	350.7	349.7	356.7
2009	333.3	331.1	330.1	335.2	339.5	347.9	350.1	349.7	344.5	339.2	336.1	334.5	339.3
2010	323.1	322.6	325.4	331.1	336.2	344.3	348.0	348.8	343.9	339.8	335.2	334.9	336.1
2011	324.3	324.7	327.8	334.2	340.5	348.3	353.5	351.9	346.8	343.2	339.1	337.8	339.3
Goods-Producing													
2000	45.1	44.9	46.1	47.7	49.4	51.3	51.5	52.0	51.2	51.4	49.9	47.9	49.0
2001	45.3	45.0	45.6	47.0	49.1	50.9	51.8	52.3	51.4	51.0	49.3	47.5	48.9
2002	44.0	43.5	43.4	45.3	47.8	50.1	50.9	51.6	50.6	50.5	49.0	47.5	47.9
2003	44.3	43.7	43.9	46.6	49.0	50.8	51.2	51.2	50.6	50.9	48.9	47.6	48.2
2004	45.0	45.0	46.4	50.0	51.2	53.4	54.7	54.8	53.9	54.3	53.2	52.2	51.2
2005	48.0	49.4	50.6	52.8	54.7	56.6	58.4	59.2	58.1	58.7	57.5	55.1	54.9
2006	52.7	52.8	53.8	55.8	58.9	62.0	62.4	62.5	61.5	61.4	60.1	59.2	58.6
2007	56.1	55.8	57.8	59.8	62.2	64.4	64.3	64.9	63.2	63.0	61.8	59.8	61.1
2008	55.6	55.1	56.0	57.0	59.1	60.5	61.4	61.2	59.5	58.8	56.5	53.8	57.9
2009	47.8	46.1	45.1	47.3	48.6	50.5	50.9	51.1	50.0	49.8	48.3	45.7	48.4
2010	42.2	41.6	42.4	44.9	46.7	48.3	49.5	50.0	49.5	49.8	47.9	45.1	46.5
2011	41.6	41.6	42.5	45.5	47.5	49.7	51.9	52.2	52.1	51.8	49.8	46.8	47.8
Mining and Logging													
2000	5.9	5.8	5.8	5.6	5.9	6.3	6.1	6.2	6.0	6.3	6.3	6.1	6.0
2001	6.0	6.0	5.8	5.7	6.0	6.4	6.5	6.5	6.5	6.7	6.5	6.3	6.2
2002	5.9	5.9	5.8	5.8	6.0	6.3	6.4	6.5	6.4	6.5	6.3	6.3	6.2
2003	6.0	5.9	5.7	5.4	5.8	6.2	6.3	6.3	6.3	6.6	6.7	6.7	6.2
2004	6.6	6.5	6.6	6.8	7.0	7.3	7.6	7.5	7.4	7.4	7.5	7.4	7.1
2005	7.3	7.5	7.4	7.2	7.5	7.9	8.1	8.2	8.0	8.0	7.9	7.9	7.7
2006	7.8	7.8	7.9	7.8	8.2	8.6	8.7	8.6	8.4	8.4	8.4	8.3	8.2
2007	8.1	8.1	8.3	8.1	8.2	8.6	8.7	8.7	8.4	8.4	8.3	8.3	8.4
2008	7.9	7.9	7.9	7.8	8.0	8.4	8.6	8.8	8.8	8.8	8.8	8.4	8.3
2009	7.7	7.1	6.9	6.8	6.8	6.9	7.2	7.2	7.0	7.1	7.0	7.0	7.1
2010	6.9	6.9	7.0	7.1	7.3	7.5	7.7	7.9	7.8	7.8	7.7	7.5	7.4
2011	7.4	7.5	7.6	7.6	7.8	8.0	8.2	8.3	8.1	8.1	8.1	7.9	7.9
Construction													
2000	17.0	16.9	18.0	19.9	21.1	22.4	22.7	23.0	22.3	22.2	20.7	19.4	20.5
2001	17.7	17.4	18.4	20.2	21.9	23.1	23.7	24.0	23.4	22.8	21.9	20.4	21.2
2002	18.2	18.0	18.1	19.9	21.9	23.5	24.1	24.5	24.0	23.7	22.7	21.5	21.7
2003	19.2	19.0	19.4	22.4	24.1	25.4	25.7	25.9	25.5	25.4	23.3	21.9	23.1
2004	19.8	19.9	21.1	24.4	25.2	26.8	27.6	27.8	27.1	27.4	26.2	25.2	24.9
2005	21.7	22.8	24.0	26.3	27.8	29.0	30.5	31.1	30.6	30.7	29.6	27.2	27.6
2006	25.3	25.3	26.2	28.2	30.6	32.9	33.2	33.5	32.8	32.5	31.1	30.2	30.2
2007	27.8	27.6	29.1	31.5	33.7	35.1	35.0	35.6	34.4	34.0	32.8	30.9	32.3
2008	27.6	27.2	28.1	29.1	30.8	31.7	32.5	32.2	31.0	30.1	28.3	26.3	29.6
2009	22.1	21.5	21.2	23.2	24.3	26.0	26.3	26.5	25.8	25.2	24.0	21.5	24.0
2010	18.9	18.4	19.3	21.7	23.1	24.3	25.2	25.4	25.1	25.2	23.3	20.8	22.6
2011	17.9	17.8	18.5	21.3	23.0	24.7	26.7	26.9	27.0	26.5	24.4	21.8	23.0
Manufacturing													
2000	22.2	22.2	22.3	22.2	22.4	22.6	22.7	22.8	22.9	22.9	22.9	22.4	22.5
2001	21.6	21.6	21.4	21.1	21.2	21.4	21.6	21.8	21.5	21.5	20.9	20.8	21.4
2002	19.9	19.6	19.5	19.6	19.9	20.3	20.4	20.6	20.2	20.3	20.0	19.7	20.0
2003	19.1	18.8	18.8	18.8	19.1	19.2	19.2	19.0	18.8	18.9	18.9	19.0	19.0
2004	18.6	18.6	18.7	18.8	19.0	19.3	19.5	19.5	19.4	19.5	19.5	19.6	19.2
2005	19.0	19.1	19.2	19.3	19.4	19.7	19.8	19.9	19.5	20.0	20.0	20.0	19.6
2006	19.6	19.7	19.7	19.8	20.1	20.5	20.5	20.4	20.3	20.5	20.6	20.7	20.2
2007	20.2	20.1	20.4	20.2	20.3	20.7	20.6	20.6	20.4	20.6	20.7	20.6	20.5
2008	20.1	20.0	20.0	20.1	20.3	20.4	20.3	20.2	19.7	19.9	19.4	19.1	20.0
2009	18.0	17.5	17.0	17.3	17.5	17.6	17.4	17.4	17.2	17.5	17.3	17.2	17.4
2010	16.4	16.3	16.1	16.1	16.3	16.5	16.6	16.7	16.6	16.8	16.9	16.8	16.5
2011	16.3	16.3	16.4	16.6	16.7	17.0	17.0	17.0	17.0	17.2	17.3	17.1	16.8

1. Employment by Industry: Montana, Selected Years, 2000–2011—*Continued*

(Numbers in thousands, not seasonally adjusted)

Industry and year	January	February	March	April	May	June	July	August	September	October	November	December	Annual average
Service-Providing													
2000	331.3	333.4	339.3	339.6	346.7	347.3	344.0	346.1	348.5	343.6	343.5	342.4	342.1
2001	334.3	335.9	339.3	340.8	346.8	349.4	343.2	344.7	345.7	344.0	343.1	343.3	342.5
2002	337.4	339.5	341.9	345.1	350.8	354.3	349.1	350.0	353.1	350.6	350.3	351.8	347.8
2003	341.7	344.6	346.1	350.1	354.7	355.9	352.8	356.0	357.2	355.7	354.2	355.8	352.1
2004	345.0	348.8	352.5	358.6	362.7	367.4	363.8	363.0	364.7	362.8	362.4	363.8	359.6
2005	352.1	355.9	359.4	361.3	366.0	371.2	369.2	368.6	370.9	369.4	369.4	371.0	365.4
2006	361.2	365.6	369.4	373.2	378.0	384.5	383.5	379.8	378.3	377.0	376.8	379.2	375.5
2007	370.1	373.5	377.9	379.3	384.7	388.9	387.8	388.0	386.2	386.6	385.3	387.3	383.0
2008	377.1	380.4	383.2	384.4	390.7	393.5	391.0	392.1	390.8	388.3	386.0	386.0	387.0
2009	372.3	373.9	374.6	378.1	383.0	387.7	384.6	384.5	383.6	382.2	380.4	381.1	380.5
2010	371.1	372.4	376.2	378.9	385.5	389.1	387.2	387.5	386.1	383.2	380.1	382.3	381.6
2011	372.1	374.1	377.2	380.5	383.3	388.1	383.2	382.7	380.6	378.9	376.0	377.2	379.9
Trade, Transportation, and Utilities													
2000	84.4	83.8	84.3	85.2	86.5	87.8	87.5	88.0	86.9	85.9	86.7	87.3	86.2
2001	83.7	82.8	83.3	84.4	85.7	86.2	85.9	86.0	84.9	84.7	85.3	85.6	84.9
2002	82.3	81.8	82.3	83.6	84.9	85.7	85.9	85.7	85.0	84.9	85.4	86.0	84.5
2003	82.1	81.4	81.8	82.4	84.0	84.8	84.5	85.0	84.8	85.1	86.0	86.5	84.0
2004	83.4	83.1	83.8	85.0	86.2	86.9	86.8	86.4	85.6	86.1	87.2	87.9	85.7
2005	84.4	84.0	84.9	85.7	86.8	87.9	88.3	88.2	87.5	87.6	88.3	89.5	86.9
2006	86.0	85.8	86.4	87.4	88.7	89.9	89.5	89.7	89.1	89.3	90.6	91.7	88.7
2007	88.8	88.6	89.4	89.8	91.4	92.0	92.9	92.5	92.2	92.5	93.9	94.6	91.6
2008	91.0	90.1	90.6	90.8	91.4	92.1	91.9	92.1	91.4	90.9	91.1	91.4	91.2
2009	86.9	85.7	85.1	86.2	87.1	88.0	87.9	87.9	87.2	86.7	87.3	87.7	87.0
2010	84.3	83.6	84.1	85.0	86.0	86.9	86.7	86.8	86.0	85.9	86.5	87.2	85.8
2011	84.1	83.6	83.7	85.2	86.4	87.4	87.9	86.6	86.3	87.0	88.2	88.3	86.2
Wholesale Trade													
2000	15.5	15.5	15.6	15.9	16.0	16.1	15.9	15.8	15.7	15.4	15.3	15.4	15.7
2001	15.2	15.0	15.2	15.5	15.7	15.8	15.6	15.6	15.3	15.3	15.3	15.2	15.4
2002	14.9	14.8	14.9	15.3	15.5	15.6	15.7	15.6	15.4	15.4	15.4	15.5	15.3
2003	15.0	14.9	15.0	15.4	15.6	15.7	15.6	15.6	15.5	15.5	15.6	15.7	15.4
2004	15.5	15.5	15.7	16.0	16.1	16.3	16.5	16.4	16.2	16.1	16.3	16.3	16.1
2005	15.8	15.9	16.1	16.3	16.5	16.6	16.6	16.5	16.3	16.2	16.2	16.4	16.3
2006	16.0	16.1	16.3	16.3	16.6	16.8	16.8	16.8	16.7	16.7	16.8	16.8	16.6
2007	16.4	16.6	16.7	16.8	17.1	17.1	17.3	17.1	17.1	17.0	17.0	17.1	16.9
2008	16.5	16.5	16.7	16.8	16.9	17.0	16.9	16.9	16.7	16.6	16.5	16.5	16.7
2009	16.0	15.9	15.8	16.1	16.1	16.2	16.2	16.0	15.8	15.7	15.7	15.7	15.9
2010	15.3	15.3	15.5	15.7	15.7	15.8	15.8	15.8	15.6	15.5	15.5	15.5	15.6
2011	15.2	15.2	15.3	15.6	15.8	15.8	15.7	15.6	15.7	15.7	15.8	15.7	15.6
Retail Trade													
2000	52.4	51.8	52.2	52.6	53.5	54.9	55.0	55.4	54.5	53.6	54.6	55.1	53.8
2001	52.6	51.9	52.0	52.6	53.5	54.2	54.6	54.8	53.9	53.5	54.3	54.6	53.5
2002	52.0	51.6	51.9	52.8	53.7	54.4	54.7	54.6	54.1	53.9	54.7	55.1	53.6
2003	52.2	51.7	52.0	52.3	53.4	54.1	54.3	54.6	54.1	54.3	55.2	55.7	53.7
2004	53.2	53.0	53.4	54.1	55.1	55.6	55.6	55.3	54.5	54.7	55.6	56.2	54.7
2005	53.6	53.1	53.7	54.3	55.1	56.0	56.4	56.4	55.7	55.8	56.5	57.2	55.3
2006	54.5	54.1	54.4	55.2	56.1	57.0	57.0	57.1	56.2	56.5	57.8	58.6	56.2
2007	56.5	56.0	56.7	56.9	58.0	58.8	59.5	59.4	58.9	59.1	60.5	60.9	58.4
2008	58.7	57.9	58.1	58.1	58.7	59.3	59.5	59.6	58.7	58.4	58.7	58.8	58.7
2009	55.5	54.5	54.1	54.7	55.5	56.4	56.6	56.7	55.8	55.3	56.0	56.1	55.6
2010	53.7	53.0	53.2	53.9	54.7	55.6	55.5	55.6	54.6	54.7	55.3	55.6	54.6
2011	53.2	52.7	52.8	53.8	54.6	55.5	56.2	55.2	54.5	55.0	56.0	56.1	54.6
Transportation and Utilities													
2000	16.5	16.5	16.5	16.7	17.0	16.8	16.6	16.8	16.7	16.9	16.8	16.8	16.7
2001	15.9	15.9	16.1	16.3	16.5	16.2	15.7	15.6	15.7	15.9	15.7	15.8	15.9
2002	15.4	15.4	15.5	15.5	15.7	15.7	15.5	15.5	15.5	15.6	15.3	15.4	15.5
2003	14.9	14.8	14.8	14.7	15.0	15.0	14.6	14.8	15.2	15.3	15.2	15.1	15.0
2004	14.7	14.6	14.7	14.9	15.0	15.0	14.7	14.7	14.9	15.3	15.3	15.4	14.9
2005	15.0	15.0	15.1	15.1	15.2	15.3	15.3	15.3	15.5	15.6	15.6	15.9	15.3
2006	15.5	15.6	15.7	15.9	16.0	16.1	15.7	15.8	16.2	16.1	16.0	16.3	15.9
2007	15.9	16.0	16.0	16.1	16.3	16.1	16.1	16.0	16.2	16.4	16.4	16.6	16.2
2008	15.8	15.7	15.8	15.9	15.8	15.8	15.5	15.6	16.0	15.9	15.9	16.1	15.8
2009	15.4	15.3	15.2	15.4	15.5	15.4	15.1	15.2	15.6	15.7	15.6	15.9	15.4
2010	15.3	15.3	15.4	15.4	15.6	15.5	15.4	15.4	15.8	15.7	15.7	16.1	15.6
2011	15.7	15.7	15.6	15.8	16.0	16.1	16.0	15.8	16.1	16.3	16.4	16.5	16.0
Information													
2000	7.9	7.9	8.0	8.0	8.1	8.1	7.8	7.8	7.8	8.0	8.0	8.0	8.0
2001	7.9	8.0	7.9	7.8	7.9	8.0	7.9	8.0	7.8	7.9	8.0	7.8	7.9
2002	7.8	7.8	7.8	7.8	7.9	7.9	8.0	7.9	7.8	7.7	7.8	7.8	7.8
2003	7.7	7.8	7.7	7.6	7.6	7.6	7.6	7.7	7.6	7.7	7.7	7.6	7.7
2004	7.6	7.6	7.7	7.7	7.8	7.9	8.0	8.1	7.8	7.7	7.8	7.8	7.8
2005	7.7	7.8	7.8	7.7	7.8	7.9	7.9	7.9	7.7	7.7	7.7	7.8	7.8
2006	7.7	7.8	7.7	7.7	7.8	7.9	7.8	7.8	7.7	7.6	7.6	7.7	7.7
2007	7.4	7.5	7.5	7.5	7.6	7.6	7.6	7.7	7.6	7.5	7.6	7.6	7.6
2008	7.6	7.6	7.6	7.7	7.7	7.8	7.7	7.7	7.8	7.7	7.7	7.7	7.7
2009	7.5	7.6	7.5	7.4	7.5	7.6	7.5	7.4	7.4	7.3	7.3	7.3	7.4
2010	7.3	7.4	7.4	7.3	7.3	7.5	7.4	7.3	7.2	7.2	7.2	7.2	7.3
2011	7.1	7.2	7.2	7.2	7.2	7.3	7.4	7.4	7.3	7.3	7.3	7.4	7.3

1. Employment by Industry: Montana, Selected Years, 2000–2011—*Continued*

(Numbers in thousands, not seasonally adjusted)

Industry and year	January	February	March	April	May	June	July	August	September	October	November	December	Annual average
Financial Activities													
2000	18.1	18.2	18.3	18.5	18.7	19.0	19.0	19.0	18.7	18.4	18.4	18.6	18.6
2001	18.4	18.3	18.4	18.5	18.8	19.1	19.3	19.2	19.1	18.8	18.8	19.0	18.8
2002	18.8	18.9	19.0	19.2	19.4	19.6	19.3	19.3	19.1	19.6	19.6	19.9	19.3
2003	19.9	19.9	20.0	19.9	20.0	20.4	20.6	20.8	20.5	20.5	20.5	20.7	20.3
2004	20.7	20.7	20.8	20.8	21.0	21.3	21.5	21.5	21.2	21.1	21.0	21.3	21.1
2005	20.8	20.8	20.8	21.0	21.2	21.5	21.8	21.8	21.7	21.8	21.9	22.2	21.4
2006	21.7	21.8	21.9	22.0	21.9	22.3	22.3	22.2	21.9	21.8	21.7	21.9	22.0
2007	21.4	21.4	21.6	21.5	21.7	21.9	22.0	22.1	21.8	21.9	21.8	22.2	21.8
2008	21.7	21.7	21.7	21.8	21.8	22.1	22.1	22.2	21.7	21.8	21.7	21.7	21.8
2009	21.1	21.0	21.0	21.1	21.3	21.6	21.8	21.8	21.6	21.6	21.6	22.0	21.5
2010	21.0	21.0	21.1	21.0	21.1	21.4	21.5	21.4	21.1	21.2	20.9	21.2	21.2
2011	20.7	20.7	20.8	20.7	20.7	21.1	21.2	20.9	20.7	21.1	20.6	21.1	20.9
Professional and Business Services													
2000	28.6	29.1	29.9	30.2	30.7	31.7	31.9	31.9	31.6	31.6	31.8	31.3	30.9
2001	30.4	31.0	31.4	31.7	32.1	32.8	32.4	32.6	32.0	31.8	31.6	31.7	31.8
2002	31.3	31.6	31.7	31.9	32.0	32.8	33.0	33.4	33.3	32.9	32.3	31.7	32.3
2003	31.2	31.3	31.7	32.6	32.9	33.4	33.6	33.8	32.9	32.9	32.1	32.0	32.5
2004	30.4	31.0	31.6	33.2	33.8	34.7	34.9	34.9	34.3	34.2	33.9	33.3	33.4
2005	32.1	32.7	33.3	34.4	34.7	35.8	36.6	36.8	36.2	36.4	36.5	36.2	35.1
2006	35.5	35.9	36.6	37.5	38.2	39.6	39.4	40.2	39.2	39.0	38.5	38.6	38.2
2007	38.1	38.5	39.3	40.3	41.0	42.1	42.0	42.5	41.2	41.5	40.8	40.3	40.6
2008	39.1	39.6	39.7	40.8	41.6	41.8	42.2	42.2	40.9	40.4	39.5	39.3	40.6
2009	37.9	37.7	37.9	38.7	38.8	39.5	39.9	39.6	38.9	38.9	39.0	38.0	38.7
2010	37.1	37.4	37.7	38.9	39.2	40.0	40.6	40.6	39.8	40.5	39.7	39.7	39.3
2011	38.6	38.8	39.3	40.5	41.0	41.6	42.6	42.4	41.4	41.8	41.4	40.7	40.8
Education and Health Services													
2000	48.6	49.0	49.2	48.9	49.2	48.9	48.2	48.6	49.2	49.1	49.5	49.6	49.0
2001	48.4	48.7	49.3	49.5	49.6	49.4	48.7	49.3	50.0	50.4	51.1	51.4	49.7
2002	51.4	51.6	51.9	52.2	52.4	51.9	50.6	50.9	51.8	52.8	53.3	53.3	52.0
2003	53.2	53.6	53.5	53.3	53.4	52.6	51.5	52.2	52.6	53.5	53.9	54.1	53.1
2004	53.5	53.7	54.3	54.5	54.4	54.0	53.1	53.3	54.6	55.1	55.7	56.1	54.4
2005	55.5	55.7	56.1	55.5	55.7	55.8	54.9	55.0	56.1	56.5	56.9	56.9	55.9
2006	56.4	56.9	57.3	57.7	57.6	57.2	56.4	56.8	57.9	58.0	58.4	58.7	57.4
2007	58.2	58.7	59.0	58.9	59.0	58.5	57.6	58.0	59.3	59.4	59.5	60.0	58.8
2008	60.0	60.6	60.9	60.9	61.0	60.3	59.6	60.2	61.3	61.7	62.0	62.5	60.9
2009	61.8	62.3	62.3	62.5	62.4	62.2	61.4	61.6	62.5	63.2	63.4	63.8	62.5
2010	63.1	63.3	63.5	63.9	63.9	63.8	63.1	63.2	64.0	64.3	64.4	64.6	63.8
2011	63.9	64.2	64.3	64.1	64.5	64.2	63.3	63.9	64.1	64.4	64.4	64.9	64.2
Leisure and Hospitality													
2000	46.2	46.2	47.5	47.4	49.7	54.2	56.4	56.6	53.8	48.7	47.3	47.4	50.1
2001	45.9	46.2	47.1	47.1	48.9	53.3	54.9	55.3	51.9	48.7	47.0	46.9	49.4
2002	46.7	47.1	47.8	48.7	50.5	55.0	56.7	57.4	54.3	50.2	48.3	49.1	51.0
2003	48.6	49.0	49.4	49.8	51.3	56.0	58.4	58.8	55.2	51.0	49.3	50.2	52.3
2004	49.0	49.3	50.1	52.1	53.3	58.0	60.5	60.6	57.2	53.1	50.6	51.9	53.8
2005	50.4	51.1	52.2	52.7	54.7	59.1	61.7	61.9	58.8	54.5	52.5	53.2	55.2
2006	52.6	53.2	54.2	55.1	56.4	61.2	62.7	62.7	58.9	55.4	53.3	55.0	56.7
2007	53.7	54.0	54.9	55.9	57.5	62.3	65.0	65.2	61.4	56.5	54.9	56.7	58.2
2008	55.2	55.6	56.6	56.7	58.8	63.5	66.1	66.1	62.2	57.0	54.7	55.9	59.0
2009	53.5	53.7	54.2	55.0	56.7	61.3	63.5	63.4	59.9	54.7	52.3	53.1	56.8
2010	51.5	51.7	52.4	53.4	55.2	59.4	62.4	62.8	59.6	54.2	52.0	53.3	55.7
2011	51.9	52.1	53.3	54.2	56.2	59.9	62.1	62.2	58.5	53.9	51.4	52.6	55.7
Other Services													
2000	15.0	15.1	15.4	15.5	15.6	15.6	15.5	15.3	15.5	15.2	15.3	15.2	15.4
2001	15.5	15.6	15.9	16.1	16.3	16.5	16.1	16.0	16.1	15.9	15.9	16.0	16.0
2002	15.5	15.6	15.7	15.9	16.1	16.3	16.3	16.3	16.3	16.2	16.2	16.3	16.1
2003	15.9	15.9	16.0	16.4	16.4	16.4	16.4	16.3	16.5	16.6	16.5	16.7	16.3
2004	16.3	16.4	16.6	16.7	16.8	16.9	17.0	17.1	17.0	16.9	16.8	16.9	16.8
2005	16.4	16.6	16.7	16.7	16.8	17.0	16.7	16.8	16.8	16.6	16.6	16.8	16.7
2006	16.5	16.6	16.9	17.0	17.1	17.3	17.1	17.1	17.1	17.1	17.0	17.1	17.0
2007	16.8	16.8	17.2	17.3	17.2	17.5	17.2	17.1	17.1	17.2	17.2	17.2	17.2
2008	17.1	17.3	17.6	17.6	17.6	17.8	17.7	17.6	17.5	17.6	17.5	17.3	17.5
2009	16.8	17.0	17.0	17.0	17.1	17.2	17.2	16.9	17.0	17.0	16.9	16.9	17.0
2010	16.6	16.6	16.8	16.7	16.8	17.0	16.8	16.7	16.7	16.7	16.6	16.6	16.7
2011	16.4	16.5	16.7	16.8	17.0	17.1	17.1	16.3	16.4	15.9	16.0	16.0	16.5
Government													
2000	82.5	84.1	86.7	85.9	88.2	82.0	77.7	78.9	85.0	86.7	86.5	85.0	84.1
2001	84.1	85.3	86.0	85.7	87.5	84.1	78.0	78.3	83.9	85.8	85.4	84.9	84.1
2002	83.6	85.1	85.7	85.8	87.6	85.1	79.3	79.1	85.5	86.3	87.4	87.7	84.9
2003	83.1	85.7	86.0	88.1	89.1	84.7	80.2	81.4	87.1	88.4	88.2	88.0	85.8
2004	84.1	87.0	87.6	88.6	89.4	87.7	82.0	81.1	87.0	88.6	89.4	88.6	86.8
2005	84.8	87.2	87.6	87.6	88.3	86.2	81.3	80.2	86.1	88.3	89.0	88.4	86.3
2006	84.8	87.6	88.4	88.8	90.3	89.1	88.3	83.3	86.5	88.8	89.7	88.5	87.8
2007	85.7	88.0	89.0	88.1	89.3	87.0	83.5	82.9	85.6	90.1	89.6	88.7	87.3
2008	85.4	87.9	88.5	88.1	90.8	88.1	83.7	84.0	88.0	91.2	91.8	90.1	88.1
2009	86.8	88.9	89.6	90.2	92.1	90.3	85.4	85.9	89.1	92.8	92.6	92.3	89.7
2010	90.2	91.4	93.2	92.7	96.0	93.1	88.7	88.7	91.7	93.2	92.8	92.5	92.0
2011	89.4	91.0	91.9	91.8	90.3	89.5	81.6	83.0	85.9	87.5	86.7	86.2	88.3

2. Average Weekly Hours by Selected Industry: Montana, 2007–2011

(Not seasonally adjusted)

Industry and year	January	February	March	April	May	June	July	August	September	October	November	December	Annual average
Total Private													
2007	31.8	32.0	31.9	32.9	43.0	42.4	42.2	41.0	33.0	32.2	31.8	32.6	35.6
2008	31.8	31.7	32.4	31.6	32.0	32.8	32.8	33.1	32.5	32.3	32.8	32.2	32.3
2009	30.0	30.7	30.5	30.4	30.9	31.0	31.3	32.1	31.6	31.8	32.2	31.4	31.2
2010	31.5	31.7	31.8	32.1	33.1	32.6	32.9	33.9	33.2	32.9	32.7	32.8	32.6
2011	33.0	32.7	32.6	33.1	33.6	33.1	33.2	33.3	33.0	33.4	32.4	32.3	33.0
Goods-Producing													
2007	37.2	38.5	38.1	38.5	39.6	39.8	39.6	39.7	36.8	37.3	36.0	35.8	38.1
2008	36.2	34.7	35.5	35.0	36.5	37.1	38.2	39.7	38.6	36.9	37.2	36.6	36.9
2009	36.1	36.1	35.4	36.4	36.3	38.1	38.1	39.4	37.2	38.1	37.9	35.5	37.1
2010	36.7	36.2	36.9	37.4	38.9	37.8	38.6	39.3	38.3	38.9	38.2	39.4	38.1
2011	39.8	38.7	38.7	39.9	40.0	40.1	39.9	39.9	39.0	39.4	37.6	37.7	39.2
Construction													
2007	36.6	39.3	39.1	39.1	41.2	38.8	39.0	38.9	33.8	35.2	32.7	33.0	37.2
2008	33.2	32.3	32.3	31.4	35.7	33.9	36.4	37.1	37.4	34.0	34.7	34.3	34.5
2009	33.1	33.1	32.0	32.8	33.6	35.5	35.0	38.3	33.4	34.6	34.7	29.6	34.0
2010	31.9	31.7	33.0	33.3	36.6	34.5	36.2	38.0	36.8	37.5	36.6	30.6	35.0
2011	31.6	31.3	32.4	34.8	34.9	36.2	36.7	37.1	36.3	36.6	34.4	33.2	34.9
Trade, Transportation, and Utilities													
2007	31.3	32.0	32.4	33.2	33.3	34.1	33.2	33.7	32.8	31.7	31.5	32.8	32.7
2008	31.2	32.2	32.5	30.9	32.3	33.3	33.2	33.9	32.7	32.5	32.8	33.2	32.6
2009	33.2	32.3	32.1	32.3	32.9	32.8	32.4	33.3	32.9	32.8	32.9	32.9	32.7
2010	32.7	33.1	33.1	32.2	33.8	33.4	33.9	34.6	33.8	34.1	34.1	34.5	33.6
2011	34.8	34.3	34.3	34.9	34.5	34.7	34.3	34.4	33.7	33.5	32.6	33.4	34.1
Financial Activities													
2007	37.4	37.0	38.6	38.7	37.2	37.4	37.7	37.2	36.2	36.6	36.2	38.8	37.4
2008	37.9	36.9	37.1	36.7	36.1	36.9	36.3	35.1	35.8	36.8	37.2	38.2	36.7
2009	37.0	38.2	38.4	38.5	37.7	37.6	36.6	36.8	36.5	36.5	37.2	35.8	37.2
2010	36.6	36.5	37.0	37.4	37.7	37.7	37.6	38.0	37.0	36.9	36.7	35.9	37.1
2011	37.1	36.3	36.4	36.7	37.6	36.6	36.7	36.8	37.3	38.3	36.7	35.8	36.9
Professional and Business Services													
2007	33.7	33.6	33.8	34.2	36.1	34.0	34.2	33.4	33.5	33.5	33.1	33.3	33.9
2008	33.4	33.8	35.2	35.0	33.0	34.5	34.6	33.9	33.9	34.4	33.9	33.1	34.1
2009	18.8	20.5	22.0	22.6	23.1	24.0	25.7	26.0	26.5	27.0	28.1	27.3	24.3
2010	28.5	29.3	29.5	30.4	31.6	30.9	30.3	33.3	32.0	32.9	32.5	32.4	31.2
2011	33.5	33.0	33.0	33.5	34.2	33.0	32.8	32.7	33.6	34.2	33.8	33.3	33.4
Education and Health Services													
2007	31.4	31.6	29.8	32.1	31.3	31.2	32.6	32.3	34.2	32.1	32.1	33.2	32.0
2008	32.3	32.0	32.9	32.4	32.1	33.0	32.2	32.3	31.9	32.3	33.0	32.8	32.4
2009	32.2	33.0	33.1	32.4	33.0	32.3	32.8	32.7	32.9	32.9	33.4	33.0	32.8
2010	32.7	32.9	32.9	32.9	33.5	33.1	33.1	33.6	33.4	33.6	33.7	34.1	33.3
2011	33.8	33.9	33.7	33.7	34.0	32.9	33.1	32.6	33.0	33.5	33.2	32.9	33.4
Leisure and Hospitality													
2007	24.0	23.6	25.0	25.7	43.0	43.8	44.8	42.4	25.4	24.1	24.0	24.8	31.4
2008	23.3	24.1	24.2	23.1	24.1	25.4	25.7	25.8	24.7	23.7	25.0	23.0	24.4
2009	23.4	24.4	24.0	22.9	24.4	24.1	25.2	27.0	25.3	25.0	25.7	24.5	24.7
2010	24.1	24.4	24.5	24.8	25.5	25.4	26.8	27.9	26.0	21.9	21.3	21.4	24.6
2011	21.3	21.4	21.3	21.7	22.8	22.7	24.2	24.9	23.4	23.8	22.4	22.4	22.8

3. Average Hourly Earnings by Selected Industry: Montana, 2007–2011

(Dollars, not seasonally adjusted)

Industry and year	January	February	March	April	May	June	July	August	September	October	November	December	Annual average
Total Private													
2007	18.02	17.91	17.89	18.05	17.72	17.38	17.53	17.62	17.86	17.83	18.06	18.11	17.80
2008	18.20	18.28	18.17	18.26	18.55	18.24	18.05	18.33	18.78	18.54	18.91	18.94	18.44
2009	20.27	20.26	20.00	19.98	19.58	19.57	19.49	19.74	19.61	19.77	20.26	19.89	19.86
2010	20.05	19.93	19.83	20.28	20.47	19.67	19.68	20.29	20.46	20.50	20.80	20.32	20.19
2011	20.54	20.44	20.58	20.75	20.83	20.41	20.62	20.33	20.82	21.07	21.16	20.54	20.68
Goods-Producing													
2007	21.37	21.77	21.91	22.43	22.13	22.50	22.45	22.54	22.67	21.78	22.03	22.41	22.18
2008	22.22	23.02	22.78	22.52	23.00	22.59	21.77	22.16	22.64	21.83	22.42	22.47	22.44
2009	22.70	23.34	22.65	23.37	22.18	22.54	22.36	23.12	23.06	22.69	23.42	22.96	22.86
2010	23.04	23.71	23.75	24.33	24.45	23.49	23.80	24.81	25.50	24.37	24.57	24.87	24.26
2011	24.90	24.98	25.77	24.63	24.69	24.30	24.55	23.84	24.03	24.13	24.02	23.61	24.42
Construction													
2007	22.01	22.24	22.11	22.76	22.29	22.85	21.97	22.44	22.64	23.06	23.21	23.95	22.61
2008	24.19	23.72	23.54	23.22	23.67	22.43	22.80	22.43	24.06	22.42	22.30	23.36	23.15
2009	22.65	22.59	22.47	24.48	23.24	23.61	23.73	24.55	22.62	23.44	23.96	24.20	23.50
2010	23.34	23.74	23.39	24.33	24.12	22.70	21.83	23.03	23.51	24.23	23.99	24.32	23.51
2011	24.37	24.15	23.76	24.56	24.77	24.34	24.37	24.45	24.90	24.67	23.96	24.04	24.40
Trade, Transportation, and Utilities													
2007	14.91	14.66	15.56	14.86	14.50	14.04	14.89	15.23	14.68	14.52	15.05	14.85	14.81
2008	15.04	15.51	15.43	15.62	15.80	15.73	15.84	16.77	16.45	16.55	17.03	17.06	16.08
2009	17.68	17.54	17.53	17.47	17.78	17.88	17.48	18.44	17.93	18.33	17.97	18.02	17.84
2010	18.64	18.30	18.32	18.70	18.55	18.07	18.24	18.24	18.24	18.23	18.34	18.24	18.34
2011	18.51	18.50	18.55	19.03	18.87	18.65	18.50	18.34	18.44	18.51	18.30	18.36	18.55
Financial Activities													
2007	20.69	19.28	18.29	19.09	18.75	18.99	19.13	19.02	19.64	19.40	19.75	20.28	19.36
2008	20.24	19.04	19.55	19.49	19.98	20.17	19.34	19.67	19.87	19.97	19.19	19.66	19.68
2009	20.92	20.24	20.44	19.80	19.95	20.11	20.50	20.80	19.99	20.46	20.33	21.10	20.38
2010	21.03	20.85	20.47	21.66	21.03	20.50	20.25	20.92	21.87	21.39	20.84	20.52	20.94
2011	20.52	21.09	21.12	22.00	21.77	20.96	22.00	21.86	22.92	23.48	22.50	20.44	21.73
Professional and Business Services													
2007	21.03	20.47	20.30	20.63	21.15	19.42	19.03	19.22	19.53	19.15	19.54	20.21	19.96
2008	19.83	19.89	19.69	19.43	19.58	19.60	19.23	19.33	19.86	19.57	20.58	20.28	19.73
2009	26.15	26.21	25.65	24.73	24.27	23.28	23.05	23.15	22.73	22.58	22.63	22.39	23.73
2010	21.10	21.45	20.94	20.72	20.77	20.41	20.64	20.51	20.55	20.80	20.94	21.21	20.83
2011	21.62	21.19	21.10	21.36	21.29	20.97	21.09	21.25	21.51	22.04	21.85	22.45	21.48
Education and Health Services													
2007	18.70	18.74	18.98	19.16	19.00	19.00	19.33	19.19	17.88	18.64	18.74	18.54	18.82
2008	18.84	18.63	18.46	18.78	19.16	18.51	19.24	18.84	19.27	18.74	19.09	19.27	18.90
2009	20.01	19.61	19.76	19.81	19.54	19.82	20.13	20.18	19.99	20.15	20.06	18.75	19.81
2010	19.81	19.22	19.54	20.19	21.76	20.35	20.48	22.21	21.35	20.97	22.38	20.95	20.78
2011	21.78	21.34	21.48	22.14	23.20	22.91	23.60	23.59	23.69	23.78	25.03	23.08	22.96
Leisure and Hospitality													
2007	11.21	11.49	10.82	10.81	10.93	10.47	10.71	10.66	11.46	11.48	11.49	11.57	10.99
2008	11.46	11.68	11.59	11.63	11.55	11.43	11.12	11.49	12.92	13.09	13.23	13.27	12.01
2009	13.38	13.40	13.07	13.50	13.49	13.27	13.45	13.58	14.35	14.80	14.90	15.67	13.89
2010	15.27	15.11	14.64	14.41	14.10	13.67	13.58	13.44	13.57	13.67	13.63	13.11	13.99
2011	13.35	13.48	13.31	13.06	12.86	12.59	12.54	12.28	12.52	12.45	12.45	12.63	12.76

4. Average Weekly Earnings by Selected Industry: Montana, 2007–2011

(Dollars, not seasonally adjusted)

Industry and year	January	February	March	April	May	June	July	August	September	October	November	December	Annual average
Total Private													
2007	573.04	573.12	570.69	593.85	761.96	736.91	739.77	722.42	589.38	574.13	574.31	590.39	634.58
2008	578.76	579.48	588.71	577.02	593.60	598.27	592.04	606.72	610.35	598.84	620.25	609.87	596.26
2009	608.10	621.98	610.00	607.39	605.02	606.67	610.04	633.65	619.68	628.69	652.37	624.55	618.85
2010	631.58	631.78	630.59	650.99	677.56	641.24	647.47	687.83	679.27	674.45	680.16	666.50	658.75
2011	677.82	668.39	670.91	686.83	699.89	675.57	684.58	676.99	687.06	703.74	685.58	663.44	681.30
Goods-Producing													
2007	794.96	838.15	834.77	863.56	876.35	895.50	889.02	894.84	834.26	812.39	793.08	802.28	845.14
2008	804.36	798.79	808.69	788.20	839.50	838.09	831.61	879.75	873.90	805.53	834.02	822.40	827.79
2009	819.47	842.57	801.81	850.67	805.13	858.77	851.92	910.93	857.83	864.49	887.62	815.08	848.09
2010	845.57	858.30	876.38	909.94	951.11	887.92	918.68	975.03	976.65	947.99	938.57	979.88	924.10
2011	991.02	966.73	997.30	982.74	987.60	974.43	979.55	951.22	937.17	950.72	903.15	890.10	958.60
Construction													
2007	805.57	874.03	864.50	889.92	918.35	886.58	856.83	872.92	765.23	811.71	758.97	790.35	841.49
2008	803.11	766.16	760.34	729.11	845.02	760.38	829.92	832.15	899.84	762.28	773.81	801.25	798.25
2009	749.72	747.73	719.04	802.94	780.86	838.16	830.55	940.27	755.51	811.02	831.41	716.32	798.12
2010	744.55	752.56	771.87	810.19	882.79	783.15	790.25	875.14	865.17	908.63	878.03	744.19	821.89
2011	770.09	755.90	769.82	854.69	864.47	881.11	894.38	907.10	903.87	902.92	824.22	798.13	851.84
Trade, Transportation, and Utilities													
2007	466.68	469.12	504.14	493.35	482.85	478.76	494.35	513.25	481.50	460.28	474.08	487.08	483.81
2008	469.25	499.42	501.48	482.66	510.34	523.81	525.89	568.50	537.92	537.88	558.58	566.39	523.58
2009	586.98	566.54	562.71	564.28	584.96	586.46	566.35	614.05	589.90	601.22	591.21	592.86	584.00
2010	609.53	605.73	606.39	602.14	626.99	603.54	618.34	631.10	616.51	621.64	625.39	629.28	616.44
2011	644.15	634.55	636.27	664.15	651.02	647.16	634.55	630.90	621.43	620.09	596.58	613.22	632.57
Financial Activities													
2007	773.81	713.36	705.99	738.78	697.50	710.23	721.20	707.54	710.97	710.04	714.95	786.86	724.28
2008	767.10	702.58	725.31	715.28	721.28	744.27	702.04	690.42	711.35	734.90	713.87	751.01	723.22
2009	774.04	773.17	784.90	762.30	752.12	756.14	750.30	765.44	729.64	746.79	756.28	755.38	758.68
2010	769.70	761.03	757.39	810.08	792.83	772.85	761.40	794.96	809.19	789.29	764.83	736.67	777.03
2011	761.29	765.57	768.77	807.40	818.55	767.14	807.40	804.45	854.92	899.28	825.75	731.75	800.88
Professional and Business Services													
2007	708.71	687.79	686.14	705.55	763.52	660.28	650.83	641.95	654.26	641.53	646.77	672.99	676.15
2008	662.32	672.28	693.09	680.05	646.14	676.20	665.36	655.29	673.25	673.21	697.66	671.27	672.00
2009	491.62	537.31	564.30	558.90	560.64	558.72	592.39	601.90	602.35	609.66	635.90	611.25	577.42
2010	601.35	628.49	617.73	629.89	656.33	630.67	625.39	682.98	657.60	684.32	680.55	687.20	649.20
2011	724.27	699.27	696.30	715.56	728.12	692.01	691.75	694.88	722.74	753.77	738.53	747.59	716.91
Education and Health Services													
2007	587.18	592.18	565.60	615.04	594.70	592.80	630.16	619.84	611.50	598.34	601.55	615.53	602.00
2008	608.53	596.16	607.33	608.47	615.04	610.83	619.53	608.53	614.71	605.30	629.97	632.06	613.11
2009	644.32	647.13	654.06	641.84	644.82	640.19	660.26	659.89	657.67	662.94	670.00	618.75	650.28
2010	647.79	632.34	642.87	664.25	728.96	673.59	677.89	746.26	713.09	704.59	754.21	714.40	691.87
2011	736.16	723.43	723.88	746.12	788.80	753.74	781.16	769.03	781.77	796.63	831.00	759.33	766.00
Leisure and Hospitality													
2007	269.04	271.16	270.50	277.82	469.99	458.59	479.81	451.98	291.08	276.67	275.76	286.94	344.75
2008	267.02	281.49	280.48	268.65	278.36	290.32	285.78	296.44	319.12	310.23	330.75	305.21	292.87
2009	313.09	326.96	313.68	309.15	329.16	319.81	338.94	366.66	363.06	370.00	382.93	383.92	343.15
2010	368.01	368.68	358.68	357.37	359.55	347.22	363.94	374.98	352.82	299.37	290.32	280.55	344.25
2011	284.36	288.47	283.50	283.40	293.21	285.79	303.47	305.77	292.97	296.31	278.88	282.91	290.34

NEBRASKA
At a Glance

Population:
    2000 census: 1,711,230
    2010 census: 1,826,341
    2011 estimate: 1,842,641

Percent change in population:
    2000–2010: 6.7%
    2010–2011: 0.9%

Percent change in total nonfarm employment:
    2000–2010: 3.3%
    2010–2011: 0.4%

Industry with the largest growth in employment, 2000–2011 (thousands):
    Education and Health Services, 29.9

Industry with the largest decline or smallest growth in employment, 2000–2011 (thousands):
    Manufacturing, -20.8

Civilian labor force:
    2000: 949,762
    2010: 988,509
    2011: 1,005,455

Unemployment rate and rank among states (lowest to highest):
    2000: 2.8%, 8th
    2010: 4.7%, 2nd
    2011: 4.4%, 2nd

Over-the-year change in unemployment rates:
    2010–2011: -0.3%

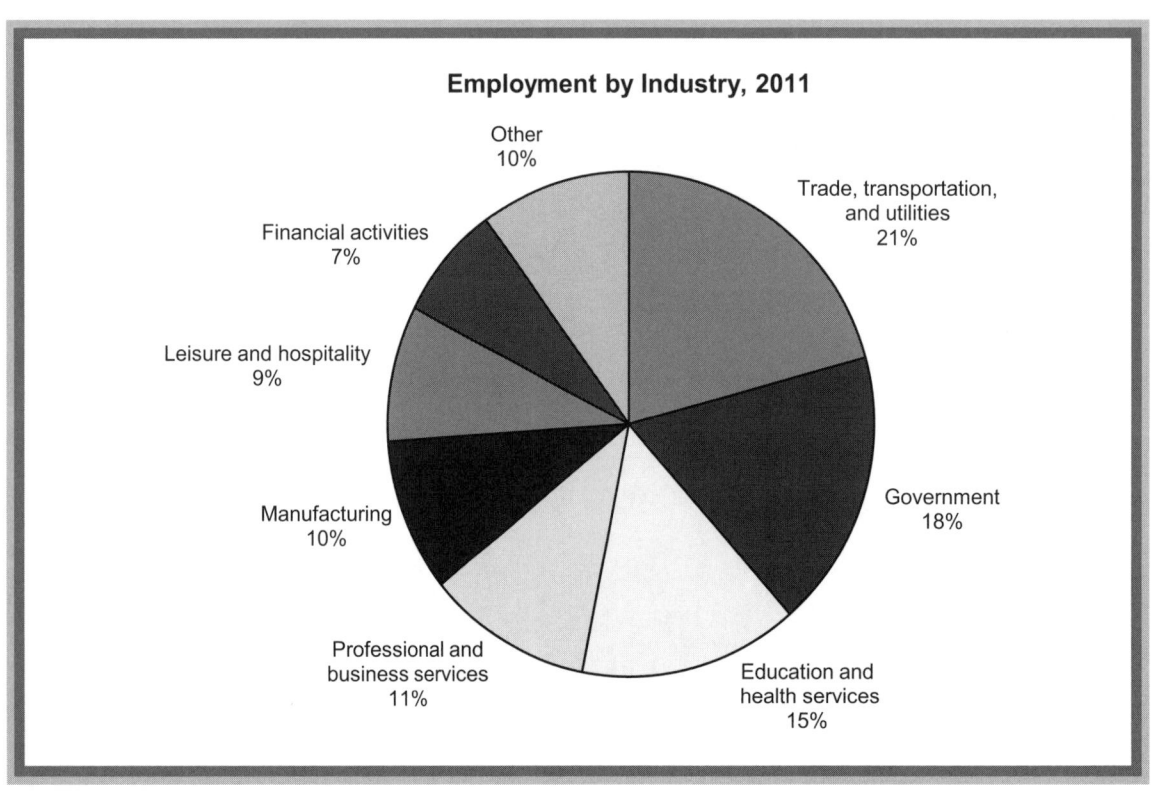

Employment by Industry, 2011

- Other 10%
- Trade, transportation, and utilities 21%
- Financial activities 7%
- Government 18%
- Leisure and hospitality 9%
- Manufacturing 10%
- Education and health services 15%
- Professional and business services 11%

1. Employment by Industry: Nebraska, Selected Years, 2000–2011

(Numbers in thousands, not seasonally adjusted)

Industry and year	January	February	March	April	May	June	July	August	September	October	November	December	Annual average
Total Nonfarm													
2000	888.7	891.7	901.1	906.8	917.6	926.5	910.8	911.9	914.6	915.9	920.8	919.5	910.5
2001	897.8	899.7	906.5	916.5	926.1	932.7	917.1	920.2	919.8	917.6	923.9	921.7	916.6
2002	889.7	893.1	899.1	909.3	916.8	922.0	907.3	907.7	911.4	911.3	913.7	914.3	908.0
2003	895.5	895.4	899.5	911.9	919.0	923.5	907.0	908.1	912.0	916.4	917.9	918.6	910.4
2004	896.0	894.0	903.0	915.9	925.0	930.2	918.7	919.7	924.6	926.2	929.3	929.9	917.7
2005	905.6	910.7	919.3	929.0	936.9	942.3	930.8	930.7	936.3	938.5	942.2	940.5	930.2
2006	918.9	924.1	930.8	937.5	947.2	954.2	939.7	940.7	947.4	949.0	954.2	953.7	941.5
2007	932.2	935.3	942.1	952.3	964.3	969.8	957.2	961.2	965.7	968.2	971.1	969.2	957.4
2008	949.1	950.6	956.8	965.2	975.4	975.0	962.1	964.9	968.0	973.7	971.4	967.3	965.0
2009	940.1	939.2	941.6	946.4	954.3	952.4	943.1	941.4	943.3	946.4	946.5	939.9	944.6
2010	916.8	920.2	926.4	939.7	949.4	951.6	942.0	942.8	943.0	950.7	949.6	948.7	940.1
2011	923.1	926.2	933.4	946.7	954.2	953.4	941.4	944.2	946.5	953.7	952.7	952.1	944.0
Total Private													
2000	735.9	737.7	744.6	751.0	758.2	768.3	762.3	763.6	761.3	761.7	764.9	763.6	756.1
2001	745.0	744.4	749.9	758.8	765.4	772.5	767.0	768.9	762.6	759.1	762.9	761.6	759.8
2002	733.3	733.6	738.9	748.8	754.0	760.3	755.7	756.8	753.5	749.7	751.5	752.7	749.1
2003	735.8	734.7	738.8	748.4	754.0	759.7	755.7	758.5	755.6	754.9	756.4	757.3	750.8
2004	737.9	734.4	742.5	754.2	761.7	767.9	765.7	767.2	764.1	764.0	766.7	767.4	757.8
2005	746.6	749.7	757.4	766.4	772.3	779.0	777.1	777.6	774.5	774.6	778.0	777.2	769.2
2006	758.4	761.6	767.5	773.7	781.2	789.0	786.0	786.6	784.7	784.5	789.0	789.4	779.3
2007	770.5	772.0	778.4	788.1	797.3	804.1	804.3	807.1	803.5	803.4	805.8	805.1	795.0
2008	786.2	787.3	793.2	799.7	807.4	809.3	806.7	809.1	803.9	806.1	803.5	800.0	801.0
2009	774.4	771.2	772.9	775.7	781.8	782.6	779.6	779.2	775.3	775.5	774.8	770.0	776.1
2010	749.8	750.7	755.0	767.7	774.1	779.5	779.6	780.3	775.2	778.8	777.6	777.5	770.5
2011	755.8	756.7	763.6	775.3	781.9	785.3	782.3	783.3	780.0	782.3	781.2	781.4	775.8
Goods-Producing													
2000	153.0	153.3	156.2	158.4	160.4	163.7	162.4	162.1	160.5	160.3	159.0	157.3	158.9
2001	152.8	152.1	152.9	156.2	158.5	160.5	159.8	159.4	156.9	156.3	155.3	153.9	156.2
2002	148.2	147.4	148.5	151.1	153.2	155.6	155.9	155.6	154.3	153.4	152.2	151.0	152.2
2003	145.7	144.5	145.1	148.4	150.8	152.9	153.2	153.4	151.6	151.8	150.7	149.8	149.8
2004	144.6	143.2	145.8	148.6	150.9	153.2	153.6	153.0	151.0	150.5	149.8	148.9	149.4
2005	142.7	143.2	145.7	148.3	150.0	152.7	153.3	152.8	151.5	150.9	150.3	148.3	149.1
2006	144.9	145.2	146.6	148.9	150.2	153.0	153.1	152.7	152.1	151.5	150.5	149.2	149.8
2007	144.7	144.4	146.6	149.7	152.1	155.0	156.7	156.9	155.8	155.0	153.9	151.7	151.9
2008	147.4	147.2	149.0	151.9	154.1	155.2	155.2	155.2	153.2	152.6	150.1	146.6	151.5
2009	140.2	138.7	138.9	140.3	142.3	143.2	143.5	142.9	141.7	139.8	138.2	134.2	140.3
2010	128.9	128.9	129.5	133.9	135.6	138.0	137.9	137.5	136.6	136.2	135.4	133.3	134.3
2011	128.6	128.3	130.7	134.0	136.1	137.9	137.8	136.7	136.0	135.5	134.9	133.2	134.1
Mining, Logging, and Construction													
2000	40.5	40.4	42.3	44.7	46.4	48.4	48.0	48.2	47.0	46.4	44.7	42.9	45.0
2001	39.7	39.4	40.6	44.1	46.7	48.5	48.6	48.9	47.4	47.2	46.6	45.3	45.3
2002	41.2	40.8	42.4	45.3	47.2	48.8	49.3	49.1	48.3	47.9	46.9	45.8	46.1
2003	42.7	41.8	42.7	46.0	48.3	50.2	51.0	51.2	49.8	49.6	48.6	47.3	47.4
2004	43.6	42.4	44.9	48.3	50.1	51.8	52.2	51.7	50.2	49.7	48.7	47.3	48.4
2005	43.0	42.7	44.7	47.1	49.0	50.9	51.4	51.1	50.1	49.2	48.5	46.2	47.8
2006	43.4	43.5	44.9	47.4	49.2	51.2	51.3	51.1	50.8	50.1	49.4	48.0	48.4
2007	44.7	44.0	46.2	49.1	50.9	53.0	54.7	55.0	54.1	53.2	51.7	49.2	50.5
2008	45.5	45.0	46.7	49.9	51.9	53.1	53.5	53.4	52.3	51.7	49.9	48.0	50.1
2009	43.4	43.0	44.1	46.5	48.7	50.1	51.3	50.9	49.8	48.2	46.4	42.8	47.1
2010	38.4	38.1	38.6	42.5	43.8	45.8	45.7	45.5	44.6	44.2	43.0	40.7	42.6
2011	36.8	36.4	38.3	41.0	42.7	43.9	44.0	43.1	42.9	42.6	41.9	39.0	41.1
Manufacturing													
2000	112.5	112.9	113.9	113.7	114.0	115.3	114.4	113.9	113.5	113.9	114.3	114.4	113.9
2001	113.1	112.7	112.3	112.1	111.8	112.0	111.2	110.5	109.5	109.1	108.7	108.6	111.0
2002	107.0	106.6	106.1	105.8	106.0	106.8	106.6	106.5	106.0	105.5	105.3	105.2	106.1
2003	103.0	102.7	102.4	102.4	102.5	102.7	102.2	102.2	101.8	102.2	102.1	102.5	102.4
2004	101.0	100.8	100.9	100.3	100.8	101.4	101.4	101.3	100.8	100.8	101.1	101.6	101.0
2005	99.7	100.5	101.0	101.2	101.0	101.8	101.9	101.7	101.4	101.7	101.8	102.1	101.3
2006	101.5	101.7	101.7	101.5	101.0	101.8	101.8	101.6	101.3	101.4	101.1	101.2	101.5
2007	100.0	100.4	100.4	100.6	101.2	102.0	102.0	101.9	101.7	101.8	102.2	102.5	101.4
2008	101.9	102.2	102.3	102.0	102.2	102.1	101.7	101.8	100.9	100.9	100.2	98.6	101.4
2009	96.8	95.7	94.8	93.8	93.6	93.1	92.2	92.0	91.9	91.6	91.8	91.4	93.2
2010	90.5	90.8	90.9	91.4	91.8	92.2	92.2	92.0	92.0	92.0	92.4	92.6	91.7
2011	91.8	91.9	92.4	93.0	93.4	94.0	93.8	93.6	93.1	92.9	93.0	94.2	93.1
Service-Providing													
2000	735.7	738.4	744.9	748.4	757.2	762.8	748.4	749.8	754.1	755.6	761.8	762.2	751.6
2001	745.0	747.6	753.6	760.3	767.6	772.2	757.3	760.8	762.9	761.3	768.6	767.8	760.4
2002	741.5	745.7	750.6	758.2	763.6	766.4	751.4	752.1	757.1	757.9	761.5	763.3	755.8
2003	749.8	750.9	754.4	763.5	768.2	770.6	753.8	754.7	760.4	764.6	767.2	768.8	760.6
2004	751.4	750.8	757.2	767.3	774.1	777.0	765.1	766.7	773.6	775.7	779.5	781.0	768.3
2005	762.9	767.5	773.6	780.7	786.9	789.6	777.5	777.9	784.8	787.6	791.9	792.2	781.1
2006	774.0	778.9	784.2	788.6	797.0	801.2	786.6	788.0	795.3	797.5	803.7	804.5	791.6
2007	787.5	790.9	795.5	802.6	812.2	814.8	800.5	804.3	809.9	813.2	817.2	817.5	805.5
2008	801.7	803.4	807.8	813.3	821.3	819.8	806.9	809.7	814.8	821.1	821.3	820.7	813.5
2009	799.9	800.5	802.7	806.1	812.0	809.2	799.6	798.5	801.6	806.6	808.3	805.7	804.2
2010	787.9	791.3	796.9	805.8	813.8	813.6	804.1	805.3	806.4	814.5	814.2	815.4	805.8
2011	794.5	797.9	802.7	812.7	818.1	815.5	803.6	807.5	810.5	818.2	817.8	818.9	809.8

1. Employment by Industry: Nebraska, Selected Years, 2000–2011—*Continued*

(Numbers in thousands, not seasonally adjusted)

Industry and year	January	February	March	April	May	June	July	August	September	October	November	December	Annual average
Trade, Transportation, and Utilities													
2000	195.8	194.4	195.1	196.2	197.1	199.0	197.4	197.7	196.9	198.6	201.5	203.6	197.8
2001	197.0	195.0	195.6	197.2	199.2	199.4	198.0	198.0	197.4	197.7	201.2	202.7	198.2
2002	194.9	192.4	193.1	194.3	196.0	196.1	194.8	194.8	195.1	194.4	198.1	200.1	195.3
2003	193.0	191.5	192.5	193.6	194.8	195.2	193.4	194.1	194.1	195.4	197.9	199.9	194.6
2004	192.8	190.3	191.7	194.3	196.6	197.5	196.8	197.7	197.8	199.2	201.6	203.7	196.7
2005	197.1	196.5	198.1	198.6	200.9	201.0	200.1	200.1	199.7	200.4	203.4	205.1	200.1
2006	196.8	196.0	197.1	197.9	200.3	200.7	200.0	200.5	200.8	202.1	206.0	208.1	200.5
2007	200.9	199.9	201.1	202.4	205.0	205.4	204.9	205.3	205.1	205.9	209.5	211.1	204.7
2008	203.9	202.2	203.7	203.3	205.4	205.5	203.9	204.4	203.5	206.4	208.6	210.0	205.1
2009	200.6	198.1	198.1	197.4	198.8	198.1	196.6	196.5	195.8	197.6	199.8	200.5	198.2
2010	192.8	191.4	192.5	194.6	196.3	196.3	195.7	195.6	194.5	197.5	200.1	202.6	195.8
2011	193.8	192.7	193.8	196.1	197.5	197.6	195.3	194.6	192.8	194.9	198.5	201.7	195.8
Wholesale Trade													
2000	41.7	41.8	41.9	41.6	41.7	42.0	42.1	42.1	41.6	41.4	41.3	41.2	41.7
2001	42.1	42.1	42.3	42.6	43.1	43.3	43.2	42.8	42.3	42.2	42.0	41.9	42.5
2002	41.1	40.9	41.3	41.6	42.0	42.2	42.5	42.0	41.6	41.0	41.0	41.1	41.5
2003	40.4	40.3	40.5	41.0	41.3	41.6	41.5	41.4	41.2	41.2	40.8	41.0	41.0
2004	40.0	39.9	40.3	41.0	41.2	41.3	41.6	41.1	40.8	40.9	40.7	40.7	40.8
2005	40.0	40.0	40.4	40.5	40.9	41.0	41.3	40.8	40.4	40.5	40.4	40.5	40.6
2006	40.2	40.2	40.4	40.8	41.2	41.4	41.3	40.9	40.7	40.6	40.6	40.9	40.8
2007	39.9	39.8	40.2	40.8	41.2	41.7	41.7	41.2	41.2	41.5	41.6	41.8	41.1
2008	41.2	41.2	41.5	41.9	42.5	42.8	42.5	42.1	41.9	42.3	42.1	42.1	42.0
2009	41.2	40.9	41.0	41.2	41.5	41.6	41.5	41.0	40.8	41.4	41.2	41.3	41.2
2010	39.9	39.8	40.1	40.9	41.2	41.4	41.2	40.7	40.4	40.7	40.4	40.5	40.6
2011	39.8	39.8	40.1	40.7	41.1	41.3	40.9	40.4	39.9	40.6	40.5	40.4	40.5
Retail Trade													
2000	109.9	108.5	108.9	109.7	110.8	112.3	110.3	110.4	110.0	111.8	114.7	116.9	111.2
2001	110.1	108.0	108.2	109.1	110.6	110.8	109.5	110.0	109.8	110.4	113.9	115.3	110.5
2002	108.5	106.3	106.6	107.4	108.7	108.8	107.8	108.0	108.9	109.0	112.3	114.2	108.9
2003	106.7	104.9	105.6	106.2	106.8	106.9	105.9	106.2	106.3	107.7	110.7	112.3	107.2
2004	106.3	104.2	104.5	105.3	106.7	107.1	106.1	106.5	106.1	107.5	110.6	112.4	106.9
2005	106.0	105.0	105.9	106.5	107.7	107.4	106.8	106.8	106.3	107.2	109.8	111.1	107.2
2006	105.0	103.8	104.4	104.8	106.1	106.1	105.7	105.9	105.7	107.0	110.5	111.9	106.4
2007	105.6	104.5	105.2	106.1	107.9	107.7	107.2	107.5	106.9	107.7	110.9	112.4	107.5
2008	107.3	105.7	106.5	105.9	106.8	106.9	106.0	106.1	105.4	107.1	109.5	110.9	107.0
2009	105.0	103.2	103.3	103.5	104.6	104.4	103.7	103.9	103.2	104.1	106.6	106.8	104.4
2010	102.4	101.2	101.9	102.8	104.1	104.2	103.7	103.6	102.5	104.7	107.1	108.5	103.9
2011	102.8	101.9	102.4	103.6	104.6	104.5	103.9	103.2	102.6	103.5	107.3	108.7	104.1
Transportation and Utilities													
2000	44.2	44.1	44.3	44.9	44.6	44.7	45.0	45.2	45.3	45.4	45.5	45.5	44.9
2001	44.8	44.9	45.1	45.5	45.5	45.3	45.3	45.2	45.3	45.1	45.3	45.5	45.2
2002	45.3	45.2	45.2	45.3	45.3	45.1	44.5	44.8	44.6	44.4	44.8	44.8	44.9
2003	45.9	46.3	46.4	46.4	46.7	46.7	46.0	46.5	46.6	46.5	46.4	46.6	46.4
2004	46.5	46.2	46.9	48.0	48.7	49.1	49.1	50.1	50.9	50.8	50.3	50.6	48.9
2005	51.1	51.5	51.8	51.6	52.3	52.6	52.0	52.5	53.0	52.7	53.2	53.5	52.3
2006	51.6	52.0	52.3	52.3	53.0	53.2	53.0	53.7	54.4	54.5	54.9	55.3	53.4
2007	55.4	55.6	55.7	55.5	55.9	56.0	56.0	56.6	57.0	56.7	57.0	56.9	56.2
2008	55.4	55.3	55.7	55.5	56.1	55.8	55.4	56.2	56.2	57.0	57.0	57.0	56.1
2009	54.4	54.0	53.8	52.7	52.7	52.1	51.4	51.6	51.8	52.1	52.0	52.4	52.6
2010	50.5	50.4	50.5	50.9	51.0	50.7	50.8	51.3	51.6	52.1	52.6	53.6	51.3
2011	51.2	51.0	51.3	51.8	51.8	51.8	50.5	51.0	50.3	50.8	50.7	52.6	51.2
Information													
2000	27.5	27.1	26.7	27.2	26.8	27.0	27.0	26.7	26.4	26.4	26.6	26.6	26.8
2001	26.3	26.2	26.3	26.5	26.2	26.3	25.8	25.4	25.2	25.2	25.2	25.3	25.8
2002	24.5	24.3	24.0	23.8	23.5	23.3	23.0	22.8	22.5	22.3	22.0	21.8	23.2
2003	21.5	21.5	21.5	21.4	21.4	21.6	21.5	21.3	21.2	21.4	21.5	21.7	21.5
2004	21.3	21.3	21.3	21.2	21.1	21.2	21.2	21.0	20.9	20.8	20.9	20.7	21.1
2005	20.4	20.5	20.4	20.3	20.0	20.3	20.2	20.2	20.0	20.0	20.0	20.1	20.2
2006	19.7	19.6	19.6	19.6	19.5	19.7	19.6	19.5	19.3	19.1	19.2	19.3	19.5
2007	19.1	19.1	19.1	19.4	19.3	19.6	19.6	19.6	19.4	19.4	19.5	19.4	19.4
2008	19.2	19.2	19.1	19.1	18.8	18.8	18.7	18.5	18.2	18.2	18.2	18.1	18.7
2009	17.7	17.7	17.6	17.4	17.3	17.6	17.5	17.5	17.3	17.2	17.4	17.4	17.5
2010	17.2	17.1	17.0	16.9	17.0	17.1	17.0	17.0	16.9	16.9	17.0	17.1	17.0
2011	16.9	16.9	16.8	16.8	16.7	16.8	17.0	17.0	16.9	16.9	17.0	17.1	16.9
Financial Activities													
2000	60.4	60.2	60.1	60.3	60.4	60.9	60.3	60.3	60.1	59.9	60.1	60.4	60.3
2001	59.1	59.2	59.3	59.7	60.1	61.0	60.8	60.8	60.5	60.3	60.5	61.0	60.2
2002	60.6	60.7	60.9	61.0	61.3	61.9	61.9	61.8	61.4	61.6	61.7	62.2	61.4
2003	61.8	61.9	62.0	62.0	62.3	62.9	63.0	62.9	62.3	62.3	62.3	62.8	62.4
2004	62.2	62.1	62.6	62.8	63.1	63.6	63.7	63.8	63.4	63.5	63.8	64.2	63.2
2005	63.5	63.8	63.9	64.1	64.5	64.9	64.9	65.0	64.7	64.8	64.7	65.0	64.5
2006	64.6	64.9	65.2	65.7	66.4	67.2	67.4	67.6	67.2	67.4	67.8	68.5	66.7
2007	67.7	68.2	68.4	68.4	69.1	69.4	69.4	69.1	68.7	68.6	68.6	68.8	68.7
2008	68.5	68.9	69.0	69.0	69.3	69.7	69.7	69.6	69.0	69.2	69.1	69.5	69.2
2009	68.6	68.8	68.8	68.4	68.5	68.7	68.4	68.4	67.9	68.1	68.2	68.5	68.4
2010	68.0	68.1	68.3	68.4	68.6	69.3	69.5	69.6	69.1	69.4	69.4	69.6	68.9
2011	69.3	69.2	69.4	69.8	70.0	70.1	69.9	69.9	68.8	69.1	69.2	69.3	69.5

1. Employment by Industry: Nebraska, Selected Years, 2000–2011—*Continued*

(Numbers in thousands, not seasonally adjusted)

Industry and year	January	February	March	April	May	June	July	August	September	October	November	December	Annual average
Professional and Business Services													
2000	92.0	92.5	93.6	95.4	95.7	97.8	97.5	97.7	97.3	97.9	98.4	98.8	96.2
2001	95.8	96.1	96.7	97.2	97.9	99.2	98.2	98.8	97.4	96.4	96.7	95.8	97.2
2002	89.0	89.8	91.4	92.9	92.7	93.1	91.3	91.2	90.8	90.9	90.9	90.5	91.2
2003	88.3	89.0	89.7	92.0	91.8	92.9	92.9	93.8	94.4	94.2	93.7	93.8	92.2
2004	91.1	91.1	92.3	94.7	94.8	96.0	95.2	95.7	94.7	95.3	95.4	95.1	94.3
2005	93.9	94.5	95.7	97.3	97.5	98.5	98.5	99.0	98.9	100.3	100.5	100.5	97.9
2006	97.9	98.7	100.4	101.2	102.3	104.4	103.8	103.4	102.9	102.5	102.5	102.1	101.8
2007	100.5	101.2	102.0	103.2	103.8	105.7	105.8	106.2	105.5	105.2	105.8	106.4	104.3
2008	103.8	104.4	105.2	106.6	106.8	107.2	106.7	106.7	106.5	106.6	105.3	104.2	105.8
2009	101.1	100.7	100.3	100.8	100.5	101.4	100.5	100.0	99.1	100.1	99.4	99.2	100.3
2010	97.5	97.7	98.0	100.6	100.7	102.0	103.0	102.7	102.7	103.3	102.4	102.6	101.1
2011	99.2	99.7	100.3	102.2	102.3	103.0	104.4	105.4	107.6	107.8	105.5	104.2	103.5
Education and Health Services													
2000	104.2	106.0	106.6	104.5	106.5	106.9	105.7	106.4	109.0	109.5	111.4	109.9	107.2
2001	109.2	110.6	111.9	112.4	111.2	112.5	111.6	113.0	114.6	114.5	116.1	115.4	112.8
2002	112.1	113.9	114.7	115.4	115.1	115.9	114.9	115.6	116.8	116.9	117.6	118.0	115.6
2003	118.0	118.6	118.7	119.4	119.1	119.3	118.0	118.6	119.6	119.3	120.8	120.6	119.2
2004	119.6	120.2	120.6	121.7	121.2	121.1	120.1	120.7	122.1	122.3	123.6	123.3	121.4
2005	121.3	122.5	122.9	124.0	123.2	123.5	122.7	122.8	124.2	124.5	126.1	125.8	123.6
2006	123.7	125.2	125.4	125.3	125.5	125.6	124.3	125.3	126.5	126.4	128.5	127.4	125.8
2007	125.7	127.1	127.3	128.0	128.5	128.3	127.9	129.2	130.3	131.0	131.7	131.9	128.9
2008	130.3	132.1	132.1	132.2	132.8	131.5	131.6	133.1	133.9	134.2	135.2	135.0	132.8
2009	133.1	133.9	133.8	133.8	133.9	132.1	132.3	132.6	134.2	135.3	135.8	135.8	133.9
2010	133.8	135.3	135.5	135.6	135.8	135.3	135.2	135.8	135.7	136.7	136.7	136.9	135.7
2011	135.8	136.8	136.9	137.3	137.4	136.9	135.1	136.2	136.9	138.1	138.6	139.2	137.1
Leisure and Hospitality													
2000	71.5	72.4	74.2	76.9	79.0	80.5	79.8	80.5	79.1	77.0	75.9	75.1	76.8
2001	72.6	72.8	74.5	77.0	79.4	80.6	79.7	80.5	78.0	75.9	75.1	74.8	76.7
2002	71.9	72.6	73.8	76.8	78.7	80.8	80.2	81.6	79.4	77.0	76.0	76.0	77.1
2003	73.9	74.0	75.3	77.5	79.7	80.6	79.7	80.6	78.7	76.9	75.9	75.2	77.3
2004	72.9	72.7	74.5	77.0	79.9	80.9	80.6	80.9	79.7	77.8	77.0	76.6	77.5
2005	73.9	74.4	76.3	79.3	81.5	83.2	82.5	83.1	81.1	79.4	78.8	78.2	79.3
2006	76.8	77.8	78.7	80.5	82.5	83.6	83.0	83.3	81.6	80.9	80.0	80.4	80.8
2007	77.7	77.8	79.2	82.1	84.4	85.6	85.1	86.1	84.1	83.3	81.8	80.8	82.3
2008	78.5	78.5	80.1	82.4	84.7	85.8	85.6	86.4	84.6	83.1	81.4	80.8	82.7
2009	77.8	77.9	79.9	81.7	84.3	84.9	84.2	84.7	82.8	80.9	79.2	77.6	81.3
2010	75.3	75.8	77.3	80.7	83.0	84.3	84.1	85.1	83.1	82.2	80.1	78.7	80.8
2011	76.1	76.8	79.0	82.3	84.9	85.8	86.3	87.0	85.0	83.5	81.0	79.6	82.3
Other Services													
2000	31.5	31.8	32.1	32.1	32.3	32.5	32.2	32.2	32.0	32.1	32.0	31.9	32.1
2001	32.2	32.4	32.7	32.6	32.9	33.0	33.1	33.0	32.6	32.8	32.8	32.7	32.7
2002	32.1	32.5	32.5	33.5	33.5	33.6	33.7	33.4	33.2	33.2	33.0	33.1	33.1
2003	33.6	33.7	34.0	34.1	34.1	34.3	34.0	33.8	33.7	33.6	33.6	33.5	33.8
2004	33.4	33.5	33.7	33.9	34.1	34.4	34.5	34.4	34.5	34.6	34.6	34.9	34.2
2005	33.8	34.3	34.4	34.5	34.7	34.9	34.9	34.6	34.4	34.3	34.2	34.2	34.4
2006	34.0	34.2	34.5	34.6	34.5	34.8	34.8	34.3	34.3	34.6	34.5	34.4	34.5
2007	34.2	34.3	34.7	34.9	35.1	35.1	34.9	34.7	34.6	35.0	35.0	35.0	34.8
2008	34.6	34.8	35.0	35.2	35.5	35.6	35.3	35.2	35.0	35.8	35.6	35.8	35.3
2009	35.3	35.4	35.5	35.9	36.2	36.6	36.6	36.6	36.5	36.5	36.8	36.8	36.2
2010	36.3	36.4	36.9	37.0	37.1	37.2	37.2	37.0	36.6	36.6	36.5	36.7	36.8
2011	36.1	36.3	36.7	36.8	37.0	37.2	36.5	36.5	36.0	36.5	36.5	37.1	36.6
Government													
2000	152.8	154.0	156.5	155.8	159.4	158.2	148.5	148.3	153.3	154.2	155.9	155.9	154.4
2001	152.8	155.3	156.6	157.7	160.7	160.2	150.1	151.3	157.2	158.5	161.0	160.1	156.8
2002	156.4	159.5	160.2	160.5	162.8	161.7	151.6	150.9	157.9	161.6	162.2	161.6	158.9
2003	159.7	160.7	160.7	163.5	165.0	163.8	151.3	149.6	156.4	161.5	161.5	161.3	159.6
2004	158.1	159.6	160.5	161.7	163.3	162.3	153.0	152.5	160.5	162.2	162.6	162.5	159.9
2005	159.0	161.0	161.9	162.6	164.6	163.3	153.7	153.1	161.8	163.9	164.2	163.3	161.0
2006	160.5	162.5	163.3	163.8	166.0	165.2	153.7	154.1	162.7	164.5	165.2	164.3	162.2
2007	161.7	163.3	163.7	164.2	167.0	165.7	152.9	154.1	162.2	164.8	165.3	164.1	162.4
2008	162.9	163.3	163.6	165.5	168.0	165.7	155.4	155.8	164.1	167.6	167.9	167.3	163.9
2009	165.7	168.0	168.7	170.7	172.5	169.8	163.5	162.2	168.0	170.9	171.7	169.9	168.5
2010	167.0	169.5	171.4	172.0	175.3	172.1	162.4	162.5	167.8	171.9	172.0	171.2	169.6
2011	167.3	169.5	169.8	171.4	172.3	168.1	159.1	160.9	166.5	171.4	171.5	170.7	168.2

2. Average Weekly Hours by Selected Industry: Nebraska, 2007–2011

(Not seasonally adjusted)

Industry and year	January	February	March	April	May	June	July	August	September	October	November	December	Annual average
Total Private													
2007	33.1	33.0	33.2	33.6	33.4	33.9	34.2	33.7	33.9	33.5	33.4	33.6	33.5
2008	33.1	33.1	33.9	33.5	33.6	34.5	34.2	34.1	33.3	33.6	33.9	33.5	33.7
2009	33.3	33.7	33.8	33.4	33.7	33.9	33.9	34.3	33.3	33.7	34.1	33.1	33.7
2010	33.6	33.7	33.7	33.9	34.4	34.3	34.3	34.8	34.3	34.3	34.1	33.8	34.1
2011	34.0	33.8	33.9	34.0	34.5	34.3	34.3	34.1	34.0	34.7	33.9	33.8	34.1
Goods-Producing													
2007	40.7	39.7	41.5	40.9	41.4	41.6	42.4	42.2	41.8	41.8	41.6	39.8	41.3
2008	39.3	39.3	40.6	40.7	41.1	41.4	41.4	41.8	39.3	39.9	40.1	39.6	40.4
2009	38.5	38.4	38.7	38.5	39.6	39.5	40.4	40.6	39.6	40.7	40.6	38.7	39.5
2010	40.0	39.8	40.1	40.4	40.4	40.9	40.7	41.2	40.2	41.1	40.8	39.6	40.4
2011	39.5	39.7	40.2	40.4	40.3	41.0	41.1	40.8	41.2	41.1	40.4	39.9	40.5
Mining, Logging, and Construction													
2007	38.1	36.4	39.9	39.4	41.4	41.6	44.2	43.3	42.1	42.3	43.0	38.6	41.0
2008	39.0	38.7	39.9	38.3	40.4	42.3	42.1	41.9	38.7	39.6	40.0	41.1	40.2
2009	38.3	38.5	37.7	39.7	40.6	40.5	42.5	42.3	40.9	41.9	42.2	37.0	40.3
2010	38.9	38.8	38.8	40.4	40.0	40.8	41.5	41.3	40.0	40.8	39.3	38.3	40.0
2011	37.4	37.5	37.8	38.7	38.7	39.8	40.4	39.3	40.4	41.2	39.9	38.5	39.2
Manufacturing													
2007	41.9	41.2	42.2	41.6	41.4	41.6	41.4	41.6	41.7	41.5	40.9	40.4	41.4
2008	39.5	39.6	40.9	41.8	41.4	41.0	41.1	41.7	39.6	40.0	40.1	38.8	40.5
2009	38.6	38.3	39.2	37.9	39.0	39.0	39.2	39.7	38.9	40.0	39.8	39.5	39.1
2010	40.4	40.3	40.6	40.4	40.5	40.9	40.3	41.2	40.3	41.2	41.5	40.2	40.7
2011	40.4	40.6	41.2	41.2	41.0	41.6	41.4	41.5	41.6	41.0	40.6	40.5	41.1
Trade, Transportation, and Utilities													
2007	30.8	31.2	31.0	31.0	31.5	32.0	32.1	31.8	32.0	31.3	31.5	31.7	31.5
2008	31.9	31.5	32.0	31.7	32.0	32.5	32.6	32.4	31.8	32.1	31.7	32.1	32.0
2009	31.6	32.0	32.3	31.9	32.0	32.5	32.1	32.7	31.6	32.0	32.1	32.1	32.1
2010	32.5	32.8	32.3	33.0	33.4	33.6	33.1	33.2	32.9	33.3	32.9	33.0	33.0
2011	32.2	32.1	32.5	32.6	33.3	33.4	33.2	33.1	33.2	34.2	33.5	33.8	33.1
Financial Activities													
2007	36.9	36.9	36.7	38.0	36.6	36.6	37.8	35.8	37.0	36.2	35.7	38.0	36.8
2008	36.5	36.4	37.9	36.5	36.2	38.0	36.5	36.1	35.9	35.5	37.0	35.8	36.5
2009	36.8	38.3	38.0	36.2	36.1	36.4	36.4	37.7	36.2	36.4	38.1	36.5	36.9
2010	36.6	36.6	36.8	36.4	38.1	36.7	36.8	38.4	36.9	36.9	36.8	36.9	37.0
2011	39.1	37.3	36.7	37.8	38.2	36.8	37.6	38.3	36.9	39.4	36.9	36.6	37.6
Professional and Business Services													
2007	31.2	31.9	31.9	32.5	32.0	32.5	32.7	32.7	33.5	32.4	32.8	33.7	32.5
2008	33.1	33.0	34.2	33.5	33.3	34.5	34.6	34.6	34.2	34.3	34.9	34.4	34.1
2009	34.6	34.9	34.9	35.0	35.1	35.7	35.5	36.0	35.1	35.2	35.5	34.4	35.2
2010	34.8	34.5	34.9	35.0	35.2	35.0	34.9	35.3	34.9	35.0	34.8	34.6	34.9
2011	34.9	34.6	34.3	34.3	34.8	34.5	34.5	34.5	34.6	35.6	34.8	35.1	34.7
Education and Health Services													
2007	32.2	32.3	32.5	33.6	32.3	33.0	32.7	32.0	32.7	32.4	31.9	33.7	32.6
2008	32.9	33.0	33.5	33.1	33.3	34.2	33.8	33.6	33.3	33.5	33.7	32.9	33.4
2009	33.0	32.7	32.6	32.8	33.1	32.4	32.3	32.4	32.1	32.2	32.5	31.8	32.5
2010	32.1	32.1	32.4	32.8	33.1	33.4	32.9	33.3	32.5	32.3	32.5	32.2	32.6
2011	32.1	32.2	32.3	32.5	32.9	32.7	32.2	31.6	31.6	31.9	31.8	31.5	32.1
Leisure and Hospitality													
2007	20.1	20.9	20.1	20.7	20.9	21.7	22.0	21.6	20.9	20.7	20.8	20.7	20.9
2008	20.5	20.6	20.6	20.7	21.0	22.3	21.9	22.0	21.2	21.7	21.6	21.2	21.3
2009	21.3	22.4	22.1	21.1	21.5	22.4	22.4	22.6	20.4	21.1	21.4	20.6	21.6
2010	21.1	21.8	22.0	21.9	22.6	22.5	22.6	22.7	22.5	22.6	22.3	22.0	22.2
2011	21.8	22.6	22.5	22.3	22.6	22.9	22.5	22.5	22.4	22.4	22.4	22.2	22.4

3. Average Hourly Earnings by Selected Industry: Nebraska, 2007–2011

(Dollars, not seasonally adjusted)

Industry and year	January	February	March	April	May	June	July	August	September	October	November	December	Annual average
Total Private													
2007	19.91	19.91	19.91	20.31	19.96	20.06	19.77	19.73	19.75	19.74	19.64	20.33	19.92
2008	19.97	20.11	20.02	19.58	19.71	19.49	19.25	19.50	19.84	19.89	20.09	20.12	19.79
2009	20.08	20.40	20.27	20.25	19.80	19.86	19.82	20.24	20.24	20.23	20.48	20.61	20.19
2010	20.63	20.67	20.81	20.98	21.09	20.86	20.83	20.99	20.97	20.94	20.89	20.92	20.89
2011	21.08	21.06	20.82	20.70	20.73	20.55	20.55	20.65	20.90	21.10	20.84	21.13	20.84
Goods-Producing													
2007	17.96	18.14	17.98	18.49	18.25	18.31	18.15	18.27	18.21	18.56	18.57	19.54	18.37
2008	18.69	18.62	18.80	18.30	18.15	18.49	18.32	18.73	19.17	19.19	19.46	19.94	18.81
2009	19.84	20.27	19.94	19.97	19.58	19.73	19.66	19.70	19.68	19.67	20.01	20.09	19.84
2010	20.00	20.02	19.95	19.71	19.78	19.72	19.78	19.75	19.90	19.84	19.89	20.10	19.87
2011	20.04	20.08	20.12	19.76	19.64	19.51	19.58	19.60	19.65	19.83	19.74	20.06	19.79
Mining, Logging, and Construction													
2007	18.69	18.83	18.41	18.48	18.10	18.67	18.11	18.09	18.05	18.72	18.71	19.31	18.49
2008	19.54	19.35	19.17	18.92	18.53	18.65	18.66	18.80	19.33	19.45	19.49	20.67	19.19
2009	20.49	21.14	20.58	19.50	19.29	19.40	19.19	19.37	19.43	19.59	19.84	20.37	19.79
2010	20.87	20.99	21.34	20.56	20.71	20.41	20.34	20.47	20.49	20.55	20.70	21.33	20.70
2011	21.34	21.64	21.55	20.66	20.35	20.28	20.27	20.41	20.18	20.50	20.42	21.42	20.71
Manufacturing													
2007	17.66	17.87	17.79	18.49	18.32	18.13	18.18	18.37	18.30	18.47	18.50	19.65	18.31
2008	18.31	18.31	18.63	18.02	17.96	18.40	18.13	18.70	19.09	19.06	19.45	19.57	18.62
2009	19.55	19.87	19.66	20.21	19.74	19.92	19.95	19.90	19.83	19.71	20.10	19.97	19.87
2010	19.65	19.63	19.39	19.31	19.34	19.38	19.49	19.40	19.61	19.50	19.53	19.59	19.48
2011	19.56	19.51	19.57	19.39	19.34	19.16	19.27	19.25	19.41	19.52	19.44	19.53	19.41
Trade, Transportation, and Utilities													
2007	16.61	16.45	16.45	16.92	16.67	17.81	16.57	16.36	16.57	16.20	16.39	17.97	16.75
2008	17.37	17.58	17.39	17.26	17.14	17.05	16.52	17.17	17.01	17.32	17.58	17.29	17.22
2009	17.31	17.26	17.18	17.44	17.34	17.15	17.26	17.86	17.75	17.71	17.90	18.10	17.52
2010	17.87	17.91	17.83	18.16	18.35	18.15	18.11	18.14	18.13	18.04	17.87	17.66	18.02
2011	18.05	18.03	17.91	17.82	17.99	18.55	18.33	18.53	19.02	18.56	18.22	18.25	18.27
Financial Activities													
2007	25.58	25.95	25.01	26.27	25.27	25.09	25.83	25.58	25.43	25.44	25.83	26.25	25.63
2008	26.43	27.74	26.81	26.32	26.63	26.81	26.08	25.60	25.94	26.10	26.42	25.93	26.40
2009	26.20	26.51	26.91	26.81	26.39	26.58	26.28	27.71	27.19	26.71	26.98	26.65	26.75
2010	26.42	26.41	26.33	26.94	27.10	26.79	26.57	26.86	26.33	26.27	26.05	26.08	26.51
2011	26.24	26.16	25.67	26.03	26.57	25.85	25.68	25.52	26.00	26.29	26.07	26.52	26.05
Professional and Business Services													
2007	24.10	23.77	24.40	24.37	24.60	24.55	24.44	25.09	24.61	24.54	24.01	24.14	24.39
2008	24.44	24.10	23.63	23.36	23.26	22.16	22.56	22.76	23.11	23.08	23.31	23.29	23.24
2009	22.65	24.11	23.81	23.45	22.15	22.10	22.06	22.42	22.57	22.93	23.36	23.43	22.91
2010	23.68	23.90	23.49	23.81	24.29	23.90	23.96	24.29	24.27	24.25	24.37	24.23	24.04
2011	24.22	24.06	24.07	24.13	24.15	23.79	23.62	23.91	24.02	24.61	24.70	25.02	24.20
Education and Health Services													
2007	21.98	21.99	22.40	22.28	22.26	21.63	21.69	21.36	21.29	21.69	21.22	20.73	21.70
2008	20.69	20.60	20.66	20.46	20.48	20.98	20.66	20.84	21.28	20.84	20.82	20.96	20.77
2009	20.79	20.48	20.25	20.19	19.90	20.20	20.10	20.32	20.30	20.00	20.01	20.16	20.22
2010	20.38	20.59	20.41	20.67	20.68	20.57	20.62	20.53	20.63	20.84	20.79	20.76	20.62
2011	20.52	20.50	20.15	19.98	20.04	19.99	20.37	20.46	20.73	21.00	20.57	20.89	20.43
Leisure and Hospitality													
2007	9.76	9.86	9.81	10.05	9.76	9.65	9.77	9.84	10.27	10.31	10.26	10.51	9.98
2008	10.42	10.51	10.49	10.56	10.34	10.43	10.49	10.62	10.58	10.67	10.70	10.86	10.56
2009	10.81	10.82	10.77	10.80	10.75	10.57	10.48	10.82	11.22	11.36	11.45	11.40	10.92
2010	11.45	11.37	11.43	11.48	11.54	11.41	11.44	11.62	11.46	11.41	11.43	11.48	11.46
2011	11.42	11.47	11.28	11.40	11.43	11.17	11.31	11.41	11.74	11.74	11.76	12.33	11.53

4. Average Weekly Earnings by Selected Industry: Nebraska, 2007–2011

(Dollars, not seasonally adjusted)

Industry and year	January	February	March	April	May	June	July	August	September	October	November	December	Annual average
Total Private													
2007	659.02	657.03	661.01	682.42	666.66	680.03	676.13	664.90	669.53	661.29	655.98	683.09	668.13
2008	661.01	665.64	678.68	655.93	662.26	672.41	658.35	664.95	660.67	668.30	681.05	674.02	666.78
2009	668.66	687.48	685.13	676.35	667.26	673.25	671.90	694.23	673.99	681.75	698.37	682.19	680.27
2010	693.17	696.58	701.30	711.22	725.50	715.50	714.47	730.45	719.27	718.24	712.35	707.10	712.08
2011	716.72	711.83	705.80	703.80	715.19	704.87	704.87	704.17	710.60	732.17	706.48	714.19	711.04
Goods-Producing													
2007	730.97	720.16	746.17	756.24	755.55	761.70	769.56	770.99	761.18	775.81	772.51	777.69	758.67
2008	734.52	731.77	763.28	744.81	745.97	765.49	758.45	782.91	753.38	765.68	780.35	789.62	759.58
2009	763.84	778.37	771.68	768.85	775.37	779.34	794.26	799.82	779.33	800.57	812.41	777.48	783.45
2010	800.00	796.80	800.00	796.28	799.11	806.55	805.05	813.70	799.98	815.42	811.51	795.96	803.39
2011	791.58	797.18	808.82	798.30	791.49	799.91	804.74	799.68	809.58	815.01	797.50	800.39	801.31
Mining, Logging, and Construction													
2007	712.09	685.41	734.56	728.11	749.34	776.67	800.46	783.30	759.91	791.86	804.53	745.37	758.25
2008	762.06	748.85	764.88	724.64	748.61	788.90	785.59	787.72	748.07	770.22	779.60	849.54	771.70
2009	784.77	813.89	775.87	774.15	783.17	785.70	815.58	819.35	794.69	820.82	837.25	753.69	797.11
2010	811.84	814.41	827.99	830.62	828.40	832.73	844.11	845.41	819.60	838.44	813.51	816.94	827.62
2011	798.12	811.50	814.59	799.54	787.55	807.14	818.91	802.11	815.27	844.60	814.76	824.67	811.47
Manufacturing													
2007	739.95	736.24	750.74	769.18	758.45	754.21	752.65	764.19	763.11	766.51	756.65	793.86	758.88
2008	723.25	725.08	761.97	753.24	743.54	754.40	745.14	779.79	755.96	762.40	779.95	759.32	753.60
2009	754.63	761.02	770.67	765.96	769.86	776.88	782.04	790.03	771.39	788.40	799.98	788.82	776.55
2010	793.86	791.09	787.23	780.12	783.27	792.64	785.45	799.28	790.28	803.40	810.50	787.52	792.15
2011	790.22	792.11	806.28	798.87	792.94	797.06	797.78	798.88	807.46	800.32	789.26	790.97	796.83
Trade, Transportation, and Utilities													
2007	511.59	513.24	509.95	524.52	525.11	569.92	531.90	520.25	530.24	507.06	516.29	569.65	527.64
2008	554.10	553.77	556.48	547.14	548.48	554.13	538.55	556.31	540.92	555.97	557.29	555.01	551.54
2009	547.00	552.32	554.91	556.34	554.88	557.38	554.05	584.02	560.90	566.72	574.59	581.01	561.98
2010	580.78	587.45	575.91	599.28	612.89	609.84	599.44	602.25	596.48	600.73	587.92	582.78	594.66
2011	581.21	578.76	582.08	580.93	599.07	619.57	608.56	613.34	631.46	634.75	610.37	616.85	604.83
Financial Activities													
2007	943.90	957.56	917.87	998.26	924.88	918.29	976.37	915.76	940.91	920.93	922.13	997.50	944.51
2008	964.70	1,009.74	1,016.10	960.68	964.01	1,018.78	951.92	924.16	931.25	926.55	977.54	928.29	964.45
2009	964.16	1,015.33	1,022.58	970.52	952.68	967.51	956.59	1,044.67	984.28	972.24	1,027.94	972.73	987.60
2010	966.97	966.61	968.94	980.62	1,032.51	983.19	977.78	1,031.42	971.58	969.36	958.64	962.35	980.39
2011	1,025.98	975.77	942.09	983.93	1,014.97	951.28	965.57	977.42	959.40	1,035.83	961.98	970.63	980.27
Professional and Business Services													
2007	751.92	758.26	778.36	792.03	787.20	797.88	799.19	820.44	824.44	795.10	787.53	813.52	792.51
2008	808.96	795.30	808.15	782.56	774.56	764.52	780.58	787.50	790.36	791.64	813.52	801.18	791.45
2009	783.69	841.44	830.97	820.75	777.47	788.97	783.13	807.12	792.21	807.14	829.28	805.99	805.79
2010	824.06	824.55	819.80	833.35	855.01	836.50	836.20	857.44	847.02	848.75	848.08	838.36	838.97
2011	845.28	832.48	825.60	827.66	840.42	820.76	814.89	824.90	831.09	876.12	859.56	878.20	840.09
Education and Health Services													
2007	707.76	710.28	728.00	748.61	719.00	713.79	709.26	683.52	696.18	702.76	676.92	698.60	707.74
2008	680.70	679.80	692.11	677.23	681.98	717.52	698.31	700.22	708.62	698.14	701.63	689.58	693.85
2009	686.07	669.70	660.15	662.23	658.69	654.48	649.23	658.37	651.63	644.00	650.33	641.09	657.09
2010	654.20	660.94	661.28	677.98	684.51	687.04	678.40	683.65	670.48	673.13	675.68	668.47	672.96
2011	658.69	660.10	650.85	649.35	659.32	653.67	655.91	646.54	655.07	669.90	654.13	658.04	655.89
Leisure and Hospitality													
2007	196.18	206.07	197.18	208.04	203.98	209.41	214.94	212.54	214.64	213.42	213.41	217.56	209.08
2008	213.61	216.51	216.09	218.59	217.14	232.59	229.73	233.64	224.30	231.54	231.12	230.23	224.74
2009	230.25	242.37	238.02	227.88	231.13	236.77	234.75	244.53	228.89	239.70	245.03	234.84	236.17
2010	241.60	247.87	251.46	251.41	260.80	256.73	258.54	263.77	257.85	257.87	254.89	252.56	254.80
2011	248.96	259.22	253.80	254.22	258.32	255.79	254.48	256.73	262.98	262.98	263.42	273.73	258.72

NEVADA
At a Glance

Population:
  2000 census: 1,998,250
  2010 census: 2,700,551
  2011 estimate: 2,723,322

Percent change in population:
  2000–2010: 35.1%
  2010–2011: 0.8%

Percent change in total nonfarm employment:
  2000–2010: 8.8%
  2010–2011: 0.7%

Industry with the largest growth in employment, 2000–2011 (thousands):
  Education and Health Services, 40.5

Industry with the largest decline or smallest growth in employment, 2000–2011 (thousands):
  Information, -6.6

Civilian labor force:
  2000: 1,062,845
  2010: 1,385,729
  2011: 1,385,872

Unemployment rate and rank among states (lowest to highest):
  2000: 4.5%, 38th
  2010: 13.7%, 51st
  2011: 13.5%, 51st

Over-the-year change in unemployment rates:
  2010–2011: -0.2%

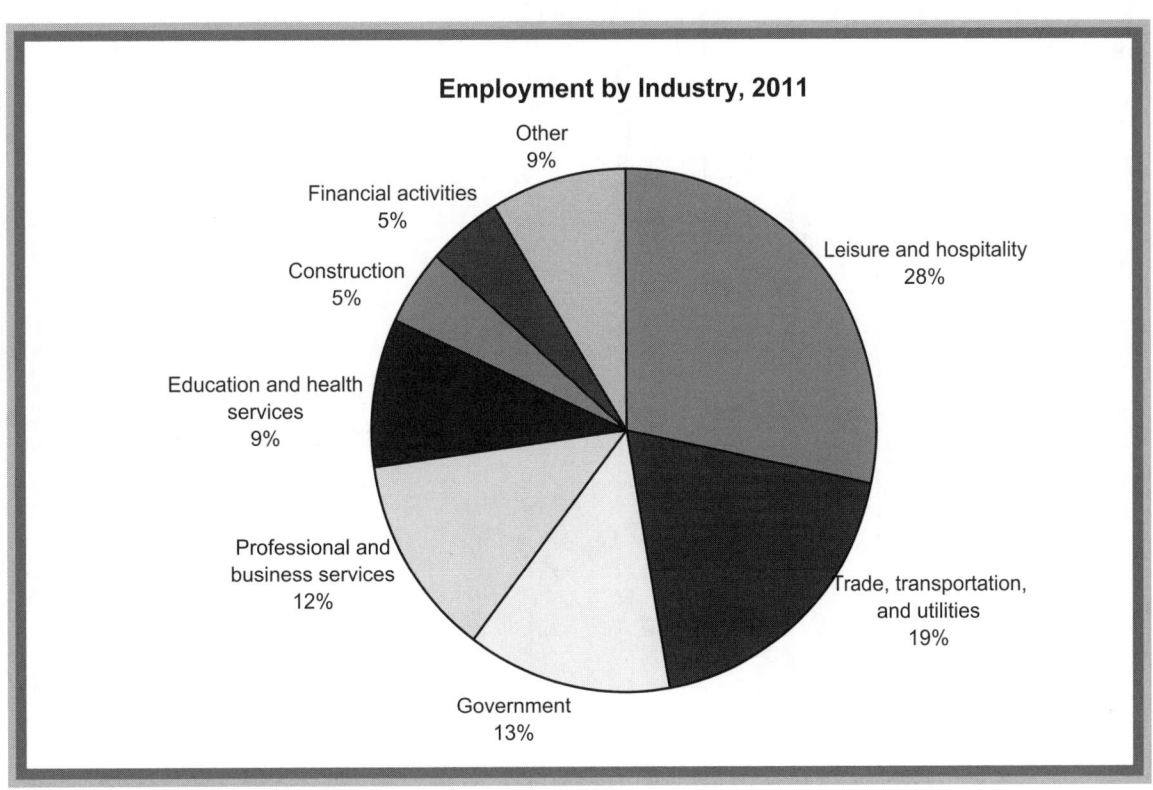

Employment by Industry, 2011

Other 9%
Financial activities 5%
Construction 5%
Education and health services 9%
Professional and business services 12%
Government 13%
Leisure and hospitality 28%
Trade, transportation, and utilities 19%

1. Employment by Industry: Nevada, Selected Years, 2000–2011

(Numbers in thousands, not seasonally adjusted)

Industry and year	January	February	March	April	May	June	July	August	September	October	November	December	Annual average
Total Nonfarm													
2000	991.6	997.5	1,007.4	1,014.8	1,028.0	1,027.7	1,024.8	1,038.3	1,043.6	1,046.7	1,051.1	1,051.3	1,026.9
2001	1,033.8	1,043.2	1,051.7	1,053.1	1,060.2	1,062.4	1,052.3	1,058.6	1,063.1	1,048.0	1,047.0	1,043.4	1,051.4
2002	1,019.1	1,025.9	1,037.4	1,046.2	1,055.6	1,053.6	1,049.2	1,057.5	1,063.6	1,070.5	1,072.2	1,072.7	1,052.0
2003	1,053.5	1,062.9	1,071.8	1,074.1	1,084.1	1,083.6	1,083.2	1,093.2	1,103.9	1,114.3	1,115.2	1,119.9	1,088.3
2004	1,101.5	1,108.3	1,122.0	1,140.2	1,148.3	1,153.7	1,153.6	1,158.8	1,174.0	1,189.2	1,189.4	1,193.0	1,152.7
2005	1,166.7	1,179.5	1,195.0	1,216.5	1,221.8	1,226.7	1,225.7	1,229.5	1,246.4	1,250.3	1,256.3	1,261.5	1,223.0
2006	1,239.8	1,255.0	1,268.3	1,276.3	1,286.3	1,291.2	1,279.8	1,282.9	1,292.6	1,292.0	1,294.8	1,295.6	1,279.6
2007	1,268.2	1,283.3	1,290.9	1,294.5	1,303.8	1,302.1	1,287.2	1,288.1	1,292.3	1,297.7	1,301.0	1,300.4	1,292.5
2008	1,269.1	1,272.9	1,275.8	1,281.0	1,286.2	1,279.5	1,265.2	1,260.6	1,261.6	1,252.5	1,238.1	1,221.1	1,263.6
2009	1,180.8	1,171.7	1,163.3	1,158.5	1,155.9	1,147.6	1,133.5	1,128.1	1,135.5	1,135.5	1,134.6	1,134.1	1,148.3
2010	1,104.1	1,105.5	1,108.7	1,120.6	1,128.0	1,123.6	1,116.2	1,113.6	1,115.4	1,123.3	1,125.0	1,124.0	1,117.3
2011	1,106.2	1,108.8	1,113.8	1,124.8	1,129.1	1,126.2	1,119.3	1,121.1	1,133.3	1,139.1	1,141.8	1,137.1	1,125.1
Total Private													
2000	874.0	876.6	884.7	891.7	900.8	910.5	910.2	920.1	922.2	920.9	925.1	925.4	905.2
2001	911.0	915.9	923.6	923.5	931.5	936.9	933.5	939.3	934.4	917.9	916.3	912.0	924.7
2002	893.2	895.0	906.4	915.4	923.9	925.3	927.5	935.5	933.5	935.3	936.4	936.5	922.0
2003	923.1	927.4	935.5	938.0	947.1	950.9	957.5	967.7	970.0	977.0	977.6	981.7	954.5
2004	968.8	971.3	982.7	1,000.9	1,007.9	1,018.2	1,024.7	1,030.4	1,035.2	1,046.0	1,045.8	1,049.1	1,015.1
2005	1,028.6	1,036.3	1,049.7	1,071.3	1,075.7	1,085.2	1,090.8	1,095.7	1,102.9	1,102.1	1,107.0	1,111.9	1,079.8
2006	1,096.6	1,105.9	1,118.3	1,125.0	1,134.5	1,144.0	1,139.6	1,143.2	1,143.0	1,136.9	1,138.5	1,139.2	1,130.4
2007	1,117.8	1,126.4	1,133.4	1,135.4	1,144.2	1,147.4	1,140.0	1,142.1	1,136.8	1,137.0	1,139.4	1,138.1	1,136.5
2008	1,112.8	1,110.6	1,112.6	1,116.7	1,121.2	1,119.7	1,111.7	1,108.3	1,100.7	1,086.8	1,072.2	1,055.6	1,102.4
2009	1,022.5	1,009.5	1,001.1	996.6	994.7	991.7	983.8	979.9	979.2	977.4	976.8	976.8	990.8
2010	951.8	948.5	950.9	962.7	966.8	969.9	968.6	968.8	963.5	969.8	971.1	970.2	963.6
2011	955.1	954.2	959.4	970.4	974.1	978.7	977.6	980.1	985.8	990.1	992.7	988.0	975.5
Goods-Producing													
2000	137.3	137.9	140.4	141.1	142.9	145.9	145.8	146.7	145.1	144.2	144.0	143.9	142.9
2001	139.4	140.2	142.0	143.0	145.5	148.4	148.4	150.0	148.2	147.0	144.5	140.9	144.8
2002	136.1	136.6	139.0	141.9	144.1	144.7	147.1	149.6	148.2	148.2	147.0	145.6	144.0
2003	142.4	144.0	146.7	148.0	150.9	153.3	155.3	157.9	157.9	160.3	158.9	159.0	152.9
2004	155.8	158.8	161.6	168.2	170.8	174.7	178.5	180.6	182.5	185.4	183.8	183.9	173.7
2005	176.8	181.1	185.5	190.0	191.0	193.7	197.8	199.7	201.9	201.2	200.5	201.1	193.4
2006	196.3	200.1	202.5	205.6	208.7	211.5	210.0	210.5	208.5	204.4	201.3	198.9	204.9
2007	191.9	193.5	196.9	197.1	200.2	200.8	199.7	200.5	197.1	193.9	191.1	187.8	195.9
2008	179.8	179.9	179.3	179.7	181.6	182.5	182.8	181.2	177.6	173.1	165.6	158.5	176.8
2009	149.4	144.9	141.6	138.5	134.4	133.2	131.3	129.7	127.6	126.1	122.4	117.3	133.0
2010	108.6	107.1	107.1	109.7	110.6	111.5	111.3	111.3	109.6	110.1	109.0	107.1	109.4
2011	102.7	102.7	101.3	102.7	103.6	105.1	105.9	106.9	107.8	105.8	107.0	104.3	104.7
Mining and Logging													
2000	10.9	11.2	11.2	10.6	10.7	10.8	10.8	10.7	10.6	10.6	10.5	10.4	10.8
2001	9.9	9.9	9.8	9.6	9.8	9.7	9.7	9.6	9.4	9.4	9.3	9.2	9.6
2002	9.0	8.9	8.8	8.8	8.8	8.9	8.9	8.9	8.8	8.8	8.6	8.7	8.8
2003	8.2	8.6	8.7	8.6	8.7	8.9	9.1	9.1	8.9	9.1	9.1	9.2	8.9
2004	9.0	9.1	9.2	9.2	9.3	9.5	9.9	10.0	10.0	9.9	9.8	9.8	9.6
2005	9.8	9.8	10.1	10.5	10.4	10.8	11.1	11.2	11.1	11.2	11.0	11.0	10.7
2006	11.0	10.9	11.1	11.3	11.5	11.7	11.9	12.0	11.9	11.8	11.8	11.8	11.6
2007	11.8	11.7	11.9	11.9	12.0	12.3	12.3	12.4	12.1	11.9	12.0	11.9	12.0
2008	11.9	11.9	11.9	11.9	12.0	12.2	12.5	12.6	12.5	12.2	12.2	12.0	12.2
2009	11.6	11.5	11.5	11.4	11.5	11.9	11.9	11.9	11.7	11.7	11.6	11.6	11.7
2010	11.5	11.5	11.7	11.7	12.0	12.4	12.7	12.7	12.4	12.4	12.7	12.8	12.2
2011	12.8	13.0	13.2	13.4	13.7	14.3	14.3	14.5	14.4	14.6	14.7	14.8	14.0
Construction													
2000	84.7	84.8	87.0	88.4	89.9	92.3	92.1	93.0	91.5	90.1	89.8	89.5	89.4
2001	85.7	86.4	88.0	89.3	91.5	94.0	94.2	95.9	94.7	94.0	92.0	88.7	91.2
2002	85.0	85.6	88.1	90.8	92.6	92.9	94.8	97.3	96.1	95.7	94.7	93.3	92.2
2003	91.2	92.4	94.9	96.3	98.7	100.8	102.3	104.6	105.0	106.8	105.4	105.4	100.3
2004	102.8	105.2	107.5	113.6	115.6	118.9	122.2	123.9	126.1	128.8	127.1	127.3	118.3
2005	120.2	124.3	128.1	131.8	132.9	134.8	138.4	140.3	142.2	141.4	141.0	141.5	134.7
2006	136.9	140.2	141.9	144.2	146.7	148.8	146.9	147.3	145.3	141.9	138.8	136.3	142.9
2007	130.3	132.0	134.7	134.7	137.5	137.6	136.7	137.5	134.6	132.1	129.4	126.7	133.7
2008	118.9	119.2	118.7	119.0	120.6	121.2	121.3	119.8	117.0	113.3	107.1	101.3	116.5
2009	94.4	91.2	88.6	86.2	82.7	81.5	79.8	78.5	76.7	75.4	71.9	67.0	81.2
2010	59.3	57.9	57.7	60.0	60.6	60.9	60.5	60.6	59.2	59.9	58.5	56.4	59.3
2011	52.4	52.1	50.2	51.3	51.8	52.5	53.2	54.1	55.2	53.0	54.3	51.7	52.7
Manufacturing													
2000	41.7	41.9	42.2	42.1	42.3	42.8	42.9	43.0	43.0	43.5	43.7	44.0	42.8
2001	43.8	43.9	44.2	44.1	44.2	44.7	44.5	44.5	44.1	43.6	43.2	43.0	44.0
2002	42.1	42.1	42.1	42.3	42.7	42.9	43.4	43.4	43.3	43.7	43.7	43.6	42.9
2003	43.0	43.0	43.1	43.1	43.5	43.6	43.9	44.2	44.0	44.4	44.4	44.4	43.7
2004	44.0	44.5	44.9	45.4	45.9	46.3	46.4	46.7	46.4	46.7	46.9	46.8	45.9
2005	46.8	47.0	47.3	47.7	47.7	48.1	48.3	48.2	48.6	48.6	48.5	48.6	48.0
2006	48.4	49.0	49.5	50.1	50.5	51.0	51.2	51.2	51.3	50.7	50.7	50.8	50.4
2007	49.8	49.8	50.3	50.5	50.7	50.9	50.7	50.6	50.4	49.9	49.7	49.2	50.2
2008	49.0	48.8	48.7	48.8	49.0	49.1	49.0	48.8	48.1	47.6	46.3	45.2	48.2
2009	43.4	42.2	41.5	40.9	40.2	39.8	39.6	39.3	39.2	39.0	38.9	38.7	40.2
2010	37.8	37.7	37.7	38.0	38.0	38.2	38.1	38.0	38.0	37.8	37.8	37.9	37.9
2011	37.5	37.6	37.9	38.0	38.1	38.3	38.4	38.3	38.2	38.2	38.0	37.8	38.0

1. Employment by Industry: Nevada, Selected Years, 2000–2011—*Continued*

(Numbers in thousands, not seasonally adjusted)

Industry and year	January	February	March	April	May	June	July	August	September	October	November	December	Annual average
Service-Providing													
2000	854.3	859.6	867.0	873.7	885.1	881.8	879.0	891.6	898.5	902.5	907.1	907.4	884.0
2001	894.4	903.0	909.7	910.1	914.7	914.0	903.9	908.6	914.9	901.0	902.5	902.5	906.6
2002	883.0	889.3	898.4	904.3	911.5	908.9	902.1	907.9	915.4	922.3	925.2	927.1	908.0
2003	911.1	918.9	925.1	926.1	933.2	930.3	927.9	935.3	946.0	954.0	956.3	960.9	935.4
2004	945.7	949.5	960.4	972.0	977.5	979.0	975.1	978.2	991.5	1,003.8	1,005.6	1,009.1	979.0
2005	989.9	998.4	1,009.5	1,026.5	1,030.8	1,033.0	1,027.9	1,029.8	1,044.5	1,049.1	1,055.8	1,060.4	1,029.6
2006	1,043.5	1,054.9	1,065.8	1,070.7	1,077.6	1,079.7	1,069.8	1,072.4	1,084.1	1,087.6	1,093.5	1,096.7	1,074.7
2007	1,076.3	1,089.8	1,094.0	1,097.4	1,103.6	1,101.3	1,087.5	1,087.6	1,095.2	1,103.8	1,109.9	1,112.6	1,096.6
2008	1,089.3	1,093.0	1,096.5	1,101.3	1,104.6	1,097.0	1,082.4	1,079.4	1,084.0	1,079.4	1,072.5	1,062.6	1,086.8
2009	1,031.4	1,026.8	1,021.7	1,020.0	1,021.5	1,014.4	1,002.2	998.4	1,007.9	1,009.4	1,012.2	1,016.8	1,015.2
2010	995.5	998.4	1,001.6	1,010.9	1,017.4	1,012.1	1,004.9	1,002.3	1,005.8	1,013.2	1,016.0	1,016.9	1,007.9
2011	1,003.5	1,006.1	1,012.5	1,022.1	1,025.5	1,021.1	1,013.4	1,014.2	1,025.5	1,033.3	1,034.8	1,032.8	1,020.4
Trade, Transportation, and Utilities													
2000	179.4	178.7	178.9	180.8	181.9	183.4	184.1	186.6	188.2	189.6	193.7	197.1	185.2
2001	188.2	186.5	186.8	188.1	189.6	191.0	191.3	191.9	191.7	191.8	193.8	194.9	190.5
2002	187.5	185.6	186.4	188.9	190.1	190.7	191.4	191.4	192.0	194.6	197.0	199.3	191.2
2003	190.2	189.7	191.3	190.5	191.8	193.0	193.7	195.9	197.6	201.3	204.8	207.9	195.6
2004	197.9	197.5	199.1	200.7	202.0	204.2	204.7	205.3	205.8	209.2	213.1	215.6	204.6
2005	207.6	207.5	208.9	211.0	211.9	213.5	215.1	215.8	217.9	219.4	223.6	226.2	214.9
2006	220.4	220.2	222.6	223.0	224.2	225.4	225.1	226.1	226.9	228.6	233.1	235.9	226.0
2007	228.6	227.5	228.8	229.6	231.1	232.1	231.6	232.8	232.9	234.1	239.7	242.6	232.6
2008	233.7	231.3	231.8	231.3	231.3	231.6	232.2	232.3	231.1	230.2	231.2	230.1	231.5
2009	219.2	215.0	213.6	211.8	211.8	212.1	211.5	211.0	211.4	212.2	216.0	217.0	213.6
2010	208.6	206.3	206.5	207.1	208.2	209.1	209.9	210.3	209.8	211.8	216.0	217.5	210.1
2011	209.1	207.5	208.0	209.5	210.4	211.1	211.9	212.2	213.4	214.8	219.3	219.9	212.3
Wholesale Trade													
2000	32.6	32.8	33.1	33.4	33.8	34.1	34.2	34.4	34.5	34.5	35.0	35.3	34.0
2001	34.5	34.7	34.8	35.0	35.2	35.5	35.3	35.3	35.2	35.1	34.9	34.9	35.0
2002	34.4	34.6	35.0	35.0	35.0	35.1	34.9	34.9	34.7	34.7	34.6	34.7	34.8
2003	34.0	34.2	34.2	34.1	34.1	34.2	34.4	34.3	34.3	34.6	34.6	34.7	34.3
2004	34.4	34.5	34.7	34.9	35.1	35.4	35.9	35.8	35.9	36.2	36.1	36.3	35.4
2005	36.1	36.5	36.7	37.0	37.2	37.4	37.6	37.6	37.8	37.7	37.8	38.0	37.3
2006	37.8	38.1	38.4	38.5	38.7	38.9	38.9	39.0	39.1	39.1	39.1	39.3	38.7
2007	38.9	39.1	39.3	39.3	39.4	39.6	39.5	39.6	39.5	39.4	39.4	39.4	39.4
2008	39.0	39.1	39.1	39.1	39.2	39.2	39.2	39.1	38.9	38.5	37.9	37.4	38.8
2009	36.5	36.0	35.6	35.0	34.7	34.4	34.2	34.0	33.7	33.6	33.4	33.3	34.5
2010	32.7	32.6	32.7	32.9	33.1	33.1	33.0	33.0	32.9	33.1	32.9	33.0	32.9
2011	32.5	32.6	32.7	32.7	32.8	32.9	32.9	32.9	33.0	33.1	32.8	33.6	32.9
Retail Trade													
2000	106.8	105.8	105.3	106.4	107.3	108.0	108.3	110.2	111.3	112.0	115.3	118.3	109.6
2001	112.3	110.4	110.3	111.0	111.9	113.0	113.3	114.0	114.1	114.5	117.1	118.3	113.4
2002	112.3	110.6	111.1	112.5	113.7	114.4	114.3	114.1	114.9	117.0	120.7	123.2	114.9
2003	115.4	114.5	115.8	115.2	116.4	117.4	118.0	120.0	121.2	123.9	127.3	129.9	119.6
2004	120.9	120.4	121.4	122.9	123.9	125.5	125.1	125.7	126.1	128.2	132.2	134.6	125.6
2005	127.3	126.5	127.3	128.1	128.5	129.5	130.8	131.2	132.5	134.0	137.5	139.3	131.0
2006	134.1	133.6	135.2	135.2	135.8	136.1	135.7	136.2	136.6	138.1	141.7	143.5	136.8
2007	137.5	136.3	137.0	137.8	138.8	139.1	139.2	139.7	139.5	140.1	145.0	147.4	139.8
2008	140.4	138.3	138.7	138.2	137.8	138.1	138.3	138.3	137.6	137.3	139.0	138.7	138.4
2009	130.9	127.7	126.9	125.9	126.2	126.7	126.6	126.4	127.2	128.2	132.0	133.0	128.1
2010	126.1	124.1	124.3	124.8	125.4	126.0	126.7	127.1	126.8	128.5	132.7	133.5	127.2
2011	126.8	125.1	125.4	126.2	127.0	127.3	128.0	128.3	128.5	129.0	132.8	132.6	128.1
Transportation and Utilities													
2000	40.0	40.1	40.5	41.0	40.8	41.3	41.6	42.0	42.4	43.1	43.4	43.5	41.6
2001	41.4	41.4	41.7	42.1	42.5	42.5	42.7	42.6	42.4	42.2	41.8	41.7	42.1
2002	40.8	40.4	40.3	41.4	41.4	41.3	42.2	42.4	42.4	42.9	41.7	41.4	41.6
2003	40.8	41.0	41.3	41.2	41.3	41.4	41.3	41.6	42.1	42.8	42.9	43.3	41.8
2004	42.6	42.6	43.0	42.9	43.0	43.3	43.7	43.8	43.8	44.8	44.8	44.7	43.6
2005	44.2	44.5	44.9	45.9	46.2	46.6	46.7	47.0	47.6	47.7	48.3	48.9	46.5
2006	48.5	48.5	49.0	49.3	49.7	50.4	50.5	50.9	51.2	51.4	52.3	53.1	50.4
2007	52.2	52.1	52.5	52.5	52.9	53.4	52.9	53.5	53.9	54.6	55.3	55.8	53.5
2008	54.3	53.9	54.0	54.0	54.3	54.3	54.7	54.9	54.6	54.4	54.3	54.0	54.3
2009	51.8	51.3	51.1	50.9	50.9	51.0	50.7	50.6	50.5	50.4	50.6	50.7	50.9
2010	49.8	49.6	49.5	49.4	49.7	50.0	50.2	50.2	50.1	50.2	50.4	51.0	50.0
2011	49.8	49.8	49.9	50.6	50.6	50.9	51.0	51.0	51.9	52.7	53.7	53.7	51.3
Information													
2000	19.1	18.6	19.0	18.7	19.5	19.4	19.1	19.5	19.3	19.7	19.8	19.2	19.2
2001	19.9	21.5	21.3	19.8	19.7	19.0	18.0	17.7	17.3	17.7	18.0	17.6	19.0
2002	17.5	17.3	17.1	17.1	17.3	16.9	16.7	16.8	16.7	16.4	16.5	16.5	16.9
2003	16.1	16.0	15.8	15.8	15.9	15.8	15.4	15.2	15.1	15.0	15.1	15.2	15.5
2004	14.9	14.6	14.5	15.7	15.0	14.9	14.8	14.6	14.5	14.8	14.8	14.6	14.8
2005	15.0	14.4	14.4	15.0	15.4	14.7	14.5	14.4	14.2	14.7	14.6	14.5	14.7
2006	14.8	15.2	14.7	15.1	15.2	15.2	15.6	15.7	15.2	15.2	15.1	15.0	15.2
2007	15.3	15.8	15.6	15.7	16.0	15.8	15.2	15.6	15.2	15.5	15.6	15.3	15.6
2008	15.2	15.2	15.1	15.4	15.9	15.2	14.8	14.8	14.9	14.9	14.4	14.1	15.0
2009	13.5	13.6	13.6	13.0	13.2	13.1	13.1	13.2	12.8	12.8	12.9	12.9	13.1
2010	12.3	12.4	12.3	12.6	12.6	12.5	12.8	12.5	12.3	12.4	12.6	12.5	12.5
2011	12.4	12.3	12.4	12.6	12.7	12.7	12.7	12.6	12.5	12.6	12.6	12.6	12.6

1. Employment by Industry: Nevada, Selected Years, 2000–2011—*Continued*

(Numbers in thousands, not seasonally adjusted)

Industry and year	January	February	March	April	May	June	July	August	September	October	November	December	Annual average
Financial Activities													
2000	51.0	51.2	51.6	51.8	52.1	52.7	53.1	53.3	53.2	53.0	53.6	54.1	52.6
2001	53.9	54.3	54.8	54.7	54.8	55.4	55.3	55.8	55.9	55.4	55.2	55.8	55.1
2002	54.4	55.1	55.4	55.5	55.6	55.8	55.9	56.3	56.0	56.5	57.0	57.2	55.9
2003	56.6	56.9	57.0	57.6	58.4	58.5	59.2	59.3	59.6	59.7	59.6	60.0	58.5
2004	59.5	59.7	60.1	60.5	60.7	61.4	62.0	62.2	62.3	63.1	63.2	64.0	61.6
2005	63.0	63.0	63.6	63.7	64.0	64.5	64.3	64.8	65.0	64.8	65.0	65.3	64.3
2006	64.2	64.2	64.8	64.8	65.2	65.7	65.7	65.8	66.1	65.5	65.8	66.2	65.3
2007	65.0	65.1	65.5	65.0	65.3	65.4	64.7	64.5	64.4	63.9	63.4	63.5	64.6
2008	62.2	62.3	62.4	62.2	62.0	61.9	61.5	61.0	60.8	60.5	59.9	59.3	61.3
2009	57.3	57.0	56.6	56.3	55.8	55.8	54.7	54.8	54.2	54.2	53.8	53.6	55.3
2010	52.9	52.5	52.5	53.3	53.0	52.9	53.0	52.7	52.5	53.1	52.8	53.0	52.9
2011	52.4	52.1	52.1	52.4	52.2	52.3	52.0	51.6	51.4	51.7	51.4	52.4	52.0
Professional and Business Services													
2000	104.5	105.4	106.3	108.3	110.2	111.2	108.7	111.5	115.1	114.4	115.0	113.3	110.3
2001	113.4	115.1	116.1	114.3	115.1	114.8	111.8	113.9	112.6	111.0	111.6	109.6	113.3
2002	110.7	110.7	112.6	112.5	113.5	112.6	112.5	116.3	116.8	116.5	117.5	116.2	114.0
2003	117.4	117.8	118.1	118.7	119.2	118.2	120.2	123.8	124.2	126.7	126.4	126.3	121.4
2004	128.0	126.4	127.8	130.5	131.4	132.3	132.7	134.9	136.2	140.9	139.1	138.2	133.2
2005	139.4	140.1	141.9	144.4	144.4	145.4	145.5	147.8	148.9	150.9	153.4	154.3	146.4
2006	153.6	154.8	157.3	157.8	158.8	159.8	157.4	159.0	158.6	158.9	159.8	159.1	157.9
2007	158.4	161.3	159.6	160.3	160.4	159.7	156.9	158.5	156.8	159.8	159.2	157.4	159.0
2008	156.5	155.2	155.4	156.0	156.8	154.4	150.7	150.7	151.0	147.6	146.1	143.3	152.0
2009	141.7	139.3	137.1	134.9	135.3	134.1	130.7	131.4	133.8	133.9	136.1	136.6	135.4
2010	134.8	133.2	133.4	135.3	135.8	136.2	134.8	137.0	134.9	137.6	138.0	137.9	135.7
2011	138.6	137.0	137.4	138.8	138.5	139.3	136.9	138.8	141.5	142.0	141.4	139.8	139.2
Education and Health Services													
2000	60.6	61.4	62.3	62.1	62.3	63.0	62.9	63.2	64.1	64.8	65.3	66.0	63.2
2001	66.1	66.7	67.4	67.2	67.9	68.3	67.8	68.7	69.0	69.2	69.6	70.0	68.2
2002	69.1	70.0	71.7	72.5	73.1	73.0	72.6	73.3	73.6	74.4	74.8	75.0	72.8
2003	74.5	75.4	75.7	75.9	76.3	76.1	75.9	76.4	77.3	77.6	78.3	78.5	76.5
2004	78.2	79.0	79.9	80.4	80.3	80.4	81.0	81.1	82.5	82.8	83.1	83.6	81.0
2005	82.9	83.9	84.7	85.5	85.6	85.8	85.2	85.2	85.8	85.6	86.1	86.9	85.3
2006	86.0	87.1	87.8	87.7	88.1	88.7	87.8	88.4	89.6	90.3	91.0	91.6	88.7
2007	90.7	92.2	92.6	92.2	92.9	92.9	92.6	92.9	93.4	94.2	94.5	94.2	92.9
2008	94.2	95.3	95.6	96.8	97.0	96.9	96.7	96.8	97.1	97.9	98.2	98.2	96.7
2009	97.1	97.4	97.4	97.8	98.1	98.2	98.3	98.5	98.5	100.3	100.2	100.2	98.5
2010	99.6	99.9	100.3	101.3	101.4	101.0	100.6	100.6	100.8	102.3	102.6	102.9	101.1
2011	102.2	103.2	103.8	103.6	103.6	103.6	103.4	102.6	104.1	105.4	105.2	104.1	103.7
Leisure and Hospitality													
2000	296.2	297.2	299.5	302.1	304.8	307.4	309.0	311.7	309.6	307.8	306.4	304.4	304.7
2001	302.2	303.4	306.5	307.1	309.1	309.5	311.0	311.2	309.6	296.3	294.5	294.0	304.5
2002	288.9	290.3	294.3	297.1	300.0	301.1	301.6	302.0	300.8	299.4	297.4	297.6	297.5
2003	296.5	298.0	300.9	301.8	304.6	305.3	307.1	308.4	307.6	305.8	303.7	303.7	303.6
2004	303.1	303.2	306.5	311.4	313.7	315.5	317.3	318.0	317.6	315.4	314.7	315.1	312.6
2005	311.5	313.6	317.5	328.5	329.9	333.5	334.2	333.6	334.6	331.0	329.1	328.5	327.1
2006	327.4	330.0	333.6	336.0	338.8	341.8	342.0	341.4	341.7	337.9	336.4	336.6	337.0
2007	332.7	335.7	338.4	339.4	341.8	343.6	342.3	340.2	340.0	338.9	339.0	340.1	339.3
2008	334.6	334.9	336.2	338.7	339.4	340.0	336.1	334.4	331.6	326.1	321.0	317.0	332.5
2009	310.6	308.9	307.6	310.4	311.9	310.9	310.1	307.2	306.9	304.5	302.2	306.2	308.1
2010	302.4	304.4	305.8	310.4	312.1	313.6	312.8	311.2	310.6	309.5	307.8	307.3	309.0
2011	306.1	307.6	312.4	318.0	320.1	321.4	320.4	320.8	320.6	323.5	321.7	321.0	317.8
Other Services													
2000	25.9	26.2	26.7	26.8	27.1	27.5	27.5	27.6	27.6	27.4	27.3	27.4	27.1
2001	27.9	28.2	28.7	29.3	29.8	30.5	29.9	30.1	30.1	29.5	29.1	29.2	29.4
2002	29.0	29.4	29.9	29.9	30.2	30.5	29.7	29.8	29.4	29.3	29.2	29.1	29.6
2003	29.4	29.6	30.0	29.7	30.0	30.7	30.7	30.8	30.7	30.6	30.8	31.1	30.3
2004	31.4	32.1	33.2	33.5	34.0	34.8	33.7	33.7	33.8	34.4	34.0	34.1	33.6
2005	32.4	32.7	33.2	33.2	33.5	34.1	34.2	34.4	34.6	34.5	34.7	35.1	33.9
2006	33.9	34.3	35.0	35.0	35.5	35.9	36.0	36.3	36.4	36.1	36.0	35.9	35.5
2007	35.2	35.3	36.0	36.1	36.5	37.1	37.0	37.1	37.0	36.7	36.9	37.2	36.5
2008	36.6	36.5	36.8	36.6	37.2	37.2	36.9	37.1	37.0	36.5	35.8	35.1	36.6
2009	33.7	33.4	33.6	33.9	34.2	34.3	34.1	34.1	34.0	33.4	33.2	33.0	33.7
2010	32.6	32.7	33.0	33.0	33.1	33.1	33.4	33.2	33.0	33.0	32.3	32.0	32.9
2011	31.6	31.8	32.0	32.8	33.0	33.2	34.4	34.6	34.5	34.3	34.1	33.9	33.4
Government													
2000	117.6	120.9	122.7	123.1	127.2	117.2	114.6	118.2	121.4	125.8	126.0	125.9	121.7
2001	122.8	127.3	128.1	129.6	128.7	125.5	118.8	119.3	128.7	130.1	130.7	131.4	126.8
2002	125.9	130.9	131.0	130.8	131.7	128.3	121.7	122.0	130.1	135.2	135.8	136.2	130.0
2003	130.4	135.5	136.3	136.1	137.0	132.7	125.7	125.5	133.9	137.3	137.6	138.2	133.9
2004	132.7	137.0	139.3	139.3	140.4	135.5	128.9	128.4	138.8	143.2	143.6	143.9	137.6
2005	138.1	143.2	145.3	145.2	146.1	141.5	134.9	133.8	143.5	148.2	149.3	149.6	143.2
2006	143.2	149.1	150.0	151.3	151.8	147.2	140.2	139.7	149.6	155.1	156.3	156.4	149.2
2007	150.4	156.9	157.5	159.1	159.6	154.7	147.2	146.0	155.5	160.7	161.6	162.3	156.0
2008	156.3	162.3	163.2	164.3	165.0	159.8	153.5	152.3	160.9	165.7	165.9	165.5	161.2
2009	158.3	162.2	162.2	161.9	161.2	155.9	149.7	148.2	156.3	158.1	157.8	157.3	157.4
2010	152.3	157.0	157.8	157.9	161.2	153.7	147.6	144.8	151.9	153.5	153.9	153.8	153.8
2011	151.1	154.6	154.4	154.4	155.0	147.5	141.7	141.0	147.5	149.0	149.1	149.1	149.5

2. Average Weekly Hours by Selected Industry: Nevada, 2007–2011

(Not seasonally adjusted)

Industry and year	January	February	March	April	May	June	July	August	September	October	November	December	Annual average
Total Private													
2007	37.6	37.5	37.4	37.5	37.4	37.5	37.6	36.9	37.0	36.9	36.9	37.0	37.3
2008	36.9	37.1	37.1	37.0	37.1	37.3	37.1	37.2	37.1	37.0	36.7	36.5	37.0
2009	36.4	36.3	36.3	36.2	36.1	35.8	35.8	35.7	35.7	35.2	35.3	35.1	35.8
2010	34.9	34.8	34.7	34.6	34.6	34.5	34.5	34.4	34.3	34.2	34.3	34.6	34.5
2011	34.6	34.5	34.6	34.7	34.8	34.3	34.1	34.5	34.4	34.7	34.0	33.5	34.4
Goods-Producing													
2007	40.0	40.1	40.0	39.8	40.0	40.3	40.2	40.1	40.3	40.3	40.1	40.2	40.1
2008	39.9	39.9	40.0	40.1	40.3	40.4	40.2	40.4	40.2	40.1	37.9	37.8	39.8
2009	38.0	37.7	37.7	37.5	37.8	37.7	37.7	37.7	37.3	36.8	36.9	37.0	37.5
2010	36.6	36.3	36.2	36.2	36.2	36.2	36.2	36.2	36.1	36.0	36.1	36.0	36.2
2011	35.7	35.8	36.4	36.6	36.6	36.8	37.2	37.8	37.8	39.0	36.4	36.7	36.9
Construction													
2007	37.8	37.9	37.7	37.4	37.6	37.9	37.6	37.6	37.7	37.6	37.4	37.5	37.6
2008	37.3	37.2	37.5	37.5	37.7	37.9	37.7	37.5	37.3	37.1	36.9	36.7	37.4
2009	36.7	36.4	36.5	36.2	36.4	36.1	35.9	36.0	35.4	35.2	34.8	34.9	35.9
2010	34.7	34.5	34.3	34.3	34.4	34.3	34.1	34.2	34.0	33.8	33.6	33.4	34.1
2011	33.2	33.3	33.9	34.8	34.7	35.9	36.0	36.3	35.6	35.7	34.8	35.2	35.0
Trade, Transportation, and Utilities													
2007	37.7	37.8	37.9	38.0	38.0	38.1	38.1	38.2	38.2	38.0	38.0	38.1	38.0
2008	37.9	37.9	37.8	37.5	37.6	37.8	37.6	37.7	37.6	37.3	37.5	37.6	37.7
2009	37.2	37.1	37.1	37.1	37.0	36.9	36.8	36.7	37.1	36.5	36.6	36.8	36.9
2010	36.1	36.0	35.7	35.7	35.9	35.9	35.9	35.9	36.0	35.7	35.8	36.1	35.9
2011	35.5	35.3	34.7	35.9	35.4	34.9	34.6	35.3	35.2	34.6	34.4	34.3	35.0
Financial Activities													
2007	38.4	38.2	38.3	38.5	38.4	38.4	38.5	38.2	38.1	38.1	38.2	38.4	38.3
2008	38.2	38.2	38.1	38.0	38.1	38.2	37.9	38.0	37.9	37.9	37.8	37.3	38.0
2009	37.2	37.3	37.2	37.0	37.0	36.9	37.1	36.6	37.5	37.3	36.9	37.1	37.1
2010	37.3	37.2	37.0	37.0	37.1	36.9	36.8	36.7	36.8	36.7	36.5	36.5	36.9
2011	36.6	36.5	36.8	36.4	38.2	37.8	37.3	37.7	38.5	38.7	37.3	36.3	37.3
Professional and Business Services													
2007	37.7	37.9	37.4	37.6	37.5	37.2	37.3	37.0	37.1	37.3	37.4	37.5	37.4
2008	37.6	37.5	37.6	37.3	37.3	37.0	36.9	37.1	37.0	37.2	36.0	35.8	37.0
2009	35.9	35.7	35.7	35.5	35.4	35.0	34.7	34.7	33.5	33.2	33.7	33.3	34.7
2010	32.8	32.6	32.6	32.4	32.2	32.2	32.0	32.0	32.1	32.2	32.4	32.6	32.3
2011	32.4	32.2	33.0	32.9	33.0	32.2	32.3	33.5	32.9	34.0	33.4	33.7	33.0
Leisure and Hospitality													
2007	35.2	34.9	35.3	35.1	34.8	35.1	35.3	35.1	34.8	34.6	34.5	34.6	34.9
2008	34.5	34.3	34.1	34.1	34.2	34.6	34.4	34.5	34.3	34.2	34.5	34.2	34.3
2009	34.2	34.3	34.3	34.3	34.2	34.0	34.0	34.0	33.7	33.2	33.3	32.5	33.8
2010	32.5	32.5	32.3	32.3	32.3	32.2	32.2	32.2	32.1	31.8	31.7	31.4	32.1
2011	31.5	31.6	31.5	31.3	31.4	30.9	30.7	31.0	31.1	31.4	30.9	29.5	31.1

3. Average Hourly Earnings by Selected Industry: Nevada, 2007–2011

(Dollars, not seasonally adjusted)

Industry and year	January	February	March	April	May	June	July	August	September	October	November	December	Annual average
Total Private													
2007	19.36	19.59	19.72	19.48	19.14	19.59	19.63	19.83	19.89	19.84	19.80	19.85	19.64
2008	19.69	19.72	19.70	19.75	19.69	19.82	19.81	19.80	19.79	19.76	19.71	19.72	19.75
2009	19.76	19.74	19.71	19.67	19.65	19.66	19.57	19.56	19.37	19.36	19.34	19.30	19.56
2010	19.20	19.16	19.14	19.14	19.14	19.13	19.12	19.12	19.10	19.09	19.09	19.11	19.13
2011	19.11	19.10	19.12	19.28	19.57	19.23	19.44	19.56	19.50	19.62	19.35	19.36	19.36
Goods-Producing													
2007	23.31	23.47	23.92	24.05	23.64	24.03	24.18	24.27	24.28	24.27	24.28	24.28	24.00
2008	24.23	24.25	24.23	24.18	24.15	24.28	24.31	24.26	24.25	24.25	24.29	24.34	24.25
2009	24.37	24.40	24.39	24.41	24.39	24.49	24.50	24.47	23.94	23.99	24.00	23.62	24.26
2010	23.58	23.55	23.57	23.58	23.59	23.56	23.57	23.55	23.59	23.60	23.61	23.62	23.58
2011	23.59	23.60	23.80	24.81	24.64	24.78	25.20	25.32	25.15	25.38	24.70	23.99	24.60
Construction													
2007	24.54	25.53	25.21	25.15	24.96	25.52	25.67	25.70	25.84	25.80	25.84	25.85	25.47
2008	25.69	25.73	25.77	25.70	25.78	25.85	25.87	25.82	25.82	25.81	25.86	25.88	25.80
2009	25.94	25.99	25.96	25.98	25.99	26.08	26.05	26.01	25.50	25.79	25.78	24.92	25.86
2010	24.88	24.84	24.83	24.83	24.79	24.79	24.77	24.74	24.78	24.77	24.76	24.73	24.79
2011	24.70	24.71	24.55	26.00	25.78	25.52	26.28	26.40	25.17	25.61	25.48	26.10	25.54
Trade, Transportation, and Utilities													
2007	17.97	17.99	17.90	17.54	17.07	17.71	17.86	17.89	17.87	17.63	17.61	17.62	17.72
2008	17.56	17.55	17.61	17.66	17.42	17.62	17.55	17.55	17.60	17.54	17.59	17.57	17.57
2009	17.67	17.68	17.67	17.65	17.69	17.73	17.69	17.64	17.48	17.35	17.36	17.38	17.58
2010	17.35	17.33	17.31	17.30	17.31	17.28	17.25	17.21	17.17	17.13	17.14	17.16	17.24
2011	17.13	17.11	17.19	17.24	17.38	16.84	17.44	17.21	17.11	17.19	17.09	17.15	17.17
Financial Activities													
2007	24.22	24.42	24.41	24.16	23.61	24.04	23.75	23.71	24.02	23.73	23.78	23.88	23.98
2008	23.85	23.86	23.83	23.81	23.81	23.83	23.75	23.78	23.77	23.75	23.75	23.72	23.79
2009	23.45	23.43	23.41	23.39	23.39	23.39	23.47	23.46	22.24	22.10	22.14	22.11	23.01
2010	21.97	21.98	21.97	21.99	21.95	21.95	21.95	21.95	21.93	21.91	21.91	21.91	21.95
2011	21.92	21.91	22.05	21.67	21.48	21.21	21.03	20.94	20.59	20.87	20.83	20.91	21.28
Professional and Business Services													
2007	26.00	26.41	26.15	24.99	24.45	25.48	25.37	25.38	25.59	25.63	25.74	25.89	25.59
2008	25.96	25.86	25.97	25.87	25.43	25.90	25.90	25.92	25.92	26.00	26.31	26.50	25.95
2009	26.29	26.20	26.19	26.00	25.94	25.74	25.63	25.64	25.30	25.43	25.40	25.35	25.77
2010	25.41	25.38	25.33	25.32	25.29	25.29	25.28	25.29	25.27	25.29	25.30	25.35	25.32
2011	25.33	25.30	24.89	24.62	25.05	24.21	23.82	23.87	23.58	23.79	23.52	23.45	24.27
Leisure and Hospitality													
2007	14.53	14.73	14.69	14.77	14.55	14.84	14.63	14.69	14.91	14.98	14.91	14.90	14.76
2008	14.88	15.00	14.97	14.95	14.97	14.94	14.94	14.94	14.91	14.88	14.83	14.82	14.92
2009	14.61	14.65	14.65	14.63	14.62	14.53	14.42	14.33	14.19	14.14	14.03	14.01	14.41
2010	13.93	13.91	13.88	13.86	13.84	13.83	13.83	13.81	13.81	13.79	13.77	13.70	13.83
2011	13.66	13.68	13.62	13.60	13.82	13.50	13.62	13.67	13.83	14.01	14.14	14.14	13.77

4. Average Weekly Earnings by Selected Industry: Nevada, 2007–2011

(Dollars, not seasonally adjusted)

Industry and year	January	February	March	April	May	June	July	August	September	October	November	December	Annual average
Total Private													
2007	727.94	734.63	737.53	730.50	715.84	734.63	738.09	731.73	735.93	732.10	730.62	734.45	731.88
2008	726.56	731.61	730.87	730.75	730.50	739.29	734.95	736.56	734.21	731.12	723.36	719.78	730.92
2009	719.26	716.56	715.47	712.05	709.37	703.83	700.61	698.29	691.51	681.47	682.70	677.43	701.22
2010	670.08	666.77	664.16	662.24	662.24	659.99	659.64	657.73	655.13	652.88	654.79	661.21	660.77
2011	661.21	658.95	661.55	669.02	681.04	659.59	662.90	674.82	670.80	680.81	657.90	648.56	665.86
Goods-Producing													
2007	932.40	941.15	956.80	957.19	945.60	968.41	972.04	973.23	978.48	978.08	973.63	976.06	962.77
2008	966.78	967.58	969.20	969.62	973.25	980.91	977.26	980.10	974.85	972.43	920.59	920.05	965.14
2009	926.06	919.88	919.50	915.38	921.94	923.27	923.65	922.52	892.96	882.83	885.60	873.94	909.86
2010	863.03	854.87	853.23	853.60	853.96	852.87	853.23	852.51	851.60	849.60	852.32	850.32	853.33
2011	842.16	844.88	866.32	908.05	901.82	911.90	937.44	957.10	950.67	989.82	899.08	880.43	908.01
Construction													
2007	927.61	967.59	950.42	940.61	938.50	967.21	965.19	966.32	974.17	970.08	966.42	969.38	958.60
2008	958.24	957.16	966.38	963.75	971.91	979.72	975.30	968.25	963.09	957.55	954.23	949.80	964.12
2009	952.00	946.04	947.54	940.48	946.04	941.49	935.20	936.36	902.70	907.81	897.14	869.71	929.05
2010	863.34	856.98	851.67	851.67	852.78	850.30	844.66	846.11	842.52	837.23	831.94	825.98	846.16
2011	820.04	822.84	832.25	904.80	894.57	916.17	946.08	958.32	896.05	914.28	886.70	918.72	892.90
Trade, Transportation, and Utilities													
2007	677.47	680.02	678.41	666.52	648.66	674.75	680.47	683.40	682.63	669.94	669.18	671.32	673.54
2008	665.52	665.15	665.66	662.25	654.99	666.04	659.88	661.64	661.76	654.24	659.63	660.63	661.46
2009	657.32	655.93	655.56	654.82	654.53	654.24	650.99	647.39	648.51	633.28	635.38	639.58	648.89
2010	626.34	623.88	617.97	617.61	621.43	620.35	619.28	617.84	618.12	611.54	613.61	619.48	619.01
2011	608.12	603.98	596.49	618.92	615.25	587.72	603.42	607.51	602.27	594.77	587.90	588.25	601.24
Financial Activities													
2007	930.05	932.84	934.90	930.16	906.62	923.14	914.38	905.72	915.16	904.11	908.40	916.99	918.61
2008	911.07	911.45	907.92	904.78	907.16	910.31	900.13	903.64	900.88	900.13	897.75	884.76	903.43
2009	872.34	873.94	870.85	865.43	865.43	863.09	870.74	858.64	824.33	816.97	820.28	820.28	853.44
2010	819.48	817.66	812.89	813.63	814.35	809.96	807.76	805.57	807.02	804.10	799.72	799.72	809.19
2011	802.27	799.72	811.44	788.79	820.54	801.74	784.42	789.44	792.72	807.67	776.96	759.03	794.56
Professional and Business Services													
2007	980.20	1,000.94	978.01	939.62	916.88	947.86	946.30	939.06	949.39	956.00	962.68	970.88	957.34
2008	976.10	969.75	976.47	964.95	948.54	958.30	955.71	961.63	959.04	967.20	947.16	948.70	961.28
2009	943.81	935.34	934.98	923.00	918.28	900.90	889.36	889.71	847.55	844.28	855.98	844.16	894.38
2010	833.45	827.39	825.76	820.37	814.34	814.34	808.96	809.28	811.17	814.34	819.72	826.41	818.75
2011	820.69	814.66	821.37	810.00	826.65	779.56	769.39	799.65	775.78	808.86	785.57	790.27	800.08
Leisure and Hospitality													
2007	511.46	514.08	518.56	518.43	506.34	520.88	516.44	515.62	518.87	518.31	514.40	515.54	515.75
2008	513.36	514.50	510.48	509.80	511.97	516.92	513.94	515.43	511.41	508.90	511.64	506.84	512.13
2009	499.66	502.50	502.50	501.81	500.00	494.02	490.28	487.22	478.20	469.45	467.20	455.33	487.40
2010	452.73	452.08	448.32	447.68	447.03	445.33	445.33	444.68	443.30	438.52	436.51	430.18	444.33
2011	430.29	432.29	429.03	425.68	433.95	417.15	418.13	423.77	430.11	439.91	436.93	417.13	427.81

NEW HAMPSHIRE
At a Glance

Population:
2000 census: 1,235,807
2010 census: 1,316,470
2011 estimate: 1,318,194

Percent change in population:
2000–2010: 6.5%
2010–2011: 0.1%

Percent change in total nonfarm employment:
2000–2010: 0.3%
2010–2011: 0.4%

Industry with the largest growth in employment, 2000–2011 (thousands):
Education and Health Services, 29.7

Industry with the largest decline or smallest growth in employment, 2000–2011 (thousands):
Manufacturing, -36.0

Civilian labor force:
2000: 694,254
2010: 739,349
2011: 738,281

Unemployment rate and rank among states (lowest to highest):
2000: 2.7%, 3rd
2010: 6.1%, 4th
2011: 5.4%, 4th

Over-the-year change in unemployment rates:
2010–2011: -0.7%

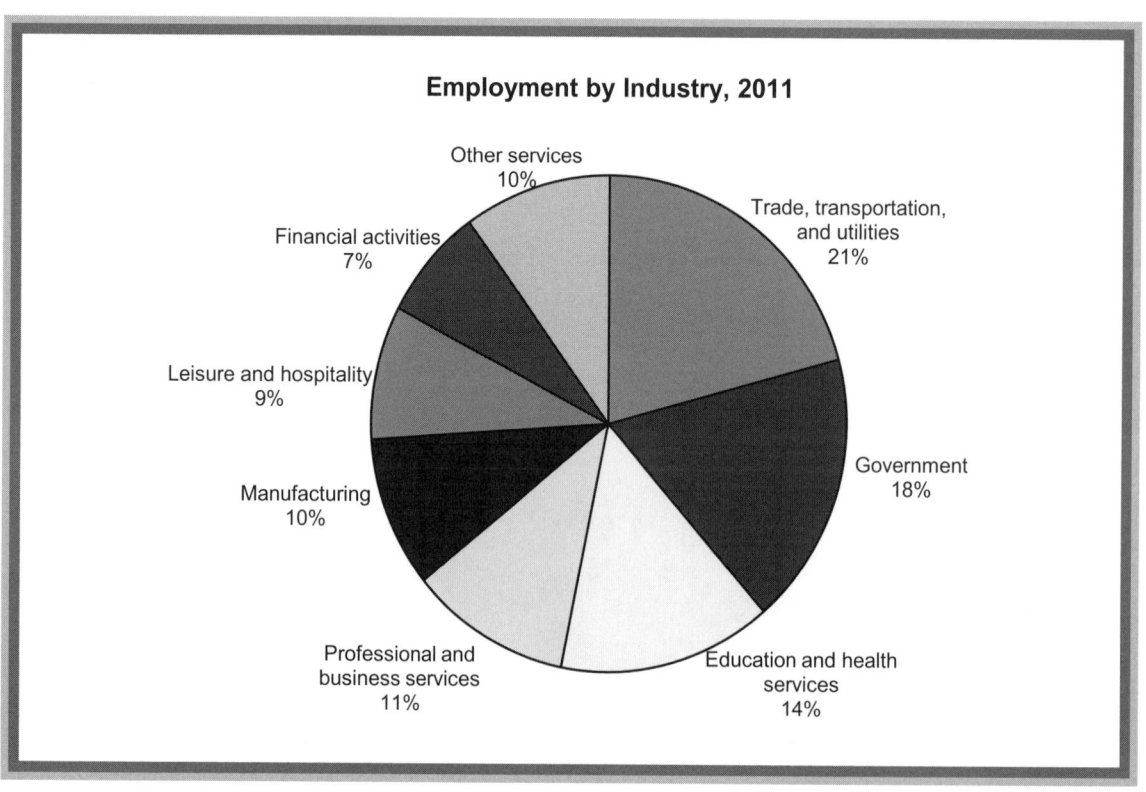

Employment by Industry, 2011

Other services 10%

Trade, transportation, and utilities 21%

Financial activities 7%

Leisure and hospitality 9%

Manufacturing 10%

Government 18%

Professional and business services 11%

Education and health services 14%

1. Employment by Industry: New Hampshire, Selected Years, 2000–2011

(Numbers in thousands, not seasonally adjusted)

Industry and year	January	February	March	April	May	June	July	August	September	October	November	December	Annual average
Total Nonfarm													
2000	603.3	605.6	609.6	615.8	623.4	631.4	625.1	624.6	628.9	628.6	631.5	637.1	622.1
2001	622.1	622.8	623.6	625.3	633.4	638.4	627.4	627.4	628.3	626.0	624.6	627.4	627.2
2002	608.3	607.7	610.7	613.9	620.7	626.9	621.1	621.9	623.7	621.0	620.4	624.2	618.4
2003	603.5	602.7	605.1	608.9	617.4	625.4	621.1	624.3	624.6	625.8	626.0	629.4	617.9
2004	608.0	609.2	615.4	621.4	630.1	635.4	632.3	632.2	635.9	635.7	634.8	638.2	627.4
2005	621.4	620.3	622.1	630.9	638.3	644.2	641.1	639.9	645.5	642.7	643.7	648.8	636.6
2006	625.8	627.6	631.0	639.0	644.2	652.1	647.1	645.8	650.4	648.9	648.3	653.7	642.8
2007	633.3	635.2	637.2	640.0	650.2	658.2	652.1	651.3	653.7	652.4	653.2	657.3	647.8
2008	640.0	639.3	640.5	644.0	653.1	659.2	652.9	653.6	654.9	653.6	649.7	648.8	649.1
2009	627.9	624.7	621.6	623.4	632.4	635.7	624.5	625.0	629.7	630.6	627.6	630.6	627.8
2010	609.3	611.7	614.3	618.6	628.7	632.5	624.7	624.7	629.3	630.5	629.1	632.9	623.9
2011	613.1	615.7	617.7	622.5	628.6	633.7	631.1	630.1	629.0	631.9	631.9	631.0	626.4
Total Private													
2000	520.7	519.7	522.9	529.4	536.2	549.3	550.7	551.7	544.9	542.6	544.3	550.5	538.6
2001	537.4	535.0	535.2	537.7	545.1	554.2	552.8	553.2	540.8	535.7	533.5	536.1	541.4
2002	521.4	517.4	519.6	523.9	531.6	540.2	541.9	543.7	535.1	528.7	526.8	530.5	530.1
2003	514.8	510.5	512.4	516.4	526.3	536.3	540.1	544.4	534.5	531.8	531.3	534.2	527.8
2004	518.9	517.4	521.8	528.3	536.9	547.6	552.4	553.6	545.0	541.1	539.9	543.1	537.2
2005	528.5	526.2	527.2	536.8	543.4	555.8	561.1	561.0	552.7	548.1	548.1	553.0	545.2
2006	535.6	532.8	535.6	543.6	548.9	563.1	565.6	566.1	555.8	552.5	551.8	556.4	550.7
2007	541.2	538.8	540.5	543.5	554.1	567.3	570.1	570.2	559.4	554.7	555.4	559.3	554.5
2008	546.3	542.2	542.2	546.2	555.4	566.0	569.7	569.6	557.3	553.9	548.6	547.8	553.8
2009	531.6	525.6	522.0	523.8	532.5	539.9	540.8	541.0	532.8	530.0	526.2	529.2	531.3
2010	514.1	511.3	512.8	518.3	527.1	537.8	541.8	542.3	533.4	532.3	530.0	534.0	527.9
2011	521.1	518.8	520.5	526.8	532.5	544.0	550.0	550.0	536.1	536.4	535.4	534.1	533.8
Goods-Producing													
2000	124.8	124.2	125.2	127.1	128.4	130.0	129.3	130.8	129.9	130.4	131.0	131.3	128.5
2001	128.4	128.0	127.6	128.4	129.3	129.1	126.1	126.4	123.7	122.0	119.8	118.7	125.6
2002	114.5	113.2	113.2	114.4	115.5	115.5	114.4	114.9	113.7	112.8	111.6	112.2	113.8
2003	108.3	106.7	107.3	108.9	110.9	112.2	111.0	112.7	111.6	111.7	111.3	110.5	110.3
2004	106.7	105.8	106.7	109.6	111.3	112.9	113.2	113.4	112.6	111.7	110.8	110.3	110.4
2005	107.1	106.6	106.9	110.1	111.4	112.9	112.2	112.9	111.9	112.0	112.2	111.3	110.6
2006	106.5	105.4	106.2	108.8	109.8	111.0	110.0	111.1	110.2	109.8	108.6	107.4	108.7
2007	104.1	102.9	103.4	105.0	107.2	108.4	108.2	108.6	107.2	106.9	106.5	105.4	106.2
2008	102.2	101.3	101.6	102.6	104.0	105.2	105.2	105.5	103.8	103.2	101.6	99.2	103.0
2009	94.1	92.1	90.6	91.3	92.2	92.3	91.4	92.1	91.7	91.4	89.6	88.4	91.4
2010	84.5	83.7	84.3	86.6	88.4	89.4	90.1	90.7	90.0	90.3	89.7	89.1	88.1
2011	86.2	85.7	86.6	88.8	89.9	91.1	92.0	91.4	90.2	90.3	89.6	89.0	89.2
Mining and Logging													
2000	1.0	1.0	1.0	0.9	1.0	1.1	1.1	1.1	1.1	1.1	1.1	1.1	1.1
2001	1.0	1.0	1.0	0.9	1.0	1.0	1.0	1.0	1.0	1.0	1.0	1.0	1.0
2002	0.9	0.9	0.9	0.9	0.9	1.0	1.0	1.0	1.0	1.0	0.9	0.9	0.9
2003	0.9	0.8	0.9	0.9	0.9	1.0	1.0	1.0	1.0	1.0	1.0	0.9	0.9
2004	0.8	0.9	0.9	0.9	1.0	1.0	1.0	1.0	1.1	1.1	1.0	1.0	1.0
2005	0.9	0.9	1.0	1.0	1.0	1.1	1.1	1.1	1.1	1.1	1.1	1.1	1.0
2006	0.9	0.9	1.0	1.0	1.1	1.1	1.2	1.2	1.2	1.2	1.1	1.1	1.1
2007	1.0	1.0	1.0	1.1	1.1	1.2	1.2	1.2	1.2	1.2	1.2	1.1	1.1
2008	1.0	1.0	1.0	1.0	1.0	1.1	1.1	1.1	1.1	1.1	1.0	0.9	1.0
2009	0.8	0.8	0.8	0.8	0.9	1.0	1.0	1.0	1.0	1.0	1.0	0.9	0.9
2010	0.8	0.8	0.8	0.9	0.9	1.0	1.0	1.0	1.0	1.0	0.9	0.9	0.9
2011	0.8	0.8	0.8	0.8	0.9	0.9	1.0	1.0	1.0	1.0	0.9	0.9	0.9
Construction													
2000	22.4	21.8	22.5	24.0	25.1	26.3	26.7	26.8	26.2	26.1	26.0	25.5	25.0
2001	23.8	23.5	23.8	25.8	27.7	28.8	29.6	29.7	28.8	28.7	28.3	28.1	27.2
2002	26.2	25.4	25.7	27.4	28.9	29.0	28.8	29.4	28.8	28.9	28.2	28.0	27.9
2003	25.7	24.9	25.2	27.4	29.4	30.5	31.2	31.4	30.8	30.9	30.2	29.4	28.9
2004	26.4	25.7	26.2	28.8	30.3	31.2	31.8	31.6	31.0	30.5	29.7	29.0	29.4
2005	26.3	25.8	26.0	28.9	30.1	31.0	31.5	31.5	30.9	30.7	30.7	29.8	29.4
2006	27.2	26.5	27.1	29.2	30.2	31.3	31.3	31.3	30.9	30.3	29.2	28.0	29.4
2007	25.6	24.6	24.8	26.2	28.4	29.1	29.5	29.4	28.7	28.2	27.8	26.6	27.4
2008	24.2	23.6	23.9	25.5	26.7	27.3	28.2	28.0	27.2	27.0	26.0	24.5	26.0
2009	21.5	20.6	20.3	21.6	22.9	23.4	23.7	23.9	24.3	24.1	22.9	21.9	22.6
2010	18.9	18.2	18.6	20.4	21.7	22.2	23.0	23.2	22.9	23.1	22.6	21.7	21.4
2011	19.6	19.1	19.7	21.6	22.5	23.1	23.7	22.9	22.5	22.7	22.6	22.2	21.9
Manufacturing													
2000	101.4	101.4	101.7	102.2	102.3	102.6	101.5	102.9	102.6	103.2	103.9	104.7	102.5
2001	103.6	103.5	102.8	101.7	100.6	99.3	95.5	95.7	93.9	92.3	90.5	89.6	97.4
2002	87.4	86.9	86.6	86.1	85.7	85.5	84.6	84.5	83.9	82.9	82.5	83.3	85.0
2003	81.7	81.0	81.2	80.6	80.6	80.7	78.8	80.3	79.8	79.8	80.1	80.2	80.4
2004	79.5	79.2	79.6	79.9	80.0	80.7	80.4	80.8	80.5	80.1	80.1	80.3	80.1
2005	79.9	79.9	79.9	80.2	80.3	80.8	79.6	80.3	79.9	80.2	80.4	80.4	80.2
2006	78.4	78.0	78.1	78.6	78.5	78.6	77.5	78.6	78.1	78.3	78.3	78.3	78.3
2007	77.5	77.3	77.6	77.7	77.7	78.1	77.5	78.0	77.3	77.5	77.5	77.7	77.6
2008	77.0	76.7	76.7	76.1	76.3	76.8	75.9	76.4	75.5	75.1	74.6	73.8	75.9
2009	71.8	70.7	69.5	68.9	68.4	67.9	66.7	67.2	66.4	66.3	65.7	65.6	67.9
2010	64.8	64.7	64.9	65.3	65.8	66.2	66.1	66.5	66.1	66.3	66.2	66.5	65.8
2011	65.8	65.8	66.1	66.4	66.5	67.1	67.3	67.5	66.7	66.6	66.1	65.9	66.5

1. Employment by Industry: New Hampshire, Selected Years, 2000–2011—*Continued*

(Numbers in thousands, not seasonally adjusted)

Industry and year	January	February	March	April	May	June	July	August	September	October	November	December	Annual average
Service-Providing													
2000	478.5	481.4	484.4	488.7	495.0	501.4	495.8	493.8	499.0	498.2	500.5	505.8	493.5
2001	493.7	494.8	496.0	496.9	504.1	509.3	501.3	501.0	504.6	504.0	504.8	508.7	501.6
2002	493.8	494.5	497.5	499.5	505.2	511.4	506.7	507.0	510.0	508.2	508.8	512.0	504.6
2003	495.2	496.0	497.8	500.0	506.5	513.2	510.1	511.6	513.0	514.1	514.7	518.9	507.6
2004	501.3	503.4	508.7	511.8	518.8	522.5	519.1	518.8	523.3	524.0	524.0	527.9	517.0
2005	514.3	513.7	515.2	520.8	526.9	531.3	528.9	527.0	533.6	530.7	531.5	537.5	526.0
2006	519.3	522.2	524.8	530.2	534.4	541.1	537.1	534.7	540.2	539.1	539.7	546.3	534.1
2007	529.2	532.3	533.8	535.0	543.0	549.8	543.9	542.7	546.5	545.5	546.7	551.9	541.7
2008	537.8	538.0	538.9	541.4	549.1	554.0	547.7	548.1	551.1	550.4	548.1	549.6	546.2
2009	533.8	532.6	531.0	532.1	540.2	543.4	533.1	532.9	538.0	539.2	538.0	542.2	536.4
2010	524.8	528.0	530.0	532.0	540.3	543.1	534.6	534.0	539.3	540.2	539.4	543.8	535.8
2011	526.9	530.0	531.1	533.7	538.7	542.6	539.1	538.7	538.8	541.6	542.3	542.0	537.1
Trade, Transportation, and Utilities													
2000	135.6	133.0	133.3	134.8	136.3	138.6	137.0	137.1	136.3	137.4	141.0	144.8	137.1
2001	137.3	134.2	133.7	134.8	136.7	138.6	137.4	137.6	136.4	137.7	140.6	143.1	137.3
2002	137.1	133.6	134.3	135.9	137.3	139.5	138.6	139.2	138.9	138.7	141.0	144.6	138.2
2003	136.0	133.3	134.3	135.2	136.9	139.2	139.2	140.0	138.9	140.3	142.9	144.7	138.4
2004	137.1	135.2	136.3	137.5	139.2	140.9	140.5	140.1	139.5	140.6	143.0	145.7	139.6
2005	139.2	136.7	136.6	137.8	139.5	141.8	141.5	141.7	140.2	141.7	144.2	146.8	140.6
2006	140.2	137.5	138.3	140.1	141.1	143.0	142.2	142.3	140.7	141.5	144.9	147.7	141.6
2007	141.5	138.0	138.5	138.9	140.9	142.9	142.6	142.0	139.7	140.5	144.2	146.5	141.4
2008	140.9	137.6	137.4	137.2	139.4	141.4	141.0	140.8	138.6	139.8	141.4	142.7	139.9
2009	136.1	132.8	131.6	131.7	134.0	135.4	133.6	133.2	132.5	133.2	135.5	137.3	133.9
2010	131.5	129.2	129.3	130.1	132.3	134.3	133.6	133.5	131.8	133.5	136.2	138.8	132.8
2011	132.7	130.3	130.5	131.7	133.0	135.3	135.2	135.0	131.3	132.0	135.4	137.0	133.3
Wholesale Trade													
2000	24.5	24.6	24.8	24.9	25.8	26.2	26.3	26.4	26.2	26.3	26.4	26.7	25.8
2001	26.3	26.3	26.3	26.5	26.6	26.9	27.0	26.9	26.7	26.9	26.6	26.8	26.7
2002	26.5	26.4	26.5	26.4	26.4	26.7	26.7	26.7	26.6	26.8	26.6	26.8	26.6
2003	26.2	26.1	26.0	26.4	26.6	27.0	27.2	27.3	26.9	26.9	26.9	26.9	26.7
2004	26.6	26.6	26.9	27.2	27.3	27.5	27.7	27.8	27.4	27.3	27.1	27.2	27.2
2005	27.1	26.9	27.0	27.4	27.6	27.7	27.8	27.7	27.4	27.8	27.7	27.7	27.5
2006	27.5	27.4	27.6	27.9	28.2	28.4	28.3	28.4	28.2	28.2	28.1	28.3	28.0
2007	28.2	28.0	28.2	28.3	28.4	28.5	28.5	28.4	28.2	28.1	28.1	28.1	28.3
2008	28.0	27.9	27.9	28.1	28.3	28.4	28.4	28.3	28.0	28.0	27.8	27.6	28.1
2009	27.1	26.7	26.5	26.6	26.7	26.6	26.4	26.4	26.1	26.2	26.1	26.1	26.5
2010	25.6	25.6	25.6	25.7	25.9	26.0	26.1	26.1	25.8	26.0	26.1	26.0	25.9
2011	25.8	25.9	26.0	26.2	26.3	26.4	26.6	26.6	26.4	26.5	26.9	26.4	26.3
Retail Trade													
2000	94.2	91.7	91.9	93.1	93.7	95.2	94.6	94.6	93.3	94.0	97.8	101.2	94.6
2001	95.4	92.2	91.9	92.5	94.0	95.5	95.0	95.4	93.7	94.8	98.2	100.5	94.9
2002	95.3	92.0	92.5	93.7	94.9	96.6	96.2	96.9	96.3	95.8	98.4	101.6	95.9
2003	94.1	91.8	92.7	93.2	94.4	96.2	96.5	97.4	96.0	97.2	99.9	101.7	95.9
2004	95.1	93.4	94.2	95.0	96.3	97.6	97.8	97.6	96.4	97.3	100.2	102.8	97.0
2005	96.6	94.4	94.2	95.0	96.3	98.1	98.3	98.6	96.9	98.1	100.7	103.0	97.5
2006	97.5	94.9	95.4	96.7	97.2	98.6	98.5	98.6	96.6	97.6	101.1	103.2	98.0
2007	98.0	94.9	95.1	95.3	97.0	98.6	98.8	98.4	95.8	96.9	100.9	102.5	97.7
2008	97.9	95.0	94.8	94.3	95.8	97.6	97.7	97.6	95.3	96.6	98.6	99.6	96.7
2009	94.4	91.6	90.7	90.8	92.7	93.9	93.4	93.2	91.7	92.3	94.8	96.1	93.0
2010	91.7	89.4	89.5	90.2	91.8	93.4	93.6	93.6	91.2	92.5	95.1	97.2	92.4
2011	92.3	90.0	90.0	90.9	91.8	93.7	94.2	94.1	90.1	90.7	93.9	95.5	92.3
Transportation and Utilities													
2000	16.9	16.7	16.6	16.8	16.8	17.2	16.1	16.1	16.8	17.1	16.8	16.9	16.7
2001	15.6	15.7	15.5	15.8	16.1	16.2	15.4	15.3	16.0	16.0	15.8	15.8	15.8
2002	15.3	15.2	15.3	15.8	16.0	16.2	15.7	15.6	16.0	16.1	16.0	16.2	15.8
2003	15.7	15.4	15.6	15.6	15.9	16.0	15.5	15.3	16.0	16.2	16.1	16.1	15.8
2004	15.4	15.2	15.2	15.3	15.6	15.8	15.0	14.7	15.7	16.0	15.7	15.7	15.4
2005	15.5	15.4	15.4	15.4	15.6	16.0	15.4	15.4	15.9	15.8	15.8	16.1	15.6
2006	15.2	15.2	15.3	15.5	15.7	16.0	15.4	15.3	15.9	15.7	15.7	16.2	15.6
2007	15.3	15.1	15.2	15.3	15.5	15.8	15.3	15.2	15.7	15.5	15.2	15.9	15.4
2008	15.0	14.7	14.7	14.8	15.3	15.4	14.9	14.9	15.3	15.2	15.0	15.5	15.1
2009	14.6	14.5	14.4	14.3	14.6	14.9	13.8	13.6	14.7	14.7	14.6	15.1	14.5
2010	14.2	14.2	14.2	14.2	14.6	14.9	13.9	13.8	14.8	15.0	15.0	15.6	14.5
2011	14.6	14.4	14.5	14.6	14.9	15.2	14.4	14.3	14.8	14.8	14.6	15.1	14.7
Information													
2000	13.3	13.3	13.4	13.7	14.0	14.2	14.2	13.6	14.1	14.5	14.6	14.6	14.0
2001	14.3	14.2	14.1	13.8	13.7	13.8	13.7	13.6	13.5	13.4	13.4	13.4	13.7
2002	13.4	13.3	13.1	13.0	12.9	12.9	12.8	12.7	12.7	12.7	12.7	12.6	12.9
2003	12.4	12.2	12.2	12.1	12.1	12.2	12.2	12.1	11.9	12.0	12.2	12.3	12.2
2004	12.1	12.3	12.4	12.6	12.6	12.6	12.7	12.7	12.5	12.6	12.7	12.8	12.6
2005	12.5	12.5	12.5	12.7	12.8	12.8	12.9	12.9	12.7	12.7	12.9	12.9	12.7
2006	12.8	12.6	12.7	12.7	12.6	12.7	12.9	12.6	12.3	12.1	12.1	12.2	12.5
2007	12.3	12.2	12.1	12.3	12.3	12.5	12.6	12.8	12.4	12.4	12.5	12.5	12.4
2008	12.7	12.6	12.5	12.7	12.6	12.8	12.8	12.8	12.5	12.5	12.5	12.5	12.6
2009	12.5	12.4	12.3	12.7	12.6	12.5	12.4	12.2	12.2	12.1	12.0	12.0	12.3
2010	11.8	11.7	11.6	11.5	11.4	11.5	11.4	11.3	11.1	11.1	11.1	11.0	11.4
2011	11.0	10.9	11.0	11.0	11.1	11.2	11.4	11.3	11.1	11.2	11.2	11.2	11.1

1. Employment by Industry: New Hampshire, Selected Years, 2000–2011—*Continued*

(Numbers in thousands, not seasonally adjusted)

Industry and year	January	February	March	April	May	June	July	August	September	October	November	December	Annual average
Financial Activities													
2000	34.1	33.9	33.8	33.7	33.8	34.3	34.3	34.4	34.1	34.1	34.4	34.8	34.1
2001	34.9	35.1	35.3	35.4	35.7	36.1	36.1	36.3	35.8	35.6	35.8	36.3	35.7
2002	36.3	36.2	36.2	36.1	36.3	36.7	36.8	37.0	36.8	36.7	36.7	36.8	36.6
2003	36.8	36.8	36.7	37.1	37.3	37.5	37.5	37.5	36.8	36.6	36.6	36.8	37.0
2004	36.7	36.7	37.1	37.1	37.3	37.7	37.8	38.0	37.4	37.6	37.6	38.0	37.4
2005	38.2	38.1	38.3	38.9	39.1	39.8	40.3	40.4	40.0	39.7	39.6	40.0	39.4
2006	39.1	39.2	39.3	39.3	39.2	39.8	40.0	39.7	39.3	39.2	39.0	39.2	39.4
2007	38.1	38.1	38.2	38.1	38.4	38.8	39.1	39.1	38.4	38.1	38.2	38.4	38.4
2008	38.0	38.0	38.0	38.1	38.2	38.6	38.6	38.5	37.8	37.8	37.6	37.7	38.1
2009	37.3	36.9	36.7	36.7	36.8	37.2	36.9	36.5	36.1	35.9	35.8	35.8	36.6
2010	35.6	35.2	35.2	35.2	35.1	35.5	35.6	35.4	34.9	34.8	34.7	34.8	35.2
2011	34.4	34.2	34.2	34.3	34.2	34.7	35.1	35.6	35.3	35.0	34.8	34.4	34.7
Professional and Business Services													
2000	55.4	56.1	57.1	58.1	58.4	59.8	59.4	60.0	59.3	59.5	60.0	60.3	58.6
2001	57.4	56.9	57.1	57.3	58.0	58.5	57.7	57.9	56.6	55.6	55.2	55.2	57.0
2002	53.0	52.8	53.1	53.9	54.7	55.0	55.4	55.7	55.0	54.5	54.6	53.9	54.3
2003	52.5	52.3	52.3	54.0	54.5	55.5	55.6	56.3	55.7	55.7	56.0	56.0	54.7
2004	54.3	54.6	55.6	57.2	57.6	58.0	58.2	59.2	58.0	58.3	58.5	58.5	57.3
2005	56.6	56.7	56.9	58.9	59.0	60.0	60.4	60.6	60.1	60.0	60.4	60.3	59.2
2006	58.3	58.8	58.8	61.6	61.7	63.4	63.2	63.4	63.0	63.2	63.1	63.4	61.8
2007	62.4	63.2	63.1	64.7	65.6	66.6	66.5	67.1	66.3	66.6	66.5	67.3	65.5
2008	65.4	65.0	64.8	67.3	67.7	67.9	67.3	67.5	67.0	66.4	65.8	64.6	66.4
2009	63.2	62.2	61.6	62.5	62.6	63.1	63.0	62.9	62.6	63.2	63.6	63.6	62.8
2010	61.3	61.3	61.7	64.1	64.5	64.9	65.2	65.4	64.6	65.7	65.9	65.4	64.2
2011	64.1	64.1	63.9	66.3	66.2	67.1	66.0	66.6	65.0	65.5	65.9	65.1	65.5
Education and Health Services													
2000	81.8	82.8	83.3	84.3	84.1	84.2	83.2	83.4	85.1	84.8	85.4	85.5	84.0
2001	86.9	88.3	88.4	88.3	88.2	88.4	88.3	88.6	89.6	90.2	91.0	91.5	89.0
2002	90.4	91.5	92.2	92.1	92.4	92.1	91.0	91.0	92.4	91.8	92.4	92.3	91.8
2003	92.1	92.9	93.2	92.8	92.9	92.8	91.9	91.9	92.3	93.4	93.7	94.4	93.1
2004	93.6	94.5	94.9	95.1	95.0	94.8	94.0	94.0	95.4	96.0	96.5	96.2	95.0
2005	95.7	96.7	97.0	98.0	97.9	97.9	97.7	97.6	99.3	99.3	99.6	100.3	98.1
2006	99.3	100.1	100.5	100.7	100.7	101.1	100.5	100.5	101.7	102.3	102.9	103.7	101.2
2007	102.3	103.9	104.4	104.3	104.5	105.2	104.1	103.8	105.4	105.8	106.3	106.7	104.7
2008	105.7	106.4	107.1	107.5	107.8	107.9	107.9	107.6	108.9	109.7	110.2	110.8	108.1
2009	109.8	110.6	110.8	110.8	111.0	110.5	110.5	109.9	109.8	110.8	111.6	111.9	110.8
2010	111.4	111.9	112.4	112.1	112.3	112.2	111.4	111.0	112.3	112.7	113.0	113.3	112.2
2011	112.6	113.3	113.8	113.5	113.5	113.2	113.2	112.5	113.6	115.1	115.5	114.5	113.7
Leisure and Hospitality													
2000	52.3	52.9	53.2	53.9	57.2	63.8	68.8	68.3	61.8	57.9	53.8	55.1	58.3
2001	54.4	54.6	54.5	55.4	59.1	65.4	69.5	69.4	62.3	58.7	55.1	55.6	59.5
2002	54.8	54.9	55.7	56.6	60.4	66.3	70.9	71.1	64.1	60.6	57.1	57.5	60.8
2003	56.3	56.0	55.9	55.9	61.1	66.2	71.4	72.2	65.4	61.3	57.3	58.9	61.5
2004	57.8	57.9	58.2	58.5	62.9	69.3	74.3	74.6	68.2	63.3	59.7	60.5	63.8
2005	58.5	58.2	58.1	59.0	62.3	69.0	74.3	73.1	67.0	61.6	58.1	60.1	63.3
2006	58.5	58.3	58.8	59.1	62.3	70.1	74.8	74.3	67.0	62.9	59.6	61.2	63.9
2007	59.2	59.1	59.2	58.7	63.3	70.3	74.2	74.1	67.9	62.3	59.2	60.4	64.0
2008	59.4	59.5	59.1	59.2	63.7	69.8	74.4	74.3	66.6	62.5	57.9	58.8	63.8
2009	57.5	57.5	57.3	56.9	61.8	67.2	71.9	72.3	65.6	61.4	56.7	58.4	62.0
2010	56.9	57.2	57.1	57.4	61.5	67.9	72.2	72.6	66.8	62.2	57.4	59.5	62.4
2011	58.0	58.1	58.0	58.8	61.9	68.2	73.9	75.0	66.7	64.2	59.5	60.3	63.6
Other Services													
2000	23.4	23.5	23.6	23.8	24.0	24.4	24.5	24.1	24.3	24.0	24.1	24.1	24.0
2001	23.8	23.7	24.5	24.3	24.4	24.3	24.0	23.4	22.9	22.5	22.6	22.3	23.6
2002	21.9	21.9	21.8	21.9	22.1	22.2	22.0	22.1	21.5	20.9	20.7	20.6	21.6
2003	20.4	20.3	20.5	20.4	20.6	20.7	21.3	21.3	20.8	20.5	20.6	20.7	20.7
2004	20.6	20.4	20.6	20.7	21.0	21.4	21.7	21.6	21.4	21.0	21.1	21.1	21.1
2005	20.7	20.7	20.9	21.4	21.4	21.6	21.8	21.8	21.5	21.1	21.1	21.3	21.3
2006	20.9	20.9	21.0	21.3	21.5	22.0	22.3	22.3	21.6	21.5	21.6	21.6	21.5
2007	21.3	21.4	21.6	21.5	21.9	22.6	22.8	22.7	22.1	22.1	22.0	22.1	22.0
2008	22.0	21.8	21.7	21.7	22.0	22.4	22.5	22.6	22.1	22.0	21.6	21.5	22.0
2009	21.1	21.1	21.1	21.2	21.5	21.7	21.7	21.7	21.9	21.3	21.2	21.2	21.3
2010	21.1	21.1	21.2	21.3	21.6	22.1	22.3	22.4	21.9	22.0	22.1	22.1	21.8
2011	22.1	22.2	22.5	22.4	22.7	23.2	23.2	22.6	22.9	23.1	23.5	22.6	22.8
Government													
2000	82.6	85.9	86.7	86.4	87.2	82.1	74.4	72.9	84.0	86.0	87.2	86.6	83.5
2001	84.7	87.8	88.4	87.6	88.3	84.2	74.6	74.2	87.5	90.3	91.1	91.3	85.8
2002	86.9	90.3	91.1	90.0	89.1	86.7	79.2	78.2	88.6	92.3	93.6	93.7	88.3
2003	88.7	92.2	92.7	92.5	91.1	89.1	81.0	79.9	90.1	94.0	94.7	95.2	90.1
2004	89.1	91.8	93.6	93.1	93.2	87.8	79.9	78.6	90.9	94.6	94.9	95.1	90.2
2005	92.9	94.1	94.9	94.1	94.9	88.4	80.0	78.9	92.8	94.6	95.6	95.8	91.4
2006	90.2	94.8	95.4	95.4	95.3	89.0	81.5	79.7	94.6	96.4	96.5	97.3	92.2
2007	92.1	96.4	96.7	96.5	96.1	90.9	82.0	81.1	94.3	97.7	97.8	98.0	93.3
2008	93.7	97.1	98.3	97.8	97.7	93.2	83.2	84.0	97.6	99.7	101.1	101.0	95.4
2009	96.3	99.1	99.6	99.6	99.9	95.8	83.7	84.0	96.9	100.6	101.4	101.4	96.5
2010	95.2	100.4	101.5	100.3	101.6	94.7	82.9	82.4	95.9	98.2	99.1	98.9	95.9
2011	92.0	96.9	97.2	95.7	96.1	89.7	81.1	80.1	92.9	95.5	96.5	96.9	92.6

2. Average Weekly Hours by Selected Industry: New Hampshire, 2007–2011

(Not seasonally adjusted)

Industry and year	January	February	March	April	May	June	July	August	September	October	November	December	Annual average
Total Private													
2007	33.2	33.0	33.2	33.3	33.5	33.4	33.5	33.5	33.4	33.3	33.1	33.3	33.3
2008	32.6	32.8	32.9	32.7	32.7	32.7	32.7	32.7	33.1	33.0	32.8	32.3	32.8
2009	32.5	32.6	32.5	32.7	32.7	32.0	32.8	33.1	32.6	33.1	33.1	33.1	32.7
2010	32.8	32.7	32.8	33.1	33.4	32.6	33.3	33.4	33.0	33.4	33.6	33.5	33.1
2011	32.8	33.0	33.1	33.2	33.2	32.8	33.3	33.5	33.3	33.4	33.2	33.2	33.2
Goods-Producing													
2007	39.5	38.7	39.3	39.8	39.5	39.1	39.1	39.4	39.5	39.2	39.7	40.2	39.4
2008	39.7	39.3	39.5	39.4	39.3	39.5	38.9	39.2	40.4	39.0	39.3	38.5	39.3
2009	39.4	38.3	38.2	38.4	38.3	38.4	38.7	38.4	37.8	39.2	39.2	39.8	38.7
2010	39.9	37.9	39.6	40.0	40.2	39.4	39.0	38.7	38.9	39.0	39.3	39.6	39.3
2011	38.8	38.3	38.6	38.8	39.0	39.1	38.9	39.3	39.5	38.2	39.9	39.6	39.0
Manufacturing													
2007	41.0	40.3	40.5	41.0	40.7	40.3	40.0	40.3	40.7	40.3	40.7	41.2	40.6
2008	40.8	40.3	40.6	40.7	40.4	40.7	40.1	40.4	40.6	39.8	40.1	39.5	40.3
2009	40.6	39.0	39.2	39.2	38.9	39.1	39.1	38.8	38.1	39.4	39.6	40.4	39.3
2010	41.1	39.1	41.1	41.5	41.2	40.5	39.7	39.4	38.9	39.0	39.4	39.7	40.0
2011	39.0	38.2	38.8	38.8	38.7	38.9	38.8	39.3	39.3	38.4	40.2	40.4	39.1
Trade, Transportation, and Utilities													
2007	31.9	32.3	32.1	31.6	31.8	32.0	31.2	31.3	30.9	31.1	30.4	30.9	31.5
2008	30.1	30.6	30.8	30.4	30.1	29.9	29.8	29.6	30.0	29.8	30.4	30.0	30.1
2009	30.0	30.5	30.9	31.9	31.9	31.1	32.1	32.0	32.5	32.2	32.4	32.4	31.7
2010	31.7	32.6	32.5	32.7	32.5	32.2	32.9	32.5	32.3	32.6	32.8	33.0	32.5
2011	32.2	33.2	33.4	33.7	34.0	33.9	34.4	34.4	34.2	35.1	34.3	34.5	33.9
Professional and Business Services													
2007	36.2	35.1	36.3	37.1	37.8	36.9	37.5	36.6	36.6	36.4	36.4	36.8	36.6
2008	34.7	35.1	36.3	35.4	36.2	36.4	36.4	36.3	36.8	37.3	36.7	35.9	36.1
2009	35.7	36.4	36.0	36.5	35.6	34.9	34.5	35.4	34.9	35.3	35.0	35.1	35.4
2010	35.1	34.5	34.9	34.8	36.0	35.0	35.0	35.2	35.2	35.5	36.1	34.8	35.2
2011	34.6	33.3	33.7	33.9	33.3	32.9	32.7	32.9	32.9	33.6	33.5	32.9	33.3
Education and Health Services													
2007	31.7	31.6	31.8	31.8	32.1	31.8	32.1	32.2	32.2	32.0	31.9	31.5	31.9
2008	31.1	31.4	31.1	30.9	30.8	30.8	31.2	30.9	31.4	31.5	31.8	31.6	31.2
2009	31.7	31.6	31.7	31.5	31.5	31.1	32.0	32.2	31.8	32.2	32.3	32.3	31.8
2010	32.3	32.6	31.9	32.0	31.9	32.0	32.3	32.7	32.4	32.7	33.2	32.6	32.4
2011	32.3	32.5	32.7	32.4	32.7	32.3	32.0	32.8	32.8	32.9	33.0	32.9	32.6
Leisure and Hospitality													
2007	24.1	24.9	24.6	24.3	25.6	26.1	26.8	26.7	25.6	25.3	24.8	24.0	25.3
2008	24.3	24.3	24.0	24.3	24.6	24.7	25.4	25.6	23.6	24.0	23.0	22.1	24.2
2009	22.5	23.7	22.9	23.2	23.1	23.3	25.2	26.1	24.3	24.3	24.6	23.3	23.9
2010	23.4	23.1	22.5	23.3	24.0	24.1	26.1	26.7	24.7	24.6	24.2	23.3	24.3
2011	23.1	23.4	23.4	23.6	23.8	23.9	26.5	26.6	24.3	24.3	22.9	22.4	24.1

3. Average Hourly Earnings by Selected Industry: New Hampshire, 2007–2011

(Dollars, not seasonally adjusted)

Industry and year	January	February	March	April	May	June	July	August	September	October	November	December	Annual average
Total Private													
2007	21.93	22.11	22.05	22.40	22.05	21.86	21.79	21.75	22.21	22.09	22.05	22.44	22.06
2008	22.41	22.44	22.61	22.54	22.45	22.29	22.26	22.50	23.13	23.00	23.05	23.22	22.66
2009	23.11	22.98	22.85	22.75	22.67	22.56	22.35	22.30	22.50	22.64	22.74	22.92	22.70
2010	22.91	22.76	22.91	23.07	23.24	23.04	22.87	22.76	22.98	23.18	23.05	23.03	22.98
2011	23.23	23.08	23.09	23.39	23.02	22.73	22.46	22.33	23.19	23.12	23.25	23.19	23.00
Goods-Producing													
2007	25.15	25.43	25.25	25.17	25.12	24.93	24.71	24.71	24.69	24.29	23.86	24.19	24.79
2008	24.23	24.36	24.73	24.70	24.02	24.12	24.52	24.69	25.18	25.01	25.26	25.63	24.70
2009	25.55	25.47	25.56	25.76	25.56	25.48	25.33	25.44	25.59	25.50	25.44	25.64	25.53
2010	25.44	25.64	25.44	25.39	25.58	25.39	25.56	25.42	25.62	25.82	26.02	26.06	25.62
2011	26.26	26.43	26.10	26.50	26.25	25.56	25.64	26.02	26.35	26.34	25.94	25.79	26.09
Manufacturing													
2007	26.23	26.34	26.16	25.95	25.81	25.62	25.40	25.29	25.22	24.69	24.17	24.50	25.45
2008	24.35	24.43	24.89	24.77	23.79	23.88	24.41	24.70	24.98	24.96	25.13	25.22	24.62
2009	25.26	25.21	25.22	25.08	25.01	25.08	25.12	25.32	25.50	25.53	25.73	25.83	25.32
2010	25.74	25.94	25.74	25.76	25.96	25.78	25.98	26.02	26.22	26.42	26.62	26.73	26.07
2011	26.93	27.08	26.66	27.30	27.01	26.12	26.28	26.51	26.95	26.89	26.43	26.09	26.68
Trade, Transportation, and Utilities													
2007	17.10	17.08	16.58	16.72	16.81	16.63	16.48	16.31	16.50	16.63	16.57	16.27	16.64
2008	16.56	17.22	17.51	17.57	17.58	17.49	17.35	17.34	17.99	17.96	17.92	18.86	17.61
2009	19.02	19.21	19.01	19.17	19.19	19.33	19.50	19.68	19.88	19.99	20.13	19.93	19.51
2010	20.13	19.93	19.94	20.14	20.17	19.97	19.81	19.67	19.67	19.68	19.48	18.61	19.76
2011	18.81	18.71	19.09	19.44	19.11	19.00	19.14	18.95	19.79	19.64	19.74	19.34	19.23
Professional and Business Services													
2007	30.30	31.18	31.29	31.73	30.25	30.65	30.50	29.97	30.25	29.94	29.68	29.91	30.46
2008	29.37	28.85	29.56	29.20	29.43	29.41	29.09	29.85	30.62	30.64	30.24	29.82	29.68
2009	29.99	29.79	29.82	29.62	29.47	29.66	29.66	29.46	29.26	29.06	28.86	28.79	29.45
2010	28.92	28.72	28.52	28.36	28.47	28.32	28.26	28.46	28.32	28.35	28.15	28.35	28.43
2011	28.37	28.17	28.37	28.53	27.69	27.75	27.26	26.87	27.22	27.07	27.13	27.44	27.66
Education and Health Services													
2007	20.25	20.28	20.44	20.84	20.70	20.98	21.05	20.92	21.39	21.38	21.66	21.79	20.98
2008	21.73	21.36	21.46	21.35	21.12	21.21	21.19	21.19	21.54	21.49	22.04	21.81	21.46
2009	21.78	21.76	21.81	21.87	21.99	22.00	21.87	21.87	22.02	22.17	22.21	22.21	21.95
2010	22.04	22.09	22.29	22.41	22.60	22.52	22.46	22.29	22.49	22.57	22.79	22.99	22.46
2011	22.98	23.18	23.34	23.73	23.83	24.29	24.67	24.10	24.74	24.91	25.01	25.18	24.17
Leisure and Hospitality													
2007	11.79	12.12	12.17	12.15	12.17	11.73	11.20	11.25	11.38	11.57	11.60	11.69	11.70
2008	11.71	11.99	12.08	11.92	12.46	12.29	12.41	12.39	12.92	12.93	12.92	13.40	12.44
2009	13.21	13.16	13.32	13.41	13.54	13.34	13.34	13.23	13.43	13.44	13.62	13.47	13.37
2010	13.42	13.27	13.24	13.44	13.45	13.25	13.10	13.25	13.44	13.40	13.20	13.38	13.31
2011	13.23	13.34	13.30	13.45	13.35	13.16	12.69	12.82	13.44	13.66	13.83	13.57	13.29

4. Average Weekly Earnings by Selected Industry: New Hampshire, 2007–2011

(Dollars, not seasonally adjusted)

Industry and year	January	February	March	April	May	June	July	August	September	October	November	December	Annual average
Total Private													
2007	728.08	729.63	732.06	745.92	738.68	730.12	729.97	728.63	741.81	735.60	729.86	747.25	734.92
2008	730.57	736.03	743.87	737.06	734.12	728.88	727.90	735.75	765.60	759.00	756.04	750.01	742.09
2009	751.08	749.15	742.63	743.93	741.31	721.92	733.08	738.13	733.50	749.38	752.69	758.65	742.83
2010	751.45	744.25	751.45	763.62	776.22	751.10	761.57	760.18	758.34	774.21	774.48	771.51	761.47
2011	761.94	761.64	764.28	776.55	764.26	745.54	747.92	748.06	772.23	772.21	771.90	769.91	762.66
Goods-Producing													
2007	993.43	984.14	992.33	1,001.77	992.24	974.76	966.16	973.57	975.26	952.17	947.24	972.44	976.99
2008	961.93	957.35	976.84	973.18	943.99	952.74	953.83	967.85	1,017.27	975.39	992.72	986.76	971.54
2009	1,006.67	975.50	976.39	989.18	978.95	978.43	980.27	976.90	967.30	999.60	997.25	1,020.47	987.24
2010	1,015.06	971.76	1,007.42	1,015.60	1,028.32	1,000.37	996.84	983.75	996.62	1,006.98	1,022.59	1,031.98	1,006.54
2011	1,018.89	1,012.27	1,007.46	1,028.20	1,023.75	999.40	997.40	1,022.59	1,040.83	1,006.19	1,035.01	1,021.28	1,017.39
Manufacturing													
2007	1,075.43	1,061.50	1,059.48	1,063.95	1,050.47	1,032.49	1,016.00	1,019.19	1,026.45	995.01	983.72	1,009.40	1,032.75
2008	993.48	984.53	1,010.53	1,008.14	961.12	971.92	978.84	997.88	1,014.19	993.41	1,007.71	996.19	993.10
2009	1,025.56	983.19	988.62	983.14	972.89	980.63	982.19	982.42	971.55	1,005.88	1,018.91	1,043.53	994.91
2010	1,057.91	1,014.25	1,057.91	1,069.04	1,069.55	1,044.09	1,031.41	1,025.19	1,019.96	1,030.38	1,048.83	1,061.18	1,044.02
2011	1,050.27	1,034.46	1,034.41	1,059.24	1,045.29	1,016.07	1,019.66	1,041.84	1,059.14	1,032.58	1,062.49	1,054.04	1,042.34
Trade, Transportation, and Utilities													
2007	545.49	551.68	532.22	528.35	534.56	532.16	514.18	510.50	509.85	517.19	503.73	502.74	523.39
2008	498.46	526.93	539.31	534.13	529.16	522.95	517.03	513.26	539.70	544.77	565.80	565.80	530.57
2009	570.60	585.91	587.41	611.52	612.16	601.16	625.95	629.76	646.10	643.68	652.21	645.73	617.80
2010	638.12	649.72	648.05	658.58	655.53	643.03	651.75	639.28	635.34	641.57	638.94	614.13	642.84
2011	605.68	621.17	637.61	655.13	649.74	644.10	658.42	651.88	676.82	689.36	677.08	667.23	652.86
Professional and Business Services													
2007	1,096.86	1,094.42	1,135.83	1,177.18	1,143.45	1,130.99	1,143.75	1,096.90	1,107.15	1,089.82	1,080.35	1,100.69	1,116.36
2008	1,019.14	1,012.64	1,073.03	1,033.68	1,065.37	1,070.52	1,058.88	1,083.56	1,126.82	1,142.87	1,109.81	1,070.54	1,072.37
2009	1,070.64	1,084.36	1,073.52	1,081.13	1,049.13	1,035.13	1,023.27	1,042.88	1,021.17	1,025.82	1,010.10	1,010.53	1,043.67
2010	1,015.09	990.84	995.35	986.93	1,024.92	991.20	989.10	1,001.79	996.86	1,006.43	1,016.22	986.58	999.92
2011	981.60	938.06	956.07	967.17	922.08	912.98	891.40	884.02	895.54	909.55	908.86	902.78	922.14
Education and Health Services													
2007	641.93	640.85	649.99	662.71	664.47	667.16	675.71	673.62	688.76	684.16	690.95	686.39	669.01
2008	675.80	670.70	667.41	659.72	650.50	653.27	661.13	654.77	676.36	676.94	700.87	689.20	669.79
2009	690.43	687.62	691.38	688.91	692.69	684.20	702.40	704.21	700.24	713.87	710.92	717.38	698.73
2010	711.89	720.13	711.05	717.12	720.94	720.64	725.46	728.88	728.68	738.04	756.63	749.47	727.43
2011	742.25	753.35	763.22	768.85	779.24	784.57	789.44	790.48	811.47	819.54	825.33	828.42	788.21
Leisure and Hospitality													
2007	284.14	301.79	299.38	295.25	311.55	306.15	300.16	300.38	291.33	292.72	287.68	280.56	296.23
2008	284.55	291.36	289.92	289.66	306.52	303.56	315.21	317.18	304.91	310.32	297.16	296.14	301.32
2009	297.23	311.89	305.03	311.11	312.77	310.82	336.17	345.30	326.35	326.59	335.05	313.85	320.03
2010	314.03	306.54	297.90	313.15	322.80	319.33	341.91	353.78	331.97	329.64	319.44	311.75	323.13
2011	305.61	312.16	311.22	317.42	317.73	314.52	336.29	341.01	326.59	331.94	316.71	303.97	320.43

NEW JERSEY
At a Glance

Population:
2000 census: 8,414,764
2010 census: 8,791,894
2011 estimate: 8,821,155

Percent change in population:
2000–2010: 4.5%
2010–2011: 0.3%

Percent change in total nonfarm employment:
2000–2010: -3.6%
2010–2011: 0.1%

Industry with the largest growth in employment, 2000–2011 (thousands):
Education and Health Services, 114.0

Industry with the largest decline or smallest growth in employment, 2000–2011 (thousands):
Manufacturing, -167.5

Civilian labor force:
2000: 4,287,783
2010: 4,554,076
2011: 4,556,186

Unemployment rate and rank among states (lowest to highest):
2000: 3.7%, 22nd
2010: 9.6%, 33rd
2011: 9.3%, 37th

Over-the-year change in unemployment rates:
2010–2011: -0.3%

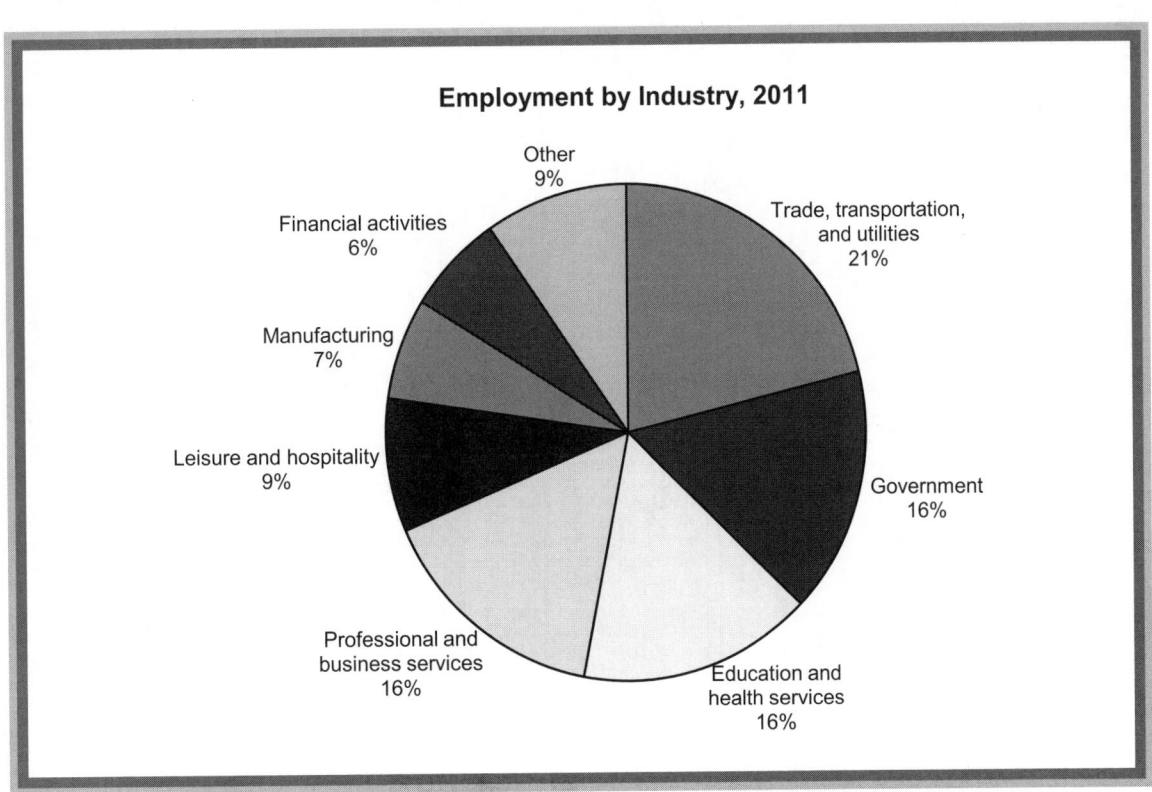

Employment by Industry, 2011

Other 9%

Financial activities 6%

Manufacturing 7%

Leisure and hospitality 9%

Professional and business services 16%

Trade, transportation, and utilities 21%

Government 16%

Education and health services 16%

1. Employment by Industry: New Jersey, Selected Years, 2000–2011

(Numbers in thousands, not seasonally adjusted)

Industry and year	January	February	March	April	May	June	July	August	September	October	November	December	Annual average
Total Nonfarm													
2000	3,887.9	3,896.4	3,942.9	3,975.9	4,006.9	4,060.6	4,020.0	4,002.5	4,014.9	4,017.6	4,042.4	4,066.5	3,994.5
2001	3,922.5	3,931.9	3,957.0	3,994.2	4,026.2	4,073.3	4,008.6	3,990.9	3,995.1	4,010.2	4,023.7	4,032.5	3,997.2
2002	3,932.8	3,940.2	3,968.8	3,982.7	4,007.4	4,042.7	3,982.8	3,970.8	3,974.7	3,983.2	4,006.5	4,014.6	3,983.9
2003	3,908.0	3,898.5	3,922.2	3,956.5	3,993.1	4,032.1	4,003.2	3,986.4	3,991.5	4,006.7	4,019.9	4,027.9	3,978.8
2004	3,905.8	3,907.6	3,944.2	3,969.9	4,014.9	4,063.0	4,023.0	4,005.1	4,014.9	4,026.9	4,050.2	4,064.0	3,999.1
2005	3,946.0	3,951.3	3,975.3	4,024.8	4,057.6	4,111.9	4,066.0	4,048.7	4,054.4	4,059.1	4,082.2	4,091.9	4,039.1
2006	3,984.6	3,992.5	4,028.4	4,050.8	4,090.9	4,143.4	4,091.5	4,076.5	4,075.3	4,088.1	4,107.4	4,122.3	4,071.0
2007	3,997.0	3,993.2	4,024.6	4,053.9	4,103.9	4,159.6	4,101.8	4,086.0	4,076.5	4,103.4	4,118.8	4,128.4	4,078.9
2008	4,017.7	4,018.0	4,043.9	4,063.3	4,094.1	4,138.3	4,073.8	4,043.9	4,038.3	4,035.7	4,026.0	4,017.3	4,050.9
2009	3,883.2	3,868.9	3,874.3	3,890.0	3,929.0	3,964.0	3,895.4	3,873.0	3,878.3	3,883.1	3,895.4	3,904.0	3,894.9
2010	3,776.6	3,768.0	3,798.8	3,849.9	3,895.4	3,939.2	3,869.2	3,843.5	3,843.7	3,863.8	3,876.6	3,882.8	3,850.6
2011	3,756.3	3,763.8	3,793.4	3,839.1	3,872.2	3,925.7	3,885.4	3,863.9	3,864.0	3,889.0	3,911.0	3,910.9	3,856.2
Total Private													
2000	3,307.4	3,306.1	3,346.9	3,379.8	3,406.3	3,463.7	3,451.2	3,444.9	3,439.0	3,421.2	3,439.2	3,462.4	3,405.7
2001	3,330.1	3,326.5	3,350.1	3,385.9	3,419.5	3,465.1	3,431.4	3,421.9	3,400.4	3,394.7	3,400.8	3,408.4	3,394.6
2002	3,320.8	3,317.8	3,343.0	3,358.9	3,384.4	3,421.7	3,397.7	3,395.3	3,376.2	3,362.9	3,378.7	3,387.5	3,370.4
2003	3,291.6	3,271.1	3,291.4	3,325.1	3,362.4	3,402.2	3,403.9	3,401.0	3,383.6	3,375.9	3,382.9	3,391.8	3,356.9
2004	3,281.0	3,271.3	3,303.1	3,329.6	3,375.4	3,422.0	3,414.1	3,406.7	3,391.5	3,381.9	3,399.4	3,412.6	3,365.7
2005	3,309.8	3,302.7	3,325.3	3,373.0	3,409.0	3,461.0	3,450.0	3,443.0	3,426.1	3,409.3	3,425.5	3,435.4	3,397.5
2006	3,340.7	3,336.1	3,370.0	3,392.0	3,435.5	3,486.1	3,469.4	3,465.5	3,445.1	3,433.0	3,447.6	3,462.8	3,423.7
2007	3,351.8	3,336.6	3,364.8	3,394.6	3,446.0	3,499.1	3,485.3	3,476.3	3,446.7	3,447.8	3,457.9	3,467.6	3,431.2
2008	3,369.0	3,358.5	3,381.9	3,402.2	3,432.9	3,476.1	3,449.8	3,435.7	3,405.8	3,381.9	3,367.3	3,359.0	3,401.7
2009	3,233.6	3,209.3	3,211.3	3,225.4	3,264.5	3,299.4	3,269.5	3,258.3	3,241.1	3,225.4	3,231.4	3,241.2	3,242.5
2010	3,129.3	3,113.8	3,141.5	3,191.0	3,226.3	3,275.5	3,251.2	3,247.2	3,231.6	3,232.6	3,238.9	3,249.2	3,210.7
2011	3,139.1	3,135.0	3,162.4	3,207.1	3,243.6	3,296.6	3,293.4	3,283.0	3,260.4	3,260.4	3,277.1	3,277.9	3,236.3
Goods-Producing													
2000	556.8	555.3	565.1	573.8	577.5	583.6	574.7	577.5	578.0	578.5	578.6	577.6	573.1
2001	554.7	556.1	560.5	566.4	571.3	574.5	564.2	566.0	563.4	559.2	554.6	549.9	561.7
2002	527.3	526.6	529.5	534.1	537.7	540.0	532.7	535.9	533.9	530.2	528.0	523.7	531.6
2003	503.7	498.3	501.0	511.0	517.3	521.4	518.6	520.3	519.0	515.6	513.2	509.9	512.4
2004	490.6	487.4	495.3	501.6	508.7	514.5	513.9	514.9	514.8	511.2	509.0	506.9	505.7
2005	487.8	484.1	488.5	498.4	504.7	509.5	507.4	509.4	510.2	505.7	506.6	502.7	501.3
2006	489.5	488.7	494.8	501.9	505.9	509.2	506.5	507.0	505.3	501.1	498.7	495.9	500.4
2007	477.3	470.4	475.8	483.9	489.6	494.7	493.4	493.6	490.3	488.4	485.2	480.1	485.2
2008	463.7	460.3	464.3	469.8	472.4	475.6	472.3	471.4	467.6	462.0	454.8	445.0	464.9
2009	416.6	409.4	408.3	408.3	410.8	411.9	407.8	406.5	403.0	400.8	398.2	395.2	406.4
2010	377.6	373.6	377.7	387.2	391.7	395.1	394.6	393.9	392.8	392.5	392.1	387.4	388.0
2011	369.0	366.7	373.1	381.2	386.1	391.1	394.1	396.1	393.2	392.2	391.6	386.8	385.1
Mining and Logging													
2000	1.9	1.7	1.8	2.0	2.0	2.0	2.0	2.0	2.1	2.0	2.0	1.9	2.0
2001	1.6	1.5	1.6	1.8	1.8	1.9	1.9	1.9	1.9	1.8	1.8	1.8	1.8
2002	1.6	1.6	1.7	1.5	1.5	1.6	1.5	1.5	1.5	1.6	1.7	1.7	1.6
2003	1.4	1.4	1.5	1.5	1.6	1.6	1.6	1.6	1.6	1.6	1.6	1.6	1.6
2004	1.5	1.4	1.5	1.6	1.7	1.7	1.7	1.7	1.7	1.7	1.7	1.7	1.6
2005	1.6	1.5	1.6	1.7	1.8	1.8	1.8	1.8	1.8	1.8	1.8	1.8	1.7
2006	1.6	1.6	1.7	1.8	1.8	1.8	1.8	1.7	1.7	1.7	1.7	1.6	1.7
2007	1.6	1.5	1.6	1.7	1.7	1.7	1.7	1.7	1.7	1.7	1.7	1.7	1.7
2008	1.6	1.5	1.6	1.6	1.7	1.7	1.7	1.7	1.7	1.7	1.7	1.6	1.7
2009	1.4	1.4	1.4	1.4	1.5	1.5	1.5	1.6	1.6	1.6	1.5	1.5	1.5
2010	1.2	1.3	1.3	1.4	1.4	1.4	1.4	1.4	1.4	1.4	1.4	1.4	1.4
2011	1.2	1.2	1.2	1.3	1.3	1.4	1.4	1.4	1.4	1.4	1.4	1.4	1.3
Construction													
2000	138.2	135.3	143.2	148.7	151.6	154.7	153.9	155.1	154.8	153.6	153.6	152.0	149.6
2001	141.8	142.6	147.0	155.2	160.5	163.7	164.5	166.4	165.1	167.7	166.2	164.4	158.8
2002	153.0	152.2	155.2	160.7	164.1	166.9	167.5	169.2	167.5	166.9	165.7	161.8	162.6
2003	149.1	144.3	147.1	157.1	162.9	165.8	168.2	169.1	167.8	167.1	165.3	162.0	160.5
2004	151.0	148.0	154.9	162.4	167.8	171.4	173.4	174.7	173.9	173.0	171.2	169.0	165.9
2005	155.4	151.4	154.7	166.0	171.6	174.8	176.6	178.0	178.5	174.7	176.0	172.0	169.1
2006	161.5	161.2	166.5	175.4	178.8	180.9	181.0	182.2	181.1	178.3	176.7	175.2	174.9
2007	161.2	155.4	160.7	169.9	175.7	179.5	179.6	181.0	179.1	178.1	175.5	171.5	172.3
2008	158.7	156.7	160.1	165.4	168.8	171.1	171.1	170.8	168.5	166.2	161.4	154.9	164.5
2009	137.2	134.1	135.7	139.0	141.9	143.0	142.7	142.5	139.8	138.1	136.3	133.4	138.6
2010	119.8	116.7	120.8	129.2	132.4	134.2	135.2	134.8	133.7	134.2	133.9	128.8	129.5
2011	114.2	112.4	118.3	126.9	131.0	134.4	137.8	139.4	138.4	136.2	136.0	130.8	129.7
Manufacturing													
2000	416.7	418.3	420.1	423.1	423.9	426.9	418.8	420.4	421.1	422.9	423.0	423.7	421.6
2001	411.3	412.0	411.9	409.4	409.0	408.9	397.8	397.7	396.4	389.7	386.6	383.7	401.2
2002	372.7	372.8	372.6	371.9	372.1	371.5	363.7	365.2	364.9	361.7	360.6	360.2	367.5
2003	353.2	352.6	352.4	352.4	352.8	354.0	348.8	349.6	349.6	346.9	346.3	346.3	350.4
2004	338.1	338.0	338.9	337.6	339.2	341.4	338.8	338.5	339.2	336.5	336.1	336.2	338.2
2005	330.8	331.2	332.2	330.7	331.3	332.9	329.0	329.6	329.9	329.2	328.8	328.9	330.4
2006	326.4	325.9	326.6	324.7	325.3	326.5	323.7	323.1	322.5	321.1	320.3	319.1	323.8
2007	314.5	313.5	313.5	312.3	312.2	313.5	312.1	310.9	309.5	308.6	308.0	306.9	311.3
2008	303.4	302.1	302.6	302.8	301.9	302.8	299.5	298.9	297.4	294.1	291.7	288.5	298.8
2009	278.0	273.9	271.2	267.9	267.4	267.4	263.6	262.4	261.6	261.1	260.4	260.3	266.3
2010	256.6	255.6	255.6	256.6	257.9	259.5	258.0	257.7	257.7	256.9	256.8	257.2	257.2
2011	253.6	253.1	253.6	253.0	253.8	255.3	254.9	255.3	253.4	254.6	254.2	254.6	254.1

1. Employment by Industry: New Jersey, Selected Years, 2000–2011—*Continued*

(Numbers in thousands, not seasonally adjusted)

Industry and year	January	February	March	April	May	June	July	August	September	October	November	December	Annual average
Service-Providing													
2000	3,331.1	3,341.1	3,377.8	3,402.1	3,429.4	3,477.0	3,445.3	3,425.0	3,436.9	3,439.1	3,463.8	3,488.9	3,421.5
2001	3,367.8	3,375.8	3,396.5	3,427.8	3,454.9	3,498.8	3,444.4	3,424.9	3,431.7	3,451.0	3,469.1	3,482.6	3,435.4
2002	3,405.5	3,413.6	3,439.3	3,448.6	3,469.7	3,502.7	3,450.1	3,434.9	3,440.8	3,453.0	3,478.5	3,490.9	3,452.3
2003	3,404.3	3,400.2	3,421.2	3,445.5	3,475.8	3,510.7	3,484.6	3,466.1	3,472.5	3,491.1	3,506.7	3,518.0	3,466.4
2004	3,415.2	3,420.2	3,448.9	3,468.3	3,506.2	3,548.5	3,509.1	3,490.2	3,500.1	3,515.7	3,541.2	3,557.1	3,493.4
2005	3,458.2	3,467.2	3,486.8	3,526.4	3,552.9	3,602.4	3,558.6	3,539.3	3,544.2	3,553.4	3,575.6	3,589.2	3,537.9
2006	3,495.1	3,503.8	3,533.6	3,548.9	3,585.0	3,634.2	3,585.0	3,569.5	3,570.0	3,587.0	3,608.7	3,626.4	3,570.6
2007	3,519.7	3,522.8	3,548.8	3,570.0	3,614.3	3,664.9	3,608.4	3,592.4	3,586.2	3,615.0	3,633.6	3,648.3	3,593.7
2008	3,554.0	3,557.7	3,579.6	3,593.5	3,621.7	3,662.7	3,601.5	3,572.5	3,570.7	3,573.7	3,571.2	3,572.3	3,585.9
2009	3,466.6	3,459.5	3,466.0	3,481.7	3,518.2	3,552.1	3,487.6	3,466.5	3,475.3	3,482.3	3,497.2	3,508.8	3,488.5
2010	3,399.0	3,394.4	3,421.1	3,462.7	3,503.7	3,544.1	3,474.6	3,449.6	3,450.9	3,471.3	3,484.5	3,495.4	3,462.6
2011	3,387.3	3,397.1	3,420.3	3,457.9	3,486.1	3,534.6	3,491.3	3,467.8	3,470.8	3,496.8	3,519.4	3,524.1	3,471.1
Trade, Transportation, and Utilities													
2000	885.2	876.5	882.5	887.9	892.7	899.8	896.9	896.5	900.5	905.8	922.7	941.1	899.0
2001	895.2	881.3	883.1	887.5	891.9	899.7	886.1	883.0	883.5	886.0	899.6	911.3	890.7
2002	879.3	869.5	874.8	873.0	877.3	887.4	875.0	873.2	877.8	882.3	896.1	910.7	881.4
2003	873.8	863.9	865.2	867.1	873.7	881.0	871.0	869.0	873.5	880.1	891.5	904.4	876.2
2004	866.8	859.3	863.2	860.7	872.4	882.2	871.0	869.5	872.0	879.7	893.2	906.5	874.7
2005	870.8	862.3	864.9	868.4	875.7	885.6	876.7	873.6	875.4	877.1	890.8	906.2	877.3
2006	870.9	858.6	863.1	862.4	871.8	880.5	871.5	868.9	870.8	877.4	894.0	908.8	874.9
2007	870.2	856.7	859.5	860.2	873.0	884.4	873.8	869.8	870.7	875.5	892.4	907.2	874.5
2008	870.6	857.0	859.8	857.3	864.9	873.1	861.6	857.7	857.1	857.2	863.4	870.4	862.5
2009	829.5	815.2	811.8	807.2	816.9	824.7	812.1	808.2	812.4	813.4	826.8	837.8	818.0
2010	800.7	789.3	792.1	799.9	807.5	817.9	809.0	808.7	808.5	815.3	828.3	842.4	810.0
2011	807.2	797.8	800.5	805.5	811.9	821.9	814.0	814.3	814.4	819.3	837.2	847.6	816.0
Wholesale Trade													
2000	237.3	237.7	239.0	240.9	242.5	241.2	244.1	243.2	243.6	242.8	242.9	245.2	241.7
2001	241.7	242.1	242.7	243.5	243.3	244.1	242.7	242.1	241.7	239.5	239.4	239.5	241.9
2002	238.5	238.2	239.3	237.8	237.7	238.1	235.5	234.8	234.4	234.8	234.5	234.9	236.5
2003	232.3	232.0	232.1	233.5	233.6	234.4	234.0	232.6	232.1	231.6	231.6	232.1	232.7
2004	228.7	228.9	230.5	230.1	231.2	232.5	232.9	233.4	233.0	233.7	233.5	234.3	231.9
2005	232.7	233.2	233.2	233.8	234.3	236.0	234.7	234.9	234.1	232.9	232.9	233.3	233.8
2006	230.7	230.9	231.4	231.8	233.4	234.8	234.4	233.8	233.0	232.8	233.4	234.4	232.9
2007	230.8	230.3	230.8	231.3	232.6	234.9	234.3	234.1	233.2	233.8	233.8	234.6	232.9
2008	231.5	231.3	231.8	231.2	232.3	233.1	231.7	230.5	229.1	228.0	226.2	225.2	230.2
2009	221.5	219.5	218.1	217.6	217.6	218.1	215.7	214.7	214.0	213.8	213.8	214.1	216.5
2010	208.9	207.8	208.0	209.1	209.5	211.0	210.5	210.2	209.6	209.9	210.3	210.6	209.6
2011	208.0	207.2	208.3	209.3	210.6	211.6	210.0	209.8	208.7	209.7	208.5	209.8	209.3
Retail Trade													
2000	457.9	448.7	452.7	453.8	457.5	464.8	463.2	465.2	462.0	463.8	479.9	495.4	463.7
2001	465.5	451.0	452.4	455.3	459.3	466.9	460.2	460.2	454.9	459.1	475.2	487.5	462.3
2002	461.2	451.7	455.7	455.1	459.4	468.1	464.3	464.4	461.9	462.8	477.1	491.9	464.5
2003	461.9	453.3	454.1	456.5	462.3	468.5	465.3	466.1	462.7	467.9	479.6	491.1	465.8
2004	461.5	453.8	455.3	455.1	463.3	471.1	468.5	468.2	463.0	468.7	481.9	494.2	467.1
2005	466.1	457.3	457.7	460.8	466.7	473.3	472.5	470.7	465.1	467.2	479.7	492.3	469.1
2006	465.7	452.9	456.7	456.3	462.1	469.1	466.7	465.7	459.9	466.0	481.0	491.9	466.2
2007	464.8	452.7	454.2	455.5	463.4	470.9	469.1	466.6	459.7	463.3	479.3	489.9	465.8
2008	463.7	450.0	451.3	449.7	455.3	462.5	460.5	458.3	452.2	454.5	462.4	469.5	457.5
2009	439.4	427.9	426.7	425.0	432.7	439.2	436.5	435.7	432.6	434.9	447.0	456.1	436.1
2010	430.7	421.1	423.7	427.5	434.1	441.9	440.6	441.3	434.5	440.3	451.6	461.9	437.4
2011	435.8	427.7	428.7	432.7	436.8	444.6	443.9	445.5	440.9	444.2	459.9	466.9	442.3
Transportation and Utilities													
2000	190.0	190.1	190.8	193.2	192.7	193.8	189.6	188.1	194.9	199.2	199.9	200.5	193.6
2001	188.0	188.2	188.0	188.7	189.3	188.7	183.2	180.7	186.9	187.4	185.0	184.3	186.5
2002	179.6	179.6	179.8	180.1	180.2	181.2	175.2	174.0	181.5	184.7	184.5	183.9	180.4
2003	179.6	178.6	179.0	177.1	177.8	178.1	171.7	170.3	178.7	180.6	180.3	181.2	177.8
2004	176.6	176.6	177.4	175.5	177.9	178.6	169.6	167.9	176.0	177.3	177.8	178.0	175.8
2005	172.0	171.8	174.0	173.8	174.7	176.3	169.5	168.0	176.2	177.0	178.2	180.6	174.3
2006	174.5	174.8	175.0	174.3	176.3	176.6	170.4	169.4	177.9	178.6	179.6	182.5	175.8
2007	174.6	173.7	174.5	173.4	177.0	178.6	170.4	169.1	177.8	178.4	179.3	182.7	175.8
2008	175.4	175.7	176.7	176.4	177.3	177.5	169.4	168.9	175.8	174.7	174.8	175.7	174.9
2009	168.6	167.8	167.0	166.1	166.6	167.4	159.9	157.8	165.8	164.7	166.0	167.6	165.3
2010	161.1	160.4	160.4	163.3	163.9	165.0	157.9	157.2	164.4	165.1	166.4	169.9	162.9
2011	163.4	162.9	163.5	163.5	164.5	165.7	160.1	159.0	164.8	165.4	168.8	170.9	164.4
Information													
2000	126.6	126.3	127.4	126.2	126.8	128.5	128.0	123.7	127.4	126.2	127.4	128.6	126.9
2001	127.2	127.8	128.4	127.0	127.3	128.1	126.1	123.5	126.3	124.5	125.3	125.3	126.4
2002	121.0	120.3	120.3	116.3	116.5	115.7	111.4	111.0	109.4	104.6	106.1	105.6	113.2
2003	102.8	102.4	102.8	102.0	102.1	102.5	102.3	102.9	101.0	101.1	101.4	101.2	102.0
2004	100.1	98.7	99.6	98.2	98.0	97.9	97.3	97.1	96.2	96.9	97.5	97.9	98.0
2005	96.7	96.4	97.0	96.2	96.6	97.8	97.4	97.2	96.7	96.9	97.8	98.3	97.1
2006	97.4	98.1	98.2	97.0	97.4	98.3	97.6	98.0	97.8	96.3	96.1	96.4	97.4
2007	96.3	97.1	97.5	96.7	96.5	96.7	96.5	97.2	95.4	94.0	94.3	93.9	96.0
2008	93.7	94.2	94.2	92.8	92.2	92.7	91.0	90.8	89.7	88.4	88.3	87.8	91.3
2009	86.5	85.9	86.1	84.5	84.8	85.0	84.0	84.7	83.1	82.0	82.1	82.4	84.3
2010	80.4	80.3	80.5	79.5	79.4	80.3	78.7	78.8	78.7	78.4	76.6	79.0	79.2
2011	75.5	75.3	75.4	76.2	76.3	77.3	77.6	72.2	72.7	70.5	71.1	69.7	74.2

1. Employment by Industry: New Jersey, Selected Years, 2000–2011—*Continued*

(Numbers in thousands, not seasonally adjusted)

Industry and year	January	February	March	April	May	June	July	August	September	October	November	December	Annual average
Financial Activities													
2000	262.5	263.0	264.1	264.9	266.1	271.1	272.4	271.6	268.8	265.8	265.4	266.7	266.9
2001	262.0	261.9	262.2	265.5	267.1	271.1	270.0	269.1	266.8	280.9	279.9	281.3	269.8
2002	277.3	276.2	275.1	275.7	276.1	277.7	279.4	278.9	276.6	275.1	275.8	276.4	276.7
2003	274.5	273.8	274.3	274.0	275.0	278.2	279.5	279.6	276.9	276.3	276.1	275.8	276.2
2004	273.1	272.7	273.6	275.6	276.9	279.5	280.9	280.4	277.0	277.2	277.7	278.1	276.9
2005	275.8	275.1	275.9	277.5	278.7	281.8	284.0	284.4	281.7	279.6	280.8	281.0	279.7
2006	276.8	276.5	277.3	278.3	279.6	281.9	283.6	283.0	279.1	278.4	278.1	278.3	279.2
2007	274.9	274.3	274.3	274.8	276.1	278.7	279.9	279.0	274.7	274.0	274.0	273.9	275.7
2008	272.0	271.9	272.3	271.7	272.4	274.2	273.5	272.7	268.4	265.7	264.6	264.0	270.3
2009	258.6	257.7	256.8	257.1	257.3	258.2	257.5	256.1	253.8	252.0	251.5	251.7	255.7
2010	250.4	250.0	250.5	250.6	251.1	254.1	253.7	253.7	251.7	250.7	250.7	251.4	251.6
2011	248.3	248.1	248.6	249.1	250.2	253.1	253.3	252.7	251.6	250.6	251.9	253.5	250.9
Professional and Business Services													
2000	575.8	579.3	591.6	595.6	597.6	610.9	608.7	610.3	608.5	598.7	601.0	604.3	598.5
2001	580.7	582.0	590.9	597.3	599.8	607.5	599.2	599.6	595.0	588.9	586.3	582.4	592.5
2002	569.0	570.8	581.0	584.2	583.6	588.2	584.9	587.8	582.2	580.1	581.9	579.9	581.1
2003	562.2	559.0	565.2	572.0	575.1	581.0	585.4	589.1	587.6	586.8	586.8	587.6	578.2
2004	564.0	562.7	572.1	582.0	585.3	592.1	592.1	593.0	591.5	592.3	593.9	592.8	584.5
2005	570.0	571.5	577.0	593.0	594.2	604.3	600.3	601.6	599.8	600.7	600.3	597.4	592.5
2006	577.8	583.3	592.3	598.2	603.9	613.7	611.9	616.0	613.1	614.2	615.6	615.1	604.6
2007	588.8	590.1	599.1	610.3	616.5	626.5	628.0	630.7	626.3	627.6	628.9	626.9	616.6
2008	605.5	606.8	612.7	618.9	620.0	626.5	625.5	626.2	620.4	615.0	611.1	605.5	616.2
2009	583.3	578.3	578.1	585.3	586.3	591.5	587.9	588.4	585.5	584.1	584.0	582.4	584.6
2010	559.9	562.3	569.6	582.9	586.5	596.6	593.3	595.8	594.3	596.5	597.6	596.9	586.0
2011	579.8	580.8	586.8	600.4	603.5	612.1	611.8	613.6	612.6	608.9	608.8	604.0	601.9
Education and Health Services													
2000	484.3	488.2	490.7	494.2	494.7	496.8	493.3	491.0	497.9	503.1	506.2	509.2	495.8
2001	492.6	496.4	499.3	504.4	507.8	511.1	503.6	501.6	505.8	510.3	514.3	517.1	505.4
2002	517.6	522.9	524.4	526.2	528.8	529.4	524.7	522.0	526.6	531.3	535.6	536.2	527.1
2003	532.3	532.5	536.2	537.3	540.9	540.2	536.5	531.8	537.3	541.6	544.1	544.8	538.0
2004	537.4	539.9	543.6	544.5	548.9	549.6	543.2	540.1	545.6	552.5	554.7	556.4	546.4
2005	549.3	552.9	555.3	556.9	561.3	561.0	555.3	551.2	557.1	565.0	567.6	568.1	558.4
2006	560.8	563.2	567.1	566.1	571.1	571.3	563.7	562.0	567.3	572.7	575.9	579.1	568.4
2007	571.6	575.6	580.1	577.4	583.8	582.0	575.1	571.4	577.2	586.7	586.1	589.6	579.7
2008	583.7	587.7	590.5	590.3	592.2	593.2	584.9	581.7	587.8	593.1	595.3	599.8	590.0
2009	590.5	594.5	597.0	597.7	600.4	601.3	590.8	587.5	594.7	602.6	605.3	609.9	597.7
2010	599.7	599.9	603.8	603.8	604.9	603.6	592.7	588.7	596.0	605.7	607.4	607.3	601.1
2011	597.8	603.1	607.0	606.5	608.7	610.1	604.0	599.2	608.9	622.5	625.0	625.2	609.8
Leisure and Hospitality													
2000	278.0	278.5	285.1	295.4	308.3	328.1	330.8	329.3	315.5	301.5	296.3	292.6	303.3
2001	278.9	281.6	285.4	296.0	310.6	327.2	334.2	332.4	315.6	299.1	294.6	294.2	304.2
2002	283.3	285.0	290.8	302.2	316.0	333.2	338.8	336.5	322.4	310.8	306.8	306.0	311.0
2003	293.7	292.7	297.3	310.3	325.8	342.8	354.8	352.9	334.9	321.0	316.2	314.0	321.4
2004	298.1	299.2	303.5	314.0	330.3	349.5	358.5	355.3	340.5	318.1	319.3	319.5	325.5
2005	305.1	305.3	311.3	324.2	338.8	359.8	367.5	364.9	348.2	327.7	324.5	323.9	333.4
2006	310.7	310.8	319.0	327.5	343.7	366.5	371.5	368.7	352.7	333.2	329.2	328.1	338.5
2007	313.2	312.8	318.2	328.0	345.6	367.9	371.9	369.2	349.7	337.9	333.4	332.1	340.0
2008	317.3	317.9	325.0	336.2	352.2	371.7	373.4	368.9	351.7	337.7	327.5	324.4	342.0
2009	309.1	308.3	313.0	323.8	344.8	361.3	365.7	363.7	348.7	330.3	323.1	321.6	334.5
2010	303.4	302.0	309.6	326.7	343.4	362.7	365.7	364.5	349.7	333.1	325.9	323.5	334.2
2011	303.7	305.2	311.7	327.2	344.3	364.4	370.7	365.5	344.4	331.5	325.0	324.2	334.8
Other Services													
2000	138.2	139.0	140.4	141.8	142.6	144.9	146.4	145.0	142.4	141.6	141.6	142.3	142.2
2001	138.8	139.4	140.3	141.8	143.7	145.9	148.0	146.7	144.0	145.8	146.2	146.9	144.0
2002	146.0	146.5	147.1	147.2	148.4	150.1	150.8	150.0	147.3	148.5	148.4	149.0	148.3
2003	148.6	148.5	149.4	151.4	152.5	155.1	155.8	155.4	153.4	153.4	153.6	154.1	152.6
2004	150.9	151.4	152.2	153.0	154.9	156.7	157.2	156.4	153.9	154.0	154.1	154.5	154.1
2005	154.3	155.1	155.4	158.4	159.0	161.2	161.4	160.7	157.0	156.6	157.1	157.8	157.8
2006	156.8	156.9	158.2	160.6	162.1	164.7	163.1	161.9	159.0	159.7	160.0	161.1	160.3
2007	159.5	159.6	160.3	163.3	164.9	168.2	166.7	165.4	162.4	163.7	163.6	163.9	163.5
2008	162.5	162.7	163.1	163.6	166.6	169.1	167.6	166.3	163.1	162.8	162.3	162.1	164.5
2009	159.5	160.0	160.2	161.5	163.2	165.5	163.7	163.2	159.9	160.2	160.4	160.2	161.5
2010	157.2	156.4	157.7	160.4	161.8	165.2	163.5	163.1	159.9	160.4	160.3	161.3	160.6
2011	157.8	158.0	159.3	161.0	162.6	166.6	167.9	169.4	162.6	164.9	166.5	166.9	163.6
Government													
2000	580.5	590.3	596.0	596.1	600.6	596.9	568.8	557.6	575.9	596.4	603.2	604.1	588.9
2001	592.4	605.4	606.9	608.3	606.7	608.2	577.2	569.0	594.7	615.5	622.9	624.1	602.6
2002	612.0	622.4	625.8	623.8	623.0	621.0	585.1	575.5	598.5	620.3	627.8	627.1	613.5
2003	616.4	627.4	630.8	631.4	630.7	629.9	599.3	585.4	607.9	630.8	637.0	636.1	621.9
2004	624.8	636.3	641.1	640.3	639.5	641.0	608.9	598.4	623.4	645.0	650.8	651.4	633.4
2005	636.2	648.6	650.0	651.8	648.6	650.9	616.0	605.7	628.3	649.8	656.7	656.5	641.6
2006	643.9	656.4	658.4	658.8	655.4	657.3	622.1	611.0	630.2	655.1	659.8	659.5	647.3
2007	645.2	656.6	659.8	659.3	657.9	660.5	616.5	609.7	629.8	655.6	660.9	660.8	647.7
2008	648.7	659.5	662.0	661.1	661.2	662.2	624.0	608.2	632.5	653.8	658.7	658.3	649.2
2009	649.6	659.6	663.0	664.6	664.5	664.6	625.9	614.7	637.2	657.7	664.0	662.8	652.4
2010	647.3	654.2	657.3	658.9	669.1	663.7	618.0	596.3	612.1	631.2	637.7	633.6	640.0
2011	617.2	628.8	631.0	632.0	628.6	629.1	592.0	580.9	603.6	628.6	633.9	633.0	619.9

2. Average Weekly Hours by Selected Industry: New Jersey, 2007–2011

(Not seasonally adjusted)

Industry and year	January	February	March	April	May	June	July	August	September	October	November	December	Annual average
Total Private													
2007	33.8	33.7	33.8	34.0	34.2	34.2	34.3	34.1	34.2	33.9	33.9	34.3	34.0
2008	33.3	33.3	33.8	33.9	33.8	34.0	33.8	33.7	33.4	33.4	33.7	33.3	33.6
2009	33.0	33.4	33.3	33.1	33.5	33.5	33.8	33.9	33.7	33.9	33.9	33.9	33.6
2010	33.5	32.9	33.3	33.6	33.9	33.7	33.8	34.4	34.0	34.2	34.3	34.3	33.8
2011	34.3	34.4	34.2	34.4	34.6	33.5	33.6	33.5	33.5	33.8	33.5	33.8	33.9
Goods-Producing													
2007	39.1	39.0	39.4	38.9	39.3	39.6	39.5	38.9	39.0	39.0	38.8	39.6	39.2
2008	39.6	38.8	39.5	39.7	39.2	40.0	39.2	39.4	39.1	38.9	38.5	38.6	39.2
2009	38.3	38.1	38.4	37.6	38.6	38.2	38.3	36.9	36.5	36.8	37.4	37.9	37.8
2010	37.2	35.1	38.0	38.6	38.4	38.5	38.3	38.6	38.7	38.7	38.5	38.8	38.1
2011	38.3	38.6	38.5	38.4	38.7	38.9	38.5	38.5	38.5	38.5	39.1	39.4	38.7
Construction													
2007	38.2	36.2	37.5	37.2	38.6	38.5	38.3	37.9	38.3	38.1	37.1	37.4	37.8
2008	37.9	36.4	37.1	37.2	35.8	37.4	36.8	37.4	37.4	37.1	36.1	35.8	36.9
2009	35.8	36.3	36.7	35.6	37.5	36.1	36.1	36.5	35.3	35.3	35.6	36.2	36.2
2010	35.4	33.8	35.1	35.7	35.3	35.9	35.4	35.7	35.8	35.9	35.7	35.6	35.5
2011	35.2	35.5	35.9	35.4	36.0	36.3	36.1	36.3	36.2	37.0	36.3	37.4	36.2
Manufacturing													
2007	39.4	40.0	40.1	39.6	39.5	40.1	40.1	39.6	39.4	39.6	39.9	40.5	39.8
2008	38.6	39.9	40.3	40.6	40.7	41.1	40.2	40.3	39.9	39.8	39.8	40.0	40.1
2009	39.6	39.1	39.4	38.8	39.3	39.5	39.0	39.4	39.3	39.5	39.7	40.0	39.4
2010	39.2	37.8	39.0	39.1	39.1	39.0	39.2	39.3	39.3	39.5	39.4	39.3	39.1
2011	39.0	39.2	39.0	39.2	39.3	39.6	39.2	39.2	39.4	40.0	39.9	40.5	39.5
Trade, Transportation, and Utilities													
2007	34.2	34.0	34.4	34.7	35.0	35.2	35.5	35.2	35.1	34.5	34.5	34.7	34.8
2008	33.3	33.3	34.0	33.8	33.5	34.2	33.1	33.0	32.6	32.6	33.0	33.4	33.3
2009	32.5	32.9	33.0	32.3	32.8	33.3	33.7	33.8	33.3	33.7	33.8	34.0	33.3
2010	33.4	32.9	33.6	33.6	34.0	34.1	34.1	34.3	33.8	34.1	34.2	34.5	33.9
2011	33.8	34.1	34.0	34.5	34.4	34.1	34.5	34.5	34.7	34.5	34.0	34.7	34.3
Financial Activities													
2007	36.2	35.9	37.1	37.6	36.5	36.2	36.4	36.4	36.7	36.5	36.7	37.2	36.6
2008	36.4	36.2	36.9	36.9	37.8	37.7	37.8	37.3	37.1	37.0	36.8	36.6	37.0
2009	36.9	37.1	37.0	37.3	36.5	36.3	36.2	36.5	36.4	36.0	36.9	36.4	36.6
2010	36.7	37.0	37.6	36.9	37.8	36.9	36.9	37.2	37.3	37.8	37.8	37.7	37.3
2011	38.4	37.8	37.4	37.2	37.7	37.0	36.5	36.3	36.6	37.6	36.4	36.0	37.1
Professional and Business Services													
2007	34.7	35.1	34.5	35.0	34.9	35.2	35.0	34.8	34.9	35.2	35.1	35.6	35.0
2008	33.5	33.8	34.2	34.5	34.4	35.2	33.8	33.9	34.0	34.6	34.5	34.4	34.2
2009	33.9	34.9	34.9	34.8	36.3	35.7	35.0	36.2	36.0	36.3	36.5	35.7	35.5
2010	35.7	34.6	35.7	35.9	36.3	35.6	35.5	36.0	34.8	35.4	35.3	35.4	35.5
2011	35.1	35.4	35.1	35.4	36.2	35.5	35.3	35.4	35.4	35.7	35.4	35.7	35.5
Education and Health Services													
2007	30.6	30.6	30.7	30.7	31.0	30.9	30.9	30.6	31.3	31.0	30.8	31.2	30.9
2008	30.2	30.3	30.6	30.5	30.4	30.6	30.5	30.4	30.6	30.6	30.8	31.1	30.6
2009	31.1	31.3	30.9	31.1	31.1	31.1	31.7	31.8	31.3	32.5	32.7	32.3	31.6
2010	32.2	32.0	32.2	32.3	32.8	32.5	32.6	32.9	32.7	32.8	33.0	32.9	32.6
2011	32.6	32.5	32.3	32.4	32.2	31.8	31.5	31.7	31.4	31.5	31.6	31.6	31.9
Leisure and Hospitality													
2007	28.8	28.8	28.7	29.3	29.5	29.2	29.9	29.8	29.1	28.6	28.8	28.5	29.1
2008	28.1	28.2	28.3	28.2	28.2	28.9	29.8	29.4	28.1	27.9	26.6	26.0	28.2
2009	26.3	26.7	26.1	26.0	26.7	26.8	28.2	28.3	27.9	26.7	26.5	25.9	26.9
2010	25.8	25.6	26.3	26.6	26.8	26.6	28.0	28.1	26.6	25.9	26.1	25.3	26.5
2011	25.2	25.7	25.8	26.1	26.3	25.8	26.1	26.2	25.3	26.2	26.4	26.1	25.9
Other Services													
2007	30.5	30.6	29.6	30.5	31.2	30.8	32.0	32.4	31.3	31.0	31.5	31.9	31.1
2008	32.5	32.1	32.4	32.0	32.0	33.0	32.4	33.2	32.7	32.3	33.7	33.1	32.6
2009	32.8	33.0	32.9	32.4	32.4	32.3	32.5	33.8	33.9	33.2	33.4	33.3	33.0
2010	33.0	31.6	32.6	32.4	32.6	32.4	32.2	32.8	32.3	31.9	32.1	32.0	32.3
2011	32.1	31.6	31.3	31.5	32.0	31.2	31.8	31.6	31.9	31.9	31.1	31.6	31.6

3. Average Hourly Earnings by Selected Industry: New Jersey, 2007–2011

(Dollars, not seasonally adjusted)

Industry and year	January	February	March	April	May	June	July	August	September	October	November	December	Annual average
Total Private													
2007	25.90	25.46	25.03	25.14	24.63	24.51	24.47	24.29	24.64	24.73	24.68	24.69	24.84
2008	25.58	25.47	25.51	25.51	25.15	25.19	24.98	25.27	25.47	25.26	24.77	25.71	25.32
2009	25.56	25.71	26.05	25.83	25.63	25.49	25.53	25.63	26.09	26.05	26.84	26.66	25.92
2010	26.56	26.89	26.29	26.19	26.04	25.78	25.67	25.45	25.62	25.65	25.67	25.80	25.96
2011	26.02	25.82	25.73	25.72	25.68	25.39	25.20	25.20	25.59	26.00	25.71	25.59	25.64
Goods-Producing													
2007	27.04	26.60	26.08	26.62	27.39	27.14	27.48	27.61	27.85	27.84	27.58	27.30	27.22
2008	27.30	27.03	27.37	27.45	27.28	27.32	27.21	27.30	27.69	27.44	27.66	28.09	27.42
2009	27.42	28.16	28.22	27.63	27.61	27.66	27.18	28.06	28.04	27.84	27.86	28.64	27.85
2010	28.32	29.38	28.40	28.49	28.84	28.91	28.84	28.46	28.39	28.41	28.54	28.60	28.63
2011	28.64	28.52	28.56	28.46	28.33	28.41	28.56	28.29	28.32	28.08	28.02	28.06	28.35
Construction													
2007	31.94	32.42	31.48	31.98	34.72	34.68	35.25	35.37	35.35	35.35	35.38	34.20	34.09
2008	33.26	33.43	33.46	34.01	33.84	33.87	33.70	34.04	35.08	34.45	34.33	34.84	34.03
2009	33.62	34.51	34.19	33.62	33.25	33.83	33.34	33.19	33.28	33.18	33.73	33.96	33.64
2010	34.02	34.30	34.10	34.09	33.96	33.87	33.84	33.64	33.69	33.68	33.68	33.76	33.88
2011	33.53	33.72	33.51	33.32	33.05	33.44	33.81	34.05	33.59	33.11	32.93	32.78	33.40
Manufacturing													
2007	24.95	24.46	23.93	24.39	24.05	23.72	23.86	23.86	24.18	24.15	24.07	24.25	24.16
2008	23.74	24.07	24.22	24.12	23.99	24.02	23.85	23.73	23.99	23.66	24.39	24.84	24.05
2009	24.53	25.19	25.25	24.63	24.79	24.60	23.85	23.87	23.82	23.67	23.69	24.03	24.33
2010	23.98	24.78	23.99	23.88	24.60	24.72	24.75	24.73	24.60	24.64	24.72	24.77	24.51
2011	24.90	24.76	24.65	24.68	24.61	24.50	24.48	23.90	24.38	24.41	24.53	24.82	24.55
Trade, Transportation, and Utilities													
2007	24.33	24.00	22.97	23.61	22.80	22.71	22.86	22.50	22.95	23.00	22.72	22.55	23.07
2008	25.16	24.51	24.59	24.27	23.82	23.80	24.11	24.58	24.69	24.53	24.53	24.27	24.40
2009	24.52	24.01	24.35	23.93	23.98	23.44	23.69	23.57	23.59	23.35	24.11	23.26	23.81
2010	23.00	22.98	22.44	22.48	22.56	21.82	22.46	22.66	22.83	22.74	22.67	22.51	22.59
2011	22.98	22.82	22.53	22.53	22.44	21.96	22.03	21.96	22.53	22.65	22.45	22.08	22.41
Financial Activities													
2007	30.93	28.53	28.37	28.67	27.48	29.82	29.43	29.27	28.85	28.79	29.08	29.12	29.03
2008	28.74	28.48	28.60	28.91	28.48	28.70	27.61	28.02	27.99	27.99	28.43	28.40	28.36
2009	28.21	28.57	30.80	32.35	31.43	31.35	33.03	34.30	33.08	32.99	33.00	32.55	31.79
2010	32.32	33.00	32.90	33.54	34.20	33.81	33.26	33.06	32.92	32.31	32.30	32.71	33.03
2011	33.86	33.25	33.29	34.04	34.31	33.51	33.29	33.51	33.77	37.04	35.71	35.37	34.25
Professional and Business Services													
2007	28.73	28.79	29.36	28.06	27.28	26.87	27.02	26.95	27.13	26.81	27.31	27.70	27.65
2008	28.19	28.91	29.32	28.56	28.36	28.60	28.79	28.89	28.51	28.23	29.19	30.04	28.80
2009	29.66	30.50	30.41	29.79	28.79	28.72	29.09	28.77	28.78	29.03	30.36	30.46	29.52
2010	30.84	32.00	31.74	31.05	30.86	30.31	30.32	30.57	30.96	30.99	30.90	31.18	30.97
2011	32.83	31.94	31.94	31.99	31.96	31.56	31.72	31.40	31.23	32.13	31.09	30.85	31.71
Education and Health Services													
2007	25.50	25.52	24.85	25.42	24.93	24.89	25.09	24.97	24.88	25.37	25.36	25.25	25.17
2008	25.55	25.15	25.37	25.35	25.11	25.11	25.33	25.46	25.48	25.29	25.43	25.44	25.34
2009	25.25	25.17	25.55	25.46	25.51	25.37	25.31	25.50	25.61	25.27	25.70	25.93	25.47
2010	25.81	25.43	25.17	25.06	24.87	24.80	24.87	24.61	25.24	25.39	25.34	25.53	25.18
2011	24.92	24.88	24.75	24.87	24.61	24.64	24.59	24.57	24.88	24.42	24.66	24.74	24.71
Leisure and Hospitality													
2007	20.44	19.60	19.13	18.64	18.18	17.59	16.97	16.64	16.95	16.93	16.83	17.08	17.86
2008	16.69	16.74	17.06	16.81	16.49	16.17	15.54	15.57	15.82	15.49	15.30	15.59	16.09
2009	15.33	15.52	15.29	15.68	16.84	17.97	17.35	16.96	16.65	16.42	16.63	16.33	16.47
2010	15.99	15.74	15.58	15.53	15.41	15.28	14.77	14.72	14.77	14.87	14.77	15.08	15.18
2011	14.71	14.47	14.52	14.35	15.18	16.34	14.28	15.98	15.27	14.26	14.33	14.32	14.86
Other Services													
2007	19.08	19.85	20.29	19.45	18.77	18.51	17.91	17.82	18.41	18.57	18.68	18.89	18.83
2008	18.75	18.70	18.84	18.49	18.48	18.88	18.43	18.20	18.55	19.28	19.42	19.48	18.79
2009	20.33	21.02	21.16	21.63	21.63	21.97	21.59	22.27	22.67	23.43	23.61	23.13	22.04
2010	24.06	24.11	23.54	24.31	23.20	23.66	22.76	22.92	23.60	23.54	23.32	24.08	23.59
2011	24.23	24.05	23.89	23.34	23.16	23.01	21.97	21.84	22.20	22.29	22.66	22.45	22.91

4. Average Weekly Earnings by Selected Industry: New Jersey, 2007–2011

(Dollars, not seasonally adjusted)

Industry and year	January	February	March	April	May	June	July	August	September	October	November	December	Annual average
Total Private													
2007	875.42	858.00	846.01	854.76	842.35	838.24	839.32	828.29	842.69	838.35	836.65	846.87	845.50
2008	851.81	848.15	862.24	864.79	850.07	856.46	844.32	851.60	850.70	843.68	834.75	856.14	851.11
2009	843.48	858.71	867.47	854.97	858.61	853.92	862.91	868.86	879.23	883.10	909.88	903.77	870.21
2010	889.76	884.68	875.46	879.98	882.76	868.79	867.65	875.48	871.08	877.23	880.48	884.94	878.11
2011	892.49	888.21	879.97	884.77	888.53	850.57	846.72	844.20	857.27	878.80	861.29	864.94	869.50
Goods-Producing													
2007	1,057.26	1,037.40	1,027.55	1,035.52	1,076.43	1,074.74	1,085.46	1,074.03	1,086.15	1,085.76	1,070.10	1,081.08	1,066.19
2008	1,081.08	1,048.76	1,081.12	1,089.77	1,069.38	1,092.80	1,066.63	1,075.62	1,082.68	1,067.42	1,064.91	1,084.27	1,075.41
2009	1,050.19	1,072.90	1,083.65	1,038.89	1,065.75	1,056.61	1,040.99	1,035.41	1,023.46	1,024.51	1,041.96	1,085.46	1,051.64
2010	1,053.50	1,031.24	1,079.20	1,099.71	1,107.46	1,113.04	1,104.57	1,098.56	1,098.69	1,099.47	1,098.79	1,109.68	1,091.51
2011	1,096.91	1,100.87	1,099.56	1,092.86	1,096.37	1,105.15	1,099.56	1,089.17	1,090.32	1,097.93	1,084.37	1,105.56	1,096.52
Construction													
2007	1,220.11	1,173.60	1,180.50	1,189.66	1,340.19	1,335.18	1,350.08	1,340.52	1,353.91	1,346.84	1,312.60	1,279.08	1,288.32
2008	1,260.55	1,216.85	1,241.37	1,265.17	1,211.47	1,266.74	1,240.16	1,273.10	1,311.99	1,278.10	1,239.31	1,247.27	1,254.66
2009	1,203.60	1,252.71	1,254.77	1,196.87	1,246.88	1,221.26	1,236.91	1,211.44	1,174.78	1,171.25	1,200.79	1,229.35	1,216.65
2010	1,204.31	1,159.34	1,196.91	1,217.01	1,198.79	1,215.93	1,197.94	1,200.95	1,206.10	1,209.11	1,202.38	1,201.86	1,201.19
2011	1,180.26	1,197.06	1,203.01	1,179.53	1,189.80	1,213.87	1,220.54	1,236.02	1,215.96	1,225.07	1,195.36	1,225.97	1,207.69
Manufacturing													
2007	983.03	978.40	959.59	965.84	949.98	951.17	956.79	944.86	952.69	956.34	960.39	982.13	961.77
2008	916.36	960.39	976.07	979.27	976.39	987.22	958.77	956.32	957.20	941.67	970.72	993.60	964.43
2009	971.39	984.93	994.85	955.64	974.25	971.70	930.15	940.48	936.13	934.97	940.49	961.20	958.28
2010	940.02	936.68	935.61	933.71	961.86	964.08	970.20	971.89	971.70	970.82	971.50	975.94	958.69
2011	971.10	970.59	961.35	967.46	967.17	970.20	959.62	936.88	960.57	976.40	978.75	1,005.21	968.79
Trade, Transportation, and Utilities													
2007	832.09	816.00	790.17	819.27	798.00	799.39	811.53	792.00	805.55	793.50	783.84	782.49	801.85
2008	837.83	816.18	836.06	820.33	797.97	813.96	798.04	811.14	804.89	799.68	809.49	810.62	813.03
2009	796.90	789.93	803.55	772.94	786.54	780.55	798.35	796.67	785.55	786.90	814.92	790.84	791.99
2010	768.20	756.04	753.98	755.33	767.04	744.06	765.89	777.24	771.65	775.43	775.31	776.60	765.64
2011	776.72	778.16	766.02	777.29	771.94	748.84	760.04	757.62	781.79	781.43	763.30	766.18	769.05
Financial Activities													
2007	1,119.67	1,024.23	1,052.53	1,077.99	1,003.02	1,079.48	1,071.25	1,065.43	1,058.80	1,050.84	1,067.24	1,083.26	1,062.83
2008	1,046.14	1,030.98	1,055.34	1,066.78	1,076.54	1,081.99	1,043.66	1,045.15	1,038.43	1,035.63	1,046.22	1,039.44	1,050.62
2009	1,040.95	1,059.95	1,139.60	1,206.66	1,147.20	1,138.01	1,195.69	1,251.95	1,204.11	1,187.64	1,217.70	1,184.82	1,164.28
2010	1,186.14	1,221.00	1,237.04	1,237.63	1,292.76	1,247.59	1,227.29	1,229.83	1,227.92	1,221.32	1,220.94	1,233.17	1,231.95
2011	1,300.22	1,256.85	1,245.05	1,266.29	1,293.49	1,239.87	1,215.09	1,216.41	1,235.98	1,392.70	1,299.84	1,273.32	1,269.42
Professional and Business Services													
2007	996.93	1,010.53	1,012.92	982.10	952.07	945.82	945.70	937.86	946.84	943.71	958.58	986.12	967.71
2008	944.37	977.16	1,002.74	985.32	975.58	1,006.72	973.10	979.37	969.34	976.76	1,007.06	1,033.38	985.88
2009	1,005.47	1,064.45	1,061.31	1,036.69	1,045.08	1,025.30	1,018.15	1,041.47	1,036.08	1,053.79	1,108.14	1,087.42	1,048.49
2010	1,100.99	1,107.20	1,133.12	1,114.70	1,120.22	1,079.04	1,076.36	1,100.52	1,077.41	1,097.05	1,090.77	1,103.77	1,099.88
2011	1,152.33	1,130.68	1,121.09	1,132.45	1,156.95	1,120.38	1,119.72	1,111.56	1,105.54	1,147.04	1,100.59	1,101.35	1,124.85
Education and Health Services													
2007	780.30	780.91	762.90	780.39	772.83	769.10	775.28	764.08	778.74	786.47	781.09	787.80	776.69
2008	771.61	762.05	776.32	773.18	763.34	768.37	772.57	773.98	779.69	773.87	783.24	791.18	774.15
2009	785.28	787.82	789.50	791.81	793.36	789.01	802.33	810.90	801.59	821.28	840.39	837.54	804.33
2010	831.08	813.76	810.47	809.44	815.74	806.00	810.76	809.67	825.35	832.79	836.22	839.94	820.15
2011	812.39	808.60	799.43	805.79	792.44	783.55	774.59	778.87	781.23	769.23	779.26	781.78	788.83
Leisure and Hospitality													
2007	588.67	564.48	549.03	546.15	536.31	513.63	507.40	495.87	493.25	484.20	484.70	486.78	519.68
2008	468.99	472.07	482.80	474.04	465.02	467.31	463.09	457.76	444.54	432.17	406.98	405.34	453.59
2009	403.18	414.38	399.07	407.68	449.63	481.60	489.27	479.97	464.54	438.41	440.70	422.95	442.76
2010	412.54	402.94	409.75	413.10	412.99	406.45	413.56	413.63	392.88	385.13	385.50	381.52	402.65
2011	370.69	371.88	374.62	374.54	399.23	421.57	372.71	418.68	386.33	373.61	378.31	373.75	385.44
Other Services													
2007	581.94	607.41	600.58	593.23	585.62	570.11	573.12	577.37	576.23	575.67	588.42	602.59	585.91
2008	609.38	600.27	610.42	591.68	591.36	623.04	597.13	604.24	606.59	622.74	654.45	644.79	612.90
2009	666.82	693.66	696.16	700.81	700.81	709.63	701.68	752.73	768.51	777.88	788.57	770.23	727.26
2010	793.98	761.88	767.40	787.64	756.32	766.58	732.87	751.78	762.28	750.93	748.57	770.56	762.53
2011	777.78	759.98	747.76	735.21	741.12	717.91	698.65	690.14	708.18	711.05	704.73	709.42	724.69

NEW MEXICO
At a Glance

Population:
    2000 census: 1,819,017
    2010 census: 2,059,179
    2011 estimate: 2,082,224

Percent change in population:
    2000–2010: 13.2%
    2010–2011: 1.1%

Percent change in total nonfarm employment:
    2000–2010: 7.8%
    2010–2011: 0.1%

Industry with the largest growth in employment, 2000–2011 (thousands):
    Education and Health Services, 40.9

Industry with the largest decline or smallest growth in employment, 2000–2011 (thousands):
    Manufacturing, -12.3

Civilian labor force:
    2000: 852,293
    2010: 934,380
    2011: 927,785

Unemployment rate and rank among states (lowest to highest):
    2000: 5.0%, 44th
    2010: 7.9%, 16th
    2011: 7.4%, 18th

Over-the-year change in unemployment rates:
    2010–2011: -0.5%

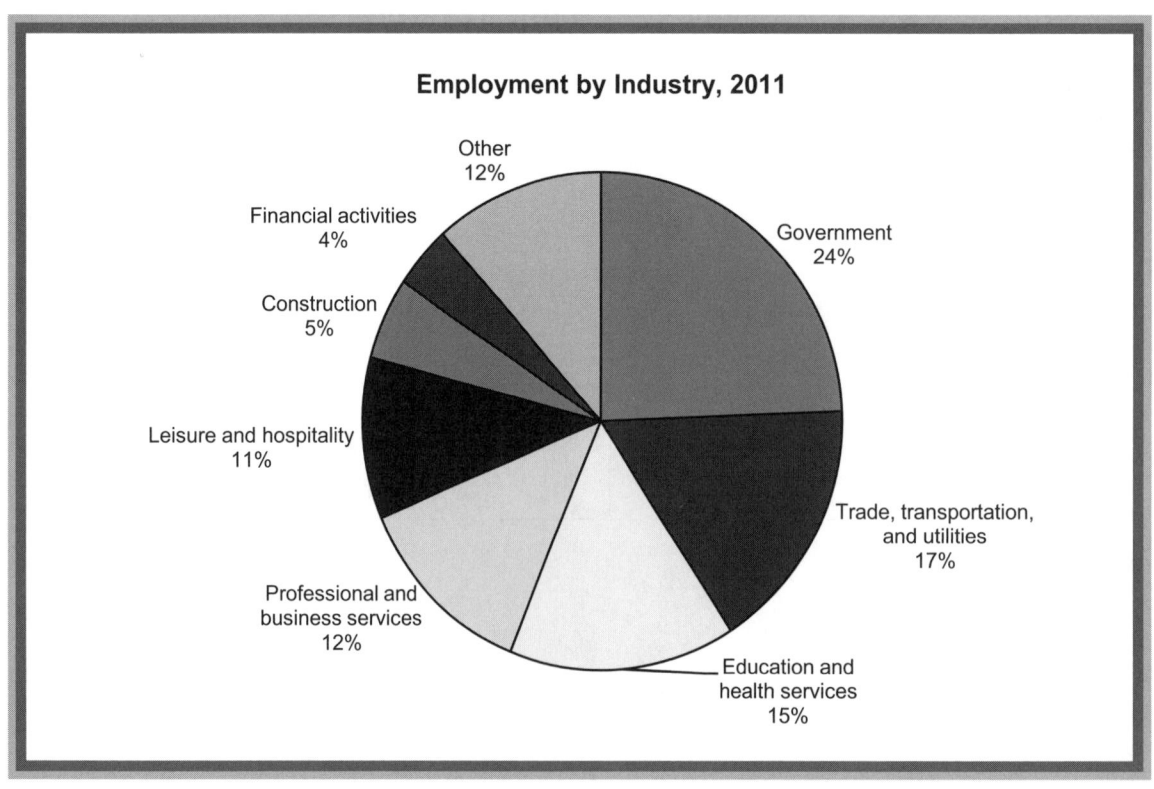

Employment by Industry, 2011

Other 12%
Financial activities 4%
Construction 5%
Leisure and hospitality 11%
Professional and business services 12%
Government 24%
Trade, transportation, and utilities 17%
Education and health services 15%

1. Employment by Industry: New Mexico, Selected Years, 2000–2011

(Numbers in thousands, not seasonally adjusted)

Industry and year	January	February	March	April	May	June	July	August	September	October	November	December	Annual average
Total Nonfarm													
2000	722.5	730.2	738.0	741.0	747.3	746.2	742.3	748.3	754.9	752.3	755.5	759.1	744.8
2001	739.8	748.1	755.1	756.4	762.3	762.5	754.7	759.6	763.9	759.9	761.1	762.6	757.2
2002	748.5	754.1	760.9	764.2	770.0	769.4	763.7	768.3	774.1	770.6	773.7	776.2	766.1
2003	759.5	765.2	769.9	772.6	777.2	776.5	772.1	776.7	781.4	783.8	784.8	787.4	775.6
2004	769.8	778.0	783.8	788.7	792.6	791.1	787.0	789.5	795.3	801.5	802.5	805.2	790.4
2005	786.5	793.6	799.1	806.9	810.1	808.6	805.2	809.7	818.8	818.5	822.3	824.5	808.7
2006	809.2	819.7	827.1	828.6	835.2	837.3	828.0	832.0	842.5	839.5	842.9	844.3	832.2
2007	824.4	833.9	842.3	840.2	845.6	845.9	837.8	843.2	850.2	851.9	853.9	855.3	843.7
2008	834.0	843.3	847.5	848.8	852.8	850.2	841.7	846.8	854.7	852.2	847.2	842.4	846.8
2009	816.9	818.2	816.7	816.0	817.0	811.7	803.5	807.6	812.4	811.3	808.8	808.5	812.4
2010	789.4	795.8	801.1	807.2	810.5	807.2	799.8	801.7	803.6	807.8	806.2	807.1	803.1
2011	787.9	795.7	800.4	807.7	808.7	806.5	799.6	804.4	810.2	811.0	809.2	808.0	804.1
Total Private													
2000	543.8	546.3	551.4	554.5	559.3	566.9	565.1	570.8	570.8	567.6	570.8	573.5	561.7
2001	560.5	562.5	567.7	568.8	574.2	578.4	576.2	579.6	574.6	571.6	572.6	573.8	571.7
2002	563.4	563.4	568.8	572.1	576.9	579.1	579.2	582.5	580.3	576.7	579.0	581.0	575.2
2003	569.0	569.9	573.4	575.3	580.6	582.8	583.8	587.4	584.6	584.6	585.8	588.3	580.5
2004	576.8	578.5	583.1	587.9	592.3	594.5	596.3	597.5	595.9	599.3	599.7	602.8	592.1
2005	590.3	591.5	595.7	603.2	606.0	609.1	611.4	614.9	615.4	613.9	617.3	620.1	607.4
2006	610.4	614.1	620.8	623.2	629.3	645.7	642.5	645.1	647.0	642.8	645.9	647.4	634.5
2007	633.8	637.9	644.6	643.4	648.9	653.2	651.3	655.5	653.9	653.7	654.7	655.9	648.9
2008	640.8	644.6	647.8	649.3	652.4	654.5	652.4	656.3	654.9	650.8	645.3	640.8	649.2
2009	621.2	617.3	615.0	613.4	614.8	614.3	612.5	615.6	613.4	609.7	606.8	606.7	613.4
2010	595.0	595.2	597.8	602.1	603.7	606.9	606.8	609.0	606.4	606.5	605.3	607.0	603.5
2011	595.4	597.3	600.5	606.7	608.7	611.4	614.2	616.5	613.8	613.0	611.2	610.3	608.3
Goods-Producing													
2000	95.4	96.2	97.6	98.7	100.4	102.4	103.4	105.9	105.7	104.7	104.0	103.9	101.5
2001	101.6	101.7	103.3	103.8	105.2	106.4	105.9	107.1	105.3	103.6	102.3	100.9	103.9
2002	97.6	96.6	97.5	98.0	98.8	99.2	99.4	100.5	98.9	98.5	97.2	96.3	98.2
2003	94.4	94.1	94.9	95.9	97.4	99.0	99.7	100.9	99.6	100.1	99.2	98.4	97.8
2004	96.1	96.0	97.2	99.0	100.6	102.1	104.2	104.4	103.9	104.8	103.6	104.1	101.3
2005	101.4	101.4	103.0	104.5	105.7	107.4	109.8	110.7	111.2	111.3	111.6	111.4	107.5
2006	110.1	111.7	113.1	113.8	115.3	117.2	117.5	118.3	118.4	118.3	116.5	115.7	115.5
2007	112.5	113.1	114.4	114.5	115.9	117.6	117.2	118.1	117.0	117.1	115.8	114.9	115.7
2008	112.0	112.5	113.1	114.2	114.9	115.9	115.1	116.6	115.9	114.3	111.6	108.3	113.7
2009	102.2	99.6	97.4	95.8	95.3	95.5	95.0	95.5	93.9	93.9	92.1	90.7	95.6
2010	88.6	88.2	88.4	89.9	90.7	91.7	92.6	93.3	93.1	93.7	92.6	91.8	91.2
2011	89.5	89.3	91.1	92.4	92.9	94.1	95.5	96.5	95.3	96.3	94.2	92.3	93.3
Mining and Logging													
2000	13.9	14.2	14.3	14.6	14.8	14.8	14.9	15.3	15.4	15.2	15.3	15.6	14.9
2001	15.6	15.7	15.8	15.8	16.0	15.8	16.0	16.1	15.8	15.3	14.9	14.9	15.6
2002	14.6	14.4	14.3	14.0	14.0	13.9	13.8	13.9	13.7	13.9	13.8	13.8	14.0
2003	13.8	13.9	14.0	14.1	14.3	14.4	14.4	14.4	14.4	14.6	14.7	14.8	14.3
2004	14.4	14.3	14.5	14.7	14.8	15.0	15.1	15.4	15.4	15.6	15.7	16.1	15.1
2005	15.9	15.9	16.1	16.2	16.4	16.6	17.2	17.4	17.8	17.8	17.7	17.7	16.9
2006	17.8	18.0	18.1	18.3	18.5	18.8	18.8	19.1	19.1	19.2	19.1	19.2	18.7
2007	19.3	19.0	19.1	19.2	19.4	19.7	19.9	20.0	19.6	19.7	19.9	19.9	19.6
2008	19.8	19.8	20.0	20.6	21.0	21.3	21.5	22.1	22.1	22.1	21.9	21.3	21.1
2009	19.9	19.1	18.3	17.8	17.5	17.5	17.5	17.5	17.1	17.3	17.5	17.5	17.9
2010	17.4	17.6	17.6	17.9	18.3	18.7	18.9	18.9	18.8	19.2	19.3	19.6	18.5
2011	19.7	20.0	20.2	20.6	20.9	21.3	21.5	21.7	21.7	22.0	21.9	22.1	21.1
Construction													
2000	41.1	41.4	42.5	43.4	44.4	45.7	46.4	47.2	47.0	46.7	46.5	46.3	44.9
2001	44.5	44.7	45.9	46.7	47.9	49.4	49.1	49.4	48.2	47.6	48.0	46.9	47.4
2002	44.7	44.3	45.1	45.8	46.3	46.5	46.1	46.8	45.8	46.2	46.0	45.6	45.8
2003	44.4	44.2	44.9	46.0	47.1	48.0	48.4	48.9	47.8	48.4	48.0	47.7	47.0
2004	46.7	46.8	47.7	48.9	50.0	50.9	52.6	52.1	51.5	52.3	51.7	51.9	50.3
2005	50.2	50.3	51.6	52.8	53.7	55.0	56.5	56.6	56.5	56.4	56.9	56.8	54.4
2006	55.9	56.8	58.1	58.5	59.8	60.9	60.4	60.4	60.4	60.4	59.4	58.7	59.1
2007	56.0	56.8	58.1	58.6	59.6	60.8	60.2	60.5	59.9	60.6	59.7	59.0	59.2
2008	57.0	57.5	58.1	58.5	58.6	59.1	58.0	58.3	57.6	57.2	55.7	53.6	57.4
2009	50.7	49.6	48.9	48.1	48.1	48.1	47.7	47.9	46.9	46.6	45.4	44.0	47.7
2010	42.7	42.2	42.3	43.4	43.5	43.9	44.6	44.6	44.3	44.4	43.9	43.0	43.6
2011	40.9	40.5	41.9	42.7	42.9	43.4	44.4	44.8	43.4	44.2	42.5	40.8	42.7
Manufacturing													
2000	40.4	40.6	40.8	40.7	41.2	41.9	42.1	43.4	43.3	42.8	42.2	42.0	41.8
2001	41.5	41.3	41.6	41.3	41.3	41.2	40.8	41.6	41.3	40.7	39.4	39.1	40.9
2002	38.3	37.9	38.1	38.2	38.5	38.8	38.8	39.5	39.8	39.4	38.4	37.4	38.4
2003	36.2	36.0	36.0	35.8	36.0	36.6	36.9	37.6	37.4	37.1	36.5	35.9	36.5
2004	35.0	34.9	35.0	35.4	35.8	36.2	36.5	36.9	37.0	36.9	36.2	36.1	36.0
2005	35.3	35.2	35.3	35.5	35.6	35.8	36.1	36.7	36.9	37.1	37.0	36.9	36.1
2006	36.4	36.9	36.9	37.0	37.0	37.5	38.3	38.8	38.9	38.7	38.0	37.8	37.7
2007	37.2	37.3	37.2	36.7	36.9	37.1	37.1	37.6	37.5	36.8	36.2	36.0	37.0
2008	35.2	35.2	35.0	35.1	35.3	35.5	35.6	36.2	36.2	35.0	34.0	33.4	35.1
2009	31.6	30.9	30.2	29.9	29.7	29.9	29.8	30.1	29.9	30.0	29.2	29.2	30.0
2010	28.5	28.4	28.5	28.6	28.9	29.1	29.1	29.8	30.0	30.1	29.4	29.2	29.1
2011	28.9	28.8	29.0	29.1	29.1	29.4	29.6	30.0	30.2	30.1	29.8	29.4	29.5

1. Employment by Industry: New Mexico, Selected Years, 2000–2011—*Continued*

(Numbers in thousands, not seasonally adjusted)

Industry and year	January	February	March	April	May	June	July	August	September	October	November	December	Annual average
Service-Providing													
2000	627.1	634.0	640.4	642.3	646.9	643.8	638.9	642.4	649.2	647.6	651.5	655.2	643.3
2001	638.2	646.4	651.8	652.6	657.1	656.1	648.8	652.5	658.6	656.3	658.8	661.7	653.2
2002	650.9	657.5	663.4	666.2	671.2	670.2	664.3	667.8	675.2	672.1	676.5	679.9	667.9
2003	665.1	671.1	675.0	676.7	679.8	677.5	672.4	675.8	681.8	683.7	685.6	689.0	677.8
2004	673.7	682.0	686.6	689.7	692.0	689.0	682.8	685.1	691.4	696.7	698.9	701.1	689.1
2005	685.1	692.2	696.1	702.4	704.4	701.2	695.4	699.0	707.6	707.2	710.7	713.1	701.2
2006	699.1	708.0	714.0	714.8	719.9	720.1	710.5	713.7	724.1	721.2	726.4	728.6	716.7
2007	711.9	720.8	727.9	725.7	729.7	728.3	720.6	725.1	733.2	734.8	738.1	740.4	728.0
2008	722.0	730.8	734.4	734.6	737.9	734.3	726.6	730.2	738.8	737.9	735.6	734.1	733.1
2009	714.7	718.6	719.3	720.2	721.7	716.2	708.5	712.1	718.5	717.4	716.7	717.8	716.8
2010	700.8	707.6	712.7	717.3	719.8	715.5	707.2	708.4	710.5	714.1	713.6	715.3	711.9
2011	698.4	706.4	709.3	715.3	715.8	712.4	704.1	707.9	714.9	714.7	715.0	715.7	710.8
Trade, Transportation, and Utilities													
2000	134.8	134.0	134.4	135.5	137.1	137.7	136.3	137.6	137.8	138.4	141.2	142.3	137.3
2001	136.4	134.4	134.7	134.3	135.5	135.4	135.0	135.8	134.8	134.7	137.0	138.5	135.5
2002	133.9	132.7	133.1	133.7	135.3	135.7	135.0	136.0	135.8	135.9	138.2	139.9	135.4
2003	134.1	133.3	134.1	134.1	135.2	134.8	134.7	135.9	135.8	136.9	139.0	140.6	135.7
2004	135.9	135.4	136.2	136.5	137.4	137.2	137.1	137.3	136.9	138.5	140.7	142.2	137.6
2005	137.5	136.9	137.4	138.0	139.2	138.9	139.5	140.4	140.0	140.5	143.0	144.5	139.7
2006	139.6	138.5	139.8	140.0	141.3	141.4	141.6	142.3	142.0	142.0	144.9	146.3	141.6
2007	142.3	141.8	143.2	142.4	144.1	143.8	144.3	145.2	145.0	146.3	149.1	150.5	144.8
2008	145.8	145.1	145.8	144.9	145.0	144.3	144.1	144.5	143.7	143.3	143.7	144.2	144.5
2009	138.7	136.5	136.3	134.8	135.3	135.2	134.7	135.1	135.0	134.8	135.7	136.6	135.7
2010	132.0	131.0	131.8	132.0	132.6	132.7	133.0	133.7	132.5	133.6	135.2	136.2	133.0
2011	131.9	131.0	131.3	132.5	133.4	133.3	133.7	133.5	133.1	132.4	133.9	136.3	133.0
Wholesale Trade													
2000	21.9	22.0	22.3	22.6	22.9	23.0	22.8	22.9	22.9	22.9	22.8	22.8	22.7
2001	22.7	22.7	22.8	22.7	22.9	23.1	23.0	23.0	23.0	22.7	22.7	22.7	22.8
2002	22.5	22.5	22.5	22.5	22.6	22.8	22.9	22.8	22.5	22.5	22.5	22.5	22.6
2003	21.9	21.9	22.2	22.2	22.1	22.2	22.2	22.2	22.0	22.0	21.9	22.0	22.1
2004	21.7	21.8	22.1	22.3	22.3	22.4	22.4	22.3	22.2	22.3	22.2	22.4	22.2
2005	22.2	22.4	22.5	22.6	22.8	22.9	23.0	22.9	22.8	22.8	22.9	23.0	22.7
2006	22.6	22.7	22.9	23.1	23.3	23.6	23.7	23.7	23.6	23.5	23.5	23.5	23.3
2007	23.4	23.4	23.4	23.5	23.6	23.9	24.1	24.0	23.9	24.1	24.1	24.2	23.8
2008	23.9	23.8	23.8	23.9	23.9	23.9	23.9	23.8	23.4	23.3	23.0	22.7	23.6
2009	22.3	22.1	22.0	21.7	21.7	22.0	21.8	21.6	21.5	21.7	21.6	21.8	21.8
2010	21.5	21.5	21.6	21.7	21.7	21.9	21.8	21.6	21.2	21.2	21.0	21.0	21.5
2011	20.7	20.6	20.7	20.8	21.1	21.3	21.4	21.3	21.2	21.0	21.0	21.4	21.0
Retail Trade													
2000	89.7	88.7	88.9	89.2	90.2	91.2	90.6	91.1	90.7	91.2	94.1	95.2	90.9
2001	90.2	88.7	88.8	88.7	89.6	90.1	90.0	90.1	88.7	88.8	91.3	92.7	89.8
2002	88.7	87.6	88.2	88.5	89.9	90.8	90.1	90.4	90.2	90.1	92.4	94.1	90.1
2003	89.5	88.7	89.2	89.2	90.3	90.4	90.4	91.1	90.7	91.6	93.9	95.3	90.9
2004	90.9	90.4	90.8	91.1	91.9	92.2	92.1	92.0	91.4	92.7	95.1	96.3	92.2
2005	92.3	91.5	91.6	92.2	93.1	93.4	93.9	94.2	93.6	94.1	96.4	97.3	93.6
2006	93.1	91.9	93.1	93.1	94.0	94.2	94.3	94.6	94.1	94.3	97.0	97.8	94.3
2007	94.2	93.6	95.0	94.2	95.6	95.7	96.2	96.3	95.8	96.6	99.3	100.2	96.1
2008	96.5	96.1	96.7	96.1	96.0	96.5	96.6	96.5	96.0	95.9	96.7	97.3	96.4
2009	92.7	90.9	91.1	90.5	90.8	91.4	91.4	91.7	91.7	91.2	92.2	92.7	91.5
2010	88.9	88.0	88.7	88.7	89.2	89.6	89.8	90.3	89.2	90.1	91.9	92.6	89.8
2011	89.0	88.1	88.5	89.5	89.9	89.9	90.1	91.1	90.2	89.8	90.8	92.2	89.9
Transportation and Utilities													
2000	23.2	23.3	23.2	23.7	24.0	23.5	22.9	23.6	24.2	24.3	24.3	24.3	23.7
2001	23.5	23.0	23.1	22.9	23.0	22.2	22.0	22.7	23.1	23.2	23.0	23.1	22.9
2002	22.7	22.6	22.4	22.7	22.8	22.1	22.0	22.8	23.1	23.3	23.3	23.3	22.8
2003	22.7	22.7	22.7	22.7	22.8	22.2	22.1	22.6	23.1	23.3	23.2	23.3	22.8
2004	23.3	23.2	23.3	23.1	23.2	22.6	22.5	23.0	23.3	23.5	23.4	23.5	23.2
2005	23.0	23.0	23.3	23.2	23.3	22.6	22.6	23.3	23.6	23.6	23.7	24.2	23.3
2006	23.9	23.9	23.8	23.8	24.0	23.6	23.6	24.0	24.3	24.2	24.4	25.0	24.0
2007	24.7	24.8	24.8	24.7	24.9	24.2	24.0	24.9	25.3	25.6	25.7	26.1	25.0
2008	25.4	25.2	25.3	24.9	25.1	23.9	23.6	24.2	24.3	24.1	24.0	24.2	24.5
2009	23.7	23.5	23.2	22.6	22.8	21.8	21.5	21.8	21.8	21.9	21.9	22.1	22.4
2010	21.6	21.5	21.5	21.6	21.7	21.2	21.4	21.8	22.1	22.3	22.3	22.6	21.8
2011	22.2	22.3	22.1	22.2	22.4	22.1	22.2	21.1	21.7	21.6	22.1	22.7	22.1
Information													
2000	16.3	16.3	16.4	16.3	16.4	16.7	16.9	17.2	17.3	16.7	16.7	17.2	16.7
2001	17.3	17.6	17.5	16.9	17.1	17.0	16.8	16.9	17.0	16.9	17.0	17.0	17.1
2002	16.8	17.1	17.2	17.0	17.0	16.8	17.0	16.8	16.6	16.4	16.8	16.8	16.9
2003	16.3	16.1	16.3	15.8	16.0	16.0	15.7	15.5	15.5	15.2	15.3	15.3	15.8
2004	14.9	15.2	15.0	14.7	15.0	14.9	14.7	14.7	14.3	14.9	15.1	15.0	14.9
2005	13.9	14.1	14.1	15.3	15.1	14.7	14.8	14.8	14.5	14.9	15.0	15.4	14.7
2006	14.5	15.4	15.9	15.0	15.6	17.4	15.1	15.9	17.1	14.9	15.9	16.9	15.8
2007	14.5	15.5	15.8	14.4	14.8	16.3	15.3	16.5	17.4	16.8	17.1	17.1	16.0
2008	15.6	16.3	16.1	15.1	15.4	16.2	16.0	15.8	16.5	16.3	16.3	15.6	15.9
2009	14.0	14.4	14.3	14.5	14.8	15.1	14.6	15.0	15.5	15.0	15.0	14.4	14.7
2010	14.2	14.6	14.7	15.3	14.7	15.0	13.8	14.1	14.1	13.7	14.0	14.3	14.4
2011	13.8	13.4	13.6	14.4	14.7	14.4	14.0	14.2	14.5	14.3	14.6	14.5	14.2

1. Employment by Industry: New Mexico, Selected Years, 2000–2011—*Continued*

(Numbers in thousands, not seasonally adjusted)

Industry and year	January	February	March	April	May	June	July	August	September	October	November	December	Annual average
Financial Activities													
2000	33.5	33.5	33.6	33.3	33.4	33.5	33.4	33.3	33.2	33.3	33.5	33.8	33.4
2001	33.1	33.3	33.4	33.3	33.3	33.5	33.5	33.4	33.1	33.1	33.1	33.5	33.3
2002	33.4	33.3	33.4	33.3	33.3	33.4	33.7	33.9	33.6	33.4	33.5	33.8	33.5
2003	33.3	33.4	33.4	33.5	33.8	34.0	34.2	34.5	34.2	34.1	34.0	34.4	33.9
2004	34.3	34.1	34.4	34.1	34.1	34.4	34.5	34.4	34.4	34.5	34.5	34.9	34.4
2005	34.7	34.6	34.6	34.7	34.8	35.1	35.2	35.1	35.0	34.9	35.0	35.6	34.9
2006	35.2	35.2	35.2	35.1	35.2	35.3	35.2	35.1	35.0	34.9	34.9	35.3	35.1
2007	34.9	35.0	35.3	35.1	35.2	35.4	35.5	35.5	35.2	35.2	35.1	35.3	35.2
2008	34.7	34.8	34.8	34.7	34.7	34.8	34.9	34.8	34.7	34.4	34.1	34.3	34.6
2009	33.7	33.5	33.2	33.8	33.9	33.7	33.7	33.6	33.5	33.9	33.5	33.8	33.7
2010	33.3	33.1	33.3	32.9	33.7	33.0	33.0	32.9	32.6	32.7	32.7	33.0	33.0
2011	32.5	32.4	32.4	32.6	32.5	32.5	33.1	33.8	33.2	33.3	33.7	33.4	33.0
Professional and Business Services													
2000	82.7	83.4	84.1	85.4	85.3	86.7	86.5	87.0	87.7	87.6	88.6	89.0	86.2
2001	86.4	87.4	88.4	88.7	88.9	89.7	89.3	89.4	88.3	89.1	88.4	88.6	88.6
2002	87.7	87.8	88.9	88.6	89.0	89.2	90.1	90.0	89.9	89.3	89.7	90.2	89.2
2003	87.7	88.6	88.8	88.6	88.6	88.4	88.5	88.8	88.2	88.6	88.2	88.7	88.5
2004	87.0	87.6	88.6	89.6	90.0	90.2	90.5	90.8	91.0	92.1	91.3	91.7	90.0
2005	90.2	90.5	90.7	92.8	92.4	93.3	93.2	93.6	94.0	93.5	94.3	94.3	92.7
2006	93.6	94.5	95.2	96.0	96.6	108.1	107.3	107.6	107.5	107.7	107.6	107.9	102.5
2007	106.3	107.6	108.3	108.3	108.7	109.3	109.5	110.3	109.2	108.6	108.4	108.2	108.6
2008	106.5	107.5	107.4	108.1	108.5	109.0	109.2	110.3	109.7	109.1	107.5	107.0	108.3
2009	104.1	103.4	102.4	102.4	102.0	102.4	102.8	103.5	102.7	101.8	101.1	101.1	102.5
2010	99.3	99.6	99.1	100.3	99.5	100.6	101.1	101.4	101.0	101.1	100.5	100.7	100.4
2011	98.8	101.0	99.6	100.2	99.9	100.5	101.7	101.4	100.0	99.9	99.1	98.6	100.1
Education and Health Services													
2000	81.2	82.3	82.8	82.4	82.2	80.5	78.8	79.7	83.1	83.5	84.4	84.6	82.1
2001	85.1	86.6	87.2	87.5	88.0	85.3	84.9	86.1	89.5	89.8	91.0	91.2	87.7
2002	91.7	92.6	93.5	94.6	94.6	91.3	90.4	91.7	95.9	96.4	97.6	97.3	94.0
2003	97.7	98.5	98.6	99.2	99.2	95.8	95.9	96.7	100.5	100.8	101.9	102.0	98.9
2004	101.6	102.4	102.4	103.1	103.0	99.7	99.0	100.0	103.5	104.1	105.4	104.8	102.4
2005	104.0	104.6	105.1	105.4	105.6	102.0	101.5	102.7	106.7	107.1	107.6	107.6	105.0
2006	106.9	107.4	108.4	108.3	108.7	105.6	104.5	105.2	109.4	109.7	110.8	110.6	108.0
2007	110.1	110.9	111.8	112.4	112.8	109.2	107.9	108.6	112.0	113.2	113.8	114.2	111.4
2008	112.6	114.1	114.8	115.8	116.3	113.0	111.9	113.2	116.9	117.8	118.3	118.7	115.3
2009	117.8	118.9	119.4	119.3	119.6	115.5	114.6	115.9	119.2	119.5	120.0	120.0	118.3
2010	119.4	119.9	120.4	120.1	120.1	117.8	117.0	117.0	120.3	120.9	121.4	121.6	119.7
2011	120.5	121.0	121.6	122.2	122.4	121.7	121.9	121.9	125.1	125.7	125.9	125.9	123.0
Leisure and Hospitality													
2000	73.4	73.8	75.7	76.1	77.3	80.2	80.6	81.1	79.4	77.0	75.9	76.2	77.2
2001	74.8	75.3	76.8	77.9	79.5	81.9	81.5	82.1	79.7	77.8	77.1	77.3	78.5
2002	75.7	76.3	78.0	79.6	81.3	83.6	83.6	83.9	81.9	79.1	78.4	79.1	80.0
2003	78.0	78.3	79.6	80.7	82.5	84.6	84.7	85.0	82.6	80.8	80.1	80.7	81.5
2004	79.1	79.7	81.1	82.8	83.8	85.3	85.4	85.3	83.4	82.0	80.8	81.8	82.5
2005	80.6	81.1	82.5	84.1	84.6	86.7	86.3	86.7	85.2	83.3	82.3	82.7	83.8
2006	82.6	83.0	84.6	86.3	87.6	89.3	89.9	89.7	88.4	86.3	86.3	86.0	86.7
2007	84.9	85.3	86.9	87.6	88.4	90.2	90.3	90.6	89.2	87.5	86.5	86.7	87.8
2008	84.9	85.1	86.5	87.2	87.9	89.0	89.1	89.4	87.8	85.7	84.3	83.9	86.7
2009	82.4	82.5	83.5	84.5	85.4	86.2	86.5	86.8	85.3	82.9	81.5	82.1	84.1
2010	80.7	81.1	82.4	83.8	84.6	86.2	86.1	86.3	84.9	83.3	81.8	82.4	83.6
2011	81.4	82.0	83.5	84.9	85.3	86.3	85.9	86.7	85.5	84.3	83.3	83.1	84.4
Other Services													
2000	26.5	26.8	26.8	26.8	27.2	29.2	29.2	29.0	26.6	26.4	26.5	26.5	27.3
2001	25.8	26.2	26.4	26.4	26.7	29.2	29.3	28.8	26.9	26.6	26.7	26.8	27.2
2002	26.6	27.0	27.2	27.3	27.6	29.9	30.0	29.7	27.7	27.7	27.6	27.6	28.0
2003	27.5	27.6	27.7	27.5	27.9	30.2	30.4	30.1	28.2	28.1	28.1	28.2	28.5
2004	27.9	28.1	28.2	28.1	28.4	30.7	30.9	30.6	28.5	28.4	28.3	28.3	28.9
2005	28.0	28.3	28.3	28.4	28.6	31.0	31.1	30.9	28.8	28.4	28.5	28.6	29.1
2006	27.9	28.4	28.6	28.7	29.0	31.4	31.4	31.0	29.2	29.0	29.0	28.7	29.4
2007	28.3	28.7	28.9	28.7	29.0	31.4	31.3	30.7	28.9	29.0	28.9	29.0	29.4
2008	28.7	29.2	29.3	29.3	29.7	32.3	32.1	31.7	29.7	29.9	29.5	28.8	30.0
2009	28.3	28.5	28.5	28.3	28.5	30.7	30.6	30.2	28.3	27.9	27.9	28.0	28.8
2010	27.5	27.7	27.7	27.8	27.8	29.9	30.2	30.3	27.9	27.5	27.1	27.0	28.2
2011	27.0	27.2	27.4	27.5	27.6	28.6	28.4	28.5	27.1	26.8	26.5	26.2	27.4
Government													
2000	178.7	183.9	186.6	186.5	188.0	179.3	177.2	177.5	184.1	184.7	184.7	185.6	183.1
2001	179.3	185.6	187.4	187.6	188.1	184.1	178.5	180.0	189.3	188.3	188.5	188.8	185.5
2002	185.1	190.7	192.1	192.1	193.1	190.3	184.5	185.8	193.8	193.9	194.7	195.2	190.9
2003	190.5	195.3	196.5	197.3	196.6	193.7	188.3	189.3	196.8	199.2	199.0	199.1	195.1
2004	193.0	199.5	200.7	200.8	200.3	196.6	190.7	192.0	199.4	202.2	202.8	202.4	198.4
2005	196.2	202.1	203.4	203.7	204.1	199.5	193.8	194.8	203.4	204.6	205.0	204.4	201.3
2006	198.8	205.6	206.3	205.4	205.9	191.6	185.5	186.9	195.5	196.7	197.0	196.9	197.7
2007	190.6	196.0	197.7	196.8	196.7	192.7	186.5	187.7	196.3	198.2	199.2	199.4	194.8
2008	193.2	198.7	199.7	199.5	200.4	195.7	189.3	190.5	199.8	201.4	201.9	201.6	197.6
2009	195.7	200.9	201.7	202.6	202.2	197.4	191.0	192.0	199.0	201.6	202.0	201.8	199.0
2010	194.4	200.6	203.3	205.1	206.8	200.3	193.0	192.7	197.2	201.3	200.9	200.1	199.6
2011	192.5	198.4	199.9	201.0	200.0	195.1	185.4	187.9	196.4	198.0	198.0	197.7	195.9

2. Average Weekly Hours by Selected Industry: New Mexico, 2007–2011

(Not seasonally adjusted)

Industry and year	January	February	March	April	May	June	July	August	September	October	November	December	Annual average
Total Private													
2007	34.4	34.2	34.1	34.8	34.4	34.5	35.0	34.7	34.8	34.5	34.3	35.2	34.6
2008	34.6	34.6	34.9	35.1	35.3	35.6	35.7	35.6	35.6	35.9	36.2	35.3	35.4
2009	35.7	35.5	35.0	34.8	34.9	35.2	35.2	35.4	34.7	34.9	35.4	34.7	35.1
2010	34.4	34.4	34.8	34.9	35.4	34.8	34.7	35.9	35.1	35.2	35.4	35.1	35.0
2011	35.7	35.0	34.9	34.9	35.2	35.2	35.2	35.1	34.8	35.7	34.9	34.1	35.1
Goods-Producing													
2007	38.7	38.5	38.2	38.7	39.2	38.8	38.9	38.9	38.6	39.8	39.0	39.8	38.9
2008	38.5	37.7	37.5	38.8	39.8	39.4	39.4	40.1	39.7	40.7	39.2	39.0	39.2
2009	42.5	39.8	38.3	38.4	39.6	39.2	39.3	39.8	38.0	39.2	39.7	39.2	39.4
2010	39.8	38.7	39.1	39.6	39.6	40.2	40.3	41.2	40.2	41.3	40.6	39.6	40.0
2011	40.6	40.4	40.3	41.2	41.2	41.9	41.8	42.4	41.9	42.1	42.3	41.3	41.5
Construction													
2007	38.1	38.3	37.9	39.1	40.6	40.4	40.4	40.2	39.5	41.4	40.5	39.7	39.7
2008	39.5	39.0	38.0	39.4	41.1	42.6	42.3	43.1	40.1	40.6	40.4	39.1	40.4
2009	39.5	39.0	38.3	38.4	39.2	39.1	39.2	39.6	36.9	39.2	40.1	38.8	39.0
2010	39.5	37.8	37.9	38.5	38.5	39.7	39.7	40.4	39.0	40.4	39.4	38.9	39.2
2011	40.2	38.8	39.1	40.1	39.6	40.5	40.4	41.0	40.4	40.7	40.8	39.0	40.1
Trade, Transportation, and Utilities													
2007	35.4	35.9	36.2	36.4	36.1	36.8	36.8	36.9	36.3	36.0	34.4	35.0	36.0
2008	34.6	34.9	35.2	35.2	35.4	35.7	35.1	35.6	35.7	36.1	36.7	35.9	35.5
2009	35.8	35.2	34.2	34.1	34.0	35.3	34.8	35.4	34.5	34.8	35.1	34.8	34.8
2010	34.3	34.3	34.3	34.4	35.3	34.9	35.1	35.3	34.7	34.5	34.8	35.0	34.7
2011	35.3	33.6	34.6	34.3	34.9	34.5	34.7	34.7	34.6	35.2	33.8	32.4	34.4
Professional and Business Services													
2007	36.6	35.4	35.7	36.6	35.5	36.2	36.5	36.4	36.6	35.5	36.0	36.5	36.1
2008	36.7	36.3	36.6	35.9	35.8	37.0	36.7	36.0	36.2	35.8	37.5	37.2	36.5
2009	35.9	36.5	35.8	36.1	36.0	36.7	35.6	35.9	35.7	36.0	36.8	36.0	36.1
2010	35.1	35.9	36.2	36.1	36.3	36.4	35.4	35.8	36.0	36.2	37.0	36.7	36.1
2011	36.8	36.6	36.6	37.0	37.1	36.8	36.2	36.0	36.0	37.1	36.4	35.8	36.5
Education and Health Services													
2007	33.5	33.2	32.9	34.0	33.7	33.4	34.0	33.5	33.9	33.6	33.7	34.6	33.7
2008	35.2	35.5	35.4	35.6	35.1	35.0	36.1	35.0	35.2	35.7	36.1	35.5	35.5
2009	36.0	37.1	36.5	35.7	35.7	36.2	36.5	36.2	36.0	35.7	36.3	35.7	36.1
2010	36.2	36.2	36.0	35.8	36.4	35.9	35.6	36.4	35.1	35.7	35.6	35.9	35.9
2011	36.6	35.2	34.7	34.9	35.0	34.9	34.9	34.8	34.0	35.0	35.2	34.1	34.9
Leisure and Hospitality													
2007	25.2	26.3	26.4	26.5	26.7	26.4	28.5	28.2	27.2	26.7	26.5	24.9	26.6
2008	25.6	26.1	27.5	27.8	29.0	29.6	29.1	29.4	27.7	27.8	27.9	26.0	27.8
2009	26.2	27.0	26.7	25.8	26.8	26.3	27.1	27.2	26.6	26.2	26.5	25.9	26.5
2010	25.8	25.7	26.5	26.7	27.5	26.8	27.5	28.2	27.4	26.7	26.6	25.4	26.7
2011	25.3	25.9	25.5	25.0	25.6	26.3	26.7	26.6	25.8	26.5	25.2	25.1	25.8

3. Average Hourly Earnings by Selected Industry: New Mexico, 2007–2011

(Dollars, not seasonally adjusted)

Industry and year	January	February	March	April	May	June	July	August	September	October	November	December	Annual average
Total Private													
2007	18.34	18.64	18.43	18.75	18.67	18.58	18.72	18.32	18.69	18.61	18.53	18.50	18.57
2008	18.54	18.58	18.87	18.75	18.74	18.83	18.73	18.72	18.36	18.76	18.92	19.01	18.73
2009	18.77	18.80	18.73	18.66	18.83	18.69	18.83	18.91	19.19	19.12	19.32	19.19	18.92
2010	19.51	19.76	19.72	19.59	19.46	19.38	19.25	19.68	19.49	19.40	19.81	19.79	19.57
2011	19.96	19.84	19.79	19.74	19.82	19.65	19.78	19.44	19.69	19.48	19.50	19.77	19.70
Goods-Producing													
2007	19.66	19.58	19.77	19.74	19.65	19.41	19.75	19.21	19.36	19.31	19.45	19.97	19.57
2008	20.38	20.80	20.95	20.77	20.56	20.29	20.63	21.06	20.86	20.95	21.68	22.43	20.94
2009	21.73	21.90	21.53	21.02	21.59	21.21	21.40	21.30	21.16	21.54	21.80	21.52	21.48
2010	21.85	21.60	21.25	21.18	21.29	21.28	21.27	21.37	20.99	21.53	21.80	22.53	21.49
2011	21.78	22.25	22.30	22.15	21.96	21.80	22.01	21.90	22.23	22.40	22.17	23.69	22.22
Construction													
2007	18.93	18.37	19.41	18.45	18.29	18.03	18.43	18.35	18.90	18.82	18.92	19.06	18.66
2008	18.70	18.44	19.17	18.79	19.07	18.96	19.48	19.58	19.92	20.05	20.30	22.03	19.52
2009	20.94	21.00	21.07	20.71	20.98	20.72	21.41	21.22	21.09	21.52	21.58	21.61	21.15
2010	22.04	21.59	21.34	21.00	20.97	20.98	21.06	21.37	21.33	21.94	21.72	22.43	21.48
2011	21.18	21.67	21.77	21.80	21.36	21.07	21.07	21.19	21.45	21.42	21.26	21.06	21.35
Trade, Transportation, and Utilities													
2007	15.86	16.22	16.24	16.58	16.84	17.07	16.75	16.31	16.45	16.84	16.67	16.33	16.52
2008	16.30	16.46	16.80	17.45	16.89	16.91	17.15	17.14	17.03	16.77	16.92	16.72	16.88
2009	17.22	17.85	17.24	17.10	17.31	17.46	17.93	18.07	18.46	17.70	18.07	17.75	17.68
2010	17.15	17.44	17.50	17.85	17.48	17.28	17.26	17.88	17.51	16.86	17.07	16.59	17.32
2011	16.86	17.01	16.61	16.33	16.65	16.67	17.05	16.47	16.73	16.64	17.02	16.47	16.71
Professional and Business Services													
2007	24.58	27.55	25.40	26.44	26.36	26.01	26.28	25.68	25.48	25.02	24.63	25.26	25.72
2008	25.11	24.46	24.95	24.81	24.68	25.80	25.12	23.08	22.89	23.89	23.72	23.21	24.31
2009	23.28	23.05	22.74	22.96	22.52	21.95	21.93	22.12	22.35	22.14	22.03	21.84	22.41
2010	21.95	22.72	23.12	21.91	22.18	22.16	22.69	22.60	22.18	21.52	23.61	23.71	22.53
2011	23.92	23.82	23.79	24.10	24.65	24.59	24.94	24.01	24.43	22.95	22.95	23.65	23.99
Education and Health Services													
2007	15.94	15.54	16.47	16.70	16.66	16.60	16.27	16.54	17.08	17.37	16.93	16.64	16.57
2008	16.47	16.48	17.17	16.87	17.02	16.99	17.18	18.14	17.91	17.90	17.89	18.01	17.34
2009	16.79	16.60	17.03	17.50	17.22	17.72	18.00	18.05	18.61	18.97	18.90	19.18	17.88
2010	21.04	21.06	21.04	20.99	20.88	21.20	20.88	21.13	20.70	20.54	20.91	20.52	20.91
2011	20.23	20.21	20.07	20.02	19.86	19.94	20.01	19.95	19.89	19.73	19.61	19.74	19.94
Leisure and Hospitality													
2007	10.38	10.25	10.42	10.48	10.59	10.51	10.72	10.76	11.17	11.28	11.60	11.58	10.81
2008	10.98	10.94	11.00	11.02	11.19	11.04	10.96	11.03	11.11	11.63	11.05	11.17	11.09
2009	11.53	11.55	11.60	11.19	11.75	11.61	11.62	11.48	12.19	11.98	12.24	12.00	11.73
2010	11.85	11.99	11.84	11.74	11.60	11.83	11.93	12.05	11.98	12.23	12.27	12.48	11.98
2011	12.28	11.97	12.26	12.09	11.92	11.80	11.83	11.52	11.60	11.73	11.70	11.61	11.85

4. Average Weekly Earnings by Selected Industry: New Mexico, 2007–2011

(Dollars, not seasonally adjusted)

Industry and year	January	February	March	April	May	June	July	August	September	October	November	December	Annual average
Total Private													
2007	630.90	637.49	628.46	652.50	642.25	641.01	655.20	635.70	650.41	642.05	635.58	651.20	642.10
2008	641.48	642.87	658.56	658.13	661.52	670.35	668.66	666.43	653.62	673.48	684.90	671.05	662.66
2009	670.09	667.40	655.55	649.37	657.17	657.89	662.82	669.41	665.89	667.29	683.93	665.89	664.19
2010	671.14	679.74	686.26	683.69	688.88	674.42	667.98	706.51	684.10	682.88	701.27	694.63	685.15
2011	712.57	694.40	690.67	688.93	697.66	691.68	696.26	682.34	685.21	695.44	680.55	674.16	690.95
Goods-Producing													
2007	760.84	753.83	755.21	763.94	770.28	753.11	768.28	747.27	747.30	768.54	758.55	794.81	761.80
2008	784.63	784.16	785.63	805.88	818.29	799.43	812.82	844.51	828.14	852.67	849.86	874.77	819.92
2009	923.53	871.62	824.60	807.17	854.96	831.43	841.02	847.74	804.08	844.37	865.46	843.58	847.33
2010	869.63	835.92	830.88	838.73	843.08	855.46	857.18	880.44	843.80	889.19	885.08	892.19	860.45
2011	884.27	898.90	898.69	912.58	904.75	913.42	920.02	928.56	931.44	943.04	937.79	978.40	921.24
Construction													
2007	721.23	703.57	735.64	721.40	742.57	728.41	744.57	737.67	746.55	779.15	766.26	756.68	740.61
2008	738.65	719.16	728.46	740.33	783.78	807.70	824.00	843.90	798.79	814.03	820.12	861.37	789.56
2009	827.13	819.00	806.98	795.26	822.42	810.15	839.27	840.31	778.22	843.58	865.36	838.47	823.74
2010	870.58	816.10	808.79	808.50	807.35	832.91	836.08	863.35	831.87	886.38	855.77	872.53	841.13
2011	851.44	840.80	851.21	874.18	845.86	853.34	851.23	868.79	866.58	871.79	867.41	821.34	855.76
Trade, Transportation, and Utilities													
2007	561.44	582.30	587.89	603.51	607.92	628.18	616.40	601.84	597.14	606.24	573.45	571.55	594.74
2008	563.98	574.45	591.36	614.24	597.91	603.69	601.97	610.18	607.97	605.40	620.96	600.25	599.31
2009	616.48	628.32	589.61	583.11	588.54	616.34	623.96	639.68	636.87	615.96	634.26	617.70	615.93
2010	588.25	598.19	600.25	614.04	617.04	603.07	605.83	631.16	607.60	581.67	594.04	580.65	601.80
2011	595.16	571.54	574.71	560.12	581.09	575.12	591.64	571.51	578.86	585.73	575.28	533.63	574.47
Professional and Business Services													
2007	899.63	975.27	906.78	967.70	935.78	941.56	959.22	934.75	932.57	888.21	886.68	921.99	929.24
2008	921.54	887.90	913.17	890.68	883.54	954.60	921.90	830.88	828.62	855.26	889.50	863.41	886.60
2009	835.75	841.33	814.09	828.86	810.72	805.57	780.71	794.11	797.90	797.04	810.70	786.24	808.69
2010	770.45	815.65	836.94	790.95	805.13	806.62	803.23	809.08	798.48	779.02	873.57	870.16	813.34
2011	880.26	871.81	870.71	891.70	914.52	904.91	902.83	864.36	879.48	851.45	835.38	846.67	876.24
Education and Health Services													
2007	533.99	515.93	541.86	567.80	561.44	554.44	553.18	554.09	579.01	583.63	570.54	575.74	557.81
2008	579.74	585.04	607.82	600.57	597.40	594.65	620.20	634.90	630.43	639.03	645.83	639.36	614.84
2009	604.44	615.86	621.60	624.75	614.75	641.46	657.00	653.41	669.96	677.23	686.07	684.73	646.02
2010	761.65	762.37	757.44	751.44	760.03	761.08	743.33	769.13	726.57	733.28	744.40	736.67	750.44
2011	740.42	711.39	696.43	698.70	695.10	695.91	698.35	694.26	676.26	690.55	690.27	673.13	696.50
Leisure and Hospitality													
2007	261.58	269.58	275.09	277.72	282.75	277.46	305.52	303.43	303.82	301.18	307.40	288.34	288.00
2008	281.09	285.53	302.50	306.36	324.51	326.78	318.94	324.28	307.75	323.31	308.30	290.42	308.55
2009	302.09	311.85	309.72	288.70	314.90	305.34	314.90	312.26	324.25	313.88	324.36	310.80	311.09
2010	305.73	308.14	313.76	313.46	319.00	317.04	328.08	339.81	328.25	326.54	326.38	316.99	320.36
2011	310.68	310.02	312.63	302.25	305.15	310.34	315.86	306.43	299.28	310.85	294.84	291.41	305.82

NEW YORK
At a Glance

Population:
2000 census: 18,977,026
2010 census: 19,378,102
2011 estimate: 19,465,197

Percent change in population:
2000–2010: 2.1%
2010–2011: 0.4%

Percent change in total nonfarm employment:
2000–2010: -0.8%
2010–2011: 1.4%

Industry with the largest growth in employment, 2000–2011 (thousands):
Education and Health Services, 348.4

Industry with the largest decline or smallest growth in employment, 2000–2011 (thousands):
Manufacturing, -291.3

Civilian labor force:
2000: 9,166,972
2010: 9,586,931
2011: 9,504,239

Unemployment rate and rank among states (lowest to highest):
2000: 4.5%, 38th
2010: 8.6%, 27th
2011: 8.2%, 27th

Over-the-year change in unemployment rates:
2010–2011: -0.4%

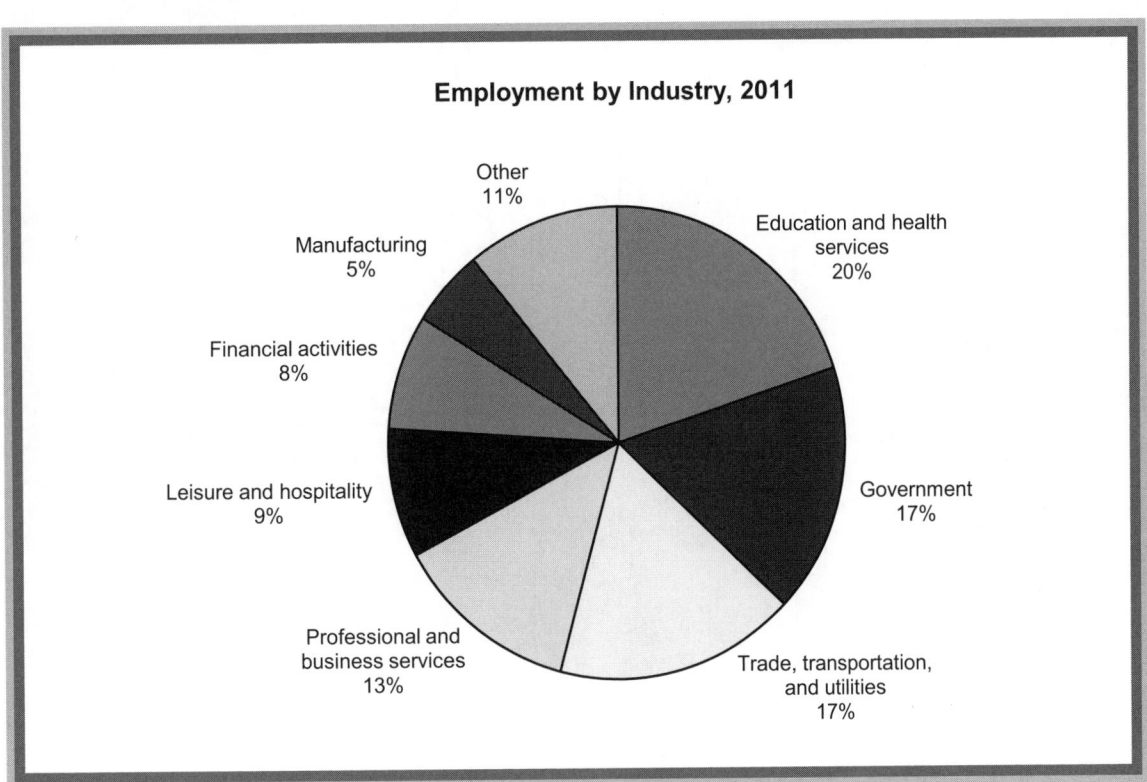

Employment by Industry, 2011

Other
11%

Manufacturing
5%

Financial activities
8%

Leisure and hospitality
9%

Professional and
business services
13%

Education and health
services
20%

Government
17%

Trade, transportation,
and utilities
17%

1. Employment by Industry: New York, Selected Years, 2000–2011

(Numbers in thousands, not seasonally adjusted)

Industry and year	January	February	March	April	May	June	July	August	September	October	November	December	Annual average
Total Nonfarm													
2000	8,394.3	8,445.9	8,520.5	8,590.8	8,676.1	8,719.4	8,648.1	8,606.1	8,666.5	8,754.1	8,800.9	8,834.3	8,638.1
2001	8,524.0	8,560.6	8,605.5	8,608.2	8,688.6	8,721.1	8,587.9	8,552.4	8,553.9	8,550.7	8,585.0	8,598.3	8,594.7
2002	8,294.5	8,342.3	8,395.5	8,430.7	8,510.8	8,540.3	8,459.3	8,444.2	8,446.4	8,528.8	8,563.5	8,586.0	8,461.9
2003	8,267.3	8,300.4	8,344.2	8,368.1	8,447.0	8,479.5	8,387.5	8,365.6	8,399.9	8,483.9	8,523.9	8,551.0	8,409.9
2004	8,235.8	8,292.3	8,365.8	8,401.2	8,499.7	8,543.9	8,481.0	8,453.3	8,485.2	8,571.3	8,607.1	8,642.4	8,464.9
2005	8,332.3	8,372.2	8,417.3	8,512.4	8,567.1	8,617.4	8,541.0	8,526.6	8,568.7	8,614.2	8,666.6	8,709.9	8,537.1
2006	8,405.4	8,446.8	8,511.8	8,568.7	8,647.5	8,704.8	8,608.5	8,585.0	8,634.3	8,715.1	8,771.9	8,822.0	8,618.5
2007	8,533.0	8,571.6	8,628.0	8,663.7	8,761.0	8,825.8	8,732.5	8,702.4	8,739.3	8,842.6	8,888.3	8,921.6	8,734.2
2008	8,636.0	8,679.9	8,720.3	8,786.1	8,849.5	8,891.8	8,819.4	8,780.9	8,795.6	8,856.3	8,852.1	8,845.9	8,792.8
2009	8,506.0	8,522.9	8,525.1	8,530.9	8,593.6	8,602.5	8,557.8	8,509.7	8,504.7	8,584.9	8,606.3	8,623.8	8,555.7
2010	8,339.8	8,388.8	8,444.3	8,558.1	8,646.0	8,660.3	8,562.9	8,529.9	8,568.6	8,675.4	8,710.3	8,719.9	8,567.0
2011	8,453.2	8,515.8	8,560.1	8,668.3	8,725.7	8,758.0	8,726.4	8,685.2	8,696.3	8,778.6	8,824.3	8,809.2	8,683.4
Total Private													
2000	6,949.2	6,981.7	7,041.8	7,099.0	7,162.8	7,239.6	7,194.4	7,195.4	7,240.0	7,277.3	7,315.6	7,353.7	7,170.9
2001	7,071.5	7,088.2	7,127.2	7,120.5	7,204.3	7,246.2	7,161.2	7,149.5	7,113.8	7,064.4	7,082.3	7,099.3	7,127.4
2002	6,817.9	6,840.6	6,885.6	6,929.6	7,001.4	7,034.9	6,989.1	6,996.1	6,993.1	7,031.6	7,049.4	7,067.8	6,969.8
2003	6,788.5	6,798.0	6,837.6	6,866.2	6,942.0	6,976.2	6,934.3	6,933.3	6,948.8	6,991.8	7,016.3	7,038.0	6,922.6
2004	6,764.9	6,799.3	6,865.9	6,904.9	6,991.4	7,040.3	7,026.7	7,020.9	7,036.7	7,081.1	7,103.4	7,137.7	6,981.1
2005	6,853.1	6,874.7	6,918.2	7,007.3	7,057.9	7,108.8	7,079.4	7,085.4	7,107.5	7,121.4	7,161.7	7,199.3	7,047.9
2006	6,930.1	6,953.6	7,016.2	7,069.9	7,143.5	7,203.7	7,156.6	7,154.6	7,176.7	7,220.3	7,265.5	7,307.5	7,133.2
2007	7,043.5	7,062.6	7,116.9	7,154.4	7,243.3	7,308.8	7,265.9	7,252.1	7,264.4	7,329.8	7,365.5	7,390.4	7,233.1
2008	7,140.6	7,164.0	7,200.5	7,256.3	7,315.9	7,358.4	7,320.1	7,309.8	7,307.9	7,330.1	7,317.0	7,306.8	7,277.3
2009	6,998.9	6,991.4	6,990.7	6,993.0	7,051.0	7,071.5	7,026.6	7,006.0	7,029.4	7,060.9	7,074.0	7,089.8	7,031.9
2010	6,838.9	6,864.2	6,914.6	7,022.0	7,068.4	7,106.2	7,090.3	7,089.0	7,105.5	7,168.7	7,194.5	7,208.0	7,055.9
2011	6,977.5	7,018.3	7,060.0	7,168.0	7,217.2	7,260.4	7,264.8	7,236.4	7,240.6	7,280.9	7,318.8	7,300.8	7,195.3
Goods-Producing													
2000	1,044.9	1,043.2	1,056.8	1,068.0	1,084.5	1,102.1	1,093.2	1,103.4	1,106.0	1,103.3	1,095.9	1,084.1	1,082.1
2001	1,034.1	1,032.3	1,038.3	1,044.9	1,060.3	1,072.4	1,055.1	1,056.3	1,045.8	1,036.3	1,024.7	1,010.4	1,042.6
2002	954.6	951.1	959.0	970.9	986.0	995.9	989.6	998.5	992.4	988.7	980.3	965.3	977.7
2003	917.3	910.3	919.6	926.6	943.6	954.1	946.7	954.1	951.7	945.8	939.9	926.8	936.4
2004	882.3	881.6	896.3	908.1	927.3	941.5	940.3	948.4	946.0	942.9	938.3	927.4	923.4
2005	879.8	873.7	881.3	900.1	914.8	928.2	926.5	934.2	931.1	923.5	922.8	910.6	910.6
2006	874.0	870.5	879.6	899.1	915.6	930.9	925.6	932.8	929.1	927.5	921.7	913.3	910.0
2007	877.1	867.8	877.5	894.1	915.9	931.2	928.8	933.1	928.8	929.1	924.1	912.2	910.0
2008	876.4	869.9	876.3	891.0	908.4	919.2	920.7	924.7	916.4	910.0	892.8	868.0	897.8
2009	815.3	801.0	798.6	803.1	812.7	817.6	818.2	817.8	810.0	803.8	793.3	777.9	805.8
2010	737.3	729.9	739.5	762.2	773.0	783.6	789.2	793.9	789.3	786.2	780.0	764.3	769.0
2011	729.0	726.7	736.4	758.4	774.9	788.6	795.9	799.3	794.7	790.3	785.3	759.5	769.9
Mining and Logging													
2000	4.7	4.6	5.1	5.4	5.7	5.9	5.9	6.0	6.0	5.8	5.7	5.2	5.5
2001	4.6	4.7	5.0	5.2	5.6	5.6	5.7	5.7	5.5	5.7	5.5	5.2	5.3
2002	4.4	4.4	4.6	5.0	5.4	5.4	5.5	5.5	5.4	5.4	5.3	4.9	5.1
2003	4.4	4.4	4.6	5.0	5.5	5.6	5.7	5.8	5.8	5.7	5.6	5.4	5.3
2004	4.7	4.6	5.0	5.4	5.8	6.0	6.1	6.2	6.2	6.1	6.0	5.7	5.7
2005	4.9	4.8	5.0	5.7	6.0	6.3	6.4	6.5	6.4	6.4	6.2	5.9	5.9
2006	5.0	5.1	5.4	6.1	6.4	6.6	6.7	6.7	6.7	6.8	6.6	6.1	6.2
2007	5.2	5.3	5.5	5.9	6.4	6.7	6.8	6.7	6.7	6.7	6.6	6.2	6.2
2008	5.3	5.2	5.5	6.0	6.6	6.9	7.1	7.0	6.9	6.8	6.3	5.8	6.3
2009	4.8	4.8	4.9	5.2	5.6	5.8	5.9	5.8	5.7	5.7	5.6	5.2	5.4
2010	4.4	4.5	4.7	5.3	5.6	5.7	5.7	5.8	5.8	5.6	5.5	5.1	5.3
2011	4.3	4.4	4.5	5.1	5.4	5.6	5.7	5.7	5.6	5.6	5.4	4.9	5.2
Construction													
2000	289.5	286.9	299.6	312.3	327.4	338.5	343.3	348.1	349.3	349.0	346.3	337.6	327.3
2001	302.2	300.3	306.4	322.0	339.2	348.0	347.7	349.3	342.8	341.9	337.6	328.8	330.5
2002	293.8	291.5	297.1	311.3	323.9	332.0	338.4	342.7	338.5	337.4	332.7	323.2	321.9
2003	291.4	286.3	293.2	307.3	323.0	331.2	337.9	340.1	336.9	333.9	328.9	319.6	319.1
2004	285.6	283.7	293.6	309.8	325.3	334.6	341.6	344.5	342.4	340.4	336.9	327.9	322.2
2005	295.0	290.1	294.8	314.6	328.6	337.8	341.7	346.8	345.1	339.4	340.0	329.1	325.3
2006	303.3	300.3	308.0	326.3	340.6	350.8	353.1	358.6	356.2	356.0	351.1	344.9	337.4
2007	318.8	310.5	318.8	336.9	355.9	367.7	370.5	374.2	371.7	373.1	369.5	358.8	352.2
2008	334.9	330.1	335.9	351.3	366.3	373.1	379.8	383.3	377.3	374.5	363.6	345.8	359.7
2009	310.9	305.3	307.8	318.0	329.6	335.6	342.3	342.6	335.5	331.2	324.4	310.5	324.5
2010	280.1	273.2	281.2	302.5	310.7	317.5	325.5	329.4	324.2	320.1	315.2	300.2	306.7
2011	273.3	270.7	278.9	296.2	310.3	319.9	327.7	329.4	326.9	326.0	322.6	299.4	306.8
Manufacturing													
2000	750.7	751.7	752.1	750.3	751.4	757.7	744.0	749.3	750.7	748.5	743.9	741.3	749.3
2001	727.3	727.3	726.9	717.7	715.5	718.8	701.7	701.3	697.5	688.7	681.6	676.4	706.7
2002	656.4	655.2	657.3	654.6	656.7	658.5	645.7	650.3	648.5	645.9	642.3	637.2	650.7
2003	621.5	619.6	621.8	614.3	615.1	617.3	603.1	608.2	609.0	606.2	605.4	601.8	611.9
2004	592.0	593.3	597.7	592.9	596.2	600.9	592.6	597.7	597.4	596.4	595.4	593.8	595.5
2005	579.9	578.8	581.5	579.8	580.2	584.1	578.4	580.9	579.6	577.7	576.6	575.6	579.4
2006	565.7	565.1	566.2	566.7	568.6	573.5	565.8	567.5	566.2	564.7	564.0	562.3	566.4
2007	553.1	552.0	553.2	551.3	553.6	556.8	551.5	552.2	550.4	549.3	548.0	547.2	551.6
2008	536.2	534.6	534.9	533.7	535.5	539.2	533.8	534.4	532.2	528.7	522.9	516.4	531.9
2009	499.6	490.9	485.9	479.9	477.5	476.2	470.0	469.4	468.8	466.9	463.3	462.2	475.9
2010	452.8	452.2	453.6	454.4	456.7	460.4	458.0	458.7	459.3	460.5	459.3	459.0	457.1
2011	451.4	451.6	453.0	457.1	459.2	463.1	462.5	464.2	462.2	458.7	457.3	455.2	458.0

1. Employment by Industry: New York, Selected Years, 2000–2011—*Continued*

(Numbers in thousands, not seasonally adjusted)

Industry and year	January	February	March	April	May	June	July	August	September	October	November	December	Annual average
Service-Providing													
2000	7,349.4	7,402.7	7,463.7	7,522.8	7,591.6	7,617.3	7,554.9	7,502.7	7,560.5	7,650.8	7,705.0	7,750.2	7,556.0
2001	7,489.9	7,528.3	7,567.2	7,563.3	7,628.3	7,648.7	7,532.8	7,496.1	7,508.1	7,514.4	7,560.3	7,587.9	7,552.1
2002	7,339.9	7,391.2	7,436.5	7,459.8	7,524.8	7,544.4	7,469.7	7,445.7	7,454.0	7,540.1	7,583.2	7,620.7	7,484.2
2003	7,350.0	7,390.1	7,424.6	7,441.5	7,503.4	7,525.4	7,440.8	7,411.5	7,448.2	7,538.1	7,584.0	7,624.2	7,473.5
2004	7,353.5	7,410.7	7,469.5	7,493.1	7,572.4	7,602.4	7,540.7	7,504.9	7,539.2	7,628.4	7,668.8	7,715.0	7,541.6
2005	7,452.5	7,498.5	7,536.0	7,612.3	7,652.3	7,689.2	7,614.5	7,592.4	7,637.6	7,690.7	7,743.8	7,799.3	7,626.6
2006	7,531.4	7,576.3	7,632.2	7,669.6	7,731.9	7,773.9	7,682.9	7,652.2	7,705.2	7,787.6	7,850.2	7,908.7	7,708.5
2007	7,655.9	7,703.8	7,750.5	7,769.6	7,845.1	7,894.6	7,803.7	7,769.3	7,810.5	7,913.5	7,964.2	8,009.4	7,824.2
2008	7,759.6	7,810.0	7,844.0	7,895.1	7,941.1	7,972.6	7,898.7	7,856.2	7,879.2	7,946.3	7,959.3	7,977.9	7,895.0
2009	7,690.7	7,721.9	7,726.5	7,727.8	7,780.9	7,784.9	7,739.6	7,691.9	7,694.7	7,781.1	7,813.0	7,845.9	7,749.9
2010	7,602.5	7,658.9	7,704.8	7,795.9	7,873.0	7,876.7	7,773.7	7,736.0	7,779.3	7,889.2	7,930.3	7,955.6	7,798.0
2011	7,724.2	7,789.1	7,823.7	7,909.9	7,950.8	7,969.4	7,930.5	7,885.9	7,901.6	7,988.3	8,039.0	8,049.7	7,913.5
Trade, Transportation, and Utilities													
2000	1,524.8	1,508.2	1,514.6	1,515.2	1,528.8	1,548.6	1,527.7	1,534.8	1,547.9	1,559.1	1,588.7	1,618.7	1,543.1
2001	1,533.9	1,511.8	1,513.8	1,502.5	1,519.2	1,533.3	1,501.0	1,497.9	1,498.6	1,499.1	1,522.3	1,543.6	1,514.8
2002	1,467.3	1,447.0	1,455.7	1,457.0	1,471.9	1,489.0	1,466.1	1,467.2	1,481.0	1,491.1	1,514.8	1,541.6	1,479.1
2003	1,464.5	1,445.7	1,449.5	1,449.1	1,465.4	1,480.5	1,460.0	1,462.4	1,474.4	1,491.4	1,515.2	1,538.7	1,474.7
2004	1,457.1	1,443.2	1,451.3	1,453.1	1,476.2	1,494.2	1,481.3	1,481.5	1,493.2	1,512.2	1,536.1	1,562.0	1,486.8
2005	1,480.5	1,463.3	1,468.3	1,479.3	1,492.8	1,509.4	1,492.5	1,494.3	1,503.6	1,510.7	1,537.6	1,568.9	1,500.1
2006	1,493.2	1,469.8	1,477.9	1,483.4	1,499.0	1,519.9	1,498.1	1,496.5	1,506.6	1,524.1	1,556.5	1,583.2	1,509.0
2007	1,513.3	1,489.6	1,496.6	1,494.7	1,517.8	1,538.4	1,517.5	1,510.2	1,521.9	1,535.7	1,569.7	1,593.5	1,524.9
2008	1,526.1	1,502.1	1,507.4	1,508.7	1,520.7	1,536.7	1,515.0	1,512.2	1,521.1	1,525.8	1,541.1	1,556.7	1,522.8
2009	1,471.3	1,447.7	1,441.3	1,432.9	1,450.6	1,464.9	1,442.2	1,440.8	1,450.5	1,459.5	1,483.8	1,504.3	1,457.5
2010	1,437.6	1,418.7	1,425.6	1,442.1	1,455.5	1,474.8	1,456.5	1,457.5	1,465.1	1,482.6	1,507.6	1,527.3	1,462.6
2011	1,467.0	1,449.8	1,452.3	1,468.1	1,480.0	1,500.3	1,481.6	1,480.1	1,486.4	1,487.7	1,521.3	1,544.9	1,485.0
Wholesale Trade													
2000	369.7	370.9	373.4	370.5	372.3	375.3	372.8	374.0	374.7	375.0	375.3	377.3	373.4
2001	369.5	370.3	370.7	367.3	368.5	370.4	366.7	366.1	364.1	362.9	362.2	362.7	366.8
2002	352.8	353.0	354.0	353.5	355.2	356.7	353.6	355.4	354.9	357.2	357.9	358.8	355.3
2003	350.5	350.3	351.7	350.5	353.4	355.3	354.1	354.3	354.3	354.5	356.0	357.4	353.5
2004	347.8	348.2	350.3	351.2	353.4	355.8	355.9	355.4	354.2	356.6	357.2	359.0	353.8
2005	348.2	349.0	350.0	351.4	352.8	354.5	354.5	355.4	355.0	355.2	356.3	358.7	353.4
2006	348.9	348.8	350.9	352.2	354.0	357.0	355.5	356.2	355.1	356.2	356.6	359.9	354.3
2007	353.2	353.0	354.4	354.1	356.1	359.1	358.0	357.0	356.0	358.5	358.2	359.8	356.5
2008	352.4	352.1	352.5	352.4	353.1	354.9	353.3	352.2	351.0	349.9	348.2	347.0	351.6
2009	338.4	335.2	333.3	329.9	330.0	330.6	327.7	327.2	325.8	325.6	325.5	326.3	329.6
2010	319.6	319.2	320.9	323.0	325.0	327.6	328.2	328.2	327.5	329.2	330.2	331.3	325.8
2011	325.6	325.2	326.7	329.5	331.1	334.0	331.5	332.4	329.7	326.8	331.1	331.8	329.6
Retail Trade													
2000	877.9	860.3	863.1	866.3	875.6	890.2	881.2	887.6	887.5	894.6	924.5	950.7	888.3
2001	880.9	858.6	859.6	854.1	863.3	874.6	859.1	861.2	853.2	856.9	885.7	907.7	867.9
2002	850.1	830.7	837.7	837.8	847.9	862.1	854.2	856.8	857.1	862.0	886.5	912.0	857.9
2003	848.6	830.9	832.1	836.0	846.6	859.1	851.2	854.4	854.0	867.1	890.1	911.4	856.8
2004	849.0	835.3	840.0	841.0	856.8	870.7	867.6	869.1	870.1	881.6	905.6	928.9	868.0
2005	868.4	850.7	853.8	862.2	870.8	882.8	878.3	880.3	876.0	883.8	907.7	932.0	878.9
2006	875.6	853.2	857.8	862.4	871.5	886.0	883.1	880.5	875.8	891.8	922.1	940.4	883.2
2007	889.1	866.1	870.7	869.9	885.2	899.7	894.9	891.6	887.9	897.6	930.6	948.7	894.3
2008	899.6	876.8	880.4	879.7	888.2	899.9	896.0	895.4	891.0	897.7	914.2	926.3	895.4
2009	865.2	846.3	843.2	839.4	854.0	867.0	860.9	861.7	860.2	868.8	891.3	906.8	863.7
2010	859.5	843.2	847.4	856.5	866.0	881.0	877.3	879.1	872.2	886.6	908.4	923.3	875.0
2011	877.6	862.9	863.1	873.8	881.8	896.4	896.1	894.7	889.5	895.3	922.5	944.0	891.5
Transportation and Utilities													
2000	277.2	277.0	278.1	278.4	280.9	283.1	273.7	273.2	285.7	289.5	288.9	290.7	281.4
2001	283.5	282.9	283.5	281.1	287.4	288.3	275.2	270.6	281.3	279.3	274.4	273.2	280.1
2002	264.4	263.3	264.0	265.7	268.8	270.2	258.3	255.0	269.0	271.9	270.4	270.8	266.0
2003	265.4	264.5	265.7	262.6	265.4	266.1	254.7	253.7	266.6	269.8	269.1	269.9	264.5
2004	260.3	259.7	261.0	260.9	266.0	267.7	257.8	257.0	268.9	274.0	273.3	274.1	265.1
2005	263.9	263.6	264.5	265.7	269.2	272.1	259.7	258.6	272.6	271.7	273.6	278.2	267.8
2006	268.7	267.8	269.2	268.8	273.5	276.9	261.3	259.8	275.7	276.1	277.8	282.9	271.5
2007	271.0	270.5	271.5	270.7	276.5	279.6	264.6	261.6	278.0	279.6	280.9	285.0	274.1
2008	274.1	273.2	274.5	276.6	279.4	281.9	265.7	264.6	279.1	278.2	278.7	283.4	275.8
2009	267.7	266.2	264.8	263.6	266.6	267.3	253.6	251.9	264.5	265.1	267.0	271.2	264.1
2010	258.5	256.3	257.3	262.6	264.5	266.2	251.0	250.2	265.4	266.8	269.0	272.7	261.7
2011	263.8	261.7	262.5	264.8	267.1	269.9	254.0	253.0	267.2	265.6	267.7	269.1	263.9
Information													
2000	303.7	308.4	311.6	314.7	318.8	323.5	322.9	301.5	326.9	329.4	332.2	333.6	318.9
2001	326.8	329.8	330.3	327.8	330.6	330.8	326.6	324.5	318.8	317.1	320.3	318.1	325.1
2002	300.0	303.9	299.7	299.1	306.0	303.5	293.1	295.4	289.9	291.1	293.3	291.8	297.2
2003	278.2	282.3	279.5	276.5	281.9	278.2	273.8	277.6	274.1	276.5	280.5	279.3	278.2
2004	269.6	271.2	272.7	271.6	272.1	271.7	271.3	273.0	273.2	272.5	275.3	273.4	272.3
2005	267.1	269.3	270.2	270.6	272.4	276.6	273.9	274.9	274.6	275.5	276.7	280.0	273.5
2006	271.3	271.4	272.8	270.0	272.1	274.7	272.4	272.8	270.7	268.8	270.8	272.5	271.7
2007	265.6	267.2	267.6	267.3	270.0	272.6	271.2	271.8	270.4	268.9	271.2	272.5	269.7
2008	265.8	267.7	268.2	266.8	269.6	272.9	270.8	271.6	271.1	269.9	270.9	272.1	269.8
2009	263.3	261.2	261.8	260.5	260.9	260.8	259.5	258.4	257.1	256.1	256.6	257.3	259.5
2010	249.2	249.4	250.8	250.1	251.6	253.2	254.5	254.9	253.8	255.7	256.6	258.6	253.2
2011	251.4	252.2	253.7	256.3	256.8	258.3	260.8	244.8	259.7	257.9	255.5	251.2	254.9

1. Employment by Industry: New York, Selected Years, 2000–2011—*Continued*

(Numbers in thousands, not seasonally adjusted)

Industry and year	January	February	March	April	May	June	July	August	September	October	November	December	Annual average
Financial Activities													
2000	738.9	740.9	742.4	740.7	742.8	754.6	752.4	752.9	748.2	747.4	748.4	753.6	746.9
2001	739.9	740.2	742.4	737.7	738.0	747.2	745.4	742.4	733.3	704.1	701.7	707.8	731.7
2002	705.5	705.5	705.4	703.4	703.7	710.2	710.5	709.5	699.6	700.3	700.7	703.4	704.8
2003	692.2	690.1	689.7	689.9	693.5	701.6	704.7	704.0	696.7	695.6	696.8	702.8	696.5
2004	692.0	692.7	695.5	694.2	695.8	705.1	711.5	710.5	702.5	705.0	705.6	712.5	701.9
2005	701.0	701.2	703.4	707.1	707.2	717.6	723.6	723.6	716.3	716.4	718.2	723.8	713.3
2006	712.8	714.7	717.8	719.4	722.6	732.5	736.7	737.3	728.6	727.7	729.8	735.1	726.3
2007	723.0	724.4	726.4	725.2	726.0	737.9	741.3	739.0	729.3	731.9	733.3	735.8	731.1
2008	723.3	723.0	723.6	720.9	720.9	728.5	730.6	729.6	715.6	711.5	708.5	708.7	720.4
2009	692.9	687.5	683.9	677.7	676.3	678.8	678.9	675.7	669.2	667.2	665.8	668.3	676.9
2010	657.1	657.9	659.8	664.8	666.0	675.3	678.7	678.7	671.5	672.2	673.9	678.4	669.5
2011	672.4	673.3	674.6	677.2	678.5	688.5	691.6	693.9	689.8	688.9	689.5	686.7	683.7
Professional and Business Services													
2000	1,067.0	1,078.4	1,090.7	1,103.4	1,114.1	1,131.3	1,133.5	1,141.2	1,139.2	1,144.8	1,146.4	1,150.2	1,120.0
2001	1,101.8	1,105.9	1,109.1	1,103.9	1,109.8	1,117.5	1,110.0	1,107.4	1,096.6	1,077.0	1,075.1	1,075.8	1,099.2
2002	1,032.6	1,036.5	1,042.1	1,051.6	1,055.7	1,066.0	1,062.8	1,063.1	1,057.5	1,061.1	1,062.3	1,062.8	1,054.5
2003	1,019.0	1,018.6	1,028.2	1,038.2	1,041.1	1,052.3	1,048.6	1,048.6	1,045.8	1,051.9	1,054.3	1,058.8	1,042.1
2004	1,016.2	1,024.1	1,036.5	1,050.7	1,056.6	1,071.8	1,069.5	1,069.4	1,064.3	1,068.7	1,073.0	1,080.7	1,056.8
2005	1,043.1	1,044.7	1,050.7	1,074.0	1,075.1	1,089.9	1,093.0	1,095.3	1,094.2	1,093.6	1,100.6	1,107.3	1,080.1
2006	1,067.6	1,072.1	1,085.3	1,096.7	1,100.3	1,118.4	1,115.9	1,119.4	1,113.2	1,117.6	1,126.2	1,133.8	1,105.5
2007	1,095.8	1,101.1	1,112.7	1,121.0	1,128.1	1,148.3	1,148.3	1,151.1	1,138.6	1,151.0	1,155.3	1,160.9	1,134.4
2008	1,125.0	1,131.6	1,138.2	1,153.0	1,153.9	1,168.7	1,170.0	1,167.6	1,154.6	1,152.9	1,147.6	1,143.1	1,150.5
2009	1,094.7	1,090.3	1,089.6	1,090.2	1,088.5	1,098.8	1,094.5	1,089.4	1,083.0	1,086.5	1,089.0	1,091.2	1,090.5
2010	1,058.3	1,064.1	1,071.6	1,095.1	1,095.6	1,110.0	1,114.4	1,113.6	1,103.9	1,115.7	1,117.9	1,119.0	1,098.3
2011	1,091.1	1,096.8	1,105.2	1,129.7	1,130.2	1,148.1	1,156.0	1,150.5	1,137.4	1,151.3	1,155.7	1,162.2	1,134.5
Education and Health Services													
2000	1,359.7	1,379.7	1,390.4	1,398.8	1,390.2	1,368.7	1,348.5	1,342.0	1,373.6	1,402.3	1,420.3	1,426.4	1,383.4
2001	1,401.2	1,425.6	1,438.9	1,441.3	1,443.2	1,417.3	1,395.7	1,391.0	1,429.5	1,461.7	1,471.7	1,475.7	1,432.7
2002	1,433.3	1,461.4	1,474.8	1,477.4	1,475.8	1,446.1	1,434.8	1,428.9	1,470.0	1,503.2	1,511.4	1,512.9	1,469.2
2003	1,474.0	1,501.9	1,512.8	1,511.5	1,507.9	1,478.7	1,457.2	1,447.8	1,492.4	1,525.9	1,534.6	1,535.0	1,498.3
2004	1,494.0	1,526.4	1,539.2	1,536.0	1,536.0	1,501.5	1,483.5	1,472.7	1,514.7	1,553.6	1,561.2	1,564.1	1,523.6
2005	1,514.9	1,548.2	1,557.2	1,562.5	1,553.4	1,518.0	1,497.3	1,490.9	1,540.3	1,573.6	1,584.0	1,585.7	1,543.8
2006	1,541.0	1,576.0	1,586.8	1,589.2	1,584.4	1,549.0	1,521.4	1,513.0	1,571.2	1,608.1	1,618.2	1,623.9	1,573.5
2007	1,571.8	1,605.0	1,616.0	1,613.4	1,606.0	1,572.8	1,545.2	1,537.6	1,594.8	1,637.0	1,643.7	1,647.3	1,599.2
2008	1,600.0	1,637.2	1,644.0	1,647.4	1,638.6	1,606.7	1,576.0	1,571.0	1,627.1	1,665.3	1,677.7	1,683.9	1,631.2
2009	1,637.5	1,674.8	1,680.2	1,678.7	1,670.1	1,637.5	1,609.3	1,603.5	1,657.4	1,699.4	1,710.8	1,717.3	1,664.7
2010	1,672.1	1,709.5	1,720.5	1,727.1	1,714.7	1,674.1	1,644.6	1,638.5	1,695.1	1,736.8	1,750.9	1,754.0	1,703.2
2011	1,701.9	1,744.4	1,750.8	1,758.9	1,747.0	1,697.3	1,678.5	1,671.0	1,718.4	1,761.5	1,777.6	1,774.1	1,731.8
Leisure and Hospitality													
2000	581.7	591.1	600.2	621.4	644.5	670.4	676.6	680.4	658.0	647.6	639.7	641.5	637.8
2001	594.8	601.1	610.4	619.2	656.8	679.0	681.8	685.2	650.1	625.9	621.0	621.3	637.2
2002	584.3	592.8	603.8	624.0	653.4	674.0	683.3	686.0	656.9	646.2	635.2	638.0	639.8
2003	598.7	603.4	610.1	625.7	657.0	678.0	692.4	690.0	666.4	654.7	644.4	648.8	647.1
2004	608.7	613.3	624.3	640.0	672.5	697.8	714.6	712.7	690.3	670.5	657.8	659.5	663.5
2005	617.5	623.5	634.1	656.3	683.3	708.6	714.9	716.8	692.0	671.8	664.0	663.3	670.5
2006	620.7	628.4	641.7	656.6	690.7	717.5	728.6	727.1	700.3	686.7	681.6	682.4	680.2
2007	640.9	649.8	659.8	677.3	713.5	739.7	750.3	748.2	719.4	711.0	702.0	700.9	701.1
2008	662.3	669.8	678.2	701.8	733.7	754.4	767.4	765.0	734.9	724.7	708.8	704.8	717.2
2009	662.2	666.1	671.2	686.6	725.2	745.5	757.8	756.5	739.7	723.5	709.1	707.3	712.6
2010	670.4	677.4	687.3	717.8	746.5	768.6	784.3	784.9	762.6	751.1	739.1	736.9	735.6
2011	701.2	709.8	719.9	747.8	775.3	803.5	824.3	821.2	788.7	774.2	767.8	755.2	765.7
Other Services													
2000	328.5	331.8	335.1	336.8	339.1	340.4	339.6	339.2	340.2	343.4	344.0	345.6	338.6
2001	339.0	341.5	344.0	343.2	346.4	348.7	345.6	344.8	341.1	343.2	345.5	346.6	344.1
2002	340.3	342.4	345.1	346.2	348.9	350.2	348.9	347.5	345.8	349.9	351.4	352.0	347.4
2003	344.6	345.7	348.2	348.7	351.6	352.8	350.9	348.8	347.3	350.0	350.6	351.8	349.3
2004	345.0	346.8	350.1	351.2	354.9	356.7	354.7	352.7	352.5	355.7	356.1	358.1	352.9
2005	349.2	350.8	353.0	357.4	358.9	360.5	357.7	355.4	355.4	356.3	357.8	359.7	356.0
2006	349.5	350.7	354.3	355.5	358.8	360.8	357.9	355.7	357.0	359.8	360.7	363.3	357.0
2007	356.0	357.7	360.3	361.4	366.0	367.9	363.3	361.1	361.2	365.2	366.2	367.3	362.8
2008	361.7	362.7	364.6	366.7	370.1	371.3	369.6	368.1	367.1	370.0	369.7	369.5	367.6
2009	361.7	362.8	364.1	363.3	366.7	367.6	366.2	363.9	362.5	364.9	365.6	366.2	364.6
2010	356.9	357.3	359.5	362.8	365.5	366.6	368.1	367.0	364.2	368.4	368.5	369.5	364.5
2011	363.5	365.3	367.1	371.6	374.5	375.8	376.1	375.6	365.5	369.1	366.1	367.0	369.8
Government													
2000	1,445.1	1,464.2	1,478.7	1,491.8	1,513.3	1,479.8	1,453.7	1,410.7	1,426.5	1,476.8	1,485.3	1,480.6	1,467.2
2001	1,452.5	1,472.4	1,478.3	1,487.7	1,484.3	1,474.9	1,426.7	1,402.9	1,440.1	1,486.3	1,502.7	1,499.0	1,467.3
2002	1,476.6	1,501.7	1,509.9	1,501.1	1,509.4	1,505.4	1,470.2	1,448.1	1,453.3	1,497.2	1,514.1	1,518.2	1,492.1
2003	1,478.8	1,502.4	1,506.6	1,501.9	1,505.0	1,503.3	1,453.2	1,432.3	1,451.1	1,492.1	1,507.6	1,513.0	1,487.3
2004	1,470.9	1,493.0	1,499.9	1,496.3	1,508.3	1,503.6	1,454.3	1,432.4	1,448.5	1,490.2	1,503.7	1,504.7	1,483.8
2005	1,479.2	1,497.5	1,499.1	1,505.1	1,509.2	1,508.6	1,461.6	1,441.2	1,461.2	1,492.8	1,504.9	1,510.6	1,489.3
2006	1,475.3	1,493.2	1,495.6	1,498.8	1,504.0	1,501.1	1,451.9	1,430.4	1,457.6	1,494.8	1,506.4	1,514.5	1,485.3
2007	1,489.5	1,509.0	1,511.1	1,509.3	1,517.7	1,517.0	1,466.6	1,450.3	1,474.9	1,512.8	1,522.8	1,531.2	1,501.0
2008	1,495.4	1,515.9	1,519.8	1,529.8	1,533.6	1,533.4	1,499.3	1,471.1	1,487.7	1,526.2	1,535.1	1,539.1	1,515.5
2009	1,507.1	1,531.5	1,534.4	1,537.9	1,542.6	1,531.0	1,531.2	1,503.7	1,475.3	1,524.0	1,532.3	1,534.0	1,523.8
2010	1,500.9	1,524.6	1,529.7	1,536.1	1,577.6	1,554.1	1,472.6	1,440.9	1,463.1	1,506.7	1,515.8	1,511.9	1,511.2
2011	1,475.7	1,497.5	1,500.1	1,500.3	1,508.5	1,497.6	1,461.6	1,448.8	1,455.7	1,497.7	1,505.5	1,508.4	1,488.1

2. Average Weekly Hours by Selected Industry: New York, 2007–2011

(Not seasonally adjusted)

Industry and year	January	February	March	April	May	June	July	August	September	October	November	December	Annual average
Total Private													
2007	33.7	33.6	33.8	34.0	33.9	34.2	34.3	34.1	34.5	34.2	34.3	34.6	34.1
2008	34.0	34.1	34.3	34.1	34.2	34.5	34.2	34.4	34.1	33.9	34.2	33.7	34.1
2009	33.6	34.0	33.8	33.5	33.7	33.6	33.7	34.1	33.7	33.7	34.0	33.7	33.7
2010	33.6	33.5	33.7	33.8	34.0	33.8	34.1	34.4	33.9	34.0	34.1	34.1	33.9
2011	33.9	33.8	33.7	34.0	34.2	34.2	34.4	34.3	34.2	34.3	34.1	34.2	34.1
Goods-Producing													
2007	38.1	37.0	37.5	37.8	38.1	38.2	37.8	37.8	38.2	37.7	37.8	38.1	37.8
2008	37.5	37.5	37.9	37.5	37.6	37.9	37.4	37.8	37.6	37.3	37.5	37.3	37.6
2009	36.8	36.9	37.0	36.3	37.2	37.5	37.3	37.8	37.2	37.7	38.1	37.9	37.3
2010	37.6	36.6	37.7	38.0	38.2	38.5	38.2	38.6	38.0	38.6	39.1	38.7	38.2
2011	37.8	38.4	38.4	38.8	39.0	39.0	39.0	38.9	38.9	38.9	39.1	39.1	38.8
Construction													
2007	36.1	34.7	35.7	35.7	36.6	36.9	36.5	36.4	36.8	36.3	36.1	35.9	36.2
2008	35.9	35.7	35.9	35.6	36.0	36.4	36.5	36.4	36.5	36.2	36.4	36.1	36.1
2009	36.1	36.0	36.3	35.7	36.4	36.2	36.6	36.7	35.3	36.0	36.8	36.1	36.2
2010	36.2	34.0	35.8	36.0	36.3	36.8	36.4	37.1	36.3	36.9	37.3	36.9	36.4
2011	35.6	36.8	37.0	37.5	38.0	38.2	38.4	37.9	37.8	37.9	38.1	37.5	37.6
Manufacturing													
2007	39.1	38.1	38.5	39.0	39.1	39.1	38.8	38.7	39.2	38.7	38.9	39.4	38.9
2008	38.4	38.5	39.1	38.7	38.6	38.8	38.0	38.6	38.3	37.9	38.1	37.9	38.4
2009	37.1	37.3	37.3	36.8	37.7	38.3	37.6	38.3	38.3	38.5	38.6	39.0	37.9
2010	38.4	38.1	38.8	39.2	39.3	39.5	39.2	39.4	39.0	39.5	40.0	39.7	39.2
2011	39.0	39.4	39.4	39.8	39.9	39.8	39.6	39.8	39.8	39.8	39.9	40.3	39.7
Trade, Transportation, and Utilities													
2007	34.6	34.5	35.0	34.9	35.1	35.4	35.0	34.7	35.3	35.0	34.9	35.4	35.0
2008	34.3	34.5	34.7	34.3	34.4	34.8	34.3	34.2	34.1	33.9	34.1	33.9	34.3
2009	33.4	33.7	33.7	33.6	33.9	33.8	34.0	34.2	34.1	33.9	34.3	34.3	33.9
2010	33.7	33.9	34.4	34.4	34.8	34.5	34.7	34.8	34.3	34.4	34.5	34.6	34.4
2011	33.8	33.8	34.0	34.3	34.5	34.9	34.8	34.9	35.2	35.1	34.9	35.5	34.6
Information													
2007	32.0	32.3	32.7	32.7	32.5	32.7	33.8	33.2	34.1	33.5	33.7	34.4	33.1
2008	33.7	33.9	34.5	33.9	34.1	34.5	34.6	34.6	34.6	34.6	35.0	33.9	34.3
2009	33.7	34.8	34.2	33.9	33.9	33.9	33.8	34.7	33.9	33.8	34.8	32.7	34.0
2010	32.7	32.9	32.9	33.3	33.6	33.3	33.3	34.5	33.9	33.7	34.0	34.0	33.5
2011	34.4	34.4	34.2	34.6	35.3	34.9	34.9	34.9	35.0	35.3	35.3	35.0	34.9
Financial Activities													
2007	36.4	36.3	36.2	37.1	36.2	36.5	37.2	37.0	37.6	37.1	37.3	37.3	36.9
2008	36.8	36.9	37.0	36.8	37.1	37.2	36.9	37.0	36.8	36.8	37.3	36.4	36.9
2009	36.7	37.7	37.0	36.5	36.4	36.6	36.6	37.2	36.8	36.9	36.9	36.4	36.8
2010	36.6	37.0	36.9	36.8	37.2	37.0	36.8	37.5	36.8	37.1	36.8	36.6	36.9
2011	37.0	36.6	36.6	36.9	37.3	37.2	37.4	37.6	37.6	37.9	37.3	37.0	37.2
Professional and Business Services													
2007	34.7	35.1	34.9	35.5	34.9	35.2	35.5	34.8	35.7	35.0	35.1	35.9	35.2
2008	35.1	35.1	35.8	35.3	35.4	36.0	35.3	35.8	35.7	35.1	35.8	34.9	35.4
2009	35.0	35.7	35.4	34.6	34.8	34.7	34.3	34.9	34.3	34.5	35.2	34.6	34.8
2010	34.9	34.7	34.7	34.8	35.5	34.7	34.8	35.4	34.9	35.1	35.1	35.2	35.0
2011	35.3	35.0	34.8	35.1	35.4	35.0	35.0	34.9	34.8	35.5	35.0	35.1	35.1
Education and Health Services													
2007	32.0	32.2	32.7	32.7	32.6	33.1	33.1	33.2	33.4	33.1	33.4	33.3	32.9
2008	33.4	33.3	33.3	33.2	33.4	33.6	33.4	33.7	33.4	33.3	33.6	33.3	33.4
2009	33.4	33.4	33.2	33.1	33.1	33.0	33.2	33.1	33.1	32.9	32.9	32.7	33.1
2010	32.8	32.5	32.4	32.5	32.5	32.5	32.8	32.9	32.9	32.6	32.9	32.9	32.7
2011	33.1	32.8	32.8	32.9	33.0	32.8	33.1	32.8	32.7	32.8	32.6	32.6	32.8
Leisure and Hospitality													
2007	27.4	27.4	27.5	27.3	28.0	28.2	28.5	28.7	28.2	28.3	28.4	28.0	28.0
2008	27.8	28.0	28.1	28.3	28.4	28.6	28.8	28.7	27.9	27.9	27.8	27.6	28.2
2009	26.9	27.4	27.2	27.5	28.1	27.5	28.3	28.6	27.9	28.1	28.1	28.0	27.8
2010	27.6	27.7	27.8	28.1	28.0	28.0	28.8	28.7	27.8	28.1	28.0	27.6	28.0
2011	26.9	27.2	27.0	27.3	27.5	28.4	29.0	28.8	27.6	27.7	27.5	27.5	27.7
Other Services													
2007	29.8	29.8	29.3	30.3	29.7	29.7	30.3	30.4	30.1	29.8	29.9	30.5	30.0
2008	30.4	30.5	30.7	30.7	30.6	30.8	30.8	30.9	30.2	29.9	30.0	29.7	30.4
2009	29.9	30.2	30.2	30.3	30.6	30.9	31.5	31.8	30.6	30.8	30.9	31.0	30.7
2010	31.3	31.0	31.2	31.6	31.9	31.7	33.1	34.0	33.4	33.2	32.7	32.9	32.3
2011	32.6	32.6	32.3	32.6	32.8	32.2	32.3	32.1	32.0	31.9	31.7	32.0	32.3

3. Average Hourly Earnings by Selected Industry: New York, 2007–2011

(Dollars, not seasonally adjusted)

Industry and year	January	February	March	April	May	June	July	August	September	October	November	December	Annual average
Total Private													
2007	25.43	25.54	25.34	25.58	25.12	25.10	25.27	25.16	25.23	25.08	25.08	25.25	25.26
2008	25.33	25.44	25.67	25.50	25.39	25.37	25.33	25.42	25.51	25.46	25.65	25.66	25.48
2009	25.67	25.79	25.72	25.52	25.35	25.60	25.56	25.71	25.80	25.75	25.98	25.96	25.70
2010	26.09	26.11	26.04	26.12	26.18	25.82	25.82	25.93	25.93	26.14	26.23	26.35	26.06
2011	26.74	26.36	26.43	26.36	26.54	26.10	26.20	26.08	26.57	26.95	26.73	26.71	26.48
Goods-Producing													
2007	24.69	24.94	25.16	25.09	25.13	24.91	25.06	25.08	25.22	24.90	25.16	25.23	25.05
2008	25.23	25.20	25.20	25.31	25.23	25.20	25.09	25.03	25.06	25.28	25.56	25.68	25.25
2009	25.48	25.52	25.84	26.00	25.91	25.81	26.37	26.31	26.61	26.36	26.40	26.45	26.09
2010	26.54	26.59	26.71	26.67	26.70	26.28	26.85	27.10	26.91	27.04	26.90	26.92	26.77
2011	26.72	26.51	27.08	27.01	27.15	27.07	27.64	27.57	27.75	28.02	28.49	28.39	27.47
Construction													
2007	29.66	30.65	30.29	29.85	29.74	29.09	29.35	29.47	29.66	29.73	29.99	30.27	29.79
2008	30.33	30.40	30.28	29.97	29.97	29.86	29.88	30.09	30.05	30.01	30.45	30.46	30.14
2009	30.60	30.45	30.54	30.42	30.31	30.42	31.08	31.02	31.69	31.27	31.23	31.80	30.91
2010	32.20	32.26	32.60	32.41	32.20	31.73	32.60	33.09	32.81	32.94	32.93	33.03	32.58
2011	32.71	32.11	32.75	31.89	31.43	31.27	31.65	31.70	32.02	32.18	32.69	32.74	32.07
Manufacturing													
2007	22.30	22.37	22.70	22.77	22.66	22.67	22.75	22.73	22.80	22.34	22.69	22.81	22.63
2008	22.85	22.88	22.92	23.03	22.78	22.73	22.60	22.49	22.56	22.88	23.02	23.32	22.84
2009	23.00	23.07	23.24	23.46	23.23	22.96	23.27	23.20	23.48	23.32	23.39	23.36	23.25
2010	23.43	23.78	23.50	23.37	23.50	23.12	23.34	23.32	23.30	23.45	23.23	23.39	23.39
2011	23.59	23.54	23.81	23.93	24.36	24.33	25.00	24.91	25.10	25.39	25.86	25.85	24.65
Trade, Transportation, and Utilities													
2007	21.34	21.59	21.39	21.56	21.11	21.30	21.30	21.46	21.34	21.27	21.26	21.17	21.34
2008	21.57	21.48	21.72	21.53	21.60	21.43	21.53	21.61	21.54	21.27	21.34	21.26	21.49
2009	21.57	21.57	21.53	21.53	21.26	21.40	21.29	21.59	21.50	21.55	21.45	21.55	21.48
2010	21.64	21.63	21.40	21.66	21.64	21.35	21.41	21.19	21.48	21.46	21.42	21.54	21.48
2011	22.12	22.01	22.04	21.96	22.02	21.59	21.62	21.55	21.93	21.91	21.66	21.51	21.82
Information													
2007	34.14	33.65	32.38	32.63	32.36	33.12	32.53	32.65	32.64	32.75	32.80	32.87	32.87
2008	33.06	32.86	33.16	33.89	33.30	33.40	33.27	33.51	33.93	33.79	34.18	35.36	33.65
2009	34.87	35.05	34.67	34.07	34.76	35.47	35.81	35.38	35.66	35.80	35.86	36.02	35.28
2010	36.43	36.65	36.67	36.54	37.59	37.21	37.59	37.64	38.99	38.94	38.91	38.73	37.68
2011	40.67	39.07	39.03	39.11	39.22	39.05	39.09	38.80	39.22	39.99	39.81	40.01	39.42
Financial Activities													
2007	35.50	35.47	35.46	35.90	35.26	35.28	35.55	35.21	35.09	34.48	34.35	35.15	35.22
2008	35.01	35.55	35.78	35.24	34.80	34.99	34.50	34.84	34.62	34.53	34.74	34.28	34.91
2009	34.13	34.33	34.79	34.59	34.53	34.56	34.47	34.98	34.71	34.78	35.85	35.49	34.76
2010	35.12	35.47	35.63	35.86	35.86	34.97	34.72	34.76	34.03	34.66	34.96	35.16	35.10
2011	35.86	34.83	34.75	34.61	35.04	34.62	34.33	34.14	34.75	35.81	35.08	34.84	34.89
Professional and Business Services													
2007	30.43	31.17	30.52	31.32	30.90	30.65	31.12	30.88	31.15	31.44	31.36	31.65	31.06
2008	31.78	32.40	32.56	32.21	32.18	32.28	32.37	32.34	32.48	33.00	33.18	33.34	32.51
2009	33.30	33.86	33.50	33.07	32.59	33.17	33.43	33.59	33.42	33.75	33.94	34.04	33.47
2010	34.49	34.19	34.18	34.39	34.38	33.78	34.01	34.49	33.94	34.31	34.34	34.48	34.25
2011	35.11	34.41	34.32	34.07	34.56	33.74	33.79	33.53	33.97	34.45	33.84	34.06	34.15
Education and Health Services													
2007	23.24	22.99	22.86	22.71	22.35	22.13	22.03	22.04	21.87	21.70	21.69	21.73	22.27
2008	21.66	21.52	21.94	21.94	21.91	21.77	22.00	21.81	22.00	21.88	22.01	22.10	21.88
2009	22.11	22.10	21.95	22.00	22.05	22.09	22.09	21.99	22.23	22.10	22.28	22.28	22.11
2010	22.32	22.43	22.36	22.44	22.50	22.56	22.76	22.65	22.72	22.90	23.10	23.17	22.66
2011	23.19	23.11	23.18	23.23	23.32	23.45	23.83	23.72	23.92	24.17	24.07	24.10	23.61
Leisure and Hospitality													
2007	16.76	16.50	16.71	16.96	16.49	16.76	17.36	16.65	17.20	17.38	17.42	17.64	16.99
2008	17.39	17.58	17.67	17.57	17.41	17.40	16.88	17.63	18.10	17.71	17.93	18.32	17.62
2009	17.53	17.54	17.38	16.95	16.96	18.00	17.39	17.38	18.03	17.43	17.76	18.15	17.54
2010	17.92	17.59	17.52	17.30	17.42	16.86	16.41	16.50	17.02	17.33	17.61	17.99	17.26
2011	17.27	17.24	17.29	17.21	17.31	15.79	15.57	15.78	16.87	17.36	17.33	17.65	16.85
Other Services													
2007	22.73	22.41	22.64	22.72	22.62	22.45	22.14	22.10	22.56	22.18	22.11	22.08	22.39
2008	21.82	21.83	21.87	21.67	21.74	21.50	21.45	21.40	21.81	21.70	21.79	21.70	21.69
2009	21.66	21.44	21.39	21.08	21.20	21.07	20.19	20.86	21.75	21.60	21.84	21.74	21.31
2010	21.55	21.91	21.88	21.78	21.69	21.75	20.13	20.30	21.00	20.99	21.42	21.57	21.31
2011	21.61	21.57	21.68	21.80	22.01	21.73	21.41	21.35	21.89	21.87	22.24	22.60	21.81

4. Average Weekly Earnings by Selected Industry: New York, 2007–2011

(Dollars, not seasonally adjusted)

Industry and year	January	February	March	April	May	June	July	August	September	October	November	December	Annual average
Total Private													
2007	856.99	858.14	856.49	869.72	851.57	858.42	866.76	857.96	870.44	857.74	860.24	873.65	861.67
2008	861.22	867.50	880.48	869.55	868.34	875.27	866.29	874.45	869.89	863.09	877.23	864.74	869.91
2009	862.51	876.86	869.34	854.92	854.30	860.16	861.37	876.71	869.46	867.78	883.32	874.85	867.35
2010	876.62	874.69	877.55	882.86	890.12	872.72	880.46	891.99	879.03	888.76	894.44	898.54	884.28
2011	906.49	890.97	890.69	896.24	907.67	892.62	901.28	894.54	908.69	924.39	911.49	913.48	903.30
Goods-Producing													
2007	940.69	922.78	943.50	948.40	957.45	951.56	947.27	948.02	963.40	938.73	951.05	961.26	948.00
2008	946.13	945.00	955.08	949.13	948.65	955.08	938.37	946.13	942.26	942.94	958.50	957.86	948.70
2009	937.66	941.69	956.08	943.80	963.85	967.88	983.60	994.52	989.89	993.77	1,005.84	1,002.46	973.28
2010	997.90	973.19	1,006.97	1,013.46	1,019.94	1,011.78	1,025.67	1,046.06	1,022.58	1,043.74	1,051.79	1,041.80	1,021.74
2011	1,010.02	1,017.98	1,039.87	1,047.99	1,058.85	1,055.73	1,077.96	1,072.47	1,079.48	1,089.98	1,113.96	1,110.05	1,065.27
Construction													
2007	1,070.73	1,063.56	1,081.35	1,065.65	1,088.48	1,073.42	1,071.28	1,072.71	1,091.49	1,079.20	1,082.64	1,086.69	1,077.52
2008	1,088.85	1,085.28	1,087.05	1,066.93	1,078.92	1,086.90	1,090.62	1,095.28	1,096.83	1,086.36	1,108.38	1,099.61	1,089.36
2009	1,104.66	1,096.20	1,108.60	1,085.99	1,103.28	1,101.20	1,137.53	1,138.43	1,118.66	1,125.72	1,149.26	1,147.98	1,118.37
2010	1,165.64	1,096.84	1,167.08	1,166.76	1,168.86	1,167.66	1,186.64	1,227.64	1,191.00	1,215.49	1,228.29	1,218.81	1,184.91
2011	1,164.48	1,181.65	1,211.75	1,195.88	1,194.34	1,194.51	1,215.36	1,201.43	1,210.36	1,219.62	1,245.49	1,227.75	1,205.98
Manufacturing													
2007	871.93	852.30	873.95	888.03	886.01	886.40	882.70	879.65	893.76	864.56	882.64	898.71	880.04
2008	877.44	880.88	896.17	891.26	879.31	881.92	858.80	868.11	864.05	867.15	877.06	883.83	877.17
2009	853.30	860.51	866.85	863.33	875.77	879.37	874.95	888.56	899.28	897.82	902.85	911.04	880.75
2010	899.71	906.02	911.80	916.10	923.55	913.24	914.93	918.81	908.70	926.28	929.20	928.58	916.46
2011	920.01	927.48	938.11	952.41	971.96	968.33	990.00	991.42	998.98	1,010.52	1,031.81	1,041.76	978.75
Trade, Transportation, and Utilities													
2007	738.36	744.86	748.65	752.44	740.96	754.02	745.50	744.66	753.30	744.45	741.97	749.42	746.55
2008	739.85	741.06	753.68	738.48	743.04	745.76	738.48	739.06	734.51	721.05	727.69	720.71	736.89
2009	720.44	726.91	725.56	723.41	720.71	723.32	723.86	738.38	733.15	730.55	735.74	739.17	728.46
2010	729.27	733.26	736.16	745.10	753.07	736.58	742.93	737.41	736.76	738.22	738.99	745.28	739.49
2011	747.66	743.94	749.36	753.23	759.69	753.49	752.38	752.10	771.94	769.04	755.93	763.61	756.11
Information													
2007	1,092.48	1,086.90	1,058.83	1,067.00	1,051.70	1,083.02	1,099.51	1,083.98	1,113.02	1,097.13	1,105.36	1,130.73	1,089.21
2008	1,114.12	1,113.95	1,144.02	1,148.87	1,135.53	1,152.30	1,151.14	1,159.45	1,173.98	1,169.13	1,196.30	1,198.70	1,154.93
2009	1,175.12	1,219.74	1,185.71	1,154.97	1,178.36	1,202.43	1,210.38	1,227.69	1,208.87	1,210.04	1,247.93	1,177.85	1,199.75
2010	1,191.26	1,205.79	1,206.44	1,216.78	1,263.02	1,239.09	1,251.75	1,298.58	1,321.76	1,312.28	1,322.94	1,316.82	1,262.67
2011	1,399.05	1,344.01	1,334.83	1,353.21	1,384.47	1,362.85	1,364.24	1,354.12	1,372.70	1,411.65	1,405.29	1,400.35	1,373.95
Financial Activities													
2007	1,292.20	1,287.56	1,283.65	1,331.89	1,276.41	1,287.72	1,322.46	1,302.77	1,319.38	1,279.21	1,281.26	1,311.10	1,298.00
2008	1,288.37	1,311.80	1,323.86	1,296.83	1,291.08	1,301.63	1,273.05	1,289.08	1,274.02	1,270.70	1,295.80	1,247.79	1,288.75
2009	1,252.57	1,294.24	1,287.23	1,262.54	1,256.89	1,264.90	1,261.60	1,301.26	1,277.33	1,283.38	1,322.87	1,291.84	1,279.61
2010	1,285.39	1,312.39	1,314.75	1,319.65	1,333.99	1,293.89	1,277.70	1,303.50	1,252.30	1,285.89	1,286.53	1,286.86	1,295.94
2011	1,326.82	1,274.78	1,271.85	1,277.11	1,306.99	1,287.86	1,283.94	1,283.66	1,306.60	1,357.20	1,308.48	1,289.08	1,297.90
Professional and Business Services													
2007	1,055.92	1,094.07	1,065.15	1,111.86	1,078.41	1,078.88	1,104.76	1,074.62	1,112.06	1,100.40	1,100.74	1,136.24	1,092.98
2008	1,115.48	1,137.24	1,165.65	1,137.01	1,139.17	1,162.08	1,142.66	1,157.77	1,159.54	1,158.30	1,187.84	1,163.57	1,152.26
2009	1,165.50	1,208.80	1,185.90	1,144.22	1,134.13	1,151.00	1,146.65	1,172.29	1,146.31	1,164.38	1,194.69	1,177.78	1,166.00
2010	1,203.70	1,186.39	1,186.05	1,196.77	1,220.49	1,172.17	1,183.55	1,220.95	1,184.51	1,204.28	1,205.33	1,213.70	1,198.21
2011	1,239.38	1,204.35	1,194.34	1,195.86	1,223.42	1,180.90	1,182.65	1,170.20	1,182.16	1,222.98	1,184.40	1,195.51	1,197.72
Education and Health Services													
2007	743.68	740.28	747.52	742.62	728.61	732.50	729.19	731.73	730.46	718.27	724.45	723.61	732.69
2008	723.44	716.62	730.60	728.41	731.79	731.47	734.80	735.00	734.80	728.60	739.54	735.93	730.93
2009	738.47	738.14	728.74	728.20	729.86	728.97	733.39	727.87	735.81	727.09	733.01	728.56	731.50
2010	732.10	728.98	724.46	729.30	731.25	733.20	746.53	745.19	747.49	746.54	759.99	762.29	740.68
2011	767.59	758.01	760.30	764.27	769.56	769.16	788.77	778.02	782.18	792.78	784.68	785.66	775.08
Leisure and Hospitality													
2007	459.22	452.10	459.53	463.01	461.72	472.63	494.76	477.86	485.04	491.85	494.73	493.92	476.04
2008	483.44	492.24	496.53	497.23	494.44	497.64	486.14	505.98	504.99	494.11	498.45	505.63	496.50
2009	471.56	480.60	472.74	466.13	476.58	495.00	492.14	497.07	503.04	489.78	499.06	508.20	488.05
2010	494.59	487.24	487.06	486.13	487.76	472.08	472.61	473.55	473.16	486.97	493.08	496.52	483.94
2011	464.56	468.93	466.83	469.83	476.03	448.44	451.53	454.46	465.61	480.87	476.58	485.38	467.16
Other Services													
2007	677.35	667.82	663.35	688.42	671.81	666.77	670.84	671.84	679.06	660.96	661.09	673.44	671.04
2008	663.33	665.82	671.41	665.27	665.24	662.20	660.66	661.26	658.66	648.83	653.70	644.49	660.04
2009	647.63	647.49	645.98	638.72	648.72	651.06	635.99	663.35	665.55	665.28	674.86	673.94	654.89
2010	674.52	679.21	682.66	688.25	691.91	689.48	666.30	690.20	701.40	696.87	700.43	709.65	689.32
2011	704.49	703.18	700.26	710.68	721.93	699.71	691.54	685.34	700.48	697.65	705.01	723.20	703.53

NORTH CAROLINA
At a Glance

Population:
    2000 census: 8,046,346
    2010 census: 9,535,483
    2011 estimate: 9,656,401

Percent change in population:
    2000–2010: 18.5%
    2010–2011: 1.3%

Percent change in total nonfarm employment:
    2000–2010: -1.0%
    2010–2011: 1.1%

Industry with the largest growth in employment, 2000–2011 (thousands):
    Education and Health Services, 161.9

Industry with the largest decline or smallest growth in employment, 2000–2011 (thousands):
    Manufacturing, -324.3

Civilian labor force:
    2000: 4,123,812
    2010: 4,616,767
    2011: 4,653,911

Unemployment rate and rank among states (lowest to highest):
    2000: 3.7%, 22nd
    2010: 10.9%, 45th
    2011: 10.5%, 46th

Over-the-year change in unemployment rates:
    2010–2011: -0.4%

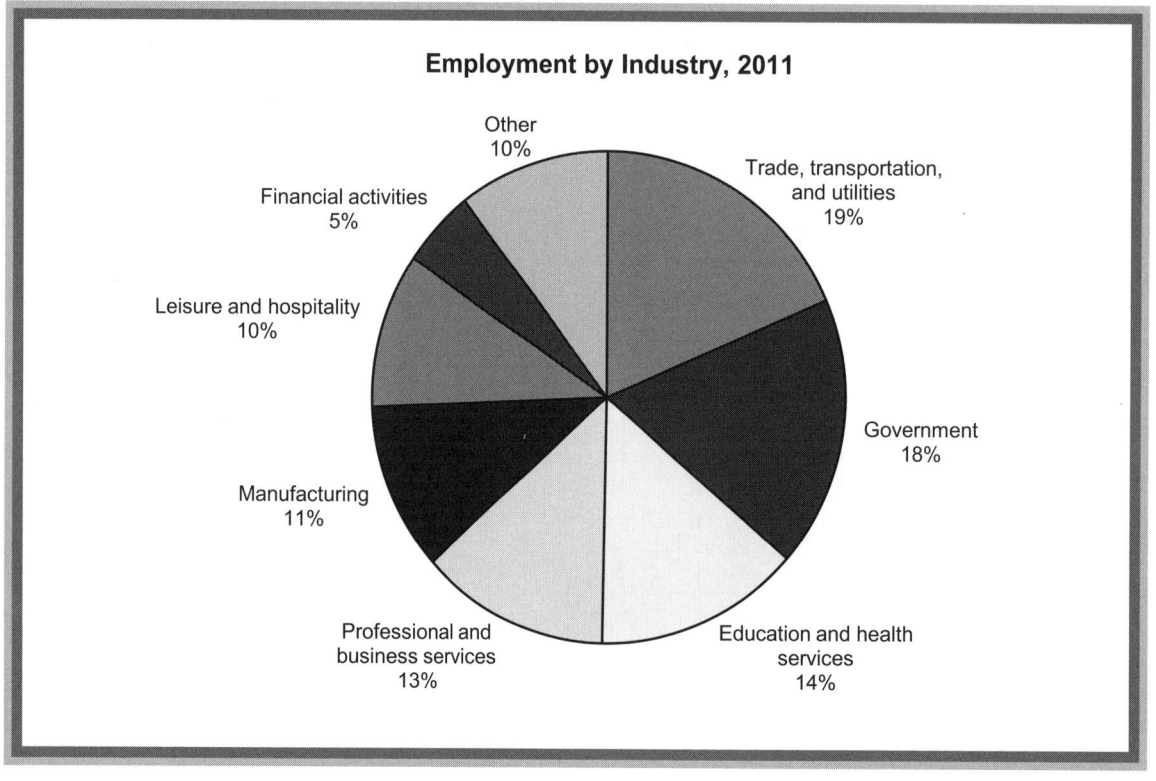

Employment by Industry, 2011

- Other 10%
- Trade, transportation, and utilities 19%
- Financial activities 5%
- Government 18%
- Leisure and hospitality 10%
- Manufacturing 11%
- Professional and business services 13%
- Education and health services 14%

1. Employment by Industry: North Carolina, Selected Years, 2000–2011

(Numbers in thousands, not seasonally adjusted)

Industry and year	January	February	March	April	May	June	July	August	September	October	November	December	Annual average
Total Nonfarm													
2000	3,825.9	3,846.7	3,892.5	3,915.1	3,944.8	3,963.9	3,886.6	3,936.5	3,953.8	3,949.1	3,958.7	3,954.4	3,919.0
2001	3,888.7	3,900.6	3,918.3	3,921.4	3,936.2	3,927.9	3,849.3	3,891.4	3,894.3	3,889.5	3,881.4	3,870.6	3,897.5
2002	3,786.1	3,802.6	3,831.3	3,855.9	3,878.2	3,861.1	3,795.7	3,846.0	3,856.0	3,861.3	3,856.7	3,849.6	3,840.0
2003	3,753.5	3,756.4	3,779.8	3,800.4	3,827.8	3,812.2	3,720.5	3,780.5	3,804.8	3,825.8	3,821.5	3,825.8	3,792.4
2004	3,742.6	3,752.8	3,789.4	3,822.5	3,854.9	3,848.2	3,801.2	3,862.5	3,891.1	3,895.2	3,904.6	3,914.0	3,839.9
2005	3,835.6	3,851.9	3,882.7	3,909.2	3,929.1	3,913.3	3,857.6	3,929.4	3,965.3	3,972.7	3,987.4	3,990.0	3,918.7
2006	3,925.7	3,940.5	3,976.6	4,023.4	4,055.5	4,052.5	3,995.2	4,067.6	4,093.0	4,115.1	4,141.8	4,147.2	4,044.5
2007	4,057.6	4,080.8	4,121.1	4,130.6	4,168.2	4,171.8	4,085.0	4,163.7	4,190.2	4,193.1	4,211.3	4,214.4	4,149.0
2008	4,117.4	4,137.1	4,157.9	4,160.4	4,186.1	4,167.8	4,075.7	4,143.7	4,163.2	4,139.5	4,120.9	4,098.1	4,139.0
2009	3,956.1	3,944.6	3,937.8	3,930.7	3,945.8	3,918.6	3,827.5	3,888.8	3,912.1	3,899.0	3,902.4	3,892.1	3,913.0
2010	3,801.2	3,806.8	3,842.7	3,875.9	3,916.5	3,895.7	3,819.8	3,886.6	3,902.7	3,930.5	3,940.6	3,930.2	3,879.1
2011	3,835.6	3,871.0	3,901.0	3,938.0	3,954.8	3,940.7	3,862.3	3,936.1	3,941.0	3,962.0	3,970.4	3,955.7	3,922.4
Total Private													
2000	3,222.0	3,235.6	3,272.1	3,292.2	3,315.8	3,349.3	3,331.6	3,335.5	3,329.5	3,317.1	3,323.8	3,322.3	3,303.9
2001	3,261.2	3,266.3	3,280.7	3,287.8	3,300.0	3,317.6	3,281.2	3,283.3	3,258.1	3,238.2	3,227.6	3,221.2	3,268.6
2002	3,147.6	3,157.1	3,181.4	3,208.2	3,229.0	3,244.9	3,225.1	3,236.9	3,219.5	3,208.1	3,206.3	3,203.7	3,205.7
2003	3,118.6	3,116.1	3,135.1	3,157.4	3,181.6	3,196.5	3,157.9	3,173.4	3,162.5	3,161.8	3,165.1	3,171.7	3,158.1
2004	3,099.2	3,104.4	3,136.3	3,170.4	3,200.1	3,225.1	3,230.1	3,240.1	3,228.4	3,228.3	3,235.5	3,245.9	3,195.3
2005	3,176.6	3,186.5	3,213.2	3,240.2	3,257.9	3,278.8	3,285.6	3,298.8	3,295.3	3,298.4	3,310.0	3,314.6	3,263.0
2006	3,255.5	3,264.0	3,294.8	3,339.2	3,367.6	3,394.0	3,408.3	3,421.0	3,410.5	3,424.1	3,440.3	3,447.5	3,372.2
2007	3,370.9	3,387.4	3,422.5	3,432.1	3,465.6	3,497.3	3,483.9	3,497.9	3,486.1	3,488.2	3,499.0	3,503.4	3,461.2
2008	3,415.3	3,427.3	3,442.9	3,443.7	3,464.8	3,474.4	3,461.0	3,463.2	3,437.6	3,412.2	3,388.7	3,367.9	3,433.3
2009	3,238.6	3,223.2	3,211.2	3,200.3	3,216.0	3,219.9	3,208.0	3,206.5	3,189.8	3,181.3	3,181.5	3,173.6	3,204.2
2010	3,092.9	3,092.7	3,122.4	3,150.1	3,172.5	3,192.9	3,205.0	3,212.1	3,197.2	3,212.5	3,217.7	3,210.9	3,173.2
2011	3,127.5	3,156.4	3,181.9	3,217.3	3,237.1	3,257.4	3,257.1	3,268.3	3,240.1	3,246.7	3,250.3	3,240.8	3,223.4
Goods-Producing													
2000	989.4	990.3	998.7	997.4	1,001.2	1,008.2	1,002.1	998.8	1,001.5	989.5	991.6	987.8	996.4
2001	972.9	968.5	965.4	959.8	953.4	953.0	938.3	934.8	927.3	916.2	905.6	898.4	941.1
2002	879.4	878.8	879.3	876.8	877.6	875.7	870.2	871.8	866.5	860.9	855.0	850.1	870.2
2003	834.6	829.2	830.0	829.1	828.9	827.9	810.4	810.5	808.0	806.2	802.4	799.9	818.1
2004	787.7	786.4	792.9	798.9	803.3	809.3	810.6	810.1	809.3	808.3	806.8	806.8	802.5
2005	794.6	795.6	798.5	800.7	803.8	807.7	805.9	807.7	808.2	802.8	802.6	800.8	802.4
2006	789.2	788.7	793.6	805.2	807.8	812.8	813.0	815.0	812.8	810.7	808.9	809.8	805.6
2007	797.6	797.8	801.5	796.8	799.6	807.4	801.9	804.1	802.5	799.0	797.5	795.7	800.1
2008	776.2	775.2	775.0	767.5	768.3	766.8	762.7	759.4	755.0	743.9	732.4	720.8	758.6
2009	685.1	673.9	662.2	651.9	646.9	644.8	639.3	636.8	634.5	629.8	625.5	622.7	646.1
2010	606.3	603.0	608.0	612.0	614.6	618.5	620.8	620.4	620.4	618.3	616.0	613.7	614.3
2011	597.4	603.2	608.0	611.6	616.0	619.4	619.3	623.0	624.1	620.7	618.5	616.8	614.8
Mining and Logging													
2000	8.4	8.3	8.5	8.4	8.5	8.5	8.5	8.5	8.5	8.4	8.4	8.4	8.4
2001	8.2	8.1	8.1	8.2	8.2	8.2	8.1	8.1	8.1	8.0	8.0	8.0	8.1
2002	8.0	8.0	8.1	8.0	8.0	7.9	7.8	7.8	7.8	7.8	7.7	7.7	7.9
2003	7.6	7.5	7.6	7.6	7.6	7.6	7.1	7.2	7.1	7.2	7.0	7.0	7.3
2004	6.8	6.8	6.9	6.9	6.9	7.0	6.9	7.0	7.1	6.9	6.9	6.9	6.9
2005	6.8	6.8	6.8	6.7	6.6	6.7	6.6	6.6	6.6	6.7	6.7	6.6	6.7
2006	6.6	6.6	6.7	6.7	6.7	6.8	6.9	7.0	7.0	6.9	6.9	6.9	6.8
2007	6.9	6.9	7.0	7.1	7.1	7.1	7.0	7.1	7.0	6.9	6.9	6.9	7.0
2008	6.8	6.8	6.7	6.6	6.6	6.6	6.6	6.6	6.6	6.5	6.5	6.4	6.6
2009	6.1	6.0	6.0	5.8	5.8	5.9	5.9	5.9	5.9	5.8	5.7	5.6	5.9
2010	5.6	5.5	5.6	5.6	5.6	5.6	5.8	5.7	5.7	5.7	5.6	5.6	5.6
2011	5.5	5.6	5.6	5.6	5.6	5.7	5.7	5.7	5.7	5.6	5.6	5.5	5.6
Construction													
2000	220.0	219.3	227.4	228.1	231.2	235.2	233.8	235.2	235.0	232.4	232.0	230.7	230.0
2001	223.6	224.7	230.0	230.3	233.1	235.8	233.1	232.6	230.0	227.4	224.9	222.3	229.0
2002	214.4	214.4	216.9	221.0	223.3	224.1	222.7	223.3	220.1	217.2	214.5	213.7	218.8
2003	206.1	204.6	206.8	209.7	214.2	215.4	212.5	212.8	212.2	215.3	214.0	213.3	211.4
2004	206.0	205.0	210.1	214.9	218.2	221.0	223.7	223.9	222.9	224.3	223.9	224.6	218.2
2005	219.3	220.2	223.4	227.2	230.4	233.5	237.2	238.0	238.5	235.6	235.5	234.5	231.1
2006	230.2	231.2	236.4	242.1	244.7	248.7	251.5	253.5	252.5	251.9	252.5	252.7	245.7
2007	246.5	247.0	252.0	253.7	256.0	259.8	258.6	259.2	258.4	256.6	255.0	253.0	254.7
2008	242.1	241.6	242.3	239.9	241.0	240.6	240.2	237.3	234.7	229.9	223.9	218.4	236.0
2009	202.2	199.6	197.5	193.6	193.7	194.1	193.7	191.9	189.8	186.6	183.6	182.1	192.4
2010	171.8	169.7	173.8	177.3	178.5	179.9	180.7	180.2	178.5	177.7	176.2	173.5	176.5
2011	162.5	167.2	170.7	174.1	176.6	178.1	178.2	180.8	181.9	180.6	179.8	176.7	175.6
Manufacturing													
2000	761.0	762.7	762.8	760.9	761.5	764.5	759.8	755.1	758.0	748.7	751.2	748.7	757.9
2001	741.1	735.7	727.3	721.3	712.1	709.0	697.1	694.1	689.2	680.8	672.7	668.1	704.0
2002	657.0	656.4	654.3	647.8	646.3	643.7	639.7	640.7	638.6	635.9	632.8	628.7	643.5
2003	620.9	617.1	615.6	611.8	607.1	604.9	590.8	590.5	588.7	583.7	581.4	579.6	599.3
2004	574.9	574.6	575.9	577.1	578.2	581.3	580.0	579.2	579.3	577.1	576.0	575.3	577.4
2005	568.5	568.6	568.3	566.8	566.8	567.5	562.1	563.1	563.1	560.5	560.4	559.7	564.6
2006	552.4	550.9	550.5	556.4	556.4	557.3	554.6	554.5	553.3	551.9	549.5	550.2	553.2
2007	544.2	543.9	542.5	536.0	536.5	540.5	536.3	537.8	537.1	535.5	535.6	535.8	538.5
2008	527.3	526.8	526.0	521.0	520.7	519.6	515.9	515.5	513.7	507.5	502.0	496.0	516.0
2009	476.8	468.3	458.7	452.5	447.4	444.8	439.7	439.0	438.8	437.4	436.2	435.0	447.9
2010	428.9	427.8	428.6	429.1	430.5	433.0	434.3	434.5	436.2	434.9	434.2	434.6	432.2
2011	429.4	430.4	431.7	431.9	433.8	435.6	435.4	436.5	436.5	434.5	433.1	434.6	433.6

1. Employment by Industry: North Carolina, Selected Years, 2000–2011—*Continued*

(Numbers in thousands, not seasonally adjusted)

Industry and year	January	February	March	April	May	June	July	August	September	October	November	December	Annual average
Service-Providing													
2000	2,836.5	2,856.4	2,893.8	2,917.7	2,943.6	2,955.7	2,884.5	2,937.7	2,952.3	2,959.6	2,967.1	2,966.6	2,922.6
2001	2,915.8	2,932.1	2,952.9	2,961.6	2,982.8	2,974.9	2,911.0	2,956.6	2,967.0	2,973.3	2,975.8	2,972.2	2,956.3
2002	2,906.7	2,923.8	2,952.0	2,979.1	3,000.6	2,985.4	2,925.5	2,974.2	2,989.5	3,000.4	3,001.7	2,999.5	2,969.9
2003	2,918.9	2,927.2	2,949.8	2,971.3	2,998.9	2,984.3	2,910.1	2,970.0	2,996.8	3,019.6	3,019.1	3,025.9	2,974.3
2004	2,954.9	2,966.4	2,996.5	3,023.6	3,051.6	3,038.9	2,990.6	3,052.4	3,081.8	3,086.9	3,097.8	3,107.2	3,037.4
2005	3,041.0	3,056.3	3,084.2	3,108.5	3,125.3	3,105.6	3,051.7	3,121.7	3,157.1	3,169.9	3,184.8	3,189.2	3,116.3
2006	3,136.5	3,151.8	3,183.0	3,218.2	3,247.7	3,239.7	3,182.2	3,252.6	3,280.2	3,304.4	3,332.9	3,337.4	3,238.9
2007	3,260.0	3,283.0	3,319.6	3,333.8	3,368.6	3,364.4	3,283.1	3,359.6	3,387.7	3,394.1	3,413.8	3,418.7	3,348.9
2008	3,341.2	3,361.9	3,382.9	3,392.9	3,417.8	3,401.0	3,313.0	3,384.3	3,408.2	3,395.6	3,388.5	3,377.3	3,380.4
2009	3,271.0	3,270.7	3,275.6	3,278.8	3,298.9	3,273.8	3,188.2	3,252.0	3,277.6	3,269.2	3,276.9	3,269.4	3,266.8
2010	3,194.9	3,203.8	3,234.7	3,263.9	3,301.9	3,277.2	3,199.0	3,266.2	3,282.3	3,312.2	3,324.6	3,316.5	3,264.8
2011	3,238.2	3,267.8	3,293.0	3,326.4	3,338.8	3,321.3	3,243.0	3,313.1	3,316.9	3,341.3	3,351.9	3,338.9	3,307.6
Trade, Transportation, and Utilities													
2000	735.4	734.6	741.8	746.9	753.2	759.2	751.1	753.8	752.6	755.6	765.1	772.7	751.8
2001	746.2	740.9	745.0	742.6	745.6	748.4	739.8	738.9	737.3	735.4	742.0	746.3	742.4
2002	715.3	710.2	716.6	720.1	723.8	728.4	725.0	727.4	724.9	725.2	738.2	745.0	725.0
2003	710.8	707.9	710.5	712.0	716.0	720.6	714.4	717.4	716.3	721.2	731.9	739.0	718.2
2004	710.2	706.9	712.6	718.7	724.7	728.4	727.7	729.9	728.5	731.5	743.2	751.9	726.2
2005	723.0	722.9	727.7	733.2	736.5	738.6	741.2	741.7	739.5	748.4	761.2	769.2	740.3
2006	739.5	734.4	740.4	749.8	755.0	756.1	761.6	763.4	761.4	767.9	784.5	791.4	758.8
2007	765.6	761.8	770.5	770.4	777.3	779.9	779.0	779.1	776.4	780.0	795.1	802.1	778.1
2008	771.0	768.0	772.6	769.1	771.7	773.3	770.6	768.9	763.0	763.3	767.5	768.9	769.0
2009	729.5	721.0	720.1	715.6	720.4	722.2	718.9	717.7	713.7	715.8	723.8	727.0	720.5
2010	699.9	696.6	703.0	706.5	712.2	714.9	715.8	717.1	712.1	717.7	730.3	735.9	713.5
2011	709.5	709.9	715.0	721.5	725.3	728.2	729.4	727.6	723.1	726.3	738.6	743.6	724.8
Wholesale Trade													
2000	160.7	161.6	162.9	163.9	164.6	165.7	165.2	165.8	165.6	166.1	165.3	166.1	164.5
2001	162.1	162.1	162.8	161.6	162.0	162.8	163.0	162.8	162.8	162.6	161.9	162.0	162.4
2002	160.1	160.1	160.7	162.3	162.7	163.6	163.4	163.4	163.6	164.0	164.2	164.2	162.7
2003	162.0	161.9	162.8	163.2	163.6	164.6	163.8	164.3	163.8	165.1	165.5	166.1	163.9
2004	164.5	164.2	165.3	165.6	166.2	167.0	167.0	167.6	167.7	167.9	168.0	168.8	166.7
2005	166.3	166.9	166.8	168.9	169.9	170.2	171.2	171.6	171.8	173.4	174.3	174.8	170.5
2006	171.7	172.1	172.9	175.5	176.3	176.7	177.7	177.7	177.7	177.7	178.6	179.1	176.1
2007	179.1	180.0	181.3	181.7	182.4	183.7	183.6	183.1	182.8	183.0	183.2	183.6	182.3
2008	181.3	182.1	182.8	180.8	181.4	181.3	180.4	179.8	178.4	178.3	176.7	175.2	179.9
2009	170.6	169.9	168.8	167.4	166.9	166.4	165.4	165.0	164.1	164.6	164.2	164.0	166.4
2010	161.7	162.2	163.4	164.1	164.5	164.4	165.0	165.2	164.4	165.5	166.0	166.1	164.4
2011	164.2	165.3	166.0	167.6	168.0	168.9	167.3	166.0	164.6	164.4	164.9	164.8	166.0
Retail Trade													
2000	442.4	440.1	445.1	448.3	453.5	457.5	450.2	451.9	450.7	451.6	463.0	470.3	452.1
2001	448.9	442.8	446.1	444.5	447.1	449.4	442.5	443.0	442.3	441.5	451.0	455.6	446.2
2002	431.0	426.5	431.8	433.6	436.2	438.6	434.9	436.5	434.7	433.7	446.4	453.4	436.4
2003	424.7	421.2	423.6	425.0	428.2	431.5	427.0	428.7	427.0	430.6	441.5	446.9	429.7
2004	423.3	419.4	423.4	427.4	432.1	434.2	432.6	434.2	432.5	435.4	446.6	453.5	432.9
2005	430.7	429.7	434.0	437.0	438.9	439.9	442.6	442.3	439.5	445.6	456.5	462.9	441.6
2006	440.1	434.5	438.6	445.3	448.9	448.9	452.3	453.4	450.9	457.0	472.3	478.1	451.7
2007	456.3	452.3	458.7	458.7	464.4	465.7	465.8	466.3	464.1	468.2	482.7	488.0	465.9
2008	463.4	459.7	463.6	462.1	463.4	465.0	464.0	462.7	459.0	459.4	465.3	467.0	462.9
2009	438.4	432.4	433.2	431.8	437.1	439.0	437.9	437.4	434.4	436.5	444.7	447.0	437.5
2010	426.7	423.0	427.4	429.3	433.4	435.7	435.4	436.4	432.0	436.1	447.4	452.2	434.6
2011	430.1	428.9	432.3	436.3	439.6	440.9	444.3	442.9	439.8	443.4	454.0	456.7	440.8
Transportation and Utilities													
2000	132.3	132.9	133.8	134.7	135.1	136.0	135.7	136.1	136.3	137.9	136.8	136.3	135.3
2001	135.2	136.0	136.1	136.5	136.5	136.2	134.3	133.1	132.2	131.3	129.1	128.7	133.8
2002	124.2	123.6	124.1	124.2	124.9	126.2	126.7	127.5	126.6	127.5	127.6	127.4	125.9
2003	124.1	124.8	124.1	123.8	124.2	124.5	123.6	124.4	125.5	125.5	124.9	126.0	124.6
2004	122.4	123.3	123.9	125.7	126.4	127.2	128.1	128.1	128.3	128.2	128.6	129.6	126.7
2005	126.0	126.3	126.9	127.3	127.7	128.5	127.4	127.8	128.2	129.4	130.4	131.5	128.1
2006	127.7	127.8	128.9	129.0	129.8	130.5	131.6	132.3	132.8	133.2	133.6	134.2	131.0
2007	130.2	129.5	130.5	130.0	130.5	130.5	129.6	129.7	129.5	128.8	129.2	130.5	129.9
2008	126.3	126.2	126.2	126.2	126.9	127.0	126.2	126.4	125.6	125.6	125.5	126.7	126.2
2009	120.5	118.7	118.1	116.4	116.4	116.8	115.6	115.3	115.2	114.7	114.9	116.0	116.6
2010	111.5	111.4	112.2	113.1	114.3	114.8	115.4	115.5	115.7	116.1	116.9	117.6	114.5
2011	115.2	115.7	116.7	117.6	117.7	118.4	117.8	118.7	118.7	118.5	119.7	122.1	118.1
Information													
2000	72.3	72.7	73.5	75.0	75.4	76.6	77.1	77.6	77.6	78.0	78.6	78.5	76.1
2001	76.9	78.2	78.0	76.5	76.9	76.6	75.6	75.7	74.0	73.8	74.3	73.1	75.8
2002	73.8	73.6	73.8	73.5	73.7	73.6	72.8	72.4	71.7	71.9	71.9	72.1	72.9
2003	70.4	70.3	70.0	68.6	69.0	69.4	68.9	68.9	67.8	67.7	67.8	67.9	68.9
2004	67.2	66.7	67.0	66.4	66.3	67.1	67.1	67.2	66.7	68.1	69.3	69.7	67.4
2005	69.6	69.4	69.6	70.1	70.4	71.0	71.4	72.1	72.5	72.8	73.2	74.5	71.4
2006	74.1	74.0	73.9	72.7	72.9	73.5	72.6	72.7	72.3	72.5	72.5	72.9	73.1
2007	72.2	72.6	72.4	72.5	72.7	73.1	73.0	72.7	72.4	72.7	72.9	72.8	72.7
2008	72.0	72.3	72.2	72.2	72.4	72.6	72.2	72.2	71.5	72.2	72.5	72.4	72.2
2009	71.3	71.1	70.6	70.4	70.3	70.1	69.6	69.1	68.5	68.6	68.8	68.7	69.8
2010	67.7	67.7	67.9	67.8	68.3	68.6	68.7	68.6	68.4	68.3	68.7	68.8	68.3
2011	67.9	67.9	67.9	68.4	68.4	68.9	69.1	69.3	68.3	68.3	68.6	68.5	68.5

1. Employment by Industry: North Carolina, Selected Years, 2000–2011—*Continued*

(Numbers in thousands, not seasonally adjusted)

Industry and year	January	February	March	April	May	June	July	August	September	October	November	December	Annual average
Financial Activities													
2000	185.7	186.5	187.7	187.7	189.1	191.5	191.7	192.0	190.9	191.6	190.9	192.3	189.8
2001	188.4	189.0	189.9	190.2	191.0	193.0	193.1	193.3	191.8	191.2	191.1	191.3	191.1
2002	189.2	189.8	191.0	190.4	191.1	193.4	194.4	194.9	194.0	194.3	193.5	194.0	192.5
2003	191.0	191.6	192.8	193.9	195.2	197.0	194.7	195.9	195.2	195.8	193.8	195.2	194.3
2004	193.3	193.7	194.4	195.6	195.9	198.1	199.8	200.1	199.4	197.5	197.1	197.7	196.9
2005	195.3	196.1	196.8	199.7	200.5	202.8	204.5	204.7	203.8	203.5	202.9	203.7	201.2
2006	200.5	201.9	203.3	207.4	208.6	210.8	214.5	214.9	213.1	213.3	212.7	213.0	209.5
2007	210.5	211.6	213.0	215.0	216.1	218.4	218.0	218.1	216.4	216.2	215.2	215.7	215.4
2008	213.0	214.2	214.8	216.5	216.6	218.5	217.5	217.5	215.0	214.2	212.4	212.5	215.2
2009	208.1	207.5	206.7	206.1	206.8	207.2	207.3	206.3	203.9	202.9	202.7	202.9	205.7
2010	200.5	200.7	201.5	201.1	201.6	203.4	204.6	204.8	203.6	203.5	203.3	203.5	202.7
2011	201.3	201.8	202.1	203.0	204.3	206.1	205.8	205.5	201.2	202.0	201.0	201.4	203.0
Professional and Business Services													
2000	406.2	410.8	417.7	421.7	421.9	426.7	425.0	428.3	427.4	427.8	426.9	422.2	421.9
2001	413.3	418.1	419.6	424.6	426.8	428.9	419.5	422.4	419.0	419.6	415.7	416.1	420.3
2002	405.6	411.9	416.4	421.7	425.6	428.8	422.9	429.6	429.5	427.1	424.4	423.8	422.3
2003	412.6	414.2	419.4	424.6	427.9	428.9	418.3	423.7	423.4	427.6	427.9	427.1	423.0
2004	417.8	421.7	426.5	429.6	432.8	435.8	437.0	441.3	440.0	444.7	442.6	442.7	434.4
2005	435.6	437.4	441.4	446.8	443.5	445.4	450.1	454.4	457.2	460.9	460.0	458.9	449.3
2006	455.4	458.7	463.4	470.3	473.7	479.4	483.4	488.7	489.8	493.9	492.6	492.6	478.6
2007	477.4	484.4	490.1	495.1	498.6	505.6	502.4	507.1	508.7	510.9	508.7	508.7	499.8
2008	497.3	501.1	502.8	505.7	506.8	508.9	504.2	508.4	504.2	502.2	492.4	486.0	501.7
2009	470.5	467.8	463.5	461.3	459.8	460.2	461.5	464.8	466.4	472.6	474.2	473.3	466.3
2010	461.7	464.7	469.7	477.9	477.8	482.6	489.2	493.3	494.4	505.5	503.9	503.1	485.3
2011	490.4	500.2	503.6	510.3	509.2	513.3	515.3	520.9	514.6	521.0	516.2	510.6	510.5
Education and Health Services													
2000	375.1	379.0	381.2	382.0	382.9	384.1	384.3	386.1	388.2	389.5	391.1	391.9	384.6
2001	394.6	398.2	401.1	403.7	405.2	405.9	405.8	409.4	411.0	413.2	415.2	416.6	406.7
2002	414.6	418.5	420.2	425.3	426.0	424.6	421.6	425.1	427.0	430.4	431.6	431.7	424.7
2003	427.4	430.5	432.5	434.0	435.1	434.3	433.9	438.3	440.8	442.4	443.6	445.4	436.5
2004	439.8	442.7	445.9	450.3	451.9	451.3	451.6	455.5	458.7	460.1	462.4	463.9	452.8
2005	460.2	463.7	467.3	468.4	469.9	468.4	469.9	474.8	479.1	479.8	482.6	482.4	472.2
2006	482.4	486.5	489.2	490.8	492.9	493.0	493.4	498.1	501.7	506.0	509.5	511.1	496.2
2007	506.1	512.5	516.2	518.9	521.7	521.4	518.7	524.5	527.7	532.3	535.1	536.2	522.6
2008	528.2	533.3	533.8	533.5	536.0	533.8	530.9	534.6	538.0	538.8	542.6	542.7	535.5
2009	537.1	541.5	541.5	542.1	543.8	541.5	537.8	541.1	542.5	544.9	546.3	545.2	542.1
2010	539.2	541.2	543.0	543.7	544.1	539.5	538.4	540.3	539.0	546.8	548.6	546.1	542.5
2011	538.3	544.6	544.8	548.1	547.5	543.1	540.5	543.8	544.2	551.3	556.9	554.8	546.5
Leisure and Hospitality													
2000	306.2	308.3	316.6	326.0	335.6	344.3	341.7	341.2	334.2	328.4	323.0	320.2	327.1
2001	312.4	315.7	322.9	331.9	340.8	349.0	345.9	346.4	336.3	327.8	322.3	318.1	330.8
2002	311.4	315.1	324.0	338.2	348.3	356.1	356.3	356.4	348.8	340.1	334.8	332.7	338.5
2003	319.0	319.3	326.6	339.0	351.3	357.9	356.5	358.5	350.8	344.9	342.2	340.6	342.2
2004	326.0	328.0	336.7	350.8	362.2	369.1	372.7	373.7	365.4	357.2	353.1	351.8	353.9
2005	337.9	339.8	349.4	358.9	368.7	377.4	377.7	378.4	371.3	365.1	362.0	359.3	362.2
2006	349.3	353.1	362.3	377.0	388.3	396.3	401.2	400.9	394.2	390.7	388.8	386.9	382.4
2007	372.8	376.6	386.8	394.6	408.4	417.2	415.6	417.6	409.3	402.6	400.0	397.5	399.9
2008	384.7	389.2	397.6	403.3	415.3	420.7	422.6	423.0	414.3	402.8	395.0	391.7	405.0
2009	374.3	376.8	382.9	390.4	404.7	409.9	410.1	408.9	401.6	389.7	384.2	379.4	392.7
2010	364.3	365.4	374.8	387.3	399.0	408.7	410.7	411.6	404.8	397.0	391.8	385.5	391.7
2011	369.8	375.0	385.9	399.3	410.4	419.6	420.3	421.2	408.8	400.9	394.3	389.7	399.6
Other Services													
2000	151.7	153.4	154.9	155.5	156.5	158.7	158.6	157.7	157.1	156.7	156.6	156.7	156.2
2001	156.5	157.7	158.8	158.5	160.3	162.8	163.2	162.4	161.4	161.0	161.4	161.3	160.4
2002	158.3	159.2	160.1	162.2	162.9	164.3	161.9	159.3	157.1	158.2	156.9	154.3	159.6
2003	152.8	153.1	153.3	156.2	158.2	160.5	160.8	160.2	160.2	156.0	155.5	156.6	157.0
2004	157.2	158.3	160.3	160.1	163.0	166.0	163.6	162.3	160.4	160.9	161.0	161.4	161.2
2005	160.4	161.6	162.5	162.4	164.6	167.5	164.9	165.0	163.7	165.1	165.5	165.8	164.1
2006	165.1	166.7	168.7	166.0	168.4	171.7	168.6	167.3	165.2	169.1	169.5	169.8	168.0
2007	168.7	170.1	172.0	168.8	171.2	174.3	175.3	174.7	172.7	174.5	174.5	174.7	172.6
2008	172.9	174.0	174.1	175.9	177.7	179.8	180.3	179.2	176.6	174.8	173.9	172.9	176.0
2009	162.7	163.6	163.7	162.5	163.3	164.0	163.5	161.8	158.7	157.0	156.0	154.4	160.9
2010	153.3	153.4	154.5	153.8	154.9	156.7	156.8	156.0	154.5	155.4	155.1	154.3	154.9
2011	152.9	153.8	154.6	155.1	156.0	158.8	157.4	157.0	155.8	156.2	156.2	155.4	155.8
Government													
2000	603.9	611.1	620.4	622.9	629.0	614.6	555.0	601.0	624.3	632.0	634.9	632.1	615.1
2001	627.5	634.3	637.6	633.6	636.2	610.3	568.1	608.1	636.2	651.3	653.8	649.4	628.9
2002	638.5	645.5	649.9	647.7	649.2	616.2	570.6	609.1	636.5	653.2	650.4	645.9	634.4
2003	634.9	640.3	644.7	643.0	646.2	615.7	562.6	607.1	642.3	664.0	656.4	654.1	634.3
2004	643.4	648.4	653.1	652.1	654.8	623.1	571.1	622.4	662.7	666.9	669.1	668.1	644.6
2005	659.0	665.4	669.5	669.0	671.2	634.5	572.0	630.6	670.0	674.3	677.4	675.4	655.7
2006	670.2	676.5	681.8	684.2	687.9	658.5	586.9	646.6	682.5	691.0	701.5	699.7	672.3
2007	686.7	693.4	698.6	698.5	702.6	674.5	601.1	665.8	704.1	704.9	712.3	711.0	687.8
2008	702.1	709.8	715.0	716.7	721.3	693.4	614.7	680.5	725.6	727.3	732.2	730.2	705.7
2009	717.5	721.4	726.6	730.4	729.8	698.7	619.5	682.3	722.3	717.7	720.9	718.5	708.8
2010	708.3	714.1	720.3	725.8	744.0	702.8	614.8	674.5	705.5	718.0	722.9	719.3	705.9
2011	708.1	714.6	719.1	720.7	717.7	683.3	605.2	667.8	700.9	715.3	720.1	714.9	699.0

2. Average Weekly Hours by Selected Industry: North Carolina, 2007–2011

(Not seasonally adjusted)

Industry and year	January	February	March	April	May	June	July	August	September	October	November	December	Annual average
Total Private													
2007	34.4	34.4	34.8	35.0	34.9	35.1	35.2	34.8	35.1	34.6	34.3	34.7	34.8
2008	33.8	33.9	34.6	34.3	34.1	34.7	34.4	34.1	34.1	34.5	34.5	34.1	34.3
2009	33.6	34.0	33.7	33.5	33.8	33.8	33.8	34.0	33.9	34.0	34.0	33.8	33.8
2010	33.4	33.5	33.5	33.9	34.2	34.3	34.1	34.5	34.1	34.4	34.4	34.3	34.0
2011	33.7	34.1	34.1	34.4	34.6	34.3	34.3	34.2	34.2	34.6	34.3	34.4	34.3
Goods-Producing													
2007	39.7	39.5	40.0	40.3	40.3	40.5	40.5	40.6	40.6	40.2	40.1	40.4	40.2
2008	39.6	38.7	40.3	39.4	39.0	39.8	38.8	39.6	38.8	39.3	38.4	38.1	39.2
2009	37.5	37.6	37.5	37.1	38.0	38.4	38.7	38.7	38.6	38.6	38.5	38.5	38.1
2010	38.3	37.9	38.2	39.5	40.0	40.0	39.2	39.9	39.8	40.2	40.1	39.8	39.4
2011	39.2	38.8	39.2	39.8	39.9	40.1	39.8	39.7	39.8	40.0	40.1	40.3	39.7
Construction													
2007	38.2	37.1	38.7	38.6	39.1	38.9	39.5	40.4	40.0	39.8	39.2	40.0	39.1
2008	39.3	37.5	40.4	39.0	38.8	38.9	38.6	39.2	37.9	38.7	37.3	37.3	38.6
2009	36.9	37.6	37.3	37.2	37.8	38.4	38.5	38.0	37.7	37.1	36.1	36.1	37.4
2010	35.8	35.6	36.4	38.9	39.6	39.8	39.2	39.6	39.1	39.0	38.7	38.7	38.4
2011	37.8	38.0	38.2	39.7	39.4	39.4	39.6	39.1	39.0	38.8	38.9	39.1	38.9
Manufacturing													
2007	40.3	40.6	40.6	41.0	40.8	41.1	40.8	40.6	40.8	40.3	40.5	40.5	40.7
2008	39.8	39.4	40.2	39.7	39.1	40.3	38.8	39.8	39.2	39.6	39.0	38.6	39.5
2009	37.9	37.8	37.7	37.2	38.2	38.5	38.6	38.9	39.1	39.3	39.7	40.0	38.6
2010	39.8	39.3	39.4	40.2	40.6	40.5	39.6	40.4	40.4	41.0	40.9	41.0	40.3
2011	40.5	40.3	40.6	40.7	40.9	41.1	40.6	40.5	40.6	40.9	40.9	41.0	40.7
Trade, Transportation, and Utilities													
2007	34.0	34.0	34.2	34.5	34.4	34.7	34.7	34.1	34.8	34.0	34.3	34.4	34.3
2008	33.7	34.8	35.6	34.9	35.1	35.4	35.7	34.2	35.0	35.5	35.3	35.9	35.1
2009	34.6	34.5	34.3	33.9	34.4	34.7	34.8	35.1	35.0	35.3	34.7	34.8	34.7
2010	34.9	35.0	35.1	35.3	35.4	36.1	35.8	35.9	35.6	35.7	35.6	35.7	35.5
2011	34.8	35.3	35.1	35.1	35.1	34.8	34.7	34.6	34.8	34.8	34.2	34.5	34.8
Information													
2007	36.1	35.5	35.8	36.2	35.3	35.4	35.9	35.2	35.3	35.1	35.3	35.6	35.6
2008	35.9	35.7	36.9	36.1	37.0	37.4	37.3	37.6	37.9	36.4	36.5	35.9	36.7
2009	35.6	34.8	35.3	35.0	34.7	34.7	35.0	35.1	35.0	35.2	35.8	35.8	35.2
2010	35.3	35.5	36.1	36.3	35.6	36.3	36.3	36.5	35.4	35.6	36.2	36.3	35.9
2011	36.0	36.0	36.4	35.9	36.7	36.5	36.8	36.5	36.9	37.9	37.0	36.7	36.6
Financial Activities													
2007	35.8	35.9	35.8	37.1	35.4	35.8	36.7	36.4	37.7	38.3	35.3	37.0	36.4
2008	34.8	35.8	36.3	36.1	35.4	37.4	35.9	35.7	35.6	36.7	39.3	38.2	36.4
2009	38.0	38.4	37.9	37.2	36.8	36.7	36.0	36.1	35.8	35.8	36.5	35.6	36.7
2010	36.3	36.8	36.1	36.7	38.0	37.2	37.1	38.2	37.5	37.9	37.8	36.8	37.2
2011	37.4	37.9	37.3	37.4	37.9	37.2	37.4	36.8	37.1	39.0	37.7	37.7	37.6
Professional and Business Services													
2007	34.3	34.7	35.2	35.1	34.7	35.5	36.0	35.4	36.0	35.2	35.1	35.9	35.3
2008	34.1	34.6	35.3	35.5	35.3	36.2	34.4	35.5	35.3	35.5	36.0	34.8	35.2
2009	34.8	35.8	35.5	35.6	35.4	35.0	34.7	35.0	34.9	35.3	35.7	35.1	35.2
2010	32.0	32.5	32.8	33.2	33.7	33.8	33.3	34.3	34.0	34.1	34.2	34.4	33.5
2011	33.5	34.1	34.1	35.3	36.1	35.6	35.3	35.5	35.4	36.1	35.7	35.9	35.2
Education and Health Services													
2007	33.1	33.1	33.5	33.7	34.0	33.1	33.0	33.3	33.2	32.6	32.4	33.0	33.2
2008	31.9	31.7	31.6	31.6	32.2	32.4	32.8	32.7	32.4	32.3	32.8	32.0	32.2
2009	31.8	32.2	31.9	31.9	32.3	31.9	31.9	32.0	31.9	32.1	32.1	31.6	32.0
2010	31.9	31.8	31.7	31.8	32.3	31.9	32.1	32.3	32.1	32.3	32.3	32.1	32.0
2011	32.0	32.3	32.2	32.3	32.7	32.2	32.2	32.1	32.1	32.4	32.2	32.3	32.3
Leisure and Hospitality													
2007	25.4	25.7	25.9	26.2	26.6	27.0	26.9	26.6	25.7	25.5	25.1	25.2	26.0
2008	24.4	26.0	25.7	25.6	25.6	26.0	26.4	25.8	25.8	25.7	25.4	25.4	25.7
2009	24.5	26.2	25.7	26.3	26.3	26.6	26.6	26.7	26.4	26.3	26.1	26.0	26.2
2010	25.6	26.3	26.3	26.4	26.2	26.2	26.6	26.6	25.6	25.9	25.8	25.7	26.1
2011	25.1	26.0	25.9	26.1	25.9	25.7	26.0	25.9	25.2	25.8	25.4	25.1	25.7
Other Services													
2007	33.1	33.1	33.7	33.2	34.0	34.5	34.2	32.4	32.0	31.3	31.4	31.1	32.8
2008	31.0	28.1	30.2	30.4	28.2	29.2	30.6	27.7	28.9	30.0	29.3	28.7	29.4
2009	29.1	29.6	29.1	29.3	29.0	28.9	29.3	29.5	29.5	29.5	29.6	29.5	29.3
2010	29.7	30.3	29.0	29.1	29.2	29.9	30.5	30.2	29.6	29.8	29.8	29.7	29.7
2011	29.6	30.7	30.5	30.6	30.9	30.6	31.3	31.3	31.3	31.1	32.0	31.8	31.0

3. Average Hourly Earnings by Selected Industry: North Carolina, 2007–2011

(Dollars, not seasonally adjusted)

Industry and year	January	February	March	April	May	June	July	August	September	October	November	December	Annual average
Total Private													
2007	19.26	19.43	19.50	19.40	19.08	19.01	19.09	18.81	19.45	19.22	19.30	19.50	19.25
2008	19.50	19.47	19.44	20.05	19.62	19.83	19.65	19.84	19.69	20.34	20.88	20.67	19.91
2009	20.85	20.70	20.70	20.60	20.37	20.45	20.40	20.46	20.52	20.55	20.82	20.67	20.59
2010	20.99	21.04	20.96	20.79	20.61	20.31	20.45	20.48	20.40	20.44	20.41	20.54	20.61
2011	20.84	20.74	20.56	20.66	20.77	20.59	20.77	20.77	21.07	21.36	21.25	21.32	20.89
Goods-Producing													
2007	18.35	18.47	18.92	18.34	18.50	18.43	18.49	18.45	18.63	18.49	18.43	18.70	18.52
2008	18.48	18.64	18.48	18.82	18.67	19.17	18.44	18.71	18.59	18.97	19.45	19.74	18.84
2009	19.76	19.83	19.95	20.09	19.90	19.89	19.83	19.90	19.89	19.77	19.93	19.90	19.89
2010	20.41	20.58	20.35	20.22	19.98	19.61	20.21	20.01	19.69	19.53	19.72	19.96	20.01
2011	20.16	20.33	20.04	20.13	20.28	20.14	20.22	20.09	20.32	20.46	20.52	20.65	20.28
Construction													
2007	18.09	18.98	18.55	18.27	18.27	18.30	18.50	18.35	18.59	18.40	18.39	18.96	18.47
2008	17.97	19.36	19.41	19.39	19.48	21.04	18.85	18.82	19.30	19.42	19.80	20.48	19.43
2009	20.42	20.34	20.48	20.64	20.51	20.25	19.99	20.12	20.22	20.23	20.56	20.66	20.36
2010	20.64	20.82	20.51	20.15	19.64	19.70	19.91	19.75	19.69	19.96	19.88	19.91	20.03
2011	20.17	20.36	20.36	20.31	20.43	20.11	20.14	20.03	20.05	20.55	20.77	20.66	20.33
Manufacturing													
2007	18.54	18.33	19.15	18.43	18.65	18.54	18.53	18.54	18.68	18.55	18.48	18.62	18.59
2008	18.74	18.35	18.08	18.61	18.36	18.33	18.32	18.72	18.30	18.79	19.33	19.43	18.61
2009	19.50	19.62	19.75	19.75	19.55	19.54	19.56	19.62	19.60	19.42	19.53	19.49	19.58
2010	20.23	20.39	20.20	20.16	20.05	19.64	20.41	20.19	19.77	19.43	19.72	19.70	19.99
2011	20.40	20.23	19.83	19.98	20.15	20.08	20.17	20.05	20.38	20.40	20.40	20.62	20.22
Trade, Transportation, and Utilities													
2007	17.60	17.50	17.29	16.99	16.85	17.05	17.17	16.87	17.78	17.59	17.65	17.45	17.32
2008	17.78	17.56	17.55	18.87	17.95	18.05	19.47	18.38	18.33	19.91	19.98	19.61	18.63
2009	20.16	19.90	20.04	19.39	19.03	19.44	19.17	19.32	19.42	19.42	19.49	19.13	19.49
2010	19.60	19.55	19.73	19.29	18.79	18.83	18.89	18.85	18.79	18.98	18.87	19.01	19.09
2011	19.51	19.46	19.14	19.60	19.47	19.46	19.54	19.42	19.67	20.00	19.87	19.71	19.57
Information													
2007	29.47	29.36	29.46	30.30	29.24	29.49	29.59	28.41	30.30	28.75	29.90	30.57	29.57
2008	29.53	29.25	30.17	29.69	30.17	29.76	30.29	30.87	29.32	27.73	29.38	27.74	29.50
2009	28.16	28.00	28.16	27.36	27.78	27.54	27.55	27.66	27.48	28.35	29.07	28.12	27.94
2010	28.37	29.26	28.06	28.07	28.68	27.80	27.68	27.53	28.32	29.10	28.70	28.27	28.31
2011	28.55	29.08	28.19	28.86	28.96	28.53	29.79	29.29	29.82	30.39	30.66	30.29	29.38
Financial Activities													
2007	27.85	29.54	31.51	30.48	28.64	27.81	28.01	27.11	28.01	26.53	25.98	26.27	28.13
2008	25.69	27.72	28.06	27.64	28.01	27.90	26.27	27.27	27.23	26.51	27.20	25.81	27.11
2009	25.50	25.07	25.00	24.97	25.29	25.42	25.93	25.99	25.88	25.66	26.36	25.51	25.54
2010	25.34	25.78	25.81	25.52	25.54	25.75	25.99	25.86	25.72	26.16	26.15	26.28	25.83
2011	26.19	26.34	26.01	25.90	25.75	25.19	25.69	26.50	26.84	26.79	26.83	26.91	26.24
Professional and Business Services													
2007	24.50	24.63	23.98	24.99	23.93	23.92	24.40	24.03	24.59	24.08	24.62	24.86	24.38
2008	25.23	23.96	23.99	24.22	23.79	24.05	23.59	23.77	24.02	25.47	26.83	26.63	24.62
2009	26.65	26.41	26.57	26.91	26.59	26.85	26.88	26.89	26.90	26.80	27.38	27.43	26.86
2010	29.04	28.82	28.68	28.20	27.80	26.73	26.84	26.96	26.95	26.80	26.38	26.53	27.43
2011	27.69	26.88	26.48	26.11	26.56	26.06	26.52	26.27	26.45	26.73	26.33	26.45	26.53
Education and Health Services													
2007	18.30	18.42	18.43	18.36	18.40	18.72	18.09	17.61	18.28	18.47	18.81	18.99	18.41
2008	19.25	19.92	19.79	21.01	20.56	20.62	20.48	21.31	20.24	20.59	20.57	20.69	20.42
2009	20.73	20.74	20.69	20.50	20.32	20.42	20.39	20.29	20.37	20.39	20.47	20.56	20.49
2010	20.31	20.27	20.14	20.31	20.41	20.35	20.37	20.34	20.03	20.04	20.13	20.21	20.24
2011	20.01	19.94	20.40	20.44	20.35	20.52	20.56	20.67	21.08	21.49	21.42	21.47	20.70
Leisure and Hospitality													
2007	11.35	11.39	11.39	11.43	12.06	11.16	11.18	11.16	11.46	11.62	11.53	11.80	11.46
2008	11.58	11.44	11.48	11.84	11.20	11.18	10.66	11.50	11.77	11.72	12.01	11.95	11.52
2009	11.90	11.98	11.30	11.84	11.71	11.57	11.58	11.66	11.77	11.87	11.89	11.84	11.74
2010	11.64	11.64	11.52	11.67	11.82	11.63	11.47	11.67	11.88	11.65	11.66	11.58	11.65
2011	11.24	11.39	11.54	11.64	11.85	11.90	11.96	12.19	12.43	12.61	12.56	12.93	12.02
Other Services													
2007	16.68	16.93	16.38	16.70	16.30	15.92	16.03	16.23	16.63	16.49	16.76	17.18	16.51
2008	16.90	15.97	15.81	15.88	15.69	15.79	15.56	15.74	16.31	16.06	16.57	16.72	16.08
2009	16.50	16.43	16.30	16.33	16.38	15.94	15.92	15.99	16.01	16.05	16.16	16.37	16.20
2010	16.19	16.33	16.43	16.74	17.07	16.78	16.48	16.82	16.71	16.73	16.70	16.74	16.64
2011	16.64	16.30	16.15	16.39	16.95	16.47	16.45	16.53	16.90	16.83	16.58	16.84	16.59

4. Average Weekly Earnings by Selected Industry: North Carolina, 2007–2011

(Dollars, not seasonally adjusted)

Industry and year	January	February	March	April	May	June	July	August	September	October	November	December	Annual average
Total Private													
2007	662.54	668.39	678.60	679.00	665.89	667.25	671.97	654.59	682.70	665.01	661.99	676.65	669.49
2008	659.10	660.03	672.62	687.72	669.04	688.10	675.96	676.54	671.43	701.73	720.36	704.85	682.39
2009	700.56	703.80	697.59	690.10	688.51	691.21	689.52	695.64	695.63	698.70	707.88	698.65	696.52
2010	701.07	704.84	702.16	704.78	704.86	696.63	697.35	706.56	695.64	703.14	702.10	704.52	701.81
2011	702.31	707.23	701.10	710.70	718.64	706.24	712.41	710.33	720.59	739.06	728.88	733.41	716.12
Goods-Producing													
2007	728.50	729.57	756.80	739.10	745.55	746.42	748.85	749.07	756.38	743.30	739.04	755.48	744.85
2008	731.81	721.37	744.74	741.51	728.13	762.97	715.47	740.92	721.29	745.52	746.88	752.09	737.61
2009	741.00	745.61	748.13	745.34	756.20	763.78	767.42	770.13	767.75	763.12	767.31	766.15	758.23
2010	781.70	779.98	777.37	798.69	799.20	784.40	792.23	798.40	783.66	785.11	790.77	794.41	788.89
2011	790.27	788.80	785.57	801.17	809.17	807.61	804.76	797.57	808.74	818.40	822.85	832.20	805.69
Construction													
2007	691.04	704.16	717.89	705.22	714.36	711.87	730.75	741.34	743.60	732.32	720.89	758.40	722.82
2008	706.22	726.00	784.16	756.21	755.82	818.46	727.61	737.74	731.47	751.55	738.54	763.90	749.80
2009	753.50	764.78	763.90	767.81	775.28	777.60	769.62	764.56	762.29	750.53	742.22	745.83	761.63
2010	738.91	741.19	746.56	783.84	777.74	784.06	780.47	782.10	769.88	778.44	769.36	770.52	768.85
2011	762.43	773.68	777.75	806.31	804.94	792.33	797.54	783.17	781.95	797.34	807.95	807.81	791.41
Manufacturing													
2007	747.16	744.20	777.49	755.63	760.92	761.99	756.02	752.72	762.14	747.57	748.44	754.11	755.70
2008	745.85	722.99	726.82	738.82	717.88	738.70	710.82	745.06	717.36	744.08	753.87	750.00	734.23
2009	739.05	741.64	744.58	734.70	746.81	752.29	755.02	763.22	766.36	763.21	775.34	779.60	754.82
2010	805.15	801.33	795.88	810.43	814.03	795.42	808.24	815.68	798.71	796.63	806.55	807.70	804.66
2011	826.20	815.27	805.10	813.19	824.14	825.29	818.90	812.03	827.43	834.36	834.36	845.42	823.47
Trade, Transportation, and Utilities													
2007	598.40	595.00	591.32	586.16	579.64	591.64	595.80	575.27	618.74	598.06	605.40	600.28	594.67
2008	599.19	611.09	624.78	658.56	630.05	638.97	695.08	628.60	641.55	706.81	705.29	704.00	653.60
2009	697.54	686.55	687.37	657.32	654.63	674.57	667.12	678.13	679.70	685.53	676.30	665.72	675.88
2010	684.04	684.25	692.52	680.94	665.17	679.76	676.26	676.72	668.92	677.59	671.77	678.66	678.03
2011	678.95	686.94	671.81	687.96	683.40	677.21	678.04	671.93	684.52	696.00	679.55	680.00	681.34
Information													
2007	1,063.87	1,042.28	1,054.67	1,096.86	1,032.17	1,043.95	1,062.28	1,000.03	1,069.59	1,009.13	1,055.47	1,088.29	1,051.53
2008	1,060.13	1,044.23	1,113.27	1,071.81	1,116.29	1,113.02	1,129.82	1,160.71	1,111.23	1,009.37	1,072.37	995.87	1,083.15
2009	1,002.50	974.40	994.05	957.60	963.97	955.64	964.25	970.87	961.80	997.92	1,040.71	1,006.70	982.41
2010	1,001.46	1,038.73	1,012.97	1,018.94	1,021.01	1,009.14	1,004.78	1,004.85	1,002.53	1,035.96	1,038.94	1,026.20	1,017.84
2011	1,027.80	1,046.88	1,026.12	1,036.07	1,062.83	1,041.35	1,096.27	1,069.09	1,100.36	1,151.78	1,134.42	1,111.64	1,075.53
Financial Activities													
2007	997.03	1,060.49	1,128.06	1,130.81	1,013.86	995.60	1,027.97	986.80	1,055.98	1,016.10	917.09	971.99	1,025.10
2008	894.01	992.38	1,018.58	997.80	991.55	1,043.46	943.09	973.54	969.39	972.92	1,068.96	985.94	987.78
2009	969.00	962.69	947.50	928.88	930.67	932.91	933.48	938.24	926.50	918.63	962.14	908.16	938.34
2010	919.84	948.70	931.74	936.58	970.52	957.90	964.23	987.85	964.50	991.46	988.47	967.10	960.80
2011	979.51	998.29	970.17	968.66	975.93	937.07	960.81	975.20	995.76	1,044.81	1,011.49	1,014.51	985.83
Professional and Business Services													
2007	840.35	854.66	844.10	877.15	830.37	849.16	878.40	850.66	885.24	847.62	864.16	892.47	859.69
2008	860.34	829.02	846.85	859.81	839.79	870.61	811.50	843.84	847.91	904.19	965.88	926.72	866.82
2009	927.42	945.48	943.24	958.00	941.29	939.75	932.74	941.15	938.81	946.04	977.47	962.79	946.28
2010	929.28	936.65	940.70	936.24	936.86	903.47	893.77	924.73	916.30	913.88	902.20	912.63	920.24
2011	927.62	916.61	902.97	921.68	958.82	927.74	936.16	932.59	936.33	964.95	939.98	949.56	934.76
Education and Health Services													
2007	605.73	609.70	617.41	618.73	625.60	619.63	596.97	586.41	606.90	602.12	609.44	626.67	610.46
2008	614.08	631.46	625.36	663.92	662.03	668.09	671.74	696.84	655.78	665.06	674.70	662.08	657.67
2009	659.21	667.83	660.01	653.95	656.34	651.40	650.44	649.28	649.80	654.52	657.09	649.70	654.95
2010	647.89	644.59	638.44	645.86	659.24	649.17	653.88	656.98	642.96	647.29	650.20	648.74	648.74
2011	640.32	644.06	656.88	660.21	665.45	660.74	662.03	663.51	676.67	696.28	689.72	693.48	667.58
Leisure and Hospitality													
2007	288.29	292.72	295.00	299.47	320.80	301.32	300.74	296.86	294.52	296.31	289.40	297.36	297.87
2008	282.55	297.44	295.04	303.10	286.72	290.68	281.42	296.70	303.67	301.20	305.05	303.53	295.53
2009	291.55	313.88	290.41	311.39	307.97	307.76	308.03	311.32	310.73	312.18	310.33	307.84	307.02
2010	297.98	306.13	302.98	308.09	309.68	304.71	305.10	310.42	304.13	301.74	300.83	297.61	304.19
2011	282.12	296.14	298.89	303.80	306.92	305.83	310.96	315.72	313.24	325.34	319.02	324.54	308.79
Other Services													
2007	552.11	560.38	552.01	554.44	554.20	549.24	548.23	525.85	532.16	516.14	526.26	534.30	541.99
2008	523.90	448.76	477.46	482.75	442.46	461.07	476.14	436.00	471.36	481.80	485.50	479.86	472.07
2009	480.15	486.33	474.33	478.47	475.02	460.67	466.46	471.71	472.30	473.48	478.34	482.92	475.02
2010	480.84	494.80	476.47	487.13	498.44	501.72	502.64	507.96	494.62	498.55	497.66	497.18	494.82
2011	492.54	500.41	492.58	501.53	523.76	503.98	514.89	517.39	528.97	523.41	530.56	535.51	513.86

NORTH DAKOTA
At a Glance

Population:
  2000 census: 642,237
  2010 census: 672,591
  2011 estimate: 683,932

Percent change in population:
  2000–2010: 4.7%
  2010–2011: 1.7%

Percent change in total nonfarm employment:
  2000–2010: 14.8%
  2010–2011: 4.8%

Industry with the largest growth in employment, 2000–2011 (thousands):
  Trade, Transportation, and Utilities, 13.6

Industry with the largest decline or smallest growth in employment, 2000–2011 (thousands):
  Information, -1.3

Civilian labor force:
  2000: 345,881
  2010: 375,728
  2011: 382,944

Unemployment rate and rank among states (lowest to highest):
  2000: 2.9%, 10th
  2010: 3.8%, 1st
  2011: 3.5%, 1st

Over-the-year change in unemployment rates:
  2010–2011: -0.3%

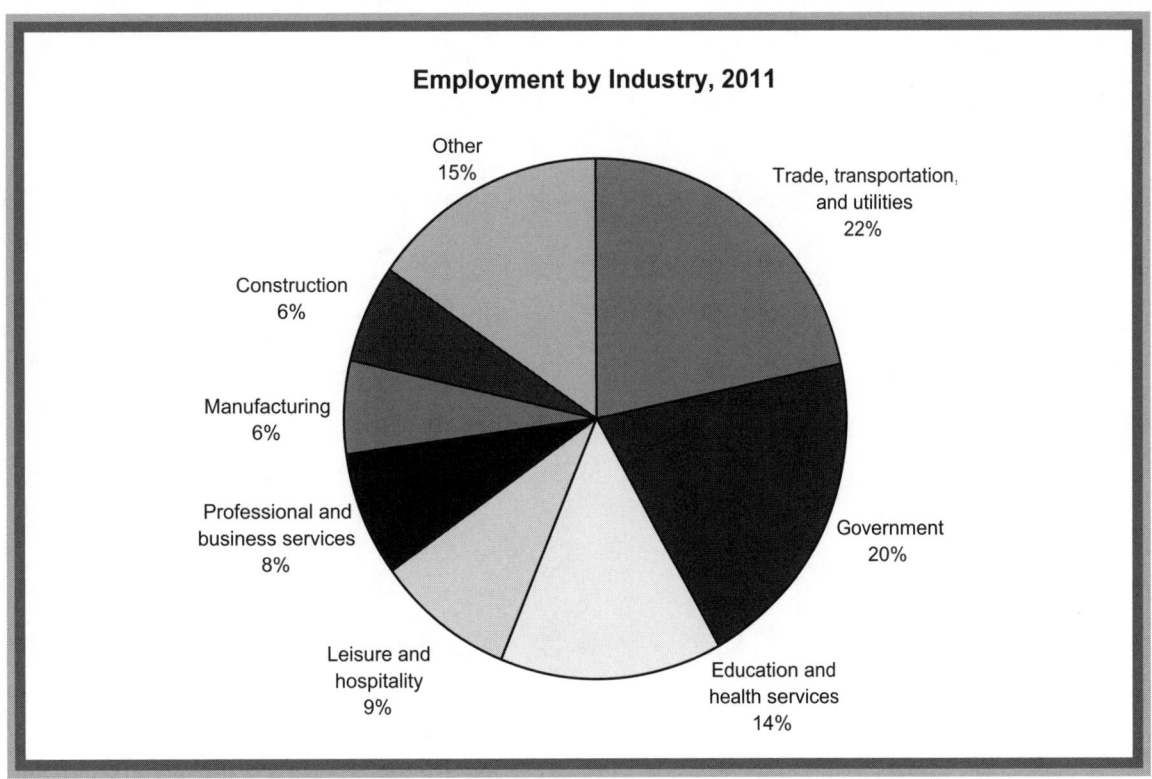

Employment by Industry, 2011

Other 15%
Trade, transportation, and utilities 22%
Construction 6%
Manufacturing 6%
Professional and business services 8%
Leisure and hospitality 9%
Education and health services 14%
Government 20%

1. Employment by Industry: North Dakota, Selected Years, 2000–2011

(Numbers in thousands, not seasonally adjusted)

Industry and year	January	February	March	April	May	June	July	August	September	October	November	December	Annual average
Total Nonfarm													
2000	319.2	320.4	323.2	327.1	332.8	329.0	327.6	327.2	331.5	332.9	330.9	330.9	327.7
2001	322.5	324.2	326.3	330.1	335.3	333.6	324.9	325.5	333.9	335.0	333.2	332.1	329.7
2002	322.6	323.9	323.9	328.6	333.8	333.4	325.1	327.0	334.2	335.5	334.5	334.5	329.8
2003	323.9	325.3	327.2	331.7	336.9	335.4	326.7	330.9	338.7	340.1	337.7	337.2	332.6
2004	326.5	328.2	330.6	337.1	342.0	341.2	334.9	336.2	343.7	346.1	344.8	343.9	337.9
2005	333.4	336.1	338.3	345.7	349.7	348.3	339.5	342.3	351.4	350.7	350.5	350.8	344.7
2006	341.1	343.7	347.0	352.2	357.0	356.2	345.6	349.1	358.6	358.8	358.3	359.0	352.2
2007	348.5	349.6	352.6	356.2	362.7	362.7	352.9	354.2	364.2	365.8	365.8	365.6	358.4
2008	356.9	359.0	361.6	365.9	371.8	371.2	363.0	364.0	373.7	374.9	373.6	372.1	367.3
2009	358.6	359.9	360.6	362.9	370.7	372.0	361.9	362.5	372.7	374.2	372.7	372.1	366.7
2010	360.1	362.7	366.0	374.2	379.0	379.8	371.2	373.2	383.2	388.5	387.6	387.6	376.1
2011	377.7	379.5	382.9	388.9	395.8	397.9	389.6	392.3	402.1	406.5	407.3	410.4	394.2
Total Private													
2000	246.4	246.0	248.3	252.5	257.4	260.1	261.1	260.8	258.5	258.5	256.7	256.1	255.2
2001	248.5	249.1	251.1	254.9	260.4	263.0	261.8	261.5	259.7	259.4	257.8	256.3	257.0
2002	247.5	247.8	247.9	252.3	257.3	261.3	260.7	261.0	258.6	258.3	257.2	256.2	255.5
2003	248.5	247.8	249.3	253.4	258.4	262.5	262.0	263.9	261.8	261.8	259.8	259.0	257.4
2004	251.0	251.6	253.8	259.9	265.0	268.9	270.6	270.2	267.5	268.3	267.2	266.0	263.3
2005	257.8	258.4	260.4	267.3	271.6	275.2	275.5	276.2	274.7	273.1	272.8	272.8	269.7
2006	264.9	266.0	268.8	273.7	278.6	282.5	281.4	282.8	281.7	280.3	279.8	280.1	276.7
2007	272.0	271.8	274.6	277.8	284.2	288.0	287.7	287.9	287.2	287.5	287.1	286.8	282.7
2008	279.9	280.6	283.4	287.4	292.5	296.4	296.9	297.0	296.0	295.6	294.3	292.5	291.0
2009	281.1	281.2	281.5	283.2	290.0	294.0	293.6	293.4	293.3	292.9	291.4	290.3	288.8
2010	280.7	281.7	284.1	292.1	296.1	299.8	301.0	302.6	302.7	306.3	305.4	305.2	296.5
2011	297.5	298.1	301.4	307.4	313.9	318.4	320.2	322.6	322.4	325.0	325.7	328.6	315.1
Goods-Producing													
2000	38.9	38.7	39.3	41.3	44.3	46.3	46.8	46.5	45.5	44.8	42.2	40.7	42.9
2001	38.9	38.5	39.6	41.0	43.7	45.4	46.3	46.1	46.2	45.2	43.1	41.1	42.9
2002	38.4	38.2	38.4	40.2	42.7	44.4	45.0	45.3	44.2	43.7	42.4	40.9	42.0
2003	38.5	38.0	38.4	40.2	43.2	45.4	45.9	46.7	46.2	45.7	43.6	42.1	42.8
2004	39.5	39.5	40.5	43.6	46.1	48.6	49.5	49.4	48.6	48.1	46.6	44.6	45.4
2005	42.0	42.3	43.2	45.8	48.2	50.1	51.1	51.2	50.4	49.6	48.8	47.3	47.5
2006	44.4	44.4	45.1	48.0	50.1	52.0	52.4	52.7	52.0	50.9	50.1	49.0	49.3
2007	45.9	45.3	46.4	48.2	50.9	52.9	53.7	53.6	53.2	53.1	52.1	50.4	50.5
2008	48.1	48.3	49.6	51.4	54.3	57.0	58.0	58.0	57.7	57.1	55.3	53.0	54.0
2009	47.6	47.7	47.7	48.5	51.2	53.7	54.6	54.9	54.7	54.1	52.4	50.2	51.4
2010	46.6	47.1	48.1	52.0	54.7	56.3	58.0	59.0	59.4	60.2	59.2	58.0	54.9
2011	54.9	55.0	56.5	59.8	63.2	65.8	67.3	68.6	69.4	69.6	68.6	67.7	63.9
Mining and Logging													
2000	3.0	3.0	3.0	3.1	3.4	3.4	3.6	3.7	3.7	3.5	3.3	3.2	3.3
2001	3.1	3.1	3.3	3.3	3.5	3.7	3.8	3.7	3.7	3.7	3.5	3.3	3.5
2002	2.9	2.8	2.9	3.1	3.3	3.4	3.4	3.4	3.3	3.4	3.3	3.1	3.2
2003	2.9	2.9	3.0	3.2	3.5	3.6	3.6	3.6	3.5	3.6	3.4	3.3	3.3
2004	3.2	3.2	3.3	3.4	3.5	3.6	3.7	3.8	3.8	3.7	3.7	3.6	3.5
2005	3.6	3.7	3.7	3.9	4.1	4.2	4.3	4.5	4.4	4.3	4.4	4.4	4.1
2006	4.1	4.3	4.3	4.6	4.8	4.7	4.7	4.9	5.0	5.1	5.1	5.0	4.7
2007	4.8	4.7	4.8	4.9	5.1	5.2	5.3	5.3	5.3	5.3	5.3	5.5	5.1
2008	5.4	5.6	5.9	6.2	6.5	6.8	6.9	7.3	7.5	7.8	8.0	7.9	6.8
2009	7.4	7.2	7.1	6.7	6.8	6.9	6.7	6.7	6.8	6.9	7.1	7.4	7.0
2010	7.6	8.3	8.8	9.4	10.0	10.6	11.2	11.7	12.1	12.5	12.7	13.2	10.7
2011	13.5	14.0	14.5	15.1	15.7	16.2	16.6	17.1	17.4	17.9	18.5	18.8	16.3
Construction													
2000	13.2	12.9	13.3	14.9	17.1	18.5	18.9	18.6	17.3	16.9	14.8	13.5	15.8
2001	12.1	11.8	12.5	13.8	16.0	17.3	18.1	18.4	17.8	17.4	15.8	14.1	15.4
2002	12.4	12.2	12.2	13.6	15.7	16.9	17.6	17.8	17.1	16.4	15.3	14.2	15.1
2003	12.4	12.2	12.4	13.9	16.3	17.9	18.4	19.1	18.9	18.2	16.6	15.1	16.0
2004	13.1	13.0	13.7	16.3	18.2	19.8	20.4	20.1	19.5	19.0	17.6	15.9	17.2
2005	13.6	13.6	14.1	16.3	18.2	19.5	20.4	20.3	19.7	19.0	18.1	16.6	17.5
2006	14.8	14.7	15.2	17.6	19.4	20.9	21.0	21.2	20.6	20.2	18.8	17.6	18.5
2007	15.6	15.3	16.1	17.7	19.9	21.2	21.8	22.0	21.6	21.4	20.4	18.6	19.3
2008	16.7	16.6	17.5	18.9	21.4	23.3	24.3	24.2	23.7	22.7	21.0	19.3	20.8
2009	16.7	16.3	16.5	17.9	20.8	23.2	24.4	24.8	24.6	23.9	22.2	20.0	20.9
2010	17.2	16.9	17.4	20.4	22.4	23.1	24.1	24.6	24.2	24.4	23.2	21.5	21.6
2011	18.5	18.1	18.9	21.1	23.8	25.7	27.0	27.9	28.4	27.7	26.0	24.4	24.0
Manufacturing													
2000	22.7	22.8	23.0	23.3	23.8	24.4	24.3	24.2	24.5	24.4	24.1	24.0	23.8
2001	23.7	23.6	23.8	23.9	24.2	24.4	24.4	24.0	24.7	24.1	23.8	23.7	24.0
2002	23.1	23.2	23.3	23.5	23.7	24.1	24.0	24.1	23.8	23.9	23.8	23.6	23.7
2003	23.2	22.9	23.0	23.1	23.4	23.9	23.9	24.0	23.8	23.9	23.6	23.7	23.5
2004	23.2	23.3	23.5	23.9	24.4	25.2	25.4	25.5	25.3	25.4	25.3	25.1	24.6
2005	24.8	25.0	25.4	25.6	25.9	26.4	26.4	26.4	26.3	26.3	26.3	26.3	25.9
2006	25.5	25.4	25.6	25.8	25.9	26.4	26.7	26.6	26.4	25.6	26.2	26.4	26.0
2007	25.5	25.3	25.5	25.6	25.9	26.5	26.6	26.3	26.3	26.4	26.4	26.3	26.1
2008	26.0	26.1	26.2	26.3	26.4	26.9	26.8	26.5	26.5	26.6	26.3	25.8	26.4
2009	23.5	24.2	24.1	23.9	23.6	23.6	23.5	23.4	23.3	23.3	23.1	22.8	23.5
2010	21.8	21.9	21.9	22.2	22.3	22.6	22.7	22.7	23.1	23.3	23.3	23.3	22.6
2011	22.9	22.9	23.1	23.6	23.7	23.9	23.7	23.6	23.6	24.0	24.1	24.5	23.6

1. Employment by Industry: North Dakota, Selected Years, 2000–2011—*Continued*

(Numbers in thousands, not seasonally adjusted)

Industry and year	January	February	March	April	May	June	July	August	September	October	November	December	Annual average
Service-Providing													
2000	280.3	281.7	283.9	285.8	288.5	282.7	280.8	280.7	286.0	288.1	288.7	290.2	284.8
2001	283.6	285.7	286.7	289.1	291.6	288.2	278.6	279.4	287.7	289.8	290.1	291.0	286.8
2002	284.2	285.7	285.5	288.4	291.1	289.0	280.1	281.7	290.0	291.8	292.1	293.6	287.8
2003	285.4	287.3	288.8	291.5	293.7	290.0	280.8	284.2	292.5	294.4	294.1	295.1	289.8
2004	287.0	288.7	290.1	293.5	295.9	292.6	285.4	286.8	295.1	298.0	298.2	299.3	292.6
2005	291.4	293.8	295.1	299.9	301.5	298.2	288.4	291.1	301.0	301.1	301.7	303.5	297.2
2006	296.7	299.3	301.9	304.2	306.9	304.2	293.2	296.4	306.6	307.9	308.2	310.0	303.0
2007	302.6	304.3	306.2	308.0	311.8	309.8	299.2	300.6	311.0	312.7	313.7	315.2	307.9
2008	308.8	310.7	312.0	314.5	317.5	314.2	305.0	306.0	316.0	317.8	318.3	319.1	313.3
2009	311.0	312.2	312.9	314.4	319.5	318.3	307.3	307.6	318.0	320.1	320.3	321.9	315.3
2010	313.5	315.6	317.9	322.2	324.3	323.5	313.2	314.2	323.8	328.3	328.4	329.6	321.2
2011	322.8	324.5	326.4	329.1	332.6	332.1	322.3	323.7	332.7	336.9	338.7	342.7	330.4
Trade, Transportation, and Utilities													
2000	71.5	70.7	70.8	71.9	72.6	72.2	71.9	72.1	71.8	72.7	73.6	74.3	72.2
2001	71.3	70.7	71.0	71.9	73.1	72.7	72.0	71.9	71.3	71.7	72.8	73.1	72.0
2002	71.0	70.3	70.3	70.9	72.2	72.4	71.7	71.5	71.2	71.8	72.9	73.6	71.7
2003	70.9	70.2	70.4	71.5	72.3	72.3	71.5	72.0	71.6	72.6	73.5	74.1	71.9
2004	71.3	71.0	71.3	72.4	73.5	73.4	73.0	72.9	72.5	73.5	74.8	75.6	72.9
2005	72.3	72.3	72.8	74.3	75.0	74.9	74.4	74.2	74.4	74.8	75.7	76.5	74.3
2006	74.0	73.9	74.6	76.0	76.9	76.9	76.1	76.3	76.2	76.4	77.4	78.0	76.1
2007	75.4	75.0	75.1	75.9	77.0	76.8	76.7	76.4	76.2	77.1	78.3	78.9	76.6
2008	76.6	76.3	76.7	77.4	78.1	78.0	78.1	77.9	77.9	78.4	79.3	79.7	77.9
2009	77.0	76.5	76.6	76.9	78.5	78.5	78.2	77.8	77.8	78.7	79.8	80.1	78.0
2010	77.7	77.6	77.8	79.7	80.6	80.9	80.9	81.1	81.0	82.4	83.5	84.2	80.6
2011	82.2	82.2	82.6	84.1	85.6	86.1	86.0	86.4	86.2	87.9	89.2	90.8	85.8
Wholesale Trade													
2000	18.1	17.9	18.0	18.5	18.7	18.6	18.3	18.3	18.1	18.2	18.2	18.2	18.3
2001	18.0	18.0	18.2	18.4	19.1	18.9	18.6	18.5	18.1	18.2	18.1	18.0	18.3
2002	17.8	17.7	17.7	18.0	18.4	18.6	18.2	18.1	17.8	18.0	17.9	17.8	18.0
2003	17.5	17.3	17.4	18.1	18.4	18.4	18.2	18.1	17.8	18.1	18.0	18.0	17.9
2004	17.8	17.8	18.0	18.6	18.8	18.8	18.7	18.6	18.2	18.4	18.5	18.6	18.4
2005	18.1	18.1	18.3	19.0	19.3	19.3	19.1	19.0	18.8	19.0	18.9	19.0	18.8
2006	18.6	18.6	18.8	19.3	19.6	19.6	19.2	19.2	19.0	19.1	19.0	19.0	19.1
2007	18.8	18.7	18.9	19.4	19.8	19.8	19.5	19.4	19.2	19.5	19.5	19.4	19.3
2008	19.1	19.2	19.4	19.9	20.3	20.2	20.2	20.1	19.9	20.0	20.0	20.0	19.9
2009	19.7	19.7	19.8	20.0	20.7	20.8	20.5	20.4	20.1	20.3	20.4	20.4	20.2
2010	20.1	20.2	20.3	21.1	21.3	21.4	21.4	21.4	21.3	21.5	21.6	21.8	21.1
2011	21.5	21.5	21.8	22.3	22.9	23.2	22.0	22.5	22.0	22.6	22.8	22.9	22.3
Retail Trade													
2000	40.6	40.1	40.0	40.5	40.9	40.8	40.9	40.9	40.6	41.1	42.1	42.8	40.9
2001	40.3	39.8	40.0	40.4	41.0	40.7	40.4	40.4	40.2	40.5	41.6	42.0	40.6
2002	40.3	39.8	39.8	40.0	40.8	40.8	40.5	40.5	40.4	40.7	41.9	42.6	40.7
2003	40.3	39.9	39.9	40.3	40.9	41.0	40.5	41.0	40.7	41.2	42.2	42.8	40.9
2004	40.6	40.2	40.4	40.8	41.5	41.5	41.2	41.2	41.0	41.5	42.7	43.3	41.3
2005	41.1	41.0	41.2	41.9	42.3	42.3	42.1	42.0	42.1	42.3	43.3	43.8	42.1
2006	41.9	41.7	42.1	43.0	43.6	43.6	43.3	43.3	43.3	43.4	44.5	44.9	43.2
2007	42.9	42.5	42.4	42.6	43.1	43.1	43.2	42.9	42.7	43.1	44.2	44.8	43.1
2008	43.0	42.5	42.6	42.8	43.0	43.0	43.2	42.9	42.9	43.1	44.0	44.3	43.1
2009	42.4	41.9	41.9	42.0	42.7	42.7	42.8	42.6	42.7	43.2	44.2	44.4	42.8
2010	42.7	42.4	42.4	42.9	43.4	43.5	43.5	43.4	43.2	44.0	44.9	45.2	43.5
2011	43.5	43.3	43.2	43.8	44.3	44.2	44.9	44.8	44.9	45.6	46.7	47.7	44.7
Transportation and Utilities													
2000	12.8	12.7	12.8	12.9	13.0	12.8	12.7	12.9	13.1	13.4	13.3	13.3	13.0
2001	13.0	12.9	12.8	13.1	13.0	13.1	13.0	13.0	13.0	13.0	13.1	13.1	13.0
2002	12.9	12.8	12.8	12.9	13.0	13.0	13.0	12.9	13.0	13.1	13.1	13.2	13.0
2003	13.1	13.0	13.1	13.1	13.0	12.9	12.8	12.9	13.1	13.3	13.3	13.3	13.1
2004	12.9	13.0	12.9	13.0	13.2	13.1	13.1	13.1	13.3	13.6	13.6	13.7	13.2
2005	13.1	13.2	13.3	13.4	13.4	13.3	13.2	13.2	13.5	13.5	13.5	13.7	13.4
2006	13.5	13.6	13.7	13.7	13.7	13.7	13.6	13.8	13.9	13.9	13.9	14.1	13.8
2007	13.7	13.8	13.8	13.9	14.1	13.9	14.0	14.1	14.3	14.5	14.6	14.7	14.1
2008	14.5	14.6	14.7	14.7	14.8	14.8	14.7	14.9	15.1	15.3	15.3	15.4	14.9
2009	14.9	14.9	14.9	14.9	15.1	15.0	14.9	14.8	15.0	15.2	15.2	15.3	15.0
2010	14.9	15.0	15.1	15.7	15.9	16.0	16.0	16.3	16.5	16.9	17.0	17.2	16.0
2011	17.2	17.4	17.6	18.0	18.4	18.7	19.1	19.1	19.3	19.7	19.7	20.2	18.7
Information													
2000	8.4	8.4	8.5	8.5	8.5	8.5	8.5	8.3	8.4	8.4	8.4	8.5	8.4
2001	8.4	8.4	8.4	8.4	8.5	8.6	8.5	8.5	8.5	8.6	8.5	8.4	8.5
2002	8.0	8.0	7.9	7.9	8.0	8.0	8.0	7.9	7.8	7.8	7.8	7.9	7.9
2003	7.7	7.6	7.7	7.7	7.7	7.7	7.7	7.7	7.7	7.7	7.7	7.7	7.7
2004	7.6	7.6	7.6	7.6	7.7	7.7	7.8	7.8	7.7	7.8	7.8	7.7	7.7
2005	7.6	7.6	7.5	7.6	7.6	7.6	7.6	7.6	7.6	7.4	7.4	7.5	7.6
2006	7.4	7.4	7.4	7.4	7.4	7.5	7.5	7.6	7.5	7.5	7.6	7.6	7.5
2007	7.6	7.6	7.6	7.6	7.7	7.6	7.6	7.7	7.5	7.5	7.5	7.5	7.6
2008	7.4	7.4	7.4	7.4	7.5	7.6	7.6	7.6	7.6	7.6	7.6	7.6	7.5
2009	7.7	7.7	7.6	7.5	7.5	7.5	7.5	7.5	7.4	7.3	7.3	7.3	7.5
2010	7.3	7.3	7.3	7.3	7.3	7.4	7.3	7.3	7.2	7.2	7.2	7.2	7.3
2011	7.1	7.1	7.1	7.1	7.1	7.2	7.2	7.0	7.1	7.1	7.2	7.3	7.1

1. Employment by Industry: North Dakota, Selected Years, 2000–2011—*Continued*

(Numbers in thousands, not seasonally adjusted)

Industry and year	January	February	March	April	May	June	July	August	September	October	November	December	Annual average
Financial Activities													
2000	16.9	16.9	16.9	16.7	17.0	17.0	17.1	17.2	17.2	17.2	17.3	17.5	17.1
2001	17.4	17.4	17.4	17.5	17.6	17.7	17.7	17.8	17.8	17.9	17.8	18.0	17.7
2002	17.7	17.8	17.8	17.8	17.9	18.1	18.1	18.3	18.1	18.3	18.3	18.4	18.1
2003	18.2	18.1	18.3	18.2	18.3	18.4	18.5	18.6	18.5	18.4	18.4	18.5	18.4
2004	18.5	18.6	18.7	18.5	18.6	18.7	18.7	18.6	18.6	18.6	18.7	18.8	18.6
2005	18.6	18.6	18.7	18.7	18.8	18.8	18.9	19.1	18.8	18.9	18.8	19.1	18.8
2006	18.9	19.0	19.1	19.0	19.1	19.3	19.4	19.4	19.3	19.2	19.3	19.6	19.2
2007	19.3	19.4	19.5	19.5	19.8	19.9	20.0	20.0	19.9	20.0	19.9	20.2	19.8
2008	19.9	20.0	20.1	20.1	20.2	20.4	20.5	20.5	20.4	20.5	20.5	20.7	20.3
2009	20.2	20.1	20.1	20.1	20.1	20.2	20.3	20.3	20.1	20.2	20.1	20.5	20.2
2010	20.1	20.1	20.1	20.4	20.5	20.7	20.7	20.8	20.7	20.8	20.8	21.2	20.6
2011	20.8	20.8	20.8	20.9	21.1	21.2	21.0	21.1	20.9	21.1	21.5	21.7	21.1
Professional and Business Services													
2000	23.2	23.7	24.2	24.5	24.7	25.2	25.6	25.3	25.0	25.2	25.1	25.2	24.7
2001	24.5	25.5	25.1	25.5	25.6	26.1	25.4	25.3	25.0	25.2	25.1	25.0	25.3
2002	23.1	23.5	23.6	24.1	24.1	25.0	24.6	24.7	24.7	24.4	24.0	23.8	24.1
2003	23.2	23.5	23.3	23.5	23.5	24.1	23.8	24.3	24.1	23.9	23.8	23.6	23.7
2004	22.9	23.3	23.4	24.2	24.5	25.0	25.0	25.1	24.7	25.6	25.1	25.2	24.5
2005	24.5	24.7	24.7	26.4	26.6	27.1	27.4	27.7	27.4	27.3	27.2	27.3	26.5
2006	26.8	27.1	27.5	27.8	28.4	29.1	28.9	28.9	29.1	29.0	28.7	28.6	28.3
2007	28.1	28.3	28.8	29.0	29.5	29.9	29.7	29.9	30.0	29.9	29.7	29.8	29.4
2008	29.3	29.5	29.8	30.3	30.6	31.0	30.8	30.9	30.7	30.4	30.0	29.7	30.3
2009	28.8	28.8	28.7	28.7	29.2	29.7	29.3	29.2	29.8	29.0	28.8	28.5	29.0
2010	27.5	27.8	27.9	28.4	28.1	28.8	28.4	28.6	28.6	29.2	28.8	28.7	28.4
2011	28.0	28.1	28.6	29.2	29.2	29.8	30.9	31.2	31.3	31.8	31.9	32.4	30.2
Education and Health Services													
2000	44.7	44.7	45.0	44.9	45.0	45.3	45.4	45.5	45.3	45.8	46.0	46.1	45.3
2001	45.5	45.8	45.9	45.8	46.0	46.2	46.3	46.2	45.8	46.1	46.4	46.6	46.1
2002	46.2	46.3	46.0	46.4	46.6	46.9	46.9	46.9	46.7	47.0	47.1	47.2	46.7
2003	46.9	47.0	47.1	47.4	47.5	48.1	48.1	47.9	47.7	47.8	48.0	48.3	47.7
2004	47.9	47.9	48.1	48.5	48.5	48.7	48.8	48.7	48.3	48.3	48.4	48.5	48.4
2005	48.2	48.2	48.2	48.5	48.4	49.1	48.9	49.0	49.0	49.0	49.1	49.4	48.8
2006	49.1	49.3	49.7	49.6	49.4	50.0	49.8	49.9	49.8	50.0	50.0	50.3	49.7
2007	50.0	50.1	50.3	50.3	50.6	51.2	51.0	51.2	51.3	51.4	51.4	51.7	50.9
2008	51.3	51.6	51.6	52.1	52.1	52.2	52.2	52.1	52.2	52.6	52.5	52.8	52.1
2009	52.2	52.8	52.7	52.8	53.1	53.6	53.3	53.3	53.6	54.2	53.9	54.4	53.3
2010	54.1	54.2	54.6	54.8	54.6	55.1	55.2	55.2	55.3	55.9	55.7	55.8	55.0
2011	55.8	56.0	56.0	56.2	56.3	56.4	56.7	56.8	56.6	57.1	57.0	57.6	56.5
Leisure and Hospitality													
2000	27.7	27.7	28.3	29.3	30.0	30.4	30.6	30.7	30.1	29.1	28.8	28.5	29.3
2001	27.5	27.7	28.5	29.4	30.5	31.0	30.5	30.5	29.8	29.4	28.8	28.7	29.4
2002	28.0	28.4	28.6	29.6	30.4	31.1	31.2	31.2	30.7	30.1	29.4	29.2	29.8
2003	28.1	28.2	28.9	29.6	30.6	31.3	31.4	31.5	30.6	30.4	29.6	29.4	30.0
2004	28.5	28.7	29.2	30.0	31.0	31.6	32.7	32.6	32.1	31.3	30.7	30.5	30.7
2005	29.7	29.7	30.1	30.8	31.8	32.5	32.3	32.5	32.2	31.2	30.9	30.7	31.2
2006	29.5	30.0	30.4	30.9	32.2	32.8	32.4	32.9	32.8	32.2	31.4	31.6	31.6
2007	30.7	31.1	31.7	32.1	33.5	34.4	33.9	34.1	33.9	33.3	32.9	33.0	32.9
2008	32.1	32.2	32.7	33.2	34.1	34.7	34.4	34.7	34.2	33.7	33.7	33.6	33.6
2009	32.4	32.4	32.8	33.2	34.8	35.4	35.0	35.2	34.8	34.1	33.8	33.8	34.0
2010	32.3	32.4	33.0	34.1	34.9	35.2	35.1	35.3	35.1	35.0	34.6	34.6	34.3
2011	33.4	33.5	34.2	34.5	35.7	36.3	35.9	36.0	35.3	34.7	34.6	35.1	34.9
Other Services													
2000	15.1	15.2	15.3	15.4	15.3	15.2	15.2	15.2	15.2	15.3	15.3	15.3	15.3
2001	15.0	15.1	15.2	15.4	15.4	15.3	15.1	15.2	15.3	15.3	15.3	15.4	15.3
2002	15.1	15.3	15.3	15.4	15.4	15.4	15.2	15.2	15.2	15.2	15.3	15.2	15.3
2003	15.0	15.2	15.2	15.3	15.3	15.2	15.1	15.2	15.4	15.3	15.2	15.3	15.2
2004	14.8	15.0	15.0	15.1	15.1	15.2	15.1	15.1	15.0	15.1	15.1	15.1	15.1
2005	14.9	15.0	15.2	15.2	15.2	15.1	14.9	14.9	14.9	14.9	14.9	15.0	15.0
2006	14.8	14.9	15.0	15.0	15.1	14.9	14.9	15.1	15.0	15.1	15.3	15.4	15.0
2007	15.0	15.0	15.2	15.2	15.2	15.3	15.1	15.0	15.2	15.2	15.3	15.3	15.2
2008	15.2	15.3	15.5	15.5	15.6	15.5	15.3	15.3	15.3	15.3	15.4	15.4	15.4
2009	15.2	15.2	15.3	15.5	15.6	15.4	15.4	15.2	15.1	15.3	15.3	15.5	15.3
2010	15.1	15.2	15.3	15.4	15.4	15.4	15.4	15.3	15.4	15.6	15.6	15.5	15.4
2011	15.3	15.4	15.6	15.6	15.7	15.6	15.2	15.5	15.6	15.7	15.7	16.0	15.6
Government													
2000	72.8	74.4	74.9	74.6	75.4	68.9	66.5	66.4	73.0	74.4	74.2	74.8	72.5
2001	74.0	75.1	75.2	75.2	74.9	70.6	63.1	64.0	74.2	75.6	75.4	75.8	72.8
2002	75.1	76.1	76.0	76.3	76.5	72.1	64.4	66.0	75.6	77.2	77.3	78.3	74.2
2003	75.4	77.5	77.9	78.3	78.5	72.9	64.7	67.0	76.9	78.3	77.9	78.2	75.3
2004	75.5	76.6	76.8	77.2	77.0	72.3	64.3	66.0	76.2	77.8	77.6	77.9	74.6
2005	75.6	77.7	77.9	78.4	78.1	73.1	64.0	66.1	76.7	77.6	77.7	78.0	75.1
2006	76.2	77.7	78.2	78.5	78.4	73.7	64.2	66.3	76.9	78.5	78.5	78.9	75.5
2007	76.5	77.8	78.0	78.4	78.5	74.7	65.2	66.3	77.0	78.3	78.7	78.8	75.7
2008	77.0	78.4	78.2	78.5	79.3	74.8	66.1	67.0	77.7	79.3	79.3	79.6	76.3
2009	77.5	78.7	79.1	79.7	80.7	78.0	68.3	69.1	79.4	81.3	81.3	81.8	77.9
2010	79.4	81.0	81.9	82.1	82.9	80.0	70.2	70.6	80.5	82.2	82.2	82.4	79.6
2011	80.2	81.4	81.5	81.5	81.9	79.5	69.4	69.7	79.7	81.5	81.6	81.8	79.1

2. Average Weekly Hours by Selected Industry: North Dakota, 2007–2011

(Not seasonally adjusted)

Industry and year	January	February	March	April	May	June	July	August	September	October	November	December	Annual average
Total Private													
2007	32.3	32.4	32.4	32.8	33.1	33.8	34.0	33.4	34.1	32.7	32.5	32.6	33.0
2008	31.8	31.7	32.4	32.2	32.7	33.3	33.0	32.9	32.7	32.3	32.2	31.7	32.4
2009	31.4	31.9	31.3	31.3	31.9	32.5	32.5	33.1	32.1	31.9	32.4	31.6	32.0
2010	31.3	31.3	31.6	32.1	32.9	33.0	33.2	34.1	33.3	33.1	32.9	32.7	32.7
2011	33.1	33.0	32.9	33.2	34.1	34.4	34.7	35.2	34.5	35.1	34.2	34.0	34.1
Goods-Producing													
2007	38.7	38.7	39.8	39.7	41.6	40.9	41.6	41.4	40.9	40.7	39.5	38.0	40.2
2008	36.6	36.1	37.3	37.1	39.0	38.1	39.6	40.0	40.0	39.9	37.5	37.1	38.3
2009	35.4	35.8	35.1	36.7	38.5	39.9	39.3	40.4	38.9	38.9	39.3	38.0	38.1
2010	36.5	35.9	37.2	37.9	39.0	39.8	40.8	41.0	40.4	40.5	39.1	37.8	38.9
2011	36.5	37.5	37.8	38.3	39.1	39.4	40.2	42.4	42.9	43.2	41.9	41.0	40.2
Construction													
2007	35.6	35.3	34.5	35.9	42.0	41.5	44.0	43.7	43.9	42.6	40.7	37.6	40.2
2008	35.0	33.4	35.2	36.0	41.9	38.5	42.6	42.5	42.9	41.8	37.2	36.4	39.0
2009	32.4	32.7	32.2	34.7	38.8	41.6	41.2	42.6	40.6	40.7	42.0	37.6	38.7
2010	34.0	33.3	35.0	36.0	37.6	40.8	42.6	41.8	41.6	42.2	40.5	36.5	38.9
2011	35.3	36.2	35.6	37.7	39.0	40.4	42.8	45.2	45.6	44.6	42.8	40.7	41.0
Manufacturing													
2007	39.6	39.7	41.8	40.9	40.8	39.8	39.7	39.4	38.3	38.8	37.8	37.0	39.5
2008	36.3	36.4	37.2	36.9	37.4	38.1	38.0	38.7	38.4	38.7	37.4	37.1	37.6
2009	35.8	36.0	35.0	36.4	37.4	37.8	37.4	38.3	37.7	37.8	37.5	37.8	37.1
2010	36.9	36.8	37.7	38.1	38.7	38.2	38.4	39.2	39.1	39.7	38.5	38.8	38.3
2011	38.3	38.8	39.3	39.2	39.1	38.6	37.7	40.1	40.6	41.6	41.3	40.8	39.6
Trade, Transportation, and Utilities													
2007	34.3	33.9	33.8	33.5	34.3	35.4	35.5	34.0	33.2	32.6	32.8	34.2	34.0
2008	32.9	32.8	33.4	33.2	33.6	34.5	33.6	33.3	32.6	32.6	33.5	33.2	33.3
2009	32.7	33.3	33.1	32.8	33.7	34.9	34.3	35.2	34.5	34.1	34.8	33.9	34.0
2010	33.7	33.8	33.9	34.6	34.7	34.5	34.4	35.3	34.2	33.8	33.2	33.4	34.1
2011	33.9	33.2	33.5	33.7	35.4	35.7	35.0	35.2	33.0	34.3	33.7	33.2	34.2
Financial Activities													
2007	35.3	35.4	34.7	37.3	35.9	36.4	36.9	36.0	36.8	35.9	35.6	36.9	36.1
2008	36.0	36.1	37.0	36.5	35.8	37.7	36.6	36.5	36.0	36.5	36.1	36.9	36.5
2009	39.3	39.6	37.4	36.4	35.8	35.9	35.7	37.6	35.2	34.9	36.7	35.1	36.6
2010	37.7	35.3	34.5	35.9	37.7	36.3	36.1	38.9	36.8	35.6	35.1	35.5	36.3
2011	38.1	36.0	35.0	34.3	35.1	35.8	36.2	37.2	37.0	36.6	33.7	35.6	35.9
Professional and Business Services													
2007	34.3	34.6	34.5	34.4	34.4	35.2	34.7	35.6	35.5	34.5	34.4	35.2	34.8
2008	34.3	33.0	34.8	34.5	35.4	34.7	34.8	35.1	34.2	33.6	33.0	33.6	34.3
2009	32.2	33.0	33.3	32.5	31.7	32.8	33.6	33.3	31.5	32.0	32.7	31.9	32.6
2010	32.3	32.0	32.0	32.2	34.0	34.1	34.4	35.0	33.2	34.0	34.4	34.5	33.5
2011	35.4	36.0	35.2	35.0	37.0	36.8	36.4	37.2	37.7	38.3	37.4	37.9	36.8
Education and Health Services													
2007	30.6	31.0	30.8	31.0	30.5	31.4	31.4	30.6	33.9	30.9	31.2	30.8	31.2
2008	31.0	31.0	31.1	30.9	31.2	31.3	30.3	30.1	30.5	30.1	30.5	30.4	30.7
2009	30.6	30.9	30.5	30.4	30.5	30.9	30.8	30.9	30.7	30.8	31.3	31.3	30.8
2010	30.7	31.0	31.6	31.2	31.3	31.5	31.3	31.6	31.8	32.0	32.8	32.5	31.6
2011	33.1	32.8	32.5	32.8	33.2	33.1	34.1	33.3	32.9	33.3	33.4	33.5	33.1
Leisure and Hospitality													
2007	20.2	20.4	20.9	21.2	21.3	22.8	23.7	23.3	22.9	22.1	21.9	22.5	22.0
2008	21.0	21.2	22.0	21.9	22.1	23.5	23.0	22.8	21.8	21.4	21.5	20.1	21.9
2009	20.5	20.8	20.5	20.5	21.2	21.5	21.9	22.9	20.8	20.3	20.5	20.0	21.0
2010	19.6	20.5	20.9	21.0	22.1	22.0	22.4	23.5	21.8	21.1	21.0	20.7	21.4
2011	21.4	21.0	20.7	21.6	22.4	22.6	23.3	23.9	22.2	22.6	21.9	21.9	22.1
Other Services													
2007	25.5	25.0	24.0	25.2	26.2	27.0	26.3	26.9	25.5	24.8	23.9	24.8	25.4
2008	23.9	24.4	25.1	24.5	24.9	25.7	26.5	25.6	24.5	23.4	23.8	23.3	24.6
2009	22.7	23.3	22.8	23.2	24.1	25.0	24.5	24.4	23.8	23.5	23.9	23.1	23.7
2010	23.7	23.8	22.9	24.6	25.6	25.3	24.2	26.2	25.1	24.6	24.4	24.4	24.6
2011	25.1	25.4	24.2	24.9	25.3	26.1	25.7	26.6	26.0	26.7	25.6	25.4	25.6

3. Average Hourly Earnings by Selected Industry: North Dakota, 2007–2011

(Dollars, not seasonally adjusted)

Industry and year	January	February	March	April	May	June	July	August	September	October	November	December	Annual average
Total Private													
2007	18.55	18.32	18.29	18.55	18.20	17.95	18.31	18.15	18.17	18.34	18.41	18.90	18.34
2008	18.50	18.59	18.54	18.58	18.30	18.43	18.65	18.84	19.32	19.07	19.09	19.14	18.75
2009	19.21	19.11	19.18	19.11	19.02	18.89	19.09	19.32	19.47	19.40	19.42	19.28	19.21
2010	19.50	19.65	19.39	20.04	20.19	19.77	20.05	20.20	20.59	20.69	20.94	21.03	20.19
2011	20.85	21.05	20.93	21.35	21.28	21.11	21.24	21.46	21.78	21.89	21.88	22.23	21.44
Goods-Producing													
2007	19.71	19.71	19.69	19.79	19.49	19.59	19.47	19.83	20.12	19.95	20.10	20.01	19.79
2008	19.83	20.13	20.51	19.99	19.97	19.75	20.33	20.88	21.29	21.07	20.82	21.05	20.49
2009	21.41	21.45	21.91	21.70	21.39	21.24	21.18	21.24	20.89	21.27	21.42	21.24	21.34
2010	21.22	21.05	21.14	21.48	21.89	21.70	21.93	21.78	22.18	22.35	22.21	22.33	21.82
2011	22.79	22.61	22.60	23.04	23.27	23.22	23.07	23.20	23.75	23.67	23.44	23.79	23.25
Construction													
2007	22.06	22.61	22.07	21.90	21.33	20.90	21.02	20.66	20.60	20.20	20.19	20.29	21.02
2008	19.96	20.05	20.31	19.28	19.12	18.82	19.26	19.56	19.63	19.43	19.52	20.32	19.55
2009	20.59	20.29	20.70	19.98	20.01	19.91	20.27	20.34	19.29	19.94	20.41	20.41	20.13
2010	19.46	19.68	19.82	19.78	20.21	20.65	20.92	20.88	21.45	21.90	21.77	21.77	20.83
2011	22.13	22.56	22.72	22.88	23.59	23.75	23.71	24.82	24.89	24.48	24.33	24.52	23.89
Manufacturing													
2007	17.36	17.36	17.45	17.69	17.43	17.74	17.46	18.23	18.56	18.71	18.57	18.26	17.89
2008	18.26	18.67	18.80	18.78	18.66	18.35	18.50	19.16	19.69	19.71	19.42	19.44	18.96
2009	19.44	19.46	20.06	20.07	19.54	19.43	19.31	19.36	19.70	19.66	19.59	19.61	19.60
2010	19.77	19.54	19.53	19.73	20.11	19.35	19.49	19.36	19.73	19.67	19.12	19.42	19.57
2011	19.69	19.28	19.29	19.73	19.99	19.93	20.51	19.89	20.29	20.59	20.29	20.86	20.04
Trade, Transportation, and Utilities													
2007	18.68	18.56	18.29	19.21	18.98	18.06	18.52	18.72	19.17	18.84	18.76	19.09	18.74
2008	18.91	18.70	18.71	19.12	18.97	18.90	18.97	18.94	19.24	19.57	19.35	18.99	19.03
2009	19.08	19.10	18.81	18.76	18.86	19.01	19.15	20.12	20.42	20.67	20.33	19.89	19.53
2010	20.38	20.00	20.09	20.25	19.96	19.59	19.67	19.60	20.03	20.19	20.06	20.08	19.99
2011	20.33	20.56	20.57	21.46	20.98	20.73	21.45	21.33	21.04	21.42	21.41	22.05	21.12
Financial Activities													
2007	19.58	17.92	17.93	18.35	17.99	18.36	20.14	18.54	19.12	18.97	19.14	19.09	18.77
2008	15.69	16.65	16.45	16.60	17.12	17.12	16.95	17.48	17.99	17.65	17.65	17.41	17.07
2009	17.07	17.26	17.34	17.41	17.82	17.82	18.22	18.82	18.46	18.58	18.89	18.78	18.02
2010	18.00	19.86	19.37	19.23	19.41	19.38	19.33	19.29	19.30	19.66	20.06	19.50	19.36
2011	18.97	20.52	19.77	19.96	19.80	19.58	19.36	19.45	19.72	19.90	20.64	20.01	19.80
Professional and Business Services													
2007	19.57	19.49	19.32	19.99	19.22	19.28	20.25	18.65	19.44	19.14	19.32	24.52	19.86
2008	22.88	23.49	22.79	22.19	21.54	21.63	21.01	21.08	20.97	20.83	21.82	21.06	21.76
2009	21.81	21.85	22.23	22.70	22.60	21.92	21.78	22.80	23.10	22.48	23.15	23.10	22.45
2010	22.84	22.84	23.03	23.04	23.39	22.56	22.62	23.09	23.05	23.00	22.91	23.41	22.98
2011	23.34	23.72	24.05	23.47	24.25	23.61	24.41	24.41	25.29	25.72	25.92	27.79	24.74
Education and Health Services													
2007	19.19	18.99	18.98	18.80	18.26	18.07	18.24	18.33	17.37	18.46	18.60	18.95	18.51
2008	18.92	18.85	18.75	18.93	17.92	18.62	19.06	19.02	19.92	19.10	19.26	19.53	18.99
2009	19.44	19.08	19.23	19.32	19.05	19.02	19.54	19.48	19.89	19.62	19.49	19.54	19.39
2010	20.08	20.57	19.99	21.19	21.49	20.62	21.22	22.03	22.28	22.25	23.52	23.48	21.59
2011	23.95	24.05	23.43	23.41	23.12	22.91	22.40	23.12	23.06	23.00	22.84	22.68	23.16
Leisure and Hospitality													
2007	9.70	9.59	9.54	9.86	9.69	9.51	9.49	9.66	9.74	10.04	10.00	10.04	9.74
2008	10.16	10.12	10.09	10.10	10.19	9.92	10.07	10.32	10.39	10.36	10.42	10.47	10.21
2009	10.44	10.47	10.66	10.63	10.57	10.43	10.68	10.72	10.88	11.01	11.02	11.24	10.73
2010	11.20	11.23	11.08	10.87	11.02	10.73	10.75	10.58	10.85	10.89	11.02	11.28	10.95
2011	11.21	11.24	11.21	11.29	11.26	11.23	11.20	11.37	11.74	11.82	12.08	12.25	11.49
Other Services													
2007	15.24	15.11	16.53	15.00	15.73	14.70	14.40	11.83	12.06	12.31	12.40	12.45	13.98
2008	12.46	12.38	12.54	12.66	12.99	13.11	12.85	13.24	13.40	13.42	13.52	14.04	13.04
2009	14.04	13.95	14.69	14.66	15.11	15.56	15.72	16.18	16.00	15.98	16.00	16.18	15.35
2010	16.15	16.15	15.77	15.91	16.02	15.96	16.08	16.17	16.33	16.19	15.90	16.05	16.06
2011	16.04	16.08	16.51	17.25	17.49	17.19	17.61	17.96	17.96	17.81	17.61	17.65	17.28

4. Average Weekly Earnings by Selected Industry: North Dakota, 2007–2011

(Dollars, not seasonally adjusted)

Industry and year	January	February	March	April	May	June	July	August	September	October	November	December	Annual average
Total Private													
2007	599.17	593.57	592.60	608.44	602.42	606.71	622.54	606.21	619.60	599.72	598.33	616.14	605.54
2008	588.30	589.30	600.70	598.28	598.41	613.72	615.45	619.84	631.76	615.96	614.70	606.74	607.86
2009	603.19	609.61	600.33	598.14	606.74	613.93	620.43	639.49	624.99	618.86	629.21	609.25	614.76
2010	610.35	615.05	612.72	643.28	664.25	652.41	665.66	688.82	685.65	684.84	688.93	687.68	659.34
2011	690.14	694.65	688.60	708.82	725.65	726.18	737.03	755.39	751.41	768.34	748.30	755.82	730.13
Goods-Producing													
2007	762.78	762.78	783.66	785.66	810.78	801.23	809.95	820.96	822.91	811.97	793.95	760.38	795.00
2008	725.78	726.69	765.02	741.63	778.83	752.48	805.07	835.20	851.60	840.69	780.75	780.96	784.34
2009	757.91	767.91	769.04	796.39	823.52	847.48	832.37	858.10	812.62	827.40	841.81	807.12	813.72
2010	774.53	755.70	786.41	814.09	853.71	863.66	894.74	892.98	896.07	905.18	868.41	844.07	849.62
2011	831.84	847.88	854.28	882.43	909.86	914.87	927.41	983.68	1,018.88	1,022.54	982.14	975.39	934.27
Construction													
2007	785.34	798.13	761.42	786.21	895.86	867.35	924.88	902.84	904.34	860.52	821.73	762.90	845.34
2008	698.60	669.67	714.91	694.08	801.13	724.57	820.48	831.30	842.13	812.17	726.14	739.65	762.87
2009	667.12	663.48	666.54	693.31	776.39	828.26	835.12	866.48	783.17	811.56	857.22	767.42	779.43
2010	661.64	655.34	693.70	712.08	759.90	842.52	891.19	872.78	892.32	924.18	881.69	794.61	810.29
2011	781.19	816.67	808.83	862.58	920.01	959.50	1,014.79	1,121.86	1,134.98	1,091.81	1,041.32	997.96	980.00
Manufacturing													
2007	687.46	689.19	729.41	723.52	711.14	706.05	693.16	718.26	710.85	725.95	701.95	675.62	706.04
2008	662.84	679.59	699.36	692.98	697.88	699.14	703.00	741.49	756.10	762.78	726.31	721.22	712.00
2009	695.95	700.56	702.10	730.55	730.80	734.45	722.19	741.49	742.69	743.15	734.63	741.26	726.42
2010	729.51	719.07	736.28	751.71	778.26	739.17	748.42	758.91	771.44	780.90	736.12	753.50	750.14
2011	754.13	748.06	758.10	773.42	781.61	769.30	773.23	797.59	823.77	856.54	837.98	851.09	793.89
Trade, Transportation, and Utilities													
2007	640.72	629.18	618.20	643.54	651.01	639.32	657.46	636.48	636.44	614.18	615.33	652.88	636.26
2008	622.14	613.36	624.91	634.78	637.39	652.05	637.39	630.70	627.22	637.98	648.23	630.47	633.14
2009	623.92	636.03	622.61	615.33	635.58	663.45	656.85	708.22	704.49	704.85	707.48	674.27	663.11
2010	686.81	676.00	681.05	700.65	692.61	675.86	676.65	691.88	685.03	682.42	665.99	670.67	681.93
2011	689.19	682.59	689.10	723.20	742.69	740.06	750.75	750.82	694.32	734.71	721.52	732.06	721.44
Financial Activities													
2007	691.17	634.37	622.17	684.46	645.84	668.30	743.17	667.44	703.62	681.02	681.38	704.42	677.49
2008	564.84	601.07	608.65	605.90	612.90	645.42	620.37	638.02	647.64	644.23	637.17	642.43	622.63
2009	670.85	683.50	648.52	633.72	637.96	639.74	650.45	707.63	649.79	648.44	693.26	659.18	660.14
2010	678.60	701.06	668.27	690.36	731.76	703.49	697.81	750.38	710.24	699.90	704.11	692.25	702.45
2011	722.76	738.72	691.95	684.63	694.98	700.96	700.83	723.54	729.64	728.34	695.57	712.36	710.20
Professional and Business Services													
2007	671.25	674.35	666.54	687.66	661.17	678.66	702.68	663.94	690.12	660.33	664.61	863.10	690.61
2008	784.78	775.17	793.09	765.56	762.52	750.56	731.15	739.91	717.17	699.89	720.06	707.62	745.42
2009	702.28	721.05	740.26	737.75	716.42	718.98	731.81	759.24	727.65	719.36	757.01	736.89	730.90
2010	737.73	730.88	736.96	741.89	795.26	769.30	778.13	808.15	765.26	782.00	788.10	807.65	770.72
2011	826.24	853.92	846.56	821.45	897.25	868.85	888.52	908.05	953.43	985.08	969.41	1,053.24	909.37
Education and Health Services													
2007	587.21	588.69	584.58	582.80	556.93	567.40	572.74	560.90	588.84	570.41	580.32	583.66	577.01
2008	586.52	584.35	583.13	584.94	559.10	582.81	577.52	572.50	607.56	574.91	587.43	593.71	582.88
2009	594.86	589.57	586.52	587.33	581.03	587.72	601.83	601.93	610.62	604.30	610.04	611.60	597.33
2010	616.46	637.67	631.68	661.13	672.64	649.53	664.19	696.15	708.50	712.00	771.46	763.10	682.60
2011	792.75	788.84	761.48	767.85	767.58	758.32	763.84	769.90	758.67	765.90	762.86	759.78	767.52
Leisure and Hospitality													
2007	195.94	195.64	199.39	209.03	206.40	216.83	224.91	225.08	223.05	221.88	219.00	225.90	213.92
2008	213.36	214.54	221.98	221.19	225.20	233.12	231.61	235.30	226.50	221.70	224.03	210.45	223.40
2009	214.02	217.78	218.53	217.92	224.08	224.25	233.89	245.49	226.30	223.50	225.91	224.80	224.78
2010	219.52	230.22	231.57	228.27	243.54	236.06	240.80	248.63	236.53	229.78	231.42	233.50	234.29
2011	239.89	236.04	232.05	243.86	252.22	253.80	260.96	271.74	260.63	267.13	264.55	268.28	254.43
Other Services													
2007	388.62	377.75	396.72	378.00	412.13	396.90	378.72	318.23	307.53	305.29	296.36	308.76	355.35
2008	297.79	302.07	314.75	310.17	323.45	336.93	340.53	385.14	328.30	314.03	321.78	327.13	321.34
2009	318.71	325.04	334.93	340.11	364.15	389.00	385.14	394.79	380.80	375.53	382.40	373.76	363.19
2010	382.76	384.37	361.13	391.39	410.11	403.79	389.14	423.65	409.88	398.27	387.96	391.62	395.06
2011	402.60	408.43	399.54	429.53	442.50	448.66	452.58	477.74	466.96	475.53	450.82	448.31	442.13

OHIO
At a Glance

Population:
  2000 census: 11,353,336
  2010 census: 11,536,504
  2011 estimate: 11,544,951

Percent change in population:
  2000–2010: 1.6%
  2010–2011: 0.1%

Percent change in total nonfarm employment:
  2000–2010: -10.5%
  2010–2011: 1.0%

Industry with the largest growth in employment, 2000–2011 (thousands):
  Education and Health Services, 169.8

Industry with the largest decline or smallest growth in employment, 2000–2011 (thousands):
  Manufacturing, -382.6

Civilian labor force:
  2000: 5,807,036
  2010: 5,864,025
  2011: 5,806,467

Unemployment rate and rank among states (lowest to highest):
  2000: 4.0%, 28th
  2010: 10.0%, 36th
  2011: 8.6%, 29th

Over-the-year change in unemployment rates:
  2010–2011: -1.4%

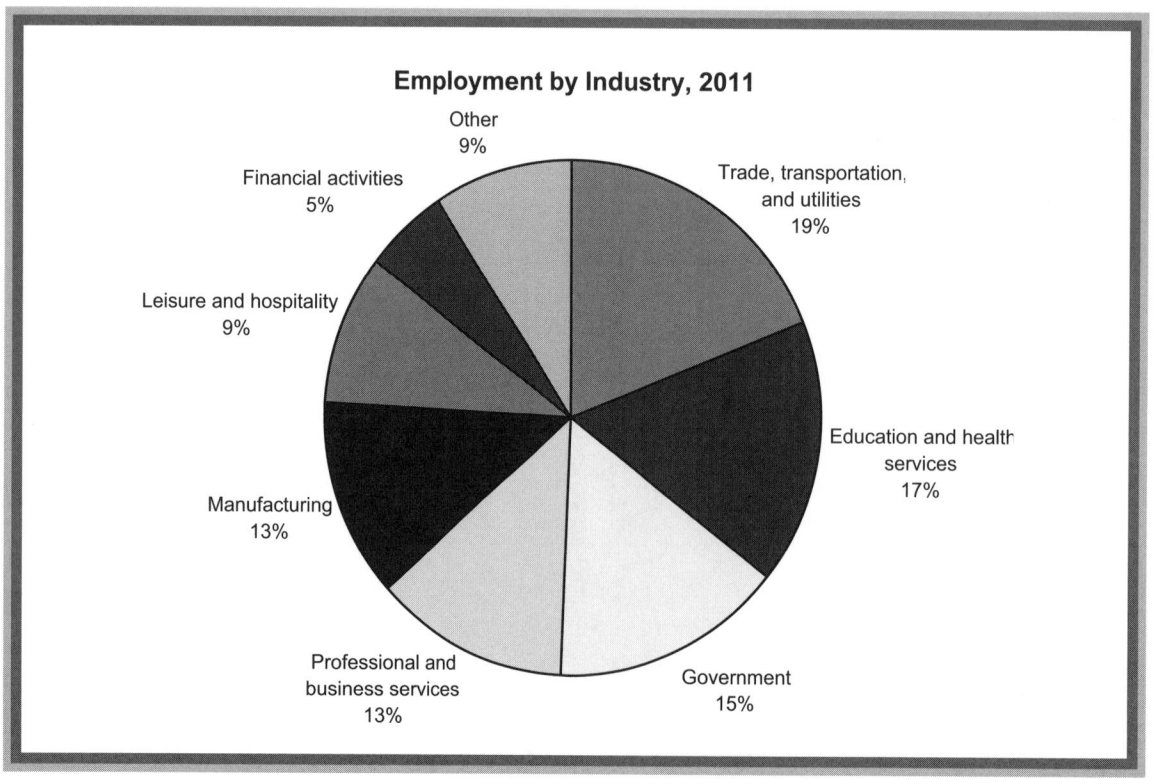

Employment by Industry, 2011

Other 9%

Financial activities 5%

Leisure and hospitality 9%

Manufacturing 13%

Professional and business services 13%

Government 15%

Education and health services 17%

Trade, transportation, and utilities 19%

1. Employment by Industry: Ohio, Selected Years, 2000–2011

(Numbers in thousands, not seasonally adjusted)

Industry and year	January	February	March	April	May	June	July	August	September	October	November	December	Annual average
Total Nonfarm													
2000	5,503.9	5,524.9	5,573.4	5,610.8	5,668.2	5,690.3	5,624.0	5,629.5	5,643.3	5,661.2	5,680.4	5,686.0	5,624.7
2001	5,488.3	5,501.1	5,532.2	5,560.1	5,596.3	5,612.1	5,529.5	5,533.5	5,530.6	5,539.3	5,546.9	5,541.5	5,542.6
2002	5,348.7	5,363.6	5,398.0	5,429.2	5,480.1	5,492.5	5,443.4	5,456.6	5,469.5	5,479.1	5,492.6	5,486.2	5,445.0
2003	5,309.8	5,307.0	5,338.5	5,390.0	5,439.9	5,440.2	5,389.2	5,405.0	5,414.5	5,441.1	5,446.5	5,450.7	5,397.7
2004	5,277.0	5,292.7	5,342.6	5,395.2	5,438.4	5,454.9	5,417.2	5,423.5	5,439.9	5,466.1	5,476.4	5,476.5	5,408.4
2005	5,287.2	5,313.9	5,354.0	5,424.3	5,465.4	5,472.4	5,431.2	5,440.1	5,469.1	5,476.8	5,494.6	5,491.3	5,426.7
2006	5,326.3	5,347.0	5,389.7	5,434.8	5,478.6	5,494.3	5,428.9	5,441.3	5,461.6	5,466.4	5,480.0	5,480.9	5,435.8
2007	5,324.2	5,321.0	5,369.0	5,417.4	5,474.8	5,493.7	5,424.3	5,438.6	5,452.2	5,465.3	5,482.7	5,472.4	5,428.0
2008	5,316.7	5,325.9	5,325.7	5,384.6	5,435.2	5,428.4	5,368.7	5,372.4	5,376.2	5,370.7	5,341.3	5,303.2	5,362.4
2009	5,099.9	5,084.7	5,078.5	5,093.8	5,119.0	5,091.7	5,036.7	5,033.8	5,053.8	5,066.8	5,063.3	5,050.6	5,072.7
2010	4,905.0	4,909.5	4,945.3	5,022.4	5,080.3	5,075.9	5,042.4	5,045.7	5,067.6	5,104.2	5,113.9	5,104.0	5,034.7
2011	4,956.1	4,977.9	5,011.7	5,087.8	5,124.1	5,122.0	5,092.6	5,096.4	5,112.9	5,141.6	5,147.2	5,126.7	5,083.1
Total Private													
2000	4,728.7	4,734.3	4,778.0	4,814.6	4,856.1	4,906.7	4,879.5	4,892.8	4,865.9	4,861.7	4,875.2	4,881.8	4,839.6
2001	4,702.0	4,697.6	4,724.2	4,754.3	4,788.2	4,822.7	4,781.2	4,788.2	4,742.2	4,728.3	4,729.7	4,724.3	4,748.6
2002	4,553.9	4,550.4	4,580.5	4,615.3	4,663.4	4,697.5	4,684.8	4,704.0	4,677.7	4,667.0	4,673.4	4,668.8	4,644.7
2003	4,511.5	4,493.9	4,520.9	4,573.2	4,619.6	4,642.1	4,625.4	4,648.1	4,621.8	4,627.1	4,627.3	4,630.3	4,595.1
2004	4,481.7	4,477.4	4,522.3	4,577.3	4,618.2	4,654.6	4,654.9	4,666.9	4,650.1	4,653.7	4,660.3	4,662.2	4,606.6
2005	4,494.9	4,501.5	4,539.6	4,611.7	4,646.7	4,677.6	4,672.1	4,683.9	4,677.7	4,664.1	4,676.8	4,678.1	4,627.1
2006	4,530.8	4,536.0	4,575.6	4,622.7	4,659.8	4,697.9	4,669.9	4,684.4	4,668.9	4,653.5	4,663.0	4,666.6	4,635.8
2007	4,530.4	4,513.3	4,557.7	4,606.7	4,660.4	4,697.6	4,667.4	4,683.5	4,662.9	4,656.0	4,669.4	4,665.7	4,630.9
2008	4,523.9	4,515.2	4,516.7	4,574.7	4,620.5	4,636.2	4,614.4	4,619.4	4,588.7	4,560.8	4,526.6	4,497.3	4,566.2
2009	4,309.7	4,279.6	4,273.1	4,286.1	4,310.3	4,306.8	4,291.7	4,292.1	4,275.6	4,267.7	4,262.8	4,259.5	4,284.6
2010	4,126.5	4,118.8	4,152.3	4,225.2	4,265.5	4,293.0	4,305.0	4,314.1	4,302.3	4,314.9	4,321.3	4,315.4	4,254.5
2011	4,191.2	4,198.5	4,229.8	4,305.6	4,342.3	4,363.3	4,367.8	4,373.5	4,353.2	4,364.0	4,365.2	4,348.1	4,316.9
Goods-Producing													
2000	1,258.9	1,259.4	1,273.0	1,281.2	1,292.7	1,307.1	1,290.3	1,294.2	1,285.7	1,280.7	1,276.0	1,261.8	1,280.1
2001	1,216.9	1,211.9	1,215.5	1,216.5	1,219.6	1,227.9	1,214.5	1,216.8	1,200.1	1,190.3	1,180.5	1,166.9	1,206.5
2002	1,117.8	1,113.3	1,118.0	1,125.1	1,137.5	1,150.8	1,143.4	1,155.9	1,147.0	1,138.8	1,131.9	1,119.6	1,133.3
2003	1,080.0	1,069.0	1,073.5	1,082.7	1,096.8	1,103.5	1,089.1	1,099.7	1,092.0	1,088.9	1,081.9	1,075.1	1,086.0
2004	1,037.2	1,034.8	1,047.9	1,063.5	1,074.5	1,086.1	1,083.6	1,089.1	1,083.2	1,079.8	1,073.5	1,066.3	1,068.3
2005	1,025.7	1,024.2	1,032.4	1,052.7	1,062.5	1,074.1	1,071.5	1,075.6	1,071.7	1,066.2	1,062.3	1,050.5	1,055.8
2006	1,018.1	1,016.0	1,024.1	1,039.4	1,046.3	1,059.4	1,049.0	1,054.1	1,048.8	1,039.3	1,032.4	1,024.5	1,037.6
2007	990.4	982.2	993.7	1,003.5	1,017.5	1,028.9	1,016.4	1,027.0	1,019.7	1,009.6	1,007.2	996.9	1,007.8
2008	962.1	957.8	952.7	964.4	976.3	986.1	978.0	978.8	971.5	960.6	940.5	915.9	962.1
2009	855.4	842.4	832.9	826.4	824.2	819.8	814.9	819.9	816.0	813.1	803.7	797.9	822.2
2010	765.2	760.9	768.4	787.8	801.3	812.6	818.3	821.8	819.6	821.9	819.2	810.1	800.6
2011	785.3	784.2	794.0	811.3	821.5	833.8	844.2	849.0	845.8	847.7	843.3	826.9	823.9
Mining and Logging													
2000	12.5	12.5	12.8	12.9	13.1	13.3	13.0	13.0	13.0	13.0	13.0	12.8	12.9
2001	12.2	12.4	12.7	12.8	13.0	13.3	13.3	13.3	13.3	13.0	12.9	12.7	12.9
2002	12.0	12.0	12.1	12.4	12.0	12.3	12.2	12.3	12.2	12.2	12.0	11.9	12.1
2003	11.5	11.3	11.4	11.6	11.7	11.8	11.8	11.9	11.8	11.8	11.8	11.6	11.7
2004	11.3	11.3	11.5	11.6	11.8	11.9	11.9	11.9	11.9	11.7	11.6	11.6	11.7
2005	10.8	10.8	10.9	11.3	11.4	11.5	11.7	11.6	11.6	11.7	11.7	11.5	11.4
2006	11.0	11.0	11.2	11.6	11.6	11.8	11.8	11.9	11.7	11.7	11.7	11.6	11.6
2007	11.3	11.0	11.2	11.6	11.8	11.9	12.0	12.1	11.9	11.8	11.9	11.7	11.7
2008	11.3	11.2	11.1	11.5	11.9	12.0	12.4	12.5	12.4	12.5	12.5	12.1	12.0
2009	11.6	11.4	11.5	11.8	12.0	12.0	12.1	12.0	11.8	11.6	11.5	11.3	11.7
2010	10.5	10.5	10.5	11.2	11.4	11.5	11.7	11.6	11.7	11.6	11.5	11.3	11.3
2011	10.8	10.8	11.1	11.5	11.7	11.8	12.0	12.1	12.0	12.3	12.2	12.0	11.7
Construction													
2000	220.7	219.5	232.7	242.8	253.6	263.6	264.3	263.2	257.0	252.8	247.6	235.8	246.1
2001	212.5	213.1	221.4	232.6	243.1	252.8	258.7	260.3	253.8	252.3	247.8	238.1	240.5
2002	212.2	210.4	216.8	226.3	236.9	246.5	253.8	255.7	250.8	249.0	243.4	232.2	236.2
2003	207.5	200.8	207.5	224.0	234.2	242.6	246.0	248.7	245.2	245.5	240.1	232.8	231.2
2004	208.5	205.6	216.0	229.0	238.3	246.8	252.0	250.7	247.6	246.4	241.1	232.8	234.6
2005	204.9	203.9	209.5	228.3	237.6	246.0	250.4	250.3	247.3	244.9	241.4	230.0	232.9
2006	208.1	207.5	215.2	227.2	234.9	241.5	243.4	244.0	240.5	237.2	232.4	225.0	229.7
2007	204.3	195.6	206.1	219.2	231.3	238.7	239.7	240.2	237.2	235.9	230.7	218.6	224.8
2008	196.4	192.2	194.6	208.3	218.3	223.7	226.0	225.9	221.3	219.6	210.8	196.8	211.2
2009	173.5	168.9	172.0	175.8	185.9	190.9	193.9	192.1	187.1	185.4	179.3	168.8	181.1
2010	147.4	142.8	149.6	162.8	170.2	176.7	183.1	183.4	181.0	182.5	178.6	167.9	168.8
2011	150.1	147.9	154.2	166.8	174.8	182.8	190.4	190.1	189.0	189.7	182.8	167.7	173.9
Manufacturing													
2000	1,025.7	1,027.4	1,027.5	1,025.5	1,026.0	1,030.2	1,013.0	1,018.0	1,015.7	1,014.9	1,015.4	1,013.2	1,021.0
2001	992.2	986.4	981.4	971.1	963.5	961.8	942.5	943.2	933.0	925.0	919.8	916.1	953.0
2002	893.6	890.9	889.1	886.4	888.6	892.0	877.4	887.9	884.0	877.6	876.5	875.5	885.0
2003	861.0	856.9	854.6	847.1	850.9	849.1	831.3	839.1	835.0	831.6	830.0	830.7	843.1
2004	817.4	817.9	820.4	822.9	824.4	827.4	819.7	826.5	823.7	821.7	820.8	821.9	822.1
2005	810.0	809.5	812.0	813.1	813.5	816.6	809.4	813.7	812.8	809.6	809.2	809.0	811.5
2006	799.0	797.5	797.7	800.6	799.8	806.1	793.8	798.2	796.6	790.4	788.3	787.9	796.3
2007	774.8	775.6	776.4	772.7	774.4	778.3	764.7	774.7	770.6	761.9	764.6	766.6	771.3
2008	754.4	754.4	747.0	744.6	746.1	750.4	739.6	740.4	737.8	728.5	717.2	707.0	739.0
2009	670.3	662.1	649.4	638.8	626.3	616.9	608.9	615.8	617.1	616.1	612.9	617.8	629.4
2010	607.3	607.6	608.3	613.8	619.7	624.4	623.5	626.8	626.9	627.8	629.1	630.9	620.5
2011	624.4	625.5	628.7	633.0	635.0	639.2	641.8	646.8	644.8	645.7	648.3	647.2	638.4

1. Employment by Industry: Ohio, Selected Years, 2000–2011—*Continued*

(Numbers in thousands, not seasonally adjusted)

Industry and year	January	February	March	April	May	June	July	August	September	October	November	December	Annual average
Service-Providing													
2000	4,245.0	4,265.5	4,300.4	4,329.6	4,375.5	4,383.2	4,333.7	4,335.3	4,357.6	4,380.5	4,404.4	4,424.2	4,344.6
2001	4,271.4	4,289.2	4,316.7	4,343.6	4,376.7	4,384.2	4,315.0	4,316.7	4,330.5	4,349.0	4,366.4	4,374.6	4,336.2
2002	4,230.9	4,250.3	4,280.0	4,304.1	4,342.6	4,341.7	4,300.0	4,300.7	4,322.5	4,340.3	4,360.7	4,366.6	4,311.7
2003	4,229.8	4,238.0	4,265.0	4,307.3	4,343.1	4,336.7	4,300.1	4,305.3	4,322.5	4,352.2	4,364.6	4,375.6	4,311.7
2004	4,239.8	4,257.9	4,294.7	4,331.7	4,363.9	4,368.8	4,333.6	4,334.4	4,356.7	4,386.3	4,402.9	4,410.2	4,340.1
2005	4,261.5	4,289.7	4,321.6	4,371.6	4,402.9	4,398.3	4,359.7	4,364.5	4,397.4	4,410.6	4,432.3	4,440.8	4,370.9
2006	4,308.2	4,331.0	4,365.6	4,395.4	4,432.3	4,434.9	4,379.9	4,387.2	4,412.8	4,427.1	4,447.6	4,456.4	4,398.2
2007	4,333.8	4,338.8	4,375.3	4,413.9	4,457.3	4,464.8	4,407.9	4,411.6	4,432.5	4,455.7	4,475.5	4,475.5	4,420.2
2008	4,354.6	4,368.1	4,373.0	4,420.2	4,458.9	4,442.3	4,390.7	4,393.6	4,404.7	4,410.1	4,400.8	4,387.3	4,400.4
2009	4,244.5	4,242.3	4,245.6	4,267.4	4,294.8	4,271.9	4,221.8	4,213.9	4,237.8	4,253.7	4,259.6	4,252.7	4,250.5
2010	4,139.8	4,148.6	4,176.9	4,234.6	4,279.0	4,263.3	4,224.1	4,223.9	4,248.0	4,282.3	4,294.7	4,293.9	4,234.1
2011	4,170.8	4,193.7	4,217.7	4,276.5	4,302.6	4,288.2	4,248.4	4,247.4	4,267.1	4,293.9	4,303.9	4,299.8	4,259.2
Trade, Transportation, and Utilities													
2000	1,107.9	1,097.0	1,100.2	1,101.8	1,107.7	1,113.5	1,107.4	1,108.6	1,103.9	1,123.9	1,145.8	1,165.8	1,115.3
2001	1,105.8	1,089.5	1,091.8	1,094.0	1,098.7	1,102.3	1,088.2	1,086.3	1,081.2	1,087.4	1,107.2	1,117.0	1,095.8
2002	1,058.2	1,045.3	1,050.2	1,053.2	1,060.1	1,064.7	1,061.5	1,061.5	1,053.5	1,057.7	1,077.5	1,089.2	1,061.1
2003	1,034.7	1,023.7	1,026.8	1,035.9	1,042.4	1,044.6	1,040.2	1,042.7	1,039.2	1,051.1	1,067.2	1,078.6	1,043.9
2004	1,026.0	1,015.1	1,021.0	1,025.4	1,033.0	1,039.8	1,039.7	1,041.7	1,036.1	1,049.2	1,068.6	1,080.9	1,039.7
2005	1,028.2	1,020.4	1,027.2	1,035.0	1,041.3	1,043.1	1,042.8	1,042.2	1,038.5	1,044.5	1,066.3	1,082.4	1,042.7
2006	1,034.4	1,024.5	1,029.7	1,034.6	1,043.6	1,047.5	1,043.7	1,044.9	1,041.5	1,047.3	1,071.5	1,085.1	1,045.7
2007	1,038.6	1,024.8	1,033.8	1,038.8	1,050.5	1,054.8	1,052.5	1,051.1	1,047.2	1,053.2	1,076.6	1,088.0	1,050.8
2008	1,038.7	1,024.4	1,025.5	1,032.1	1,039.9	1,040.2	1,036.6	1,037.2	1,028.3	1,028.0	1,035.5	1,041.0	1,034.0
2009	985.6	970.0	966.3	963.5	968.6	967.7	962.8	960.1	953.3	957.3	971.6	979.3	967.2
2010	934.4	924.6	929.8	937.6	945.9	950.2	949.1	950.2	944.0	954.4	970.7	980.8	947.6
2011	936.7	931.3	934.4	947.4	953.3	957.6	954.4	953.9	949.7	960.3	977.5	987.3	953.7
Wholesale Trade													
2000	244.2	244.9	246.1	246.4	247.6	249.2	248.0	247.8	247.2	248.5	248.7	250.0	247.4
2001	247.6	247.6	248.4	248.2	248.8	249.3	247.9	247.1	244.6	243.8	242.8	243.1	246.6
2002	238.4	237.7	238.6	239.3	240.2	240.9	240.7	240.2	238.3	237.7	237.6	238.3	239.0
2003	233.7	233.5	234.1	234.4	235.1	235.3	235.1	234.7	232.5	232.9	232.4	232.4	233.8
2004	228.1	228.0	229.0	229.9	231.5	233.1	234.5	234.7	233.0	234.8	235.4	236.4	232.4
2005	232.0	232.1	232.9	234.9	235.7	237.0	238.1	237.6	236.2	235.9	236.6	237.4	235.5
2006	234.7	235.1	235.7	237.0	238.2	239.9	239.5	239.3	237.6	237.5	237.9	238.8	237.6
2007	236.5	236.1	237.1	237.7	239.1	240.3	240.2	239.6	237.8	238.0	237.9	238.5	238.2
2008	235.5	235.2	235.2	236.8	238.2	238.8	238.5	238.0	235.7	235.1	233.1	231.7	236.0
2009	226.8	224.6	223.3	221.7	221.1	220.7	220.2	219.0	217.0	216.9	216.6	216.7	220.4
2010	213.3	213.1	213.6	214.9	215.5	216.5	217.2	216.9	215.1	215.5	215.1	214.8	215.1
2011	212.7	213.1	213.8	216.3	217.7	218.7	217.7	218.0	217.9	219.0	220.9	222.1	217.3
Retail Trade													
2000	669.8	658.8	661.1	660.0	664.2	668.5	663.5	664.9	660.4	675.2	697.0	715.9	671.6
2001	665.9	651.0	652.6	652.8	656.8	660.4	648.7	647.5	645.4	651.5	673.3	684.4	657.5
2002	637.4	626.1	630.3	631.1	635.8	639.8	635.8	634.9	629.4	631.3	650.7	662.9	637.1
2003	618.8	609.4	612.3	619.4	623.8	626.1	622.5	624.4	622.5	629.8	646.2	657.5	626.1
2004	616.4	607.0	611.2	612.4	616.9	621.1	617.8	618.5	613.7	619.1	637.0	647.6	619.9
2005	607.0	598.8	603.4	608.7	613.0	613.0	609.7	608.7	604.3	607.2	624.6	637.6	611.3
2006	599.9	589.8	593.6	596.1	602.0	603.4	600.6	600.4	595.9	601.1	621.4	630.8	602.9
2007	594.7	583.3	590.4	592.8	601.0	602.6	601.2	598.7	595.2	599.2	619.1	627.5	600.5
2008	592.2	579.7	581.1	585.5	590.8	592.2	591.2	591.0	584.9	586.0	595.8	·603.5	589.5
2009	563.3	552.4	552.2	554.7	561.0	561.6	558.4	557.3	553.5	556.6	570.8	577.6	560.0
2010	543.0	534.9	539.1	544.4	550.4	552.7	552.0	552.5	547.4	555.9	571.2	579.1	551.9
2011	544.0	538.5	540.6	549.2	552.6	555.4	554.8	553.2	548.3	557.4	570.5	577.9	553.5
Transportation and Utilities													
2000	193.9	193.3	193.0	195.4	195.9	195.8	195.9	195.9	196.3	200.2	200.1	199.9	196.3
2001	192.3	190.9	190.8	193.0	193.1	192.6	191.6	191.7	191.2	192.1	191.1	189.5	191.7
2002	182.4	181.5	181.3	182.8	184.1	184.0	185.0	186.4	185.8	188.7	189.2	188.0	184.9
2003	182.2	180.8	180.4	182.1	183.5	183.2	182.6	183.6	184.2	188.4	188.6	188.7	184.0
2004	181.5	180.1	180.8	183.1	184.6	185.6	187.4	188.5	189.4	195.3	196.2	196.9	187.5
2005	189.2	189.5	190.9	191.4	192.6	193.1	195.0	196.0	198.0	201.4	205.1	207.4	195.8
2006	199.8	199.6	200.4	201.5	203.4	204.2	203.6	205.2	208.0	208.7	212.2	215.5	205.2
2007	207.4	205.4	206.3	208.3	210.4	211.9	211.1	212.8	214.2	216.0	219.6	222.0	212.1
2008	211.0	209.5	209.2	209.8	210.9	209.2	206.9	208.2	207.7	206.9	206.6	205.8	208.5
2009	195.5	193.0	190.8	187.1	186.5	185.4	184.2	183.8	182.8	183.8	184.2	185.0	186.8
2010	178.1	176.6	177.1	178.3	180.0	181.0	179.9	180.8	181.5	183.0	184.4	186.9	180.6
2011	180.0	179.7	180.0	181.9	183.0	183.5	181.9	182.7	183.5	183.9	186.1	187.3	182.8
Information													
2000	106.7	106.8	107.6	106.4	106.6	107.7	107.1	107.6	106.8	107.2	107.8	108.5	107.2
2001	108.4	108.3	108.0	106.1	106.4	107.3	106.8	106.3	104.8	104.3	104.4	104.6	106.3
2002	103.5	102.5	102.2	101.9	101.7	101.9	101.3	100.8	99.5	98.4	99.1	99.2	101.0
2003	98.2	97.7	97.7	97.4	97.6	97.4	97.0	96.5	94.8	94.4	94.5	94.6	96.5
2004	93.4	93.0	92.9	92.4	92.6	93.3	92.9	92.3	90.8	90.5	91.5	91.1	92.2
2005	89.9	89.5	89.5	90.0	90.6	90.8	90.6	90.3	89.7	89.0	89.4	89.8	89.9
2006	88.8	88.6	88.7	88.3	88.6	88.9	88.8	88.6	87.8	87.5	87.8	88.0	88.4
2007	87.3	87.4	87.0	87.8	88.4	88.9	88.8	88.5	87.3	86.9	87.1	87.4	87.7
2008	86.3	86.2	86.1	86.4	86.4	86.4	86.5	86.4	84.8	84.5	84.9	84.8	85.8
2009	83.6	83.1	82.2	81.2	81.3	81.1	80.9	80.4	79.1	78.5	78.7	79.0	80.8
2010	78.5	78.1	77.9	77.4	77.6	77.5	77.9	77.9	77.0	76.8	77.1	77.2	77.6
2011	76.1	75.8	75.3	75.8	76.2	76.2	76.9	76.3	76.2	76.7	77.6	78.0	76.4

1. Employment by Industry: Ohio, Selected Years, 2000–2011—*Continued*

(Numbers in thousands, not seasonally adjusted)

Industry and year	January	February	March	April	May	June	July	August	September	October	November	December	Annual average
Financial Activities													
2000	304.2	304.1	304.5	304.7	305.2	307.4	305.9	305.9	304.6	303.2	305.3	307.7	305.2
2001	302.6	303.8	304.9	305.5	306.9	310.8	310.4	310.7	307.7	306.5	308.3	309.4	307.3
2002	305.6	306.9	307.5	306.4	307.5	309.6	310.7	310.3	307.9	308.0	309.6	311.1	308.4
2003	307.9	308.7	309.6	309.4	311.5	314.1	314.3	315.2	312.8	311.9	311.9	313.8	311.8
2004	309.8	310.5	311.3	310.4	311.1	313.5	313.5	313.3	309.6	308.8	308.8	309.9	310.9
2005	305.7	305.8	305.9	306.8	308.0	310.6	310.9	311.2	309.2	309.0	309.1	309.8	308.5
2006	305.6	305.5	306.3	306.1	306.5	307.9	307.3	306.1	304.2	304.5	304.1	303.5	305.6
2007	301.5	301.2	300.0	301.8	302.3	301.7	301.5	301.0	297.9	297.1	295.5	295.8	299.8
2008	292.1	291.6	291.3	291.4	292.1	292.5	291.7	291.2	288.3	287.4	286.9	286.8	290.3
2009	282.9	281.5	280.8	280.4	281.1	281.7	281.5	280.1	277.8	277.2	277.2	277.0	279.9
2010	274.4	273.9	273.6	274.9	275.8	277.3	278.9	278.8	277.1	278.2	278.6	279.3	276.7
2011	277.4	277.5	277.4	278.2	279.4	279.7	281.8	281.8	278.1	276.2	274.5	275.1	278.1
Professional and Business Services													
2000	618.5	622.4	630.9	642.7	645.4	655.2	653.3	657.6	656.0	654.1	653.0	649.5	644.9
2001	621.3	622.0	628.0	633.5	635.3	640.2	636.0	636.6	629.8	625.9	620.8	618.7	629.0
2002	596.8	597.0	603.2	610.5	613.8	618.9	621.4	626.3	625.4	627.1	625.2	621.5	615.6
2003	597.8	597.4	602.2	609.5	611.2	614.1	615.2	620.7	616.6	619.9	619.9	615.8	611.7
2004	600.5	601.1	608.6	620.0	622.0	631.1	634.0	639.7	640.2	641.9	640.4	638.8	626.5
2005	615.1	619.0	625.2	639.8	640.5	646.4	649.6	656.4	658.5	659.4	657.1	657.2	643.7
2006	633.4	636.0	642.2	653.4	654.9	663.6	661.2	668.9	666.4	666.0	664.3	664.4	656.4
2007	645.1	646.7	653.4	664.2	667.3	676.8	674.1	677.7	676.0	680.2	680.6	678.8	668.4
2008	660.5	662.1	661.9	673.3	674.0	677.2	678.2	680.1	674.1	668.9	660.4	652.6	668.6
2009	625.7	619.0	614.1	616.9	615.4	614.6	613.8	616.2	613.9	616.0	618.3	614.5	616.5
2010	596.2	598.1	603.0	621.6	622.6	630.1	634.4	639.3	636.6	642.4	643.6	641.9	625.8
2011	624.5	628.1	634.3	649.1	648.3	651.0	655.2	654.2	654.4	658.7	656.7	648.2	646.9
Education and Health Services													
2000	666.9	674.9	677.9	677.8	677.3	677.5	676.0	679.3	685.6	687.0	690.4	693.4	680.3
2001	680.1	690.2	691.7	696.2	693.5	688.6	680.3	683.6	695.4	706.7	710.5	711.2	694.0
2002	698.2	708.9	709.8	711.8	710.6	703.2	697.2	700.2	714.0	724.7	728.7	728.9	711.4
2003	719.1	725.2	727.2	730.1	726.9	719.6	717.7	719.9	734.4	743.8	746.9	747.2	729.8
2004	734.7	741.5	744.1	748.3	744.0	736.3	734.6	732.9	749.7	760.0	763.2	766.2	746.3
2005	748.6	757.1	760.2	763.3	759.8	753.3	748.7	750.2	768.6	775.8	780.0	781.4	762.3
2006	766.8	777.6	781.0	782.0	778.5	769.8	763.5	765.6	783.1	789.3	792.3	792.1	778.5
2007	779.9	785.2	789.5	792.5	791.6	785.0	780.7	783.9	801.7	809.2	814.0	814.1	793.9
2008	803.9	811.5	812.6	815.1	813.3	803.7	799.2	802.1	818.9	826.5	829.9	829.9	813.9
2009	818.6	825.7	827.3	829.5	826.8	817.0	815.4	817.0	832.6	841.7	844.5	844.4	828.4
2010	833.6	839.1	842.4	843.2	839.1	827.2	826.6	828.0	845.1	853.7	856.0	853.6	840.6
2011	841.5	849.7	850.6	854.5	851.3	838.3	832.9	838.2	853.1	861.9	865.6	863.8	850.1
Leisure and Hospitality													
2000	446.7	448.7	460.8	476.8	496.8	512.9	515.2	515.4	499.6	482.1	473.4	471.3	483.3
2001	443.8	447.6	458.5	474.7	498.0	514.6	515.4	516.6	495.2	478.5	469.0	467.3	481.6
2002	448.2	449.9	461.1	477.9	502.0	516.7	519.4	518.4	502.5	484.5	473.9	471.2	485.5
2003	449.1	447.1	456.7	480.5	504.2	519.3	523.1	524.7	506.0	490.3	479.5	479.3	488.3
2004	457.4	457.8	470.1	489.8	512.1	524.4	527.0	529.2	513.9	496.3	487.9	484.0	495.8
2005	460.6	463.2	475.1	498.4	517.5	531.8	531.7	532.0	517.8	496.6	488.7	483.7	499.8
2006	463.8	467.4	479.5	496.2	517.2	533.9	531.9	532.6	514.9	497.6	489.1	486.8	500.9
2007	468.3	466.4	478.4	495.9	519.4	535.5	529.3	530.9	512.5	498.5	487.6	483.9	500.6
2008	462.6	463.3	467.8	491.8	516.6	527.1	522.3	522.2	503.7	485.8	471.1	469.6	492.0
2009	445.5	445.2	455.9	474.4	497.9	509.7	507.8	505.4	491.8	472.8	458.9	457.0	476.9
2010	436.7	437.3	448.5	472.0	492.3	505.5	506.7	506.1	492.6	476.8	466.2	462.4	475.3
2011	442.6	444.6	455.6	479.2	500.9	514.2	511.0	507.2	486.8	472.5	460.5	457.6	477.7
Other Services													
2000	218.9	221.0	223.1	223.2	224.4	225.4	224.3	224.2	223.7	223.5	223.5	223.8	223.3
2001	223.1	224.3	225.8	227.8	229.8	231.0	229.6	231.3	228.0	228.7	229.0	229.2	228.1
2002	225.6	226.6	228.5	228.5	230.2	231.7	229.9	230.6	227.9	227.8	227.5	228.1	228.6
2003	224.7	225.1	227.2	227.7	229.0	229.5	228.8	228.7	226.0	226.8	225.5	225.9	227.1
2004	222.7	223.6	226.4	227.5	228.9	230.1	229.6	228.7	226.6	227.2	226.4	225.0	226.9
2005	221.1	222.3	224.1	225.7	226.5	227.5	226.3	226.0	223.7	223.6	223.9	223.3	224.5
2006	219.9	220.4	222.1	222.7	224.2	226.9	224.5	223.6	222.2	222.0	221.5	222.2	222.7
2007	219.3	219.4	221.9	222.2	223.4	226.0	224.1	223.4	220.6	221.3	220.8	220.8	221.9
2008	217.7	218.3	218.8	220.2	221.9	223.0	221.9	221.4	219.1	219.1	217.4	216.7	219.6
2009	212.4	212.7	213.6	213.8	215.0	215.2	214.6	213.0	211.1	211.1	209.9	210.4	212.7
2010	207.5	206.8	208.7	210.7	210.9	212.6	213.1	212.0	210.3	210.7	209.9	210.1	210.3
2011	207.1	207.3	208.2	210.1	211.4	212.5	211.4	212.9	209.1	210.0	209.5	211.2	210.1
Government													
2000	775.2	790.6	795.4	796.2	812.1	783.6	744.5	736.7	777.4	799.5	805.2	804.2	785.1
2001	786.3	803.5	808.0	805.8	808.1	789.4	748.3	745.3	788.4	811.0	817.2	817.2	794.0
2002	794.8	813.2	817.5	813.9	816.7	795.0	758.6	752.6	791.8	812.1	819.2	817.4	800.2
2003	798.3	813.1	817.6	816.8	820.3	798.1	763.8	756.9	792.7	814.0	819.2	820.4	802.6
2004	795.3	815.3	820.3	817.9	820.2	800.3	762.3	756.6	789.8	812.4	816.1	814.3	801.7
2005	792.3	812.4	814.4	812.6	818.7	794.8	759.1	756.2	791.4	812.7	817.8	813.2	799.6
2006	795.5	811.0	814.1	812.1	818.8	796.4	759.0	756.9	792.7	812.9	817.0	814.3	800.1
2007	793.8	807.7	811.3	810.7	814.4	796.1	756.9	755.1	789.3	809.3	813.3	806.7	797.1
2008	792.8	810.7	809.0	809.9	814.7	792.2	754.3	753.0	787.5	809.9	814.7	805.9	796.2
2009	790.2	805.1	805.4	807.7	808.7	784.9	745.0	741.7	778.2	799.1	800.5	791.1	788.1
2010	778.5	790.7	793.0	797.2	814.8	782.9	737.4	731.6	765.3	789.3	792.6	788.6	780.2
2011	764.9	779.4	781.9	782.2	781.8	758.7	724.8	722.9	759.7	777.6	782.0	778.6	766.2

2. Average Weekly Hours by Selected Industry: Ohio, 2007–2011

(Not seasonally adjusted)

Industry and year	January	February	March	April	May	June	July	August	September	October	November	December	Annual average
Total Private													
2007	33.5	32.9	33.9	34.2	34.0	34.2	34.3	34.2	34.4	34.1	33.9	33.9	33.9
2008	33.6	33.7	34.0	34.0	34.0	34.3	34.0	34.2	34.0	34.0	34.0	33.4	33.9
2009	32.5	33.0	32.9	32.5	32.8	32.9	32.9	33.3	33.0	33.0	33.5	33.2	33.0
2010	33.1	32.9	33.4	33.5	33.5	33.4	33.5	33.8	33.4	33.8	33.7	33.5	33.5
2011	33.4	33.4	33.4	33.7	33.9	33.7	33.6	33.7	33.8	34.3	34.0	33.9	33.7
Goods-Producing													
2007	38.6	36.7	39.3	39.0	39.4	39.7	39.1	39.3	39.9	39.8	39.7	39.6	39.2
2008	38.8	39.1	39.7	39.6	39.7	39.8	39.0	40.2	40.1	39.7	39.3	38.9	39.5
2009	36.2	36.7	36.5	36.5	37.2	37.7	37.5	38.2	37.6	37.9	38.5	38.8	37.4
2010	38.8	38.7	39.4	39.8	39.8	40.0	39.5	40.1	39.6	40.4	40.3	39.8	39.7
2011	39.3	39.7	39.7	39.9	39.9	39.9	39.7	40.5	40.3	40.4	40.6	40.5	40.0
Construction													
2007	36.8	35.3	37.5	37.1	38.8	39.5	38.9	39.0	39.0	38.5	37.8	36.5	38.0
2008	36.9	36.8	36.5	36.1	36.1	37.1	37.1	37.6	37.7	38.3	37.3	36.8	37.0
2009	35.3	36.3	35.8	35.1	36.5	37.3	38.0	38.8	38.3	37.7	38.1	37.5	37.1
2010	37.2	37.1	37.2	37.8	37.2	37.7	37.8	38.4	37.6	38.8	38.5	37.6	37.8
2011	37.4	37.6	37.2	38.1	38.4	39.1	40.1	40.4	40.0	39.1	39.8	38.4	38.9
Manufacturing													
2007	39.1	37.0	39.8	39.6	39.7	39.8	39.2	39.0	40.7	40.5	40.4	40.5	39.6
2008	39.4	39.7	40.3	40.5	40.6	40.5	39.4	40.5	40.4	40.1	39.9	39.5	40.1
2009	37.6	37.7	37.8	37.9	38.1	38.4	37.9	38.9	38.5	38.8	39.2	39.6	38.4
2010	39.5	39.5	39.8	40.1	40.5	40.4	39.7	40.3	40.0	40.8	40.7	40.3	40.1
2011	39.5	40.0	40.0	40.1	40.1	40.0	39.4	40.4	40.2	40.6	40.6	40.8	40.1
Trade, Transportation, and Utilities													
2007	33.1	32.7	33.3	34.1	34.0	34.1	34.0	33.7	34.1	34.1	33.7	32.8	33.6
2008	33.2	33.1	33.1	33.3	33.4	33.8	33.6	33.8	33.7	34.0	33.7	33.4	33.5
2009	33.1	33.5	33.3	33.1	33.6	33.7	33.6	33.9	33.9	33.6	33.6	33.6	33.5
2010	33.3	33.5	33.8	33.6	33.9	33.9	34.3	34.6	34.6	34.7	34.5	35.0	34.1
2011	34.6	34.1	34.2	34.6	34.8	34.7	34.6	34.3	34.8	35.3	34.6	35.0	34.6
Financial Activities													
2007	36.6	36.2	36.4	36.8	36.0	36.3	37.6	37.2	37.8	36.9	36.8	37.7	36.9
2008	36.8	36.9	37.6	37.0	36.6	36.9	36.1	36.6	35.9	36.6	37.6	36.8	36.8
2009	36.8	37.3	36.7	36.1	36.4	36.5	36.1	36.7	36.4	36.1	36.9	36.5	36.5
2010	36.2	36.2	36.1	36.4	36.5	36.2	35.8	36.7	36.5	36.7	36.7	36.5	36.4
2011	37.1	36.0	36.1	36.6	37.7	37.1	36.8	36.6	36.9	37.5	36.8	36.9	36.8
Professional and Business Services													
2007	34.9	35.1	35.6	36.3	36.2	35.9	36.1	35.6	35.8	35.6	35.4	35.4	35.7
2008	35.1	35.1	35.9	35.8	35.6	35.9	35.7	35.6	35.6	35.8	35.9	34.8	35.6
2009	34.7	34.8	34.7	34.7	34.5	34.4	34.2	34.6	34.2	34.0	34.6	34.2	34.5
2010	34.4	34.3	34.6	34.8	35.0	34.7	35.0	35.3	34.6	35.2	34.8	34.8	34.8
2011	34.9	34.5	34.6	34.6	34.9	34.1	33.9	34.3	34.1	35.4	34.5	34.3	34.5
Education and Health Services													
2007	32.5	32.1	32.7	32.7	32.4	32.6	32.2	32.2	32.5	32.0	32.1	32.0	32.3
2008	31.8	32.4	32.4	32.3	32.4	32.6	32.6	32.6	32.6	32.5	32.8	32.7	32.5
2009	32.2	32.7	32.8	32.1	32.9	32.6	32.7	33.0	32.9	32.8	33.2	32.8	32.7
2010	32.6	32.3	32.6	32.5	32.2	32.0	32.2	32.1	32.1	32.3	32.3	32.2	32.3
2011	32.4	32.4	32.4	32.6	32.5	32.3	32.7	32.2	32.4	32.6	32.6	32.5	32.5
Leisure and Hospitality													
2007	22.8	22.5	23.3	23.5	23.4	24.5	24.7	24.6	24.3	24.3	23.5	23.3	23.8
2008	23.0	23.3	23.2	23.8	23.9	24.4	24.6	24.5	23.8	24.0	23.9	23.3	23.8
2009	22.3	22.4	22.5	22.2	22.8	23.3	23.6	23.6	23.3	23.2	23.4	23.6	23.0
2010	23.1	23.4	23.9	23.8	24.0	24.3	24.4	24.7	23.8	24.1	24.0	23.6	23.9
2011	22.8	23.5	23.6	23.9	23.8	24.1	24.0	23.9	23.6	24.0	23.9	23.6	23.7
Other Services													
2007	32.6	31.3	31.4	31.5	32.0	31.7	32.2	32.5	31.5	31.4	31.4	31.1	31.7
2008	31.6	31.9	31.8	31.7	32.0	31.5	31.8	31.6	31.5	31.6	32.1	31.7	31.7
2009	31.2	30.6	30.4	29.7	29.9	29.7	29.9	30.3	29.9	30.3	30.3	30.2	30.2
2010	30.4	30.2	30.4	30.2	30.4	29.7	29.6	29.9	29.8	29.9	30.8	30.3	30.1
2011	30.8	30.5	30.5	30.4	30.6	30.4	30.1	29.7	29.9	30.2	29.8	29.8	30.2

3. Average Hourly Earnings by Selected Industry: Ohio, 2007–2011

(Dollars, not seasonally adjusted)

Industry and year	January	February	March	April	May	June	July	August	September	October	November	December	Annual average
Total Private													
2007	20.08	20.51	20.24	20.39	19.96	19.99	20.06	20.07	20.30	20.29	20.35	20.39	20.22
2008	19.95	20.03	20.19	20.08	19.83	19.96	19.94	20.02	20.31	20.22	20.31	20.52	20.11
2009	20.02	20.01	19.95	19.98	19.85	19.76	19.73	19.74	19.95	20.03	20.11	20.24	19.95
2010	20.11	20.17	20.06	20.19	20.14	20.01	20.11	20.19	20.25	20.31	20.39	20.62	20.21
2011	20.85	20.94	20.83	20.85	21.03	20.77	20.93	21.11	21.31	21.44	21.38	21.40	21.07
Goods-Producing													
2007	22.50	23.39	23.32	22.94	22.81	22.72	22.94	22.64	22.79	22.84	22.87	22.90	22.88
2008	22.22	22.26	22.26	21.99	21.57	21.95	22.04	22.22	22.49	22.19	22.12	22.61	22.16
2009	21.80	22.11	21.92	21.93	21.86	21.82	21.80	21.47	21.65	21.54	21.67	21.56	21.76
2010	21.42	21.45	21.49	21.56	21.73	21.69	21.84	21.82	21.93	21.90	21.86	22.07	21.74
2011	22.19	22.43	22.65	22.81	22.85	22.91	22.99	23.21	23.58	23.51	23.57	23.90	23.07
Construction													
2007	23.23	23.87	23.13	23.29	23.52	23.53	23.49	23.57	23.92	24.23	24.40	24.56	23.73
2008	23.67	23.88	24.36	24.30	24.46	24.83	24.54	25.07	25.38	25.00	24.81	24.92	24.62
2009	24.64	24.88	24.93	24.78	25.19	24.91	24.70	24.68	24.79	24.90	25.00	25.12	24.87
2010	25.09	25.14	25.09	24.95	25.07	25.10	25.00	25.04	24.87	24.84	24.67	24.89	24.97
2011	24.95	25.09	25.57	25.14	25.02	25.16	25.10	25.42	25.64	25.61	25.81	26.07	25.39
Manufacturing													
2007	22.33	23.22	23.39	22.89	22.61	22.48	22.78	23.66	22.61	22.42	22.37	22.47	22.77
2008	21.84	21.85	21.74	21.95	21.44	21.74	21.83	22.17	22.36	22.31	22.23	22.31	21.98
2009	21.89	21.93	21.86	21.85	21.63	21.56	21.54	21.13	21.28	21.17	21.36	21.22	21.54
2010	21.16	21.16	21.15	21.26	21.36	21.19	21.37	21.32	21.47	21.40	21.46	22.13	21.37
2011	22.20	22.34	22.51	22.70	22.79	22.73	22.77	22.93	23.23	23.20	23.19	23.38	22.84
Trade, Transportation, and Utilities													
2007	17.37	17.80	17.48	17.81	17.43	17.67	17.66	17.77	17.88	17.93	17.81	17.97	17.72
2008	17.92	18.08	18.29	18.19	18.12	18.35	18.15	18.04	18.17	18.15	18.20	17.89	18.13
2009	18.30	18.46	18.49	18.40	18.41	18.34	18.48	18.56	18.50	18.44	18.46	18.29	18.43
2010	18.37	18.46	18.41	18.52	18.33	18.47	18.56	18.66	18.68	18.83	18.62	18.81	18.56
2011	19.00	19.02	18.91	18.38	18.52	18.55	19.00	19.03	19.09	19.09	19.01	18.69	18.86
Financial Activities													
2007	24.08	23.76	23.65	23.68	23.75	23.82	24.01	24.17	24.16	24.20	24.05	23.89	23.94
2008	24.27	24.14	24.40	24.62	24.62	24.30	24.04	24.10	24.00	23.77	23.72	23.84	24.15
2009	23.50	23.75	23.55	23.71	23.54	23.31	23.49	23.42	23.42	23.35	23.27	23.35	23.47
2010	23.25	24.33	24.38	24.41	24.48	24.35	24.34	24.31	24.35	24.54	24.74	24.99	24.38
2011	24.80	24.53	24.08	24.37	24.66	24.26	24.80	24.56	24.68	25.10	24.92	25.27	24.67
Professional and Business Services													
2007	23.90	23.96	23.55	24.06	24.07	24.23	24.35	23.78	24.04	23.66	23.79	23.89	23.94
2008	23.61	24.07	23.97	23.62	23.88	23.99	23.94	23.92	24.04	24.11	24.07	24.26	23.96
2009	24.42	24.07	24.08	23.92	23.60	23.67	23.61	23.72	23.56	23.78	23.89	24.00	23.86
2010	24.14	24.17	24.06	23.90	24.01	23.85	23.72	23.81	23.79	23.74	24.00	23.94	23.92
2011	24.20	24.11	23.74	24.35	24.33	24.04	24.24	24.02	24.23	24.83	24.69	24.60	24.29
Education and Health Services													
2007	18.91	18.67	18.48	18.69	18.77	18.89	18.69	18.50	18.73	18.83	18.78	18.83	18.73
2008	19.26	19.10	19.42	19.35	18.87	18.88	19.14	19.18	19.36	19.24	19.44	19.54	19.23
2009	19.47	19.41	19.67	19.89	20.19	20.25	20.06	20.03	20.23	20.34	20.29	20.44	20.03
2010	20.44	20.32	20.41	20.57	20.46	20.47	20.66	20.62	20.72	21.01	20.65	20.90	20.60
2011	21.11	21.32	21.30	21.33	21.71	21.23	21.14	21.34	21.34	21.51	21.51	21.47	21.36
Leisure and Hospitality													
2007	10.91	11.26	11.16	11.16	10.86	11.20	11.11	11.02	10.99	11.02	11.10	11.12	11.07
2008	11.21	11.12	11.09	11.01	11.12	10.97	10.85	10.92	11.11	11.01	11.03	10.99	11.03
2009	11.12	11.10	11.05	10.99	10.90	10.84	10.86	10.88	10.99	11.13	11.28	11.26	11.03
2010	11.32	11.30	11.20	11.30	11.21	11.16	11.00	10.94	11.13	11.15	11.87	11.96	11.29
2011	11.78	11.77	11.67	11.72	11.74	11.60	11.56	11.66	11.65	11.66	11.81	11.95	11.71
Other Services													
2007	15.37	15.31	15.30	15.40	15.62	16.04	16.15	16.28	16.16	16.23	16.33	16.38	15.88
2008	15.95	16.14	16.08	15.87	15.82	16.17	16.19	16.33	16.30	16.33	16.48	16.30	16.16
2009	16.32	16.39	16.19	15.86	15.72	15.79	15.63	16.29	16.35	16.17	16.19	16.22	16.09
2010	16.12	16.31	16.23	16.30	16.36	16.21	16.29	16.37	16.24	16.40	16.26	16.49	16.30
2011	16.83	17.03	17.17	17.01	17.42	17.38	17.64	17.76	17.97	17.91	18.03	18.41	17.54

4. Average Weekly Earnings by Selected Industry: Ohio, 2007–2011

(Dollars, not seasonally adjusted)

Industry and year	January	February	March	April	May	June	July	August	September	October	November	December	Annual average
Total Private													
2007	672.68	674.78	686.14	697.34	678.64	683.66	688.06	686.39	698.32	691.89	689.87	691.22	686.37
2008	670.32	675.01	686.46	682.72	674.22	684.63	677.96	684.68	690.54	687.48	690.54	685.37	682.65
2009	650.65	660.33	656.36	649.35	651.08	650.10	649.12	657.34	658.35	660.99	673.69	671.97	657.39
2010	665.64	663.59	670.00	676.37	674.69	668.33	673.69	682.42	676.35	686.48	687.14	690.77	676.46
2011	696.39	699.40	695.72	702.65	712.92	699.95	703.25	711.41	720.28	735.39	726.92	725.46	710.70
Goods-Producing													
2007	868.50	858.41	916.48	894.66	898.71	901.98	896.95	889.75	909.32	909.03	907.94	906.84	896.65
2008	862.14	870.37	883.72	870.80	856.33	873.61	859.56	893.24	901.85	880.94	869.32	879.53	875.10
2009	789.16	811.44	800.08	800.45	813.19	822.61	817.50	820.15	814.04	816.37	834.30	836.53	814.44
2010	831.10	830.12	846.71	858.09	864.85	867.60	862.68	874.98	868.43	884.76	880.96	878.39	862.85
2011	872.07	890.47	899.21	910.12	911.72	914.11	912.70	940.01	950.27	949.80	956.94	967.95	923.57
Construction													
2007	854.86	842.61	867.38	864.06	912.58	929.44	913.76	919.23	932.88	932.86	922.32	896.44	901.01
2008	873.42	878.78	889.14	877.23	883.01	921.19	910.43	942.63	956.83	957.50	925.41	917.06	912.15
2009	869.79	903.14	892.49	869.78	919.44	929.14	938.60	957.58	949.46	938.73	952.50	942.00	922.74
2010	933.35	932.69	933.35	943.11	932.60	946.27	945.00	961.54	935.11	963.79	949.80	935.86	943.29
2011	933.13	943.38	951.20	957.83	960.77	983.76	1,006.51	1,026.97	1,025.60	1,001.35	1,027.24	1,001.09	987.47
Manufacturing													
2007	873.10	859.14	930.92	906.44	897.62	894.70	892.98	922.74	920.23	908.01	903.75	910.04	901.62
2008	860.50	867.45	876.12	888.98	870.46	880.47	860.10	897.89	903.34	894.63	886.98	881.25	880.58
2009	823.06	826.76	826.31	828.12	824.10	827.90	816.37	821.96	819.28	821.40	837.31	840.31	826.07
2010	835.82	835.82	841.77	852.53	865.08	856.08	848.39	859.20	858.80	873.12	873.42	891.84	857.87
2011	876.90	893.60	900.40	910.27	913.88	909.20	897.14	926.37	933.85	941.92	941.51	953.90	916.82
Trade, Transportation, and Utilities													
2007	574.95	582.06	582.08	607.32	592.62	602.55	600.44	598.85	609.71	611.41	600.20	589.42	596.01
2008	594.94	598.45	605.40	605.73	605.21	620.23	609.84	609.75	612.33	617.10	613.34	597.53	607.49
2009	605.73	618.41	615.72	609.04	618.58	618.06	620.93	629.18	627.15	619.58	620.26	614.54	618.05
2010	611.72	618.41	622.26	622.27	621.39	626.13	636.61	645.64	646.33	653.40	642.39	658.35	633.92
2011	657.40	648.58	646.72	635.95	644.50	643.69	657.40	652.73	664.33	673.88	657.75	654.15	653.13
Financial Activities													
2007	881.33	860.11	860.86	871.42	855.00	864.67	902.78	899.12	913.25	892.98	885.04	900.65	882.19
2008	893.14	890.77	917.44	910.94	901.09	896.67	867.84	882.06	861.60	869.98	891.87	877.31	888.45
2009	864.80	885.88	864.29	855.93	856.86	850.82	847.99	859.51	852.49	842.94	858.66	852.28	857.77
2010	841.65	880.75	880.12	888.52	893.52	881.47	871.37	892.18	888.78	900.62	907.96	912.14	886.67
2011	920.08	883.08	869.29	891.94	929.68	900.05	912.64	898.90	910.69	941.25	917.06	932.46	908.84
Professional and Business Services													
2007	834.11	841.00	838.38	873.38	871.33	869.86	879.04	846.57	860.63	842.30	842.17	845.71	853.80
2008	828.71	844.86	860.52	845.60	850.13	861.24	854.66	851.55	855.82	863.14	864.11	844.25	852.08
2009	847.37	837.64	835.58	830.02	814.20	814.25	807.46	820.71	805.75	808.52	826.59	820.80	822.47
2010	830.42	829.03	832.48	831.72	840.35	827.60	830.20	840.49	823.13	835.65	835.20	833.11	832.48
2011	844.58	831.80	821.40	842.51	849.12	819.76	821.74	823.89	826.24	878.98	851.81	843.78	838.02
Education and Health Services													
2007	614.58	599.31	604.30	611.16	608.15	615.81	601.82	595.70	608.73	602.56	602.84	602.56	605.61
2008	612.47	618.84	629.21	625.01	611.39	615.49	623.96	625.27	631.14	625.30	637.63	638.96	624.63
2009	626.93	634.71	645.18	638.47	664.25	660.15	655.96	660.99	665.57	667.15	673.63	670.43	655.39
2010	666.34	656.34	665.37	668.53	658.81	655.04	665.25	661.90	665.11	678.62	667.00	672.98	665.17
2011	683.96	690.77	690.12	695.36	705.58	685.73	691.28	687.15	691.42	701.23	701.23	697.78	693.52
Leisure and Hospitality													
2007	248.75	253.35	260.03	262.26	254.12	274.40	274.42	271.09	267.06	267.79	260.85	259.10	263.07
2008	257.83	259.10	257.29	262.04	265.77	267.67	266.91	267.54	264.42	264.24	263.62	256.07	262.88
2009	247.98	248.64	248.63	243.98	248.52	252.57	256.30	256.77	256.07	258.22	263.95	265.74	253.96
2010	261.49	264.42	267.68	268.94	269.04	271.19	268.40	270.22	264.89	268.72	284.88	282.26	270.20
2011	268.58	276.60	275.41	280.11	279.41	279.56	277.44	278.67	274.94	279.84	282.26	282.02	277.97
Other Services													
2007	501.06	479.20	480.42	485.10	499.84	508.47	520.03	529.10	509.04	509.62	512.76	509.42	503.72
2008	504.02	514.87	511.34	503.08	506.24	509.36	514.84	516.03	513.45	516.03	529.01	516.71	512.89
2009	509.18	501.53	492.18	471.04	470.03	468.96	467.34	493.59	488.87	489.95	490.56	489.84	486.03
2010	490.05	492.56	493.39	492.26	497.34	481.44	482.18	489.46	483.95	490.36	500.81	499.65	491.14
2011	518.36	519.42	523.69	517.10	533.05	528.35	530.96	527.47	537.30	540.88	537.29	548.62	530.18

OKLAHOMA
At a Glance

Population:
    2000 census: 3,450,451
    2010 census: 3,751,351
    2011 estimate: 3,791,508

Percent change in population:
    2000–2010: 8.7%
    2010–2011: 1.1%

Percent change in total nonfarm employment:
    2000–2010: 3.6%
    2010–2011: 1.3%

Industry with the largest growth in employment, 2000–2011 (thousands):
    Government, 48.3

Industry with the largest decline or smallest growth in employment, 2000–2011 (thousands):
    Manufacturing, -47.9

Civilian labor force:
    2000: 1,661,045
    2010: 1,771,234
    2011: 1,770,822

Unemployment rate and rank among states (lowest to highest):
    2000: 3.1%, 12th
    2010: 6.9%, 7th
    2011: 6.2%, 8th

Over-the-year change in unemployment rates:
    2010–2011: -0.7%

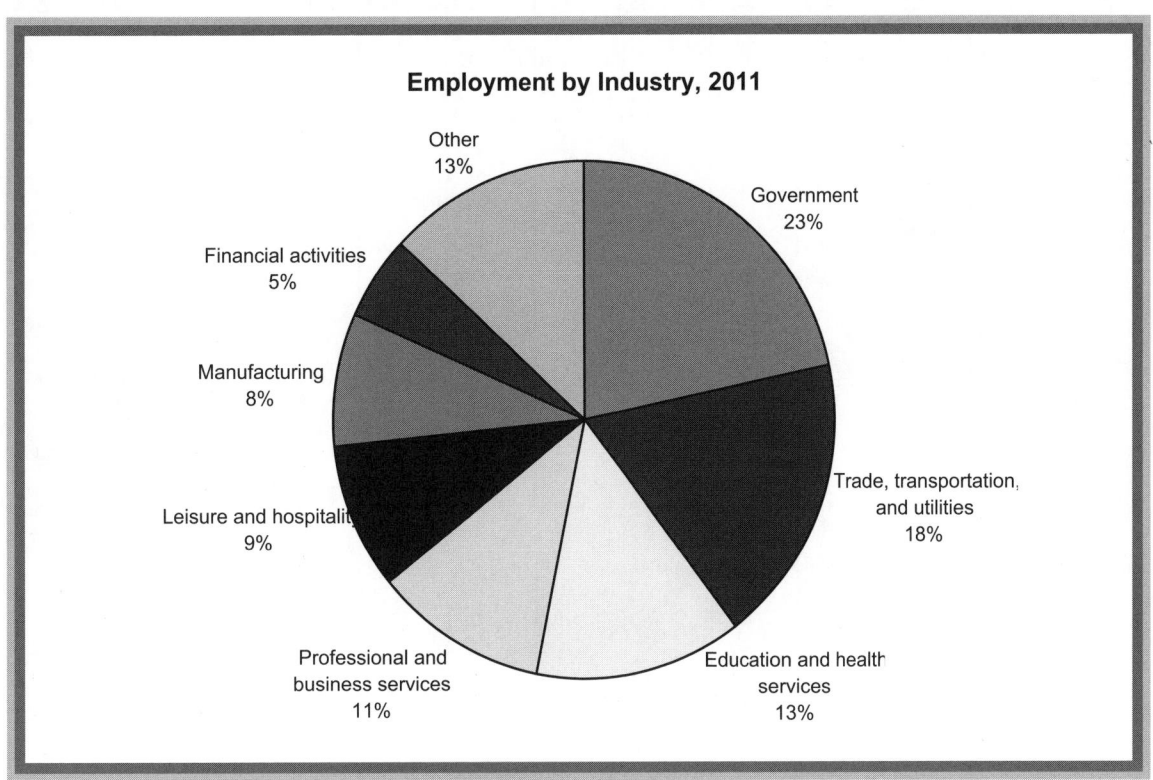

Employment by Industry, 2011

Other 13%
Financial activities 5%
Manufacturing 8%
Leisure and hospitality 9%
Professional and business services 11%
Education and health services 13%
Trade, transportation, and utilities 18%
Government 23%

1. Employment by Industry: Oklahoma, Selected Years, 2000–2011

(Numbers in thousands, not seasonally adjusted)

Industry and year	January	February	March	April	May	June	July	August	September	October	November	December	Annual average
Total Nonfarm													
2000	1,434.7	1,443.9	1,460.3	1,470.7	1,487.0	1,485.2	1,467.3	1,476.2	1,491.9	1,495.1	1,504.2	1,504.2	1,476.7
2001	1,467.5	1,480.1	1,493.8	1,503.2	1,512.3	1,507.0	1,481.0	1,488.9	1,499.2	1,492.9	1,501.9	1,498.5	1,493.9
2002	1,455.6	1,463.9	1,474.7	1,483.8	1,495.9	1,480.8	1,461.2	1,469.9	1,475.5	1,471.6	1,476.4	1,473.8	1,473.6
2003	1,435.2	1,439.2	1,442.6	1,448.2	1,457.5	1,440.4	1,429.2	1,435.7	1,448.0	1,453.3	1,456.4	1,457.7	1,445.3
2004	1,426.8	1,435.4	1,450.3	1,460.1	1,467.4	1,458.9	1,450.7	1,458.1	1,472.6	1,480.9	1,485.3	1,490.6	1,461.4
2005	1,452.6	1,467.0	1,483.9	1,497.8	1,506.5	1,500.3	1,486.3	1,497.6	1,514.3	1,520.0	1,531.1	1,536.5	1,499.5
2006	1,503.3	1,517.5	1,534.0	1,533.8	1,547.5	1,545.4	1,525.4	1,539.5	1,554.2	1,554.0	1,559.9	1,565.6	1,540.0
2007	1,528.8	1,543.8	1,565.0	1,563.3	1,574.2	1,573.2	1,553.3	1,569.2	1,582.2	1,588.2	1,596.7	1,592.2	1,569.2
2008	1,566.3	1,581.2	1,592.5	1,596.5	1,606.5	1,592.3	1,578.0	1,589.5	1,601.3	1,603.6	1,603.4	1,601.5	1,592.7
2009	1,555.6	1,556.5	1,559.3	1,554.2	1,554.1	1,542.4	1,524.9	1,524.9	1,531.8	1,532.2	1,533.8	1,532.1	1,541.8
2010	1,495.9	1,502.8	1,518.1	1,531.4	1,544.0	1,538.3	1,524.1	1,525.0	1,532.7	1,546.1	1,550.4	1,554.2	1,530.3
2011	1,516.1	1,515.7	1,539.2	1,554.2	1,557.2	1,551.5	1,536.8	1,542.5	1,562.6	1,573.2	1,577.9	1,577.0	1,550.3
Total Private													
2000	1,151.8	1,155.1	1,167.8	1,179.4	1,189.1	1,200.2	1,197.3	1,205.1	1,205.1	1,200.6	1,208.0	1,208.6	1,189.0
2001	1,175.5	1,181.6	1,193.4	1,203.1	1,209.4	1,217.4	1,203.2	1,208.3	1,201.3	1,188.5	1,194.8	1,192.6	1,197.4
2002	1,157.3	1,159.9	1,169.0	1,177.9	1,186.4	1,185.3	1,176.9	1,183.1	1,175.7	1,165.0	1,169.1	1,166.6	1,172.7
2003	1,140.1	1,138.1	1,141.8	1,148.0	1,155.3	1,151.3	1,150.7	1,156.1	1,152.4	1,151.7	1,153.9	1,154.5	1,149.5
2004	1,132.3	1,133.6	1,146.7	1,156.1	1,161.3	1,164.1	1,166.3	1,167.5	1,166.1	1,169.5	1,173.8	1,177.6	1,159.6
2005	1,147.4	1,154.4	1,169.1	1,181.3	1,187.5	1,193.5	1,193.5	1,199.0	1,199.9	1,198.1	1,207.8	1,213.2	1,187.1
2006	1,188.5	1,194.6	1,209.6	1,210.1	1,220.8	1,230.8	1,223.3	1,230.4	1,229.7	1,224.0	1,229.4	1,235.5	1,218.9
2007	1,206.8	1,215.1	1,234.5	1,234.2	1,243.1	1,253.9	1,249.4	1,257.9	1,253.6	1,255.1	1,262.5	1,259.8	1,243.8
2008	1,245.2	1,252.6	1,262.2	1,263.4	1,270.1	1,272.6	1,269.6	1,273.7	1,269.6	1,264.3	1,263.1	1,261.1	1,264.0
2009	1,223.9	1,217.9	1,217.7	1,210.5	1,208.3	1,209.9	1,199.3	1,195.8	1,189.9	1,183.2	1,184.4	1,183.5	1,202.0
2010	1,158.1	1,159.5	1,171.8	1,184.9	1,191.6	1,198.3	1,196.2	1,199.9	1,198.4	1,204.4	1,208.4	1,211.7	1,190.3
2011	1,183.3	1,178.0	1,199.5	1,213.6	1,216.6	1,221.9	1,220.3	1,221.7	1,222.2	1,230.0	1,233.5	1,231.4	1,214.3
Goods-Producing													
2000	260.4	260.7	263.2	262.6	264.7	267.6	267.7	269.1	267.9	266.0	266.7	268.5	265.4
2001	263.0	264.7	266.8	267.1	269.0	272.5	268.2	267.1	265.7	259.2	259.2	257.7	265.0
2002	246.6	246.3	246.7	245.8	248.1	248.7	247.1	246.8	243.7	241.2	240.1	239.6	245.1
2003	237.2	235.6	236.0	236.0	236.6	235.6	238.0	239.2	237.8	236.8	235.0	235.2	236.6
2004	231.8	230.9	233.9	234.8	236.9	237.5	241.0	240.8	240.2	241.3	240.5	242.2	237.7
2005	236.8	238.3	241.7	243.9	244.7	246.3	249.6	250.4	250.5	251.7	252.8	255.9	246.9
2006	253.8	255.4	258.7	256.7	259.7	263.8	263.3	265.6	265.0	264.5	264.4	266.0	261.4
2007	260.7	261.2	265.1	264.9	266.9	271.4	272.0	273.9	271.8	273.4	275.1	274.6	269.3
2008	272.3	273.7	275.6	276.8	279.0	280.9	281.5	281.7	280.1	277.9	275.2	273.2	277.3
2009	263.8	258.3	253.7	246.5	243.2	242.1	238.3	235.4	232.4	229.9	228.3	227.7	241.6
2010	224.2	223.9	226.6	230.2	232.4	235.4	236.8	237.7	237.7	240.8	240.7	242.6	234.1
2011	237.8	237.1	242.2	245.9	246.9	250.7	250.2	250.5	253.3	255.4	254.5	255.8	248.4
Mining and Logging													
2000	26.5	26.6	26.6	25.5	26.0	26.3	27.2	27.4	27.5	27.3	27.6	28.6	26.9
2001	27.9	28.6	28.9	28.7	29.2	30.2	29.8	29.8	29.2	29.0	29.0	28.8	29.1
2002	28.1	28.1	28.1	28.2	28.7	29.0	28.9	28.9	28.3	27.9	27.8	27.9	28.3
2003	28.7	28.8	28.9	28.9	29.3	29.9	30.0	30.4	30.5	30.5	30.5	30.8	29.8
2004	30.8	30.9	31.3	31.6	32.1	32.8	32.9	33.0	32.9	33.5	33.9	34.4	32.5
2005	34.4	34.5	34.8	34.8	35.3	35.8	36.1	36.5	36.8	37.2	37.5	37.9	36.0
2006	38.4	39.2	40.0	40.7	41.3	42.4	42.5	43.5	43.6	43.4	43.9	44.5	42.0
2007	44.3	44.2	44.8	44.9	45.3	46.4	47.2	47.9	47.6	48.6	49.2	49.3	46.6
2008	49.6	49.9	50.2	50.5	51.4	52.5	52.9	53.5	53.3	53.8	53.3	52.7	52.0
2009	50.4	48.9	47.3	44.7	43.4	42.8	41.9	41.3	40.4	39.8	39.9	40.3	43.4
2010	40.5	40.6	41.3	42.2	42.8	43.9	44.4	45.0	45.1	46.0	46.1	47.1	43.8
2011	47.3	47.8	48.6	49.4	50.0	51.2	52.3	51.8	52.6	53.2	53.5	54.3	51.0
Construction													
2000	58.1	58.1	59.7	61.1	62.2	63.2	62.8	63.6	62.9	63.1	62.5	62.2	61.6
2001	60.6	62.5	65.0	66.3	67.6	69.4	68.9	69.5	67.6	66.3	65.1	64.4	66.1
2002	63.1	63.3	63.7	63.6	65.2	65.9	66.5	66.4	64.8	64.0	63.3	63.1	64.4
2003	62.0	61.3	61.8	63.7	64.6	65.9	65.9	65.7	64.3	63.6	62.1	62.3	63.6
2004	59.7	59.2	61.3	61.7	62.6	64.0	65.2	64.8	64.5	64.3	63.1	63.4	62.8
2005	61.1	61.4	63.6	65.5	65.3	66.9	68.1	68.1	68.0	68.1	68.0	68.8	66.1
2006	67.7	68.1	69.7	69.6	70.1	72.1	71.1	71.5	71.3	71.0	70.4	70.5	70.3
2007	67.5	67.7	70.2	70.0	70.7	73.0	72.4	73.5	72.4	72.8	73.3	72.2	71.3
2008	71.6	72.3	73.8	74.8	76.2	77.0	78.0	78.0	77.7	76.8	75.7	74.7	75.6
2009	71.4	70.7	70.7	69.4	69.3	70.4	69.8	69.0	68.0	67.0	65.9	65.2	68.9
2010	62.9	62.5	64.2	65.9	66.9	68.0	68.4	68.6	68.6	70.0	69.0	69.1	67.0
2011	65.1	63.7	66.8	68.3	68.2	69.6	69.3	69.1	70.7	71.4	69.2	68.6	68.3
Manufacturing													
2000	175.8	176.0	176.9	176.0	176.5	178.1	177.7	178.1	177.5	175.6	176.6	177.7	176.9
2001	174.5	173.6	172.9	172.1	172.2	172.9	169.5	167.8	168.9	163.9	165.1	164.5	169.8
2002	155.4	154.9	154.9	154.0	154.2	153.8	151.7	151.5	150.6	149.3	149.0	148.6	152.3
2003	146.5	145.5	145.3	143.4	142.7	139.8	142.1	143.1	143.0	142.7	142.4	142.1	143.2
2004	141.3	140.8	141.3	141.5	142.2	140.7	142.9	143.0	142.8	143.5	143.5	144.4	142.3
2005	141.3	142.4	143.3	143.6	144.1	143.6	145.4	145.8	145.7	146.4	147.3	149.2	144.8
2006	147.7	148.1	149.0	146.4	148.3	149.3	149.7	150.6	150.1	150.1	150.1	151.0	149.2
2007	148.9	149.3	150.1	150.0	150.9	152.0	152.4	152.5	151.8	152.0	152.6	153.1	151.3
2008	151.1	151.5	151.6	151.5	151.4	151.4	150.6	150.2	149.1	147.3	146.2	145.8	149.8
2009	142.0	138.7	135.7	132.4	130.5	128.9	126.6	125.1	124.0	123.1	122.5	122.2	129.3
2010	120.8	120.8	121.1	122.1	122.7	123.5	124.0	124.1	124.0	124.8	125.6	126.4	123.3
2011	125.4	125.6	126.8	128.2	128.7	129.9	128.6	129.6	130.0	130.8	131.8	132.9	129.0

1. Employment by Industry: Oklahoma, Selected Years, 2000–2011—*Continued*

(Numbers in thousands, not seasonally adjusted)

Industry and year	January	February	March	April	May	June	July	August	September	October	November	December	Annual average
Service-Providing													
2000	1,174.3	1,183.2	1,197.1	1,208.1	1,222.3	1,217.6	1,199.6	1,207.1	1,224.0	1,229.1	1,237.5	1,235.7	1,211.3
2001	1,204.5	1,215.4	1,227.0	1,236.1	1,243.3	1,234.5	1,212.8	1,221.8	1,233.5	1,233.7	1,242.7	1,240.8	1,228.8
2002	1,209.0	1,217.6	1,228.0	1,238.0	1,247.8	1,232.1	1,214.1	1,223.1	1,231.8	1,230.4	1,236.3	1,234.2	1,228.5
2003	1,198.0	1,203.6	1,206.6	1,212.2	1,220.9	1,204.8	1,191.2	1,196.5	1,210.2	1,216.5	1,221.4	1,222.5	1,208.7
2004	1,195.0	1,204.5	1,216.4	1,225.3	1,230.5	1,221.4	1,209.7	1,217.3	1,232.4	1,239.6	1,244.8	1,248.4	1,223.8
2005	1,215.8	1,228.7	1,242.2	1,253.9	1,261.8	1,254.0	1,236.7	1,247.2	1,263.8	1,268.3	1,278.3	1,280.6	1,252.6
2006	1,249.5	1,262.1	1,275.3	1,277.1	1,287.8	1,281.6	1,262.1	1,273.9	1,289.2	1,289.5	1,295.5	1,299.6	1,278.6
2007	1,268.1	1,282.6	1,299.9	1,298.4	1,307.3	1,301.8	1,281.3	1,295.3	1,310.4	1,314.8	1,321.6	1,317.6	1,299.9
2008	1,294.0	1,307.5	1,316.9	1,319.7	1,327.5	1,311.4	1,296.5	1,307.8	1,321.2	1,325.7	1,328.2	1,328.3	1,315.4
2009	1,291.8	1,298.2	1,305.6	1,307.7	1,310.9	1,300.3	1,286.6	1,289.5	1,299.4	1,302.3	1,305.5	1,304.4	1,300.2
2010	1,271.7	1,278.9	1,291.5	1,301.2	1,311.6	1,302.9	1,287.3	1,287.3	1,295.0	1,305.3	1,309.7	1,311.6	1,296.2
2011	1,278.3	1,278.6	1,297.0	1,308.3	1,310.3	1,300.8	1,286.6	1,292.0	1,309.3	1,317.8	1,323.4	1,321.2	1,302.0
Trade, Transportation, and Utilities													
2000	287.0	285.0	286.3	288.9	291.6	294.1	292.2	294.7	294.7	295.7	302.0	304.2	293.0
2001	290.7	287.7	289.2	289.8	291.1	292.2	287.9	288.5	286.5	286.7	291.2	293.0	289.5
2002	283.5	281.3	283.9	283.9	285.1	284.9	282.5	283.1	281.8	280.7	285.5	287.3	283.6
2003	275.9	273.8	274.9	275.4	277.0	276.1	274.6	276.0	275.2	277.0	281.5	284.5	276.8
2004	273.3	271.1	274.0	274.1	275.7	276.0	273.6	273.4	272.1	274.1	279.1	282.4	274.9
2005	272.1	271.8	274.3	276.7	278.1	278.5	279.0	280.3	280.5	282.3	287.6	290.6	279.3
2006	278.1	278.1	280.3	281.8	284.4	284.9	282.8	283.8	283.7	284.0	288.8	292.8	283.6
2007	282.8	282.6	288.3	285.2	287.3	288.2	286.7	287.3	286.4	287.8	293.1	294.1	287.5
2008	285.8	285.2	287.9	287.8	288.9	289.4	289.3	290.0	289.3	289.9	293.4	295.0	289.3
2009	284.2	282.2	282.7	282.3	282.8	282.5	279.9	279.4	278.5	277.8	281.2	282.5	281.3
2010	272.8	271.3	274.0	275.4	277.3	278.5	277.9	277.8	275.8	278.3	282.9	285.2	277.3
2011	275.8	274.2	278.4	280.7	281.4	281.8	281.7	280.2	278.4	282.5	288.2	289.9	281.1
Wholesale Trade													
2000	55.7	55.8	56.2	56.2	56.5	58.1	57.0	57.5	57.4	57.3	57.3	57.4	56.9
2001	56.0	55.9	56.4	56.6	56.9	57.7	57.0	57.1	56.9	56.8	56.7	57.0	56.8
2002	56.4	56.1	56.5	56.2	56.6	57.0	56.8	56.9	56.6	56.0	56.1	56.1	56.4
2003	54.9	54.5	54.9	54.6	55.0	55.3	54.6	54.5	54.6	54.9	54.6	54.7	54.8
2004	54.1	53.7	53.9	54.0	54.7	55.3	55.1	55.1	54.8	55.2	55.4	55.7	54.8
2005	54.9	55.1	55.5	56.0	56.3	56.9	57.1	57.2	57.0	57.3	57.4	57.7	56.5
2006	57.2	57.6	58.0	57.8	58.4	58.9	58.7	58.8	58.8	58.6	58.7	58.9	58.4
2007	58.4	58.6	59.4	59.3	59.5	60.3	59.5	59.2	59.0	59.6	59.7	59.7	59.4
2008	59.2	59.1	59.3	59.2	59.5	59.9	59.6	59.3	59.1	59.1	59.1	58.9	59.3
2009	58.0	57.8	57.5	57.1	56.6	56.5	56.0	55.4	55.0	55.0	54.7	54.7	56.2
2010	54.2	54.2	54.6	55.1	55.6	56.1	55.9	55.8	55.9	56.6	56.8	56.8	55.6
2011	56.2	56.4	57.3	57.5	57.7	58.0	58.4	58.2	58.4	59.7	60.2	60.6	58.2
Retail Trade													
2000	174.8	172.9	173.8	175.4	177.5	177.9	177.3	179.1	179.5	180.3	186.6	188.7	178.7
2001	176.2	173.6	174.5	174.6	175.5	175.9	172.8	173.4	172.5	173.2	177.9	179.8	175.0
2002	172.0	170.2	172.2	172.5	173.2	172.5	170.2	170.9	170.1	169.7	174.7	176.9	172.1
2003	167.6	165.8	166.6	167.9	169.1	168.5	167.8	169.1	168.7	170.0	174.8	177.6	169.5
2004	167.6	165.9	168.2	168.7	169.4	168.8	166.5	166.3	165.3	166.7	171.5	173.9	168.2
2005	165.5	164.9	166.7	168.1	169.0	168.5	168.6	169.5	170.0	171.6	176.4	178.5	169.8
2006	167.6	167.2	168.7	169.7	171.1	170.8	168.9	169.3	168.8	169.1	173.5	176.3	170.1
2007	167.8	167.1	171.7	169.5	170.1	170.7	169.9	170.9	170.5	171.6	176.7	177.3	171.2
2008	170.7	170.3	172.6	172.1	172.5	172.3	172.3	173.1	172.5	172.9	176.4	177.7	173.0
2009	169.8	168.4	169.4	169.3	170.6	170.4	168.9	169.4	169.2	168.3	171.9	172.8	169.9
2010	166.0	164.5	166.7	167.4	168.7	169.3	168.9	169.0	166.8	168.7	172.9	174.3	168.6
2011	167.2	165.3	168.2	169.9	170.2	169.8	169.7	168.6	166.7	169.1	174.5	175.0	169.5
Transportation and Utilities													
2000	56.5	56.3	56.3	57.3	57.6	58.1	57.9	58.1	57.8	58.1	58.1	58.1	57.5
2001	58.5	58.2	58.3	58.6	58.7	58.6	58.1	58.0	57.1	56.7	56.6	56.2	57.8
2002	55.1	55.0	55.2	55.2	55.3	55.4	55.5	55.3	55.1	55.0	54.7	54.3	55.1
2003	53.4	53.5	53.4	52.9	52.9	52.3	52.2	52.4	51.9	52.1	52.1	52.2	52.6
2004	51.6	51.5	51.9	51.4	51.6	51.9	52.0	52.0	52.0	52.2	52.2	52.8	51.9
2005	51.7	51.8	52.1	52.6	52.8	53.1	53.3	53.6	53.5	53.4	53.8	54.4	53.0
2006	53.3	53.3	53.6	54.3	54.9	55.2	55.2	55.7	56.1	56.3	56.6	57.6	55.2
2007	56.6	56.9	57.2	56.4	56.8	57.2	57.3	57.2	56.9	56.6	56.7	57.1	56.9
2008	55.9	55.8	56.0	56.5	56.9	57.2	57.4	57.6	57.7	57.9	57.9	58.4	57.1
2009	56.4	56.0	55.8	55.9	55.6	55.6	55.0	54.6	54.3	54.5	54.6	55.0	55.3
2010	52.6	52.6	52.7	52.9	53.0	53.1	53.1	53.0	53.1	53.0	53.2	54.1	53.0
2011	52.4	52.5	52.9	53.3	53.5	54.0	53.6	53.4	53.3	53.7	53.5	54.3	53.4
Information													
2000	33.9	34.4	34.5	34.8	35.0	35.6	36.0	36.2	36.6	36.1	36.5	36.7	35.5
2001	36.7	37.0	36.5	36.9	36.7	36.4	36.6	37.4	37.5	37.5	38.0	37.8	37.1
2002	36.8	36.9	36.4	35.6	35.4	35.1	35.0	34.9	34.5	34.3	34.4	34.0	35.3
2003	33.5	33.2	32.9	32.7	32.8	32.4	32.0	31.6	31.3	31.7	31.9	32.2	32.4
2004	31.6	31.6	31.4	31.2	31.1	31.4	31.4	30.9	30.1	30.5	30.4	30.5	31.0
2005	30.2	30.4	30.1	30.4	30.4	30.4	30.5	30.2	29.9	29.8	30.0	30.3	30.2
2006	30.0	30.0	30.0	29.7	29.8	29.8	29.9	29.8	29.6	29.3	29.3	30.2	29.8
2007	29.2	29.0	28.6	28.6	28.8	28.8	28.8	28.8	28.6	28.8	28.9	29.0	28.8
2008	28.7	28.9	28.8	29.0	29.1	29.0	29.1	28.8	28.4	28.2	28.2	28.2	28.7
2009	27.8	27.8	27.7	27.5	27.4	27.2	27.1	26.7	26.1	25.9	25.9	25.9	26.9
2010	25.5	25.2	25.0	25.2	25.2	25.0	25.1	24.7	24.6	24.4	24.6	24.6	24.9
2011	24.3	24.1	24.0	24.1	24.2	24.2	23.9	24.0	24.8	24.2	24.3	24.0	24.2

1. Employment by Industry: Oklahoma, Selected Years, 2000–2011—*Continued*

(Numbers in thousands, not seasonally adjusted)

Industry and year	January	February	March	April	May	June	July	August	September	October	November	December	Annual average
Financial Activities													
2000	80.1	80.3	80.4	81.0	81.6	82.7	81.8	82.2	81.9	81.6	81.5	82.0	81.4
2001	80.8	81.2	81.7	82.3	82.8	83.6	83.3	83.7	83.1	82.7	82.6	82.6	82.5
2002	82.9	82.6	82.6	82.7	83.3	84.0	83.8	83.8	82.9	82.4	82.5	82.5	83.0
2003	81.6	81.7	82.0	82.7	83.2	83.8	83.7	84.0	83.6	83.8	83.8	84.0	83.2
2004	83.1	83.3	83.9	84.1	84.1	84.7	84.2	84.2	83.6	83.7	83.7	84.0	83.9
2005	82.3	82.4	82.8	82.4	83.0	83.7	83.8	83.8	83.4	82.8	83.0	84.0	83.1
2006	83.5	83.5	84.0	83.0	83.5	84.0	83.4	83.5	83.1	82.9	82.9	83.0	83.4
2007	82.8	83.3	83.5	82.4	82.6	83.1	83.0	83.1	82.7	82.9	82.9	83.0	82.9
2008	83.0	83.0	83.1	83.1	83.4	83.5	83.8	83.3	83.0	82.8	82.8	83.2	83.2
2009	81.7	81.4	81.5	81.8	82.0	82.2	82.0	81.7	81.1	80.7	80.6	80.9	81.5
2010	79.8	79.8	79.9	79.9	80.2	80.5	80.1	80.0	79.5	79.6	79.6	80.0	79.9
2011	78.7	78.5	79.1	79.3	79.5	79.8	80.4	80.6	79.9	79.9	79.6	79.4	79.6
Professional and Business Services													
2000	154.9	156.0	159.6	162.8	164.3	166.3	167.0	168.7	168.3	168.2	168.3	167.1	164.3
2001	160.8	163.1	166.0	168.7	169.1	171.1	168.2	168.9	167.1	163.9	164.0	163.6	166.2
2002	156.5	158.3	160.7	163.9	165.6	165.1	162.2	164.2	163.5	161.4	160.7	160.5	161.9
2003	154.3	154.8	154.8	156.6	158.1	157.9	158.3	158.8	159.0	158.5	158.3	157.7	157.3
2004	154.2	155.8	157.0	161.3	161.3	162.5	165.0	165.8	166.3	167.9	168.4	168.1	162.8
2005	162.2	164.9	166.9	169.7	170.1	171.6	171.2	173.2	174.4	172.7	174.6	173.8	170.4
2006	170.1	172.1	174.8	174.7	175.8	178.0	176.5	178.4	178.9	176.5	177.3	176.6	175.8
2007	173.6	176.4	179.7	180.3	181.3	182.9	182.0	184.9	184.6	184.2	184.6	184.2	181.6
2008	181.6	183.9	184.8	185.0	184.8	184.9	183.2	184.8	184.2	182.7	181.4	179.3	183.4
2009	171.0	171.1	170.0	168.0	166.7	167.7	166.1	166.2	166.2	166.8	166.8	167.1	167.8
2010	162.9	164.3	166.0	168.5	168.9	170.8	172.1	173.0	172.9	174.3	173.9	173.2	170.1
2011	168.7	167.8	171.0	173.1	172.7	173.0	174.6	174.7	174.7	176.1	174.7	173.9	172.9
Education and Health Services													
2000	157.2	159.2	160.1	162.2	162.6	162.2	162.2	163.0	165.0	164.2	166.2	165.4	162.5
2001	163.2	164.8	165.9	167.1	166.9	165.4	164.8	167.2	169.1	169.1	171.1	170.9	167.1
2002	169.2	170.8	171.1	173.1	172.6	171.2	171.6	174.8	176.3	175.3	178.4	177.3	173.5
2003	175.2	175.9	175.7	176.3	175.9	173.6	173.3	174.7	176.4	175.8	177.4	175.7	175.5
2004	176.7	177.9	178.8	180.2	179.1	177.1	177.6	178.3	180.5	180.9	181.8	181.4	179.2
2005	178.6	179.4	181.1	183.0	183.5	183.4	182.6	184.2	186.0	185.7	187.4	187.7	183.6
2006	184.0	184.7	186.3	186.8	187.7	188.3	186.4	187.7	189.6	189.3	190.6	190.3	187.6
2007	186.8	188.6	190.0	192.5	193.0	193.7	192.3	194.0	195.2	196.3	196.4	195.9	192.9
2008	194.4	196.6	197.2	197.7	198.3	196.5	195.8	197.5	198.4	198.9	199.7	199.7	197.6
2009	198.2	198.5	199.4	200.1	200.6	201.2	201.3	202.2	203.1	203.4	203.9	203.7	201.3
2010	201.7	202.4	203.2	204.5	204.5	203.8	202.6	203.9	205.3	206.8	207.2	207.3	204.4
2011	203.3	202.4	204.3	205.1	205.4	204.6	204.4	206.2	208.3	209.6	210.9	210.2	206.2
Leisure and Hospitality													
2000	119.1	120.2	123.7	126.2	128.0	129.4	128.8	129.6	128.8	127.4	125.4	122.8	125.8
2001	119.2	121.4	124.6	129.3	131.3	132.6	131.0	132.0	129.3	126.5	125.9	124.3	127.3
2002	120.2	121.8	125.2	128.1	131.3	131.1	130.2	131.3	129.4	127.4	125.4	123.5	127.1
2003	120.9	121.4	123.8	127.6	130.5	130.1	129.4	130.6	128.3	127.6	125.7	124.5	126.7
2004	121.5	122.6	126.5	129.1	131.5	132.6	131.9	132.8	132.5	130.6	129.4	128.3	129.1
2005	124.9	126.5	130.9	134.2	136.5	138.0	135.1	135.6	134.1	132.1	131.4	129.9	132.4
2006	128.7	130.2	134.3	136.2	138.0	139.2	138.7	139.4	137.8	135.6	134.1	134.4	135.6
2007	129.4	131.9	136.6	137.2	139.8	141.3	140.8	142.1	140.6	138.7	138.5	136.3	137.8
2008	136.8	138.2	141.3	140.2	142.7	144.2	142.9	143.6	142.7	140.3	139.4	139.7	141.0
2009	135.3	136.7	140.5	142.4	143.5	144.6	142.6	142.7	141.2	137.9	136.9	135.3	140.0
2010	131.4	132.7	136.7	140.5	142.1	142.8	141.0	142.0	141.9	139.6	139.0	138.4	139.0
2011	135.2	134.5	140.4	144.7	145.8	146.5	145.2	145.6	143.0	143.0	142.4	139.5	142.2
Other Services													
2000	59.2	59.3	60.0	60.9	61.3	62.3	61.6	61.6	61.9	61.4	61.4	61.9	61.1
2001	61.1	61.7	62.7	61.9	62.5	63.6	63.2	63.5	63.0	62.9	62.8	62.7	62.6
2002	61.6	61.9	62.4	64.8	65.0	65.2	64.5	64.2	63.6	62.3	62.1	61.9	63.3
2003	61.5	61.7	61.7	60.7	61.2	61.8	61.4	61.2	60.8	60.5	60.3	60.7	61.1
2004	60.1	60.4	61.2	61.3	61.6	62.3	61.6	61.3	60.8	60.5	60.5	60.7	61.0
2005	60.3	60.7	61.3	61.0	61.2	61.6	61.7	61.3	61.1	61.0	61.0	61.0	61.1
2006	60.3	60.6	61.2	61.2	61.9	62.8	62.3	62.2	62.0	61.9	62.0	62.2	61.7
2007	61.5	62.1	62.7	63.1	63.4	64.5	63.8	63.8	63.7	63.0	63.0	62.7	63.1
2008	62.6	63.1	63.5	63.8	63.9	64.2	64.0	64.0	63.5	63.6	63.0	62.8	63.5
2009	61.9	61.9	62.2	61.9	62.1	62.4	62.0	61.5	61.3	60.8	60.8	60.4	61.6
2010	59.8	59.9	60.4	60.7	61.0	61.5	60.6	60.8	60.7	60.6	60.5	60.4	60.6
2011	59.5	59.4	60.1	60.7	60.7	61.3	59.9	59.9	59.8	59.3	58.9	58.7	59.9
Government													
2000	282.9	288.8	292.5	291.3	297.9	285.0	270.0	271.1	286.8	294.5	296.2	295.6	287.7
2001	292.0	298.5	300.4	300.1	302.9	289.6	277.8	280.6	297.9	304.4	307.1	305.9	296.4
2002	298.3	304.0	305.7	305.9	309.5	295.5	284.3	286.8	299.8	306.6	307.3	307.2	300.9
2003	295.1	301.1	300.8	300.2	302.2	289.1	278.5	279.6	295.6	301.6	302.5	303.2	295.8
2004	294.5	301.8	303.6	304.0	306.1	294.8	284.4	290.6	306.5	311.4	311.5	313.0	301.9
2005	305.2	312.6	314.8	316.5	319.0	306.8	292.8	298.6	314.4	321.9	323.3	323.3	312.4
2006	314.8	322.9	324.4	323.7	326.7	314.6	302.1	309.1	324.5	330.0	330.5	330.1	321.1
2007	322.0	328.7	330.5	329.1	331.1	319.3	303.9	311.3	328.6	333.1	334.2	332.4	325.4
2008	321.1	328.6	330.3	333.1	336.4	319.7	308.4	315.8	331.7	339.3	340.3	340.4	328.8
2009	331.7	338.6	341.6	343.7	345.8	332.5	325.6	329.1	341.9	349.0	349.4	348.6	339.8
2010	337.8	343.3	346.3	346.5	352.4	340.0	327.9	325.1	334.3	341.7	342.0	342.5	340.0
2011	332.8	337.7	339.7	340.6	340.6	329.6	316.5	320.8	340.4	343.2	344.4	345.6	336.0

2. Average Weekly Hours by Selected Industry: Oklahoma, 2007–2011

(Not seasonally adjusted)

Industry and year	January	February	March	April	May	June	July	August	September	October	November	December	Annual average
Total Private													
2007	34.7	34.9	34.8	35.4	34.1	35.1	35.3	35.1	35.2	35.3	35.2	35.2	35.0
2008	34.9	35.0	35.9	35.4	35.7	36.6	35.6	36.0	35.3	35.0	35.6	35.2	35.5
2009	34.8	35.3	35.0	34.3	34.2	35.0	35.2	36.0	35.1	34.9	36.2	35.4	35.1
2010	35.2	35.3	35.5	36.1	36.0	35.9	36.1	36.3	35.1	35.3	34.9	35.3	35.6
2011	35.5	34.1	35.5	35.7	36.2	35.7	35.4	35.4	35.4	36.0	35.1	35.3	35.4
Goods-Producing													
2007	40.9	41.7	41.0	43.1	40.6	42.5	42.2	43.7	42.1	43.1	43.3	40.9	42.1
2008	42.2	41.8	42.2	42.7	43.0	43.5	43.5	42.5	41.7	41.6	41.4	41.7	42.3
2009	40.1	40.6	40.0	40.4	39.4	41.3	42.3	41.9	40.9	40.4	42.2	41.8	40.9
2010	40.5	40.3	41.0	42.5	40.5	41.3	42.1	42.5	42.0	41.9	41.1	41.7	41.5
2011	40.8	39.8	43.1	43.4	42.6	42.5	41.7	42.0	41.7	41.9	41.1	41.2	41.8
Construction													
2007	39.1	39.5	38.2	41.7	36.0	39.0	42.1	46.0	43.5	43.8	45.0	40.3	41.2
2008	42.6	41.5	41.7	41.3	42.1	41.5	42.1	41.3	40.0	39.8	40.5	40.4	41.2
2009	39.0	39.2	39.0	39.9	39.3	40.7	40.8	41.5	39.5	39.7	41.6	40.0	40.0
2010	39.1	38.1	39.9	41.5	39.5	40.5	40.9	42.0	41.5	42.0	40.1	42.1	40.6
2011	40.0	38.0	44.0	45.1	43.5	43.0	42.9	41.3	41.3	41.0	40.4	40.9	41.8
Manufacturing													
2007	42.4	43.3	42.9	44.4	43.5	44.8	41.8	42.2	40.3	41.7	41.8	40.1	42.4
2008	41.6	40.7	41.1	42.8	42.8	44.2	44.0	42.0	41.7	42.0	40.8	41.9	42.1
2009	39.8	40.6	40.2	40.5	38.8	40.6	41.8	39.8	40.6	40.2	41.5	42.6	40.6
2010	40.5	41.2	41.9	42.7	41.3	42.1	42.1	41.8	41.6	41.2	41.2	40.9	41.5
2011	39.4	40.4	42.2	42.0	42.1	42.2	41.7	42.1	41.9	42.1	41.4	41.7	41.6
Trade, Transportation, and Utilities													
2007	31.5	31.9	32.9	32.5	31.7	33.6	33.0	32.6	33.0	33.2	32.5	33.3	32.6
2008	32.8	32.8	34.0	33.6	34.0	36.0	34.5	34.0	34.5	34.2	35.1	34.6	34.2
2009	34.7	34.8	34.4	34.2	34.6	34.9	35.0	35.8	35.9	35.8	35.7	35.9	35.1
2010	35.8	36.6	36.7	37.2	37.0	36.6	35.9	36.7	35.0	35.5	34.8	35.4	36.1
2011	35.9	34.4	35.2	35.9	36.6	36.3	35.7	35.2	35.2	36.0	35.1	35.2	35.6
Financial Activities													
2007	37.1	34.8	36.5	36.8	35.2	36.0	37.3	35.3	37.3	36.4	34.7	37.0	36.2
2008	34.5	34.2	35.9	35.5	34.7	37.0	35.3	37.3	37.5	37.9	38.4	37.3	36.3
2009	36.4	38.1	38.1	36.4	36.6	37.6	37.1	38.1	37.0	35.6	37.1	35.7	37.0
2010	35.0	35.0	35.0	35.3	37.0	35.4	35.6	37.3	35.5	34.8	35.3	35.0	35.5
2011	36.7	34.9	35.8	36.1	38.2	36.0	36.3	36.1	37.0	38.8	36.9	37.1	36.7
Professional and Business Services													
2007	36.5	36.8	35.2	37.2	36.4	36.9	37.4	35.7	35.4	35.2	35.7	35.2	36.1
2008	35.7	36.1	36.5	36.9	36.4	36.9	37.3	37.4	35.9	36.5	37.7	36.7	36.7
2009	36.7	38.5	38.3	36.6	37.2	38.4	37.0	38.4	36.8	37.4	38.4	37.1	37.6
2010	37.3	36.8	37.1	37.6	38.0	37.3	37.5	38.2	37.1	37.7	37.1	37.0	37.4
2011	37.8	36.5	37.3	37.0	37.9	37.5	37.5	37.7	37.4	37.7	36.6	36.8	37.3
Education and Health Services													
2007	36.2	35.9	35.0	34.9	33.2	33.4	34.3	33.3	34.2	33.4	32.8	33.8	34.2
2008	32.7	33.7	34.7	32.9	33.9	34.0	32.2	34.4	33.7	32.8	33.2	32.9	33.4
2009	32.5	32.5	32.6	31.6	31.6	31.8	32.6	33.9	32.4	32.2	33.8	32.2	32.5
2010	32.4	32.7	32.6	33.2	33.6	33.1	34.3	32.8	32.0	31.9	31.9	32.5	32.7
2011	33.0	31.4	32.6	33.0	33.8	33.0	33.1	33.2	33.5	34.0	33.4	33.4	33.1
Leisure and Hospitality													
2007	23.5	24.3	24.8	24.7	24.8	25.7	26.2	26.1	25.2	25.3	27.2	27.0	25.4
2008	25.9	26.8	27.5	27.2	27.5	28.0	26.5	26.0	25.6	25.1	26.7	25.9	26.6
2009	26.5	27.3	27.1	26.3	26.1	26.7	26.7	26.7	25.6	25.8	26.4	25.8	26.4
2010	25.2	26.2	26.6	25.8	26.3	27.4	26.8	26.7	25.5	26.6	26.8	26.4	26.4
2011	25.9	24.7	26.0	25.9	26.4	26.5	25.6	25.6	25.2	25.9	25.2	25.1	25.7

3. Average Hourly Earnings by Selected Industry: Oklahoma, 2007–2011

(Dollars, not seasonally adjusted)

Industry and year	January	February	March	April	May	June	July	August	September	October	November	December	Annual average
Total Private													
2007	17.39	17.25	16.98	17.18	17.43	17.15	17.49	17.40	17.47	17.30	17.41	17.58	17.34
2008	17.34	17.24	17.21	17.17	17.34	17.39	17.38	17.34	17.63	17.59	17.95	17.64	17.43
2009	17.80	17.94	17.87	17.89	18.03	17.87	18.03	18.19	18.25	18.29	18.40	18.34	18.07
2010	18.78	18.56	18.38	18.88	18.84	18.62	18.83	19.49	19.97	19.85	20.05	20.06	19.20
2011	20.08	20.76	20.41	20.43	20.19	20.13	20.32	20.15	20.32	20.19	20.39	20.97	20.36
Goods-Producing													
2007	19.57	19.05	18.77	18.51	18.96	18.66	18.94	19.20	19.34	19.08	19.33	19.87	19.11
2008	19.13	19.29	19.58	19.25	19.71	19.33	19.35	20.01	20.62	20.42	21.17	20.46	19.85
2009	20.66	20.77	20.57	20.43	21.25	20.70	20.78	21.34	20.92	21.02	21.15	20.88	20.87
2010	21.55	21.52	21.08	20.97	21.58	21.26	21.84	22.50	23.27	22.18	22.71	22.46	21.93
2011	22.56	23.19	22.41	22.00	21.83	21.97	22.17	22.07	21.89	21.97	22.45	22.56	22.24
Construction													
2007	18.60	18.71	17.26	17.21	18.05	17.50	17.77	17.24	17.55	17.60	17.70	19.58	17.87
2008	17.98	18.32	18.58	18.64	18.39	18.72	18.64	19.04	18.79	18.81	18.92	19.26	18.67
2009	19.63	20.11	19.78	19.91	20.47	19.64	19.87	19.93	20.06	20.37	19.72	20.03	19.96
2010	20.73	21.03	20.49	20.36	20.47	20.01	20.52	20.62	20.39	20.70	21.07	20.62	20.58
2011	20.64	21.03	20.27	19.68	19.75	19.43	19.70	19.92	19.76	20.00	19.77	20.08	19.98
Manufacturing													
2007	19.70	18.62	19.02	18.44	18.50	18.18	18.39	19.33	19.68	18.96	19.30	18.56	18.88
2008	18.39	18.64	18.73	18.35	19.27	18.02	18.26	19.17	20.32	20.03	20.40	19.58	19.08
2009	19.25	18.85	18.52	18.30	19.21	18.60	18.49	19.36	18.74	18.74	19.67	18.93	18.88
2010	18.86	18.65	18.36	18.47	19.21	18.39	18.21	18.39	18.26	18.19	18.11	18.18	18.44
2011	18.71	18.89	18.58	18.49	18.19	18.14	18.75	18.85	18.83	18.77	19.13	19.46	18.73
Trade, Transportation, and Utilities													
2007	15.91	15.72	15.06	15.52	15.28	15.83	16.69	16.35	16.80	16.43	16.40	16.40	16.04
2008	16.43	16.09	15.94	16.33	16.32	16.87	16.94	16.56	16.86	17.00	17.03	17.18	16.64
2009	17.47	17.58	17.60	17.74	17.55	17.68	17.79	17.99	17.93	17.98	18.21	17.89	17.79
2010	18.26	18.44	17.86	18.17	17.44	17.20	18.04	18.46	18.27	18.61	19.32	18.97	18.25
2011	18.53	19.45	18.07	18.47	18.43	18.47	18.93	18.66	19.29	18.69	18.81	19.86	18.80
Financial Activities													
2007	19.63	19.87	19.70	20.08	19.55	17.67	17.71	17.56	17.38	17.43	18.34	17.87	18.56
2008	18.48	17.94	17.94	17.93	17.61	17.47	16.66	16.85	17.05	17.23	17.85	16.97	17.49
2009	17.55	17.93	17.83	17.61	18.03	18.33	18.26	18.70	18.79	18.57	18.98	18.78	18.28
2010	19.47	19.15	18.95	19.88	20.32	20.42	20.76	20.35	20.80	20.74	20.61	21.63	20.26
2011	22.24	21.97	20.58	21.45	20.68	20.85	21.57	21.43	21.70	21.43	21.79	21.81	21.46
Professional and Business Services													
2007	19.65	19.72	19.63	19.90	22.03	20.15	20.31	19.79	19.76	19.44	19.38	20.29	20.01
2008	19.43	19.54	19.29	19.54	19.82	19.08	19.36	19.69	19.06	19.53	19.89	19.68	19.49
2009	19.91	20.50	20.60	20.85	20.42	19.84	20.01	20.29	20.01	19.72	20.12	20.12	20.20
2010	20.85	20.58	20.31	20.61	20.92	20.99	20.63	21.02	21.10	21.92	21.58	21.41	21.00
2011	21.49	21.38	21.04	21.29	21.12	20.86	20.64	20.44	20.54	20.94	21.17	22.06	21.08
Education and Health Services													
2007	17.07	17.20	17.42	17.65	17.45	17.84	17.77	17.76	17.53	17.65	17.49	17.63	17.54
2008	17.35	17.00	16.88	16.77	17.00	17.11	17.44	16.57	17.09	16.69	16.94	16.64	16.95
2009	16.71	16.97	17.07	17.24	17.49	17.45	17.87	17.09	17.87	17.93	17.54	17.83	17.42
2010	17.94	17.19	17.71	18.10	17.57	17.35	16.85	17.60	18.17	18.23	18.46	18.30	17.78
2011	18.27	19.18	18.29	18.59	18.51	19.01	19.27	19.38	19.90	19.60	19.78	20.83	19.23
Leisure and Hospitality													
2007	8.94	9.25	9.00	8.97	8.85	9.06	9.24	9.42	9.48	9.44	9.88	9.93	9.30
2008	9.92	9.77	9.72	9.62	10.06	10.26	9.76	10.01	10.16	10.30	10.54	10.53	10.05
2009	10.56	10.41	10.42	10.53	10.52	10.39	10.28	10.53	10.53	11.05	10.69	10.78	10.55
2010	10.87	10.91	10.82	10.94	11.08	10.79	10.87	10.93	11.24	11.12	11.14	11.16	10.99
2011	11.12	11.26	10.87	10.87	10.93	10.59	10.64	10.76	10.87	10.94	10.87	11.02	10.89

4. Average Weekly Earnings by Selected Industry: Oklahoma, 2007–2011

(Dollars, not seasonally adjusted)

Industry and year	January	February	March	April	May	June	July	August	September	October	November	December	Annual average
Total Private													
2007	603.43	602.03	590.90	608.17	594.36	601.97	617.40	610.74	614.94	610.69	612.83	618.82	607.21
2008	605.17	603.40	617.84	607.82	619.04	636.47	618.73	624.24	622.34	615.65	639.02	620.93	619.08
2009	619.44	633.28	625.45	613.63	616.63	625.45	634.66	654.84	640.58	638.32	666.08	649.24	634.58
2010	661.06	655.17	652.49	681.57	678.24	668.46	679.76	707.49	700.95	700.71	699.75	708.12	682.84
2011	712.84	707.92	724.56	729.35	730.88	718.64	719.33	713.31	719.33	726.84	715.69	740.24	721.67
Goods-Producing													
2007	800.41	794.39	769.57	797.78	769.78	793.05	799.27	839.04	814.21	822.35	836.99	812.68	804.38
2008	807.29	806.32	826.28	821.98	847.53	840.86	841.73	850.43	859.85	849.47	876.44	853.18	840.21
2009	828.47	843.26	822.80	825.37	837.25	854.91	878.99	894.15	855.63	849.21	892.53	872.78	853.84
2010	872.78	867.26	864.28	891.23	873.99	878.04	919.46	956.25	977.34	929.34	933.38	936.58	909.08
2011	920.45	922.96	965.87	954.80	929.96	933.73	924.49	926.94	912.81	920.54	922.70	929.47	930.25
Construction													
2007	727.26	739.05	659.33	717.66	649.80	682.50	748.12	793.04	763.43	770.88	796.50	789.07	736.95
2008	765.95	760.28	774.79	769.83	774.22	776.88	784.74	786.35	751.60	748.64	766.26	778.10	769.86
2009	765.57	788.31	771.42	794.41	804.47	799.35	810.70	827.10	792.37	808.69	820.35	801.20	798.45
2010	810.54	801.24	817.55	844.94	808.57	810.41	839.27	866.04	846.19	869.40	844.91	868.10	836.03
2011	825.60	799.14	891.88	887.57	859.13	835.49	845.13	822.70	816.09	820.00	798.71	821.27	835.17
Manufacturing													
2007	835.28	806.25	815.96	818.74	804.75	814.46	768.70	815.73	793.10	790.63	806.74	744.26	801.08
2008	765.02	758.65	769.80	785.38	824.76	796.48	803.44	805.14	847.34	841.26	832.32	820.40	803.89
2009	766.15	765.31	744.50	741.15	745.35	755.16	772.88	770.53	760.84	753.35	816.31	806.42	765.95
2010	763.83	768.38	769.28	788.67	793.37	774.22	766.64	768.70	759.62	749.43	746.13	743.56	765.89
2011	737.17	763.16	784.08	776.58	765.80	765.51	781.88	793.59	788.98	790.22	791.98	811.48	779.46
Trade, Transportation, and Utilities													
2007	501.17	501.47	495.47	504.40	484.38	531.89	550.77	533.01	554.40	545.48	533.00	546.12	523.58
2008	538.90	527.75	541.96	548.69	554.88	607.32	584.43	563.04	581.67	581.40	597.75	594.43	568.70
2009	606.21	611.78	605.44	606.71	607.23	617.03	622.65	644.04	643.69	643.68	650.10	642.25	624.97
2010	653.71	674.90	655.46	675.92	645.28	629.52	647.64	677.48	639.45	660.66	672.34	671.54	658.68
2011	665.23	669.08	636.06	663.07	674.54	670.46	675.80	656.83	679.01	672.84	660.23	699.07	668.65
Financial Activities													
2007	728.27	691.48	719.05	738.94	688.16	636.12	660.58	619.87	648.27	634.45	636.40	661.19	671.88
2008	637.56	613.55	644.05	636.52	611.07	646.39	588.10	628.51	639.38	653.02	685.44	632.98	634.66
2009	638.82	683.13	679.32	641.00	659.90	689.21	677.45	712.47	695.23	661.09	704.16	670.45	675.92
2010	681.45	670.25	663.25	701.76	751.84	722.87	739.06	759.06	738.40	721.75	727.53	757.05	719.52
2011	816.21	766.75	736.76	774.35	789.98	750.60	782.99	773.62	802.90	831.48	804.05	809.15	786.64
Professional and Business Services													
2007	717.23	725.70	690.98	740.28	801.89	743.54	759.59	706.50	699.50	684.29	691.87	714.21	722.85
2008	693.65	705.39	704.09	721.03	721.45	704.05	722.13	736.41	684.25	712.85	749.85	722.26	714.75
2009	730.70	789.25	788.98	763.11	759.62	761.86	740.37	779.14	736.37	737.53	772.61	746.45	758.96
2010	777.71	757.34	753.50	774.94	794.96	782.93	773.63	802.96	782.81	826.38	800.62	792.17	785.24
2011	812.32	780.37	784.79	787.73	800.45	782.25	774.00	770.59	768.20	789.44	774.82	811.81	786.31
Education and Health Services													
2007	617.93	617.48	609.70	615.99	579.34	595.86	609.51	591.41	599.53	589.51	573.67	595.89	599.49
2008	567.35	572.90	585.74	551.73	576.30	581.74	561.57	570.01	575.93	547.43	562.41	547.46	566.68
2009	543.08	551.53	556.48	544.78	552.68	554.91	582.56	579.35	578.99	577.35	592.85	574.13	565.88
2010	581.26	562.11	577.35	600.92	590.35	574.29	577.96	577.28	581.44	581.54	588.87	594.75	582.37
2011	602.91	602.25	596.25	613.47	625.64	627.33	637.84	643.42	666.65	666.40	660.65	695.72	636.73
Leisure and Hospitality													
2007	210.09	224.78	223.20	221.56	219.48	232.84	242.09	245.86	238.90	238.83	268.74	268.11	236.39
2008	256.93	261.84	267.30	261.66	276.65	287.28	258.64	260.26	260.10	258.53	281.42	272.73	266.99
2009	279.84	284.19	282.38	276.94	274.57	277.41	274.48	281.15	269.57	285.09	282.22	278.12	278.76
2010	273.92	285.84	287.81	282.25	291.40	295.65	291.32	291.83	286.62	295.79	298.55	294.62	289.75
2011	288.01	278.12	282.62	281.53	288.55	280.64	272.38	275.46	273.92	283.35	273.92	276.60	279.60

OREGON

At a Glance

Population:
　2000 census: 3,421,524
　2010 census: 3,831,074
　2011 estimate: 3,871,859

Percent change in population:
　2000–2010: 12.0%
　2010–2011: 1.1%

Percent change in total nonfarm employment:
　2000–2010: -1.0%
　2010–2011: 1.0%

Industry with the largest growth in employment, 2000–2011 (thousands):
　Education and Health Services, 62.8

Industry with the largest decline or smallest growth in employment, 2000–2011 (thousands):
　Manufacturing, -58.5

Civilian labor force:
　2000: 1,810,150
　2010: 1,983,572
　2011: 1,991,873

Unemployment rate and rank among states (lowest to highest):
　2000: 5.1%, 47th
　2010: 10.7%, 44th
　2011: 9.5%, 38th

Over-the-year change in unemployment rates:
　2010–2011: -1.2%

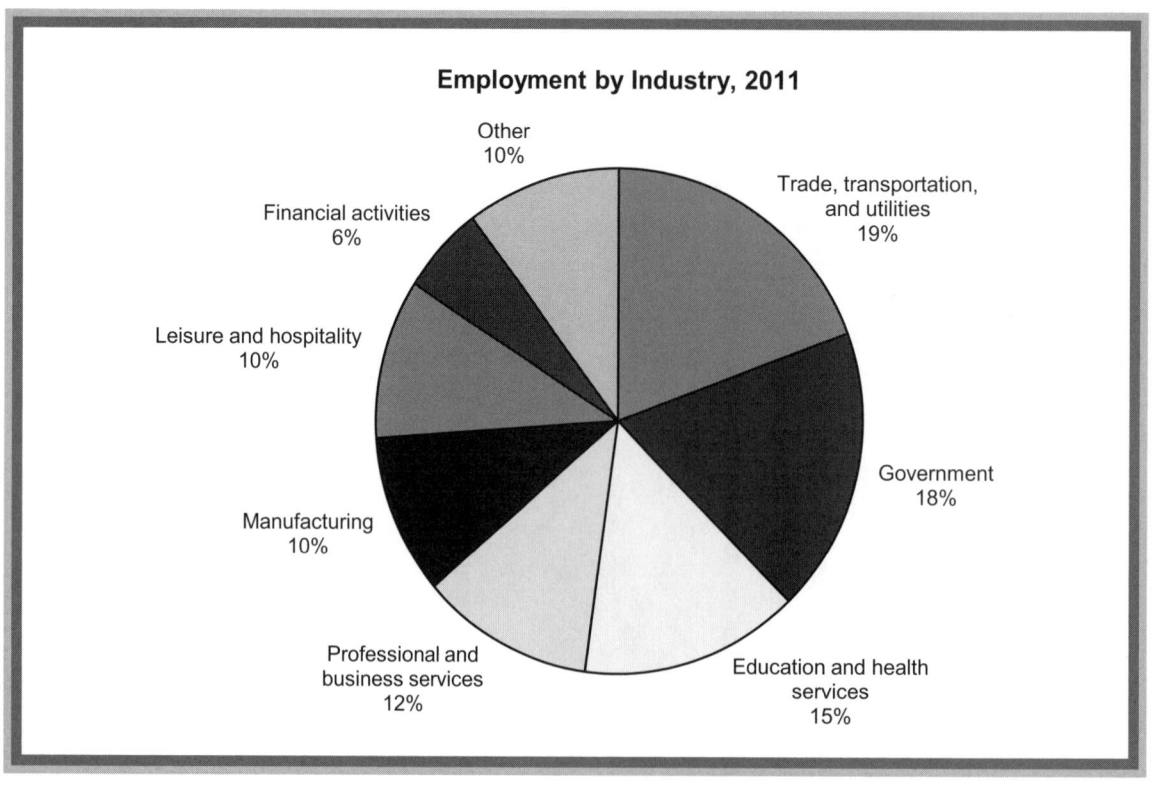

Employment by Industry, 2011

- Other 10%
- Trade, transportation, and utilities 19%
- Financial activities 6%
- Government 18%
- Leisure and hospitality 10%
- Manufacturing 10%
- Education and health services 15%
- Professional and business services 12%

1. Employment by Industry: Oregon, Selected Years, 2000–2011

(Numbers in thousands, not seasonally adjusted)

Industry and year	January	February	March	April	May	June	July	August	September	October	November	December	Annual average
Total Nonfarm													
2000	1,567.9	1,581.4	1,591.8	1,603.5	1,621.7	1,638.0	1,614.6	1,620.9	1,635.2	1,644.0	1,650.2	1,645.1	1,617.9
2001	1,593.1	1,600.9	1,606.0	1,607.5	1,616.3	1,629.4	1,597.3	1,600.1	1,606.0	1,610.0	1,603.1	1,596.3	1,605.5
2002	1,548.1	1,558.8	1,567.2	1,575.9	1,589.5	1,602.4	1,584.7	1,591.6	1,599.8	1,607.0	1,603.6	1,595.2	1,585.3
2003	1,552.9	1,557.7	1,561.6	1,561.2	1,572.4	1,582.6	1,561.4	1,570.9	1,582.1	1,597.8	1,595.8	1,595.5	1,574.3
2004	1,542.4	1,558.7	1,574.6	1,591.5	1,604.9	1,622.4	1,610.1	1,615.9	1,628.5	1,642.6	1,643.7	1,644.5	1,606.7
2005	1,598.9	1,613.8	1,628.4	1,640.2	1,651.2	1,668.0	1,651.3	1,658.6	1,673.0	1,683.6	1,691.7	1,694.7	1,654.5
2006	1,648.2	1,665.2	1,678.0	1,690.6	1,707.3	1,722.7	1,700.4	1,707.1	1,720.7	1,732.3	1,735.5	1,734.4	1,703.5
2007	1,688.3	1,704.5	1,717.7	1,721.0	1,736.3	1,748.9	1,723.2	1,732.5	1,740.8	1,755.0	1,755.9	1,751.7	1,731.3
2008	1,702.9	1,714.8	1,721.7	1,728.3	1,735.6	1,740.5	1,718.2	1,718.9	1,724.6	1,724.6	1,706.1	1,684.5	1,718.4
2009	1,626.0	1,621.3	1,613.0	1,615.2	1,620.1	1,623.6	1,600.8	1,595.3	1,606.0	1,615.0	1,610.3	1,603.8	1,612.5
2010	1,562.8	1,570.8	1,579.3	1,596.7	1,611.6	1,621.5	1,597.7	1,598.6	1,607.6	1,629.2	1,626.9	1,621.2	1,602.0
2011	1,583.6	1,596.6	1,603.4	1,617.8	1,624.5	1,635.0	1,611.6	1,615.9	1,626.7	1,638.4	1,636.0	1,627.6	1,618.1
Total Private													
2000	1,291.1	1,299.5	1,308.5	1,319.5	1,330.5	1,348.5	1,355.2	1,364.1	1,368.0	1,360.5	1,364.7	1,361.3	1,339.3
2001	1,314.7	1,315.9	1,318.7	1,320.8	1,325.7	1,338.2	1,336.8	1,340.7	1,333.7	1,320.2	1,311.6	1,307.1	1,323.7
2002	1,262.7	1,267.8	1,274.3	1,284.4	1,295.1	1,307.1	1,318.0	1,326.8	1,323.6	1,317.2	1,311.9	1,306.6	1,299.6
2003	1,267.3	1,269.3	1,273.4	1,274.6	1,284.0	1,295.4	1,305.3	1,314.2	1,314.7	1,313.8	1,309.9	1,312.0	1,294.5
2004	1,263.4	1,273.7	1,286.7	1,304.6	1,315.4	1,330.1	1,346.4	1,353.1	1,354.7	1,353.1	1,356.0	1,356.0	1,324.3
2005	1,312.8	1,323.4	1,337.0	1,348.3	1,357.7	1,372.6	1,387.1	1,394.9	1,398.7	1,395.1	1,399.5	1,405.5	1,369.4
2006	1,363.7	1,374.6	1,385.9	1,399.4	1,412.2	1,426.2	1,435.1	1,442.4	1,444.6	1,440.9	1,440.2	1,443.6	1,417.4
2007	1,401.7	1,412.4	1,423.5	1,426.7	1,437.1	1,448.4	1,454.4	1,464.4	1,462.3	1,458.4	1,455.9	1,453.6	1,441.6
2008	1,408.1	1,414.7	1,419.7	1,425.9	1,429.9	1,433.7	1,438.4	1,440.6	1,436.3	1,420.3	1,398.1	1,379.3	1,420.4
2009	1,325.0	1,315.4	1,306.3	1,307.5	1,309.9	1,314.7	1,319.9	1,317.6	1,321.2	1,312.4	1,305.4	1,301.5	1,313.1
2010	1,264.1	1,267.4	1,274.4	1,289.2	1,296.7	1,307.1	1,316.3	1,320.9	1,324.0	1,326.4	1,320.7	1,319.7	1,302.2
2011	1,284.0	1,293.0	1,299.6	1,313.2	1,317.6	1,327.8	1,337.5	1,344.2	1,347.7	1,340.7	1,336.1	1,331.1	1,322.7
Goods-Producing													
2000	306.6	308.0	309.7	311.1	314.5	323.1	327.4	329.5	329.9	323.1	320.3	317.3	318.4
2001	307.7	306.7	305.0	304.4	304.8	310.5	314.8	314.3	309.4	304.0	294.3	290.1	305.5
2002	280.5	280.5	281.6	283.7	287.0	292.7	299.6	301.3	298.3	294.0	287.7	283.5	289.2
2003	276.2	275.7	275.0	272.9	275.7	281.5	286.2	290.0	288.7	287.8	283.4	281.4	281.2
2004	272.1	275.4	278.4	284.2	288.3	295.0	304.0	306.2	304.9	303.4	298.4	296.3	292.2
2005	289.2	291.4	294.4	296.8	300.1	305.9	313.4	315.9	314.8	313.2	309.2	307.9	304.4
2006	302.3	305.4	308.0	311.1	315.0	321.4	328.6	330.2	328.3	325.1	319.5	316.8	317.6
2007	309.7	311.2	312.9	312.1	315.4	319.9	325.6	328.9	325.5	322.1	316.0	311.3	317.6
2008	301.1	300.7	299.7	299.6	300.5	302.4	306.0	306.4	302.2	296.3	284.7	274.7	297.9
2009	259.8	252.2	247.3	245.3	245.0	248.0	253.1	251.9	250.8	246.9	239.6	235.7	248.0
2010	229.2	228.2	229.5	232.3	235.3	239.6	246.4	247.6	247.2	246.2	240.3	236.4	238.2
2011	230.8	232.9	234.5	238.5	241.0	245.0	250.6	251.8	252.3	248.3	242.6	238.7	242.3
Mining and Logging													
2000	9.2	9.3	9.1	9.3	9.7	10.2	10.3	10.4	10.3	10.4	10.0	9.7	9.8
2001	9.2	9.1	8.8	8.6	9.0	9.6	9.9	10.1	9.8	9.7	9.2	8.8	9.3
2002	8.7	8.7	8.7	8.6	9.0	9.5	9.9	9.9	9.8	9.8	9.7	9.5	9.3
2003	8.9	8.9	8.8	8.9	9.1	9.6	9.9	9.9	9.8	9.8	9.5	9.3	9.4
2004	8.8	9.0	9.2	9.4	9.6	10.0	10.2	10.2	10.1	10.0	9.7	9.7	9.7
2005	9.2	9.4	9.3	9.1	9.2	9.6	10.1	10.1	9.9	9.8	9.6	9.4	9.6
2006	8.8	9.0	8.9	9.0	9.3	9.7	9.9	10.0	9.9	9.8	9.4	9.2	9.4
2007	8.7	8.9	8.9	9.1	9.3	9.6	9.7	9.7	9.6	9.4	9.2	8.8	9.2
2008	8.4	8.4	8.3	8.3	8.5	8.8	9.1	9.3	9.2	9.0	8.7	8.1	8.7
2009	7.1	7.0	6.7	6.7	6.6	6.9	7.0	7.0	7.0	6.9	6.6	6.3	6.8
2010	6.2	6.2	6.3	6.4	6.6	6.9	7.3	7.2	7.2	7.0	6.7	6.5	6.7
2011	6.2	6.5	6.4	6.6	6.8	7.0	7.4	7.4	7.4	7.2	7.0	6.7	6.9
Construction													
2000	77.9	78.4	79.2	80.3	82.0	85.5	86.8	88.9	89.3	86.7	84.8	83.3	83.6
2001	78.6	78.4	78.9	78.6	79.7	82.2	83.6	85.0	83.2	81.7	78.8	76.8	80.5
2002	72.6	72.9	73.9	75.0	77.2	79.9	82.6	84.9	83.3	81.8	79.1	76.5	78.3
2003	72.1	72.0	72.1	72.6	74.6	76.9	79.9	82.4	81.7	81.6	79.5	78.1	77.0
2004	72.4	74.2	76.2	79.2	81.4	84.2	87.9	89.0	88.9	88.1	85.9	85.2	82.7
2005	80.8	82.0	84.0	86.1	88.5	91.4	95.2	97.3	98.0	96.9	95.3	95.1	90.9
2006	91.3	93.3	94.7	97.2	100.2	103.2	105.7	107.2	106.9	105.7	103.5	101.9	100.9
2007	97.4	98.9	100.5	101.5	104.2	105.8	109.4	110.8	109.2	107.4	104.5	101.3	104.2
2008	94.4	94.3	94.2	94.7	95.8	96.9	98.7	98.6	96.9	93.1	87.9	83.4	94.1
2009	76.9	74.2	72.6	72.4	73.1	75.0	77.1	77.1	76.3	74.4	70.5	68.1	74.0
2010	63.4	62.7	63.4	65.0	66.6	68.4	71.8	72.6	72.1	71.5	68.1	66.1	67.6
2011	62.1	62.9	63.6	66.2	67.7	69.8	72.7	73.2	74.6	73.5	70.7	69.0	68.8
Manufacturing													
2000	219.5	220.3	221.4	221.5	222.8	227.4	230.3	230.2	230.3	226.0	225.5	224.3	225.0
2001	219.9	219.2	217.3	217.2	216.1	218.7	221.3	219.2	216.4	212.6	206.3	204.5	215.7
2002	199.2	198.9	199.0	200.1	200.8	203.3	207.1	206.5	205.2	202.4	198.9	197.5	201.6
2003	195.2	194.8	194.1	191.4	192.0	195.0	196.4	197.7	197.2	196.4	194.4	194.0	194.9
2004	190.9	192.2	193.0	195.6	197.3	200.8	205.9	207.0	205.9	205.3	202.8	201.4	199.8
2005	199.2	200.0	201.1	201.6	202.4	204.9	208.1	208.5	206.9	206.5	204.3	203.4	203.9
2006	202.2	203.1	204.4	204.9	205.5	208.5	213.0	213.0	211.5	209.6	206.6	205.7	207.3
2007	203.6	203.4	203.5	201.5	201.9	204.5	206.5	208.4	206.7	205.3	202.3	201.2	204.1
2008	198.3	198.0	197.2	196.6	196.2	196.7	198.2	198.5	196.1	194.2	188.1	183.2	195.1
2009	175.8	171.0	168.0	166.2	165.3	166.1	169.0	167.8	167.5	165.6	162.5	161.3	167.2
2010	159.6	159.3	159.8	160.9	162.1	164.3	167.3	167.8	167.9	167.7	165.5	163.8	163.8
2011	162.5	163.5	164.5	165.7	166.5	168.2	170.5	171.2	170.3	167.6	164.9	163.0	166.5

1. Employment by Industry: Oregon, Selected Years, 2000–2011—*Continued*

(Numbers in thousands, not seasonally adjusted)

Industry and year	January	February	March	April	May	June	July	August	September	October	November	December	Annual average
Service-Providing													
2000	1,261.3	1,273.4	1,282.1	1,292.4	1,307.2	1,314.9	1,287.2	1,291.4	1,305.3	1,320.9	1,329.9	1,327.8	1,299.5
2001	1,285.4	1,294.2	1,301.0	1,303.1	1,311.5	1,318.9	1,282.5	1,285.8	1,296.6	1,306.0	1,308.8	1,306.2	1,300.0
2002	1,267.6	1,278.3	1,285.6	1,292.2	1,302.5	1,309.7	1,285.1	1,290.3	1,301.5	1,313.0	1,315.9	1,311.7	1,296.1
2003	1,276.7	1,282.0	1,286.6	1,288.3	1,296.7	1,301.1	1,275.2	1,280.9	1,293.4	1,310.0	1,312.4	1,314.1	1,293.1
2004	1,270.3	1,283.3	1,296.2	1,307.3	1,316.6	1,327.4	1,306.1	1,309.7	1,323.6	1,339.2	1,345.3	1,348.2	1,314.4
2005	1,309.7	1,322.4	1,334.0	1,343.4	1,351.1	1,362.1	1,337.9	1,342.7	1,358.2	1,370.4	1,382.5	1,386.8	1,350.1
2006	1,345.9	1,359.8	1,370.0	1,379.5	1,392.3	1,401.3	1,371.8	1,376.9	1,392.4	1,407.2	1,416.0	1,417.6	1,385.9
2007	1,378.6	1,393.3	1,404.8	1,408.9	1,420.9	1,429.0	1,397.6	1,403.6	1,415.3	1,432.9	1,439.9	1,440.4	1,413.8
2008	1,401.8	1,414.1	1,422.0	1,428.7	1,435.1	1,438.1	1,412.2	1,412.5	1,422.4	1,428.3	1,421.4	1,409.8	1,420.5
2009	1,366.2	1,369.1	1,365.7	1,369.9	1,375.1	1,375.6	1,347.7	1,343.4	1,355.2	1,368.1	1,370.7	1,368.1	1,364.6
2010	1,333.6	1,342.6	1,349.8	1,364.4	1,376.3	1,381.9	1,351.3	1,351.0	1,360.4	1,383.0	1,386.6	1,384.8	1,363.8
2011	1,352.8	1,363.7	1,368.9	1,379.3	1,383.5	1,390.0	1,361.0	1,364.1	1,374.4	1,390.1	1,393.4	1,388.9	1,375.8
Trade, Transportation, and Utilities													
2000	318.9	317.7	318.2	320.5	322.5	326.0	325.9	327.6	328.1	331.2	339.8	340.4	326.4
2001	320.7	316.9	317.6	317.6	318.9	321.4	321.2	321.7	321.0	320.5	325.4	326.7	320.8
2002	309.7	307.4	308.6	310.5	312.5	314.9	316.8	317.2	317.8	318.4	323.2	326.3	315.3
2003	310.4	308.3	308.4	308.6	310.9	312.9	314.8	315.9	316.5	319.4	324.7	326.5	314.8
2004	311.7	309.1	310.9	313.7	316.3	319.2	322.4	323.2	323.9	325.9	331.9	335.1	320.3
2005	319.1	317.8	320.5	321.6	323.1	327.0	329.2	331.3	332.9	334.1	341.2	345.5	328.6
2006	328.4	326.9	328.3	329.5	332.7	335.0	335.9	337.3	338.4	339.3	345.6	349.7	335.6
2007	334.4	332.3	333.8	334.4	336.3	339.2	340.3	342.2	343.5	344.0	350.7	352.9	340.3
2008	336.9	334.6	335.0	335.3	335.4	336.1	337.2	337.6	337.2	335.4	335.3	334.6	335.9
2009	317.7	312.9	309.9	309.0	310.4	310.5	310.8	310.8	312.3	311.2	314.0	316.3	312.2
2010	303.1	300.8	301.2	303.7	305.0	307.1	308.9	310.6	311.4	313.2	317.5	320.6	308.6
2011	307.1	305.1	305.4	307.7	309.8	311.5	313.5	314.6	313.9	314.9	321.5	323.7	312.4
Wholesale Trade													
2000	75.5	75.8	76.0	75.9	76.0	76.6	77.3	77.3	77.2	77.5	77.4	77.2	76.6
2001	74.7	74.8	75.2	75.0	74.8	75.3	75.7	75.4	75.2	74.1	73.6	73.2	74.8
2002	72.7	72.8	72.8	73.1	73.2	73.7	74.7	74.7	74.6	75.0	74.7	74.7	73.9
2003	73.7	74.0	74.0	74.0	74.2	74.4	75.6	75.1	75.4	75.2	75.1	74.9	74.6
2004	73.7	74.1	74.3	74.6	75.0	75.5	76.7	76.7	76.7	76.5	76.7	76.9	75.6
2005	76.1	76.6	76.9	77.1	76.9	77.7	78.5	78.6	79.1	78.7	78.9	78.9	77.8
2006	78.1	78.9	79.0	79.2	79.8	80.1	80.4	80.4	80.4	80.8	80.8	80.7	79.9
2007	80.1	80.6	80.5	80.4	80.5	80.8	81.4	81.2	81.0	81.3	81.2	81.0	80.8
2008	80.0	80.6	80.7	80.5	80.7	80.7	81.3	81.0	80.9	80.8	79.9	79.1	80.5
2009	77.4	76.9	76.1	75.8	75.7	75.4	75.4	74.8	74.6	74.1	73.7	73.3	75.3
2010	72.1	72.3	72.2	72.9	73.2	73.2	73.8	73.7	74.0	74.2	73.8	73.7	73.3
2011	72.7	73.2	73.3	73.8	74.4	74.4	74.8	75.8	75.1	74.3	75.4	75.8	74.4
Retail Trade													
2000	186.7	185.1	185.4	187.5	189.3	191.6	191.7	192.7	192.3	195.2	203.5	204.9	192.2
2001	189.5	185.7	186.2	186.6	187.4	189.5	189.2	189.0	188.4	188.5	194.3	196.2	189.2
2002	181.7	179.3	180.5	181.7	183.3	184.9	186.3	186.1	186.6	186.8	192.2	195.4	185.4
2003	181.2	179.0	179.4	179.7	181.6	183.1	184.1	184.8	184.7	187.3	192.9	195.0	184.4
2004	182.4	179.6	180.9	183.0	185.0	187.3	189.1	189.6	189.2	190.7	196.8	199.9	187.8
2005	186.8	184.8	186.7	187.9	189.6	192.3	194.2	195.7	195.7	197.5	204.3	207.4	193.6
2006	193.2	190.5	191.7	192.7	194.9	196.1	197.7	198.8	198.8	199.3	205.6	208.8	197.3
2007	196.6	193.9	195.3	195.9	197.5	199.3	201.0	202.6	202.9	202.9	209.3	210.9	200.7
2008	198.3	195.2	195.6	195.6	195.4	196.2	197.7	197.9	197.1	195.8	197.9	197.9	196.7
2009	185.1	181.6	180.0	179.9	181.2	181.8	183.0	183.4	183.8	183.8	187.6	189.5	183.4
2010	179.6	177.3	177.8	179.0	180.0	181.6	183.6	184.9	184.4	185.9	190.8	193.1	183.2
2011	182.0	179.6	179.7	181.4	182.5	184.0	185.2	184.5	184.7	186.7	192.3	193.2	184.7
Transportation and Utilities													
2000	56.7	56.8	56.8	57.1	57.2	57.8	56.9	57.6	58.6	58.5	58.9	58.3	57.6
2001	56.5	56.4	56.2	56.0	56.7	56.6	56.3	57.3	57.4	57.9	57.5	57.3	56.8
2002	55.3	55.3	55.3	55.7	56.0	56.3	55.8	56.4	56.6	56.6	56.3	56.2	56.0
2003	55.5	55.3	55.0	54.9	55.1	55.4	55.1	56.0	56.4	56.9	56.7	56.6	55.7
2004	55.6	55.4	55.7	56.1	56.3	56.4	56.6	56.9	58.0	58.7	58.4	58.3	56.9
2005	56.2	56.4	56.9	56.6	56.6	57.0	56.5	57.0	58.1	57.9	58.0	59.2	57.2
2006	57.1	57.5	57.6	57.6	58.0	58.8	57.8	58.1	59.2	59.2	59.2	60.2	58.4
2007	57.7	57.8	58.0	58.1	58.3	59.1	57.9	58.4	59.6	59.8	60.2	61.0	58.8
2008	58.6	58.8	58.7	59.2	59.3	59.2	58.2	58.7	59.2	58.8	57.5	57.6	58.7
2009	55.2	54.4	53.8	53.3	53.5	53.3	52.4	52.6	53.9	53.3	52.7	53.5	53.5
2010	51.4	51.2	51.2	51.8	51.8	52.3	51.5	52.0	53.0	53.1	52.9	53.8	52.2
2011	52.4	52.3	52.4	52.5	52.9	53.1	53.5	54.3	54.1	53.9	53.8	54.7	53.3
Information													
2000	38.1	38.2	38.6	38.6	39.2	39.6	40.4	40.4	40.5	41.1	41.2	41.8	39.8
2001	41.1	40.9	40.8	41.2	41.1	41.8	39.3	39.1	38.5	38.4	38.5	38.5	39.9
2002	38.1	38.2	37.5	36.0	36.0	35.9	35.7	35.7	35.4	35.4	35.3	36.0	36.3
2003	35.0	34.7	34.5	33.7	33.9	33.4	32.9	33.1	32.7	32.9	33.3	33.1	33.6
2004	32.7	32.8	32.6	32.8	33.1	33.2	33.1	33.2	32.9	32.8	33.2	33.1	33.0
2005	32.6	33.0	32.9	33.2	33.5	33.6	33.7	33.6	33.8	34.1	34.4	35.1	33.6
2006	34.1	34.5	34.5	34.2	34.5	34.8	35.0	35.1	35.1	35.3	35.3	35.9	34.9
2007	34.9	35.3	35.8	35.9	36.2	36.5	36.0	36.2	36.0	35.8	36.2	37.2	36.0
2008	36.1	36.3	36.3	35.9	36.1	36.3	35.6	35.7	35.4	34.8	34.5	34.2	35.6
2009	33.4	33.5	33.3	32.9	33.2	34.3	33.1	33.1	32.6	32.0	32.6	32.8	33.1
2010	31.7	31.8	32.0	31.8	32.3	32.7	31.9	32.3	32.2	31.8	32.2	32.2	32.1
2011	31.8	32.0	32.3	32.2	32.0	32.0	32.4	32.7	32.3	32.1	32.6	32.6	32.3

1. Employment by Industry: Oregon, Selected Years, 2000–2011—*Continued*

(Numbers in thousands, not seasonally adjusted)

Industry and year	January	February	March	April	May	June	July	August	September	October	November	December	Annual average
Financial Activities													
2000	94.2	94.1	94.4	95.3	95.9	96.4	96.4	96.5	95.8	94.8	94.7	95.4	95.3
2001	93.2	93.7	94.2	94.5	95.0	95.8	96.5	96.3	95.8	95.7	95.7	95.8	95.2
2002	93.7	94.1	93.9	93.6	94.1	94.5	96.5	96.9	96.5	96.4	96.3	97.1	95.3
2003	95.2	95.5	96.2	96.9	97.1	98.0	98.8	99.1	98.1	97.0	96.3	96.4	97.1
2004	94.1	94.4	94.9	95.9	96.9	98.0	98.7	99.2	98.8	99.1	99.1	99.9	97.4
2005	98.0	98.8	99.5	100.4	101.1	102.0	103.9	104.3	103.9	103.8	104.3	105.1	102.1
2006	103.2	103.8	104.3	105.1	105.8	106.8	107.4	107.9	107.6	107.0	106.9	107.6	106.1
2007	105.8	106.5	107.1	106.4	106.8	107.4	107.9	107.5	105.8	105.6	105.1	105.3	106.4
2008	102.5	102.8	102.6	102.9	102.8	102.5	102.5	102.4	101.2	100.7	99.7	99.5	101.8
2009	96.4	96.2	95.7	95.7	95.5	95.3	96.1	96.0	95.3	95.6	94.9	95.2	95.7
2010	92.4	92.1	92.1	93.1	93.2	93.8	94.2	94.1	93.5	93.4	92.8	93.5	93.2
2011	91.3	91.7	91.4	91.6	91.8	92.4	92.6	92.6	92.4	92.7	91.2	91.8	92.0
Professional and Business Services													
2000	172.9	175.4	178.1	180.8	182.0	185.0	187.2	189.4	190.1	188.6	187.9	186.2	183.6
2001	180.1	179.4	179.5	178.0	177.9	179.7	178.2	179.4	177.5	173.5	172.2	170.3	177.1
2002	164.6	166.7	168.4	170.4	171.7	174.0	176.1	179.4	177.5	176.4	174.1	171.0	172.5
2003	164.5	165.7	166.7	167.8	169.5	170.8	173.3	175.2	175.6	174.6	172.2	173.7	170.8
2004	165.5	168.1	171.0	173.9	174.5	177.0	179.8	181.2	180.5	181.2	180.4	181.7	176.2
2005	174.8	177.9	180.0	182.7	183.1	186.1	188.9	190.5	190.6	190.0	190.3	191.9	185.6
2006	184.2	187.0	188.8	191.6	193.0	196.2	197.8	199.5	199.7	199.5	198.0	197.4	194.4
2007	190.6	193.0	195.3	196.1	196.6	198.9	199.2	201.3	200.2	200.5	198.0	197.1	197.2
2008	191.4	193.9	195.3	197.5	197.8	198.5	200.6	201.6	199.6	196.7	191.9	188.5	196.1
2009	182.1	180.8	179.1	180.1	179.0	179.8	181.2	180.2	180.1	179.7	179.2	179.2	180.0
2010	173.6	175.6	177.2	181.3	181.4	182.8	185.5	186.5	185.8	187.0	185.9	185.7	182.4
2011	180.1	182.1	183.8	186.8	185.7	187.6	188.4	189.8	188.5	188.3	185.1	185.2	186.0
Education and Health Services													
2000	167.9	171.4	172.2	172.6	172.4	169.5	166.8	168.5	173.9	176.8	177.8	177.9	172.3
2001	174.4	178.7	179.4	179.7	179.3	176.6	173.2	174.3	179.1	182.4	183.9	184.5	178.8
2002	180.5	184.0	185.1	186.6	186.4	183.4	180.4	180.9	185.2	189.5	190.7	190.1	185.2
2003	186.7	189.4	190.1	189.9	189.7	186.1	183.3	183.3	188.2	192.3	193.0	193.6	188.8
2004	187.0	191.8	193.1	193.8	193.0	190.2	187.5	187.7	193.9	197.5	198.9	199.1	192.8
2005	193.9	197.8	199.0	199.7	198.8	196.1	194.0	193.8	199.8	202.7	204.4	204.0	198.8
2006	200.1	204.1	205.5	206.8	206.7	202.7	198.5	199.0	205.2	208.9	210.9	211.0	205.0
2007	206.3	211.3	212.4	212.8	212.7	209.3	205.2	206.2	212.3	217.1	218.0	218.0	211.8
2008	213.7	218.8	219.8	220.8	220.1	217.3	213.8	214.2	220.7	224.7	225.3	225.4	219.6
2009	219.7	223.8	224.1	225.3	224.5	221.2	217.5	217.5	224.3	228.1	228.9	228.2	223.6
2010	225.0	228.4	229.5	230.3	229.5	226.2	222.2	222.3	229.1	234.3	235.5	235.1	229.0
2011	230.9	234.6	235.8	236.3	234.9	231.4	228.1	229.4	236.5	240.1	242.8	240.0	235.1
Leisure and Hospitality													
2000	138.8	140.2	142.2	145.3	148.3	153.2	156.2	156.8	153.7	148.9	147.1	146.7	148.1
2001	141.4	142.6	145.0	148.3	151.4	154.9	156.9	158.9	155.6	149.2	145.6	145.5	149.6
2002	140.8	141.6	143.6	147.4	150.8	155.1	156.6	159.0	156.3	150.5	148.1	146.4	149.7
2003	143.7	144.1	146.2	148.4	150.3	156.0	159.2	160.6	157.3	152.7	150.2	150.4	151.6
2004	144.9	145.9	148.8	153.1	156.0	159.5	162.9	164.6	161.6	156.0	154.0	154.0	155.1
2005	149.4	150.1	153.9	156.7	159.5	164.1	166.4	167.9	165.2	159.6	158.2	158.4	159.1
2006	154.6	155.5	158.4	162.5	165.2	169.4	172.6	173.9	170.8	166.2	164.6	165.6	164.9
2007	161.5	163.2	166.2	169.0	172.4	176.1	179.8	181.4	178.4	172.5	171.2	171.1	171.9
2008	166.6	167.2	170.2	172.8	175.5	178.9	181.6	181.7	178.6	171.1	167.0	163.3	172.9
2009	158.1	158.1	159.2	161.4	164.2	167.7	170.0	170.2	168.0	161.7	159.1	157.3	162.9
2010	153.2	154.4	156.5	160.3	163.1	167.4	170.2	170.9	167.9	163.6	160.2	160.0	162.3
2011	156.2	158.3	159.9	163.4	165.5	170.6	174.4	175.5	172.4	165.0	161.3	161.2	165.3
Other Services													
2000	53.7	54.5	55.1	55.3	55.7	55.7	54.9	55.4	56.0	56.0	55.9	55.6	55.3
2001	56.1	57.0	57.2	57.1	57.3	57.5	56.7	56.7	56.8	56.5	56.0	55.7	56.7
2002	54.8	55.3	55.6	56.2	56.6	56.6	56.3	56.4	56.6	56.6	56.5	56.2	56.1
2003	55.6	55.9	56.3	56.4	56.9	56.7	56.8	57.0	57.6	57.1	56.8	56.9	56.7
2004	55.4	56.2	57.0	57.2	57.3	58.0	58.0	57.8	58.2	58.7	57.2	56.8	57.3
2005	55.8	56.6	56.8	57.2	57.5	57.8	57.6	57.6	57.7	57.6	57.5	57.6	57.3
2006	56.8	57.4	58.1	58.6	59.3	59.9	59.3	59.5	59.5	59.6	59.4	59.6	58.9
2007	58.5	59.6	60.0	60.0	60.7	61.1	60.4	60.7	60.6	60.8	60.7	60.7	60.3
2008	59.8	60.4	60.8	61.1	61.7	61.7	61.1	61.0	61.4	60.6	59.7	59.1	60.7
2009	57.8	57.9	57.7	57.8	58.1	57.9	58.1	57.9	57.8	57.2	57.1	56.8	57.7
2010	55.9	56.1	56.4	56.4	56.9	57.5	57.0	56.6	56.9	56.9	56.3	56.2	56.6
2011	55.8	56.3	56.5	56.7	56.9	57.3	57.5	57.8	59.4	59.3	59.0	57.9	57.5
Government													
2000	276.8	281.9	283.3	284.0	291.2	289.5	259.4	256.8	267.2	283.5	285.5	283.8	278.6
2001	278.4	285.0	287.3	286.7	290.6	291.2	260.5	259.4	272.3	289.8	291.5	289.2	281.8
2002	285.4	291.0	292.9	291.5	294.4	295.3	266.7	264.8	276.2	289.8	291.7	288.6	285.7
2003	285.6	288.4	288.2	286.6	288.4	287.2	256.1	256.7	267.4	284.0	285.9	283.5	279.8
2004	279.0	285.0	287.9	286.9	289.5	292.3	263.7	262.8	273.8	288.0	290.6	288.5	282.3
2005	286.1	290.4	291.4	291.9	293.5	295.4	264.2	263.7	274.3	288.5	289.2	289.2	285.1
2006	284.5	290.6	292.1	291.2	295.1	296.5	265.3	264.7	276.1	291.4	295.3	290.8	286.1
2007	286.6	292.1	294.2	294.3	299.2	300.5	268.8	268.1	278.5	296.6	300.0	298.1	289.8
2008	294.8	300.1	302.0	302.4	305.7	306.8	279.8	278.3	288.3	304.3	308.0	305.2	298.0
2009	301.0	305.9	306.7	307.7	310.2	308.9	280.9	277.7	284.8	302.6	304.9	302.3	299.5
2010	298.7	303.4	304.9	307.5	314.9	314.4	281.4	277.7	283.6	302.8	306.2	301.5	299.8
2011	299.6	303.6	303.8	304.6	306.9	307.2	274.1	271.7	279.0	297.7	299.9	296.5	295.4

2. Average Weekly Hours by Selected Industry: Oregon, 2007–2011

(Not seasonally adjusted)

Industry and year	January	February	March	April	May	June	July	August	September	October	November	December	Annual average
Total Private													
2007	33.1	34.0	33.8	34.8	33.9	34.4	35.0	34.3	35.1	33.8	33.4	34.6	34.2
2008	32.9	33.6	34.4	33.7	33.8	34.9	33.8	34.2	33.7	33.5	34.2	32.7	33.8
2009	32.8	33.7	33.4	32.9	32.7	33.0	32.9	34.1	33.3	33.3	34.0	33.0	33.2
2010	33.0	33.4	33.1	33.4	34.3	33.4	33.6	34.8	33.6	33.7	33.3	33.6	33.6
2011	34.1	33.6	33.3	33.8	34.4	33.6	33.8	33.9	33.9	34.1	33.6	33.6	33.8
Goods-Producing													
2007	37.0	38.8	38.8	39.5	39.5	39.7	39.6	39.5	39.5	39.1	38.3	39.2	39.0
2008	37.0	37.6	38.0	37.7	38.4	38.9	37.9	38.5	38.0	37.7	38.0	37.0	37.9
2009	36.7	36.9	37.1	37.0	37.4	38.0	37.4	38.0	37.0	37.5	37.3	37.2	37.3
2010	37.3	37.3	37.1	37.6	38.0	37.6	37.7	38.5	38.0	38.6	37.6	37.5	37.7
2011	37.0	37.3	37.2	37.6	38.1	37.9	37.7	38.5	38.7	38.8	38.6	38.9	38.0
Construction													
2007	34.9	36.9	36.8	37.0	37.7	38.3	37.7	38.1	38.0	37.7	36.2	36.8	37.2
2008	34.1	35.4	35.5	35.8	37.3	37.7	36.9	38.0	37.7	37.1	36.5	36.2	36.5
2009	36.4	35.8	35.0	35.0	34.9	35.5	35.9	36.3	34.8	35.3	35.3	34.6	35.4
2010	34.9	34.8	34.2	34.8	35.2	35.8	36.8	37.3	35.5	35.9	34.7	35.0	35.4
2011	34.5	34.5	34.1	34.7	35.8	35.3	35.7	36.4	36.8	36.1	36.1	36.3	35.6
Manufacturing													
2007	38.1	39.8	39.9	40.8	40.5	40.4	40.6	40.2	40.2	40.0	39.5	40.6	40.1
2008	38.7	38.9	39.5	39.0	39.2	39.7	38.7	38.8	38.3	38.1	38.8	37.6	38.8
2009	37.2	37.4	38.1	38.0	38.5	39.1	38.3	38.9	38.0	38.6	38.4	38.3	38.2
2010	38.2	38.3	38.4	39.0	39.4	38.7	38.2	39.2	39.4	40.0	39.0	38.8	38.9
2011	38.2	38.6	38.5	38.8	39.1	39.0	38.7	39.5	39.8	40.0	39.9	40.1	39.2
Trade, Transportation, and Utilities													
2007	33.3	34.3	33.7	35.0	34.1	34.6	35.3	34.7	35.8	34.2	34.0	34.8	34.5
2008	33.5	34.0	34.8	34.2	34.2	35.3	34.8	35.2	34.9	34.5	34.8	34.0	34.5
2009	33.8	34.5	34.1	33.7	33.5	34.0	34.2	35.1	34.7	33.9	34.1	33.8	34.1
2010	33.4	34.0	33.8	34.2	35.2	34.5	34.7	35.7	34.8	34.6	34.2	35.1	34.5
2011	35.3	34.5	34.4	35.1	36.0	35.1	35.3	35.5	35.4	35.5	34.8	35.0	35.2
Financial Activities													
2007	36.2	36.6	35.7	37.0	35.2	35.8	37.0	35.6	37.3	35.2	35.4	37.1	36.2
2008	34.7	36.0	37.7	36.0	36.0	37.6	35.6	36.6	35.8	36.1	38.3	36.1	36.4
2009	36.7	37.9	37.2	35.8	35.5	35.3	35.1	37.4	35.7	35.8	37.9	35.7	36.3
2010	36.6	36.1	36.2	35.6	37.8	35.6	35.6	37.6	35.2	36.0	35.9	34.9	36.1
2011	37.8	36.0	35.9	35.8	37.3	35.7	35.5	36.7	36.7	37.8	37.4	37.3	36.7
Professional and Business Services													
2007	33.3	34.4	34.5	35.3	34.2	34.8	35.6	34.4	35.8	34.4	34.1	35.7	34.7
2008	33.9	34.5	35.5	34.6	34.7	36.1	34.5	34.8	34.6	34.5	35.2	33.7	34.7
2009	33.9	35.2	35.0	34.3	33.8	34.0	34.1	35.2	33.1	33.6	34.9	34.2	34.3
2010	34.5	35.1	34.6	34.9	35.3	34.5	34.9	36.1	34.8	34.9	34.7	34.6	34.9
2011	35.6	35.3	34.5	35.3	35.3	34.3	34.6	34.1	34.2	35.0	34.4	34.2	34.7
Education and Health Services													
2007	31.2	31.7	31.3	32.4	31.3	31.6	32.4	31.1	32.7	31.5	31.2	32.5	31.7
2008	31.9	32.3	33.0	32.5	32.1	33.2	32.0	32.0	31.9	31.4	32.2	30.3	32.1
2009	30.4	31.3	30.9	30.4	30.0	30.0	29.7	30.8	30.2	30.1	31.2	29.8	30.4
2010	30.0	30.4	30.0	30.4	31.3	30.5	30.6	31.3	30.7	30.6	30.5	30.5	30.6
2011	31.8	30.8	30.7	31.1	31.6	30.9	31.3	31.1	31.3	31.4	30.9	30.5	31.1
Leisure and Hospitality													
2007	24.5	24.5	24.8	25.6	24.2	24.9	26.2	25.5	26.0	24.0	23.7	24.6	24.9
2008	23.1	23.8	24.8	24.4	24.6	26.2	25.4	26.1	24.7	24.2	24.7	22.9	24.6
2009	23.6	25.1	25.0	24.5	24.7	25.0	25.3	27.2	24.9	24.7	25.1	23.9	24.9
2010	23.3	24.2	23.9	24.5	26.2	24.9	25.4	27.6	25.3	24.9	24.3	24.9	25.0
2011	25.4	25.0	24.9	26.0	26.7	25.6	26.6	26.2	25.7	25.7	24.9	24.4	25.6
Other Services													
2007	28.3	29.4	28.9	30.5	28.5	30.4	29.2	29.3	29.3	27.7	27.3	27.9	28.9
2008	25.7	27.7	28.4	27.3	27.9	28.4	27.0	28.3	27.8	27.9	29.2	27.1	27.7
2009	27.2	28.7	28.3	27.7	28.0	28.3	28.4	30.4	34.1	34.6	35.1	33.3	30.3
2010	33.3	33.3	32.1	31.9	32.5	31.6	31.8	32.7	30.2	30.4	30.8	31.0	31.8
2011	31.3	30.6	29.0	30.3	30.7	29.8	29.8	29.7	29.8	30.0	29.3	29.9	30.0

3. Average Hourly Earnings by Selected Industry: Oregon, 2007–2011

(Dollars, not seasonally adjusted)

Industry and year	January	February	March	April	May	June	July	August	September	October	November	December	Annual average
Total Private													
2007	20.92	20.70	20.67	20.77	20.44	20.45	20.57	20.28	20.60	20.55	20.48	20.87	20.61
2008	20.85	20.86	20.82	20.88	20.81	20.79	20.84	20.94	20.93	21.04	21.17	21.34	20.93
2009	21.42	21.68	21.63	21.31	21.27	21.06	20.95	21.21	21.25	21.21	21.39	21.52	21.33
2010	21.52	21.56	21.74	21.64	21.59	21.42	21.55	21.47	21.49	21.55	21.54	21.66	21.56
2011	21.95	21.75	21.68	21.69	21.57	21.53	21.66	21.52	21.68	21.91	21.89	22.15	21.75
Goods-Producing													
2007	21.23	20.84	20.93	21.04	20.89	21.22	20.91	20.98	21.33	20.95	20.77	21.42	21.04
2008	21.32	21.18	21.20	21.25	21.38	21.67	21.76	21.95	21.56	21.77	21.84	22.12	21.58
2009	22.32	22.40	22.55	22.43	22.53	22.23	22.44	22.47	22.26	22.37	22.50	22.42	22.41
2010	22.39	22.58	22.71	22.76	22.88	22.93	23.20	23.19	23.00	23.09	23.07	23.10	22.92
2011	23.31	23.11	23.14	23.47	23.36	23.41	23.66	23.47	23.69	23.96	23.91	24.30	23.57
Construction													
2007	23.03	22.62	22.98	23.05	23.30	23.39	22.92	23.56	23.59	23.42	23.07	23.74	23.23
2008	24.04	23.72	23.82	23.89	23.94	24.12	25.03	24.83	24.61	24.76	25.01	25.19	24.41
2009	25.24	25.33	25.71	25.62	25.92	25.54	25.70	25.84	26.01	25.95	26.04	26.40	25.77
2010	26.30	26.57	26.76	26.13	26.33	26.71	26.64	27.28	27.19	27.06	26.85	27.27	26.77
2011	26.96	27.02	27.09	27.20	26.96	27.18	27.01	27.08	27.16	27.47	27.29	28.37	27.24
Manufacturing													
2007	20.39	20.00	19.94	20.08	19.64	20.12	19.87	19.59	20.18	19.66	19.67	20.37	19.96
2008	20.21	20.07	20.04	20.07	20.15	20.48	20.14	20.52	20.06	20.34	20.48	20.85	20.28
2009	21.02	21.17	21.13	21.09	21.15	20.80	20.96	21.01	20.71	20.90	21.11	21.07	21.01
2010	21.17	21.38	21.46	21.49	21.71	21.54	21.85	21.56	21.39	21.55	21.72	21.65	21.54
2011	22.14	21.84	21.92	22.30	22.22	22.20	22.61	22.13	22.42	22.65	22.69	22.78	22.33
Trade, Transportation, and Utilities													
2007	17.23	17.32	17.57	17.40	17.05	17.34	17.58	17.24	17.73	17.65	17.77	18.07	17.50
2008	18.10	18.48	18.62	18.31	18.33	18.21	18.32	18.43	18.37	18.66	19.00	19.03	18.49
2009	19.34	19.51	20.32	19.51	19.57	19.24	19.36	19.50	19.22	19.11	19.24	19.49	19.45
2010	19.67	19.30	19.67	19.32	19.32	19.18	19.29	19.16	19.16	19.34	19.11	19.22	19.31
2011	19.91	19.71	19.79	19.53	19.50	19.53	19.70	19.42	19.58	19.78	19.35	19.13	19.57
Financial Activities													
2007	26.82	27.26	25.78	26.16	25.23	24.32	24.70	24.37	24.04	25.12	24.39	25.27	25.29
2008	25.02	24.53	23.48	25.21	24.72	23.71	23.93	24.40	23.88	24.25	24.13	23.74	24.24
2009	23.93	25.51	24.41	24.37	24.82	24.64	25.46	25.60	25.42	25.35	25.66	26.38	25.13
2010	25.60	27.68	26.20	27.20	26.37	26.36	26.62	26.57	26.57	26.17	26.07	26.15	26.46
2011	25.52	25.31	25.20	25.16	24.84	24.41	24.55	24.49	24.67	24.44	24.96	24.72	24.85
Professional and Business Services													
2007	25.07	23.27	24.05	23.80	23.62	23.33	23.39	23.12	23.62	23.44	23.38	23.95	23.66
2008	24.03	24.16	24.28	24.06	24.01	24.70	24.95	24.92	24.89	25.02	24.85	25.19	24.59
2009	25.29	25.33	24.62	24.55	24.04	23.94	23.92	24.08	24.18	24.05	24.45	24.44	24.41
2010	24.43	24.35	24.62	24.81	25.18	24.50	24.53	24.79	24.48	24.61	24.62	25.03	24.67
2011	25.18	25.02	24.71	24.79	24.92	24.60	24.36	24.52	24.36	24.82	24.97	24.98	24.77
Education and Health Services													
2007	22.66	22.99	22.50	23.24	22.72	23.33	23.90	22.97	22.95	22.79	23.11	22.70	22.99
2008	22.27	22.04	22.28	22.23	21.99	21.99	22.01	22.21	22.20	21.95	21.93	22.17	22.11
2009	21.87	21.62	21.61	21.47	21.61	21.67	21.77	21.74	22.09	21.93	21.63	21.78	21.73
2010	21.82	21.60	21.86	21.77	21.65	21.62	21.89	21.69	21.72	21.61	21.80	22.07	21.76
2011	22.31	22.20	22.25	22.49	22.26	22.32	22.75	22.47	22.57	22.54	22.60	22.68	22.45
Leisure and Hospitality													
2007	14.31	14.04	14.12	13.82	14.04	13.42	13.49	13.17	13.00	12.94	12.75	12.83	13.48
2008	12.81	12.97	12.66	12.71	12.59	12.50	12.52	12.55	12.64	12.70	12.79	13.07	12.70
2009	13.08	13.10	13.06	12.84	12.84	12.62	12.59	12.57	12.78	13.04	13.10	13.17	12.89
2010	13.19	12.97	13.03	12.80	12.80	12.62	12.55	12.45	12.77	13.03	13.03	13.34	12.87
2011	13.14	13.27	13.00	13.03	12.92	12.88	13.01	13.00	13.16	13.20	13.26	13.36	13.10
Other Services													
2007	18.18	18.03	18.12	18.18	17.82	17.17	17.03	16.86	17.60	17.60	17.20	17.29	17.59
2008	17.40	17.41	17.25	17.37	17.37	17.01	16.70	16.97	17.51	17.58	17.64	17.99	17.35
2009	17.99	18.08	18.02	17.84	17.78	17.89	17.72	17.76	17.95	17.63	18.13	18.19	17.92
2010	18.12	18.07	18.44	18.41	18.80	18.15	18.05	18.42	18.10	17.99	18.21	18.37	18.26
2011	18.50	18.75	19.00	18.96	19.44	19.45	19.49	19.22	19.29	19.64	19.95	20.25	19.33

4. Average Weekly Earnings by Selected Industry: Oregon, 2007–2011

(Dollars, not seasonally adjusted)

Industry and year	January	February	March	April	May	June	July	August	September	October	November	December	Annual average
Total Private													
2007	692.45	703.80	698.65	722.80	692.92	703.48	719.95	695.60	723.06	694.59	684.03	722.10	704.68
2008	685.97	700.90	716.21	703.66	703.38	725.57	704.39	716.15	705.34	704.84	724.01	697.82	707.29
2009	702.58	730.62	722.44	701.10	695.53	694.98	689.26	723.26	707.63	706.29	727.26	710.16	708.74
2010	710.16	720.10	719.59	722.78	740.54	715.43	724.08	747.16	722.06	726.24	717.28	727.78	724.69
2011	748.50	730.80	721.94	733.12	742.01	723.41	732.11	729.53	734.95	747.13	735.50	744.24	735.19
Goods-Producing													
2007	785.51	808.59	812.08	831.08	825.16	842.43	828.04	828.71	842.54	819.15	795.49	839.66	821.70
2008	788.84	796.37	805.60	801.13	820.99	842.96	824.70	845.08	819.28	820.73	829.92	818.44	817.85
2009	819.14	826.56	836.61	829.91	842.62	844.74	839.26	853.86	823.62	838.88	839.25	834.02	835.55
2010	835.15	842.23	842.54	855.78	869.44	862.17	874.64	892.82	874.00	891.27	867.43	866.25	864.75
2011	862.47	862.00	860.81	882.47	890.02	887.24	891.98	903.60	916.80	929.65	922.93	945.27	896.82
Construction													
2007	803.75	834.68	845.66	852.85	878.41	895.84	864.08	897.64	896.42	882.93	835.13	873.63	864.32
2008	819.76	839.69	845.61	855.26	892.96	909.32	923.61	943.54	927.80	918.60	912.87	911.88	891.83
2009	918.74	906.81	899.85	896.70	904.61	906.67	922.63	937.99	905.15	916.04	919.21	913.44	912.20
2010	917.87	924.64	915.19	909.32	926.82	956.22	980.35	1,017.54	965.25	971.45	931.70	954.45	948.39
2011	930.12	932.19	923.77	943.84	965.17	959.45	964.26	985.71	999.49	991.67	985.17	1,029.83	969.48
Manufacturing													
2007	776.86	796.00	795.61	819.26	795.42	812.85	806.72	787.52	811.24	786.40	776.97	827.02	799.29
2008	782.13	780.72	791.58	782.73	789.88	813.06	779.42	796.18	768.30	774.95	794.62	783.96	786.46
2009	781.94	791.76	805.05	801.42	814.28	813.28	802.77	817.29	786.98	806.74	810.62	806.98	803.03
2010	808.69	818.85	824.06	838.11	855.37	833.60	834.67	845.15	842.77	862.00	847.08	840.02	837.71
2011	845.75	843.02	843.92	865.24	868.80	865.80	875.01	874.14	892.32	906.00	905.33	913.48	874.94
Trade, Transportation, and Utilities													
2007	573.76	594.08	592.11	609.00	581.41	599.96	620.57	598.23	634.73	603.63	604.18	628.84	603.57
2008	606.35	628.32	647.98	626.20	626.89	642.81	637.54	648.74	641.11	643.77	661.20	647.02	638.15
2009	653.69	673.10	692.91	657.49	655.60	654.16	662.11	684.45	666.93	647.83	656.08	658.76	663.57
2010	656.98	656.20	664.85	660.74	680.06	661.71	669.36	684.01	666.77	669.16	653.56	674.62	666.63
2011	702.82	680.00	680.78	685.50	702.00	685.50	695.41	689.41	693.13	702.19	673.38	669.55	688.17
Financial Activities													
2007	970.88	997.72	920.35	967.92	888.10	870.66	913.90	867.57	896.69	884.22	863.41	937.52	914.87
2008	868.19	883.08	885.20	907.56	889.92	891.50	851.91	893.04	854.90	875.43	924.18	857.01	881.84
2009	878.23	966.83	908.05	872.45	881.11	869.79	893.65	957.44	907.49	907.53	972.51	941.77	912.99
2010	936.96	999.25	948.44	968.32	996.79	938.42	947.67	999.03	935.26	942.12	935.91	912.64	955.05
2011	964.66	911.16	904.68	900.73	926.53	871.44	871.53	898.78	905.39	923.83	933.50	922.06	911.09
Professional and Business Services													
2007	834.83	800.49	829.73	840.14	807.80	811.88	832.68	795.33	845.60	806.34	797.26	855.02	821.37
2008	814.62	833.52	861.94	832.48	833.15	891.67	860.78	867.22	861.19	863.19	874.72	848.90	853.76
2009	857.33	891.62	861.70	842.07	812.55	813.96	815.67	847.62	800.36	808.08	853.31	835.85	836.79
2010	842.84	854.69	851.85	865.87	888.85	845.25	856.10	894.92	851.90	858.89	854.31	866.04	861.13
2011	896.41	883.21	852.50	875.09	879.68	843.78	842.86	836.13	833.11	868.70	858.97	854.32	860.21
Education and Health Services													
2007	706.99	728.78	704.25	752.98	711.14	737.23	774.36	714.37	750.47	717.89	721.03	737.75	729.70
2008	710.41	711.89	735.24	722.48	708.13	730.07	704.32	710.72	708.18	689.23	706.15	671.75	708.91
2009	664.85	676.71	667.75	652.69	648.30	650.10	646.57	669.59	667.12	660.09	674.86	649.04	660.65
2010	654.60	656.64	655.80	661.81	677.65	659.41	669.83	678.90	666.80	661.27	664.90	673.14	665.05
2011	709.46	683.76	683.08	699.44	703.42	689.69	712.08	698.82	706.44	707.76	698.34	691.74	698.64
Leisure and Hospitality													
2007	350.60	343.98	350.18	353.79	339.77	334.16	353.44	335.84	338.00	310.56	302.18	315.62	335.58
2008	295.91	308.69	313.97	310.12	309.71	327.50	318.01	327.56	312.21	307.34	315.91	299.30	312.43
2009	308.69	328.81	326.50	314.58	317.15	315.50	318.53	341.90	318.22	322.09	328.81	314.76	321.32
2010	307.33	313.87	311.42	313.60	335.36	314.24	318.77	343.62	323.08	324.45	316.63	332.17	321.38
2011	333.76	331.75	323.70	338.78	344.96	329.73	346.07	340.60	338.21	339.24	330.17	325.98	335.40
Other Services													
2007	514.49	530.08	523.67	554.49	507.87	521.97	497.28	494.00	515.68	487.52	469.56	482.39	508.15
2008	447.18	482.26	489.90	474.20	484.62	483.08	450.90	480.25	486.78	490.48	515.09	487.53	481.00
2009	489.33	518.90	509.97	494.17	497.84	506.29	503.25	539.90	612.10	610.00	636.36	605.73	543.19
2010	603.40	601.73	591.92	587.28	611.00	573.54	573.99	602.33	546.62	546.90	560.87	569.47	580.83
2011	579.05	573.75	551.00	574.49	596.81	579.61	580.80	570.83	574.84	589.20	584.54	605.48	580.12

PENNSYLVANIA
At a Glance

Population:
2000 census: 12,280,548
2010 census: 12,702,379
2011 estimate: 12,742,886

Percent change in population:
2000–2010: 3.4%
2010–2011: 0.3%

Percent change in total nonfarm employment:
2000–2010: -1.2%
2010–2011: 1.1%

Industry with the largest growth in employment, 2000–2011 (thousands):
Education and Health Services, 238.1

Industry with the largest decline or smallest growth in employment, 2000–2011 (thousands):
Manufacturing, -300.1

Civilian labor force:
2000: 6,805,833
2010: 6,389,594
2011: 6,385,714

Unemployment rate and rank among states (lowest to highest):
2000: 4.2%, 33rd
2010: 8.5%, 24th
2011: 7.9%, 23rd

Over-the-year change in unemployment rates:
2010–2011: -0.6%

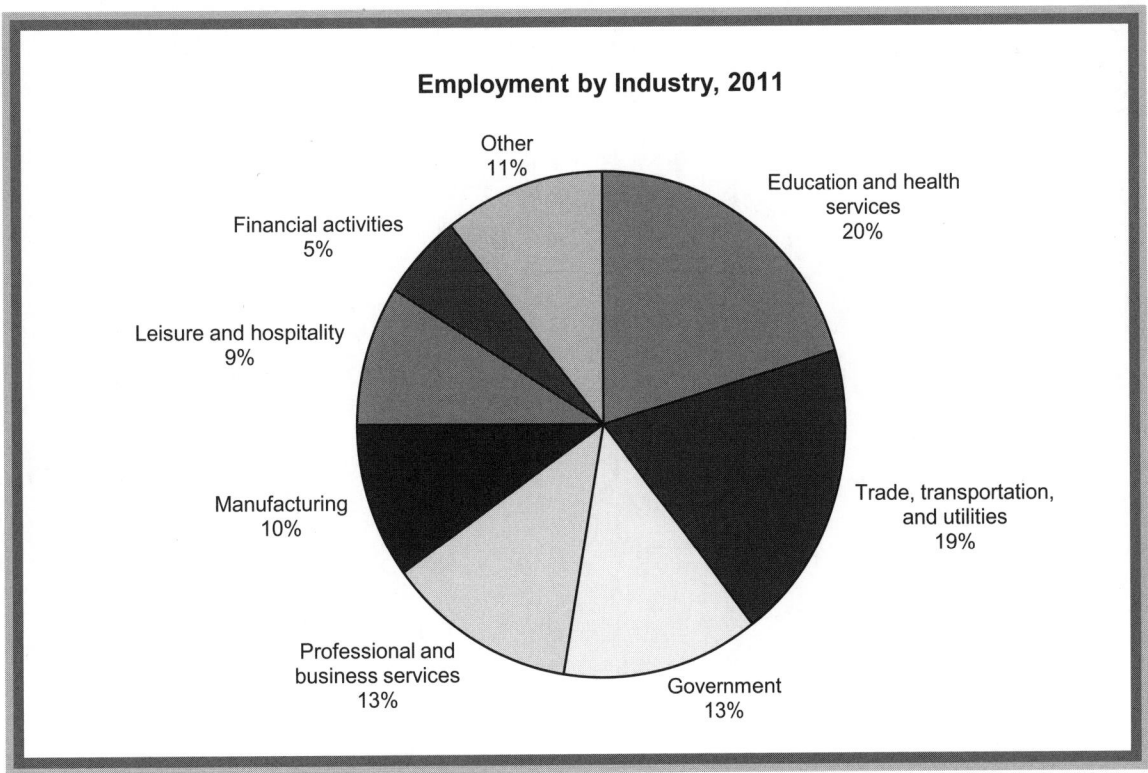

Employment by Industry, 2011

Other 11%
Education and health services 20%
Financial activities 5%
Leisure and hospitality 9%
Manufacturing 10%
Trade, transportation, and utilities 19%
Professional and business services 13%
Government 13%

1. Employment by Industry: Pennsylvania, Selected Years, 2000–2011

(Numbers in thousands, not seasonally adjusted)

Industry and year	January	February	March	April	May	June	July	August	September	October	November	December	Annual average
Total Nonfarm													
2000	5,549.9	5,579.7	5,638.4	5,692.8	5,733.1	5,742.9	5,691.0	5,676.4	5,737.1	5,747.5	5,769.3	5,769.8	5,694.0
2001	5,615.8	5,643.8	5,679.2	5,705.0	5,731.8	5,741.4	5,655.1	5,657.5	5,693.6	5,695.6	5,706.1	5,697.6	5,685.2
2002	5,552.3	5,577.7	5,616.5	5,649.7	5,683.5	5,695.1	5,617.0	5,616.9	5,664.5	5,683.7	5,691.9	5,672.7	5,643.5
2003	5,525.2	5,533.1	5,572.0	5,612.0	5,650.9	5,659.6	5,578.6	5,582.2	5,631.0	5,671.3	5,678.7	5,673.9	5,614.0
2004	5,509.8	5,533.1	5,584.9	5,636.6	5,677.5	5,694.6	5,631.1	5,624.8	5,681.9	5,721.7	5,735.1	5,731.4	5,646.9
2005	5,571.0	5,600.9	5,631.5	5,710.9	5,742.5	5,750.3	5,694.8	5,687.3	5,744.4	5,767.0	5,784.3	5,774.2	5,704.9
2006	5,624.6	5,658.7	5,703.4	5,762.9	5,797.9	5,803.0	5,734.2	5,732.3	5,790.0	5,823.8	5,837.8	5,836.9	5,758.8
2007	5,681.8	5,693.0	5,744.4	5,795.5	5,840.2	5,855.9	5,787.6	5,779.3	5,821.0	5,863.5	5,877.9	5,867.8	5,800.7
2008	5,714.6	5,734.8	5,763.2	5,829.5	5,864.8	5,858.5	5,786.1	5,780.0	5,822.1	5,848.0	5,825.6	5,797.4	5,802.1
2009	5,603.4	5,607.3	5,606.6	5,636.7	5,662.5	5,643.7	5,570.1	5,551.2	5,600.0	5,647.4	5,652.6	5,634.3	5,618.0
2010	5,473.6	5,484.9	5,542.3	5,623.7	5,678.9	5,674.5	5,607.0	5,602.9	5,652.6	5,705.0	5,724.1	5,714.0	5,623.6
2011	5,557.1	5,589.7	5,632.6	5,704.2	5,733.3	5,733.5	5,670.7	5,661.8	5,700.2	5,757.2	5,758.7	5,746.0	5,687.1
Total Private													
2000	4,828.7	4,840.6	4,891.3	4,943.4	4,973.9	5,020.4	5,010.1	5,005.5	5,014.5	5,009.2	5,025.2	5,031.7	4,966.2
2001	4,892.5	4,901.0	4,933.6	4,955.4	4,986.1	5,020.2	4,978.1	4,981.6	4,962.0	4,945.9	4,950.1	4,944.6	4,954.3
2002	4,814.1	4,819.6	4,856.6	4,887.4	4,926.4	4,960.3	4,932.1	4,938.9	4,925.2	4,924.7	4,925.0	4,912.3	4,901.9
2003	4,783.0	4,768.3	4,803.1	4,842.9	4,886.3	4,910.5	4,885.3	4,893.6	4,888.6	4,906.3	4,909.6	4,911.0	4,865.7
2004	4,766.0	4,770.3	4,817.1	4,866.1	4,911.1	4,947.5	4,942.8	4,942.1	4,938.5	4,959.5	4,965.8	4,970.5	4,899.8
2005	4,824.9	4,835.7	4,862.5	4,938.7	4,979.1	5,005.1	5,003.0	5,002.1	5,000.7	5,005.0	5,016.6	5,012.7	4,957.2
2006	4,882.1	4,894.6	4,936.4	4,994.2	5,031.1	5,058.0	5,042.2	5,044.1	5,043.9	5,060.1	5,066.3	5,071.5	5,010.5
2007	4,937.1	4,929.0	4,977.1	5,027.5	5,076.2	5,110.9	5,095.8	5,090.3	5,078.4	5,101.0	5,110.0	5,104.4	5,053.2
2008	4,968.9	4,970.5	4,995.5	5,059.0	5,101.3	5,110.6	5,095.3	5,086.7	5,067.3	5,073.6	5,046.9	5,025.2	5,050.1
2009	4,851.2	4,834.4	4,831.5	4,854.8	4,890.0	4,887.5	4,864.3	4,851.6	4,840.9	4,869.1	4,868.3	4,856.8	4,858.4
2010	4,722.6	4,712.5	4,764.0	4,840.0	4,886.7	4,904.8	4,900.2	4,902.5	4,898.1	4,931.7	4,944.8	4,941.8	4,862.5
2011	4,805.7	4,821.2	4,862.6	4,932.7	4,972.1	4,986.8	4,983.1	4,980.1	4,968.1	5,005.5	5,001.5	4,996.2	4,943.0
Goods-Producing													
2000	1,099.9	1,092.8	1,112.0	1,126.0	1,135.2	1,153.7	1,153.5	1,155.8	1,150.1	1,140.3	1,132.3	1,122.0	1,131.1
2001	1,096.3	1,090.4	1,095.9	1,101.6	1,105.7	1,114.7	1,105.2	1,105.1	1,093.7	1,077.5	1,063.6	1,051.0	1,091.7
2002	1,017.1	1,012.9	1,019.0	1,027.7	1,036.0	1,048.0	1,043.2	1,045.1	1,035.1	1,027.3	1,014.5	999.1	1,027.1
2003	972.6	959.4	965.5	975.1	985.1	992.8	989.3	989.0	982.4	977.7	969.0	957.8	976.3
2004	928.9	922.5	935.8	950.6	963.6	977.5	981.6	981.1	976.3	972.4	965.9	958.2	959.5
2005	928.9	921.9	928.3	948.9	961.6	973.7	975.6	976.2	969.3	964.4	961.4	947.7	954.8
2006	924.4	921.9	934.4	948.8	958.0	969.8	969.5	971.8	965.6	959.8	952.1	944.1	951.7
2007	921.6	906.3	922.4	936.4	948.7	962.5	962.5	961.8	955.2	953.5	945.6	933.0	942.5
2008	910.1	901.9	909.4	923.2	934.9	943.3	941.0	939.6	930.2	922.3	905.7	885.8	920.6
2009	844.8	828.2	822.9	824.5	825.5	828.2	824.0	821.3	816.3	815.3	807.0	793.8	821.0
2010	766.8	759.2	773.7	797.2	807.8	818.8	823.4	823.5	819.2	818.8	816.2	804.7	802.4
2011	781.5	778.9	793.4	811.5	823.3	834.4	839.3	842.1	835.4	837.0	830.1	823.5	819.2
Mining and Logging													
2000	18.9	18.8	19.2	19.2	19.3	19.7	19.9	19.9	19.9	19.6	19.4	19.0	19.4
2001	18.6	18.6	18.9	19.2	19.7	20.0	20.1	20.2	20.0	19.9	19.7	19.3	19.5
2002	18.7	18.7	18.8	18.9	19.2	19.4	18.9	19.3	18.9	18.8	18.4	17.8	18.8
2003	17.2	17.1	17.3	17.5	17.8	18.1	18.3	18.3	18.4	18.4	18.3	17.9	17.9
2004	17.2	17.2	17.7	18.4	18.7	19.2	19.5	19.5	19.3	19.3	19.3	19.1	18.7
2005	18.6	18.6	18.6	19.6	19.8	20.3	20.5	20.4	20.4	20.2	20.1	19.6	19.7
2006	19.2	19.3	19.7	20.3	20.6	20.9	21.0	20.9	20.8	20.7	20.7	20.3	20.4
2007	19.9	19.8	20.2	20.8	21.2	21.7	21.9	21.9	21.6	21.5	21.4	21.0	21.1
2008	20.6	20.5	20.9	21.6	22.2	22.8	22.9	23.1	23.1	23.4	23.3	22.5	22.2
2009	21.8	21.5	21.2	21.7	21.9	22.4	22.6	22.6	22.7	22.9	23.1	22.7	22.3
2010	22.4	22.8	23.6	25.3	26.0	26.8	27.5	27.9	28.6	28.9	29.6	29.4	26.6
2011	29.4	30.2	30.8	31.7	32.5	33.4	34.2	35.1	35.5	36.4	36.5	36.2	33.5
Construction													
2000	220.5	215.9	230.3	245.0	254.5	261.7	263.9	265.3	262.3	258.6	252.8	241.6	247.7
2001	226.2	225.4	232.7	244.7	255.7	263.9	266.3	267.8	263.1	259.4	253.2	245.1	250.3
2002	225.3	224.8	231.9	243.9	253.4	260.8	264.0	265.8	260.4	258.6	252.2	240.7	248.5
2003	224.1	218.6	226.4	239.4	250.6	256.5	261.7	263.1	259.2	258.0	252.7	242.2	246.0
2004	223.8	219.9	231.3	243.7	254.1	262.0	266.7	266.5	264.9	262.4	257.1	249.5	250.2
2005	229.3	225.4	230.6	250.9	260.8	268.2	272.7	273.7	270.8	267.8	265.3	253.4	255.7
2006	237.2	236.4	245.3	258.1	265.9	272.3	274.8	276.6	274.2	270.4	263.7	256.6	261.0
2007	241.8	232.9	244.0	257.3	267.9	275.9	278.1	278.7	276.0	274.3	266.5	253.9	262.3
2008	239.1	234.0	240.3	255.2	264.3	269.3	270.2	269.8	264.7	260.9	250.5	236.9	254.6
2009	215.4	211.8	215.9	224.5	230.6	234.3	235.5	234.3	230.8	229.9	222.1	210.6	224.6
2010	191.4	185.5	196.3	215.2	222.2	227.4	231.3	231.2	227.9	226.9	223.3	212.1	215.9
2011	194.7	192.5	203.5	217.9	226.0	232.3	236.9	237.3	234.5	234.6	230.0	221.4	221.8
Manufacturing													
2000	860.5	858.1	862.5	861.8	861.4	872.3	869.7	870.6	867.9	862.1	860.1	861.4	864.0
2001	851.5	846.4	844.3	837.7	830.3	830.8	818.8	817.1	810.6	798.2	790.7	786.6	821.9
2002	773.1	769.4	768.3	764.9	763.4	767.8	760.3	760.0	755.8	749.9	743.9	740.6	759.8
2003	731.3	723.7	721.8	718.2	716.7	718.2	709.3	707.6	704.8	701.3	698.0	697.7	712.4
2004	687.9	685.4	686.8	688.5	690.8	696.3	695.4	695.1	692.1	690.7	689.5	689.6	690.7
2005	681.0	677.9	679.1	678.4	681.0	685.2	682.4	682.1	678.1	676.4	676.0	674.7	679.4
2006	668.0	666.2	669.4	670.4	671.5	676.6	673.7	674.3	670.6	668.7	667.7	667.2	670.4
2007	659.9	653.6	658.2	658.3	659.6	664.9	662.5	661.2	657.6	657.7	657.7	658.1	659.2
2008	650.4	647.4	648.2	646.4	648.4	651.2	647.9	646.7	642.4	638.0	631.9	626.4	643.8
2009	607.6	594.9	585.8	578.3	573.0	571.5	565.9	564.4	562.8	562.5	561.8	560.5	574.1
2010	553.0	550.9	553.8	556.7	559.6	564.6	564.6	564.4	562.7	563.0	563.3	563.2	560.0
2011	557.4	556.2	559.1	561.9	564.8	568.7	568.2	569.7	565.4	566.0	563.6	565.9	563.9

1. Employment by Industry: Pennsylvania, Selected Years, 2000–2011—*Continued*

(Numbers in thousands, not seasonally adjusted)

Industry and year	January	February	March	April	May	June	July	August	September	October	November	December	Annual average
Service-Providing													
2000	4,450.0	4,486.9	4,526.4	4,566.8	4,597.9	4,589.2	4,537.5	4,520.6	4,587.0	4,607.2	4,637.0	4,647.8	4,562.9
2001	4,519.5	4,553.4	4,583.3	4,603.4	4,626.1	4,626.7	4,549.9	4,552.4	4,599.9	4,618.1	4,642.5	4,646.6	4,593.5
2002	4,535.2	4,564.8	4,597.5	4,622.0	4,647.5	4,647.1	4,573.8	4,571.8	4,629.4	4,656.4	4,677.4	4,673.6	4,616.4
2003	4,552.6	4,573.7	4,606.5	4,636.9	4,665.8	4,666.8	4,589.3	4,593.2	4,648.6	4,693.6	4,709.7	4,716.1	4,637.7
2004	4,580.9	4,610.6	4,649.1	4,686.0	4,713.9	4,717.1	4,649.5	4,643.7	4,705.6	4,749.3	4,769.2	4,773.2	4,687.3
2005	4,642.1	4,679.0	4,703.2	4,762.0	4,780.9	4,776.6	4,719.2	4,711.1	4,775.1	4,802.6	4,822.9	4,826.5	4,750.1
2006	4,700.2	4,736.8	4,769.0	4,814.1	4,839.9	4,833.2	4,764.7	4,760.5	4,824.4	4,864.0	4,885.7	4,892.8	4,807.1
2007	4,760.2	4,786.7	4,822.0	4,859.1	4,891.5	4,893.4	4,825.1	4,817.5	4,865.9	4,910.0	4,932.3	4,934.8	4,858.2
2008	4,804.5	4,832.9	4,853.8	4,906.3	4,929.9	4,915.2	4,845.1	4,840.4	4,891.9	4,925.7	4,919.9	4,911.6	4,881.4
2009	4,758.6	4,779.1	4,783.7	4,812.2	4,837.0	4,815.5	4,746.1	4,729.9	4,783.7	4,832.1	4,845.6	4,840.5	4,797.0
2010	4,706.8	4,725.7	4,768.6	4,826.5	4,871.1	4,855.7	4,783.6	4,779.4	4,833.4	4,886.2	4,907.9	4,909.3	4,821.2
2011	4,775.6	4,810.8	4,839.2	4,892.7	4,910.0	4,899.1	4,831.4	4,819.7	4,864.8	4,920.2	4,928.6	4,922.5	4,867.9
Trade, Transportation, and Utilities													
2000	1,112.0	1,101.1	1,106.2	1,119.0	1,125.0	1,131.0	1,119.1	1,123.4	1,131.5	1,142.5	1,164.7	1,179.3	1,129.6
2001	1,129.5	1,112.2	1,116.1	1,115.9	1,121.7	1,125.5	1,108.4	1,110.1	1,116.2	1,123.7	1,143.8	1,155.0	1,123.2
2002	1,111.4	1,094.5	1,101.1	1,101.7	1,111.9	1,115.5	1,102.3	1,104.8	1,109.1	1,117.9	1,135.7	1,148.5	1,112.9
2003	1,101.4	1,085.7	1,090.7	1,096.8	1,105.6	1,110.6	1,095.6	1,098.9	1,105.5	1,120.6	1,137.1	1,150.4	1,108.2
2004	1,102.3	1,091.8	1,097.7	1,101.9	1,111.3	1,115.4	1,104.6	1,105.2	1,110.1	1,123.9	1,142.2	1,157.3	1,113.6
2005	1,108.9	1,097.7	1,102.0	1,110.1	1,119.2	1,121.5	1,113.6	1,113.9	1,118.5	1,127.7	1,147.6	1,162.9	1,120.3
2006	1,119.6	1,103.2	1,110.5	1,115.2	1,122.7	1,123.7	1,113.6	1,115.2	1,122.2	1,135.0	1,156.5	1,172.3	1,125.8
2007	1,130.6	1,110.6	1,119.1	1,122.9	1,134.2	1,137.3	1,126.6	1,123.9	1,127.6	1,137.1	1,162.1	1,174.4	1,133.9
2008	1,133.4	1,114.2	1,118.3	1,121.9	1,130.8	1,130.3	1,117.6	1,115.4	1,119.4	1,126.7	1,136.3	1,146.5	1,125.9
2009	1,093.5	1,077.3	1,072.5	1,071.9	1,082.5	1,081.8	1,065.4	1,064.2	1,070.9	1,081.1	1,099.3	1,109.5	1,080.8
2010	1,068.3	1,050.1	1,060.3	1,067.3	1,079.4	1,084.2	1,071.5	1,072.9	1,078.3	1,091.2	1,110.6	1,126.1	1,080.0
2011	1,084.0	1,073.5	1,076.6	1,086.4	1,094.5	1,095.2	1,085.6	1,087.1	1,088.5	1,100.5	1,118.6	1,131.2	1,093.5
Wholesale Trade													
2000	221.0	221.3	223.0	227.6	227.6	229.4	228.5	228.7	227.7	228.4	228.6	228.9	226.7
2001	227.0	226.7	227.4	227.8	228.1	229.8	229.8	229.5	228.1	226.6	226.6	227.7	227.9
2002	225.4	224.3	225.2	225.3	226.8	228.3	227.9	227.3	225.9	226.5	226.8	227.5	226.4
2003	225.4	225.2	226.7	226.9	228.2	228.7	228.2	228.1	227.0	227.3	227.7	228.6	227.3
2004	225.7	225.4	227.1	227.9	229.0	231.1	231.8	231.8	230.5	231.1	231.3	232.4	229.6
2005	229.9	230.0	231.2	233.2	234.6	235.7	236.2	236.2	235.2	235.3	235.5	236.5	234.1
2006	233.3	233.8	235.0	236.7	238.2	239.9	239.7	239.9	238.6	239.0	239.0	239.3	237.7
2007	236.5	235.6	237.2	238.3	239.3	241.2	241.5	240.7	239.2	239.7	240.6	240.8	239.2
2008	237.8	237.7	238.4	239.3	240.5	241.2	241.2	240.3	238.1	237.7	235.6	234.5	238.5
2009	230.0	228.0	227.1	226.3	226.7	226.8	225.5	224.7	223.0	223.1	222.6	222.7	225.5
2010	219.8	218.7	220.3	221.8	223.5	224.7	225.3	225.7	224.3	225.4	225.3	225.7	223.4
2011	223.7	223.8	224.9	226.8	228.0	229.0	227.1	228.2	226.0	227.3	227.1	228.6	226.7
Retail Trade													
2000	671.6	661.0	663.0	670.3	675.2	680.7	675.8	680.3	679.8	684.9	707.2	722.3	681.0
2001	679.7	663.3	666.5	663.8	668.0	672.5	664.3	667.3	664.7	668.9	689.9	701.6	672.5
2002	666.2	651.2	656.1	655.1	662.5	666.8	661.7	664.4	659.9	663.1	682.0	695.3	665.4
2003	657.1	642.8	646.4	650.7	656.7	662.4	657.3	660.4	657.8	667.2	683.7	697.0	661.6
2004	657.9	647.9	650.8	652.7	659.8	663.0	660.9	661.6	656.4	666.6	684.3	696.8	663.2
2005	658.2	647.0	648.6	652.9	658.7	661.2	661.3	660.9	653.5	661.0	678.4	690.0	661.0
2006	655.8	639.6	643.9	646.6	650.0	652.6	649.8	650.3	645.6	656.0	676.7	688.2	654.6
2007	655.7	637.7	642.8	644.6	653.1	655.7	655.1	653.3	646.6	655.6	678.2	687.9	655.5
2008	656.7	638.4	641.7	642.6	648.8	650.1	647.2	645.8	639.5	646.6	658.1	667.6	648.6
2009	628.5	616.0	613.4	613.8	623.3	625.4	621.8	621.8	616.5	624.9	642.3	649.7	624.8
2010	620.1	604.1	611.2	615.3	623.5	627.3	625.0	625.4	618.0	628.2	646.1	656.4	625.1
2011	624.4	613.5	614.7	621.1	626.5	628.1	628.2	628.3	619.8	630.2	646.1	655.1	628.0
Transportation and Utilities													
2000	219.4	218.8	220.2	221.1	222.2	220.9	214.8	214.4	224.0	229.2	228.9	228.1	221.8
2001	222.8	222.2	222.2	224.3	225.6	223.2	214.3	213.3	223.4	228.2	227.3	225.7	222.7
2002	219.8	219.0	219.8	221.3	222.6	220.4	212.7	213.1	223.3	228.3	226.9	225.7	221.1
2003	218.9	217.7	217.6	219.2	220.7	219.5	210.1	210.4	220.7	226.1	225.7	224.8	219.3
2004	218.7	218.5	219.8	221.3	222.5	221.3	211.9	211.8	223.2	226.2	226.6	228.1	220.8
2005	220.8	220.7	222.2	224.0	225.9	224.6	216.1	216.8	229.8	231.4	233.7	236.4	225.2
2006	230.5	229.8	231.6	231.9	234.5	231.2	224.1	225.0	238.0	240.0	240.8	244.8	233.5
2007	238.4	237.3	239.1	240.0	241.8	240.4	230.0	229.9	241.8	241.8	243.3	245.7	239.1
2008	238.9	238.1	238.2	240.0	241.5	239.0	229.2	229.3	241.8	242.4	242.6	244.4	238.8
2009	235.0	233.3	232.0	231.8	232.5	229.6	218.1	217.7	231.4	233.1	234.4	237.1	230.5
2010	228.4	227.3	228.8	230.2	232.4	232.2	221.2	221.8	236.0	237.6	239.2	244.0	231.6
2011	235.9	236.2	237.0	238.5	240.0	238.1	230.3	230.6	242.7	243.0	245.4	247.5	238.8
Information													
2000	132.5	133.2	133.8	133.3	134.7	136.8	138.6	129.4	138.9	138.6	140.2	141.3	135.9
2001	138.2	138.1	138.1	136.4	136.5	136.8	136.5	135.4	133.2	132.6	132.8	132.9	135.6
2002	130.6	130.2	130.9	129.3	129.9	129.6	128.3	127.9	126.3	125.7	126.0	125.9	128.4
2003	124.3	123.7	124.5	122.8	122.4	122.1	120.6	119.8	118.1	116.7	116.6	115.6	120.6
2004	114.1	113.4	113.4	112.7	112.8	113.2	113.1	112.2	110.8	110.4	110.3	110.2	112.2
2005	109.1	108.8	109.0	109.4	110.0	110.5	109.6	109.4	111.6	108.1	108.8	109.1	109.5
2006	107.6	108.0	107.7	108.1	108.7	108.9	108.6	108.4	108.3	108.0	107.5	108.3	108.2
2007	106.8	106.5	106.4	106.6	107.3	109.0	108.1	108.0	108.1	107.0	107.6	108.9	107.5
2008	107.2	106.8	106.5	108.1	108.3	107.8	106.2	105.3	103.9	103.7	103.4	103.2	105.9
2009	101.6	101.0	100.8	100.5	100.3	100.4	99.8	98.7	97.9	98.5	97.8	98.2	99.6
2010	94.1	93.3	93.3	93.3	93.6	94.7	94.7	93.6	93.3	91.5	91.8	92.0	93.3
2011	90.6	90.6	90.7	90.9	91.2	91.6	90.8	88.0	89.6	89.9	89.3	89.6	90.2

1. Employment by Industry: Pennsylvania, Selected Years, 2000–2011—*Continued*

(Numbers in thousands, not seasonally adjusted)

Industry and year	January	February	March	April	May	June	July	August	September	October	November	December	Annual average
Financial Activities													
2000	335.9	335.4	335.9	337.0	338.0	342.2	342.1	341.4	338.4	337.8	338.8	341.1	338.7
2001	339.4	339.3	340.6	338.9	339.3	342.1	341.3	340.8	337.0	335.8	335.4	336.8	338.9
2002	334.7	334.5	335.5	335.1	336.3	339.7	340.1	340.6	337.4	335.4	335.7	337.1	336.8
2003	335.9	335.8	336.7	336.9	338.9	341.4	342.2	342.2	338.6	337.5	337.5	338.5	338.5
2004	336.5	335.4	336.4	335.4	337.0	339.0	339.8	338.6	334.3	333.4	333.2	335.2	336.2
2005	332.3	332.4	332.9	333.9	335.5	338.2	339.4	339.9	336.0	335.0	335.6	337.1	335.7
2006	333.9	333.7	334.1	334.9	335.9	339.3	338.9	337.4	333.6	332.7	332.6	333.2	335.0
2007	330.4	330.4	330.6	331.0	332.3	335.9	337.2	336.4	332.5	331.8	332.3	332.3	332.8
2008	328.2	328.7	329.3	329.9	331.1	333.7	334.2	333.6	328.5	327.0	326.5	326.6	329.8
2009	321.5	320.4	319.9	319.3	319.9	321.3	321.0	319.0	315.5	314.8	314.1	313.9	318.4
2010	311.4	310.2	310.9	310.5	311.9	313.3	313.0	312.5	308.8	309.5	309.5	310.0	311.0
2011	308.1	306.9	307.2	307.9	308.7	310.7	311.1	313.0	309.5	310.6	311.0	309.6	309.5
Professional and Business Services													
2000	589.1	592.4	603.4	611.1	611.4	619.9	623.4	625.3	621.9	616.9	616.9	616.4	612.3
2001	603.7	606.9	612.2	618.1	619.2	625.0	615.7	620.4	616.0	611.9	608.5	603.5	613.4
2002	589.0	589.9	596.7	604.8	607.0	613.3	611.6	615.5	611.1	610.6	610.4	608.4	605.7
2003	589.6	587.3	592.9	603.1	607.3	611.7	612.7	620.1	621.2	624.8	627.1	627.7	610.5
2004	610.1	611.8	620.1	631.1	634.9	644.3	645.4	649.1	647.9	654.0	654.3	653.6	638.1
2005	634.3	638.1	642.4	657.9	659.1	666.6	668.6	671.3	669.9	672.9	673.0	671.3	660.5
2006	653.8	658.9	666.9	679.1	682.6	692.3	693.0	697.3	696.1	701.4	701.8	700.4	685.3
2007	679.9	681.6	688.1	701.8	706.3	716.3	715.2	717.4	713.7	715.8	716.8	715.8	705.7
2008	695.7	695.5	699.7	713.3	714.8	719.0	720.0	721.0	713.8	713.1	706.8	699.5	709.4
2009	675.9	671.1	669.7	674.4	673.5	675.8	672.8	674.3	670.5	679.5	680.9	679.3	674.8
2010	661.4	662.9	669.3	686.8	689.0	694.8	696.0	698.7	696.4	705.3	709.1	709.0	689.9
2011	690.8	692.7	699.1	714.2	716.8	721.0	717.0	718.7	712.2	713.9	712.3	710.6	709.9
Education and Health Services													
2000	902.4	925.8	924.8	924.3	916.3	903.7	897.5	895.7	919.4	933.6	940.4	938.8	918.6
2001	917.5	941.2	946.0	944.9	937.2	928.4	923.7	922.6	944.2	956.0	963.8	962.7	940.7
2002	948.9	971.2	974.9	971.6	963.3	953.0	945.4	942.8	965.3	980.6	985.7	976.8	965.0
2003	965.6	985.5	989.7	988.8	979.6	967.6	957.9	954.2	977.9	998.2	1,002.1	998.7	980.5
2004	975.1	997.4	1,003.4	1,005.0	996.7	983.7	980.8	975.5	1,000.7	1,021.3	1,026.9	1,024.1	999.2
2005	1,005.1	1,029.6	1,030.2	1,037.9	1,027.7	1,010.3	1,010.4	1,006.5	1,034.4	1,055.3	1,058.7	1,054.4	1,030.0
2006	1,032.7	1,057.6	1,058.7	1,064.2	1,056.1	1,036.7	1,033.0	1,029.4	1,057.2	1,074.8	1,078.3	1,073.8	1,054.4
2007	1,052.3	1,076.0	1,081.2	1,082.6	1,074.8	1,056.6	1,053.5	1,050.9	1,075.9	1,100.0	1,101.3	1,096.3	1,075.1
2008	1,074.5	1,103.0	1,102.9	1,110.2	1,099.9	1,080.5	1,078.7	1,077.8	1,103.2	1,125.1	1,129.3	1,126.4	1,101.0
2009	1,104.6	1,128.2	1,127.0	1,130.3	1,120.7	1,100.4	1,098.6	1,092.3	1,114.9	1,138.2	1,142.8	1,136.9	1,119.6
2010	1,115.3	1,136.0	1,139.5	1,143.4	1,137.1	1,115.9	1,111.9	1,108.4	1,134.0	1,159.1	1,161.7	1,157.3	1,135.0
2011	1,131.6	1,159.1	1,161.3	1,163.1	1,155.1	1,134.3	1,132.9	1,127.1	1,159.0	1,185.0	1,190.3	1,181.7	1,156.7
Leisure and Hospitality													
2000	413.2	415.2	426.7	442.4	462.2	478.8	481.1	481.0	463.7	448.9	440.8	440.9	449.6
2001	420.3	424.2	431.7	445.8	470.1	487.9	488.1	488.7	466.5	452.7	445.6	444.9	455.5
2002	428.0	430.6	440.8	458.6	481.8	497.6	497.9	499.8	482.0	468.3	458.3	457.0	466.7
2003	437.4	435.1	444.7	460.4	486.3	500.4	502.9	506.4	485.2	470.9	460.7	461.8	471.0
2004	441.1	440.1	449.1	467.6	491.1	506.5	508.9	512.9	493.9	479.6	469.0	467.6	477.3
2005	446.1	446.5	455.6	477.9	502.4	518.3	519.6	521.4	501.6	483.0	473.1	472.5	484.8
2006	454.4	455.5	466.8	485.0	506.9	524.6	525.0	524.0	503.4	491.4	481.2	483.1	491.8
2007	463.0	464.8	474.9	490.6	515.5	533.5	532.3	533.6	510.5	501.2	489.6	489.4	499.9
2008	468.5	469.5	478.2	498.6	525.8	537.7	538.8	536.7	513.5	501.7	485.9	485.0	503.3
2009	461.4	460.2	469.5	484.8	515.9	525.6	528.7	529.7	506.9	493.4	478.5	477.0	494.3
2010	459.4	456.1	469.6	492.9	516.8	529.2	535.1	538.7	517.5	505.2	494.7	491.9	500.6
2011	471.3	471.0	484.1	506.3	528.7	542.4	547.9	545.8	519.5	512.4	493.1	493.0	509.6
Other Services													
2000	243.7	244.7	248.5	250.3	251.1	254.3	254.8	253.5	250.6	250.6	251.1	251.9	250.4
2001	247.6	248.7	253.0	253.7	256.4	259.8	259.2	258.5	255.2	255.7	256.6	257.8	255.2
2002	254.4	255.8	257.7	258.6	260.2	263.6	263.3	262.4	258.9	258.9	258.7	259.5	259.3
2003	256.2	255.8	258.4	259.0	261.1	263.9	264.1	263.0	259.7	259.9	259.5	260.5	260.1
2004	257.9	257.9	261.2	261.8	263.7	267.9	268.6	267.5	264.5	264.5	264.0	264.3	263.7
2005	260.2	260.7	262.1	262.7	263.6	266.0	266.2	263.5	259.4	258.6	258.4	257.7	261.6
2006	255.7	255.8	257.3	258.9	260.2	262.7	262.6	260.6	257.5	257.0	256.3	256.3	258.4
2007	252.5	252.8	254.4	255.6	257.1	259.8	260.4	258.3	254.9	254.6	254.7	254.3	255.8
2008	251.3	250.9	251.2	253.8	255.7	258.3	258.8	257.3	254.8	254.0	253.0	252.2	254.3
2009	247.9	248.0	249.2	249.1	251.7	254.0	254.0	252.1	248.0	248.3	247.9	248.2	249.9
2010	245.9	244.7	247.4	248.6	251.1	253.9	254.6	254.2	250.6	251.1	251.2	250.8	250.3
2011	247.8	248.5	250.2	252.4	253.8	257.2	258.5	258.3	254.4	256.2	256.8	257.0	254.3
Government													
2000	721.2	739.1	747.1	749.4	759.2	722.5	680.9	670.9	722.6	738.3	744.1	738.1	727.8
2001	723.3	742.8	745.6	749.7	745.7	721.2	677.0	675.9	731.6	749.7	756.0	753.0	731.0
2002	738.2	758.1	759.9	762.3	757.1	734.8	684.9	678.0	739.3	759.0	766.9	760.4	741.6
2003	742.2	764.8	768.9	769.1	764.6	749.1	693.3	688.6	742.4	765.0	769.1	762.9	748.3
2004	743.8	762.8	767.8	770.5	766.4	747.1	688.3	682.7	743.4	762.2	769.3	760.9	747.1
2005	746.1	765.2	769.0	772.2	763.4	745.2	691.8	685.2	743.7	762.0	767.7	761.5	747.8
2006	742.5	764.1	767.0	768.7	766.8	745.0	690.0	688.2	746.1	763.7	771.5	765.4	748.3
2007	744.7	764.0	767.3	768.0	764.0	745.0	691.8	689.0	742.7	762.5	767.9	763.4	747.5
2008	745.7	764.3	767.7	770.5	763.5	747.9	690.8	693.3	754.8	774.4	778.7	772.2	752.0
2009	752.2	772.9	775.1	781.9	772.5	756.2	705.8	699.6	759.1	778.3	784.3	777.5	759.6
2010	751.0	772.4	778.3	783.7	792.2	769.7	706.8	700.4	754.5	773.3	779.3	772.2	761.2
2011	751.4	768.5	770.0	771.5	761.2	746.7	687.6	681.7	732.1	751.7	757.2	749.8	744.1

2. Average Weekly Hours by Selected Industry: Pennsylvania, 2007–2011

(Not seasonally adjusted)

Industry and year	January	February	March	April	May	June	July	August	September	October	November	December	Annual average
Total Private													
2007	33.3	33.0	33.4	33.9	33.9	34.0	34.2	34.0	34.1	33.8	33.9	34.2	33.8
2008	33.6	33.5	34.0	33.9	33.7	34.0	33.8	33.8	33.7	33.7	33.8	33.3	33.7
2009	33.0	33.4	33.1	32.9	33.0	32.9	33.0	33.2	32.9	32.9	33.3	33.1	33.0
2010	33.0	32.2	33.1	33.3	33.5	33.3	33.4	33.7	33.5	33.6	33.7	33.6	33.3
2011	33.5	33.3	33.4	33.6	33.7	33.5	33.4	33.4	33.4	33.6	33.6	33.5	33.5
Goods-Producing													
2007	38.6	37.4	38.3	38.8	39.2	39.4	39.4	39.4	39.7	39.6	39.7	40.0	39.1
2008	39.7	39.2	40.1	40.2	39.4	39.8	39.4	39.4	38.4	38.8	38.6	38.1	39.3
2009	37.7	37.8	37.8	37.1	37.6	38.0	37.9	38.5	37.8	38.2	38.6	38.4	37.9
2010	38.8	36.4	39.0	39.3	39.5	39.2	38.9	39.6	39.5	39.6	40.0	39.1	39.1
2011	39.0	38.9	38.9	39.2	39.4	39.3	39.3	39.2	39.2	39.5	39.6	39.3	39.2
Construction													
2007	37.1	34.8	36.4	37.6	39.0	39.0	38.8	38.2	38.9	38.5	38.2	38.0	37.9
2008	38.5	36.8	38.6	39.1	38.0	39.2	39.1	39.1	38.1	38.7	37.8	36.7	38.3
2009	36.1	36.5	37.4	36.8	37.6	37.3	37.9	37.9	36.5	36.9	36.8	36.6	37.0
2010	36.5	33.4	36.6	37.7	37.2	37.3	37.8	38.4	37.8	37.7	38.2	36.9	37.2
2011	36.9	37.0	37.0	37.5	38.8	39.3	38.9	38.8	38.1	38.4	38.7	38.1	38.2
Manufacturing													
2007	39.0	38.1	38.8	39.1	39.1	39.4	39.6	39.8	40.1	40.0	40.3	40.5	39.5
2008	40.1	40.0	40.6	40.6	40.0	40.2	39.7	40.0	40.2	40.4	40.3	39.7	40.2
2009	39.2	39.0	38.7	38.0	38.5	39.0	38.6	39.3	38.7	39.0	39.5	39.3	38.9
2010	39.8	37.5	39.9	39.7	40.2	39.7	39.0	39.8	39.9	40.1	40.3	39.5	39.6
2011	39.4	39.3	39.5	39.6	39.4	39.1	39.2	39.2	39.6	39.8	39.8	39.6	39.5
Trade, Transportation, and Utilities													
2007	33.3	32.6	33.3	33.8	33.8	34.2	34.3	34.0	33.9	33.5	33.7	34.0	33.7
2008	32.9	32.8	33.7	33.3	33.6	33.9	33.9	34.1	34.1	33.8	33.7	33.7	33.6
2009	33.2	33.4	33.1	33.3	33.7	33.6	33.5	33.6	33.9	33.5	33.6	33.7	33.5
2010	33.2	32.2	33.1	33.5	33.9	33.9	33.9	34.0	34.0	33.9	33.8	34.4	33.7
2011	33.6	33.8	34.0	34.3	34.3	34.4	34.2	34.1	34.0	34.1	34.0	34.2	34.1
Information													
2007	34.8	34.5	33.5	34.8	33.5	33.7	34.5	33.3	34.1	33.6	33.7	34.8	34.1
2008	33.5	33.9	35.3	34.6	33.7	33.8	32.6	32.6	32.1	32.2	32.2	32.1	33.2
2009	32.1	32.0	32.1	31.6	31.4	31.9	31.9	32.2	31.4	31.1	31.9	31.5	31.8
2010	31.5	31.4	32.6	32.3	32.6	32.7	32.5	32.7	32.9	32.9	33.1	33.3	32.5
2011	33.3	32.5	32.9	33.0	32.0	32.3	32.8	31.6	32.0	31.3	31.7	31.2	32.2
Financial Activities													
2007	34.6	34.6	35.3	35.6	35.0	35.0	35.8	35.7	36.1	35.9	36.4	37.2	35.6
2008	37.0	36.9	36.6	36.0	35.8	35.3	34.6	34.7	35.1	35.4	36.1	35.7	35.8
2009	36.0	36.3	36.3	35.3	35.8	35.4	35.3	35.5	35.0	35.2	36.0	35.6	35.6
2010	35.4	35.5	35.9	35.5	35.9	35.5	35.5	36.0	35.4	35.6	35.6	35.8	35.6
2011	36.5	36.1	36.1	36.5	36.6	36.2	36.2	36.1	36.4	36.8	36.5	36.3	36.4
Professional and Business Services													
2007	34.5	34.5	34.3	35.4	35.1	35.1	35.5	35.2	35.7	34.8	34.8	35.5	35.0
2008	34.3	34.6	35.0	35.1	35.0	35.3	35.1	35.3	35.2	35.2	35.6	34.3	35.0
2009	34.0	34.8	34.5	34.0	34.3	34.0	34.1	34.6	33.7	34.1	34.6	34.2	34.2
2010	34.2	33.6	34.3	34.6	34.9	34.6	34.9	35.5	35.0	35.6	35.7	35.7	34.9
2011	35.8	35.3	35.3	35.4	35.7	35.2	34.9	35.1	35.0	35.6	35.3	35.4	35.3
Education and Health Services													
2007	32.3	32.6	32.7	33.0	32.7	33.1	33.2	32.8	32.9	32.5	32.7	32.9	32.8
2008	32.7	32.8	33.0	32.6	32.5	32.8	32.6	32.5	32.6	32.5	32.9	32.3	32.6
2009	32.0	32.4	32.4	32.4	32.0	31.7	32.1	32.2	31.8	31.8	32.1	32.0	32.1
2010	31.9	31.6	31.8	32.1	32.1	32.0	32.1	32.0	32.0	32.0	32.0	31.9	32.0
2011	32.1	31.9	32.0	32.0	32.1	31.8	31.7	31.6	31.7	31.8	31.7	31.9	31.9
Leisure and Hospitality													
2007	24.0	24.5	25.1	25.8	26.3	26.0	25.8	26.1	25.4	25.4	25.2	25.4	25.4
2008	24.3	24.4	24.2	24.8	25.1	25.5	25.5	25.3	25.0	25.4	24.5	24.4	24.9
2009	23.6	24.8	24.0	24.1	24.3	24.0	24.2	24.3	23.8	23.7	23.7	23.6	24.0
2010	23.3	23.2	23.9	24.2	24.1	24.0	24.8	24.8	24.3	24.4	24.3	24.0	24.1
2011	23.5	23.9	23.9	24.1	24.2	24.5	24.6	24.5	24.2	24.4	24.5	24.2	24.2
Other Services													
2007	29.2	29.3	29.6	30.0	29.6	29.6	29.9	29.9	29.8	29.7	29.4	29.2	29.6
2008	29.3	29.3	30.2	30.3	30.1	30.7	31.3	31.3	31.8	31.3	31.7	31.7	30.8
2009	31.6	31.3	30.7	30.5	30.4	30.5	30.9	31.4	30.9	31.4	31.8	31.3	31.1
2010	31.4	31.0	31.2	31.4	31.6	31.2	31.4	31.6	31.2	30.8	30.6	30.3	31.1
2011	30.5	29.6	30.0	30.2	30.4	30.4	30.4	30.2	30.6	30.8	30.4	30.1	30.3

3. Average Hourly Earnings by Selected Industry: Pennsylvania, 2007–2011

(Dollars, not seasonally adjusted)

Industry and year	January	February	March	April	May	June	July	August	September	October	November	December	Annual average
Total Private													
2007	20.15	20.12	20.01	20.10	19.94	19.92	19.98	20.00	20.14	20.11	20.14	20.28	20.07
2008	20.30	20.34	20.37	20.37	20.32	20.35	20.40	20.39	20.51	20.55	20.68	20.58	20.43
2009	20.65	20.65	20.70	20.68	20.64	20.62	20.64	20.76	20.82	20.88	20.95	20.96	20.75
2010	21.07	21.15	21.12	21.16	21.15	21.08	21.14	21.21	21.25	21.35	21.36	21.44	21.21
2011	21.60	21.61	21.70	21.77	21.80	21.64	21.77	21.78	21.95	22.07	22.12	22.26	21.84
Goods-Producing													
2007	21.34	21.27	21.21	21.41	21.26	21.32	21.24	21.32	21.41	21.46	21.56	21.64	21.37
2008	21.71	21.69	21.82	21.85	21.90	21.92	21.95	22.06	22.18	22.29	22.32	22.13	21.98
2009	22.15	22.25	22.37	22.42	22.38	22.39	22.49	22.60	22.62	22.74	22.79	22.91	22.51
2010	22.93	22.96	22.84	22.92	22.88	22.83	22.93	22.94	22.85	22.80	22.87	23.00	22.89
2011	23.18	23.26	23.37	23.46	23.65	23.55	23.66	23.81	23.87	23.89	24.03	24.13	23.66
Construction													
2007	24.23	23.96	23.82	23.86	23.70	23.72	23.56	23.80	23.65	23.80	24.06	23.96	23.83
2008	24.04	23.81	23.96	23.97	24.08	24.04	23.82	23.93	23.84	23.98	23.92	24.21	23.96
2009	24.18	24.32	24.28	24.26	24.43	24.51	24.53	24.79	24.75	24.89	24.89	24.99	24.57
2010	25.07	25.09	25.04	25.02	25.12	25.12	25.22	25.32	25.15	25.26	25.24	25.37	25.17
2011	25.49	25.57	25.59	25.62	25.62	25.51	25.80	26.19	26.01	25.92	26.02	26.03	25.79
Manufacturing													
2007	20.52	20.57	20.47	20.67	20.54	20.60	20.54	20.57	20.73	20.73	20.70	20.81	20.62
2008	20.88	20.91	21.05	21.10	21.04	21.07	21.17	21.19	21.24	21.32	21.41	21.32	21.14
2009	21.42	21.49	21.62	21.70	21.64	21.64	21.77	21.74	21.80	21.81	21.90	22.06	21.71
2010	22.06	22.09	21.91	22.04	21.92	21.84	21.97	21.94	21.97	21.83	21.90	22.06	21.96
2011	22.30	22.30	22.42	22.56	22.72	22.61	22.63	22.68	22.86	22.97	23.13	23.30	22.71
Trade, Transportation, and Utilities													
2007	17.56	17.70	17.57	17.67	17.47	17.56	17.58	17.75	17.84	17.81	17.60	17.76	17.66
2008	17.74	17.84	17.87	17.91	17.79	17.85	17.94	17.82	17.97	18.06	18.26	18.20	17.94
2009	18.34	18.39	18.46	18.46	18.50	18.39	18.39	18.58	18.69	18.61	18.67	18.59	18.51
2010	18.73	18.81	18.86	18.98	18.87	18.78	18.91	18.93	18.98	19.10	18.91	18.87	18.90
2011	19.01	19.12	19.31	19.12	19.05	18.98	19.06	19.00	19.05	19.14	19.09	19.18	19.09
Information													
2007	24.24	23.93	23.80	23.61	23.45	23.20	23.00	22.88	22.87	23.01	22.91	22.97	23.32
2008	23.07	23.20	23.22	23.23	23.02	23.26	23.32	23.51	23.31	23.14	22.93	22.91	23.18
2009	22.79	22.58	22.51	22.61	22.26	22.45	22.35	22.25	22.14	22.23	22.18	22.16	22.38
2010	22.27	22.40	22.33	22.43	22.57	22.60	22.67	22.87	22.83	22.93	23.06	23.12	22.68
2011	23.13	22.96	22.66	22.24	22.38	21.93	21.71	21.70	21.84	21.74	21.38	21.52	22.11
Financial Activities													
2007	25.28	25.24	25.36	25.55	25.61	25.58	25.59	25.53	25.64	25.66	25.65	25.76	25.54
2008	25.50	25.74	25.83	25.70	25.80	26.01	26.03	26.12	26.23	26.30	26.45	26.47	26.01
2009	26.62	26.78	26.74	26.88	26.68	26.69	26.78	26.87	26.88	26.89	27.04	27.11	26.83
2010	27.26	27.42	27.32	27.46	27.53	27.64	27.73	27.82	27.88	27.98	27.86	28.01	27.66
2011	28.16	28.09	28.15	28.34	28.51	27.98	28.02	27.83	27.89	28.12	28.31	28.54	28.16
Professional and Business Services													
2007	25.01	25.21	25.04	25.07	24.84	24.68	24.71	24.62	24.72	24.61	24.72	24.95	24.84
2008	24.92	24.98	25.06	24.92	24.95	24.95	24.78	24.94	24.99	25.12	25.34	25.41	25.03
2009	25.50	25.69	25.73	25.76	25.94	25.89	25.89	26.10	26.15	26.24	26.35	26.42	25.97
2010	26.51	26.64	26.68	26.58	26.76	26.71	26.62	26.78	26.83	26.97	27.07	27.24	26.79
2011	27.33	27.14	27.25	27.34	27.38	27.03	27.27	27.24	27.49	27.85	28.09	28.34	27.48
Education and Health Services													
2007	19.13	18.92	18.86	18.94	18.97	18.92	19.11	19.12	19.25	19.13	19.23	19.34	19.08
2008	19.37	19.24	19.21	19.35	19.34	19.44	19.63	19.42	19.53	19.49	19.51	19.42	19.41
2009	19.31	19.14	19.16	19.16	19.17	19.23	19.31	19.36	19.47	19.43	19.40	19.43	19.30
2010	19.57	19.69	19.63	19.71	19.73	19.65	19.79	19.87	19.98	20.00	20.06	20.13	19.82
2011	20.23	20.35	20.49	20.82	20.88	21.03	21.37	21.26	21.53	21.52	21.44	21.61	21.05
Leisure and Hospitality													
2007	12.67	12.71	12.61	12.62	12.52	12.45	12.44	12.41	12.52	12.59	12.68	12.80	12.58
2008	12.67	12.78	12.86	12.74	12.82	12.67	12.72	12.66	12.88	12.84	12.83	12.84	12.77
2009	12.75	12.60	12.55	12.53	12.40	12.33	12.25	12.23	12.39	12.51	12.53	12.54	12.46
2010	12.45	12.40	12.35	12.37	12.44	12.33	12.32	12.25	12.32	12.47	12.51	12.69	12.41
2011	12.57	12.62	12.65	12.62	12.59	12.20	12.19	12.25	12.39	12.45	12.45	12.63	12.46
Other Services													
2007	18.04	17.81	17.80	17.56	17.31	17.17	17.29	17.14	17.25	17.30	17.45	17.56	17.47
2008	17.67	17.91	17.70	17.83	17.88	17.96	18.13	18.26	18.29	18.09	18.09	18.28	18.01
2009	18.39	18.39	18.49	18.62	18.48	18.39	18.32	18.21	18.24	18.28	18.32	18.38	18.37
2010	18.28	18.39	18.35	18.34	18.39	18.33	18.32	18.25	18.34	18.27	18.35	18.39	18.33
2011	18.50	18.53	18.30	18.52	18.65	18.64	18.50	18.65	18.84	18.97	19.03	19.27	18.70

4. Average Weekly Earnings by Selected Industry: Pennsylvania, 2007–2011

(Dollars, not seasonally adjusted)

Industry and year	January	February	March	April	May	June	July	August	September	October	November	December	Annual average
Total Private													
2007	671.00	663.96	668.33	681.39	675.97	677.28	683.32	680.00	686.77	679.72	682.75	693.58	678.78
2008	682.08	681.39	692.58	690.54	684.78	691.90	689.52	689.18	691.19	692.54	698.98	685.31	689.53
2009	681.45	689.71	685.17	680.37	681.12	678.40	681.12	689.23	684.98	686.95	697.64	693.78	685.48
2010	695.31	681.03	699.07	704.63	708.53	701.96	706.08	714.78	711.88	717.36	719.83	720.38	706.84
2011	723.60	719.61	724.78	731.47	734.66	724.94	727.12	727.45	733.13	741.55	743.23	745.71	731.49
Goods-Producing													
2007	823.72	795.50	812.34	830.71	833.39	840.01	836.86	840.01	849.98	849.82	855.93	865.60	836.41
2008	861.89	850.25	874.98	878.37	862.86	872.42	864.83	869.16	851.71	864.85	861.55	843.15	863.10
2009	835.06	841.05	845.59	831.78	841.49	850.82	852.37	870.10	855.04	868.67	879.69	879.74	854.10
2010	889.68	835.74	890.76	900.76	903.76	894.94	891.98	908.42	902.58	902.88	914.80	899.30	895.04
2011	904.02	904.81	909.09	919.63	931.81	925.52	929.84	933.35	935.70	943.66	951.59	948.31	928.47
Construction													
2007	898.93	833.81	867.05	897.14	924.30	925.08	914.13	909.16	919.99	916.30	919.09	910.48	904.19
2008	925.54	876.21	924.86	937.23	915.04	942.37	931.36	935.66	908.30	928.03	904.18	888.51	918.76
2009	872.90	887.68	908.07	892.77	918.57	914.22	929.69	939.54	903.38	918.44	915.95	914.63	910.08
2010	915.06	838.01	916.46	943.25	934.46	936.98	953.32	972.29	950.67	952.30	964.17	936.15	936.52
2011	940.58	946.09	946.83	960.75	994.06	1,002.54	1,003.62	1,016.17	990.98	995.33	1,006.97	991.74	984.64
Manufacturing													
2007	800.28	783.72	794.24	808.20	803.11	811.64	813.38	818.69	831.27	829.20	834.21	842.81	814.29
2008	837.29	836.40	854.63	856.66	841.60	847.01	840.45	847.60	853.85	861.33	862.82	846.40	848.79
2009	839.66	838.11	836.69	824.60	833.14	843.96	840.32	854.38	843.66	850.59	865.05	866.96	844.61
2010	877.99	828.38	874.21	874.99	881.18	867.05	856.83	873.21	876.60	875.38	882.57	871.37	870.03
2011	878.62	876.39	885.59	893.38	895.17	884.05	887.10	889.06	905.26	914.21	920.57	922.68	896.07
Trade, Transportation, and Utilities													
2007	584.75	577.02	585.08	597.25	590.49	600.55	602.99	603.50	604.78	596.64	593.12	603.84	595.05
2008	583.65	585.15	602.22	596.40	597.74	605.12	608.17	607.66	612.78	610.43	615.36	613.34	603.19
2009	608.89	614.23	611.03	614.72	623.45	617.90	616.07	624.29	633.59	623.44	627.31	626.48	620.11
2010	621.84	605.68	624.27	635.83	639.69	636.64	641.05	643.62	645.32	647.49	639.16	649.13	635.96
2011	638.74	646.26	656.54	655.82	653.42	652.91	651.85	647.90	647.70	652.67	649.06	655.96	650.75
Information													
2007	843.55	825.59	797.30	821.63	785.58	781.84	793.50	761.90	779.87	773.14	772.07	799.36	794.52
2008	772.85	786.48	819.67	803.76	775.77	786.19	760.23	766.43	748.25	745.11	738.35	735.41	770.22
2009	731.56	722.56	722.57	714.48	698.96	716.16	712.97	716.45	695.20	691.35	707.54	698.04	710.76
2010	701.51	703.36	727.96	724.49	735.78	739.02	736.78	747.85	751.11	754.40	763.29	769.90	737.84
2011	770.23	746.20	745.51	733.92	716.16	708.34	712.09	685.72	698.88	680.46	677.75	671.42	712.34
Financial Activities													
2007	874.69	873.30	895.21	909.58	896.35	895.30	916.12	911.42	925.60	921.19	933.66	958.27	909.26
2008	943.50	949.81	945.38	925.20	923.64	918.15	900.64	906.36	920.67	931.02	954.85	944.98	930.24
2009	958.32	972.11	970.66	948.86	955.14	944.83	945.33	953.89	940.80	946.53	973.44	965.12	956.27
2010	965.00	973.41	980.79	974.83	988.33	981.22	984.42	1,001.52	986.95	996.09	991.82	1,002.76	985.56
2011	1,027.84	1,014.05	1,016.22	1,034.41	1,043.47	1,012.88	1,014.32	1,004.66	1,015.20	1,034.82	1,033.32	1,036.00	1,023.86
Professional and Business Services													
2007	862.85	869.75	858.87	887.48	871.88	866.27	877.21	866.62	882.50	856.43	860.26	885.73	870.52
2008	854.76	864.31	877.10	874.69	873.25	880.74	869.78	880.38	879.65	884.22	902.10	871.56	876.10
2009	867.00	894.01	887.69	875.84	889.74	880.26	882.85	903.06	881.26	894.78	911.71	903.56	889.33
2010	906.64	895.10	915.12	919.67	933.92	924.17	929.04	950.69	939.05	960.13	966.40	972.47	934.88
2011	978.41	958.04	961.93	967.84	977.47	951.46	951.72	956.12	962.15	991.46	991.58	1,003.24	970.93
Education and Health Services													
2007	617.90	616.79	616.72	625.02	620.32	626.25	634.45	627.14	633.33	621.73	628.82	636.29	625.40
2008	633.40	631.07	633.93	630.81	628.55	637.63	639.94	631.15	636.68	633.43	641.88	627.27	633.80
2009	617.92	620.14	620.78	620.78	613.44	609.59	619.85	623.39	619.15	617.87	622.74	621.76	618.98
2010	624.28	622.20	624.23	632.69	633.33	628.80	635.26	635.84	639.36	640.00	641.92	642.15	633.39
2011	649.38	649.17	655.68	666.24	670.25	668.75	677.43	671.82	682.50	684.34	679.65	689.36	670.48
Leisure and Hospitality													
2007	304.08	311.40	316.51	325.60	329.28	323.70	320.95	323.90	318.01	319.79	319.54	325.12	320.04
2008	307.88	311.83	311.21	315.95	321.78	323.09	324.36	320.30	322.00	326.14	314.34	313.30	317.93
2009	300.90	312.48	301.20	301.97	301.32	295.92	296.45	297.19	294.88	296.49	296.96	295.94	299.18
2010	290.09	287.68	295.17	299.35	299.80	295.92	305.54	303.80	299.38	304.27	303.99	304.56	299.34
2011	295.40	301.62	302.34	304.14	304.68	298.90	299.87	300.13	299.84	303.78	305.03	305.65	301.77
Other Services													
2007	526.77	521.83	526.88	526.80	512.38	508.23	516.97	512.49	514.05	513.81	513.03	512.75	517.13
2008	517.73	524.76	534.54	540.25	538.19	551.37	567.47	571.54	581.62	566.22	573.45	579.48	553.98
2009	581.12	575.61	567.64	567.91	561.79	560.90	566.09	571.79	563.62	573.99	582.58	575.29	570.65
2010	573.99	570.09	572.52	575.88	581.12	571.90	575.25	576.70	572.21	562.72	561.51	557.22	570.92
2011	564.25	548.49	549.00	559.30	566.96	566.66	562.40	563.23	576.50	584.28	578.51	580.03	566.76

RHODE ISLAND
At a Glance

Population:
   2000 census: 1,048,259
   2010 census: 1,052,567
   2011 estimate: 1,051,302

Percent change in population:
   2000–2010: 0.4%
   2010–2011: -0.1%

Percent change in total nonfarm employment:
   2000–2010: -3.7%
   2010–2011: 0.2%

Industry with the largest growth in employment, 2000–2011 (thousands):
   Education and Health Services, 20.3

Industry with the largest decline or smallest growth in employment, 2000–2011 (thousands):
   Manufacturing, -30.5

Civilian labor force:
   2000: 543,404
   2010: 570,301
   2011: 563,413

Unemployment rate and rank among states (lowest to highest):
   2000: 4.2%, 33rd
   2010: 11.7%, 48th
   2011: 11.3%, 49th

Over-the-year change in unemployment rates:
   2010–2011: -0.4%

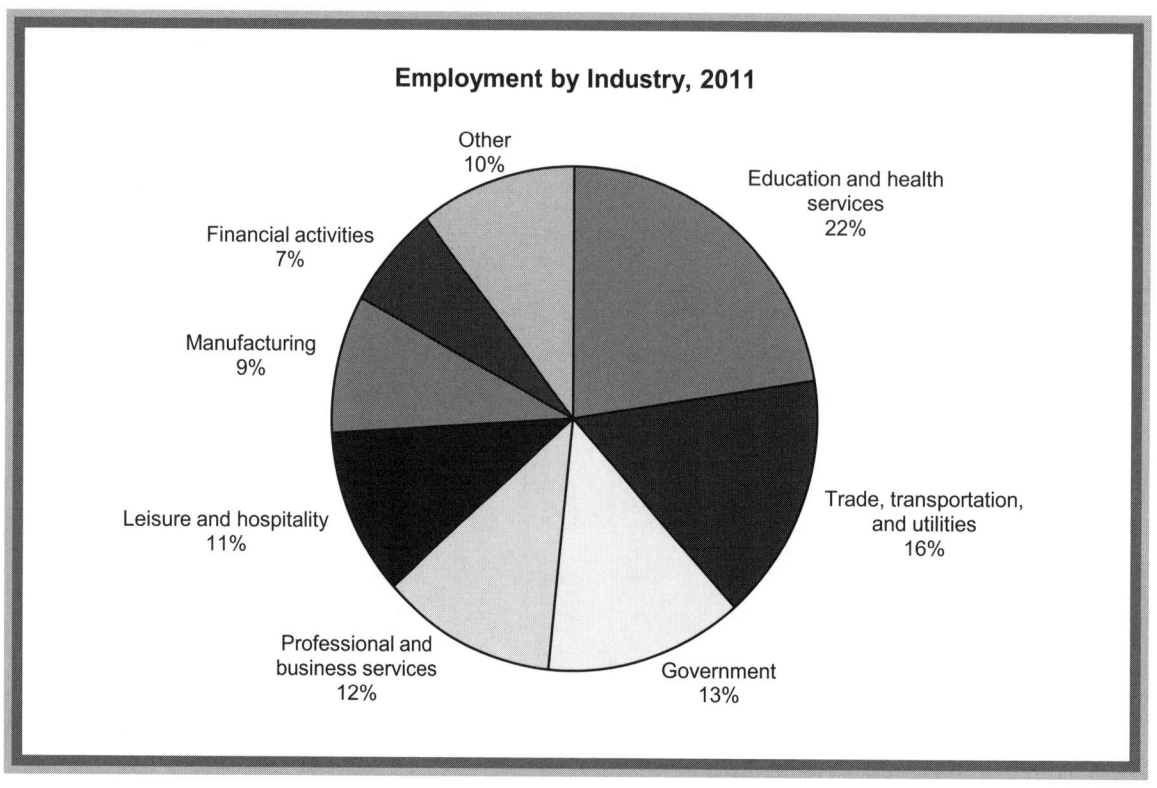

Employment by Industry, 2011

- Other 10%
- Education and health services 22%
- Financial activities 7%
- Manufacturing 9%
- Trade, transportation, and utilities 16%
- Leisure and hospitality 11%
- Professional and business services 12%
- Government 13%

1. Employment by Industry: Rhode Island, Selected Years, 2000–2011

(Numbers in thousands, not seasonally adjusted)

Industry and year	January	February	March	April	May	June	July	August	September	October	November	December	Annual average
Total Nonfarm													
2000	460.2	462.3	467.3	475.0	482.0	481.8	474.1	476.1	482.2	485.3	486.7	487.6	476.7
2001	468.4	471.0	472.8	479.1	483.2	484.2	474.1	478.5	481.8	482.6	482.1	483.1	478.4
2002	466.0	467.1	471.4	478.6	484.3	485.3	475.4	479.5	484.7	486.0	487.1	487.2	479.4
2003	469.9	469.9	473.5	482.0	489.4	490.7	482.7	485.1	490.5	492.1	492.8	492.4	484.3
2004	473.2	475.5	478.5	486.0	494.4	494.7	487.7	489.3	494.7	496.4	496.5	495.3	488.5
2005	475.8	478.6	481.0	491.0	495.7	498.1	491.2	492.8	497.5	496.7	497.8	496.1	491.0
2006	475.5	478.5	482.9	494.0	497.3	500.6	491.4	493.8	500.6	501.5	501.9	501.3	493.3
2007	481.9	483.5	485.9	493.2	499.5	501.3	492.9	492.7	495.9	496.0	495.0	493.4	492.6
2008	474.3	476.4	478.2	484.9	489.9	490.5	480.3	481.2	485.3	483.8	480.9	477.2	481.9
2009	455.2	456.5	456.0	459.7	466.1	466.3	457.6	457.1	462.2	464.4	463.5	461.5	460.5
2010	444.5	446.8	450.2	457.3	464.6	464.9	460.5	460.9	464.6	465.3	465.7	463.5	459.1
2011	445.5	448.9	451.8	461.1	466.5	468.1	464.9	462.0	464.1	465.9	463.8	459.4	460.2
Total Private													
2000	395.8	397.9	402.1	409.8	414.5	417.7	412.7	415.9	418.8	420.0	420.9	421.8	412.3
2001	403.0	405.4	407.0	413.2	416.8	418.6	412.4	417.3	417.3	416.4	415.1	415.9	413.2
2002	399.3	400.3	404.3	411.4	416.6	418.6	413.5	417.8	419.4	419.1	419.7	419.6	413.3
2003	402.8	402.8	406.1	414.8	421.7	422.9	420.7	423.0	424.8	425.4	426.0	425.5	418.0
2004	407.1	409.2	411.6	419.8	427.4	428.0	425.7	427.5	429.5	430.5	430.0	429.5	423.0
2005	410.3	412.8	415.1	425.2	429.6	432.2	429.7	432.1	433.4	430.9	431.7	430.2	426.1
2006	410.1	412.6	417.0	428.4	431.5	435.0	430.1	432.8	435.9	435.8	435.5	435.3	428.3
2007	416.7	418.1	420.6	427.9	433.5	436.4	431.4	431.5	432.0	431.3	430.2	428.4	428.2
2008	409.7	411.9	413.3	420.1	424.4	426.0	420.1	421.7	422.9	420.7	416.9	413.5	418.4
2009	392.2	393.2	392.7	396.3	402.4	403.3	399.7	399.5	400.9	401.6	400.5	398.7	398.4
2010	382.3	384.5	387.5	394.6	399.8	401.9	402.0	402.7	404.1	403.7	403.6	401.5	397.4
2011	384.1	387.5	390.0	399.3	404.3	406.6	408.0	405.2	404.0	404.7	402.6	398.4	399.6
Goods-Producing													
2000	87.1	87.2	88.2	88.6	90.0	91.5	86.6	90.8	91.3	91.6	91.1	90.7	89.6
2001	87.8	87.7	87.8	88.5	88.3	88.4	83.8	87.3	87.3	86.8	85.4	85.0	87.0
2002	81.1	81.0	81.9	82.1	83.0	83.6	79.4	82.8	82.7	82.2	82.0	80.9	81.9
2003	77.5	76.3	77.0	79.2	80.3	81.0	78.5	81.3	81.8	81.3	81.1	79.9	79.6
2004	75.5	75.0	75.4	77.5	78.5	79.5	77.8	79.8	79.9	80.3	79.9	79.1	78.2
2005	74.8	74.2	74.5	77.1	78.0	79.1	76.4	78.7	78.6	77.6	77.8	76.8	77.0
2006	73.1	72.8	73.4	76.0	76.7	77.8	75.5	77.5	77.3	76.9	76.4	76.0	75.8
2007	72.6	71.6	71.9	73.0	74.2	74.8	72.7	74.3	74.1	73.8	73.1	71.7	73.2
2008	68.4	67.4	67.9	69.3	70.2	70.8	68.4	70.0	69.8	68.5	67.2	65.5	68.6
2009	60.9	59.0	58.5	59.3	59.7	59.9	58.7	59.5	59.2	59.1	58.5	57.5	59.2
2010	54.2	53.7	54.0	55.5	56.8	57.7	57.1	58.2	57.9	57.9	57.8	56.8	56.5
2011	54.0	53.4	53.9	55.8	56.7	57.6	57.3	57.8	57.8	58.1	58.4	57.5	56.5
Mining and Logging													
2000	0.2	0.2	0.2	0.2	0.2	0.2	0.2	0.2	0.2	0.3	0.3	0.2	0.2
2001	0.2	0.2	0.2	0.2	0.3	0.3	0.3	0.3	0.2	0.3	0.2	0.2	0.2
2002	0.2	0.2	0.2	0.2	0.2	0.2	0.3	0.2	0.2	0.2	0.2	0.2	0.2
2003	0.2	0.1	0.2	0.2	0.2	0.2	0.2	0.2	0.2	0.2	0.2	0.2	0.2
2004	0.2	0.2	0.2	0.2	0.2	0.2	0.2	0.2	0.3	0.3	0.3	0.3	0.2
2005	0.2	0.2	0.2	0.3	0.3	0.3	0.3	0.3	0.3	0.3	0.3	0.3	0.3
2006	0.2	0.2	0.2	0.3	0.3	0.3	0.3	0.3	0.3	0.3	0.3	0.3	0.3
2007	0.2	0.2	0.2	0.3	0.3	0.3	0.3	0.3	0.3	0.3	0.3	0.2	0.3
2008	0.2	0.2	0.2	0.2	0.3	0.3	0.3	0.3	0.3	0.3	0.2	0.2	0.3
2009	0.2	0.1	0.2	0.2	0.2	0.2	0.2	0.2	0.2	0.2	0.2	0.2	0.2
2010	0.1	0.1	0.1	0.2	0.2	0.2	0.2	0.2	0.2	0.2	0.2	0.2	0.2
2011	0.1	0.1	0.1	0.2	0.2	0.2	0.2	0.2	0.2	0.2	0.2	0.2	0.2
Construction													
2000	16.4	15.8	17.0	17.8	18.3	18.9	19.1	19.1	19.1	19.0	18.9	18.4	18.2
2001	16.6	16.5	16.9	18.6	19.2	19.8	20.3	20.5	20.3	20.0	19.8	19.5	19.0
2002	17.4	17.3	18.0	19.1	19.9	20.4	20.4	20.6	20.5	20.1	19.9	19.4	19.4
2003	17.2	16.6	17.3	19.6	21.1	21.8	22.8	23.0	23.0	22.7	22.4	21.5	20.8
2004	18.6	18.0	18.4	20.3	21.1	21.8	22.5	22.4	22.3	22.4	22.2	21.6	21.0
2005	18.8	18.3	18.6	21.3	22.3	23.4	23.5	23.6	23.5	22.8	23.1	22.2	21.8
2006	19.8	19.4	20.0	22.5	23.3	24.3	24.4	24.7	24.4	24.0	23.7	23.3	22.8
2007	21.0	19.9	20.4	21.6	22.8	23.4	23.6	23.4	23.0	22.8	22.5	21.4	22.2
2008	18.8	18.3	18.7	20.3	21.3	21.9	21.9	22.0	21.9	21.7	20.9	20.2	20.4
2009	16.4	15.9	15.9	17.1	17.8	18.0	18.2	18.2	17.8	17.6	17.1	16.3	17.2
2010	13.9	13.5	13.9	15.5	16.4	16.9	17.3	17.5	17.0	16.9	16.7	15.8	15.9
2011	13.6	13.0	13.4	15.0	15.9	16.5	16.9	16.5	16.4	16.9	17.5	16.4	15.7
Manufacturing													
2000	70.5	71.2	71.0	70.6	71.5	72.4	67.3	71.5	72.0	72.3	71.9	72.1	71.2
2001	71.0	71.0	70.7	69.7	68.8	68.3	63.2	66.5	66.8	66.5	65.4	65.3	67.8
2002	63.5	63.5	63.7	62.8	62.9	63.0	58.7	62.0	62.0	61.9	61.9	61.3	62.3
2003	60.1	59.6	59.5	59.4	59.0	59.0	55.5	58.1	58.6	58.4	58.5	58.2	58.7
2004	56.7	56.8	56.8	57.0	57.2	57.5	55.1	57.2	57.3	57.6	57.4	57.2	57.0
2005	55.8	55.7	55.7	55.5	55.4	55.4	52.6	54.8	54.8	54.5	54.4	54.3	54.9
2006	53.1	53.2	53.2	53.2	53.1	53.2	50.8	52.5	52.6	52.6	52.4	52.4	52.7
2007	51.4	51.5	51.3	51.1	51.1	51.1	48.8	50.6	50.8	50.7	50.3	50.1	50.7
2008	49.4	48.9	49.0	48.8	48.6	48.6	46.1	47.8	47.8	47.3	46.7	46.3	47.9
2009	44.3	43.0	42.4	42.0	41.7	41.7	40.3	41.1	41.2	41.3	41.2	41.0	41.8
2010	40.2	40.1	40.0	39.8	40.2	40.6	39.6	40.5	40.7	40.8	40.9	40.8	40.4
2011	40.3	40.3	40.4	40.6	40.6	40.9	40.2	41.1	41.2	41.0	40.7	40.9	40.7

1. Employment by Industry: Rhode Island, Selected Years, 2000–2011—*Continued*

(Numbers in thousands, not seasonally adjusted)

Industry and year	January	February	March	April	May	June	July	August	September	October	November	December	Annual average
Service-Providing													
2000	373.1	375.1	379.1	386.4	392.0	390.3	387.5	385.3	390.9	393.7	395.6	396.9	387.2
2001	380.6	383.3	385.0	390.6	394.9	395.8	390.3	391.2	394.5	395.8	396.7	398.1	391.4
2002	384.9	386.1	389.5	396.5	401.3	401.7	396.0	396.7	402.0	403.8	405.1	406.3	397.5
2003	392.4	393.6	396.5	402.8	409.1	409.7	404.2	403.8	408.7	410.8	411.7	412.5	404.7
2004	397.7	400.5	403.1	408.5	415.9	415.2	409.9	409.5	414.8	416.1	416.6	416.2	410.3
2005	401.0	404.4	406.5	413.9	417.7	419.0	414.8	414.1	418.9	419.1	420.0	419.3	414.1
2006	402.4	405.7	409.5	418.0	420.6	422.8	415.9	416.3	423.3	424.6	425.5	425.3	417.5
2007	409.3	411.9	414.0	420.2	425.3	426.5	420.2	418.4	421.8	422.2	421.9	421.7	419.5
2008	405.9	409.0	410.3	415.6	419.7	419.7	411.9	411.2	415.5	413.7	411.7	413.3	413.3
2009	394.3	397.5	397.5	400.4	406.4	406.4	398.9	397.6	403.0	405.3	405.0	404.0	401.4
2010	390.3	393.1	396.2	401.8	407.8	407.2	403.4	402.7	406.7	407.4	407.9	406.7	402.6
2011	391.5	395.5	397.9	405.3	409.8	410.5	407.6	404.2	406.3	407.8	405.4	401.9	403.6
Trade, Transportation, and Utilities													
2000	77.5	76.9	77.1	79.0	79.1	79.3	78.3	79.2	80.3	81.3	83.0	84.2	79.6
2001	78.9	77.9	77.7	78.5	78.6	79.7	78.7	78.8	79.2	79.8	81.4	82.4	79.3
2002	79.0	77.7	77.9	79.1	79.9	81.0	80.0	80.1	81.2	82.0	83.3	84.5	80.5
2003	79.6	78.5	78.6	79.3	80.4	81.3	80.2	80.4	81.3	81.9	83.4	84.3	80.8
2004	79.7	78.9	78.8	78.3	80.2	80.8	79.8	79.6	80.2	81.1	82.2	83.1	80.2
2005	78.9	78.3	78.3	79.3	79.9	80.7	79.8	80.0	80.1	80.7	82.1	83.1	80.1
2006	78.6	77.7	78.0	79.2	79.5	80.2	79.0	79.0	79.9	80.6	82.1	83.2	79.8
2007	79.1	78.0	78.2	78.9	79.8	80.7	79.8	79.6	79.7	79.8	81.2	82.2	79.8
2008	77.8	76.7	76.6	77.0	77.4	78.3	77.2	77.3	77.3	77.4	77.6	78.0	77.7
2009	73.8	72.8	72.4	71.8	73.1	73.7	72.8	72.6	73.3	73.5	74.4	75.0	73.3
2010	72.0	71.5	71.9	71.4	71.8	72.9	72.3	72.4	73.0	73.5	74.5	75.2	72.7
2011	72.2	71.7	71.9	72.8	73.6	74.2	73.6	73.2	73.2	73.5	73.9	73.7	73.1
Wholesale Trade													
2000	15.7	15.9	16.0	16.5	16.5	16.7	16.5	16.7	16.8	17.0	17.1	17.2	16.6
2001	16.0	16.2	16.3	16.5	16.5	16.6	16.6	16.7	16.6	16.7	16.7	16.8	16.5
2002	16.5	16.3	16.4	16.5	16.6	16.7	16.4	16.4	16.3	16.4	16.5	16.4	16.5
2003	16.4	16.2	16.3	16.4	16.6	16.7	16.5	16.4	16.4	16.4	16.4	16.3	16.4
2004	16.1	16.0	16.1	16.3	16.4	16.6	16.6	16.6	16.5	16.6	16.6	16.7	16.4
2005	16.3	16.4	16.5	16.8	16.9	17.0	16.9	17.0	16.9	16.9	16.9	17.0	16.8
2006	16.7	16.7	16.8	17.0	17.0	17.1	17.1	17.1	17.1	17.2	17.2	17.2	17.0
2007	17.0	16.9	16.9	17.2	17.3	17.4	17.4	17.3	17.1	17.2	17.3	17.4	17.2
2008	16.9	16.9	16.9	16.9	17.0	17.1	17.0	16.9	16.9	16.9	16.8	16.7	16.9
2009	16.3	16.2	16.1	16.0	16.0	16.1	15.9	15.9	15.9	16.0	15.9	16.0	16.0
2010	15.6	15.6	15.7	15.6	15.9	16.0	15.9	16.0	16.0	16.0	16.0	16.1	15.9
2011	15.8	15.8	15.9	16.0	16.2	16.3	16.3	16.5	16.4	16.7	16.6	16.5	16.3
Retail Trade													
2000	51.1	50.4	50.4	51.5	51.5	51.5	51.2	51.7	52.3	53.0	54.7	55.8	52.1
2001	52.0	50.7	50.4	50.7	50.9	51.8	51.3	51.4	51.3	51.7	53.3	54.4	51.7
2002	51.7	50.9	51.0	51.8	52.4	53.1	53.1	53.3	53.7	54.2	55.5	56.8	53.1
2003	52.4	51.5	51.3	51.8	52.4	53.1	52.9	53.3	53.3	54.0	55.5	56.5	53.2
2004	52.6	52.0	51.8	51.7	52.5	53.0	52.9	52.8	52.5	53.5	54.7	55.4	53.0
2005	52.1	51.4	51.3	51.7	52.0	52.5	52.2	52.2	51.9	52.6	54.0	54.8	52.4
2006	51.3	50.4	50.6	51.3	51.4	51.8	51.4	51.3	51.4	52.1	53.6	54.6	51.8
2007	51.3	50.5	50.7	50.7	51.3	51.9	51.7	51.6	51.1	51.2	52.5	53.2	51.5
2008	50.1	49.1	49.0	49.1	49.3	49.9	49.6	49.6	49.1	49.5	50.0	50.2	49.5
2009	47.3	46.5	46.3	45.9	46.9	47.3	47.3	47.0	46.9	47.2	48.1	48.5	47.1
2010	46.5	46.0	46.3	45.6	45.6	46.3	46.5	46.6	46.2	46.7	47.7	48.0	46.5
2011	46.0	45.5	45.6	46.2	46.7	47.0	47.0	46.4	45.9	45.9	46.4	45.9	46.2
Transportation and Utilities													
2000	10.7	10.6	10.7	11.0	11.1	11.1	10.6	10.8	11.2	11.3	11.2	11.2	11.0
2001	10.9	11.0	11.0	11.3	11.2	11.3	10.8	10.7	11.3	11.4	11.4	11.2	11.1
2002	10.8	10.5	10.5	10.8	10.9	11.2	10.5	10.4	11.2	11.4	11.3	11.3	10.9
2003	10.8	10.8	11.0	11.1	11.4	11.5	10.8	10.7	11.6	11.5	11.5	11.5	11.2
2004	11.0	10.9	10.9	10.3	11.3	11.2	10.3	10.2	11.2	11.0	10.9	11.0	10.9
2005	10.5	10.5	10.5	10.8	11.0	11.2	10.7	10.8	11.3	11.2	11.2	11.3	10.9
2006	10.6	10.6	10.6	10.9	11.1	11.3	10.5	10.6	11.4	11.3	11.3	11.4	11.0
2007	10.8	10.6	10.6	11.0	11.2	11.4	10.7	10.7	11.5	11.4	11.4	11.6	11.1
2008	10.8	10.7	10.7	11.0	11.1	11.3	10.6	10.8	11.3	11.0	10.8	11.1	10.9
2009	10.2	10.1	10.0	9.9	10.2	10.3	9.6	9.7	10.5	10.3	10.4	10.5	10.1
2010	9.9	9.9	9.9	10.2	10.3	10.6	9.9	9.8	10.8	10.8	10.8	11.1	10.3
2011	10.4	10.4	10.4	10.6	10.7	10.9	10.3	10.3	10.9	10.9	10.9	11.3	10.7
Information													
2000	10.8	10.9	10.8	10.9	11.0	11.2	11.2	10.0	11.1	11.1	11.1	11.1	10.9
2001	11.1	11.1	11.1	11.2	11.4	11.4	11.4	11.3	11.3	11.2	11.2	11.3	11.3
2002	11.3	11.2	11.3	11.2	11.2	11.3	11.3	11.2	11.2	10.9	11.1	11.2	11.2
2003	11.1	11.1	11.0	11.0	11.0	11.2	11.0	11.0	10.8	11.0	10.9	10.9	11.0
2004	11.1	11.0	11.1	11.1	11.0	10.9	10.7	10.7	10.6	10.6	11.0	10.9	10.8
2005	10.8	10.8	10.7	10.7	10.7	10.7	10.8	10.8	10.7	10.8	10.9	11.0	10.8
2006	11.0	10.9	11.0	11.3	11.3	11.4	10.8	10.7	10.7	10.6	10.9	10.9	11.0
2007	10.5	10.4	10.5	10.5	10.6	10.6	10.6	10.7	10.6	10.5	10.8	10.8	10.6
2008	10.6	10.9	10.9	10.8	10.6	10.9	10.9	10.9	10.8	10.8	10.5	10.4	10.7
2009	10.4	10.3	10.2	10.3	10.4	10.4	10.0	10.0	9.9	9.7	9.9	9.9	10.1
2010	9.8	9.8	9.9	9.9	9.8	9.8	9.9	10.2	10.3	10.2	10.2	10.2	10.0
2011	9.8	9.8	10.0	10.1	10.4	10.4	10.4	9.6	10.4	10.4	10.5	10.5	10.2

1. Employment by Industry: Rhode Island, Selected Years, 2000–2011—*Continued*

(Numbers in thousands, not seasonally adjusted)

Industry and year	January	February	March	April	May	June	July	August	September	October	November	December	Annual average
Financial Activities													
2000	30.0	30.0	30.2	30.7	30.5	31.4	32.0	31.7	31.6	31.5	31.7	32.0	31.1
2001	32.0	32.1	32.3	32.0	32.0	32.5	32.5	32.3	32.2	32.2	32.2	32.4	32.2
2002	32.3	32.3	32.2	32.6	32.6	32.9	33.3	33.2	33.1	33.2	33.3	33.6	32.9
2003	33.1	33.2	33.5	33.2	33.5	33.9	34.0	34.0	33.8	33.8	33.9	34.1	33.7
2004	33.8	33.8	33.8	33.9	34.2	34.3	34.2	34.2	34.0	34.1	34.1	34.1	34.0
2005	33.7	33.8	33.8	34.3	34.3	34.5	34.7	34.7	34.5	34.2	34.3	34.6	34.3
2006	34.2	34.1	34.4	34.5	34.8	34.9	35.2	35.6	35.7	35.6	35.7	36.1	35.1
2007	35.2	35.3	35.2	35.3	35.4	35.3	35.0	34.7	34.6	34.1	34.1	34.0	34.9
2008	33.6	33.7	33.5	33.4	33.5	33.5	33.3	33.2	33.3	32.4	32.3	32.3	33.2
2009	31.9	31.9	31.6	31.2	31.3	31.5	31.3	30.9	30.7	30.7	30.9	30.8	31.2
2010	30.3	30.4	30.6	30.4	30.5	30.6	30.8	30.7	30.8	31.0	31.0	31.1	30.7
2011	30.5	30.6	30.6	30.7	30.6	31.0	31.1	31.0	30.8	30.4	30.6	31.0	30.7
Professional and Business Services													
2000	48.2	48.4	49.5	50.9	51.5	52.2	51.0	51.4	51.8	51.9	51.7	51.9	50.9
2001	48.4	48.9	49.0	50.6	50.7	51.1	50.7	51.5	51.6	51.8	50.9	50.6	50.5
2002	47.2	47.0	47.7	49.4	49.4	50.1	48.9	49.3	49.7	49.7	49.4	48.8	48.9
2003	46.4	46.5	47.0	49.2	49.8	50.9	50.9	51.5	51.4	52.2	52.0	52.0	50.0
2004	49.9	50.3	50.9	53.2	53.7	54.5	54.3	55.0	55.4	55.6	55.2	54.7	53.6
2005	51.8	52.2	52.7	55.2	55.3	55.9	56.2	56.9	57.2	56.2	56.2	55.8	55.1
2006	52.6	53.0	53.6	56.6	56.8	57.9	56.9	57.8	58.7	58.4	57.8	57.3	56.5
2007	54.3	54.0	54.3	56.4	56.9	58.0	56.8	56.8	56.6	56.2	56.0	55.7	56.0
2008	53.2	52.9	53.1	55.2	55.3	56.2	55.4	55.5	55.9	55.5	54.8	53.6	54.7
2009	51.1	51.0	51.1	52.5	52.7	53.5	53.0	53.2	53.4	53.3	53.2	52.5	52.5
2010	50.1	50.2	51.1	54.0	54.2	54.9	54.4	54.5	54.6	54.8	54.6	53.6	53.4
2011	51.5	51.8	52.2	54.1	54.4	54.8	55.5	55.3	55.2	55.5	55.3	54.3	54.2
Education and Health Services													
2000	81.1	83.2	84.0	84.8	84.8	80.2	80.3	80.0	83.2	85.0	86.1	86.1	83.2
2001	83.0	85.4	86.2	86.1	86.3	82.0	81.2	82.1	84.8	86.5	87.5	88.0	84.9
2002	85.6	87.7	88.7	88.9	89.1	84.6	84.0	85.1	88.4	90.3	91.5	92.2	88.0
2003	89.6	91.6	92.6	93.0	93.2	88.0	87.1	86.6	90.3	92.6	93.4	93.7	91.0
2004	90.8	93.3	94.4	95.0	95.2	89.9	89.1	88.9	92.7	94.6	95.4	95.9	92.9
2005	92.7	95.2	96.2	96.7	96.6	92.5	92.0	91.7	96.0	97.9	98.5	97.8	95.3
2006	94.0	97.4	98.6	99.2	98.2	94.4	93.4	93.1	96.8	99.7	100.5	100.0	97.1
2007	96.9	100.1	101.0	101.2	100.9	96.7	95.6	95.1	98.8	101.2	101.9	101.3	99.2
2008	97.8	101.4	102.1	102.0	101.5	97.3	95.9	96.0	99.4	102.2	102.5	102.5	100.1
2009	98.7	102.2	102.6	102.3	102.0	98.2	97.3	96.7	100.2	103.6	104.2	103.9	101.0
2010	100.8	103.3	104.0	104.1	103.9	99.5	99.0	98.6	102.3	104.3	105.0	105.2	102.5
2011	100.6	103.9	104.7	105.8	105.6	101.1	100.7	99.9	103.0	105.8	106.2	105.2	103.5
Leisure and Hospitality													
2000	41.1	41.2	41.9	44.3	47.0	50.8	52.0	51.4	48.6	46.6	45.4	44.8	46.3
2001	41.1	41.7	42.2	45.4	48.4	51.8	52.4	52.2	49.8	47.0	45.2	44.8	46.8
2002	41.7	42.3	43.4	46.6	49.6	52.7	53.9	53.5	51.0	48.5	45.8	45.8	48.0
2003	43.3	43.4	44.0	47.1	50.4	53.1	55.2	54.6	52.3	49.6	47.9	47.2	49.0
2004	43.6	44.1	44.3	47.7	51.2	54.4	55.8	55.5	53.4	50.7	49.0	48.5	49.9
2005	44.7	45.4	45.8	48.8	51.4	55.1	55.8	55.3	53.2	50.5	48.8	48.1	50.2
2006	44.4	44.5	45.6	48.7	51.1	54.8	55.6	55.5	53.7	50.7	48.9	48.6	50.2
2007	45.5	46.0	46.7	49.6	52.4	56.4	57.1	56.7	54.6	52.6	50.0	49.5	51.4
2008	45.9	46.4	46.7	49.7	53.0	55.8	55.9	55.5	53.7	51.2	49.4	48.7	51.0
2009	43.6	44.1	44.4	46.8	51.0	53.6	53.8	54.0	52.3	49.5	47.2	47.0	48.9
2010	43.6	44.0	44.4	47.6	50.8	54.3	55.5	55.2	53.1	50.0	48.3	47.3	49.5
2011	44.0	44.6	45.0	48.0	50.8	54.8	56.1	55.0	51.4	49.2	46.4	45.2	49.2
Other Services													
2000	20.0	20.1	20.4	20.6	20.6	21.1	21.3	21.4	20.9	21.0	20.8	21.0	20.8
2001	20.7	20.6	20.7	20.9	21.1	21.7	21.7	21.8	21.1	21.1	21.3	21.4	21.2
2002	21.1	21.1	21.2	21.5	21.8	22.4	22.7	22.6	22.1	22.3	22.3	22.6	22.0
2003	22.2	22.2	22.4	22.8	23.1	23.5	23.8	23.6	23.1	23.0	23.3	23.4	23.0
2004	22.7	22.8	22.9	23.1	23.4	23.7	24.0	23.8	23.3	23.5	23.6	23.5	23.4
2005	22.9	22.9	23.1	23.1	23.4	23.7	24.0	24.0	23.1	23.0	23.1	23.0	23.3
2006	22.2	22.2	22.4	22.9	23.1	23.6	23.7	23.6	23.1	23.3	23.3	23.2	23.1
2007	22.6	22.7	22.8	23.0	23.3	23.9	23.8	23.6	23.0	23.1	23.1	23.2	23.2
2008	22.4	22.5	22.5	22.7	22.9	23.2	23.4	23.2	22.7	22.7	22.6	22.5	22.8
2009	21.8	21.9	21.9	22.1	22.2	22.5	22.8	22.6	21.9	22.2	22.2	22.1	22.2
2010	21.5	21.6	21.6	21.7	22.0	22.2	23.0	22.9	22.1	22.0	22.2	22.1	22.1
2011	21.5	21.7	21.7	22.0	22.2	22.7	23.3	23.4	22.2	21.8	21.3	21.0	22.1
Government													
2000	64.4	64.4	65.2	65.2	67.5	64.1	61.4	60.2	63.4	65.3	65.8	65.8	64.4
2001	65.4	65.6	65.8	65.9	66.4	65.6	61.7	61.2	64.5	66.2	67.0	67.2	65.2
2002	66.7	66.8	67.1	67.2	67.7	66.7	61.9	61.7	65.3	66.9	67.4	67.6	66.1
2003	67.1	67.1	67.4	67.2	67.7	67.8	62.0	62.1	65.7	66.7	66.8	66.9	66.2
2004	66.1	66.3	66.9	66.2	67.0	66.7	62.0	61.8	65.2	65.9	66.5	65.8	65.5
2005	65.5	65.8	65.9	65.8	66.1	65.9	61.5	60.7	64.1	65.8	66.1	65.9	64.9
2006	65.4	65.9	65.9	65.6	65.8	65.6	61.3	61.0	64.7	65.7	66.4	66.0	64.9
2007	65.2	65.4	65.3	65.3	66.0	64.9	61.5	61.2	63.9	64.7	64.8	65.0	64.4
2008	64.6	64.5	64.9	64.8	65.5	64.5	60.2	59.5	62.4	63.1	64.0	63.7	63.5
2009	63.0	63.3	63.3	63.4	63.7	63.0	57.9	57.6	61.3	62.8	63.0	62.8	62.1
2010	62.2	62.3	62.7	62.7	64.8	63.0	58.5	58.2	60.5	61.6	62.1	62.0	61.7
2011	61.4	61.4	61.8	61.8	62.2	61.5	56.9	56.8	60.1	61.2	61.2	61.0	60.6

2. Average Weekly Hours by Selected Industry: Rhode Island, 2007–2011

(Not seasonally adjusted)

Industry and year	January	February	March	April	May	June	July	August	September	October	November	December	Annual average
Total Private													
2007	33.3	33.6	33.8	33.4	33.4	33.8	33.5	33.7	33.4	33.1	33.9	33.7	33.5
2008	33.7	33.8	34.2	33.9	34.2	34.5	34.3	34.3	34.0	34.0	34.0	33.8	34.1
2009	33.5	33.8	33.6	33.8	33.7	33.6	33.8	34.0	34.0	34.0	34.1	34.1	33.9
2010	33.9	33.6	34.1	34.1	34.4	34.0	34.2	34.0	33.8	33.7	33.4	33.7	33.9
2011	33.0	33.3	33.2	33.1	33.3	32.9	33.1	32.9	33.0	33.0	32.9	33.0	33.0
Goods-Producing													
2007	37.8	38.0	38.4	37.8	38.9	38.2	37.3	38.0	38.3	37.7	38.2	38.0	38.1
2008	38.5	37.7	38.5	37.6	39.4	39.7	38.9	38.8	38.8	38.3	37.9	37.4	38.5
2009	36.4	36.3	36.0	35.9	35.7	35.6	36.0	35.9	35.8	36.1	35.7	36.7	36.0
2010	35.6	35.1	36.3	36.4	37.2	36.9	37.0	36.8	37.0	37.0	37.0	37.4	36.7
2011	36.6	36.4	36.7	36.9	37.3	37.1	36.8	36.3	36.5	36.5	37.1	38.2	36.9
Construction													
2007	36.2	36.0	36.9	36.4	38.1	37.4	37.2	36.9	36.6	35.5	35.7	35.3	36.5
2008	34.1	34.3	35.4	34.9	37.5	38.0	38.1	37.4	36.8	37.8	36.2	36.1	36.5
2009	33.9	34.0	34.3	35.1	35.9	34.8	36.8	36.4	36.2	35.6	35.5	36.0	35.4
2010	34.9	34.4	35.0	34.9	36.1	35.9	36.4	36.0	35.6	35.6	35.3	35.6	35.5
2011	34.9	35.1	35.4	35.0	35.9	36.0	36.6	35.7	36.3	36.1	37.3	38.5	36.1
Manufacturing													
2007	38.5	38.7	39.0	38.4	39.4	38.7	37.6	38.6	39.1	38.7	39.3	38.9	38.7
2008	39.8	38.7	39.4	39.1	40.3	40.6	38.9	39.3	39.7	39.0	39.3	38.8	39.4
2009	38.7	38.3	38.0	37.3	36.9	37.4	37.4	38.4	38.2	38.5	37.9	38.6	38.0
2010	37.5	37.1	38.5	38.5	38.9	38.4	38.2	38.2	38.6	38.6	38.6	38.5	38.3
2011	38.1	38.4	38.5	38.8	38.9	38.6	37.9	37.5	37.5	38.0	38.3	38.9	38.3
Trade, Transportation, and Utilities													
2007	33.7	33.7	33.4	33.5	34.0	34.8	34.1	34.7	34.4	33.5	34.0	34.1	34.0
2008	34.1	34.4	35.5	34.7	35.1	34.8	35.0	35.0	34.7	34.1	33.8	34.8	34.7
2009	34.2	34.6	34.0	34.2	34.5	34.5	34.9	35.6	34.6	35.1	35.7	35.2	34.8
2010	34.9	35.3	35.5	36.6	36.8	36.2	36.3	36.0	35.3	35.4	35.2	35.4	35.7
2011	34.8	35.2	35.4	34.9	35.2	34.9	34.9	34.7	34.7	33.8	33.4	34.4	34.7
Professional and Business Services													
2007	34.6	36.3	36.4	36.5	37.1	36.0	35.6	34.4	35.0	35.1	35.7	35.5	35.7
2008	36.7	36.9	37.4	36.8	36.1	36.7	36.1	35.2	35.3	35.8	35.0	35.2	36.1
2009	36.1	36.1	35.7	36.4	36.5	36.7	37.1	37.2	37.2	37.3	36.9	36.0	36.6
2010	35.7	35.3	35.6	36.1	36.6	36.4	36.0	36.0	36.1	36.3	36.3	36.1	36.1
2011	35.6	35.9	36.0	35.8	35.7	36.0	36.0	36.1	36.0	35.6	35.2	35.7	35.8
Education and Health Services													
2007	32.3	32.4	32.4	31.7	31.4	32.4	31.9	31.8	31.7	31.8	32.9	31.9	32.1
2008	32.1	31.8	32.2	32.5	32.3	32.1	32.3	32.3	32.2	32.5	33.3	32.2	32.3
2009	32.2	32.8	33.2	33.4	33.8	34.2	34.1	33.9	33.9	33.7	34.1	32.9	33.5
2010	32.9	32.6	32.2	32.0	32.0	31.4	31.9	31.4	31.5	31.8	31.7	31.4	31.9
2011	31.1	31.7	31.5	31.3	31.2	31.1	31.0	30.7	30.5	31.2	31.3	30.7	31.1
Leisure and Hospitality													
2007	22.0	23.2	23.8	23.8	24.0	25.4	26.0	25.3	24.6	24.3	23.8	24.5	24.3
2008	24.0	24.5	24.4	23.9	24.3	25.0	25.6	24.9	24.3	24.9	24.8	24.0	24.6
2009	24.4	24.7	24.9	26.0	26.1	25.9	26.8	27.3	26.6	26.1	26.2	26.3	26.0
2010	26.4	25.9	26.1	26.5	26.5	26.2	26.9	26.3	25.6	25.7	25.6	25.8	26.1
2011	25.3	25.8	25.4	25.9	26.1	25.8	26.8	26.8	25.7	25.6	25.4	25.3	25.9

3. Average Hourly Earnings by Selected Industry: Rhode Island, 2007–2011

(Dollars, not seasonally adjusted)

Industry and year	January	February	March	April	May	June	July	August	September	October	November	December	Annual average
Total Private													
2007	22.14	22.37	22.20	22.19	21.97	22.00	22.29	21.92	22.43	22.05	22.08	22.39	22.17
2008	22.75	22.61	22.47	22.58	22.15	22.29	22.47	22.15	22.37	22.59	22.73	22.86	22.50
2009	22.81	22.63	22.98	22.64	22.49	22.34	22.19	22.31	22.36	22.44	22.58	22.52	22.52
2010	22.42	22.66	22.50	22.41	22.52	22.64	22.60	22.70	22.78	22.89	22.90	22.95	22.67
2011	23.04	22.96	23.13	23.06	23.40	23.41	23.88	24.02	24.12	24.49	24.67	24.47	23.73
Goods-Producing													
2007	21.65	21.85	21.79	22.20	22.27	22.98	23.06	22.45	22.42	22.01	22.19	22.37	22.27
2008	22.56	22.28	22.19	22.33	22.34	22.34	22.40	22.13	22.14	23.09	22.94	23.14	22.48
2009	22.74	22.51	22.54	23.19	23.33	23.28	23.79	24.04	23.75	23.80	23.93	23.74	23.38
2010	24.04	24.08	23.94	24.13	24.23	24.33	24.35	24.45	24.42	24.52	24.51	24.38	24.29
2011	24.42	24.41	24.58	24.55	24.69	24.79	25.64	25.78	25.40	25.42	25.48	25.74	25.09
Construction													
2007	25.82	27.26	26.98	27.62	27.23	27.96	27.09	26.54	27.05	26.41	26.13	26.24	26.87
2008	26.09	26.63	26.77	26.73	26.95	27.49	27.70	27.09	27.51	27.06	27.50	27.15	27.09
2009	26.06	26.54	27.05	27.29	27.38	26.95	27.27	27.63	27.56	27.54	27.40	27.42	27.20
2010	27.64	27.73	27.76	27.61	27.67	27.56	27.59	27.67	27.73	27.83	27.78	27.70	27.69
2011	27.70	27.73	28.33	28.42	28.02	28.02	28.17	28.62	28.03	28.17	28.69	28.77	28.25
Manufacturing													
2007	20.14	20.28	20.26	20.58	20.60	21.23	21.59	21.00	20.86	20.78	20.89	21.20	20.78
2008	21.32	21.27	21.33	21.40	21.41	21.39	21.63	21.36	21.10	21.30	20.94	21.29	21.31
2009	20.96	21.15	21.00	21.56	21.80	21.63	22.13	22.19	22.20	22.28	22.36	22.04	21.76
2010	22.08	21.97	21.80	22.00	22.09	22.17	22.18	22.20	22.03	22.08	22.13	22.17	22.08
2011	22.26	22.20	22.41	22.61	22.94	23.08	23.98	24.14	24.19	24.27	24.16	24.48	23.39
Trade, Transportation, and Utilities													
2007	18.99	19.58	19.19	19.49	19.10	19.34	19.65	19.45	19.74	19.41	19.69	20.04	19.48
2008	20.15	20.35	20.34	20.24	20.29	20.40	20.46	20.15	20.38	19.89	20.18	20.03	20.24
2009	19.51	19.81	20.24	19.68	19.51	19.46	19.19	19.70	20.04	20.07	20.26	20.04	19.79
2010	19.56	19.87	19.80	19.65	19.76	19.70	19.74	19.78	19.87	19.94	19.90	19.86	19.79
2011	19.95	19.96	20.41	20.02	20.23	20.41	20.29	20.72	20.74	21.23	20.99	20.86	20.48
Professional and Business Services													
2007	28.52	28.75	27.94	28.14	28.66	28.01	28.96	28.84	28.77	28.67	28.63	28.48	28.53
2008	28.73	28.79	28.87	28.46	28.57	28.49	28.55	28.47	28.58	28.40	28.92	28.99	28.65
2009	29.10	29.13	28.50	27.88	27.72	27.56	27.00	26.88	26.79	26.83	26.86	27.03	27.58
2010	27.06	27.12	27.27	27.13	27.20	27.27	27.32	27.45	27.44	27.50	27.54	27.59	27.33
2011	27.69	27.64	27.66	27.31	28.08	28.24	29.85	29.48	29.64	29.95	30.65	30.32	28.89
Education and Health Services													
2007	23.04	23.37	23.14	22.91	22.87	23.05	23.07	22.89	22.92	22.95	22.89	22.74	22.99
2008	23.15	23.05	23.12	23.18	23.03	23.09	23.19	22.91	22.61	22.96	23.05	23.46	23.07
2009	23.41	23.91	23.73	23.69	23.70	23.24	23.04	23.17	23.26	23.34	23.40	24.08	23.50
2010	23.26	23.39	23.14	23.06	23.24	23.32	23.25	23.21	23.20	23.23	23.25	23.35	23.24
2011	23.34	23.36	23.37	23.51	23.34	23.16	23.29	23.24	23.51	23.27	23.55	23.51	23.37
Leisure and Hospitality													
2007	13.83	14.38	14.66	14.24	14.62	13.57	13.68	14.01	14.73	14.60	14.89	15.68	14.39
2008	14.97	14.72	14.77	14.67	14.58	14.60	14.47	14.32	15.00	14.80	14.88	15.31	14.74
2009	15.39	15.49	15.63	15.23	15.25	15.06	14.59	14.42	14.49	14.42	14.47	14.57	14.89
2010	14.50	14.41	14.43	14.16	14.09	14.03	13.98	13.93	13.87	13.91	13.88	13.89	14.08
2011	13.92	13.90	13.99	13.97	13.98	13.89	13.62	13.77	13.92	13.96	14.32	14.09	13.93

4. Average Weekly Earnings by Selected Industry: Rhode Island, 2007–2011

(Dollars, not seasonally adjusted)

Industry and year	January	February	March	April	May	June	July	August	September	October	November	December	Annual average
Total Private													
2007	737.26	751.63	750.36	741.15	733.80	743.60	746.72	738.70	749.16	729.86	748.51	754.54	743.45
2008	766.68	764.22	768.47	765.46	757.53	769.01	770.72	759.75	760.58	768.06	772.82	772.67	766.54
2009	764.14	764.89	772.13	765.23	757.91	750.62	750.02	758.54	760.24	762.96	769.98	767.93	762.52
2010	760.04	761.38	767.25	764.18	774.69	769.76	772.92	771.80	769.96	771.39	764.86	773.42	768.25
2011	760.32	764.57	767.92	763.29	779.22	770.19	790.43	790.26	795.96	808.17	811.64	807.51	784.17
Goods-Producing													
2007	818.37	830.30	836.74	839.16	866.30	877.84	860.14	853.10	858.69	829.78	847.66	850.06	847.48
2008	868.56	839.96	854.32	839.61	880.20	886.90	871.36	858.64	859.03	884.35	869.43	865.44	864.89
2009	827.74	817.11	811.44	832.52	832.88	828.77	856.44	863.04	850.25	859.18	854.30	871.26	842.04
2010	855.82	845.21	869.02	878.33	901.36	897.78	900.95	899.76	903.54	907.24	906.87	911.81	890.58
2011	893.77	888.52	902.09	905.90	920.94	919.71	943.55	935.81	927.10	927.83	945.31	983.27	925.21
Construction													
2007	934.68	981.36	995.56	1,005.37	1,037.46	1,045.70	1,007.75	979.33	990.03	937.56	932.84	926.27	981.80
2008	889.67	913.41	947.66	932.88	1,010.63	1,044.62	1,055.37	1,013.17	1,012.37	1,022.87	995.50	980.12	987.70
2009	883.43	902.36	927.82	957.88	982.94	937.86	1,003.54	1,005.73	997.67	980.42	972.70	987.12	962.61
2010	964.64	953.91	971.60	963.59	998.89	989.40	1,004.28	996.12	987.19	990.75	980.63	986.12	983.61
2011	966.73	973.32	1,002.88	994.70	1,005.92	1,008.72	1,031.02	1,021.73	1,017.49	1,016.94	1,070.14	1,107.65	1,021.06
Manufacturing													
2007	775.39	784.84	790.14	790.27	811.64	821.60	811.78	810.60	815.63	804.19	820.98	824.68	805.02
2008	848.54	823.15	840.40	836.74	862.82	868.43	841.41	839.45	837.67	830.70	822.94	826.05	839.99
2009	811.15	810.05	798.00	804.19	804.42	808.96	827.66	852.10	848.04	857.78	847.44	850.74	826.45
2010	828.00	815.09	839.30	847.00	859.30	851.33	847.28	848.04	850.36	852.29	854.22	853.55	845.70
2011	848.11	852.48	862.79	877.27	892.37	890.89	908.84	905.25	907.13	922.26	925.33	952.27	895.52
Trade, Transportation, and Utilities													
2007	639.96	659.85	640.95	652.92	649.40	673.03	670.07	674.92	679.06	650.24	669.46	683.36	662.07
2008	687.12	700.04	722.07	702.33	712.18	709.92	716.10	705.25	707.19	678.25	682.08	697.04	701.60
2009	667.24	685.43	688.16	673.06	673.10	671.37	669.73	701.32	693.38	704.46	723.28	705.41	688.11
2010	682.64	701.41	702.90	719.19	727.17	713.14	716.56	712.08	701.41	705.88	700.48	703.04	707.08
2011	694.26	702.59	722.51	698.70	712.10	712.31	708.12	718.98	719.68	717.57	701.07	717.58	710.21
Professional and Business Services													
2007	986.79	1,043.63	1,017.02	1,027.11	1,063.29	1,008.36	1,030.98	992.10	1,006.95	1,006.32	1,022.09	1,011.04	1,017.99
2008	1,054.39	1,062.35	1,079.74	1,047.33	1,031.38	1,045.58	1,030.66	1,002.14	1,008.87	1,016.72	1,012.20	1,020.45	1,034.03
2009	1,050.51	1,051.59	1,017.45	1,014.83	1,011.78	1,011.45	1,001.70	999.94	996.59	1,000.76	991.13	973.08	1,009.45
2010	966.04	957.34	970.81	979.39	995.52	992.63	983.52	988.20	990.58	998.25	999.70	996.00	985.59
2011	985.76	992.28	995.76	977.70	1,002.46	1,016.64	1,074.60	1,064.23	1,067.04	1,066.22	1,078.88	1,082.42	1,034.59
Education and Health Services													
2007	744.19	757.19	749.74	726.25	718.12	746.82	735.93	727.90	726.56	729.81	753.08	725.41	736.75
2008	743.12	732.99	744.46	753.35	743.87	741.19	749.04	739.99	728.04	746.20	767.57	755.41	745.53
2009	753.80	784.25	787.84	791.25	801.06	794.81	785.66	785.46	788.51	786.56	797.94	792.23	787.45
2010	765.25	762.51	745.11	737.92	743.68	732.25	741.68	728.79	730.80	738.71	737.03	733.19	741.36
2011	725.87	740.51	736.16	735.86	728.21	720.28	721.99	713.47	717.06	726.02	737.12	721.76	727.16
Leisure and Hospitality													
2007	304.26	333.62	348.91	338.91	350.88	344.68	355.68	354.45	362.36	354.78	354.38	384.16	349.55
2008	359.28	360.64	360.39	350.61	354.29	365.00	370.43	356.57	364.50	368.52	369.02	367.44	362.29
2009	375.52	382.60	389.19	395.98	398.03	390.05	391.01	393.67	385.43	376.36	379.11	383.19	386.78
2010	382.80	373.22	376.62	375.24	373.39	367.59	376.06	366.36	355.07	357.49	355.33	358.36	367.86
2011	352.18	358.62	355.35	361.82	364.88	358.36	365.02	369.04	357.74	357.38	363.73	356.48	360.19

SOUTH CAROLINA
At a Glance

Population:
2000 census: 4,012,023
2010 census: 4,625,364
2011 estimate: 4,679,230

Percent change in population:
2000–2010: 15.3%
2010–2011: 1.2%

Percent change in total nonfarm employment:
2000–2010: -2.7%
2010–2011: 1.1%

Industry with the largest growth in employment, 2000–2011 (thousands):
Education and Health Services, 60.6

Industry with the largest decline or smallest growth in employment, 2000–2011 (thousands):
Manufacturing, -120.1

Civilian labor force:
2000: 1,988,159
2010: 2,150,576
2011: 2,157,266

Unemployment rate and rank among states (lowest to highest):
2000: 3.6%, 20th
2010: 11.2%, 46th
2011: 10.3%, 44th

Over-the-year change in unemployment rates:
2010–2011: -0.9%

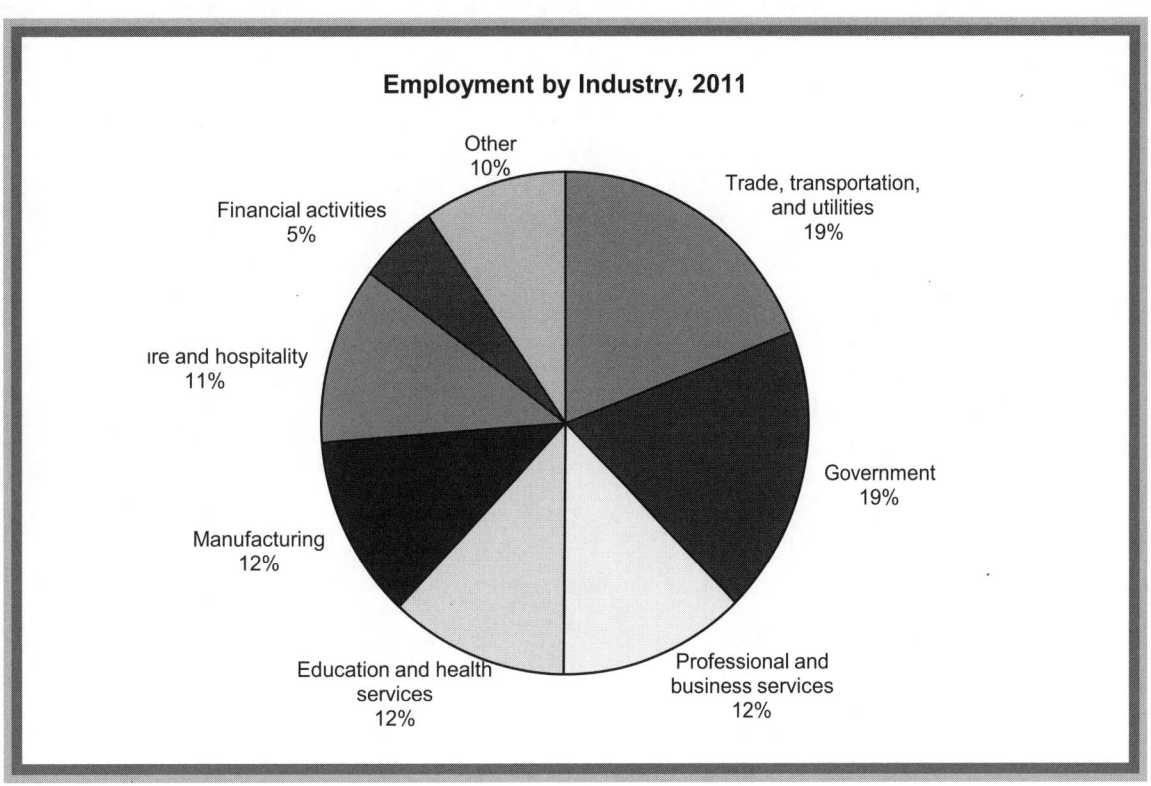

Employment by Industry, 2011

Other
10%

Trade, transportation,
and utilities
19%

Financial activities
5%

ıre and hospitality
11%

Government
19%

Manufacturing
12%

Professional and
business services
12%

Education and health
services
12%

1. Employment by Industry: South Carolina, Selected Years, 2000–2011

(Numbers in thousands, not seasonally adjusted)

Industry and year	January	February	March	April	May	June	July	August	September	October	November	December	Annual average
Total Nonfarm													
2000	1,826.0	1,838.7	1,864.4	1,870.4	1,889.1	1,902.5	1,848.8	1,853.9	1,853.5	1,863.2	1,866.4	1,868.3	1,862.1
2001	1,809.5	1,817.8	1,833.8	1,838.1	1,843.7	1,843.1	1,821.9	1,828.1	1,827.2	1,813.0	1,815.2	1,812.4	1,825.3
2002	1,762.6	1,774.0	1,795.3	1,813.5	1,824.8	1,830.5	1,802.5	1,814.9	1,814.9	1,815.3	1,814.8	1,814.7	1,806.5
2003	1,777.7	1,790.6	1,807.2	1,813.7	1,823.3	1,822.5	1,803.1	1,813.0	1,815.5	1,815.1	1,815.1	1,818.3	1,809.6
2004	1,782.0	1,791.7	1,816.8	1,836.6	1,849.0	1,852.3	1,834.7	1,843.7	1,847.2	1,853.5	1,858.7	1,858.4	1,835.4
2005	1,821.5	1,834.9	1,846.9	1,870.5	1,881.0	1,870.3	1,870.2	1,881.9	1,880.0	1,887.6	1,896.3	1,885.7	1,868.9
2006	1,860.4	1,878.8	1,899.7	1,917.0	1,926.1	1,906.7	1,893.8	1,903.7	1,911.1	1,932.8	1,936.7	1,944.0	1,909.2
2007	1,905.3	1,917.2	1,940.6	1,948.4	1,961.7	1,969.8	1,942.8	1,952.2	1,957.6	1,955.6	1,960.4	1,958.4	1,947.5
2008	1,919.9	1,930.4	1,945.5	1,948.7	1,962.3	1,956.8	1,922.5	1,923.6	1,925.3	1,914.1	1,906.2	1,890.4	1,928.8
2009	1,828.8	1,823.6	1,827.7	1,831.5	1,836.2	1,828.8	1,805.2	1,806.7	1,802.5	1,801.6	1,803.1	1,796.4	1,816.0
2010	1,761.4	1,771.5	1,789.6	1,816.7	1,837.8	1,834.5	1,818.8	1,823.2	1,818.7	1,821.8	1,825.7	1,825.3	1,812.1
2011	1,779.6	1,798.8	1,819.1	1,841.7	1,851.1	1,851.1	1,840.7	1,839.6	1,832.6	1,840.4	1,847.7	1,842.8	1,832.1
Total Private													
2000	1,504.4	1,514.1	1,535.9	1,543.3	1,556.1	1,572.4	1,541.7	1,542.0	1,532.6	1,537.2	1,538.6	1,540.1	1,538.2
2001	1,486.8	1,491.0	1,505.9	1,511.2	1,517.1	1,521.1	1,516.2	1,514.5	1,501.2	1,484.2	1,484.5	1,480.4	1,501.2
2002	1,437.2	1,445.2	1,465.3	1,483.4	1,494.2	1,506.1	1,494.5	1,495.7	1,486.4	1,484.4	1,481.4	1,481.1	1,479.6
2003	1,449.5	1,457.6	1,473.6	1,480.3	1,490.9	1,497.9	1,492.8	1,496.7	1,487.7	1,486.0	1,484.6	1,486.8	1,482.0
2004	1,455.6	1,463.6	1,487.0	1,506.0	1,518.7	1,529.2	1,528.2	1,527.7	1,519.9	1,523.2	1,527.0	1,526.5	1,509.4
2005	1,494.5	1,504.6	1,515.3	1,538.4	1,549.0	1,543.9	1,559.7	1,564.2	1,547.4	1,552.3	1,558.5	1,547.7	1,539.6
2006	1,529.5	1,543.6	1,560.6	1,578.2	1,587.2	1,580.3	1,582.2	1,585.3	1,579.5	1,594.5	1,597.8	1,603.9	1,576.9
2007	1,569.3	1,578.0	1,599.1	1,608.4	1,620.8	1,633.0	1,622.8	1,624.0	1,615.8	1,609.6	1,611.3	1,610.0	1,608.5
2008	1,574.2	1,581.4	1,595.4	1,597.8	1,609.3	1,608.5	1,593.8	1,592.9	1,575.7	1,560.1	1,550.0	1,534.9	1,581.2
2009	1,479.6	1,472.8	1,476.3	1,478.2	1,483.4	1,481.7	1,472.8	1,469.6	1,457.4	1,451.7	1,451.9	1,445.7	1,468.4
2010	1,414.5	1,421.8	1,438.1	1,464.3	1,475.3	1,483.1	1,483.7	1,484.7	1,475.5	1,476.5	1,479.8	1,479.7	1,464.8
2011	1,438.7	1,455.2	1,474.3	1,496.4	1,506.5	1,510.9	1,515.2	1,510.1	1,493.2	1,497.6	1,503.5	1,501.6	1,491.9
Goods-Producing													
2000	453.4	455.9	458.6	458.3	460.0	463.9	454.7	455.0	454.0	454.6	453.9	454.0	456.4
2001	443.1	441.5	441.6	439.4	438.3	435.8	430.3	427.5	424.0	418.2	417.6	414.9	431.0
2002	405.9	405.7	406.8	408.4	409.6	410.6	406.8	407.0	404.6	403.1	399.8	398.4	405.6
2003	396.4	396.9	397.6	395.3	394.1	392.7	391.5	390.7	390.0	389.4	387.0	386.2	392.3
2004	382.0	381.7	385.6	386.9	388.1	389.8	389.6	388.8	388.1	386.5	385.4	384.9	386.5
2005	381.6	382.2	383.3	383.6	384.3	382.3	382.1	382.5	379.6	380.2	380.2	377.2	381.6
2006	376.7	378.0	380.0	382.4	384.1	382.3	381.1	380.8	379.4	382.3	381.8	383.6	381.0
2007	377.9	378.8	381.8	380.2	381.5	383.7	380.1	379.4	378.3	374.9	373.9	373.4	378.7
2008	367.3	365.7	366.0	361.1	361.6	360.3	356.2	354.1	351.3	345.8	341.7	336.3	355.6
2009	325.6	320.0	316.0	309.3	306.3	304.8	299.7	297.7	296.2	293.1	292.5	291.6	304.4
2010	286.3	286.1	287.4	290.0	291.4	292.5	292.2	291.6	291.5	291.1	291.6	293.0	290.4
2011	287.3	291.0	294.2	295.4	296.5	297.8	299.4	299.8	297.6	298.0	298.9	300.4	296.4
Mining and Logging													
2000	5.6	5.7	5.7	5.6	5.7	5.5	5.6	5.4	5.3	5.4	5.4	5.4	5.5
2001	5.2	5.2	5.2	5.2	5.2	5.2	5.2	5.2	5.2	5.2	5.2	5.2	5.2
2002	5.1	5.1	5.1	5.1	5.1	5.1	5.0	5.0	5.0	5.0	5.0	5.0	5.1
2003	5.1	5.1	5.1	5.0	5.0	5.0	5.0	5.0	5.0	5.0	5.0	5.0	5.0
2004	5.1	5.1	5.1	5.1	5.1	5.1	5.1	5.1	5.1	5.0	5.0	5.0	5.1
2005	4.9	4.9	4.9	4.9	4.9	4.9	4.8	4.8	4.7	4.7	4.7	4.7	4.8
2006	4.7	4.7	4.7	4.7	4.7	4.7	4.7	4.7	4.7	4.7	4.7	4.8	4.7
2007	4.7	4.7	4.7	4.6	4.6	4.7	4.6	4.6	4.6	4.6	4.6	4.6	4.6
2008	4.5	4.5	4.5	4.4	4.4	4.3	4.3	4.3	4.3	4.3	4.3	4.3	4.4
2009	4.2	4.1	4.1	4.1	4.1	4.1	4.1	4.1	4.1	4.0	4.0	4.0	4.1
2010	4.0	4.0	4.0	4.0	4.0	4.0	4.0	4.0	4.0	4.0	3.9	3.9	4.0
2011	3.9	3.9	4.0	3.9	4.0	4.0	3.9	3.9	3.9	3.8	3.8	3.8	3.9
Construction													
2000	112.7	113.4	116.1	115.4	116.7	118.9	113.3	113.3	112.4	114.4	114.0	114.1	114.6
2001	111.2	111.1	112.9	114.2	115.4	116.0	114.3	114.2	113.0	112.4	112.2	110.9	113.2
2002	107.5	108.8	110.4	112.0	113.4	114.2	113.9	113.8	112.8	112.5	111.8	111.0	111.8
2003	110.7	111.1	112.3	110.9	111.7	112.6	112.5	113.0	113.3	114.5	113.4	113.0	112.4
2004	110.8	110.9	113.2	114.4	115.3	115.7	116.4	116.0	115.6	115.5	114.7	113.8	114.4
2005	112.5	112.9	114.0	115.1	117.4	116.8	118.7	119.4	118.2	119.5	120.4	118.2	116.9
2006	119.3	120.8	122.5	123.8	125.4	123.9	125.7	126.2	125.8	128.1	127.7	127.6	124.7
2007	124.2	124.4	126.7	125.8	126.6	127.7	126.7	126.1	125.6	122.9	121.8	120.8	125.0
2008	116.3	115.7	116.0	112.5	112.6	112.5	109.9	109.0	107.3	104.4	102.1	99.4	109.8
2009	94.6	92.4	92.5	89.7	89.3	88.9	86.9	85.5	84.2	82.7	81.8	81.3	87.5
2010	77.6	77.1	78.2	80.1	80.6	81.2	81.2	80.3	79.8	79.4	79.1	78.5	79.4
2011	74.0	75.6	76.7	77.1	77.7	77.9	77.9	77.0	75.3	75.4	75.3	75.6	76.3
Manufacturing													
2000	335.1	336.8	336.8	337.3	337.6	339.5	335.8	336.3	336.3	334.8	334.5	334.5	336.3
2001	326.7	325.2	323.5	320.0	317.7	314.6	310.8	308.1	305.8	300.6	300.2	298.8	312.7
2002	293.3	291.8	291.3	291.3	291.1	291.3	287.9	288.2	286.8	285.6	283.0	282.4	288.7
2003	280.6	280.7	280.2	279.4	277.4	275.1	274.0	272.7	271.7	269.9	268.6	268.2	274.9
2004	266.1	265.7	267.3	267.4	267.7	269.0	268.1	267.7	267.4	266.0	265.7	266.1	267.0
2005	264.2	264.4	264.4	263.6	262.0	260.6	258.6	258.3	256.7	256.0	255.1	254.3	259.9
2006	252.7	252.5	252.8	253.9	254.0	253.7	250.7	249.9	248.9	249.5	249.4	251.2	251.6
2007	249.0	249.7	250.4	249.8	250.3	251.3	248.8	248.1	248.1	247.4	247.5	248.0	249.0
2008	246.5	245.5	245.5	244.2	244.6	243.5	242.0	240.8	239.7	237.1	235.3	232.6	241.4
2009	226.8	223.5	219.4	215.5	212.9	211.8	208.7	208.1	207.9	206.4	206.7	206.3	212.8
2010	204.7	205.0	205.2	205.9	206.8	207.3	207.0	207.3	207.7	207.7	208.6	210.6	207.0
2011	209.4	211.5	213.5	214.4	214.8	215.9	217.6	218.9	218.4	218.8	219.8	221.0	216.2

1. Employment by Industry: South Carolina, Selected Years, 2000–2011—*Continued*

(Numbers in thousands, not seasonally adjusted)

Industry and year	January	February	March	April	May	June	July	August	September	October	November	December	Annual average
Service-Providing													
2000	1,372.6	1,382.8	1,405.8	1,412.1	1,429.1	1,438.6	1,394.1	1,398.9	1,399.5	1,408.6	1,412.5	1,414.3	1,405.7
2001	1,366.4	1,376.3	1,392.2	1,398.7	1,405.4	1,407.3	1,391.6	1,400.6	1,403.2	1,394.8	1,397.6	1,397.5	1,394.3
2002	1,356.7	1,368.3	1,388.5	1,405.1	1,415.2	1,419.9	1,395.7	1,407.9	1,410.3	1,412.2	1,415.0	1,416.3	1,400.9
2003	1,381.3	1,393.7	1,409.6	1,418.4	1,429.2	1,429.8	1,411.6	1,422.3	1,425.5	1,425.7	1,428.1	1,432.1	1,417.3
2004	1,400.0	1,410.0	1,431.2	1,449.7	1,460.9	1,462.5	1,445.1	1,454.9	1,459.1	1,467.0	1,473.3	1,473.5	1,448.9
2005	1,439.9	1,452.7	1,463.6	1,486.9	1,496.7	1,488.0	1,488.1	1,499.4	1,500.4	1,507.4	1,516.1	1,508.5	1,487.3
2006	1,483.7	1,500.8	1,519.7	1,534.6	1,542.0	1,524.4	1,512.7	1,522.9	1,531.7	1,550.5	1,554.9	1,560.4	1,528.2
2007	1,527.4	1,538.4	1,558.8	1,568.2	1,580.2	1,586.1	1,562.7	1,572.8	1,579.3	1,580.7	1,586.5	1,585.0	1,568.8
2008	1,552.6	1,564.7	1,579.5	1,587.6	1,600.7	1,596.5	1,566.3	1,569.5	1,574.0	1,568.3	1,564.5	1,554.1	1,573.2
2009	1,503.2	1,503.6	1,511.7	1,522.2	1,529.9	1,524.0	1,505.5	1,509.0	1,506.3	1,508.5	1,510.6	1,504.8	1,511.6
2010	1,475.1	1,485.4	1,502.2	1,526.7	1,546.4	1,542.0	1,526.6	1,531.6	1,527.2	1,530.7	1,534.1	1,532.3	1,521.7
2011	1,492.3	1,507.8	1,524.9	1,546.3	1,554.6	1,553.3	1,541.3	1,539.8	1,535.0	1,542.4	1,548.8	1,542.4	1,535.7
Trade, Transportation, and Utilities													
2000	360.1	360.0	364.7	363.3	366.7	369.2	363.2	364.0	362.6	364.9	371.1	373.7	365.3
2001	353.6	350.7	353.9	353.0	355.3	356.2	355.3	354.8	352.5	350.7	354.9	356.7	354.0
2002	340.9	340.0	344.3	346.8	348.6	350.5	347.8	347.5	346.3	347.1	352.5	356.1	347.4
2003	342.7	341.9	344.5	344.5	347.2	349.9	348.3	349.2	347.8	348.6	353.2	357.5	347.9
2004	346.1	345.4	349.8	351.0	354.2	354.8	357.0	357.2	355.7	358.2	364.0	367.7	355.1
2005	355.2	355.0	356.5	359.7	363.4	361.1	364.5	365.2	360.7	364.9	370.7	373.1	362.5
2006	361.4	364.7	368.7	368.8	368.9	367.5	367.5	369.0	368.6	374.1	382.0	385.0	370.5
2007	370.1	369.4	374.9	374.8	377.8	380.0	379.5	379.0	378.2	379.5	385.9	388.9	378.2
2008	375.5	374.4	377.1	375.9	375.8	376.0	374.0	373.2	370.5	368.5	370.5	371.2	373.6
2009	353.0	348.4	348.6	349.4	350.9	351.3	348.9	348.3	346.0	345.0	349.1	350.6	349.1
2010	339.0	337.9	341.5	343.6	345.8	347.4	347.2	347.8	345.3	347.7	353.1	355.8	346.0
2011	341.7	342.5	345.0	348.8	350.5	352.6	353.6	352.0	348.6	351.7	358.2	359.6	350.4
Wholesale Trade													
2000	62.8	63.0	63.9	63.5	63.9	64.2	63.5	63.4	63.5	63.8	63.9	64.2	63.6
2001	63.5	63.7	64.0	64.0	64.0	64.4	64.3	64.0	63.8	63.2	63.1	62.7	63.7
2002	61.7	62.4	63.1	63.3	63.3	64.0	63.5	63.1	62.8	63.5	63.6	63.4	63.1
2003	62.7	63.1	63.3	63.3	63.7	63.9	63.6	63.6	63.4	63.5	63.5	63.9	63.5
2004	63.5	63.7	64.4	64.8	65.3	65.6	66.2	66.5	66.4	66.6	67.0	67.0	65.6
2005	67.6	68.0	68.0	67.7	68.7	67.9	68.3	68.5	68.2	68.8	68.9	68.6	68.3
2006	69.0	69.5	69.7	70.6	70.7	70.5	69.4	69.8	70.2	71.4	71.6	71.7	70.3
2007	70.7	71.1	71.8	71.9	71.9	72.4	72.1	71.9	71.9	72.2	72.1	72.5	71.9
2008	71.9	72.4	72.6	72.3	72.4	72.5	72.3	72.2	71.9	72.0	71.5	70.8	72.1
2009	68.5	67.8	67.2	67.0	66.8	66.2	65.7	65.6	65.0	65.1	65.0	64.8	66.2
2010	64.0	64.0	64.2	64.5	64.7	64.7	64.7	64.8	64.2	64.4	64.4	64.3	64.4
2011	63.4	64.1	64.2	64.5	64.6	64.9	64.7	64.8	65.7	66.0	67.0	66.1	65.0
Retail Trade													
2000	233.3	232.2	235.4	235.0	237.5	239.3	234.0	234.6	233.8	235.0	240.9	243.1	236.2
2001	228.3	225.3	227.8	227.4	229.1	229.8	228.5	228.0	226.2	225.0	229.4	232.0	228.1
2002	219.1	216.9	220.5	222.1	223.7	225.4	223.7	223.3	222.4	221.8	226.6	230.7	223.0
2003	218.9	217.4	219.6	220.1	222.0	224.3	223.4	224.0	222.9	223.1	227.5	231.1	222.9
2004	221.6	220.4	223.8	225.2	227.1	227.2	227.9	227.2	226.1	228.1	233.3	237.1	227.1
2005	225.8	225.0	226.3	229.1	230.9	229.8	232.0	232.2	228.1	231.7	237.1	239.3	230.6
2006	228.5	230.7	234.4	233.7	233.4	231.8	233.3	234.0	233.1	236.8	244.3	246.4	235.0
2007	234.5	232.8	237.3	236.9	239.4	240.7	241.0	240.3	239.5	240.1	246.0	248.0	239.7
2008	237.7	235.8	238.6	237.5	237.5	237.8	236.6	235.7	234.1	231.6	234.3	235.4	236.1
2009	222.4	219.2	220.2	221.9	223.7	224.6	223.9	223.3	221.6	221.0	225.8	226.8	222.9
2010	217.5	216.4	219.1	220.7	222.5	223.6	223.1	223.5	221.6	223.3	228.3	230.5	222.5
2011	219.1	219.2	221.2	224.5	225.6	226.9	227.4	225.8	221.5	223.1	228.0	229.2	224.3
Transportation and Utilities													
2000	64.0	64.8	65.4	64.8	65.3	65.7	65.7	66.0	65.3	66.1	66.3	66.4	65.5
2001	61.8	61.7	62.1	61.6	62.2	62.0	62.5	62.8	62.5	62.5	62.4	62.0	62.2
2002	60.1	60.7	60.7	61.4	61.6	61.1	60.6	61.1	61.1	61.8	62.3	62.0	61.2
2003	61.1	61.4	61.6	61.1	61.5	61.7	61.3	61.6	61.5	62.0	62.2	62.5	61.6
2004	61.0	61.3	61.6	61.0	61.8	62.0	62.9	63.5	63.2	63.5	63.7	63.6	62.4
2005	61.8	62.0	62.2	62.9	63.8	63.4	64.2	64.5	64.4	64.4	64.7	65.2	63.6
2006	63.9	64.5	64.6	64.5	64.8	65.2	64.8	65.2	65.3	65.9	66.1	66.9	65.1
2007	64.9	65.5	65.8	66.0	66.5	66.9	66.4	66.8	66.8	67.2	67.8	68.4	66.6
2008	65.9	66.2	65.9	66.1	65.9	65.7	65.1	65.3	64.5	64.9	64.7	65.0	65.4
2009	62.1	61.4	61.2	60.5	60.4	60.5	59.3	59.4	59.4	58.9	58.3	59.0	60.0
2010	57.5	57.5	58.2	58.4	58.6	59.1	59.4	59.5	59.5	60.0	60.4	61.0	59.1
2011	59.2	59.2	59.6	59.8	60.3	60.8	61.5	61.4	61.4	62.6	63.2	64.3	61.1
Information													
2000	30.0	30.0	30.4	29.9	30.2	31.0	30.5	30.8	30.7	30.6	30.8	31.2	30.5
2001	29.7	29.8	29.8	29.1	29.1	29.2	28.7	28.7	28.4	27.9	28.1	28.0	28.9
2002	27.7	27.6	27.8	27.5	28.0	28.1	27.8	27.9	27.4	27.9	28.3	28.3	27.9
2003	27.5	27.6	27.5	26.7	26.9	26.9	27.1	27.1	26.9	26.7	26.8	26.9	27.1
2004	26.8	26.5	26.5	26.5	26.9	27.0	27.0	26.9	26.6	26.8	26.7	27.2	26.8
2005	26.6	26.7	26.6	27.0	27.3	27.2	27.2	27.1	26.9	26.9	27.1	27.4	27.0
2006	27.2	27.6	27.4	27.5	27.6	27.7	27.5	27.4	27.1	27.3	27.8	27.9	27.5
2007	27.1	27.2	27.4	27.6	27.9	28.5	28.7	28.5	28.0	28.1	28.2	28.4	28.0
2008	28.1	28.2	28.2	28.6	28.8	29.0	29.1	28.9	28.4	28.2	28.2	28.3	28.5
2009	27.9	27.7	27.9	27.5	27.4	27.4	27.6	26.9	26.5	26.5	26.4	26.3	27.2
2010	26.3	26.3	26.3	25.5	25.6	26.0	26.3	25.7	25.4	25.5	25.7	26.1	25.9
2011	26.0	25.7	25.9	25.7	25.6	25.7	25.8	25.8	25.6	26.1	26.6	26.3	25.9

1. Employment by Industry: South Carolina, Selected Years, 2000–2011—*Continued*

(Numbers in thousands, not seasonally adjusted)

Industry and year	January	February	March	April	May	June	July	August	September	October	November	December	Annual average
Financial Activities													
2000	85.9	86.4	87.0	87.6	88.3	89.7	87.9	88.1	86.7	87.4	87.1	87.3	87.5
2001	85.9	86.5	87.0	87.8	88.1	89.3	90.4	89.9	88.5	87.8	88.2	87.8	88.1
2002	86.4	86.7	87.5	88.9	89.7	90.8	90.4	90.0	89.3	89.2	89.2	89.6	89.0
2003	88.8	88.8	89.5	91.1	92.3	93.4	92.8	93.6	91.9	91.9	91.5	91.9	91.5
2004	90.3	91.0	92.0	93.1	93.8	95.4	95.0	95.2	94.9	95.2	95.3	95.9	93.9
2005	95.4	95.7	95.9	96.9	98.1	98.4	99.7	99.8	99.1	98.4	98.5	99.0	97.9
2006	99.4	100.0	100.3	102.0	102.6	103.2	104.0	104.5	104.0	104.5	104.3	104.8	102.8
2007	104.1	104.1	105.0	105.4	106.2	107.2	106.9	106.9	106.2	106.2	106.2	106.6	105.9
2008	105.2	106.0	106.3	106.2	106.7	107.6	106.9	106.7	105.2	104.7	104.1	104.0	105.8
2009	101.7	101.6	101.6	101.4	101.8	102.1	102.2	101.5	100.0	98.9	98.3	98.1	100.8
2010	96.6	96.6	97.0	97.4	97.8	98.5	98.7	98.2	96.8	96.8	96.6	96.3	97.3
2011	94.9	94.9	95.1	96.0	96.7	97.1	96.9	96.3	95.3	96.3	96.5	96.6	96.1
Professional and Business Services													
2000	187.9	189.2	193.1	196.9	198.8	201.9	198.1	199.1	198.8	198.2	196.9	196.7	196.3
2001	186.3	188.3	189.8	190.6	189.9	189.8	188.7	190.4	188.9	186.0	184.1	183.1	188.0
2002	175.4	177.7	180.4	184.7	185.4	187.6	185.3	188.2	187.5	188.8	186.9	186.4	184.5
2003	181.4	184.0	187.7	188.2	188.6	188.7	187.2	189.4	188.5	191.8	192.1	192.2	188.3
2004	186.1	188.4	192.8	196.5	196.3	198.8	198.9	200.3	199.2	201.9	201.8	200.4	196.8
2005	196.5	198.6	198.7	204.3	205.1	204.4	206.8	210.3	210.4	213.3	214.6	211.6	206.2
2006	212.6	214.6	216.1	218.9	220.2	218.0	217.3	219.3	220.7	223.7	221.7	224.3	219.0
2007	220.9	223.6	225.2	227.0	228.5	230.0	226.7	229.2	229.2	227.9	227.5	226.5	226.9
2008	220.7	223.3	224.6	225.3	227.5	225.5	221.2	223.5	220.7	218.6	216.6	210.6	221.5
2009	201.0	199.9	200.2	199.2	199.0	198.2	198.5	199.9	199.5	203.8	205.3	203.5	200.7
2010	200.0	202.8	205.5	214.4	216.0	218.0	219.2	221.2	221.0	222.6	223.1	223.0	215.6
2011	217.8	222.0	225.1	230.1	230.3	230.5	230.4	229.1	229.3	229.9	230.9	229.2	227.9
Education and Health Services													
2000	154.6	155.5	156.5	156.4	156.7	156.8	153.2	154.1	156.0	157.7	158.4	159.2	156.3
2001	158.7	160.1	161.3	161.4	162.4	163.3	163.7	165.3	167.9	168.0	169.4	170.4	164.3
2002	168.9	170.2	172.1	171.8	172.4	171.6	171.6	172.5	174.1	174.1	175.2	174.9	172.5
2003	173.2	174.5	175.4	176.4	176.9	176.2	175.6	177.4	179.6	179.0	179.2	179.6	176.9
2004	178.3	179.5	180.2	181.1	181.8	180.5	179.8	181.0	182.2	183.0	184.1	184.3	181.3
2005	182.6	184.3	184.7	187.5	187.8	184.7	187.2	187.8	189.2	190.5	191.0	189.9	187.3
2006	189.2	191.4	191.8	192.7	193.0	189.6	189.9	191.5	193.8	197.9	198.2	199.0	193.2
2007	196.0	198.1	199.1	199.7	200.2	199.7	199.6	200.6	202.6	203.4	204.1	204.0	200.6
2008	204.1	206.2	207.2	205.8	207.2	206.1	205.2	206.5	208.1	209.1	209.5	209.1	207.0
2009	206.0	207.5	207.4	208.0	208.7	207.0	207.0	208.4	208.8	210.3	211.2	210.5	208.4
2010	209.8	211.7	211.9	213.6	214.1	212.3	212.1	213.5	214.2	216.6	217.0	216.9	213.6
2011	213.3	216.2	216.7	217.4	217.5	215.6	216.0	216.5	217.1	218.9	219.0	218.4	216.9
Leisure and Hospitality													
2000	175.1	179.0	186.5	191.2	195.3	199.9	195.8	192.8	185.8	184.6	181.6	179.5	187.3
2001	169.1	173.2	180.4	187.6	191.3	194.8	196.7	195.2	188.4	183.0	179.2	176.5	184.6
2002	169.4	173.9	181.7	191.1	195.6	201.3	200.6	197.9	191.9	190.5	185.7	183.4	188.6
2003	176.1	180.0	186.7	194.0	200.1	204.8	205.4	204.1	197.7	193.3	189.2	186.5	193.2
2004	181.0	185.5	193.6	202.0	207.6	211.4	211.8	209.0	203.5	201.0	197.9	194.1	199.9
2005	185.5	189.7	196.5	206.7	209.7	212.9	217.3	215.9	206.1	202.7	200.7	194.6	203.2
2006	191.1	194.7	200.1	209.8	214.5	216.1	218.7	217.0	210.6	210.0	207.7	205.0	207.9
2007	199.8	203.0	211.3	219.4	224.1	229.3	227.9	227.4	220.9	217.9	214.0	210.6	217.1
2008	203.1	207.2	214.7	223.2	229.3	231.5	229.0	228.0	219.9	214.0	208.5	204.8	217.8
2009	195.0	198.1	204.8	213.5	219.1	220.8	219.1	217.7	211.2	205.1	200.5	196.7	208.5
2010	189.1	192.7	200.1	211.0	215.6	219.2	219.3	218.3	212.7	207.5	204.2	200.3	207.5
2011	190.2	195.0	203.7	214.2	220.4	222.5	224.1	221.3	210.4	207.7	204.5	201.4	209.6
Other Services													
2000	57.4	58.1	59.1	59.7	60.1	60.0	58.3	58.1	58.0	59.2	58.8	58.5	58.8
2001	60.4	60.9	62.1	62.3	62.7	62.7	62.4	62.7	62.6	62.6	63.0	63.0	62.3
2002	62.6	63.4	64.7	64.2	64.9	65.6	64.2	64.7	65.3	63.7	63.8	64.0	64.3
2003	63.4	63.9	64.7	64.1	64.8	65.3	64.9	65.2	65.3	65.3	65.6	66.0	64.9
2004	65.0	65.6	66.5	68.9	70.0	71.5	69.1	69.3	69.7	70.6	71.8	72.0	69.2
2005	71.1	72.4	73.1	72.7	73.3	72.9	74.9	75.6	75.4	75.4	75.7	74.9	74.0
2006	71.9	72.6	76.2	76.1	76.3	75.9	76.2	75.8	75.3	74.7	74.3	74.3	75.0
2007	73.4	73.8	74.4	74.3	74.6	74.6	73.4	73.0	72.4	71.7	71.5	71.6	73.2
2008	70.2	70.4	71.3	71.7	72.4	72.5	72.2	72.0	71.6	71.2	70.9	70.5	71.4
2009	69.4	69.6	69.8	69.9	70.2	70.1	69.8	69.2	69.2	69.0	68.6	68.4	69.4
2010	67.4	67.7	68.4	68.8	69.0	69.2	68.7	68.4	68.6	68.7	68.5	68.3	68.5
2011	67.5	67.9	68.6	68.8	69.0	69.1	69.0	69.3	69.3	69.0	68.9	69.7	68.8
Government													
2000	321.6	324.6	328.5	327.1	333.0	330.1	307.1	311.9	320.9	326.0	327.8	328.2	323.9
2001	322.7	326.8	327.9	326.9	326.6	322.0	305.7	313.6	326.0	328.8	330.7	332.0	324.1
2002	325.4	328.8	330.0	330.1	330.6	324.4	308.0	319.2	328.5	330.9	333.4	333.6	326.9
2003	328.2	333.0	333.6	333.4	332.4	324.6	310.3	316.3	327.8	329.1	330.5	331.5	327.6
2004	326.4	328.1	329.8	330.6	330.3	323.1	306.5	316.0	327.3	330.3	331.7	331.9	326.0
2005	327.0	330.3	331.6	332.1	332.0	326.4	310.5	317.7	332.6	335.3	337.8	338.0	329.3
2006	330.9	335.2	339.1	338.8	338.9	326.4	311.6	318.4	331.6	338.3	338.9	340.1	332.4
2007	336.0	339.2	341.5	340.0	340.9	336.8	320.0	328.2	341.8	346.0	349.1	348.4	339.0
2008	345.7	349.0	350.1	350.9	353.0	348.3	328.7	330.7	349.6	354.0	356.2	355.5	347.6
2009	349.2	350.8	351.4	353.3	352.8	347.1	332.4	337.1	345.1	349.9	351.2	350.7	347.6
2010	346.9	349.7	351.5	352.4	362.5	351.4	335.1	338.5	343.2	345.3	345.9	345.6	347.3
2011	340.9	343.6	344.8	345.3	344.6	340.2	325.5	329.5	339.4	342.8	344.2	341.2	340.2

2. Average Weekly Hours by Selected Industry: South Carolina, 2007–2011

(Not seasonally adjusted)

Industry and year	January	February	March	April	May	June	July	August	September	October	November	December	Annual average
Total Private													
2007	36.2	36.0	36.4	36.1	35.9	36.2	36.2	36.2	35.9	35.5	35.8	36.1	36.0
2008	35.2	35.3	36.1	35.6	35.9	37.0	35.8	35.6	34.8	35.1	35.5	35.3	35.6
2009	34.8	34.9	35.0	34.6	34.8	34.8	34.6	34.9	34.2	34.4	34.7	35.0	34.7
2010	34.7	34.4	34.5	34.8	34.9	34.7	34.9	35.3	34.7	34.9	34.8	34.7	34.8
2011	33.6	34.8	34.8	35.0	35.1	35.1	34.9	34.9	34.7	35.0	34.7	34.8	34.8
Goods-Producing													
2007	39.5	39.7	40.2	39.6	40.6	41.0	39.9	40.6	41.0	41.3	42.0	42.1	40.6
2008	41.0	41.1	41.0	40.3	42.1	43.2	40.3	40.4	39.1	40.2	40.5	40.7	40.8
2009	39.9	40.0	40.2	39.4	40.9	40.9	40.7	41.0	40.3	40.2	40.5	41.1	40.4
2010	41.5	40.6	40.8	41.3	41.6	41.3	40.8	41.7	40.9	40.9	41.2	41.2	41.1
2011	38.2	40.4	40.6	40.8	41.1	41.5	40.7	41.1	41.0	40.9	41.3	41.2	40.7
Construction													
2007	36.9	36.6	37.4	36.9	37.9	38.8	37.9	38.8	38.6	39.4	38.7	38.9	38.1
2008	38.7	37.9	38.4	37.5	37.6	39.5	39.2	38.6	35.0	37.9	38.8	37.1	38.0
2009	37.3	37.4	36.6	36.0	36.5	37.5	37.7	37.6	36.3	35.9	36.6	37.3	36.9
2010	39.1	37.8	36.4	37.0	36.8	37.5	37.9	38.8	37.3	38.9	38.8	37.6	37.8
2011	34.3	36.7	37.1	37.8	39.0	39.2	38.4	39.2	37.7	37.1	40.0	39.2	38.0
Manufacturing													
2007	41.1	41.9	42.1	41.5	42.4	42.5	41.3	41.9	42.7	42.6	44.3	44.3	42.4
2008	42.7	43.1	43.0	42.2	44.7	45.3	41.1	41.5	41.7	41.7	41.6	42.8	42.6
2009	41.6	41.6	41.9	40.6	42.7	42.1	42.0	42.5	42.1	42.2	42.5	42.8	42.0
2010	41.2	40.3	41.3	41.6	42.1	41.6	40.7	41.5	41.2	40.7	41.3	41.5	41.2
2011	39.2	40.9	41.1	41.2	41.2	41.7	40.9	41.3	41.7	41.8	41.5	41.6	41.2
Trade, Transportation, and Utilities													
2007	35.0	35.1	35.4	35.4	34.9	35.6	35.2	34.6	34.7	34.3	34.1	34.7	34.9
2008	34.6	34.3	34.8	35.3	34.9	35.1	34.9	34.4	34.0	33.7	34.4	34.1	34.5
2009	34.1	34.2	34.4	34.4	34.8	34.7	34.4	34.5	34.2	34.5	34.5	34.8	34.5
2010	34.7	34.7	35.1	35.1	35.2	34.9	35.3	35.3	35.2	35.2	34.9	34.6	35.0
2011	34.0	34.9	35.1	35.0	34.9	34.7	34.5	34.7	34.2	34.4	33.7	34.2	34.5
Financial Activities													
2007	36.0	36.9	37.0	37.7	37.2	37.9	38.0	37.5	38.2	37.5	37.3	38.3	37.5
2008	36.6	37.4	38.4	36.7	36.4	37.1	36.4	36.4	36.0	36.0	37.3	35.7	36.7
2009	35.8	36.7	36.5	36.4	36.9	36.6	36.9	37.6	35.7	36.7	37.5	36.7	36.7
2010	36.5	36.2	36.6	36.4	36.6	36.1	36.8	37.2	36.6	36.8	37.1	37.0	36.7
2011	37.8	37.4	37.3	37.9	38.0	37.6	38.2	34.6	35.1	35.8	35.3	36.2	36.8
Professional and Business Services													
2007	42.7	41.7	43.1	43.3	42.1	41.9	42.9	43.4	41.1	39.9	39.9	40.0	41.8
2008	37.8	37.8	41.0	41.5	42.2	41.2	40.8	39.8	39.4	39.7	40.4	40.8	40.2
2009	38.3	37.5	38.4	37.1	36.7	37.6	37.1	37.4	37.0	36.3	36.2	37.4	37.2
2010	35.6	34.9	34.5	35.5	35.9	35.5	35.1	36.2	34.9	34.9	34.6	35.5	35.3
2011	34.0	35.4	35.6	36.8	37.0	36.7	36.8	36.9	36.6	36.6	35.7	35.8	36.2
Education and Health Services													
2007	37.0	34.8	35.4	33.9	33.7	35.2	35.2	34.5	35.0	34.0	35.6	35.6	35.0
2008	34.7	35.1	34.7	32.7	32.7	34.1	32.8	32.4	32.4	32.9	33.1	32.8	33.4
2009	32.4	33.1	32.9	32.6	31.8	31.9	32.0	32.1	31.7	31.7	32.8	33.0	32.3
2010	34.5	34.3	33.7	33.7	34.1	33.7	33.7	33.9	34.0	34.0	33.6	33.4	33.9
2011	32.7	33.6	32.2	32.4	32.5	32.6	32.3	32.8	32.8	33.6	33.8	33.8	32.9
Leisure and Hospitality													
2007	24.6	24.9	25.7	25.9	25.4	26.2	26.8	26.7	24.7	24.8	24.5	24.4	25.4
2008	24.0	24.9	26.0	25.9	25.9	26.9	26.6	26.7	24.6	25.1	24.8	24.5	25.5
2009	24.7	25.4	25.9	26.4	26.4	26.9	27.0	27.0	25.2	25.4	25.3	25.0	25.9
2010	24.9	25.0	25.5	26.2	25.9	26.5	27.3	27.2	26.3	26.2	26.2	25.7	26.1
2011	24.6	25.8	26.1	26.5	26.4	26.6	27.0	27.2	26.4	26.7	26.2	25.6	26.3
Other Services													
2007	37.2	36.5	36.3	35.7	35.5	34.7	35.8	36.5	35.9	36.3	35.7	37.1	36.1
2008	35.8	35.4	36.4	35.0	34.5	35.1	32.2	34.3	33.1	32.4	32.5	32.4	34.1
2009	31.9	31.8	31.9	32.3	31.2	30.2	30.6	30.8	30.9	30.8	30.8	31.2	31.2
2010	31.5	30.8	32.2	32.3	32.3	32.5	32.3	32.3	31.8	32.6	31.8	31.4	32.0
2011	30.6	32.3	32.5	32.9	33.9	34.0	34.0	33.4	33.9	34.5	33.2	32.8	33.2

3. Average Hourly Earnings by Selected Industry: South Carolina, 2007–2011

(Dollars, not seasonally adjusted)

Industry and year	January	February	March	April	May	June	July	August	September	October	November	December	Annual average
Total Private													
2007	18.77	19.12	18.78	19.01	18.82	18.63	18.65	18.38	18.77	18.59	18.62	19.03	18.76
2008	19.00	19.04	19.42	18.54	18.37	18.36	18.62	18.59	18.74	18.69	18.99	19.25	18.80
2009	19.16	19.33	18.74	18.74	18.70	18.67	18.78	19.40	19.70	19.41	19.72	19.77	19.17
2010	19.98	20.11	19.63	19.55	19.65	19.44	19.56	19.81	20.02	20.19	20.25	20.54	19.89
2011	21.00	20.80	20.90	20.90	20.71	20.44	20.54	20.25	20.53	20.37	20.28	20.29	20.58
Goods-Producing													
2007	17.69	17.95	17.76	18.48	18.27	18.33	18.64	18.25	18.35	18.28	18.31	19.06	18.28
2008	18.55	19.10	19.38	19.41	18.91	18.87	19.33	19.35	19.14	19.56	19.63	20.19	19.27
2009	20.26	20.07	20.29	20.43	20.22	20.09	20.16	20.06	20.08	20.13	20.81	20.70	20.27
2010	20.75	21.23	20.80	20.74	20.48	20.27	20.68	20.39	20.83	20.84	20.81	21.29	20.76
2011	21.73	21.22	21.21	21.23	20.98	20.73	20.84	20.74	20.98	20.68	20.64	21.01	20.99
Construction													
2007	18.21	18.24	18.14	17.46	17.72	17.77	17.95	17.44	17.64	17.97	18.48	19.30	18.02
2008	18.17	19.24	18.65	18.86	19.05	18.86	19.53	19.75	19.13	20.24	19.69	21.35	19.34
2009	20.98	20.15	20.24	20.35	21.42	21.46	21.29	21.20	21.18	21.19	21.56	21.39	21.02
2010	21.25	22.11	21.37	21.24	20.97	20.52	20.34	20.19	20.49	20.41	20.79	21.12	20.89
2011	21.77	21.25	21.58	21.65	21.36	21.06	21.01	21.07	21.43	21.44	21.37	21.41	21.36
Manufacturing													
2007	17.40	17.80	17.58	19.76	19.28	19.32	19.64	19.26	19.28	18.96	18.65	19.33	18.86
2008	19.10	18.92	19.04	19.14	18.43	18.49	18.89	18.85	18.88	19.00	19.41	19.50	18.96
2009	19.67	19.67	19.98	20.18	19.89	19.68	19.88	19.70	19.73	19.77	20.26	20.21	19.88
2010	20.40	20.67	20.38	20.36	20.23	20.22	20.85	20.74	21.15	21.22	20.96	21.29	20.71
2011	21.72	21.16	21.04	21.06	20.82	20.56	20.74	20.59	20.78	20.37	20.32	20.83	20.82
Trade, Transportation, and Utilities													
2007	17.82	17.96	18.09	17.86	18.40	18.29	18.68	18.20	18.95	18.70	18.21	18.64	18.32
2008	18.17	18.99	19.02	16.72	16.91	17.06	17.36	17.34	17.67	17.32	17.57	17.46	17.63
2009	17.57	17.66	18.01	17.28	17.17	17.30	17.34	17.70	17.65	17.71	17.90	17.76	17.59
2010	18.04	18.25	18.10	17.44	17.38	17.51	17.76	17.97	18.18	18.35	18.16	18.43	17.96
2011	18.88	18.74	18.48	18.33	18.44	18.21	18.09	18.13	18.61	18.68	18.52	17.90	18.41
Financial Activities													
2007	21.59	21.94	19.93	20.48	20.88	20.35	20.98	20.43	20.36	20.05	20.56	20.30	20.65
2008	22.24	20.59	20.93	21.03	21.61	22.70	22.88	22.46	22.76	22.99	22.82	22.44	22.11
2009	22.26	22.37	20.55	20.56	20.70	20.98	21.34	21.62	21.96	22.03	22.49	22.26	21.59
2010	22.80	22.81	22.68	22.90	23.57	23.87	23.39	23.88	24.00	24.37	24.08	25.37	23.65
2011	24.89	25.30	23.75	23.80	23.40	22.99	22.80	22.49	22.72	22.73	22.76	22.30	23.34
Professional and Business Services													
2007	26.05	27.00	26.32	26.85	25.56	24.65	23.95	23.31	24.16	23.62	23.85	25.06	25.04
2008	24.99	24.25	25.88	23.77	23.05	23.00	22.82	22.51	22.55	21.80	22.64	23.20	23.37
2009	23.27	24.46	23.56	23.94	23.88	23.37	23.01	25.41	25.64	23.62	23.65	23.49	23.94
2010	22.45	22.65	21.93	21.06	21.44	20.97	21.08	21.54	21.77	22.12	22.13	21.62	21.72
2011	22.82	22.42	21.74	22.33	22.05	21.87	22.23	21.90	22.26	22.56	22.09	22.36	22.21
Education and Health Services													
2007	17.32	18.34	19.00	18.71	17.60	18.84	18.89	19.36	19.08	19.17	19.19	19.16	18.72
2008	19.73	19.64	19.46	19.66	19.40	18.79	19.44	19.74	19.44	19.34	19.91	20.42	19.58
2009	19.75	20.48	20.80	20.77	21.22	21.22	21.87	21.79	22.19	22.16	22.03	22.90	21.43
2010	22.03	23.24	22.98	22.93	23.46	23.12	23.39	23.23	23.09	23.38	24.08	23.93	23.24
2011	24.46	24.63	25.50	25.50	25.49	25.34	25.94	25.24	25.02	24.27	24.52	24.02	24.98
Leisure and Hospitality													
2007	10.51	10.49	10.10	10.46	10.25	10.21	10.26	10.18	10.39	10.40	10.62	10.64	10.37
2008	10.70	10.57	10.60	10.59	10.54	10.39	10.63	10.80	10.64	10.64	10.82	10.90	10.65
2009	10.79	10.96	10.87	10.90	10.80	10.76	10.90	11.05	11.16	11.00	11.09	11.11	10.95
2010	11.10	11.19	11.20	11.31	11.37	11.26	11.21	11.31	11.30	11.51	11.80	11.87	11.37
2011	12.13	11.89	11.87	11.93	11.80	11.77	11.91	11.90	11.99	11.93	11.85	12.05	11.91
Other Services													
2007	15.72	16.44	16.01	16.08	16.51	16.04	16.24	17.08	16.57	16.35	17.29	16.45	16.39
2008	16.78	16.57	16.72	16.92	16.63	16.32	16.61	16.28	17.43	17.17	17.13	16.89	16.78
2009	16.63	17.03	16.44	16.14	15.91	15.90	15.68	16.00	16.08	15.74	16.04	16.04	16.14
2010	16.09	16.38	16.27	16.57	16.41	16.35	16.28	16.72	16.98	16.59	17.09	17.25	16.58
2011	17.43	17.63	16.76	17.45	17.59	17.96	18.56	18.29	18.41	18.22	17.77	18.16	17.86

4. Average Weekly Earnings by Selected Industry: South Carolina, 2007–2011

(Dollars, not seasonally adjusted)

Industry and year	January	February	March	April	May	June	July	August	September	October	November	December	Annual average
Total Private													
2007	679.47	688.32	683.59	686.26	675.64	674.41	675.13	665.36	673.84	659.95	666.60	686.98	676.26
2008	668.80	672.11	701.06	660.02	659.48	679.32	666.60	661.80	652.15	656.02	674.15	679.53	669.28
2009	666.77	674.62	655.90	648.40	650.76	649.72	649.79	677.06	673.74	667.70	684.28	691.95	665.74
2010	693.31	691.78	677.24	680.34	685.79	674.57	682.64	699.29	694.69	704.63	704.70	712.74	691.69
2011	705.60	723.84	727.32	731.50	726.92	717.44	716.85	706.73	712.39	712.95	703.72	706.09	715.49
Goods-Producing													
2007	698.76	712.62	713.95	731.81	741.76	751.53	743.74	740.95	752.35	754.96	769.02	802.43	742.77
2008	760.55	785.01	794.58	782.22	796.11	815.18	779.00	781.74	748.37	786.31	795.02	821.73	787.06
2009	808.37	802.80	815.66	804.94	827.00	821.68	820.51	822.46	809.22	809.23	842.81	850.77	819.34
2010	861.13	861.94	848.64	856.56	851.97	837.15	843.74	850.26	851.95	852.36	857.37	877.15	854.13
2011	830.09	857.29	861.13	866.18	862.28	860.30	848.19	852.41	860.18	845.81	852.43	865.61	855.17
Construction													
2007	671.95	667.58	678.44	644.27	671.59	689.48	680.31	676.67	680.90	708.02	715.18	750.77	685.94
2008	703.18	729.20	716.16	707.25	716.28	744.97	765.58	762.35	669.55	767.10	763.97	792.09	735.48
2009	782.55	753.61	740.78	732.60	781.83	804.75	802.63	797.12	768.83	760.72	789.10	797.85	775.62
2010	830.88	835.76	777.87	785.88	771.70	769.50	770.89	783.37	764.28	793.95	806.65	794.11	790.12
2011	746.71	779.88	800.62	818.37	833.04	825.55	806.78	825.94	807.91	795.42	854.80	839.27	811.29
Manufacturing													
2007	715.14	745.82	740.12	820.04	817.47	821.10	811.13	806.99	823.26	807.70	826.20	856.32	799.32
2008	815.57	815.45	818.72	807.71	823.82	837.60	776.38	782.28	787.30	792.30	807.46	834.60	808.40
2009	818.27	818.27	837.16	819.31	849.30	828.53	834.96	837.25	830.63	834.29	861.05	864.99	835.93
2010	840.48	833.00	841.69	846.98	851.68	841.15	848.60	860.71	871.38	863.65	865.65	883.54	854.07
2011	851.42	865.44	864.74	867.67	857.78	857.35	848.27	850.37	866.53	851.47	843.28	866.53	857.53
Trade, Transportation, and Utilities													
2007	623.70	630.40	640.39	632.24	642.16	651.12	657.54	629.72	657.57	641.41	620.96	646.81	639.49
2008	628.68	651.36	661.90	590.22	590.16	598.81	605.86	596.50	600.78	583.68	604.41	595.39	609.00
2009	599.14	603.97	619.54	594.43	597.52	600.31	596.50	610.65	603.63	611.00	617.55	618.05	606.03
2010	625.99	633.28	635.31	612.14	611.78	611.10	626.93	634.34	639.94	645.92	633.78	637.68	629.05
2011	641.92	654.03	648.65	641.55	643.56	631.89	624.11	629.11	636.46	642.59	624.12	612.18	635.70
Financial Activities													
2007	777.24	809.59	737.41	772.10	776.74	771.27	797.24	766.13	777.75	751.88	766.89	777.49	773.45
2008	813.98	770.07	803.71	771.80	786.60	842.17	832.83	817.54	819.36	827.64	851.19	801.11	811.47
2009	796.91	820.98	750.08	748.38	763.83	767.87	787.45	812.91	783.97	808.50	843.38	816.94	791.47
2010	832.20	825.72	830.09	833.56	862.66	861.71	860.75	888.34	878.40	896.82	893.37	938.69	866.87
2011	940.84	946.22	885.88	902.02	889.20	864.42	870.96	778.15	797.47	813.73	803.43	807.26	858.17
Professional and Business Services													
2007	1,112.34	1,125.90	1,134.39	1,162.61	1,076.08	1,032.84	1,027.46	1,011.65	992.98	942.44	951.62	1,002.40	1,046.98
2008	944.62	916.65	1,061.08	986.46	972.71	947.60	931.06	895.90	888.47	865.46	914.66	946.56	939.32
2009	891.24	917.25	904.70	888.17	876.40	878.71	853.67	950.33	948.68	857.41	856.13	878.53	891.61
2010	799.22	790.49	756.59	747.63	769.70	744.44	739.91	779.75	759.77	771.99	765.70	767.51	765.75
2011	775.88	793.67	773.94	821.74	815.85	802.63	818.06	808.11	814.72	825.70	788.61	800.49	803.52
Education and Health Services													
2007	640.84	638.23	672.60	634.27	593.12	663.17	664.93	667.92	667.80	651.78	683.16	682.10	655.12
2008	684.63	689.36	675.26	642.88	634.38	640.74	637.63	639.58	629.86	636.29	659.02	669.78	653.25
2009	639.90	677.89	684.32	677.10	674.80	676.92	699.84	699.46	703.42	702.47	722.58	755.70	693.03
2010	760.04	797.13	774.43	772.74	799.99	779.14	788.24	787.50	785.06	794.92	809.09	799.26	787.40
2011	799.84	827.57	821.10	826.20	828.43	826.08	837.86	827.87	820.66	815.47	828.78	811.88	822.69
Leisure and Hospitality													
2007	258.55	261.20	259.57	270.91	260.35	267.50	274.97	271.81	256.63	257.92	260.19	259.62	263.42
2008	256.80	263.19	275.60	274.28	272.99	279.49	282.76	288.36	261.74	267.06	268.34	267.05	271.78
2009	266.51	278.38	281.53	287.76	285.12	289.44	294.30	298.35	281.23	279.40	280.58	277.75	283.64
2010	276.39	279.75	285.60	296.32	294.48	298.39	306.03	307.63	297.19	301.56	309.16	305.06	296.79
2011	298.40	306.76	309.81	316.15	311.52	313.08	321.57	323.68	316.54	318.53	310.47	308.48	313.16
Other Services													
2007	584.78	600.06	581.16	574.06	586.11	556.59	581.39	623.42	594.86	593.51	617.25	610.30	591.76
2008	600.72	586.58	608.61	592.20	573.74	572.83	534.84	558.40	576.93	556.31	556.73	547.24	572.04
2009	530.50	541.55	524.44	521.32	496.39	480.18	479.81	492.80	496.87	484.79	494.03	500.45	503.59
2010	506.84	504.50	523.89	535.21	530.04	531.38	525.84	540.06	539.96	540.83	543.46	541.65	530.27
2011	533.36	569.45	544.70	574.11	596.30	610.64	631.04	610.89	624.10	628.59	589.96	595.65	592.54

SOUTH DAKOTA
At a Glance

Population:
  2000 census: 754,858
  2010 census: 814,180
  2011 estimate: 824,082

Percent change in population:
  2000–2010: 7.9%
  2010–2011: 1.2%

Percent change in total nonfarm employment:
  2000–2010: 6.7%
  2010–2011: 0.7%

Industry with the largest growth in employment, 2000–2011 (thousands):
  Education and Health Services, 14.1

Industry with the largest decline or smallest growth in employment, 2000–2011 (thousands):
  Manufacturing, -4.9

Civilian labor force:
  2000: 408,685
  2010: 443,444
  2011: 446,254

Unemployment rate and rank among states (lowest to highest):
  2000: 2.7%, 3rd
  2010: 5.0%, 3rd
  2011: 4.7%, 3rd

Over-the-year change in unemployment rates:
  2010–2011: -0.3%

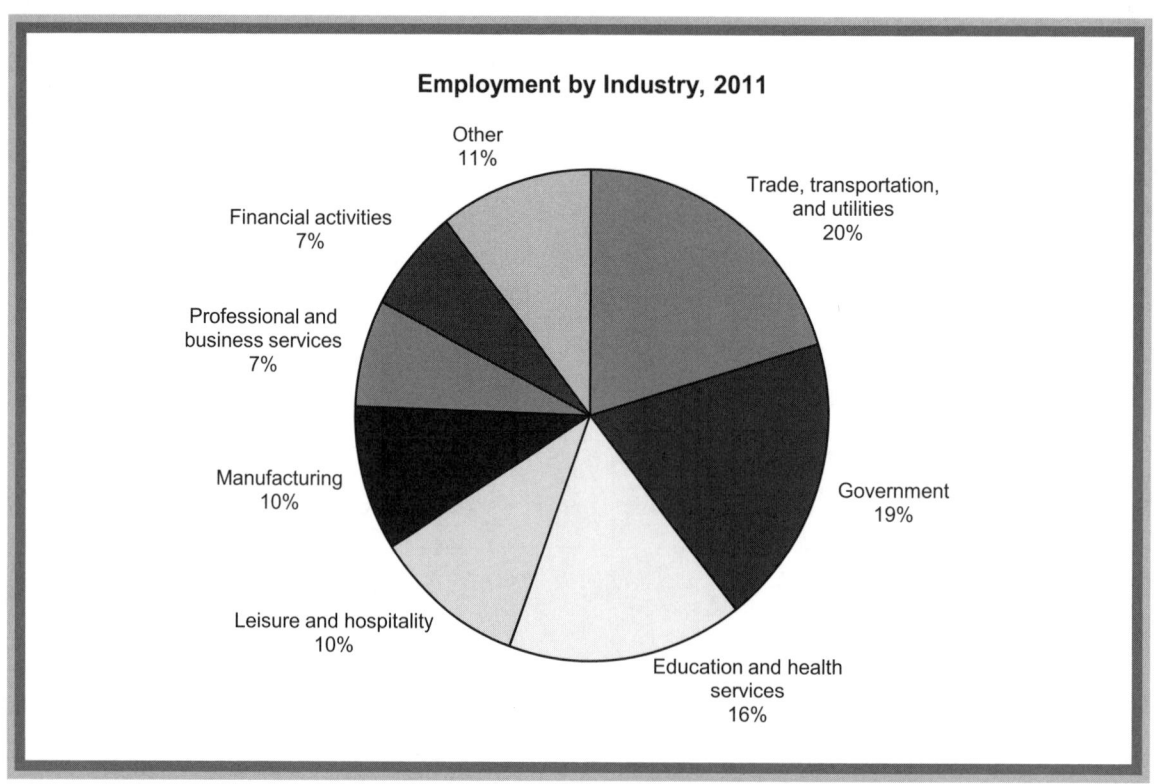

Employment by Industry, 2011

Other 11%
Trade, transportation, and utilities 20%
Financial activities 7%
Professional and business services 7%
Manufacturing 10%
Government 19%
Leisure and hospitality 10%
Education and health services 16%

1. Employment by Industry: South Dakota, Selected Years, 2000–2011

(Numbers in thousands, not seasonally adjusted)

Industry and year	January	February	March	April	May	June	July	August	September	October	November	December	Annual average
Total Nonfarm													
2000	367.1	367.7	371.8	376.7	383.5	388.3	381.8	382.2	380.3	379.9	377.6	377.3	377.9
2001	369.2	369.5	371.4	376.3	385.1	389.6	383.8	384.5	380.5	379.4	378.1	376.8	378.7
2002	365.7	365.7	367.3	373.6	382.9	388.1	383.2	384.7	381.1	380.9	378.7	378.6	377.5
2003	367.9	367.2	368.9	375.0	383.0	387.8	383.4	386.0	381.2	381.1	380.2	379.5	378.4
2004	369.7	370.0	372.1	381.0	388.9	394.1	388.4	391.2	388.9	388.0	386.3	385.4	383.7
2005	375.3	376.3	379.6	386.8	393.9	399.8	395.6	398.2	395.7	393.7	393.2	393.5	390.1
2006	384.0	385.0	388.1	393.3	402.7	408.8	404.0	407.4	403.4	402.6	401.8	401.9	398.6
2007	391.9	392.8	396.4	401.5	411.6	416.7	413.3	415.8	411.0	410.4	409.1	407.8	406.5
2008	399.6	401.1	403.5	407.1	416.5	420.9	416.6	420.1	415.3	414.8	411.6	409.7	411.4
2009	397.5	396.9	397.2	399.0	409.2	413.0	408.9	409.1	406.2	404.4	402.8	399.9	403.7
2010	388.2	389.1	392.1	399.4	407.5	413.1	409.1	411.6	407.9	408.8	406.8	405.0	403.2
2011	393.0	394.4	396.8	403.4	411.3	416.9	413.6	414.3	407.9	409.1	407.1	406.7	406.2
Total Private													
2000	296.8	296.5	299.3	304.1	309.6	315.4	314.6	314.7	309.5	308.1	305.8	305.2	306.6
2001	296.9	296.5	298.9	302.8	309.7	313.7	313.8	314.0	307.2	305.1	303.5	301.9	305.3
2002	292.4	291.6	293.1	299.3	306.8	311.8	312.0	313.2	307.1	305.9	303.5	303.0	303.3
2003	294.0	292.4	293.8	299.7	306.5	311.6	312.4	314.2	306.9	305.7	304.9	304.0	303.8
2004	295.4	295.1	297.0	304.9	311.7	317.3	317.2	320.1	313.8	312.1	310.1	309.1	308.7
2005	300.4	300.9	303.7	310.7	316.6	322.8	323.8	326.7	320.4	317.7	317.0	317.5	314.9
2006	309.6	309.5	312.3	317.4	325.2	331.5	332.1	335.4	328.5	326.5	325.4	325.8	323.3
2007	317.7	317.0	320.6	325.7	334.0	339.9	340.7	343.0	335.7	334.0	332.5	331.5	331.0
2008	324.9	324.6	327.0	330.5	338.1	344.0	344.5	346.8	339.3	337.2	333.9	332.1	335.2
2009	321.4	319.6	319.4	320.4	328.8	334.2	334.1	334.4	328.1	325.3	323.5	321.5	325.9
2010	311.1	310.7	312.7	319.6	326.3	332.8	333.9	336.3	329.2	329.1	327.0	325.6	324.5
2011	315.4	315.4	317.7	324.0	331.5	337.0	339.4	341.0	330.9	330.2	328.3	327.8	328.2
Goods-Producing													
2000	59.8	59.5	60.4	62.1	63.4	65.8	66.7	66.2	64.9	64.5	62.7	60.9	63.1
2001	59.1	58.3	58.5	60.1	61.6	63.7	63.7	63.3	61.4	60.7	59.3	57.7	60.6
2002	55.0	54.0	54.2	56.3	58.8	60.6	61.3	60.9	59.6	59.3	58.0	56.9	57.9
2003	54.3	53.6	54.2	56.7	59.1	60.6	61.0	61.0	59.5	59.3	58.4	56.9	57.9
2004	54.7	54.4	55.3	58.7	60.6	62.4	63.1	62.8	61.7	61.5	60.7	59.5	59.6
2005	56.9	56.8	57.7	60.5	62.3	64.3	64.9	64.7	63.7	63.7	63.0	61.5	61.7
2006	59.9	59.6	60.5	62.8	65.1	67.1	67.8	67.6	66.4	65.9	64.9	64.1	64.3
2007	61.5	60.6	61.9	63.6	65.9	67.8	68.4	68.1	67.2	66.9	66.1	64.6	65.2
2008	62.7	62.3	63.2	64.8	67.4	68.8	69.1	68.7	67.7	67.3	65.9	63.4	65.9
2009	59.6	58.4	57.8	57.7	60.3	62.1	62.2	61.2	60.1	59.7	58.4	56.2	59.5
2010	53.1	52.7	53.3	56.2	58.1	60.2	61.2	61.3	60.6	60.7	59.8	57.9	57.9
2011	54.9	54.6	55.4	58.1	61.0	62.8	63.6	63.7	62.1	62.2	60.9	58.2	59.8
Mining, Logging, and Construction													
2000	16.1	15.8	16.7	18.6	20.1	21.7	22.3	22.1	21.2	20.5	18.8	17.7	19.3
2001	16.2	15.9	16.4	18.2	20.3	22.2	22.6	22.6	21.6	21.0	19.9	18.6	19.6
2002	16.4	16.1	16.3	18.1	20.5	21.9	22.2	22.1	21.2	20.9	19.9	19.0	19.6
2003	16.8	16.4	16.8	19.1	21.4	22.7	23.1	23.0	22.0	21.6	20.5	19.3	20.2
2004	17.1	16.7	17.4	20.0	21.7	22.9	23.5	23.4	22.4	22.2	21.4	20.5	20.8
2005	18.1	17.9	18.6	21.0	22.7	24.2	24.7	24.7	23.7	23.5	22.7	21.2	21.9
2006	19.5	19.3	19.8	21.8	23.7	25.1	25.7	25.5	24.4	23.7	22.7	21.8	22.8
2007	19.7	19.0	20.0	21.5	23.9	25.4	26.1	26.0	25.2	24.6	23.9	22.5	23.2
2008	20.6	20.0	20.5	22.2	24.5	25.6	25.9	25.7	24.9	24.4	23.3	21.6	23.3
2009	19.0	18.7	18.9	19.9	22.6	24.4	25.3	24.3	23.2	22.9	21.9	20.0	21.8
2010	17.3	16.8	17.2	19.9	21.4	23.1	23.7	23.9	23.2	23.2	22.3	20.3	21.0
2011	17.4	16.9	17.4	19.6	21.7	23.3	24.0	23.9	22.9	22.6	21.4	19.4	20.9
Manufacturing													
2000	43.7	43.7	43.7	43.5	43.3	44.1	44.4	44.1	43.7	44.0	43.9	43.2	43.8
2001	42.9	42.4	42.1	41.9	41.3	41.5	41.1	40.7	39.8	39.7	39.4	39.1	41.0
2002	38.6	37.9	37.9	38.2	38.3	38.7	39.1	38.8	38.4	38.4	38.1	37.9	38.4
2003	37.5	37.2	37.4	37.6	37.7	37.9	37.9	38.0	37.5	37.7	37.9	37.6	37.7
2004	37.6	37.7	37.9	38.7	38.9	39.5	39.6	39.4	39.3	39.3	39.3	39.0	38.9
2005	38.8	38.9	39.1	39.5	39.6	40.1	40.2	40.0	40.0	40.2	40.3	40.3	39.8
2006	40.4	40.3	40.7	41.0	41.4	42.0	42.1	42.1	42.0	42.2	42.2	42.3	41.6
2007	41.8	41.6	41.9	42.1	42.0	42.4	42.3	42.1	42.0	42.3	42.2	42.1	42.1
2008	42.1	42.3	42.7	42.6	42.9	43.2	43.2	43.0	42.8	42.9	42.6	41.8	42.7
2009	40.6	39.7	38.9	37.8	37.7	37.7	36.9	36.9	36.9	36.8	36.5	36.2	37.7
2010	35.8	35.9	36.1	36.3	36.7	37.1	37.5	37.4	37.4	37.5	37.5	37.6	36.9
2011	37.5	37.7	38.0	38.5	39.3	39.5	39.6	39.8	39.2	39.6	39.5	38.8	38.9
Service-Providing													
2000	307.3	308.2	311.4	314.6	320.1	322.5	315.1	316.0	315.4	315.4	314.9	316.4	314.8
2001	310.1	311.2	312.9	316.2	323.5	325.9	320.1	321.2	319.1	318.7	318.8	319.1	318.1
2002	310.7	311.7	313.1	317.3	324.1	327.5	321.9	323.8	321.5	321.6	320.7	321.7	319.6
2003	313.6	313.6	314.7	318.3	323.9	327.2	322.4	325.0	321.7	321.8	321.8	322.6	320.6
2004	315.0	315.6	316.8	322.3	328.3	331.7	325.3	328.4	327.2	326.5	325.6	325.9	324.1
2005	318.4	319.5	321.9	326.3	331.6	335.5	330.7	333.5	332.0	330.0	330.2	332.0	328.5
2006	324.1	325.4	327.6	330.5	337.6	341.7	336.2	339.8	337.0	336.7	336.9	337.8	334.3
2007	330.4	332.2	334.5	337.9	345.7	348.9	344.9	347.7	343.8	343.5	343.0	343.2	341.3
2008	336.9	338.8	340.3	342.3	349.1	352.1	347.5	351.4	347.6	347.5	345.7	346.3	345.5
2009	337.9	338.5	339.4	341.3	348.9	350.9	346.7	347.9	346.1	344.7	344.4	343.7	344.2
2010	335.1	336.4	338.8	343.2	349.4	352.9	347.9	350.3	347.3	348.1	347.0	347.1	345.3
2011	338.1	339.8	341.4	345.3	350.3	354.1	350.0	350.6	345.8	346.9	346.2	348.5	346.4

1. Employment by Industry: South Dakota, Selected Years, 2000–2011—*Continued*

(Numbers in thousands, not seasonally adjusted)

Industry and year	January	February	March	April	May	June	July	August	September	October	November	December	Annual average
Trade, Transportation, and Utilities													
2000	75.1	74.7	75.0	76.9	77.7	78.0	77.3	77.4	76.5	77.2	78.1	78.4	76.9
2001	75.7	75.7	76.3	76.5	77.9	78.0	77.4	77.4	76.2	77.0	77.9	78.4	77.0
2002	75.0	74.3	74.3	75.9	77.2	77.8	77.0	77.4	76.4	77.1	77.7	78.2	76.5
2003	75.1	74.3	74.5	76.0	77.0	77.4	77.0	77.2	75.9	76.5	77.3	78.0	76.4
2004	75.2	74.4	74.7	76.2	77.7	78.2	77.8	78.7	77.1	77.8	78.7	79.3	77.2
2005	76.4	76.4	76.9	78.3	79.4	79.6	79.6	80.5	79.2	79.2	80.2	81.0	78.9
2006	78.3	77.7	78.3	79.0	80.4	81.2	80.7	81.6	80.1	80.5	81.4	82.2	80.1
2007	79.5	78.7	79.5	80.2	81.7	82.3	82.3	82.6	81.2	81.6	82.4	82.9	81.2
2008	81.0	80.3	80.6	81.1	82.3	83.0	83.3	83.7	82.2	82.6	82.6	83.1	82.2
2009	80.0	79.2	79.1	79.4	81.1	81.6	81.4	81.8	80.5	80.6	81.5	81.7	80.7
2010	78.8	78.1	78.6	79.7	80.9	81.7	81.6	82.0	80.4	81.2	82.0	82.3	80.6
2011	79.7	79.3	79.6	80.9	82.1	82.7	83.7	84.2	82.2	83.0	83.7	84.7	82.2
Wholesale Trade													
2000	16.3	16.4	16.5	16.7	16.7	16.7	16.5	16.5	16.4	16.5	16.5	16.5	16.5
2001	16.5	16.5	16.6	16.8	17.0	16.9	16.7	16.6	16.4	16.7	16.7	16.7	16.7
2002	16.6	16.6	16.6	16.9	16.9	17.0	16.7	16.6	16.3	16.6	16.6	16.6	16.7
2003	16.4	16.3	16.4	16.8	16.9	16.8	16.7	16.6	16.6	16.9	16.9	16.9	16.7
2004	16.6	16.6	16.9	17.2	17.3	17.3	17.1	17.1	16.9	17.4	17.3	17.4	17.1
2005	17.1	17.1	17.1	17.5	17.7	17.7	17.6	17.8	17.6	17.8	17.8	17.8	17.6
2006	18.0	18.0	18.1	18.3	18.6	18.6	18.3	18.3	18.0	18.2	18.1	18.1	18.2
2007	18.0	17.9	18.1	18.3	18.6	18.6	18.5	18.6	18.4	18.5	18.6	18.6	18.4
2008	18.6	18.6	18.7	18.8	19.0	19.0	18.9	18.9	18.6	18.8	18.4	18.6	18.7
2009	18.1	18.1	18.1	18.2	18.6	18.5	18.5	18.5	18.1	18.4	18.4	18.3	18.3
2010	18.1	18.1	18.2	18.6	18.8	18.8	18.8	18.8	18.6	18.8	18.8	18.7	18.6
2011	18.5	18.5	18.7	18.9	19.2	19.3	19.4	19.2	18.7	19.4	19.6	19.5	19.1
Retail Trade													
2000	46.9	46.5	46.8	48.3	48.9	49.4	49.0	49.0	47.9	48.4	49.3	49.6	48.3
2001	47.3	47.3	47.7	47.6	48.7	49.0	48.8	49.0	47.7	48.0	49.0	49.5	48.3
2002	46.8	46.1	46.1	47.2	48.3	48.9	48.7	49.1	48.2	48.7	49.4	49.8	48.1
2003	47.2	46.6	46.7	47.8	48.5	49.0	48.8	49.1	47.8	48.1	48.9	49.6	48.2
2004	47.4	46.7	46.7	47.7	48.9	49.3	49.2	50.0	48.4	48.5	49.5	50.1	48.5
2005	47.7	47.7	48.2	49.0	49.7	49.9	49.9	50.5	49.2	49.0	50.0	50.6	49.3
2006	48.0	47.4	47.8	48.2	49.0	49.8	49.7	50.3	49.1	49.3	50.4	51.0	49.2
2007	48.8	48.2	48.8	49.1	50.1	50.7	50.9	51.0	49.6	49.9	50.7	51.2	49.9
2008	49.4	48.7	48.9	49.2	50.0	50.7	51.1	51.5	50.2	50.4	50.9	51.2	50.2
2009	48.9	48.2	48.2	48.5	49.6	50.2	50.3	50.6	49.6	49.5	50.5	50.8	49.6
2010	48.5	47.9	48.2	48.7	49.5	50.2	50.3	50.6	49.1	49.7	50.5	50.9	49.5
2011	48.9	48.5	48.6	49.4	50.2	50.7	51.5	51.6	50.5	51.0	51.7	52.8	50.5
Transportation and Utilities													
2000	11.9	11.8	11.7	11.9	12.1	11.9	11.8	11.9	12.2	12.3	12.3	12.3	12.0
2001	11.9	11.9	12.0	12.1	12.2	12.1	11.9	11.8	12.1	12.3	12.2	12.2	12.1
2002	11.6	11.6	11.6	11.8	12.0	11.9	11.6	11.7	11.9	11.8	11.7	11.8	11.8
2003	11.5	11.4	11.4	11.4	11.6	11.6	11.5	11.5	11.5	11.5	11.5	11.5	11.5
2004	11.2	11.1	11.1	11.3	11.5	11.6	11.5	11.6	11.8	11.9	11.9	11.8	11.5
2005	11.6	11.6	11.6	11.8	12.0	12.0	12.1	12.2	12.4	12.4	12.4	12.6	12.1
2006	12.3	12.3	12.4	12.5	12.8	12.8	12.7	13.0	13.0	13.0	12.9	13.1	12.7
2007	12.7	12.6	12.6	12.8	13.0	13.0	12.9	13.0	13.2	13.2	13.1	13.1	12.9
2008	13.0	13.0	13.0	13.1	13.3	13.3	13.3	13.3	13.4	13.4	13.3	13.3	13.2
2009	13.0	12.9	12.8	12.7	12.9	12.9	12.6	12.7	12.8	12.7	12.6	12.6	12.8
2010	12.2	12.1	12.2	12.4	12.6	12.7	12.5	12.6	12.7	12.7	12.7	12.7	12.5
2011	12.3	12.3	12.3	12.6	12.7	12.7	12.8	13.4	13.0	12.6	12.4	12.4	12.6
Information													
2000	6.8	6.7	6.8	6.9	7.0	7.0	7.0	6.9	6.9	6.8	6.9	6.9	6.9
2001	6.8	6.8	6.8	6.7	6.9	6.9	6.9	6.8	6.8	6.8	6.8	6.8	6.8
2002	6.8	6.7	6.8	6.7	6.8	6.9	6.9	6.8	6.7	6.9	6.9	6.9	6.8
2003	6.8	6.7	6.7	6.6	6.7	6.8	6.7	6.8	6.7	6.8	6.9	6.9	6.8
2004	6.8	6.8	6.8	6.7	6.8	6.7	6.8	6.8	6.7	6.6	6.6	6.6	6.7
2005	6.6	6.6	6.5	6.5	6.7	6.8	6.9	6.9	6.9	6.9	6.9	6.9	6.8
2006	6.8	6.9	6.9	6.8	6.9	7.0	7.1	7.1	7.0	6.9	6.9	7.0	6.9
2007	7.0	7.1	7.0	7.3	7.4	7.5	7.1	7.2	7.0	7.0	7.0	7.0	7.1
2008	7.0	7.0	6.9	6.8	6.9	7.0	7.0	7.1	6.9	6.9	6.9	6.9	6.9
2009	6.8	6.8	6.7	6.6	6.8	6.7	6.7	6.7	6.7	6.7	6.7	6.7	6.7
2010	6.6	6.6	6.5	6.5	6.5	6.6	6.6	6.6	6.5	6.4	6.5	6.5	6.5
2011	6.4	6.4	6.4	6.3	6.4	6.4	6.5	6.5	6.3	6.3	6.3	6.4	6.4
Financial Activities													
2000	25.6	25.6	25.7	25.9	26.0	26.4	26.5	26.4	26.3	26.5	26.7	27.2	26.2
2001	27.5	27.7	27.8	27.8	28.0	28.3	28.4	28.2	28.1	27.9	28.0	28.1	28.0
2002	28.0	28.0	27.9	27.9	27.9	28.1	28.0	28.0	27.7	27.6	27.7	28.0	27.9
2003	27.6	27.6	27.8	27.5	27.4	27.6	27.8	27.8	27.6	27.7	27.7	28.0	27.7
2004	27.7	27.6	27.8	27.5	27.7	28.0	27.9	28.0	27.9	27.8	27.8	28.1	27.8
2005	28.2	28.0	28.2	27.9	28.2	28.8	28.6	28.6	28.7	28.5	28.6	29.2	28.5
2006	29.0	29.0	29.1	29.0	29.2	29.5	29.7	29.9	29.8	29.8	29.9	30.2	29.5
2007	30.2	30.4	30.7	30.6	30.8	31.3	31.3	31.2	31.1	31.2	31.2	31.2	30.9
2008	31.0	31.0	31.3	30.9	31.2	31.5	31.4	31.1	31.0	30.6	30.6	30.7	31.0
2009	30.7	30.8	30.9	30.7	30.6	30.9	30.6	30.3	30.0	29.9	29.8	29.9	30.4
2010	29.3	29.1	28.9	28.8	28.9	29.0	29.0	28.9	28.5	28.6	28.6	28.7	28.9
2011	28.3	28.3	28.3	28.1	28.1	28.2	28.0	27.5	27.5	27.6	27.4	28.3	28.0

1. Employment by Industry: South Dakota, Selected Years, 2000–2011—*Continued*

(Numbers in thousands, not seasonally adjusted)

Industry and year	January	February	March	April	May	June	July	August	September	October	November	December	Annual average
Professional and Business Services													
2000	26.8	27.1	27.2	27.4	27.4	28.0	27.9	27.7	27.3	27.3	26.7	27.0	27.3
2001	26.1	25.9	25.9	26.4	26.5	26.6	26.4	26.3	25.6	25.5	25.1	24.9	25.9
2002	24.2	24.6	24.7	25.1	25.1	25.5	25.1	25.4	24.7	24.9	25.0	24.9	24.9
2003	24.2	24.4	24.2	24.2	24.3	24.5	24.5	24.6	24.0	24.2	24.5	24.2	24.3
2004	23.2	23.8	23.4	24.3	24.5	24.5	24.5	25.2	24.7	24.5	24.1	24.0	24.2
2005	23.2	23.7	23.9	24.6	24.4	24.7	25.0	25.2	24.6	24.6	24.8	25.3	24.5
2006	24.6	25.0	25.0	25.5	25.7	26.0	26.1	26.1	25.8	26.1	26.1	26.4	25.7
2007	26.0	26.4	26.6	27.4	28.0	28.5	28.5	28.6	27.9	27.6	27.5	27.8	27.6
2008	27.4	27.6	27.8	28.2	28.2	28.6	28.5	28.8	28.1	27.8	27.7	27.8	28.0
2009	27.1	27.0	26.7	26.7	27.0	27.2	27.2	27.1	26.6	26.5	26.5	26.6	26.9
2010	26.2	26.4	26.6	27.6	27.6	27.9	28.2	28.2	27.7	28.1	27.8	28.0	27.5
2011	27.4	27.6	27.8	28.6	28.7	29.0	29.0	28.9	28.7	29.0	28.6	28.8	28.5
Education and Health Services													
2000	50.8	51.1	51.3	51.5	51.5	51.0	50.3	50.4	51.2	51.9	52.0	52.4	51.3
2001	51.7	52.3	52.7	52.8	52.9	52.1	51.9	52.0	52.5	53.1	53.7	53.6	52.6
2002	53.1	53.5	53.8	54.2	54.1	53.7	53.2	53.4	54.1	54.7	54.9	55.0	54.0
2003	54.9	54.8	54.9	55.2	55.3	54.9	55.0	55.2	55.4	56.2	56.4	56.5	55.4
2004	55.8	56.2	56.4	56.6	56.5	56.4	55.8	55.7	56.4	57.0	57.3	57.5	56.5
2005	56.8	57.0	57.3	57.5	57.3	57.2	56.6	57.0	57.6	57.9	58.2	58.4	57.4
2006	57.8	58.0	58.3	58.4	58.4	58.2	57.9	58.2	58.9	59.0	59.5	59.6	58.5
2007	58.9	59.1	59.5	59.8	60.1	59.8	59.6	59.9	60.5	60.9	61.2	61.3	60.1
2008	61.2	61.5	61.7	61.6	62.0	61.9	61.4	61.9	62.2	62.7	63.0	63.4	62.0
2009	62.6	62.7	62.9	63.0	63.2	63.2	62.7	62.6	63.1	63.7	64.1	64.5	63.2
2010	63.5	63.8	64.1	64.2	64.6	64.5	64.3	64.1	64.5	65.0	65.2	65.6	64.5
2011	64.5	64.7	65.0	65.1	65.5	65.5	65.3	65.1	65.4	66.1	66.4	66.6	65.4
Leisure and Hospitality													
2000	34.9	35.1	35.8	36.8	39.8	42.5	42.7	43.6	40.6	37.8	36.6	36.3	38.5
2001	34.5	34.3	35.3	36.9	40.1	42.2	43.1	44.0	40.8	38.2	36.9	36.6	38.6
2002	34.7	34.9	35.7	37.4	40.8	43.1	44.3	45.2	41.9	39.4	37.5	37.4	39.4
2003	35.6	35.5	36.0	37.8	40.9	43.9	44.5	45.7	42.0	39.3	38.0	37.7	39.7
2004	36.4	36.3	36.9	39.0	41.8	45.0	45.2	46.8	43.3	40.7	38.8	38.5	40.7
2005	37.0	37.0	37.8	39.9	42.7	45.7	46.5	48.1	44.1	41.5	39.8	39.7	41.7
2006	37.9	38.0	38.8	40.4	43.8	46.7	46.9	49.0	44.7	42.6	41.0	40.6	42.5
2007	39.0	39.1	39.7	41.1	44.2	46.7	47.5	49.5	45.0	43.1	41.5	41.0	43.1
2008	39.1	39.3	39.9	41.3	44.1	47.1	47.6	49.3	45.2	43.3	41.4	41.0	43.2
2009	39.0	39.1	39.8	40.7	44.0	46.6	47.4	48.9	45.5	42.6	41.0	40.3	42.9
2010	38.2	38.6	39.2	41.0	44.0	47.0	47.1	49.4	45.4	43.5	41.7	41.1	43.0
2011	38.9	39.2	39.8	41.4	44.0	46.5	47.4	49.3	43.2	40.8	39.6	39.2	42.4
Other Services													
2000	17.0	16.7	17.1	16.6	16.8	16.7	16.2	16.1	15.8	16.1	16.1	16.1	16.4
2001	15.5	15.5	15.6	15.6	15.8	15.9	16.0	16.0	15.8	15.9	15.8	15.8	15.8
2002	15.6	15.6	15.7	15.8	16.1	16.1	16.2	16.1	16.0	16.0	15.8	15.8	15.9
2003	15.5	15.5	15.5	15.7	15.8	15.9	15.9	15.9	15.8	15.7	15.7	15.8	15.7
2004	15.6	15.6	15.7	15.9	16.1	16.1	16.1	16.1	16.0	16.2	16.1	15.6	15.9
2005	15.3	15.4	15.4	15.5	15.6	15.7	15.7	15.7	15.6	15.4	15.5	15.5	15.5
2006	15.3	15.3	15.4	15.5	15.7	15.8	15.9	15.9	15.8	15.7	15.7	15.7	15.6
2007	15.6	15.6	15.7	15.7	15.9	16.0	16.0	15.9	15.8	15.7	15.6	15.7	15.8
2008	15.5	15.6	15.6	15.8	16.0	16.1	16.2	16.2	16.0	16.0	15.8	15.8	15.9
2009	15.6	15.6	15.5	15.6	15.8	15.9	15.9	15.8	15.6	15.6	15.5	15.6	15.7
2010	15.4	15.4	15.5	15.6	15.7	15.9	15.9	15.8	15.6	15.6	15.4	15.5	15.6
2011	15.3	15.3	15.4	15.5	15.7	15.9	15.9	15.8	15.5	15.2	15.4	15.6	15.5
Government													
2000	70.3	71.2	72.5	72.6	73.9	72.9	67.2	67.5	70.8	71.8	71.8	72.1	71.2
2001	72.3	73.0	72.5	73.5	75.4	75.9	70.0	70.5	73.3	74.3	74.6	74.9	73.4
2002	73.3	74.1	74.2	74.3	76.1	76.3	71.2	71.5	74.0	75.0	75.2	75.6	74.2
2003	73.9	74.8	75.1	75.3	76.5	76.2	71.0	71.8	74.3	75.4	75.3	75.5	74.6
2004	74.3	74.9	75.1	76.1	77.2	76.8	71.2	71.1	75.1	75.9	76.2	76.3	75.0
2005	74.9	75.4	75.9	76.1	77.3	77.0	71.8	71.5	75.3	76.0	76.2	76.0	75.3
2006	74.4	75.5	75.8	75.9	77.5	77.3	71.9	72.0	74.9	76.1	76.4	76.1	75.3
2007	74.2	75.8	75.8	75.8	77.6	76.8	72.6	72.8	75.3	76.4	76.6	76.3	75.5
2008	74.7	76.5	76.5	76.6	78.4	76.9	72.1	73.3	76.0	77.6	77.7	77.6	76.2
2009	76.1	77.3	77.8	78.6	80.4	78.8	74.8	74.7	78.1	79.1	79.3	78.4	77.8
2010	77.1	78.4	79.4	79.8	81.2	80.3	75.2	75.3	78.7	79.7	79.8	79.4	78.7
2011	77.6	79.0	79.1	79.4	79.8	79.9	74.2	73.3	77.0	78.9	78.8	78.9	78.0

2. Average Weekly Hours by Selected Industry: South Dakota, 2007–2011

(Not seasonally adjusted)

Industry and year	January	February	March	April	May	June	July	August	September	October	November	December	Annual average
Total Private													
2007	31.9	32.4	33.4	32.7	32.5	33.6	34.0	33.2	33.4	32.8	32.4	33.0	33.0
2008	32.4	32.5	32.7	32.6	32.8	33.7	33.2	33.2	32.9	32.8	32.8	32.7	32.9
2009	32.4	32.8	32.9	32.3	33.2	33.1	33.9	34.5	34.1	33.1	33.9	33.5	33.3
2010	33.2	33.7	33.3	33.6	33.8	34.0	34.2	34.5	33.8	33.9	34.2	33.7	33.8
2011	33.8	33.7	33.7	33.8	34.1	34.1	34.0	33.9	33.9	34.3	34.0	33.8	33.9
Goods-Producing													
2007	36.7	38.7	39.9	39.3	39.6	40.8	41.0	38.9	39.9	39.8	39.4	38.9	39.4
2008	38.5	38.8	38.3	38.6	39.6	39.6	39.6	40.1	40.9	40.4	39.6	38.8	39.4
2009	36.3	36.6	35.6	34.8	37.3	36.3	37.7	38.6	37.7	37.5	38.7	37.6	37.1
2010	37.1	37.3	36.9	39.1	37.7	38.4	39.0	39.2	39.3	39.8	39.7	38.8	38.6
2011	38.2	38.1	39.2	39.6	40.0	39.7	39.6	39.8	40.1	40.5	40.2	39.8	39.6
Mining, Logging, and Construction													
2007	36.9	39.2	42.1	40.8	43.0	44.0	44.8	43.1	43.0	42.5	41.4	39.1	41.8
2008	38.0	38.1	38.7	39.1	42.0	41.7	41.5	41.4	43.1	41.5	38.0	38.1	40.2
2009	36.6	37.2	37.6	37.9	40.4	39.1	41.6	41.8	40.3	38.6	39.9	37.0	39.2
2010	36.7	36.2	35.6	40.4	36.6	38.5	40.2	41.1	40.0	41.9	40.5	37.4	38.9
2011	36.8	36.7	37.7	38.9	38.9	40.1	39.9	40.2	40.0	41.1	41.0	38.6	39.3
Manufacturing													
2007	36.6	38.4	38.9	38.5	37.7	38.9	38.7	36.3	38.0	38.2	38.2	38.8	38.1
2008	38.7	39.1	38.1	38.4	38.2	38.4	38.5	39.3	39.6	39.7	40.4	39.2	39.0
2009	36.1	36.3	34.6	33.2	35.5	34.5	35.1	36.4	36.0	36.9	37.9	38.0	35.8
2010	37.4	37.7	37.6	38.4	38.4	38.3	38.2	38.0	38.9	38.5	39.2	39.5	38.4
2011	38.9	38.7	39.9	39.9	40.6	39.4	39.4	39.5	40.2	40.1	39.7	40.4	39.7
Trade, Transportation, and Utilities													
2007	29.8	30.1	30.5	29.4	31.2	32.3	33.5	33.4	33.3	31.8	31.9	32.5	31.7
2008	30.9	31.2	31.7	31.1	31.5	31.9	31.4	31.7	31.3	31.2	31.5	32.4	31.5
2009	31.5	32.3	32.2	31.6	33.3	33.0	33.1	33.1	32.9	32.7	33.5	33.4	32.7
2010	32.8	33.6	33.4	33.2	34.0	34.1	34.2	34.6	33.7	33.8	33.5	32.6	33.6
2011	33.2	33.1	32.9	33.0	33.6	33.5	33.2	33.0	32.9	33.3	32.7	32.5	33.1
Professional and Business Services													
2007	32.1	31.1	31.7	32.4	28.1	28.4	28.4	27.5	29.0	30.8	30.8	30.9	30.1
2008	32.0	31.8	32.4	32.2	31.7	33.4	33.6	32.9	32.1	32.1	32.4	32.2	32.4
2009	32.8	33.4	34.5	33.1	32.2	33.1	33.5	34.3	33.5	33.7	34.4	34.1	33.5
2010	34.6	35.7	35.4	36.0	35.9	37.2	36.8	37.0	36.1	36.6	37.2	36.3	36.2
2011	37.5	37.2	37.2	37.6	38.7	38.4	37.7	38.3	37.6	39.2	38.1	37.8	37.9
Education and Health Services													
2007	36.3	36.2	39.9	37.1	36.1	37.0	35.3	34.9	35.7	33.9	33.7	34.5	35.9
2008	33.7	33.9	33.5	33.4	32.8	34.0	32.5	32.8	31.8	31.6	31.7	31.6	32.8
2009	33.8	33.0	35.4	35.2	34.9	35.2	37.1	37.0	37.2	33.5	34.0	34.5	35.1
2010	32.7	32.9	32.2	32.2	32.7	32.6	33.5	32.3	32.0	32.3	32.6	32.3	32.5
2011	32.0	31.7	31.3	31.3	30.6	31.2	31.6	30.9	31.5	30.9	31.4	30.6	31.2
Leisure and Hospitality													
2007	21.8	22.8	22.9	23.8	23.4	25.8	27.1	26.4	25.0	24.1	22.4	23.1	24.2
2008	22.4	22.5	23.3	22.9	23.5	25.9	24.8	24.1	23.1	22.5	22.5	21.7	23.3
2009	21.9	23.5	22.9	22.2	23.1	24.1	25.0	25.5	23.9	22.7	23.2	22.3	23.4
2010	22.5	22.7	23.0	22.6	23.8	24.1	24.6	26.4	23.9	23.1	22.8	22.5	23.6
2011	22.9	22.7	23.1	22.7	23.3	23.8	24.5	25.3	23.0	23.4	22.8	22.7	23.4

3. Average Hourly Earnings by Selected Industry: South Dakota, 2007–2011

(Dollars, not seasonally adjusted)

Industry and year	January	February	March	April	May	June	July	August	September	October	November	December	Annual average
Total Private													
2007	16.81	16.90	16.56	17.76	16.59	16.24	15.96	16.02	16.47	16.12	16.22	16.12	16.47
2008	16.31	16.46	16.36	16.42	16.46	16.31	16.13	16.37	16.51	16.61	17.11	17.39	16.53
2009	17.72	17.78	17.89	17.69	17.80	17.60	18.10	17.78	18.10	18.13	18.30	18.43	17.94
2010	18.78	18.63	18.53	18.68	18.41	18.14	18.55	18.16	18.65	18.64	18.73	18.75	18.55
2011	19.20	19.14	19.14	19.21	18.96	18.66	18.72	18.74	18.98	19.19	19.26	19.45	19.05
Goods-Producing													
2007	18.18	18.41	17.36	17.59	18.05	17.29	17.06	16.76	16.83	17.21	16.80	16.83	17.34
2008	17.48	17.30	17.19	17.30	17.14	17.08	17.07	17.10	16.97	17.10	17.13	17.75	17.21
2009	17.73	18.31	18.35	18.28	17.86	18.13	18.16	17.95	18.09	18.15	17.82	17.88	18.06
2010	18.32	18.73	18.32	18.94	18.55	18.39	18.70	18.74	18.81	18.85	18.82	19.47	18.73
2011	19.75	19.68	19.55	19.44	19.12	19.02	18.97	18.99	19.09	19.11	18.80	18.96	19.19
Mining, Logging, and Construction													
2007	18.66	20.22	19.71	19.25	19.89	18.48	18.00	18.04	18.35	18.76	18.18	18.37	18.76
2008	19.13	19.17	18.70	18.82	18.34	18.51	18.28	18.54	18.53	18.68	19.14	19.76	18.76
2009	20.40	21.09	20.43	19.88	19.56	19.25	19.32	19.31	19.05	19.28	19.64	19.63	19.67
2010	20.53	21.17	20.89	21.14	20.22	19.76	20.15	20.15	20.15	20.16	20.47	21.29	20.45
2011	21.15	21.16	21.23	20.71	20.38	19.82	19.68	19.36	19.48	19.39	19.41	19.93	20.04
Manufacturing													
2007	17.95	17.56	16.14	16.69	16.85	16.49	16.39	15.82	15.80	16.20	15.96	16.00	16.48
2008	16.68	16.44	16.46	16.50	16.39	16.16	16.29	16.19	15.99	16.16	16.10	16.74	16.34
2009	16.47	16.96	17.25	17.32	16.70	17.31	17.22	16.93	17.42	17.41	16.66	16.94	17.04
2010	17.27	17.63	17.17	17.67	17.62	17.54	17.73	17.77	17.95	17.96	17.80	18.53	17.73
2011	19.13	19.05	18.83	18.81	18.46	18.54	18.53	18.76	18.87	18.95	18.46	18.49	18.74
Trade, Transportation, and Utilities													
2007	13.78	13.46	14.00	13.60	13.65	13.46	13.68	13.77	14.81	13.74	14.35	14.22	13.88
2008	14.61	14.70	14.66	14.90	14.86	14.96	14.76	15.08	15.04	15.22	16.20	16.84	15.16
2009	17.50	17.71	18.13	17.98	18.41	18.25	18.50	18.51	19.37	19.60	20.34	20.13	18.72
2010	20.57	19.98	19.77	20.23	19.58	19.18	19.73	19.08	19.74	19.78	19.60	19.16	19.69
2011	19.20	19.40	19.43	19.83	19.54	18.70	18.82	18.97	19.00	19.22	19.10	18.96	19.18
Professional and Business Services													
2007	22.40	22.07	21.95	21.78	22.23	22.50	21.23	21.75	21.58	21.10	22.04	21.38	21.83
2008	21.28	21.49	21.98	21.60	22.38	21.35	21.13	21.87	21.99	21.60	23.37	22.16	21.84
2009	22.42	21.94	21.32	20.68	21.38	20.63	20.78	21.46	20.81	21.02	21.13	21.23	21.23
2010	20.95	20.56	20.50	19.88	20.08	19.63	20.09	20.32	20.81	20.90	21.04	21.16	20.49
2011	23.46	22.89	23.01	22.93	22.70	22.34	22.79	22.63	23.54	23.95	24.19	23.98	23.20
Education and Health Services													
2007	16.36	16.25	16.71	17.11	16.62	16.80	16.41	16.09	16.13	16.05	15.81	15.75	16.35
2008	15.68	15.91	15.81	15.72	16.19	16.59	16.32	16.37	16.80	17.04	17.42	16.95	16.39
2009	17.25	17.03	17.78	17.98	17.67	18.01	19.02	18.58	18.67	18.21	18.22	18.38	18.08
2010	18.52	18.51	18.84	19.05	18.99	19.54	19.25	18.27	18.96	19.16	19.04	18.34	18.87
2011	18.65	18.52	18.50	18.44	18.00	17.80	18.28	18.04	18.00	18.09	18.31	18.05	18.22
Leisure and Hospitality													
2007	11.16	10.88	10.93	10.72	10.64	10.14	10.54	10.96	11.13	11.27	11.06	11.17	10.86
2008	11.16	11.20	11.05	11.36	11.21	10.85	10.86	10.83	11.05	11.22	11.28	11.69	11.13
2009	11.58	11.56	11.30	11.43	11.29	10.94	10.78	11.26	10.00	10.23	10.47	10.83	10.96
2010	10.68	10.90	10.88	10.88	10.56	10.26	10.34	10.45	10.75	10.73	10.72	11.17	10.67
2011	11.05	10.99	10.90	10.81	10.74	10.42	10.47	10.91	10.89	10.85	11.18	11.30	10.86

4. Average Weekly Earnings by Selected Industry: South Dakota, 2007–2011

(Dollars, not seasonally adjusted)

Industry and year	January	February	March	April	May	June	July	August	September	October	November	December	Annual average
Total Private													
2007	536.24	547.56	553.10	580.75	539.18	545.66	542.64	531.86	550.10	528.74	525.53	531.96	542.83
2008	528.44	534.95	534.97	535.29	539.89	549.65	535.52	543.48	543.18	544.81	561.21	568.65	543.30
2009	574.13	583.18	588.58	571.39	590.96	582.56	613.59	613.41	617.21	600.10	620.37	617.41	598.13
2010	623.50	627.83	617.05	627.65	622.26	616.76	634.41	626.52	630.37	631.90	640.57	631.88	627.92
2011	648.96	645.02	645.02	649.30	646.54	636.31	636.48	635.29	643.42	658.22	654.84	657.41	646.45
Goods-Producing													
2007	667.21	712.47	692.66	691.29	714.78	705.43	699.46	651.96	671.52	684.96	661.92	654.69	683.78
2008	672.98	671.24	658.38	667.78	678.74	676.37	675.97	685.71	694.07	690.84	678.35	688.70	678.36
2009	643.60	670.15	653.26	636.14	666.18	658.12	684.63	692.87	681.99	680.63	689.63	672.29	669.09
2010	679.67	698.63	676.01	740.55	699.34	706.18	729.30	734.61	739.23	750.23	747.15	755.44	722.30
2011	754.45	749.81	766.36	769.82	764.80	755.09	751.21	755.80	765.51	773.96	755.76	754.61	759.57
Mining, Logging, and Construction													
2007	688.55	792.62	829.79	785.40	855.27	813.12	806.40	777.52	789.05	797.30	752.65	718.27	785.13
2008	726.94	730.38	723.69	735.86	770.28	771.87	758.62	767.56	798.64	775.22	727.32	752.86	754.91
2009	746.64	784.55	768.17	753.45	790.22	752.68	803.71	807.16	767.72	744.21	783.64	726.31	770.18
2010	753.45	766.35	743.68	854.06	740.05	760.76	810.03	828.17	806.00	844.70	829.04	796.25	796.56
2011	778.32	776.57	800.37	805.62	792.78	794.78	785.23	778.27	779.20	796.93	795.81	769.30	788.15
Manufacturing													
2007	656.97	674.30	627.85	642.57	635.25	641.46	634.29	574.27	600.40	618.84	609.67	620.80	628.00
2008	645.52	642.80	627.13	633.60	626.10	620.54	627.17	636.27	633.20	641.55	641.55	626.21	636.63
2009	594.57	615.65	596.85	575.02	592.85	597.20	604.42	616.25	627.12	642.43	631.41	643.72	610.77
2010	645.90	664.65	645.59	678.53	676.61	671.78	677.29	675.26	698.26	691.46	697.76	731.94	679.99
2011	744.16	737.24	751.32	750.52	749.48	730.48	730.08	741.02	758.57	759.90	732.86	747.00	744.23
Trade, Transportation, and Utilities													
2007	410.64	405.15	427.00	399.84	425.88	434.76	458.28	459.92	493.17	436.93	457.77	462.15	439.59
2008	451.45	458.64	464.72	463.39	468.00	477.22	463.46	478.04	470.75	474.86	510.30	545.62	477.38
2009	551.25	572.03	583.79	568.17	613.05	602.25	612.35	612.68	637.27	640.92	681.39	672.34	612.72
2010	674.70	671.33	660.32	671.64	665.72	654.04	674.77	660.17	665.24	668.56	656.60	624.62	662.38
2011	637.44	642.14	639.25	654.39	656.54	626.45	624.82	626.01	625.10	640.03	624.57	616.20	634.27
Professional and Business Services													
2007	719.04	686.38	695.82	705.67	624.66	639.00	602.93	598.13	625.82	649.88	678.83	660.64	656.23
2008	680.96	683.38	712.15	695.52	709.45	713.09	709.97	719.52	705.88	693.36	757.19	713.55	707.90
2009	735.38	732.80	735.54	684.51	688.44	682.85	696.13	736.08	697.14	708.37	726.87	723.94	712.26
2010	724.87	733.99	725.70	715.68	720.87	730.24	739.31	751.84	751.24	764.94	782.69	768.11	742.63
2011	879.75	851.51	855.97	862.17	878.49	857.86	859.18	866.73	885.10	938.84	921.64	906.44	880.38
Education and Health Services													
2007	593.87	588.25	666.73	634.78	599.98	621.60	579.27	561.54	575.84	544.10	532.80	543.38	586.53
2008	528.42	539.35	529.64	525.05	531.03	564.06	530.40	536.94	534.24	538.46	552.21	535.62	537.15
2009	583.05	561.99	629.41	632.90	616.68	633.95	705.64	687.46	694.52	610.04	619.48	634.11	634.18
2010	605.60	608.98	606.65	613.41	620.97	637.00	644.88	590.12	606.72	618.87	620.70	592.38	613.84
2011	596.80	587.08	579.05	577.17	550.80	555.36	577.65	557.44	567.00	558.98	574.93	552.33	569.43
Leisure and Hospitality													
2007	243.29	248.06	250.30	255.14	248.98	261.61	285.63	289.34	278.25	271.61	247.74	258.03	262.49
2008	249.98	252.00	257.47	260.14	263.44	281.02	269.33	261.00	255.26	252.45	253.80	253.67	259.57
2009	253.60	271.66	258.77	253.75	260.80	263.65	269.50	287.13	239.00	232.22	242.90	241.51	256.70
2010	240.30	247.43	250.24	245.89	251.33	247.27	254.36	275.88	256.93	247.86	244.42	251.33	251.60
2011	253.05	249.47	251.79	245.39	250.24	248.00	256.52	276.02	250.47	253.89	254.90	256.51	254.16

TENNESSEE
At a Glance

Population:
    2000 census: 5,689,427
    2010 census: 6,346,105
    2011 estimate: 6,403,353

Percent change in population:
    2000–2010: 11.5%
    2010–2011: 0.9%

Percent change in total nonfarm employment:
    2000–2010: -4.3%
    2010–2011: 1.6%

Industry with the largest growth in employment, 2000–2011 (thousands):
    Education and Health Services, 101.5

Industry with the largest decline or smallest growth in employment, 2000–2011 (thousands):
    Manufacturing, -193.1

Civilian labor force:
    2000: 2,871,539
    2010: 3,084,127
    2011: 3,132,742

Unemployment rate and rank among states (lowest to highest):
    2000: 4.0%, 28th
    2010: 9.8%, 34th
    2011: 9.2%, 35th

Over-the-year change in unemployment rates:
    2010–2011: -0.6%

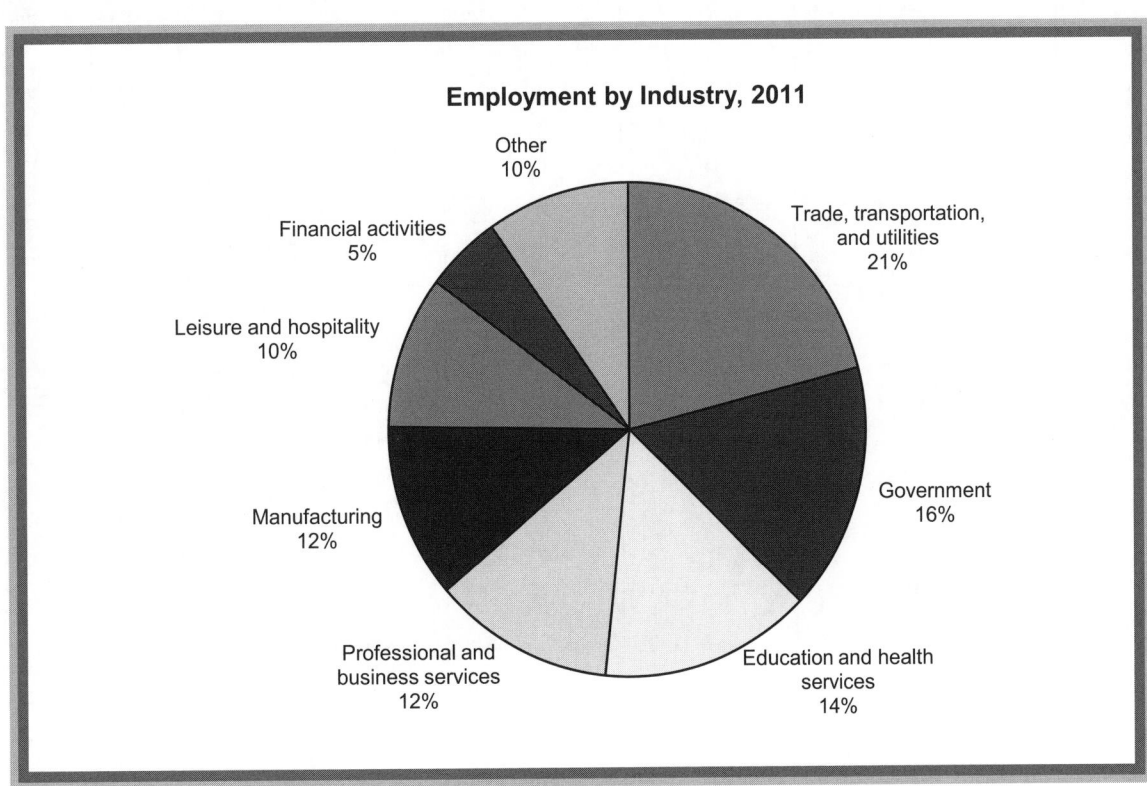

Employment by Industry, 2011

Other
10%

Trade, transportation, and utilities
21%

Financial activities
5%

Leisure and hospitality
10%

Government
16%

Manufacturing
12%

Professional and business services
12%

Education and health services
14%

1. Employment by Industry: Tennessee, Selected Years, 2000–2011

(Numbers in thousands, not seasonally adjusted)

Industry and year	January	February	March	April	May	June	July	August	September	October	November	December	Annual average
Total Nonfarm													
2000	2,668.3	2,687.4	2,731.0	2,729.2	2,744.7	2,749.4	2,723.3	2,741.6	2,752.8	2,750.2	2,757.4	2,759.0	2,732.9
2001	2,673.4	2,683.1	2,701.2	2,705.5	2,708.1	2,703.2	2,666.2	2,684.1	2,691.2	2,676.8	2,683.3	2,683.0	2,688.3
2002	2,611.9	2,622.8	2,643.7	2,660.0	2,670.2	2,672.0	2,657.2	2,674.7	2,684.2	2,684.6	2,693.5	2,698.1	2,664.4
2003	2,619.8	2,627.9	2,646.0	2,662.8	2,671.8	2,668.1	2,637.3	2,661.8	2,675.7	2,683.5	2,694.7	2,702.4	2,662.7
2004	2,637.4	2,668.4	2,678.9	2,700.4	2,706.7	2,710.6	2,693.6	2,716.3	2,725.5	2,732.6	2,746.2	2,756.2	2,706.1
2005	2,671.3	2,696.1	2,718.4	2,739.5	2,746.5	2,743.7	2,731.8	2,753.6	2,776.3	2,767.1	2,784.7	2,788.3	2,743.1
2006	2,727.1	2,734.8	2,765.3	2,781.4	2,791.6	2,791.4	2,769.8	2,796.8	2,810.2	2,793.8	2,811.4	2,818.6	2,782.7
2007	2,744.9	2,753.7	2,784.0	2,787.9	2,799.3	2,798.0	2,782.4	2,811.2	2,821.7	2,815.9	2,833.6	2,836.4	2,797.4
2008	2,762.4	2,771.9	2,790.1	2,797.1	2,805.4	2,784.3	2,758.6	2,779.0	2,779.4	2,766.1	2,758.6	2,745.1	2,774.8
2009	2,647.6	2,636.8	2,634.6	2,629.9	2,630.3	2,599.4	2,582.6	2,600.3	2,609.7	2,616.3	2,629.2	2,622.1	2,619.9
2010	2,557.1	2,562.5	2,585.2	2,614.9	2,638.0	2,613.2	2,600.4	2,619.3	2,635.2	2,645.4	2,656.9	2,655.2	2,615.3
2011	2,587.1	2,609.1	2,631.5	2,655.2	2,663.2	2,645.5	2,644.9	2,664.5	2,680.1	2,691.8	2,704.8	2,697.8	2,656.3
Total Private													
2000	2,278.2	2,289.2	2,312.1	2,325.9	2,336.7	2,356.9	2,345.1	2,353.6	2,356.6	2,346.6	2,352.1	2,353.2	2,333.9
2001	2,275.2	2,276.0	2,292.1	2,295.6	2,300.6	2,309.2	2,285.7	2,292.7	2,286.5	2,266.7	2,269.9	2,270.9	2,285.1
2002	2,205.5	2,208.0	2,226.9	2,240.8	2,255.1	2,266.4	2,271.0	2,278.9	2,275.1	2,268.9	2,274.5	2,278.7	2,254.2
2003	2,211.4	2,212.6	2,228.4	2,242.6	2,254.1	2,263.6	2,248.4	2,263.4	2,264.1	2,267.5	2,277.7	2,284.7	2,251.5
2004	2,226.3	2,235.3	2,257.8	2,279.7	2,289.2	2,303.1	2,301.8	2,313.8	2,310.2	2,313.6	2,325.0	2,334.3	2,290.8
2005	2,261.1	2,278.4	2,299.4	2,322.9	2,331.4	2,343.9	2,339.8	2,352.1	2,358.0	2,347.1	2,363.1	2,367.6	2,330.4
2006	2,315.1	2,317.2	2,345.0	2,359.3	2,371.0	2,387.0	2,371.8	2,386.7	2,387.4	2,370.0	2,385.1	2,393.4	2,365.8
2007	2,326.8	2,331.2	2,358.7	2,365.2	2,376.0	2,392.8	2,382.1	2,396.7	2,394.0	2,384.5	2,400.3	2,405.3	2,376.1
2008	2,337.7	2,341.8	2,357.7	2,363.8	2,371.5	2,378.6	2,352.7	2,360.0	2,348.8	2,327.3	2,318.6	2,306.5	2,347.1
2009	2,219.7	2,204.1	2,200.1	2,193.8	2,195.1	2,195.7	2,178.0	2,183.2	2,178.1	2,176.3	2,188.1	2,184.4	2,191.4
2010	2,126.5	2,127.6	2,148.4	2,174.1	2,188.2	2,199.6	2,191.4	2,198.2	2,196.9	2,204.9	2,215.7	2,217.1	2,182.4
2011	2,155.9	2,172.6	2,193.9	2,218.4	2,229.8	2,242.6	2,243.2	2,244.1	2,240.3	2,244.6	2,256.2	2,251.5	2,224.4
Goods-Producing													
2000	627.6	628.9	633.6	632.3	635.6	640.5	632.1	632.8	630.6	622.3	617.9	615.4	629.1
2001	593.0	588.5	591.4	588.8	586.8	587.6	579.3	578.8	574.3	565.2	561.8	558.5	579.5
2002	544.6	543.1	544.3	546.3	551.1	554.0	552.0	554.1	552.4	547.8	543.1	543.2	548.0
2003	530.3	528.2	530.3	532.4	534.7	537.0	532.0	534.9	534.5	533.6	532.3	533.5	532.8
2004	522.0	522.8	526.7	531.8	536.5	539.8	537.3	539.1	538.9	534.1	533.2	533.0	532.9
2005	526.0	527.4	531.2	532.4	535.0	538.4	534.3	538.1	539.7	535.6	536.5	533.3	534.0
2006	530.3	529.7	535.0	536.7	538.4	541.8	535.4	538.5	537.7	529.6	527.4	525.2	533.8
2007	517.8	517.4	522.1	520.0	518.2	522.0	517.1	519.4	518.5	515.5	513.6	512.2	517.8
2008	502.0	502.2	503.6	501.9	502.8	503.9	494.7	496.3	491.5	482.8	473.2	464.9	493.3
2009	443.7	435.5	430.9	423.0	418.3	415.0	413.5	413.9	413.2	409.6	408.1	403.8	419.0
2010	393.2	391.5	396.4	402.6	404.6	409.3	408.2	409.8	409.9	408.7	407.8	406.5	404.0
2011	397.2	400.6	404.9	409.6	412.3	416.7	420.5	418.9	420.7	421.6	422.3	419.4	413.7
Mining, Logging, and Construction													
2000	126.5	127.6	132.2	131.5	134.2	136.3	134.2	134.8	135.1	131.9	130.3	128.8	132.0
2001	120.0	120.9	124.8	125.8	127.4	129.3	128.7	128.4	126.6	124.5	124.6	122.4	125.3
2002	114.5	114.3	115.9	117.9	120.5	122.5	122.4	122.7	122.3	121.1	119.9	120.1	119.5
2003	113.6	112.4	115.0	118.5	120.9	122.5	122.5	123.3	123.2	121.8	120.7	120.8	119.6
2004	115.3	115.2	117.8	120.2	122.8	124.8	124.8	124.4	123.8	122.0	121.8	120.9	121.2
2005	117.0	117.6	120.3	121.4	124.2	127.0	128.1	129.4	130.1	129.4	129.2	129.1	125.2
2006	126.4	126.9	131.6	133.3	135.2	138.3	137.4	138.4	138.6	136.5	135.5	134.8	134.4
2007	129.9	130.1	135.0	136.5	138.6	141.5	140.3	141.6	141.5	141.0	139.9	138.5	137.9
2008	132.7	132.6	134.0	134.3	135.6	136.3	134.7	134.7	133.0	130.2	127.1	123.2	132.4
2009	113.2	111.1	111.4	110.3	110.1	111.1	110.7	110.1	110.1	108.2	107.0	104.9	109.9
2010	97.5	96.8	100.1	104.8	105.6	108.2	108.5	108.8	108.9	108.9	107.3	105.9	105.1
2011	97.8	99.8	103.1	107.1	108.5	111.6	113.8	114.1	114.5	114.8	115.9	114.0	109.6
Manufacturing													
2000	501.1	501.3	501.4	500.8	501.4	504.2	497.9	498.0	495.5	490.4	487.6	486.6	497.2
2001	473.0	467.6	466.6	463.0	459.4	458.3	450.6	450.4	447.7	440.7	437.2	436.1	454.2
2002	430.1	428.8	428.4	428.4	430.6	431.5	429.6	431.4	430.1	426.7	423.2	423.1	428.5
2003	416.7	415.8	415.3	413.9	413.8	414.5	409.5	411.6	411.3	411.8	411.6	412.7	413.2
2004	406.7	407.6	408.9	411.6	413.7	415.0	412.5	414.7	415.1	412.1	411.4	412.1	411.8
2005	409.0	409.8	410.9	411.0	410.8	411.4	406.2	408.7	409.6	406.2	407.3	404.2	408.8
2006	403.9	402.8	403.4	403.4	403.2	403.5	398.0	400.1	399.1	393.1	391.9	390.4	399.4
2007	387.9	387.3	387.1	383.5	379.6	380.5	376.8	377.8	377.0	374.5	373.7	373.7	380.0
2008	369.3	369.6	369.6	367.6	367.2	367.6	360.0	361.6	358.5	352.6	346.1	341.7	361.0
2009	330.5	324.4	319.5	312.7	308.2	303.9	302.8	303.8	303.1	301.4	301.1	298.9	309.2
2010	295.7	294.7	296.3	297.8	299.0	301.1	299.7	301.0	301.0	299.8	300.5	300.6	298.9
2011	299.4	300.8	301.8	302.5	303.8	305.1	306.7	304.8	306.2	306.8	306.4	305.4	304.1
Service-Providing													
2000	2,040.7	2,058.5	2,097.4	2,096.9	2,109.1	2,108.9	2,091.2	2,108.8	2,122.2	2,127.9	2,139.5	2,143.6	2,103.7
2001	2,080.4	2,094.6	2,109.8	2,116.7	2,121.3	2,115.6	2,086.9	2,105.3	2,116.9	2,111.6	2,121.5	2,124.5	2,108.8
2002	2,067.3	2,079.7	2,099.4	2,113.7	2,119.1	2,118.0	2,105.2	2,120.6	2,131.8	2,136.8	2,150.4	2,154.9	2,116.4
2003	2,089.5	2,099.7	2,115.7	2,130.4	2,137.1	2,131.1	2,105.3	2,126.9	2,141.2	2,149.9	2,162.4	2,168.9	2,129.8
2004	2,115.4	2,145.6	2,152.2	2,168.6	2,170.2	2,170.8	2,156.3	2,177.2	2,186.6	2,198.5	2,213.0	2,223.2	2,173.1
2005	2,145.3	2,168.7	2,187.2	2,207.1	2,211.5	2,205.3	2,197.5	2,215.5	2,236.6	2,231.5	2,248.2	2,255.0	2,209.1
2006	2,196.8	2,205.1	2,230.3	2,244.7	2,253.2	2,249.6	2,234.4	2,258.3	2,272.5	2,264.2	2,284.0	2,293.4	2,248.9
2007	2,227.1	2,236.3	2,261.9	2,267.9	2,281.1	2,276.0	2,265.3	2,291.8	2,303.2	2,300.4	2,320.0	2,324.2	2,279.6
2008	2,260.4	2,269.7	2,286.5	2,295.2	2,302.6	2,280.4	2,263.9	2,282.7	2,287.9	2,283.3	2,285.4	2,280.2	2,281.5
2009	2,203.9	2,201.3	2,203.7	2,206.9	2,212.0	2,184.4	2,169.1	2,186.4	2,196.5	2,206.7	2,221.1	2,218.3	2,200.9
2010	2,163.9	2,171.0	2,188.8	2,212.3	2,233.4	2,203.9	2,192.2	2,209.5	2,225.3	2,236.7	2,249.1	2,248.7	2,211.2
2011	2,189.9	2,208.5	2,226.6	2,245.6	2,250.9	2,228.8	2,224.4	2,245.6	2,259.4	2,270.2	2,282.5	2,278.4	2,242.6

1. Employment by Industry: Tennessee, Selected Years, 2000–2011—*Continued*

(Numbers in thousands, not seasonally adjusted)

Industry and year	January	February	March	April	May	June	July	August	September	October	November	December	Annual average
Trade, Transportation, and Utilities													
2000	580.5	582.0	586.8	590.1	590.8	596.0	593.9	592.1	592.7	596.4	604.9	608.2	592.9
2001	593.1	589.1	591.6	590.6	592.3	592.2	584.8	586.5	586.2	585.5	593.4	596.6	590.2
2002	569.4	566.1	570.1	570.3	572.3	573.6	576.6	576.6	577.5	581.3	590.2	597.1	576.8
2003	571.2	569.0	572.1	573.4	574.5	576.4	574.4	578.0	579.5	584.7	593.3	598.1	578.7
2004	575.9	574.8	580.0	582.0	583.1	586.0	584.9	587.3	587.6	594.5	604.9	613.0	587.8
2005	578.4	585.4	590.5	593.6	595.8	595.8	599.5	600.2	601.7	602.0	613.5	620.0	598.0
2006	598.3	596.2	602.2	603.5	606.1	607.0	604.2	607.7	608.6	607.4	619.4	626.6	607.3
2007	603.8	600.6	607.1	606.3	609.1	609.6	606.8	609.5	610.3	611.2	623.5	628.4	610.5
2008	605.4	602.4	606.1	602.9	602.5	601.5	598.3	599.3	596.7	591.7	596.4	598.1	600.1
2009	571.7	564.4	561.8	557.0	557.7	557.1	553.8	555.1	553.1	554.2	562.0	565.8	559.5
2010	546.5	543.9	547.4	550.4	552.5	554.2	554.7	556.1	554.5	558.8	568.5	573.2	555.1
2011	550.4	550.2	553.9	559.3	561.1	563.3	561.9	558.1	555.5	556.9	567.6	569.2	559.0
Wholesale Trade													
2000	133.3	134.0	134.9	133.7	133.2	133.4	132.8	132.5	132.4	131.5	131.4	131.5	132.9
2001	128.0	128.1	128.6	128.2	128.1	128.0	126.5	126.9	127.4	126.8	126.9	126.7	127.5
2002	124.7	125.0	125.2	125.4	125.8	126.1	127.0	127.2	127.0	127.8	128.1	128.9	126.5
2003	126.7	127.0	127.2	127.2	127.4	127.2	125.9	126.0	125.9	125.8	126.2	126.1	126.6
2004	124.9	125.4	126.6	127.2	127.5	128.4	128.7	129.1	129.0	129.5	129.9	130.2	128.0
2005	128.4	128.8	129.7	130.1	130.7	130.4	130.5	130.6	131.0	130.7	131.1	131.4	130.3
2006	130.0	130.6	131.4	131.7	132.3	132.5	132.6	132.9	133.0	132.4	132.5	132.5	132.0
2007	131.0	131.4	132.3	132.7	133.0	133.4	133.1	133.3	133.8	134.0	133.7	133.9	133.0
2008	132.5	132.9	133.1	132.8	133.1	132.5	131.8	131.9	131.7	130.5	129.3	128.2	131.7
2009	124.9	123.9	123.0	122.0	121.4	121.0	119.8	119.3	118.6	118.7	118.3	118.1	120.8
2010	116.6	116.5	117.2	117.2	117.3	117.2	116.9	116.8	116.3	116.6	116.5	116.3	116.8
2011	115.4	116.0	116.5	117.4	117.8	118.5	118.5	117.3	116.7	116.3	115.1	115.0	116.7
Retail Trade													
2000	311.1	310.6	313.3	315.8	316.7	320.5	319.4	319.6	320.6	323.6	332.2	335.8	319.9
2001	322.1	318.4	320.5	319.4	320.0	319.8	314.7	314.8	314.1	314.7	323.7	327.5	319.1
2002	307.8	304.8	307.5	307.7	309.0	310.0	311.2	310.6	312.4	313.9	322.3	328.9	312.2
2003	307.3	304.9	307.0	308.1	308.7	310.2	309.5	312.0	313.5	318.6	326.5	331.9	313.2
2004	313.7	312.2	314.8	315.5	316.3	317.9	316.3	317.4	317.5	322.7	332.4	337.0	319.5
2005	311.7	318.1	321.0	322.2	323.5	323.7	324.1	323.7	324.1	324.8	334.9	339.7	324.3
2006	323.2	320.8	324.7	325.9	327.0	327.4	325.7	327.1	326.7	327.6	338.6	343.7	328.2
2007	327.1	323.5	328.3	327.1	329.0	329.1	327.3	328.0	328.3	330.0	342.3	346.5	330.5
2008	328.7	325.9	329.6	326.5	325.5	325.2	323.6	323.6	321.3	320.4	325.9	327.6	325.3
2009	310.6	305.9	305.1	303.7	305.1	305.4	304.5	305.5	304.2	305.1	313.1	316.2	307.0
2010	301.9	299.7	302.2	304.6	306.0	307.0	306.0	306.8	304.0	307.5	316.1	319.0	306.7
2011	303.3	302.1	304.5	307.5	308.5	309.6	308.2	306.2	303.8	304.8	315.4	316.0	307.5
Transportation and Utilities													
2000	136.1	137.4	138.6	140.6	140.9	142.1	141.7	140.0	139.7	141.3	141.3	140.9	140.1
2001	143.0	142.6	142.5	143.0	144.2	144.4	143.6	144.8	144.7	144.0	142.8	142.4	143.5
2002	136.9	136.3	137.4	137.2	137.5	137.5	138.4	138.8	138.1	139.6	139.8	139.3	138.1
2003	137.2	137.1	137.9	138.1	138.4	139.0	139.0	140.0	140.1	140.3	140.6	140.1	139.0
2004	137.3	137.2	138.6	139.3	139.3	139.7	139.9	140.8	141.1	142.3	142.6	145.8	140.3
2005	138.3	138.5	139.8	141.3	141.6	141.7	144.9	145.9	146.6	146.5	147.5	148.9	143.5
2006	145.1	144.8	146.1	145.9	146.8	147.1	145.9	147.7	148.9	147.4	148.3	150.4	147.0
2007	145.7	145.7	146.5	146.5	147.1	147.1	146.4	148.2	148.2	147.2	147.5	148.0	147.0
2008	144.2	143.6	143.4	143.6	143.9	143.8	142.9	143.8	143.7	140.8	141.2	142.3	143.1
2009	136.2	134.6	133.7	131.3	131.2	130.7	129.5	130.3	130.3	130.4	130.6	131.5	131.7
2010	128.0	127.7	128.0	128.6	129.2	130.0	131.8	132.5	134.2	134.7	135.9	137.9	131.5
2011	131.7	132.1	132.9	134.4	134.8	135.2	135.2	134.6	135.0	135.8	137.1	138.2	134.8
Information													
2000	55.1	55.2	55.6	54.6	54.7	55.2	54.6	54.9	55.0	55.2	56.4	56.8	55.3
2001	56.0	56.3	56.5	55.2	55.2	55.7	55.3	55.3	54.5	54.6	55.1	55.4	55.4
2002	54.1	53.9	54.4	53.6	53.8	53.3	52.9	53.0	52.4	52.7	53.1	52.9	53.3
2003	52.1	51.9	51.8	51.7	51.4	51.1	50.5	50.4	49.9	50.6	51.3	51.4	51.2
2004	50.1	49.9	49.7	49.7	49.4	49.6	49.5	49.5	48.3	49.0	49.3	50.0	49.5
2005	49.7	49.7	49.6	49.5	49.7	49.9	49.4	49.2	48.8	48.8	49.3	49.3	49.4
2006	49.1	49.2	49.4	49.9	50.1	50.2	49.3	49.2	49.4	49.4	49.8	50.0	49.6
2007	49.1	49.3	49.2	49.6	50.1	50.4	50.7	50.6	50.6	50.6	51.2	51.8	50.3
2008	51.0	51.0	51.2	50.9	51.1	51.2	50.7	50.3	49.9	49.7	49.5	49.7	50.5
2009	49.1	48.8	48.3	47.6	47.3	46.8	46.2	46.1	45.8	45.5	45.9	45.7	46.9
2010	45.4	46.3	45.5	44.8	44.7	44.8	44.7	44.3	44.3	44.9	45.1	45.3	45.0
2011	44.3	44.1	44.1	44.0	44.1	44.4	44.3	44.2	43.9	43.6	43.8	44.4	44.1
Financial Activities													
2000	140.2	140.2	140.4	140.3	140.8	141.9	141.3	141.0	140.7	139.9	140.0	140.7	140.6
2001	137.7	138.0	138.6	138.6	138.8	139.9	139.4	139.3	138.3	137.7	137.8	137.6	138.5
2002	137.2	137.6	137.9	137.7	138.2	138.9	138.2	138.5	137.6	138.0	138.8	139.1	138.1
2003	137.9	137.9	138.5	138.8	139.4	140.1	140.5	140.9	140.2	140.4	141.2	142.0	139.8
2004	140.6	140.4	140.8	141.0	141.5	142.0	142.3	142.5	142.1	142.8	143.1	144.0	141.9
2005	141.3	141.7	142.4	142.9	143.4	144.3	143.9	144.1	144.0	143.5	143.7	144.1	143.3
2006	142.5	142.8	143.5	143.1	143.6	144.3	143.7	144.2	143.7	143.2	143.5	144.2	143.5
2007	142.0	142.8	143.8	143.8	145.0	146.1	145.8	146.0	145.5	145.2	145.6	146.3	144.8
2008	144.5	144.9	145.2	145.1	145.6	146.3	145.8	145.7	144.9	144.3	144.1	144.0	145.0
2009	141.8	141.6	141.1	141.1	141.5	141.2	140.3	140.6	139.6	139.1	139.4	139.6	140.6
2010	137.7	137.6	137.5	138.6	138.5	137.9	137.5	137.3	135.9	135.6	135.7	135.6	137.1
2011	134.8	134.7	134.7	135.2	136.0	135.9	136.1	136.2	135.9	135.6	135.6	134.8	135.5

1. Employment by Industry: Tennessee, Selected Years, 2000–2011—*Continued*

(Numbers in thousands, not seasonally adjusted)

Industry and year	January	February	March	April	May	June	July	August	September	October	November	December	Annual average
Professional and Business Services													
2000	295.4	298.7	302.7	302.2	302.5	304.8	304.2	308.4	310.4	307.2	305.7	305.6	304.0
2001	299.2	300.5	301.0	299.8	298.3	298.7	296.2	299.4	301.2	297.9	297.4	299.8	299.1
2002	292.3	293.4	297.3	297.4	297.4	297.6	297.8	300.4	298.6	296.2	295.8	293.4	296.5
2003	281.3	282.2	284.0	284.0	286.0	286.7	282.8	288.9	290.9	292.6	294.8	295.5	287.5
2004	288.5	291.8	294.5	299.2	298.9	301.7	301.5	306.5	307.4	312.4	313.6	314.4	302.5
2005	300.6	304.4	306.5	309.9	308.7	310.6	308.3	315.1	319.6	319.8	322.6	325.6	312.6
2006	310.9	311.3	314.9	316.2	316.0	319.6	315.4	321.6	324.3	321.9	327.2	329.1	319.0
2007	310.8	312.6	316.0	318.0	319.3	322.6	321.9	326.5	328.6	328.2	332.7	333.7	322.6
2008	318.1	319.3	321.2	325.0	324.1	327.4	317.8	321.2	322.1	321.3	319.4	316.2	321.1
2009	297.9	296.8	294.1	291.0	291.0	290.7	284.5	289.5	291.4	297.3	302.0	301.1	293.9
2010	291.6	293.8	297.1	300.0	307.7	306.3	301.0	304.7	307.4	311.2	313.7	314.3	304.1
2011	304.5	311.2	315.4	319.1	318.9	320.4	321.0	328.1	328.0	330.4	330.7	334.6	321.9
Education and Health Services													
2000	274.2	276.9	279.5	280.9	279.8	278.8	279.1	280.2	285.4	287.3	288.5	288.8	281.6
2001	278.0	281.7	283.6	284.7	285.0	284.0	284.4	286.0	289.5	289.9	291.0	291.9	285.8
2002	288.7	291.2	293.8	296.3	297.8	297.6	299.7	301.8	306.3	307.7	309.6	310.5	300.1
2003	307.2	310.5	311.3	312.7	312.3	311.3	310.1	311.6	314.8	316.9	316.9	317.5	312.8
2004	313.6	316.5	318.6	319.4	318.8	318.5	320.7	322.2	323.5	324.9	326.0	326.6	320.8
2005	323.1	325.2	325.9	329.6	329.5	329.1	330.0	331.7	334.0	334.3	335.2	335.8	330.3
2006	332.6	334.3	336.5	338.9	339.6	339.9	340.1	341.9	344.7	345.5	346.6	347.2	340.7
2007	342.7	345.7	347.4	347.4	348.0	347.6	349.4	352.1	354.9	353.9	354.3	355.0	349.9
2008	351.1	353.3	354.4	356.6	357.2	356.8	357.2	360.0	362.4	364.3	365.5	366.2	358.8
2009	361.0	362.3	362.3	365.5	364.8	365.4	364.9	365.3	368.4	369.7	370.5	371.0	365.9
2010	366.4	368.2	370.1	374.1	371.8	370.4	372.0	373.5	377.3	380.6	381.2	381.4	373.9
2011	376.0	379.9	380.7	381.9	382.1	380.8	380.6	383.1	386.2	389.1	389.6	387.7	383.1
Leisure and Hospitality													
2000	218.3	219.4	224.1	233.9	240.2	247.0	247.1	247.4	243.7	237.4	235.9	234.1	235.7
2001	219.0	220.8	228.0	236.5	242.1	247.6	245.4	246.3	240.9	235.4	232.9	231.3	235.5
2002	220.6	223.1	228.9	239.0	243.1	248.7	250.8	252.3	247.4	242.3	241.2	239.7	239.8
2003	229.9	231.6	238.2	247.0	252.6	257.6	255.6	256.6	252.2	247.0	246.2	245.0	246.6
2004	234.8	237.6	244.7	254.6	259.0	262.7	263.2	264.7	261.0	254.9	253.9	252.7	253.7
2005	243.0	244.8	252.0	263.6	268.0	273.4	272.9	272.9	269.3	263.1	261.8	259.6	262.0
2006	252.7	254.3	262.7	270.2	275.3	280.2	280.8	280.8	276.1	270.9	269.0	268.6	270.1
2007	258.9	260.5	268.9	276.2	281.2	288.3	285.9	288.2	281.7	276.0	275.5	274.1	276.3
2008	262.4	264.3	270.7	276.6	282.2	285.1	283.1	282.5	277.4	269.3	267.2	264.4	273.8
2009	253.2	253.0	259.1	266.0	271.8	275.5	271.8	270.6	265.4	259.7	258.8	256.9	263.5
2010	247.2	247.4	254.5	263.7	267.7	274.2	270.9	270.3	265.8	262.7	261.3	258.0	262.0
2011	249.0	251.5	259.0	267.9	273.3	277.7	277.3	274.5	268.3	265.5	264.8	260.7	265.8
Other Services													
2000	86.9	87.9	89.4	91.6	92.3	92.7	92.8	96.8	98.1	100.9	102.8	103.6	94.7
2001	99.2	101.1	101.4	101.4	102.1	103.5	100.9	101.1	101.6	100.5	100.5	99.8	101.1
2002	98.6	99.6	100.2	100.2	101.4	102.7	103.0	102.2	102.9	102.9	102.7	102.8	101.6
2003	101.5	101.3	102.2	102.6	103.2	103.4	102.5	102.1	102.1	101.7	101.7	101.7	102.2
2004	100.8	101.5	102.8	102.0	102.0	102.8	102.4	102.0	101.4	101.0	101.0	100.6	101.7
2005	99.0	99.8	101.3	101.4	101.3	102.4	101.5	100.8	100.9	100.0	100.5	99.9	100.7
2006	98.7	99.4	100.8	100.8	101.9	104.0	102.9	102.8	102.9	102.1	102.2	102.5	101.8
2007	101.7	102.3	104.2	103.9	105.1	106.2	104.5	104.4	103.9	103.9	103.9	103.8	104.0
2008	103.2	104.4	105.3	104.8	106.0	106.4	105.1	104.7	103.9	103.9	103.3	103.0	104.5
2009	101.3	101.7	102.5	102.6	102.7	104.0	103.0	102.1	101.2	101.2	101.4	100.5	102.0
2010	98.5	98.9	99.9	99.9	100.7	102.5	102.4	102.2	101.8	102.4	102.4	102.8	101.2
2011	99.7	100.4	101.2	101.4	102.0	103.4	101.5	101.0	101.8	101.9	101.8	100.7	101.4
Government													
2000	390.1	398.2	418.9	403.3	408.0	392.5	378.2	388.0	396.2	403.6	405.3	405.8	399.0
2001	398.2	407.1	409.1	409.9	407.5	394.0	380.5	391.4	404.7	410.1	413.4	412.1	403.2
2002	406.4	414.8	416.8	419.2	415.1	405.6	386.2	395.8	409.1	415.7	419.0	419.4	410.3
2003	408.4	415.3	417.6	420.2	417.7	404.5	388.9	398.4	411.6	416.0	417.0	417.7	411.1
2004	411.1	433.1	421.1	420.7	417.5	407.5	391.8	402.5	415.3	419.0	421.2	421.9	415.2
2005	410.2	417.7	419.0	416.6	415.1	399.8	392.0	401.5	418.3	420.0	421.6	420.7	412.7
2006	412.0	417.6	420.3	422.1	420.6	404.4	398.0	410.1	422.8	423.8	426.3	425.2	416.9
2007	418.1	422.5	425.3	422.7	423.3	405.2	400.3	414.5	427.7	431.4	433.3	431.1	421.3
2008	424.7	430.1	432.4	433.3	433.9	405.7	405.9	419.0	430.6	438.8	440.0	438.6	427.8
2009	427.9	432.7	434.5	436.1	435.2	403.7	404.6	417.1	431.6	440.0	441.1	437.7	428.5
2010	430.6	434.9	436.8	440.8	449.8	413.6	409.0	421.1	438.3	440.5	441.2	438.1	432.9
2011	431.2	436.5	437.6	436.8	433.4	402.9	401.7	420.4	439.8	447.2	448.6	446.3	431.9

2. Average Weekly Hours by Selected Industry: Tennessee, 2007–2011

(Not seasonally adjusted)

Industry and year	January	February	March	April	May	June	July	August	September	October	November	December	Annual average
Total Private													
2007	34.8	35.2	35.3	35.2	35.2	35.4	35.3	35.2	35.6	35.3	35.1	35.5	35.3
2008	34.8	34.8	35.2	35.0	35.2	35.8	35.1	35.4	35.1	35.3	35.5	35.0	35.2
2009	34.6	35.2	34.9	34.7	35.0	35.3	35.1	35.7	35.1	35.5	35.8	35.4	35.2
2010	35.0	35.0	35.2	35.5	35.7	35.5	35.5	35.6	35.0	35.2	35.2	35.0	35.3
2011	34.5	34.8	35.3	35.2	35.5	35.3	35.1	35.3	35.0	35.6	35.0	35.2	35.2
Goods-Producing													
2007	38.1	39.1	39.3	39.2	39.9	39.4	38.8	40.2	39.9	39.6	39.7	38.9	39.3
2008	38.5	38.5	38.8	39.0	39.3	40.1	39.1	39.8	39.5	39.3	39.4	38.8	39.2
2009	37.9	38.6	38.4	38.7	38.9	40.0	39.8	40.6	40.0	40.5	41.0	40.7	39.6
2010	40.7	40.2	40.9	41.8	41.6	41.6	41.0	41.6	41.2	41.8	41.8	41.0	41.3
2011	39.7	40.6	41.5	41.0	40.9	41.3	40.3	41.3	41.0	41.4	41.3	41.4	41.0
Mining, Logging, and Construction													
2007	35.9	36.4	37.6	37.2	37.9	38.0	37.6	38.2	38.8	38.9	38.5	37.1	37.7
2008	36.4	37.5	37.3	37.8	37.5	38.6	37.9	38.4	38.1	38.0	37.6	36.1	37.6
2009	36.3	36.4	36.6	36.4	36.4	37.4	37.5	38.0	36.3	35.9	36.8	36.4	36.7
2010	35.5	34.3	35.9	37.1	37.4	37.8	37.2	38.5	37.5	38.3	38.2	36.9	37.1
2011	35.1	36.9	37.6	38.6	39.6	39.9	39.4	40.0	39.0	39.4	39.3	38.9	38.7
Manufacturing													
2007	38.8	40.0	39.9	39.9	40.6	39.9	39.2	41.0	40.3	39.9	40.1	39.5	39.9
2008	39.2	38.8	39.3	39.5	39.9	40.7	39.5	40.3	40.0	39.8	40.1	39.8	39.7
2009	38.5	39.3	39.0	39.5	39.8	41.0	40.7	41.6	41.3	42.1	42.5	42.2	40.6
2010	42.4	42.2	42.6	43.5	43.1	43.0	42.4	42.8	42.5	43.0	43.1	42.4	42.7
2011	41.2	41.9	42.8	41.8	41.4	41.8	40.6	41.8	41.8	42.2	42.1	42.3	41.8
Trade, Transportation, and Utilities													
2007	35.4	35.5	35.8	34.9	34.8	35.2	34.9	34.7	35.0	34.7	34.3	34.9	35.0
2008	34.6	34.3	34.7	34.2	34.7	35.2	34.6	34.7	34.8	35.1	35.7	35.5	34.8
2009	34.9	35.7	35.3	34.7	35.0	34.9	34.5	35.0	35.4	36.2	35.9	36.0	35.3
2010	35.5	35.6	35.5	35.6	35.8	35.6	35.8	36.1	35.6	35.4	35.6	35.6	35.6
2011	34.6	35.1	35.5	35.5	35.8	35.8	35.6	35.7	34.5	34.7	34.2	34.8	35.2
Information													
2007	34.9	36.9	35.8	35.4	35.5	35.7	36.4	34.9	35.5	35.6	37.2	36.4	35.9
2008	35.5	35.9	35.8	36.1	36.3	36.3	35.8	36.1	36.0	37.3	36.9	35.6	36.1
2009	35.9	37.2	37.0	36.4	36.6	36.6	36.8	37.8	36.8	36.5	37.1	36.7	36.8
2010	36.0	36.5	36.0	36.2	36.8	36.9	37.0	37.3	36.9	36.9	37.0	37.0	36.7
2011	37.2	37.5	37.0	37.6	38.0	37.5	37.2	37.5	37.4	38.1	37.1	36.9	37.4
Financial Activities													
2007	37.3	37.6	38.1	38.4	37.5	38.1	38.8	37.8	39.0	37.6	37.2	38.5	38.0
2008	37.6	37.2	37.6	37.2	36.7	37.4	36.8	37.1	36.6	36.7	37.4	37.1	37.1
2009	37.1	37.5	37.3	36.5	36.9	37.0	37.1	38.1	36.8	37.0	37.4	36.7	37.1
2010	36.4	36.2	36.2	36.6	37.8	37.0	37.4	38.6	37.5	37.4	37.1	37.1	37.1
2011	37.7	36.7	36.4	36.6	37.5	37.0	36.9	37.1	37.0	38.3	37.2	37.1	37.1
Professional and Business Services													
2007	35.1	35.0	35.9	36.1	36.0	36.3	36.5	36.2	36.8	36.5	35.9	37.8	36.2
2008	36.5	36.6	37.3	36.6	37.4	37.3	37.0	37.6	36.7	37.1	37.4	36.6	37.0
2009	36.2	36.9	36.3	35.9	37.6	37.8	36.9	37.9	36.7	36.7	37.5	36.6	36.9
2010	36.0	36.3	36.3	36.7	36.9	36.2	36.4	36.9	36.2	36.4	36.4	36.1	36.4
2011	36.0	36.0	36.4	36.4	36.8	36.3	35.9	36.1	36.4	36.5	35.5	35.6	36.2
Education and Health Services													
2007	33.4	34.2	33.5	33.8	34.0	34.4	34.3	33.9	34.5	33.9	34.1	34.7	34.1
2008	33.6	34.2	34.4	34.2	34.1	34.7	34.5	34.5	34.2	34.0	34.3	33.4	34.2
2009	34.3	34.3	34.4	34.2	34.0	34.2	34.6	35.0	34.4	34.6	34.6	33.8	34.4
2010	33.7	33.3	33.6	34.0	34.5	34.3	34.6	32.9	32.8	33.0	33.0	33.0	33.6
2011	33.4	33.1	33.5	33.9	34.4	34.0	34.5	34.1	34.2	34.9	34.3	34.5	34.1
Leisure and Hospitality													
2007	27.4	27.4	27.4	27.9	27.3	28.3	28.3	27.3	27.2	27.5	27.3	26.9	27.5
2008	26.2	26.5	26.5	27.1	26.8	27.8	26.7	26.7	26.2	26.9	26.5	26.2	26.7
2009	25.7	26.8	26.7	26.6	26.7	27.4	27.2	27.1	26.4	26.6	26.6	26.3	26.7
2010	25.6	26.4	26.7	26.6	26.3	26.8	26.8	26.7	25.6	25.8	25.6	25.2	26.2
2011	24.6	25.8	26.2	26.4	26.1	26.2	26.1	26.3	25.9	27.1	26.2	26.3	26.1
Other Services													
2007	33.0	33.3	33.5	33.5	33.0	33.6	34.1	32.6	35.7	34.6	34.6	35.5	33.9
2008	35.4	34.6	35.7	35.1	35.8	36.4	35.5	35.9	35.3	35.5	35.7	34.9	35.5
2009	33.5	33.5	33.4	33.6	33.1	33.2	32.8	34.2	32.1	32.5	33.4	33.0	33.2
2010	33.0	32.7	33.1	33.3	33.6	33.2	32.9	33.1	32.8	33.3	33.2	32.5	33.1
2011	32.2	32.3	32.9	32.4	32.9	32.1	32.4	32.1	31.8	33.6	32.8	33.3	32.6

3. Average Hourly Earnings by Selected Industry: Tennessee, 2007–2011

(Dollars, not seasonally adjusted)

Industry and year	January	February	March	April	May	June	July	August	September	October	November	December	Annual average
Total Private													
2007	18.98	19.04	19.03	19.14	18.78	18.92	19.09	18.88	19.15	18.85	18.91	19.33	19.01
2008	19.35	19.43	19.23	19.11	19.34	19.36	19.47	19.39	19.48	19.46	19.62	19.60	19.40
2009	19.41	19.65	19.59	19.50	19.39	19.39	19.47	19.60	19.65	19.53	19.59	19.50	19.52
2010	19.54	19.78	19.74	19.79	19.84	19.74	19.88	20.06	20.18	20.23	20.18	20.26	19.94
2011	20.52	20.34	20.15	20.12	20.08	19.92	20.13	20.07	20.25	20.48	20.17	20.24	20.20
Goods-Producing													
2007	19.64	19.07	19.42	19.38	18.98	19.03	19.52	19.41	19.59	19.68	19.59	20.19	19.46
2008	20.21	20.44	20.28	19.75	20.04	19.77	19.81	19.91	19.98	19.96	20.10	20.06	20.02
2009	20.04	20.51	20.51	20.69	20.56	20.86	20.98	21.24	21.42	21.30	21.25	21.01	20.86
2010	21.15	21.44	21.45	21.34	21.52	21.45	21.63	21.54	21.76	21.73	21.73	22.17	21.58
2011	22.33	22.00	21.98	21.45	21.43	21.28	21.14	21.09	20.85	20.74	20.79	20.95	21.32
Mining, Logging, and Construction													
2007	18.49	18.32	18.14	17.92	18.04	18.25	18.65	18.91	19.27	19.95	19.08	19.39	18.72
2008	19.19	19.50	19.48	19.32	19.45	19.31	19.21	19.01	19.29	19.27	19.15	19.42	19.30
2009	19.71	19.78	20.00	20.12	20.18	20.01	19.95	20.29	20.24	20.49	20.07	20.37	20.10
2010	20.62	20.71	20.38	19.99	20.24	20.17	20.01	19.99	20.21	20.30	20.15	20.56	20.26
2011	21.01	20.76	20.63	20.45	20.15	20.34	20.34	20.19	20.23	20.37	20.67	20.84	20.48
Manufacturing													
2007	20.00	19.30	19.84	19.87	19.30	19.30	19.83	19.58	19.70	19.58	19.78	20.47	19.71
2008	20.55	20.77	20.56	19.90	20.24	19.93	20.02	20.23	20.22	20.21	20.43	20.27	20.28
2009	20.15	20.74	20.68	20.87	20.69	21.15	21.33	21.55	21.79	21.55	21.61	21.21	21.11
2010	21.29	21.63	21.75	21.75	21.91	21.85	22.14	22.04	22.25	22.19	22.23	22.66	21.98
2011	22.70	22.36	22.39	21.78	21.87	21.61	21.43	21.41	21.07	20.87	20.83	20.99	21.60
Trade, Transportation, and Utilities													
2007	17.90	18.21	18.82	18.84	18.32	19.09	18.79	18.09	18.27	17.84	17.83	17.97	18.33
2008	18.00	18.36	18.12	18.14	18.71	18.92	19.32	19.00	19.14	18.97	19.13	19.46	18.77
2009	19.01	19.10	19.06	19.01	18.67	18.54	18.60	18.60	18.35	17.99	18.05	17.96	18.58
2010	17.76	18.20	18.41	18.60	18.52	18.45	18.64	18.55	18.50	18.53	18.41	18.34	18.41
2011	18.77	18.28	18.24	18.38	18.22	18.00	18.50	18.30	18.55	18.76	18.20	18.27	18.37
Information													
2007	19.94	20.26	20.10	20.98	20.65	20.09	20.18	21.07	21.40	21.01	21.32	20.93	20.67
2008	20.73	20.51	20.75	20.60	20.47	20.94	21.01	21.20	21.43	21.67	22.06	22.17	21.12
2009	22.46	23.05	22.82	22.35	22.86	22.70	22.43	23.53	23.18	23.36	23.51	23.24	22.95
2010	23.12	23.45	23.28	23.32	24.06	23.53	23.90	24.10	24.61	24.45	24.65	24.61	23.93
2011	24.68	24.31	23.72	23.40	23.61	23.48	23.93	23.23	23.04	23.89	24.11	23.19	23.72
Financial Activities													
2007	21.11	21.77	20.61	21.57	20.79	20.55	21.82	21.52	21.36	21.49	21.11	21.59	21.28
2008	21.11	20.78	20.90	20.89	20.63	20.72	20.67	20.72	20.83	21.20	21.47	21.11	20.92
2009	21.35	21.89	21.63	21.24	21.26	21.24	21.20	21.25	21.17	21.39	21.43	21.33	21.37
2010	21.46	21.71	21.74	22.19	22.01	22.24	22.09	22.65	22.51	22.78	22.59	22.57	22.21
2011	22.88	23.11	22.86	22.91	22.96	22.77	23.37	23.55	23.36	23.67	23.28	23.47	23.18
Professional and Business Services													
2007	22.38	22.71	21.91	22.16	22.12	21.87	22.56	22.38	23.01	22.37	23.01	23.40	22.50
2008	23.90	23.06	22.92	23.05	22.91	23.07	23.18	22.94	22.97	22.61	22.69	22.24	22.96
2009	22.39	22.92	22.79	22.52	22.33	22.29	22.63	22.26	22.47	22.28	22.35	22.55	22.48
2010	22.74	22.96	22.70	22.65	22.98	22.75	23.10	23.03	23.13	23.13	23.17	23.18	22.96
2011	23.36	23.80	23.43	23.96	24.24	24.04	24.23	24.02	24.55	25.38	24.86	24.76	24.23
Education and Health Services													
2007	21.08	20.87	20.58	20.53	20.25	20.57	19.94	20.08	20.27	19.92	19.97	20.40	20.37
2008	20.42	20.63	20.21	20.17	20.38	20.58	20.34	20.33	20.45	20.72	20.82	20.91	20.50
2009	20.38	20.48	20.67	20.59	20.65	20.69	20.58	20.77	21.06	20.98	21.03	21.00	20.74
2010	21.07	21.21	21.05	21.24	20.83	20.96	21.01	22.04	22.25	22.35	22.09	22.02	21.51
2011	21.99	21.90	21.60	21.65	21.31	21.29	21.49	21.36	21.64	21.54	21.15	21.22	21.51
Leisure and Hospitality													
2007	10.74	11.19	11.02	11.32	11.22	11.14	11.55	11.24	11.73	10.80	10.77	11.22	11.17
2008	10.98	11.17	11.00	11.32	11.52	11.72	11.72	11.60	11.60	11.62	11.75	11.88	11.49
2009	11.27	11.33	11.27	11.22	11.42	11.35	11.46	11.95	11.87	11.89	11.98	11.87	11.57
2010	11.87	11.86	11.60	11.40	11.63	11.46	11.55	11.65	11.55	11.51	11.67	11.65	11.61
2011	11.94	11.73	11.56	11.51	11.54	11.44	11.57	11.69	11.80	12.14	12.07	12.04	11.75
Other Services													
2007	17.31	17.42	17.38	17.45	16.97	16.67	16.37	16.54	16.25	16.62	16.70	17.31	16.91
2008	17.10	17.87	17.59	17.45	17.58	17.08	17.18	17.18	16.94	16.93	17.16	16.44	17.21
2009	16.61	16.49	16.25	16.41	16.27	16.19	16.38	16.26	16.16	16.34	16.46	16.51	16.36
2010	16.26	16.35	16.54	16.22	16.67	16.55	16.40	16.53	16.56	16.60	16.80	17.11	16.55
2011	16.99	17.21	17.07	16.99	17.17	17.24	17.05	17.45	17.49	18.47	18.20	18.64	17.50

4. Average Weekly Earnings by Selected Industry: Tennessee, 2007–2011

(Dollars, not seasonally adjusted)

Industry and year	January	February	March	April	May	June	July	August	September	October	November	December	Annual average
Total Private													
2007	660.50	670.21	671.76	673.73	661.06	669.77	673.88	664.58	681.74	665.41	663.74	686.22	670.09
2008	673.38	676.16	676.90	668.85	680.77	693.09	683.40	686.41	683.75	686.94	696.51	686.00	682.78
2009	671.59	691.68	683.69	676.65	678.65	684.47	683.40	699.72	689.72	693.32	701.32	690.30	686.92
2010	683.90	692.30	694.85	702.55	708.29	700.77	705.74	714.14	706.30	712.10	710.34	709.10	703.65
2011	707.94	707.83	711.30	708.22	712.84	703.18	706.56	708.47	708.75	729.09	705.95	712.45	710.39
Goods-Producing													
2007	748.28	745.64	763.21	759.70	757.30	749.78	757.38	780.28	781.64	779.33	777.72	785.39	765.20
2008	778.09	786.94	786.86	770.25	787.57	792.78	774.57	792.42	789.21	784.43	791.94	778.33	784.30
2009	759.52	791.69	787.58	800.70	799.78	834.40	835.00	862.34	856.80	862.65	871.25	855.11	825.49
2010	860.81	861.89	877.31	892.01	895.23	892.32	886.83	896.06	896.51	908.31	908.31	908.97	890.59
2011	886.50	893.20	912.17	879.45	876.49	878.86	851.94	871.02	854.85	858.64	858.63	867.33	873.88
Mining, Logging, and Construction													
2007	663.79	666.85	682.06	666.62	683.72	693.50	701.24	722.36	747.68	776.06	734.58	719.37	705.54
2008	698.52	731.25	726.60	730.30	729.38	745.37	728.06	729.98	734.95	732.26	720.04	701.06	725.87
2009	715.47	719.99	732.00	732.37	734.55	748.37	748.13	771.02	734.71	735.59	738.58	741.47	737.59
2010	732.01	710.35	731.64	741.63	756.98	762.43	744.37	769.62	757.88	777.49	769.73	758.66	751.77
2011	737.45	766.04	775.69	789.37	797.94	811.57	801.40	807.60	788.97	802.58	812.33	810.68	792.88
Manufacturing													
2007	776.00	772.00	791.62	792.81	783.58	770.07	777.34	802.78	793.91	781.24	793.18	808.57	786.85
2008	805.56	805.88	808.01	786.05	807.58	811.15	790.79	815.27	808.80	804.36	819.24	806.75	805.73
2009	775.78	815.08	806.52	824.37	823.46	867.15	868.13	896.48	899.93	907.26	918.43	895.06	856.73
2010	902.70	912.79	926.55	946.13	944.32	939.55	938.74	943.31	945.63	954.17	958.11	960.78	939.40
2011	935.24	936.88	958.29	910.40	905.42	903.30	870.06	894.94	880.73	880.71	876.94	887.88	903.06
Trade, Transportation, and Utilities													
2007	633.66	646.46	673.76	657.52	637.54	671.97	655.77	627.72	639.45	619.05	611.57	627.15	641.68
2008	622.80	629.75	628.76	620.39	649.24	665.98	668.47	659.30	666.07	665.85	682.94	690.83	654.09
2009	663.45	681.87	672.82	659.65	653.45	647.05	641.70	651.00	649.59	651.24	648.00	646.56	655.55
2010	630.48	647.92	653.56	662.16	663.02	656.82	667.31	669.66	658.60	655.96	655.40	652.90	656.17
2011	649.44	641.63	647.52	652.49	652.28	644.40	658.60	653.31	639.98	650.97	622.44	635.80	645.75
Information													
2007	695.91	747.59	719.58	742.69	733.08	717.21	734.55	735.34	759.70	747.96	793.10	761.85	740.96
2008	735.92	736.31	742.85	743.66	743.06	760.12	752.16	765.32	771.48	808.29	814.01	789.25	763.24
2009	806.31	857.46	844.34	813.54	836.68	830.82	825.42	889.43	853.02	852.64	872.22	852.91	844.17
2010	832.32	855.93	838.08	844.18	885.41	868.26	884.30	898.93	908.11	902.21	912.05	910.57	878.28
2011	918.10	911.63	877.64	879.84	897.18	880.50	890.20	871.13	861.70	910.21	894.48	855.71	887.36
Financial Activities													
2007	787.40	818.55	785.24	828.29	779.63	782.96	846.62	813.46	833.04	808.02	785.29	831.22	808.35
2008	793.74	773.02	785.84	777.11	757.12	774.93	760.66	768.71	762.38	778.04	802.98	783.18	776.44
2009	792.09	820.88	806.80	775.26	784.49	785.88	786.52	809.63	779.06	791.43	801.48	782.81	792.94
2010	781.14	785.90	786.99	812.15	831.98	822.88	826.17	874.29	844.13	851.97	838.09	837.35	824.29
2011	862.58	848.14	832.10	838.51	861.00	842.49	862.35	873.71	864.32	906.56	866.02	870.74	860.79
Professional and Business Services													
2007	785.54	794.85	786.57	799.98	796.32	793.88	823.44	810.16	846.77	816.51	826.06	884.52	814.21
2008	872.35	844.00	854.92	843.63	856.83	860.51	857.66	862.54	843.00	838.83	848.61	813.98	849.78
2009	810.52	845.75	827.28	808.47	839.61	842.56	835.05	843.65	824.65	817.68	838.13	825.33	829.86
2010	818.64	833.45	824.01	831.26	847.96	823.55	840.84	849.81	837.31	841.93	843.39	836.80	835.88
2011	840.96	856.80	852.85	872.14	892.03	872.65	869.86	867.12	893.62	926.37	882.53	881.46	876.17
Education and Health Services													
2007	704.07	713.75	689.43	693.91	688.50	707.61	683.94	680.71	699.32	675.29	680.98	707.88	693.73
2008	686.11	705.55	695.22	689.81	694.96	714.13	701.73	701.39	699.39	704.48	714.13	698.39	700.49
2009	699.03	702.46	711.05	704.18	702.10	707.60	712.07	726.95	724.46	725.91	727.64	709.80	712.82
2010	710.06	706.29	707.28	722.16	718.64	718.93	726.95	725.12	729.80	737.55	728.97	726.66	721.68
2011	734.47	724.89	723.60	733.94	733.06	723.86	741.41	728.38	740.09	751.75	725.45	732.09	732.76
Leisure and Hospitality													
2007	294.28	306.61	301.95	315.83	306.31	315.26	326.87	306.85	319.06	297.00	294.02	301.82	307.35
2008	287.68	296.01	291.50	306.77	308.74	325.82	312.92	309.72	303.92	312.58	311.38	311.26	306.70
2009	289.64	303.64	300.91	298.45	304.91	310.99	311.71	323.85	313.37	316.27	318.67	312.18	308.83
2010	303.87	313.10	309.72	303.24	305.87	307.13	309.54	311.06	295.68	296.96	298.75	293.58	304.02
2011	293.72	302.63	302.87	303.86	301.19	299.73	301.98	307.45	305.62	328.99	316.23	316.65	306.76
Other Services													
2007	571.23	580.09	582.23	584.58	560.01	560.11	558.22	539.20	580.13	575.05	577.82	614.51	573.53
2008	605.34	618.30	627.96	612.50	629.36	621.71	609.89	616.76	597.98	601.02	612.61	573.76	610.71
2009	556.44	552.42	542.75	551.38	538.54	537.26	537.26	556.09	518.74	531.05	549.76	544.83	543.05
2010	536.58	534.65	547.47	540.13	560.11	549.46	539.56	547.14	543.17	552.78	557.76	556.08	547.13
2011	547.08	555.88	561.60	550.48	564.89	553.40	552.42	560.15	556.18	620.59	596.96	620.71	569.97

TEXAS
At a Glance

Population:
   2000 census: 20,851,028
   2010 census: 25,145,561
   2011 estimate: 25,674,681

Percent change in population:
   2000–2010: 20.6%
   2010–2011: 2.1%

Percent change in total nonfarm employment:
   2000–2010: 9.6%
   2010–2011: 2.1%

Industry with the largest growth in employment, 2000–2011 (thousands):
   Education and Health Services, 419.6

Industry with the largest decline or smallest growth in employment, 2000–2011 (thousands):
   Manufacturing, -231.8

Civilian labor force:
   2000: 10,347,847
   2010: 12,269,727
   2011: 12,451,504

Unemployment rate and rank among states (lowest to highest):
   2000: 4.4%, 37th
   2010: 8.2%, 21st
   2011: 7.9%, 23rd

Over-the-year change in unemployment rates:
   2010–2011: -0.3%

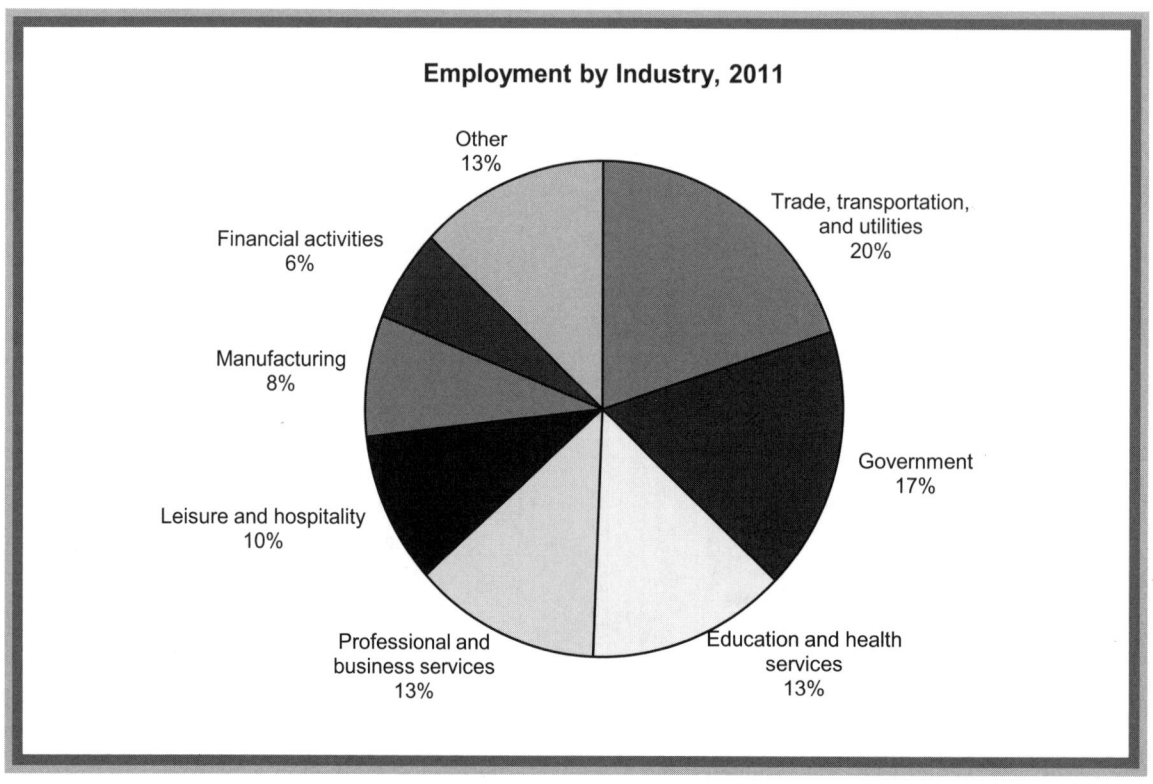

Employment by Industry, 2011

- Other 13%
- Trade, transportation, and utilities 20%
- Financial activities 6%
- Government 17%
- Manufacturing 8%
- Leisure and hospitality 10%
- Education and health services 13%
- Professional and business services 13%

1. Employment by Industry: Texas, Selected Years, 2000–2011

(Numbers in thousands, not seasonally adjusted)

Industry and year	January	February	March	April	May	June	July	August	September	October	November	December	Annual average
Total Nonfarm													
2000	9,195.5	9,275.1	9,357.0	9,369.8	9,444.6	9,472.4	9,388.0	9,455.5	9,521.5	9,522.2	9,564.5	9,614.1	9,431.7
2001	9,423.4	9,493.2	9,550.0	9,547.5	9,574.6	9,583.4	9,460.8	9,511.2	9,532.1	9,488.6	9,498.4	9,502.6	9,513.8
2002	9,306.0	9,360.0	9,417.2	9,423.0	9,469.0	9,451.9	9,347.7	9,400.8	9,450.5	9,428.7	9,461.3	9,472.9	9,415.8
2003	9,280.6	9,326.8	9,360.9	9,374.3	9,402.1	9,379.8	9,281.2	9,336.8	9,394.5	9,403.8	9,432.2	9,465.1	9,369.8
2004	9,306.7	9,371.4	9,433.7	9,480.1	9,506.5	9,506.9	9,450.3	9,496.0	9,545.2	9,584.7	9,621.0	9,658.2	9,496.7
2005	9,492.3	9,563.1	9,633.2	9,700.0	9,730.0	9,735.7	9,696.9	9,750.5	9,833.0	9,845.9	9,925.7	9,967.5	9,739.5
2006	9,808.6	9,891.2	9,979.8	10,004.0	10,059.6	10,088.7	9,992.9	10,072.1	10,157.0	10,176.3	10,247.9	10,297.5	10,064.6
2007	10,110.0	10,210.5	10,305.8	10,337.0	10,395.9	10,433.9	10,350.4	10,402.8	10,456.9	10,512.0	10,582.3	10,616.9	10,392.9
2008	10,437.3	10,532.9	10,577.3	10,607.2	10,654.3	10,654.6	10,571.0	10,609.6	10,606.8	10,657.8	10,678.7	10,667.0	10,604.5
2009	10,400.8	10,396.5	10,392.1	10,351.8	10,352.8	10,319.1	10,197.3	10,189.3	10,215.4	10,254.8	10,285.3	10,298.2	10,304.5
2010	10,115.6	10,175.3	10,263.9	10,314.7	10,396.2	10,394.2	10,295.0	10,320.9	10,364.0	10,443.6	10,489.3	10,517.9	10,340.9
2011	10,325.6	10,390.7	10,486.7	10,556.2	10,576.4	10,601.8	10,545.5	10,550.0	10,595.8	10,653.6	10,697.8	10,707.3	10,557.3
Total Private													
2000	7,648.4	7,698.9	7,773.1	7,785.5	7,837.1	7,935.4	7,912.8	7,955.8	7,957.1	7,938.5	7,972.1	8,022.3	7,869.8
2001	7,857.7	7,898.5	7,950.0	7,946.3	7,972.6	8,023.7	7,966.6	7,988.4	7,929.0	7,864.5	7,862.1	7,871.8	7,927.6
2002	7,700.6	7,722.0	7,772.1	7,778.3	7,821.6	7,852.3	7,817.4	7,850.0	7,818.0	7,760.6	7,783.4	7,801.3	7,789.8
2003	7,637.8	7,649.0	7,684.8	7,696.9	7,724.9	7,747.7	7,725.8	7,766.3	7,752.3	7,739.7	7,758.9	7,801.4	7,723.8
2004	7,666.5	7,697.0	7,757.6	7,803.4	7,827.9	7,870.3	7,882.5	7,910.0	7,883.6	7,900.2	7,927.5	7,970.1	7,841.4
2005	7,826.3	7,862.9	7,930.7	7,995.4	8,023.7	8,076.0	8,100.2	8,132.9	8,143.6	8,131.0	8,198.9	8,253.2	8,056.2
2006	8,113.3	8,163.5	8,251.0	8,278.8	8,333.7	8,406.2	8,385.3	8,438.8	8,447.2	8,436.7	8,499.5	8,556.7	8,359.2
2007	8,395.4	8,464.2	8,553.2	8,585.2	8,641.2	8,718.5	8,706.0	8,749.3	8,727.6	8,743.2	8,798.6	8,837.6	8,660.0
2008	8,677.9	8,741.6	8,777.9	8,814.5	8,857.7	8,893.3	8,879.6	8,910.9	8,835.8	8,851.2	8,853.0	8,846.9	8,828.4
2009	8,599.7	8,567.2	8,556.0	8,506.7	8,508.2	8,510.7	8,465.3	8,461.3	8,410.4	8,398.8	8,416.7	8,437.6	8,486.6
2010	8,283.0	8,310.3	8,386.4	8,425.6	8,472.7	8,520.2	8,513.4	8,548.5	8,532.6	8,569.2	8,604.2	8,646.1	8,484.4
2011	8,485.4	8,526.0	8,621.6	8,691.2	8,718.8	8,778.2	8,801.8	8,825.2	8,821.9	8,853.8	8,888.1	8,906.0	8,743.2
Goods-Producing													
2000	1,737.3	1,753.3	1,771.5	1,763.5	1,774.2	1,797.0	1,790.0	1,794.1	1,794.7	1,785.1	1,782.1	1,785.3	1,777.3
2001	1,765.6	1,778.5	1,787.3	1,775.9	1,777.1	1,784.6	1,767.1	1,768.6	1,752.0	1,731.2	1,718.3	1,705.7	1,759.3
2002	1,672.4	1,673.1	1,679.6	1,668.8	1,673.4	1,680.3	1,667.4	1,670.0	1,657.8	1,639.3	1,630.0	1,621.5	1,661.1
2003	1,600.5	1,600.7	1,600.3	1,600.0	1,605.3	1,609.0	1,600.1	1,603.2	1,600.0	1,589.5	1,580.5	1,582.1	1,597.6
2004	1,565.5	1,568.7	1,577.3	1,580.6	1,583.1	1,593.7	1,596.5	1,598.8	1,596.1	1,597.9	1,596.6	1,599.7	1,587.9
2005	1,583.7	1,591.8	1,605.5	1,615.9	1,620.9	1,635.0	1,642.4	1,645.4	1,650.9	1,648.1	1,655.0	1,664.2	1,629.9
2006	1,654.1	1,670.3	1,690.4	1,690.8	1,706.9	1,731.2	1,725.9	1,735.3	1,742.7	1,739.6	1,745.6	1,751.9	1,715.4
2007	1,733.0	1,750.5	1,766.9	1,772.3	1,783.5	1,807.1	1,799.9	1,808.6	1,807.0	1,812.6	1,818.0	1,819.0	1,789.9
2008	1,799.2	1,817.6	1,822.7	1,825.7	1,835.0	1,843.8	1,840.9	1,846.0	1,836.4	1,838.4	1,825.4	1,806.3	1,828.1
2009	1,750.9	1,727.1	1,700.5	1,661.6	1,645.9	1,633.6	1,615.2	1,608.6	1,594.7	1,582.2	1,571.9	1,569.0	1,638.4
2010	1,553.3	1,552.9	1,565.4	1,569.5	1,576.2	1,586.6	1,594.5	1,600.2	1,598.0	1,601.4	1,597.3	1,599.1	1,582.9
2011	1,578.5	1,590.3	1,605.8	1,615.1	1,621.9	1,642.6	1,648.0	1,654.3	1,655.6	1,653.0	1,654.1	1,652.3	1,631.0
Mining and Logging													
2000	140.6	140.5	141.5	139.5	140.6	142.2	143.3	144.1	144.6	146.1	146.3	149.4	143.2
2001	146.9	148.7	150.4	151.2	152.3	155.2	155.9	156.8	155.7	155.1	154.1	153.6	153.0
2002	147.7	146.8	146.0	144.5	145.3	146.2	144.9	145.5	145.5	143.7	143.8	144.1	145.3
2003	142.6	143.3	144.4	144.6	145.9	147.3	148.2	149.3	148.8	147.8	147.8	149.5	146.6
2004	149.2	149.3	150.6	150.2	151.2	152.9	153.8	154.6	154.6	155.6	156.3	157.5	153.0
2005	158.4	159.1	160.1	161.6	163.1	165.9	168.1	169.1	169.7	170.9	172.0	174.0	166.0
2006	173.2	175.6	177.5	179.3	181.4	185.9	188.0	190.3	192.5	194.3	195.5	197.1	185.9
2007	197.6	199.3	201.4	202.6	204.3	208.2	209.9	211.2	211.2	213.3	215.1	216.9	207.6
2008	218.6	221.6	222.9	224.4	226.5	230.7	233.6	235.9	236.0	238.8	237.8	235.8	230.2
2009	227.7	221.5	215.4	205.3	200.3	197.7	195.5	193.9	192.2	191.0	191.5	193.2	202.1
2010	193.2	195.4	197.6	200.6	203.1	206.9	208.6	210.9	211.7	213.9	215.0	217.7	206.2
2011	218.3	220.9	223.9	227.5	229.6	235.3	240.8	240.3	244.1	248.0	249.7	253.7	236.0
Construction													
2000	539.4	550.4	562.9	561.1	567.3	579.6	577.1	579.9	578.2	571.2	567.6	567.3	566.8
2001	564.2	575.5	584.4	581.4	586.5	591.5	586.2	590.4	583.7	576.5	574.1	568.5	580.2
2002	556.3	562.9	572.5	569.4	575.2	579.5	574.0	577.4	571.0	563.7	558.7	552.8	567.8
2003	545.5	547.1	549.7	551.0	557.9	559.4	555.5	558.5	556.3	551.9	543.5	543.4	551.6
2004	534.1	535.4	541.8	543.6	543.1	548.1	548.9	549.5	548.5	548.9	545.9	546.6	544.5
2005	540.1	545.5	555.3	564.6	565.9	570.6	573.6	574.8	579.3	576.6	577.9	581.1	567.1
2006	575.8	586.0	599.5	594.7	602.9	614.8	609.3	613.4	617.4	615.6	617.5	619.8	605.6
2007	609.2	622.2	635.2	637.7	644.9	657.9	652.2	658.7	659.4	665.3	668.5	666.3	648.1
2008	653.8	667.0	672.5	675.3	679.8	681.8	678.0	681.4	676.6	680.2	671.7	661.4	673.3
2009	634.0	627.8	620.5	606.9	603.8	602.1	595.6	591.0	582.0	576.2	569.3	565.0	597.9
2010	554.6	552.4	560.6	563.9	565.0	568.1	572.2	573.6	570.8	569.8	562.7	559.4	564.4
2011	543.5	549.4	557.6	559.5	561.6	569.4	566.0	567.8	567.1	560.6	558.1	553.0	559.5
Manufacturing													
2000	1,057.3	1,062.4	1,067.1	1,062.9	1,066.3	1,075.2	1,069.6	1,070.1	1,071.9	1,067.8	1,068.2	1,068.6	1,067.3
2001	1,054.5	1,054.3	1,052.5	1,043.3	1,038.3	1,037.9	1,025.0	1,021.4	1,012.6	999.6	990.1	983.6	1,026.1
2002	968.4	963.4	961.1	954.9	952.9	954.6	948.5	947.1	941.3	931.9	927.5	924.6	948.0
2003	912.4	910.3	906.2	904.4	901.5	902.3	896.4	895.4	894.9	889.8	889.2	889.2	899.3
2004	882.2	884.0	884.9	886.8	888.8	892.7	893.8	894.7	893.0	893.4	894.4	895.6	890.4
2005	885.2	887.2	890.1	889.7	891.9	898.5	900.7	901.5	901.9	900.6	905.1	909.1	896.8
2006	905.1	908.7	913.4	916.8	922.6	930.5	928.6	931.6	932.8	929.7	932.6	935.0	924.0
2007	926.2	929.0	930.3	932.0	934.3	941.0	937.8	938.0	936.4	934.0	934.4	935.8	934.1
2008	926.8	929.0	927.3	926.0	928.7	931.3	929.3	928.7	923.8	919.4	915.9	909.1	924.6
2009	889.2	877.8	864.6	849.4	841.8	833.8	824.1	823.7	820.5	815.0	811.1	810.8	838.5
2010	805.5	805.1	807.2	805.0	808.1	811.6	813.7	815.7	815.5	817.7	819.6	822.0	812.2
2011	816.7	820.0	824.3	828.1	830.7	837.9	841.2	846.2	844.4	844.4	846.3	845.6	835.5

1. Employment by Industry: Texas, Selected Years, 2000–2011—*Continued*

(Numbers in thousands, not seasonally adjusted)

Industry and year	January	February	March	April	May	June	July	August	September	October	November	December	Annual average
Service-Providing													
2000	7,458.2	7,521.8	7,585.5	7,606.3	7,670.4	7,675.4	7,598.0	7,661.4	7,726.8	7,737.1	7,782.4	7,828.8	7,654.3
2001	7,657.8	7,714.7	7,762.7	7,771.6	7,797.5	7,798.3	7,693.7	7,742.6	7,780.1	7,757.4	7,780.1	7,796.9	7,754.5
2002	7,633.6	7,686.9	7,737.6	7,754.2	7,795.6	7,771.6	7,680.3	7,730.8	7,792.7	7,789.4	7,831.3	7,851.4	7,754.6
2003	7,680.1	7,726.1	7,760.6	7,774.3	7,796.8	7,770.8	7,681.1	7,733.6	7,794.5	7,814.3	7,851.7	7,883.0	7,772.2
2004	7,741.2	7,802.7	7,856.4	7,899.5	7,923.4	7,913.2	7,853.8	7,897.2	7,949.1	7,986.8	8,024.4	8,058.5	7,908.9
2005	7,908.6	7,971.3	8,027.7	8,084.1	8,109.1	8,100.7	8,054.5	8,105.1	8,182.1	8,197.8	8,270.7	8,303.3	8,109.6
2006	8,154.5	8,220.9	8,289.4	8,313.2	8,352.7	8,357.5	8,267.0	8,336.8	8,414.3	8,436.7	8,502.3	8,545.6	8,349.2
2007	8,377.0	8,460.0	8,538.9	8,564.7	8,612.4	8,626.8	8,550.5	8,594.2	8,649.9	8,699.4	8,764.3	8,797.9	8,603.0
2008	8,638.1	8,715.3	8,754.6	8,781.5	8,819.3	8,810.8	8,730.1	8,763.6	8,770.4	8,819.4	8,853.3	8,860.7	8,776.4
2009	8,649.9	8,669.4	8,691.6	8,690.2	8,706.9	8,685.5	8,582.1	8,580.7	8,620.7	8,672.6	8,713.4	8,729.2	8,666.0
2010	8,562.3	8,622.4	8,698.5	8,745.2	8,820.0	8,807.6	8,700.5	8,720.7	8,766.0	8,842.2	8,892.0	8,918.8	8,758.0
2011	8,747.1	8,800.4	8,880.9	8,941.1	8,954.5	8,959.2	8,897.5	8,895.7	8,940.2	9,000.6	9,043.7	9,055.0	8,926.3
Trade, Transportation, and Utilities													
2000	1,942.2	1,938.4	1,945.0	1,942.9	1,954.0	1,974.7	1,967.7	1,986.4	1,980.9	1,992.0	2,029.3	2,064.0	1,976.5
2001	1,986.1	1,974.2	1,981.3	1,977.6	1,982.7	1,991.1	1,982.3	1,990.1	1,978.9	1,975.6	1,993.1	2,014.0	1,985.6
2002	1,944.8	1,932.4	1,939.5	1,937.8	1,945.6	1,950.2	1,945.3	1,950.0	1,942.4	1,937.5	1,964.9	1,989.7	1,948.3
2003	1,910.7	1,896.0	1,898.8	1,896.9	1,897.7	1,903.4	1,900.7	1,915.7	1,914.0	1,922.6	1,951.5	1,978.6	1,915.6
2004	1,913.6	1,907.7	1,917.9	1,925.5	1,931.9	1,935.8	1,941.6	1,956.1	1,945.8	1,956.9	1,990.0	2,018.0	1,945.1
2005	1,954.1	1,942.7	1,954.5	1,964.7	1,973.4	1,983.5	1,992.8	2,007.1	2,004.3	2,006.5	2,055.0	2,086.1	1,993.7
2006	2,013.7	2,004.8	2,022.0	2,022.9	2,031.7	2,040.4	2,039.5	2,056.4	2,054.2	2,062.6	2,104.0	2,135.6	2,049.0
2007	2,071.9	2,064.4	2,084.8	2,084.7	2,095.3	2,107.8	2,111.1	2,121.9	2,118.8	2,130.9	2,171.2	2,198.5	2,113.4
2008	2,129.7	2,124.1	2,132.0	2,127.5	2,133.2	2,142.1	2,143.8	2,157.0	2,136.7	2,142.2	2,166.1	2,182.6	2,143.1
2009	2,098.3	2,072.7	2,070.5	2,054.5	2,052.9	2,051.2	2,044.1	2,050.0	2,041.6	2,041.3	2,064.4	2,085.9	2,060.6
2010	2,019.8	2,009.1	2,023.9	2,027.7	2,038.1	2,047.2	2,048.2	2,060.2	2,053.0	2,067.8	2,101.6	2,129.7	2,052.2
2011	2,064.2	2,055.5	2,072.0	2,086.9	2,089.1	2,099.2	2,111.5	2,110.9	2,108.3	2,121.9	2,147.0	2,173.1	2,103.3
Wholesale Trade													
2000	459.4	461.5	462.9	463.6	465.5	470.2	470.6	471.3	472.2	471.3	472.6	475.1	468.0
2001	472.6	474.2	476.4	475.5	475.5	476.8	475.7	475.3	472.6	469.7	467.2	467.8	473.3
2002	460.6	460.4	463.0	461.4	463.0	465.1	465.0	465.6	464.7	462.6	463.5	464.4	463.3
2003	456.9	456.5	457.7	456.9	457.9	460.1	459.0	459.5	459.4	458.0	458.5	460.2	458.4
2004	454.7	455.4	457.9	460.1	461.6	463.9	466.1	466.5	466.1	467.7	468.3	469.7	463.2
2005	465.1	466.1	468.7	472.7	474.9	477.7	480.9	481.8	483.8	482.9	485.1	488.8	477.4
2006	485.4	488.2	492.1	492.6	495.5	499.9	499.1	501.3	503.1	503.1	505.9	509.2	498.0
2007	504.7	508.1	511.4	513.1	516.2	521.7	521.8	523.5	523.3	526.4	527.0	530.2	519.0
2008	525.0	527.4	527.6	529.0	530.4	532.6	531.6	532.2	529.2	529.1	527.2	526.2	529.0
2009	515.7	510.5	507.1	501.6	499.8	498.4	496.3	495.0	492.6	492.2	490.8	491.7	499.3
2010	489.3	489.6	490.9	492.7	495.2	498.1	499.0	500.0	499.7	500.9	501.7	503.8	496.7
2011	500.2	503.5	506.5	510.3	513.1	516.3	519.9	520.6	517.4	519.0	514.3	517.9	513.3
Retail Trade													
2000	1,086.0	1,078.2	1,083.3	1,080.6	1,088.0	1,100.1	1,093.4	1,108.0	1,100.7	1,111.1	1,145.1	1,171.7	1,103.9
2001	1,107.6	1,095.2	1,100.3	1,099.0	1,102.1	1,107.8	1,100.7	1,107.1	1,099.9	1,099.8	1,125.6	1,147.0	1,107.7
2002	1,093.7	1,082.7	1,087.6	1,087.9	1,092.0	1,093.5	1,087.3	1,089.3	1,084.8	1,080.1	1,107.4	1,130.7	1,093.1
2003	1,065.8	1,053.0	1,055.0	1,054.5	1,055.7	1,058.6	1,056.9	1,067.8	1,066.2	1,073.3	1,101.1	1,122.2	1,069.2
2004	1,068.7	1,060.4	1,067.1	1,070.6	1,074.4	1,075.5	1,076.1	1,089.6	1,079.9	1,087.0	1,118.0	1,139.1	1,083.9
2005	1,088.2	1,077.6	1,085.3	1,090.2	1,094.9	1,102.1	1,106.1	1,115.9	1,109.7	1,111.9	1,154.2	1,176.0	1,109.3
2006	1,118.6	1,106.5	1,117.1	1,116.8	1,120.5	1,122.5	1,122.5	1,134.1	1,127.9	1,135.3	1,172.0	1,191.0	1,132.1
2007	1,142.8	1,130.4	1,144.0	1,142.9	1,148.3	1,152.4	1,156.9	1,162.8	1,158.4	1,167.5	1,206.5	1,224.5	1,161.5
2008	1,171.3	1,161.4	1,169.0	1,162.1	1,163.4	1,168.7	1,171.2	1,180.6	1,164.8	1,171.7	1,197.3	1,210.6	1,174.3
2009	1,152.4	1,136.8	1,138.1	1,132.8	1,134.2	1,134.6	1,132.1	1,139.6	1,133.4	1,133.9	1,157.8	1,172.2	1,141.5
2010	1,119.7	1,108.9	1,119.9	1,120.9	1,127.1	1,131.0	1,129.7	1,138.7	1,130.2	1,142.9	1,174.1	1,193.8	1,136.4
2011	1,140.3	1,127.4	1,138.0	1,148.6	1,149.5	1,155.2	1,160.9	1,158.0	1,154.8	1,164.0	1,192.6	1,205.6	1,157.9
Transportation and Utilities													
2000	396.8	398.7	398.8	398.7	400.5	404.4	403.7	407.1	408.0	409.6	411.6	417.2	404.6
2001	405.9	404.8	404.6	403.1	405.1	406.5	405.9	407.7	406.4	406.1	400.3	399.2	404.6
2002	390.5	389.3	388.9	388.5	390.6	391.6	393.0	395.1	392.9	394.8	394.0	394.6	392.0
2003	388.0	386.5	386.1	385.5	384.1	384.7	384.8	388.4	388.4	391.3	391.9	396.2	388.0
2004	390.2	391.9	392.9	394.8	395.9	396.4	399.4	400.0	399.8	402.2	403.7	409.2	398.0
2005	400.8	399.0	400.5	401.8	403.6	403.7	405.8	409.4	410.8	411.7	415.7	421.3	407.0
2006	409.7	410.1	412.8	413.5	415.7	418.0	417.9	421.0	423.2	424.2	426.1	435.4	419.0
2007	424.4	425.9	429.4	428.7	430.8	433.7	432.4	435.6	437.1	437.0	437.7	443.8	433.0
2008	433.4	435.3	435.4	436.4	439.4	440.8	441.0	444.2	442.7	441.4	441.6	445.8	439.8
2009	430.2	425.4	425.3	420.1	418.9	418.2	415.7	415.4	415.6	415.2	415.8	422.0	419.8
2010	410.8	410.6	413.1	414.1	415.8	418.1	419.5	421.5	423.1	424.0	425.8	432.1	419.0
2011	423.7	424.6	427.5	428.0	426.5	427.7	430.7	432.3	436.1	438.9	440.1	449.6	432.1
Information													
2000	258.0	259.5	262.1	266.3	269.6	275.3	276.5	278.5	279.7	278.1	280.4	280.5	272.0
2001	273.2	274.5	274.7	273.6	273.1	273.5	269.5	268.5	266.3	264.6	263.9	261.7	269.8
2002	258.1	256.0	255.0	251.7	251.5	251.2	247.7	246.5	244.2	243.7	243.0	242.4	249.3
2003	238.4	237.7	237.3	235.2	235.1	235.1	234.1	232.9	230.3	229.2	229.6	229.2	233.7
2004	227.4	225.5	227.2	225.8	226.1	226.8	225.2	224.2	222.3	222.4	222.6	223.2	224.9
2005	221.8	222.1	222.5	222.8	223.1	224.6	224.1	223.9	223.9	222.0	223.1	223.7	223.1
2006	221.2	222.1	222.3	221.9	222.7	223.9	221.7	221.4	221.0	219.9	220.6	221.3	221.7
2007	219.4	220.7	220.7	220.0	221.9	222.4	221.9	222.2	220.4	220.0	221.1	221.0	221.0
2008	219.0	219.2	219.2	218.3	219.3	219.3	218.2	217.3	214.4	213.8	214.3	214.3	217.2
2009	211.2	210.2	209.2	207.0	206.1	205.3	203.2	201.5	198.9	198.9	199.3	199.7	204.2
2010	196.8	195.9	196.0	196.5	196.2	197.5	195.6	195.4	193.9	193.8	195.1	195.3	195.7
2011	194.6	194.2	194.6	194.8	195.6	196.2	197.0	196.4	195.5	194.9	196.2	195.5	195.5

1. Employment by Industry: Texas, Selected Years, 2000–2011—*Continued*

(Numbers in thousands, not seasonally adjusted)

Industry and year	January	February	March	April	May	June	July	August	September	October	November	December	Annual average
Financial Activities													
2000	558.4	560.1	563.0	563.9	565.2	570.0	571.2	571.3	570.2	570.3	571.2	575.2	567.5
2001	569.1	572.1	574.5	575.7	577.5	582.3	582.2	582.2	579.1	577.9	577.0	579.9	577.5
2002	574.8	575.5	576.8	576.2	579.6	582.4	582.7	583.3	580.4	579.9	581.5	582.7	579.7
2003	577.4	579.4	580.8	582.2	584.8	587.5	589.0	590.9	587.8	587.8	587.6	590.2	585.5
2004	586.1	587.0	588.5	591.2	592.0	596.1	599.4	600.4	599.1	600.2	600.1	604.3	595.4
2005	597.0	598.7	600.2	602.4	603.7	608.2	613.9	616.1	616.8	617.1	618.7	621.6	609.5
2006	614.2	616.8	620.7	624.0	626.6	631.9	630.5	633.4	633.2	633.5	634.4	638.9	628.2
2007	633.7	636.8	639.8	640.1	643.6	648.1	648.3	649.7	646.4	645.6	646.7	648.4	643.9
2008	641.7	645.2	644.7	647.8	650.6	652.9	652.4	651.7	646.9	644.3	642.4	643.2	647.0
2009	632.9	632.4	630.9	628.8	629.1	629.9	629.1	627.6	624.0	622.9	622.9	624.5	627.9
2010	618.3	619.9	621.4	621.0	623.7	626.6	626.8	627.0	625.0	629.3	631.4	634.1	625.4
2011	629.0	631.4	634.3	636.1	637.0	639.1	640.7	643.0	642.8	642.0	645.5	647.6	639.0
Professional and Business Services													
2000	1,058.6	1,069.4	1,085.2	1,091.2	1,097.2	1,119.8	1,120.9	1,129.4	1,134.0	1,130.2	1,129.1	1,134.3	1,108.3
2001	1,107.3	1,113.1	1,119.1	1,115.5	1,113.3	1,120.6	1,110.0	1,112.7	1,101.2	1,084.8	1,081.0	1,079.5	1,104.8
2002	1,048.5	1,053.4	1,061.0	1,066.7	1,068.5	1,072.8	1,070.7	1,080.7	1,075.2	1,067.2	1,066.7	1,064.5	1,066.3
2003	1,039.3	1,043.6	1,049.9	1,055.6	1,056.0	1,057.0	1,056.1	1,064.9	1,065.5	1,067.2	1,070.3	1,078.9	1,058.7
2004	1,060.7	1,069.5	1,078.1	1,094.1	1,095.1	1,104.2	1,110.4	1,116.0	1,112.3	1,120.1	1,122.0	1,125.4	1,100.7
2005	1,108.5	1,122.3	1,131.7	1,150.6	1,148.1	1,157.8	1,163.1	1,172.9	1,183.6	1,193.1	1,200.3	1,208.5	1,161.7
2006	1,189.0	1,204.1	1,219.6	1,225.8	1,231.8	1,244.4	1,245.8	1,257.2	1,261.9	1,261.7	1,272.2	1,279.6	1,241.1
2007	1,250.9	1,269.0	1,283.0	1,287.8	1,292.6	1,307.3	1,307.0	1,319.3	1,319.4	1,326.1	1,330.0	1,335.8	1,302.4
2008	1,313.4	1,327.2	1,330.8	1,338.7	1,339.8	1,345.3	1,341.7	1,351.3	1,338.9	1,345.3	1,336.4	1,327.3	1,336.3
2009	1,280.1	1,272.3	1,266.4	1,254.4	1,249.2	1,250.6	1,241.2	1,240.5	1,232.9	1,242.7	1,249.0	1,249.2	1,252.4
2010	1,231.0	1,240.6	1,253.0	1,264.0	1,265.5	1,275.5	1,279.3	1,287.7	1,288.5	1,301.7	1,304.8	1,310.9	1,275.2
2011	1,288.3	1,301.9	1,318.0	1,333.4	1,330.1	1,340.6	1,343.0	1,355.0	1,362.7	1,369.9	1,366.0	1,361.5	1,339.2
Education and Health Services													
2000	980.2	988.3	993.8	995.3	999.3	998.9	996.0	1,005.3	1,018.0	1,015.6	1,019.1	1,021.4	1,002.6
2001	1,013.0	1,023.7	1,029.5	1,031.2	1,036.2	1,040.7	1,038.3	1,047.3	1,053.6	1,055.6	1,059.9	1,062.5	1,041.0
2002	1,054.0	1,065.4	1,070.2	1,073.7	1,079.6	1,076.3	1,076.8	1,089.3	1,100.4	1,096.2	1,102.2	1,104.9	1,082.4
2003	1,098.0	1,107.0	1,111.6	1,113.1	1,116.3	1,108.7	1,110.5	1,120.8	1,132.9	1,134.8	1,136.4	1,136.2	1,118.9
2004	1,124.0	1,135.0	1,140.3	1,143.7	1,145.3	1,141.1	1,143.0	1,150.0	1,159.1	1,169.1	1,170.8	1,173.8	1,149.6
2005	1,156.8	1,167.1	1,173.4	1,176.6	1,178.8	1,175.9	1,180.3	1,188.5	1,200.0	1,198.3	1,203.3	1,206.3	1,183.8
2006	1,192.5	1,201.1	1,205.3	1,205.9	1,209.3	1,209.4	1,207.2	1,220.5	1,230.4	1,231.8	1,235.8	1,239.6	1,215.7
2007	1,221.9	1,237.0	1,245.2	1,246.1	1,251.4	1,251.1	1,250.7	1,259.9	1,267.1	1,268.4	1,273.3	1,274.8	1,253.9
2008	1,258.1	1,272.6	1,273.2	1,278.9	1,286.2	1,282.0	1,281.9	1,291.0	1,295.7	1,304.0	1,308.6	1,314.4	1,287.2
2009	1,296.5	1,307.0	1,313.6	1,324.3	1,332.3	1,332.8	1,338.3	1,345.1	1,352.0	1,363.2	1,365.5	1,368.2	1,336.6
2010	1,353.4	1,364.4	1,373.9	1,379.3	1,385.5	1,384.1	1,379.6	1,387.7	1,395.1	1,402.9	1,404.8	1,407.4	1,384.8
2011	1,390.5	1,396.7	1,405.2	1,413.5	1,416.6	1,413.8	1,413.1	1,425.3	1,440.0	1,450.4	1,452.6	1,449.0	1,422.2
Leisure and Hospitality													
2000	775.4	789.0	808.1	817.1	830.4	847.3	839.3	840.2	829.2	818.6	813.1	813.2	818.4
2001	793.1	809.7	827.1	840.1	854.0	867.5	860.5	862.4	844.7	825.5	819.3	819.1	835.3
2002	800.6	815.4	834.4	847.4	864.2	876.2	868.4	871.4	859.7	842.4	839.2	839.8	846.6
2003	820.9	830.9	847.7	857.4	872.2	885.0	877.0	880.4	867.0	858.2	852.7	854.4	858.7
2004	838.3	850.4	869.8	884.3	897.3	912.2	908.8	909.7	897.7	886.1	880.1	880.4	884.6
2005	861.4	874.1	893.6	912.2	925.0	936.6	930.7	928.6	916.1	902.1	899.7	898.7	906.6
2006	887.8	901.8	923.9	938.3	954.4	970.3	964.3	965.5	955.8	940.7	939.2	942.0	940.3
2007	919.8	937.3	960.9	980.6	996.6	1,013.0	1,007.7	1,008.7	991.8	982.7	980.8	982.6	980.2
2008	961.6	977.8	995.7	1,014.8	1,028.8	1,039.2	1,032.4	1,028.8	1,004.9	999.4	996.4	996.3	1,006.3
2009	971.2	984.8	1,003.7	1,014.6	1,029.4	1,040.3	1,029.2	1,025.7	1,008.3	990.2	985.3	983.6	1,005.5
2010	956.3	971.8	994.5	1,007.9	1,025.1	1,036.5	1,025.3	1,027.0	1,018.5	1,011.8	1,009.5	1,009.2	1,007.8
2011	983.4	996.8	1,028.7	1,046.0	1,061.5	1,075.4	1,073.8	1,065.9	1,044.9	1,046.4	1,049.9	1,051.1	1,043.7
Other Services													
2000	338.3	340.9	344.4	345.3	347.2	352.4	351.2	350.6	350.4	348.6	347.8	348.4	347.1
2001	350.3	352.7	356.5	356.7	358.7	363.4	356.7	356.6	353.2	349.3	349.6	349.4	354.4
2002	347.4	350.8	355.6	356.0	359.2	362.9	358.4	358.8	357.9	354.4	355.9	355.8	356.1
2003	352.6	353.7	358.4	356.5	357.5	362.0	358.3	357.5	354.8	350.4	350.3	351.8	355.3
2004	350.9	353.2	358.5	358.2	357.1	360.4	357.6	354.8	351.2	347.5	345.3	345.3	353.3
2005	343.0	344.1	349.3	350.2	350.7	354.4	352.9	350.4	348.0	343.8	343.8	344.1	347.9
2006	340.8	342.5	346.8	349.2	350.3	354.7	350.4	349.1	348.0	346.9	347.7	347.8	347.9
2007	344.8	348.5	351.9	353.6	356.3	361.7	359.4	359.0	356.7	356.9	357.5	357.5	355.3
2008	355.2	357.9	359.6	362.8	364.8	368.7	368.3	367.8	361.9	363.8	363.4	362.5	363.1
2009	358.6	360.7	361.2	361.5	363.3	367.0	365.0	362.3	358.0	357.4	358.4	357.5	360.9
2010	354.1	355.7	358.3	359.7	362.4	366.2	364.1	363.3	360.6	360.5	359.7	360.4	360.4
2011	356.9	359.2	363.0	365.4	367.0	371.3	374.7	374.4	372.1	375.3	376.8	375.9	369.3
Government													
2000	1,547.1	1,576.2	1,583.9	1,584.3	1,607.5	1,537.0	1,475.2	1,499.7	1,564.4	1,583.7	1,592.4	1,591.8	1,561.9
2001	1,565.7	1,594.7	1,600.0	1,601.2	1,602.0	1,559.7	1,494.2	1,522.8	1,603.1	1,624.1	1,636.3	1,630.8	1,586.2
2002	1,605.4	1,638.0	1,645.1	1,644.7	1,647.4	1,599.6	1,530.3	1,550.8	1,632.5	1,668.1	1,677.9	1,671.6	1,626.0
2003	1,642.8	1,677.8	1,676.1	1,677.4	1,677.2	1,632.1	1,555.4	1,570.5	1,642.2	1,664.1	1,673.3	1,663.7	1,646.1
2004	1,640.2	1,674.4	1,676.1	1,676.7	1,678.6	1,636.6	1,567.8	1,586.0	1,661.6	1,684.5	1,693.5	1,688.1	1,655.3
2005	1,666.0	1,700.2	1,702.5	1,704.6	1,706.3	1,659.7	1,596.7	1,617.6	1,689.4	1,714.9	1,726.8	1,714.3	1,683.3
2006	1,695.3	1,727.7	1,728.8	1,725.2	1,725.9	1,682.5	1,607.6	1,633.3	1,709.8	1,739.6	1,748.4	1,740.8	1,705.4
2007	1,714.6	1,746.3	1,752.6	1,751.8	1,754.7	1,715.4	1,644.4	1,653.5	1,729.3	1,768.8	1,783.7	1,779.3	1,732.9
2008	1,759.4	1,791.3	1,799.4	1,792.7	1,796.6	1,761.3	1,691.4	1,698.7	1,771.0	1,806.6	1,825.7	1,820.1	1,776.2
2009	1,801.1	1,829.3	1,836.1	1,845.1	1,844.6	1,808.4	1,732.0	1,728.0	1,805.0	1,856.0	1,868.6	1,860.6	1,817.9
2010	1,832.6	1,865.0	1,877.5	1,889.1	1,923.5	1,874.0	1,781.6	1,772.4	1,831.4	1,874.4	1,885.1	1,871.8	1,856.5
2011	1,840.2	1,864.7	1,865.1	1,865.0	1,857.6	1,823.6	1,743.7	1,724.8	1,773.9	1,799.8	1,809.7	1,801.3	1,814.1

2. Average Weekly Hours by Selected Industry: Texas, 2007–2011

(Not seasonally adjusted)

Industry and year	January	February	March	April	May	June	July	August	September	October	November	December	Annual average
Total Private													
2007	35.5	36.3	36.2	36.7	36.2	36.7	36.6	36.6	36.8	36.4	36.5	37.0	36.5
2008	36.0	36.4	36.7	36.4	36.2	36.9	36.3	36.2	35.3	36.2	36.4	36.1	36.2
2009	35.4	35.5	35.3	35.0	35.0	35.1	35.0	35.5	34.8	35.1	35.8	35.4	35.2
2010	35.1	35.0	35.7	35.7	36.4	35.9	36.1	36.8	35.7	36.1	36.0	36.4	35.9
2011	36.8	36.1	36.7	36.6	37.0	36.8	36.6	36.7	36.7	37.3	37.0	36.9	36.8
Goods-Producing													
2007	41.2	41.7	41.4	43.0	42.4	42.3	42.2	42.9	42.8	43.2	43.6	42.6	42.4
2008	42.6	42.9	42.5	42.7	42.1	43.0	43.1	42.5	41.2	43.1	42.3	42.2	42.5
2009	41.1	40.0	39.1	39.6	40.5	40.6	40.7	40.8	39.9	40.5	41.8	41.0	40.5
2010	40.5	39.0	40.8	41.1	41.5	41.5	41.9	42.7	41.2	42.0	41.6	42.8	41.4
2011	43.1	42.4	44.0	43.9	43.2	43.7	43.1	43.2	43.1	43.2	43.3	42.7	43.2
Construction													
2007	44.7	45.2	44.3	45.9	44.7	44.6	44.7	44.6	43.1	44.9	45.2	42.7	44.5
2008	43.2	43.3	42.1	42.9	41.9	43.0	42.8	41.3	39.4	41.4	41.7	41.5	42.0
2009	41.7	40.1	38.3	39.3	40.9	41.3	42.1	41.5	41.0	42.0	42.0	41.0	40.9
2010	40.1	39.6	40.6	41.1	41.3	42.1	42.2	42.9	42.1	44.1	42.7	42.8	41.8
2011	43.2	42.7	44.5	44.4	43.2	44.5	43.8	44.1	43.8	43.4	43.5	42.2	43.6
Manufacturing													
2007	39.8	40.9	40.5	40.7	41.3	41.3	40.8	42.1	42.4	42.2	42.7	42.2	41.4
2008	41.8	42.3	42.0	42.0	41.9	42.8	42.3	42.3	41.5	42.6	41.3	41.9	42.1
2009	40.5	38.9	38.9	39.2	39.7	39.7	39.1	39.7	39.4	39.6	40.3	39.9	39.6
2010	39.8	38.7	38.8	39.4	39.9	39.8	39.6	40.5	40.3	40.2	40.4	41.2	39.9
2011	40.9	40.3	40.8	40.9	40.6	40.9	40.5	40.6	40.9	41.3	41.8	41.8	40.9
Trade, Transportation, and Utilities													
2007	38.6	40.3	38.5	42.5	42.6	45.0	43.4	42.5	42.9	41.4	41.0	40.8	41.6
2008	39.8	39.7	40.7	40.6	40.1	40.0	39.2	39.5	40.4	39.9	41.2	39.6	40.1
2009	38.4	38.5	38.0	37.5	37.3	37.3	37.0	37.0	36.9	36.3	36.8	36.8	37.3
2010	36.2	36.1	36.1	36.2	36.5	36.9	37.2	37.3	36.0	36.4	36.6	37.2	36.6
2011	36.7	36.6	36.8	37.1	37.3	36.9	36.9	37.3	37.2	37.6	37.0	37.2	37.1
Financial Activities													
2007	37.5	37.9	37.7	39.1	38.1	38.1	39.3	38.4	39.1	38.0	37.8	39.2	38.4
2008	37.4	37.4	38.0	37.2	37.5	38.3	37.3	37.5	37.0	37.6	38.5	37.5	37.6
2009	37.8	38.3	37.8	37.9	36.8	36.9	37.2	38.0	37.1	37.9	38.4	37.7	37.7
2010	38.1	38.2	38.4	37.8	38.9	38.5	38.2	39.1	38.6	38.3	38.3	38.4	38.4
2011	38.8	38.7	38.8	39.0	40.3	38.7	38.9	38.1	38.6	40.1	39.4	39.5	39.1
Professional and Business Services													
2007	36.1	37.5	37.0	37.3	36.3	36.8	36.4	36.6	36.7	36.0	36.3	37.3	36.7
2008	35.6	36.4	37.1	36.0	35.7	36.8	35.7	35.8	34.9	35.9	36.5	35.5	36.0
2009	34.6	35.1	35.0	34.7	34.6	35.2	34.5	35.2	34.2	34.5	35.5	34.7	34.8
2010	34.5	34.4	35.1	35.4	36.5	36.6	36.8	37.8	37.2	38.1	37.8	37.5	36.5
2011	37.6	37.3	37.9	37.7	38.4	38.6	38.2	38.1	37.9	38.8	38.0	37.6	38.0
Education and Health Services													
2007	33.0	33.5	33.5	34.2	33.8	35.2	34.7	34.2	34.7	34.3	34.1	35.5	34.2
2008	34.5	34.6	34.9	34.4	34.7	35.4	35.1	34.5	34.7	35.2	35.5	35.0	34.9
2009	34.8	35.4	35.8	35.0	35.0	34.8	34.9	35.0	34.8	34.5	35.2	34.6	35.0
2010	34.5	34.5	34.1	34.3	34.6	33.9	34.0	34.5	34.2	34.0	33.7	33.9	34.2
2011	34.6	34.0	34.2	34.1	34.6	33.9	34.0	33.6	33.9	34.4	33.6	33.9	34.1
Leisure and Hospitality													
2007	27.8	28.9	28.4	28.0	28.1	28.3	27.8	27.7	27.0	26.8	26.5	27.0	27.7
2008	26.0	26.9	26.9	26.8	26.8	27.2	26.6	27.0	26.0	26.7	27.1	26.9	26.7
2009	26.3	27.2	27.3	26.5	26.3	26.6	26.3	27.0	25.9	26.8	26.5	26.8	26.6
2010	26.2	27.3	27.4	27.4	28.0	27.8	27.8	28.0	27.1	27.8	27.7	28.2	27.6
2011	27.8	28.0	28.7	27.9	28.8	28.1	28.2	28.1	27.6	28.4	27.7	27.9	28.1
Other Services													
2007	28.1	31.1	30.3	30.5	30.7	30.1	30.1	30.4	31.5	31.6	32.7	33.2	30.9
2008	31.6	32.7	33.4	32.8	32.6	33.6	32.8	32.8	32.0	32.9	33.9	33.5	32.9
2009	32.7	33.5	33.2	32.9	33.1	33.4	33.9	34.1	33.6	34.5	34.9	34.3	33.7
2010	34.0	33.6	34.7	33.9	35.0	34.5	34.1	35.1	34.3	34.4	34.1	34.3	34.3
2011	34.8	34.1	35.5	35.1	35.9	35.1	35.3	35.8	36.0	36.6	35.4	35.9	35.5

3. Average Hourly Earnings by Selected Industry: Texas, 2007–2011

(Dollars, not seasonally adjusted)

Industry and year	January	February	March	April	May	June	July	August	September	October	November	December	Annual average
Total Private													
2007	21.30	20.96	21.07	21.30	21.05	20.94	21.20	21.05	21.08	20.84	20.76	21.34	21.07
2008	20.97	21.12	21.47	21.46	21.39	21.47	21.18	21.15	21.27	21.29	21.41	21.36	21.30
2009	21.32	21.37	21.26	21.22	21.30	21.26	21.39	21.47	21.50	21.47	21.76	21.41	21.39
2010	21.31	21.41	21.31	21.42	21.39	21.17	21.29	21.37	21.43	21.44	21.48	21.32	21.36
2011	21.95	22.00	21.84	21.92	22.02	21.74	21.90	21.86	21.94	22.21	22.15	22.09	21.97
Goods-Producing													
2007	23.08	22.48	22.74	22.68	21.92	22.29	22.44	21.86	22.05	21.72	21.64	23.64	22.37
2008	22.71	22.61	23.79	22.75	22.89	22.81	22.62	22.70	22.62	22.79	22.60	22.72	22.80
2009	22.68	22.63	22.65	22.60	22.70	22.74	22.85	22.88	22.80	23.04	23.12	23.06	22.81
2010	22.80	22.90	22.68	22.61	22.69	22.61	22.88	22.90	22.86	23.03	22.86	21.25	22.67
2011	22.70	22.76	22.33	22.79	22.82	22.48	22.74	22.79	22.99	23.39	23.43	23.64	22.91
Construction													
2007	22.33	21.11	22.13	21.18	21.15	21.22	21.17	21.10	21.13	21.12	21.08	21.03	21.30
2008	20.27	19.99	19.89	19.80	19.77	19.70	19.63	19.53	19.43	19.45	19.38	19.35	19.69
2009	19.19	19.36	19.72	19.60	19.48	19.50	19.48	19.52	19.77	19.86	19.63	19.66	19.56
2010	19.49	19.56	19.55	19.45	19.66	19.81	19.78	19.85	19.89	19.67	19.70	19.78	19.69
2011	19.70	19.74	19.18	19.35	19.86	19.76	19.55	20.03	20.38	20.80	20.99	21.19	20.04
Manufacturing													
2007	22.64	22.54	22.21	22.57	22.57	22.50	22.45	22.40	22.41	22.31	22.21	22.11	22.41
2008	22.21	22.43	22.73	22.98	23.40	23.45	23.40	23.37	23.35	23.25	23.15	23.05	23.06
2009	22.92	22.96	23.14	23.21	23.28	23.40	23.30	23.40	23.45	23.51	23.54	23.57	23.30
2010	23.53	23.51	23.56	23.73	23.87	23.82	23.77	23.74	23.67	23.79	23.87	23.82	23.73
2011	23.69	23.71	23.23	23.87	24.39	23.96	24.36	23.91	23.91	24.15	24.12	24.32	23.97
Trade, Transportation, and Utilities													
2007	28.56	28.52	28.41	28.66	28.77	28.72	28.79	28.68	28.73	28.48	28.66	28.70	28.64
2008	27.72	27.74	27.49	27.53	27.37	27.54	27.49	27.54	27.61	27.54	27.44	27.52	27.54
2009	27.65	27.60	27.55	27.58	27.64	27.60	27.73	27.68	27.60	27.64	27.41	27.47	27.60
2010	27.68	27.43	27.87	27.74	27.68	27.97	27.94	27.92	27.82	27.86	27.88	27.90	27.81
2011	27.84	27.87	27.24	26.50	26.18	25.58	25.22	24.67	24.15	24.40	23.56	23.52	25.53
Financial Activities													
2007	25.78	25.71	25.60	25.32	25.26	25.65	25.98	25.53	25.52	25.43	25.77	25.43	25.58
2008	25.24	25.15	25.20	25.48	25.20	25.24	25.20	25.14	25.17	25.25	25.33	25.42	25.25
2009	25.32	25.54	25.37	25.24	25.47	25.48	25.59	25.42	25.47	25.20	25.34	25.20	25.39
2010	25.36	25.42	25.32	25.53	25.73	25.53	25.73	25.81	25.77	25.57	25.37	25.17	25.53
2011	25.37	25.11	25.14	25.00	25.18	24.68	24.50	24.81	24.61	25.23	24.73	24.41	24.90
Professional and Business Services													
2007	25.22	25.46	25.63	25.54	25.51	25.29	25.57	25.41	25.43	25.30	25.16	25.23	25.40
2008	24.95	25.08	25.16	25.21	25.25	25.37	25.11	25.33	25.21	25.37	25.44	25.65	25.26
2009	25.86	26.18	26.32	26.53	26.26	26.00	26.25	26.39	26.45	26.27	26.22	26.14	26.24
2010	26.12	26.40	26.20	26.34	26.46	26.26	26.12	26.32	26.13	26.17	26.20	26.31	26.25
2011	26.39	26.33	26.00	25.85	26.00	25.15	25.20	25.05	25.34	25.56	25.48	25.74	25.67
Education and Health Services													
2007	24.55	24.47	24.04	23.77	23.69	23.56	23.81	23.70	23.30	23.04	22.89	22.67	23.61
2008	22.54	22.59	22.45	22.32	22.25	22.15	22.06	22.02	22.13	22.03	22.09	21.95	22.21
2009	21.81	21.64	21.60	21.74	21.74	21.62	21.76	21.82	21.85	21.95	21.85	21.97	21.78
2010	21.87	21.98	21.91	22.00	21.97	22.07	21.97	21.97	21.95	22.02	22.10	22.08	21.99
2011	21.91	22.02	21.84	21.77	21.80	21.87	22.36	22.37	22.43	22.48	22.58	22.57	22.17
Leisure and Hospitality													
2007	10.95	11.05	11.01	11.10	11.13	11.17	11.16	11.01	11.27	11.30	11.52	11.74	11.20
2008	11.44	11.41	11.35	11.31	11.33	11.34	11.22	11.27	11.40	11.52	11.62	11.69	11.41
2009	11.60	11.69	11.71	11.65	11.58	11.48	11.58	11.50	11.69	11.73	11.88	11.93	11.67
2010	11.80	11.75	11.63	11.76	11.69	11.59	11.62	11.70	11.76	11.73	11.77	11.91	11.72
2011	11.98	11.95	11.89	11.86	11.82	11.91	11.85	11.91	11.89	11.95	12.08	12.07	11.93
Other Services													
2007	16.51	16.59	16.62	16.64	16.51	16.40	16.13	16.27	16.04	16.09	15.95	16.30	16.33
2008	15.71	15.68	15.80	15.92	15.77	15.76	15.91	16.03	16.12	16.30	16.41	16.52	16.00
2009	16.65	16.78	16.90	16.84	16.70	16.71	16.76	16.74	16.82	16.89	16.75	16.84	16.78
2010	16.83	16.83	16.97	17.06	17.11	17.19	17.30	17.41	17.52	17.64	17.77	17.85	17.29
2011	18.00	17.93	18.40	18.56	19.05	19.16	19.12	20.26	20.21	21.00	20.84	20.87	19.48

4. Average Weekly Earnings by Selected Industry: Texas, 2007–2011

(Dollars, not seasonally adjusted)

Industry and year	January	February	March	April	May	June	July	August	September	October	November	December	Annual average
Total Private													
2007	756.15	760.85	762.73	781.71	762.01	768.50	775.92	770.43	775.74	758.58	757.74	789.58	768.26
2008	754.92	768.77	787.95	781.14	774.32	792.24	768.83	765.63	750.83	770.70	779.32	771.10	771.90
2009	754.73	758.64	750.48	742.70	745.50	746.23	748.65	762.19	748.20	753.60	779.01	757.91	754.09
2010	747.98	749.35	760.77	764.69	778.60	760.00	768.57	786.42	765.05	773.98	773.28	776.05	767.41
2011	807.76	794.20	801.53	802.27	814.74	800.03	801.54	802.26	805.20	828.43	819.55	815.12	807.68
Goods-Producing													
2007	950.90	937.42	941.44	975.24	929.41	942.87	946.97	937.79	943.74	938.30	943.50	1,007.06	949.60
2008	967.45	969.97	1,011.08	971.43	963.67	980.83	974.92	964.75	931.94	982.25	955.98	958.78	969.42
2009	932.15	905.20	885.62	894.96	919.35	923.24	930.00	933.50	909.72	933.12	966.42	945.46	922.80
2010	923.40	893.10	925.34	929.27	941.64	938.32	958.67	977.83	941.83	967.26	950.98	909.50	938.25
2011	978.37	965.02	982.52	1,000.48	985.82	982.38	980.09	984.53	990.87	1,010.45	1,014.52	1,009.43	990.47
Construction													
2007	998.15	954.17	980.36	972.16	945.41	946.41	946.30	941.06	910.70	948.29	952.82	897.98	948.96
2008	875.66	865.57	837.37	849.42	828.36	847.10	840.16	806.59	765.54	805.23	808.15	803.03	827.54
2009	800.22	776.34	755.28	770.28	796.73	805.35	820.11	810.08	810.57	834.12	824.46	806.06	800.24
2010	781.55	774.58	793.73	799.40	811.96	834.00	834.72	851.57	837.37	867.45	841.19	846.58	823.12
2011	851.04	842.90	853.51	859.14	857.95	879.32	856.29	883.32	892.64	902.72	913.07	894.22	873.89
Manufacturing													
2007	901.07	921.89	899.51	918.60	932.14	929.25	915.96	943.04	950.18	941.48	948.37	933.04	927.92
2008	928.38	948.79	954.66	965.16	980.46	1,003.66	989.82	988.55	969.03	990.45	956.10	965.80	970.09
2009	928.26	893.14	900.15	909.83	924.22	928.98	911.03	928.98	923.93	931.00	948.66	940.44	922.11
2010	936.49	909.84	914.13	934.96	952.41	948.04	941.29	961.47	953.90	956.36	964.35	981.38	946.28
2011	968.92	955.51	947.78	976.28	990.23	979.96	986.58	970.75	977.92	997.40	1,008.22	1,016.58	981.47
Trade, Transportation, and Utilities													
2007	1,102.42	1,149.36	1,093.79	1,218.05	1,225.60	1,292.40	1,249.49	1,218.90	1,232.52	1,179.07	1,175.06	1,170.96	1,192.46
2008	1,103.26	1,101.28	1,118.84	1,117.72	1,097.54	1,101.60	1,077.61	1,087.83	1,115.44	1,098.85	1,130.53	1,089.79	1,103.34
2009	1,061.76	1,062.60	1,046.90	1,034.25	1,030.97	1,029.48	1,026.01	1,024.16	1,018.44	1,003.33	1,008.69	1,010.90	1,029.86
2010	1,002.02	990.22	1,006.11	1,004.19	1,010.32	1,032.09	1,039.37	1,041.42	1,001.52	1,014.10	1,020.41	1,037.88	1,016.80
2011	1,021.73	1,020.04	1,002.43	983.15	976.51	943.90	930.62	920.19	898.38	917.44	871.72	874.94	945.98
Financial Activities													
2007	966.75	974.41	965.12	990.01	962.41	977.27	1,021.01	980.35	997.83	966.34	974.11	996.86	981.10
2008	943.98	940.61	957.60	947.86	945.00	966.69	939.96	942.75	931.29	949.40	975.21	953.25	949.45
2009	957.10	978.18	958.99	956.60	937.30	940.21	951.95	965.96	944.94	955.08	973.06	950.04	955.81
2010	966.22	971.04	972.29	965.03	1,000.90	982.91	982.89	1,009.17	994.72	979.33	971.67	966.53	980.19
2011	984.36	971.76	975.43	975.00	1,014.75	955.12	953.05	945.26	949.95	1,011.72	974.36	964.20	972.86
Professional and Business Services													
2007	910.44	954.75	948.31	952.64	926.01	930.67	930.75	930.01	933.28	910.80	913.31	941.08	931.78
2008	888.22	912.91	933.44	907.56	901.43	933.62	896.43	906.81	879.83	910.78	928.56	910.58	909.20
2009	894.76	918.92	921.20	920.59	908.60	915.20	905.63	928.93	904.59	906.32	930.81	907.06	913.53
2010	901.14	908.16	919.62	932.44	965.79	961.12	961.22	994.90	972.04	997.08	990.36	986.63	958.13
2011	992.26	982.11	985.40	974.55	998.40	970.79	962.64	954.41	960.39	991.73	968.24	967.82	975.60
Education and Health Services													
2007	810.15	819.75	805.34	812.93	800.72	829.31	826.21	810.54	808.51	790.27	780.55	804.79	808.17
2008	777.63	781.61	783.51	767.81	772.08	784.11	774.31	759.69	767.91	775.46	784.20	768.25	774.69
2009	758.99	766.06	773.28	760.90	760.90	752.38	759.42	763.70	760.38	757.28	769.12	760.16	761.88
2010	754.52	758.31	747.13	754.60	760.16	748.17	746.98	757.97	750.69	748.68	744.77	748.51	751.67
2011	758.09	748.68	746.93	742.36	754.28	741.39	760.24	751.63	760.38	773.31	758.69	765.12	755.17
Leisure and Hospitality													
2007	304.41	319.35	312.68	310.80	312.75	316.11	310.25	304.98	304.29	302.84	305.28	316.98	310.05
2008	297.44	306.93	305.32	303.11	303.64	308.45	298.45	304.29	296.40	307.58	314.90	314.46	305.08
2009	305.08	317.97	319.68	308.73	304.55	305.37	304.55	310.50	302.77	314.36	314.82	319.72	310.60
2010	309.16	320.78	318.66	322.22	327.32	322.20	323.04	327.60	318.70	326.09	326.03	335.86	323.22
2011	333.04	334.60	341.24	330.89	340.42	334.67	334.17	334.67	328.16	339.38	334.62	336.75	335.23
Other Services													
2007	463.93	515.95	503.59	507.52	506.86	493.64	485.51	494.61	505.26	508.44	521.57	541.16	504.07
2008	496.44	512.74	527.72	522.18	514.10	529.54	521.85	525.78	515.84	536.27	556.30	553.42	526.08
2009	544.46	562.13	561.08	554.04	552.77	558.11	568.16	570.83	565.15	582.71	584.58	577.61	565.10
2010	572.22	565.49	588.86	578.33	598.85	593.06	589.93	611.09	600.94	606.82	605.96	612.26	593.74
2011	626.40	611.41	653.20	651.46	683.90	672.52	674.94	725.31	727.56	768.60	737.74	749.23	690.95

UTAH
At a Glance

Population:
    2000 census: 2,233,183
    2010 census: 2,763,885
    2011 estimate: 2,817,222

Percent change in population:
    2000–2010: 23.8%
    2010–2011: 1.9%

Percent change in total nonfarm employment:
    2000–2010: 10.0%
    2010–2011: 2.2%

Industry with the largest growth in employment, 2000–2011 (thousands):
    Education and Health Services, 55.0

Industry with the largest decline or smallest growth in employment, 2000–2011 (thousands):
    Manufacturing, -11.4

Civilian labor force:
    2000: 1,136,036
    2010: 1,361,756
    2011: 1,338,259

Unemployment rate and rank among states (lowest to highest):
    2000: 3.4%, 17th
    2010: 8.0%, 18th
    2011: 6.7%, 11th

Over-the-year change in unemployment rates:
    2010–2011: -1.3%

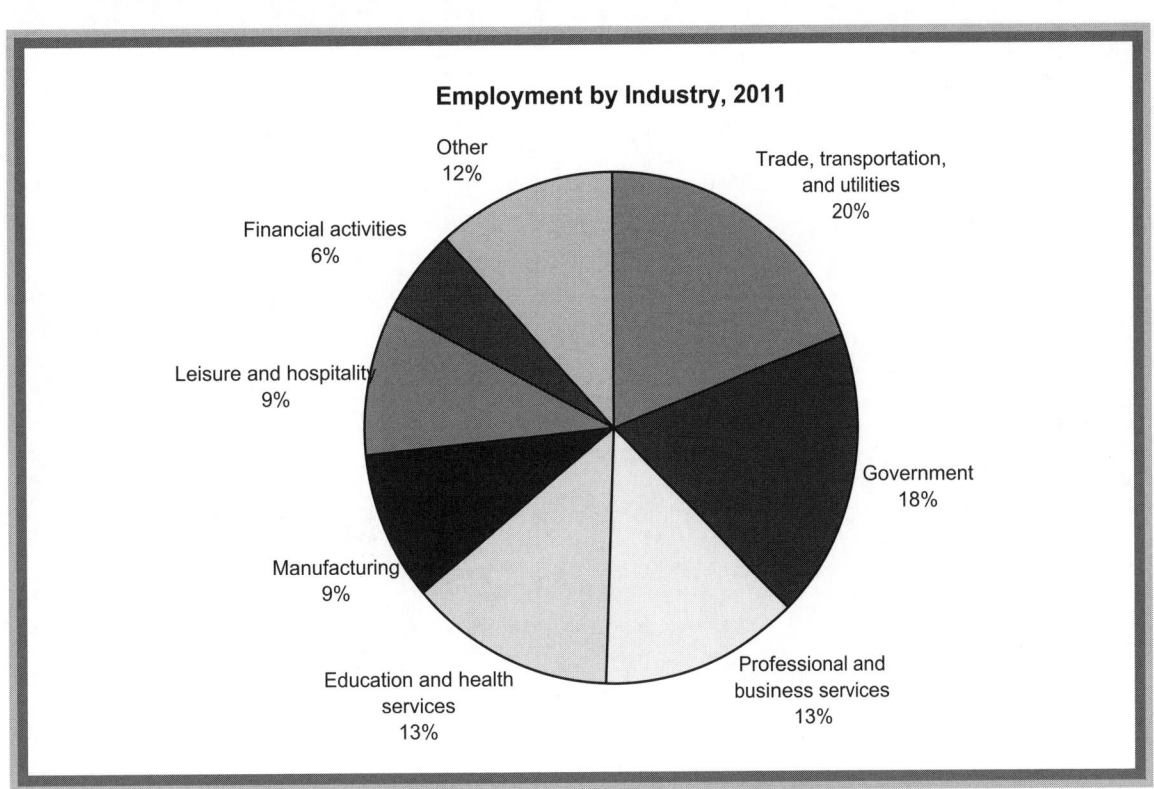

Employment by Industry, 2011

- Other 12%
- Trade, transportation, and utilities 20%
- Financial activities 6%
- Leisure and hospitality 9%
- Government 18%
- Manufacturing 9%
- Education and health services 13%
- Professional and business services 13%

1. Employment by Industry: Utah, Selected Years, 2000–2011

(Numbers in thousands, not seasonally adjusted)

Industry and year	January	February	March	April	May	June	July	August	September	October	November	December	Annual average
Total Nonfarm													
2000	1,044.9	1,053.3	1,063.1	1,071.1	1,074.0	1,083.5	1,067.3	1,073.8	1,088.4	1,089.0	1,094.5	1,101.7	1,075.4
2001	1,069.2	1,072.9	1,080.2	1,083.5	1,084.3	1,091.3	1,073.4	1,078.4	1,088.4	1,083.5	1,085.3	1,085.7	1,081.3
2002	1,062.8	1,069.6	1,065.7	1,073.4	1,072.0	1,077.1	1,063.3	1,066.5	1,079.1	1,080.3	1,084.4	1,087.1	1,073.4
2003	1,058.2	1,059.0	1,062.3	1,069.2	1,069.9	1,076.0	1,062.8	1,070.0	1,082.4	1,087.8	1,092.2	1,099.2	1,074.1
2004	1,072.3	1,077.7	1,086.2	1,098.8	1,100.1	1,109.8	1,096.9	1,102.9	1,117.1	1,123.1	1,130.3	1,136.4	1,104.3
2005	1,110.8	1,118.0	1,126.8	1,138.4	1,139.7	1,149.0	1,140.1	1,152.1	1,168.0	1,170.0	1,177.9	1,185.3	1,148.0
2006	1,162.9	1,171.5	1,182.5	1,192.9	1,196.1	1,211.1	1,196.1	1,208.2	1,222.5	1,222.8	1,234.6	1,243.3	1,203.7
2007	1,219.2	1,226.7	1,238.5	1,247.0	1,250.3	1,261.9	1,244.6	1,256.2	1,266.5	1,270.5	1,276.6	1,281.0	1,253.3
2008	1,244.5	1,248.0	1,253.3	1,259.1	1,256.6	1,261.4	1,242.8	1,252.3	1,261.4	1,254.9	1,249.1	1,246.7	1,252.5
2009	1,203.3	1,197.0	1,195.9	1,194.2	1,189.7	1,190.4	1,168.5	1,174.4	1,187.3	1,187.8	1,187.5	1,190.0	1,188.8
2010	1,159.7	1,159.9	1,168.9	1,182.2	1,183.9	1,187.1	1,171.9	1,179.1	1,193.1	1,198.2	1,201.4	1,204.7	1,182.5
2011	1,177.1	1,182.2	1,190.7	1,206.1	1,201.7	1,208.7	1,198.9	1,210.4	1,227.2	1,230.3	1,228.9	1,234.6	1,208.1
Total Private													
2000	863.7	866.4	874.6	880.7	882.2	895.7	894.7	901.7	902.7	900.5	905.2	912.1	890.0
2001	882.6	881.0	887.5	889.5	890.1	898.0	896.4	901.3	897.1	890.1	890.4	890.7	891.2
2002	868.5	874.6	867.7	874.5	874.4	879.3	878.9	883.6	883.3	882.5	885.9	888.7	878.5
2003	860.1	859.3	862.4	868.1	870.1	878.0	879.3	886.3	885.7	888.4	892.8	899.9	877.5
2004	873.9	877.7	885.1	895.8	898.6	909.4	911.4	915.8	916.8	920.1	926.9	933.5	905.4
2005	908.5	914.0	922.1	932.4	934.7	944.7	951.3	960.4	964.3	964.5	971.8	979.8	945.7
2006	958.9	965.3	975.6	985.2	989.5	1,004.0	1,004.8	1,014.0	1,016.5	1,015.3	1,026.2	1,035.7	999.3
2007	1,013.2	1,018.7	1,029.8	1,037.0	1,040.8	1,052.3	1,052.3	1,060.2	1,057.9	1,059.5	1,064.7	1,070.0	1,046.4
2008	1,034.4	1,035.9	1,040.3	1,044.7	1,042.3	1,047.8	1,046.5	1,051.3	1,046.7	1,038.0	1,031.6	1,030.1	1,040.8
2009	988.9	980.7	979.4	974.9	971.2	973.8	969.7	971.6	970.7	968.8	968.5	971.8	974.2
2010	943.4	942.2	950.2	961.2	959.2	966.5	969.6	973.1	973.3	975.9	979.2	983.8	964.8
2011	958.1	961.0	968.0	982.2	978.8	987.7	996.7	1,004.2	1,004.1	1,005.0	1,004.3	1,011.2	988.4
Goods-Producing													
2000	200.2	199.7	200.9	203.6	205.4	209.6	208.8	210.2	209.4	207.3	206.0	204.5	205.5
2001	198.4	197.1	198.5	198.5	201.3	204.2	204.9	205.5	204.1	202.0	199.6	194.7	200.8
2002	185.4	182.0	183.2	185.6	188.6	190.8	191.9	192.8	192.5	192.3	191.2	188.9	188.8
2003	181.3	179.8	180.4	182.8	186.2	188.7	189.4	191.0	190.2	191.2	190.1	189.0	186.7
2004	182.4	182.5	185.3	190.1	194.1	197.6	199.9	200.9	200.6	200.3	200.0	199.5	194.4
2005	194.0	195.4	196.9	202.8	206.4	210.4	213.3	215.6	216.4	215.3	216.4	216.0	208.2
2006	212.0	214.5	218.1	222.0	227.1	232.0	233.0	235.6	236.3	236.1	237.1	237.2	228.4
2007	231.6	232.8	236.7	239.8	243.9	248.6	248.5	250.3	248.2	247.9	244.7	241.6	242.9
2008	231.0	228.9	229.8	230.1	231.7	233.6	233.1	233.0	230.5	226.7	221.5	215.8	228.8
2009	202.1	196.4	194.8	192.3	194.2	195.5	195.3	195.1	193.7	192.9	190.4	187.7	194.2
2010	180.2	178.4	179.6	183.3	186.0	188.3	190.0	191.5	191.6	191.8	190.6	188.4	186.6
2011	181.4	181.2	182.9	186.5	188.4	191.9	195.4	196.9	196.9	199.5	195.5	195.5	191.0
Mining and Logging													
2000	7.2	7.2	7.3	7.5	7.6	7.7	7.7	7.7	7.7	7.4	7.3	7.3	7.5
2001	7.2	7.2	7.3	7.3	7.5	7.5	7.4	7.5	7.3	7.1	7.1	7.0	7.3
2002	6.7	6.7	6.7	6.9	7.0	7.1	7.1	7.1	7.2	7.1	7.1	7.0	7.0
2003	6.6	6.5	6.6	6.7	6.8	6.9	6.9	6.8	6.8	6.9	6.8	6.8	6.8
2004	6.7	6.6	6.6	6.9	7.1	7.3	7.4	7.4	7.5	7.6	7.6	7.7	7.2
2005	7.6	7.8	7.8	8.2	8.4	8.6	8.8	8.9	9.0	9.0	9.2	9.2	8.5
2006	9.0	9.2	9.4	9.7	9.9	10.2	10.4	10.5	10.5	10.6	10.7	10.8	10.1
2007	10.6	10.6	10.8	10.9	11.1	11.2	11.3	11.4	11.1	11.4	11.4	11.4	11.1
2008	11.4	11.4	11.5	11.8	12.3	12.6	12.8	13.4	13.5	13.6	13.5	13.2	12.6
2009	12.1	11.8	11.5	10.9	10.6	10.6	10.5	10.3	10.3	10.1	10.1	10.0	10.7
2010	9.8	9.8	10.0	10.2	10.4	10.6	10.6	10.8	10.8	11.0	11.0	11.0	10.5
2011	10.8	10.9	11.1	11.3	11.4	11.7	11.8	12.0	12.0	12.1	12.1	12.1	11.6
Construction													
2000	68.0	67.9	68.9	71.0	72.8	75.8	75.5	76.5	75.4	74.1	72.7	71.3	72.5
2001	65.9	65.4	66.8	68.3	71.2	74.1	75.2	77.0	75.7	75.0	73.7	70.5	71.6
2002	63.9	61.5	62.9	65.1	67.6	69.5	70.8	71.6	71.4	71.3	70.4	68.3	67.9
2003	62.6	62.0	62.5	64.4	67.2	69.1	70.2	71.7	71.1	71.4	70.1	68.8	67.6
2004	63.9	63.8	66.1	69.8	72.5	75.2	77.1	77.9	77.6	77.1	76.1	75.2	72.7
2005	71.1	72.1	73.7	78.1	80.5	83.3	85.5	86.9	87.5	86.8	86.9	86.0	81.5
2006	83.0	84.5	87.3	90.4	94.6	98.4	99.1	101.1	101.6	100.9	100.9	100.3	95.2
2007	96.0	96.5	99.3	102.1	105.2	108.6	108.3	109.7	108.0	107.2	103.2	99.7	103.7
2008	91.2	89.3	90.3	91.1	92.6	94.0	93.6	93.9	92.0	89.1	85.3	81.7	90.3
2009	72.1	69.3	69.1	68.4	70.9	72.0	72.5	72.6	71.9	71.2	69.2	66.4	70.5
2010	60.5	59.3	60.4	62.6	64.9	66.2	67.4	68.4	68.8	69.1	67.6	65.1	65.0
2011	59.4	58.8	60.0	62.6	64.0	66.5	69.4	69.4	69.0	70.6	67.4	66.9	65.3
Manufacturing													
2000	125.0	124.6	124.7	125.1	125.0	126.1	125.6	126.0	126.3	125.8	126.0	125.9	125.5
2001	125.3	124.5	124.4	122.9	122.6	122.6	122.3	122.0	121.1	119.9	118.8	117.2	122.0
2002	114.8	113.8	113.6	113.6	114.0	114.2	114.0	114.1	113.9	113.9	113.7	113.6	113.9
2003	112.1	111.3	111.3	111.7	112.2	112.7	112.3	112.5	112.3	112.9	113.2	113.4	112.3
2004	111.8	112.1	112.6	113.4	114.5	115.1	115.4	115.6	115.5	115.6	116.3	116.6	114.5
2005	115.3	115.5	115.4	116.5	117.5	118.5	119.0	119.8	119.9	119.5	120.3	120.8	118.2
2006	120.0	120.8	121.4	121.9	122.6	123.4	123.5	124.0	124.2	124.6	125.5	126.1	123.2
2007	125.0	125.7	126.6	126.8	127.6	128.8	128.9	129.2	129.1	129.3	130.1	130.5	128.1
2008	128.4	128.2	128.0	127.2	126.8	127.0	126.7	125.7	125.0	124.0	122.7	120.9	125.9
2009	117.9	115.3	114.2	113.0	112.7	112.9	112.3	112.2	111.5	111.6	111.1	111.3	113.0
2010	109.9	109.3	109.2	110.5	110.7	111.5	112.0	112.3	112.0	111.7	112.0	112.3	111.1
2011	111.2	111.5	111.8	112.6	113.0	113.7	114.2	115.5	115.9	116.8	116.0	116.5	114.1

1. Employment by Industry: Utah, Selected Years, 2000–2011—*Continued*

(Numbers in thousands, not seasonally adjusted)

Industry and year	January	February	March	April	May	June	July	August	September	October	November	December	Annual average
Service-Providing													
2000	844.7	853.6	862.2	867.5	868.6	873.9	858.5	863.6	879.0	881.7	888.5	897.2	869.9
2001	870.8	875.8	881.7	885.0	883.0	887.1	868.5	871.9	884.3	881.5	885.7	891.0	880.5
2002	877.4	887.6	882.5	887.8	883.4	886.3	871.4	873.7	886.6	888.0	893.2	898.2	884.7
2003	876.9	879.2	881.9	886.4	883.7	887.3	873.4	879.0	892.2	896.6	902.1	910.2	887.4
2004	889.9	895.2	900.9	908.7	906.0	912.2	897.0	902.0	916.5	922.8	930.3	936.9	909.9
2005	916.8	922.6	929.9	935.6	933.3	938.6	926.8	936.5	951.6	954.7	961.5	969.3	939.8
2006	950.9	957.0	964.4	970.9	969.0	979.1	963.1	972.6	986.2	986.7	997.5	1,006.1	975.3
2007	987.6	993.9	1,001.8	1,007.2	1,006.4	1,013.3	996.1	1,005.9	1,018.3	1,022.6	1,031.9	1,039.4	1,010.4
2008	1,013.5	1,019.1	1,023.5	1,029.0	1,024.9	1,027.8	1,009.7	1,019.3	1,030.9	1,028.2	1,027.6	1,030.9	1,023.7
2009	1,001.2	1,000.6	1,001.1	1,001.9	995.5	994.9	973.2	979.3	993.6	994.9	997.1	1,002.3	994.6
2010	979.5	981.5	989.3	998.9	997.9	998.8	981.9	987.6	1,001.5	1,006.4	1,010.8	1,016.3	995.9
2011	995.7	1,001.0	1,007.8	1,019.6	1,013.3	1,016.8	1,003.5	1,013.5	1,030.3	1,030.8	1,033.4	1,039.1	1,017.1
Trade, Transportation, and Utilities													
2000	216.9	214.7	215.7	216.4	216.5	219.1	219.3	220.9	221.6	223.4	228.1	231.4	220.3
2001	219.8	218.1	218.6	219.0	218.7	218.9	218.4	218.8	217.6	217.1	220.7	222.4	219.0
2002	214.2	212.5	211.7	213.5	215.2	215.5	215.3	216.1	215.1	216.2	220.0	221.8	215.6
2003	211.1	209.6	210.0	210.6	212.1	212.8	212.9	214.5	213.9	215.8	220.5	223.4	213.9
2004	214.6	213.1	213.6	215.5	217.5	218.5	218.5	219.4	219.3	221.3	226.3	228.7	218.9
2005	219.7	218.8	221.2	221.8	223.0	223.8	225.1	227.5	227.6	229.7	234.2	237.3	225.8
2006	228.6	228.1	229.6	230.0	231.7	234.2	234.8	237.2	237.6	238.3	244.8	248.6	235.3
2007	240.4	239.9	241.8	241.8	243.4	244.3	245.2	246.8	247.0	248.1	253.5	256.4	245.7
2008	246.9	245.5	246.3	247.0	247.8	248.8	248.2	249.1	248.0	247.5	251.0	251.0	248.0
2009	238.6	236.0	235.1	233.2	233.9	233.6	231.6	231.8	231.8	231.8	235.4	237.1	234.2
2010	226.3	225.0	225.9	226.8	227.8	228.5	228.6	229.8	228.9	230.1	234.8	236.7	229.1
2011	227.5	226.5	227.8	230.8	231.7	232.6	233.6	236.0	233.8	234.8	238.4	240.9	232.9
Wholesale Trade													
2000	39.5	39.7	39.9	39.9	40.1	40.5	40.7	40.8	40.9	41.1	41.0	41.3	40.5
2001	40.9	41.1	41.3	41.2	41.4	41.5	41.5	41.4	41.1	40.9	40.9	40.9	41.2
2002	39.9	40.0	40.0	40.1	40.6	40.5	40.5	40.6	40.4	40.5	40.4	40.5	40.3
2003	39.8	39.8	39.9	40.1	40.4	40.5	40.2	40.3	40.2	40.3	40.4	40.5	40.2
2004	40.1	40.2	40.4	40.8	41.1	41.5	41.4	41.4	41.5	41.7	42.0	42.2	41.2
2005	41.8	42.0	42.2	42.4	42.9	43.1	43.1	43.3	43.3	43.5	43.7	43.8	42.9
2006	43.3	43.6	43.8	44.1	44.6	45.2	45.1	45.3	45.5	45.7	46.0	46.4	44.9
2007	46.2	46.4	46.6	46.6	47.2	47.5	47.6	47.9	47.8	48.0	48.2	48.5	47.4
2008	47.7	47.8	48.0	48.2	48.5	48.6	48.5	48.6	48.5	48.2	47.9	48.0	48.2
2009	46.6	46.4	46.0	45.3	45.1	45.0	44.7	44.6	44.5	44.5	44.3	44.4	45.1
2010	43.6	43.4	43.6	43.9	44.3	44.3	44.5	44.6	44.5	44.7	44.9	45.3	44.3
2011	44.8	45.1	45.4	45.8	46.1	46.3	46.4	46.7	46.7	46.9	47.1	47.2	46.2
Retail Trade													
2000	129.3	127.0	127.5	128.2	128.6	130.1	129.7	130.9	131.3	132.7	137.1	139.5	131.0
2001	131.6	129.8	130.0	130.6	130.8	131.0	130.4	130.8	129.9	129.7	133.9	135.5	131.2
2002	129.6	127.5	127.5	129.0	130.1	130.6	130.3	131.0	130.5	130.9	135.0	137.1	130.8
2003	127.7	126.3	126.7	127.1	128.1	128.8	128.9	130.2	129.8	131.1	135.8	138.5	129.9
2004	130.1	128.5	128.8	130.2	131.7	132.2	132.3	133.1	132.9	134.2	138.7	140.6	132.8
2005	132.4	130.8	132.8	132.4	133.0	133.5	134.6	136.6	136.4	137.9	142.0	144.3	135.6
2006	137.0	135.9	137.1	137.1	138.3	139.9	140.5	142.3	142.2	142.9	148.6	151.2	141.1
2007	144.3	143.4	144.7	144.8	145.6	145.9	146.5	147.5	147.3	147.8	152.7	154.5	147.1
2008	148.3	146.7	147.2	147.5	148.1	149.1	148.6	149.2	148.3	148.2	151.1	151.8	148.7
2009	142.0	140.2	140.2	139.5	140.5	140.7	139.1	139.7	139.8	139.9	143.7	144.9	140.9
2010	136.4	135.2	135.7	136.3	136.9	137.2	136.9	137.6	136.7	137.5	141.4	142.1	137.5
2011	134.8	133.6	134.4	136.7	137.3	137.6	138.4	139.2	137.3	138.4	141.5	143.8	137.8
Transportation and Utilities													
2000	48.1	48.0	48.3	48.3	47.8	48.5	48.9	49.2	49.4	49.6	50.0	50.6	48.9
2001	47.3	47.2	47.3	47.2	46.5	46.4	46.5	46.6	46.6	46.5	45.9	46.0	46.7
2002	44.7	45.0	44.2	44.4	44.5	44.4	44.5	44.5	44.2	44.8	44.6	44.2	44.5
2003	43.6	43.5	43.4	43.4	43.6	43.5	43.8	44.0	43.9	44.4	44.3	44.4	43.8
2004	44.4	44.4	44.4	44.5	44.7	44.8	44.8	44.9	44.9	45.4	45.6	45.9	44.9
2005	45.5	46.0	46.2	47.0	47.1	47.2	47.4	47.6	47.9	48.3	48.5	49.2	47.3
2006	48.3	48.6	48.7	48.8	48.8	49.1	49.2	49.6	49.9	49.7	50.2	51.0	49.3
2007	49.9	50.1	50.5	50.4	50.6	50.9	51.1	51.4	51.9	52.3	52.6	53.4	51.3
2008	50.9	51.0	51.1	51.3	51.2	51.1	51.1	51.3	51.2	51.1	51.1	51.2	51.1
2009	50.0	49.4	48.9	48.4	48.3	47.9	47.8	47.5	47.5	47.4	47.4	47.8	48.2
2010	46.3	46.4	46.6	46.6	46.6	47.0	47.2	47.6	47.7	47.9	48.5	49.3	47.3
2011	47.9	47.8	48.0	48.3	48.3	48.7	48.8	50.1	49.8	49.5	49.8	49.9	48.9
Information													
2000	34.2	34.3	34.6	34.5	35.3	35.8	35.7	36.2	36.3	35.9	36.2	36.1	35.4
2001	34.5	33.9	33.8	33.8	34.1	34.2	33.7	33.4	33.0	32.5	32.9	32.5	33.5
2002	31.8	31.7	31.1	30.9	31.3	31.1	31.0	30.7	30.5	30.5	30.8	30.7	31.0
2003	30.1	30.0	29.9	29.4	30.1	30.2	29.8	30.0	29.8	30.2	30.1	30.6	30.0
2004	29.4	30.0	30.1	30.3	30.2	30.7	30.1	30.3	30.2	30.5	31.3	31.3	30.4
2005	31.0	31.5	31.8	31.6	31.7	31.7	32.4	33.0	32.7	32.2	32.5	32.3	32.0
2006	31.7	31.5	31.5	31.9	32.8	33.0	32.1	32.5	32.2	32.0	32.5	32.0	32.1
2007	32.0	32.0	32.2	30.9	31.1	31.0	30.9	31.0	30.4	30.4	30.5	30.5	31.1
2008	29.8	30.5	30.6	30.9	31.4	31.5	31.1	31.1	30.8	30.5	30.7	30.8	30.8
2009	29.9	30.0	29.9	29.5	29.8	29.9	29.5	29.3	29.0	29.0	29.4	29.7	29.6
2010	28.7	28.9	29.3	29.4	29.3	29.4	29.3	29.0	29.0	29.0	29.8	29.9	29.3
2011	28.9	29.2	29.2	29.2	29.4	29.5	29.6	29.9	29.2	29.2	29.7	30.0	29.4

1. Employment by Industry: Utah, Selected Years, 2000–2011—*Continued*

(Numbers in thousands, not seasonally adjusted)

Industry and year	January	February	March	April	May	June	July	August	September	October	November	December	Annual average
Financial Activities													
2000	58.6	58.4	58.7	58.5	58.3	58.6	58.9	59.2	59.2	59.3	59.8	60.6	59.0
2001	61.2	61.5	61.8	61.6	61.7	62.2	62.6	63.1	63.0	62.7	63.3	63.9	62.4
2002	63.4	63.4	62.9	63.0	63.3	63.4	63.0	63.3	62.9	63.7	63.8	64.6	63.4
2003	64.1	64.8	64.4	64.6	64.9	64.6	65.1	65.2	64.6	64.4	64.3	64.9	64.7
2004	63.7	64.2	64.2	64.7	64.7	64.7	65.0	64.9	65.0	65.3	65.7	66.6	64.9
2005	65.5	66.0	65.5	66.8	66.7	67.2	67.9	68.1	68.1	68.7	69.0	70.3	67.5
2006	69.2	69.9	70.1	70.7	70.9	71.4	71.8	72.1	72.0	72.9	73.5	74.6	71.6
2007	73.7	74.4	74.6	75.0	75.2	75.6	75.6	75.7	75.2	75.7	75.9	76.6	75.3
2008	74.2	74.9	74.6	74.5	74.3	74.2	74.1	74.1	73.4	73.1	72.9	73.8	74.0
2009	72.5	72.5	72.4	71.7	71.4	71.2	70.3	70.3	69.8	69.7	69.6	70.5	71.0
2010	68.5	67.9	68.1	67.8	67.6	67.7	67.6	67.9	67.7	68.2	68.3	68.8	68.0
2011	67.4	67.6	67.7	68.2	68.0	68.5	70.1	70.4	70.3	69.8	69.9	70.5	69.0
Professional and Business Services													
2000	131.1	132.4	134.8	136.8	137.0	140.0	139.1	140.7	141.6	142.0	141.6	142.7	138.3
2001	136.8	135.9	137.0	137.3	137.9	138.1	137.4	138.3	136.3	134.7	132.9	131.8	136.2
2002	129.5	132.7	129.6	131.2	132.4	132.6	132.1	133.4	133.3	132.9	133.1	132.0	132.1
2003	126.5	126.4	127.0	129.3	131.0	132.0	132.8	134.6	134.2	135.7	136.1	136.4	131.8
2004	132.2	133.6	134.7	137.1	138.5	139.9	139.5	140.6	139.3	142.1	142.1	142.8	138.5
2005	138.2	139.5	140.9	143.4	145.3	146.1	147.4	149.0	149.1	150.1	150.5	151.1	145.9
2006	147.1	148.5	149.8	152.2	153.8	156.2	156.6	157.5	157.1	156.9	158.1	158.6	154.4
2007	153.5	154.5	156.4	160.0	163.0	164.7	164.1	165.8	165.0	167.0	168.2	167.8	162.5
2008	159.0	159.8	160.6	162.2	164.2	164.4	164.4	165.8	164.6	162.6	160.0	158.9	162.2
2009	150.5	149.6	148.8	149.1	149.5	149.4	149.0	149.0	148.9	149.9	148.9	149.0	149.3
2010	144.2	145.0	147.9	150.9	152.8	154.3	155.4	155.0	154.4	156.1	156.1	156.5	152.4
2011	151.8	153.2	155.0	157.9	158.5	159.2	160.8	163.3	162.6	163.4	164.3	165.2	159.6
Education and Health Services													
2000	99.9	102.6	103.1	103.8	103.4	102.5	101.7	102.4	105.1	106.2	107.4	108.2	103.9
2001	107.6	109.0	109.6	109.9	106.8	107.5	105.6	106.4	111.0	112.1	113.1	113.9	109.4
2002	111.7	112.9	113.4	114.5	110.8	110.7	110.0	111.6	116.3	117.6	118.1	119.2	113.9
2003	117.4	118.4	119.1	119.0	115.0	115.6	114.6	115.5	120.1	121.6	122.1	123.3	118.5
2004	121.4	122.9	123.8	123.7	120.2	121.0	120.0	120.9	125.5	126.8	127.8	128.3	123.5
2005	126.8	128.0	128.7	129.0	125.0	125.9	124.5	125.9	130.7	132.0	133.1	133.6	128.6
2006	132.6	133.5	134.6	134.8	131.2	131.6	130.2	131.9	136.5	137.6	138.6	139.1	134.4
2007	137.7	139.1	139.8	140.5	136.7	136.6	135.7	137.7	142.6	144.1	145.2	146.1	140.2
2008	145.0	146.3	146.8	147.2	143.1	142.6	141.7	143.4	148.7	150.4	151.7	152.1	146.6
2009	150.4	150.9	151.7	151.5	147.5	146.8	146.0	147.6	152.6	154.5	155.7	155.7	150.9
2010	154.6	155.3	156.0	156.4	152.1	151.4	150.7	151.7	157.1	158.6	158.9	158.4	155.1
2011	157.6	158.8	159.0	160.7	155.8	155.3	153.2	154.9	161.4	163.7	163.2	163.4	158.9
Leisure and Hospitality													
2000	92.5	94.2	96.7	96.8	95.9	99.2	100.0	100.9	98.8	96.4	95.9	98.4	97.1
2001	94.9	96.0	98.5	99.2	98.9	101.4	101.5	102.1	100.2	97.1	95.7	99.1	98.7
2002	100.5	106.3	103.3	103.1	100.0	102.1	102.1	102.2	99.9	96.8	96.1	99.0	101.0
2003	97.7	98.4	99.5	100.1	98.4	101.3	101.7	102.3	100.6	97.6	97.6	100.2	99.6
2004	98.4	99.4	100.9	101.8	100.5	103.9	104.4	104.9	103.9	101.0	100.9	103.5	102.0
2005	100.9	102.2	104.0	103.7	103.2	106.0	106.1	106.8	105.8	103.1	102.5	105.4	104.1
2006	104.5	105.8	107.8	109.5	107.4	110.4	110.8	111.6	109.6	106.9	107.0	110.6	108.5
2007	109.9	111.2	111.3	111.8	111.6	115.2	115.7	116.0	113.6	110.6	111.1	115.4	113.1
2008	113.7	114.9	116.3	117.4	114.2	116.8	117.3	117.7	114.9	112.2	109.9	112.9	114.9
2009	111.0	111.3	112.6	113.5	110.7	112.9	113.0	113.6	111.1	107.4	105.7	108.7	111.0
2010	107.8	108.5	109.8	113.1	110.0	113.0	113.4	113.9	111.2	108.7	107.4	111.8	110.7
2011	110.5	111.2	113.0	115.2	112.9	116.3	118.5	118.3	116.3	110.7	109.4	111.9	113.7
Other Services													
2000	30.3	30.1	30.1	30.3	30.4	30.9	31.2	31.2	30.7	30.0	30.2	30.2	30.5
2001	29.4	29.5	29.7	30.2	30.7	31.5	32.3	32.7	31.9	31.9	32.2	32.4	31.2
2002	32.0	33.1	32.5	32.7	32.8	33.1	33.5	33.5	32.8	32.5	32.8	32.5	32.8
2003	31.9	31.9	32.1	32.3	32.4	32.8	33.0	33.2	32.3	31.9	32.0	32.1	32.3
2004	31.8	32.0	32.5	32.6	32.9	33.1	34.0	33.9	33.0	32.8	32.8	32.8	32.9
2005	32.4	32.6	33.1	33.3	33.4	33.6	34.6	34.5	33.9	33.4	33.6	33.8	33.5
2006	33.2	33.5	34.1	34.1	34.6	35.2	35.5	35.6	35.2	34.6	34.6	35.0	34.6
2007	34.4	34.8	35.0	35.2	35.9	36.3	36.6	36.9	35.9	35.7	35.6	35.6	35.7
2008	34.8	35.1	35.3	35.4	35.6	35.9	36.6	37.1	35.8	35.0	34.8	34.8	35.5
2009	33.9	34.0	34.1	34.1	34.2	34.5	35.0	34.9	33.8	33.6	33.4	33.4	34.1
2010	33.1	33.2	33.6	33.5	33.6	33.9	34.6	34.3	33.4	33.4	33.3	33.3	33.6
2011	33.0	33.3	33.4	33.7	34.1	34.4	35.5	34.5	33.6	33.9	33.9	33.8	33.9
Government													
2000	181.2	186.9	188.5	190.4	191.8	187.8	172.6	172.1	185.7	188.5	189.3	189.6	185.4
2001	186.6	191.9	192.7	194.0	194.2	193.3	177.0	177.1	191.3	193.4	194.9	195.0	190.1
2002	194.3	195.0	198.0	198.9	197.6	197.8	184.4	182.9	195.8	197.8	198.5	198.4	195.0
2003	198.1	199.7	199.9	201.1	199.8	198.0	183.5	183.7	196.7	199.4	199.4	199.3	196.6
2004	198.4	200.0	201.0	203.0	201.5	200.4	185.5	187.1	200.3	203.0	203.4	202.9	198.9
2005	202.3	204.0	204.7	206.0	205.0	204.3	188.8	191.7	203.7	205.5	206.1	205.5	202.3
2006	204.0	206.2	206.9	207.7	206.6	207.1	191.3	194.2	206.0	207.5	208.4	207.6	204.5
2007	206.0	208.0	208.7	210.0	209.5	209.6	192.3	196.0	208.6	211.0	211.9	211.0	206.9
2008	210.1	212.1	213.0	214.4	214.3	213.6	196.3	201.0	214.7	216.9	217.5	216.6	211.7
2009	214.4	216.3	216.5	219.3	218.5	216.6	198.8	202.8	216.6	219.0	219.0	218.2	214.7
2010	216.3	217.7	218.7	221.0	224.7	220.6	202.3	206.0	219.8	222.3	222.2	220.9	217.7
2011	219.0	221.2	222.7	223.9	222.9	221.0	202.2	206.2	223.1	225.3	224.6	223.4	219.6

2. Average Weekly Hours by Selected Industry: Utah, 2007–2011

(Not seasonally adjusted)

Industry and year	January	February	March	April	May	June	July	August	September	October	November	December	Annual average
Total Private													
2007	34.6	34.6	35.1	35.5	35.1	35.1	35.5	34.6	35.3	34.7	34.3	34.7	34.9
2008	33.7	34.3	34.6	33.9	34.4	35.0	34.8	35.2	35.0	34.8	35.0	34.5	34.6
2009	34.1	34.9	34.9	35.9	36.0	36.1	36.2	36.7	36.1	36.1	36.6	36.1	35.8
2010	35.9	36.0	35.3	34.7	35.6	35.4	35.4	36.3	35.4	35.4	35.1	35.3	35.5
2011	35.1	34.8	34.8	34.8	35.3	35.0	34.9	35.0	34.7	35.7	34.9	34.7	35.0
Goods-Producing													
2007	38.2	38.0	39.2	39.4	39.6	39.5	39.8	39.5	39.1	38.7	38.5	38.6	39.0
2008	37.3	37.4	37.9	37.6	37.7	37.8	38.4	39.7	38.5	38.5	37.6	37.7	38.0
2009	36.8	37.1	37.5	37.0	37.8	37.3	37.9	38.5	37.1	39.1	39.4	38.5	37.8
2010	40.4	40.7	40.9	38.3	39.2	38.3	38.3	39.5	38.7	40.9	39.5	40.0	39.6
2011	39.6	39.2	39.2	39.3	39.7	39.4	38.9	39.6	38.9	39.7	40.1	39.5	39.4
Construction													
2007	36.2	37.5	38.1	38.2	38.9	38.1	38.8	38.5	37.4	37.4	37.3	36.2	37.7
2008	34.6	35.6	35.5	34.0	34.1	35.2	36.2	36.7	35.4	35.7	34.5	35.3	35.2
2009	35.2	34.6	35.0	35.1	36.9	36.4	36.9	37.5	35.2	38.5	38.0	35.4	36.2
2010	36.9	35.7	37.1	36.8	37.0	37.3	37.0	37.7	36.5	38.9	37.5	38.2	37.2
2011	36.9	37.4	37.7	38.4	38.4	38.8	38.2	38.5	38.2	38.4	38.7	37.3	38.1
Manufacturing													
2007	39.8	38.4	40.3	40.2	40.3	40.1	40.8	40.5	40.4	40.0	39.2	40.4	40.0
2008	39.4	38.3	39.6	39.3	39.4	39.3	38.8	39.5	39.1	38.9	38.1	37.8	39.0
2009	36.6	37.9	38.1	37.3	37.6	37.1	37.8	38.4	37.8	39.1	39.8	39.9	38.1
2010	40.3	40.2	40.3	40.3	40.7	40.0	39.2	39.2	39.0	39.0	39.7	39.5	39.8
2011	39.5	39.1	39.0	38.9	39.6	39.0	38.7	39.5	38.5	39.7	40.1	39.9	39.3
Trade, Transportation, and Utilities													
2007	31.1	31.2	31.8	31.9	30.5	30.7	31.0	30.0	31.0	30.7	30.0	31.3	30.9
2008	29.9	30.3	29.7	28.7	29.4	30.5	30.2	30.5	30.1	30.2	30.8	30.9	30.1
2009	30.5	31.3	31.8	31.1	31.4	31.5	31.9	32.6	31.8	31.8	31.9	32.2	31.6
2010	31.2	32.2	31.1	31.6	32.3	32.5	32.6	33.3	32.9	33.0	33.0	33.5	32.4
2011	33.6	33.5	34.0	34.1	34.2	34.2	34.1	34.0	33.6	34.4	33.4	33.6	33.9
Information													
2007	35.7	35.3	35.4	36.8	35.8	36.2	36.1	35.3	36.2	35.7	34.8	35.7	35.7
2008	33.8	33.5	34.2	33.4	33.9	35.7	34.0	34.0	34.0	34.2	35.3	33.7	34.1
2009	33.3	36.3	35.9	34.2	34.5	34.5	34.4	35.4	33.7	33.6	34.5	32.8	34.4
2010	32.7	32.8	32.7	32.3	32.9	31.3	32.3	33.1	32.1	31.7	31.9	32.3	32.3
2011	32.6	32.1	32.4	31.8	33.6	32.2	33.1	33.1	33.5	34.8	34.2	34.1	33.1
Financial Activities													
2007	35.6	35.8	36.0	36.6	36.0	35.8	36.3	36.0	35.6	36.1	35.0	36.5	35.9
2008	35.7	36.7	37.4	36.9	36.5	37.2	36.4	36.5	35.6	36.2	36.7	36.1	36.5
2009	34.1	34.6	34.0	34.0	34.1	35.8	34.1	34.9	34.5	34.6	36.6	35.3	34.7
2010	35.0	35.0	35.0	35.0	35.3	34.9	34.6	35.0	34.7	34.3	34.6	34.9	34.9
2011	35.1	34.9	34.8	35.4	36.1	35.3	35.2	35.1	35.3	36.1	35.4	35.7	35.4
Professional and Business Services													
2007	32.8	32.8	34.0	34.1	33.5	33.6	34.2	33.3	34.2	33.9	33.4	33.2	33.6
2008	31.7	32.3	33.9	33.5	33.5	34.1	33.4	33.8	33.7	33.6	34.3	34.1	33.5
2009	33.4	35.3	34.9	36.0	36.2	36.7	36.2	36.9	35.7	35.5	36.3	36.5	35.8
2010	37.3	36.9	35.8	36.4	37.3	37.3	37.0	37.8	36.2	35.7	35.6	35.5	36.6
2011	35.2	35.9	35.8	35.8	36.5	36.2	35.4	35.9	35.8	36.7	35.3	34.7	35.8
Education and Health Services													
2007	40.0	40.4	39.8	39.9	40.5	40.1	40.5	40.0	40.6	39.8	40.3	39.7	40.1
2008	39.2	39.6	39.2	38.5	38.9	39.7	39.6	39.1	40.4	39.8	40.4	39.5	39.5
2009	39.7	40.0	39.6	39.3	39.1	39.0	39.3	39.6	41.0	39.5	39.8	39.9	39.7
2010	39.7	39.8	39.0	38.5	39.1	39.4	39.2	39.7	41.0	40.3	40.7	40.6	39.8
2011	40.2	40.2	39.8	39.5	39.8	39.3	39.3	39.0	38.8	39.4	39.0	39.1	39.4
Leisure and Hospitality													
2007	24.3	24.3	24.6	25.0	23.6	24.3	25.0	24.1	24.6	23.5	22.0	23.9	24.1
2008	23.2	24.2	24.4	23.3	24.2	24.9	24.5	24.9	24.0	23.7	23.4	22.5	23.9
2009	23.9	24.4	24.7	22.8	23.6	24.3	24.5	26.4	24.5	24.5	24.3	23.4	24.3
2010	24.5	25.2	24.7	25.0	26.0	26.7	27.1	27.2	25.1	25.2	24.2	24.3	25.4
2011	26.0	25.9	25.4	25.3	25.5	24.7	25.5	25.2	24.4	26.0	24.2	23.8	25.2

3. Average Hourly Earnings by Selected Industry: Utah, 2007–2011

(Dollars, not seasonally adjusted)

Industry and year	January	February	March	April	May	June	July	August	September	October	November	December	Annual average
Total Private													
2007	21.74	22.84	21.89	22.20	21.77	21.72	20.97	21.05	20.44	20.26	20.73	21.37	21.41
2008	20.95	21.28	20.84	20.65	20.75	20.91	20.96	21.15	21.25	21.23	21.44	21.75	21.10
2009	21.48	22.01	22.14	22.69	22.46	22.44	22.09	22.16	22.20	21.95	22.11	25.96	22.48
2010	25.51	25.55	24.64	24.48	24.13	24.08	23.92	23.88	23.86	23.80	24.12	23.76	24.31
2011	23.90	23.85	24.68	23.30	23.03	22.58	22.75	22.44	22.63	22.70	22.73	22.80	23.10
Goods-Producing													
2007	20.72	21.72	20.74	21.20	21.03	20.64	20.80	20.78	21.35	21.27	22.19	23.12	21.29
2008	21.89	21.81	22.05	21.83	22.21	22.34	22.85	23.77	23.43	23.01	23.27	24.52	22.75
2009	23.61	23.95	23.94	24.06	23.80	23.72	23.39	23.64	24.01	23.61	23.47	23.68	23.74
2010	23.52	23.95	23.39	23.63	23.41	23.25	22.85	23.45	23.36	23.16	23.78	23.22	23.41
2011	23.64	23.47	23.27	23.47	23.41	22.90	23.11	22.91	22.99	23.14	22.99	23.21	23.20
Construction													
2007	21.69	21.26	21.19	22.44	22.10	21.71	22.23	22.04	22.79	22.62	23.80	24.03	22.32
2008	22.55	22.02	22.58	22.24	23.32	22.29	22.17	22.93	22.21	22.26	22.62	24.36	22.61
2009	24.01	24.09	24.09	24.48	24.29	24.21	23.32	23.62	23.81	23.95	23.47	24.75	23.99
2010	24.27	24.66	24.24	23.94	24.17	23.66	23.29	24.19	24.02	24.21	24.50	24.07	24.09
2011	24.37	23.94	23.62	23.50	24.00	23.36	23.30	23.58	23.11	23.27	23.12	23.03	23.50
Manufacturing													
2007	19.73	20.36	19.15	19.30	19.37	19.52	19.58	19.61	20.02	19.94	20.58	20.56	19.81
2008	20.90	21.12	21.12	20.85	20.80	21.50	20.32	21.16	21.61	21.08	21.42	21.72	21.13
2009	20.80	20.28	21.55	21.76	21.69	21.84	21.91	22.30	22.94	22.31	22.50	21.98	21.82
2010	22.32	22.90	22.32	22.86	22.71	23.02	22.66	23.01	22.97	22.50	22.77	22.05	22.67
2011	22.27	21.99	21.84	22.40	21.97	21.53	21.94	21.49	21.88	21.91	21.79	22.21	21.93
Trade, Transportation, and Utilities													
2007	18.41	19.42	18.32	19.00	18.61	18.90	18.91	18.94	19.18	18.88	19.43	19.37	18.95
2008	19.75	20.75	19.71	19.72	19.43	19.69	19.72	19.81	19.74	19.55	20.02	19.61	19.79
2009	18.85	20.31	19.41	20.24	19.42	19.43	18.55	19.13	18.91	19.09	19.46	19.29	19.34
2010	19.49	19.46	18.37	19.36	19.38	19.06	19.08	19.03	19.05	19.23	19.65	19.70	19.24
2011	19.91	20.74	20.66	20.64	20.53	20.32	20.84	20.40	20.65	20.89	20.69	20.58	20.57
Information													
2007	27.13	28.25	27.91	26.04	25.61	25.13	26.66	26.64	27.78	27.18	27.11	27.51	26.91
2008	27.05	26.50	26.30	25.41	25.22	25.41	25.42	25.56	25.71	25.77	26.20	26.31	25.90
2009	26.62	26.78	26.63	26.78	26.32	26.26	26.68	28.11	27.31	27.69	28.15	27.60	27.07
2010	27.65	26.51	26.91	28.23	27.64	27.55	27.85	27.66	26.92	27.57	27.41	27.92	27.49
2011	27.67	26.73	26.70	26.77	25.96	25.65	26.50	26.06	27.42	28.69	28.09	27.94	27.03
Financial Activities													
2007	22.31	21.95	22.36	21.80	21.95	22.09	22.41	22.51	22.86	22.58	22.67	23.31	22.40
2008	21.85	22.07	22.24	22.08	22.26	22.39	22.57	23.15	23.07	23.89	23.71	23.59	22.73
2009	25.58	25.30	25.77	26.06	25.77	25.87	28.09	26.55	26.20	25.95	25.38	25.48	25.99
2010	26.40	26.06	25.67	26.26	26.16	25.26	25.49	25.23	25.02	24.86	24.49	24.59	25.46
2011	24.97	25.11	24.95	24.88	24.66	25.12	25.61	25.90	26.24	25.64	25.98	26.30	25.46
Professional and Business Services													
2007	41.92	42.46	41.25	42.70	41.50	42.54	42.25	41.75	42.16	41.20	40.94	40.52	41.76
2008	40.47	40.19	39.43	37.46	36.69	36.18	35.56	33.95	33.71	33.40	33.00	32.00	35.95
2009	32.25	31.54	31.33	31.44	31.33	31.12	29.43	30.50	30.02	29.04	29.57	27.93	30.44
2010	29.12	30.58	29.71	29.14	29.26	27.83	27.26	26.10	26.02	26.33	26.78	27.49	27.94
2011	27.30	26.43	26.16	26.01	25.82	25.41	25.14	24.67	25.13	25.84	25.60	25.80	25.76
Education and Health Services													
2007	17.76	18.80	16.65	16.73	16.47	16.50	16.81	16.82	17.55	17.06	17.15	18.04	17.20
2008	17.72	17.62	18.11	17.96	18.06	18.29	18.40	18.37	18.74	18.60	18.76	19.47	18.35
2009	18.85	19.01	19.16	19.33	19.22	19.39	19.25	19.22	19.65	19.23	19.31	19.11	19.23
2010	18.45	19.47	19.36	19.71	19.68	19.37	19.55	19.64	19.86	20.02	20.11	19.79	19.59
2011	19.00	20.01	19.65	17.67	17.77	17.47	18.24	18.29	18.39	18.85	18.77	19.49	18.64
Leisure and Hospitality													
2007	11.32	11.47	11.38	11.28	10.93	11.06	11.03	11.28	11.35	11.45	11.49	11.66	11.31
2008	11.75	11.74	11.83	11.60	11.42	11.54	11.38	11.49	11.91	11.87	11.91	12.26	11.72
2009	12.26	11.64	11.92	11.47	11.47	11.49	11.43	11.75	12.01	12.07	12.32	12.63	11.87
2010	12.79	12.60	12.51	12.02	11.69	11.73	11.83	11.65	11.91	11.90	12.21	12.62	12.11
2011	12.83	12.73	12.87	12.25	12.03	11.84	11.75	11.73	11.84	11.68	12.01	12.25	12.15

4. Average Weekly Earnings by Selected Industry: Utah, 2007–2011

(Dollars, not seasonally adjusted)

Industry and year	January	February	March	April	May	June	July	August	September	October	November	December	Annual average
Total Private													
2007	752.20	790.26	768.34	788.10	764.13	762.37	744.44	728.33	721.53	703.02	711.04	741.54	747.80
2008	706.02	729.90	721.06	700.04	713.80	731.85	729.41	744.48	743.75	738.80	750.40	750.38	730.03
2009	732.47	768.15	772.69	814.57	808.56	810.08	799.66	813.27	801.42	792.40	809.23	937.16	804.82
2010	915.81	919.80	869.79	849.46	859.03	852.43	846.77	866.84	844.64	842.52	846.61	838.73	862.42
2011	838.89	829.98	858.86	810.84	812.96	790.30	793.98	785.40	785.26	810.39	793.28	791.16	808.54
Goods-Producing													
2007	791.50	825.36	813.01	835.28	832.79	815.28	827.84	820.81	834.79	823.15	854.32	892.43	830.67
2008	816.50	815.69	835.70	820.81	837.32	844.45	877.44	943.67	902.06	885.89	874.95	924.40	864.61
2009	868.85	888.55	897.75	890.22	899.64	884.76	886.48	910.14	890.77	923.15	924.72	911.68	897.71
2010	950.21	974.77	956.65	905.03	917.67	890.48	875.16	926.28	904.03	947.24	939.31	928.80	926.03
2011	936.14	920.02	912.18	922.37	929.38	902.26	898.98	907.24	894.31	918.66	921.90	916.80	914.85
Construction													
2007	785.18	797.25	807.34	857.21	859.69	827.15	862.52	848.54	852.35	845.99	887.74	869.89	842.46
2008	780.23	783.91	801.59	756.16	795.21	784.61	802.55	841.53	786.23	794.68	780.39	859.91	796.90
2009	845.15	833.51	843.15	859.25	896.30	881.24	860.51	885.75	838.11	922.08	891.86	876.15	869.24
2010	895.56	880.36	899.30	880.99	894.29	882.52	861.73	911.96	876.73	941.77	918.75	919.47	897.44
2011	899.25	895.36	890.47	902.40	921.60	906.37	890.06	907.83	882.80	893.57	894.74	859.02	895.21
Manufacturing													
2007	785.25	781.82	771.75	775.86	780.61	782.75	798.86	794.21	808.81	797.60	806.74	830.62	793.07
2008	823.46	808.90	836.35	819.41	819.52	844.95	788.42	835.82	844.95	820.01	816.10	821.02	823.24
2009	761.28	768.61	821.06	811.65	815.54	810.26	828.20	856.32	867.13	872.32	895.50	877.00	831.42
2010	899.50	920.58	899.50	921.26	924.30	920.80	888.27	901.99	895.83	877.50	903.97	870.98	902.06
2011	879.67	859.81	851.76	871.36	870.01	839.67	849.08	848.86	842.38	869.83	873.78	886.18	861.82
Trade, Transportation, and Utilities													
2007	572.55	605.90	582.58	606.10	567.61	580.23	586.21	568.20	594.58	579.62	582.90	606.28	586.10
2008	590.53	628.73	585.39	565.96	571.24	600.55	595.54	604.21	594.17	590.41	616.62	605.95	595.80
2009	574.93	635.70	617.24	629.46	609.79	612.05	591.75	623.64	601.34	607.06	620.77	621.14	612.04
2010	608.09	626.61	571.31	611.78	625.97	619.45	622.01	633.70	626.75	634.59	648.45	659.95	624.25
2011	668.98	694.79	702.44	703.82	702.13	694.94	710.64	693.60	693.84	718.62	691.05	691.49	697.17
Information													
2007	968.54	997.23	988.01	958.27	916.84	909.71	962.43	940.39	1,005.64	970.33	943.43	982.11	962.01
2008	914.29	887.75	899.46	848.69	854.96	907.14	864.28	869.04	874.14	881.33	924.86	886.65	884.24
2009	886.45	972.11	956.02	915.88	908.04	905.97	917.79	995.09	920.35	930.38	971.18	905.28	932.18
2010	904.16	869.53	879.96	911.83	909.36	862.32	899.56	915.55	864.13	873.97	874.38	901.82	888.97
2011	902.04	858.03	865.08	851.29	872.26	825.93	877.15	862.59	918.57	998.41	960.68	952.75	895.54
Financial Activities													
2007	794.24	785.81	804.96	797.88	790.20	790.82	813.48	810.36	813.82	815.14	793.45	850.82	805.19
2008	780.05	809.97	831.78	814.75	812.49	832.91	821.55	844.98	821.29	864.82	870.16	851.60	829.57
2009	872.28	875.38	876.18	886.04	878.76	926.15	957.87	926.60	903.90	897.87	928.91	899.44	902.23
2010	924.00	912.10	898.45	919.10	923.45	881.57	881.95	883.05	868.19	852.70	847.35	858.19	887.30
2011	876.45	876.34	868.26	880.75	890.23	886.74	901.47	909.09	926.27	925.60	919.69	938.91	900.35
Professional and Business Services													
2007	1,374.98	1,392.69	1,402.50	1,456.07	1,390.25	1,429.34	1,444.95	1,390.28	1,441.87	1,396.68	1,367.40	1,345.26	1,402.61
2008	1,282.90	1,298.14	1,336.68	1,254.91	1,229.12	1,233.74	1,187.70	1,147.51	1,136.03	1,122.24	1,131.90	1,091.20	1,204.09
2009	1,077.15	1,113.36	1,093.42	1,131.84	1,134.15	1,142.10	1,065.37	1,125.45	1,071.71	1,030.92	1,073.39	1,019.45	1,089.70
2010	1,086.18	1,128.40	1,063.62	1,060.70	1,091.40	1,038.06	1,008.62	986.58	941.92	939.98	953.37	975.90	1,021.39
2011	960.96	948.84	936.53	931.16	942.43	919.84	889.96	885.65	899.65	948.33	903.68	895.26	921.43
Education and Health Services													
2007	710.40	759.52	662.67	667.53	667.04	661.65	680.81	672.80	712.53	678.99	691.15	716.19	690.29
2008	694.62	697.75	709.91	691.46	702.53	726.11	728.64	718.27	757.10	740.28	757.90	769.07	724.84
2009	748.35	760.40	758.74	759.67	751.50	756.21	756.53	761.11	805.65	759.59	768.54	762.49	762.43
2010	732.47	774.91	755.04	758.84	769.49	763.18	766.36	779.71	814.26	806.81	818.48	803.47	778.83
2011	763.80	804.40	782.07	697.97	707.25	686.57	716.83	713.31	713.53	742.69	732.03	762.06	735.44
Leisure and Hospitality													
2007	275.08	278.72	279.95	282.00	257.95	268.76	275.75	271.85	279.21	269.08	252.78	278.67	272.54
2008	272.60	284.11	288.65	270.28	276.36	287.35	278.81	286.10	285.84	281.32	278.69	275.85	280.53
2009	293.01	284.02	294.42	261.52	270.69	279.21	280.04	310.20	294.25	295.72	299.38	295.54	288.02
2010	313.36	317.52	309.00	300.50	303.94	313.19	320.59	316.88	298.94	299.88	295.48	306.67	308.02
2011	333.58	329.71	326.90	309.93	306.77	292.45	299.63	295.60	288.90	303.68	290.64	291.55	305.59

VERMONT
At a Glance

Population:
    2000 census: 608,613
    2010 census: 625,741
    2011 estimate: 626,431

Percent change in population:
    2000–2010: 2.8%
    2010–2011: 0.1%

Percent change in total nonfarm employment:
    2000–2010: -0.4%
    2010–2011: 0.7%

Industry with the largest growth in employment, 2000–2011 (thousands):
    Education and Health Services, 14.2

Industry with the largest decline or smallest growth in employment, 2000–2011 (thousands):
    Manufacturing, -15.4

Civilian labor force:
    2000: 335,798
    2010: 359,844
    2011: 359,166

Unemployment rate and rank among states (lowest to highest):
    2000: 2.7%, 3rd
    2010: 6.4%, 6th
    2011: 5.6%, 5th

Over-the-year change in unemployment rates:
    2010–2011: -0.8%

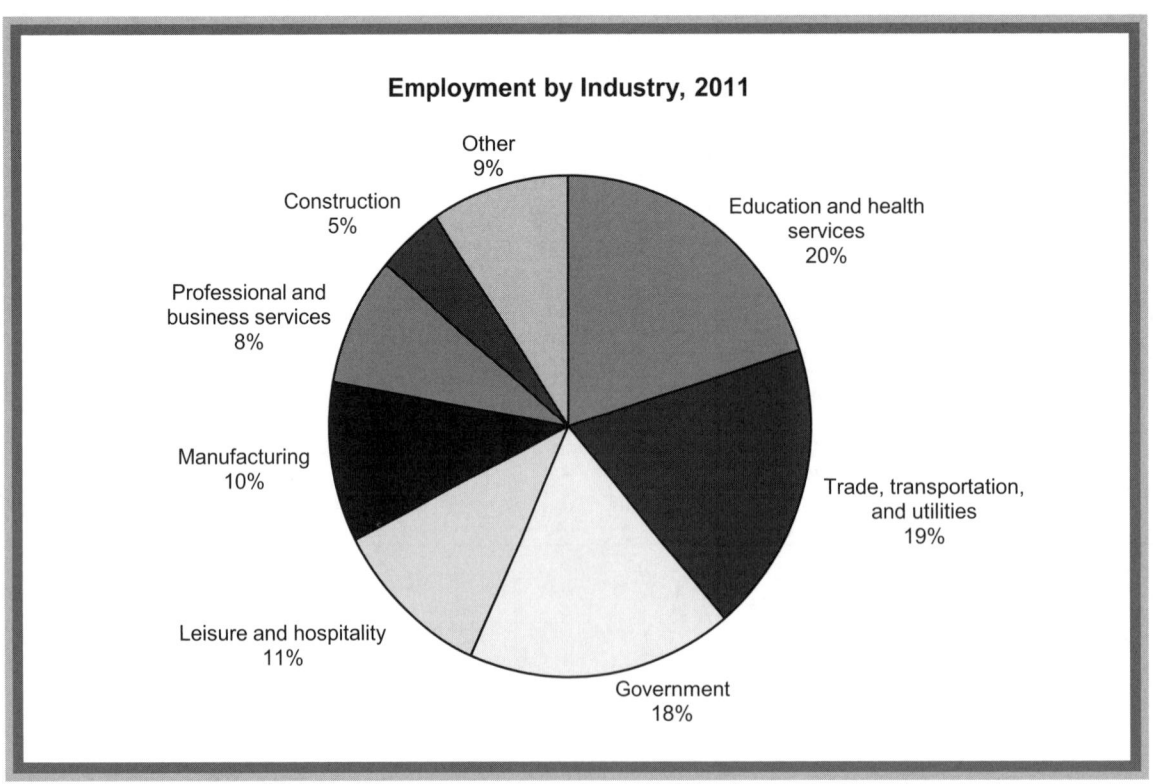

Employment by Industry, 2011

Other 9%
Construction 5%
Professional and business services 8%
Manufacturing 10%
Leisure and hospitality 11%
Government 18%
Education and health services 20%
Trade, transportation, and utilities 19%

1. Employment by Industry: Vermont, Selected Years, 2000–2011

(Numbers in thousands, not seasonally adjusted)

Industry and year	January	February	March	April	May	June	July	August	September	October	November	December	Annual average
Total Nonfarm													
2000	293.7	296.9	299.0	293.6	297.2	300.0	293.6	293.8	301.3	304.2	302.4	308.7	298.7
2001	301.7	302.6	302.0	299.6	301.2	304.6	297.8	297.5	303.7	305.3	303.1	306.0	302.1
2002	299.4	299.4	299.1	297.1	299.4	302.1	294.0	293.9	300.8	302.6	300.2	304.1	299.3
2003	297.2	297.8	296.9	293.6	298.0	301.1	294.2	294.9	301.7	304.4	302.5	307.9	299.2
2004	298.7	300.6	300.1	298.8	302.8	305.2	298.8	298.9	306.9	308.2	306.3	310.3	303.0
2005	302.9	304.0	303.5	302.4	305.1	307.1	300.7	301.1	308.4	309.5	308.1	313.6	305.5
2006	305.3	306.4	306.1	303.5	306.8	310.5	301.9	302.6	310.6	312.6	311.5	314.9	307.7
2007	306.2	307.2	306.8	303.3	308.2	311.6	303.7	303.5	310.8	312.1	311.3	315.5	308.4
2008	307.0	308.4	306.6	304.5	308.6	309.0	301.7	301.5	309.2	311.9	307.9	310.3	307.2
2009	299.1	300.9	297.2	293.8	297.8	297.3	290.2	290.8	297.6	301.5	298.4	302.4	297.3
2010	293.4	296.1	295.0	295.4	297.3	297.2	294.5	292.4	299.3	304.8	301.1	305.0	297.6
2011	296.5	299.2	297.9	295.5	298.4	299.6	293.1	294.3	302.1	306.0	304.0	308.1	299.6
Total Private													
2000	244.8	246.1	246.7	242.1	244.8	251.1	252.4	252.8	251.4	252.5	250.2	256.4	249.3
2001	251.6	251.0	250.3	247.9	249.4	254.7	256.1	255.8	252.6	251.9	249.6	252.4	251.9
2002	248.1	246.8	246.4	244.2	246.7	251.1	252.2	251.8	249.6	248.6	245.8	250.7	248.5
2003	245.1	243.9	243.1	239.7	244.1	249.2	250.9	252.0	248.9	249.5	247.3	252.8	247.2
2004	246.2	246.3	245.8	244.3	248.5	254.1	255.6	255.6	253.4	252.8	250.3	254.7	250.6
2005	249.5	248.9	248.3	247.3	250.1	255.2	255.2	256.9	254.3	253.3	251.6	257.3	252.5
2006	250.9	250.4	250.1	247.5	251.1	257.3	258.1	258.6	256.1	255.9	254.5	258.1	254.1
2007	251.4	250.8	250.4	247.3	252.0	257.9	259.4	259.4	256.2	255.6	254.7	258.7	254.5
2008	251.5	252.0	250.3	248.2	252.4	255.6	257.1	256.9	254.3	254.6	250.3	252.9	253.0
2009	244.1	243.9	240.6	236.3	240.1	243.2	245.3	245.8	242.9	243.8	240.8	245.5	242.7
2010	238.2	239.2	237.5	238.1	238.7	242.7	249.4	247.7	245.0	247.7	244.1	248.4	243.1
2011	241.8	242.8	241.5	239.3	242.0	246.9	250.4	251.7	249.3	250.3	248.0	253.0	246.4
Goods-Producing													
2000	58.8	58.6	59.2	60.7	62.1	64.1	64.2	64.5	63.8	64.0	63.6	63.0	62.2
2001	60.9	60.1	60.2	61.1	62.6	64.1	64.4	63.8	62.6	61.8	60.6	60.1	61.9
2002	56.5	55.3	55.1	56.2	57.6	58.4	58.1	57.0	56.4	56.2	55.3	54.0	56.3
2003	51.7	51.0	51.1	52.2	54.4	55.5	55.9	56.1	54.6	55.0	54.5	53.7	53.8
2004	51.1	51.1	51.0	53.1	55.2	56.6	57.0	57.0	56.3	56.0	55.3	54.5	54.5
2005	51.6	51.1	51.0	52.9	54.9	56.4	57.1	57.1	56.2	56.1	55.4	54.3	54.5
2006	51.7	51.1	51.1	53.3	54.9	56.2	56.8	56.8	56.0	55.9	55.4	54.6	54.5
2007	51.7	50.8	50.9	51.9	54.6	55.7	55.9	55.7	54.7	54.4	53.6	52.7	53.6
2008	50.0	49.6	49.2	50.1	52.2	53.4	53.9	53.5	52.9	52.7	51.4	49.2	51.5
2009	45.6	44.7	43.7	44.2	45.6	46.4	46.9	47.4	46.8	46.7	45.9	44.8	45.7
2010	41.9	41.7	41.6	43.8	45.5	46.1	47.1	47.0	46.4	46.7	45.9	44.7	44.9
2011	42.4	42.5	42.0	43.3	45.1	46.9	48.1	47.9	46.8	47.2	46.2	45.4	45.3
Mining and Logging													
2000	1.0	0.9	1.0	1.1	1.1	1.1	1.1	1.2	1.1	1.1	1.1	1.1	1.1
2001	1.0	1.0	1.1	1.0	1.1	1.1	1.2	1.2	1.2	1.2	1.1	1.1	1.1
2002	0.9	0.9	0.9	1.0	1.0	1.1	1.1	1.1	1.1	1.0	1.0	0.9	1.0
2003	0.8	0.8	0.9	0.9	1.0	1.0	1.0	1.0	1.0	1.0	1.0	0.9	0.9
2004	0.8	0.8	0.8	0.9	1.0	1.0	0.9	0.9	0.9	0.9	0.9	0.9	0.9
2005	0.7	0.7	0.8	0.8	0.8	0.9	0.9	0.9	0.9	0.9	0.9	0.8	0.8
2006	0.8	0.7	0.8	0.9	0.9	0.9	0.9	0.9	0.9	0.9	0.9	0.9	0.9
2007	0.8	0.8	0.8	0.8	0.9	0.9	0.9	0.9	0.9	0.9	0.8	0.8	0.8
2008	0.8	0.8	0.8	0.8	0.9	0.9	0.9	0.9	0.9	0.9	0.9	0.8	0.9
2009	0.7	0.7	0.7	0.8	0.8	0.8	0.8	0.8	0.8	0.8	0.8	0.7	0.8
2010	0.7	0.7	0.7	0.7	0.8	0.8	0.8	0.8	0.8	0.8	0.8	0.7	0.8
2011	0.7	0.7	0.7	0.7	0.8	0.8	0.8	0.8	0.8	0.8	0.8	0.7	0.8
Construction													
2000	12.7	12.3	12.5	13.9	15.2	16.3	16.7	16.6	16.1	16.0	15.3	14.6	14.9
2001	13.2	12.7	12.8	13.8	15.5	16.6	17.2	17.2	16.5	16.1	15.6	15.1	15.2
2002	13.4	12.9	12.8	13.9	15.3	15.8	16.3	16.3	15.8	15.8	15.3	14.3	14.8
2003	13.0	12.4	12.5	13.7	15.6	16.6	17.2	17.4	16.9	17.0	16.5	15.8	15.4
2004	14.1	13.8	13.9	15.7	17.3	18.3	18.8	18.7	18.2	17.9	17.3	16.2	16.7
2005	14.4	13.8	13.8	15.4	17.3	18.3	19.2	19.1	18.5	18.3	17.6	16.6	16.9
2006	14.9	14.5	14.7	16.4	17.8	18.8	19.4	19.4	18.9	18.6	18.0	17.1	17.4
2007	15.1	14.2	14.4	15.3	17.7	18.5	18.8	18.7	18.1	17.8	17.0	16.0	16.8
2008	14.1	13.5	13.3	14.2	16.2	17.1	17.5	17.3	16.9	16.9	15.9	14.3	15.6
2009	12.3	11.6	11.4	12.4	14.0	14.9	15.3	15.6	15.2	15.1	14.4	13.2	13.8
2010	11.4	10.9	10.9	12.8	14.2	14.4	15.2	15.2	14.9	15.0	14.3	13.1	13.5
2011	11.5	11.1	11.0	12.1	13.7	14.9	15.7	15.7	15.1	15.3	14.3	13.5	13.7
Manufacturing													
2000	45.1	45.4	45.7	45.7	45.8	46.7	46.4	46.7	46.6	46.9	47.2	47.3	46.3
2001	46.7	46.4	46.3	46.3	46.0	46.4	46.0	45.4	44.9	44.5	43.9	43.9	45.6
2002	42.2	41.5	41.4	41.3	41.3	41.5	40.7	39.6	39.5	39.4	39.0	38.8	40.5
2003	37.9	37.8	37.7	37.6	37.8	37.9	37.7	37.7	36.7	37.0	37.0	37.0	37.5
2004	36.2	36.5	36.3	36.5	36.9	37.3	37.3	37.4	37.2	37.2	37.1	37.4	36.9
2005	36.5	36.6	36.4	36.7	36.8	36.8	37.0	37.1	36.8	36.9	36.9	36.9	36.8
2006	36.0	35.9	35.6	36.0	36.2	36.5	36.5	36.5	36.2	36.4	36.5	36.6	36.2
2007	35.8	35.8	35.7	35.8	36.0	36.3	36.2	36.1	35.7	35.8	35.8	35.9	35.9
2008	35.1	35.3	35.1	35.1	35.1	35.4	35.5	35.3	35.1	34.9	34.6	34.1	35.1
2009	32.6	32.4	31.6	31.0	30.8	30.7	30.8	31.0	30.8	30.8	30.7	30.9	31.2
2010	29.8	30.1	30.0	30.3	30.5	30.9	31.1	31.0	30.7	30.9	30.8	30.9	30.6
2011	30.2	30.7	30.3	30.5	30.6	31.2	31.6	31.4	30.9	31.1	31.1	31.2	30.9

1. Employment by Industry: Vermont, Selected Years, 2000–2011—*Continued*

(Numbers in thousands, not seasonally adjusted)

Industry and year	January	February	March	April	May	June	July	August	September	October	November	December	Annual average
Service-Providing													
2000	234.9	238.3	239.8	232.9	235.1	235.9	229.4	229.3	237.5	240.2	238.8	245.7	236.5
2001	240.8	242.5	241.8	238.5	238.6	240.5	233.4	233.7	241.1	243.5	242.5	245.9	240.2
2002	242.9	244.1	244.0	240.9	241.8	243.7	235.9	236.9	244.4	246.4	244.9	250.1	243.0
2003	245.5	246.8	245.8	241.4	243.6	245.6	238.3	238.8	247.1	249.4	248.0	254.2	245.4
2004	247.6	249.5	249.1	245.7	247.6	248.6	241.8	241.9	250.6	252.2	251.0	255.8	248.5
2005	251.3	252.9	252.5	249.5	250.2	250.7	243.6	244.0	252.2	253.4	252.7	259.3	251.0
2006	253.6	255.3	255.0	250.2	251.9	254.3	245.1	245.8	254.6	256.7	256.1	260.3	253.2
2007	254.5	256.4	255.9	251.4	253.6	255.9	247.8	247.8	256.1	257.7	257.7	262.8	254.8
2008	257.0	258.8	257.4	254.4	256.4	255.6	247.8	248.0	256.3	259.2	256.5	261.1	255.7
2009	253.5	256.2	253.5	249.6	252.2	250.9	243.3	243.4	250.8	254.8	252.5	257.6	251.5
2010	251.5	254.4	253.4	251.6	251.8	251.1	247.4	245.4	252.9	258.1	255.2	260.3	252.8
2011	254.1	256.7	255.9	252.2	253.3	252.7	245.0	246.4	255.3	258.8	257.8	262.7	254.2
Trade, Transportation, and Utilities													
2000	57.2	57.0	56.9	56.9	57.2	57.9	58.0	58.1	58.0	58.7	59.5	60.5	58.0
2001	58.1	57.6	57.5	57.7	58.4	58.9	58.4	58.5	58.3	59.2	60.1	61.1	58.7
2002	58.3	57.7	57.9	57.9	58.7	59.2	59.1	59.2	58.7	59.1	59.7	60.5	58.8
2003	57.9	57.4	56.8	57.0	57.6	58.4	57.9	58.1	57.8	59.1	59.9	61.1	58.3
2004	57.9	57.4	57.5	57.8	58.7	59.3	59.1	59.0	58.6	59.8	60.8	61.4	58.9
2005	59.0	58.6	58.1	58.6	59.1	59.7	59.4	59.4	59.2	59.8	60.6	61.6	59.4
2006	58.9	58.3	58.2	58.4	59.4	59.9	59.4	59.5	59.4	60.1	61.1	61.9	59.5
2007	59.2	58.4	58.0	57.8	58.9	59.7	59.3	59.0	58.9	59.9	61.2	61.8	59.3
2008	59.0	58.7	58.1	58.2	59.1	59.6	58.8	58.9	58.3	58.9	59.3	59.8	58.9
2009	56.5	56.1	55.1	55.0	56.0	56.5	55.8	56.0	55.5	56.3	56.8	57.8	56.1
2010	54.8	54.5	54.0	54.7	54.9	55.7	56.6	56.4	56.0	57.2	57.7	58.4	55.9
2011	55.6	55.3	54.9	55.1	55.9	56.6	56.6	56.7	56.3	57.3	57.9	58.9	56.4
Wholesale Trade													
2000	9.7	9.7	9.8	9.9	9.8	9.8	9.9	9.9	9.8	9.8	9.9	9.9	9.8
2001	9.9	10.0	10.0	10.1	10.0	10.1	10.1	10.1	10.1	10.1	10.1	10.3	10.1
2002	9.9	9.9	10.0	10.0	10.1	10.1	10.2	10.2	10.3	10.2	10.3	10.4	10.1
2003	10.1	10.1	10.1	10.1	10.2	10.3	10.3	10.3	10.3	10.5	10.4	10.4	10.3
2004	10.1	10.1	10.2	10.2	10.3	10.4	10.4	10.1	10.0	10.1	10.2	9.9	10.2
2005	9.9	9.9	9.8	10.0	10.0	10.1	10.2	10.3	10.2	10.2	10.3	10.3	10.1
2006	10.2	10.1	10.2	10.2	10.3	10.2	10.4	10.5	10.5	10.5	10.5	10.6	10.4
2007	10.4	10.3	10.3	10.3	10.4	10.4	10.4	10.4	10.4	10.4	10.5	10.5	10.4
2008	10.2	10.2	10.3	10.3	10.3	10.3	10.2	10.2	10.1	10.0	10.0	9.9	10.2
2009	9.8	9.7	9.7	9.7	9.7	9.7	9.6	9.6	9.5	9.5	9.5	9.5	9.6
2010	9.2	9.2	9.2	9.3	9.3	9.4	9.6	9.6	9.5	9.7	9.7	9.6	9.4
2011	9.4	9.4	9.4	9.4	9.5	9.5	9.7	9.8	9.9	9.9	10.0	10.0	9.7
Retail Trade													
2000	38.9	38.7	38.5	38.5	38.9	39.5	39.6	39.8	39.4	40.0	40.7	41.8	39.5
2001	39.6	39.0	39.0	39.0	39.8	40.0	39.9	40.0	39.4	40.2	41.1	41.9	39.9
2002	39.7	39.2	39.3	39.2	39.8	40.3	40.5	40.5	39.7	40.0	40.5	41.2	40.0
2003	39.2	38.8	38.3	38.4	38.9	39.4	39.6	39.7	39.0	39.9	40.9	42.0	39.5
2004	39.2	38.7	38.8	39.1	39.8	40.3	40.3	40.4	39.8	40.6	41.5	42.4	40.1
2005	40.1	39.8	39.4	39.8	40.3	40.7	40.8	40.7	40.2	40.6	41.2	42.1	40.5
2006	39.9	39.5	39.3	39.5	40.3	40.9	40.7	40.7	40.1	40.7	41.6	42.2	40.5
2007	40.0	39.4	39.1	39.0	39.7	40.4	40.5	40.2	39.6	40.4	41.5	42.0	40.2
2008	40.1	39.9	39.3	39.4	40.0	40.4	40.2	40.2	39.4	40.1	40.4	40.8	40.0
2009	38.3	38.0	37.2	37.2	38.0	38.5	38.2	38.3	37.6	38.2	38.6	39.3	38.1
2010	37.3	37.0	36.5	37.2	37.2	37.8	38.6	38.4	37.7	38.6	39.1	39.5	37.9
2011	37.5	37.3	36.9	37.1	37.6	38.2	38.1	38.1	37.4	38.3	38.7	39.5	37.9
Transportation and Utilities													
2000	8.6	8.6	8.6	8.5	8.5	8.6	8.5	8.4	8.8	8.9	8.9	8.8	8.6
2001	8.6	8.6	8.5	8.6	8.6	8.8	8.4	8.4	8.8	8.9	8.9	8.9	8.7
2002	8.7	8.6	8.6	8.7	8.8	8.8	8.4	8.5	8.7	8.9	8.9	8.9	8.7
2003	8.6	8.5	8.4	8.5	8.5	8.7	8.0	8.1	8.5	8.7	8.6	8.7	8.5
2004	8.6	8.6	8.5	8.5	8.6	8.8	8.4	8.5	8.8	9.1	9.1	9.1	8.7
2005	9.0	8.9	8.9	8.8	8.8	8.9	8.4	8.4	8.8	9.0	9.1	9.2	8.9
2006	8.8	8.7	8.7	8.7	8.8	8.8	8.3	8.3	8.8	8.9	9.0	9.1	8.7
2007	8.8	8.7	8.6	8.5	8.8	8.9	8.4	8.4	8.9	9.1	9.2	9.3	8.8
2008	8.7	8.6	8.5	8.5	8.8	8.9	8.4	8.5	8.8	8.8	8.9	9.1	8.7
2009	8.4	8.4	8.2	8.1	8.3	8.3	8.0	8.1	8.4	8.6	8.7	9.0	8.4
2010	8.3	8.3	8.3	8.2	8.4	8.5	8.4	8.4	8.8	8.9	8.9	9.3	8.6
2011	8.7	8.6	8.6	8.6	8.8	8.9	8.8	8.8	9.0	9.1	9.2	9.4	8.9
Information													
2000	6.7	6.8	6.8	6.8	6.8	6.9	6.9	6.3	6.9	6.9	7.0	7.0	6.8
2001	6.9	7.0	6.8	6.8	6.8	6.9	6.7	6.7	6.6	6.7	6.8	6.8	6.8
2002	6.7	6.7	6.7	6.8	6.7	6.7	6.7	6.7	6.6	6.5	6.6	6.6	6.7
2003	6.5	6.4	6.5	6.4	6.5	6.6	6.5	6.5	6.5	6.5	6.5	6.5	6.5
2004	6.4	6.4	6.4	6.4	6.4	6.4	6.4	6.4	6.2	6.3	6.3	6.3	6.4
2005	6.3	6.2	6.2	6.2	6.2	6.2	6.3	6.2	6.2	6.2	6.2	6.3	6.2
2006	6.1	6.1	6.2	6.0	6.0	6.0	6.0	6.0	6.0	5.9	6.0	6.0	6.0
2007	6.0	5.9	5.9	5.9	5.9	5.9	6.0	6.0	5.9	5.8	5.8	5.8	5.9
2008	5.8	5.8	5.8	5.8	5.8	5.7	5.8	5.8	5.8	5.7	5.7	5.7	5.8
2009	5.6	5.6	5.6	5.6	5.5	5.6	5.5	5.5	5.5	5.4	5.4	5.4	5.5
2010	5.4	5.4	5.4	5.4	5.4	5.4	5.3	5.3	5.3	5.3	5.3	5.3	5.4
2011	5.2	5.3	5.2	5.0	4.9	5.0	5.0	5.0	4.9	4.9	4.9	4.9	5.0

1. Employment by Industry: Vermont, Selected Years, 2000–2011—*Continued*

(Numbers in thousands, not seasonally adjusted)

Industry and year	January	February	March	April	May	June	July	August	September	October	November	December	Annual average
Financial Activities													
2000	13.0	12.9	13.0	12.8	13.0	13.1	12.9	13.0	12.7	13.0	12.9	13.2	13.0
2001	12.9	13.0	13.1	12.9	13.1	13.4	13.4	13.4	13.3	13.2	13.2	13.3	13.2
2002	13.0	13.0	13.0	12.9	13.1	13.3	13.5	13.5	13.2	13.2	13.0	13.2	13.2
2003	13.0	13.0	13.0	13.0	13.2	13.4	13.5	13.5	13.3	13.3	13.2	13.5	13.2
2004	13.3	13.1	13.1	13.1	13.3	13.4	13.5	13.5	13.3	13.1	13.1	13.4	13.3
2005	13.1	13.1	13.1	13.0	13.1	13.4	13.4	13.4	13.2	13.2	13.1	13.3	13.2
2006	13.2	13.2	13.2	13.1	13.2	13.4	13.4	13.4	13.2	13.1	13.1	13.2	13.2
2007	13.2	13.1	13.2	13.1	13.2	13.4	13.4	13.3	13.1	13.0	13.0	13.0	13.2
2008	12.8	12.8	12.8	12.8	12.9	13.0	13.1	13.0	12.8	12.7	12.6	12.7	12.8
2009	12.5	12.4	12.4	12.2	12.4	12.5	12.6	12.5	12.3	12.3	12.2	12.2	12.4
2010	12.1	12.1	12.0	12.1	12.0	12.3	12.4	12.4	12.1	12.2	12.1	12.2	12.2
2011	12.1	12.0	12.0	11.9	12.1	12.2	12.3	12.3	12.1	12.1	12.0	12.0	12.1
Professional and Business Services													
2000	19.5	19.8	20.3	20.7	21.0	21.5	21.4	21.3	20.9	21.0	20.7	20.9	20.8
2001	20.1	20.3	20.4	20.7	21.3	21.4	21.4	21.3	20.8	20.5	20.2	20.0	20.7
2002	19.2	19.2	19.3	20.0	20.5	20.6	20.7	20.9	21.0	20.9	20.4	20.3	20.3
2003	19.3	19.4	19.3	20.0	20.6	21.0	21.0	21.0	20.7	20.7	20.6	20.7	20.4
2004	20.0	20.0	20.3	21.4	21.2	21.7	21.8	21.9	21.8	21.8	21.6	21.8	21.3
2005	20.8	20.9	21.2	21.7	22.0	22.3	22.4	22.4	22.1	22.2	22.1	22.2	21.9
2006	21.5	21.5	21.6	22.0	22.3	22.8	22.8	22.9	22.5	22.4	21.9	22.0	22.2
2007	21.2	21.3	21.6	22.1	22.6	23.1	23.1	23.2	22.9	22.8	22.5	22.7	22.4
2008	21.8	21.9	21.7	22.4	23.3	23.5	23.5	23.3	23.1	23.3	22.7	22.4	22.7
2009	21.3	21.3	21.1	21.8	22.4	22.8	22.9	23.0	22.4	22.9	22.9	22.6	22.3
2010	21.8	21.8	22.0	23.1	23.2	23.6	24.3	24.4	24.1	24.4	24.0	23.6	23.4
2011	23.0	23.2	23.4	24.0	24.7	25.2	25.3	26.0	26.1	26.2	26.1	25.8	24.9
Education and Health Services													
2000	45.1	46.2	46.2	46.0	45.5	44.7	44.9	44.8	46.3	47.1	47.3	47.4	46.0
2001	46.8	47.5	47.7	47.7	47.7	47.2	47.1	46.8	48.6	49.0	49.2	49.7	47.9
2002	49.0	49.7	50.0	50.1	50.3	49.5	49.5	49.2	50.7	50.9	51.3	51.5	50.1
2003	50.9	51.4	51.8	52.0	52.2	51.7	51.8	51.7	53.0	53.0	52.9	53.3	52.1
2004	51.9	52.7	53.1	53.1	53.5	52.9	52.5	52.1	53.8	53.4	53.7	53.8	53.0
2005	53.3	53.9	54.2	54.5	54.6	53.7	53.5	53.2	54.7	54.3	54.6	55.2	54.1
2006	54.2	55.1	55.3	55.0	55.1	55.0	55.0	54.8	56.1	56.1	56.3	56.8	55.4
2007	55.7	56.7	56.8	57.1	57.0	57.1	57.1	56.8	58.1	58.0	58.6	58.4	57.3
2008	57.3	58.2	58.6	58.7	59.1	58.0	58.3	58.2	59.3	59.6	59.5	59.6	58.7
2009	58.1	59.5	59.7	59.5	60.1	59.0	59.5	58.8	59.5	59.4	59.1	59.2	59.3
2010	58.0	59.1	59.1	59.7	58.9	58.2	59.5	58.5	59.4	59.9	59.6	59.7	59.1
2011	58.5	59.6	59.8	60.4	59.9	59.2	59.6	59.3	61.0	61.5	61.7	61.4	60.2
Leisure and Hospitality													
2000	35.1	35.3	34.7	28.6	29.5	33.0	34.2	34.9	33.1	32.1	29.6	34.7	32.9
2001	36.1	35.8	34.9	31.2	29.6	32.6	34.3	35.1	32.5	31.5	29.5	31.4	32.9
2002	35.6	35.5	34.6	30.4	29.8	33.0	34.1	34.9	32.7	31.7	29.5	34.4	33.0
2003	35.9	35.4	34.6	29.1	29.5	32.2	34.0	34.8	32.8	31.7	29.6	33.7	32.8
2004	35.5	35.5	34.4	29.3	30.0	33.4	35.0	35.5	33.3	32.3	29.6	33.5	33.1
2005	35.6	35.3	34.7	30.4	30.1	33.2	35.0	35.1	32.8	31.7	29.8	34.5	33.2
2006	35.6	35.4	34.8	29.9	30.3	33.9	34.5	35.1	32.9	32.4	30.8	33.7	33.3
2007	34.6	34.8	34.2	29.7	29.9	32.9	34.5	35.3	32.7	31.7	30.1	34.3	32.9
2008	35.1	35.3	34.4	30.4	30.1	32.4	33.8	34.4	32.3	31.9	29.4	33.8	32.8
2009	35.0	34.8	33.6	28.5	28.5	30.6	32.3	32.9	31.3	31.0	28.8	33.7	31.8
2010	34.5	34.9	33.7	29.4	29.0	31.5	34.0	33.6	31.7	32.0	29.7	34.7	32.4
2011	35.3	35.2	34.5	29.8	29.5	31.9	33.6	34.7	32.2	31.2	29.4	34.8	32.7
Other Services													
2000	9.4	9.5	9.6	9.6	9.7	9.9	9.9	9.9	9.7	9.7	9.6	9.7	9.7
2001	9.8	9.7	9.7	9.8	9.9	10.2	10.4	10.2	9.9	10.0	10.0	10.0	10.0
2002	9.8	9.7	9.8	9.9	10.0	10.4	10.5	10.4	10.3	10.1	10.0	10.2	10.1
2003	9.9	9.9	10.0	10.0	10.1	10.4	10.3	10.3	10.2	10.2	10.1	10.3	10.1
2004	10.1	10.1	10.0	10.1	10.2	10.4	10.3	10.2	10.1	10.1	9.9	10.0	10.1
2005	9.8	9.8	9.8	10.0	10.1	10.3	10.2	10.1	9.9	9.8	9.8	9.9	10.0
2006	9.7	9.7	9.7	9.8	9.9	10.1	10.2	10.1	10.0	10.0	9.9	9.9	9.9
2007	9.8	9.8	9.8	9.7	9.9	10.1	10.1	10.1	9.9	10.0	9.9	10.0	9.9
2008	9.7	9.7	9.7	9.8	9.9	10.0	9.9	9.8	9.8	9.8	9.7	9.7	9.8
2009	9.5	9.5	9.4	9.5	9.6	9.8	9.8	9.7	9.7	9.8	9.7	9.8	9.7
2010	9.7	9.7	9.7	9.9	9.8	9.9	10.2	10.1	10.0	10.0	9.8	9.8	9.9
2011	9.7	9.7	9.7	9.8	9.9	9.9	9.9	9.8	9.9	9.9	9.8	9.8	9.8
Government													
2000	48.9	50.8	52.3	51.5	52.4	48.9	41.2	41.0	49.9	51.7	52.2	52.3	49.4
2001	50.1	51.6	51.7	51.7	51.8	49.9	41.7	41.7	51.1	53.4	53.5	53.6	50.2
2002	51.3	52.6	52.7	52.9	52.7	51.0	41.8	42.1	51.2	54.0	54.4	53.4	50.8
2003	52.1	53.9	53.8	53.9	53.9	51.9	43.3	42.9	52.8	54.9	55.2	55.1	52.0
2004	52.5	54.3	54.3	54.5	54.3	51.1	43.2	43.3	53.5	55.4	56.0	55.6	52.3
2005	53.4	55.1	55.2	55.1	55.0	51.9	43.4	44.2	54.1	56.2	56.5	56.3	53.0
2006	54.4	56.0	56.0	56.0	55.7	53.2	43.8	44.0	54.5	56.7	57.0	56.8	53.7
2007	54.8	56.4	56.4	56.0	56.2	53.7	44.3	44.1	54.6	56.5	56.6	56.8	53.9
2008	55.5	56.4	56.3	56.3	56.2	53.4	44.6	44.6	54.9	57.3	57.6	57.4	54.2
2009	55.0	57.0	56.6	57.5	57.7	54.1	44.9	45.0	54.7	57.7	57.6	56.9	54.6
2010	55.2	56.9	57.5	57.3	58.6	54.5	45.1	44.7	54.3	57.1	57.0	56.6	54.6
2011	54.7	56.4	56.4	56.2	56.4	52.7	42.7	42.6	52.8	55.7	56.0	55.1	53.1

2. Average Weekly Hours by Selected Industry: Vermont, 2007–2011

(Not seasonally adjusted)

Industry and year	January	February	March	April	May	June	July	August	September	October	November	December	Annual average
Total Private													
2007	33.2	33.0	33.2	33.7	34.1	34.7	34.6	34.7	34.9	34.5	34.3	34.2	34.1
2008	33.9	33.8	33.9	34.2	34.6	35.2	34.9	35.0	34.7	34.5	34.1	33.5	34.4
2009	34.1	33.8	33.5	33.7	34.1	34.2	34.3	34.9	34.3	34.5	34.4	33.5	34.1
2010	33.5	33.7	33.2	33.8	34.6	34.4	34.9	34.8	34.8	34.6	34.0	33.9	34.2
2011	33.6	33.5	33.3	33.2	33.9	33.7	34.2	34.1	33.9	34.2	33.7	33.5	33.7
Goods-Producing													
2007	38.8	36.2	37.4	38.0	38.9	39.4	37.5	38.7	38.4	38.1	37.9	38.3	38.1
2008	38.1	38.0	37.9	38.4	39.0	39.0	38.9	39.5	39.4	38.5	37.5	37.3	38.5
2009	37.4	36.9	36.7	35.8	36.8	37.4	37.5	38.4	37.7	38.4	37.6	36.6	37.3
2010	37.5	38.1	37.1	37.7	38.4	38.6	38.9	39.2	39.3	39.1	38.6	38.5	38.5
2011	37.7	38.2	37.6	38.5	38.7	38.2	38.9	38.6	39.0	38.4	38.6	38.6	38.4
Construction													
2007	40.0	35.6	35.8	37.0	40.1	39.8	39.7	40.5	39.5	39.7	39.1	39.3	39.0
2008	37.8	36.8	37.3	38.0	39.6	40.1	40.0	41.3	41.0	40.4	38.9	37.7	39.2
2009	36.9	36.9	36.1	36.6	39.8	40.2	40.4	41.0	40.2	41.2	40.4	39.8	39.3
2010	40.0	39.2	39.9	40.4	40.7	40.6	40.6	41.0	41.5	40.7	40.0	39.1	40.4
2011	38.2	38.1	37.0	38.8	40.3	39.1	40.4	40.2	40.8	39.8	40.1	39.9	39.5
Manufacturing													
2007	38.4	36.6	38.2	38.6	38.4	39.4	36.4	37.9	38.0	37.4	37.5	38.0	37.9
2008	38.3	38.4	38.1	38.6	38.8	38.6	38.5	38.6	38.6	37.5	36.8	37.0	38.2
2009	37.9	37.0	37.0	35.6	35.8	36.5	36.1	36.9	36.3	37.2	36.9	36.4	36.6
2010	37.1	37.9	37.2	37.7	38.5	38.7	39.1	39.3	39.1	39.1	38.8	38.9	38.5
2011	38.4	39.0	38.7	39.1	38.6	38.3	38.5	38.4	38.7	38.2	38.6	38.7	38.6
Trade, Transportation, and Utilities													
2007	32.1	31.9	32.4	32.4	32.2	33.9	35.0	35.2	35.0	34.3	34.0	34.6	33.6
2008	34.2	33.7	34.1	33.9	34.0	34.1	34.0	33.7	33.3	33.0	33.0	33.1	33.7
2009	32.9	31.5	31.6	32.2	32.6	32.9	32.9	33.6	33.3	33.3	33.2	33.4	32.8
2010	32.6	32.8	32.4	32.6	32.4	32.3	33.0	32.9	33.0	32.5	32.2	33.2	32.7
2011	32.5	32.3	32.3	32.4	32.6	32.9	33.6	33.6	33.2	33.6	33.4	33.8	33.0
Professional and Business Services													
2007	35.0	35.3	35.7	35.6	36.0	36.3	36.4	36.0	37.7	35.9	36.6	36.5	36.1
2008	36.2	35.8	36.0	36.4	36.2	37.0	36.5	36.8	37.4	37.0	37.1	37.0	36.6
2009	37.4	39.5	39.2	39.2	37.7	37.9	37.1	37.6	36.9	36.9	36.9	36.2	37.7
2010	37.2	36.7	36.7	37.7	37.1	36.4	35.9	35.0	35.7	36.1	36.5	35.7	36.4
2011	36.0	35.2	35.1	34.9	36.2	36.0	36.5	35.3	35.1	36.4	35.6	35.8	35.7
Education and Health Services													
2007	32.0	31.5	31.4	31.3	31.5	31.6	31.5	32.0	32.1	32.2	32.0	32.6	31.8
2008	32.5	32.6	32.8	32.9	33.0	32.9	33.0	33.0	33.2	33.2	33.1	33.1	32.9
2009	33.7	33.3	32.8	32.8	33.1	32.7	32.9	32.8	32.8	32.6	32.8	33.1	32.9
2010	32.8	32.8	32.9	32.7	32.8	33.2	33.2	33.4	33.3	33.4	32.9	33.1	33.0
2011	33.2	32.8	32.8	32.6	32.9	32.9	33.0	33.4	33.4	33.2	33.1	33.2	33.0
Leisure and Hospitality													
2007	25.7	28.2	26.4	25.6	26.7	27.3	28.4	27.7	26.4	27.1	26.3	23.8	26.6
2008	24.6	26.2	25.4	24.4	26.9	27.0	26.9	27.2	25.5	26.0	24.2	21.5	25.5
2009	24.7	25.0	23.7	23.8	25.3	25.8	26.7	27.1	26.2	27.0	26.2	25.2	25.6
2010	26.3	26.9	25.9	26.2	26.8	26.3	27.3	27.0	26.1	26.2	25.8	25.7	26.4
2011	26.2	26.2	25.1	24.5	25.9	25.8	27.5	27.6	25.7	26.3	24.6	24.4	25.8

3. Average Hourly Earnings by Selected Industry: Vermont, 2007–2011

(Dollars, not seasonally adjusted)

Industry and year	January	February	March	April	May	June	July	August	September	October	November	December	Annual average
Total Private													
2007	20.01	20.15	20.88	20.43	20.22	19.89	20.16	20.12	20.74	20.63	20.90	20.95	20.42
2008	20.89	21.22	21.27	21.24	20.85	21.05	21.22	21.09	21.51	21.62	22.13	22.16	21.35
2009	21.54	22.11	22.49	22.32	22.23	22.37	22.34	22.29	22.51	22.93	23.17	22.66	22.41
2010	23.04	22.91	23.10	23.39	23.32	22.75	22.76	22.71	22.73	23.09	22.93	23.46	23.01
2011	23.65	23.14	23.23	23.53	23.32	22.80	22.57	22.53	22.93	23.07	23.03	22.66	23.03
Goods-Producing													
2007	20.48	20.59	20.36	20.23	19.91	19.94	20.43	20.08	20.46	20.23	20.38	21.06	20.34
2008	21.15	21.27	21.22	21.05	20.56	20.68	20.68	20.75	20.96	21.28	21.77	21.87	21.09
2009	21.40	21.83	21.87	21.48	22.23	21.39	21.42	21.33	21.30	21.59	21.60	22.14	21.62
2010	21.87	22.43	22.75	22.45	22.11	21.85	21.99	22.32	22.09	22.39	22.41	22.43	22.25
2011	22.67	21.91	22.10	21.94	21.90	21.76	21.93	22.00	22.53	22.64	22.35	22.39	22.18
Construction													
2007	21.18	20.41	20.44	20.16	20.02	20.52	20.44	20.96	20.71	20.20	20.46	21.21	20.56
2008	21.88	22.08	21.80	21.64	20.57	20.94	20.88	21.02	21.35	21.50	21.97	22.72	21.47
2009	23.29	23.00	23.22	22.41	21.81	21.95	21.93	21.40	20.83	21.24	21.48	22.16	21.96
2010	21.59	21.88	21.91	21.30	20.64	20.35	20.81	20.77	20.67	21.16	21.71	21.64	21.15
2011	21.65	21.37	21.23	20.92	20.83	20.73	20.69	20.96	21.75	21.61	21.57	22.40	21.30
Manufacturing													
2007	20.21	20.79	20.45	20.34	19.89	19.61	20.48	19.59	20.35	20.28	20.34	20.97	20.27
2008	20.81	20.94	20.95	20.76	20.25	20.28	20.34	20.38	20.55	20.99	21.49	21.34	20.75
2009	20.69	21.28	21.23	21.12	21.69	21.53	21.58	21.67	21.95	22.11	21.88	22.22	21.57
2010	22.05	22.64	23.10	22.98	22.89	22.64	22.67	23.16	22.87	22.52	22.34	22.44	22.69
2011	22.88	22.49	22.80	22.70	22.74	22.57	22.89	22.81	23.04	23.30	22.94	22.60	22.81
Trade, Transportation, and Utilities													
2007	16.51	16.95	17.07	16.85	17.37	17.01	17.46	17.19	17.35	17.40	17.63	17.41	17.19
2008	17.69	18.33	18.07	18.12	18.06	18.22	17.97	17.84	17.89	18.01	18.11	19.07	18.11
2009	18.61	19.50	19.56	18.94	18.95	18.90	18.78	18.92	19.01	19.07	18.99	19.40	19.05
2010	19.90	19.36	19.68	19.78	19.27	18.80	18.74	18.83	18.66	18.77	18.37	18.50	19.04
2011	18.77	18.51	19.04	19.00	18.88	18.52	18.31	18.10	18.38	18.27	18.15	18.00	18.48
Professional and Business Services													
2007	23.02	24.08	23.57	23.65	23.47	22.95	22.75	23.33	23.52	23.78	23.86	24.80	23.56
2008	23.96	24.45	24.62	24.98	24.23	22.97	23.45	23.65	23.52	23.41	24.42	24.08	23.96
2009	21.82	22.92	23.76	23.80	24.21	25.03	25.48	25.43	26.04	26.56	26.57	26.34	24.84
2010	25.91	26.50	26.51	26.10	26.94	26.04	26.94	26.31	26.24	26.89	26.75	27.61	26.56
2011	28.14	27.68	27.70	29.04	29.02	28.71	28.43	29.35	29.54	29.35	29.99	28.99	28.86
Education and Health Services													
2007	23.51	23.54	23.83	23.93	23.78	23.70	24.02	23.91	24.59	24.53	25.30	25.14	24.16
2008	25.19	25.06	25.01	24.83	24.62	25.03	25.46	25.12	25.75	25.94	26.33	26.28	25.39
2009	25.93	26.12	26.17	25.88	25.37	25.63	25.39	25.63	25.96	25.77	26.60	25.66	25.84
2010	26.42	26.45	26.32	26.53	26.87	26.73	26.76	26.72	26.69	27.56	27.06	27.95	26.84
2011	27.16	27.06	26.83	26.69	26.10	25.98	25.78	25.25	25.57	25.82	25.80	25.29	26.10
Leisure and Hospitality													
2007	14.37	14.40	14.42	15.87	15.35	14.35	14.85	15.11	15.71	16.00	16.10	14.67	15.07
2008	14.70	14.60	14.54	15.37	15.20	14.86	14.64	14.83	15.65	16.00	16.32	14.87	15.10
2009	14.51	14.63	14.59	15.23	14.80	15.67	15.24	14.96	15.38	15.40	15.21	14.51	15.00
2010	14.19	13.97	14.14	15.15	14.21	14.93	13.93	14.17	14.80	15.06	14.93	14.23	14.45
2011	14.02	14.14	14.44	14.43	14.35	14.30	14.00	14.08	14.57	15.05	15.04	14.98	14.43

4. Average Weekly Earnings by Selected Industry: Vermont, 2007–2011

(Dollars, not seasonally adjusted)

Industry and year	January	February	March	April	May	June	July	August	September	October	November	December	Annual average
Total Private													
2007	664.33	664.95	693.22	688.49	689.50	690.18	697.54	698.16	723.83	711.74	716.87	716.49	696.20
2008	708.17	717.24	721.05	726.41	721.41	740.96	740.58	738.15	746.40	745.89	754.63	742.36	733.46
2009	734.51	747.32	753.42	752.18	758.04	765.05	766.26	777.92	772.09	791.09	797.05	759.11	764.19
2010	771.84	772.07	766.92	790.58	806.87	782.60	794.32	790.31	791.00	798.91	779.62	795.29	786.67
2011	794.64	775.19	773.56	781.20	790.55	768.36	771.89	768.27	777.33	788.99	776.11	759.11	776.80
Goods-Producing													
2007	794.62	745.36	761.46	768.74	774.50	785.64	766.13	777.10	785.66	770.76	772.40	806.60	775.87
2008	805.82	808.26	804.24	808.32	801.84	806.52	804.45	819.63	825.82	819.28	816.38	815.75	811.42
2009	800.36	805.53	802.63	768.98	818.06	799.99	803.25	819.07	803.01	829.06	812.16	810.32	806.69
2010	820.13	854.58	844.03	846.37	849.02	843.41	855.41	874.94	868.14	875.45	865.03	863.56	855.72
2011	854.66	836.96	830.96	844.69	847.53	831.23	853.08	849.20	878.67	869.38	862.71	864.25	852.31
Construction													
2007	847.20	726.60	731.75	745.92	802.80	816.70	811.47	848.88	818.05	801.94	799.99	833.55	801.22
2008	827.06	812.54	813.14	822.32	814.57	839.69	835.20	868.13	875.35	868.60	854.63	856.54	842.00
2009	859.40	848.70	838.24	820.21	868.04	882.39	885.97	877.40	837.37	875.09	867.79	881.97	862.90
2010	863.60	857.70	874.21	860.52	840.05	826.21	844.89	851.57	857.81	861.21	868.40	846.12	854.37
2011	827.03	814.20	785.51	811.70	839.45	810.54	835.88	842.59	887.40	860.08	864.96	893.76	841.62
Manufacturing													
2007	776.06	760.91	781.19	785.12	763.78	772.63	745.47	742.46	773.30	758.47	762.75	796.86	768.22
2008	797.02	804.10	798.20	801.34	786.86	781.65	783.09	786.67	793.23	787.13	790.83	789.58	791.64
2009	784.15	787.36	785.51	751.87	776.50	785.85	779.04	799.62	796.79	822.49	807.37	808.81	790.56
2010	818.06	858.06	859.32	866.35	881.27	876.17	886.40	910.19	894.22	880.53	866.79	872.92	872.83
2011	878.59	877.11	882.36	887.57	877.76	864.43	881.27	875.90	891.65	890.06	885.48	874.62	880.57
Trade, Transportation, and Utilities													
2007	529.97	540.71	553.07	545.94	559.31	576.64	611.10	605.09	607.25	596.82	599.42	602.39	577.62
2008	605.00	617.72	616.19	614.27	614.04	621.30	610.98	601.21	595.74	594.33	597.63	631.22	610.00
2009	612.27	614.25	618.10	609.87	617.77	621.81	617.86	635.71	633.03	635.03	630.47	647.96	624.64
2010	648.74	635.01	637.63	644.83	624.35	607.24	618.42	619.51	615.78	610.03	591.51	614.20	622.12
2011	610.03	597.87	614.99	615.60	615.49	609.31	615.22	608.16	610.22	613.87	606.21	608.40	610.44
Professional and Business Services													
2007	805.70	850.02	841.45	841.94	844.92	833.09	828.10	839.88	886.70	853.70	873.28	905.20	850.57
2008	867.35	875.31	886.32	909.27	877.13	849.89	855.93	870.32	879.65	866.17	905.98	890.96	877.63
2009	816.07	905.34	931.39	932.96	912.72	948.64	945.31	956.17	960.88	980.06	980.43	953.51	935.96
2010	963.85	972.55	972.92	983.97	999.47	947.86	967.15	920.85	936.77	970.73	976.38	985.68	966.78
2011	1,013.04	974.34	972.27	1,013.50	1,050.52	1,033.56	1,037.70	1,036.06	1,036.85	1,068.34	1,067.64	1,037.84	1,029.70
Education and Health Services													
2007	752.32	741.51	748.26	749.01	749.07	748.92	756.63	765.12	789.34	789.87	809.60	819.56	768.57
2008	818.68	816.96	820.33	816.91	812.46	823.49	840.18	828.96	854.90	861.21	871.52	869.87	836.47
2009	873.84	869.80	858.38	848.86	839.75	838.10	835.33	840.66	851.49	840.10	872.48	849.35	851.43
2010	866.58	867.56	865.93	867.53	881.34	887.44	888.43	892.45	888.78	920.50	890.27	925.15	886.97
2011	901.71	887.57	880.02	870.09	858.69	854.74	850.74	843.35	854.04	857.22	853.98	839.63	862.47
Leisure and Hospitality													
2007	369.31	406.08	380.69	406.27	409.85	391.76	421.74	418.55	414.74	433.60	423.43	349.15	401.55
2008	361.62	382.52	369.32	375.03	408.88	401.22	393.82	403.38	399.08	416.00	394.94	319.71	384.88
2009	358.40	365.75	345.78	362.47	374.44	404.29	406.91	405.42	402.96	415.80	398.50	365.65	383.35
2010	373.20	375.79	366.23	396.93	380.83	392.66	380.29	382.59	386.28	394.57	385.19	365.71	381.27
2011	367.32	370.47	362.44	353.54	371.67	368.94	385.00	388.61	374.45	395.82	369.98	365.51	373.00

VIRGINIA
At a Glance

Population:
  2000 census: 7,079,057
  2010 census: 8,001,024
  2011 estimate: 8,096,604

Percent change in population:
  2000–2010: 13.0%
  2010–2011: 1.2%

Percent change in total nonfarm employment:
  2000–2010: 3.5%
  2010–2011: 1.2%

Industry with the largest growth in employment, 2000–2011 (thousands):
  Education and Health Services, 136.2

Industry with the largest decline or smallest growth in employment, 2000–2011 (thousands):
  Manufacturing, -134.6

Civilian labor force:
  2000: 3,584,037
  2010: 4,255,162
  2011: 4,306,174

Unemployment rate and rank among states (lowest to highest):
  2000: 2.3%, 1st
  2010: 6.9%, 7th
  2011: 6.2%, 8th

Over-the-year change in unemployment rates:
  2010–2011: -0.7%

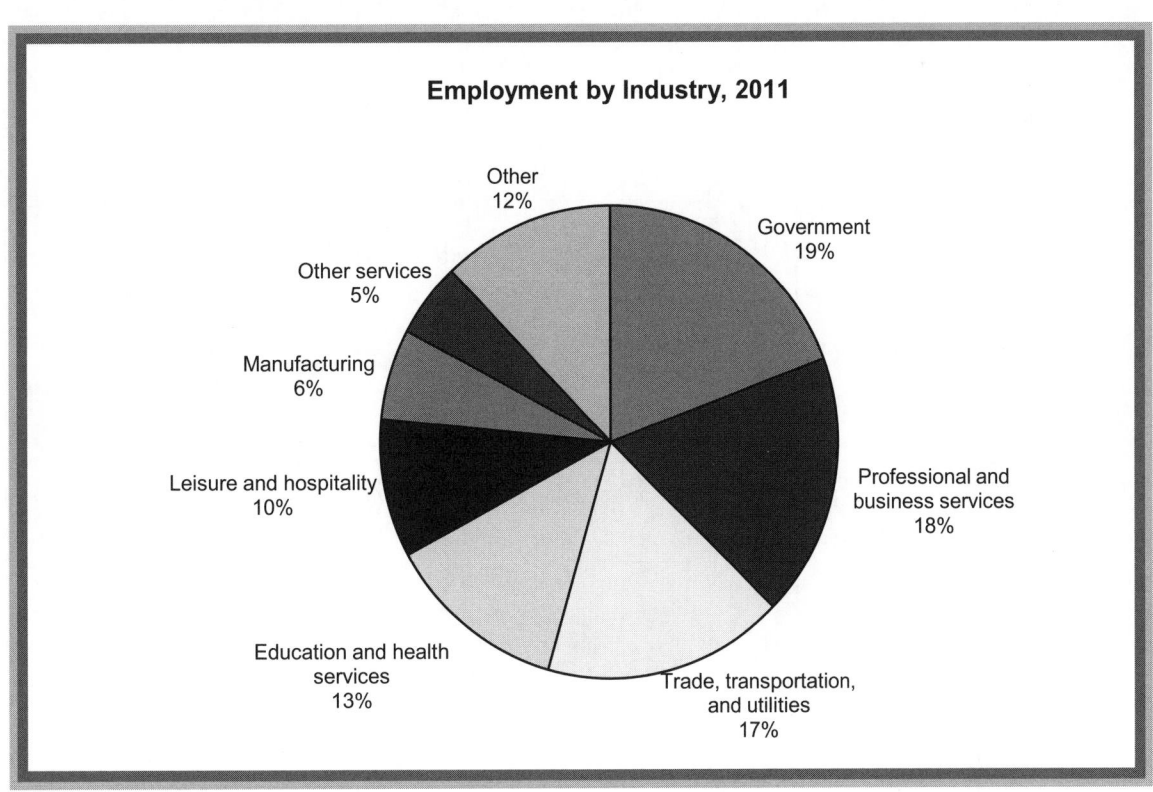

Employment by Industry, 2011

Other 12%
Government 19%
Other services 5%
Manufacturing 6%
Leisure and hospitality 10%
Professional and business services 18%
Education and health services 13%
Trade, transportation, and utilities 17%

1. Employment by Industry: Virginia, Selected Years, 2000–2011

(Numbers in thousands, not seasonally adjusted)

Industry and year	January	February	March	April	May	June	July	August	September	October	November	December	Annual average
Total Nonfarm													
2000	3,408.6	3,423.7	3,469.8	3,492.2	3,520.4	3,557.5	3,517.3	3,521.2	3,545.7	3,560.5	3,584.4	3,596.9	3,516.5
2001	3,472.6	3,484.7	3,514.3	3,519.6	3,537.9	3,568.1	3,516.5	3,515.7	3,520.6	3,507.4	3,522.0	3,525.0	3,517.0
2002	3,433.6	3,444.5	3,472.7	3,490.6	3,510.2	3,538.4	3,484.7	3,487.0	3,504.9	3,509.3	3,524.1	3,529.5	3,494.1
2003	3,439.0	3,435.7	3,460.8	3,476.6	3,502.5	3,529.0	3,485.9	3,492.6	3,512.8	3,527.5	3,548.8	3,558.4	3,497.5
2004	3,483.3	3,495.8	3,535.3	3,565.7	3,588.0	3,621.2	3,586.7	3,585.8	3,607.1	3,627.7	3,647.5	3,660.0	3,583.7
2005	3,573.4	3,588.8	3,614.4	3,651.0	3,671.6	3,701.3	3,667.3	3,668.2	3,698.5	3,695.0	3,717.0	3,725.8	3,664.4
2006	3,654.1	3,664.7	3,700.7	3,714.0	3,743.3	3,777.6	3,724.7	3,720.5	3,734.8	3,744.6	3,763.4	3,775.2	3,726.5
2007	3,699.8	3,705.7	3,737.1	3,753.1	3,777.8	3,808.8	3,760.0	3,752.5	3,770.2	3,776.9	3,795.3	3,799.5	3,761.4
2008	3,719.8	3,728.1	3,749.0	3,772.8	3,790.1	3,811.1	3,765.0	3,759.9	3,767.3	3,770.5	3,764.7	3,756.1	3,762.9
2009	3,643.0	3,631.6	3,638.3	3,648.0	3,666.4	3,679.4	3,619.8	3,611.0	3,628.0	3,640.7	3,651.3	3,648.6	3,642.2
2010	3,558.5	3,543.5	3,586.1	3,641.9	3,673.1	3,690.4	3,641.0	3,630.3	3,653.0	3,673.1	3,683.1	3,683.7	3,638.1
2011	3,603.0	3,620.8	3,647.4	3,687.8	3,701.2	3,720.1	3,672.7	3,667.9	3,690.4	3,714.9	3,722.7	3,715.4	3,680.4
Total Private													
2000	2,794.6	2,802.8	2,841.6	2,857.5	2,883.8	2,925.5	2,912.5	2,919.6	2,927.7	2,929.3	2,946.5	2,960.4	2,891.8
2001	2,847.3	2,849.4	2,877.9	2,882.5	2,904.7	2,933.8	2,907.0	2,911.8	2,898.8	2,874.6	2,880.4	2,885.7	2,887.8
2002	2,803.3	2,807.2	2,832.3	2,849.1	2,870.5	2,898.5	2,870.3	2,877.0	2,875.5	2,865.1	2,876.7	2,885.2	2,859.2
2003	2,805.1	2,795.6	2,819.1	2,833.5	2,861.3	2,886.6	2,870.6	2,881.3	2,876.4	2,884.0	2,896.8	2,909.2	2,860.0
2004	2,840.8	2,845.1	2,879.9	2,907.2	2,933.6	2,966.7	2,958.1	2,961.6	2,959.9	2,967.2	2,979.1	2,993.8	2,932.8
2005	2,919.5	2,927.5	2,950.3	2,980.6	3,003.4	3,033.8	3,027.1	3,033.1	3,037.2	3,025.3	3,040.1	3,052.1	3,002.5
2006	2,988.1	2,989.9	3,020.4	3,031.9	3,061.6	3,096.4	3,070.0	3,071.2	3,065.6	3,062.0	3,075.0	3,088.2	3,051.7
2007	3,020.7	3,017.9	3,047.8	3,061.5	3,089.2	3,121.8	3,098.0	3,097.6	3,092.9	3,088.9	3,098.5	3,106.2	3,078.4
2008	3,033.4	3,031.3	3,047.9	3,073.3	3,091.5	3,114.7	3,094.7	3,090.6	3,077.8	3,065.8	3,053.8	3,047.1	3,068.5
2009	2,946.8	2,927.7	2,930.1	2,937.6	2,957.5	2,972.9	2,949.1	2,942.1	2,934.6	2,933.6	2,935.5	2,938.1	2,942.1
2010	2,858.4	2,838.5	2,875.1	2,925.4	2,949.4	2,971.5	2,963.6	2,961.1	2,952.0	2,964.0	2,969.8	2,972.0	2,933.4
2011	2,899.3	2,904.9	2,928.1	2,967.1	2,984.8	3,005.6	2,991.8	2,992.5	2,982.9	2,994.4	2,995.7	2,992.0	2,969.9
Goods-Producing													
2000	574.0	573.8	581.4	582.2	585.7	591.0	585.6	589.4	591.8	588.7	589.1	588.9	585.1
2001	571.2	569.7	573.6	572.5	573.1	576.6	572.3	575.4	570.4	562.4	560.2	556.8	569.5
2002	539.1	538.5	542.5	544.4	547.9	551.4	546.9	550.1	547.5	545.6	543.4	541.2	544.9
2003	528.3	525.1	529.1	528.9	534.0	535.5	534.9	537.8	535.4	534.9	534.3	532.4	532.6
2004	522.6	522.4	529.6	536.0	539.8	545.8	546.4	547.5	546.9	547.5	546.9	547.0	539.9
2005	538.0	537.4	539.8	546.3	549.4	555.3	557.8	560.2	557.3	553.9	553.6	552.8	550.2
2006	543.1	543.0	547.4	549.9	553.7	558.6	554.9	554.9	548.8	543.6	540.4	539.2	548.1
2007	526.8	525.1	529.8	531.2	532.9	537.0	534.0	533.2	529.3	524.1	521.0	518.3	528.6
2008	504.5	500.1	500.4	505.0	504.4	506.5	504.8	503.2	498.7	493.7	486.3	478.9	498.9
2009	456.4	446.7	443.8	441.3	440.0	441.0	440.3	438.5	435.9	434.3	430.7	429.4	439.9
2010	414.1	407.8	415.2	424.5	428.1	429.3	431.6	430.5	429.0	428.0	425.8	423.0	423.9
2011	409.7	410.3	414.1	418.5	420.4	423.7	421.6	423.4	420.8	423.3	420.5	416.3	418.6
Mining and Logging													
2000	11.4	11.3	11.4	11.4	11.4	11.5	11.5	11.5	11.5	11.5	11.5	11.6	11.5
2001	11.2	11.3	11.3	11.4	11.5	11.6	11.5	11.6	11.5	11.4	11.4	11.3	11.4
2002	11.0	10.9	11.0	10.7	10.8	10.7	10.5	10.4	10.4	10.2	10.2	10.2	10.6
2003	10.0	9.9	10.1	9.9	10.1	10.2	10.2	10.2	10.1	10.2	10.2	10.3	10.1
2004	10.0	10.1	10.2	10.2	10.3	10.4	10.3	10.3	10.3	10.3	10.4	10.4	10.3
2005	10.4	10.4	10.1	10.3	10.4	10.8	10.9	10.9	10.9	10.9	11.0	11.1	10.7
2006	11.0	11.0	11.2	11.0	11.2	11.5	11.5	11.5	11.3	11.2	11.3	11.3	11.3
2007	11.3	11.2	11.4	10.7	10.8	10.8	11.0	11.0	10.6	10.7	10.6	10.8	10.9
2008	10.6	10.9	10.8	10.9	11.0	11.1	11.2	11.2	11.3	11.5	11.5	11.4	11.1
2009	10.8	10.5	10.4	10.2	10.1	10.1	10.0	10.1	10.1	10.2	10.2	10.2	10.2
2010	9.9	9.8	10.0	10.3	10.3	10.4	10.5	10.6	10.6	10.7	10.7	10.6	10.4
2011	10.7	10.6	10.7	10.8	10.8	10.9	10.9	11.0	11.0	11.1	11.1	11.0	10.9
Construction													
2000	196.0	196.9	204.4	207.4	210.3	214.6	214.7	216.4	216.1	215.2	215.1	214.4	210.1
2001	205.9	207.7	213.1	215.9	219.8	223.4	223.3	224.3	221.5	217.7	216.1	214.5	216.9
2002	205.0	206.0	210.0	213.0	216.4	218.9	219.7	220.5	217.7	216.5	214.5	212.9	214.3
2003	204.4	202.6	208.1	211.6	218.3	220.2	224.2	225.7	223.7	225.0	223.5	222.8	217.5
2004	215.3	215.4	221.4	227.3	231.4	235.6	238.6	238.0	236.7	237.6	237.0	236.6	230.9
2005	230.5	230.1	232.9	239.6	242.7	247.5	252.5	253.1	250.9	248.5	248.2	247.1	243.6
2006	240.8	241.7	246.8	248.5	252.1	256.0	254.8	254.0	251.1	247.9	246.0	245.3	248.8
2007	236.1	233.3	237.6	240.9	243.3	246.0	244.9	245.2	242.6	238.7	236.1	233.6	239.9
2008	223.7	222.0	223.9	226.2	226.8	228.6	228.3	227.1	223.8	220.4	214.9	209.6	222.9
2009	195.4	190.8	190.2	190.6	191.1	192.4	192.9	192.2	189.9	188.4	185.6	184.0	190.3
2010	173.9	168.6	175.5	184.1	186.4	187.6	190.2	189.4	187.9	186.4	185.0	181.7	183.1
2011	171.7	171.9	174.5	178.4	179.7	181.5	181.1	183.0	180.6	181.7	181.0	178.4	178.6
Manufacturing													
2000	366.6	365.6	365.6	363.4	364.0	364.9	359.4	361.5	364.2	362.0	362.5	362.9	363.6
2001	354.1	350.7	349.2	345.2	341.8	341.6	337.5	339.5	337.4	333.3	332.7	331.0	341.2
2002	323.1	321.6	321.5	320.7	320.7	321.8	316.7	319.2	319.4	318.9	318.7	318.1	320.0
2003	313.9	312.6	310.9	307.4	305.6	305.1	300.5	301.9	301.6	299.7	300.6	299.3	304.9
2004	297.3	296.9	298.0	298.5	298.1	299.8	297.5	299.2	299.9	299.6	299.5	300.0	298.7
2005	297.1	296.9	296.8	296.4	296.3	297.0	294.4	296.2	295.5	294.5	294.4	294.6	295.8
2006	291.3	290.3	289.4	290.4	290.4	291.1	288.6	289.4	286.4	284.5	283.1	282.6	288.1
2007	279.4	280.6	280.8	279.6	278.8	280.2	278.1	277.0	276.1	274.7	274.3	273.9	277.8
2008	270.2	267.2	265.7	267.9	266.6	266.8	265.3	264.9	263.6	261.8	259.9	257.9	264.8
2009	250.2	245.4	243.2	240.5	238.8	238.5	237.4	236.2	235.9	235.7	234.9	235.2	239.3
2010	230.3	229.4	229.7	230.1	231.4	231.3	230.9	230.5	230.5	230.9	230.1	230.7	230.5
2011	227.3	227.8	228.9	229.3	229.9	231.3	229.6	229.4	229.2	230.5	228.4	226.9	229.0

1. Employment by Industry: Virginia, Selected Years, 2000–2011—*Continued*

(Numbers in thousands, not seasonally adjusted)

Industry and year	January	February	March	April	May	June	July	August	September	October	November	December	Annual average
Service-Providing													
2000	2,834.6	2,849.9	2,888.4	2,910.0	2,934.7	2,966.5	2,931.7	2,931.8	2,953.9	2,971.8	2,995.3	3,008.0	2,931.4
2001	2,901.4	2,915.0	2,940.7	2,947.1	2,964.8	2,991.5	2,944.2	2,940.3	2,950.2	2,945.0	2,961.8	2,968.2	2,947.5
2002	2,894.5	2,906.0	2,930.2	2,946.2	2,962.3	2,987.0	2,937.8	2,936.9	2,957.4	2,963.7	2,980.7	2,988.3	2,949.3
2003	2,910.7	2,910.6	2,931.7	2,947.7	2,968.5	2,993.5	2,951.0	2,954.8	2,977.4	2,992.6	3,014.5	3,026.0	2,964.9
2004	2,960.7	2,973.4	3,005.7	3,029.7	3,048.2	3,075.4	3,040.3	3,038.3	3,060.2	3,080.2	3,100.6	3,113.0	3,043.8
2005	3,035.4	3,051.4	3,074.6	3,104.7	3,122.2	3,146.0	3,109.5	3,108.0	3,141.2	3,141.1	3,163.4	3,173.0	3,114.2
2006	3,111.0	3,121.7	3,153.3	3,164.1	3,189.6	3,219.0	3,169.8	3,165.6	3,186.0	3,201.0	3,223.0	3,236.0	3,178.3
2007	3,173.0	3,180.6	3,207.3	3,221.9	3,244.9	3,271.8	3,226.0	3,219.3	3,240.9	3,252.8	3,274.3	3,281.2	3,232.8
2008	3,215.3	3,228.0	3,248.6	3,267.8	3,285.7	3,304.6	3,260.2	3,256.7	3,268.6	3,276.8	3,278.4	3,277.2	3,264.0
2009	3,186.6	3,184.9	3,194.5	3,206.7	3,226.4	3,238.4	3,179.5	3,172.5	3,192.1	3,206.4	3,220.6	3,219.2	3,202.3
2010	3,144.4	3,135.7	3,170.9	3,217.4	3,245.0	3,261.1	3,209.4	3,199.8	3,224.0	3,245.1	3,257.3	3,260.7	3,214.2
2011	3,193.3	3,210.5	3,233.3	3,269.3	3,280.8	3,296.4	3,251.1	3,244.5	3,269.6	3,291.6	3,302.2	3,299.1	3,261.8
Trade, Transportation, and Utilities													
2000	637.7	633.8	638.1	637.3	642.8	648.1	645.3	649.2	651.3	661.3	676.8	686.8	650.7
2001	644.0	634.8	638.3	635.0	640.7	645.2	642.9	643.8	641.6	646.0	658.7	664.9	644.7
2002	632.9	623.7	625.5	626.3	630.8	636.2	634.6	636.3	634.8	639.2	652.9	663.7	636.4
2003	625.3	618.4	621.0	622.9	628.5	632.7	632.8	636.0	634.0	643.7	657.8	669.2	635.2
2004	635.8	630.2	633.3	636.0	641.4	646.4	646.3	647.6	644.4	652.5	666.4	676.5	646.4
2005	646.9	640.6	643.6	648.1	651.6	655.1	656.1	657.2	655.6	662.7	678.4	689.4	657.1
2006	659.2	648.1	653.4	652.9	659.0	663.6	660.3	661.0	658.1	665.9	682.0	692.1	663.0
2007	663.5	654.2	658.5	657.6	664.4	668.4	668.2	667.2	665.7	669.1	686.2	694.4	668.1
2008	663.4	653.3	655.3	654.2	658.0	661.5	660.0	659.4	655.7	654.8	663.8	669.7	659.1
2009	633.3	622.3	619.7	618.1	623.6	624.9	620.9	619.8	617.9	620.1	631.9	638.8	624.3
2010	611.2	601.0	607.0	614.2	620.3	623.6	622.6	623.6	618.6	625.9	638.2	647.3	621.1
2011	619.6	614.5	616.8	623.3	626.9	629.8	631.9	633.7	627.7	631.6	644.7	648.5	629.1
Wholesale Trade													
2000	111.2	111.8	112.7	113.5	114.0	114.9	113.9	114.4	114.5	116.3	116.7	117.4	114.3
2001	113.9	114.1	115.1	115.2	115.1	115.9	115.2	115.0	114.4	114.1	114.3	114.4	114.7
2002	112.4	112.2	112.6	112.8	113.0	113.4	112.8	113.0	112.6	112.7	113.1	113.5	112.8
2003	112.3	112.3	112.6	112.5	113.3	113.5	113.5	113.7	113.1	113.6	113.8	114.5	113.2
2004	113.0	113.1	113.9	114.1	114.4	115.1	115.5	115.2	114.5	115.2	115.4	115.9	114.6
2005	114.7	115.0	115.6	116.8	117.2	117.4	117.9	118.2	117.8	118.1	118.7	119.1	117.2
2006	117.4	117.8	118.5	119.1	119.7	120.5	119.9	120.1	119.8	120.5	120.8	121.2	119.6
2007	120.0	120.4	121.1	120.7	121.2	121.8	121.2	121.4	120.9	120.7	120.6	121.0	120.9
2008	119.6	119.7	119.7	120.0	120.4	120.6	120.3	120.1	119.2	119.0	118.1	117.6	119.5
2009	115.4	114.7	114.2	113.8	113.6	113.1	112.2	112.0	111.1	110.6	110.2	110.2	112.6
2010	107.9	107.6	108.2	109.5	110.0	110.2	110.7	110.9	110.5	111.2	111.5	111.7	110.0
2011	110.6	110.7	111.1	111.9	112.2	112.7	113.1	112.8	112.2	112.3	111.5	110.4	111.8
Retail Trade													
2000	401.9	397.4	400.5	398.9	403.6	407.3	404.6	407.9	410.2	415.8	431.2	440.8	410.0
2001	405.2	395.9	398.2	395.6	400.6	404.0	402.3	404.0	402.9	407.9	421.9	429.1	405.6
2002	402.8	394.7	396.1	396.4	400.1	403.6	401.6	402.8	402.2	405.3	418.1	428.6	404.4
2003	395.8	389.6	391.3	392.8	397.1	400.4	398.9	402.1	401.6	409.4	424.2	434.5	403.1
2004	407.6	401.7	403.5	405.1	409.3	412.6	410.7	411.5	409.2	415.5	428.9	437.0	412.7
2005	412.3	405.9	407.3	410.4	413.3	416.1	416.8	417.7	417.1	422.6	436.5	445.5	418.5
2006	422.2	412.9	416.6	415.8	420.6	423.1	421.2	421.5	418.6	425.3	440.7	447.6	423.8
2007	425.5	416.2	419.2	418.7	424.3	426.4	426.5	425.4	424.4	428.1	444.5	450.3	427.5
2008	425.9	415.8	418.1	415.8	418.5	421.0	420.0	419.2	417.1	417.4	426.7	431.5	420.6
2009	403.5	394.4	392.8	392.4	397.4	399.0	396.2	395.6	394.3	397.3	408.6	414.0	398.8
2010	393.1	383.8	388.5	393.3	398.0	400.0	398.3	398.9	394.4	400.0	410.9	417.9	398.1
2011	396.1	391.4	392.9	398.1	400.7	402.5	402.4	404.8	399.1	403.2	413.1	417.2	401.8
Transportation and Utilities													
2000	124.6	124.6	124.9	124.9	125.2	125.9	126.8	126.9	126.6	129.2	128.9	128.6	126.4
2001	124.9	124.8	125.0	124.2	125.0	125.3	125.4	124.8	124.3	124.0	122.5	121.4	124.3
2002	117.7	116.8	116.8	117.1	117.7	119.2	120.2	120.5	120.0	121.2	121.7	121.6	119.2
2003	117.2	116.5	117.1	117.6	118.1	118.8	120.4	120.2	119.3	120.7	119.8	120.2	118.8
2004	115.2	115.4	115.9	116.8	117.7	118.7	120.1	120.9	120.7	121.8	122.1	123.6	119.1
2005	119.9	119.7	120.7	120.9	121.1	121.6	121.4	121.3	120.7	122.0	123.2	124.8	121.4
2006	119.6	117.4	118.3	118.0	118.7	120.0	119.2	119.4	119.7	120.1	120.5	123.3	119.5
2007	118.0	117.6	118.2	118.2	118.9	120.2	120.5	120.4	120.4	120.3	121.1	123.1	119.7
2008	117.9	117.8	117.5	118.4	119.1	119.9	119.7	120.1	119.4	118.4	119.0	120.6	119.0
2009	114.4	113.2	112.7	111.9	112.6	112.8	112.5	112.2	112.5	112.2	113.1	114.6	112.9
2010	110.2	109.6	110.3	111.4	112.3	113.4	113.6	113.8	113.7	114.7	115.8	117.7	113.0
2011	112.9	112.4	112.8	113.3	114.0	114.6	116.4	116.1	116.4	116.1	120.1	120.9	115.5
Information													
2000	112.6	113.5	114.7	115.5	117.7	120.0	121.2	116.4	123.3	123.4	124.3	125.3	119.0
2001	123.9	124.2	124.0	121.3	121.2	119.7	119.2	118.0	116.6	114.4	113.4	112.8	119.1
2002	109.9	109.4	108.8	107.4	107.5	107.3	104.9	104.4	102.6	102.2	102.9	102.6	105.8
2003	101.3	101.6	101.5	100.7	101.2	102.2	102.2	101.8	100.9	100.5	101.3	101.5	101.4
2004	101.1	100.7	101.2	99.4	99.1	99.1	98.8	97.7	96.2	95.4	95.5	95.0	98.3
2005	93.5	93.4	93.4	93.0	93.0	93.3	92.9	92.6	91.8	91.6	91.9	92.0	92.7
2006	91.3	91.7	91.8	91.4	91.8	91.8	92.9	91.8	91.3	90.4	90.8	90.8	91.6
2007	91.9	91.3	90.7	90.5	91.0	90.9	90.3	89.8	89.7	89.6	89.7	89.5	90.4
2008	88.7	88.7	88.5	88.1	88.2	88.4	88.0	87.5	86.4	85.6	85.4	84.9	87.4
2009	84.0	83.8	83.1	82.1	81.9	81.8	81.1	80.1	79.1	79.0	78.7	78.5	81.1
2010	77.4	76.7	76.7	75.7	75.7	76.0	75.8	75.8	75.5	75.5	75.5	75.7	76.0
2011	74.7	74.5	74.6	74.2	74.5	74.8	74.5	69.9	73.9	74.5	74.1	74.3	74.0

1. Employment by Industry: Virginia, Selected Years, 2000–2011—*Continued*

(Numbers in thousands, not seasonally adjusted)

Industry and year	January	February	March	April	May	June	July	August	September	October	November	December	Annual average
Financial Activities													
2000	173.8	174.3	175.3	176.4	178.0	180.7	180.1	181.0	180.4	181.3	181.8	183.4	178.9
2001	176.9	177.8	178.9	179.0	180.2	182.6	182.5	183.0	181.1	178.2	178.9	179.9	179.9
2002	179.0	179.7	180.4	180.3	181.6	184.0	183.9	183.9	182.6	182.4	183.4	184.4	182.1
2003	182.6	183.3	184.2	184.9	186.4	188.9	190.0	190.3	188.1	186.3	185.6	186.7	186.4
2004	184.8	185.0	186.0	188.2	189.0	191.1	191.9	191.9	190.0	189.5	189.8	190.8	189.0
2005	188.7	189.4	189.9	191.2	192.2	194.5	195.9	195.9	194.2	192.3	192.1	193.5	192.5
2006	191.9	192.6	193.6	193.6	195.0	197.6	197.0	197.1	194.8	194.4	194.3	195.5	194.8
2007	193.7	193.9	194.7	194.0	195.1	196.6	196.0	195.1	193.0	191.3	190.2	190.3	193.7
2008	189.3	189.5	189.6	189.1	189.1	190.5	191.1	190.1	187.7	186.7	185.5	185.6	188.7
2009	182.1	181.1	181.1	181.0	180.6	181.6	181.0	180.8	178.4	177.4	177.0	177.5	180.0
2010	176.3	175.6	176.4	177.4	178.3	180.8	181.7	181.6	179.9	180.1	180.2	180.7	179.1
2011	178.4	178.6	179.0	180.7	181.6	183.1	184.7	185.1	183.9	184.9	184.9	184.6	182.5
Professional and Business Services													
2000	542.0	548.4	558.0	563.1	564.1	575.2	572.9	575.6	576.1	578.1	579.3	583.4	568.0
2001	554.8	557.8	563.1	561.2	561.2	567.0	563.5	565.2	559.6	554.4	552.2	554.3	559.5
2002	537.1	541.5	547.3	548.4	548.5	552.0	550.3	551.7	548.1	545.7	546.1	546.9	547.0
2003	535.9	535.9	541.4	544.3	545.7	549.9	550.4	554.8	552.8	557.9	560.5	562.6	549.3
2004	551.7	556.7	563.7	570.0	573.5	581.0	586.0	590.5	587.7	592.1	592.9	596.4	578.5
2005	584.8	590.4	595.1	599.4	600.7	607.0	612.8	615.8	616.5	616.1	616.3	618.7	606.1
2006	610.5	615.0	621.1	622.3	625.4	632.4	633.2	636.0	634.3	636.1	637.2	639.0	628.5
2007	628.4	631.9	638.2	642.1	643.6	650.6	650.9	653.7	649.9	655.0	655.3	656.4	646.3
2008	644.9	647.3	650.3	656.4	657.0	662.5	663.2	665.6	661.1	662.0	658.3	655.8	657.0
2009	640.3	639.0	639.2	638.0	636.7	639.7	639.5	640.8	636.9	642.4	644.6	643.7	640.1
2010	631.2	631.1	636.0	648.7	648.4	652.4	657.5	658.3	655.1	661.7	662.5	661.7	650.4
2011	652.7	655.3	659.5	666.7	664.8	666.4	665.9	663.7	659.7	665.9	665.3	665.5	662.6
Education and Health Services													
2000	326.3	329.1	331.8	329.1	330.7	330.8	330.3	330.5	335.0	336.7	338.0	339.2	332.3
2001	339.5	342.8	344.6	345.2	346.5	346.7	331.6	332.1	350.0	353.7	355.1	356.6	345.4
2002	355.9	360.2	362.1	363.8	363.5	363.0	343.9	345.4	367.4	370.8	373.0	372.9	361.8
2003	370.2	370.3	370.0	372.7	372.3	371.7	352.9	354.5	373.5	375.6	377.5	378.5	370.0
2004	376.4	379.1	383.0	382.6	383.0	381.6	364.4	365.1	385.7	389.7	391.7	393.0	381.3
2005	387.3	391.3	393.0	395.3	396.9	395.4	377.0	377.9	401.7	400.6	402.8	403.1	393.5
2006	400.4	403.8	406.1	406.0	407.8	408.5	387.7	387.6	410.7	412.9	415.7	416.8	405.3
2007	412.0	414.9	417.7	420.3	422.8	423.9	403.9	405.7	426.7	430.4	432.9	435.0	420.5
2008	430.3	436.1	437.4	441.9	442.7	441.6	423.7	424.5	445.2	448.7	449.8	450.4	439.4
2009	445.5	447.5	448.9	451.1	453.0	451.0	434.5	434.2	453.2	456.3	457.9	458.5	449.3
2010	452.6	452.3	456.3	459.9	461.0	458.1	443.1	442.3	458.5	465.3	466.8	465.5	456.8
2011	461.3	464.2	465.9	469.8	470.1	467.2	452.9	458.1	473.9	480.1	480.4	478.1	468.5
Leisure and Hospitality													
2000	272.2	273.1	283.9	294.2	304.6	317.7	314.8	315.2	307.7	297.3	294.5	290.4	297.1
2001	275.1	279.5	289.9	299.8	311.9	324.4	324.0	323.2	309.9	296.9	291.1	289.1	301.2
2002	275.8	279.2	289.3	301.5	312.3	324.5	326.4	326.2	314.4	302.7	298.5	296.2	303.9
2003	283.5	282.7	292.0	303.2	316.9	328.4	330.4	329.7	316.7	310.2	304.8	303.0	308.5
2004	292.4	294.4	304.8	316.3	328.3	340.4	341.9	340.4	329.6	321.0	316.2	314.9	320.1
2005	302.3	305.9	315.6	326.2	337.6	349.9	350.8	350.6	338.4	328.1	324.9	322.2	329.4
2006	313.2	316.7	326.7	335.3	345.4	360.2	360.4	359.4	345.7	336.8	332.7	332.3	338.7
2007	322.3	323.9	333.7	341.0	353.3	367.0	367.2	366.3	353.1	343.2	337.0	335.4	345.3
2008	327.2	329.7	339.2	349.7	362.1	372.7	372.9	369.6	354.3	344.6	336.2	333.6	349.3
2009	320.2	321.9	328.4	339.7	355.0	364.9	364.0	361.1	348.3	339.0	330.3	327.2	341.7
2010	313.3	312.5	323.8	339.8	351.6	364.2	364.5	363.0	351.2	342.7	336.4	334.0	341.4
2011	319.9	323.5	333.0	347.1	359.2	371.5	372.5	371.7	355.1	346.6	338.3	337.6	348.0
Other Services													
2000	156.0	156.8	158.4	159.7	160.2	162.0	162.3	162.3	162.1	162.5	162.7	163.0	160.7
2001	161.9	162.8	165.5	168.5	169.9	171.6	171.0	171.1	169.6	168.6	170.8	171.3	168.6
2002	173.6	175.0	176.4	177.0	178.4	180.1	179.4	179.0	178.1	176.5	176.5	177.3	177.3
2003	178.0	178.3	179.9	175.9	176.3	177.3	177.0	176.4	175.0	174.9	175.0	175.3	176.6
2004	176.0	176.6	178.3	178.7	179.5	181.3	182.4	180.9	179.4	179.5	179.7	180.2	179.4
2005	178.0	179.1	179.9	181.1	182.0	183.3	183.8	182.9	181.7	180.0	180.1	180.4	181.0
2006	178.5	179.0	180.3	180.8	181.9	183.7	183.6	183.4	181.9	181.9	181.9	182.5	181.6
2007	182.1	182.7	184.5	184.8	186.1	187.4	187.5	186.6	185.5	186.2	186.2	186.9	185.5
2008	185.1	186.6	187.2	188.9	190.0	191.0	191.0	190.7	188.7	189.7	188.5	188.2	188.8
2009	185.0	185.4	185.9	186.3	186.7	188.0	187.8	186.8	184.9	185.1	184.4	184.5	185.9
2010	182.3	181.5	183.7	185.2	186.0	187.1	186.8	186.0	184.2	184.8	184.4	184.1	184.7
2011	183.0	184.0	185.2	186.8	187.3	189.1	187.8	186.9	187.9	187.5	187.5	187.1	186.7
Government													
2000	614.0	620.9	628.2	634.7	636.6	632.0	604.8	601.6	618.0	631.2	637.9	636.5	624.7
2001	625.3	635.3	636.4	637.1	633.2	634.3	609.5	603.9	621.8	632.8	641.6	639.3	629.2
2002	630.3	637.3	640.4	641.5	639.7	639.9	614.4	610.0	629.4	644.2	647.4	644.3	634.9
2003	633.9	640.1	641.7	643.1	641.2	642.4	615.3	611.3	636.4	643.5	652.0	649.2	637.5
2004	642.5	650.7	655.4	658.5	654.4	654.5	628.6	624.2	647.2	660.5	668.4	666.2	650.9
2005	653.9	661.3	664.1	670.4	668.2	667.5	640.2	635.1	661.3	669.7	676.9	673.7	661.9
2006	666.0	674.8	680.3	682.1	681.7	681.2	654.7	649.3	669.2	682.6	688.4	687.0	674.8
2007	679.1	687.8	689.3	691.6	688.6	687.0	662.0	654.9	677.3	688.0	696.8	693.3	683.0
2008	686.4	696.8	701.1	699.5	698.6	696.4	670.3	669.3	689.5	704.7	710.9	709.0	694.4
2009	696.2	703.9	708.2	710.4	708.9	706.5	670.7	668.9	693.4	707.1	715.8	710.5	700.0
2010	700.1	705.0	711.0	716.5	723.7	718.9	677.4	669.2	701.0	709.1	713.3	711.7	704.7
2011	703.7	715.9	719.3	720.7	716.4	714.5	680.9	675.4	707.5	720.5	727.0	723.4	710.4

2. Average Weekly Hours by Selected Industry: Virginia, 2007–2011

(Not seasonally adjusted)

Industry and year	January	February	March	April	May	June	July	August	September	October	November	December	Annual average
Total Private													
2007	34.7	34.7	34.9	35.3	35.1	35.3	35.5	35.4	35.7	35.6	35.2	35.5	35.2
2008	34.4	34.6	35.4	35.1	34.8	35.3	35.0	35.1	35.0	35.2	34.7	34.8	35.0
2009	34.6	34.7	34.6	34.3	34.5	34.3	34.5	35.1	34.3	34.8	35.0	34.6	34.6
2010	34.4	34.0	35.1	35.6	36.1	35.5	35.5	36.0	35.5	35.5	35.6	35.6	35.4
2011	35.8	35.3	35.2	35.5	35.9	35.5	35.6	35.5	35.3	35.5	34.9	35.0	35.4
Goods-Producing													
2007	38.7	38.3	40.1	39.5	40.5	41.2	39.9	39.6	39.9	41.1	40.3	39.9	39.9
2008	38.9	38.8	40.5	39.9	39.2	40.3	40.0	40.4	40.4	41.1	39.9	40.1	40.0
2009	38.3	38.7	37.9	38.5	38.5	39.1	39.6	39.5	38.6	39.7	39.5	39.4	38.9
2010	38.7	36.8	38.7	39.8	40.0	39.8	39.2	39.7	39.9	40.4	40.7	39.7	39.5
2011	39.0	39.0	39.2	39.9	40.6	40.4	39.5	39.6	39.6	38.6	39.7	39.5	39.6
Construction													
2007	38.4	37.5	39.3	39.2	39.9	40.8	39.7	40.1	40.6	40.2	39.1	39.8	39.6
2008	38.9	37.8	39.1	39.1	38.8	41.0	40.1	40.8	40.4	40.8	38.6	38.4	39.5
2009	37.5	37.6	37.1	37.5	37.5	37.9	38.6	38.7	37.2	37.7	36.4	37.4	37.6
2010	37.1	35.0	37.0	39.2	38.7	38.8	38.2	38.8	38.7	38.6	39.7	38.2	38.2
2011	37.2	37.9	37.1	38.5	39.7	39.5	39.3	39.0	38.9	37.9	39.5	39.1	38.7
Manufacturing													
2007	39.0	39.2	41.0	39.8	41.1	41.5	40.0	39.1	39.3	40.7	40.3	38.8	40.0
2008	37.8	38.6	40.7	39.8	40.0	39.9	40.1	40.0	40.4	40.9	40.6	40.6	39.9
2009	37.8	38.6	38.0	38.8	38.9	39.8	40.3	40.0	39.4	40.2	40.3	40.8	39.4
2010	39.7	38.1	40.0	40.1	41.1	40.7	40.4	40.7	40.6	41.6	41.2	40.4	40.4
2011	40.2	39.6	40.8	40.7	41.0	40.9	39.2	39.7	39.9	39.1	39.7	39.7	40.0
Trade, Transportation, and Utilities													
2007	34.3	34.5	34.2	34.3	34.7	34.9	35.3	35.5	35.6	35.3	35.2	35.6	35.0
2008	34.2	34.5	35.2	35.0	34.9	35.0	34.8	35.0	34.8	34.4	34.6	34.0	34.7
2009	33.9	34.7	34.7	34.4	34.5	34.2	34.4	34.8	34.9	35.1	34.9	34.8	34.6
2010	34.6	34.4	34.5	35.0	34.7	34.4	34.7	34.6	34.1	34.2	33.4	34.1	34.4
2011	33.4	33.1	33.2	34.1	34.3	34.6	34.9	34.7	34.7	34.9	34.4	34.9	34.3
Financial Activities													
2007	35.3	35.2	35.3	35.6	35.2	35.6	35.8	35.4	35.7	35.4	35.2	35.5	35.4
2008	35.1	35.4	35.5	35.2	35.2	35.5	35.3	35.6	35.9	35.5	35.8	35.4	35.4
2009	35.5	35.9	35.9	34.6	34.8	35.5	35.9	36.9	36.2	36.3	37.2	36.0	35.9
2010	36.7	36.5	36.7	36.6	38.0	37.1	37.1	38.1	37.2	37.2	37.3	37.3	37.2
2011	39.7	39.3	38.3	38.7	39.5	37.9	38.5	37.9	38.3	39.4	38.0	38.3	38.6
Professional and Business Services													
2007	35.2	35.5	35.4	36.6	35.7	36.1	36.5	36.5	37.1	36.8	36.7	37.0	36.3
2008	36.2	36.9	37.2	36.8	36.7	36.9	36.7	37.0	37.4	37.2	36.6	37.4	36.9
2009	37.5	38.2	38.1	37.8	37.8	36.8	36.7	37.7	36.7	37.2	37.6	36.9	37.4
2010	36.9	36.6	37.2	37.5	38.1	37.1	36.9	38.0	36.9	36.7	37.0	36.8	37.1
2011	38.1	37.6	37.4	37.7	38.1	37.2	37.1	37.1	37.3	37.2	35.6	36.0	37.2
Education and Health Services													
2007	35.8	35.2	35.5	35.8	35.8	34.9	35.3	35.0	35.2	34.7	34.3	34.8	35.2
2008	34.0	33.9	34.4	34.3	34.5	34.4	34.1	33.9	33.7	33.7	34.7	33.7	34.1
2009	33.6	33.6	33.8	33.6	33.7	33.6	33.2	33.6	33.3	33.5	33.8	33.9	33.6
2010	33.8	34.2	34.1	34.2	34.2	33.9	34.2	34.7	34.2	34.2	34.2	34.3	34.2
2011	35.1	34.3	34.3	34.4	34.8	34.9	35.1	35.1	34.9	35.3	34.8	34.7	34.8
Leisure and Hospitality													
2007	25.2	25.6	25.9	25.8	25.5	25.5	25.8	25.7	25.8	25.7	25.5	25.8	25.7
2008	25.6	25.7	25.8	25.9	25.8	25.9	25.6	25.4	25.2	25.9	25.5	25.4	25.6
2009	25.4	26.3	26.1	25.9	25.9	25.8	26.3	26.1	25.6	25.8	26.1	25.5	25.9
2010	25.6	25.1	26.1	26.8	26.7	27.3	28.7	28.3	27.5	27.6	27.3	26.6	27.0
2011	26.6	26.3	26.2	26.3	26.4	26.1	27.2	26.7	26.1	26.6	26.3	26.0	26.4
Other Services													
2007	33.3	32.9	33.7	33.9	33.9	33.9	34.5	34.2	34.0	33.9	33.6	33.8	33.8
2008	32.6	32.2	32.7	33.2	32.7	33.3	33.2	33.0	33.4	32.5	32.6	32.7	32.8
2009	33.2	33.1	32.7	32.4	32.5	32.8	33.5	33.8	33.4	33.5	33.4	32.4	33.1
2010	31.9	30.9	32.2	32.4	32.9	32.4	31.8	32.2	32.6	31.9	32.6	31.8	32.1
2011	32.1	31.8	32.2	32.1	32.9	32.3	32.3	31.8	32.4	33.8	31.8	31.4	32.2

3. Average Hourly Earnings by Selected Industry: Virginia, 2007–2011

(Dollars, not seasonally adjusted)

Industry and year	January	February	March	April	May	June	July	August	September	October	November	December	Annual average
Total Private													
2007	22.43	22.45	22.32	22.70	22.33	22.25	22.57	22.36	22.49	22.37	22.58	22.65	22.46
2008	22.29	22.56	22.56	22.13	22.11	22.26	22.21	22.24	22.31	22.35	22.38	22.37	22.31
2009	22.19	22.24	22.45	22.17	22.20	22.38	22.42	22.72	22.62	22.86	23.31	23.39	22.58
2010	23.54	23.97	23.42	23.24	23.63	22.89	23.05	23.52	23.58	23.67	23.73	24.33	23.54
2011	24.46	24.54	24.36	24.49	24.54	24.32	24.47	24.39	24.72	25.39	25.10	25.12	24.66
Goods-Producing													
2007	21.35	20.74	20.98	21.17	20.78	20.96	21.03	20.92	20.85	20.80	21.31	21.46	21.03
2008	20.67	20.91	21.03	20.67	20.42	20.70	20.55	20.80	20.86	20.99	21.02	21.05	20.80
2009	20.54	20.53	20.97	20.78	20.79	20.94	20.82	21.01	20.90	20.91	21.12	21.08	20.86
2010	21.19	21.61	21.28	21.04	21.01	21.01	21.18	21.11	21.05	21.15	21.20	21.64	21.20
2011	21.58	21.50	21.47	21.68	21.77	21.66	21.80	21.75	21.79	22.01	22.04	22.11	21.76
Construction													
2007	22.56	21.99	21.97	22.20	21.75	22.02	22.30	21.78	21.55	21.35	21.29	21.49	21.85
2008	20.99	21.46	21.22	21.18	21.40	21.37	21.16	21.48	21.53	21.65	21.57	21.69	21.39
2009	20.94	20.89	21.33	21.30	21.30	21.29	21.11	21.54	21.60	21.64	21.81	21.98	21.39
2010	22.08	22.64	21.99	21.54	21.58	21.38	21.63	21.55	21.43	21.96	21.60	22.15	21.77
2011	22.06	22.00	22.06	22.19	22.04	21.93	22.18	22.13	22.23	22.62	22.53	22.42	22.20
Manufacturing													
2007	20.15	19.49	20.00	20.14	19.80	19.88	19.73	20.05	20.13	20.19	20.20	20.08	19.99
2008	19.79	19.81	20.10	19.81	19.72	20.25	20.04	20.16	20.12	20.02	20.20	20.29	20.03
2009	19.91	20.02	20.26	20.03	20.11	20.32	20.46	20.38	20.37	20.35	20.68	20.92	20.32
2010	20.94	21.21	20.97	20.84	20.77	20.86	21.01	20.85	20.90	20.51	20.89	21.24	20.91
2011	21.17	20.99	20.93	21.19	21.55	21.64	22.31	22.13	22.06	21.99	22.10	22.30	21.69
Trade, Transportation, and Utilities													
2007	18.76	18.67	18.53	18.98	19.08	18.87	18.73	18.61	18.81	18.84	18.94	18.75	18.80
2008	18.45	18.34	18.41	18.55	18.60	18.59	18.57	18.72	18.64	18.46	18.83	19.09	18.60
2009	19.24	19.67	19.53	18.64	18.81	18.87	19.03	19.34	19.61	19.08	19.45	19.32	19.22
2010	19.86	20.03	19.53	19.69	19.58	19.28	19.57	19.68	19.68	19.78	19.88	20.27	19.74
2011	20.56	20.56	20.48	20.73	20.57	20.77	20.85	20.58	20.44	20.70	20.60	20.11	20.58
Financial Activities													
2007	20.45	20.61	20.66	20.72	20.48	20.22	20.64	20.47	20.57	20.39	20.58	20.77	20.55
2008	20.40	20.65	20.84	20.93	20.97	20.92	20.83	20.96	20.97	21.12	21.15	21.33	20.92
2009	21.03	21.44	21.32	21.65	21.71	21.91	21.76	21.96	21.42	22.63	22.45	22.97	21.85
2010	22.99	23.45	23.31	25.45	25.89	24.68	24.76	24.95	25.58	25.96	25.64	25.96	24.90
2011	24.55	25.05	24.91	26.07	25.35	25.59	25.83	25.37	26.56	27.72	27.56	26.90	25.96
Professional and Business Services													
2007	32.99	33.09	33.08	33.78	33.16	32.75	33.68	33.05	33.61	33.18	33.55	33.54	33.29
2008	32.85	33.36	33.46	33.23	32.89	33.08	32.82	32.95	33.40	33.21	33.32	33.40	33.17
2009	33.03	33.74	33.70	33.68	33.38	33.69	33.73	33.44	33.49	33.51	33.78	33.62	33.57
2010	33.71	34.10	33.45	33.60	34.09	33.37	33.41	33.91	33.54	33.60	33.79	34.20	33.73
2011	34.36	34.52	34.19	33.79	34.17	33.45	33.80	33.81	33.58	34.84	34.60	35.08	34.18
Education and Health Services													
2007	18.37	18.61	18.71	18.89	18.83	19.38	19.33	19.15	19.48	19.52	19.67	19.61	19.13
2008	19.55	19.41	19.63	19.47	19.55	20.01	20.27	20.22	20.34	20.36	20.47	20.47	19.98
2009	20.35	20.58	20.65	20.62	20.43	20.25	20.48	20.57	20.87	20.93	21.14	21.14	20.67
2010	20.96	21.15	21.13	21.39	21.44	21.25	21.53	21.46	21.56	21.65	21.60	21.72	21.41
2011	21.42	21.93	21.76	22.10	22.47	22.45	23.00	22.99	23.44	23.82	23.94	23.96	22.79
Leisure and Hospitality													
2007	11.42	11.58	11.29	11.28	11.37	11.37	11.46	11.39	11.66	11.81	11.89	11.81	11.53
2008	11.72	11.85	11.97	11.96	12.07	12.08	12.04	12.14	12.17	12.21	12.03	12.14	12.03
2009	12.04	11.86	11.95	12.09	12.17	12.15	11.83	12.14	12.40	12.55	12.66	12.70	12.21
2010	12.79	13.02	13.15	12.94	12.82	13.41	13.06	12.98	13.35	13.50	13.46	13.58	13.18
2011	13.36	13.34	13.19	13.31	13.04	12.87	12.62	12.62	13.06	13.00	12.99	13.08	13.03
Other Services													
2007	21.23	21.87	21.21	21.29	21.37	21.51	21.36	21.57	21.55	21.34	21.58	21.84	21.48
2008	22.18	21.79	21.63	21.42	21.83	21.84	21.56	21.70	21.65	21.79	21.61	21.81	21.73
2009	21.51	21.41	21.60	21.66	21.66	21.50	21.60	21.67	21.66	21.47	21.69	21.60	21.59
2010	21.79	22.24	21.92	22.24	22.43	22.42	22.54	22.70	22.55	22.42	22.83	23.03	22.43
2011	23.48	23.62	23.39	24.10	24.15	24.07	24.36	24.48	24.38	25.37	24.20	25.35	24.25

4. Average Weekly Earnings by Selected Industry: Virginia, 2007–2011

(Dollars, not seasonally adjusted)

Industry and year	January	February	March	April	May	June	July	August	September	October	November	December	Annual average
Total Private													
2007	778.32	779.02	778.97	801.31	783.78	785.43	801.24	791.54	802.89	796.37	794.82	804.08	791.55
2008	766.78	780.58	798.62	776.76	769.43	785.78	777.35	780.62	780.85	786.72	776.59	778.48	779.94
2009	767.77	771.73	776.77	760.43	765.90	767.63	773.49	797.47	775.87	795.53	815.85	809.29	781.60
2010	809.78	814.98	822.04	827.34	853.04	812.60	818.28	846.72	837.09	840.29	844.79	866.15	832.99
2011	875.67	866.26	857.47	869.40	880.99	863.36	871.13	865.85	872.62	901.35	875.99	879.20	873.33
Goods-Producing													
2007	826.25	794.34	841.30	836.22	841.59	863.55	839.10	828.43	831.92	854.88	858.79	856.25	839.37
2008	804.06	811.31	851.72	824.73	800.46	834.21	822.00	840.32	842.74	862.69	838.70	844.11	831.28
2009	786.68	794.51	794.76	800.03	800.42	818.75	824.47	829.90	806.74	830.13	834.24	830.55	812.37
2010	820.05	795.25	823.54	837.39	840.40	836.20	830.26	838.07	839.90	854.46	862.84	859.11	836.59
2011	841.62	838.50	841.62	865.03	883.86	875.06	861.10	861.30	862.88	849.59	874.99	873.35	860.87
Construction													
2007	866.30	824.63	863.42	870.24	867.83	898.42	885.31	873.38	874.93	858.27	832.44	855.30	864.50
2008	816.51	811.19	829.70	828.14	830.32	876.17	848.52	876.38	869.81	883.32	832.60	832.90	844.78
2009	785.25	785.46	791.34	798.75	798.75	806.89	814.85	833.60	803.52	815.83	793.88	822.05	804.07
2010	819.17	792.40	813.63	844.37	835.15	829.54	826.27	836.14	829.34	847.66	857.52	846.13	831.77
2011	820.63	833.80	818.43	854.32	874.99	866.24	871.67	863.07	864.75	857.30	889.94	876.62	858.11
Manufacturing													
2007	785.85	764.01	820.00	801.57	813.78	825.02	789.20	783.96	791.11	821.73	814.06	779.10	799.12
2008	748.06	764.67	818.07	788.44	788.80	807.98	803.60	806.40	812.85	818.82	820.12	823.77	799.90
2009	752.60	772.77	769.88	777.16	782.28	808.74	824.54	815.20	802.58	818.07	833.40	853.54	800.41
2010	831.32	808.10	838.80	835.68	853.65	849.00	848.80	848.60	848.54	853.22	860.67	858.10	844.49
2011	851.03	831.20	853.94	862.43	883.55	885.08	874.55	878.56	880.19	859.81	877.37	885.31	868.59
Trade, Transportation, and Utilities													
2007	643.47	644.12	633.73	651.01	662.08	658.56	661.17	660.66	669.64	665.05	666.69	667.50	657.09
2008	630.99	632.73	648.03	649.25	649.14	650.65	646.24	655.20	648.67	635.02	651.52	649.06	645.55
2009	652.24	682.55	677.69	641.22	648.95	645.35	654.63	673.03	684.39	669.71	678.81	672.34	665.07
2010	687.16	689.03	673.79	689.15	679.43	663.23	679.08	680.93	671.09	676.48	663.99	691.21	678.69
2011	686.70	680.54	679.94	706.89	705.55	718.64	727.67	714.13	709.27	722.43	708.64	701.84	705.32
Financial Activities													
2007	721.89	725.47	729.30	737.63	720.90	719.83	738.91	724.64	734.35	721.81	724.42	737.34	728.03
2008	716.04	731.01	739.82	736.74	738.14	742.66	735.30	746.18	752.82	749.76	757.17	755.08	741.66
2009	746.57	769.70	765.39	749.09	755.51	777.81	781.18	810.32	775.40	821.47	835.14	826.92	784.24
2010	843.73	855.93	855.48	931.47	983.82	915.63	918.60	950.60	951.58	965.71	956.37	968.31	925.15
2011	974.64	984.47	954.05	1,008.91	1,001.33	969.86	994.46	961.52	1,017.25	1,092.17	1,047.28	1,030.27	1,003.31
Professional and Business Services													
2007	1,161.25	1,174.70	1,171.03	1,236.35	1,183.81	1,182.28	1,229.32	1,206.33	1,246.93	1,221.02	1,231.29	1,240.98	1,207.41
2008	1,189.17	1,230.98	1,244.71	1,222.86	1,207.06	1,220.65	1,204.49	1,219.15	1,249.16	1,235.41	1,219.51	1,249.16	1,224.38
2009	1,238.63	1,288.87	1,283.97	1,273.10	1,261.76	1,239.79	1,237.89	1,260.69	1,229.08	1,246.57	1,270.13	1,240.58	1,255.90
2010	1,243.90	1,248.06	1,244.34	1,260.00	1,298.83	1,238.03	1,232.83	1,288.58	1,237.63	1,233.12	1,250.23	1,258.56	1,252.90
2011	1,309.12	1,297.95	1,278.71	1,273.88	1,301.88	1,244.34	1,253.98	1,254.35	1,252.53	1,296.05	1,231.76	1,262.88	1,271.37
Education and Health Services													
2007	657.65	655.07	664.21	676.26	674.11	676.36	682.35	670.25	685.70	677.34	674.68	682.43	673.12
2008	664.70	658.00	675.27	667.82	674.48	688.34	691.21	685.46	685.46	686.13	710.31	689.84	681.50
2009	683.76	691.49	697.97	692.83	688.49	680.40	679.94	691.15	694.97	701.16	714.53	716.65	694.53
2010	708.45	723.33	720.53	731.54	733.25	720.38	736.33	744.66	737.35	740.43	738.72	745.00	731.65
2011	751.84	752.20	746.37	760.24	781.96	783.51	807.30	806.95	818.06	840.85	833.11	831.41	793.13
Leisure and Hospitality													
2007	287.78	296.45	292.41	291.02	289.94	289.94	295.67	292.72	300.83	303.52	303.20	304.70	295.65
2008	300.03	304.55	308.83	309.76	311.41	312.87	308.22	308.36	306.68	316.24	306.77	308.36	308.59
2009	305.82	311.92	311.90	313.13	315.20	313.47	311.13	316.85	317.44	323.79	330.43	323.85	316.23
2010	327.42	326.80	343.22	346.79	342.29	366.09	374.82	367.33	367.13	372.60	367.46	361.23	355.94
2011	355.38	350.84	345.58	350.05	344.26	335.91	343.26	336.95	340.87	345.80	341.64	340.08	344.01
Other Services													
2007	706.96	719.52	714.78	721.73	724.44	729.19	736.92	737.69	732.70	723.43	725.09	738.19	725.95
2008	723.07	701.64	707.30	711.14	713.84	727.27	715.79	716.10	723.11	708.18	704.49	713.19	713.78
2009	714.13	708.67	706.32	701.78	703.95	705.20	723.60	732.45	723.44	719.25	724.45	699.84	713.50
2010	695.10	687.22	705.82	720.58	737.95	726.41	716.77	730.94	735.13	715.20	744.26	732.35	720.74
2011	753.71	751.12	753.16	773.61	794.54	777.46	786.83	778.46	789.91	857.51	769.56	795.99	781.90

WASHINGTON
At a Glance

Population:
  2000 census: 5,894,281
  2010 census: 6,724,540
  2011 estimate: 6,830,038

Percent change in population:
  2000–2010: 14.1%
  2010–2011: 1.6%

Percent change in total nonfarm employment:
  2000–2010: 2.8%
  2010–2011: 1.2%

Industry with the largest growth in employment, 2000–2011 (thousands):
  Education and Health Services, 90.2

Industry with the largest decline or smallest growth in employment, 2000–2011 (thousands):
  Manufacturing, -62.7

Civilian labor force:
  2000: 3,050,021
  2010: 3,516,463
  2011: 3,484,814

Unemployment rate and rank among states (lowest to highest):
  2000: 5.0%, 44th
  2010: 9.9%, 35th
  2011: 9.2%, 35th

Over-the-year change in unemployment rates:
  2010–2011: -0.7%

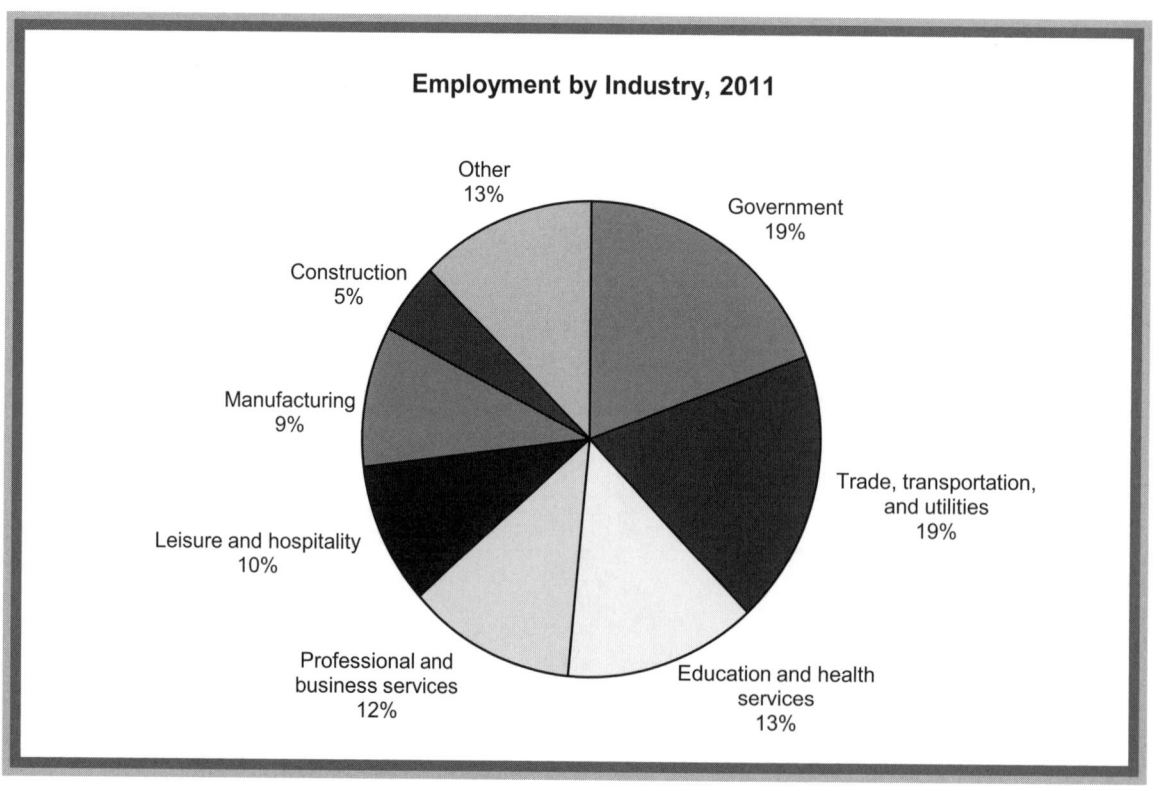

Employment by Industry, 2011

Other 13%
Government 19%
Construction 5%
Manufacturing 9%
Trade, transportation, and utilities 19%
Leisure and hospitality 10%
Professional and business services 12%
Education and health services 13%

1. Employment by Industry: Washington, Selected Years, 2000–2011

(Numbers in thousands, not seasonally adjusted)

Industry and year	January	February	March	April	May	June	July	August	September	October	November	December	Annual average
Total Nonfarm													
2000	2,638.8	2,645.3	2,688.2	2,687.0	2,721.2	2,744.6	2,709.3	2,721.1	2,739.6	2,741.6	2,749.6	2,749.1	2,711.3
2001	2,670.9	2,677.0	2,694.5	2,699.1	2,718.3	2,736.6	2,700.7	2,697.1	2,705.5	2,697.8	2,691.4	2,674.9	2,697.0
2002	2,606.2	2,611.2	2,623.0	2,637.5	2,663.7	2,679.5	2,661.2	2,660.3	2,674.7	2,678.5	2,683.4	2,669.3	2,654.0
2003	2,608.8	2,617.8	2,624.1	2,637.7	2,663.3	2,679.0	2,659.9	2,659.9	2,677.7	2,686.4	2,689.4	2,685.5	2,657.5
2004	2,613.8	2,633.5	2,659.6	2,682.4	2,704.9	2,727.5	2,710.7	2,705.8	2,725.8	2,744.5	2,753.6	2,749.6	2,701.0
2005	2,688.2	2,704.2	2,729.8	2,755.2	2,780.3	2,800.7	2,787.5	2,787.7	2,800.7	2,820.8	2,834.5	2,835.2	2,777.1
2006	2,775.7	2,796.2	2,816.9	2,832.6	2,862.7	2,893.8	2,863.5	2,867.7	2,894.5	2,897.4	2,906.6	2,903.0	2,859.2
2007	2,843.3	2,873.7	2,891.4	2,909.7	2,939.3	2,965.7	2,944.1	2,945.1	2,960.5	2,970.7	2,984.4	2,975.1	2,933.6
2008	2,916.9	2,936.9	2,949.4	2,960.3	2,981.3	2,993.4	2,977.9	2,973.6	2,979.1	2,954.4	2,958.2	2,925.2	2,958.9
2009	2,850.9	2,843.9	2,834.6	2,829.8	2,842.3	2,841.5	2,817.2	2,795.4	2,808.0	2,815.4	2,804.0	2,785.7	2,822.4
2010	2,729.4	2,736.5	2,752.9	2,777.8	2,804.1	2,809.7	2,797.4	2,779.4	2,798.9	2,821.5	2,820.1	2,808.5	2,786.4
2011	2,756.4	2,769.3	2,781.4	2,811.4	2,829.1	2,841.4	2,837.3	2,827.1	2,834.3	2,858.3	2,861.1	2,839.0	2,820.5
Total Private													
2000	2,159.5	2,158.1	2,198.6	2,198.9	2,221.6	2,249.7	2,245.5	2,266.0	2,268.7	2,255.0	2,255.9	2,258.1	2,228.0
2001	2,170.6	2,170.9	2,183.8	2,188.3	2,204.4	2,221.0	2,212.9	2,222.2	2,211.9	2,185.0	2,169.8	2,158.0	2,191.6
2002	2,093.9	2,092.1	2,102.0	2,115.8	2,139.2	2,154.8	2,163.0	2,175.3	2,170.6	2,154.9	2,150.5	2,142.7	2,137.9
2003	2,088.1	2,091.5	2,096.8	2,110.4	2,130.4	2,148.6	2,158.8	2,170.3	2,170.7	2,161.8	2,157.2	2,157.9	2,136.9
2004	2,092.1	2,105.9	2,129.3	2,152.1	2,172.7	2,193.8	2,204.3	2,213.3	2,214.0	2,215.8	2,216.0	2,218.7	2,177.3
2005	2,161.9	2,173.4	2,195.9	2,220.7	2,244.4	2,263.1	2,278.9	2,293.1	2,286.6	2,288.8	2,294.7	2,302.6	2,250.3
2006	2,246.1	2,259.7	2,278.7	2,295.8	2,323.6	2,351.9	2,354.2	2,370.9	2,376.6	2,362.3	2,364.0	2,366.7	2,329.2
2007	2,312.6	2,336.1	2,354.6	2,370.0	2,397.3	2,424.2	2,426.6	2,440.6	2,438.7	2,429.5	2,435.0	2,432.6	2,399.8
2008	2,375.6	2,387.2	2,400.2	2,410.4	2,428.5	2,440.2	2,446.9	2,454.1	2,445.3	2,398.4	2,394.0	2,369.9	2,412.6
2009	2,299.2	2,287.5	2,276.0	2,264.9	2,277.4	2,286.0	2,284.7	2,281.5	2,277.7	2,259.4	2,244.4	2,235.8	2,272.9
2010	2,178.0	2,181.4	2,196.2	2,216.6	2,231.7	2,249.2	2,261.7	2,264.0	2,268.6	2,267.4	2,261.8	2,260.0	2,236.4
2011	2,206.8	2,216.2	2,228.0	2,256.2	2,272.4	2,292.4	2,310.5	2,318.3	2,315.0	2,313.5	2,312.6	2,300.9	2,278.6
Goods-Producing													
2000	489.2	476.7	496.0	498.4	503.2	510.1	511.7	516.3	514.8	511.9	504.7	496.6	502.5
2001	483.6	480.5	483.5	483.9	488.4	493.6	494.7	498.3	494.1	484.1	471.6	459.7	484.7
2002	443.7	440.2	440.6	443.5	450.4	454.1	458.8	462.7	457.4	452.3	443.4	435.5	448.6
2003	422.4	421.7	421.3	424.8	430.2	436.0	440.5	444.2	442.8	439.0	432.1	427.7	431.9
2004	413.0	416.8	422.7	428.5	434.3	440.0	448.5	450.7	450.5	451.1	445.7	442.0	437.0
2005	431.1	435.0	442.1	448.8	455.7	462.6	472.4	476.2	464.1	477.3	472.0	470.2	459.0
2006	461.8	467.9	472.7	476.9	485.6	496.5	502.2	506.3	508.3	504.7	498.1	493.6	489.6
2007	484.5	490.4	494.5	499.8	508.0	518.5	522.5	526.8	525.9	521.8	515.4	508.1	509.7
2008	496.9	498.7	500.4	500.6	505.4	509.3	513.6	515.6	511.2	479.7	487.0	471.7	499.2
2009	451.0	444.4	436.5	430.8	431.7	433.8	434.9	434.5	432.0	424.8	412.8	404.5	431.0
2010	393.4	392.5	394.1	397.4	401.4	406.8	414.4	416.7	417.9	415.2	406.9	400.2	404.7
2011	390.1	392.9	395.6	401.8	406.9	413.7	423.4	430.0	430.3	429.0	422.2	415.7	412.6
Mining and Logging													
2000	10.0	10.1	9.8	9.7	10.1	10.4	10.3	10.4	10.2	9.9	9.7	9.5	10.0
2001	9.9	9.7	9.2	9.0	9.5	9.9	10.4	10.4	10.3	10.1	9.8	9.4	9.8
2002	9.0	9.1	8.9	8.9	9.3	9.5	9.5	9.7	9.7	9.8	9.7	9.4	9.3	9.4
2003	8.7	8.7	8.5	8.3	8.5	8.7	8.8	8.8	8.7	8.7	8.5	8.6	8.6
2004	8.5	8.7	8.6	8.8	9.0	9.2	9.5	9.6	9.7	9.5	9.3	9.2	9.1
2005	8.8	8.9	8.8	8.8	9.1	9.2	9.2	9.1	9.1	8.9	8.8	8.8	9.0
2006	8.4	8.5	8.5	8.4	8.8	9.0	9.0	8.9	8.8	8.7	8.6	8.6	8.7
2007	8.4	7.9	7.6	7.9	8.2	8.5	8.5	8.4	8.3	8.3	8.0	7.9	8.2
2008	7.4	7.4	7.3	7.3	7.5	7.6	7.9	7.9	7.8	7.8	7.4	7.2	7.5
2009	6.5	6.4	5.8	5.6	5.8	6.2	6.3	6.3	6.3	6.1	5.7	5.5	6.0
2010	5.4	5.5	5.5	5.6	5.9	6.1	6.2	6.3	6.3	6.2	5.9	5.7	5.9
2011	5.6	5.7	5.7	5.7	5.9	6.1	6.2	6.2	6.2	6.1	6.0	5.8	5.9
Construction													
2000	146.7	149.2	153.1	155.8	159.3	163.8	166.6	169.7	170.1	168.1	164.7	159.7	160.6
2001	152.0	150.9	155.4	155.5	159.4	163.3	165.4	168.6	166.5	162.5	155.6	149.8	158.7
2002	143.2	143.5	144.6	148.4	153.6	156.6	161.3	166.0	163.9	161.2	156.5	151.6	154.2
2003	144.9	145.2	145.8	149.8	154.6	158.6	163.0	166.6	165.4	164.2	160.1	156.4	156.2
2004	147.3	151.0	155.5	158.8	163.1	166.5	172.0	174.0	172.7	172.9	170.2	166.6	164.2
2005	158.4	162.0	167.0	170.8	175.0	178.7	184.5	188.2	189.3	187.7	184.5	182.8	177.4
2006	175.6	179.5	184.2	187.7	193.8	200.1	203.3	206.9	207.1	204.6	200.0	196.4	194.9
2007	190.3	194.4	199.6	203.5	210.2	215.3	216.5	220.4	218.0	214.6	210.3	205.2	208.2
2008	196.6	197.3	200.3	201.6	204.6	206.9	209.1	210.1	206.5	200.9	190.6	181.1	200.5
2009	168.4	163.7	162.4	159.9	161.8	162.8	162.6	162.3	160.6	156.7	148.9	143.3	159.5
2010	134.7	133.9	135.5	137.2	140.0	142.2	146.8	148.6	147.7	146.2	140.4	135.2	140.7
2011	126.9	127.5	129.0	132.8	136.2	139.2	145.2	147.9	146.3	145.3	140.0	133.8	137.5
Manufacturing													
2000	332.5	317.4	333.1	332.9	333.8	335.9	334.8	336.2	334.5	333.9	330.3	327.4	331.9
2001	321.7	319.9	318.9	319.4	319.5	320.4	318.9	319.3	317.3	311.5	306.2	300.5	316.1
2002	291.5	287.6	287.1	286.2	287.5	288.0	287.8	287.0	283.7	281.4	277.5	274.6	285.0
2003	268.8	267.8	267.0	266.7	267.1	268.7	268.7	268.8	268.7	266.1	263.5	262.7	267.1
2004	257.2	257.1	258.6	260.9	262.2	264.3	267.0	267.1	268.1	268.7	266.2	266.2	263.6
2005	263.9	264.1	266.3	269.2	271.6	274.7	278.7	278.9	265.7	280.7	278.7	278.6	272.6
2006	277.8	279.9	280.0	280.8	283.0	287.4	289.9	290.5	292.4	291.4	289.5	288.6	285.9
2007	285.8	288.1	287.3	288.4	289.6	294.7	297.5	298.0	299.6	298.9	297.1	295.0	293.3
2008	292.9	294.0	292.8	291.7	293.3	294.8	296.6	297.6	296.9	271.0	289.0	283.4	291.2
2009	276.1	274.3	268.3	265.3	264.1	264.8	266.0	265.9	265.1	262.0	258.2	255.7	265.5
2010	253.3	253.1	253.1	254.6	255.5	258.5	261.4	261.8	263.9	262.8	260.6	259.3	258.2
2011	257.6	259.7	260.9	263.3	264.8	268.4	272.0	275.9	277.8	277.6	276.2	276.1	269.2

1. Employment by Industry: Washington, Selected Years, 2000–2011—*Continued*

(Numbers in thousands, not seasonally adjusted)

Industry and year	January	February	March	April	May	June	July	August	September	October	November	December	Annual average
Service-Providing													
2000	2,149.6	2,168.6	2,192.2	2,188.6	2,218.0	2,234.5	2,197.6	2,204.8	2,224.8	2,229.7	2,244.9	2,252.5	2,208.8
2001	2,187.3	2,196.5	2,211.0	2,215.2	2,229.9	2,243.0	2,206.0	2,198.8	2,211.4	2,213.7	2,219.8	2,215.2	2,212.3
2002	2,162.5	2,171.0	2,182.4	2,194.0	2,213.3	2,225.4	2,202.4	2,197.6	2,217.3	2,226.2	2,240.0	2,233.8	2,205.5
2003	2,186.4	2,196.1	2,202.8	2,212.9	2,233.1	2,243.0	2,219.4	2,215.7	2,234.9	2,247.4	2,257.3	2,257.8	2,225.6
2004	2,200.8	2,216.7	2,236.9	2,253.9	2,270.6	2,287.5	2,262.2	2,255.1	2,275.3	2,293.4	2,307.9	2,307.6	2,264.0
2005	2,257.1	2,269.2	2,287.7	2,306.4	2,324.6	2,338.1	2,315.1	2,311.5	2,336.6	2,343.5	2,362.5	2,365.0	2,318.1
2006	2,313.9	2,328.3	2,344.2	2,355.7	2,377.1	2,397.3	2,361.3	2,361.4	2,386.2	2,392.7	2,408.5	2,409.4	2,369.7
2007	2,358.8	2,383.3	2,396.9	2,409.9	2,431.3	2,447.2	2,421.6	2,418.3	2,434.6	2,448.9	2,469.0	2,467.0	2,423.9
2008	2,420.0	2,438.2	2,449.0	2,459.7	2,475.9	2,484.1	2,464.3	2,458.0	2,467.9	2,474.6	2,471.2	2,453.5	2,459.7
2009	2,399.9	2,399.5	2,398.1	2,399.0	2,410.6	2,407.7	2,382.3	2,360.9	2,376.0	2,390.6	2,391.2	2,381.2	2,391.4
2010	2,336.0	2,344.0	2,358.8	2,380.4	2,402.7	2,402.9	2,383.0	2,362.7	2,381.0	2,406.3	2,413.2	2,408.3	2,381.6
2011	2,366.3	2,376.4	2,385.8	2,409.6	2,422.2	2,427.7	2,413.9	2,397.1	2,404.0	2,429.3	2,438.9	2,423.3	2,407.9
Trade, Transportation, and Utilities													
2000	520.6	518.8	523.6	522.5	527.1	533.5	530.2	533.0	533.3	539.1	548.2	552.6	531.9
2001	523.5	518.3	520.9	520.4	522.0	527.2	526.3	526.0	523.5	522.2	526.0	527.8	523.7
2002	505.1	498.9	500.1	501.2	505.7	510.0	512.4	512.0	512.7	512.6	518.3	522.1	509.3
2003	502.1	497.9	498.3	499.7	504.2	509.2	513.2	513.5	514.3	515.7	522.0	527.0	509.8
2004	501.9	500.9	504.1	509.0	513.6	519.4	521.0	523.9	523.6	527.3	535.4	540.6	518.4
2005	517.2	515.2	517.9	520.5	525.8	530.4	531.7	535.3	535.7	536.0	546.3	553.4	530.5
2006	530.4	527.2	530.4	531.4	537.4	543.5	543.0	546.0	546.0	546.2	556.2	561.5	541.6
2007	540.5	539.1	541.9	544.0	549.0	554.2	555.8	557.5	556.2	558.3	570.5	573.5	553.4
2008	552.4	548.2	549.7	549.6	552.6	554.6	557.1	557.5	554.3	553.7	555.1	555.7	553.4
2009	531.2	523.0	518.9	515.6	519.5	520.8	522.8	521.8	521.4	520.8	525.6	527.9	522.4
2010	507.7	504.0	506.3	510.4	514.0	517.6	519.5	519.1	518.6	522.7	529.9	533.8	517.0
2011	512.7	510.0	512.3	515.5	520.3	525.2	532.9	532.1	530.0	535.5	543.1	541.8	526.0
Wholesale Trade													
2000	118.0	118.8	120.2	120.0	120.6	123.3	121.7	122.4	122.0	123.1	122.6	122.1	121.2
2001	119.3	119.4	120.1	120.1	120.6	122.0	121.5	120.7	119.6	119.0	118.0	116.4	119.7
2002	114.8	115.0	115.3	114.9	115.8	116.3	116.3	116.4	116.3	116.1	115.5	114.4	115.6
2003	113.5	113.7	114.3	114.9	115.3	116.3	117.3	117.2	117.4	117.8	117.5	116.5	116.0
2004	114.9	115.7	116.9	118.6	118.8	119.8	120.7	120.7	120.8	121.6	121.4	121.1	119.3
2005	119.2	119.8	120.6	120.2	121.2	122.7	122.8	123.3	123.5	124.0	124.5	124.4	122.2
2006	123.7	124.2	125.0	124.8	126.0	127.9	128.1	127.8	127.9	128.3	128.1	127.1	126.6
2007	125.9	126.6	127.3	128.0	128.9	130.3	130.7	130.6	130.2	131.2	131.4	130.9	129.3
2008	129.0	129.6	130.0	130.1	130.7	130.7	131.4	130.8	130.7	131.3	129.4	127.7	130.1
2009	125.6	124.7	123.8	122.7	122.7	122.8	122.9	121.9	121.6	122.5	121.2	120.1	122.7
2010	118.0	118.4	118.9	120.3	120.6	120.8	121.0	120.6	120.4	121.4	121.3	120.1	120.2
2011	119.0	119.4	120.1	120.9	122.3	122.8	126.1	124.3	123.7	127.9	127.2	125.8	123.3
Retail Trade													
2000	310.0	307.1	309.5	308.9	312.9	315.4	312.6	314.4	314.8	316.7	327.3	332.9	315.2
2001	312.3	307.4	308.9	307.9	308.7	311.1	311.6	312.4	310.9	309.6	317.1	321.2	311.6
2002	303.2	297.2	298.3	299.3	302.1	304.8	306.6	306.3	306.4	306.1	314.1	319.5	305.3
2003	301.7	297.8	298.0	298.7	302.1	305.2	307.4	307.7	307.0	308.0	316.1	321.1	305.9
2004	300.9	299.2	300.5	302.9	306.6	309.0	309.8	312.5	310.7	312.2	321.6	326.7	309.4
2005	308.7	305.5	307.1	309.1	312.4	314.6	316.5	319.2	318.3	319.1	328.6	334.2	316.1
2006	315.4	311.5	313.3	314.2	317.9	320.4	320.6	323.2	322.0	322.7	333.6	337.8	321.1
2007	321.2	318.9	320.3	321.1	324.4	326.8	328.8	329.7	328.3	329.6	341.9	344.4	328.0
2008	328.7	323.5	324.8	324.3	325.7	327.2	328.8	329.7	326.6	326.3	330.6	332.2	327.4
2009	312.3	307.1	305.0	303.4	306.6	307.7	309.0	309.6	308.7	308.5	315.1	317.6	309.2
2010	303.0	299.4	300.7	302.8	305.4	308.0	308.7	309.2	308.0	311.0	319.0	322.7	308.2
2011	306.3	303.3	303.8	305.4	308.5	311.9	314.2	315.3	314.0	316.0	324.2	323.0	312.2
Transportation and Utilities													
2000	92.6	92.9	93.9	93.6	93.6	94.8	95.9	96.2	96.5	99.3	98.3	97.6	95.4
2001	91.9	91.5	91.9	92.4	92.7	94.1	93.2	92.9	93.0	93.6	90.9	90.2	92.4
2002	87.1	86.7	86.5	87.0	87.8	88.9	89.5	89.3	90.0	90.4	88.7	88.2	88.3
2003	86.9	86.4	86.0	86.1	86.8	87.7	88.5	88.6	89.9	89.9	88.4	89.4	87.9
2004	86.1	86.0	86.7	87.5	88.2	90.6	90.5	90.7	92.1	93.5	92.4	92.8	89.8
2005	89.3	89.9	90.2	91.2	92.2	93.1	92.4	92.8	93.9	92.9	93.2	94.8	92.2
2006	91.3	91.5	92.1	92.4	93.5	95.2	94.3	95.0	96.1	95.2	94.5	96.6	94.0
2007	93.4	93.6	94.3	94.9	95.7	97.1	96.3	97.2	97.7	97.5	97.2	98.2	96.1
2008	94.7	95.1	94.9	95.2	96.2	96.7	96.9	97.0	97.0	96.1	95.1	95.8	95.9
2009	93.3	91.2	90.1	89.5	90.2	90.3	90.9	90.3	91.1	89.8	89.3	90.2	90.5
2010	86.7	86.2	86.7	87.3	88.0	88.8	89.8	89.3	90.2	90.3	89.6	91.0	88.7
2011	87.4	87.3	88.4	89.2	89.5	90.5	92.6	92.5	92.3	91.6	91.7	93.0	90.5
Information													
2000	90.5	92.0	93.5	94.1	95.9	98.7	99.9	101.0	102.0	100.9	101.6	101.9	97.7
2001	101.6	101.8	101.0	99.4	99.6	100.3	99.3	99.1	97.0	96.3	96.1	96.7	99.0
2002	94.2	93.9	93.5	93.2	93.3	93.8	93.9	94.0	93.1	93.3	93.4	93.3	93.6
2003	92.2	92.0	91.5	91.0	91.6	92.1	92.2	93.1	92.4	92.6	93.0	93.6	92.3
2004	91.7	91.7	92.1	92.1	92.8	93.2	93.4	93.7	92.7	93.0	93.7	94.2	92.9
2005	92.7	93.5	93.4	94.1	94.5	94.9	95.7	96.4	95.4	94.6	95.5	96.1	94.7
2006	94.8	95.2	95.9	96.2	96.9	99.5	100.0	100.7	100.6	99.7	100.6	101.1	98.4
2007	100.4	101.3	101.0	101.5	102.4	103.5	103.7	104.0	103.3	102.0	103.1	103.3	102.5
2008	102.7	103.8	104.0	104.2	104.9	106.0	107.2	107.9	106.8	105.9	107.0	107.0	105.6
2009	104.9	105.4	105.0	103.7	104.2	104.5	104.8	104.2	102.9	102.2	102.5	102.4	103.9
2010	102.2	102.4	102.3	101.7	102.5	103.6	103.8	104.2	103.7	102.8	103.3	103.8	103.0
2011	102.8	103.4	103.1	103.2	103.5	104.6	103.9	105.5	103.9	103.4	103.3	103.2	103.7

1. Employment by Industry: Washington, Selected Years, 2000–2011—*Continued*

(Numbers in thousands, not seasonally adjusted)

Industry and year	January	February	March	April	May	June	July	August	September	October	November	December	Annual average
Financial Activities													
2000	141.9	142.6	142.5	141.7	142.2	142.6	142.6	143.0	142.9	141.3	141.6	142.7	142.3
2001	142.4	143.3	143.1	143.4	144.3	145.2	147.2	147.7	147.9	145.9	145.7	146.1	145.2
2002	143.0	143.6	144.0	144.7	145.6	146.2	147.1	148.1	147.8	147.1	148.1	148.7	146.2
2003	148.2	148.9	149.7	150.8	152.0	152.9	154.2	154.8	153.9	153.0	152.3	152.1	151.9
2004	149.9	150.2	151.4	151.0	151.6	152.3	152.8	153.0	152.3	152.2	151.9	153.3	151.8
2005	150.5	151.2	151.4	152.5	153.6	154.6	156.4	157.5	157.0	156.4	156.4	157.2	154.6
2006	155.2	155.4	155.8	156.0	156.7	157.5	157.7	157.5	156.6	155.6	155.1	155.5	156.2
2007	153.9	154.5	155.2	155.7	156.1	157.1	157.1	157.1	155.2	154.6	154.8	154.7	155.5
2008	153.3	153.5	153.5	153.2	154.2	154.0	153.2	153.4	151.8	150.3	149.4	148.5	152.4
2009	145.8	145.5	143.9	143.8	143.8	144.5	143.5	143.0	142.0	140.3	139.5	139.3	142.9
2010	137.1	136.9	137.1	137.4	137.4	137.9	138.8	138.9	138.5	138.2	137.8	138.3	137.9
2011	136.4	136.6	136.7	137.5	137.4	138.4	140.0	138.0	137.3	137.0	137.0	136.9	137.4
Professional and Business Services													
2000	290.3	293.1	298.3	298.6	300.7	305.2	305.9	311.6	312.8	309.8	309.0	310.6	303.8
2001	296.8	296.9	299.6	300.7	300.6	301.3	297.8	299.0	296.5	293.9	290.3	287.5	296.7
2002	279.8	282.3	284.6	287.1	288.6	291.5	293.2	297.2	297.1	295.3	294.9	291.3	290.2
2003	282.2	284.5	285.4	287.8	288.3	289.7	292.1	295.6	295.5	295.4	294.3	293.2	290.3
2004	286.0	289.8	294.2	298.8	299.9	303.0	306.2	308.6	308.1	309.6	309.3	307.4	301.7
2005	300.0	304.7	308.3	312.4	314.9	317.0	320.8	323.0	324.8	322.7	322.5	321.8	316.1
2006	313.6	317.4	320.6	325.6	328.5	333.3	335.1	338.8	339.2	338.3	338.6	338.0	330.6
2007	329.4	335.6	339.9	340.8	343.4	347.2	348.5	351.2	350.8	349.3	349.2	349.7	344.6
2008	340.5	344.2	346.9	351.0	352.4	353.6	354.9	355.5	353.6	349.5	342.8	337.7	348.6
2009	330.0	327.5	325.6	323.4	322.8	324.9	324.4	324.1	323.7	323.2	321.5	321.6	324.4
2010	313.2	315.3	319.1	323.3	324.0	326.9	331.6	331.0	332.0	333.8	333.0	333.6	326.4
2011	326.3	329.4	331.9	339.1	338.6	340.6	344.0	343.4	344.6	338.0	339.4	337.1	337.7
Education and Health Services													
2000	285.4	289.8	292.8	290.1	291.2	291.0	289.5	291.3	293.3	294.9	296.3	297.1	291.9
2001	292.4	296.8	298.0	298.6	299.7	298.1	291.6	292.9	299.2	302.5	305.1	305.0	298.3
2002	301.7	305.6	307.3	307.7	309.4	306.2	300.8	301.5	306.7	311.1	312.8	312.0	306.9
2003	307.8	311.4	312.6	314.0	314.7	312.1	308.1	307.8	312.6	316.8	318.3	318.3	312.9
2004	312.9	316.9	318.7	320.9	321.9	320.3	313.9	313.8	319.4	325.0	326.4	326.0	319.7
2005	322.1	325.5	328.2	331.1	332.1	328.3	322.9	323.7	331.2	334.8	336.3	335.5	329.3
2006	331.3	335.4	337.8	338.8	340.2	336.3	329.2	330.7	338.1	342.4	343.4	342.8	337.2
2007	338.9	344.7	346.9	347.7	350.4	347.1	340.9	342.2	349.3	355.9	358.0	357.5	348.3
2008	353.0	358.7	359.9	361.7	363.5	359.8	355.2	356.7	363.4	370.3	371.8	371.0	362.1
2009	369.0	373.1	374.8	374.4	375.7	371.6	365.4	364.9	370.9	376.4	377.0	376.0	372.4
2010	370.5	374.5	376.1	377.4	378.1	374.7	368.5	367.5	374.0	381.1	381.9	380.4	375.4
2011	377.2	380.9	382.6	382.8	383.1	380.0	372.9	373.4	379.7	390.4	390.9	391.1	382.1
Leisure and Hospitality													
2000	237.8	240.6	246.4	249.2	254.7	261.2	258.5	261.7	261.9	250.4	248.1	250.1	251.7
2001	235.0	237.7	241.2	245.4	252.4	256.7	257.6	260.6	256.6	243.7	238.9	239.1	247.1
2002	231.4	232.2	236.0	241.2	248.1	253.7	256.7	259.7	257.0	245.4	241.8	242.1	245.4
2003	235.7	237.2	239.6	243.7	249.9	256.2	258.4	261.3	259.8	250.7	247.1	247.6	248.9
2004	239.6	241.6	247.0	252.1	257.9	263.8	266.2	267.5	266.0	256.9	253.5	254.8	255.6
2005	248.1	247.2	252.4	259.2	265.1	271.2	274.7	276.7	274.9	264.4	263.1	265.4	263.5
2006	257.6	258.9	262.3	267.4	273.9	279.7	281.5	285.4	282.7	271.7	268.4	270.3	271.7
2007	262.9	266.7	270.5	275.9	282.5	289.8	291.5	294.8	292.0	282.1	278.3	280.1	280.6
2008	271.8	274.0	278.5	282.7	287.2	293.7	295.6	297.5	295.2	281.4	274.0	272.3	283.7
2009	261.7	262.5	264.5	266.5	272.7	278.4	281.1	281.6	278.8	266.4	260.9	259.7	269.6
2010	251.2	252.7	257.4	264.6	269.2	275.1	277.5	278.9	277.6	267.4	262.6	263.7	266.5
2011	256.1	257.0	259.5	268.6	274.0	280.0	284.5	286.9	282.3	273.5	271.1	269.5	271.9
Other Services													
2000	103.8	104.5	105.5	104.3	106.6	107.4	107.2	108.1	107.7	106.7	106.4	106.5	106.2
2001	95.3	95.6	96.5	96.5	97.4	98.6	98.4	98.6	97.1	96.4	96.1	96.1	96.9
2002	95.0	95.4	95.9	97.2	98.1	99.3	100.1	100.1	98.8	97.8	97.8	97.7	97.8
2003	97.5	97.9	98.4	98.6	99.5	100.4	100.1	100.0	99.4	98.6	98.1	98.4	98.9
2004	97.1	98.0	99.1	99.7	100.7	101.8	102.3	102.1	101.4	100.7	100.1	100.4	100.3
2005	100.2	101.1	102.2	102.1	102.7	104.1	104.3	104.3	103.5	102.6	102.6	103.0	102.7
2006	101.4	102.3	103.2	103.5	104.4	105.6	105.5	105.5	105.1	103.7	103.6	103.9	104.0
2007	102.1	103.8	104.7	104.6	105.5	106.8	106.6	107.0	106.0	105.5	105.7	105.7	105.3
2008	105.0	106.1	107.3	107.4	108.3	109.2	110.1	110.0	109.0	107.6	106.9	106.0	107.7
2009	105.6	106.1	106.8	106.7	107.0	107.5	107.8	107.4	106.0	105.3	104.6	104.4	106.3
2010	102.7	103.1	103.8	104.4	105.1	106.6	107.6	107.7	106.3	106.2	106.4	106.2	105.5
2011	105.2	106.0	106.3	107.7	108.6	109.9	108.9	109.0	106.9	106.7	105.6	105.6	107.2
Government													
2000	479.3	487.2	489.6	488.1	499.6	494.9	463.8	455.1	470.9	486.6	493.7	491.0	483.3
2001	500.3	506.1	510.7	510.8	513.9	515.6	487.8	474.9	493.6	512.8	521.6	516.9	505.4
2002	512.3	519.1	521.0	521.7	524.5	524.7	498.2	485.0	504.1	523.6	532.9	526.6	516.1
2003	520.7	526.3	527.3	527.3	532.9	530.4	501.1	489.6	507.0	524.6	532.2	527.6	520.6
2004	521.7	527.6	530.3	530.3	532.2	533.7	506.4	492.5	511.8	528.7	537.6	530.9	523.6
2005	526.3	530.8	533.9	534.5	535.9	537.6	508.6	494.6	514.1	532.0	539.8	532.6	526.7
2006	529.6	536.5	538.2	536.8	539.1	541.9	509.3	496.8	517.9	535.1	542.6	536.3	530.0
2007	530.7	537.6	536.8	539.7	542.0	541.5	517.5	504.5	521.8	541.2	549.4	542.5	533.8
2008	541.3	549.7	549.2	549.9	552.8	553.2	531.0	519.5	533.8	555.9	564.2	555.3	546.3
2009	551.7	556.4	558.6	564.9	564.9	555.5	532.5	513.9	530.3	556.0	559.6	549.9	549.5
2010	551.4	555.1	556.7	561.2	572.4	560.5	535.7	515.4	530.3	554.1	558.3	548.5	550.0
2011	549.6	553.1	553.4	555.2	556.7	549.0	526.8	508.8	519.3	544.8	548.5	538.1	541.9

2. Average Weekly Hours by Selected Industry: Washington, 2007–2011

(Not seasonally adjusted)

Industry and year	January	February	March	April	May	June	July	August	September	October	November	December	Annual average
Total Private													
2007	34.1	35.3	34.9	35.8	35.1	35.1	36.0	35.4	36.2	34.9	34.7	35.5	35.3
2008	34.2	34.7	35.3	34.6	34.5	35.5	34.7	35.0	34.2	33.8	35.2	33.8	34.6
2009	33.8	34.9	34.9	34.2	34.2	34.3	34.2	35.3	34.0	34.0	34.7	33.6	34.4
2010	33.5	33.8	33.7	33.9	35.1	33.9	34.1	35.3	34.1	34.2	34.0	34.0	34.1
2011	34.9	34.2	34.0	34.4	35.1	34.4	34.6	34.6	34.6	35.4	34.2	34.2	34.6
Goods-Producing													
2007	39.0	40.4	40.3	40.7	40.7	40.9	40.8	41.0	41.5	41.2	40.4	41.0	40.7
2008	39.8	40.6	40.9	40.8	40.7	41.1	40.5	40.9	38.8	38.2	40.8	40.7	40.3
2009	40.3	40.6	39.3	39.5	39.4	39.8	39.5	40.1	39.1	39.7	39.7	38.6	39.6
2010	37.9	38.3	38.7	38.7	39.5	39.0	39.1	39.9	39.2	39.2	39.0	39.4	39.0
2011	39.1	39.0	39.2	39.6	40.1	39.7	39.8	40.0	40.0	40.3	40.2	40.0	39.8
Construction													
2007	35.3	36.9	36.5	37.8	37.9	37.8	38.7	38.7	39.1	38.8	37.1	37.4	37.7
2008	36.1	36.6	37.4	38.0	38.3	38.0	38.1	38.8	39.0	38.3	38.1	36.6	37.8
2009	36.8	37.2	35.8	36.0	36.2	36.5	36.1	37.3	35.0	35.5	34.8	32.3	35.8
2010	32.3	32.3	32.9	33.6	34.6	34.7	35.0	36.2	34.5	33.8	33.1	33.7	33.9
2011	32.8	33.4	33.2	34.2	34.8	34.6	35.3	36.5	36.1	35.5	35.3	35.2	34.8
Manufacturing													
2007	40.7	42.0	42.1	42.0	42.0	42.4	41.8	42.0	42.6	42.3	41.9	42.6	42.0
2008	41.4	42.4	42.5	42.0	41.7	42.4	41.6	41.9	38.3	37.8	41.9	42.6	41.4
2009	41.9	42.0	40.8	41.1	41.0	41.3	41.1	41.5	41.2	41.8	41.6	41.7	41.4
2010	40.6	41.0	41.3	41.1	41.7	41.0	41.1	41.7	41.4	41.8	41.7	41.8	41.4
2011	41.5	41.1	41.5	41.6	42.1	41.7	41.6	41.4	41.6	42.1	42.0	41.7	41.7
Trade, Transportation, and Utilities													
2007	33.6	35.3	35.0	36.1	35.3	35.4	36.5	36.2	36.7	35.1	35.1	35.9	35.5
2008	34.6	34.7	35.2	35.0	34.7	35.4	34.9	35.6	35.0	34.4	35.4	34.0	34.9
2009	33.9	35.4	37.2	36.4	36.4	36.4	36.1	37.4	36.7	35.8	35.8	35.0	36.0
2010	34.5	34.9	34.7	35.0	36.0	35.2	35.6	36.8	35.8	35.5	35.0	35.3	35.4
2011	35.9	35.4	35.4	35.8	36.5	36.2	36.3	35.9	36.0	36.5	35.1	35.1	35.8
Information													
2007	39.0	38.9	38.7	41.9	38.6	38.8	41.6	38.8	41.9	38.4	41.4	41.7	40.0
2008	40.9	40.7	41.4	38.3	38.0	41.6	41.2	38.4	38.2	38.4	41.3	37.7	39.7
2009	38.4	41.7	41.7	38.4	38.3	38.3	39.0	41.6	38.3	38.4	41.9	38.5	39.5
2010	38.5	38.7	38.0	38.4	41.3	38.3	38.3	41.1	38.1	38.0	38.1	38.3	38.8
2011	41.3	38.2	38.0	38.3	40.8	38.3	37.9	37.8	37.9	40.8	38.0	37.9	38.8
Financial Activities													
2007	36.4	35.7	35.4	37.2	34.9	35.0	36.9	35.1	37.5	35.1	35.2	36.8	35.9
2008	35.0	35.9	37.4	35.9	35.7	37.6	35.7	36.9	36.6	36.6	38.2	36.0	36.5
2009	36.7	38.1	38.0	36.3	36.3	35.6	35.7	37.5	34.9	35.6	37.5	35.5	36.5
2010	38.6	38.7	38.6	38.2	40.2	37.2	37.6	38.7	36.8	36.9	37.0	35.5	37.8
2011	38.4	36.2	34.9	35.6	36.6	35.2	35.3	35.5	35.6	37.5	34.7	34.8	35.9
Professional and Business Services													
2007	35.0	35.4	35.3	36.2	35.2	35.6	35.8	35.2	35.7	35.0	34.6	35.7	35.4
2008	34.1	35.0	35.7	34.8	35.0	35.9	34.8	35.2	34.7	34.4	35.5	33.9	34.9
2009	34.0	34.8	34.5	34.1	34.2	34.5	34.2	35.0	33.6	33.8	34.5	33.5	34.2
2010	33.6	34.1	34.1	34.4	35.5	34.2	34.3	35.5	34.8	35.3	35.2	35.1	34.7
2011	35.9	35.3	35.2	35.6	36.5	35.8	35.7	35.7	35.5	37.0	35.5	35.6	35.8
Education and Health Services													
2007	32.1	33.7	32.3	33.2	33.1	32.7	34.0	33.0	34.0	32.1	31.8	32.7	32.9
2008	31.9	31.9	32.6	32.4	31.9	33.2	32.0	32.0	32.2	31.4	32.3	31.0	32.1
2009	31.1	31.9	31.9	31.3	31.3	31.5	31.6	32.8	31.8	31.6	32.6	31.9	31.8
2010	32.0	31.8	31.6	32.0	32.9	32.0	31.9	32.7	32.1	32.0	32.1	32.0	32.1
2011	33.3	32.1	32.0	31.9	32.5	31.8	31.7	31.8	32.2	32.8	32.1	32.2	32.2
Leisure and Hospitality													
2007	25.0	26.1	26.2	27.1	26.3	26.3	27.7	27.2	27.2	26.1	25.8	26.4	26.5
2008	24.3	25.2	26.0	24.9	25.1	26.6	25.8	26.3	25.5	25.2	25.5	23.9	25.4
2009	23.9	25.2	24.8	24.0	24.6	24.6	24.7	26.1	24.5	24.4	25.3	24.1	24.7
2010	23.6	24.4	24.2	24.2	25.6	24.5	24.9	26.3	24.4	24.6	24.0	23.9	24.6
2011	24.7	24.9	24.6	25.1	25.8	25.2	25.7	25.9	25.5	26.2	24.8	24.8	25.3
Other Services													
2007	32.1	35.4	34.2	33.6	33.0	32.2	32.5	32.5	32.6	31.7	31.8	32.8	32.9
2008	31.0	31.7	32.7	30.8	31.0	31.8	31.7	31.4	30.6	30.7	31.9	30.0	31.3
2009	31.0	32.3	32.2	30.9	30.8	31.0	31.5	31.0	29.0	28.4	30.1	29.0	30.6
2010	29.7	30.2	29.2	29.9	31.5	29.8	30.6	32.3	29.3	30.1	29.5	29.6	30.1
2011	31.2	30.5	29.7	30.7	31.4	30.3	31.0	30.7	30.5	30.8	29.6	29.7	30.5

3. Average Hourly Earnings by Selected Industry: Washington, 2007–2011

(Dollars, not seasonally adjusted)

Industry and year	January	February	March	April	May	June	July	August	September	October	November	December	Annual average
Total Private													
2007	24.69	24.13	24.10	24.24	23.67	23.73	24.02	23.75	24.20	24.41	24.53	24.87	24.19
2008	24.91	25.01	25.37	25.07	24.85	25.02	25.12	25.01	25.17	25.24	25.74	26.23	25.23
2009	26.23	26.48	26.48	26.25	26.10	25.95	26.50	26.07	26.06	26.25	26.65	26.84	26.32
2010	26.64	26.82	26.87	26.81	26.80	26.72	26.69	26.72	26.96	27.18	27.25	27.93	26.95
2011	27.62	27.49	27.38	27.39	27.34	27.10	26.99	26.68	27.00	27.29	27.23	27.50	27.25
Goods-Producing													
2007	27.68	26.76	27.16	27.10	27.13	27.13	27.78	27.17	27.34	27.41	27.59	28.08	27.36
2008	28.11	28.01	28.28	28.62	28.27	28.54	28.69	28.82	28.56	28.39	28.79	29.89	28.58
2009	29.69	30.09	30.99	30.69	30.55	30.27	30.14	30.00	30.43	30.20	31.48	31.67	30.50
2010	30.70	31.34	31.37	31.02	30.66	30.69	30.55	30.42	30.19	30.48	30.80	31.68	30.82
2011	30.90	30.59	31.23	31.02	30.87	30.92	30.91	30.55	30.65	30.71	30.77	31.16	30.85
Construction													
2007	26.73	25.89	26.34	26.12	26.21	26.45	28.29	26.96	27.40	27.62	27.64	28.47	27.03
2008	28.05	28.18	27.74	27.91	28.11	28.56	28.80	28.95	29.09	28.83	29.02	30.69	28.65
2009	30.08	30.10	31.73	30.90	30.38	30.31	30.28	30.20	30.88	30.53	30.65	31.09	30.58
2010	29.85	29.94	29.81	29.76	30.15	30.12	30.29	30.35	30.60	32.46	32.53	32.69	30.72
2011	31.25	30.90	30.67	30.51	30.06	30.17	29.86	29.78	29.73	29.48	29.36	29.81	30.09
Manufacturing													
2007	27.98	27.18	27.57	27.60	27.61	27.50	27.62	27.34	27.38	27.40	27.63	27.97	27.56
2008	28.23	28.00	28.59	29.04	28.44	28.64	28.74	28.86	28.27	28.19	28.76	29.64	28.62
2009	29.59	30.19	30.80	30.72	30.77	30.42	30.33	30.15	30.48	30.26	32.16	32.23	30.66
2010	32.16	32.90	32.72	32.08	31.54	31.55	31.22	30.98	31.22	30.96	31.19	31.42	31.65
2011	31.00	30.72	31.41	31.35	31.27	31.29	31.27	30.91	31.15	31.25	31.34	31.68	31.22
Trade, Transportation, and Utilities													
2007	21.33	20.21	20.33	20.13	18.76	18.97	19.12	18.85	19.17	19.23	19.27	19.76	19.58
2008	19.58	19.86	21.19	20.09	20.06	20.46	20.49	20.22	20.44	20.34	20.81	20.92	20.37
2009	21.16	21.62	20.93	20.70	20.58	20.46	20.71	20.79	20.53	20.57	20.80	21.15	20.83
2010	21.02	21.40	21.82	21.73	21.79	21.73	21.56	21.79	22.19	22.06	22.29	22.92	21.87
2011	22.26	22.21	22.06	22.28	22.26	22.06	21.98	21.62	21.82	21.85	21.84	22.02	22.02
Information													
2007	41.99	42.64	41.71	42.26	42.60	41.53	42.47	43.74	44.36	44.04	43.90	44.09	42.96
2008	43.98	44.06	44.68	43.94	43.95	44.64	44.69	44.23	46.49	46.08	48.31	48.72	45.32
2009	47.78	48.51	47.79	47.33	47.17	47.17	52.18	47.31	46.88	46.95	47.23	46.75	47.77
2010	47.03	46.92	47.20	47.51	47.90	47.28	47.05	47.97	48.80	48.79	48.75	48.58	47.82
2011	49.20	49.03	48.27	48.38	49.15	47.46	46.81	45.67	48.17	49.21	48.85	49.21	48.30
Financial Activities													
2007	24.50	24.53	24.33	24.85	23.17	23.33	23.56	23.41	23.84	23.64	23.97	24.99	24.02
2008	24.56	25.10	25.43	26.56	24.98	24.17	23.58	24.48	24.29	24.78	24.63	24.61	24.76
2009	24.69	25.55	26.55	25.80	26.11	25.88	26.14	26.69	26.15	26.81	26.63	26.63	26.13
2010	27.64	27.80	27.71	27.00	27.36	26.61	26.51	27.00	27.10	27.15	26.47	27.72	27.17
2011	27.75	28.23	27.77	28.09	28.26	27.70	27.51	27.90	27.64	28.42	28.46	28.58	28.02
Professional and Business Services													
2007	28.86	28.26	27.46	28.12	27.51	27.64	28.11	27.76	28.64	29.22	28.80	29.02	28.28
2008	29.23	29.77	29.67	29.25	28.95	29.09	28.88	28.98	29.39	29.05	29.81	30.23	29.35
2009	29.94	30.66	30.94	30.55	30.38	29.87	30.11	30.90	30.79	30.34	30.72	31.14	30.53
2010	31.21	30.93	30.72	30.84	30.95	31.33	31.11	31.55	31.85	32.29	32.30	33.33	31.55
2011	33.16	33.31	32.84	32.87	32.75	32.65	32.81	32.34	32.94	33.49	33.27	33.45	32.99
Education and Health Services													
2007	22.39	23.22	23.38	23.15	23.23	23.37	23.48	23.38	22.51	23.60	24.02	24.03	23.32
2008	23.97	23.60	23.68	23.30	23.54	23.41	24.35	24.03	24.21	25.09	24.47	24.86	24.04
2009	25.76	24.55	24.35	25.14	25.03	25.07	25.97	25.97	24.63	25.03	25.84	25.60	25.90	25.24
2010	25.59	25.59	25.44	26.07	26.03	26.15	27.06	25.97	26.10	27.23	26.68	27.14	26.26
2011	27.02	27.01	26.76	26.92	26.50	26.59	26.63	26.32	26.43	26.52	26.38	26.75	26.65
Leisure and Hospitality													
2007	14.11	14.17	13.93	14.02	13.81	13.72	13.53	13.57	15.40	15.30	15.24	15.58	14.36
2008	15.72	15.48	15.10	14.82	14.79	14.77	14.53	14.75	14.65	14.85	15.05	15.67	15.00
2009	15.12	15.01	15.09	14.96	14.87	14.79	14.60	14.62	14.52	14.73	14.80	15.29	14.86
2010	14.80	14.75	14.65	14.51	14.22	14.12	13.98	13.90	13.92	12.96	13.10	13.77	14.05
2011	13.37	13.30	13.28	13.19	13.31	13.35	13.43	13.38	13.44	13.50	13.71	14.17	13.45
Other Services													
2007	19.82	18.16	18.54	19.55	18.82	19.03	18.95	18.69	19.30	19.10	19.38	19.55	19.06
2008	19.27	19.25	19.30	19.45	19.44	19.90	19.73	19.23	19.48	20.04	20.90	22.10	19.83
2009	21.13	22.04	22.47	21.76	21.59	22.16	24.22	21.76	22.60	22.91	22.92	23.28	22.39
2010	22.35	22.76	22.86	22.60	23.10	22.59	22.32	22.74	24.00	23.88	24.76	24.66	23.21
2011	24.22	23.76	23.27	22.92	22.95	22.36	21.77	21.45	21.36	21.25	21.14	21.23	22.31

4. Average Weekly Earnings by Selected Industry: Washington, 2007–2011

(Dollars, not seasonally adjusted)

Industry and year	January	February	March	April	May	June	July	August	September	October	November	December	Annual average
Total Private													
2007	841.93	851.79	841.09	867.79	830.82	832.92	864.72	840.75	876.04	851.91	851.19	882.89	852.90
2008	851.92	867.85	895.56	867.42	857.33	888.21	871.66	875.35	860.81	853.11	906.05	886.57	873.47
2009	886.57	924.15	924.15	897.75	892.62	890.09	906.30	920.27	886.04	892.50	924.76	901.82	904.13
2010	892.44	906.52	905.52	908.86	940.68	905.81	910.13	943.22	919.34	929.56	926.50	949.62	920.28
2011	963.94	940.16	930.92	942.22	959.63	932.24	933.85	923.13	934.20	966.07	931.27	940.50	941.53
Goods-Producing													
2007	1,079.52	1,081.10	1,094.55	1,102.97	1,104.19	1,109.62	1,133.42	1,113.97	1,134.61	1,129.29	1,114.64	1,151.28	1,112.85
2008	1,118.78	1,137.21	1,156.65	1,167.70	1,150.59	1,172.99	1,161.95	1,178.74	1,108.13	1,084.50	1,174.63	1,216.52	1,152.30
2009	1,196.51	1,221.65	1,217.91	1,212.26	1,203.67	1,204.75	1,190.53	1,203.00	1,189.81	1,198.94	1,249.76	1,222.46	1,208.99
2010	1,163.53	1,200.32	1,214.02	1,200.47	1,211.07	1,196.91	1,194.51	1,213.76	1,183.45	1,194.82	1,201.20	1,248.19	1,201.83
2011	1,208.19	1,193.01	1,224.22	1,228.39	1,237.89	1,227.52	1,230.22	1,222.00	1,226.00	1,237.61	1,236.95	1,246.40	1,226.86
Construction													
2007	943.57	955.34	961.41	987.34	993.36	999.81	1,094.82	1,043.35	1,071.34	1,071.66	1,025.44	1,064.78	1,019.42
2008	1,012.61	1,031.39	1,037.48	1,060.58	1,076.61	1,085.28	1,097.28	1,123.26	1,134.51	1,104.19	1,105.66	1,123.25	1,082.77
2009	1,106.94	1,119.72	1,135.93	1,112.40	1,099.76	1,106.32	1,093.11	1,126.46	1,080.80	1,083.82	1,066.62	1,004.21	1,095.75
2010	964.16	967.06	980.75	999.94	1,043.19	1,045.16	1,060.15	1,098.67	1,055.70	1,097.15	1,076.74	1,101.65	1,042.07
2011	1,025.00	1,032.06	1,018.24	1,043.44	1,046.09	1,043.88	1,054.06	1,086.97	1,073.25	1,046.54	1,036.41	1,049.31	1,047.10
Manufacturing													
2007	1,138.79	1,141.56	1,160.70	1,159.20	1,159.62	1,166.00	1,154.52	1,148.28	1,166.39	1,159.02	1,157.70	1,191.52	1,158.68
2008	1,168.72	1,187.20	1,215.08	1,219.68	1,185.95	1,214.34	1,195.58	1,209.23	1,082.74	1,065.58	1,205.04	1,262.66	1,184.76
2009	1,239.82	1,267.98	1,256.64	1,262.59	1,261.57	1,256.35	1,246.56	1,251.23	1,255.78	1,264.87	1,337.86	1,343.99	1,269.93
2010	1,305.70	1,348.90	1,351.34	1,318.49	1,315.22	1,293.55	1,283.14	1,291.87	1,292.51	1,294.13	1,300.62	1,313.36	1,308.84
2011	1,286.50	1,262.59	1,303.52	1,304.16	1,316.47	1,304.79	1,300.83	1,279.67	1,295.84	1,315.63	1,316.28	1,321.06	1,300.86
Trade, Transportation, and Utilities													
2007	716.69	713.41	711.55	726.69	662.23	671.54	697.88	682.37	703.54	674.97	676.38	709.38	695.39
2008	677.47	689.14	745.89	703.15	696.08	724.28	715.10	719.83	715.40	699.70	736.67	711.28	711.19
2009	717.32	765.35	778.60	753.48	749.11	744.74	747.63	777.55	753.45	736.41	744.64	740.25	750.64
2010	725.19	746.86	757.15	760.55	784.44	764.90	767.54	801.87	794.40	783.13	780.15	809.08	773.22
2011	799.13	786.23	780.92	797.62	812.49	798.57	797.87	776.16	785.52	797.53	766.58	772.90	789.16
Information													
2007	1,637.61	1,658.70	1,614.18	1,770.69	1,644.36	1,611.36	1,766.75	1,697.11	1,858.68	1,691.14	1,817.46	1,838.55	1,717.67
2008	1,798.78	1,793.24	1,849.75	1,682.90	1,670.10	1,857.02	1,841.23	1,698.43	1,775.92	1,769.47	1,995.20	1,836.74	1,797.66
2009	1,834.75	2,022.87	1,992.84	1,817.47	1,806.61	1,806.61	2,035.02	1,968.10	1,795.50	1,802.88	1,978.94	1,799.88	1,888.93
2010	1,810.66	1,815.80	1,793.60	1,824.38	1,978.27	1,810.82	1,802.02	1,971.57	1,859.28	1,854.02	1,857.38	1,860.61	1,853.01
2011	2,031.96	1,872.95	1,834.26	1,852.95	2,005.32	1,817.72	1,774.10	1,726.33	1,825.64	2,007.77	1,856.30	1,865.06	1,872.27
Financial Activities													
2007	891.80	875.72	861.28	924.42	808.63	816.55	869.36	821.69	894.00	829.76	843.74	919.63	862.93
2008	859.60	901.09	951.08	953.50	891.79	908.79	841.81	903.31	889.01	906.95	940.87	885.96	902.78
2009	906.12	973.46	1,008.90	936.54	947.79	921.33	933.20	1,000.88	912.64	954.44	998.63	945.37	953.08
2010	1,066.90	1,075.86	1,069.61	1,031.40	1,099.87	989.89	996.78	1,044.90	997.28	1,001.84	979.39	984.06	1,028.02
2011	1,065.60	1,021.93	969.17	1,000.00	1,034.32	975.04	971.10	990.45	983.98	1,065.75	987.56	994.58	1,004.84
Professional and Business Services													
2007	1,010.10	1,000.40	969.34	1,017.94	968.35	983.98	1,006.34	977.15	1,022.45	1,022.70	996.48	1,036.01	1,000.99
2008	996.74	1,041.95	1,059.22	1,017.90	1,013.25	1,044.33	1,005.02	1,020.10	1,019.83	999.32	1,058.26	1,024.80	1,025.00
2009	1,017.96	1,066.97	1,067.43	1,041.76	1,039.00	1,030.52	1,029.76	1,081.50	1,034.54	1,025.49	1,059.84	1,043.19	1,044.81
2010	1,048.66	1,054.71	1,047.55	1,060.90	1,098.73	1,071.49	1,067.07	1,120.03	1,108.38	1,139.84	1,136.96	1,169.88	1,094.44
2011	1,190.44	1,175.84	1,155.97	1,170.17	1,195.38	1,168.87	1,171.32	1,154.54	1,169.37	1,239.13	1,181.09	1,190.82	1,180.15
Education and Health Services													
2007	718.72	782.51	755.17	768.58	768.91	764.20	798.32	771.54	765.34	757.56	763.84	785.78	766.76
2008	764.64	752.84	771.97	754.92	750.93	777.21	779.20	768.96	779.56	787.83	790.38	770.66	770.84
2009	801.14	783.15	776.77	786.88	783.44	789.71	820.65	807.86	795.95	816.54	834.56	826.21	801.90
2010	818.88	813.76	803.90	834.24	856.39	836.80	863.21	849.22	837.81	871.36	856.43	868.48	842.57
2011	899.77	867.02	856.32	858.75	861.25	845.56	844.17	836.98	851.05	869.86	846.80	861.35	858.20
Leisure and Hospitality													
2007	352.75	369.84	364.97	379.94	363.20	360.84	374.78	369.10	418.88	399.33	393.19	411.31	380.08
2008	382.00	390.10	392.60	369.02	371.23	392.88	374.87	387.93	373.58	374.22	383.78	374.51	380.54
2009	361.37	378.25	374.23	359.04	365.80	363.83	360.62	381.58	355.74	359.41	374.44	368.49	366.87
2010	349.28	359.90	354.53	351.14	364.03	345.94	348.10	365.57	339.65	318.82	314.40	329.10	345.10
2011	330.24	331.17	326.69	331.07	343.40	336.42	345.15	346.54	342.72	353.70	340.01	351.42	340.08
Other Services													
2007	636.22	642.86	634.07	656.88	621.06	612.77	615.88	607.43	629.18	605.47	616.28	641.24	626.49
2008	597.37	610.23	631.11	599.06	602.64	632.82	625.44	603.82	596.09	615.23	666.71	663.00	620.23
2009	655.03	711.89	723.53	672.38	664.97	686.96	762.93	674.56	655.40	650.64	689.89	675.12	685.38
2010	663.80	687.35	667.51	675.74	727.65	673.18	682.99	734.50	703.20	718.79	730.42	729.94	699.66
2011	755.66	724.68	691.12	703.64	720.63	677.51	674.87	658.52	651.48	654.50	625.74	630.53	680.70

WEST VIRGINIA
At a Glance

Population:
    2000 census: 1,808,193
    2010 census: 1,852,994
    2011 estimate: 1,855,364

Percent change in population:
    2000–2010: 2.5%
    2010–2011: 0.1%

Percent change in total nonfarm employment:
    2000–2010: 1.5%
    2010–2011: 1.0%

Industry with the largest growth in employment, 2000–2011 (thousands):
    Education and Health Services, 23.4

Industry with the largest decline or smallest growth in employment, 2000–2011 (thousands):
    Manufacturing, -26.4

Civilian labor force:
    2000: 808,861
    2010: 801,895
    2011: 799,883

Unemployment rate and rank among states (lowest to highest):
    2000: 5.5%, 48th
    2010: 8.5%, 24th
    2011: 8.0%, 25th

Over-the-year change in unemployment rates:
    2010–2011: -0.5%

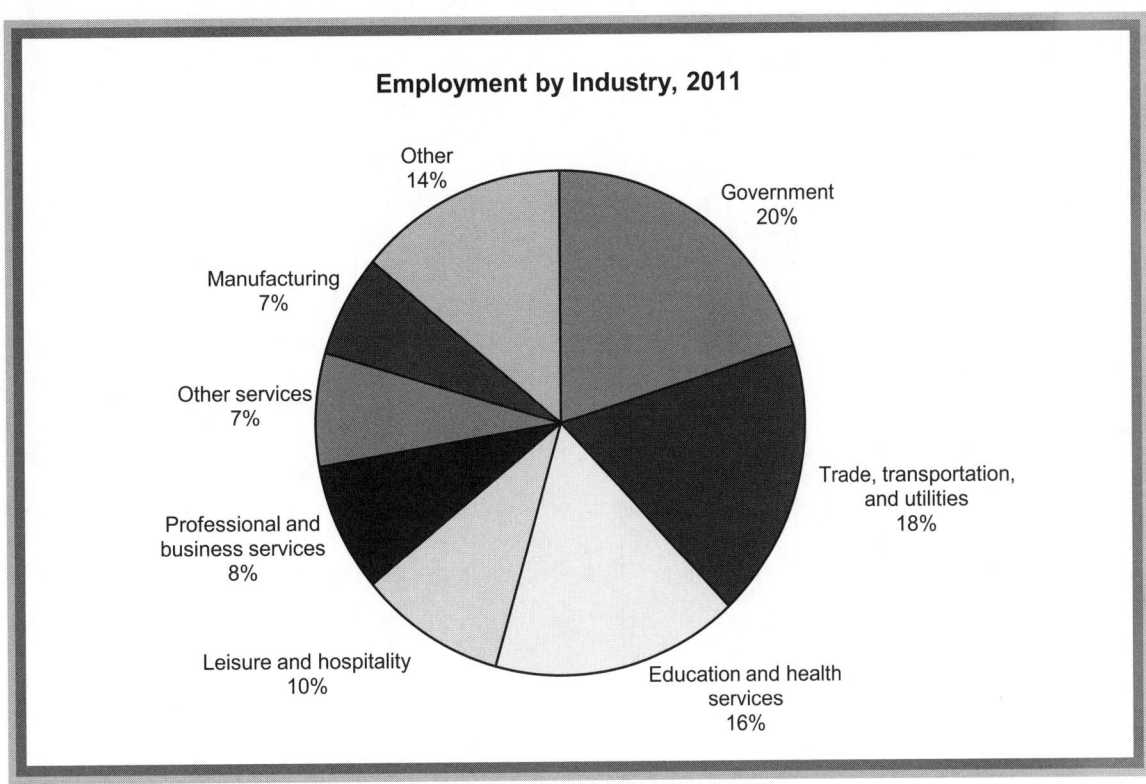

Employment by Industry, 2011

- Other 14%
- Government 20%
- Manufacturing 7%
- Trade, transportation, and utilities 18%
- Other services 7%
- Professional and business services 8%
- Leisure and hospitality 10%
- Education and health services 16%

1. Employment by Industry: West Virginia, Selected Years, 2000–2011

(Numbers in thousands, not seasonally adjusted)

Industry and year	January	February	March	April	May	June	July	August	September	October	November	December	Annual average
Total Nonfarm													
2000	714.1	714.1	728.6	733.1	751.5	741.1	742.1	733.8	739.8	741.7	744.9	744.8	735.8
2001	719.0	721.9	730.5	735.2	739.6	742.1	734.8	737.8	737.8	740.3	742.2	741.9	735.3
2002	717.2	719.9	727.5	731.5	747.3	737.1	733.8	735.4	735.6	735.9	738.2	737.2	733.1
2003	714.4	711.1	719.6	726.9	731.8	732.7	728.5	730.1	730.5	734.7	733.2	737.3	727.6
2004	716.2	717.4	728.0	736.8	742.1	741.2	739.3	739.9	742.1	746.2	745.9	747.3	736.9
2005	727.1	728.5	734.9	745.1	751.4	752.7	748.5	750.5	753.7	751.0	756.2	758.4	746.5
2006	738.2	741.3	750.4	754.3	759.3	762.5	752.8	756.8	761.6	762.1	766.4	766.1	756.0
2007	740.5	741.5	752.0	755.9	761.8	764.0	755.7	760.2	764.3	765.9	769.2	768.6	758.3
2008	746.7	750.6	754.9	760.4	766.7	763.3	761.4	763.3	768.7	770.4	770.0	767.7	762.0
2009	740.4	740.8	744.8	746.9	751.9	752.8	741.1	742.2	744.4	746.7	748.1	749.6	745.8
2010	724.6	725.0	737.4	745.0	751.7	753.2	749.4	750.0	754.2	755.8	757.9	754.4	746.6
2011	729.5	735.8	744.6	754.3	757.9	752.1	755.1	756.2	761.0	766.2	768.7	764.8	753.9
Total Private													
2000	574.9	574.0	583.7	589.6	594.1	599.1	597.1	595.6	600.7	599.9	601.7	601.7	592.7
2001	581.0	581.3	587.7	592.6	597.3	601.2	596.6	599.4	598.8	597.9	598.5	598.2	594.2
2002	578.1	578.9	583.8	588.1	592.8	594.9	596.0	597.0	595.0	592.6	593.1	592.3	590.2
2003	573.6	568.8	575.6	581.9	586.7	590.5	589.7	591.0	590.8	591.2	588.5	592.5	585.1
2004	575.8	575.4	583.3	591.6	597.1	597.9	599.3	600.0	600.3	600.4	600.5	602.2	593.7
2005	584.6	584.9	589.7	599.5	605.6	609.4	609.0	611.0	611.1	607.5	609.9	611.8	602.8
2006	596.9	596.5	603.9	607.9	612.8	618.9	613.6	615.8	617.5	615.1	618.5	618.1	611.3
2007	598.1	595.7	604.6	608.7	613.7	619.6	615.8	619.1	619.7	618.9	621.3	620.9	613.0
2008	603.4	604.1	607.0	612.3	616.3	618.8	619.2	620.1	621.4	620.6	619.6	617.2	615.0
2009	595.1	591.9	593.8	596.5	599.4	598.8	595.5	595.9	595.9	594.4	595.4	596.7	595.8
2010	575.5	573.3	582.4	590.5	593.2	599.0	600.7	601.7	602.2	602.2	603.3	600.0	593.7
2011	582.7	584.8	591.1	599.8	602.9	607.2	608.4	608.2	608.4	610.3	612.3	608.6	602.1
Goods-Producing													
2000	127.2	125.6	129.1	130.9	132.2	132.9	133.0	132.5	134.0	133.8	133.3	130.4	131.2
2001	125.0	125.1	127.6	129.9	131.2	132.4	132.0	132.9	133.2	133.8	133.0	131.1	130.6
2002	123.8	123.5	123.9	126.0	126.2	127.0	126.7	127.2	127.0	125.6	124.4	121.3	125.2
2003	116.0	113.6	116.3	118.4	119.8	121.1	121.5	121.1	121.4	121.3	120.6	118.9	119.2
2004	114.5	114.2	117.0	121.6	123.7	123.3	124.1	124.3	124.2	124.2	123.3	122.3	121.4
2005	118.3	118.8	119.9	123.4	125.6	127.3	127.1	127.9	129.0	128.7	128.1	126.8	125.1
2006	122.7	122.7	125.5	128.1	129.9	131.6	130.1	130.5	130.5	130.2	130.0	129.2	128.4
2007	123.4	121.0	124.3	125.9	127.3	129.4	128.6	128.7	128.2	128.4	127.8	125.5	126.5
2008	120.9	119.8	121.1	124.9	126.3	127.7	128.5	129.4	130.4	132.0	130.4	127.4	126.6
2009	118.9	116.8	116.8	116.3	115.9	114.3	112.7	112.7	112.0	112.7	112.1	111.6	114.4
2010	104.7	104.0	107.5	110.8	111.6	113.6	115.2	115.8	116.3	116.5	115.6	112.2	112.0
2011	107.7	108.4	110.6	114.1	115.9	118.0	118.7	119.4	120.3	121.0	120.9	116.9	116.0
Mining and Logging													
2000	21.4	21.0	21.0	21.1	21.3	21.0	21.2	21.4	21.7	21.8	21.8	21.8	21.4
2001	21.8	21.8	22.1	22.6	23.0	23.8	24.2	24.2	24.3	24.6	24.8	24.9	23.5
2002	24.4	24.1	23.6	23.3	22.9	22.9	22.6	22.8	22.8	22.7	22.9	22.5	23.1
2003	22.1	21.6	22.1	22.1	22.0	22.1	22.1	21.7	21.8	21.8	22.0	22.2	22.0
2004	22.4	22.1	22.5	23.4	23.9	24.1	24.2	24.2	24.5	24.6	24.6	24.7	23.8
2005	24.4	24.7	25.0	25.4	26.0	26.2	26.2	26.4	26.7	26.8	27.2	27.4	26.0
2006	27.2	27.4	27.7	27.8	27.9	28.3	28.3	28.2	28.3	28.0	28.3	28.4	28.0
2007	28.1	27.9	27.9	28.2	28.2	28.9	28.9	29.2	28.9	28.9	29.1	29.1	28.6
2008	28.7	28.8	29.2	29.8	30.5	31.1	31.3	31.7	32.5	33.3	33.4	33.4	31.1
2009	32.7	32.0	31.8	30.9	29.9	29.3	28.5	28.5	28.4	28.5	28.5	28.9	29.8
2010	28.2	28.4	28.8	29.2	29.4	30.1	30.5	30.9	31.1	31.2	31.6	31.6	30.1
2011	31.6	32.0	32.2	32.6	33.0	33.8	33.8	34.0	34.9	35.1	35.3	34.8	33.6
Construction													
2000	28.9	28.1	31.6	33.9	35.2	35.5	35.7	35.5	36.8	36.8	36.4	33.7	34.0
2001	29.3	29.7	32.1	34.1	35.1	35.6	35.6	37.0	37.8	38.7	37.9	35.8	34.9
2002	29.7	30.0	31.0	33.4	34.0	34.9	35.4	35.8	35.7	35.2	34.3	31.8	33.4
2003	28.4	27.1	29.3	31.3	32.9	34.1	34.6	34.9	35.3	35.5	34.9	33.6	32.7
2004	29.1	29.2	31.7	34.7	36.0	36.2	36.8	37.0	36.6	36.9	36.2	34.9	34.6
2005	31.9	32.2	33.0	35.9	37.2	38.3	38.3	38.9	39.6	39.8	39.1	37.5	36.8
2006	34.3	34.0	36.2	39.1	40.8	42.0	40.8	41.3	41.2	41.8	41.3	40.3	39.4
2007	36.2	34.2	37.2	38.7	39.9	40.8	40.2	40.3	40.2	40.9	40.3	38.3	38.9
2008	34.9	34.2	35.3	38.2	39.0	39.6	40.4	41.0	41.6	42.5	41.5	38.7	38.9
2009	32.6	32.6	33.9	33.8	35.1	34.6	34.8	34.5	34.2	34.9	34.4	33.5	34.1
2010	28.3	27.5	30.3	32.8	33.0	34.0	35.0	35.1	35.8	36.0	34.6	31.1	32.8
2011	27.4	27.7	29.2	32.2	33.3	34.1	35.0	35.5	35.6	36.2	36.2	33.0	33.0
Manufacturing													
2000	76.9	76.5	76.5	75.9	75.7	76.4	76.1	75.6	75.5	75.2	75.1	74.9	75.9
2001	73.9	73.6	73.4	73.2	73.1	73.0	72.2	71.7	71.1	70.5	70.3	70.4	72.2
2002	69.7	69.4	69.3	69.3	69.3	69.2	68.7	68.6	68.5	67.7	67.2	67.0	68.7
2003	65.5	64.9	64.9	65.0	64.9	64.9	64.8	64.5	64.3	64.0	63.7	63.1	64.5
2004	63.0	62.9	62.8	63.5	63.8	63.0	63.1	63.1	63.1	62.7	62.5	62.7	63.0
2005	62.0	61.9	61.9	62.1	62.4	62.8	62.6	62.6	62.7	62.1	61.8	61.9	62.2
2006	61.2	61.3	61.6	61.2	61.2	61.3	61.0	61.0	61.0	60.4	60.4	60.5	61.0
2007	59.1	58.9	59.2	59.0	59.2	59.7	59.5	59.2	59.1	58.6	58.4	58.1	59.0
2008	57.3	56.8	56.6	56.9	56.8	57.0	56.8	56.7	56.3	56.2	55.5	55.3	56.5
2009	53.6	52.2	51.1	51.6	50.9	50.4	49.4	49.7	49.4	49.3	49.2	49.2	50.5
2010	48.2	48.1	48.4	48.8	49.2	49.5	49.7	49.8	49.4	49.3	49.4	49.5	49.1
2011	48.7	48.7	49.2	49.3	49.6	50.1	49.9	49.9	49.8	49.7	49.4	49.1	49.5

1. Employment by Industry: West Virginia, Selected Years, 2000–2011—*Continued*

(Numbers in thousands, not seasonally adjusted)

Industry and year	January	February	March	April	May	June	July	August	September	October	November	December	Annual average
Service-Providing													
2000	586.9	588.5	599.5	602.2	619.3	608.2	609.1	601.3	605.8	607.9	611.6	614.4	604.6
2001	594.0	596.8	602.9	605.3	608.4	609.7	602.8	604.9	604.6	606.5	609.2	610.8	604.7
2002	593.4	596.4	603.6	605.5	621.1	610.1	607.1	608.2	608.6	610.3	613.8	615.9	607.8
2003	598.4	597.5	603.3	608.5	612.0	611.6	607.0	609.0	609.1	613.4	612.6	618.4	608.4
2004	601.7	603.2	611.0	615.2	618.4	617.9	615.2	615.6	617.9	622.0	622.6	625.0	615.5
2005	608.8	609.7	615.0	621.7	625.8	625.4	621.4	622.6	624.7	622.3	628.1	631.6	621.4
2006	615.5	618.6	624.9	626.2	629.4	630.9	622.7	626.3	631.1	631.9	636.4	636.9	627.6
2007	617.1	620.5	627.7	630.0	634.5	634.6	627.1	631.5	636.1	637.5	641.4	643.1	631.8
2008	625.8	630.8	633.8	635.5	640.4	635.6	632.9	633.9	638.3	638.4	639.6	640.3	635.4
2009	621.5	624.0	628.0	630.6	636.0	638.5	628.4	629.5	632.4	634.0	636.0	638.0	631.4
2010	619.9	621.0	629.9	634.2	640.1	639.6	634.2	634.2	637.9	639.3	642.3	642.2	634.6
2011	621.8	627.4	634.0	640.2	642.0	634.1	636.4	636.8	640.7	645.2	647.8	647.9	637.9
Trade, Transportation, and Utilities													
2000	142.6	141.3	142.6	142.9	144.3	145.5	144.9	145.4	145.1	145.0	147.9	148.8	144.7
2001	140.1	138.4	139.0	139.5	140.5	141.3	139.6	140.0	139.5	139.1	141.3	142.1	140.0
2002	136.1	134.9	135.9	136.2	137.4	137.7	137.1	136.9	136.2	136.6	138.6	139.7	136.9
2003	133.5	131.7	132.9	134.3	135.5	136.1	135.8	136.3	136.2	136.8	136.7	140.2	135.5
2004	134.7	133.3	134.2	135.3	136.5	137.0	137.4	137.9	138.0	139.0	141.4	142.3	137.3
2005	136.9	136.1	136.7	138.1	139.6	139.7	139.6	139.8	139.9	140.3	143.2	144.6	139.5
2006	139.0	138.1	139.6	140.3	141.1	142.1	141.2	141.6	142.2	143.2	146.5	147.2	141.8
2007	141.3	140.1	141.6	141.4	142.6	143.3	142.7	143.4	143.6	144.4	147.2	147.8	143.3
2008	141.7	140.8	141.5	140.9	141.4	141.9	141.7	141.5	141.5	141.0	142.6	143.3	141.7
2009	136.5	134.6	134.6	135.0	135.8	136.3	135.5	135.5	135.8	135.6	137.6	138.2	135.9
2010	132.5	131.1	132.5	133.2	134.4	134.8	134.8	134.7	134.1	135.8	138.8	139.1	134.7
2011	133.4	132.5	133.2	134.8	135.3	135.8	136.2	135.5	134.4	135.5	137.8	137.5	135.2
Wholesale Trade													
2000	23.7	23.8	24.0	24.0	24.1	24.1	24.1	24.2	24.3	24.0	24.2	24.1	24.1
2001	23.7	23.8	24.0	24.2	24.2	24.5	24.1	23.9	23.9	23.7	23.6	23.7	23.9
2002	23.0	23.2	23.4	23.5	23.5	23.4	23.3	23.2	23.1	23.0	23.0	23.0	23.2
2003	22.4	22.3	22.6	22.7	22.9	23.0	22.9	22.9	22.8	22.8	22.8	22.8	22.7
2004	22.7	22.8	23.0	23.2	23.2	23.2	23.2	23.1	23.3	23.5	23.6	23.7	23.2
2005	23.6	23.6	23.8	24.1	24.3	24.4	24.4	24.3	24.3	24.3	24.4	24.6	24.2
2006	24.3	24.3	24.5	24.7	24.8	25.3	24.9	25.0	25.1	25.2	25.5	25.6	24.9
2007	24.8	24.7	24.9	24.8	24.8	24.9	25.0	25.1	25.2	25.5	25.6	25.7	25.1
2008	24.5	24.5	24.6	24.6	24.8	24.8	24.6	24.6	24.7	24.5	24.4	24.4	24.6
2009	23.8	23.5	23.5	23.4	23.5	23.4	23.3	23.1	23.1	23.0	22.9	22.8	23.3
2010	22.4	22.3	22.5	22.7	22.7	22.8	23.0	22.9	23.0	23.3	23.4	23.3	22.9
2011	22.7	22.6	22.9	23.1	23.3	23.3	23.5	23.1	23.2	23.5	23.5	23.6	23.2
Retail Trade													
2000	91.7	90.4	91.2	91.7	92.8	93.7	93.2	93.7	93.2	93.6	96.5	97.7	93.3
2001	90.3	88.4	88.8	88.9	89.7	90.0	89.0	89.6	89.2	89.0	91.4	92.1	89.7
2002	87.2	86.0	86.9	87.1	88.1	88.3	88.2	88.1	87.8	88.2	90.4	91.5	88.2
2003	86.0	84.5	85.3	86.6	87.4	87.9	87.8	88.2	88.2	89.0	89.0	92.5	87.7
2004	87.4	85.9	86.4	87.0	88.1	88.4	88.7	89.1	88.9	89.6	92.0	92.7	88.7
2005	88.0	87.0	87.3	88.3	89.4	89.2	89.2	89.3	89.3	89.7	92.5	93.5	89.4
2006	88.8	87.9	89.0	89.2	89.7	90.0	89.7	89.9	90.4	91.3	94.2	94.6	90.4
2007	90.0	89.0	90.2	89.9	90.8	91.2	90.7	91.2	91.2	91.9	94.5	94.9	91.3
2008	90.4	89.4	90.1	89.1	89.3	89.6	89.6	89.4	89.3	89.1	90.9	91.5	89.8
2009	86.4	84.8	85.0	85.6	86.4	87.0	86.6	86.8	87.1	87.2	89.4	90.0	86.9
2010	85.3	84.0	84.9	85.4	86.3	86.5	86.5	86.5	85.9	87.2	90.1	90.2	86.6
2011	85.7	84.8	85.3	86.5	86.8	87.1	87.3	87.0	86.0	86.8	88.9	88.5	86.7
Transportation and Utilities													
2000	27.2	27.1	27.4	27.2	27.4	27.7	27.6	27.5	27.6	27.4	27.2	27.0	27.4
2001	26.1	26.2	26.2	26.4	26.6	26.8	26.5	26.5	26.4	26.4	26.3	26.3	26.4
2002	25.9	25.7	25.6	25.6	25.8	26.0	25.6	25.6	25.3	25.4	25.2	25.2	25.6
2003	25.1	24.9	25.0	25.0	25.2	25.2	25.1	25.2	25.2	25.0	24.9	24.9	25.1
2004	24.6	24.6	24.8	25.1	25.2	25.4	25.5	25.7	25.8	25.9	25.8	25.9	25.4
2005	25.3	25.5	25.6	25.7	25.9	26.1	26.0	26.2	26.3	26.3	26.3	26.5	26.0
2006	25.9	25.9	26.1	26.4	26.6	26.8	26.6	26.7	26.7	26.7	26.8	27.0	26.5
2007	26.5	26.4	26.5	26.7	27.0	27.2	27.0	27.1	27.2	27.0	27.1	27.2	26.9
2008	26.8	26.9	26.8	27.2	27.3	27.5	27.5	27.5	27.5	27.4	27.3	27.4	27.3
2009	26.3	26.3	26.1	26.0	25.9	25.9	25.6	25.6	25.6	25.4	25.3	25.4	25.8
2010	24.8	24.8	25.1	25.1	25.4	25.5	25.3	25.3	25.2	25.3	25.3	25.6	25.2
2011	25.0	25.1	25.0	25.2	25.2	25.4	25.4	25.4	25.2	25.2	25.4	25.4	25.2
Information													
2000	14.0	14.1	14.1	14.2	14.2	14.3	14.4	11.7	14.3	14.3	14.5	14.7	14.1
2001	14.2	14.3	14.3	14.2	14.2	14.3	14.1	14.1	13.9	13.8	13.8	13.8	14.1
2002	13.4	13.4	13.4	13.2	13.3	13.3	13.3	13.3	13.2	13.2	13.4	13.4	13.3
2003	12.9	12.8	12.8	12.7	12.6	12.6	12.6	12.5	12.3	12.2	12.2	12.0	12.5
2004	11.8	11.7	12.0	11.9	11.9	12.0	12.0	12.0	11.8	11.7	11.8	11.8	11.9
2005	11.6	11.4	11.5	11.5	11.7	11.8	11.9	12.0	11.8	11.8	11.9	12.0	11.7
2006	11.7	11.5	11.5	11.4	11.5	11.6	11.5	11.6	11.5	11.5	11.4	11.4	11.5
2007	11.3	11.3	11.2	11.3	11.4	11.5	11.6	11.5	11.5	11.4	11.4	11.5	11.4
2008	11.3	11.3	11.2	11.2	11.2	11.2	11.2	11.2	11.1	11.1	11.0	10.9	11.2
2009	10.9	10.7	10.7	10.6	10.5	10.4	10.3	10.2	10.3	10.2	10.2	10.2	10.4
2010	10.1	10.0	10.0	9.8	10.1	10.3	10.7	10.6	10.5	10.5	10.5	10.6	10.3
2011	10.4	10.4	10.4	10.3	10.3	10.3	10.5	10.4	10.6	10.6	10.8	10.6	10.5

1. Employment by Industry: West Virginia, Selected Years, 2000–2011—*Continued*

(Numbers in thousands, not seasonally adjusted)

Industry and year	January	February	March	April	May	June	July	August	September	October	November	December	Annual average
Service-Providing													
Financial Activities													
2000	30.7	30.8	31.2	31.1	31.3	31.6	31.3	31.4	31.1	31.1	31.2	31.6	31.2
2001	30.6	30.5	30.6	30.7	30.8	30.9	30.8	30.6	30.5	30.6	30.5	30.7	30.7
2002	30.2	30.4	30.7	30.8	31.0	31.3	31.5	31.7	31.5	31.6	31.6	31.8	31.2
2003	30.8	30.8	30.8	30.9	30.7	31.0	30.6	30.6	30.7	30.7	30.7	30.8	30.8
2004	30.3	30.1	30.4	30.5	30.5	30.7	30.7	30.4	30.1	30.1	29.9	30.0	30.3
2005	29.6	29.5	29.5	29.7	29.7	29.8	29.8	29.8	29.7	29.6	29.7	29.7	29.7
2006	29.9	29.9	30.0	30.1	30.3	30.7	30.1	30.1	30.0	30.0	29.9	30.0	30.1
2007	29.5	29.5	29.6	29.8	30.0	30.2	30.0	30.1	30.0	29.9	29.9	30.0	29.9
2008	29.8	29.8	29.7	29.9	29.8	29.9	29.9	29.7	29.6	29.6	29.6	29.6	29.7
2009	28.9	28.7	28.7	28.9	29.1	29.1	29.0	28.8	28.6	28.6	28.4	28.4	28.8
2010	28.1	28.1	28.4	28.5	28.5	28.8	28.5	28.4	28.3	28.5	28.5	28.4	28.4
2011	27.9	27.6	27.6	27.6	27.6	27.6	27.0	26.8	26.8	26.9	26.8	27.1	27.3
Professional and													
Business Services													
2000	52.9	53.6	54.8	56.5	56.1	57.2	56.6	56.5	56.8	56.3	56.6	57.0	55.9
2001	56.1	56.7	57.4	57.4	57.6	58.3	57.7	57.9	57.2	57.3	57.2	57.4	57.4
2002	54.5	54.8	55.6	56.5	56.6	57.4	57.8	58.4	57.7	56.8	57.0	57.5	56.7
2003	55.5	55.4	55.8	56.3	56.3	57.0	56.7	57.1	57.0	57.5	57.4	58.7	56.7
2004	57.3	57.2	57.6	57.7	57.6	58.4	59.0	59.2	59.0	59.1	58.5	60.1	58.4
2005	57.6	57.1	57.5	58.6	58.4	59.1	59.2	59.7	59.2	59.3	59.8	60.8	58.9
2006	59.4	59.5	59.7	60.0	59.5	60.6	60.2	60.3	60.2	59.4	59.8	59.6	59.9
2007	59.1	58.8	59.7	60.7	60.7	61.1	60.9	61.4	61.2	61.1	61.4	62.4	60.7
2008	60.2	60.4	60.4	61.4	61.3	61.5	61.4	61.3	60.8	61.1	61.1	61.3	61.0
2009	60.0	59.9	59.6	60.1	59.8	59.8	59.5	59.8	59.7	59.9	60.3	61.3	60.0
2010	59.3	59.0	59.7	60.8	59.8	60.5	61.2	61.1	60.8	61.1	61.2	61.3	60.5
2011	60.5	61.1	61.6	62.5	61.9	62.5	63.0	63.0	62.6	63.0	63.0	63.1	62.3
Education and													
Health Services													
2000	97.5	98.6	99.6	100.1	99.9	99.1	98.1	98.6	100.1	101.7	102.0	102.6	99.8
2001	100.8	101.8	102.7	102.8	102.9	102.4	101.5	102.3	103.9	105.1	105.9	106.7	103.2
2002	105.4	106.7	107.4	106.9	107.3	106.0	106.3	105.9	107.0	108.5	109.3	109.7	107.2
2003	108.4	108.2	108.7	108.6	109.0	107.9	107.0	107.6	108.6	110.3	110.5	110.8	108.8
2004	108.5	110.0	111.0	110.9	111.0	109.9	109.5	109.7	111.2	112.4	112.8	112.7	110.8
2005	110.9	112.1	112.6	113.0	113.1	113.1	112.8	113.2	114.1	113.3	113.9	114.3	113.0
2006	112.7	113.1	113.6	113.4	113.3	112.1	111.1	111.5	113.2	113.6	114.1	114.1	113.0
2007	111.3	112.7	113.5	113.1	113.6	113.5	112.6	113.5	115.5	116.2	116.8	116.4	114.1
2008	114.9	116.6	116.5	116.4	116.4	115.8	115.3	115.6	117.4	117.1	117.6	117.4	116.4
2009	115.5	117.0	117.7	118.5	119.0	118.6	118.2	118.7	120.4	120.7	121.2	121.4	118.9
2010	118.5	119.4	120.4	120.8	120.5	120.3	120.0	120.3	122.2	121.9	122.4	122.4	120.8
2011	120.2	121.5	122.3	123.3	122.8	122.7	122.6	122.7	124.7	124.8	125.1	125.5	123.2
Leisure and Hospitality													
2000	58.3	57.8	59.4	61.0	62.8	64.7	64.8	65.4	64.8	62.9	61.2	61.2	62.0
2001	59.2	59.4	60.8	62.6	64.4	65.8	65.6	66.4	65.3	63.1	61.8	61.2	63.0
2002	59.8	60.2	61.7	63.0	65.3	66.6	67.9	68.2	67.1	65.2	63.8	63.7	64.4
2003	61.8	61.7	63.3	65.4	67.6	69.3	70.0	70.4	68.9	66.9	65.4	66.0	66.4
2004	64.1	64.3	65.8	67.8	69.6	70.8	71.2	71.5	70.3	68.3	67.1	67.4	68.2
2005	65.1	65.3	66.6	68.5	70.6	72.0	72.7	73.0	71.7	69.2	68.1	68.3	69.3
2006	66.9	67.0	68.7	69.3	71.7	74.1	73.8	74.4	73.7	70.9	70.5	70.5	71.0
2007	67.0	66.9	69.0	70.9	72.6	74.6	74.0	75.3	74.3	72.1	71.3	71.9	71.7
2008	69.3	69.9	70.9	72.2	74.1	75.0	75.6	76.0	75.2	73.2	71.6	71.6	72.9
2009	68.8	68.7	70.3	71.3	73.4	74.5	74.8	75.1	73.9	71.4	70.2	70.2	71.9
2010	67.6	67.3	69.3	71.6	73.0	75.0	75.1	75.8	74.9	72.9	71.5	71.2	72.1
2011	68.5	69.0	70.8	72.5	74.3	75.3	75.3	75.3	73.7	73.6	73.1	73.0	72.9
Other Services													
2000	51.7	52.2	52.9	52.9	53.3	53.8	54.0	54.1	54.5	54.8	55.0	55.4	53.7
2001	55.0	55.1	55.3	55.5	55.7	55.8	55.3	55.2	55.3	55.1	55.0	55.2	55.3
2002	54.9	55.0	55.2	55.5	55.7	55.6	55.4	55.4	55.3	55.1	55.0	55.2	55.3
2003	54.7	54.6	55.0	55.3	55.2	55.5	55.5	55.4	55.7	55.5	55.0	55.1	55.2
2004	54.6	54.6	55.3	55.9	56.3	55.8	55.4	55.0	55.7	55.6	55.7	55.6	55.5
2005	54.6	54.6	55.4	56.7	56.9	56.6	55.9	55.6	55.7	55.3	55.2	55.3	55.5
2006	54.6	54.7	55.3	55.3	55.5	56.1	55.6	55.8	56.2	56.3	56.3	56.1	55.7
2007	55.2	55.4	55.7	55.6	55.5	56.0	55.4	55.2	55.4	55.4	55.5	55.3	55.5
2008	55.3	55.5	55.7	55.4	55.8	55.8	55.6	55.4	55.4	55.5	55.7	55.7	55.6
2009	55.6	55.5	55.4	55.8	55.9	55.8	55.5	55.1	55.2	55.3	55.4	55.4	55.5
2010	54.7	54.4	54.6	55.0	55.3	55.7	55.2	55.0	55.1	55.0	54.8	54.8	55.0
2011	54.1	54.3	54.6	54.7	54.8	55.0	55.1	55.1	55.3	54.9	54.8	54.9	54.8
Government													
2000	139.2	140.1	144.9	143.5	157.4	142.0	145.0	138.2	139.1	141.8	143.2	143.1	143.1
2001	138.0	140.6	142.8	142.6	142.3	140.9	138.2	138.4	139.0	142.4	143.7	143.7	141.1
2002	139.1	141.0	143.7	143.4	154.5	142.2	137.8	138.4	140.6	143.3	145.1	144.9	142.8
2003	140.8	142.3	144.0	145.0	145.1	142.2	138.8	139.1	139.7	143.5	144.7	144.8	142.5
2004	140.4	142.0	144.7	145.2	145.0	143.3	140.0	139.9	141.8	145.8	145.4	145.1	143.2
2005	142.5	143.6	145.2	145.6	145.8	143.3	139.5	139.5	142.6	143.5	146.3	146.6	143.7
2006	141.3	144.8	146.5	146.4	146.5	143.6	139.2	141.0	144.1	147.0	147.9	148.0	144.7
2007	142.4	145.8	147.4	147.2	148.1	144.4	139.9	141.1	144.6	147.0	147.9	147.7	145.3
2008	143.3	146.5	147.9	148.1	150.4	144.5	142.2	143.2	147.3	149.8	150.4	150.5	147.0
2009	145.3	148.9	151.0	150.4	152.5	154.0	145.6	146.3	148.5	152.3	152.7	152.9	150.0
2010	149.1	151.7	155.0	154.5	158.5	154.2	148.7	148.3	152.0	153.6	154.6	154.4	152.9
2011	146.8	151.0	153.5	154.5	155.0	144.9	146.7	148.0	152.6	155.9	156.4	156.2	151.8

2. Average Weekly Hours by Selected Industry: West Virginia, 2007–2011

(Not seasonally adjusted)

Industry and year	January	February	March	April	May	June	July	August	September	October	November	December	Annual average
Total Private													
2007	35.1	34.5	35.1	35.5	35.4	35.2	35.6	35.3	35.4	35.2	34.7	35.3	35.2
2008	35.0	34.8	35.2	35.0	35.1	35.9	35.6	35.7	35.2	35.5	35.0	34.5	35.2
2009	34.0	34.1	34.1	34.0	34.3	34.3	34.4	34.6	34.6	34.6	35.1	35.1	34.4
2010	34.4	34.2	34.6	35.2	35.3	35.1	35.0	35.1	35.1	35.2	35.1	34.8	34.9
2011	34.8	34.5	34.3	34.7	35.1	34.9	34.5	34.4	34.6	34.4	34.3	34.1	34.5
Goods-Producing													
2007	40.9	40.6	41.3	41.2	41.3	41.2	41.4	41.2	41.3	41.5	40.3	41.5	41.1
2008	40.9	40.3	40.8	41.2	40.3	42.0	41.8	42.1	41.7	41.8	41.5	40.8	41.3
2009	40.6	40.3	40.1	40.1	40.4	40.9	40.6	41.6	41.0	41.0	41.5	41.4	40.8
2010	40.7	40.0	40.6	41.5	41.3	41.6	41.2	41.6	41.1	41.2	41.2	40.7	41.1
2011	40.8	40.4	39.9	40.1	40.8	40.6	40.4	40.3	40.1	40.4	40.6	40.5	40.4
Mining and Logging													
2007	45.9	46.3	46.9	46.3	46.8	45.9	44.8	45.7	45.3	46.1	43.6	44.8	45.7
2008	45.6	45.9	46.2	46.9	45.5	46.5	44.9	45.3	45.6	46.5	46.7	46.1	46.0
2009	45.7	45.1	44.9	45.0	44.2	45.8	45.3	46.1	45.3	45.1	46.0	45.9	45.4
2010	46.4	45.6	46.0	45.5	46.3	46.8	45.5	46.6	47.0	47.4	47.0	46.1	46.4
2011	48.7	47.4	46.9	46.3	45.9	45.4	44.0	45.3	44.2	44.0	44.0	44.5	45.5
Construction													
2007	36.6	36.5	37.6	38.8	38.9	39.4	39.8	40.1	39.3	40.9	37.4	38.4	38.7
2008	36.6	34.8	36.7	37.6	36.6	38.9	39.1	40.1	40.5	40.4	38.8	36.3	38.1
2009	36.5	36.7	36.4	36.5	38.2	38.5	39.1	39.8	39.1	39.5	40.0	39.7	38.4
2010	38.1	36.4	38.2	41.3	38.9	40.2	40.0	40.5	39.9	40.0	39.1	37.4	39.3
2011	37.0	36.7	36.7	38.8	40.4	40.3	40.2	40.1	39.2	39.9	40.5	39.2	39.2
Manufacturing													
2007	41.1	40.2	40.9	40.3	40.3	40.2	40.8	39.8	40.7	39.6	40.7	41.8	40.5
2008	41.2	40.8	40.6	40.6	40.1	41.8	41.9	41.8	40.4	40.0	40.4	40.8	40.9
2009	40.1	39.7	39.5	39.5	39.6	39.7	39.0	40.2	39.9	39.7	39.9	39.3	39.7
2010	38.9	38.8	38.9	39.2	40.0	39.4	39.4	39.2	38.2	38.2	39.0	39.3	39.0
2011	37.9	37.9	37.3	36.8	37.6	37.5	38.0	37.0	37.9	38.2	38.2	38.5	37.7
Trade, Transportation, and Utilities													
2007	35.2	34.8	35.3	35.5	35.7	35.6	35.8	35.7	35.8	35.6	35.1	36.0	35.5
2008	35.2	34.0	34.4	34.3	34.0	34.8	34.5	34.6	34.8	34.6	35.1	34.8	34.6
2009	34.8	34.5	34.5	34.4	34.8	34.6	34.4	34.2	34.1	34.6	34.6	35.0	34.5
2010	34.5	34.9	35.2	36.7	36.4	36.8	36.4	36.6	36.4	36.5	36.2	35.5	36.0
2011	35.2	34.7	35.2	35.4	35.8	35.6	35.6	35.4	35.6	35.2	34.7	34.8	35.3
Financial Activities													
2007	35.6	35.3	35.0	35.6	35.7	35.1	35.5	34.3	35.5	33.7	32.9	34.8	34.9
2008	34.5	34.5	34.1	34.7	35.5	37.6	35.2	34.9	34.4	36.9	36.7	36.9	35.5
2009	35.3	35.4	35.3	35.4	35.9	35.9	35.9	36.0	35.9	36.0	36.1	35.3	35.7
2010	36.1	36.0	35.4	35.2	36.3	36.0	35.9	36.1	36.3	36.0	35.8	36.0	36.0
2011	36.3	36.2	36.0	36.5	36.8	36.3	36.0	35.5	36.7	37.4	35.6	35.1	36.2
Professional and Business Services													
2007	35.9	34.4	35.2	35.8	35.0	34.9	35.5	34.9	35.2	35.1	34.8	35.2	35.2
2008	34.2	34.8	35.5	34.8	34.2	35.4	35.2	35.8	35.2	36.2	35.5	35.1	35.2
2009	34.8	35.0	35.4	35.5	35.8	35.3	35.2	36.0	35.6	35.4	36.5	36.5	35.6
2010	36.2	36.4	36.8	36.4	37.1	36.5	36.1	37.4	36.8	36.6	36.6	36.7	36.6
2011	37.0	37.1	37.0	37.6	38.2	37.6	37.0	37.4	37.2	37.5	37.7	36.6	37.3
Education and Health Services													
2007	34.5	33.6	33.9	34.5	34.3	33.9	34.4	34.0	34.4	34.1	34.1	34.2	34.2
2008	34.6	34.7	34.8	34.5	34.9	34.9	34.7	34.5	34.2	34.5	34.6	34.1	34.6
2009	34.4	34.7	34.7	34.5	34.4	34.2	34.2	34.2	34.5	34.5	34.7	34.4	34.5
2010	34.2	34.4	34.7	34.8	35.0	34.7	34.6	34.2	34.3	34.5	34.4	34.0	34.5
2011	34.3	34.3	34.0	34.2	34.4	34.2	34.1	33.8	34.2	33.8	34.1	33.8	34.1
Leisure and Hospitality													
2007	26.8	26.9	27.8	27.8	27.7	28.2	28.3	27.7	27.1	26.6	26.1	26.0	27.3
2008	26.5	26.8	27.2	27.7	28.9	29.5	29.6	29.7	28.1	27.9	27.5	27.1	28.1
2009	26.7	27.1	27.0	27.3	27.8	28.2	28.5	27.9	27.6	27.2	27.2	26.7	27.5
2010	26.5	26.4	27.2	27.4	27.4	27.9	28.1	28.3	27.6	27.5	26.8	26.4	27.3
2011	26.4	27.0	26.7	26.5	26.8	26.9	27.4	27.1	26.4	26.7	26.1	26.0	26.7
Other Services													
2007	30.3	30.4	31.3	31.0	31.3	30.5	30.3	31.0	31.0	30.5	30.1	31.3	30.8
2008	30.6	31.3	31.8	31.4	32.5	32.6	33.1	34.0	32.1	33.4	33.2	32.2	32.4
2009	31.4	31.5	31.8	31.6	31.6	31.6	31.3	32.1	32.1	32.2	32.5	32.4	31.8
2010	31.4	31.7	31.8	33.0	32.3	32.0	32.2	31.7	31.7	31.5	31.6	31.5	31.9
2011	31.2	30.9	30.7	31.1	31.0	31.0	30.9	31.2	30.4	31.4	31.3	31.3	31.0

3. Average Hourly Earnings by Selected Industry: West Virginia, 2007–2011

(Dollars, not seasonally adjusted)

Industry and year	January	February	March	April	May	June	July	August	September	October	November	December	Annual average
Total Private													
2007	17.15	16.80	16.73	16.95	16.84	16.82	16.98	16.96	17.00	17.07	17.37	17.83	17.04
2008	17.43	17.55	17.59	17.63	17.57	17.60	17.64	17.69	17.90	17.84	17.91	17.91	17.70
2009	18.19	18.10	18.13	18.17	17.90	17.85	17.95	18.01	18.12	18.15	18.23	18.28	18.09
2010	18.41	18.63	18.49	18.52	18.72	18.69	18.78	18.83	18.68	18.58	18.62	18.88	18.65
2011	18.82	18.66	18.74	18.86	18.88	18.84	18.96	18.90	19.06	19.13	19.24	19.16	18.94
Goods-Producing													
2007	21.37	21.25	21.15	21.39	21.18	21.30	21.36	21.43	21.35	21.39	21.99	21.98	21.43
2008	21.85	22.15	22.05	21.97	21.90	22.27	22.04	22.12	22.65	22.64	23.24	22.97	22.33
2009	22.96	22.83	23.02	23.07	22.75	22.81	22.88	22.94	22.86	22.83	23.04	22.89	22.91
2010	22.93	22.74	22.67	22.65	22.74	22.82	22.75	22.85	22.83	22.66	22.70	23.20	22.79
2011	22.81	22.60	22.60	22.78	22.82	22.67	22.73	22.80	22.82	23.16	23.32	23.50	22.89
Mining and Logging													
2007	23.15	22.97	23.01	22.84	22.68	23.10	23.13	23.98	23.37	23.65	24.93	24.44	23.43
2008	23.57	23.85	24.21	24.19	24.52	25.27	24.79	25.06	25.93	26.12	26.96	26.43	25.13
2009	26.10	26.01	26.26	26.41	26.47	26.26	26.16	27.00	27.03	26.90	26.99	26.59	26.50
2010	27.01	26.77	26.76	26.66	26.73	26.24	25.88	26.04	25.60	25.42	25.52	26.26	26.22
2011	25.68	25.78	26.05	26.11	26.11	25.60	25.26	25.69	25.80	26.51	26.54	26.86	26.00
Construction													
2007	19.83	19.98	20.03	20.38	20.19	20.57	20.67	19.76	20.12	20.14	20.50	20.55	20.23
2008	20.63	21.69	20.61	20.96	20.99	20.95	21.25	21.40	22.20	22.03	22.08	22.07	21.44
2009	22.18	22.21	23.02	23.10	22.55	22.49	22.89	22.97	22.76	22.93	23.15	22.71	22.75
2010	23.12	22.64	22.63	22.36	22.30	22.60	22.61	22.96	23.14	22.89	23.12	23.77	22.84
2011	23.29	22.69	22.53	22.98	23.14	23.36	23.93	23.75	23.58	23.77	24.42	24.48	23.54
Manufacturing													
2007	21.27	20.99	20.79	21.24	21.00	20.80	20.86	21.14	21.06	21.00	21.37	21.53	21.09
2008	21.56	21.42	21.60	21.26	20.87	21.31	20.95	20.83	20.85	20.71	21.48	21.16	21.17
2009	21.21	20.98	20.74	20.78	20.44	20.71	20.68	20.25	20.22	20.09	20.32	20.51	20.58
2010	19.98	20.00	19.82	20.06	20.26	20.51	20.63	20.42	20.44	20.32	20.24	20.56	20.27
2011	20.16	19.93	19.81	19.88	19.92	19.77	19.85	19.66	19.81	19.96	19.81	20.07	19.89
Trade, Transportation, and Utilities													
2007	14.27	13.96	14.04	14.35	14.00	13.88	14.15	14.09	14.09	13.95	14.18	14.18	14.10
2008	14.28	14.93	15.12	14.94	15.40	15.12	15.09	15.04	15.26	15.90	15.31	15.31	15.15
2009	15.40	15.36	15.45	15.43	15.12	15.11	15.09	15.24	15.30	15.37	15.28	15.29	15.29
2010	15.63	16.30	16.33	16.35	16.63	16.61	16.56	16.75	16.69	16.42	16.16	16.14	16.39
2011	16.52	16.54	16.61	16.88	16.79	16.76	17.02	16.87	17.48	17.11	17.10	16.83	16.88
Financial Activities													
2007	16.09	16.36	16.53	16.48	16.44	16.56	16.59	16.64	16.66	16.59	16.92	16.28	16.51
2008	16.66	16.69	16.68	17.07	16.82	16.62	17.23	16.86	16.71	16.35	16.72	16.92	16.78
2009	17.15	17.13	17.16	17.23	17.08	17.07	17.03	16.81	16.74	16.90	17.00	17.00	17.02
2010	17.22	17.27	17.07	17.34	17.48	17.49	17.57	17.96	17.09	17.25	17.39	17.32	17.37
2011	17.23	17.18	17.33	17.41	17.48	17.14	17.63	17.95	17.80	18.16	18.28	17.86	17.62
Professional and Business Services													
2007	19.62	20.06	19.50	19.88	20.17	19.81	20.18	20.10	20.64	20.44	20.64	21.66	20.23
2008	21.12	21.00	21.25	20.92	20.48	20.18	20.00	20.01	19.76	20.40	20.42	20.09	20.46
2009	19.89	20.08	20.04	20.18	19.99	19.90	19.92	19.76	19.58	19.49	19.40	19.44	19.80
2010	20.16	20.04	20.12	19.91	20.18	19.74	19.77	19.47	19.47	19.48	19.59	19.88	19.81
2011	19.71	19.83	19.90	19.71	19.78	19.81	19.98	20.05	20.23	20.85	20.63	20.72	20.10
Education and Health Services													
2007	16.78	17.02	17.07	17.17	17.21	17.30	17.46	17.25	17.15	17.30	17.48	18.27	17.29
2008	17.62	17.39	17.28	17.50	17.42	17.48	17.80	17.90	18.11	17.41	18.38	18.12	17.70
2009	18.22	18.52	18.41	18.39	18.44	18.37	18.42	18.21	18.48	18.59	18.66	18.87	18.47
2010	18.83	18.73	18.65	18.66	18.90	19.00	19.39	19.24	19.19	18.92	19.08	19.22	18.98
2011	19.42	19.62	19.56	19.50	19.39	19.63	19.94	19.78	19.60	19.50	19.70	19.67	19.61
Leisure and Hospitality													
2007	9.30	9.33	9.31	9.20	9.07	9.09	9.09	9.14	9.26	9.49	9.46	10.74	9.36
2008	9.63	9.67	9.72	9.59	9.56	9.45	9.52	9.65	9.88	10.02	10.12	10.30	9.75
2009	10.34	10.34	10.54	10.66	10.47	10.51	10.45	10.71	10.57	10.43	10.36	10.62	10.50
2010	10.54	10.66	10.57	10.34	10.49	10.45	10.47	10.52	10.46	10.55	10.75	11.07	10.57
2011	10.92	10.85	10.68	10.56	10.61	10.55	10.51	10.54	10.51	10.59	10.64	10.67	10.63
Other Services													
2007	14.89	14.95	14.70	14.85	14.58	14.98	14.68	14.88	15.18	15.31	16.12	15.83	15.08
2008	15.44	15.78	15.68	15.20	15.07	15.72	15.51	15.67	15.92	15.90	16.97	17.28	15.85
2009	16.84	16.88	17.00	16.93	16.54	16.54	16.36	16.58	16.54	16.54	16.69	16.64	16.67
2010	16.64	16.98	16.90	16.70	16.75	16.32	16.19	16.47	16.25	16.54	16.13	15.93	16.46
2011	16.23	16.40	16.21	15.76	15.77	15.74	15.63	15.59	15.67	15.80	15.84	16.14	15.90

4. Average Weekly Earnings by Selected Industry: West Virginia, 2007–2011

(Dollars, not seasonally adjusted)

Industry and year	January	February	March	April	May	June	July	August	September	October	November	December	Annual average
Total Private													
2007	601.97	579.60	587.22	601.73	596.14	592.06	604.49	598.69	601.80	600.86	602.74	629.40	599.84
2008	610.05	610.74	619.17	617.05	616.71	631.84	627.98	631.53	630.08	633.32	633.15	617.90	623.37
2009	618.46	617.21	618.23	617.78	613.97	612.26	617.48	623.15	626.95	627.99	639.87	641.63	622.91
2010	633.30	637.15	639.75	651.90	660.82	656.02	657.30	660.93	655.67	654.02	653.56	657.02	651.68
2011	654.94	643.77	642.78	654.44	662.69	657.52	654.12	650.16	659.48	658.07	659.93	653.36	654.16
Goods-Producing													
2007	874.03	862.75	873.50	881.27	874.73	877.56	884.30	882.92	881.76	887.69	886.20	912.17	881.50
2008	893.67	892.65	899.64	905.16	882.57	935.34	921.27	931.25	944.51	946.35	964.46	937.18	921.98
2009	932.18	920.05	923.10	925.11	919.10	932.93	928.93	954.30	937.26	936.03	956.16	947.65	934.22
2010	933.25	909.60	920.40	939.98	939.16	949.31	937.30	950.56	938.31	933.59	935.24	944.24	936.43
2011	930.65	913.04	901.74	913.48	931.06	920.40	918.29	918.84	915.08	935.66	946.79	951.75	924.62
Mining and Logging													
2007	1,062.59	1,063.51	1,079.17	1,057.49	1,061.42	1,060.29	1,036.22	1,095.89	1,058.66	1,090.27	1,086.95	1,094.91	1,070.72
2008	1,074.79	1,094.72	1,118.50	1,134.51	1,115.66	1,175.06	1,113.07	1,135.22	1,182.41	1,214.58	1,259.03	1,218.42	1,155.64
2009	1,192.77	1,173.05	1,179.07	1,188.45	1,169.97	1,202.71	1,185.05	1,244.70	1,224.46	1,213.19	1,241.54	1,220.48	1,202.01
2010	1,253.26	1,220.71	1,230.96	1,213.03	1,237.60	1,228.03	1,177.54	1,213.46	1,203.20	1,204.91	1,199.44	1,210.59	1,215.66
2011	1,250.62	1,221.97	1,221.75	1,208.89	1,198.45	1,162.24	1,111.44	1,163.76	1,140.36	1,166.44	1,167.76	1,195.27	1,183.09
Construction													
2007	725.78	729.27	753.13	790.74	785.39	810.46	822.67	792.38	790.72	823.73	766.70	789.12	783.04
2008	755.06	754.81	756.39	788.10	768.23	814.96	830.88	858.14	899.10	890.01	856.70	801.14	817.61
2009	809.57	815.11	837.93	843.15	861.41	865.87	895.00	914.21	889.92	905.74	926.00	901.59	872.70
2010	880.87	824.10	864.47	923.47	867.47	908.52	904.40	929.88	923.29	915.60	903.99	889.00	897.27
2011	861.73	832.72	826.85	891.62	934.86	941.41	961.99	952.38	924.34	948.42	989.01	959.62	922.79
Manufacturing													
2007	874.20	843.80	850.31	855.97	846.30	836.16	851.09	841.37	857.14	831.60	869.76	899.95	854.72
2008	888.27	873.94	876.96	863.16	836.89	890.76	877.81	870.69	842.34	828.40	867.79	863.33	865.10
2009	850.52	832.91	819.23	820.81	809.42	822.19	806.52	814.05	806.78	797.57	810.77	818.35	817.57
2010	777.22	776.00	771.00	786.35	810.40	808.09	812.82	800.46	780.81	776.22	789.36	808.01	791.52
2011	764.06	755.35	738.91	731.58	748.99	741.38	754.30	727.42	750.80	762.47	756.74	772.70	750.26
Trade, Transportation, and Utilities													
2007	502.30	485.81	495.61	509.43	499.80	494.13	506.57	503.01	504.42	496.62	497.72	510.48	500.53
2008	502.66	507.62	520.13	512.44	523.60	526.18	520.61	520.38	531.05	550.14	539.49	532.79	523.94
2009	535.92	529.92	533.03	530.79	526.18	522.81	519.10	521.21	521.73	531.80	528.69	535.15	527.97
2010	539.24	568.87	574.82	600.05	605.33	611.25	602.78	613.05	607.52	599.33	584.99	572.97	590.00
2011	581.50	573.94	584.67	597.55	601.08	596.66	605.91	597.20	622.29	602.27	593.37	585.68	595.20
Financial Activities													
2007	572.80	577.51	578.55	586.69	586.91	581.26	588.95	570.75	591.43	559.08	556.67	566.54	576.43
2008	574.77	575.81	568.79	592.33	597.11	624.91	606.50	588.41	574.82	603.32	613.62	624.35	595.40
2009	605.40	606.40	605.75	609.94	613.17	612.81	611.38	605.16	600.97	608.40	613.70	600.10	607.51
2010	621.64	621.72	604.28	610.37	634.52	629.64	630.76	648.36	620.37	621.00	622.56	623.52	624.57
2011	625.45	621.92	623.88	635.47	643.26	622.18	634.68	637.23	653.26	679.18	650.77	626.89	637.81
Professional and Business Services													
2007	704.36	690.06	686.40	711.70	705.95	691.37	716.39	701.49	726.53	717.44	718.27	762.43	711.26
2008	722.30	730.80	754.38	728.02	700.42	714.37	704.00	716.36	695.55	738.48	724.91	705.16	719.51
2009	692.17	702.80	709.42	716.39	715.64	702.47	701.18	711.36	697.05	689.95	708.10	709.56	704.59
2010	729.79	729.46	740.42	724.72	748.68	720.51	713.70	728.18	716.50	712.97	716.99	729.60	726.17
2011	729.27	735.69	736.30	741.10	755.60	744.86	739.26	749.87	752.56	781.88	777.75	758.35	750.73
Education and Health Services													
2007	578.91	571.87	578.67	592.37	590.30	586.47	600.62	586.50	589.96	589.93	596.07	624.83	590.65
2008	609.65	603.43	601.34	603.75	607.96	610.05	617.66	617.55	619.36	600.65	635.95	617.89	612.12
2009	626.77	642.64	638.83	634.46	634.34	628.25	629.96	622.78	637.56	641.36	647.50	649.13	636.25
2010	643.99	644.31	647.16	649.37	661.50	659.30	670.89	658.01	658.22	652.74	656.35	653.48	654.75
2011	666.11	672.97	665.04	666.90	667.02	671.35	679.95	668.56	670.32	659.10	671.77	664.85	668.69
Leisure and Hospitality													
2007	249.24	250.98	258.82	255.76	251.24	256.34	257.25	253.18	250.95	252.43	246.91	279.24	255.23
2008	255.20	259.16	264.38	265.64	276.28	278.78	281.79	286.61	277.63	279.56	278.30	279.13	273.78
2009	276.08	280.21	284.58	291.02	291.07	296.38	297.83	298.81	291.73	283.70	281.79	283.55	288.29
2010	279.31	281.42	287.50	283.32	287.43	291.56	294.21	297.72	288.70	290.13	288.10	292.25	288.59
2011	288.29	292.95	285.16	279.84	284.35	283.80	287.97	285.63	277.46	282.75	277.70	277.42	283.55
Other Services													
2007	451.17	454.48	460.11	460.35	456.35	456.89	444.80	461.28	470.58	466.96	485.21	495.48	463.63
2008	472.46	493.91	498.62	477.28	489.78	512.47	513.38	532.78	511.03	531.06	563.40	556.42	512.75
2009	528.78	531.72	540.60	534.99	522.66	522.66	512.07	532.22	530.93	532.54	542.43	539.14	530.86
2010	522.50	538.27	537.42	551.10	541.03	522.24	521.32	522.10	515.13	508.10	503.39	511.88	524.59
2011	506.38	506.76	497.65	490.14	488.87	487.94	482.97	486.41	476.37	496.12	495.79	505.18	493.19

WISCONSIN
At a Glance

Population:
  2000 census: 5,363,757
  2010 census: 5,686,986
  2011 estimate: 5,711,767

Percent change in population:
  2000–2010: 6.0%
  2010–2011: 0.4%

Percent change in total nonfarm employment:
  2000–2010: -3.7%
  2010–2011: 0.4%

Industry with the largest growth in employment, 2000–2011 (thousands):
  Education and Health Services, 71.1

Industry with the largest decline or smallest growth in employment, 2000–2011 (thousands):
  Manufacturing, -151.3

Civilian labor force:
  2000: 2,996,091
  2010: 3,082,676
  2011: 3,062,259

Unemployment rate and rank among states (lowest to highest):
  2000: 3.4%, 17th
  2010: 8.5%, 24th
  2011: 7.5%, 20th

Over-the-year change in unemployment rates:
  2010–2011: -1.0%

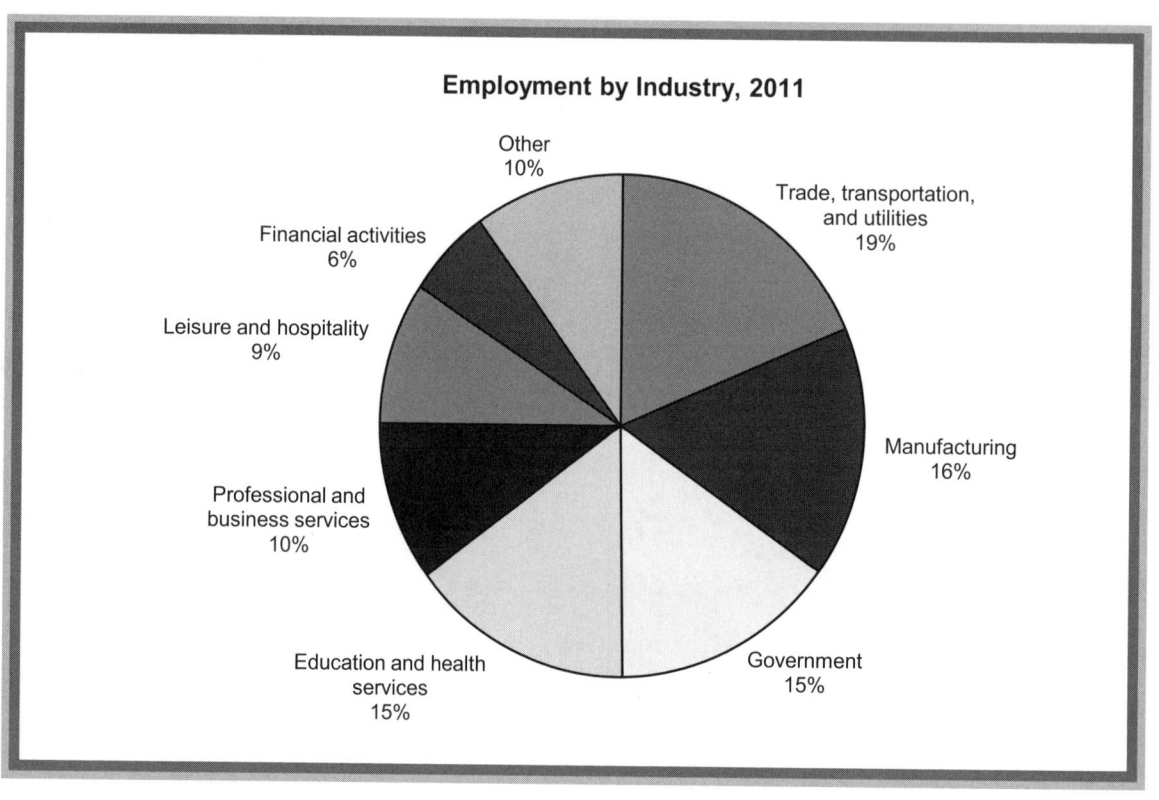

Employment by Industry, 2011

- Other 10%
- Trade, transportation, and utilities 19%
- Financial activities 6%
- Manufacturing 16%
- Leisure and hospitality 9%
- Government 15%
- Professional and business services 10%
- Education and health services 15%

1. Employment by Industry: Wisconsin, Selected Years, 2000–2011

(Numbers in thousands, not seasonally adjusted)

Industry and year	January	February	March	April	May	June	July	August	September	October	November	December	Annual average
Total Nonfarm													
2000	2,748.9	2,759.7	2,785.1	2,820.3	2,846.9	2,885.5	2,852.5	2,858.5	2,859.3	2,864.1	2,869.9	2,854.7	2,833.8
2001	2,770.7	2,776.5	2,788.9	2,813.6	2,840.1	2,861.6	2,829.3	2,829.1	2,825.0	2,820.8	2,812.6	2,798.4	2,813.9
2002	2,719.4	2,717.6	2,735.9	2,766.0	2,799.2	2,822.8	2,795.0	2,800.0	2,797.9	2,813.5	2,815.7	2,800.9	2,782.0
2003	2,709.5	2,717.4	2,725.5	2,760.3	2,794.5	2,816.8	2,780.3	2,782.3	2,791.3	2,808.5	2,801.5	2,798.1	2,773.8
2004	2,716.0	2,725.1	2,742.0	2,781.5	2,814.8	2,845.2	2,831.8	2,836.1	2,833.9	2,844.7	2,844.1	2,838.4	2,804.5
2005	2,754.0	2,765.5	2,780.1	2,827.2	2,851.3	2,876.7	2,858.0	2,860.2	2,873.0	2,870.0	2,871.8	2,872.0	2,838.3
2006	2,785.6	2,789.4	2,807.2	2,846.9	2,875.8	2,912.2	2,880.9	2,882.0	2,891.0	2,889.9	2,889.9	2,887.7	2,861.5
2007	2,808.9	2,804.4	2,824.3	2,856.6	2,898.4	2,936.8	2,900.2	2,901.5	2,901.7	2,902.8	2,904.0	2,900.3	2,878.3
2008	2,821.6	2,817.3	2,830.1	2,858.6	2,900.8	2,921.9	2,890.3	2,889.1	2,892.3	2,892.4	2,879.9	2,857.4	2,871.0
2009	2,747.3	2,734.3	2,726.4	2,738.5	2,767.9	2,778.2	2,741.3	2,735.2	2,734.9	2,747.1	2,742.8	2,734.9	2,744.1
2010	2,649.3	2,654.0	2,668.4	2,713.8	2,746.5	2,765.3	2,744.4	2,748.9	2,751.2	2,772.0	2,772.8	2,758.1	2,728.7
2011	2,681.6	2,688.9	2,705.0	2,742.4	2,772.0	2,786.3	2,765.2	2,755.6	2,755.3	2,763.9	2,747.6	2,724.2	2,740.7
Total Private													
2000	2,349.3	2,350.9	2,373.0	2,401.6	2,429.5	2,472.2	2,471.9	2,480.1	2,461.6	2,454.1	2,452.2	2,442.6	2,428.2
2001	2,368.4	2,358.8	2,367.9	2,388.5	2,415.6	2,445.5	2,441.9	2,445.1	2,413.4	2,396.8	2,386.0	2,374.1	2,400.2
2002	2,310.8	2,296.1	2,309.7	2,337.8	2,373.1	2,409.5	2,411.3	2,419.9	2,393.9	2,386.8	2,382.9	2,374.7	2,367.2
2003	2,305.2	2,292.5	2,299.3	2,331.4	2,369.5	2,396.5	2,397.3	2,402.4	2,392.1	2,388.1	2,379.2	2,377.9	2,361.0
2004	2,312.8	2,304.8	2,320.0	2,358.8	2,392.6	2,430.6	2,447.2	2,454.3	2,427.9	2,424.0	2,417.9	2,416.9	2,392.3
2005	2,343.1	2,340.9	2,356.3	2,400.0	2,425.3	2,462.4	2,472.3	2,478.7	2,458.7	2,446.9	2,446.4	2,445.0	2,423.0
2006	2,375.5	2,369.7	2,382.6	2,419.4	2,449.8	2,493.6	2,493.6	2,498.7	2,477.1	2,468.5	2,465.0	2,462.2	2,446.3
2007	2,398.7	2,387.6	2,401.8	2,429.6	2,471.3	2,514.7	2,511.9	2,516.7	2,487.7	2,479.0	2,477.7	2,471.5	2,462.4
2008	2,404.9	2,395.1	2,402.9	2,429.0	2,468.3	2,499.7	2,497.9	2,502.1	2,469.3	2,459.9	2,438.5	2,421.4	2,449.1
2009	2,328.7	2,303.0	2,293.7	2,303.6	2,332.2	2,356.4	2,348.9	2,350.1	2,326.4	2,321.0	2,311.6	2,303.1	2,323.2
2010	2,234.0	2,228.9	2,240.9	2,278.3	2,309.0	2,343.9	2,354.4	2,364.6	2,340.1	2,343.2	2,338.9	2,331.6	2,309.0
2011	2,269.5	2,262.3	2,276.9	2,310.1	2,342.2	2,378.0	2,381.4	2,380.2	2,350.5	2,344.8	2,328.3	2,308.9	2,327.8
Goods-Producing													
2000	701.3	700.7	708.0	716.5	724.4	742.7	741.7	742.5	734.2	729.5	722.6	711.8	723.0
2001	689.5	682.5	683.2	687.1	694.4	706.8	706.1	705.6	694.6	685.4	674.5	664.8	689.5
2002	643.5	634.9	638.6	646.8	658.0	671.8	673.1	675.7	667.4	662.4	657.0	645.7	656.2
2003	621.1	613.0	614.0	623.2	635.8	646.3	647.7	648.2	640.8	637.2	631.1	623.9	631.9
2004	607.0	603.4	608.7	623.3	634.0	646.1	654.6	655.8	648.5	644.1	640.0	634.3	633.3
2005	612.0	611.3	615.0	628.4	637.1	652.2	656.4	657.0	649.0	644.4	640.5	633.2	636.4
2006	618.8	613.9	617.2	629.7	638.8	656.0	656.7	656.9	648.4	642.9	636.5	630.2	637.2
2007	614.4	607.4	612.2	620.8	633.6	649.2	650.1	650.0	640.9	636.2	632.3	623.2	630.9
2008	606.8	601.7	603.6	610.3	621.3	633.8	633.5	632.1	621.9	616.0	605.5	590.1	614.7
2009	561.4	546.8	538.3	536.2	540.5	546.9	546.2	545.7	541.8	536.5	531.3	521.7	541.1
2010	504.3	500.9	504.7	517.5	526.3	540.1	546.2	548.7	542.8	540.1	536.7	527.8	528.0
2011	515.0	512.5	517.3	529.0	539.8	554.1	559.4	558.4	549.5	542.3	533.4	523.5	536.2
Mining and Logging													
2000	3.5	3.6	3.7	3.9	4.3	4.4	4.4	4.4	4.3	4.2	4.1	3.6	4.0
2001	3.2	3.3	3.4	3.6	4.1	4.3	4.3	4.3	4.2	4.2	4.0	3.7	3.9
2002	3.2	3.2	3.3	3.6	4.1	4.2	4.2	4.2	4.2	4.1	3.9	3.6	3.8
2003	3.2	3.1	3.2	3.5	4.0	4.1	4.1	4.1	4.1	4.0	3.9	3.7	3.8
2004	3.1	3.2	3.3	3.7	4.0	4.1	4.2	4.2	4.1	4.2	4.1	3.9	3.8
2005	3.3	3.3	3.5	3.8	4.1	4.3	4.4	4.4	4.3	4.2	4.1	3.8	4.0
2006	3.4	3.4	3.5	3.8	4.2	4.3	4.3	4.3	4.2	4.1	3.9	3.7	3.9
2007	3.2	3.2	3.3	3.5	3.9	3.9	4.0	4.0	3.9	3.8	3.7	3.3	3.6
2008	3.0	2.9	3.0	3.1	3.5	3.7	3.7	3.8	3.7	3.6	3.5	3.1	3.4
2009	2.6	2.6	2.6	2.7	3.1	3.2	3.3	3.3	3.3	3.3	3.1	2.8	3.0
2010	2.4	2.4	2.5	2.8	3.1	3.2	3.3	3.3	3.2	3.2	3.1	2.7	2.9
2011	2.5	2.5	2.6	2.7	3.0	3.2	3.3	3.3	3.3	3.3	3.2	2.8	3.0
Construction													
2000	107.6	106.1	111.2	121.3	128.7	135.3	137.3	137.5	133.6	131.7	127.7	119.9	124.8
2001	109.3	108.0	110.1	118.1	128.0	134.6	138.1	138.8	134.8	133.3	129.0	122.3	125.4
2002	108.7	105.7	108.0	117.9	127.2	133.4	136.7	136.7	133.1	132.0	129.2	120.9	124.1
2003	108.6	105.0	106.6	116.2	127.8	133.6	136.0	136.5	133.3	132.8	129.1	123.4	124.1
2004	110.4	107.6	110.9	122.2	129.6	135.4	139.7	138.7	135.7	134.0	131.4	125.4	126.8
2005	112.1	109.5	111.8	123.2	130.5	136.5	139.5	138.9	136.2	134.6	132.2	125.2	127.5
2006	114.3	111.9	113.4	124.0	131.1	137.8	138.5	138.1	134.9	132.9	129.3	123.6	127.5
2007	112.5	107.9	113.0	120.0	130.2	135.7	137.0	136.9	133.8	132.8	130.0	121.2	125.9
2008	108.0	104.9	106.8	113.8	123.9	127.9	129.4	129.0	125.6	124.1	118.4	108.9	118.4
2009	93.9	91.4	91.0	98.0	105.7	109.5	110.8	109.5	107.6	106.2	102.7	94.3	101.7
2010	82.1	79.9	81.6	92.1	97.1	101.7	103.6	103.9	102.1	102.3	98.5	90.0	94.6
2011	79.2	76.8	79.5	87.7	95.1	100.6	102.4	99.7	97.1	96.0	90.7	80.6	90.5
Manufacturing													
2000	590.2	591.0	593.1	591.3	591.4	603.0	600.0	600.6	596.3	593.6	590.8	588.3	594.1
2001	577.0	571.2	569.7	565.4	562.3	567.9	563.7	562.5	555.6	547.9	541.5	538.8	560.3
2002	531.6	526.0	527.3	525.3	526.7	534.2	532.2	534.8	530.1	526.3	523.9	521.2	528.3
2003	509.3	504.9	504.2	503.5	504.0	508.6	507.6	507.6	503.4	500.4	498.1	496.8	504.0
2004	493.5	492.6	494.5	497.4	500.4	506.6	510.7	512.9	508.7	505.9	504.5	505.0	502.7
2005	496.6	498.5	499.7	501.4	502.5	511.4	512.5	513.7	508.5	505.6	504.2	504.2	504.9
2006	501.1	498.6	500.3	501.9	503.5	513.9	513.9	514.5	509.3	505.9	503.3	502.9	505.8
2007	498.7	496.3	495.9	497.3	499.5	509.6	509.1	509.1	503.2	499.6	498.6	498.7	501.3
2008	495.8	493.9	493.8	493.4	493.9	502.2	500.4	499.3	492.6	488.3	483.6	478.1	492.9
2009	464.9	452.8	444.7	435.5	431.7	434.2	432.1	432.9	430.9	427.0	425.5	424.6	436.4
2010	419.8	418.6	420.6	422.6	426.1	435.2	439.3	441.5	437.5	434.6	435.1	435.1	430.5
2011	433.3	433.2	435.2	438.6	441.7	450.3	453.7	455.4	449.1	443.0	439.5	440.1	442.8

1. Employment by Industry: Wisconsin, Selected Years, 2000–2011—*Continued*

(Numbers in thousands, not seasonally adjusted)

Industry and year	January	February	March	April	May	June	July	August	September	October	November	December	Annual average
Service-Providing													
2000	2,047.6	2,059.0	2,077.1	2,103.8	2,122.5	2,142.8	2,110.8	2,116.0	2,125.1	2,134.6	2,147.3	2,142.9	2,110.8
2001	2,081.2	2,094.0	2,105.7	2,126.5	2,145.7	2,154.8	2,123.2	2,125.5	2,130.4	2,135.4	2,138.1	2,133.6	2,124.3
2002	2,075.9	2,082.7	2,097.3	2,119.2	2,141.2	2,151.0	2,121.9	2,124.3	2,130.5	2,151.1	2,158.7	2,155.2	2,125.8
2003	2,088.4	2,104.4	2,111.5	2,137.1	2,158.7	2,170.5	2,132.6	2,134.1	2,150.5	2,171.3	2,170.4	2,174.2	2,142.0
2004	2,109.0	2,121.7	2,133.3	2,158.2	2,180.8	2,199.1	2,177.2	2,180.3	2,185.4	2,200.6	2,204.1	2,204.1	2,171.2
2005	2,142.0	2,154.2	2,165.1	2,198.8	2,214.2	2,224.5	2,201.6	2,203.2	2,224.0	2,225.6	2,231.3	2,238.8	2,201.9
2006	2,166.8	2,175.5	2,190.0	2,217.2	2,237.0	2,256.2	2,224.2	2,225.1	2,242.6	2,247.0	2,253.4	2,257.5	2,224.4
2007	2,194.5	2,197.0	2,212.1	2,235.8	2,264.8	2,287.6	2,250.1	2,251.5	2,260.8	2,266.6	2,271.7	2,277.1	2,247.5
2008	2,214.8	2,215.6	2,226.5	2,248.3	2,279.5	2,288.1	2,256.8	2,257.0	2,270.4	2,276.4	2,274.4	2,267.3	2,256.3
2009	2,185.9	2,187.5	2,188.1	2,202.3	2,227.4	2,231.3	2,195.1	2,189.5	2,193.1	2,210.6	2,211.5	2,213.2	2,203.0
2010	2,145.0	2,153.1	2,163.7	2,196.3	2,220.2	2,225.2	2,198.2	2,200.2	2,208.4	2,231.9	2,236.1	2,230.3	2,200.7
2011	2,166.6	2,176.4	2,187.7	2,213.4	2,232.2	2,232.2	2,205.8	2,197.2	2,205.8	2,221.6	2,214.2	2,200.7	2,204.5
Trade, Transportation, and Utilities													
2000	541.4	535.8	539.4	543.9	548.4	550.6	549.2	552.0	555.7	564.7	574.9	578.7	552.9
2001	549.2	540.0	541.7	544.1	549.2	549.8	543.5	546.2	544.2	548.0	557.2	558.8	547.7
2002	533.0	524.7	527.4	528.9	535.8	538.2	533.5	534.9	535.4	540.8	552.4	555.9	536.7
2003	528.3	521.9	521.8	528.4	535.8	540.1	533.3	535.6	537.7	543.7	551.8	557.7	536.3
2004	529.5	522.5	524.7	529.2	537.1	543.0	539.9	540.6	540.0	545.7	555.6	559.5	538.9
2005	532.0	526.7	529.0	535.4	541.3	543.8	542.1	543.9	544.1	551.7	561.4	566.8	543.2
2006	536.0	529.6	532.7	536.8	542.9	548.0	542.9	544.3	544.4	549.3	561.4	565.8	544.5
2007	541.3	533.5	536.3	538.3	547.7	552.3	547.5	547.2	546.5	550.0	561.0	563.0	547.1
2008	539.9	531.4	533.2	536.6	543.2	546.3	541.6	542.1	538.8	541.5	546.4	547.7	540.7
2009	520.6	511.9	510.2	512.3	519.0	523.1	515.9	515.7	513.6	517.8	523.2	524.6	517.3
2010	501.3	494.4	496.4	501.7	507.6	512.1	508.0	509.0	507.2	514.7	521.6	524.0	508.2
2011	502.1	495.6	497.8	503.5	508.5	511.7	509.9	511.2	507.1	511.8	518.3	523.5	508.4
Wholesale Trade													
2000	114.1	114.2	114.9	115.2	115.7	117.1	117.5	117.4	116.3	116.4	116.6	117.0	116.0
2001	115.4	115.2	115.5	115.4	116.4	117.5	117.2	116.8	115.4	115.3	114.8	114.9	115.8
2002	113.2	112.7	113.2	113.9	114.8	115.5	116.1	115.6	114.4	113.6	113.7	113.6	114.2
2003	111.3	111.1	111.3	112.5	113.2	114.4	114.1	114.1	113.2	113.7	113.2	113.9	113.0
2004	112.3	111.8	112.4	112.9	113.6	114.9	116.6	117.0	115.0	115.7	116.0	116.5	114.6
2005	115.0	114.7	114.9	116.9	117.8	119.3	119.8	119.6	118.4	118.9	119.1	119.8	117.9
2006	118.5	118.1	118.8	119.9	120.6	122.6	122.8	122.5	121.2	121.3	121.4	121.9	120.8
2007	120.0	119.7	120.0	121.1	122.2	124.1	124.3	123.5	122.3	122.2	122.6	122.9	122.1
2008	121.1	120.4	120.9	122.0	123.2	124.3	124.2	123.6	121.5	121.1	120.7	120.1	121.9
2009	117.6	116.5	116.0	115.6	116.2	117.0	116.3	115.3	113.4	113.8	113.3	113.1	115.3
2010	110.6	110.0	110.3	112.0	112.7	114.0	114.7	114.5	112.4	113.3	113.4	113.4	112.6
2011	111.8	111.6	112.1	113.3	114.5	115.7	117.0	116.4	115.3	117.0	117.3	116.5	114.9
Retail Trade													
2000	325.0	319.2	321.3	323.5	326.2	328.5	328.3	330.5	331.6	338.2	349.1	353.2	331.2
2001	326.4	317.7	318.8	319.6	322.4	323.6	320.4	323.0	319.6	323.1	333.6	336.3	323.7
2002	317.1	309.9	311.3	310.5	314.5	317.6	315.8	317.4	315.0	319.8	331.5	336.4	318.1
2003	314.2	308.0	307.2	310.7	315.6	318.3	315.9	318.3	316.7	321.2	330.6	336.6	317.8
2004	313.8	307.3	308.1	310.4	315.6	319.7	317.9	318.5	316.1	318.9	329.1	333.4	317.4
2005	311.7	306.2	307.4	310.2	314.0	315.4	315.7	317.7	315.1	321.9	331.5	336.1	316.9
2006	310.4	303.9	305.5	307.6	311.4	314.4	312.5	314.0	311.2	315.5	328.0	331.4	313.8
2007	313.5	305.6	307.6	307.9	314.0	316.1	315.7	315.0	311.9	314.9	325.6	327.4	314.6
2008	310.3	302.5	303.8	305.9	309.9	312.0	311.2	312.0	307.9	310.7	316.8	319.1	310.2
2009	299.4	292.4	291.4	292.5	296.9	299.8	297.8	298.4	294.7	298.5	305.4	307.1	297.9
2010	290.3	283.9	285.3	287.3	291.7	294.5	293.3	294.8	291.6	297.4	304.7	307.0	293.5
2011	290.6	284.6	286.0	289.5	292.2	295.0	296.0	297.2	291.4	293.4	300.5	306.4	293.6
Transportation and Utilities													
2000	102.3	102.4	103.2	105.2	106.5	105.0	103.4	104.1	107.8	110.1	109.2	108.5	105.6
2001	107.4	107.1	107.4	109.1	110.4	108.7	105.9	106.4	109.2	109.6	108.8	107.6	108.1
2002	102.7	102.1	102.9	104.5	106.5	105.1	101.6	101.9	106.0	107.4	107.2	105.9	104.5
2003	102.8	102.8	103.3	105.2	107.0	107.4	103.3	103.2	107.8	108.8	108.0	107.2	105.6
2004	103.4	103.4	104.2	105.9	107.9	108.4	105.4	105.1	108.9	111.1	110.5	109.6	107.0
2005	105.3	105.8	106.7	108.3	109.5	109.1	106.6	106.6	110.6	110.9	110.8	110.9	108.4
2006	107.1	107.6	108.4	109.3	110.9	111.0	107.6	107.8	112.0	112.5	112.0	112.5	109.9
2007	107.8	108.2	108.7	109.3	111.5	112.1	107.5	108.7	112.3	112.9	112.8	112.7	110.4
2008	108.5	108.5	108.5	108.7	110.1	110.0	106.2	106.5	109.4	109.7	108.9	108.5	108.6
2009	103.6	103.0	102.8	104.2	105.9	106.3	101.8	102.0	105.5	105.5	104.5	104.4	104.1
2010	100.4	100.5	100.8	102.4	103.2	103.6	100.0	99.7	103.2	104.0	103.5	103.6	102.1
2011	99.7	99.4	99.7	100.7	101.8	101.0	96.9	97.6	100.4	101.4	100.5	100.6	100.0
Information													
2000	52.5	52.4	52.5	52.6	52.9	53.4	53.8	53.9	53.8	54.6	55.6	55.6	53.6
2001	53.8	53.6	53.8	54.0	53.4	53.7	53.3	53.1	52.6	52.5	52.8	52.5	53.3
2002	51.8	51.3	51.2	51.1	51.0	51.1	51.1	51.2	50.6	50.8	51.2	51.4	51.2
2003	50.7	50.1	50.1	49.9	49.9	50.2	50.2	50.4	50.4	50.3	50.8	51.0	50.3
2004	50.2	49.8	49.9	49.6	49.6	49.7	50.2	50.3	49.7	49.6	50.0	50.1	49.9
2005	49.6	49.4	49.3	49.6	49.7	50.1	49.8	50.0	49.6	49.6	50.0	50.1	49.7
2006	49.6	49.3	49.1	48.9	48.9	49.1	49.2	49.4	48.9	49.3	49.8	50.0	49.3
2007	49.8	49.5	49.4	49.7	49.9	50.4	50.6	50.8	50.3	50.6	50.8	50.9	50.2
2008	50.3	50.0	49.9	50.1	50.9	50.7	50.5	50.5	49.8	49.7	49.9	49.9	50.2
2009	49.1	48.9	48.3	48.0	48.1	48.1	48.1	48.0	47.4	46.9	47.4	47.6	48.0
2010	46.6	46.2	46.1	45.9	46.1	46.7	47.1	47.2	46.8	46.5	47.4	47.4	46.7
2011	46.9	46.6	46.4	46.5	46.5	46.4	46.6	46.2	46.0	46.2	46.6	46.0	46.4

1. Employment by Industry: Wisconsin, Selected Years, 2000–2011—*Continued*

(Numbers in thousands, not seasonally adjusted)

Industry and year	January	February	March	April	May	June	July	August	September	October	November	December	Annual average
Financial Activities													
2000	146.7	146.6	146.8	148.1	148.6	150.6	151.0	150.8	149.8	149.7	150.0	150.9	149.1
2001	150.0	150.0	151.0	150.6	151.5	153.4	153.8	153.6	152.2	151.4	151.7	151.8	151.8
2002	151.4	151.7	151.7	152.4	153.1	154.8	155.6	156.0	154.5	154.2	154.8	155.5	153.8
2003	154.3	154.9	155.0	155.9	157.1	158.7	158.7	158.8	157.2	156.9	156.9	157.8	156.9
2004	156.7	156.5	156.7	157.7	158.3	159.9	160.8	161.0	158.9	159.1	159.1	160.4	158.8
2005	158.3	157.7	158.1	158.8	159.3	161.0	161.8	161.8	160.4	159.9	159.9	161.0	159.8
2006	159.5	159.2	159.2	160.6	161.7	163.2	164.2	163.9	162.6	162.3	162.3	163.3	161.8
2007	162.1	161.9	161.5	162.3	162.7	164.6	164.5	164.0	162.3	163.5	164.3	164.3	163.1
2008	163.1	163.4	163.0	163.8	164.9	165.7	166.4	166.0	163.5	163.0	162.8	163.3	164.1
2009	162.1	161.5	160.8	161.6	161.9	162.7	162.6	162.4	159.9	159.7	159.4	159.7	161.2
2010	157.9	157.6	157.8	157.9	158.4	159.6	160.1	160.0	158.6	158.8	158.8	159.7	158.8
2011	158.1	157.9	158.3	158.6	158.9	159.8	158.6	158.8	157.7	157.4	156.4	156.1	158.1
Professional and Business Services													
2000	236.5	238.7	242.0	245.5	248.8	252.4	250.0	253.0	252.1	250.4	249.4	245.0	247.0
2001	235.3	235.4	235.1	239.0	240.5	242.4	242.3	244.1	240.2	238.5	235.7	233.1	238.5
2002	228.8	229.5	233.1	239.8	241.5	244.2	245.1	247.1	244.6	244.5	240.8	238.7	239.8
2003	234.9	236.4	238.3	243.1	243.6	245.9	247.6	248.8	249.3	249.5	247.3	247.1	244.3
2004	240.0	241.0	243.3	249.5	250.8	256.3	258.4	262.6	258.7	260.7	257.8	257.2	253.0
2005	249.6	251.6	254.7	262.3	261.4	265.3	268.5	271.2	270.2	267.7	267.1	267.5	263.1
2006	257.2	260.2	261.6	270.1	270.7	275.4	275.1	277.5	276.6	276.9	275.4	273.6	270.9
2007	265.5	267.2	269.2	275.8	278.1	284.0	283.8	286.8	284.1	284.0	283.6	284.5	278.9
2008	274.4	276.8	276.0	280.6	282.4	285.9	286.6	289.7	286.5	283.6	278.5	276.0	281.4
2009	260.0	255.6	252.7	255.1	255.8	257.5	258.6	260.3	258.7	262.1	262.6	262.9	258.5
2010	253.2	256.6	257.0	266.3	268.1	271.9	276.1	280.3	278.7	282.8	283.1	283.3	271.5
2011	274.4	274.7	277.6	281.2	282.5	288.7	288.8	289.8	286.1	287.6	284.2	277.7	282.8
Education and Health Services													
2000	331.2	334.3	336.6	338.8	338.0	340.2	339.7	340.7	341.3	342.6	345.2	346.3	339.6
2001	341.9	347.6	349.0	349.5	349.3	349.0	347.9	347.9	350.0	352.6	355.2	355.3	349.6
2002	350.3	352.3	353.0	355.5	355.9	358.4	356.1	357.4	357.5	360.2	362.7	362.1	356.8
2003	358.8	360.6	360.8	362.7	362.6	358.1	358.8	359.0	366.3	370.1	370.1	369.5	363.1
2004	366.5	369.1	369.7	372.4	371.9	372.6	372.2	372.0	372.7	374.7	376.6	377.0	372.3
2005	373.9	375.8	376.9	379.2	378.8	380.3	378.7	379.0	381.1	382.3	384.4	384.4	379.6
2006	381.5	383.9	384.2	385.3	386.4	387.4	386.3	386.7	388.5	390.8	392.3	392.1	387.1
2007	387.6	389.8	390.7	391.2	392.7	393.5	392.3	393.5	394.7	394.5	395.2	396.2	392.7
2008	392.3	394.3	395.7	396.5	398.1	398.5	397.8	399.5	400.8	405.3	406.5	408.4	399.5
2009	403.7	405.7	407.4	405.9	406.3	406.1	404.4	405.0	405.2	408.9	409.0	409.3	406.4
2010	405.4	407.5	409.3	406.5	407.1	406.1	405.5	406.0	406.2	409.5	410.5	411.0	407.6
2011	405.2	407.5	408.4	409.9	410.6	409.2	407.8	409.2	413.1	415.9	416.6	415.5	410.7
Leisure and Hospitality													
2000	215.5	216.9	221.6	230.1	242.4	254.8	259.6	261.3	248.3	235.9	228.0	226.4	236.7
2001	219.4	220.1	223.0	233.9	246.7	257.7	263.0	262.4	247.8	236.8	227.6	224.7	238.6
2002	221.0	220.7	222.5	231.4	245.8	256.9	264.2	265.0	251.9	241.7	232.0	232.1	240.4
2003	225.6	224.0	226.6	235.8	252.2	262.6	267.5	268.2	257.5	248.3	239.5	237.9	245.5
2004	230.3	229.4	232.6	242.7	256.2	265.9	275.0	275.6	263.4	252.9	243.4	242.6	250.8
2005	233.8	233.9	237.7	250.3	261.5	271.9	278.0	278.8	267.7	255.2	247.7	245.6	255.2
2006	239.0	239.6	243.4	252.6	264.4	276.5	282.1	283.1	271.0	260.6	251.4	250.2	259.5
2007	242.9	242.8	246.0	254.2	268.6	281.0	284.1	286.1	271.4	261.9	253.6	251.0	262.0
2008	242.2	241.1	244.2	252.7	268.3	277.9	281.2	282.2	268.7	259.6	249.2	246.1	259.5
2009	235.1	235.6	237.9	246.3	262.0	271.9	274.0	274.3	262.2	251.5	241.5	239.6	252.7
2010	230.8	230.7	233.6	245.4	258.1	268.8	273.1	275.4	262.8	253.0	244.1	241.2	251.4
2011	232.7	232.4	235.0	244.7	258.0	269.4	274.0	270.9	255.1	248.5	239.0	232.9	249.4
Other Services													
2000	124.2	125.5	126.1	126.1	126.0	127.5	126.4	125.9	126.4	126.7	126.5	127.9	126.3
2001	129.3	129.6	131.1	130.3	130.6	132.7	132.0	132.2	131.8	131.6	131.3	133.1	131.3
2002	131.0	131.0	132.2	131.9	132.0	134.1	132.6	132.6	132.0	132.2	132.0	133.3	132.2
2003	131.5	131.6	132.7	132.4	132.5	134.6	133.5	133.4	132.9	132.1	131.7	133.0	132.7
2004	132.6	133.1	134.4	134.4	134.7	137.1	136.1	136.4	136.0	137.2	135.4	135.8	135.3
2005	133.9	134.5	135.6	136.0	136.2	137.8	137.0	137.0	136.6	136.1	135.4	136.4	136.0
2006	133.9	134.0	135.2	135.4	136.0	138.0	137.1	136.9	136.7	136.4	135.9	137.0	136.0
2007	135.1	135.5	136.5	137.3	138.0	139.7	139.0	138.3	137.5	138.3	137.8	138.4	137.6
2008	135.9	136.4	137.3	138.4	139.2	140.9	140.3	140.0	139.3	141.2	139.7	139.9	139.0
2009	136.7	137.0	138.1	138.2	138.6	140.1	139.1	138.7	137.6	137.6	137.2	137.7	138.1
2010	134.5	135.0	136.0	137.1	137.3	138.6	138.3	138.0	137.0	137.8	136.7	137.2	137.0
2011	135.1	135.1	136.1	136.7	137.4	138.7	136.3	135.7	135.9	135.1	133.8	133.7	135.8
Government													
2000	399.6	408.8	412.1	418.7	417.4	413.3	381.1	378.4	397.7	410.0	417.7	412.1	405.6
2001	402.3	417.7	421.0	425.1	424.5	416.1	387.4	384.0	411.6	424.0	426.6	424.3	413.7
2002	408.6	421.5	426.2	428.2	426.1	413.3	383.7	380.1	404.0	426.7	432.8	426.2	414.8
2003	404.3	424.9	426.2	428.9	425.0	420.3	383.0	379.9	399.2	420.4	422.3	420.2	412.9
2004	403.2	420.3	422.0	422.7	422.2	414.6	384.6	381.8	406.0	420.7	426.2	421.5	412.2
2005	410.9	424.6	423.8	427.2	426.0	414.3	385.7	381.5	414.3	423.1	425.4	427.0	415.3
2006	410.1	419.7	424.6	427.5	426.0	418.6	387.3	383.3	413.9	421.4	424.9	425.5	415.2
2007	410.2	416.8	422.5	427.0	427.1	422.1	388.3	384.8	414.0	423.8	426.3	428.8	416.0
2008	416.7	422.2	427.2	429.6	432.5	422.2	392.4	387.0	423.0	432.5	441.4	436.3	421.9
2009	418.6	431.3	432.7	434.9	435.7	421.8	392.4	385.1	408.5	426.1	431.2	431.8	420.8
2010	415.3	425.1	427.5	435.5	437.5	421.4	390.0	384.3	411.1	428.8	433.9	426.5	419.7
2011	412.1	426.6	428.1	432.3	429.8	408.3	383.8	375.4	404.8	419.1	419.3	415.3	412.9

2. Average Weekly Hours by Selected Industry: Wisconsin, 2007–2011

(Not seasonally adjusted)

Industry and year	January	February	March	April	May	June	July	August	September	October	November	December	Annual average
Total Private													
2007	32.2	32.1	32.5	32.6	32.6	33.1	33.4	33.2	33.4	33.0	33.1	33.4	32.9
2008	32.8	32.7	33.1	32.8	33.0	33.3	33.1	33.4	33.0	32.8	33.1	32.4	33.0
2009	31.8	32.2	31.9	31.6	31.8	32.0	32.4	32.8	32.2	32.4	33.2	32.3	32.2
2010	32.4	32.4	32.5	32.6	32.9	32.8	32.9	33.4	32.8	33.0	32.9	32.6	32.8
2011	32.9	32.4	32.8	32.9	33.3	33.1	33.2	33.3	33.3	33.7	33.2	33.3	33.1
Goods-Producing													
2007	37.7	37.5	37.7	38.0	38.7	38.7	38.8	38.8	39.0	38.8	38.5	39.0	38.4
2008	38.3	38.0	38.3	37.9	38.4	38.2	38.3	38.7	39.1	38.6	38.7	38.0	38.4
2009	36.8	37.3	36.9	37.0	37.6	37.7	37.8	38.0	37.6	38.6	39.4	38.3	37.7
2010	38.4	38.2	38.5	38.6	38.6	39.0	38.9	39.2	38.8	39.4	39.4	38.8	38.8
2011	38.8	38.4	39.1	39.3	39.6	39.8	39.6	40.1	40.7	40.3	40.0	40.2	39.7
Construction													
2007	35.9	35.0	36.6	36.9	39.3	39.8	39.9	39.2	38.6	39.5	38.7	38.4	38.3
2008	35.9	36.1	36.6	35.7	38.6	38.2	38.7	40.1	39.5	39.0	38.9	35.8	37.9
2009	34.4	35.6	34.7	36.2	37.6	36.7	38.2	38.3	37.8	38.0	38.4	35.0	36.8
2010	37.5	37.2	37.1	37.9	36.7	37.4	38.2	38.2	38.0	39.4	38.3	35.3	37.7
2011	35.7	34.8	35.5	36.8	37.9	38.0	38.3	38.1	38.1	37.6	35.6	36.6	37.0
Manufacturing													
2007	38.1	38.1	38.0	38.2	38.4	38.3	38.4	38.6	39.0	38.4	38.3	39.0	38.4
2008	38.8	38.4	38.7	38.5	38.3	38.1	38.1	38.2	38.9	38.4	38.5	38.4	38.4
2009	37.3	37.2	36.8	36.6	37.0	37.5	37.3	37.6	37.2	38.2	38.8	38.8	37.5
2010	38.3	38.2	38.7	38.6	38.9	39.3	38.9	39.6	39.1	39.5	39.8	39.7	39.1
2011	39.6	39.2	39.9	39.8	39.9	40.2	39.5	40.3	40.8	40.4	40.6	40.5	40.1
Trade, Transportation, and Utilities													
2007	32.6	33.1	33.4	33.3	33.5	34.6	34.8	34.5	34.5	34.1	34.0	34.4	33.9
2008	32.9	32.9	33.3	33.3	33.3	33.9	33.6	33.6	33.2	33.2	33.2	32.8	33.3
2009	31.6	32.4	32.3	31.7	31.9	32.5	32.7	33.1	32.5	32.7	33.8	32.6	32.5
2010	31.9	32.1	32.7	32.7	33.0	32.7	33.1	33.8	33.1	33.5	32.8	32.6	32.8
2011	32.0	31.6	31.9	32.1	32.6	32.7	32.6	32.5	32.7	32.7	32.5	32.6	32.4
Financial Activities													
2007	36.8	35.0	35.2	35.9	34.8	35.1	35.8	35.3	36.2	35.4	35.7	36.2	35.6
2008	36.0	35.6	36.3	35.2	35.2	36.5	35.6	35.8	35.6	35.6	37.5	35.5	35.9
2009	36.6	37.3	36.8	35.9	35.7	35.8	35.6	37.5	35.5	35.9	37.0	36.0	36.3
2010	36.8	36.0	35.9	36.2	37.3	36.7	36.9	38.0	36.3	36.5	36.2	36.4	36.6
2011	36.8	34.8	34.8	35.3	36.8	35.2	35.8	35.6	36.0	37.1	35.8	35.6	35.8
Professional and Business Services													
2007	33.3	33.6	34.6	34.3	33.8	34.2	33.7	34.1	34.7	34.3	34.5	34.1	34.1
2008	34.3	34.7	35.0	34.5	35.1	35.5	34.0	34.8	34.2	33.4	33.5	32.1	34.3
2009	31.9	32.2	32.1	31.7	31.6	31.5	31.0	32.3	31.0	31.9	32.5	31.6	31.8
2010	31.9	33.0	32.5	32.8	33.2	33.1	33.1	33.5	33.4	33.1	33.3	33.4	33.0
2011	34.2	33.2	33.3	33.6	34.2	33.6	33.2	33.5	33.2	34.1	33.4	33.0	33.5
Education and Health Services													
2007	28.9	28.6	28.8	29.3	29.0	29.6	30.2	30.4	30.7	30.3	30.5	30.6	29.7
2008	31.0	30.3	30.6	30.7	30.9	31.2	31.1	31.3	30.6	30.9	31.5	30.8	30.9
2009	31.0	31.3	31.1	30.9	31.3	31.3	31.3	31.6	31.4	31.1	31.6	31.0	31.2
2010	31.0	31.0	30.9	31.1	31.2	31.2	31.0	31.4	31.2	30.9	30.7	30.6	31.0
2011	30.9	30.7	30.5	30.6	30.8	30.9	31.2	31.0	31.1	31.8	31.5	31.9	31.1
Leisure and Hospitality													
2007	20.7	20.9	21.2	21.0	21.0	22.4	23.3	22.4	21.9	21.1	21.3	20.9	21.5
2008	20.7	21.0	21.1	21.7	21.8	22.4	22.9	23.5	22.2	21.2	21.5	21.5	21.8
2009	20.4	21.2	20.6	20.1	20.4	20.8	22.6	22.8	21.4	20.6	21.1	20.8	21.1
2010	20.8	21.5	21.4	21.7	22.1	22.0	22.8	23.0	21.9	22.1	21.4	21.4	21.9
2011	21.3	22.0	22.1	22.2	22.6	23.7	24.6	23.6	22.7	22.8	22.0	21.9	22.7
Other Services													
2007	25.7	25.6	26.0	25.9	27.1	26.8	27.2	26.7	26.7	26.0	26.4	26.3	26.4
2008	25.8	26.0	27.0	26.6	26.8	27.6	27.6	28.0	27.3	27.0	26.9	26.6	26.9
2009	26.1	26.0	26.2	25.9	25.3	25.7	27.0	26.6	25.0	25.5	26.2	25.3	25.9
2010	26.0	25.7	25.8	25.6	26.0	25.8	27.1	27.5	25.9	25.7	26.0	25.3	26.0
2011	26.7	26.2	27.4	26.9	27.5	26.6	27.6	28.6	26.7	28.3	27.7	27.6	27.3

3. Average Hourly Earnings by Selected Industry: Wisconsin, 2007–2011

(Dollars, not seasonally adjusted)

Industry and year	January	February	March	April	May	June	July	August	September	October	November	December	Annual average
Total Private													
2007	20.27	20.44	20.56	20.99	20.44	20.23	20.25	20.03	20.62	20.59	20.44	20.61	20.45
2008	20.64	20.76	20.86	20.58	20.50	20.46	20.61	20.53	20.84	20.60	20.80	20.94	20.67
2009	21.04	21.37	21.23	21.17	20.99	20.90	21.03	20.95	20.96	21.23	21.17	21.48	21.13
2010	21.37	21.39	21.26	21.38	21.38	21.06	21.23	21.06	21.30	21.53	21.48	21.79	21.35
2011	21.98	22.05	21.78	21.94	21.92	21.50	21.76	21.61	21.75	22.07	21.86	21.94	21.84
Goods-Producing													
2007	23.18	22.95	23.17	22.94	22.89	22.87	22.88	22.61	22.73	22.87	22.68	22.85	22.88
2008	22.16	22.52	22.43	22.40	22.80	23.09	22.83	22.93	23.13	23.00	23.02	22.95	22.78
2009	22.99	23.34	23.20	22.97	23.07	22.83	22.89	22.60	22.82	22.78	22.86	23.08	22.95
2010	23.13	22.62	22.77	22.83	23.04	22.66	22.73	22.64	22.99	23.03	22.65	23.16	22.85
2011	23.04	23.06	22.69	22.96	22.86	22.49	22.89	22.46	22.58	22.78	22.53	22.57	22.74
Construction													
2007	31.74	31.45	30.65	30.55	29.73	29.71	29.54	28.98	29.30	28.71	28.20	28.26	29.64
2008	27.41	27.74	27.53	27.14	27.81	27.64	27.96	28.00	28.75	28.31	27.86	28.04	27.87
2009	27.63	28.33	28.34	28.37	28.50	28.19	28.25	28.21	27.81	28.61	27.92	28.86	28.25
2010	28.36	27.65	27.86	27.80	27.51	27.43	27.37	27.83	27.92	27.89	27.60	28.55	27.80
2011	28.50	29.11	29.01	28.44	27.73	27.27	27.91	27.55	27.79	27.90	27.47	28.21	28.01
Manufacturing													
2007	21.04	20.96	21.33	21.00	20.98	20.88	20.92	20.74	20.80	21.12	21.07	21.40	21.02
2008	20.91	21.29	21.21	21.21	21.25	21.68	21.16	21.18	21.29	21.25	21.49	21.59	21.29
2009	21.78	22.05	21.85	21.52	21.49	21.28	21.28	20.92	21.38	21.08	21.45	21.78	21.49
2010	21.97	21.44	21.55	21.49	21.71	21.23	21.32	21.13	21.59	21.60	21.35	22.05	21.53
2011	21.96	21.93	21.53	21.78	21.68	21.29	21.63	21.23	21.31	21.55	21.43	21.39	21.55
Trade, Transportation, and Utilities													
2007	18.75	18.44	19.03	20.59	18.86	18.89	18.45	18.53	18.85	18.77	18.15	17.46	18.72
2008	18.80	18.84	19.55	18.94	18.37	18.33	19.50	18.84	18.87	18.21	18.31	18.63	18.76
2009	19.00	18.81	18.93	18.97	18.77	18.63	18.51	18.55	18.45	18.39	18.26	18.59	18.65
2010	18.79	18.64	18.46	18.73	18.51	18.36	18.55	18.12	18.29	18.88	18.26	18.58	18.51
2011	19.36	19.11	18.90	19.20	19.05	18.75	19.17	19.07	19.17	19.76	19.22	19.06	19.15
Financial Activities													
2007	21.37	23.25	22.10	22.95	22.69	22.40	22.79	22.60	23.25	23.31	23.15	24.37	22.85
2008	23.72	24.91	24.52	24.52	24.93	23.95	23.51	24.72	24.63	24.63	24.48	24.43	24.41
2009	24.02	26.44	25.21	24.62	24.72	25.21	25.75	26.75	25.55	26.01	25.99	26.17	25.54
2010	25.16	27.00	26.23	25.89	26.26	25.46	25.37	25.99	26.07	25.96	26.39	26.38	26.01
2011	26.23	27.96	27.64	27.30	27.35	27.40	27.73	27.93	27.67	28.52	28.38	28.65	27.73
Professional and Business Services													
2007	24.01	24.16	25.07	24.93	24.29	23.79	23.71	22.42	24.43	23.54	23.78	23.98	24.00
2008	23.26	23.08	23.13	22.71	22.52	23.02	22.51	22.29	22.76	22.73	23.20	23.57	22.89
2009	23.62	24.45	24.64	24.25	24.36	24.10	23.54	23.06	23.69	24.01	24.43	25.82	24.17
2010	25.22	24.70	24.57	25.26	25.06	24.34	24.67	24.58	24.86	25.14	25.30	26.05	24.98
2011	26.31	26.16	26.02	26.04	26.07	25.82	26.01	25.55	25.97	26.05	26.01	26.64	26.05
Education and Health Services													
2007	19.08	19.32	19.33	19.49	19.45	19.11	19.85	19.31	19.90	19.69	19.78	20.00	19.53
2008	20.27	19.93	20.14	19.89	19.62	19.59	19.91	19.79	20.24	20.03	20.53	20.63	20.05
2009	20.59	20.67	20.67	21.29	20.81	21.24	21.67	21.65	21.40	21.88	21.54	21.66	21.26
2010	21.40	21.73	21.62	21.81	21.76	21.69	21.99	21.54	21.48	21.65	22.02	22.01	21.72
2011	21.95	22.27	22.03	22.27	22.40	22.30	22.63	22.57	22.38	22.55	22.48	22.63	22.37
Leisure and Hospitality													
2007	11.52	10.94	11.19	11.19	11.10	10.85	11.00	10.96	11.23	11.33	11.25	11.65	11.17
2008	11.65	11.44	11.34	11.24	11.26	10.98	11.22	11.63	11.76	11.28	11.51	11.44	11.39
2009	11.36	11.37	11.66	11.60	11.52	11.18	11.27	11.16	11.32	11.82	11.82	11.85	11.48
2010	11.95	11.75	11.72	11.56	11.62	11.36	11.42	11.25	11.54	11.72	12.14	12.28	11.67
2011	12.02	12.07	11.94	11.95	11.96	11.70	11.61	11.58	11.82	11.80	11.92	11.94	11.85
Other Services													
2007	16.90	17.06	17.00	17.55	17.36	17.58	17.57	17.73	17.78	17.52	17.51	17.70	17.44
2008	17.96	17.97	17.88	17.62	17.59	17.49	17.40	17.06	17.88	17.47	17.63	17.73	17.63
2009	17.52	17.57	17.45	17.60	17.56	17.10	16.68	17.09	17.60	17.46	17.60	17.90	17.42
2010	17.75	17.80	17.74	17.89	18.08	18.15	17.62	17.77	18.29	18.30	18.35	19.19	18.07
2011	18.95	18.66	18.68	18.53	18.55	18.25	18.41	18.23	18.51	18.42	18.59	19.06	18.57

4. Average Weekly Earnings by Selected Industry: Wisconsin, 2007–2011

(Dollars, not seasonally adjusted)

Industry and year	January	February	March	April	May	June	July	August	September	October	November	December	Annual average
Total Private													
2007	652.69	656.12	668.20	684.27	666.34	669.61	676.35	665.00	688.71	679.47	676.56	688.37	672.79
2008	676.99	678.85	690.47	675.02	676.50	681.32	682.19	685.70	687.72	675.68	688.48	678.46	681.68
2009	669.07	688.11	677.24	668.97	667.48	668.80	681.37	687.16	674.91	687.85	702.84	693.80	680.51
2010	692.39	693.04	690.95	696.99	703.40	690.77	698.47	703.40	698.64	710.49	706.69	710.35	699.62
2011	723.14	714.42	714.38	721.83	729.94	711.65	722.43	719.61	724.28	743.76	725.75	730.60	723.74
Goods-Producing													
2007	873.89	860.63	873.51	871.72	885.84	885.07	887.74	877.27	886.47	887.36	873.18	891.15	879.61
2008	848.73	855.76	859.07	848.96	875.52	882.04	874.39	887.39	904.38	887.80	890.87	872.10	874.09
2009	846.03	870.58	856.08	849.89	867.43	860.69	865.24	858.80	858.03	879.31	900.68	883.96	866.29
2010	888.19	864.08	876.65	881.24	889.34	883.74	884.20	887.49	892.01	907.38	892.41	898.61	887.31
2011	893.95	885.50	887.18	902.33	905.26	895.10	906.44	900.65	919.01	918.03	901.20	907.31	901.96
Construction													
2007	1,139.47	1,100.75	1,121.79	1,127.30	1,168.39	1,182.46	1,178.65	1,136.02	1,130.98	1,134.05	1,091.34	1,085.18	1,134.28
2008	984.02	1,001.41	1,007.60	968.90	1,073.47	1,055.85	1,082.05	1,122.80	1,135.63	1,104.09	1,083.75	1,003.83	1,055.38
2009	950.47	1,008.55	983.40	1,026.99	1,071.60	1,034.57	1,079.15	1,080.44	1,051.22	1,087.18	1,072.13	1,010.10	1,040.60
2010	1,063.50	1,028.58	1,033.61	1,053.62	1,009.62	1,025.88	1,045.53	1,063.11	1,060.96	1,098.87	1,057.08	1,007.82	1,046.63
2011	1,017.45	1,013.03	1,029.86	1,046.59	1,050.97	1,036.26	1,068.95	1,049.66	1,058.80	1,049.04	977.93	1,032.49	1,036.97
Manufacturing													
2007	801.62	798.58	810.54	802.20	805.63	799.70	803.33	800.56	811.20	811.01	806.98	834.60	807.14
2008	811.31	817.54	820.83	816.59	813.88	826.01	806.20	809.08	828.18	816.00	827.37	829.06	818.44
2009	812.39	820.26	804.08	787.63	795.13	798.00	793.74	786.59	795.34	805.26	832.26	845.06	806.31
2010	841.45	819.01	833.99	829.51	844.52	834.34	829.35	836.75	844.17	853.20	849.73	875.39	841.02
2011	869.62	859.66	859.05	866.84	865.03	855.86	854.39	855.57	869.45	870.62	870.06	866.30	863.50
Trade, Transportation, and Utilities													
2007	611.25	610.36	635.60	685.65	631.81	653.59	642.06	639.29	650.33	640.06	617.10	600.62	634.71
2008	618.52	619.84	651.02	630.70	611.72	621.39	655.20	633.02	626.48	604.57	607.89	611.06	624.22
2009	600.40	609.44	611.44	601.35	598.76	605.48	605.28	614.01	599.63	601.35	617.19	606.03	605.91
2010	599.40	598.34	603.64	612.47	610.83	600.37	614.01	612.46	605.40	632.48	598.93	605.71	607.88
2011	619.52	603.88	602.91	616.32	621.03	613.13	624.94	619.78	626.86	646.15	624.65	621.36	620.13
Financial Activities													
2007	786.42	813.75	777.92	823.91	789.61	786.24	815.88	797.78	841.65	825.17	826.46	882.19	813.97
2008	853.92	886.80	890.08	863.10	877.54	874.18	836.96	884.98	876.83	876.83	918.00	867.27	875.48
2009	879.13	986.21	927.73	883.86	882.50	902.52	916.70	1,003.13	907.03	933.76	961.63	942.12	927.08
2010	925.89	972.00	941.66	937.22	979.50	934.38	936.15	987.62	946.34	947.54	955.32	960.23	951.98
2011	965.26	973.01	961.87	963.69	1,006.48	964.48	992.73	994.31	996.12	1,058.09	1,016.00	1,019.94	992.51
Professional and Business Services													
2007	799.53	811.78	867.42	855.10	821.00	813.62	799.03	764.52	847.72	807.42	820.41	817.72	818.56
2008	797.82	800.88	809.55	783.50	790.45	817.21	765.34	775.69	778.39	759.18	777.20	756.60	784.25
2009	753.48	787.29	790.94	768.73	769.78	759.15	729.74	744.84	734.39	765.92	793.98	815.91	767.78
2010	804.52	815.10	798.53	828.53	831.99	805.65	816.58	823.43	830.32	832.13	842.49	870.07	825.44
2011	899.80	868.51	866.47	874.94	891.59	867.55	863.53	855.93	862.20	888.31	868.73	879.12	873.83
Education and Health Services													
2007	551.41	552.55	556.70	571.06	564.05	565.66	599.47	587.02	610.93	596.61	603.29	612.00	581.03
2008	628.37	603.88	616.28	610.62	606.26	611.21	619.20	619.43	619.34	618.93	646.70	635.40	619.69
2009	638.29	646.97	642.84	657.86	651.35	664.81	678.27	684.14	671.96	680.47	680.66	671.46	664.11
2010	663.40	673.63	668.06	678.29	678.91	676.73	681.69	676.36	670.18	668.99	676.01	673.51	673.79
2011	678.26	683.69	671.92	681.46	689.92	689.07	706.06	699.67	696.02	717.09	708.12	721.90	695.38
Leisure and Hospitality													
2007	238.46	228.65	237.23	234.99	233.10	243.04	256.30	245.50	245.94	239.06	239.63	243.49	240.72
2008	241.16	240.24	239.27	243.91	245.47	245.95	256.94	273.31	261.07	239.14	247.47	245.96	248.73
2009	231.74	241.04	240.20	233.16	235.01	232.54	254.70	254.45	242.25	243.49	249.40	246.48	242.15
2010	248.56	252.63	250.81	250.85	256.80	249.92	260.38	258.75	252.73	259.01	259.80	262.79	255.32
2011	256.03	265.54	263.87	265.29	270.30	277.29	285.61	273.29	268.31	269.04	262.24	261.49	268.58
Other Services													
2007	434.33	436.74	442.00	454.55	470.46	471.14	477.90	473.39	474.73	455.52	462.26	465.51	460.00
2008	463.37	467.22	482.76	468.69	471.41	482.72	480.24	477.68	488.12	471.69	474.25	471.62	475.02
2009	457.27	456.82	457.19	455.84	444.27	439.47	450.36	454.59	440.00	445.23	461.12	452.87	451.18
2010	461.50	457.46	457.69	457.98	470.08	468.27	477.50	488.68	473.71	470.31	477.10	485.51	470.56
2011	505.97	488.89	511.83	498.46	510.13	485.45	508.12	521.38	494.22	521.29	514.94	526.06	507.14

WYOMING
At a Glance

Population:
   2000 census: 493,786
   2010 census: 563,626
   2011 estimate: 568,158

Percent change in population:
   2000–2010: 14.1%
   2010–2011: 0.8%

Percent change in total nonfarm employment:
   2000–2010: 18.2%
   2010–2011: 1.0%

Industry with the largest growth in employment, 2000–2011 (thousands):
   Education and Health Services, 12.5

Industry with the largest decline or smallest growth in employment, 2000–2011 (thousands):
   Manufacturing, -1.4

Civilian labor force:
   2000: 266,882
   2010: 303,215
   2011: 304,242

Unemployment rate and rank among states (lowest to highest):
   2000: 3.8%, 25th
   2010: 7.0%, 11th
   2011: 6.0%, 7th

Over-the-year change in unemployment rates:
   2010–2011: -1.0%

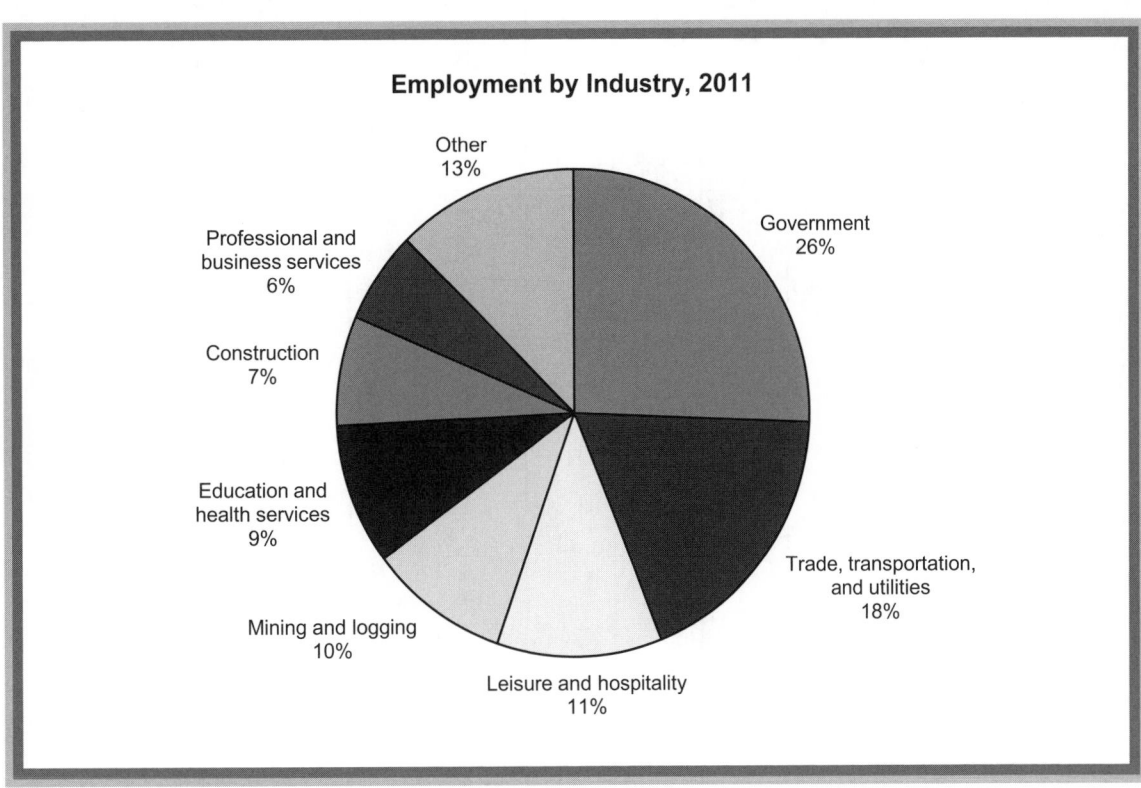

Employment by Industry, 2011

Other 13%
Government 26%
Professional and business services 6%
Construction 7%
Education and health services 9%
Mining and logging 10%
Leisure and hospitality 11%
Trade, transportation, and utilities 18%

1. Employment by Industry: Wyoming, Selected Years, 2000–2011

(Numbers in thousands, not seasonally adjusted)

Industry and year	January	February	March	April	May	June	July	August	September	October	November	December	Annual average
Total Nonfarm													
2000	227.8	228.5	232.2	234.1	241.7	248.8	246.4	247.1	245.0	242.9	238.2	239.3	239.3
2001	233.1	233.5	236.8	239.4	247.2	256.6	252.8	254.5	251.4	248.8	245.5	245.3	245.4
2002	237.9	237.7	240.2	242.4	250.2	258.2	255.7	255.4	254.2	250.5	246.5	246.1	247.9
2003	238.9	238.4	240.0	243.2	250.8	260.3	257.5	258.7	257.2	255.0	249.9	250.4	250.0
2004	243.9	244.3	246.9	250.8	256.4	266.0	263.2	262.8	260.1	258.4	255.4	256.0	255.0
2005	249.6	250.7	254.0	257.1	264.0	273.5	271.6	272.2	271.5	269.4	266.0	267.4	263.9
2006	262.4	264.3	267.5	269.8	277.8	288.7	284.3	284.6	284.7	281.9	279.3	281.9	277.3
2007	275.1	276.9	280.3	280.6	289.3	299.0	295.4	295.8	295.9	293.7	291.6	292.4	288.8
2008	286.1	287.9	289.7	290.4	299.1	308.1	305.8	305.3	306.4	304.0	298.5	297.1	298.2
2009	286.8	285.0	284.9	283.0	290.3	294.5	289.6	288.3	290.3	284.6	279.8	279.2	286.4
2010	271.1	272.2	274.4	277.2	284.9	292.2	288.2	289.5	291.6	288.8	282.5	282.7	282.9
2011	273.9	275.6	278.0	279.3	287.4	295.8	294.7	292.9	292.7	288.6	284.7	284.6	285.7
Total Private													
2000	167.7	167.9	169.9	172.1	178.1	187.5	190.1	190.6	184.8	180.8	176.2	177.3	178.6
2001	172.3	172.1	174.6	177.4	184.1	193.3	195.4	196.6	190.2	186.1	182.8	181.9	183.9
2002	176.0	175.4	176.8	179.4	186.1	194.1	197.2	197.0	191.5	186.3	182.2	181.0	185.3
2003	175.6	174.7	175.5	179.0	185.6	195.1	198.3	199.6	194.3	190.1	185.4	185.3	186.5
2004	179.7	179.7	181.6	185.3	189.9	199.6	202.4	202.4	196.4	192.8	189.9	190.3	190.8
2005	184.9	185.5	188.2	191.3	196.9	206.9	210.6	211.1	206.4	202.9	199.8	201.0	198.8
2006	197.6	198.7	201.3	203.7	210.7	221.3	223.0	223.7	219.2	215.0	212.8	214.9	211.8
2007	209.0	210.0	212.9	213.2	220.5	230.3	232.9	233.3	227.9	224.6	222.5	223.4	221.7
2008	218.7	219.2	220.4	220.9	227.7	236.8	240.9	241.0	235.7	232.1	226.7	225.2	228.8
2009	216.7	213.2	212.4	210.1	215.9	221.3	223.6	222.5	217.6	211.4	206.9	206.2	214.8
2010	199.9	199.5	200.5	203.7	208.7	217.2	221.2	222.8	218.5	214.7	208.9	209.0	210.4
2011	202.2	202.2	203.9	205.3	211.7	221.1	224.4	223.6	219.1	213.9	210.6	210.5	212.4
Goods-Producing													
2000	42.1	42.0	42.7	43.7	45.2	46.6	47.3	48.0	47.4	47.4	45.6	45.2	45.3
2001	43.0	43.0	43.9	45.6	47.7	49.9	50.6	51.3	50.4	51.2	50.3	48.1	47.9
2002	45.5	44.2	44.7	45.9	48.2	49.0	49.4	50.2	49.4	48.7	47.0	45.1	47.3
2003	42.9	42.3	42.6	44.5	46.8	48.3	49.4	50.9	50.5	50.4	48.8	47.6	47.1
2004	44.6	44.6	45.4	47.1	48.9	50.7	51.4	51.5	50.6	51.0	50.5	49.5	48.8
2005	47.6	47.8	49.0	50.8	52.6	54.4	55.6	56.2	56.0	56.5	56.1	55.3	53.2
2006	54.6	54.8	55.7	58.2	60.8	62.8	62.8	64.1	63.8	63.9	63.3	62.9	60.6
2007	59.7	59.4	60.6	61.7	63.8	65.8	66.3	67.0	65.9	66.5	66.9	65.6	64.1
2008	63.9	63.6	63.9	64.6	66.9	68.7	70.3	71.1	70.2	70.4	69.0	66.2	67.4
2009	61.6	59.3	58.3	57.7	59.0	58.9	59.4	59.2	58.3	57.6	56.7	55.0	58.4
2010	52.3	51.9	52.5	54.2	55.8	56.9	58.3	59.7	59.3	59.7	57.9	56.1	56.2
2011	52.9	52.7	53.2	54.5	56.4	58.5	59.1	59.6	60.2	59.9	59.2	57.1	56.9
Mining and Logging													
2000	16.1	16.1	16.0	15.5	15.8	16.1	16.4	16.8	16.7	16.7	16.7	16.9	16.3
2001	16.6	16.8	17.3	17.4	18.0	18.8	19.0	19.3	19.3	19.5	19.3	19.1	18.4
2002	18.4	18.1	17.9	17.4	17.7	18.0	18.3	18.4	18.0	17.8	17.5	17.3	17.9
2003	17.1	17.2	17.2	17.4	17.8	18.3	18.9	19.1	18.9	19.1	19.0	19.2	18.3
2004	18.9	19.0	19.1	19.2	19.4	20.2	20.6	20.9	20.9	21.0	21.3	21.3	20.2
2005	21.0	21.3	21.6	21.8	22.1	22.9	23.2	23.4	23.5	23.6	23.9	24.3	22.7
2006	24.6	25.0	25.4	25.8	26.2	27.0	27.3	27.6	27.5	27.5	27.4	27.6	26.6
2007	27.0	26.9	26.8	26.8	27.2	27.7	27.6	27.7	27.5	27.6	27.8	27.9	27.4
2008	28.1	28.1	28.1	28.0	28.6	29.3	29.8	30.2	30.2	30.5	30.5	30.3	29.3
2009	29.2	28.1	27.2	25.8	25.2	24.8	24.6	24.4	24.2	24.1	24.2	24.2	25.5
2010	24.0	24.0	24.1	24.2	24.6	25.1	25.6	25.9	25.8	26.1	26.3	26.5	25.2
2011	26.2	26.2	26.3	26.4	26.7	27.3	27.6	27.5	27.8	27.8	27.8	28.2	27.2
Construction													
2000	15.9	15.8	16.7	18.0	19.1	20.0	20.3	20.7	20.3	19.8	18.1	17.5	18.5
2001	16.1	16.0	16.5	18.2	19.9	21.2	21.6	22.0	21.2	21.4	20.9	19.3	19.5
2002	17.6	17.0	17.5	19.2	21.1	21.5	21.6	22.2	21.9	21.2	19.8	18.2	19.9
2003	16.6	16.2	16.6	18.1	19.9	20.7	21.1	22.3	22.2	21.6	20.1	18.7	19.5
2004	16.5	16.6	17.2	18.7	20.3	20.9	21.2	21.0	20.2	20.2	19.5	18.5	19.2
2005	17.0	17.2	18.0	19.5	21.0	21.8	22.7	23.0	22.7	22.8	22.1	21.0	20.7
2006	20.2	20.1	20.6	22.6	24.6	25.5	25.1	26.2	26.0	25.9	25.4	24.8	23.9
2007	22.4	22.4	23.6	24.9	26.5	28.0	28.6	29.2	28.3	28.6	28.7	27.4	26.6
2008	25.8	25.6	26.2	26.8	28.5	29.4	30.5	30.9	30.1	29.6	28.2	25.9	28.1
2009	22.8	22.0	22.1	23.0	24.9	25.2	25.8	25.8	25.0	24.4	23.5	21.9	23.9
2010	19.7	19.5	19.9	21.6	22.8	23.2	24.0	24.9	24.6	24.5	22.4	20.5	22.3
2011	17.9	17.8	18.3	19.3	20.8	22.0	22.3	22.9	23.3	22.8	22.2	19.8	20.8
Manufacturing													
2000	10.1	10.1	10.0	10.2	10.3	10.5	10.6	10.5	10.4	10.9	10.8	10.8	10.4
2001	10.3	10.2	10.1	10.0	9.8	9.9	10.0	10.0	9.9	10.3	10.1	9.7	10.0
2002	9.5	9.1	9.3	9.3	9.4	9.5	9.5	9.6	9.5	9.7	9.7	9.6	9.5
2003	9.2	8.9	8.8	9.0	9.1	9.3	9.4	9.5	9.4	9.7	9.7	9.7	9.3
2004	9.2	9.0	9.1	9.2	9.2	9.6	9.6	9.6	9.5	9.8	9.7	9.7	9.4
2005	9.6	9.3	9.4	9.5	9.5	9.7	9.7	9.8	9.8	10.1	10.1	10.0	9.7
2006	9.8	9.7	9.7	9.8	10.0	10.3	10.4	10.3	10.3	10.5	10.5	10.5	10.2
2007	10.3	10.1	10.2	10.0	10.1	10.1	10.1	10.1	10.1	10.3	10.4	10.3	10.2
2008	10.0	9.9	9.6	9.8	9.8	10.0	10.0	10.0	9.9	10.3	10.3	10.0	10.0
2009	9.6	9.2	9.0	8.9	8.9	8.9	9.0	9.0	9.1	9.1	9.0	8.9	9.1
2010	8.6	8.4	8.5	8.4	8.4	8.6	8.7	8.9	8.9	9.1	9.2	9.1	8.7
2011	8.8	8.7	8.6	8.8	8.9	9.2	9.2	9.2	9.1	9.3	9.2	9.1	9.0

1. Employment by Industry: Wyoming, Selected Years, 2000–2011—*Continued*

(Numbers in thousands, not seasonally adjusted)

Industry and year	January	February	March	April	May	June	July	August	September	October	November	December	Annual average
Service-Providing													
2000	185.7	186.5	189.5	190.4	196.5	202.2	199.1	199.1	197.6	195.5	192.6	194.1	194.1
2001	190.1	190.5	192.9	193.8	199.5	206.7	202.2	203.2	201.0	197.6	195.2	197.2	197.5
2002	192.4	193.5	195.5	196.5	202.0	209.2	206.3	205.2	204.8	201.8	199.5	201.0	200.6
2003	196.0	196.1	197.4	198.7	204.0	212.0	208.1	207.8	206.7	204.6	201.1	202.8	202.9
2004	199.3	199.7	201.5	203.7	207.5	215.3	211.8	211.3	209.5	207.4	204.9	206.5	206.5
2005	202.0	202.9	205.0	206.3	211.4	219.1	216.0	216.0	215.5	212.9	209.9	212.1	210.8
2006	207.8	209.5	211.8	211.6	217.0	225.9	221.5	220.5	220.9	218.0	216.0	219.0	216.6
2007	215.4	217.5	219.7	218.9	225.5	233.2	229.1	228.8	230.0	227.2	224.7	226.8	224.7
2008	222.2	224.3	225.8	225.8	232.2	239.4	235.5	234.2	236.2	233.6	229.5	230.9	230.8
2009	225.2	225.7	226.6	225.3	231.3	235.6	230.2	229.1	232.0	227.0	223.1	224.2	227.9
2010	218.8	220.3	221.9	223.0	229.1	235.3	229.9	229.8	232.3	229.1	224.6	226.6	226.7
2011	221.0	222.9	224.8	224.8	231.0	237.3	235.6	233.3	232.5	228.7	225.5	227.5	228.7
Trade, Transportation, and Utilities													
2000	46.3	46.0	45.9	46.6	47.7	48.9	49.7	50.0	49.1	48.7	49.1	49.4	48.1
2001	47.5	46.9	47.3	47.8	49.0	50.2	50.2	50.1	49.1	48.1	48.1	48.6	48.6
2002	47.0	46.4	46.7	47.2	48.5	49.7	50.0	50.0	49.1	48.7	49.0	49.2	48.5
2003	47.1	46.5	46.5	47.2	48.2	49.5	50.1	50.2	49.4	48.9	48.6	49.1	48.4
2004	47.5	47.4	47.6	48.3	49.1	50.5	51.0	50.8	49.9	49.4	49.5	50.0	49.3
2005	48.2	48.2	48.7	49.3	50.4	52.0	52.4	52.5	51.8	51.5	51.5	52.2	50.7
2006	50.7	50.6	51.1	51.0	52.1	53.9	54.2	54.0	53.3	52.8	53.4	54.0	52.6
2007	53.0	53.2	53.8	53.4	54.7	56.3	56.8	56.9	56.1	55.7	56.0	56.7	55.2
2008	55.0	54.7	54.8	54.8	55.8	56.9	57.4	57.3	56.7	56.0	56.0	56.4	56.0
2009	54.1	53.5	53.3	52.8	53.5	54.5	54.5	54.4	53.6	52.5	52.4	52.6	53.5
2010	50.6	50.3	50.3	50.9	51.6	52.9	53.2	53.1	52.5	52.1	52.2	52.7	51.9
2011	50.8	50.7	51.0	51.3	52.2	53.3	53.7	53.6	53.1	52.9	53.2	53.9	52.5
Wholesale Trade													
2000	6.1	6.2	6.2	6.3	6.3	6.5	6.5	6.5	6.5	6.4	6.4	6.5	6.4
2001	6.5	6.5	6.6	6.8	6.9	7.0	7.0	7.1	7.0	7.0	7.0	7.1	6.9
2002	7.0	7.0	7.0	7.0	7.0	7.1	7.1	7.1	7.0	7.0	7.0	7.0	7.0
2003	6.9	6.8	6.8	6.9	6.9	7.0	7.1	7.1	7.0	7.0	7.0	7.1	7.0
2004	7.1	7.2	7.2	7.3	7.4	7.4	7.5	7.4	7.4	7.3	7.4	7.4	7.3
2005	7.3	7.4	7.5	7.6	7.8	7.9	7.9	7.9	7.9	7.9	7.9	8.0	7.8
2006	7.8	7.9	8.0	8.0	8.2	8.4	8.3	8.3	8.3	8.3	8.4	8.4	8.2
2007	8.4	8.5	8.6	8.7	8.8	9.0	8.8	8.9	8.8	8.7	8.8	8.9	8.7
2008	8.8	8.8	8.9	9.0	9.2	9.2	9.2	9.2	9.2	9.2	9.2	9.2	9.1
2009	9.0	9.0	8.9	8.8	8.8	8.9	8.7	8.6	8.5	8.4	8.4	8.4	8.7
2010	8.3	8.3	8.4	8.4	8.5	8.6	8.5	8.5	8.5	8.5	8.6	8.6	8.5
2011	8.5	8.6	8.7	8.7	8.8	8.9	8.9	8.9	8.9	8.9	9.0	9.0	8.8
Retail Trade													
2000	28.7	28.4	28.3	28.8	29.9	30.7	31.5	31.7	31.0	30.5	30.8	31.0	30.1
2001	29.5	29.2	29.5	29.7	30.8	31.7	31.6	31.4	30.6	29.7	29.8	30.2	30.3
2002	28.9	28.4	28.7	29.1	30.3	31.2	31.5	31.4	30.7	30.1	30.4	30.6	30.1
2003	28.8	28.3	28.3	28.9	29.7	30.7	31.2	31.2	30.6	30.1	30.1	30.4	29.9
2004	28.8	28.6	28.8	28.8	29.9	31.0	31.3	31.2	30.4	30.0	30.1	30.4	30.0
2005	28.9	28.7	29.0	29.2	30.1	31.4	31.7	31.7	31.1	30.7	30.7	31.0	30.4
2006	29.8	29.5	29.8	29.7	30.5	31.8	32.2	32.0	31.3	30.9	31.4	31.7	30.9
2007	30.8	30.8	31.2	30.7	31.7	32.6	33.3	33.1	32.4	32.2	32.4	32.8	32.0
2008	31.6	31.3	31.3	31.2	31.8	32.8	33.3	33.1	32.7	32.2	32.2	32.4	32.2
2009	30.7	30.1	30.1	30.0	30.7	31.4	31.7	31.6	31.0	30.3	30.2	30.3	30.7
2010	28.8	28.7	28.7	28.9	29.5	30.3	30.5	30.2	29.6	29.3	29.3	29.6	29.5
2011	28.2	27.9	28.1	28.4	29.0	29.8	30.1	30.0	29.7	29.5	29.8	30.3	29.2
Transportation and Utilities													
2000	11.5	11.4	11.4	11.5	11.5	11.7	11.7	11.8	11.6	11.8	11.9	11.9	11.6
2001	11.5	11.2	11.2	11.3	11.3	11.5	11.6	11.6	11.5	11.4	11.3	11.3	11.4
2002	11.1	11.0	11.0	11.1	11.2	11.4	11.4	11.5	11.4	11.6	11.6	11.6	11.3
2003	11.4	11.4	11.4	11.4	11.6	11.8	11.8	11.9	11.8	11.8	11.5	11.6	11.6
2004	11.6	11.6	11.6	11.8	11.8	12.1	12.2	12.2	12.1	12.1	12.0	12.2	11.9
2005	12.0	12.1	12.2	12.5	12.5	12.7	12.8	12.9	12.8	12.9	12.9	13.2	12.6
2006	13.1	13.2	13.3	13.3	13.4	13.7	13.7	13.7	13.7	13.6	13.6	13.9	13.5
2007	13.8	13.9	14.0	14.0	14.2	14.7	14.7	14.9	14.9	14.8	14.8	15.0	14.5
2008	14.6	14.6	14.6	14.6	14.8	14.9	14.9	15.0	14.8	14.6	14.6	14.8	14.7
2009	14.4	14.4	14.3	14.0	14.0	14.2	14.1	14.2	14.1	13.8	13.8	13.9	14.1
2010	13.5	13.3	13.2	13.6	13.6	14.0	14.2	14.4	14.4	14.3	14.3	14.5	13.9
2011	14.1	14.2	14.2	14.2	14.4	14.6	14.7	14.7	14.5	14.5	14.4	14.6	14.4
Information													
2000	4.0	3.9	3.9	4.0	4.0	4.1	4.1	4.0	4.0	3.9	4.0	4.0	4.0
2001	4.0	3.9	3.9	3.9	4.0	4.1	4.1	4.2	4.2	4.1	4.2	4.2	4.1
2002	4.2	4.2	4.2	4.2	4.1	4.2	4.2	4.1	4.1	4.0	4.1	4.1	4.1
2003	4.1	4.1	4.2	4.1	4.2	4.3	4.3	4.3	4.2	4.3	4.3	4.3	4.2
2004	4.3	4.3	4.3	4.2	4.2	4.3	4.4	4.4	4.4	4.2	4.3	4.3	4.3
2005	4.3	4.3	4.3	4.3	4.3	4.4	4.3	4.3	4.3	4.2	4.3	4.3	4.3
2006	4.3	4.3	4.2	4.1	4.1	4.2	4.1	4.1	4.1	4.0	4.0	4.1	4.1
2007	4.0	4.0	4.0	4.0	4.0	4.1	4.1	4.1	4.0	4.0	4.0	4.1	4.0
2008	4.0	4.0	4.0	4.0	4.0	4.0	4.1	4.1	4.0	4.0	4.0	4.0	4.0
2009	4.0	4.0	4.0	3.9	4.0	4.0	4.0	4.0	3.9	3.9	3.9	3.9	4.0
2010	3.9	3.9	3.9	3.9	3.9	3.9	3.9	3.9	3.9	3.8	3.8	3.8	3.9
2011	3.8	3.8	3.8	3.8	3.9	3.9	3.9	3.9	3.8	3.8	3.9	3.9	3.9

1. Employment by Industry: Wyoming, Selected Years, 2000–2011—*Continued*

(Numbers in thousands, not seasonally adjusted)

Industry and year	January	February	March	April	May	June	July	August	September	October	November	December	Annual average
Financial Activities													
2000	9.0	8.9	9.1	9.1	9.2	9.4	9.3	9.4	9.2	9.2	9.1	9.3	9.2
2001	9.0	9.0	9.1	9.3	9.4	9.7	9.7	9.9	9.7	9.6	9.6	9.6	9.5
2002	9.6	9.7	9.7	9.8	10.0	10.3	10.4	10.4	10.3	10.0	9.9	9.9	10.0
2003	9.8	9.8	10.0	10.0	10.1	10.4	10.3	10.4	10.3	10.3	10.2	10.2	10.2
2004	10.2	10.2	10.3	10.3	10.5	10.6	10.6	10.7	10.5	10.4	10.5	10.6	10.5
2005	10.5	10.4	10.6	10.6	10.8	11.0	11.0	11.0	10.9	10.8	10.8	11.0	10.8
2006	10.9	10.9	11.0	11.0	11.1	11.3	11.3	11.3	11.2	11.1	11.2	11.3	11.1
2007	11.0	11.0	11.1	11.2	11.3	11.6	11.6	11.6	11.5	11.5	11.4	11.5	11.4
2008	11.4	11.4	11.4	11.5	11.6	11.8	11.9	11.9	11.7	11.7	11.6	11.6	11.6
2009	11.3	11.3	11.2	11.2	11.3	11.4	11.3	11.3	11.1	11.0	10.9	11.0	11.2
2010	10.7	10.7	10.7	10.8	10.9	10.9	10.9	10.8	10.7	10.8	10.7	10.8	10.8
2011	10.7	10.6	10.6	10.7	10.7	10.8	10.9	10.6	10.6	10.5	10.6	10.5	10.7
Professional and Business Services													
2000	13.6	13.8	14.2	14.6	15.0	15.5	15.5	15.4	15.0	14.8	14.6	14.4	14.7
2001	14.9	15.0	15.3	15.8	16.0	16.3	16.4	16.5	15.9	15.6	15.4	15.1	15.7
2002	14.5	14.8	15.0	15.5	15.7	16.2	16.6	16.4	15.7	15.8	15.5	15.2	15.6
2003	14.3	14.5	14.5	15.3	15.7	16.5	16.7	16.8	16.0	16.1	15.2	14.9	15.5
2004	14.3	14.3	14.4	15.2	15.4	16.2	16.4	16.5	15.7	15.6	15.1	14.8	15.3
2005	14.5	14.6	14.9	15.5	15.8	16.6	16.8	17.0	16.4	16.3	15.9	15.6	15.8
2006	15.4	15.7	15.9	16.7	17.3	17.9	18.0	18.1	17.8	17.4	17.2	17.3	17.1
2007	16.8	17.1	17.5	17.9	18.8	19.6	19.5	19.5	19.0	18.8	18.0	17.8	18.4
2008	17.3	17.5	17.7	18.2	18.9	19.7	19.8	19.8	19.2	19.0	18.3	18.0	18.6
2009	17.3	17.0	17.0	17.1	17.6	17.9	18.0	18.0	17.5	17.2	16.7	16.3	17.3
2010	16.0	15.8	16.1	16.8	17.2	17.9	18.3	18.6	18.0	17.5	17.0	16.7	17.2
2011	16.4	16.4	16.6	17.2	17.8	18.4	18.9	18.9	17.9	17.4	17.4	16.9	17.5
Education and Health Services													
2000	17.6	17.9	18.1	18.0	18.2	18.3	18.2	18.4	18.3	18.7	18.5	18.7	18.2
2001	18.8	18.9	19.2	19.1	19.2	19.2	19.3	19.6	19.3	19.5	19.8	19.6	19.3
2002	19.3	19.7	19.8	19.7	19.9	20.0	20.0	20.1	20.0	19.9	20.1	20.2	19.9
2003	20.4	20.5	20.4	20.7	20.7	20.9	20.9	20.8	20.9	20.8	21.1	21.1	20.8
2004	21.2	21.1	21.2	21.3	21.2	21.5	21.5	21.7	21.6	21.5	22.0	22.0	21.5
2005	21.7	21.7	21.9	21.8	21.9	22.0	22.1	22.2	22.1	22.2	22.5	22.4	22.0
2006	22.1	22.2	22.5	22.3	22.6	22.8	22.7	22.8	22.7	22.7	23.0	22.8	22.6
2007	22.7	22.9	23.0	22.9	23.2	23.4	23.4	23.5	23.5	23.6	24.0	23.8	23.3
2008	23.7	24.1	24.1	24.2	24.2	24.6	24.7	24.7	24.8	25.1	25.1	25.0	24.5
2009	25.2	25.3	25.4	25.4	25.8	25.6	25.8	25.7	25.7	25.9	26.2	26.2	25.7
2010	25.7	26.0	26.1	26.2	26.2	26.4	26.4	26.5	26.4	26.7	26.9	26.7	26.4
2011	26.5	26.8	27.0	26.8	27.0	26.8	26.7	26.7	26.6	26.6	26.6	26.7	26.7
Leisure and Hospitality													
2000	26.2	26.4	26.9	27.0	29.6	35.4	36.7	36.1	32.7	29.0	26.2	27.2	30.0
2001	26.3	26.5	26.9	26.8	29.5	34.5	35.7	35.5	32.2	28.6	26.0	27.2	29.6
2002	26.6	27.0	27.2	27.5	29.9	34.9	36.7	35.9	33.2	29.6	27.1	27.7	30.3
2003	27.5	27.5	27.7	27.8	30.3	35.5	36.8	36.4	33.5	29.8	27.7	28.5	30.8
2004	28.1	28.2	28.8	29.2	30.8	36.0	37.1	36.8	34.0	31.1	28.4	29.4	31.5
2005	28.7	28.9	29.2	29.3	31.3	36.5	38.1	37.6	34.8	31.4	28.7	30.0	32.0
2006	29.3	29.8	30.2	29.6	31.6	37.0	38.4	37.8	35.0	31.8	29.4	31.0	32.6
2007	30.5	31.0	31.3	30.5	32.6	37.4	39.1	38.6	36.0	32.6	30.4	31.9	33.5
2008	31.6	32.0	32.5	31.6	34.1	38.8	40.3	39.7	36.9	33.8	30.6	31.9	34.5
2009	31.1	30.8	31.2	30.1	32.5	36.8	38.5	38.0	35.8	31.8	28.7	29.8	32.9
2010	29.4	29.6	29.6	29.4	31.6	36.7	38.5	38.5	36.1	32.6	28.9	30.8	32.6
2011	29.8	29.8	30.2	29.3	32.0	37.4	39.1	38.3	35.0	30.9	27.5	29.4	32.4
Other Services													
2000	8.9	9.0	9.1	9.1	9.2	9.3	9.3	9.3	9.1	9.1	9.1	9.1	9.1
2001	8.8	8.9	9.0	9.1	9.3	9.4	9.4	9.5	9.4	9.4	9.4	9.5	9.3
2002	9.3	9.4	9.5	9.6	9.8	9.8	9.9	9.9	9.7	9.6	9.5	9.6	9.6
2003	9.5	9.5	9.6	9.4	9.6	9.7	9.8	9.8	9.5	9.5	9.5	9.6	9.6
2004	9.5	9.6	9.6	9.7	9.8	9.8	10.0	10.0	9.7	9.6	9.6	9.7	9.7
2005	9.4	9.6	9.6	9.7	9.8	10.0	10.3	10.3	10.1	10.0	10.0	10.2	9.9
2006	10.3	10.4	10.7	10.8	11.1	11.4	11.5	11.5	11.3	11.3	11.3	11.5	11.1
2007	11.3	11.4	11.6	11.6	12.1	12.1	12.1	12.1	11.9	11.9	11.8	12.0	11.8
2008	11.8	11.9	12.0	12.0	12.2	12.3	12.4	12.4	12.2	12.1	12.1	12.1	12.1
2009	12.1	12.0	12.0	11.9	12.2	12.2	12.1	11.9	11.7	11.5	11.4	11.4	11.9
2010	11.3	11.3	11.3	11.5	11.5	11.6	11.7	11.7	11.6	11.5	11.5	11.4	11.5
2011	11.3	11.4	11.5	11.7	11.7	12.0	12.1	12.0	11.9	11.9	12.2	12.1	11.8
Government													
2000	60.1	60.6	62.3	62.0	63.6	61.3	56.3	56.5	60.2	62.1	62.0	62.0	60.8
2001	60.8	61.4	62.2	62.0	63.1	63.3	57.4	57.9	61.2	62.7	62.7	63.4	61.5
2002	61.9	62.3	63.4	63.0	64.1	64.1	58.5	58.4	62.7	64.2	64.3	65.1	62.7
2003	63.3	63.7	64.5	64.2	65.2	65.2	59.2	59.1	62.9	64.9	64.5	65.1	63.5
2004	64.2	64.6	65.3	65.5	66.5	66.4	60.8	60.4	63.7	65.6	65.5	65.7	64.5
2005	64.7	65.2	65.8	65.8	67.1	66.6	61.0	61.1	65.1	66.5	66.2	66.4	65.1
2006	64.8	65.6	66.2	66.1	67.1	67.4	61.3	60.9	65.5	66.9	66.5	67.0	65.4
2007	66.1	66.9	67.4	67.4	68.8	68.7	62.5	62.5	68.0	69.1	69.1	69.0	67.1
2008	67.4	68.7	69.3	69.5	71.4	71.3	64.9	64.3	70.7	71.9	71.8	71.9	69.4
2009	70.1	71.8	72.5	72.9	74.4	73.2	66.0	65.8	72.7	73.2	72.9	73.0	71.5
2010	71.2	72.7	73.9	73.5	76.2	75.0	67.0	66.7	73.1	74.1	73.6	73.7	72.6
2011	71.7	73.4	74.1	74.0	75.7	74.7	70.3	69.3	73.6	74.7	74.1	74.1	73.3

2. Average Weekly Hours by Selected Industry: Wyoming, 2007–2011

(Not seasonally adjusted)

Industry and year	January	February	March	April	May	June	July	August	September	October	November	December	Annual average
Total Private													
2007	34.7	36.0	35.8	36.1	35.9	36.8	37.4	37.5	36.1	35.6	35.7	36.5	36.2
2008	36.1	36.1	36.6	36.3	36.3	37.3	37.1	37.3	37.0	36.7	37.0	36.2	36.7
2009	35.8	36.3	35.5	35.1	35.3	35.2	35.5	36.7	35.2	35.1	36.1	34.9	35.5
2010	35.4	35.5	35.2	35.3	35.7	36.0	36.6	37.2	36.2	36.1	36.1	35.3	35.9
2011	35.8	35.3	35.1	36.4	36.2	36.4	36.5	36.5	36.5	37.1	35.9	35.5	36.1
Goods-Producing													
2007	39.3	42.2	41.5	40.9	42.2	42.6	43.4	44.0	43.1	43.5	42.7	43.3	42.4
2008	42.6	42.9	43.3	43.2	43.6	44.2	43.8	43.9	44.0	43.5	43.5	42.9	43.5
2009	41.9	41.9	41.0	40.8	41.2	39.8	41.3	42.9	40.9	40.8	41.8	41.1	41.3
2010	42.1	41.1	40.8	41.4	41.6	42.5	43.4	44.2	43.3	43.5	43.5	42.6	42.6
2011	42.2	41.9	41.9	42.9	42.8	43.4	43.4	43.5	43.2	43.9	43.3	42.2	42.9
Mining and Logging													
2007	42.4	45.8	44.1	44.5	45.1	45.5	46.0	46.4	46.1	45.2	46.0	47.1	45.4
2008	46.7	47.2	47.1	46.6	45.3	46.2	46.6	46.0	46.8	45.9	46.6	45.3	46.3
2009	44.4	43.5	42.8	42.6	41.6	41.4	42.6	43.7	44.2	44.2	44.7	44.8	43.4
2010	45.6	45.3	44.1	43.7	44.0	44.1	44.7	46.1	46.3	46.4	46.8	46.5	45.3
2011	46.3	45.4	44.0	45.0	43.9	45.0	45.2	46.1	46.2	48.0	47.1	45.5	45.7
Construction													
2007	37.6	40.9	40.5	39.1	41.6	41.9	43.0	44.0	42.7	43.7	42.1	41.8	41.7
2008	41.0	41.5	42.1	42.3	43.3	43.7	43.0	43.4	43.0	42.6	42.0	41.6	42.5
2009	41.0	41.6	39.9	40.0	41.2	38.8	41.0	42.9	39.8	39.5	40.8	39.2	40.5
2010	40.5	39.6	40.0	41.4	41.0	41.9	42.7	43.7	42.0	42.3	41.9	41.0	41.6
2011	39.9	40.0	41.7	42.8	42.7	44.3	44.3	44.3	43.4	43.3	42.7	41.4	42.7
Trade, Transportation, and Utilities													
2007	34.9	35.7	36.6	36.9	36.4	36.6	36.4	37.2	35.7	34.0	34.8	36.3	36.0
2008	35.5	35.1	35.8	35.6	35.0	36.3	36.5	36.4	36.0	36.1	36.5	35.7	35.9
2009	35.7	36.6	36.7	37.1	36.5	36.6	36.0	37.3	36.0	36.0	36.9	35.7	36.4
2010	36.1	36.5	36.3	36.3	36.3	36.9	37.0	37.1	37.1	36.8	36.9	35.8	36.6
2011	36.4	36.1	35.7	36.7	36.5	36.1	36.5	36.0	35.7	37.0	35.5	35.1	36.1
Professional and Business Services													
2007	32.7	32.6	31.2	31.6	31.1	32.2	34.8	35.7	36.8	35.8	35.4	35.7	33.8
2008	34.5	34.9	34.3	33.8	33.4	34.6	34.2	33.8	34.6	34.1	35.1	34.1	34.3
2009	34.9	34.7	33.9	34.1	34.5	34.9	35.2	35.8	34.8	34.4	35.1	33.9	34.7
2010	33.8	34.6	33.5	34.6	34.1	34.3	34.5	35.4	34.6	34.0	33.6	33.3	34.2
2011	34.2	33.7	32.8	37.3	37.5	36.5	36.8	36.8	36.4	37.9	34.4	34.8	35.8
Education and Health Services													
2007	31.4	33.3	33.8	34.1	33.8	35.1	35.8	34.4	32.6	31.7	31.8	32.5	33.4
2008	32.2	31.9	32.9	31.8	32.4	33.4	33.0	33.4	33.0	32.4	33.1	32.7	32.7
2009	32.4	33.1	32.9	31.9	33.2	33.9	33.5	34.6	33.8	33.7	34.5	33.5	33.4
2010	33.6	33.6	33.4	33.8	33.9	34.1	34.5	35.1	34.2	33.6	34.1	34.1	34.0
2011	35.1	34.3	33.9	35.2	34.9	35.4	35.3	34.9	35.9	35.6	35.4	35.2	35.1
Leisure and Hospitality													
2007	25.1	26.2	24.8	25.7	25.0	27.0	28.1	27.3	26.1	24.8	24.9	25.4	26.0
2008	25.8	26.4	26.9	26.8	26.5	27.5	27.9	28.3	27.3	25.8	25.6	25.2	26.7
2009	25.5	25.8	25.0	24.7	25.5	27.4	27.7	29.2	27.3	26.7	26.6	25.9	26.5
2010	26.4	27.1	27.2	26.3	26.7	27.6	29.1	29.9	27.7	27.0	25.8	25.6	27.3
2011	26.6	25.8	25.8	25.6	25.7	26.8	27.4	27.8	26.5	25.7	24.1	23.5	26.0
Other Services													
2007	31.1	33.2	33.1	32.5	32.6	32.8	32.7	33.8	32.3	31.1	30.8	31.0	32.3
2008	31.1	31.1	31.0	30.4	30.1	31.3	30.4	30.1	28.7	29.0	29.7	28.1	30.1
2009	29.9	29.5	29.8	30.2	30.4	29.5	28.9	29.8	27.3	27.8	29.1	28.0	29.2
2010	28.0	28.0	28.6	27.4	28.3	28.0	28.3	29.0	26.9	27.2	27.7	28.5	28.0
2011	29.8	29.3	30.0	31.4	31.8	33.5	33.1	33.3	33.7	33.8	32.2	33.9	32.2

3. Average Hourly Earnings by Selected Industry: Wyoming, 2007–2011

(Dollars, not seasonally adjusted)

Industry and year	January	February	March	April	May	June	July	August	September	October	November	December	Annual average
Total Private													
2007	19.61	19.59	19.69	19.95	19.68	19.92	20.06	20.14	19.93	20.33	20.60	20.91	20.04
2008	20.40	20.46	20.82	20.67	20.86	20.55	20.51	20.68	21.03	21.14	21.38	21.50	20.83
2009	21.27	21.26	21.25	21.25	21.09	20.51	20.46	20.69	20.84	21.22	21.35	21.69	21.06
2010	21.49	21.42	21.45	21.68	21.68	21.09	21.11	21.10	21.43	21.62	21.63	21.81	21.45
2011	22.00	21.84	21.76	22.69	22.68	21.97	22.02	21.79	22.14	22.36	22.26	22.53	22.17
Goods-Producing													
2007	23.09	22.63	22.82	22.90	22.80	23.43	23.69	23.82	23.64	24.25	24.94	25.39	23.66
2008	24.77	24.53	24.47	24.56	24.68	24.49	24.66	24.66	24.86	24.74	24.87	25.31	24.72
2009	25.17	25.14	25.72	25.89	25.55	25.32	24.96	25.39	25.29	25.57	25.66	26.03	25.47
2010	25.80	25.75	25.63	25.90	25.99	25.49	25.69	25.52	25.68	25.41	25.29	25.84	25.66
2011	26.33	26.05	26.09	26.10	26.52	25.84	25.86	25.48	25.73	25.43	25.42	26.02	25.89
Mining and Logging													
2007	27.61	26.61	27.16	27.72	27.60	28.28	29.04	28.71	26.28	26.50	27.43	27.35	27.53
2008	27.68	27.13	27.52	27.71	28.20	28.11	27.91	27.92	28.18	28.41	27.98	28.28	27.92
2009	28.04	28.26	28.46	29.10	28.96	28.99	28.83	29.00	29.02	28.77	28.96	28.64	28.73
2010	28.57	28.49	28.70	28.99	29.34	28.87	29.05	29.02	28.74	28.31	27.62	28.05	28.63
2011	28.58	27.74	27.60	27.50	27.79	27.63	27.99	27.35	27.48	27.84	27.52	28.23	27.77
Construction													
2007	21.11	20.93	21.07	20.92	20.69	21.31	21.25	21.70	23.09	24.10	24.75	25.64	22.32
2008	24.60	24.55	23.88	23.99	24.03	23.47	23.47	23.51	23.71	23.75	24.05	24.69	23.94
2009	24.29	24.07	24.44	24.56	24.26	23.84	23.22	23.84	23.54	24.10	24.01	24.23	24.02
2010	24.08	24.15	24.08	24.52	24.74	23.89	24.17	23.92	24.17	23.84	24.02	24.65	24.18
2011	25.19	25.21	25.35	24.99	25.75	24.48	24.08	23.91	24.61	23.94	23.98	24.63	24.62
Trade, Transportation, and Utilities													
2007	19.01	19.23	19.53	20.11	19.62	19.30	19.55	19.34	20.06	20.20	20.18	20.86	19.75
2008	19.87	20.47	21.22	21.07	21.55	20.71	20.34	20.42	20.62	20.57	20.61	20.98	20.70
2009	20.39	20.38	20.41	21.07	20.64	19.64	19.79	20.29	20.12	20.84	20.29	20.55	20.36
2010	20.69	20.67	21.19	21.28	20.98	20.15	19.95	20.05	20.13	20.43	20.56	20.58	20.55
2011	20.95	20.73	20.77	21.38	20.96	20.63	20.81	20.99	21.05	21.65	21.10	21.71	21.06
Professional and Business Services													
2007	24.65	24.71	23.84	24.47	24.14	24.19	24.65	24.71	22.39	22.34	22.04	22.26	23.66
2008	21.98	22.04	22.72	22.23	22.26	22.38	22.37	22.84	22.95	23.47	24.07	24.10	22.79
2009	24.37	24.74	24.87	24.42	23.92	23.84	23.41	23.81	23.79	24.33	24.45	24.58	24.20
2010	24.71	24.56	24.96	24.78	24.97	24.53	24.75	24.93	25.76	26.49	26.78	27.06	25.35
2011	26.36	26.25	25.87	29.65	28.51	27.02	26.37	26.72	26.68	27.30	27.93	28.02	27.24
Education and Health Services													
2007	17.22	17.16	16.76	17.07	16.58	17.69	17.40	17.49	16.74	16.66	16.87	17.52	17.10
2008	17.76	17.94	18.03	17.61	17.83	18.11	17.96	18.23	18.71	19.07	19.00	19.08	18.29
2009	19.36	19.11	18.83	18.97	19.09	18.83	18.98	19.37	19.48	19.59	19.67	20.08	19.29
2010	20.05	19.88	19.47	19.49	19.66	19.24	19.53	19.45	19.38	19.62	19.51	19.74	19.58
2011	20.03	20.06	19.74	19.83	20.43	19.81	19.87	20.02	20.57	20.32	20.03	20.25	20.08
Leisure and Hospitality													
2007	11.30	10.98	11.29	11.47	11.14	11.14	11.21	11.27	11.29	11.52	11.26	11.51	11.28
2008	11.17	10.92	10.98	10.94	11.13	11.12	11.34	11.52	11.52	11.56	11.53	11.54	11.28
2009	12.18	12.47	12.42	12.48	12.34	11.92	12.11	12.37	12.92	12.73	12.91	13.24	12.49
2010	13.33	13.57	13.35	13.17	13.14	12.77	12.60	12.77	13.22	13.07	12.97	13.06	13.06
2011	12.87	12.75	12.68	12.28	12.40	11.90	11.87	11.77	12.09	11.98	12.00	12.35	12.21
Other Services													
2007	17.09	17.80	18.52	18.65	18.50	18.44	18.11	18.64	19.50	18.98	18.68	19.46	18.54
2008	18.48	18.44	18.68	18.70	18.77	18.35	18.77	18.83	19.04	18.75	19.39	19.48	18.80
2009	19.03	18.80	19.26	19.28	19.41	19.40	18.85	18.81	18.50	18.98	19.52	19.99	19.15
2010	19.30	19.37	19.20	19.28	19.31	19.33	19.24	19.12	19.42	19.21	19.52	19.57	19.32
2011	19.91	19.71	20.61	20.59	20.17	20.47	20.33	21.48	21.28	21.72	22.06	21.52	20.85

4. Average Weekly Earnings by Selected Industry: Wyoming, 2007–2011

(Dollars, not seasonally adjusted)

Industry and year	January	February	March	April	May	June	July	August	September	October	November	December	Annual average
Total Private													
2007	680.47	705.24	704.90	720.20	706.51	733.06	750.24	755.25	719.47	723.75	735.42	763.22	725.63
2008	736.44	738.61	762.01	750.32	757.22	766.52	760.92	771.36	778.11	775.84	791.06	778.30	764.15
2009	761.47	771.74	754.38	745.88	744.48	721.95	726.33	759.32	733.57	744.82	770.74	756.98	748.79
2010	760.75	760.41	755.04	765.30	773.98	759.24	772.63	784.92	775.77	780.48	780.84	769.89	770.07
2011	787.60	770.95	763.78	825.92	821.02	799.71	803.73	795.34	808.11	829.56	799.13	799.82	800.57
Goods-Producing													
2007	907.44	954.99	947.03	936.61	962.16	998.12	1,028.15	1,048.08	1,018.88	1,054.88	1,064.94	1,099.39	1,003.88
2008	1,055.20	1,052.34	1,059.55	1,060.99	1,076.05	1,082.46	1,080.11	1,082.57	1,093.84	1,076.19	1,081.85	1,085.80	1,074.35
2009	1,054.62	1,053.37	1,054.52	1,056.31	1,052.66	1,007.74	1,030.85	1,089.23	1,034.36	1,043.26	1,072.59	1,069.83	1,051.43
2010	1,086.18	1,058.33	1,045.70	1,072.26	1,081.18	1,083.33	1,114.95	1,127.98	1,111.94	1,105.34	1,100.12	1,100.78	1,092.03
2011	1,111.13	1,091.50	1,093.17	1,119.69	1,135.06	1,121.46	1,122.32	1,108.38	1,111.54	1,116.38	1,100.69	1,098.04	1,111.15
Mining and Logging													
2007	1,170.66	1,218.74	1,197.76	1,233.54	1,244.76	1,286.74	1,335.84	1,332.14	1,211.51	1,197.80	1,261.78	1,288.19	1,248.75
2008	1,292.66	1,280.54	1,296.19	1,291.29	1,277.46	1,298.68	1,300.61	1,284.32	1,318.82	1,304.02	1,303.87	1,281.08	1,294.29
2009	1,244.98	1,229.31	1,218.09	1,239.66	1,204.74	1,200.19	1,228.16	1,267.30	1,282.68	1,271.63	1,294.51	1,283.07	1,246.19
2010	1,302.79	1,290.60	1,265.67	1,266.86	1,290.96	1,273.17	1,298.54	1,337.82	1,330.66	1,313.58	1,292.62	1,304.33	1,297.55
2011	1,323.25	1,259.40	1,214.40	1,237.50	1,219.98	1,243.35	1,265.15	1,260.84	1,269.58	1,336.32	1,296.19	1,284.47	1,268.21
Construction													
2007	793.74	856.04	853.34	817.97	860.70	892.89	913.75	954.80	985.94	1,053.17	1,041.98	1,071.75	930.88
2008	1,008.60	1,018.83	1,005.35	1,014.78	1,040.50	1,025.64	1,009.21	1,020.33	1,019.53	1,011.75	1,010.10	1,027.10	1,017.72
2009	995.89	1,001.31	975.16	982.40	999.51	924.99	952.02	1,022.74	936.89	951.95	979.61	949.82	972.12
2010	975.24	956.34	963.20	1,015.13	1,014.34	1,000.99	1,032.06	1,045.30	1,015.14	1,008.43	1,006.44	1,010.65	1,006.35
2011	1,005.08	1,008.40	1,057.10	1,069.57	1,099.53	1,084.46	1,066.74	1,059.21	1,068.07	1,036.60	1,023.95	1,019.68	1,052.17
Trade, Transportation, and Utilities													
2007	663.45	686.51	714.80	742.06	714.17	706.38	711.62	719.45	716.14	686.80	702.26	757.22	710.31
2008	705.39	718.50	759.68	750.09	754.25	751.77	742.41	743.29	742.32	742.58	752.27	748.99	742.70
2009	727.92	745.91	749.05	781.70	753.36	718.82	712.44	756.82	724.32	750.24	754.79	733.64	742.11
2010	746.91	754.46	769.20	772.46	774.16	745.55	740.15	743.86	740.78	753.87	758.66	736.76	752.77
2011	762.58	748.35	741.49	784.65	765.04	744.74	759.57	755.64	751.49	801.05	749.05	762.02	760.25
Professional and Business Services													
2007	806.06	805.55	743.81	773.25	750.75	778.92	857.82	882.15	823.95	799.77	780.22	794.68	800.57
2008	758.31	769.20	779.30	751.37	743.48	774.35	765.05	771.99	794.07	800.33	844.86	821.81	781.08
2009	850.51	858.48	843.09	832.72	825.24	832.02	824.03	852.40	827.89	836.95	858.20	833.26	839.75
2010	835.20	849.78	836.16	857.39	851.48	841.38	853.88	882.52	891.30	900.66	899.81	901.10	866.78
2011	901.51	884.63	848.54	1,105.95	1,069.13	986.23	970.42	983.30	971.15	1,034.67	960.79	975.10	975.00
Education and Health Services													
2007	540.71	571.43	566.49	582.09	560.40	620.92	622.92	601.66	545.72	528.12	536.47	569.40	570.49
2008	571.87	572.29	593.19	560.00	577.69	604.87	592.68	608.88	617.43	617.87	628.90	623.92	597.81
2009	627.26	632.54	619.51	605.14	633.79	638.34	635.83	670.20	658.42	660.18	678.62	672.68	644.91
2010	673.68	667.97	650.30	658.76	666.47	656.08	673.79	682.70	662.80	659.23	665.29	673.13	665.85
2011	703.05	688.06	669.19	698.02	713.01	701.27	701.41	698.70	738.46	723.39	709.06	712.80	704.71
Leisure and Hospitality													
2007	283.63	287.68	279.99	294.78	278.50	300.78	315.00	307.67	294.67	285.70	280.37	292.35	292.65
2008	288.19	288.29	295.36	293.19	294.95	305.80	316.39	326.02	314.50	298.25	295.17	290.81	301.61
2009	310.59	321.73	310.50	308.26	314.67	326.61	335.45	361.20	352.72	339.89	343.41	342.92	331.31
2010	351.91	367.75	363.12	346.37	350.84	352.45	366.66	381.82	366.19	352.89	334.63	334.34	356.88
2011	342.34	328.95	327.14	314.37	318.68	318.92	325.24	327.21	320.39	307.89	289.20	290.23	318.07
Other Services													
2007	531.50	590.96	613.01	606.13	603.10	604.83	592.20	630.03	629.85	590.28	575.34	603.26	597.87
2008	574.73	573.48	579.08	568.48	564.98	574.36	570.61	566.78	546.45	543.75	575.88	547.39	565.47
2009	569.00	554.60	573.95	582.26	590.06	572.30	544.77	560.54	505.05	527.64	568.03	559.72	559.32
2010	540.40	542.36	549.12	528.27	546.47	541.24	544.49	554.48	522.40	522.51	540.70	557.75	540.85
2011	593.32	577.50	618.30	646.53	641.41	685.75	672.92	715.28	717.14	734.14	710.33	729.53	671.08

PART B

METROPOLITAN STATISTICAL AREA (MSA) DATA

METROPOLITAN STATISTICAL AREA (MSA) NOTES

Part B provides employment data for the 75 largest (of the 372) metropolitan statistical areas (MSAs) and New England city and town areas (NECTAs) in the United States from 2000 through 2011. As mentioned in the technical notes, all employment data are for MSAs unless otherwise noted. NECTAs are similar to MSAs but are defined by cities and towns rather than counties in the New England region.

According to the 2010 Census and the 2011 estimates from the Census Bureau, New York–Northern New Jersey–Long Island, NY–NJ–PA, was again the largest MSA in the United States—a population of 19,015,900—larger than the population of all but four states. Los Angeles–Long Beach–Santa Ana, CA, followed with a population of 12,944,801. Although the New York area was the most populated MSA, it was not among the fastest growing. Many of the MSAs that experienced rapid growth were in the south and the west. From 2000 to 2011 Raleigh, NC, grew the most quickly, increasing 46.0 percent, followed by Las Vegas–Paradise, NV, which grew at a rate of 43.2 percent. New Orleans–Metairie–Kenner, LA, experienced the slowest growth, decreasing 9.5 percent.

According to the 2011 unemployment ratings from the Bureau of Labor Statistics, unemployment rates decreased in all of the 75 largest MSAs except one, El Paso, TX, where it increased 0.5 percent. Unemployment rate increases ranged from 5.0 percent in Omaha–Council Bluffs, NE–IA, to a high of 16.5 percent in Fresno, CA—0.3 percent lower than the high in 2010. Of the MSAs with population of 1,000,000 or more, four areas reported unemployment rates lower than 6 percent, Washington–Arlington–Alexandria, DC–VA–MD–WV, 5.8 percent; Oklahoma City, OK, 5.7 percent; Honolulu, HI, 5.7 percent; and Omaha–Council Bluffs, NE–IA, mentioned earlier with 5.0 percent.

When compared with the years 1990-2000, total nonfarm employment slowed considerably between 2000 and 2011. In McAllen–Edinburg–Mission, TX, total nonfarm employment increased 43.8 percent from 2000 to 2011; however, employment in this MSA was higher than in all the 75 largest MSAs by more than 24 percentage points. Bakersfield–Delano, CA, was the closest follower with a 19.1 percent increase in nonfarm employment from 2000 through 2011.

Employment increased in the vast majority of MSAs from 2000 to 2011; however it declined most significantly in the following areas: Detroit–Warren–Livonia, MI; San Jose–Sunnyvale–Santa Clara, CA; New Orleans–Metairie–Kenner, LA; Dayton, OH; and Cleveland–Elyria–Mentor, OH, where nonfarm employment declined between 12 percent and 19 percent in each area.

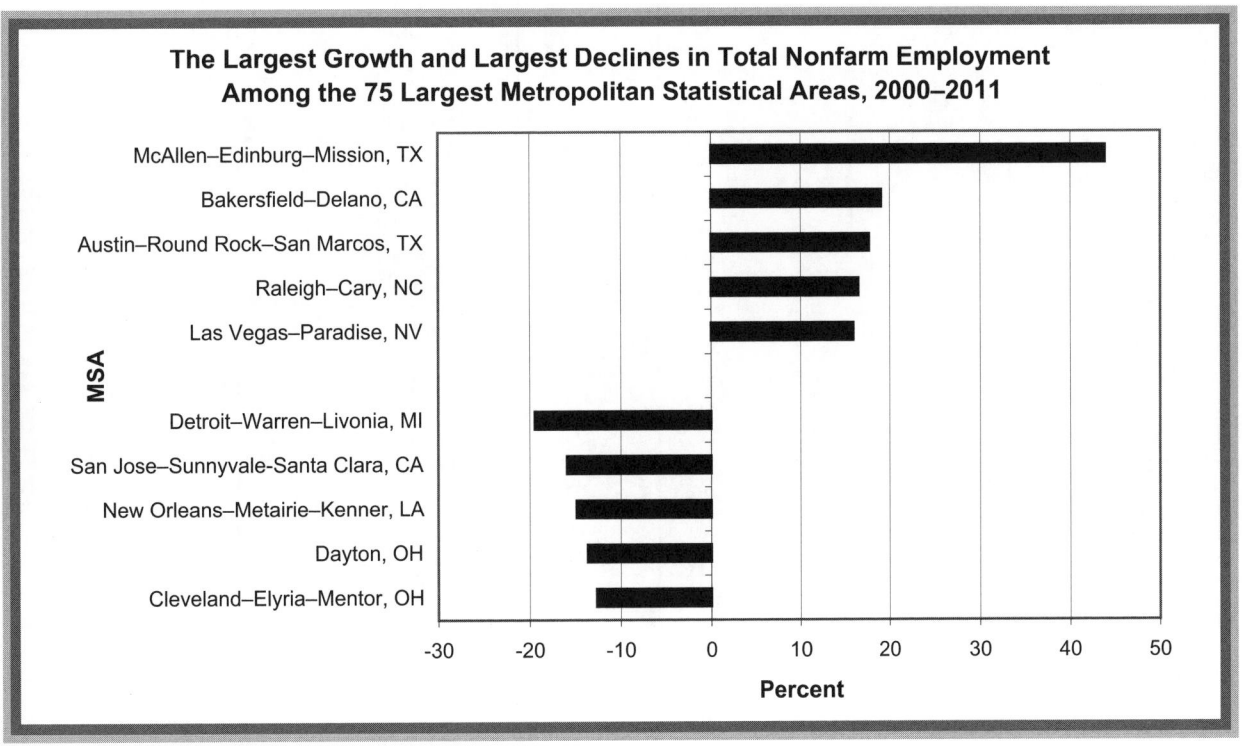

The Largest Growth and Largest Declines in Total Nonfarm Employment Among the 75 Largest Metropolitan Statistical Areas, 2000–2011

Metropolitan Statistical Areas: Employment and Unemployment Rates

Seventy-five largest; ranked by population

Rank	Metropolitan statistical area	2011 Census population estimates[1]	Total nonfarm employment, 2000	Total nonfarm employment, 2011	Percent change in total nonfarm employment, 2000–2011	Unemployment rate, 2010	Unemployment rate, 2011
1	New York–Northern New Jersey–Long Island, NY–NJ–PA	19,015,900	8,397.3	8,403.9	0.1	9.0	8.5
2	Los Angeles–Long Beach–Santa Ana, CA................	12,944,801	5,461.0	5,162.2	-5.5	11.8	11.4
3	Chicago–Joliet–Naperville, IL–IN–WI	9,504,753	4,571.4	4,291.4	-6.1	10.4	9.8
4	Dallas–Fort Worth–Arlington, TX	6,526,548	2,761.0	2,921.7	5.8	8.2	7.8
5	Houston–Sugar Land–Baytown, TX......................	6,086,538	2,250.6	2,593.1	15.2	8.5	8.1
6	Philadelphia–Camden–Wilmington, PA–NJ–DE–MD..............	5,992,414	2,744.8	2,705.9	-1.4	8.9	8.6
7	Washington–Arlington–Alexandria, DC–VA–MD–WV	5,703,948	2,678.8	2,995.5	11.8	6.3	5.8
8	Miami–Fort Lauderdale–Pompano Beach, FL.................	5,670,125	2,153.3	2,218.3	3.0	11.3	10.5
9	Atlanta–Sandy Springs–Marietta, GA...................	5,359,205	2,292.2	2,302.9	0.5	10.2	9.6
10	Boston–Cambridge–Quincy, MA–NH, NECTA..............	4,591,112	2,538.8	2,443.3	-3.8	7.6	6.6
11	San Francisco–Oakland–Fremont, CA	4,391,037	2,126.7	1,894.3	-10.9	10.3	9.4
12	Riverside–San Bernardino–Ontario, CA	4,304,997	988.4	1,129.7	14.3	14.3	13.4
13	Detroit–Warren–Livonia, MI........................	4,285,832	2,203.0	1,775.3	-19.4	13.9	11.5
14	Phoenix–Mesa–Glendale, AZ........................	4,263,236	1,578.4	1,712.8	8.5	9.8	8.6
15	Seattle–Tacoma–Bellevue, WA	3,500,026	1,646.8	1,666.1	1.2	9.7	8.7
16	Minneapolis–St. Paul–Bloomington, MN–WI..............	3,318,486	1,748.0	1,727.1	-1.2	7.3	6.3
17	San Diego–Carlsbad–San Marcos, CA	3,140,069	1,193.8	1,231.2	3.1	10.5	10.0
18	Tampa–St. Petersburg–Clearwater, FL	2,824,724	1,148.1	1,132.3	-1.4	11.8	10.9
19	St. Louis, MO–IL	2,817,355	1,338.3	1,295.4	-3.2	9.8	8.9
20	Baltimore–Towson, MD	2,729,110	1,250.3	1,293.5	3.5	8.3	7.5
21	Denver–Aurora–Broomfield, CO	2,599,504	1,211.2	1,211.6	0.0	9.0	8.3
22	Pittsburgh, PA................................	2,359,746	1,147.0	1,148.6	0.1	7.8	7.2
23	Portland–Vancouver–Hillsboro, OR–WA	2,262,605	973.3	986.1	1.3	10.5	9.1
24	San Antonio–New Braunfels, TX	2,194,927	745.2	853.2	14.5	7.4	7.4
25	Sacramento–Arden–Arcade–Roseville, CA	2,176,235	797.2	802.0	0.6	12.5	11.9
26	Orlando–Kissimmee–Sanford, FL	2,171,360	909.1	1,011.0	11.2	11.2	10.4
27	Cincinnati–Middletown, OH–KY–IN	2,138,038	1,017.4	989.4	-2.8	9.6	8.6
28	Cleveland–Elyria–Mentor, OH	2,068,283	1,136.0	992.7	-12.6	8.7	7.7
29	Kansas City, MO–KS	2,052,676	980.6	981.4	0.1	8.9	8.1
30	Las Vegas–Paradise, NV	1,969,975	697.7	808.3	15.9	14.1	13.9
31	San Jose–Sunnyvale–Santa Clara, CA	1,865,450	1,044.3	878.2	-15.9	11.2	9.9
32	Columbus, OH	1,858,464	915.4	916.9	0.2	8.7	7.5
33	Charlotte–Gastonia–Rock Hill, NC–SC	1,795,472	766.8	826.7	7.8	11.9	10.9
34	Austin–Round Rock–San Marcos, TX	1,783,519	672.7	791.4	17.6	7.1	6.8
35	Indianapolis–Carmel, IN..........................	1,778,568	853.5	881.2	3.2	9.1	8.4
36	Virginia Beach–Norfolk–Newport News, VA–NC	1,679,894	720.3	735.2	2.1	7.3	7.0
37	Nashville–Davidson–Murfreesboro–Franklin, TN	1,617,142	698.2	751.7	7.7	8.7	8.0
38	Providence–Fall River–Warwick, RI–MA, NECTA	1,600,224	576.2	542.8	-5.8	11.7	11.2
39	Milwaukee–Waukesha–West Allis, WI	1,562,216	867.9	814.1	-6.2	8.9	7.9
40	Jacksonville, FL...............................	1,360,251	564.9	589.6	4.4	10.9	10.1
41	Memphis, TN–MS–AR	1,325,605	624.4	595.4	-4.6	10.1	9.9
42	Louisville–Jefferson County, KY–IN	1,294,849	620.4	599.0	-3.4	10.2	9.7
43	Oklahoma City, OK.............................	1,278,053	535.8	569.6	6.3	6.5	5.7
44	Richmond, VA	1,269,380	587.3	609.5	3.8	7.8	6.9
45	Hartford–West Hartford–East Hartford, CT, NECTA	1,213,255	556.7	538.9	-3.2	9.4	8.8
46	New Orleans–Metairie–Kenner, LA	1,191,089	617.7	526.0	-14.8	7.3	7.2
47	Raleigh–Cary, NC	1,163,515	436.8	508.6	16.4	9.0	8.6
48	Salt Lake City, UT	1,145,905	565.6	622.0	10.0	7.8	6.5
49	Buffalo–Niagara Falls, NY	1,134,039	559.1	542.7	-2.9	8.5	8.0
50	Birmingham–Hoover, AL..........................	1,132,264	516.9	488.6	-5.5	8.9	8.3
51	Rochester, NY................................	1,055,278	530.9	508.7	-4.2	8.2	7.7
52	Tucson, AZ..................................	989,569	346.9	354.6	2.2	9.4	8.4
53	Honolulu, HI.................................	963,607	411.9	438.4	6.4	5.8	5.7
54	Tulsa, OK...................................	946,962	407.7	407.4	-0.1	7.7	6.9
55	Fresno, CA..................................	942,904	270.6	279.9	3.4	16.8	16.5
56	Bridgeport–Stamford–Norwalk, CT, NECTA	925,899	426.4	399.1	-6.4	8.6	8.2
57	Albuquerque, NM..............................	898,642	357.4	371.7	4.0	8.3	7.8
58	Omaha–Council Bluffs, NE–IA	877,110	441.6	460.4	4.3	5.2	5.0
59	Albany–Schenectady–Troy, NY	871,478	436.2	436.3	0.0	7.4	7.2
60	New Haven, CT, NECTA	861,113	274.5	267.1	-2.7	9.5	9.2
61	Bakersfield–Delano, CA..........................	851,710	194.1	231.1	19.1	15.9	14.9
62	Dayton, OH	845,388	435.3	376.1	-13.6	10.7	9.2
63	Oxnard–Thousand Oaks–Ventura, CA..................	831,771	275.0	274.6	-0.1	10.8	10.1
64	Allentown–Bethlehem–Easton, PA–NJ	824,916	323.5	338.0	4.5	9.2	8.7
65	El Paso, TX	820,790	256.4	280.3	9.3	9.8	10.3
66	Baton Rouge, LA..............................	808,242	339.2	367.4	8.3	7.5	7.4
67	Worcester, MA, NECTA	801,227	245.1	243.0	-0.9	8.9	7.8
68	McAllen–Edinburg–Mission, TX	797,810	156.9	225.7	43.8	12.1	12.0
69	Grand Rapids–Wyoming, MI........................	779,604	403.7	371.9	-7.9	10.5	8.3
70	Columbia, SC................................	777,116	341.9	345.8	1.1	9.4	8.9
71	Greensboro–High Point, NC	730,966	367.0	341.7	-6.9	11.5	11.0
72	Little Rock–North Little Rock–Conway, AR	709,901	321.6	337.4	4.9	7.0	7.0
73	North Port–Bradenton–Sarasota, FL...................	709,355	236.4	240.1	1.6	12.0	10.8
74	Knoxville, TN................................	704,500	302.9	329.5	8.8	7.9	7.3
75	Akron, OH	701,456	330.8	318.4	-3.7	9.9	8.4

1. Population estimates are from July 1, 2010, to July 1, 2011.

Employment by Industry: Akron, OH, Selected Years, 2000–2011

(Numbers in thousands, not seasonally adjusted)

Industry and year	January	February	March	April	May	June	July	August	September	October	November	December	Annual average
Total Nonfarm													
2000	322.2	325.8	328.8	331.8	335.8	332.4	330.1	328.6	331.9	334.0	334.5	333.2	330.8
2001	321.6	323.4	325.5	328.2	329.9	330.2	324.8	325.3	328.5	329.9	330.8	330.0	327.3
2002	316.4	317.4	320.0	320.5	321.7	323.2	321.7	321.2	326.1	326.9	326.0	325.6	322.2
2003	317.3	318.6	320.8	326.5	329.0	326.7	326.3	327.0	331.2	332.2	332.5	333.3	326.8
2004	320.8	323.2	326.2	330.5	332.4	331.6	330.9	331.0	335.2	337.1	338.1	338.5	331.3
2005	328.0	330.8	332.9	337.8	340.7	336.4	336.7	337.3	341.1	341.9	342.7	342.2	337.4
2006	330.4	332.4	334.6	338.6	342.4	338.8	338.1	339.3	342.9	342.1	343.3	342.7	338.8
2007	332.0	333.1	334.8	338.5	340.5	341.6	340.6	341.3	344.1	344.6	346.3	346.6	340.3
2008	335.8	337.9	337.9	340.1	340.9	339.8	339.2	339.6	341.6	340.8	339.8	338.0	339.3
2009	323.7	322.3	321.7	320.3	320.0	317.1	315.0	314.8	317.9	318.4	319.1	318.1	319.0
2010	308.5	309.9	312.5	315.4	316.2	316.7	315.4	315.9	318.9	322.1	323.1	322.7	316.4
2011	311.8	313.1	315.0	318.5	320.0	318.5	317.7	318.6	319.8	324.1	323.3	320.2	318.4
Total Private													
2000	275.7	275.4	278.4	281.2	284.1	288.3	287.1	287.2	284.3	284.2	284.4	284.8	282.9
2001	273.8	273.3	274.4	277.3	282.0	285.3	281.3	283.2	280.0	279.7	280.0	280.7	279.3
2002	268.7	267.4	269.1	269.7	273.8	277.4	278.1	279.0	276.9	275.8	274.4	274.8	273.8
2003	269.0	268.1	269.3	273.9	278.0	280.2	281.0	282.2	280.6	280.1	280.0	280.7	276.9
2004	271.2	270.9	273.6	278.1	282.0	285.6	285.8	286.8	285.2	285.2	285.8	286.4	281.4
2005	277.7	278.7	280.7	285.8	288.7	291.1	292.2	292.6	290.9	290.7	290.8	290.7	287.6
2006	280.8	280.9	283.1	287.3	290.7	294.4	294.3	295.4	292.6	291.0	292.1	292.6	289.6
2007	283.8	281.9	283.6	287.4	291.9	295.9	295.8	295.6	293.8	293.3	294.8	295.4	291.1
2008	287.3	286.4	286.3	288.7	292.4	293.8	293.6	293.5	291.0	289.1	288.1	286.7	289.7
2009	274.4	271.1	270.4	269.3	271.5	271.3	270.2	269.8	268.1	267.9	268.2	268.0	270.0
2010	260.2	259.9	262.6	265.4	268.1	271.5	271.8	272.2	270.6	272.4	273.2	273.1	268.4
2011	264.0	264.3	265.9	269.7	273.0	275.4	275.1	276.0	272.3	275.0	273.9	271.0	271.3
Goods-Producing													
2000	72.1	72.1	72.5	73.8	74.7	75.6	74.8	74.5	73.5	73.6	73.2	72.1	73.5
2001	68.5	68.1	68.2	68.7	69.1	69.6	67.8	68.7	67.5	66.9	66.2	65.9	67.9
2002	62.1	61.6	62.0	62.2	63.7	64.4	65.2	65.4	64.8	64.3	63.7	63.1	63.5
2003	61.5	61.4	61.8	63.4	64.0	64.3	64.5	64.8	64.4	64.5	63.8	63.4	63.5
2004	60.7	60.6	61.5	62.7	63.8	64.5	64.6	65.3	64.8	64.6	64.2	63.7	63.4
2005	60.9	61.4	61.8	63.2	64.0	64.4	64.5	64.5	64.1	63.6	63.7	62.7	63.2
2006	60.4	60.6	61.7	62.8	63.5	64.2	63.4	63.8	63.6	63.2	62.8	62.4	62.7
2007	60.1	59.1	59.6	60.3	61.4	62.1	62.3	61.8	61.4	60.9	61.0	60.2	60.9
2008	57.4	57.0	56.8	57.4	58.6	59.1	59.2	59.0	58.5	58.2	57.4	55.8	57.9
2009	52.5	51.3	50.4	50.0	50.4	49.8	49.8	49.7	49.4	49.5	49.2	48.7	50.1
2010	46.8	47.0	47.5	48.0	48.9	49.5	49.8	50.1	49.6	49.6	49.7	49.3	48.8
2011	47.4	47.3	47.5	48.6	49.6	50.5	51.6	52.9	52.6	53.1	52.7	50.8	50.4
Mining, Logging, and Construction													
2000	13.1	13.1	13.9	14.9	15.7	16.2	16.1	16.0	15.9	15.7	15.2	14.3	15.0
2001	12.7	12.7	13.3	14.1	15.1	15.8	16.1	16.1	15.5	15.4	14.9	14.3	14.7
2002	12.3	12.1	12.5	12.7	13.9	14.6	15.2	15.4	15.0	14.6	14.2	13.5	13.8
2003	12.1	11.7	12.2	13.5	14.3	14.7	14.9	15.2	15.0	14.9	14.4	13.8	13.9
2004	11.8	11.6	12.3	13.3	14.2	14.8	15.4	15.4	15.1	15.0	14.5	13.8	13.9
2005	12.0	12.0	12.2	13.7	14.7	15.3	15.6	15.7	15.6	15.3	15.3	14.4	14.3
2006	12.7	12.6	13.5	14.7	15.5	16.0	16.0	16.1	16.0	15.8	15.3	14.7	14.9
2007	12.9	12.3	13.0	13.8	14.7	15.3	15.5	15.3	15.1	15.0	14.8	13.8	14.3
2008	12.1	11.8	11.8	12.6	13.7	14.2	14.4	14.4	14.3	14.2	13.7	12.5	13.3
2009	11.0	10.9	11.1	11.7	12.6	12.7	13.1	12.8	12.5	12.5	12.0	11.1	12.0
2010	10.0	10.1	10.4	10.8	11.5	12.0	12.0	12.1	11.9	11.8	11.7	10.9	11.3
2011	9.5	9.3	9.5	10.4	11.2	11.8	12.4	12.7	12.5	12.6	12.1	10.9	11.2
Manufacturing													
2000	59.0	59.0	58.6	58.9	59.0	59.4	58.7	58.5	57.6	57.9	58.0	57.8	58.5
2001	55.8	55.4	54.9	54.6	54.0	53.8	51.7	52.6	52.0	51.5	51.3	51.6	53.3
2002	49.8	49.5	49.5	49.5	49.8	49.8	50.0	50.0	49.8	49.7	49.5	49.6	49.7
2003	49.4	49.7	49.6	49.9	49.7	49.6	49.6	49.6	49.4	49.6	49.4	49.6	49.6
2004	48.9	49.0	49.2	49.4	49.6	49.7	49.2	49.9	49.7	49.6	49.7	49.9	49.5
2005	48.9	49.4	49.6	49.5	49.3	49.1	48.9	48.8	48.5	48.3	48.4	48.3	48.9
2006	47.7	48.0	48.2	48.1	48.0	48.2	47.4	47.7	47.6	47.4	47.5	47.7	47.8
2007	47.2	46.8	46.6	46.5	46.7	46.8	46.8	46.5	46.3	45.9	46.2	46.4	46.6
2008	45.3	45.2	45.0	44.8	44.9	44.9	44.8	44.6	44.2	44.0	43.7	43.3	44.6
2009	41.5	40.4	39.3	38.3	37.8	37.1	36.7	36.9	36.9	37.0	37.2	37.6	38.1
2010	36.8	36.9	37.1	37.2	37.4	37.5	37.8	38.0	37.7	37.8	38.0	38.4	37.6
2011	37.9	38.0	38.0	38.2	38.4	38.7	39.2	40.2	40.1	40.5	40.6	39.9	39.1
Service-Providing													
2000	250.1	253.7	256.3	258.0	261.1	256.8	255.3	254.1	258.4	260.4	261.3	261.1	257.2
2001	253.1	255.3	257.3	259.5	260.8	260.6	257.0	256.6	261.0	263.0	264.6	264.1	259.4
2002	254.3	255.8	258.0	258.3	258.0	258.8	256.5	255.8	261.3	262.6	262.3	262.5	258.7
2003	255.8	257.2	259.0	263.1	265.0	262.4	261.8	262.2	266.8	267.7	268.7	269.9	263.3
2004	260.1	262.6	264.7	267.8	268.6	267.1	266.3	265.7	270.4	272.5	273.9	274.8	267.9
2005	267.1	269.4	271.1	274.6	276.7	272.0	272.2	272.8	277.0	278.3	279.0	279.5	274.1
2006	270.0	271.8	272.9	275.8	278.9	274.6	274.7	275.5	279.3	278.9	280.5	280.3	276.1
2007	271.9	274.0	275.2	278.2	279.1	279.5	278.3	279.5	282.7	283.7	285.3	286.4	279.5
2008	278.4	280.9	281.1	282.7	282.3	280.7	280.0	280.6	283.1	282.6	282.4	282.2	281.4
2009	271.2	271.0	271.3	270.3	269.6	267.3	265.2	265.1	268.5	268.9	269.9	269.4	269.0
2010	261.7	262.9	265.0	267.4	267.3	267.2	265.6	265.8	269.3	272.5	273.4	273.4	267.6
2011	264.4	265.8	267.5	269.9	270.4	268.0	266.1	265.7	267.2	271.0	270.6	269.4	268.0

Employment by Industry: Akron, OH, Selected Years, 2000–2011—*Continued*

(Numbers in thousands, not seasonally adjusted)

Industry and year	January	February	March	April	May	June	July	August	September	October	November	December	Annual average
Trade, Transportation, and Utilities													
2000	65.5	65.0	65.4	65.7	66.0	66.5	66.1	66.5	66.4	67.3	68.7	69.7	66.6
2001	68.6	67.4	67.5	67.9	68.6	68.9	67.6	67.4	66.9	67.0	67.7	68.4	67.8
2002	65.5	64.5	64.7	64.7	65.0	65.3	64.9	65.1	64.6	64.9	65.9	66.4	65.1
2003	64.5	63.7	64.1	64.5	65.0	65.4	65.1	65.4	65.6	66.3	67.4	68.1	65.4
2004	64.8	64.5	64.7	65.3	65.8	66.1	66.0	66.4	66.6	67.6	68.7	69.4	66.3
2005	66.7	66.7	67.1	68.0	68.0	68.1	67.9	67.6	67.3	67.6	68.8	69.5	67.8
2006	67.0	66.3	66.3	66.4	66.8	67.6	67.5	67.8	67.4	68.1	69.7	70.4	67.6
2007	67.7	66.6	66.8	66.9	67.7	67.9	67.8	67.9	67.9	68.8	70.3	71.3	68.1
2008	68.5	67.0	66.8	67.1	67.2	67.3	67.2	67.2	66.8	66.7	67.3	67.5	67.2
2009	63.9	62.5	62.4	61.3	61.4	61.6	61.6	61.4	61.3	61.9	62.8	63.4	62.1
2010	60.8	60.1	60.8	60.6	61.1	61.5	61.4	61.3	61.0	62.0	63.0	63.5	61.4
2011	61.0	60.9	61.0	61.6	62.0	62.2	61.9	61.8	61.7	62.6	63.5	64.2	62.0
Wholesale Trade													
2000	16.6	16.6	16.8	16.8	16.8	16.9	16.9	16.9	16.8	16.8	16.8	16.8	16.8
2001	17.5	17.4	17.4	17.3	17.6	17.6	17.3	17.4	17.2	17.0	16.9	17.0	17.3
2002	16.5	16.3	16.4	16.3	16.1	16.0	15.9	15.8	15.7	15.6	15.5	15.6	16.0
2003	16.1	16.1	16.2	16.1	16.1	16.2	16.1	16.2	16.2	16.2	16.3	16.3	16.2
2004	15.9	16.0	16.1	16.1	16.2	16.3	16.4	16.5	16.6	16.7	16.8	17.0	16.4
2005	17.0	17.1	17.2	17.3	17.3	17.4	17.4	17.3	17.3	17.5	17.6	17.7	17.3
2006	17.6	17.7	17.7	17.7	17.8	18.1	18.0	18.2	18.1	18.3	18.4	18.4	18.0
2007	18.4	18.3	18.4	18.3	18.4	18.4	18.3	18.3	18.2	18.4	18.3	18.4	18.3
2008	18.2	18.1	18.1	18.2	18.1	18.1	18.1	18.1	17.9	17.9	17.7	17.6	18.0
2009	17.3	17.1	16.9	16.9	16.8	16.8	17.0	16.9	16.7	16.6	16.6	16.9	16.9
2010	16.7	16.6	17.0	16.9	17.0	17.1	17.0	17.1	17.1	17.1	17.0	17.1	17.0
2011	17.1	17.3	17.3	17.5	17.6	17.6	17.6	17.6	17.6	17.7	17.8	17.9	17.6
Retail Trade													
2000	40.4	40.0	40.2	40.0	40.2	40.7	40.0	40.4	40.3	40.8	42.2	43.1	40.7
2001	40.8	40.0	40.0	40.3	40.7	40.9	40.1	39.8	39.5	39.9	40.8	41.4	40.4
2002	38.5	37.9	38.0	38.0	38.3	38.6	38.3	38.5	38.3	38.8	39.9	40.5	38.6
2003	37.9	37.5	37.7	37.9	38.3	38.5	38.4	38.5	38.7	39.2	40.3	41.0	38.7
2004	38.6	38.2	38.3	38.5	38.7	38.8	38.5	38.6	38.7	39.3	40.2	40.7	38.9
2005	38.3	38.1	38.3	38.9	39.0	38.9	38.6	38.5	38.2	38.6	39.6	40.2	38.8
2006	38.3	37.6	37.7	37.7	37.9	38.3	38.3	38.4	38.1	38.5	40.0	40.6	38.5
2007	38.5	37.6	37.7	37.6	38.3	38.4	38.5	38.5	38.7	39.3	41.0	41.8	38.8
2008	39.7	38.4	38.3	38.3	38.3	38.3	38.2	38.1	37.9	37.8	38.6	39.0	38.4
2009	36.2	35.3	35.4	34.3	34.5	34.7	34.6	34.5	34.6	35.2	36.2	36.5	35.2
2010	34.5	34.0	34.2	33.9	34.2	34.5	34.5	34.4	34.2	35.1	36.3	36.7	34.7
2011	34.5	34.1	34.3	34.5	34.7	34.9	34.7	34.5	34.4	35.1	35.9	36.6	34.9
Transportation and Utilities													
2000	8.5	8.4	8.4	8.9	9.0	8.9	9.2	9.2	9.3	9.7	9.7	9.8	9.1
2001	10.3	10.0	10.1	10.3	10.3	10.4	10.2	10.2	10.2	10.1	10.0	10.0	10.2
2002	10.5	10.3	10.3	10.4	10.6	10.7	10.7	10.8	10.6	10.5	10.5	10.3	10.5
2003	10.5	10.1	10.2	10.5	10.6	10.7	10.6	10.7	10.7	10.9	10.8	10.8	10.6
2004	10.3	10.3	10.3	10.7	10.9	11.0	11.1	11.3	11.3	11.6	11.7	11.7	11.0
2005	11.4	11.5	11.6	11.8	11.7	11.8	11.9	11.8	11.8	11.5	11.6	11.6	11.7
2006	11.1	11.0	10.9	11.0	11.1	11.2	11.2	11.2	11.2	11.3	11.3	11.4	11.2
2007	10.8	10.7	10.7	11.0	11.0	11.1	11.0	11.1	11.0	11.1	11.0	11.1	11.0
2008	10.6	10.5	10.4	10.6	10.8	10.9	10.9	11.0	11.0	11.0	11.0	10.9	10.8
2009	10.4	10.1	10.1	10.1	10.1	10.1	10.0	10.0	10.0	10.1	10.0	10.0	10.1
2010	9.6	9.5	9.6	9.8	9.9	9.9	9.9	9.8	9.7	9.8	9.7	9.7	9.7
2011	9.4	9.5	9.4	9.6	9.7	9.7	9.6	9.7	9.7	9.8	9.8	9.7	9.6
Information													
2000	5.0	5.1	5.1	5.2	5.1	5.2	5.3	5.3	5.4	5.4	5.4	5.4	5.2
2001	5.1	5.2	5.1	5.0	5.0	5.0	5.0	5.1	5.0	5.1	5.1	5.1	5.1
2002	5.5	5.5	5.4	5.3	5.3	5.4	5.5	5.5	5.5	5.5	5.5	5.6	5.5
2003	5.5	5.5	5.5	5.5	5.5	5.4	5.2	5.2	5.0	4.8	4.8	4.7	5.2
2004	4.8	4.7	4.6	4.6	4.6	4.6	4.5	4.4	4.3	4.3	4.3	4.4	4.5
2005	4.4	4.4	4.4	4.4	4.5	4.5	4.5	4.5	4.5	4.5	4.5	4.5	4.5
2006	4.5	4.5	4.5	4.6	4.6	4.6	4.7	4.6	4.5	4.4	4.4	4.5	4.5
2007	4.5	4.5	4.5	4.6	4.6	4.6	4.6	4.6	4.5	4.5	4.5	4.5	4.5
2008	4.5	4.5	4.4	4.4	4.4	4.5	4.5	4.5	4.4	4.3	4.4	4.4	4.4
2009	4.4	4.3	4.3	4.2	4.2	4.2	4.2	4.2	4.1	4.1	4.1	4.1	4.2
2010	4.2	4.1	4.1	4.0	4.0	4.0	4.0	4.0	4.0	3.9	3.9	3.9	4.0
2011	3.8	3.8	3.8	3.8	3.8	3.9	3.9	3.8	3.8	3.8	3.8	3.8	3.8
Financial Activities													
2000	14.5	14.4	14.6	14.3	14.6	14.9	14.7	14.8	14.8	14.6	14.6	14.7	14.6
2001	14.1	14.5	14.5	14.4	14.5	14.8	14.7	14.8	14.7	14.6	14.6	14.6	14.6
2002	14.1	14.2	14.2	13.9	14.1	14.2	14.2	14.3	14.3	14.3	14.4	14.4	14.2
2003	14.2	14.2	14.3	14.6	14.7	14.7	14.7	14.7	14.6	14.5	14.5	14.6	14.5
2004	14.5	14.4	14.6	14.6	14.8	14.9	14.9	14.9	14.8	14.7	14.9	15.0	14.8
2005	14.9	14.9	14.9	14.8	14.8	14.8	14.8	14.8	14.8	14.6	14.6	14.5	14.8
2006	14.5	14.4	14.4	14.6	14.5	14.6	14.5	14.5	14.3	14.4	14.4	14.4	14.5
2007	14.2	14.2	14.0	14.1	14.1	14.0	13.9	14.0	13.9	13.8	13.7	13.8	14.0
2008	13.9	13.9	13.9	13.9	14.0	14.1	14.0	14.0	13.9	13.9	13.8	13.9	13.9
2009	13.6	13.4	13.4	13.3	13.4	13.5	13.5	13.5	13.5	13.3	13.3	13.4	13.4
2010	13.1	13.2	13.2	13.3	13.4	13.5	13.5	13.5	13.5	13.5	13.5	13.6	13.4
2011	13.5	13.5	13.5	13.6	13.7	13.7	13.7	13.7	13.6	13.5	13.5	13.5	13.6

Employment by Industry: Akron, OH, Selected Years, 2000–2011—*Continued*

(Numbers in thousands, not seasonally adjusted)

Industry and year	January	February	March	April	May	June	July	August	September	October	November	December	Annual average
Professional and Business Services													
2000	37.3	37.1	38.0	39.2	38.8	39.6	39.4	39.5	39.4	39.3	38.7	38.3	38.7
2001	36.2	36.1	36.5	37.4	38.7	39.4	38.9	39.5	39.9	40.8	41.4	41.3	38.8
2002	38.7	38.7	39.2	39.0	39.1	39.6	40.0	40.5	40.8	41.0	40.1	40.1	39.7
2003	40.1	40.5	40.2	40.9	41.7	42.0	42.5	43.0	43.0	42.7	43.0	43.0	41.9
2004	41.9	42.0	42.8	43.8	43.9	44.9	45.1	45.1	45.2	45.1	45.4	45.5	44.2
2005	44.4	44.8	44.9	46.3	46.8	47.3	48.1	48.6	48.5	49.5	49.1	49.2	47.3
2006	47.0	47.4	47.8	49.4	50.0	50.7	51.3	51.8	51.3	50.6	50.4	50.4	49.8
2007	48.4	48.6	48.6	50.7	51.4	52.3	52.3	52.5	52.7	52.5	52.7	52.9	51.3
2008	52.2	52.9	52.9	53.7	53.8	53.6	53.5	53.5	53.1	52.4	52.0	51.6	52.9
2009	49.2	48.9	48.4	48.7	48.5	48.2	47.6	47.5	47.1	46.8	46.9	46.4	47.9
2010	45.6	45.6	45.9	47.2	47.4	48.1	48.7	48.8	48.5	50.0	50.2	49.9	48.0
2011	47.4	47.5	48.1	49.0	49.4	49.7	48.9	49.4	48.7	49.9	48.5	47.6	48.7
Education and Health Services													
2000	38.3	38.6	38.9	38.1	38.3	38.2	38.4	38.6	38.9	39.3	39.5	39.7	38.7
2001	39.0	39.3	39.6	39.8	40.0	39.9	39.5	39.9	40.3	40.6	40.9	41.3	40.0
2002	40.3	40.6	40.8	40.6	40.7	40.5	40.5	40.6	41.0	41.2	41.5	41.6	40.8
2003	41.2	41.2	41.2	41.2	41.3	41.2	41.2	41.3	42.0	42.1	42.3	42.5	41.6
2004	41.8	42.1	42.3	42.8	43.0	43.0	42.8	43.0	43.1	43.6	43.8	44.0	42.9
2005	43.3	43.4	43.7	43.9	44.0	43.8	44.1	44.2	44.6	45.3	45.3	45.5	44.3
2006	44.6	44.7	44.9	45.2	45.4	45.3	44.8	44.9	45.4	45.9	46.1	46.2	45.3
2007	45.9	46.0	46.3	46.5	46.9	47.1	47.2	47.3	47.6	48.0	48.3	48.3	47.1
2008	48.1	48.1	48.3	48.3	48.6	48.7	48.7	48.8	49.1	49.5	49.8	49.8	48.8
2009	49.0	49.1	49.4	49.3	49.5	49.2	49.0	49.2	49.3	49.7	49.8	49.8	49.4
2010	49.5	49.5	49.9	50.1	50.1	50.3	50.0	50.2	50.5	50.6	50.7	50.5	50.2
2011	50.2	50.5	50.5	50.7	50.8	50.7	50.2	50.3	50.4	50.6	51.7	51.4	50.7
Leisure and Hospitality													
2000	29.3	29.3	30.0	31.3	32.9	34.3	34.5	34.3	32.2	31.1	30.7	31.1	31.8
2001	28.2	28.4	28.8	29.8	31.7	33.2	33.3	33.3	31.4	30.4	29.9	29.8	30.7
2002	28.6	28.4	28.8	29.9	31.7	33.6	33.6	33.5	31.9	30.6	29.5	29.6	30.8
2003	28.1	27.7	28.2	29.8	31.7	33.0	33.7	33.8	32.2	31.4	30.4	30.6	30.9
2004	29.1	29.0	29.4	30.6	32.3	33.6	34.0	33.9	32.6	31.4	30.6	30.3	31.4
2005	29.3	29.1	29.8	31.1	32.4	33.9	34.1	34.2	33.1	31.6	30.8	30.7	31.7
2006	29.2	29.3	29.7	30.6	32.1	33.4	34.3	34.1	32.3	30.7	30.5	30.5	31.4
2007	29.4	29.4	30.1	30.7	32.1	34.1	33.9	33.7	32.2	30.9	30.4	30.4	31.4
2008	28.9	29.1	29.3	30.0	31.8	32.4	32.4	32.4	31.3	30.3	29.6	29.9	30.6
2009	28.2	28.1	28.5	29.0	30.6	31.2	30.9	30.8	30.2	29.3	28.6	28.9	29.5
2010	27.2	27.4	28.0	29.2	30.2	31.3	31.1	31.0	30.3	29.5	28.9	29.0	29.4
2011	27.5	27.6	28.2	29.1	30.4	31.3	31.6	30.8	28.4	28.4	27.1	26.5	28.9
Other Services													
2000	13.7	13.8	13.9	13.6	13.7	14.0	13.9	13.7	13.7	13.6	13.6	13.8	13.8
2001	14.1	14.3	14.2	14.3	14.4	14.5	14.5	14.5	14.3	14.3	14.2	14.3	14.3
2002	13.9	13.9	14.0	14.1	14.2	14.4	14.2	14.1	14.0	14.0	13.9	14.0	14.1
2003	13.9	13.9	14.0	14.0	14.1	14.2	14.1	14.0	13.8	13.8	13.8	13.8	14.0
2004	13.6	13.6	13.7	13.7	13.8	14.0	13.9	13.8	13.8	13.9	13.9	14.1	13.8
2005	13.8	14.0	14.1	14.1	14.2	14.3	14.2	14.2	14.0	14.0	14.0	14.1	14.1
2006	13.6	13.7	13.8	13.7	13.8	14.0	13.8	13.9	13.8	13.7	13.8	13.8	13.8
2007	13.6	13.5	13.7	13.6	13.7	13.8	13.8	13.8	13.6	13.9	13.9	14.0	13.7
2008	13.8	13.9	13.9	13.9	14.0	14.1	14.1	14.1	13.9	13.8	13.8	13.8	13.9
2009	13.6	13.5	13.6	13.5	13.5	13.6	13.6	13.5	13.4	13.3	13.4	13.4	13.5
2010	13.0	13.0	13.2	13.0	13.0	13.3	13.3	13.3	13.2	13.3	13.3	13.4	13.2
2011	13.2	13.2	13.3	13.3	13.3	13.4	13.3	13.3	13.1	13.1	13.1	13.2	13.2
Government													
2000	46.5	50.4	50.4	50.6	51.7	44.1	43.0	41.4	47.6	49.8	50.1	48.4	47.8
2001	47.8	50.1	51.1	50.9	47.9	44.9	43.5	42.1	48.5	50.2	50.8	49.3	48.1
2002	47.7	50.0	50.9	50.8	47.9	45.8	43.6	42.2	49.2	51.1	51.6	50.8	48.5
2003	48.3	50.5	51.5	52.6	51.0	46.5	45.3	44.8	50.6	52.1	52.5	52.6	49.9
2004	49.6	52.3	52.6	52.4	50.4	46.0	45.1	44.2	50.0	51.9	52.3	52.1	49.9
2005	50.3	52.1	52.2	52.0	52.0	45.3	44.5	44.7	50.2	51.2	51.9	51.5	49.8
2006	49.6	51.5	51.5	51.3	51.7	44.4	43.8	43.9	50.3	51.1	51.2	50.1	49.2
2007	48.2	51.2	51.2	51.1	48.6	45.7	44.8	45.7	50.3	51.3	51.5	51.2	49.2
2008	48.5	51.5	51.6	51.4	48.5	46.0	45.6	46.1	50.6	51.7	51.7	51.3	49.5
2009	49.3	51.2	51.3	51.0	48.5	45.8	44.8	45.0	49.8	50.5	50.9	50.1	49.0
2010	48.3	50.0	49.9	50.0	48.1	45.2	43.6	43.7	48.3	49.7	49.9	49.6	48.0
2011	47.8	48.8	49.1	48.8	47.0	43.1	42.6	42.6	47.5	49.1	49.4	49.2	47.1

Employment by Industry: Albany–Schenectady–Troy, NY, Selected Years, 2000–2011

(Numbers in thousands, not seasonally adjusted)

Industry and year	January	February	March	April	May	June	July	August	September	October	November	December	Annual average
Total Nonfarm													
2000	423.7	427.0	429.4	434.6	438.3	441.6	433.2	433.6	438.0	442.4	445.6	446.6	436.2
2001	432.2	434.4	436.9	439.3	443.6	445.0	438.2	441.3	439.2	441.8	444.9	443.8	440.1
2002	427.1	431.8	435.3	439.2	441.3	442.3	435.6	438.3	440.5	442.8	444.2	443.1	438.5
2003	427.8	431.4	432.4	435.5	439.8	440.1	435.2	437.7	438.7	442.4	445.1	444.7	437.6
2004	430.7	434.1	437.0	440.4	447.5	446.3	441.4	441.9	443.4	446.7	448.2	449.1	442.2
2005	435.0	437.8	438.2	445.1	446.5	447.8	443.3	444.3	446.0	448.7	450.4	449.8	444.4
2006	434.8	439.1	442.2	446.3	448.5	449.4	442.6	443.2	445.5	450.5	452.6	453.7	445.7
2007	437.6	440.4	442.9	444.3	450.2	452.6	444.6	445.7	448.6	453.7	455.9	456.1	447.7
2008	440.9	444.6	445.5	450.8	456.1	457.2	450.3	450.2	451.0	455.5	455.8	453.5	451.0
2009	436.6	440.8	440.9	443.4	446.0	445.7	437.9	437.0	438.9	443.5	444.7	442.6	441.5
2010	427.2	431.6	432.9	439.2	442.6	441.6	433.7	432.4	435.3	439.3	441.6	439.7	436.4
2011	424.0	430.4	431.0	438.8	439.5	439.9	437.5	434.2	436.0	441.1	441.7	441.6	436.3
Total Private													
2000	318.6	319.5	321.9	326.4	329.4	333.1	330.7	331.9	331.7	334.7	336.8	338.7	329.5
2001	325.8	325.3	328.0	329.9	334.2	336.8	334.2	336.8	332.2	332.8	334.6	334.5	332.1
2002	319.9	321.5	325.0	328.5	330.7	332.4	331.8	335.1	331.9	332.9	333.7	332.8	329.7
2003	319.8	321.2	322.8	326.5	330.8	331.9	332.3	335.5	331.9	333.9	336.4	335.9	329.9
2004	324.6	325.8	328.6	331.3	338.0	337.0	337.9	339.2	337.2	338.5	339.6	340.6	334.9
2005	327.8	329.3	329.6	336.0	337.4	339.4	340.5	342.2	340.1	340.4	341.9	341.2	337.2
2006	328.7	331.0	334.1	337.7	340.0	341.8	340.3	341.9	340.6	342.6	344.1	344.5	338.9
2007	330.7	331.5	334.3	335.5	340.8	343.4	342.1	343.0	342.5	344.3	346.1	345.2	340.0
2008	333.8	335.4	336.5	340.3	344.8	346.4	345.1	346.1	343.8	345.1	345.3	342.5	342.1
2009	329.3	330.7	331.3	332.3	335.0	335.5	333.6	334.2	333.1	334.4	335.0	332.7	333.1
2010	320.0	322.7	324.4	330.1	331.7	331.4	332.4	333.3	333.1	335.1	336.8	335.1	330.5
2011	323.3	327.1	327.9	335.2	335.8	336.3	338.9	336.7	336.0	337.5	337.9	337.8	334.2
Goods-Producing													
2000	43.8	43.1	43.9	45.4	47.0	47.8	47.3	47.8	47.3	47.3	46.9	46.2	46.2
2001	43.8	43.4	43.6	44.9	46.4	47.3	47.0	47.2	46.4	45.9	45.0	43.4	45.4
2002	40.4	39.7	40.3	41.5	42.7	43.4	43.9	44.1	43.6	43.0	42.4	40.8	42.2
2003	38.6	37.8	37.9	38.9	40.5	41.4	41.8	42.4	41.9	42.0	41.3	40.2	40.4
2004	38.0	37.5	37.9	39.6	41.1	41.8	42.7	42.9	42.3	42.0	41.7	40.4	40.7
2005	38.8	38.1	38.3	40.5	41.8	42.6	43.3	43.4	42.8	42.4	42.3	40.9	41.3
2006	39.1	38.5	39.1	40.9	42.1	42.9	43.0	43.3	42.7	42.7	42.0	40.8	41.4
2007	38.8	37.8	38.6	39.9	41.9	42.8	43.4	43.4	42.9	43.0	42.2	40.9	41.3
2008	38.7	37.8	38.1	39.5	41.3	42.3	42.7	42.9	42.4	42.3	41.3	39.6	40.7
2009	36.7	35.8	35.7	36.8	37.8	38.8	39.3	39.5	38.9	38.7	38.3	36.9	37.8
2010	34.7	34.0	34.4	36.1	37.0	37.9	38.0	38.2	38.5	38.1	37.7	36.8	36.8
2011	35.2	34.8	35.1	37.1	38.2	39.4	40.5	40.2	39.8	40.1	40.5	38.6	38.3
Mining, Logging, and Construction													
2000	15.4	14.9	15.5	16.7	18.1	18.8	19.1	19.4	19.0	18.7	18.5	17.4	17.6
2001	15.8	15.4	15.6	17.0	18.5	19.2	19.6	19.9	19.4	19.1	18.5	17.3	17.9
2002	15.3	14.8	15.3	16.7	17.9	18.4	19.1	19.3	18.9	18.5	18.3	17.1	17.5
2003	15.5	14.9	15.0	16.1	17.7	18.6	19.5	19.8	19.3	19.3	18.6	17.6	17.7
2004	15.8	15.4	15.7	17.1	18.5	19.0	19.6	19.5	19.2	19.0	18.6	17.4	17.9
2005	16.0	15.4	15.5	17.4	18.6	19.3	20.0	20.0	19.6	19.4	19.2	17.9	18.2
2006	16.1	15.6	16.1	17.6	18.7	19.4	19.6	19.8	19.4	19.4	18.6	17.6	18.2
2007	16.0	15.1	15.7	16.8	18.8	19.4	20.0	20.1	19.8	19.9	19.2	17.9	18.2
2008	16.1	15.5	15.7	17.2	18.7	19.4	20.0	20.2	19.9	19.9	19.0	17.5	18.3
2009	15.3	14.7	14.9	16.1	17.2	18.0	18.7	18.9	18.3	18.1	17.7	16.4	17.0
2010	14.5	14.0	14.3	15.9	16.7	17.4	18.1	18.4	18.1	17.6	17.0	16.2	16.5
2011	14.7	14.2	14.4	15.9	16.9	17.8	18.9	18.8	18.5	18.6	18.7	17.1	17.0
Manufacturing													
2000	28.4	28.2	28.4	28.7	28.9	29.0	28.2	28.4	28.3	28.6	28.4	28.8	28.5
2001	28.0	28.0	28.0	27.9	27.9	28.1	27.4	27.3	27.0	26.8	26.5	26.1	27.4
2002	25.1	24.9	25.0	24.8	24.8	25.0	24.8	24.8	24.7	24.5	24.1	23.7	24.7
2003	23.1	22.9	22.9	22.8	22.8	22.8	22.3	22.6	22.6	22.7	22.7	22.6	22.7
2004	22.2	22.1	22.2	22.5	22.6	22.8	23.1	23.4	23.1	23.0	23.1	23.0	22.8
2005	22.8	22.7	22.8	23.1	23.2	23.3	23.3	23.4	23.2	23.0	23.1	23.0	23.1
2006	23.0	22.9	23.0	23.3	23.4	23.5	23.4	23.5	23.3	23.3	23.4	23.2	23.3
2007	22.8	22.7	22.9	23.1	23.1	23.4	23.4	23.3	23.1	23.1	23.0	23.0	23.1
2008	22.6	22.3	22.4	22.3	22.6	22.9	22.7	22.7	22.5	22.4	22.3	22.1	22.5
2009	21.4	21.1	20.8	20.7	20.6	20.8	20.6	20.6	20.6	20.6	20.6	20.5	20.7
2010	20.2	20.0	20.1	20.2	20.3	20.5	19.9	19.8	20.4	20.5	20.7	20.6	20.3
2011	20.5	20.6	20.7	21.2	21.3	21.6	21.6	21.4	21.3	21.5	21.8	21.5	21.3
Service-Providing													
2000	379.9	383.9	385.5	389.2	391.3	393.8	385.9	385.8	390.7	395.1	398.7	400.4	390.0
2001	388.4	391.0	393.3	394.4	397.2	397.7	391.2	394.1	392.8	395.9	399.9	400.4	394.7
2002	386.7	392.1	395.0	397.7	398.6	398.9	391.7	394.2	396.9	399.8	401.8	402.3	396.3
2003	389.2	393.6	394.5	396.6	399.3	398.7	393.4	395.3	396.8	400.4	403.8	404.5	397.2
2004	392.7	396.6	399.1	400.8	406.4	404.5	398.7	399.0	401.1	404.7	406.5	408.7	401.6
2005	396.2	399.7	399.9	404.6	404.7	405.2	400.0	400.9	403.2	406.3	408.1	408.9	403.1
2006	395.7	400.6	403.1	405.4	406.4	406.5	399.6	399.9	402.8	407.8	410.6	412.9	404.3
2007	398.8	402.6	404.3	404.4	408.3	409.8	401.2	402.3	405.7	410.7	413.7	415.2	406.4
2008	402.2	406.8	407.4	411.3	414.8	414.9	407.6	407.3	408.6	413.2	414.5	413.9	410.2
2009	399.9	405.0	405.2	406.6	408.2	406.9	398.6	397.5	400.0	404.8	406.4	405.7	403.7
2010	392.5	397.6	398.5	403.1	405.6	403.7	395.7	394.2	396.8	401.2	403.9	402.9	399.6
2011	388.8	395.6	395.9	401.7	401.3	400.5	397.0	394.0	396.2	401.0	401.2	403.0	398.0

Employment by Industry: Albany–Schenectady–Troy, NY, Selected Years, 2000–2011—*Continued*

(Numbers in thousands, not seasonally adjusted)

Industry and year	January	February	March	April	May	June	July	August	September	October	November	December	Annual average
Trade, Transportation, and Utilities													
2000	77.3	76.3	76.6	76.8	77.7	78.5	78.3	79.4	79.3	80.6	82.8	84.6	79.0
2001	78.8	77.6	77.4	76.8	77.6	78.5	77.3	77.5	76.7	77.9	80.5	81.5	78.2
2002	76.8	75.6	76.0	76.4	76.8	77.7	77.1	77.2	77.0	77.4	79.3	80.9	77.4
2003	77.4	76.4	76.5	76.4	77.3	78.4	77.5	78.0	78.1	79.5	81.8	83.2	78.4
2004	78.7	78.0	78.2	77.8	79.0	79.8	78.8	79.0	79.0	80.4	82.3	83.7	79.6
2005	79.4	78.0	77.9	78.6	79.1	79.7	79.8	80.1	79.6	80.2	82.0	83.5	79.8
2006	78.8	77.4	77.7	78.0	79.0	79.6	78.4	78.5	77.8	78.9	81.1	82.4	79.0
2007	77.9	76.1	76.8	75.9	77.2	77.8	77.1	76.8	76.7	77.6	79.4	80.3	77.5
2008	76.4	74.9	75.0	75.2	76.1	76.8	76.1	76.2	75.8	76.5	77.4	78.5	76.2
2009	74.1	72.9	72.5	72.4	73.3	74.1	73.0	73.1	72.6	73.1	74.6	75.6	73.4
2010	71.7	70.2	70.7	71.3	71.8	72.6	72.0	72.5	71.8	72.4	73.9	75.0	72.2
2011	71.3	70.2	70.4	71.3	71.7	72.5	71.8	71.7	71.7	72.1	73.1	74.3	71.8
Wholesale Trade													
2000	16.2	16.2	16.4	16.5	16.5	16.5	16.5	16.6	16.5	16.5	16.6	16.7	16.5
2001	16.3	16.3	16.2	16.4	16.4	16.6	16.8	16.6	16.5	16.3	16.2	16.3	16.4
2002	16.3	16.2	16.2	16.2	16.3	16.3	16.4	16.3	16.2	16.1	16.2	16.2	16.2
2003	16.5	16.5	16.5	16.4	16.5	16.6	16.6	16.6	16.6	16.6	16.8	17.0	16.6
2004	16.7	16.9	16.9	16.9	16.8	16.7	16.4	16.4	16.3	16.2	16.2	16.2	16.6
2005	15.9	15.7	15.7	15.7	15.6	15.6	15.9	15.8	15.6	15.6	15.7	15.7	15.7
2006	15.3	15.2	15.2	14.9	14.9	15.0	14.9	14.9	14.7	14.7	14.6	14.8	14.9
2007	14.7	14.6	14.8	14.7	14.7	14.8	14.6	14.5	14.2	14.2	14.1	14.1	14.5
2008	13.7	13.7	13.7	13.7	13.8	13.9	14.0	14.0	13.9	13.9	13.9	14.0	13.9
2009	13.6	13.6	13.5	13.5	13.4	13.4	13.4	13.4	13.2	13.1	13.1	13.2	13.4
2010	12.7	12.7	12.7	12.9	13.0	13.0	13.0	13.1	13.1	13.2	13.3	13.2	13.0
2011	13.1	13.1	13.1	13.3	13.3	13.3	13.2	13.2	13.1	13.1	13.1	13.2	13.2
Retail Trade													
2000	49.2	48.1	48.1	48.1	48.5	49.2	49.2	50.0	49.9	50.9	52.9	54.5	49.9
2001	49.3	48.2	48.1	47.2	47.7	48.4	47.5	47.7	46.9	48.1	50.8	51.7	48.5
2002	47.8	46.8	47.2	47.5	47.7	48.5	48.2	48.3	47.9	48.2	50.0	51.6	48.3
2003	48.1	47.0	47.1	47.3	48.0	49.0	48.6	49.0	48.8	50.1	52.2	53.5	49.1
2004	49.9	48.8	48.9	48.5	49.4	50.2	49.8	50.1	49.8	51.0	52.9	54.3	50.3
2005	50.6	49.3	49.2	49.5	49.9	50.3	50.3	50.5	49.8	50.5	52.0	53.5	50.5
2006	49.8	48.5	48.7	49.4	50.2	50.7	50.1	50.0	49.2	50.2	52.6	53.6	50.3
2007	50.0	48.4	48.7	48.1	49.1	49.6	49.3	49.2	49.0	49.8	51.6	52.4	49.6
2008	49.6	48.2	48.2	48.3	48.8	49.3	48.8	48.9	48.3	48.8	49.7	50.6	49.0
2009	47.3	46.2	45.9	45.8	46.6	47.4	46.7	46.8	46.2	46.8	48.2	49.0	46.9
2010	46.2	44.8	45.1	45.5	45.9	46.7	46.2	46.6	45.9	46.5	47.8	48.9	46.3
2011	46.1	45.0	45.3	45.9	46.1	46.9	46.6	46.5	46.3	46.6	47.6	48.7	46.5
Transportation and Utilities													
2000	11.9	12.0	12.1	12.2	12.7	12.8	12.6	12.8	12.9	13.2	13.3	13.4	12.7
2001	13.2	13.1	13.1	13.2	13.5	13.5	13.0	13.2	13.3	13.5	13.5	13.5	13.3
2002	12.7	12.6	12.6	12.7	12.8	12.9	12.5	12.6	12.9	13.1	13.1	13.1	12.8
2003	12.8	12.9	12.9	12.7	12.8	12.8	12.3	12.4	12.7	12.8	12.8	12.7	12.7
2004	12.1	12.3	12.4	12.4	12.8	12.9	12.6	12.5	12.9	13.2	13.2	13.2	12.7
2005	12.9	13.0	13.0	13.4	13.6	13.8	13.6	13.8	14.2	14.1	14.3	14.3	13.7
2006	13.7	13.7	13.8	13.7	13.9	13.9	13.4	13.6	13.9	14.0	13.9	14.0	13.8
2007	13.2	13.1	13.3	13.1	13.4	13.4	13.2	13.1	13.5	13.6	13.7	13.8	13.4
2008	13.1	13.0	13.1	13.2	13.5	13.6	13.3	13.3	13.6	13.8	13.8	13.9	13.4
2009	13.2	13.1	13.1	13.1	13.3	13.3	12.9	12.9	13.2	13.2	13.3	13.4	13.2
2010	12.8	12.7	12.9	12.9	12.9	12.9	12.8	12.8	12.8	12.7	12.8	12.9	12.8
2011	12.1	12.1	12.0	12.1	12.3	12.3	12.0	12.0	12.3	12.4	12.4	12.4	12.2
Information													
2000	11.8	11.9	12.0	12.3	12.3	12.5	12.3	10.7	12.3	12.0	12.1	12.2	12.0
2001	12.2	12.1	12.2	12.2	12.3	12.4	12.1	12.1	12.1	12.0	12.0	12.0	12.1
2002	11.9	11.9	12.0	12.0	12.1	12.1	11.9	11.9	11.8	11.9	12.0	12.0	12.0
2003	11.6	11.7	12.0	12.0	11.8	11.5	11.2	11.1	10.8	10.6	10.4	10.2	11.2
2004	11.1	11.1	11.5	11.0	10.7	10.7	10.8	10.8	10.8	10.6	10.7	10.5	10.9
2005	10.5	10.6	10.8	11.1	11.0	11.1	11.0	11.1	10.9	10.9	10.8	10.9	10.9
2006	10.8	10.7	10.7	10.6	10.6	10.6	10.5	10.4	10.1	10.2	10.2	10.2	10.5
2007	10.1	10.0	10.0	9.9	10.0	10.0	10.0	10.0	9.8	9.7	9.7	9.8	9.9
2008	9.4	9.4	9.4	9.5	9.8	9.9	9.9	9.9	9.7	9.8	9.8	9.8	9.7
2009	9.8	9.7	9.6	9.6	9.6	9.7	9.6	9.6	9.4	9.2	9.3	9.3	9.5
2010	9.0	9.0	9.0	8.8	8.9	8.9	9.0	9.0	8.8	8.8	8.8	8.8	8.9
2011	8.8	8.7	8.7	8.8	8.8	8.9	8.9	8.1	8.7	8.7	8.6	8.6	8.7
Financial Activities													
2000	24.6	24.7	24.7	24.9	25.0	25.3	25.2	25.3	24.9	24.8	24.9	25.3	25.0
2001	24.5	24.6	24.7	24.4	24.6	25.1	25.0	25.0	24.7	24.8	24.8	24.9	24.8
2002	24.4	24.7	24.9	24.8	25.1	25.4	25.0	25.3	24.8	25.2	25.3	25.4	25.0
2003	25.3	25.3	25.4	25.5	25.8	26.3	26.3	26.3	25.9	26.0	26.1	26.1	25.9
2004	25.8	25.6	25.9	25.7	25.8	26.5	26.6	26.5	26.4	26.3	26.1	26.3	26.1
2005	25.9	25.9	26.0	26.1	26.2	26.6	26.8	26.8	26.5	26.5	26.4	26.6	26.4
2006	26.2	26.3	26.5	26.7	26.6	27.0	27.1	27.0	26.6	26.7	26.7	26.7	26.7
2007	26.3	26.0	26.0	26.1	26.2	26.7	26.5	26.4	26.0	26.0	26.1	26.1	26.2
2008	25.9	25.8	25.9	25.9	26.0	26.4	26.4	26.4	25.8	25.6	25.5	25.4	25.9
2009	25.3	25.2	25.2	24.9	25.0	25.3	25.1	25.1	24.6	24.5	24.4	24.4	24.9
2010	24.3	24.2	24.3	24.3	24.3	24.7	24.8	24.7	24.3	24.5	24.4	24.6	24.5
2011	24.3	24.3	24.3	24.4	24.5	24.8	24.9	24.9	24.8	24.7	24.8	24.9	24.6

Employment by Industry: Albany–Schenectady–Troy, NY, Selected Years, 2000–2011—*Continued*

(Numbers in thousands, not seasonally adjusted)

Industry and year	January	February	March	April	May	June	July	August	September	October	November	December	Annual average
Professional and Business Services													
2000	48.4	48.5	48.8	49.8	50.1	50.9	50.6	51.1	50.3	50.9	51.2	51.3	50.2
2001	50.6	50.9	50.8	51.3	51.7	52.1	51.9	52.1	50.9	50.3	50.0	50.3	51.1
2002	47.7	47.5	48.0	48.7	48.4	49.2	49.0	49.3	48.7	48.6	48.0	47.6	48.4
2003	45.9	45.8	46.1	47.2	47.9	48.7	48.9	49.2	48.4	48.3	48.8	49.0	47.9
2004	47.6	47.6	48.1	49.3	49.9	50.8	50.9	51.0	50.3	49.6	49.8	49.8	49.6
2005	49.5	49.7	49.6	50.7	50.5	51.7	52.2	51.9	52.0	51.3	51.5	50.8	51.0
2006	50.6	50.8	51.4	52.3	51.7	52.5	53.0	53.0	52.8	52.4	52.9	53.0	52.2
2007	51.3	51.8	52.1	52.4	52.5	54.0	54.2	54.2	53.6	53.5	53.9	54.0	53.1
2008	54.0	54.1	54.4	55.1	54.9	56.0	55.8	56.0	55.0	54.8	54.5	54.1	54.9
2009	52.9	52.3	52.6	52.3	51.7	51.8	51.6	51.2	50.9	51.2	50.8	50.5	51.7
2010	49.1	49.2	49.5	50.5	50.6	51.0	51.9	51.5	50.7	51.1	51.2	50.9	50.6
2011	50.0	50.2	50.3	51.6	51.3	51.7	51.4	51.5	51.4	51.9	50.6	52.3	51.2
Education and Health Services													
2000	68.7	70.5	70.8	70.7	70.1	69.3	68.7	68.8	70.1	72.7	72.9	73.0	70.5
2001	71.3	72.2	74.1	74.0	73.2	71.2	71.2	71.1	73.6	74.8	75.3	75.3	73.1
2002	72.9	75.8	76.5	76.7	75.4	73.5	73.7	73.7	76.2	77.4	77.6	77.6	75.6
2003	74.8	77.6	77.8	78.2	77.6	75.1	74.4	74.1	76.6	77.9	78.7	78.3	76.8
2004	75.9	78.4	78.5	79.0	80.3	75.3	75.5	74.9	77.8	79.4	79.5	80.2	77.9
2005	76.3	79.2	78.8	79.5	78.2	75.9	75.6	75.0	77.4	79.0	79.2	78.8	77.7
2006	76.3	79.4	79.5	79.9	79.0	76.7	75.9	75.6	79.4	80.8	81.1	81.2	78.7
2007	77.9	81.0	81.1	81.2	80.6	78.4	77.3	77.0	81.1	82.4	83.4	83.2	80.4
2008	80.3	83.7	83.3	83.6	83.3	80.8	79.1	78.5	82.2	83.5	84.9	84.2	82.3
2009	81.5	85.3	85.6	85.5	84.4	81.8	80.4	80.1	84.0	85.7	86.4	85.2	83.8
2010	82.9	87.0	87.1	87.8	86.3	83.1	82.0	81.7	86.1	87.7	88.7	87.4	85.7
2011	84.3	88.8	88.7	89.6	87.8	84.6	84.7	84.1	85.7	87.5	87.8	87.4	86.8
Leisure and Hospitality													
2000	27.3	27.7	28.2	29.3	30.0	31.4	31.1	31.5	30.4	29.0	28.4	28.4	29.4
2001	27.3	27.2	27.8	29.1	31.0	32.6	32.5	34.6	30.6	29.8	29.4	29.4	30.1
2002	28.5	28.8	29.6	30.5	32.3	33.2	33.4	35.8	32.0	31.3	30.7	30.2	31.4
2003	28.0	28.4	28.9	30.1	31.7	32.3	33.8	36.0	32.0	31.2	30.8	30.5	31.1
2004	29.2	29.2	30.0	30.4	32.6	33.7	34.2	35.8	32.5	31.6	30.9	31.2	31.8
2005	29.1	29.3	29.8	31.1	32.3	33.6	33.8	35.9	32.9	31.9	31.4	31.5	31.9
2006	29.2	29.9	30.9	31.1	32.7	34.2	34.2	36.0	33.1	32.5	31.7	31.7	32.3
2007	30.2	30.4	31.2	31.8	33.9	35.2	35.6	37.2	34.4	33.8	33.0	32.4	33.3
2008	30.7	31.2	31.9	33.1	34.9	35.7	36.5	37.7	34.6	33.9	33.1	32.2	33.8
2009	30.4	30.7	31.2	32.2	34.4	35.3	36.0	37.3	34.6	33.7	33.0	32.6	33.5
2010	30.7	31.4	31.7	33.5	34.9	35.5	36.8	37.7	35.3	34.8	34.4	33.7	34.2
2011	31.8	32.4	32.7	34.5	35.6	36.7	39.0	38.5	36.5	34.8	34.8	34.0	35.1
Other Services													
2000	16.7	16.8	16.9	17.2	17.2	17.4	17.2	17.3	17.1	17.4	17.6	17.7	17.2
2001	17.3	17.3	17.4	17.2	17.4	17.6	17.2	17.2	17.2	17.3	17.6	17.7	17.4
2002	17.3	17.5	17.7	17.9	17.9	17.9	17.8	17.8	17.8	18.1	18.4	18.3	17.9
2003	18.2	18.2	18.2	18.2	18.2	18.2	18.4	18.4	18.2	18.4	18.5	18.4	18.3
2004	18.3	18.4	18.5	18.5	18.6	18.4	18.4	18.3	18.1	18.6	18.6	18.5	18.4
2005	18.3	18.5	18.4	18.4	18.3	18.2	18.0	18.0	18.0	18.2	18.3	18.2	18.2
2006	17.7	18.0	18.3	18.2	18.3	18.3	18.2	18.1	18.1	18.4	18.4	18.5	18.2
2007	18.2	18.4	18.5	18.3	18.5	18.5	18.0	18.0	18.0	18.3	18.4	18.5	18.3
2008	18.4	18.5	18.5	18.4	18.5	18.5	18.6	18.6	18.3	18.7	18.8	18.7	18.5
2009	18.6	18.8	18.9	18.6	18.8	18.7	18.6	18.3	18.1	18.3	18.2	18.2	18.5
2010	17.6	17.7	17.7	17.8	17.9	17.7	17.9	18.0	17.6	17.7	17.7	17.9	17.8
2011	17.6	17.7	17.7	17.9	17.9	17.7	17.7	17.7	17.4	17.7	17.7	17.7	17.7
Government													
2000	105.1	107.5	107.5	108.2	108.9	108.5	102.5	101.7	106.3	107.7	108.8	107.9	106.7
2001	106.4	109.1	108.9	109.4	109.4	108.2	104.0	104.5	107.0	109.0	110.3	109.3	108.0
2002	107.2	110.3	110.3	110.7	110.6	109.9	103.8	103.2	108.6	109.9	110.5	110.3	108.8
2003	108.0	110.2	109.6	109.0	109.0	108.2	102.9	102.2	106.8	108.5	108.7	108.8	107.7
2004	106.1	108.3	108.4	109.1	109.5	109.3	103.5	102.7	106.2	108.2	108.6	108.5	107.4
2005	107.2	108.5	108.6	109.1	109.1	108.4	102.8	102.1	105.9	108.3	108.5	108.6	107.3
2006	106.1	108.1	108.1	108.6	108.5	107.6	102.3	101.3	104.9	107.9	108.5	109.2	106.8
2007	106.9	108.9	108.6	108.8	109.4	109.2	102.5	102.7	106.1	109.4	109.8	110.9	107.8
2008	107.1	109.2	109.0	110.5	111.3	110.8	105.2	104.1	107.2	110.4	110.5	111.0	108.9
2009	107.3	110.1	109.6	111.1	111.0	110.2	104.3	102.8	105.8	109.1	109.7	109.9	108.4
2010	107.2	108.9	108.5	109.1	110.9	110.2	101.3	99.1	102.2	104.2	104.8	104.6	105.9
2011	100.7	103.3	103.1	103.6	103.7	103.6	98.6	97.5	100.0	103.6	103.8	103.8	102.1

Employment by Industry: Albuquerque, NM, Selected Years, 2000–2011

(Numbers in thousands, not seasonally adjusted)

Industry and year	January	February	March	April	May	June	July	August	September	October	November	December	Annual average
Total Nonfarm													
2000	346.2	349.2	352.8	355.0	358.4	357.9	356.3	357.7	362.6	361.9	364.4	365.9	357.4
2001	356.5	359.8	362.3	363.3	365.0	365.7	361.0	361.3	361.7	361.6	363.2	364.4	362.2
2002	355.5	357.2	359.9	360.7	363.3	364.0	361.4	361.7	364.7	362.1	364.0	366.1	361.7
2003	356.6	359.5	362.0	362.5	364.0	364.4	361.9	363.5	365.0	364.5	365.6	368.0	363.1
2004	360.2	364.5	367.5	369.6	371.3	371.1	369.1	369.4	371.4	375.1	376.0	376.9	370.2
2005	367.5	370.5	373.0	376.4	377.9	378.4	376.5	378.4	381.6	382.2	385.0	387.0	377.9
2006	381.5	385.2	389.6	389.8	391.8	393.8	390.1	391.2	394.8	395.2	397.2	397.8	391.5
2007	388.0	391.6	395.9	395.4	397.7	397.5	393.9	396.0	397.2	398.0	399.1	399.5	395.8
2008	390.1	392.8	394.6	396.7	398.0	396.3	394.0	396.7	398.3	396.9	393.2	390.7	394.9
2009	380.5	379.5	379.3	379.8	379.6	377.1	374.3	376.7	378.2	377.6	376.5	376.4	378.0
2010	367.7	368.7	370.3	373.5	374.3	372.8	369.2	370.0	371.4	373.8	373.7	374.3	371.6
2011	365.6	369.8	370.1	373.3	373.5	371.9	370.6	371.1	373.3	372.9	374.4	373.3	371.7
Total Private													
2000	279.2	279.9	282.8	285.0	287.6	290.0	289.2	291.1	292.9	292.4	294.6	296.1	288.4
2001	289.4	289.9	292.0	292.6	294.1	295.4	292.8	293.4	290.7	290.5	291.5	291.7	292.0
2002	285.6	284.7	287.1	287.9	290.5	290.8	290.2	290.9	291.3	289.3	290.8	292.3	289.3
2003	285.8	286.1	288.1	288.7	290.4	290.9	290.0	291.6	291.0	290.5	291.3	292.9	289.8
2004	288.6	289.5	292.0	294.3	296.1	296.6	296.7	297.0	296.3	298.9	299.4	300.0	295.5
2005	293.7	294.1	296.4	300.0	301.7	302.7	302.8	304.4	304.8	304.4	307.1	308.5	301.7
2006	305.1	306.7	310.7	311.2	313.3	316.0	314.2	314.1	315.4	315.4	317.1	317.4	313.1
2007	310.6	312.1	315.4	315.7	318.1	319.0	317.4	318.2	316.8	316.9	317.6	318.0	316.3
2008	311.4	311.8	313.1	315.2	315.9	315.9	315.5	316.9	315.9	313.8	310.2	307.7	313.6
2009	299.3	296.3	295.6	296.0	296.4	295.6	295.3	296.4	295.4	293.5	292.5	292.1	295.4
2010	286.2	285.1	286.1	288.5	288.9	289.8	289.2	289.4	288.4	289.4	289.3	289.7	288.3
2011	283.7	285.8	285.5	288.6	289.3	289.2	290.5	290.6	290.5	289.4	290.9	289.7	288.6
Goods-Producing													
2000	47.5	48.0	48.7	49.2	50.5	51.3	52.4	53.1	53.4	53.1	53.2	53.3	51.1
2001	52.4	52.5	52.9	52.7	52.9	53.3	52.2	52.2	51.1	50.5	50.1	49.6	51.9
2002	48.4	47.9	48.2	48.2	48.3	48.8	49.1	49.1	48.4	47.7	47.2	47.3	48.2
2003	46.8	46.7	46.9	47.0	47.5	47.9	48.3	48.6	48.0	47.5	47.1	47.1	47.5
2004	46.2	46.4	46.9	47.5	48.1	49.1	50.1	50.0	49.6	49.8	49.6	49.6	48.6
2005	48.9	49.1	49.6	50.5	51.0	51.5	52.2	52.3	52.4	52.8	53.3	53.6	51.4
2006	53.5	54.3	55.0	54.9	55.5	56.4	56.4	56.4	56.2	56.2	55.4	55.5	55.5
2007	53.6	54.0	54.6	54.6	55.1	55.4	54.9	54.8	53.9	53.6	53.1	52.2	54.2
2008	50.9	50.9	51.1	51.3	51.4	51.9	51.3	51.0	50.5	49.2	48.1	46.9	50.4
2009	44.6	43.3	42.5	42.4	42.1	42.3	42.2	42.3	41.6	41.2	40.5	39.8	42.1
2010	38.8	38.3	38.2	38.6	39.0	39.2	39.9	39.6	39.3	39.0	38.7	38.3	38.9
2011	37.3	37.1	37.8	38.2	38.2	38.5	39.2	39.8	38.9	38.6	38.3	37.9	38.3
Mining, Logging, and Construction													
2000	20.9	21.2	21.8	22.2	23.2	23.8	24.3	24.9	25.2	25.0	25.2	25.1	23.6
2001	24.3	24.3	24.6	24.8	25.1	25.7	25.3	25.4	24.7	24.4	24.5	24.1	24.8
2002	23.4	23.1	23.4	23.3	23.4	23.7	23.8	23.9	23.4	23.2	23.1	23.2	23.4
2003	23.1	23.0	23.2	23.5	24.1	24.5	24.8	25.0	24.6	24.4	24.4	24.5	24.1
2004	24.0	24.3	24.7	25.0	25.4	26.3	27.1	27.0	26.7	27.0	26.9	26.9	25.9
2005	26.3	26.6	27.1	27.8	28.2	28.8	29.5	29.5	29.5	29.6	30.0	30.2	28.6
2006	30.2	30.5	31.2	31.0	31.6	32.2	32.0	32.0	31.7	31.7	31.3	31.4	31.4
2007	29.8	29.9	30.6	30.8	31.2	31.4	30.9	30.8	30.3	30.5	30.1	29.4	30.5
2008	28.6	28.6	28.8	29.0	29.0	29.4	28.9	28.5	28.1	27.8	27.1	26.2	28.3
2009	24.7	24.0	23.8	24.0	24.0	24.2	24.2	24.5	24.1	23.8	23.2	22.4	23.9
2010	21.5	21.0	20.9	21.1	21.3	21.5	22.1	21.9	21.6	21.3	21.1	20.7	21.3
2011	19.8	19.7	20.3	20.5	20.6	20.8	21.4	21.9	20.9	20.6	20.2	19.8	20.5
Manufacturing													
2000	26.6	26.8	26.9	27.0	27.3	27.5	28.1	28.2	28.2	28.1	28.0	28.2	27.6
2001	28.1	28.2	28.3	27.9	27.8	27.6	26.9	26.8	26.4	26.1	25.6	25.5	27.1
2002	25.0	24.8	24.8	24.9	24.9	25.1	25.3	25.2	25.0	24.5	24.1	24.1	24.8
2003	23.7	23.7	23.7	22.5	23.4	23.4	23.5	23.6	23.4	23.1	22.7	22.6	23.4
2004	22.2	22.1	22.2	22.5	22.7	22.8	23.0	23.0	22.9	22.8	22.7	22.7	22.6
2005	22.6	22.5	22.5	22.7	22.8	22.7	22.7	22.8	22.9	23.2	23.3	23.4	22.8
2006	23.3	23.8	23.8	23.9	23.9	24.2	24.4	24.4	24.5	24.5	24.1	24.1	24.1
2007	23.8	24.1	24.0	23.8	23.9	24.0	24.0	24.0	23.6	23.1	23.0	22.8	23.7
2008	22.3	22.3	22.3	22.3	22.4	22.5	22.4	22.5	22.4	21.4	21.0	20.7	22.0
2009	19.9	19.3	18.7	18.4	18.1	18.1	18.0	17.8	17.5	17.4	17.3	17.4	18.2
2010	17.3	17.3	17.3	17.5	17.7	17.7	17.8	17.7	17.7	17.7	17.6	17.6	17.6
2011	17.5	17.4	17.5	17.7	17.6	17.7	17.8	17.9	18.0	18.0	18.1	18.1	17.8
Service-Providing													
2000	298.7	301.2	304.1	305.8	307.9	306.6	303.9	304.6	309.2	308.8	311.2	312.6	306.2
2001	304.1	307.3	309.4	310.6	312.1	312.4	308.8	309.1	310.6	311.1	313.1	314.8	310.3
2002	307.1	309.3	311.7	312.5	315.0	315.2	312.3	312.6	316.3	314.4	316.8	318.8	313.5
2003	309.8	312.8	315.1	315.5	316.5	316.5	313.6	314.9	317.0	317.0	318.5	320.9	315.7
2004	314.0	318.1	320.6	322.1	323.2	322.0	319.0	319.4	321.8	325.3	326.4	327.3	321.6
2005	318.6	321.4	323.4	325.9	326.9	326.9	324.3	326.1	329.2	329.4	331.7	333.4	326.4
2006	328.0	330.9	334.6	334.9	336.3	337.4	333.7	334.8	338.6	339.0	341.8	342.3	336.0
2007	334.4	337.6	341.3	340.8	342.6	342.1	339.0	341.2	343.3	344.4	346.0	347.3	341.7
2008	339.2	341.9	343.5	345.4	346.6	344.4	342.7	345.7	347.8	347.7	345.1	343.8	344.5
2009	335.9	336.2	336.8	337.4	337.5	334.8	332.1	334.4	336.6	336.4	336.0	336.6	335.9
2010	328.9	330.4	332.1	334.9	335.3	333.6	329.3	330.4	332.1	334.8	335.0	336.0	332.7
2011	328.3	332.7	332.3	335.1	335.3	333.4	331.4	331.3	334.4	334.3	336.1	335.4	333.3

Employment by Industry: Albuquerque, NM, Selected Years, 2000–2011—*Continued*

(Numbers in thousands, not seasonally adjusted)

Industry and year	January	February	March	April	May	June	July	August	September	October	November	December	Annual average
Trade, Transportation, and Utilities													
2000	65.2	64.6	64.8	65.3	66.0	65.9	65.2	66.0	66.2	66.7	69.1	69.6	66.2
2001	66.7	65.9	65.8	65.4	65.8	65.6	65.2	65.8	65.4	65.5	67.1	67.9	66.0
2002	65.6	64.5	64.5	64.9	65.8	65.5	65.3	65.7	65.9	66.1	67.8	68.9	65.9
2003	65.6	64.8	65.4	65.2	65.4	65.0	64.7	65.3	65.2	65.7	67.2	68.3	65.7
2004	65.8	65.4	65.6	65.8	65.8	65.5	65.6	65.8	65.6	66.6	68.1	68.8	66.2
2005	66.2	65.9	65.9	66.0	66.6	66.0	66.4	67.1	66.9	67.4	68.8	69.7	66.9
2006	66.7	66.0	66.5	66.6	67.2	66.9	67.1	67.5	67.6	67.8	69.5	70.2	67.5
2007	68.2	67.7	67.9	67.7	68.5	68.4	68.4	68.8	68.7	69.2	70.9	72.0	68.9
2008	69.5	68.6	68.6	68.4	68.3	67.9	68.0	68.2	68.0	67.8	67.9	68.2	68.3
2009	64.9	63.5	63.2	62.6	62.7	62.7	62.8	62.8	63.0	63.1	63.9	64.5	63.3
2010	62.0	61.2	61.5	61.2	61.6	61.5	61.7	62.1	61.5	62.2	63.3	63.9	62.0
2011	61.6	61.2	61.1	61.7	62.1	61.4	61.3	61.9	61.8	61.4	62.7	63.2	61.8
Wholesale Trade													
2000	13.9	14.0	14.1	14.2	14.3	14.2	14.1	14.3	14.3	14.1	14.2	14.1	14.2
2001	14.0	14.0	14.0	13.9	14.0	13.9	13.8	13.8	13.8	13.6	13.6	13.6	13.8
2002	13.6	13.5	13.5	13.4	13.5	13.4	13.5	13.4	13.4	13.4	13.4	13.3	13.4
2003	13.0	12.9	13.3	13.2	13.0	13.0	12.9	13.0	13.0	12.8	12.8	12.9	13.0
2004	12.8	12.8	13.0	13.2	12.9	12.8	12.9	12.7	12.7	12.7	12.7	12.7	12.8
2005	12.7	12.9	12.9	12.9	13.0	12.9	13.0	13.0	13.0	13.0	13.1	13.1	13.0
2006	12.9	13.0	13.1	13.2	13.3	13.3	13.3	13.3	13.4	13.4	13.3	13.4	13.2
2007	13.3	13.2	13.2	13.2	13.2	13.3	13.4	13.4	13.4	13.5	13.4	13.6	13.3
2008	13.5	13.3	13.2	13.2	13.2	13.1	13.2	13.1	12.9	12.8	12.6	12.5	13.1
2009	12.2	12.1	12.0	11.9	11.8	11.8	12.0	11.9	12.0	12.0	12.0	12.0	12.0
2010	11.9	11.8	11.8	11.8	11.8	11.8	11.8	11.7	11.6	11.6	11.5	11.5	11.7
2011	11.4	11.4	11.4	11.5	11.6	11.5	11.6	11.6	11.5	11.5	11.5	11.6	11.5
Retail Trade													
2000	40.6	40.0	40.1	40.3	40.8	41.1	40.7	41.1	41.2	41.8	44.0	44.7	41.4
2001	42.1	41.2	41.2	40.9	41.2	41.5	41.2	41.3	40.9	41.1	42.8	43.6	41.6
2002	41.4	40.4	40.6	41.0	41.8	41.8	41.5	41.6	41.8	41.9	43.5	44.6	41.8
2003	42.0	41.4	41.6	41.5	41.9	41.7	41.6	41.8	41.7	42.3	43.8	44.8	42.2
2004	42.4	41.9	42.0	42.0	42.3	42.5	42.5	42.6	42.4	43.3	44.9	45.5	42.9
2005	43.1	42.6	42.6	42.8	43.2	43.2	43.4	43.7	43.4	43.9	45.3	45.9	43.6
2006	43.3	42.6	43.0	43.0	43.4	43.3	43.5	43.6	43.6	43.8	45.5	45.8	43.7
2007	44.1	43.6	43.9	43.7	44.4	44.5	44.5	44.5	44.3	44.6	46.4	47.0	44.6
2008	44.9	44.3	44.5	44.3	44.2	44.4	44.4	44.4	44.4	44.6	44.9	45.2	44.5
2009	42.4	41.2	41.2	41.0	41.1	41.4	41.5	41.5	41.6	41.6	42.4	42.9	41.7
2010	40.7	40.0	40.3	40.1	40.4	40.4	40.6	41.0	40.4	41.0	42.1	42.6	40.8
2011	40.6	40.2	40.3	40.8	41.0	40.6	40.4	41.0	40.9	40.5	41.7	41.9	40.8
Transportation and Utilities													
2000	10.7	10.6	10.6	10.8	10.9	10.6	10.4	10.6	10.7	10.8	10.9	10.8	10.7
2001	10.6	10.7	10.6	10.6	10.6	10.2	10.2	10.7	10.7	10.8	10.7	10.7	10.6
2002	10.6	10.6	10.4	10.5	10.5	10.3	10.3	10.7	10.7	10.8	10.9	11.0	10.6
2003	10.6	10.5	10.5	10.5	10.5	10.3	10.2	10.5	10.5	10.6	10.6	10.6	10.5
2004	10.6	10.7	10.6	10.6	10.6	10.2	10.2	10.5	10.5	10.6	10.5	10.6	10.5
2005	10.4	10.4	10.4	10.3	10.4	9.9	10.0	10.4	10.5	10.5	10.4	10.7	10.4
2006	10.5	10.4	10.4	10.4	10.5	10.3	10.3	10.6	10.6	10.6	10.7	11.0	10.5
2007	10.8	10.9	10.8	10.8	10.9	10.6	10.5	10.9	11.0	11.1	11.1	11.4	10.9
2008	11.1	11.0	10.9	10.9	10.9	10.4	10.4	10.7	10.7	10.4	10.4	10.5	10.7
2009	10.3	10.2	10.0	9.7	9.8	9.5	9.3	9.4	9.4	9.5	9.5	9.6	9.7
2010	9.4	9.4	9.4	9.3	9.4	9.3	9.3	9.4	9.5	9.6	9.7	9.8	9.5
2011	9.6	9.6	9.4	9.4	9.5	9.3	9.3	9.3	9.4	9.4	9.5	9.7	9.5
Information													
2000	11.1	10.9	11.1	11.0	11.0	11.1	10.9	11.0	11.1	11.0	11.0	11.4	11.1
2001	11.5	11.7	11.6	11.2	11.2	11.2	11.4	11.5	11.6	11.4	11.5	11.5	11.4
2002	11.2	11.4	11.5	11.3	11.4	11.1	10.9	10.7	10.4	10.5	10.8	10.8	11.0
2003	10.5	10.5	10.5	10.3	10.3	10.3	10.2	10.0	10.1	9.9	9.9	10.0	10.2
2004	9.9	9.9	9.9	9.6	9.8	9.6	9.4	9.3	9.0	9.4	9.5	9.5	9.6
2005	8.5	8.5	8.6	8.7	8.8	8.7	8.7	8.7	8.5	8.7	8.8	9.0	8.7
2006	8.7	9.3	9.5	9.1	9.2	9.9	9.2	9.3	9.7	9.4	9.9	10.0	9.4
2007	8.7	8.9	9.2	9.1	9.3	9.8	9.1	9.1	9.1	9.3	9.3	9.3	9.2
2008	9.4	9.4	9.3	9.1	9.0	9.0	9.7	9.6	9.6	9.4	9.4	9.3	9.4
2009	8.8	8.7	8.7	8.9	8.8	8.9	9.2	9.4	9.4	9.0	9.1	9.1	9.0
2010	8.9	8.6	8.3	9.2	8.7	9.2	8.7	8.8	8.3	8.3	8.6	8.6	8.7
2011	8.4	8.4	8.4	8.6	8.8	8.6	8.5	8.6	8.6	8.5	8.8	8.8	8.6
Financial Activities													
2000	19.2	19.2	19.2	19.4	19.4	19.4	19.5	19.4	19.5	19.6	19.7	19.8	19.4
2001	19.5	19.5	19.7	19.8	19.7	19.8	19.7	19.7	19.4	19.4	19.3	19.5	19.6
2002	18.7	18.6	18.7	18.7	18.8	18.9	19.0	19.1	19.0	19.0	18.9	19.0	18.9
2003	18.5	18.6	18.7	18.7	18.8	18.9	19.0	19.2	19.0	18.8	18.8	18.9	18.8
2004	18.8	18.8	19.0	19.0	19.0	19.1	19.1	19.1	19.1	19.1	19.2	19.3	19.1
2005	19.1	19.1	19.2	19.2	19.3	19.5	19.5	19.4	19.3	19.4	19.4	19.6	19.3
2006	19.3	19.3	19.3	19.3	19.3	19.4	19.3	19.2	19.1	19.1	19.1	19.2	19.2
2007	19.0	19.1	19.2	19.2	19.2	19.3	19.3	19.3	19.2	19.3	19.1	19.1	19.2
2008	18.8	18.8	18.7	18.8	18.7	18.7	18.9	18.9	18.8	18.6	18.4	18.4	18.7
2009	18.0	18.0	17.9	18.1	18.2	18.3	18.3	18.3	18.3	18.3	18.4	18.4	18.2
2010	18.1	18.0	18.1	17.8	17.8	17.9	17.8	17.8	17.6	17.6	17.5	17.6	17.8
2011	17.3	17.3	17.2	17.3	17.3	17.3	17.4	17.4	17.2	17.2	17.1	17.2	17.3

Employment by Industry: Albuquerque, NM, Selected Years, 2000–2011—*Continued*

(Numbers in thousands, not seasonally adjusted)

Industry and year	January	February	March	April	May	June	July	August	September	October	November	December	Annual average
Professional and Business Services													
2000	56.6	56.8	57.4	58.6	58.8	59.6	59.1	59.5	60.0	59.4	59.3	59.8	58.7
2001	57.6	58.2	58.7	58.8	59.0	59.6	59.0	59.0	57.7	58.5	58.4	58.1	58.6
2002	57.2	57.1	57.8	57.1	57.7	57.9	58.0	58.0	58.5	57.8	57.9	58.4	57.8
2003	56.8	57.3	57.6	57.0	57.1	57.5	57.4	57.7	57.6	57.8	57.8	57.9	57.5
2004	57.4	57.8	58.5	58.6	59.0	59.3	59.4	59.6	59.7	60.8	60.1	60.1	59.2
2005	59.3	59.3	59.5	60.6	60.3	61.2	61.1	61.4	61.6	60.8	61.5	61.4	60.7
2006	61.7	62.2	62.7	62.9	62.8	63.8	62.8	62.8	62.9	63.3	63.3	63.6	62.9
2007	62.8	63.6	64.0	63.8	64.2	64.8	64.9	65.6	64.7	64.3	64.2	64.4	64.3
2008	63.5	63.9	63.8	64.0	64.3	64.4	64.8	66.1	65.4	65.1	63.6	63.2	64.3
2009	61.9	61.2	60.6	60.5	60.2	60.1	60.1	60.5	59.7	59.0	58.3	58.2	60.0
2010	57.0	57.1	56.7	57.3	56.8	57.6	57.4	57.6	57.7	58.1	57.7	57.8	57.4
2011	56.4	58.5	56.8	57.0	56.9	57.3	58.2	57.2	56.1	56.0	56.2	55.7	56.9
Education and Health Services													
2000	37.5	37.8	38.0	37.5	37.4	36.7	36.2	36.0	37.3	37.6	37.8	37.9	37.3
2001	38.3	38.6	39.0	39.2	39.4	39.0	38.7	38.6	39.7	40.0	40.2	40.4	39.3
2002	40.8	41.1	41.4	41.4	41.6	40.8	40.2	40.5	41.8	41.8	42.1	41.9	41.3
2003	42.4	42.7	42.9	43.0	43.0	42.2	41.5	41.9	43.2	43.2	43.4	43.5	42.7
2004	44.2	44.4	44.7	45.3	45.3	44.5	43.9	44.4	45.4	45.7	46.1	45.9	45.0
2005	45.7	45.9	46.5	46.5	46.7	45.8	45.2	45.6	46.7	46.9	47.1	47.1	46.3
2006	47.2	47.2	48.4	48.0	48.3	47.6	47.2	47.0	48.5	48.3	48.5	48.4	47.9
2007	48.5	48.8	49.5	49.6	49.7	48.5	48.1	47.9	48.8	49.4	49.7	49.8	49.0
2008	49.4	50.0	50.7	51.5	51.8	51.0	50.3	50.6	51.7	52.3	52.5	52.6	51.2
2009	53.0	53.5	54.1	54.0	54.2	52.9	52.5	52.8	53.8	54.0	54.2	54.1	53.6
2010	54.2	54.4	54.9	55.0	55.1	54.2	53.7	53.6	54.9	55.3	55.5	55.6	54.7
2011	55.4	55.5	55.7	55.9	56.1	55.8	56.0	55.9	58.8	58.8	59.4	59.3	56.9
Leisure and Hospitality													
2000	31.4	31.8	32.8	33.3	33.7	34.8	34.7	35.0	34.6	34.1	33.5	33.3	33.6
2001	32.5	32.7	33.3	34.4	34.9	35.3	35.1	35.2	34.7	34.2	33.9	33.6	34.2
2002	32.8	33.0	33.8	34.9	35.5	36.0	35.9	36.0	35.7	34.9	34.6	34.5	34.8
2003	33.7	34.0	34.5	36.0	36.7	37.2	36.9	37.0	36.2	35.9	35.5	35.6	35.8
2004	34.7	35.2	35.8	36.9	37.3	37.4	37.0	36.7	36.1	35.8	35.1	35.2	36.1
2005	34.4	34.7	35.4	36.8	37.2	37.8	37.4	37.7	37.5	36.6	36.4	36.3	36.5
2006	36.3	36.6	37.4	38.3	38.9	39.5	39.7	39.6	39.3	39.0	39.2	38.6	38.5
2007	37.9	38.0	38.8	39.6	39.9	40.3	40.2	40.5	40.3	39.6	39.1	39.0	39.4
2008	37.8	37.9	38.6	39.8	40.0	40.1	39.7	39.9	39.4	38.7	37.8	37.1	38.9
2009	36.2	36.1	36.6	37.6	38.2	38.1	38.1	38.3	37.9	37.2	36.5	36.2	37.3
2010	35.5	35.8	36.7	37.7	38.2	38.1	38.0	37.9	37.4	37.1	36.5	36.4	37.1
2011	35.8	36.1	36.8	38.1	38.2	38.3	38.1	38.0	37.5	37.2	36.9	36.1	37.3
Other Services													
2000	10.7	10.8	10.8	10.7	10.8	11.2	11.2	11.1	10.8	10.9	11.0	11.0	10.9
2001	10.9	10.8	11.0	11.1	11.2	11.6	11.5	11.4	11.1	11.0	11.0	11.1	11.1
2002	10.9	11.1	11.2	11.4	11.4	11.8	11.8	11.8	11.6	11.5	11.5	11.5	11.5
2003	11.5	11.5	11.6	11.5	11.6	11.9	12.0	11.9	11.7	11.7	11.6	11.6	11.7
2004	11.6	11.6	11.6	11.6	11.8	12.1	12.2	12.1	11.8	11.7	11.6	11.6	11.8
2005	11.6	11.6	11.7	11.7	11.8	12.2	12.3	12.2	11.9	11.8	11.8	11.8	11.9
2006	11.7	11.8	11.9	12.1	12.1	12.5	12.5	12.3	12.1	12.3	12.2	11.9	12.1
2007	11.9	12.0	12.2	12.1	12.2	12.5	12.5	12.2	12.1	12.2	12.2	12.2	12.2
2008	12.1	12.3	12.3	12.3	12.4	12.9	12.8	12.6	12.5	12.7	12.5	12.0	12.5
2009	11.9	12.0	12.0	11.9	12.0	12.3	12.1	12.0	11.7	11.7	11.7	11.8	11.9
2010	11.7	11.7	11.7	11.7	11.7	12.1	12.0	12.0	11.7	11.8	11.5	11.5	11.8
2011	11.5	11.7	11.7	11.8	11.7	12.0	11.8	11.8	11.6	11.7	11.5	11.5	11.7
Government													
2000	67.0	69.3	70.0	70.0	70.8	67.9	67.1	66.6	69.7	69.5	69.8	69.8	69.0
2001	67.1	69.9	70.3	70.7	70.9	70.3	68.2	67.9	71.0	71.1	71.7	72.7	70.2
2002	69.9	72.5	72.8	72.8	72.8	73.2	71.2	70.8	73.4	72.8	73.2	73.8	72.4
2003	70.8	73.4	73.9	73.8	73.6	73.5	71.9	71.9	74.0	74.0	74.3	75.1	73.4
2004	71.6	75.0	75.5	75.3	75.2	74.5	72.4	72.4	75.1	76.2	76.6	76.9	74.7
2005	73.8	76.4	76.6	76.4	76.2	75.7	73.7	74.0	76.8	77.8	77.9	78.5	76.2
2006	76.4	78.5	78.9	78.6	78.5	77.8	75.9	77.1	79.4	79.8	80.1	80.4	78.5
2007	77.4	79.5	80.5	79.7	79.6	78.5	76.5	77.8	80.4	81.1	81.5	81.5	79.5
2008	78.7	81.0	81.5	81.5	82.1	80.4	78.5	79.8	82.4	83.1	83.0	83.0	81.3
2009	81.2	83.2	83.7	83.8	83.2	81.5	79.0	80.3	82.8	84.1	84.0	84.3	82.6
2010	81.5	83.6	84.2	85.0	85.4	83.0	80.0	80.6	83.0	84.4	84.4	84.6	83.3
2011	81.9	84.0	84.6	84.7	84.2	82.7	80.1	80.5	82.8	83.5	83.5	83.6	83.0

Employment by Industry: Allentown–Bethlehem–Easton, PA–NJ, Selected Years, 2000–2011

(Numbers in thousands, not seasonally adjusted)

Industry and year	January	February	March	April	May	June	July	August	September	October	November	December	Annual average
Total Nonfarm													
2000	314.4	315.7	319.2	321.1	325.4	328.6	324.3	324.1	324.3	326.2	328.3	329.8	323.5
2001	322.8	323.3	326.7	326.0	329.2	331.3	324.9	326.2	325.8	325.6	325.4	325.6	326.1
2002	318.9	319.2	323.1	322.7	326.4	327.4	323.0	324.1	327.1	327.4	327.1	327.4	324.5
2003	320.7	319.8	322.8	324.9	329.0	329.9	321.4	322.1	328.4	330.3	330.9	330.8	325.9
2004	321.6	323.1	327.2	329.6	333.1	334.9	326.5	326.5	331.1	335.0	334.9	334.2	329.8
2005	325.8	328.1	331.1	336.7	339.5	340.7	334.9	334.1	339.1	340.6	341.4	341.1	336.1
2006	332.7	334.4	339.3	341.6	344.2	346.0	338.4	340.2	344.9	347.0	346.4	346.7	341.8
2007	336.7	337.0	341.8	343.3	348.0	350.2	342.5	342.4	346.5	350.0	349.5	349.4	344.8
2008	338.6	339.3	342.5	344.8	348.7	349.7	342.6	342.4	344.8	346.7	343.7	343.6	344.0
2009	331.0	331.0	332.5	333.4	337.9	337.4	330.3	330.1	332.9	335.5	335.8	335.2	333.6
2010	324.7	326.0	329.9	334.1	338.4	338.6	330.5	330.9	335.3	338.0	339.1	341.3	333.9
2011	328.9	331.2	334.9	339.9	343.5	343.9	338.1	335.4	337.4	338.7	341.1	342.5	338.0
Total Private													
2000	276.7	277.3	280.3	282.2	285.3	288.9	287.4	287.5	287.5	287.3	289.1	290.4	285.0
2001	284.9	284.4	287.5	286.9	289.8	292.4	289.2	290.0	287.9	286.2	285.9	285.8	287.6
2002	280.2	279.7	283.3	283.0	286.3	288.2	287.4	288.9	288.6	287.6	287.2	287.4	285.7
2003	281.3	279.2	281.9	284.0	287.7	289.0	286.7	287.9	288.5	289.4	289.3	289.5	286.2
2004	281.6	281.8	285.6	288.1	291.0	293.2	290.9	291.2	290.9	293.4	293.2	292.6	289.5
2005	285.5	286.3	289.2	293.9	297.0	299.2	299.2	299.2	298.5	299.0	299.4	299.0	295.5
2006	291.5	292.3	296.9	299.2	301.5	304.1	302.6	304.1	303.8	304.8	303.5	303.9	300.7
2007	295.2	294.3	298.9	300.3	304.3	307.0	305.2	305.3	304.4	306.8	305.8	305.6	302.8
2008	296.6	296.0	299.0	301.3	304.9	305.6	304.2	304.0	302.2	302.7	299.3	299.3	301.3
2009	288.8	287.1	288.2	288.7	293.0	293.3	291.7	291.5	290.3	291.4	291.2	290.7	290.5
2010	282.0	282.0	285.6	289.4	292.6	293.7	292.4	293.5	293.6	295.6	296.2	298.6	291.3
2011	287.7	288.7	292.1	297.0	300.6	301.4	301.1	298.6	297.4	297.4	299.2	300.7	296.8
Goods-Producing													
2000	67.9	67.2	68.4	68.3	68.8	70.2	69.7	70.9	70.5	69.8	70.3	70.4	69.4
2001	69.4	69.2	69.6	70.2	70.3	70.8	69.3	69.8	68.7	67.1	66.0	65.5	68.8
2002	64.5	64.2	64.7	64.6	65.1	65.5	64.6	64.6	63.7	62.6	61.9	61.1	63.9
2003	59.2	58.2	58.4	58.7	59.2	59.7	58.8	58.8	58.3	58.2	57.7	57.1	58.5
2004	56.0	55.7	56.5	57.0	57.7	58.7	58.6	59.1	58.7	58.5	58.6	58.3	57.8
2005	56.8	56.4	56.8	58.1	58.7	59.6	59.2	59.3	59.0	58.6	58.4	57.8	58.2
2006	56.1	56.1	56.8	57.2	57.2	58.4	57.6	58.2	57.5	57.4	56.8	56.6	57.2
2007	55.5	54.9	55.7	56.2	57.0	57.8	57.4	57.5	57.3	57.0	56.6	55.7	56.6
2008	54.4	54.1	54.8	55.4	56.2	56.8	56.1	56.2	55.9	55.4	54.1	53.0	55.2
2009	50.9	49.8	49.6	49.6	49.7	49.7	49.6	49.2	48.7	48.2	48.1	47.4	49.2
2010	45.8	45.1	45.8	46.8	47.6	48.4	48.5	48.6	48.5	48.4	48.2	47.8	47.5
2011	46.2	45.8	46.9	47.9	48.8	49.5	49.3	48.9	48.5	48.7	48.3	47.7	48.0
Mining, Logging, and Construction													
2000	13.5	12.9	13.6	14.0	14.4	14.9	15.4	15.5	15.3	15.0	15.0	14.6	14.5
2001	13.9	13.6	13.8	14.4	14.8	15.3	15.6	15.7	15.4	15.0	14.7	14.5	14.7
2002	13.5	13.5	14.0	14.9	15.3	15.8	16.0	15.7	15.3	15.0	15.0	14.6	14.9
2003	13.4	13.0	13.4	14.3	15.0	15.6	15.9	16.0	15.7	15.7	15.5	15.1	14.9
2004	14.5	14.3	15.0	15.5	16.2	16.7	16.9	17.0	16.8	16.6	16.5	16.4	16.0
2005	15.3	15.1	15.3	16.6	17.1	17.8	18.0	17.9	17.6	17.3	17.4	16.9	16.9
2006	15.8	15.8	16.2	16.9	17.1	17.7	17.7	17.9	17.5	17.3	16.9	16.7	17.0
2007	15.6	14.9	15.4	16.2	17.0	17.5	17.7	17.8	17.4	17.0	16.6	15.8	16.6
2008	14.9	14.6	15.0	15.6	16.4	16.9	16.8	16.5	16.2	15.9	15.1	14.3	15.7
2009	13.0	12.6	12.8	13.3	13.6	13.6	13.6	13.4	13.1	13.0	12.7	12.1	13.1
2010	10.8	10.5	11.0	12.0	12.5	12.9	13.0	13.1	13.1	13.0	12.7	12.1	12.2
2011	10.9	10.7	11.4	12.2	12.8	13.1	13.2	13.1	12.8	12.8	12.5	12.0	12.3
Manufacturing													
2000	54.4	54.3	54.8	54.3	54.4	55.3	54.3	55.4	55.2	54.8	55.3	55.8	54.9
2001	55.5	55.6	55.8	55.8	55.5	55.5	53.7	54.1	53.3	52.1	51.3	51.0	54.1
2002	51.0	50.7	50.7	49.7	49.8	49.7	48.6	48.9	48.4	47.6	46.9	46.5	49.0
2003	45.8	45.2	45.0	44.4	44.2	44.1	42.9	42.8	42.6	42.5	42.2	42.0	43.6
2004	41.5	41.4	41.5	41.5	41.5	42.0	41.7	42.1	41.9	41.9	42.1	41.9	41.8
2005	41.5	41.3	41.5	41.5	41.6	41.8	41.2	41.4	41.4	41.3	41.0	40.9	41.4
2006	40.3	40.3	40.6	40.3	40.1	40.7	39.9	40.3	40.0	40.1	39.9	39.9	40.2
2007	39.9	40.0	40.3	40.0	40.0	40.3	39.7	39.7	39.9	40.0	40.0	39.9	40.0
2008	39.5	39.5	39.8	39.8	39.8	39.9	39.3	39.7	39.7	39.5	39.0	38.7	39.5
2009	37.9	37.2	36.8	36.3	36.1	36.1	36.0	35.8	35.6	35.2	35.4	35.3	36.1
2010	35.0	34.6	34.8	34.8	35.1	35.5	35.5	35.5	35.4	35.4	35.5	35.7	35.2
2011	35.3	35.1	35.5	35.7	36.0	36.4	36.1	35.8	35.7	35.9	35.8	35.7	35.8
Service-Providing													
2000	246.5	248.5	250.8	252.8	256.6	258.4	254.6	253.2	253.8	256.4	258.0	259.4	254.1
2001	253.4	254.1	257.1	255.8	258.9	260.5	255.6	256.4	257.1	258.5	259.4	260.1	257.2
2002	254.4	255.0	258.4	258.1	261.3	261.9	258.4	259.5	263.4	264.8	265.2	266.3	260.6
2003	261.5	261.6	264.4	266.2	269.8	270.2	262.6	263.3	270.1	272.1	273.2	273.7	267.4
2004	265.6	267.4	270.7	272.6	275.4	276.2	267.9	267.4	272.4	276.5	276.3	275.9	272.0
2005	269.0	271.7	274.3	278.6	280.8	281.1	275.7	274.8	280.1	282.0	283.0	283.3	277.9
2006	276.6	278.3	282.5	284.4	287.0	287.6	280.8	282.0	287.4	289.6	289.6	290.1	284.7
2007	281.2	282.1	286.1	287.1	291.0	292.4	285.1	284.9	289.2	293.0	292.9	293.7	288.2
2008	284.2	285.2	287.7	289.4	292.5	292.9	286.5	286.2	288.9	291.3	289.6	290.6	288.8
2009	280.1	281.2	282.9	283.8	288.2	287.7	280.7	280.9	284.2	287.3	287.7	287.8	284.4
2010	278.9	280.9	284.1	287.3	290.8	290.2	282.0	282.3	286.8	289.6	290.9	293.5	286.4
2011	282.7	285.4	288.0	292.0	294.7	294.4	288.8	286.5	288.9	290.0	292.8	294.8	289.9

Employment by Industry: Allentown–Bethlehem–Easton, PA–NJ, Selected Years, 2000–2011—*Continued*

(Numbers in thousands, not seasonally adjusted)

Industry and year	January	February	March	April	May	June	July	August	September	October	November	December	Annual average
Trade, Transportation, and Utilities													
2000	60.5	60.1	60.7	60.8	61.0	61.5	60.8	61.1	61.4	62.5	63.9	64.8	61.6
2001	62.5	61.3	61.9	61.5	61.9	63.1	62.4	62.9	62.4	63.2	64.7	65.5	62.8
2002	63.2	62.2	62.9	62.2	63.0	63.1	63.3	63.9	64.8	64.9	66.3	67.4	63.9
2003	65.0	63.7	64.1	64.4	65.1	65.6	64.3	64.5	64.9	65.8	66.7	67.7	65.2
2004	64.5	63.6	64.5	64.6	64.9	65.2	64.1	64.2	64.4	65.2	66.5	68.1	65.0
2005	66.1	65.5	65.9	66.7	67.5	68.0	67.6	67.7	67.6	68.3	70.0	70.9	67.7
2006	68.9	68.0	68.5	69.3	69.7	70.3	69.9	70.3	70.5	71.1	72.4	73.2	70.2
2007	70.3	68.9	69.3	69.3	70.2	70.7	70.2	70.1	69.9	71.0	72.8	73.5	70.5
2008	70.9	69.3	69.5	69.4	70.1	70.4	69.6	69.5	69.5	70.0	70.7	71.2	70.0
2009	67.9	66.8	66.5	65.9	67.0	67.3	66.6	66.4	66.4	67.3	68.2	68.7	67.1
2010	66.1	64.9	65.6	65.9	66.4	67.0	67.1	67.5	67.7	68.7	69.9	71.0	67.3
2011	68.1	67.3	67.7	68.1	68.8	69.6	69.5	69.1	69.2	69.6	70.3	71.0	69.0
Wholesale Trade													
2000	10.7	10.8	11.0	11.2	11.1	11.1	11.3	11.3	11.2	11.6	11.6	11.6	11.2
2001	11.6	11.4	11.6	11.3	11.3	11.6	11.4	11.6	11.3	11.2	11.4	11.4	11.4
2002	11.3	11.1	11.2	11.1	11.2	11.3	11.3	11.2	11.1	11.0	11.1	11.2	11.2
2003	11.2	11.1	11.2	11.1	11.2	11.3	11.3	11.4	11.3	11.4	11.5	11.6	11.3
2004	11.3	11.2	11.4	11.6	11.6	11.8	11.7	11.6	11.7	11.8	11.9	12.1	11.6
2005	12.1	12.1	12.3	12.6	12.6	12.6	12.6	12.5	12.3	12.3	12.3	12.3	12.4
2006	12.5	12.7	12.9	13.3	13.5	13.7	13.7	13.8	13.7	13.8	13.8	13.9	13.4
2007	13.4	13.4	13.5	13.6	13.8	14.0	14.1	14.0	13.9	14.1	14.1	14.1	13.8
2008	13.8	13.8	13.8	14.0	14.1	14.2	14.3	14.2	14.0	14.0	13.9	13.8	14.0
2009	13.4	13.3	13.3	13.4	13.4	13.5	13.4	13.3	13.3	13.5	13.4	13.4	13.4
2010	13.0	12.9	13.0	13.3	13.3	13.5	13.5	13.5	13.5	13.6	13.6	13.6	13.4
2011	13.2	13.2	13.4	13.5	13.6	13.7	13.6	13.6	13.5	13.6	13.6	13.6	13.5
Retail Trade													
2000	37.9	37.4	37.6	37.6	37.8	38.2	38.1	38.3	38.0	38.6	40.0	41.0	38.4
2001	38.6	37.6	37.8	37.6	38.0	39.0	38.9	39.2	38.4	39.2	40.6	41.4	38.9
2002	39.6	38.8	39.1	38.7	39.3	39.5	40.0	40.5	40.4	40.4	41.7	42.7	40.1
2003	40.4	39.4	39.6	39.8	40.3	40.7	40.3	40.5	40.4	41.0	41.9	42.9	40.6
2004	40.4	39.6	40.1	40.1	40.8	41.0	40.3	40.5	40.0	40.7	41.8	43.1	40.7
2005	41.2	40.6	40.6	40.8	41.4	41.8	41.6	41.6	40.9	41.2	42.5	43.3	41.5
2006	41.3	40.1	40.4	40.5	40.8	41.3	41.5	41.2	41.7	43.0	43.7		41.4
2007	41.5	40.2	40.4	40.2	40.8	41.2	41.1	41.1	40.5	41.2	42.9	43.6	41.2
2008	41.8	40.4	40.5	40.3	40.8	41.0	40.5	40.4	40.1	40.5	41.3	42.0	40.8
2009	39.5	38.8	38.6	38.2	38.9	39.3	39.1	39.1	38.5	38.9	40.0	40.5	39.1
2010	38.9	37.9	38.3	38.3	38.7	39.1	39.0	39.0	38.6	39.3	40.4	41.4	39.1
2011	39.3	38.5	38.7	38.9	39.2	39.6	40.1	39.9	39.4	39.5	40.2	40.9	39.5
Transportation and Utilities													
2000	11.9	11.9	12.1	12.0	12.1	12.2	11.4	11.5	12.2	12.3	12.3	12.2	12.0
2001	12.3	12.3	12.5	12.6	12.6	12.5	12.1	12.1	12.7	12.8	12.7	12.7	12.5
2002	12.3	12.3	12.6	12.4	12.5	12.3	12.0	12.2	13.3	13.5	13.5	13.5	12.7
2003	13.4	13.2	13.3	13.5	13.6	13.6	12.7	12.6	13.2	13.4	13.3	13.2	13.3
2004	12.8	12.8	13.0	12.9	12.5	12.4	12.1	12.1	12.7	12.7	12.8	12.9	12.6
2005	12.8	12.8	13.0	13.3	13.5	13.6	13.4	13.6	14.4	14.8	15.2	15.3	13.8
2006	15.1	15.2	15.2	15.5	15.4	15.3	14.9	15.0	15.6	15.6	15.6	15.6	15.3
2007	15.4	15.3	15.4	15.5	15.6	15.5	15.0	15.0	15.5	15.7	15.8	15.8	15.5
2008	15.3	15.1	15.2	15.1	15.2	15.2	14.8	14.9	15.4	15.5	15.5	15.4	15.2
2009	15.0	14.7	14.6	14.3	14.7	14.5	14.1	14.0	14.6	14.9	14.8	14.8	14.6
2010	14.2	14.1	14.3	14.3	14.4	14.4	14.6	15.0	15.6	15.8	15.9	16.0	14.9
2011	15.6	15.6	15.6	15.7	16.0	16.3	15.8	15.6	16.3	16.5	16.5	16.5	16.0
Information													
2000	8.7	8.7	8.9	8.9	9.0	9.3	9.3	9.0	8.9	9.0	9.1	9.3	9.0
2001	9.4	9.3	9.2	9.1	9.1	9.0	9.0	8.7	8.4	8.4	8.2	8.2	8.8
2002	7.8	7.8	7.8	7.8	7.8	7.9	7.8	7.7	7.6	7.6	7.7	7.8	7.7
2003	7.6	7.7	7.8	7.8	7.8	7.9	7.7	7.7	7.6	7.6	7.7	7.8	7.7
2004	7.6	7.6	7.6	7.7	7.7	7.8	7.8	7.7	7.6	7.7	7.7	7.8	7.7
2005	7.6	7.6	7.6	7.6	7.6	7.6	7.6	7.6	7.4	7.4	7.4	7.4	7.5
2006	7.4	7.4	7.4	7.4	7.5	7.6	7.5	7.5	7.5	7.4	7.4	7.5	7.5
2007	7.4	7.3	7.3	7.3	7.4	7.5	7.5	7.5	7.4	7.4	7.4	7.5	7.4
2008	7.4	7.4	7.4	7.5	7.6	7.5	7.5	7.4	7.3	7.3	7.1	7.2	7.4
2009	7.1	7.0	6.9	6.7	6.7	6.6	6.5	6.3	6.2	6.1	5.9	5.9	6.5
2010	5.6	5.5	5.5	5.6	5.6	5.7	5.7	5.7	5.7	5.6	5.6	5.6	5.6
2011	5.5	5.6	5.6	5.6	5.7	5.7	5.6	5.4	5.6	5.5	5.5	5.5	5.6
Financial Activities													
2000	15.7	15.7	15.9	15.9	16.0	16.2	16.2	16.2	16.1	16.2	16.3	16.5	16.1
2001	16.9	16.8	17.0	16.5	16.4	16.8	16.9	17.0	16.9	16.8	16.8	16.9	16.8
2002	16.6	16.6	16.6	16.6	16.5	16.8	16.9	17.0	16.8	16.5	16.5	16.6	16.7
2003	16.7	16.7	16.7	16.6	16.7	16.8	16.8	16.8	16.5	16.5	16.5	16.6	16.7
2004	16.3	16.1	16.2	16.3	16.5	16.5	16.4	16.4	16.2	16.4	16.4	16.5	16.4
2005	16.3	16.3	16.3	16.5	16.6	16.7	16.7	16.8	16.6	16.5	16.6	16.6	16.5
2006	16.4	16.5	16.6	16.6	16.6	16.8	16.7	16.7	16.6	16.4	16.4	16.5	16.6
2007	16.3	16.4	16.4	16.2	16.2	16.3	16.2	16.2	16.0	16.0	15.9	15.8	16.2
2008	15.7	15.8	15.8	15.9	15.9	15.9	16.0	15.9	16.2	15.6	15.7	15.7	15.8
2009	15.5	15.6	15.5	15.6	15.7	15.8	15.8	15.7	15.6	15.6	15.6	15.6	15.6
2010	15.6	15.6	15.5	15.4	15.4	15.4	15.4	15.4	15.2	15.3	15.3	15.4	15.4
2011	15.2	15.2	15.2	15.2	15.2	15.2	15.2	15.3	15.1	15.1	15.1	15.1	15.2

Employment by Industry: Allentown–Bethlehem–Easton, PA–NJ, Selected Years, 2000–2011—*Continued*

(Numbers in thousands, not seasonally adjusted)

Industry and year	January	February	March	April	May	June	July	August	September	October	November	December	Annual average
Professional and Business Services													
2000	35.9	35.9	36.5	37.4	37.5	38.0	38.4	37.7	37.7	37.6	37.5	37.4	37.3
2001	36.8	36.7	37.1	37.7	37.9	38.1	37.2	37.0	36.8	37.0	36.8	36.8	37.2
2002	36.1	35.9	36.6	37.0	36.8	37.3	37.5	38.0	37.7	38.1	37.9	37.9	37.2
2003	36.7	36.6	37.1	38.0	38.6	39.1	39.4	40.4	40.9	41.0	41.3	41.5	39.2
2004	40.1	39.9	40.4	41.1	41.1	41.4	41.4	41.6	41.3	42.2	41.9	41.5	41.2
2005	40.0	40.4	40.4	41.3	41.4	42.0	42.5	42.7	42.6	43.3	43.5	43.1	41.9
2006	41.4	41.6	42.3	42.6	43.0	43.7	44.0	44.5	44.3	44.9	44.4	44.1	43.4
2007	42.7	42.6	43.1	43.6	43.7	44.3	44.0	43.6	43.8	44.6	44.2	44.0	43.7
2008	42.2	41.5	41.9	42.6	42.7	42.7	43.2	43.2	42.7	42.9	42.4	42.7	42.6
2009	40.5	39.9	40.0	40.1	40.3	41.0	40.4	41.2	41.2	41.6	42.3	42.5	40.9
2010	41.0	40.9	41.6	42.5	42.6	42.8	42.2	42.3	42.6	43.9	45.1	46.6	42.8
2011	43.3	43.6	44.2	45.4	45.6	45.1	45.5	46.0	46.4	46.8	48.5	49.0	45.8
Education and Health Services													
2000	48.8	50.3	50.6	51.1	51.4	50.3	49.7	49.7	51.6	52.1	52.8	52.3	50.9
2001	50.5	51.8	52.7	52.3	52.1	50.9	50.8	51.3	53.2	53.4	54.0	53.7	52.2
2002	51.9	52.8	53.7	53.4	53.5	52.1	52.2	52.2	54.5	55.6	56.1	55.0	53.6
2003	54.5	55.0	55.9	56.0	55.8	54.3	54.1	54.2	56.3	57.4	57.9	57.5	55.7
2004	55.6	57.3	58.3	58.0	57.9	56.7	56.2	56.0	57.6	59.3	59.4	58.1	57.5
2005	57.4	58.1	59.3	59.6	59.2	57.8	58.1	57.7	59.5	60.8	60.9	60.5	59.1
2006	59.2	60.2	61.8	61.5	60.9	59.2	59.2	59.3	61.4	62.9	62.6	62.3	60.9
2007	60.6	61.6	63.3	63.2	63.0	61.3	61.2	62.0	63.5	65.0	64.7	64.5	62.8
2008	62.6	64.3	65.3	65.3	64.0	62.9	62.9	63.4	64.6	65.8	66.1	65.9	64.4
2009	64.6	65.6	66.6	66.4	65.6	64.0	64.0	64.3	65.8	67.3	67.6	67.2	65.8
2010	65.0	67.5	68.2	67.8	67.8	65.9	65.4	66.0	67.3	68.2	68.4	68.2	67.1
2011	66.6	68.0	68.6	68.5	68.5	67.0	66.4	65.3	66.9	67.1	68.1	68.4	67.5
Leisure and Hospitality													
2000	24.9	24.9	24.9	25.5	27.2	28.7	28.7	28.3	27.0	25.8	24.7	25.2	26.3
2001	25.0	24.9	25.3	24.9	27.2	28.5	28.3	28.2	26.8	25.7	24.6	24.4	26.2
2002	25.4	25.5	26.2	26.5	28.6	30.3	29.8	30.3	28.7	27.6	26.2	26.6	27.6
2003	27.0	26.7	27.1	27.7	29.5	30.4	30.3	30.4	29.1	28.0	26.6	26.4	28.3
2004	26.8	26.8	27.2	28.3	30.0	31.4	30.9	30.9	30.0	28.9	27.5	27.0	28.8
2005	26.2	26.7	27.5	28.9	30.6	31.9	31.9	32.0	30.6	29.2	27.7	27.7	29.2
2006	27.4	27.7	28.6	29.5	31.3	32.7	32.3	32.3	30.9	29.8	28.6	28.6	30.0
2007	27.6	27.8	28.7	29.4	31.5	33.7	33.2	33.0	31.3	30.8	29.2	29.4	30.5
2008	28.5	28.6	29.3	30.1	33.2	33.9	33.5	33.2	31.5	30.8	28.4	28.7	30.8
2009	27.8	27.8	28.5	29.7	33.2	34.0	34.0	33.7	32.1	31.0	29.2	29.1	30.8
2010	28.9	28.6	29.3	31.2	33.0	34.1	33.8	33.7	32.6	31.5	29.7	29.9	31.4
2011	29.0	29.4	30.0	32.2	33.8	34.8	35.1	34.2	31.6	30.5	29.3	29.8	31.6
Other Services													
2000	14.3	14.5	14.4	14.3	14.4	14.7	14.6	14.6	14.3	14.3	14.5	14.5	14.5
2001	14.4	14.4	14.7	14.7	14.9	15.2	15.3	15.1	14.7	14.6	14.8	14.8	14.8
2002	14.7	14.7	14.8	14.9	15.0	15.2	15.3	15.2	14.8	14.7	14.7	14.9	14.9
2003	14.6	14.6	14.8	14.8	15.0	15.2	15.3	15.1	14.9	14.9	14.9	14.9	14.9
2004	14.7	14.8	14.9	15.1	15.2	15.5	15.5	15.3	15.1	15.2	15.2	15.3	15.2
2005	15.1	15.3	15.4	15.2	15.4	15.6	15.6	15.4	15.2	14.9	14.9	15.0	15.3
2006	14.7	14.8	14.9	15.1	15.3	15.4	15.4	15.3	15.1	14.9	14.9	15.1	15.1
2007	14.8	14.8	15.1	15.1	15.3	15.4	15.5	15.4	15.2	15.0	15.0	15.2	15.2
2008	14.9	15.0	15.0	15.1	15.2	15.5	15.4	15.2	15.0	14.9	14.8	14.9	15.1
2009	14.5	14.6	14.6	14.7	14.8	14.9	14.8	14.7	14.3	14.3	14.3	14.3	14.6
2010	14.0	13.9	14.1	14.2	14.2	14.4	14.3	14.3	14.0	14.0	14.0	14.1	14.1
2011	13.8	13.8	13.9	14.1	14.2	14.5	14.5	14.4	14.1	14.1	14.1	14.2	14.1
Government													
2000	37.7	38.4	38.9	38.9	40.1	39.7	36.9	36.6	36.8	38.9	39.2	39.4	38.5
2001	37.9	38.9	39.2	39.1	39.4	38.9	35.7	36.2	37.9	39.4	39.5	39.8	38.5
2002	38.7	39.5	39.8	39.7	40.1	39.2	35.6	35.2	38.5	39.8	39.9	40.0	38.8
2003	39.4	40.6	40.9	40.9	41.3	40.9	34.7	34.2	39.9	40.9	41.6	41.3	39.7
2004	40.0	41.3	41.6	41.5	42.1	41.7	35.6	35.3	40.2	41.6	41.7	41.6	40.4
2005	40.3	41.8	41.9	42.8	42.5	41.5	35.7	34.9	40.6	41.6	42.0	42.1	40.6
2006	41.2	42.1	42.4	42.4	42.7	41.9	35.8	36.1	41.1	42.2	42.9	42.8	41.1
2007	41.5	42.7	42.9	43.0	43.7	43.2	37.3	37.1	42.1	43.2	43.7	43.8	42.0
2008	42.0	43.3	43.5	43.5	44.1	43.4	38.4	38.4	42.6	44.0	44.4	44.3	42.7
2009	42.2	43.9	44.3	44.7	44.9	44.1	38.6	38.6	42.6	44.1	44.6	44.5	43.1
2010	42.7	44.0	44.3	44.7	45.8	44.9	38.1	37.4	41.7	42.4	42.9	42.7	42.6
2011	41.2	42.5	42.8	42.9	42.9	42.5	37.0	36.8	40.0	41.3	41.9	41.8	41.1

Employment by Industry: Atlanta–Sandy Springs–Marietta, GA, Selected Years, 2000–2011

(Numbers in thousands, not seasonally adjusted)

Industry and year	January	February	March	April	May	June	July	August	September	October	November	December	Annual average
Total Nonfarm													
2000	2,238.7	2,253.0	2,275.3	2,275.4	2,289.5	2,307.3	2,288.1	2,301.0	2,306.4	2,314.5	2,323.7	2,333.7	2,292.2
2001	2,278.5	2,287.7	2,304.3	2,310.2	2,312.9	2,316.5	2,302.6	2,315.4	2,313.6	2,300.7	2,302.3	2,302.0	2,303.9
2002	2,235.6	2,238.1	2,257.2	2,268.7	2,275.9	2,278.2	2,245.1	2,266.1	2,265.2	2,259.6	2,270.6	2,274.6	2,261.2
2003	2,209.9	2,220.1	2,233.6	2,230.3	2,237.7	2,233.6	2,222.2	2,246.6	2,249.4	2,249.1	2,262.0	2,270.3	2,238.7
2004	2,218.8	2,231.3	2,248.6	2,259.4	2,265.0	2,260.8	2,263.3	2,283.7	2,276.0	2,297.0	2,308.7	2,315.4	2,269.0
2005	2,280.4	2,292.2	2,299.2	2,329.5	2,341.4	2,331.7	2,330.2	2,354.8	2,356.4	2,369.7	2,387.3	2,392.1	2,338.7
2006	2,355.5	2,365.4	2,378.8	2,390.6	2,402.6	2,403.7	2,388.7	2,411.9	2,415.2	2,440.1	2,454.7	2,461.3	2,405.7
2007	2,422.4	2,435.3	2,447.3	2,445.6	2,457.2	2,450.7	2,446.0	2,469.6	2,465.5	2,466.2	2,478.7	2,480.6	2,455.4
2008	2,435.5	2,447.1	2,448.6	2,448.8	2,456.3	2,440.9	2,417.2	2,430.8	2,416.1	2,412.1	2,405.7	2,393.3	2,429.4
2009	2,334.0	2,328.4	2,318.8	2,312.3	2,309.7	2,290.9	2,268.0	2,271.3	2,265.9	2,271.8	2,278.4	2,276.3	2,293.9
2010	2,233.4	2,241.2	2,253.0	2,271.6	2,289.8	2,280.3	2,272.3	2,278.1	2,271.2	2,294.4	2,303.5	2,299.7	2,274.0
2011	2,238.1	2,272.5	2,287.6	2,312.6	2,317.9	2,306.5	2,298.8	2,309.6	2,304.3	2,319.8	2,332.6	2,334.1	2,302.9
Total Private													
2000	1,969.0	1,980.6	2,001.5	2,001.8	2,015.8	2,034.9	2,025.9	2,033.2	2,033.1	2,038.3	2,046.2	2,055.3	2,019.6
2001	1,999.8	2,005.6	2,020.8	2,028.0	2,029.2	2,035.9	2,030.9	2,031.4	2,025.4	2,010.2	2,009.8	2,010.7	2,019.8
2002	1,946.5	1,949.2	1,963.7	1,972.6	1,979.7	1,987.2	1,966.3	1,973.8	1,965.9	1,961.3	1,970.5	1,977.0	1,967.8
2003	1,912.3	1,920.9	1,932.7	1,930.5	1,939.9	1,945.2	1,943.3	1,956.7	1,952.0	1,950.2	1,962.9	1,971.7	1,943.2
2004	1,920.4	1,927.5	1,944.2	1,955.6	1,963.1	1,969.6	1,979.7	1,984.6	1,971.1	1,992.9	2,002.9	2,012.3	1,968.7
2005	1,977.8	1,985.2	1,991.6	2,021.3	2,033.6	2,034.6	2,041.6	2,049.2	2,047.6	2,057.8	2,074.5	2,080.0	2,032.9
2006	2,044.1	2,050.4	2,062.1	2,075.6	2,088.4	2,094.8	2,092.5	2,099.3	2,096.3	2,118.3	2,130.5	2,137.6	2,090.8
2007	2,100.8	2,109.4	2,120.2	2,119.7	2,130.0	2,133.9	2,135.6	2,145.2	2,136.2	2,137.5	2,148.3	2,150.3	2,130.8
2008	2,105.1	2,111.4	2,111.2	2,112.1	2,120.3	2,112.3	2,100.4	2,100.9	2,085.2	2,074.5	2,064.9	2,055.1	2,096.1
2009	1,996.2	1,987.2	1,976.7	1,971.1	1,972.5	1,963.5	1,953.7	1,948.7	1,934.7	1,941.2	1,947.7	1,946.9	1,961.7
2010	1,905.3	1,911.0	1,921.9	1,939.7	1,952.6	1,951.9	1,958.2	1,961.7	1,952.7	1,974.6	1,979.6	1,980.1	1,949.1
2011	1,922.2	1,953.2	1,966.6	1,993.0	1,999.9	1,995.0	1,998.8	2,000.8	1,987.6	2,003.1	2,014.8	2,017.0	1,987.7
Goods-Producing													
2000	331.3	333.3	336.9	336.4	337.9	341.6	340.3	340.5	340.6	339.7	338.0	337.6	337.8
2001	329.7	330.1	331.0	331.9	331.0	333.2	331.7	330.2	328.2	323.8	320.3	318.1	328.3
2002	311.0	311.0	313.4	314.3	314.0	315.4	314.4	314.5	312.4	308.7	307.7	305.3	311.8
2003	299.1	301.7	303.0	300.1	302.1	302.9	302.2	303.8	303.4	304.2	303.0	303.8	302.4
2004	297.6	300.7	302.3	303.2	303.4	306.0	308.1	308.6	307.1	308.2	308.5	308.7	305.2
2005	304.5	306.0	305.8	310.3	312.6	312.9	312.9	314.0	315.8	314.0	316.3	315.5	311.7
2006	312.3	314.1	314.5	314.7	316.9	319.5	319.3	322.1	321.2	322.5	319.3	317.8	317.9
2007	316.0	317.6	318.3	317.1	317.9	318.6	317.2	318.1	315.7	315.2	314.4	312.5	316.6
2008	306.9	307.2	305.7	302.3	302.1	301.1	298.2	296.0	292.8	289.2	284.3	278.6	297.0
2009	266.9	263.7	259.5	255.1	253.0	249.9	244.3	242.4	240.6	239.5	238.2	236.4	249.1
2010	233.6	233.5	233.7	234.5	236.0	236.5	238.2	237.9	237.2	238.2	237.3	235.5	236.0
2011	228.1	234.3	236.2	238.8	239.5	240.0	242.2	243.5	240.7	239.2	237.1	240.9	238.4
Mining and Logging													
2000	2.1	2.2	2.2	2.1	2.1	2.1	2.1	2.2	2.1	2.3	2.3	2.2	2.2
2001	2.2	2.2	2.2	2.2	2.2	2.2	2.2	2.1	2.2	2.2	2.2	2.1	2.2
2002	2.2	2.1	2.1	2.1	2.1	2.1	2.1	2.2	2.2	2.1	2.1	2.0	2.1
2003	2.0	2.0	2.0	2.0	2.0	2.0	2.0	2.0	2.0	2.1	2.0	2.0	2.0
2004	2.0	2.0	2.0	2.0	2.0	2.1	2.1	2.1	2.1	2.0	2.1	2.1	2.1
2005	1.9	1.9	1.9	2.1	2.1	2.1	2.1	2.1	2.1	2.1	2.1	2.1	2.1
2006	2.2	2.1	2.1	2.1	2.1	2.1	2.1	2.1	2.0	2.1	2.1	2.1	2.1
2007	2.1	2.0	2.1	2.0	2.0	2.0	2.0	2.0	2.0	2.0	2.0	1.9	2.0
2008	1.8	1.8	1.8	1.7	1.6	1.6	1.5	1.5	1.5	1.5	1.5	1.5	1.6
2009	1.3	1.4	1.3	1.3	1.3	1.3	1.3	1.3	1.3	1.3	1.3	1.3	1.3
2010	1.3	1.3	1.3	1.3	1.3	1.3	1.3	1.3	1.4	1.4	1.3	1.3	1.3
2011	1.3	1.3	1.3	1.3	1.3	1.3	1.3	1.3	1.3	1.3	1.3	1.3	1.3
Construction													
2000	121.1	122.7	125.9	127.0	128.6	131.0	131.4	131.4	132.0	131.5	130.1	129.5	128.5
2001	124.9	126.3	127.3	129.6	130.2	131.8	132.5	131.7	130.5	129.2	127.8	126.0	129.0
2002	122.7	123.7	125.0	125.1	124.8	125.1	124.7	124.7	123.8	122.7	122.1	120.6	123.8
2003	117.4	118.0	119.3	119.1	120.1	121.2	122.1	123.2	123.6	123.6	123.4	123.8	121.2
2004	121.0	121.2	122.6	124.1	124.1	126.5	129.0	128.2	127.2	127.9	128.1	128.2	125.7
2005	125.9	127.1	127.0	130.1	132.1	132.5	133.3	134.1	135.0	134.5	135.0	133.8	131.7
2006	131.2	132.8	133.5	134.7	136.5	138.4	140.5	141.4	141.2	141.7	141.2	139.7	137.7
2007	137.0	138.7	139.6	139.1	139.9	140.4	139.8	140.5	139.1	139.1	138.4	136.7	139.0
2008	132.7	133.3	132.2	130.4	130.6	130.0	128.9	127.5	125.7	123.3	120.2	116.9	127.6
2009	110.5	109.3	106.9	104.9	104.2	102.7	99.7	97.8	96.6	96.0	95.4	93.7	101.5
2010	91.1	91.4	91.3	92.2	92.7	92.6	93.2	93.0	92.5	92.6	91.8	89.6	92.0
2011	84.1	88.2	89.8	91.7	91.6	91.9	92.6	94.2	91.6	90.2	88.6	91.5	90.5
Manufacturing													
2000	208.1	208.4	208.8	207.3	207.2	208.5	206.8	206.9	206.5	205.9	205.6	205.9	207.2
2001	202.6	201.6	201.5	200.1	198.6	199.2	197.0	196.4	195.5	192.4	190.3	190.0	197.1
2002	186.1	185.2	186.3	187.1	187.1	188.2	187.6	187.6	186.4	183.9	183.5	182.7	186.0
2003	179.7	181.7	181.7	179.0	180.0	179.7	178.1	178.6	177.8	178.5	177.6	178.0	179.2
2004	174.6	177.5	177.7	177.1	177.3	177.4	177.0	178.3	177.8	178.3	178.3	178.4	177.5
2005	176.7	177.0	176.9	178.1	178.4	178.3	177.5	177.8	178.7	177.4	179.2	179.6	178.0
2006	178.9	179.2	178.9	177.9	178.3	179.0	176.7	178.6	178.0	178.7	176.0	176.0	178.0
2007	176.9	176.9	176.6	176.0	176.0	176.2	175.4	175.6	174.6	174.1	174.0	173.9	175.5
2008	172.4	172.1	171.7	170.2	169.9	169.5	167.8	167.0	165.6	164.4	162.6	160.2	167.8
2009	155.1	153.0	151.3	148.9	147.5	145.9	143.3	143.3	142.7	142.2	141.5	141.4	146.3
2010	141.2	140.8	141.1	141.0	142.0	142.6	143.7	143.6	143.3	144.2	144.2	144.6	142.7
2011	142.7	144.8	145.1	145.8	146.6	146.8	148.3	148.0	147.8	147.7	147.2	148.1	146.6

Employment by Industry: Atlanta–Sandy Springs–Marietta, GA, Selected Years, 2000–2011—*Continued*
(Numbers in thousands, not seasonally adjusted)

Industry and year	January	February	March	April	May	June	July	August	September	October	November	December	Annual average
Service-Providing													
2000	1,907.4	1,919.7	1,938.4	1,939.0	1,951.6	1,965.7	1,947.8	1,960.5	1,965.8	1,974.8	1,985.7	1,996.1	1,954.4
2001	1,948.8	1,957.6	1,973.3	1,978.3	1,981.9	1,983.3	1,970.9	1,985.2	1,985.4	1,976.9	1,982.0	1,983.9	1,975.6
2002	1,924.6	1,927.1	1,943.8	1,954.4	1,961.9	1,962.8	1,930.7	1,951.6	1,952.8	1,950.9	1,962.9	1,969.3	1,949.4
2003	1,910.8	1,918.4	1,930.6	1,930.2	1,935.6	1,930.7	1,920.0	1,942.8	1,946.0	1,944.9	1,959.0	1,966.5	1,936.3
2004	1,921.2	1,930.6	1,946.3	1,956.2	1,961.6	1,954.8	1,955.2	1,975.1	1,968.9	1,988.8	2,000.2	2,006.7	1,963.8
2005	1,975.9	1,986.2	1,993.4	2,019.2	2,028.8	2,018.8	2,017.3	2,040.8	2,040.6	2,055.7	2,071.0	2,076.6	2,027.0
2006	2,043.2	2,051.3	2,064.3	2,075.9	2,085.7	2,084.2	2,069.4	2,089.8	2,094.0	2,117.6	2,135.4	2,143.5	2,087.9
2007	2,106.4	2,117.7	2,129.0	2,128.5	2,139.3	2,132.1	2,128.8	2,151.5	2,149.8	2,151.0	2,164.3	2,168.1	2,138.9
2008	2,128.6	2,139.9	2,142.9	2,146.5	2,154.2	2,139.8	2,119.0	2,134.8	2,123.3	2,122.9	2,121.4	2,114.7	2,132.3
2009	2,067.1	2,064.7	2,059.3	2,057.2	2,056.7	2,041.0	2,023.7	2,028.9	2,025.3	2,032.3	2,040.2	2,039.9	2,044.8
2010	1,999.8	2,007.7	2,019.3	2,037.1	2,053.8	2,043.8	2,034.1	2,040.2	2,034.0	2,056.2	2,066.2	2,064.2	2,038.0
2011	2,010.0	2,038.2	2,051.4	2,073.8	2,078.4	2,066.5	2,056.6	2,066.1	2,063.6	2,080.6	2,095.5	2,093.2	2,064.5
Trade, Transportation, and Utilities													
2000	541.1	541.4	546.0	546.7	548.9	551.3	547.0	550.3	549.6	556.7	566.4	574.1	551.6
2001	551.9	548.9	552.2	547.7	547.9	549.3	547.5	546.5	546.3	546.1	552.0	557.1	549.5
2002	530.8	525.8	528.1	528.9	530.8	533.1	525.1	526.5	526.0	529.2	538.3	546.1	530.7
2003	516.7	513.6	514.9	511.7	514.0	514.1	514.2	516.8	516.1	518.2	528.2	533.5	517.7
2004	513.1	509.8	512.6	511.4	513.6	514.9	517.7	518.5	515.3	522.1	531.9	538.3	518.3
2005	522.1	521.0	522.7	529.7	532.3	532.6	538.3	537.0	535.1	541.2	553.0	559.8	535.4
2006	540.4	537.8	540.9	545.2	548.5	549.5	547.7	548.9	550.5	559.7	572.4	580.1	551.8
2007	560.4	556.4	557.1	557.4	560.8	561.0	561.4	561.2	561.2	563.4	573.8	578.4	562.7
2008	560.2	557.9	558.1	554.5	555.7	553.6	553.2	552.0	549.6	546.8	549.8	551.4	553.6
2009	529.7	523.8	520.2	515.8	516.2	514.9	513.2	513.1	510.8	509.9	517.7	521.2	517.2
2010	507.2	505.4	506.4	508.2	511.4	512.1	512.8	513.7	510.2	518.8	526.5	530.8	513.6
2011	510.0	514.0	516.4	520.1	522.1	522.0	523.0	521.8	522.3	528.9	539.5	541.6	523.5
Wholesale Trade													
2000	157.9	159.3	160.3	160.0	160.7	161.4	161.6	162.0	161.3	161.8	162.0	162.1	160.9
2001	161.0	161.2	161.8	162.3	162.1	163.3	163.0	161.8	160.8	159.2	158.2	158.2	161.1
2002	155.0	154.7	155.5	155.0	154.7	154.5	151.9	151.8	150.9	152.4	152.1	152.1	153.4
2003	151.1	151.4	151.9	150.9	151.3	151.3	151.3	151.1	150.5	150.1	151.0	151.7	151.1
2004	149.9	150.1	150.8	151.4	151.2	151.5	152.7	152.6	151.3	152.0	152.3	152.8	151.6
2005	153.2	154.0	154.4	155.3	155.2	155.2	155.8	156.2	155.9	155.4	155.5	156.1	155.2
2006	154.6	155.3	155.6	157.2	158.1	158.3	159.3	159.2	159.3	160.7	160.0	161.2	158.2
2007	159.2	159.6	159.6	160.1	159.9	159.7	160.6	160.6	160.1	160.1	160.0	160.4	160.0
2008	159.7	160.2	159.9	159.6	159.7	159.1	159.4	159.2	158.6	157.6	156.2	155.0	158.7
2009	152.3	150.7	148.9	147.7	146.5	145.5	145.2	144.6	144.0	144.0	143.8	143.7	146.4
2010	143.0	143.4	143.3	144.0	144.5	144.4	144.4	144.3	143.2	144.7	144.7	144.1	144.0
2011	142.6	143.9	144.0	145.1	145.8	145.3	146.6	145.3	145.0	146.2	146.8	147.5	145.3
Retail Trade													
2000	258.5	257.6	260.6	260.0	261.6	263.2	258.5	260.7	260.3	264.8	274.0	281.4	263.4
2001	264.2	261.3	264.1	260.3	260.7	260.8	257.1	257.7	258.9	260.1	269.4	274.6	262.4
2002	256.8	252.7	254.3	253.9	255.4	256.3	252.8	253.5	254.3	254.8	263.7	271.6	256.7
2003	246.8	243.8	244.8	244.2	246.1	246.3	245.7	248.0	248.0	250.1	258.7	263.5	248.8
2004	245.9	242.6	244.0	241.6	243.5	244.7	245.2	245.9	244.7	250.0	259.0	264.7	247.7
2005	249.3	246.2	247.3	253.9	256.2	256.8	259.3	258.2	256.3	262.5	272.1	277.3	258.0
2006	263.2	259.8	261.7	263.7	265.3	265.6	262.2	263.0	263.3	271.2	283.8	288.0	267.6
2007	275.2	270.4	270.6	270.3	271.6	270.8	271.5	271.0	270.9	273.3	283.4	286.3	273.8
2008	271.6	268.4	268.7	265.7	266.2	264.8	264.7	263.8	262.4	261.6	266.3	267.7	266.0
2009	251.9	248.6	247.1	245.9	247.0	246.6	245.2	245.8	244.0	243.5	251.0	253.6	247.5
2010	242.0	240.0	240.9	242.1	243.8	244.2	244.6	244.9	242.7	247.8	254.8	257.8	245.5
2011	243.5	244.7	246.0	248.8	249.3	249.2	248.7	248.4	250.2	254.0	263.9	265.3	251.0
Transportation and Utilities													
2000	124.7	124.5	125.1	126.7	126.6	126.7	126.9	127.6	128.0	130.1	130.4	130.6	127.3
2001	126.7	126.4	126.3	125.1	125.1	125.2	127.4	127.0	126.6	126.8	124.4	124.3	125.9
2002	119.0	118.4	118.3	120.0	120.7	122.3	120.4	121.2	120.8	122.0	122.5	122.4	120.7
2003	118.8	118.4	118.2	116.6	116.6	116.5	117.2	117.7	117.6	118.0	118.5	118.3	117.7
2004	117.3	117.1	117.8	118.4	118.9	118.7	119.8	120.0	119.3	120.1	120.6	120.8	119.1
2005	119.6	120.8	121.0	120.5	120.9	120.6	123.2	122.6	122.9	123.3	125.4	126.4	122.3
2006	122.6	122.7	123.6	124.3	125.1	125.6	126.2	126.7	127.9	127.8	128.6	130.9	126.0
2007	126.0	126.4	126.9	127.0	129.3	130.5	129.3	129.6	130.2	130.0	130.4	131.7	128.9
2008	128.9	129.3	129.5	129.2	129.8	129.7	129.1	129.0	128.6	127.6	127.3	128.7	128.9
2009	125.5	124.5	124.2	122.2	122.7	122.8	122.8	122.7	122.8	122.4	122.9	123.9	123.3
2010	122.2	122.0	122.2	122.1	123.1	123.5	123.8	124.5	124.3	126.3	127.0	128.9	124.2
2011	123.9	125.4	126.4	126.2	127.0	127.5	127.7	128.1	127.1	128.7	128.8	128.8	127.1
Information													
2000	103.7	103.7	105.2	104.5	105.5	107.3	107.2	107.7	107.9	108.8	109.4	110.9	106.8
2001	108.8	109.0	109.6	109.0	108.8	108.9	107.3	106.6	105.8	105.1	104.7	104.8	107.4
2002	104.4	103.5	104.6	101.2	100.2	100.1	99.6	99.1	98.0	98.0	97.5	97.4	100.3
2003	92.5	92.6	92.8	91.2	90.7	91.1	90.5	91.1	90.0	90.2	91.2	91.2	91.3
2004	88.9	88.4	88.9	88.4	88.1	88.5	88.0	87.6	87.0	86.5	87.2	87.1	87.9
2005	85.3	85.3	85.8	85.8	84.8	86.3	85.7	84.4	85.0	85.4	86.2	86.6	85.6
2006	85.0	85.4	85.8	85.4	85.9	85.5	85.0	84.7	84.6	84.8	85.7	85.9	85.3
2007	86.3	86.1	86.1	85.3	85.8	85.8	85.5	85.6	85.7	84.7	85.1	85.2	85.6
2008	83.2	83.7	84.0	84.0	84.5	84.4	83.9	83.7	83.1	82.3	82.5	82.4	83.5
2009	82.3	82.2	81.7	81.3	81.1	80.7	80.0	79.7	79.2	78.4	78.5	79.0	80.3
2010	77.7	77.6	77.8	78.3	78.8	78.5	78.7	78.5	77.9	77.8	78.1	78.2	78.2
2011	79.1	79.2	79.1	80.0	80.0	79.7	80.0	79.7	79.2	78.7	78.4	79.0	79.3

Employment by Industry: Atlanta–Sandy Springs–Marietta, GA, Selected Years, 2000–2011—*Continued*

(Numbers in thousands, not seasonally adjusted)

Industry and year	January	February	March	April	May	June	July	August	September	October	November	December	Annual average
Financial Activities													
2000	146.0	146.5	146.7	149.1	149.5	150.4	149.2	149.3	147.8	148.3	148.4	149.4	148.4
2001	147.4	147.6	148.4	150.9	150.8	151.4	152.5	152.6	152.2	152.1	152.5	152.5	150.9
2002	149.9	150.1	149.8	150.5	150.9	151.2	151.0	151.7	150.7	150.4	150.8	151.3	150.7
2003	149.1	149.7	150.3	150.4	151.5	152.3	152.6	153.3	152.9	150.1	150.4	150.8	151.1
2004	149.1	149.7	150.1	151.7	152.0	151.6	152.6	152.8	152.2	154.1	154.1	154.8	152.1
2005	155.0	155.4	155.4	156.1	157.0	157.3	156.7	157.7	157.7	159.9	160.1	161.4	157.5
2006	158.2	159.1	159.6	161.5	162.1	162.5	162.4	163.2	163.1	164.6	164.4	165.1	162.2
2007	162.1	163.6	163.9	163.2	163.1	162.9	163.0	162.9	161.6	161.4	161.3	161.0	162.5
2008	157.3	157.8	157.3	157.0	157.0	156.3	156.3	155.3	153.5	154.0	152.4	151.7	155.5
2009	149.3	148.5	147.7	146.9	147.1	146.8	146.1	145.2	144.0	143.6	143.3	143.4	146.0
2010	141.5	141.4	141.3	141.0	141.5	141.4	141.2	141.7	141.1	142.6	142.8	143.2	141.7
2011	140.5	141.0	141.3	142.3	142.3	142.1	141.9	140.3	138.5	138.9	139.7	138.8	140.6
Professional and Business Services													
2000	385.6	389.6	393.0	389.8	392.9	399.6	396.9	400.1	401.8	400.2	399.4	401.1	395.8
2001	385.6	387.4	390.2	392.8	390.3	389.5	389.5	391.8	388.6	382.7	379.3	379.1	387.2
2002	362.8	366.4	367.4	371.5	372.9	373.6	370.5	372.8	370.8	369.6	369.4	368.7	369.7
2003	357.6	361.3	361.9	363.6	361.4	362.6	362.5	365.9	365.1	366.8	367.7	368.8	363.8
2004	358.1	361.7	366.1	370.4	370.7	371.0	376.5	376.3	373.3	383.0	382.3	383.1	372.7
2005	377.8	381.3	382.0	385.6	386.2	386.7	391.4	394.7	396.1	397.9	399.0	397.4	389.7
2006	393.0	394.4	396.8	399.5	399.7	402.8	403.2	402.8	401.7	405.6	405.9	407.1	401.0
2007	401.3	404.8	408.5	405.2	407.4	408.9	412.7	416.1	415.3	415.5	416.8	417.7	410.9
2008	409.5	410.2	407.9	412.4	411.5	412.4	407.3	408.3	405.0	405.1	401.0	398.4	407.4
2009	381.0	378.4	375.4	374.2	373.0	374.1	375.8	372.9	370.5	379.5	381.3	381.8	376.5
2010	371.2	374.0	377.3	384.3	385.3	386.9	389.2	388.7	387.1	393.8	393.5	393.5	385.4
2011	381.6	390.8	393.3	401.0	399.9	400.3	400.8	403.9	404.9	409.1	412.1	411.7	400.8
Education and Health Services													
2000	189.9	191.8	192.7	194.1	194.7	194.4	191.6	192.4	195.1	198.5	199.5	198.7	194.5
2001	196.7	199.2	200.8	201.7	202.4	202.3	203.8	205.2	207.4	208.1	209.4	209.8	203.9
2002	205.6	208.6	211.1	210.8	211.5	211.3	210.5	213.6	214.8	216.0	217.8	217.8	212.5
2003	214.7	217.1	218.6	218.4	219.7	218.3	217.4	220.2	221.1	222.2	223.6	224.4	219.6
2004	222.8	224.3	225.3	226.4	227.3	225.7	226.5	229.1	229.2	233.1	234.0	234.6	228.2
2005	233.4	234.7	232.6	237.6	239.0	236.0	237.2	240.0	241.1	243.8	244.6	244.7	238.7
2006	245.3	247.0	247.1	247.5	248.2	245.3	245.9	248.4	250.5	255.8	256.5	256.4	249.5
2007	254.0	256.6	256.8	258.3	258.3	255.9	256.5	260.8	262.5	265.3	266.3	266.3	259.8
2008	262.9	266.5	266.6	267.5	268.9	263.9	264.4	269.0	269.5	271.6	272.6	272.9	268.0
2009	271.0	272.7	271.7	272.4	273.7	268.7	267.5	271.1	271.0	275.4	276.3	276.2	272.3
2010	273.6	276.5	277.7	278.6	280.3	276.3	277.8	281.3	281.8	286.3	286.4	286.0	280.2
2011	280.9	285.5	286.5	288.6	287.9	283.0	284.6	290.3	289.4	293.6	294.5	294.1	288.2
Leisure and Hospitality													
2000	184.9	187.1	193.0	193.2	197.6	200.7	203.7	203.2	200.9	198.4	197.5	195.6	196.3
2001	188.5	191.6	196.2	201.4	204.9	207.4	203.4	203.9	199.6	199.1	198.0	195.9	199.2
2002	189.7	191.7	196.8	203.1	207.2	209.6	203.4	203.8	201.7	199.5	199.4	201.0	200.6
2003	191.7	193.7	199.3	203.6	208.1	210.8	210.7	212.2	210.5	206.1	206.3	206.9	205.0
2004	199.3	201.5	206.1	211.6	215.1	218.4	216.6	218.0	214.5	213.9	212.8	213.7	211.8
2005	206.4	207.5	212.9	220.7	225.6	226.8	223.0	223.8	221.1	220.2	219.9	219.1	218.9
2006	214.6	217.1	221.8	224.8	229.4	231.7	230.6	231.4	228.1	228.7	229.7	229.1	226.4
2007	224.5	227.8	232.6	235.2	240.0	241.7	240.0	241.3	236.6	234.1	233.0	232.2	234.9
2008	227.8	229.8	233.4	236.3	241.4	241.2	238.6	238.1	234.3	228.8	226.1	224.2	233.3
2009	217.4	219.0	222.3	226.3	229.5	230.1	228.3	227.3	223.6	220.0	218.4	216.1	223.2
2010	208.9	210.6	215.6	221.7	225.4	226.9	226.2	226.2	224.1	222.9	220.9	219.9	220.8
2011	210.8	215.5	220.8	227.9	233.2	233.0	231.3	226.9	220.1	222.0	221.6	219.6	223.6
Other Services													
2000	86.5	87.2	88.0	88.0	88.8	89.6	90.0	89.7	89.4	87.7	87.6	87.9	88.4
2001	91.2	91.8	92.4	92.6	93.1	93.9	95.2	94.6	97.3	93.2	93.6	93.4	93.5
2002	92.3	92.1	92.5	92.3	92.2	92.9	91.8	91.8	91.5	89.9	89.6	89.4	91.5
2003	90.9	91.2	91.9	91.5	92.4	93.1	93.2	93.4	92.9	92.4	92.5	92.3	92.3
2004	91.5	91.4	92.8	92.5	92.9	93.5	93.7	93.7	92.5	92.0	92.1	92.0	92.6
2005	93.3	94.0	94.4	95.5	96.1	96.0	96.4	97.6	95.7	95.4	95.4	95.5	95.4
2006	95.3	95.5	95.6	97.0	97.7	98.0	98.4	97.8	96.6	96.6	96.6	96.1	96.8
2007	96.2	96.5	96.9	98.0	98.7	99.1	99.3	99.2	97.6	97.9	97.6	97.0	97.8
2008	97.3	98.3	98.2	98.1	99.2	99.1	98.5	98.5	97.4	96.7	96.2	95.5	97.8
2009	98.6	98.9	98.2	99.1	98.9	98.3	98.5	97.0	95.0	94.9	94.0	92.8	97.0
2010	91.6	92.0	92.1	93.1	93.9	93.3	94.1	93.7	93.3	94.2	94.1	93.0	93.2
2011	91.2	92.9	93.0	94.3	95.0	94.9	95.0	94.4	92.5	92.7	91.9	91.3	93.3
Government													
2000	269.7	272.4	273.8	273.6	273.7	272.4	262.2	267.8	273.3	276.2	277.5	278.4	272.6
2001	278.7	282.1	283.5	282.2	283.7	280.6	271.7	284.0	288.2	290.5	292.5	291.3	284.1
2002	289.1	288.9	293.5	296.1	296.2	291.0	278.8	292.3	299.3	298.3	300.1	297.6	293.4
2003	297.6	299.2	300.9	299.8	297.8	288.4	278.9	289.9	297.4	298.9	299.1	298.6	295.5
2004	298.4	303.8	304.4	303.8	301.9	291.2	283.6	299.1	304.9	304.1	305.8	303.1	300.3
2005	302.6	307.0	307.6	308.2	307.8	297.1	288.6	305.6	308.8	311.9	312.8	312.1	305.8
2006	311.4	315.0	316.7	315.0	314.2	308.9	296.2	312.6	318.9	321.8	324.2	323.7	314.9
2007	321.6	325.9	327.1	325.9	325.2	316.8	310.4	324.4	329.3	328.7	330.4	330.3	324.7
2008	330.4	335.7	337.4	336.7	336.0	328.6	316.8	329.9	330.9	337.6	340.8	338.2	333.3
2009	337.8	341.2	342.1	341.2	337.2	327.4	314.3	322.6	331.2	330.6	330.7	329.4	332.1
2010	328.1	330.2	331.1	331.9	337.2	328.4	314.1	316.4	318.5	319.8	323.9	319.6	324.9
2011	315.9	319.3	321.0	319.6	318.0	311.5	300.0	308.8	316.7	316.7	317.8	317.1	315.2

Employment by Industry: Austin–Round Rock–San Marcos, TX, Selected Years, 2000–2011

(Numbers in thousands, not seasonally adjusted)

Industry and year	January	February	March	April	May	June	July	August	September	October	November	December	Annual average
Total Nonfarm													
2000	646.2	655.5	662.7	663.8	670.4	674.8	670.2	679.9	682.3	685.9	690.3	690.1	672.7
2001	675.2	679.8	682.8	679.2	678.3	677.7	666.7	672.6	671.5	669.6	669.2	666.2	674.1
2002	652.4	656.5	659.8	661.0	662.5	656.9	652.2	658.1	659.1	658.9	662.7	660.4	658.4
2003	646.5	648.7	649.4	653.6	654.8	653.2	649.3	652.8	654.3	656.3	658.0	659.1	653.0
2004	648.5	655.5	661.0	665.5	667.1	666.9	664.2	669.3	671.5	676.9	680.8	681.8	667.4
2005	672.2	679.2	684.4	690.3	692.8	693.4	690.1	693.7	698.4	699.1	705.7	706.9	692.2
2006	696.4	704.2	710.8	717.0	720.8	723.5	715.9	724.1	734.8	737.7	744.6	748.6	723.2
2007	731.7	743.5	751.5	754.7	758.8	761.6	753.8	757.9	762.7	767.8	773.1	773.4	757.5
2008	763.9	771.8	773.9	776.5	779.2	778.7	770.0	774.3	778.3	780.7	783.4	779.0	775.8
2009	760.2	760.6	760.8	762.7	763.8	761.2	751.0	752.5	754.3	758.5	762.5	760.7	759.1
2010	749.9	755.3	763.7	767.4	771.8	773.2	764.3	767.8	769.4	780.6	786.1	784.7	769.5
2011	772.7	780.3	787.2	793.9	793.6	795.3	787.8	793.6	794.9	799.4	798.9	799.3	791.4
Total Private													
2000	511.2	517.0	523.6	525.1	531.0	540.4	540.5	544.9	545.2	547.2	550.5	553.4	535.8
2001	538.6	540.0	541.9	538.4	537.9	540.5	533.8	533.8	528.2	525.1	522.8	523.1	533.7
2002	509.7	510.9	513.0	513.9	516.4	517.8	514.4	516.7	514.1	510.7	512.9	512.8	513.6
2003	499.9	499.6	500.8	503.8	506.2	508.5	508.2	510.7	510.4	511.7	513.1	515.6	507.4
2004	504.8	508.5	512.9	516.7	519.0	523.1	525.8	528.0	526.8	528.6	531.1	534.5	521.7
2005	525.3	528.5	533.5	538.6	541.1	545.8	546.9	549.3	550.6	548.6	553.5	557.2	543.2
2006	547.0	551.1	557.1	562.6	566.9	573.3	573.9	578.2	580.2	581.6	588.6	594.2	571.2
2007	577.7	586.1	592.9	595.8	600.0	606.0	604.7	607.0	606.6	607.7	611.9	614.5	600.9
2008	603.9	608.4	608.1	613.3	616.2	617.6	615.5	618.5	615.6	616.4	616.8	614.4	613.7
2009	595.6	592.7	592.0	592.5	593.8	593.6	591.7	592.6	588.2	589.8	591.2	591.8	592.1
2010	581.3	584.5	589.8	594.1	597.3	600.5	601.2	604.3	603.0	609.3	613.4	615.0	599.5
2011	604.6	608.9	615.4	621.9	623.5	626.1	626.5	631.8	628.8	631.3	629.0	631.9	623.3
Goods-Producing													
2000	117.6	119.2	121.8	121.9	122.9	125.9	126.1	126.8	126.7	126.6	126.8	126.8	124.1
2001	125.0	124.8	124.5	120.9	120.0	120.4	117.6	116.6	113.7	111.9	109.8	108.8	117.8
2002	105.4	104.7	104.7	103.0	103.0	103.7	102.1	101.4	99.5	98.6	97.5	96.8	101.7
2003	96.0	95.2	95.2	95.2	95.4	96.0	95.7	95.4	94.8	94.5	94.1	94.0	95.1
2004	92.4	92.6	93.2	94.1	94.4	95.6	96.6	96.7	96.3	96.7	96.4	96.1	95.1
2005	95.1	95.4	96.0	96.4	96.7	98.0	98.7	98.6	98.4	98.1	98.5	99.0	97.4
2006	98.5	99.5	101.0	101.5	102.4	104.5	105.2	105.5	105.3	105.3	105.9	106.9	103.5
2007	104.9	106.2	107.2	108.2	108.9	110.3	110.0	110.2	109.3	109.6	109.7	109.0	108.6
2008	106.8	107.4	107.0	106.6	106.7	106.8	105.9	105.2	103.5	101.4	99.7	98.0	104.6
2009	93.1	91.5	89.6	90.3	89.9	90.0	89.5	88.6	88.0	87.2	86.5	86.8	89.3
2010	85.0	85.1	85.8	86.8	86.7	87.8	88.5	89.3	88.8	89.2	89.0	88.9	87.6
2011	87.6	87.9	88.4	88.6	88.7	89.5	89.3	90.9	91.8	91.0	90.4	89.5	89.5
Mining, Logging, and Construction													
2000	38.3	39.2	40.5	40.9	41.4	42.6	42.3	42.6	42.7	42.1	41.7	41.5	41.3
2001	40.4	41.4	42.0	42.0	42.6	43.3	42.7	42.6	41.8	40.8	39.7	39.2	41.5
2002	37.6	38.0	38.7	38.5	38.8	39.4	39.2	39.0	37.9	37.6	37.1	36.5	38.2
2003	36.6	36.5	36.6	37.3	37.8	38.3	38.3	38.3	37.9	37.5	37.1	36.9	37.4
2004	35.9	36.1	36.4	37.2	37.2	37.9	38.8	38.7	38.5	38.9	38.5	38.2	37.7
2005	37.8	38.2	38.8	39.3	39.8	40.5	41.2	41.1	41.3	41.0	41.3	41.5	40.2
2006	41.2	41.9	42.9	43.5	44.1	45.3	45.7	45.9	46.0	45.7	46.1	46.8	44.6
2007	45.7	46.7	47.5	48.2	48.9	49.9	49.8	50.2	49.9	50.3	50.7	49.9	49.0
2008	48.0	48.4	48.3	48.3	48.5	48.6	48.1	48.0	47.2	46.0	44.9	44.0	47.4
2009	42.4	42.0	41.4	40.7	40.8	41.4	41.2	40.5	40.2	39.6	39.6	39.7	40.8
2010	38.2	38.0	38.7	39.7	39.6	40.3	41.0	41.5	40.9	41.0	40.6	40.3	40.0
2011	39.3	39.3	39.5	39.2	39.1	39.5	39.0	40.1	41.1	40.2	39.5	38.6	39.5
Manufacturing													
2000	79.3	80.0	81.3	81.0	81.5	83.3	83.8	84.2	84.0	84.5	85.1	85.3	82.8
2001	84.6	83.4	82.5	78.9	77.4	77.1	74.9	74.0	71.9	71.1	70.1	69.6	76.3
2002	67.8	66.7	66.0	64.5	64.2	64.3	62.9	62.4	61.6	61.0	60.4	60.3	63.5
2003	59.4	58.7	58.6	57.9	57.6	57.7	57.4	57.1	56.9	57.0	57.0	57.1	57.7
2004	56.5	56.5	56.8	56.9	57.2	57.7	57.8	58.0	57.8	57.8	57.9	57.9	57.4
2005	57.3	57.2	57.2	57.1	56.9	57.5	57.5	57.5	57.1	57.1	57.2	57.5	57.3
2006	57.3	57.6	58.1	58.0	58.3	59.2	59.5	59.6	59.3	59.6	59.8	60.1	58.9
2007	59.2	59.5	59.7	60.0	60.0	60.4	60.2	60.0	59.4	59.3	59.0	59.1	59.7
2008	58.8	59.0	58.7	58.3	58.2	58.2	57.8	57.2	56.3	55.4	54.8	54.0	57.2
2009	50.7	49.5	48.2	49.6	49.1	48.6	48.3	48.1	47.8	47.6	46.9	47.1	48.5
2010	46.8	47.1	47.1	47.1	47.1	47.5	47.5	47.8	47.9	48.2	48.4	48.6	47.6
2011	48.3	48.6	48.9	49.4	49.6	50.0	50.3	50.8	50.7	50.8	50.9	50.9	49.9
Service-Providing													
2000	528.6	536.3	540.9	541.9	547.5	548.9	544.1	553.1	555.6	559.3	563.5	563.3	548.6
2001	550.2	555.0	558.3	558.3	558.3	557.3	549.1	556.0	557.8	557.7	559.4	557.4	556.2
2002	547.0	551.8	555.1	558.0	559.5	553.2	550.1	556.7	559.6	560.3	565.2	563.6	556.7
2003	550.5	553.5	554.2	558.4	559.4	557.2	553.6	557.4	559.5	561.8	563.9	565.1	557.9
2004	556.1	562.9	567.8	571.4	572.7	571.3	567.6	572.6	575.2	580.2	584.4	585.7	572.3
2005	577.1	583.8	588.4	593.9	596.1	595.4	591.4	595.1	600.0	601.0	607.2	607.9	594.8
2006	597.9	604.7	609.8	615.5	618.4	619.0	610.7	618.6	629.5	632.4	638.7	641.7	619.7
2007	626.8	637.3	644.3	646.5	649.9	651.3	643.8	647.7	653.4	658.2	663.4	664.4	648.9
2008	657.1	664.4	666.9	669.9	672.5	671.9	664.1	669.1	674.8	679.3	683.7	681.0	671.2
2009	667.1	669.1	671.2	672.4	673.9	671.2	661.5	663.9	666.3	671.3	676.0	673.9	669.8
2010	664.9	670.2	677.9	680.6	685.1	685.4	675.8	678.5	680.6	691.4	697.1	695.8	681.9
2011	685.1	692.4	698.8	705.3	704.9	705.8	698.5	702.7	703.1	708.4	708.5	709.8	701.9

Employment by Industry: Austin–Round Rock–San Marcos, TX, Selected Years, 2000–2011—*Continued*

(Numbers in thousands, not seasonally adjusted)

Industry and year	January	February	March	April	May	June	July	August	September	October	November	December	Annual average
Trade, Transportation, and Utilities													
2000	111.4	111.6	111.9	111.9	112.8	114.0	114.6	116.2	116.0	117.6	120.5	122.5	115.1
2001	118.6	116.8	116.4	116.6	116.7	116.2	115.5	115.7	115.3	115.9	116.9	118.6	116.6
2002	113.8	112.7	112.7	112.9	113.0	113.1	112.6	113.0	112.2	112.4	114.7	116.6	113.3
2003	110.9	109.7	109.6	109.7	109.9	110.4	111.6	112.7	112.8	113.8	116.1	117.9	112.1
2004	113.5	113.1	113.5	113.0	113.3	113.8	115.1	116.1	115.9	117.0	119.6	121.9	115.5
2005	117.8	117.7	118.6	119.1	120.2	121.4	122.4	123.4	123.1	123.0	126.1	128.3	121.8
2006	123.2	122.7	123.4	124.4	125.2	126.5	127.3	128.4	128.2	129.4	133.4	136.5	127.4
2007	131.9	132.2	133.3	134.0	134.5	136.1	136.4	136.6	136.4	137.8	140.0	143.0	136.0
2008	138.4	137.8	137.5	137.8	137.7	138.3	138.5	139.7	138.9	140.0	141.7	142.5	139.1
2009	136.9	133.0	133.0	131.1	131.2	131.0	131.2	132.2	131.3	132.2	134.4	136.0	132.8
2010	133.0	131.9	132.4	133.4	133.8	134.2	134.4	135.5	135.2	136.8	140.0	142.2	135.2
2011	137.5	137.2	138.2	139.1	139.6	139.4	138.5	138.9	137.7	138.9	141.4	142.6	139.1
Wholesale Trade													
2000	33.0	33.5	33.5	33.8	34.1	35.0	35.1	35.4	35.7	36.2	36.6	36.9	34.9
2001	37.0	36.5	36.1	36.5	36.3	35.4	35.5	35.1	34.6	34.5	34.3	34.5	35.5
2002	33.9	33.9	34.0	33.9	33.9	34.2	34.2	34.1	34.0	33.8	33.7	33.7	33.9
2003	33.4	33.4	33.3	33.3	33.5	33.7	33.9	33.9	33.8	33.8	34.1	34.5	33.7
2004	34.4	34.7	34.8	34.8	34.9	35.3	35.7	35.8	35.8	35.9	36.1	36.5	35.4
2005	36.5	36.8	36.8	37.0	37.3	37.5	38.0	38.1	38.0	37.5	37.4	37.4	37.4
2006	37.1	37.3	37.5	37.6	37.8	38.3	38.6	38.7	38.8	39.1	40.0	40.8	38.5
2007	40.4	40.7	40.9	41.0	41.4	42.4	42.1	41.8	41.4	41.5	40.4	41.6	41.3
2008	41.3	41.3	41.2	41.1	41.1	41.5	41.6	41.7	41.6	41.7	41.7	41.6	41.5
2009	41.2	38.2	38.2	37.3	37.1	36.9	37.5	37.4	37.1	37.1	37.2	37.3	37.7
2010	39.1	39.0	39.1	39.5	39.6	39.8	39.9	40.0	39.9	40.5	40.7	40.8	39.8
2011	40.7	41.1	41.4	41.5	41.8	42.0	42.4	42.4	42.3	42.4	42.3	42.5	41.9
Retail Trade													
2000	67.6	67.3	67.6	67.7	68.2	68.7	69.0	70.0	69.4	70.5	72.9	74.4	69.4
2001	70.3	69.1	69.1	68.9	69.1	69.6	68.8	69.3	69.3	69.9	71.2	72.7	69.8
2002	68.7	67.7	67.6	67.9	68.0	67.9	67.3	67.7	67.2	67.5	69.9	71.8	68.3
2003	67.0	65.9	65.9	66.0	66.0	66.3	67.2	68.2	68.4	69.2	71.2	72.6	67.8
2004	68.6	67.8	68.1	67.5	67.7	67.8	68.4	69.1	68.8	69.7	72.0	73.7	69.1
2005	69.9	69.5	70.2	70.6	71.3	72.3	72.9	73.6	73.2	73.7	76.7	78.5	72.7
2006	74.2	73.4	73.7	74.5	74.9	75.8	76.2	77.0	76.5	77.3	80.3	82.2	76.3
2007	78.6	78.5	79.1	79.9	79.9	80.5	81.2	81.4	81.5	82.7	85.9	87.5	81.4
2008	83.7	83.0	82.8	83.4	83.3	83.5	83.9	84.7	83.9	85.0	86.6	87.4	84.3
2009	82.8	82.0	82.1	81.1	81.4	81.4	81.2	82.1	81.4	82.1	84.1	85.2	82.2
2010	81.2	80.2	80.5	81.2	81.4	81.7	82.0	82.8	82.3	83.4	86.2	87.8	82.6
2011	83.5	82.8	83.5	84.3	84.3	84.4	83.1	83.4	82.2	83.2	85.7	86.4	83.9
Transportation and Utilities													
2000	10.8	10.8	10.8	10.4	10.5	10.3	10.5	10.8	10.9	10.9	11.0	11.2	10.7
2001	11.3	11.2	11.2	11.2	11.3	11.2	11.2	11.3	11.4	11.5	11.4	11.4	11.3
2002	11.2	11.1	11.1	11.1	11.1	11.0	11.1	11.2	11.0	11.1	11.1	11.1	11.1
2003	10.5	10.4	10.4	10.4	10.4	10.4	10.5	10.6	10.6	10.8	10.8	10.8	10.6
2004	10.5	10.6	10.6	10.7	10.7	10.7	11.0	11.2	11.3	11.4	11.5	11.7	11.0
2005	11.4	11.4	11.6	11.5	11.6	11.6	11.5	11.7	11.9	11.8	12.0	12.4	11.7
2006	11.9	12.0	12.2	12.3	12.5	12.4	12.5	12.7	12.9	13.0	13.1	13.5	12.6
2007	12.9	13.0	13.3	13.1	13.2	13.2	13.1	13.4	13.5	13.6	13.7	13.9	13.3
2008	13.4	13.5	13.5	13.3	13.3	13.3	13.0	13.3	13.4	13.3	13.4	13.5	13.4
2009	12.9	12.8	12.7	12.7	12.7	12.7	12.5	12.7	12.8	13.0	13.1	13.5	12.8
2010	12.7	12.7	12.8	12.7	12.8	12.7	12.5	12.7	13.0	12.9	13.1	13.6	12.9
2011	13.3	13.3	13.3	13.3	13.5	13.0	13.0	13.1	13.2	13.3	13.4	13.7	13.3
Information													
2000	21.9	22.3	22.7	23.5	24.1	25.0	25.5	25.7	25.5	25.0	25.1	25.3	24.3
2001	24.1	23.8	23.2	23.0	23.0	23.0	23.3	23.3	23.2	23.0	23.1	23.0	23.3
2002	23.0	22.9	23.0	22.9	22.8	23.0	22.7	22.5	22.3	22.1	22.0	21.8	22.6
2003	21.5	21.4	21.3	20.9	20.9	21.1	20.8	20.7	20.5	20.4	20.2	20.2	20.8
2004	20.1	20.1	20.3	20.2	20.4	20.7	20.6	20.7	20.6	20.6	20.9	21.0	20.5
2005	21.0	21.1	21.3	21.2	21.4	21.6	21.7	21.5	22.1	21.5	21.7	21.9	21.5
2006	21.8	21.8	21.8	21.8	21.7	21.7	21.5	21.6	21.6	21.8	22.1	22.2	21.8
2007	21.9	22.1	22.1	22.2	22.3	22.3	21.7	21.6	21.6	21.5	21.8	21.6	21.9
2008	21.3	21.0	20.9	20.8	21.0	21.1	21.1	21.1	20.8	20.8	21.0	20.9	21.0
2009	20.4	20.3	20.2	19.9	19.9	19.6	19.6	19.6	19.4	19.2	19.3	19.4	19.7
2010	19.2	19.2	19.2	19.2	19.3	19.4	19.5	19.6	19.5	19.8	19.9	20.0	19.5
2011	19.7	19.8	19.9	19.9	20.0	20.2	20.2	20.2	20.2	20.2	20.3	20.3	20.1
Financial Activities													
2000	34.6	34.9	34.9	35.0	35.0	35.4	35.4	35.6	35.4	35.6	35.5	35.8	35.3
2001	35.5	35.9	36.1	36.3	36.5	36.9	37.0	36.8	36.4	36.6	36.4	36.9	36.4
2002	36.7	36.9	37.0	37.4	37.7	38.1	38.2	38.4	38.5	38.7	38.9	39.1	38.0
2003	38.5	38.6	38.7	39.1	39.4	39.6	39.8	40.0	39.9	40.0	40.1	40.2	39.5
2004	39.3	39.4	39.5	39.7	39.7	40.0	40.0	40.1	40.1	40.4	40.5	40.8	40.0
2005	40.0	40.3	40.5	40.6	40.8	41.1	41.4	41.7	41.7	41.9	41.9	42.4	41.2
2006	41.9	42.2	42.5	42.6	42.9	43.3	43.4	43.7	43.9	44.1	44.1	44.6	43.3
2007	43.8	44.1	44.5	44.5	44.9	45.1	45.0	45.0	44.8	44.6	44.9	45.2	44.7
2008	44.5	44.9	44.8	45.1	45.2	45.4	45.4	45.4	45.4	45.2	45.2	45.2	45.1
2009	43.8	43.9	43.7	43.8	43.8	43.9	43.7	43.6	43.3	43.3	43.2	43.3	43.6
2010	42.2	42.3	42.4	42.4	42.6	42.6	42.6	42.6	42.3	42.7	42.8	42.8	42.5
2011	42.7	42.9	43.3	43.7	43.8	44.4	44.7	44.4	44.5	44.7	45.3	45.3	44.1

Employment by Industry: Austin–Round Rock–San Marcos, TX, Selected Years, 2000–2011—*Continued*

(Numbers in thousands, not seasonally adjusted)

Industry and year	January	February	March	April	May	June	July	August	September	October	November	December	Annual average
Professional and Business Services													
2000	86.5	87.0	88.6	88.9	90.3	92.7	93.5	94.2	94.4	95.0	95.4	95.8	91.9
2001	92.7	93.0	93.7	92.6	91.8	91.5	91.4	91.6	90.3	89.6	89.1	88.8	91.3
2002	86.3	86.4	86.7	87.0	87.4	88.0	87.6	88.8	87.7	86.9	87.1	86.6	87.2
2003	84.6	84.6	84.8	85.4	86.0	86.1	86.1	86.0	86.0	86.2	85.6	86.0	85.6
2004	84.9	86.1	87.1	88.0	88.5	89.4	90.4	91.2	90.9	90.9	90.8	91.4	89.1
2005	90.3	91.2	92.1	93.1	93.2	94.4	95.2	95.8	95.8	95.4	96.2	96.6	94.1
2006	94.7	95.6	96.9	97.5	98.6	99.7	100.2	101.1	101.4	102.1	103.5	103.7	99.6
2007	100.8	102.9	104.4	103.9	104.8	106.3	106.8	108.0	108.0	108.3	108.8	108.7	106.0
2008	108.7	109.5	109.1	111.0	111.8	112.0	111.4	112.3	111.7	112.3	111.6	110.7	111.0
2009	108.2	107.8	107.7	107.5	107.5	107.7	106.5	106.8	105.5	107.0	107.0	106.4	107.1
2010	105.1	106.1	107.7	107.9	108.6	109.7	109.9	110.2	110.2	112.4	112.5	112.9	109.4
2011	112.1	113.6	115.1	116.0	115.8	116.8	118.7	120.1	117.1	118.1	115.1	116.5	116.3
Education and Health Services													
2000	60.3	61.2	61.5	61.8	62.6	62.6	61.4	62.3	63.5	63.6	63.5	63.5	62.3
2001	61.5	62.7	63.3	63.5	63.3	64.5	62.5	62.8	63.7	63.8	63.8	63.7	63.3
2002	62.7	63.9	64.0	64.7	64.9	64.1	64.0	64.7	65.7	65.7	66.1	65.8	64.7
2003	64.6	65.4	65.1	65.9	65.9	65.2	65.0	65.8	66.9	67.3	67.3	67.2	66.0
2004	66.2	67.3	67.5	68.5	68.4	67.9	67.7	68.0	68.8	70.0	70.4	70.3	68.4
2005	69.4	70.3	70.8	71.2	71.3	70.5	69.9	70.4	72.1	72.1	72.2	72.5	71.1
2006	71.5	72.5	72.8	73.3	73.4	73.0	72.8	73.8	75.0	75.8	75.7	75.6	73.8
2007	73.6	75.5	76.3	76.2	76.9	76.5	76.7	77.2	78.7	79.1	79.5	79.7	77.2
2008	78.7	80.1	80.0	80.6	81.0	80.0	79.7	80.6	81.5	82.2	82.5	82.7	80.8
2009	80.6	81.9	82.5	83.2	83.6	82.8	82.9	83.6	83.6	84.6	84.8	84.9	83.3
2010	84.1	85.6	86.0	87.0	87.5	86.9	87.4	87.8	88.2	89.3	89.7	89.3	87.4
2011	88.2	89.3	89.6	90.8	91.0	90.5	89.1	91.6	91.4	93.7	92.9	92.4	90.9
Leisure and Hospitality													
2000	57.1	58.9	60.1	59.9	60.9	62.1	61.5	61.7	61.3	61.4	61.3	61.1	60.6
2001	58.6	60.2	61.7	62.1	63.0	64.0	63.0	63.5	62.5	61.3	60.7	60.4	61.8
2002	58.8	60.1	61.4	62.4	63.5	63.6	63.1	63.6	63.6	62.3	62.4	62.3	62.3
2003	60.3	61.0	62.2	63.7	64.6	65.4	64.7	65.3	64.8	64.3	64.3	64.6	63.8
2004	62.8	63.9	65.4	67.1	68.2	69.4	69.4	69.1	68.4	67.5	66.8	67.1	67.1
2005	65.8	66.5	68.0	70.3	70.9	71.7	70.9	71.1	70.6	70.4	70.6	70.1	69.7
2006	69.3	70.4	72.0	74.0	74.9	76.4	75.3	75.9	76.4	75.1	75.7	76.3	74.3
2007	73.7	75.3	77.0	78.6	79.2	80.5	79.8	80.2	79.6	78.6	78.7	78.7	78.3
2008	77.3	78.8	79.9	81.6	82.5	83.2	82.2	82.5	82.0	82.7	82.9	81.7	81.4
2009	79.9	80.9	81.9	83.2	84.2	84.4	84.6	84.7	84.0	83.3	83.0	82.1	83.0
2010	80.0	81.3	83.1	84.6	85.8	86.6	85.6	85.8	85.7	86.0	86.5	86.1	84.8
2011	84.1	85.3	87.7	90.4	91.1	91.5	92.3	91.9	92.4	91.1	89.9	91.6	89.9
Other Services													
2000	21.8	21.9	22.1	22.2	22.4	22.7	22.5	22.4	22.4	22.4	22.4	22.6	22.3
2001	22.6	22.8	23.0	23.4	23.6	24.0	23.5	23.5	23.1	23.0	23.0	22.9	23.2
2002	23.0	23.3	23.5	23.6	24.1	24.2	24.1	24.3	24.6	24.0	24.2	23.8	23.9
2003	23.5	23.7	23.9	23.9	24.1	24.7	24.5	24.8	24.7	25.2	25.4	25.5	24.5
2004	25.6	26.0	26.4	26.1	26.1	26.3	26.0	26.1	25.8	25.5	25.7	25.9	26.0
2005	25.9	26.0	26.2	26.7	26.6	27.1	26.7	26.8	26.8	26.2	26.3	26.4	26.5
2006	26.1	26.4	26.7	27.5	27.8	28.2	28.2	28.2	28.4	28.0	28.2	28.4	27.7
2007	27.1	27.8	28.1	28.2	28.5	28.9	28.3	28.2	28.2	28.2	28.5	28.6	28.2
2008	28.2	28.9	28.9	29.8	30.3	30.8	31.3	31.7	32.0	32.1	32.4	32.7	30.8
2009	32.7	33.4	33.4	33.5	33.7	34.2	33.7	33.5	33.1	33.0	33.0	32.9	33.3
2010	32.7	33.0	33.2	32.8	33.0	33.3	33.3	33.5	33.1	33.1	33.0	32.8	33.1
2011	32.7	32.9	33.2	33.4	33.5	33.8	33.7	33.8	33.7	33.6	33.7	33.7	33.5
Government													
2000	135.0	138.5	139.1	138.7	139.4	134.4	129.7	135.0	137.1	138.7	139.8	136.7	136.8
2001	136.6	139.8	140.9	140.8	140.4	137.2	132.9	138.8	143.3	144.5	146.4	143.1	140.4
2002	142.7	145.6	146.8	147.1	146.1	139.1	137.8	141.4	145.0	148.2	149.8	147.6	144.8
2003	146.6	149.1	148.6	149.8	148.6	144.7	141.1	142.1	143.9	144.6	144.9	143.5	145.6
2004	143.7	147.0	148.1	148.8	148.1	143.8	138.4	141.3	144.7	148.3	149.7	147.3	145.8
2005	146.9	150.7	150.9	151.7	151.7	147.6	143.2	144.4	147.8	150.5	152.2	149.7	148.9
2006	149.4	153.1	153.7	154.4	153.9	150.2	142.0	145.9	154.6	156.1	156.0	154.4	152.0
2007	154.0	157.4	158.6	158.9	158.8	155.6	149.1	150.9	156.1	160.1	161.2	158.9	156.6
2008	160.0	163.4	165.8	163.2	163.0	161.1	154.5	155.8	162.7	164.3	166.6	164.6	162.1
2009	164.6	167.9	168.8	170.2	170.0	167.6	159.3	159.9	166.1	168.7	171.3	168.9	166.9
2010	168.6	170.8	173.9	173.3	174.5	172.7	163.1	163.5	166.4	171.3	172.7	169.7	170.0
2011	168.1	171.4	171.8	172.0	170.1	169.2	161.3	161.8	166.1	168.1	169.9	167.4	168.1

Employment by Industry: Bakersfield–Delano, CA, Selected Years, 2000–2011

(Numbers in thousands, not seasonally adjusted)

Industry and year	January	February	March	April	May	June	July	August	September	October	November	December	Annual average
Total Nonfarm													
2000	189.8	190.8	192.7	193.0	195.1	196.0	191.3	191.0	195.0	196.9	198.4	199.2	194.1
2001	199.3	200.1	201.5	202.2	202.9	205.3	197.9	200.1	201.8	204.2	205.8	205.8	202.2
2002	202.2	202.8	205.3	205.8	206.7	208.2	201.8	202.4	203.2	206.2	208.0	208.5	205.1
2003	204.9	205.2	207.8	207.0	208.0	208.1	205.0	205.4	206.4	208.4	209.3	209.8	207.1
2004	205.1	206.2	208.3	211.7	212.5	215.9	210.3	210.2	212.0	215.0	216.6	217.2	211.8
2005	214.6	215.9	217.4	220.1	222.3	223.8	220.6	221.8	224.6	226.5	228.1	229.0	222.1
2006	227.1	228.6	229.9	230.9	233.6	235.1	230.8	233.1	235.5	237.8	238.7	238.9	233.3
2007	235.3	236.3	237.7	239.9	240.6	240.9	235.2	237.1	239.4	240.2	241.0	241.2	238.7
2008	236.0	237.5	238.3	239.8	240.7	241.6	235.9	235.5	237.4	239.6	240.4	238.9	238.5
2009	232.9	232.1	232.1	231.7	231.5	231.7	220.4	223.7	225.4	224.7	225.5	225.0	228.1
2010	221.7	221.9	224.9	229.3	229.9	229.7	220.3	223.5	226.3	228.1	229.4	230.5	226.3
2011	226.8	228.1	230.1	232.0	234.2	234.0	225.9	229.9	229.4	232.4	234.6	235.6	231.1
Total Private													
2000	137.9	138.9	139.9	140.3	141.8	143.0	144.6	145.0	144.4	143.7	144.5	145.7	142.5
2001	146.1	146.2	147.3	147.6	148.3	149.7	149.5	149.8	149.3	149.4	150.2	150.1	148.6
2002	147.1	147.5	148.8	149.2	150.4	151.1	150.0	150.7	150.3	150.5	151.1	151.7	149.9
2003	148.4	149.1	151.0	151.0	152.4	152.8	153.6	154.0	154.2	154.7	154.5	155.2	152.6
2004	151.4	152.2	154.0	157.0	157.9	158.9	159.0	159.9	159.6	160.2	161.1	161.7	157.7
2005	159.3	159.9	161.1	163.9	165.9	167.1	168.6	168.5	170.0	169.1	170.6	171.7	166.3
2006	169.6	170.9	172.0	172.9	175.8	177.0	176.9	178.0	178.5	178.1	178.9	179.3	175.7
2007	175.8	176.7	178.0	178.1	179.0	179.2	179.7	180.7	180.8	178.9	179.2	179.3	178.8
2008	174.5	175.3	175.8	177.4	178.4	178.9	177.7	178.2	177.8	176.9	176.8	176.0	177.0
2009	170.6	169.2	168.9	168.6	168.8	168.8	166.3	167.2	165.9	164.6	164.4	164.0	167.3
2010	161.5	161.0	162.4	165.1	165.7	166.2	166.9	167.7	167.5	167.2	167.8	168.8	165.7
2011	166.3	167.0	168.3	170.5	172.6	172.5	171.8	173.5	171.5	173.1	175.1	176.1	171.5
Goods-Producing													
2000	28.5	28.9	29.5	29.8	30.4	30.9	31.4	31.5	31.6	31.5	31.5	31.9	30.6
2001	31.6	31.8	32.2	32.6	32.8	33.1	33.2	33.5	33.3	32.9	32.6	32.3	32.7
2002	31.9	31.9	32.2	32.2	32.4	32.8	33.0	33.2	33.3	33.5	33.5	33.6	32.8
2003	33.5	33.7	33.8	33.6	33.8	33.9	34.5	34.7	34.9	34.7	34.3	34.6	34.2
2004	34.5	34.7	35.3	36.1	36.2	36.8	36.8	36.9	37.2	37.2	36.7	37.2	36.3
2005	36.6	37.0	37.4	38.1	38.5	39.2	40.0	39.7	40.7	40.5	40.6	40.7	39.1
2006	40.6	41.2	41.5	41.5	42.3	42.8	43.2	43.2	43.5	43.1	42.6	42.5	42.3
2007	41.0	41.3	41.6	41.0	41.2	41.4	42.0	42.3	42.2	41.7	41.2	40.9	41.5
2008	40.0	40.0	39.9	40.5	40.7	41.4	41.5	41.5	41.7	41.5	41.1	41.2	40.9
2009	39.0	37.8	37.5	36.6	36.1	36.1	35.5	35.4	35.3	34.7	34.6	34.4	36.1
2010	34.2	33.7	34.3	35.0	35.8	35.9	36.5	36.8	37.0	37.1	37.0	37.4	35.9
2011	36.9	37.1	37.3	38.4	38.8	39.6	39.7	40.4	41.6	42.2	42.0	42.9	39.7
Mining and Logging													
2000	7.6	7.8	8.0	7.8	7.9	8.0	8.4	8.6	8.6	8.5	8.6	8.7	8.2
2001	8.5	8.5	8.6	8.6	8.6	8.7	8.7	8.8	8.7	8.7	8.6	8.5	8.6
2002	8.2	8.0	7.9	7.8	7.7	7.8	7.9	7.9	7.9	7.9	7.9	7.9	7.9
2003	7.8	7.9	7.9	7.9	8.0	7.9	8.1	8.1	8.0	8.1	8.0	8.2	8.0
2004	8.0	8.1	8.2	8.1	8.2	8.3	8.1	8.2	8.1	8.1	8.1	8.2	8.1
2005	8.1	8.2	8.3	8.4	8.4	8.4	8.5	8.6	8.7	8.7	8.7	8.8	8.5
2006	8.9	8.9	9.0	9.1	9.2	9.4	9.4	9.6	9.6	9.7	9.7	9.7	9.4
2007	9.5	9.6	9.6	9.6	9.6	9.6	9.9	10.0	9.9	9.9	9.9	10.0	9.8
2008	10.1	10.2	10.3	10.3	10.4	10.5	10.9	10.9	10.9	11.2	11.3	11.2	10.7
2009	10.7	10.4	10.2	10.0	9.9	10.0	9.7	9.5	9.5	9.3	9.3	9.5	9.8
2010	9.4	9.1	9.2	9.5	10.2	10.2	10.6	10.7	10.8	10.7	10.8	11.1	10.2
2011	11.1	11.2	11.4	11.7	11.9	12.0	12.1	12.3	12.5	12.7	12.8	12.8	12.0
Construction													
2000	10.6	10.7	10.8	11.1	11.5	11.8	12.0	12.0	12.1	12.1	12.1	12.3	11.6
2001	12.1	12.3	12.7	13.0	13.1	13.2	13.3	13.6	13.4	13.1	13.0	12.9	13.0
2002	12.9	13.1	13.4	13.3	13.4	13.5	13.4	13.5	13.3	13.3	13.5	13.4	13.3
2003	13.2	13.2	13.3	13.2	13.3	13.4	13.7	13.9	13.9	13.9	13.9	14.0	13.6
2004	14.0	14.1	14.6	15.2	15.2	15.8	15.9	16.0	15.8	16.1	16.0	16.3	15.4
2005	15.9	16.3	16.8	17.4	17.8	18.5	19.0	18.7	19.2	19.3	19.5	19.5	18.2
2006	19.0	19.5	19.7	19.8	20.4	20.7	20.8	20.4	20.4	20.0	19.8	19.7	20.0
2007	18.8	18.9	19.1	18.5	18.7	18.7	18.5	18.6	18.2	18.2	17.7	17.4	18.4
2008	16.5	16.4	16.2	16.6	16.6	16.9	16.9	16.8	16.7	16.5	16.0	16.1	16.5
2009	14.8	14.0	14.0	13.4	13.1	13.1	12.7	12.6	12.4	12.3	12.4	12.2	13.1
2010	12.1	12.0	12.4	12.6	12.7	12.9	12.9	13.0	12.8	12.9	12.9	13.1	12.7
2011	12.8	13.0	13.0	13.6	13.8	14.2	14.2	14.4	15.1	15.5	15.4	16.1	14.3
Manufacturing													
2000	10.3	10.4	10.7	10.9	11.0	11.1	11.0	10.9	10.9	10.9	10.8	10.9	10.8
2001	11.0	11.0	10.9	11.0	11.1	11.2	11.2	11.1	11.2	11.1	11.0	10.9	11.1
2002	10.8	10.8	10.9	11.1	11.3	11.5	11.7	11.8	12.1	12.3	12.1	12.3	11.6
2003	12.5	12.6	12.6	12.5	12.5	12.6	12.7	12.7	13.0	12.7	12.4	12.4	12.6
2004	12.5	12.5	12.5	12.8	12.8	12.7	12.8	12.7	13.3	13.0	12.6	12.7	12.7
2005	12.6	12.5	12.3	12.3	12.3	12.3	12.5	12.4	12.8	12.5	12.4	12.4	12.4
2006	12.7	12.8	12.8	12.6	12.7	12.7	13.0	13.2	13.5	13.4	13.1	13.1	13.0
2007	12.7	12.8	12.9	12.9	12.9	13.1	13.6	13.7	14.1	13.6	13.6	13.5	13.3
2008	13.4	13.4	13.4	13.6	13.7	14.0	13.7	13.8	14.1	13.8	13.8	13.9	13.7
2009	13.5	13.4	13.3	13.2	13.1	13.0	13.1	13.3	13.4	13.1	12.9	12.7	13.2
2010	12.7	12.6	12.7	12.9	12.9	12.8	13.0	13.1	13.4	13.5	13.3	13.2	13.0
2011	13.0	12.9	12.9	13.1	13.1	13.4	13.4	13.7	14.0	14.0	13.8	14.0	13.4

Employment by Industry: Bakersfield–Delano, CA, Selected Years, 2000–2011—*Continued*

(Numbers in thousands, not seasonally adjusted)

Industry and year	January	February	March	April	May	June	July	August	September	October	November	December	Annual average
Service-Providing													
2000	161.3	161.9	163.2	163.2	164.7	165.1	159.9	159.5	163.4	165.4	166.9	167.3	163.5
2001	167.7	168.3	169.3	169.6	170.1	172.2	164.7	166.6	168.5	171.3	173.2	173.5	169.6
2002	170.3	170.9	173.1	173.6	174.3	175.4	168.8	169.2	169.9	172.7	174.5	174.9	172.3
2003	171.4	171.5	174.0	173.4	174.2	174.2	170.5	170.7	171.5	173.7	175.0	175.2	172.9
2004	170.6	171.5	173.0	175.6	176.3	179.1	173.5	173.3	174.8	177.8	179.9	180.0	175.5
2005	178.0	178.9	180.0	182.0	183.8	184.6	180.6	182.1	183.9	186.0	187.5	188.3	183.0
2006	186.5	187.4	188.4	189.4	191.3	192.3	187.6	189.9	192.0	194.7	196.1	196.4	191.0
2007	194.3	195.0	196.1	198.9	199.4	199.5	193.2	194.8	197.2	198.5	199.8	200.3	197.3
2008	196.0	197.5	198.4	199.3	200.0	200.2	194.4	194.0	195.7	198.1	199.3	197.7	197.6
2009	193.9	194.3	194.6	195.1	195.4	195.6	184.9	188.3	190.1	190.0	190.9	190.6	192.0
2010	187.5	188.2	190.6	194.3	194.1	193.8	183.8	186.7	189.3	191.0	192.4	193.1	190.4
2011	189.9	191.0	192.8	193.6	195.4	194.4	186.2	189.5	187.8	190.2	192.6	192.7	191.3
Trade, Transportation, and Utilities													
2000	36.2	36.2	36.3	36.5	36.9	37.0	37.6	37.8	37.6	37.6	38.3	38.8	37.2
2001	38.3	37.8	38.0	38.1	38.2	38.6	38.4	38.2	38.1	38.6	39.2	39.3	38.4
2002	38.0	37.8	38.1	38.5	38.8	39.1	39.3	39.3	39.4	39.3	39.9	40.4	39.0
2003	38.6	38.7	39.2	39.3	39.5	39.7	39.9	39.7	39.6	40.3	40.5	41.0	39.7
2004	39.2	38.9	39.4	40.4	40.8	41.2	41.6	42.0	41.6	42.1	42.8	42.7	41.1
2005	41.5	41.6	41.9	42.4	43.3	43.3	43.7	43.9	44.3	44.6	45.6	46.5	43.6
2006	45.1	44.8	45.1	45.0	46.2	46.3	46.3	46.6	46.7	46.6	47.8	48.2	46.2
2007	46.0	45.6	46.1	46.2	46.8	46.6	46.6	46.7	46.6	46.6	47.4	47.6	46.6
2008	45.5	45.0	45.1	45.2	45.9	45.7	45.1	45.1	45.0	44.5	44.9	44.8	45.2
2009	42.9	42.7	42.3	42.6	43.2	42.9	43.1	43.7	42.6	42.4	42.4	42.5	42.8
2010	41.4	41.2	41.1	41.5	41.8	41.9	42.7	43.1	43.0	42.1	42.8	43.4	42.2
2011	42.1	41.9	41.9	42.6	43.5	43.4	42.8	42.9	42.1	42.4	43.6	43.4	42.7
Wholesale Trade													
2000	5.5	5.5	5.5	5.6	5.7	5.7	5.8	5.8	5.7	5.8	5.8	5.8	5.7
2001	5.7	5.7	5.7	5.9	5.9	6.0	5.9	5.9	5.9	6.0	6.0	6.0	5.9
2002	6.0	6.0	6.0	6.0	6.0	6.1	6.3	6.3	6.3	6.2	6.0	6.1	6.1
2003	5.9	5.9	6.0	6.1	6.2	6.2	6.3	6.2	6.2	6.3	6.4	6.5	6.2
2004	6.2	6.2	6.2	6.3	6.4	6.5	6.7	6.7	6.6	6.6	6.6	6.6	6.5
2005	6.6	6.6	6.6	6.8	6.8	6.9	6.9	6.9	6.9	7.0	7.0	7.1	6.8
2006	7.2	7.3	7.4	7.4	7.6	7.7	7.7	7.7	7.8	7.8	7.9	7.9	7.6
2007	7.8	7.8	7.9	8.0	8.0	8.1	8.2	8.1	8.1	8.2	8.1	8.0	8.0
2008	8.0	8.0	8.0	8.1	8.2	8.3	8.3	8.3	8.4	8.2	8.2	8.0	8.2
2009	8.1	8.3	8.0	8.1	8.3	8.1	9.0	9.5	8.3	7.9	7.5	7.2	8.2
2010	7.4	7.4	7.1	7.6	7.6	8.0	8.9	9.1	9.1	7.8	7.7	7.7	8.0
2011	7.7	7.6	7.4	7.8	7.9	8.0	8.0	8.0	7.9	8.0	8.0	8.0	7.9
Retail Trade													
2000	22.7	22.6	22.7	22.6	22.9	23.0	23.1	23.2	23.2	23.3	24.1	24.6	23.2
2001	24.3	23.9	24.0	24.0	24.0	24.3	24.0	23.8	23.8	24.2	24.8	25.1	24.2
2002	24.0	23.7	24.0	24.4	24.6	24.8	24.5	24.5	24.6	24.6	25.4	25.9	24.6
2003	24.4	24.4	24.5	24.3	24.5	24.6	24.6	24.5	24.5	25.2	25.5	26.0	24.8
2004	24.8	24.5	24.9	25.6	25.7	25.9	25.8	26.0	25.9	26.3	27.2	27.2	25.8
2005	26.3	26.2	26.5	26.8	27.0	27.2	27.5	27.7	28.0	28.1	29.3	30.1	27.6
2006	28.9	28.4	28.6	28.5	28.9	29.1	29.1	29.4	29.4	29.4	30.5	30.8	29.3
2007	29.1	28.6	28.8	28.8	28.9	28.8	28.7	28.7	28.8	28.5	29.6	29.9	28.9
2008	28.2	27.7	27.8	27.6	27.7	27.7	27.3	27.2	26.9	26.6	27.1	27.3	27.4
2009	25.6	25.3	25.3	25.5	25.7	25.7	25.1	25.2	25.3	25.8	26.4	26.8	25.6
2010	25.7	25.5	25.7	25.6	25.6	25.5	25.3	25.5	25.4	25.7	26.6	27.4	25.8
2011	26.2	26.0	26.2	26.4	26.7	26.8	26.3	26.3	25.7	25.8	27.0	26.8	26.4
Transportation and Utilities													
2000	8.0	8.1	8.1	8.3	8.3	8.3	8.7	8.8	8.7	8.5	8.4	8.4	8.4
2001	8.3	8.2	8.3	8.2	8.3	8.3	8.5	8.5	8.4	8.4	8.4	8.2	8.3
2002	8.0	8.1	8.1	8.1	8.2	8.2	8.5	8.5	8.5	8.5	8.5	8.4	8.3
2003	8.3	8.4	8.7	8.9	8.8	8.9	9.0	9.0	8.9	8.8	8.6	8.5	8.7
2004	8.2	8.2	8.3	8.5	8.7	8.8	9.1	9.3	9.1	9.2	9.0	8.9	8.8
2005	8.6	8.8	8.8	8.8	9.5	9.2	9.3	9.3	9.4	9.5	9.3	9.3	9.2
2006	9.0	9.1	9.1	9.1	9.7	9.5	9.5	9.5	9.5	9.4	9.4	9.5	9.4
2007	9.1	9.2	9.4	9.4	9.9	9.7	9.7	9.8	9.8	9.9	9.7	9.7	9.6
2008	9.3	9.3	9.3	9.5	10.0	9.7	9.5	9.6	9.7	9.7	9.6	9.5	9.6
2009	9.2	9.1	9.0	9.0	9.2	9.1	9.0	9.0	9.0	8.7	8.5	8.5	8.9
2010	8.3	8.3	8.3	8.3	8.6	8.4	8.5	8.5	8.5	8.6	8.5	8.3	8.4
2011	8.2	8.3	8.3	8.4	8.9	8.6	8.5	8.6	8.5	8.6	8.6	8.6	8.5
Information													
2000	2.5	2.5	2.5	2.5	2.5	2.5	2.6	2.5	2.5	2.5	2.5	2.5	2.5
2001	2.5	2.5	2.5	2.6	2.6	2.7	2.6	2.5	2.5	2.5	2.5	2.5	2.5
2002	2.6	2.6	2.6	2.6	2.6	2.6	2.5	2.4	2.4	2.5	2.5	2.5	2.5
2003	2.6	2.6	2.6	2.6	2.6	2.5	2.5	2.5	2.5	2.5	2.5	2.5	2.5
2004	2.5	2.5	2.5	2.5	2.5	2.6	2.6	2.5	2.5	2.5	2.5	2.6	2.5
2005	2.5	2.5	2.5	2.5	2.5	2.5	2.6	2.5	2.6	2.5	2.6	2.6	2.5
2006	2.6	2.7	2.6	2.6	2.7	2.7	2.7	2.7	2.6	2.6	2.7	2.7	2.7
2007	2.8	2.8	2.7	2.8	2.8	2.9	2.8	2.9	2.8	2.8	2.9	2.9	2.8
2008	2.9	3.0	3.0	3.1	3.1	3.1	3.0	3.0	3.0	3.0	3.0	2.9	3.0
2009	2.8	2.8	2.8	2.8	2.8	2.8	2.8	2.7	2.7	2.7	2.7	2.7	2.7
2010	2.7	2.6	2.6	2.6	2.6	2.6	2.9	2.8	2.7	2.7	2.7	2.8	2.7
2011	2.7	2.6	2.6	2.6	2.6	2.6	2.6	2.7	2.6	2.6	2.7	2.7	2.6

Employment by Industry: Bakersfield–Delano, CA, Selected Years, 2000–2011—*Continued*

(Numbers in thousands, not seasonally adjusted)

Industry and year	January	February	March	April	May	June	July	August	September	October	November	December	Annual average
Financial Activities													
2000	7.6	7.7	7.7	7.5	7.6	7.5	7.6	7.5	7.5	7.5	7.5	7.6	7.6
2001	7.6	7.6	7.6	7.7	7.7	7.9	7.8	7.8	7.8	7.8	7.8	7.9	7.8
2002	7.7	7.8	7.9	8.0	8.0	8.0	8.0	8.0	8.0	8.0	8.1	8.2	8.0
2003	8.1	8.1	8.2	8.2	8.3	8.4	8.4	8.5	8.4	8.4	8.4	8.4	8.3
2004	8.4	8.4	8.5	8.7	8.6	8.6	8.7	8.7	8.7	8.6	8.6	8.6	8.6
2005	8.6	8.5	8.6	8.6	8.7	8.8	8.9	8.9	8.8	8.7	8.8	8.8	8.7
2006	8.9	8.9	8.9	8.9	9.1	9.1	9.0	9.0	8.9	9.0	9.0	9.0	9.0
2007	9.1	9.2	9.2	9.1	9.1	9.2	9.1	9.1	9.0	9.0	8.9	8.9	9.1
2008	8.8	8.8	8.9	9.0	9.0	8.9	8.9	8.9	8.9	8.8	8.8	8.8	8.9
2009	8.6	8.6	8.6	8.6	8.5	8.5	8.5	8.5	8.4	8.4	8.2	8.3	8.5
2010	8.2	8.3	8.3	8.4	8.4	8.3	8.2	8.1	8.0	7.9	7.9	7.9	8.2
2011	7.8	7.9	8.0	8.1	8.3	8.2	8.2	8.3	8.1	8.2	8.2	8.3	8.1
Professional and Business Services													
2000	22.1	22.1	22.1	21.9	21.9	22.2	22.2	22.5	22.2	22.0	22.4	22.5	22.2
2001	23.1	23.1	23.2	22.7	22.7	23.0	22.6	23.0	22.7	23.2	23.5	23.5	23.0
2002	23.2	23.3	23.4	22.8	22.6	22.6	21.9	22.3	21.9	21.6	21.4	21.3	22.4
2003	20.7	20.7	21.2	21.3	21.5	21.8	21.8	22.1	22.3	22.1	22.3	22.3	21.7
2004	21.1	21.5	21.6	21.8	21.8	21.7	21.5	21.9	21.6	21.9	22.1	22.2	21.7
2005	22.1	22.1	22.0	22.8	22.8	23.0	23.4	23.6	23.9	23.4	23.8	23.6	23.0
2006	23.7	24.0	24.1	24.3	24.8	25.0	25.3	25.6	25.9	26.0	25.8	25.7	25.0
2007	26.0	26.3	26.2	26.5	26.5	26.3	26.2	26.5	26.7	25.3	25.3	25.4	26.1
2008	24.7	25.2	25.2	25.4	25.1	25.1	25.0	25.1	25.1	25.0	24.9	24.5	25.0
2009	24.6	24.0	24.0	23.8	23.8	23.9	23.3	23.5	23.6	23.2	23.6	23.3	23.7
2010	23.3	23.1	23.4	24.3	24.0	24.2	23.6	23.6	23.6	24.2	24.4	24.4	23.8
2011	24.4	24.7	25.1	25.1	25.0	24.6	24.6	24.8	24.5	24.9	25.0	25.1	24.8
Education and Health Services													
2000	18.6	18.9	19.0	19.1	19.2	19.4	19.5	19.4	19.5	19.2	19.2	19.3	19.2
2001	20.1	20.3	20.3	19.9	19.9	20.0	20.3	20.3	20.3	20.3	20.4	20.5	20.2
2002	20.1	20.3	20.4	20.7	20.9	21.0	20.6	20.8	20.8	20.9	21.0	21.1	20.7
2003	20.9	21.1	21.2	21.2	21.4	21.3	21.3	21.4	21.4	21.4	21.4	21.5	21.3
2004	21.2	21.2	21.4	21.5	21.6	21.7	21.7	21.8	21.7	21.6	21.7	21.9	21.6
2005	21.7	21.9	22.0	22.2	22.3	22.2	22.4	22.4	22.2	22.3	22.3	22.4	22.2
2006	22.4	22.6	22.7	22.7	22.7	23.0	22.7	23.0	23.1	23.5	23.7	23.8	23.0
2007	23.9	24.3	24.3	24.2	24.1	24.2	24.6	24.7	24.8	24.8	24.9	25.0	24.5
2008	25.0	25.2	25.4	25.4	25.4	25.4	25.4	25.7	25.6	25.7	25.8	25.8	25.5
2009	25.4	25.7	25.9	25.9	25.9	26.2	25.6	25.9	25.8	26.0	25.8	25.8	25.8
2010	25.4	25.4	25.5	25.7	25.6	25.5	25.9	26.0	25.9	26.1	26.1	26.3	25.8
2011	26.1	26.2	26.4	26.4	26.6	26.4	26.5	26.8	26.3	26.6	26.7	26.8	26.5
Leisure and Hospitality													
2000	15.9	16.1	16.2	16.4	16.7	16.9	17.1	16.9	16.7	16.6	16.4	16.4	16.5
2001	16.4	16.5	16.9	17.2	17.5	17.6	17.7	17.6	17.5	17.2	17.3	17.3	17.2
2002	16.8	16.9	17.3	17.6	18.1	18.2	17.9	17.9	17.8	17.7	17.6	17.7	17.6
2003	17.3	17.4	17.9	17.9	18.3	18.3	18.4	18.3	18.1	18.3	18.2	18.0	18.0
2004	17.6	18.1	18.4	19.0	19.4	19.4	19.3	19.3	19.3	19.1	19.3	19.4	19.0
2005	19.3	19.3	19.6	20.1	20.5	20.9	20.6	20.5	20.3	20.0	20.1	20.3	20.1
2006	19.6	19.9	20.2	20.9	21.0	21.3	21.0	20.9	20.9	20.6	20.7	20.9	20.7
2007	20.5	20.7	21.2	21.7	21.9	22.1	21.7	21.7	21.8	21.7	21.6	21.6	21.5
2008	20.9	21.2	21.4	21.8	22.0	22.1	22.0	21.9	21.5	21.2	21.2	21.0	21.5
2009	20.6	20.8	21.1	21.5	21.7	21.7	21.0	20.8	20.8	20.4	20.4	20.4	20.9
2010	19.7	20.0	20.4	20.8	20.8	21.1	20.7	20.7	20.7	20.5	20.4	20.1	20.5
2011	19.8	20.1	20.4	20.7	21.1	21.1	20.9	21.0	19.8	19.7	20.4	20.4	20.5
Other Services													
2000	6.5	6.5	6.6	6.6	6.6	6.6	6.6	6.9	6.8	6.8	6.7	6.7	6.7
2001	6.5	6.6	6.6	6.8	6.9	6.8	6.9	6.9	7.1	6.9	6.9	6.8	6.8
2002	6.8	6.9	6.9	6.8	7.0	6.8	6.8	6.8	6.7	7.0	7.1	6.9	6.9
2003	6.7	6.8	6.9	6.9	7.0	6.9	6.8	6.8	7.0	7.0	6.9	6.9	6.9
2004	6.9	6.9	6.9	7.0	7.0	6.9	6.8	6.8	7.0	7.2	7.4	7.1	7.0
2005	7.0	7.0	7.1	7.2	7.3	7.2	7.0	7.0	7.2	7.1	6.8	6.8	7.1
2006	6.7	6.8	6.9	7.0	7.0	6.8	6.7	7.0	6.9	6.7	6.6	6.5	6.8
2007	6.5	6.5	6.7	6.6	6.6	6.5	6.7	6.8	6.9	7.0	7.0	7.0	6.7
2008	6.7	6.9	6.9	7.0	7.2	7.2	6.8	7.0	7.0	7.2	7.1	7.0	7.0
2009	6.7	6.8	6.7	6.8	6.8	6.7	6.5	6.7	6.7	6.8	6.7	6.6	6.7
2010	6.6	6.7	6.8	6.8	6.7	6.7	6.4	6.6	6.6	6.6	6.5	6.5	6.6
2011	6.5	6.5	6.6	6.6	6.7	6.6	6.5	6.6	6.5	6.5	6.5	6.5	6.6
Government													
2000	51.9	51.9	52.8	52.7	53.3	53.0	46.7	46.0	50.6	53.2	53.9	53.5	51.6
2001	53.2	53.9	54.2	54.6	54.6	55.6	48.4	50.3	52.5	54.8	55.6	55.7	53.6
2002	55.1	55.3	56.5	56.6	56.3	57.1	51.8	51.7	52.9	55.7	56.9	56.8	55.2
2003	56.5	56.1	56.8	56.0	55.6	55.3	51.4	51.4	52.2	53.7	54.8	54.6	54.5
2004	53.7	54.0	54.3	54.7	54.6	57.0	51.3	50.3	52.4	54.8	55.5	55.5	54.0
2005	55.3	56.0	56.3	56.2	56.4	56.7	52.0	53.3	54.6	57.4	57.5	57.3	55.8
2006	57.5	57.7	57.9	58.0	57.8	58.1	53.9	55.1	57.0	59.7	59.8	59.6	57.7
2007	59.5	59.6	59.7	61.8	61.6	61.7	55.5	56.4	58.6	61.3	61.8	61.9	60.0
2008	61.5	62.2	62.5	62.4	62.3	62.7	58.2	57.3	59.6	62.7	63.6	62.9	61.5
2009	62.3	62.9	63.2	63.1	62.7	62.9	54.1	56.5	59.5	60.1	61.1	61.0	60.8
2010	60.2	60.9	62.5	64.2	64.2	63.5	53.4	55.8	58.8	60.9	61.6	61.7	60.6
2011	60.5	61.1	61.8	61.5	61.6	61.5	54.1	56.4	57.9	59.3	59.5	59.5	59.6

Employment by Industry: Baltimore–Towson, MD, Selected Years, 2000–2011

(Numbers in thousands, not seasonally adjusted)

Industry and year	January	February	March	April	May	June	July	August	September	October	November	December	Annual average
Total Nonfarm													
2000	1,209.0	1,212.3	1,230.4	1,243.3	1,254.6	1,264.2	1,253.1	1,251.4	1,259.4	1,266.8	1,275.4	1,284.1	1,250.3
2001	1,231.9	1,238.9	1,249.8	1,255.3	1,262.8	1,271.9	1,260.7	1,257.4	1,257.8	1,260.2	1,268.1	1,271.3	1,257.2
2002	1,227.8	1,234.3	1,246.7	1,248.7	1,259.1	1,265.6	1,253.2	1,250.3	1,251.8	1,254.2	1,260.1	1,261.1	1,251.1
2003	1,225.6	1,222.7	1,235.1	1,247.4	1,256.9	1,252.5	1,241.7	1,253.1	1,255.7	1,260.2	1,266.1	1,269.4	1,248.9
2004	1,234.5	1,234.9	1,250.8	1,258.2	1,266.8	1,277.3	1,267.6	1,267.0	1,267.0	1,275.7	1,281.6	1,284.8	1,263.9
2005	1,248.8	1,255.2	1,263.3	1,278.5	1,287.6	1,294.7	1,292.7	1,288.1	1,300.3	1,300.3	1,306.5	1,311.1	1,285.6
2006	1,275.3	1,280.3	1,295.2	1,303.9	1,312.6	1,318.6	1,307.7	1,306.5	1,310.0	1,316.9	1,323.0	1,329.9	1,306.7
2007	1,292.7	1,293.0	1,309.0	1,315.1	1,325.6	1,330.4	1,320.8	1,320.8	1,320.9	1,323.8	1,330.1	1,333.7	1,318.0
2008	1,298.7	1,301.8	1,311.4	1,320.5	1,326.6	1,327.5	1,319.2	1,316.5	1,313.1	1,316.7	1,312.9	1,311.1	1,314.7
2009	1,266.2	1,263.7	1,268.4	1,276.7	1,283.8	1,287.3	1,272.4	1,267.6	1,270.8	1,277.1	1,277.8	1,277.9	1,274.1
2010	1,242.9	1,229.8	1,259.5	1,278.2	1,286.6	1,291.1	1,278.1	1,276.1	1,276.0	1,287.7	1,290.4	1,291.2	1,274.0
2011	1,257.4	1,264.3	1,278.6	1,293.6	1,298.8	1,302.5	1,299.4	1,289.7	1,295.9	1,312.2	1,315.1	1,314.4	1,293.5
Total Private													
2000	993.1	994.1	1,008.3	1,021.8	1,030.2	1,043.8	1,040.8	1,042.9	1,045.2	1,044.7	1,053.4	1,061.7	1,031.7
2001	1,014.6	1,017.5	1,026.9	1,032.3	1,040.9	1,053.1	1,047.2	1,046.8	1,040.4	1,038.2	1,044.3	1,047.9	1,037.5
2002	1,007.3	1,010.1	1,020.4	1,025.4	1,035.3	1,044.6	1,037.9	1,038.4	1,031.8	1,029.6	1,035.0	1,037.5	1,029.4
2003	1,007.2	1,000.5	1,011.0	1,024.0	1,034.3	1,037.1	1,031.9	1,036.4	1,038.3	1,039.5	1,044.7	1,049.3	1,029.5
2004	1,019.7	1,018.6	1,031.6	1,038.2	1,047.7	1,060.3	1,059.9	1,059.7	1,054.2	1,057.7	1,061.4	1,065.4	1,047.9
2005	1,035.2	1,037.1	1,045.2	1,058.6	1,066.8	1,076.6	1,082.6	1,082.3	1,083.2	1,078.3	1,082.5	1,087.7	1,068.0
2006	1,060.1	1,060.2	1,073.1	1,080.5	1,089.0	1,099.2	1,094.4	1,094.0	1,091.3	1,092.1	1,096.3	1,102.8	1,086.1
2007	1,073.6	1,069.1	1,082.6	1,089.8	1,099.6	1,108.9	1,106.2	1,106.5	1,101.5	1,098.5	1,103.0	1,107.1	1,095.5
2008	1,079.4	1,076.9	1,084.9	1,092.0	1,097.9	1,103.5	1,100.4	1,098.8	1,090.1	1,086.7	1,082.3	1,080.5	1,089.5
2009	1,043.0	1,035.3	1,038.2	1,044.6	1,051.9	1,059.3	1,050.5	1,048.4	1,046.0	1,042.5	1,043.4	1,044.1	1,045.6
2010	1,016.1	998.3	1,024.1	1,040.6	1,047.8	1,055.8	1,051.6	1,051.1	1,047.3	1,051.5	1,052.5	1,055.7	1,041.0
2011	1,027.9	1,029.2	1,039.4	1,053.0	1,060.4	1,067.4	1,069.5	1,064.8	1,060.1	1,068.5	1,071.3	1,070.4	1,056.8
Goods-Producing													
2000	163.6	162.2	165.9	166.9	168.4	170.8	170.4	171.3	171.6	170.4	170.6	170.4	168.5
2001	162.6	163.9	165.8	166.4	166.3	169.1	168.8	169.0	167.7	165.9	165.1	164.7	166.3
2002	156.2	157.2	158.4	159.6	160.4	162.1	160.3	160.8	159.3	157.8	157.5	156.4	158.8
2003	152.9	150.9	151.9	153.2	154.3	155.9	155.4	156.1	155.4	154.9	154.8	154.6	154.2
2004	150.0	149.0	152.0	154.1	155.4	157.4	158.5	159.1	158.2	158.1	158.1	158.6	155.7
2005	154.2	153.6	154.9	158.0	159.1	160.9	161.1	161.7	161.7	160.3	160.8	160.9	158.9
2006	157.0	156.5	158.6	159.3	159.9	161.9	161.8	161.8	160.9	159.1	158.4	158.1	159.4
2007	154.4	152.5	155.0	155.9	157.4	159.3	159.8	159.9	158.5	156.8	156.2	155.3	156.8
2008	152.4	151.3	151.9	151.8	151.9	153.3	153.8	153.5	151.7	149.6	147.8	145.6	151.2
2009	138.7	136.6	135.9	135.3	135.8	137.1	136.7	136.1	134.8	133.8	132.8	132.1	135.5
2010	127.6	123.1	126.7	130.1	131.0	132.6	132.5	132.5	131.5	130.9	130.4	130.0	129.9
2011	126.8	126.2	127.5	129.8	130.5	132.0	132.8	132.8	131.1	132.4	131.5	130.2	130.3
Mining, Logging, and Construction													
2000	68.6	67.3	70.6	72.0	73.4	74.9	75.5	76.3	76.2	75.2	75.2	74.6	73.3
2001	70.4	71.2	73.3	74.2	75.1	76.9	76.5	77.0	76.0	75.0	74.6	74.1	74.5
2002	69.6	70.1	71.7	73.1	74.1	75.5	76.0	76.4	75.5	75.2	75.0	74.1	73.9
2003	71.3	69.6	70.6	72.2	73.9	75.4	76.6	77.5	77.3	77.3	77.4	77.4	74.7
2004	74.0	73.1	76.0	77.9	79.1	80.9	81.8	82.4	81.9	81.9	81.9	82.2	79.4
2005	78.9	78.1	79.4	82.3	83.6	85.3	85.9	86.3	86.3	85.6	86.0	85.9	83.6
2006	83.2	82.9	84.7	85.8	86.7	88.4	88.4	88.6	88.0	87.1	86.6	86.3	86.4
2007	83.2	81.5	83.9	84.9	86.2	87.7	88.2	88.4	87.4	86.0	85.5	84.3	85.6
2008	82.1	81.1	81.9	82.4	82.5	83.6	84.4	84.2	83.0	81.8	80.5	78.5	82.2
2009	73.2	72.0	71.6	71.7	72.2	73.4	73.5	72.9	71.7	70.8	70.0	69.2	71.9
2010	65.2	61.7	64.9	68.1	68.9	70.1	69.9	69.9	69.4	69.2	69.1	68.5	67.9
2011	64.8	64.2	65.4	67.3	68.1	69.3	69.9	70.4	68.9	69.9	69.5	68.2	68.0
Manufacturing													
2000	95.0	94.9	95.3	94.9	95.0	95.9	94.9	95.0	95.4	95.2	95.4	95.8	95.2
2001	92.2	92.7	92.5	92.2	91.2	92.2	92.3	92.0	91.7	90.9	90.5	90.6	91.8
2002	86.6	87.1	86.7	86.5	86.3	86.6	84.3	84.4	83.8	82.6	82.5	82.3	85.0
2003	81.6	81.3	81.3	81.0	80.4	80.5	78.8	78.6	78.1	77.6	77.4	77.2	79.5
2004	76.0	75.9	76.0	76.2	76.3	76.5	76.7	76.7	76.3	76.2	76.2	76.4	76.3
2005	75.3	75.5	75.5	75.7	75.5	75.6	75.2	75.4	75.4	74.7	74.8	75.0	75.3
2006	73.8	73.6	73.9	73.5	73.2	73.5	73.4	73.2	72.9	72.0	71.8	71.8	73.1
2007	71.2	71.0	71.1	71.0	71.2	71.6	71.6	71.5	71.1	70.8	70.7	71.0	71.2
2008	70.3	70.2	70.0	69.4	69.4	69.7	69.4	69.3	68.7	67.8	67.3	67.1	69.1
2009	65.5	64.6	64.3	63.6	63.6	63.7	63.2	63.2	63.1	63.0	62.8	62.9	63.6
2010	62.4	61.4	61.8	62.0	62.1	62.5	62.6	62.6	62.1	61.7	61.3	61.5	62.0
2011	62.0	62.0	62.1	62.5	62.4	62.7	62.9	62.4	62.2	62.5	62.0	62.0	62.3
Service-Providing													
2000	1,045.4	1,050.1	1,064.5	1,076.4	1,086.2	1,093.4	1,082.7	1,080.1	1,087.8	1,096.4	1,104.8	1,113.7	1,081.8
2001	1,069.3	1,075.0	1,084.0	1,088.9	1,096.5	1,102.8	1,091.9	1,088.4	1,090.1	1,094.3	1,103.0	1,106.6	1,090.9
2002	1,071.6	1,077.1	1,088.3	1,089.1	1,098.7	1,103.5	1,092.9	1,089.5	1,092.5	1,096.4	1,102.6	1,104.7	1,092.2
2003	1,072.7	1,071.8	1,083.2	1,094.2	1,102.6	1,096.6	1,086.3	1,097.0	1,100.3	1,105.3	1,111.3	1,114.8	1,094.7
2004	1,084.5	1,085.9	1,098.8	1,104.1	1,111.4	1,119.9	1,109.1	1,107.9	1,108.8	1,117.6	1,123.5	1,126.2	1,108.1
2005	1,094.6	1,101.6	1,108.4	1,120.5	1,128.5	1,133.8	1,131.6	1,126.4	1,138.6	1,140.0	1,145.7	1,150.2	1,126.7
2006	1,118.3	1,123.8	1,136.6	1,144.6	1,152.7	1,156.7	1,145.9	1,144.7	1,149.1	1,157.8	1,164.6	1,171.8	1,147.2
2007	1,138.3	1,140.5	1,154.0	1,159.2	1,168.2	1,171.1	1,161.0	1,160.9	1,162.4	1,167.0	1,173.9	1,178.4	1,161.2
2008	1,146.3	1,150.5	1,159.5	1,168.7	1,174.7	1,174.2	1,165.4	1,163.0	1,161.4	1,167.1	1,165.1	1,165.5	1,163.5
2009	1,127.5	1,127.1	1,132.5	1,141.4	1,148.0	1,150.2	1,135.7	1,131.5	1,136.0	1,143.3	1,145.0	1,145.8	1,138.7
2010	1,115.3	1,106.7	1,132.8	1,148.1	1,155.6	1,158.5	1,145.6	1,143.6	1,144.5	1,156.8	1,160.0	1,161.2	1,144.1
2011	1,130.6	1,138.1	1,151.1	1,163.8	1,168.3	1,170.5	1,166.6	1,156.9	1,164.8	1,179.8	1,183.6	1,184.2	1,163.2

Employment by Industry: Baltimore–Towson, MD, Selected Years, 2000–2011—*Continued*

(Numbers in thousands, not seasonally adjusted)

Industry and year	January	February	March	April	May	June	July	August	September	October	November	December	Annual average
Trade, Transportation, and Utilities													
2000	238.2	236.4	237.8	239.9	242.0	244.0	243.0	245.1	245.7	248.6	254.6	259.8	244.6
2001	243.6	240.2	241.1	240.7	242.3	243.6	239.9	240.1	240.8	241.7	245.9	249.5	242.5
2002	236.5	233.4	235.4	236.2	238.1	239.9	236.4	236.3	237.3	237.8	241.3	245.6	237.9
2003	234.2	231.2	233.0	234.0	236.5	238.3	236.1	237.8	238.9	241.1	246.2	250.1	238.1
2004	239.5	237.6	239.2	239.0	240.4	242.8	239.8	239.8	239.9	242.0	246.2	249.9	241.3
2005	239.1	237.1	238.1	239.2	240.9	242.7	242.8	242.2	243.4	244.4	248.4	253.1	242.6
2006	243.7	241.4	243.3	243.6	245.2	246.8	244.2	244.0	243.8	246.6	251.9	256.5	245.9
2007	246.3	242.3	244.4	243.7	246.9	247.9	246.2	245.3	244.8	246.1	251.2	255.7	246.7
2008	244.1	240.4	241.4	240.2	241.2	242.4	240.5	239.9	238.6	238.8	240.4	242.7	240.9
2009	231.5	227.5	226.8	226.5	227.4	229.0	225.0	224.8	225.6	226.2	230.3	231.8	227.7
2010	221.5	216.1	220.9	224.7	225.7	226.4	224.8	224.8	224.4	228.1	231.7	235.0	225.3
2011	226.1	224.2	225.7	227.5	228.9	229.9	226.8	225.5	224.7	227.5	230.1	232.5	227.5
Wholesale Trade													
2000	52.4	52.7	53.4	53.8	54.1	54.9	55.3	55.7	55.6	55.6	55.9	56.4	54.7
2001	55.4	55.6	56.1	56.4	56.5	56.5	56.2	56.1	56.0	55.7	55.5	55.7	56.0
2002	54.6	54.6	54.6	54.2	54.3	54.4	54.3	54.5	54.4	54.2	54.1	54.3	54.4
2003	53.3	52.9	53.3	53.2	53.4	53.6	53.3	53.3	53.3	53.1	53.1	53.2	53.3
2004	52.6	52.9	53.3	53.5	53.6	53.9	53.9	53.9	53.8	54.1	54.0	54.2	53.6
2005	54.3	54.4	54.5	54.8	55.1	55.6	55.9	55.7	55.8	56.0	56.1	56.5	55.4
2006	56.0	56.3	56.4	56.7	56.7	57.0	56.8	56.8	56.7	56.7	56.6	56.9	56.6
2007	55.9	56.0	56.0	56.2	56.4	56.5	56.4	56.3	56.1	55.8	55.8	56.1	56.1
2008	55.5	55.3	55.7	55.7	55.9	56.0	55.5	55.3	55.0	54.8	54.4	54.2	55.3
2009	53.6	53.3	52.9	52.7	52.5	52.4	51.8	51.7	51.6	51.6	51.4	51.3	52.2
2010	50.3	50.1	50.5	51.0	51.2	51.1	51.2	51.0	50.6	51.1	51.2	51.3	50.9
2011	50.9	51.1	51.3	51.7	52.0	52.1	50.9	50.4	51.0	51.1	50.4	49.8	51.1
Retail Trade													
2000	143.6	141.6	142.2	143.2	144.8	145.8	145.1	146.1	145.5	147.9	153.6	157.8	146.4
2001	144.9	141.5	141.9	140.8	142.1	143.3	142.0	142.4	142.0	142.9	147.7	150.9	143.5
2002	141.0	138.2	140.1	139.7	140.8	142.6	141.3	140.9	141.0	141.3	145.3	148.9	141.8
2003	140.1	137.7	138.4	139.8	141.2	142.8	142.2	143.7	143.5	144.8	149.9	153.3	143.1
2004	144.4	142.3	143.4	142.3	143.2	145.1	143.0	143.2	142.2	143.9	148.2	151.3	144.4
2005	140.7	138.7	139.3	140.6	141.6	142.5	143.2	143.2	142.9	143.7	147.7	151.2	142.9
2006	143.6	140.6	142.1	141.9	143.1	144.0	142.8	142.6	141.6	144.4	149.8	153.1	144.1
2007	145.1	141.2	142.8	142.1	144.4	144.9	144.4	144.1	143.0	144.6	149.7	153.2	145.0
2008	143.8	140.3	141.1	140.6	141.0	141.8	141.0	140.7	139.0	139.6	141.7	143.4	141.2
2009	135.0	131.8	131.7	131.8	132.9	133.7	132.4	132.3	131.8	132.7	136.5	138.2	133.4
2010	130.1	125.7	129.0	130.5	131.7	132.3	131.9	132.1	130.9	133.4	137.1	139.7	132.0
2011	132.4	130.5	131.6	132.5	133.5	134.3	135.2	135.2	132.6	135.0	138.8	141.4	134.4
Transportation and Utilities													
2000	42.2	42.1	42.2	42.9	43.1	43.3	42.6	43.3	44.6	45.1	45.1	45.6	43.5
2001	43.3	43.1	43.1	43.5	43.7	43.8	41.7	41.6	42.8	43.1	42.7	42.9	42.9
2002	40.9	40.6	40.7	42.3	43.0	42.9	40.8	40.9	41.9	42.3	41.9	42.4	41.7
2003	40.8	40.6	41.3	41.0	41.9	41.9	40.6	40.8	42.1	43.2	43.2	43.6	41.8
2004	42.5	42.4	42.5	43.2	43.6	43.8	42.9	42.7	43.9	44.0	44.0	44.4	43.3
2005	44.1	44.0	44.3	43.8	44.2	44.6	43.7	43.3	44.7	44.7	44.6	45.4	44.3
2006	44.1	44.5	44.8	45.0	45.4	45.8	44.6	44.6	45.5	45.5	45.5	46.5	45.2
2007	45.3	45.1	45.6	45.4	46.1	46.5	45.4	44.9	45.7	45.7	45.7	46.4	45.7
2008	44.8	44.8	44.6	43.9	44.3	44.6	44.0	43.9	44.6	44.4	44.3	45.1	44.4
2009	42.9	42.4	42.2	42.0	42.0	42.9	40.8	40.8	42.2	41.9	42.4	42.3	42.1
2010	41.1	40.3	41.4	43.2	42.8	43.0	41.7	41.7	42.9	43.6	43.4	44.0	42.4
2011	42.8	42.6	42.8	43.3	43.4	43.5	40.7	39.9	41.1	41.4	40.9	41.3	42.0
Information													
2000	24.5	24.3	24.5	24.1	24.4	25.0	25.0	22.5	25.3	25.3	25.8	26.5	24.8
2001	25.8	26.1	26.0	25.1	25.2	25.2	24.3	24.3	23.7	23.5	23.6	23.4	24.7
2002	22.5	22.5	22.4	22.3	22.3	22.2	21.7	21.8	21.2	20.6	21.1	20.8	21.8
2003	20.8	20.8	20.8	21.1	21.4	21.2	21.2	21.0	20.7	20.7	21.2	21.3	21.0
2004	21.2	20.8	21.1	21.0	21.2	21.5	21.0	21.3	21.0	21.0	21.2	21.0	21.1
2005	20.8	20.9	21.0	21.2	21.3	21.6	22.2	22.6	22.2	22.2	22.2	22.2	21.7
2006	21.6	21.8	21.9	21.9	22.1	22.3	22.1	22.2	22.3	22.2	22.7	22.9	22.2
2007	22.4	22.6	23.1	23.1	23.3	24.0	23.7	24.1	24.1	23.1	23.6	23.6	23.4
2008	23.1	23.1	23.4	23.2	23.3	22.9	22.7	23.0	22.8	22.1	22.4	22.3	22.9
2009	21.3	21.3	21.5	20.6	20.5	20.8	20.1	20.3	19.9	19.5	19.7	19.6	20.4
2010	19.4	19.8	21.1	20.8	20.9	21.3	20.0	19.3	19.3	18.9	18.5	19.3	19.9
2011	17.7	18.1	18.2	17.8	17.9	17.6	17.4	16.1	17.4	17.4	17.4	17.4	17.5
Financial Activities													
2000	76.7	77.1	77.6	77.0	77.5	78.7	79.0	79.1	78.7	78.7	79.2	79.9	78.3
2001	77.4	77.9	78.5	78.5	78.9	80.0	80.3	80.4	80.1	80.0	80.8	81.1	79.5
2002	79.0	79.1	79.3	79.5	79.8	80.6	80.6	80.7	80.8	80.5	81.0	81.3	80.2
2003	81.0	81.0	81.5	81.8	82.3	83.2	83.4	83.7	83.1	82.0	82.3	82.5	82.3
2004	81.4	81.6	82.1	82.1	82.2	82.4	82.2	82.3	81.7	82.0	81.9	82.0	82.0
2005	81.0	81.7	81.7	82.3	82.4	83.0	83.7	84.1	83.7	83.0	83.2	83.6	82.8
2006	82.8	82.9	83.2	82.9	82.7	83.3	83.1	82.8	82.4	82.0	81.8	82.4	82.7
2007	81.6	81.6	81.7	81.7	81.8	82.2	82.1	81.7	80.8	80.4	80.2	80.5	81.4
2008	79.2	79.5	79.7	79.2	79.3	79.7	79.1	78.8	78.1	78.2	77.5	77.7	78.8
2009	75.9	75.7	75.4	75.3	75.2	75.5	74.8	74.8	74.4	74.5	74.6	74.6	75.1
2010	73.4	72.9	73.3	73.2	73.4	74.0	74.2	74.3	74.0	74.4	74.5	75.0	73.9
2011	73.7	73.6	73.9	73.8	74.0	74.3	74.8	74.1	73.7	73.8	73.9	73.9	74.0

Employment by Industry: Baltimore–Towson, MD, Selected Years, 2000–2011—*Continued*

(Numbers in thousands, not seasonally adjusted)

Industry and year	January	February	March	April	May	June	July	August	September	October	November	December	Annual average
Professional and Business Services													
2000	161.0	162.1	166.1	173.0	174.0	176.6	175.8	177.3	175.7	176.5	176.1	175.9	172.5
2001	173.5	174.4	175.9	177.6	179.5	179.7	181.9	182.0	179.2	177.5	178.9	178.0	178.2
2002	171.2	171.8	174.0	174.4	176.5	177.5	177.2	178.7	176.1	175.1	175.3	175.0	175.2
2003	168.8	166.8	169.5	173.9	175.2	176.1	174.1	175.9	174.9	177.1	176.5	177.0	173.8
2004	171.4	172.0	174.9	175.8	178.3	180.4	181.8	181.9	180.0	181.8	181.8	181.7	178.5
2005	177.3	178.5	181.2	183.0	184.6	185.7	189.8	190.4	190.5	189.5	188.8	188.3	185.6
2006	182.0	183.5	186.6	188.9	190.1	191.5	191.6	192.0	191.4	191.3	190.8	191.3	189.3
2007	185.5	185.5	188.1	191.1	191.7	193.5	193.1	194.9	194.5	194.6	195.1	195.1	191.9
2008	190.4	190.6	192.4	194.7	195.6	195.9	196.1	196.8	194.7	193.5	191.0	188.9	193.4
2009	182.0	180.0	180.4	183.1	182.9	184.7	184.8	185.4	184.2	184.6	183.7	183.3	183.3
2010	177.9	175.6	180.7	184.6	185.0	188.0	186.9	188.0	187.0	189.7	189.1	189.0	185.1
2011	184.2	184.2	186.7	191.0	191.5	193.8	196.0	197.8	196.0	197.4	197.6	195.7	192.7
Education and Health Services													
2000	182.6	184.9	185.7	188.0	187.5	187.2	187.3	187.4	190.4	191.1	192.5	194.1	188.2
2001	185.6	188.2	189.2	190.3	191.0	191.9	189.8	189.1	190.4	193.1	194.9	195.9	190.8
2002	192.1	195.7	196.5	195.3	195.6	195.0	194.1	193.1	194.9	198.0	200.1	200.2	195.9
2003	196.0	197.7	198.8	199.4	199.8	193.0	192.8	193.0	200.1	201.8	202.9	203.5	198.2
2004	201.7	202.2	203.2	203.2	203.8	204.4	205.2	203.8	205.1	206.9	208.1	207.8	204.6
2005	204.6	206.8	207.0	208.4	209.0	208.2	208.6	208.1	211.0	213.5	214.9	215.8	209.7
2006	212.6	214.4	215.8	216.2	216.8	215.7	214.3	214.1	216.8	220.0	221.0	222.1	216.7
2007	218.6	220.6	222.1	222.8	223.0	222.1	221.5	220.9	223.1	225.2	225.6	226.3	222.7
2008	224.4	226.2	227.4	229.1	229.0	228.2	227.8	227.5	230.5	232.7	233.8	234.6	229.3
2009	232.1	233.4	234.3	235.7	235.6	234.9	232.9	232.0	234.7	236.8	237.8	238.5	234.9
2010	237.0	234.6	238.8	239.7	239.7	238.4	238.1	236.8	238.8	241.3	242.2	242.3	239.0
2011	240.3	243.2	243.4	244.3	243.9	242.5	242.2	239.7	245.5	253.3	253.7	253.5	245.5
Leisure and Hospitality													
2000	96.7	96.9	99.9	102.0	104.9	109.1	108.2	108.0	105.5	102.5	102.9	103.2	103.3
2001	94.2	94.3	97.2	100.9	104.1	109.0	107.7	107.5	105.1	103.0	101.5	101.4	102.2
2002	97.0	97.2	100.5	103.8	107.8	111.9	111.9	112.1	107.5	105.2	103.9	103.3	105.2
2003	99.7	98.2	100.7	106.1	109.9	113.7	113.7	114.4	111.2	107.9	106.9	106.3	107.4
2004	101.7	101.9	105.1	108.3	111.4	115.8	115.9	116.5	113.5	111.5	109.6	109.6	110.1
2005	104.4	104.3	106.6	111.4	114.2	118.6	118.9	117.9	115.8	110.8	109.5	108.8	111.8
2006	105.9	105.0	108.5	111.7	115.8	120.8	120.5	120.4	117.1	114.6	113.2	112.9	113.9
2007	108.7	108.0	111.5	115.4	119.0	122.7	122.4	123.0	119.3	115.9	114.5	113.9	116.2
2008	110.0	109.7	112.2	117.1	120.8	123.7	123.4	122.6	117.3	115.5	113.2	112.7	116.5
2009	106.4	105.8	108.5	112.7	118.7	121.2	120.2	119.2	116.9	111.5	108.9	108.5	113.2
2010	104.8	102.5	107.4	112.1	116.3	119.1	119.0	119.6	116.7	112.8	110.6	109.8	112.6
2011	104.5	105.0	108.8	113.4	118.0	121.0	121.1	120.1	114.8	109.6	108.9	108.9	112.8
Other Services													
2000	49.8	50.2	50.8	50.9	51.5	52.4	52.1	52.2	52.3	51.6	51.7	51.9	51.5
2001	51.9	52.5	53.2	52.8	53.6	54.6	54.5	54.4	53.4	53.5	53.6	53.9	53.5
2002	52.8	53.2	53.9	54.3	54.8	55.4	55.7	54.9	54.7	54.6	54.8	54.9	54.5
2003	53.8	53.9	54.8	54.5	54.9	55.7	55.2	54.5	54.0	54.0	53.9	54.0	54.4
2004	52.8	53.5	54.0	54.7	55.0	55.6	55.5	55.0	54.8	54.4	54.5	54.8	54.6
2005	53.8	54.2	54.7	55.1	55.3	55.9	55.5	55.3	54.9	54.6	54.7	55.0	54.9
2006	54.5	54.7	55.2	56.0	56.4	56.9	56.8	56.7	56.6	56.3	56.5	56.6	56.1
2007	56.1	56.0	56.7	56.1	56.5	57.2	57.4	56.7	56.4	56.4	56.6	56.7	56.6
2008	55.8	56.1	56.5	56.7	56.8	57.4	57.0	56.7	56.4	56.3	56.2	56.0	56.5
2009	55.1	55.0	55.4	55.4	55.8	56.1	56.0	55.8	55.5	55.6	55.6	55.7	55.6
2010	54.5	53.7	55.2	55.4	55.8	56.0	56.1	55.8	55.6	55.4	55.5	55.3	55.4
2011	54.6	54.7	55.2	55.4	55.7	56.3	58.4	58.7	56.9	57.1	58.2	58.3	56.6
Government													
2000	215.9	218.2	222.1	221.5	224.4	220.4	212.3	208.5	214.2	222.1	222.0	222.4	218.7
2001	217.3	221.4	222.9	223.0	221.9	218.8	213.5	210.6	217.4	222.0	223.8	223.4	219.7
2002	220.5	224.2	226.3	223.3	223.8	221.0	215.3	211.9	220.0	224.6	225.1	223.6	221.6
2003	218.4	222.2	224.1	223.4	222.6	215.4	209.8	216.7	217.4	220.7	221.4	220.1	219.4
2004	214.8	216.3	219.2	220.0	219.1	217.0	207.7	207.3	212.8	218.0	220.2	219.4	216.0
2005	213.6	218.1	218.1	219.9	220.8	218.1	210.1	205.8	217.1	222.0	224.0	223.4	217.6
2006	215.2	220.1	222.1	223.4	223.6	219.4	213.3	212.5	218.7	224.8	226.7	227.1	220.6
2007	219.1	223.9	226.4	225.3	226.0	221.5	214.6	214.3	219.4	225.3	227.1	226.6	222.5
2008	219.3	224.9	226.5	228.5	228.7	224.0	218.8	217.7	223.0	230.0	230.6	230.6	225.2
2009	223.2	228.4	230.2	232.1	231.9	228.0	221.9	219.2	224.8	234.6	234.4	233.8	228.5
2010	226.8	231.5	235.4	237.6	238.8	235.3	226.5	225.0	228.7	236.2	237.9	235.5	232.9
2011	229.5	235.1	239.2	240.6	238.4	235.1	229.9	224.9	235.8	243.7	243.8	244.0	236.7

Employment by Industry: Baton Rouge, LA, Selected Years, 2000–2011

(Numbers in thousands, not seasonally adjusted)

Industry and year	January	February	March	April	May	June	July	August	September	October	November	December	Annual average
Total Nonfarm													
2000	335.0	337.6	339.9	344.0	344.5	346.6	332.9	334.6	339.8	337.3	338.6	339.3	339.2
2001	333.6	332.9	334.5	336.3	339.4	339.4	328.6	331.4	334.2	337.1	338.0	337.7	335.3
2002	332.4	333.4	334.3	336.3	337.9	337.0	329.5	331.8	336.4	338.5	339.3	338.2	335.4
2003	331.5	335.3	336.2	339.6	340.7	339.1	336.3	336.5	340.2	343.5	342.7	340.9	338.5
2004	336.6	340.6	344.5	344.9	342.4	343.6	339.9	338.8	341.1	342.3	345.7	344.5	342.1
2005	337.7	343.0	346.1	352.6	350.8	350.4	350.2	351.7	358.1	360.2	364.7	364.0	352.5
2006	356.1	361.5	364.7	363.1	363.2	358.9	349.9	356.5	361.4	362.2	363.9	366.2	360.6
2007	360.1	365.5	369.5	370.6	371.5	372.3	370.7	373.9	378.3	378.9	380.9	382.3	372.9
2008	369.7	374.7	376.1	374.2	374.0	374.6	369.8	372.6	369.5	377.3	380.3	380.9	374.5
2009	368.7	372.1	373.4	373.3	372.7	369.3	367.5	368.3	371.5	369.2	370.6	368.4	370.4
2010	358.2	360.2	363.1	363.1	364.3	363.7	359.4	362.3	363.6	366.4	367.2	366.6	363.2
2011	362.6	366.7	368.5	370.3	369.7	365.9	362.9	363.1	367.8	369.5	370.6	371.4	367.4
Total Private													
2000	268.6	271.1	273.5	276.6	277.1	278.7	272.2	274.1	274.1	270.8	272.2	273.1	273.5
2001	267.1	266.4	268.0	269.4	271.9	271.5	267.9	270.4	267.9	269.6	269.8	269.9	269.2
2002	264.0	263.9	264.5	266.5	267.5	266.9	266.8	268.5	267.5	268.5	268.4	267.7	266.7
2003	260.2	261.2	261.9	265.8	266.8	266.3	265.4	266.2	266.5	269.0	268.2	268.4	265.5
2004	265.5	266.5	270.2	270.2	268.9	270.1	267.3	266.5	266.2	266.6	269.9	270.3	268.2
2005	265.1	267.8	270.7	277.3	277.1	276.9	278.7	279.1	282.6	283.3	287.3	287.9	277.8
2006	283.6	286.3	289.3	289.2	289.8	290.5	283.2	284.8	287.4	288.0	289.3	292.6	287.8
2007	287.6	290.3	293.6	293.8	295.5	296.7	297.5	298.0	299.1	300.5	301.9	303.9	296.5
2008	294.2	296.2	297.9	296.1	296.8	298.0	294.9	297.3	293.5	298.1	300.6	302.1	297.1
2009	292.4	293.0	294.2	294.4	294.9	292.5	292.7	293.7	292.7	290.1	291.3	290.0	292.7
2010	281.9	282.4	285.0	285.3	286.2	287.3	286.4	286.8	286.0	288.3	289.0	289.2	286.2
2011	287.7	289.7	291.8	293.3	292.9	290.8	289.9	290.6	291.1	291.9	293.0	294.2	291.4
Goods-Producing													
2000	70.7	71.6	72.8	72.9	73.2	72.2	68.2	69.4	68.3	67.6	67.2	66.7	70.1
2001	65.1	65.1	65.9	66.9	68.6	67.2	66.6	67.5	65.0	67.0	66.7	65.9	66.5
2002	64.1	63.2	62.4	63.4	63.5	62.3	62.6	63.3	63.2	65.4	63.3	61.8	63.2
2003	61.0	61.4	61.2	61.8	62.8	62.1	62.0	61.9	62.4	63.4	61.6	61.0	61.9
2004	62.7	62.7	64.9	62.3	61.2	61.1	58.9	58.2	58.9	59.9	61.0	60.7	61.0
2005	58.4	60.5	61.5	65.1	65.1	64.3	63.7	63.8	64.2	63.5	64.8	64.5	63.3
2006	65.6	66.1	67.0	67.4	66.9	66.7	62.6	63.2	64.4	65.4	65.4	66.8	65.6
2007	65.5	66.7	67.5	68.3	69.2	69.2	69.2	68.6	68.8	70.6	70.7	71.3	68.8
2008	66.2	67.0	67.5	67.3	67.7	68.2	67.1	68.3	67.8	69.0	69.5	69.9	68.0
2009	67.6	68.0	68.4	68.3	68.6	67.4	68.5	68.7	68.4	66.2	65.8	64.1	67.5
2010	63.7	63.6	63.7	63.0	62.8	64.0	64.7	64.9	64.8	65.0	64.3	64.3	64.1
2011	64.8	66.0	66.8	66.9	65.9	65.0	66.2	67.1	68.9	68.4	69.1	67.8	66.9
Mining and Logging													
2005	1.5	1.5	1.5	1.6	1.5	1.6	1.5	1.5	1.6	1.8	1.8	1.8	1.6
2006	1.6	1.6	1.6	1.5	1.5	1.5	1.5	1.4	1.5	1.4	1.4	1.4	1.5
2007	1.6	1.7	1.7	1.8	1.9	1.9	1.8	1.9	1.9	1.9	1.9	1.9	1.8
2008	1.6	1.6	1.7	1.7	1.7	1.7	1.6	1.6	1.6	1.6	1.6	1.6	1.6
2009	1.6	1.5	1.5	1.6	1.5	1.5	1.5	1.5	1.6	1.5	1.5	1.6	1.5
2010	1.7	1.9	1.9	2.1	1.9	1.9	1.9	1.9	2.0	2.0	2.0	1.9	1.9
2011	2.0	2.1	2.2	2.1	1.8	1.9	2.0	1.9	2.0	2.0	2.0	2.0	2.0
Construction													
2005	31.4	33.4	34.2	37.5	37.6	36.9	36.2	36.4	36.8	36.0	37.3	36.9	35.9
2006	38.5	39.0	39.7	40.4	39.9	39.5	36.0	36.6	37.5	38.5	38.4	39.7	38.6
2007	38.1	39.1	39.8	40.4	41.0	40.6	40.6	40.6	40.8	42.1	42.0	42.5	40.6
2008	38.8	39.4	39.8	39.6	39.9	40.4	39.5	40.7	40.4	41.3	41.8	42.0	40.3
2009	40.4	40.9	41.4	41.1	41.5	40.5	42	42.3	42.1	40.1	39.8	38	40.8
2010	37.4	37.0	37.1	36.3	36.1	37.2	37.9	38.1	37.9	37.9	37.2	37.2	37.3
2011	37.6	38.7	39.4	39.6	38.7	37.7	39.0	40.0	41.8	41.2	41.9	40.5	39.7
Manufacturing													
2000	29.4	29.5	29.4	29.7	29.8	29.8	29.6	29.7	29.7	30.2	30.3	30.4	29.8
2001	30.2	30.1	30.2	29.9	30.1	30.3	29.9	30.0	29.9	29.9	29.7	29.6	30.0
2002	28.5	28.1	28.2	27.9	27.9	28.1	27.8	27.9	27.8	28.0	27.8	27.7	28.0
2003	27.5	27.4	27.5	27.4	27.5	27.5	26.9	26.8	26.8	27.1	27.0	27.0	27.2
2004	26.8	26.8	26.8	26.6	26.5	26.6	26.2	26.1	26.1	26.0	26.0	26.1	26.4
2005	25.5	25.6	25.8	26.0	26.0	25.8	26.0	25.9	25.8	25.7	25.7	25.8	25.8
2006	25.5	25.5	25.7	25.5	25.5	25.7	25.1	25.2	25.4	25.5	25.6	25.7	25.5
2007	25.8	25.9	26.0	26.1	26.3	26.7	26.8	26.1	26.1	26.6	26.8	26.9	26.3
2008	25.8	26.0	26.0	26.0	26.1	26.1	26.0	26.0	25.8	26.1	26.1	26.3	26.0
2009	25.6	25.6	25.5	25.6	25.6	25.4	25.0	24.9	24.7	24.6	24.5	24.5	25.1
2010	24.6	24.7	24.7	24.6	24.8	24.9	24.9	24.9	24.9	25.1	25.1	25.2	24.9
2011	25.2	25.2	25.2	25.2	25.4	25.4	25.2	25.2	25.1	25.2	25.2	25.3	25.2
Service-Providing													
2000	264.3	266.0	267.1	271.1	271.3	274.4	264.7	265.2	271.5	269.7	271.4	272.6	269.1
2001	268.5	267.8	268.6	269.4	270.8	272.2	262.0	263.9	269.2	270.1	271.3	271.8	268.8
2002	268.3	270.2	271.9	272.9	274.4	274.7	266.9	268.5	273.2	273.1	276.0	276.4	272.2
2003	270.5	273.9	275.0	277.8	277.9	277.0	274.3	274.6	277.8	280.1	281.1	279.9	276.7
2004	273.9	277.9	279.6	282.6	281.2	282.5	281.0	280.6	282.2	282.4	284.7	283.8	281.0
2005	279.3	282.5	284.6	287.5	285.7	286.1	286.5	287.9	293.9	296.7	299.9	299.5	289.2
2006	290.5	295.4	297.7	295.7	296.3	292.2	287.3	293.3	297.0	296.8	298.5	299.4	295.0
2007	294.6	298.8	302.0	302.3	302.3	303.1	301.5	305.3	309.5	308.3	310.2	311.0	304.1
2008	303.5	307.7	308.6	306.9	306.3	306.4	302.7	304.3	301.7	308.3	310.8	311.0	306.5
2009	301.1	304.1	305.0	305.0	304.1	301.9	299.0	299.6	303.1	303.0	304.8	304.3	302.9
2010	294.5	296.6	299.4	300.1	301.5	299.7	294.7	297.4	298.8	301.4	302.9	302.3	299.1
2011	297.8	300.7	301.7	303.4	303.8	300.9	296.7	296.0	298.9	301.1	301.5	303.6	300.5

Employment by Industry: Baton Rouge, LA, Selected Years, 2000–2011—*Continued*

(Numbers in thousands, not seasonally adjusted)

Industry and year	January	February	March	April	May	June	July	August	September	October	November	December	Annual average
Trade, Transportation, and Utilities													
2000	65.1	65.2	65.7	66.0	66.1	66.9	66.7	66.8	67.2	66.7	68.3	69.1	66.7
2001	66.8	66.0	66.2	65.9	66.0	66.1	65.1	65.7	65.6	65.7	66.7	67.4	66.1
2002	65.1	65.1	65.3	65.8	65.9	66.0	65.5	65.9	65.8	65.4	67.1	67.9	65.9
2003	63.1	62.9	63.1	64.0	63.9	64.0	63.5	63.7	63.7	64.1	65.1	65.9	63.9
2004	63.3	63.2	63.5	63.6	63.7	64.0	63.3	63.4	63.2	64.3	64.9		63.6
2005	62.3	62.3	62.8	63.1	63.6	63.7	64.7	64.9	65.7	66.5	68.6	69.4	64.8
2006	66.4	66.2	67.0	66.1	66.5	66.3	65.6	65.6	65.8	65.9	67.2	68.2	66.4
2007	65.7	65.5	66.3	65.4	65.9	66.1	66.7	67.2	67.6	67.7	69.4	70.2	67.0
2008	67.7	67.1	67.7	66.7	66.8	66.9	66.8	67.3	66.4	66.8	67.9	68.8	67.2
2009	66.1	65.5	65.6	65.8	65.7	65.3	65.3	65.3	65.3	64.9	66.0	66.6	65.6
2010	64.0	63.9	64.5	64.9	65.0	64.9	64.4	64.5	64.3	65.2	66.5	67.2	64.9
2011	65.0	64.8	65.0	65.4	65.4	65.0	64.9	64.6	64.4	64.7	66.0	66.8	65.2
Wholesale Trade													
2000	13.9	13.9	14.0	14.2	14.2	14.4	14.2	14.2	14.1	14.0	14.0	14.1	14.1
2001	14.1	14.2	14.3	14.2	14.2	14.3	14.1	14.0	14.1	14.0	14.0	14.0	14.1
2002	13.7	13.7	13.7	13.6	13.7	13.8	13.7	13.7	13.7	13.5	13.6	13.6	13.7
2003	13.5	13.4	13.5	13.4	13.4	13.5	13.4	13.4	13.4	13.3	13.3	13.2	13.4
2004	13.2	13.2	13.3	13.3	13.2	13.2	12.9	13.0	12.9	12.6	12.7	12.8	13.0
2005	12.6	12.5	12.6	12.7	12.8	12.8	13.1	13.1	13.1	12.9	12.9	13.0	12.8
2006	12.7	12.7	12.8	12.8	12.9	13.0	12.9	12.8	12.9	12.9	13.0	13.0	12.9
2007	13.2	13.2	13.3	13.2	13.3	13.5	13.7	13.8	13.8	13.8	13.9	14.0	13.6
2008	13.6	13.6	13.7	13.4	13.5	13.4	13.4	13.4	13.5	13.5	13.4	13.4	13.5
2009	13.2	13.2	13.1	13.3	13.2	13.1	12.7	12.6	12.7	12.6	12.7	12.7	12.9
2010	12.4	12.4	12.4	12.5	12.5	12.4	12.4	12.5	12.4	12.7	12.6	12.6	12.5
2011	12.7	12.7	12.7	12.6	12.6	12.6	12.6	12.7	12.6	12.7	12.8	12.8	12.7
Retail Trade													
2000	39.4	39.4	40.0	39.8	39.9	40.2	40.0	40.2	40.7	40.2	41.7	42.4	40.3
2001	40.1	39.2	39.3	38.9	39.0	38.9	38.5	39.1	38.9	39.0	40.1	40.7	39.3
2002	38.7	38.4	38.4	38.5	38.4	38.3	38.0	38.2	38.2	38.0	39.5	40.3	38.6
2003	36.4	36.2	36.3	37.1	36.9	37.0	36.7	36.8	36.7	37.2	38.1	39.0	37.0
2004	37.0	36.8	37.0	37.2	37.4	37.8	37.5	37.5	37.5	37.8	38.9	39.5	37.7
2005	37.5	37.5	37.9	37.9	38.2	38.4	39.1	39.3	40.1	41.1	43.0	43.6	39.5
2006	41.5	41.2	41.9	41.1	41.2	40.9	40.2	40.3	40.3	40.5	41.6	42.4	41.1
2007	40.3	40.0	40.8	40.0	40.3	40.3	40.6	40.7	41.0	41.4	42.9	43.6	41.0
2008	41.5	40.9	41.4	40.8	40.7	41.0	40.9	41.1	40.2	40.9	42.1	42.9	41.2
2009	40.6	40.3	40.5	40.8	40.8	40.8	41.1	41.0	40.9	40.4	41.5	41.9	40.9
2010	40.0	39.9	40.4	40.5	40.6	40.6	40.2	40.1	40.0	40.5	41.9	42.3	40.6
2011	40.2	39.9	40.2	40.7	40.7	40.4	40.3	39.8	39.6	39.8	41.1	41.7	40.4
Transportation and Utilities													
2000	11.8	11.9	11.7	12.0	12.0	12.3	12.5	12.4	12.4	12.5	12.6	12.6	12.2
2001	12.6	12.6	12.6	12.8	12.8	12.9	12.5	12.6	12.6	12.7	12.6	12.7	12.7
2002	12.7	13.0	13.2	13.7	13.8	13.9	13.8	14.0	13.9	13.9	14.0	14.0	13.7
2003	13.2	13.3	13.3	13.5	13.6	13.5	13.4	13.5	13.6	13.6	13.7	13.7	13.5
2004	13.1	13.2	13.2	13.1	13.1	13.0	12.9	12.9	12.8	12.8	12.7	12.6	13.0
2005	12.2	12.3	12.3	12.5	12.6	12.5	12.5	12.5	12.5	12.5	12.7	12.8	12.5
2006	12.2	12.3	12.3	12.2	12.4	12.4	12.5	12.5	12.6	12.5	12.6	12.8	12.4
2007	12.2	12.3	12.2	12.2	12.3	12.3	12.4	12.7	12.8	12.5	12.6	12.6	12.4
2008	12.6	12.6	12.6	12.5	12.6	12.5	12.5	12.8	12.7	12.4	12.4	12.5	12.6
2009	12.3	12.0	12.0	11.7	11.7	11.4	11.5	11.7	11.7	11.9	11.8	12.0	11.8
2010	11.6	11.6	11.7	11.9	11.9	11.9	11.8	11.9	11.9	12.0	12.0	12.3	11.9
2011	12.1	12.2	12.1	12.1	12.1	12.0	12.0	12.1	12.2	12.2	12.1	12.3	12.1
Information													
2000	4.8	4.8	5.0	5.3	5.2	5.3	5.5	5.6	5.6	5.6	5.6	5.6	5.3
2001	5.2	5.2	5.3	5.7	5.7	5.7	5.5	5.5	5.4	5.3	5.2	5.2	5.4
2002	5.2	5.2	5.3	5.0	5.1	5.1	5.2	5.2	5.2	5.0	5.0	5.0	5.1
2003	4.9	4.9	5.0	5.2	5.3	5.3	5.4	5.6	5.6	5.6	5.6	5.7	5.3
2004	5.6	5.6	5.6	5.6	5.6	5.6	5.5	5.5	5.4	5.4	5.5	5.5	5.5
2005	5.8	5.7	5.7	5.9	5.6	5.5	5.6	5.5	5.4	5.4	5.6	5.5	5.6
2006	5.6	5.6	5.7	5.7	5.6	5.5	5.4	5.3	5.2	5.4	5.5	5.4	5.5
2007	5.5	5.5	5.5	5.7	5.8	5.6	6.0	5.9	5.8	6.6	5.9	5.8	5.8
2008	5.6	6.0	5.8	6.4	6.2	6.4	5.8	5.8	5.6	5.6	6.0	6.0	5.9
2009	5.5	5.4	5.2	5.1	5.0	4.9	4.7	4.8	4.6	4.7	4.7	4.7	4.9
2010	4.6	4.6	4.6	4.8	4.8	4.8	4.7	4.6	4.4	4.7	4.7	5.0	4.7
2011	4.8	4.9	4.8	4.9	4.8	4.8	4.6	4.4	4.4	4.4	4.4	4.3	4.6
Financial Activities													
2000	15.8	15.9	16.0	16.2	16.2	16.4	16.0	16.0	16.0	15.8	15.8	16.0	16.0
2001	16.0	16.1	16.1	16.4	16.3	16.5	16.4	16.5	16.4	16.3	16.5	16.5	16.3
2002	16.7	16.7	16.5	17.0	17.0	17.0	17.1	17.2	17.0	17.3	17.2	17.4	17.0
2003	16.7	16.8	16.8	17.4	17.3	17.4	17.5	17.6	17.6	17.9	17.9	18.0	17.4
2004	17.9	17.9	18.0	18.2	18.2	18.2	18.1	18.1	17.9	17.8	17.8	18.0	18.0
2005	17.9	18.0	18.0	18.1	18.2	18.2	18.5	18.5	18.5	18.5	18.6	18.7	18.3
2006	18.5	18.5	18.6	18.6	18.6	18.6	18.4	18.5	18.5	18.7	18.7	18.8	18.6
2007	19.1	19.2	18.9	18.9	18.8	18.8	18.7	18.7	18.5	18.4	18.5	18.6	18.8
2008	18.3	18.3	18.4	18.2	18.2	18.3	18.1	18.1	17.9	18.0	17.9	17.9	18.1
2009	17.5	17.4	17.4	17.6	17.7	17.6	17.4	17.4	17.2	17.2	17.5	17.5	17.5
2010	17.3	17.3	17.4	17.3	17.3	17.3	17.0	17.1	16.9	17.0	17.1	17.1	17.2
2011	17.1	17.2	17.1	17.0	17.0	16.9	16.8	16.9	16.8	16.9	16.9	17.0	17.0

Employment by Industry: Baton Rouge, LA, Selected Years, 2000–2011—*Continued*

(Numbers in thousands, not seasonally adjusted)

Industry and year	January	February	March	April	May	June	July	August	September	October	November	December	Annual average
Professional and Business Services													
2000	38.9	39.6	39.6	40.2	40.2	40.7	40.0	40.3	40.7	40.5	40.5	40.4	40.1
2001	40.3	39.6	39.5	39.1	39.0	39.6	38.8	39.2	39.0	39.3	39.1	39.6	39.3
2002	39.0	39.0	39.2	39.1	38.9	38.9	38.7	38.8	38.4	38.6	38.6	38.7	38.8
2003	37.6	37.2	37.6	38.3	37.9	37.9	37.2	37.3	36.7	36.8	36.9	37.0	37.4
2004	36.8	37.2	37.5	38.1	37.3	37.6	37.6	37.4	36.9	36.6	36.8	36.8	37.2
2005	37.6	37.7	38.1	39.7	38.5	38.4	38.8	39.1	40.5	41.3	42.0	42.4	39.5
2006	41.1	41.8	42.3	42.7	42.7	43.0	42.5	42.6	43.1	43.4	43.0	43.8	42.7
2007	43.8	44.2	44.9	45.1	44.4	45.0	45.4	45.8	46.3	46.7	47.0	47.3	45.5
2008	47.0	46.7	46.7	45.9	45.8	45.8	44.9	45.2	45.6	46.3	46.3	46.4	46.1
2009	44.8	44.7	44.7	44.6	44.5	44.1	43.0	43.3	42.7	42.3	42.3	42.4	43.6
2010	41.0	41.1	41.5	41.7	41.8	41.9	41.8	41.9	41.5	41.9	41.6	41.7	41.6
2011	41.6	41.9	42.3	42.8	42.7	42.5	42.5	42.0	41.8	41.9	41.5	42.1	42.1
Education and Health Services													
2000	34.9	35.0	35.0	35.6	35.4	35.6	34.9	35.1	35.5	35.2	35.2	35.4	35.2
2001	34.8	34.9	35.0	34.9	35.0	35.0	34.8	35.1	35.5	35.4	35.6	35.5	35.1
2002	34.9	35.1	35.5	35.2	35.4	35.6	35.5	36.0	36.4	36.0	36.3	36.4	35.7
2003	35.8	36.1	36.1	36.2	36.4	36.5	37.2	37.4	37.7	38.1	38.1	38.2	37.0
2004	37.7	38.0	38.0	38.5	38.5	38.5	38.9	39.0	39.2	39.4	39.5	39.5	38.7
2005	39.4	39.6	39.7	40.1	40.4	40.4	41.3	41.2	41.6	42.4	42.4	42.0	40.9
2006	41.7	42.1	42.4	42.8	43.0	43.2	42.8	43.3	43.7	43.9	43.8	43.7	43.0
2007	42.9	43.3	43.5	44.0	44.6	44.5	44.3	44.8	44.7	44.3	44.4	44.8	44.2
2008	44.2	44.8	45.0	45.2	45.3	45.6	45.6	46.2	45.3	46.0	46.1	46.3	45.5
2009	45.7	46.2	46.4	46.7	46.6	46.3	47.4	47.5	47.8	48.5	48.6	48.6	47.2
2010	47.7	47.9	48.4	48.9	49.2	48.8	48.8	48.8	49.2	49.6	49.8	49.5	48.9
2011	49.6	49.9	50.0	49.6	49.8	49.5	49.2	50.2	49.9	50.7	50.1	51.0	50.0
Leisure and Hospitality													
2000	26.8	27.3	27.6	28.5	28.7	29.5	28.8	28.8	28.7	27.7	27.9	28.2	28.2
2001	27.1	27.6	28.1	28.3	29.1	29.0	28.6	28.8	28.8	28.4	28.1	27.9	28.3
2002	26.8	27.3	27.9	28.3	28.8	29.0	29.0	29.1	28.6	27.9	28.0	27.7	28.2
2003	28.3	29.1	29.3	29.9	30.1	30.0	29.8	29.9	30.0	30.0	30.0	29.7	29.7
2004	28.9	29.2	29.9	30.2	30.7	31.1	30.9	30.9	30.7	30.6	31.2	31.2	30.5
2005	30.2	30.5	31.1	31.5	31.9	32.4	32.0	32.0	32.6	32.0	31.7	31.7	31.6
2006	31.3	32.4	32.7	32.3	32.8	33.2	32.1	32.5	32.7	31.7	32.0	32.1	32.3
2007	31.3	32.0	33.0	32.5	33.0	33.4	32.9	32.8	33.2	32.3	32.3	32.1	32.6
2008	31.7	32.5	32.9	33.3	33.6	33.5	33.2	33.3	32.1	32.9	33.4	33.4	33.0
2009	32.0	32.6	33.3	33.0	33.5	33.4	32.8	33.2	33.0	32.4	32.5	32.1	32.8
2010	31.0	31.3	32.2	32.4	32.9	33.1	32.7	32.8	32.8	32.4	32.6	32.1	32.4
2011	32.5	32.6	33.3	34.1	34.8	34.4	33.1	32.9	32.4	32.4	32.5	32.7	33.1
Other Services													
2000	11.6	11.7	11.8	11.9	12.1	12.1	12.1	12.1	12.1	11.7	11.7	11.7	11.9
2001	11.8	11.9	11.9	12.2	12.2	12.4	12.1	12.1	12.2	12.2	11.9	11.9	12.1
2002	12.2	12.3	12.4	12.7	12.9	13.0	13.2	13.0	12.9	12.9	12.9	12.8	12.8
2003	12.8	12.8	12.8	13.0	13.1	13.1	12.8	12.8	12.8	13.1	13.0	12.9	12.9
2004	12.6	12.7	12.8	13.7	13.7	14.0	14.1	14.0	14.0	13.7	13.8	13.7	13.6
2005	13.5	13.5	13.8	13.8	13.8	14.0	14.1	14.1	13.7	13.6	13.7	13.7	13.8
2006	13.4	13.6	13.6	13.6	13.7	14.0	13.8	13.8	14.0	13.6	13.7	13.8	13.7
2007	13.8	13.9	14.0	13.9	13.8	14.1	14.3	14.2	14.2	13.9	13.7	13.8	14.0
2008	13.5	13.8	13.9	13.1	13.2	13.3	13.4	13.1	12.8	13.5	13.5	13.4	13.4
2009	13.2	13.2	13.2	13.3	13.3	13.5	13.6	13.5	13.7	13.9	13.9	14.0	13.5
2010	12.6	12.7	12.7	12.3	12.4	12.5	12.3	12.2	12.1	12.5	12.4	12.3	12.4
2011	12.3	12.4	12.5	12.6	12.5	12.7	12.6	12.5	12.5	12.5	12.5	12.5	12.5
Government													
2000	66.4	66.5	66.4	67.4	67.4	67.9	60.7	60.5	65.7	66.5	66.4	66.2	65.7
2001	66.5	66.5	66.5	66.9	67.5	67.9	60.7	61.0	66.3	67.5	68.2	67.8	66.1
2002	68.4	69.5	69.8	69.8	70.4	70.1	62.7	63.3	68.9	70.0	70.9	70.5	68.7
2003	71.3	74.1	74.3	73.8	73.9	72.8	70.9	70.3	73.7	74.5	74.5	72.5	73.1
2004	71.1	74.1	74.3	74.7	73.5	73.5	72.6	72.3	74.9	75.7	75.8	74.2	73.9
2005	72.6	75.2	75.4	75.3	73.7	73.5	71.5	72.6	75.5	76.9	77.4	76.1	74.6
2006	72.5	75.2	75.4	73.9	73.4	68.4	66.7	71.7	74.0	74.2	74.6	73.6	72.8
2007	72.5	75.2	75.9	76.8	76.0	75.6	73.2	75.9	79.2	78.4	79.0	78.4	76.3
2008	75.5	78.5	78.2	78.1	77.2	76.6	74.9	75.3	76.0	79.2	79.7	78.8	77.3
2009	76.3	79.1	79.2	78.9	77.8	76.8	74.8	74.6	78.8	79.1	79.3	78.4	77.8
2010	76.3	77.8	78.1	77.8	78.1	76.4	73.0	75.5	77.6	78.1	78.2	77.4	77.0
2011	74.9	77.0	76.7	77.0	76.8	75.1	73.0	72.5	76.7	77.6	77.6	77.2	76.0

Employment by Industry: Birmingham–Hoover, AL, Selected Years, 2000–2011

(Numbers in thousands, not seasonally adjusted)

Industry and year	January	February	March	April	May	June	July	August	September	October	November	December	Annual average
Total Nonfarm													
2000	509.4	511.3	514.8	514.8	518.3	518.3	516.3	515.4	519.6	520.2	522.0	522.7	516.9
2001	513.4	514.1	517.4	517.5	518.7	520.1	513.8	513.0	513.2	514.5	516.1	517.2	515.8
2002	506.5	507.1	510.2	509.7	510.2	509.3	507.5	506.4	508.1	508.6	511.6	511.1	508.9
2003	498.9	501.0	503.5	504.5	505.3	504.8	503.4	504.8	506.0	508.3	511.1	513.1	505.4
2004	503.5	505.4	508.2	509.9	510.6	511.6	510.2	509.8	510.3	513.2	516.5	517.7	510.6
2005	509.1	511.1	514.0	517.7	518.3	519.1	517.7	518.2	520.3	521.5	524.4	525.3	518.1
2006	517.8	520.0	523.1	525.6	527.6	531.8	526.9	528.3	530.3	530.2	533.1	534.1	527.4
2007	526.4	528.9	532.2	529.1	532.1	534.5	529.5	531.2	532.2	532.5	535.6	536.9	531.8
2008	525.4	526.9	527.7	529.5	531.8	533.0	527.5	527.5	526.1	525.7	524.2	523.3	527.4
2009	505.7	504.0	502.4	500.6	500.9	499.4	493.9	491.8	492.2	492.5	494.6	494.1	497.7
2010	485.0	485.8	487.2	489.9	493.4	492.8	489.1	487.6	487.0	490.5	492.9	492.9	489.5
2011	482.5	484.7	487.7	489.6	490.9	492.7	489.7	487.5	488.6	489.3	489.6	490.7	488.6
Total Private													
2000	434.3	436.0	438.9	438.9	440.9	444.3	443.4	444.0	444.5	444.0	446.0	446.5	441.8
2001	437.6	437.8	441.1	441.4	442.3	444.8	440.7	440.3	437.9	437.9	439.4	440.6	440.2
2002	430.5	430.8	433.6	433.0	433.1	433.4	434.2	433.5	431.7	430.9	433.4	432.9	432.6
2003	421.4	422.9	425.1	425.5	426.2	427.6	428.0	429.3	427.7	429.5	432.0	433.7	427.4
2004	424.5	426.3	429.3	430.4	431.5	433.3	433.7	433.3	431.6	434.1	436.9	438.2	431.9
2005	430.3	431.8	434.5	437.9	438.4	439.7	440.8	440.7	440.6	440.8	443.5	444.6	438.6
2006	436.4	438.4	441.4	443.4	445.2	449.5	447.8	448.7	448.0	447.2	449.9	450.8	445.6
2007	443.5	445.6	448.7	445.6	448.3	450.9	449.5	450.5	448.9	448.6	451.5	452.9	448.7
2008	441.8	442.9	443.5	445.1	447.1	448.3	446.4	445.9	442.5	440.7	439.3	438.1	443.5
2009	421.2	419.4	417.8	415.6	416.1	414.6	413.3	410.9	409.1	408.6	410.3	409.9	413.9
2010	401.1	401.7	402.6	404.9	406.1	406.8	407.2	406.4	404.0	406.6	409.0	408.9	405.4
2011	398.8	400.9	403.8	405.7	406.9	409.0	409.2	407.6	406.2	407.1	408.0	409.4	406.1
Goods-Producing													
2000	86.5	86.9	87.6	88.6	89.1	90.1	89.6	89.6	89.7	89.2	89.0	88.5	88.7
2001	87.2	86.4	87.2	86.7	86.5	86.5	84.8	84.5	83.9	83.5	82.9	82.8	85.2
2002	80.1	79.4	80.1	80.7	80.4	80.3	80.2	80.3	79.9	80.4	80.1	79.2	80.1
2003	77.7	77.7	78.4	78.4	78.3	78.2	78.2	78.7	78.5	79.9	80.1	80.0	78.7
2004	78.4	79.0	79.5	79.3	79.1	78.9	79.0	78.9	79.0	80.0	80.0	79.8	79.2
2005	78.4	78.4	78.7	79.7	79.4	79.3	80.1	80.4	80.5	80.9	81.1	80.6	79.8
2006	79.7	79.9	80.6	81.3	82.0	82.9	82.8	82.5	82.9	82.5	82.1	81.8	81.8
2007	81.1	81.7	82.2	81.4	81.5	82.2	81.5	81.8	81.7	81.2	80.7	80.5	81.5
2008	79.0	79.0	78.6	78.9	79.2	79.3	79.4	78.6	78.2	76.6	75.5	74.5	78.1
2009	70.4	69.3	68.6	67.0	66.9	66.0	65.9	65.3	64.9	64.0	63.9	63.9	66.3
2010	62.2	61.8	61.6	62.1	62.0	61.9	62.3	62.3	61.7	61.3	61.5	61.4	61.8
2011	60.3	60.8	61.8	62.0	62.5	62.9	62.5	61.7	62.5	62.1	61.2	61.0	61.8
Mining and Logging													
2000	3.0	3.0	3.1	3.2	3.2	3.4	3.3	3.3	3.4	3.3	3.3	3.2	3.2
2001	3.1	3.2	3.2	3.3	3.3	3.3	3.3	3.3	3.3	3.3	3.2	3.2	3.3
2002	3.0	3.0	3.1	3.2	3.2	3.2	3.1	3.2	3.2	3.4	3.4	3.2	3.2
2003	3.1	3.0	3.0	3.0	3.0	3.0	2.9	2.8	2.8	2.8	2.8	2.8	2.9
2004	2.7	2.7	2.7	2.8	2.8	2.9	2.9	3.0	3.0	3.0	3.0	3.1	2.9
2005	3.0	3.0	3.1	3.1	3.2	3.2	3.3	3.3	3.3	3.3	3.3	3.3	3.2
2006	3.1	3.1	3.1	3.0	3.1	3.1	3.2	3.1	3.2	3.1	3.1	3.2	3.1
2007	3.1	3.1	3.1	3.0	3.0	2.9	2.9	3.0	3.0	3.0	3.0	3.1	3.0
2008	3.0	3.0	3.0	3.0	3.0	3.0	3.1	3.1	3.1	3.1	3.1	3.1	3.1
2009	2.9	2.9	2.9	2.9	2.9	2.8	2.8	2.7	2.8	2.8	2.8	2.8	2.8
2010	2.8	2.8	2.8	2.9	2.9	3.0	3.0	3.1	2.9	3.1	3.1	3.1	3.0
2011	3.1	3.1	3.2	3.3	3.3	3.4	3.4	3.4	3.4	3.4	3.4	3.4	3.3
Construction													
2000	31.0	31.2	31.6	31.9	32.2	32.9	33.0	33.0	33.1	32.6	32.6	32.5	32.3
2001	31.9	31.9	32.5	32.6	32.8	33.0	32.4	32.3	32.1	32.0	31.8	31.9	32.3
2002	30.3	30.6	31.0	31.7	31.6	31.4	31.8	31.8	31.7	32.2	32.0	31.5	31.5
2003	31.1	31.3	32.0	32.1	31.9	31.9	32.6	33.3	33.3	34.8	34.8	34.5	32.8
2004	34.0	34.5	34.9	34.3	33.8	33.3	33.3	33.1	33.2	33.9	33.6	33.1	33.8
2005	32.4	32.6	32.6	33.6	32.9	32.7	33.3	33.3	33.3	34.1	34.0	33.4	33.2
2006	33.0	33.0	33.7	34.3	34.6	35.2	34.8	34.9	35.0	34.9	34.7	34.2	34.4
2007	33.8	34.3	34.8	34.1	34.1	34.4	34.2	34.4	34.7	34.7	34.2	33.9	34.3
2008	33.2	33.0	32.9	33.4	33.8	33.5	33.7	33.2	32.8	31.7	31.0	30.6	32.7
2009	28.5	28.0	28.0	27.1	27.2	27.3	27.1	26.7	26.4	25.2	25.1	25.0	26.8
2010	24.1	23.9	24.0	24.2	24.3	24.4	24.6	24.7	24.3	23.9	23.7	23.7	24.2
2011	22.8	23.2	23.9	23.9	24.2	24.4	23.9	22.9	23.5	23.4	22.5	22.5	23.4
Manufacturing													
2000	52.5	52.7	52.9	53.5	53.7	53.8	53.3	53.3	53.2	53.3	53.1	52.8	53.2
2001	52.2	51.3	51.5	50.8	50.4	50.2	49.1	48.9	48.5	48.2	47.9	47.7	49.7
2002	46.8	45.8	46.0	45.8	45.6	45.7	45.3	45.3	45.0	44.8	44.7	44.5	45.4
2003	43.5	43.4	43.4	43.3	43.4	43.3	42.7	42.6	42.4	42.3	42.5	42.7	43.0
2004	41.7	41.8	41.9	42.2	42.5	42.7	42.8	42.8	42.8	43.1	43.4	43.6	42.6
2005	43.0	42.8	43.0	43.0	43.3	43.4	43.5	43.8	43.9	43.5	43.8	43.9	43.4
2006	43.6	43.8	43.8	44.0	44.3	44.6	44.8	44.5	44.7	44.5	44.3	44.4	44.3
2007	44.2	44.3	44.3	44.3	44.4	44.9	44.4	44.4	44.0	43.5	43.5	43.5	44.1
2008	42.8	43.0	42.7	42.5	42.4	42.8	42.6	42.3	42.3	41.8	41.4	40.8	42.3
2009	39.0	38.4	37.7	37.0	36.8	35.9	36.0	35.9	35.7	36.0	36.0	36.1	36.7
2010	35.3	35.1	34.8	35.0	34.8	34.5	34.7	34.5	34.5	34.3	34.7	34.6	34.7
2011	34.4	34.5	34.7	34.8	35.0	35.1	35.2	35.4	35.6	35.3	35.3	35.1	35.0

Employment by Industry: Birmingham–Hoover, AL, Selected Years, 2000–2011—*Continued*

(Numbers in thousands, not seasonally adjusted)

Industry and year	January	February	March	April	May	June	July	August	September	October	November	December	Annual average
Service-Providing													
2000	422.9	424.4	427.2	426.2	429.2	428.2	426.7	425.8	429.9	431.0	433.0	434.2	428.2
2001	426.2	427.7	430.2	430.8	432.2	433.6	429.0	428.5	429.3	431.0	433.2	434.4	430.5
2002	426.4	427.7	430.1	429.0	429.8	429.0	427.3	426.1	428.2	428.2	431.5	431.9	428.8
2003	421.2	423.3	425.1	426.1	427.0	426.6	425.2	426.1	427.5	428.4	431.0	433.1	426.7
2004	425.1	426.4	428.7	430.6	431.5	432.7	431.2	430.9	431.3	433.2	436.5	437.9	431.3
2005	430.7	432.7	435.3	438.0	438.9	439.8	437.6	437.8	439.8	440.6	443.3	444.7	438.3
2006	438.1	440.1	442.5	444.3	445.6	448.9	444.1	445.8	447.4	447.7	451.0	452.3	445.7
2007	445.3	447.2	450.0	447.7	450.6	452.3	448.0	449.4	450.5	451.3	454.9	456.4	450.3
2008	446.4	447.9	449.1	450.6	452.6	453.7	448.1	448.9	447.9	449.1	448.7	448.8	449.3
2009	435.3	434.7	433.8	433.6	434.0	433.4	428.0	426.5	427.3	428.5	430.7	430.2	431.3
2010	422.8	424.0	425.6	427.8	431.4	430.9	426.8	425.3	425.3	429.2	431.4	431.5	427.7
2011	422.2	423.9	425.9	427.6	428.4	429.8	427.2	425.8	426.1	427.2	428.4	429.7	426.9
Trade, Transportation, and Utilities													
2000	114.1	113.3	113.6	112.4	113.3	113.4	112.9	112.9	114.0	114.4	116.4	117.4	114.0
2001	113.6	112.4	113.0	112.0	112.7	113.2	112.0	111.8	111.1	111.5	113.6	114.9	112.7
2002	110.9	110.2	110.7	109.3	109.7	109.6	109.9	109.8	108.9	109.6	112.0	113.5	110.3
2003	108.9	108.5	109.0	108.8	109.2	109.8	110.4	110.5	110.3	111.0	112.9	114.4	110.3
2004	110.9	110.8	111.5	111.3	111.6	111.6	111.2	111.1	110.7	111.3	113.4	115.3	111.7
2005	110.5	110.2	110.6	111.0	111.3	111.7	111.4	111.8	111.6	112.2	114.0	115.7	111.8
2006	112.4	112.1	112.9	112.9	113.3	114.0	113.5	114.0	113.8	115.0	117.2	118.7	114.2
2007	114.7	114.4	115.5	114.5	115.5	116.4	116.2	115.8	115.9	116.1	118.4	119.7	116.1
2008	115.7	115.1	115.5	115.2	115.2	115.3	114.9	115.0	114.4	114.2	115.2	115.9	115.1
2009	110.4	109.4	108.8	107.9	107.9	107.3	106.8	106.3	106.0	106.1	107.0	107.8	107.6
2010	104.3	104.1	104.6	104.5	105.1	105.2	105.2	105.3	105.0	106.3	107.9	108.8	105.5
2011	104.9	104.9	105.1	105.0	105.0	105.4	105.9	106.1	105.9	107.8	109.5	111.1	106.4
Wholesale Trade													
2000	31.2	31.3	31.4	30.7	30.8	30.9	30.9	30.9	31.1	31.0	31.1	31.1	31.0
2001	31.1	31.2	31.3	31.0	31.0	31.0	30.7	30.5	30.5	30.2	30.1	30.0	30.7
2002	30.0	29.9	29.9	29.7	29.6	29.6	29.6	29.7	29.4	29.3	29.4	29.4	29.6
2003	29.1	29.1	29.1	29.1	29.2	29.3	29.5	29.4	29.5	29.7	29.9	30.1	29.4
2004	29.8	29.9	30.0	30.0	30.2	30.2	30.3	30.4	30.2	30.3	30.4	30.5	30.2
2005	30.1	30.2	30.2	30.3	30.2	30.3	30.4	30.5	30.6	30.4	30.4	30.6	30.4
2006	30.6	30.8	31.0	31.1	31.2	31.5	31.5	31.6	31.5	31.5	31.6	31.7	31.3
2007	31.4	31.6	31.8	31.4	31.4	31.7	31.5	31.5	31.6	31.6	31.7	31.8	31.6
2008	31.5	31.6	31.6	31.6	31.6	31.5	31.4	31.5	31.5	31.5	31.2	31.2	31.5
2009	30.4	30.2	30.0	29.7	29.6	29.4	29.4	29.3	29.2	29.3	28.9	28.9	29.5
2010	28.3	28.3	28.3	28.3	28.4	28.3	28.3	28.4	28.2	28.5	28.4	28.4	28.3
2011	27.9	28.1	28.0	28.2	28.1	28.1	28.3	28.4	28.5	28.7	28.5	28.7	28.3
Retail Trade													
2000	61.8	61.1	61.3	61.2	61.7	62.0	61.3	61.5	62.3	62.8	64.6	65.7	62.3
2001	61.9	60.6	61.1	60.5	61.1	61.6	60.8	60.8	60.3	60.9	63.2	64.4	61.4
2002	61.4	60.9	61.3	60.4	60.6	60.6	60.9	60.6	60.1	61.0	63.2	64.6	61.3
2003	60.7	60.3	60.8	60.8	61.0	61.4	61.8	62.2	62.1	62.4	64.1	65.4	61.9
2004	62.3	62.1	62.6	62.4	62.5	62.4	61.8	61.6	61.5	62.0	64.0	65.6	62.6
2005	61.5	61.0	61.2	61.5	61.8	62.0	61.7	62.0	61.6	62.2	64.1	65.5	62.2
2006	62.3	61.8	62.3	62.0	62.2	62.3	61.7	62.0	61.8	62.7	64.8	66.0	62.7
2007	62.8	62.2	62.9	62.4	63.2	63.6	63.4	62.9	62.8	63.1	65.2	66.2	63.4
2008	63.0	62.4	62.8	62.3	62.3	62.5	62.1	61.9	61.4	61.5	62.9	63.6	62.4
2009	59.3	58.6	58.4	58.0	58.1	57.8	57.4	56.9	56.7	56.7	58.0	58.5	57.9
2010	55.9	55.6	56.1	56.0	56.2	56.3	55.9	55.9	55.7	56.7	58.4	59.2	56.5
2011	56.1	55.7	55.9	56.2	56.3	56.6	56.9	57.1	56.9	58.5	60.4	61.7	57.4
Transportation and Utilities													
2000	21.1	20.9	20.9	20.5	20.8	20.5	20.7	20.5	20.6	20.6	20.7	20.6	20.7
2001	20.6	20.6	20.6	20.5	20.6	20.6	20.5	20.5	20.3	20.4	20.3	20.5	20.5
2002	19.5	19.4	19.5	19.2	19.5	19.4	19.4	19.5	19.5	19.4	19.3	19.4	19.4
2003	19.1	19.1	19.1	18.9	19.0	19.1	19.1	18.9	18.7	18.9	18.9	18.9	19.0
2004	18.8	18.8	18.9	18.9	18.9	19.0	19.1	19.1	19.0	19.0	19.0	19.2	19.0
2005	18.9	19.0	19.2	19.2	19.3	19.4	19.3	19.3	19.4	19.6	19.5	19.6	19.3
2006	19.5	19.5	19.6	19.8	19.9	20.2	20.3	20.4	20.5	20.8	20.8	21.0	20.2
2007	20.5	20.6	20.8	20.7	20.9	21.1	21.3	21.4	21.5	21.4	21.5	21.7	21.1
2008	21.2	21.1	21.1	21.3	21.3	21.3	21.4	21.6	21.5	21.2	21.1	21.1	21.3
2009	20.7	20.6	20.4	20.2	20.2	20.1	20.0	20.1	20.1	20.1	20.1	20.4	20.3
2010	20.1	20.2	20.2	20.2	20.5	20.6	21.0	21.0	21.1	21.1	21.1	21.2	20.7
2011	20.9	21.1	21.2	20.6	20.6	20.7	20.7	20.6	20.5	20.6	20.6	20.7	20.7
Information													
2000	40.3	40.4	40.5	40.7	40.7	40.9	41.4	41.4	41.2	40.9	40.9	41.0	40.9
2001	40.5	40.7	40.7	41.1	41.2	41.5	41.4	41.5	41.2	41.2	41.1	41.2	41.1
2002	41.0	40.8	40.7	40.8	41.0	41.0	41.0	41.0	40.8	40.9	41.0	41.2	40.9
2003	40.1	40.0	39.9	40.2	40.2	40.4	40.5	40.3	40.2	40.2	40.3	40.4	40.2
2004	40.0	40.1	40.1	40.1	40.2	40.4	40.3	40.3	40.1	40.4	40.4	40.5	40.2
2005	39.9	40.1	40.3	40.4	40.3	40.4	40.4	40.2	40.2	40.4	40.2	40.4	40.3
2006	39.9	40.0	40.0	40.0	40.0	40.1	40.1	40.0	39.8	40.0	40.2	40.4	40.0
2007	40.1	40.2	40.4	39.4	39.6	39.8	39.7	39.7	39.8	39.8	40.0	40.1	39.9
2008	39.5	39.6	39.7	39.7	39.6	39.6	39.8	39.9	39.4	39.3	39.2	39.2	39.5
2009	38.8	38.9	38.7	38.5	38.4	38.4	38.2	37.9	37.7	37.6	37.4	37.3	38.2
2010	36.8	36.9	37.0	36.9	37.0	37.0	37.0	36.9	36.9	37.6	37.8	37.9	37.1
2011	37.6	37.6	37.6	37.6	37.5	37.1	37.4	37.4	37.5	37.3	37.4	37.6	37.5

Employment by Industry: Birmingham–Hoover, AL, Selected Years, 2000–2011—*Continued*

(Numbers in thousands, not seasonally adjusted)

Industry and year	January	February	March	April	May	June	July	August	September	October	November	December	Annual average
Financial Activities													
2000	40.3	40.4	40.5	40.7	40.7	40.9	41.4	41.4	41.2	40.9	40.9	41.0	40.9
2001	40.5	40.7	40.7	41.1	41.2	41.5	41.4	41.5	41.2	41.2	41.1	41.2	41.1
2002	41.0	40.8	40.7	40.8	41.0	41.0	41.0	41.0	40.8	40.9	41.0	41.2	40.9
2003	40.1	40.0	39.9	40.2	40.2	40.4	40.5	40.3	40.2	40.2	40.3	40.4	40.2
2004	40.0	40.1	40.1	40.1	40.2	40.4	40.3	40.3	40.1	40.4	40.4	40.5	40.2
2005	39.9	40.1	40.3	40.4	40.3	40.4	40.4	40.2	40.2	40.4	40.5	40.7	40.3
2006	39.9	40.0	40.0	40.0	40.0	40.1	40.1	40.0	39.8	40.0	40.2	40.4	40.0
2007	40.1	40.2	40.4	39.4	39.6	39.8	39.7	39.7	39.8	39.8	40.0	40.1	39.9
2008	39.5	39.6	39.7	39.7	39.6	39.6	39.8	39.9	39.4	39.3	39.2	39.2	39.5
2009	38.8	38.9	38.7	38.5	38.4	38.4	38.2	37.9	37.7	37.6	37.4	37.3	38.2
2010	36.8	36.9	37.0	36.9	37.0	37.0	37.0	36.9	36.9	37.6	37.8	37.9	37.1
2011	37.6	37.6	37.6	37.6	37.5	37.1	37.4	37.4	37.5	37.3	37.4	37.6	37.5
Professional and Business Services													
2000	61.6	62.1	62.6	62.9	62.7	63.6	63.3	63.8	64.0	63.5	63.5	63.2	63.1
2001	62.4	62.7	63.4	63.9	64.0	64.8	64.5	64.6	64.2	64.2	64.0	64.0	63.9
2002	62.8	63.0	63.8	63.6	63.2	63.4	62.4	62.6	62.1	61.5	61.3	61.0	62.6
2003	59.6	60.2	60.5	60.3	60.4	60.7	60.8	61.3	60.8	61.0	60.8	61.0	60.6
2004	59.7	59.9	60.1	60.8	61.2	61.8	62.7	62.8	62.6	63.4	63.5	63.6	61.8
2005	63.7	64.5	64.8	65.2	65.2	65.4	66.4	66.2	66.7	67.1	67.5	67.5	65.9
2006	66.8	67.2	67.7	67.9	67.7	69.0	68.6	69.1	69.2	68.9	69.0	69.1	68.4
2007	68.1	68.8	68.7	68.0	68.1	68.3	67.5	67.9	67.7	67.8	68.5	68.1	68.1
2008	66.3	66.6	66.2	66.5	66.7	67.0	65.9	65.9	65.6	65.6	65.4	64.9	66.1
2009	62.0	61.6	61.0	60.5	60.1	59.8	59.3	59.0	58.6	59.4	59.6	59.1	60.0
2010	58.9	59.1	59.2	60.0	59.8	59.4	60.2	60.0	59.3	59.9	59.7	59.5	59.6
2011	58.6	59.2	59.4	60.2	60.2	60.8	61.1	61.5	61.2	61.5	61.5	62.1	60.6
Education and Health Services													
2000	54.5	55.1	55.2	55.4	55.4	55.3	56.1	56.2	56.4	56.6	56.8	56.6	55.8
2001	55.6	56.5	56.6	57.0	56.8	56.6	56.5	56.3	57.0	57.5	58.1	58.0	56.9
2002	57.1	58.3	58.5	58.7	58.4	58.2	59.6	59.1	60.2	59.9	60.2	59.7	59.0
2003	59.0	59.8	60.1	60.1	59.8	59.4	59.4	59.5	59.7	60.1	60.7	60.5	59.8
2004	59.8	60.4	60.7	60.8	60.6	60.5	60.5	60.6	61.0	61.1	61.5	61.4	60.7
2005	60.9	61.4	61.7	62.0	62.1	61.9	62.2	62.1	62.1	62.4	62.5	62.5	62.0
2006	61.2	61.9	61.9	62.2	62.2	62.1	62.1	62.3	62.5	62.8	63.5	63.0	62.3
2007	62.2	62.7	62.8	63.3	63.6	63.7	64.0	64.5	64.3	64.6	64.7	64.9	63.8
2008	64.0	64.5	64.7	64.6	65.1	65.0	65.0	65.1	65.2	65.8	65.2	65.1	64.9
2009	63.9	64.1	64.1	64.5	64.6	64.2	65.1	65.0	65.1	65.4	66.3	65.6	64.8
2010	65.0	65.6	65.3	65.6	65.7	65.6	65.7	65.6	65.6	65.9	66.2	65.6	65.6
2011	64.6	64.9	65.5	65.4	65.6	65.2	65.2	65.0	65.5	65.1	65.3	64.8	65.2
Leisure and Hospitality													
2000	38.2	38.9	39.6	39.5	40.4	41.0	39.7	39.8	39.3	39.1	39.1	39.2	39.5
2001	38.2	38.9	39.8	40.2	40.6	41.5	40.7	40.8	40.0	39.4	39.2	39.3	39.9
2002	38.0	38.4	38.9	39.4	39.9	40.3	40.2	40.1	39.7	38.5	38.7	38.6	39.2
2003	37.4	38.0	38.6	39.7	40.3	40.8	40.5	40.9	40.5	39.8	39.8	40.1	39.7
2004	38.7	39.2	40.3	41.1	41.8	42.7	42.5	42.4	41.6	41.3	41.3	40.9	41.2
2005	40.5	40.9	42.1	43.2	43.8	44.5	43.8	43.8	43.5	42.0	42.2	42.0	42.7
2006	41.2	42.1	42.9	43.8	44.7	45.5	45.1	45.4	44.7	43.2	42.9	42.8	43.7
2007	42.4	42.9	43.9	43.8	44.7	45.1	45.1	45.3	44.4	44.0	43.9	44.2	44.1
2008	42.2	42.8	43.4	44.7	45.8	46.3	45.6	45.7	44.6	44.2	44.0	43.8	44.4
2009	41.4	41.9	42.4	43.2	44.1	44.3	43.5	43.3	43.4	42.7	42.8	42.8	43.0
2010	40.7	41.0	41.6	42.7	43.3	43.8	43.0	42.8	42.7	42.5	43.0	43.0	42.5
2011	40.7	41.3	42.1	43.2	43.7	44.8	44.3	43.4	41.5	41.2	41.0	40.8	42.3
Other Services													
2000	24.8	25.0	25.4	25.3	25.2	25.7	25.7	25.5	25.2	25.3	25.2	25.4	25.3
2001	25.0	25.0	25.0	25.2	25.1	25.3	25.5	25.5	25.4	25.4	25.3	25.3	25.3
2002	25.5	25.7	25.7	25.5	25.6	25.7	25.9	25.8	25.5	25.3	25.4	25.2	25.6
2003	24.6	24.6	24.6	24.8	24.9	25.1	25.0	25.0	24.6	24.4	24.2	24.1	24.7
2004	23.8	23.9	24.0	23.9	23.9	24.2	24.3	24.2	23.8	23.7	23.8	23.8	23.9
2005	23.5	23.5	23.5	23.6	23.6	23.8	23.8	23.6	23.3	23.2	23.2	23.1	23.5
2006	23.0	23.1	23.2	23.3	23.3	23.9	23.7	23.6	23.4	23.1	23.3	23.3	23.4
2007	23.3	23.3	23.6	23.7	23.8	23.9	24.1	24.0	23.7	23.8	23.9	24.0	23.8
2008	24.0	24.2	24.2	24.3	24.3	24.7	24.8	24.6	24.2	24.1	24.0	23.9	24.3
2009	23.8	23.8	23.8	23.7	23.9	24.4	24.4	24.1	23.5	23.5	23.5	23.5	23.8
2010	23.4	23.5	23.6	23.6	23.7	24.3	24.4	24.1	23.5	23.8	23.6	23.4	23.7
2011	22.9	23.1	23.2	23.3	23.4	23.8	23.8	23.6	23.2	23.2	23.3	23.2	23.3
Government													
2000	75.1	75.3	75.9	75.9	77.4	74.0	72.9	71.4	75.1	76.2	76.0	76.2	75.1
2001	75.8	76.3	76.3	76.1	76.4	75.3	73.1	72.7	75.3	76.6	76.7	76.6	75.6
2002	76.0	76.3	76.6	76.7	77.1	75.9	73.3	72.9	76.4	77.7	78.2	78.2	76.3
2003	77.5	78.1	78.4	79.0	79.1	77.2	75.4	75.5	78.3	78.8	79.1	79.4	78.0
2004	79.0	79.1	78.9	79.5	79.1	78.3	76.5	76.5	78.7	79.1	79.6	79.5	78.7
2005	78.8	79.3	79.5	79.8	79.9	79.4	76.9	77.5	79.7	80.7	80.9	80.7	79.4
2006	81.4	81.6	81.7	82.2	82.4	82.3	79.1	79.6	82.3	83.0	83.2	83.3	81.8
2007	82.9	83.3	83.5	83.5	83.8	83.6	80.0	80.7	83.3	83.9	84.1	84.0	83.1
2008	83.6	84.0	84.2	84.4	84.7	84.7	81.1	81.6	83.6	85.0	84.9	85.2	83.9
2009	84.5	84.6	84.6	85.0	84.8	84.8	80.6	80.9	83.1	83.9	84.3	84.2	83.8
2010	83.9	84.1	84.6	85.0	87.3	86.0	81.9	81.2	83.0	83.9	83.9	84.0	84.1
2011	83.7	83.8	83.9	83.9	84.0	83.7	80.5	79.9	82.4	82.2	81.6	81.3	82.6

Employment by Industry: Boston–Cambridge–Quincy, MA–NH, NECTA, Selected Years, 2000–2011

(Numbers in thousands, not seasonally adjusted)

Industry and year	January	February	March	April	May	June	July	August	September	October	November	December	Annual average
Total Nonfarm													
2000	2,469.0	2,480.9	2,499.9	2,523.4	2,535.3	2,559.3	2,531.5	2,525.8	2,558.7	2,578.2	2,595.4	2,608.4	2,538.8
2001	2,531.3	2,535.2	2,539.7	2,553.7	2,557.2	2,565.7	2,523.3	2,515.2	2,521.8	2,524.1	2,524.7	2,526.4	2,534.9
2002	2,451.2	2,444.9	2,457.0	2,472.1	2,480.6	2,487.1	2,450.7	2,443.9	2,464.3	2,472.6	2,480.8	2,482.4	2,465.6
2003	2,394.3	2,384.3	2,392.5	2,413.6	2,423.7	2,430.4	2,401.9	2,391.6	2,414.1	2,419.9	2,429.6	2,426.5	2,410.2
2004	2,353.9	2,359.2	2,373.7	2,401.3	2,412.9	2,423.8	2,405.6	2,395.0	2,417.0	2,430.1	2,438.3	2,443.9	2,404.6
2005	2,370.7	2,379.7	2,385.6	2,421.4	2,431.1	2,443.3	2,422.7	2,415.8	2,439.2	2,447.9	2,462.1	2,468.4	2,424.0
2006	2,398.5	2,403.8	2,417.9	2,442.0	2,451.9	2,471.9	2,448.9	2,443.0	2,468.5	2,480.3	2,490.6	2,498.2	2,451.3
2007	2,435.2	2,436.4	2,446.3	2,474.5	2,493.4	2,510.1	2,483.9	2,478.1	2,497.2	2,511.9	2,524.1	2,524.8	2,484.7
2008	2,463.8	2,467.0	2,476.0	2,499.6	2,513.0	2,523.7	2,496.8	2,487.5	2,503.6	2,516.1	2,509.4	2,499.3	2,496.3
2009	2,413.0	2,407.1	2,402.3	2,423.7	2,428.4	2,429.6	2,396.9	2,388.9	2,411.5	2,430.7	2,433.5	2,436.2	2,416.8
2010	2,384.7	2,384.4	2,394.0	2,423.1	2,440.3	2,439.6	2,420.9	2,414.1	2,430.6	2,458.0	2,462.2	2,466.6	2,426.5
2011	2,397.7	2,404.6	2,416.6	2,449.7	2,456.3	2,463.1	2,447.5	2,434.7	2,447.5	2,467.8	2,469.2	2,464.3	2,443.3
Total Private													
2000	2,168.6	2,177.1	2,194.1	2,216.6	2,223.7	2,251.5	2,245.9	2,245.6	2,257.3	2,274.4	2,289.9	2,303.0	2,237.3
2001	2,227.2	2,228.2	2,232.6	2,245.9	2,248.9	2,259.6	2,236.9	2,231.0	2,217.0	2,218.3	2,217.9	2,218.8	2,231.9
2002	2,146.7	2,138.0	2,149.7	2,165.7	2,173.9	2,181.9	2,167.3	2,164.1	2,159.2	2,170.0	2,175.6	2,177.5	2,164.1
2003	2,093.5	2,081.1	2,089.6	2,110.3	2,120.8	2,128.9	2,119.1	2,115.3	2,114.4	2,122.0	2,130.6	2,128.1	2,112.8
2004	2,059.5	2,060.8	2,075.0	2,101.9	2,114.3	2,127.4	2,131.3	2,126.9	2,122.1	2,133.3	2,139.8	2,145.7	2,111.5
2005	2,075.3	2,079.5	2,085.5	2,120.6	2,130.1	2,145.9	2,146.7	2,145.7	2,143.2	2,148.3	2,160.4	2,167.9	2,129.1
2006	2,101.0	2,101.8	2,115.6	2,139.4	2,148.9	2,171.9	2,169.9	2,170.7	2,169.7	2,178.3	2,186.9	2,195.2	2,154.1
2007	2,134.7	2,132.5	2,141.9	2,169.2	2,187.1	2,207.8	2,205.1	2,205.5	2,196.4	2,207.0	2,217.2	2,218.6	2,185.3
2008	2,160.1	2,159.1	2,167.8	2,190.1	2,203.0	2,216.4	2,213.7	2,210.5	2,198.7	2,206.9	2,198.8	2,189.2	2,192.9
2009	2,107.2	2,095.8	2,091.5	2,109.2	2,116.2	2,121.8	2,116.4	2,111.3	2,106.9	2,120.9	2,123.3	2,124.7	2,112.1
2010	2,077.4	2,074.6	2,083.5	2,111.0	2,122.8	2,130.4	2,138.6	2,134.6	2,125.8	2,149.7	2,151.6	2,156.0	2,121.3
2011	2,095.3	2,096.4	2,108.1	2,141.8	2,148.0	2,158.5	2,166.7	2,160.2	2,147.0	2,163.1	2,163.7	2,157.0	2,142.2
Goods-Producing													
2000	380.9	379.9	384.4	390.4	394.0	401.6	397.6	401.2	401.1	401.8	402.8	402.2	394.8
2001	392.1	390.6	390.7	396.4	397.9	399.4	393.9	392.6	388.4	384.8	379.2	374.8	390.1
2002	362.4	356.6	357.9	362.0	365.7	367.2	362.6	363.0	360.5	360.1	358.0	352.8	360.7
2003	340.7	333.4	334.0	339.6	343.4	345.7	342.4	342.9	340.4	337.9	337.0	332.5	339.2
2004	319.9	318.2	322.2	329.7	335.3	340.0	339.7	340.9	338.3	335.2	334.1	331.6	332.1
2005	320.1	317.7	318.3	326.2	330.3	335.1	335.6	336.7	334.7	332.3	332.0	329.2	329.0
2006	318.9	316.5	317.8	324.2	327.3	331.7	332.1	333.4	331.6	329.6	327.2	325.1	326.3
2007	315.8	311.9	313.5	317.8	323.8	328.9	329.2	329.6	327.2	325.2	323.6	319.7	322.2
2008	309.7	306.9	308.4	312.7	316.7	320.1	320.6	320.4	317.0	314.0	309.6	302.9	313.3
2009	286.3	280.1	277.1	279.5	280.5	282.4	282.1	281.6	279.1	278.5	276.8	273.8	279.8
2010	264.9	261.9	263.3	268.3	272.8	276.7	279.6	279.4	277.6	278.6	277.5	275.2	273.0
2011	265.6	263.3	265.1	272.4	275.6	280.0	281.4	282.5	279.3	280.0	279.1	276.9	275.1
Mining and Logging													
2000	0.8	0.7	0.8	1.0	1.0	1.1	0.9	1.0	1.0	1.0	1.0	0.9	0.9
2001	0.8	0.8	0.8	0.9	1.0	1.0	1.0	1.0	1.0	1.0	1.0	1.0	0.9
2002	0.8	0.8	0.9	1.0	1.1	1.1	1.1	1.1	1.1	1.1	1.1	1.1	1.0
2003	1.0	0.9	0.9	1.1	1.2	1.2	1.3	1.2	1.3	1.3	1.3	1.2	1.2
2004	1.0	1.0	1.0	1.2	1.3	1.3	1.3	1.3	1.3	1.3	1.3	1.3	1.2
2005	1.1	1.0	1.0	1.3	1.3	1.4	1.4	1.3	1.3	1.3	1.3	1.1	1.2
2006	1.0	1.0	1.0	1.1	1.2	1.2	1.3	1.2	1.2	1.2	1.2	1.1	1.1
2007	0.9	0.8	0.9	1.0	1.1	1.1	1.1	1.1	1.1	1.0	1.0	0.9	1.0
2008	0.7	0.7	0.7	0.8	0.9	0.9	0.9	0.8	0.8	0.8	0.8	0.7	0.8
2009	0.7	0.6	0.6	0.7	0.8	0.8	0.8	0.8	0.8	0.8	0.8	0.7	0.7
2010	0.6	0.5	0.6	0.7	0.7	0.7	0.6	0.6	0.6	0.6	0.6	0.5	0.6
2011	0.4	0.4	0.4	0.5	0.6	0.6	0.6	0.6	0.6	0.6	0.6	0.5	0.5
Construction													
2000	84.7	83.3	86.9	93	96.2	100.2	103	104	102.7	103.1	102.7	100.8	96.7
2001	93.7	92.6	94.0	100.7	104.7	107.6	109.7	109.7	107.4	107.8	106.3	103.5	103.1
2002	96.7	93.9	95.9	102.6	106.8	108.1	109.1	109.3	107.6	108.9	107.8	102.9	104.1
2003	95.0	90.5	91.6	98.6	103.0	104.8	105.8	106.0	104.5	103.2	102.4	98.9	100.4
2004	90.0	88.6	91.6	97.9	103.0	106.0	107.5	107.6	105.9	104.4	103.7	101.1	100.6
2005	91.5	89.2	90.3	98.5	102.4	105.7	108.2	108.6	107.7	105.5	105.4	102.5	101.3
2006	94.4	92.5	94.0	100.9	103.6	106.3	107.7	108.1	106.6	105.2	102.9	100.2	101.9
2007	92.4	88.9	90.5	95.5	100.8	104.3	106.1	106.3	105.1	104.1	102.9	98.9	99.7
2008	90.8	88.7	90.5	95.3	98.9	100.9	102.7	102.3	100.3	98.7	95.6	91.0	96.3
2009	80.1	76.6	75.9	80.0	82.4	84.1	85.1	84.9	83.5	83.0	80.8	77.7	81.2
2010	71.1	68.8	70.0	75.1	78.6	81.2	83.7	83.5	82.2	82.0	80.9	78.5	78.0
2011	71.7	69.9	71.3	77.5	80.6	83.5	84.7	85.2	82.5	82.6	81.7	78.8	79.2
Manufacturing													
2000	295.4	295.9	296.7	296.4	296.8	300.3	293.7	296.2	297.4	297.7	299.1	300.5	297.2
2001	297.6	297.2	295.9	294.8	292.2	290.8	283.2	281.9	280.0	276.0	271.9	270.3	286.0
2002	264.9	261.9	261.1	258.4	257.8	258.0	252.4	252.6	251.8	250.1	249.1	248.8	255.6
2003	244.7	242.0	241.5	239.9	239.2	239.7	235.3	235.7	234.6	233.4	233.3	232.4	237.6
2004	228.9	228.6	229.6	230.6	231.0	232.7	230.9	232.0	231.1	229.5	229.1	229.2	230.3
2005	227.5	227.5	227.0	226.4	226.6	228.0	226.0	226.8	225.7	225.5	225.3	225.6	226.5
2006	223.5	223.0	222.8	222.2	222.5	224.2	223.1	224.1	223.8	223.2	223.1	223.8	223.3
2007	222.5	222.2	222.1	221.3	221.9	223.5	222.0	222.2	221.0	220.1	219.7	219.9	221.5
2008	218.2	217.5	217.2	216.6	216.9	218.3	217.0	217.3	215.9	214.5	213.2	211.2	216.2
2009	205.5	202.9	200.6	198.8	197.3	197.5	196.2	195.9	194.8	194.7	195.2	195.4	197.9
2010	193.2	192.6	192.7	192.5	193.5	194.8	195.3	195.3	194.8	196.0	196.0	196.2	194.4
2011	193.5	193	193.4	194.4	194.4	195.9	196.1	196.7	196.2	196.8	196.8	197.6	195.4

Employment by Industry: Boston–Cambridge–Quincy, MA–NH, NECTA, Selected Years, 2000–2011—*Continued*

(Numbers in thousands, not seasonally adjusted)

Industry and year	January	February	March	April	May	June	July	August	September	October	November	December	Annual average
Service-Providing													
2000	2,088.1	2,101.0	2,115.5	2,133.0	2,141.3	2,157.7	2,133.9	2,124.6	2,157.6	2,176.4	2,192.6	2,206.2	2,144.0
2001	2,139.2	2,144.6	2,149.0	2,157.3	2,159.3	2,166.3	2,129.4	2,122.6	2,133.4	2,139.3	2,145.5	2,151.6	2,144.8
2002	2,088.8	2,088.3	2,099.1	2,110.1	2,114.9	2,119.9	2,088.1	2,080.9	2,103.8	2,112.5	2,122.8	2,129.6	2,104.9
2003	2,053.6	2,050.9	2,058.5	2,074.0	2,080.3	2,084.7	2,059.5	2,048.7	2,073.7	2,082.0	2,092.6	2,094.0	2,071.0
2004	2,034.0	2,041.0	2,051.5	2,071.6	2,077.6	2,083.8	2,065.9	2,054.1	2,078.7	2,094.9	2,104.2	2,112.3	2,072.5
2005	2,050.6	2,062.0	2,067.3	2,095.2	2,100.8	2,108.2	2,087.1	2,079.1	2,104.5	2,115.6	2,130.1	2,139.2	2,095.0
2006	2,079.6	2,087.3	2,100.1	2,117.8	2,124.6	2,140.2	2,116.8	2,109.6	2,136.9	2,150.7	2,163.4	2,173.1	2,125.0
2007	2,119.4	2,124.5	2,132.8	2,156.7	2,169.6	2,181.2	2,154.7	2,148.5	2,170.0	2,186.7	2,200.5	2,205.1	2,162.5
2008	2,154.1	2,160.1	2,167.6	2,186.9	2,196.3	2,203.6	2,176.2	2,167.1	2,186.6	2,202.1	2,199.8	2,196.4	2,183.1
2009	2,126.7	2,127.0	2,125.2	2,144.2	2,147.9	2,147.2	2,114.8	2,107.3	2,132.4	2,152.2	2,156.7	2,162.4	2,137.0
2010	2,119.8	2,122.5	2,130.7	2,154.8	2,167.5	2,162.9	2,141.3	2,134.7	2,153.0	2,179.4	2,184.7	2,191.4	2,153.6
2011	2,132.1	2,141.3	2,151.5	2,177.3	2,180.7	2,183.1	2,166.1	2,152.2	2,168.2	2,187.8	2,190.1	2,187.4	2,168.2
Trade, Transportation, and Utilities													
2000	446.1	441.2	441.7	443.6	445.2	450.3	443.6	443.6	446.7	454.0	464.2	474.4	449.6
2001	450.4	442.5	442.2	442.4	443.5	448.4	440.4	439.2	438.8	441.7	449.9	455.9	444.6
2002	434.4	426.5	427.5	428.5	431.2	436.0	430.0	428.5	430.6	433.3	441.0	449.4	433.1
2003	426.0	419.3	420.7	421.5	423.9	428.5	422.7	422.2	424.3	428.5	436.7	442.0	426.4
2004	422.9	417.4	417.9	417.8	420.4	424.8	419.8	418.4	417.9	425.5	433.0	440.5	423.0
2005	420.1	415.8	414.8	417.6	420.2	423.8	418.8	418.5	417.7	420.9	428.5	437.5	421.2
2006	419.6	411.2	413.1	414.5	416.7	421.8	416.1	416.2	417.3	421.4	430.1	438.4	419.7
2007	419.3	411.1	411.9	412.0	417.1	422.4	416.8	415.9	415.7	420.3	430.1	435.9	419.0
2008	421.1	411.6	412.0	413.2	416.6	420.9	416.4	415.9	414.4	417.3	421.1	425.9	417.2
2009	404.2	395.8	392.7	392.3	395.7	400.0	393.9	392.6	394.4	399.6	406.0	411.1	398.2
2010	397.4	390.5	390.8	393.5	397.1	401.1	397.8	397.2	395.3	402.0	408.2	416.1	398.9
2011	399.8	394.2	394.5	398.6	400.8	404.9	403.2	405.8	401.9	407.3	412.5	418.7	403.5
Wholesale Trade													
2000	109.3	109.3	109.8	109.9	110.6	112.1	111.0	111.1	111.3	112.4	113.0	114.2	111.2
2001	111.9	112.0	112.1	111.8	111.4	111.8	111.5	110.8	109.5	109.2	108.7	108.7	110.8
2002	107.1	106.6	106.9	105.9	106.0	106.7	105.7	105.2	104.4	104.7	104.7	105.2	105.8
2003	104.7	104.2	104.1	103.7	103.9	104.4	104.5	104.4	103.6	103.8	104.2	104.7	104.2
2004	102.8	102.6	103.2	102.9	102.6	103.2	102.8	102.5	101.3	101.3	101.2	101.3	102.3
2005	100.8	100.6	100.2	100.9	101.5	102.1	102.8	102.8	102.3	103.1	103.4	104.1	102.1
2006	103.0	102.6	102.8	103.4	103.5	104.7	104.9	105.2	104.5	104.8	104.9	105.4	104.1
2007	104.3	103.9	104.2	103.8	104.1	105.1	104.9	104.6	103.7	103.8	103.5	103.6	104.1
2008	102.6	101.6	101.5	101.9	101.9	102.6	102.5	101.9	100.8	100.3	99.7	99.4	101.4
2009	97.0	95.6	94.9	94.2	93.8	94.0	93.3	92.8	91.6	92.2	91.8	91.7	93.6
2010	90.6	90.3	90.4	90.5	91.2	91.7	92.1	92.0	91.1	91.5	91.5	91.6	91.2
2011	90.9	90.7	91.0	91.8	92.0	92.5	93.9	95.5	93.9	94.1	94.6	94.8	93.0
Retail Trade													
2000	263.7	258.7	259.0	259.1	260.0	262.8	259.5	259.4	260.1	265.3	275.5	284.9	264.0
2001	265.5	257.4	257.5	257.0	258.2	262.2	257.5	257.5	256.2	259.6	269.9	277.0	261.3
2002	259.7	252.6	253.5	255.1	257.0	260.6	258.3	257.8	257.8	259.5	267.5	276.0	259.6
2003	255.0	249.2	250.5	251.7	253.2	257.1	254.3	254.4	254.2	258.5	266.3	271.5	256.3
2004	256.6	251.8	251.7	251.1	253.4	257.1	254.9	254.5	253.2	259.6	267.5	275.3	257.2
2005	257.2	253.1	252.6	254.3	255.7	258.3	254.8	255.0	252.9	256.4	263.8	271.4	257.1
2006	256.7	248.8	250.2	250.7	252.0	254.8	251.0	251.3	249.5	253.8	262.5	269.3	254.2
2007	253.2	245.9	246.1	246.5	250.4	253.6	251.1	250.8	248.5	253.2	263.7	268.6	252.6
2008	256.7	248.7	248.8	249.2	251.4	254.3	252.6	253.4	249.9	253.9	258.9	263.1	253.4
2009	246.9	240.3	238.1	238.1	241.3	244.8	242.5	242.8	241.7	246.3	253.2	257.2	244.4
2010	246.6	240.4	240.5	242.5	244.6	247.5	246.9	247.4	243.4	249.4	255.8	262.1	247.3
2011	249.2	244.0	243.7	246.3	247.6	250.2	249.7	250.1	245.8	250.6	256.9	261.3	249.6
Transportation and Utilities													
2000	73.1	73.2	72.9	74.6	74.6	75.4	73.1	73.1	75.3	76.3	75.7	75.3	74.4
2001	73.0	73.1	72.6	73.6	73.9	74.4	71.4	70.9	73.1	72.9	71.3	70.2	72.5
2002	67.6	67.3	67.1	67.5	68.2	68.7	66.0	65.5	68.4	69.1	68.8	68.2	67.7
2003	66.3	65.9	66.1	66.1	66.8	67.0	63.9	63.4	66.5	66.2	66.2	65.8	65.9
2004	63.5	63.0	63.0	63.8	64.4	64.5	62.1	61.4	63.4	64.6	64.3	63.9	63.5
2005	62.1	62.1	62.0	62.4	63.0	63.4	61.2	60.7	62.5	61.4	61.3	62.0	62.0
2006	59.9	59.8	60.1	60.4	61.2	62.3	60.2	59.7	63.3	62.8	62.7	63.7	61.3
2007	61.8	61.3	61.6	61.7	62.6	63.7	60.8	60.5	63.5	63.3	62.9	63.7	62.3
2008	61.8	61.3	61.7	62.1	63.3	64.0	61.3	60.6	63.7	63.1	62.5	63.4	62.4
2009	60.3	59.9	59.7	60.0	60.6	61.2	58.1	57.0	61.1	61.1	61.0	62.2	60.2
2010	60.2	59.8	59.9	60.5	61.3	61.9	58.8	57.8	60.8	61.1	60.9	62.4	60.5
2011	59.7	59.5	59.8	60.5	61.2	62.2	59.6	60.2	62.2	62.6	61.0	62.6	60.9
Information													
2000	89.5	90.4	92.1	93.5	95.0	97.4	99.3	93.6	99.5	99.7	100.3	100.9	95.9
2001	99.8	99.7	99.0	99.4	98.0	97.9	96.2	95.2	93.3	91.3	90.5	89.8	95.8
2002	88.2	87.5	87.2	85.6	84.9	84.7	84.1	84.3	82.0	82.0	81.8	81.9	84.5
2003	79.5	79.1	79.0	78.0	77.6	78.0	76.9	76.5	75.7	75.4	75.2	75.2	77.2
2004	73.8	73.4	74.0	73.3	73.5	73.7	73.9	73.9	73.5	73.4	73.8	74.1	73.7
2005	73.4	73.6	73.6	73.7	73.8	74.4	74.6	74.3	73.7	73.8	74.0	74.3	73.9
2006	74.0	74.1	74.1	73.7	74.0	74.6	74.4	74.5	73.6	74.5	74.6	74.9	74.3
2007	73.6	73.8	74.0	74.2	74.5	75.3	75.5	75.5	75.0	74.5	74.7	74.9	74.6
2008	74.8	75.2	75.4	75.1	75.1	76.0	76.4	76.5	75.7	75.3	75.0	75.0	75.5
2009	74.8	73.6	73.3	72.7	72.6	72.8	72.7	72.9	72.6	72.8	72.9	73.1	73.1
2010	73.3	73.2	73.1	73.3	73.4	74.1	73.7	73.4	72.6	71.8	72.0	72.2	73.0
2011	71.5	71.6	71.8	71.8	72.1	72.8	73.9	68.5	73.6	73.0	73.1	72.9	72.2

Employment by Industry: Boston–Cambridge–Quincy, MA–NH, NECTA, Selected Years, 2000–2011—*Continued*

(Numbers in thousands, not seasonally adjusted)

Industry and year	January	February	March	April	May	June	July	August	September	October	November	December	Annual average
Financial Activities													
2000	189.0	188.4	188.9	189.1	189.1	192.7	193.0	193.6	192.4	193.6	194.2	196.3	191.7
2001	195.9	196.0	197.1	194.2	193.9	196.4	197.4	197.4	194.7	193.8	194.3	195.3	195.5
2002	195.0	193.7	193.1	190.6	190.9	192.7	193.1	192.6	189.8	190.4	189.8	190.5	191.9
2003	188.5	187.3	187.2	187.1	187.3	188.4	188.3	188.2	184.9	183.7	184.0	184.4	186.6
2004	181.8	182.1	182.3	182.5	182.7	184.9	186.1	185.5	183.4	182.1	182.1	183.1	183.2
2005	182.5	182.4	182.6	183.2	184.1	186.9	189.7	189.9	188.6	187.0	187.8	189.4	186.2
2006	185.7	185.6	185.9	186.1	186.8	189.3	191.6	191.1	189.4	188.9	189.4	190.9	188.4
2007	188.5	188.5	188.5	188.5	189.0	191.3	191.8	191.8	188.7	187.5	187.2	188.2	189.1
2008	186.0	185.6	185.8	185.6	185.9	187.7	188.7	188.4	185.6	184.9	184.3	184.4	186.1
2009	181.8	180.6	179.9	178.9	178.8	179.8	179.6	178.7	176.2	175.8	175.8	176.0	178.5
2010	174.1	173.3	173.0	172.8	173.6	175.0	175.9	175.7	173.4	173.3	173.0	174.1	173.9
2011	171.9	171.6	171.6	172.1	172.4	173.8	174.6	174.0	172.3	171.7	170.4	171.1	172.3
Professional and Business Services													
2000	395.0	398.2	403.5	409.9	411.5	422.0	425.3	427.9	427.3	426.7	428.6	429.9	417.2
2001	416.7	414.9	415.6	417.6	416.7	418.7	410.8	409.2	403.3	399.6	396.3	395.2	409.6
2002	382.0	378.7	380.0	385.3	384.9	387.5	385.2	384.4	381.1	381.2	380.2	379.0	382.5
2003	363.4	359.4	359.7	367.0	367.7	370.5	371.8	371.6	369.9	371.2	372.4	371.9	368.0
2004	361.4	361.4	364.1	373.5	374.7	380.0	383.2	383.9	382.8	383.4	383.7	385.0	376.4
2005	372.6	373.1	374.8	384.2	384.9	390.2	391.4	392.2	390.9	390.9	393.3	393.4	386.0
2006	382.5	383.8	386.3	393.5	395.2	402.6	402.1	403.1	401.2	402.4	403.9	403.9	396.7
2007	393.5	395.3	397.6	406.9	409.8	415.4	415.2	417.2	412.9	415.0	416.5	417.0	409.4
2008	408.1	408.9	409.8	415.9	417.9	422.1	421.2	419.9	416.6	416.9	413.3	409.0	415.0
2009	395.4	391.0	389.3	393.0	391.4	393.7	392.2	391.1	387.9	389.8	389.7	390.2	391.2
2010	384.0	384.2	385.7	394.3	394.6	397.4	400.7	400.0	395.3	400.1	399.6	398.7	394.6
2011	391.3	391.1	391.4	401.8	401.3	405.2	405.1	406.2	404.3	406.6	405.9	401.9	401.0
Education and Health Services													
2000	404.1	413.1	414.2	412.9	406.2	395.9	393.3	392.9	403.9	413.2	417.3	417.7	407.1
2001	402.8	413.6	413.8	415.7	410.2	400.7	400.2	399.8	410.2	421.5	425.1	426.1	411.6
2002	413.5	423.2	426.2	427.2	421.0	410.3	408.9	407.8	420.1	430.0	435.1	434.9	421.5
2003	419.3	427.6	430.5	431.7	425.1	414.8	413.3	411.0	424.0	432.9	436.7	436.2	425.3
2004	423.9	433.3	435.5	437.1	430.6	420.3	420.8	418.0	429.0	439.0	442.1	441.7	430.9
2005	429.0	438.9	440.1	443.8	437.0	426.4	426.5	424.9	436.6	447.2	451.2	451.4	437.8
2006	439.2	449.7	453.0	453.8	448.3	440.4	438.5	437.1	450.2	458.9	462.6	462.8	449.5
2007	455.5	463.8	464.9	470.8	464.6	454.0	454.8	452.9	463.9	474.7	478.0	478.3	464.7
2008	464.4	476.5	478.9	481.4	474.9	465.0	465.2	463.4	473.9	485.2	488.1	488.5	475.6
2009	476.6	486.3	488.5	492.4	485.2	473.7	476.2	475.1	486.2	496.1	499.5	499.9	486.3
2010	490.2	499.8	502.3	499.9	493.4	479.8	481.9	480.5	493.0	504.1	507.4	507.2	495.0
2011	494.7	505.4	508.5	507.4	500.9	487.3	489.1	484.0	492.1	504.0	507.0	505.4	498.8
Leisure and Hospitality													
2000	181.8	183.2	186.1	193.6	198.5	206.0	207.7	207.0	202.4	200.6	197.4	196.1	196.7
2001	185.5	186.6	189.3	194.9	202.6	210.7	210.1	209.8	202.4	199.5	196.1	194.8	198.5
2002	185.9	186.4	191.4	200.0	207.9	215.2	214.7	215.0	208.7	206.1	202.6	201.6	203.0
2003	190.5	189.6	192.2	199.3	209.1	215.5	215.8	215.7	209.4	206.9	202.5	199.9	203.9
2004	190.8	190.2	193.3	202.3	210.8	217.3	220.5	219.3	212.2	209.7	205.6	203.9	206.3
2005	193.2	193.5	196.1	205.6	213.3	221.4	221.7	221.2	214.4	210.4	207.4	205.7	208.7
2006	195.4	195.7	199.1	207.0	213.7	223.2	226.0	226.1	219.3	215.4	212.5	211.7	212.1
2007	202.3	201.5	204.2	211.3	219.3	229.6	230.1	230.9	223.7	220.9	217.5	215.0	217.2
2008	206.1	206.4	209.0	217.2	226.2	233.4	232.7	233.6	225.8	223.8	218.0	214.4	220.6
2009	200.7	201.2	202.8	211.3	221.9	226.8	226.6	226.6	221.2	219.3	213.7	211.6	215.3
2010	205.8	204.2	207.0	219.4	227.1	232.8	233.7	233.6	227.5	228.8	222.7	220.8	222.0
2011	210.6	208.8	213.4	224.7	231.3	238.6	241.0	241.3	227.8	224.5	219.2	215.0	224.7
Other Services													
2000	82.2	82.7	83.2	83.6	84.2	85.6	86.1	85.8	84.0	84.8	85.1	85.5	84.4
2001	84.0	84.3	84.9	85.3	86.1	87.4	87.9	87.8	85.9	86.1	86.5	86.9	86.1
2002	85.3	85.4	86.4	86.5	87.4	88.3	88.7	88.5	86.4	86.9	87.1	87.4	87.0
2003	85.6	85.4	86.3	86.1	86.7	87.5	87.9	87.2	85.8	85.5	86.1	86.0	86.3
2004	85.0	84.8	85.7	85.7	86.3	86.4	87.3	87.0	85.0	85.0	85.4	85.8	85.8
2005	84.4	84.5	85.2	86.3	86.5	87.7	88.4	88.0	86.6	85.8	86.2	87.0	86.4
2006	85.7	85.2	86.3	86.6	86.9	88.3	89.1	89.2	87.1	87.2	87.1	87.5	87.2
2007	86.2	86.6	87.3	87.7	89.0	90.9	91.7	91.7	89.3	88.9	89.6	89.6	89.0
2008	87.9	88.0	88.5	89.0	89.7	91.2	92.5	92.4	89.7	89.5	89.4	89.1	89.7
2009	87.4	87.2	87.9	89.1	90.1	92.6	93.1	92.7	89.3	89.0	88.9	89.0	89.7
2010	87.7	87.5	88.3	89.5	90.8	93.5	95.3	94.8	91.1	91.0	91.2	91.7	91.0
2011	89.9	90.4	91.8	93.0	93.6	95.9	98.4	97.9	95.7	96.0	96.5	95.1	94.5
Government													
2000	300.4	303.8	305.8	306.8	311.6	307.8	285.6	280.2	301.4	303.8	305.5	305.4	301.5
2001	304.1	307.0	307.1	307.8	308.3	306.1	286.4	284.2	304.8	305.8	306.8	307.6	303.0
2002	304.5	306.9	307.3	306.4	306.7	305.2	283.4	279.8	305.1	302.6	305.2	304.9	301.5
2003	300.8	303.2	302.9	303.3	302.9	301.5	282.8	276.3	299.7	297.9	299.0	298.4	297.4
2004	294.4	298.4	298.7	299.4	298.6	296.4	274.3	268.1	294.9	296.8	298.5	298.2	293.1
2005	295.4	300.2	300.1	300.8	301.0	297.4	276.0	270.1	296.0	299.6	301.7	300.5	294.9
2006	297.5	302.0	302.3	302.6	303.0	300.0	279.0	272.3	298.8	302.0	303.7	303.0	297.2
2007	300.5	303.9	304.4	305.3	306.3	302.3	278.8	272.6	300.8	304.9	306.9	306.2	299.4
2008	303.7	307.9	308.2	309.5	310.0	302.7	283.1	277.0	304.9	309.2	310.6	311.5	303.5
2009	305.8	311.3	310.8	314.5	312.2	307.8	280.5	277.6	304.6	309.8	310.2	311.5	304.7
2010	307.3	309.8	310.5	312.1	317.5	309.2	282.3	279.5	304.8	308.3	310.6	310.6	305.2
2011	302.4	308.2	308.5	307.9	308.3	304.6	280.8	274.5	300.5	304.7	305.5	307.3	301.1

Employment by Industry: Bridgeport–Stamford–Norwalk, CT, NECTA, Selected Years, 2000–2011

(Numbers in thousands, not seasonally adjusted)

Industry and year	January	February	March	April	May	June	July	August	September	October	November	December	Annual average
Total Nonfarm													
2000	416.3	416.6	420.0	423.9	427.4	433.3	427.2	424.6	430.2	430.1	431.8	434.9	426.4
2001	420.2	418.8	420.2	422.4	426.0	429.4	420.8	417.4	420.3	422.5	424.4	423.8	422.2
2002	410.6	409.5	412.5	416.8	418.9	421.5	410.7	408.9	412.0	414.7	417.8	418.9	414.4
2003	406.0	404.8	407.1	409.8	413.0	415.5	411.6	406.7	409.7	412.5	413.6	414.1	410.4
2004	402.5	402.1	405.8	407.2	411.4	415.2	412.1	408.2	410.5	412.9	415.1	416.3	409.9
2005	402.0	402.9	404.7	411.0	413.8	417.2	414.2	410.1	411.8	413.1	415.8	418.4	411.3
2006	408.4	408.9	408.8	415.6	418.9	422.1	417.8	414.3	416.0	418.1	421.4	425.2	416.3
2007	412.1	411.7	413.3	417.1	422.0	425.7	424.1	419.6	419.2	421.5	424.0	426.8	419.8
2008	414.3	413.1	415.6	418.0	421.4	424.6	419.2	415.1	415.6	416.3	417.1	416.9	417.3
2009	402.0	399.3	399.2	396.8	400.9	403.2	398.2	394.2	396.3	396.6	398.1	399.8	398.7
2010	385.5	384.2	386.7	392.8	401.0	403.7	403.3	399.3	398.4	399.8	400.8	403.2	396.6
2011	391.2	392.1	394.1	398.6	403.4	406.2	404.1	398.6	397.6	400.0	400.3	402.4	399.1
Total Private													
2000	370.6	370.0	373.3	377.5	380.6	386.5	385.5	383.2	383.4	383.7	384.8	387.7	380.6
2001	373.6	371.8	373.4	375.3	378.6	382.2	378.9	376.3	372.0	374.2	375.3	374.8	375.5
2002	362.9	361.4	364.2	368.0	369.9	372.4	369.8	367.5	365.1	366.3	368.6	369.9	367.2
2003	357.9	356.5	358.6	361.8	364.7	367.1	366.5	364.1	363.5	365.4	365.9	366.6	363.2
2004	355.0	354.1	357.3	359.7	363.8	367.7	367.6	365.2	363.8	365.1	366.9	368.8	362.9
2005	355.4	355.9	357.6	363.0	365.5	368.8	368.7	366.1	364.9	365.7	368.3	370.6	364.2
2006	361.1	361.1	360.8	367.8	370.9	375.2	373.5	371.4	369.5	370.9	373.7	377.7	369.5
2007	365.2	364.1	365.7	369.6	373.5	378.4	377.8	374.9	372.4	373.5	375.6	378.7	372.5
2008	366.5	364.5	367.2	370.0	372.6	376.9	374.2	371.5	368.4	368.1	368.0	368.4	369.7
2009	354.5	351.4	351.1	349.9	352.5	355.1	353.5	350.6	349.4	349.4	350.4	352.6	351.7
2010	339.0	337.6	340.1	347.1	352.0	356.6	357.9	355.8	352.8	354.1	354.7	356.8	350.4
2011	345.6	345.9	347.9	353.5	356.6	360.7	361.2	356.6	352.1	353.9	353.5	355.9	353.6
Goods-Producing													
2000	64.1	63.8	64.6	65.0	65.6	66.5	65.9	65.9	66.1	65.4	65.3	65.1	65.3
2001	63.1	62.7	63.0	64.1	64.7	64.9	63.3	63.3	63.0	62.1	61.7	61.4	63.1
2002	59.6	59.2	59.5	60.4	60.5	60.9	59.9	60.0	59.7	59.2	58.9	58.3	59.7
2003	56.7	56.2	56.3	56.9	57.5	57.8	56.8	57.2	56.9	57.0	56.8	56.4	56.9
2004	54.8	54.4	55.0	56.2	56.6	57.2	56.8	56.8	56.9	57.2	56.9	56.8	56.3
2005	55.2	54.9	54.9	56.3	56.7	57.2	57.1	56.7	56.3	56.4	56.4	55.9	56.2
2006	54.9	55.1	52.3	56.4	56.6	57.2	57.2	57.1	56.8	56.7	56.5	56.3	56.1
2007	55.0	54.7	55.1	55.7	56.1	57.0	57.0	56.8	56.5	56.1	55.9	55.7	56.0
2008	54.1	53.5	54.0	54.7	55.4	55.7	55.3	55.1	54.9	54.2	53.7	52.8	54.5
2009	50.8	49.8	49.5	49.6	49.5	49.8	49.2	48.6	48.4	48.0	47.7	47.3	49.0
2010	45.3	44.9	45.2	46.4	46.9	47.8	48.0	47.9	47.5	47.2	46.8	46.5	46.7
2011	45.3	45.3	45.5	46.5	47.1	47.7	47.0	47.4	46.9	46.7	46.2	46.0	46.5
Mining, Logging, and Construction													
2000	13.1	12.8	13.6	14.2	14.7	15.1	15.3	15.3	15.2	15.1	15	14.6	14.5
2001	13.1	12.8	13.2	14.7	15.3	15.6	15.7	15.7	15.3	15.0	14.8	14.6	14.7
2002	13.6	13.4	13.8	14.5	14.8	15.2	15.2	15.2	15.0	14.7	14.6	14.0	14.5
2003	13.0	12.7	12.9	13.9	14.6	14.7	15.0	15.1	14.9	14.9	14.7	14.2	14.2
2004	12.9	12.5	12.9	14.2	14.7	15.0	15.3	15.4	15.2	15.3	15.1	14.8	14.4
2005	13.6	13.4	13.5	15.1	15.5	15.7	16.0	15.9	15.6	15.6	15.6	15.0	15.0
2006	14.3	14.2	14.6	15.5	15.8	16.0	16.4	16.3	16.1	16.0	15.8	15.5	15.5
2007	14.6	14.1	14.4	15.6	16.0	16.4	16.6	16.6	16.3	16.2	16.0	15.7	15.7
2008	14.3	14.1	14.3	15.2	15.7	15.8	15.8	15.8	15.6	15.1	14.7	14.0	15.0
2009	12.6	12.2	12.0	12.3	12.5	12.6	12.6	12.3	12.1	12.0	11.8	11.4	12.2
2010	9.7	9.5	9.7	11.0	11.3	11.7	11.9	12.0	11.8	11.6	11.5	11.1	11.1
2011	9.9	9.9	10.0	11.1	11.6	11.9	11.4	12.0	11.6	11.5	10.8	10.7	11.0
Manufacturing													
2000	51.0	51.0	51.0	50.8	50.9	51.4	50.6	50.6	50.9	50.3	50.3	50.5	50.8
2001	50.0	49.9	49.8	49.4	49.4	49.3	47.6	47.6	47.7	47.1	46.9	46.8	48.5
2002	46.0	45.8	45.7	45.9	45.7	45.7	44.7	44.8	44.7	44.5	44.3	44.3	45.2
2003	43.7	43.5	43.4	43.0	42.9	43.1	41.8	42.1	42.0	42.1	42.1	42.2	42.7
2004	41.9	41.9	42.1	42.0	41.9	42.2	41.5	41.4	41.7	41.9	41.8	42.0	41.9
2005	41.6	41.5	41.4	41.2	41.2	41.5	41.1	40.8	40.7	40.8	40.8	40.9	41.1
2006	40.6	40.9	37.7	40.9	40.8	41.2	40.8	40.8	40.7	40.7	40.7	40.8	40.6
2007	40.4	40.6	40.7	40.1	40.1	40.6	40.4	40.2	40.2	39.9	39.9	40.0	40.3
2008	39.8	39.4	39.7	39.5	39.7	39.9	39.5	39.3	39.3	39.1	39.0	38.8	39.4
2009	38.2	37.6	37.5	37.3	37.0	37.2	36.6	36.3	36.3	36.0	35.9	35.9	36.8
2010	35.6	35.4	35.5	35.4	35.6	36.1	36.1	35.9	35.7	35.6	35.3	35.4	35.6
2011	35.4	35.4	35.5	35.4	35.5	35.8	35.6	35.4	35.3	35.2	35.4	35.3	35.4
Service-Providing													
2000	352.2	352.8	355.4	358.9	361.8	366.8	361.3	358.7	364.1	364.7	366.5	369.8	361.1
2001	357.1	356.1	357.2	358.3	361.3	364.5	357.5	354.1	357.3	360.4	362.7	362.4	359.1
2002	351.0	350.3	353.0	356.4	358.4	360.6	350.8	348.9	352.3	355.5	358.9	360.6	354.7
2003	349.3	348.6	350.8	352.9	355.5	357.7	354.8	349.5	352.8	355.5	356.8	357.7	353.5
2004	347.7	347.7	350.8	351.0	354.8	358.0	355.3	351.4	353.6	355.7	358.2	359.5	353.6
2005	346.8	348.0	349.8	354.7	357.1	360.0	357.1	353.4	355.5	356.7	359.4	362.5	355.1
2006	353.5	353.8	356.5	359.2	362.3	364.9	360.6	357.2	359.2	361.4	364.9	368.9	360.2
2007	357.1	357.0	358.2	361.4	365.9	368.7	367.1	362.8	362.7	365.4	368.1	371.1	363.8
2008	360.2	359.6	361.6	363.3	366.0	368.9	363.9	360.0	360.7	362.1	363.4	364.1	362.8
2009	351.2	349.5	349.7	347.2	351.4	353.4	349.0	345.6	347.9	348.6	350.4	352.5	349.7
2010	340.2	339.3	341.5	346.4	354.1	355.9	355.3	351.4	350.9	352.6	354.0	356.7	349.9
2011	345.9	346.8	348.6	352.1	356.3	358.5	357.1	351.2	350.7	353.3	354.1	356.4	352.6

Employment by Industry: Bridgeport–Stamford–Norwalk, CT, NECTA, Selected Years, 2000–2011—*Continued*

(Numbers in thousands, not seasonally adjusted)

Industry and year	January	February	March	April	May	June	July	August	September	October	November	December	Annual average
Trade, Transportation, and Utilities													
2000	79.2	78.7	79.1	79.5	79.9	80.5	79.2	78.4	79.6	80.3	82.0	84.0	80.0
2001	80.2	77.8	77.6	77.9	78.4	79.2	77.9	77.2	77.2	78.4	78.9	80.6	78.4
2002	77.4	75.9	76.4	76.9	77.3	78.3	76.4	75.7	76.4	75.5	78.1	79.6	77.0
2003	75.5	74.1	74.5	74.1	74.7	75.3	74.2	73.4	74.4	75.1	76.5	78.0	75.0
2004	74.8	73.6	73.7	73.6	74.5	75.3	74.3	73.5	74.4	75.2	77.1	78.5	74.9
2005	75.3	74.1	74.2	74.2	74.7	75.3	74.1	73.8	74.7	75.5	77.4	79.5	75.2
2006	76.4	75.1	75.3	75.3	75.7	76.6	75.1	74.6	74.9	75.8	78.1	80.0	76.1
2007	76.1	74.3	74.6	74.6	75.8	77.0	75.6	75.3	75.6	76.1	78.6	80.8	76.2
2008	77.1	75.3	75.5	75.1	75.7	76.5	74.9	74.6	74.9	74.7	76.1	77.4	75.7
2009	73.2	71.5	71.2	69.9	70.7	71.4	69.8	69.2	69.7	70.2	71.9	73.5	71.0
2010	69.6	68.3	68.6	68.7	70.3	71.5	70.5	70.2	70.2	71.0	72.8	74.6	70.5
2011	71.0	69.9	69.9	70.9	71.4	72.3	71.0	69.6	69.6	70.4	71.6	73.8	71.0
Wholesale Trade													
2000	16.4	16.4	16.4	16.3	16.4	16.5	16.3	16.2	16.2	15.9	16.0	16.2	16.3
2001	15.7	15.7	15.8	15.9	15.9	15.9	15.9	15.8	15.7	15.8	15.9	15.9	15.8
2002	15.8	15.6	15.7	15.6	15.6	15.5	15.5	15.5	15.4	15.4	15.4	15.5	15.5
2003	15.1	15.0	15.0	14.9	14.9	15.0	15.0	14.9	14.9	14.8	14.9	15.0	15.0
2004	14.9	14.8	14.8	14.7	14.8	15.0	14.9	14.9	14.7	14.7	14.8	14.8	14.8
2005	14.7	14.7	14.7	14.6	14.7	14.8	14.7	14.7	14.6	14.7	14.6	14.8	14.7
2006	14.6	14.7	14.7	14.6	14.6	14.6	14.6	14.4	14.4	14.5	14.5	14.6	14.6
2007	14.4	14.4	14.5	14.4	14.4	14.6	14.6	14.7	14.6	14.6	14.7	14.9	14.6
2008	14.8	14.7	14.8	14.8	14.8	14.9	14.8	14.8	14.7	14.7	14.7	14.8	14.8
2009	14.4	14.3	14.2	13.9	13.8	13.9	13.8	13.6	13.6	13.6	13.4	13.5	13.8
2010	13.1	13.1	13.2	13.3	13.4	13.6	13.5	13.5	13.4	13.4	13.5	13.6	13.4
2011	13.5	13.4	13.5	13.7	13.8	14.0	13.9	13.9	13.9	13.9	14.0	14.0	13.8
Retail Trade													
2000	52.0	51.4	51.8	52.0	52.2	52.7	52.1	51.7	52.0	52.7	54.3	56.0	52.6
2001	53.0	50.7	50.5	50.6	51.0	51.8	51.1	50.9	50.4	51.2	51.8	53.4	51.4
2002	50.7	49.4	49.8	50.2	50.6	51.6	50.5	50.1	50.0	49.9	51.5	52.9	50.6
2003	49.6	48.3	48.6	48.8	49.3	49.7	49.4	49.0	49.0	49.6	50.9	52.3	49.5
2004	49.5	48.5	48.6	48.5	49.2	49.7	49.5	49.1	49.3	49.8	51.6	53.0	49.7
2005	50.1	49.0	49.0	49.1	49.5	50.0	49.6	49.6	49.6	50.1	52.0	53.7	50.1
2006	51.1	49.7	49.9	49.9	50.1	50.9	50.2	50.0	49.4	50.0	52.2	53.6	50.6
2007	50.3	48.6	48.8	48.8	49.9	50.7	50.2	50.0	49.6	50.1	52.3	54.0	50.3
2008	51.0	49.3	49.4	48.9	49.4	50.0	49.4	49.4	49.1	49.1	50.4	51.4	49.7
2009	47.9	46.4	46.2	45.7	46.4	47.0	46.2	46.1	45.8	46.3	48.2	49.3	46.8
2010	46.5	45.2	45.4	45.6	46.7	47.5	47.3	47.1	46.5	47.3	48.8	50.1	47.0
2011	47.2	46.2	46.1	46.7	47.1	47.7	47.1	45.8	45.1	45.9	46.7	48.5	46.7
Transportation and Utilities													
2000	10.8	10.9	10.9	11.2	11.3	11.3	10.8	10.5	11.4	11.7	11.7	11.8	11.2
2001	11.5	11.4	11.3	11.4	11.5	11.5	10.9	10.5	11.1	11.4	11.2	11.3	11.3
2002	10.9	10.9	10.9	11.1	11.1	11.2	10.4	10.1	11.0	10.2	11.2	11.2	10.9
2003	10.8	10.8	10.9	10.4	10.5	10.6	9.8	9.5	10.5	10.7	10.7	10.7	10.5
2004	10.4	10.3	10.3	10.4	10.5	10.6	9.9	9.5	10.4	10.7	10.7	10.7	10.4
2005	10.5	10.4	10.5	10.5	10.5	10.5	9.8	9.5	10.5	10.7	10.8	11.0	10.4
2006	10.7	10.7	10.7	10.8	11.0	11.1	10.3	10.2	11.1	11.3	11.4	11.8	10.9
2007	11.4	11.3	11.3	11.4	11.5	11.7	10.8	10.6	11.4	11.4	11.6	11.9	11.4
2008	11.3	11.3	11.3	11.4	11.5	11.6	10.7	10.4	11.1	10.9	11.0	11.2	11.1
2009	10.9	10.8	10.8	10.3	10.5	10.5	9.8	9.5	10.3	10.3	10.3	10.7	10.4
2010	10.0	10.0	10.0	9.8	10.2	10.4	9.7	9.6	10.3	10.3	10.5	10.9	10.1
2011	10.3	10.3	10.3	10.5	10.5	10.6	10.0	9.9	10.6	10.6	10.9	11.3	10.5
Information													
2000	14.8	14.8	14.8	14.8	14.9	15.2	15.3	15.1	15.0	15.0	15.1	15.2	15.0
2001	14.8	14.8	14.8	14.7	14.5	14.5	13.9	13.9	13.6	13.5	13.4	13.4	14.2
2002	13.2	13.0	13.0	12.8	12.7	12.7	12.7	12.6	12.4	12.4	12.4	12.4	12.7
2003	12.3	12.2	12.3	12.2	12.2	12.2	12.2	12.2	12.0	12.0	12.1	12.1	12.2
2004	12.2	12.1	12.0	12.0	12.1	12.2	12.1	12.1	11.9	11.7	11.8	11.7	12.0
2005	11.6	11.6	11.6	11.6	11.6	11.6	11.5	11.5	11.3	11.4	11.4	11.4	11.5
2006	11.3	11.2	11.4	11.3	11.4	11.4	11.3	11.2	11.2	11.1	11.2	11.4	11.3
2007	11.3	11.4	11.5	11.3	11.5	11.5	11.8	11.8	12.1	11.8	11.2	11.3	11.5
2008	11.3	11.3	11.4	11.3	11.3	11.5	11.5	11.6	11.5	11.5	11.6	11.7	11.5
2009	11.8	11.7	11.6	11.5	11.4	11.4	11.3	11.2	11.1	10.9	11.0	11.0	11.3
2010	10.8	10.8	10.8	10.9	11.0	10.9	10.8	10.8	10.7	10.7	10.8	10.9	10.8
2011	10.8	10.8	10.8	10.8	10.8	10.8	10.8	10.8	10.8	10.8	10.8	10.9	10.8
Financial Activities													
2000	40.2	40.2	40.3	40.4	40.7	41.4	41.5	41.6	41.2	41.3	41.4	41.8	41.0
2001	40.6	40.7	40.7	40.8	40.9	41.3	41.1	41.1	40.5	40.5	40.5	40.6	40.8
2002	40.0	40.1	39.8	40.3	40.4	40.8	41.0	41.1	40.7	41.0	41.2	41.7	40.7
2003	41.1	41.1	41.3	41.3	41.5	41.8	42.0	41.9	41.3	41.2	41.2	41.4	41.4
2004	40.9	41.0	41.2	41.0	41.3	41.8	42.2	42.2	41.9	42.0	42.1	42.3	41.7
2005	42.1	42.3	42.6	42.7	42.7	43.1	43.4	43.3	42.8	42.9	43.0	43.2	42.8
2006	43.1	43.1	43.4	43.3	43.7	44.2	44.4	44.8	44.4	44.6	45.0	45.2	44.1
2007	45.0	45.0	45.1	45.0	45.3	45.9	46.3	46.1	45.4	45.6	45.6	45.8	45.5
2008	45.2	45.3	45.5	45.4	45.4	46.0	45.8	45.9	45.1	45.0	44.9	45.0	45.4
2009	44.0	44.0	44.0	43.0	42.9	43.3	43.5	43.4	42.9	42.9	42.9	43.1	43.3
2010	42.3	42.3	42.4	42.4	42.5	43.2	43.4	43.5	42.8	42.7	42.7	43.0	42.8
2011	42.7	42.7	42.7	42.7	42.6	42.6	42.8	42.5	42.1	42.1	41.8	41.6	42.4

Employment by Industry: Bridgeport–Stamford–Norwalk, CT, NECTA, Selected Years, 2000–2011—*Continued*

(Numbers in thousands, not seasonally adjusted)

Industry and year	January	February	March	April	May	June	July	August	September	October	November	December	Annual average
Professional and Business Services													
2000	75.7	75.8	77.1	78.0	78.4	79.9	79.9	79.5	79.9	79.5	79.1	79.1	78.5
2001	76.2	76.0	76.6	75.8	77.0	77.6	76.8	76.4	75.3	75.5	74.3	73.3	75.9
2002	70.4	70.3	71.1	71.8	71.7	72.2	70.9	71.0	70.5	71.1	70.8	70.5	71.0
2003	68.8	68.8	68.9	70.7	70.6	71.0	70.6	71.0	71.4	71.2	70.8	70.5	70.4
2004	67.7	67.8	68.8	69.3	70.1	71.1	70.5	70.4	69.9	69.6	69.8	70.2	69.6
2005	66.6	67.1	67.9	69.4	69.6	70.4	70.2	70.3	71.0	70.7	71.2	71.4	69.7
2006	68.6	69.3	70.5	71.5	71.7	72.6	71.1	71.2	71.2	70.9	71.1	72.0	71.0
2007	68.6	68.5	68.7	70.6	71.0	71.7	70.4	70.2	69.9	70.4	70.3	70.4	70.1
2008	67.5	66.8	67.4	68.8	68.7	69.2	68.5	68.2	67.3	67.1	66.5	66.1	67.7
2009	63.7	63.0	63.0	63.3	63.1	63.6	63.0	62.9	62.6	62.8	62.5	62.6	63.0
2010	60.0	60.4	61.3	63.8	64.1	64.8	65.3	65.2	64.9	65.3	64.8	64.5	63.7
2011	62.4	63.1	63.7	65.3	65.8	66.4	67.5	66.3	66.0	65.4	65.0	64.4	65.1
Education and Health Services													
2000	53.1	53.5	53.5	53.8	53.8	53.6	53.6	53.2	54.1	55.0	55.3	55.5	54.0
2001	54.1	55.2	55.4	55.7	54.8	54.8	55.1	54.5	55.2	57.1	59.6	58.0	55.8
2002	56.6	57.6	58.3	58.3	58.3	57.2	57.2	56.4	57.4	59.4	59.8	59.7	58.0
2003	58.0	58.7	59.1	58.9	58.8	57.9	58.3	57.2	58.5	60.1	60.2	60.0	58.8
2004	58.4	59.1	59.8	59.4	59.2	58.5	58.7	58.2	58.9	60.2	60.5	60.1	59.3
2005	58.4	59.6	59.4	59.8	59.8	58.7	59.1	58.2	59.0	59.9	60.3	60.3	59.4
2006	59.6	60.3	60.2	60.6	60.8	59.9	60.0	59.1	60.0	61.2	61.8	62.2	60.5
2007	60.6	62.0	61.9	62.3	61.9	61.5	61.3	60.4	61.5	62.8	63.3	63.7	61.9
2008	62.3	63.6	64.0	64.0	63.5	63.5	63.1	62.1	63.4	64.7	65.2	65.4	63.7
2009	63.8	64.6	64.6	64.4	64.7	63.7	63.8	63.2	64.3	65.2	65.7	66.1	64.5
2010	64.8	65.0	65.2	66.1	66.2	65.4	65.7	64.8	65.8	66.8	67.1	67.3	65.9
2011	66.2	66.7	67.1	67.4	67.2	66.8	66.1	65.2	65.2	67.8	69.0	69.9	67.1
Leisure and Hospitality													
2000	27.5	27.3	27.9	29.6	30.8	32.6	32.8	32.4	30.9	30.4	29.9	30.1	30.2
2001	28.3	28.2	28.8	29.6	31.5	32.9	33.3	32.6	30.5	30.2	30.0	30.5	30.5
2002	28.8	28.4	29.2	30.5	31.8	33.0	34.2	33.4	31.3	30.9	30.5	30.7	31.1
2003	29.0	28.9	29.6	31.0	32.7	34.3	35.2	34.3	32.5	32.2	31.8	31.7	31.9
2004	29.8	29.7	30.3	31.6	33.3	34.7	35.6	34.8	33.3	32.6	32.1	32.5	32.5
2005	29.8	29.8	30.3	32.1	33.4	35.3	35.8	35.2	33.1	32.2	31.8	31.9	32.6
2006	30.4	30.3	30.9	32.5	34.0	36.1	36.6	36.0	34.1	33.5	32.9	33.4	33.4
2007	31.5	31.2	31.7	33.0	34.7	36.4	37.5	36.8	34.4	33.9	33.9	34.2	34.1
2008	32.3	32.2	32.8	34.0	35.8	37.3	37.6	36.7	34.6	34.2	33.3	33.3	34.5
2009	31.0	30.7	31.0	32.1	33.9	35.3	36.0	35.4	34.2	33.2	32.4	32.6	33.2
2010	30.3	30.1	30.7	32.7	34.6	36.2	37.1	36.3	34.6	34.1	33.3	33.6	33.6
2011	31.2	31.3	32.0	33.6	35.2	37.3	38.9	37.9	35.1	34.3	32.7	32.8	34.4
Other Services													
2000	16.0	15.9	16.0	16.4	16.5	16.8	17.3	17.1	16.6	16.8	16.7	16.9	16.6
2001	16.3	16.4	16.5	16.7	16.8	17.0	17.5	17.3	16.7	16.9	16.9	17.0	16.8
2002	16.9	16.9	16.9	17.0	17.2	17.3	17.5	17.3	16.7	16.8	16.9	17.0	17.0
2003	16.5	16.5	16.6	16.7	16.7	16.8	17.2	16.9	16.5	16.6	16.5	16.5	16.7
2004	16.4	16.4	16.5	16.6	16.7	16.9	17.4	17.2	16.6	16.6	16.6	16.7	16.7
2005	16.4	16.5	16.7	16.9	17.0	17.2	17.5	17.1	16.7	16.7	16.8	17.0	16.9
2006	16.8	16.7	16.8	16.9	17.0	17.2	17.8	17.4	16.9	17.1	17.1	17.2	17.1
2007	17.1	17.0	17.1	17.1	17.2	17.4	17.9	17.5	17.0	16.8	16.8	16.8	17.1
2008	16.7	16.5	16.6	16.7	16.8	17.2	17.5	17.3	16.7	16.7	16.7	16.7	16.8
2009	16.2	16.1	16.2	16.1	16.3	16.6	16.9	16.7	16.2	16.2	16.3	16.4	16.4
2010	15.9	15.8	15.9	16.1	16.4	16.8	17.1	17.1	16.3	16.3	16.4	16.4	16.4
2011	16.0	16.1	16.2	16.3	16.5	16.8	17.1	16.9	16.4	16.4	16.4	16.5	16.5
Government													
2000	45.7	46.6	46.7	46.4	46.8	46.8	41.7	41.4	46.8	46.4	47.0	47.2	45.8
2001	46.6	47.0	46.8	47.1	47.4	47.2	41.9	41.1	48.3	48.3	49.1	49.0	46.7
2002	47.7	48.1	48.3	48.8	49.0	49.1	40.9	41.4	46.9	48.4	49.2	49.0	47.2
2003	48.1	48.3	48.5	48.0	48.3	48.4	45.1	42.6	46.2	47.1	47.7	47.5	47.2
2004	47.5	48.0	48.5	47.5	47.6	47.5	44.5	43.0	46.7	47.8	48.2	47.5	47.0
2005	46.6	47.0	47.1	48.0	48.3	48.4	45.5	44.0	46.9	47.4	47.5	47.8	47.0
2006	47.3	47.8	48.0	47.8	48.0	46.9	44.3	42.9	46.5	47.2	47.7	47.5	46.8
2007	46.9	47.6	47.6	47.5	48.5	47.3	46.3	44.7	46.8	48.0	48.4	48.1	47.3
2008	47.8	48.6	48.4	48.0	48.8	47.7	45.0	43.6	47.2	48.2	49.1	48.5	47.6
2009	47.5	47.9	48.1	46.9	48.4	48.1	44.7	43.6	46.9	47.2	47.7	47.2	47.0
2010	46.5	46.6	46.6	45.7	49.0	47.1	45.4	43.5	45.6	45.7	46.1	46.4	46.2
2011	45.6	46.2	46.2	45.1	46.8	45.5	42.9	42.0	45.5	46.1	46.8	46.5	45.4

Employment by Industry: Buffalo–Niagra Falls, NY, Selected Years, 2000–2011

(Numbers in thousands, not seasonally adjusted)

Industry and year	January	February	March	April	May	June	July	August	September	October	November	December	Annual average
Total Nonfarm													
2000	545.9	548.9	551.4	555.6	562.1	563.9	558.1	559.1	561.7	567.6	568.7	565.9	559.1
2001	546.9	548.3	550.0	546.6	556.3	558.5	546.6	546.6	547.4	551.1	551.7	550.2	550.0
2002	537.2	539.2	541.2	543.1	550.9	553.4	546.2	548.1	549.2	554.5	554.8	555.7	547.8
2003	535.7	537.5	540.2	542.1	547.6	550.3	541.0	541.8	548.0	551.7	555.1	555.4	545.5
2004	535.2	539.1	543.8	542.6	551.7	551.9	543.6	545.4	551.5	556.4	557.1	558.4	548.1
2005	535.0	538.0	538.9	545.2	550.1	551.1	540.8	544.0	552.1	555.6	556.2	555.5	546.9
2006	534.3	537.5	540.3	544.8	551.0	552.2	541.6	544.8	548.1	548.7	554.9	556.4	546.2
2007	534.7	537.6	541.3	540.9	550.9	552.1	542.6	545.5	550.5	557.4	558.9	559.0	547.6
2008	539.1	541.4	542.9	549.5	556.4	559.1	551.1	552.4	556.3	562.1	559.1	556.2	552.1
2009	531.8	532.2	533.1	535.0	540.2	540.8	536.0	536.4	539.2	545.0	545.2	543.0	538.2
2010	524.6	526.6	529.5	537.0	543.0	542.5	533.2	535.6	540.5	548.3	549.1	548.4	538.2
2011	530.3	532.8	533.7	541.1	545.7	548.8	542.2	544.2	546.4	550.7	550.2	546.5	542.7
Total Private													
2000	456.7	457.8	459.5	463.5	469.0	473.5	471.0	472.7	473.3	474.2	475.1	474.6	468.4
2001	456.5	455.7	457.3	454.2	463.1	467.2	459.9	460.1	457.4	458.0	458.1	457.3	458.7
2002	445.4	445.2	446.7	450.3	457.0	460.8	457.0	458.8	458.8	460.2	460.3	461.0	455.1
2003	442.6	441.9	443.2	446.2	451.4	454.9	450.7	451.9	455.0	456.8	457.0	457.2	450.7
2004	439.6	441.2	445.2	446.8	453.9	457.3	454.0	456.0	459.1	460.5	459.8	461.7	452.9
2005	440.4	441.3	443.5	449.9	454.4	457.8	452.8	456.2	459.5	460.3	460.5	460.0	453.1
2006	441.7	443.0	445.9	450.2	456.0	458.2	452.8	456.2	455.9	453.9	459.5	460.8	452.8
2007	441.1	442.4	445.8	446.0	455.3	457.3	453.8	455.4	457.5	461.2	462.2	462.4	453.4
2008	445.3	445.5	446.7	452.9	459.7	463.1	460.4	461.2	462.0	464.4	461.2	458.7	456.8
2009	437.0	436.0	436.6	438.3	442.9	445.1	444.1	444.5	445.3	447.8	447.6	445.9	442.6
2010	429.4	429.8	432.2	439.9	444.0	445.9	445.1	447.1	449.0	452.1	452.2	451.7	443.2
2011	435.8	437.2	438.5	445.6	450.1	454.3	451.9	453.9	453.6	454.6	453.7	450.3	448.3
Goods-Producing													
2000	100.5	100.0	100.6	102.5	104.4	105.9	105.5	106.5	105.9	105.7	104.9	103.0	103.8
2001	98.3	97.3	97.3	98.0	98.6	100.7	100.5	99.6	99.1	98.2	97.1	95.6	98.4
2002	89.2	88.7	89.2	91.4	93.4	94.4	94.4	94.2	93.3	93.6	93.1	90.8	92.1
2003	87.0	85.6	86.4	86.2	88.0	89.2	88.3	89.0	89.2	88.7	87.7	86.3	87.6
2004	82.5	82.2	83.7	84.9	86.8	88.0	87.4	88.6	88.5	87.9	87.4	86.3	86.2
2005	81.8	80.9	81.0	82.3	83.9	84.8	83.8	85.4	84.8	84.5	84.3	82.3	83.3
2006	79.8	79.0	79.5	81.5	83.1	84.3	83.3	84.3	83.5	82.1	82.2	80.8	82.0
2007	77.7	76.5	77.3	78.2	81.0	82.4	81.6	82.3	81.6	81.1	80.5	79.0	79.9
2008	75.2	74.7	74.3	76.4	79.3	80.8	80.9	81.6	80.8	80.3	78.3	76.1	78.2
2009	70.6	69.0	68.4	69.6	70.7	70.5	70.8	71.2	70.9	70.4	69.7	67.9	70.0
2010	64.5	63.8	64.2	66.9	68.7	69.8	70.8	71.3	71.1	71.2	70.6	69.0	68.5
2011	66.7	66.4	67.0	69.5	71.3	73.2	74.2	74.9	74.8	74.9	74.9	71.4	71.6
Mining, Logging, and Construction													
2000	17.7	17.2	17.9	19.7	21.4	22.2	23.0	23.4	22.9	22.4	21.7	19.6	20.8
2001	17.6	17.3	17.8	19.5	21.5	22.5	23.2	23.3	22.7	22.3	21.6	20.6	20.8
2002	17.1	16.7	17.4	19.4	21.2	22.0	22.9	23.1	22.4	22.4	21.7	20.2	20.5
2003	17.3	16.6	16.9	18.2	20.1	20.9	21.9	22.5	22.0	22.0	20.8	19.8	19.9
2004	16.7	16.6	17.4	19.1	21.0	21.9	22.7	22.9	22.6	22.8	22.1	20.6	20.5
2005	17.4	17.0	16.7	18.7	20.2	21.2	21.7	22.3	21.7	21.6	21.3	19.6	20.0
2006	17.2	16.7	17.1	19.2	20.8	21.8	21.9	22.3	21.7	21.3	21.1	19.9	20.1
2007	17.6	16.3	17.2	18.3	20.8	21.9	22.1	22.4	21.7	21.6	20.8	19.6	20.0
2008	17.3	16.5	16.9	19.0	21.4	22.3	23.5	23.8	23.3	23.1	21.6	20.0	20.7
2009	17.1	16.6	17.0	18.3	19.9	20.5	21.2	21.5	20.8	20.5	19.8	17.9	19.3
2010	15.5	15.0	15.3	18.1	19.5	20.2	21.1	21.3	20.9	21.0	20.5	18.5	18.9
2011	16.5	16.1	16.7	18.6	20.3	21.4	22.5	22.8	22.6	22.6	22.4	18.9	20.1
Manufacturing													
2000	82.8	82.8	82.7	82.8	83.0	83.7	82.5	83.1	83.0	83.3	83.2	83.4	83.0
2001	80.7	80.0	79.5	78.5	77.1	78.2	77.3	76.3	76.4	75.9	75.5	75.0	77.5
2002	72.1	72.0	71.8	72.0	72.2	72.4	71.5	71.1	70.9	71.2	71.4	70.6	71.6
2003	69.7	69.0	69.5	68.0	67.9	68.3	66.4	66.5	67.2	66.7	66.9	66.5	67.7
2004	65.8	65.6	66.3	65.8	65.8	66.1	64.7	65.7	65.9	65.1	65.3	65.7	65.7
2005	64.4	63.9	64.3	63.6	63.7	63.6	62.1	63.1	63.1	62.9	63.0	62.7	63.4
2006	62.6	62.3	62.4	62.3	62.3	62.5	61.4	62.0	61.8	60.8	61.1	60.9	61.9
2007	60.1	60.2	60.1	59.9	60.2	60.5	59.5	59.9	59.9	59.5	59.7	59.4	59.9
2008	57.9	58.2	57.4	57.4	57.9	58.5	57.4	57.8	57.5	57.2	56.7	56.1	57.5
2009	53.5	52.4	51.4	51.3	50.8	50.0	49.6	49.7	50.1	49.9	49.9	50.0	50.7
2010	49.0	48.8	48.9	48.8	49.2	49.6	49.7	50.0	50.2	50.2	50.1	50.5	49.6
2011	50.2	50.3	50.3	50.9	51.0	51.8	51.7	52.1	52.2	52.3	52.5	52.5	51.5
Service-Providing													
2000	445.4	448.9	450.8	453.1	457.7	458	452.6	452.6	455.8	461.9	463.8	462.9	455.3
2001	448.6	451.0	452.7	448.6	457.7	457.8	446.1	447.0	448.3	452.9	454.6	454.6	451.7
2002	448.0	450.5	452.0	451.7	457.5	459.0	451.8	453.9	455.9	460.9	461.7	464.9	455.7
2003	448.7	451.9	453.8	455.9	459.6	461.1	452.7	452.8	458.8	463.0	467.4	469.1	457.9
2004	452.7	456.9	460.1	457.7	464.9	463.9	456.2	456.8	463.0	468.5	469.7	472.1	461.9
2005	453.2	457.1	457.9	462.9	466.2	466.3	457.0	458.6	467.3	471.1	471.9	473.2	463.6
2006	454.5	458.5	460.8	463.3	467.9	467.9	458.3	460.5	464.6	466.6	472.7	475.6	464.3
2007	457.0	461.1	464.0	462.7	469.9	469.7	461.0	463.2	468.9	476.3	478.4	480.0	467.7
2008	463.9	466.7	468.6	473.1	477.1	478.3	470.2	470.8	475.5	481.8	480.8	480.1	473.9
2009	461.2	463.2	464.7	465.4	469.5	470.3	465.2	465.2	468.3	474.6	475.5	475.1	468.2
2010	460.1	462.8	465.3	470.1	474.3	472.7	462.4	464.3	469.4	477.1	478.5	479.4	469.7
2011	463.6	466.4	466.7	471.6	474.4	475.6	468.0	469.3	471.6	475.8	475.3	475.1	471.1

Employment by Industry: Buffalo–Niagra Falls, NY, Selected Years, 2000–2011—*Continued*

(Numbers in thousands, not seasonally adjusted)

Industry and year	January	February	March	April	May	June	July	August	September	October	November	December	Annual average
Trade, Transportation, and Utilities													
2000	108.6	107.4	107.4	106.7	108.1	109.7	108.2	109.3	109.5	109.9	112.6	114.2	109.3
2001	110.1	108.1	108.2	105.9	107.7	108.6	106.0	105.8	105.6	106.2	108.2	109.5	107.5
2002	105.2	103.1	103.2	103.1	104.3	105.9	103.9	104.0	104.4	105.2	106.6	108.0	104.7
2003	102.4	100.4	100.5	100.7	102.1	103.2	102.1	102.3	102.9	103.7	105.4	106.7	102.7
2004	100.8	99.4	99.7	99.9	102.0	102.9	101.9	102.5	103.1	103.9	105.8	107.5	102.5
2005	102.0	100.7	101.8	102.4	103.3	104.3	103.1	103.3	103.6	103.9	105.2	107.1	103.4
2006	102.1	99.5	100.0	100.9	102.2	103.7	102.2	102.7	102.8	103.7	106.1	107.5	102.8
2007	102.7	100.9	101.2	100.8	102.9	104.1	102.9	103.0	104.3	104.9	107.0	108.9	103.6
2008	103.4	101.1	101.2	101.8	103.1	104.4	102.5	102.5	103.3	103.7	104.3	105.0	103.0
2009	98.4	96.9	96.6	96.1	97.6	98.4	97.7	97.7	98.2	98.8	100.4	101.2	98.2
2010	96.4	95.0	95.1	96.1	97.4	98.4	96.9	97.3	98.3	99.3	101.3	101.9	97.8
2011	97.3	95.8	96.0	97.2	98.1	99.5	98.7	98.0	97.3	98.2	100.3	102.2	98.2
Wholesale Trade													
2000	24.1	24.3	24.1	23.6	23.7	23.9	23.9	24.0	23.7	23.7	23.9	23.9	23.9
2001	24.0	24.0	24.0	23.8	23.9	24.1	23.9	23.7	23.5	23.6	23.5	23.5	23.8
2002	23.2	23.2	23.1	23.0	23.1	23.3	23.2	23.1	23.1	23.3	23.3	23.3	23.2
2003	22.5	22.4	22.5	22.4	22.8	22.7	23.0	23.0	22.9	22.9	23.0	23.1	22.8
2004	22.8	22.7	22.8	22.9	23.1	23.2	23.3	23.4	23.2	23.4	23.6	23.8	23.2
2005	23.4	23.4	23.5	23.6	23.6	23.7	23.8	23.6	23.5	23.3	23.5	23.5	23.5
2006	23.3	23.2	23.3	23.3	23.4	23.6	23.3	23.3	23.1	23.3	23.4	23.6	23.3
2007	23.6	23.5	23.5	23.5	23.6	23.9	23.9	23.8	23.7	23.8	23.8	24.0	23.7
2008	23.4	23.2	23.2	23.1	23.1	23.2	23.2	23.0	22.7	22.6	22.5	22.4	23.0
2009	22.1	21.8	21.7	21.5	21.5	21.5	21.4	21.2	21.2	21.1	21.1	21.1	21.4
2010	20.9	20.8	20.8	21.0	21.1	21.2	21.3	21.3	21.2	21.3	21.4	21.4	21.1
2011	21.2	21.0	21.1	21.3	21.5	21.7	21.6	21.6	21.4	21.4	21.5	21.7	21.4
Retail Trade													
2000	65.3	64.0	64.2	63.8	64.7	65.8	65.4	66.2	65.9	65.9	68.5	70.1	65.8
2001	65.8	64.1	64.1	62.7	63.8	64.4	63.1	63.2	62.5	63.0	65.2	66.5	64.0
2002	62.9	61.2	61.6	61.3	62.0	63.1	62.2	62.3	61.9	62.5	64.0	65.4	62.5
2003	61.2	59.6	59.6	60.0	60.8	61.9	61.4	61.7	61.5	62.3	64.1	65.5	61.6
2004	60.8	59.5	59.7	59.6	61.1	62.0	61.6	62.1	61.9	62.6	64.4	65.8	61.8
2005	61.4	60.2	61.1	61.5	62.0	62.7	62.3	62.6	62.4	62.8	64.2	65.8	62.4
2006	61.8	59.6	59.8	60.5	61.2	62.1	61.6	61.9	61.2	62.0	64.3	65.2	61.8
2007	61.2	59.6	59.8	59.2	60.8	61.5	61.3	61.6	61.7	62.3	64.5	65.9	61.6
2008	62.0	60.1	60.2	60.4	61.4	62.3	62.1	62.2	62.1	62.8	63.6	64.3	62.0
2009	59.7	58.6	58.6	58.4	59.6	60.4	60.2	60.6	60.7	61.3	62.9	63.5	60.4
2010	59.8	58.7	58.8	59.4	60.3	60.9	60.4	60.8	60.8	60.8	61.8	63.5	60.8
2011	60.4	59.3	59.5	60.4	60.8	61.7	61.6	60.9	59.6	60.6	62.6	64.3	61.0
Transportation and Utilities													
2000	19.2	19.1	19.1	19.3	19.7	20.0	18.9	19.1	19.9	20.3	20.2	20.2	19.6
2001	20.3	20.0	20.1	19.4	20.0	20.1	19.0	18.9	19.6	19.6	19.5	19.5	19.7
2002	19.1	18.7	18.5	18.8	19.2	19.5	18.5	18.6	19.4	19.4	19.3	19.3	19.0
2003	18.7	18.4	18.4	18.3	18.5	18.6	17.7	17.6	18.5	18.5	18.3	18.1	18.3
2004	17.2	17.2	17.2	17.4	17.8	17.7	17.0	17.0	18.0	17.9	17.8	17.9	17.5
2005	17.2	17.1	17.2	17.3	17.7	17.9	17.0	17.1	17.7	17.8	17.5	17.8	17.4
2006	17.0	16.7	16.9	17.1	17.6	18.0	17.3	17.5	18.5	18.4	18.4	18.7	17.7
2007	17.9	17.8	17.9	18.1	18.5	18.7	17.7	17.6	18.9	18.8	18.7	19.0	18.3
2008	18.0	17.8	17.8	18.3	18.6	18.9	17.2	17.3	18.5	18.3	18.2	18.3	18.1
2009	16.6	16.5	16.3	16.2	16.5	16.5	16.1	15.9	16.3	16.4	16.4	16.6	16.4
2010	15.7	15.5	15.5	15.7	16.0	16.3	15.2	15.2	16.3	16.2	16.4	16.5	15.9
2011	15.7	15.5	15.4	15.5	15.8	16.1	15.5	15.5	16.3	16.2	16.2	16.2	15.8
Information													
2000	9.7	9.8	9.7	10.0	10.1	10.1	10.2	9.0	10.3	10.1	10.1	10.2	9.9
2001	11.0	11.0	11.1	11.0	11.2	11.3	11.0	10.8	10.7	10.4	10.4	10.5	10.9
2002	10.4	10.5	10.6	10.6	10.9	10.9	10.7	10.9	10.9	10.8	10.2	10.3	10.6
2003	9.8	9.9	9.9	9.9	9.9	9.8	9.8	10.1	9.8	9.9	9.9	10.0	9.9
2004	9.8	9.8	9.9	9.9	9.9	9.9	9.8	9.9	9.7	9.7	9.6	9.6	9.8
2005	9.5	9.4	9.4	9.5	9.5	9.5	9.7	9.7	9.6	9.6	9.6	9.7	9.6
2006	9.4	9.3	9.3	9.2	9.3	9.3	9.2	9.1	8.9	8.6	8.6	8.6	9.1
2007	8.5	8.5	8.5	8.4	8.6	8.6	8.6	8.5	8.4	8.3	8.4	8.4	8.5
2008	8.3	8.3	8.3	8.3	8.6	8.6	8.6	8.7	8.5	8.4	8.4	8.5	8.5
2009	8.3	8.2	8.3	8.4	8.4	8.5	8.4	8.3	8.1	8.2	8.1	8.1	8.3
2010	7.9	7.8	7.9	7.7	7.7	7.8	7.9	7.9	7.8	7.8	7.8	7.7	7.8
2011	7.6	7.6	7.6	7.7	7.7	7.8	7.8	6.9	7.7	7.6	7.6	7.6	7.6
Financial Activities													
2000	29.3	29.3	29.5	29.4	29.8	30.3	30.3	30.3	30.1	30.0	30.2	30.3	29.9
2001	30.2	30.2	30.5	30.3	30.8	30.9	31.5	31.6	31.6	32.1	31.9	32.5	31.2
2002	33.1	33.1	32.9	32.8	32.9	33.3	33.4	33.3	32.9	33.4	33.7	33.8	33.2
2003	33.2	32.8	32.4	33.7	33.8	34.2	34.2	34.4	34.3	34.4	34.5	34.6	33.9
2004	34.4	34.4	34.7	34.1	34.1	34.2	34.5	34.3	34.0	34.0	34.0	34.1	34.2
2005	33.4	33.3	33.3	34.0	34.1	34.7	34.8	34.9	34.8	34.8	35.0	35.2	34.4
2006	35.0	35.1	35.2	34.9	35.1	35.2	35.1	35.0	34.5	34.0	34.0	34.3	34.8
2007	33.3	33.4	33.6	32.9	33.0	33.5	33.5	33.4	33.0	33.3	33.4	33.9	33.4
2008	32.8	32.7	32.6	32.7	32.9	33.1	33.0	32.9	32.5	32.5	32.5	32.8	32.8
2009	31.4	31.3	31.3	31.4	31.5	31.7	31.7	31.4	31.0	31.0	30.9	31.1	31.3
2010	30.3	30.3	30.4	30.4	30.4	30.6	30.7	30.5	30.2	30.5	30.6	31.1	30.5
2011	31.1	31.1	31.2	31.2	30.8	31.1	30.5	32.0	31.9	31.9	32.0	32.0	31.4

Employment by Industry: Buffalo–Niagra Falls, NY, Selected Years, 2000–2011—*Continued*

(Numbers in thousands, not seasonally adjusted)

Industry and year	January	February	March	April	May	June	July	August	September	October	November	December	Annual average
Professional and Business Services													
2000	60.2	60.8	60.9	61.5	62.3	62.9	63.6	63.7	63.0	63.0	62.4	61.5	62.2
2001	60.3	60.5	60.7	61.3	62.7	62.9	62.7	63.2	62.1	61.7	60.9	60.1	61.6
2002	60.3	60.4	60.3	60.9	61.9	63.0	63.4	64.2	64.3	64.0	63.9	63.7	62.5
2003	61.3	62.0	61.9	62.9	63.0	64.0	64.6	64.4	64.4	64.4	64.2	64.2	63.4
2004	62.0	62.5	63.1	64.3	65.0	66.6	66.4	66.6	66.2	66.3	66.0	65.9	65.1
2005	63.4	63.7	63.8	65.7	66.0	67.8	67.5	68.2	68.9	68.8	68.1	67.8	66.6
2006	65.7	66.1	66.4	67.9	68.2	69.4	68.8	69.9	68.9	69.1	70.5	70.4	68.4
2007	67.1	67.6	68.3	68.9	69.6	70.9	70.8	71.5	71.0	71.4	71.5	71.3	70.0
2008	69.4	70.0	70.4	72.9	73.3	74.6	74.8	74.6	73.7	73.2	72.4	71.6	72.6
2009	69.4	69.3	69.7	69.9	70.4	72.1	72.2	72.0	71.2	71.5	71.2	70.5	70.8
2010	69.2	68.9	69.4	71.6	71.7	72.5	73.5	73.5	72.8	72.6	71.5	71.5	71.6
2011	70.1	70.3	70.1	71.9	72.5	73.7	73.7	73.6	73.8	73.6	71.6	69.6	72.0
Education and Health Services													
2000	82.7	83.3	83.4	83.9	83.8	82.7	81.7	81.3	83.5	85.6	85.1	85.4	83.5
2001	80.3	80.7	80.4	80.3	80.8	79.7	78.1	78.0	80.2	81.4	81.8	81.5	80.3
2002	80.5	81.7	82.0	81.9	81.8	80.5	79.0	79.0	82.1	83.4	83.7	83.9	81.6
2003	81.5	83.2	83.8	83.5	83.2	81.8	79.9	79.8	83.7	85.2	85.6	85.7	83.1
2004	83.0	84.9	85.2	84.8	84.5	83.3	82.2	81.4	85.0	87.3	87.4	87.6	84.7
2005	83.4	86.2	86.1	86.6	86.1	83.9	81.6	81.2	85.4	86.8	87.2	86.8	85.1
2006	82.9	86.0	86.5	86.2	86.1	83.7	82.2	82.3	85.8	86.8	87.4	87.5	85.3
2007	83.6	86.1	86.9	86.5	86.4	83.8	82.2	82.0	85.9	88.0	88.1	88.1	85.6
2008	85.8	87.7	88.3	88.6	87.6	85.7	84.6	84.3	87.9	90.2	90.5	90.6	87.7
2009	88.0	90.2	90.7	89.9	89.5	87.5	86.1	85.7	89.3	91.9	92.4	92.5	89.5
2010	89.6	91.8	92.3	92.6	92.0	89.7	87.5	87.4	91.0	93.1	93.6	93.3	91.2
2011	90.5	92.8	92.9	93.0	92.3	89.9	89.0	89.4	91.1	91.9	93.0	93.3	91.6
Leisure and Hospitality													
2000	43.4	44.5	44.9	46.2	47.3	48.7	48.1	49.1	48.0	46.8	46.8	46.7	46.7
2001	43.0	44.4	45.3	43.9	47.5	48.9	46.9	47.8	45.1	44.7	44.4	43.9	45.5
2002	43.9	44.6	45.1	46.3	48.5	49.5	49.1	50.1	48.2	47.1	46.2	47.5	47.2
2003	44.7	45.1	45.2	45.9	48.0	49.2	48.5	49.0	47.8	47.6	46.8	46.7	47.0
2004	44.7	45.2	45.7	45.8	48.1	49.3	49.0	49.8	49.5	48.3	46.4	47.3	47.4
2005	44.2	44.4	44.8	46.4	48.3	49.7	49.5	50.7	49.6	49.0	48.2	48.0	47.7
2006	44.5	45.6	46.1	46.8	48.9	49.6	49.2	49.9	48.6	46.6	47.6	48.3	47.6
2007	45.6	46.5	46.8	47.2	50.5	50.6	50.8	51.2	50.1	50.6	49.8	49.2	49.1
2008	47.1	47.6	47.9	48.5	51.0	52.0	51.9	52.4	51.5	51.8	50.8	50.1	50.2
2009	47.5	47.5	47.8	49.0	50.8	52.4	53.2	54.2	52.9	52.0	51.0	51.0	50.8
2010	48.6	49.2	49.8	51.4	52.9	53.8	53.6	54.7	54.7	54.3	53.5	53.8	52.5
2011	49.7	50.2	50.7	51.9	54.1	55.7	54.6	55.7	54.0	53.2	51.1	50.9	52.7
Other Services													
2000	22.3	22.7	23.1	23.3	23.2	23.2	23.4	23.5	23.0	23.1	23.0	23.3	23.1
2001	23.3	23.5	23.8	23.5	23.8	24.2	23.2	23.3	23.0	23.3	23.4	23.7	23.5
2002	22.8	23.1	23.4	23.3	23.3	23.3	23.1	23.1	22.7	22.7	22.9	23.0	23.1
2003	22.7	22.9	23.1	23.4	23.4	23.5	23.3	22.9	22.9	22.9	22.9	23.0	23.1
2004	22.4	22.8	23.2	23.1	23.5	23.1	22.8	22.9	23.1	23.1	23.2	23.4	23.1
2005	22.7	22.7	23.3	23.0	23.2	23.1	22.8	22.8	22.8	22.9	22.9	23.1	22.9
2006	22.3	22.4	22.9	22.8	23.1	23.0	22.8	23.0	22.9	23.0	23.1	23.4	22.9
2007	22.6	22.9	23.2	23.1	23.3	23.4	23.4	23.5	23.2	23.6	23.5	23.6	23.3
2008	23.3	23.4	23.7	23.7	23.9	23.9	24.1	24.2	23.8	24.3	24.0	24.0	23.9
2009	23.4	23.6	23.8	24.0	24.0	24.0	24.0	24.0	23.7	24.0	23.9	23.6	23.8
2010	22.9	23.0	23.1	23.2	23.2	23.3	24.2	24.5	23.1	23.3	23.3	23.4	23.4
2011	22.8	23.0	23.0	23.2	23.3	23.4	23.4	23.4	23.0	23.3	23.2	23.3	23.2
Government													
2000	89.2	91.1	91.9	92.1	93.1	90.4	87.1	86.4	88.4	93.4	93.6	91.3	90.7
2001	90.4	92.6	92.7	92.4	93.2	91.3	86.7	86.5	90.0	93.1	93.6	92.9	91.3
2002	91.8	94.0	94.5	92.8	93.9	92.6	89.2	89.3	90.4	94.3	94.5	94.7	92.7
2003	93.1	95.6	97.0	95.9	96.2	95.4	90.3	89.9	93.0	94.9	98.1	98.2	94.8
2004	95.6	97.9	98.6	95.8	97.8	94.6	89.6	89.4	92.4	95.9	97.3	96.7	95.1
2005	94.6	96.7	95.4	95.3	95.7	93.3	88.0	87.8	92.6	95.3	95.7	95.5	93.8
2006	92.6	94.5	94.4	94.6	95.0	94.0	88.8	88.6	92.2	94.8	95.4	95.6	93.4
2007	93.6	95.2	95.5	94.9	95.6	94.8	88.8	90.1	93.0	96.2	96.7	96.6	94.3
2008	93.8	95.9	96.2	96.6	96.7	96.0	90.7	91.2	94.3	97.7	97.9	97.5	95.4
2009	94.8	96.2	96.5	96.7	97.3	95.7	91.9	91.9	93.9	97.2	97.6	97.1	95.6
2010	95.2	96.8	97.3	97.1	99.0	96.6	88.1	88.5	91.5	96.2	96.9	96.7	95.0
2011	94.5	95.6	95.2	95.5	95.6	94.5	90.3	90.3	92.8	96.1	96.5	96.2	94.4

Employment by Industry: Charlotte–Gastonia–Rock Hill, NC–SC, Selected Years, 2000–2011

(Numbers in thousands, not seasonally adjusted)

Industry and year	January	February	March	April	May	June	July	August	September	October	November	December	Annual average
Total Nonfarm													
2000	748.5	750.3	758.7	766.0	769.8	774.6	759.9	767.2	771.4	778.5	778.0	779.0	766.8
2001	763.0	766.7	771.5	775.7	777.7	777.4	761.1	769.4	771.3	774.6	773.8	771.5	771.1
2002	757.4	761.1	767.3	768.2	771.5	773.8	761.3	770.8	775.2	777.0	777.9	776.3	769.8
2003	758.7	759.2	765.5	767.3	773.6	771.0	744.2	756.3	766.4	772.6	773.7	774.2	765.2
2004	756.0	757.9	764.1	766.2	772.6	771.7	755.6	770.1	778.8	786.4	788.1	787.4	771.2
2005	772.5	776.5	782.5	787.1	791.6	788.4	773.8	790.8	799.9	808.9	810.7	811.1	791.2
2006	801.7	805.1	813.1	821.3	827.0	822.0	808.8	828.8	837.7	844.0	850.2	851.2	825.9
2007	838.8	844.1	853.3	856.9	863.7	858.4	840.9	862.7	867.6	875.3	877.7	879.4	859.9
2008	858.2	863.0	868.3	866.2	870.8	863.7	840.7	862.0	865.0	863.1	857.4	855.4	861.2
2009	824.5	821.9	820.7	814.9	815.8	807.3	786.4	805.5	805.6	805.1	805.7	805.0	809.9
2010	791.2	793.1	801.1	806.3	815.1	806.6	786.8	807.8	809.8	822.0	824.4	825.5	807.5
2011	807.2	816.2	823.1	830.2	833.5	827.7	810.2	831.5	834.0	836.8	836.2	833.2	826.7
Total Private													
2000	660.1	661.6	668.8	676.1	680.2	687.2	681.8	683.8	683.3	686.3	686.4	687.5	678.6
2001	673.2	675.4	679.9	683.5	685.6	688.4	681.3	683.0	679.5	679.5	676.5	675.6	680.1
2002	663.4	665.6	671.0	672.7	676.1	681.2	678.5	682.3	680.7	678.5	679.0	678.9	675.7
2003	663.0	662.6	668.2	670.1	675.8	677.2	667.3	670.5	670.1	670.4	671.9	673.5	670.1
2004	657.2	658.1	664.2	666.2	672.4	675.6	677.5	681.9	678.8	683.2	684.4	684.9	673.7
2005	671.9	675.0	680.5	684.3	689.1	690.6	694.4	696.9	697.0	703.3	705.0	705.9	691.2
2006	697.4	700.2	707.8	715.7	721.3	724.9	728.8	732.5	731.5	736.5	740.9	741.9	723.3
2007	730.6	734.4	743.5	747.9	754.0	758.2	757.1	759.3	757.5	763.2	764.2	765.6	753.0
2008	744.8	748.4	753.2	751.1	755.3	755.9	750.7	751.8	747.0	745.4	738.4	735.7	748.1
2009	706.4	703.2	701.5	695.5	697.2	694.5	692.2	691.2	687.7	686.8	686.9	685.9	694.1
2010	670.8	671.4	678.5	683.7	689.2	691.8	691.7	694.5	694.1	700.7	702.7	703.6	689.4
2011	687.7	695.8	701.9	708.5	711.9	715.7	715.6	717.9	717.7	719.3	718.4	715.3	710.5
Goods-Producing													
2000	157.5	157.1	158.3	159.7	160.3	161.6	160.0	160.2	160.8	159.1	158.9	158.4	159.3
2001	155.4	155.8	156.4	156.3	156.3	156.6	154.8	154.7	154.5	152.7	150.9	150.1	154.5
2002	149.5	149.1	149.5	148.9	149.7	150.5	149.4	149.7	148.9	147.6	146.6	144.6	148.7
2003	142.5	141.8	142.5	140.7	140.8	140.6	136.3	135.9	135.4	135.6	135.0	134.5	138.5
2004	131.7	131.8	132.9	133.8	135.0	135.9	136.3	136.8	136.3	136.4	135.9	135.5	134.9
2005	133.9	134.6	135.3	134.8	135.7	136.5	136.9	137.1	137.0	136.8	136.8	136.6	136.0
2006	135.4	135.6	137.1	138.7	139.3	140.2	140.9	141.9	141.3	141.5	141.1	141.7	139.6
2007	139.9	140.3	140.7	141.4	141.4	142.2	142.3	142.5	142.0	141.4	140.7	140.2	141.3
2008	137.1	136.8	136.8	135.6	135.7	135.3	134.6	134.1	132.9	130.7	128.0	125.3	133.6
2009	118.9	117.1	115.6	112.8	111.9	111.0	110.7	109.6	108.9	107.5	106.7	106.4	111.4
2010	103.2	102.8	103.3	104.2	103.9	104.4	104.3	103.8	103.4	103.2	103.1	102.7	103.5
2011	100.0	101.5	102.1	103.6	104.3	105.0	105.6	105.6	107.5	106.1	106.0	105.6	104.4
Mining, Logging, and Construction													
2000	48.3	48.3	49.6	50.3	51.0	51.7	51.6	51.8	51.8	51.5	51.4	51.2	50.7
2001	49.5	49.8	50.9	51.2	51.7	52.3	52.4	52.4	52.4	51.3	50.5	49.9	51.2
2002	50.0	49.8	50.7	50.9	51.6	51.9	52.1	52.2	51.2	50.2	49.7	49.4	50.8
2003	47.8	47.5	47.9	47.1	47.9	48.3	48.4	48.6	48.6	49.1	49.1	49.0	48.3
2004	47.4	47.3	48.1	48.9	49.8	50.3	50.7	51.0	50.5	51.4	51.3	51.3	49.8
2005	50.5	50.7	51.3	51.1	51.7	52.6	54.0	54.4	54.5	53.9	54.1	54.0	52.7
2006	53.3	53.6	54.8	56.0	56.5	57.4	58.1	58.8	58.5	58.7	58.5	58.7	56.9
2007	57.6	58.1	58.9	59.6	59.7	60.6	60.7	60.8	60.4	60.0	59.3	58.6	59.5
2008	56.3	56.1	56.0	55.6	55.8	55.6	55.1	54.6	53.8	52.3	50.7	49.3	54.3
2009	45.9	45.1	44.3	43.1	43.0	43.0	43.0	42.4	41.7	40.6	40.0	39.7	42.7
2010	37.3	37.0	37.6	38.2	38.0	38.5	38.4	38.1	37.7	37.6	37.4	36.9	37.7
2011	34.4	35.7	36.2	37.1	37.4	37.7	38.3	38.6	39.9	38.8	38.6	37.5	37.5
Manufacturing													
2000	109.2	108.8	108.7	109.4	109.3	109.9	108.4	108.4	109.0	107.6	107.5	107.2	108.6
2001	105.9	106.0	105.5	105.1	104.6	104.3	102.4	102.3	102.1	101.4	100.4	100.2	103.4
2002	99.5	99.3	98.8	98.0	98.1	98.6	97.3	97.5	97.7	97.4	96.9	95.2	97.9
2003	94.7	94.3	94.6	93.6	92.9	92.3	87.9	87.3	86.8	86.5	85.9	85.5	90.2
2004	84.3	84.5	84.8	84.9	85.2	85.6	85.6	85.8	85.8	85.0	84.6	84.2	85.0
2005	83.4	83.9	84.0	83.7	84.0	83.9	82.9	82.7	82.5	82.9	82.7	82.6	83.3
2006	82.1	82.0	82.3	82.7	82.8	82.8	82.8	83.1	82.8	82.8	82.6	83.0	82.7
2007	82.3	82.2	81.8	81.8	81.7	81.6	81.6	81.7	81.6	81.4	81.4	81.6	81.7
2008	80.8	80.7	80.8	80.0	79.9	79.7	79.5	79.5	79.1	78.4	77.3	76.0	79.3
2009	73.0	72.0	71.3	69.7	68.9	68.0	67.7	67.2	67.2	66.9	66.7	66.7	68.8
2010	65.9	65.8	65.7	66.0	65.9	65.9	65.9	65.7	65.7	65.6	65.7	65.8	65.8
2011	65.6	65.8	65.9	66.5	66.9	67.3	67.3	67.0	67.6	67.3	67.4	68.1	66.9
Service-Providing													
2000	591.0	593.2	600.4	606.3	609.5	613.0	599.9	607.0	610.6	619.4	619.1	620.6	607.5
2001	607.6	610.9	615.1	619.4	621.4	620.8	606.3	614.7	616.8	621.9	622.9	621.4	616.6
2002	607.9	612.0	617.8	619.3	621.8	623.3	611.9	621.1	626.3	629.4	631.3	631.7	621.2
2003	616.2	617.4	623.0	626.6	632.8	630.4	607.9	620.4	631.0	637.0	638.7	639.7	626.8
2004	624.3	626.1	631.2	632.4	637.6	635.8	619.3	633.3	642.5	650.0	652.2	651.9	636.4
2005	638.6	641.9	647.2	652.3	655.9	651.9	636.9	653.7	662.9	672.1	673.9	674.5	655.2
2006	666.3	669.5	676.0	682.6	687.7	681.8	667.9	686.9	696.4	702.5	709.1	709.5	686.4
2007	698.9	703.8	712.6	715.5	722.3	716.2	698.6	720.2	725.6	733.9	737.0	739.2	718.7
2008	721.1	726.2	731.5	730.6	735.1	728.4	706.1	727.9	732.1	732.4	729.4	730.1	727.6
2009	705.6	704.8	705.1	702.1	703.9	696.3	675.7	695.9	696.7	697.6	699.0	698.6	698.4
2010	688.0	690.3	697.8	702.1	711.2	702.2	682.5	704.0	706.4	718.8	721.3	722.8	704.0
2011	707.2	714.7	721.0	726.6	729.2	722.7	704.6	725.9	726.5	730.7	730.2	727.6	722.2

Employment by Industry: Charlotte–Gastonia–Rock Hill, NC–SC, Selected Years, 2000–2011—*Continued*

(Numbers in thousands, not seasonally adjusted)

Industry and year	January	February	March	April	May	June	July	August	September	October	November	December	Annual average
Trade, Transportation, and Utilities													
2000	163.0	163.0	164.3	165.3	166.3	167.9	166.2	166.5	166.5	167.7	170.2	171.7	166.6
2001	167.5	166.7	167.3	169.0	169.3	169.9	167.8	167.8	167.7	168.4	169.7	170.6	168.5
2002	164.4	163.2	164.3	163.3	163.3	164.0	163.6	164.4	163.8	163.8	167.1	168.8	164.5
2003	161.2	160.8	160.9	161.1	161.4	162.1	160.5	161.3	161.8	163.0	165.9	167.7	162.3
2004	162.0	161.8	161.9	163.6	165.0	165.0	164.7	166.0	165.4	166.2	168.6	170.4	165.1
2005	165.5	166.0	167.0	167.4	167.4	166.8	166.7	166.8	166.1	169.5	172.2	174.5	168.0
2006	168.8	167.7	168.8	171.1	172.2	172.1	172.4	172.8	172.5	175.1	179.5	180.9	172.8
2007	176.2	175.4	177.5	178.1	179.2	179.4	180.0	180.2	180.1	181.8	185.7	187.2	180.1
2008	180.6	179.5	180.4	178.8	179.1	178.9	177.4	177.4	176.1	176.7	177.8	178.2	178.4
2009	172.5	170.3	169.6	167.1	167.8	167.3	166.5	166.5	165.5	166.1	167.8	168.6	168.0
2010	163.2	162.2	163.6	163.8	165.0	165.1	165.1	165.7	164.7	166.5	169.5	171.3	165.5
2011	165.2	165.2	166.4	167.2	167.8	167.8	167.1	168.7	167.6	168.9	171.9	174.9	168.2
Wholesale Trade													
2000	46.2	46.4	46.8	47.1	47.4	47.8	47.6	47.7	47.8	47.8	48.0	48.1	47.4
2001	48.6	48.6	48.9	49.2	48.9	49.0	48.8	48.6	48.5	48.1	47.9	47.6	48.6
2002	46.8	46.7	46.9	46.8	46.5	46.4	46.5	46.5	46.5	46.4	46.5	46.4	46.6
2003	46.0	46.0	45.9	46.2	46.1	46.1	45.8	45.7	45.6	46.5	46.6	46.7	46.1
2004	47.3	47.4	47.5	46.9	46.9	46.8	47.1	47.1	46.9	46.0	45.7	45.6	46.8
2005	46.0	46.0	46.1	46.7	46.8	46.4	46.5	46.5	46.4	47.0	47.3	47.3	46.6
2006	47.5	47.6	47.8	48.2	48.3	48.2	47.5	47.5	47.3	47.3	47.4	47.5	47.7
2007	47.7	48.0	48.5	49.0	48.9	49.1	49.4	49.3	49.2	49.8	49.7	49.7	49.0
2008	49.2	49.5	50.0	49.2	49.2	49.0	48.3	48.5	48.2	48.3	48.0	48.0	48.8
2009	47.2	47.1	46.6	45.6	45.2	44.8	44.5	44.3	43.8	44.1	43.8	43.7	45.1
2010	43.3	43.5	43.8	43.6	43.7	43.5	43.7	43.8	43.6	44.0	43.9	44.1	43.7
2011	43.5	43.8	44.0	43.9	44.0	44.0	43.8	45.0	45.2	44.9	45.7	45.7	44.5
Retail Trade													
2000	83.7	83.3	83.7	84.2	84.9	86.0	84.2	84.1	83.9	84.3	86.9	88.4	84.8
2001	84.2	82.8	83.5	83.7	84.2	84.8	82.9	83.0	83.0	83.3	85.4	86.7	84.0
2002	82.1	81.2	82.1	81.7	81.8	82.2	81.4	81.8	81.5	81.8	85.0	86.6	82.4
2003	80.5	79.8	80.5	80.7	80.9	81.5	80.7	81.2	81.2	81.8	84.6	85.7	81.6
2004	81.0	80.3	80.7	81.7	82.8	82.9	81.8	82.8	82.6	84.3	86.8	88.4	83.0
2005	83.8	84.2	85.0	84.8	84.6	84.1	84.6	84.7	84.3	86.7	89.0	90.7	85.5
2006	85.9	84.7	85.4	87.2	88.1	87.9	88.7	88.9	89.0	91.5	95.7	96.8	89.2
2007	92.8	91.8	93.1	93.2	94.3	94.3	94.6	95.0	95.0	96.2	100.3	101.5	95.2
2008	95.9	94.7	95.4	94.1	94.2	94.3	93.7	93.4	92.7	93.2	94.7	94.9	94.3
2009	91.3	89.8	89.4	88.5	89.6	89.5	89.2	89.6	89.0	89.7	91.8	92.4	90.0
2010	88.4	87.4	88.3	88.5	89.3	89.5	89.3	89.9	89.0	90.3	93.1	94.4	89.8
2011	89.4	89.0	89.7	90.3	90.7	90.7	90.7	90.7	89.4	91.2	93.1	95.0	90.8
Transportation and Utilities													
2000	33.1	33.3	33.8	34.0	34.0	34.1	34.4	34.7	34.8	35.6	35.3	35.2	34.4
2001	34.7	35.3	34.9	36.1	36.2	36.1	36.1	36.2	36.2	37.0	36.4	36.3	36.0
2002	35.5	35.3	35.3	34.8	35.0	35.4	35.7	36.1	35.8	35.6	35.6	35.8	35.5
2003	34.7	35.0	34.5	34.2	34.4	34.5	34.0	34.4	35.0	34.7	34.7	35.3	34.6
2004	33.7	34.1	33.7	35.0	35.3	35.3	35.8	36.1	35.9	35.9	36.1	36.4	35.3
2005	35.7	35.8	35.9	35.9	36.0	36.3	35.6	35.6	35.4	35.8	35.9	36.5	35.9
2006	35.4	35.4	35.6	35.7	35.8	36.0	36.2	36.4	36.2	36.3	36.4	36.6	36.0
2007	35.7	35.6	35.9	35.9	36.0	36.0	36.0	35.9	35.9	35.8	35.7	36.0	35.9
2008	35.5	35.3	35.0	35.5	35.7	35.6	35.4	35.5	35.2	35.2	35.1	35.3	35.4
2009	34.0	33.4	33.6	33.0	33.0	33.0	32.8	32.6	32.7	32.3	32.2	32.5	32.9
2010	31.5	31.3	31.5	31.7	32.0	32.1	32.1	32.0	32.1	32.2	32.5	32.8	32.0
2011	32.3	32.4	32.7	33.0	33.1	33.1	32.6	33.0	33.0	32.8	33.1	34.2	32.9
Information													
2000	23.8	23.9	24.0	24.1	23.8	24.0	24.0	24.1	24.2	24.3	24.7	24.4	24.1
2001	24.0	24.1	24.2	23.4	23.3	23.5	23.5	23.2	22.6	23.2	23.2	22.9	23.4
2002	23.1	23.0	23.2	22.8	22.8	23.0	22.9	22.8	22.7	23.0	23.0	23.2	23.0
2003	22.5	22.3	22.4	22.1	22.0	22.3	22.0	21.9	21.8	21.9	21.9	22.0	22.1
2004	22.0	21.9	22.0	21.8	21.6	21.8	21.1	20.9	20.6	21.0	21.1	20.8	21.4
2005	20.5	20.4	20.5	20.8	21.0	21.1	21.2	21.2	21.2	21.3	21.7	22.1	21.1
2006	22.2	22.2	22.2	21.9	22.0	22.1	21.7	22.1	22.0	21.9	22.1	22.3	22.1
2007	22.0	22.0	21.9	21.9	22.0	22.4	22.3	22.3	22.2	22.1	22.3	22.4	22.2
2008	21.8	22.0	22.1	22.0	22.1	22.2	22.1	22.0	22.0	22.3	22.3	22.4	22.1
2009	21.6	21.5	21.5	21.5	21.4	21.3	21.2	21.1	21.0	20.9	21.0	21.0	21.3
2010	20.9	20.9	21.0	20.9	21.0	21.1	21.1	21.2	21.3	21.4	21.5	21.6	21.2
2011	21.3	21.4	21.4	21.5	21.4	21.7	21.7	21.7	21.5	21.6	21.7	21.7	21.6
Financial Activities													
2000	54.5	54.8	54.8	56.1	56.6	57.5	57.2	57.4	57.2	57.4	57.5	57.8	56.6
2001	57.7	58.1	58.4	58.8	59.0	59.3	59.9	60.3	60.3	60.2	60.8	61.0	59.5
2002	61.5	61.8	62.3	62.8	63.1	63.8	64.7	65.2	65.1	65.8	66.2	66.4	64.1
2003	66.4	66.7	66.9	67.0	67.1	67.6	66.3	66.7	66.7	66.7	66.6	67.0	66.8
2004	66.8	67.0	67.1	67.1	67.1	67.5	68.7	69.0	68.9	69.1	69.3	69.3	68.1
2005	69.4	69.8	69.8	70.3	70.8	71.5	72.6	72.4	72.3	72.7	73.0	73.7	71.5
2006	73.8	74.7	75.2	76.1	76.2	76.6	78.2	78.1	77.7	77.2	77.1	77.2	76.5
2007	76.7	77.3	77.5	77.9	78.0	78.1	77.5	77.3	76.8	77.2	77.0	77.1	77.4
2008	75.8	76.1	76.1	76.5	75.8	75.9	74.8	74.8	74.1	73.9	73.4	73.8	75.1
2009	71.9	71.8	71.5	70.9	70.9	70.4	70.0	69.4	68.6	68.5	68.5	68.6	70.1
2010	68.7	69.3	69.4	68.8	69.1	69.4	68.9	69.7	70.2	70.8	71.1	71.3	69.7
2011	71.8	72.2	72.3	71.8	72.2	72.5	73.0	71.9	71.7	71.5	70.8	71.0	71.9

Employment by Industry: Charlotte–Gastonia–Rock Hill, NC–SC, Selected Years, 2000–2011—*Continued*

(Numbers in thousands, not seasonally adjusted)

Industry and year	January	February	March	April	May	June	July	August	September	October	November	December	Annual average
Professional and Business Services													
2000	113.5	114.2	116.5	120.4	120.4	121.1	121.3	122.2	122.3	123.6	122.2	122.2	120.0
2001	119.4	119.7	120.7	119.5	119.1	117.9	116.3	116.4	115.2	115.3	113.1	113.4	117.2
2002	110.2	112.2	112.9	113.3	114.4	114.9	114.0	116.1	116.2	114.9	113.7	112.8	113.8
2003	111.9	111.5	113.0	114.0	114.9	114.4	113.9	115.9	116.2	115.4	114.9	114.1	114.2
2004	110.1	111.9	113.5	111.3	111.5	113.1	113.8	115.3	115.1	117.5	117.1	115.2	113.8
2005	112.9	113.5	114.2	115.7	116.3	115.8	117.8	118.5	120.4	121.9	121.0	119.3	117.3
2006	117.5	118.7	120.1	122.5	123.9	124.5	125.9	127.3	128.4	129.8	130.2	128.1	124.7
2007	125.5	127.2	129.9	131.7	133.2	134.3	134.1	135.7	136.4	138.2	137.3	136.8	133.4
2008	133.5	136.0	137.1	137.2	138.6	138.9	137.2	137.7	137.2	136.1	133.0	131.6	136.2
2009	126.5	126.3	125.8	124.8	123.9	123.2	123.6	123.9	124.4	126.1	126.6	126.5	125.1
2010	123.6	124.2	126.6	128.3	128.9	129.6	130.3	131.6	132.1	135.4	135.0	135.1	130.1
2011	131.7	135.5	136.6	138.8	138.2	139.3	138.6	139.4	140.4	142.4	141.6	140.9	138.6
Education and Health Services													
2000	53.1	53.7	53.9	53.7	53.6	53.6	53.2	53.5	54.4	55.4	55.7	55.8	54.1
2001	54.4	55.2	55.9	55.5	55.8	56.6	55.8	56.6	57.1	57.7	58.2	58.2	56.4
2002	57.2	58.1	58.2	57.8	58.4	58.9	59.2	60.1	60.8	61.4	61.8	62.8	59.6
2003	62.0	62.7	63.2	63.3	63.8	63.9	63.4	64.2	64.2	65.0	65.2	65.9	63.9
2004	64.6	63.0	63.3	64.0	64.1	63.7	64.4	64.9	65.0	65.7	66.0	67.1	64.7
2005	65.7	65.8	66.5	67.0	67.0	66.8	67.2	67.9	68.3	69.1	69.3	69.3	67.5
2006	70.6	71.2	71.5	70.9	70.9	71.6	71.8	72.5	73.1	74.4	74.8	75.4	72.4
2007	74.7	75.7	76.1	76.7	76.9	77.1	77.1	77.7	77.9	79.3	79.2	79.7	77.3
2008	77.6	78.3	78.5	78.2	78.3	78.3	78.1	79.0	79.4	81.2	81.8	82.4	79.3
2009	80.3	80.9	80.7	81.0	81.1	80.9	80.4	81.4	81.3	81.9	82.5	82.4	81.2
2010	81.4	81.9	82.0	83.1	83.4	82.4	83.0	83.5	83.4	85.1	85.7	85.6	83.4
2011	84.7	85.9	85.8	86.0	85.9	84.9	85.4	85.3	85.6	87.4	88.0	87.3	86.0
Leisure and Hospitality													
2000	65.6	65.5	67.3	67.0	69.4	71.2	69.6	69.8	67.8	68.1	66.5	66.3	67.8
2001	64.3	64.8	65.5	69.2	70.3	71.6	70.1	70.6	68.5	68.2	66.5	65.0	67.9
2002	62.9	63.5	65.6	68.8	69.8	71.2	70.7	70.5	69.7	68.5	67.2	67.6	68.0
2003	64.8	65.3	67.7	69.7	73.3	73.8	72.3	72.2	71.3	71.2	70.8	70.7	70.3
2004	68.0	68.7	71.0	72.5	75.5	75.6	75.7	76.4	75.2	74.3	73.4	73.3	73.3
2005	71.1	71.9	73.9	75.3	77.3	78.2	78.2	79.3	78.0	78.2	77.3	76.7	76.3
2006	75.3	75.8	78.3	80.6	82.3	82.7	83.7	83.6	82.5	82.4	81.9	81.9	80.9
2007	81.3	81.9	84.7	86.1	88.8	89.9	89.0	88.8	87.5	87.8	86.6	86.7	86.6
2008	84.4	85.7	88.3	89.6	91.9	92.6	92.9	93.2	92.4	91.8	89.6	89.7	90.2
2009	83.5	83.9	85.5	86.5	89.2	89.6	89.0	88.7	88.0	86.0	84.0	83.0	86.4
2010	80.7	80.9	83.1	85.3	88.3	89.9	89.0	88.7	88.6	87.7	86.1	85.2	86.1
2011	82.2	82.9	85.9	88.1	90.4	92.6	92.8	93.5	91.9	89.8	87.1	82.2	88.3
Other Services													
2000	29.1	29.4	29.7	29.8	29.8	30.3	30.3	30.1	30.1	30.7	30.7	30.9	30.1
2001	30.5	31.0	31.5	31.8	32.5	33.0	33.1	33.4	33.6	33.8	34.1	34.4	32.7
2002	34.6	34.7	35.0	35.0	34.6	34.9	34.0	33.5	33.5	33.5	33.4	32.7	34.1
2003	31.7	31.5	31.6	32.2	32.5	32.5	32.6	32.4	32.7	31.6	31.6	31.6	32.0
2004	32.0	32.0	32.5	32.1	32.6	33.0	32.8	32.6	32.3	33.0	33.0	33.3	32.6
2005	32.9	33.0	33.3	33.0	33.6	33.9	33.8	33.7	33.7	33.8	33.7	33.7	33.5
2006	33.8	34.3	34.6	33.9	34.5	35.1	34.2	34.2	34.0	34.2	34.2	34.4	34.3
2007	34.3	34.6	35.2	34.1	34.5	34.8	34.8	34.8	34.6	35.4	35.4	35.5	34.8
2008	34.0	34.0	33.9	33.2	33.8	33.8	33.6	33.6	32.9	32.7	32.5	32.3	33.4
2009	31.2	31.4	31.3	30.9	31.0	30.8	30.8	30.6	30.0	29.8	29.8	29.4	30.6
2010	29.1	29.2	29.5	29.3	29.6	29.9	30.0	30.3	30.4	30.6	30.7	30.8	30.0
2011	30.8	31.2	31.4	31.5	31.7	31.9	31.4	31.8	31.5	31.6	31.3	31.7	31.5
Government													
2000	88.4	88.7	89.9	89.9	89.6	87.4	78.1	83.4	88.1	92.2	91.6	91.5	88.2
2001	89.8	91.3	91.6	92.2	92.1	89.0	79.8	86.4	91.8	95.1	97.3	95.9	91.0
2002	94.0	95.5	96.3	95.5	95.4	92.6	82.8	88.5	94.5	98.5	98.9	97.4	94.2
2003	95.7	96.6	97.3	97.2	97.8	93.8	76.9	85.8	96.3	102.2	101.8	100.7	95.2
2004	98.8	99.8	99.9	100.0	100.2	96.1	78.1	88.2	100.0	103.2	103.7	102.5	97.5
2005	100.6	101.5	102.0	102.8	102.5	97.8	79.4	93.9	102.9	105.6	105.7	105.2	100.0
2006	104.3	104.9	105.3	105.6	105.7	97.1	80.0	96.3	106.2	107.5	109.3	109.3	102.6
2007	108.2	109.7	109.8	109.0	109.7	100.2	83.8	103.4	110.1	112.1	113.5	113.8	106.9
2008	113.4	114.6	115.1	115.1	115.5	107.8	90.0	110.2	118.0	117.7	119.0	119.7	113.0
2009	118.1	118.7	119.2	119.4	118.6	112.8	94.2	114.3	117.9	118.3	118.8	119.1	115.8
2010	120.4	121.7	122.6	122.6	125.9	114.8	95.1	113.3	115.7	121.3	121.7	121.9	118.1
2011	119.5	120.4	121.2	121.7	121.6	112.0	94.6	113.6	116.3	117.5	117.8	117.9	116.2

Employment by Industry: Chicago–Joliet–Naperville, IL–IN–WI, Selected Years, 2000–2011

(Numbers in thousands, not seasonally adjusted)

Industry and year	January	February	March	April	May	June	July	August	September	October	November	December	Annual average
Total Nonfarm													
2000	4,445.7	4,464.9	4,509.8	4,543.2	4,586.9	4,626.3	4,585.9	4,606.9	4,608.4	4,613.6	4,631.5	4,633.8	4,571.4
2001	4,491.0	4,498.8	4,529.9	4,552.3	4,590.7	4,625.9	4,568.8	4,571.4	4,555.9	4,528.8	4,527.6	4,529.0	4,547.5
2002	4,377.2	4,372.5	4,395.3	4,436.4	4,471.8	4,501.6	4,477.9	4,489.7	4,475.4	4,476.2	4,487.2	4,484.5	4,453.8
2003	4,342.1	4,338.0	4,359.0	4,392.0	4,432.9	4,461.7	4,447.9	4,451.7	4,437.1	4,428.7	4,427.4	4,437.1	4,413.0
2004	4,296.5	4,299.2	4,334.5	4,383.3	4,431.5	4,465.8	4,450.2	4,450.7	4,447.1	4,464.7	4,475.0	4,479.5	4,414.8
2005	4,339.5	4,347.2	4,372.8	4,440.5	4,474.7	4,496.9	4,498.1	4,497.4	4,505.1	4,510.7	4,526.5	4,527.0	4,461.4
2006	4,401.0	4,413.7	4,446.4	4,495.0	4,533.5	4,577.3	4,549.4	4,554.0	4,557.2	4,560.6	4,574.5	4,576.1	4,519.9
2007	4,451.8	4,450.3	4,490.0	4,531.2	4,580.0	4,614.5	4,588.7	4,590.8	4,583.8	4,591.7	4,606.9	4,605.4	4,557.1
2008	4,472.5	4,469.4	4,489.7	4,536.3	4,576.2	4,594.2	4,563.3	4,565.2	4,541.0	4,536.8	4,514.2	4,484.2	4,529.0
2009	4,317.3	4,293.6	4,285.4	4,295.6	4,321.1	4,328.5	4,288.4	4,276.8	4,270.5	4,280.2	4,281.1	4,267.5	4,292.2
2010	4,141.9	4,148.8	4,170.3	4,223.3	4,278.5	4,294.4	4,253.7	4,263.9	4,268.5	4,300.6	4,311.7	4,303.5	4,246.6
2011	4,182.7	4,188.9	4,220.4	4,278.3	4,313.0	4,341.6	4,319.7	4,315.2	4,318.2	4,343.2	4,346.0	4,329.3	4,291.4
Total Private													
2000	3,910.7	3,916.9	3,956.5	3,992.6	4,019.7	4,061.1	4,042.2	4,061.0	4,056.6	4,057.3	4,073.4	4,075.0	4,018.6
2001	3,946.8	3,940.8	3,969.6	3,994.9	4,025.3	4,062.5	4,018.4	4,024.7	4,002.3	3,965.2	3,962.3	3,961.7	3,989.5
2002	3,821.9	3,806.5	3,826.7	3,864.6	3,895.8	3,927.7	3,915.4	3,930.1	3,915.2	3,903.1	3,911.8	3,908.9	3,885.6
2003	3,778.7	3,764.3	3,782.8	3,818.6	3,855.6	3,886.2	3,875.2	3,888.1	3,875.1	3,862.7	3,861.4	3,873.6	3,843.5
2004	3,742.5	3,736.5	3,769.5	3,816.9	3,861.1	3,897.7	3,897.9	3,903.6	3,892.5	3,896.7	3,904.4	3,914.7	3,852.8
2005	3,783.2	3,780.6	3,802.0	3,868.9	3,900.1	3,927.7	3,941.2	3,947.2	3,943.9	3,943.4	3,956.0	3,961.3	3,896.3
2006	3,844.8	3,847.2	3,877.7	3,923.7	3,958.5	4,003.8	3,995.6	4,004.9	3,992.0	3,991.8	4,002.9	4,008.8	3,954.3
2007	3,894.0	3,881.7	3,918.8	3,958.6	4,005.0	4,042.6	4,033.9	4,038.5	4,018.6	4,022.6	4,035.7	4,037.9	3,990.7
2008	3,912.8	3,899.4	3,917.0	3,962.0	3,996.4	4,018.5	4,008.2	4,008.9	3,971.5	3,960.2	3,937.3	3,910.7	3,958.6
2009	3,754.9	3,724.0	3,712.7	3,718.1	3,739.9	3,753.6	3,731.9	3,726.7	3,703.1	3,702.9	3,703.4	3,695.6	3,722.2
2010	3,579.3	3,578.7	3,599.8	3,648.2	3,685.8	3,715.9	3,703.9	3,720.7	3,710.1	3,733.9	3,743.6	3,743.4	3,680.3
2011	3,633.0	3,631.4	3,660.8	3,717.9	3,748.2	3,784.4	3,777.0	3,780.2	3,767.2	3,784.8	3,786.7	3,775.5	3,737.3
Goods-Producing													
2000	827.6	828.9	841.2	851.5	856.4	862.3	858.0	863.7	862.0	861.1	859.1	847.8	851.6
2001	811.7	811.1	815.9	821.9	826.9	831.3	816.9	819.6	815.9	808.4	802.0	792.4	814.5
2002	754.9	750.8	755.5	765.6	771.1	778.3	773.0	777.0	775.8	772.5	768.7	758.9	766.8
2003	725.4	720.7	725.1	735.9	744.3	749.5	743.8	748.3	745.7	737.3	730.9	723.9	735.9
2004	691.4	687.1	696.5	709.1	719.0	726.5	727.3	728.8	728.6	727.2	724.4	717.9	715.3
2005	686.9	686.6	691.8	708.6	715.2	721.8	721.9	723.8	723.9	723.3	721.1	711.4	711.4
2006	688.8	688.7	692.6	709.1	715.2	724.5	720.1	721.9	721.0	720.0	715.6	708.8	710.5
2007	682.3	673.7	686.0	697.8	706.9	716.3	712.7	712.4	710.5	708.9	704.5	696.0	700.7
2008	667.2	660.6	666.3	677.3	685.2	690.0	688.2	688.0	682.1	675.9	662.7	642.8	673.9
2009	601.8	593.3	588.6	586.3	585.3	588.1	582.3	581.3	577.5	573.6	567.2	555.3	581.7
2010	528.2	527.0	533.5	546.6	554.3	560.5	555.9	565.5	563.0	567.3	563.7	553.0	551.5
2011	533.3	531.7	540.5	554.6	563.2	569.6	571.6	571.3	566.3	565.2	564.2	554.4	557.2
Mining and Logging													
2000	2.1	2.1	2.2	2.3	2.3	2.4	2.4	2.4	2.4	2.5	2.4	2.4	2.3
2001	2.1	2.1	2.2	2.4	2.4	2.4	2.4	2.4	2.4	2.4	2.3	2.3	2.3
2002	2.0	2.0	2.2	2.2	2.2	2.4	2.4	2.4	2.4	2.3	2.3	2.3	2.3
2003	1.9	2.0	2.1	2.3	2.3	2.3	2.3	2.3	2.3	2.3	2.2	2.1	2.2
2004	1.8	1.9	2.1	2.2	2.2	2.2	2.2	2.3	2.3	2.3	2.3	2.2	2.2
2005	2.0	2.0	2.1	2.3	2.3	2.4	2.5	2.4	2.4	2.5	2.4	2.3	2.3
2006	2.0	2.0	2.1	2.4	2.5	2.6	2.6	2.6	2.6	2.5	2.6	2.4	2.4
2007	2.3	2.1	2.4	2.3	2.4	2.4	2.4	2.4	2.3	2.3	2.3	2.1	2.3
2008	1.9	1.8	1.9	2.1	2.1	2.2	2.2	2.2	2.1	2.0	1.9	1.8	2.0
2009	1.4	1.5	1.6	1.8	1.8	1.8	1.8	1.8	1.9	1.7	1.7	1.6	1.7
2010	1.3	1.3	1.3	1.5	1.6	1.6	1.6	1.6	1.6	1.6	1.6	1.4	1.5
2011	1.3	1.2	1.4	1.4	1.5	1.5	1.5	1.5	1.5	1.5	1.5	1.5	1.4
Construction													
2000	188.5	188.4	197.8	209.4	215.1	219.8	222.4	224.2	223.0	222.9	221.1	211.8	212.0
2001	189.7	191.6	198.2	211.6	220.4	225.6	227.0	229.1	227.2	226.9	226.3	220.7	216.2
2002	194.3	193.0	198.2	209.9	217.3	223.2	227.4	229.4	228.6	228.0	225.8	217.1	216.0
2003	196.2	192.8	198.1	210.5	221.0	226.6	229.7	232.8	231.1	225.8	220.9	214.6	216.7
2004	189.5	186.1	193.6	206.8	214.6	220.1	224.7	224.5	223.8	223.9	221.6	215.2	212.0
2005	189.3	188.8	192.9	209.0	215.2	220.3	224.3	225.5	226.0	226.2	223.8	214.1	213.0
2006	197.9	197.5	203.2	216.6	223.9	229.7	229.0	230.9	228.2	227.8	223.9	216.6	218.8
2007	196.3	188.3	199.4	211.9	220.9	227.1	227.2	227.2	225.6	224.1	221.1	210.7	215.0
2008	188.1	184.6	189.7	201.2	209.3	212.7	215.2	215.9	212.3	209.3	200.0	185.6	202.0
2009	157.4	155.6	157.1	163.4	167.2	170.7	171.1	170.9	167.6	166.1	161.1	149.4	163.1
2010	128.2	126.7	132.3	144.1	149.8	153.6	150.0	157.4	155.4	157.2	152.9	141.9	145.8
2011	125.8	124.1	130.4	142.2	149.8	153.8	156.5	156.6	152.6	153.6	149.7	139.3	144.5
Manufacturing													
2000	637.0	638.4	641.2	639.8	639.0	640.1	633.2	637.1	636.6	635.7	635.6	633.6	637.3
2001	619.9	617.4	615.5	607.9	604.1	603.3	587.5	588.1	586.3	579.1	573.4	569.4	596.0
2002	558.6	555.8	555.1	553.5	551.6	552.7	543.2	545.2	544.8	542.2	540.6	539.5	548.6
2003	527.3	525.9	524.9	523.1	521.0	520.6	511.8	513.2	512.3	509.2	507.8	507.2	517.0
2004	500.1	499.1	500.8	500.1	502.2	504.2	500.4	502.0	502.5	501.1	500.5	500.5	501.1
2005	495.6	495.8	496.8	497.3	497.7	499.1	495.1	495.9	495.5	494.6	494.9	495.0	496.1
2006	488.9	489.2	487.3	490.1	488.8	492.2	488.5	488.4	490.2	489.7	489.1	489.8	489.4
2007	483.7	483.3	484.2	483.6	483.6	486.8	483.1	482.8	482.6	482.5	481.1	483.2	483.4
2008	477.2	474.2	474.7	474.0	473.8	475.1	470.8	469.9	467.7	464.6	460.8	455.4	469.9
2009	443.0	436.2	429.9	421.1	416.3	415.6	409.4	408.6	408.0	405.8	404.4	404.3	416.9
2010	398.7	399.0	399.9	401.0	402.9	405.3	404.3	406.5	406.0	408.5	409.2	409.7	404.3
2011	406.2	406.4	408.7	411.0	411.9	414.3	413.6	413.2	412.2	410.1	413.0	413.6	411.2

Employment by Industry: Chicago–Joliet–Naperville, IL–IN–WI, Selected Years, 2000–2011—*Continued*

(Numbers in thousands, not seasonally adjusted)

Industry and year	January	February	March	April	May	June	July	August	September	October	November	December	Annual average
Service-Providing													
2000	3,618.1	3,636.0	3,668.6	3,691.7	3,730.5	3,764.0	3,727.9	3,743.2	3,746.4	3,752.5	3,772.4	3,786.0	3,719.8
2001	3,679.3	3,687.7	3,714.0	3,730.4	3,763.8	3,794.6	3,751.9	3,751.8	3,740.0	3,720.4	3,725.6	3,736.6	3,733.0
2002	3,622.3	3,621.7	3,639.8	3,670.8	3,700.7	3,723.3	3,704.9	3,712.7	3,699.6	3,703.7	3,718.5	3,725.6	3,687.0
2003	3,616.7	3,617.3	3,633.9	3,656.1	3,688.6	3,712.2	3,704.1	3,703.4	3,691.4	3,691.4	3,696.5	3,713.2	3,677.1
2004	3,605.1	3,612.1	3,638.0	3,674.2	3,712.5	3,739.3	3,722.9	3,721.9	3,718.5	3,737.5	3,750.6	3,761.6	3,699.5
2005	3,652.6	3,660.6	3,681.0	3,731.9	3,759.5	3,775.1	3,776.2	3,773.6	3,781.2	3,787.4	3,805.4	3,815.6	3,750.0
2006	3,712.2	3,725.0	3,753.8	3,785.9	3,818.3	3,852.8	3,829.3	3,832.1	3,836.2	3,840.6	3,858.9	3,867.3	3,809.4
2007	3,769.5	3,776.6	3,804.0	3,833.4	3,873.1	3,898.2	3,876.0	3,878.4	3,873.3	3,882.8	3,902.4	3,909.4	3,856.4
2008	3,805.3	3,808.8	3,823.4	3,859.0	3,891.0	3,904.2	3,880.1	3,877.2	3,858.9	3,860.9	3,851.5	3,841.4	3,855.1
2009	3,715.5	3,700.3	3,696.8	3,709.3	3,735.8	3,740.4	3,706.1	3,695.5	3,693.0	3,706.6	3,713.9	3,712.2	3,710.5
2010	3,613.7	3,621.8	3,636.8	3,676.7	3,724.2	3,733.9	3,697.8	3,698.4	3,705.5	3,733.3	3,748.0	3,750.5	3,695.1
2011	3,649.4	3,657.2	3,679.9	3,723.7	3,749.8	3,772.0	3,748.1	3,743.9	3,751.9	3,778.0	3,781.8	3,774.9	3,734.2
Trade, Transportation, and Utilities													
2000	940.8	933.7	937.5	938.0	943.4	950.3	949.5	955.0	954.3	961.6	980.8	993.8	953.2
2001	957.5	944.4	947.0	950.5	954.7	961.2	950.2	949.2	947.1	939.4	952.7	963.6	951.5
2002	921.2	907.3	910.3	913.1	918.1	922.1	916.8	918.8	918.3	921.6	938.0	949.5	921.3
2003	904.3	895.3	897.3	897.3	903.5	908.0	900.1	902.3	904.0	907.8	921.7	935.3	906.4
2004	895.3	886.8	891.3	895.7	905.8	911.8	907.0	908.4	909.4	915.7	930.8	944.8	908.6
2005	902.6	892.9	896.2	902.3	909.3	913.9	911.6	913.8	915.0	918.9	934.5	949.5	913.4
2006	911.6	903.0	908.2	911.1	918.3	925.1	919.3	920.1	919.0	922.8	942.0	954.7	921.3
2007	923.9	912.0	918.3	916.4	926.9	934.1	928.5	928.4	927.4	931.8	954.1	966.0	930.7
2008	931.5	918.2	920.7	921.0	927.6	930.7	923.7	922.7	917.5	918.9	927.1	931.9	924.3
2009	890.1	875.7	870.2	863.7	868.5	869.7	859.9	859.5	855.8	858.4	869.3	876.6	868.1
2010	843.0	835.6	838.0	843.9	851.5	856.6	853.5	855.7	853.0	861.7	877.1	889.0	854.9
2011	857.4	849.3	852.3	860.4	866.3	872.8	866.1	865.5	867.5	873.0	886.7	894.3	867.6
Wholesale Trade													
2000	251.1	252.3	253.0	251.6	252.9	255.1	254.7	255.3	254.4	255.3	255.9	256.9	254.0
2001	255.5	255.1	255.2	258.2	259.6	261.5	261.4	260.9	260.1	255.9	254.7	255.5	257.8
2002	250.8	250.7	251.0	251.2	251.4	252.9	251.2	251.1	250.1	250.0	250.6	250.6	251.0
2003	248.6	248.5	249.0	247.5	247.9	248.6	247.2	246.2	245.1	243.2	243.9	244.6	246.7
2004	240.9	240.4	241.5	242.4	243.9	245.3	244.7	244.6	243.8	244.5	245.1	246.3	243.6
2005	241.1	240.9	241.7	243.4	244.5	246.2	246.4	245.9	246.0	246.3	247.5	249.1	244.9
2006	246.0	246.0	247.2	247.7	248.8	250.8	249.7	249.3	248.4	248.5	248.6	250.1	248.4
2007	247.7	247.7	248.8	248.9	250.2	252.4	252.0	251.3	250.5	251.7	252.0	253.4	250.6
2008	250.3	249.7	250.4	250.8	251.9	252.9	251.0	250.4	249.1	248.6	247.6	247.0	250.0
2009	241.3	239.2	237.7	235.1	234.2	233.8	231.2	230.7	228.7	229.1	228.3	228.6	233.2
2010	225.5	225.1	226.3	227.6	229.0	230.0	230.2	230.3	228.9	229.9	230.1	230.8	228.6
2011	229.0	229.2	230.0	231.6	232.3	234.3	235.1	235.2	234.2	233.6	234.1	233.0	232.6
Retail Trade													
2000	475.2	467.3	470.4	470.3	473.3	477.8	477.5	481.1	479.8	484.5	501.9	512.9	481.0
2001	484.3	473.1	475.1	477.2	479.2	485.3	477.0	477.0	474.5	472.4	489.2	501.2	480.5
2002	469.7	457.6	461.1	461.3	466.1	470.6	466.9	467.9	466.8	469.2	485.8	497.6	470.1
2003	459.5	452.1	453.7	454.6	459.1	463.9	459.2	461.2	460.5	464.7	477.7	490.2	463.0
2004	458.7	451.4	454.1	455.5	462.2	468.5	463.9	465.0	463.6	467.3	481.8	494.2	465.5
2005	462.9	453.2	454.8	458.1	463.3	467.2	467.9	469.7	467.5	470.0	483.5	495.2	467.8
2006	466.8	457.6	460.1	461.7	466.0	471.6	469.2	469.9	465.1	469.8	487.8	496.6	470.2
2007	474.5	462.6	466.7	465.6	472.5	478.0	475.8	475.3	471.3	474.2	495.0	502.9	476.2
2008	477.9	465.2	466.3	466.4	470.2	474.2	471.8	469.7	463.5	465.8	475.3	479.7	470.5
2009	452.6	441.8	439.1	437.2	442.1	445.1	441.9	441.4	436.9	439.1	450.9	456.3	443.7
2010	431.7	424.5	425.6	428.2	433.1	437.8	436.9	437.1	432.3	438.6	452.6	461.0	436.6
2011	437.0	428.6	430.2	435.0	438.8	443.8	440.9	439.4	434.0	438.9	450.4	459.6	439.7
Transportation and Utilities													
2000	214.5	214.1	214.1	216.1	217.2	217.4	217.3	218.6	220.1	221.8	223.0	224.0	218.2
2001	217.7	216.2	216.7	215.1	215.9	214.4	211.8	211.3	212.5	211.1	208.8	206.9	213.2
2002	200.7	199.0	198.2	200.6	200.6	198.6	198.7	199.8	201.4	202.4	201.6	201.3	200.2
2003	196.2	194.7	194.6	195.2	196.5	195.5	193.7	194.9	198.4	199.9	200.1	200.5	196.7
2004	195.7	195.0	195.7	197.8	199.7	198.0	198.4	198.8	202.0	203.9	203.9	204.3	199.4
2005	198.6	198.8	199.7	200.8	201.5	200.5	197.3	198.2	201.5	202.6	203.5	205.2	200.7
2006	198.8	199.4	200.9	201.7	203.5	202.7	200.4	200.9	205.5	204.5	205.6	208.0	202.7
2007	201.7	201.7	202.8	201.9	204.2	203.7	200.7	201.8	205.6	205.9	207.1	209.7	203.9
2008	203.3	203.3	204.0	203.8	205.5	203.6	200.9	202.6	204.9	204.5	204.2	205.2	203.8
2009	196.2	194.7	193.4	191.4	192.2	190.8	186.8	187.4	190.2	190.2	190.1	191.7	191.3
2010	185.8	186.0	186.1	188.1	189.4	188.8	186.4	188.3	191.8	193.2	194.4	197.2	189.6
2011	191.4	191.5	192.1	193.8	195.2	194.7	190.1	190.9	199.3	200.5	202.2	201.7	195.3
Information													
2000	114.4	115.1	116.3	115.2	115.9	117.5	117.3	117.5	117.0	117.6	118.2	118.8	116.7
2001	117.9	118.1	118.4	117.4	118.0	119.1	117.7	117.7	116.1	114.0	114.0	114.1	116.9
2002	111.3	110.7	110.5	110.0	110.1	110.1	107.9	107.6	105.9	105.5	105.0	104.7	108.3
2003	102.1	102.2	101.2	100.3	100.2	100.4	99.8	98.9	97.8	97.5	97.1	96.9	99.5
2004	96.1	96.0	95.8	95.4	95.4	95.7	95.2	94.7	93.5	93.9	93.8	94.5	95.0
2005	93.4	93.1	93.1	93.4	93.1	93.4	93.6	92.8	92.0	91.8	91.7	91.7	92.8
2006	91.4	91.2	91.2	91.3	91.6	92.0	91.7	91.4	90.6	90.8	90.7	91.0	91.2
2007	90.4	90.8	90.5	90.5	90.8	91.3	91.6	91.7	91.0	91.0	91.0	91.1	91.0
2008	90.7	90.9	90.9	90.8	91.1	91.0	90.9	90.7	89.0	88.4	88.0	87.9	90.0
2009	86.6	85.8	84.8	84.1	83.9	83.8	83.4	83.2	82.6	82.4	82.1	82.3	83.8
2010	81.5	80.8	80.5	80.4	80.5	81.0	80.8	80.7	79.8	80.2	80.1	79.9	80.5
2011	79.5	79.2	79.0	79.2	79.3	79.8	79.8	79.7	78.8	79.4	79.1	79.3	79.3

Employment by Industry: Chicago–Joliet–Naperville, IL–IN–WI, Selected Years, 2000–2011—*Continued*

(Numbers in thousands, not seasonally adjusted)

Industry and year	January	February	March	April	May	June	July	August	September	October	November	December	Annual average
Financial Activities													
2000	318.0	318.2	317.9	318.2	318.3	321.7	320.5	320.6	317.2	318.5	318.9	321.9	319.2
2001	321.6	322.3	324.6	325.0	326.1	329.4	328.6	328.0	324.2	322.8	323.7	325.4	325.1
2002	320.5	319.9	320.6	319.8	320.9	324.4	323.9	324.2	322.0	322.5	323.7	325.7	322.3
2003	323.9	323.6	324.6	325.3	326.7	330.4	330.7	330.9	328.3	324.9	325.2	326.6	326.8
2004	321.8	321.5	323.0	322.3	323.5	326.7	327.5	327.5	324.1	323.7	323.5	325.7	324.2
2005	323.1	322.8	323.4	325.2	326.2	329.1	331.4	331.4	329.6	329.7	330.0	332.1	327.8
2006	327.6	327.9	328.9	329.8	330.7	333.8	334.7	334.7	333.1	332.1	331.8	333.2	331.5
2007	329.8	329.5	329.3	329.4	330.0	332.2	331.2	329.8	325.7	324.8	323.9	324.2	328.3
2008	318.7	318.6	318.6	318.0	318.5	320.0	318.4	317.8	313.6	312.4	310.7	310.6	316.3
2009	304.4	302.4	300.7	299.8	299.4	300.1	298.6	297.6	294.4	293.6	293.0	293.5	298.1
2010	288.8	288.4	288.4	288.0	288.2	290.1	289.3	289.1	286.0	287.3	286.7	287.1	288.1
2011	283.1	282.8	282.6	283.1	283.5	285.9	286.5	284.9	281.9	283.0	282.0	283.4	283.6
Professional and Business Services													
2000	698.9	702.9	713.4	725.2	730.5	742.4	740.3	746.7	746.5	743.5	741.9	738.2	730.9
2001	704.4	701.8	705.5	709.0	714.2	721.9	711.1	714.1	708.6	703.1	694.3	690.9	706.6
2002	662.1	660.9	662.9	676.0	678.9	684.9	685.5	692.3	690.0	683.8	680.7	673.5	677.6
2003	647.0	644.9	646.9	659.1	663.4	668.0	667.7	673.2	675.7	676.4	671.0	671.8	663.8
2004	645.8	648.7	655.3	671.8	680.2	691.8	690.9	695.9	696.6	703.1	700.8	696.9	681.5
2005	672.0	675.2	680.8	698.7	702.5	711.7	714.5	719.5	721.8	728.2	727.7	723.5	706.3
2006	695.2	698.7	707.9	722.2	726.7	738.8	739.0	745.8	744.2	747.8	745.2	740.0	729.3
2007	711.4	713.9	721.1	739.0	744.9	753.1	754.2	760.1	755.0	757.8	755.4	753.0	743.2
2008	723.5	725.2	724.9	739.4	743.2	746.4	744.5	747.8	739.3	736.9	727.3	717.5	734.7
2009	681.9	674.2	666.8	672.1	675.4	677.3	675.5	676.5	672.4	677.3	678.0	674.5	675.2
2010	652.8	656.0	657.1	677.5	681.8	690.6	692.7	697.7	695.6	703.3	702.8	700.9	684.1
2011	675.0	678.6	682.8	702.1	703.2	713.8	715.1	720.7	719.4	728.8	722.2	714.9	706.4
Education and Health Services													
2000	486.9	491.1	493.1	496.0	497.0	496.1	486.9	487.2	495.6	500.5	503.9	504.9	494.9
2001	504.3	509.5	514.9	516.3	516.8	517.1	511.8	514.6	521.0	521.9	525.3	525.5	516.6
2002	518.9	524.0	526.9	528.3	530.3	527.1	521.5	523.0	529.9	533.9	537.0	537.4	528.2
2003	529.7	532.6	535.5	536.6	538.4	534.9	533.2	534.0	540.1	545.0	547.2	548.5	538.0
2004	539.9	543.7	545.9	549.5	549.6	545.1	542.4	542.2	548.6	554.1	556.9	560.1	548.2
2005	552.9	556.2	556.6	562.1	562.7	556.2	555.9	554.7	561.9	566.3	569.0	570.1	560.4
2006	563.0	569.8	572.3	573.1	574.8	571.7	568.6	569.9	578.1	581.9	585.3	585.3	574.5
2007	578.7	586.2	588.8	589.1	591.9	588.8	585.1	584.1	592.7	599.5	603.0	603.8	591.0
2008	596.8	602.4	603.2	608.0	609.0	606.6	604.1	604.7	612.3	618.4	622.6	623.3	609.3
2009	614.8	620.1	622.3	622.3	623.0	619.4	616.6	615.4	621.2	628.6	631.4	631.9	622.3
2010	624.9	630.4	634.0	636.1	638.4	634.6	630.7	630.0	637.4	645.3	649.5	650.5	636.8
2011	643.0	648.4	651.7	651.1	651.3	648.3	643.9	643.7	650.6	661.5	663.4	662.7	651.6
Leisure and Hospitality													
2000	340.9	342.9	351.5	361.8	371.3	380.7	379.5	380.1	374.2	367.0	363.0	361.6	364.5
2001	342.7	346.0	354.0	365.0	378.0	388.3	387.0	387.4	377.5	366.5	360.4	359.4	367.7
2002	345.8	345.7	351.6	363.0	376.9	387.9	389.8	389.9	382.4	373.0	367.9	367.8	370.1
2003	351.6	350.2	355.5	369.0	382.7	395.4	394.7	394.6	387.4	377.7	372.8	374.2	375.5
2004	358.1	357.8	365.3	377.3	390.8	400.8	403.3	402.8	395.3	382.9	378.1	377.1	382.5
2005	360.6	361.6	367.0	384.2	396.4	404.7	408.7	408.0	402.6	389.7	385.6	385.1	387.9
2006	370.8	372.6	379.4	392.3	405.1	418.9	419.7	418.5	409.6	399.9	395.6	397.1	398.3
2007	382.9	381.1	387.8	400.4	415.6	426.0	425.5	426.9	417.8	410.8	405.4	404.4	407.1
2008	387.9	386.3	394.0	409.1	421.8	431.5	430.5	429.5	417.9	409.7	399.9	397.4	409.6
2009	380.9	378.0	383.8	395.1	408.3	416.8	414.5	412.8	405.7	394.7	387.9	386.4	397.1
2010	369.4	369.9	376.6	389.4	403.7	413.2	412.6	413.8	408.1	400.3	394.9	393.7	395.5
2011	375.5	374.7	383.6	398.2	410.4	421.0	420.0	420.4	411.4	403.2	398.6	394.8	401.0
Other Services													
2000	183.2	184.1	185.6	186.7	186.9	190.1	190.2	190.2	189.8	187.5	187.6	188.0	187.5
2001	186.7	187.6	189.3	189.8	190.6	194.2	195.1	194.1	191.9	189.1	189.9	190.4	190.7
2002	187.2	187.2	188.4	188.8	189.5	192.9	197.0	197.3	190.9	190.3	190.8	191.4	191.0
2003	194.7	194.8	196.7	195.1	196.4	199.6	205.2	205.9	196.1	196.1	195.5	196.4	197.7
2004	194.1	194.9	196.4	195.8	196.8	199.3	204.3	203.3	196.4	196.1	196.1	197.7	197.6
2005	191.7	192.2	193.1	194.4	194.7	196.9	203.6	203.2	197.1	195.5	196.4	197.9	196.4
2006	196.4	195.3	197.2	194.8	196.1	199.0	202.5	202.6	196.4	196.5	196.7	198.7	197.7
2007	194.6	194.5	197.0	196.0	198.0	200.8	205.1	205.1	198.5	198.0	198.4	199.4	198.8
2008	196.5	197.2	198.4	198.4	200.0	202.3	207.9	207.7	199.8	199.6	199.0	199.3	200.5
2009	194.4	194.5	195.5	194.7	196.1	198.4	201.1	200.4	193.5	194.3	194.5	195.1	196.0
2010	190.7	190.6	191.7	186.3	187.4	189.3	188.4	188.2	187.2	188.5	188.8	189.3	188.9
2011	186.2	186.7	188.3	189.2	191.0	193.2	194.0	194.0	191.3	190.7	190.5	191.7	190.6
Government													
2000	535.0	548.0	553.3	550.6	567.2	565.2	543.7	545.9	551.8	556.3	558.1	558.8	552.8
2001	544.2	558.0	560.3	557.4	565.4	563.4	550.4	546.7	553.6	563.6	565.3	567.3	558.0
2002	555.3	566.0	568.6	571.8	576.0	573.9	562.5	559.6	560.2	573.1	575.4	575.6	568.2
2003	563.4	573.7	576.2	573.4	577.3	575.5	572.7	563.6	562.0	566.0	566.0	563.5	569.4
2004	554.0	562.7	565.0	566.4	570.4	568.1	552.3	547.1	554.6	568.0	570.6	564.8	562.0
2005	556.3	566.6	570.8	571.6	574.6	569.2	556.9	550.2	561.2	567.3	570.5	565.7	565.1
2006	556.2	566.5	568.7	571.3	575.0	573.5	553.8	549.1	565.2	568.8	571.6	567.3	565.6
2007	557.8	568.6	571.2	572.6	575.0	571.9	554.8	552.3	565.2	569.1	571.2	567.5	566.4
2008	559.7	570.0	572.7	574.3	579.8	575.7	560.1	556.3	569.5	576.6	576.9	573.5	570.4
2009	562.4	569.6	572.7	577.5	581.2	574.9	556.5	550.1	567.4	577.3	577.7	571.9	569.9
2010	562.6	570.1	570.5	575.1	592.7	578.5	549.8	543.2	558.4	566.7	568.1	560.1	566.3
2011	549.7	557.5	559.6	560.4	564.8	557.2	542.7	535.0	551.0	558.4	559.3	553.8	554.1

Employment by Industry: Cincinnati–Middletown, OH–KY–IN, Selected Years, 2000–2011

(Numbers in thousands, not seasonally adjusted)

Industry and year	January	February	March	April	May	June	July	August	September	October	November	December	Annual average
Total Nonfarm													
2000	995.4	1,001.6	1,011.7	1,015.2	1,025.2	1,027.4	1,016.7	1,017.9	1,020.3	1,022.1	1,025.2	1,029.9	1,017.4
2001	998.1	1,001.5	1,008.7	1,010.2	1,017.5	1,020.2	1,010.4	1,013.0	1,013.0	1,014.8	1,015.1	1,016.0	1,011.5
2002	988.2	991.4	998.7	1,004.3	1,013.3	1,014.3	1,009.0	1,012.8	1,014.4	1,015.6	1,019.8	1,021.9	1,008.6
2003	998.9	998.0	1,007.4	1,017.6	1,023.6	1,024.0	1,013.9	1,020.9	1,019.1	1,020.8	1,022.9	1,026.0	1,016.1
2004	997.8	999.8	1,012.1	1,022.3	1,029.9	1,034.2	1,029.4	1,033.7	1,033.1	1,034.4	1,037.7	1,039.4	1,025.3
2005	1,004.3	1,010.2	1,021.1	1,033.7	1,041.7	1,044.5	1,037.1	1,039.2	1,044.3	1,041.0	1,045.8	1,048.7	1,034.3
2006	1,017.3	1,020.9	1,028.1	1,036.5	1,043.9	1,046.8	1,036.4	1,041.7	1,043.1	1,040.5	1,044.4	1,047.1	1,037.2
2007	1,022.8	1,023.1	1,036.3	1,045.6	1,057.9	1,059.8	1,045.9	1,050.0	1,050.9	1,055.3	1,058.4	1,060.4	1,047.2
2008	1,032.9	1,034.4	1,037.1	1,051.2	1,059.6	1,055.1	1,046.7	1,048.1	1,041.6	1,042.1	1,037.3	1,034.7	1,043.4
2009	997.2	993.4	993.1	995.4	1,002.3	998.4	985.6	988.5	987.2	987.8	989.4	989.2	992.3
2010	959.0	959.2	969.5	984.6	995.3	993.2	980.2	981.1	981.6	988.2	989.8	987.8	980.8
2011	962.1	965.2	975.0	990.8	998.5	997.3	989.6	995.0	997.8	1,000.6	1,001.4	999.0	989.4
Total Private													
2000	872.1	873.8	882.8	885.7	893.4	901.1	898.7	900.6	896.5	895.0	897.0	901.4	891.5
2001	871.9	871.8	878.2	878.9	885.6	892.9	891.1	892.7	885.6	884.7	883.9	884.6	883.5
2002	858.9	858.6	864.7	870.5	878.8	885.6	886.9	888.7	885.2	882.9	886.5	889.2	878.0
2003	866.9	863.4	871.5	881.1	886.9	892.8	890.3	894.2	886.9	884.9	886.6	890.0	883.0
2004	865.7	864.4	875.3	885.2	892.4	901.6	905.9	907.9	901.5	899.2	902.0	904.6	892.1
2005	873.2	876.2	886.1	898.3	905.8	912.8	913.8	914.1	912.7	906.1	910.4	914.0	902.0
2006	886.0	886.4	892.3	900.5	907.1	915.4	913.4	916.6	911.1	905.5	909.1	912.0	904.6
2007	890.6	887.9	899.8	909.4	920.6	926.7	921.9	924.1	919.4	920.8	921.9	924.7	914.0
2008	901.5	898.8	901.6	915.5	922.5	923.9	922.8	922.2	910.4	907.4	900.8	899.1	910.5
2009	865.0	858.7	858.6	859.9	866.5	867.0	863.9	864.6	857.2	855.0	856.3	857.1	860.8
2010	829.5	827.5	836.8	850.8	858.2	862.5	861.2	861.3	855.7	859.7	859.6	858.2	851.8
2011	836.3	837.1	846.0	861.5	869.6	873.2	872.1	874.9	871.7	872.7	872.9	870.7	863.2
Goods-Producing													
2000	194.8	195.3	197.8	197.8	199.9	200.8	200.6	200.2	199.2	198.4	197.7	196.8	198.3
2001	190.6	190.7	192.0	191.3	192.4	193.3	191.9	192.6	190.5	188.8	186.8	185.2	190.5
2002	178.2	177.3	177.7	177.8	178.7	180.2	180.5	181.4	180.7	180.2	179.6	177.7	179.2
2003	174.2	172.8	174.9	177.4	178.4	179.3	178.0	178.8	177.5	176.6	175.8	175.5	176.6
2004	171.3	170.9	173.4	176.2	177.8	180.1	179.6	179.4	178.6	177.8	177.2	176.2	176.5
2005	169.7	170.1	172.3	174.6	176.8	178.0	178.5	178.6	178.5	177.4	177.1	175.7	175.6
2006	170.4	170.5	169.4	173.3	174.8	176.5	175.7	176.7	175.2	172.9	172.3	172.1	173.3
2007	167.8	166.8	170.0	172.1	174.0	174.8	174.0	174.3	173.2	172.3	171.2	169.9	171.7
2008	165.5	164.7	165.0	167.9	169.2	169.9	169.3	169.0	166.8	165.5	162.9	160.1	166.3
2009	151.8	149.2	148.2	146.4	147.0	146.7	145.5	146.3	144.8	144.2	143.3	141.9	146.3
2010	135.4	134.0	136.1	139.0	140.1	140.9	142.2	142.1	141.9	142.7	142.0	139.7	139.7
2011	135.9	136.1	137.7	141.1	142.9	144.1	147.0	148.7	150.4	149.2	147.7	145.8	143.9
Mining, Logging, and Construction													
2000	47.5	47.3	49.4	49.9	51.4	52.8	53.0	52.9	51.8	51.2	50.6	49.6	50.6
2001	46.6	46.9	48.4	50.2	51.7	53.3	53.7	54.0	53.1	52.7	51.9	50.8	51.1
2002	46.1	46.0	46.8	47.7	48.9	50.6	51.2	51.6	51.0	50.8	50.4	48.7	49.2
2003	45.3	44.4	46.1	49.0	50.2	51.5	51.4	52.3	51.6	51.6	50.9	50.4	49.6
2004	48.3	48.0	49.9	51.7	53.0	54.8	55.2	55.1	54.4	53.6	52.9	51.8	52.4
2005	47.4	48.1	49.6	51.6	53.2	54.3	55.1	55.1	54.9	54.1	53.7	52.1	52.4
2006	48.5	48.8	49.9	52.0	53.0	54.1	54.2	54.8	53.6	52.1	51.4	50.5	51.9
2007	47.3	45.8	48.0	50.4	52.0	52.7	53.0	53.0	52.4	52.2	51.2	49.6	50.6
2008	45.4	44.6	45.1	47.3	48.7	49.4	49.7	49.5	48.2	47.9	46.6	44.7	47.3
2009	40.0	39.1	39.4	39.2	40.7	40.9	40.9	41.1	40.2	39.8	39.1	37.8	39.9
2010	33.0	31.9	33.4	35.9	36.7	37.4	38.3	38.4	38.0	38.9	38.3	36.5	36.4
2011	33.4	33.4	34.7	37.1	38.2	38.9	41	41.3	41.2	39.9	38.3	36.2	37.8
Manufacturing													
2000	147.3	148.0	148.4	147.9	148.5	148.0	147.6	147.3	147.4	147.2	147.1	147.2	147.7
2001	144.0	143.8	143.6	141.1	140.7	140.0	138.2	138.6	137.4	136.1	134.9	134.4	139.4
2002	132.1	131.3	130.9	130.1	129.8	129.6	129.3	129.8	129.7	129.4	129.2	129.0	130.0
2003	128.9	128.4	128.8	128.4	128.2	127.8	126.6	126.5	125.9	125.0	124.9	125.1	127.0
2004	123.0	122.9	123.5	124.5	124.8	125.3	124.4	124.3	124.2	124.2	124.3	124.4	124.2
2005	122.3	122.0	122.7	123.0	123.6	123.7	123.4	123.5	123.6	123.3	123.4	123.6	123.2
2006	121.9	121.7	119.5	121.3	121.8	122.4	121.5	121.9	121.6	120.8	120.9	121.6	121.4
2007	120.5	121.0	122.0	121.7	122.0	122.1	121.0	121.3	120.8	120.1	120.0	120.3	121.1
2008	120.1	120.1	119.9	120.6	120.5	120.5	119.6	119.5	118.6	117.6	116.3	115.4	119.1
2009	111.8	110.1	108.8	107.2	106.3	105.8	104.6	105.2	104.6	104.4	104.2	104.1	106.4
2010	102.4	102.1	102.7	103.1	103.4	103.5	103.9	103.7	103.9	103.8	103.7	103.2	103.3
2011	102.5	102.7	103.0	104.0	104.7	105.2	106.0	107.4	109.2	109.3	109.4	109.6	106.1
Service-Providing													
2000	800.6	806.3	813.9	817.4	825.3	826.6	816.1	817.7	821.1	823.7	827.5	833.1	819.1
2001	807.5	810.8	816.7	818.9	825.1	826.9	818.5	820.4	822.5	826.0	828.3	830.8	821.0
2002	810.0	814.1	821.0	826.5	834.6	834.1	828.5	831.4	833.7	835.4	840.2	844.2	829.5
2003	824.7	825.2	832.5	840.2	845.2	844.7	835.9	842.1	841.6	844.2	847.1	850.5	839.5
2004	826.5	828.9	838.7	846.1	852.1	854.1	849.8	854.3	854.5	856.6	860.5	863.2	848.8
2005	834.6	840.1	848.8	859.1	864.9	866.5	858.6	860.6	865.8	863.6	868.7	873.0	858.7
2006	846.9	850.4	858.7	863.2	869.1	870.3	860.7	865.0	867.9	867.6	872.1	875.0	863.9
2007	855.0	856.3	866.3	873.5	883.9	885.0	871.9	875.7	877.7	883.0	887.2	890.5	875.5
2008	867.4	869.7	872.1	883.3	890.4	885.2	877.4	879.1	874.8	876.6	874.4	874.6	877.1
2009	845.4	844.2	844.9	849.0	855.3	851.7	840.1	842.2	842.4	843.6	846.1	847.3	846.0
2010	823.6	825.2	833.4	845.6	855.2	852.3	838.0	839.0	839.7	845.5	847.8	848.1	841.1
2011	826.2	829.1	837.3	849.7	855.6	853.2	842.6	846.3	847.4	851.4	853.7	853.2	845.5

Employment by Industry: Cincinnati–Middletown, OH–KY–IN, Selected Years, 2000–2011—*Continued*

(Numbers in thousands, not seasonally adjusted)

Industry and year	January	February	March	April	May	June	July	August	September	October	November	December	Annual average
Trade, Transportation, and Utilities													
2000	216.8	215.3	216.5	215.9	217.3	217.5	215.6	215.9	215.7	219.6	223.4	227.4	218.1
2001	217.6	214.8	215.4	212.6	213.5	214.3	215.2	215.1	215.0	216.9	220.3	222.8	216.1
2002	212.5	210.9	211.7	212.1	213.1	213.6	213.0	212.9	213.0	212.5	217.3	221.2	213.7
2003	210.3	208.6	209.5	209.7	210.5	210.6	209.1	210.2	209.4	211.1	214.7	217.4	210.9
2004	207.3	205.3	206.5	207.2	208.3	209.4	210.5	212.2	210.5	211.9	216.1	218.8	210.3
2005	208.2	206.7	208.1	209.1	210.4	210.5	211.5	210.6	210.9	209.9	213.5	217.0	210.5
2006	208.6	206.3	207.0	207.2	209.0	209.5	208.7	209.2	209.6	210.5	214.9	217.5	209.8
2007	210.3	208.3	210.1	210.5	212.9	213.3	212.8	212.6	212.9	214.3	218.5	221.2	213.1
2008	212.2	209.9	210.2	210.9	212.4	211.8	210.9	211.3	209.5	209.4	211.2	212.8	211.0
2009	202.2	199.5	198.2	196.1	197.4	196.6	195.6	196.7	195.8	197.7	200.8	202.5	198.3
2010	193.3	192.6	193.5	194.6	196.2	196.3	194.7	194.7	193.8	196.2	200.2	201.4	195.6
2011	193.0	191.9	192.9	194.7	195.5	196.0	193.2	194.3	193.1	196.0	199.6	200.7	195.1
Wholesale Trade													
2000	58.6	58.9	59.1	59.4	59.6	59.4	59.3	59.2	59.4	59.6	59.6	59.8	59.3
2001	58.6	58.6	58.6	58.9	58.9	58.9	59.0	58.8	58.5	58.8	58.8	58.9	58.8
2002	57.6	57.7	57.7	57.9	58.0	58.2	58.7	58.4	58.5	58.7	58.8	59.0	58.3
2003	57.8	57.7	57.9	57.5	57.6	57.9	56.9	56.9	56.3	56.4	56.6	56.8	57.2
2004	55.6	55.5	55.6	55.6	55.8	56.2	57.8	57.9	57.7	57.1	57.4	57.9	56.7
2005	56.7	56.6	56.8	57.2	57.5	58.0	58.6	58.9	59.4	58.6	58.9	59.2	58.0
2006	58.9	58.9	59.0	59.1	59.3	59.8	59.6	59.8	59.5	59.4	59.5	59.9	59.4
2007	60.5	60.4	60.6	60.7	60.8	61.3	61.1	61.1	61.2	61.3	61.3	61.7	61.0
2008	61.3	61.4	61.5	61.3	61.5	61.8	61.6	61.3	60.7	60.8	60.6	60.4	61.2
2009	59.1	58.6	58.0	56.4	56.3	55.8	55.6	55.4	55.0	55.2	55.2	55.4	56.3
2010	54.8	54.8	54.8	54.7	54.8	55.1	54.9	54.7	54.3	54.5	54.6	54.5	54.7
2011	54.5	54.6	54.9	55.3	55.6	55.8	54.9	55.3	54.4	54.9	55.7	55.5	55.1
Retail Trade													
2000	114.6	113.2	113.9	113.7	114.5	115.3	114.0	114.2	113.5	116.4	120.1	123.9	115.6
2001	115.8	113.2	114.0	113.5	114.4	115.6	113.9	113.9	113.4	114.3	118.0	120.5	115.0
2002	111.9	110.5	111.2	111.4	112.2	113.2	112.1	112.1	111.7	111.1	115.3	118.6	112.6
2003	109.4	107.7	108.2	109.0	109.8	110.4	110.0	110.6	110.3	111.0	114.4	116.7	110.6
2004	109.5	107.9	108.9	109.3	109.9	110.9	110.3	111.3	109.7	111.0	114.6	116.7	110.8
2005	108.8	107.0	107.9	108.5	109.3	109.1	109.7	108.6	108.1	108.4	111.6	114.9	109.3
2006	108.1	106.2	106.9	107.4	108.7	108.8	108.6	108.8	108.4	109.2	112.8	114.4	109.0
2007	108.1	106.4	108.0	108.5	110.0	109.9	109.9	109.3	108.7	109.5	113.0	114.5	109.7
2008	108.5	106.4	106.7	107.6	108.6	108.4	108.2	108.3	107.1	107.0	108.9	110.3	108.0
2009	103.3	101.7	101.5	101.5	102.8	102.8	101.9	102.0	101.6	102.8	105.4	106.5	102.8
2010	100.0	99.4	100.3	101.3	102.4	102.0	101.9	101.7	100.9	102.6	105.8	106.6	102.1
2011	100.4	99.5	99.9	101.1	101.5	102.0	100.6	100.3	99.6	101.7	103.8	104.5	101.2
Transportation and Utilities													
2000	43.6	43.2	43.5	42.8	43.2	42.8	42.3	42.5	42.8	43.6	43.7	43.7	43.1
2001	43.2	43.0	42.8	40.2	40.2	39.8	42.3	42.4	43.1	43.8	43.5	43.4	42.3
2002	43.0	42.7	42.8	42.8	42.9	42.2	42.2	42.4	42.8	42.7	43.2	43.6	42.8
2003	43.1	43.2	43.4	43.2	43.1	42.3	42.2	42.7	42.8	43.7	43.7	43.9	43.1
2004	42.2	41.9	42.0	42.3	42.6	42.3	42.4	43.0	43.1	43.8	44.1	44.2	42.8
2005	42.7	43.1	43.4	43.4	43.6	43.4	43.2	43.1	43.4	42.9	43.0	42.9	43.2
2006	41.6	41.2	41.1	40.7	41.0	40.9	40.5	40.6	41.7	41.9	42.6	43.2	41.4
2007	41.7	41.5	41.5	41.3	42.1	42.1	41.8	42.2	43.0	43.5	44.2	45.0	42.5
2008	42.4	42.1	42.0	42.0	42.3	41.6	41.1	41.7	41.7	41.6	41.7	42.1	41.9
2009	39.8	39.2	38.7	38.2	38.3	38.0	38.1	39.3	39.2	39.7	40.2	40.6	39.1
2010	38.5	38.4	38.4	38.6	39.0	39.2	37.9	38.3	38.6	39.1	39.8	40.3	38.8
2011	38.1	37.8	38.1	38.3	38.4	38.2	37.7	38.7	39.1	39.4	40.1	40.7	38.7
Information													
2000	20.3	20.1	20.7	20.5	20.6	20.7	20.1	20.3	20.0	20.0	19.8	19.9	20.3
2001	20.1	19.9	20.0	19.5	19.6	19.7	19.4	19.3	18.9	18.8	18.6	18.5	19.4
2002	18.4	18.1	18.1	17.9	17.9	18.2	18.1	17.8	17.4	16.9	17.1	17.1	17.8
2003	16.4	16.2	16.3	16.3	16.5	16.4	16.5	16.3	16.0	15.7	15.9	16.0	16.2
2004	15.9	15.7	15.7	16.0	16.1	16.2	16.2	16.2	16.0	16.1	16.1	16.1	16.0
2005	15.9	15.9	15.9	15.8	16.0	15.9	15.9	15.8	15.7	15.8	15.9	16.1	15.9
2006	15.7	15.6	15.7	15.8	15.7	15.8	15.8	15.8	15.5	15.5	15.6	15.6	15.7
2007	15.3	15.4	15.3	15.5	15.6	15.7	15.7	15.7	15.3	15.2	15.2	15.2	15.4
2008	15.1	15.1	15.2	15.1	15.1	15.2	15.3	15.3	15.1	15.2	15.1	15.1	15.2
2009	15.0	14.9	14.9	14.8	14.8	14.8	14.8	14.6	14.4	14.3	14.4	14.3	14.7
2010	14.2	14.0	14.0	14.0	14.1	14.1	14.2	14.2	14.1	14.0	14.1	14.0	14.1
2011	14.0	13.9	13.9	13.9	14.0	14.0	14.0	14.0	13.8	13.8	13.8	13.8	13.9
Financial Activities													
2000	58.8	58.9	58.8	58.9	59.1	59.5	59.1	59.2	58.6	58.9	59.2	59.8	59.1
2001	59.5	59.8	59.6	60.4	60.6	61.3	61.2	61.6	61.3	61.5	61.7	62.3	60.9
2002	62.4	62.9	62.9	63.3	63.9	64.4	64.5	64.7	64.3	64.7	65.1	65.7	64.1
2003	65.6	65.9	65.9	65.6	65.9	66.2	66.3	66.6	66.1	65.9	65.8	66.0	66.0
2004	64.8	64.9	65.0	65.0	65.0	65.5	65.5	65.5	64.8	64.5	64.6	65.0	65.0
2005	64.7	64.8	64.8	65.0	65.2	65.8	65.6	65.6	65.0	64.9	65.0	65.5	65.2
2006	64.6	64.7	64.9	65.2	65.5	65.7	65.4	65.4	64.9	64.9	64.9	65.2	65.1
2007	65.0	65.2	65.3	65.4	65.7	66.0	66.3	66.0	65.5	65.3	65.1	65.6	65.5
2008	65.2	65.1	65.2	65.7	65.9	66.1	66.2	66.0	65.3	65.1	65.1	64.9	65.5
2009	64.1	63.8	63.7	63.5	63.9	63.8	63.8	63.1	62.6	62.6	62.5	62.3	63.3
2010	61.9	61.7	61.7	62.5	62.7	63.0	63.7	63.6	63.4	63.5	63.6	63.8	62.9
2011	63.6	63.6	63.7	63.6	63.7	63.8	63.2	62.5	61.4	60.5	60.4	60.9	62.6

Employment by Industry: Cincinnati–Middletown, OH–KY–IN, Selected Years, 2000–2011—*Continued*

(Numbers in thousands, not seasonally adjusted)

Industry and year	January	February	March	April	May	June	July	August	September	October	November	December	Annual average
Professional and Business Services													
2000	134.4	135.2	137.3	137.6	138.1	141.1	140.7	141.8	141.2	141.2	140.7	140.1	139.1
2001	136.1	136.6	137.8	139.4	139.4	140.5	138.9	139.5	139.6	141.3	139.9	137.9	138.9
2002	134.9	134.3	135.4	137.0	137.9	139.6	140.5	142.1	142.5	144.2	144.1	143.1	139.6
2003	141.7	141.3	142.7	144.3	144.0	144.7	143.8	144.8	144.5	146.3	145.6	145.2	144.1
2004	142.6	141.3	143.3	144.1	144.2	146.7	149.2	150.3	150.6	150.2	150.6	150.8	147.0
2005	145.0	146.3	148.3	150.5	150.9	153.5	153.9	155.7	157.2	156.8	157.3	158.0	152.8
2006	151.3	151.8	153.8	154.3	153.5	154.6	155.9	156.6	156.3	154.9	154.9	154.7	154.4
2007	150.8	151.0	153.8	155.7	155.8	157.7	156.6	157.7	157.7	160.5	161.3	161.3	156.7
2008	157.8	157.1	157.2	159.3	158.5	159.2	160.3	160.5	159.0	159.6	157.6	156.5	158.6
2009	149.9	148.7	147.9	147.2	146.3	146.1	146.0	146.7	145.8	146.0	147.2	147.9	147.1
2010	143.9	143.7	145.4	148.5	148.2	149.7	149.6	150.3	149.8	151.8	151.6	151.1	148.6
2011	149.1	149.5	151.3	154.2	153.6	154.1	154.4	153.0	151.9	153.1	154.3	154.0	152.7
Education and Health Services													
2000	116.9	118.2	118.5	119.3	119.9	119.3	119.6	119.9	121.1	120.1	120.9	121.3	119.6
2001	118.1	119.6	120.1	120.1	120.3	119.4	120.5	120.9	122.2	123.2	123.7	124.3	121.0
2002	121.4	122.6	122.8	123.9	124.4	123.5	123.4	124.4	126.0	127.2	127.8	128.4	124.7
2003	125.5	125.7	125.8	126.2	126.2	125.5	126.4	127.2	128.4	128.9	130.0	130.3	127.2
2004	128.8	129.7	130.3	131.0	130.9	130.4	130.8	130.6	131.6	132.5	133.4	133.6	131.1
2005	131.5	132.8	133.3	135.1	134.8	134.2	133.3	134.1	134.9	135.7	136.3	136.5	134.4
2006	135.1	136.2	137.0	138.1	138.1	137.7	136.6	137.6	138.9	140.1	140.8	141.0	138.1
2007	139.3	139.9	140.9	141.6	142.2	141.0	139.7	140.3	142.9	144.0	145.0	144.9	141.8
2008	143.3	144.2	144.9	146.1	146.5	144.0	144.4	144.6	145.4	146.2	146.8	146.6	145.3
2009	144.2	144.7	145.3	147.0	147.2	145.4	145.7	145.5	146.0	147.3	148.3	147.9	146.2
2010	145.1	146.0	147.0	148.6	148.8	146.8	146.2	146.2	147.2	148.7	149.2	149.1	147.4
2011	146.2	147.3	147.9	149.6	150.5	148.7	148.6	150.4	151.0	152.0	153.2	150.2	149.6
Leisure and Hospitality													
2000	88.9	89.5	91.8	94.2	96.8	100.7	101.7	102.2	99.7	96.0	94.6	95.5	96.0
2001	90.0	90.3	92.9	95.1	98.8	103.1	103.2	102.6	97.9	93.9	92.6	93.3	96.1
2002	90.7	91.8	95.1	97.4	101.5	104.2	105.3	104.0	100.7	96.8	95.1	95.6	98.2
2003	92.1	91.5	94.4	99.4	102.8	107.3	107.6	107.8	103.0	98.4	96.9	97.5	99.9
2004	93.4	94.7	98.6	102.7	106.8	109.7	110.7	110.2	106.1	103.2	101.2	101.2	103.2
2005	96.2	97.3	100.7	105.0	108.4	111.5	111.9	110.7	107.8	102.9	102.7	102.5	104.8
2006	98.5	99.5	102.3	104.3	107.8	112.5	112.1	112.1	107.7	104.0	103.1	103.1	105.6
2007	99.8	99.0	101.4	105.4	110.8	113.9	112.9	113.4	108.6	105.5	101.9	102.9	106.3
2008	99.1	99.4	100.3	106.7	110.9	113.3	112.4	111.7	106.3	103.1	99.1	100.0	105.2
2009	95.4	95.5	97.7	102.4	107.1	110.7	109.6	109.0	105.5	100.5	97.8	98.1	102.4
2010	94.3	94.3	97.5	102.7	107.3	110.6	109.4	109.1	104.9	102.2	98.6	98.9	102.5
2011	94.6	95.1	98.5	103.9	108.4	111.5	111.2	111.6	109.9	107.9	104.1	104.5	105.1
Other Services													
2000	41.2	41.3	41.4	41.5	41.7	41.5	41.3	41.1	41.0	40.8	40.7	40.6	41.2
2001	39.9	40.1	40.4	40.5	41.0	41.3	40.8	41.1	40.2	40.3	40.3	40.3	40.5
2002	40.4	40.7	41.0	41.1	41.4	41.9	41.6	41.4	40.6	40.4	40.4	40.4	40.9
2003	41.1	41.4	42.0	42.2	42.6	42.8	42.6	42.5	42.0	42.0	41.9	42.1	42.1
2004	41.6	41.9	42.5	43.0	43.3	43.6	43.4	43.5	43.3	43.0	42.8	42.9	42.9
2005	42.0	42.3	42.7	43.2	43.3	43.4	43.2	43.0	42.7	42.7	42.6	42.7	42.8
2006	41.8	41.8	42.2	42.3	42.7	43.1	43.2	43.2	43.0	42.7	42.6	42.8	42.6
2007	42.3	42.3	43.0	43.2	43.6	44.3	43.9	44.1	43.3	43.7	43.7	43.7	43.4
2008	43.3	43.3	43.6	43.8	44.0	44.4	44.0	43.8	43.0	43.3	43.0	43.1	43.6
2009	42.4	42.4	42.7	42.5	42.8	42.9	42.9	42.7	42.3	42.4	42.0	42.2	42.5
2010	41.4	41.2	41.6	40.9	40.8	41.1	41.2	41.1	40.6	40.6	40.3	40.2	40.9
2011	39.9	39.7	40.1	40.5	41.0	41.0	40.5	40.4	40.2	40.2	39.8	40.8	40.3
Government													
2000	123.3	127.8	128.9	129.5	131.8	126.3	118.0	117.3	123.8	127.1	128.2	128.5	125.9
2001	126.2	129.7	130.5	131.3	131.9	127.3	119.3	120.3	127.4	130.1	131.2	131.4	128.1
2002	129.3	132.8	134.0	133.8	134.5	128.7	122.1	124.1	129.2	132.7	133.3	132.7	130.6
2003	132.0	134.6	135.9	136.5	136.7	131.2	123.6	126.7	132.2	135.9	136.3	136.0	133.1
2004	132.1	135.4	136.8	137.1	137.5	132.6	123.5	125.8	131.6	135.2	135.7	134.8	133.2
2005	131.1	134.0	135.0	135.4	135.9	131.7	122.3	125.1	131.6	134.9	135.4	134.7	132.3
2006	131.3	134.5	135.8	136.0	136.8	131.4	123.0	125.1	132.0	135.0	135.3	135.1	132.6
2007	132.2	135.2	136.5	136.2	137.3	133.1	124.0	125.9	131.5	134.5	136.5	135.7	133.2
2008	131.4	135.6	135.5	135.7	137.1	131.2	123.9	125.9	131.2	134.7	136.5	135.6	132.9
2009	132.2	134.7	134.5	135.5	135.8	131.4	121.7	123.9	130.0	132.8	133.1	132.1	131.5
2010	129.5	131.7	132.7	133.8	137.1	130.7	119.0	119.8	125.9	128.5	130.2	129.6	129.0
2011	125.8	128.1	129.0	129.3	128.9	124.1	117.5	120.1	126.1	127.9	128.5	128.3	126.1

Employment by Industry: Cleveland–Elyria–Mentor, OH, Selected Years, 2000–2011

(Numbers in thousands, not seasonally adjusted)

Industry and year	January	February	March	April	May	June	July	August	September	October	November	December	Annual average
Total Nonfarm													
2000	1,113.8	1,118.2	1,126.4	1,132.1	1,144.5	1,149.7	1,138.4	1,139.9	1,140.5	1,140.0	1,143.4	1,145.2	1,136.0
2001	1,112.7	1,114.3	1,121.1	1,121.6	1,129.4	1,133.6	1,120.0	1,119.0	1,110.3	1,109.3	1,110.0	1,108.3	1,117.5
2002	1,069.6	1,072.2	1,078.5	1,078.7	1,087.5	1,091.2	1,081.7	1,084.1	1,084.5	1,087.0	1,086.8	1,085.9	1,082.3
2003	1,057.1	1,058.1	1,063.8	1,072.1	1,083.4	1,085.0	1,076.1	1,076.3	1,077.1	1,079.8	1,080.4	1,081.1	1,074.2
2004	1,047.3	1,050.5	1,059.9	1,067.7	1,076.8	1,082.6	1,076.2	1,076.4	1,077.1	1,082.0	1,084.8	1,084.0	1,072.1
2005	1,044.9	1,051.2	1,058.1	1,068.6	1,075.5	1,082.0	1,075.4	1,077.2	1,079.8	1,082.7	1,085.3	1,085.3	1,072.2
2006	1,053.6	1,057.6	1,065.4	1,074.8	1,082.1	1,088.9	1,076.9	1,078.4	1,079.1	1,080.2	1,081.1	1,081.3	1,075.0
2007	1,052.8	1,052.6	1,061.5	1,070.4	1,080.2	1,090.2	1,075.6	1,076.9	1,073.8	1,076.6	1,079.4	1,077.4	1,072.3
2008	1,049.9	1,050.4	1,048.2	1,060.9	1,072.8	1,075.8	1,064.3	1,062.6	1,060.8	1,058.9	1,052.6	1,044.9	1,058.5
2009	1,009.3	1,006.1	1,003.5	1,004.9	1,008.6	1,006.7	996.0	992.5	994.2	995.9	997.3	994.8	1,000.8
2010	969.2	970.0	973.2	986.4	998.6	1,000.2	996.4	995.8	995.6	1,002.4	1,003.6	1,001.4	991.1
2011	971.4	977.2	981.6	996.7	1,004.1	1,005.9	1,002.6	1,000.3	992.1	994.3	995.9	989.7	992.7
Total Private													
2000	975.4	977.3	984.4	990.9	999.0	1,008.5	1,002.9	1,003.7	999.5	996.8	999.5	1,000.7	994.9
2001	971.7	970.6	976.0	977.1	984.2	990.6	982.5	981.1	966.4	963.4	963.5	961.3	974.0
2002	927.5	926.0	931.4	932.8	940.4	946.4	945.3	946.6	940.7	940.6	940.0	939.6	938.1
2003	914.7	912.8	917.4	926.2	937.4	941.5	939.8	942.5	935.9	935.1	934.9	935.3	931.1
2004	906.0	905.8	914.1	922.0	930.4	938.6	941.0	942.6	937.7	939.0	940.9	940.6	929.9
2005	905.8	908.4	914.7	924.9	931.1	938.8	940.7	943.7	940.9	940.5	943.0	942.7	931.3
2006	914.8	915.8	922.3	931.7	938.1	946.6	943.0	945.3	940.3	938.2	937.9	938.2	934.4
2007	913.0	909.3	916.8	925.2	934.3	942.9	936.1	938.6	933.7	932.9	935.1	934.1	929.3
2008	908.6	906.2	904.8	916.9	926.3	928.6	924.8	924.7	920.6	915.3	909.0	902.6	915.7
2009	868.9	863.4	860.8	861.8	864.5	863.9	860.0	857.9	855.9	854.7	855.9	854.8	860.2
2010	831.4	829.4	833.1	845.8	853.9	859.1	861.7	863.6	860.4	863.3	864.4	863.1	852.4
2011	838.6	840.0	843.9	858.5	866.5	869.4	872.3	871.7	860.9	861.8	862.4	856.8	858.6
Goods-Producing													
2000	237.4	238.8	241.1	241.3	243.2	246.1	243.6	243.8	241.6	240.7	240.3	237.3	241.3
2001	229.6	228.1	228.2	226.4	227.3	227.8	225.3	224.7	219.6	217.0	216.4	213.8	223.7
2002	203.0	201.5	202.4	202.4	204.4	206.7	206.8	207.2	205.4	204.8	203.4	200.8	204.1
2003	195.1	194.0	195.0	195.8	199.5	200.5	198.5	199.0	197.4	197.5	196.7	194.5	197.0
2004	187.3	187.5	189.9	193.0	195.7	198.0	198.0	198.1	197.4	197.4	196.4	194.2	194.4
2005	185.8	185.4	187.1	191.6	193.4	195.9	195.3	195.8	195.4	194.7	194.1	191.2	192.1
2006	185.5	184.3	185.3	189.0	190.1	193.0	192.6	192.8	191.9	190.9	188.7	184.7	189.1
2007	180.8	178.8	181.1	182.9	186.4	188.5	184.2	186.8	185.5	184.8	184.4	181.9	183.8
2008	176.1	175.3	174.9	177.8	180.3	181.7	181.5	179.6	179.4	178.1	173.4	167.8	177.2
2009	158.6	156.9	154.6	152.9	151.9	151.5	149.8	149.5	149.4	148.6	149.1	147.1	151.7
2010	142.1	141.6	143.1	145.1	148.4	150.9	150.6	151.8	151.2	151.9	151.1	149.0	148.1
2011	145.2	145.2	146.4	149.4	151.6	152.8	154.8	155.4	152.8	152.3	152.6	151.8	150.9
Mining, Logging, and Construction													
2000	40.5	40.3	42.6	44.4	46.7	49.0	49.3	49.3	47.6	47.0	46.3	43.7	45.6
2001	39.1	38.8	40.0	42.0	44.6	46.2	47.2	47.8	46.2	46.0	44.9	42.9	43.8
2002	37.8	37.2	38.3	40.3	42.6	44.5	45.9	46.3	45.5	45.5	44.3	42.0	42.5
2003	38.0	37.1	38.4	41.4	44.1	45.9	46.3	46.9	46.1	46.5	45.4	43.3	43.3
2004	38.3	38.4	40.1	42.4	44.8	46.4	47.3	47.0	46.6	46.7	45.6	43.5	43.9
2005	37.1	37.0	37.8	42.2	44.0	45.9	46.4	46.5	45.9	45.7	44.5	41.5	42.9
2006	37.0	36.5	37.5	40.7	42.5	43.7	44.7	44.8	44.3	44.0	43.0	40.7	41.6
2007	36.6	34.9	36.6	39.6	43.0	44.4	43.9	44.2	43.5	43.3	42.4	39.9	41.0
2008	35.1	34.4	34.5	37.1	39.7	40.9	42.0	41.9	40.9	40.6	38.5	35.6	38.4
2009	30.6	29.9	30.6	31.9	34.0	35.2	35.8	35.5	34.9	34.9	33.6	31.6	33.2
2010	27.3	26.6	27.9	30.2	31.9	33.4	34.7	34.6	34.1	34.2	33.3	30.8	31.6
2011	27.6	27.2	28.1	30.1	31.8	33.6	34.5	34.0	34.2	32.8	31.6	29.7	31.3
Manufacturing													
2000	196.9	198.5	198.5	196.9	196.5	197.1	194.3	194.5	194.0	193.7	194.0	193.6	195.7
2001	190.5	189.3	188.2	184.4	182.7	181.6	178.1	176.9	173.4	171.0	171.5	170.9	179.9
2002	165.2	164.3	164.1	162.1	161.8	162.2	160.9	160.9	159.9	159.3	159.1	158.8	161.6
2003	157.1	156.9	156.6	154.4	155.4	154.6	152.2	152.1	151.3	151.0	151.3	151.2	153.7
2004	149.0	149.1	149.8	150.6	150.9	151.6	150.7	151.1	150.8	150.7	150.8	150.7	150.5
2005	148.7	148.4	149.3	149.4	149.4	150.0	148.9	149.3	149.5	149.0	149.6	149.7	149.3
2006	148.5	147.8	147.8	148.3	147.6	149.3	147.9	148.0	147.6	146.9	145.7	144.0	147.5
2007	144.2	143.9	144.5	143.3	143.4	144.1	140.3	142.6	142.0	141.5	142.0	142.0	142.8
2008	141.0	140.9	140.4	140.7	140.6	140.8	139.5	137.7	138.5	137.5	134.9	132.2	138.7
2009	128.0	127.0	124.0	121.0	117.9	116.3	114.0	114.0	114.5	113.7	115.5	115.5	118.5
2010	114.8	115.0	115.2	114.9	116.5	117.5	115.9	117.2	117.1	117.7	117.8	118.2	116.5
2011	117.6	118.0	118.3	119.3	119.8	119.2	120.3	121.4	118.6	119.5	121.0	122.1	119.6
Service-Providing													
2000	876.4	879.4	885.3	890.8	901.3	903.6	894.8	896.1	898.9	899.3	903.1	907.9	894.7
2001	883.1	886.2	892.9	895.2	902.1	905.8	894.7	894.3	890.7	892.3	893.6	894.5	893.8
2002	866.6	870.7	876.1	876.3	883.1	884.5	874.9	876.9	879.1	882.2	883.4	885.1	878.2
2003	862.0	864.1	868.8	876.3	883.9	884.5	877.6	877.3	879.7	882.3	883.7	886.6	877.2
2004	860.0	863.0	870.0	874.7	881.1	884.6	878.2	878.3	879.7	884.6	888.4	889.8	877.7
2005	859.1	865.8	871.0	877.0	882.1	886.1	880.1	881.4	884.4	888.0	891.2	894.1	880.0
2006	868.1	873.3	880.1	885.8	892.0	895.9	884.3	885.6	887.2	889.3	892.4	896.6	885.9
2007	872.0	873.8	880.4	887.5	893.8	901.7	891.4	890.1	888.3	891.8	895.0	895.5	888.4
2008	873.8	875.1	873.3	883.1	892.5	894.1	882.8	883.0	881.4	880.8	879.2	877.1	881.4
2009	850.7	849.2	848.9	852.0	856.7	855.2	846.2	843.0	844.8	847.3	848.2	847.7	849.2
2010	827.1	828.4	830.1	841.3	850.2	849.3	845.8	844.0	844.4	850.5	852.5	852.4	843.0
2011	826.2	832.0	835.2	847.3	852.5	853.1	847.8	844.9	839.3	842.0	843.3	837.9	841.8

Employment by Industry: Cleveland–Elyria–Mentor, OH, Selected Years, 2000–2011—*Continued*

(Numbers in thousands, not seasonally adjusted)

Industry and year	January	February	March	April	May	June	July	August	September	October	November	December	Annual average
Trade, Transportation, and Utilities													
2000	219.1	216.7	217.2	217.5	219.0	220.3	219.0	219.2	218.5	221.3	225.3	229.1	220.2
2001	216.9	213.9	214.5	214.3	214.8	215.5	212.3	211.5	209.4	210.3	213.1	214.2	213.4
2002	204.6	201.3	202.6	200.9	202.5	203.3	202.9	202.9	200.9	202.6	204.9	207.5	203.1
2003	200.4	197.9	197.4	200.2	201.9	202.7	202.1	201.9	200.6	202.8	205.5	208.7	201.8
2004	199.3	197.2	198.0	197.8	199.0	200.4	199.6	199.6	197.5	199.8	203.7	206.1	199.8
2005	197.0	195.5	196.3	196.5	198.0	198.8	199.1	199.0	197.7	198.7	202.0	205.2	198.7
2006	197.6	196.0	197.1	198.5	199.6	200.4	198.9	199.3	198.2	199.3	203.1	206.5	199.5
2007	198.2	195.4	196.8	197.4	198.6	199.8	199.0	198.1	196.6	197.6	201.3	204.0	198.6
2008	196.5	193.2	192.6	193.9	195.4	195.4	194.9	195.2	192.9	192.7	193.9	195.7	194.4
2009	185.7	182.9	182.2	180.7	181.3	181.4	179.9	179.0	177.1	177.6	179.6	181.5	180.7
2010	174.3	172.3	172.6	173.6	175.0	176.4	176.8	177.3	175.5	176.9	179.5	182.1	176.0
2011	174.0	172.9	173.5	175.7	176.9	177.7	177.7	178.1	176.0	178.4	180.2	182.1	176.9
Wholesale Trade													
2000	56.8	56.9	57.0	57.2	57.5	57.7	57.8	57.9	58.2	58.5	58.7	58.9	57.8
2001	58.6	58.8	59.2	58.6	58.3	58.5	57.7	57.4	56.6	56.4	56.2	55.6	57.7
2002	55.5	55.1	55.4	54.9	54.9	54.6	54.6	54.3	53.6	53.5	53.2	53.5	54.4
2003	54.6	54.5	54.4	54.7	55.1	55.1	55.1	55.0	54.6	54.7	54.8	55.0	54.8
2004	54.1	54.1	54.3	54.2	54.5	54.9	54.9	54.9	54.3	54.9	55.1	55.4	54.6
2005	54.6	54.6	54.8	54.9	55.0	55.5	55.7	55.8	55.6	55.3	55.4	55.8	55.3
2006	55.5	55.6	55.9	56.2	56.3	56.6	56.5	56.3	56.1	55.8	55.9	56.2	56.1
2007	55.4	55.4	55.5	55.3	55.3	55.4	55.2	54.8	54.1	53.9	53.8	53.8	54.8
2008	53.7	53.5	53.3	53.7	53.9	53.8	53.5	53.3	52.7	52.5	52.0	51.5	53.1
2009	50.6	50.0	49.5	48.9	48.7	48.4	48.0	47.7	47.2	47.1	46.9	46.6	48.3
2010	46.2	46.1	46.0	46.2	46.3	46.5	47.1	47.1	46.8	46.8	46.7	46.8	46.6
2011	47.1	47.1	47.2	47.7	48.0	48.2	48.4	48.4	47.9	48.6	48.6	48.6	48.0
Retail Trade													
2000	124.5	122.3	122.6	121.9	123.0	124.1	122.8	123.1	122.1	123.9	127.8	131.5	124.1
2001	122.0	119.2	119.3	118.9	119.3	119.8	118.0	117.6	116.6	117.7	121.6	123.9	119.5
2002	115.9	112.9	114.0	112.4	113.6	114.5	114.1	114.2	113.0	114.0	116.8	119.5	114.6
2003	113.4	111.5	111.5	113.4	114.3	115.1	114.6	114.7	114.0	115.1	117.8	120.9	114.7
2004	113.5	111.5	111.9	111.8	112.6	113.3	112.4	112.2	110.6	111.6	115.1	117.4	112.8
2005	110.2	108.5	108.9	109.2	110.3	110.7	110.5	110.3	109.2	110.1	113.1	115.5	110.5
2006	109.0	107.4	108.0	108.7	109.6	109.9	108.9	109.1	107.8	109.3	112.8	115.4	109.7
2007	108.9	106.3	107.3	107.5	109.0	110.0	109.8	109.2	108.1	109.1	112.8	115.2	109.4
2008	108.9	106.1	105.9	106.4	107.4	107.9	107.8	108.1	106.6	106.8	108.7	110.6	107.6
2009	103.1	100.9	101.1	100.9	101.9	102.4	101.8	101.4	100.1	100.7	103.2	105.0	101.9
2010	99.1	97.3	97.7	98.4	99.6	100.5	100.4	100.7	99.3	100.6	103.4	105.5	100.2
2011	98.3	97.3	97.7	99.1	99.8	100.3	99.7	100.1	98.6	100.3	102.0	103.1	99.7
Transportation and Utilities													
2000	37.8	37.5	37.6	38.4	38.5	38.5	38.4	38.2	38.2	38.9	38.8	38.7	38.3
2001	36.3	35.9	36.0	36.8	37.2	37.2	36.6	36.5	36.2	36.2	35.3	34.7	36.2
2002	33.2	33.3	33.2	33.6	34.0	34.2	34.2	34.4	34.3	35.1	34.9	34.5	34.1
2003	32.4	31.9	31.5	32.1	32.5	32.5	32.4	32.2	32.0	33.0	32.9	32.8	32.4
2004	31.7	31.6	31.8	31.8	31.9	32.2	32.3	32.5	32.6	33.3	33.5	33.3	32.4
2005	32.2	32.4	32.6	32.4	32.7	32.6	32.9	32.9	32.9	33.3	33.5	33.9	32.9
2006	33.1	33.0	33.2	33.6	33.7	33.9	33.5	33.9	34.3	34.2	34.4	34.9	33.8
2007	33.9	33.7	34.0	34.6	34.3	34.4	34.0	34.1	34.4	34.6	34.7	35.0	34.3
2008	33.9	33.6	33.4	33.8	34.1	33.7	33.6	33.8	33.6	33.4	33.2	33.6	33.6
2009	32.0	32.0	31.6	30.9	30.7	30.6	30.1	29.9	29.8	29.8	29.5	29.9	30.6
2010	29.0	28.9	28.9	29.0	29.1	29.4	29.3	29.5	29.4	29.5	29.4	29.8	29.3
2011	28.6	28.5	28.6	28.9	29.1	29.2	29.6	29.6	29.5	29.5	29.6	30.4	29.3
Information													
2000	23.9	24.0	24.0	24.1	24.1	24.2	24.1	24.2	24.3	24.4	24.5	24.5	24.2
2001	24.5	24.5	24.6	24.3	24.2	24.3	24.2	23.9	23.5	23.3	23.3	23.3	24.0
2002	23.3	23.0	22.9	22.1	21.9	21.9	21.6	21.4	21.2	21.1	21.1	21.0	21.9
2003	21.3	21.2	21.2	21.0	21.0	20.9	20.7	20.5	20.2	20.2	20.2	20.4	20.7
2004	20.1	20.0	20.1	20.0	20.0	20.1	20.1	20.0	19.7	19.7	19.8	19.6	19.9
2005	19.5	19.5	19.4	19.7	19.7	19.6	19.5	19.5	19.2	19.2	19.3	19.2	19.4
2006	19.2	19.1	19.1	18.8	18.9	18.9	18.9	18.9	18.7	18.6	18.7	18.7	18.9
2007	18.4	18.5	18.3	18.5	18.6	18.6	18.7	18.5	18.4	18.3	18.4	18.4	18.5
2008	18.2	18.0	18.0	18.0	18.0	17.9	17.8	17.7	17.2	17.2	17.3	17.3	17.7
2009	17.1	17.0	16.7	16.5	16.5	16.6	16.5	16.4	16.1	16.1	16.2	16.2	16.5
2010	16.0	15.9	15.8	15.8	15.9	15.8	15.8	15.9	15.5	15.6	15.6	15.7	15.8
2011	15.4	15.3	15.2	15.3	15.4	15.3	15.3	15.3	15.1	15.1	15.1	15.1	15.2
Financial Activities													
2000	75.6	75.2	75.6	74.8	74.5	75.3	74.8	75.0	74.9	74.2	74.9	75.5	75.0
2001	75.5	75.9	76.1	76.1	76.0	77.1	77.1	77.1	76.0	75.8	76.5	76.9	76.3
2002	75.7	76.0	76.0	75.9	75.8	75.7	75.6	75.4	74.6	74.4	75.1	75.5	75.5
2003	75.8	75.9	76.2	76.0	76.5	77.5	77.7	77.9	77.2	76.6	76.9	77.6	76.8
2004	76.7	76.9	77.1	76.6	76.8	77.8	77.7	77.7	76.7	76.3	76.3	76.4	76.9
2005	75.5	75.4	75.2	74.4	74.3	75.3	75.1	75.0	74.2	74.9	74.7	74.6	74.9
2006	73.6	73.7	73.8	73.5	73.5	74.0	74.4	74.2	73.7	73.5	73.7	73.8	73.8
2007	73.1	73.0	72.9	72.8	72.9	72.8	72.7	72.3	71.3	71.0	70.7	70.5	72.2
2008	69.7	69.3	69.3	69.1	69.2	69.2	69.4	69.2	68.2	67.9	67.9	67.7	68.8
2009	66.9	66.5	66.2	65.9	65.9	66.1	66.1	65.8	65.3	64.9	64.9	64.9	65.8
2010	64.4	64.3	64.1	64.5	64.6	64.8	65.1	65.0	64.3	64.7	64.6	64.6	64.6
2011	64.4	64.3	64.0	64.3	64.5	64.5	64.7	64.2	63.9	64.4	64.8	64.9	64.4

Employment by Industry: Cleveland–Elyria–Mentor, OH, Selected Years, 2000–2011—*Continued*

(Numbers in thousands, not seasonally adjusted)

Industry and year	January	February	March	April	May	June	July	August	September	October	November	December	Annual average
Professional and Business Services													
2000	140.2	140.8	141.9	146.5	147.1	149.3	148.8	149.2	148.3	147.4	146.6	145.8	146.0
2001	143.6	143.7	145.2	145.4	145.9	146.7	145.6	145.1	141.3	140.3	138.6	137.4	143.2
2002	132.5	132.8	134.1	134.3	134.3	135.7	135.2	136.0	134.1	135.7	134.3	133.6	134.4
2003	131.5	131.6	132.9	134.5	135.3	136.6	137.1	138.7	136.5	135.5	134.6	133.1	134.8
2004	129.3	129.8	131.3	135.8	136.9	139.1	140.1	141.7	141.1	140.9	139.8	139.0	137.1
2005	133.2	134.9	136.2	139.4	139.5	141.3	143.0	144.3	144.2	144.6	144.3	143.1	140.7
2006	138.6	139.4	140.8	143.4	143.8	145.8	145.8	147.2	146.4	146.1	145.3	145.3	144.0
2007	140.2	140.4	141.0	143.3	144.1	146.4	146.2	147.0	146.0	146.1	146.0	145.3	144.3
2008	142.1	142.2	141.5	144.3	145.6	146.5	146.6	147.5	145.9	143.3	141.7	139.0	143.9
2009	134.1	132.3	131.3	131.4	131.5	132.0	131.5	131.7	131.1	131.7	131.6	129.9	131.7
2010	126.4	126.1	126.5	131.3	132.1	133.9	134.7	135.0	134.4	134.8	135.0	134.5	132.1
2011	130.9	132.1	133.1	137.5	138.4	139.1	142.0	141.6	140.2	140.2	137.9	135.0	137.3
Education and Health Services													
2000	147.4	149.5	150.2	149.9	150.0	149.4	147.7	147.9	150.7	150.8	151.4	152.0	149.7
2001	150.5	153.0	153.7	154.8	155.2	154.5	152.9	153.4	157.0	159.5	160.5	161.0	155.5
2002	158.8	162.2	162.5	162.6	162.4	161.1	160.3	160.7	164.3	165.9	166.8	167.1	162.9
2003	161.5	163.6	164.1	164.1	163.9	161.5	161.5	161.1	164.4	166.0	166.4	165.5	163.6
2004	163.0	165.1	165.7	164.2	163.5	161.5	162.9	161.8	166.0	168.2	168.7	169.3	165.0
2005	164.9	167.5	167.8	166.6	166.2	165.4	164.6	164.9	169.2	170.1	171.3	172.0	167.5
2006	168.5	171.7	172.2	171.3	170.7	169.9	168.0	167.7	170.8	172.5	173.4	173.3	170.8
2007	171.3	172.8	173.9	174.7	174.0	173.2	172.1	172.3	176.6	178.4	179.2	179.5	174.8
2008	176.9	179.2	179.0	179.8	179.0	177.3	174.7	175.4	180.6	183.4	184.1	184.3	179.5
2009	182.1	184.1	184.5	184.8	183.7	181.4	180.8	181.0	185.6	187.6	188.2	188.1	184.3
2010	186.9	188.3	188.4	188.1	187.1	184.3	184.7	184.2	188.8	190.5	191.0	190.3	187.7
2011	187.0	188.7	188.6	188.9	188.6	186.5	185.2	185.3	186.6	188.5	189.1	187.2	187.5
Leisure and Hospitality													
2000	86.9	87.1	88.9	91.7	95.7	98.4	99.5	99.1	95.8	92.6	91.1	90.9	93.1
2001	86.2	86.5	88.6	90.3	95.0	98.2	98.6	98.6	93.3	91.3	89.1	88.5	92.0
2002	84.1	83.6	85.0	88.8	93.0	95.4	96.4	96.7	94.2	90.7	89.1	88.8	90.5
2003	85.0	84.5	86.2	90.2	94.7	96.8	97.7	98.8	95.4	92.5	90.8	91.5	92.0
2004	86.6	85.6	87.6	90.1	93.8	96.6	97.5	98.9	94.9	92.3	91.8	91.7	92.3
2005	86.3	86.4	88.6	92.3	95.6	97.8	99.3	100.6	96.8	94.2	93.1	93.0	93.7
2006	88.1	87.9	90.2	93.5	97.4	99.7	99.8	101.0	96.7	93.5	91.3	91.8	94.2
2007	87.6	87.0	89.0	91.6	95.5	98.7	98.3	99.0	95.2	92.8	91.2	90.5	93.0
2008	85.7	85.4	86.0	90.6	95.1	96.7	96.2	96.5	93.2	89.7	87.8	87.8	90.9
2009	82.1	81.4	82.9	87.1	91.1	92.4	92.8	92.2	89.4	86.3	84.6	85.2	87.3
2010	80.2	80.0	81.4	86.0	89.5	91.4	92.3	92.9	89.5	87.5	86.3	85.4	86.9
2011	80.8	80.7	82.3	86.2	89.8	92.0	91.5	90.6	85.0	82.2	82.2	80.0	85.3
Other Services													
2000	44.9	45.2	45.5	45.1	45.4	45.5	45.4	45.3	45.4	45.4	45.4	45.6	45.3
2001	44.9	45.0	45.1	45.5	45.8	46.5	46.5	46.8	46.3	45.9	46.0	46.2	45.9
2002	45.5	45.6	45.9	45.8	46.1	46.6	46.5	46.3	46.0	45.4	45.3	45.3	45.9
2003	44.1	44.1	44.4	44.4	44.6	45.0	44.5	44.6	44.2	44.0	43.8	44.0	44.3
2004	43.7	43.7	44.4	44.5	44.7	45.1	45.1	44.8	44.4	44.4	44.4	44.3	44.5
2005	43.6	43.8	44.1	44.4	44.4	44.7	44.8	44.6	44.2	44.1	44.2	44.4	44.3
2006	43.7	43.7	43.8	43.7	44.1	44.9	44.6	44.2	43.9	43.8	43.7	44.1	44.0
2007	43.4	43.4	43.8	44.0	44.2	44.9	44.9	44.6	44.1	43.9	43.9	44.0	44.1
2008	43.4	43.6	43.5	43.4	43.7	43.9	43.7	43.6	43.2	43.0	42.9	43.0	43.4
2009	42.3	42.3	42.4	42.5	42.6	42.5	42.6	42.3	41.9	41.9	41.7	41.9	42.2
2010	41.1	40.9	41.2	41.4	41.3	41.6	41.7	41.5	41.2	41.4	41.3	41.5	41.3
2011	40.9	40.8	40.8	41.2	41.3	41.5	41.1	41.2	41.3	40.7	40.5	40.7	41.0
Government													
2000	138.4	140.9	142.0	141.2	145.5	141.2	135.5	136.2	141.0	143.2	143.9	144.5	141.1
2001	141.0	143.7	145.1	144.5	145.2	143.0	137.5	137.9	143.9	145.9	146.5	147.0	143.4
2002	142.1	146.2	147.1	145.9	147.1	144.8	136.4	137.5	143.8	146.4	146.8	146.3	144.2
2003	142.4	145.3	146.4	145.9	146.0	143.5	136.3	133.8	141.2	144.7	145.5	145.8	143.1
2004	141.3	144.7	145.8	145.7	146.4	144.0	135.2	133.8	139.4	143.0	143.9	143.4	142.2
2005	139.1	142.8	143.4	143.7	144.4	143.2	134.7	133.5	138.9	142.2	142.3	142.6	140.9
2006	138.8	141.8	143.1	143.1	144.0	142.3	133.9	133.1	138.8	142.0	143.2	143.1	140.6
2007	139.8	143.3	144.7	145.2	145.9	147.3	139.5	138.3	140.1	143.7	144.3	143.3	143.0
2008	141.3	144.2	143.4	144.0	146.5	147.2	139.5	137.9	140.2	143.6	143.6	142.3	142.8
2009	140.4	142.7	142.7	143.1	144.1	142.8	136.0	134.6	138.3	141.2	141.4	140.0	140.6
2010	137.8	140.6	140.1	140.6	144.7	141.1	134.7	132.2	135.2	139.1	139.2	138.3	138.6
2011	132.8	137.2	137.7	138.2	137.6	136.5	130.3	128.6	131.2	132.5	133.5	132.9	134.1

Employment by Industry: Columbia, SC, Selected Years, 2000–2011

(Numbers in thousands, not seasonally adjusted)

Industry and year	January	February	March	April	May	June	July	August	September	October	November	December	Annual average
Total Nonfarm													
2000	334.8	336.6	340.8	342.0	343.9	344.8	337.2	339.7	342.8	345.4	346.5	347.7	341.9
2001	336.8	338.4	340.6	339.7	341.2	341.3	335.2	337.6	338.5	338.2	339.9	340.3	339.0
2002	330.7	332.2	334.8	336.6	338.4	338.0	334.7	337.7	339.1	341.7	342.0	343.4	337.4
2003	334.5	335.7	336.7	336.9	338.8	337.4	332.9	337.1	338.6	341.6	342.2	344.2	338.1
2004	337.4	338.0	340.9	344.2	345.6	346.0	342.4	345.6	347.7	350.1	350.1	352.1	345.0
2005	347.6	350.3	350.5	351.7	351.6	348.7	348.9	353.7	353.4	355.7	358.4	359.0	352.5
2006	354.7	356.8	358.3	359.7	361.5	357.7	354.0	358.6	360.4	361.3	363.8	366.2	359.4
2007	359.2	361.6	363.5	365.4	368.2	368.7	364.2	366.1	368.0	368.7	369.2	369.9	366.1
2008	364.4	365.9	366.4	366.8	368.4	365.8	360.8	363.8	363.3	362.0	362.2	361.3	364.3
2009	349.8	348.9	349.1	347.9	348.1	345.7	342.4	342.5	343.2	344.9	345.6	344.8	346.1
2010	340.0	341.7	343.2	345.2	347.3	346.0	341.7	342.3	343.6	346.6	348.2	347.0	344.4
2011	338.5	342.6	344.6	347.3	347.4	345.4	342.8	343.5	345.7	349.0	353.1	349.7	345.8
Total Private													
2000	259.4	260.0	263.3	264.9	266.4	269.0	264.2	264.0	265.2	267.2	268.2	269.2	265.1
2001	259.4	260.2	261.9	261.6	263.2	265.2	261.7	262.0	261.4	261.4	262.6	262.6	261.9
2002	254.0	255.1	257.4	259.8	261.4	263.3	262.2	262.9	262.4	264.8	264.6	265.8	261.1
2003	257.3	257.9	258.7	259.7	261.7	262.5	261.0	263.1	262.5	265.3	265.4	267.1	261.9
2004	260.4	261.3	263.7	267.1	268.4	270.7	269.8	270.8	271.0	273.6	273.4	275.1	268.8
2005	271.6	273.7	273.6	274.4	274.5	273.8	276.5	278.0	276.1	278.1	280.4	281.1	276.0
2006	277.4	278.8	279.8	282.0	283.9	282.3	281.2	283.4	283.6	284.4	286.3	288.6	282.6
2007	282.2	283.7	285.3	287.5	290.0	291.7	289.3	290.0	289.9	289.7	289.5	290.2	288.3
2008	284.5	285.6	286.0	285.9	287.4	286.7	284.6	285.4	282.4	280.8	280.4	279.6	284.1
2009	269.2	267.7	267.9	266.5	267.1	266.6	264.7	264.3	263.7	264.6	265.0	264.1	266.0
2010	260.2	261.3	262.4	264.0	264.8	265.2	264.0	264.7	264.5	266.7	267.8	266.9	264.4
2011	259.3	262.6	264.3	267.2	268.3	267.7	267.9	267.4	267.1	269.1	272.6	271.4	267.1
Goods-Producing													
2000	56.4	56.4	56.9	57.2	57.4	58.0	57.8	57.6	57.6	57.5	57.2	57.4	57.3
2001	56.1	56.3	56.4	56.0	56.3	56.3	55.7	55.3	55.3	54.6	54.7	54.1	55.6
2002	53.3	53.3	53.3	53.7	54.5	54.5	54.4	54.7	54.2	54.0	53.5	53.4	53.9
2003	53.0	52.7	53.2	52.8	53.2	53.2	53.0	53.0	52.5	52.6	52.2	52.0	52.8
2004	51.0	51.0	51.3	51.9	51.9	52.3	52.3	52.4	52.5	52.4	52.3	52.5	52.0
2005	52.1	52.2	52.1	52.3	52.9	52.2	52.2	52.2	51.7	51.8	52.0	51.7	52.1
2006	51.7	52.0	52.2	53.3	53.7	53.9	53.4	53.5	53.2	52.9	53.0	52.6	53.0
2007	52.1	52.4	52.6	52.9	53.4	53.8	53.7	53.8	53.2	52.9	52.8	52.7	53.0
2008	51.6	51.2	51.0	50.4	50.4	50.8	50.5	50.4	49.8	49.0	48.8	48.3	50.2
2009	46.4	45.6	45.0	44.5	44.5	44.4	44.0	43.5	43.1	42.9	42.8	42.6	44.1
2010	42.1	42.1	42.0	41.8	41.9	42.3	42.3	41.9	42.0	42.1	42.2	42.0	42.1
2011	41.1	41.6	42.0	42.2	42.5	42.7	42.7	43.3	42.6	42.7	42.5	43.5	42.5
Mining, Logging, and Construction													
2000	19.2	19.1	19.5	19.7	19.9	20.3	20.4	20.4	20.3	20.1	19.9	20.1	19.9
2001	19.6	19.6	19.9	19.9	20.3	20.5	20.1	20.1	20.2	19.7	19.7	19.2	19.9
2002	18.8	18.9	19.1	19.5	19.8	20.0	19.8	19.9	19.7	19.6	19.7	19.7	19.5
2003	20.0	20.0	20.2	19.7	20.1	20.3	20.5	20.6	20.6	20.8	20.5	20.5	20.3
2004	20.1	20.1	20.3	20.6	20.8	21.0	20.7	20.7	20.9	20.8	20.7	20.7	20.6
2005	20.2	20.2	20.0	20.6	21.1	20.5	20.7	20.7	20.4	20.6	20.8	20.6	20.5
2006	20.7	20.9	21.1	22.1	22.4	22.4	22.4	22.5	22.3	22.1	22.2	21.7	21.9
2007	21.0	21.2	21.4	21.6	21.9	22.1	22.1	22.0	21.7	21.4	21.3	21.2	21.6
2008	20.3	20.3	20.2	19.6	19.6	19.9	19.7	19.7	19.4	18.9	18.7	18.4	19.6
2009	17.6	17.2	17.1	17.1	17.1	17.0	16.7	16.4	16.0	15.9	15.8	15.6	16.6
2010	15.3	15.2	15.3	15.1	15.0	15.2	15.2	14.9	14.8	14.8	14.7	14.6	15.0
2011	13.9	14.2	14.5	14.5	14.6	14.7	14.7	14.8	14.5	14.4	14.3	14.6	14.5
Manufacturing													
2000	37.2	37.3	37.4	37.5	37.5	37.7	37.4	37.2	37.3	37.4	37.3	37.3	37.4
2001	36.5	36.7	36.5	36.1	36.0	35.8	35.6	35.2	35.1	34.9	35.0	34.9	35.7
2002	34.5	34.4	34.2	34.2	34.7	34.5	34.6	34.8	34.5	34.4	33.8	33.7	34.4
2003	33.0	32.7	33.0	33.1	33.1	32.9	32.5	32.4	31.9	31.8	31.7	31.5	32.5
2004	30.9	30.9	31.0	31.3	31.1	31.3	31.6	31.7	31.6	31.6	31.6	31.8	31.4
2005	31.9	32.0	32.1	31.7	31.8	31.7	31.5	31.5	31.3	31.2	31.2	31.1	31.6
2006	31.0	31.1	31.1	31.2	31.3	31.5	31.0	31.0	30.9	30.8	30.8	30.9	31.1
2007	31.1	31.2	31.2	31.3	31.5	31.7	31.6	31.8	31.5	31.5	31.5	31.5	31.5
2008	31.3	30.9	30.8	30.8	30.8	30.9	30.8	30.7	30.4	30.1	30.1	29.9	30.6
2009	28.8	28.4	27.9	27.4	27.4	27.4	27.3	27.1	27.1	27.0	27.0	27.0	27.5
2010	26.8	26.9	26.7	26.7	26.9	27.1	27.1	27.0	27.2	27.3	27.5	27.4	27.1
2011	27.2	27.4	27.5	27.7	27.9	28.0	28.0	28.5	28.1	28.3	28.2	28.9	28.0
Service-Providing													
2000	278.4	280.2	283.9	284.8	286.5	286.8	279.4	282.1	285.2	287.9	289.3	290.3	284.6
2001	280.7	282.1	284.2	283.7	284.9	285.0	279.5	282.3	283.2	283.6	285.2	286.2	283.4
2002	277.4	278.9	281.5	282.9	283.9	283.5	280.3	283.0	284.9	287.7	288.5	290.0	283.5
2003	281.5	283.0	283.5	284.1	285.6	284.2	279.9	284.1	286.1	289.0	290.0	292.2	285.3
2004	286.4	287.0	289.6	292.3	293.7	293.7	290.1	293.2	295.2	297.7	297.8	299.6	293.0
2005	295.5	298.1	298.4	299.4	298.7	296.5	296.7	301.5	301.7	303.9	306.4	307.3	300.3
2006	303.0	304.8	306.1	306.4	307.8	303.8	300.6	305.1	307.2	308.4	310.8	313.6	306.5
2007	307.1	309.2	310.9	312.5	314.8	314.9	310.5	312.3	314.8	315.8	316.4	317.2	313.0
2008	312.8	314.7	315.4	316.4	318.0	315.0	310.3	313.4	313.5	313.0	313.4	313.0	314.1
2009	303.4	303.3	304.1	303.4	303.6	301.3	298.4	299.0	300.1	302.0	302.8	302.2	302.0
2010	297.9	299.6	301.2	303.4	305.4	303.7	299.4	300.4	301.6	304.5	306.0	305.0	302.3
2011	297.4	301.0	302.6	305.1	304.9	302.7	300.1	300.2	303.1	306.3	310.6	306.2	303.4

Employment by Industry: Columbia, SC, Selected Years, 2000–2011—*Continued*

(Numbers in thousands, not seasonally adjusted)

Industry and year	January	February	March	April	May	June	July	August	September	October	November	December	Annual average
Trade, Transportation, and Utilities													
2000	65.8	65.6	66.3	66.6	66.9	67.3	65.7	66.2	66.2	67.4	68.6	69.3	66.8
2001	65.8	65.0	65.3	64.8	65.3	65.8	64.2	63.9	63.7	63.9	64.8	65.7	64.9
2002	61.7	61.9	62.4	63.2	63.6	64.2	63.6	63.4	63.5	63.8	65.2	66.2	63.6
2003	61.0	61.5	61.9	62.3	62.7	63.5	62.4	62.8	63.2	64.0	65.2	66.3	63.1
2004	63.4	63.0	63.5	63.5	64.2	64.1	64.8	65.0	64.6	65.2	66.2	67.5	64.6
2005	65.4	65.2	65.5	65.9	65.8	65.4	66.1	66.2	65.7	66.8	68.2	69.1	66.3
2006	66.8	66.8	67.4	67.1	67.5	67.1	66.8	67.2	67.6	68.2	69.8	71.2	67.8
2007	68.8	68.9	69.1	69.3	69.8	69.9	69.5	69.6	69.4	69.8	70.8	71.4	69.7
2008	69.6	69.6	69.6	69.7	69.5	69.4	69.0	68.6	68.0	66.8	67.3	68.1	68.8
2009	64.6	63.6	63.2	63.1	63.4	63.3	63.2	63.1	63.0	62.9	63.7	64.5	63.5
2010	62.5	62.1	62.3	62.4	62.4	62.4	62.2	62.5	61.8	62.3	63.2	64.0	62.5
2011	61.4	61.7	61.8	62.4	62.5	62.8	62.4	61.4	62.0	62.7	65.4	65.1	62.6
Wholesale Trade													
2000	14.8	14.9	15.0	15.1	15.2	15.2	15.0	15.1	15.1	15.1	15.1	15.1	15.1
2001	15.2	15.1	15.2	15.1	15.2	15.3	15.0	14.9	14.9	14.8	14.6	14.8	15.0
2002	14.4	14.8	14.9	15.1	15.1	15.2	15.0	14.9	14.8	14.6	14.6	14.6	14.8
2003	13.6	13.6	13.6	13.9	14.0	14.2	13.9	14.0	14.1	14.1	14.2	14.3	14.0
2004	14.4	14.4	14.6	14.6	14.8	14.8	15.1	15.2	15.0	15.0	15.1	15.2	14.9
2005	16.0	15.9	16.0	15.9	16.0	15.9	16.2	16.2	16.1	16.2	16.2	16.3	16.1
2006	16.5	16.6	16.8	16.9	16.9	16.8	16.9	16.9	17.1	17.0	17.0	17.1	16.9
2007	17.4	17.9	17.7	17.3	17.1	17.1	16.9	16.8	16.7	16.7	16.6	16.6	17.1
2008	16.8	16.9	16.7	16.8	16.9	16.8	16.7	16.3	16.0	15.9	15.8	15.9	16.5
2009	15.2	15.0	14.9	14.8	14.8	14.7	14.5	14.4	14.4	14.4	14.3	14.3	14.6
2010	14.0	14.0	14.0	14.0	13.9	13.9	13.8	13.7	13.5	13.7	13.7	13.7	13.8
2011	13.5	13.6	13.6	13.7	13.7	13.7	13.7	13.7	13.7	13.8	13.8	13.7	13.7
Retail Trade													
2000	39.3	39.0	39.5	39.6	39.8	40.0	38.9	39.2	39.3	40.3	41.5	42.2	39.9
2001	39.1	38.4	38.6	38.4	38.8	39.1	38.0	38.0	37.9	38.0	39.1	39.8	38.6
2002	37.2	36.9	37.2	37.7	38.1	38.4	37.8	37.8	38.0	38.3	39.7	40.7	38.2
2003	37.3	37.8	38.1	38.1	38.3	38.8	38.1	38.3	38.5	39.0	40.1	40.9	38.6
2004	38.3	37.8	38.1	38.2	38.5	38.2	38.4	38.4	38.2	38.9	39.6	40.6	38.6
2005	38.2	38.1	38.1	38.7	38.4	38.1	38.4	38.4	38.0	38.8	40.0	40.6	38.7
2006	38.7	38.5	38.8	38.5	38.5	38.5	38.2	38.4	38.5	39.5	40.8	41.7	39.1
2007	39.7	39.3	39.7	40.2	40.7	40.6	40.5	40.7	40.5	40.9	41.8	42.1	40.6
2008	41.2	41.0	41.2	41.2	40.9	40.9	40.5	40.7	40.6	39.8	40.3	40.7	40.8
2009	38.7	37.9	37.8	37.9	38.1	38.1	38.1	38.2	38.1	38.0	39.0	39.5	38.3
2010	38.0	37.6	37.8	38.2	38.3	38.2	37.9	38.3	37.9	38.1	39.0	39.7	38.3
2011	37.5	37.6	37.7	38.1	38.2	38.3	38.0	37.0	37.8	38.0	40.5	40.0	38.2
Transportation and Utilities													
2000	11.7	11.7	11.8	11.9	11.9	12.1	11.8	11.9	11.8	12.0	12.0	12.0	11.9
2001	11.5	11.5	11.5	11.3	11.3	11.4	11.2	11.0	10.9	11.1	11.1	11.1	11.2
2002	10.1	10.2	10.3	10.4	10.4	10.6	10.8	10.7	10.7	10.9	10.9	10.9	10.6
2003	10.1	10.1	10.2	10.3	10.4	10.5	10.4	10.5	10.6	10.9	10.9	11.1	10.5
2004	10.7	10.8	10.8	10.7	10.9	11.1	11.3	11.4	11.4	11.3	11.5	11.7	11.1
2005	11.2	11.2	11.4	11.3	11.4	11.4	11.5	11.6	11.6	11.8	12.0	12.2	11.6
2006	11.6	11.7	11.8	11.7	11.8	11.8	11.7	11.9	12.0	11.7	12.0	12.4	11.8
2007	11.7	11.7	11.7	11.8	12.0	12.2	12.1	12.1	12.2	12.2	12.4	12.7	12.1
2008	11.6	11.7	11.7	11.7	11.7	11.7	11.8	11.6	11.4	11.1	11.2	11.5	11.6
2009	10.7	10.7	10.5	10.4	10.5	10.5	10.6	10.5	10.5	10.5	10.4	10.7	10.5
2010	10.5	10.5	10.5	10.2	10.2	10.3	10.5	10.5	10.4	10.5	10.5	10.6	10.4
2011	10.4	10.5	10.5	10.6	10.6	10.8	10.7	10.7	10.5	10.9	11.1	11.4	10.7
Information													
2000	7.6	7.6	7.6	7.6	7.5	7.7	7.4	7.4	7.4	7.2	7.2	7.2	7.5
2001	6.9	6.7	6.7	6.6	6.6	6.7	6.3	6.3	6.2	6.3	6.3	6.4	6.5
2002	6.4	6.3	6.4	6.3	6.4	6.5	6.4	6.5	6.3	6.5	6.6	6.6	6.4
2003	6.2	6.1	6.2	6.1	6.3	6.2	6.4	6.3	6.3	6.2	6.2	6.3	6.2
2004	6.1	6.1	6.1	6.0	6.0	6.0	6.1	6.0	6.0	6.0	5.9	6.0	6.0
2005	6.0	6.1	6.0	6.1	6.1	6.2	6.2	6.1	6.0	6.1	6.1	6.1	6.1
2006	6.2	6.2	6.2	6.2	6.2	6.2	6.2	6.1	6.1	6.1	6.3	6.4	6.2
2007	6.1	6.1	6.1	6.1	6.2	6.2	6.1	6.0	6.0	6.2	6.1	6.2	6.1
2008	5.8	5.9	5.9	5.9	5.9	6.0	6.0	6.0	5.9	5.9	5.9	5.9	5.9
2009	5.9	5.8	5.9	5.8	5.8	5.8	5.7	5.7	5.7	5.7	5.7	5.6	5.8
2010	5.6	5.6	5.6	5.6	5.6	5.5	5.6	5.7	5.6	5.6	5.7	5.6	5.6
2011	5.4	5.4	5.4	5.3	5.4	5.4	5.4	5.5	5.5	5.6	5.6	5.6	5.5
Financial Activities													
2000	23.6	23.8	23.9	23.6	23.9	24.2	24.4	24.5	24.4	25.0	25.2	25.3	24.3
2001	24.6	24.6	24.6	25.2	25.3	25.9	25.6	25.6	25.5	25.7	26.2	25.9	25.4
2002	25.4	25.6	25.7	25.2	25.3	25.5	25.8	25.8	26.0	26.6	26.7	26.7	25.9
2003	26.3	26.0	26.6	26.2	26.5	26.6	26.2	26.6	26.3	26.5	26.6	26.7	26.4
2004	26.3	26.5	26.6	26.7	26.8	27.1	26.9	27.0	27.3	27.8	27.8	28.1	27.1
2005	28.5	28.9	28.7	28.5	28.9	29.0	29.2	29.2	29.1	29.3	29.7	29.0	29.0
2006	29.4	29.5	29.5	29.3	29.6	29.6	29.7	29.7	29.8	29.9	30.0	30.5	29.7
2007	30.4	30.4	30.3	30.4	30.5	30.6	30.2	29.8	30.0	30.0	30.2	30.3	30.3
2008	30.0	30.1	30.2	30.1	30.1	30.2	29.8	29.8	29.7	29.8	29.9	30.0	30.0
2009	29.3	29.5	29.5	29.0	29.1	28.9	28.8	28.6	28.3	27.9	27.8	27.6	28.7
2010	27.4	27.4	27.3	27.0	27.0	27.0	26.7	26.7	26.5	26.7	26.7	26.7	26.9
2011	26.6	26.6	26.7	26.8	26.9	26.8	26.9	27.0	26.8	27.0	27.2	27.3	26.9

Employment by Industry: Columbia, SC, Selected Years, 2000–2011—*Continued*

(Numbers in thousands, not seasonally adjusted)

Industry and year	January	February	March	April	May	June	July	August	September	October	November	December	Annual average
Professional and Business Services													
2000	36.1	36.2	36.8	38.6	38.9	39.6	38.4	38.4	38.8	38.7	38.3	38.2	38.1
2001	36.4	37.1	37.5	37.9	38.0	38.0	37.8	38.2	37.9	36.7	36.4	36.3	37.4
2002	34.4	34.4	35.1	36.4	36.2	36.7	36.3	36.8	36.5	36.7	36.2	36.3	36.0
2003	35.2	35.4	33.8	35.8	35.8	35.9	35.8	36.3	36.0	37.0	37.0	37.1	35.9
2004	36.1	36.6	37.2	39.5	39.3	41.0	40.1	40.4	40.5	40.8	40.3	40.0	39.3
2005	39.5	40.2	39.5	40.0	39.3	40.5	40.9	42.1	42.3	42.5	43.2	43.3	41.1
2006	42.6	42.4	42.2	43.4	43.9	42.8	43.0	44.3	43.9	43.0	43.0	43.4	43.2
2007	42.5	42.8	43.0	43.2	43.4	43.8	43.4	44.1	44.4	44.2	43.5	43.4	43.5
2008	41.9	42.3	41.9	41.6	42.8	41.4	41.2	42.5	41.0	41.3	41.2	40.2	41.6
2009	38.3	37.7	37.9	37.6	37.4	37.4	37.0	37.3	37.1	38.8	38.9	38.4	37.8
2010	38.1	38.8	39.1	39.8	40.0	40.4	40.2	40.6	40.9	41.5	41.2	40.9	40.1
2011	40.1	41.1	41.3	42.5	42.4	42.3	43.4	42.4	43.2	43.6	44.1	43.3	42.5
Education and Health Services													
2000	31.9	31.9	32.2	32.4	32.4	32.5	32.1	32.0	32.4	32.6	32.9	33.1	32.4
2001	32.5	32.9	33.1	32.5	32.6	33.0	33.1	33.2	33.8	34.5	34.7	34.9	33.4
2002	34.8	35.1	35.4	35.6	35.7	35.7	36.1	36.2	36.5	36.4	36.7	37.1	35.9
2003	37.1	37.2	37.5	37.2	37.2	37.2	37.2	37.5	37.9	38.1	38.2	38.5	37.6
2004	37.7	37.9	38.2	38.2	38.2	38.0	38.0	38.1	38.3	38.3	38.6	38.6	38.2
2005	39.0	39.3	39.6	38.8	38.8	37.9	38.7	38.7	38.6	39.3	39.4	39.3	39.0
2006	39.2	39.9	39.8	39.5	39.5	39.3	39.3	39.4	39.7	41.0	41.0	41.1	39.9
2007	40.4	40.8	41.0	41.7	42.1	42.5	42.1	41.9	42.4	42.2	42.2	42.1	41.8
2008	42.7	43.1	43.3	43.2	43.3	43.3	43.1	43.0	43.3	43.2	43.3	43.3	43.2
2009	42.1	42.4	42.5	42.3	42.4	42.1	42.2	42.3	42.7	42.6	42.8	42.6	42.4
2010	42.3	42.6	42.6	42.8	43.0	42.9	42.8	42.8	42.9	43.5	43.5	43.3	42.9
2011	42.5	43.1	43.1	43.2	43.3	43.1	42.5	42.4	42.3	42.5	42.6	42.3	42.7
Leisure and Hospitality													
2000	26.7	27.1	27.9	27.4	27.6	27.7	27.0	26.8	27.0	27.4	27.4	27.6	27.3
2001	26.0	26.5	27.0	27.2	27.6	27.8	27.6	28.0	27.5	28.2	27.8	27.6	27.4
2002	26.5	27.1	27.5	27.5	27.8	28.1	28.0	27.9	27.8	28.8	27.8	27.6	27.7
2003	27.0	27.5	27.8	27.7	28.2	28.1	28.4	28.9	28.6	29.1	28.3	28.4	28.2
2004	28.2	28.5	29.1	29.4	29.9	29.9	29.3	29.5	29.4	30.5	29.7	29.7	29.4
2005	28.8	29.2	29.4	30.1	30.0	29.8	30.2	30.3	29.6	30.0	29.6	29.3	29.7
2006	28.8	29.2	29.8	30.4	30.5	30.4	30.2	30.4	30.3	30.7	30.5	30.7	30.2
2007	29.3	29.7	30.3	31.2	31.7	32.0	31.5	31.9	31.8	31.7	31.2	31.1	31.1
2008	30.0	30.5	31.0	31.9	32.3	32.6	31.9	32.0	31.8	31.8	31.1	31.0	31.5
2009	29.8	30.4	31.1	31.5	31.8	32.0	31.1	31.2	31.3	31.3	30.8	30.4	31.1
2010	29.7	30.2	30.8	31.9	32.1	31.8	31.5	31.9	32.1	32.1	32.6	31.7	31.5
2011	29.8	30.7	31.5	32.3	32.7	32.0	32.0	32.8	32.1	32.4	32.6	31.7	31.9
Other Services													
2000	11.3	11.4	11.7	11.5	11.8	12.0	11.4	11.1	11.4	11.4	11.4	11.1	11.5
2001	11.1	11.1	11.3	11.4	11.5	11.7	11.4	11.5	11.5	11.5	11.7	11.7	11.5
2002	11.5	11.4	11.6	11.9	11.9	12.1	11.6	11.6	11.6	12.0	11.9	11.9	11.8
2003	11.5	11.5	11.7	11.6	11.8	11.8	11.6	11.7	11.7	11.8	11.7	11.8	11.7
2004	11.6	11.7	11.7	11.9	12.1	12.3	12.3	12.4	12.4	12.6	12.6	12.7	12.2
2005	12.3	12.6	12.8	12.7	12.7	12.8	13.0	13.2	13.0	12.5	12.6	12.6	12.7
2006	12.7	12.8	12.7	12.8	13.0	13.0	12.6	12.8	13.0	12.6	12.7	12.7	12.8
2007	12.6	12.6	12.9	12.7	12.9	12.9	12.8	12.9	12.7	12.7	12.7	13.0	12.8
2008	12.9	12.9	13.1	13.1	13.1	13.0	13.1	13.1	12.9	13.0	12.9	12.8	13.0
2009	12.8	12.7	12.8	12.7	12.7	12.7	12.7	12.6	12.5	12.5	12.5	12.4	12.6
2010	12.5	12.5	12.7	12.7	12.8	12.9	12.7	12.6	12.7	12.9	12.7	12.7	12.7
2011	12.4	12.4	12.5	12.5	12.6	12.6	12.6	12.6	12.6	12.6	12.6	12.6	12.6
Government													
2000	75.4	76.6	77.5	77.1	77.5	75.8	73.0	75.7	77.6	78.2	78.3	78.5	76.8
2001	77.4	78.2	78.7	78.1	78.0	76.1	73.5	75.6	77.1	76.8	77.3	77.7	77.0
2002	76.7	77.1	77.4	76.8	77.0	74.7	72.5	74.8	76.7	76.9	77.4	77.6	76.3
2003	77.2	77.8	78.0	77.2	77.1	74.9	71.9	74.0	76.1	76.3	76.8	77.1	76.2
2004	77.0	76.7	77.2	77.1	77.2	75.3	72.6	74.8	76.7	76.5	76.7	77.0	76.2
2005	76.0	76.6	76.9	77.3	77.1	74.9	72.4	75.7	77.3	77.6	78.0	77.9	76.5
2006	77.3	78.0	78.5	77.7	77.6	75.4	72.8	75.2	76.8	76.9	77.5	77.6	76.8
2007	77.0	77.9	78.2	77.9	78.2	77.0	74.9	76.1	78.1	79.0	79.7	79.7	77.8
2008	79.9	80.3	80.4	80.9	81.0	79.1	76.2	78.4	80.9	81.2	81.8	81.7	80.2
2009	80.6	81.2	81.2	81.4	81.0	79.1	77.7	78.2	79.5	80.3	80.6	80.7	80.1
2010	79.8	80.4	80.8	81.2	82.5	80.8	77.7	77.6	79.1	79.9	80.4	80.1	80.0
2011	79.2	80.0	80.3	80.1	79.1	77.7	74.9	76.1	78.6	79.9	80.5	78.3	78.7

Employment by Industry: Columbus, OH, Selected Years, 2000–2011

(Numbers in thousands, not seasonally adjusted)

Industry and year	January	February	March	April	May	June	July	August	September	October	November	December	Annual average
Total Nonfarm													
2000	892.8	896.5	902.1	908.6	914.2	922.2	919.0	920.3	916.4	924.7	931.9	935.6	915.4
2001	912.4	914.3	918.3	921.1	924.3	927.6	919.2	917.7	912.6	919.7	924.6	926.6	919.9
2002	903.9	904.7	909.3	911.3	916.3	919.8	913.4	913.4	911.7	917.0	921.5	921.1	913.6
2003	901.3	898.8	902.2	907.5	912.0	914.3	910.8	911.8	908.0	916.8	921.8	922.6	910.7
2004	894.5	895.1	902.8	909.5	916.8	921.5	917.4	920.0	917.0	928.8	934.2	934.8	916.0
2005	902.7	903.7	909.3	917.7	923.4	926.9	923.2	925.2	925.8	933.9	939.8	940.5	922.7
2006	911.9	915.2	921.8	927.8	934.0	937.8	931.5	933.1	932.5	940.5	946.9	949.5	931.9
2007	926.1	922.5	929.5	938.4	947.0	951.9	943.9	943.8	943.1	950.6	957.2	956.2	942.5
2008	932.1	931.8	931.0	939.9	946.1	946.7	942.5	942.1	938.4	945.0	943.0	939.3	939.8
2009	911.1	906.0	905.3	908.0	912.0	909.7	901.0	901.0	898.3	906.6	907.7	905.1	906.0
2010	884.3	884.1	888.6	899.8	907.8	908.1	903.3	905.8	904.4	915.2	919.6	919.0	903.3
2011	897.7	901.1	905.5	917.8	923.5	924.2	918.0	913.7	916.1	924.6	931.0	929.9	916.9
Total Private													
2000	749.7	752.3	757.4	763.7	769.0	775.4	776.0	778.1	772.4	777.9	784.1	786.7	770.2
2001	766.8	766.8	770.0	773.1	775.4	778.3	773.2	773.0	765.7	769.3	773.1	774.5	771.6
2002	753.4	753.6	758.1	760.6	765.2	767.7	766.1	767.0	763.7	766.2	768.9	768.1	763.2
2003	749.3	746.2	749.6	755.2	759.0	760.9	761.2	763.6	759.1	764.7	768.5	768.8	758.8
2004	741.9	741.8	749.0	756.3	762.6	766.3	766.2	768.9	765.6	773.4	777.6	778.4	762.3
2005	748.2	747.5	752.8	761.4	766.4	769.1	769.4	771.4	772.8	776.6	781.8	782.8	766.7
2006	755.8	757.7	763.9	770.5	775.6	780.3	777.9	779.2	779.2	782.9	788.5	791.0	775.2
2007	769.1	765.0	771.6	780.5	788.1	792.5	790.6	791.5	788.1	791.4	797.0	796.5	785.2
2008	773.5	771.9	771.6	780.9	785.5	786.6	787.5	787.8	783.0	784.7	782.8	780.0	781.3
2009	753.1	747.1	746.3	748.6	752.0	751.1	748.6	749.5	743.6	746.8	747.8	746.8	748.4
2010	727.0	725.9	730.6	740.6	745.0	748.2	751.3	754.3	749.9	755.8	759.8	758.9	745.6
2011	740.0	742.9	747.2	760.3	765.3	768.2	768.7	763.9	764.2	770.0	775.7	775.6	761.8
Goods-Producing													
2000	138.7	138.7	141.1	142.2	143.9	146.2	146.2	146.1	144.8	144.2	143.3	141.9	143.1
2001	136.6	136.4	137.2	138.3	138.7	139.8	139.9	139.7	137.4	136.2	134.8	133.0	137.3
2002	128.2	127.8	128.5	129.2	130.9	132.6	131.9	133.1	132.5	131.2	129.7	127.9	130.3
2003	123.1	121.5	122.0	124.2	125.1	126.2	126.4	126.8	126.1	125.9	125.0	124.2	124.7
2004	118.6	118.0	119.2	121.8	123.5	123.8	123.7	123.8	123.1	122.1	121.5	120.7	121.7
2005	114.5	114.0	114.8	117.7	119.3	121.0	121.8	121.9	121.7	120.8	120.6	119.3	119.0
2006	114.2	114.3	115.3	117.4	118.3	119.9	119.6	119.9	119.6	118.5	117.2	116.6	117.6
2007	113.0	111.1	112.5	114.1	115.9	117.6	117.5	117.6	116.8	115.2	114.6	113.2	114.9
2008	109.4	108.5	108.1	109.5	111.0	112.2	112.1	111.7	111.1	109.6	107.8	105.4	109.7
2009	99.8	97.4	96.7	96.6	96.9	97.3	96.1	96.2	94.7	93.5	92.4	91.1	95.7
2010	87.4	86.5	87.4	89.5	91.1	92.2	92.9	93.1	92.6	93.3	92.8	91.3	90.8
2011	88.2	88.4	89.4	91.9	93.1	94.5	94.6	94.7	96.0	97.6	96.9	94.8	93.3
Mining, Logging, and Construction													
2000	37.8	37.7	39.7	41.9	43.3	44.8	45.0	44.9	44.1	43.0	42.3	40.8	42.1
2001	37.8	38.2	39.5	41.6	42.7	44.4	45.2	45.5	44.4	43.2	42.6	41.3	42.2
2002	37.7	37.4	38.4	39.8	41.2	42.4	43.3	43.5	43.0	42.5	41.9	40.5	41.0
2003	37.1	36.1	36.8	39.6	40.8	42.0	42.7	43.0	42.6	42.5	41.9	41.1	40.5
2004	37.1	36.5	37.5	40.1	41.7	42.4	43.1	42.9	42.5	41.8	41.3	40.3	40.6
2005	35.7	35.3	36.2	39.1	40.7	41.8	42.9	43.0	42.6	41.8	41.5	40.1	40.1
2006	36.6	36.5	37.4	39.3	40.3	41.2	41.6	41.6	41.3	40.7	39.8	38.9	39.6
2007	35.9	34.4	35.8	37.2	38.9	40.3	40.5	40.4	39.8	39.2	38.3	36.7	38.1
2008	33.8	32.9	33.0	35.2	36.6	37.3	36.9	36.7	36.2	35.7	34.2	32.3	35.1
2009	28.9	28.2	28.7	29.1	30.2	31.3	31.6	31.6	30.5	29.3	28.5	27.1	29.6
2010	24.7	23.8	24.6	26.5	27.8	28.7	29.4	29.5	29.3	29.5	28.9	27.4	27.5
2011	25.1	25.1	25.9	27.7	28.8	29.8	29.4	29.3	30.1	31.2	30.5	28.6	28.5
Manufacturing													
2000	100.9	101.0	101.4	100.3	100.6	101.4	101.2	101.2	100.7	101.2	101.0	101.1	101.0
2001	98.8	98.2	97.7	96.7	96.0	95.4	94.7	94.2	93.0	93.0	92.2	91.7	95.1
2002	90.5	90.4	90.1	89.4	89.7	90.2	88.6	89.6	89.5	88.7	87.8	87.4	89.3
2003	86.0	85.4	85.2	84.6	84.3	84.2	83.7	83.8	83.5	83.4	83.1	83.1	84.2
2004	81.5	81.5	81.7	81.7	81.8	81.4	80.6	80.9	80.6	80.3	80.2	80.4	81.1
2005	78.8	78.7	78.6	78.6	78.6	79.2	78.9	78.9	79.1	79.0	79.1	79.2	78.9
2006	77.6	77.8	77.9	78.1	78.0	78.7	78.0	78.3	78.3	77.8	77.4	77.7	78.0
2007	77.1	76.7	76.7	76.9	77.0	77.3	77.0	77.2	77.0	76.0	76.3	76.5	76.8
2008	75.6	75.6	75.1	74.3	74.4	74.9	75.2	75.0	74.9	73.9	73.6	73.1	74.6
2009	70.9	69.2	68.0	67.5	66.7	66.0	64.5	64.6	64.2	64.2	63.9	64.0	66.1
2010	62.7	62.7	62.8	63.0	63.3	63.5	63.5	63.6	63.3	63.8	63.9	63.9	63.3
2011	63.1	63.3	63.5	64.2	64.3	64.7	65.2	65.4	65.9	66.4	66.4	66.2	64.9
Service-Providing													
2000	754.1	757.8	761.0	766.4	770.3	776.0	772.8	774.2	771.6	780.5	788.6	793.7	772.3
2001	775.8	777.9	781.1	782.8	785.6	787.8	779.3	778.0	775.2	783.5	789.8	793.6	782.5
2002	775.7	776.9	780.8	782.1	785.4	787.2	781.5	780.3	779.2	785.8	791.8	793.2	783.3
2003	778.2	777.3	780.2	783.3	786.9	788.1	784.4	785.0	781.9	790.9	796.8	798.4	786.0
2004	775.9	777.1	783.6	787.7	793.3	797.7	793.7	796.2	793.9	806.7	812.7	814.1	794.4
2005	788.2	789.7	794.5	800.0	804.1	805.9	801.4	803.3	804.1	813.1	819.2	821.2	803.7
2006	797.7	800.9	806.5	810.4	815.7	817.9	811.9	813.2	812.9	822.0	829.7	832.9	814.3
2007	813.1	811.4	817.0	824.3	831.1	834.3	826.4	826.2	826.3	835.4	842.6	843.0	827.6
2008	822.7	823.3	822.9	830.4	835.1	834.5	830.4	830.4	827.3	835.4	835.2	833.9	830.1
2009	811.3	808.6	808.6	811.4	815.1	812.4	804.9	804.8	803.6	813.1	815.3	814.0	810.3
2010	796.9	797.6	801.2	810.3	816.7	815.9	810.4	812.7	811.8	821.9	826.8	827.7	812.5
2011	809.5	812.7	816.1	825.9	830.4	829.7	823.4	819.0	820.1	827.0	834.1	835.1	823.6

Employment by Industry: Columbus, OH, Selected Years, 2000–2011—*Continued*

(Numbers in thousands, not seasonally adjusted)

Industry and year	January	February	March	April	May	June	July	August	September	October	November	December	Annual average
Trade, Transportation, and Utilities													
2000	193.3	191.7	191.5	193.4	193.8	194.5	194.8	195.1	193.9	199.1	206.3	210.9	196.5
2001	198.6	194.5	194.5	194.6	194.5	194.3	191.7	191.2	191.2	194.6	199.9	203.4	195.3
2002	191.0	189.0	189.9	189.5	190.0	189.5	189.2	188.9	188.0	189.2	192.1	194.4	190.1
2003	185.1	182.8	183.4	184.2	184.6	184.6	184.3	185.2	184.5	187.1	191.1	193.6	185.9
2004	182.4	179.9	181.4	180.4	181.7	183.6	184.2	184.6	184.2	188.6	193.9	197.3	185.2
2005	185.8	183.2	184.1	184.2	184.8	184.3	184.1	184.2	184.7	187.8	193.3	197.2	186.5
2006	185.8	183.8	184.1	184.4	186.1	186.0	185.9	185.7	185.8	189.1	196.1	199.3	187.7
2007	189.2	185.9	187.1	187.7	189.7	189.9	190.5	190.6	190.8	193.6	199.7	201.7	191.4
2008	190.8	187.6	187.4	188.7	189.7	189.1	190.0	190.6	189.7	191.5	194.2	196.0	190.4
2009	183.5	179.7	178.4	178.7	179.2	178.4	178.0	178.3	177.2	178.9	182.7	184.7	179.8
2010	175.3	173.1	173.1	173.9	175.4	175.7	174.9	175.6	174.8	177.9	181.5	183.7	176.2
2011	176.1	175.7	175.7	178.1	178.9	179.1	178.4	177.3	175.3	179.1	183.7	185.8	178.6
Wholesale Trade													
2000	38.1	38.5	38.6	39.1	39.2	39.7	39.7	39.9	40.0	39.7	39.8	39.8	39.3
2001	39.4	39.5	39.8	40.0	40.0	40.0	39.8	39.7	39.3	39.5	39.2	39.7	39.7
2002	39.1	39.1	39.3	38.8	38.8	38.7	38.8	38.8	38.6	38.6	38.6	38.7	38.8
2003	38.1	38.1	38.3	38.2	38.1	37.8	37.8	37.8	37.2	37.4	37.3	37.3	37.8
2004	36.8	36.6	36.4	36.5	36.8	36.9	37.3	37.5	37.2	37.4	37.5	37.4	37.0
2005	37.0	37.0	37.0	37.3	37.3	37.2	37.7	37.5	37.5	37.4	37.7	37.7	37.4
2006	37.4	37.6	37.5	37.6	37.8	37.8	37.8	37.7	37.6	37.7	38.1	38.1	37.7
2007	37.8	37.8	38.0	38.2	38.7	38.8	38.8	38.8	38.7	38.8	38.8	38.8	38.5
2008	38.9	38.9	38.9	39.2	39.4	39.4	39.5	39.6	39.3	39.0	38.8	38.6	39.1
2009	38.4	38.2	38.2	37.7	37.5	37.4	37.4	37.2	36.7	36.6	36.6	36.5	37.4
2010	36.9	37.1	36.9	37.3	37.4	37.5	37.4	37.5	37.1	37.2	37.3	37.1	37.2
2011	37.1	37.2	37.2	37.6	37.8	37.8	37.3	37.0	37.4	37.7	37.9	38.1	37.5
Retail Trade													
2000	120.8	118.9	119.0	119.5	120.0	120.4	120.2	120.4	119.2	123.3	130.4	135.2	122.3
2001	123.5	119.6	119.8	119.1	119.2	119.3	116.4	116.0	116.6	119.0	124.6	127.9	120.1
2002	116.5	114.8	115.6	115.8	116.3	115.7	114.4	113.7	113.2	113.8	116.5	118.8	115.4
2003	110.7	108.4	108.9	109.4	109.7	109.9	109.4	109.9	109.5	111.2	115.0	117.4	110.8
2004	108.0	106.1	107.3	105.9	106.7	108.0	107.6	107.8	107.6	109.6	114.3	117.6	108.9
2005	108.4	106.1	106.8	106.6	107.0	106.5	105.4	105.4	105.4	106.7	110.5	114.3	107.4
2006	104.7	102.7	103.0	102.8	103.9	103.5	103.1	102.6	101.8	103.4	108.3	110.7	104.2
2007	102.2	99.9	100.9	101.2	102.1	101.8	102.4	102.2	101.8	103.0	107.2	108.9	102.8
2008	101.4	99.2	98.9	100.2	101.4	101.3	102.5	102.9	101.8	103.3	105.5	107.7	102.2
2009	98.9	96.6	95.9	96.7	97.5	97.1	96.7	96.9	96.3	97.7	100.9	102.9	97.8
2010	95.0	93.3	93.6	94.6	95.5	95.8	95.6	96.2	95.5	98.0	100.7	102.5	96.4
2011	95.9	95.4	95.4	97.0	97.3	97.5	98.7	97.7	95.3	98.2	101.6	103.0	97.8
Transportation and Utilities													
2000	34.4	34.3	33.9	34.8	34.6	34.4	34.9	34.8	34.7	36.1	36.1	35.9	34.9
2001	35.7	35.4	34.9	35.5	35.3	35.0	35.5	35.5	35.3	36.1	36.1	35.8	35.5
2002	35.4	35.1	35.0	34.9	34.9	35.1	36.0	36.4	36.2	36.8	37.0	36.9	35.8
2003	36.3	36.3	36.2	36.6	36.8	36.9	37.1	37.5	37.8	38.5	38.8	38.9	37.3
2004	37.6	37.2	37.7	38.0	38.2	38.7	39.3	39.3	39.4	41.6	42.1	42.3	39.3
2005	40.4	40.1	40.3	40.3	40.5	40.6	41.0	41.3	41.8	43.7	45.1	45.2	41.7
2006	43.7	43.5	43.6	44.0	44.4	44.7	45.0	45.4	46.4	48.0	49.7	50.5	45.7
2007	49.2	48.2	48.2	48.3	48.9	49.3	49.3	49.6	50.3	51.8	53.7	54.0	50.1
2008	50.5	49.5	49.6	49.3	48.9	48.4	48.0	48.1	48.6	49.2	49.9	49.7	49.1
2009	46.2	44.9	44.3	44.3	44.2	43.9	43.9	44.2	44.2	44.6	45.2	45.3	44.6
2010	43.4	42.7	42.6	42.0	42.5	42.4	41.9	41.9	42.2	42.7	43.5	44.1	42.7
2011	43.1	43.1	43.1	43.5	43.8	43.8	42.4	42.6	42.6	43.2	44.2	44.7	43.3
Information													
2000	22.0	22.2	22.3	22.0	22.2	22.4	22.5	22.7	22.6	23.1	23.1	23.1	22.5
2001	23.4	23.3	23.0	22.7	22.8	22.9	22.5	22.5	22.0	21.7	21.7	21.5	22.5
2002	21.8	21.5	21.5	21.1	21.1	21.2	21.3	21.4	21.3	21.1	21.2	21.2	21.3
2003	21.1	21.1	20.8	20.7	20.6	20.6	20.4	20.4	20.1	20.2	20.2	20.1	20.5
2004	19.8	19.8	19.6	19.5	19.6	19.8	19.9	19.7	19.7	19.6	19.6	19.5	19.7
2005	19.4	19.2	19.3	19.3	19.4	19.4	19.4	19.5	19.6	19.2	19.2	19.2	19.3
2006	19.1	19.0	19.0	18.8	18.9	18.9	18.8	18.7	18.5	18.4	18.5	18.5	18.8
2007	18.7	18.8	18.7	18.8	18.8	18.8	18.8	18.6	18.3	18.0	18.0	18.0	18.5
2008	17.6	17.7	17.7	17.8	17.7	17.7	17.7	17.7	17.5	17.5	17.6	17.6	17.7
2009	17.6	17.5	17.3	17.1	17.1	17.0	17.1	16.9	16.6	16.5	16.5	16.7	17.0
2010	16.8	16.8	16.7	16.5	16.6	16.6	16.7	16.7	16.6	16.5	16.8	16.8	16.7
2011	16.6	16.6	16.5	16.8	16.9	16.9	16.9	16.9	16.8	16.7	16.8	16.8	16.8
Financial Activities													
2000	75.8	75.9	75.6	75.3	75.5	75.9	75.8	75.6	75.5	75.6	76.1	76.7	75.8
2001	76.0	76.4	77.0	77.1	77.2	77.9	77.4	77.3	77.1	76.4	76.8	77.2	77.0
2002	76.7	77.1	77.3	77.3	77.1	76.9	77.0	77.0	76.8	77.4	77.9	78.1	77.2
2003	76.1	76.6	76.6	75.9	75.9	76.1	75.8	75.9	75.4	74.9	75.0	75.1	75.8
2004	74.3	74.4	74.4	74.3	74.1	74.3	74.1	73.9	73.2	73.3	73.2	73.1	73.9
2005	72.3	72.3	72.3	72.3	72.5	72.8	73.1	73.2	73.3	73.3	73.5	73.8	72.9
2006	73.1	73.0	73.1	73.2	73.3	73.8	74.3	73.9	74.0	74.6	74.7	74.5	73.8
2007	74.1	74.0	73.4	74.2	73.7	73.0	72.9	72.9	72.2	72.2	71.8	71.8	73.0
2008	71.2	71.4	71.2	71.0	71.1	71.0	70.6	70.7	70.3	70.5	70.2	70.3	70.8
2009	69.6	69.5	69.5	69.1	69.1	68.9	69.1	68.9	68.5	68.7	69.1	69.0	69.1
2010	68.2	68.2	68.1	68.8	68.7	68.9	69.3	69.2	68.9	69.4	69.5	69.6	68.9
2011	69.7	69.7	69.8	69.8	70.0	70.1	71.1	70.8	71.2	71.2	71.2	71.4	70.5

Employment by Industry: Columbus, OH, Selected Years, 2000–2011—*Continued*

(Numbers in thousands, not seasonally adjusted)

Industry and year	January	February	March	April	May	June	July	August	September	October	November	December	Annual average
Professional and Business Services													
2000	125.2	126.4	127.7	128.4	128.8	130.1	130.8	131.2	131.1	131.6	131.4	131.1	129.5
2001	133.0	133.4	133.8	133.8	132.6	132.3	132.3	132.0	130.5	131.3	130.5	130.5	132.2
2002	129.1	129.2	129.5	129.4	128.4	128.8	128.8	129.0	128.5	129.5	130.1	129.6	129.2
2003	131.4	130.6	131.3	130.9	130.4	129.7	130.5	131.1	130.3	132.2	133.1	132.0	131.1
2004	129.1	129.9	131.4	133.5	133.6	134.5	134.2	136.3	136.2	139.1	138.9	139.1	134.7
2005	134.3	135.0	136.0	136.9	137.0	137.4	137.8	139.6	140.4	142.0	141.7	141.9	138.3
2006	137.5	138.4	140.0	142.2	142.2	144.1	143.7	145.2	145.1	146.1	146.6	147.7	143.2
2007	143.9	144.1	145.9	148.5	149.1	151.0	151.0	151.5	151.2	152.9	153.7	154.2	149.8
2008	151.3	151.6	151.8	154.3	153.6	153.9	155.3	155.0	153.6	153.9	152.9	152.1	153.3
2009	148.9	147.1	146.1	146.4	145.9	145.1	144.8	145.7	143.6	145.1	144.8	143.2	145.6
2010	141.3	141.6	142.4	145.9	145.2	146.5	148.1	149.5	147.4	149.1	149.8	149.9	146.4
2011	145.8	146.4	147.6	150.0	149.4	150.0	152.7	150.2	149.4	150.0	151.1	150.0	149.4
Education and Health Services													
2000	86.6	87.7	87.7	88.1	88.0	87.6	87.3	88.4	88.4	89.2	89.4	89.9	88.2
2001	87.9	89.8	90.4	90.4	90.7	90.7	89.5	89.8	90.0	92.6	93.5	93.7	90.8
2002	92.4	93.7	94.1	94.3	94.5	93.7	93.2	93.2	94.4	96.7	97.2	97.3	94.6
2003	95.6	96.7	97.0	97.9	98.0	96.9	96.5	96.7	98.1	100.2	101.0	100.9	98.0
2004	98.4	100.0	100.7	102.1	102.2	100.8	100.6	100.4	101.9	104.0	104.4	104.5	101.7
2005	102.0	103.4	103.9	105.4	104.8	103.5	103.5	103.5	105.5	107.2	107.9	107.7	104.9
2006	105.7	107.6	108.4	108.8	108.1	106.4	105.4	105.6	108.4	109.6	110.1	109.8	107.8
2007	108.5	109.4	110.2	111.2	111.4	110.5	109.8	110.1	111.7	113.0	113.9	113.5	111.1
2008	112.6	114.3	114.1	114.5	114.3	113.2	112.9	113.2	115.0	116.4	117.2	117.2	114.6
2009	116.4	117.8	118.0	118.6	118.7	117.9	118.0	118.6	120.7	122.5	122.9	123.4	119.5
2010	122.5	123.6	124.8	125.1	124.9	123.0	123.8	124.9	126.5	127.5	128.0	127.4	125.2
2011	126.5	128.1	128.3	130.1	130.0	128.5	128.2	128.1	131.2	132.2	133.0	134.5	129.9
Leisure and Hospitality													
2000	74.8	76.0	77.6	80.0	82.3	84.0	83.9	84.2	81.7	80.8	80.2	78.9	80.4
2001	77.3	78.5	79.4	80.9	83.3	84.6	84.2	84.6	82.1	81.0	80.0	79.4	81.3
2002	78.8	79.4	81.2	83.2	86.1	87.6	87.4	87.0	85.1	84.1	83.5	82.3	83.8
2003	79.7	79.5	80.9	83.7	86.5	88.5	89.1	89.3	86.9	86.5	85.4	85.0	85.1
2004	81.6	81.8	83.7	86.1	89.3	90.6	90.5	91.3	88.9	88.0	87.0	86.5	87.1
2005	82.8	83.0	84.7	88.0	90.8	92.8	92.2	91.8	90.4	88.7	87.5	86.5	88.3
2006	83.4	84.4	86.5	88.1	91.0	92.9	92.3	92.3	90.3	89.0	87.8	87.3	88.8
2007	84.7	84.6	86.5	89.0	92.1	94.1	92.7	93.0	90.6	89.8	88.7	87.7	89.5
2008	84.7	84.8	85.2	88.7	91.5	92.6	91.8	91.7	89.0	87.8	86.1	85.4	88.3
2009	81.8	82.2	84.3	86.1	88.7	90.2	89.5	89.1	87.1	86.2	84.2	83.5	86.1
2010	80.4	80.9	82.7	85.6	87.8	89.7	89.7	89.5	87.8	86.6	86.0	84.8	86.0
2011	82.4	83.2	85.1	88.4	91.6	93.5	91.9	90.6	89.7	88.2	88.2	86.7	88.3
Other Services													
2000	33.3	33.7	33.9	34.3	34.5	34.7	34.7	34.8	34.4	34.3	34.3	34.2	34.3
2001	34.0	34.5	34.7	35.3	35.6	35.8	35.7	35.9	35.4	35.5	35.9	35.8	35.3
2002	35.4	35.9	36.1	36.6	37.1	37.4	37.3	37.4	37.1	37.0	37.2	37.3	36.8
2003	37.2	37.4	37.6	37.7	37.9	38.3	38.2	38.2	37.7	37.7	37.7	37.9	37.8
2004	37.7	38.0	38.6	38.6	38.6	38.9	39.0	38.9	38.4	38.7	39.1	37.7	38.5
2005	37.1	37.4	37.7	37.6	37.8	37.9	37.5	37.7	37.2	37.6	38.1	37.2	37.6
2006	37.0	37.2	37.5	37.6	37.7	38.3	37.9	37.9	37.5	37.6	37.5	37.3	37.6
2007	37.0	37.1	37.3	37.0	37.4	37.6	37.4	37.2	36.5	36.7	36.6	36.4	37.0
2008	35.9	36.0	36.1	36.4	36.6	36.9	37.1	37.2	36.8	37.5	36.8	36.0	36.6
2009	35.5	35.9	36.0	36.0	36.4	36.3	36.0	35.8	35.2	35.4	35.2	35.2	35.7
2010	35.1	35.2	35.4	35.3	35.3	35.6	35.9	35.8	35.3	35.5	35.4	35.4	35.4
2011	34.7	34.8	34.8	35.2	35.4	35.6	34.9	35.3	34.6	35.0	34.8	35.6	35.1
Government													
2000	143.1	144.2	144.7	144.9	145.2	146.8	143.0	142.2	144.0	146.8	147.8	148.9	145.1
2001	145.6	147.5	148.3	148.0	148.9	149.3	146.0	144.7	146.9	150.4	151.5	152.1	148.3
2002	150.5	151.1	151.2	150.7	151.1	152.1	147.3	146.4	148.0	150.8	152.6	153.0	150.4
2003	152.0	152.6	152.6	152.3	153.0	153.4	149.6	148.2	148.9	152.1	153.3	153.8	151.8
2004	152.6	153.3	153.8	153.2	154.2	155.2	151.2	151.1	151.4	155.4	156.6	156.4	153.7
2005	154.5	156.2	156.5	156.3	157.0	157.8	153.8	153.8	153.0	157.3	158.0	157.7	156.0
2006	156.1	157.5	157.9	157.3	158.4	157.5	153.6	153.9	153.3	157.6	158.4	158.5	156.7
2007	157.0	157.5	157.9	157.9	158.9	159.4	153.3	152.3	155.0	159.2	160.2	159.7	157.4
2008	158.6	159.9	159.4	159.0	160.6	160.1	155.0	154.3	155.4	160.3	160.2	159.3	158.5
2009	158.0	158.9	159.0	159.4	160.0	158.6	152.4	151.5	154.7	159.8	159.9	158.3	157.5
2010	157.3	158.2	158.0	159.2	162.8	159.9	152.0	151.5	154.5	159.4	159.8	160.1	157.7
2011	157.7	158.2	158.3	157.5	158.2	156.0	149.3	149.8	151.9	154.6	155.3	154.3	155.1

Employment by Industry: Dallas–Forth Worth–Arlington, TX, Selected Years, 2000–2011

(Numbers in thousands, not seasonally adjusted)

Industry and year	January	February	March	April	May	June	July	August	September	October	November	December	Annual average
Total Nonfarm													
2000	2,681.5	2,698.9	2,723.5	2,737.8	2,759.4	2,782.7	2,763.6	2,777.6	2,790.6	2,794.2	2,804.0	2,818.5	2,761.0
2001	2,761.8	2,774.8	2,790.5	2,792.9	2,795.2	2,803.3	2,768.1	2,778.3	2,771.0	2,750.6	2,744.9	2,741.9	2,772.8
2002	2,687.5	2,694.2	2,708.7	2,709.0	2,718.4	2,718.5	2,689.7	2,700.8	2,704.0	2,696.2	2,703.2	2,704.1	2,702.9
2003	2,644.4	2,652.0	2,657.9	2,663.1	2,668.2	2,666.4	2,644.5	2,656.1	2,666.4	2,673.9	2,681.9	2,685.7	2,663.4
2004	2,638.5	2,652.3	2,670.5	2,688.3	2,695.3	2,694.6	2,688.5	2,702.7	2,712.0	2,727.6	2,735.6	2,745.5	2,696.0
2005	2,686.9	2,704.8	2,723.3	2,748.8	2,757.9	2,763.5	2,761.7	2,777.1	2,794.7	2,802.5	2,822.0	2,827.9	2,764.3
2006	2,780.4	2,800.1	2,821.3	2,837.7	2,852.7	2,866.0	2,843.3	2,867.3	2,881.7	2,886.6	2,910.1	2,923.1	2,855.9
2007	2,859.6	2,887.3	2,915.0	2,921.5	2,937.1	2,950.4	2,925.4	2,945.4	2,955.9	2,970.9	2,990.1	2,999.1	2,938.1
2008	2,941.5	2,963.3	2,973.7	2,979.4	2,996.2	2,994.6	2,971.3	2,977.9	2,974.0	2,975.3	2,970.1	2,967.7	2,973.8
2009	2,888.5	2,882.7	2,881.0	2,875.8	2,878.4	2,869.4	2,842.5	2,844.0	2,839.8	2,850.5	2,854.6	2,859.8	2,863.9
2010	2,802.5	2,813.5	2,836.2	2,848.6	2,871.2	2,877.7	2,854.7	2,861.5	2,865.3	2,890.7	2,899.2	2,910.1	2,860.9
2011	2,857.8	2,870.2	2,896.8	2,916.5	2,927.2	2,940.4	2,919.3	2,924.3	2,941.7	2,943.4	2,961.3	2,961.3	2,921.7
Total Private													
2000	2,369.1	2,383.2	2,406.9	2,420.2	2,436.1	2,467.0	2,463.5	2,473.7	2,474.3	2,473.7	2,480.9	2,492.3	2,445.1
2001	2,441.2	2,448.9	2,464.2	2,467.9	2,470.0	2,482.0	2,463.3	2,468.2	2,447.0	2,419.5	2,410.9	2,408.7	2,449.3
2002	2,359.9	2,358.2	2,371.8	2,374.2	2,382.0	2,387.6	2,377.2	2,381.6	2,369.0	2,353.3	2,356.5	2,358.4	2,369.1
2003	2,307.5	2,305.8	2,312.5	2,317.1	2,320.8	2,324.2	2,322.1	2,332.7	2,324.3	2,327.9	2,333.1	2,340.0	2,322.3
2004	2,297.4	2,304.2	2,324.1	2,339.9	2,344.9	2,351.3	2,360.2	2,366.6	2,358.4	2,373.0	2,377.8	2,388.4	2,348.9
2005	2,335.0	2,345.6	2,365.0	2,389.5	2,397.5	2,411.9	2,426.0	2,432.9	2,434.3	2,438.5	2,454.7	2,466.7	2,408.1
2006	2,421.4	2,434.0	2,456.5	2,472.0	2,486.1	2,507.5	2,498.1	2,515.3	2,516.8	2,515.6	2,536.8	2,552.4	2,492.7
2007	2,492.9	2,513.8	2,540.7	2,549.0	2,562.6	2,583.5	2,575.6	2,591.4	2,585.3	2,592.0	2,608.0	2,618.3	2,567.8
2008	2,565.3	2,579.6	2,588.8	2,594.8	2,609.7	2,615.5	2,606.2	2,610.6	2,592.8	2,585.2	2,576.5	2,573.9	2,591.6
2009	2,501.9	2,489.2	2,486.6	2,480.9	2,483.0	2,482.8	2,471.3	2,472.7	2,456.1	2,455.5	2,457.1	2,465.9	2,475.3
2010	2,413.2	2,416.8	2,438.2	2,450.6	2,462.5	2,476.5	2,473.8	2,483.9	2,478.8	2,493.5	2,500.2	2,511.8	2,466.7
2011	2,464.7	2,472.9	2,499.1	2,519.6	2,529.8	2,547.6	2,543.3	2,549.3	2,555.9	2,553.1	2,568.0	2,566.9	2,530.9
Goods-Producing													
2000	507.1	511.2	516.5	516.2	519.6	526.1	524.5	524.0	523.1	520.3	518.0	516.4	518.6
2001	512.3	513.7	515.6	513.0	513.4	516.2	509.2	509.2	502.7	493.0	487.5	482.6	505.7
2002	473.5	472.4	474.0	472.7	474.0	477.3	475.0	474.0	469.4	461.9	459.7	456.2	470.0
2003	448.0	448.2	448.0	448.6	450.3	452.5	451.3	451.9	449.9	447.4	446.0	445.2	448.9
2004	441.2	442.6	446.0	448.7	449.9	452.2	455.1	454.6	453.3	451.4	449.4	449.4	449.5
2005	443.0	446.8	450.4	453.8	456.4	461.9	465.6	466.0	465.4	464.4	464.3	465.1	458.6
2006	459.2	463.4	468.0	469.5	474.2	480.7	477.7	480.5	482.1	478.8	480.5	480.9	474.6
2007	473.3	478.1	483.1	481.7	483.9	490.2	486.6	488.8	489.2	485.8	486.0	486.6	484.4
2008	479.4	483.8	485.0	482.8	484.9	487.2	484.8	485.4	482.5	478.1	472.5	468.5	481.2
2009	454.2	449.5	444.3	437.6	433.9	430.3	423.9	424.5	419.4	411.9	408.8	407.2	428.8
2010	401.9	399.6	403.2	404.8	406.9	410.9	411.4	412.5	410.8	409.7	408.8	409.1	407.5
2011	401.8	403.8	407.7	409.8	411.6	416.5	415.8	416.4	415.7	410.9	410.9	409.1	410.8
Mining, Logging, and Construction													
2000	154.6	158.0	162.6	162.7	165.4	170.3	171.4	171.7	171.1	168.8	167.4	167.2	165.9
2001	164.8	166.4	169.0	169.7	171.9	174.7	172.6	173.5	170.1	166.1	163.8	162.0	168.7
2002	157.7	158.2	160.2	160.4	161.9	164.5	163.5	163.9	160.7	156.9	156.3	154.3	159.9
2003	150.0	150.2	151.0	152.2	154.2	156.2	157.4	157.8	156.4	154.8	153.9	153.2	153.9
2004	150.8	151.0	153.7	155.6	156.6	158.2	160.6	160.9	160.3	158.9	157.7	157.6	156.8
2005	155.8	157.4	160.1	163.1	165.0	168.4	169.6	169.9	170.5	169.6	168.8	169.0	165.6
2006	165.6	167.8	171.2	171.6	174.9	179.0	177.2	178.9	180.4	179.4	180.4	181.4	175.7
2007	176.9	179.9	184.3	184.7	186.4	191.1	188.9	191.9	192.9	192.0	192.9	192.9	187.9
2008	189.0	192.9	195.2	194.6	196.2	198.7	197.0	197.5	195.9	193.2	189.7	187.2	193.9
2009	179.0	177.6	175.5	172.2	171.0	171.2	169.1	167.3	163.2	157.8	156.3	155.5	168.0
2010	151.6	150.7	153.9	155.1	156.1	158.6	159.4	160.1	158.8	157.9	156.7	156.5	156.3
2011	152.1	153.0	155.7	156.8	157.8	160.7	159.0	159.1	158.0	154.0	153.6	152.6	156.0
Manufacturing													
2000	352.5	353.2	353.9	353.5	354.2	355.8	353.1	352.3	352.0	351.5	350.6	349.2	352.7
2001	347.5	347.3	346.6	343.3	341.5	341.5	336.6	335.7	332.6	326.9	323.7	320.6	337.0
2002	315.8	314.2	313.8	312.3	312.1	312.8	311.5	310.1	308.7	305.0	303.4	301.9	310.1
2003	298.0	298.0	297.0	296.4	296.1	296.3	293.9	294.1	293.5	292.6	292.1	292.0	295.0
2004	290.4	291.6	292.3	293.1	293.3	294.0	294.5	293.7	293.0	292.5	291.7	291.8	292.7
2005	287.2	289.4	290.3	290.7	291.4	293.5	296.0	296.1	294.9	294.8	295.5	296.1	293.0
2006	293.6	295.6	296.8	297.9	299.3	301.7	300.5	301.6	301.7	299.4	300.1	299.5	299.0
2007	296.4	298.2	298.8	297.0	297.5	299.1	297.7	296.9	296.3	293.8	293.1	293.7	296.5
2008	290.4	290.9	289.8	288.2	288.7	288.5	287.8	287.9	286.6	284.9	282.8	281.3	287.3
2009	275.2	271.9	268.8	265.4	262.9	259.1	254.8	257.2	256.2	254.1	252.5	251.7	260.8
2010	250.3	248.9	249.3	249.7	250.8	252.3	252.0	252.4	252.0	251.8	252.1	252.6	251.2
2011	249.7	250.8	252.0	253.0	253.8	255.8	256.8	257.3	257.7	256.9	257.3	256.5	254.8
Service-Providing													
2000	2,174.4	2,187.7	2,207.0	2,221.6	2,239.8	2,256.6	2,239.1	2,253.6	2,267.5	2,273.9	2,286.0	2,302.1	2,242.4
2001	2,249.5	2,261.1	2,274.9	2,279.9	2,281.8	2,287.1	2,258.9	2,269.1	2,268.3	2,257.6	2,257.4	2,259.3	2,267.1
2002	2,214.0	2,221.8	2,234.7	2,236.3	2,244.4	2,241.2	2,214.7	2,226.8	2,234.6	2,234.3	2,243.5	2,247.9	2,232.9
2003	2,196.4	2,203.8	2,209.9	2,214.5	2,217.9	2,213.9	2,193.2	2,204.2	2,216.5	2,226.5	2,235.9	2,240.5	2,214.4
2004	2,197.3	2,209.7	2,224.5	2,239.6	2,245.4	2,242.4	2,233.4	2,248.1	2,258.7	2,276.2	2,286.2	2,296.1	2,246.5
2005	2,243.9	2,258.0	2,272.9	2,295.0	2,301.5	2,301.6	2,296.1	2,311.1	2,329.3	2,338.1	2,357.7	2,362.8	2,305.7
2006	2,321.2	2,336.7	2,353.3	2,368.2	2,378.5	2,385.3	2,365.6	2,386.8	2,399.6	2,407.8	2,429.6	2,442.2	2,381.2
2007	2,386.3	2,409.2	2,431.9	2,439.8	2,453.2	2,460.2	2,438.8	2,456.6	2,466.7	2,485.1	2,504.1	2,512.5	2,453.7
2008	2,462.1	2,479.5	2,488.7	2,496.6	2,511.3	2,507.4	2,486.5	2,492.5	2,491.5	2,497.2	2,497.6	2,499.2	2,492.5
2009	2,434.3	2,433.2	2,436.7	2,438.2	2,444.5	2,439.1	2,418.6	2,419.5	2,420.4	2,438.6	2,445.8	2,452.6	2,435.1
2010	2,400.6	2,413.9	2,433.0	2,443.8	2,464.3	2,466.8	2,443.3	2,449.0	2,454.5	2,481.0	2,490.4	2,501.0	2,453.5
2011	2,456.0	2,466.4	2,489.1	2,506.7	2,515.6	2,523.9	2,503.5	2,507.9	2,526.0	2,532.5	2,550.4	2,552.2	2,510.9

Employment by Industry: Dallas–Forth Worth–Arlington, TX, Selected Years, 2000–2011—*Continued*

(Numbers in thousands, not seasonally adjusted)

Industry and year	January	February	March	April	May	June	July	August	September	October	November	December	Annual average
Trade, Transportation, and Utilities													
2000	612.4	611.5	614.4	615.4	619.6	627.3	626.1	631.9	631.4	637.0	649.5	660.2	628.1
2001	637.9	634.0	636.7	634.2	634.0	636.8	634.5	637.2	634.8	631.2	633.2	637.7	635.2
2002	618.2	613.7	615.4	613.6	614.1	614.9	615.3	615.7	612.3	610.4	616.8	624.0	615.4
2003	598.5	592.7	592.3	588.8	587.0	585.8	583.2	588.1	586.0	588.8	596.1	601.2	590.7
2004	582.5	580.1	583.3	583.8	586.5	587.2	590.0	594.8	591.6	595.2	604.7	611.5	590.9
2005	591.7	586.6	590.7	591.6	593.8	596.9	600.1	604.3	604.1	605.0	618.8	626.6	600.9
2006	604.4	601.1	605.2	606.5	608.9	611.0	609.6	614.0	611.7	613.8	626.6	635.3	612.3
2007	614.5	612.1	617.3	616.4	618.4	621.8	622.0	624.0	622.7	628.0	640.2	647.2	623.7
2008	627.3	624.6	626.4	623.9	625.6	626.9	626.2	629.2	624.1	623.9	628.1	632.6	626.6
2009	609.2	601.3	599.9	594.4	593.9	591.8	590.6	591.0	588.3	589.2	595.3	601.6	595.5
2010	582.3	578.9	583.0	583.7	586.9	588.8	588.9	590.9	588.5	593.2	602.9	609.0	589.8
2011	589.9	587.3	591.7	595.8	597.5	600.1	601.8	607.3	607.8	609.8	618.9	625.0	602.7
Wholesale Trade													
2000	166.8	167.1	169.1	170.9	171.4	172.9	171.5	171.8	171.8	172.2	172.7	173.2	171.0
2001	173.3	174.2	175.0	173.9	173.2	173.9	172.8	172.6	171.2	170.2	168.9	168.6	172.3
2002	166.3	166.1	167.1	166.0	166.0	166.5	166.6	166.5	166.2	165.2	165.3	165.7	166.1
2003	162.6	162.1	162.6	161.9	161.3	161.5	160.9	160.6	159.9	159.6	159.1	159.3	161.0
2004	157.7	157.7	158.5	158.1	158.3	158.4	159.1	159.0	158.4	159.2	159.0	159.3	158.6
2005	157.2	157.5	158.2	159.3	159.7	160.2	161.6	162.0	162.4	161.8	162.4	163.5	160.5
2006	162.3	162.8	163.7	164.3	165.0	166.0	166.1	166.9	167.3	167.6	168.5	169.2	165.8
2007	166.9	168.0	168.9	168.8	169.5	171.0	170.8	171.1	171.0	173.1	174.0	174.3	170.6
2008	172.5	173.0	172.8	172.6	172.7	172.7	171.9	171.9	170.9	170.3	169.6	169.0	171.7
2009	165.8	164.9	163.2	161.3	160.7	159.6	159.1	158.4	157.6	157.2	156.3	156.6	160.1
2010	154.8	154.7	155.0	154.5	155.2	155.6	156.5	156.5	156.1	156.7	156.8	157.3	155.8
2011	155.7	156.8	157.2	157.9	159.0	159.7	159.0	161.7	162.1	161.6	161.4	162.4	159.5
Retail Trade													
2000	309.9	308.3	308.9	307.5	310.2	315.0	315.1	319.2	318.0	322.1	332.9	341.5	317.4
2001	323.6	319.3	321.1	319.9	319.7	321.1	319.8	321.5	321.2	320.6	327.0	332.2	322.3
2002	316.7	313.1	313.2	312.2	312.0	311.9	312.0	312.0	309.5	307.9	315.1	322.4	313.2
2003	302.2	297.6	296.9	294.3	293.7	293.3	292.2	296.3	295.1	297.1	304.7	309.5	297.7
2004	293.4	290.9	292.9	293.6	295.9	296.3	297.3	301.6	298.9	301.5	311.7	317.4	299.3
2005	300.8	297.1	299.0	300.1	301.3	303.8	304.8	307.4	306.0	307.5	319.7	325.7	306.1
2006	308.0	303.9	306.4	306.6	307.5	307.9	306.3	308.7	305.2	306.4	317.6	323.1	309.0
2007	307.8	303.9	307.4	306.7	307.3	308.4	309.6	310.4	308.5	311.6	322.7	328.1	311.0
2008	313.1	309.8	311.9	308.9	309.9	311.3	311.9	313.5	309.2	310.5	315.5	319.4	312.1
2009	303.1	298.0	298.2	296.2	296.8	296.3	296.0	297.4	295.3	297.0	303.6	308.5	298.9
2010	294.7	291.5	294.7	296.5	298.7	299.7	298.8	300.6	298.2	302.2	311.0	316.0	300.2
2011	300.7	296.6	299.8	303.0	303.4	305.2	307.4	308.7	307.6	309.5	317.2	321.1	306.7
Transportation and Utilities													
2000	135.7	136.1	136.4	137.0	138.0	139.4	139.5	140.9	141.6	142.7	143.9	145.5	139.7
2001	141.0	140.5	140.6	140.4	141.1	141.8	141.9	143.1	142.4	140.4	137.3	136.9	140.6
2002	135.2	134.5	135.1	135.4	136.1	136.5	136.7	137.2	136.6	137.3	136.4	135.9	136.1
2003	133.7	133.0	132.8	132.6	132.0	131.0	130.1	131.2	131.0	132.1	132.3	132.4	132.0
2004	131.4	131.5	131.9	132.1	132.3	132.5	133.6	134.2	134.3	134.5	134.0	134.8	133.1
2005	133.7	132.0	133.5	132.2	132.8	132.9	133.7	134.9	135.7	135.7	137.4	137.4	134.3
2006	134.1	134.4	135.1	135.6	136.4	137.1	137.2	138.4	139.2	139.8	140.5	143.0	137.6
2007	139.8	140.2	141.0	140.9	141.6	142.4	141.6	142.5	143.2	143.3	143.5	144.8	142.1
2008	141.7	141.8	141.7	142.4	143.0	142.9	142.4	143.8	144.0	143.1	143.0	144.2	142.8
2009	140.3	138.4	138.5	136.9	136.4	135.9	135.5	135.2	135.4	135.0	135.4	136.5	136.6
2010	132.8	132.7	133.3	132.7	133.0	133.5	133.6	133.8	134.2	134.3	135.1	135.7	133.7
2011	133.5	133.9	134.7	134.9	135.1	135.2	135.4	136.9	138.1	138.7	140.3	141.5	136.5
Information													
2000	116.1	117.7	118.8	119.9	120.7	123.0	123.5	124.2	124.7	125.1	126.2	126.2	122.2
2001	122.8	122.9	124.0	123.1	122.6	122.2	120.4	119.8	118.3	117.5	116.7	115.5	120.5
2002	114.2	113.0	112.6	110.1	109.3	108.6	106.2	105.3	104.1	103.5	103.0	102.4	107.7
2003	100.6	100.4	100.1	98.9	98.5	98.2	98.0	97.5	96.4	96.7	96.3	96.3	98.2
2004	96.1	94.7	96.1	94.8	94.9	94.7	94.0	93.4	92.7	92.9	92.8	93.0	94.2
2005	92.5	92.5	92.7	92.4	92.2	92.5	92.8	92.5	92.7	92.2	92.4	92.2	92.5
2006	91.5	92.4	92.3	91.0	90.3	90.3	89.4	88.5	87.9	86.6	86.1	85.8	89.3
2007	87.8	88.4	88.5	88.2	88.8	88.9	89.4	90.0	89.5	89.9	90.3	89.8	89.1
2008	89.1	89.2	89.2	88.9	88.8	88.6	88.2	87.8	86.4	86.0	86.1	86.0	87.9
2009	85.4	84.8	84.1	83.6	83.4	83.2	82.3	82.3	81.6	80.7	80.8	81.0	82.7
2010	79.6	79.1	79.2	79.8	79.4	79.8	79.4	79.3	78.7	78.5	78.7	78.7	79.2
2011	78.9	78.6	78.6	78.4	78.9	79.2	79.0	78.9	78.7	78.8	79.1	78.9	78.8
Financial Activities													
2000	204.8	205.0	206.3	208.1	208.3	209.2	209.6	209.2	208.6	208.8	208.7	210.0	208.1
2001	207.2	208.3	209.0	209.7	210.3	212.4	212.3	212.8	211.9	212.4	212.9	213.9	211.1
2002	212.3	212.4	212.8	212.2	212.8	213.3	213.2	213.4	212.4	211.7	212.3	212.1	212.6
2003	210.4	211.2	210.7	211.1	211.9	212.7	213.4	214.2	213.4	213.0	212.9	213.7	212.4
2004	212.0	212.0	212.7	213.6	213.7	214.6	216.2	216.8	216.1	217.5	217.6	218.7	215.1
2005	216.5	217.0	217.3	218.3	218.8	220.4	222.5	223.6	224.2	224.3	225.2	226.4	221.2
2006	224.3	225.4	227.4	229.0	229.4	230.7	229.5	230.6	230.3	230.4	231.1	232.5	229.2
2007	229.3	230.3	231.6	232.4	233.2	235.1	234.3	235.4	234.3	233.7	233.9	234.3	233.2
2008	231.7	232.8	233.0	234.5	235.5	236.1	234.7	235.4	232.6	231.4	230.3	229.9	233.1
2009	227.0	226.8	226.6	228.8	229.4	229.5	228.9	228.9	227.2	227.1	227.3	228.3	228.0
2010	226.1	226.7	227.2	227.3	227.9	229.0	229.7	229.7	229.5	231.2	231.3	232.6	229.0
2011	231.6	232.3	233.4	234.0	234.1	235.3	236.9	237.2	236.8	237.1	239.1	240.0	235.7

Employment by Industry: Dallas–Forth Worth–Arlington, TX, Selected Years, 2000–2011—*Continued*

(Numbers in thousands, not seasonally adjusted)

Industry and year	January	February	March	April	May	June	July	August	September	October	November	December	Annual average
Professional and Business Services													
2000	367.1	370.8	376.3	380.8	382.7	392.3	390.5	393.7	396.9	393.5	392.8	393.4	385.9
2001	380.3	381.2	382.6	384.0	382.8	383.5	379.4	379.8	375.4	366.5	364.0	362.3	376.8
2002	352.2	351.7	354.0	355.4	356.6	357.3	356.1	359.6	357.8	355.4	355.2	353.8	355.4
2003	344.0	343.5	345.4	349.3	349.8	351.5	353.7	356.6	357.3	358.5	361.0	364.5	352.9
2004	354.8	357.3	360.5	366.3	366.3	368.3	371.5	373.1	371.2	376.6	376.4	377.3	368.3
2005	366.4	370.4	373.7	383.0	382.2	385.1	389.7	392.3	395.5	400.1	402.9	405.3	387.2
2006	395.9	399.9	404.4	409.4	411.3	415.3	416.3	421.9	424.1	426.2	431.4	433.9	415.8
2007	422.3	428.3	433.2	435.2	436.2	441.5	440.7	446.8	447.7	451.8	453.8	456.6	441.2
2008	444.1	446.4	448.5	449.9	451.8	453.9	452.2	454.3	450.5	449.2	445.1	440.0	448.8
2009	422.9	418.3	416.3	413.5	413.5	415.5	415.3	415.9	412.7	417.4	418.6	418.7	416.6
2010	409.9	412.3	415.7	420.5	421.3	424.3	426.3	430.2	431.5	435.8	437.1	438.6	425.3
2011	431.8	435.4	440.0	445.4	445.4	449.3	448.6	451.5	459.3	459.3	456.7	450.6	447.8
Education and Health Services													
2000	239.0	240.1	242.0	242.3	243.5	242.7	243.2	244.5	246.9	246.5	246.9	247.5	243.8
2001	245.7	248.3	249.8	250.9	252.3	253.9	254.4	255.8	257.0	257.0	257.6	258.0	253.4
2002	256.0	258.5	259.3	260.7	262.2	260.8	260.9	263.7	265.4	265.1	266.5	266.8	262.2
2003	266.4	268.2	268.9	269.5	270.0	267.9	269.6	270.7	272.2	274.2	274.4	272.6	270.4
2004	268.5	272.2	273.1	274.4	274.4	271.5	274.0	274.9	277.3	283.0	283.2	284.1	275.9
2005	277.6	280.8	281.9	285.0	285.4	284.7	288.6	289.1	291.0	293.8	294.3	294.8	287.3
2006	293.0	295.2	295.8	296.7	297.3	298.3	298.1	302.4	305.0	306.6	307.9	310.3	300.6
2007	303.6	308.7	311.7	312.7	314.1	314.0	313.6	316.7	319.0	320.5	322.2	322.7	315.0
2008	318.9	323.8	324.6	325.1	327.8	325.6	326.5	328.6	330.7	331.9	333.3	335.7	327.7
2009	331.0	333.7	336.6	338.5	340.6	339.9	341.9	344.0	346.7	350.2	350.6	351.9	342.1
2010	344.6	347.5	351.1	353.6	354.9	353.9	353.1	355.4	356.9	360.3	360.6	362.4	354.5
2011	357.5	358.3	362.1	364.4	365.4	365.2	363.8	361.7	361.6	361.8	364.2	362.7	362.4
Leisure and Hospitality													
2000	222.8	226.2	230.5	234.7	238.6	242.1	242.3	242.6	239.8	239.7	236.3	236.1	236.0
2001	231.9	236.5	241.0	247.7	249.4	250.1	248.8	249.4	244.0	240.5	237.2	236.8	242.8
2002	232.5	234.6	239.7	244.6	247.8	249.3	246.0	245.6	243.6	241.9	239.2	239.3	242.0
2003	234.9	236.1	239.1	243.7	246.2	247.6	245.3	246.5	242.8	244.6	241.7	241.0	242.5
2004	237.1	239.0	243.4	250.6	252.3	255.0	253.5	254.2	252.7	254.1	251.5	251.5	249.6
2005	244.9	248.0	251.9	258.6	261.1	262.2	261.3	260.2	257.2	256.3	254.1	253.1	255.7
2006	250.4	253.1	257.4	262.5	267.2	272.0	268.7	268.9	267.2	265.7	264.8	265.0	263.6
2007	258.7	262.7	268.7	276.8	281.4	283.5	282.8	283.6	277.9	279.0	278.3	278.0	276.0
2008	272.1	275.6	278.8	285.8	290.4	291.3	289.2	286.4	282.0	282.0	278.5	278.6	282.6
2009	271.2	273.1	277.1	282.3	285.8	289.0	286.2	284.9	280.3	278.4	274.4	276.1	279.9
2010	268.7	272.1	277.3	280.0	284.0	287.3	283.6	284.5	282.2	284.1	280.1	280.4	280.4
2011	273.2	276.4	283.7	289.2	293.8	297.6	293.9	292.9	293.3	293.0	296.4	297.8	290.1
Other Services													
2000	99.8	100.7	102.1	102.8	103.1	104.3	103.8	103.6	102.9	102.8	102.5	102.5	102.6
2001	103.1	104.0	105.5	105.3	105.2	106.9	104.3	104.2	102.9	101.4	101.8	101.9	103.9
2002	101.0	101.9	104.0	104.9	105.2	106.1	104.5	104.3	104.0	103.4	103.8	103.8	103.9
2003	104.7	105.5	108.0	107.2	107.1	108.0	107.6	107.2	106.3	104.7	104.7	105.5	106.4
2004	105.2	106.3	109.0	107.7	106.9	107.8	105.9	104.8	103.5	102.3	102.2	102.9	105.4
2005	102.4	103.5	106.4	106.8	107.6	108.2	105.4	104.9	104.2	102.4	102.7	103.2	104.8
2006	102.7	103.5	106.0	107.4	107.5	109.2	108.8	108.5	108.5	107.5	108.4	108.7	107.2
2007	103.4	105.2	106.6	105.6	106.6	108.5	106.2	106.1	105.0	103.3	103.3	103.1	105.2
2008	102.7	103.4	103.3	103.9	104.9	105.9	104.4	104.4	104.0	102.7	102.6	102.6	103.7
2009	101.0	101.7	101.7	102.2	102.5	103.6	102.2	101.9	100.8	100.5	101.2	101.1	101.7
2010	100.1	100.6	101.5	100.9	101.2	102.5	101.4	101.4	100.7	100.7	100.7	101.0	101.1
2011	100.0	100.8	101.9	102.6	103.1	104.4	103.5	103.4	102.7	102.4	102.7	102.8	102.5
Government													
2000	312.4	315.7	316.6	317.6	323.3	315.7	300.1	303.9	316.3	320.5	323.1	326.2	316.0
2001	320.6	325.9	326.3	325.0	325.2	321.3	304.8	310.1	324.0	331.1	334.0	333.2	323.5
2002	327.6	336.0	336.9	334.8	336.4	330.9	312.5	319.2	335.0	342.9	346.7	345.7	333.7
2003	336.9	346.2	345.4	346.0	347.4	342.2	322.4	323.4	342.1	346.0	348.8	345.7	341.0
2004	341.1	348.1	346.4	348.4	350.4	343.3	328.3	336.1	353.6	354.6	357.8	357.1	347.1
2005	351.9	359.2	358.3	359.3	360.4	351.6	335.7	344.2	360.4	364.0	367.3	361.2	356.1
2006	359.0	366.1	364.8	365.7	366.6	358.5	345.2	352.0	364.9	371.0	373.3	370.7	363.2
2007	366.7	373.5	374.3	372.5	374.5	366.9	349.8	354.0	370.6	378.9	382.1	380.8	370.4
2008	376.2	383.7	384.9	384.6	386.5	379.1	365.1	367.3	381.2	390.1	393.6	393.8	382.2
2009	386.6	393.5	394.4	394.9	395.4	386.6	371.2	371.3	383.7	395.0	397.5	393.9	388.7
2010	389.3	396.7	398.0	398.0	408.7	401.2	380.9	377.6	386.5	397.2	399.0	398.3	394.3
2011	393.1	397.3	397.7	396.9	397.4	392.8	376.0	375.0	385.8	390.3	393.3	394.4	390.8

Employment by Industry: Dayton, OH, Selected Years, 2000–2011

(Numbers in thousands, not seasonally adjusted)

Industry and year	January	February	March	April	May	June	July	August	September	October	November	December	Annual average
Total Nonfarm													
2000	426.4	429.3	432.1	434.5	439.6	437.7	430.5	433.0	435.7	439.6	441.8	443.1	435.3
2001	426.6	429.6	431.9	432.9	433.1	432.3	424.2	425.1	426.0	427.6	428.4	427.4	428.8
2002	418.1	420.4	421.8	421.4	422.2	422.1	417.3	418.3	421.2	420.6	422.3	421.4	420.6
2003	411.5	410.6	413.2	416.8	417.2	418.0	412.8	414.1	416.1	418.1	418.8	418.9	415.5
2004	406.0	406.8	409.1	413.3	413.5	414.6	410.2	411.8	413.8	414.2	414.2	414.4	411.8
2005	404.1	405.6	408.0	412.1	412.3	411.5	407.0	408.9	412.7	412.3	413.0	413.0	410.0
2006	401.9	404.4	407.9	410.1	412.2	412.0	404.5	406.2	408.3	408.5	410.1	411.2	408.1
2007	396.6	399.3	402.4	404.9	406.4	407.0	400.4	402.2	404.7	405.7	406.1	404.7	403.4
2008	394.7	395.4	393.7	395.8	397.3	397.9	392.7	394.2	395.3	394.3	392.3	390.1	394.5
2009	375.5	374.5	374.4	373.3	374.5	372.1	367.6	368.1	371.9	372.7	373.2	372.2	372.5
2010	363.0	363.5	366.5	370.8	373.1	371.6	367.3	368.9	372.7	374.4	376.2	376.2	370.4
2011	367.3	368.8	371.5	376.0	377.1	376.7	375.8	377.8	379.4	381.7	382.3	379.3	376.1
Total Private													
2000	362.3	363.0	365.4	367.4	371.0	369.6	365.9	368.9	369.1	371.4	373.3	374.2	368.5
2001	360.5	361.8	363.7	365.1	364.5	364.0	359.8	361.3	359.5	359.6	360.1	358.9	361.6
2002	351.3	352.2	353.7	353.9	353.8	354.3	352.3	353.8	354.5	352.7	354.0	353.4	353.3
2003	346.3	344.3	347.1	350.9	350.5	351.7	349.6	351.5	351.7	352.2	352.8	352.8	350.1
2004	341.3	341.2	343.3	347.6	347.0	348.7	347.3	349.2	349.4	348.6	348.4	348.8	346.7
2005	339.8	339.9	342.5	346.6	346.1	346.8	344.4	346.6	348.1	347.1	347.7	348.4	345.3
2006	337.9	338.9	342.4	344.7	345.8	346.2	341.6	343.6	344.5	343.1	344.7	345.8	343.3
2007	332.5	334.5	337.4	340.1	340.8	342.1	338.7	340.5	340.8	340.7	342.0	341.6	339.3
2008	331.9	330.9	329.1	331.1	331.5	333.7	331.1	332.6	331.1	329.0	326.6	325.5	330.3
2009	311.0	309.4	308.9	307.5	307.2	306.1	305.1	305.6	306.5	305.9	306.6	307.0	307.2
2010	297.8	297.6	300.1	304.0	304.6	305.0	304.9	306.2	307.7	307.9	309.8	310.0	304.6
2011	302.2	302.8	305.2	309.8	310.2	311.2	313.0	315.1	314.1	315.1	315.6	314.5	310.7
Goods-Producing													
2000	94.5	93.6	94.4	95.0	95.9	96.2	94.2	95.7	95.8	95.8	95.4	94.8	95.1
2001	88.4	88.6	88.1	86.9	86.6	87.0	85.6	85.9	84.5	84.3	83.5	82.8	86.0
2002	81.4	81.6	81.1	81.7	81.9	82.7	81.6	82.3	81.4	80.8	80.3	79.9	81.4
2003	77.9	76.5	76.6	77.7	78.3	78.8	76.6	77.8	76.9	76.7	76.4	76.0	77.2
2004	73.7	73.2	73.6	74.2	74.6	75.4	74.8	75.5	74.9	74.5	73.8	73.8	74.3
2005	71.4	71.1	71.3	72.7	72.9	74.1	73.4	74.1	73.8	73.2	72.5	71.9	72.7
2006	69.4	69.7	70.5	71.1	71.4	72.3	70.1	71.0	70.4	69.7	69.2	69.3	70.3
2007	63.8	65.6	66.2	66.9	67.3	68.3	67.0	68.0	67.4	66.5	66.6	65.9	66.6
2008	63.5	62.9	60.5	60.5	61.1	63.9	63.3	64.0	62.5	61.8	60.0	58.5	61.9
2009	53.3	52.4	51.7	50.9	50.6	50.1	50.0	50.4	50.0	50.0	49.4	49.4	50.7
2010	47.3	47.0	47.6	48.8	49.6	50.2	50.7	51.2	51.0	50.7	50.7	50.5	49.6
2011	49.3	49.3	50.1	50.6	51.3	52.0	52.9	53.4	51.8	51.9	51.3	50.9	51.2
Mining, Logging, and Construction													
2000	14.8	14.6	15.5	16.0	16.7	17.3	17.4	17.2	16.7	16.4	16.0	15.5	16.2
2001	13.8	13.7	14.2	14.6	15.0	15.7	16.0	16.1	15.7	15.8	15.7	15.3	15.1
2002	14.1	14.1	14.4	14.9	15.3	15.8	16.2	16.2	15.8	15.9	15.4	15.0	15.3
2003	13.8	13.3	13.7	14.7	15.3	15.8	16.1	16.3	15.9	16.1	15.9	15.6	15.2
2004	14.5	14.1	14.5	15.2	15.7	16.3	16.8	16.5	16.2	16.0	15.7	15.5	15.6
2005	14.0	13.7	14.2	15.2	15.7	16.3	16.6	16.3	16.1	15.7	15.6	15.0	15.4
2006	14.1	14.0	14.4	15.0	15.4	16.1	16.2	16.2	15.7	15.1	14.8	14.5	15.1
2007	13.4	12.8	13.5	14.5	15.2	15.9	15.9	15.7	15.2	14.9	15.0	14.3	14.7
2008	13.0	12.8	12.9	13.6	14.3	14.5	14.7	14.5	14.0	13.7	13.1	12.5	13.6
2009	11.2	11.1	11.3	11.4	11.9	12.2	12.5	12.2	11.8	11.8	11.5	11.2	11.7
2010	10.0	9.6	10.1	10.8	11.1	11.5	11.8	11.8	11.5	11.3	11.2	10.7	11.0
2011	9.8	9.7	10.1	10.6	11.3	11.7	12.2	12.1	11.8	11.8	11.5	10.7	11.1
Manufacturing													
2000	79.7	79.0	78.9	79.0	79.2	78.9	76.8	78.5	79.1	79.4	79.4	79.3	78.9
2001	74.6	74.9	73.9	72.3	71.6	71.3	69.6	69.8	68.8	68.5	67.8	67.5	70.9
2002	67.3	67.5	66.7	66.8	66.6	66.9	65.4	66.1	65.6	64.9	64.9	64.9	66.1
2003	64.1	63.2	62.9	63.0	63.0	63.0	60.5	61.5	61.0	60.6	60.5	60.4	62.0
2004	59.2	59.1	59.1	59.0	58.9	59.1	58.0	59.0	58.7	58.5	58.1	58.3	58.8
2005	57.4	57.4	57.1	57.5	57.2	57.8	56.8	57.8	57.7	57.5	56.9	56.9	57.3
2006	55.3	55.7	56.1	56.1	56.0	56.2	53.9	54.8	54.7	54.6	54.4	54.8	55.2
2007	50.4	52.8	52.7	52.4	52.1	52.4	51.1	52.3	52.2	51.6	51.6	51.6	51.9
2008	50.5	50.1	47.6	46.9	46.8	49.4	48.6	49.5	48.5	48.1	46.9	46.0	48.2
2009	42.1	41.3	40.4	39.5	38.7	37.9	37.5	38.2	38.2	38.2	37.9	38.2	39.0
2010	37.3	37.4	37.5	38.0	38.5	38.7	38.9	39.4	39.5	39.4	39.5	39.8	38.7
2011	39.5	39.6	40.0	40.0	40.0	40.3	40.7	41.3	40.1	40.1	39.8	40.2	40.1
Service-Providing													
2000	331.9	335.7	337.7	339.5	343.7	341.5	336.3	337.3	339.9	343.8	346.4	348.3	340.2
2001	338.2	341.0	343.8	346.0	346.5	345.3	338.6	339.2	341.5	343.3	344.9	344.6	342.7
2002	336.7	338.8	340.7	339.7	340.3	339.4	335.7	336.0	339.8	339.8	342.0	341.5	339.2
2003	333.6	334.1	336.6	339.1	338.9	339.2	336.2	336.3	339.2	341.4	342.4	342.9	338.3
2004	332.3	333.6	335.5	339.1	338.9	339.2	335.4	336.3	338.9	339.7	340.4	340.6	337.5
2005	332.7	334.5	336.7	339.4	339.4	337.4	333.6	334.8	338.9	339.1	340.5	341.1	337.3
2006	332.5	334.7	337.4	339.0	340.8	339.7	334.4	335.2	337.9	338.8	340.9	341.9	337.8
2007	332.8	333.7	336.2	338.0	339.1	338.7	333.4	334.2	337.3	339.2	339.5	338.8	336.7
2008	331.2	332.5	333.2	335.3	336.2	334.0	329.4	330.2	332.8	332.5	332.3	331.6	332.6
2009	322.2	322.1	322.7	322.4	323.9	322.0	317.6	317.7	321.9	322.7	323.8	322.8	321.8
2010	315.7	316.5	318.9	322.0	323.5	321.4	316.6	317.7	321.7	323.7	325.5	325.7	320.7
2011	318.0	319.5	321.4	325.4	325.8	324.7	322.9	324.4	327.6	329.8	331.0	328.4	324.9

Employment by Industry: Dayton, OH, Selected Years, 2000–2011—*Continued*

(Numbers in thousands, not seasonally adjusted)

Industry and year	January	February	March	April	May	June	July	August	September	October	November	December	Annual average
Trade, Transportation, and Utilities													
2000	81.0	80.4	80.6	80.9	81.7	81.2	80.3	80.3	80.2	82.2	84.1	85.6	81.5
2001	80.6	79.5	79.4	79.9	79.6	79.4	78.2	77.8	77.3	77.7	79.4	79.6	79.0
2002	75.9	75.2	75.4	74.8	75.1	75.5	74.8	74.2	74.0	73.6	75.2	76.0	75.0
2003	72.7	71.5	71.9	72.6	72.8	72.4	72.0	72.1	72.2	72.7	74.1	74.7	72.6
2004	70.4	69.9	70.4	71.3	71.6	72.0	71.5	71.4	71.5	72.2	73.3	73.9	71.6
2005	70.3	70.2	70.8	71.5	71.5	71.5	71.0	70.9	70.7	70.8	72.2	73.1	71.2
2006	69.6	69.1	69.8	69.9	70.6	70.4	69.7	69.9	69.0	69.2	70.7	71.5	70.0
2007	68.1	67.3	68.1	68.7	69.0	69.0	68.9	68.5	68.4	68.6	70.0	70.6	68.8
2008	67.3	66.4	66.6	67.0	67.2	67.5	66.7	66.9	66.5	66.1	66.7	67.5	66.9
2009	63.9	63.1	63.2	63.1	63.5	63.3	62.7	62.6	62.3	62.4	63.5	64.2	63.2
2010	61.1	60.5	61.0	61.5	61.7	61.9	61.3	61.5	61.3	62.0	63.7	64.7	61.9
2011	61.8	61.0	61.5	62.4	62.7	62.8	62.4	61.8	61.7	62.6	64.0	64.4	62.4
Wholesale Trade													
2000	14.8	14.8	14.9	15.0	15.1	15.1	14.8	14.8	14.9	15.0	15.0	15.0	14.9
2001	15.2	15.0	15.0	15.3	15.3	15.0	15.0	15.1	15.2	15.3	15.3	15.3	15.2
2002	15.3	15.4	15.3	15.3	15.2	15.1	15.2	15.0	15.1	15.3	15.2	15.2	15.2
2003	14.8	14.7	14.7	14.6	14.6	14.6	14.6	14.5	14.4	14.5	14.5	14.4	14.6
2004	14.1	14.0	14.1	14.2	14.3	14.4	14.5	14.4	14.4	14.5	14.4	14.4	14.3
2005	14.0	14.1	14.1	14.2	14.2	14.3	14.3	14.2	14.1	14.1	14.0	14.1	14.1
2006	13.8	13.8	13.9	13.9	14.1	14.1	14.1	14.0	14.0	14.0	14.0	14.1	14.0
2007	13.9	13.9	14.0	14.0	14.0	14.1	14.2	14.1	14.0	14.1	14.0	14.1	14.0
2008	14.0	13.9	14.0	14.0	14.0	13.9	13.8	13.7	13.6	13.4	13.3	13.2	13.7
2009	13.1	13.0	12.9	12.8	12.6	12.6	12.5	12.4	12.2	12.0	12.0	12.1	12.5
2010	12.0	12.0	12.0	12.0	12.0	12.1	12.1	12.1	12.0	12.0	12.0	12.1	12.0
2011	12.2	12.2	12.3	12.4	12.5	12.5	12.5	12.5	12.5	12.5	12.6	12.6	12.4
Retail Trade													
2000	51.2	50.4	50.6	50.7	51.3	50.9	50.5	50.5	50.1	51.5	53.5	55.0	51.4
2001	50.2	49.3	49.3	49.5	49.5	49.6	48.4	48.0	47.8	48.2	50.0	50.4	49.2
2002	47.1	46.4	46.8	46.3	46.6	47.0	46.3	46.0	45.8	45.5	47.0	47.9	46.6
2003	45.4	44.4	45.0	45.7	45.8	45.5	45.2	45.4	45.6	45.8	47.1	47.7	45.7
2004	44.6	44.0	44.4	45.1	45.2	45.3	44.8	44.7	44.8	45.2	46.3	46.9	45.1
2005	44.1	43.8	44.3	45.0	44.9	44.7	44.0	43.9	43.8	44.0	45.3	46.0	44.5
2006	43.3	42.6	43.1	43.0	43.4	43.1	42.7	42.9	42.8	43.1	44.6	45.2	43.3
2007	42.6	41.8	42.4	43.0	43.2	43.0	42.8	42.5	42.5	42.7	44.2	44.6	42.9
2008	42.0	41.2	41.5	41.9	41.9	42.0	41.4	41.5	41.3	41.2	41.9	42.7	41.7
2009	39.9	39.2	39.5	39.8	40.4	40.2	39.6	39.6	39.4	39.6	40.6	41.1	39.9
2010	38.7	38.1	38.6	39.0	39.2	39.2	38.7	38.8	38.6	39.1	40.6	41.1	39.1
2011	38.8	38.1	38.5	39.1	39.2	39.4	39.1	38.4	38.3	39.1	40.3	40.7	39.1
Transportation and Utilities													
2000	15.0	15.2	15.1	15.2	15.3	15.2	15.0	15.0	15.2	15.7	15.6	15.6	15.3
2001	15.2	15.2	15.1	15.1	14.8	14.8	14.8	14.7	14.3	14.2	14.1	13.9	14.7
2002	13.5	13.4	13.3	13.2	13.3	13.4	13.3	13.2	13.1	12.8	13.0	12.9	13.2
2003	12.5	12.4	12.2	12.3	12.4	12.3	12.2	12.2	12.2	12.4	12.5	12.6	12.4
2004	11.7	11.9	11.9	12.0	12.1	12.3	12.2	12.3	12.3	12.5	12.6	12.6	12.2
2005	12.2	12.3	12.4	12.3	12.4	12.5	12.7	12.8	12.8	12.7	12.9	13.0	12.6
2006	12.5	12.7	12.8	13.0	13.1	13.2	12.9	13.0	12.2	12.1	12.1	12.2	12.7
2007	11.6	11.6	11.7	11.7	11.8	11.9	11.9	11.9	11.9	11.8	11.8	11.9	11.8
2008	11.3	11.3	11.1	11.1	11.3	11.6	11.5	11.7	11.6	11.5	11.5	11.6	11.4
2009	10.9	10.9	10.8	10.5	10.5	10.5	10.6	10.6	10.7	10.8	10.9	11.0	10.7
2010	10.4	10.4	10.4	10.5	10.5	10.6	10.5	10.6	10.7	10.9	11.1	11.5	10.7
2011	10.8	10.7	10.7	10.9	11.0	10.9	10.8	10.9	10.9	11.0	11.1	11.1	10.9
Information													
2000	11.4	11.4	11.4	11.2	11.3	11.2	11.2	11.2	11.4	11.6	11.9	12.1	11.4
2001	12.5	12.6	12.7	12.5	12.5	12.7	12.8	12.6	12.5	12.5	12.5	12.7	12.6
2002	12.8	12.7	12.7	12.6	12.6	12.6	12.6	12.7	12.7	12.7	12.6	12.6	12.7
2003	12.8	12.7	12.7	12.6	12.5	12.6	12.6	12.5	12.3	12.4	12.4	12.4	12.5
2004	12.2	12.0	12.0	12.1	12.0	12.3	12.4	12.5	12.3	12.3	12.4	12.4	12.2
2005	12.3	12.2	12.2	12.2	12.2	12.3	12.2	12.0	11.8	11.7	11.7	11.8	12.1
2006	11.7	11.7	11.7	11.7	11.7	11.8	11.9	12.0	11.9	12.0	12.0	12.1	11.9
2007	12.1	12.1	12.0	12.1	12.2	12.2	12.1	12.1	12.0	12.0	12.1	12.1	12.1
2008	12.2	12.1	12.1	12.1	12.0	11.9	12.2	12.1	11.7	11.6	11.6	11.5	11.9
2009	11.4	11.4	11.2	11.0	11.0	10.9	10.8	10.8	10.7	10.7	10.7	10.8	11.0
2010	10.7	10.7	10.7	10.5	10.4	10.4	10.3	10.2	10.2	10.0	9.9	9.9	10.3
2011	9.8	9.9	9.8	9.9	9.8	9.9	9.9	9.8	9.8	9.9	9.8	9.8	9.8
Financial Activities													
2000	17.2	17.1	17.1	17.3	17.4	17.3	17.3	17.2	17.0	17.2	17.4	17.6	17.3
2001	17.4	17.5	17.8	17.9	18.1	18.1	18.2	18.2	18.2	18.3	18.2	18.2	18.0
2002	18.0	18.1	18.2	18.3	18.3	18.4	18.5	18.6	18.5	18.4	18.4	18.4	18.3
2003	18.4	18.5	18.6	18.7	18.9	19.1	19.1	19.1	18.9	18.8	18.8	18.8	18.8
2004	18.6	18.6	18.8	18.9	19.1	19.2	19.3	19.3	19.1	19.2	19.1	19.2	19.0
2005	18.8	18.9	18.8	19.1	19.2	19.4	19.5	19.6	19.6	19.7	19.7	19.8	19.3
2006	19.7	19.9	20.0	20.1	20.1	20.2	20.2	20.2	20.1	20.2	20.2	20.2	20.1
2007	19.9	20.0	20.0	20.1	20.1	19.9	19.8	19.7	19.4	19.3	19.2	19.1	19.7
2008	19.0	18.7	18.6	18.5	18.4	18.3	18.1	18.0	17.7	17.5	17.4	17.4	18.1
2009	17.3	17.1	16.9	16.9	16.9	17.0	17.0	16.8	16.6	16.7	16.7	16.6	16.9
2010	16.6	16.6	16.6	16.9	17.0	16.9	17.1	17.0	16.9	17.1	17.1	17.1	16.9
2011	16.9	16.9	16.9	17.0	17.1	17.1	17.1	17.1	16.9	16.9	16.9	16.9	17.0

Employment by Industry: Dayton, OH, Selected Years, 2000–2011—*Continued*

(Numbers in thousands, not seasonally adjusted)

Industry and year	January	February	March	April	May	June	July	August	September	October	November	December	Annual average
Professional and Business Services													
2000	50.3	51.2	51.6	52.7	53.0	52.8	52.2	52.6	53.0	53.6	53.2	53.0	52.4
2001	54.2	54.7	55.7	55.8	55.7	55.6	54.6	55.1	54.7	54.4	53.9	53.4	54.8
2002	53.1	53.1	53.6	53.3	53.0	52.9	52.7	52.6	52.7	51.8	52.0	51.3	52.7
2003	52.7	52.3	52.9	54.0	53.9	54.2	54.6	54.8	54.3	54.7	54.4	54.3	53.9
2004	52.5	52.4	52.5	53.6	53.7	54.0	53.4	53.5	54.1	53.3	52.9	52.8	53.2
2005	52.0	51.6	52.0	52.2	52.1	52.0	51.8	52.4	52.4	53.0	52.7	52.9	52.3
2006	51.2	51.1	51.6	52.3	52.7	53.1	52.7	52.9	52.6	52.4	52.4	52.6	52.3
2007	51.6	51.8	52.0	52.2	52.1	52.7	52.3	52.5	52.4	52.9	52.6	52.6	52.3
2008	51.2	51.5	51.6	51.8	51.5	51.7	51.1	50.9	50.4	49.9	48.9	48.8	50.8
2009	46.7	45.9	45.5	45.4	45.0	45.3	45.5	45.6	45.4	45.3	45.4	45.4	45.5
2010	44.0	44.3	44.5	45.8	45.8	46.4	46.3	47.1	46.7	46.6	46.9	46.6	45.9
2011	46.1	46.2	46.6	47.5	47.0	47.3	48.7	49.9	49.8	50.1	50.2	50.4	48.3
Education and Health Services													
2000	57.7	58.6	58.5	58.1	58.1	57.4	57.5	58.1	58.5	58.8	59.3	59.4	58.3
2001	58.6	59.7	59.5	60.4	59.0	57.4	56.7	57.1	59.4	60.8	61.4	61.1	59.3
2002	60.2	61.2	61.4	61.3	59.9	58.6	58.3	58.8	61.9	63.0	63.4	63.2	60.9
2003	61.2	62.0	62.4	62.5	60.1	59.4	59.2	59.4	62.8	63.8	64.1	63.6	61.7
2004	62.3	63.1	63.0	63.7	61.1	60.7	60.5	60.9	62.6	64.0	63.9	64.0	62.5
2005	63.4	64.1	64.5	64.8	63.3	61.9	61.7	61.9	65.2	65.7	66.1	66.1	64.1
2006	64.7	65.5	65.8	65.7	64.5	62.7	61.9	62.5	65.8	66.6	67.1	66.9	65.0
2007	65.5	66.2	66.5	66.5	65.6	64.7	64.0	64.8	67.5	68.4	68.7	68.9	66.4
2008	67.8	68.5	68.6	68.5	67.5	66.4	66.0	66.7	69.3	69.9	70.2	70.3	68.3
2009	68.7	69.7	69.8	69.0	68.0	66.8	66.4	66.7	69.6	70.1	70.3	70.1	68.8
2010	68.9	69.5	69.8	69.2	68.1	66.5	66.4	66.5	69.5	70.5	70.7	70.8	68.9
2011	69.4	70.3	70.5	70.6	69.8	68.7	67.8	68.8	70.2	70.6	71.2	70.3	69.9
Leisure and Hospitality													
2000	34.4	34.6	35.5	35.8	37.1	37.3	37.1	37.3	36.8	35.9	35.6	35.5	36.1
2001	33.1	33.5	34.6	35.4	36.6	37.3	37.4	37.5	36.5	35.1	34.7	34.7	35.5
2002	33.7	33.8	34.6	35.4	36.4	37.0	37.0	37.2	36.6	35.8	35.4	35.3	35.7
2003	34.2	34.3	35.2	36.0	37.2	38.1	38.4	38.3	37.4	36.3	36.0	36.3	36.5
2004	35.3	35.5	36.3	37.0	38.0	38.2	38.5	38.8	38.1	36.5	36.4	36.2	37.1
2005	35.2	35.4	36.3	37.4	38.1	38.7	38.2	38.6	38.0	36.7	36.6	36.6	37.2
2006	35.6	35.8	36.8	37.4	38.3	39.0	38.7	38.8	38.3	36.9	37.0	37.1	37.5
2007	35.7	35.7	36.5	37.5	38.4	39.0	38.6	38.9	37.8	37.1	36.9	36.6	37.4
2008	35.4	35.3	35.6	37.2	38.2	38.5	38.2	38.5	37.6	36.9	36.5	36.2	37.0
2009	34.8	34.9	35.7	36.3	37.2	37.8	37.8	37.7	36.9	35.8	35.6	35.4	36.3
2010	34.2	34.1	34.8	36.1	36.8	37.4	37.5	37.5	36.9	35.9	35.7	35.4	36.0
2011	34.1	34.3	34.9	36.6	37.3	38.1	38.9	39.0	38.7	38.0	37.1	36.7	37.0
Other Services													
2000	15.8	16.1	16.3	16.4	16.5	16.2	16.1	16.5	16.4	16.3	16.4	16.2	16.3
2001	15.7	15.7	15.9	16.3	16.4	16.5	16.3	17.1	16.4	16.5	16.5	16.4	16.3
2002	16.2	16.5	16.7	16.5	16.6	16.6	16.8	17.4	16.7	16.6	16.7	16.7	16.7
2003	16.4	16.5	16.8	16.8	16.8	17.1	17.1	17.5	16.9	16.8	16.6	16.7	16.8
2004	16.3	16.5	16.7	16.8	16.9	16.9	16.9	17.3	16.8	16.6	16.6	16.5	16.7
2005	16.4	16.4	16.6	16.7	16.8	16.9	16.6	17.1	16.6	16.3	16.2	16.2	16.6
2006	16.0	16.1	16.2	16.5	16.5	16.7	16.4	16.3	16.4	16.1	16.1	16.1	16.3
2007	15.8	15.8	16.1	16.1	16.1	16.3	16.0	16.0	15.9	15.9	15.9	15.8	16.0
2008	15.5	15.5	15.5	15.5	15.6	15.5	15.5	15.5	15.4	15.3	15.3	15.3	15.5
2009	14.9	14.9	14.9	14.9	15.0	14.9	14.9	15.0	15.0	14.9	15.0	15.1	14.9
2010	15.0	14.9	15.1	15.2	15.2	15.3	15.3	15.2	15.2	15.1	15.1	15.0	15.1
2011	14.8	14.9	14.9	15.2	15.2	15.3	15.3	15.3	15.2	15.1	15.1	15.1	15.1
Government													
2000	64.1	66.3	66.7	67.1	68.6	68.1	64.6	64.1	66.6	68.2	68.5	68.9	66.8
2001	66.1	67.8	68.2	67.8	68.6	68.3	64.4	63.8	66.5	68.0	68.3	68.5	67.2
2002	66.8	68.2	68.1	67.5	68.4	67.8	65.0	64.5	66.7	67.9	68.3	68.0	67.3
2003	65.2	66.3	66.1	65.9	66.7	66.3	63.2	62.6	64.4	65.9	66.0	66.1	65.4
2004	64.7	65.6	65.8	65.7	66.5	65.9	62.9	62.6	64.4	65.6	65.8	65.6	65.1
2005	64.3	65.7	65.5	65.5	66.2	64.7	62.6	62.3	64.6	65.2	65.3	64.6	64.7
2006	64.0	65.5	65.5	65.4	66.4	65.8	62.9	62.6	63.8	65.4	65.4	65.4	64.8
2007	64.1	64.8	65.0	64.8	65.6	64.9	61.7	61.7	63.9	65.0	64.1	63.1	64.1
2008	62.8	64.5	64.6	64.7	65.8	64.2	61.6	61.6	64.2	65.3	65.7	64.6	64.1
2009	64.5	65.1	65.5	65.8	67.3	66.0	62.5	62.5	65.4	66.8	66.6	65.2	65.3
2010	65.2	65.9	66.4	66.8	68.5	66.6	62.4	62.7	65.0	66.5	66.4	66.2	65.7
2011	65.1	66.0	66.3	66.2	66.9	65.5	62.8	62.7	65.3	66.6	66.7	64.8	65.4

Employment by Industry: Denver–Aurora–Broomfield, CO, Selected Years, 2000–2011

(Numbers in thousands, not seasonally adjusted)

Industry and year	January	February	March	April	May	June	July	August	September	October	November	December	Annual average
Total Nonfarm													
2000	1,168.0	1,177.6	1,188.3	1,196.6	1,210.5	1,223.8	1,221.1	1,225.8	1,227.2	1,224.1	1,231.3	1,239.7	1,211.2
2001	1,204.6	1,207.2	1,211.2	1,212.1	1,219.0	1,230.0	1,216.8	1,216.3	1,207.7	1,196.7	1,194.2	1,192.4	1,209.0
2002	1,152.5	1,155.8	1,159.9	1,170.2	1,181.1	1,188.8	1,177.7	1,182.1	1,175.0	1,172.1	1,175.3	1,177.4	1,172.3
2003	1,148.6	1,148.1	1,147.2	1,151.4	1,160.4	1,168.5	1,160.7	1,164.9	1,159.6	1,161.1	1,161.6	1,165.0	1,158.1
2004	1,135.2	1,138.3	1,148.1	1,162.3	1,170.2	1,180.8	1,175.3	1,177.3	1,176.0	1,177.6	1,180.8	1,186.1	1,167.3
2005	1,154.5	1,161.8	1,170.6	1,180.2	1,190.2	1,201.5	1,198.9	1,199.0	1,203.6	1,202.6	1,206.2	1,212.1	1,190.1
2006	1,182.1	1,187.7	1,196.4	1,204.2	1,217.1	1,231.8	1,222.3	1,225.8	1,225.3	1,225.3	1,229.6	1,234.1	1,215.1
2007	1,202.6	1,209.0	1,221.4	1,230.3	1,244.0	1,257.7	1,249.5	1,252.7	1,252.9	1,254.2	1,258.6	1,261.1	1,241.2
2008	1,231.3	1,237.2	1,244.5	1,252.2	1,261.9	1,271.6	1,261.7	1,265.9	1,259.4	1,256.2	1,251.2	1,244.5	1,253.1
2009	1,206.6	1,198.3	1,197.5	1,199.2	1,206.7	1,210.6	1,199.8	1,198.0	1,194.6	1,197.0	1,195.6	1,193.8	1,199.8
2010	1,162.0	1,167.2	1,174.6	1,185.9	1,199.8	1,206.8	1,202.5	1,202.9	1,199.5	1,206.1	1,207.5	1,206.9	1,193.5
2011	1,180.4	1,183.8	1,191.4	1,207.1	1,216.3	1,225.2	1,217.2	1,219.6	1,221.5	1,224.4	1,227.6	1,224.8	1,211.6
Total Private													
2000	1,018.4	1,024.1	1,033.2	1,040.8	1,051.5	1,067.8	1,071.3	1,074.9	1,070.3	1,067.5	1,073.5	1,081.0	1,056.2
2001	1,050.2	1,049.0	1,053.5	1,053.8	1,059.8	1,070.9	1,062.9	1,061.5	1,047.0	1,035.6	1,031.3	1,029.6	1,050.4
2002	993.0	993.1	995.8	1,005.8	1,015.4	1,024.2	1,018.8	1,021.7	1,010.7	1,006.0	1,008.4	1,010.9	1,008.7
2003	986.8	983.1	981.7	986.0	993.0	1,002.6	1,001.7	1,005.0	995.4	996.8	997.0	1,001.3	994.2
2004	976.1	975.7	984.2	997.0	1,004.3	1,016.0	1,017.4	1,019.1	1,011.8	1,012.1	1,014.6	1,020.1	1,004.0
2005	994.1	997.3	1,005.7	1,013.7	1,023.0	1,035.9	1,039.3	1,040.3	1,037.4	1,035.9	1,039.1	1,045.1	1,025.6
2006	1,019.5	1,021.2	1,028.8	1,037.1	1,048.4	1,063.5	1,061.2	1,063.9	1,057.5	1,057.3	1,060.7	1,064.9	1,048.7
2007	1,038.7	1,040.0	1,051.1	1,059.6	1,072.2	1,086.9	1,086.1	1,088.4	1,081.2	1,081.7	1,085.2	1,088.1	1,071.6
2008	1,063.4	1,064.9	1,070.9	1,078.0	1,085.6	1,097.1	1,094.0	1,095.4	1,084.0	1,078.8	1,072.9	1,067.2	1,079.4
2009	1,033.8	1,022.4	1,020.2	1,020.9	1,026.4	1,032.8	1,030.8	1,027.9	1,017.4	1,017.4	1,016.7	1,016.1	1,023.6
2010	990.1	989.6	995.8	1,006.1	1,014.6	1,026.6	1,029.7	1,031.5	1,020.9	1,025.0	1,026.0	1,027.4	1,015.3
2011	1,006.5	1,004.5	1,011.4	1,025.9	1,033.9	1,045.4	1,046.6	1,049.4	1,044.3	1,045.9	1,049.0	1,047.4	1,034.2
Goods-Producing													
2000	173.5	176.0	179.1	179.5	182.0	185.6	186.0	186.6	186.1	185.7	183.9	183.3	182.3
2001	178.6	178.8	180.2	180.0	181.5	183.3	181.9	181.6	179.4	175.9	172.3	169.0	178.5
2002	163.3	164.0	165.9	167.5	169.9	171.4	171.0	170.6	167.7	164.4	163.6	161.1	166.9
2003	157.9	156.7	156.1	156.5	158.4	160.6	160.0	159.5	157.5	157.4	155.7	154.1	157.5
2004	151.0	150.7	153.2	155.6	157.2	160.1	161.1	161.2	160.1	160.8	159.7	158.5	157.4
2005	154.3	155.7	158.1	158.9	160.8	164.6	166.8	167.3	166.8	166.2	165.6	164.3	162.5
2006	161.4	162.6	164.8	165.8	167.9	171.0	170.1	169.8	169.0	167.6	165.8	163.9	166.6
2007	157.3	158.0	161.1	162.5	164.7	168.0	168.6	168.7	167.2	167.6	166.2	163.3	164.4
2008	159.7	159.7	160.9	161.5	163.0	165.6	164.9	165.0	162.8	161.7	158.1	153.9	161.4
2009	146.7	143.2	141.4	140.0	140.0	141.5	141.3	139.7	137.9	136.9	135.6	132.7	139.7
2010	127.8	127.2	128.0	129.9	131.1	133.3	134.2	133.6	132.0	132.0	130.8	129.8	130.8
2011	125.8	125.1	127.2	130.3	130.7	133.6	133.5	135.2	135.0	134.0	133.8	133.2	131.5
Mining, Logging, and Construction													
2000	86.4	88.7	91.5	92.9	95.5	98.5	98.9	99.6	99.4	99.1	97.6	96.9	95.4
2001	94.2	94.5	96.3	97.4	99.0	101.3	100.9	101.2	100.1	97.8	95.0	92.3	97.5
2002	88.3	89.2	91.1	93.2	95.5	96.9	96.8	96.6	94.1	92.9	90.8	88.5	92.8
2003	85.4	84.4	84.3	84.9	86.9	89.0	88.8	88.5	86.8	86.8	85.0	83.4	86.2
2004	80.6	80.1	82.3	84.3	85.8	88.1	88.7	88.5	87.9	88.4	87.3	86.2	85.7
2005	82.8	83.9	86.1	87.0	88.8	92.3	94.1	94.7	94.4	93.6	93.2	91.9	90.2
2006	89.7	90.8	92.7	93.7	95.7	98.4	97.4	97.1	96.5	95.3	93.6	92.0	94.4
2007	86.1	87.1	90.1	91.7	93.4	96.1	96.7	96.8	95.4	95.7	94.3	91.5	92.9
2008	88.7	89.3	90.5	91.4	92.9	95.1	94.5	94.8	93.0	92.3	89.7	86.2	91.5
2009	80.7	78.5	77.3	76.4	76.9	78.5	78.4	77.2	76.0	75.1	73.8	71.2	76.7
2010	67.5	66.9	67.6	69.4	70.0	71.7	72.5	71.9	70.5	70.5	69.3	68.3	69.7
2011	64.6	64.0	65.8	68.6	68.7	71.2	70.5	72.6	73.0	72.8	72.7	71.9	69.7
Manufacturing													
2000	87.1	87.3	87.6	86.6	86.5	87.1	87.1	87.0	86.7	86.6	86.3	86.4	86.9
2001	84.4	84.3	83.9	82.6	82.5	82.0	81.0	80.4	79.3	78.1	77.3	76.7	81.0
2002	75.0	74.8	74.8	74.3	74.4	74.5	74.2	74.0	73.6	73.5	72.8	72.6	74.0
2003	72.5	72.3	71.8	71.6	71.5	71.6	71.2	71.0	70.7	70.6	70.7	70.7	71.4
2004	70.4	70.6	70.9	71.3	71.4	72.0	72.4	72.7	72.2	72.4	72.4	72.3	71.8
2005	71.5	71.8	72.0	71.9	72.0	72.3	72.7	72.6	72.4	72.6	72.4	72.4	72.2
2006	71.7	71.8	72.1	72.1	72.2	72.6	72.7	72.7	72.5	72.3	72.2	71.9	72.2
2007	71.2	70.9	71.0	70.8	71.3	71.9	71.9	71.9	71.8	71.9	71.9	71.8	71.5
2008	71.0	70.4	70.4	70.1	70.1	70.5	70.4	70.2	69.8	69.4	68.4	67.7	69.9
2009	66.0	64.7	64.1	63.6	63.1	63.0	62.9	62.5	61.9	61.8	61.8	61.5	63.1
2010	60.3	60.3	60.4	60.5	61.1	61.6	61.7	61.7	61.5	61.5	61.5	61.5	61.1
2011	61.2	61.1	61.4	61.7	62.0	62.4	63.0	62.6	62.0	61.2	61.1	61.3	61.8
Service-Providing													
2000	994.5	1,001.6	1,009.2	1,017.1	1,028.5	1,038.2	1,035.1	1,039.2	1,041.1	1,038.4	1,047.4	1,056.4	1,028.9
2001	1,026.0	1,028.4	1,031.0	1,032.1	1,037.5	1,046.7	1,034.9	1,034.7	1,028.3	1,020.8	1,021.9	1,023.4	1,030.5
2002	989.2	991.8	994.0	1,002.7	1,011.2	1,017.4	1,006.7	1,011.5	1,007.3	1,005.7	1,011.7	1,016.3	1,005.5
2003	990.7	991.4	991.1	994.9	1,002.0	1,007.9	1,000.7	1,005.4	1,002.1	1,003.7	1,005.9	1,010.9	1,000.6
2004	984.2	987.6	994.9	1,006.7	1,013.0	1,020.7	1,014.2	1,016.1	1,015.9	1,016.8	1,021.1	1,027.6	1,009.9
2005	1,000.2	1,006.1	1,012.5	1,021.3	1,029.4	1,036.9	1,032.1	1,031.7	1,036.8	1,036.4	1,040.6	1,047.8	1,027.7
2006	1,020.7	1,025.1	1,031.6	1,038.4	1,049.2	1,060.8	1,052.2	1,056.0	1,056.3	1,057.7	1,063.8	1,070.2	1,048.5
2007	1,045.3	1,051.0	1,060.3	1,067.8	1,079.3	1,089.7	1,080.9	1,084.0	1,085.7	1,086.6	1,092.4	1,097.8	1,076.7
2008	1,071.6	1,077.5	1,083.6	1,090.7	1,098.9	1,106.0	1,096.8	1,100.9	1,096.6	1,094.5	1,093.1	1,090.6	1,091.7
2009	1,059.9	1,055.1	1,056.1	1,059.2	1,066.7	1,069.1	1,058.5	1,058.3	1,056.7	1,060.1	1,060.0	1,061.1	1,060.1
2010	1,034.2	1,040.0	1,046.6	1,056.0	1,068.7	1,073.5	1,068.3	1,069.3	1,067.5	1,074.1	1,076.7	1,077.1	1,062.7
2011	1,054.6	1,058.7	1,064.2	1,076.8	1,085.6	1,091.6	1,083.7	1,084.4	1,086.5	1,090.4	1,093.8	1,091.6	1,080.2

Employment by Industry: Denver–Aurora–Broomfield, CO, Selected Years, 2000–2011—*Continued*

(Numbers in thousands, not seasonally adjusted)

Industry and year	January	February	March	April	May	June	July	August	September	October	November	December	Annual average
Trade, Transportation, and Utilities													
2000	240.3	240.4	239.2	241.2	243.4	245.3	245.9	246.7	246.1	248.1	256.2	261.1	246.2
2001	249.6	246.2	246.3	245.3	246.8	248.9	247.6	247.1	245.4	244.8	247.2	247.5	246.9
2002	233.5	231.1	230.7	232.5	235.5	237.6	236.7	236.8	235.0	235.7	241.6	245.2	236.0
2003	235.2	232.9	231.6	229.8	230.0	230.7	230.5	231.2	230.5	232.2	236.6	239.6	232.6
2004	229.6	227.3	228.3	229.7	231.3	232.7	233.0	233.2	231.8	233.8	238.6	242.4	232.6
2005	232.4	231.3	232.2	232.5	234.3	236.1	236.6	236.3	237.8	239.6	244.2	247.2	236.7
2006	236.6	233.5	234.3	235.3	236.8	238.8	238.4	239.0	238.6	241.4	246.8	250.8	239.2
2007	242.2	239.4	240.1	241.0	242.8	244.3	244.5	244.5	243.8	245.6	251.2	253.8	244.4
2008	245.8	243.0	244.1	244.3	245.0	246.2	245.9	245.5	243.5	243.0	244.7	246.3	244.8
2009	235.7	231.7	229.8	229.1	229.9	230.7	229.5	229.1	227.9	229.3	231.7	234.1	230.7
2010	225.0	223.9	224.0	224.9	226.5	228.2	228.8	229.2	227.7	229.6	232.9	235.3	228.0
2011	226.4	224.6	225.4	227.5	228.9	230.3	231.0	232.9	232.6	233.6	236.1	238.8	230.7
Wholesale Trade													
2000	65.4	66.8	67.3	68.1	68.6	69.0	68.4	67.8	67.6	68.3	68.6	69.0	67.9
2001	68.9	69.5	69.7	69.2	68.9	69.0	68.6	67.6	67.2	66.9	66.8	66.8	68.4
2002	65.4	65.3	65.3	65.1	65.2	65.2	64.9	64.5	64.0	63.9	63.7	63.8	64.7
2003	63.7	63.4	63.3	63.0	62.9	62.9	62.6	62.3	61.9	62.1	61.9	62.0	62.7
2004	61.3	61.5	61.9	62.0	62.1	62.4	62.2	62.2	61.9	62.0	62.1	62.3	62.0
2005	61.6	61.9	62.2	62.4	62.6	63.0	63.1	63.2	63.3	63.3	63.5	63.8	62.8
2006	63.3	63.6	64.0	64.3	64.7	65.4	65.3	65.5	65.3	65.6	65.9	66.4	64.9
2007	65.0	65.4	65.8	65.8	66.3	66.7	66.6	66.7	66.4	66.8	66.9	66.8	66.3
2008	66.5	66.7	66.8	67.0	67.2	67.4	67.4	67.1	66.8	66.4	66.1	66.0	66.8
2009	64.8	64.2	63.5	62.8	62.6	62.5	62.1	61.8	61.3	61.4	61.2	61.4	62.5
2010	60.9	60.7	60.8	60.9	61.1	61.5	61.7	61.7	61.5	61.7	61.7	61.8	61.3
2011	61.3	61.4	61.7	62.1	62.3	62.6	62.9	62.8	62.6	62.1	61.9	62.9	62.2
Retail Trade													
2000	123.3	121.9	121.2	120.9	122.2	123.7	123.6	125.1	124.4	125.7	130.9	135.2	124.8
2001	125.4	122.2	122.2	121.8	122.9	124.4	123.2	122.8	122.5	123.3	127.6	129.4	124.0
2002	121.1	118.5	118.7	119.9	121.5	123.2	122.4	122.5	121.3	121.8	127.0	129.8	122.3
2003	121.3	119.3	118.3	118.1	119.0	120.0	119.7	120.6	120.4	121.4	125.3	127.8	120.9
2004	119.8	117.3	117.7	118.5	119.7	120.5	120.7	121.2	120.3	122.3	126.9	129.7	121.2
2005	121.9	120.3	121.0	121.2	122.9	123.9	124.1	123.7	125.2	126.7	131.0	133.2	124.6
2006	124.4	121.1	121.3	122.3	123.2	123.9	123.9	124.3	124.0	126.4	131.3	133.4	125.0
2007	127.0	124.2	124.5	125.1	126.3	127.2	127.5	127.2	126.8	127.7	132.4	134.0	127.5
2008	127.7	125.3	126.2	126.3	126.7	127.6	127.3	127.7	126.7	127.1	128.8	129.6	127.3
2009	122.5	119.8	118.9	118.3	119.6	120.5	119.8	119.8	119.4	120.6	123.5	124.7	120.6
2010	118.3	117.1	117.4	118.6	120.0	121.2	121.8	122.1	120.8	122.1	125.1	126.3	120.9
2011	119.8	118.4	118.8	120.3	121.5	122.5	122.5	124.3	124.2	125.7	128.6	129.7	123.0
Transportation and Utilities													
2000	51.6	51.7	50.7	52.2	52.6	52.6	53.9	53.8	54.1	54.1	56.7	56.9	53.4
2001	55.3	54.5	54.4	54.3	55.0	55.5	55.8	56.0	55.3	54.3	52.7	51.3	54.5
2002	47.0	47.3	46.7	47.5	48.8	49.2	49.4	49.8	49.7	50.0	50.9	51.6	49.0
2003	50.2	50.2	50.0	48.7	48.1	47.8	48.2	48.3	48.2	48.7	49.4	49.8	49.0
2004	48.5	48.5	48.7	49.2	49.5	49.8	50.1	49.8	49.6	49.5	49.6	50.4	49.4
2005	48.9	49.1	49.0	48.9	48.8	49.2	49.4	49.4	49.3	49.6	49.7	50.2	49.3
2006	48.9	48.8	49.0	48.7	48.9	49.5	49.2	49.2	49.3	49.4	49.6	51.0	49.3
2007	50.2	49.8	49.8	50.1	50.2	50.4	50.4	50.6	50.6	51.1	51.9	53.0	50.7
2008	51.6	51.0	51.1	51.0	51.1	51.2	51.2	50.7	50.0	49.5	49.8	50.7	50.7
2009	48.4	47.7	47.4	48.0	47.7	47.7	47.6	47.5	47.2	47.3	47.0	48.0	47.6
2010	45.8	46.1	45.8	45.4	45.4	45.5	45.3	45.4	45.4	45.8	46.1	47.2	45.8
2011	45.3	44.8	44.9	45.1	45.1	45.2	45.6	45.8	45.8	45.8	45.6	46.2	45.4
Information													
2000	68.6	69.3	70.1	70.9	71.1	71.9	72.8	73.0	72.9	72.9	72.8	73.2	71.6
2001	72.9	72.8	72.4	71.3	70.8	70.5	68.5	67.8	66.6	65.2	64.8	64.0	69.0
2002	62.3	62.0	61.3	60.6	59.6	59.3	58.2	57.9	57.2	56.9	56.9	56.6	59.1
2003	56.1	55.9	55.4	54.7	54.5	54.2	54.0	53.8	53.5	53.2	53.3	53.2	54.3
2004	52.5	52.6	52.3	51.9	52.0	51.9	51.3	51.1	50.4	50.1	50.2	50.0	51.4
2005	49.2	49.0	48.9	48.4	48.4	48.2	47.9	47.7	47.5	47.4	47.7	47.9	48.2
2006	47.7	47.8	48.0	47.7	47.9	48.0	47.8	47.4	47.1	47.2	47.5	47.4	47.6
2007	47.0	47.2	47.2	47.9	48.1	48.5	48.3	48.3	48.0	48.3	48.7	48.9	48.0
2008	48.5	48.7	48.6	48.6	48.5	48.7	48.7	48.5	48.0	48.0	48.2	48.2	48.4
2009	47.5	47.2	47.1	46.7	46.4	46.4	46.2	45.9	45.5	45.3	45.4	45.4	46.3
2010	45.1	44.9	44.9	44.7	44.8	45.1	45.0	45.0	44.9	45.0	45.5	45.5	45.0
2011	45.3	45.2	44.8	45.1	45.0	45.1	44.8	43.8	43.0	43.2	44.2	43.9	44.5
Financial Activities													
2000	95.0	95.4	96.0	95.5	95.8	96.6	96.8	96.9	96.6	96.5	96.8	97.7	96.3
2001	96.1	96.3	96.2	96.1	96.1	96.6	95.8	95.4	94.6	94.6	94.6	95.0	95.6
2002	93.5	93.9	93.9	93.5	93.8	94.6	94.5	95.1	95.0	95.8	96.7	97.4	94.8
2003	96.5	96.8	96.9	97.5	98.0	98.7	99.1	99.5	98.9	98.5	98.1	98.6	98.1
2004	97.1	97.4	97.5	97.7	97.9	98.5	98.5	98.4	98.2	98.1	98.0	98.6	98.0
2005	97.3	97.9	98.5	98.8	99.2	99.7	100.3	100.5	100.7	100.6	101.0	101.8	99.7
2006	99.6	99.8	100.0	100.1	100.8	101.4	101.3	101.3	100.9	100.5	100.5	101.1	100.6
2007	99.4	99.9	99.9	100.0	100.1	100.5	100.4	100.0	99.1	98.8	98.7	98.8	99.6
2008	97.5	97.7	98.1	97.8	97.6	98.0	97.9	97.3	96.4	96.0	95.5	95.6	97.1
2009	93.7	93.5	93.0	93.2	93.3	93.0	92.9	92.6	92.0	92.0	91.7	92.1	92.8
2010	90.5	90.4	90.4	90.5	90.5	90.9	91.2	91.2	90.8	91.0	90.9	91.4	90.8
2011	90.2	90.1	90.1	90.2	90.3	90.9	90.3	90.3	90.1	90.7	90.4	90.9	90.4

Employment by Industry: Denver–Aurora–Broomfield, CO, Selected Years, 2000–2011—*Continued*

(Numbers in thousands, not seasonally adjusted)

Industry and year	January	February	March	April	May	June	July	August	September	October	November	December	Annual average
Professional and Business Services													
2000	189.7	190.1	192.6	195.6	197.6	200.6	201.1	202.3	202.5	201.5	201.1	202.1	198.1
2001	193.9	194.9	195.6	197.3	197.2	198.4	197.4	196.8	192.9	189.6	187.0	187.5	194.0
2002	178.9	179.8	180.3	183.5	184.6	185.3	183.6	185.4	183.3	181.2	180.1	180.3	182.2
2003	175.3	175.2	175.5	177.6	178.8	181.1	181.1	182.8	180.7	181.6	180.2	182.1	179.3
2004	176.1	177.8	179.8	184.7	184.9	187.7	188.9	189.2	188.3	187.7	187.0	188.8	185.1
2005	184.3	184.8	186.7	191.1	191.8	194.5	195.9	196.5	195.8	195.1	194.8	196.9	192.4
2006	190.2	192.2	193.8	197.0	199.6	203.5	203.4	204.7	203.9	203.8	203.3	204.6	200.0
2007	201.6	202.7	205.5	208.3	211.1	215.3	215.3	216.6	216.5	215.3	214.3	215.5	211.5
2008	209.7	211.5	212.3	216.3	216.3	218.7	218.0	219.8	217.8	216.2	214.2	212.8	215.3
2009	205.7	202.8	202.7	203.4	203.4	204.1	203.3	202.6	200.9	201.2	201.4	201.3	202.7
2010	195.5	196.4	198.4	201.8	203.5	205.7	206.8	207.1	204.0	205.8	205.6	204.9	203.0
2011	202.6	202.8	203.5	208.7	210.6	211.9	213.8	214.0	213.6	214.9	215.5	214.0	210.5
Education and Health Services													
2000	99.8	100.5	100.6	101.4	101.7	102.7	102.4	103.1	103.7	103.7	104.5	105.2	102.4
2001	104.3	105.2	105.7	105.8	106.2	106.3	106.0	106.7	106.4	108.2	108.8	109.1	106.6
2002	108.0	108.6	109.0	109.8	110.0	109.7	109.6	110.2	110.4	111.0	111.4	111.8	110.0
2003	111.3	112.2	112.3	113.1	113.1	113.1	113.0	113.1	113.4	114.1	114.4	114.6	113.1
2004	114.2	115.2	115.7	115.9	116.2	116.1	115.6	116.2	117.0	117.9	118.3	118.5	116.4
2005	117.0	118.6	119.1	119.2	119.8	119.6	118.8	119.3	119.7	119.9	120.6	120.9	119.4
2006	120.3	121.7	122.0	122.7	123.1	123.0	122.3	122.9	123.5	124.7	125.1	125.5	123.1
2007	124.5	126.0	126.8	127.2	127.9	127.8	127.3	127.9	128.5	129.6	130.7	131.5	128.0
2008	130.0	131.8	132.0	132.5	133.4	133.3	132.8	133.8	134.5	136.1	137.1	136.8	133.7
2009	135.7	136.8	136.9	137.3	137.7	137.7	137.5	137.9	138.1	139.5	140.3	140.7	138.0
2010	139.6	140.8	141.7	142.1	142.7	142.7	142.1	143.0	143.4	144.5	145.4	145.7	142.8
2011	144.8	145.9	146.4	147.0	147.5	147.3	146.9	147.8	148.7	149.6	151.1	149.5	147.7
Leisure and Hospitality													
2000	108.1	109.3	112.0	113.8	116.7	120.9	121.9	122.0	118.6	115.5	114.6	114.5	115.7
2001	111.4	111.9	113.7	114.7	117.6	122.6	121.7	122.0	118.1	113.9	113.1	113.9	116.2
2002	109.8	110.0	110.8	114.3	117.8	121.6	120.4	120.9	118.0	115.2	114.2	114.6	115.6
2003	110.4	109.7	110.3	112.9	116.1	119.4	119.4	120.6	117.2	116.0	114.8	115.0	115.2
2004	111.4	110.8	113.2	117.1	120.0	123.5	123.4	124.0	120.5	118.2	117.5	117.9	118.1
2005	114.2	114.9	116.9	119.5	123.3	127.3	127.4	127.1	123.9	122.1	120.5	121.1	121.5
2006	118.0	118.1	120.0	122.4	126.0	130.7	131.2	132.0	128.1	125.9	125.5	125.2	125.3
2007	120.4	120.5	123.7	125.8	130.4	134.8	134.3	134.9	130.9	129.2	128.2	128.8	128.5
2008	124.4	124.6	126.7	129.1	133.5	137.9	136.8	136.4	132.1	129.1	126.8	125.8	130.3
2009	120.9	119.9	121.9	124.2	128.2	131.6	132.2	132.3	127.8	125.9	123.5	122.7	125.9
2010	119.5	119.1	121.4	125.3	128.2	132.9	133.6	134.3	130.6	129.8	127.4	127.4	127.5
2011	124.0	123.5	126.4	129.2	132.7	137.5	137.3	135.9	131.8	129.5	127.8	127.1	130.2
Other Services													
2000	43.4	43.1	43.6	42.9	43.2	44.2	44.4	44.3	43.8	43.6	43.6	43.9	43.7
2001	43.4	42.9	43.4	43.3	43.6	44.3	44.0	44.1	43.6	43.4	43.5	43.6	43.6
2002	43.7	43.7	43.9	44.1	44.2	44.7	44.8	44.8	44.1	43.8	43.9	43.9	44.1
2003	44.1	43.7	43.6	43.9	44.1	44.8	44.6	44.5	43.7	43.8	43.9	44.1	44.1
2004	44.2	43.9	44.2	44.4	44.8	45.5	45.6	45.8	45.5	45.5	45.3	45.4	45.0
2005	45.4	45.1	45.3	45.3	45.4	45.9	45.6	45.6	45.2	45.0	44.7	45.0	45.3
2006	45.7	45.5	45.9	46.1	46.3	47.1	46.7	46.8	46.4	46.2	46.2	46.4	46.3
2007	46.3	46.3	46.8	46.9	47.1	47.7	47.4	47.5	47.2	47.3	47.2	47.5	47.1
2008	47.8	47.9	48.2	47.9	48.3	48.7	49.0	49.1	48.9	48.7	48.3	47.8	48.4
2009	47.9	47.3	47.4	47.0	47.5	47.8	47.9	47.8	47.3	47.3	47.1	47.1	47.5
2010	47.1	46.9	47.0	46.9	47.3	47.8	48.0	48.1	47.5	47.3	47.5	47.4	47.4
2011	47.4	47.3	47.6	47.9	48.2	48.8	49.0	49.5	49.5	50.4	50.1	50.0	48.8
Government													
2000	149.6	153.5	155.1	155.8	159.0	156.0	149.8	150.9	156.9	156.6	157.8	158.7	155.0
2001	154.4	158.2	157.7	158.3	159.2	159.1	153.9	154.8	160.7	161.1	162.9	162.8	158.6
2002	159.5	162.7	164.1	164.4	165.7	164.6	158.9	160.4	164.3	166.1	166.9	166.5	163.7
2003	161.8	165.0	165.5	165.4	167.4	165.9	159.0	159.9	164.2	164.3	164.6	163.7	163.9
2004	159.1	162.6	163.9	165.3	165.9	164.8	157.9	158.2	164.2	165.5	166.2	166.0	163.3
2005	160.4	164.5	164.9	166.5	167.2	165.6	159.6	158.7	166.2	166.7	167.1	167.0	164.5
2006	162.6	166.5	167.6	167.1	168.7	168.3	161.1	161.9	167.8	168.0	168.9	169.2	166.5
2007	163.9	169.0	170.3	170.7	171.8	170.8	163.4	164.3	171.7	172.5	173.4	173.0	169.6
2008	167.9	172.3	173.6	174.2	176.3	174.5	167.7	170.5	175.4	177.4	178.3	177.3	173.8
2009	172.8	175.9	177.3	178.3	180.3	177.8	169.0	170.1	177.2	179.6	178.9	177.7	176.2
2010	171.9	177.6	178.8	179.8	185.2	180.2	172.8	171.4	178.6	181.1	181.5	179.5	178.2
2011	173.9	179.3	180.0	181.2	182.4	179.8	170.6	170.2	177.2	178.5	178.6	177.4	177.4

Employment by Industry: Detroit–Warren–Livonia, MI, Selected Years, 2000–2011

(Numbers in thousands, not seasonally adjusted)

Industry and year	January	February	March	April	May	June	July	August	September	October	November	December	Annual average
Total Nonfarm													
2000	2,158.6	2,160.9	2,175.0	2,208.6	2,235.9	2,247.7	2,169.3	2,190.1	2,200.8	2,223.1	2,232.1	2,233.6	2,203.0
2001	2,122.8	2,139.7	2,149.1	2,154.7	2,173.7	2,179.9	2,094.6	2,108.0	2,119.8	2,127.2	2,130.2	2,137.5	2,136.4
2002	2,046.9	2,056.7	2,068.8	2,086.2	2,111.8	2,119.1	2,058.0	2,078.2	2,091.4	2,103.0	2,111.8	2,114.5	2,087.2
2003	2,050.2	2,049.9	2,059.7	2,065.3	2,092.2	2,100.9	2,016.8	2,045.5	2,060.6	2,071.2	2,078.5	2,080.6	2,064.3
2004	2,008.9	2,010.1	2,022.3	2,045.9	2,069.3	2,072.2	1,990.9	2,033.4	2,058.5	2,069.7	2,080.3	2,078.8	2,045.0
2005	2,004.8	2,019.9	2,020.4	2,046.3	2,070.7	2,072.0	2,000.1	2,029.2	2,059.5	2,058.4	2,072.1	2,065.8	2,043.3
2006	1,987.5	1,990.7	1,998.7	2,010.8	2,029.2	2,034.6	1,952.8	1,981.3	2,000.4	1,994.2	2,009.2	2,006.2	1,999.6
2007	1,935.2	1,947.8	1,951.7	1,964.8	1,989.7	1,993.3	1,927.8	1,956.3	1,966.2	1,959.5	1,976.9	1,969.5	1,961.6
2008	1,907.0	1,908.5	1,904.3	1,908.1	1,928.2	1,936.7	1,866.3	1,886.5	1,893.7	1,893.3	1,885.0	1,866.0	1,898.6
2009	1,751.3	1,760.5	1,757.2	1,757.4	1,749.4	1,738.5	1,706.1	1,716.3	1,733.7	1,744.6	1,743.7	1,739.8	1,741.5
2010	1,694.9	1,698.9	1,702.5	1,726.7	1,751.0	1,758.7	1,724.2	1,728.1	1,751.1	1,768.1	1,771.8	1,768.6	1,737.1
2011	1,732.5	1,738.4	1,751.2	1,769.4	1,787.8	1,795.6	1,764.5	1,774.8	1,783.4	1,802.3	1,803.7	1,799.9	1,775.3
Total Private													
2000	1,924.3	1,924.5	1,935.9	1,968.1	1,992.6	2,009.6	1,967.7	1,992.9	1,976.0	1,983.1	1,989.9	1,992.2	1,971.4
2001	1,887.0	1,900.0	1,908.3	1,913.1	1,931.7	1,942.6	1,890.5	1,907.0	1,891.8	1,886.2	1,887.2	1,893.9	1,903.3
2002	1,812.7	1,817.6	1,828.0	1,846.7	1,870.2	1,880.0	1,852.5	1,875.9	1,863.3	1,860.5	1,868.4	1,871.7	1,854.1
2003	1,810.7	1,805.9	1,815.7	1,820.1	1,846.4	1,857.2	1,802.0	1,834.0	1,831.6	1,822.0	1,829.4	1,832.3	1,825.6
2004	1,769.6	1,766.8	1,777.7	1,802.4	1,824.3	1,832.1	1,780.1	1,825.7	1,824.1	1,827.7	1,836.0	1,837.2	1,808.6
2005	1,769.8	1,779.0	1,779.4	1,804.8	1,827.4	1,834.0	1,793.0	1,823.6	1,826.2	1,820.3	1,831.5	1,828.3	1,809.8
2006	1,756.2	1,753.8	1,760.6	1,773.2	1,790.5	1,800.3	1,745.4	1,777.6	1,773.6	1,760.5	1,773.7	1,773.5	1,769.9
2007	1,706.7	1,716.0	1,717.6	1,732.1	1,754.3	1,762.1	1,722.9	1,752.6	1,746.0	1,733.5	1,750.4	1,744.4	1,736.6
2008	1,687.1	1,684.6	1,679.9	1,684.1	1,702.5	1,714.0	1,663.9	1,683.0	1,676.3	1,670.1	1,660.9	1,645.0	1,679.3
2009	1,534.7	1,540.1	1,535.8	1,534.4	1,528.0	1,519.5	1,508.5	1,519.0	1,522.1	1,527.8	1,526.6	1,525.1	1,526.8
2010	1,485.3	1,485.2	1,488.2	1,510.8	1,532.1	1,545.0	1,530.2	1,539.0	1,548.2	1,560.8	1,565.1	1,563.5	1,529.5
2011	1,533.3	1,534.9	1,547.6	1,566.1	1,587.7	1,597.0	1,583.5	1,594.8	1,587.8	1,601.0	1,602.3	1,601.5	1,578.1
Goods-Producing													
2000	473.0	474.9	477.7	491.5	498.8	502.6	485.5	497.6	491.5	491.5	489.1	483.7	488.1
2001	446.5	457.9	457.7	459.1	462.5	464.4	445.1	452.5	452.3	448.0	443.9	444.3	452.9
2002	409.5	415.4	416.5	422.0	426.5	431.3	420.1	430.3	426.7	424.9	424.1	420.9	422.4
2003	400.0	396.1	398.2	395.2	403.9	409.2	378.9	403.4	402.5	395.9	397.9	395.3	398.0
2004	377.2	375.8	380.8	386.5	391.9	392.0	357.3	393.1	393.2	392.0	391.9	386.1	384.8
2005	363.8	369.9	365.1	369.1	379.9	381.7	353.8	375.5	379.5	377.0	379.5	371.7	372.2
2006	345.9	346.3	349.9	356.2	362.0	362.0	326.5	350.9	350.2	342.2	347.4	341.3	348.4
2007	316.6	328.1	328.3	331.0	336.1	338.5	317.7	337.6	335.1	322.3	328.8	323.5	328.6
2008	306.4	307.7	301.8	298.7	302.5	314.1	283.6	300.6	299.8	296.7	293.5	282.0	299.0
2009	233.9	243.6	243.7	241.1	228.9	226.2	226.6	236.2	239.8	241.0	236.1	232.8	235.8
2010	226.4	224.1	224.2	231.9	237.9	243.4	241.9	240.8	249.9	251.1	249.8	247.1	239.0
2011	241.7	243.2	245.4	251.9	258.6	264.3	258.1	264.8	265.9	265.9	264.7	262.2	257.2
Mining, Logging, and Construction													
2000	85.5	85.2	88.5	95.5	99.6	102.5	103.9	102.8	101.8	100.5	98.4	93.7	96.5
2001	84.7	84.0	86.1	90.3	95.8	98.3	99.3	99.2	97.9	97.0	95.7	93.3	93.5
2002	83.5	81.8	82.7	87.0	92.3	94.9	95.8	95.4	93.1	92.0	89.9	86.2	89.6
2003	76.0	73.8	74.3	79.5	87.8	91.9	93.0	91.9	90.8	90.3	88.4	85.3	85.3
2004	75.2	74.0	75.8	82.0	87.2	90.8	93.2	92.3	91.0	90.7	89.5	85.7	85.6
2005	76.6	74.8	75.8	81.2	86.5	89.9	92.0	90.4	88.9	87.6	85.9	80.7	84.2
2006	71.5	70.1	70.9	74.6	80.0	82.6	82.8	81.8	79.8	78.5	76.8	72.8	76.9
2007	64.9	62.4	64.4	67.1	72.7	75.5	77.9	77.7	76.4	74.0	71.8	68.1	71.1
2008	61.0	58.6	58.6	61.6	66.8	68.9	69.2	68.9	67.4	66.5	63.3	57.8	64.1
2009	49.8	48.4	48.1	49.7	53.7	54.8	55.2	54.7	53.6	54.0	52.3	49.0	51.9
2010	43.5	42.0	43.7	47.4	51.0	53.1	55.5	56.1	55.4	55.8	54.5	51.5	50.8
2011	46.6	45.3	46.3	49.8	54.3	58.1	59.5	61.6	60.6	59.2	57.1	52.5	54.2
Manufacturing													
2000	387.5	389.7	389.2	396.0	399.2	400.1	381.6	394.8	389.7	391.0	390.7	390.0	391.6
2001	361.8	373.9	371.6	368.8	366.7	366.1	345.8	353.3	354.4	351.0	348.2	351.0	359.4
2002	326.0	333.6	333.8	335.0	334.2	336.4	324.3	334.9	333.6	332.9	334.2	334.7	332.8
2003	324.0	322.3	323.9	315.7	316.1	317.3	285.9	311.5	311.7	305.6	309.5	310.0	312.8
2004	302.0	301.8	305.0	304.5	304.7	301.2	264.1	300.8	302.2	301.3	302.4	300.4	299.2
2005	287.2	295.1	289.3	287.9	293.4	291.8	261.8	285.1	290.6	289.4	293.6	291.0	288.0
2006	274.4	276.2	279.0	281.6	282.0	279.4	243.7	269.1	270.4	263.7	270.6	268.5	271.6
2007	251.7	265.7	263.9	263.9	263.4	263.0	239.8	259.9	258.7	248.3	257.0	255.4	257.6
2008	245.4	249.1	243.2	237.1	235.7	245.2	214.4	231.7	232.4	230.2	230.2	224.2	234.9
2009	184.1	195.2	195.6	191.4	175.2	171.4	171.4	181.5	186.2	187.0	183.8	183.8	183.9
2010	182.9	182.1	180.5	184.5	186.9	190.3	186.4	184.7	194.5	195.3	195.3	195.6	188.3
2011	195.1	197.9	199.1	202.1	204.3	206.2	198.6	203.2	205.3	206.7	207.6	209.7	203.0
Service-Providing													
2000	1,685.6	1,686.0	1,697.3	1,717.1	1,737.1	1,745.1	1,683.8	1,692.5	1,709.3	1,731.6	1,743.0	1,749.9	1,714.9
2001	1,676.3	1,681.8	1,691.4	1,695.6	1,711.2	1,715.5	1,649.5	1,655.5	1,667.5	1,679.2	1,686.3	1,693.2	1,683.6
2002	1,637.4	1,641.3	1,652.3	1,664.2	1,685.3	1,687.8	1,637.9	1,647.9	1,664.7	1,678.1	1,687.7	1,693.6	1,664.9
2003	1,650.2	1,653.8	1,661.5	1,670.1	1,688.3	1,691.7	1,637.9	1,642.1	1,658.1	1,675.3	1,680.6	1,685.3	1,666.2
2004	1,631.7	1,634.3	1,641.5	1,659.4	1,677.4	1,680.2	1,633.6	1,640.3	1,665.3	1,677.7	1,688.4	1,692.7	1,660.2
2005	1,641.0	1,650.0	1,655.3	1,677.2	1,690.8	1,690.3	1,646.3	1,653.7	1,680.0	1,681.4	1,692.6	1,694.1	1,671.1
2006	1,641.6	1,644.4	1,648.8	1,654.6	1,667.2	1,672.6	1,626.3	1,630.4	1,650.2	1,652.0	1,661.8	1,664.9	1,651.2
2007	1,618.6	1,619.7	1,623.4	1,633.8	1,653.6	1,654.8	1,610.1	1,618.7	1,631.1	1,637.2	1,648.1	1,646.0	1,632.9
2008	1,600.6	1,600.8	1,602.5	1,609.4	1,625.7	1,622.6	1,582.7	1,585.9	1,593.9	1,596.6	1,591.5	1,584.0	1,599.7
2009	1,517.4	1,516.9	1,513.5	1,516.3	1,520.5	1,512.3	1,479.5	1,480.1	1,493.9	1,503.6	1,507.6	1,507.0	1,505.7
2010	1,468.5	1,474.8	1,478.3	1,494.8	1,513.1	1,515.3	1,482.3	1,487.3	1,501.2	1,517.0	1,522.0	1,521.5	1,498.0
2011	1,490.8	1,495.2	1,505.8	1,517.5	1,529.2	1,531.3	1,506.4	1,510	1,517.5	1,536.4	1,539	1,537.7	1,518.1

Employment by Industry: Detroit–Warren–Livonia, MI, Selected Years, 2000–2011—*Continued*

(Numbers in thousands, not seasonally adjusted)

Industry and year	January	February	March	April	May	June	July	August	September	October	November	December	Annual average
Trade, Transportation, and Utilities													
2000	412.6	408.7	409.7	412.3	416.2	420.1	410.6	414.2	413.1	421.5	431.6	440.9	417.6
2001	415.7	411.0	411.6	409.5	411.5	412.7	405.0	406.2	403.8	403.9	411.4	417.4	410.0
2002	394.6	389.4	392.0	390.9	396.3	398.2	393.0	394.8	395.3	394.2	402.6	408.2	395.8
2003	388.7	385.1	385.4	384.3	387.4	388.8	381.6	384.3	384.8	388.4	394.2	399.5	387.7
2004	379.9	376.8	376.9	378.9	383.7	385.1	378.8	380.8	378.7	383.2	391.4	396.9	382.6
2005	376.0	373.5	374.8	376.4	380.0	380.8	378.2	379.5	376.9	379.3	387.1	391.1	379.5
2006	371.8	367.6	368.7	369.7	372.8	374.4	368.8	370.9	369.4	371.5	379.6	384.1	372.4
2007	366.2	361.7	361.5	362.2	366.6	366.8	362.1	365.2	364.4	366.5	375.2	378.7	366.4
2008	363.3	358.3	358.9	357.0	359.7	360.5	356.2	356.4	355.5	354.4	357.2	358.3	358.0
2009	336.6	332.5	330.1	325.9	328.1	327.1	323.2	323.6	323.4	325.7	331.1	334.4	328.5
2010	320.2	317.3	318.8	321.7	325.8	327.6	325.8	327.4	325.7	332.1	337.7	341.3	326.8
2011	327.9	325.0	325.8	329.0	333.3	335.5	332.7	333.8	332.2	334.4	340.0	342.4	332.7
Wholesale Trade													
2000	101.4	101.6	101.8	103.0	103.8	104.6	103.3	103.2	102.5	103.1	102.9	103.7	102.9
2001	101.9	102.8	102.6	102.9	103.2	102.7	101.3	100.9	99.8	99.3	99.2	99.6	101.4
2002	98.1	98.5	98.6	98.5	99.1	99.6	98.5	98.8	98.4	97.4	97.7	98.3	98.5
2003	97.3	97.4	97.6	97.6	97.1	97.7	96.1	96.2	95.7	96.0	95.5	95.9	96.7
2004	93.5	93.5	93.9	94.3	94.7	95.0	94.7	94.4	93.7	93.9	93.9	94.1	94.1
2005	93.2	93.2	93.5	93.7	94.2	94.1	93.8	93.5	93.0	93.7	93.4	93.7	93.6
2006	92.4	92.5	92.7	93.0	93.3	93.8	93.0	92.7	91.9	91.8	91.7	91.9	92.6
2007	90.5	90.0	89.8	89.9	90.5	90.4	90.2	89.9	89.4	89.9	89.3	89.7	90.0
2008	89.2	88.8	88.9	89.0	89.3	89.2	88.7	88.5	88.2	87.7	86.7	86.0	88.4
2009	84.1	83.0	81.9	80.8	80.1	78.5	77.6	77.8	77.3	77.4	77.2	77.6	79.4
2010	76.1	76.4	76.7	77.2	77.9	78.3	78.3	78.9	78.5	79.5	79.6	80.0	78.1
2011	79.0	79.1	79.4	80.4	81.3	81.7	81.9	82.5	83.2	84.2	84.4	84.8	81.8
Retail Trade													
2000	240.9	237.0	237.9	237.9	241.1	243.8	238.5	241.0	240.9	246.6	256.9	265.6	244.0
2001	244.6	239.8	240.6	236.9	238.7	239.9	235.3	236.3	235.3	236.1	244.6	249.9	239.8
2002	230.8	225.3	226.9	225.9	229.9	231.0	228.0	228.5	229.4	228.9	237.2	242.9	230.4
2003	223.4	220.0	220.2	219.5	223.1	224.0	220.2	221.9	222.8	225.8	232.3	237.1	224.2
2004	221.9	218.6	218.7	219.9	224.3	225.1	220.3	221.6	220.1	223.1	231.3	236.3	223.4
2005	218.7	215.5	216.3	218.7	221.3	222.1	219.8	219.7	218.2	219.9	227.2	230.8	220.7
2006	215.1	210.9	211.5	212.3	214.7	215.7	213.8	214.4	213.5	216.2	223.8	226.6	215.7
2007	212.2	207.0	207.3	207.7	210.7	210.6	209.1	210.2	209.9	212.2	220.7	223.0	211.7
2008	211.3	206.4	206.6	205.6	208.0	207.8	206.6	206.7	205.7	206.3	210.0	211.4	207.7
2009	197.5	193.3	192.3	190.8	194.5	195.8	193.1	192.6	191.9	194.2	199.7	201.5	194.8
2010	190.4	187.4	188.1	190.8	193.8	194.6	193.5	194.0	192.1	196.5	201.6	203.9	193.9
2011	192.7	189.9	190.3	192.1	194.5	195.4	193.0	192.9	191.4	192.6	197.9	199.5	193.5
Transportation and Utilities													
2000	70.3	70.1	70.0	71.4	71.3	71.7	68.8	70.0	69.7	71.8	71.8	71.6	70.7
2001	69.2	68.4	68.4	69.7	69.6	70.1	68.4	69.0	68.7	68.5	67.6	67.9	68.8
2002	65.7	65.6	66.5	66.5	67.3	67.6	66.5	67.5	67.5	67.9	67.7	67.0	66.9
2003	68.0	67.7	67.6	67.2	67.2	67.1	65.3	66.2	66.3	66.6	66.4	66.5	66.8
2004	64.5	64.7	64.3	64.7	64.7	65.0	63.8	64.8	64.9	66.2	66.2	66.5	65.0
2005	64.1	64.8	65.0	64.0	64.5	64.6	64.6	66.3	65.7	65.7	66.5	66.6	65.2
2006	64.3	64.2	64.5	64.4	64.8	64.9	62.0	63.8	64.0	63.5	64.1	65.6	64.2
2007	63.5	64.7	64.4	64.6	65.4	65.8	62.8	65.1	65.1	64.4	65.2	66.0	64.8
2008	62.8	63.1	63.4	62.4	62.4	63.5	60.9	61.2	61.6	60.4	60.5	60.9	61.9
2009	55.0	56.2	55.9	54.3	53.5	52.8	52.5	53.2	54.2	54.1	54.2	55.3	54.3
2010	53.7	53.5	54.0	53.7	54.1	54.7	54.0	54.5	55.1	56.1	56.5	57.4	54.8
2011	56.2	56.0	56.1	56.5	57.5	58.4	57.8	58.4	57.6	57.6	57.7	58.1	57.3
Information													
2000	14.1	14.1	14.3	14.0	14.0	14.1	14.2	14.3	14.3	14.5	14.7	14.8	14.3
2001	14.6	14.6	14.6	14.4	14.4	14.5	14.2	14.1	14.0	13.9	14.1	13.9	14.3
2002	13.9	13.8	13.8	13.5	13.3	13.1	13.4	13.2	13.1	13.1	13.1	13.0	13.4
2003	13.6	13.5	13.7	12.9	12.9	13.0	12.7	12.8	12.9	12.8	12.9	12.8	13.0
2004	13.0	12.9	12.9	12.8	12.9	12.8	12.6	12.6	12.4	12.5	12.5	12.5	12.7
2005	12.4	12.2	12.2	12.1	12.2	12.3	12.3	12.2	12.2	11.9	12.0	12.0	12.2
2006	12.5	12.6	12.4	12.4	12.4	12.4	12.2	12.2	12.1	12.3	12.2	12.2	12.3
2007	12.3	12.3	12.2	12.1	12.2	12.2	12.2	12.1	12.1	12.2	12.2	12.0	12.2
2008	12.2	12.2	11.9	11.9	12.0	11.9	11.8	11.8	11.7	11.8	12.3	12.1	12.0
2009	11.9	12.0	11.7	11.6	11.5	11.3	11.0	11.1	11.0	10.7	10.7	10.7	11.3
2010	10.4	10.3	10.1	10.2	10.0	10.2	9.7	9.6	9.7	9.7	9.6	9.4	9.9
2011	9.7	9.6	9.4	9.4	9.4	9.2	9.1	9.1	9.1	9.1	9.1	8.9	9.3
Financial Activities													
2000	115.6	115.3	115.3	114.6	115.2	116.9	116.8	116.0	114.7	113.0	112.7	113.8	115.0
2001	112.7	114.1	114.6	113.9	115.2	116.3	115.6	115.6	113.9	112.8	113.0	115.4	114.4
2002	115.7	115.7	115.3	115.6	116.2	116.4	116.5	117.2	115.6	115.1	115.7	116.3	115.9
2003	116.7	116.7	116.7	118.7	119.8	120.7	120.3	120.2	118.2	116.9	116.3	116.9	118.2
2004	114.7	114.5	115.0	116.3	117.0	118.0	117.8	117.5	116.4	115.8	115.9	116.7	116.3
2005	116.1	116.2	116.2	116.7	116.9	118.1	117.4	117.4	116.1	115.7	115.7	115.7	116.5
2006	114.0	113.9	113.4	113.2	113.9	114.8	114.1	114.0	112.4	111.7	111.5	112.2	113.3
2007	111.0	110.8	110.5	111.1	111.4	112.2	112.1	111.1	109.0	108.0	107.6	107.5	110.2
2008	106.8	106.7	106.2	105.8	106.7	106.7	105.9	105.0	103.5	102.7	101.9	101.6	105.0
2009	99.9	99.4	98.8	98.8	99.2	99.2	98.8	98.3	97.0	96.0	95.6	95.6	98.1
2010	95.1	94.9	94.2	93.8	95.0	96.1	96.4	96.8	95.7	96.0	96.3	96.9	95.6
2011	96.5	96.7	97.3	97.5	97.8	98.9	99.1	99.3	98.5	98.3	97.5	98.7	98.0

Employment by Industry: Detroit–Warren–Livonia, MI, Selected Years, 2000–2011—*Continued*

(Numbers in thousands, not seasonally adjusted)

Industry and year	January	February	March	April	May	June	July	August	September	October	November	December	Annual average
Professional and Business Services													
2000	395.1	392.8	395.6	404.3	410.9	413.4	405.7	414.6	410.7	408.5	406.2	404.3	405.2
2001	382.8	383.9	385.2	385.3	387.1	389.1	375.9	383.6	378.6	376.5	373.2	371.6	381.1
2002	361.6	362.6	364.0	367.7	371.3	373.1	363.9	372.5	370.1	371.5	371.5	370.5	368.4
2003	361.6	360.2	361.3	365.9	370.2	372.1	361.9	368.2	367.0	360.4	362.0	361.7	364.4
2004	350.4	349.4	349.9	358.4	363.7	367.0	361.8	368.7	369.0	372.7	373.1	373.5	363.1
2005	363.2	363.7	363.0	371.2	373.7	375.7	370.1	375.7	377.4	373.8	374.3	373.6	371.3
2006	361.2	357.7	356.6	358.8	360.4	364.6	358.1	363.9	362.4	361.5	363.2	362.2	360.9
2007	349.0	349.0	346.4	353.2	354.9	357.0	351.5	357.7	355.7	356.3	359.2	355.1	353.8
2008	343.3	343.0	341.6	346.6	348.5	346.7	337.0	338.3	335.7	338.2	333.4	329.0	340.1
2009	306.9	305.5	301.8	301.0	297.1	293.0	291.5	292.7	296.3	299.1	299.4	298.6	298.6
2010	293.1	295.6	294.9	301.5	304.4	306.7	301.0	305.5	310.8	315.7	316.9	313.8	305.0
2011	312.7	314.9	318.8	323.8	327.6	325.4	323.7	327.4	324.7	333.1	334.0	330.7	324.7
Education and Health Services													
2000	232.7	235.3	236.4	238.0	237.7	238.7	236.0	236.3	237.3	238.9	241.7	240.5	237.5
2001	235.4	237.8	239.3	241.3	242.8	244.5	240.7	241.4	241.9	244.3	246.6	246.2	241.9
2002	243.4	245.4	246.3	250.0	250.5	252.2	247.9	248.1	247.6	251.1	252.8	252.3	249.0
2003	250.9	253.5	253.7	252.0	252.1	250.7	249.5	249.0	251.9	254.5	256.3	255.7	252.5
2004	252.6	255.0	255.8	258.0	258.1	255.9	256.5	256.0	258.9	261.7	263.4	263.8	258.0
2005	259.5	262.7	263.8	265.5	265.5	263.4	262.2	262.9	267.1	270.8	272.7	273.3	265.8
2006	269.0	271.0	272.8	270.7	272.0	271.0	268.2	267.9	273.1	272.7	274.2	275.2	271.5
2007	272.5	275.2	276.4	275.9	277.3	277.8	273.4	273.3	277.4	278.9	280.7	280.8	276.6
2008	277.8	279.9	280.2	280.5	282.2	280.8	278.3	278.1	281.0	283.3	284.1	284.1	280.9
2009	279.8	283.0	283.9	283.3	284.7	284.2	280.2	280.5	281.6	284.6	286.4	285.6	283.2
2010	281.3	283.9	284.7	283.9	284.8	283.7	282.2	282.2	283.5	288.4	289.4	289.3	284.8
2011	285.8	287.8	288.8	288.9	288.9	287.6	286.4	287.0	287.7	291.3	291.4	292.4	288.7
Leisure and Hospitality													
2000	169.6	170.8	172.5	177.6	183.2	186.1	182.0	182.4	178.3	179.9	177.6	177.3	178.1
2001	167.5	167.7	170.7	175.1	182.1	184.9	179.3	179.1	175.5	176.8	174.0	173.3	175.5
2002	165.5	166.3	169.6	175.3	182.3	182.9	183.5	184.7	181.3	180.4	178.5	178.4	177.4
2003	171.6	171.2	174.5	180.0	187.9	190.5	185.2	183.8	183.3	182.7	179.6	179.9	180.9
2004	172.7	172.9	175.8	181.3	187.5	189.9	187.6	188.6	186.1	182.2	178.9	178.5	181.8
2005	171.6	173.1	176.0	183.8	189.4	191.0	188.3	189.7	186.9	182.1	180.1	180.1	182.7
2006	174.3	176.9	178.7	184.3	188.3	191.8	189.5	189.8	186.8	182.3	179.0	179.4	183.4
2007	174.0	173.7	176.8	181.1	189.3	190.6	187.8	189.2	186.7	184.1	181.6	181.3	183.0
2008	174.0	173.3	175.7	179.7	186.0	188.0	186.0	187.5	183.9	179.4	176.1	175.9	180.5
2009	166.0	164.3	166.3	173.2	178.1	177.5	176.7	176.8	174.3	171.1	167.5	167.1	171.6
2010	160.6	160.7	162.6	169.5	174.8	177.5	174.3	176.2	173.4	170.7	168.5	168.4	169.8
2011	163.0	161.9	165.7	169.8	175.5	178.4	177.6	176.6	173.7	171.2	168.3	168.8	170.9
Other Services													
2000	88.9	89.9	91.6	93.1	93.4	94.4	93.4	94.0	92.9	92.4	93.0	93.3	92.5
2001	89.2	90.3	91.8	91.7	93.1	93.3	91.5	92.2	90.0	89.0	89.7	90.6	91.0
2002	87.9	88.5	90.0	91.6	93.2	94.1	93.5	94.5	93.5	90.6	90.4	91.6	91.6
2003	88.0	89.8	92.5	91.3	92.2	92.0	92.0	92.7	91.9	91.1	90.7	90.9	91.3
2004	90.2	90.6	91.8	91.1	90.3	91.8	88.1	88.9	90.0	88.3	89.3	89.5	90.0
2005	87.7	88.4	89.0	90.7	90.4	91.7	91.5	91.6	91.4	91.1	91.3	91.9	90.6
2006	89.5	89.7	90.2	90.2	90.7	91.3	90.0	90.1	89.7	88.9	89.0	89.2	89.9
2007	87.3	87.6	88.0	87.6	88.4	89.0	88.3	88.6	88.1	87.8	87.6	87.9	88.0
2008	85.8	86.0	86.2	86.6	87.5	87.7	87.7	87.6	87.1	86.4	85.5	85.3	86.6
2009	83.4	83.5	83.5	83.6	84.3	84.6	84.0	83.7	82.7	83.2	83.0	83.3	83.6
2010	81.7	81.9	82.1	81.7	82.4	82.8	81.8	81.5	80.8	80.4	80.2	80.2	81.5
2011	79.3	79.3	79.7	79.7	80.2	81.0	80.2	80.1	79.5	81.1	80.4	80.4	80.1
Government													
2000	234.3	236.4	239.1	240.5	243.3	238.1	201.6	197.2	224.8	240.0	242.2	241.4	231.6
2001	235.8	239.7	240.8	241.6	242.0	237.3	204.1	201.0	228.0	241.0	243.0	243.6	233.2
2002	234.2	239.1	240.8	239.5	241.6	237.1	205.5	202.3	228.1	242.5	243.4	242.8	233.1
2003	239.5	244.0	244.0	245.2	245.8	243.7	214.8	211.5	229.0	249.2	249.1	248.3	238.7
2004	239.3	243.3	244.6	243.5	245.0	240.1	210.8	207.7	234.4	242.0	244.3	241.6	236.4
2005	235.0	240.9	241.0	241.5	243.3	238.0	207.1	205.6	233.3	238.1	240.6	237.5	233.5
2006	231.3	236.9	238.1	237.6	238.7	234.3	207.4	203.7	226.8	233.7	235.5	232.7	229.7
2007	228.5	231.8	234.1	232.7	235.4	231.2	204.9	203.7	220.2	226.0	226.5	225.1	225.0
2008	219.9	223.9	224.4	224.0	225.7	222.7	202.4	203.5	217.4	223.2	224.1	221.0	219.4
2009	216.6	220.4	221.4	223.0	221.4	219.0	197.6	197.3	211.6	216.8	217.1	214.7	214.7
2010	209.6	213.7	214.3	215.9	218.9	213.7	194.0	189.1	202.9	207.3	206.7	205.1	207.6
2011	199.2	203.5	203.6	203.3	200.1	198.6	181.0	180.0	195.6	201.3	201.4	198.4	197.2

Employment by Industry: El Paso, TX, Selected Years, 2000–2011

(Numbers in thousands, not seasonally adjusted)

Industry and year	January	February	March	April	May	June	July	August	September	October	November	December	Annual average
Total Nonfarm													
2000	252.0	253.6	255.4	255.0	256.3	255.9	254.3	256.7	259.1	257.9	259.5	260.7	256.4
2001	254.9	255.6	257.6	255.1	256.3	255.5	251.4	254.7	257.0	253.9	254.8	254.7	255.1
2002	251.6	251.9	254.7	255.3	255.7	254.7	251.7	256.1	261.0	258.6	260.2	261.1	256.1
2003	254.3	255.1	255.4	255.7	254.8	251.2	249.9	253.4	257.4	257.0	258.0	258.3	255.0
2004	254.3	255.8	256.0	256.1	257.3	255.5	255.3	255.7	258.9	259.8	260.7	260.5	257.2
2005	255.2	256.6	258.3	260.1	260.9	260.5	257.3	259.5	264.2	264.2	265.4	266.0	260.7
2006	261.2	262.9	265.4	263.9	264.8	263.5	259.8	262.6	267.7	267.7	269.4	271.3	265.0
2007	265.5	267.0	269.0	270.1	271.5	269.7	266.9	269.0	274.5	277.5	279.0	281.2	271.7
2008	277.4	279.2	279.8	278.3	279.8	276.8	272.5	274.9	277.5	280.5	280.5	280.3	278.1
2009	274.9	274.1	273.8	274.6	273.9	273.1	268.0	269.2	272.6	274.9	276.0	277.0	273.5
2010	273.1	274.6	277.5	278.8	280.2	279.3	272.2	274.3	278.5	279.2	280.8	282.1	277.6
2011	278.1	278.7	279.9	281.6	281.1	279.3	276.3	277.4	281.9	281.5	283.0	284.3	280.3
Total Private													
2000	196.0	196.5	198.2	197.5	198.7	200.6	198.9	201.1	202.8	200.8	202.3	203.3	199.7
2001	197.4	197.2	199.1	196.5	197.6	198.4	197.0	198.8	198.3	195.3	195.7	196.5	197.3
2002	193.2	192.5	195.5	196.6	197.9	199.0	198.3	201.1	201.6	198.4	199.8	201.7	198.0
2003	195.0	194.4	194.8	195.2	195.3	194.6	194.4	196.4	196.9	196.6	197.4	198.8	195.8
2004	194.2	194.7	195.0	195.2	195.9	197.0	197.8	198.8	198.3	197.9	198.9	199.6	196.9
2005	194.0	194.6	196.3	198.3	199.0	201.2	200.8	202.5	203.6	202.5	203.9	205.3	200.2
2006	200.2	200.9	203.3	202.2	203.0	205.1	203.8	206.1	206.3	204.9	206.4	208.2	204.2
2007	202.4	203.3	205.2	205.2	206.4	207.6	207.4	209.4	209.6	211.1	212.4	214.7	207.9
2008	211.4	211.8	212.5	213.1	213.8	213.4	213.2	215.5	213.2	213.7	213.7	213.5	213.2
2009	207.9	206.6	206.4	205.7	205.4	206.3	206.1	207.2	205.4	205.2	206.3	207.5	206.3
2010	203.7	204.4	207.3	208.1	208.8	210.3	208.2	209.7	209.2	209.6	210.9	212.3	208.5
2011	208.8	209.2	210.5	211.7	211.4	211.4	212.8	214.4	215.6	215.0	216.2	218.1	212.9
Goods-Producing													
2000	51.5	51.5	51.4	50.2	50.5	50.7	49.4	50.7	51.0	49.6	49.5	49.2	50.4
2001	47.7	47.7	47.7	46.0	46.1	46.2	45.7	46.3	46.3	44.9	44.2	44.1	46.1
2002	42.9	41.6	42.4	42.1	41.7	42.0	41.6	43.1	43.2	41.5	40.9	40.8	42.0
2003	39.7	39.6	39.4	39.0	38.3	37.8	37.3	37.7	37.8	36.8	36.4	36.1	38.0
2004	35.3	35.5	35.4	35.4	35.6	35.7	35.6	36.0	36.1	36.3	36.0	35.3	35.7
2005	34.2	34.3	34.6	34.7	35.2	35.2	34.7	35.0	35.6	34.8	34.8	34.7	34.8
2006	34.3	34.2	34.4	34.4	34.7	35.5	34.8	34.8	34.7	34.3	34.1	34.4	34.6
2007	33.7	33.9	34.2	34.4	34.5	34.8	34.7	35.4	35.5	35.7	35.8	35.8	34.9
2008	35.3	35.3	35.2	35.6	35.7	35.5	35.4	35.6	35.4	35.0	34.8	34.3	35.3
2009	33.7	33.2	32.6	32.7	32.6	32.2	32.3	32.9	32.4	32.6	32.2	32.3	32.6
2010	31.8	31.9	32.0	32.2	32.1	32.1	32.3	33.1	32.7	32.0	31.8	31.5	32.1
2011	31.0	30.9	31.2	31.2	31.2	31.1	31.2	31.5	31.4	31.3	31.2	31.1	31.2
Mining, Logging, and Construction													
2000	12.9	12.8	12.9	12.6	12.8	12.9	12.5	12.6	12.7	12.5	12.5	12.6	12.7
2001	12.5	12.5	12.7	11.6	11.8	11.8	11.9	12.0	12.3	11.9	11.8	11.8	12.1
2002	11.7	11.7	12.0	11.6	11.5	11.8	11.7	12.0	12.0	11.7	11.7	11.6	11.8
2003	11.9	11.9	11.9	11.8	11.8	11.8	11.6	11.7	11.7	11.6	11.5	11.5	11.7
2004	11.1	11.2	11.3	11.3	11.4	11.6	11.7	11.6	11.6	11.9	11.8	11.8	11.5
2005	11.5	11.6	11.6	11.7	12.0	12.1	12.0	12.1	12.5	12.3	12.3	12.2	12.0
2006	12.2	12.2	12.4	12.5	12.6	12.9	12.8	12.8	12.9	12.9	13.0	13.2	12.7
2007	13.3	13.6	14.0	14.2	14.3	14.6	14.5	15.0	15.1	15.5	15.6	15.6	14.6
2008	15.2	15.2	15.3	15.7	15.8	15.6	15.7	15.9	15.9	15.8	15.7	15.6	15.6
2009	15.3	15.2	15.4	15.3	15.4	15.1	15.4	15.6	15.3	15.7	15.5	15.6	15.4
2010	15.5	15.6	15.7	15.8	15.7	15.6	15.5	15.6	15.3	14.7	14.6	14.3	15.3
2011	14.0	13.9	14.0	13.9	13.8	13.6	13.6	13.7	13.7	13.7	13.6	13.6	13.8
Manufacturing													
2000	38.6	38.7	38.5	37.6	37.7	37.8	36.9	38.1	38.3	37.1	37.0	36.6	37.7
2001	35.2	35.2	35.0	34.4	34.3	34.4	33.8	34.3	34.0	33.0	32.4	32.3	34.0
2002	31.2	29.9	30.4	30.5	30.2	30.2	29.9	31.1	31.2	29.8	29.2	29.2	30.2
2003	27.8	27.7	27.5	27.2	26.5	26.0	25.7	26.0	26.1	25.2	24.9	24.6	26.3
2004	24.2	24.3	24.1	24.1	24.2	24.1	23.9	24.4	24.5	24.4	24.2	23.5	24.2
2005	22.7	22.7	23.0	23.0	23.2	23.2	22.7	22.9	23.1	22.5	22.5	22.5	22.8
2006	22.1	22.0	22.0	21.9	22.1	22.6	22.0	22.0	21.8	21.4	21.1	21.2	21.9
2007	20.4	20.3	20.2	20.2	20.2	20.2	20.2	20.4	20.4	20.2	20.2	20.2	20.3
2008	20.1	20.1	19.9	19.9	19.9	19.9	19.7	19.7	19.5	19.2	19.1	18.7	19.6
2009	18.4	18.0	17.2	17.4	17.2	17.1	16.9	17.3	17.1	16.9	16.7	16.7	17.2
2010	16.3	16.3	16.3	16.4	16.4	16.5	16.8	17.5	17.4	17.3	17.2	17.2	16.8
2011	17.0	17.0	17.2	17.3	17.4	17.5	17.6	17.8	17.7	17.6	17.6	17.5	17.4
Service-Providing													
2000	200.5	202.1	204.0	204.8	205.8	205.2	204.9	206.0	208.1	208.3	210.0	211.5	205.9
2001	207.2	207.9	209.9	209.1	210.2	209.3	205.7	208.4	210.7	209.0	210.6	210.6	209.1
2002	208.7	210.3	212.3	213.2	214.0	212.7	210.1	213.0	217.8	217.1	219.3	220.3	214.1
2003	214.6	215.5	216.0	216.7	216.5	213.4	212.6	215.7	219.6	220.2	221.6	222.2	217.1
2004	219.0	220.3	220.6	220.7	221.7	219.8	219.7	219.7	222.8	223.5	224.7	225.2	221.5
2005	221.0	222.3	223.7	225.4	225.7	225.2	222.6	224.5	228.6	229.4	230.6	231.3	225.9
2006	226.9	228.7	231.0	229.5	230.1	228.0	225.0	227.8	233.0	233.4	235.3	236.9	230.5
2007	231.8	233.1	234.8	235.7	237.0	234.9	232.2	233.6	239.0	241.8	243.2	245.4	236.9
2008	242.1	243.9	244.6	242.7	244.1	241.3	237.1	239.3	242.1	245.5	245.7	246.0	242.9
2009	241.2	240.9	241.2	241.9	241.3	240.9	235.7	236.3	240.2	242.3	243.8	244.7	240.9
2010	241.3	242.7	245.5	246.6	248.1	247.2	239.9	241.2	245.8	247.2	249.0	250.6	245.4
2011	247.1	247.8	248.7	250.4	249.9	248.2	245.1	245.9	250.5	250.2	251.8	253.2	249.1

Employment by Industry: El Paso, TX, Selected Years, 2000–2011—*Continued*

(Numbers in thousands, not seasonally adjusted)

Industry and year	January	February	March	April	May	June	July	August	September	October	November	December	Annual average
Trade, Transportation, and Utilities													
2000	53.4	52.7	53.2	53.2	53.8	54.2	53.9	54.3	54.7	55.0	56.3	57.0	54.3
2001	54.6	53.6	54.2	53.7	53.8	53.7	53.7	53.8	53.1	52.9	54.1	54.8	53.8
2002	53.0	52.2	53.0	53.2	53.8	54.1	53.7	54.1	54.4	54.6	55.6	56.7	54.0
2003	54.3	53.4	53.9	54.5	54.6	54.6	54.8	55.6	55.6	56.0	57.3	58.1	55.2
2004	55.7	55.4	55.6	54.8	54.9	55.1	55.1	55.3	54.9	55.5	56.8	57.5	55.6
2005	54.9	54.5	54.9	55.3	55.4	55.8	56.1	56.7	56.9	57.0	58.7	59.2	56.3
2006	56.9	56.8	57.6	57.3	57.5	57.7	57.7	58.4	58.5	58.3	59.7	60.4	58.1
2007	58.0	57.6	58.2	58.4	58.6	58.7	58.7	59.2	59.6	60.3	61.4	62.2	59.2
2008	59.9	59.2	59.3	58.9	58.8	58.8	58.9	59.5	58.7	59.0	59.4	59.6	59.2
2009	56.5	55.4	55.4	54.6	54.4	54.6	54.6	54.7	54.8	54.7	55.6	56.4	55.1
2010	54.3	54.2	54.7	55.1	55.3	55.2	55.5	55.8	55.8	56.4	57.6	58.8	55.7
2011	56.2	55.7	56.0	56.4	56.4	56.5	57.0	57.3	57.7	57.8	58.8	59.9	57.1
Wholesale Trade													
2000	10.4	10.3	10.4	10.4	10.5	10.5	10.3	10.3	10.3	10.2	10.2	10.3	10.3
2001	10.1	10.1	10.2	10.1	10.1	10.1	10.1	10.1	10.1	9.9	9.9	9.9	10.1
2002	9.7	9.7	9.8	9.8	9.9	9.9	9.8	9.9	9.8	9.7	9.6	9.7	9.8
2003	9.6	9.5	9.6	9.7	9.8	9.8	9.9	10.0	10.0	10.1	10.2	10.3	9.9
2004	10.4	10.3	10.4	10.2	10.2	10.3	10.4	10.4	10.3	10.5	10.5	10.4	10.4
2005	10.1	10.1	10.2	10.2	10.3	10.3	10.3	10.4	10.5	10.4	10.5	10.6	10.3
2006	10.5	10.5	10.6	10.5	10.6	10.6	10.6	10.6	10.6	10.5	10.5	10.5	10.6
2007	10.5	10.5	10.6	10.8	10.8	10.9	10.8	10.9	10.9	11.0	11.0	11.1	10.8
2008	10.8	10.8	10.6	10.9	10.7	10.6	10.8	10.8	10.6	10.6	10.2	10.1	10.6
2009	9.8	9.7	9.6	9.4	9.3	9.3	9.4	9.3	9.3	9.3	9.3	9.4	9.4
2010	9.4	9.4	9.5	9.6	9.6	9.6	9.7	9.7	9.6	9.6	9.6	9.6	9.6
2011	9.5	9.5	9.6	9.6	9.7	9.7	9.9	9.9	9.9	9.9	9.9	10.0	9.8
Retail Trade													
2000	30.8	30.1	30.5	30.6	30.9	31.1	31.1	31.4	31.7	32.3	33.5	34.0	31.5
2001	32.3	31.5	32.0	31.6	31.6	31.5	31.7	32.0	31.2	31.3	32.5	33.1	31.9
2002	31.7	30.9	31.5	31.6	32.0	32.3	31.8	32.1	32.5	32.6	33.6	34.5	32.3
2003	32.6	31.9	32.2	32.6	32.6	32.6	32.7	33.4	33.3	33.6	34.8	35.5	33.2
2004	33.1	32.8	32.8	32.2	32.2	32.2	32.0	32.3	31.9	32.1	33.2	34.0	32.6
2005	31.9	31.4	31.6	31.9	31.9	32.2	32.4	32.8	32.8	33.2	34.6	35.1	32.7
2006	33.1	32.9	33.5	33.4	33.4	33.4	33.4	34.0	34.1	34.0	35.4	36.0	33.9
2007	34.0	33.5	34.0	33.9	34.1	34.1	34.2	34.6	35.0	35.8	36.8	37.4	34.8
2008	35.7	35.0	35.3	34.6	34.6	34.8	34.8	35.2	34.9	35.1	35.9	36.2	35.2
2009	33.9	33.0	33.1	32.7	32.6	32.8	32.6	32.9	33.0	33.0	33.9	34.4	33.2
2010	32.7	32.5	32.9	33.1	33.3	33.2	33.4	33.7	33.8	34.3	35.6	36.6	33.8
2011	34.3	33.7	33.9	34.2	34.2	34.3	34.5	34.7	35.0	35.1	36.1	36.9	34.7
Transportation and Utilities													
2000	12.2	12.3	12.3	12.2	12.4	12.6	12.5	12.6	12.7	12.5	12.6	12.7	12.5
2001	12.2	12.0	12.0	12.0	12.1	12.1	11.9	11.7	11.8	11.7	11.7	11.8	11.9
2002	11.6	11.6	11.7	11.8	11.9	11.9	12.1	12.1	12.1	12.3	12.4	12.5	12.0
2003	12.1	12.0	12.1	12.2	12.2	12.2	12.2	12.2	12.3	12.3	12.3	12.3	12.2
2004	12.2	12.3	12.4	12.4	12.5	12.6	12.7	12.6	12.7	12.9	13.1	13.1	12.6
2005	12.9	13.0	13.1	13.2	13.2	13.3	13.4	13.5	13.6	13.4	13.6	13.5	13.3
2006	13.3	13.4	13.5	13.4	13.5	13.7	13.7	13.8	13.8	13.8	13.8	13.9	13.6
2007	13.5	13.6	13.6	13.7	13.7	13.7	13.7	13.7	13.7	13.5	13.6	13.7	13.6
2008	13.4	13.4	13.4	13.4	13.5	13.4	13.3	13.5	13.2	13.3	13.3	13.3	13.4
2009	12.8	12.7	12.7	12.5	12.5	12.5	12.6	12.5	12.5	12.4	12.4	12.6	12.6
2010	12.2	12.3	12.3	12.4	12.4	12.4	12.4	12.4	12.4	12.5	12.4	12.6	12.4
2011	12.4	12.5	12.5	12.6	12.5	12.5	12.6	12.7	12.8	12.8	12.8	13.0	12.6
Information													
2000	4.9	4.8	4.9	4.9	4.9	4.9	4.9	4.9	4.9	4.8	4.9	5.0	4.9
2001	4.8	4.8	4.8	4.9	5.0	5.1	4.9	4.9	5.0	4.9	5.0	4.9	4.9
2002	5.0	4.9	4.9	5.0	5.0	5.0	5.1	5.2	5.2	5.2	5.3	5.5	5.1
2003	5.5	5.5	5.4	5.5	5.5	5.4	5.4	5.4	5.3	5.5	5.6	5.3	5.4
2004	5.1	5.1	5.0	4.9	4.9	4.9	4.9	4.9	4.8	4.9	4.8	4.9	4.9
2005	4.7	4.7	4.7	4.8	4.8	4.9	4.8	4.8	4.7	4.7	4.8	4.7	4.8
2006	4.7	4.7	4.9	4.6	4.7	4.9	4.6	4.6	4.7	4.8	4.8	5.0	4.8
2007	4.9	5.0	5.0	5.0	5.0	5.0	5.3	5.3	5.2	5.5	5.5	5.5	5.2
2008	5.7	5.7	5.7	5.6	5.8	5.8	5.5	5.5	5.4	5.4	5.4	5.4	5.6
2009	5.3	5.4	5.3	5.3	5.2	5.2	5.1	5.0	4.9	4.8	4.8	4.9	5.1
2010	5.0	5.0	5.0	5.1	5.1	5.3	5.2	5.1	5.0	5.0	5.1	5.0	5.1
2011	5.0	4.9	4.9	4.9	4.8	4.9	4.9	4.9	4.9	4.8	4.8	4.9	4.9
Financial Activities													
2000	10.2	10.1	10.1	10.1	10.1	10.3	10.3	10.3	10.3	10.3	10.3	10.4	10.2
2001	10.9	10.9	11.2	11.0	11.1	11.3	11.6	11.7	11.7	11.7	11.7	11.8	11.4
2002	11.8	11.9	12.0	11.8	11.8	11.8	11.8	11.7	11.7	11.8	12.0	12.0	11.8
2003	12.0	12.0	12.1	11.9	11.9	11.9	12.0	11.9	11.8	11.7	11.7	11.6	11.9
2004	11.5	11.6	11.6	11.4	11.3	11.4	11.4	11.4	11.4	11.4	11.3	11.4	11.4
2005	11.2	11.2	11.3	11.4	11.4	11.4	11.5	11.5	11.5	11.5	11.4	11.5	11.4
2006	11.2	11.3	11.3	11.0	11.0	11.1	11.1	11.2	11.3	11.3	11.4	11.5	11.2
2007	11.3	11.3	11.4	11.5	11.6	11.6	11.6	11.7	11.7	11.7	11.8	12.1	11.6
2008	12.1	12.2	12.2	11.9	12.0	12.1	12.2	12.3	12.2	12.3	12.2	12.2	12.2
2009	12.1	12.1	12.1	12.0	12.0	11.8	11.8	11.9	11.9	11.9	11.9	11.9	12.0
2010	11.5	11.5	11.5	11.6	11.6	11.6	11.8	11.8	11.7	11.9	11.9	12.0	11.7
2011	12.0	12.0	12.0	12.3	12.2	12.2	12.3	12.4	12.5	12.5	12.5	12.6	12.3

Employment by Industry: El Paso, TX, Selected Years, 2000–2011—*Continued*

(Numbers in thousands, not seasonally adjusted)

Industry and year	January	February	March	April	May	June	July	August	September	October	November	December	Annual average
Professional and Business Services													
2000	23.8	24.6	25.4	25.2	25.2	25.6	25.0	25.3	25.8	26.0	26.3	26.5	25.4
2001	25.3	25.5	25.7	25.3	25.1	25.2	24.4	24.9	24.9	25.1	24.6	24.7	25.1
2002	24.9	25.5	25.8	26.1	26.1	26.3	26.5	26.8	27.1	27.4	27.3	27.9	26.5
2003	25.6	25.5	24.8	25.0	25.0	24.5	24.8	25.3	26.0	26.6	26.5	27.4	25.6
2004	26.6	26.5	26.1	27.2	27.1	27.4	28.0	28.1	27.8	26.9	26.9	26.9	27.1
2005	25.6	25.8	25.9	26.2	25.8	26.4	26.8	27.3	27.8	27.9	28.1	28.7	26.9
2006	28.2	28.3	28.6	28.6	28.7	29.2	29.3	30.7	30.9	31.0	31.4	31.6	29.7
2007	30.5	30.9	30.8	30.1	29.9	29.8	29.8	30.3	30.2	30.9	30.8	31.4	30.5
2008	30.7	31.0	31.0	31.1	30.8	30.7	31.2	32.4	31.6	32.1	31.8	31.8	31.4
2009	31.2	30.7	30.7	30.8	29.7	29.9	29.7	30.1	30.0	30.4	30.7	30.8	30.4
2010	30.7	30.7	31.6	30.9	30.7	30.4	30.6	30.7	30.7	31.2	31.2	31.3	30.9
2011	30.9	31.3	31.1	31.0	30.5	30.0	30.4	30.8	31.2	31.2	31.2	31.4	30.9
Education and Health Services													
2000	23.6	24.0	24.0	23.8	24.0	24.1	24.4	24.7	25.1	25.1	25.3	25.5	24.5
2001	25.1	25.3	25.6	25.6	25.8	26.2	26.1	26.3	26.5	26.0	26.2	26.4	25.9
2002	26.3	26.6	26.8	27.2	27.6	27.7	28.1	28.5	28.5	27.6	27.8	28.0	27.6
2003	27.7	28.0	28.3	28.5	28.6	28.7	28.7	29.0	29.2	29.1	29.2	29.3	28.7
2004	28.8	29.1	29.4	29.6	29.9	30.0	30.4	30.6	31.0	31.5	31.7	32.0	30.3
2005	31.8	32.1	32.3	32.4	32.5	32.9	33.0	33.1	33.2	33.2	33.3	33.5	32.8
2006	33.3	33.5	33.6	32.9	32.4	32.2	32.0	32.4	32.0	31.3	31.5	31.4	32.4
2007	31.0	31.3	31.5	31.5	31.8	32.2	32.1	32.4	32.3	32.1	32.3	32.7	31.9
2008	32.3	32.7	32.9	32.6	32.9	32.9	32.7	33.0	33.1	33.2	33.5	33.7	33.0
2009	33.5	33.9	33.9	33.9	34.2	35.3	35.9	35.9	35.1	35.2	35.2	35.2	34.8
2010	35.1	35.1	35.7	35.9	36.1	37.7	35.7	35.9	36.1	36.2	36.4	36.6	36.0
2011	36.5	36.8	36.8	37.3	37.4	37.4	37.8	38.1	38.6	38.6	38.7	38.9	37.7
Leisure and Hospitality													
2000	21.3	21.4	21.7	22.6	22.8	23.2	23.3	23.2	23.3	22.3	22.1	22.2	22.5
2001	21.5	21.8	22.2	22.3	22.9	22.9	22.9	23.0	23.0	22.0	22.1	22.0	22.4
2002	21.6	22.0	22.6	23.2	23.8	24.0	23.6	23.8	23.7	22.6	23.1	23.1	23.1
2003	22.7	22.8	23.3	23.3	23.9	24.1	23.9	24.0	23.8	23.2	23.2	23.5	23.5
2004	23.6	23.7	24.0	24.6	24.8	25.0	25.0	25.0	24.9	24.0	24.0	24.1	24.4
2005	24.2	24.6	25.0	25.7	26.0	26.5	26.2	26.3	26.1	25.6	25.2	25.5	25.6
2006	24.5	24.9	25.6	25.8	26.3	26.7	26.4	26.2	26.4	25.9	25.6	26.0	25.9
2007	25.6	25.8	26.5	26.6	27.1	27.4	27.1	26.9	26.8	26.6	26.4	26.5	26.6
2008	26.8	26.8	27.2	27.9	28.2	28.0	27.8	27.7	27.3	27.3	27.2	27.1	27.4
2009	26.4	26.7	27.1	27.1	28.0	27.9	27.4	27.5	27.1	26.3	26.6	26.8	27.1
2010	26.2	26.8	27.5	28.1	28.7	28.7	28.0	28.1	28.0	27.6	27.7	27.8	27.8
2011	28.0	28.3	29.1	29.1	29.5	29.8	29.7	29.8	29.7	29.2	29.3	29.6	29.3
Other Services													
2000	7.3	7.4	7.5	7.5	7.4	7.6	7.7	7.7	7.7	7.7	7.6	7.5	7.6
2001	7.5	7.6	7.7	7.7	7.8	7.8	7.7	7.9	7.8	7.8	7.8	7.8	7.7
2002	7.7	7.8	8.0	8.0	8.1	8.1	7.9	7.9	7.8	7.7	7.8	7.7	7.9
2003	7.5	7.6	7.6	7.5	7.5	7.6	7.5	7.5	7.4	7.7	7.5	7.5	7.5
2004	7.6	7.8	7.9	7.3	7.4	7.5	7.4	7.5	7.4	7.4	7.4	7.5	7.5
2005	7.4	7.4	7.6	7.8	7.9	8.0	7.7	7.8	7.8	7.8	7.6	7.5	7.7
2006	7.1	7.2	7.3	7.6	7.7	7.8	7.9	7.8	7.8	8.0	7.9	7.9	7.7
2007	7.4	7.5	7.6	7.7	7.9	8.1	8.1	8.2	8.3	8.3	8.4	8.5	8.0
2008	8.6	8.9	9.0	9.5	9.6	9.6	9.5	9.5	9.5	9.4	9.4	9.4	9.3
2009	9.2	9.2	9.3	9.3	9.3	9.4	9.3	9.2	9.2	9.3	9.3	9.2	9.3
2010	9.1	9.2	9.3	9.2	9.2	9.3	9.1	9.2	9.2	9.3	9.2	9.3	9.2
2011	9.2	9.3	9.4	9.5	9.4	9.5	9.5	9.6	9.6	9.6	9.7	9.7	9.5
Government													
2000	56.0	57.1	57.2	57.5	57.6	55.3	55.4	55.6	56.3	57.1	57.2	57.4	56.6
2001	57.5	58.4	58.5	58.6	58.7	57.1	54.4	55.9	58.7	58.6	59.1	58.2	57.8
2002	58.4	59.4	59.2	58.7	57.8	55.7	53.4	55.0	59.4	60.2	60.4	59.4	58.1
2003	59.3	60.7	60.6	60.5	59.5	56.6	55.5	57.0	60.5	60.4	60.6	59.5	59.2
2004	60.1	61.1	61.0	60.9	61.4	58.5	57.5	56.9	60.6	61.9	61.8	60.9	60.2
2005	61.2	62.0	62.0	61.8	61.9	59.3	56.5	57.0	60.6	61.7	61.5	60.7	60.5
2006	61.0	62.0	62.1	61.7	61.8	58.4	56.0	56.5	61.4	62.8	63.0	63.1	60.8
2007	63.1	63.7	63.8	64.9	65.1	62.1	59.5	59.6	64.9	66.4	66.6	66.5	63.9
2008	66.0	67.4	67.3	65.2	66.0	63.4	59.3	59.4	64.3	66.8	66.8	66.8	64.9
2009	67.0	67.5	67.4	68.9	68.5	66.8	61.9	62.0	67.2	69.7	69.7	69.5	67.2
2010	69.4	70.2	70.2	70.7	71.4	69.0	64.0	64.6	69.3	69.6	69.9	69.8	69.0
2011	69.3	69.5	69.4	69.9	69.7	67.9	63.5	63.0	66.3	66.5	66.8	66.2	67.3

Employment by Industry: Fresno, CA, Selected Years, 2000–2011

(Numbers in thousands, not seasonally adjusted)

Industry and year	January	February	March	April	May	June	July	August	September	October	November	December	Annual average
Total Nonfarm													
2000	261.7	264.7	267.0	268.4	271.2	271.8	272.1	272.1	274.3	274.3	274.8	275.2	270.6
2001	268.0	270.4	273.1	274.3	276.0	277.3	277.5	279.7	278.1	278.3	279.2	278.9	275.9
2002	271.8	275.0	277.7	280.3	283.6	284.2	282.9	285.4	286.1	285.2	286.6	284.8	282.0
2003	276.3	277.6	280.2	280.5	284.4	286.9	282.5	283.3	285.1	285.7	285.2	284.1	282.7
2004	277.9	281.2	282.0	285.6	288.9	287.6	286.8	289.2	291.2	291.5	291.3	289.9	286.9
2005	284.3	287.5	289.6	294.1	295.2	295.3	293.2	295.5	296.5	299.2	299.8	301.6	294.3
2006	293.7	297.7	301.1	301.7	304.8	303.7	300.7	302.9	306.2	306.1	306.4	306.2	302.6
2007	299.4	302.8	306.0	308.1	309.0	308.7	307.0	308.6	308.5	307.0	306.2	305.4	306.6
2008	298.5	302.1	303.7	305.9	308.4	306.6	300.5	301.8	303.7	303.8	301.6	299.4	303.0
2009	289.2	290.2	290.7	290.9	292.1	287.8	282.2	281.5	283.2	284.2	283.4	281.3	286.4
2010	273.1	276.8	278.9	280.7	283.8	283.1	275.1	276.9	279.5	283.5	282.1	280.0	279.5
2011	274.4	278.7	281.2	282.1	283.2	281.7	276.3	275.1	278.6	282.7	282.4	282.2	279.9
Total Private													
2000	198.1	199.5	201.1	202.2	204.0	207.0	209.0	210.4	210.4	207.8	208.0	208.7	205.5
2001	201.2	202.9	204.6	205.7	207.9	208.9	211.7	214.5	212.2	210.1	210.0	210.3	208.3
2002	203.6	205.4	207.2	209.2	211.9	213.6	216.0	219.2	219.2	216.0	216.6	216.1	212.8
2003	208.0	208.3	210.7	210.6	214.7	217.1	216.6	219.9	220.6	218.5	217.9	217.9	215.1
2004	211.5	213.2	213.8	216.7	221.1	220.8	223.3	225.8	226.0	224.3	223.9	223.3	220.3
2005	217.8	219.5	220.5	224.7	225.9	227.0	229.3	232.0	231.5	232.1	232.5	234.9	227.3
2006	227.2	229.5	231.1	231.8	234.5	235.9	237.0	239.3	240.2	237.6	237.9	238.3	235.0
2007	231.8	233.0	234.8	236.1	237.5	238.7	241.2	243.1	241.2	237.2	236.3	235.9	237.2
2008	229.5	230.4	231.0	232.6	235.8	234.9	235.5	236.5	235.6	233.5	231.3	230.0	233.1
2009	221.0	219.9	219.4	218.4	220.3	218.6	216.4	217.2	216.3	215.2	215.2	214.1	217.7
2010	206.7	207.2	208.2	210.1	213.3	214.2	213.0	215.1	215.2	216.1	215.3	214.0	212.4
2011	209.0	210.7	212.2	212.4	214.4	215.0	215.0	215.5	215.9	216.8	216.6	217.4	214.2
Goods-Producing													
2000	40.7	40.6	40.8	41.2	41.7	43.0	46.2	46.5	45.8	44.0	43.6	43.0	43.1
2001	41.2	41.4	41.9	42.1	43.0	43.4	45.5	47.3	46.5	44.3	42.5	42.4	43.5
2002	40.9	41.2	41.8	42.0	43.5	44.1	45.5	48.0	48.2	45.2	44.3	43.4	44.0
2003	42.0	42.0	42.8	42.6	44.9	46.6	46.5	49.1	49.5	47.6	45.8	45.2	45.4
2004	43.7	43.9	44.2	45.8	48.4	47.4	50.5	52.0	51.5	49.2	48.0	47.3	47.7
2005	45.3	46.0	46.1	47.1	47.6	48.4	51.5	52.7	51.6	50.7	50.0	50.5	49.0
2006	48.7	49.3	49.3	49.3	50.6	51.2	52.6	53.8	53.6	51.6	50.4	49.8	50.9
2007	48.2	48.1	48.6	48.7	49.3	49.7	52.9	53.6	51.7	48.3	46.7	45.9	49.3
2008	44.1	44.2	44.3	44.7	46.4	46.2	47.1	47.3	46.7	45.0	42.9	41.8	45.1
2009	39.8	38.8	38.8	38.5	40.0	39.2	40.2	40.9	39.9	38.0	37.2	36.3	39.0
2010	34.8	34.3	34.6	35.2	36.9	37.4	37.5	38.2	38.2	37.7	36.0	35.2	36.3
2011	33.9	34.0	34.1	34.4	35.6	36.3	36.3	37.4	36.7	37.4	36.2	35.7	35.7
Mining and Logging													
2000	0.3	0.3	0.3	0.3	0.4	0.4	0.4	0.4	0.4	0.4	0.4	0.3	0.4
2001	0.3	0.3	0.3	0.3	0.3	0.4	0.4	0.4	0.4	0.4	0.3	0.3	0.3
2002	0.3	0.3	0.2	0.3	0.3	0.3	0.2	0.3	0.3	0.2	0.3	0.2	0.3
2003	0.2	0.2	0.2	0.2	0.2	0.2	0.2	0.2	0.2	0.2	0.2	0.2	0.2
2004	0.2	0.2	0.2	0.2	0.2	0.2	0.2	0.2	0.2	0.2	0.2	0.2	0.2
2005	0.2	0.2	0.2	0.2	0.2	0.2	0.2	0.2	0.2	0.2	0.2	0.2	0.2
2006	0.2	0.2	0.2	0.2	0.2	0.2	0.2	0.2	0.2	0.2	0.2	0.1	0.2
2007	0.1	0.1	0.1	0.1	0.1	0.1	0.2	0.2	0.2	0.2	0.2	0.1	0.1
2008	0.1	0.1	0.1	0.1	0.1	0.1	0.2	0.1	0.1	0.2	0.2	0.1	0.1
2009	0.2	0.2	0.2	0.2	0.2	0.2	0.2	0.2	0.2	0.3	0.3	0.2	0.2
2010	0.2	0.2	0.2	0.2	0.2	0.2	0.2	0.2	0.2	0.2	0.2	0.2	0.2
2011	0.2	0.2	0.2	0.2	0.2	0.2	0.2	0.2	0.2	0.2	0.2	0.2	0.2
Construction													
2000	14.1	14.0	14.1	14.6	14.9	15.5	15.6	15.8	16.1	15.5	15.7	15.7	15.1
2001	14.6	14.8	15.1	15.5	16.0	16.6	16.4	16.8	16.5	16.6	16.2	16.2	15.9
2002	16.0	16.2	16.6	16.7	17.1	17.1	17.2	17.4	17.1	17.1	17.2	17.0	16.9
2003	16.5	16.5	17.2	17.6	18.1	18.8	18.6	18.8	18.8	18.8	18.5	18.4	18.1
2004	18.4	18.7	19.0	19.7	19.8	20.1	20.5	20.8	20.8	20.7	20.3	20.3	19.9
2005	19.3	19.8	20.2	20.7	20.9	21.6	22.4	22.7	22.7	22.7	22.9	23.1	21.6
2006	22.3	22.6	22.6	22.8	23.4	23.7	23.8	24.0	23.6	23.3	23.0	22.9	23.2
2007	21.7	21.5	21.9	21.8	21.7	21.9	21.7	21.4	20.4	20.0	19.7	19.0	21.1
2008	17.9	18.1	18.1	18.6	18.6	18.4	18.5	18.3	17.7	17.4	16.7	16.0	17.9
2009	14.6	14.1	14.3	14.1	14.2	14.1	14.1	13.9	13.4	12.8	12.6	12.0	13.7
2010	11.7	11.5	11.7	11.9	12.3	12.4	12.5	12.4	12.2	12.1	11.8	11.6	12.0
2011	11.0	11.1	11.4	11.4	11.5	11.7	11.7	11.9	11.7	12.0	11.7	11.5	11.6
Manufacturing													
2000	26.3	26.3	26.4	26.3	26.4	27.1	30.2	30.3	29.3	28.1	27.5	27.0	27.6
2001	26.3	26.3	26.5	26.3	26.7	26.4	28.7	30.1	29.6	27.3	26.0	25.9	27.2
2002	24.6	24.7	25.0	25.0	26.1	26.7	28.1	30.3	30.8	27.9	26.8	26.2	26.9
2003	25.3	25.3	25.4	24.8	26.6	27.6	27.7	30.1	30.5	28.6	27.1	26.6	27.1
2004	25.1	25.0	25.0	25.9	28.4	27.1	29.8	31.0	30.5	28.3	27.5	26.8	27.5
2005	25.8	26.0	25.7	26.2	26.5	26.6	28.9	29.8	28.7	27.8	26.9	27.2	27.2
2006	26.2	26.5	26.5	26.3	27.0	27.3	28.6	29.6	29.8	28.1	27.2	26.8	27.5
2007	26.4	26.5	26.6	26.8	27.5	27.7	31.0	32.0	31.1	28.1	26.8	26.8	28.1
2008	26.1	26.0	26.1	26.0	27.7	27.7	28.4	28.9	28.9	27.4	26.0	25.7	27.1
2009	25.0	24.5	24.3	24.2	25.6	24.9	25.9	26.8	26.3	24.9	24.3	24.1	25.1
2010	22.9	22.6	22.7	23.1	24.4	24.8	24.8	25.6	25.8	25.4	24.0	23.4	24.1
2011	22.7	22.7	22.5	22.8	23.9	24.4	24.4	25.3	24.8	25.2	24.3	24.0	23.9

Employment by Industry: Fresno, CA, Selected Years, 2000–2011—*Continued*

(Numbers in thousands, not seasonally adjusted)

Industry and year	January	February	March	April	May	June	July	August	September	October	November	December	Annual average
Service-Providing													
2000	221.0	224.1	226.2	227.2	229.5	228.8	225.9	225.6	228.5	230.3	231.2	232.2	227.5
2001	226.8	229.0	231.2	232.2	233.0	233.9	232.0	232.4	231.6	234.0	236.7	236.5	232.4
2002	230.9	233.8	235.9	238.3	240.1	240.1	237.4	237.4	237.9	240.0	242.3	241.4	238.0
2003	234.3	235.6	237.4	237.9	239.5	240.3	236.0	234.2	235.6	238.1	239.4	238.9	237.3
2004	234.2	237.3	237.8	239.8	240.5	240.2	236.3	237.2	239.7	242.3	243.3	242.6	239.3
2005	239.0	241.5	243.5	247.0	247.6	246.9	241.7	242.8	244.9	248.5	249.8	251.1	245.4
2006	245.0	248.4	251.8	252.4	254.2	252.5	248.1	249.1	252.6	254.5	256.0	256.4	251.8
2007	251.2	254.7	257.4	259.4	259.7	259.0	254.1	255.0	256.8	258.7	259.5	259.5	257.1
2008	254.4	257.9	259.4	261.2	262.0	260.4	253.4	254.5	257.0	258.8	258.7	257.6	257.9
2009	249.4	251.4	251.9	252.4	252.1	248.6	242.0	240.6	243.3	246.2	246.2	245.0	247.4
2010	238.3	242.5	244.3	245.5	246.9	245.7	237.6	238.7	241.3	245.8	246.1	244.8	243.1
2011	240.5	244.7	247.1	247.7	247.6	245.4	240.0	237.7	241.9	245.3	246.2	246.5	244.2
Trade, Transportation, and Utilities													
2000	51.3	51.3	51.7	51.5	52.2	52.9	53.1	53.5	53.9	53.7	54.9	55.3	52.9
2001	52.3	52.2	52.6	53.1	53.5	53.9	54.2	54.6	54.5	54.6	55.6	55.7	53.9
2002	53.0	52.7	52.7	53.5	53.5	54.6	55.2	55.7	55.8	56.1	57.5	57.9	54.9
2003	54.3	53.9	54.3	55.1	55.6	56.5	56.4	56.5	56.5	56.5	57.3	57.9	55.9
2004	54.5	54.3	54.0	54.6	55.4	56.2	56.0	56.1	56.4	56.5	57.3	57.6	55.7
2005	55.7	55.1	55.3	55.8	56.2	56.9	57.3	57.9	58.0	58.4	59.1	60.0	57.1
2006	56.8	56.4	57.0	56.9	57.5	58.4	58.7	59.0	59.5	59.6	60.8	60.9	58.5
2007	58.7	58.2	58.8	59.1	59.9	60.6	61.1	61.4	61.3	61.1	62.0	62.6	60.4
2008	58.8	58.0	58.0	57.8	59.2	59.3	59.4	59.7	60.0	59.8	60.1	60.0	59.2
2009	56.4	55.6	55.1	54.7	55.3	55.4	54.6	55.0	55.9	55.8	56.8	56.9	55.6
2010	53.6	53.3	53.3	53.7	54.1	54.8	54.7	55.6	56.1	56.7	57.7	58.0	55.1
2011	55.6	55.5	55.2	55.5	55.9	56.1	56.3	56.3	57.2	57.4	58.2	58.6	56.5
Wholesale Trade													
2000	11.7	11.8	12.0	12.0	12.1	12.2	12.3	12.4	12.2	12.0	12.0	12.0	12.1
2001	11.6	11.7	11.8	12.0	12.0	12.1	12.4	12.6	12.3	12.1	12.0	11.8	12.0
2002	11.8	11.8	11.9	12.3	12.3	12.7	12.8	12.9	12.8	13.0	12.9	12.9	12.5
2003	12.2	12.2	12.3	12.6	12.7	12.9	12.7	12.7	12.6	12.6	12.3	12.2	12.5
2004	11.6	11.8	11.7	11.9	12.2	12.4	12.6	12.7	12.7	12.6	12.3	12.2	12.2
2005	12.0	12.0	12.1	12.3	12.4	12.8	13.0	13.1	13.2	13.1	13.0	12.9	12.7
2006	12.7	12.8	12.9	12.9	13.1	13.7	13.6	13.6	13.6	13.6	13.3	13.0	13.2
2007	12.9	13.0	13.3	13.3	13.6	14.0	14.0	14.0	13.8	13.5	13.3	13.0	13.5
2008	12.5	12.5	12.6	12.9	13.1	13.4	13.3	13.2	13.1	12.8	12.6	12.3	12.9
2009	11.9	11.8	11.7	11.7	11.8	12.1	11.9	11.9	12.0	11.9	11.9	11.6	11.9
2010	11.1	11.1	11.1	11.1	11.2	11.6	11.7	11.8	11.7	12.0	11.8	11.6	11.5
2011	12.1	12.2	12.2	12.1	12.2	12.4	12.4	12.4	12.4	12.4	12.4	12.3	12.3
Retail Trade													
2000	31.0	30.9	31.1	30.8	31.2	31.7	31.5	31.6	32.1	32.3	33.6	34.1	31.8
2001	32.0	31.8	32.0	32.1	32.4	32.6	32.3	32.4	32.6	32.8	34.0	34.5	32.6
2002	32.4	32.1	32.0	32.1	32.2	32.7	32.7	32.9	33.0	33.2	34.6	35.2	32.9
2003	33.0	32.6	32.7	33.0	33.2	33.7	33.8	33.8	34.0	34.0	35.4	36.1	33.8
2004	33.6	33.2	32.9	33.2	33.6	34.0	33.7	33.7	34.0	34.2	35.4	35.8	33.9
2005	34.6	34.0	34.0	34.4	34.5	34.6	34.7	35.1	35.1	35.6	36.6	37.7	35.1
2006	35.0	34.5	34.8	34.6	34.7	34.7	34.8	35.1	35.2	35.5	36.7	37.3	35.2
2007	35.7	35.1	35.3	35.5	35.9	36.0	36.2	36.4	36.4	36.6	37.7	38.5	36.3
2008	35.8	35.1	35.0	35.0	35.0	34.8	34.9	35.0	35.2	35.6	36.3	36.6	35.4
2009	33.8	33.2	32.9	32.5	32.8	32.6	32.3	32.5	33.0	33.1	34.2	34.8	33.1
2010	32.3	32.0	32.0	32.2	32.3	32.4	32.2	32.6	33.1	33.4	34.4	35.0	32.8
2011	32.7	32.5	32.2	32.4	32.6	32.6	32.8	32.7	33.5	33.7	34.5	35.0	33.1
Transportation and Utilities													
2000	8.6	8.6	8.6	8.7	8.9	9.0	9.3	9.5	9.6	9.4	9.3	9.2	9.1
2001	8.7	8.7	8.8	9.0	9.1	9.2	9.5	9.6	9.6	9.7	9.6	9.4	9.2
2002	8.8	8.8	8.8	9.1	9.0	9.2	9.7	9.9	10.0	9.9	10.0	9.8	9.4
2003	9.1	9.1	9.3	9.5	9.7	9.9	9.9	10.0	9.9	9.9	9.6	9.6	9.6
2004	9.3	9.3	9.4	9.5	9.6	9.8	9.7	9.7	9.7	9.7	9.6	9.6	9.6
2005	9.1	9.1	9.2	9.1	9.3	9.5	9.6	9.7	9.7	9.7	9.5	9.4	9.4
2006	9.1	9.1	9.3	9.4	9.7	10.0	10.3	10.3	10.7	10.5	10.8	10.6	10.0
2007	10.1	10.1	10.2	10.3	10.4	10.6	10.9	11.0	11.1	11.0	11.0	11.1	10.7
2008	10.5	10.4	10.4	9.9	11.1	11.1	11.2	11.5	11.7	11.4	11.2	11.1	11.0
2009	10.7	10.6	10.5	10.5	10.7	10.7	10.4	10.6	10.9	10.8	10.7	10.5	10.6
2010	10.2	10.2	10.2	10.4	10.6	10.8	10.8	11.2	11.3	11.3	11.5	11.4	10.8
2011	10.8	10.8	10.8	11.0	11.1	11.1	11.1	11.2	11.3	11.3	11.3	11.3	11.1
Information													
2000	4.8	4.9	4.9	4.9	4.9	5.0	5.1	5.1	5.1	5.1	5.1	5.1	5.0
2001	5.5	5.4	5.4	5.1	5.1	5.0	5.1	5.0	4.9	4.7	4.8	4.8	5.1
2002	4.9	4.8	4.9	4.8	4.7	4.7	4.6	4.6	4.5	4.6	4.6	4.5	4.7
2003	4.0	4.1	4.0	4.0	4.0	4.1	4.2	4.3	4.2	4.4	4.5	4.6	4.2
2004	4.5	4.5	4.5	4.5	4.6	4.6	4.6	4.6	4.6	4.7	4.5	4.5	4.6
2005	4.4	4.5	4.4	4.4	4.4	4.4	4.3	4.3	4.2	4.2	4.3	4.2	4.3
2006	4.2	4.2	4.2	4.2	4.2	4.2	4.2	4.2	4.2	4.2	4.2	4.2	4.2
2007	4.1	4.2	4.1	4.1	4.2	4.2	4.2	4.2	4.2	4.2	4.2	4.2	4.2
2008	4.5	4.5	4.4	4.8	4.8	4.8	4.9	4.8	4.8	4.8	4.8	4.8	4.7
2009	4.6	4.6	4.5	4.3	4.2	4.2	4.0	3.9	3.8	3.8	3.7	3.7	4.1
2010	3.6	3.6	3.5	3.4	3.3	3.4	3.4	3.4	3.3	3.3	3.3	3.2	3.4
2011	3.2	3.2	3.2	3.1	3.1	3.1	3.1	3.2	3.1	3.1	3.2	3.2	3.2

Employment by Industry: Fresno, CA, Selected Years, 2000–2011—*Continued*

(Numbers in thousands, not seasonally adjusted)

Industry and year	January	February	March	April	May	June	July	August	September	October	November	December	Annual average
Financial Activities													
2000	13.4	13.6	13.6	13.2	13.2	13.5	13.4	13.4	13.5	13.4	13.4	13.6	13.4
2001	13.8	14.0	14.1	14.1	14.2	14.3	14.4	14.3	14.2	13.9	13.9	14.0	14.1
2002	13.7	13.7	13.8	14.1	14.2	14.2	14.5	14.5	14.4	14.1	14.2	14.2	14.1
2003	13.7	13.7	13.8	13.8	13.9	13.9	13.7	13.7	13.6	13.6	13.5	13.5	13.7
2004	13.5	13.6	13.7	13.7	13.9	14.0	14.0	14.0	14.1	14.2	14.2	14.3	13.9
2005	14.3	14.2	14.3	14.5	14.5	14.6	14.8	14.8	15.0	15.1	15.2	15.3	14.7
2006	15.2	15.3	15.3	15.5	15.6	15.6	15.7	15.7	15.7	15.5	15.5	15.6	15.5
2007	15.3	15.4	15.4	15.5	15.5	15.6	15.4	15.3	15.3	14.9	15.0	15.0	15.3
2008	14.9	14.9	14.9	14.8	14.9	14.9	14.7	14.8	14.6	14.6	14.6	14.5	14.8
2009	14.2	14.1	14.0	14.0	13.9	13.8	13.7	13.6	13.5	13.5	13.5	13.5	13.8
2010	13.4	13.4	13.3	13.4	13.4	13.4	13.4	13.4	13.3	13.4	13.4	13.3	13.4
2011	13.2	13.2	13.2	13.1	13.1	13.1	13.1	13.1	13.1	13.2	13.2	13.2	13.2
Professional and Business Services													
2000	24.7	24.7	24.8	26.2	26.0	26.3	25.4	25.6	25.7	25.9	25.4	25.8	25.5
2001	23.4	23.5	23.4	23.4	23.5	24.0	23.2	23.4	23.1	23.7	23.8	24.0	23.5
2002	23.8	24.3	24.2	25.0	25.2	25.3	25.2	25.6	25.5	26.1	26.1	26.1	25.2
2003	26.2	26.0	26.3	25.8	26.2	26.0	26.2	26.6	26.8	26.6	26.9	26.8	26.4
2004	26.7	27.1	27.2	27.4	27.4	27.4	27.6	28.1	28.1	28.3	28.6	28.2	27.7
2005	27.7	28.4	28.6	29.2	29.3	29.0	28.6	28.9	28.6	29.0	29.0	29.3	28.8
2006	28.7	29.1	29.4	29.8	29.5	29.4	29.3	29.9	29.8	29.9	29.7	29.7	29.5
2007	29.3	29.6	29.9	30.0	29.8	30.0	30.2	30.2	30.3	30.6	30.1	29.9	30.0
2008	30.3	30.6	30.4	30.8	30.4	30.3	31.2	31.2	31.1	30.7	30.3	30.5	30.7
2009	29.6	29.4	29.3	28.8	28.3	28.0	28.0	27.5	27.2	27.5	27.3	27.1	28.2
2010	26.0	26.3	26.6	27.2	27.3	27.2	26.9	26.8	26.4	26.7	26.7	26.3	26.7
2011	26.7	27.3	27.3	27.2	27.2	27.0	27.3	26.6	26.6	26.7	26.6	27.1	27.0
Education and Health Services													
2000	30.2	30.8	31.0	30.7	30.8	30.9	30.4	30.6	31.0	31.2	31.3	31.5	30.9
2001	31.2	31.6	31.9	32.5	32.3	32.1	32.4	32.7	33.1	33.1	33.5	33.4	32.5
2002	32.6	33.2	33.7	33.9	33.9	33.8	34.0	33.7	34.3	34.2	34.6	34.6	33.9
2003	34.0	34.3	34.7	34.8	34.7	34.7	34.5	34.6	35.2	35.7	35.9	35.9	34.9
2004	35.2	35.8	35.9	35.9	35.6	35.2	35.2	35.3	35.7	36.4	36.4	36.5	35.8
2005	35.7	36.0	36.2	36.9	36.6	36.4	36.1	36.2	37.0	37.4	37.4	37.5	36.6
2006	36.7	37.3	37.4	37.3	37.3	37.2	37.0	37.0	37.7	37.9	38.4	38.6	37.5
2007	38.1	38.7	38.8	39.0	38.6	38.6	38.3	38.7	39.1	39.6	39.6	39.7	38.9
2008	39.1	39.8	40.2	40.8	40.6	40.1	39.3	39.6	39.7	40.4	40.6	40.8	40.1
2009	40.0	40.6	40.7	40.9	40.6	40.1	39.0	39.1	39.7	40.6	40.8	40.7	40.2
2010	39.9	40.3	40.5	41.0	40.8	40.5	40.0	40.3	40.9	41.1	41.4	41.4	40.7
2011	40.7	41.0	42.0	42.0	41.7	41.2	41.0	41.0	41.6	41.6	41.9	42.3	41.5
Leisure and Hospitality													
2000	23.2	23.4	23.8	24.0	24.7	25.1	25.3	25.3	24.7	24.1	23.9	23.9	24.3
2001	23.4	23.9	24.4	24.1	24.7	25.0	25.6	25.3	24.4	24.4	24.4	24.5	24.5
2002	23.7	23.9	24.3	23.8	24.6	25.0	25.0	24.7	24.2	23.9	23.6	23.5	24.2
2003	22.6	23.0	23.3	23.2	24.0	24.3	24.5	24.3	23.8	23.3	23.4	23.2	23.6
2004	23.0	23.3	23.5	23.8	24.7	25.2	24.9	24.9	24.7	24.6	24.6	24.5	24.3
2005	24.4	24.8	25.1	25.8	26.3	26.3	26.1	26.1	26.0	26.3	26.5	27.0	25.9
2006	26.5	27.1	27.5	27.8	28.5	28.9	28.7	28.7	28.7	28.1	28.2	28.6	28.1
2007	27.5	27.9	28.3	28.6	28.9	29.1	28.3	28.5	28.2	27.6	27.7	27.7	28.2
2008	27.3	27.7	28.0	28.1	28.7	28.5	28.5	28.4	28.1	27.6	27.5	27.1	28.0
2009	26.2	26.5	26.6	26.9	27.5	27.4	27.2	27.1	26.3	26.0	25.9	25.9	26.6
2010	25.5	25.9	26.3	26.2	27.4	27.4	27.4	27.5	27.1	27.2	26.8	26.7	26.8
2011	26.0	26.6	27.3	27.1	27.8	28.1	28.0	28.0	27.7	27.5	27.4	27.4	27.4
Other Services													
2000	9.8	10.2	10.5	10.5	10.5	10.3	10.1	10.4	10.7	10.4	10.4	10.5	10.4
2001	10.4	10.9	10.9	11.3	11.6	11.2	11.3	11.9	11.5	11.4	11.5	11.5	11.3
2002	11.0	11.6	11.8	12.1	12.3	11.9	12.0	12.4	12.3	11.8	11.7	11.9	11.9
2003	11.2	11.3	11.5	11.3	11.4	11.0	10.6	10.8	11.0	10.8	10.6	10.8	11.0
2004	10.4	10.7	10.8	11.0	11.1	10.8	10.5	10.8	10.9	10.4	10.3	10.4	10.7
2005	10.3	10.5	10.5	11.0	11.0	11.0	10.6	11.1	11.0	11.0	11.0	11.1	10.8
2006	10.4	10.8	11.0	11.0	11.3	11.0	10.8	11.0	11.0	10.8	10.7	10.9	10.9
2007	10.6	10.9	10.9	11.1	11.3	10.9	10.8	11.2	11.1	10.9	11.0	10.9	11.0
2008	10.5	10.7	10.8	10.8	10.8	10.8	10.4	10.6	10.6	10.6	10.5	10.5	10.6
2009	10.2	10.3	10.4	10.3	10.5	10.5	9.7	10.1	10.0	10.0	10.0	10.0	10.2
2010	9.9	10.1	10.1	10.0	10.1	10.1	9.7	9.9	9.9	10.0	10.0	9.9	10.0
2011	9.7	9.9	9.9	10.0	10.0	10.1	9.9	9.9	9.9	9.9	9.9	9.9	9.9
Government													
2000	63.6	65.2	65.9	66.2	67.2	64.8	63.1	61.7	63.9	66.5	66.8	66.5	65.1
2001	66.8	67.5	68.5	68.6	68.1	68.4	65.8	65.2	65.9	68.2	69.2	68.6	67.6
2002	68.2	69.6	70.5	71.1	71.7	70.6	66.9	66.2	66.9	69.2	70.0	68.7	69.1
2003	68.3	69.3	69.5	69.9	69.7	69.8	65.9	63.4	64.5	67.2	67.3	66.2	67.6
2004	66.4	68.0	68.2	68.9	67.8	66.8	63.5	63.4	65.2	67.2	67.4	66.6	66.6
2005	66.5	68.0	69.1	69.4	69.3	68.3	63.9	63.5	65.0	67.1	67.3	66.7	67.0
2006	66.5	68.2	70.0	69.9	70.3	67.8	63.7	63.6	66.0	68.5	68.5	67.9	67.6
2007	67.6	69.8	71.2	72.0	71.5	70.0	65.8	65.5	67.3	69.8	69.9	69.5	69.2
2008	69.0	71.7	72.7	73.3	72.6	71.7	65.0	65.3	68.1	70.3	70.3	69.4	70.0
2009	68.2	70.3	71.3	72.5	71.8	69.2	65.8	64.3	66.9	69.0	68.2	67.2	68.7
2010	66.4	69.6	70.7	70.6	70.5	68.9	62.1	61.8	64.3	67.4	66.8	66.0	67.1
2011	65.4	68.0	69.0	69.7	68.8	66.7	61.3	59.6	62.7	65.9	65.8	64.8	65.6

Employment by Industry: Grand Rapids–Wyoming, MI, Selected Years, 2000–2011

(Numbers in thousands, not seasonally adjusted)

Industry and year	January	February	March	April	May	June	July	August	September	October	November	December	Annual average
Total Nonfarm													
2000	396.7	400.8	404.0	401.2	405.0	404.4	397.2	398.4	405.9	409.8	410.3	411.0	403.7
2001	396.8	396.0	397.1	402.3	406.5	404.3	392.5	395.2	399.6	400.1	399.0	398.9	399.0
2002	385.1	386.1	388.2	391.3	397.1	396.0	387.3	390.1	395.5	397.4	398.2	398.0	392.5
2003	376.4	376.9	376.6	377.2	386.7	384.0	375.1	379.9	384.7	389.2	391.7	392.9	382.6
2004	378.6	379.1	379.8	386.2	390.9	388.4	379.6	382.7	388.4	390.6	392.2	391.6	385.7
2005	378.5	381.0	383.8	388.1	392.9	390.1	385.1	388.0	394.0	394.2	395.5	395.0	388.9
2006	379.9	382.0	384.3	389.0	394.2	391.9	381.2	384.9	391.1	390.5	392.1	392.3	387.8
2007	379.5	381.7	383.4	385.9	391.8	391.5	382.9	386.0	391.3	391.8	393.8	394.6	387.9
2008	382.7	383.5	383.9	386.3	392.3	390.0	377.3	381.2	384.0	383.5	382.2	379.4	383.9
2009	359.8	360.7	360.0	364.3	368.6	361.8	349.3	351.4	359.8	362.1	363.7	363.3	360.4
2010	351.6	354.4	354.7	359.5	366.4	366.7	360.0	360.9	368.2	369.7	371.0	370.6	362.8
2011	361.4	363.5	365.9	370.8	376.6	374.7	369.7	371.5	376.4	376.8	379.5	376.5	371.9
Total Private													
2000	359.7	362.2	365.2	362.8	365.4	367.1	364.9	366.9	368.3	370.8	371.3	372.2	366.4
2001	358.3	356.5	357.3	363.3	366.7	367.2	360.4	363.4	362.1	361.2	360.1	359.8	361.4
2002	346.7	347.0	348.9	352.9	357.8	359.4	355.6	358.6	358.2	357.6	358.0	357.6	354.9
2003	337.2	337.1	336.8	338.1	346.5	346.2	342.1	346.2	346.9	349.6	351.9	353.0	344.3
2004	339.4	339.6	340.0	346.9	350.9	351.9	347.8	350.5	350.9	351.4	352.9	352.2	347.9
2005	340.5	341.7	344.4	348.8	352.8	352.3	352.9	355.5	357.0	355.2	356.4	356.3	351.2
2006	342.1	342.9	345.1	350.0	354.4	354.4	349.2	352.5	354.8	352.3	354.1	354.3	350.5
2007	343.1	344.5	346.1	348.8	354.3	355.1	351.1	353.5	355.3	355.1	357.2	357.9	351.8
2008	347.0	347.1	347.3	349.7	355.5	353.8	345.7	348.4	348.1	346.5	345.5	342.9	348.1
2009	323.5	324.1	323.2	327.3	331.4	326.1	317.6	319.8	324.4	326.1	327.6	327.5	324.9
2010	316.2	318.9	319.2	323.9	329.8	331.2	328.6	330.0	333.9	334.3	335.4	335.6	328.1
2011	326.9	329.0	331.0	335.9	341.6	340.6	339.9	342.1	342.9	342.7	345.3	342.8	338.4
Goods-Producing													
2000	109.0	109.6	110.4	109.3	109.9	111.6	110.8	111.5	111.4	112.8	112.0	111.5	110.8
2001	108.0	106.6	106.1	106.6	107.3	108.0	106.8	108.0	107.5	105.5	104.3	103.6	106.5
2002	98.5	97.8	97.7	98.7	100.2	100.7	99.4	99.9	99.2	99.2	98.4	97.8	99.0
2003	93.7	92.8	92.5	91.3	94.9	95.0	92.9	95.0	94.5	94.4	94.2	94.2	93.8
2004	92.1	91.1	91.2	92.8	93.6	94.5	92.9	94.4	94.1	94.0	93.2	93.2	93.1
2005	91.2	90.5	91.5	91.6	92.5	93.4	92.6	93.7	93.3	93.4	93.1	92.7	92.5
2006	90.1	89.5	89.8	91.5	92.6	93.4	91.1	92.7	92.1	90.8	90.0	89.7	91.1
2007	86.8	86.5	86.5	87.8	88.9	90.0	88.6	90.0	89.4	88.8	88.8	88.4	88.4
2008	86.2	85.3	84.8	84.7	86.0	87.4	84.2	86.0	85.0	83.1	81.6	79.7	84.5
2009	72.0	71.5	70.7	70.8	70.7	70.8	69.7	71.6	72.1	71.5	70.6	70.3	71.0
2010	67.7	67.8	68.4	70.3	71.6	72.9	73.4	73.9	73.9	73.6	73.2	73.2	71.7
2011	71.9	72.0	72.3	73.7	75.1	76.5	76.5	77.5	76.0	76.0	75.8	75.4	74.9
Mining, Logging, and Construction													
2000	18.6	18.4	19.2	20.4	21.1	22.1	21.7	21.7	21.5	21.3	20.8	20.2	20.6
2001	18.2	18.1	18.6	19.9	20.9	21.7	22.3	22.4	22.2	21.6	21.2	20.5	20.6
2002	19.0	18.8	19.1	20.0	21.2	21.5	21.8	21.7	21.1	20.9	20.3	19.6	20.4
2003	17.2	16.8	16.8	18.1	19.0	19.7	20.3	20.4	19.9	19.6	19.3	19.1	18.9
2004	17.4	16.9	17.2	19.0	19.6	20.2	20.4	20.2	19.9	19.5	19.0	18.7	19.0
2005	17.1	16.6	16.9	18.3	19.0	19.5	19.8	19.8	19.5	19.1	18.7	18.0	18.5
2006	16.5	16.2	16.5	17.9	18.8	19.5	19.3	19.3	18.9	18.4	17.9	17.4	18.1
2007	15.9	15.5	15.7	16.7	17.6	18.2	18.3	18.3	18.0	17.6	17.2	16.7	17.1
2008	15.6	15.3	15.5	16.1	17.1	17.6	17.5	17.6	17.1	16.4	15.7	14.9	16.4
2009	13.2	12.9	12.9	13.6	14.2	14.4	14.6	14.5	14.2	13.9	13.3	12.8	13.7
2010	11.6	11.6	11.9	12.7	13.3	13.7	14.0	14.1	13.7	13.4	13.0	12.5	13.0
2011	11.7	11.5	11.7	12.5	13.3	13.9	14.2	14.5	13.7	13.6	12.7	11.7	12.9
Manufacturing													
2000	90.4	91.2	91.2	88.9	88.8	89.5	89.1	89.8	89.9	91.5	91.2	91.3	90.2
2001	89.8	88.5	87.5	86.7	86.4	86.3	84.5	85.6	85.3	83.9	83.1	83.1	85.9
2002	79.5	79.0	78.6	78.7	79.0	79.2	77.6	78.2	78.1	78.3	78.1	78.2	78.5
2003	76.5	76.0	75.7	73.2	75.9	75.3	72.6	74.6	74.6	74.8	74.9	75.1	74.9
2004	74.7	74.2	74.0	73.8	74.0	74.3	72.5	74.2	74.2	74.5	74.2	74.5	74.1
2005	74.1	73.9	74.6	73.3	73.5	73.9	72.8	73.9	73.8	74.3	74.4	74.7	73.9
2006	73.6	73.3	73.3	73.6	73.8	73.9	71.8	73.4	73.2	72.4	72.1	72.3	73.1
2007	70.9	71.0	70.8	71.1	71.3	71.8	70.3	71.7	71.4	71.2	71.6	71.7	71.2
2008	70.6	70.0	69.3	68.6	68.9	69.8	66.7	68.4	67.9	66.7	65.9	64.8	68.1
2009	58.8	58.6	57.8	57.2	56.5	56.4	55.1	57.1	57.9	57.6	57.3	57.5	57.3
2010	56.1	56.2	56.5	57.6	58.3	59.2	59.4	59.8	60.2	60.2	60.2	60.7	58.7
2011	60.2	60.5	60.6	61.2	61.8	62.6	62.3	63.0	62.3	62.4	63.1	63.7	62.0
Service-Providing													
2000	287.7	291.2	293.6	291.9	295.1	292.8	286.4	286.9	294.5	297.0	298.3	299.5	292.9
2001	288.8	289.4	291.0	295.7	299.2	296.3	285.7	287.2	292.1	294.6	294.7	295.3	292.5
2002	286.6	288.3	290.5	292.6	296.9	295.3	287.9	290.2	296.3	298.2	299.8	300.2	293.6
2003	282.7	284.1	284.1	285.9	291.8	289.0	282.2	284.9	290.2	294.8	297.5	298.7	288.8
2004	286.5	288.0	288.6	293.4	297.3	293.9	286.7	288.3	294.3	296.6	299.0	298.4	292.6
2005	287.3	290.5	292.3	296.5	300.4	296.7	292.5	294.3	300.7	300.8	302.4	302.3	296.4
2006	289.8	292.5	294.5	297.5	301.6	298.5	290.1	292.2	299.0	299.7	302.1	302.6	296.7
2007	292.7	295.2	296.9	298.1	302.9	301.5	294.3	296.0	301.9	303.0	305.0	306.2	299.5
2008	296.5	298.2	299.1	301.6	306.3	302.6	293.1	295.2	299.0	300.4	300.6	299.7	299.4
2009	287.8	289.2	289.3	293.5	297.9	291.0	279.6	279.8	287.7	290.6	293.1	293.0	289.4
2010	283.9	286.6	286.3	289.2	294.8	293.8	286.6	287.0	294.3	296.1	297.8	297.4	291.2
2011	289.5	291.5	293.6	297.1	301.5	298.2	293.2	294.0	300.4	300.8	303.7	301.1	297.1

Employment by Industry: Grand Rapids–Wyoming, MI, Selected Years, 2000–2011—*Continued*

(Numbers in thousands, not seasonally adjusted)

Industry and year	January	February	March	April	May	June	July	August	September	October	November	December	Annual average
Trade, Transportation, and Utilities													
2000	81.0	81.0	81.6	81.4	81.7	81.0	79.5	79.8	80.6	82.0	83.2	84.4	81.4
2001	82.1	81.1	80.9	81.6	81.9	81.1	78.9	78.9	78.4	79.1	79.9	80.2	80.3
2002	76.9	76.3	76.4	76.5	77.1	77.5	77.0	77.5	77.3	77.4	78.2	79.3	77.3
2003	75.5	74.4	74.3	74.8	75.8	76.3	75.5	75.4	75.4	76.1	77.4	78.1	75.8
2004	74.3	73.3	73.1	74.6	75.1	75.3	74.9	74.9	74.6	75.2	76.6	77.0	74.9
2005	73.7	73.2	73.5	74.6	75.5	75.8	75.8	75.8	75.4	75.4	76.5	76.9	75.2
2006	73.2	72.6	72.7	73.2	73.8	73.9	73.6	73.4	73.3	73.7	75.1	75.7	73.7
2007	73.4	72.4	72.6	73.0	73.9	74.2	73.8	73.6	73.6	73.9	75.1	75.4	73.7
2008	72.8	72.0	72.1	71.9	72.8	73.0	72.0	72.0	71.3	71.1	71.6	71.6	72.0
2009	68.5	67.5	67.1	68.0	68.5	68.5	67.5	67.4	67.1	67.8	68.3	68.5	67.9
2010	66.0	65.5	65.5	66.3	67.0	67.5	66.9	66.8	66.5	67.6	68.5	68.7	66.9
2011	66.1	65.7	65.5	66.7	67.4	67.6	67.1	67.1	67.3	67.8	69.6	69.4	67.3
Wholesale Trade													
2000	23.7	24.0	23.9	24.1	24.0	24.1	24.0	23.8	24.0	24.0	23.8	24.2	24.0
2001	24.3	23.9	24.1	24.3	24.0	23.8	23.3	23.2	23.0	23.0	22.9	22.8	23.6
2002	23.2	22.9	22.9	22.9	23.1	23.2	23.0	23.0	22.7	22.9	22.8	22.9	23.0
2003	22.6	22.4	22.3	22.4	22.6	22.5	22.2	22.1	22.0	22.3	22.3	22.3	22.3
2004	21.7	21.7	21.6	22.1	22.2	22.4	22.3	22.1	22.1	22.1	22.2	22.2	22.1
2005	21.7	21.7	21.8	22.0	22.3	22.4	22.4	22.4	22.3	22.4	22.3	22.4	22.2
2006	22.0	22.0	22.0	22.2	22.4	22.5	22.5	22.4	22.4	22.5	22.4	22.4	22.3
2007	22.2	22.1	22.2	22.5	22.6	22.7	22.8	22.7	22.7	22.7	22.6	22.6	22.5
2008	22.2	22.2	22.3	22.3	22.4	22.5	22.3	22.4	22.3	22.0	21.8	21.6	22.2
2009	21.0	20.8	20.6	20.7	20.8	20.7	20.6	20.6	20.5	20.6	20.6	20.6	20.7
2010	20.2	20.2	20.3	20.4	20.5	20.7	20.6	20.6	20.5	20.6	20.5	20.6	20.5
2011	20.3	20.3	20.2	20.6	20.9	21.1	21.0	21.0	20.9	21.0	20.9	21.0	20.8
Retail Trade													
2000	46.2	45.9	46.7	46.1	46.6	45.6	44.2	44.6	45.2	46.3	47.7	48.5	46.1
2001	46.3	45.8	45.4	45.6	46.1	45.6	44.0	44.0	43.8	44.3	45.5	46.0	45.2
2002	42.5	42.2	42.2	42.4	42.8	43.1	42.9	43.3	43.5	43.2	44.2	45.2	43.1
2003	42.7	42.0	42.0	42.1	42.8	43.3	43.1	43.2	43.3	43.6	45.0	45.6	43.2
2004	42.6	41.7	41.5	42.0	42.4	42.4	42.2	42.3	41.8	42.1	43.5	44.0	42.4
2005	41.6	41.1	41.2	41.9	42.4	42.4	42.4	42.3	42.0	42.0	43.2	43.4	42.2
2006	40.5	40.0	40.1	40.4	40.7	40.6	40.3	40.3	40.1	40.4	41.9	42.4	40.6
2007	40.6	39.8	39.8	39.9	40.5	40.5	40.1	40.1	40.1	40.5	41.7	42.0	40.5
2008	40.2	39.5	39.6	39.2	39.8	39.8	39.2	39.1	38.6	38.7	39.6	39.8	39.4
2009	37.7	37.1	37.0	37.5	37.8	37.9	37.3	37.2	37.1	37.6	38.2	38.4	37.6
2010	36.4	36.0	35.9	36.4	36.9	37.1	36.7	36.8	36.4	37.4	38.3	38.5	36.9
2011	36.4	36.0	35.9	36.5	36.9	36.8	36.5	36.5	36.8	37.2	39.1	38.8	37.0
Transportation and Utilities													
2000	11.1	11.1	11.0	11.2	11.1	11.3	11.3	11.4	11.4	11.7	11.7	11.7	11.3
2001	11.5	11.4	11.4	11.7	11.8	11.7	11.6	11.7	11.6	11.8	11.5	11.4	11.6
2002	11.2	11.2	11.3	11.2	11.2	11.2	11.1	11.2	11.1	11.3	11.2	11.2	11.2
2003	10.2	10.0	10.0	10.3	10.4	10.5	10.2	10.1	10.1	10.2	10.1	10.2	10.2
2004	10.0	9.9	10.0	10.5	10.5	10.5	10.4	10.5	10.7	11.0	10.9	10.8	10.5
2005	10.4	10.4	10.5	10.7	10.8	11.0	11.0	11.1	11.1	11.0	11.0	11.1	10.8
2006	10.7	10.6	10.6	10.6	10.7	10.8	10.8	10.7	10.8	10.8	10.8	10.9	10.7
2007	10.6	10.5	10.6	10.6	10.8	11.0	10.9	10.8	10.8	10.7	10.8	10.8	10.7
2008	10.4	10.3	10.2	10.4	10.6	10.7	10.5	10.5	10.4	10.4	10.2	10.2	10.4
2009	9.8	9.6	9.5	9.8	9.9	9.9	9.6	9.6	9.5	9.6	9.5	9.5	9.7
2010	9.4	9.3	9.3	9.5	9.6	9.7	9.6	9.4	9.6	9.6	9.7	9.6	9.5
2011	9.4	9.4	9.4	9.6	9.6	9.7	9.6	9.6	9.6	9.6	9.6	9.6	9.6
Information													
2000	6.1	6.0	6.0	6.0	6.1	6.1	6.2	6.3	6.2	6.1	6.1	6.2	6.1
2001	5.8	5.9	5.9	6.1	6.1	6.3	6.1	6.0	6.0	6.1	6.5	6.5	6.1
2002	6.5	6.5	6.6	6.1	6.1	6.1	6.0	6.0	5.9	6.1	6.1	6.2	6.2
2003	6.1	6.0	6.0	5.9	6.0	5.9	5.5	5.5	5.4	5.5	5.5	5.5	5.7
2004	5.6	5.6	5.6	5.6	5.5	5.6	5.6	5.5	5.4	5.3	5.4	5.4	5.5
2005	5.5	5.6	5.6	5.7	5.6	5.7	5.6	5.6	5.5	5.7	5.9	5.9	5.7
2006	5.7	5.7	5.7	5.6	5.6	5.7	5.5	5.5	5.4	5.4	5.4	5.4	5.6
2007	5.3	5.3	5.2	5.2	5.3	5.3	5.2	5.2	5.0	5.0	5.1	5.1	5.2
2008	5.0	4.9	4.8	4.8	4.9	4.9	4.9	4.9	4.8	4.8	4.8	4.8	4.9
2009	4.7	4.7	4.6	4.6	4.6	4.6	4.6	4.4	4.4	4.4	4.4	4.4	4.5
2010	4.3	4.2	4.2	4.3	4.4	4.5	4.5	4.5	4.5	4.3	4.3	4.3	4.4
2011	4.2	4.2	4.2	4.1	4.2	4.2	4.2	4.2	4.2	4.2	4.2	4.2	4.2
Financial Activities													
2000	20.8	20.9	20.8	19.4	19.4	19.4	19.2	19.2	19.3	19.6	19.7	19.8	19.8
2001	19.1	19.1	19.2	19.1	19.4	19.4	19.3	19.3	19.2	19.9	19.7	19.9	19.4
2002	19.7	19.9	20.1	19.7	19.7	19.5	19.4	19.5	19.3	19.7	19.5	19.6	19.6
2003	19.6	19.5	19.5	19.7	19.7	19.7	19.8	19.8	19.8	20.0	19.9	20.1	19.8
2004	20.1	20.0	20.2	20.3	20.4	20.4	20.3	20.3	20.2	19.9	20.0	20.1	20.2
2005	20.1	20.4	20.1	20.3	20.4	20.4	20.5	20.6	20.6	20.5	20.6	20.7	20.5
2006	20.9	20.9	20.8	20.9	20.9	20.9	20.8	20.8	20.7	20.5	20.5	20.4	20.8
2007	20.1	20.1	20.0	20.5	20.6	20.4	20.5	20.1	19.9	20.4	20.2	20.3	20.3
2008	20.3	20.4	20.2	20.3	20.4	20.0	20.0	19.9	20.0	19.8	19.9	19.7	20.1
2009	19.4	19.4	19.2	19.6	19.6	19.5	19.4	19.4	18.8	19.0	19.0	18.8	19.3
2010	18.9	18.9	18.8	18.8	19.0	19.0	19.2	19.2	19.3	19.5	19.5	19.8	19.2
2011	19.3	19.5	19.4	19.4	19.5	19.5	19.6	19.5	19.4	19.5	19.4	19.6	19.5

Employment by Industry: Grand Rapids–Wyoming, MI, Selected Years, 2000–2011—*Continued*

(Numbers in thousands, not seasonally adjusted)

Industry and year	January	February	March	April	May	June	July	August	September	October	November	December	Annual average
Professional and Business Services													
2000	52.1	52.4	52.9	53.3	53.6	54.9	56.2	56.9	56.6	56.1	56.0	55.9	54.7
2001	51.4	50.7	50.7	53.4	54.6	55.3	53.4	54.8	54.2	52.6	51.9	51.1	52.8
2002	49.7	50.0	50.4	52.6	54.0	54.5	54.5	55.7	54.8	54.2	54.4	53.8	53.2
2003	46.6	46.3	45.9	47.5	49.0	49.3	50.4	52.1	51.4	52.1	52.9	52.8	49.7
2004	47.9	48.7	48.5	51.0	52.3	52.6	52.1	53.6	52.7	52.2	52.0	51.3	51.2
2005	48.2	48.3	49.0	51.0	52.1	52.6	54.8	55.8	55.9	54.5	54.6	53.8	52.6
2006	50.1	50.9	50.7	52.6	53.9	55.2	54.7	56.1	56.5	55.5	56.2	56.6	54.1
2007	53.3	54.6	55.4	55.3	57.1	57.7	57.1	58.3	59.5	58.6	59.4	59.6	57.2
2008	57.6	58.1	58.3	58.5	59.7	57.7	55.9	56.5	57.7	58.3	58.0	57.6	57.8
2009	52.7	53.4	53.6	54.0	55.9	52.1	47.0	47.6	51.7	51.9	53.9	54.3	52.3
2010	50.5	52.8	52.0	53.5	55.7	56.0	53.9	54.7	58.7	58.0	59.0	58.9	55.3
2011	56.4	58.2	59.3	60.7	62.8	60.9	60.4	61.5	62.5	62.6	63.3	62.1	60.9
Education and Health Services													
2000	43.9	44.8	45.5	45.7	45.7	44.8	43.9	44.3	45.4	46.0	46.4	46.6	45.3
2001	46.3	47.0	47.8	48.4	48.3	48.0	47.1	46.9	48.0	49.3	49.8	50.0	48.1
2002	49.2	50.1	50.8	51.0	51.1	50.9	49.4	49.7	50.7	51.1	52.0	51.4	50.6
2003	49.1	51.5	51.4	51.3	51.9	50.2	49.2	49.3	50.9	52.8	53.7	53.7	51.3
2004	52.4	53.6	53.7	54.3	54.2	53.3	51.9	52.0	54.4	55.6	56.7	56.3	54.0
2005	54.0	55.5	56.0	56.5	56.2	53.4	53.4	53.4	55.7	56.4	56.7	56.7	55.3
2006	54.8	55.4	56.8	57.0	56.9	54.6	53.3	53.7	56.6	57.1	58.1	58.0	56.0
2007	57.0	58.2	58.5	58.9	58.8	57.3	56.3	56.6	58.4	59.3	59.9	60.0	58.3
2008	58.5	59.7	60.0	60.6	61.0	59.7	58.9	59.0	60.2	61.1	62.1	61.7	60.2
2009	60.1	61.1	61.1	62.2	62.3	60.4	59.7	60.0	61.1	62.9	63.4	63.2	61.5
2010	61.8	62.5	62.6	62.3	62.3	60.9	60.9	60.9	61.4	62.4	62.9	62.4	61.9
2011	61.9	62.3	62.7	62.9	62.7	61.7	61.6	62.1	64.7	66.0	66.4	65.4	63.4
Leisure and Hospitality													
2000	30.8	31.5	31.8	31.6	32.9	33.1	32.8	32.7	32.8	32.0	31.7	31.5	32.1
2001	29.6	30.0	30.4	31.5	32.5	32.4	32.2	32.9	32.4	32.0	31.4	31.7	31.6
2002	29.9	30.0	30.4	31.6	32.8	33.2	32.7	33.2	33.8	32.7	32.3	32.3	32.1
2003	29.7	29.6	29.9	30.8	32.2	32.6	31.7	31.9	32.1	31.6	31.2	31.2	31.2
2004	30.0	30.1	30.3	31.3	32.7	33.0	32.8	32.7	32.5	32.1	32.0	31.9	31.8
2005	30.6	30.8	31.2	32.4	33.7	33.9	33.2	33.8	34.1	33.0	32.7	33.3	32.7
2006	31.2	31.6	32.2	32.4	33.8	33.6	33.4	33.6	33.7	32.8	32.4	32.0	32.7
2007	31.1	31.3	31.6	31.7	33.2	33.5	33.0	33.2	33.2	32.7	32.3	32.6	32.5
2008	30.4	30.5	30.8	32.1	33.8	33.9	32.9	33.0	32.5	31.2	30.5	30.7	31.9
2009	29.1	29.4	29.6	30.3	32.0	32.3	31.9	31.8	31.7	31.0	30.5	30.4	30.8
2010	29.6	29.7	30.2	31.0	32.4	32.7	32.2	32.5	32.4	31.5	30.7	30.9	31.3
2011	29.9	30.0	30.4	31.3	32.6	33.0	33.4	33.2	31.9	29.6	29.7	29.7	31.2
Other Services													
2000	16.0	16.0	16.2	16.1	16.1	16.2	16.3	16.2	16.0	16.2	16.2	16.3	16.2
2001	16.0	16.1	16.3	16.6	16.6	16.7	16.6	16.6	16.4	16.6	16.6	16.8	16.5
2002	16.3	16.4	16.5	16.7	16.8	17.0	17.2	17.1	17.2	17.2	17.1	17.2	16.9
2003	16.9	17.0	17.3	16.8	17.0	17.2	17.1	17.2	17.4	17.1	17.1	17.4	17.1
2004	17.0	17.2	17.4	17.0	17.1	17.2	17.3	17.1	17.0	17.1	17.0	17.0	17.1
2005	17.2	17.4	17.5	16.7	16.8	17.0	16.9	16.8	16.6	16.2	16.3	16.3	16.8
2006	16.1	16.3	16.4	16.8	16.9	17.1	16.8	16.7	16.5	16.5	16.4	16.5	16.6
2007	16.1	16.1	16.3	16.4	16.5	16.7	16.6	16.5	16.3	16.4	16.4	16.5	16.4
2008	16.2	16.2	16.3	16.8	16.9	17.2	17.0	17.0	16.8	17.0	17.0	17.1	16.8
2009	17.0	17.1	17.3	17.8	17.8	17.9	17.8	17.6	17.5	17.6	17.5	17.6	17.5
2010	17.4	17.5	17.5	17.4	17.4	17.7	17.6	17.5	17.2	17.4	17.3	17.4	17.4
2011	17.2	17.1	17.2	17.1	17.3	17.2	17.1	17.0	16.9	17.0	16.9	17.0	17.1
Government													
2000	37.0	38.6	38.8	38.4	39.6	37.3	32.3	31.5	37.6	39.0	39.0	38.8	37.3
2001	38.5	39.5	39.8	39.0	39.8	37.1	32.1	31.8	37.5	38.9	38.9	39.1	37.7
2002	38.4	39.1	39.3	38.4	39.3	36.6	31.7	31.5	37.3	39.8	40.2	40.4	37.7
2003	39.2	39.8	39.8	39.1	40.2	37.8	33.0	33.7	37.8	39.6	39.8	39.9	38.3
2004	39.2	39.5	39.8	39.3	40.0	36.5	31.8	32.2	37.5	39.2	39.3	39.4	37.8
2005	38.0	39.3	39.4	39.3	40.1	37.8	32.2	32.5	37.0	39.0	39.1	38.7	37.7
2006	37.8	39.1	39.2	39.0	39.8	37.5	32.0	32.4	36.3	38.2	38.0	38.0	37.3
2007	36.4	37.2	37.3	37.1	37.5	36.4	31.8	32.5	36.0	36.7	36.6	36.7	36.0
2008	35.7	36.4	36.6	36.6	36.8	36.2	31.6	32.8	35.9	37.0	36.7	36.5	35.7
2009	36.3	36.6	36.8	37.0	37.2	35.7	31.7	31.6	35.4	36.0	36.1	35.8	35.5
2010	35.4	35.5	35.5	35.6	36.6	35.5	31.4	30.9	34.3	35.4	35.6	35.0	34.7
2011	34.5	34.5	34.9	34.9	35.0	34.1	29.8	29.4	33.5	34.1	34.2	33.7	33.6

Employment by Industry: Greensboro–High Point, NC, Selected Years, 2000–2011

(Numbers in thousands, not seasonally adjusted)

Industry and year	January	February	March	April	May	June	July	August	September	October	November	December	Annual average
Total Nonfarm													
2000	359.6	361.3	365.0	366.2	367.7	369.3	363.0	367.8	369.0	370.4	372.2	372.7	367.0
2001	363.4	364.7	364.9	365.9	366.6	366.5	357.3	360.6	361.0	360.6	361.0	360.4	362.7
2002	351.4	352.6	354.6	359.7	360.8	361.4	355.5	360.1	361.8	363.8	365.2	364.7	359.3
2003	356.4	356.9	358.9	358.8	358.2	357.2	346.5	350.1	352.2	355.3	354.4	353.8	354.9
2004	347.6	348.7	352.1	358.1	359.8	359.9	352.8	356.8	359.5	361.5	362.0	363.3	356.8
2005	357.0	359.6	362.3	364.5	364.4	363.8	357.5	362.7	363.9	365.3	366.2	366.8	362.8
2006	362.0	363.5	366.7	370.4	373.2	370.3	364.7	370.2	370.6	374.3	376.1	377.5	370.0
2007	367.8	369.0	372.6	373.3	374.8	373.3	366.2	371.9	372.9	375.7	376.1	376.5	372.5
2008	369.7	370.2	371.6	370.1	370.3	367.5	360.6	366.6	368.5	368.6	366.8	361.8	367.7
2009	350.2	349.1	346.1	345.3	344.3	342.5	335.7	340.1	342.8	342.2	342.0	340.7	343.4
2010	334.4	334.5	337.3	338.7	340.5	340.4	336.3	340.1	340.6	344.7	342.8	343.0	339.4
2011	335.8	338.6	340.6	343.6	344.6	342.0	336.2	339.7	341.0	344.3	346.8	347.2	341.7
Total Private													
2000	321.4	322.9	325.9	327.0	328.5	330.1	329.3	330.5	330.4	330.6	331.4	331.6	328.3
2001	323.7	324.7	324.7	325.7	326.1	326.5	323.6	323.6	322.1	320.2	319.4	319.4	323.3
2002	311.1	312.0	313.5	318.1	319.3	321.0	321.0	322.5	321.5	322.2	322.6	322.6	319.0
2003	315.4	315.4	317.2	316.7	315.8	316.6	311.1	312.2	311.3	312.2	312.1	311.5	314.0
2004	306.3	307.2	310.1	315.7	317.3	318.8	317.6	318.4	318.3	318.9	319.6	320.5	315.7
2005	315.0	317.2	319.6	321.6	321.3	322.5	321.8	322.7	321.7	321.4	322.8	323.2	320.9
2006	319.3	320.4	323.0	326.3	328.9	328.5	328.2	329.5	327.7	330.2	331.5	332.5	327.2
2007	324.2	325.2	328.3	328.8	330.1	331.0	329.0	329.0	329.3	330.7	330.7	331.5	329.1
2008	324.7	324.8	325.8	324.1	323.9	323.7	322.1	324.0	322.5	322.3	320.3	315.8	322.8
2009	304.5	303.0	299.7	298.4	297.6	297.1	296.3	296.8	295.8	296.1	295.7	294.9	298.0
2010	288.7	288.7	290.9	291.8	292.3	294.4	296.2	297.2	295.4	298.5	297.0	297.4	294.0
2011	290.8	293.4	295.1	298.0	299.0	300.2	299.7	299.5	297.9	300.0	302.0	302.6	298.2
Goods-Producing													
2000	99.6	99.7	100.1	99.4	100.1	100.1	100.8	100.8	100.6	99.5	99.2	98.8	99.9
2001	97.1	96.4	96.0	95.6	95.1	95.1	93.8	93.4	92.8	91.7	91.0	90.4	94.0
2002	89.4	88.9	89.2	89.9	90.2	90.8	91.0	91.5	91.2	90.4	89.6	89.0	90.1
2003	88.8	88.6	88.4	87.5	87.4	87.4	85.1	85.2	85.0	84.3	84.1	84.3	86.3
2004	83.0	82.7	83.3	84.1	84.6	85.4	84.9	85.4	85.7	85.2	85.4	85.5	84.6
2005	85.3	85.4	85.5	86.0	86.1	86.4	85.6	85.4	84.9	84.1	84.0	84.1	85.2
2006	82.8	83.0	83.3	83.9	84.0	83.8	83.1	83.6	83.2	83.3	83.2	83.4	83.4
2007	82.4	82.1	82.5	82.6	82.3	82.6	81.9	81.9	81.5	81.8	81.7	82.1	82.1
2008	80.6	80.4	80.4	79.2	79.3	79.0	78.4	78.3	78.0	77.0	76.3	74.8	78.5
2009	71.4	70.2	68.5	68.0	67.0	66.7	66.2	66.1	65.9	65.2	64.9	64.9	67.1
2010	63.3	63.1	63.6	64.1	64.0	64.7	64.9	65.0	64.8	64.7	64.3	64.5	64.3
2011	63.5	64.0	64.4	65.0	65.4	66.0	65.9	66.4	66.2	66.7	66.7	67.6	65.7
Mining, Logging, and Construction													
2000	18.8	18.7	19.0	18.7	18.9	19.0	19.2	19.6	19.8	19.7	19.5	19.3	19.2
2001	18.7	18.6	18.9	19.0	19.1	19.4	19.5	19.3	19.2	18.9	18.6	18.4	19.0
2002	17.4	17.4	17.6	17.7	17.7	17.9	18.1	18.1	17.9	17.5	17.3	17.1	17.6
2003	17.3	17.3	17.5	17.7	18.0	18.1	17.9	18.0	18.2	18.4	18.4	18.6	18.0
2004	17.8	17.5	17.9	18.3	18.5	18.9	18.8	19.0	19.0	18.9	18.9	18.9	18.5
2005	18.6	18.5	18.6	19.1	19.3	19.5	19.5	19.5	19.5	19.2	19.2	19.1	19.1
2006	18.6	18.6	18.9	19.2	19.3	19.5	19.6	19.7	19.6	19.5	19.5	19.5	19.3
2007	19.0	18.9	19.3	19.3	19.3	19.5	19.5	19.4	19.2	19.3	19.3	19.3	19.3
2008	18.5	18.5	18.7	18.3	18.3	18.3	18.3	18.1	18.1	17.9	17.7	17.1	18.2
2009	15.9	15.6	15.3	15.2	14.9	14.9	14.8	14.7	14.5	14.1	14.0	13.9	14.8
2010	13.0	12.8	13.1	13.5	13.3	13.6	13.5	13.5	13.4	13.6	13.5	13.4	13.4
2011	12.6	13.0	13.3	13.7	13.9	14.2	14.2	14.4	14.4	14.4	14.4	14.6	13.9
Manufacturing													
2000	80.8	81.0	81.1	80.7	81.2	81.1	81.6	81.2	80.8	79.8	79.7	79.5	80.7
2001	78.4	77.8	77.1	76.6	76.0	75.7	74.3	74.1	73.6	72.8	72.4	72.0	75.1
2002	72.0	71.5	71.6	72.2	72.5	72.9	72.9	73.4	73.3	72.9	72.3	71.9	72.5
2003	71.5	71.3	70.9	69.8	69.4	69.3	67.2	67.2	66.8	65.9	65.7	65.7	68.4
2004	65.2	65.2	65.4	65.8	66.1	66.5	66.1	66.4	66.7	66.3	66.5	66.6	66.1
2005	66.7	66.9	66.9	66.9	66.8	66.9	66.1	65.9	65.4	64.9	64.8	65.0	66.1
2006	64.2	64.4	64.4	64.7	64.7	64.3	63.5	63.9	63.6	63.8	63.7	63.9	64.1
2007	63.4	63.2	63.2	63.3	63.0	63.1	62.4	62.5	62.3	62.5	62.4	62.8	62.8
2008	62.1	61.9	61.7	60.9	61.0	60.7	60.1	60.2	59.9	59.1	58.6	57.7	60.3
2009	55.5	54.6	53.2	52.8	52.1	51.8	51.4	51.4	51.4	51.1	50.9	51.0	52.3
2010	50.3	50.3	50.5	50.6	50.7	51.1	51.4	51.5	51.4	51.1	50.8	51.1	50.9
2011	50.9	51.0	51.1	51.3	51.5	51.8	51.7	52.0	51.8	52.3	52.3	53.0	51.7
Service-Providing													
2000	260.0	261.6	264.9	266.8	267.6	269.2	262.2	267.0	268.4	270.9	273.0	273.9	267.1
2001	266.3	268.3	268.9	270.3	271.5	271.4	263.5	267.2	268.2	268.9	270.0	270.0	268.7
2002	262.0	263.7	265.4	269.8	270.6	270.6	264.5	268.6	270.6	273.4	275.6	275.7	269.2
2003	267.6	268.3	270.5	271.3	270.8	269.8	261.4	264.9	267.2	271.0	270.3	269.5	268.6
2004	264.6	266.0	268.8	274.0	275.2	274.5	267.9	271.4	273.8	276.3	276.6	277.8	272.2
2005	271.7	274.2	276.8	278.5	278.3	277.4	271.9	277.3	279.0	281.2	282.2	282.7	277.6
2006	279.2	280.5	283.4	286.5	289.2	286.5	281.6	286.6	287.4	291.0	292.9	294.1	286.6
2007	285.4	286.9	290.1	290.7	292.5	290.7	284.3	290.0	291.4	293.9	294.4	294.4	290.4
2008	289.1	289.8	291.2	290.9	291.0	288.5	282.2	288.3	290.5	291.6	290.5	287.0	289.2
2009	278.8	278.9	277.6	277.3	277.3	275.8	269.5	274.0	276.9	277.0	277.1	275.8	276.3
2010	271.1	271.4	273.7	274.6	276.5	275.7	271.4	275.1	275.8	280.0	278.5	278.5	275.2
2011	272.3	274.6	276.2	278.6	279.2	276.0	270.3	273.3	274.8	277.6	280.1	279.6	276.1

Employment by Industry: Greensboro–High Point, NC, Selected Years, 2000–2011—*Continued*

(Numbers in thousands, not seasonally adjusted)

Industry and year	January	February	March	April	May	June	July	August	September	October	November	December	Annual average
Trade, Transportation, and Utilities													
2000	79.0	79.1	79.7	80.3	80.4	80.6	80.0	80.3	80.2	81.1	82.0	82.7	80.5
2001	79.6	79.1	79.1	80.2	80.3	80.1	79.2	78.9	78.4	78.3	78.5	78.9	79.2
2002	74.9	74.3	74.5	75.0	75.1	75.1	74.2	74.4	73.9	74.3	75.7	76.4	74.8
2003	73.5	73.3	73.7	73.5	73.0	73.4	72.1	72.1	72.0	72.4	73.5	73.8	73.0
2004	71.8	71.2	71.8	72.0	72.3	72.3	72.5	72.6	72.3	72.9	74.3	75.4	72.6
2005	72.1	72.2	72.6	73.0	73.1	73.2	73.5	73.7	73.3	74.8	76.1	76.9	73.7
2006	75.4	75.0	75.1	75.8	76.2	75.4	75.6	75.7	75.7	76.3	78.1	78.9	76.1
2007	76.1	75.7	76.5	76.3	76.8	76.6	76.5	76.9	76.7	77.0	78.0	78.9	76.8
2008	75.3	74.8	74.8	74.6	74.8	74.7	73.8	73.8	73.7	74.0	74.2	74.4	74.4
2009	70.9	70.2	70.0	69.1	69.2	68.9	68.5	68.5	68.6	68.5	69.2	69.5	69.3
2010	67.4	67.2	67.5	67.9	68.1	68.0	68.1	68.2	68.0	68.8	69.4	70.3	68.2
2011	67.8	68.1	68.3	68.8	69.0	68.9	68.7	68.4	68.4	68.8	69.6	70.1	68.7
Wholesale Trade													
2000	19.0	19.2	19.3	19.6	19.7	19.7	19.8	19.8	19.8	19.8	19.7	19.8	19.6
2001	19.6	19.8	19.8	19.7	19.6	19.6	19.5	19.5	19.2	19.2	19.0	19.0	19.5
2002	18.8	19.0	18.9	19.2	19.1	19.2	19.3	19.3	19.3	19.3	19.4	19.4	19.2
2003	18.9	19.0	19.1	19.0	18.8	18.9	18.5	18.5	18.4	18.5	18.5	18.5	18.7
2004	18.6	18.5	18.6	18.9	18.8	18.8	18.5	18.5	18.3	18.3	18.3	18.3	18.5
2005	18.5	18.5	18.5	18.5	18.6	18.5	18.8	18.9	18.8	18.8	18.8	18.8	18.7
2006	18.9	19.1	19.1	19.4	19.6	19.5	19.5	19.6	19.7	19.8	19.9	20.0	19.5
2007	20.1	20.1	20.3	20.3	20.4	20.5	20.6	20.6	20.6	20.6	20.6	20.7	20.5
2008	20.4	20.4	20.4	20.2	20.3	20.2	20.0	19.9	19.9	19.8	19.6	19.3	20.0
2009	18.8	18.7	18.5	18.5	18.5	18.3	18.2	18.4	18.2	18.2	18.2	18.2	18.4
2010	18.0	18.0	18.2	18.2	18.2	18.1	18.1	18.2	18.0	18.0	18.0	18.0	18.1
2011	17.8	18.0	18.0	18.1	18.2	18.1	18.1	18.3	18.3	18.3	18.4	18.4	18.2
Retail Trade													
2000	39.4	39.3	39.8	39.7	39.8	39.9	38.9	39.1	39.1	39.3	40.3	41.0	39.6
2001	39.2	38.7	38.8	38.9	39.2	39.2	39.0	39.0	39.0	39.1	39.8	40.3	39.2
2002	38.2	37.7	38.0	38.1	38.3	38.3	37.7	37.9	37.5	37.6	38.8	39.5	38.1
2003	37.3	36.8	37.0	36.8	36.7	36.6	36.1	36.1	35.9	36.3	37.4	37.7	36.7
2004	35.9	35.5	35.8	36.2	36.6	36.5	36.4	36.6	36.5	37.0	38.3	39.2	36.7
2005	36.6	36.7	37.0	37.3	37.2	37.3	37.4	37.3	36.9	38.4	39.5	40.4	37.7
2006	39.4	38.9	38.9	39.2	39.4	38.8	38.9	39.1	38.9	39.5	41.2	41.8	39.5
2007	39.6	39.3	39.7	39.6	39.9	39.7	39.5	39.6	39.4	39.7	40.6	40.9	39.8
2008	38.7	38.2	38.1	38.1	38.0	37.9	37.7	37.7	37.5	37.9	38.2	38.5	38.0
2009	36.5	36.1	36.2	35.6	35.8	35.7	35.6	35.5	35.6	35.6	36.2	36.4	35.9
2010	34.8	34.6	34.7	34.9	35.0	34.9	34.8	34.8	34.7	35.1	35.9	36.3	35.0
2011	34.6	34.5	34.7	35.0	35.1	35.0	34.9	34.5	34.5	34.9	35.5	35.8	34.9
Transportation and Utilities													
2000	20.6	20.6	20.6	21.0	20.9	21.0	21.3	21.4	21.3	22.0	22.0	21.9	21.2
2001	20.8	20.6	20.5	21.6	21.5	21.3	20.7	20.4	20.2	20.0	19.7	19.6	20.6
2002	17.9	17.6	17.6	17.7	17.7	17.6	17.2	17.2	17.1	17.4	17.5	17.5	17.5
2003	17.3	17.5	17.6	17.7	17.5	17.9	17.5	17.5	17.7	17.6	17.6	17.6	17.6
2004	17.3	17.2	17.4	16.9	16.9	17.0	17.6	17.5	17.5	17.6	17.7	17.9	17.4
2005	17.0	17.0	17.1	17.2	17.3	17.4	17.3	17.5	17.6	17.6	17.8	17.7	17.4
2006	17.1	17.0	17.1	17.2	17.2	17.1	17.2	17.0	17.1	17.0	17.0	17.1	17.1
2007	16.4	16.3	16.5	16.4	16.5	16.4	16.4	16.7	16.7	16.7	16.8	17.3	16.6
2008	16.2	16.2	16.3	16.3	16.5	16.6	16.1	16.2	16.3	16.3	16.4	16.6	16.3
2009	15.6	15.4	15.3	15.0	14.9	14.9	14.7	14.6	14.8	14.7	14.8	14.9	15.0
2010	14.6	14.6	14.6	14.8	14.9	15.0	15.2	15.2	15.3	15.7	15.5	16.0	15.1
2011	15.4	15.6	15.6	15.7	15.7	15.8	15.7	15.6	15.6	15.6	15.7	15.9	15.7
Information													
2000	7.6	7.6	7.6	7.8	7.9	8.0	8.3	8.3	8.3	8.3	8.3	8.3	8.0
2001	8.4	8.3	8.4	8.3	8.4	8.5	8.6	8.4	8.4	8.0	8.0	8.1	8.3
2002	7.8	7.7	7.6	7.7	7.9	7.8	7.8	7.7	7.6	7.6	7.7	7.7	7.7
2003	7.5	7.4	7.4	7.4	7.6	7.5	7.5	7.6	7.5	7.4	7.5	7.5	7.5
2004	7.1	6.9	6.9	6.8	6.8	6.7	6.7	6.6	6.5	6.5	6.5	6.5	6.7
2005	6.5	6.4	6.5	6.6	6.6	6.6	6.6	6.6	6.6	6.5	6.5	6.6	6.6
2006	6.6	6.5	6.5	6.3	6.4	6.3	6.3	6.3	6.3	6.4	6.4	6.5	6.4
2007	6.3	6.3	6.2	6.3	6.2	6.2	6.2	6.2	6.2	6.2	6.3	6.3	6.2
2008	6.2	6.1	6.2	6.2	6.2	6.3	6.2	6.1	6.0	6.0	6.2	6.2	6.2
2009	5.9	5.8	5.8	5.8	5.8	5.7	5.6	5.6	5.5	5.5	5.5	5.6	5.7
2010	5.6	5.5	5.5	5.5	5.5	5.5	5.6	5.6	5.5	5.5	5.5	5.6	5.5
2011	5.5	5.5	5.5	5.5	5.5	5.5	5.5	5.5	5.4	5.4	5.5	5.5	5.5
Financial Activities													
2000	20.6	20.7	20.9	20.9	20.9	21.1	21.0	20.9	20.9	21.0	20.9	21.1	20.9
2001	20.8	20.8	20.9	20.9	20.9	21.1	21.3	21.5	21.4	21.3	21.3	21.4	21.1
2002	21.0	21.0	20.9	21.0	20.9	21.0	21.2	21.2	21.1	21.4	21.1	21.2	21.1
2003	21.6	21.6	21.8	21.4	21.1	20.9	20.7	20.5	20.3	20.1	19.8	19.7	20.8
2004	19.8	19.9	19.9	20.9	20.7	20.8	21.2	21.1	21.1	21.2	21.2	21.3	20.8
2005	21.1	21.2	21.3	21.4	21.4	21.5	21.7	21.7	21.7	21.4	21.5	21.5	21.5
2006	21.5	21.6	21.8	21.8	22.0	22.1	22.3	22.4	22.4	22.5	22.5	22.6	22.1
2007	22.3	22.5	22.5	22.5	22.4	22.6	22.4	22.3	22.4	22.4	22.4	22.2	22.4
2008	21.9	22.0	22.0	22.1	22.2	22.3	22.4	22.2	22.1	22.2	22.1	22.1	22.1
2009	21.6	21.6	21.4	21.4	21.4	21.3	21.1	21.2	21.1	21.1	21.0	20.8	21.3
2010	20.5	20.4	20.3	20.2	20.0	20.0	20.1	20.1	20.1	20.1	20.0	20.1	20.2
2011	19.8	19.8	19.9	19.9	19.8	19.8	19.7	19.8	19.7	19.8	19.7	19.7	19.8

Employment by Industry: Greensboro–High Point, NC, Selected Years, 2000–2011—*Continued*

(Numbers in thousands, not seasonally adjusted)

Industry and year	January	February	March	April	May	June	July	August	September	October	November	December	Annual average
Professional and Business Services													
2000	44.5	45.4	46.2	46.4	46.2	46.3	45.4	45.9	46.0	45.9	45.8	45.5	45.8
2001	43.8	44.1	44.2	43.5	43.4	43.3	42.1	42.6	42.8	42.1	41.6	40.9	42.9
2002	39.2	40.2	40.4	41.1	41.3	41.2	41.0	41.8	42.0	42.0	42.1	42.0	41.2
2003	39.9	40.3	41.2	41.4	41.3	41.4	40.8	41.4	41.8	42.9	42.5	41.7	41.4
2004	41.3	42.0	42.6	43.9	44.2	44.1	44.1	44.4	44.8	45.0	44.6	44.5	43.8
2005	44.7	45.8	46.2	45.9	45.0	45.1	45.2	45.6	46.0	45.3	45.4	45.2	45.5
2006	44.2	44.5	45.6	47.4	48.2	47.9	48.1	48.5	47.8	49.0	48.7	48.3	47.4
2007	45.3	46.2	47.0	47.0	47.2	47.4	47.0	48.2	48.5	48.7	48.1	47.8	47.4
2008	47.2	47.3	47.7	47.6	46.8	46.5	47.1	48.6	48.6	49.1	47.1	44.9	47.4
2009	42.9	42.6	41.7	41.2	40.7	41.3	41.8	42.6	43.1	44.6	43.8	43.4	42.5
2010	43.2	43.5	44.1	44.0	43.9	44.7	46.0	46.6	46.5	47.7	46.7	46.3	45.3
2011	45.4	46.3	46.9	47.4	47.4	47.6	47.2	47.7	47.6	47.7	48.2	47.9	47.3
Education and Health Services													
2000	36.1	36.2	36.4	36.0	36.2	36.5	36.7	37.1	37.3	37.6	38.1	37.9	36.8
2001	37.5	38.1	38.1	38.4	38.4	38.6	38.4	38.6	38.8	39.8	40.1	40.5	38.8
2002	39.8	40.2	40.5	40.7	40.7	40.9	40.8	40.9	41.1	41.8	41.9	41.8	40.9
2003	41.2	41.6	41.7	41.5	41.4	41.3	41.1	41.3	41.5	42.0	41.9	41.8	41.5
2004	41.6	42.1	42.1	42.6	42.6	42.6	42.3	42.7	42.9	43.6	43.7	43.8	42.7
2005	43.3	43.8	44.2	44.4	44.4	44.3	44.5	44.8	45.1	45.3	45.5	45.4	44.6
2006	45.6	46.0	46.1	46.0	45.9	45.9	45.8	46.1	46.1	46.4	46.5	46.6	46.1
2007	46.6	47.0	47.1	46.8	47.0	46.7	46.3	46.4	46.1	46.9	46.7	46.7	46.7
2008	46.3	46.5	46.5	47.0	46.9	46.9	46.5	47.0	47.0	47.9	48.4	48.0	47.1
2009	47.7	48.1	47.5	47.9	47.7	47.4	47.2	47.3	46.7	47.5	47.7	47.5	47.5
2010	47.0	46.9	47.1	47.0	47.0	46.9	46.9	47.0	46.5	47.7	47.6	47.5	47.1
2011	46.7	47.0	46.8	47.3	47.2	47.0	46.9	46.4	46.5	47.3	47.7	47.7	47.0
Leisure and Hospitality													
2000	25.1	25.0	25.5	26.5	26.8	27.3	26.8	26.7	26.4	26.4	26.1	26.1	26.2
2001	25.2	26.3	26.1	26.8	27.3	27.4	27.5	27.5	26.7	26.1	25.8	25.8	26.5
2002	25.5	25.9	26.4	28.3	28.7	29.3	29.7	29.6	29.4	29.3	29.1	29.2	28.4
2003	27.8	27.5	28.0	28.8	29.0	29.6	29.1	29.4	28.5	28.6	28.3	28.2	28.6
2004	27.2	27.8	28.7	29.9	30.5	31.2	30.8	30.9	30.4	29.7	29.4	29.0	29.6
2005	27.7	27.9	28.8	29.7	30.2	30.8	30.2	30.5	29.8	29.6	29.4	29.0	29.5
2006	28.9	29.4	30.0	30.8	31.6	32.6	32.8	32.9	32.3	32.0	31.9	31.9	31.4
2007	31.0	31.2	32.1	32.6	33.4	34.0	33.6	33.7	33.1	32.6	32.6	32.5	32.7
2008	32.3	32.7	33.2	32.5	33.0	33.2	32.9	33.1	32.4	31.5	31.2	30.7	32.4
2009	29.6	29.9	30.2	30.5	31.4	31.5	31.6	31.3	30.8	29.7	29.7	29.3	30.5
2010	28.1	28.4	29.1	29.5	30.2	30.9	30.9	31.1	30.6	30.5	30.1	29.8	29.9
2011	28.8	29.3	30.0	30.7	31.3	31.8	32.2	31.8	30.7	30.8	31.1	30.6	30.8
Other Services													
2000	8.9	9.2	9.5	9.7	10.0	10.2	10.3	10.5	10.7	10.8	11.0	11.2	10.2
2001	11.3	11.6	11.9	12.0	12.3	12.4	12.7	12.7	12.8	12.9	13.1	13.4	12.4
2002	13.5	13.8	14.0	14.4	14.5	14.9	15.3	15.4	15.2	15.4	15.4	15.3	14.8
2003	15.1	15.1	15.0	15.2	15.0	15.1	15.0	14.7	14.7	14.5	14.5	14.5	14.9
2004	14.5	14.6	14.8	15.5	15.6	15.7	15.1	14.7	14.6	14.8	14.5	14.5	14.9
2005	14.3	14.5	14.5	14.6	14.5	14.6	14.5	14.4	14.3	14.4	14.4	14.5	14.5
2006	14.3	14.4	14.6	14.3	14.6	14.5	14.2	14.0	13.9	14.3	14.2	14.3	14.3
2007	14.2	14.2	14.4	14.7	14.8	14.9	15.1	14.9	14.8	15.1	14.9	15.0	14.8
2008	14.9	15.0	15.0	14.9	14.7	14.8	15.0	14.9	14.7	14.7	14.7	14.7	14.8
2009	14.5	14.6	14.6	14.5	14.4	14.3	14.3	14.2	14.1	14.0	13.9	13.9	14.3
2010	13.6	13.7	13.7	13.6	13.6	13.7	13.7	13.6	13.4	13.5	13.4	13.3	13.6
2011	13.3	13.4	13.3	13.4	13.4	13.6	13.6	13.5	13.4	13.5	13.5	13.5	13.5
Government													
2000	38.2	38.4	39.1	39.2	39.2	39.2	33.7	37.3	38.6	39.8	40.8	41.1	38.7
2001	39.7	40.0	40.2	40.2	40.5	40.0	33.7	37.0	38.9	40.4	41.6	41.0	39.4
2002	40.3	40.6	41.1	41.6	41.5	40.4	34.5	37.6	40.3	41.6	42.6	42.1	40.4
2003	41.0	41.5	41.7	42.1	42.4	40.6	35.1	37.9	40.9	43.1	42.3	42.3	40.9
2004	41.3	41.5	42.0	42.4	42.5	41.1	35.2	38.4	41.2	42.6	42.4	42.8	41.1
2005	42.0	42.4	42.7	42.9	43.1	41.3	35.7	40.0	42.2	43.9	43.4	43.6	41.9
2006	42.7	43.1	43.7	44.1	44.3	41.8	36.5	40.7	42.9	44.1	44.6	45.0	42.8
2007	43.6	43.8	44.3	44.5	44.7	42.3	37.2	41.4	43.6	45.0	45.4	45.0	43.4
2008	45.0	45.4	45.8	46.0	46.4	43.8	38.5	42.6	46.0	46.3	46.5	46.0	44.9
2009	45.7	46.1	46.4	46.9	46.7	45.4	39.4	43.3	47.0	46.1	46.3	45.8	45.4
2010	45.7	45.8	46.4	46.9	48.2	46.0	40.1	42.9	45.2	46.2	45.8	45.6	45.4
2011	45.0	45.2	45.5	45.6	45.6	41.8	36.5	40.2	43.1	44.3	44.8	44.6	43.5

Employment by Industry: Hartford–West Hartford–East Hartford, CT, NECTA, Selected Years, 2000–2011

(Numbers in thousands, not seasonally adjusted)

Industry and year	January	February	March	April	May	June	July	August	September	October	November	December	Annual average
Total Nonfarm													
2000	547.6	550.9	554.5	555.4	557.4	559.5	554.4	548.8	558.0	561.6	564.5	568.2	556.7
2001	552.4	552.5	554.1	554.9	555.8	557.7	550.2	547.5	552.4	554.2	556.4	557.5	553.8
2002	542.7	544.0	545.8	546.3	549.3	549.6	539.2	536.3	543.2	544.3	546.9	547.9	544.6
2003	534.3	533.2	533.3	536.5	539.0	538.1	529.2	526.4	533.5	539.0	540.9	541.3	535.4
2004	528.3	529.2	531.3	537.5	540.0	541.0	534.0	531.0	539.8	543.3	546.4	548.6	537.5
2005	535.0	536.2	537.3	545.0	546.6	548.8	539.9	538.0	546.8	547.7	552.4	553.2	543.9
2006	541.2	541.8	543.7	549.7	551.8	553.0	547.5	545.4	552.6	557.2	559.5	560.4	550.3
2007	547.0	548.7	550.2	554.8	558.5	561.9	553.3	551.0	558.2	561.2	565.1	564.5	556.2
2008	552.2	555.1	557.1	560.7	562.2	565.1	555.7	551.9	559.9	561.8	560.4	556.7	558.2
2009	541.4	543.1	540.9	541.6	543.3	542.5	533.3	529.9	538.5	541.3	541.8	540.8	539.9
2010	521.5	523.4	525.9	533.5	535.5	535.6	528.8	526.6	537.3	542.2	544.4	544.1	533.2
2011	530.8	533.3	533.8	541.5	540.7	541.3	532.2	530.9	539.5	546.3	548.1	548.1	538.9
Total Private													
2000	461.5	461.5	464.6	465.5	467.5	472.9	474.3	470.6	471.7	473.2	475.2	479.5	469.8
2001	465.8	462.9	464.4	465.1	466.7	471.6	469.4	467.3	465.0	464.3	465.0	466.4	466.2
2002	454.8	452.8	454.4	455.5	458.9	462.0	458.2	455.4	454.7	454.6	456.0	457.2	456.2
2003	447.3	443.2	443.8	447.5	451.1	452.7	450.6	448.6	449.9	452.2	453.7	454.2	449.6
2004	444.5	442.2	444.2	449.7	453.4	456.8	455.9	453.8	455.7	456.3	458.4	461.0	452.7
2005	450.6	449.0	450.5	456.8	459.3	464.0	460.4	459.4	460.0	459.3	462.1	464.6	458.0
2006	455.8	454.0	456.0	460.5	463.3	467.6	466.7	465.5	464.9	466.7	467.8	470.2	463.3
2007	459.6	458.6	460.2	464.3	470.6	476.3	472.5	471.1	470.7	470.9	473.9	475.2	468.7
2008	465.8	464.9	466.9	469.9	474.0	479.0	474.3	471.5	472.2	471.6	470.2	468.8	470.8
2009	456.1	452.7	450.8	450.5	455.2	456.8	453.5	450.9	451.1	450.6	450.7	451.0	452.5
2010	437.0	436.1	438.3	445.6	449.5	453.1	450.9	450.0	451.9	454.0	456.1	456.9	448.3
2011	445.9	446.2	446.9	454.0	456.9	460.8	456.7	456.7	456.8	460.5	462.1	463.5	455.6
Goods-Producing													
2000	93.7	93.3	94.5	96.0	96.5	97.7	98.6	98.4	99.1	99.2	99.2	99.3	97.1
2001	96.1	95.0	95.2	95.9	96.2	96.6	95.3	95.2	94.5	93.4	92.5	92.3	94.9
2002	89.6	88.7	89.2	90.2	90.8	91.2	90.0	89.7	89.4	88.8	88.1	87.3	89.4
2003	84.5	83.0	83.2	84.5	85.1	85.6	85.6	85.6	85.6	85.5	85.6	85.1	84.9
2004	82.4	81.8	82.6	84.5	85.4	86.6	86.9	86.8	86.9	86.6	86.7	86.3	85.3
2005	83.8	83.1	83.5	85.4	86.2	87.7	87.1	86.9	86.6	86.3	86.4	85.9	85.7
2006	84.1	83.8	84.2	86.1	86.8	88.1	88.6	88.6	88.1	88.0	87.8	87.6	86.8
2007	85.2	84.5	84.9	86.5	87.9	88.9	88.9	88.9	88.0	87.8	87.7	86.9	87.2
2008	84.4	84.0	83.9	85.6	86.1	87.2	86.8	86.5	86.1	85.2	83.9	82.5	85.2
2009	79.8	78.2	77.3	77.1	77.5	77.8	77.4	76.9	76.9	75.7	75.2	74.8	77.1
2010	71.4	70.4	70.6	72.6	73.6	74.7	74.7	74.7	75.0	75.2	75.3	75.0	73.6
2011	72.4	72.2	72.5	73.6	74.6	76.1	76.2	75.7	74.4	74.8	74.8	72.9	74.2
Mining, Logging, and Construction													
2000	19.3	19.0	19.9	21.0	21.6	22.3	22.8	23.0	22.8	22.5	22.5	22.2	21.6
2001	20.1	19.8	20.2	21.5	22.4	22.9	22.8	22.9	22.4	21.8	21.2	20.7	21.6
2002	19.6	19.3	19.7	20.9	21.6	21.9	21.8	21.8	21.4	21.2	20.9	20.1	20.9
2003	18.5	17.7	17.9	19.2	20.1	20.6	21.5	21.6	21.4	21.3	21.4	20.7	20.2
2004	18.5	18.1	18.6	20.5	21.3	22.0	22.6	23.0	22.8	22.7	22.6	22.1	21.2
2005	20.1	19.5	19.8	21.3	22.0	23.0	23.1	23.2	22.8	22.4	22.4	21.7	21.8
2006	20.3	19.9	20.2	21.6	22.3	22.9	23.5	23.8	23.3	23.2	23.0	22.5	22.2
2007	20.8	20.1	20.5	22.1	23.4	23.9	24.1	24.2	23.8	23.6	23.3	22.4	22.7
2008	20.4	20.1	20.2	21.4	21.9	22.4	22.5	22.3	21.9	21.4	20.6	19.6	21.2
2009	17.7	17.1	17.1	17.9	18.7	19.1	19.3	19.4	19.2	18.7	18.4	17.9	18.4
2010	15.3	14.5	14.6	16.6	17.3	17.9	18.1	18.3	18.1	18.2	18.1	17.5	17.0
2011	15.6	15.3	15.4	16.6	17.4	18.2	18.8	18.4	17.4	17.6	17.4	16.1	17.0
Manufacturing													
2000	74.4	74.3	74.6	75.0	74.9	75.4	75.8	75.4	76.3	76.7	76.7	77.1	75.6
2001	76.0	75.2	75.0	74.4	73.8	73.7	72.5	72.3	72.1	71.6	71.3	71.6	73.3
2002	70.0	69.4	69.5	69.3	69.2	69.3	68.2	67.9	68.0	67.6	67.2	67.2	68.6
2003	66.0	65.3	65.3	65.3	65.0	65.0	64.1	64.0	64.2	64.2	64.2	64.4	64.8
2004	63.9	63.7	64.0	64.0	64.1	64.6	64.3	63.8	64.1	63.9	64.1	64.2	64.1
2005	63.7	63.6	63.7	64.1	64.2	64.7	64.0	63.7	63.8	63.9	64.0	64.2	64.0
2006	63.8	63.9	64.0	64.5	64.5	65.2	65.1	64.8	64.8	64.8	64.8	65.1	64.6
2007	64.4	64.4	64.4	64.4	64.5	65.0	64.8	64.7	64.2	64.2	64.4	64.5	64.5
2008	64.0	63.9	63.7	64.2	64.2	64.8	64.3	64.2	64.2	63.8	63.3	62.9	64.0
2009	62.1	61.1	60.2	59.2	58.8	58.7	58.1	57.5	57.7	57.0	56.8	56.9	58.7
2010	56.1	55.9	56.0	56.0	56.3	56.8	56.6	56.4	56.9	57.0	57.2	57.5	56.6
2011	56.8	56.9	57.1	57.0	57.2	57.9	57.4	57.3	57.0	57.2	57.4	56.8	57.2
Service-Providing													
2000	453.9	457.6	460.0	459.4	460.9	461.8	455.8	450.4	458.9	462.4	465.3	468.9	459.6
2001	456.3	457.5	458.9	459.0	459.6	461.1	454.9	452.3	457.9	460.8	463.9	465.2	459.0
2002	453.1	455.3	456.6	456.1	458.5	458.4	449.2	446.6	453.8	455.5	458.8	460.6	455.2
2003	449.8	450.2	450.1	452.0	453.9	452.5	443.6	440.8	447.9	453.5	455.3	456.2	450.5
2004	445.9	447.4	448.7	453.0	454.6	454.4	447.1	444.2	452.9	456.7	459.7	462.3	452.2
2005	451.2	453.1	453.8	459.6	460.4	461.1	452.8	451.1	460.2	461.4	466.0	467.3	458.2
2006	457.1	458.0	459.5	463.6	465.0	464.9	458.9	456.8	464.5	469.2	471.7	472.8	463.5
2007	461.8	464.2	465.3	468.3	470.6	473.0	464.4	462.1	470.2	473.4	477.4	477.6	469.0
2008	467.8	471.1	473.2	475.1	476.1	477.9	468.9	465.4	473.8	476.6	476.5	474.2	473.1
2009	461.6	464.9	463.6	464.5	465.8	464.7	455.9	453.0	461.6	465.6	466.6	466.0	462.8
2010	450.1	453.0	455.3	460.9	461.9	460.9	454.1	451.9	462.3	467.0	469.1	469.1	459.6
2011	458.4	461.1	461.3	467.9	466.1	465.2	456.0	455.2	465.1	471.5	473.3	475.2	464.7

Employment by Industry: Hartford–West Hartford–East Hartford, CT, NECTA, Selected Years, 2000–2011—*Continued*

(Numbers in thousands, not seasonally adjusted)

Industry and year	January	February	March	April	May	June	July	August	September	October	November	December	Annual average
Trade, Transportation, and Utilities													
2000	93.7	92.5	92.9	91.7	92.0	92.5	91.2	90.6	92.0	92.7	94.8	96.2	92.7
2001	91.8	89.9	90.3	91.1	91.5	91.9	90.6	90.0	91.1	91.7	93.4	94.3	91.5
2002	91.0	89.6	89.8	89.1	89.4	90.6	88.2	87.7	88.6	88.3	89.8	91.3	89.5
2003	88.1	86.7	87.0	86.8	87.3	87.7	86.3	86.0	87.5	88.7	90.0	90.8	87.7
2004	88.0	87.1	87.3	88.0	88.6	89.2	88.0	87.5	89.1	90.0	92.3	94.0	89.1
2005	90.2	89.1	89.3	90.1	90.2	90.8	88.4	88.2	89.8	89.7	92.0	93.6	90.1
2006	90.1	88.1	88.6	89.4	89.7	89.9	87.8	87.6	89.0	89.6	91.4	93.0	89.5
2007	89.1	87.6	88.1	87.9	89.6	90.6	88.8	88.3	89.8	90.9	93.1	94.8	89.9
2008	91.3	89.9	90.2	90.1	90.9	91.6	89.3	88.8	90.2	90.5	91.4	92.4	90.6
2009	88.2	86.4	85.8	84.6	86.0	86.4	84.6	84.2	85.6	86.0	87.4	88.3	86.1
2010	84.7	83.4	83.8	83.9	85.1	86.1	84.5	84.2	84.8	86.0	87.6	89.2	85.3
2011	85.5	84.8	84.8	86.1	86.4	87.2	86.1	85.6	86.1	87.1	88.8	90.4	86.6
Wholesale Trade													
2000	20.3	20.2	20.3	20.1	20.1	20.1	20.2	20.1	20.1	20.0	20.2	20.3	20.2
2001	20.1	20.1	20.1	20.2	20.1	20.2	20.2	20.1	19.9	20.1	19.9	20.0	20.1
2002	19.7	19.6	19.6	19.4	19.3	19.3	19.4	19.3	19.2	19.1	19.0	19.1	19.3
2003	19.5	19.4	19.6	19.5	19.5	19.6	19.4	19.4	19.3	19.2	18.9	19.4
2004	18.7	18.6	18.7	18.9	18.9	19.1	19.2	19.2	19.1	19.0	19.1	19.2	19.0
2005	19.1	19.0	19.1	19.4	19.5	19.7	19.5	19.5	19.6	19.5	19.6	19.6	19.4
2006	19.6	19.5	19.6	19.8	19.7	19.9	19.7	19.7	19.6	19.6	19.5	19.5	19.6
2007	19.5	19.5	19.6	19.6	19.8	19.9	20.1	20.0	20.0	20.0	20.0	20.2	19.9
2008	20.0	20.0	20.2	20.1	20.3	20.4	20.2	20.1	20.0	19.9	19.7	19.5	20.0
2009	19.4	19.1	19.0	18.8	18.8	18.8	18.8	18.7	18.6	18.4	18.4	18.4	18.8
2010	18.0	17.9	18.0	18.2	18.3	18.4	18.5	18.5	18.3	18.3	18.4	18.4	18.3
2011	18.0	18.0	18.1	18.4	18.5	18.7	18.6	18.6	18.7	18.6	18.6	18.6	18.5
Retail Trade													
2000	57.3	56.2	56.5	55.5	55.8	56.3	55.4	55.3	55.3	55.8	57.7	59.2	56.4
2001	55.7	54.3	54.7	55.5	56.1	56.5	56.0	56.0	55.9	56.1	58.0	58.9	56.1
2002	56.4	55.2	55.6	55.5	55.8	57.0	55.7	55.7	55.4	54.8	56.4	57.8	55.9
2003	54.6	53.4	53.5	53.6	54.0	54.3	53.9	54.0	54.2	55.0	56.2	57.4	54.5
2004	55.2	54.4	54.5	54.7	55.2	55.5	55.2	55.0	55.3	55.7	57.8	59.4	55.7
2005	56.2	55.4	55.4	55.8	55.8	56.0	55.0	55.1	55.3	55.3	57.2	58.5	55.9
2006	55.8	54.0	54.5	55.1	55.3	55.3	54.5	54.4	54.6	55.1	56.9	58.1	55.3
2007	54.9	53.5	53.9	54.0	55.3	56.0	55.1	55.2	55.1	55.9	58.0	59.2	55.5
2008	56.4	54.9	55.0	55.0	55.4	55.9	54.8	54.9	54.6	54.8	55.8	56.7	55.4
2009	53.4	52.0	51.6	51.3	52.0	52.5	51.9	51.9	51.9	52.4	53.8	54.6	52.4
2010	51.9	50.8	51.0	51.3	51.9	52.7	52.3	52.1	51.6	52.7	54.0	55.4	52.3
2011	52.8	51.9	51.8	52.7	52.7	53.2	53.3	53.1	52.1	53.2	54.8	56.2	53.2
Transportation and Utilities													
2000	16.1	16.1	16.1	16.1	16.1	16.1	15.6	15.2	16.6	16.9	16.9	16.7	16.2
2001	16.0	15.5	15.5	15.4	15.3	15.2	14.4	13.9	15.3	15.5	15.5	15.4	15.2
2002	14.9	14.8	14.6	14.2	14.3	14.3	13.1	12.7	14.0	14.4	14.4	14.4	14.2
2003	14.0	13.9	13.9	13.7	13.8	13.8	13.0	12.6	14.0	14.5	14.6	14.5	13.9
2004	14.1	14.1	14.1	14.4	14.5	14.6	13.6	13.3	14.7	15.3	15.4	15.4	14.5
2005	14.9	14.7	14.8	14.9	14.9	15.1	13.9	13.6	14.9	14.9	15.2	15.5	14.8
2006	14.7	14.6	14.5	14.5	14.7	14.7	13.6	13.5	14.8	14.9	15.0	15.4	14.6
2007	14.7	14.6	14.6	14.3	14.5	14.7	13.6	13.1	14.7	15.0	15.1	15.4	14.5
2008	14.9	15.0	15.0	15.0	15.2	15.3	14.3	13.8	15.6	15.8	15.9	16.2	15.2
2009	15.4	15.3	15.2	14.5	15.2	15.1	13.9	13.6	15.1	15.2	15.2	15.3	14.9
2010	14.8	14.7	14.8	14.4	14.9	15.0	13.7	13.6	14.9	15.0	15.2	15.4	14.7
2011	14.7	14.9	14.9	15.0	15.2	15.3	14.2	13.9	15.3	15.3	15.4	15.6	15.0
Information													
2000	12.5	12.6	12.7	12.8	12.9	13.0	13.2	13.2	13.2	13.3	13.4	13.4	13.0
2001	13.0	13.1	12.8	11.9	11.8	11.7	12.2	12.2	12.0	11.9	12.0	11.8	12.2
2002	11.4	11.3	11.3	11.4	11.4	11.5	11.4	11.3	11.2	11.2	11.2	11.2	11.3
2003	11.3	11.3	11.3	11.1	11.1	11.3	11.2	11.2	11.0	11.0	11.0	11.0	11.2
2004	11.3	11.2	11.3	11.3	11.3	11.4	11.4	11.4	11.3	11.3	11.4	11.4	11.3
2005	11.5	11.4	11.4	11.4	11.5	11.6	11.6	11.6	11.5	11.6	11.7	11.8	11.6
2006	12.0	12.0	12.0	11.9	11.9	12.1	12.1	12.0	11.8	11.9	11.9	11.9	12.0
2007	11.9	12.0	12.0	12.1	12.1	12.3	12.4	12.3	12.2	12.1	12.2	12.3	12.2
2008	12.4	12.4	12.4	12.4	12.4	12.6	12.6	12.4	12.1	12.1	12.2	12.1	12.3
2009	12.0	12.0	11.8	11.8	11.7	11.7	11.7	11.6	11.5	11.3	11.2	11.2	11.6
2010	11.1	11.0	11.0	11.0	11.0	11.1	11.1	11.2	11.2	11.2	11.3	11.3	11.1
2011	11.3	11.3	11.3	11.2	11.2	11.2	11.3	11.3	11.2	11.3	11.3	11.3	11.3
Financial Activities													
2000	69.3	69.2	69.6	69.1	69.2	70.2	70.5	70.5	69.8	69.7	69.8	70.2	69.8
2001	70.0	69.7	69.9	70.1	70.4	71.4	71.5	71.4	70.7	70.2	70.2	70.5	70.5
2002	70.2	69.7	69.7	69.3	69.6	70.3	70.6	70.5	69.9	69.5	69.7	69.7	69.9
2003	69.4	68.9	68.6	69.7	69.9	70.6	70.1	69.7	69.1	68.7	68.7	68.8	69.4
2004	68.2	67.6	67.4	67.4	67.3	68.2	68.8	68.7	68.2	67.8	68.0	68.2	68.0
2005	68.1	67.8	67.0	67.9	67.6	68.4	68.4	68.4	67.8	67.5	67.4	67.7	67.8
2006	67.8	67.6	67.5	67.1	67.2	67.9	68.2	68.0	67.4	67.3	67.4	67.6	67.6
2007	67.6	67.1	66.9	66.6	66.7	67.5	67.2	67.1	66.4	66.1	66.1	66.2	66.8
2008	65.9	66.0	66.6	65.9	66.0	66.8	66.6	66.7	65.7	65.3	65.4	65.2	66.0
2009	64.7	64.5	64.4	63.9	63.9	64.2	63.8	63.4	62.6	62.2	62.1	61.9	63.5
2010	61.6	61.6	62.0	61.3	61.3	62.3	62.3	62.5	61.8	62.0	62.1	62.2	61.9
2011	62.1	61.8	62.0	61.6	61.6	62.1	62.2	62.3	61.9	61.6	61.7	61.8	61.9

Employment by Industry: Hartford–West Hartford–East Hartford, CT, NECTA, Selected Years, 2000–2011—*Continued*

(Numbers in thousands, not seasonally adjusted)

Industry and year	January	February	March	April	May	June	July	August	September	October	November	December	Annual average
Professional and Business Services													
2000	58.7	58.7	59.0	59.9	59.6	61.0	61.2	61.1	60.6	60.7	60.7	61.1	60.2
2001	59.2	59.0	59.5	60.0	59.6	60.3	59.3	59.0	58.4	58.4	57.9	57.4	59.0
2002	56.5	56.6	57.5	57.7	57.6	57.9	57.1	57.0	56.7	56.9	57.0	56.8	57.1
2003	55.5	55.1	55.2	56.0	55.9	56.1	55.9	56.0	56.2	56.3	56.7	56.3	55.9
2004	55.7	55.4	55.8	57.1	56.9	57.5	57.5	57.7	57.8	57.8	58.0	58.1	57.1
2005	56.8	56.8	57.5	58.2	58.1	59.3	59.5	59.5	59.6	59.0	59.3	59.6	58.6
2006	58.3	58.6	58.9	60.0	59.8	60.7	60.7	60.8	60.6	60.7	60.5	60.6	60.0
2007	58.8	59.1	59.4	61.0	61.3	62.4	61.7	61.9	61.4	61.0	61.4	62.1	61.0
2008	61.3	61.5	61.8	62.1	62.4	63.3	62.9	62.6	62.1	61.6	61.3	60.5	62.0
2009	59.3	58.6	58.2	58.7	59.0	58.9	58.2	58.4	57.8	58.3	58.3	58.0	58.5
2010	56.1	56.8	56.8	59.3	59.4	59.8	59.5	59.4	59.2	59.7	59.6	59.4	58.8
2011	58.4	58.6	58.3	60.1	60.2	60.9	60.0	60.4	60.1	61.5	61.1	62.2	60.2
Education and Health Services													
2000	77.6	78.8	79.2	78.1	77.8	77.7	78.6	77.0	78.1	79.0	79.4	80.5	78.5
2001	79.3	80.0	79.9	79.5	78.4	79.8	80.4	79.9	80.4	81.4	82.4	83.1	80.4
2002	81.3	82.0	82.0	81.6	82.2	81.5	81.1	80.4	81.7	82.8	83.6	83.9	82.0
2003	82.6	82.7	82.5	82.5	82.7	81.7	81.5	80.5	82.3	83.7	84.2	84.3	82.6
2004	82.9	83.2	83.5	83.6	84.3	83.2	82.4	81.6	83.4	84.4	84.7	85.0	83.5
2005	83.6	84.1	84.2	84.6	84.8	83.9	83.3	83.0	84.4	85.9	86.1	86.3	84.5
2006	85.3	85.8	85.8	86.2	86.4	85.7	86.1	85.7	86.7	88.1	88.6	88.7	86.6
2007	88.2	89.2	89.6	89.8	89.9	89.6	88.9	88.1	90.1	91.0	91.8	91.5	89.8
2008	91.1	91.6	91.9	92.4	92.2	92.3	91.9	91.1	93.2	94.3	94.9	94.9	92.7
2009	93.8	94.5	94.8	95.1	94.7	94.3	95.1	94.4	95.5	96.5	96.5	96.7	95.2
2010	95.5	95.9	96.6	97.3	96.7	96.0	95.1	94.7	96.8	97.9	98.5	98.5	96.6
2011	97.9	98.4	98.8	99.8	99.2	98.3	96.7	96.7	100.6	101.3	101.2	101.4	99.2
Leisure and Hospitality													
2000	34.7	35.1	35.2	36.3	37.8	38.9	39.0	38.1	37.3	36.8	36.2	37.0	36.9
2001	35.1	34.9	35.3	35.0	37.2	38.0	38.1	37.8	36.5	35.6	34.8	35.1	36.1
2002	33.5	33.6	33.4	34.7	36.3	37.3	38.1	37.5	36.2	35.9	35.3	35.6	35.6
2003	35.2	34.8	35.1	36.0	38.1	38.5	38.8	38.7	37.5	37.6	36.9	37.2	37.0
2004	35.5	35.4	35.7	37.1	38.9	39.7	39.9	39.3	38.4	37.7	36.6	37.3	37.6
2005	36.2	36.3	37.1	38.4	40.2	41.2	41.2	41.1	39.8	38.7	38.6	39.0	39.0
2006	37.7	37.6	38.4	39.0	40.6	42.1	42.1	41.9	40.5	40.2	39.4	40.0	40.0
2007	38.1	38.4	38.6	39.5	42.2	43.7	43.6	43.6	42.0	41.1	40.8	40.6	41.0
2008	38.8	38.8	39.3	40.5	43.0	44.0	43.4	42.9	42.1	41.9	40.4	40.7	41.3
2009	37.9	38.4	38.4	39.1	42.1	43.1	42.6	42.0	41.2	40.5	40.0	39.9	40.4
2010	36.7	37.2	37.7	40.3	42.2	42.7	43.4	43.1	42.8	41.7	41.3	41.1	40.9
2011	38.3	39.1	39.1	41.4	43.3	44.1	44.0	44.8	42.5	42.4	42.9	43.0	42.1
Other Services													
2000	21.3	21.3	21.5	21.6	21.7	21.9	22.0	21.7	21.6	21.8	21.7	21.8	21.7
2001	21.3	21.3	21.5	21.6	21.6	21.9	22.0	21.8	21.4	21.7	21.8	21.9	21.7
2002	21.3	21.3	21.5	21.5	21.6	21.7	21.7	21.3	21.0	21.2	21.3	21.4	21.4
2003	20.7	20.7	20.9	20.9	21.0	21.2	21.2	20.9	20.7	20.7	20.6	20.7	20.9
2004	20.5	20.5	20.6	20.7	20.7	21.0	21.0	20.8	20.6	20.7	20.7	20.7	20.7
2005	20.4	20.4	20.5	20.8	20.7	21.1	20.9	20.7	20.5	20.6	20.6	20.7	20.7
2006	20.5	20.5	20.6	20.8	20.9	21.1	21.1	20.9	20.8	20.9	20.8	20.8	20.8
2007	20.7	20.7	20.7	20.9	20.9	21.3	21.0	20.9	20.8	20.9	20.8	20.8	20.9
2008	20.6	20.7	20.8	20.9	21.0	21.2	20.6	20.5	20.7	20.7	20.7	20.5	20.7
2009	20.4	20.1	20.1	20.2	20.3	20.4	20.1	20.0	20.0	20.1	20.0	20.2	20.2
2010	19.9	19.8	19.8	19.9	20.2	20.4	20.3	20.2	20.3	20.3	20.4	20.2	20.1
2011	20.0	20.0	20.1	20.2	20.4	20.9	20.2	19.9	20.0	20.5	20.3	20.5	20.3
Government													
2000	86.1	89.4	89.9	89.9	89.9	86.6	80.1	78.2	86.3	88.4	89.3	88.7	86.9
2001	86.6	89.6	89.7	89.8	89.1	86.1	80.8	80.2	87.4	89.9	91.4	91.1	87.6
2002	87.9	91.2	91.4	90.8	90.4	87.6	81.0	80.9	88.5	89.7	90.9	90.7	88.4
2003	87.0	90.0	89.5	89.0	87.9	85.4	78.6	77.8	83.6	86.8	87.2	87.1	85.8
2004	83.8	87.0	87.1	87.8	86.6	84.2	78.1	77.2	84.1	87.0	88.0	87.6	84.9
2005	84.4	87.2	86.8	88.2	87.3	84.8	79.5	78.6	86.8	88.4	90.3	88.6	85.9
2006	85.4	87.8	87.7	89.2	88.5	85.4	80.8	79.9	87.7	90.5	91.7	90.2	87.1
2007	87.4	90.1	90.0	90.5	87.9	85.6	80.8	79.9	87.5	90.3	91.2	89.3	87.5
2008	86.4	90.2	90.2	90.8	88.2	86.1	81.4	80.4	87.7	90.2	90.2	87.9	87.5
2009	85.3	90.4	90.1	91.1	88.1	85.7	79.8	79.0	87.4	90.7	91.1	89.8	87.4
2010	84.5	87.3	87.6	87.9	86.0	82.5	77.9	76.6	85.4	88.2	88.3	87.2	85.0
2011	84.9	87.1	86.9	87.5	83.8	80.5	75.5	74.2	82.7	85.8	86.0	84.6	83.3

Employment by Industry: Honolulu, HI, Selected Years, 2000–2011

(Numbers in thousands, not seasonally adjusted)

Industry and year	January	February	March	April	May	June	July	August	September	October	November	December	Annual average
Total Nonfarm													
2000	399.1	406.3	409.9	409.6	412.9	416.0	407.5	409.0	413.0	415.2	420.3	424.4	411.9
2001	405.9	415.3	418.0	413.0	414.3	419.2	409.4	410.7	412.4	408.4	410.8	413.4	412.6
2002	401.8	408.4	411.0	405.0	414.7	419.5	408.0	409.0	413.0	416.5	421.3	426.2	412.9
2003	414.2	418.8	421.0	416.6	421.2	420.8	414.1	414.6	417.2	420.9	426.4	429.8	419.6
2004	419.0	423.2	425.9	426.3	429.8	430.3	424.7	425.9	429.3	435.2	442.5	444.1	429.7
2005	429.9	437.3	440.0	440.4	443.5	444.3	437.6	441.0	444.2	446.2	451.1	456.3	442.7
2006	440.0	449.6	452.7	448.9	453.5	454.9	445.5	448.7	453.9	451.8	460.1	461.4	451.8
2007	447.2	454.2	457.2	449.9	457.3	458.9	448.3	449.7	456.2	458.0	462.3	465.8	455.4
2008	450.9	456.6	459.0	451.6	457.3	455.5	445.7	447.2	449.4	450.1	455.7	454.3	452.8
2009	440.4	443.4	444.5	439.3	440.4	439.0	429.1	427.6	431.9	435.2	436.3	439.6	437.2
2010	428.0	432.8	434.8	434.0	437.1	433.2	428.8	425.0	433.1	438.0	442.9	445.4	434.4
2011	431.9	439.4	442.0	438.7	439.3	437.1	433.1	429.4	437.0	441.8	444.1	446.5	438.4
Total Private													
2000	310.8	313.8	316.0	315.7	317.3	321.7	320.6	322.5	324.9	323.9	326.7	329.5	320.3
2001	320.4	322.3	324.2	321.0	322.7	325.3	323.4	323.8	323.2	316.3	315.7	317.3	321.3
2002	310.7	313.1	314.5	314.6	317.4	319.8	319.9	320.3	322.2	321.6	324.8	328.2	318.9
2003	319.5	321.5	323.2	322.1	323.5	324.1	324.3	325.5	326.7	325.5	329.4	332.4	324.8
2004	324.7	326.6	327.9	329.0	331.1	333.5	334.5	335.4	336.4	339.2	343.4	346.0	334.0
2005	337.8	340.5	342.4	343.6	345.4	347.6	348.0	349.8	351.7	350.7	354.1	358.3	347.5
2006	348.8	352.5	354.7	351.8	354.6	357.5	355.7	357.6	358.7	354.6	358.7	361.7	355.6
2007	352.6	355.4	357.7	355.4	357.7	360.9	358.2	359.8	360.6	360.2	362.9	365.5	358.9
2008	355.4	357.4	358.6	356.1	356.2	356.2	353.6	353.4	352.4	349.8	351.3	352.5	354.4
2009	342.1	343.1	342.7	337.9	337.7	338.3	335.7	335.5	336.2	336.7	336.8	339.5	338.5
2010	332.2	333.8	334.5	333.3	334.7	334.3	334.7	335.1	337.1	338.9	340.4	344.5	336.1
2011	335.2	338.9	341.0	338.1	338.0	338.1	339.6	340.0	340.7	342.6	343.4	345.2	340.1
Goods-Producing													
2000	28.7	28.8	29.4	29.5	29.9	30.3	30.6	31.0	31.2	31.0	30.8	31.0	30.2
2001	30.1	30.1	30.0	29.8	29.9	30.1	30.0	30.1	29.9	29.2	29.1	29.2	29.8
2002	28.7	28.6	29.1	28.9	29.2	30.0	30.1	30.3	30.0	29.9	30.1	30.2	29.6
2003	29.6	29.7	30.2	30.3	30.7	30.9	31.2	31.4	31.4	31.7	31.8	31.7	30.9
2004	31.2	31.3	30.7	31.7	32.3	32.9	33.1	33.2	33.4	33.4	33.4	33.7	32.5
2005	33.1	33.5	34.0	34.4	34.8	35.2	35.4	35.9	36.3	36.1	36.2	36.5	35.1
2006	35.5	35.7	35.7	35.5	36.2	36.7	36.9	37.3	37.7	37.3	37.8	38.1	36.7
2007	37.0	37.3	37.4	37.4	37.9	38.6	38.7	39.0	39.2	39.0	39.3	39.3	38.3
2008	38.4	38.6	38.7	38.2	38.0	37.8	38.0	37.9	37.7	36.9	36.9	36.5	37.8
2009	34.8	34.5	34.3	33.6	33.6	33.6	33.5	33.2	33.0	32.7	32.3	32.5	33.5
2010	32.0	31.8	31.8	31.7	31.7	31.5	31.8	31.7	31.9	32.4	32.4	32.6	31.9
2011	31.5	31.9	32.1	32.1	32.0	32.5	32.8	33.1	32.6	33.1	31.8	32.1	32.3
Mining, Logging, and Construction													
2000	16.4	16.5	16.8	17.0	17.3	17.6	17.9	18.1	18.2	18.0	17.9	18.1	17.5
2001	17.3	17.2	17.2	16.9	17.0	17.1	17.1	17.2	17.0	16.7	16.6	16.7	17.0
2002	16.5	16.5	16.9	17.1	17.4	18.1	18.4	18.7	18.5	18.5	18.7	18.7	17.8
2003	18.3	18.4	18.8	19.0	19.3	19.4	19.7	19.8	19.8	19.9	19.9	19.7	19.3
2004	19.3	19.4	18.9	19.7	20.3	20.7	21.1	21.2	21.4	21.5	21.5	21.8	20.6
2005	21.4	21.6	22.1	22.6	23.0	23.4	23.7	24.0	24.4	24.3	24.4	24.6	23.3
2006	23.9	24.0	24.0	23.9	24.5	24.8	25.0	25.3	25.7	25.5	25.8	26.1	24.9
2007	25.2	25.4	25.6	25.7	26.1	26.7	26.9	27.1	27.3	27.3	27.4	27.3	26.5
2008	26.6	26.8	26.8	26.4	26.1	26.0	26.2	26.1	26.0	25.5	25.4	25.0	26.1
2009	23.7	23.4	23.2	22.7	22.7	22.7	22.8	22.4	22.2	22.0	21.6	21.7	22.6
2010	21.4	21.3	21.3	21.3	21.3	21.2	21.5	21.3	21.4	21.9	21.8	21.9	21.5
2011	20.9	21.2	21.3	21.4	21.3	21.9	22.0	22.2	22.0	22.6	21.1	21.4	21.6
Manufacturing													
2000	12.3	12.3	12.6	12.5	12.6	12.7	12.7	12.9	13.0	13.0	12.9	12.9	12.7
2001	12.8	12.9	12.8	12.9	12.9	13.0	12.9	12.9	12.9	12.5	12.5	12.5	12.8
2002	12.2	12.1	12.2	11.8	11.8	11.9	11.7	11.6	11.5	11.4	11.4	11.5	11.8
2003	11.3	11.3	11.4	11.3	11.4	11.5	11.5	11.6	11.6	11.8	11.9	12.0	11.6
2004	11.9	11.9	11.8	12.0	12.0	12.2	12.0	12.0	12.0	11.9	11.9	11.9	12.0
2005	11.7	11.9	11.9	11.8	11.8	11.8	11.7	11.9	11.9	11.8	11.8	11.9	11.8
2006	11.6	11.7	11.7	11.6	11.7	11.9	11.9	12.0	12.0	11.8	12.0	12.0	11.8
2007	11.8	11.9	11.8	11.7	11.8	11.9	11.8	11.9	11.9	11.7	11.9	12.0	11.8
2008	11.8	11.8	11.9	11.8	11.9	11.8	11.8	11.8	11.7	11.4	11.5	11.5	11.7
2009	11.1	11.1	11.1	10.9	10.9	10.9	10.7	10.8	10.8	10.7	10.7	10.8	10.9
2010	10.6	10.5	10.5	10.4	10.4	10.3	10.3	10.4	10.5	10.5	10.6	10.7	10.5
2011	10.6	10.7	10.8	10.7	10.7	10.6	10.8	10.9	10.6	10.5	10.7	10.7	10.7
Service-Providing													
2000	370.4	377.5	380.5	380.1	383.0	385.7	376.9	378.0	381.8	384.2	389.5	393.4	381.8
2001	375.8	385.2	388.0	383.2	384.4	389.1	379.4	380.6	382.5	379.2	381.7	384.2	382.8
2002	373.1	379.8	381.9	376.1	385.5	389.5	377.9	378.7	383.0	386.6	391.2	396.0	383.3
2003	384.6	389.1	390.8	386.3	390.5	389.9	382.9	383.2	385.8	389.2	394.6	398.1	388.8
2004	387.8	391.9	395.2	394.6	397.5	397.4	391.6	392.7	395.9	401.8	409.1	410.4	397.2
2005	396.8	403.8	406.0	406.0	408.7	409.1	402.2	405.1	407.9	410.1	414.9	419.8	407.5
2006	404.5	413.9	417.0	413.4	417.3	418.2	408.6	411.4	416.2	414.5	422.3	423.3	415.1
2007	410.2	416.9	419.8	412.5	419.4	420.3	409.6	410.7	417.0	419.0	423.0	426.5	417.1
2008	412.5	418.0	420.3	413.4	419.3	417.7	407.7	409.3	411.7	413.2	418.8	417.8	415.0
2009	405.6	408.9	410.2	405.7	406.8	405.4	395.6	394.4	398.9	402.5	404.0	407.1	403.8
2010	396.0	401.0	403.0	402.3	405.4	401.7	397.0	393.3	401.2	405.6	410.5	412.8	402.5
2011	400.4	407.5	409.9	406.6	407.3	404.6	400.3	396.3	404.4	408.7	412.3	414.4	406.1

Employment by Industry: Honolulu, HI, Selected Years, 2000–2011—*Continued*

(Numbers in thousands, not seasonally adjusted)

Industry and year	January	February	March	April	May	June	July	August	September	October	November	December	Annual average
Trade, Transportation, and Utilities													
2000	80.5	80.4	80.1	79.7	79.9	81.0	81.1	81.6	81.8	81.8	84.1	85.0	81.4
2001	82.3	81.7	81.8	81.1	81.3	81.8	81.7	81.7	81.5	79.1	77.9	79.0	80.9
2002	75.9	75.3	75.1	75.3	75.8	76.3	76.6	76.8	76.7	76.9	78.2	79.6	76.5
2003	76.6	76.3	76.1	75.7	75.6	76.0	76.3	76.5	76.5	76.6	78.1	79.6	76.7
2004	77.2	76.7	76.9	77.7	78.2	79.0	79.2	79.6	80.0	81.5	83.3	84.3	79.5
2005	81.8	81.7	81.9	82.3	83.1	83.9	84.6	85.1	85.4	85.3	86.7	88.1	84.2
2006	85.3	85.0	85.7	85.2	85.5	86.4	86.0	86.7	86.7	85.7	87.7	88.9	86.2
2007	86.3	85.3	85.8	85.0	85.3	85.5	85.5	85.6	85.4	85.9	88.0	89.7	86.1
2008	86.2	84.9	84.9	83.7	83.7	83.4	82.7	82.9	82.4	81.7	82.6	83.2	83.5
2009	80.6	80.0	79.4	78.3	78.3	78.5	78.2	78.1	78.3	78.4	79.7	80.9	79.1
2010	78.3	77.6	77.4	77.7	77.3	77.9	78.3	78.5	78.2	78.7	80.3	81.6	78.5
2011	79.2	78.7	78.7	78.3	78.3	78.5	78.9	78.6	78.3	78.9	79.8	80.8	78.9
Wholesale Trade													
2000	13.1	13.2	13.2	13.2	13.2	13.4	13.5	13.6	13.5	13.5	13.6	13.6	13.4
2001	13.5	13.6	13.6	13.5	13.6	13.7	13.6	13.7	13.6	13.4	13.4	13.5	13.6
2002	13.3	13.3	13.3	13.3	13.5	13.5	13.5	13.5	13.6	13.6	13.7	13.8	13.5
2003	13.5	13.6	13.6	13.7	13.7	13.7	13.7	13.7	13.7	13.6	13.7	13.7	13.7
2004	13.6	13.6	13.7	13.7	13.8	13.9	13.9	13.8	13.8	13.9	14.0	14.0	13.8
2005	13.8	13.9	14.0	14.0	14.1	14.1	14.2	14.3	14.4	14.4	14.4	14.5	14.2
2006	14.2	14.2	14.2	14.3	14.3	14.5	14.4	14.6	14.5	14.6	14.7	14.9	14.5
2007	14.6	14.6	14.7	14.7	14.8	14.9	14.9	15.0	15.0	15.0	15.1	15.3	14.9
2008	15.0	15.0	15.1	15.1	15.1	15.1	15.1	15.1	15.1	15.0	15.0	15.0	15.1
2009	14.7	14.6	14.5	14.4	14.4	14.3	14.3	14.3	14.3	14.2	14.2	14.3	14.4
2010	14.1	14.1	14.1	14.2	14.2	14.2	14.3	14.3	14.2	14.3	14.3	14.4	14.2
2011	14.1	14.0	14.0	14.0	14.0	14.0	14.1	14.1	13.8	14.0	13.6	13.7	14.0
Retail Trade													
2000	46.2	45.8	45.4	45.1	45.3	45.8	46.0	46.3	46.4	46.4	48.3	49.0	46.3
2001	46.7	46.0	46.0	45.5	45.4	45.6	45.6	45.6	45.6	44.6	45.0	46.0	45.6
2002	43.7	43.0	42.7	42.7	42.9	43.2	43.6	43.6	43.5	43.6	44.6	46.0	43.6
2003	43.4	42.9	42.7	42.4	42.5	43.0	43.3	43.4	43.3	43.6	44.9	46.4	43.5
2004	44.2	43.7	43.7	43.5	43.8	44.3	44.5	44.9	45.1	46.1	47.6	48.8	45.0
2005	46.3	45.9	45.9	45.7	45.8	46.1	46.7	46.9	46.9	47.3	48.6	49.9	46.8
2006	47.5	47.1	47.2	46.6	46.5	46.9	46.6	46.7	46.5	46.5	48.2	49.0	47.1
2007	47.0	46.3	46.5	45.9	46.0	46.2	46.1	46.1	46.0	46.3	48.2	49.3	46.7
2008	46.7	46.3	46.9	46.1	46.0	46.3	46.4	46.5	46.3	45.9	46.8	47.5	46.5
2009	45.7	45.2	44.8	44.1	44.0	44.3	44.2	44.1	44.5	44.8	46.0	46.9	44.9
2010	44.8	44.2	44.1	44.1	43.8	44.2	44.5	44.6	44.5	44.8	46.3	47.3	44.8
2011	45.5	45.0	45.0	44.8	44.8	44.8	45.2	44.9	44.8	45.2	46.4	47.1	45.3
Transportation and Utilities													
2000	21.2	21.4	21.5	21.4	21.4	21.8	21.6	21.7	21.9	21.9	22.2	22.4	21.7
2001	22.1	22.1	22.2	22.1	22.3	22.5	22.5	22.4	22.3	21.1	19.5	19.5	21.7
2002	18.9	19.0	19.1	19.3	19.4	19.6	19.5	19.7	19.6	19.7	19.9	19.8	19.5
2003	19.7	19.8	19.8	19.6	19.4	19.3	19.3	19.4	19.5	19.4	19.5	19.5	19.5
2004	19.4	19.4	19.5	20.5	20.6	20.8	20.8	20.9	21.1	21.5	21.7	21.5	20.6
2005	21.7	21.9	22.0	22.6	23.2	23.7	23.7	23.9	24.1	23.6	23.7	23.7	23.2
2006	23.6	23.7	24.3	24.3	24.7	25.0	25.0	25.4	25.7	24.6	24.8	25.0	24.7
2007	24.7	24.4	24.6	24.4	24.5	24.4	24.5	24.5	24.4	24.6	24.7	25.1	24.6
2008	24.5	23.6	22.9	22.5	22.6	22.0	21.2	21.3	21.0	20.8	20.8	20.7	22.0
2009	20.2	20.2	20.1	19.8	19.9	19.9	19.7	19.7	19.5	19.4	19.5	19.7	19.8
2010	19.4	19.3	19.2	19.4	19.3	19.5	19.5	19.6	19.5	19.6	19.7	19.9	19.5
2011	19.6	19.7	19.7	19.5	19.5	19.7	19.6	19.6	19.7	19.7	19.8	20.0	19.7
Information													
2000	9.2	9.2	9.3	10.1	10.1	10.9	10.1	10.7	11.4	11.0	10.5	10.3	10.2
2001	10.2	10.2	10.4	9.8	10.2	10.0	9.8	10.0	9.7	9.7	9.8	9.7	10.0
2002	9.8	9.7	9.7	9.5	9.5	9.3	9.1	9.2	9.9	9.1	9.1	9.7	9.5
2003	8.9	9.0	9.0	8.8	9.4	9.2	8.3	8.2	8.2	8.1	8.3	8.2	8.6
2004	8.4	8.4	8.7	8.5	9.0	8.8	9.2	9.2	9.2	9.3	9.8	9.7	9.0
2005	8.6	8.8	8.6	8.9	9.0	8.7	8.7	9.1	9.1	9.1	9.3	9.8	9.0
2006	9.0	9.3	9.2	8.4	9.2	8.9	8.5	8.7	9.2	8.4	8.8	9.0	8.9
2007	8.4	8.9	8.9	8.6	9.3	9.2	8.5	9.0	8.6	8.4	8.5	8.6	8.7
2008	7.8	8.3	8.6	8.7	9.0	9.4	8.0	7.8	7.8	7.6	8.1	8.3	8.3
2009	7.4	7.9	7.7	7.7	7.3	7.4	7.0	7.2	7.3	7.6	7.3	7.3	7.4
2010	7.3	8.1	8.3	7.7	8.9	8.3	7.0	7.5	9.4	8.3	7.9	8.8	8.1
2011	6.9	7.9	8.7	6.6	6.5	6.3	6.2	6.3	6.3	6.2	6.2	6.6	6.7
Financial Activities													
2000	22.9	22.9	23.0	22.7	22.7	22.7	22.7	22.8	22.6	22.4	22.3	22.4	22.7
2001	22.0	22.2	22.3	22.0	22.0	22.2	21.9	21.9	21.8	21.7	21.6	21.6	21.9
2002	21.1	21.3	21.4	21.3	21.5	21.5	21.6	21.5	21.5	21.6	21.7	21.8	21.5
2003	21.3	21.5	21.6	21.5	21.7	21.9	22.0	22.1	22.1	22.1	22.1	22.2	21.8
2004	22.0	22.0	22.1	22.1	22.2	22.2	22.2	22.1	22.0	22.3	22.3	22.4	22.2
2005	22.1	22.3	22.3	22.2	22.4	22.5	22.5	22.6	22.7	22.6	22.8	22.9	22.5
2006	22.5	22.7	22.9	22.8	22.9	23.2	23.0	23.0	22.8	22.9	22.9	23.0	22.9
2007	22.8	22.7	23.0	22.8	22.9	23.1	23.1	23.0	22.9	23.1	23.0	23.1	23.0
2008	22.6	22.7	22.9	22.9	22.9	22.8	22.7	22.7	22.5	22.3	22.3	22.3	22.6
2009	21.7	21.6	21.5	21.4	21.5	21.4	21.3	21.1	21.1	21.1	21.0	21.0	21.3
2010	20.6	20.7	20.7	20.6	20.6	20.5	20.7	20.6	20.6	20.6	20.5	20.7	20.6
2011	20.3	20.4	20.3	20.3	20.2	20.3	21.0	20.7	20.6	20.8	21.2	21.1	20.6

Employment by Industry: Honolulu, HI, Selected Years, 2000–2011—*Continued*

(Numbers in thousands, not seasonally adjusted)

Industry and year	January	February	March	April	May	June	July	August	September	October	November	December	Annual average
Professional and Business Services													
2000	48.1	48.6	49.3	49.5	49.5	50.1	50.3	50.5	51.0	51.2	51.6	52.1	50.2
2001	51.3	51.8	52.5	51.9	52.2	52.8	52.8	53.0	53.0	52.1	52.8	52.8	52.4
2002	52.4	53.5	53.7	54.0	54.5	55.3	55.7	56.3	56.4	56.4	56.5	58.1	55.2
2003	56.6	56.5	56.8	56.5	56.4	56.8	56.9	57.6	57.9	56.5	57.4	58.0	57.0
2004	56.6	57.2	57.5	57.1	56.3	56.9	57.2	57.6	57.2	57.7	58.3	59.1	57.4
2005	58.0	58.5	59.0	59.2	58.7	59.4	59.9	60.4	60.3	60.9	61.7	62.5	59.9
2006	61.0	62.5	62.8	62.0	61.7	62.5	62.2	62.3	61.6	60.2	60.4	61.1	61.7
2007	59.3	59.8	60.2	59.4	59.4	60.9	60.5	60.8	61.1	61.3	61.2	61.8	60.5
2008	60.2	60.6	60.8	60.6	60.1	60.2	60.4	60.6	60.2	60.1	60.0	60.9	60.4
2009	59.3	59.3	59.4	57.9	57.5	57.6	57.1	57.0	57.0	57.8	57.4	58.1	58.0
2010	57.0	57.3	57.4	57.5	57.5	57.6	58.1	58.0	58.1	58.6	58.7	59.3	57.9
2011	59.0	60.0	60.5	60.3	59.9	60.0	60.1	60.4	60.5	60.6	60.9	60.9	60.3
Education and Health Services													
2000	46.8	47.9	48.4	47.9	48.1	48.2	47.7	47.5	48.3	48.2	48.9	49.4	48.1
2001	47.8	48.7	49.1	48.9	49.3	49.4	49.0	48.7	49.2	49.2	49.9	50.0	49.1
2002	48.6	49.7	49.8	50.0	50.4	50.2	50.1	49.6	50.6	50.9	52.0	51.2	50.3
2003	50.3	51.6	51.9	51.9	52.1	51.7	51.9	51.7	52.6	52.7	53.4	53.6	52.1
2004	52.0	52.8	53.2	53.2	53.9	53.7	53.3	53.1	54.0	54.3	55.1	55.4	53.7
2005	54.4	55.1	55.5	55.3	55.7	55.5	54.9	54.6	55.5	55.3	55.7	56.1	55.3
2006	54.4	55.2	55.7	55.7	56.3	56.6	55.8	55.9	56.7	56.7	57.2	57.6	56.2
2007	56.3	57.3	57.6	57.6	57.8	58.2	57.2	57.0	57.8	57.8	58.1	58.1	57.6
2008	56.9	57.9	58.2	58.0	58.3	58.5	58.0	57.8	58.3	58.5	59.0	59.3	58.2
2009	58.0	58.7	59.0	58.4	58.5	58.6	57.8	57.7	58.3	58.5	58.7	59.2	58.5
2010	58.1	58.8	59.0	58.7	59.1	58.7	58.6	58.3	58.3	59.5	59.7	60.1	58.9
2011	58.1	59.5	59.6	59.5	59.8	59.1	58.8	58.7	58.9	59.0	59.3	59.1	59.1
Leisure and Hospitality													
2000	57.3	58.1	58.4	58.2	58.9	60.0	59.7	59.9	60.0	59.5	59.5	60.4	59.2
2001	58.2	58.9	59.3	58.6	58.9	59.8	59.1	59.5	59.2	56.7	56.0	56.3	58.4
2002	55.7	56.4	56.9	56.8	57.6	58.3	57.8	57.8	58.1	57.9	58.1	58.5	57.5
2003	57.5	57.9	58.5	58.1	58.3	58.3	58.5	58.8	58.8	58.6	59.0	59.8	58.5
2004	58.6	59.3	59.6	59.7	60.0	60.7	61.2	61.5	61.7	61.4	61.9	62.1	60.6
2005	60.8	61.5	61.9	61.8	61.9	62.7	62.4	62.4	62.6	61.7	61.8	62.3	62.0
2006	61.2	62.0	62.4	62.0	62.4	62.8	63.0	63.2	63.5	62.9	63.2	63.4	62.7
2007	62.5	63.7	64.2	64.2	64.6	64.9	64.2	64.8	64.8	63.8	63.9	64.0	64.1
2008	62.8	63.4	63.3	62.8	62.9	63.1	63.0	62.9	62.5	61.7	61.4	61.1	62.6
2009	60.2	60.7	61.0	61.0	60.8	61.1	60.7	60.9	60.8	60.2	60.0	60.1	60.6
2010	59.0	59.3	59.6	59.4	59.6	59.9	60.2	60.4	60.6	60.7	60.9	61.4	60.1
2011	60.5	60.6	61.2	61.1	61.2	61.4	61.8	62.2	63.4	63.8	64.0	64.4	62.1
Other Services													
2000	17.3	17.9	18.1	18.1	18.2	18.5	18.4	18.5	18.6	18.8	19.0	18.9	18.4
2001	18.5	18.7	18.8	18.9	18.9	19.2	19.1	18.9	18.9	18.6	18.6	18.7	18.8
2002	18.5	18.6	18.8	18.8	18.9	18.9	18.9	18.8	19.0	19.2	19.1	19.1	18.9
2003	18.7	19.0	19.1	19.3	19.3	19.3	19.2	19.2	19.2	19.2	19.3	19.3	19.2
2004	18.7	18.9	19.2	19.0	19.2	19.3	19.1	19.1	18.9	19.3	19.3	19.3	19.1
2005	19.0	19.1	19.2	19.5	19.8	19.7	19.6	19.7	19.8	19.7	19.9	20.1	19.6
2006	19.9	20.1	20.3	20.2	20.4	20.4	20.3	20.5	20.5	20.5	20.7	20.6	20.4
2007	20.0	20.4	20.6	20.4	20.5	20.5	20.5	20.6	20.8	20.9	20.9	20.9	20.6
2008	20.5	21.0	21.2	21.2	21.3	21.0	20.8	20.8	21.0	21.0	21.0	20.9	21.0
2009	20.1	20.4	20.4	20.2	20.2	20.1	20.1	20.3	20.4	20.4	20.4	20.4	20.3
2010	19.9	20.2	20.3	20.0	20.0	19.9	20.0	20.1	20.0	20.1	20.0	20.0	20.0
2011	19.7	19.9	19.9	19.9	20.1	20.0	20.0	20.0	20.1	20.2	20.2	20.2	20.0
Government													
2000	88.3	92.5	93.9	93.9	95.6	94.3	86.9	86.5	88.1	91.3	93.6	94.9	91.7
2001	85.5	93.0	93.8	92.0	91.6	93.9	86.0	86.9	89.2	92.1	95.1	96.1	91.3
2002	91.1	95.3	96.5	90.4	97.3	99.7	88.1	88.7	90.8	94.9	96.5	98.0	93.9
2003	94.7	97.3	97.8	94.5	97.7	96.7	89.8	89.1	90.5	95.4	97.0	97.4	94.8
2004	94.3	96.6	98.0	97.3	98.7	96.8	90.2	90.5	92.9	96.0	99.1	98.1	95.7
2005	92.1	96.8	97.6	96.8	98.1	96.7	89.6	91.2	92.5	95.5	97.0	98.0	95.2
2006	91.2	97.1	98.0	97.1	98.9	97.4	89.8	91.1	95.2	97.2	101.4	99.7	96.2
2007	94.6	98.8	99.5	94.5	99.6	98.0	90.1	89.9	95.6	97.8	99.4	100.3	96.5
2008	95.5	99.2	100.4	95.5	101.1	99.3	92.1	93.8	97.0	100.3	104.4	101.8	98.4
2009	98.3	100.3	101.8	101.4	102.7	100.7	93.4	92.1	95.7	98.5	99.5	100.1	98.7
2010	95.8	99.0	100.3	100.7	102.4	98.9	94.1	89.9	96.0	99.1	102.5	100.9	98.3
2011	96.7	100.5	101.0	100.6	101.3	99.0	93.5	89.4	96.3	99.2	100.7	101.3	98.3

Employment by Industry: Houston–Sugar Land–Baytown, TX, Selected Years, 2000–2011

(Numbers in thousands, not seasonally adjusted)

Industry and year	January	February	March	April	May	June	July	August	September	October	November	December	Annual average
Total Nonfarm													
2000	2,194.2	2,214.7	2,231.6	2,233.5	2,250.0	2,258.7	2,243.0	2,254.4	2,272.3	2,273.2	2,282.7	2,298.5	2,250.6
2001	2,252.6	2,273.6	2,286.1	2,289.0	2,298.8	2,300.4	2,281.3	2,294.5	2,300.2	2,294.8	2,301.4	2,302.1	2,289.6
2002	2,259.2	2,274.7	2,284.6	2,282.1	2,294.5	2,294.4	2,272.8	2,283.0	2,290.1	2,287.1	2,292.6	2,298.9	2,284.5
2003	2,257.1	2,266.6	2,274.2	2,271.0	2,277.1	2,277.9	2,250.1	2,262.5	2,273.0	2,271.4	2,274.6	2,287.5	2,270.3
2004	2,252.9	2,264.3	2,275.6	2,279.7	2,283.5	2,289.2	2,275.8	2,283.1	2,290.8	2,299.8	2,310.2	2,325.0	2,285.8
2005	2,292.7	2,305.1	2,324.1	2,335.1	2,342.5	2,346.7	2,341.3	2,354.6	2,369.8	2,376.0	2,397.5	2,414.2	2,350.0
2006	2,375.0	2,395.9	2,420.2	2,420.1	2,437.7	2,449.4	2,439.3	2,456.5	2,474.2	2,480.9	2,501.3	2,520.0	2,447.5
2007	2,474.8	2,498.2	2,522.1	2,527.4	2,546.2	2,562.9	2,545.4	2,554.1	2,562.4	2,576.3	2,595.2	2,608.8	2,547.8
2008	2,556.9	2,578.9	2,590.2	2,596.2	2,607.9	2,615.0	2,603.2	2,610.9	2,592.0	2,611.6	2,626.5	2,628.3	2,601.5
2009	2,564.9	2,565.1	2,561.9	2,545.8	2,546.1	2,540.7	2,511.0	2,504.2	2,507.7	2,511.3	2,515.1	2,520.9	2,532.9
2010	2,475.5	2,490.3	2,508.0	2,520.4	2,539.3	2,539.8	2,524.1	2,526.8	2,534.5	2,549.0	2,560.0	2,569.7	2,528.1
2011	2,527.8	2,543.7	2,567.2	2,585.7	2,588.8	2,601.0	2,592.7	2,593.4	2,602.8	2,625.0	2,642.9	2,646.5	2,593.1
Total Private													
2000	1,888.2	1,902.7	1,918.8	1,919.8	1,930.2	1,953.9	1,950.6	1,961.2	1,958.6	1,959.3	1,969.0	1,984.9	1,941.4
2001	1,945.3	1,960.3	1,971.5	1,972.8	1,982.5	1,994.4	1,984.2	1,991.2	1,979.0	1,971.7	1,976.3	1,977.7	1,975.6
2002	1,938.9	1,947.2	1,956.0	1,953.6	1,965.0	1,973.7	1,963.4	1,970.7	1,960.2	1,949.6	1,954.9	1,961.6	1,957.9
2003	1,925.5	1,928.2	1,935.4	1,932.5	1,938.8	1,947.8	1,935.4	1,943.6	1,939.5	1,933.2	1,935.3	1,949.4	1,937.1
2004	1,917.7	1,924.3	1,935.2	1,940.3	1,944.4	1,956.8	1,958.0	1,962.7	1,954.6	1,960.4	1,970.0	1,984.8	1,950.8
2005	1,957.4	1,963.8	1,981.5	1,991.9	1,999.4	2,014.9	2,016.9	2,027.2	2,028.9	2,030.2	2,048.5	2,066.1	2,010.6
2006	2,031.6	2,046.4	2,070.0	2,072.7	2,089.9	2,111.4	2,113.6	2,125.7	2,127.5	2,128.4	2,147.0	2,167.0	2,102.6
2007	2,128.2	2,144.3	2,166.7	2,170.7	2,189.3	2,216.2	2,211.6	2,218.3	2,210.1	2,215.8	2,230.9	2,244.8	2,195.6
2008	2,195.7	2,213.3	2,223.0	2,230.1	2,242.2	2,258.8	2,255.8	2,264.5	2,229.4	2,245.4	2,255.4	2,258.1	2,239.3
2009	2,198.6	2,193.2	2,188.4	2,169.4	2,170.9	2,173.9	2,158.6	2,155.2	2,139.8	2,131.4	2,133.1	2,140.1	2,162.7
2010	2,103.1	2,109.0	2,124.5	2,134.7	2,145.3	2,159.3	2,160.1	2,166.3	2,159.8	2,166.3	2,175.7	2,188.4	2,149.4
2011	2,150.1	2,162.0	2,184.3	2,202.2	2,207.9	2,228.6	2,234.6	2,241.4	2,235.1	2,249.4	2,265.9	2,270.6	2,219.3
Goods-Producing													
2000	448.9	455.2	459.5	457.2	459.9	464.7	463.0	465.5	466.2	465.3	466.2	468.1	461.6
2001	465.5	472.5	475.3	476.5	478.0	477.5	473.9	476.0	474.4	473.1	472.6	468.8	473.7
2002	462.0	464.8	466.3	463.5	464.1	464.6	461.4	462.3	460.1	458.8	455.4	453.2	461.4
2003	449.0	448.9	448.1	446.1	446.9	448.1	442.9	443.4	444.3	441.8	437.4	438.0	444.6
2004	435.4	435.6	436.7	436.7	434.8	437.0	436.3	436.6	435.0	437.8	439.0	440.1	436.8
2005	442.5	444.8	448.9	449.7	449.1	453.2	454.2	456.0	458.2	458.4	461.2	464.3	453.4
2006	463.7	469.8	475.6	474.6	480.3	487.2	486.6	490.0	493.3	496.5	499.9	502.5	485.0
2007	500.5	506.3	510.3	509.7	515.4	522.6	521.1	521.0	520.6	526.4	529.3	530.4	517.8
2008	520.6	527.6	528.5	531.6	534.5	536.9	537.0	538.7	535.3	541.8	541.1	536.7	534.2
2009	523.1	518.3	508.9	496.6	492.9	489.0	483.3	480.3	476.3	472.7	467.9	466.6	489.7
2010	463.9	464.0	465.4	466.4	468.4	471.0	472.4	474.0	473.7	475.4	473.7	474.1	470.2
2011	468.4	474.5	477.8	480.5	481.4	489.2	493.3	496.4	494.9	493.1	492.9	492.5	486.2
Mining and Logging													
2000	55.7	55.7	56.3	56.4	56.9	57.3	58.4	58.6	58.7	59.4	59.6	61.6	57.9
2001	59.0	59.8	60.3	60.4	60.8	61.5	62.2	62.5	62.0	62.1	62.5	62.2	61.3
2002	59.1	58.7	58.3	58.5	58.7	59.4	59.7	59.8	59.4	59.6	59.8	59.8	59.2
2003	59.5	59.5	59.8	60.0	60.4	60.9	61.7	61.9	61.5	61.4	61.3	62.4	60.9
2004	62.0	61.8	62.3	62.7	62.9	63.2	64.2	64.3	64.0	64.9	65.2	65.5	63.6
2005	65.5	65.9	66.2	65.3	65.7	67.0	67.6	67.8	68.0	68.7	68.9	68.9	67.1
2006	69.6	70.2	70.2	71.2	71.8	73.4	74.6	75.5	76.2	77.6	77.9	78.7	73.9
2007	78.6	79.0	79.3	78.9	79.6	80.8	81.0	81.0	80.3	81.3	81.8	82.1	80.3
2008	82.0	83.0	83.2	83.7	84.5	86.4	87.3	87.8	87.4	88.6	88.5	88.3	85.9
2009	86.7	85.2	84.0	81.4	80.3	80.0	80.1	79.5	78.7	78.1	77.5	77.8	80.8
2010	77.5	77.9	78.1	79.3	80.1	81.6	81.9	82.4	82.2	82.8	83.3	83.7	80.9
2011	83.4	84.5	84.9	85.8	85.9	88.6	89.7	89.9	90.5	91.5	91.9	92.8	88.3
Construction													
2000	166.0	170.4	173.0	170.8	172.4	175.2	172.4	173.9	174.5	173.1	172.4	171.6	172.1
2001	172.4	177.0	179.0	180.4	181.2	179.4	177.0	179.3	179.1	179.8	180.5	178.4	178.6
2002	177.5	180.8	183.4	181.8	182.9	182.2	180.2	181.1	180.8	180.9	178.4	176.4	180.5
2003	175.4	176.4	176.1	174.8	176.4	175.8	171.8	173.0	173.9	173.4	168.6	168.2	173.7
2004	166.0	166.4	166.7	166.9	164.8	165.3	163.3	163.4	163.6	165.8	165.3	165.7	165.3
2005	169.4	170.8	173.7	174.6	172.7	172.9	172.9	174.2	176.0	176.0	177.0	179.0	174.1
2006	178.2	183.0	187.3	183.1	185.8	188.6	187.0	188.3	191.0	192.5	193.8	194.3	187.7
2007	193.5	198.5	200.9	200.5	203.6	207.1	204.9	204.9	205.3	209.3	210.1	210.0	204.1
2008	201.4	206.6	207.0	207.9	208.3	206.8	205.1	206.3	203.8	208.7	207.3	203.3	206.0
2009	196.3	194.9	191.2	185.9	185.4	183.5	180.3	179.4	177.3	176.9	173.6	171.8	183.0
2010	170.6	169.8	170.7	171.3	172.0	172.1	172.6	173.2	173.0	173.5	170.6	169.4	171.6
2011	164.4	168.1	169.4	169.6	169.8	172.4	173.5	176.2	175.2	172.1	170.6	168.9	170.9
Manufacturing													
2000	227.2	229.1	230.2	230.0	230.6	232.2	232.2	233.0	233.0	232.8	234.2	234.9	231.6
2001	234.1	235.7	236.0	235.7	236.0	236.6	234.7	234.2	233.3	231.2	229.6	228.2	233.8
2002	225.4	225.3	224.6	223.2	222.5	223.0	221.5	221.4	219.9	218.3	217.2	217.0	221.6
2003	214.1	213.0	212.2	211.3	210.1	211.4	209.4	208.5	208.9	207.0	207.5	207.4	210.1
2004	207.4	207.4	207.7	207.1	207.1	208.5	208.8	208.9	207.4	207.1	208.5	208.9	207.9
2005	207.6	208.1	209.0	209.8	210.7	213.3	213.7	214.0	214.2	213.7	215.3	216.4	212.2
2006	215.9	216.6	218.1	220.3	222.7	225.2	225.0	226.2	226.1	226.4	228.2	229.5	223.4
2007	228.4	228.8	230.1	230.3	232.2	234.7	235.2	235.1	235.0	235.8	237.4	238.3	233.4
2008	237.2	238.0	238.3	240.0	241.7	243.7	244.6	244.6	244.1	244.5	245.3	245.1	242.3
2009	240.1	238.2	233.7	229.3	227.2	225.5	222.9	221.4	220.3	217.7	216.8	217.0	225.8
2010	215.8	216.3	216.6	215.8	216.3	217.3	217.9	218.4	218.5	219.1	219.8	221.0	217.7
2011	220.6	221.9	223.5	225.1	225.7	228.2	230.1	230.3	229.2	229.5	230.4	230.8	227.1

Employment by Industry: Houston–Sugar Land–Baytown, TX, Selected Years, 2000–2011—*Continued*

(Numbers in thousands, not seasonally adjusted)

Industry and year	January	February	March	April	May	June	July	August	September	October	November	December	Annual average
Service-Providing													
2000	1,745.3	1,759.5	1,772.1	1,776.3	1,790.1	1,794.0	1,780.0	1,788.9	1,806.1	1,807.9	1,816.5	1,830.4	1,788.9
2001	1,787.1	1,801.1	1,810.8	1,812.5	1,820.8	1,822.9	1,807.4	1,818.5	1,825.8	1,821.7	1,828.8	1,833.3	1,815.9
2002	1,797.2	1,809.9	1,818.3	1,818.6	1,830.4	1,829.8	1,811.4	1,820.7	1,830.0	1,828.3	1,837.2	1,845.7	1,823.1
2003	1,808.1	1,817.7	1,826.1	1,824.9	1,830.2	1,829.8	1,807.2	1,819.1	1,828.7	1,829.6	1,837.2	1,849.5	1,825.7
2004	1,817.5	1,828.7	1,838.9	1,843.0	1,848.7	1,852.2	1,839.5	1,846.5	1,855.8	1,862.0	1,871.2	1,884.9	1,849.1
2005	1,850.2	1,860.3	1,875.2	1,885.4	1,893.4	1,893.5	1,887.1	1,898.6	1,911.6	1,917.6	1,936.3	1,949.9	1,896.6
2006	1,911.3	1,926.1	1,944.6	1,945.5	1,957.4	1,962.2	1,952.7	1,966.5	1,980.9	1,984.4	2,001.4	2,017.5	1,962.5
2007	1,974.3	1,991.9	2,011.8	2,017.7	2,030.8	2,040.3	2,024.3	2,033.1	2,041.8	2,049.9	2,065.9	2,078.4	2,030.0
2008	2,036.3	2,051.3	2,061.7	2,064.6	2,073.4	2,078.4	2,066.2	2,072.2	2,056.7	2,069.8	2,085.4	2,091.6	2,067.3
2009	2,041.8	2,046.8	2,053.0	2,049.2	2,053.2	2,051.7	2,027.7	2,023.9	2,031.4	2,038.6	2,047.2	2,054.3	2,043.2
2010	2,011.6	2,026.3	2,042.6	2,054.0	2,070.9	2,068.8	2,051.7	2,052.8	2,060.8	2,073.6	2,086.3	2,095.6	2,057.9
2011	2,059.4	2,069.2	2,089.4	2,105.2	2,107.4	2,111.8	2,099.4	2,097.0	2,107.9	2,131.9	2,150.0	2,154.0	2,106.9
Trade, Transportation, and Utilities													
2000	480.7	479.2	481.0	479.8	481.7	486.0	485.1	488.9	485.5	489.5	497.4	507.6	486.9
2001	487.7	485.9	486.6	485.4	487.9	491.1	490.8	493.0	489.7	491.4	495.9	500.2	490.5
2002	484.0	482.3	483.4	481.2	482.9	484.2	482.3	483.5	481.0	480.2	487.2	494.7	483.9
2003	473.2	468.1	468.2	467.2	466.0	468.9	468.4	470.7	469.0	469.3	476.4	484.8	470.9
2004	466.6	464.5	467.0	469.9	469.9	472.1	472.5	475.2	471.6	474.1	482.5	491.8	473.1
2005	473.6	470.7	472.5	476.6	478.8	482.0	483.9	487.4	485.8	488.0	500.0	511.2	484.2
2006	491.0	489.2	493.5	493.5	495.0	498.4	499.1	502.5	501.9	504.1	513.0	522.8	500.3
2007	506.2	504.4	509.7	510.1	513.7	519.6	520.4	523.3	522.5	525.6	535.6	544.3	519.6
2008	525.9	525.5	528.1	526.8	528.7	532.8	533.7	536.9	529.3	530.7	540.8	548.2	532.3
2009	525.7	521.3	521.0	517.6	516.9	517.4	514.7	516.2	513.7	512.7	517.9	525.7	518.4
2010	509.1	506.7	509.6	509.9	511.8	515.4	515.9	518.8	516.4	519.5	528.3	537.7	516.6
2011	520.4	518.0	522.1	525.2	523.6	527.8	527.8	527.4	525.5	530.3	540.0	543.5	527.6
Wholesale Trade													
2000	116.8	117.3	117.8	118.0	118.1	118.9	118.9	118.9	118.9	117.9	118.0	118.6	118.2
2001	118.1	118.8	119.7	118.8	119.1	119.8	120.2	120.5	120.1	119.7	119.4	119.4	119.5
2002	117.6	118.0	118.6	117.8	118.2	118.4	118.2	118.5	118.5	118.1	118.5	118.4	118.2
2003	117.1	116.9	117.1	116.4	117.0	117.7	117.8	118.0	118.5	118.1	118.3	118.9	117.7
2004	116.8	117.0	117.8	118.2	118.6	119.4	119.4	119.4	119.6	120.0	120.2	120.8	118.9
2005	119.9	120.1	120.8	121.8	122.2	123.2	123.3	123.6	124.4	124.7	124.9	126.0	122.9
2006	125.3	126.5	127.8	127.5	128.1	129.3	129.3	129.8	130.5	130.7	131.0	131.6	129.0
2007	130.0	131.3	132.3	132.5	133.3	134.8	134.9	135.6	135.7	136.2	136.4	137.1	134.2
2008	136.2	137.5	137.8	138.2	138.9	139.9	139.5	139.9	139.2	139.0	138.9	138.9	138.7
2009	135.5	135.4	134.6	132.9	132.3	132.1	131.0	130.8	130.4	130.1	130.0	130.4	132.1
2010	129.8	129.9	130.3	130.2	130.7	131.5	131.9	132.1	132.0	131.7	131.8	132.3	131.2
2011	132.2	132.9	133.7	134.8	135.4	136.5	138.2	138.1	137.4	137.3	137.0	137.0	135.9
Retail Trade													
2000	247.0	243.4	245.0	243.0	244.4	246.6	245.6	248.4	245.4	249.3	256.7	263.8	248.2
2001	247.6	245.0	245.6	245.5	246.5	248.4	247.6	249.0	246.4	247.4	254.1	260.2	248.6
2002	247.4	245.7	247.5	246.4	247.4	247.8	245.3	245.9	244.4	244.0	250.9	257.2	247.5
2003	240.0	236.9	237.5	237.3	237.4	239.1	238.0	240.0	239.1	240.1	247.0	252.4	240.4
2004	239.7	236.8	238.6	241.3	240.1	241.2	240.4	243.6	240.9	241.9	248.7	254.8	242.3
2005	240.7	237.0	238.3	240.8	241.9	244.0	245.1	247.4	245.6	246.9	257.1	263.6	245.7
2006	248.8	245.8	247.9	248.4	248.6	249.9	250.6	252.8	251.2	252.4	260.8	265.6	251.9
2007	255.4	251.6	255.2	255.4	257.6	260.7	261.2	262.6	261.4	264.0	273.5	278.1	261.4
2008	264.2	261.8	264.2	262.8	263.1	265.1	265.6	268.0	262.5	263.9	273.6	278.3	266.1
2009	264.8	261.2	261.7	260.8	261.2	262.0	261.3	263.1	261.5	261.3	266.7	271.0	263.1
2010	258.5	256.1	258.2	258.1	259.4	261.4	260.8	263.1	260.6	264.0	272.4	277.7	262.5
2011	264.8	261.8	264.5	267.1	267.4	269.8	267.8	268.8	267.8	272.5	280.7	281.7	269.6
Transportation and Utilities													
2000	116.9	118.5	118.2	118.8	119.2	120.5	120.6	121.6	121.2	122.3	122.7	125.2	120.5
2001	122.0	122.1	121.3	121.1	122.3	122.9	123.0	123.5	123.2	124.3	122.4	120.6	122.4
2002	119.0	118.6	117.3	117.0	117.3	118.0	118.8	119.1	118.1	118.1	117.8	119.1	118.2
2003	116.1	114.3	113.6	113.5	111.6	112.1	112.6	112.7	111.4	111.1	111.1	113.5	112.8
2004	110.1	110.7	110.6	110.4	111.2	111.5	112.7	112.2	111.1	112.2	113.6	116.2	111.9
2005	113.0	113.6	113.4	114.0	114.7	114.8	115.5	116.4	115.8	116.4	118.0	121.6	115.6
2006	116.9	116.9	117.8	117.6	118.3	119.2	119.2	119.9	120.2	121.0	121.2	125.6	119.5
2007	120.8	121.5	122.2	122.2	122.8	124.1	124.3	125.1	125.4	125.4	125.7	129.1	124.1
2008	125.5	126.2	126.1	125.8	126.7	127.8	128.6	129.0	127.6	127.8	128.3	131.0	127.5
2009	125.4	124.7	124.7	123.9	123.4	123.3	122.4	122.3	121.8	121.3	121.2	124.3	123.2
2010	120.8	120.7	121.1	121.6	121.7	122.5	123.2	123.6	123.8	123.8	124.1	127.7	122.9
2011	123.4	123.3	123.9	123.3	120.8	121.5	121.8	120.5	120.3	120.5	122.3	124.8	122.2
Information													
2000	45.7	46.0	46.2	46.7	47.1	47.6	47.8	48.0	48.1	48.2	48.5	48.7	47.4
2001	47.8	48.1	48.2	48.0	47.5	47.4	45.8	45.6	44.7	44.4	44.3	43.8	46.3
2002	42.6	42.2	42.0	41.1	41.1	41.3	40.8	40.5	40.1	39.9	39.6	39.5	40.9
2003	39.3	39.2	39.2	38.9	38.8	38.8	38.9	38.6	38.2	37.8	37.8	37.8	38.6
2004	37.7	37.7	37.6	37.5	37.6	38.0	37.4	37.3	36.9	36.5	36.5	36.5	37.3
2005	36.9	36.9	37.1	36.2	36.2	36.5	36.1	36.2	35.8	35.4	35.6	35.7	36.2
2006	35.4	35.5	35.5	35.9	36.2	36.5	36.5	36.5	36.2	36.3	36.5	36.6	36.1
2007	36.6	36.8	36.7	36.5	36.9	37.2	37.1	37.2	36.9	36.7	36.8	36.8	36.9
2008	36.6	36.8	36.7	36.5	36.7	36.7	36.8	36.5	35.9	35.8	35.8	35.9	36.4
2009	35.2	35.2	35.2	34.7	34.5	34.6	34.1	33.9	33.4	33.5	33.5	33.5	34.3
2010	32.7	32.4	32.2	32.1	32.0	32.5	32.0	31.9	31.5	31.6	31.8	31.9	32.1
2011	31.9	31.8	31.7	31.7	31.8	31.9	31.7	31.7	31.5	31.3	31.5	31.5	31.7

Employment by Industry: Houston–Sugar Land–Baytown, TX, Selected Years, 2000–2011—*Continued*
(Numbers in thousands, not seasonally adjusted)

Industry and year	January	February	March	April	May	June	July	August	September	October	November	December	Annual average
Financial Activities													
2000	130.3	130.6	130.9	131.4	131.6	132.9	134.2	134.1	134.2	134.1	134.5	135.1	132.8
2001	133.7	134.3	134.7	134.6	134.8	135.4	135.3	135.0	134.2	133.2	132.7	132.9	134.2
2002	132.1	132.3	132.3	132.2	132.7	133.4	133.2	133.2	132.2	132.6	132.6	132.7	132.6
2003	131.0	131.4	132.0	132.9	133.7	134.4	134.5	135.4	134.6	135.7	135.5	135.9	133.9
2004	134.8	135.2	135.5	136.2	136.5	137.3	137.9	137.9	137.4	137.7	137.0	137.9	136.8
2005	136.3	136.7	137.1	137.3	137.4	138.4	139.8	140.4	140.3	139.5	139.9	139.9	138.6
2006	138.4	138.7	139.5	139.2	139.7	140.9	141.2	141.8	141.6	141.8	141.6	142.5	140.6
2007	141.4	142.3	143.0	142.3	143.1	144.6	145.0	145.5	144.8	145.0	145.1	145.3	144.0
2008	143.3	144.5	144.2	144.0	144.6	145.2	145.1	145.3	143.8	143.0	142.9	143.0	144.1
2009	140.5	140.4	140.1	139.5	139.6	139.9	139.4	138.9	138.1	136.8	136.6	136.7	138.9
2010	135.2	135.5	135.8	135.5	135.7	136.3	136.4	136.4	135.7	136.4	136.6	137.0	136.0
2011	135.9	136.0	136.5	136.8	136.8	137.1	136.5	137.7	137.5	138.6	139.5	140.3	137.4
Professional and Business Services													
2000	300.7	304.2	307.8	308.8	310.2	317.5	318.5	321.9	323.1	322.4	322.1	324.1	315.1
2001	316.2	319.1	320.6	320.8	320.3	323.3	321.4	321.4	318.8	316.1	316.5	315.9	319.2
2002	308.5	309.5	311.7	311.9	312.9	313.9	312.2	314.7	312.2	309.6	309.4	309.1	311.3
2003	305.2	306.4	307.3	307.9	306.5	306.9	304.8	306.7	306.8	306.0	306.0	309.2	306.6
2004	303.2	306.1	307.7	311.4	312.0	315.3	317.7	319.0	319.0	321.1	322.9	324.3	315.0
2005	321.1	324.9	328.4	330.8	331.3	333.8	335.7	337.8	341.0	345.1	346.7	348.2	335.4
2006	342.3	346.8	351.7	351.2	354.4	359.5	361.2	363.4	363.9	363.9	367.8	370.1	358.0
2007	362.6	366.6	370.7	374.0	376.1	381.3	382.1	382.5	380.5	380.9	380.7	381.8	376.7
2008	374.8	379.4	381.4	382.9	383.2	387.2	386.5	388.1	381.4	387.2	384.4	381.4	383.2
2009	368.9	366.2	364.6	360.1	358.6	359.1	357.4	355.7	353.4	353.4	353.9	354.1	358.8
2010	347.3	349.7	352.8	357.7	359.0	362.9	365.1	365.8	364.7	366.1	366.7	368.5	360.5
2011	364.1	368.2	372.8	378.8	379.1	383.9	383.1	385.6	383.2	386.6	388.5	390.2	380.3
Education and Health Services													
2000	219.0	220.5	222.3	222.9	223.3	222.8	222.5	223.4	225.3	224.6	225.3	226.2	223.2
2001	223.9	226.1	227.4	227.8	229.9	229.9	229.9	233.1	235.4	236.2	237.5	238.4	231.3
2002	237.1	239.4	240.2	241.0	241.9	242.2	241.7	244.3	245.4	243.8	245.3	245.5	242.3
2003	243.6	246.4	248.0	247.7	249.1	247.7	247.3	249.6	251.9	251.9	252.0	252.5	249.0
2004	250.2	252.1	252.8	251.8	252.7	251.9	251.8	254.1	256.0	258.4	258.8	259.9	254.2
2005	256.5	257.9	259.6	260.0	261.0	260.3	260.4	263.2	265.2	265.3	266.7	267.6	262.0
2006	264.6	266.6	267.8	269.0	270.2	269.8	269.4	271.7	273.6	273.8	274.4	276.1	270.6
2007	274.2	276.6	278.0	279.0	280.4	280.0	279.4	281.3	282.3	283.2	283.8	284.2	280.2
2008	279.8	281.7	281.0	283.0	284.0	284.6	284.0	286.8	284.3	287.7	289.3	290.5	284.7
2009	287.4	290.2	291.4	293.2	295.3	296.5	297.0	299.2	299.9	302.0	302.6	303.1	296.5
2010	301.5	303.8	305.5	307.3	308.8	308.1	308.0	309.8	311.1	312.5	313.3	313.7	308.6
2011	309.7	311.0	312.4	314.1	315.2	314.7	317.3	321.8	327.2	330.7	330.1	331.0	319.6
Leisure and Hospitality													
2000	174.2	177.5	181.2	183.0	186.2	190.8	187.7	188.0	184.7	183.6	183.1	182.9	183.6
2001	179.0	182.4	185.9	186.9	190.9	195.9	194.4	194.6	189.8	185.5	185.0	185.8	188.0
2002	181.4	184.7	187.5	190.5	196.1	199.8	198.0	198.5	195.8	191.7	192.1	193.3	192.5
2003	188.6	191.9	195.6	196.3	201.6	205.5	202.5	203.2	199.1	197.0	196.6	197.1	197.9
2004	195.5	198.1	201.5	202.3	206.3	209.7	210.0	209.5	206.0	203.7	202.4	203.0	204.0
2005	198.8	199.9	204.8	208.0	212.1	215.8	213.7	214.0	211.0	208.1	207.9	208.7	208.6
2006	206.4	209.3	215.1	216.6	220.7	223.7	224.8	225.2	222.6	217.9	219.3	221.2	218.6
2007	215.4	218.9	224.8	226.9	230.8	236.5	233.7	234.8	230.5	226.9	228.3	230.4	228.2
2008	224.5	227.1	232.2	233.8	238.1	241.6	239.0	238.4	228.4	227.2	228.9	230.5	232.5
2009	226.3	229.6	235.0	235.4	240.4	243.8	239.9	239.4	234.4	229.8	230.0	229.9	234.5
2010	223.5	226.4	232.2	235.5	238.4	241.2	238.4	238.6	236.3	234.3	234.8	235.0	234.6
2011	230.0	232.3	240.0	243.6	247.4	250.4	249.9	247.2	241.5	243.6	247.9	245.9	243.3
Other Services													
2000	88.7	89.5	89.9	90.0	90.2	91.6	91.8	91.4	91.5	91.6	91.9	92.2	90.9
2001	91.5	91.9	92.8	92.8	93.2	93.9	92.7	92.5	92.0	91.8	91.8	91.9	92.4
2002	91.2	92.0	92.6	92.2	93.3	94.3	93.8	93.7	93.4	93.0	93.3	93.6	93.0
2003	95.6	95.9	97.0	95.5	96.2	97.5	96.1	96.0	95.6	93.7	93.6	94.1	95.6
2004	94.3	95.0	96.4	94.5	94.6	95.5	94.4	93.1	92.7	91.1	90.9	91.3	93.7
2005	91.7	92.0	93.1	93.3	93.5	94.9	93.1	92.2	91.6	90.4	90.5	90.5	92.2
2006	89.8	90.5	91.3	92.7	93.4	95.4	94.8	94.6	94.4	94.1	94.5	95.2	93.4
2007	91.3	92.4	93.5	92.2	92.9	94.4	92.8	92.7	92.0	91.1	91.3	91.6	92.4
2008	90.2	90.7	90.9	91.5	92.4	93.8	93.7	93.8	91.0	92.0	92.2	91.9	92.0
2009	91.5	92.0	92.2	92.3	92.7	93.6	92.8	91.6	90.6	90.5	90.7	90.5	91.8
2010	89.9	90.5	91.0	90.3	91.2	91.9	91.9	91.0	90.4	90.5	90.5	90.5	90.8
2011	89.7	90.2	91.0	91.5	92.6	93.6	95.0	93.6	93.8	95.2	95.5	95.7	93.1
Government													
2000	306.0	312.0	312.8	313.7	319.8	304.8	292.4	293.2	313.7	313.9	313.7	313.6	309.1
2001	307.3	313.3	314.6	316.2	316.3	306.0	297.1	303.3	321.2	323.1	325.1	324.4	314.0
2002	320.3	327.5	328.6	328.5	329.5	320.7	309.4	312.3	329.9	337.5	337.7	337.3	326.6
2003	331.6	338.4	338.8	338.5	338.3	330.1	314.7	318.9	333.5	338.2	339.3	338.1	333.2
2004	335.2	340.0	340.4	339.4	339.1	332.4	317.8	320.4	336.2	339.4	340.2	340.2	335.1
2005	335.3	341.3	342.6	343.2	343.1	331.8	324.4	327.4	340.9	345.8	349.0	348.1	339.4
2006	343.4	349.5	350.2	347.4	347.8	338.0	325.7	330.8	346.7	352.5	354.3	353.0	344.9
2007	346.6	353.9	355.4	356.7	356.9	346.7	333.8	335.8	352.3	360.5	364.3	364.0	352.2
2008	361.2	365.6	367.2	366.1	365.7	356.5	347.4	346.4	362.6	366.2	371.1	370.2	362.2
2009	366.3	371.9	373.5	376.4	375.2	366.8	352.4	349.0	367.9	379.9	382.0	380.8	370.2
2010	372.4	381.3	383.5	385.7	394.0	380.5	364.0	360.5	374.7	382.7	384.3	381.3	378.7
2011	377.7	381.7	382.9	383.5	380.9	372.4	358.1	352.0	367.7	375.6	377.0	375.9	373.8

Employment by Industry: Indianapolis–Carmel, IN, Selected Years, 2000–2011

(Numbers in thousands, not seasonally adjusted)

Industry and year	January	February	March	April	May	June	July	August	September	October	November	December	Annual average
Total Nonfarm													
2000	832.9	839.3	849.3	850.3	860.2	862.8	848.9	857.2	861.6	861.1	858.4	859.5	853.5
2001	842.7	845.1	854.1	861.5	869.7	870.7	857.0	868.0	867.0	865.6	864.9	864.6	860.9
2002	838.6	841.4	847.0	854.0	865.0	864.9	852.6	861.9	863.1	865.8	868.3	868.1	857.6
2003	845.0	843.9	849.2	863.8	873.3	869.4	860.5	869.2	871.5	879.7	881.3	878.9	865.5
2004	851.5	851.2	862.3	874.5	883.7	882.2	879.0	882.4	887.2	891.6	894.2	892.7	877.7
2005	862.8	868.2	875.5	886.2	896.6	892.9	886.9	891.3	899.6	896.7	901.0	897.3	887.9
2006	875.1	881.0	890.2	898.8	911.6	908.2	896.6	903.9	911.7	914.5	919.1	918.2	902.4
2007	891.6	890.3	905.0	912.5	925.0	923.9	909.7	919.4	925.2	929.2	932.6	930.9	916.3
2008	897.8	901.4	907.7	913.7	927.3	922.2	914.4	923.5	921.0	920.8	915.5	907.0	914.4
2009	874.4	871.4	871.9	872.6	878.4	873.1	862.6	871.0	873.2	873.9	877.4	874.2	872.8
2010	849.7	848.6	857.2	871.4	879.4	875.3	867.6	877.6	874.8	883.4	885.3	882.6	871.1
2011	861.3	861.5	872.3	882.7	891.5	885.7	876.8	882.5	887.5	890.3	891.2	890.8	881.2
Total Private													
2000	725.3	728.4	737.6	739.9	748.9	756.8	750.9	753.9	749.3	749.6	746.2	747.2	744.5
2001	734.0	734.1	742.3	750.0	757.1	763.4	757.8	764.0	754.4	752.9	752.3	752.0	751.2
2002	729.5	728.4	733.7	740.6	750.6	756.1	751.7	756.1	749.1	750.0	751.7	751.5	745.8
2003	731.4	728.3	733.0	748.1	757.1	759.2	755.6	759.4	756.2	763.7	765.6	763.2	751.7
2004	736.9	735.0	745.7	758.7	767.4	772.6	777.1	776.2	771.0	774.1	776.7	775.2	763.9
2005	747.1	749.5	757.4	769.6	779.7	784.5	784.8	785.2	783.0	780.6	784.6	781.1	773.9
2006	759.9	762.2	771.0	779.6	791.3	797.9	792.4	795.0	792.8	793.7	798.0	796.6	785.9
2007	774.0	769.2	783.0	791.2	802.5	808.7	802.2	804.6	802.3	805.4	808.0	806.0	796.4
2008	776.8	776.0	781.4	788.3	800.4	802.3	798.6	800.9	794.9	793.5	788.0	779.6	790.1
2009	749.9	744.2	744.4	746.9	751.9	756.1	750.0	750.8	748.8	748.4	752.0	748.6	749.3
2010	725.6	722.5	731.2	745.1	750.3	755.8	754.9	758.3	752.1	758.6	760.4	758.4	747.8
2011	738.1	737.5	748.0	759.1	767.1	769.1	761.8	764.1	763.4	765.7	766.5	766.4	758.9
Goods-Producing													
2000	155.9	156.4	158.2	159.5	161.2	163.6	163.2	163.8	162.6	160.5	158.8	157.5	160.1
2001	154.8	154.7	156.1	157.9	159.5	161.4	160.4	161.9	159.9	158.1	156.6	155.3	158.1
2002	150.5	149.6	150.6	151.9	154.1	156.3	156.6	157.4	155.9	154.1	153.4	152.0	153.5
2003	148.0	146.9	147.6	150.0	152.0	153.6	153.3	153.7	152.6	153.5	153.1	151.6	151.3
2004	147.1	146.4	148.7	151.6	154.8	156.6	155.4	156.3	155.5	155.4	154.3	153.2	152.9
2005	148.1	147.7	149.4	151.9	153.1	155.3	154.4	155.7	155.0	154.4	154.5	152.8	152.7
2006	148.7	148.8	150.5	153.5	154.7	157.6	155.6	157.1	155.6	154.9	154.3	152.6	153.7
2007	147.6	144.7	148.0	150.4	152.4	154.3	153.9	154.7	153.8	152.0	151.0	149.5	151.0
2008	145.2	145.0	145.7	146.2	148.2	149.2	148.4	148.0	145.2	143.8	141.1	137.2	145.3
2009	130.4	127.5	126.4	125.9	125.5	125.9	125.7	125.9	124.7	123.5	122.7	120.7	125.4
2010	116.7	115.6	117.6	120.5	121.7	123.5	124.1	123.6	122.3	122.2	120.9	118.7	120.6
2011	114.3	113.8	116.2	118.8	120.6	123.3	125.8	126.2	126.6	126.3	125.0	123.1	121.7
Mining and Logging													
2005	0.8	0.8	0.8	0.8	0.8	0.8	0.8	0.8	0.8	0.8	0.8	0.8	0.8
2006	0.8	0.8	0.8	0.8	0.8	0.8	0.8	0.8	0.8	0.8	0.8	0.8	0.8
2007	0.8	0.7	0.8	0.8	0.8	0.8	0.8	0.8	0.8	0.8	0.8	0.8	0.8
2008	0.7	0.7	0.8	0.8	0.8	0.8	0.8	0.8	0.8	0.8	0.8	0.8	0.8
2009	0.7	0.7	0.7	0.7	0.7	0.7	0.8	0.8	0.8	0.7	0.7	0.7	0.7
2010	0.7	0.7	0.7	0.7	0.7	0.7	0.7	0.7	0.7	0.7	0.7	0.7	0.7
2011	0.6	0.6	0.6	0.7	0.7	0.7	0.7	0.7	0.7	0.7	0.7	0.7	0.7
Construction													
2005	46.3	46.1	47.7	50.1	51.0	52.5	53.2	53.3	53.1	53.2	52.9	51.4	50.9
2006	47.7	48.0	49.4	52.0	53.2	54.9	54.8	55.0	54.5	54.2	53.5	52.5	52.5
2007	48.6	46.5	49.4	51.9	53.9	55.2	55.5	55.9	55.1	54.6	53.8	51.4	52.7
2008	47.7	47.4	48.3	49.8	51.1	51.4	52.0	51.2	50.1	48.8	47.6	44.9	49.2
2009	40.2	39.4	39.8	40.5	41.0	41.5	41.9	41.6	40.9	40.3	39.6	37.5	40.4
2010	34.2	33.2	34.9	37.8	38.9	40.2	40.9	40.7	39.7	39.7	38.9	36.8	38.0
2011	33.8	33.5	35.3	37.5	39.1	41.1	42.9	43.8	44.6	44.1	42.8	41.3	40.0
Manufacturing													
2000	111.1	111.5	111.3	111.1	111.8	113.2	112.8	113.6	113.1	112.6	111.8	112.0	112.2
2001	111.1	110.3	110.0	109.6	109.9	110.2	108.6	109.6	108.4	107.6	106.6	106.3	109.0
2002	104.5	104.0	104.2	103.5	104.2	105.4	104.6	105.4	104.8	103.9	103.8	103.5	104.3
2003	102.5	102.4	102.2	102.0	102.4	102.8	101.7	101.8	101.0	101.5	101.4	101.1	101.9
2004	100.1	100.0	100.3	100.3	101.2	102.2	101.2	102.4	102.0	101.9	102.0	102.1	101.3
2005	101.0	100.8	100.9	101.0	101.3	102.0	100.4	101.6	101.1	100.4	100.8	100.6	101.0
2006	100.2	100.0	100.3	100.7	100.7	101.9	100.0	101.3	100.3	99.9	100.0	99.3	100.4
2007	98.2	97.5	97.8	97.7	97.7	98.3	97.6	98.0	97.9	96.6	96.4	97.3	97.6
2008	96.8	96.9	96.6	95.6	96.3	97.0	95.6	96.0	94.3	94.2	92.7	91.5	95.3
2009	89.5	87.4	85.9	84.7	83.8	83.7	83.0	83.5	83.0	82.5	82.4	82.5	84.3
2010	81.8	81.7	82.0	82.0	82.1	82.6	82.5	82.2	81.9	81.8	81.3	81.2	81.9
2011	79.9	79.7	80.3	80.6	80.8	81.5	82.2	81.7	81.3	81.5	81.5	81.1	81.0

Employment by Industry: Indianapolis–Carmel, IN, Selected Years, 2000–2011—*Continued*

(Numbers in thousands, not seasonally adjusted)

Industry and year	January	February	March	April	May	June	July	August	September	October	November	December	Annual average
Service-Providing													
2000	677.0	682.9	691.1	690.8	699.0	699.2	685.7	693.4	699.0	700.6	699.6	702.0	693.4
2001	687.9	690.4	698.0	703.6	710.2	709.3	696.6	706.1	707.1	707.5	708.3	709.3	702.9
2002	688.1	691.8	696.4	702.1	710.9	708.6	696.0	704.5	707.2	711.7	714.9	716.1	704.0
2003	697.0	697.0	701.6	713.8	721.3	715.8	707.2	715.5	718.9	726.2	728.2	727.3	714.2
2004	704.4	704.8	713.6	722.9	728.9	725.6	723.6	726.1	731.7	736.2	739.9	739.5	724.8
2005	714.7	720.5	726.1	734.3	743.5	737.6	732.5	735.6	744.6	742.3	746.5	744.5	735.2
2006	726.4	732.2	739.7	745.3	756.9	750.6	741.0	746.8	756.1	759.6	764.8	765.6	748.8
2007	744.0	745.6	757.0	762.1	772.6	769.6	755.8	764.7	771.4	777.2	781.6	781.4	765.3
2008	752.6	756.4	762.0	767.5	779.1	773.0	766.0	775.5	775.8	777.0	774.4	769.8	769.1
2009	744.0	743.9	745.5	746.7	752.9	747.2	736.9	745.1	748.5	750.4	754.7	753.5	747.4
2010	733.0	733.0	739.6	750.9	757.7	751.8	743.5	754.0	752.5	761.2	764.4	763.9	750.5
2011	747.0	747.7	756.1	763.9	770.9	762.4	751.0	756.3	760.9	764.0	766.2	767.7	759.5
Trade, Transportation, and Utilities													
2000	188.9	188.4	190.0	188.3	189.6	190.6	191.6	191.1	190.3	193.3	195.8	199.4	191.4
2001	194.7	191.6	192.3	194.0	194.1	194.3	194.7	195.0	193.8	195.2	198.2	200.8	194.9
2002	191.4	189.5	190.0	190.5	191.7	192.4	191.1	191.6	190.6	190.7	194.7	196.9	191.8
2003	189.6	186.6	188.1	189.2	189.3	189.5	188.6	189.1	188.4	190.1	193.9	195.4	189.8
2004	185.7	183.7	185.2	186.7	188.3	188.4	190.4	190.9	188.9	192.3	196.2	198.2	189.7
2005	189.1	189.0	190.4	192.3	193.6	193.9	194.6	195.2	194.6	196.3	199.9	201.0	194.2
2006	192.8	191.4	193.0	192.7	194.3	195.2	195.0	194.8	194.3	195.7	200.2	202.1	195.1
2007	193.5	190.9	193.9	193.8	196.3	197.8	196.8	196.1	195.7	196.3	200.9	202.6	196.2
2008	193.7	192.2	193.4	193.5	196.4	196.7	195.7	196.3	194.9	195.8	196.9	197.3	195.2
2009	187.9	185.4	185.1	184.3	186.1	186.4	185.3	185.0	183.7	185.0	187.8	188.3	185.9
2010	181.4	179.6	181.3	182.8	184.6	185.4	185.7	186.2	184.4	186.9	190.2	191.4	185.0
2011	184.6	183.7	184.5	186.4	188.3	188.9	186.7	185.9	184.3	185.4	187.5	189.2	186.3
Wholesale Trade													
2000	47.6	47.9	48.3	48.1	48.4	48.8	48.8	48.8	48.6	48.8	48.6	48.7	48.5
2001	49.0	49.0	49.0	49.0	49.0	49.1	49.0	48.9	48.6	48.5	48.3	48.4	48.8
2002	47.4	47.7	47.5	47.4	47.7	47.7	47.3	47.2	46.8	46.8	46.7	46.8	47.3
2003	46.3	46.2	46.2	45.8	45.9	46.0	45.7	45.6	45.4	45.6	45.7	45.8	45.9
2004	45.4	45.6	46.0	46.0	46.2	46.6	46.9	46.7	46.3	46.6	46.6	46.5	46.3
2005	46.2	46.4	46.6	46.8	46.8	47.0	47.2	47.2	47.0	47.1	47.1	47.3	46.9
2006	46.9	46.9	47.0	47.1	47.4	47.7	47.5	47.3	47.2	47.5	47.4	47.6	47.3
2007	47.2	47.2	47.6	47.5	47.7	48.1	48.5	48.0	47.8	47.8	48.1	48.2	47.8
2008	47.8	47.9	48.2	48.2	48.5	48.5	48.4	48.1	47.9	47.9	47.8	47.6	48.1
2009	46.4	46.0	45.7	45.2	45.1	45.0	45.1	44.6	44.1	44.3	44.2	44.2	45.0
2010	43.8	43.6	44.0	44.0	44.1	44.1	44.6	44.5	44.2	44.3	44.2	44.1	44.1
2011	44.3	44.5	44.6	45.0	45.3	45.4	44.4	44.5	44.2	44.4	43.7	43.6	44.5
Retail Trade													
2000	96.0	94.9	95.8	94.9	96.0	96.8	96.0	96.1	95.6	98.0	101.0	103.4	97.0
2001	99.7	97.4	97.5	97.7	98.2	98.7	97.8	97.6	97.3	98.2	101.9	103.2	98.8
2002	97.8	96.2	96.9	96.4	97.4	98.1	96.8	96.8	96.4	96.0	99.3	101.4	97.5
2003	96.1	94.2	95.4	95.5	96.6	97.0	95.8	96.4	95.8	96.6	100.2	101.8	96.8
2004	95.2	93.0	93.6	94.2	95.4	96.0	95.9	96.2	95.0	97.1	100.9	102.5	96.3
2005	95.2	94.5	95.4	96.4	97.6	97.4	97.5	97.4	96.8	98.1	101.0	102.4	97.5
2006	96.1	94.7	95.8	95.4	96.2	96.5	96.6	96.3	95.6	96.4	100.1	101.6	96.8
2007	95.3	93.1	94.7	94.6	96.3	97.0	96.2	95.7	95.1	95.6	98.9	100.3	96.1
2008	93.9	92.4	92.7	92.6	94.7	94.9	94.9	95.1	94.3	95.1	96.1	96.5	94.4
2009	90.4	88.7	88.9	89.2	90.7	91.2	90.3	90.1	89.1	89.9	92.5	92.9	90.3
2010	88.5	87.1	88.0	88.8	90.1	90.6	90.4	90.5	88.9	90.7	93.5	94.2	90.1
2011	89.7	88.4	89.2	90.3	91.6	91.9	90.9	89.8	88.5	89.0	90.5	91.2	90.1
Transportation and Utilities													
2000	45.3	45.6	45.9	45.3	45.2	45.0	46.8	46.2	46.1	46.5	46.2	47.3	46.0
2001	46.0	45.2	45.8	47.3	46.9	46.5	47.9	48.5	47.9	48.5	48.0	49.2	47.3
2002	46.2	45.6	45.6	46.7	46.6	46.6	47.0	47.6	47.4	47.9	48.7	48.7	47.1
2003	47.2	46.2	46.5	47.9	46.8	46.5	47.1	47.1	47.2	47.9	48.0	47.8	47.2
2004	45.1	45.1	45.6	46.5	46.7	46.8	47.6	48.0	47.6	48.6	48.7	49.2	47.1
2005	47.7	48.1	48.4	49.1	49.2	49.5	49.9	50.6	50.8	51.1	51.8	51.3	49.8
2006	49.8	49.8	50.2	50.2	50.7	51.0	50.9	51.2	51.5	51.8	52.7	52.9	51.1
2007	51.0	50.6	51.6	51.7	52.3	52.7	52.1	52.4	52.8	52.9	53.9	54.1	52.3
2008	52.0	51.9	52.5	52.7	53.2	53.3	52.4	53.1	52.7	52.8	53.0	53.2	52.7
2009	51.1	50.7	50.5	49.9	50.3	50.2	49.9	50.3	50.5	50.8	51.1	51.2	50.5
2010	49.1	48.9	49.3	50.0	50.4	50.7	50.7	51.2	51.3	51.9	52.5	53.1	50.8
2011	50.6	50.8	50.7	51.1	51.4	51.6	51.4	51.6	51.6	52.0	53.3	54.4	51.7
Information													
2000	17.0	17.1	17.4	16.9	17.0	17.4	17.5	17.7	17.4	17.5	17.6	17.7	17.4
2001	17.6	17.4	17.6	17.0	17.2	17.4	17.2	17.0	16.8	16.7	16.7	16.7	17.1
2002	16.5	16.4	16.6	16.4	16.6	16.7	16.6	16.6	16.4	16.3	16.2	16.2	16.5
2003	16.0	15.9	16.1	15.9	16.2	16.6	16.6	16.8	16.5	16.3	16.4	16.4	16.3
2004	16.3	16.3	16.3	16.2	16.5	16.8	16.8	16.8	16.4	16.6	16.5	16.6	16.5
2005	16.1	16.3	16.3	16.3	16.5	16.7	16.6	16.6	16.2	16.1	16.2	16.4	16.4
2006	15.8	16.0	16.0	16.2	16.3	16.4	16.4	16.3	16.1	16.0	16.1	16.1	16.1
2007	16.1	16.2	16.1	16.2	16.4	16.6	16.7	16.7	16.6	16.5	16.5	16.7	16.4
2008	16.7	16.7	16.7	16.7	16.9	17.0	17.0	16.9	16.6	16.4	16.3	16.3	16.7
2009	16.1	16.1	15.9	15.7	15.8	16.0	15.7	15.7	15.5	15.3	15.2	15.3	15.7
2010	15.0	14.9	14.9	14.9	15.1	15.3	15.1	15.1	14.8	14.6	14.6	14.7	14.9
2011	14.3	14.2	14.3	14.2	14.4	14.6	14.5	14.5	14.2	14.2	14.2	14.2	14.3

Employment by Industry: Indianapolis–Carmel, IN, Selected Years, 2000–2011—*Continued*

(Numbers in thousands, not seasonally adjusted)

Industry and year	January	February	March	April	May	June	July	August	September	October	November	December	Annual average
Financial Activities													
2000	63.1	63.1	62.9	63.0	63.5	64.1	63.5	63.2	62.7	62.6	62.2	62.4	63.0
2001	61.9	62.1	62.3	62.9	63.2	63.9	63.2	62.9	62.2	61.2	61.5	61.8	62.4
2002	62.0	62.0	61.8	61.9	62.2	62.8	62.5	62.6	62.2	62.6	62.8	62.9	62.4
2003	62.7	62.8	62.9	63.2	63.6	64.2	64.2	64.2	63.9	63.9	63.7	63.7	63.6
2004	62.9	63.2	63.2	63.1	63.5	63.9	63.8	63.8	63.1	63.1	63.0	63.4	63.3
2005	62.4	62.5	62.4	62.8	62.8	63.3	63.8	63.8	63.4	63.3	63.2	63.4	63.1
2006	62.5	62.6	62.6	62.7	63.1	63.5	63.4	63.5	62.9	62.7	62.5	62.7	62.9
2007	61.5	61.9	62.0	62.3	62.4	63.0	63.3	63.1	62.7	62.4	62.2	62.3	62.4
2008	60.6	60.7	60.6	60.5	60.7	61.1	61.3	60.8	60.0	59.9	59.3	59.4	60.4
2009	58.8	58.8	58.6	58.5	58.5	58.6	58.5	58.3	57.6	57.6	57.4	57.6	58.2
2010	57.5	57.3	57.4	57.5	57.7	58.2	58.7	58.6	58.1	58.5	58.5	58.6	58.1
2011	58.2	58.3	58.5	58.4	58.7	59.0	59.3	59.3	58.3	57.3	57.1	57.6	58.3
Professional and Business Services													
2000	104.1	104.7	106.9	108.0	110.0	111.5	109.0	109.6	109.8	108.5	107.7	106.6	108.0
2001	103.4	104.1	106.3	108.2	108.5	109.3	108.6	109.8	107.2	106.9	106.1	104.6	106.9
2002	104.1	104.4	105.3	107.2	108.2	108.8	108.9	109.2	108.2	109.3	108.5	107.7	107.5
2003	105.0	105.1	105.2	107.8	110.1	110.7	111.2	111.9	111.5	113.7	114.6	113.1	110.0
2004	106.9	107.3	110.4	115.2	116.4	117.5	122.3	121.5	120.5	119.8	120.5	119.3	116.5
2005	115.4	115.8	117.2	118.9	119.5	120.1	121.8	121.2	121.1	122.2	122.2	120.3	119.6
2006	116.8	117.6	119.5	122.1	124.1	125.0	124.7	127.0	126.4	126.6	127.5	126.0	123.6
2007	123.9	123.3	126.5	129.2	131.1	130.7	130.1	131.8	131.8	134.3	134.1	132.0	129.9
2008	127.2	126.3	127.3	129.5	130.4	130.6	129.9	131.9	130.7	132.2	129.6	125.9	129.3
2009	118.3	117.1	116.8	117.5	117.1	118.8	116.6	118.6	119.3	121.7	123.7	123.3	119.1
2010	115.1	114.4	116.3	121.3	121.1	122.4	123.0	124.6	122.6	126.2	126.6	127.5	121.8
2011	122.6	121.9	124.3	127.2	127.9	127.0	125.2	130.8	130.6	131.9	131.5	133.4	127.9
Education and Health Services													
2000	90.5	91.8	92.6	91.4	91.3	90.8	90.7	91.1	92.3	92.4	92.3	92.6	91.7
2001	92.3	93.4	93.8	94.2	94.6	93.7	93.5	94.8	97.3	97.0	97.9	98.3	95.1
2002	96.4	96.9	97.5	97.5	97.8	96.8	96.0	96.8	98.8	100.0	100.8	101.0	98.0
2003	99.5	100.1	100.4	105.7	104.8	101.5	101.0	100.8	105.0	107.5	107.5	107.4	103.4
2004	107.1	107.1	107.9	107.6	105.6	103.9	104.6	102.0	105.5	107.3	107.3	106.4	106.0
2005	102.8	104.1	104.9	105.8	108.7	107.2	106.8	104.3	109.1	106.5	107.0	106.2	106.1
2006	106.1	107.6	108.6	108.3	111.1	110.2	109.3	107.0	111.6	113.5	113.7	113.5	110.0
2007	112.2	113.3	114.2	115.1	115.0	115.0	113.6	112.2	116.3	118.3	118.9	119.3	115.3
2008	113.8	115.1	115.7	116.7	117.3	116.8	116.9	115.6	119.2	120.6	121.2	121.5	117.5
2009	120.7	121.5	121.4	122.9	122.9	122.9	122.5	121.6	125.2	125.4	126.2	126.0	123.3
2010	125.7	126.4	126.7	127.7	126.6	125.7	124.2	124.6	127.9	129.0	129.4	128.7	126.9
2011	128.5	129.5	130.6	131.5	131.0	129.6	124.8	121.9	126.2	128.0	129.0	127.6	128.2
Leisure and Hospitality													
2000	73.5	74.3	76.6	79.9	83.2	85.3	82.2	84.2	81.7	82.0	79.2	78.4	80.0
2001	76.9	78.1	80.7	82.7	86.4	89.1	86.0	88.6	84.3	84.9	82.3	81.5	83.5
2002	76.2	76.9	78.8	81.6	85.7	87.4	85.3	87.4	83.4	83.4	81.6	81.2	82.4
2003	77.4	77.4	79.0	82.5	86.9	88.4	86.1	88.5	84.6	85.0	82.8	82.2	83.4
2004	77.6	77.5	80.1	84.0	87.6	89.5	88.6	89.7	86.5	85.2	84.7	84.0	84.6
2005	79.3	79.9	82.2	86.8	90.3	92.5	91.2	92.7	88.7	86.9	86.8	86.2	87.0
2006	82.8	83.5	85.8	88.7	92.0	93.6	92.0	93.3	90.4	89.0	88.4	88.3	89.0
2007	84.2	83.8	86.8	88.4	92.6	94.4	91.0	93.7	89.6	89.8	88.8	88.0	89.3
2008	84.5	84.6	86.6	89.2	94.0	94.1	92.5	94.9	92.3	89.1	88.0	86.8	89.7
2009	82.9	83.2	85.4	87.3	90.9	91.9	90.4	91.0	88.7	85.8	85.0	83.5	87.2
2010	80.5	80.7	82.9	86.2	89.1	90.3	89.1	90.9	87.7	86.8	85.8	84.7	86.2
2011	81.7	82.2	85.2	88.1	91.5	91.6	90.5	90.8	88.9	88.4	88.0	87.3	87.9
Other Services													
2000	32.3	32.6	33.0	32.9	33.1	33.5	33.2	33.2	32.5	32.8	32.6	32.6	32.9
2001	32.4	32.7	33.2	33.1	33.6	34.3	34.2	34.0	32.9	32.9	33.0	33.0	33.3
2002	32.4	32.7	33.1	33.6	34.3	34.9	34.7	34.5	33.6	33.6	33.7	33.6	33.7
2003	33.2	33.5	33.7	33.8	34.2	34.7	34.6	34.4	33.7	33.7	33.6	33.4	33.9
2004	33.3	33.5	33.9	34.3	34.7	35.0	35.2	35.2	34.6	34.4	34.2	34.1	34.4
2005	33.9	34.2	34.6	34.8	35.2	35.5	35.6	35.7	34.9	34.9	34.8	34.8	34.9
2006	34.4	34.7	35.0	35.4	35.7	36.4	36.0	36.0	35.5	35.3	35.3	35.3	35.4
2007	35.0	35.1	35.5	35.8	36.3	36.9	36.8	36.3	35.8	35.8	35.6	35.6	35.9
2008	35.1	35.4	35.4	36.0	36.5	36.8	36.9	36.5	36.0	35.7	35.6	35.2	35.9
2009	34.8	34.6	34.8	34.8	35.1	35.6	35.3	34.7	34.1	34.1	34.0	33.9	34.7
2010	33.7	33.6	34.1	34.2	34.4	35.0	35.0	34.7	34.3	34.4	34.4	34.1	34.3
2011	33.9	33.9	34.4	34.5	34.7	35.1	35.0	34.7	34.3	34.2	34.2	34.0	34.4
Government													
2000	107.6	110.9	111.7	110.4	111.3	106.0	98.0	103.3	112.3	111.5	112.2	112.3	109.0
2001	108.7	111.0	111.8	111.5	112.6	107.3	99.2	104.0	112.6	112.7	112.6	112.6	109.7
2002	109.1	113.0	113.3	113.4	114.4	108.8	100.9	105.8	114.0	115.8	116.6	116.6	111.8
2003	113.6	115.6	116.2	115.7	116.2	110.2	104.9	109.8	115.3	116.0	115.7	115.7	113.7
2004	114.6	116.2	116.6	115.8	116.3	109.6	101.9	106.2	116.2	117.5	117.5	117.5	113.8
2005	115.7	118.7	118.1	116.6	116.9	108.4	102.1	106.1	116.6	116.6	116.4	116.2	114.0
2006	115.2	118.8	119.2	119.2	120.3	110.3	104.2	108.9	118.9	120.8	121.1	121.6	116.5
2007	117.6	121.1	122.0	121.3	122.5	115.2	107.5	114.8	122.9	123.8	124.6	124.9	119.9
2008	121.0	125.4	126.3	125.4	126.9	119.9	115.8	122.6	126.1	127.3	127.5	127.4	124.3
2009	124.5	127.2	127.5	125.7	126.5	117.0	112.6	120.2	124.4	125.5	125.4	125.6	123.5
2010	124.1	126.1	126.0	126.3	129.1	119.5	112.7	119.3	122.7	124.8	124.9	124.2	123.3
2011	123.2	124.0	124.3	123.6	124.4	116.6	115.0	118.4	124.1	124.6	124.7	124.4	122.3

Employment by Industry: Jacksonville, FL, Selected Years, 2000–2011

(Numbers in thousands, not seasonally adjusted)

Industry and year	January	February	March	April	May	June	July	August	September	October	November	December	Annual average
Total Nonfarm													
2000	553.6	556.5	561.6	564.5	568.5	565.5	560.1	567.5	567.3	569.3	570.5	574.0	564.9
2001	553.5	560.2	566.7	567.8	568.6	565.4	560.1	571.1	569.3	565.3	566.5	567.7	565.2
2002	555.8	557.9	563.4	563.3	565.3	559.6	552.5	560.7	558.6	559.8	563.6	566.4	560.6
2003	555.9	558.6	565.1	564.3	566.9	560.9	555.7	563.4	562.3	565.3	568.1	572.1	563.2
2004	564.3	567.2	573.0	577.2	579.0	576.4	573.4	580.1	579.3	583.3	591.1	597.9	578.5
2005	590.0	595.0	598.1	599.7	602.1	598.5	598.2	608.0	610.2	609.4	616.5	620.4	603.8
2006	612.0	617.7	623.7	621.5	625.6	620.8	617.9	626.1	627.2	629.7	637.0	639.0	624.9
2007	628.3	631.7	637.6	636.9	639.1	633.9	626.4	632.8	631.8	632.6	637.6	637.8	633.9
2008	626.5	629.6	630.9	630.2	630.7	622.0	613.8	616.3	615.6	614.3	615.7	613.1	621.6
2009	595.6	595.3	594.6	591.1	590.6	582.9	577.3	579.5	578.7	582.1	585.9	585.7	586.6
2010	574.0	576.7	579.9	582.1	586.3	579.5	578.2	581.4	583.3	588.8	592.7	594.2	583.1
2011	583.7	587.4	591.8	592.7	593.5	586.9	582.2	585.6	585.9	588.4	596.6	600.6	589.6
Total Private													
2000	484.9	486.9	491.6	494.2	496.4	499.8	495.6	497.6	497.6	498.8	500.1	503.3	495.6
2001	484.3	489.6	495.8	496.5	497.1	499.1	495.1	499.6	498.0	494.1	494.8	495.6	495.0
2002	485.6	487.0	492.5	491.8	493.6	493.1	487.5	489.3	487.4	488.1	491.3	493.7	490.1
2003	484.1	486.8	493.1	492.0	493.9	492.6	488.8	491.5	490.3	492.4	494.8	498.6	491.6
2004	491.7	494.0	499.5	503.5	505.1	507.0	505.4	506.7	505.5	508.4	515.6	521.7	505.3
2005	515.0	519.1	522.0	524.3	526.3	527.5	529.1	533.3	535.1	534.5	541.4	545.2	529.4
2006	537.6	542.5	548.4	547.1	551.4	551.0	549.6	552.5	552.9	554.3	560.6	562.5	550.9
2007	552.7	555.1	560.8	559.9	561.9	560.9	555.7	556.3	554.9	555.2	559.4	559.7	557.7
2008	549.5	551.7	552.9	552.7	553.0	549.0	542.2	540.4	538.6	536.9	537.0	535.0	544.9
2009	519.3	517.9	517.1	513.5	512.7	509.8	505.0	503.6	502.0	504.8	508.4	508.7	510.2
2010	497.0	499.2	502.4	504.2	505.8	505.3	504.6	505.4	506.4	511.1	514.5	516.3	506.0
2011	505.9	509.1	513.5	514.6	515.4	513.3	509.9	510.0	509.8	511.7	519.5	523.4	513.0
Goods-Producing													
2000	70.3	70.9	71.8	71.7	72.1	72.9	73.0	72.9	72.9	72.5	71.7	72.2	72.1
2001	68.6	69.3	69.4	69.3	69.0	69.7	69.8	69.4	68.8	68.8	68.7	68.5	69.1
2002	67.7	67.7	68.3	67.6	68.4	68.9	68.3	68.5	68.3	69.0	69.7	69.8	68.5
2003	69.5	70.1	70.9	69.3	69.9	70.7	69.5	69.7	69.7	69.7	70.2	70.8	70.0
2004	70.4	71.4	72.5	72.9	73.4	74.4	74.9	75.1	75.3	75.7	76.5	77.4	74.2
2005	76.2	76.5	77.3	77.7	78.0	79.0	79.5	80.0	80.6	80.0	80.9	81.5	78.9
2006	80.7	81.9	82.8	83.1	83.9	84.9	84.1	84.5	84.3	83.4	83.4	83.2	83.4
2007	81.6	81.5	82.4	81.4	82.5	83.4	82.8	82.9	82.0	80.5	80.4	80.1	81.8
2008	77.7	78.0	77.8	76.3	76.3	76.2	74.8	74.2	74.0	72.4	71.3	70.1	74.9
2009	67.2	66.2	65.3	62.8	61.7	61.5	60.5	60.0	59.4	58.1	57.8	57.5	61.5
2010	55.2	55.0	55.5	55.6	55.6	55.7	56.0	55.6	55.8	55.6	55.4	55.0	55.5
2011	53.1	53.0	53.6	53.8	53.7	53.8	53.3	53.3	53.1	52.5	53.9	53.0	53.3
Mining and Logging													
2000	0.4	0.4	0.4	0.4	0.4	0.5	0.5	0.5	0.5	0.5	0.5	0.5	0.5
2001	0.4	0.5	0.5	0.4	0.4	0.5	0.5	0.5	0.5	0.5	0.5	0.5	0.5
2002	0.5	0.5	0.5	0.4	0.5	0.5	0.5	0.5	0.5	0.5	0.5	0.5	0.5
2003	0.5	0.5	0.5	0.5	0.5	0.5	0.5	0.5	0.5	0.5	0.5	0.5	0.5
2004	0.5	0.4	0.4	0.4	0.4	0.4	0.4	0.4	0.4	0.4	0.4	0.4	0.4
2005	0.4	0.4	0.4	0.4	0.4	0.4	0.4	0.4	0.4	0.4	0.4	0.4	0.4
2006	0.4	0.4	0.4	0.4	0.4	0.4	0.4	0.4	0.4	0.4	0.4	0.4	0.4
2007	0.4	0.4	0.4	0.4	0.4	0.4	0.4	0.4	0.4	0.4	0.4	0.4	0.4
2008	0.4	0.4	0.4	0.4	0.4	0.4	0.4	0.4	0.4	0.4	0.4	0.4	0.4
2009	0.4	0.4	0.4	0.4	0.4	0.4	0.3	0.4	0.4	0.3	0.3	0.3	0.4
2010	0.3	0.3	0.3	0.3	0.3	0.4	0.3	0.3	0.3	0.4	0.4	0.4	0.3
2011	0.3	0.3	0.3	0.3	0.3	0.3	0.3	0.3	0.3	0.3	0.3	0.3	0.3
Construction													
2000	30.9	31.2	31.9	31.7	32.0	32.4	32.5	32.6	32.8	32.7	32.5	32.8	32.2
2001	31.6	32.0	31.9	31.9	31.9	32.5	32.8	32.9	32.8	33.1	33.1	33.0	32.5
2002	32.3	32.2	32.9	32.8	33.6	34.0	33.5	33.8	33.8	34.4	35.0	35.2	33.6
2003	35.0	35.4	36.2	35.7	36.0	36.5	36.0	36.4	36.3	36.3	36.8	37.2	36.2
2004	37.3	38.2	39.1	39.4	39.7	40.4	41.0	41.3	41.6	41.9	42.6	43.3	40.5
2005	42.5	42.5	43.2	43.8	44.2	45.0	45.4	46.0	46.5	46.2	47.0	47.5	45.0
2006	46.9	48.1	48.9	49.5	50.1	50.9	50.3	50.8	50.6	50.0	50.1	49.9	49.7
2007	48.4	48.2	49.1	48.8	49.8	50.5	49.9	49.9	49.0	47.7	47.6	47.2	48.8
2008	44.9	45.2	45.1	43.7	43.7	43.7	42.4	42.0	41.8	40.6	39.6	38.5	42.6
2009	36.0	35.7	35.1	33.3	32.7	32.6	31.9	31.4	31.0	30.0	29.7	29.5	32.4
2010	27.7	27.8	28.4	28.6	28.6	28.6	28.8	28.5	28.5	28.0	27.8	27.3	28.2
2011	25.9	25.9	26.5	26.7	26.5	26.6	26.3	26.4	26.1	25.5	26.9	25.9	26.3
Manufacturing													
2000	39.0	39.3	39.5	39.6	39.7	40.0	40.0	39.8	39.6	39.3	38.7	38.9	39.5
2001	36.6	36.8	37.0	37.0	36.7	36.7	36.5	36.0	35.5	35.2	35.1	35.0	36.2
2002	34.9	35.0	34.9	34.4	34.3	34.4	34.3	34.2	34.0	34.1	34.2	34.1	34.4
2003	34.0	34.2	34.2	33.1	33.4	33.7	33.0	32.8	32.9	32.9	32.9	33.1	33.4
2004	32.6	32.8	33.0	33.1	33.3	33.6	33.5	33.4	33.3	33.4	33.5	33.7	33.3
2005	33.3	33.6	33.7	33.5	33.4	33.6	33.7	33.6	33.7	33.4	33.5	33.6	33.6
2006	33.4	33.4	33.5	33.2	33.4	33.6	33.4	33.3	33.3	33.0	32.9	32.9	33.3
2007	32.8	32.9	32.9	32.2	32.3	32.5	32.5	32.6	32.6	32.4	32.4	32.5	32.6
2008	32.4	32.4	32.3	32.2	32.2	32.1	32.0	31.8	31.8	31.4	31.3	31.2	31.9
2009	30.8	30.1	29.8	29.1	28.6	28.5	28.3	28.2	28.0	27.8	27.8	27.7	28.7
2010	27.2	26.9	26.8	26.7	26.7	26.7	26.9	26.8	27.0	27.2	27.2	27.3	27.0
2011	26.9	26.8	26.8	26.8	26.9	26.9	26.7	26.6	26.7	26.7	26.7	26.8	26.8

Employment by Industry: Jacksonville, FL, Selected Years, 2000–2011—*Continued*

(Numbers in thousands, not seasonally adjusted)

Industry and year	January	February	March	April	May	June	July	August	September	October	November	December	Annual average
Service-Providing													
2000	483.3	485.6	489.8	492.8	496.4	492.6	487.1	494.6	494.4	496.8	498.8	501.8	492.8
2001	484.9	490.9	497.3	498.5	499.6	495.7	490.3	501.7	500.5	496.5	497.8	499.2	496.1
2002	488.1	490.2	495.1	495.7	496.9	490.7	484.2	492.2	490.3	490.8	493.9	496.6	492.1
2003	486.4	488.5	494.2	495.0	497.0	490.2	486.2	493.7	492.6	495.6	497.9	501.3	493.2
2004	493.9	495.8	500.5	504.3	505.6	502.0	498.5	505.0	504.0	507.6	514.6	520.5	504.4
2005	513.8	518.5	520.8	522.0	524.1	519.5	518.7	528.0	529.6	529.4	535.6	538.9	524.9
2006	531.3	535.8	540.9	538.4	541.7	535.9	533.8	541.6	542.9	546.3	553.6	555.8	541.5
2007	546.7	550.2	555.2	555.5	556.6	550.5	543.6	549.9	549.8	552.1	557.2	557.7	552.1
2008	548.8	551.6	553.1	553.9	554.4	545.8	539.0	542.1	541.6	541.9	544.4	543.0	546.6
2009	528.4	529.1	529.3	528.3	528.9	521.4	516.8	519.5	519.3	524.0	528.1	528.2	525.1
2010	518.8	521.7	524.4	526.5	530.7	523.8	522.2	525.8	527.5	533.2	537.3	539.2	527.6
2011	530.6	534.4	538.2	538.9	539.8	533.1	528.9	532.3	532.8	535.9	542.7	547.6	536.3
Trade, Transportation, and Utilities													
2000	128.4	128.6	130.2	129.7	130.1	131.6	127.7	129.0	129.1	129.1	131.1	131.8	129.7
2001	125.9	124.9	126.1	125.3	125.3	125.3	124.3	125.5	125.3	124.5	126.0	128.0	125.5
2002	122.9	122.7	124.1	124.0	124.2	124.0	123.2	124.1	124.1	124.3	126.5	128.9	124.4
2003	124.7	123.9	124.7	124.1	124.2	123.1	123.4	124.4	124.1	125.4	127.8	129.9	125.0
2004	125.5	125.5	126.4	127.5	127.4	126.7	127.0	127.9	127.3	128.9	132.3	134.5	128.1
2005	130.0	130.6	131.5	131.8	132.3	131.8	132.0	132.8	132.9	133.0	135.9	138.0	132.7
2006	133.8	133.6	135.1	135.1	135.8	135.8	135.8	137.1	137.4	138.7	141.2	143.1	136.9
2007	138.0	137.6	139.1	138.9	139.3	138.7	137.9	138.1	138.1	139.1	142.4	143.3	139.2
2008	138.5	138.0	138.3	137.2	137.1	136.0	135.3	135.5	134.2	134.2	135.5	136.0	136.3
2009	130.3	128.9	128.3	126.8	126.8	126.2	125.3	125.0	124.9	125.2	127.1	128.2	126.9
2010	124.3	123.4	123.7	123.7	123.7	123.7	123.1	123.9	123.3	124.5	126.7	128.2	124.4
2011	123.0	123.2	123.9	124.4	123.9	124.2	123.1	124.1	124.5	125.2	127.7	129.4	124.7
Wholesale Trade													
2000	26.1	26.3	26.7	26.2	26.3	26.3	26.4	26.3	26.1	26.3	26.5	26.6	26.3
2001	26.1	26.2	26.4	26.1	26.1	26.3	26.4	26.5	26.5	26.1	26.0	25.9	26.2
2002	25.1	25.3	25.4	25.5	25.6	25.9	25.9	26.1	26.2	26.3	26.6	26.9	25.9
2003	27.1	27.1	27.1	26.8	26.7	26.7	26.7	26.7	26.6	26.6	26.7	26.8	26.8
2004	26.4	26.7	26.8	26.7	26.7	26.9	27.0	26.9	26.7	27.1	27.2	27.2	26.9
2005	27.0	27.3	27.2	27.3	27.5	27.7	27.9	28.0	28.1	28.3	28.4	28.7	27.8
2006	29.0	29.1	29.3	29.4	29.6	29.9	29.8	30.1	30.3	30.6	30.7	30.9	29.9
2007	30.2	30.4	30.6	30.4	30.3	30.4	30.3	30.2	30.0	30.1	29.8	29.7	30.2
2008	29.0	29.0	29.0	28.8	28.7	28.8	28.8	28.7	28.5	28.2	28.0	27.9	28.6
2009	27.7	27.4	27.1	27.0	26.8	26.8	26.6	26.4	26.2	26.2	26.1	26.0	26.7
2010	25.7	25.5	25.4	25.5	25.6	25.7	25.8	25.9	25.7	25.6	25.5	25.5	25.6
2011	24.8	25.0	25.1	25.2	25.3	25.3	25.3	25.3	25.2	25.3	25.3	25.4	25.2
Retail Trade													
2000	69.3	69.4	70.6	70.3	70.6	71.4	68.7	69.8	69.8	70.1	72.0	73.3	70.4
2001	68.0	67.2	67.9	67.2	67.5	67.4	66.8	67.2	67.0	66.9	68.6	69.7	67.6
2002	67.0	66.5	67.4	67.5	68.0	68.2	67.6	68.0	67.9	68.0	69.7	71.2	68.1
2003	68.6	67.9	68.2	67.8	68.2	68.3	68.2	68.4	68.3	68.9	70.8	72.2	68.8
2004	69.4	69.0	69.7	70.5	70.8	70.7	70.9	70.8	70.3	71.5	74.5	75.8	71.2
2005	72.2	72.4	73.3	73.4	73.6	73.8	73.9	73.9	73.7	73.6	75.8	77.0	73.9
2006	72.9	72.8	73.7	73.7	74.0	74.6	74.7	74.9	74.7	75.5	77.7	78.6	74.8
2007	75.5	75.0	76.2	75.7	76.2	76.0	75.7	76.0	75.7	76.2	79.2	80.2	76.5
2008	77.1	76.5	76.8	75.9	76.0	75.5	74.7	74.5	74.0	73.8	75.2	75.3	75.4
2009	70.8	70.0	70.0	69.1	69.4	69.3	68.8	68.7	68.4	68.6	70.4	71.0	69.5
2010	68.8	68.2	68.5	68.5	68.4	68.3	67.9	68.1	67.7	68.6	70.7	71.3	68.8
2011	67.9	67.8	68.3	68.7	68.8	69.2	68.4	69.2	69.5	69.9	72.3	73.3	69.4
Transportation and Utilities													
2000	33.0	32.9	32.9	33.2	33.2	33.9	32.6	32.9	33.2	32.7	32.6	31.9	32.9
2001	31.8	31.5	31.8	32.0	31.7	31.6	31.1	31.8	31.8	31.5	31.4	32.4	31.7
2002	30.8	30.9	31.3	31.0	30.6	29.9	29.7	30.0	30.0	30.0	30.2	30.8	30.4
2003	29.0	28.9	29.4	29.5	29.3	28.1	28.5	29.3	29.2	29.9	30.3	30.9	29.4
2004	29.7	29.8	29.9	30.3	29.9	29.1	29.1	30.2	30.3	30.3	30.6	31.5	30.1
2005	30.8	30.9	31.0	31.1	31.2	30.3	30.2	30.9	31.1	31.1	31.7	32.3	31.1
2006	31.9	31.7	32.1	32.0	32.2	31.3	31.3	32.1	32.4	32.6	32.8	33.6	32.2
2007	32.3	32.2	32.3	32.8	32.8	32.3	31.9	31.9	32.4	32.8	33.4	33.4	32.5
2008	32.4	32.5	32.5	32.5	32.4	31.7	31.8	32.3	31.7	32.2	32.3	32.8	32.3
2009	31.8	31.5	31.2	30.7	30.6	30.1	29.9	29.9	30.3	30.4	30.6	31.2	30.7
2010	29.8	29.7	29.8	29.7	29.7	29.7	29.4	29.9	29.9	30.3	30.5	31.4	30.0
2011	30.3	30.4	30.5	30.5	29.8	29.7	29.4	29.6	29.8	30.0	30.1	30.7	30.1
Information													
2000	15.3	15.3	15.3	15.0	15.2	15.2	15.3	15.2	15.3	15.0	15.3	15.6	15.3
2001	15.0	15.0	15.0	14.9	14.7	14.6	14.5	14.2	14.1	13.7	13.6	13.5	14.4
2002	13.8	13.6	13.7	13.6	13.4	13.2	13.2	13.0	12.9	12.9	12.8	12.8	13.2
2003	12.7	12.8	12.8	12.5	12.8	12.3	12.4	12.3	12.2	12.1	12.1	12.2	12.4
2004	12.0	11.5	11.5	11.3	11.4	11.6	11.5	11.6	11.5	11.7	11.9	12.1	11.6
2005	12.0	12.0	11.9	11.8	12.0	12.0	12.1	12.2	12.0	11.7	11.8	11.4	11.9
2006	11.5	11.5	11.5	11.4	11.3	11.4	11.4	11.1	10.6	10.5	10.4	10.5	11.1
2007	10.1	10.1	10.2	10.2	10.2	10.3	10.2	10.2	10.2	10.1	10.0	10.0	10.2
2008	9.9	9.9	10.0	10.1	10.1	10.2	10.4	10.3	10.4	10.4	10.5	10.5	10.2
2009	10.4	10.4	10.4	10.5	10.5	10.5	10.4	10.4	10.2	10.1	10.2	10.2	10.4
2010	10.2	10.2	10.4	10.4	10.3	10.2	10.2	10.2	10.1	10.0	10.0	9.9	10.2
2011	9.7	9.6	9.6	9.6	9.6	9.5	9.5	9.5	9.4	9.5	9.6	9.6	9.6

Employment by Industry: Jacksonville, FL, Selected Years, 2000–2011—*Continued*

(Numbers in thousands, not seasonally adjusted)

Industry and year	January	February	March	April	May	June	July	August	September	October	November	December	Annual average
Financial Activities													
2000	55.8	55.8	55.9	56.5	56.8	57.1	57.1	56.7	56.4	56.4	56.6	57.0	56.5
2001	56.3	56.6	57.0	57.2	57.4	57.9	58.3	58.4	58.5	58.7	58.9	59.1	57.9
2002	58.6	58.0	57.9	57.9	57.8	57.7	57.6	57.5	57.2	57.3	57.4	57.4	57.7
2003	57.1	56.7	56.9	57.1	57.4	57.6	57.9	58.2	58.2	58.0	58.0	58.4	57.6
2004	57.9	57.8	57.8	58.4	58.5	58.6	58.5	58.7	58.6	58.5	58.7	59.1	58.4
2005	58.8	58.9	59.2	59.1	59.0	59.0	58.9	59.0	58.9	59.5	60.1	60.9	59.3
2006	59.7	60.1	60.3	60.4	60.4	60.2	59.9	59.6	59.4	59.1	59.3	59.6	59.8
2007	58.9	59.1	59.4	59.5	59.8	60.1	60.5	60.8	60.7	60.7	61.1	61.1	60.1
2008	60.7	60.7	60.8	60.7	60.5	60.3	60.0	59.6	59.1	58.6	58.0	57.9	59.7
2009	56.9	56.7	56.5	55.7	55.8	55.7	55.8	55.5	55.0	55.1	55.1	55.2	55.8
2010	54.9	55.0	55.0	54.9	55.2	55.5	56.1	56.2	56.3	56.8	57.3	57.9	55.9
2011	57.6	57.9	58.3	57.9	58.0	58.3	58.5	57.6	57.0	57.3	57.9	58.4	57.9
Professional and Business Services													
2000	83.9	84.2	85.2	86.9	86.7	87.2	89.4	90.1	90.3	93.0	92.2	92.6	88.5
2001	88.9	92.3	94.6	94.7	94.5	93.6	91.5	93.4	93.1	90.7	89.4	87.8	92.0
2002	86.1	87.5	88.8	88.2	87.9	86.5	84.2	83.9	83.5	82.9	82.1	81.6	85.3
2003	81.0	83.1	85.7	86.4	85.6	84.0	81.9	81.9	81.0	81.7	81.0	80.4	82.8
2004	80.2	81.1	82.9	83.5	83.6	84.6	83.0	82.1	81.7	81.3	82.5	83.7	82.5
2005	83.9	85.6	85.1	85.7	86.0	86.7	88.1	89.6	90.5	91.2	92.5	93.1	88.2
2006	92.4	94.2	95.6	94.2	95.5	94.1	94.2	94.9	95.5	97.0	99.3	99.1	95.5
2007	97.6	97.8	98.4	98.0	96.5	94.8	92.6	91.7	91.2	92.0	91.4	90.6	94.4
2008	88.8	90.0	90.4	90.8	91.4	89.6	85.8	85.7	86.5	86.4	86.1	85.9	88.1
2009	83.2	83.9	83.5	83.4	83.3	82.8	81.0	81.1	81.9	84.2	85.2	85.8	83.3
2010	83.0	84.3	84.9	84.8	85.3	85.3	85.0	85.6	87.1	89.4	89.7	89.7	86.2
2011	89.1	91.0	91.8	91.0	91.6	90.7	90.1	90.0	91.2	92.6	94.3	96.6	91.7
Education and Health Services													
2000	59.9	60.1	60.3	59.8	60.1	60.2	58.8	59.2	59.5	59.0	59.2	59.6	59.6
2001	59.0	59.6	60.1	60.1	60.5	61.1	60.8	61.4	61.9	62.6	62.8	63.1	61.1
2002	62.6	62.9	63.3	63.3	63.6	63.7	63.2	63.6	63.7	63.9	64.1	64.3	63.5
2003	63.5	64.0	64.4	64.0	64.4	64.3	64.2	64.6	65.2	66.0	65.9	66.2	64.7
2004	65.8	66.4	66.5	67.4	67.8	67.8	67.5	68.0	68.5	69.3	69.9	70.4	67.9
2005	70.1	70.4	70.6	70.7	71.2	70.8	70.8	71.3	72.3	72.1	72.3	72.7	71.3
2006	72.9	73.5	73.9	73.8	74.0	73.6	73.6	74.5	75.1	76.0	76.4	76.4	74.5
2007	76.2	77.1	77.5	77.4	77.6	77.3	77.0	77.6	78.6	78.9	79.4	79.9	77.9
2008	80.6	81.0	80.9	81.8	81.5	80.9	80.8	80.9	81.5	82.8	83.9	83.8	81.7
2009	82.5	83.2	83.5	83.3	83.4	82.9	82.6	82.9	83.7	85.2	85.9	85.6	83.7
2010	84.5	85.0	85.2	85.4	85.5	84.9	84.4	84.7	85.4	87.3	87.7	87.7	85.6
2011	86.8	87.3	87.4	87.7	87.6	86.4	85.9	86.4	87.4	87.8	88.1	88.8	87.3
Leisure and Hospitality													
2000	48.7	49.1	49.8	50.4	51.3	51.2	50.0	50.3	50.2	50.1	50.2	50.6	50.2
2001	47.7	48.6	50.1	51.5	52.2	52.7	51.6	52.8	52.1	50.9	51.2	51.6	51.1
2002	49.8	50.4	51.7	52.7	53.6	54.1	52.5	53.1	52.5	52.6	53.3	53.5	52.5
2003	50.7	51.1	52.4	53.1	53.9	54.4	53.6	54.6	54.1	53.6	53.9	54.5	53.3
2004	53.6	54.1	55.4	56.1	56.5	56.5	56.4	56.7	56.4	57.0	57.8	58.3	56.2
2005	57.8	58.7	59.9	60.7	60.9	61.0	60.5	61.4	60.8	60.4	61.2	61.0	60.4
2006	60.0	60.7	61.9	61.9	63.0	63.2	62.7	63.0	62.7	61.7	62.5	62.3	62.1
2007	62.0	63.4	64.9	66.1	67.5	67.5	66.4	67.0	66.4	66.1	66.8	66.8	65.9
2008	65.6	66.2	66.8	68.2	68.6	68.5	68.5	67.9	67.2	66.8	66.8	66.4	67.3
2009	64.7	64.5	65.5	66.8	67.0	66.1	65.5	64.8	63.2	62.9	63.0	62.2	64.7
2010	61.2	62.4	63.8	65.4	66.2	65.9	65.8	65.4	64.8	63.6	63.9	64.3	64.4
2011	63.2	63.5	65.2	66.5	67.4	66.8	66.1	65.9	64.2	63.8	65.0	64.6	65.2
Other Services													
2000	22.6	22.9	23.1	24.2	24.1	24.4	24.3	24.2	23.9	23.7	23.8	23.9	23.8
2001	22.9	23.3	23.5	23.5	23.5	24.2	24.3	24.5	24.2	24.2	24.2	24.0	23.9
2002	24.1	24.2	24.7	24.5	24.7	25.0	25.3	25.6	25.2	25.2	25.4	25.4	24.9
2003	24.9	25.1	25.3	25.5	25.7	26.2	25.9	25.8	25.8	25.9	25.9	26.2	25.7
2004	26.3	26.2	26.5	26.4	26.5	26.8	26.6	26.6	26.2	26.0	26.0	26.2	26.4
2005	26.2	26.4	26.5	26.8	26.9	27.2	27.2	27.0	27.1	26.6	26.7	26.6	26.8
2006	26.6	27.0	27.3	27.2	27.5	27.8	27.9	27.8	27.9	27.9	28.1	28.3	27.6
2007	28.3	28.5	28.9	28.4	28.5	28.8	28.3	28.0	27.7	27.8	27.9	27.9	28.3
2008	27.7	27.9	27.9	27.6	27.5	27.3	26.6	26.3	25.7	25.3	24.9	24.4	26.6
2009	24.1	24.1	24.1	24.2	24.2	24.1	23.9	23.9	23.7	24.0	24.1	24.0	24.0
2010	23.7	23.9	23.9	24.0	24.0	24.1	24.0	23.8	23.6	23.9	23.8	23.6	23.9
2011	23.4	23.6	23.7	23.7	23.6	23.6	23.4	23.2	23.0	23.0	23.0	23.0	23.4
Government													
2000	68.7	69.6	70.0	70.3	72.1	65.7	64.5	69.9	69.7	70.5	70.4	70.7	69.3
2001	69.2	70.6	70.9	71.3	71.5	66.3	65.0	71.5	71.3	71.2	71.7	72.1	70.2
2002	70.2	70.9	70.9	71.5	71.7	66.5	65.0	71.4	71.2	71.7	72.3	72.7	70.5
2003	71.8	71.8	72.0	72.3	73.0	68.3	66.9	71.9	72.0	72.9	73.3	73.5	71.6
2004	72.6	73.2	73.5	73.7	73.9	69.4	68.0	73.4	73.8	74.9	75.5	76.2	73.2
2005	75.0	75.9	76.1	75.4	75.8	71.0	69.1	74.7	75.1	74.9	75.1	75.2	74.4
2006	74.4	75.2	75.3	74.4	74.2	69.8	68.3	73.6	74.3	75.4	76.4	76.5	74.0
2007	75.6	76.6	76.8	77.0	77.2	73.0	70.7	76.5	76.9	77.4	78.2	78.1	76.2
2008	77.0	77.9	78.0	77.5	77.7	73.0	71.6	75.9	77.0	77.4	78.7	78.1	76.7
2009	76.3	77.4	77.5	77.6	77.9	73.1	72.3	75.5	76.7	77.3	77.5	77.0	76.4
2010	77.0	77.5	77.5	77.9	80.5	74.2	73.6	76.0	76.9	77.7	78.2	77.9	77.1
2011	77.8	78.3	78.3	78.1	78.1	73.6	72.3	75.6	76.1	76.7	77.1	77.2	76.6

Employment by Industry: Kansas City, MO–KS, Selected Years, 2000–2011

(Numbers in thousands, not seasonally adjusted)

Industry and year	January	February	March	April	May	June	July	August	September	October	November	December	Annual average
Total Nonfarm													
2000	963.9	966.8	977.1	984.5	988.2	996.9	965.7	973.7	987.2	988.5	986.3	987.9	980.6
2001	970.0	971.6	980.8	983.1	987.2	992.7	960.2	967.1	976.5	975.7	973.0	973.5	976.0
2002	955.9	954.9	964.8	973.7	977.2	979.4	944.0	949.4	960.3	959.7	964.5	966.6	962.5
2003	945.9	946.0	951.4	959.3	963.7	969.4	948.8	953.6	963.7	966.3	967.3	968.3	958.6
2004	944.7	942.8	955.7	969.5	973.0	979.8	964.4	964.1	974.3	978.6	979.8	981.5	967.4
2005	955.0	960.8	972.6	983.0	986.0	990.7	972.9	974.1	984.1	986.1	990.2	992.3	979.0
2006	970.8	975.7	985.1	994.9	999.7	1,004.7	986.3	990.5	1,002.0	1,001.7	1,007.1	1,011.0	994.1
2007	988.3	991.6	1,007.1	1,013.0	1,019.2	1,023.7	1,014.2	1,017.7	1,020.5	1,018.8	1,024.4	1,021.2	1,013.3
2008	1,001.5	1,004.3	1,013.7	1,025.4	1,024.9	1,027.9	1,016.5	1,015.4	1,018.0	1,019.2	1,013.9	1,008.6	1,015.8
2009	981.6	979.4	981.7	988.1	988.5	989.2	974.7	973.1	974.9	974.1	973.2	970.7	979.1
2010	944.7	947.7	956.5	978.6	985.3	986.2	966.0	967.0	977.8	983.4	983.4	982.7	971.6
2011	956.1	959.1	971.9	984.8	990.1	989.7	981.1	976.5	992.8	993.0	993.4	987.8	981.4
Total Private													
2000	828.4	828.0	836.9	844.2	848.3	856.7	846.5	851.1	849.8	849.7	846.2	847.7	844.5
2001	829.3	828.7	836.9	839.5	843.3	850.3	837.8	842.2	837.5	834.4	830.8	830.1	836.7
2002	813.6	811.7	820.2	829.4	832.6	836.3	820.9	824.1	821.0	817.9	821.9	822.8	822.7
2003	803.4	801.0	805.3	812.5	816.9	824.0	816.7	823.4	821.3	822.3	823.1	824.0	816.2
2004	802.4	798.1	810.1	822.4	826.4	833.8	827.3	830.3	829.7	833.8	834.2	835.9	823.7
2005	811.8	814.7	824.9	834.0	838.7	845.3	837.7	841.6	839.7	840.8	843.8	845.9	834.9
2006	826.7	827.2	835.5	846.0	850.3	857.8	851.5	857.3	854.5	853.2	857.6	862.5	848.3
2007	841.0	840.6	854.6	859.0	865.9	871.7	869.3	873.7	869.9	867.1	871.3	869.8	862.8
2008	851.4	850.9	858.5	869.3	868.4	872.7	872.1	870.1	864.7	864.5	859.1	853.9	863.0
2009	828.9	822.6	824.7	829.5	829.2	832.6	829.7	828.7	820.6	819.1	818.3	816.3	825.0
2010	793.2	792.8	800.0	820.2	824.3	828.3	827.0	829.0	825.6	831.1	830.7	830.7	819.4
2011	806.1	806.7	816.9	829.0	834.8	836.6	839.8	837.2	842.5	841.4	841.3	835.6	830.7
Goods-Producing													
2000	142.4	142.1	143.2	145.0	146.0	148.7	143.2	147.1	145.9	145.4	143.8	142.3	144.6
2001	138.2	138.0	140.4	142.3	143.5	145.8	140.8	144.4	142.9	140.2	139.3	138.1	141.2
2002	133.0	131.9	133.5	135.2	135.9	137.7	133.6	137.5	135.6	134.6	133.7	133.0	134.6
2003	130.2	130.3	132.2	132.5	134.7	135.7	131.0	136.0	135.4	135.6	134.8	132.7	133.4
2004	129.5	126.9	131.3	134.6	135.3	138.0	134.5	137.7	137.4	137.5	136.9	136.2	134.7
2005	129.3	130.5	134.2	135.9	137.4	139.1	135.4	138.7	137.8	137.7	137.7	136.7	135.9
2006	133.4	133.8	136.7	137.9	138.8	141.8	137.4	140.7	137.7	136.8	138.3	138.2	137.6
2007	133.0	130.4	135.2	135.4	136.7	138.2	136.1	138.2	137.7	134.8	135.9	133.2	135.4
2008	129.2	128.5	131.4	133.0	131.3	133.3	134.4	133.2	132.3	131.6	129.7	126.3	131.2
2009	119.6	117.0	117.9	118.4	117.3	119.0	118.9	117.6	116.0	115.7	114.0	110.9	116.9
2010	106.3	105.9	108.3	111.7	112.0	114.0	113.1	115.2	114.6	114.7	113.6	112.2	111.8
2011	105.7	105.0	108.0	110.1	111.1	112.3	114.0	113.5	115.1	114.2	112.8	110.7	111.0
Mining, Logging, and Construction													
2000	48.2	48.1	49.0	50.6	51.5	53.4	53.3	53.5	52.4	52.2	50.8	48.8	51.0
2001	46.4	45.9	48.2	50.6	51.8	53.6	53.8	53.4	52.1	50.8	50.6	49.8	50.6
2002	46.8	46.1	48.1	49.3	50.1	51.9	52.6	52.6	51.4	51.0	50.4	49.9	50.0
2003	47.6	47.5	48.8	50.9	51.6	52.6	52.9	52.9	52.3	52.5	51.5	49.3	50.9
2004	46.3	44.3	48.0	50.7	51.3	52.9	53.8	53.6	53.2	53.4	52.2	51.5	50.9
2005	46.1	47.2	50.3	52.0	53.6	55.1	55.9	55.7	55.1	54.8	54.2	53.0	52.8
2006	51.3	51.8	53.4	54.5	55.1	56.9	56.0	56.0	55.7	54.5	53.9	53.3	54.4
2007	50.3	47.8	51.9	52.6	53.9	55.0	55.6	55.1	54.9	54.1	53.6	51.2	53.0
2008	47.7	46.9	49.4	50.7	52.0	52.6	52.5	52.2	51.2	51.1	49.9	47.1	50.3
2009	42.9	42.6	43.3	43.9	45.1	45.5	45.6	44.1	42.8	42.3	41.4	38.8	43.2
2010	34.0	33.7	36.0	39.1	39.1	40.5	41.1	41.2	40.5	40.7	39.9	38.2	38.7
2011	33.3	32.7	35.5	37.7	38.4	39.1	41.3	38.9	39.4	38.3	36.7	34.5	37.2
Manufacturing													
2000	94.2	94.0	94.2	94.4	94.5	95.3	89.9	93.6	93.5	93.2	93.0	93.5	93.6
2001	91.8	92.1	92.2	91.7	91.7	92.2	87.0	91.0	90.8	89.4	88.7	88.3	90.6
2002	86.2	85.8	85.4	85.9	85.8	85.8	81.0	84.9	84.2	83.6	83.3	83.1	84.6
2003	82.6	82.8	83.4	81.6	83.1	83.1	78.1	83.1	83.1	83.1	83.3	83.4	82.6
2004	83.2	82.6	83.3	83.9	84.0	85.1	80.7	84.1	84.2	84.1	84.7	84.7	83.7
2005	83.2	83.3	83.9	83.9	83.8	84.0	79.5	83.0	82.7	82.9	83.5	83.7	83.1
2006	82.1	82.0	83.3	83.4	83.7	84.9	81.4	84.7	82.0	82.3	84.4	84.9	83.3
2007	82.7	82.6	83.3	82.8	82.8	83.2	80.5	83.1	82.8	80.7	82.3	82.0	82.4
2008	81.5	81.6	82.0	82.3	79.3	80.7	81.9	81.0	81.1	80.5	79.8	79.2	80.9
2009	76.7	74.4	74.6	74.5	72.2	73.5	73.3	73.5	73.2	73.4	72.6	72.1	73.7
2010	72.3	72.2	72.3	72.6	72.9	73.5	72.0	74.0	74.1	74.0	73.7	74.0	73.1
2011	72.4	72.3	72.5	72.4	72.7	73.2	72.7	74.6	75.7	75.9	76.1	76.2	73.9
Service-Providing													
2000	821.5	824.7	833.9	839.5	842.2	848.2	822.5	826.6	841.3	843.1	842.5	845.6	836.0
2001	831.8	833.6	840.4	840.8	843.7	846.9	819.4	822.7	833.6	835.5	833.7	835.4	834.8
2002	822.9	823.0	831.3	838.5	841.3	841.7	810.4	811.9	824.7	825.1	830.8	833.6	827.9
2003	815.7	815.7	819.2	826.8	829.0	833.7	817.8	817.6	828.3	830.7	832.5	835.6	825.2
2004	815.2	815.9	824.4	834.9	837.7	841.8	829.9	826.4	836.9	841.1	842.9	845.3	832.7
2005	825.7	830.3	838.4	847.1	848.6	851.6	837.5	835.4	846.3	848.4	852.5	855.6	843.1
2006	837.4	841.9	848.4	857.0	860.9	862.9	848.9	849.8	864.3	864.9	868.8	872.8	856.5
2007	855.3	861.2	871.9	877.6	882.5	885.5	878.1	879.5	882.8	884.0	888.5	888.0	877.9
2008	872.3	875.8	882.3	892.4	893.6	894.6	882.1	882.2	885.7	887.6	884.2	882.3	884.6
2009	862.0	862.4	863.8	869.7	871.2	870.2	855.8	855.5	858.9	858.4	859.2	859.8	862.2
2010	838.4	841.8	848.2	866.9	873.3	872.2	852.9	851.8	863.2	868.7	869.8	870.5	859.8
2011	850.4	854.1	863.9	874.7	879.0	877.4	867.1	863.0	877.7	878.8	880.6	877.1	870.3

Employment by Industry: Kansas City, MO–KS, Selected Years, 2000–2011—*Continued*

(Numbers in thousands, not seasonally adjusted)

Industry and year	January	February	March	April	May	June	July	August	September	October	November	December	Annual average
Trade, Transportation, and Utilities													
2000	206.8	204.8	205.5	208.3	209.5	208.0	206.0	206.1	208.7	209.8	213.4	214.9	208.5
2001	207.7	205.3	205.4	205.8	207.2	206.2	204.8	205.3	206.5	207.1	209.2	210.0	206.7
2002	204.4	201.7	203.5	204.2	205.0	203.6	200.4	200.3	201.2	202.6	206.5	207.7	203.4
2003	200.4	198.8	199.1	199.0	199.1	199.9	199.3	201.1	201.9	203.9	207.4	209.2	201.6
2004	200.6	198.5	199.6	201.0	202.4	202.5	200.8	200.6	201.8	204.7	208.5	211.2	202.7
2005	202.5	201.1	202.2	202.5	203.6	203.6	201.5	201.8	202.2	204.3	208.3	210.5	203.7
2006	203.5	201.9	203.1	203.6	204.6	204.6	202.8	203.9	205.1	205.7	209.4	212.2	205.0
2007	204.9	204.0	206.0	206.4	207.3	207.3	207.0	207.6	208.0	208.7	212.9	214.3	207.9
2008	206.2	204.6	204.8	205.9	206.2	205.7	205.4	204.9	204.3	206.8	208.1	208.4	205.9
2009	200.0	197.4	196.8	196.6	196.5	196.6	195.3	195.3	194.3	195.5	198.1	198.2	196.7
2010	191.3	189.7	190.6	193.0	194.5	195.2	194.7	195.2	194.5	196.9	199.9	201.0	194.7
2011	194.2	192.8	194.4	196.6	197.7	197.2	196.8	196.0	196.1	197.1	199.9	200.6	196.6
Wholesale Trade													
2000	48.9	48.7	48.9	50.0	50.0	50.2	50.1	49.7	50.1	49.5	49.7	49.8	49.6
2001	49.5	49.3	49.3	49.5	49.4	49.5	49.0	48.5	48.6	48.7	48.2	48.2	49.0
2002	48.8	48.6	48.7	48.9	48.5	48.6	47.5	47.6	47.2	47.2	47.2	47.3	48.0
2003	47.3	47.5	47.4	47.2	47.1	47.3	47.0	47.0	46.5	46.6	46.5	46.5	47.0
2004	45.4	45.5	46.0	46.3	46.5	46.8	47.1	47.0	46.8	47.5	47.6	47.9	46.7
2005	48.1	48.2	48.5	49.3	49.4	49.6	49.3	49.4	49.2	49.0	49.3	49.4	49.1
2006	48.8	48.8	49.1	48.7	49.1	49.4	49.2	49.5	49.5	49.9	50.0	50.7	49.4
2007	50.2	50.4	51.1	50.7	50.7	51.2	51.3	51.5	51.5	51.8	51.8	51.9	51.2
2008	51.5	51.5	51.3	51.7	51.6	51.6	51.9	51.8	51.4	52.5	52.2	51.9	51.7
2009	51.1	50.6	50.2	49.7	49.1	49.0	48.7	48.2	47.9	48.0	47.9	47.6	49.0
2010	47.2	47.2	47.4	48.7	48.8	49.0	48.9	48.8	48.5	48.8	48.6	48.6	48.4
2011	48.1	48.1	48.3	48.7	49.1	49.1	49.2	49.2	49.1	49.4	49.3	49.0	48.9
Retail Trade													
2000	110.0	108.4	108.8	109.5	110.1	110.4	109.1	109.5	109.3	110.6	114.3	116.0	110.5
2001	110.5	108.8	108.7	108.7	109.6	110.2	109.7	110.4	109.9	110.7	113.5	114.9	110.5
2002	109.1	107.2	108.8	108.7	109.6	110.0	109.0	109.0	109.1	109.5	113.4	115.1	109.9
2003	108.2	106.5	107.0	106.8	107.2	107.9	108.3	109.4	110.0	111.5	115.0	116.6	109.5
2004	110.7	108.4	109.0	109.1	110.0	110.4	109.7	109.2	109.9	110.9	114.6	116.9	110.7
2005	110.2	108.5	109.0	108.8	109.3	109.4	108.9	108.2	107.9	109.5	113.0	114.6	109.8
2006	108.8	107.4	108.2	108.5	109.0	109.2	108.3	108.2	108.3	108.4	111.8	113.2	109.1
2007	107.4	106.5	107.6	108.0	108.7	108.9	108.5	108.2	107.6	108.5	112.2	113.4	108.8
2008	107.5	105.4	106.1	106.4	106.9	107.2	106.9	106.4	105.4	106.4	108.0	108.6	106.8
2009	103.2	101.4	101.9	102.0	102.6	103.2	102.9	102.9	102.2	103.1	105.9	106.2	103.1
2010	100.9	99.6	100.2	101.7	102.8	103.3	103.0	103.0	102.1	103.6	106.5	107.4	102.8
2011	102.3	100.9	102.1	103.5	104.2	104.3	103.9	102.9	102.7	103.6	106.2	106.9	103.6
Transportation and Utilities													
2000	47.9	47.7	47.8	48.8	49.4	47.4	46.8	46.9	49.3	49.7	49.4	49.1	48.4
2001	47.7	47.2	47.4	47.6	48.2	46.5	46.1	46.4	48.0	47.7	47.5	46.9	47.3
2002	46.5	45.9	46.0	46.6	46.9	45.0	43.9	43.7	44.9	45.9	45.9	45.3	45.5
2003	44.9	44.8	44.7	45.0	44.8	44.7	44.0	44.7	45.4	45.8	45.9	46.1	45.1
2004	44.5	44.6	44.6	45.6	45.9	45.3	44.0	44.4	45.1	46.3	46.3	46.4	45.3
2005	44.2	44.4	44.7	44.4	44.9	44.6	43.3	44.2	45.1	45.8	46.0	46.5	44.8
2006	45.9	45.7	45.8	46.4	46.5	46.0	45.3	46.2	47.3	47.4	47.6	48.3	46.5
2007	47.3	47.1	47.3	47.7	47.9	47.2	47.2	47.9	48.9	48.4	48.9	49.0	47.9
2008	47.2	47.7	47.4	47.8	47.7	46.9	46.6	46.7	47.5	47.9	47.9	47.9	47.4
2009	45.7	45.4	44.7	44.9	44.8	44.4	43.7	44.2	44.2	44.4	44.3	44.4	44.6
2010	43.2	42.9	43.0	42.6	42.9	42.9	42.8	43.4	43.9	44.5	44.8	45.0	43.5
2011	43.8	43.8	44.0	44.4	44.4	43.8	43.7	43.9	44.3	44.1	44.4	44.7	44.1
Information													
2000	53.4	55.2	55.3	55.6	55.7	56.4	57.4	57.4	57.3	56.3	56.3	56.1	56.0
2001	55.1	54.6	54.1	54.0	53.3	55.0	53.9	54.0	53.6	52.6	52.9	51.5	53.7
2002	51.0	51.3	51.6	50.8	51.7	52.0	51.3	50.9	50.1	48.6	49.8	50.3	50.8
2003	49.1	48.5	48.3	48.5	48.2	48.5	47.7	47.6	46.9	46.8	46.6	46.7	47.8
2004	46.5	46.1	45.8	45.8	45.7	45.8	45.4	45.3	44.7	43.6	43.8	43.3	45.2
2005	43.2	43.1	43.1	43.0	42.9	43.1	42.8	42.3	42.0	41.1	40.9	40.8	42.4
2006	40.9	40.8	41.1	42.4	42.4	42.8	42.6	42.6	42.6	41.6	41.8	42.2	42.0
2007	42.2	42.1	42.0	42.0	42.3	42.4	42.8	42.6	42.4	42.8	42.9	43.0	42.5
2008	43.0	42.7	42.7	42.0	42.1	42.1	42.0	41.7	41.0	40.5	40.1	39.8	41.6
2009	39.6	39.3	39.1	39.1	38.6	38.3	38.0	37.5	36.7	34.3	33.9	33.9	37.4
2010	32.0	31.6	31.7	32.4	32.3	31.9	31.2	30.9	30.6	30.5	30.3	29.9	31.3
2011	28.8	28.8	28.7	28.8	28.8	28.8	28.5	28.4	28.1	27.9	27.8	27.9	28.4
Financial Activities													
2000	69.8	69.5	70.1	69.3	69.5	70.3	70.2	70.1	69.5	70.1	70.3	70.7	70.0
2001	70.0	70.2	70.6	70.5	70.8	71.2	71.1	71.1	70.5	70.5	70.5	70.9	70.7
2002	70.9	70.7	70.9	71.6	71.7	71.7	71.9	71.3	70.8	70.8	70.9	71.2	71.2
2003	69.8	69.8	69.7	69.9	69.8	70.0	70.0	70.2	69.4	69.1	68.8	68.9	69.6
2004	68.7	68.6	69.2	68.9	68.9	69.9	70.1	69.9	69.6	69.8	69.8	70.3	69.5
2005	70.0	70.1	70.3	70.8	71.0	71.4	71.8	71.6	71.4	71.6	71.7	72.2	71.2
2006	72.0	72.2	72.2	72.5	73.0	73.4	74.1	73.9	73.6	73.1	73.4	73.9	73.1
2007	73.5	73.8	74.5	73.7	73.8	74.4	75.1	74.9	74.3	74.0	74.0	74.2	74.2
2008	73.2	73.5	73.4	73.8	73.8	73.5	73.7	73.3	72.3	71.9	71.3	70.9	72.9
2009	70.3	70.0	70.3	71.0	71.0	71.5	72.0	72.0	70.9	71.0	71.1	70.9	71.0
2010	70.9	71.1	71.2	71.8	72.1	72.1	71.9	71.5	70.9	71.2	71.1	71.2	71.4
2011	70.5	70.7	70.7	72.0	72.5	72.5	72.5	71.6	71.6	71.6	71.0	70.2	71.5

Employment by Industry: Kansas City, MO–KS, Selected Years, 2000–2011—*Continued*

(Numbers in thousands, not seasonally adjusted)

Industry and year	January	February	March	April	May	June	July	August	September	October	November	December	Annual average
Professional and Business Services													
2000	135.0	134.0	137.5	136.9	136.6	138.6	135.9	136.8	136.6	136.9	134.5	135.6	136.2
2001	133.9	134.6	136.7	133.7	133.6	133.9	130.2	130.7	130.6	129.5	127.3	127.9	131.9
2002	125.4	126.8	128.0	128.7	128.0	127.7	123.1	122.8	122.8	122.4	122.7	123.1	125.1
2003	121.0	120.6	120.7	123.2	123.2	125.6	124.5	124.9	124.9	124.7	125.6	127.9	123.9
2004	124.1	124.7	127.6	130.1	129.7	131.5	130.8	131.5	131.9	133.0	133.3	133.7	130.2
2005	131.1	132.9	135.2	137.3	137.0	138.8	138.8	139.6	139.8	139.8	140.8	142.0	137.8
2006	135.9	137.6	139.2	141.1	140.4	141.9	141.6	142.6	143.0	144.8	145.3	146.3	141.6
2007	142.7	143.7	145.7	146.0	147.3	148.6	148.5	149.9	149.8	150.2	151.0	151.2	147.9
2008	147.3	147.9	149.4	151.8	149.4	150.6	150.5	150.2	150.3	148.4	147.8	147.2	149.2
2009	144.1	143.2	142.9	143.2	141.7	141.6	140.8	140.4	139.2	139.2	140.0	141.2	141.5
2010	138.6	138.5	140.0	146.2	145.4	145.6	146.2	145.9	145.3	147.4	147.4	148.4	144.6
2011	145.1	146.3	148.1	150.9	151.0	151.3	151.6	150.7	152.8	153.0	155.3	154.0	150.8
Education and Health Services													
2000	98.7	99.7	99.6	100.2	100.1	100.2	100.7	100.2	101.1	101.2	101.5	101.7	100.4
2001	100.5	101.9	102.4	103.0	103.0	103.4	102.6	102.8	103.3	103.3	104.2	104.4	102.9
2002	103.5	104.1	104.5	105.8	106.2	106.4	105.7	106.1	106.7	107.2	107.6	107.7	106.0
2003	106.5	106.7	106.7	108.0	108.4	107.3	107.6	107.1	108.3	108.6	108.8	108.5	107.7
2004	107.0	107.8	108.0	109.0	109.1	108.6	109.1	108.8	109.8	111.2	111.1	110.7	109.2
2005	109.6	110.4	110.4	111.5	111.8	111.5	110.7	110.7	111.8	112.9	113.1	113.2	111.5
2006	111.6	112.7	112.7	114.0	114.3	114.1	114.1	114.2	115.8	116.4	116.8	117.3	114.5
2007	115.4	116.7	117.4	118.1	118.4	118.3	118.6	118.8	119.5	120.6	120.9	120.8	118.6
2008	120.5	122.0	122.2	123.9	123.9	124.0	123.8	123.7	124.1	126.1	126.4	126.3	123.9
2009	124.2	125.0	125.3	126.6	126.7	126.4	127.4	127.1	127.9	129.3	129.8	129.9	127.1
2010	128.1	129.3	129.3	128.3	128.6	128.4	129.1	129.1	130.2	131.6	132.0	132.4	129.7
2011	130.2	131.7	132.2	132.8	132.7	131.4	133.3	132.6	134.0	134.6	133.5	133.7	132.7
Leisure and Hospitality													
2000	84.3	84.5	86.4	89.6	91.6	93.7	92.7	93.2	91.4	90.7	87.6	86.6	89.4
2001	84.5	84.5	87.1	89.9	91.4	93.1	92.9	93.3	90.2	90.7	87.7	86.8	89.3
2002	85.1	85.0	87.3	91.2	92.3	93.7	92.4	92.9	91.3	90.1	89.0	87.6	89.8
2003	85.0	85.1	87.1	90.0	91.9	94.8	94.2	94.5	93.3	92.6	90.3	89.4	90.7
2004	86.1	85.7	88.5	92.6	95.0	96.7	95.9	96.1	94.4	93.7	90.8	90.5	92.2
2005	86.4	86.7	89.3	93.3	95.4	97.7	96.3	96.6	94.8	93.9	91.9	91.1	92.8
2006	88.7	88.7	91.0	94.8	96.9	98.9	98.6	99.2	96.9	95.2	93.0	92.8	94.6
2007	89.8	90.2	93.8	96.1	98.6	100.4	98.9	99.6	96.7	94.8	92.7	92.2	95.3
2008	90.6	90.3	93.0	97.2	99.8	101.4	100.2	101.2	98.7	97.5	94.1	93.7	96.5
2009	89.8	89.4	91.4	93.2	96.1	97.6	95.9	97.7	95.0	93.3	90.7	90.8	93.4
2010	85.8	86.5	88.8	92.8	95.4	96.9	96.3	96.9	95.7	94.6	92.3	91.5	92.8
2011	87.6	87.6	90.6	93.4	96.5	98.4	98.4	99.8	100.6	98.7	96.8	94.4	95.2
Other Services													
2000	38.0	38.2	39.3	39.3	39.3	40.8	40.4	40.2	39.3	39.3	38.8	39.8	39.4
2001	39.4	39.6	40.2	40.3	40.5	41.7	41.5	40.6	39.9	40.5	39.7	40.5	40.4
2002	40.3	40.2	40.9	41.9	41.8	43.5	42.5	42.3	42.5	41.6	41.7	42.2	41.8
2003	41.4	41.2	41.5	41.4	41.6	42.2	42.4	42.0	41.2	41.0	40.8	40.7	41.5
2004	39.9	39.8	40.1	40.4	40.3	40.8	40.7	40.4	40.1	40.3	40.0	40.0	40.2
2005	39.7	39.9	40.2	39.7	39.6	40.1	40.4	40.3	39.9	39.5	39.4	39.4	39.8
2006	40.7	39.5	39.5	39.7	39.9	40.3	40.3	40.2	39.8	39.6	39.6	39.6	39.9
2007	39.5	39.7	40.0	41.3	41.5	42.1	42.3	42.1	41.5	41.2	41.0	40.9	41.1
2008	41.4	41.4	41.6	41.7	41.9	42.1	42.1	41.9	41.7	41.7	41.6	41.3	41.7
2009	41.3	41.3	41.0	41.4	41.3	41.6	41.4	41.1	40.6	40.8	40.7	40.5	41.1
2010	40.2	40.2	40.1	44.0	44.0	44.2	44.5	44.3	43.8	44.2	44.1	44.1	43.1
2011	44.0	43.8	44.2	44.4	44.5	44.7	44.7	44.6	44.2	44.3	44.2	44.1	44.3
Government													
2000	135.5	138.8	140.2	140.3	139.9	140.2	119.2	122.6	137.4	138.8	140.1	140.2	136.1
2001	140.7	142.9	143.9	143.6	143.9	142.4	122.4	124.9	139.0	141.3	142.2	143.4	139.2
2002	142.3	143.2	144.6	144.3	144.6	143.1	123.1	125.3	139.3	141.8	142.6	143.8	139.8
2003	142.5	145.0	146.1	146.8	146.8	145.4	132.1	130.2	142.4	144.0	144.2	144.3	142.5
2004	142.3	144.7	145.6	147.1	146.6	146.0	137.1	133.8	144.6	144.8	145.6	145.6	143.7
2005	143.2	146.1	147.7	149.0	147.3	145.4	135.2	132.5	144.4	145.3	146.4	146.4	144.1
2006	144.1	148.5	149.6	148.9	149.4	146.9	134.8	133.2	147.5	148.5	149.5	148.5	145.8
2007	147.3	151.0	152.5	154.0	153.3	152.0	144.9	144.0	150.6	151.7	153.1	151.4	150.5
2008	150.1	153.4	155.2	156.1	156.5	155.2	144.4	145.3	153.3	154.7	154.8	154.7	152.8
2009	152.7	156.8	157.0	158.6	159.3	156.6	145.0	144.4	154.3	155.0	154.9	154.4	154.1
2010	151.5	154.9	156.5	158.4	161.0	157.9	139.0	138.0	152.2	152.3	152.7	152.0	152.2
2011	150.0	152.4	155.0	155.8	155.3	153.1	141.3	139.3	150.3	151.6	152.1	152.2	150.7

Employment by Industry: Knoxville, TN, Selected Years, 2000–2011

(Numbers in thousands, not seasonally adjusted)

Industry and year	January	February	March	April	May	June	July	August	September	October	November	December	Annual average
Total Nonfarm													
2000	294.9	296.9	300.7	302.3	305.2	306.5	301.7	302.7	305.7	304.9	305.8	307.0	302.9
2001	302.4	303.8	306.8	308.4	309.3	310.7	306.2	305.8	308.1	307.9	309.0	310.2	307.4
2002	303.5	304.2	307.2	312.0	313.9	315.7	312.8	314.0	315.8	318.8	319.2	321.5	313.2
2003	311.2	311.4	313.7	316.8	318.2	318.9	314.0	316.1	316.8	319.0	320.3	320.8	316.4
2004	315.1	317.9	319.8	321.8	322.8	322.8	323.1	324.3	325.2	325.2	327.6	327.5	322.8
2005	321.7	321.9	324.7	325.4	326.5	327.1	325.0	326.5	329.3	328.3	329.7	330.9	326.4
2006	325.3	326.9	329.9	331.4	332.3	332.0	331.1	334.5	337.6	335.3	336.4	338.2	332.6
2007	331.6	332.5	335.4	336.2	336.7	335.4	334.1	337.6	339.1	337.9	340.0	338.7	336.3
2008	333.5	334.6	335.2	336.8	338.5	336.7	333.1	336.5	338.2	339.1	337.6	335.6	336.3
2009	324.9	323.6	321.8	321.5	321.1	318.8	316.5	317.8	320.2	322.0	324.3	321.6	321.2
2010	314.8	316.1	317.8	322.4	324.9	321.2	321.7	324.1	325.9	325.7	326.9	326.4	322.3
2011	320.6	323.3	325.3	329.1	330.0	327.3	326.1	331.9	333.2	334.7	336.9	335.9	329.5
Total Private													
2000	244.2	245.4	248.9	249.9	252.0	254.4	252.1	252.4	253.5	252.6	253.5	254.5	251.1
2001	251.2	251.7	254.6	256.2	257.2	258.9	256.2	255.8	256.1	254.8	255.9	257.0	255.5
2002	251.4	251.8	254.7	258.0	259.8	262.0	262.0	263.0	263.4	265.2	265.6	267.4	260.4
2003	259.0	258.9	260.9	263.6	265.0	266.3	263.9	265.7	266.1	265.8	267.1	268.0	264.2
2004	262.1	262.9	265.9	269.0	270.6	270.8	272.1	272.9	273.0	271.5	273.8	274.1	269.9
2005	269.3	268.9	271.9	272.6	274.2	275.6	275.0	276.4	277.3	275.4	276.7	277.6	274.2
2006	273.4	274.1	277.3	278.9	280.2	281.8	280.8	283.5	284.5	281.7	282.9	284.2	280.3
2007	279.2	279.3	282.2	283.3	284.5	285.5	284.9	287.3	286.9	285.5	287.5	287.8	284.5
2008	282.8	283.4	284.5	285.7	287.9	288.5	285.4	286.9	286.4	286.2	285.2	284.1	285.6
2009	274.2	272.2	270.6	270.2	270.2	270.2	269.0	270.0	269.9	270.1	271.5	270.4	270.7
2010	264.1	264.3	266.2	270.2	271.3	272.1	273.1	274.3	274.4	273.8	275.1	275.2	271.2
2011	270.4	272.8	275.0	277.6	278.6	279.3	279.7	282.6	281.8	282.3	284.0	284.4	279.0
Goods-Producing													
2000	59.4	59.6	60.4	59.8	59.8	60.1	59.4	59.6	59.6	58.9	58.7	58.9	59.5
2001	58.1	57.7	58.3	57.7	57.4	57.7	56.5	56.4	56.1	55.5	55.4	55.4	56.9
2002	54.5	54.4	55.0	55.3	55.7	56.2	56.6	56.6	56.4	57.0	56.6	56.7	55.9
2003	55.7	55.3	55.9	56.0	56.1	55.7	55.1	55.1	55.0	55.1	55.0	54.9	55.4
2004	54.2	54.3	54.8	55.2	55.3	55.1	55.6	55.6	55.6	55.2	55.4	55.1	55.1
2005	55.2	54.7	55.1	54.9	55.0	55.2	55.5	55.7	55.7	55.4	55.3	55.5	55.3
2006	55.6	55.5	56.2	56.6	56.7	57.3	56.8	57.3	57.5	56.4	56.1	55.8	56.5
2007	55.5	55.2	55.8	55.9	56.0	56.3	56.1	56.4	56.6	56.0	55.7	55.4	55.9
2008	53.9	54.0	54.2	54.0	54.5	55.0	54.1	54.2	53.7	53.3	51.9	50.5	53.6
2009	48.6	47.8	47.3	45.9	45.7	45.6	45.3	45.2	45.4	45.7	45.5	44.8	46.1
2010	43.5	43.5	44.1	45.1	45.3	45.9	46.3	46.3	46.4	46.4	46.2	46.1	45.4
2011	45.3	45.7	46.2	46.4	46.6	47.3	48.0	48.2	48.7	49.4	49.9	49.9	47.6
Mining, Logging, and Construction													
2000	15.0	15.2	15.9	15.5	15.4	15.6	15.6	15.7	15.8	15.4	15.3	15.4	15.5
2001	14.4	14.6	15.1	15.2	15.3	15.7	15.2	15.1	15.1	15.0	15.1	15.2	15.1
2002	14.0	14.1	14.5	14.8	15.1	15.3	15.6	15.6	15.5	16.0	15.6	15.6	15.1
2003	15.1	14.7	15.4	15.7	16.0	15.9	15.6	15.7	15.8	16.1	16.0	16.2	15.7
2004	15.6	15.6	16.0	16.4	16.6	16.4	16.7	16.8	16.9	16.9	17.0	16.6	16.5
2005	16.6	16.4	16.6	16.5	16.5	16.7	16.8	17.0	17.1	16.9	16.8	16.7	16.7
2006	16.7	16.8	17.5	17.8	18.0	18.6	18.5	18.9	19.3	19.0	18.8	18.4	18.2
2007	18.0	18.0	18.6	18.8	19.0	19.2	19.1	19.4	19.5	19.3	19.1	18.8	18.9
2008	17.6	17.7	18.2	18.4	18.8	19.0	18.8	18.9	18.9	19.0	18.6	17.7	18.5
2009	16.2	16.0	16.1	15.8	16.1	16.4	16.5	16.4	16.5	16.6	16.4	15.8	16.2
2010	14.7	14.8	15.3	15.9	15.9	16.3	16.7	16.7	16.8	16.8	16.6	16.5	16.1
2011	15.2	15.5	15.9	16.1	16.1	16.7	17.3	17.4	17.9	18.0	18.3	18.1	16.9
Manufacturing													
2000	44.4	44.4	44.5	44.3	44.4	44.5	43.8	43.9	43.8	43.5	43.4	43.5	44.0
2001	43.7	43.1	43.2	42.5	42.1	42.0	41.3	41.3	41.0	40.5	40.3	40.2	41.8
2002	40.5	40.3	40.5	40.5	40.6	40.9	41.0	41.0	40.9	41.0	41.0	41.1	40.8
2003	40.6	40.6	40.5	40.3	40.1	39.8	39.5	39.4	39.2	39.0	39.0	38.7	39.7
2004	38.6	38.7	38.8	38.8	38.7	38.7	38.9	38.8	38.7	38.3	38.4	38.5	38.7
2005	38.6	38.3	38.5	38.4	38.5	38.5	38.7	38.7	38.6	38.5	38.5	38.8	38.6
2006	38.9	38.7	38.7	38.8	38.7	38.7	38.3	38.4	38.2	37.4	37.3	37.4	38.3
2007	37.5	37.2	37.2	37.1	37.0	37.1	37.0	37.0	37.1	36.7	36.6	36.6	37.0
2008	36.3	36.3	36.0	35.6	35.7	36.0	35.3	35.3	34.8	34.3	33.3	32.8	35.1
2009	32.4	31.8	31.2	30.1	29.6	29.2	28.8	28.8	28.9	29.1	29.1	29.0	29.8
2010	28.8	28.7	28.8	29.2	29.4	29.6	29.6	29.6	29.6	29.6	29.6	29.6	29.3
2011	30.1	30.2	30.3	30.3	30.5	30.6	30.7	30.8	30.8	31.4	31.6	31.8	30.8
Service-Providing													
2000	235.5	237.3	240.3	242.5	245.4	246.4	242.3	243.1	246.1	246.0	247.1	248.1	243.3
2001	244.3	246.1	248.5	250.7	251.9	253.0	249.7	249.4	252.0	252.4	253.6	254.8	250.5
2002	249.0	249.8	252.2	256.7	258.2	259.5	256.2	257.4	259.4	261.8	262.6	264.8	257.3
2003	255.5	256.1	257.8	260.8	262.1	263.2	258.9	261.0	261.8	263.9	265.3	265.9	261.0
2004	260.9	263.6	265.0	266.6	267.5	267.7	267.5	268.7	269.6	270.0	272.2	272.4	267.6
2005	266.5	267.2	269.6	270.5	271.5	271.9	269.5	270.8	273.6	272.9	274.4	275.4	271.2
2006	269.7	271.4	273.7	274.8	275.6	274.7	274.3	277.2	280.1	278.9	280.3	282.4	276.1
2007	276.1	277.3	279.6	280.3	280.7	279.1	278.0	281.2	282.5	281.9	284.3	283.3	280.4
2008	279.6	280.6	281.0	282.8	284.0	281.7	279.0	282.3	284.5	285.8	285.7	285.1	282.7
2009	276.3	275.8	274.5	275.6	275.4	273.2	271.2	272.6	274.8	276.3	278.8	276.8	275.1
2010	271.3	272.6	273.7	277.3	279.6	275.3	275.4	277.8	279.5	279.3	280.7	280.3	276.9
2011	275.3	277.6	279.1	282.7	283.4	280.0	278.1	283.7	284.5	285.3	287.0	286.0	281.9

Employment by Industry: Knoxville, TN, Selected Years, 2000–2011—*Continued*

(Numbers in thousands, not seasonally adjusted)

Industry and year	January	February	March	April	May	June	July	August	September	October	November	December	Annual average
Trade, Transportation, and Utilities													
2000	61.6	61.8	62.3	63.2	63.3	63.8	63.9	63.7	64.1	64.4	65.3	66.3	63.6
2001	64.5	64.3	64.6	65.1	65.2	65.3	64.5	64.5	64.7	65.3	66.0	66.8	65.1
2002	64.7	64.5	65.3	65.4	65.2	65.2	65.7	65.9	66.0	66.9	67.7	68.9	66.0
2003	65.4	65.1	65.2	65.4	65.8	66.4	66.0	66.6	66.6	67.1	68.3	69.2	66.4
2004	66.8	66.9	67.7	67.6	68.1	68.0	68.0	68.4	68.5	69.0	70.3	70.9	68.4
2005	69.0	68.7	69.4	68.9	69.4	69.3	69.4	69.8	69.7	69.2	70.5	71.3	69.6
2006	69.5	69.4	70.2	70.2	70.6	70.8	70.6	71.5	72.0	71.5	72.8	74.2	71.1
2007	72.0	71.5	72.3	72.6	73.0	72.8	72.5	73.1	73.1	73.2	74.9	75.2	73.0
2008	73.4	72.7	72.8	72.6	72.3	72.2	71.7	72.0	71.7	72.5	72.9	72.9	72.5
2009	69.3	68.0	67.1	66.7	66.5	66.6	66.1	66.3	66.2	66.6	67.5	68.1	67.1
2010	66.0	65.5	65.5	65.8	66.0	65.9	66.5	66.8	66.6	67.0	68.3	68.6	66.5
2011	66.3	66.2	66.5	67.0	67.2	67.4	67.2	67.2	67.2	67.4	68.3	68.2	67.2
Wholesale Trade													
2000	13.3	13.4	13.5	13.6	13.6	13.9	13.8	13.6	13.8	13.8	13.7	13.9	13.7
2001	14.0	14.1	14.1	13.9	14.0	14.0	13.9	13.8	13.9	14.0	13.9	13.9	14.0
2002	13.8	13.9	14.0	14.0	14.1	14.2	14.6	14.7	14.7	15.0	15.1	15.3	14.5
2003	14.9	14.9	14.9	14.9	14.9	15.1	15.2	15.3	15.3	15.4	15.5	15.6	15.2
2004	15.4	15.5	15.8	15.8	15.9	15.8	16.2	16.2	16.0	16.1	16.2	16.2	15.9
2005	16.0	16.0	16.0	15.8	15.7	15.8	15.8	15.8	15.7	15.5	15.4	15.4	15.7
2006	15.5	15.6	15.7	15.8	15.9	15.9	16.0	16.0	16.1	16.1	16.0	16.2	15.9
2007	16.3	16.2	16.2	16.2	16.4	16.4	16.5	16.7	16.6	16.7	16.7	16.7	16.5
2008	16.6	16.6	16.6	16.8	17.0	17.0	16.9	17.0	17.1	17.2	17.1	17.1	16.9
2009	16.8	16.6	16.3	16.2	16.1	16.0	16.0	15.9	15.9	16.1	16.0	16.0	16.2
2010	16.0	15.9	15.9	15.8	15.7	15.7	15.7	15.6	15.5	15.4	15.4	15.2	15.7
2011	15.2	15.3	15.3	15.6	15.6	15.7	15.7	15.6	15.6	15.7	15.7	15.7	15.6
Retail Trade													
2000	38.9	38.9	39.1	39.5	39.7	40.0	40.4	40.3	40.4	40.8	41.8	42.7	40.2
2001	40.6	40.2	40.4	40.7	40.7	40.8	40.2	40.2	40.4	40.5	41.5	42.3	40.7
2002	40.6	40.3	40.9	40.9	40.8	40.7	40.6	40.6	40.8	41.1	41.9	42.9	41.0
2003	40.5	40.0	40.2	40.4	40.7	41.0	40.7	41.0	41.0	41.2	42.3	43.1	41.0
2004	41.2	41.2	41.6	41.5	41.8	41.8	41.6	41.8	42.0	42.4	43.6	44.0	42.0
2005	42.6	42.3	42.8	42.8	43.2	43.1	42.9	43.1	43.0	42.9	44.2	44.8	43.1
2006	43.2	43.0	43.4	43.5	43.6	43.8	43.7	44.3	44.6	44.3	45.6	46.5	44.1
2007	44.8	44.3	44.9	45.3	45.4	45.2	45.0	45.2	45.3	45.4	47.0	47.3	45.4
2008	45.7	45.0	45.2	44.7	44.2	44.1	43.8	43.8	43.4	44.1	44.5	44.5	44.4
2009	42.1	41.2	40.7	40.7	40.5	40.7	40.3	40.3	40.2	40.4	41.4	41.7	40.9
2010	40.0	39.6	39.6	39.9	40.0	40.0	40.0	40.3	40.1	40.6	41.8	42.0	40.3
2011	40.2	39.9	40.1	40.2	40.3	40.4	40.3	40.3	40.3	40.3	41.1	40.9	40.4
Transportation and Utilities													
2000	9.4	9.5	9.7	10.1	10.0	9.9	9.7	9.8	9.9	9.8	9.8	9.7	9.8
2001	9.9	10.0	10.1	10.5	10.5	10.5	10.4	10.5	10.4	10.8	10.6	10.6	10.4
2002	10.3	10.3	10.4	10.5	10.3	10.3	10.5	10.6	10.5	10.8	10.7	10.7	10.5
2003	10.0	10.2	10.1	10.1	10.2	10.3	10.1	10.3	10.3	10.5	10.5	10.5	10.3
2004	10.2	10.2	10.3	10.3	10.4	10.4	10.2	10.4	10.5	10.5	10.5	10.7	10.4
2005	10.4	10.4	10.6	10.3	10.5	10.4	10.7	10.9	11.0	10.8	10.9	11.1	10.7
2006	10.8	10.8	11.1	10.9	11.1	11.1	10.9	11.2	11.3	11.1	11.2	11.5	11.1
2007	10.9	11.0	11.2	11.1	11.2	11.2	11.0	11.2	11.2	11.1	11.2	11.2	11.1
2008	11.1	11.1	11.0	11.1	11.1	11.1	11.0	11.2	11.2	11.2	11.3	11.3	11.1
2009	10.4	10.2	10.1	9.8	9.9	9.9	9.8	10.1	10.1	10.1	10.1	10.4	10.1
2010	10.0	10.0	10.0	10.1	10.3	10.2	10.8	10.9	11.0	11.0	11.1	11.4	10.6
2011	10.9	11.0	11.1	11.2	11.3	11.3	11.2	11.3	11.3	11.4	11.5	11.6	11.3
Information													
2000	6.1	6.1	6.2	6.0	6.0	6.0	6.0	5.9	5.9	5.9	5.9	5.9	6.0
2001	5.8	5.8	5.8	5.7	5.6	5.7	5.7	5.6	5.6	5.8	5.8	5.8	5.7
2002	5.8	5.8	5.8	5.9	5.9	5.8	5.9	5.9	5.8	6.0	6.0	6.1	5.9
2003	5.9	5.9	5.9	5.9	5.9	6.0	6.0	6.0	6.0	6.0	6.2	6.2	6.0
2004	6.2	6.1	6.2	6.2	6.2	6.1	6.2	6.0	5.9	5.9	5.9	5.8	6.1
2005	5.8	5.8	5.9	5.9	5.9	5.9	6.0	5.9	5.9	5.9	5.9	5.9	5.9
2006	6.0	6.1	6.1	6.1	6.0	6.0	6.0	5.9	5.8	5.8	5.9	5.8	6.0
2007	5.6	5.6	5.6	5.6	5.7	5.7	5.7	5.7	5.6	5.5	5.6	5.6	5.6
2008	5.6	5.6	5.6	5.6	5.7	5.7	5.6	5.5	5.5	5.6	5.6	5.6	5.6
2009	5.6	5.5	5.5	5.5	5.5	5.5	5.5	5.4	5.4	5.4	5.4	5.4	5.5
2010	5.4	5.4	5.4	5.4	5.4	5.5	5.5	5.5	5.4	5.6	5.6	5.6	5.5
2011	5.7	5.7	5.7	5.7	5.7	5.6	5.6	5.6	5.6	5.6	5.6	5.7	5.7
Financial Activities													
2000	13.9	13.9	14.0	13.9	14.0	14.1	13.9	13.9	13.8	13.9	14.0	14.1	14.0
2001	13.9	14.0	14.0	14.1	14.2	14.3	14.4	14.3	14.2	14.3	14.4	14.4	14.2
2002	14.3	14.4	14.4	14.5	14.7	14.9	14.9	14.9	15.1	15.3	15.6	15.8	14.9
2003	15.6	15.7	15.8	15.9	16.1	16.3	16.3	16.5	16.5	16.4	16.4	16.5	16.2
2004	16.4	16.4	16.5	16.6	16.7	16.7	16.8	16.8	16.8	16.8	16.9	17.0	16.7
2005	16.9	16.9	17.0	17.1	17.2	17.4	17.2	17.3	17.2	17.2	17.2	17.3	17.2
2006	17.2	17.2	17.3	17.2	17.3	17.3	17.4	17.6	17.5	17.4	17.5	17.5	17.4
2007	17.3	17.3	17.4	17.4	17.5	17.6	17.6	17.6	17.6	17.6	17.7	17.7	17.5
2008	17.4	17.5	17.6	17.6	17.7	17.9	17.9	18.0	17.9	18.0	18.0	18.0	17.8
2009	17.5	17.6	17.4	17.4	17.4	17.2	17.2	17.1	17.1	17.0	16.9	16.9	17.2
2010	16.9	16.9	16.9	17.1	17.1	17.1	17.0	16.9	16.8	16.8	16.8	16.8	16.9
2011	16.7	16.7	16.7	16.8	16.8	16.8	16.8	16.8	16.7	16.7	16.7	16.7	16.7

Employment by Industry: Knoxville, TN, Selected Years, 2000–2011—*Continued*

(Numbers in thousands, not seasonally adjusted)

Industry and year	January	February	March	April	May	June	July	August	September	October	November	December	Annual average
Professional and Business Services													
2000	35.1	35.7	36.8	36.7	37.0	37.9	36.8	37.3	37.6	37.1	37.1	37.0	36.8
2001	37.1	37.2	37.7	38.2	38.0	37.9	38.0	37.7	38.0	37.1	37.4	37.9	37.7
2002	37.4	37.2	37.9	38.2	38.3	38.5	38.5	38.8	38.8	38.6	37.9	37.8	38.2
2003	37.5	37.6	37.9	39.1	38.9	38.8	38.1	38.8	39.0	38.8	38.4	38.4	38.4
2004	37.3	37.4	38.0	39.2	39.0	39.4	39.4	39.8	39.9	39.4	39.4	39.6	39.0
2005	38.0	38.2	38.8	39.2	39.1	39.1	38.7	39.4	40.0	39.5	39.3	39.3	39.1
2006	38.5	38.8	39.3	39.8	40.0	39.8	39.6	40.3	40.8	40.5	40.5	40.6	39.9
2007	39.7	40.2	40.4	40.8	40.5	40.2	40.2	41.2	41.0	41.0	41.1	41.4	40.6
2008	41.1	41.4	41.3	42.2	42.2	42.0	42.0	42.8	43.4	43.6	43.7	44.0	42.5
2009	42.6	42.2	41.5	41.4	41.2	40.9	41.1	41.9	42.3	42.6	43.2	42.9	42.0
2010	42.3	42.4	42.6	44.3	44.4	43.9	44.8	45.9	46.0	46.4	46.7	46.9	44.7
2011	46.7	47.8	48.3	48.7	48.7	48.0	47.9	49.3	49.0	49.0	49.5	49.8	48.6
Education and Health Services													
2000	30.8	31.3	31.4	31.5	31.8	31.8	31.5	31.7	31.9	32.2	32.5	32.5	31.7
2001	32.0	32.4	32.8	33.1	33.3	33.6	33.1	33.3	33.4	33.7	34.0	34.1	33.2
2002	33.8	34.1	34.2	34.8	35.0	35.5	35.1	35.4	35.7	36.0	36.3	36.3	35.2
2003	35.5	35.6	35.8	36.0	36.2	36.5	36.5	36.6	37.2	37.4	37.6	37.7	36.6
2004	36.7	36.9	37.1	37.3	37.5	37.7	37.9	38.1	38.2	38.2	38.4	38.5	37.7
2005	38.2	38.1	38.5	38.7	39.0	39.3	39.3	39.5	39.7	40.1	40.2	40.3	39.2
2006	39.9	39.8	40.3	40.2	40.4	40.8	40.8	41.0	41.0	41.1	41.1	41.3	40.6
2007	40.9	40.9	41.1	41.3	41.4	41.7	41.9	42.2	42.4	42.6	42.7	42.8	41.8
2008	42.8	43.0	42.9	43.4	43.7	43.8	43.4	43.5	43.4	43.9	44.0	44.2	43.5
2009	43.3	43.4	43.3	44.0	44.3	44.3	44.6	44.7	44.6	44.3	44.2	44.4	44.1
2010	44.0	44.2	44.5	44.7	44.8	44.8	44.7	44.8	45.1	44.9	45.1	45.1	44.7
2011	44.7	45.1	45.3	45.8	45.9	46.0	46.5	47.7	47.4	47.4	47.4	47.5	46.4
Leisure and Hospitality													
2000	25.8	26.0	26.7	27.2	28.5	28.7	28.5	28.3	28.9	28.2	28.1	27.9	27.7
2001	27.8	28.2	28.8	30.2	31.3	31.9	31.4	31.5	31.5	30.8	30.5	30.2	30.3
2002	28.4	28.8	29.3	31.0	31.9	32.6	32.1	32.3	32.2	32.1	32.2	32.3	31.3
2003	29.8	30.0	30.7	31.6	32.2	32.5	31.8	32.2	31.9	31.2	31.4	31.2	31.4
2004	30.7	31.1	31.7	33.0	33.9	33.8	34.3	34.4	34.3	33.4	33.9	33.6	33.2
2005	32.7	33.0	33.6	34.2	34.9	35.5	35.0	35.0	35.3	34.4	34.6	34.2	34.4
2006	33.1	33.6	34.1	35.0	35.3	35.6	35.4	35.8	35.8	35.1	35.0	35.0	34.9
2007	34.1	34.4	35.3	35.6	36.1	36.6	36.4	36.7	36.2	35.2	35.4	35.3	35.6
2008	34.3	34.6	35.4	35.7	36.6	36.9	36.0	36.2	36.1	34.7	34.6	34.4	35.5
2009	32.9	33.3	33.9	34.3	35.1	35.3	34.6	34.7	34.5	33.8	33.8	33.5	34.1
2010	31.9	32.2	32.9	33.8	34.5	35.0	34.6	34.6	34.9	33.7	33.6	33.3	33.8
2011	32.5	33.1	33.7	34.5	35.0	35.2	34.8	35.0	34.4	34.0	33.8	33.8	34.2
Other Services													
2000	11.5	11.0	11.1	11.6	11.6	12.0	12.1	12.0	11.7	12.0	11.9	11.9	11.7
2001	12.0	12.1	12.6	12.1	12.2	12.5	12.6	12.5	12.6	12.3	12.4	12.4	12.4
2002	12.5	12.6	12.8	12.9	13.1	13.3	13.2	13.2	13.4	13.3	13.3	13.5	13.1
2003	13.6	13.7	13.7	13.7	13.8	14.1	14.1	13.9	13.9	13.8	13.8	13.9	13.8
2004	13.8	13.8	13.9	13.9	13.9	14.0	13.9	13.8	13.8	13.6	13.6	13.6	13.8
2005	13.5	13.5	13.6	13.7	13.7	13.9	13.9	13.8	13.8	13.7	13.7	13.8	13.7
2006	13.6	13.7	13.8	13.8	13.9	14.2	14.2	14.1	14.1	13.9	14.0	14.0	13.9
2007	14.1	14.2	14.3	14.1	14.3	14.6	14.5	14.4	14.4	14.4	14.4	14.4	14.3
2008	14.3	14.6	14.7	14.6	15.2	15.0	14.7	14.7	14.7	14.6	14.5	14.5	14.7
2009	14.4	14.4	14.6	15.0	14.5	14.8	14.7	14.7	14.5	14.8	15.0	14.4	14.7
2010	14.1	14.2	14.3	14.0	13.8	14.0	13.7	13.5	13.2	13.0	12.8	12.8	13.6
2011	12.5	12.5	12.6	12.7	12.7	13.0	12.9	12.8	12.8	12.8	12.8	12.8	12.7
Government													
2000	50.7	51.5	51.8	52.4	53.2	52.1	49.6	50.3	52.2	52.3	52.3	52.5	51.7
2001	51.2	52.1	52.2	52.2	52.1	51.8	50.0	50.0	52.0	53.1	53.1	53.2	51.9
2002	52.1	52.4	52.5	54.0	54.1	53.7	50.8	51.0	52.4	53.6	53.6	54.1	52.9
2003	52.2	52.5	52.8	53.2	53.2	52.6	50.1	50.4	50.7	53.2	53.2	52.8	52.2
2004	53.0	55.0	53.9	52.8	52.2	52.0	51.0	51.4	52.2	53.7	53.8	53.4	52.9
2005	52.4	53.0	52.8	52.8	52.3	51.5	50.0	50.1	52.0	52.9	53.0	53.3	52.2
2006	51.9	52.8	52.6	52.5	52.1	50.2	50.3	51.0	53.1	53.6	53.5	54.0	52.3
2007	52.4	53.2	53.2	52.9	52.2	49.9	49.2	50.3	52.2	52.4	52.5	50.9	51.8
2008	50.7	51.2	50.7	51.1	50.6	48.2	47.7	49.6	51.8	52.9	52.4	51.5	50.7
2009	50.7	51.4	51.2	51.3	50.9	48.6	47.5	47.8	50.3	51.9	52.8	51.2	50.5
2010	50.7	51.8	51.6	52.2	53.6	49.1	48.6	49.8	51.5	51.9	51.8	51.2	51.2
2011	50.2	50.5	50.3	51.5	51.4	48.0	46.4	49.3	51.4	52.4	52.9	51.5	50.5

Employment by Industry: Las Vegas–Paradise, NV, Selected Years, 2000–2011

(Numbers in thousands, not seasonally adjusted)

Industry and year	January	February	March	April	May	June	July	August	September	October	November	December	Annual average
Total Nonfarm													
2000	675.1	678.0	685.1	688.9	698.4	694.9	692.5	705.4	708.2	711.5	717.1	716.8	697.7
2001	716.4	723.5	728.8	728.8	732.5	731.9	725.3	731.1	735.7	722.3	722.8	720.8	726.7
2002	709.8	714.2	722.6	727.9	734.2	730.5	726.8	731.6	736.8	743.4	746.1	746.7	730.9
2003	738.2	743.4	749.5	750.0	756.4	754.2	754.0	761.8	770.3	778.8	780.9	785.0	760.2
2004	777.9	781.8	790.7	803.5	808.2	810.4	811.2	815.2	827.4	840.5	841.3	843.9	812.7
2005	832.4	840.6	850.5	867.3	869.9	872.4	870.3	873.4	887.4	892.6	899.2	903.3	871.6
2006	891.4	900.9	910.7	916.0	922.3	923.8	915.7	917.5	925.3	926.7	929.3	927.9	917.3
2007	913.2	923.9	927.9	930.4	936.7	933.3	921.2	921.1	924.6	932.2	935.3	936.3	928.0
2008	919.5	921.4	923.6	926.2	929.6	923.0	910.2	906.7	910.0	903.5	893.5	880.6	912.3
2009	855.7	850.0	842.6	836.1	832.2	824.2	811.1	807.2	815.5	815.6	815.6	816.9	826.9
2010	798.1	798.6	799.5	808.2	811.6	807.6	800.4	799.5	799.7	806.3	807.8	805.4	803.6
2011	797.2	797.3	803.4	809.8	811.4	806.7	802.4	802.5	813.5	818.7	821.7	814.9	808.3
Total Private													
2000	606.5	608.5	614.5	618.0	624.1	628.6	626.6	635.7	637.7	638.4	643.0	642.6	627.0
2001	644.7	649.6	654.6	653.0	658.1	659.6	656.7	662.2	659.9	645.8	646.0	644.0	652.9
2002	635.7	637.1	645.0	650.7	656.5	655.2	655.1	659.7	659.8	662.3	664.3	664.8	653.9
2003	659.9	662.2	667.9	668.5	674.5	675.5	678.9	687.1	689.8	695.9	697.6	701.4	679.9
2004	697.7	699.2	706.6	719.4	723.4	729.4	733.8	738.5	742.8	753.3	753.7	756.2	729.5
2005	748.4	753.5	761.9	778.5	780.8	786.9	788.5	792.6	799.9	801.3	806.9	810.7	784.2
2006	802.8	809.0	818.4	822.5	828.6	833.8	829.8	832.1	833.1	830.2	831.8	830.4	825.2
2007	819.4	826.1	829.6	830.5	836.6	837.3	829.6	831.0	827.5	831.0	833.3	833.9	830.5
2008	820.9	819.1	820.6	822.1	825.6	823.6	814.3	812.1	808.3	797.9	787.8	775.0	810.6
2009	755.1	747.5	740.2	734.3	731.4	727.7	718.0	715.5	717.3	716.5	717.1	718.8	728.3
2010	702.5	700.4	701.1	709.5	710.7	712.3	707.2	708.3	703.9	709.5	710.9	708.6	707.1
2011	702.0	700.5	706.5	713.2	714.4	716.5	713.5	714.3	720.3	725.2	728.3	721.5	714.7
Goods-Producing													
2000	83.6	84.0	86.1	86.5	87.4	89.2	88.9	89.3	88.1	87.3	87.7	87.8	87.2
2001	86.2	87.1	88.1	88.5	89.9	91.7	91.9	93.3	92.5	91.6	90.3	88.4	90.0
2002	85.4	85.8	87.5	89.5	91.0	91.1	92.2	93.6	92.9	93.1	92.4	91.8	90.5
2003	90.8	91.3	93.0	94.0	95.6	97.0	98.1	100.0	100.5	102.3	101.8	102.2	97.2
2004	100.5	102.6	104.1	108.4	109.7	112.1	115.1	116.6	118.5	120.8	119.7	120.5	112.4
2005	117.7	120.5	122.3	124.6	124.6	126.0	128.4	129.9	131.9	131.6	131.8	132.9	126.9
2006	130.8	133.6	135.8	137.3	138.5	139.9	138.8	139.3	138.2	135.6	133.7	132.3	136.2
2007	128.1	129.6	131.9	131.0	132.7	132.1	131.5	132.0	129.5	127.9	126.5	125.5	129.9
2008	121.3	121.4	120.9	120.7	121.7	122.0	121.9	120.6	118.0	114.7	109.7	104.8	118.1
2009	99.3	96.8	94.0	90.8	86.5	84.8	82.9	82.2	81.2	79.8	77.2	73.7	85.8
2010	66.8	65.3	64.6	66.8	66.7	66.3	65.2	65.0	63.6	63.0	61.6	60.1	64.6
2011	57.7	57.5	57.2	57.5	57.0	57.0	57.5	58.2	59.0	58.6	59.9	58.4	58.0
Mining and Logging													
2000	0.5	0.5	0.6	0.6	0.6	0.6	0.6	0.6	0.6	0.6	0.5	0.5	0.6
2001	0.6	0.5	0.5	0.5	0.5	0.5	0.5	0.5	0.5	0.4	0.3	0.3	0.5
2002	0.4	0.3	0.4	0.3	0.3	0.3	0.3	0.3	0.3	0.3	0.3	0.3	0.3
2003	0.3	0.3	0.3	0.3	0.4	0.4	0.4	0.4	0.4	0.4	0.4	0.4	0.4
2004	0.4	0.4	0.4	0.4	0.4	0.4	0.4	0.4	0.4	0.4	0.4	0.4	0.4
2005	0.4	0.4	0.4	0.4	0.4	0.4	0.4	0.4	0.4	0.4	0.4	0.4	0.4
2006	0.4	0.4	0.4	0.4	0.4	0.5	0.5	0.5	0.5	0.5	0.5	0.5	0.5
2007	0.5	0.5	0.5	0.5	0.5	0.5	0.5	0.5	0.5	0.5	0.4	0.4	0.5
2008	0.4	0.4	0.4	0.4	0.4	0.4	0.4	0.4	0.4	0.3	0.3	0.3	0.4
2009	0.3	0.3	0.3	0.3	0.3	0.3	0.3	0.3	0.3	0.3	0.3	0.3	0.3
2010	0.3	0.3	0.2	0.3	0.3	0.3	0.3	0.3	0.3	0.3	0.3	0.2	0.3
2011	0.2	0.2	0.2	0.2	0.2	0.2	0.2	0.2	0.2	0.2	0.2	0.2	0.2
Construction													
2000	63.3	63.6	65.3	65.9	66.7	68.4	68.2	68.6	67.3	66.3	66.8	66.7	66.4
2001	65.0	65.8	66.9	67.2	68.4	70.0	70.3	71.5	70.8	70.2	69.0	67.2	68.5
2002	64.5	64.9	66.5	68.5	69.8	69.7	70.6	71.9	71.3	71.0	70.3	69.6	69.1
2003	69.1	69.6	71.3	72.2	73.6	74.8	75.7	77.4	77.9	79.4	78.7	79.1	74.9
2004	77.8	79.7	80.9	85.1	86.1	88.3	91.1	92.4	94.3	96.4	95.2	96.1	88.6
2005	93.2	96.0	97.5	99.5	99.4	100.6	102.9	104.3	105.9	105.6	105.7	106.8	101.5
2006	104.6	107.1	108.9	110.0	110.9	112.0	110.8	111.3	110.0	107.7	105.9	104.4	108.6
2007	100.9	102.4	104.5	103.6	105.2	104.4	104.0	104.6	102.3	101.1	99.8	99.0	102.7
2008	95.0	95.2	94.7	94.5	95.4	95.6	95.7	94.6	92.3	89.5	85.2	80.8	92.4
2009	76.2	74.2	71.8	69.0	65.2	63.8	62.0	61.2	60.2	59.1	56.7	53.3	64.4
2010	46.8	45.5	45.0	46.8	46.8	46.4	45.4	45.4	43.9	43.3	41.8	40.5	44.8
2011	38.1	37.9	37.5	37.8	37.4	37.3	37.7	38.3	39.1	38.6	40.0	38.4	38.2
Manufacturing													
2000	19.8	19.9	20.2	20.0	20.1	20.2	20.1	20.1	20.2	20.4	20.4	20.6	20.2
2001	20.6	20.8	20.7	20.8	21.0	21.2	21.1	21.3	21.2	21.0	21.0	20.9	21.0
2002	20.5	20.6	20.6	20.7	20.9	21.1	21.3	21.4	21.3	21.8	21.8	21.9	21.2
2003	21.4	21.4	21.4	21.5	21.6	21.8	22.0	22.2	22.2	22.5	22.7	22.7	22.0
2004	22.3	22.5	22.8	22.9	23.2	23.4	23.6	23.8	23.8	24.0	24.1	24.0	23.4
2005	24.1	24.1	24.4	24.7	24.8	25.0	25.1	25.2	25.6	25.6	25.7	25.7	25.0
2006	25.8	26.1	26.5	26.9	27.2	27.4	27.5	27.5	27.7	27.4	27.3	27.4	27.1
2007	26.7	26.7	26.9	26.9	27.0	27.2	27.0	26.9	26.7	26.3	26.3	26.1	26.7
2008	25.9	25.8	25.8	25.8	25.9	26.0	25.8	25.6	25.3	24.9	24.2	23.7	25.4
2009	22.8	22.3	21.9	21.5	21.0	20.7	20.6	20.7	20.7	20.4	20.2	20.1	21.1
2010	19.7	19.5	19.4	19.7	19.6	19.6	19.5	19.3	19.4	19.4	19.5	19.4	19.5
2011	19.4	19.4	19.5	19.5	19.4	19.5	19.6	19.7	19.7	19.8	19.7	19.8	19.6

Employment by Industry: Las Vegas–Paradise, NV, Selected Years, 2000–2011—*Continued*

(Numbers in thousands, not seasonally adjusted)

Industry and year	January	February	March	April	May	June	July	August	September	October	November	December	Annual average
Service-Providing													
2000	591.5	594.0	599.0	602.4	611.0	605.7	603.6	616.1	620.1	624.2	629.4	629.0	610.5
2001	630.2	636.4	640.7	640.3	642.6	640.2	633.4	637.8	643.2	630.7	632.5	632.4	636.7
2002	624.4	628.4	635.1	638.4	643.2	639.4	634.6	638.0	643.9	650.3	653.7	654.9	640.4
2003	647.4	652.1	656.5	656.0	660.8	657.2	655.9	661.8	669.8	676.5	679.1	682.8	663.0
2004	677.4	679.2	686.6	695.1	698.5	698.3	691.1	698.6	708.9	719.7	721.6	723.4	700.3
2005	714.7	720.1	728.2	742.7	745.3	746.4	741.9	743.5	755.5	761.0	767.4	770.4	744.8
2006	760.6	767.3	774.9	778.7	783.8	783.9	776.9	778.2	787.1	791.1	795.6	795.6	781.1
2007	785.1	794.3	796.0	799.4	804.0	801.2	789.7	789.1	795.1	804.3	808.8	810.8	798.2
2008	798.2	800.0	802.7	805.5	807.9	801.0	788.3	786.1	792.0	788.8	783.8	775.8	794.2
2009	756.4	753.2	748.6	745.3	745.7	739.4	728.2	725.0	734.3	735.8	738.4	743.2	741.1
2010	731.3	733.3	734.9	741.4	744.9	741.3	735.2	734.5	736.1	743.3	746.2	745.3	739.0
2011	739.5	739.8	746.2	752.3	754.4	749.7	744.9	744.3	754.5	760.1	761.8	756.5	750.3
Trade, Transportation, and Utilities													
2000	117.1	116.6	116.2	117.3	118.1	118.7	118.9	121.2	122.3	123.9	126.5	128.9	120.5
2001	125.9	125.0	125.2	126.3	127.0	128.0	128.1	128.3	128.3	128.0	129.8	130.8	127.6
2002	126.3	125.2	125.9	128.0	128.2	128.5	128.5	128.6	129.3	131.4	133.2	135.3	129.0
2003	129.3	129.1	130.3	129.4	130.0	130.6	130.9	132.7	134.0	136.9	139.8	142.2	132.9
2004	135.2	135.0	136.4	137.1	137.9	139.6	139.8	140.5	141.1	143.7	146.8	149.0	140.2
2005	143.7	143.2	144.0	145.6	146.2	147.3	148.2	149.0	150.6	151.8	155.2	157.2	148.5
2006	152.6	152.1	153.7	153.8	154.8	155.3	155.3	155.9	156.8	158.0	161.4	163.3	156.1
2007	158.4	157.7	158.4	158.8	160.0	160.7	160.0	161.0	161.0	162.1	166.6	168.9	161.1
2008	163.2	161.2	161.6	161.0	160.9	160.9	161.1	161.1	160.3	159.5	160.4	160.0	160.9
2009	152.8	150.0	149.0	147.5	147.4	147.4	146.6	146.5	147.1	147.9	151.1	152.2	148.8
2010	146.5	144.7	144.8	145.1	145.8	146.5	146.7	147.3	146.9	148.4	151.8	152.9	147.3
2011	147.0	145.7	146.0	147.3	147.7	148.1	149.1	149.3	150.6	151.5	155.5	154.8	149.4
Wholesale Trade													
2000	17.1	17.1	17.3	17.7	17.8	17.9	17.8	18.0	18.0	17.9	18.1	18.2	17.7
2001	19.0	19.1	19.3	19.6	19.7	20.0	19.8	19.9	19.9	19.8	19.8	19.9	19.7
2002	19.5	19.7	19.9	20.0	20.0	20.1	19.9	20.0	20.0	20.1	20.1	20.2	20.0
2003	19.7	19.8	19.8	19.7	19.7	19.8	19.9	19.8	19.8	20.0	20.1	20.2	19.9
2004	19.9	20.0	20.1	20.2	20.2	20.4	20.7	20.7	20.8	21.1	21.1	21.2	20.5
2005	21.2	21.4	21.6	21.9	22.0	22.2	22.4	22.5	22.7	22.6	22.7	22.9	22.2
2006	22.8	23.0	23.2	23.4	23.6	23.6	23.7	23.8	24.0	23.9	23.9	24.1	23.6
2007	23.8	23.9	24.0	24.0	24.2	24.3	24.2	24.3	24.3	24.2	24.2	24.2	24.1
2008	24.0	24.0	24.1	23.9	24.0	24.0	24.1	24.1	24.0	23.7	23.4	23.1	23.9
2009	22.5	22.2	21.9	21.6	21.3	21.2	21.1	21.0	20.9	20.9	20.8	20.8	21.4
2010	20.4	20.3	20.4	20.4	20.5	20.5	20.4	20.5	20.4	20.6	20.5	20.5	20.5
2011	20.1	20.1	20.1	20.2	20.2	20.2	20.3	20.4	20.7	20.6	20.6	20.9	20.4
Retail Trade													
2000	73.0	72.4	71.5	72.4	73.2	73.5	73.5	75.3	76.0	77.2	79.3	81.7	74.9
2001	78.5	77.3	77.2	77.8	78.2	78.9	79.1	79.3	79.5	79.6	81.7	82.8	79.2
2002	79.0	77.9	78.3	79.4	79.8	80.2	80.0	79.9	80.4	82.1	85.0	87.3	80.8
2003	81.9	81.3	82.3	81.6	82.3	82.7	83.0	84.6	85.5	87.8	90.4	92.4	84.7
2004	85.9	85.4	86.3	87.2	87.9	89.1	88.7	89.3	89.7	91.3	94.5	96.7	89.3
2005	91.6	90.7	91.1	91.7	91.9	92.6	93.5	93.9	94.9	96.1	99.0	100.5	94.0
2006	96.1	95.4	96.3	96.1	96.6	97.0	96.7	97.1	97.4	98.7	101.6	103.1	97.7
2007	98.7	97.8	98.1	98.5	99.2	99.5	99.4	99.9	99.6	100.2	104.1	106.2	100.1
2008	101.6	99.9	100.0	99.6	99.2	99.4	99.4	99.3	98.8	98.5	99.8	100.0	99.6
2009	94.5	92.2	91.6	90.6	90.8	90.9	90.6	90.7	91.6	92.5	95.5	96.7	92.4
2010	91.6	90.1	90.2	90.6	91.1	91.6	92.0	92.5	92.2	93.5	96.8	97.6	92.5
2011	92.7	91.3	91.5	92.1	92.6	92.8	93.7	93.7	94.1	94.9	98.6	97.7	93.8
Transportation and Utilities													
2000	27.0	27.1	27.4	27.2	27.1	27.3	27.6	27.9	28.3	28.8	29.1	29.0	27.8
2001	28.4	28.6	28.7	28.9	29.1	29.1	29.2	29.1	28.9	28.6	28.3	28.1	28.8
2002	27.8	27.6	27.7	28.6	28.4	28.2	28.6	28.7	28.9	29.2	28.1	27.8	28.3
2003	27.7	28.0	28.2	28.1	28.0	28.1	28.0	28.3	28.7	29.1	29.3	29.6	28.4
2004	29.4	29.6	30.0	29.7	29.8	30.1	30.4	30.5	30.6	31.3	31.2	31.1	30.3
2005	30.9	31.1	31.3	32.0	32.3	32.5	32.3	32.6	33.0	33.1	33.5	33.8	32.4
2006	33.7	33.7	34.2	34.3	34.6	34.7	34.9	35.0	35.4	35.4	35.9	36.1	34.8
2007	35.9	36.0	36.3	36.3	36.6	36.9	36.4	36.8	37.1	37.7	38.3	38.5	36.9
2008	37.6	37.3	37.5	37.5	37.7	37.5	37.6	37.7	37.5	37.3	37.2	36.9	37.4
2009	35.8	35.6	35.5	35.3	35.3	35.3	34.9	34.8	34.6	34.5	34.8	34.7	35.1
2010	34.5	34.3	34.2	34.1	34.2	34.4	34.3	34.3	34.3	34.3	34.5	34.8	34.4
2011	34.2	34.3	34.4	35.0	34.9	35.1	35.1	35.2	35.8	36.0	36.3	36.2	35.2
Information													
2000	13.1	12.7	13.1	12.9	13.7	13.4	13.1	13.4	13.2	13.6	13.8	13.1	13.3
2001	14.0	15.6	15.4	14.1	14.0	13.3	12.4	12.2	11.8	12.2	12.6	12.1	13.3
2002	12.1	11.9	11.6	11.7	11.8	11.4	11.2	11.2	11.2	11.0	11.1	11.0	11.4
2003	10.6	10.4	10.3	10.4	10.6	10.5	10.2	10.0	10.0	10.1	10.2	10.3	10.3
2004	10.2	10.0	10.0	11.1	10.5	10.4	10.4	10.2	10.1	10.5	10.4	10.1	10.3
2005	10.5	10.1	10.1	10.6	11.0	10.4	10.1	10.2	10.2	10.6	10.5	10.3	10.4
2006	10.8	10.8	10.5	10.9	10.9	11.0	11.5	11.5	11.1	11.1	11.0	10.8	11.0
2007	11.3	11.6	11.3	11.4	11.6	11.5	10.9	11.3	10.9	11.4	11.4	11.1	11.3
2008	11.0	11.1	11.1	11.3	11.8	11.2	10.8	10.8	10.7	11.0	10.6	10.2	11.0
2009	9.8	9.9	10.0	9.5	9.5	9.6	9.5	9.6	9.3	9.4	9.4	9.4	9.6
2010	9.0	9.0	8.9	9.3	9.1	9.1	9.4	9.2	9.0	9.1	9.3	9.3	9.1
2011	9.2	9.0	9.1	9.4	9.4	9.4	9.5	9.4	9.2	9.3	9.3	9.3	9.3

Employment by Industry: Las Vegas–Paradise, NV, Selected Years, 2000–2011—*Continued*

(Numbers in thousands, not seasonally adjusted)

Industry and year	January	February	March	April	May	June	July	August	September	October	November	December	Annual average
Financial Activities													
2000	36.9	37.0	37.4	37.4	37.5	37.9	38.3	38.5	38.6	38.3	38.9	39.2	38.0
2001	40.0	40.2	40.7	40.5	40.7	41.0	41.1	41.7	41.8	41.3	41.0	41.6	41.0
2002	40.5	41.0	41.2	41.3	41.3	41.5	41.6	41.5	41.4	41.8	42.3	42.3	41.5
2003	42.1	42.3	42.5	42.8	43.5	43.5	43.9	44.1	44.3	44.4	44.3	44.5	43.5
2004	44.6	44.8	44.9	45.3	45.4	45.8	46.5	46.6	46.7	47.6	47.7	48.4	46.2
2005	47.7	47.6	48.3	48.2	48.4	48.9	48.9	49.1	49.7	49.4	49.6	49.9	48.8
2006	49.0	49.0	49.6	49.6	50.0	50.4	50.5	50.6	50.9	50.6	50.8	51.3	50.2
2007	50.4	50.4	50.7	50.2	50.5	50.6	50.0	49.8	49.7	49.4	48.9	49.0	50.0
2008	48.0	48.1	48.2	48.0	47.9	48.0	47.5	47.1	47.0	46.9	46.4	45.9	47.4
2009	44.1	43.9	43.5	43.1	42.9	42.9	41.7	41.7	41.3	41.4	41.0	40.9	42.4
2010	40.3	39.9	40.0	40.5	40.3	40.1	40.2	39.9	39.8	40.3	40.2	40.3	40.2
2011	39.8	39.6	39.8	39.8	39.7	39.7	39.4	38.9	39.0	39.1	38.8	39.0	39.4
Professional and Business Services													
2000	70.9	71.9	72.5	73.7	74.8	74.9	72.5	75.1	77.9	77.1	78.1	76.0	74.6
2001	80.8	82.4	82.6	80.6	81.6	80.5	78.3	80.6	79.9	78.3	78.7	76.8	80.1
2002	80.0	79.7	81.2	80.5	81.3	80.0	79.7	82.3	82.9	82.4	83.2	81.9	81.3
2003	85.4	85.7	85.4	84.8	85.1	83.5	85.1	87.8	88.0	89.5	88.7	88.3	86.4
2004	93.6	92.2	92.6	94.4	95.1	95.0	95.2	97.0	97.6	101.5	99.3	97.8	95.9
2005	101.5	102.4	103.6	104.9	104.6	105.0	104.4	106.3	107.0	109.7	112.2	112.1	106.1
2006	113.0	114.2	115.3	115.5	116.3	116.6	114.4	115.6	115.2	115.6	116.2	114.0	115.2
2007	116.9	119.5	117.5	117.9	117.9	116.9	113.6	115.3	113.8	116.3	115.3	113.1	116.2
2008	115.9	115.1	115.0	115.0	116.0	113.6	109.8	110.0	110.8	107.9	106.7	103.0	111.6
2009	105.5	103.6	101.4	99.2	99.5	98.4	94.7	95.4	97.6	97.6	99.0	98.5	99.2
2010	100.2	99.1	98.6	99.7	99.6	100.2	98.2	100.4	98.3	100.8	100.6	99.2	99.6
2011	102.7	101.0	101.5	101.9	101.5	101.7	99.1	100.1	102.0	102.4	101.6	100.9	101.4
Education and Health Services													
2000	39.1	39.5	39.9	39.9	40.2	40.4	40.6	40.8	41.5	42.1	42.5	43.0	40.8
2001	43.3	43.8	44.2	44.5	44.9	45.2	45.0	45.8	46.0	46.0	46.2	46.6	45.1
2002	46.0	46.6	47.1	47.4	48.0	47.8	47.8	48.0	48.2	48.8	49.1	49.2	47.8
2003	48.7	49.5	49.7	50.0	50.4	50.3	50.1	50.6	51.2	51.4	52.0	52.2	50.5
2004	51.9	52.6	53.2	53.6	53.5	53.6	54.0	54.3	55.2	55.6	55.7	56.0	54.1
2005	55.8	56.4	57.0	57.7	57.9	58.1	57.6	57.7	58.1	58.0	58.4	59.0	57.6
2006	58.5	59.1	59.8	59.4	59.6	60.2	59.3	59.8	60.7	61.2	61.7	62.1	60.1
2007	61.5	62.4	62.7	62.6	63.2	63.4	63.3	63.5	64.0	64.6	64.9	64.7	63.4
2008	64.6	65.3	65.6	66.3	66.5	66.6	66.2	66.5	67.0	67.2	67.5	67.6	66.4
2009	66.4	66.9	66.9	66.9	67.3	67.5	67.4	67.7	67.7	68.8	68.9	69.0	67.6
2010	68.3	68.6	69.1	69.7	69.8	69.7	69.1	69.3	69.6	70.7	71.1	71.3	69.7
2011	70.8	71.4	71.9	72.0	72.0	72.1	71.7	70.8	72.1	72.2	72.6	72.2	71.8
Leisure and Hospitality													
2000	228.1	228.8	230.9	232.0	233.8	235.2	235.5	238.5	237.2	237.2	236.6	235.7	234.1
2001	235.7	236.4	238.9	238.7	239.8	239.3	239.8	239.8	239.1	228.5	227.8	228.1	236.0
2002	225.6	226.8	230.0	232.0	234.3	234.2	233.7	234.0	233.6	233.6	233.0	233.3	232.0
2003	233.3	234.0	236.5	237.2	239.2	239.6	240.1	241.3	241.2	240.9	240.2	240.9	238.7
2004	240.8	240.5	243.2	247.1	248.4	249.4	249.9	250.4	250.5	251.0	250.8	251.0	247.7
2005	249.2	250.7	253.7	263.9	264.8	267.5	267.2	266.6	268.3	266.2	265.0	264.8	262.3
2006	264.4	266.3	269.4	271.7	273.8	275.3	274.9	274.1	274.7	272.8	271.8	271.5	271.7
2007	268.3	270.4	272.1	273.4	275.1	276.1	274.4	272.1	272.6	273.5	273.8	275.4	273.1
2008	271.1	271.3	272.4	274.1	274.7	275.1	271.1	271.1	269.9	268.4	265.0	261.4	258.9	269.5
2009	253.7	253.0	251.9	253.6	254.4	253.2	251.6	248.7	249.4	248.3	247.5	252.1	251.5
2010	248.8	251.1	252.1	255.1	256.0	257.0	254.9	253.6	253.2	253.6	253.2	252.6	253.4
2011	252.1	253.3	257.8	261.4	263.1	264.3	263.0	263.3	264.1	267.9	266.5	262.9	261.6
Other Services													
2000	17.7	18.0	18.4	18.3	18.6	18.9	18.8	18.9	18.9	18.9	18.9	18.9	18.6
2001	18.8	19.1	19.5	19.8	20.2	20.6	20.1	20.5	20.5	19.9	19.6	19.6	19.9
2002	19.8	20.1	20.5	20.3	20.6	20.7	20.4	20.5	20.3	20.2	20.0	20.0	20.3
2003	19.7	19.9	20.2	19.9	20.1	20.5	20.5	20.6	20.6	20.4	20.6	20.8	20.3
2004	20.9	21.5	22.2	22.4	22.9	23.5	22.9	22.9	23.1	23.5	23.3	23.4	22.7
2005	22.3	22.6	22.9	23.0	23.3	23.7	23.7	23.8	24.1	24.0	24.2	24.5	23.5
2006	23.7	23.9	24.3	24.3	24.7	25.1	25.1	25.3	25.5	25.3	25.2	25.1	24.8
2007	24.5	24.5	25.0	25.2	25.6	26.0	25.9	26.0	26.0	25.8	25.9	26.2	25.6
2008	25.8	25.6	25.8	25.7	26.1	26.2	25.9	26.1	26.1	25.7	25.1	24.6	25.7
2009	23.5	23.4	23.5	23.7	23.9	23.9	23.6	23.7	23.7	23.3	23.0	23.0	23.5
2010	22.6	22.7	23.0	23.3	23.4	23.4	23.5	23.6	23.5	23.6	23.1	22.9	23.2
2011	22.7	23.0	23.2	23.9	24.0	24.2	24.2	24.3	24.3	24.2	24.1	24.0	23.8
Government													
2000	68.6	69.5	70.6	70.9	74.3	66.3	65.9	69.7	70.5	73.1	74.1	74.2	70.6
2001	71.7	73.9	74.2	75.8	74.4	72.3	68.6	68.9	75.8	76.5	76.8	76.8	73.8
2002	74.1	77.1	77.6	77.2	77.7	75.3	71.7	71.9	77.0	81.1	81.8	81.9	77.0
2003	78.3	81.2	81.6	81.5	81.9	78.7	75.1	74.7	80.5	82.9	83.3	83.6	80.3
2004	80.2	82.6	84.1	84.1	84.8	81.0	77.4	76.7	84.6	87.2	87.6	87.7	83.2
2005	84.0	87.1	88.6	88.8	89.1	85.5	81.8	80.8	87.5	91.3	92.3	92.6	87.5
2006	88.6	91.9	92.3	93.5	93.7	90.0	85.9	85.4	92.2	96.5	97.5	97.5	92.1
2007	93.8	97.8	98.3	99.9	100.1	96.0	91.6	90.1	97.1	101.2	102.0	102.4	97.5
2008	98.6	102.3	103.0	104.1	104.0	99.4	95.9	94.6	101.7	105.6	105.7	105.6	101.7
2009	100.6	102.5	102.4	101.8	100.8	96.5	93.1	91.7	98.2	99.1	98.5	98.1	98.6
2010	95.6	98.2	98.4	98.7	100.9	95.3	93.2	91.2	95.8	96.8	96.9	96.8	96.5
2011	95.2	96.8	96.9	96.6	97.0	90.2	88.9	88.2	93.2	93.5	93.4	93.4	93.6

Employment by Industry: Little Rock–North Little Rock–Conway, AR, Selected Years, 2000–2011

(Numbers in thousands, not seasonally adjusted)

Industry and year	January	February	March	April	May	June	July	August	September	October	November	December	Annual average
Total Nonfarm													
2000	318.6	318.8	321.1	321.4	321.7	323.4	319.1	320.9	323.2	323.5	323.7	323.2	321.6
2001	322.7	324.5	326.4	325.6	325.9	326.5	322.3	323.8	324.2	323.7	323.5	323.0	324.3
2002	316.5	317.5	319.8	320.1	322.4	322.4	318.6	319.7	322.5	322.3	322.9	324.3	320.8
2003	318.2	319.2	321.2	322.1	323.8	324.0	321.2	324.8	326.2	326.5	326.3	328.3	323.5
2004	322.1	323.4	325.6	326.3	327.7	329.0	327.6	329.8	330.8	330.5	331.8	333.2	328.2
2005	325.4	327.7	330.3	332.8	333.6	334.6	331.3	332.8	335.8	334.8	337.2	338.9	332.9
2006	333.9	336.3	339.9	341.0	341.6	342.8	338.8	340.7	343.6	343.1	343.9	345.6	340.9
2007	339.7	341.2	344.7	345.3	345.7	348.0	343.7	347.0	349.3	348.3	349.7	350.6	346.1
2008	345.4	347.1	348.5	348.6	350.5	349.7	346.1	347.9	349.3	347.4	347.4	346.7	347.9
2009	339.8	340.8	341.4	340.5	339.6	338.8	335.8	335.5	336.1	335.8	337.4	338.0	338.3
2010	331.0	330.8	334.8	336.0	339.0	341.4	337.0	337.1	339.6	340.9	341.5	341.9	337.6
2011	333.9	334.1	337.8	341.2	339.3	338.1	335.5	334.4	336.4	336.7	339.2	341.6	337.4
Total Private													
2000	256.9	256.9	259.0	259.0	259.7	261.9	261.3	262.0	261.2	261.1	260.9	260.4	260.0
2001	260.1	261.3	262.8	261.8	262.7	264.1	262.5	263.1	261.3	259.9	259.3	258.8	261.5
2002	252.9	253.2	255.2	255.6	257.9	259.0	258.2	258.6	258.8	257.9	258.0	259.2	257.0
2003	253.8	254.5	256.4	257.0	259.4	260.1	259.3	262.1	262.0	261.4	260.8	263.2	259.2
2004	257.7	258.3	260.3	261.9	263.4	265.1	265.0	266.3	265.7	265.0	266.0	267.5	263.5
2005	260.7	262.4	264.9	266.5	268.2	269.5	269.1	269.2	270.0	268.6	270.8	272.9	267.7
2006	268.0	269.3	272.7	273.5	274.8	276.4	274.3	275.0	275.7	275.3	276.4	278.2	274.1
2007	272.8	273.5	276.7	276.7	277.9	280.2	279.3	280.0	280.1	278.7	280.0	281.3	278.1
2008	277.3	277.9	279.2	279.1	280.5	280.5	279.6	280.3	279.7	277.3	277.1	276.4	278.7
2009	270.4	270.1	270.6	269.5	269.1	268.7	267.1	267.0	265.8	264.0	265.5	266.1	267.8
2010	259.9	259.2	262.9	264.2	266.4	269.9	268.2	268.3	268.5	269.3	269.7	270.0	266.4
2011	263.4	262.5	266.0	269.4	267.8	267.6	267.5	265.7	265.3	265.0	267.0	269.3	266.4
Goods-Producing													
2000	49.4	49.4	50.1	49.7	49.8	50.4	50.3	50.3	49.8	49.3	49.1	48.8	49.7
2001	48.4	48.5	49.0	48.1	48.2	48.3	47.5	47.7	47.2	46.7	45.4	45.1	47.5
2002	44.5	44.3	44.4	44.5	44.9	45.0	45.1	45.2	44.7	44.4	43.7	43.5	44.5
2003	42.8	42.9	43.3	43.4	43.8	44.1	43.8	43.8	43.3	42.7	41.6	42.2	43.1
2004	41.3	41.1	41.5	42.5	43.0	43.6	43.4	43.5	43.3	42.9	42.8	42.6	42.6
2005	42.0	42.1	42.5	42.7	43.0	43.4	43.5	43.7	43.6	43.2	43.2	43.2	43.0
2006	42.9	43.0	43.3	43.5	43.9	44.5	44.1	44.6	44.6	44.2	44.0	44.0	43.9
2007	43.3	43.4	44.3	44.1	44.2	45.0	45.0	45.0	44.7	44.4	44.4	44.4	44.4
2008	43.9	43.5	43.5	43.3	43.9	44.4	44.5	44.6	44.1	43.2	42.6	42.3	43.7
2009	41.4	41.0	40.7	39.8	39.4	39.3	39.4	39.5	39.0	38.0	37.8	37.5	39.4
2010	36.3	35.8	36.2	36.5	37.1	38.3	38.1	37.9	37.7	37.4	37.2	37.1	37.1
2011	35.9	35.6	36.2	36.7	36.5	36.9	37.1	36.5	36.0	36.0	35.7	36.0	36.3
Mining, Logging, and Construction													
2000	16.1	16.2	16.4	16.3	16.5	16.9	16.9	16.9	16.7	16.6	16.6	16.5	16.6
2001	16.3	16.4	17.0	16.7	17.1	17.4	17.5	17.6	17.4	17.1	16.9	16.8	17.0
2002	16.3	16.3	16.5	16.7	17.1	17.5	17.7	17.6	17.4	17.3	16.9	16.8	17.0
2003	16.9	16.9	17.3	17.4	17.8	18.1	18.0	18.0	17.7	17.5	17.1	17.0	17.5
2004	16.5	16.3	16.7	17.5	17.8	18.2	18.0	18.0	18.0	17.5	17.3	17.2	17.4
2005	16.7	16.9	17.3	17.5	18.0	18.1	18.1	18.3	18.2	17.7	17.8	17.9	17.7
2006	17.6	17.7	18.1	18.3	18.7	19.1	18.8	19.2	19.3	18.9	18.7	18.8	18.6
2007	18.3	18.4	19.3	19.2	19.4	20.1	20.0	20.1	19.9	19.7	19.6	19.5	19.5
2008	19.1	19.1	19.2	19.1	19.5	19.8	19.9	20.0	19.6	18.8	18.4	18.2	19.2
2009	17.6	17.5	17.5	17.3	17.1	17.2	17.6	17.6	17.3	16.8	16.8	16.6	17.2
2010	15.9	15.6	16.0	16.5	17.0	17.7	17.8	17.7	17.6	17.4	17.2	17.2	17.0
2011	16.2	15.9	16.4	16.9	16.7	17.1	17.4	16.8	16.5	16.7	16.4	16.7	16.6
Manufacturing													
2000	33.3	33.2	33.7	33.4	33.3	33.5	33.4	33.4	33.1	32.7	32.5	32.3	33.2
2001	32.1	32.1	32.0	31.4	31.1	30.9	30.0	30.1	29.8	29.6	28.5	28.3	30.5
2002	28.2	28.0	27.9	27.8	27.8	27.5	27.4	27.6	27.3	27.1	26.8	26.7	27.5
2003	25.9	26.0	26.0	26.0	26.0	26.0	25.8	25.8	25.6	25.2	24.5	25.2	25.7
2004	24.8	24.8	24.8	25.0	25.2	25.4	25.4	25.5	25.3	25.4	25.5	25.4	25.2
2005	25.3	25.2	25.2	25.2	25.0	25.3	25.4	25.4	25.4	25.5	25.4	25.3	25.3
2006	25.3	25.3	25.2	25.2	25.2	25.4	25.3	25.4	25.3	25.3	25.3	25.2	25.3
2007	25.0	25.0	25.0	24.9	24.8	24.9	25.0	24.9	24.8	24.7	24.8	24.9	24.9
2008	24.8	24.4	24.3	24.2	24.4	24.6	24.6	24.6	24.5	24.4	24.2	24.1	24.4
2009	23.8	23.5	23.2	22.5	22.3	22.1	21.8	21.9	21.7	21.2	21.0	20.9	22.2
2010	20.4	20.2	20.2	20.0	20.1	20.6	20.3	20.2	20.1	20.0	20.0	19.9	20.2
2011	19.7	19.7	19.8	19.8	19.8	19.8	19.7	19.7	19.5	19.3	19.3	19.3	19.6
Service-Providing													
2000	269.2	269.4	271.0	271.7	271.9	273.0	268.8	270.6	273.4	274.2	274.6	274.4	271.9
2001	274.3	276.0	277.4	277.5	277.7	278.2	274.8	276.1	277.0	277.0	278.1	277.9	276.8
2002	272.0	273.2	275.4	275.6	275.5	277.4	273.5	274.5	277.8	277.9	279.2	280.8	276.2
2003	275.4	276.3	277.9	278.7	280.0	279.9	277.4	281.0	282.9	283.8	284.7	286.1	280.3
2004	280.8	282.3	284.1	283.8	284.7	285.4	284.2	286.3	287.5	287.6	289.0	290.6	285.5
2005	283.4	285.6	287.8	290.1	290.6	291.2	287.8	289.1	292.2	291.6	294.0	295.7	289.9
2006	291.0	293.3	296.6	297.5	297.7	298.3	294.7	296.1	299.0	298.9	299.9	301.6	297.1
2007	296.4	297.8	300.4	301.2	301.5	303.0	298.7	302.0	304.6	303.9	305.3	306.2	301.8
2008	301.5	303.6	305.0	305.3	306.6	305.3	301.6	303.3	305.2	304.2	304.8	304.4	304.2
2009	298.4	299.8	300.7	300.7	300.2	299.5	296.4	296.0	297.1	297.8	299.6	300.5	298.9
2010	294.7	295.0	298.6	299.5	301.9	303.1	298.9	299.2	301.9	303.5	304.3	304.8	300.5
2011	298.0	298.5	301.6	304.5	302.8	301.2	298.4	297.9	300.4	300.7	303.5	305.6	301.1

Employment by Industry: Little Rock–North Little Rock–Conway, AR, Selected Years, 2000–2011—*Continued*

(Numbers in thousands, not seasonally adjusted)

Industry and year	January	February	March	April	May	June	July	August	September	October	November	December	Annual average
Trade, Transportation, and Utilities													
2000	70.3	69.8	69.6	69.8	69.7	70.0	70.0	70.2	70.1	70.8	71.4	72.3	70.3
2001	70.7	70.1	70.5	70.4	70.5	70.8	70.1	70.1	69.9	69.8	70.8	71.1	70.4
2002	68.6	68.2	68.7	68.8	69.0	69.0	68.2	68.1	68.2	68.0	69.1	69.9	68.7
2003	67.7	67.3	67.4	67.4	67.6	67.6	67.2	67.7	68.3	69.3	69.7	70.7	68.2
2004	68.0	67.9	68.1	68.0	68.3	68.6	68.7	69.3	69.2	69.3	70.2	71.3	68.9
2005	68.6	68.5	68.7	69.0	69.1	69.0	69.1	69.2	69.8	69.7	71.1	71.9	69.5
2006	69.5	69.3	69.9	70.1	70.5	70.2	69.9	70.3	70.5	70.7	71.8	72.7	70.5
2007	70.1	69.7	70.6	70.0	70.3	70.4	70.2	70.3	70.3	70.0	71.2	72.0	70.4
2008	69.7	69.4	69.7	69.4	69.8	69.7	69.3	69.4	69.2	68.7	69.4	69.4	69.4
2009	66.9	66.4	66.5	65.6	65.2	64.7	63.9	64.1	64.0	63.8	64.9	65.4	65.1
2010	62.8	62.3	63.3	63.6	63.9	64.4	64.2	64.2	64.1	65.6	66.6	67.1	64.3
2011	64.8	64.0	64.7	65.2	64.9	64.9	64.8	65.1	64.3	63.3	65.4	68.8	65.0
Wholesale Trade													
2000	15.5	15.6	15.8	15.9	16.0	16.2	16.3	16.4	16.5	16.5	16.3	16.4	16.1
2001	16.6	16.6	16.6	16.6	16.6	16.8	16.7	16.7	16.7	16.3	16.3	16.3	16.6
2002	16.2	16.2	16.3	16.3	16.3	16.3	16.2	16.2	16.1	16.0	15.9	16.0	16.2
2003	15.9	16.0	15.9	16.0	16.2	16.2	16.3	16.3	16.4	16.5	16.5	16.6	16.2
2004	16.3	16.4	16.5	16.7	16.8	16.9	16.9	16.9	16.9	16.8	16.7	16.9	16.7
2005	16.7	16.8	16.8	16.9	16.9	17.1	17.2	17.2	17.3	17.2	17.3	17.4	17.1
2006	17.3	17.3	17.3	17.5	17.6	17.7	17.6	17.6	17.6	17.4	17.5	17.6	17.5
2007	17.1	17.2	17.3	17.3	17.3	17.4	17.4	17.4	17.3	17.4	17.3	17.4	17.3
2008	17.4	17.5	17.5	17.6	17.7	17.7	17.8	17.9	17.9	17.8	17.7	17.7	17.7
2009	17.6	17.6	17.6	17.5	17.4	17.2	17.0	16.9	16.7	16.7	16.6	16.6	17.1
2010	16.2	16.2	16.4	16.7	16.7	16.8	16.7	16.4	16.2	16.6	16.5	16.4	16.5
2011	15.9	15.9	15.9	16.2	16.1	16.0	16.0	16.1	16.1	15.9	15.9	16.3	16.0
Retail Trade													
2000	36.2	35.6	35.2	35.2	35.3	35.5	35.1	35.3	35.1	35.8	36.6	37.4	35.7
2001	35.9	35.5	35.9	35.8	36.0	36.1	35.4	35.3	35.2	35.4	36.6	37.1	35.9
2002	35.0	34.7	35.1	35.1	35.4	35.5	35.0	34.8	34.9	34.8	36.0	36.7	35.3
2003	34.5	34.1	34.2	34.3	34.4	34.5	34.1	34.5	34.9	35.6	36.2	37.1	34.9
2004	35.0	34.9	35.3	35.3	35.4	35.6	35.5	35.9	35.7	36.0	36.9	37.6	35.8
2005	35.8	35.5	35.6	35.7	35.7	35.7	35.6	35.6	35.8	36.0	37.2	37.8	36.0
2006	35.8	35.5	36.0	35.9	36.0	35.8	35.7	36.1	36.0	36.4	37.5	38.1	36.2
2007	36.5	35.9	36.6	36.1	36.4	36.5	36.4	36.4	36.4	36.3	37.6	38.2	36.6
2008	36.4	36.2	36.5	36.0	36.2	36.4	36.5	36.5	35.9	36.7	36.9	38.2	36.4
2009	35.0	34.7	34.9	34.8	34.9	34.9	34.6	34.8	34.8	34.9	36.1	36.5	35.1
2010	34.7	34.2	34.9	35.0	35.3	35.7	35.5	35.7	35.5	36.6	37.7	38.1	35.7
2011	36.4	35.7	36.2	36.4	36.1	36.1	36.0	36.1	35.2	34.7	36.7	39.3	36.2
Transportation and Utilities													
2000	18.6	18.6	18.6	18.7	18.4	18.3	18.6	18.5	18.5	18.5	18.5	18.5	18.5
2001	18.2	18.0	18.0	18.0	17.9	17.9	18.0	18.1	18.0	18.1	17.9	17.7	18.0
2002	17.4	17.3	17.3	17.4	17.3	17.2	17.0	17.1	17.2	17.2	17.2	17.2	17.2
2003	17.3	17.2	17.3	17.1	17.0	16.9	16.8	16.9	17.0	17.2	17.0	17.0	17.1
2004	16.7	16.6	16.3	16.0	16.1	16.1	16.3	16.5	16.6	16.5	16.6	16.8	16.4
2005	16.1	16.2	16.3	16.4	16.5	16.2	16.3	16.4	16.7	16.5	16.6	16.7	16.4
2006	16.4	16.5	16.6	16.7	16.9	16.7	16.6	16.6	16.9	16.9	16.8	17.0	16.7
2007	16.5	16.6	16.7	16.6	16.6	16.5	16.4	16.5	16.6	16.3	16.3	16.4	16.5
2008	15.9	15.7	15.7	15.8	15.9	15.6	15.0	15.0	15.1	15.0	15.0	14.8	15.4
2009	14.3	14.1	14.0	13.3	12.9	12.6	12.3	12.4	12.5	12.2	12.2	12.3	12.9
2010	11.9	11.9	12.0	11.9	11.9	11.9	12.0	12.1	12.4	12.4	12.4	12.6	12.1
2011	12.5	12.4	12.6	12.6	12.7	12.8	12.8	12.9	13.0	12.7	12.8	13.2	12.8
Information													
2000	8.8	8.9	8.9	8.9	9.0	9.2	9.2	9.4	9.4	9.5	9.6	9.5	9.2
2001	9.4	9.4	9.2	9.0	9.1	9.1	9.3	9.3	9.3	9.2	9.2	9.1	9.2
2002	9.2	9.2	9.1	9.1	9.1	9.2	9.1	9.1	9.1	9.3	9.3	9.3	9.2
2003	9.3	9.3	9.3	9.3	9.4	9.5	9.4	9.5	9.4	9.4	9.5	9.5	9.4
2004	9.6	9.4	9.5	9.5	9.5	9.5	9.5	9.5	9.5	9.4	9.5	9.4	9.5
2005	9.3	9.4	9.3	9.2	9.3	9.4	9.4	9.4	9.3	9.3	9.3	9.4	9.3
2006	9.3	9.3	9.3	9.3	9.3	9.4	9.3	9.3	9.3	9.1	9.2	9.1	9.3
2007	9.4	9.4	9.3	9.4	9.4	9.5	9.4	9.3	9.3	9.3	9.3	9.3	9.4
2008	9.1	9.1	9.1	9.4	9.0	9.1	9.1	9.1	8.9	8.8	8.8	8.8	9.0
2009	8.7	8.6	8.6	8.6	8.6	8.6	8.5	8.4	8.2	8.0	7.9	7.9	8.4
2010	7.7	7.9	7.9	7.9	7.9	8.2	7.8	7.8	7.8	7.8	7.8	7.9	7.9
2011	7.8	7.8	7.8	7.7	7.7	7.6	7.6	7.6	7.5	7.5	7.5	7.4	7.6
Financial Activities													
2000	18.9	18.9	18.9	18.7	18.7	18.8	18.9	18.9	18.7	18.5	18.4	18.6	18.7
2001	19.1	19.1	19.2	19.2	19.3	19.4	19.4	19.3	19.2	19.0	19.1	19.3	19.2
2002	19.1	19.1	19.2	19.1	19.1	19.2	19.3	19.3	19.3	19.2	19.2	19.4	19.2
2003	19.2	19.2	19.2	19.3	19.5	19.7	19.7	19.7	19.7	19.6	19.6	19.9	19.5
2004	19.6	19.7	19.7	19.7	19.7	19.7	19.7	19.7	19.7	19.0	19.0	19.1	19.5
2005	18.8	18.8	18.8	19.5	19.6	19.7	19.8	19.8	19.8	19.7	19.8	20.0	19.5
2006	19.7	19.8	19.8	19.9	20.0	20.0	20.1	20.2	20.1	20.1	20.2	20.3	20.0
2007	20.2	20.2	20.2	20.2	20.2	20.3	20.3	20.2	20.2	20.1	20.0	20.2	20.2
2008	20.1	20.1	20.1	19.8	19.9	19.8	19.9	19.9	19.9	19.8	19.8	19.9	19.9
2009	19.7	19.6	19.6	19.6	19.6	19.7	19.5	19.5	19.4	19.4	19.4	19.5	19.5
2010	19.0	19.0	18.9	18.8	18.8	19.0	19.1	19.1	19.0	19.1	19.2	19.3	19.0
2011	19.1	19.0	19.0	19.1	19.0	19.1	19.0	19.0	19.0	18.9	18.9	19.0	19.0

Employment by Industry: Little Rock–North Little Rock–Conway, AR, Selected Years, 2000–2011—*Continued*

(Numbers in thousands, not seasonally adjusted)

Industry and year	January	February	March	April	May	June	July	August	September	October	November	December	Annual average
Professional and Business Services													
2000	38.1	38.3	39.0	38.4	38.8	39.1	39.4	40.1	40.1	40.1	40.0	39.0	39.2
2001	39.5	40.3	40.1	39.6	39.5	39.4	39.8	40.2	39.8	39.1	38.8	38.5	39.6
2002	37.3	37.2	37.8	37.8	38.3	38.9	39.0	39.4	39.7	39.9	39.3	39.8	38.7
2003	38.9	39.0	39.6	39.2	39.7	39.2	39.5	41.3	41.0	41.1	40.8	41.1	40.0
2004	40.4	40.4	40.9	40.3	40.5	40.5	41.0	41.5	41.2	42.1	42.1	42.4	41.1
2005	40.8	41.2	41.8	41.5	41.4	41.7	41.6	41.6	41.7	41.6	42.1	42.9	41.7
2006	41.7	42.5	43.6	43.1	43.2	43.2	43.1	42.8	43.5	43.1	43.2	43.8	43.1
2007	42.7	43.0	43.2	43.4	43.4	43.6	42.9	43.6	43.8	43.4	43.5	43.7	43.4
2008	43.5	44.1	44.1	43.7	43.7	43.3	42.8	43.0	43.1	42.9	42.8	42.6	43.3
2009	41.4	41.5	41.1	41.4	41.4	41.2	41.0	41.3	41.1	41.4	41.9	42.2	41.4
2010	42.1	42.2	43.2	43.1	43.3	43.9	43.7	43.9	43.9	44.1	44.0	44.0	43.5
2011	42.8	43.1	43.8	44.6	44.0	44.2	44.0	43.6	44.1	44.2	43.2	43.1	43.7
Education and Health Services													
2000	36.8	37.0	37.1	37.2	37.2	37.1	36.9	36.6	37.1	37.1	37.1	37.0	37.0
2001	37.6	38.1	38.3	38.5	38.5	38.7	38.6	38.8	39.0	39.5	39.6	39.5	38.7
2002	38.9	39.3	39.6	39.5	39.8	39.5	39.6	39.7	40.6	40.3	40.5	40.5	39.8
2003	40.0	40.5	40.8	40.9	41.0	41.0	40.8	41.0	41.8	41.8	41.8	41.9	41.1
2004	41.2	41.5	41.6	42.2	42.1	42.1	42.1	42.1	42.8	43.1	43.0	42.9	42.2
2005	42.4	42.9	43.1	43.6	43.6	43.6	43.5	43.5	44.1	44.4	44.4	44.3	43.6
2006	44.2	44.7	45.1	45.0	45.0	45.2	44.9	45.1	45.9	45.7	45.8	46.0	45.2
2007	45.6	46.1	46.5	46.7	46.8	46.9	47.2	47.3	48.0	47.3	47.4	47.3	46.9
2008	47.2	47.7	47.9	48.1	48.0	47.9	47.9	48.1	48.7	48.8	48.7	48.7	48.1
2009	48.5	49.1	49.5	49.4	49.2	49.1	49.0	48.7	49.4	49.4	49.7	50.0	49.3
2010	49.3	49.4	49.8	50.0	49.9	50.1	49.8	49.8	50.7	50.5	50.6	50.4	50.0
2011	49.8	49.8	50.3	50.6	50.4	49.5	49.5	49.3	49.3	50.0	50.7	50.2	50.0
Leisure and Hospitality													
2000	22.8	22.8	23.5	24.4	24.5	25.0	24.5	24.4	24.1	24.1	23.6	23.5	23.9
2001	23.5	23.9	24.3	24.9	25.4	25.8	25.4	25.3	24.6	24.5	24.3	24.1	24.7
2002	23.2	23.8	24.2	24.6	25.3	25.5	25.2	25.1	24.6	24.5	24.5	24.5	24.6
2003	23.7	24.0	24.3	24.9	25.6	25.9	25.8	25.9	25.3	24.3	24.4	24.3	24.9
2004	24.0	24.5	25.2	25.8	26.4	26.8	26.5	26.7	26.1	25.6	25.6	25.9	25.8
2005	25.1	25.7	26.7	26.9	28.0	28.3	27.8	27.7	27.4	26.8	26.9	27.1	27.0
2006	26.6	26.5	27.4	28.2	28.4	29.1	28.1	28.0	27.3	27.9	27.8	27.9	27.8
2007	27.3	27.5	28.3	28.5	29.1	29.5	29.3	29.3	28.8	29.2	29.0	29.1	28.7
2008	28.4	28.5	29.1	29.6	30.2	30.1	29.8	29.9	29.7	29.3	29.3	28.9	29.4
2009	28.2	28.3	29.0	29.6	30.1	30.3	30.1	30.0	29.4	29.1	29.0	28.7	29.3
2010	28.0	28.0	28.9	29.4	30.5	30.7	30.4	30.6	30.3	29.9	29.4	29.3	29.6
2011	28.3	28.3	29.1	30.2	30.1	30.0	30.2	29.3	29.9	30.1	30.6	29.8	29.7
Other Services													
2000	11.8	11.8	11.9	11.9	12.0	12.3	12.1	12.1	11.9	11.7	11.7	11.7	11.9
2001	11.9	11.9	12.2	12.1	12.2	12.6	12.4	12.4	12.3	12.1	12.1	12.1	12.2
2002	12.1	12.1	12.2	12.2	12.4	12.7	12.7	12.7	12.6	12.3	12.4	12.3	12.4
2003	12.2	12.3	12.5	12.6	12.8	13.1	13.1	13.2	13.2	13.2	13.4	13.6	12.9
2004	13.6	13.8	13.8	13.9	13.9	14.3	14.1	14.0	13.9	13.6	13.8	13.8	13.9
2005	13.7	13.8	14.0	14.1	14.2	14.4	14.4	14.3	14.3	13.9	14.0	14.1	14.1
2006	14.1	14.2	14.3	14.4	14.5	14.8	14.8	14.7	14.6	14.5	14.4	14.4	14.5
2007	14.2	14.2	14.3	14.4	14.5	15.0	15.0	15.0	15.0	15.0	15.2	15.3	14.8
2008	15.4	15.5	15.7	15.8	16.0	16.2	16.3	16.3	16.1	15.8	15.7	15.8	15.9
2009	15.6	15.6	15.6	15.5	15.6	15.8	15.7	15.5	15.3	14.9	14.9	14.9	15.4
2010	14.7	14.6	14.7	14.9	15.0	15.3	15.1	15.0	15.0	14.9	14.9	14.9	14.9
2011	14.9	14.9	15.1	15.3	15.2	15.4	15.3	15.3	15.2	15.0	15.0	15.0	15.1
Government													
2000	61.7	61.9	62.1	62.4	62.0	61.5	57.8	58.9	62.0	62.4	62.8	62.8	61.5
2001	62.6	63.2	63.6	63.8	63.2	62.4	59.8	60.7	62.9	63.8	64.2	64.2	62.9
2002	63.6	64.3	64.6	64.5	64.5	63.4	60.4	61.1	63.7	64.4	64.9	65.1	63.7
2003	64.4	64.7	64.8	65.1	64.4	63.9	61.9	62.7	64.2	65.1	65.5	65.1	64.3
2004	64.4	65.1	65.3	64.4	64.3	63.9	62.6	63.5	65.1	65.5	65.8	65.7	64.6
2005	64.7	65.3	65.4	66.3	65.4	65.1	62.2	63.6	65.8	66.2	66.4	66.0	65.2
2006	65.9	67.0	67.2	67.5	66.8	66.4	64.5	65.7	67.9	67.8	67.5	67.4	66.8
2007	66.9	67.7	68.0	68.6	67.8	67.8	64.4	67.0	69.2	69.6	69.7	69.3	68.0
2008	68.1	69.2	69.3	69.5	70.0	69.2	66.5	67.6	69.6	70.1	70.3	70.3	69.1
2009	69.4	70.7	70.8	71.0	70.5	70.1	68.7	68.5	70.3	71.8	71.9	71.9	70.5
2010	71.1	71.6	71.9	71.8	72.6	71.5	68.8	68.8	71.1	71.6	71.8	71.9	71.2
2011	70.5	71.6	71.8	71.8	71.5	70.5	68.0	68.7	71.1	71.7	72.2	72.3	71.0

Employment by Industry: Los Angeles–Long Beach–Santa Ana, CA, Selected Years, 2000–2011

(Numbers in thousands, not seasonally adjusted)

Industry and year	January	February	March	April	May	June	July	August	September	October	November	December	Annual average
Total Nonfarm													
2000	5,343.5	5,395.6	5,437.4	5,446.6	5,475.9	5,477.2	5,425.2	5,440.1	5,490.1	5,499.1	5,534.7	5,566.3	5,461.0
2001	5,471.1	5,503.6	5,546.3	5,518.1	5,515.8	5,522.8	5,431.0	5,438.0	5,459.8	5,471.7	5,474.8	5,494.6	5,487.3
2002	5,364.4	5,393.4	5,441.9	5,436.3	5,453.6	5,456.5	5,374.2	5,389.0	5,427.0	5,455.5	5,481.4	5,492.1	5,430.4
2003	5,367.1	5,390.9	5,419.8	5,410.3	5,425.1	5,425.1	5,366.6	5,376.4	5,392.4	5,442.0	5,454.0	5,473.3	5,411.9
2004	5,376.1	5,406.6	5,441.4	5,447.3	5,469.6	5,467.4	5,429.9	5,415.9	5,439.8	5,493.3	5,522.6	5,528.7	5,453.2
2005	5,417.9	5,452.7	5,481.9	5,498.8	5,510.0	5,523.8	5,477.6	5,487.7	5,531.4	5,566.2	5,603.0	5,630.6	5,515.1
2006	5,519.6	5,566.8	5,597.4	5,597.5	5,613.8	5,635.0	5,576.7	5,581.2	5,619.9	5,652.9	5,675.2	5,700.9	5,611.4
2007	5,578.5	5,615.8	5,649.5	5,626.9	5,638.8	5,656.0	5,611.6	5,600.5	5,633.1	5,657.2	5,679.5	5,705.4	5,637.7
2008	5,548.8	5,583.2	5,603.7	5,605.1	5,605.8	5,600.1	5,534.3	5,504.2	5,521.9	5,528.7	5,503.1	5,488.9	5,552.3
2009	5,316.1	5,294.7	5,288.0	5,241.3	5,232.8	5,214.0	5,114.2	5,078.0	5,096.0	5,149.9	5,157.2	5,172.3	5,196.2
2010	5,063.9	5,076.1	5,098.9	5,135.6	5,160.5	5,156.8	5,086.2	5,074.4	5,102.5	5,167.2	5,188.1	5,211.0	5,126.8
2011	5,109.8	5,136.8	5,156.2	5,162.1	5,171.5	5,173.0	5,118.9	5,085.9	5,143.0	5,211.4	5,231.7	5,245.6	5,162.2
Total Private													
2000	4,625.3	4,667.5	4,700.9	4,707.1	4,716.9	4,743.3	4,727.4	4,751.7	4,772.5	4,767.8	4,792.5	4,824.8	4,733.1
2001	4,730.8	4,755.7	4,787.6	4,758.2	4,753.9	4,758.8	4,713.6	4,723.9	4,721.8	4,713.1	4,711.6	4,728.7	4,738.1
2002	4,605.3	4,630.0	4,667.8	4,662.9	4,677.1	4,682.9	4,644.0	4,667.3	4,677.5	4,687.5	4,708.3	4,720.6	4,669.3
2003	4,604.3	4,624.4	4,646.0	4,641.7	4,657.0	4,658.0	4,632.6	4,660.0	4,660.6	4,693.0	4,700.8	4,723.0	4,658.5
2004	4,629.1	4,658.3	4,686.6	4,693.7	4,714.8	4,714.7	4,711.8	4,715.1	4,715.9	4,752.0	4,775.5	4,785.1	4,712.7
2005	4,679.6	4,707.2	4,731.7	4,751.0	4,759.8	4,773.7	4,762.5	4,781.7	4,806.8	4,824.4	4,853.3	4,882.2	4,776.2
2006	4,778.2	4,818.1	4,842.7	4,843.5	4,857.3	4,878.7	4,852.0	4,869.2	4,886.5	4,899.9	4,914.9	4,942.4	4,865.3
2007	4,826.9	4,858.0	4,885.6	4,864.1	4,873.8	4,890.8	4,879.0	4,880.7	4,891.2	4,895.5	4,909.9	4,936.6	4,882.7
2008	4,786.1	4,812.6	4,828.3	4,828.9	4,825.8	4,821.8	4,794.2	4,776.0	4,774.7	4,760.2	4,728.2	4,717.4	4,787.9
2009	4,549.2	4,524.1	4,512.1	4,463.7	4,457.7	4,440.0	4,386.5	4,373.6	4,384.4	4,401.8	4,407.0	4,425.1	4,443.8
2010	4,322.9	4,332.3	4,350.2	4,378.7	4,389.7	4,399.6	4,385.3	4,397.6	4,408.1	4,439.6	4,454.5	4,480.3	4,394.9
2011	4,384.9	4,409.0	4,421.8	4,428.5	4,436.9	4,438.1	4,431.3	4,431.0	4,462.3	4,494.0	4,506.0	4,524.7	4,447.4
Goods-Producing													
2000	1,028.3	1,036.0	1,045.3	1,043.0	1,045.4	1,056.5	1,046.9	1,047.8	1,052.5	1,042.0	1,041.4	1,047.0	1,044.3
2001	1,025.4	1,027.3	1,032.7	1,025.8	1,024.1	1,024.8	1,009.8	1,009.7	1,003.2	990.2	979.7	973.5	1,010.5
2002	947.5	951.1	958.5	952.2	954.1	955.1	939.8	943.4	942.9	936.7	933.6	931.0	945.6
2003	912.8	912.0	915.4	909.7	912.1	914.7	903.9	907.4	906.2	902.6	901.8	903.9	908.5
2004	894.3	897.9	904.8	905.5	907.9	913.0	911.4	910.8	911.5	908.9	903.5	901.3	905.9
2005	887.0	895.3	900.2	906.3	910.1	914.5	916.1	918.6	920.4	917.3	916.1	915.4	909.8
2006	904.4	912.5	916.4	915.4	917.7	923.2	918.7	920.5	921.6	914.6	910.9	908.0	915.3
2007	892.2	897.9	902.2	898.3	899.7	906.0	901.8	899.5	895.2	889.5	882.5	878.3	895.3
2008	863.0	864.6	863.9	861.5	860.1	859.2	855.3	852.2	847.0	836.6	823.4	812.2	849.9
2009	787.0	772.9	766.0	753.1	749.1	744.7	730.9	725.3	719.8	715.0	711.2	705.7	740.1
2010	696.7	695.1	697.5	699.5	702.6	705.7	704.9	704.9	701.8	701.9	700.3	697.9	700.7
2011	688.3	690.6	693.4	695.4	698.2	700.8	700.0	698.4	694.5	697.0	693.8	693.2	695.3
Mining and Logging													
2000	4.0	4.0	4.0	3.9	4.0	4.0	3.9	3.9	4.0	4.0	3.9	4.3	4.0
2001	4.5	4.4	4.4	4.4	4.4	4.4	4.4	4.4	4.4	4.4	4.4	4.4	4.4
2002	4.4	4.4	4.4	4.1	4.2	4.2	4.2	4.2	4.2	4.2	4.4	4.4	4.3
2003	4.3	4.4	4.4	4.3	4.3	4.3	4.3	4.4	4.2	4.4	4.4	4.4	4.3
2004	4.3	4.3	4.4	4.4	4.3	4.4	4.3	4.3	4.3	4.6	4.6	4.6	4.4
2005	4.5	4.5	4.5	4.3	4.3	4.3	4.4	4.4	4.4	4.3	4.4	4.4	4.4
2006	4.5	4.5	4.5	4.5	4.6	4.7	4.7	4.7	4.7	4.7	4.7	4.7	4.6
2007	4.9	5.0	5.0	4.9	4.9	5.0	5.0	4.9	5.0	5.0	5.1	5.0	5.0
2008	5.0	5.0	5.0	4.9	4.9	5.0	5.0	5.0	5.0	5.1	5.0	5.0	5.0
2009	4.9	4.8	4.8	4.7	4.7	4.7	4.5	4.5	4.4	4.5	4.5	4.3	4.6
2010	4.6	4.7	4.7	4.7	4.7	4.7	4.7	4.6	4.6	4.6	4.5	4.5	4.6
2011	4.5	4.5	4.4	4.5	4.5	4.5	4.5	4.5	4.5	4.5	4.6	4.5	4.5
Construction													
2000	198.3	199.1	202.1	203.3	206.6	211.6	208.8	212.9	215.2	214.4	215.0	216.5	208.7
2001	208.7	209.3	212.1	213.5	216.9	220.3	221.2	225.3	223.9	221.9	219.2	217.8	217.5
2002	208.8	209.5	211.8	209.7	211.7	213.2	212.5	217.9	218.2	217.3	216.6	216.5	213.6
2003	210.3	208.2	211.3	212.3	216.3	219.8	220.0	223.6	223.9	224.1	224.2	225.2	218.3
2004	221.9	222.1	224.7	228.2	230.4	234.1	236.6	239.2	240.5	238.7	236.2	235.3	232.3
2005	226.2	232.9	236.3	241.8	246.4	250.7	254.9	258.5	259.4	259.2	258.8	258.3	248.6
2006	253.9	257.0	259.1	260.0	263.5	267.3	267.9	271.0	272.0	267.9	265.6	264.2	264.1
2007	255.1	257.9	261.6	260.1	261.9	265.8	266.7	266.1	263.8	260.6	255.6	252.7	260.7
2008	242.9	243.3	243.6	241.4	240.6	239.3	237.9	237.9	234.7	230.5	224.9	220.1	236.4
2009	209.1	202.1	201.3	196.0	195.1	193.6	188.3	187.6	184.9	182.7	180.9	176.3	191.5
2010	171.3	169.4	170.9	172.3	173.4	173.9	173.7	174.6	172.7	173.4	173.1	171.2	172.5
2011	167.2	167.8	169.1	170.9	172.7	174.4	174.3	173.4	171.6	173.8	174.0	172.2	171.8
Manufacturing													
2000	826.0	832.9	839.2	835.8	834.8	840.9	834.2	831.0	833.3	823.6	822.5	826.2	831.7
2001	812.2	813.6	816.2	807.9	802.8	800.1	784.2	780.0	774.9	763.9	756.1	751.3	788.6
2002	734.3	738.2	742.3	738.4	738.2	737.7	723.1	721.3	720.5	715.2	712.6	710.1	727.7
2003	698.2	699.4	699.7	693.1	691.5	690.6	679.6	679.4	678.1	674.1	673.2	674.3	685.9
2004	668.1	671.5	675.7	672.9	673.2	674.5	670.5	667.3	666.7	665.6	662.7	661.4	669.2
2005	656.3	657.9	659.4	660.2	659.4	659.5	656.8	655.7	656.6	653.8	652.9	652.7	656.8
2006	646.0	651.0	652.8	650.9	649.6	651.2	646.1	644.8	644.9	642.0	640.6	639.1	646.6
2007	632.2	635.0	635.6	633.3	632.9	635.2	630.1	628.5	626.4	623.9	621.8	620.6	629.6
2008	615.1	616.3	615.3	615.2	614.6	614.9	612.4	609.3	607.3	601.0	593.5	587.1	608.5
2009	573.0	566.0	559.9	552.4	549.3	546.4	538.1	533.2	530.5	527.8	525.8	525.1	544.0
2010	520.8	521.0	521.9	522.5	524.5	527.1	526.5	525.7	524.5	523.9	522.7	522.2	523.6
2011	516.6	518.3	519.9	520.0	521.0	521.9	521.2	520.5	518.4	518.7	515.2	516.5	519.0

Employment by Industry: Los Angeles–Long Beach–Santa Ana, CA, Selected Years, 2000–2011—*Continued*

(Numbers in thousands, not seasonally adjusted)

Industry and year	January	February	March	April	May	June	July	August	September	October	November	December	Annual average
Service-Providing													
2000	4,315.2	4,359.6	4,392.1	4,403.6	4,430.5	4,420.7	4,378.3	4,392.3	4,437.6	4,457.1	4,493.3	4,519.3	4,416.6
2001	4,445.7	4,476.3	4,513.6	4,492.3	4,491.7	4,498.0	4,421.2	4,428.3	4,456.6	4,481.5	4,495.1	4,521.1	4,476.8
2002	4,416.9	4,441.3	4,483.4	4,484.1	4,499.5	4,501.4	4,434.4	4,445.6	4,484.1	4,518.8	4,547.8	4,561.1	4,484.9
2003	4,454.3	4,478.9	4,504.4	4,500.6	4,513.0	4,510.4	4,462.7	4,469.0	4,486.2	4,539.4	4,552.2	4,569.4	4,503.4
2004	4,481.8	4,508.7	4,536.6	4,541.8	4,561.7	4,554.4	4,518.5	4,505.1	4,528.3	4,584.4	4,619.1	4,627.4	4,547.3
2005	4,530.9	4,557.4	4,581.7	4,592.5	4,599.9	4,609.3	4,561.5	4,569.1	4,611.0	4,648.9	4,686.9	4,715.2	4,605.4
2006	4,615.2	4,654.3	4,681.0	4,682.1	4,696.1	4,711.8	4,658.0	4,660.7	4,698.3	4,738.3	4,764.3	4,792.9	4,696.1
2007	4,686.3	4,717.9	4,747.3	4,728.6	4,739.1	4,750.0	4,709.8	4,701.0	4,737.9	4,767.7	4,797.0	4,827.1	4,742.5
2008	4,685.8	4,718.7	4,739.8	4,743.6	4,745.7	4,740.9	4,679.0	4,652.0	4,674.9	4,692.1	4,679.7	4,676.7	4,702.4
2009	4,529.1	4,521.8	4,522.0	4,488.2	4,483.7	4,469.3	4,383.3	4,352.7	4,376.2	4,434.9	4,446.0	4,466.6	4,456.2
2010	4,367.2	4,381.0	4,401.4	4,436.1	4,457.9	4,451.1	4,381.3	4,369.5	4,400.7	4,465.3	4,487.8	4,513.1	4,426.0
2011	4,421.5	4,446.2	4,462.8	4,466.7	4,473.3	4,472.2	4,418.9	4,387.5	4,448.5	4,514.4	4,537.9	4,552.4	4,466.9
Trade, Transportation, and Utilities													
2000	1,031.5	1,029.3	1,031.0	1,027.2	1,029.3	1,035.7	1,034.1	1,038.7	1,042.6	1,051.0	1,068.8	1,088.2	1,042.3
2001	1,057.9	1,050.1	1,053.3	1,048.4	1,047.6	1,051.9	1,044.2	1,044.6	1,046.4	1,046.8	1,057.8	1,074.4	1,052.0
2002	1,033.5	1,027.9	1,030.3	1,032.1	1,036.2	1,042.0	1,037.0	1,040.4	1,044.3	1,045.8	1,063.6	1,084.5	1,043.1
2003	1,037.3	1,031.4	1,031.8	1,027.5	1,029.8	1,033.6	1,027.6	1,028.5	1,033.2	1,045.8	1,054.5	1,070.1	1,037.8
2004	1,028.2	1,024.3	1,029.5	1,032.4	1,037.1	1,043.0	1,039.9	1,041.0	1,042.7	1,053.3	1,074.2	1,086.2	1,044.3
2005	1,052.2	1,045.9	1,045.5	1,046.0	1,049.2	1,054.2	1,057.5	1,060.4	1,064.1	1,073.5	1,093.8	1,114.4	1,063.1
2006	1,072.3	1,067.4	1,071.2	1,068.7	1,071.7	1,077.1	1,077.9	1,082.3	1,086.4	1,093.5	1,115.2	1,132.6	1,084.7
2007	1,092.0	1,083.1	1,081.0	1,080.6	1,082.5	1,086.8	1,092.2	1,091.5	1,092.6	1,100.6	1,122.1	1,141.4	1,095.5
2008	1,093.6	1,085.0	1,080.7	1,076.9	1,076.1	1,076.6	1,072.8	1,067.3	1,062.9	1,064.5	1,068.5	1,073.5	1,074.9
2009	1,027.2	1,010.2	1,001.9	988.7	988.7	985.2	973.4	972.6	975.4	980.6	994.6	1,007.3	992.2
2010	977.1	970.7	969.1	974.4	979.3	981.5	979.5	982.1	980.5	989.3	1,006.9	1,020.5	984.2
2011	987.4	983.9	981.4	982.0	985.9	987.4	988.8	992.2	997.2	1,001.9	1,021.7	1,029.3	994.9
Wholesale Trade													
2000	295.9	297.3	298.0	295.9	295.9	297.1	297.2	297.8	298.1	298.4	298.7	299.6	297.5
2001	300.5	302.7	303.1	302.8	301.6	303.6	301.2	299.8	299.6	300.4	298.6	299.2	301.1
2002	294.0	295.4	297.4	297.1	297.4	298.4	297.9	298.5	299.1	298.1	298.7	300.0	297.7
2003	295.7	296.3	297.1	295.8	295.8	296.6	294.6	294.4	294.5	293.7	293.0	294.7	295.2
2004	292.2	293.3	295.0	294.9	295.6	297.3	295.8	294.9	294.5	296.9	297.2	297.1	295.4
2005	295.8	296.7	297.8	299.6	300.5	301.3	300.4	300.4	300.6	301.7	301.9	304.5	300.1
2006	301.3	303.5	304.8	305.3	306.3	307.7	308.1	308.1	309.2	309.7	310.0	312.3	307.2
2007	311.0	312.5	313.9	313.4	313.3	313.8	314.0	313.6	314.0	315.3	315.0	316.8	313.9
2008	313.9	314.6	315.0	314.6	313.0	312.8	310.6	308.7	307.9	306.7	303.7	302.4	310.3
2009	295.4	292.9	290.7	287.0	285.6	284.6	279.8	278.4	277.4	278.6	277.6	278.6	283.9
2010	277.0	277.4	278.1	280.1	281.2	281.6	281.3	281.5	281.4	283.5	283.5	284.3	280.9
2011	281.1	282.3	282.3	283.6	284.6	284.4	284.9	286.1	286.9	287.8	288.2	288.6	285.1
Retail Trade													
2000	533.9	529.5	530.4	527.2	529.0	533.9	533.6	536.7	539.6	544.0	561.2	579.0	539.8
2001	549.5	540.5	541.3	536.5	537.7	540.8	537.2	539.6	540.7	541.8	558.3	575.1	544.9
2002	545.3	536.9	540.0	539.1	541.9	546.5	543.5	545.1	548.6	551.4	569.0	587.4	549.6
2003	549.1	542.9	543.0	540.9	543.1	546.3	543.5	545.5	547.9	564.6	571.3	587.2	552.1
2004	548.9	544.2	546.2	548.6	552.3	556.1	554.0	556.1	556.4	561.7	581.9	596.7	558.6
2005	566.7	558.9	558.6	556.1	559.0	563.2	566.8	570.2	573.3	579.7	600.4	617.4	572.5
2006	580.6	572.7	574.5	571.9	573.5	576.6	576.6	580.8	581.9	588.2	608.6	622.7	584.1
2007	587.4	576.9	576.5	573.4	575.5	579.2	583.0	585.1	583.0	589.1	610.6	626.3	587.2
2008	588.6	577.0	575.6	571.2	569.7	570.5	567.8	564.5	563.3	564.7	573.4	579.4	572.1
2009	546.5	534.4	528.9	522.2	523.4	522.3	517.8	519.2	521.7	524.9	539.9	550.2	529.3
2010	525.2	517.9	516.5	519.3	520.5	521.7	521.4	523.3	521.6	526.4	544.2	554.9	526.1
2011	529.8	523.1	521.9	522.3	524.2	526.0	527.5	529.2	532.9	536.3	554.8	561.4	532.5
Transportation and Utilities													
2000	201.7	202.5	202.6	204.1	204.4	204.7	203.3	204.2	204.9	208.6	208.9	209.6	205.0
2001	207.9	206.9	208.9	209.1	208.3	207.5	205.8	205.2	206.1	204.6	200.9	200.1	205.9
2002	194.2	195.6	192.9	195.9	196.9	197.1	195.6	196.8	196.6	196.3	195.9	197.1	195.9
2003	192.5	192.2	191.7	190.8	190.9	190.7	189.5	188.6	190.8	190.2	190.2	188.2	190.5
2004	187.1	186.8	188.3	188.9	189.2	189.6	190.1	190.0	191.8	194.7	195.1	192.4	190.3
2005	189.7	190.3	189.1	190.3	189.7	189.7	190.3	189.8	190.2	192.1	191.5	192.5	190.4
2006	190.4	191.2	191.9	191.5	191.9	192.8	193.2	193.4	195.3	195.6	196.6	197.6	193.5
2007	193.6	193.7	190.6	193.8	193.7	193.8	195.2	192.8	195.6	196.2	196.5	198.3	194.5
2008	191.1	193.4	190.1	191.1	193.4	193.3	194.4	194.1	191.7	193.1	191.4	191.7	192.4
2009	185.3	182.9	182.3	179.5	179.7	178.3	175.8	175.0	176.3	177.1	177.1	178.5	179.0
2010	174.9	175.4	174.5	175.0	177.6	178.2	176.8	177.3	177.5	179.4	179.2	181.3	177.3
2011	176.5	178.5	177.2	176.1	177.1	177.0	176.4	176.9	177.4	177.8	178.7	179.3	177.4
Information													
2000	272.2	277.9	280.3	279.4	282.0	282.0	283.6	290.3	288.6	291.6	299.4	294.2	285.1
2001	282.1	285.8	287.3	277.0	265.3	264.8	256.9	256.3	257.3	253.3	255.4	255.9	266.5
2002	247.2	249.4	257.3	245.3	244.6	245.1	235.2	242.3	235.5	242.6	250.0	234.3	244.1
2003	237.1	241.5	239.6	233.7	237.1	229.3	230.1	241.8	230.9	241.9	246.8	240.9	237.6
2004	246.6	249.6	245.5	241.4	249.4	238.3	241.4	243.1	235.2	249.2	257.1	248.1	245.6
2005	238.6	240.3	245.0	237.9	236.7	236.7	234.5	240.5	240.8	241.0	247.8	244.3	240.3
2006	238.9	245.8	245.1	239.0	239.5	240.9	234.5	235.3	232.2	230.4	230.9	236.8	237.4
2007	234.7	241.2	248.9	237.6	241.1	243.4	240.2	244.2	244.5	233.5	238.0	244.6	241.0
2008	226.6	234.8	243.4	242.6	246.6	248.9	240.1	241.4	245.3	242.4	236.5	237.7	240.4
2009	218.5	221.8	225.4	217.8	216.7	219.3	215.3	216.6	220.9	212.4	215.2	222.6	218.5
2010	211.8	212.4	216.0	210.5	211.4	215.2	215.5	220.4	222.4	216.1	218.7	225.0	216.3
2011	219.0	218.4	219.6	216.7	215.4	215.2	214.9	219.7	219.8	220.4	223.5	229.7	219.4

Employment by Industry: Los Angeles–Long Beach–Santa Ana, CA, Selected Years, 2000–2011—*Continued*

(Numbers in thousands, not seasonally adjusted)

Industry and year	January	February	March	April	May	June	July	August	September	October	November	December	Annual average
Financial Activities													
2000	321.4	323.5	323.8	323.5	323.7	325.2	322.0	324.0	323.5	323.7	323.2	326.5	323.7
2001	327.9	330.8	333.2	331.3	331.6	333.5	331.1	334.1	333.7	335.6	336.1	338.9	333.2
2002	334.2	336.5	337.6	337.8	338.7	340.5	340.7	342.3	342.9	344.3	346.7	349.4	341.0
2003	349.1	351.3	353.7	356.5	358.9	360.9	362.1	364.8	364.7	365.5	365.7	367.8	360.1
2004	367.3	368.7	370.6	370.6	370.4	371.5	372.9	373.2	372.3	374.0	374.9	376.6	371.9
2005	373.0	374.6	376.4	378.1	379.0	379.8	380.7	382.1	382.8	385.0	385.6	388.4	380.5
2006	384.4	385.4	386.4	385.7	386.5	385.5	384.4	384.6	383.9	383.8	383.1	384.9	384.9
2007	380.0	381.1	381.4	377.6	375.3	373.1	371.5	369.4	364.8	363.6	361.0	359.1	371.5
2008	353.8	353.7	352.8	350.7	349.5	348.4	346.9	344.9	341.5	339.4	337.6	337.5	346.4
2009	330.7	328.6	327.8	324.9	322.5	322.1	319.4	317.5	314.8	315.3	314.3	315.4	321.1
2010	310.8	310.9	311.8	311.9	311.9	313.0	313.5	313.5	313.1	314.1	314.2	316.6	312.9
2011	312.7	312.9	313.7	311.4	311.8	313.0	314.8	314.1	312.2	314.1	313.5	315.9	313.3
Professional and Business Services													
2000	809.0	818.1	825.1	832.5	829.5	836.7	839.8	847.0	850.0	849.5	850.9	853.1	836.8
2001	836.5	841.7	848.1	835.6	841.1	838.5	833.6	839.5	835.8	830.7	826.9	829.1	836.4
2002	812.1	815.5	824.2	823.0	823.9	824.3	820.3	826.7	827.7	829.3	828.3	830.6	823.8
2003	806.4	808.9	816.0	812.7	811.7	812.2	808.7	815.7	813.0	813.8	813.8	817.1	812.5
2004	794.8	801.0	808.3	810.0	814.5	818.9	820.8	823.9	821.4	828.9	831.5	834.1	817.3
2005	820.8	827.2	829.6	835.1	834.9	838.7	838.4	845.0	849.0	852.5	855.4	859.0	840.5
2006	846.1	856.3	862.1	865.2	866.4	875.7	875.8	882.6	883.5	889.4	889.0	888.8	873.4
2007	866.5	875.9	881.5	871.5	872.0	878.8	876.4	881.1	882.8	885.4	884.8	887.9	878.7
2008	851.0	859.8	862.1	859.9	855.2	854.8	851.6	850.4	845.9	842.7	831.4	825.6	849.2
2009	795.2	790.6	785.0	771.9	767.8	765.2	754.8	755.8	754.9	766.0	766.4	766.0	770.0
2010	752.1	758.0	759.8	765.8	765.7	770.3	767.5	772.4	770.6	790.8	789.1	789.5	771.0
2011	771.1	779.1	781.1	779.8	779.5	784.6	782.3	784.7	795.0	804.2	799.0	805.3	787.1
Education and Health Services													
2000	519.6	530.2	534.9	537.4	535.3	528.2	520.5	522.0	533.6	536.6	537.9	540.4	531.4
2001	531.1	543.3	548.9	548.4	548.4	541.6	537.3	539.6	551.0	561.7	564.3	566.5	548.5
2002	554.6	564.9	568.8	574.2	573.8	566.1	558.5	559.9	573.1	582.1	585.1	586.3	570.6
2003	572.1	583.1	587.8	592.3	591.3	583.8	577.1	578.3	591.7	600.5	601.7	603.7	588.6
2004	590.4	601.7	606.1	606.6	603.9	594.6	586.2	587.0	599.8	606.8	607.4	608.6	599.9
2005	596.7	605.9	608.3	612.2	610.8	603.1	590.6	592.3	608.7	615.7	617.4	618.8	606.7
2006	605.9	617.8	620.8	622.6	621.1	613.5	601.7	603.8	620.9	629.7	631.2	632.5	618.5
2007	620.9	632.9	636.6	634.4	635.8	626.6	620.7	620.6	639.6	649.1	652.1	653.2	635.4
2008	643.0	655.1	657.7	660.6	658.0	648.1	641.9	641.0	659.6	668.3	671.7	673.0	656.5
2009	656.5	668.0	671.1	671.5	670.0	659.4	651.3	649.4	665.4	677.9	679.3	681.4	666.8
2010	665.4	674.9	680.3	685.5	681.8	670.7	659.0	661.2	678.3	687.7	691.1	694.0	677.5
2011	682.5	694.9	698.5	699.1	696.2	683.5	678.7	676.9	695.2	704.8	707.3	705.1	693.6
Leisure and Hospitality													
2000	463.7	471.5	477.0	480.2	486.9	491.7	495.3	497.0	495.7	488.9	486.5	490.6	485.4
2001	484.9	490.1	495.3	502.9	506.1	512.4	512.3	512.4	506.4	505.5	503.0	502.4	502.8
2002	490.7	495.7	501.5	507.9	513.4	516.5	519.9	520.1	517.7	513.0	508.2	511.2	509.7
2003	499.7	505.0	509.3	516.9	522.7	528.8	531.6	532.2	528.1	527.5	524.7	527.5	521.2
2004	518.4	524.6	529.4	531.9	538.0	541.1	546.6	544.9	540.3	539.0	535.4	538.2	535.7
2005	522.0	526.6	533.5	541.5	544.9	551.2	552.9	551.3	548.0	546.7	544.9	549.3	542.7
2006	536.4	541.3	547.8	554.7	560.5	567.3	567.0	568.1	563.8	564.8	560.8	565.1	558.1
2007	550.4	553.3	560.0	568.0	572.7	579.6	581.7	580.2	575.9	577.4	573.8	576.6	570.8
2008	562.8	566.3	573.2	581.5	585.0	590.6	592.2	588.0	581.1	576.5	569.4	569.3	578.0
2009	550.6	548.8	551.2	554.3	561.0	562.0	562.6	559.3	555.9	554.7	547.4	548.3	554.7
2010	533.3	534.9	539.1	551.7	556.7	562.1	565.3	564.6	561.5	559.0	554.7	558.2	553.4
2011	547.5	551.2	555.6	564.8	570.1	573.6	574.2	569.1	572.4	574.1	570.3	568.4	565.9
Other Services													
2000	179.6	181.0	183.5	183.9	184.8	187.3	185.2	184.9	186.0	184.5	184.4	184.8	184.2
2001	185.0	186.6	188.8	188.8	189.7	191.3	188.4	187.7	188.0	189.3	188.4	188.0	188.3
2002	185.5	188.0	189.6	190.4	192.4	193.3	192.6	192.2	193.4	193.7	192.8	193.3	191.4
2003	189.8	191.2	192.4	192.4	193.4	194.7	191.5	191.3	192.8	192.7	191.8	192.0	192.2
2004	189.1	190.5	192.4	192.6	193.6	194.3	192.6	191.2	192.7	191.9	191.5	192.0	192.0
2005	189.3	191.4	193.2	193.9	194.2	195.5	191.8	191.5	193.0	192.7	192.3	192.6	192.6
2006	189.8	191.6	192.9	192.2	193.9	195.5	192.0	192.0	194.2	193.7	193.8	193.7	192.9
2007	190.2	192.6	194.0	194.1	194.7	196.5	194.5	194.2	195.8	196.4	195.6	195.5	194.5
2008	192.3	193.3	194.5	195.2	195.3	195.2	193.4	190.8	191.4	191.7	189.7	188.6	192.6
2009	183.5	183.2	183.7	181.5	181.9	182.1	178.8	177.1	177.3	179.9	178.6	178.4	180.5
2010	175.7	175.4	176.6	179.4	180.3	181.1	180.1	178.5	179.9	180.7	179.5	178.6	178.8
2011	176.4	178.0	178.5	179.3	179.8	180.0	177.6	175.9	176.0	177.5	176.9	177.8	177.8
Government													
2000	718.2	728.1	736.5	739.5	759.0	733.9	697.8	688.4	717.6	731.3	742.2	741.5	727.8
2001	740.3	747.9	758.7	759.9	761.9	764.0	717.4	714.1	738.0	758.6	763.2	765.9	749.2
2002	759.1	763.4	774.1	773.4	776.5	773.6	730.2	721.7	749.5	768.0	773.1	771.5	761.2
2003	762.8	766.5	773.8	768.6	768.1	767.1	734.0	716.4	731.8	749.0	753.2	750.3	753.5
2004	747.0	748.3	754.8	753.6	754.8	752.7	718.1	700.8	723.9	741.3	747.1	743.6	740.5
2005	738.3	745.5	750.2	747.8	750.2	750.1	715.1	706.0	724.6	741.8	749.7	748.4	739.0
2006	741.4	748.7	754.7	754.0	756.5	756.3	724.7	712.0	733.4	753.0	760.3	758.5	746.1
2007	751.6	757.8	763.9	762.8	765.0	765.2	732.6	719.8	741.9	761.7	769.6	768.8	755.1
2008	762.7	770.7	775.4	776.2	780.0	778.3	740.1	728.2	747.2	768.5	774.9	771.5	764.5
2009	766.9	770.6	775.9	777.6	775.1	774.0	727.7	704.4	711.6	748.1	750.2	747.2	752.4
2010	741.0	743.8	748.7	756.9	770.8	757.2	700.9	676.8	694.4	727.6	733.6	730.7	731.9
2011	724.9	727.8	734.4	733.6	734.6	734.9	687.6	654.9	680.7	717.4	725.7	720.9	714.8

Employment by Industry: Louisville–Jefferson County, KY–IN, Selected Years, 2000–2011

(Numbers in thousands, not seasonally adjusted)

Industry and year	January	February	March	April	May	June	July	August	September	October	November	December	Annual average
Total Nonfarm													
2000	609.9	612.0	617.4	619.6	624.7	629.6	620.7	623.6	622.3	621.1	622.3	621.7	620.4
2001	605.0	606.0	608.3	611.5	615.9	615.1	606.3	609.6	607.0	605.5	605.7	602.4	608.2
2002	586.1	587.1	591.2	596.0	601.4	601.9	594.6	600.6	599.9	600.6	602.5	602.7	597.1
2003	585.5	585.5	590.9	594.2	599.0	601.7	591.3	596.9	598.1	599.3	601.4	603.5	595.6
2004	586.4	587.7	593.2	597.5	599.5	602.9	593.2	603.1	604.2	606.2	609.6	609.3	599.4
2005	591.4	594.4	598.1	604.2	608.2	613.2	601.9	609.7	612.5	613.6	617.2	615.9	606.7
2006	600.9	603.3	611.4	615.7	621.8	625.3	611.1	620.3	622.7	616.5	619.5	626.4	616.2
2007	611.6	611.7	615.0	623.4	631.6	635.8	623.1	626.3	628.8	627.2	633.0	630.7	624.9
2008	615.2	615.6	617.8	623.2	633.0	631.7	619.5	624.4	619.5	618.4	621.5	615.5	621.3
2009	592.0	591.4	593.0	597.4	599.6	599.0	592.6	595.0	595.1	596.0	597.4	595.3	595.3
2010	579.0	573.7	584.5	592.0	599.0	599.2	591.0	593.9	595.5	599.2	602.7	604.5	592.9
2011	584.0	585.9	591.0	598.1	600.5	603.5	595.7	601.2	603.0	607.7	608.1	609.8	599.0
Total Private													
2000	534.7	534.9	539.6	540.6	543.9	549.0	547.0	547.6	545.7	544.3	545.5	545.1	543.2
2001	528.9	528.9	530.9	533.4	537.5	538.4	533.9	534.1	529.0	527.8	527.3	524.8	531.2
2002	510.3	510.1	514.1	518.3	524.1	525.8	523.6	526.5	523.6	523.6	525.4	525.7	520.9
2003	509.9	509.0	513.8	515.6	520.4	523.3	520.1	522.8	521.4	522.1	523.9	526.7	519.1
2004	511.1	510.9	516.0	519.8	522.1	525.7	520.6	528.4	526.7	528.9	531.9	532.4	522.9
2005	514.8	517.0	520.3	526.1	529.7	535.1	527.8	533.6	533.9	534.9	538.2	537.2	529.1
2006	523.1	524.5	532.3	536.2	541.9	546.0	535.6	542.1	541.6	536.5	539.3	546.6	537.1
2007	533.2	532.5	535.4	542.4	550.3	554.8	546.5	547.4	548.2	547.2	552.6	550.2	545.1
2008	535.1	534.5	536.4	541.9	551.3	550.5	542.8	545.6	538.7	537.1	540.0	534.4	540.7
2009	512.0	511.3	512.4	515.8	517.5	517.8	514.7	514.7	512.3	512.4	514.2	513.1	514.0
2010	497.6	492.0	501.1	507.5	512.6	514.7	511.2	513.5	513.5	516.8	520.4	523.0	510.3
2011	503.0	504.3	509.1	516.7	519.3	523.1	518.8	521.9	521.9	526.1	526.5	528.9	518.3
Goods-Producing													
2000	128.6	128.4	129.9	130.0	130.3	131.3	132.1	131.7	131.6	131.6	131.4	131.3	130.7
2001	126.6	126.9	127.2	128.1	128.4	128.6	126.7	126.0	124.8	124.5	123.0	121.5	126.0
2002	117.5	117.2	117.5	118.6	118.5	119.6	119.6	120.6	120.4	119.8	119.1	118.8	118.9
2003	114.3	113.7	114.3	114.4	114.8	115.5	115.3	115.8	115.7	116.7	115.7	116.5	115.2
2004	113.9	112.7	113.7	115.6	115.9	116.6	110.6	117.2	117.3	116.8	117.0	116.2	115.3
2005	112.8	112.9	113.7	114.9	115.2	116.9	111.3	116.0	115.5	115.4	115.7	114.5	114.6
2006	112.1	111.8	112.5	113.3	114.3	115.6	109.4	115.2	114.7	109.6	109.3	113.3	112.6
2007	110.2	109.4	107.8	112.1	113.7	115.3	109.5	110.6	113.6	109.2	112.7	109.7	111.2
2008	108.0	108.2	108.5	108.2	111.6	110.5	105.8	108.4	106.1	105.0	107.3	102.7	107.5
2009	97.0	97.1	95.9	96.9	95.9	95.7	94.2	95.1	94.6	94.1	93.4	92.3	95.2
2010	88.9	84.0	88.7	89.5	90.3	91.0	88.6	91.0	91.4	91.2	91.0	90.4	89.7
2011	86.6	86.7	87.6	89.2	89.6	91.1	88.0	89.8	90.6	89.8	87.7	89.1	88.8
Mining and Logging													
2000	31.8	31.9	33.4	34.0	34.5	35.1	35.5	35.0	34.9	34.4	34.0	33.8	34.0
2001	31.0	31.6	32.2	33.9	34.7	35.5	35.5	35.0	34.1	33.8	33.1	32.2	33.6
2002	30.4	30.7	31.1	31.9	32.6	33.6	33.9	34.2	34.3	33.8	33.6	33.1	32.8
2003	30.8	30.3	31.2	32.1	32.4	32.9	33.4	33.4	33.2	34.2	33.6	33.6	32.6
2004	31.6	31.0	32.1	33.7	34.1	35.0	36.0	35.6	35.7	35.3	35.0	34.4	34.1
2005	31.5	32.1	32.8	34.1	34.7	36.2	37.1	36.2	35.8	35.9	35.5	34.8	34.7
2006	32.5	32.2	32.9	33.4	34.1	34.6	34.7	34.4	34.1	33.6	33.2	33.0	33.6
2007	30.7	30.2	31.8	33.2	34.3	35.2	35.8	35.6	35.5	35.2	35.0	34.3	33.9
2008	32.2	31.9	32.4	34.0	35.2	35.8	35.8	35.8	35.5	35.3	34.6	33.8	34.4
2009	31.3	30.6	30.5	30.9	30.8	31.0	31.2	31.0	30.8	30.8	30.0	28.8	30.6
2010	26.1	25.1	25.8	26.8	26.8	27.3	27.9	27.4	27.0	26.7	26.2	25.3	26.5
2011	23.2	23.1	24.3	25.3	25.6	26.6	25.9	26.0	26.1	25.7	24.9	25.6	25.2
Construction													
2000	143.1	141.6	142.1	142.4	143.0	143.8	143.7	143.9	142.7	143.1	145.2	146.3	143.4
2001	142.3	140.6	139.9	139.3	139.7	139.3	139.1	139.1	138.0	139.2	140.4	140.7	139.8
2002	135.1	133.8	134.6	134.6	135.4	136.0	135.5	135.9	135.1	134.9	137.3	138.4	135.6
2003	131.2	130.3	130.7	130.1	131.0	131.1	130.5	131.4	131.3	132.3	134.3	136.1	131.7
2004	130.5	129.5	130.2	129.6	130.4	131.2	131.3	131.7	131.4	132.6	134.2	135.4	131.5
2005	130.9	130.0	130.9	131.6	132.4	132.8	132.8	133.0	133.5	134.7	137.8	139.4	133.3
2006	133.9	133.0	135.0	135.5	137.1	138.0	136.4	136.9	137.0	137.5	140.6	142.9	137.0
2007	138.1	136.9	137.8	137.9	139.2	140.7	139.3	139.6	139.8	141.5	143.5	145.2	140.0
2008	138.5	136.6	136.4	136.9	138.4	138.1	136.9	137.4	135.4	135.3	137.6	139.8	137.3
2009	131.1	129.3	129.3	128.7	129.4	129.6	128.2	128.0	127.7	128.4	130.8	132.7	129.4
2010	126.2	125.0	126.1	127.7	128.7	129.3	129.5	130.3	130.1	132.1	135.1	138.5	129.9
2011	130.6	130.0	130.9	131.6	132.0	133.1	132.8	132.6	132.6	133.0	135.0	138.3	132.7
Manufacturing													
2000	31.4	31.5	31.6	31.4	31.5	31.5	31.2	31.3	31.2	31.4	31.4	31.3	31.4
2001	31.1	31.1	31.0	30.7	30.8	30.6	30.6	30.4	30.3	30.3	29.6	29.5	30.5
2002	29.3	29.3	29.2	29.2	29.3	29.1	29.1	29.6	28.9	29.0	28.9	28.9	29.2
2003	28.5	28.7	28.7	28.5	28.7	28.8	28.7	28.8	29.0	28.9	29.1	29.5	28.8
2004	29.1	29.1	29.2	29.2	29.2	29.3	29.5	29.5	29.3	29.4	29.4	29.5	29.3
2005	29.3	29.4	29.5	29.4	29.5	29.6	29.7	29.6	29.6	29.6	29.7	29.8	29.6
2006	29.9	29.9	30.1	30.0	30.2	30.4	30.1	30.2	30.1	30.2	30.3	30.4	30.2
2007	30.3	30.4	30.5	30.3	30.3	30.4	30.2	30.2	30.2	30.3	30.1	30.2	30.3
2008	29.9	30.0	29.9	30.0	30.1	30.1	30.0	30.0	29.9	29.8	29.6	29.5	29.9
2009	28.7	28.5	28.3	28.3	28.2	28.0	27.9	27.9	28.0	28.0	27.9	27.9	28.1
2010	27.5	27.5	27.7	27.6	27.7	27.8	28.0	28.1	28.0	28.1	28.1	28.0	27.8
2011	27.9	28.0	28.1	28.0	28.1	28.3	27.7	27.9	27.6	27.7	28.1	28.4	28.0

Employment by Industry: Louisville–Jefferson County, KY–IN, Selected Years, 2000–2011—*Continued*

(Numbers in thousands, not seasonally adjusted)

Industry and year	January	February	March	April	May	June	July	August	September	October	November	December	Annual average
Service-Providing													
2000	481.3	483.6	487.5	489.6	494.4	498.3	488.6	491.9	490.7	489.5	490.9	490.4	489.7
2001	478.4	479.1	481.1	483.4	487.5	486.5	479.6	483.6	482.2	481.0	482.7	480.9	482.2
2002	468.6	469.9	473.7	477.4	482.9	482.3	475.0	480.0	479.5	480.8	483.4	483.9	478.1
2003	471.2	471.8	476.6	479.8	484.2	486.2	476.0	481.1	482.4	482.6	485.7	487.0	480.4
2004	472.5	475.0	479.5	481.9	483.6	486.3	482.6	485.9	486.9	489.4	492.6	493.1	484.1
2005	478.6	481.5	484.4	489.3	493.0	496.3	490.6	493.7	497.0	498.2	501.5	501.4	492.1
2006	488.8	491.5	498.9	502.4	507.5	509.7	501.7	505.1	508.0	506.9	510.2	513.1	503.7
2007	501.4	502.3	507.2	511.3	517.9	520.5	513.6	515.7	515.2	518.0	520.3	521.0	513.7
2008	507.2	507.4	509.3	515.0	521.4	521.2	513.7	516.0	513.4	513.4	514.2	512.8	513.8
2009	495.0	494.3	497.1	500.5	503.7	503.3	498.4	499.9	500.5	501.9	504.0	503.0	500.1
2010	490.1	489.7	495.8	502.5	508.7	508.2	502.4	502.9	504.1	508.0	511.7	514.1	503.2
2011	497.4	499.2	503.4	508.9	510.9	512.4	507.7	511.4	512.4	517.9	520.4	520.7	510.2
Trade, Transportation, and Utilities													
2000	70.5	69.5	70.0	69.3	70.1	71.2	69.8	70.2	69.7	68.8	71.3	72.8	70.3
2001	69.0	67.8	67.8	67.6	68.4	68.7	67.8	68.1	67.6	68.4	70.3	71.2	68.6
2002	66.7	65.8	66.7	66.7	67.4	68.2	67.5	67.3	67.1	66.7	69.4	70.7	67.5
2003	65.4	64.4	64.8	64.7	65.5	65.7	65.2	65.6	65.4	65.9	68.0	69.3	65.8
2004	64.9	64.0	64.5	64.2	64.8	65.3	65.2	65.4	65.3	65.7	67.5	68.7	65.5
2005	65.0	63.9	64.4	64.8	65.3	65.5	65.2	65.0	64.9	65.7	67.9	69.2	65.6
2006	65.2	64.3	65.2	65.3	65.7	65.4	64.7	64.3	63.8	64.4	66.7	67.7	65.2
2007	64.7	63.7	64.4	64.3	65.1	65.7	65.6	65.3	65.0	65.2	67.3	67.9	65.4
2008	64.6	63.7	64.2	63.8	64.6	64.6	64.4	64.4	63.3	63.5	65.0	65.6	64.3
2009	61.6	60.4	60.7	60.7	61.3	61.5	61.0	60.7	60.3	61.0	62.7	63.4	61.3
2010	59.9	59.1	59.8	60.0	60.5	60.6	60.6	60.8	60.1	61.3	62.9	63.6	60.8
2011	60.2	59.6	60.2	60.9	61.1	61.1	61.9	61.6	61.5	62.1	63.3	64.7	61.5
Wholesale Trade													
2000	41.2	40.6	40.5	41.7	41.4	41.1	42.7	42.4	41.8	42.9	42.5	42.2	41.8
2001	42.2	41.7	41.1	41.0	40.5	40.0	40.7	40.6	40.1	40.5	40.5	40.0	40.7
2002	39.1	38.7	38.7	38.7	38.7	38.7	38.9	39.0	39.1	39.2	39.0	38.8	38.9
2003	37.3	37.2	37.2	36.9	36.8	36.6	36.6	37.0	36.9	37.5	37.2	37.3	37.0
2004	36.5	36.4	36.5	36.2	36.4	36.6	36.6	36.8	36.8	37.5	37.3	37.2	36.7
2005	36.6	36.7	37.0	37.4	37.6	37.7	37.9	38.4	39.0	39.4	40.2	40.4	38.2
2006	38.8	38.8	39.7	40.2	41.2	42.2	41.6	42.4	43.1	42.9	43.6	44.8	41.6
2007	43.1	42.8	42.9	43.3	43.8	44.6	43.5	44.1	44.6	46.0	46.1	47.1	44.3
2008	44.0	42.9	42.3	43.1	43.7	43.4	42.5	43.0	42.2	42.0	43.0	44.7	43.1
2009	40.8	40.4	40.3	39.7	39.9	40.1	39.3	39.4	39.4	39.4	40.2	41.4	40.0
2010	38.8	38.4	38.6	40.1	40.5	40.9	40.9	41.4	42.0	42.7	44.1	46.9	41.3
2011	42.5	42.4	42.6	42.7	42.8	43.7	43.2	43.1	43.5	43.2	43.6	45.2	43.2
Retail Trade													
2000	12.1	12.0	12.0	12.0	12.0	12.1	12.0	12.0	12.0	12.0	12.0	12.0	12.0
2001	11.9	11.9	12.0	11.9	11.9	11.9	11.9	11.9	11.9	11.9	11.9	11.9	11.9
2002	11.9	11.9	12.0	11.5	11.3	11.4	11.4	11.2	11.2	11.1	11.2	11.3	11.5
2003	11.2	11.2	11.4	10.9	11.0	11.0	11.0	10.8	10.6	10.6	10.5	10.6	10.9
2004	10.4	10.4	10.3	10.2	10.2	10.3	10.3	10.2	10.1	10.0	10.1	10.2	10.2
2005	9.8	9.8	9.8	9.9	10.0	10.1	10.2	10.2	10.1	10.0	10.1	10.2	10.0
2006	9.9	10.0	10.0	10.0	10.1	10.2	10.2	10.2	10.1	10.3	10.3	10.5	10.2
2007	10.5	10.5	10.5	10.5	10.6	10.6	10.7	10.6	10.5	10.4	10.4	10.4	10.5
2008	10.4	10.3	10.4	10.4	10.6	10.9	10.8	10.7	10.5	10.3	10.3	10.2	10.5
2009	10.1	10.0	10.0	9.8	9.9	9.9	9.9	9.9	9.7	9.6	9.7	9.7	9.9
2010	9.4	9.4	9.5	9.5	9.5	9.6	9.5	9.5	9.4	9.3	9.4	9.5	9.5
2011	9.4	9.3	9.3	9.4	9.5	9.4	9.4	9.3	9.2	9.2	9.2	9.2	9.3
Transportation and Utilities													
2000	38.0	38.2	37.8	37.8	37.8	38.8	37.3	37.5	37.2	36.9	37.0	37.0	37.6
2001	37.1	37.0	37.3	37.4	37.6	38.0	37.9	38.0	37.7	37.7	37.7	37.9	37.6
2002	38.0	38.2	38.2	38.4	38.6	38.6	37.8	37.9	38.3	38.1	38.2	38.3	38.2
2003	37.7	37.7	38.0	38.2	38.6	39.1	39.2	39.4	39.5	39.3	39.3	39.5	38.8
2004	39.2	39.2	39.3	39.1	39.0	39.1	39.3	39.2	38.8	38.7	39.0	39.4	39.1
2005	39.1	39.1	39.0	39.2	39.2	39.9	39.7	40.1	40.1	40.3	40.4	40.6	39.7
2006	40.8	41.1	41.4	41.5	41.8	42.2	41.9	42.0	42.2	42.1	42.5	43.1	41.9
2007	43.0	43.0	43.1	43.3	43.3	43.6	43.7	43.6	43.3	43.5	43.5	43.5	43.4
2008	43.2	43.4	43.3	43.3	43.5	43.4	43.5	43.6	43.4	43.2	43.3	43.2	43.4
2009	42.9	42.7	42.6	42.6	42.6	42.6	42.7	42.7	42.4	42.1	41.9	41.8	42.4
2010	41.5	41.3	41.1	40.7	40.8	40.8	40.7	40.5	40.0	40.3	40.5	40.7	40.7
2011	40.4	40.6	40.6	40.5	40.7	40.9	40.7	40.6	40.5	40.5	40.7	40.8	40.6
Information													
2000	62.6	63.2	64.8	63.5	63.9	64.5	65.5	66.0	66.4	66.8	66.7	66.3	65.0
2001	62.4	62.6	63.2	62.6	62.7	62.8	62.2	63.5	62.9	62.8	62.9	61.8	62.7
2002	60.4	60.5	61.4	61.8	63.4	63.1	62.5	63.9	63.0	63.5	63.8	63.3	62.6
2003	62.6	62.6	63.6	63.8	64.9	64.5	63.2	64.5	64.7	64.7	65.5	65.4	64.2
2004	61.2	62.0	63.2	63.2	63.8	63.8	64.9	66.4	66.9	68.2	69.3	68.9	65.2
2005	65.3	65.9	66.7	67.7	68.0	68.8	68.2	69.0	70.0	70.8	71.8	71.2	68.6
2006	68.0	68.7	71.6	71.2	71.5	72.3	71.5	72.2	73.1	73.0	73.0	73.2	71.6
2007	70.5	71.2	72.6	72.7	74.4	74.6	73.9	74.2	73.9	75.2	75.8	75.2	73.7
2008	72.1	72.2	72.5	74.0	75.3	76.1	74.9	74.7	74.7	74.8	74.5	72.9	74.1
2009	68.6	69.4	69.4	69.6	69.3	69.3	69.9	70.2	70.3	71.5	72.3	71.5	70.1
2010	69.7	69.9	70.7	72.4	72.8	73.2	73.0	72.7	73.9	73.9	74.6	75.2	72.7
2011	70.9	71.8	72.6	73.2	73.6	74.0	74.5	76.5	76.7	79.8	80.1	78.5	75.2

Employment by Industry: Louisville–Jefferson County, KY–IN, Selected Years, 2000–2011—*Continued*

(Numbers in thousands, not seasonally adjusted)

Industry and year	January	February	March	April	May	June	July	August	September	October	November	December	Annual average
Financial Activities													
2000	65.9	66.4	66.2	65.7	65.8	65.8	66.2	66.7	67.0	66.6	66.5	66.5	66.3
2001	66.9	67.1	67.5	67.4	67.4	67.6	67.2	67.2	67.4	68.1	68.1	68.3	67.5
2002	68.3	68.7	68.8	69.6	69.6	69.9	70.6	70.9	71.0	72.1	72.5	72.7	70.4
2003	72.6	72.9	73.4	73.5	73.3	73.3	73.0	73.3	73.8	73.8	73.9	74.2	73.4
2004	74.1	74.3	74.5	74.6	74.5	74.8	75.1	75.0	75.2	76.5	76.6	77.0	75.2
2005	75.5	76.9	76.3	76.4	76.7	76.7	76.7	76.7	76.8	77.0	76.6	76.6	76.6
2006	75.9	76.2	76.5	77.1	76.9	77.0	76.8	76.6	76.8	77.0	76.9	77.4	76.8
2007	76.7	77.1	77.4	77.7	78.3	78.6	79.2	78.8	78.8	79.6	79.4	79.6	78.4
2008	79.2	79.1	79.3	80.3	80.4	80.4	80.3	80.5	80.4	80.9	80.8	80.9	80.2
2009	80.6	80.5	81.0	81.5	81.6	81.8	81.5	82.4	82.7	83.3	83.2	83.4	82.0
2010	82.7	82.8	83.4	83.5	84.0	83.6	83.8	83.9	84.2	84.7	84.9	85.0	83.9
2011	84.3	84.3	84.6	85.1	85.2	85.2	85.1	85.1	85.3	85.8	86.5	85.9	85.2
Professional and Business Services													
2000	55.1	55.4	57.0	59.7	61.6	62.7	61.3	60.9	60.0	58.2	57.5	56.4	58.8
2001	52.8	53.8	54.6	57.6	60.6	60.6	59.4	59.1	57.2	55.1	54.8	53.7	56.6
2002	50.7	51.3	52.9	54.8	58.2	57.5	56.9	56.9	55.6	55.0	54.2	53.6	54.8
2003	51.6	51.9	53.4	55.7	57.6	58.9	58.5	58.3	56.9	55.8	55.9	55.3	55.8
2004	53.3	54.0	55.6	58.1	58.8	60.0	59.8	59.4	58.2	57.5	57.3	56.6	57.4
2005	53.2	54.0	55.3	58.2	59.6	61.1	60.6	60.3	59.7	58.4	57.5	56.3	57.9
2006	54.6	55.6	56.9	59.4	61.9	61.9	61.1	60.9	59.9	59.2	59.0	58.2	59.1
2007	56.5	56.7	58.3	60.1	62.4	62.7	62.1	61.9	60.4	60.0	59.5	58.6	59.9
2008	56.4	57.3	58.5	61.1	63.4	62.9	63.0	62.5	61.2	60.2	59.1	57.8	60.3
2009	55.4	56.0	57.8	60.4	62.6	62.4	62.1	60.7	59.5	58.4	57.9	56.4	59.1
2010	54.4	54.8	56.4	58.9	61.0	61.3	60.5	60.1	59.3	59.9	59.5	58.2	58.7
2011	55.6	56.3	58.0	62.0	63.0	63.3	62.6	62.4	61.7	62.7	62.1	61.8	61.0
Education and Health Services													
2000	29.3	29.7	29.8	29.5	29.5	30.0	28.9	28.9	28.8	29.1	29.2	29.3	29.3
2001	28.9	29.0	29.2	29.1	29.2	29.6	29.5	29.3	29.1	28.5	28.5	29.0	29.1
2002	28.4	28.5	28.7	29.0	29.1	29.7	29.3	29.2	29.0	29.1	29.1	29.3	29.0
2003	28.7	28.7	29.0	29.0	29.2	29.9	29.4	29.3	28.9	28.9	28.8	29.1	29.1
2004	28.5	28.8	29.2	29.4	29.5	29.9	29.3	29.3	28.8	28.6	28.4	28.7	29.0
2005	28.2	28.4	28.6	28.2	28.6	28.8	28.3	28.3	28.2	28.3	28.3	28.4	28.4
2006	27.9	28.1	28.4	28.2	28.3	28.8	28.3	28.1	27.8	27.8	27.7	28.0	28.1
2007	27.7	27.7	27.9	28.1	28.4	28.7	28.1	28.1	27.9	27.8	27.8	28.0	28.0
2008	27.3	27.4	27.5	27.7	28.1	28.2	27.6	27.6	27.0	27.4	27.1	26.9	27.5
2009	26.3	26.3	26.4	26.3	26.2	26.5	26.2	26.0	25.7	25.2	25.1	25.1	25.9
2010	24.8	24.8	25.2	25.3	25.5	25.9	25.6	25.5	25.2	25.4	25.4	25.5	25.3
2011	25.2	25.3	25.5	25.7	25.7	26.1	25.7	25.6	25.3	25.3	25.2	25.3	25.5
Leisure and Hospitality													
2000	75.2	77.1	77.8	79.0	80.8	80.6	73.7	76.0	76.6	76.8	76.8	76.6	77.3
2001	76.1	77.1	77.4	78.1	78.4	76.7	72.4	75.5	78.0	77.7	78.4	77.6	77.0
2002	75.8	77.0	77.1	77.7	77.3	76.1	71.0	74.1	76.3	77.0	77.1	77.0	76.1
2003	75.6	76.5	77.1	78.6	78.6	78.4	71.2	74.1	76.7	77.2	77.5	76.8	76.5
2004	75.3	76.8	77.2	77.7	77.4	77.2	72.6	74.7	77.5	77.3	77.7	76.9	76.5
2005	76.6	77.4	77.8	78.1	78.5	78.1	74.1	76.1	78.6	78.7	79.0	78.7	77.6
2006	77.8	78.8	79.1	79.5	79.9	79.3	75.5	78.2	81.1	80.0	80.2	79.8	79.1
2007	78.4	79.2	79.6	81.0	81.3	81.0	76.6	78.9	80.6	80.0	80.4	80.5	79.8
2008	80.1	81.1	81.4	81.3	81.7	81.2	76.7	78.8	80.8	81.3	81.5	81.1	80.6
2009	80.0	80.1	80.6	81.6	82.1	81.2	77.9	80.3	82.8	83.6	83.2	82.2	81.3
2010	81.4	81.7	83.4	84.5	86.4	84.5	79.8	80.4	82.0	82.4	82.3	81.5	82.5
2011	81.0	81.6	81.9	81.4	81.2	80.4	76.9	79.3	81.1	81.6	81.6	80.9	80.7
Other Services													
2000	179.6	181.0	183.5	183.9	184.8	187.3	185.2	184.9	186.0	184.5	184.4	184.8	184.2
2001	185.0	186.6	188.8	188.8	189.7	191.3	188.4	187.7	188.0	189.3	188.4	188.0	188.3
2002	185.5	188.0	189.6	190.4	192.4	193.3	192.6	192.2	193.4	193.7	192.8	193.3	191.4
2003	189.8	191.2	192.4	192.4	193.4	194.7	191.5	191.3	192.8	192.7	191.8	192.0	192.2
2004	189.1	190.5	192.4	192.6	193.6	194.3	192.6	191.2	192.7	191.9	191.5	192.0	192.0
2005	189.3	191.4	193.2	193.9	194.2	195.5	191.8	191.5	193.0	192.7	192.3	192.6	192.6
2006	189.8	191.6	192.9	192.2	193.9	195.5	192.0	192.0	194.2	193.7	193.8	193.7	192.9
2007	190.2	192.6	194.0	194.1	194.7	196.5	194.5	194.2	195.8	196.4	195.6	195.5	194.5
2008	192.3	193.3	194.5	195.2	195.3	195.2	193.4	190.8	191.4	191.7	189.7	188.6	192.6
2009	183.5	183.2	183.7	181.5	181.9	182.1	178.8	177.1	177.3	179.9	178.6	178.4	180.5
2010	175.7	175.4	176.6	179.4	180.3	181.1	180.1	178.5	179.9	180.7	179.5	178.6	178.8
2011	176.4	178.0	178.5	179.3	179.8	180.0	177.6	175.9	176.0	177.5	176.9	177.8	177.8
Government													
2000	718.2	728.1	736.5	739.5	759.0	733.9	697.8	688.4	717.6	731.3	742.2	741.5	727.8
2001	740.3	747.9	758.7	759.9	761.9	764.0	717.4	714.1	738.0	758.6	763.2	765.9	749.2
2002	759.1	763.4	774.1	773.4	776.5	773.6	730.2	721.7	749.5	768.0	773.1	771.5	761.2
2003	762.8	766.5	773.8	768.6	768.1	767.1	734.0	716.4	731.8	749.0	753.2	750.3	753.5
2004	747.0	748.3	754.8	753.6	754.8	752.7	718.1	700.8	723.9	741.3	747.1	743.6	740.5
2005	738.3	745.5	750.2	747.8	750.2	750.1	715.1	706.0	724.6	741.8	749.7	748.4	739.0
2006	741.4	748.7	754.7	754.0	756.5	756.3	724.7	712.0	733.4	753.0	760.3	758.5	746.1
2007	751.6	757.8	763.9	762.8	765.0	765.2	732.6	719.8	741.9	761.7	769.6	768.8	755.1
2008	762.7	770.7	775.4	776.2	780.0	778.3	740.1	728.2	747.2	768.5	774.9	771.5	764.5
2009	766.9	770.6	775.9	777.6	775.1	774.0	727.7	704.4	711.6	748.1	750.2	747.2	752.4
2010	741.0	743.8	748.7	756.9	770.8	757.2	700.9	676.8	694.4	727.6	733.6	730.7	731.9
2011	724.9	727.8	734.4	733.6	734.6	734.9	687.6	654.9	680.7	717.4	725.7	720.9	714.8

Employment by Industry: McAllen–Edinburg–Mission, TX, Selected Years, 2000–2011

(Numbers in thousands, not seasonally adjusted)

Industry and year	January	February	March	April	May	June	July	August	September	October	November	December	Annual average
Total Nonfarm													
2000	152.9	155.2	157.3	157.1	157.5	157.2	153.0	154.5	157.2	158.2	160.7	162.4	156.9
2001	160.1	161.2	163.0	163.5	163.7	162.9	156.4	158.8	161.6	163.6	165.4	167.3	162.3
2002	165.1	166.1	168.1	168.1	168.1	168.0	161.3	165.6	168.4	170.2	172.9	173.7	168.0
2003	172.1	173.8	174.6	174.9	175.6	175.0	170.0	172.7	176.0	178.0	180.9	183.0	175.6
2004	181.4	182.6	184.0	184.9	186.1	184.7	179.3	183.0	185.2	188.0	191.0	192.6	185.2
2005	189.7	191.9	193.3	196.0	195.4	194.8	187.5	192.3	195.1	198.0	199.9	201.8	194.6
2006	200.8	201.7	202.7	202.2	201.6	201.6	192.8	198.2	201.5	205.4	208.4	209.8	202.2
2007	208.1	208.7	209.9	211.8	211.5	210.6	206.3	210.3	211.9	215.8	218.0	219.4	211.9
2008	218.9	219.9	220.3	221.2	220.9	218.4	212.8	215.4	216.3	221.4	222.1	222.9	219.2
2009	218.7	217.9	217.9	219.2	219.3	216.3	211.6	213.8	215.3	219.1	220.5	220.9	217.5
2010	218.6	218.8	220.2	219.7	221.6	219.9	210.5	214.1	217.7	221.3	223.5	225.3	219.3
2011	222.7	223.3	224.9	226.1	226.3	225.4	217.5	222.2	225.7	229.2	232.6	232.9	225.7
Total Private													
2000	113.1	114.5	115.4	115.8	116.3	116.9	115.5	116.1	116.6	116.5	118.4	119.9	116.3
2001	118.4	118.4	120.2	121.0	121.0	121.1	118.6	119.9	119.8	120.3	121.7	123.5	120.3
2002	122.0	122.4	124.0	124.2	124.1	124.5	123.7	125.7	125.6	125.4	127.5	128.4	124.8
2003	127.0	128.5	129.3	129.3	129.8	130.2	130.2	131.4	131.6	132.1	134.1	136.1	130.8
2004	134.9	135.6	136.8	137.6	138.5	138.3	138.0	139.1	138.8	140.3	142.7	144.5	138.8
2005	142.0	143.3	144.6	147.3	146.7	146.7	146.5	147.0	147.5	148.7	150.2	152.1	146.9
2006	150.8	151.0	152.1	152.5	152.0	151.9	151.7	152.4	153.5	154.9	157.4	158.9	153.3
2007	157.9	157.9	158.8	161.2	160.8	160.2	161.3	162.5	161.9	163.9	165.5	166.6	161.5
2008	166.6	167.0	167.1	168.1	167.1	165.9	165.6	166.2	164.4	167.4	167.2	167.8	166.7
2009	164.4	163.1	163.0	164.5	164.2	162.5	163.0	162.9	162.2	164.2	165.0	165.3	163.7
2010	163.6	163.1	164.2	163.3	165.0	164.2	162.2	164.0	165.1	166.3	168.0	170.0	164.9
2011	167.3	167.5	169.2	170.4	170.6	170.2	167.5	169.9	171.0	172.7	175.4	175.7	170.6
Goods-Producing													
2000	21.8	22.0	21.9	21.9	22.0	21.9	21.6	21.7	21.9	22.1	22.2	22.3	21.9
2001	22.4	22.6	22.5	22.2	22.2	22.2	21.2	21.1	20.9	21.3	21.4	21.5	21.8
2002	21.0	21.0	21.2	20.6	20.3	20.5	20.4	20.8	20.4	20.1	20.2	20.2	20.6
2003	20.2	20.3	20.3	20.5	20.6	20.4	20.3	20.5	20.5	19.9	20.2	20.3	20.3
2004	19.9	19.9	20.1	19.8	20.0	19.6	19.4	19.4	19.3	19.4	19.4	19.6	19.7
2005	18.8	18.9	19.0	18.8	18.9	19.0	18.6	18.6	18.8	18.9	19.0	19.1	18.9
2006	18.9	19.0	19.2	19.0	18.9	18.9	18.6	18.8	18.9	18.6	19.0	19.2	18.9
2007	19.0	18.9	19.0	19.3	19.3	19.2	18.9	19.5	19.5	19.4	19.4	19.4	19.2
2008	19.3	19.1	19.0	18.7	18.4	18.2	17.6	17.8	17.4	17.9	17.5	17.6	18.2
2009	16.9	16.6	16.3	15.7	15.6	15.4	15.2	15.2	15.0	15.2	15.0	14.9	15.6
2010	15.0	14.7	15.0	14.7	14.8	14.4	14.0	14.3	14.3	14.4	14.5	14.6	14.6
2011	14.6	14.5	14.7	14.4	14.4	14.4	14.4	14.6	14.5	14.5	14.5	14.5	14.5
Mining, Logging, and Construction													
2000	9.3	9.4	9.6	9.9	9.9	9.9	9.9	9.9	9.9	9.9	9.9	10.0	9.8
2001	10.1	10.3	10.2	10.2	10.3	10.5	10.5	10.4	10.1	10.3	10.3	10.5	10.3
2002	10.2	10.2	10.4	10.4	10.5	10.8	10.8	11.0	11.0	10.8	10.9	11.0	10.7
2003	10.9	10.9	11.0	11.2	11.3	11.4	11.3	11.4	11.3	11.1	11.1	11.2	11.2
2004	10.8	10.8	11.0	10.9	10.9	10.8	10.8	10.8	10.9	10.7	10.5	10.6	10.8
2005	10.3	10.5	10.5	10.6	10.7	10.9	10.6	10.6	10.7	10.5	10.6	10.6	10.6
2006	10.4	10.6	10.9	10.7	10.8	10.9	11.0	11.1	11.0	10.9	10.9	11.0	10.9
2007	10.9	10.9	11.0	11.1	11.1	11.3	11.4	11.7	11.6	11.3	11.3	11.3	11.2
2008	11.3	11.2	11.1	11.1	10.9	10.8	10.7	10.8	10.6	10.7	10.5	10.5	10.9
2009	10.2	10.0	9.7	9.6	9.4	9.2	9.2	9.0	8.8	8.8	8.7	8.6	9.3
2010	8.6	8.5	8.6	8.5	8.6	8.6	8.4	8.5	8.5	8.4	8.4	8.4	8.5
2011	8.4	8.4	8.6	8.5	8.6	8.6	8.6	8.7	8.7	8.6	8.6	8.6	8.6
Manufacturing													
2000	12.5	12.6	12.3	12.0	12.1	12.0	11.7	11.8	12.0	12.2	12.3	12.3	12.2
2001	12.3	12.3	12.3	12.0	11.9	11.7	10.7	10.7	10.8	11.0	11.1	11.0	11.5
2002	10.8	10.8	10.8	10.2	9.8	9.7	9.6	9.8	9.4	9.3	9.3	9.2	9.9
2003	9.3	9.4	9.3	9.3	9.3	9.0	9.0	9.1	9.2	8.8	9.1	9.1	9.2
2004	9.1	9.1	9.1	8.9	9.1	8.8	8.6	8.6	8.4	8.7	8.9	9.0	8.9
2005	8.5	8.4	8.5	8.2	8.2	8.1	8.0	8.0	8.1	8.4	8.4	8.5	8.3
2006	8.5	8.4	8.3	8.3	8.1	8.0	7.6	7.7	7.9	7.7	8.1	8.2	8.1
2007	8.1	8.0	8.0	8.2	8.2	7.9	7.5	7.8	7.9	8.1	8.1	8.1	8.0
2008	8.0	7.9	7.9	7.6	7.5	7.4	6.9	7.0	6.8	7.2	7.0	7.1	7.4
2009	6.7	6.6	6.6	6.1	6.2	6.2	6.0	6.2	6.2	6.4	6.3	6.3	6.3
2010	6.4	6.2	6.4	6.2	6.2	5.8	5.6	5.8	5.8	6.0	6.1	6.2	6.1
2011	6.2	6.1	6.1	5.9	5.8	5.8	5.8	5.9	5.8	5.9	5.9	5.9	5.9
Service-Providing													
2000	131.1	133.2	135.4	135.2	135.5	135.3	131.4	132.8	135.3	136.1	138.5	140.1	135.0
2001	137.7	138.6	140.5	141.3	141.5	140.7	135.2	137.7	140.7	142.3	144.0	145.8	140.5
2002	144.1	145.1	146.9	147.5	147.8	147.5	140.9	144.8	148.0	150.1	152.7	153.5	147.4
2003	151.9	153.5	154.3	154.4	155.0	154.6	149.7	152.2	155.5	158.1	160.7	162.7	155.2
2004	161.5	162.7	163.9	165.1	166.1	165.1	159.9	163.6	165.9	168.6	171.6	173.0	165.6
2005	170.9	173.0	174.3	177.2	176.5	175.8	168.9	173.7	176.3	179.1	180.9	182.7	175.8
2006	181.9	182.7	183.5	183.2	182.7	182.7	174.2	179.4	182.6	186.8	189.4	190.6	183.3
2007	189.1	189.8	190.9	192.5	192.2	191.4	187.4	190.8	192.4	196.4	198.6	200.0	192.6
2008	199.6	200.8	201.3	202.5	202.5	200.2	195.2	197.6	198.9	203.5	204.6	205.3	201.0
2009	201.8	201.3	201.6	203.5	203.7	200.9	196.4	198.6	200.3	203.9	205.5	206.0	202.0
2010	203.6	204.1	205.2	205.0	206.8	205.5	196.5	199.8	203.4	206.9	209.0	210.7	204.7
2011	208.1	208.8	210.2	211.7	211.9	211.0	203.1	207.6	211.2	214.7	218.1	218.4	211.2

Employment by Industry: McAllen–Edinburg–Mission, TX, Selected Years, 2000–2011—*Continued*

(Numbers in thousands, not seasonally adjusted)

Industry and year	January	February	March	April	May	June	July	August	September	October	November	December	Annual average
Trade, Transportation, and Utilities													
2000	34.9	34.9	35.4	35.2	35.2	34.9	34.4	34.8	34.8	34.8	35.9	37.0	35.2
2001	35.5	35.0	35.4	35.8	35.4	35.1	34.2	34.3	34.1	34.0	34.7	35.6	34.9
2002	34.5	34.2	34.7	34.8	34.9	34.9	34.7	35.1	35.1	35.0	36.2	37.0	35.1
2003	35.5	35.5	35.8	36.1	36.2	36.3	36.2	36.2	36.2	36.6	37.9	39.2	36.5
2004	38.4	38.3	38.5	39.1	39.1	38.7	38.4	38.7	38.2	38.5	39.7	40.7	38.9
2005	39.4	39.2	39.6	40.8	40.6	40.6	40.7	40.8	40.5	40.8	42.0	42.9	40.7
2006	41.8	41.4	41.9	42.4	42.3	42.1	42.3	42.7	43.2	43.8	45.3	46.0	42.9
2007	44.7	44.3	45.0	45.5	45.2	44.8	45.5	45.8	45.5	46.0	47.3	47.9	45.6
2008	47.0	46.2	46.5	46.7	46.4	46.2	46.3	46.5	45.9	46.5	46.9	47.5	46.6
2009	45.4	44.5	44.6	45.4	45.3	44.9	44.9	45.5	45.1	45.4	46.1	46.7	45.3
2010	44.7	44.1	44.4	44.8	45.2	45.2	44.7	45.3	45.1	45.8	46.9	48.1	45.4
2011	46.1	45.6	46.0	46.6	46.7	46.7	45.7	46.3	46.5	47.1	48.2	48.7	46.7
Wholesale Trade													
2000	5.7	5.9	6.1	6.2	6.0	5.8	5.5	5.4	5.4	5.6	5.8	6.0	5.8
2001	5.9	5.9	6.1	6.5	6.3	6.0	5.6	5.5	5.4	5.3	5.4	5.5	5.8
2002	5.6	5.6	5.8	5.8	5.7	5.7	5.6	5.6	5.6	5.6	5.6	5.8	5.7
2003	5.9	6.0	6.1	6.3	6.3	6.3	6.0	5.9	5.9	5.9	6.0	6.3	6.1
2004	6.2	6.2	6.3	6.8	6.9	6.7	6.5	6.5	6.5	6.4	6.6	6.9	6.5
2005	6.8	6.7	6.7	6.9	6.7	6.7	6.6	6.4	6.5	6.6	6.7	6.8	6.7
2006	6.8	6.9	7.0	7.0	6.9	6.8	6.7	6.6	6.6	6.4	6.4	6.5	6.7
2007	6.3	6.4	6.6	6.9	6.8	6.6	6.7	6.6	6.7	7.0	7.0	7.0	6.7
2008	7.1	6.8	6.9	7.2	7.1	6.9	6.7	6.4	6.3	6.8	6.6	6.7	6.8
2009	6.5	6.4	6.3	6.8	6.6	6.3	6.2	6.2	6.1	6.3	6.2	6.2	6.3
2010	6.1	6.1	6.0	6.2	6.3	6.3	6.1	6.1	6.2	6.3	6.3	6.5	6.2
2011	6.3	6.3	6.5	6.6	6.6	6.5	6.1	6.1	6.1	6.2	6.2	6.2	6.3
Retail Trade													
2000	24.7	24.4	24.5	24.3	24.3	24.4	24.2	24.7	24.6	24.7	25.6	26.3	24.7
2001	24.9	24.4	24.6	24.6	24.5	24.5	24.1	24.3	24.1	23.9	24.5	25.3	24.5
2002	24.3	24.1	24.3	24.4	24.6	24.6	24.5	24.8	24.9	24.8	25.9	26.5	24.8
2003	25.0	24.8	25.0	24.9	25.0	25.0	25.2	25.2	25.3	25.7	26.8	27.8	25.5
2004	27.0	26.9	26.9	27.0	26.9	26.7	26.5	26.8	26.3	26.7	27.7	28.3	27.0
2005	27.1	27.0	27.3	28.2	28.1	28.0	28.1	28.4	28.0	28.4	29.4	30.1	28.2
2006	28.8	28.3	28.5	29.0	28.9	28.6	29.0	29.4	29.9	30.6	32.0	32.5	29.6
2007	31.6	31.0	31.5	31.7	31.4	31.1	31.7	32.1	31.6	32.1	33.5	34.0	31.9
2008	33.0	32.5	32.6	32.4	32.1	32.1	32.5	33.0	32.5	32.9	33.5	33.9	32.8
2009	32.1	31.4	31.5	31.8	31.8	31.6	31.8	32.3	32.1	32.1	32.9	33.4	32.1
2010	31.8	31.2	31.6	31.7	31.8	31.8	31.7	32.2	31.9	32.5	33.6	34.4	32.2
2011	33.0	32.4	32.5	32.9	32.9	33.0	32.5	33.0	33.1	33.5	34.6	35.0	33.2
Transportation and Utilities													
2000	4.5	4.6	4.8	4.7	4.9	4.7	4.7	4.7	4.8	4.5	4.5	4.7	4.7
2001	4.7	4.7	4.7	4.7	4.6	4.6	4.5	4.5	4.6	4.8	4.8	4.8	4.7
2002	4.6	4.5	4.6	4.6	4.6	4.6	4.6	4.7	4.6	4.6	4.7	4.7	4.6
2003	4.6	4.7	4.7	4.9	4.9	5.0	5.0	5.1	5.0	5.0	5.1	5.1	4.9
2004	5.2	5.2	5.3	5.3	5.3	5.3	5.4	5.4	5.4	5.4	5.4	5.5	5.3
2005	5.5	5.5	5.6	5.7	5.8	5.9	6.0	6.0	6.0	5.8	5.9	6.0	5.8
2006	6.2	6.2	6.4	6.4	6.5	6.7	6.6	6.7	6.7	6.8	6.9	7.0	6.6
2007	6.8	6.9	6.9	6.9	7.0	7.1	7.1	7.1	7.2	6.9	6.8	6.9	7.0
2008	6.9	6.9	7.0	7.1	7.2	7.2	7.1	7.1	7.1	6.8	6.8	6.9	7.0
2009	6.8	6.7	6.8	6.8	6.9	7.0	6.9	7.0	6.9	7.0	7.0	7.1	6.9
2010	6.8	6.8	6.8	6.9	7.1	7.1	6.9	7.0	7.0	7.0	7.0	7.2	7.0
2011	6.8	6.9	7.0	7.1	7.2	7.2	7.1	7.2	7.3	7.4	7.4	7.5	7.2
Information													
2000	1.3	1.3	1.2	1.3	1.3	1.4	1.4	1.4	1.4	1.3	1.3	1.3	1.3
2001	1.1	1.1	1.1	1.1	1.1	1.2	1.1	1.1	1.1	1.1	1.1	1.1	1.1
2002	1.1	1.1	1.1	1.0	1.1	1.1	1.0	1.0	1.0	0.9	1.0	1.0	1.0
2003	1.0	1.0	1.0	1.0	1.1	1.3	1.4	1.4	1.4	1.5	1.6	1.7	1.3
2004	1.9	1.8	1.8	1.9	1.9	2.0	2.0	2.0	2.0	2.1	2.1	2.1	2.0
2005	2.0	2.0	2.0	2.1	2.1	2.2	2.2	2.2	2.3	2.3	2.3	2.3	2.2
2006	2.2	2.2	2.3	2.2	2.2	2.2	2.1	2.1	2.1	2.3	2.3	2.2	2.2
2007	2.2	2.2	2.2	2.3	2.3	2.3	2.2	2.2	2.1	2.1	2.1	2.2	2.2
2008	2.2	2.2	2.2	2.2	2.2	2.3	2.3	2.3	2.2	2.2	2.3	2.3	2.2
2009	2.2	2.2	2.2	2.2	2.1	2.1	2.2	2.1	2.1	2.0	2.0	2.0	2.1
2010	2.1	2.0	2.0	2.0	2.0	2.0	1.9	1.9	1.9	1.9	1.9	2.0	2.0
2011	2.1	2.0	2.0	2.1	2.1	2.1	2.1	2.1	2.1	2.1	2.1	2.1	2.1
Financial Activities													
2000	6.0	5.9	6.0	6.2	6.1	6.1	6.1	6.1	6.1	6.1	6.1	6.2	6.1
2001	6.1	6.1	6.2	6.2	6.2	6.3	6.4	6.4	6.4	6.4	6.5	6.5	6.3
2002	6.5	6.5	6.5	6.6	6.7	6.7	6.7	6.7	6.7	6.8	6.9	7.0	6.7
2003	7.0	7.1	7.1	7.1	7.2	7.3	7.3	7.3	7.3	7.4	7.4	7.4	7.2
2004	7.5	7.5	7.6	7.6	7.5	7.7	7.8	7.7	7.7	7.8	7.9	7.9	7.7
2005	7.9	7.9	8.0	8.1	8.0	8.1	8.2	8.2	8.2	8.3	8.3	8.3	8.1
2006	8.3	8.3	8.4	8.2	8.2	8.3	8.4	8.4	8.4	8.6	8.6	8.7	8.4
2007	8.7	8.7	8.7	8.8	8.8	8.8	8.8	8.8	8.8	8.8	8.9	8.8	8.8
2008	8.9	8.9	8.8	8.9	8.8	8.8	8.8	8.7	8.6	8.5	8.5	8.4	8.7
2009	8.3	8.1	8.1	8.0	7.9	7.9	8.0	8.0	7.9	8.0	8.0	8.0	8.0
2010	7.9	7.9	7.9	7.9	8.0	8.0	8.0	8.0	8.1	8.2	8.3	8.4	8.1
2011	8.3	8.3	8.4	8.4	8.4	8.4	8.3	8.4	8.5	8.5	8.6	8.6	8.4

Employment by Industry: McAllen–Edinburg–Mission, TX, Selected Years, 2000–2011—*Continued*

(Numbers in thousands, not seasonally adjusted)

Industry and year	January	February	March	April	May	June	July	August	September	October	November	December	Annual average
Professional and Business Services													
2000	8.3	8.7	8.9	9.0	9.2	9.6	9.2	9.3	9.2	9.1	9.1	8.9	9.0
2001	9.0	8.9	9.6	10.0	10.1	10.3	10.0	10.4	10.6	10.7	11.0	11.2	10.2
2002	11.1	11.1	11.3	11.3	11.0	11.0	10.7	10.9	10.9	11.3	11.4	11.2	11.1
2003	10.9	11.5	11.2	11.1	11.0	11.1	11.0	11.5	11.6	11.7	11.8	12.0	11.4
2004	11.4	11.5	11.4	11.6	11.8	12.0	12.0	12.3	12.1	12.2	12.4	12.5	11.9
2005	12.3	12.8	13.1	13.4	13.2	13.3	13.3	13.5	13.5	13.5	13.6	13.8	13.3
2006	13.8	14.1	14.3	14.0	13.9	14.1	13.8	13.8	13.9	14.0	14.2	14.6	14.0
2007	14.5	14.6	14.8	14.7	14.7	14.7	14.6	14.6	14.7	14.7	14.8	15.0	14.7
2008	15.2	15.4	15.2	14.8	14.7	14.6	14.6	14.6	14.4	14.9	14.9	14.8	14.8
2009	14.6	14.5	14.3	14.4	14.4	14.2	14.1	13.5	13.4	13.5	13.7	13.5	14.0
2010	13.7	13.8	13.7	13.6	13.6	13.8	13.6	13.7	13.7	13.9	14.0	14.2	13.8
2011	14.1	14.3	14.4	15.1	15.0	14.8	14.6	14.8	15.0	15.1	15.6	15.5	14.9
Education and Health Services													
2000	23.3	23.7	23.7	24.0	24.2	24.1	24.3	24.4	24.8	24.8	25.3	25.3	24.3
2001	25.5	25.8	26.1	26.1	26.3	26.4	26.5	27.1	27.4	27.7	27.7	28.0	26.7
2002	28.2	28.4	28.8	29.4	29.7	29.9	30.4	31.0	31.4	31.6	32.1	32.2	30.3
2003	32.4	32.7	33.0	32.9	32.9	32.7	33.1	33.7	34.0	34.3	34.6	34.8	33.4
2004	35.1	35.6	36.0	36.1	36.7	36.8	37.4	37.9	38.7	39.5	40.1	40.5	37.5
2005	40.4	41.0	41.2	41.6	41.7	41.6	41.9	42.3	42.9	43.3	43.5	44.0	42.1
2006	43.6	43.9	43.8	43.9	44.0	44.0	44.0	44.5	44.9	45.0	45.3	45.5	44.4
2007	46.0	46.3	46.3	47.1	47.3	47.1	47.3	47.8	48.2	48.4	48.9	49.0	47.5
2008	49.2	50.1	50.1	50.8	51.0	50.5	50.8	51.0	51.3	52.2	52.5	52.9	51.0
2009	52.4	52.6	52.8	53.7	54.0	53.4	54.0	54.2	54.5	55.5	55.7	55.8	54.1
2010	55.6	55.7	56.0	55.6	56.3	55.9	55.6	56.1	57.1	57.2	57.5	57.7	56.4
2011	57.3	57.6	57.9	58.1	58.3	58.0	57.2	58.3	59.1	59.8	60.4	60.3	58.5
Leisure and Hospitality													
2000	13.5	13.9	14.2	14.1	14.2	14.8	14.3	14.3	14.2	14.1	14.3	14.6	14.2
2001	14.5	14.6	15.0	15.1	15.2	15.1	14.8	15.0	14.9	14.8	14.9	15.2	14.9
2002	15.3	15.7	16.0	15.9	15.9	15.9	15.4	15.8	15.8	15.3	15.3	15.4	15.6
2003	15.5	15.9	16.3	16.1	16.2	16.6	16.5	16.4	16.2	16.3	16.2	16.3	16.2
2004	16.2	16.5	16.8	17.0	16.9	16.9	16.4	16.5	16.3	16.3	16.5	16.6	16.6
2005	16.6	16.9	17.0	17.6	17.3	17.0	16.9	16.7	16.6	16.8	16.7	17.0	16.9
2006	17.6	17.5	17.5	17.9	17.6	17.4	17.4	17.1	16.9	17.4	17.4	17.4	17.4
2007	17.9	17.9	17.7	18.3	18.0	18.0	18.6	18.4	17.8	18.9	18.6	18.7	18.2
2008	19.0	19.2	19.3	19.9	19.7	19.4	19.2	19.3	18.8	19.3	18.8	18.7	19.2
2009	19.0	19.0	19.1	19.3	19.1	18.8	18.9	18.8	18.6	18.9	18.8	18.8	18.9
2010	19.0	19.3	19.5	19.1	19.4	19.2	18.9	19.2	19.3	19.2	19.2	19.4	19.2
2011	19.2	19.5	20.0	20.0	20.0	20.1	19.6	19.8	19.7	19.9	20.3	20.3	19.9
Other Services													
2000	4.0	4.1	4.1	4.1	4.1	4.1	4.2	4.1	4.2	4.2	4.2	4.3	4.1
2001	4.3	4.3	4.3	4.5	4.5	4.5	4.4	4.5	4.4	4.3	4.4	4.4	4.4
2002	4.3	4.4	4.4	4.6	4.5	4.5	4.4	4.4	4.3	4.4	4.4	4.4	4.4
2003	4.5	4.5	4.6	4.5	4.6	4.5	4.4	4.4	4.4	4.4	4.4	4.4	4.5
2004	4.5	4.5	4.6	4.5	4.6	4.6	4.6	4.6	4.5	4.5	4.6	4.6	4.6
2005	4.6	4.6	4.7	4.9	4.9	4.9	4.7	4.7	4.7	4.8	4.8	4.7	4.8
2006	4.6	4.6	4.7	4.9	4.9	4.9	5.1	5.0	5.2	5.2	5.3	5.3	5.0
2007	4.9	5.0	5.1	5.2	5.2	5.3	5.4	5.4	5.3	5.6	5.5	5.6	5.3
2008	5.8	5.9	6.0	6.1	5.9	5.9	6.0	6.0	5.8	5.9	5.8	5.6	5.9
2009	5.6	5.6	5.6	5.8	5.7	5.8	5.7	5.6	5.6	5.7	5.7	5.6	5.7
2010	5.6	5.6	5.7	5.6	5.7	5.7	5.5	5.5	5.6	5.7	5.7	5.6	5.6
2011	5.6	5.7	5.8	5.7	5.7	5.7	5.6	5.6	5.6	5.7	5.7	5.7	5.7
Government													
2000	39.8	40.7	41.9	41.3	41.2	40.3	37.5	38.4	40.6	41.7	42.3	42.5	40.7
2001	41.7	42.8	42.8	42.5	42.7	41.8	37.8	38.9	41.8	43.3	43.7	43.8	42.0
2002	43.1	43.7	44.1	43.9	44.0	43.5	37.6	39.9	42.8	44.8	45.4	45.3	43.2
2003	45.1	45.3	45.3	45.6	45.8	44.8	39.8	41.3	44.4	45.9	46.8	46.9	44.8
2004	46.5	47.0	47.2	47.3	47.6	46.4	41.3	43.9	46.4	47.7	48.3	48.1	46.5
2005	47.7	48.6	48.7	48.7	48.7	48.1	41.0	45.3	47.6	49.3	49.7	49.7	47.8
2006	50.0	50.7	50.6	49.7	49.6	49.7	41.1	45.8	48.0	50.5	51.0	50.9	49.0
2007	50.2	50.8	51.1	50.6	50.7	50.4	45.0	47.8	50.0	51.9	52.5	52.8	50.3
2008	52.3	52.9	53.2	53.1	53.8	52.5	47.2	49.2	51.9	54.0	54.9	55.1	52.5
2009	54.3	54.8	54.9	54.7	55.1	53.8	48.6	50.9	53.1	54.9	55.5	55.6	53.9
2010	55.0	55.7	56.0	56.4	56.6	55.7	48.3	50.1	52.6	55.0	55.5	55.3	54.4
2011	55.4	55.8	55.7	55.7	55.7	55.2	50.0	52.3	54.7	56.5	57.2	57.2	55.1

Employment by Industry: Memphis, TN–MS–AR, Selected Years, 2000–2011

(Numbers in thousands, not seasonally adjusted)

Industry and year	January	February	March	April	May	June	July	August	September	October	November	December	Annual average
Total Nonfarm													
2000	610.6	614.7	623.3	623.5	626.1	627.3	622.3	629.4	628.3	628.7	629.4	629.5	624.4
2001	613.4	615.4	618.7	625.7	623.4	622.7	618.3	621.9	620.0	617.5	616.2	615.2	619.0
2002	603.4	606.9	609.7	613.0	612.6	611.7	610.0	614.2	614.1	618.9	621.5	621.1	613.1
2003	613.0	615.0	618.3	619.6	618.9	614.8	609.0	614.2	616.2	619.9	620.7	620.2	616.7
2004	605.4	610.4	611.5	616.6	614.1	613.3	614.7	620.1	620.9	622.4	624.5	625.3	616.6
2005	610.8	614.7	618.6	625.0	625.6	622.5	626.3	630.9	636.5	632.5	638.0	639.0	626.7
2006	627.8	627.5	632.3	634.2	634.9	633.6	635.5	640.6	643.8	641.2	648.4	649.3	637.4
2007	631.1	632.1	638.1	639.8	641.2	639.8	638.1	643.1	645.3	643.6	648.7	649.2	640.8
2008	632.3	631.3	634.0	636.7	637.6	632.3	631.2	634.2	632.2	630.6	630.9	626.9	632.5
2009	607.9	606.8	605.3	604.2	603.0	600.0	596.2	596.7	596.6	596.7	601.1	598.1	601.1
2010	582.6	584.1	588.5	589.7	595.2	589.8	585.6	589.1	587.9	593.8	596.5	595.3	589.8
2011	582.5	584.6	587.9	592.8	593.0	590.5	591.9	598.0	599.1	600.4	611.4	612.8	595.4
Total Private													
2000	528.1	529.8	534.2	537.4	540.6	544.6	543.1	546.3	544.4	542.3	542.8	542.8	539.7
2001	528.7	527.9	530.9	537.4	537.6	540.6	537.1	537.5	533.9	528.6	527.3	527.2	532.9
2002	516.4	516.9	519.4	522.2	523.9	526.9	527.9	528.3	525.6	527.8	529.3	530.3	524.6
2003	522.1	522.0	524.6	527.0	528.7	530.5	526.2	527.8	527.0	528.9	529.6	529.6	527.0
2004	515.3	516.6	519.7	525.4	525.4	528.4	531.7	532.9	530.5	531.3	533.1	535.0	527.1
2005	521.6	524.2	527.9	534.0	536.4	537.8	542.9	543.9	547.2	542.2	547.4	549.2	537.9
2006	539.3	538.4	542.9	545.2	548.0	550.5	552.7	554.7	554.4	550.2	557.9	558.9	549.4
2007	541.3	541.8	548.1	550.5	553.0	556.3	554.8	556.3	556.0	552.9	557.7	559.0	552.3
2008	542.7	540.3	542.9	545.5	547.3	547.4	546.8	546.3	542.6	540.1	540.5	537.7	543.3
2009	519.7	517.7	516.1	515.2	514.5	515.1	511.6	511.5	508.6	508.1	512.1	510.1	513.4
2010	496.4	495.9	500.0	501.2	505.1	506.0	502.5	503.7	500.2	505.2	507.9	508.6	502.7
2011	495.3	495.9	499.3	504.6	506.6	509.1	510.5	512.4	510.4	511.5	521.9	524.0	508.5
Goods-Producing													
2000	90.1	90.3	91.2	91.0	91.8	92.4	91.6	91.8	91.2	89.6	88.8	88.2	90.7
2001	85.6	85.4	86.0	86.6	87.0	88.1	86.8	86.7	85.5	83.3	82.5	81.8	85.4
2002	79.0	78.8	79.5	79.9	80.6	81.5	82.0	81.9	81.8	81.0	80.0	79.6	80.5
2003	77.9	78.2	78.5	79.1	79.6	79.9	79.7	79.5	79.5	79.4	78.8	78.4	79.0
2004	76.7	77.1	78.1	78.9	79.3	80.7	80.9	81.0	80.6	79.2	78.9	77.4	79.1
2005	76.5	77.5	78.5	79.6	80.5	81.4	81.8	80.4	82.6	81.6	81.6	79.2	80.1
2006	79.9	80.4	81.3	81.4	82.0	83.0	82.7	82.6	82.5	80.5	79.9	77.5	81.1
2007	77.5	77.9	79.6	79.4	79.8	80.6	80.0	79.4	78.9	78.4	78.0	77.0	78.9
2008	75.6	75.1	75.9	76.5	77.0	77.2	76.4	76.5	75.9	74.5	73.5	72.3	75.5
2009	70.6	69.2	68.8	68.1	68.1	68.4	67.8	67.8	67.7	66.1	66.6	64.6	67.8
2010	62.5	62.8	63.7	63.9	64.3	64.8	65.0	64.9	64.5	63.6	63.9	63.6	64.0
2011	62.8	62.4	62.7	63.5	64.2	65.2	66.4	66.9	66.3	65.2	64.9	64.8	64.6
Mining, Logging, and Construction													
2000	26.1	26.4	27.5	27.2	28.0	28.6	27.9	28.1	28.2	27.2	26.8	26.4	27.4
2001	25.6	25.8	26.8	27.0	27.3	27.7	27.6	27.5	27.0	25.6	25.7	25.4	26.6
2002	24.5	24.1	24.6	25.0	25.7	26.2	26.5	26.3	26.6	25.9	25.6	25.5	25.5
2003	24.3	24.2	24.6	25.2	25.7	25.9	26.0	26.1	26.2	26.0	25.8	25.8	25.5
2004	24.9	25.0	25.7	25.9	26.0	26.8	27.2	27.1	27.0	25.7	25.6	25.1	26.0
2005	23.7	24.1	24.7	25.3	26.0	26.7	26.9	27.2	27.6	26.9	26.8	26.7	26.1
2006	25.8	26.0	26.7	27.1	27.7	28.2	28.3	28.2	28.0	27.0	26.5	26.3	27.2
2007	25.5	25.5	26.0	26.3	26.8	27.3	26.9	27.0	26.8	26.5	26.3	26.2	26.4
2008	24.5	24.5	25.0	25.5	25.7	25.8	25.2	25.1	24.7	23.8	23.4	22.9	24.7
2009	21.7	21.4	21.5	21.5	21.5	22.0	21.7	21.7	21.4	20.5	20.6	20.1	21.3
2010	19.0	18.7	19.2	19.2	19.3	19.7	19.8	19.8	19.6	19.4	19.1	18.9	19.3
2011	18.1	18.2	18.5	19.0	19.4	20.1	21.3	21.7	21.4	20.7	20.6	20.7	20.0
Manufacturing													
2000	64.0	63.9	63.7	63.8	63.8	63.8	63.7	63.7	63.0	62.4	62.0	61.8	63.3
2001	60.0	59.6	59.2	59.6	59.7	60.4	59.2	59.2	58.5	57.7	56.8	56.4	58.9
2002	54.5	54.7	54.9	54.9	54.9	55.3	55.5	55.6	55.2	55.1	54.4	54.1	54.9
2003	53.6	54.0	53.9	53.9	53.9	54.0	53.7	53.4	53.3	53.4	53.0	52.6	53.6
2004	51.8	52.1	52.4	53.0	53.3	53.9	53.7	53.9	53.6	53.5	53.3	52.3	53.1
2005	52.8	53.4	53.8	54.3	54.5	54.7	54.9	53.2	55.0	54.7	54.8	52.5	54.1
2006	54.1	54.4	54.6	54.3	54.3	54.8	54.4	54.4	54.5	53.5	53.4	51.2	54.0
2007	52.0	52.4	53.6	53.1	53.0	53.3	53.1	52.4	52.1	51.9	51.7	50.8	52.5
2008	51.1	50.6	50.9	51.0	51.3	51.4	51.2	51.4	51.2	50.7	50.1	49.4	50.9
2009	48.9	47.8	47.3	46.6	46.6	46.4	46.1	46.1	46.3	45.6	46.0	44.5	46.5
2010	43.5	44.1	44.5	44.7	45.0	45.1	45.2	45.1	44.9	44.2	44.8	44.7	44.7
2011	44.7	44.2	44.2	44.5	44.8	45.1	45.1	45.2	44.9	44.5	44.3	44.1	44.6
Service-Providing													
2000	520.5	524.4	532.1	532.5	534.3	534.9	530.7	537.6	537.1	539.1	540.6	541.3	533.8
2001	527.8	530.0	532.7	539.1	536.4	534.6	531.5	535.2	534.5	534.2	533.7	533.4	533.6
2002	524.4	528.1	530.2	533.1	532.0	530.2	528.0	532.3	532.3	537.9	541.5	541.5	532.6
2003	535.1	536.8	539.8	540.5	539.3	534.9	529.3	534.7	536.7	540.5	541.9	541.8	537.6
2004	528.7	533.3	533.4	537.7	534.8	532.6	533.8	539.1	540.3	543.2	545.6	547.9	537.5
2005	534.3	537.2	540.1	545.4	545.1	541.1	544.5	550.5	553.9	550.9	556.4	559.8	546.6
2006	547.9	547.1	551.0	552.8	552.9	550.6	552.8	558.0	561.3	560.7	568.5	571.8	556.3
2007	553.6	554.2	558.5	560.4	561.4	559.2	558.1	563.7	566.4	565.2	570.7	572.2	562.0
2008	556.7	556.2	558.1	560.2	560.6	555.1	554.8	557.7	556.3	556.1	557.4	554.6	557.0
2009	537.3	537.6	536.5	536.1	534.9	531.6	528.4	528.9	528.9	530.6	534.5	533.5	533.2
2010	520.1	521.3	524.8	525.8	530.9	525.0	520.6	524.2	523.4	530.2	532.6	531.7	525.9
2011	519.7	522.2	525.2	529.3	528.8	525.3	525.5	531.1	532.8	535.2	546.5	548.0	530.8

Employment by Industry: Memphis, TN–MS–AR, Selected Years, 2000–2011—*Continued*

(Numbers in thousands, not seasonally adjusted)

Industry and year	January	February	March	April	May	June	July	August	September	October	November	December	Annual average
Trade, Transportation, and Utilities													
2000	174.3	174.2	175.1	177.2	177.4	178.9	174.8	175.6	175.1	176.9	179.0	180.3	176.6
2001	176.9	174.3	173.9	175.5	175.2	175.3	174.0	174.7	173.9	173.4	174.4	174.7	174.7
2002	169.1	166.8	167.5	168.0	168.3	168.7	169.7	169.5	169.5	170.7	173.8	175.4	169.8
2003	171.4	170.2	170.8	170.9	170.7	170.8	169.8	170.0	170.3	171.1	173.3	174.1	171.1
2004	167.7	167.4	167.8	168.0	168.0	168.5	170.3	170.0	168.9	170.1	172.7	175.3	169.6
2005	169.8	168.7	169.7	170.0	170.5	170.5	173.5	173.2	173.5	172.9	176.2	178.4	172.2
2006	173.6	172.4	173.0	173.3	174.0	173.7	174.7	175.1	174.9	174.7	178.2	179.9	174.8
2007	173.3	172.5	173.8	174.7	175.5	175.6	175.3	175.3	175.6	174.8	178.0	179.1	175.3
2008	172.8	171.4	171.7	171.7	171.6	171.3	170.8	170.2	169.3	168.3	169.9	170.4	170.8
2009	164.4	163.0	162.3	161.0	161.0	160.5	159.8	159.3	158.6	158.2	159.6	160.7	160.7
2010	157.1	156.3	156.7	157.8	158.0	158.1	158.4	158.3	156.9	158.4	160.8	162.1	158.2
2011	156.7	156.0	156.4	157.6	158.1	158.7	158.2	157.4	157.2	158.7	162.9	163.9	158.5
Wholesale Trade													
2000	38.2	38.4	38.2	38.1	38.0	38.2	38.2	38.4	38.4	38.3	38.4	38.5	38.3
2001	36.5	36.4	36.5	37.2	37.0	36.9	36.5	36.8	36.7	36.6	36.6	36.1	36.7
2002	36.1	36.0	36.1	36.1	36.2	36.4	36.3	36.2	36.2	36.9	37.1	37.3	36.4
2003	37.9	38.1	38.0	37.7	37.5	37.6	36.7	36.6	36.4	36.2	36.4	36.3	37.1
2004	35.8	35.9	36.2	36.5	36.6	36.9	37.3	37.3	37.1	36.8	36.8	36.8	36.7
2005	36.7	36.8	37.1	37.3	37.4	37.5	37.9	38.0	37.7	37.6	37.6	37.7	37.4
2006	37.3	37.4	37.5	37.5	37.7	37.8	37.8	37.9	37.7	37.3	37.5	37.4	37.6
2007	37.0	37.2	37.3	37.5	37.6	37.6	37.5	37.5	37.6	37.3	37.1	37.0	37.4
2008	36.2	36.0	35.9	36.3	36.1	35.8	35.2	35.2	35.0	34.9	34.7	34.3	35.5
2009	33.6	33.6	33.3	33.4	33.3	33.2	32.8	32.7	32.4	32.3	32.2	32.2	32.9
2010	32.0	32.0	32.0	32.8	32.7	32.8	32.7	32.8	32.5	32.6	32.8	32.8	32.5
2011	32.6	32.7	32.6	32.8	32.9	33.3	32.6	32.9	32.8	33.1	32.7	32.3	32.8
Retail Trade													
2000	69.6	68.9	69.6	70.2	70.6	70.8	69.9	69.9	69.6	70.8	72.9	74.2	70.6
2001	73.2	71.7	72.2	72.0	72.0	72.0	71.3	70.5	69.5	70.0	71.8	72.7	71.6
2002	70.4	69.0	69.4	69.6	69.8	70.1	70.4	70.1	70.4	70.4	73.1	74.8	70.6
2003	70.3	69.3	69.8	69.9	69.9	69.8	69.5	69.4	69.9	71.1	73.0	74.3	70.5
2004	69.4	69.3	69.4	69.3	69.4	69.6	70.8	70.3	69.7	70.8	73.0	74.5	70.5
2005	70.5	69.6	69.8	69.8	70.0	70.1	71.5	71.0	71.4	71.4	74.2	75.8	71.3
2006	72.4	71.2	71.8	71.6	71.9	71.8	72.9	72.7	72.6	72.5	75.3	76.3	72.8
2007	72.0	71.0	71.9	72.2	72.5	72.9	72.7	71.8	71.8	71.7	74.8	75.6	72.6
2008	71.6	70.6	71.1	70.5	70.5	70.4	70.5	69.5	68.8	68.4	69.6	69.9	70.1
2009	66.8	65.9	65.8	65.2	65.5	65.7	65.8	65.2	64.8	65.0	66.9	67.7	65.9
2010	64.5	63.9	64.4	64.3	64.5	64.4	64.6	64.0	62.9	63.8	65.7	66.4	64.5
2011	62.4	61.7	61.8	62.3	62.5	62.5	62.6	61.5	61.2	62.3	66.9	67.8	63.0
Transportation and Utilities													
2000	66.5	66.9	67.3	68.9	68.8	69.9	66.7	67.3	67.1	67.8	67.7	67.6	67.7
2001	67.2	66.2	65.2	66.3	66.2	66.4	66.2	67.4	67.7	66.8	66.0	65.9	66.5
2002	62.6	61.8	62.0	62.3	62.3	62.2	63.0	63.2	62.9	63.4	63.6	63.3	62.7
2003	63.2	62.8	63.0	63.3	63.3	63.4	63.6	64.0	64.0	63.8	63.9	63.5	63.5
2004	62.5	62.2	62.2	62.2	62.0	62.0	62.2	62.4	62.1	62.5	62.9	64.0	62.4
2005	62.6	62.3	62.8	62.9	63.1	62.9	64.1	64.2	64.4	63.9	64.4	64.9	63.5
2006	63.9	63.8	63.7	64.2	64.4	64.1	64.0	64.5	64.6	64.9	65.4	66.2	64.5
2007	64.3	64.3	64.6	65.0	65.4	65.1	65.1	66.0	66.2	65.8	66.1	66.5	65.4
2008	65.0	64.8	64.7	64.9	65.0	65.1	65.1	65.5	65.5	65.0	65.6	66.2	65.2
2009	64.0	63.5	63.2	62.4	62.2	61.6	61.2	61.4	61.4	60.9	60.5	60.8	61.9
2010	60.6	60.4	60.3	60.7	60.8	60.9	61.1	61.5	61.5	62.0	62.3	62.9	61.3
2011	61.7	61.6	62.0	62.5	62.7	62.9	63.0	63.0	63.2	63.3	63.3	63.8	62.8
Information													
2000	10.1	10.1	10.2	10.2	10.3	10.4	10.1	10.4	10.3	10.3	10.5	10.6	10.3
2001	9.4	9.3	9.4	9.6	9.6	9.9	9.6	9.9	9.8	9.9	9.9	9.9	9.7
2002	10.2	10.1	10.2	10.1	10.1	10.0	9.6	10.0	9.8	10.0	10.1	10.0	10.0
2003	9.9	9.8	9.8	9.9	9.7	9.6	9.5	9.5	9.2	9.4	9.3	9.4	9.6
2004	9.0	8.9	8.8	8.8	8.6	8.6	8.5	8.6	8.6	8.6	8.6	8.4	8.7
2005	8.2	8.1	8.2	8.2	8.2	8.0	7.8	7.7	7.6	7.7	7.6	7.4	7.9
2006	7.3	7.3	7.3	7.4	7.5	7.5	7.5	7.5	7.8	7.7	7.8	7.9	7.5
2007	7.4	7.4	7.3	7.4	7.4	7.5	7.5	7.4	7.3	7.3	7.4	7.4	7.4
2008	7.4	7.4	7.4	7.4	7.4	7.4	7.2	7.2	7.2	7.3	7.2	7.3	7.3
2009	7.2	7.1	7.0	6.9	6.9	6.8	6.8	6.7	6.7	6.6	6.6	6.6	6.8
2010	6.4	6.3	6.3	6.2	6.3	6.3	6.2	6.2	6.2	6.2	6.2	6.3	6.3
2011	6.2	6.1	6.1	6.1	6.2	6.1	6.1	6.1	6.1	6.0	6.0	6.0	6.1
Financial Activities													
2000	32.6	32.4	32.5	32.8	33.0	33.2	33.7	33.5	33.3	32.6	32.5	32.7	32.9
2001	32.3	32.2	32.2	32.4	32.4	32.5	32.4	32.6	32.5	32.7	32.7	32.4	32.4
2002	32.3	32.4	32.6	32.5	32.6	32.6	32.2	32.3	31.9	32.1	32.3	32.3	32.3
2003	32.5	32.5	32.6	32.7	32.8	32.8	33.0	33.0	32.8	32.8	33.1	33.1	32.8
2004	32.8	32.7	32.6	33.1	33.2	33.2	33.6	33.6	33.4	33.4	33.4	33.5	33.2
2005	32.8	32.7	32.9	32.9	32.9	32.9	32.9	33.0	32.9	32.7	32.8	32.8	32.9
2006	32.7	32.8	32.9	32.7	32.8	33.2	33.1	33.1	33.0	32.5	33.0	33.1	32.9
2007	32.4	32.8	33.0	33.0	33.3	33.6	33.5	33.7	33.5	33.1	33.2	33.2	33.2
2008	32.8	32.7	33.0	32.9	33.0	32.9	32.6	32.5	32.1	32.0	31.9	31.4	32.5
2009	31.2	31.2	31.1	31.1	31.2	31.1	30.8	30.7	30.5	30.2	30.4	30.3	30.8
2010	29.7	29.5	29.4	29.1	29.1	28.9	28.8	28.8	28.5	28.2	28.0	28.0	28.8
2011	27.5	27.3	27.2	27.3	27.4	27.3	27.1	27.5	27.3	27.3	27.4	27.4	27.3

Employment by Industry: Memphis, TN–MS–AR, Selected Years, 2000–2011—*Continued*

(Numbers in thousands, not seasonally adjusted)

Industry and year	January	February	March	April	May	June	July	August	September	October	November	December	Annual average
Professional and Business Services													
2000	70.8	71.2	72.4	70.9	71.8	72.8	76.9	78.5	79.3	78.5	77.6	77.4	74.8
2001	75.3	76.5	77.2	78.5	77.7	77.8	78.4	77.8	78.0	76.4	75.9	76.7	77.2
2002	75.5	77.0	75.8	75.6	74.5	74.9	74.6	74.0	73.6	74.2	74.0	74.2	74.8
2003	72.4	72.3	72.3	73.0	73.6	73.5	71.8	72.9	73.8	74.2	73.8	73.2	73.1
2004	70.2	70.6	70.7	71.9	71.6	72.1	72.9	73.9	73.9	76.1	76.7	77.6	73.2
2005	73.8	75.5	75.2	77.1	77.3	77.2	78.3	80.2	81.3	80.3	81.2	83.8	78.4
2006	79.2	78.9	79.3	79.6	80.0	80.2	81.9	83.5	84.1	83.4	87.2	88.8	82.2
2007	80.4	80.5	81.3	82.0	81.9	81.7	82.7	84.0	85.3	85.4	87.0	87.5	83.3
2008	81.5	81.1	81.0	81.9	81.6	81.5	83.6	84.0	84.1	85.1	85.1	84.0	82.9
2009	77.9	77.8	76.8	75.9	75.0	74.4	73.7	74.7	74.5	76.6	77.9	77.4	76.1
2010	73.8	73.2	73.8	73.0	75.8	75.5	72.6	74.4	75.3	79.3	80.2	80.5	75.6
2011	76.6	77.8	78.7	79.9	80.0	80.0	82.0	83.0	81.9	83.4	87.4	89.6	81.7
Education and Health Services													
2000	61.7	62.1	62.4	63.0	63.0	63.1	63.2	63.3	64.0	64.6	65.0	64.8	63.4
2001	63.9	64.4	64.5	64.9	65.1	64.8	65.0	65.4	66.1	65.5	65.6	65.9	65.1
2002	65.8	66.3	66.9	67.3	67.4	66.8	67.2	67.9	68.9	69.5	69.9	69.9	67.8
2003	69.9	70.5	70.6	70.2	70.4	69.9	69.1	69.9	70.4	71.3	71.0	71.2	70.4
2004	70.0	70.8	71.0	71.6	71.5	71.3	71.3	71.6	72.2	72.7	72.6	72.7	71.6
2005	72.4	73.1	73.3	73.7	73.9	73.4	73.4	74.5	75.1	74.5	75.0	74.7	73.9
2006	75.0	74.7	75.4	75.4	75.2	75.2	75.2	75.6	76.1	76.2	76.1	76.2	75.5
2007	76.1	76.3	77.1	76.9	77.4	77.1	77.0	77.8	78.1	78.3	78.4	79.1	77.5
2008	78.6	78.8	79.3	79.2	79.6	79.2	78.5	78.8	79.2	79.7	79.9	79.8	79.2
2009	78.5	79.3	79.5	80.4	79.8	79.6	79.1	79.4	80.1	81.2	81.8	81.7	80.0
2010	80.1	80.7	81.3	81.2	80.9	80.4	80.3	80.7	80.6	81.3	81.5	81.4	80.9
2011	80.2	80.6	81.1	81.4	81.2	80.9	80.9	83.0	84.1	84.4	85.3	85.3	82.4
Leisure and Hospitality													
2000	62.2	62.7	63.9	65.4	66.4	68.8	68.8	68.6	66.9	65.3	64.9	64.3	65.7
2001	61.4	61.8	63.4	65.8	66.4	67.8	66.9	66.5	64.4	63.9	62.8	62.3	64.5
2002	61.6	62.6	63.9	65.6	67.0	68.7	68.5	68.8	66.3	66.5	65.4	64.9	65.8
2003	64.2	64.5	65.7	66.8	67.6	69.3	68.8	68.4	66.7	66.5	66.1	66.0	66.7
2004	64.9	65.0	66.3	68.8	68.8	69.1	69.4	69.5	68.1	66.6	65.5	65.3	67.3
2005	63.9	64.2	65.5	67.8	68.4	69.4	70.4	70.3	69.6	68.1	68.6	68.6	67.9
2006	67.5	67.7	69.3	71.0	72.1	72.8	72.9	72.7	71.5	71.2	71.7	71.6	71.0
2007	70.5	70.7	71.9	72.8	73.2	75.3	74.3	74.3	73.1	71.5	71.7	71.7	72.6
2008	70.1	69.8	70.5	71.7	72.5	72.8	72.7	72.1	69.9	68.3	68.1	67.5	70.5
2009	65.1	65.2	65.7	66.9	67.4	69.0	68.5	68.0	65.7	64.6	64.7	64.4	66.3
2010	62.4	62.8	64.3	65.2	66.0	67.3	66.9	66.4	64.6	64.3	63.8	63.4	64.8
2011	62.3	62.6	63.9	65.4	66.1	67.3	66.3	65.3	64.2	63.2	64.8	64.1	64.6
Other Services													
2000	26.3	26.8	26.5	26.9	26.9	25.0	24.0	24.6	24.3	24.5	24.5	24.5	25.4
2001	23.9	24.0	24.3	24.1	24.2	24.4	24.0	23.9	23.7	23.5	23.5	23.5	23.9
2002	22.9	22.9	23.0	23.2	23.4	23.7	24.1	23.9	23.8	23.8	23.8	24.0	23.5
2003	23.9	24.0	24.3	24.4	24.3	24.7	24.5	24.6	24.3	24.2	24.2	24.2	24.3
2004	24.0	24.1	24.4	24.3	24.4	24.9	24.8	24.7	24.8	24.6	24.7	24.8	24.5
2005	24.2	24.4	24.6	24.7	24.7	25.0	24.8	24.6	24.6	24.4	24.4	24.3	24.6
2006	24.1	24.2	24.4	24.4	24.4	24.9	24.7	24.6	24.5	24.0	24.0	23.9	24.3
2007	23.7	23.7	24.1	24.3	24.5	24.9	24.5	24.4	24.2	24.1	24.0	24.0	24.2
2008	23.9	24.0	24.1	24.2	24.6	25.1	25.0	25.0	24.9	24.9	24.9	25.0	24.6
2009	24.8	24.9	24.9	24.9	25.1	25.3	25.1	24.9	24.8	24.6	24.5	24.4	24.9
2010	24.4	24.3	24.5	24.8	24.7	24.7	24.3	24.0	23.6	23.9	23.5	23.3	24.2
2011	23.0	23.1	23.2	23.4	23.4	23.6	23.5	23.2	23.3	23.3	23.2	22.9	23.3
Government													
2000	82.5	84.9	89.1	86.1	85.5	82.7	79.2	83.1	83.9	86.4	86.6	86.7	84.7
2001	84.7	87.5	87.8	88.3	85.8	82.1	81.2	84.4	86.1	88.9	88.9	88.0	86.1
2002	87.0	90.0	90.3	90.8	88.7	84.8	82.1	85.9	88.5	91.1	92.2	90.8	88.5
2003	90.9	93.0	93.7	92.6	90.2	84.3	82.8	86.4	89.2	91.0	91.1	90.6	89.7
2004	90.1	93.8	91.8	91.2	88.7	84.9	83.0	87.2	90.4	91.1	91.4	90.3	89.5
2005	89.2	90.5	90.7	91.0	89.2	84.7	83.4	87.0	89.3	90.3	90.6	89.8	88.8
2006	88.5	89.1	89.4	89.0	86.9	83.1	82.8	85.9	89.4	91.0	90.5	90.4	88.0
2007	89.8	90.3	90.0	89.3	88.2	83.5	83.3	86.8	89.3	90.7	91.0	90.2	88.5
2008	89.6	91.0	91.1	91.2	90.3	84.9	84.4	87.9	89.6	90.5	90.4	89.2	89.2
2009	88.2	89.1	89.2	89.0	88.5	84.9	84.6	85.2	88.0	88.6	89.0	88.0	87.7
2010	86.2	88.2	88.5	88.5	90.1	83.8	83.1	85.4	87.7	88.6	88.6	86.7	87.1
2011	87.2	88.7	88.6	88.2	86.4	81.4	81.4	85.6	88.7	88.9	89.5	88.8	87.0

Employment by Industry: Miami–Fort Lauderdale–Pompano Beach, FL, Selected Years, 2000–2011

(Numbers in thousands, not seasonally adjusted)

Industry and year	January	February	March	April	May	June	July	August	September	October	November	December	Annual average
Total Nonfarm													
2000	2,114.4	2,127.6	2,146.5	2,145.1	2,156.0	2,153.7	2,115.2	2,128.9	2,162.3	2,165.2	2,199.2	2,225.9	2,153.3
2001	2,182.8	2,201.0	2,217.6	2,200.5	2,201.7	2,197.3	2,150.0	2,157.9	2,185.4	2,183.7	2,202.7	2,222.4	2,191.9
2002	2,181.2	2,190.7	2,209.8	2,193.7	2,198.7	2,190.3	2,144.8	2,154.2	2,185.9	2,193.8	2,218.2	2,242.1	2,192.0
2003	2,195.6	2,211.6	2,223.9	2,206.0	2,203.0	2,188.8	2,143.5	2,150.9	2,181.7	2,199.2	2,209.1	2,236.8	2,195.8
2004	2,209.9	2,229.6	2,246.8	2,251.8	2,252.3	2,242.9	2,211.5	2,221.5	2,237.1	2,272.5	2,303.6	2,331.8	2,250.9
2005	2,287.4	2,311.2	2,321.9	2,336.9	2,339.3	2,312.0	2,298.6	2,338.3	2,354.1	2,349.2	2,368.0	2,401.0	2,334.8
2006	2,357.3	2,380.7	2,401.6	2,388.0	2,398.5	2,375.1	2,344.0	2,383.4	2,393.2	2,396.6	2,428.2	2,454.3	2,391.7
2007	2,406.7	2,425.2	2,441.0	2,419.9	2,428.0	2,399.6	2,357.9	2,397.7	2,405.7	2,401.6	2,432.6	2,454.2	2,414.2
2008	2,397.5	2,411.5	2,417.8	2,388.6	2,382.7	2,338.9	2,291.7	2,317.1	2,312.9	2,306.1	2,318.3	2,326.7	2,350.8
2009	2,256.1	2,250.6	2,245.3	2,222.9	2,214.8	2,176.9	2,143.7	2,166.8	2,168.7	2,181.5	2,204.3	2,217.4	2,204.1
2010	2,171.4	2,183.2	2,191.0	2,189.9	2,198.2	2,162.8	2,140.7	2,168.9	2,171.7	2,193.3	2,219.3	2,237.0	2,185.6
2011	2,201.7	2,214.0	2,220.0	2,230.9	2,227.9	2,194.9	2,177.2	2,207.6	2,210.5	2,229.9	2,245.1	2,260.4	2,218.3
Total Private													
2000	1,827.7	1,839.8	1,856.4	1,849.1	1,854.1	1,862.5	1,843.4	1,856.1	1,868.7	1,867.8	1,899.9	1,925.1	1,862.6
2001	1,884.2	1,900.4	1,915.3	1,897.0	1,897.4	1,898.7	1,871.4	1,877.7	1,881.7	1,876.3	1,893.1	1,911.9	1,892.1
2002	1,873.3	1,881.6	1,897.6	1,883.1	1,886.1	1,885.5	1,860.5	1,867.8	1,874.7	1,881.6	1,903.4	1,925.6	1,885.1
2003	1,881.9	1,895.8	1,906.2	1,889.6	1,884.4	1,878.4	1,853.6	1,859.3	1,867.4	1,882.6	1,892.5	1,920.6	1,884.4
2004	1,894.6	1,912.9	1,929.3	1,933.3	1,933.0	1,930.8	1,919.5	1,927.0	1,919.5	1,951.1	1,982.0	2,009.8	1,936.9
2005	1,967.2	1,989.8	1,999.4	2,012.2	2,013.9	2,015.0	2,005.7	2,017.5	2,030.2	2,023.2	2,042.7	2,075.3	2,016.0
2006	2,033.0	2,055.2	2,074.6	2,062.6	2,072.6	2,077.4	2,050.5	2,061.3	2,067.4	2,069.4	2,097.9	2,124.7	2,070.6
2007	2,080.2	2,097.3	2,110.8	2,089.5	2,096.8	2,097.5	2,060.1	2,069.9	2,074.1	2,071.4	2,100.0	2,120.7	2,089.0
2008	2,066.7	2,078.2	2,084.8	2,057.0	2,050.1	2,035.8	1,993.1	1,991.7	1,985.7	1,979.5	1,989.7	1,996.9	2,025.8
2009	1,928.2	1,924.2	1,918.7	1,895.9	1,889.3	1,879.5	1,849.0	1,850.3	1,849.7	1,860.5	1,882.4	1,895.7	1,885.3
2010	1,853.1	1,864.3	1,872.2	1,870.0	1,869.2	1,867.2	1,851.6	1,858.7	1,860.3	1,879.6	1,905.2	1,923.5	1,872.9
2011	1,889.7	1,900.4	1,907.9	1,917.7	1,916.2	1,909.4	1,894.7	1,901.2	1,902.8	1,918.4	1,934.7	1,949.0	1,911.8
Goods-Producing													
2000	250.0	251.7	254.2	252.2	254.1	254.9	251.7	253.0	254.4	253.8	255.0	255.4	253.4
2001	249.7	250.4	250.5	247.0	247.0	247.4	243.1	244.2	243.8	242.5	242.1	242.2	245.8
2002	235.9	235.9	236.2	233.9	234.7	235.0	231.4	232.5	233.1	232.9	233.2	233.4	234.0
2003	227.9	228.1	228.3	225.1	225.6	225.9	223.5	225.6	227.1	227.2	226.1	228.0	226.5
2004	225.1	226.7	229.3	229.6	231.2	233.0	233.0	235.4	235.1	237.7	239.7	241.4	233.1
2005	238.5	240.6	242.3	244.3	246.8	249.4	250.5	252.8	255.8	256.0	257.3	259.7	249.5
2006	255.8	259.3	261.9	263.3	266.4	269.3	267.0	268.5	270.3	268.8	269.7	270.4	265.9
2007	264.7	266.0	267.1	261.7	262.7	265.7	258.5	259.2	259.1	255.0	254.3	253.5	260.6
2008	244.1	243.0	241.6	234.5	233.1	232.1	225.0	223.6	221.7	217.3	213.8	210.6	228.4
2009	198.8	196.0	193.2	187.1	185.5	183.9	179.2	177.8	176.7	174.4	172.8	171.7	183.1
2010	164.2	164.7	164.6	164.1	164.7	165.4	165.0	165.5	165.3	164.8	164.3	163.9	164.7
2011	159.8	160.4	160.5	160.8	160.9	161.3	158.4	159.6	159.8	159.4	160.2	160.1	160.1
Mining and Logging													
2000	0.4	0.3	0.4	0.4	0.4	0.4	0.4	0.4	0.4	0.4	0.4	0.4	0.4
2001	0.5	0.4	0.5	0.5	0.5	0.5	0.5	0.5	0.5	0.5	0.5	0.5	0.5
2002	0.5	0.5	0.5	0.5	0.5	0.5	0.5	0.5	0.5	0.5	0.5	0.5	0.5
2003	0.5	0.4	0.4	0.4	0.4	0.4	0.4	0.4	0.4	0.4	0.4	0.4	0.4
2004	0.4	0.4	0.4	0.4	0.5	0.5	0.5	0.5	0.5	0.5	0.5	0.5	0.5
2005	0.5	0.6	0.6	0.6	0.8	0.8	0.8	0.8	0.7	0.7	0.7	0.6	0.7
2006	0.6	0.7	0.7	0.7	0.7	0.8	0.8	0.8	0.8	0.8	0.9	0.9	0.8
2007	0.9	0.9	0.9	0.9	0.9	0.9	0.9	0.9	0.9	1.0	1.0	1.0	0.9
2008	0.8	0.8	0.9	0.9	0.9	0.8	0.7	0.7	0.7	0.7	0.7	0.7	0.8
2009	0.7	0.7	0.6	0.6	0.6	0.6	0.6	0.6	0.6	0.6	0.6	0.6	0.6
2010	0.6	0.6	0.6	0.6	0.6	0.6	0.6	0.6	0.6	0.6	0.6	0.6	0.6
2011	0.7	0.7	0.7	0.7	0.7	0.7	0.7	0.7	0.7	0.7	0.7	0.7	0.7
Construction													
2000	113.2	114.1	115.9	116.3	117.7	119.0	118.7	120.1	121.3	121.7	122.4	123.2	118.6
2001	120.3	120.8	121.2	119.7	120.6	122.0	121.2	122.2	122.3	122.9	122.7	122.5	121.5
2002	119.0	118.9	119.5	118.9	119.9	120.6	119.1	120.5	121.0	122.0	121.8	121.8	120.3
2003	118.7	119.2	119.8	119.2	120.5	121.2	121.7	123.1	124.3	124.8	124.3	125.4	121.9
2004	123.8	124.7	126.5	127.0	127.9	130.3	131.5	133.4	133.6	136.0	137.7	138.9	130.9
2005	137.8	139.2	140.3	142.2	143.8	145.9	147.8	149.4	151.9	153.1	154.2	155.7	146.8
2006	153.3	156.3	159.1	161.3	164.0	166.4	165.5	166.6	167.9	167.6	168.0	167.7	163.6
2007	163.2	164.0	165.0	161.0	161.7	164.2	159.7	159.9	159.7	155.9	154.7	153.7	160.2
2008	146.0	144.8	144.1	138.4	137.4	136.8	132.1	130.9	129.2	126.1	123.4	121.1	134.2
2009	111.9	110.1	108.9	104.7	103.9	102.8	100.2	98.8	98.1	96.1	94.3	93.4	101.9
2010	87.6	88.0	87.9	87.8	88.2	88.5	88.9	89.0	89.0	88.2	87.4	86.7	88.1
2011	83.7	84.1	84.3	84.3	84.0	84.2	82.3	82.6	82.4	81.8	82.0	81.4	83.1
Manufacturing													
2000	136.4	137.3	137.9	135.5	136.0	135.5	132.6	132.5	132.7	131.7	132.2	131.8	134.3
2001	128.9	129.2	128.8	126.8	125.9	124.9	121.4	121.5	121.0	119.1	118.9	119.2	123.8
2002	116.4	116.5	116.2	114.5	114.3	113.9	111.8	111.5	111.6	110.4	110.9	111.1	113.3
2003	108.7	108.5	108.1	105.5	104.7	104.3	101.4	102.1	102.4	102.0	101.4	102.2	104.3
2004	100.9	101.6	102.4	102.2	102.8	102.2	101.0	101.5	101.0	101.2	101.5	102.0	101.7
2005	100.2	100.8	101.4	101.5	102.2	102.7	101.9	102.6	103.2	102.2	102.4	103.4	102.0
2006	101.9	102.3	102.1	101.3	101.7	102.1	100.7	101.1	101.6	100.4	100.8	101.8	101.5
2007	100.6	101.1	101.2	99.8	100.1	100.6	97.9	98.4	98.5	98.1	98.6	98.8	99.5
2008	97.3	97.4	96.6	95.2	94.8	94.5	92.2	92.0	91.8	90.5	89.7	88.8	93.4
2009	86.2	85.2	83.7	81.8	81.0	80.5	78.4	78.4	78.0	77.7	77.9	77.7	80.5
2010	76.0	76.1	76.1	75.7	75.9	76.3	75.5	75.9	75.7	76.0	76.3	76.6	76.0
2011	75.4	75.6	75.5	75.8	76.2	76.4	75.4	76.3	76.7	76.9	77.5	78.0	76.3

Employment by Industry: Miami–Fort Lauderdale–Pompano Beach, FL, Selected Years, 2000–2011—*Continued*
(Numbers in thousands, not seasonally adjusted)

Industry and year	January	February	March	April	May	June	July	August	September	October	November	December	Annual average
Service-Providing													
2000	1,864.4	1,875.9	1,892.3	1,892.9	1,901.9	1,898.8	1,863.5	1,875.9	1,907.9	1,911.4	1,944.2	1,970.5	1,900.0
2001	1,933.1	1,950.6	1,967.1	1,953.5	1,954.7	1,949.9	1,906.9	1,913.7	1,941.6	1,941.2	1,960.6	1,980.2	1,946.1
2002	1,945.3	1,954.8	1,973.6	1,959.8	1,964.0	1,955.3	1,913.4	1,921.7	1,952.8	1,960.9	1,985.0	2,008.7	1,957.9
2003	1,967.7	1,983.5	1,995.6	1,980.9	1,977.4	1,962.9	1,920.0	1,925.3	1,954.6	1,972.0	1,983.0	2,008.8	1,969.3
2004	1,984.8	2,002.9	2,017.5	2,022.2	2,021.1	2,009.9	1,978.5	1,986.1	2,002.0	2,034.8	2,063.9	2,090.4	2,017.8
2005	2,048.9	2,070.6	2,079.6	2,092.6	2,092.5	2,062.6	2,048.1	2,085.5	2,098.3	2,093.2	2,110.7	2,141.3	2,085.3
2006	2,101.5	2,121.4	2,139.7	2,124.7	2,132.1	2,105.8	2,077.0	2,114.9	2,122.9	2,127.8	2,158.5	2,183.9	2,125.9
2007	2,142.0	2,159.2	2,173.9	2,158.2	2,165.3	2,133.9	2,099.4	2,138.5	2,146.6	2,146.6	2,178.3	2,200.7	2,153.6
2008	2,153.4	2,168.5	2,176.2	2,154.1	2,149.6	2,106.8	2,066.7	2,093.5	2,091.2	2,088.8	2,104.5	2,116.1	2,122.5
2009	2,057.3	2,054.6	2,052.1	2,035.8	2,029.3	1,993.0	1,964.5	1,989.0	1,992.0	2,007.1	2,031.5	2,045.7	2,021.0
2010	2,007.2	2,018.5	2,026.4	2,025.8	2,033.5	1,997.4	1,975.7	2,003.4	2,006.4	2,028.5	2,055.0	2,073.1	2,020.9
2011	2,041.9	2,053.6	2,059.5	2,070.1	2,067.0	2,033.6	2,018.8	2,048.0	2,050.7	2,070.5	2,084.9	2,100.3	2,058.2
Trade, Transportation, and Utilities													
2000	517.8	516.3	517.0	517.5	518.7	520.9	515.4	518.7	519.3	521.1	534.1	545.5	521.9
2001	525.1	524.6	527.8	523.3	522.4	521.0	517.4	519.0	519.4	519.0	527.7	535.6	523.5
2002	518.3	514.5	517.8	512.9	513.3	512.8	508.8	511.2	512.6	513.0	521.7	531.2	515.7
2003	512.3	509.9	509.3	507.6	506.7	505.7	503.4	504.8	506.4	509.7	518.1	528.9	510.2
2004	513.2	512.3	513.5	513.7	513.5	512.8	511.7	513.4	510.9	517.2	529.4	539.3	516.7
2005	522.6	522.6	523.1	525.9	527.2	526.6	527.6	529.9	530.8	532.4	538.7	551.4	529.9
2006	537.7	538.3	541.0	539.4	541.5	541.9	537.2	539.4	539.6	542.6	554.3	564.6	543.1
2007	546.8	546.0	548.2	544.9	548.4	548.6	542.7	544.6	545.0	546.6	561.0	570.1	549.4
2008	550.7	549.7	549.7	543.8	543.7	540.8	533.8	533.6	532.0	530.4	536.3	541.8	540.5
2009	519.1	515.0	511.8	504.2	503.5	501.0	494.9	495.0	494.2	498.3	509.6	516.9	505.3
2010	499.6	498.3	499.2	500.3	501.9	501.9	498.1	500.0	499.5	506.5	519.0	527.3	504.3
2011	511.0	510.3	511.3	514.8	515.0	515.0	514.9	517.0	515.0	518.8	531.3	538.2	517.7
Wholesale Trade													
2000	119.8	120.4	121.3	123.4	124.1	124.9	124.5	125.0	126.0	125.7	126.6	128.2	124.2
2001	129.1	130.5	131.2	131.4	132.0	131.6	130.8	131.0	131.3	131.5	132.3	133.0	131.3
2002	131.6	132.3	133.1	131.8	132.3	132.0	131.5	132.1	132.0	132.5	133.3	134.2	132.4
2003	133.0	133.4	133.3	133.3	133.3	133.3	133.5	134.2	134.6	135.4	136.3	138.2	134.3
2004	136.9	137.8	138.8	138.9	139.3	139.0	137.9	138.0	137.6	138.8	140.1	140.7	138.7
2005	139.5	140.5	140.6	141.4	142.0	141.6	140.9	141.1	141.3	141.2	141.3	142.7	141.2
2006	141.5	142.9	143.6	143.5	144.1	144.7	144.2	145.1	145.3	145.7	146.7	148.2	144.6
2007	146.8	148.4	149.0	147.9	148.6	148.4	146.2	146.5	146.7	146.6	147.4	148.5	147.6
2008	145.9	146.8	146.9	145.9	146.3	145.3	143.2	143.0	143.0	142.2	142.0	142.2	144.4
2009	138.7	138.6	137.3	135.9	135.8	134.3	132.4	132.3	131.7	132.4	133.4	134.2	134.8
2010	131.3	131.9	132.0	131.9	132.6	131.9	130.8	131.0	130.9	131.9	132.7	133.7	131.9
2011	131.5	132.5	132.7	133.5	133.3	132.9	133.0	132.8	132.9	133.5	135.5	136.4	133.4
Retail Trade													
2000	296.2	294.7	294.7	293.4	294.4	296.4	291.4	294.5	294.0	296.7	307.8	315.9	297.5
2001	297.2	295.1	296.9	293.0	292.0	291.1	287.5	289.2	289.8	290.1	298.6	305.1	293.8
2002	290.9	286.5	287.5	285.1	284.9	284.7	281.1	282.8	284.3	284.4	291.4	299.0	286.9
2003	283.7	280.9	280.9	279.8	280.1	279.3	278.1	279.1	280.2	282.9	290.4	297.8	282.8
2004	284.2	282.1	282.4	282.5	283.1	282.7	282.3	283.7	281.7	285.6	295.0	302.4	285.6
2005	288.8	287.6	288.0	289.6	290.0	290.7	292.4	295.0	295.4	297.3	302.5	312.2	294.1
2006	300.8	299.8	301.5	300.6	302.7	302.2	299.5	300.0	299.9	302.9	312.7	319.1	303.5
2007	305.1	302.8	303.9	302.0	304.9	304.8	301.7	303.0	303.0	304.1	315.9	321.6	306.1
2008	307.6	305.2	305.1	301.8	301.7	300.8	297.0	296.8	295.8	294.7	300.0	303.8	300.9
2009	288.0	284.6	282.9	278.5	278.7	278.1	274.9	275.3	275.8	278.6	287.7	292.9	281.3
2010	280.1	278.1	278.7	279.9	281.4	282.2	279.9	281.6	281.1	286.4	296.5	302.2	284.0
2011	290.1	287.7	288.2	290.4	291.2	291.3	291.9	294.1	291.3	294.5	304.3	308.5	293.6
Transportation and Utilities													
2000	101.8	101.2	101.0	100.7	100.2	99.6	99.5	99.2	99.3	98.7	99.7	101.4	100.2
2001	98.8	99.0	99.7	98.9	98.4	98.3	99.1	98.8	98.3	97.4	96.8	97.5	98.4
2002	95.8	95.7	97.2	96.0	96.1	96.1	96.2	96.3	96.3	96.1	97.0	98.0	96.4
2003	95.6	95.6	95.1	94.5	93.3	93.1	91.8	91.5	91.6	91.4	91.4	92.9	93.2
2004	92.1	92.4	92.3	92.3	91.1	91.1	91.5	91.7	91.6	92.8	94.3	96.2	92.5
2005	94.3	94.5	94.5	94.9	95.2	94.3	94.3	93.8	94.1	93.9	94.9	96.5	94.6
2006	95.4	95.6	95.9	95.3	94.7	95.0	93.5	94.3	94.4	94.0	94.9	97.3	95.0
2007	94.9	94.8	95.3	95.0	94.9	95.4	94.8	95.1	95.3	95.9	97.7	100.0	95.8
2008	97.2	97.7	97.7	96.1	95.7	94.7	93.6	93.8	93.2	93.5	94.3	95.8	95.3
2009	92.4	91.8	91.6	89.8	89.0	88.6	87.6	87.4	86.7	87.3	88.5	89.8	89.2
2010	88.2	88.3	88.5	88.5	87.9	87.8	87.4	87.4	87.5	88.2	89.8	91.4	88.4
2011	89.4	90.1	90.4	90.9	90.5	90.8	90.0	90.1	90.8	90.8	91.5	93.3	90.7
Information													
2000	57.2	57.4	58.5	58.4	59.0	60.9	62.3	63.0	63.6	63.0	63.6	64.6	61.0
2001	65.1	65.7	66.4	65.9	66.3	66.2	64.8	64.9	64.1	63.6	63.4	63.9	65.0
2002	62.5	62.6	62.8	61.8	61.7	61.9	60.9	60.3	60.0	59.2	59.0	59.1	61.0
2003	57.3	57.0	57.4	56.3	56.4	56.6	56.6	56.6	56.2	56.5	56.6	57.0	56.7
2004	55.4	55.4	55.6	55.6	55.7	55.9	55.8	55.9	55.5	55.9	56.1	56.6	55.8
2005	55.7	56.1	56.2	55.7	55.6	55.7	55.1	54.9	54.8	53.7	54.0	54.1	55.1
2006	53.0	53.4	53.5	52.7	53.1	53.0	52.5	52.3	51.7	51.3	51.3	51.4	52.4
2007	50.7	51.1	51.4	51.2	51.4	51.7	51.3	51.3	50.7	51.0	51.1	51.3	51.2
2008	50.7	50.7	50.7	50.3	50.4	50.3	49.6	49.3	48.9	48.6	48.7	48.4	49.7
2009	47.1	46.9	46.6	45.8	45.7	45.2	44.3	44.2	43.4	43.5	43.5	43.5	45.0
2010	43.1	43.1	43.5	43.4	43.6	43.7	43.6	43.8	43.5	43.9	44.0	44.1	43.6
2011	43.9	43.9	44.0	44.0	44.0	43.9	43.4	43.4	43.2	43.2	43.4	43.7	43.7

Employment by Industry: Miami–Fort Lauderdale–Pompano Beach, FL, Selected Years, 2000–2011—*Continued*

(Numbers in thousands, not seasonally adjusted)

Industry and year	January	February	March	April	May	June	July	August	September	October	November	December	Annual average
Financial Activities													
2000	155.0	155.7	156.3	156.1	155.8	158.0	156.6	157.2	157.6	156.9	157.5	158.9	156.8
2001	156.1	157.4	158.7	158.3	158.6	159.5	158.9	159.5	159.1	159.2	159.6	160.1	158.8
2002	159.9	160.7	161.5	160.9	161.0	161.1	161.4	162.2	162.0	162.4	163.2	163.7	161.7
2003	161.5	162.1	162.4	162.1	162.4	162.8	163.0	163.7	163.9	164.5	164.3	166.0	163.2
2004	164.0	165.1	166.3	167.8	168.2	168.5	170.0	169.9	169.6	171.9	172.0	173.7	168.9
2005	172.1	173.6	174.3	175.6	176.1	177.2	177.6	178.7	178.9	179.1	180.1	182.1	177.1
2006	178.7	180.8	182.0	182.0	182.7	183.4	182.1	182.8	182.0	182.8	183.5	185.5	182.4
2007	181.1	182.1	182.2	181.0	180.8	181.1	179.8	179.5	178.5	177.7	178.7	180.0	180.2
2008	175.3	175.4	175.5	173.0	172.3	171.1	168.5	167.2	165.7	164.4	163.7	163.8	169.7
2009	158.0	157.5	156.9	155.2	155.0	154.6	152.5	152.1	151.0	151.8	152.2	153.0	154.2
2010	149.6	150.1	150.6	150.2	150.4	151.3	151.1	151.1	150.5	151.9	152.9	154.0	151.1
2011	151.2	151.7	152.1	153.1	153.4	153.2	151.9	151.6	151.2	150.9	151.5	151.9	152.0
Professional and Business Services													
2000	284.4	286.9	292.4	291.6	293.3	296.6	294.2	298.5	302.4	299.4	306.2	309.6	296.3
2001	308.7	313.4	316.2	313.6	313.0	316.5	312.4	313.0	314.8	314.6	315.6	318.1	314.2
2002	311.3	313.6	319.0	318.5	320.6	322.5	319.0	318.2	317.7	319.2	323.4	328.1	319.3
2003	318.7	325.9	330.1	325.8	321.9	318.1	311.9	311.3	309.5	316.1	314.4	317.8	318.5
2004	314.5	321.6	327.0	331.4	330.0	328.9	327.6	328.1	327.0	338.4	344.6	351.6	330.9
2005	342.1	349.7	352.4	356.1	355.8	356.3	355.1	357.4	362.2	357.8	362.9	369.1	356.4
2006	356.7	362.3	367.3	364.7	368.0	370.7	366.0	367.5	370.0	369.3	373.2	379.9	368.0
2007	370.1	375.1	377.4	372.2	373.0	372.9	365.4	367.2	367.1	365.3	366.9	369.4	370.2
2008	357.6	362.4	364.3	359.7	356.7	354.4	348.0	347.8	346.8	347.3	347.1	347.8	353.3
2009	331.2	331.2	328.8	325.0	323.4	323.5	320.1	321.3	321.4	324.5	328.5	330.3	325.8
2010	323.0	327.5	329.2	327.2	325.5	326.4	326.1	327.9	328.5	332.5	335.6	340.1	329.1
2011	334.7	339.4	340.9	342.8	341.0	339.5	337.2	339.5	339.8	345.2	345.8	346.3	341.0
Education and Health Services													
2000	253.7	256.8	258.3	255.7	256.5	257.4	253.9	255.2	258.0	258.8	260.4	262.6	257.3
2001	255.5	258.9	260.8	260.8	263.0	263.8	261.2	262.9	267.0	268.0	270.0	272.7	263.7
2002	268.6	271.8	274.5	273.1	274.1	274.5	269.7	272.6	276.8	278.1	279.7	281.7	274.6
2003	278.2	281.5	283.2	282.8	283.6	283.9	279.6	282.0	286.2	288.6	287.8	290.5	284.0
2004	287.3	290.8	291.7	293.3	294.4	293.4	290.0	292.0	293.0	297.4	299.1	300.1	293.5
2005	294.2	298.4	298.9	302.0	302.0	300.3	299.4	302.5	305.1	304.1	304.5	306.4	301.5
2006	300.7	303.7	306.1	306.0	307.9	307.3	304.5	307.9	310.4	311.3	313.3	315.6	307.9
2007	312.0	315.4	316.9	317.2	319.0	318.6	314.5	317.8	321.2	322.1	324.0	326.5	318.8
2008	322.6	326.1	328.0	326.3	328.0	326.6	320.9	324.0	326.1	327.3	329.0	330.0	326.2
2009	325.4	327.2	328.7	329.4	331.5	330.2	326.3	329.0	332.2	335.6	337.0	337.0	330.8
2010	332.6	334.8	335.3	335.4	336.9	335.2	331.3	332.4	334.7	337.8	339.6	340.1	335.5
2011	337.9	340.6	340.9	343.7	344.6	342.1	340.9	343.6	349.5	352.5	355.0	355.4	345.6
Leisure and Hospitality													
2000	214.9	219.8	223.9	221.8	220.2	216.9	213.5	214.7	216.8	217.9	225.7	230.9	219.8
2001	228.1	233.7	238.1	233.1	232.5	229.9	220.8	222.1	221.5	218.4	223.3	227.5	227.4
2002	224.5	229.1	231.8	229.0	227.5	224.5	216.3	217.5	218.6	221.9	227.0	231.3	224.9
2003	230.2	234.1	237.5	232.9	230.6	227.9	221.2	221.4	223.8	225.7	230.9	236.7	229.4
2004	239.4	244.1	248.0	245.2	242.7	239.9	234.0	234.1	230.2	235.2	242.2	248.1	240.3
2005	243.3	249.1	252.6	252.8	250.7	250.1	242.2	242.9	243.8	242.5	247.0	253.1	247.5
2006	250.9	256.6	260.7	255.3	253.6	251.7	243.4	244.9	245.2	245.5	253.9	257.7	251.6
2007	255.1	260.6	265.2	261.9	261.6	258.6	249.3	251.3	252.8	252.2	260.7	265.0	257.9
2008	261.9	266.4	269.6	265.7	263.0	258.4	247.3	247.0	246.4	246.9	254.2	257.5	257.0
2009	253.7	255.6	257.9	254.8	250.7	247.6	239.4	238.8	238.8	239.8	245.7	249.5	247.7
2010	248.2	252.1	255.7	255.3	252.7	250.1	244.7	246.2	246.7	249.8	256.5	260.5	251.5
2011	258.4	260.9	264.5	264.1	262.9	260.6	255.6	255.0	252.5	255.3	254.0	258.8	258.6
Other Services													
2000	94.7	95.2	95.8	95.8	96.5	96.9	95.8	95.8	96.6	96.9	97.4	97.6	96.3
2001	95.9	96.3	96.8	95.0	94.6	94.4	92.8	92.1	92.0	91.0	91.4	91.8	93.7
2002	92.3	93.4	94.0	93.0	93.2	93.2	93.0	93.3	93.9	94.9	96.2	97.1	94.0
2003	95.8	97.2	98.0	97.0	97.2	97.5	94.4	93.9	94.3	94.3	94.3	95.7	95.8
2004	95.7	96.9	97.9	96.7	97.3	98.4	97.4	98.2	98.2	97.4	98.9	99.0	97.7
2005	98.7	99.7	99.6	99.8	99.7	99.4	98.2	98.4	98.8	97.6	98.2	99.4	99.0
2006	99.5	100.8	102.1	99.2	99.4	100.1	97.8	98.0	98.2	97.8	98.7	99.6	99.3
2007	99.7	101.0	102.4	99.4	99.9	100.3	98.6	99.0	99.7	101.5	103.3	104.9	100.8
2008	103.8	104.5	105.4	103.7	102.9	102.1	100.0	99.2	98.1	97.3	96.9	97.0	100.9
2009	94.9	94.8	94.8	94.4	94.0	93.5	92.3	92.1	92.0	92.6	93.1	93.8	93.5
2010	92.8	93.7	94.1	94.1	93.5	93.2	91.7	91.8	91.6	92.4	93.3	93.5	93.0
2011	92.8	93.2	93.7	94.4	94.4	93.8	92.4	91.5	91.8	93.1	93.5	94.6	93.3
Government													
2000	286.7	287.8	290.1	296.0	301.9	291.2	271.8	272.8	293.6	297.4	299.3	300.8	290.8
2001	298.6	300.6	302.3	303.5	304.3	298.6	278.6	280.2	303.7	307.4	309.6	310.5	299.8
2002	307.9	309.1	312.2	310.6	312.6	304.8	284.3	286.4	311.2	312.2	314.8	316.5	306.9
2003	313.7	315.8	317.7	316.4	318.6	310.4	289.9	291.6	314.3	316.6	316.6	316.2	311.5
2004	315.3	316.7	317.5	318.5	319.3	312.1	292.0	294.5	317.6	321.4	321.6	322.0	314.0
2005	320.2	321.4	322.5	324.7	325.4	297.0	292.9	320.8	323.9	326.0	325.3	325.7	318.8
2006	324.3	325.5	327.0	325.4	325.9	297.7	293.5	322.1	325.8	327.2	330.3	329.6	321.2
2007	326.5	327.9	330.2	330.4	331.2	302.1	297.8	327.8	331.6	330.2	332.6	333.5	325.2
2008	330.8	333.3	333.0	331.6	332.6	303.1	298.6	325.4	327.2	326.6	328.6	329.8	325.1
2009	327.9	326.4	326.6	327.0	325.5	297.4	294.7	316.5	319.0	321.0	321.9	321.7	318.8
2010	318.3	318.9	318.8	319.9	329.0	295.6	289.1	310.2	311.4	313.7	314.1	313.5	312.7
2011	312.0	313.6	312.1	313.2	311.7	285.5	282.5	306.4	307.7	311.5	310.4	311.4	306.5

Employment by Industry: Milwaukee–Waukesha–West Allis, WI, Selected Years, 2000–2011

(Numbers in thousands, not seasonally adjusted)

Industry and year	January	February	March	April	May	June	July	August	September	October	November	December	Annual average
Total Nonfarm													
2000	850.2	852.8	857.8	865.8	869.4	879.4	869.1	871.7	871.5	874.3	878.0	874.9	867.9
2001	856.5	856.4	858.7	863.1	864.3	866.0	856.1	855.0	853.6	853.7	850.0	849.2	856.9
2002	829.0	828.2	832.4	839.3	843.8	848.7	840.3	840.5	839.0	844.7	845.0	843.6	839.5
2003	820.0	822.8	824.9	830.9	834.0	839.6	826.8	828.8	828.4	837.1	834.8	837.0	830.4
2004	815.1	817.9	822.8	827.1	833.1	842.0	833.9	836.4	834.8	841.0	841.0	840.5	832.1
2005	822.9	825.2	827.8	839.2	842.1	849.0	843.6	844.8	847.5	847.1	849.0	850.4	840.7
2006	830.0	832.5	836.1	845.8	850.7	859.2	851.7	855.1	858.3	861.4	863.0	863.2	850.6
2007	843.3	843.0	846.0	853.0	861.8	870.8	858.9	861.8	860.1	862.3	863.2	863.5	857.3
2008	843.8	842.9	846.1	853.0	860.1	865.0	854.9	854.7	855.7	856.8	852.8	847.8	852.8
2009	820.7	815.1	810.6	813.4	816.9	819.3	806.3	805.8	810.6	811.5	809.5	808.1	812.3
2010	790.1	789.7	792.4	800.9	809.0	810.9	808.2	810.4	809.0	815.7	818.0	815.5	805.8
2011	797.3	799.4	802.8	813.5	818.1	822.7	819.4	821.6	821.3	822.8	818.6	811.7	814.1
Total Private													
2000	759.5	760.8	765.3	771.1	775.6	782.5	781.8	784.0	780.9	780.5	783.3	782.2	775.6
2001	763.6	761.0	763.4	766.7	768.9	771.7	770.0	768.5	760.7	757.8	754.4	752.8	763.3
2002	734.8	731.1	734.9	742.6	747.8	752.4	753.0	753.2	747.6	746.6	746.5	745.3	744.7
2003	726.6	725.5	728.1	733.7	739.1	744.1	742.2	743.6	740.3	742.0	740.5	742.3	737.3
2004	725.3	723.0	727.5	733.5	739.5	748.5	750.0	751.5	745.0	748.8	747.5	747.6	740.6
2005	731.3	730.4	734.2	745.5	748.7	755.5	758.5	759.4	755.2	754.1	755.5	757.6	748.8
2006	739.8	739.6	742.7	752.1	757.2	765.3	766.2	769.2	766.1	767.8	769.4	770.0	758.8
2007	753.2	751.3	754.0	760.4	768.8	777.2	773.9	776.9	768.6	770.1	771.0	770.5	766.3
2008	752.6	751.6	752.4	759.7	765.8	770.8	769.0	770.1	762.2	761.7	755.9	752.2	760.3
2009	727.5	720.1	715.7	718.1	722.3	725.7	722.7	723.2	719.1	718.5	716.4	714.9	720.4
2010	698.4	698.1	700.4	709.3	715.0	719.6	723.3	726.4	721.0	725.4	726.2	725.4	715.7
2011	708.4	706.6	710.5	719.3	724.8	730.4	731.0	734.3	732.6	733.5	729.4	723.7	723.7
Goods-Producing													
2000	195.5	195.6	196.6	199.0	200.2	202.8	202.1	202.4	200.7	199.5	199.0	197.1	199.2
2001	192.3	190.8	190.8	189.8	189.9	191.6	190.7	190.8	188.8	187.1	184.6	183.2	189.2
2002	176.5	174.9	175.4	176.8	178.1	179.8	178.4	179.4	178.0	177.5	176.7	174.6	177.2
2003	169.1	167.9	167.9	169.5	170.7	172.1	171.2	172.8	171.1	170.7	169.9	168.7	170.1
2004	163.7	163.0	163.9	166.1	167.6	170.2	171.1	171.5	170.2	169.5	169.1	168.2	167.8
2005	164.1	163.8	164.4	166.9	168.3	170.7	171.1	170.9	169.4	168.2	167.7	166.7	167.7
2006	164.1	163.0	163.5	166.3	168.1	171.1	170.9	171.8	170.3	170.3	169.7	169.1	168.2
2007	165.8	163.7	164.8	167.2	169.9	172.4	172.0	172.6	170.6	170.3	169.4	167.8	168.9
2008	164.2	163.1	163.6	165.1	167.0	168.6	167.5	167.7	165.0	164.2	162.2	159.1	164.8
2009	153.2	149.4	146.3	145.4	145.0	145.4	143.8	144.0	143.0	142.1	140.5	138.4	144.7
2010	134.9	133.3	133.7	136.4	137.6	140.1	141.8	142.7	141.2	141.4	140.4	138.7	138.5
2011	136.5	135.7	136.8	139.5	141.2	144.2	146.5	145.9	145.3	146.0	144.0	142.1	142.0
Mining and Logging													
2000	0.4	0.4	0.4	0.4	0.5	0.5	0.5	0.5	0.5	0.5	0.5	0.4	0.5
2001	0.4	0.4	0.4	0.4	0.5	0.5	0.5	0.5	0.5	0.5	0.4	0.4	0.5
2002	0.4	0.4	0.4	0.4	0.4	0.5	0.5	0.5	0.5	0.4	0.4	0.4	0.4
2003	0.4	0.4	0.4	0.4	0.4	0.5	0.5	0.5	0.5	0.5	0.4	0.5	0.4
2004	0.4	0.4	0.4	0.4	0.5	0.5	0.5	0.5	0.5	0.5	0.5	0.5	0.5
2005	0.4	0.4	0.4	0.5	0.5	0.5	0.5	0.5	0.5	0.5	0.5	0.5	0.5
2006	0.5	0.5	0.5	0.5	0.5	0.5	0.5	0.5	0.5	0.5	0.5	0.5	0.5
2007	0.5	0.4	0.5	0.5	0.5	0.5	0.5	0.5	0.5	0.5	0.5	0.5	0.5
2008	0.4	0.4	0.4	0.4	0.4	0.4	0.4	0.4	0.4	0.4	0.4	0.4	0.4
2009	0.3	0.3	0.3	0.4	0.4	0.4	0.4	0.4	0.4	0.4	0.3	0.3	0.4
2010	0.3	0.3	0.3	0.3	0.4	0.4	0.4	0.4	0.4	0.4	0.3	0.3	0.4
2011	0.3	0.3	0.3	0.3	0.3	0.4	0.4	0.4	0.4	0.4	0.3	0.3	0.3
Construction													
2000	30.3	30.0	31.0	33.2	34.7	36.1	36.3	36.5	35.7	35.1	34.4	32.7	33.8
2001	30.9	30.9	31.4	32.8	34.6	35.9	36.8	36.9	36.0	35.5	34.7	33.6	34.2
2002	29.7	28.9	29.5	32.2	34.0	35.1	35.9	36.1	35.6	35.7	34.9	33.0	33.4
2003	29.9	29.2	29.4	31.5	33.6	34.7	35.7	36.1	35.5	35.4	34.5	33.1	33.2
2004	29.7	29.2	29.9	32.0	33.3	34.7	36.0	36.0	35.4	35.1	34.7	33.5	33.3
2005	30.3	29.9	30.4	32.7	34.4	35.6	36.1	36.0	35.5	35.1	34.8	33.4	33.7
2006	31.2	30.5	31.0	33.5	35.0	36.4	36.7	36.7	36.3	36.1	35.5	34.4	34.4
2007	31.9	30.6	32.3	33.8	36.1	37.5	37.9	37.9	37.1	36.7	36.1	34.0	35.2
2008	31.0	30.2	30.9	32.6	35.0	35.9	36.1	35.9	34.8	35.0	33.6	31.4	33.5
2009	27.6	27.0	26.8	28.4	29.7	30.6	30.8	30.7	29.8	29.3	28.3	26.0	28.8
2010	23.1	22.3	22.6	25.0	25.9	27.1	27.6	28.0	27.2	27.0	25.9	23.9	25.5
2011	21.5	20.8	21.4	23.5	24.9	26.0	27.2	26.8	26.9	27.4	25.6	22.6	24.6
Manufacturing													
2000	164.8	165.2	165.2	165.4	165.0	166.2	165.3	165.4	164.5	163.9	164.1	164.0	164.9
2001	161.0	159.5	159.0	156.6	154.8	155.2	153.4	153.4	152.3	151.1	149.5	149.2	154.6
2002	146.4	145.6	145.5	144.2	143.7	144.2	142.0	142.8	141.9	141.4	141.4	141.2	143.4
2003	138.8	138.3	138.1	137.6	136.7	136.9	135.0	136.2	135.1	134.9	135.0	135.1	136.5
2004	133.6	133.4	133.6	133.7	133.8	135.0	134.6	135.0	134.3	133.9	133.9	134.2	134.1
2005	133.4	133.5	133.6	133.7	133.4	134.6	134.5	134.4	133.4	132.6	132.4	132.8	133.5
2006	132.4	132.0	132.0	132.3	132.6	134.2	133.7	134.6	133.5	133.7	133.7	134.2	133.2
2007	133.4	132.7	132.0	132.9	133.3	134.4	133.6	134.2	133.0	133.1	132.8	133.3	133.2
2008	132.8	132.5	132.3	132.1	131.6	132.3	131.0	131.4	129.8	128.8	128.2	127.3	130.8
2009	125.3	122.1	119.2	116.6	114.9	114.4	112.6	112.9	112.8	112.4	111.9	112.1	115.6
2010	111.5	110.7	110.8	111.1	111.3	112.6	113.8	114.3	113.6	114.0	114.2	114.5	112.7
2011	114.7	114.6	115.1	115.7	116.0	117.8	118.9	118.7	118.0	118.2	118.1	119.2	117.1

Employment by Industry: Milwaukee–Waukesha–West Allis, WI, Selected Years, 2000–2011—*Continued*

(Numbers in thousands, not seasonally adjusted)

Industry and year	January	February	March	April	May	June	July	August	September	October	November	December	Annual average
Service-Providing													
2000	654.7	657.2	661.2	666.8	669.2	676.6	667.0	669.3	670.8	674.8	679.0	677.8	668.7
2001	664.2	665.6	667.9	673.3	674.4	674.4	665.4	664.2	664.8	666.6	665.4	666.0	667.7
2002	652.5	653.3	657.0	662.5	665.7	668.9	661.9	661.1	661.0	667.2	668.3	669.0	662.4
2003	650.9	654.9	657.0	661.4	663.3	667.5	655.6	656.0	657.3	666.4	664.9	668.3	660.3
2004	651.4	654.9	658.9	661.0	665.5	671.8	662.8	664.9	664.6	671.5	671.9	672.3	664.3
2005	658.8	661.4	663.4	672.3	673.8	678.3	672.5	673.9	678.1	678.9	681.3	683.7	673.0
2006	665.9	669.5	672.6	679.5	682.6	688.1	680.8	683.3	688.0	691.1	693.3	694.1	682.4
2007	677.5	679.3	681.2	685.8	691.9	698.4	686.9	689.2	689.5	692.0	693.8	695.7	688.4
2008	679.6	679.8	682.5	687.9	693.1	696.4	687.4	687.0	690.7	692.6	690.6	688.7	688.0
2009	667.5	665.7	664.3	668.0	671.9	673.9	662.5	661.8	667.6	669.4	669.0	669.7	667.6
2010	655.2	656.4	658.7	664.5	671.4	670.8	666.4	667.7	667.8	674.3	677.6	676.8	667.3
2011	660.8	663.7	666.0	674.0	676.9	678.5	672.9	675.7	676.0	676.8	674.6	669.6	672.1
Trade, Transportation, and Utilities													
2000	159.9	158.0	158.3	158.9	159.5	159.3	160.0	160.8	161.6	162.8	165.2	167.1	161.0
2001	163.5	160.9	161.2	161.0	161.3	160.3	158.0	158.3	157.3	157.9	159.9	160.4	160.0
2002	155.6	152.9	153.7	153.5	154.8	154.6	153.0	152.7	153.4	153.9	157.2	159.1	154.5
2003	152.3	150.4	150.6	151.1	152.3	152.9	149.8	150.7	151.9	153.8	155.6	157.5	152.4
2004	151.4	149.8	150.6	149.7	151.6	153.2	151.3	151.7	152.1	154.1	156.5	157.6	152.5
2005	152.2	150.8	151.3	151.9	153.0	153.6	153.1	153.9	154.2	154.9	157.5	158.9	153.8
2006	153.3	151.5	152.4	152.9	154.2	155.0	153.1	153.6	154.1	155.2	158.2	159.7	154.4
2007	154.2	152.1	152.1	152.0	153.9	154.6	152.7	152.8	152.4	153.2	156.0	156.8	153.6
2008	151.8	149.4	149.5	150.5	151.2	151.8	150.7	150.7	149.8	150.2	150.9	151.4	150.7
2009	145.1	142.6	141.7	140.9	142.6	143.6	140.8	140.6	141.0	143.0	143.5	143.8	142.4
2010	138.5	136.3	136.4	136.6	138.0	138.9	137.5	138.0	138.4	141.5	142.5	143.3	138.8
2011	138.3	136.8	137.3	138.1	139.1	139.5	138.6	138.4	137.7	138.1	138.9	139.8	138.4
Wholesale Trade													
2000	42.7	42.9	42.9	43.0	43.2	43.5	43.3	43.3	42.9	42.9	43.0	43.2	43.1
2001	42.9	43.0	43.1	42.7	42.7	42.9	42.5	42.5	41.9	41.7	41.5	41.6	42.4
2002	41.1	41.0	41.0	40.8	40.9	41.0	41.1	40.9	40.5	40.2	40.2	40.2	40.7
2003	40.0	40.0	40.0	39.9	39.9	40.1	40.1	40.0	39.7	39.5	39.3	39.4	39.8
2004	38.9	38.7	38.9	38.9	38.9	39.3	39.7	39.8	39.5	39.9	40.0	40.1	39.4
2005	39.9	39.9	39.8	40.4	40.5	40.9	41.2	41.0	40.7	40.8	40.9	41.0	40.6
2006	40.4	40.5	40.6	40.8	40.9	41.4	41.6	41.5	41.3	41.4	41.4	41.6	41.1
2007	40.9	41.0	41.0	41.1	41.2	41.8	41.8	41.7	41.3	41.3	41.2	41.2	41.3
2008	40.6	40.6	40.6	40.8	40.8	40.9	41.0	40.9	40.3	39.9	39.9	39.6	40.5
2009	38.9	38.6	38.1	37.6	37.5	37.6	37.2	36.9	36.5	36.5	36.3	36.2	37.3
2010	35.4	35.2	35.1	35.0	35.2	35.5	35.8	35.8	35.4	35.7	35.6	35.6	35.4
2011	35.1	35.1	35.2	35.4	35.6	35.8	35.9	35.5	35.4	35.0	35.1	34.9	35.3
Retail Trade													
2000	84.1	82.2	82.5	82.4	82.9	83.4	84.2	84.9	84.9	85.1	87.8	89.5	84.5
2001	86.8	84.5	84.9	84.7	85.1	85.0	83.9	84.0	82.7	83.3	85.9	86.8	84.8
2002	84.3	81.9	82.5	82.5	83.5	84.2	83.0	83.0	82.5	82.9	86.3	88.2	83.7
2003	82.3	80.3	80.5	80.6	81.7	82.2	81.2	81.8	81.4	83.2	85.3	87.1	82.3
2004	82.5	81.0	81.4	81.1	82.4	83.3	82.4	82.8	82.1	82.9	85.3	86.8	82.8
2005	82.0	80.6	81.1	81.6	82.3	82.8	82.6	83.5	82.7	83.3	85.4	86.6	82.9
2006	82.5	80.6	81.1	81.4	82.4	83.0	82.1	82.7	81.9	82.9	85.9	86.9	82.8
2007	83.3	81.1	81.1	80.5	81.9	82.0	81.7	81.5	80.1	80.8	83.4	84.2	81.8
2008	81.2	78.9	79.1	79.6	80.2	80.7	80.7	80.6	79.2	79.9	81.0	81.7	80.2
2009	77.6	75.6	75.4	75.2	76.4	77.3	76.6	76.6	76.0	77.7	78.5	78.7	76.8
2010	75.4	73.6	73.9	74.3	75.3	75.7	75.3	75.7	75.3	77.5	78.5	79.1	75.8
2011	75.6	74.1	74.5	75.1	75.6	76.2	76.4	76.4	74.8	75.3	76.1	77.2	75.6
Transportation and Utilities													
2000	33.1	32.9	32.9	33.5	33.4	32.4	32.5	32.6	33.8	34.8	34.4	34.4	33.4
2001	33.8	33.4	33.2	33.6	33.5	32.4	31.6	31.8	32.7	32.9	32.5	32.0	32.8
2002	30.2	30.0	30.2	30.2	30.4	29.4	28.9	28.8	30.4	30.8	30.7	30.7	30.1
2003	30.0	30.1	30.1	30.6	30.7	30.6	28.5	28.9	30.8	31.1	31.0	30.7	30.3
2004	30.0	30.1	30.3	29.7	30.3	30.6	29.2	29.1	30.5	31.3	31.2	30.7	30.3
2005	30.3	30.3	30.4	29.9	30.2	29.9	29.3	29.4	30.8	30.8	31.2	31.3	30.3
2006	30.4	30.4	30.7	30.7	30.9	30.6	29.4	29.4	30.9	30.9	30.9	31.2	30.5
2007	30.0	30.0	30.0	30.4	30.8	30.8	29.2	29.6	31.0	31.1	31.4	31.4	30.5
2008	30.0	29.9	29.8	30.1	30.2	30.2	29.0	29.2	30.3	30.4	30.0	30.1	29.9
2009	28.6	28.4	28.2	28.1	28.7	28.7	27.0	27.1	28.5	28.8	28.7	28.9	28.3
2010	27.7	27.5	27.4	27.3	27.5	27.7	26.4	26.5	27.7	28.3	28.4	28.6	27.6
2011	27.6	27.6	27.6	27.6	27.9	27.5	26.3	26.5	27.5	27.8	27.7	27.7	27.4
Information													
2000	19.9	20.1	20.2	20.2	20.3	20.4	20.4	20.5	20.6	20.8	20.9	21.0	20.4
2001	19.7	19.7	19.9	20.1	19.9	20.0	20.0	19.9	19.8	20.0	20.0	20.0	19.9
2002	19.7	19.5	19.6	19.5	19.3	19.3	19.2	19.2	18.9	18.8	18.8	18.8	19.2
2003	18.8	18.6	18.6	18.6	18.5	18.3	18.3	18.4	18.4	18.3	18.3	18.3	18.4
2004	18.5	18.5	18.5	18.6	18.5	18.4	18.6	18.6	18.6	18.3	18.2	18.3	18.4
2005	18.2	18.1	18.1	18.2	18.2	18.3	18.1	18.2	18.1	18.1	18.2	18.3	18.2
2006	18.0	18.1	18.0	17.9	17.9	17.7	17.7	17.7	17.5	17.5	17.5	17.5	17.8
2007	17.5	17.5	17.5	17.5	17.5	17.6	17.5	17.5	17.3	17.4	17.5	17.4	17.5
2008	17.1	17.1	17.0	17.5	17.5	17.7	17.5	17.5	17.3	17.3	17.3	17.3	17.3
2009	16.9	16.9	16.8	16.7	16.5	16.5	16.5	16.4	16.3	16.2	16.2	16.1	16.5
2010	15.6	15.6	15.5	15.5	15.5	15.6	15.9	15.8	15.6	15.2	15.8	15.6	15.6
2011	15.6	15.6	15.4	15.5	15.5	15.5	15.6	15.5	15.4	15.4	15.5	15.4	15.5

Employment by Industry: Milwaukee–Waukesha–West Allis, WI, Selected Years, 2000–2011—*Continued*

(Numbers in thousands, not seasonally adjusted)

Industry and year	January	February	March	April	May	June	July	August	September	October	November	December	Annual average
Financial Activities													
2000	56.6	56.7	56.6	57.0	57.2	58.0	58.2	58.1	57.8	58.3	58.8	59.2	57.7
2001	58.5	58.2	58.3	58.4	58.5	59.1	58.8	58.5	57.9	57.4	57.5	57.2	58.2
2002	57.1	57.1	57.0	57.3	57.4	57.9	58.6	58.6	57.9	57.8	58.1	58.1	57.7
2003	57.8	58.0	58.0	58.1	58.3	58.7	58.7	58.4	57.6	57.5	57.2	57.3	58.0
2004	57.4	57.2	57.4	57.6	57.6	58.1	58.5	58.6	57.5	57.9	57.9	58.1	57.8
2005	57.1	56.8	57.1	57.2	57.2	57.4	57.9	57.7	57.1	56.9	57.1	57.3	57.2
2006	57.0	56.8	56.7	57.3	57.5	57.9	58.4	58.3	58.0	58.0	58.1	58.2	57.7
2007	57.8	57.9	57.6	58.0	58.2	58.7	58.7	58.5	57.7	58.2	58.4	58.6	58.2
2008	58.0	58.2	57.9	58.1	58.5	58.5	59.0	58.9	57.9	58.3	58.2	58.2	58.3
2009	57.7	57.5	57.2	57.6	57.6	57.6	57.8	57.7	56.6	56.8	56.8	56.5	57.3
2010	55.7	55.7	55.9	55.8	55.8	56.0	56.3	56.3	55.8	56.0	56.0	56.3	56.0
2011	55.4	55.4	55.6	55.6	55.6	55.9	55.8	56.0	56.0	55.4	55.3	54.9	55.6
Professional and Business Services													
2000	108.5	109.7	110.6	110.8	112.0	113.2	111.7	112.2	113.0	111.8	112.3	109.8	111.3
2001	106.2	105.2	105.2	107.0	106.9	106.9	107.1	107.6	105.9	104.0	102.6	102.0	105.6
2002	100.1	100.1	101.6	105.3	105.6	105.7	106.3	106.9	106.0	105.6	103.5	102.8	104.1
2003	100.9	101.3	102.5	103.7	103.2	103.6	104.2	104.0	104.5	105.4	104.4	105.4	103.6
2004	102.0	101.6	103.0	104.4	104.0	106.5	107.0	107.6	106.5	106.9	105.9	105.6	105.1
2005	103.5	103.9	104.8	107.9	107.0	108.8	110.6	110.9	111.2	110.8	110.8	111.6	108.5
2006	106.4	107.3	107.9	110.7	110.3	111.9	112.7	113.7	113.9	114.4	114.1	113.6	111.4
2007	110.4	111.0	111.8	113.2	113.8	116.2	115.9	117.7	116.2	115.9	116.1	116.5	114.6
2008	113.1	113.9	112.8	114.3	114.7	116.0	115.9	116.7	116.0	114.6	112.6	111.5	114.3
2009	105.7	103.4	101.9	102.4	102.3	102.8	103.4	103.1	102.4	103.6	103.7	104.3	103.3
2010	100.5	101.7	100.7	104.2	104.8	106.4	108.6	110.1	109.6	110.9	111.9	112.2	106.8
2011	109.1	109.3	110.4	111.1	111.2	113.8	114.3	114.3	114.2	115.3	113.8	112.8	112.5
Education and Health Services													
2000	119.8	120.9	122.0	122.5	122.4	122.1	121.8	122.6	122.7	124.5	125.2	125.9	122.7
2001	121.5	124.2	125.0	124.6	124.7	123.9	124.0	124.1	124.9	126.4	126.6	126.6	124.7
2002	124.4	125.3	125.7	125.9	126.2	125.9	126.0	126.4	126.5	127.9	128.6	128.0	126.4
2003	125.8	128.0	128.1	128.5	128.4	128.0	127.7	127.7	128.1	129.2	129.6	129.4	128.2
2004	129.2	130.0	130.3	130.9	131.2	130.5	130.3	130.5	130.9	132.5	132.8	133.0	131.0
2005	131.1	132.0	132.3	133.2	133.2	132.7	131.7	132.1	133.2	134.8	135.0	135.5	133.1
2006	134.2	135.7	135.6	136.2	136.5	136.1	135.8	136.4	138.2	140.0	140.0	139.9	137.1
2007	137.5	138.9	139.1	139.4	139.8	139.3	138.5	139.4	140.8	141.5	141.9	142.0	139.8
2008	140.0	141.4	141.9	142.3	142.6	141.5	140.6	141.4	142.3	144.6	144.7	145.1	142.4
2009	142.5	143.8	144.2	145.1	145.4	145.0	144.3	144.9	145.9	147.6	147.8	147.8	145.4
2010	146.0	147.6	148.7	148.1	148.0	146.1	145.8	145.4	145.6	147.3	147.6	147.4	147.0
2011	143.9	144.6	145.0	146.1	146.1	144.3	143.1	143.3	147.4	148.2	149.1	148.3	145.8
Leisure and Hospitality													
2000	60.1	60.2	61.0	62.5	63.7	66.1	67.3	67.3	64.3	62.4	61.4	61.3	63.1
2001	60.6	60.8	61.5	65.1	66.9	68.5	70.0	68.1	64.9	63.9	62.1	61.8	64.5
2002	60.4	60.3	60.7	63.0	65.2	67.3	70.0	68.6	65.8	63.8	62.5	62.4	64.2
2003	60.9	60.5	61.3	63.2	67.0	68.8	71.0	70.3	68.0	66.3	64.9	64.8	65.6
2004	62.3	61.9	62.7	64.8	67.7	69.5	71.1	70.9	67.7	67.0	65.3	65.2	66.3
2005	63.8	63.6	64.7	68.4	70.1	71.8	73.9	73.6	70.7	69.2	68.2	68.2	68.9
2006	66.2	66.5	67.8	69.6	71.4	73.7	75.6	75.9	72.5	70.9	70.3	70.2	70.9
2007	68.9	68.9	69.7	70.9	73.8	75.8	76.4	76.5	72.3	71.2	69.5	69.1	71.9
2008	66.7	66.5	67.6	69.3	71.6	73.5	74.6	74.2	71.5	69.6	67.4	67.0	70.0
2009	65.0	65.1	66.0	67.7	70.2	71.4	72.4	72.5	70.0	67.3	65.7	65.4	68.2
2010	63.2	63.3	64.3	67.0	69.8	70.6	71.5	72.2	69.5	67.9	66.9	66.6	67.7
2011	64.8	64.4	65.0	67.9	70.5	71.3	72.0	75.8	71.2	70.2	68.4	66.2	69.0
Other Services													
2000	39.2	39.6	40.0	40.2	40.3	40.6	40.3	40.1	40.2	40.4	40.5	40.8	40.2
2001	41.3	41.2	41.5	40.7	40.8	41.4	41.4	41.2	41.2	41.1	41.1	41.6	41.2
2002	41.0	41.0	41.2	41.3	41.2	41.9	41.5	41.4	41.1	41.3	41.1	41.5	41.3
2003	41.0	40.8	41.1	41.1	40.9	41.7	41.2	41.3	40.8	40.8	40.6	40.9	41.0
2004	40.8	41.0	41.1	41.4	41.3	42.1	42.1	42.1	41.8	42.7	41.7	41.7	41.7
2005	41.3	41.4	41.5	41.8	41.7	42.2	42.1	42.1	41.3	41.2	41.0	41.1	41.6
2006	40.6	40.7	40.8	41.2	41.3	41.9	42.0	41.8	41.6	41.5	41.5	41.8	41.4
2007	41.1	41.3	41.4	42.2	41.9	42.6	42.2	41.9	41.3	42.4	42.2	42.3	41.9
2008	41.7	42.0	42.1	42.6	42.7	43.2	43.2	43.0	42.4	42.9	42.6	42.6	42.6
2009	41.4	41.4	41.6	42.3	42.7	43.4	43.7	44.0	43.9	41.9	42.2	42.6	42.6
2010	44.0	44.6	45.2	45.7	45.5	45.9	45.9	45.9	45.3	45.2	45.1	45.3	45.3
2011	44.8	44.8	45.0	45.5	45.6	45.9	45.1	45.1	45.4	44.9	44.4	44.2	45.1
Government													
2000	90.7	92.0	92.5	94.7	93.8	96.9	87.3	87.7	90.6	93.8	94.7	92.7	92.3
2001	92.9	95.4	95.3	96.4	95.4	94.3	86.1	86.5	92.9	95.9	95.6	96.4	93.6
2002	94.2	97.1	97.5	96.7	96.0	96.3	87.3	87.3	91.4	98.1	98.5	98.3	94.9
2003	93.4	97.3	96.8	97.2	94.9	95.5	84.6	85.2	88.1	95.1	94.3	94.7	93.1
2004	89.8	94.9	95.3	93.6	93.6	93.5	83.9	84.9	89.8	92.2	93.5	92.9	91.5
2005	91.6	94.8	93.6	93.7	93.4	93.5	85.1	85.4	92.3	93.0	93.5	92.8	91.9
2006	90.2	92.9	93.4	93.7	93.5	93.9	85.5	85.9	92.2	93.6	93.6	93.2	91.8
2007	90.1	91.7	92.0	92.6	93.0	93.6	85.0	84.9	91.5	92.2	92.2	93.0	91.0
2008	91.2	91.3	93.7	93.3	94.3	94.2	85.9	84.6	93.5	95.1	96.9	95.6	92.5
2009	93.2	95.0	94.9	95.3	94.6	93.6	83.6	82.6	91.5	93.0	93.1	93.2	92.0
2010	91.7	91.6	92.0	91.6	94.0	91.3	84.9	84.0	88.0	90.3	91.8	90.1	90.1
2011	88.9	92.8	92.3	94.2	93.3	92.3	88.4	87.3	88.7	89.3	89.2	88.0	90.4

Employment by Industry: Minneapolis–St. Paul–Bloomington, MN–WI, Selected Years, 2000–2011

(Numbers in thousands, not seasonally adjusted)

Industry and year	January	February	March	April	May	June	July	August	September	October	November	December	Annual average
Total Nonfarm													
2000	1,698.8	1,705.1	1,717.7	1,736.4	1,753.8	1,769.8	1,747.2	1,754.7	1,763.2	1,771.4	1,778.2	1,779.5	1,748.0
2001	1,729.4	1,732.2	1,737.8	1,745.3	1,762.6	1,770.9	1,746.8	1,748.3	1,753.0	1,754.1	1,755.4	1,750.5	1,748.9
2002	1,695.9	1,694.5	1,697.2	1,708.2	1,729.0	1,737.9	1,720.9	1,719.7	1,733.3	1,736.2	1,742.9	1,737.2	1,721.1
2003	1,691.2	1,693.8	1,696.3	1,714.5	1,734.8	1,741.9	1,721.4	1,726.0	1,735.5	1,742.3	1,743.5	1,744.2	1,723.8
2004	1,692.9	1,694.9	1,700.0	1,732.0	1,751.3	1,765.1	1,738.3	1,738.3	1,750.8	1,764.0	1,764.0	1,767.9	1,738.3
2005	1,715.0	1,716.5	1,723.9	1,754.0	1,775.8	1,787.5	1,765.6	1,768.5	1,783.1	1,792.5	1,796.8	1,798.2	1,764.8
2006	1,754.2	1,751.1	1,760.2	1,777.9	1,797.9	1,815.8	1,787.0	1,787.2	1,794.5	1,801.1	1,809.6	1,808.1	1,787.1
2007	1,767.0	1,767.1	1,772.1	1,783.7	1,808.4	1,822.0	1,795.9	1,796.1	1,801.1	1,809.6	1,814.5	1,808.9	1,795.5
2008	1,764.4	1,766.7	1,770.6	1,780.0	1,802.2	1,812.6	1,792.9	1,791.8	1,792.3	1,795.3	1,786.2	1,772.2	1,785.6
2009	1,714.0	1,704.0	1,695.9	1,706.9	1,722.6	1,722.5	1,704.0	1,697.2	1,691.9	1,704.6	1,704.6	1,700.0	1,705.7
2010	1,652.8	1,653.5	1,659.0	1,692.6	1,712.5	1,720.2	1,699.0	1,699.8	1,706.0	1,723.2	1,725.6	1,720.4	1,697.1
2011	1,685.6	1,690.3	1,696.6	1,726.6	1,746.2	1,752.1	1,721.3	1,734.7	1,737.7	1,749.9	1,744.2	1,739.6	1,727.1
Total Private													
2000	1,464.8	1,467.3	1,477.9	1,494.8	1,509.4	1,530.9	1,530.0	1,538.1	1,532.9	1,536.3	1,539.9	1,542.0	1,513.7
2001	1,498.3	1,494.4	1,499.4	1,506.5	1,520.8	1,533.5	1,526.9	1,529.6	1,519.2	1,514.6	1,514.0	1,509.2	1,513.9
2002	1,459.0	1,452.5	1,454.7	1,465.7	1,484.4	1,498.7	1,497.5	1,504.2	1,495.4	1,494.1	1,496.0	1,492.7	1,482.9
2003	1,453.4	1,449.5	1,452.2	1,467.5	1,487.3	1,500.2	1,497.2	1,503.7	1,496.8	1,497.4	1,497.2	1,497.4	1,483.3
2004	1,452.1	1,448.5	1,454.3	1,485.9	1,503.0	1,521.3	1,517.8	1,521.5	1,513.2	1,520.2	1,518.5	1,521.6	1,498.2
2005	1,470.9	1,469.4	1,476.9	1,507.0	1,528.6	1,543.6	1,539.0	1,546.6	1,542.5	1,545.8	1,551.1	1,551.4	1,522.7
2006	1,511.1	1,506.1	1,514.9	1,532.8	1,551.8	1,572.8	1,560.5	1,566.0	1,553.6	1,554.8	1,561.9	1,560.0	1,545.5
2007	1,526.2	1,523.4	1,528.9	1,541.0	1,563.1	1,580.4	1,572.9	1,578.2	1,563.5	1,566.9	1,570.4	1,566.0	1,556.7
2008	1,524.2	1,520.8	1,525.3	1,535.0	1,554.2	1,567.1	1,564.2	1,566.0	1,549.5	1,549.4	1,538.6	1,526.0	1,543.4
2009	1,474.7	1,458.9	1,451.3	1,463.1	1,477.4	1,480.2	1,473.5	1,472.2	1,456.7	1,463.6	1,462.3	1,459.0	1,466.1
2010	1,416.1	1,412.2	1,417.7	1,448.7	1,465.0	1,477.5	1,479.6	1,483.3	1,472.7	1,482.3	1,483.0	1,479.2	1,459.8
2011	1,449.7	1,448.7	1,456.0	1,485.3	1,504.4	1,514.2	1,518.1	1,523.3	1,510.3	1,516.1	1,509.9	1,506.6	1,495.2
Goods-Producing													
2000	300.5	300.4	303.9	310.6	315.9	322.4	323.9	326.5	322.0	322.2	319.8	315.5	315.3
2001	305.1	303.4	303.7	305.7	310.2	314.0	315.2	315.3	313.8	308.7	304.3	298.7	308.2
2002	286.1	283.6	283.7	287.3	293.7	299.3	300.9	303.5	299.4	296.9	293.5	286.8	292.9
2003	277.5	274.2	274.4	279.5	286.5	292.8	292.9	295.1	291.7	289.4	287.1	282.5	285.3
2004	271.8	269.8	271.0	281.1	286.3	293.5	296.0	298.2	295.4	296.0	291.9	288.8	286.7
2005	277.1	275.7	277.3	285.5	293.1	299.8	299.2	301.0	297.8	293.9	292.2	286.5	289.9
2006	277.6	275.0	276.4	283.2	289.4	296.0	294.7	295.8	291.2	289.8	286.4	280.5	286.3
2007	272.0	269.1	269.9	272.7	280.6	286.5	285.7	286.9	281.9	280.8	278.1	272.0	278.0
2008	262.5	259.9	259.6	262.2	270.0	275.2	275.4	275.6	270.7	268.4	261.8	253.1	266.2
2009	240.6	234.1	230.2	231.7	235.5	238.5	238.0	236.8	232.8	231.1	228.2	223.2	233.4
2010	213.9	211.8	212.7	221.1	226.4	231.7	235.0	234.8	232.5	232.6	230.6	226.2	225.8
2011	220.4	219.2	220.6	226.6	233.1	239.0	241.7	242.8	238.7	238.9	236.4	228.0	232.1
Mining, Logging, and Construction													
2000	66.4	66.2	68.7	74.6	79.6	84.1	85.6	86.5	84.8	84.0	81.2	77.3	78.3
2001	71.5	70.7	72.1	76.4	82.1	87.8	90.1	91.3	89.0	87.9	85.5	80.7	82.1
2002	72.3	70.9	71.0	75.8	82.6	86.6	89.6	90.7	88.8	87.3	84.6	79.3	81.6
2003	71.5	69.5	69.9	75.2	82.1	87.0	89.3	90.3	88.5	87.6	84.5	79.8	81.3
2004	71.5	70.3	71.9	79.7	85.0	89.0	92.0	92.6	91.1	90.9	88.8	84.3	83.9
2005	74.2	73.3	74.5	81.2	86.6	91.6	93.6	93.7	91.7	89.1	87.4	82.6	85.0
2006	75.0	74.1	74.8	79.7	85.1	89.1	89.4	89.1	87.7	85.3	82.1	77.0	82.4
2007	70.8	68.7	69.9	72.1	78.8	82.7	82.8	83.1	80.7	79.4	76.5	70.8	76.4
2008	64.6	63.2	63.5	65.3	72.0	75.5	76.5	76.5	74.0	71.8	67.0	61.3	69.3
2009	52.6	51.1	50.8	54.0	59.6	61.4	62.0	61.2	59.7	58.2	55.8	51.8	56.5
2010	44.4	43.1	43.8	50.0	53.7	56.8	58.8	59.0	57.8	57.7	55.4	50.7	52.6
2011	46.4	45.7	46.9	51.0	56.0	59.7	61.3	62.6	60.5	59.8	56.8	49.4	54.7
Manufacturing													
2000	234.1	234.2	235.2	236.0	236.3	238.3	238.3	240.0	237.2	238.2	238.6	238.2	237.1
2001	233.6	232.7	231.6	229.3	228.1	226.2	225.1	224.0	224.8	220.8	218.8	218.0	226.1
2002	213.8	212.7	212.7	211.5	211.1	212.7	211.3	212.8	210.6	209.6	208.9	207.5	211.3
2003	206.0	204.7	204.5	204.3	204.4	205.8	203.6	204.8	203.2	201.8	202.6	202.7	204.0
2004	200.3	199.5	199.1	201.4	201.3	204.5	204.0	205.6	204.3	205.1	203.1	204.5	202.7
2005	202.9	202.4	202.8	204.3	206.5	208.2	205.6	207.3	206.1	204.8	204.8	203.9	205.0
2006	202.6	200.9	201.6	203.5	204.3	206.9	205.3	206.7	203.5	204.5	204.3	203.5	204.0
2007	201.2	200.4	200.0	200.6	201.8	203.8	202.9	203.8	201.2	201.4	201.6	201.2	201.7
2008	197.9	196.7	196.1	196.9	198.0	199.7	198.9	199.1	196.7	196.6	194.8	191.8	196.9
2009	188.0	183.0	179.4	177.7	175.9	177.1	176.0	175.6	173.1	172.9	172.4	171.4	176.9
2010	169.5	168.7	168.9	171.1	172.7	174.9	176.2	175.8	174.7	174.9	175.2	175.5	173.2
2011	174.0	173.5	173.7	175.6	177.1	179.3	180.4	180.2	178.2	179.1	179.6	178.6	177.4
Service-Providing													
2000	1,398.3	1,404.7	1,413.8	1,425.8	1,437.9	1,447.4	1,423.3	1,428.2	1,441.2	1,449.2	1,458.4	1,464.0	1,432.7
2001	1,424.3	1,428.8	1,434.1	1,439.6	1,452.4	1,456.9	1,431.6	1,433.0	1,439.2	1,445.4	1,451.1	1,451.8	1,440.7
2002	1,409.8	1,410.9	1,413.5	1,420.9	1,435.3	1,438.6	1,420.0	1,416.2	1,433.9	1,439.3	1,449.4	1,450.4	1,428.2
2003	1,413.7	1,419.6	1,421.9	1,435.0	1,448.3	1,449.1	1,428.5	1,430.9	1,443.8	1,452.9	1,456.4	1,461.7	1,438.5
2004	1,421.1	1,425.1	1,429.0	1,450.9	1,465.0	1,471.6	1,442.3	1,440.1	1,455.4	1,468.0	1,472.1	1,479.1	1,451.6
2005	1,437.9	1,440.8	1,446.6	1,468.5	1,482.7	1,487.7	1,466.4	1,467.5	1,485.3	1,498.6	1,504.6	1,511.7	1,474.9
2006	1,476.6	1,476.1	1,483.8	1,494.7	1,508.5	1,519.8	1,492.3	1,491.4	1,503.3	1,511.3	1,523.2	1,527.6	1,500.7
2007	1,495.0	1,498.0	1,502.2	1,511.0	1,527.8	1,535.5	1,510.2	1,509.2	1,519.2	1,528.8	1,536.4	1,536.9	1,517.5
2008	1,501.9	1,506.8	1,511.0	1,517.8	1,532.2	1,537.4	1,517.5	1,516.2	1,521.6	1,526.9	1,524.4	1,519.1	1,519.4
2009	1,473.4	1,469.9	1,465.7	1,475.2	1,487.1	1,484.0	1,466.0	1,460.4	1,459.1	1,473.5	1,476.4	1,476.8	1,472.3
2010	1,438.9	1,441.7	1,446.3	1,471.5	1,486.1	1,488.5	1,464.0	1,465.0	1,473.5	1,490.6	1,495.0	1,494.2	1,471.3
2011	1,465.2	1,471.1	1,476.0	1,500.0	1,513.1	1,513.1	1,479.6	1,491.9	1,499.0	1,511.0	1,507.8	1,511.6	1,495.0

Employment by Industry: Minneapolis–St. Paul–Bloomington, MN–WI, Selected Years, 2000–2011—*Continued*

(Numbers in thousands, not seasonally adjusted)

Industry and year	January	February	March	April	May	June	July	August	September	October	November	December	Annual average
Trade, Transportation, and Utilities													
2000	345.6	342.0	341.7	341.9	343.9	347.4	346.7	347.9	347.4	352.1	359.3	364.4	348.4
2001	352.2	347.1	346.6	346.7	349.0	350.8	348.6	347.6	344.4	346.9	351.7	353.5	348.8
2002	339.5	332.6	332.6	333.9	336.7	338.2	334.9	335.0	333.4	336.1	343.3	347.0	336.9
2003	335.4	330.5	330.2	331.2	334.2	335.0	330.9	331.8	331.4	335.3	340.2	343.0	334.1
2004	329.6	326.0	326.0	331.4	335.5	338.7	338.1	338.2	336.3	340.8	347.0	350.6	336.5
2005	335.2	331.4	332.4	337.1	340.5	340.5	338.7	339.1	337.7	342.2	348.7	352.1	339.6
2006	338.7	333.8	334.0	335.7	338.7	341.4	337.4	337.5	336.5	338.8	346.9	349.3	339.1
2007	338.1	334.9	334.1	336.3	340.0	342.5	339.2	339.2	337.8	340.6	346.6	349.5	339.9
2008	336.2	331.0	331.9	331.5	334.5	334.7	331.6	330.9	328.3	329.4	332.5	332.8	332.1
2009	318.3	312.4	310.4	310.0	312.5	313.2	309.5	308.8	306.3	307.8	313.0	314.3	311.4
2010	303.1	299.3	300.0	304.3	307.2	310.1	307.8	307.1	306.2	308.9	314.4	316.9	307.1
2011	305.2	302.1	303.2	308.8	311.8	312.9	314.0	316.8	313.8	315.0	317.9	320.1	311.8
Wholesale Trade													
2000	84.0	84.0	84.4	84.6	85.2	87.0	85.9	86.0	85.2	85.5	85.7	86.1	85.3
2001	86.9	86.8	86.8	86.5	86.4	86.9	86.8	86.3	85.3	85.2	85.3	85.1	86.2
2002	83.8	83.8	83.6	83.6	83.7	84.2	84.4	84.3	83.3	83.6	83.4	83.4	83.8
2003	83.7	83.7	83.7	82.9	83.3	83.9	84.2	84.0	83.2	83.3	83.2	83.3	83.5
2004	82.4	82.4	82.5	84.1	84.5	85.4	86.2	86.0	84.9	84.9	84.8	84.9	84.4
2005	83.8	83.7	83.6	85.9	86.5	86.8	86.4	86.5	85.7	86.3	86.3	86.6	85.7
2006	85.8	85.9	86.4	86.6	87.1	88.1	88.1	88.2	87.2	87.3	87.2	87.3	87.1
2007	86.5	86.6	86.8	87.0	87.7	88.6	88.5	88.4	87.0	86.9	87.1	87.2	87.4
2008	86.3	86.1	86.4	86.1	86.4	87.1	87.2	86.9	85.5	85.3	84.7	84.2	86.0
2009	82.2	81.3	80.4	80.4	80.3	80.6	80.7	80.0	78.2	78.4	78.4	78.2	79.9
2010	76.7	76.4	76.7	77.4	77.9	79.0	79.3	79.0	78.0	78.4	78.3	78.3	78.0
2011	77.9	77.9	78.1	79.1	79.5	80.1	81.1	83.3	81.7	81.1	80.5	80.5	80.1
Retail Trade													
2000	187.2	183.6	183.0	182.3	183.6	185.5	186.1	187.1	186.3	190.2	197.2	202.0	187.8
2001	190.7	186.3	185.7	185.6	187.8	189.4	188.2	188.8	185.8	189.3	195.6	198.6	189.3
2002	187.5	181.7	181.9	182.6	184.9	186.5	185.3	185.6	183.4	185.2	192.7	196.8	186.2
2003	185.8	181.2	181.0	182.8	185.4	186.4	183.2	184.7	183.4	186.0	191.1	194.0	185.4
2004	183.0	179.4	179.2	181.9	185.1	187.4	186.1	186.2	183.7	186.3	192.4	195.9	185.6
2005	184.0	180.1	180.7	184.2	186.4	186.6	185.1	186.1	185.1	188.9	195.2	198.5	186.7
2006	187.2	182.8	182.5	184.3	186.3	188.4	186.0	186.2	183.8	186.1	193.0	195.8	186.9
2007	187.0	183.0	182.9	184.1	186.7	188.6	186.8	186.9	184.6	187.0	192.9	194.7	187.1
2008	184.7	179.6	179.9	180.1	182.3	182.7	181.3	181.1	177.9	179.1	182.8	183.0	181.2
2009	173.7	169.3	167.8	168.1	170.8	172.2	170.2	170.8	167.3	168.7	173.3	174.5	170.6
2010	166.5	163.2	163.5	166.7	168.8	170.7	169.6	170.1	167.3	169.1	173.9	175.7	168.8
2011	166.7	163.6	164.0	167.8	170.0	171.4	172.5	172.5	169.4	171.8	175.2	176.9	170.2
Transportation and Utilities													
2000	74.4	74.4	74.3	75.0	75.1	74.9	74.7	74.8	75.9	76.4	76.4	76.3	75.2
2001	74.6	74.0	74.1	74.6	74.8	74.5	73.6	72.5	73.3	72.4	70.8	69.8	73.3
2002	68.2	67.1	67.1	67.7	68.1	67.5	65.2	65.1	66.7	67.3	67.2	66.8	67.0
2003	65.9	65.6	65.5	65.5	65.5	64.7	63.5	63.1	64.8	66.0	65.9	65.7	65.1
2004	64.2	64.2	64.3	65.4	65.9	65.9	65.8	66.0	67.7	69.6	69.8	69.8	66.6
2005	67.4	67.6	68.1	67.0	67.6	67.1	67.2	66.5	66.9	67.0	67.2	67.0	67.2
2006	65.7	65.1	65.1	64.8	65.3	64.9	63.3	63.1	65.5	65.4	66.7	66.2	65.1
2007	64.6	65.3	64.4	65.2	65.6	65.3	63.9	63.9	66.2	66.7	66.6	67.6	65.4
2008	65.2	65.3	65.6	65.3	65.8	64.9	63.1	62.9	64.9	65.0	65.0	65.6	64.9
2009	62.4	61.8	62.2	61.5	61.4	60.4	58.6	58.0	60.8	60.7	61.3	61.6	60.9
2010	59.9	59.7	59.8	60.2	60.5	60.4	58.9	58.0	60.9	61.4	62.2	62.9	60.4
2011	60.6	60.6	61.1	61.9	62.3	61.4	60.4	61.0	62.7	62.1	62.2	62.7	61.6
Information													
2000	47.7	48.1	48.3	48.9	49.2	50.5	50.9	50.8	50.2	50.3	50.5	50.7	49.7
2001	50.5	50.4	50.7	50.1	50.1	50.8	50.5	49.7	49.1	49.4	49.5	49.3	50.0
2002	48.0	47.8	47.7	48.2	48.2	48.7	48.3	47.4	46.6	46.6	46.7	47.0	47.6
2003	45.6	45.4	45.3	45.9	45.8	45.4	44.9	44.5	43.9	43.7	43.9	44.3	44.9
2004	43.5	43.3	43.5	44.2	44.3	44.1	43.4	42.7	42.2	42.2	42.7	42.9	43.3
2005	42.1	42.1	41.9	43.6	43.6	43.8	43.0	42.5	42.2	42.0	42.2	42.2	42.6
2006	41.7	41.6	41.7	41.3	41.7	41.9	41.7	41.9	41.3	41.3	41.6	41.9	41.6
2007	42.1	42.2	42.4	42.4	42.5	42.7	42.5	42.6	42.2	42.1	42.0	42.3	42.3
2008	41.9	41.7	41.8	41.7	41.7	42.0	42.2	42.1	41.9	41.4	41.5	41.2	41.8
2009	40.7	40.4	40.3	39.9	39.9	40.0	40.2	40.0	39.4	39.1	39.1	39.2	39.9
2010	39.1	38.9	38.9	39.1	38.9	39.1	39.4	39.3	38.9	39.0	38.9	38.9	39.0
2011	39.0	38.9	38.7	39.0	38.9	38.8	38.9	38.4	38.0	38.1	38.1	38.1	38.6
Financial Activities													
2000	130.1	130.1	130.5	131.4	131.9	133.7	134.1	134.4	133.6	134.0	133.9	135.1	132.7
2001	133.1	133.8	134.3	134.8	135.1	136.5	136.9	136.9	135.4	135.0	135.3	135.9	135.3
2002	134.9	135.2	135.2	135.5	135.8	136.4	138.0	138.4	137.6	137.4	138.1	138.6	136.8
2003	135.6	136.2	137.0	138.7	139.4	141.0	142.1	142.4	141.4	140.2	140.1	140.5	139.6
2004	139.9	139.5	139.3	140.1	140.3	141.5	141.5	141.6	140.4	140.7	140.7	141.3	140.6
2005	139.2	139.3	139.6	140.8	141.4	143.6	143.4	143.9	142.9	142.4	142.6	143.3	141.9
2006	142.0	142.1	142.4	141.9	142.6	143.8	143.1	142.8	141.7	141.5	141.7	142.1	142.3
2007	141.2	141.7	141.7	140.8	141.1	142.4	142.2	142.3	141.1	141.0	141.1	141.5	141.5
2008	139.2	139.5	139.6	139.4	139.4	140.2	140.9	140.4	138.9	138.5	138.2	138.8	139.4
2009	136.9	136.5	136.1	135.7	136.1	136.7	136.9	136.9	136.5	135.6	135.8	136.3	136.2
2010	134.4	134.3	134.2	134.7	135.0	136.3	136.8	137.0	136.3	137.1	137.5	137.9	136.0
2011	137.2	137.3	137.5	137.9	138.2	138.8	139.6	140.3	140.1	139.1	137.7	138.0	138.5

Employment by Industry: Minneapolis–St. Paul–Bloomington, MN–WI, Selected Years, 2000–2011—*Continued*

(Numbers in thousands, not seasonally adjusted)

Industry and year	January	February	March	April	May	June	July	August	September	October	November	December	Annual average
Professional and Business Services													
2000	255.9	255.2	258.4	263.0	264.7	270.5	269.3	271.0	269.3	270.1	269.0	267.3	265.3
2001	260.5	258.3	258.4	261.8	261.7	263.5	260.6	260.5	257.6	255.8	253.0	251.8	258.6
2002	241.8	241.0	241.0	242.2	244.2	247.3	247.8	249.2	247.5	248.4	246.7	244.6	245.1
2003	237.2	237.5	237.7	238.8	240.0	242.2	243.1	244.2	244.5	246.2	245.0	245.5	241.8
2004	236.4	237.4	238.7	244.4	245.9	249.2	249.3	249.1	248.0	249.6	248.3	247.3	245.3
2005	238.0	238.4	240.6	247.3	249.4	252.6	251.8	254.0	255.4	259.2	259.2	259.0	250.4
2006	253.2	253.7	255.0	258.3	260.9	265.9	263.4	265.2	263.9	265.4	266.4	266.3	261.5
2007	259.1	259.9	261.5	261.9	263.7	267.9	267.7	270.3	267.0	268.9	269.0	267.7	265.4
2008	260.4	260.9	260.6	262.5	264.2	266.9	268.1	268.2	266.4	267.1	263.9	261.4	264.2
2009	249.1	245.0	242.8	245.4	245.8	246.9	246.4	247.7	244.6	249.4	249.9	250.3	246.9
2010	241.9	242.4	242.0	249.3	251.1	254.0	257.4	258.8	256.0	258.7	259.5	259.1	252.5
2011	253.3	253.6	255.0	260.6	261.6	264.1	264.6	265.7	265.2	272.1	270.7	275.4	263.5
Education and Health Services													
2000	180.6	184.8	186.2	186.8	187.3	184.2	182.7	183.1	188.0	190.8	192.2	193.4	186.7
2001	185.9	189.0	190.9	191.0	192.3	189.2	187.9	188.5	193.2	197.0	198.7	199.1	191.9
2002	194.5	197.8	198.9	199.6	201.1	198.2	198.7	199.3	203.1	206.3	207.9	208.1	201.1
2003	205.7	210.0	210.9	211.4	212.5	210.5	208.8	208.7	210.5	213.5	214.7	214.3	211.0
2004	211.2	213.7	214.7	216.3	217.1	215.8	212.6	212.4	214.6	218.5	219.2	220.4	215.5
2005	216.7	220.5	221.5	222.6	224.0	222.0	221.8	223.0	225.9	228.7	230.3	231.9	224.1
2006	229.7	231.8	233.9	237.2	237.8	237.1	237.0	237.4	238.6	241.7	244.0	245.0	237.6
2007	244.7	246.6	248.1	250.7	252.0	250.4	248.7	249.4	250.1	254.1	256.4	255.8	250.6
2008	253.1	256.0	257.5	260.1	259.6	257.7	256.9	257.0	259.3	264.3	265.3	264.8	259.3
2009	262.1	264.8	265.4	268.2	268.2	263.2	262.3	261.6	263.0	267.6	268.9	269.0	265.4
2010	263.4	266.2	267.9	270.4	271.1	267.5	264.4	266.0	267.9	272.9	274.1	273.4	268.8
2011	272.1	275.1	275.8	279.0	279.6	275.0	272.4	273.4	274.8	279.0	281.2	281.0	276.5
Leisure and Hospitality													
2000	133.7	135.0	136.6	140.3	144.9	149.8	150.1	151.8	150.6	143.7	142.0	141.9	143.4
2001	138.2	139.5	141.0	143.2	148.7	154.4	153.6	157.3	153.0	147.3	144.9	145.5	147.2
2002	141.3	141.5	142.5	145.3	150.8	156.0	153.9	156.1	153.5	148.0	145.1	145.8	148.3
2003	143.1	142.3	142.8	148.2	154.6	158.1	157.1	159.5	156.6	152.6	149.4	150.5	151.2
2004	144.8	144.3	145.9	152.3	157.8	161.9	160.7	162.5	160.5	156.4	153.0	154.1	154.5
2005	148.3	147.7	149.0	153.7	159.1	164.5	164.4	165.9	163.8	160.8	159.4	159.2	158.0
2006	154.2	154.1	156.1	159.3	164.4	169.3	166.4	168.3	164.2	159.8	157.8	157.8	161.0
2007	154.5	154.6	155.5	160.7	167.2	171.4	170.0	170.7	167.7	163.5	160.4	160.1	163.0
2008	155.0	154.7	156.5	159.6	166.8	171.1	170.2	172.3	166.6	162.8	158.3	157.0	162.6
2009	152.0	150.6	151.1	156.2	163.2	164.7	164.0	164.7	160.3	157.2	152.2	151.6	157.3
2010	146.3	145.2	147.1	154.8	160.1	162.4	162.5	163.8	160.0	157.4	152.8	151.8	155.4
2011	148.2	147.9	150.2	156.4	164.1	167.8	168.7	167.9	160.5	155.2	149.2	146.5	156.9
Other Services													
2000	70.7	71.7	72.3	71.9	71.6	72.4	72.3	72.6	71.8	73.1	73.2	73.7	72.3
2001	72.8	72.9	73.8	73.2	73.7	74.3	73.6	73.8	72.7	74.5	76.6	75.4	73.9
2002	72.9	73.0	73.1	73.7	73.9	74.6	75.0	75.3	74.3	74.4	74.7	74.8	74.1
2003	73.3	73.4	73.9	73.8	74.3	75.2	77.4	77.5	76.8	76.5	76.8	76.8	75.5
2004	74.9	74.5	75.2	76.1	75.8	76.6	76.2	76.8	75.8	76.0	75.7	76.2	75.8
2005	74.3	74.3	74.6	76.4	77.5	76.8	76.7	77.2	76.8	76.6	76.5	77.2	76.2
2006	74.0	74.0	75.4	75.9	76.3	77.4	76.8	77.1	76.2	76.5	77.1	77.1	76.2
2007	74.5	74.4	75.7	75.5	76.0	76.6	76.9	76.8	75.7	75.9	76.8	77.1	76.0
2008	75.9	77.1	77.8	78.0	78.0	79.3	78.9	79.5	77.4	77.5	77.1	76.9	77.8
2009	75.0	75.1	75.0	76.0	76.2	77.0	76.2	76.1	74.7	75.6	75.2	75.1	75.6
2010	74.0	74.1	74.9	75.0	75.2	76.4	76.3	76.5	74.9	75.7	75.2	75.0	75.3
2011	74.3	74.6	75.0	77.0	77.1	77.8	78.2	78.0	79.2	78.7	78.7	79.5	77.3
Government													
2000	234.0	237.8	239.8	241.6	244.4	238.9	217.2	216.6	230.3	235.1	238.3	237.5	234.3
2001	231.1	237.8	238.4	238.8	241.8	237.4	219.9	218.7	233.8	239.5	241.4	241.3	235.0
2002	236.9	242.0	242.5	242.5	244.6	239.2	223.4	215.5	237.9	242.1	246.9	244.5	238.2
2003	237.8	244.3	244.1	247.0	247.5	241.7	224.2	222.3	238.7	244.9	246.3	246.8	240.5
2004	240.8	246.4	245.7	246.1	248.3	243.8	220.5	216.8	237.6	243.8	245.5	246.3	240.1
2005	244.1	247.1	247.0	247.0	247.2	243.9	226.6	221.9	240.6	246.7	245.7	246.8	242.1
2006	243.1	245.0	245.3	245.1	246.1	243.0	226.5	221.2	240.9	246.3	247.7	248.1	241.5
2007	240.8	243.7	243.2	242.7	245.3	241.6	223.0	217.9	237.6	242.7	244.1	242.9	238.8
2008	240.2	245.9	245.3	245.0	248.0	245.5	228.7	225.8	242.8	245.9	247.6	246.2	242.2
2009	239.3	245.1	244.6	243.8	245.2	242.3	230.5	225.0	235.2	241.0	242.3	241.0	239.6
2010	236.7	241.3	241.3	243.9	247.5	242.7	219.4	216.5	233.3	240.9	242.6	241.2	237.3
2011	235.9	241.6	240.6	241.3	241.8	237.9	203.2	211.4	227.4	233.8	234.3	233.0	231.9

Employment by Industry: Nashville–Davidson–Murfreesboro–Franklin, TN, Selected Years, 2000–2011

(Numbers in thousands, not seasonally adjusted)

Industry and year	January	February	March	April	May	June	July	August	September	October	November	December	Annual average
Total Nonfarm													
2000	683.6	688.1	699.3	696.8	700.0	700.8	693.7	698.3	701.6	703.8	705.9	706.2	698.2
2001	687.4	689.7	694.0	697.1	696.9	696.1	691.4	692.8	696.5	693.0	695.3	694.4	693.7
2002	674.5	677.8	682.7	685.1	688.1	685.8	688.5	692.9	697.0	698.2	701.6	703.0	689.6
2003	687.4	688.6	691.5	696.9	699.2	695.2	691.8	698.5	701.7	703.4	707.0	710.2	697.6
2004	695.8	701.3	705.5	711.1	711.8	709.5	712.4	719.6	721.6	727.9	732.0	735.5	715.3
2005	713.7	719.2	724.5	732.7	734.1	731.1	733.1	740.6	744.8	746.0	751.3	753.2	735.4
2006	736.9	739.4	746.9	748.8	750.0	750.3	749.6	757.5	760.0	756.1	761.7	764.2	751.8
2007	744.2	747.8	755.6	754.6	758.2	759.4	759.0	769.8	773.6	770.5	778.4	778.6	762.5
2008	756.0	758.9	762.1	762.8	767.4	761.1	753.4	760.6	764.1	760.9	760.2	759.1	760.6
2009	731.4	730.0	728.1	726.2	727.1	717.6	712.4	719.8	724.4	727.8	733.4	733.3	726.0
2010	714.7	717.3	723.7	732.0	738.6	730.6	725.2	732.9	742.4	748.8	752.8	753.0	734.3
2011	731.9	737.0	744.2	751.8	754.7	749.2	746.9	754.3	760.0	761.0	767.5	761.5	751.7
Total Private													
2000	594.5	597.5	604.7	605.5	607.5	613.1	609.5	610.4	612.6	612.5	614.0	614.4	608.0
2001	597.1	597.3	601.6	603.6	604.1	607.9	603.5	604.9	604.1	599.6	601.1	600.5	602.1
2002	582.4	583.9	587.9	591.0	594.6	597.4	602.3	604.9	604.4	604.5	607.8	608.8	597.5
2003	593.5	593.3	595.7	600.4	603.8	606.1	603.1	606.2	606.1	607.6	611.6	613.9	603.4
2004	599.8	601.2	607.0	613.0	615.2	619.9	623.0	626.5	625.8	630.8	634.6	636.9	619.5
2005	617.4	621.0	626.3	634.1	636.5	639.5	641.5	644.8	646.2	647.5	652.7	654.4	638.5
2006	638.7	639.5	646.7	648.7	651.0	657.7	656.2	660.1	659.8	655.8	660.7	662.8	653.1
2007	644.4	646.7	654.4	655.4	660.7	667.4	665.8	670.7	668.9	667.4	673.4	675.2	662.5
2008	653.6	654.7	657.8	659.0	662.5	666.0	658.5	660.7	658.5	654.4	653.0	651.0	657.5
2009	626.6	622.4	621.1	618.7	620.2	622.5	616.4	619.1	618.3	620.0	625.3	625.5	621.3
2010	609.1	610.0	615.9	623.6	628.6	632.1	629.1	631.5	633.4	639.2	643.6	644.3	628.4
2011	625.9	631.0	637.5	644.5	648.0	652.1	650.1	652.3	655.1	655.1	661.7	656.9	647.5
Goods-Producing													
2000	129.9	130.3	131.5	130.7	130.3	131.5	129.5	128.9	127.7	126.4	124.9	124.8	128.9
2001	124.7	123.5	124.0	122.9	123.0	124.1	122.7	122.8	122.2	120.6	119.6	119.5	122.5
2002	115.4	114.7	114.5	115.7	116.8	117.5	117.5	118.0	117.6	116.9	116.5	117.1	116.5
2003	114.9	114.7	114.9	115.4	116.4	117.0	116.8	117.0	117.2	117.0	116.6	116.7	116.2
2004	115.0	115.0	115.8	117.6	118.4	119.3	119.5	119.3	119.2	118.7	118.9	119.2	118.0
2005	116.5	117.3	118.2	120.1	120.7	121.7	120.7	121.9	121.8	122.0	122.2	122.5	120.5
2006	121.4	121.3	122.4	123.0	123.0	124.9	124.1	124.8	124.5	123.1	123.4	123.4	123.3
2007	120.7	120.3	121.4	121.0	121.1	122.3	121.3	121.4	121.4	120.4	120.3	119.8	121.0
2008	116.7	116.1	115.7	115.4	115.8	116.1	114.1	113.5	111.4	108.1	106.0	104.3	112.8
2009	99.3	97.8	96.6	94.9	94.0	93.7	93.1	93.1	92.5	91.8	91.6	90.8	94.1
2010	88.0	87.6	88.5	90.4	90.8	92.0	92.0	92.6	92.7	93.1	92.5	92.4	91.1
2011	89.8	90.6	92.2	93.9	94.0	95.1	95.6	95.6	96.1	96.1	97.0	96.0	94.3
Mining, Logging, and Construction													
2000	34.5	34.5	35.6	36.1	37.0	37.5	36.9	36.8	36.1	35.6	34.9	34.7	35.9
2001	32.3	32.5	33.2	33.4	33.9	34.8	34.9	35.0	34.2	33.6	33.4	33.3	33.7
2002	31.1	31.0	31.2	31.5	32.5	33.0	33.6	34.1	34.0	33.6	33.8	33.8	32.8
2003	32.7	32.6	33.2	33.9	34.7	35.4	35.7	35.6	35.5	34.9	34.5	34.6	34.4
2004	33.1	32.9	33.4	34.0	34.6	35.4	35.5	35.3	35.1	34.6	34.5	34.5	34.4
2005	32.8	33.1	34.0	35.2	36.1	37.1	37.2	37.5	37.5	37.3	37.2	37.2	36.0
2006	37.0	37.3	38.3	38.7	39.2	40.3	40.1	40.3	40.2	39.6	39.5	39.6	39.2
2007	38.8	39.3	40.8	41.1	41.7	42.9	42.8	43.1	43.1	42.7	42.4	41.9	41.7
2008	40.3	40.1	40.1	40.1	40.5	40.7	40.0	40.0	39.3	38.1	36.9	35.9	39.3
2009	33.5	32.7	32.4	31.7	31.7	31.9	31.9	31.7	31.3	30.9	30.6	30.2	31.7
2010	28.1	27.8	28.7	30.5	30.7	31.7	31.8	32.1	32.0	32.4	31.5	31.1	30.7
2011	28.6	29.2	30.4	31.8	31.9	32.8	33.4	33.9	34.1	33.5	33.7	33.1	32.2
Manufacturing													
2000	95.4	95.8	95.9	94.6	93.3	94.0	92.6	92.1	91.6	90.8	90.0	90.1	93.0
2001	92.4	91.0	90.8	89.5	89.1	89.3	87.8	87.8	88.0	87.0	86.2	86.2	88.8
2002	84.3	83.7	83.3	84.2	84.3	84.5	83.9	83.9	83.6	83.3	82.7	83.3	83.8
2003	82.2	82.1	81.7	81.5	81.7	81.6	81.1	81.4	81.7	82.1	82.1	82.1	81.8
2004	81.9	82.1	82.4	83.6	83.8	83.9	84.0	84.0	84.1	84.1	84.4	84.7	83.6
2005	83.7	84.2	84.2	84.9	84.6	84.6	83.5	84.4	84.3	84.7	85.0	85.3	84.5
2006	84.4	84.0	84.1	84.3	83.8	84.6	84.0	84.5	84.3	83.5	83.9	83.8	84.1
2007	81.9	81.0	80.6	79.9	79.4	79.4	78.5	78.3	78.5	77.7	77.9	77.9	79.3
2008	76.4	76.0	75.6	75.3	75.3	75.4	74.1	73.5	72.1	70.0	69.1	68.4	73.4
2009	65.8	65.1	64.2	63.2	62.3	61.8	61.2	61.4	61.2	60.9	61.0	60.6	62.4
2010	59.9	59.8	59.8	59.9	60.1	60.3	60.2	60.5	60.7	60.7	61.0	61.3	60.4
2011	61.2	61.4	61.8	62.1	62.1	62.3	62.2	61.7	62.0	62.6	63.3	62.9	62.1
Service-Providing													
2000	553.7	557.8	567.8	566.1	569.7	569.3	564.2	569.4	573.9	577.4	581.0	581.4	569.3
2001	562.7	566.2	570.0	574.2	573.9	572.0	568.7	570.0	574.3	572.4	575.7	574.9	571.3
2002	559.1	563.1	568.2	569.4	571.3	568.3	571.0	574.9	579.4	581.3	585.1	585.9	573.1
2003	572.5	573.9	576.6	581.5	582.8	578.2	575.0	581.5	584.5	586.4	590.4	593.5	581.4
2004	580.8	586.3	589.7	593.5	593.4	590.2	592.9	600.3	602.4	609.2	613.1	616.3	597.3
2005	597.2	601.9	606.3	612.6	613.4	609.4	612.4	618.7	623.0	624.0	629.1	630.7	614.9
2006	615.5	618.1	624.5	625.8	627.0	625.4	625.5	632.7	635.5	633.0	638.3	640.8	628.5
2007	623.5	627.5	634.2	633.6	637.1	637.1	637.7	648.4	652.0	650.1	658.1	658.8	641.5
2008	639.3	642.8	646.4	647.4	651.6	645.0	639.3	647.1	652.7	652.8	654.2	654.8	647.8
2009	632.1	632.2	631.5	631.3	633.1	623.9	619.3	626.7	631.9	636.0	641.8	642.5	631.9
2010	626.7	629.7	635.2	641.6	647.8	638.6	633.2	640.3	649.7	655.7	660.3	660.6	643.3
2011	642.1	646.4	652.0	657.9	660.7	654.1	651.3	658.7	663.9	664.9	670.5	665.5	657.3

Employment by Industry: Nashville–Davidson–Murfreesboro–Franklin, TN, Selected Years, 2000–2011—*Continued*

(Numbers in thousands, not seasonally adjusted)

Industry and year	January	February	March	April	May	June	July	August	September	October	November	December	Annual average
Trade, Transportation, and Utilities													
2000	139.8	139.6	140.3	140.5	140.3	141.1	142.1	142.8	144.1	146.5	148.6	149.4	142.9
2001	142.6	141.6	142.1	142.6	142.6	142.6	141.0	140.8	140.7	140.6	143.1	143.5	142.0
2002	136.0	134.9	136.2	134.6	135.4	136.1	137.3	137.8	138.4	140.8	143.1	145.5	138.0
2003	139.3	139.0	139.3	139.7	140.0	141.3	140.6	142.0	141.9	143.9	146.5	148.3	141.8
2004	142.5	141.8	142.9	143.0	143.7	144.8	144.9	146.1	146.6	149.2	152.2	153.7	146.0
2005	146.4	146.1	147.3	148.5	149.1	149.1	150.5	150.9	152.1	153.3	156.8	158.5	150.7
2006	151.9	151.4	152.9	152.5	153.0	153.7	152.7	153.6	153.9	153.3	156.4	158.6	153.7
2007	152.6	152.0	153.6	152.8	153.5	153.7	153.4	154.1	154.6	154.9	158.7	160.7	154.6
2008	154.3	153.9	154.8	153.7	153.9	153.9	154.2	154.4	154.4	154.3	156.1	157.5	154.6
2009	150.5	148.2	147.2	145.8	146.3	146.4	146.2	146.9	146.2	147.4	150.0	151.4	147.7
2010	145.4	144.6	145.3	145.9	146.3	147.3	146.9	147.7	147.4	149.6	152.6	154.4	147.8
2011	148.1	148.0	149.2	150.7	151.5	151.9	150.6	150.2	150.7	149.7	153.5	153.6	150.6
Wholesale Trade													
2000	35.5	35.4	35.6	35.7	35.6	35.8	36.1	36.2	36.6	37.2	37.7	37.9	36.3
2001	36.2	35.9	36.1	36.2	36.2	36.2	35.8	35.7	35.7	35.7	36.3	36.4	36.0
2002	34.5	34.2	34.6	34.2	34.3	34.5	34.8	35.0	35.1	35.7	36.3	36.9	35.0
2003	34.8	34.8	34.7	34.7	34.9	34.8	34.5	34.5	34.5	34.2	34.0	33.9	34.5
2004	33.7	33.9	34.1	34.2	34.3	34.6	34.6	35.0	35.1	35.5	35.4	35.5	34.7
2005	35.4	35.7	35.7	36.1	36.3	36.1	36.2	36.3	36.6	36.7	37.0	36.8	36.2
2006	36.4	36.5	36.5	36.4	36.5	36.6	36.5	36.7	36.9	36.3	36.2	36.3	36.5
2007	35.8	36.0	36.3	36.3	36.5	36.7	36.7	36.8	37.2	37.2	37.4	37.4	36.7
2008	37.1	37.3	37.2	37.2	37.6	37.8	38.0	38.2	38.5	38.4	38.4	38.2	37.8
2009	37.2	36.9	36.5	36.3	36.2	36.0	35.8	35.9	35.8	36.0	35.9	35.9	36.2
2010	35.3	35.3	35.4	35.5	35.7	35.6	35.7	35.9	35.8	36.3	36.3	36.5	35.8
2011	36.2	36.4	36.7	36.6	36.8	37.0	37.2	36.6	37.0	36.9	36.8	36.9	36.8
Retail Trade													
2000	77.9	77.8	78.2	78.3	78.2	78.7	79.2	79.6	80.3	81.6	82.8	83.3	79.7
2001	79.5	79.0	79.2	79.5	79.5	79.5	78.6	78.5	78.4	78.4	79.8	80.0	79.2
2002	75.8	75.2	75.9	75.0	75.5	75.9	76.6	76.8	77.2	78.5	79.8	81.1	76.9
2003	78.0	77.5	77.7	78.0	78.0	79.1	78.6	79.8	80.3	82.5	85.1	86.8	80.1
2004	81.9	80.9	81.3	81.2	81.5	82.1	81.9	82.4	82.5	84.3	87.0	88.0	82.9
2005	83.2	82.6	83.6	83.9	84.2	84.1	84.3	84.3	84.9	85.5	88.4	89.7	84.9
2006	84.8	84.3	85.3	85.5	85.8	86.0	85.3	85.8	85.6	85.8	89.1	90.6	86.2
2007	86.4	85.6	86.8	86.1	86.7	86.5	86.1	86.5	86.6	87.3	90.7	92.5	87.3
2008	87.6	87.1	88.1	86.8	86.5	86.2	86.1	86.2	85.8	85.7	87.7	88.6	86.9
2009	83.9	82.5	82.1	81.6	82.1	82.2	82.1	82.5	81.7	82.5	84.7	85.9	82.8
2010	81.9	81.2	81.6	82.3	82.3	83.0	82.5	82.9	82.2	83.3	85.7	86.9	83.0
2011	83.1	83.0	83.6	84.5	84.9	85.2	84.0	84.2	84.1	83.2	86.5	86.2	84.4
Transportation and Utilities													
2000	26.4	26.4	26.5	26.5	26.5	26.6	26.8	27.0	27.2	27.7	28.1	28.2	27.0
2001	26.9	26.7	26.8	26.9	26.9	26.9	26.6	26.6	26.6	26.5	27.0	27.1	26.8
2002	25.7	25.5	25.7	25.4	25.6	25.7	25.9	26.0	26.1	26.6	27.0	27.5	26.1
2003	26.5	26.7	26.9	27.0	27.1	27.4	27.5	27.7	27.1	27.2	27.4	27.6	27.2
2004	26.9	27.0	27.5	27.6	27.9	28.1	28.4	28.7	29.0	29.4	29.8	30.2	28.4
2005	27.8	27.8	28.0	28.5	28.6	28.9	30.0	30.3	30.6	31.1	31.4	32.0	29.6
2006	30.7	30.6	31.1	30.6	30.7	31.1	30.9	31.1	31.4	31.2	31.1	31.7	31.0
2007	30.4	30.4	30.5	30.4	30.3	30.5	30.6	30.8	30.8	30.4	30.6	30.8	30.5
2008	29.6	29.5	29.5	29.7	29.8	29.9	30.1	30.0	30.1	30.2	30.0	30.7	29.9
2009	29.4	28.8	28.6	27.9	28.0	28.2	28.3	28.5	28.7	28.9	29.4	29.6	28.7
2010	28.2	28.1	28.3	28.1	28.3	28.7	28.7	28.9	29.4	30.0	30.6	31.0	29.0
2011	28.8	28.6	28.9	29.6	29.8	29.7	29.4	29.4	29.6	29.6	30.2	30.5	29.5
Information													
2000	21.1	21.0	21.3	21.2	21.2	21.4	21.7	21.7	21.7	21.8	22.3	22.5	21.6
2001	23.9	24.1	24.1	23.4	23.4	23.4	23.0	22.7	22.5	22.8	22.9	22.9	23.3
2002	22.3	22.2	22.4	21.9	21.8	21.5	21.5	21.3	21.0	21.3	21.1	20.9	21.6
2003	20.2	20.1	20.1	19.9	20.0	19.8	19.8	19.8	19.6	19.6	19.8	19.9	19.9
2004	19.5	19.4	19.3	19.3	19.3	19.5	19.5	19.5	18.8	19.1	19.2	19.9	19.4
2005	19.8	19.9	19.8	19.5	19.5	19.7	19.7	19.6	19.6	19.7	19.8	19.8	19.7
2006	19.6	19.6	19.7	19.7	19.6	19.7	19.0	18.9	19.0	19.0	19.1	19.2	19.3
2007	19.0	19.0	19.0	19.2	19.6	19.7	19.9	20.0	20.1	20.3	20.4	20.8	19.8
2008	21.1	21.1	21.2	21.2	21.3	21.3	21.0	21.0	20.9	21.2	21.1	21.2	21.1
2009	20.8	20.7	20.6	20.3	20.2	20.0	19.8	20.0	19.8	19.4	19.5	19.4	20.0
2010	19.4	19.4	19.5	19.4	19.3	19.3	19.3	19.0	19.0	19.3	19.3	19.3	19.3
2011	18.9	18.8	18.8	18.7	18.9	18.9	18.8	18.8	18.6	18.5	18.6	18.8	18.8
Financial Activities													
2000	47.2	47.3	47.3	47.0	47.0	47.3	47.2	46.8	46.5	46.1	46.3	46.3	46.9
2001	43.9	44.2	44.4	44.6	44.6	44.8	44.8	44.6	44.1	43.7	43.5	43.2	44.2
2002	42.7	42.8	42.7	43.1	43.3	43.9	43.8	44.0	43.8	44.1	44.3	44.4	43.6
2003	44.4	44.5	44.7	44.8	44.8	45.1	44.8	44.8	44.6	44.5	44.5	44.7	44.5
2004	44.0	44.0	44.2	44.5	44.4	44.4	44.5	44.6	44.5	44.9	45.1	45.2	44.5
2005	44.4	44.5	44.7	45.1	45.3	45.4	45.5	45.6	45.6	45.4	45.6	45.7	45.2
2006	45.3	45.2	45.5	45.7	45.9	45.9	46.0	45.9	45.7	45.8	45.7	45.9	45.7
2007	45.3	45.6	45.8	46.1	46.6	46.8	46.6	46.6	46.3	46.3	46.2	46.4	46.2
2008	45.9	46.2	46.1	46.1	46.2	46.4	46.3	46.1	45.7	45.5	45.1	45.1	45.9
2009	44.8	44.7	44.5	44.6	44.8	44.9	44.9	45.3	45.1	45.2	45.5	45.8	45.0
2010	45.4	45.5	45.5	46.0	46.3	46.2	46.4	46.7	46.3	46.7	46.9	47.0	46.2
2011	46.2	46.4	46.3	46.7	47.2	46.9	46.8	47.5	47.5	47.1	47.1	46.6	46.9

Employment by Industry: Nashville–Davidson–Murfreesboro–Franklin, TN, Selected Years, 2000–2011—*Continued*
(Numbers in thousands, not seasonally adjusted)

Industry and year	January	February	March	April	May	June	July	August	September	October	November	December	Annual average
Professional and Business Services													
2000	84.9	86.4	88.2	88.0	88.7	88.9	88.0	88.9	90.0	90.2	90.2	90.2	88.6
2001	84.9	84.8	85.5	86.3	85.7	85.9	86.8	88.0	88.4	87.2	87.4	87.6	86.5
2002	84.4	85.7	86.9	87.2	87.5	87.2	88.0	88.7	88.0	86.7	87.4	86.2	87.0
2003	82.4	82.2	82.2	82.8	83.6	84.0	83.0	84.0	84.5	85.4	87.1	87.7	84.1
2004	85.7	86.6	87.7	89.4	89.7	91.0	91.5	93.0	94.0	96.5	96.6	96.5	91.5
2005	92.3	93.4	93.9	95.3	95.2	95.7	96.1	97.8	99.3	99.7	100.5	101.0	96.7
2006	95.4	95.4	96.3	96.6	96.9	99.3	98.7	101.1	102.4	100.8	102.1	102.1	98.9
2007	96.5	97.3	98.9	98.9	100.0	102.6	103.3	104.8	104.2	104.4	106.2	105.8	101.9
2008	99.2	98.9	99.3	100.2	101.1	103.5	98.8	100.5	101.8	102.0	101.9	100.0	100.6
2009	93.4	92.9	92.2	91.2	91.9	93.5	90.2	91.9	92.9	94.5	96.4	95.5	93.0
2010	92.1	92.8	94.2	96.2	100.6	100.4	98.8	99.4	101.4	101.4	103.0	103.0	98.6
2011	99.3	101.4	102.7	103.7	104.5	106.7	107.5	109.0	110.4	110.5	112.1	110.5	106.5
Education and Health Services													
2000	80.5	81.3	82.0	83.1	82.4	82.4	82.6	82.6	83.5	83.9	84.4	84.3	82.8
2001	83.3	84.3	84.7	86.0	86.0	86.5	86.7	86.7	87.0	86.8	87.1	87.7	86.1
2002	87.2	88.0	88.3	89.5	90.0	90.0	92.0	92.0	92.3	92.6	92.8	92.7	90.6
2003	93.0	93.4	93.7	94.9	94.9	94.9	95.5	95.5	95.5	95.6	95.6	95.8	94.9
2004	96.3	96.6	97.2	98.3	97.9	97.9	99.3	99.2	99.0	99.6	99.7	99.8	98.4
2005	98.7	99.4	99.5	101.2	101.7	101.6	102.5	102.5	102.3	102.2	102.3	102.5	101.4
2006	102.2	102.8	103.5	104.1	104.2	104.5	104.8	105.0	105.1	105.2	105.7	105.6	104.4
2007	104.9	105.8	106.2	107.0	107.5	107.8	108.7	109.5	110.2	109.5	109.7	110.0	108.1
2008	108.9	109.7	109.8	111.3	111.5	111.8	112.2	112.9	113.7	113.8	114.2	114.7	112.0
2009	113.6	114.0	114.0	115.1	114.6	114.1	114.5	114.3	115.7	116.0	116.4	116.6	114.9
2010	115.8	116.5	117.0	118.5	117.3	116.9	118.4	118.5	120.4	120.9	121.1	120.9	118.5
2011	119.6	120.9	121.0	122.1	121.1	120.7	120.0	120.1	121.4	122.3	122.0	120.8	121.0
Leisure and Hospitality													
2000	64.6	64.7	66.6	67.6	69.9	72.1	70.9	71.0	71.0	69.7	69.4	69.7	68.9
2001	66.4	66.8	68.4	68.9	69.7	71.0	69.5	70.2	69.4	68.0	67.9	67.4	68.6
2002	65.6	66.3	67.7	69.3	69.5	70.6	71.3	72.4	71.9	70.0	71.0	70.7	69.7
2003	68.1	68.8	70.1	71.9	73.1	73.8	73.0	73.7	73.1	71.8	71.9	71.6	71.7
2004	67.4	68.0	69.5	71.2	72.5	73.5	74.0	74.8	74.2	73.0	72.9	73.3	72.0
2005	70.4	71.3	72.7	74.6	75.4	76.3	76.7	76.8	75.6	75.4	75.4	74.7	74.6
2006	73.2	73.9	75.8	77.1	77.9	78.9	80.4	80.4	78.9	78.2	78.1	78.1	77.6
2007	75.9	76.8	79.0	80.1	81.8	83.8	82.4	83.8	81.6	81.0	81.3	81.2	80.7
2008	77.1	77.9	79.4	80.3	81.6	81.9	80.8	81.4	80.1	78.5	77.8	77.5	79.5
2009	74.4	74.0	75.5	76.8	78.2	79.1	77.5	77.7	76.7	75.9	76.1	76.4	76.5
2010	73.8	74.2	76.3	77.8	78.3	79.6	77.1	77.4	76.1	77.8	77.6	76.5	76.9
2011	73.3	73.8	75.9	77.6	79.5	79.9	79.8	79.6	78.3	78.5	78.7	77.5	77.7
Other Services													
2000	26.5	26.9	27.5	27.4	27.7	28.4	27.5	27.7	28.1	27.9	27.9	27.2	27.6
2001	27.4	28.0	28.4	28.9	29.1	29.6	29.0	29.1	29.8	29.9	29.6	28.7	29.0
2002	28.8	29.3	29.2	29.7	30.3	30.6	30.9	30.7	31.4	32.1	31.6	31.3	30.5
2003	31.2	30.6	30.7	31.0	31.0	30.2	29.6	29.4	29.7	29.8	29.6	29.3	30.2
2004	29.4	29.8	30.4	29.7	29.3	29.5	29.8	30.0	29.5	29.8	30.0	29.3	29.7
2005	28.9	29.1	30.2	29.8	29.6	30.0	29.8	29.7	29.9	29.8	30.1	29.7	29.7
2006	29.7	29.9	30.6	30.1	30.4	30.8	30.5	30.4	30.3	30.4	30.2	29.9	30.3
2007	29.5	29.9	30.5	30.3	30.6	30.7	30.2	30.5	30.3	30.6	30.6	30.5	30.4
2008	30.4	30.9	31.5	30.8	31.1	31.1	31.1	30.9	30.5	31.2	30.8	30.7	30.9
2009	29.8	30.1	30.5	30.0	30.2	30.6	30.2	29.9	29.4	29.8	29.8	29.6	30.0
2010	29.2	29.4	29.6	29.4	29.7	30.4	30.2	30.2	30.1	30.4	30.6	30.8	30.0
2011	30.7	31.1	31.4	31.1	31.3	32.0	31.0	31.5	32.1	32.4	32.7	33.1	31.7
Government													
2000	89.1	90.6	94.6	91.3	92.5	87.7	84.2	87.9	89.0	91.3	91.9	91.8	90.2
2001	90.3	92.4	92.4	93.5	92.8	88.2	87.9	87.9	92.4	93.4	94.2	93.9	91.6
2002	92.1	93.9	94.8	94.1	93.5	88.4	86.2	88.0	92.6	93.7	93.8	94.2	92.1
2003	93.9	95.3	95.8	96.5	95.4	89.1	88.7	92.3	95.6	95.8	95.4	96.3	94.2
2004	96.0	100.1	98.5	98.1	96.6	89.6	89.4	93.1	95.8	97.1	97.4	98.6	95.9
2005	96.3	98.2	98.2	98.6	97.6	91.6	91.6	95.8	98.6	98.5	98.6	98.8	96.9
2006	98.2	99.9	100.2	100.1	99.0	92.6	93.4	97.4	100.2	100.3	101.0	101.4	98.6
2007	99.8	101.1	101.2	99.2	97.5	92.0	93.2	99.1	104.7	103.1	105.0	103.4	99.9
2008	102.4	104.2	104.3	103.8	104.9	95.1	94.9	99.9	105.6	106.5	107.2	108.1	103.1
2009	104.8	107.6	107.0	107.5	106.9	95.1	96.0	100.7	106.1	107.8	108.1	107.8	104.6
2010	105.6	107.3	107.8	108.4	110.0	98.5	96.1	101.4	109.0	109.6	109.2	108.7	106.0
2011	106.0	106.0	106.7	107.3	106.7	97.1	96.8	102.0	104.9	105.9	105.8	104.6	104.2

Employment by Industry: New Haven, CT, NECTA, Selected Years, 2000–2011

(Numbers in thousands, not seasonally adjusted)

Industry and year	January	February	March	April	May	June	July	August	September	October	November	December	Annual average
Total Nonfarm													
2000	269.0	272.7	275.0	275.1	276.6	278.9	269.8	269.0	275.5	275.5	277.5	279.2	274.5
2001	268.1	270.3	271.4	273.8	275.7	279.0	269.2	269.4	275.1	275.1	276.8	278.1	273.5
2002	269.0	270.9	272.6	275.2	277.6	281.3	271.0	270.5	276.0	275.0	277.0	278.1	274.5
2003	267.5	269.0	269.0	270.6	271.6	271.7	265.8	265.1	267.7	271.4	274.6	275.5	270.0
2004	266.6	268.0	269.2	271.5	273.4	273.8	269.8	267.6	271.3	275.5	277.0	278.0	271.8
2005	268.2	270.7	269.3	275.1	275.6	277.6	270.2	268.0	274.5	274.8	277.7	278.8	273.4
2006	270.2	273.7	273.4	276.9	278.8	280.3	272.2	270.5	276.6	278.7	280.5	281.9	276.1
2007	272.3	275.0	273.8	277.8	279.7	281.8	273.8	272.6	278.4	280.9	282.5	283.4	277.7
2008	276.0	278.4	276.9	278.6	280.6	280.4	271.6	270.0	276.1	277.2	279.1	278.4	276.9
2009	268.1	269.1	265.7	266.6	269.0	268.6	260.0	258.5	265.4	266.6	268.2	269.0	266.2
2010	259.1	261.1	259.6	263.8	267.5	267.1	262.2	260.0	265.6	267.4	267.9	267.9	264.1
2011	262.0	263.7	261.8	268.1	269.1	269.7	265.2	262.6	268.5	271.9	272.8	269.6	267.1
Total Private													
2000	234.3	236.9	239.1	239.1	241.2	243.9	239.2	238.6	240.7	240.1	241.7	243.3	239.8
2001	233.0	234.6	235.8	238.0	240.0	243.7	238.4	238.2	240.9	239.5	240.1	241.5	238.6
2002	233.3	234.6	236.4	239.5	241.8	245.1	240.3	239.5	241.9	239.3	240.2	241.3	239.4
2003	231.7	232.9	232.7	234.4	235.5	237.5	234.6	234.3	233.7	236.1	238.2	239.5	235.1
2004	231.8	232.4	233.3	235.8	237.7	239.8	238.3	237.1	237.8	240.3	241.2	242.3	237.3
2005	233.9	235.5	234.2	239.4	240.2	241.8	239.8	238.2	240.8	240.1	242.3	243.3	239.1
2006	234.9	238.2	238.0	241.5	243.1	244.3	241.4	240.1	242.7	243.8	245.1	246.4	241.6
2007	237.3	239.7	238.5	242.6	244.3	245.6	243.2	242.3	244.4	245.7	246.7	247.7	243.2
2008	240.7	242.6	241.4	243.6	244.8	245.1	241.0	241.8	241.9	243.2	242.7	242.4	242.4
2009	232.9	233.8	230.5	231.7	233.3	233.9	230.2	229.4	231.5	232.7	233.5	234.7	232.3
2010	224.7	226.3	225.4	229.5	231.1	231.7	231.6	230.5	231.9	233.7	233.7	233.9	230.3
2011	228.0	229.4	228.4	233.7	234.8	235.4	236.0	234.1	236.0	238.5	238.6	235.5	234.0
Goods-Producing													
2000	50.3	50.3	50.8	50.6	51.0	51.8	51.3	51.3	51.4	51.1	50.9	50.7	51.0
2001	49.3	48.8	49.3	49.6	49.8	50.4	50.6	50.1	50.2	49.8	49.4	48.9	49.7
2002	47.5	46.9	47.2	47.4	47.7	48.1	47.7	47.5	47.3	46.8	46.5	46.1	47.2
2003	44.4	44.0	44.0	44.6	45.1	45.7	45.3	45.4	45.1	45.1	45.1	45.0	44.9
2004	43.9	43.5	44.3	45.1	45.7	46.3	46.4	46.4	46.1	45.7	45.6	45.3	45.4
2005	43.9	43.4	43.7	44.2	44.5	45.3	45.3	45.1	44.5	44.2	44.1	43.8	44.3
2006	43.3	43.1	43.3	44.0	44.4	45.0	44.9	44.7	44.1	44.0	43.9	43.7	44.0
2007	42.9	42.5	42.7	43.4	43.6	44.2	43.9	44.1	43.8	43.6	43.7	43.3	43.5
2008	42.6	42.1	42.1	42.3	42.7	42.9	42.8	42.6	42.2	41.8	41.6	40.8	42.2
2009	38.1	37.2	36.9	37.5	37.9	38.2	37.4	37.3	36.8	36.3	36.1	35.9	37.1
2010	34.2	33.8	34.1	34.7	35.4	35.8	35.9	35.9	35.7	35.2	35.1	34.8	35.1
2011	33.9	33.9	34.1	34.7	35.2	35.7	36.7	36.4	35.8	36.4	35.3	34.7	35.2
Mining, Logging, and Construction													
2000	10.1	10.0	10.4	10.7	11.2	11.7	11.7	11.7	11.6	11.4	11.2	10.9	11.1
2001	9.8	9.7	10.1	11.3	11.7	12.0	12.0	12.0	11.8	11.5	11.5	11.1	11.2
2002	10.0	10.0	10.4	11.1	11.5	11.7	11.7	11.7	11.5	11.3	11.2	10.6	11.1
2003	9.6	9.4	9.6	10.2	10.8	11.1	11.3	11.4	11.1	11.1	11.0	10.8	10.6
2004	9.9	9.7	10.3	11.3	11.8	12.1	12.3	12.3	12.0	11.7	11.5	11.1	11.3
2005	10.0	9.7	9.9	10.6	11.0	11.4	11.7	11.8	11.4	11.3	11.2	10.9	10.9
2006	10.1	10.1	10.3	11.1	11.5	11.9	12.1	12.1	12.0	11.7	11.6	11.4	11.3
2007	10.7	10.4	10.7	11.3	12.1	12.1	12.3	12.4	12.2	12.1	12.2	11.8	11.7
2008	11.0	10.8	10.9	11.1	11.5	11.6	11.7	11.7	11.4	11.1	11.0	10.5	11.2
2009	9.3	8.9	8.9	9.4	9.8	10.0	9.9	10.0	9.8	9.4	9.3	9.0	9.5
2010	7.7	7.5	7.7	8.4	8.9	9.0	9.2	9.2	9.1	9.0	9.0	8.6	8.6
2011	8.0	8.0	8.1	8.7	9.1	9.4	9.9	9.9	9.6	9.8	8.8	8.5	9.0
Manufacturing													
2000	40.2	40.3	40.4	39.9	39.8	40.1	39.6	39.6	39.8	39.7	39.7	39.8	39.9
2001	39.5	39.1	39.2	38.3	38.1	38.4	38.6	38.1	38.4	38.3	37.9	37.8	38.5
2002	37.5	36.9	36.8	36.3	36.2	36.4	36.0	35.8	35.8	35.5	35.3	35.5	36.2
2003	34.8	34.6	34.4	34.4	34.3	34.6	34.0	34.0	34.0	34.0	34.1	34.2	34.3
2004	34.0	33.8	34.0	33.8	33.9	34.2	34.1	34.1	34.1	34.0	34.1	34.2	34.0
2005	33.9	33.7	33.8	33.6	33.5	33.9	33.6	33.3	33.1	32.9	32.9	32.9	33.4
2006	33.2	33.0	33.0	32.9	32.9	33.1	32.8	32.6	32.1	32.3	32.3	32.3	32.7
2007	32.2	32.1	32.0	32.1	31.9	32.1	31.6	31.7	31.6	31.5	31.5	31.5	31.8
2008	31.6	31.3	31.2	31.2	31.2	31.3	31.1	30.9	30.8	30.7	30.6	30.3	31.0
2009	28.8	28.3	28.0	28.1	28.1	28.2	27.5	27.3	27.0	26.9	26.8	26.9	27.7
2010	26.5	26.3	26.4	26.3	26.5	26.8	26.7	26.7	26.6	26.2	26.1	26.2	26.4
2011	25.9	25.9	26.0	26.0	26.1	26.3	26.8	26.5	26.2	26.6	26.5	26.2	26.3
Service-Providing													
2000	218.7	222.4	224.2	224.5	225.6	227.1	218.5	217.7	224.1	224.4	226.6	228.5	223.5
2001	218.8	221.5	222.1	224.2	225.9	228.6	218.6	219.3	224.9	225.3	227.4	229.2	223.8
2002	221.5	224.0	225.4	227.8	229.9	233.2	223.3	223.0	228.7	228.2	230.5	232.0	227.3
2003	223.1	225.0	225.0	226.0	226.5	226.0	220.5	219.7	222.6	226.3	229.5	230.5	225.1
2004	222.7	224.5	224.9	226.4	227.7	227.5	223.4	221.2	225.2	229.8	231.4	232.7	226.5
2005	224.3	227.3	225.6	230.9	231.1	232.3	224.9	222.9	230.0	230.6	233.6	235.0	229.0
2006	226.9	230.6	230.1	232.9	234.4	235.3	227.3	225.8	232.5	234.7	236.6	238.2	232.1
2007	229.4	232.5	231.1	234.4	236.1	237.6	229.9	228.5	234.6	237.3	238.8	240.1	234.2
2008	233.4	236.3	234.8	236.3	237.9	237.5	228.8	227.4	233.9	235.4	237.5	237.6	234.7
2009	230.0	231.9	228.8	229.1	231.1	230.4	222.6	221.2	228.6	230.3	232.1	233.1	229.1
2010	224.9	227.3	225.5	229.1	232.1	231.3	226.3	224.1	229.9	232.2	232.8	233.1	229.1
2011	228.1	229.8	227.7	233.4	233.9	234.0	228.5	226.2	232.7	235.5	237.5	234.9	231.9

Employment by Industry: New Haven, CT, NECTA, Selected Years, 2000–2011—*Continued*

(Numbers in thousands, not seasonally adjusted)

Industry and year	January	February	March	April	May	June	July	August	September	October	November	December	Annual average
Trade, Transportation, and Utilities													
2000	49.1	48.6	49.1	48.8	49.0	49.3	48.8	48.8	49.4	49.8	50.8	51.7	49.4
2001	48.8	47.9	47.9	48.2	48.8	49.3	48.8	48.8	49.1	49.7	50.5	51.3	49.1
2002	49.5	48.7	49.0	50.2	50.7	51.4	50.1	49.7	50.5	50.5	51.4	52.3	50.3
2003	49.7	48.8	49.2	48.8	49.4	49.8	48.4	48.4	49.0	50.1	51.0	51.7	49.5
2004	49.8	48.9	49.3	49.2	49.7	50.3	49.7	49.6	50.4	51.2	52.1	52.9	50.3
2005	51.0	50.3	50.2	50.8	51.3	51.6	50.6	50.4	51.1	51.3	52.4	53.1	51.2
2006	51.4	50.4	50.8	51.1	51.7	52.1	50.8	50.5	51.0	51.4	52.5	53.3	51.4
2007	51.6	51.0	51.0	50.9	51.7	52.3	51.1	50.8	51.1	51.5	52.3	52.8	51.5
2008	51.7	50.6	50.6	50.5	50.8	51.2	50.3	49.9	50.2	50.1	50.8	51.2	50.7
2009	49.1	48.3	47.9	47.4	48.3	48.7	47.7	47.6	47.9	48.5	49.4	49.9	48.4
2010	47.7	46.8	46.9	46.7	47.7	48.3	47.7	47.9	47.7	48.2	49.1	49.9	47.9
2011	47.6	47.1	47.1	48.1	48.6	48.8	47.7	47.4	48.6	49.2	49.9	50.5	48.4
Wholesale Trade													
2000	11.2	11.3	11.4	11.3	11.4	11.5	11.4	11.4	11.5	11.4	11.5	11.6	11.4
2001	11.3	11.4	11.3	11.4	11.4	11.4	11.5	11.4	11.3	11.3	11.2	11.2	11.3
2002	11.1	11.0	11.0	11.3	11.4	11.4	11.1	11.1	11.1	11.0	11.0	11.0	11.1
2003	10.8	10.7	10.8	10.8	11.0	11.1	11.1	11.2	11.2	11.5	11.6	11.7	11.1
2004	11.4	11.3	11.4	11.5	11.5	11.6	11.3	11.3	11.4	11.4	11.4	11.5	11.4
2005	11.4	11.3	11.3	11.4	11.4	11.4	11.4	11.4	11.4	11.5	11.6	11.6	11.4
2006	11.5	11.5	11.5	11.6	11.7	11.8	11.7	11.7	11.6	11.5	11.5	11.5	11.6
2007	11.6	11.6	11.5	11.4	11.5	11.6	11.6	11.6	11.6	11.5	11.5	11.6	11.6
2008	11.9	11.8	11.8	11.9	11.9	12.0	12.0	12.0	12.1	12.0	12.1	12.1	12.0
2009	11.9	11.8	11.7	11.5	11.5	11.6	11.5	11.5	11.5	11.4	11.4	11.4	11.6
2010	11.2	11.2	11.2	11.2	11.3	11.4	11.4	11.4	11.3	11.3	11.3	11.4	11.3
2011	11.2	11.2	11.2	11.3	11.4	11.5	11.4	11.4	11.5	11.4	11.4	11.5	11.4
Retail Trade													
2000	30.2	29.6	30.1	29.8	29.9	30.1	30.0	30.1	30.0	30.4	31.3	32.1	30.3
2001	29.9	29.0	29.2	29.2	29.7	30.1	29.9	30.2	30.2	30.7	31.6	32.4	30.2
2002	31.0	30.2	30.6	30.9	31.2	32.0	31.5	31.3	31.4	31.4	32.3	33.2	31.4
2003	31.2	30.4	30.6	30.3	30.6	30.8	30.0	30.0	29.9	30.4	31.2	31.8	30.6
2004	30.4	29.6	29.9	29.7	30.0	30.4	30.6	30.6	30.4	30.8	31.6	32.2	30.5
2005	30.4	29.7	29.5	29.9	30.2	30.5	30.2	30.1	30.1	30.4	31.3	32.0	30.4
2006	30.7	29.8	30.1	30.3	30.8	31.2	30.8	30.7	30.5	31.1	32.2	32.8	30.9
2007	31.2	30.6	30.7	30.7	31.2	31.6	31.0	30.9	30.5	30.8	31.7	32.0	31.1
2008	30.9	29.9	29.9	29.6	29.9	30.1	29.6	29.5	29.1	29.1	29.8	30.2	29.8
2009	28.7	28.0	27.7	27.6	28.2	28.5	28.1	28.1	27.9	28.6	29.5	29.9	28.4
2010	28.2	27.4	27.5	27.3	27.9	28.3	28.2	28.3	27.8	28.3	29.2	29.7	28.2
2011	28.2	27.6	27.6	28.2	28.5	28.6	28.1	27.9	28.4	29.1	29.8	30.2	28.5
Transportation and Utilities													
2000	7.7	7.7	7.6	7.7	7.7	7.7	7.4	7.3	7.9	8.0	8.0	8.0	7.7
2001	7.6	7.5	7.4	7.6	7.7	7.8	7.4	7.2	7.6	7.7	7.7	7.7	7.6
2002	7.4	7.5	7.4	8.0	8.1	8.0	7.5	7.3	8.0	8.1	8.1	8.1	7.8
2003	7.7	7.7	7.8	7.7	7.8	7.9	7.3	7.2	7.9	8.2	8.2	8.2	7.8
2004	8.0	8.0	8.0	8.0	8.2	8.3	7.8	7.7	8.6	9.0	9.1	9.2	8.3
2005	9.2	9.3	9.4	9.5	9.7	9.7	9.0	8.9	9.6	9.4	9.5	9.5	9.4
2006	9.2	9.1	9.2	9.2	9.2	9.1	8.3	8.1	8.9	8.8	8.8	9.0	8.9
2007	8.8	8.8	8.8	8.8	9.0	9.1	8.5	8.3	9.0	9.2	9.1	9.2	8.9
2008	8.9	8.9	8.9	9.0	9.0	9.1	8.7	8.4	9.0	9.0	8.9	8.9	8.9
2009	8.5	8.5	8.5	8.3	8.6	8.6	8.1	8.0	8.5	8.5	8.5	8.6	8.4
2010	8.3	8.2	8.2	8.2	8.5	8.6	8.1	8.2	8.6	8.6	8.6	8.8	8.4
2011	8.2	8.3	8.3	8.6	8.7	8.7	8.2	8.1	8.7	8.7	8.7	8.8	8.5
Information													
2000	9.7	9.7	9.8	9.6	9.6	9.8	10.1	10.2	10.2	10.5	10.5	10.4	10.0
2001	10.6	10.6	10.5	10.2	10.2	10.2	10.1	10.2	10.1	10.1	10.1	10.3	10.3
2002	10.0	10.0	10.0	9.8	9.8	9.8	9.7	9.6	9.6	9.5	9.4	9.5	9.7
2003	9.2	9.2	9.2	9.1	9.1	9.1	9.1	9.1	9.0	8.9	9.0	9.0	9.1
2004	8.7	8.6	8.6	8.6	8.6	8.7	8.7	8.7	8.6	8.7	8.7	8.7	8.7
2005	8.6	8.8	8.5	8.4	8.4	8.5	8.4	8.3	8.3	8.2	8.3	8.2	8.4
2006	8.3	8.3	8.2	8.2	8.2	8.2	8.1	8.1	8.0	8.1	8.1	8.2	8.2
2007	8.1	8.2	8.1	8.2	8.2	8.1	8.1	8.1	8.1	8.1	8.1	8.2	8.1
2008	8.1	8.3	8.0	7.9	7.8	7.8	7.7	7.8	7.6	7.6	7.6	7.5	7.8
2009	7.3	7.3	7.0	6.8	6.7	6.6	6.5	6.4	6.2	6.2	6.1	5.9	6.6
2010	5.7	5.6	5.4	5.3	5.3	5.2	5.1	5.0	4.9	4.9	4.9	4.9	5.2
2011	4.8	4.8	4.8	4.7	4.7	4.7	4.7	4.7	4.6	4.7	4.7	4.7	4.7
Financial Activities													
2000	13.8	13.7	13.7	13.7	13.7	13.9	14.0	13.9	13.7	13.7	13.7	13.9	13.8
2001	13.9	14.0	14.0	13.8	13.9	14.1	14.2	14.2	14.1	14.1	14.1	14.2	14.1
2002	14.0	13.8	13.9	14.1	14.2	14.3	14.6	14.6	14.3	14.2	14.2	14.3	14.2
2003	14.1	14.1	14.1	14.1	14.2	14.4	14.4	14.5	14.4	14.2	14.2	14.3	14.3
2004	14.1	14.1	14.2	14.2	14.2	14.4	14.2	14.1	14.0	14.0	14.0	14.0	14.1
2005	13.8	13.8	13.8	13.9	14.1	14.3	14.3	14.3	14.1	14.0	14.1	14.1	14.1
2006	14.0	14.0	13.9	14.0	14.0	14.1	14.1	14.1	13.9	13.9	14.0	14.0	14.0
2007	13.8	13.8	13.7	13.7	13.8	13.9	13.8	13.7	13.4	13.4	13.3	13.4	13.6
2008	13.3	13.3	13.3	13.0	13.1	13.2	13.1	13.1	12.9	12.7	12.7	12.7	13.0
2009	12.5	12.5	12.5	12.4	12.5	12.6	12.4	12.3	12.1	12.2	12.2	12.3	12.4
2010	12.1	12.1	12.1	12.1	12.2	12.3	12.5	12.5	12.2	12.2	12.2	12.3	12.2
2011	12.3	12.3	12.3	12.2	12.2	12.3	12.3	12.3	12.2	12.2	12.2	12.1	12.2

Employment by Industry: New Haven, CT, NECTA, Selected Years, 2000–2011—*Continued*

(Numbers in thousands, not seasonally adjusted)

Industry and year	January	February	March	April	May	June	July	August	September	October	November	December	Annual average
Professional and Business Services													
2000	28.5	29.2	29.6	29.1	29.9	30.6	29.7	29.9	29.7	28.9	29.3	29.8	29.5
2001	27.6	27.9	28.5	28.3	29.4	29.5	28.6	28.9	29.5	27.9	27.8	28.3	28.5
2002	27.4	27.4	28.0	27.6	27.9	28.9	28.1	28.8	29.0	27.7	27.9	27.9	28.1
2003	26.5	26.7	26.6	26.4	26.6	26.8	26.4	26.6	26.5	26.5	26.8	26.9	26.6
2004	25.2	25.6	25.5	25.7	25.9	26.3	26.0	26.0	25.8	25.1	25.2	25.6	25.7
2005	24.6	24.7	24.8	25.7	25.5	26.5	26.2	26.1	25.9	25.5	25.6	25.9	25.6
2006	25.0	25.6	25.8	26.1	26.4	27.2	25.9	26.1	26.2	26.0	26.2	26.4	26.1
2007	25.4	25.6	25.8	26.0	26.3	26.8	26.4	26.7	26.7	26.6	26.6	27.1	26.3
2008	26.4	26.8	26.6	27.1	27.1	27.5	26.0	26.1	26.1	25.3	25.1	25.3	26.3
2009	24.4	23.9	23.7	23.8	23.8	23.9	23.4	23.9	23.8	24.1	24.4	25.1	24.0
2010	23.9	24.5	24.4	25.0	24.9	25.5	25.6	25.6	25.3	25.4	25.3	25.4	25.1
2011	24.9	25.2	24.9	25.8	25.6	26.1	26.0	25.9	25.5	25.3	25.7	25.0	25.5
Education and Health Services													
2000	56.3	58.4	58.8	59.3	59.3	58.2	54.8	54.3	57.3	57.5	57.8	58.0	57.5
2001	55.9	58.3	58.2	59.9	58.4	59.8	56.0	55.9	59.5	59.8	60.1	60.3	58.5
2002	58.1	60.7	60.3	61.6	61.6	61.5	58.9	58.4	61.8	61.8	62.4	62.6	60.8
2003	60.6	62.6	61.6	62.5	61.5	60.3	59.1	58.7	59.4	61.4	62.4	62.8	61.1
2004	61.5	63.2	62.1	62.8	62.0	60.9	60.2	59.2	61.2	64.7	65.1	64.8	62.3
2005	62.8	65.0	63.5	65.4	64.4	62.3	61.7	60.8	64.8	65.5	66.6	66.8	64.1
2006	62.7	66.7	65.1	66.9	65.9	64.0	63.9	63.1	67.1	68.4	68.9	68.8	66.0
2007	64.9	68.3	66.5	68.7	67.8	66.2	65.8	64.9	68.5	69.9	70.4	70.5	67.7
2008	68.0	70.8	69.4	70.9	70.1	68.4	67.7	67.0	70.1	72.2	73.4	73.0	70.1
2009	71.0	74.0	71.2	72.1	71.3	70.0	69.1	68.6	71.9	73.6	73.8	73.9	71.7
2010	72.0	73.8	72.4	74.6	73.5	71.7	71.6	70.7	73.9	76.0	75.6	74.9	73.4
2011	74.7	75.9	74.5	76.0	75.3	73.6	73.7	72.5	75.1	76.8	76.7	75.0	75.0
Leisure and Hospitality													
2000	16.8	17.1	17.4	18.0	18.7	20.2	20.4	20.2	18.9	18.5	18.5	18.6	18.6
2001	17.1	17.3	17.5	18.1	19.3	20.1	19.9	19.9	18.4	18.1	17.9	18.0	18.5
2002	16.6	16.9	17.6	18.5	19.4	20.5	20.7	20.5	19.1	18.6	18.2	18.2	18.7
2003	17.1	17.5	17.8	18.9	19.5	20.9	21.5	21.3	20.2	19.7	19.3	19.3	19.4
2004	18.4	18.4	19.0	19.8	20.8	22.0	22.1	22.0	21.0	20.3	19.8	20.1	20.3
2005	18.5	18.8	18.9	20.2	21.1	22.1	22.2	22.2	21.3	20.6	20.3	20.3	20.5
2006	19.5	19.5	20.2	20.4	21.5	22.6	22.6	22.4	21.5	20.9	20.4	20.8	21.0
2007	19.7	19.6	20.0	20.8	22.0	22.9	23.0	22.9	21.9	21.6	21.4	21.3	21.4
2008	19.9	20.0	20.5	21.1	22.3	23.0	22.7	22.7	22.0	21.5	21.3	21.3	21.5
2009	19.9	20.0	20.6	21.0	22.2	23.0	23.0	22.7	22.2	21.4	21.1	21.2	21.5
2010	19.0	19.6	19.8	20.8	21.8	22.4	22.7	22.5	21.8	21.5	21.3	21.5	21.2
2011	19.8	20.2	20.7	21.9	22.9	23.6	24.3	24.4	23.7	23.5	23.7	23.0	22.6
Other Services													
2000	9.8	9.9	9.9	10.0	10.0	10.1	10.1	10.0	10.1	10.1	10.2	10.2	10.0
2001	9.8	9.8	9.9	9.9	10.2	10.3	10.2	10.2	10.0	10.0	10.2	10.2	10.1
2002	10.2	10.2	10.4	10.3	10.5	10.6	10.5	10.4	10.3	10.2	10.2	10.4	10.4
2003	10.1	10.0	10.2	10.0	10.1	10.5	10.4	10.3	10.1	10.2	10.4	10.5	10.2
2004	10.2	10.1	10.3	10.4	10.8	10.9	11.0	11.1	10.7	10.6	10.7	10.9	10.6
2005	10.7	10.7	10.8	10.8	10.9	11.2	11.1	11.0	10.8	10.8	10.9	11.1	10.9
2006	10.7	10.6	10.7	10.8	11.0	11.1	11.1	11.1	10.9	11.1	11.1	11.2	11.0
2007	10.9	10.7	10.7	10.9	10.9	11.2	11.1	11.1	10.9	11.0	10.9	11.1	11.0
2008	10.7	10.7	10.9	10.8	10.9	11.1	10.9	10.9	10.7	10.7	10.7	10.9	10.8
2009	10.6	10.6	10.7	10.7	10.6	10.9	10.7	10.6	10.6	10.4	10.4	10.5	10.6
2010	10.1	10.1	10.3	10.3	10.3	10.5	10.5	10.4	10.4	10.3	10.2	10.3	10.3
2011	10.0	10.0	10.0	10.3	10.3	10.6	10.6	10.5	10.5	10.4	10.4	10.5	10.3
Government													
2000	34.7	35.8	35.9	36.0	35.4	35.0	30.6	30.4	34.8	35.4	35.8	35.9	34.6
2001	35.1	35.7	35.6	35.8	35.7	35.3	30.8	31.2	34.2	35.6	36.7	36.6	34.9
2002	35.7	36.3	36.2	35.7	35.8	36.2	30.7	31.0	34.1	35.7	36.8	36.8	35.1
2003	35.8	36.1	36.3	36.2	36.1	34.2	31.2	30.8	34.0	35.3	36.4	36.0	34.9
2004	34.8	35.6	35.9	35.7	35.7	34.0	31.5	30.5	33.5	35.2	35.8	35.7	34.5
2005	34.3	35.2	35.1	35.7	35.4	35.8	30.4	29.8	33.7	34.7	35.4	35.5	34.3
2006	35.3	35.5	35.4	35.4	35.7	36.0	30.8	30.4	33.9	34.9	35.4	35.5	34.5
2007	35.0	35.3	35.3	35.2	35.4	36.2	30.6	30.3	34.0	35.2	35.8	35.7	34.5
2008	35.3	35.8	35.5	35.0	35.8	35.3	30.4	29.9	34.3	35.3	35.9	35.7	34.5
2009	35.2	35.3	35.2	34.9	35.7	34.7	29.8	29.1	33.9	33.9	34.7	34.3	33.9
2010	34.4	34.8	34.2	34.3	36.4	35.4	30.6	29.5	33.7	33.7	34.2	34.0	33.8
2011	34.0	34.3	33.4	34.4	34.3	34.3	29.2	28.5	32.5	33.4	34.2	34.1	33.1

Employment by Industry: New Orleans–Metairie–Kenner, LA, Selected Years, 2000–2011

(Numbers in thousands, not seasonally adjusted)

Industry and year	January	February	March	April	May	June	July	August	September	October	November	December	Annual average
Total Nonfarm													
2000	614.0	616.7	619.5	619.6	622.9	619.7	610.8	611.8	616.8	616.8	618.8	624.4	617.7
2001	615.9	620.9	624.8	622.7	623.9	623.1	611.6	612.4	617.8	614.4	617.2	618.2	618.6
2002	603.2	605.3	608.9	612.9	611.1	614.2	601.4	602.9	607.5	606.4	612.2	612.7	608.2
2003	604.2	607.4	608.8	615.5	614.2	615.5	607.0	604.2	610.1	611.1	616.5	617.6	611.0
2004	608.1	610.2	614.5	620.6	619.7	618.4	610.0	612.0	610.1	613.9	618.1	616.0	614.3
2005	606.5	607.2	613.1	613.0	612.4	616.3	604.5	603.7	473.2	425.8	438.9	450.9	555.5
2006	446.4	456.3	469.0	472.0	477.6	484.7	480.8	485.0	489.3	496.0	503.0	507.5	480.6
2007	503.8	508.5	515.2	508.3	509.6	512.4	506.5	511.0	511.9	522.2	527.2	530.9	514.0
2008	520.9	524.8	528.4	527.4	526.8	526.2	519.0	526.3	519.3	527.6	530.2	532.3	525.8
2009	519.2	521.8	521.7	523.5	524.8	519.8	515.4	519.2	517.2	519.4	521.5	521.5	520.4
2010	512.5	514.4	518.6	521.5	521.1	520.8	513.5	515.0	518.0	521.4	525.0	527.3	519.1
2011	519.2	522.6	525.5	528.4	528.6	524.0	524.2	521.6	527.1	529.7	531.8	529.3	526.0
Total Private													
2000	510.6	512.9	515.2	515.4	518.9	516.0	511.6	512.1	513.9	514.1	516.2	520.7	514.8
2001	512.5	516.9	520.8	518.1	519.6	519.0	512.5	511.7	514.8	511.6	514.7	515.0	515.6
2002	500.3	501.4	504.8	509.0	507.6	509.3	502.1	502.2	504.9	503.2	508.0	508.2	505.1
2003	500.4	502.6	503.6	510.7	509.8	510.3	503.8	504.0	505.6	508.0	512.5	513.7	507.1
2004	504.9	506.2	510.0	513.7	512.8	512.5	506.3	509.3	504.3	509.6	513.1	510.8	509.5
2005	501.3	500.9	506.2	507.9	507.8	511.4	503.1	501.5	371.3	345.5	358.9	371.3	457.3
2006	373.7	383.5	395.5	398.6	403.8	411.3	408.8	412.4	413.4	419.9	425.8	429.5	406.4
2007	427.5	431.1	437.1	435.6	436.5	439.0	435.1	438.6	436.2	444.1	448.4	451.9	438.4
2008	443.0	446.1	449.9	446.7	446.0	446.8	440.5	445.6	437.6	445.0	447.1	449.4	445.3
2009	437.4	439.3	439.8	439.9	441.6	439.1	434.0	435.9	434.1	435.2	437.4	438.1	437.7
2010	430.2	431.6	435.2	438.2	436.3	438.1	433.2	434.1	436.5	439.4	442.7	445.5	436.8
2011	438.4	441.7	444.9	447.3	447.6	444.0	443.4	439.3	445.1	446.6	448.9	446.6	444.5
Goods-Producing													
2000	88.6	88.4	88.8	87.7	88.8	89.1	88.6	89.2	87.8	86.9	85.9	85.7	88.0
2001	85.3	86.3	88.1	85.9	86.5	86.8	86.1	85.5	85.0	83.8	82.7	81.9	85.3
2002	80.4	79.9	80.6	80.6	81.1	81.3	80.2	80.7	80.4	80.2	80.1	79.9	80.5
2003	79.4	79.4	79.4	80.5	81.2	81.5	80.3	79.9	79.3	79.4	78.5	78.7	79.8
2004	77.9	77.5	78.2	78.8	78.2	78.4	77.7	77.5	76.9	77.2	76.9	76.9	77.7
2005	75.1	75.8	76.6	76.5	76.9	77.6	77.1	77.2	60.5	65.7	68.8	71.2	73.3
2006	71.5	72.5	73.9	74.5	74.8	76.5	74.8	75.9	75.9	76.6	76.7	76.9	75.0
2007	75.1	75.5	75.8	75.8	76.1	76.8	76.7	77.0	77.1	77.2	77.1	77.4	76.5
2008	77.2	76.7	76.6	77.0	77.4	77.8	78.1	78.4	77.8	78.6	77.8	78.1	77.6
2009	76.3	75.9	75.3	75.3	75.2	75.1	74.0	73.3	72.6	72.9	72.5	71.7	74.2
2010	69.8	69.8	70.1	70.3	70.7	71.4	71.0	70.9	70.6	71.5	70.7	70.7	70.6
2011	69.7	69.9	70.1	70.4	70.3	69.5	69.7	68.5	68.8	67.9	67.3	66.3	69.0
Mining and Logging													
2005	8.3	8.4	8.6	8.3	8.4	8.6	8.4	8.5	8.1	8.3	8.3	8.4	8.4
2006	7.9	8.0	8.1	8.0	8.0	8.1	8.4	8.5	8.7	8.7	8.5	8.3	8.3
2007	7.8	8.0	8.1	8.3	8.3	8.3	8.4	8.3	8.3	8.6	8.6	8.6	8.3
2008	8.9	8.4	8.4	8.5	8.4	8.4	8.6	8.7	8.8	8.9	8.8	8.7	8.6
2009	8.6	8.5	8.4	8.3	8.2	8.3	7.8	7.8	7.7	7.8	7.7	7.8	8.1
2010	7.5	7.6	7.6	7.6	7.7	7.8	7.7	7.6	7.5	7.6	7.5	7.4	7.6
2011	7.3	7.5	7.5	7.1	7.1	6.8	6.8	6.8	6.8	6.8	6.8	6.8	7.0
Construction													
2005	29.2	29.0	29.6	29.8	30.0	30.0	29.8	29.7	21.8	25.8	28.4	29.4	28.5
2006	30.6	31.1	32.2	32.7	32.9	33.7	31.4	32.0	31.8	32.5	32.3	32.3	32.1
2007	31.6	31.6	31.9	31.7	31.9	32.1	32.0	32.4	32.2	32.2	31.9	31.8	31.9
2008	31.8	31.9	31.8	32.4	32.5	32.6	32.9	33.2	33.1	33.5	32.9	33.0	32.6
2009	31.9	31.9	31.7	31.8	32.0	32.0	31.7	31.4	31.0	31.6	31.5	30.7	31.6
2010	29.8	29.9	30.2	29.9	30.1	30.7	30.9	31.0	31.0	32.0	31.7	31.7	30.7
2011	31.0	30.9	31.3	32.3	32.0	31.6	31.7	30.9	30.9	29.7	29.1	28.0	30.8
Manufacturing													
2000	46.2	45.8	45.7	44.7	45.3	45.3	45.4	45.4	44.7	44.2	44.1	44.0	45.1
2001	44.2	44.1	44.2	43.7	44.0	44.3	43.4	43.1	43.2	42.3	42.2	42.1	43.4
2002	41.3	41.2	41.2	41.4	41.5	41.7	41.1	41.3	40.6	40.3	40.4	40.4	41.0
2003	39.5	39.4	39.3	39.1	39.3	39.4	39.3	39.3	39.1	39.3	39.0	39.4	39.3
2004	38.5	38.5	38.4	38.9	38.9	39.2	38.9	39.1	38.8	38.4	38.1	38.4	38.7
2005	37.6	38.4	38.4	38.4	38.5	39.0	38.9	39.0	30.6	31.6	32.1	33.4	36.3
2006	33.0	33.4	33.6	33.8	33.9	34.7	35.0	35.4	35.4	35.4	35.9	36.3	34.7
2007	35.7	35.9	35.8	35.8	35.9	36.4	36.3	36.3	36.6	36.4	36.6	37.0	36.2
2008	36.5	36.4	36.4	36.1	36.5	36.8	36.6	36.5	35.9	36.2	36.1	36.4	36.4
2009	35.8	35.5	35.2	35.2	35.0	34.8	34.5	34.1	33.9	33.5	33.3	33.2	34.5
2010	32.5	32.3	32.3	32.8	32.9	32.9	32.4	32.3	32.1	31.9	31.5	31.6	32.3
2011	31.4	31.5	31.3	31.0	31.2	31.1	31.2	30.8	31.1	31.4	31.4	31.5	31.2

Employment by Industry: New Orleans–Metairie–Kenner, LA, Selected Years, 2000–2011—*Continued*

(Numbers in thousands, not seasonally adjusted)

Industry and year	January	February	March	April	May	June	July	August	September	October	November	December	Annual average
Service-Providing													
2000	525.4	528.3	530.7	531.9	534.1	530.6	522.2	522.6	529.0	529.9	532.9	538.7	529.7
2001	530.6	534.6	536.7	536.8	537.4	536.3	525.5	526.9	532.8	530.6	534.5	536.3	533.3
2002	522.8	525.4	528.3	532.3	530.0	532.9	521.2	522.2	527.1	526.2	532.1	532.8	527.8
2003	524.8	528.0	529.4	535.0	533.0	534.0	526.7	524.3	530.8	531.7	538.0	538.9	531.2
2004	530.2	532.7	536.3	541.8	541.5	540.0	532.3	534.5	533.2	536.7	541.2	539.1	536.6
2005	531.4	531.4	536.5	536.5	535.5	538.7	527.4	526.5	412.7	360.1	370.1	379.7	482.2
2006	374.9	383.8	395.1	397.5	402.8	408.2	406.0	409.1	413.4	419.4	426.3	430.6	405.6
2007	428.7	433.0	439.4	432.5	433.5	435.6	429.8	434.0	434.8	445.0	450.1	453.5	437.5
2008	443.7	448.1	451.8	450.4	449.4	448.4	440.9	447.9	441.5	449.0	452.4	454.2	448.1
2009	442.9	445.9	446.4	448.2	449.6	444.7	441.4	445.9	444.6	446.5	449.0	449.8	446.2
2010	442.7	444.6	448.5	451.2	450.4	449.4	442.5	444.1	447.4	449.9	454.3	456.6	448.5
2011	449.5	452.7	455.4	458.0	458.3	454.5	454.5	453.1	458.3	461.8	464.5	463.0	457.0
Trade, Transportation, and Utilities													
2000	127.4	127.7	128.2	127.3	128.3	129.3	127.0	127.0	126.5	126.6	128.5	131.5	127.9
2001	127.1	127.2	127.8	127.3	127.3	127.8	126.2	126.8	126.5	125.7	127.3	128.8	127.2
2002	123.1	122.3	123.9	123.9	123.9	125.7	123.5	123.5	123.1	122.6	124.1	126.5	123.8
2003	121.0	120.9	121.3	121.0	120.9	121.4	121.4	121.8	121.1	121.9	124.2	125.6	121.9
2004	121.4	121.3	122.3	123.0	123.3	123.2	122.1	122.4	121.1	122.8	124.2	126.4	122.8
2005	121.5	120.7	121.7	121.3	121.6	122.0	121.1	120.6	88.6	84.1	89.9	94.3	110.6
2006	94.7	96.7	99.3	101.0	102.2	104.0	103.9	104.4	104.2	106.0	107.8	110.1	102.9
2007	107.6	107.2	108.4	107.5	107.7	108.0	107.7	107.8	107.1	109.8	112.3	114.0	108.8
2008	110.0	109.1	109.6	108.6	108.8	108.7	108.2	108.6	106.3	108.3	110.2	111.3	109.0
2009	106.4	105.6	105.5	104.8	104.8	105.1	104.1	104.0	103.6	103.2	104.5	105.2	104.7
2010	102.0	101.4	102.2	102.8	102.8	102.9	103.1	103.1	103.0	104.7	106.5	107.9	103.5
2011	106.1	105.6	105.8	106.0	106.3	106.0	105.8	105.3	104.9	105.7	106.8	107.9	106.0
Wholesale Trade													
2000	28.0	28.2	28.5	28.6	28.8	29.0	28.8	28.7	28.6	28.3	28.2	28.5	28.5
2001	28.4	28.5	28.6	28.5	28.6	28.8	28.2	28.2	28.1	28.1	27.9	27.9	28.3
2002	27.1	27.1	27.3	27.4	27.5	27.6	27.1	27.2	27.0	26.9	26.8	26.8	27.2
2003	27.0	27.1	27.1	26.6	26.6	26.6	26.6	26.6	26.3	26.8	26.7	26.6	26.7
2004	26.3	26.3	26.4	26.4	26.5	26.5	26.3	26.3	26.2	25.8	25.8	25.8	26.2
2005	25.3	25.3	25.4	25.8	25.9	26.0	26.2	26.1	21.8	21.9	22.2	22.5	24.5
2006	21.8	22.2	22.4	22.6	22.8	23.0	23.0	23.1	23.1	23.1	23.2	23.4	22.8
2007	23.6	23.7	24.0	23.8	24.0	24.2	24.6	24.8	24.5	24.9	24.9	25.0	24.3
2008	24.5	24.6	24.7	24.0	24.0	24.0	23.9	23.9	23.7	23.8	23.9	23.9	24.1
2009	23.3	23.3	23.3	23.5	23.5	23.4	22.9	22.8	22.7	22.6	22.6	22.6	23.0
2010	22.0	22.0	22.1	22.1	22.2	22.3	22.2	22.2	22.1	22.3	22.3	22.4	22.2
2011	22.8	22.9	22.9	22.4	22.6	22.7	22.7	22.6	23.0	23.2	23.2	23.5	22.9
Retail Trade													
2000	70.5	70.2	70.4	69.9	70.6	71.1	69.4	69.8	69.3	69.3	71.5	73.6	70.5
2001	69.4	68.8	69.2	68.6	68.6	68.8	68.3	68.7	68.6	68.1	70.3	71.5	69.1
2002	67.5	66.8	68.1	67.4	67.3	68.6	67.0	66.8	66.5	65.7	67.5	69.4	67.4
2003	66.1	65.9	66.5	66.3	66.5	67.0	66.7	67.3	67.0	67.3	69.5	71.0	67.3
2004	67.8	67.4	67.9	68.7	68.7	68.7	67.9	67.6	66.6	68.0	69.5	71.0	68.3
2005	67.6	66.8	67.4	67.5	67.8	68.0	67.2	66.9	44.1	41.0	45.7	48.8	59.9
2006	50.3	51.6	53.2	54.3	55.1	56.2	56.7	56.8	56.8	58.7	60.1	61.3	55.9
2007	59.4	58.9	59.7	59.1	59.4	59.4	59.4	59.0	58.9	60.5	62.8	64.1	60.1
2008	61.4	60.2	60.6	60.1	60.1	60.1	59.8	60.0	58.3	59.5	61.0	62.0	60.3
2009	58.4	58.1	58.0	57.6	57.8	58.1	57.6	57.6	57.3	56.9	58.2	58.7	57.9
2010	56.5	55.9	56.6	56.4	56.3	56.3	56.2	56.0	56.1	57.3	59.2	60.1	56.9
2011	58.1	57.8	58.0	58.4	58.3	58.1	57.9	57.4	56.6	57.0	58.2	58.6	57.9
Transportation and Utilities													
2000	28.9	29.3	29.3	28.8	28.9	29.2	28.8	28.5	28.6	29.0	28.8	29.4	29.0
2001	29.3	29.9	30.0	30.2	30.1	30.2	29.7	29.9	29.8	29.5	29.1	29.4	29.8
2002	28.5	28.4	28.5	29.1	29.1	29.5	29.4	29.5	29.6	30.0	29.8	30.3	29.3
2003	27.9	27.9	27.7	28.1	27.8	27.8	28.1	27.9	27.8	27.8	28.0	28.0	27.9
2004	27.3	27.6	28.0	27.9	28.1	28.0	27.9	28.5	28.3	29.0	28.9	29.6	28.3
2005	28.6	28.6	28.9	28.0	27.9	28.0	27.7	27.6	22.7	21.2	22.0	23.0	26.2
2006	22.6	22.9	23.7	24.1	24.3	24.8	24.2	24.5	24.3	24.2	24.5	25.4	24.1
2007	24.6	24.6	24.7	24.6	24.3	24.4	23.7	24.0	23.7	24.4	24.6	24.9	24.4
2008	24.1	24.3	24.3	24.5	24.7	24.6	24.5	24.7	24.3	25.0	25.3	25.4	24.6
2009	24.7	24.2	24.2	23.7	23.5	23.6	23.6	23.6	23.6	23.7	23.7	23.9	23.8
2010	23.5	23.5	23.5	24.3	24.3	24.3	24.7	24.9	24.8	25.1	25.0	25.4	24.4
2011	25.2	24.9	24.9	25.2	25.4	25.2	25.2	25.3	25.3	25.5	25.4	25.8	25.3
Information													
2000	10.3	10.3	10.4	10.4	10.5	10.8	11.3	11.3	11.0	10.8	10.9	11.2	10.8
2001	11.0	11.1	11.2	10.7	10.8	10.8	10.6	10.5	10.3	10.3	10.4	10.2	10.7
2002	10.0	10.0	10.0	9.6	9.5	9.7	9.6	9.6	9.5	9.3	9.3	9.4	9.6
2003	9.8	9.7	9.9	10.0	10.4	10.7	9.2	9.5	9.4	9.1	9.2	9.2	9.7
2004	9.4	9.8	9.8	10.7	10.4	10.7	9.7	11.2	10.1	11.0	12.7	10.8	10.5
2005	10.8	10.6	10.5	9.5	9.6	9.8	10.1	10.5	9.0	7.3	7.4	7.7	9.4
2006	7.1	7.3	8.8	8.1	8.4	7.5	6.7	6.8	6.9	6.9	7.4	7.5	7.5
2007	7.4	8.2	10.1	9.5	9.2	9.8	8.7	8.3	7.3	7.1	7.4	7.3	8.4
2008	8.0	9.2	11.2	9.8	10.6	11.2	7.2	8.6	8.9	6.0	7.4	7.9	8.9
2009	6.0	6.4	6.6	6.3	6.7	7.1	6.4	6.4	6.4	6.0	6.4	6.1	6.4
2010	6.8	7.3	7.2	6.9	7.5	8.3	6.0	6.3	8.7	6.5	6.9	7.1	7.1
2011	6.9	6.8	8.4	7.5	8.4	7.9	7.8	7.6	7.5	7.5	7.5	7.6	7.6

Employment by Industry: New Orleans–Metairie–Kenner, LA, Selected Years, 2000–2011—*Continued*

(Numbers in thousands, not seasonally adjusted)

Industry and year	January	February	March	April	May	June	July	August	September	October	November	December	Annual average
Financial Activities													
2000	33.5	33.7	33.8	33.8	33.7	33.5	34.0	34.0	33.7	33.4	33.4	33.6	33.7
2001	33.7	33.9	33.7	33.9	34.0	34.0	34.3	34.2	34.0	34.1	34.2	34.1	34.0
2002	33.7	33.9	34.1	34.5	34.6	34.9	34.7	35.2	35.0	35.5	35.6	35.5	34.8
2003	35.1	34.7	34.6	34.4	34.4	34.5	34.6	34.9	34.6	34.6	34.5	34.5	34.6
2004	33.9	33.8	33.8	34.2	34.1	34.2	34.7	34.7	34.3	34.3	34.1	34.2	34.2
2005	33.2	33.2	33.2	32.8	32.7	32.8	32.9	33.0	27.6	26.2	26.1	25.9	30.8
2006	25.7	25.8	26.1	25.7	26.0	26.3	26.4	26.4	26.4	26.6	26.7	26.8	26.2
2007	27.4	27.5	27.3	27.1	27.2	27.4	27.6	27.5	27.3	27.6	27.5	27.5	27.4
2008	27.0	27.2	27.2	26.9	26.9	26.9	26.6	26.4	26.0	26.2	26.1	26.1	26.6
2009	25.7	25.8	25.8	26.2	26.2	26.3	26.2	26.1	26.0	25.9	26.0	26.1	26.0
2010	25.7	25.7	25.8	25.9	26.1	26.1	26.1	26.0	25.8	26.1	26.2	26.2	26.0
2011	26.4	26.4	26.4	26.2	26.3	26.2	25.3	25.2	24.7	25.2	25.3	25.0	25.7
Professional and Business Services													
2000	72.8	72.7	73.3	74.9	74.8	74.2	73.9	74.5	75.0	74.3	75.3	75.6	74.3
2001	74.8	75.5	75.8	74.2	75.2	75.0	73.8	73.8	74.1	73.9	74.1	74.8	74.6
2002	72.8	72.8	73.1	73.4	72.1	72.2	71.5	71.9	71.3	70.4	70.4	70.8	71.9
2003	70.7	71.6	72.3	73.9	72.0	72.5	71.8	71.9	71.6	73.7	74.5	75.1	72.6
2004	72.8	73.4	73.8	75.0	74.6	74.7	71.5	71.7	71.0	73.1	73.7	73.6	73.2
2005	73.2	73.4	74.3	76.9	75.8	75.2	74.1	73.8	54.0	55.6	59.1	61.1	68.9
2006	60.7	62.8	64.4	64.5	65.1	66.3	65.6	66.6	66.2	66.7	67.0	67.4	65.3
2007	67.3	68.4	69.0	68.4	69.0	68.8	66.8	67.9	67.8	69.9	70.1	70.2	68.6
2008	67.1	68.7	69.1	69.5	69.3	68.7	68.3	69.1	67.8	68.8	68.9	69.0	68.7
2009	66.7	67.5	67.3	67.4	67.8	67.3	66.2	66.0	65.9	67.3	67.5	68.1	67.1
2010	65.8	66.6	67.3	69.3	69.2	69.5	69.0	68.6	67.6	68.2	68.4	68.3	68.2
2011	66.9	68.3	68.0	68.6	68.3	68.0	67.7	66.9	70.5	70.2	70.6	69.6	68.6
Education and Health Services													
2000	76.9	77.9	78.0	78.2	77.8	73.5	73.1	73.0	78.5	79.5	79.4	79.5	77.1
2001	78.9	79.4	79.2	81.2	80.3	78.3	76.8	76.3	81.3	81.5	83.7	82.9	80.0
2002	79.9	81.2	80.8	82.9	81.2	79.8	78.2	77.9	83.2	83.6	85.6	83.7	81.5
2003	83.0	83.4	82.5	84.0	83.5	81.6	80.9	80.5	85.3	85.3	87.5	85.9	83.6
2004	85.5	85.1	85.2	85.7	84.8	82.3	82.9	83.9	84.3	84.5	84.3	81.2	84.1
2005	81.9	81.5	82.1	82.3	81.5	82.9	79.4	78.4	64.4	51.1	50.2	50.9	72.2
2006	53.0	52.9	54.2	55.4	55.9	55.5	55.4	55.6	57.7	58.9	60.9	60.0	56.3
2007	61.5	62.2	62.8	63.1	61.9	61.7	61.6	63.3	64.5	66.3	66.9	67.1	63.6
2008	66.7	67.5	68.0	68.0	65.9	65.8	65.9	67.6	67.7	70.0	70.5	70.6	67.9
2009	71.1	71.9	72.2	72.7	73.0	70.2	70.5	72.3	72.6	74.1	74.4	74.4	72.5
2010	74.3	74.5	75.1	75.8	73.0	72.0	72.0	72.7	73.7	75.0	75.5	75.6	74.1
2011	74.2	75.3	75.8	77.6	76.3	74.4	76.0	75.6	78.8	79.2	79.7	78.8	76.8
Leisure and Hospitality													
2000	79.0	79.9	80.2	80.8	82.7	83.0	81.2	80.6	79.2	80.4	80.8	81.6	80.8
2001	80.0	81.6	82.9	82.8	83.2	83.7	82.4	82.3	81.2	79.8	79.7	79.7	81.6
2002	78.4	79.2	79.9	81.7	82.5	82.9	81.6	80.6	79.7	78.6	79.8	79.1	80.3
2003	78.5	79.8	80.5	83.2	83.5	84.9	83.1	83.0	81.9	81.0	81.1	81.7	81.9
2004	81.3	82.5	83.9	83.7	84.8	86.5	85.1	85.3	84.2	84.3	84.9	85.3	84.3
2005	83.6	83.6	85.5	86.2	87.2	88.6	85.8	85.6	51.7	42.2	44.1	46.3	72.5
2006	47.3	51.2	54.1	54.4	56.1	59.6	60.2	60.7	59.9	61.6	62.7	64.1	57.7
2007	63.5	64.0	65.4	65.1	66.1	67.0	65.9	66.5	64.8	65.5	66.4	67.6	65.7
2008	67.1	67.6	68.1	68.8	68.9	69.4	68.3	69.0	65.4	67.0	66.9	67.2	67.8
2009	66.1	67.0	67.8	67.8	68.4	68.6	67.2	68.2	67.4	66.8	67.0	67.4	67.5
2010	67.4	67.9	69.0	69.6	69.4	70.2	68.6	69.1	69.9	69.7	70.8	71.9	69.5
2011	70.4	71.5	72.5	72.9	73.6	73.7	73.0	72.0	71.8	72.6	73.4	73.0	72.5
Other Services													
2000	22.1	22.3	22.5	22.3	22.3	22.6	22.5	22.5	22.2	22.2	22.0	22.0	22.3
2001	21.7	21.9	22.1	22.1	22.3	22.6	22.3	22.3	22.4	22.5	22.6	22.6	22.3
2002	22.0	22.1	22.4	22.4	22.7	22.8	22.8	22.8	22.7	23.0	23.1	23.3	22.7
2003	22.9	23.1	23.1	23.7	23.9	23.2	22.5	22.5	22.4	23.0	23.0	23.0	23.0
2004	22.7	22.8	23.0	22.6	22.6	22.5	22.6	22.6	22.4	22.4	22.3	22.4	22.6
2005	22.0	22.1	22.3	22.4	22.5	22.5	22.6	22.4	15.5	13.3	13.3	13.9	19.6
2006	13.7	14.3	14.7	15.0	15.3	15.6	15.8	16.0	16.2	16.6	16.6	16.7	15.5
2007	17.7	18.1	18.3	19.1	19.3	19.5	20.1	20.3	20.3	20.7	20.7	20.8	19.6
2008	19.9	20.1	20.1	18.1	18.2	18.3	17.9	17.9	17.7	19.2	19.3	19.2	18.8
2009	19.1	19.2	19.3	19.4	19.5	19.4	19.4	19.6	19.6	19.0	19.1	19.1	19.3
2010	18.4	18.4	18.5	17.6	17.6	17.7	17.4	17.4	17.2	17.7	17.7	17.8	17.8
2011	17.8	17.9	17.9	18.1	18.1	18.3	18.1	18.2	18.1	18.3	18.3	18.4	18.1
Government													
2000	103.4	103.8	104.3	104.2	104.0	103.7	99.2	99.7	102.9	102.7	102.6	103.7	102.9
2001	103.4	104.0	104.0	104.6	104.3	104.1	99.1	100.7	103.0	102.8	102.5	103.2	103.0
2002	102.9	103.9	104.1	103.9	103.5	104.9	99.3	100.7	102.6	103.2	104.2	104.5	103.1
2003	103.8	104.8	105.2	104.8	104.4	105.2	103.2	100.2	104.5	103.1	104.0	103.9	103.9
2004	103.2	104.0	104.5	106.9	106.9	105.9	103.7	102.7	105.8	104.3	105.0	105.2	104.8
2005	105.2	106.3	106.9	105.1	104.6	104.9	101.4	102.2	101.9	80.3	80.0	79.6	98.2
2006	72.7	72.8	73.5	73.4	73.8	73.4	72.0	72.6	75.9	76.1	77.2	78.0	74.3
2007	76.3	77.4	78.1	72.7	73.1	73.4	71.4	72.4	75.7	78.1	78.8	79.0	75.5
2008	77.9	78.7	78.5	80.7	80.8	79.4	78.5	80.7	81.7	82.6	83.1	82.9	80.5
2009	81.8	82.5	81.9	83.6	83.2	80.7	81.4	83.3	83.1	84.2	84.1	83.4	82.8
2010	82.3	82.8	83.4	83.3	84.8	82.7	80.3	80.9	81.5	82.0	82.3	81.8	82.3
2011	80.8	80.9	80.6	81.1	81.0	80.0	80.8	82.3	82.0	83.1	82.9	82.7	81.5

Employment by Industry: New York–Northern New Jersey–Long Island, NY–NJ–PA, Selected Years, 2000–2011

(Numbers in thousands, not seasonally adjusted)

Industry and year	January	February	March	April	May	June	July	August	September	October	November	December	Annual average
Total Nonfarm													
2000	8,170.8	8,203.4	8,284.3	8,362.8	8,422.6	8,496.1	8,408.2	8,359.1	8,410.0	8,490.4	8,550.5	8,609.9	8,397.3
2001	8,327.1	8,347.0	8,402.1	8,420.8	8,474.2	8,533.6	8,451.9	8,401.1	8,359.0	8,346.4	8,395.6	8,424.2	8,406.9
2002	8,139.7	8,170.6	8,227.5	8,257.5	8,316.9	8,361.5	8,273.1	8,238.0	8,244.1	8,321.5	8,378.7	8,413.1	8,278.5
2003	8,135.2	8,142.3	8,189.7	8,216.5	8,273.1	8,317.9	8,255.3	8,214.5	8,237.7	8,316.2	8,367.0	8,401.4	8,255.6
2004	8,102.6	8,132.1	8,211.6	8,248.9	8,321.1	8,385.3	8,332.2	8,288.8	8,303.1	8,374.3	8,421.2	8,469.4	8,299.2
2005	8,171.0	8,191.5	8,244.3	8,332.0	8,379.4	8,453.8	8,378.9	8,346.6	8,378.5	8,406.0	8,476.6	8,530.6	8,357.4
2006	8,255.8	8,277.3	8,353.9	8,397.3	8,471.4	8,548.3	8,462.7	8,425.4	8,461.1	8,529.0	8,598.8	8,661.1	8,453.5
2007	8,394.4	8,413.1	8,474.7	8,519.8	8,596.6	8,679.9	8,594.8	8,545.6	8,564.4	8,654.4	8,712.3	8,757.6	8,575.6
2008	8,498.1	8,518.9	8,569.5	8,614.6	8,657.7	8,710.7	8,629.0	8,573.6	8,573.7	8,616.5	8,625.6	8,626.0	8,601.2
2009	8,297.5	8,284.5	8,292.7	8,302.9	8,357.2	8,385.0	8,298.7	8,237.4	8,246.3	8,320.5	8,357.9	8,392.6	8,314.4
2010	8,118.7	8,134.3	8,200.4	8,302.4	8,380.3	8,417.7	8,298.6	8,251.9	8,292.5	8,388.4	8,434.4	8,461.7	8,306.8
2011	8,202.9	8,238.8	8,298.0	8,396.9	8,445.3	8,499.2	8,461.6	8,396.5	8,384.8	8,463.9	8,523.3	8,535.3	8,403.9
Total Private													
2000	6,953.3	6,982.3	7,050.9	7,116.1	7,162.5	7,249.4	7,171.1	7,161.5	7,212.1	7,253.5	7,307.2	7,363.7	7,165.3
2001	7,099.4	7,116.6	7,163.4	7,173.4	7,232.1	7,289.4	7,202.4	7,177.7	7,150.4	7,102.0	7,134.9	7,159.1	7,166.7
2002	6,887.6	6,910.1	6,960.1	6,992.2	7,045.5	7,088.7	7,022.9	7,014.2	7,017.7	7,062.7	7,103.5	7,133.4	7,019.9
2003	6,872.0	6,865.7	6,909.4	6,935.7	6,992.6	7,036.0	6,996.1	6,982.6	7,004.4	7,041.7	7,079.6	7,111.2	6,985.6
2004	6,840.8	6,856.4	6,928.5	6,967.1	7,035.9	7,095.6	7,067.5	7,051.0	7,063.4	7,097.0	7,131.6	7,179.6	7,026.2
2005	6,898.7	6,908.5	6,958.4	7,039.1	7,085.2	7,152.1	7,101.9	7,096.7	7,124.3	7,124.8	7,181.4	7,230.5	7,075.1
2006	6,977.5	6,989.1	7,061.6	7,103.8	7,175.5	7,250.1	7,192.6	7,182.2	7,205.5	7,241.6	7,298.9	7,354.6	7,169.4
2007	7,107.8	7,114.1	7,171.0	7,218.1	7,289.5	7,369.2	7,313.5	7,289.0	7,296.0	7,355.3	7,402.7	7,441.2	7,280.6
2008	7,204.8	7,212.8	7,258.5	7,298.5	7,339.7	7,390.2	7,327.5	7,304.3	7,296.0	7,303.2	7,302.1	7,298.3	7,294.7
2009	6,997.4	6,973.5	6,976.6	6,981.4	7,033.0	7,065.4	6,989.8	6,958.5	6,978.6	7,014.9	7,042.9	7,076.3	7,007.4
2010	6,830.3	6,834.1	6,893.4	6,985.0	7,029.3	7,086.8	7,039.4	7,031.6	7,045.3	7,106.3	7,146.3	7,179.0	7,017.2
2011	6,948.9	6,969.0	7,024.7	7,121.1	7,171.3	7,228.5	7,211.5	7,167.8	7,166.7	7,207.7	7,256.8	7,266.9	7,145.1
Goods-Producing													
2000	924.8	928.7	945.8	958.0	967.0	979.0	961.3	969.1	976.7	976.2	975.8	970.3	961.1
2001	911.8	916.7	925.4	932.9	941.6	950.3	930.8	934.6	929.3	925.7	919.1	910.1	927.4
2002	860.2	862.2	869.3	878.1	886.0	891.1	882.5	888.3	888.0	884.6	878.9	870.4	878.3
2003	827.9	823.9	831.6	841.2	851.6	857.7	850.9	854.1	855.9	851.0	848.3	842.2	844.7
2004	800.1	800.9	815.6	822.7	834.2	846.0	842.3	845.9	847.4	842.4	839.3	835.3	831.0
2005	790.5	787.8	795.6	809.5	818.6	827.7	821.8	828.4	830.8	822.0	824.5	819.3	814.7
2006	787.7	787.5	797.5	810.0	819.8	829.2	821.9	826.9	828.2	825.1	822.2	818.1	814.5
2007	786.7	780.1	788.6	802.8	814.0	824.3	820.8	822.7	821.3	821.6	818.7	811.7	809.4
2008	782.6	779.4	786.7	795.7	800.3	805.0	802.4	803.7	799.1	791.9	780.7	762.7	790.9
2009	713.1	704.1	702.8	704.1	707.9	709.9	705.1	702.5	696.6	693.7	687.2	679.3	700.5
2010	643.4	637.8	647.3	664.9	668.3	674.2	675.0	676.3	673.8	672.4	671.2	661.7	663.9
2011	628.4	627.4	638.1	652.7	662.6	669.2	673.7	677.8	675.0	676.0	673.2	658.5	659.4
Mining, Logging, and Construction													
2000	292.1	290.4	303.7	314.3	322.1	329.0	328.0	331.7	335.2	336.0	337.5	335.2	321.3
2001	303.9	305.1	312.6	327.0	335.6	341.6	340.3	342.0	338.6	343.7	342.5	339.4	331.0
2002	309.6	310.0	315.3	326.7	332.3	337.3	340.7	343.7	342.6	342.2	339.8	334.9	331.3
2003	306.5	301.6	308.8	321.6	331.4	336.2	339.1	340.3	340.3	338.3	336.6	331.9	327.7
2004	303.5	301.9	313.3	324.8	333.9	342.0	345.2	347.7	347.6	345.0	343.2	340.1	332.4
2005	309.6	305.5	311.6	328.6	337.2	344.0	345.3	350.4	351.9	344.7	348.1	343.0	335.0
2006	320.4	320.2	329.2	342.8	351.1	358.7	359.7	364.6	365.3	363.3	361.6	359.9	349.7
2007	336.4	330.3	338.5	354.9	365.8	374.6	375.3	378.3	377.2	377.8	376.2	370.5	363.0
2008	346.9	344.6	351.0	362.1	367.9	371.2	374.2	376.1	371.8	368.7	361.2	348.4	362.0
2009	314.9	310.9	313.5	319.4	323.6	325.8	327.5	326.6	321.1	318.1	313.8	306.3	318.5
2010	278.3	272.8	281.1	297.5	300.2	303.8	307.2	309.0	306.3	304.5	303.2	293.8	296.5
2011	268.0	267.0	277.0	291.1	299.8	304.7	310.4	314.4	313.6	311.3	310.7	296.6	297.1
Manufacturing													
2000	632.7	638.3	642.1	643.7	644.9	650.0	633.3	637.4	641.5	640.2	638.3	635.1	639.8
2001	607.9	611.6	612.8	605.9	606.0	608.7	590.5	592.6	590.7	582.0	576.6	570.7	596.3
2002	550.6	552.2	554.0	551.4	553.7	553.8	541.8	544.6	545.4	542.4	539.1	535.5	547.0
2003	521.4	522.3	522.8	519.6	520.2	521.5	511.8	513.8	515.6	512.7	511.7	510.3	517.0
2004	496.6	499.0	502.3	497.9	500.3	504.0	497.1	498.2	499.8	497.4	496.1	495.2	498.7
2005	480.9	482.3	484.0	480.9	481.4	483.7	476.5	478.0	478.9	477.3	476.4	476.3	479.7
2006	467.3	467.3	468.3	467.2	468.7	470.5	462.2	462.3	462.9	461.8	460.6	458.2	464.8
2007	450.3	449.8	450.1	447.9	448.2	449.7	445.5	444.4	444.1	443.8	442.5	441.2	446.5
2008	435.7	434.8	435.7	433.6	432.4	433.8	428.2	427.6	427.3	423.2	419.5	414.3	428.8
2009	398.2	393.2	389.3	384.7	384.3	384.1	377.6	375.9	375.5	375.6	373.4	373.0	382.1
2010	365.1	365.0	366.2	367.4	368.1	370.4	367.8	367.3	367.5	367.9	368.0	367.9	367.4
2011	360.4	360.4	361.1	361.6	362.8	364.5	363.3	363.4	361.4	364.7	362.5	361.9	362.3
Service-Providing													
2000	7,246.0	7,274.7	7,338.5	7,404.8	7,455.6	7,517.1	7,446.9	7,390.0	7,433.3	7,514.2	7,574.7	7,639.6	7,436.3
2001	7,415.3	7,430.3	7,476.7	7,487.9	7,532.6	7,583.3	7,521.1	7,466.5	7,429.7	7,420.7	7,476.5	7,514.1	7,479.6
2002	7,279.5	7,308.4	7,358.2	7,379.4	7,430.9	7,470.4	7,390.6	7,349.7	7,356.1	7,436.9	7,499.8	7,542.7	7,400.2
2003	7,307.3	7,318.4	7,358.1	7,375.3	7,421.5	7,460.2	7,404.4	7,360.4	7,381.8	7,465.2	7,518.7	7,559.2	7,410.9
2004	7,302.5	7,331.2	7,396.0	7,426.2	7,486.9	7,539.3	7,489.9	7,442.9	7,455.7	7,531.9	7,581.9	7,634.1	7,468.2
2005	7,380.5	7,403.7	7,448.7	7,522.5	7,560.8	7,626.1	7,557.1	7,518.2	7,547.7	7,584.0	7,652.1	7,711.3	7,542.7
2006	7,468.1	7,489.8	7,556.4	7,587.3	7,651.6	7,719.1	7,640.8	7,598.5	7,632.9	7,703.9	7,776.6	7,843.0	7,639.0
2007	7,607.7	7,633.0	7,686.1	7,717.0	7,782.6	7,855.6	7,774.0	7,722.9	7,743.1	7,832.8	7,893.6	7,945.9	7,766.2
2008	7,715.5	7,739.5	7,782.8	7,818.9	7,857.4	7,905.7	7,826.6	7,769.9	7,774.6	7,824.6	7,844.9	7,863.3	7,810.3
2009	7,584.4	7,580.4	7,589.9	7,598.8	7,649.3	7,675.1	7,593.6	7,534.9	7,549.7	7,626.8	7,670.7	7,713.3	7,613.9
2010	7,475.3	7,496.5	7,553.1	7,637.5	7,712.0	7,743.5	7,623.6	7,575.6	7,618.7	7,716.0	7,763.2	7,800.0	7,642.9
2011	7,574.5	7,611.4	7,659.9	7,744.2	7,782.7	7,830.0	7,787.9	7,718.7	7,709.8	7,787.9	7,850.1	7,876.8	7,744.5

Employment by Industry: New York–Northern New Jersey–Long Island, NY–NJ–PA, Selected Years, 2000–2011—Continued

(Numbers in thousands, not seasonally adjusted)

Industry and year	January	February	March	April	May	June	July	August	September	October	November	December	Annual average
Trade, Transportation, and Utilities													
2000	1,610.7	1,596.4	1,604.8	1,611.2	1,617.7	1,635.0	1,606.7	1,608.4	1,627.1	1,645.0	1,679.4	1,714.5	1,629.7
2001	1,635.6	1,615.0	1,616.8	1,611.0	1,620.7	1,632.6	1,601.7	1,594.5	1,602.5	1,603.5	1,624.8	1,649.9	1,617.4
2002	1,574.0	1,558.0	1,568.4	1,563.6	1,571.7	1,587.5	1,561.9	1,558.1	1,578.3	1,590.9	1,618.9	1,649.6	1,581.7
2003	1,575.2	1,559.6	1,563.9	1,558.0	1,568.7	1,580.4	1,557.8	1,556.1	1,573.8	1,590.2	1,615.1	1,641.3	1,578.3
2004	1,562.3	1,550.4	1,558.9	1,555.8	1,572.8	1,589.2	1,570.8	1,568.4	1,583.4	1,600.8	1,625.9	1,654.4	1,582.8
2005	1,568.2	1,553.5	1,558.3	1,567.7	1,579.3	1,594.0	1,571.3	1,569.4	1,585.6	1,592.3	1,622.8	1,656.9	1,584.9
2006	1,583.2	1,562.0	1,570.6	1,573.1	1,587.3	1,604.2	1,581.5	1,577.1	1,593.5	1,611.6	1,646.7	1,677.9	1,597.4
2007	1,605.7	1,584.6	1,590.4	1,591.6	1,609.5	1,629.3	1,603.0	1,593.1	1,609.5	1,622.1	1,659.2	1,688.2	1,615.5
2008	1,615.8	1,593.9	1,600.3	1,596.4	1,605.7	1,619.2	1,594.2	1,588.8	1,599.5	1,602.5	1,620.1	1,636.6	1,606.1
2009	1,550.0	1,525.4	1,518.9	1,506.9	1,521.0	1,532.7	1,505.2	1,500.7	1,516.9	1,529.1	1,556.6	1,582.0	1,528.8
2010	1,510.4	1,492.8	1,498.6	1,511.2	1,522.3	1,540.6	1,519.9	1,519.3	1,531.7	1,548.6	1,576.3	1,602.2	1,531.2
2011	1,538.0	1,522.1	1,526.0	1,538.6	1,548.8	1,567.0	1,544.5	1,539.6	1,552.6	1,561.1	1,599.3	1,621.6	1,554.9
Wholesale Trade													
2000	440.3	441.8	444.3	443.9	444.7	448.3	444.1	445.3	446.8	447.7	448.7	451.7	445.6
2001	452.3	453.9	454.8	450.1	450.2	451.8	447.6	446.7	445.9	444.2	443.4	443.9	448.7
2002	434.4	435.0	437.4	432.2	432.5	433.4	429.2	430.2	431.0	432.7	433.4	434.9	433.0
2003	431.8	432.1	433.4	430.9	432.2	433.6	431.9	431.2	431.2	431.7	432.7	434.1	432.2
2004	425.4	426.4	428.9	427.9	429.3	432.2	432.1	431.8	431.5	432.9	433.2	435.1	430.6
2005	424.5	425.6	426.5	427.5	428.8	430.9	428.6	429.5	430.6	430.5	431.6	434.9	429.1
2006	425.3	425.6	427.5	429.4	431.7	434.5	432.9	432.6	432.4	434.4	435.4	438.4	431.7
2007	431.4	431.2	432.2	432.4	434.2	437.7	436.1	435.3	434.6	437.5	437.5	439.4	435.0
2008	432.0	432.0	432.9	431.0	431.6	433.1	430.3	428.8	427.6	425.6	423.0	421.2	429.1
2009	411.8	407.8	405.5	401.6	401.4	401.6	397.4	396.2	395.1	396.6	396.6	397.8	400.8
2010	389.5	388.7	390.2	391.0	392.5	395.4	395.2	394.6	394.4	395.7	396.9	398.5	393.6
2011	392.3	391.7	393.5	395.1	396.7	399.1	396.4	395.1	393.2	394.9	395.4	397.5	395.1
Retail Trade													
2000	834.2	818.6	823.5	828.7	833.7	845.3	831.0	834.6	837.6	847.4	879.8	910.4	843.7
2001	841.7	819.0	820.0	820.9	826.3	837.0	822.4	822.5	819.0	822.3	850.4	877.0	831.5
2002	819.4	802.7	810.2	810.2	816.8	830.6	820.2	820.3	823.8	830.6	859.0	887.9	827.6
2003	825.2	810.3	811.5	813.3	820.6	830.5	821.6	823.0	825.0	837.0	860.6	883.8	830.2
2004	823.2	810.9	815.5	816.1	827.5	839.5	834.6	834.7	835.6	847.2	872.0	897.6	837.9
2005	836.1	820.4	822.1	829.3	836.8	847.0	840.8	840.6	839.1	845.7	872.2	898.0	844.0
2006	843.8	822.7	828.0	829.3	836.7	848.4	843.6	842.0	839.6	854.6	886.1	907.7	848.5
2007	855.8	835.4	838.9	840.9	851.1	864.2	858.1	852.8	850.2	858.5	893.7	915.0	859.6
2008	863.1	841.5	844.9	842.0	848.7	858.7	854.6	852.1	847.8	854.2	873.1	887.1	855.7
2009	825.6	806.5	803.7	798.8	809.8	820.7	814.3	814.3	815.3	824.8	849.3	869.3	821.0
2010	819.3	804.5	808.4	819.2	827.2	840.5	836.6	837.6	833.2	846.8	870.6	889.1	836.1
2011	841.3	827.9	828.7	838.1	844.6	857.7	854.1	853.4	851.9	858.4	891.0	909.8	854.7
Transportation and Utilities													
2000	336.2	336.0	337.0	338.6	339.3	341.4	331.6	328.5	342.7	349.9	350.9	352.4	340.4
2001	341.6	342.1	342.0	340.0	344.2	343.8	331.7	325.3	337.6	337.0	331.0	329.0	337.1
2002	320.2	320.3	320.8	321.2	322.4	323.5	312.5	307.6	323.5	327.6	326.5	326.8	321.1
2003	318.2	317.2	319.0	313.8	315.9	316.3	304.3	301.9	317.6	321.5	321.8	323.4	315.9
2004	313.7	313.1	314.5	311.8	316.0	317.5	304.1	301.9	316.3	320.7	320.7	321.7	314.3
2005	307.6	307.5	309.7	310.9	313.7	316.1	301.9	299.3	315.9	316.1	319.0	324.0	311.8
2006	314.1	313.7	315.1	314.4	318.9	321.3	305.0	302.5	321.5	322.6	325.2	331.8	317.2
2007	318.5	318.0	319.3	318.3	324.2	327.4	308.8	305.0	324.7	326.1	328.0	333.8	321.0
2008	320.7	320.4	322.5	323.4	325.4	327.4	309.3	307.9	324.1	322.7	324.0	328.3	321.3
2009	312.6	311.1	309.7	306.5	309.8	310.4	293.5	290.2	306.5	307.7	310.7	314.9	307.0
2010	301.6	299.6	300.0	301.0	302.6	304.7	288.1	287.1	304.1	306.1	308.8	314.6	301.5
2011	304.4	302.5	303.8	305.4	307.5	310.2	294.0	291.1	307.5	307.8	312.9	314.3	305.1
Information													
2000	317.9	321.1	323.8	326.8	330.1	335.2	334.5	316.5	337.1	338.9	342.6	343.3	330.7
2001	348.3	351.4	352.0	349.6	351.8	351.9	348.0	345.0	341.0	338.2	342.2	339.4	346.6
2002	321.0	324.3	319.8	316.7	322.9	320.5	310.2	312.6	307.4	308.1	312.1	310.3	315.5
2003	296.3	299.3	296.3	293.2	297.8	295.0	292.3	296.2	292.6	294.4	298.4	296.7	295.7
2004	286.4	286.2	288.1	286.7	287.6	287.5	286.6	288.4	288.4	288.3	290.8	290.4	288.0
2005	282.4	284.1	284.9	284.1	286.2	291.0	288.6	289.7	289.7	290.1	292.1	295.0	288.2
2006	286.9	287.5	289.0	286.7	288.8	291.9	290.6	291.5	290.6	287.5	289.5	291.3	289.3
2007	284.5	286.5	286.7	285.6	287.5	289.9	288.6	288.9	287.9	286.4	288.1	289.4	287.5
2008	284.1	286.2	286.4	284.6	286.1	288.7	285.5	285.9	285.2	283.3	283.5	284.1	285.3
2009	276.9	275.1	275.8	276.6	276.5	276.1	274.5	273.3	272.6	271.7	272.0	272.3	274.5
2010	265.0	265.1	266.1	266.0	267.0	269.0	268.8	269.0	269.0	270.8	270.3	274.4	268.4
2011	265.6	266.6	268.4	271.1	271.5	273.1	274.1	256.2	271.4	270.7	270.5	270.2	269.1
Financial Activities													
2000	809.2	811.4	812.7	812.8	814.7	828.6	825.4	825.7	820.1	817.6	819.4	824.5	818.5
2001	807.3	807.0	808.3	804.7	805.0	815.1	815.0	811.0	801.1	773.0	774.4	777.9	800.0
2002	774.9	774.0	773.1	768.8	768.9	776.2	777.5	775.7	767.5	766.8	766.9	770.1	771.7
2003	764.8	762.8	762.4	760.4	762.7	770.0	773.8	772.6	765.7	764.0	765.4	770.2	766.2
2004	759.5	760.4	762.3	763.0	764.4	773.3	780.5	779.5	771.2	774.8	776.0	781.6	770.5
2005	768.0	767.7	770.3	774.4	774.1	784.3	791.0	791.3	784.1	783.2	785.2	790.1	780.3
2006	776.4	778.3	781.3	783.6	786.7	797.6	801.7	802.4	794.4	793.8	795.8	800.7	791.1
2007	788.5	789.9	791.6	791.7	792.5	804.0	807.5	804.8	795.7	797.9	799.4	801.3	797.1
2008	790.6	791.0	791.3	788.0	787.4	794.5	795.7	794.5	780.3	775.7	771.8	771.3	786.0
2009	754.9	749.9	745.8	740.6	738.5	740.4	738.9	735.1	729.6	728.0	726.7	729.1	738.1
2010	718.4	719.4	721.6	722.3	723.5	733.1	735.6	736.4	730.9	730.4	732.5	737.2	728.4
2011	727.1	728.2	729.3	731.6	733.6	743.6	747.6	749.3	745.8	742.3	744.9	743.2	738.9

Employment by Industry: New York–Northern New Jersey–Long Island, NY–NJ–PA, Selected Years, 2000–2011—*Continued*

(Numbers in thousands, not seasonally adjusted)

Industry and year	January	February	March	April	May	June	July	August	September	October	November	December	Annual average
Professional and Business Services													
2000	1,221.6	1,234.8	1,252.0	1,269.3	1,278.5	1,301.1	1,294.7	1,302.6	1,300.2	1,302.0	1,307.9	1,316.4	1,281.8
2001	1,284.1	1,291.5	1,301.1	1,299.4	1,301.8	1,314.4	1,303.0	1,298.8	1,289.6	1,264.5	1,263.4	1,259.7	1,289.3
2002	1,212.7	1,217.4	1,228.4	1,239.9	1,242.0	1,250.2	1,241.9	1,244.0	1,238.9	1,244.9	1,248.3	1,249.2	1,238.2
2003	1,195.2	1,192.4	1,205.0	1,214.5	1,218.1	1,229.6	1,227.4	1,230.6	1,230.6	1,235.3	1,238.6	1,243.5	1,221.7
2004	1,194.4	1,198.6	1,215.5	1,229.4	1,235.0	1,246.8	1,242.9	1,244.1	1,240.1	1,242.8	1,248.2	1,255.5	1,232.8
2005	1,205.8	1,206.9	1,216.2	1,240.2	1,241.9	1,258.9	1,255.5	1,259.0	1,258.0	1,256.4	1,263.8	1,268.9	1,244.3
2006	1,218.7	1,227.1	1,244.5	1,256.6	1,265.6	1,286.4	1,284.2	1,289.4	1,284.0	1,289.0	1,298.7	1,306.7	1,270.9
2007	1,260.1	1,264.8	1,280.7	1,294.9	1,304.2	1,325.1	1,328.7	1,332.7	1,321.9	1,334.0	1,338.9	1,342.2	1,310.7
2008	1,298.6	1,303.8	1,313.3	1,327.3	1,328.9	1,343.0	1,343.0	1,340.0	1,328.3	1,322.4	1,317.2	1,310.9	1,323.1
2009	1,253.1	1,246.7	1,245.2	1,247.5	1,247.4	1,257.4	1,249.8	1,245.3	1,240.2	1,244.4	1,248.4	1,251.8	1,248.1
2010	1,211.7	1,217.5	1,229.2	1,251.4	1,255.8	1,273.3	1,271.0	1,273.0	1,267.2	1,278.0	1,283.1	1,285.7	1,258.1
2011	1,251.4	1,256.8	1,269.1	1,295.3	1,299.3	1,317.9	1,324.3	1,320.4	1,315.0	1,322.3	1,323.4	1,327.8	1,301.9
Education and Health Services													
2000	1,228.9	1,241.6	1,249.9	1,253.4	1,251.3	1,239.9	1,221.7	1,216.1	1,242.0	1,268.9	1,276.5	1,285.1	1,247.9
2001	1,246.0	1,261.9	1,274.3	1,276.4	1,283.3	1,274.5	1,254.7	1,248.7	1,266.5	1,296.4	1,307.6	1,313.6	1,275.3
2002	1,281.9	1,302.5	1,314.3	1,318.0	1,323.5	1,309.9	1,295.8	1,287.5	1,309.1	1,338.7	1,349.0	1,351.0	1,315.1
2003	1,324.6	1,336.8	1,348.7	1,348.4	1,349.9	1,336.9	1,320.4	1,308.8	1,333.8	1,361.0	1,369.2	1,370.5	1,342.4
2004	1,337.8	1,354.8	1,368.2	1,366.0	1,371.4	1,355.8	1,339.4	1,328.3	1,348.2	1,380.7	1,387.9	1,393.3	1,361.0
2005	1,356.9	1,375.9	1,385.7	1,391.9	1,391.4	1,375.2	1,357.6	1,348.4	1,378.1	1,405.4	1,415.0	1,420.0	1,383.5
2006	1,387.5	1,405.6	1,417.3	1,420.1	1,423.1	1,408.0	1,383.0	1,373.7	1,406.3	1,438.3	1,447.9	1,456.6	1,414.0
2007	1,421.6	1,440.3	1,450.9	1,448.1	1,448.7	1,434.8	1,409.5	1,399.0	1,431.0	1,466.7	1,472.9	1,480.5	1,442.0
2008	1,448.8	1,469.3	1,478.1	1,480.7	1,480.1	1,465.4	1,434.5	1,428.0	1,459.7	1,491.0	1,501.8	1,509.5	1,470.6
2009	1,477.1	1,497.7	1,504.4	1,505.9	1,506.7	1,492.7	1,461.6	1,454.4	1,485.5	1,522.2	1,532.5	1,541.3	1,498.5
2010	1,508.3	1,527.4	1,539.6	1,543.6	1,540.8	1,520.0	1,490.2	1,482.5	1,514.4	1,550.5	1,562.6	1,565.0	1,528.7
2011	1,530.8	1,553.9	1,564.6	1,568.9	1,568.1	1,540.8	1,520.6	1,508.6	1,525.5	1,559.3	1,572.6	1,574.6	1,549.0
Leisure and Hospitality													
2000	515.6	521.5	532.0	552.3	568.9	593.1	590.5	589.6	575.6	569.9	569.4	571.7	562.5
2001	537.3	542.1	551.7	562.8	587.5	606.4	606.5	604.9	584.2	563.6	564.2	567.6	573.2
2002	527.6	534.5	547.0	567.1	587.0	607.2	607.9	605.6	588.8	584.4	583.1	585.3	577.1
2003	549.5	551.3	559.4	576.8	597.8	617.6	624.6	617.2	605.2	596.6	594.1	594.5	590.4
2004	560.2	563.1	574.8	592.4	615.5	638.4	646.2	639.3	627.5	611.1	606.3	609.5	607.0
2005	570.6	573.8	586.1	606.3	626.2	649.7	651.1	647.2	634.9	614.1	614.5	614.2	615.7
2006	580.6	583.2	599.7	613.9	640.3	664.2	667.6	661.6	647.3	636.0	635.6	637.5	630.6
2007	600.6	605.5	616.9	637.2	662.3	686.8	689.1	684.5	665.7	660.2	657.4	658.5	652.1
2008	622.8	626.5	638.0	660.3	682.7	703.3	704.6	698.0	679.8	671.2	661.8	658.1	667.3
2009	618.4	619.7	628.1	644.0	675.6	694.2	696.2	690.7	682.9	669.2	661.6	661.7	661.9
2010	623.5	624.7	639.1	670.1	693.2	714.7	719.3	717.0	702.4	695.4	689.8	690.9	681.7
2011	652.6	657.4	670.6	699.8	721.0	746.4	757.3	748.3	721.6	712.6	709.0	706.1	708.6
Other Services													
2000	324.6	326.8	329.9	332.3	334.3	337.5	336.3	333.5	333.3	335.0	336.2	337.9	333.1
2001	329.0	331.0	333.8	336.6	340.4	344.2	342.7	340.2	336.2	337.1	339.2	340.9	337.6
2002	335.3	337.2	339.8	340.0	343.5	346.1	345.2	342.4	339.7	344.3	346.3	347.5	342.3
2003	338.5	339.6	342.1	343.2	346.0	348.8	348.9	347.0	346.8	349.2	350.5	352.3	346.1
2004	340.1	342.0	345.1	351.1	355.0	358.6	358.8	357.1	357.2	356.1	357.2	359.6	353.2
2005	356.3	358.8	361.3	365.0	367.5	371.3	365.0	363.3	363.1	361.3	363.5	366.1	363.5
2006	356.5	357.9	361.7	359.8	363.9	368.6	362.1	359.6	361.2	360.3	362.5	365.8	361.7
2007	360.1	362.4	365.2	366.2	370.8	375.0	366.3	363.3	363.0	366.4	368.1	369.4	366.4
2008	361.5	362.7	364.4	365.5	368.5	371.1	367.6	365.4	364.1	365.3	365.2	365.1	365.4
2009	353.9	354.9	355.6	355.8	359.4	362.0	358.5	356.5	354.3	356.6	357.9	358.8	357.0
2010	349.6	349.4	351.9	355.5	358.4	361.9	359.6	358.1	355.9	360.2	360.5	361.9	356.9
2011	355.0	356.6	358.6	363.1	366.4	370.5	369.4	367.6	359.8	363.4	363.9	364.9	363.3
Government													
2000	1,217.5	1,221.1	1,233.4	1,246.7	1,260.1	1,246.7	1,237.1	1,197.6	1,197.9	1,236.9	1,243.3	1,246.2	1,232.0
2001	1,227.7	1,230.4	1,238.7	1,247.4	1,242.1	1,244.2	1,249.5	1,223.4	1,208.6	1,244.4	1,260.7	1,265.1	1,240.2
2002	1,252.1	1,260.5	1,267.4	1,265.3	1,271.4	1,272.8	1,250.2	1,223.8	1,226.4	1,258.8	1,275.2	1,279.7	1,258.6
2003	1,263.2	1,276.6	1,280.3	1,280.8	1,280.5	1,281.9	1,259.2	1,231.9	1,233.3	1,274.5	1,287.4	1,290.2	1,270.0
2004	1,261.8	1,275.7	1,283.1	1,281.8	1,285.2	1,289.7	1,264.7	1,237.8	1,239.7	1,277.3	1,289.6	1,289.8	1,273.0
2005	1,272.3	1,283.0	1,285.9	1,292.9	1,294.2	1,301.7	1,277.0	1,249.9	1,254.2	1,281.2	1,295.2	1,300.1	1,282.3
2006	1,278.3	1,288.2	1,292.3	1,293.5	1,295.9	1,298.2	1,270.1	1,243.2	1,255.6	1,287.4	1,299.9	1,306.5	1,284.1
2007	1,286.6	1,299.0	1,303.7	1,301.7	1,307.1	1,310.7	1,281.3	1,256.6	1,268.4	1,299.1	1,309.6	1,316.4	1,295.0
2008	1,293.3	1,306.1	1,311.0	1,316.1	1,318.0	1,320.5	1,301.5	1,269.3	1,277.7	1,313.2	1,323.5	1,327.7	1,306.5
2009	1,300.1	1,311.0	1,316.1	1,321.5	1,324.2	1,319.6	1,308.9	1,278.9	1,267.7	1,305.6	1,315.0	1,316.3	1,307.1
2010	1,288.4	1,300.2	1,307.0	1,317.4	1,351.0	1,330.9	1,259.2	1,220.3	1,247.2	1,282.1	1,288.1	1,282:7	1,289.5
2011	1,254.0	1,269.8	1,273.3	1,275.8	1,274.0	1,270.7	1,250.1	1,228.7	1,218.1	1,256.2	1,266.5	1,268.4	1,258.8

Employment by Industry: North Port–Bradenton–Sarasota, FL, Selected Years, 2000–2011

(Numbers in thousands, not seasonally adjusted)

Industry and year	January	February	March	April	May	June	July	August	September	October	November	December	Annual average
Total Nonfarm													
2000	231.9	234.1	236.6	238.0	237.7	236.5	232.4	235.3	235.2	237.1	239.8	241.8	236.4
2001	231.4	234.5	236.6	235.6	236.2	233.2	230.3	233.8	233.7	238.0	242.3	245.2	235.9
2002	239.7	243.1	246.5	247.8	246.5	243.2	241.0	244.6	245.0	246.2	248.4	250.5	245.2
2003	246.0	247.7	249.4	247.6	248.6	248.5	242.8	247.4	248.2	250.5	254.8	258.7	249.2
2004	253.2	255.8	259.1	259.8	261.1	259.2	259.3	262.8	263.3	267.0	270.6	274.8	262.2
2005	269.4	272.8	274.9	274.2	275.2	272.1	270.6	274.1	274.9	275.9	279.2	282.6	274.7
2006	276.9	280.6	284.6	283.1	283.9	281.8	277.4	280.5	280.8	278.9	282.0	284.0	281.2
2007	278.0	280.0	282.2	278.1	277.4	273.5	267.6	271.0	269.6	268.6	271.9	274.6	274.4
2008	269.5	272.0	273.3	267.2	265.8	260.6	255.7	257.9	256.9	254.7	255.1	256.0	262.1
2009	249.4	248.8	249.5	246.5	244.9	240.3	235.7	237.4	236.5	238.9	241.4	242.8	242.7
2010	237.4	239.0	241.0	241.2	242.8	237.4	234.1	235.9	234.6	236.1	239.5	241.4	238.4
2011	237.5	240.6	242.2	243.8	242.1	238.2	235.4	238.0	237.3	239.8	243.2	243.5	240.1
Total Private													
2000	207.6	209.6	212.0	213.3	212.3	214.0	210.2	211.0	211.1	212.7	215.1	216.9	212.2
2001	207.0	209.8	211.7	210.9	211.3	210.7	208.0	209.2	209.0	212.8	216.7	219.4	211.4
2002	214.4	217.4	220.7	222.1	220.6	219.8	217.8	219.0	219.2	220.3	222.2	224.3	219.8
2003	219.8	221.3	222.9	221.2	221.9	224.4	218.9	220.9	221.6	223.8	227.7	231.4	223.0
2004	226.5	228.8	232.1	232.7	233.8	234.6	235.0	235.8	236.5	240.0	243.4	247.4	235.6
2005	242.5	245.7	247.8	246.9	247.8	247.6	246.2	247.1	247.7	248.1	251.2	254.7	247.8
2006	249.1	252.7	256.5	254.7	255.4	256.2	252.1	252.3	252.2	250.3	252.7	254.7	253.2
2007	249.2	250.9	253.0	248.9	248.3	247.4	241.7	242.2	240.7	239.8	242.8	245.5	245.9
2008	240.5	242.8	243.8	237.7	236.3	234.1	229.4	228.7	227.7	225.7	226.3	227.2	233.4
2009	220.8	220.1	220.6	217.2	216.0	214.5	210.1	209.8	208.7	210.9	213.2	214.7	214.7
2010	209.6	211.1	213.0	213.2	213.3	211.9	208.9	209.2	207.5	208.6	211.9	213.8	211.0
2011	210.1	213.0	214.5	216.1	214.9	213.9	211.4	210.9	210.3	212.5	215.8	216.2	213.3
Goods-Producing													
2000	43.0	43.2	43.6	44.4	44.0	43.9	43.3	42.8	42.8	42.5	42.4	42.5	43.2
2001	41.6	41.4	41.5	41.4	41.6	42.0	41.8	42.0	42.2	42.6	42.8	42.9	42.0
2002	42.6	42.9	42.8	42.6	42.8	42.8	42.7	43.2	42.9	42.8	42.8	43.0	42.8
2003	42.2	42.7	42.5	41.9	42.1	42.3	42.2	42.3	42.2	42.7	42.6	42.9	42.4
2004	43.1	43.4	43.9	44.2	44.6	44.8	45.3	45.4	45.6	46.2	46.4	46.9	45.0
2005	46.2	46.9	47.2	47.1	47.8	48.0	48.5	48.8	49.4	49.5	49.9	50.4	48.3
2006	50.1	50.7	51.1	50.9	51.4	51.7	51.3	51.3	51.1	50.5	50.0	49.9	50.8
2007	48.4	48.0	47.9	46.5	46.3	45.9	44.8	44.6	43.7	42.8	42.4	42.1	45.3
2008	40.8	40.7	40.2	39.1	38.9	38.8	37.8	37.5	37.2	35.8	35.2	35.0	38.1
2009	32.6	31.7	31.4	30.7	30.6	30.3	29.6	29.4	29.1	28.9	28.7	28.7	30.1
2010	27.6	27.6	27.5	27.8	28.1	28.4	28.4	28.5	28.4	28.2	28.1	28.2	28.1
2011	27.3	27.5	27.7	27.9	28.1	28.6	28.4	28.3	28.4	28.2	28.3	28.2	28.1
Mining, Logging, and Construction													
2000	21.0	21.3	21.5	21.9	21.9	22.0	21.8	21.7	21.6	21.7	21.7	21.9	21.7
2001	21.0	21.1	21.2	21.1	21.3	21.6	21.6	21.9	22.0	22.6	22.8	22.7	21.7
2002	22.7	22.9	22.9	22.8	23.1	23.2	23.2	23.5	23.4	23.7	23.8	24.0	23.3
2003	23.5	24.0	24.0	23.7	23.9	24.0	23.9	24.0	24.0	24.4	24.4	24.6	24.0
2004	24.9	25.1	25.5	25.9	26.1	26.2	26.6	26.5	26.7	27.4	27.5	27.8	26.4
2005	27.5	28.1	28.4	28.4	28.9	29.0	29.4	29.6	30.1	30.2	30.6	31.0	29.3
2006	30.9	31.5	31.9	31.8	32.2	32.4	32.2	32.4	32.4	32.0	31.6	31.4	31.9
2007	30.2	30.0	29.9	28.7	28.5	28.1	27.0	26.9	26.1	25.3	24.9	24.6	27.5
2008	23.4	23.3	23.0	22.2	22.0	22.0	21.4	21.3	21.2	20.2	19.7	19.6	21.6
2009	18.0	17.6	17.4	17.0	17.0	16.8	16.5	16.4	16.1	16.0	15.8	15.7	16.7
2010	14.9	14.9	14.9	15.0	15.2	15.5	15.5	15.6	15.5	15.3	15.2	15.1	15.2
2011	14.5	14.6	14.8	14.8	14.8	15.0	14.9	14.8	14.9	14.7	14.7	14.6	14.8
Manufacturing													
2000	22.0	21.9	22.1	22.5	22.1	21.9	21.5	21.1	21.2	20.8	20.7	20.6	21.5
2001	20.6	20.3	20.3	20.3	20.3	20.4	20.2	20.1	20.2	20.0	20.0	20.2	20.2
2002	19.9	20.0	19.9	19.8	19.7	19.6	19.5	19.7	19.5	19.1	19.0	19.0	19.6
2003	18.7	18.7	18.5	18.2	18.2	18.3	18.3	18.3	18.2	18.3	18.2	18.3	18.4
2004	18.2	18.3	18.4	18.3	18.5	18.6	18.7	18.9	18.9	18.8	18.9	19.1	18.6
2005	18.7	18.8	18.8	18.7	18.9	19.0	19.1	19.2	19.3	19.3	19.3	19.4	19.0
2006	19.2	19.2	19.2	19.1	19.2	19.3	19.1	18.9	18.7	18.5	18.4	18.5	18.9
2007	18.2	18.0	18.0	17.8	17.8	17.8	17.8	17.7	17.6	17.5	17.5	17.5	17.8
2008	17.4	17.4	17.2	16.9	16.9	16.8	16.4	16.2	16.0	15.6	15.5	15.4	16.5
2009	14.6	14.1	14.0	13.7	13.6	13.5	13.1	13.0	13.0	12.9	12.9	13.0	13.5
2010	12.7	12.7	12.6	12.8	12.9	12.9	12.9	12.9	12.9	12.9	12.9	13.1	12.9
2011	12.8	12.9	12.9	13.1	13.3	13.6	13.5	13.5	13.5	13.5	13.6	13.6	13.3
Service-Providing													
2000	188.9	190.9	193.0	193.6	193.7	192.6	189.1	192.5	192.4	194.6	197.4	199.3	193.2
2001	189.8	193.1	195.1	194.2	194.6	191.2	188.5	191.8	191.5	195.4	199.5	202.3	193.9
2002	197.1	200.2	203.7	205.2	203.7	200.4	198.3	201.4	202.1	203.4	205.6	207.5	202.4
2003	203.8	205.0	206.9	205.7	206.5	206.2	200.6	205.1	206.0	207.8	212.2	215.8	206.8
2004	210.1	212.4	215.2	215.6	216.5	214.4	214.0	217.4	217.7	220.8	224.2	227.9	217.2
2005	223.2	225.9	227.7	227.1	227.4	224.1	222.1	225.3	225.5	226.4	229.3	232.2	226.4
2006	226.8	229.9	233.5	232.2	232.5	230.1	226.1	229.2	229.7	228.4	232.0	234.1	230.4
2007	229.6	232.0	234.3	231.6	231.1	227.6	222.8	226.4	225.9	225.8	229.5	232.5	229.1
2008	228.7	231.3	233.1	228.1	226.9	221.8	217.9	220.4	219.7	218.9	219.9	221.0	224.0
2009	216.8	217.1	218.1	215.8	214.3	210.0	206.1	208.0	207.4	210.0	212.7	214.1	212.5
2010	209.8	211.4	213.5	213.4	214.7	209.0	205.7	207.4	206.2	207.9	211.4	213.2	210.3
2011	210.2	213.1	214.5	215.9	214.0	209.6	207.0	209.7	208.9	211.6	214.9	215.3	212.1

Employment by Industry: North Port–Bradenton–Sarasota, FL, Selected Years, 2000–2011—*Continued*

(Numbers in thousands, not seasonally adjusted)

Industry and year	January	February	March	April	May	June	July	August	September	October	November	December	Annual average
Trade, Transportation, and Utilities													
2000	48.6	48.8	48.8	49.4	49.1	48.8	47.7	48.0	47.9	48.6	50.3	51.1	48.9
2001	47.7	47.8	48.2	48.1	47.7	47.2	46.5	46.5	46.4	47.5	48.9	49.9	47.7
2002	48.3	48.0	48.3	48.0	47.7	47.4	46.8	47.0	47.3	47.5	48.8	49.9	47.9
2003	48.0	47.6	48.0	47.9	47.7	47.3	46.6	47.0	47.2	47.8	49.1	50.7	47.9
2004	49.3	49.5	49.7	49.5	49.4	49.2	49.3	49.3	49.3	50.3	51.9	52.8	50.0
2005	50.8	51.2	51.5	51.6	51.5	51.1	50.6	50.5	50.5	50.6	51.7	52.5	51.2
2006	50.7	50.8	51.3	51.4	51.4	51.2	50.1	50.1	50.1	50.1	51.4	52.5	50.9
2007	51.7	51.3	51.6	50.8	50.8	50.4	49.8	49.5	49.2	49.5	50.7	52.1	50.6
2008	50.6	50.4	50.6	49.4	49.1	48.4	47.6	47.3	47.2	47.0	47.5	48.2	48.6
2009	46.3	46.0	45.7	44.9	44.6	44.1	43.3	43.1	43.2	43.4	44.6	45.3	44.5
2010	44.0	44.1	44.3	44.5	44.3	43.9	43.3	43.4	43.2	43.9	45.2	46.1	44.2
2011	45.0	45.0	45.2	45.6	45.4	45.0	44.3	44.0	44.3	45.1	46.2	46.3	45.1
Wholesale Trade													
2000	6.9	6.9	7.0	7.0	7.0	6.8	6.8	6.8	6.8	6.9	7.1	6.9	6.9
2001	6.6	6.6	6.7	7.0	7.0	6.9	6.8	6.9	6.8	7.1	7.2	7.2	6.9
2002	7.1	7.1	7.1	7.2	7.2	7.2	7.2	7.3	7.4	7.5	7.5	7.5	7.3
2003	7.2	7.2	7.4	7.4	7.4	7.3	7.2	7.3	7.4	7.3	7.4	7.5	7.3
2004	7.3	7.4	7.4	7.6	7.6	7.4	7.5	7.5	7.5	7.6	7.9	7.9	7.6
2005	7.8	8.0	8.0	8.2	8.3	8.2	8.1	8.2	8.3	8.3	8.4	8.6	8.2
2006	8.4	8.5	8.6	8.6	8.7	8.7	8.6	8.6	8.7	8.5	8.4	8.6	8.6
2007	8.7	8.7	8.7	8.8	8.9	8.9	8.8	8.8	8.7	8.7	8.7	8.8	8.8
2008	8.5	8.5	8.5	8.4	8.3	8.2	8.1	8.0	8.0	8.0	7.8	7.7	8.2
2009	7.4	7.4	7.3	7.3	7.2	7.3	7.2	7.2	7.2	7.2	7.1	7.2	7.3
2010	7.1	7.1	7.2	7.2	7.2	7.2	7.1	7.1	7.1	7.2	7.2	7.2	7.2
2011	7.3	7.3	7.4	7.4	7.3	7.3	7.3	7.3	7.3	7.4	7.4	7.4	7.3
Retail Trade													
2000	38.3	38.5	38.4	39.0	38.8	38.7	37.6	37.8	37.7	38.4	39.9	40.7	38.7
2001	37.9	37.8	38.1	37.7	37.4	37.0	36.4	36.4	36.3	37.1	38.4	39.3	37.5
2002	38.0	37.7	38.0	37.6	37.3	37.0	36.4	36.6	36.7	36.9	38.1	39.1	37.5
2003	37.6	37.3	37.5	37.3	37.1	36.8	36.1	36.4	36.5	37.2	38.3	39.5	37.3
2004	38.5	38.5	38.6	38.3	38.2	38.2	38.1	38.1	38.1	38.8	40.0	40.9	38.7
2005	39.3	39.5	39.7	39.6	39.4	39.1	38.7	38.5	38.4	38.5	39.2	39.7	39.1
2006	38.5	38.5	38.9	38.9	38.8	38.6	37.8	37.8	37.6	37.8	39.1	39.6	38.5
2007	39.1	38.9	39.1	38.3	38.3	37.9	37.5	37.3	37.1	37.4	38.5	39.5	38.2
2008	38.8	38.6	38.7	37.7	37.5	37.0	36.3	36.1	36.0	35.8	36.4	36.9	37.2
2009	35.6	35.4	35.2	34.4	34.2	33.7	33.1	32.9	32.9	33.2	34.4	34.8	34.2
2010	33.8	33.9	34.0	34.1	33.9	33.6	33.1	33.2	33.0	33.6	34.7	35.4	33.9
2011	34.4	34.4	34.5	34.9	34.8	34.4	33.8	33.5	33.7	34.4	35.5	35.5	34.5
Transportation and Utilities													
2000	3.4	3.4	3.4	3.4	3.3	3.3	3.3	3.4	3.4	3.3	3.3	3.5	3.4
2001	3.2	3.4	3.4	3.4	3.3	3.3	3.3	3.2	3.3	3.3	3.3	3.4	3.3
2002	3.2	3.2	3.2	3.2	3.2	3.2	3.2	3.1	3.2	3.1	3.2	3.3	3.2
2003	3.2	3.1	3.1	3.2	3.2	3.2	3.3	3.3	3.3	3.3	3.4	3.7	3.3
2004	3.5	3.6	3.7	3.6	3.6	3.6	3.7	3.7	3.7	3.9	4.0	4.0	3.7
2005	3.7	3.7	3.8	3.8	3.8	3.8	3.8	3.8	3.8	3.8	4.1	4.2	3.8
2006	3.8	3.8	3.8	3.9	3.9	3.8	3.7	3.7	3.8	3.8	3.9	4.3	3.9
2007	3.9	3.7	3.8	3.7	3.6	3.6	3.5	3.4	3.4	3.4	3.5	3.8	3.6
2008	3.3	3.3	3.4	3.3	3.3	3.3	3.2	3.2	3.2	3.2	3.3	3.6	3.3
2009	3.3	3.2	3.2	3.2	3.2	3.1	3.0	3.0	3.1	3.0	3.1	3.3	3.1
2010	3.1	3.1	3.1	3.2	3.2	3.1	3.1	3.1	3.1	3.1	3.3	3.5	3.2
2011	3.3	3.3	3.3	3.3	3.3	3.3	3.2	3.2	3.3	3.3	3.3	3.4	3.3
Information													
2000	4.3	4.2	4.3	4.4	4.3	4.4	4.6	4.6	4.5	4.5	4.5	4.5	4.4
2001	4.5	4.5	4.4	4.3	4.4	4.5	4.4	4.4	4.3	4.2	4.3	4.3	4.4
2002	4.3	4.3	4.3	4.3	4.3	4.3	4.3	4.2	4.2	4.3	4.3	4.3	4.3
2003	4.3	4.3	4.3	4.2	4.3	4.3	4.3	4.4	4.3	4.2	4.3	4.3	4.3
2004	4.2	4.2	4.2	4.1	4.3	4.3	4.2	4.1	4.1	4.1	4.2	4.2	4.2
2005	4.1	4.2	4.2	4.3	4.3	4.4	4.4	4.4	4.3	4.3	4.4	4.4	4.3
2006	4.2	4.3	4.3	4.3	4.3	4.3	4.4	4.5	4.4	4.6	4.6	4.6	4.4
2007	4.4	4.3	4.3	4.3	4.2	4.2	4.1	4.1	4.1	4.1	4.1	4.0	4.2
2008	4.0	4.0	4.0	3.9	3.9	3.9	3.8	3.8	3.8	3.7	3.6	3.6	3.8
2009	3.6	3.6	3.5	3.5	3.4	3.5	3.4	3.4	3.4	3.4	3.4	3.4	3.5
2010	3.4	3.4	3.3	3.3	3.4	3.4	3.4	3.4	3.4	3.4	3.5	3.5	3.4
2011	3.4	3.5	3.5	3.5	3.4	3.4	3.4	3.4	3.4	3.4	3.4	3.4	3.4
Financial Activities													
2000	12.9	12.9	13.0	13.3	13.5	13.6	13.2	13.0	12.9	13.0	13.0	13.0	13.1
2001	12.9	12.9	13.0	13.1	13.1	13.3	13.2	13.3	13.3	13.4	13.6	13.7	13.2
2002	13.7	13.7	13.7	13.6	13.5	13.7	13.7	13.8	13.7	13.7	13.8	14.0	13.7
2003	13.7	13.6	13.6	13.8	13.8	13.8	14.1	14.1	14.0	14.1	14.1	14.3	13.9
2004	14.1	14.3	14.4	14.5	14.5	14.7	15.0	15.0	15.1	15.4	15.7	15.8	14.9
2005	15.4	15.5	15.4	15.6	15.6	15.7	15.7	15.9	15.9	16.2	16.3	16.5	15.8
2006	16.1	16.2	16.3	16.2	16.2	16.3	16.2	16.1	16.1	16.3	16.3	16.5	16.2
2007	16.0	16.0	16.1	16.4	16.4	16.3	16.2	16.2	16.3	16.5	16.4	16.5	16.3
2008	16.3	16.3	16.2	15.8	15.7	15.7	15.4	15.3	15.2	15.1	15.0	15.0	15.6
2009	14.5	14.4	14.3	14.2	14.2	14.2	14.0	13.9	13.9	13.9	13.9	13.8	14.1
2010	13.6	13.6	13.6	13.7	13.6	13.6	13.7	13.7	13.6	13.7	13.8	13.9	13.7
2011	13.8	13.9	14.0	14.0	14.0	14.0	14.0	14.0	13.9	13.9	14.0	14.0	14.0

Employment by Industry: North Port–Bradenton–Sarasota, FL, Selected Years, 2000–2011—*Continued*

(Numbers in thousands, not seasonally adjusted)

Industry and year	January	February	March	April	May	June	July	August	September	October	November	December	Annual average
Professional and Business Services													
2000	21.9	22.6	23.3	21.4	21.7	23.3	24.2	25.4	25.4	25.2	25.2	25.5	23.8
2001	22.4	24.0	24.5	24.2	25.6	25.2	24.7	25.1	24.8	26.4	27.0	27.5	25.1
2002	25.6	27.9	30.0	32.8	31.9	31.0	30.7	30.5	30.6	30.5	29.1	28.3	29.9
2003	28.6	28.8	29.0	29.3	30.1	33.6	30.5	31.7	32.4	33.0	34.0	34.7	31.3
2004	31.4	32.7	33.5	34.3	35.2	36.5	36.8	37.5	38.1	38.8	38.7	40.1	36.1
2005	39.1	40.2	40.7	40.5	41.2	41.7	41.9	42.1	42.1	41.7	41.8	43.0	41.3
2006	40.9	42.2	43.7	42.4	42.8	43.7	42.7	42.5	42.8	40.9	40.8	40.4	42.2
2007	38.7	39.5	40.1	38.8	39.3	39.9	38.0	38.7	38.5	37.2	38.0	38.6	38.8
2008	36.6	37.8	38.4	36.9	37.2	37.3	36.9	37.1	37.1	36.3	36.3	35.9	37.0
2009	34.2	34.3	34.7	33.8	34.0	34.6	33.6	33.7	33.7	34.0	34.0	34.2	34.1
2010	32.4	32.6	33.0	33.0	34.4	34.5	33.3	33.5	32.6	32.4	33.1	33.5	33.2
2011	31.9	33.2	33.3	33.8	33.6	33.8	33.6	33.5	32.5	33.6	34.3	33.9	33.4
Education and Health Services													
2000	35.1	35.5	35.8	36.3	36.0	36.5	35.6	35.8	36.3	36.7	37.0	37.1	36.1
2001	35.2	35.6	35.8	35.5	35.4	35.7	35.0	35.2	35.6	35.5	35.7	36.1	35.5
2002	35.4	35.5	35.8	35.8	36.0	36.1	36.0	36.5	36.9	37.3	37.8	38.1	36.4
2003	37.4	37.8	38.1	37.8	38.1	38.0	37.4	37.7	38.1	38.3	38.6	38.6	38.0
2004	38.2	38.5	38.7	38.8	39.1	39.0	38.6	38.9	39.2	39.6	39.9	40.1	39.1
2005	39.1	39.4	39.6	39.3	39.5	39.4	39.1	39.3	39.5	39.6	39.9	40.3	39.5
2006	39.5	40.0	40.3	40.2	40.4	40.4	40.0	40.3	40.5	40.3	40.7	41.1	40.3
2007	40.8	41.6	41.5	41.3	41.3	41.3	41.0	41.3	41.6	41.7	42.0	42.2	41.5
2008	42.5	43.0	43.2	42.7	42.7	42.4	41.9	42.1	42.4	42.7	43.1	43.3	42.7
2009	43.3	43.3	43.4	43.2	43.1	42.8	42.3	42.7	42.4	43.3	43.6	43.9	43.1
2010	43.3	43.7	44.0	44.1	43.8	43.4	43.2	43.4	43.4	43.7	43.9	44.1	43.7
2011	44.0	44.4	44.6	44.8	44.8	44.5	44.2	44.4	44.8	45.0	45.4	45.6	44.7
Leisure and Hospitality													
2000	29.5	30.1	30.8	31.6	31.1	30.6	29.1	28.9	28.7	29.5	30.0	30.4	30.0
2001	30.2	30.9	31.6	31.6	30.8	30.0	29.6	29.8	29.5	30.3	31.4	31.9	30.6
2002	31.2	31.7	32.5	31.6	31.0	31.1	30.5	30.7	30.4	30.9	32.2	33.2	31.4
2003	32.2	32.9	33.8	33.1	32.6	32.0	30.9	30.9	30.5	30.8	32.1	32.9	32.1
2004	33.0	33.4	34.3	34.3	33.6	32.9	32.6	32.4	32.0	32.7	33.6	34.4	33.3
2005	34.5	35.0	35.8	35.4	34.8	34.2	33.1	33.2	32.9	33.2	34.2	34.5	34.2
2006	34.3	35.0	35.8	35.7	35.2	34.8	34.0	33.9	33.4	33.8	34.8	35.6	34.7
2007	35.4	36.4	37.5	37.1	36.4	35.5	34.3	34.2	33.6	34.0	34.9	35.5	35.4
2008	35.3	36.0	36.5	35.8	34.8	33.9	32.7	32.5	31.9	32.4	33.2	33.9	34.1
2009	34.2	34.7	35.4	34.9	34.1	33.0	32.2	31.9	31.3	32.2	33.1	33.6	33.4
2010	33.6	34.4	35.4	35.0	34.1	33.3	32.3	32.1	31.7	32.2	33.1	33.3	33.4
2011	33.7	34.5	35.2	35.3	34.4	33.5	32.6	32.4	32.1	32.4	33.2	33.7	33.6
Other Services													
2000	12.3	12.3	12.4	12.5	12.6	12.9	12.5	12.5	12.6	12.7	12.7	12.8	12.6
2001	12.5	12.7	12.7	12.7	12.7	12.8	12.8	12.9	12.9	12.9	13.0	13.1	12.8
2002	13.3	13.4	13.3	13.4	13.4	13.4	13.1	13.1	13.2	13.3	13.4	13.5	13.3
2003	13.4	13.6	13.6	13.2	13.2	13.1	12.9	12.8	12.9	12.9	12.9	13.0	13.1
2004	13.2	12.8	13.4	13.0	13.1	13.2	13.2	13.2	13.1	12.9	13.0	13.1	13.1
2005	13.3	13.3	13.4	13.1	13.1	13.1	12.9	12.9	13.1	13.0	13.0	13.1	13.1
2006	13.3	13.5	13.7	13.6	13.7	13.8	13.4	13.6	13.8	13.8	14.1	14.1	13.7
2007	13.8	13.8	14.0	13.7	13.6	13.9	13.5	13.6	13.7	14.0	14.3	14.5	13.9
2008	14.4	14.6	14.7	14.1	14.0	13.7	13.3	13.1	12.9	12.7	12.4	12.3	13.5
2009	12.1	12.1	12.2	12.0	12.0	12.0	11.7	11.7	11.7	11.8	11.9	11.8	11.9
2010	11.7	11.7	11.9	11.8	11.6	11.4	11.3	11.2	11.2	11.1	11.2	11.2	11.4
2011	11.0	11.0	11.0	11.2	11.2	11.1	10.9	10.9	10.9	10.9	11.0	11.1	11.0
Government													
2000	24.3	24.5	24.6	24.7	25.4	22.5	22.2	24.3	24.1	24.4	24.7	24.9	24.2
2001	24.4	24.7	24.9	24.7	24.9	22.5	22.3	24.6	24.7	25.2	25.6	25.8	24.5
2002	25.3	25.7	25.8	25.7	25.9	23.4	23.2	25.6	25.8	25.9	26.2	26.2	25.4
2003	26.2	26.4	26.5	26.4	26.7	24.1	23.9	26.5	26.6	26.7	27.1	27.3	26.2
2004	26.7	27.0	27.0	27.1	27.3	24.6	24.3	27.0	26.8	27.0	27.2	27.4	26.6
2005	26.9	27.1	27.1	27.3	27.4	24.5	24.4	27.0	27.2	27.8	28.0	27.9	26.9
2006	27.8	27.9	28.1	28.4	28.5	25.6	25.3	28.2	28.6	28.6	29.3	29.3	28.0
2007	28.8	29.1	29.2	29.2	29.1	26.1	25.9	28.8	28.9	28.8	29.1	29.1	28.5
2008	29.0	29.2	29.5	29.5	29.5	26.5	26.3	29.2	29.2	29.0	28.8	28.8	28.7
2009	28.6	28.7	28.9	29.3	28.9	25.8	25.6	27.6	27.8	28.0	28.2	28.1	28.0
2010	27.8	27.9	28.0	28.0	29.5	25.5	25.2	26.7	27.1	27.5	27.6	27.6	27.4
2011	27.4	27.6	27.7	27.7	27.2	24.3	24.0	27.1	27.0	27.3	27.4	27.3	26.8

Employment by Industry: Oklahoma City, OK, Selected Years, 2000–2011

(Numbers in thousands, not seasonally adjusted)

Industry and year	January	February	March	April	May	June	July	August	September	October	November	December	Annual average
Total Nonfarm													
2000	522.3	525.3	530.2	533.6	538.3	537.1	529.0	534.5	543.7	543.2	546.7	546.1	535.8
2001	532.9	535.5	540.7	544.6	547.7	548.4	534.9	539.0	546.8	544.0	547.8	547.4	542.5
2002	527.4	533.0	537.8	539.9	543.9	541.2	530.9	535.9	542.7	541.0	543.1	542.9	538.3
2003	523.1	526.0	527.3	529.5	532.3	526.2	520.9	525.1	532.7	534.9	535.7	537.2	529.2
2004	524.5	528.7	534.2	538.6	540.5	536.8	532.3	536.8	545.3	546.2	547.6	550.6	538.5
2005	532.6	539.3	545.1	551.3	552.8	550.2	545.3	549.5	557.8	557.6	562.2	564.4	550.7
2006	549.3	554.6	560.0	560.9	563.5	562.5	552.6	557.6	565.2	564.1	565.7	568.5	560.4
2007	554.8	560.4	567.7	567.3	570.0	570.0	559.9	566.1	572.8	575.3	580.3	578.6	568.6
2008	565.2	571.4	575.4	577.4	580.0	575.5	567.7	572.7	580.9	581.4	583.3	581.9	576.1
2009	567.2	565.4	566.9	563.8	562.5	558.5	551.0	551.7	556.9	556.7	558.6	558.2	559.8
2010	544.1	546.9	553.4	557.6	561.2	558.2	552.0	556.0	562.9	567.1	570.2	572.1	558.5
2011	556.0	559.1	566.9	573.1	573.2	569.6	562.6	564.4	572.6	577.8	581.4	579.0	569.6
Total Private													
2000	416.6	418.1	421.7	425.3	428.5	431.1	431.6	434.4	435.7	434.0	436.1	436.6	429.1
2001	424.9	425.9	430.3	434.6	437.0	440.7	435.3	436.2	436.0	431.3	433.8	434.0	433.3
2002	417.2	420.8	424.8	427.1	430.9	432.0	430.6	432.8	431.2	427.4	429.2	429.1	427.8
2003	414.3	414.3	416.3	418.7	421.6	419.0	421.2	423.7	423.1	423.8	424.2	425.5	420.5
2004	416.7	417.4	422.5	427.0	428.7	428.4	431.2	431.5	432.0	432.8	433.8	436.2	428.2
2005	421.7	426.1	431.5	437.1	438.2	439.8	441.8	443.8	444.5	442.4	446.3	448.7	438.5
2006	436.8	439.2	444.3	445.1	447.4	450.6	448.1	450.3	451.3	446.9	448.2	451.3	446.6
2007	440.0	443.4	450.0	449.8	452.2	455.7	452.9	456.4	456.5	456.2	460.6	459.8	452.8
2008	451.3	453.5	456.7	458.8	460.8	462.3	460.9	461.7	462.7	461.3	462.2	461.5	459.5
2009	448.4	446.4	446.7	443.3	441.7	442.4	439.9	438.8	437.6	434.4	435.6	435.3	440.9
2010	426.1	425.9	431.3	435.1	436.8	439.2	438.8	441.3	442.4	445.3	448.0	449.5	438.3
2011	438.8	438.2	445.2	451.1	451.1	452.8	451.2	452.7	454.0	457.7	460.9	458.2	451.0
Goods-Producing													
2000	79.7	80.0	80.6	80.1	80.6	81.5	81.5	82.2	82.0	81.4	81.8	82.0	81.1
2001	79.4	79.3	80.0	80.0	81.1	81.6	80.3	78.6	79.6	77.0	77.8	77.2	79.3
2002	70.6	71.7	71.9	70.9	72.2	72.4	72.4	72.2	71.5	70.4	70.1	69.9	71.4
2003	68.8	68.6	68.8	69.1	69.4	67.3	70.5	70.7	70.2	70.2	69.7	70.0	69.4
2004	69.3	69.0	69.7	70.8	71.6	70.3	73.1	73.3	73.1	72.9	72.2	73.2	71.5
2005	70.5	72.0	73.2	73.5	73.7	73.1	75.4	75.6	75.5	76.0	76.3	77.3	74.3
2006	76.3	76.7	77.5	77.1	77.5	78.4	77.5	77.9	77.7	77.7	77.3	77.9	77.5
2007	75.4	75.5	76.9	77.1	77.4	78.8	78.6	79.4	79.0	79.2	79.8	79.3	78.0
2008	78.5	79.0	79.6	80.3	81.0	82.1	82.0	82.1	81.6	81.4	80.7	79.7	80.7
2009	77.6	75.9	74.6	72.6	71.8	72.0	71.3	70.6	69.6	68.8	68.7	68.6	71.8
2010	67.6	67.1	68.1	69.1	69.7	70.6	70.9	71.4	71.6	73.1	72.8	73.6	70.5
2011	72.3	72.2	73.4	74.6	74.8	75.8	75.9	75.8	76.5	77.3	76.8	76.4	75.2
Mining and Logging													
2000	6.0	6.2	6.2	6.3	6.3	6.5	6.7	6.9	6.9	7.1	7.2	7.5	6.7
2001	7.1	7.3	7.5	7.4	7.5	7.7	7.7	7.7	7.5	7.5	7.4	7.4	7.5
2002	7.4	7.5	7.5	7.3	7.5	7.5	7.6	7.6	7.5	7.4	7.4	7.4	7.5
2003	7.5	7.5	7.5	7.7	7.7	7.8	8.1	8.2	8.2	8.3	8.3	8.4	7.9
2004	8.5	8.5	8.6	8.8	8.9	9.1	9.2	9.2	9.3	9.4	9.5	9.6	9.1
2005	9.7	9.8	10.0	10.1	10.2	10.3	10.6	10.7	10.9	11.0	11.3	11.7	10.5
2006	11.7	12.0	12.2	12.4	12.6	12.8	12.7	13.0	13.1	13.3	13.5	13.8	12.8
2007	13.7	13.7	13.7	13.9	14.0	14.2	14.6	14.9	14.9	15.1	15.3	15.3	14.4
2008	14.9	15.1	15.2	15.6	15.9	16.3	16.4	16.6	16.5	16.8	16.7	16.3	16.0
2009	15.9	15.2	14.5	13.6	13.3	13.2	12.9	12.8	12.6	12.6	12.8	13.1	13.5
2010	13.1	13.2	13.5	13.7	13.9	14.2	14.4	14.6	14.7	15.3	15.1	15.5	14.3
2011	15.6	15.9	16.0	16.6	16.8	17.1	17.3	17.4	17.5	17.7	17.8	17.9	17.0
Construction													
2000	21.5	21.4	21.9	22.2	22.7	23.2	23.0	23.3	23.0	23.1	22.8	22.5	22.6
2001	21.7	22.2	22.8	23.4	24.0	24.6	24.3	24.5	23.9	23.2	22.6	22.3	23.3
2002	21.6	21.4	21.7	21.6	22.1	22.5	22.7	22.6	22.2	22.0	21.8	21.8	22.0
2003	21.5	21.4	21.6	22.0	22.8	23.6	23.6	23.7	23.3	23.2	22.8	22.9	22.7
2004	22.3	22.1	22.7	23.1	23.4	24.0	24.5	24.5	24.3	23.9	23.4	23.9	23.5
2005	23.1	23.2	24.1	24.6	24.9	25.7	26.0	26.1	26.0	26.1	26.2	26.4	25.2
2006	25.8	25.9	26.6	26.2	26.5	27.2	26.7	26.9	26.7	26.3	26.1	26.2	26.4
2007	25.3	25.2	26.2	26.3	26.3	27.3	26.9	27.2	27.0	26.9	27.2	26.8	26.6
2008	26.6	26.9	27.4	27.5	27.9	28.4	28.5	28.3	28.1	27.7	27.4	27.1	27.7
2009	26.1	25.8	26.1	25.7	25.8	26.5	26.4	26.3	25.9	25.1	25.0	24.7	25.8
2010	23.9	23.4	24.1	24.7	25.0	25.5	25.7	25.8	25.7	26.3	26.0	26.2	25.2
2011	25.3	24.7	25.5	25.8	25.7	26.3	26.2	25.8	26.2	26.6	25.7	24.9	25.7
Manufacturing													
2000	52.2	52.4	52.5	51.6	51.6	51.8	51.8	52.0	52.1	51.2	51.8	52.0	51.9
2001	50.6	49.8	49.7	49.2	49.6	49.3	48.3	46.4	48.2	46.3	47.8	47.5	48.6
2002	41.6	42.8	42.7	42.0	42.6	42.4	42.1	42.0	41.8	41.0	40.9	40.7	41.9
2003	39.8	39.7	39.7	39.4	38.9	35.9	38.8	38.8	38.7	38.7	38.6	38.7	38.8
2004	38.5	38.4	38.4	38.9	39.3	37.2	39.4	39.6	39.5	39.6	39.3	39.7	39.0
2005	37.7	39.0	39.1	38.8	38.6	37.1	38.8	38.8	38.6	38.9	38.8	39.2	38.6
2006	38.8	38.8	38.7	38.5	38.4	38.4	38.1	38.0	37.9	38.1	37.7	37.9	38.3
2007	36.4	36.6	37.0	36.9	37.1	37.3	37.1	37.3	37.1	37.2	37.3	37.2	37.0
2008	37.0	37.0	37.0	37.2	37.2	37.4	37.1	37.2	37.0	36.9	36.6	36.3	37.0
2009	35.6	34.9	34.0	33.3	32.7	32.3	32.0	31.5	31.1	31.1	30.9	30.8	32.5
2010	30.6	30.5	30.5	30.7	30.8	30.9	30.8	31.0	31.2	31.5	31.7	31.9	31.0
2011	31.4	31.6	31.9	32.2	32.3	32.4	32.4	32.6	32.8	33.0	33.3	33.6	32.5

Employment by Industry: Oklahoma City, OK, Selected Years, 2000–2011—*Continued*

(Numbers in thousands, not seasonally adjusted)

Industry and year	January	February	March	April	May	June	July	August	September	October	November	December	Annual average
Service-Providing													
2000	442.6	445.3	449.6	453.5	457.7	455.6	447.5	452.3	461.7	461.8	464.9	464.1	454.7
2001	453.5	456.2	460.7	464.6	466.6	466.8	454.6	460.4	467.2	467.0	470.0	470.2	463.2
2002	456.8	461.3	465.9	469.0	471.7	468.8	458.5	463.7	471.2	470.6	473.0	473.0	467.0
2003	454.3	457.4	458.5	460.4	462.9	458.9	450.4	454.4	462.5	464.7	466.0	467.2	459.8
2004	455.2	459.7	464.5	467.8	468.9	466.5	459.2	463.5	472.2	473.3	475.4	477.4	467.0
2005	462.1	467.3	471.9	477.8	479.1	477.1	469.9	473.9	482.3	481.6	485.9	487.1	476.3
2006	473.0	477.9	482.5	483.8	486.0	484.1	475.1	479.7	487.5	486.4	488.4	490.6	482.9
2007	479.4	484.9	490.8	490.2	492.6	491.2	481.3	486.7	493.8	496.1	500.5	499.3	490.6
2008	486.7	492.4	495.8	497.1	499.0	493.4	485.7	490.6	499.3	500.0	502.6	502.2	495.4
2009	489.6	489.5	492.3	491.2	490.7	486.5	479.7	481.1	487.3	487.9	489.9	489.6	487.9
2010	476.5	479.8	485.3	488.5	491.5	487.6	481.1	484.6	491.3	494.0	497.4	498.5	488.0
2011	483.7	486.9	493.5	498.5	498.4	493.8	486.7	488.6	496.1	500.5	504.6	502.6	494.5
Trade, Transportation, and Utilities													
2000	101.3	99.9	99.8	100.6	101.2	101.1	101.2	102.1	102.0	102.6	105.1	106.6	102.0
2001	101.7	100.0	100.1	100.8	100.8	100.9	99.8	99.8	99.5	100.1	101.9	103.0	100.7
2002	99.0	98.3	99.3	98.7	98.9	98.9	98.7	99.1	98.8	98.0	100.3	101.2	99.1
2003	96.6	95.5	95.9	96.0	96.4	96.4	95.8	96.5	96.5	97.5	99.5	101.0	97.0
2004	96.3	95.7	96.3	96.1	96.3	96.5	96.0	95.8	95.7	96.8	99.3	100.9	96.8
2005	96.4	96.4	97.1	97.8	98.0	98.0	98.6	99.3	99.5	100.0	102.6	104.2	99.0
2006	99.1	99.0	99.5	99.3	99.7	100.1	99.4	100.1	100.4	100.4	102.5	104.0	100.3
2007	100.3	100.3	102.0	100.9	101.3	101.2	100.4	100.7	100.3	100.7	102.9	103.3	101.2
2008	100.4	99.8	100.5	99.8	99.9	100.1	100.5	100.4	100.8	100.9	102.5	102.9	100.7
2009	98.9	97.9	98.2	97.5	97.4	97.6	96.8	96.7	96.3	96.5	97.9	98.4	97.5
2010	94.8	94.4	95.5	95.9	96.4	97.2	97.4	97.6	97.1	98.3	100.3	101.5	97.2
2011	97.9	97.4	98.8	99.3	99.3	99.7	99.4	99.8	99.1	100.5	103.9	104.4	100.0
Wholesale Trade													
2000	21.9	21.8	21.8	22.0	22.0	22.1	22.1	22.4	22.3	22.0	22.1	22.2	22.1
2001	21.3	21.4	21.5	21.5	21.6	22.0	21.9	22.0	21.9	21.8	21.8	22.0	21.7
2002	21.4	21.3	21.4	21.2	21.4	21.5	21.7	21.6	21.6	21.3	21.3	21.3	21.4
2003	21.2	21.1	21.2	21.0	21.0	21.0	20.9	20.9	21.0	21.0	20.9	21.1	21.0
2004	20.8	20.7	20.6	20.6	20.8	21.2	21.2	21.1	21.0	21.2	21.3	21.4	21.0
2005	21.1	21.2	21.3	21.4	21.4	21.6	22.0	22.0	21.9	22.0	22.2	22.4	21.7
2006	22.2	22.4	22.5	22.4	22.6	22.8	22.8	22.9	23.0	23.0	23.0	23.2	22.7
2007	22.8	22.9	23.0	23.0	23.0	23.1	22.9	22.7	22.6	23.0	22.9	23.1	22.9
2008	22.9	22.8	22.9	22.9	22.9	23.1	23.1	22.9	23.0	23.0	23.0	22.9	23.0
2009	22.5	22.4	22.3	22.0	21.8	21.8	21.8	21.7	21.6	21.8	21.6	21.6	21.9
2010	21.5	21.5	21.5	21.7	21.8	22.0	22.2	22.3	22.4	22.7	22.8	22.9	22.1
2011	22.8	22.8	23.1	23.3	23.3	23.6	23.6	23.6	23.7	23.8	23.9	24.0	23.5
Retail Trade													
2000	62.2	61.0	61.0	61.3	61.7	61.7	61.8	62.4	62.4	63.2	65.6	67.0	62.6
2001	62.9	61.4	61.4	61.4	61.5	61.5	60.4	60.3	60.3	61.2	63.1	64.2	61.6
2002	61.4	60.8	61.7	61.2	61.2	61.1	60.5	61.0	60.9	60.6	63.1	64.3	61.5
2003	60.0	59.0	59.2	59.7	60.1	60.2	59.6	60.3	60.3	61.1	63.3	64.7	60.6
2004	60.2	59.8	60.3	60.2	60.2	60.0	59.5	59.4	59.2	59.9	62.3	63.6	60.4
2005	60.0	59.8	60.3	60.7	60.8	60.7	60.6	61.2	61.4	61.9	64.2	65.4	61.4
2006	61.1	60.8	61.1	61.1	61.2	61.4	60.8	61.3	61.3	61.1	63.1	64.2	61.5
2007	61.1	60.9	62.2	61.3	61.7	61.6	61.2	61.7	61.5	61.9	64.3	64.4	62.0
2008	62.5	62.0	62.4	61.5	61.5	61.4	61.8	61.9	62.2	62.3	63.8	64.1	62.3
2009	60.8	60.0	60.2	59.9	60.1	60.2	59.6	59.7	59.6	59.4	61.0	61.4	60.2
2010	58.6	58.2	59.1	59.2	59.7	60.1	60.1	60.2	59.6	60.6	62.3	63.0	60.1
2011	60.1	59.6	60.5	60.8	60.7	60.6	60.4	60.8	60.0	61.2	64.5	64.7	61.2
Transportation and Utilities													
2000	17.2	17.1	17.0	17.3	17.5	17.3	17.3	17.3	17.3	17.4	17.4	17.4	17.3
2001	17.5	17.2	17.2	17.9	17.7	17.4	17.5	17.5	17.3	17.1	17.0	16.8	17.3
2002	16.2	16.2	16.2	16.3	16.3	16.3	16.5	16.5	16.3	16.1	15.9	15.6	16.2
2003	15.4	15.4	15.5	15.3	15.3	15.2	15.3	15.3	15.2	15.4	15.3	15.2	15.3
2004	15.3	15.2	15.4	15.3	15.3	15.3	15.3	15.3	15.5	15.7	15.7	15.9	15.4
2005	15.3	15.4	15.5	15.7	15.8	15.7	16.0	16.1	16.2	16.1	16.2	16.4	15.9
2006	15.8	15.8	15.9	15.8	15.9	15.9	15.8	15.9	16.1	16.3	16.4	16.6	16.0
2007	16.4	16.5	16.8	16.6	16.6	16.5	16.3	16.3	16.2	15.8	15.7	15.8	16.3
2008	15.0	15.0	15.2	15.4	15.5	15.6	15.6	15.6	15.6	15.6	15.7	15.9	15.5
2009	15.6	15.5	15.7	15.6	15.5	15.6	15.4	15.3	15.1	15.3	15.3	15.4	15.4
2010	14.7	14.7	14.9	15.0	14.9	15.1	15.1	15.1	15.1	15.0	15.2	15.6	15.0
2011	15.0	15.0	15.2	15.2	15.3	15.5	15.4	15.4	15.4	15.5	15.5	15.7	15.3
Information													
2000	12.8	13.2	13.3	13.9	13.8	14.0	14.2	14.2	14.4	14.4	14.4	14.4	13.9
2001	14.6	14.8	14.8	14.5	14.5	14.6	14.4	14.1	14.2	14.4	14.3	14.3	14.5
2002	14.3	14.4	14.2	14.1	14.2	14.1	14.0	14.0	13.8	13.7	13.9	13.8	14.0
2003	13.6	13.5	13.5	13.4	13.5	13.4	13.4	13.4	13.3	13.4	13.5	13.7	13.5
2004	13.5	13.4	13.3	13.5	13.5	13.8	14.0	13.8	13.5	13.8	13.7	13.7	13.6
2005	13.6	13.7	13.6	13.7	13.7	13.5	13.6	13.3	13.0	12.9	13.0	13.0	13.4
2006	12.4	12.5	12.6	13.5	13.4	13.3	13.5	13.5	13.4	13.2	13.2	13.7	13.2
2007	13.1	12.7	12.4	12.4	12.4	12.5	12.4	12.4	12.4	12.4	12.5	12.5	12.5
2008	12.5	12.6	12.5	12.7	12.7	12.7	12.8	12.7	12.5	12.4	12.5	12.4	12.6
2009	12.3	12.2	12.2	12.2	12.1	11.9	11.8	11.6	11.3	11.1	11.1	11.0	11.7
2010	11.0	10.9	10.7	10.7	10.6	10.5	10.4	10.3	10.2	10.1	10.2	10.1	10.5
2011	10.2	10.1	10.0	10.1	10.1	10.1	10.0	10.0	9.9	9.8	9.8	9.8	10.0

Employment by Industry: Oklahoma City, OK, Selected Years, 2000–2011—*Continued*

(Numbers in thousands, not seasonally adjusted)

Industry and year	January	February	March	April	May	June	July	August	September	October	November	December	Annual average
Financial Activities													
2000	33.5	33.7	33.6	33.5	33.6	33.7	33.7	33.9	33.8	33.8	33.9	34.0	33.7
2001	33.4	33.6	33.8	34.1	34.3	34.6	34.6	34.9	34.7	34.8	34.8	34.8	34.4
2002	34.8	34.8	34.9	34.9	35.1	35.6	35.6	35.8	35.6	35.5	35.6	35.8	35.3
2003	34.3	34.4	34.5	34.7	34.8	35.0	35.0	35.3	35.2	35.2	35.0	35.1	34.9
2004	34.8	34.9	35.1	35.8	35.7	35.9	35.6	35.5	35.3	35.3	35.2	35.3	35.4
2005	34.1	34.1	34.3	34.3	34.5	34.8	34.9	34.8	34.7	34.2	34.3	35.0	34.5
2006	34.6	34.5	34.6	34.2	34.4	34.4	34.5	34.6	34.5	34.5	34.4	34.4	34.5
2007	34.7	35.1	34.9	34.4	34.5	34.5	34.3	34.3	33.9	33.9	33.9	33.9	34.4
2008	34.2	34.1	34.1	34.2	34.4	34.4	34.5	34.2	34.0	33.9	34.0	34.1	34.2
2009	33.3	33.2	33.3	33.2	33.3	33.4	33.3	33.3	33.1	33.1	33.1	33.3	33.2
2010	32.8	32.8	32.9	32.7	32.9	32.9	32.8	32.7	32.5	32.6	32.6	32.8	32.8
2011	32.0	32.1	32.3	32.3	32.4	32.5	32.6	32.9	32.8	32.5	32.3	32.3	32.4
Professional and Business Services													
2000	62.8	63.5	64.8	65.8	66.5	67.7	68.4	68.3	69.0	67.7	67.4	68.0	66.7
2001	65.7	66.4	67.7	69.1	68.9	70.3	68.7	70.3	70.8	68.3	68.0	68.5	68.6
2002	65.6	67.0	68.1	69.4	69.4	69.5	67.8	68.5	68.5	67.0	66.7	66.8	67.9
2003	63.3	63.5	63.7	64.5	65.2	65.0	65.0	65.5	65.7	65.6	65.3	65.1	64.8
2004	63.1	63.3	64.6	66.5	66.4	66.7	67.6	68.0	67.9	68.0	68.1	68.0	66.5
2005	65.3	66.5	67.5	70.0	69.9	71.2	71.1	72.2	72.2	70.9	71.6	71.0	70.0
2006	69.6	70.1	71.3	71.4	72.1	73.4	73.0	73.6	74.3	72.1	72.5	72.8	72.2
2007	71.3	72.6	73.7	74.0	74.6	75.9	74.6	75.7	76.4	75.6	76.7	76.9	74.8
2008	74.5	75.2	75.4	75.3	75.3	75.4	74.1	74.7	75.1	74.5	74.4	74.3	74.9
2009	71.1	71.3	70.9	69.9	68.7	68.9	68.7	68.6	69.3	68.5	68.4	68.4	69.4
2010	67.3	67.9	68.7	69.2	69.1	70.1	71.0	72.0	72.2	72.9	73.4	73.1	70.6
2011	71.1	71.0	71.9	73.4	73.2	73.1	73.8	73.1	73.2	74.2	74.6	74.0	73.1
Education and Health Services													
2000	56.7	57.2	57.5	58.5	59.1	58.6	58.4	58.9	59.8	59.3	59.6	59.3	58.6
2001	58.9	59.5	60.1	59.9	60.6	60.7	60.5	61.3	61.6	62.2	62.1	62.3	60.8
2002	61.2	62.1	62.6	63.8	64.5	64.3	64.6	65.4	65.5	65.7	66.4	66.4	64.4
2003	64.5	65.3	65.8	65.4	65.4	64.9	64.8	65.5	66.3	65.8	66.1	65.9	65.5
2004	66.8	67.4	68.1	67.9	67.7	67.1	66.6	67.1	68.0	68.5	68.5	68.6	67.7
2005	66.6	67.3	67.9	68.8	68.5	68.3	68.7	69.6	70.6	70.5	70.7	71.1	69.1
2006	68.5	69.3	69.6	70.0	70.2	70.7	70.1	70.6	71.2	70.9	70.7	70.9	70.2
2007	70.5	71.2	71.8	72.2	72.4	72.5	72.1	72.8	73.7	74.3	74.6	74.5	72.7
2008	73.4	74.3	74.4	75.4	75.7	75.1	75.3	76.0	76.5	76.8	77.0	77.0	75.6
2009	76.4	76.2	76.4	76.1	76.2	76.2	76.0	76.2	76.8	76.3	76.4	76.2	76.3
2010	75.4	75.7	76.1	76.7	76.6	76.4	75.5	76.1	77.1	77.6	77.8	77.7	76.6
2011	75.9	76.0	76.8	77.5	77.7	77.6	77.0	78.3	80.0	80.9	81.4	80.5	78.3
Leisure and Hospitality													
2000	46.3	47.1	48.4	48.9	49.6	50.1	50.0	50.5	50.3	50.6	49.7	48.0	49.1
2001	47.5	48.5	49.6	52.1	52.5	53.1	52.4	52.6	51.3	50.4	50.8	49.9	50.9
2002	48.6	49.3	50.4	51.3	52.5	52.9	53.1	53.4	53.1	53.0	52.2	51.1	51.7
2003	49.7	50.0	50.6	52.2	53.3	53.1	53.0	53.3	52.6	52.9	51.9	51.4	52.0
2004	49.9	50.6	52.0	53.0	54.0	54.4	54.8	54.8	55.4	54.7	54.0	53.6	53.4
2005	52.3	53.1	54.8	55.9	56.8	57.6	56.0	55.7	55.7	54.7	54.6	53.9	55.1
2006	53.5	54.2	56.0	56.7	56.9	56.8	56.9	57.0	56.8	55.3	54.9	54.8	55.8
2007	52.1	53.3	55.4	55.5	56.1	56.5	57.0	57.7	57.5	56.9	57.0	56.4	56.0
2008	54.7	55.1	56.6	57.2	57.8	58.3	57.6	57.5	58.1	57.4	57.2	57.3	57.1
2009	55.2	56.1	57.4	58.3	58.7	58.7	58.6	58.7	58.2	57.2	57.0	56.6	57.6
2010	54.7	54.6	56.6	58.0	58.7	58.6	58.2	58.6	59.1	58.0	58.1	57.9	57.6
2011	57.0	57.0	59.5	61.1	60.7	60.9	59.6	60.0	59.8	59.9	59.5	58.2	59.4
Other Services													
2000	23.5	23.5	23.7	24.0	24.1	24.4	24.2	24.3	24.4	24.2	24.2	24.3	24.1
2001	23.7	23.8	24.2	24.1	24.3	24.9	24.6	24.6	24.3	24.1	24.1	24.0	24.2
2002	23.1	23.2	23.4	24.0	24.1	24.3	24.4	24.4	24.4	24.1	24.0	24.1	24.0
2003	23.5	23.5	23.5	23.4	23.6	23.9	23.7	23.5	23.3	23.2	23.2	23.3	23.5
2004	23.0	23.1	23.4	23.4	23.5	23.7	23.5	23.2	23.1	22.8	22.8	22.9	23.2
2005	22.9	23.0	23.1	23.1	23.1	23.3	23.5	23.3	23.3	23.2	23.2	23.2	23.2
2006	22.8	22.9	23.2	22.9	23.2	23.5	23.2	23.0	23.0	22.8	22.7	22.8	23.0
2007	22.6	22.7	22.9	23.3	23.5	23.8	23.5	23.4	23.3	23.2	23.2	23.0	23.2
2008	23.1	23.4	23.6	23.9	24.0	24.2	24.1	24.1	24.1	24.0	23.9	23.8	23.9
2009	23.6	23.6	23.7	23.5	23.5	23.7	23.4	23.1	23.0	22.9	23.0	22.8	23.3
2010	22.5	22.5	22.7	22.8	22.8	22.9	22.6	22.6	22.6	22.7	22.8	22.8	22.7
2011	22.4	22.4	22.5	22.8	22.9	23.1	22.9	22.8	22.7	22.6	22.6	22.6	22.7
Government													
2000	105.7	107.2	108.5	108.3	109.8	106.0	97.4	100.1	108.0	109.2	110.6	109.5	106.7
2001	108.0	109.6	110.4	110.0	110.7	107.7	99.6	102.8	110.8	112.7	114.0	113.4	109.1
2002	110.2	112.2	113.0	112.8	113.0	109.2	100.3	103.1	111.5	113.6	113.9	113.8	110.6
2003	108.8	111.7	111.0	110.8	110.7	107.2	99.7	101.4	109.6	111.1	111.5	111.7	108.8
2004	107.8	111.3	111.7	111.6	111.8	108.4	101.1	105.3	113.3	113.4	113.8	114.4	110.3
2005	110.9	113.2	113.6	114.2	114.6	110.4	103.5	105.7	113.3	115.2	115.9	115.7	112.2
2006	112.5	115.4	115.7	115.8	116.1	111.9	104.5	107.3	113.9	117.2	117.5	117.2	113.8
2007	114.8	117.0	117.7	117.5	117.8	114.3	107.0	109.7	116.3	119.1	119.7	118.8	115.8
2008	113.9	117.9	118.7	118.6	119.2	113.2	106.8	111.0	118.2	120.1	121.1	120.4	116.6
2009	118.8	119.0	120.2	120.5	120.8	116.1	111.1	112.9	119.3	122.3	123.0	122.9	118.9
2010	118.0	121.0	122.1	122.5	124.4	119.0	113.2	114.7	120.5	121.8	122.2	122.6	120.2
2011	117.2	120.9	121.7	122.0	122.1	116.8	111.4	111.7	118.6	120.1	120.5	120.8	118.7

Employment by Industry: Omaha–Council Bluffs, NE–IA, Selected Years, 2000–2011

(Numbers in thousands, not seasonally adjusted)

Industry and year	January	February	March	April	May	June	July	August	September	October	November	December	Annual average
Total Nonfarm													
2000	428.5	429.8	432.1	437.5	442.9	449.1	445.0	446.0	446.6	445.7	447.8	448.6	441.6
2001	436.0	435.0	437.2	442.7	446.0	451.7	446.8	448.1	447.1	445.5	449.2	449.0	444.5
2002	432.9	434.1	435.8	440.1	443.1	446.1	440.1	440.6	439.8	438.9	441.3	440.2	439.4
2003	433.9	433.4	435.2	436.1	440.5	443.1	442.8	443.5	443.5	444.8	446.0	445.1	440.7
2004	435.2	432.8	436.9	439.4	444.0	446.8	442.7	443.5	443.3	443.9	446.9	447.2	441.9
2005	437.3	438.1	441.7	447.1	450.3	453.9	449.8	450.1	451.3	452.8	456.4	456.3	448.8
2006	444.8	446.9	450.6	454.3	459.2	462.7	457.3	457.7	460.4	460.9	463.9	463.4	456.8
2007	451.8	452.6	455.1	460.7	465.7	468.6	463.1	465.8	466.9	469.5	472.2	471.3	463.6
2008	461.3	461.7	464.1	469.0	474.5	474.5	469.3	471.3	471.1	474.3	474.1	471.5	469.8
2009	457.6	456.4	456.6	460.2	463.6	462.6	460.5	460.2	458.2	459.8	460.8	457.7	459.5
2010	446.6	445.8	449.5	456.9	461.7	462.9	459.1	460.2	456.9	462.4	462.9	462.9	457.3
2011	451.1	451.6	453.7	460.2	463.8	464.1	460.8	463.1	460.9	464.1	465.9	465.0	460.4
Total Private													
2000	373.6	374.8	377.3	381.9	387.1	393.1	391.3	392.6	391.6	389.6	391.4	392.1	386.4
2001	380.1	378.9	381.1	386.0	388.9	394.1	391.8	393.3	390.9	388.4	391.8	391.4	388.1
2002	375.9	376.5	378.4	382.7	385.4	388.3	385.3	386.0	383.4	380.9	383.2	382.4	382.4
2003	376.2	375.3	377.5	377.0	381.2	383.7	387.2	389.4	387.0	385.9	387.1	386.7	382.9
2004	376.6	374.0	377.8	380.1	384.3	387.2	385.8	386.7	384.5	383.9	386.9	387.4	382.9
2005	377.7	378.0	381.7	387.0	389.6	393.4	392.4	393.0	391.7	391.7	395.1	395.4	388.9
2006	384.1	385.9	389.6	392.7	397.2	401.0	399.7	400.0	399.6	399.2	402.0	402.1	396.1
2007	390.6	391.0	393.6	398.5	403.1	406.6	406.4	408.1	406.0	407.1	409.8	409.7	402.5
2008	399.6	399.7	402.4	406.0	411.4	412.6	411.2	412.2	409.1	410.2	409.8	408.0	407.7
2009	394.1	392.5	392.8	395.0	397.7	398.4	397.2	397.4	394.1	394.1	395.0	393.2	395.1
2010	382.1	381.0	383.7	390.4	394.4	396.4	396.5	397.2	393.2	396.0	396.5	397.2	392.1
2011	385.7	385.6	388.3	393.7	397.1	399.4	398.0	399.6	396.5	397.6	399.3	399.3	395.0
Goods-Producing													
2000	55.6	55.9	56.8	58.3	59.2	60.8	60.5	60.7	60.5	60.4	59.6	58.5	58.9
2001	56.2	55.8	56.2	58.2	59.0	60.1	60.4	60.0	59.6	58.9	58.4	57.6	58.4
2002	55.4	55.2	55.7	57.1	57.6	58.3	58.0	58.0	57.5	57.3	57.3	56.4	57.0
2003	55.9	55.3	55.6	56.7	58.1	59.2	60.7	60.9	60.2	60.1	59.6	58.8	58.4
2004	56.4	55.4	57.1	58.1	59.1	59.7	59.9	59.5	59.0	58.9	58.7	58.3	58.3
2005	56.0	55.6	57.1	58.5	58.7	60.0	60.3	60.1	59.6	59.4	59.2	58.2	58.6
2006	56.4	56.8	57.7	59.2	60.2	61.4	61.6	61.6	61.7	61.1	60.2	59.2	59.8
2007	56.6	55.7	56.2	57.6	58.7	59.8	60.2	60.6	59.9	60.5	60.2	59.1	58.8
2008	57.5	57.3	57.9	59.4	60.6	61.2	60.9	60.9	60.4	60.2	59.4	58.1	59.5
2009	54.9	54.5	54.5	55.8	56.2	56.5	56.5	56.3	55.7	55.0	54.7	53.1	55.3
2010	50.4	49.9	50.4	52.4	52.9	53.3	53.5	53.2	52.5	52.3	52.2	51.3	52.0
2011	49.0	49.0	49.8	51.1	51.7	52.7	52.9	52.2	52.3	51.9	52.3	51.3	51.4
Mining, Logging, and Construction													
2000	20.7	20.7	21.5	22.9	23.6	24.5	24.6	24.8	24.6	24.4	23.4	22.3	23.2
2001	20.4	20.3	20.8	22.8	23.8	24.5	24.8	24.8	24.3	24.2	23.8	23.1	23.1
2002	20.9	20.8	21.7	23.3	23.9	24.7	25.1	25.1	24.7	24.7	24.7	23.8	23.6
2003	23.0	22.4	22.8	24.0	25.1	25.9	27.6	27.8	27.1	27.0	26.6	25.8	25.4
2004	23.6	22.8	24.3	25.4	26.2	26.6	26.7	26.5	26.0	25.9	25.8	25.1	25.4
2005	23.1	23.0	24.3	25.5	25.9	27.0	27.2	27.3	26.8	26.7	26.4	25.3	25.7
2006	24.1	24.4	25.2	26.4	27.3	28.3	28.4	28.5	28.7	27.8	26.8	25.8	26.8
2007	23.7	22.7	23.1	24.4	25.3	26.2	26.3	26.6	26.1	26.5	26.2	25.2	25.2
2008	23.6	23.4	24.0	25.5	26.5	27.0	27.0	27.1	26.8	26.5	25.9	25.1	25.7
2009	22.6	22.4	22.8	24.4	24.8	25.2	25.3	25.1	24.5	23.8	23.3	21.8	23.8
2010	19.4	19.0	19.4	21.4	21.7	22.0	22.1	22.0	21.4	21.1	21.0	20.0	20.9
2011	18.2	18.0	18.7	19.7	20.2	21.2	21.3	20.8	20.8	20.4	20.6	19.2	19.9
Manufacturing													
2000	34.9	35.2	35.3	35.4	35.6	36.3	35.9	35.9	35.9	36.0	36.2	36.2	35.7
2001	35.8	35.5	35.4	35.4	35.2	35.6	35.6	35.2	35.3	34.7	34.6	34.5	35.2
2002	34.5	34.4	34.0	33.8	33.7	33.6	32.9	32.9	32.8	32.6	32.6	32.6	33.4
2003	32.9	32.9	32.8	32.7	33.0	33.3	33.1	33.1	33.1	33.1	33.0	33.0	33.0
2004	32.8	32.6	32.8	32.7	32.9	33.1	33.2	33.0	33.0	33.0	32.9	33.2	32.9
2005	32.9	32.6	32.8	33.0	32.8	33.0	33.1	32.8	32.8	32.7	32.8	32.9	32.9
2006	32.3	32.4	32.5	32.8	32.9	33.1	33.2	33.1	33.0	33.3	33.4	33.4	33.0
2007	32.9	33.0	33.1	33.2	33.4	33.6	33.9	34.0	33.8	34.0	34.0	33.9	33.6
2008	33.9	33.9	33.9	33.9	34.1	34.2	33.9	33.8	33.6	33.7	33.5	33.0	33.8
2009	32.3	32.1	31.7	31.4	31.4	31.3	31.2	31.2	31.2	31.2	31.4	31.3	31.5
2010	31.0	30.9	31.0	31.0	31.2	31.3	31.4	31.2	31.1	31.2	31.2	31.3	31.2
2011	30.8	31.0	31.1	31.4	31.5	31.5	31.6	31.4	31.5	31.5	31.7	32.1	31.4
Service-Providing													
2000	372.9	373.9	375.3	379.2	383.7	388.3	384.5	385.3	386.1	385.3	388.2	390.1	382.7
2001	379.8	379.2	381.0	384.5	387.0	391.6	386.4	388.1	387.5	386.6	390.8	391.4	386.2
2002	377.5	378.9	380.1	383.0	385.5	387.8	382.1	382.6	382.3	381.6	384.0	383.8	382.4
2003	378.0	378.1	379.6	379.4	382.4	383.9	382.1	382.6	383.3	384.7	386.4	386.3	382.2
2004	378.8	377.4	379.8	381.3	384.9	387.1	382.8	384.0	384.3	385.0	388.2	388.9	383.5
2005	381.3	382.5	384.6	388.6	391.6	393.9	389.5	390.0	391.7	393.4	397.2	398.1	390.2
2006	388.4	390.1	392.9	395.1	399.0	401.3	395.7	396.1	398.7	399.8	403.7	404.2	397.1
2007	395.2	396.9	398.9	403.1	407.0	408.8	402.9	405.2	407.0	409.0	412.0	412.2	404.9
2008	403.8	404.4	406.2	409.6	414.2	413.3	408.4	410.4	410.7	414.1	414.7	413.4	410.3
2009	402.7	401.9	402.1	404.4	407.4	406.1	404.0	403.9	402.5	404.8	406.1	404.6	404.2
2010	396.2	395.9	399.1	404.5	408.8	409.6	405.6	407.0	404.4	410.1	410.7	411.6	405.3
2011	402.1	402.6	403.9	409.1	412.1	411.4	407.9	410.9	408.6	412.2	413.6	413.7	409.0

Employment by Industry: Omaha–Council Bluffs, NE–IA, Selected Years, 2000–2011—*Continued*

(Numbers in thousands, not seasonally adjusted)

Industry and year	January	February	March	April	May	June	July	August	September	October	November	December	Annual average
Trade, Transportation, and Utilities													
2000	105.6	104.9	104.7	106.4	107.4	108.5	107.4	107.6	107.3	108.1	110.0	111.5	107.5
2001	107.2	106.3	106.2	106.7	107.2	107.5	106.6	107.4	107.8	107.7	110.3	111.5	107.7
2002	105.6	104.2	103.9	103.6	103.9	103.7	103.0	102.7	102.9	102.3	103.9	104.4	103.7
2003	99.3	98.2	98.9	97.2	97.8	97.9	97.9	97.9	98.0	97.9	99.2	100.1	98.4
2004	96.3	94.9	94.6	95.6	97.0	97.8	97.3	98.5	98.9	98.2	100.7	102.0	97.7
2005	98.1	97.8	98.2	98.1	99.4	99.4	98.8	99.2	99.3	99.8	101.9	102.8	99.4
2006	97.0	96.6	97.4	97.4	98.5	98.7	98.6	98.9	99.1	100.0	102.7	103.7	99.1
2007	98.6	98.1	98.7	99.2	100.0	100.1	99.8	100.3	100.4	100.6	103.2	103.9	100.2
2008	99.4	98.5	99.0	98.7	99.9	99.6	99.0	99.4	98.9	100.1	101.8	102.6	99.7
2009	96.7	95.3	95.1	94.3	95.0	94.5	94.0	94.3	93.9	94.8	96.6	97.1	95.1
2010	92.1	91.3	91.9	93.0	94.1	93.9	93.4	93.5	92.9	94.3	96.4	98.1	93.7
2011	92.6	91.9	92.4	93.1	93.7	93.4	92.6	92.6	91.8	92.6	95.4	96.6	93.2
Wholesale Trade													
2000	22.1	22.2	22.1	22.3	22.2	22.4	22.3	22.3	22.3	22.2	22.1	22.1	22.2
2001	21.6	21.7	21.7	22.0	22.0	22.1	22.0	21.7	21.6	21.6	21.5	21.4	21.7
2002	21.0	21.0	21.1	21.0	21.1	21.2	21.2	21.3	21.2	21.0	21.0	21.0	21.1
2003	20.7	20.7	20.9	20.8	20.6	20.5	20.4	20.3	20.2	19.6	19.7	19.6	20.3
2004	19.2	19.0	19.1	19.1	19.0	19.2	19.2	19.3	19.2	19.2	19.1	19.1	19.1
2005	18.6	18.6	18.8	18.6	18.6	18.6	18.7	18.5	18.3	18.4	18.4	18.4	18.5
2006	18.1	18.2	18.3	18.2	18.3	18.3	18.4	18.2	18.1	18.1	18.1	18.2	18.2
2007	17.7	17.7	17.8	18.0	18.0	18.3	18.3	18.3	18.4	18.4	18.5	18.6	18.2
2008	18.4	18.4	18.5	18.4	18.6	18.6	18.6	18.5	18.4	18.4	18.4	18.3	18.5
2009	18.0	17.9	17.8	17.9	17.9	17.9	18.0	17.9	17.7	17.8	17.9	17.9	17.9
2010	17.5	17.4	17.4	17.6	17.6	17.7	17.6	17.4	17.2	17.3	17.3	17.2	17.4
2011	16.9	16.9	17.0	17.0	17.1	17.1	17.1	16.9	17.0	17.1	17.1	17.0	17.0
Retail Trade													
2000	54.0	53.2	53.0	54.0	55.1	56.2	55.0	55.0	55.0	56.3	58.4	59.6	55.4
2001	54.8	53.5	53.7	54.4	54.9	55.1	54.7	55.6	56.1	56.6	59.1	60.0	55.7
2002	54.4	53.2	53.1	53.4	54.0	54.1	53.8	53.9	54.6	54.6	56.6	57.6	54.4
2003	53.2	52.0	52.3	51.3	51.5	51.4	51.2	51.1	51.2	52.1	53.7	54.6	52.1
2004	51.4	50.2	50.0	50.1	50.1	50.8	51.1	50.7	50.6	50.5	51.1	53.1	54.3	51.2
2005	50.8	50.1	50.2	50.6	51.2	51.0	50.8	51.0	50.9	51.8	53.6	54.4	51.4
2006	50.5	49.6	50.1	50.3	50.8	50.9	50.7	50.7	50.7	51.7	54.0	54.8	51.2
2007	50.9	50.2	50.6	51.1	51.9	51.9	51.7	51.7	51.5	52.4	54.5	55.3	52.0
2008	52.1	51.1	51.2	50.9	51.3	51.2	50.8	50.7	50.2	51.0	52.6	53.6	51.4
2009	50.1	49.1	49.0	49.1	49.8	49.8	49.5	49.5	49.2	50.0	51.5	51.6	49.9
2010	48.9	48.3	48.7	49.3	50.1	50.2	49.6	49.6	49.1	50.2	51.8	52.7	49.9
2011	49.3	48.7	49.0	49.6	50.0	49.9	49.4	49.2	48.3	48.9	51.6	52.3	49.7
Transportation and Utilities													
2000	29.5	29.5	29.6	30.1	30.1	29.9	30.1	30.3	30.0	29.6	29.5	29.8	29.8
2001	30.8	31.1	30.8	30.3	30.3	30.3	29.9	30.1	30.1	29.5	29.7	30.1	30.3
2002	30.2	30.0	29.7	29.2	28.8	28.4	28.0	27.5	27.1	26.7	26.3	25.8	28.1
2003	25.4	25.5	25.7	25.1	25.7	26.0	26.3	26.5	26.6	26.2	25.8	25.9	25.9
2004	25.7	25.7	25.5	26.4	27.2	27.5	27.4	28.6	29.2	27.9	28.5	28.6	27.4
2005	28.7	29.1	29.2	28.9	29.6	29.8	29.3	29.7	30.1	29.6	29.9	30.0	29.5
2006	28.4	28.8	29.0	28.9	29.4	29.5	29.5	30.0	30.3	30.2	30.6	30.7	29.6
2007	30.0	30.2	30.3	30.1	30.1	29.9	29.8	30.3	30.5	29.8	30.2	30.0	30.1
2008	28.9	29.0	29.3	29.4	30.0	29.8	29.6	30.2	30.3	30.7	30.8	30.7	29.9
2009	28.6	28.3	28.3	27.3	27.3	26.8	26.5	26.9	27.0	27.0	27.2	27.6	27.4
2010	25.7	25.6	25.8	26.1	26.4	26.0	26.2	26.5	26.6	26.8	27.3	28.2	26.4
2011	26.4	26.3	26.4	26.5	26.6	26.4	26.1	26.5	26.5	26.6	26.7	27.3	26.5
Information													
2000	15.7	15.5	15.3	15.3	15.1	15.0	14.9	14.9	14.8	14.8	14.9	14.9	15.1
2001	14.8	14.7	14.7	14.9	15.0	15.1	14.9	14.9	14.6	14.7	14.7	14.6	14.8
2002	14.4	14.4	14.4	14.3	14.4	14.4	14.4	14.3	14.1	14.0	14.1	14.1	14.3
2003	14.0	14.0	13.9	13.7	13.7	13.8	13.9	13.8	13.7	13.8	13.8	13.9	13.8
2004	13.6	13.6	13.6	13.4	13.5	13.5	13.6	13.5	13.4	13.4	13.4	13.5	13.5
2005	13.3	13.3	13.3	13.2	13.1	13.3	13.3	13.4	13.2	13.3	13.4	13.4	13.3
2006	13.1	13.0	13.0	13.0	13.1	13.1	13.0	12.8	12.7	12.5	12.6	12.6	12.9
2007	12.3	12.4	12.4	12.5	12.6	12.7	12.7	12.7	12.6	12.6	12.6	12.6	12.6
2008	12.3	12.3	12.3	12.4	12.4	12.3	12.3	12.1	12.0	12.0	12.0	11.9	12.2
2009	11.6	11.6	11.6	11.5	11.4	11.5	11.5	11.5	11.4	11.3	11.5	11.5	11.5
2010	11.3	11.3	11.2	11.2	11.3	11.3	11.2	11.2	11.1	11.1	11.1	11.2	11.2
2011	11.2	11.2	11.1	11.0	11.0	11.0	11.1	11.1	10.9	10.9	10.9	11.0	11.0
Financial Activities													
2000	35.2	35.2	35.3	35.3	35.6	35.9	35.7	35.8	36.0	36.0	36.0	36.4	35.7
2001	36.0	36.0	36.0	35.9	36.1	36.6	36.6	36.4	36.2	36.4	36.4	36.4	36.3
2002	35.6	35.9	36.1	36.3	36.8	37.1	37.5	37.6	37.4	37.7	38.0	38.2	37.0
2003	38.2	38.3	38.3	37.3	37.3	37.5	38.2	38.2	38.0	37.8	37.8	38.1	37.9
2004	37.6	37.6	38.0	37.3	37.4	37.6	37.5	37.4	37.1	37.5	37.4	37.5	37.5
2005	37.3	37.3	37.3	37.3	37.5	37.6	37.6	37.8	37.7	37.6	37.7	38.0	37.6
2006	37.8	38.1	38.2	38.3	38.6	39.1	39.2	39.4	39.1	39.1	39.3	39.6	38.8
2007	39.3	39.5	39.7	39.8	40.1	40.3	40.2	40.0	39.9	39.9	39.9	40.1	39.9
2008	40.2	40.5	40.7	40.5	40.8	41.0	40.9	40.7	40.6	40.7	40.8	40.8	40.7
2009	40.1	40.4	40.4	40.0	40.1	40.1	40.0	40.0	39.7	39.8	40.0	40.1	40.1
2010	40.0	40.1	40.3	40.1	40.3	40.5	40.7	40.8	40.5	40.9	40.8	40.9	40.5
2011	40.9	40.9	41.0	41.2	41.3	41.2	41.0	41.1	40.6	40.9	41.0	40.7	41.0

Employment by Industry: Omaha–Council Bluffs, NE–IA, Selected Years, 2000–2011—*Continued*

(Numbers in thousands, not seasonally adjusted)

Industry and year	January	February	March	April	May	June	July	August	September	October	November	December	Annual average
Professional and Business Services													
2000	56.4	56.8	57.6	59.3	59.4	60.9	60.8	61.3	60.7	60.0	60.2	61.2	59.6
2001	59.7	59.5	59.7	60.0	60.5	61.5	61.0	61.6	60.5	60.0	60.3	60.5	60.4
2002	58.0	58.6	59.1	59.6	59.5	60.1	58.1	58.3	57.4	57.7	57.9	57.7	58.5
2003	58.0	58.6	59.2	59.0	59.6	59.5	61.3	62.6	62.6	63.0	62.9	62.9	60.8
2004	61.2	61.0	61.7	60.9	61.1	61.3	60.5	60.9	59.7	60.0	60.3	60.2	60.7
2005	59.4	59.7	60.4	61.5	61.7	62.1	61.7	61.9	62.1	62.6	62.9	63.6	61.6
2006	61.8	62.3	63.1	63.4	63.7	64.6	64.4	64.1	63.9	63.3	63.1	63.2	63.4
2007	62.0	62.7	63.2	63.9	64.3	65.1	65.4	65.3	65.4	65.9	66.6		64.6
2008	64.8	64.8	65.1	66.1	66.3	66.4	65.8	66.1	65.5	65.5	65.2	64.7	65.5
2009	63.1	62.9	62.5	63.1	63.1	63.4	63.1	63.0	62.1	62.3	62.1	62.3	62.8
2010	61.2	60.7	60.9	62.5	62.9	63.4	63.9	64.3	63.9	64.5	64.3	64.5	63.1
2011	62.5	62.6	62.9	64.2	64.3	65.0	65.5	65.8	66.1	66.2	65.9	65.8	64.7
Education and Health Services													
2000	52.8	53.9	54.1	52.7	53.9	54.1	53.9	54.4	55.8	55.5	56.5	55.8	54.5
2001	54.3	54.7	55.4	55.8	55.3	56.1	55.4	55.9	57.0	56.9	58.0	57.6	56.0
2002	55.4	56.5	56.6	57.1	57.3	57.4	56.5	57.1	57.7	57.5	58.0	57.9	57.1
2003	58.0	58.2	58.0	58.1	58.0	58.2	57.6	58.1	58.3	58.2	59.3	59.0	58.3
2004	58.2	58.4	58.8	59.3	59.0	58.8	58.6	58.6	59.1	59.5	60.2	59.9	59.0
2005	58.5	59.1	59.3	60.3	59.9	60.0	59.9	59.8	60.5	60.8	62.0	61.9	60.2
2006	60.9	61.7	62.0	61.7	61.9	61.9	61.3	61.8	62.8	62.6	63.9	63.3	62.2
2007	62.7	63.6	63.8	64.0	64.3	64.5	64.3	65.1	65.4	65.9	66.4	66.4	64.7
2008	65.7	66.7	66.9	67.2	67.6	67.3	67.4	68.3	68.7	68.9	69.4	69.3	67.8
2009	68.6	68.9	68.8	69.0	69.0	68.4	68.4	68.7	69.2	69.8	70.1	69.9	69.1
2010	69.2	69.7	69.9	70.0	70.3	70.1	70.1	70.5	70.2	70.8	70.8	71.1	70.2
2011	70.7	71.2	71.2	71.0	71.2	71.1	70.7	72.2	72.2	73.3	74.1	74.1	71.9
Leisure and Hospitality													
2000	38.3	38.5	39.3	40.6	42.2	43.5	43.4	43.3	42.3	40.8	40.2	39.8	41.0
2001	37.7	37.9	38.5	39.8	41.0	42.1	42.1	42.4	40.7	39.1	39.0	38.6	39.9
2002	37.2	37.2	38.0	39.6	40.8	42.1	42.4	43.0	41.7	39.7	39.3	39.0	40.0
2003	38.4	38.3	39.0	39.9	41.0	41.8	41.7	42.0	40.5	39.5	38.9	38.4	40.0
2004	37.8	37.6	38.3	39.9	41.5	42.5	42.3	42.3	41.4	40.4	40.2	39.9	40.3
2005	39.2	39.2	40.1	42.1	43.2	44.7	44.4	44.5	43.3	42.1	41.9	41.5	42.2
2006	40.9	41.2	42.0	43.3	44.7	45.6	45.0	44.9	43.9	44.0	43.7	43.9	43.6
2007	42.7	42.6	43.1	44.9	46.5	47.4	47.2	47.6	46.1	45.7	45.0	44.4	45.3
2008	43.2	43.1	43.9	45.1	46.9	48.0	48.1	48.0	46.4	45.8	44.4	43.7	45.6
2009	42.4	42.2	43.2	44.4	45.9	46.8	46.4	46.4	44.9	43.8	42.6	41.7	44.2
2010	40.7	40.8	41.8	43.7	45.0	46.1	45.9	46.0	44.6	44.7	43.5	42.7	43.8
2011	41.5	41.6	42.6	44.7	46.4	47.3	46.7	47.3	45.7	45.0	42.7	42.4	44.5
Other Services													
2000	14.0	14.1	14.2	14.0	14.3	14.4	14.7	14.6	14.2	14.0	14.0	14.0	14.2
2001	14.2	14.0	14.4	14.7	14.8	15.1	14.8	14.7	14.5	14.7	14.7	14.6	14.6
2002	14.3	14.5	14.6	15.1	15.1	15.2	15.4	15.0	14.7	14.7	14.7	14.7	14.8
2003	14.4	14.4	14.6	15.1	15.7	15.8	15.9	15.9	15.7	15.6	15.6	15.5	15.4
2004	15.5	15.5	15.7	15.6	15.7	16.0	16.1	16.0	15.9	16.0	16.0	16.1	15.8
2005	15.9	16.0	16.0	16.0	16.1	16.3	16.4	16.3	16.0	16.1	16.1	16.0	16.1
2006	16.2	16.2	16.2	16.4	16.5	16.6	16.6	16.5	16.4	16.6	16.5	16.6	16.4
2007	16.4	16.4	16.5	16.6	16.6	16.7	16.6	16.5	16.4	16.5	16.6	16.6	16.5
2008	16.5	16.5	16.6	16.6	16.9	16.8	16.8	16.7	16.6	17.0	17.0	16.9	16.7
2009	16.7	16.7	16.7	16.9	17.0	17.2	17.3	17.2	17.2	17.3	17.4	17.5	17.1
2010	17.2	17.2	17.3	17.5	17.6	17.8	17.8	17.7	17.5	17.4	17.4	17.4	17.5
2011	17.3	17.2	17.3	17.4	17.5	17.7	17.5	17.3	16.9	16.8	17.0	17.4	17.3
Government													
2000	54.9	55.0	54.8	55.6	55.8	56.0	53.7	53.4	55.0	56.1	56.4	56.5	55.3
2001	55.9	56.1	56.1	56.7	57.1	57.6	55.0	54.8	56.2	57.1	57.4	57.6	56.5
2002	57.0	57.6	57.4	57.4	57.7	57.8	54.8	54.6	56.4	58.0	58.1	57.8	57.1
2003	57.7	58.1	57.7	59.1	59.3	59.4	55.6	54.1	56.5	58.9	58.9	58.4	57.8
2004	58.6	58.8	59.1	59.3	59.7	59.6	56.9	56.8	58.8	60.0	60.0	59.8	59.0
2005	59.6	60.1	60.0	60.1	60.7	60.5	57.4	57.1	59.6	61.1	61.3	60.9	59.9
2006	60.7	61.0	61.0	61.6	62.0	61.7	57.6	57.7	60.8	61.7	61.9	61.3	60.8
2007	61.2	61.6	61.5	62.2	62.6	62.0	56.7	57.7	60.9	62.4	62.4	61.6	61.1
2008	61.7	62.0	61.7	63.0	63.4	61.9	58.1	59.1	62.0	64.1	64.3	63.5	62.1
2009	63.5	63.9	63.8	65.2	65.9	64.2	63.3	62.8	64.1	65.7	65.8	64.5	64.4
2010	64.5	64.8	65.8	66.5	67.3	66.5	62.6	63.0	63.7	66.4	66.4	65.7	65.3
2011	65.4	66.0	65.4	66.5	66.7	64.7	62.8	63.5	64.4	66.5	66.6	65.7	65.4

Employment by Industry: Orlando–Kissimmee–Sanford, FL, Selected Years, 2000–2011

(Numbers in thousands, not seasonally adjusted)

Industry and year	January	February	March	April	May	June	July	August	September	October	November	December	Annual average
Total Nonfarm													
2000	892.3	902.6	910.1	908.1	912.7	909.0	896.8	908.1	913.6	911.7	919.0	925.0	909.1
2001	904.8	914.0	921.8	916.5	918.5	908.9	900.0	911.0	910.6	900.9	900.6	902.0	909.1
2002	885.3	895.2	902.2	898.8	903.0	895.4	889.8	903.2	905.7	910.5	919.7	927.5	903.0
2003	909.8	915.1	919.7	919.7	921.4	912.6	907.1	922.0	922.4	930.3	937.3	943.2	921.7
2004	937.0	945.0	951.2	960.3	963.7	956.5	955.4	966.9	966.8	979.8	991.7	999.7	964.5
2005	991.2	998.9	1,006.4	1,013.5	1,020.2	1,010.0	1,009.9	1,025.1	1,030.4	1,033.0	1,043.9	1,051.0	1,019.5
2006	1,041.0	1,048.1	1,056.9	1,062.2	1,066.6	1,057.3	1,048.3	1,066.2	1,071.1	1,071.7	1,083.7	1,091.4	1,063.7
2007	1,079.2	1,089.1	1,094.7	1,094.9	1,096.3	1,083.2	1,075.2	1,088.4	1,087.7	1,091.7	1,102.9	1,103.9	1,090.6
2008	1,085.1	1,095.3	1,098.9	1,087.7	1,085.2	1,068.3	1,058.9	1,066.9	1,060.3	1,056.3	1,054.3	1,052.4	1,072.5
2009	1,025.9	1,025.9	1,023.5	1,017.6	1,013.6	996.7	985.9	994.1	992.8	994.8	1,001.2	1,001.9	1,006.2
2010	984.6	990.8	998.4	1,004.4	1,009.4	997.5	992.9	1,002.8	998.5	1,006.8	1,013.0	1,014.5	1,001.1
2011	998.3	1,005.0	1,011.4	1,018.4	1,018.2	1,006.7	1,000.5	1,000.9	1,008.7	1,015.2	1,022.1	1,026.1	1,011.0
Total Private													
2000	800.7	809.3	816.3	814.5	816.9	824.6	814.3	816.4	820.9	818.1	824.9	830.3	817.3
2001	811.2	818.3	824.4	818.9	821.1	821.2	814.4	815.3	813.5	801.8	800.6	801.7	813.5
2002	785.2	794.1	801.0	797.0	800.5	803.7	800.0	801.8	802.7	806.0	814.6	822.0	802.4
2003	805.4	810.0	814.5	814.1	815.3	817.8	814.3	818.3	817.3	823.5	829.9	835.6	818.0
2004	830.3	837.0	843.0	852.2	855.4	859.7	860.6	860.8	858.1	869.1	880.1	888.2	857.9
2005	880.4	887.1	894.2	901.3	907.0	909.1	911.1	914.6	917.2	919.1	929.4	936.7	908.9
2006	927.1	932.8	941.7	946.0	950.6	952.2	945.5	950.9	954.3	954.3	965.6	974.1	949.6
2007	961.4	969.8	975.0	974.5	976.2	974.4	968.6	968.5	967.1	971.9	983.0	985.1	973.0
2008	966.7	976.0	978.5	967.2	964.5	959.8	952.6	948.5	940.8	936.8	934.1	932.3	954.8
2009	906.9	905.9	903.4	897.6	895.3	889.3	879.9	877.9	875.8	877.0	882.8	884.6	889.7
2010	867.3	873.3	880.7	885.8	888.0	888.9	885.7	885.4	881.5	888.4	894.6	897.3	884.7
2011	881.3	886.3	892.5	899.7	900.5	900.0	894.7	885.1	891.8	897.0	903.6	908.6	895.1
Goods-Producing													
2000	111.7	112.6	112.8	112.9	113.4	114.1	113.0	113.2	113.4	111.6	112.1	112.5	112.8
2001	111.0	110.8	111.3	110.8	110.2	110.7	110.0	110.3	109.7	108.8	108.1	107.5	109.9
2002	106.7	107.2	107.6	106.7	106.9	106.6	106.2	107.1	107.3	108.2	108.5	109.1	107.3
2003	106.9	107.7	108.3	107.8	108.5	109.4	109.1	110.3	111.0	111.8	111.9	113.2	109.7
2004	112.9	114.0	115.4	116.9	117.6	119.1	120.2	120.5	120.4	121.9	123.2	124.3	118.9
2005	124.4	125.5	126.8	128.5	129.6	130.7	131.9	132.4	133.0	132.6	133.5	134.1	130.3
2006	133.0	134.2	136.0	136.3	137.4	138.1	137.1	137.2	136.9	136.4	135.5	135.6	136.1
2007	132.2	131.9	132.4	130.9	130.9	131.1	129.6	129.9	129.4	127.9	127.5	126.0	130.0
2008	121.8	121.8	121.2	118.4	117.7	116.9	115.3	114.2	113.5	110.7	108.3	106.2	115.5
2009	102.8	100.8	99.4	95.4	94.3	93.7	91.3	90.2	88.9	88.0	87.4	86.5	93.2
2010	84.7	85.1	85.7	86.1	86.2	86.9	87.0	86.4	86.0	85.4	84.6	84.3	85.7
2011	83.1	83.2	83.0	82.9	83.0	83.0	82.1	79.0	80.0	79.3	80.8	81.5	81.7
Mining and Logging													
2000	0.5	0.5	0.5	0.5	0.5	0.5	0.5	0.4	0.5	0.5	0.5	0.4	0.5
2001	0.4	0.5	0.5	0.5	0.5	0.5	0.5	0.5	0.5	0.5	0.4	0.5	0.5
2002	0.4	0.5	0.5	0.5	0.5	0.5	0.5	0.5	0.5	0.5	0.5	0.5	0.5
2003	0.5	0.5	0.5	0.5	0.5	0.5	0.5	0.5	0.5	0.4	0.4	0.4	0.5
2004	0.4	0.4	0.4	0.4	0.4	0.4	0.4	0.4	0.4	0.4	0.3	0.4	0.4
2005	0.3	0.3	0.3	0.4	0.4	0.4	0.3	0.3	0.3	0.3	0.3	0.3	0.3
2006	0.3	0.3	0.3	0.3	0.3	0.3	0.3	0.3	0.3	0.3	0.3	0.4	0.3
2007	0.3	0.4	0.4	0.4	0.4	0.4	0.3	0.3	0.4	0.4	0.4	0.4	0.4
2008	0.4	0.4	0.4	0.4	0.4	0.3	0.3	0.3	0.3	0.3	0.2	0.2	0.3
2009	0.2	0.2	0.2	0.2	0.3	0.3	0.3	0.2	0.2	0.2	0.2	0.2	0.2
2010	0.2	0.2	0.2	0.2	0.2	0.2	0.2	0.2	0.2	0.2	0.2	0.2	0.2
2011	0.2	0.2	0.2	0.2	0.2	0.2	0.2	0.2	0.2	0.2	0.2	0.2	0.2
Construction													
2000	58.2	59.1	59.1	60.1	60.2	61.0	60.1	60.2	60.5	59.3	59.4	59.7	59.7
2001	59.1	59.0	59.5	59.2	59.1	59.9	60.2	60.7	60.6	60.4	60.3	60.0	59.8
2002	59.2	59.5	59.9	59.6	60.0	60.1	60.4	61.4	61.7	62.6	63.1	63.6	60.9
2003	62.0	62.8	63.3	63.6	64.3	65.2	65.3	66.5	67.1	68.1	68.3	69.4	65.5
2004	69.2	70.1	71.2	72.2	72.7	73.9	74.9	75.3	75.2	76.1	77.2	77.9	73.8
2005	78.4	79.4	80.5	81.7	83.0	84.0	85.4	86.2	87.0	86.9	87.9	88.8	84.1
2006	88.1	89.3	90.6	91.1	92.0	92.4	91.7	91.9	91.7	91.1	90.3	90.2	90.9
2007	87.4	86.9	87.2	85.6	85.7	85.8	84.6	85.0	84.6	83.3	82.7	81.2	85.0
2008	77.7	77.7	77.2	74.5	74.0	73.3	72.1	71.5	70.9	68.4	66.5	64.8	72.4
2009	62.3	60.7	59.6	56.3	55.2	54.5	52.7	51.8	50.7	49.9	49.2	48.6	54.3
2010	47.2	47.7	48.0	48.3	47.9	48.5	48.2	47.9	47.5	47.0	46.1	45.6	47.5
2011	44.7	44.7	44.6	44.4	44.6	44.7	44.1	41.2	42.2	41.5	42.9	43.5	43.6
Manufacturing													
2000	53.0	53.0	53.2	52.3	52.7	52.6	52.4	52.6	52.4	51.8	52.2	52.4	52.6
2001	51.5	51.3	51.3	51.1	50.6	50.3	49.3	49.1	48.6	47.9	47.4	47.0	49.6
2002	47.1	47.2	47.2	46.6	46.4	46.0	45.3	45.2	45.1	45.1	44.9	45.0	45.9
2003	44.4	44.4	44.5	43.7	43.7	43.7	43.3	43.3	43.4	43.3	43.2	43.4	43.7
2004	43.3	43.5	43.8	44.3	44.5	44.8	44.9	44.8	44.8	45.4	45.7	46.0	44.7
2005	45.7	45.8	46.0	46.4	46.2	46.3	46.2	45.9	45.7	45.4	45.3	45.0	45.8
2006	44.6	44.6	45.1	44.9	45.1	45.4	45.1	45.0	44.9	45.0	44.9	45.0	45.0
2007	44.5	44.6	44.8	44.9	44.8	44.9	44.7	44.6	44.5	44.2	44.4	44.4	44.6
2008	43.7	43.7	43.6	43.5	43.3	43.3	42.9	42.4	42.3	42.0	41.6	41.2	42.8
2009	40.3	39.9	39.6	38.9	38.8	38.9	38.3	38.2	38.0	37.9	38.0	37.7	38.7
2010	37.3	37.2	37.5	37.6	38.1	38.2	38.6	38.3	38.3	38.2	38.3	38.5	38.0
2011	38.2	38.3	38.2	38.3	38.2	38.1	37.8	37.6	37.6	37.6	37.7	37.8	38.0

Employment by Industry: Orlando–Kissimmee–Sanford, FL, Selected Years, 2000–2011—*Continued*

(Numbers in thousands, not seasonally adjusted)

Industry and year	January	February	March	April	May	June	July	August	September	October	November	December	Annual average
Service-Providing													
2000	780.6	790.0	797.3	795.2	799.3	794.9	783.8	794.9	800.2	800.1	806.9	812.5	796.3
2001	793.8	803.2	810.5	805.7	808.3	798.2	790.0	800.7	800.9	792.1	792.5	794.5	799.2
2002	778.6	788.0	794.6	792.1	796.1	788.8	783.6	796.1	798.4	802.3	811.2	818.4	795.7
2003	802.9	807.4	811.4	811.9	812.9	803.2	798.0	811.7	811.4	818.5	825.4	830.0	812.1
2004	824.1	831.0	835.8	843.4	846.1	837.4	835.2	846.4	846.4	857.9	868.5	875.4	845.6
2005	866.8	873.4	879.6	885.0	890.6	879.3	878.0	892.7	897.4	900.4	910.4	916.9	889.2
2006	908.0	913.9	920.9	925.9	929.2	919.2	911.2	929.0	934.2	935.3	948.2	955.8	927.6
2007	947.0	957.2	962.3	964.0	965.4	952.1	945.6	958.5	958.3	963.8	975.4	977.9	960.6
2008	963.3	973.5	977.7	969.3	967.5	951.4	943.6	952.7	946.8	945.6	946.0	946.2	957.0
2009	923.1	925.1	924.1	922.2	919.3	903.0	894.6	903.9	903.9	906.8	913.8	915.4	912.9
2010	899.9	905.7	912.7	918.3	923.2	910.6	905.9	916.4	912.5	921.4	928.4	930.2	915.4
2011	915.2	921.8	928.4	935.5	935.2	923.7	918.4	921.9	928.7	935.9	941.3	944.6	929.2
Trade, Transportation, and Utilities													
2000	176.7	176.7	177.7	178.0	178.3	179.6	177.9	179.3	179.9	180.1	184.4	187.4	179.7
2001	179.1	178.1	178.8	178.6	178.6	178.2	177.8	178.0	177.7	175.8	177.7	179.4	178.2
2002	171.9	170.6	171.0	170.6	170.9	170.3	169.2	170.1	170.6	170.9	174.8	178.2	171.6
2003	172.1	171.0	171.2	170.8	170.6	170.5	171.6	172.8	173.6	175.0	178.8	182.4	173.4
2004	176.9	175.7	176.6	179.0	179.9	180.5	181.3	181.8	181.2	184.5	189.4	193.1	181.7
2005	187.7	187.9	189.2	190.8	191.7	191.8	192.8	193.3	193.2	194.4	198.4	201.8	192.8
2006	196.8	196.3	197.3	197.3	198.3	198.1	197.4	198.0	197.8	198.4	203.5	207.1	198.8
2007	200.7	201.2	200.9	201.2	203.1	202.9	202.4	203.5	204.1	205.1	210.1	212.6	204.0
2008	205.7	205.1	204.7	201.9	201.3	200.4	199.0	198.6	197.5	196.3	198.6	199.9	200.8
2009	191.9	190.1	188.4	186.4	185.7	184.6	183.1	183.2	182.6	182.3	186.4	188.0	186.1
2010	182.6	182.9	182.7	183.9	184.6	185.1	185.0	185.8	185.1	187.2	192.7	195.5	186.1
2011	188.8	188.4	188.7	189.4	189.7	189.6	189.2	188.6	186.8	189.4	192.7	194.6	189.7
Wholesale Trade													
2000	38.0	38.4	38.7	40.3	40.6	41.1	41.3	41.5	41.7	41.5	41.6	41.9	40.6
2001	42.0	42.2	42.4	42.2	42.2	42.2	41.9	41.9	42.0	41.7	41.4	40.9	41.9
2002	39.9	39.9	40.0	39.7	39.7	39.4	39.2	39.2	39.3	39.4	39.5	39.4	39.6
2003	39.6	39.6	39.8	39.7	39.8	39.9	40.1	40.2	40.4	40.2	40.4	40.6	40.0
2004	40.8	41.0	41.2	41.9	42.0	42.2	42.3	42.2	42.1	42.3	42.5	42.8	41.9
2005	43.3	43.7	43.7	44.3	44.6	44.8	45.0	45.1	45.3	45.2	45.5	45.9	44.7
2006	45.7	46.1	46.2	46.2	46.8	46.5	46.4	46.0	46.2	46.1	46.1	46.3	46.2
2007	46.6	47.2	47.1	47.1	47.3	47.2	47.2	47.1	47.2	47.6	47.6	47.8	47.3
2008	47.3	48.0	47.5	46.4	46.2	46.0	45.5	45.3	45.0	44.4	44.2	43.9	45.8
2009	42.4	42.5	41.6	41.0	40.7	40.5	39.9	39.7	39.5	39.2	39.0	39.0	40.4
2010	38.4	38.9	38.7	38.7	38.8	38.5	38.1	38.1	38.0	38.2	38.1	38.1	38.4
2011	38.5	38.6	38.6	38.5	38.5	38.4	38.6	38.1	37.2	37.3	37.1	37.6	38.1
Retail Trade													
2000	109.9	109.3	109.9	108.1	108.3	109.4	107.3	108.3	108.5	108.9	112.5	114.5	109.6
2001	106.8	105.9	106.4	106.0	106.2	106.2	106.3	106.6	106.3	105.7	108.1	109.7	106.7
2002	104.9	103.7	104.0	103.4	103.8	103.6	102.7	103.6	104.0	104.5	108.1	110.7	104.8
2003	105.8	105.1	105.2	105.0	105.0	105.2	105.8	106.8	107.5	109.3	112.8	115.5	107.4
2004	110.8	109.2	109.8	111.0	111.7	112.2	113.0	113.3	112.9	115.6	119.9	122.3	113.5
2005	117.5	117.4	118.3	119.0	119.2	119.2	120.0	120.1	119.5	120.7	124.0	126.3	120.1
2006	122.1	121.2	121.3	121.6	121.6	121.6	121.0	121.3	120.6	121.3	126.1	128.4	122.3
2007	122.6	121.8	121.7	121.5	123.0	123.2	122.6	123.3	123.2	123.8	128.4	129.8	123.7
2008	124.5	123.2	123.3	121.6	121.3	121.1	120.6	120.7	120.2	120.0	122.6	123.4	121.9
2009	117.8	116.4	115.8	114.9	114.7	114.3	113.7	114.2	113.8	113.9	118.1	119.1	115.6
2010	114.9	114.3	114.3	115.5	116.0	117.0	117.3	118.1	117.5	119.4	124.6	126.7	118.0
2011	120.8	120.3	120.2	120.9	121.2	121.2	120.8	120.6	119.6	122.0	125.2	125.7	121.5
Transportation and Utilities													
2000	28.8	29.0	29.1	29.6	29.4	29.1	29.3	29.5	29.7	29.7	30.3	31.0	29.5
2001	30.3	30.0	30.0	30.4	30.2	29.8	29.6	29.5	29.4	28.4	28.2	28.8	29.6
2002	27.1	27.0	27.0	27.5	27.4	27.3	27.3	27.3	27.3	27.0	27.2	28.1	27.3
2003	26.7	26.3	26.2	26.1	25.8	25.4	25.7	25.8	25.7	25.5	25.6	26.3	25.9
2004	25.3	25.5	25.6	26.1	26.2	26.1	26.0	26.3	26.2	26.6	27.0	28.0	26.2
2005	26.9	26.8	27.2	27.5	27.9	27.8	27.8	28.1	28.4	28.5	28.9	29.6	28.0
2006	29.0	29.0	29.2	29.5	29.9	30.0	30.0	30.7	31.0	31.0	31.3	32.4	30.3
2007	31.5	32.2	32.1	32.6	32.8	32.5	32.6	33.1	33.7	33.7	34.1	35.0	33.0
2008	33.9	33.9	33.9	33.9	33.8	33.3	32.9	32.6	32.3	31.9	31.8	32.6	33.1
2009	31.7	31.2	31.0	30.5	30.3	29.8	29.5	29.3	29.3	29.2	29.3	29.9	30.1
2010	29.3	29.7	29.7	29.7	29.8	29.6	29.6	29.6	29.6	29.6	30.0	30.7	29.7
2011	29.5	29.5	29.9	30.0	30.0	30.0	29.8	29.9	30.0	30.1	30.4	31.3	30.0
Information													
2000	23.4	23.2	23.5	23.0	23.2	23.4	23.4	23.5	23.8	23.2	23.3	23.5	23.4
2001	23.1	23.2	23.0	22.8	23.0	23.0	22.9	22.8	22.7	22.5	22.7	22.9	22.9
2002	22.5	22.5	22.4	22.1	22.5	22.4	22.3	22.6	22.3	22.3	22.5	22.6	22.4
2003	22.3	22.8	22.7	22.5	23.1	23.2	22.9	23.3	23.0	23.0	23.4	23.5	23.0
2004	23.1	23.3	23.3	23.5	23.8	23.7	23.9	23.9	23.6	23.7	24.2	24.1	23.7
2005	23.7	24.1	24.0	24.1	25.0	24.8	24.7	24.8	24.8	24.8	25.1	25.3	24.6
2006	25.2	25.4	25.7	25.8	25.9	25.9	25.8	25.6	25.8	25.8	25.9	25.9	25.7
2007	26.1	26.3	26.8	27.1	27.3	27.2	26.9	26.7	26.5	26.5	26.4	26.5	26.7
2008	26.5	26.7	26.7	26.4	26.4	26.4	26.3	26.2	26.5	25.9	25.9	25.8	26.2
2009	25.8	25.9	25.7	25.1	25.1	25.0	24.7	24.4	24.1	23.9	23.9	23.9	24.8
2010	23.9	23.8	23.9	23.8	23.6	23.7	23.7	23.9	23.7	23.7	23.9	23.9	23.8
2011	23.8	23.9	23.9	23.9	24.0	23.9	23.5	23.5	23.4	23.6	23.7	23.8	23.7

Employment by Industry: Orlando–Kissimmee–Sanford, FL, Selected Years, 2000–2011—*Continued*

(Numbers in thousands, not seasonally adjusted)

Industry and year	January	February	March	April	May	June	July	August	September	October	November	December	Annual average
Financial Activities													
2000	55.2	55.6	56.1	55.1	55.5	56.0	55.5	55.6	55.6	55.2	55.4	55.8	55.6
2001	54.4	54.5	54.8	55.5	55.5	56.0	55.8	56.0	55.7	55.0	55.1	55.4	55.3
2002	54.7	54.9	55.4	54.9	55.3	55.7	56.0	56.1	56.3	56.5	56.9	57.5	55.9
2003	57.1	57.5	57.8	57.7	57.8	58.5	58.6	59.0	59.0	59.3	59.5	60.0	58.5
2004	58.5	59.1	59.2	59.8	60.1	60.6	61.0	61.4	61.0	61.7	61.9	62.8	60.6
2005	61.8	62.6	63.0	63.7	64.1	64.5	65.6	65.9	66.0	66.4	66.7	67.3	64.8
2006	66.7	67.2	67.5	67.8	68.0	68.2	67.9	68.3	68.2	68.7	69.2	69.6	68.1
2007	68.4	69.0	69.2	68.7	68.9	69.5	69.0	68.9	68.6	68.6	68.7	69.0	68.9
2008	68.0	68.3	68.4	67.8	68.3	67.9	67.7	67.7	67.1	66.7	66.6	66.7	67.6
2009	65.4	65.2	64.9	64.5	64.3	64.2	63.5	63.4	62.7	63.0	63.3	63.3	64.0
2010	62.2	62.5	62.8	62.7	63.1	63.6	63.6	63.7	63.1	63.8	63.7	64.0	63.2
2011	63.6	63.9	64.2	64.2	64.3	64.1	64.7	65.4	65.2	65.2	65.6	65.1	64.6
Professional and Business Services													
2000	136.7	139.9	142.4	141.2	142.8	144.9	142.0	143.4	146.8	147.3	148.9	148.8	143.8
2001	146.8	150.2	152.6	148.8	149.5	147.2	146.3	146.6	145.9	144.8	144.1	143.8	147.2
2002	141.8	144.9	146.8	144.4	144.5	143.9	144.3	143.9	145.1	146.9	149.0	150.4	145.5
2003	145.9	146.7	147.2	148.2	146.5	144.9	141.3	141.4	140.5	144.5	143.8	141.7	144.4
2004	143.1	145.5	146.5	149.4	149.3	149.4	147.6	148.2	148.1	151.9	153.5	154.3	148.9
2005	154.8	156.2	157.1	159.6	160.5	160.7	160.3	161.8	163.0	164.0	166.2	166.9	160.9
2006	166.2	166.4	169.0	171.9	172.9	173.7	171.0	173.5	176.3	175.9	179.0	181.0	173.1
2007	180.0	182.5	183.1	183.3	183.2	180.1	179.4	178.8	179.1	181.3	183.1	181.6	181.3
2008	179.2	183.3	182.2	180.1	178.7	176.4	175.1	175.0	175.2	175.9	173.9	172.4	177.3
2009	167.5	167.3	166.1	164.8	166.4	163.9	161.1	161.8	163.8	165.8	165.9	165.1	165.0
2010	162.1	162.4	163.8	164.5	164.2	163.0	160.7	160.8	160.5	160.7	160.4	159.8	161.9
2011	158.2	159.6	160.2	162.9	162.9	162.5	159.6	158.4	160.3	162.0	162.6	162.6	161.0
Education and Health Services													
2000	84.1	84.4	84.9	85.8	86.4	86.0	85.1	85.8	86.4	85.9	85.7	86.1	85.6
2001	84.2	85.0	85.6	86.3	86.7	86.8	86.4	87.6	88.3	88.8	89.1	89.2	87.0
2002	86.9	87.8	88.1	88.9	89.3	88.8	88.6	89.9	90.5	90.9	91.3	91.4	89.4
2003	91.5	92.0	92.1	92.7	93.4	93.3	93.1	94.1	94.9	94.8	95.3	95.5	93.6
2004	95.2	96.1	96.5	96.7	97.3	97.1	97.1	97.4	97.7	98.4	99.1	99.3	97.3
2005	99.6	100.1	100.6	100.8	101.7	100.9	101.3	102.8	103.6	104.2	105.0	105.3	102.2
2006	104.8	105.8	106.3	106.4	107.0	106.8	106.3	107.9	108.9	109.3	109.9	110.3	107.5
2007	109.5	110.6	111.0	111.7	112.5	112.3	111.5	112.7	113.7	114.8	115.8	116.1	112.7
2008	115.5	116.3	116.6	116.6	117.2	116.3	115.3	116.0	116.2	116.9	117.0	117.4	116.4
2009	116.0	116.8	117.6	117.7	118.1	117.9	118.0	118.3	118.8	120.2	121.1	121.4	118.5
2010	120.0	120.2	120.7	121.3	121.7	120.8	120.2	120.7	120.3	121.5	122.0	121.1	120.9
2011	121.1	121.9	122.2	123.5	123.8	122.8	122.3	121.1	123.9	123.9	124.8	124.5	123.0
Leisure and Hospitality													
2000	173.6	177.4	179.4	178.6	177.3	180.5	178.0	176.4	175.6	174.8	175.4	176.4	177.0
2001	172.7	175.9	177.1	174.6	175.4	176.6	172.4	171.0	170.0	162.6	159.9	159.2	170.6
2002	156.2	161.3	164.6	164.7	166.0	170.7	168.0	166.4	164.7	164.4	165.5	166.9	165.0
2003	163.9	166.3	169.1	169.0	169.8	172.3	172.2	172.0	169.6	169.5	171.6	173.5	169.9
2004	174.1	176.6	178.4	179.9	180.0	181.3	181.7	180.3	178.4	179.1	180.5	181.8	179.3
2005	180.0	182.1	184.8	184.7	184.7	185.8	184.4	183.4	182.8	182.0	183.6	184.8	183.6
2006	183.0	185.5	188.4	188.5	188.5	188.3	187.0	186.8	185.9	184.7	187.0	188.6	186.9
2007	188.0	191.1	193.9	194.7	193.5	194.8	194.2	193.0	190.8	193.1	197.1	199.3	193.6
2008	196.9	201.2	205.0	203.4	202.5	203.6	202.6	200.3	195.4	194.6	194.6	195.0	199.6
2009	189.1	191.3	192.3	194.7	192.8	191.9	190.4	189.1	187.4	186.4	187.7	189.3	190.2
2010	184.7	189.2	193.6	195.7	196.8	198.0	197.7	196.6	195.5	198.6	199.9	201.4	195.6
2011	195.7	198.2	202.8	205.2	204.8	206.2	205.6	201.6	204.6	206.0	205.9	208.9	203.8
Other Services													
2000	39.3	39.5	39.5	39.9	40.0	40.1	39.4	39.2	39.4	40.0	39.7	39.8	39.7
2001	39.9	40.6	41.2	41.5	42.2	42.7	42.8	43.0	43.5	43.5	43.9	44.3	42.4
2002	44.5	44.9	45.1	44.7	45.1	45.3	45.4	45.7	45.9	45.9	46.1	45.9	45.4
2003	45.7	46.0	46.1	45.4	45.6	45.7	45.5	45.4	45.7	45.6	45.6	45.8	45.7
2004	46.5	46.7	47.1	47.0	47.4	48.0	47.8	47.3	47.7	47.9	48.3	48.5	47.5
2005	48.4	48.6	48.7	49.1	49.7	49.9	50.1	50.2	50.8	50.7	50.9	51.2	49.9
2006	51.4	52.0	52.1	52.0	52.6	53.1	53.0	53.6	54.5	55.1	55.6	56.0	53.4
2007	56.5	57.2	57.7	56.9	56.8	56.5	55.6	55.0	54.9	54.6	54.3	54.0	55.8
2008	53.1	53.3	53.7	52.6	52.4	51.9	51.3	50.5	50.4	49.8	49.2	48.9	51.4
2009	48.4	48.5	48.8	49.0	48.6	48.1	47.8	47.5	47.5	47.4	47.1	47.1	48.0
2010	47.1	47.2	47.5	47.8	47.8	47.8	47.8	47.5	47.3	47.5	47.4	47.3	47.5
2011	47.0	47.2	47.5	47.7	48.0	47.9	47.7	47.5	47.6	47.6	47.5	47.6	47.6
Government													
2000	91.6	93.3	93.8	93.6	95.8	84.4	82.5	91.7	92.7	93.6	94.1	94.7	91.8
2001	93.6	95.7	97.4	97.6	97.4	87.7	85.6	95.7	97.1	99.1	100.0	100.3	95.6
2002	100.1	101.1	101.2	101.8	102.5	91.7	89.8	101.4	103.0	104.5	105.1	105.5	100.6
2003	104.4	105.1	105.2	105.6	106.1	94.8	92.8	103.7	105.1	106.8	107.4	107.6	103.7
2004	106.7	108.0	108.2	108.1	108.3	96.8	94.8	106.1	108.7	110.7	111.6	111.5	106.6
2005	110.8	111.8	112.2	112.2	113.2	100.9	98.8	110.5	113.2	113.9	114.5	114.3	110.5
2006	113.9	115.3	115.2	116.2	116.0	105.1	102.8	115.3	116.8	117.4	118.1	117.3	114.1
2007	117.8	119.3	119.7	120.4	120.1	108.8	106.6	119.9	120.6	119.8	119.9	118.8	117.6
2008	118.4	119.3	120.4	120.5	120.7	108.5	106.3	118.4	119.5	119.5	120.2	120.1	117.7
2009	119.0	120.0	120.1	120.0	118.3	107.4	106.0	116.2	117.0	117.8	118.4	117.3	116.5
2010	117.3	117.5	117.7	118.6	121.4	108.6	107.2	117.4	117.0	118.4	118.4	117.2	116.4
2011	117.0	118.7	118.9	118.7	117.7	106.7	105.8	115.8	116.9	118.2	118.5	117.5	115.9

Employment by Industry: Oxnard–Thousand Oaks–Ventura, CA, Selected Years, 2000–2011

(Numbers in thousands, not seasonally adjusted)

Industry and year	January	February	March	April	May	June	July	August	September	October	November	December	Annual average
Total Nonfarm													
2000	267.4	267.9	270.3	273.3	275.2	277.2	275.5	274.3	277.4	278.4	279.9	283.1	275.0
2001	277.3	277.1	278.8	279.0	280.6	280.9	279.3	277.8	279.6	281.4	283.0	284.5	279.9
2002	277.7	279.6	280.4	280.2	281.7	283.8	281.1	278.3	282.4	282.9	286.9	286.9	281.8
2003	279.7	280.1	282.4	283.5	285.9	287.5	283.1	281.7	284.3	286.7	287.7	287.9	284.2
2004	280.8	283.3	285.9	286.5	286.9	288.7	285.0	284.1	285.0	288.0	289.3	291.1	286.2
2005	285.7	288.4	290.3	291.5	292.1	293.2	289.1	288.9	291.1	292.3	294.5	296.7	291.2
2006	292.2	294.9	296.5	297.5	300.0	301.1	296.6	296.4	298.2	298.2	300.0	301.3	297.7
2007	293.7	295.4	297.3	295.7	298.2	299.7	295.6	295.5	295.8	296.4	297.9	299.1	296.7
2008	290.7	292.6	292.6	293.0	293.7	293.7	288.3	287.5	289.3	289.5	288.7	289.5	290.8
2009	280.8	278.8	277.3	277.0	277.0	276.6	268.6	269.6	270.6	272.1	274.0	274.8	274.8
2010	268.1	269.1	269.8	274.3	277.3	274.4	270.4	271.2	272.3	275.3	277.7	278.8	273.2
2011	272.6	273.7	273.8	274.9	275.2	275.1	273.1	272.9	274.9	275.0	276.0	278.2	274.6
Total Private													
2000	223.3	223.3	225.3	228.0	229.5	232.2	232.3	233.0	234.5	233.8	234.8	237.8	230.7
2001	231.5	231.5	233.4	234.3	235.7	236.7	234.4	235.1	235.4	235.8	236.4	237.7	234.8
2002	231.8	233.1	234.4	234.5	236.1	237.7	237.3	236.6	238.0	237.8	240.2	241.3	236.6
2003	234.2	234.6	236.3	237.7	239.3	241.5	240.1	240.1	240.7	241.9	242.5	244.1	239.4
2004	237.7	239.9	242.2	242.8	243.5	244.9	244.4	244.4	244.2	245.7	246.7	248.4	243.7
2005	243.5	245.7	247.5	248.8	249.0	250.3	248.9	249.0	249.3	250.1	251.6	253.9	249.0
2006	249.7	252.1	253.5	254.5	257.1	257.9	255.7	256.0	255.6	255.7	256.8	258.2	255.2
2007	251.0	252.3	254.0	252.2	254.5	255.9	254.1	254.4	252.8	253.3	254.1	255.3	253.7
2008	247.2	248.7	248.6	249.2	249.6	249.3	247.2	247.3	247.6	246.3	245.0	245.7	247.6
2009	237.6	235.2	233.7	232.8	232.7	232.0	228.6	228.9	229.0	229.3	230.7	231.7	231.9
2010	225.4	225.9	226.4	228.3	229.8	229.4	229.1	228.8	229.0	230.4	232.0	233.3	229.0
2011	227.8	228.3	228.3	229.4	230.0	230.1	231.3	229.2	229.8	229.9	230.2	232.9	229.8
Goods-Producing													
2000	55.0	54.8	55.3	56.0	56.7	57.8	58.1	58.4	59.1	58.8	58.3	58.5	57.2
2001	57.1	57.1	57.6	57.5	57.7	58.0	57.3	57.6	57.5	57.1	56.2	55.5	57.2
2002	53.9	54.7	54.7	54.4	54.8	55.2	54.4	54.0	54.2	53.7	54.2	54.0	54.4
2003	52.9	52.7	53.2	53.8	54.4	55.1	55.3	55.2	55.1	54.8	54.7	54.3	54.3
2004	54.0	54.7	55.3	55.8	56.0	56.5	56.7	56.4	56.3	56.4	56.4	56.5	55.9
2005	55.6	56.6	57.3	57.4	57.4	58.1	57.6	57.5	57.5	57.5	57.2	57.5	57.3
2006	57.7	58.8	59.1	59.3	60.2	61.2	61.1	61.2	61.1	60.2	59.8	59.2	59.9
2007	58.0	58.2	58.6	57.9	58.7	59.0	58.3	58.3	57.5	57.3	56.7	56.1	57.9
2008	54.0	54.3	54.2	54.3	54.2	54.3	54.2	53.9	53.8	53.5	52.5	52.0	53.8
2009	50.2	48.9	48.9	48.3	47.7	47.8	46.6	46.3	45.8	45.1	44.6	44.2	47.0
2010	43.6	43.6	43.7	43.7	44.3	44.5	44.6	44.1	44.0	44.1	44.0	43.6	44.0
2011	43.1	43.2	43.2	43.3	43.4	43.8	43.8	42.8	42.6	42.2	42.2	41.9	43.0
Mining and Logging													
2000	0.7	0.7	0.7	0.7	0.7	0.7	0.7	0.7	0.7	0.7	0.6	0.6	0.7
2001	0.6	0.6	0.6	0.6	0.6	0.6	0.6	0.6	0.6	0.6	0.6	0.6	0.6
2002	0.6	0.7	0.7	0.7	0.7	0.7	0.7	0.7	0.7	0.7	0.7	0.6	0.7
2003	0.6	0.6	0.6	0.6	0.6	0.6	0.6	0.6	0.6	0.6	0.6	0.6	0.6
2004	0.6	0.6	0.7	0.7	0.7	0.7	0.7	0.7	0.7	0.7	0.7	0.7	0.7
2005	0.7	0.6	0.7	0.7	0.7	0.8	0.8	0.8	0.8	0.9	0.9	0.9	0.8
2006	1.0	1.0	1.0	1.0	1.0	1.0	1.1	1.1	1.1	1.1	1.1	1.1	1.1
2007	1.1	1.1	1.1	1.1	1.1	1.1	1.0	1.0	1.0	1.1	1.1	1.1	1.1
2008	1.0	1.1	1.1	1.1	1.1	1.1	1.2	1.2	1.2	1.3	1.3	1.3	1.2
2009	1.3	1.3	1.3	1.3	1.2	1.3	1.2	1.2	1.2	1.2	1.2	1.2	1.2
2010	1.1	1.1	1.1	1.1	1.2	1.2	1.2	1.2	1.2	1.3	1.3	1.3	1.2
2011	1.2	1.3	1.3	1.2	1.2	1.2	1.2	1.2	1.2	1.1	1.1	1.1	1.2
Construction													
2000	14.2	14.0	14.2	14.7	15.2	15.9	16.0	16.2	16.6	16.1	15.8	15.9	15.4
2001	15.1	15.0	15.4	15.7	16.1	16.5	16.4	16.9	16.9	16.6	16.2	16.0	16.1
2002	15.3	15.8	15.5	15.3	15.4	15.6	15.8	15.8	15.9	16.0	16.0	15.9	15.7
2003	15.3	15.1	15.4	16.0	16.9	17.3	17.6	17.7	17.5	17.1	17.0	16.8	16.6
2004	16.4	16.4	16.5	16.5	16.5	16.9	17.3	17.1	17.2	17.4	17.3	17.5	16.9
2005	16.6	17.4	18.0	18.5	18.7	19.2	19.2	19.4	19.5	19.7	19.5	19.8	18.8
2006	19.8	20.4	20.4	20.4	21.0	21.4	21.2	21.2	21.0	20.2	19.6	19.2	20.5
2007	18.3	18.5	18.7	18.5	19.1	19.7	19.5	19.7	19.1	18.8	18.3	17.9	18.8
2008	16.9	17.1	17.0	17.2	17.1	17.2	17.0	16.7	16.6	16.2	15.7	15.4	16.7
2009	14.2	13.6	13.9	13.7	13.6	13.6	13.2	13.2	12.8	12.4	12.2	11.9	13.2
2010	11.2	11.2	11.3	11.2	11.5	11.5	11.5	11.4	11.2	11.3	11.3	11.1	11.3
2011	11.1	11.0	11.0	11.2	11.3	11.4	11.4	11.1	11.1	10.8	10.9	10.6	11.1
Manufacturing													
2000	40.1	40.1	40.4	40.6	40.8	41.2	41.4	41.5	41.8	42.0	41.9	42.0	41.2
2001	41.4	41.5	41.6	41.2	41.0	40.9	40.3	40.1	40.0	39.9	39.4	38.9	40.5
2002	38.0	38.2	38.5	38.4	38.7	38.9	37.9	37.5	37.6	37.0	37.5	37.5	38.0
2003	37.0	37.0	37.2	37.2	36.9	37.2	37.1	36.9	37.0	37.1	37.1	36.9	37.1
2004	37.0	37.7	38.1	38.6	38.8	38.9	38.7	38.6	38.4	38.3	38.4	38.3	38.3
2005	38.3	38.6	38.6	38.2	38.0	38.1	37.6	37.3	37.2	36.9	36.8	36.8	37.7
2006	36.9	37.4	37.7	37.9	38.2	38.8	38.8	38.9	39.0	38.9	39.1	38.9	38.4
2007	38.6	38.6	38.8	38.3	38.5	38.2	37.8	37.6	37.4	37.4	37.3	37.1	38.0
2008	36.1	36.1	36.1	36.0	36.0	36.0	36.0	36.0	36.0	36.0	35.5	35.3	35.9
2009	34.7	34.0	33.7	33.3	32.9	32.9	32.2	31.9	31.8	31.5	31.2	31.1	32.6
2010	31.3	31.3	31.3	31.4	31.6	31.8	31.9	31.5	31.6	31.5	31.4	31.2	31.5
2011	30.8	30.9	30.9	30.9	30.9	31.2	31.2	30.5	30.3	30.3	30.2	30.2	30.7

Employment by Industry: Oxnard–Thousand Oaks–Ventura, CA, Selected Years, 2000–2011—*Continued*

(Numbers in thousands, not seasonally adjusted)

Industry and year	January	February	March	April	May	June	July	August	September	October	November	December	Annual average
Service-Providing													
2000	212.4	213.1	215.0	217.3	218.5	219.4	217.4	215.9	218.3	219.6	221.6	224.6	217.8
2001	220.2	220.0	221.2	221.5	222.9	222.9	222.0	220.2	222.1	224.3	226.8	229.0	222.8
2002	223.8	224.9	225.7	225.8	226.9	228.6	226.7	224.3	228.2	229.2	232.7	232.9	227.5
2003	226.8	227.4	229.2	229.7	231.5	232.4	227.8	226.5	229.2	231.9	233.0	233.6	229.9
2004	226.8	228.6	230.6	230.7	230.9	232.2	228.3	227.7	228.7	231.6	232.9	234.6	230.3
2005	230.1	231.8	233.0	234.1	234.7	235.1	231.5	231.4	233.6	234.8	237.3	239.2	233.9
2006	234.5	236.1	237.4	238.2	239.8	239.9	235.5	235.2	237.1	238.0	240.2	242.1	237.8
2007	235.7	237.2	238.7	237.8	239.5	240.7	237.3	237.2	238.3	239.1	241.2	243.0	238.8
2008	236.7	238.3	238.4	238.7	239.5	239.4	234.1	233.6	235.5	236.0	236.2	237.5	237.0
2009	230.6	229.9	228.4	228.7	229.3	228.8	222.0	223.3	224.8	227.0	229.4	230.6	227.7
2010	224.5	225.5	226.1	230.6	233.0	229.9	225.8	227.1	228.3	231.2	233.7	235.2	229.2
2011	229.5	230.5	230.6	231.6	231.8	231.3	229.3	230.1	232.3	232.8	233.8	236.3	231.7
Trade, Transportation, and Utilities													
2000	48.4	48.1	48.2	48.6	48.7	49.1	49.1	49.3	49.5	49.8	51.7	53.2	49.5
2001	51.1	50.5	50.7	50.7	50.4	50.4	50.1	50.6	50.4	51.0	52.2	53.3	51.0
2002	51.9	51.5	51.5	50.6	50.9	51.4	50.8	51.0	51.1	51.7	53.0	54.2	51.6
2003	51.5	51.3	51.3	51.0	51.2	51.3	51.3	51.5	51.8	53.1	53.4	54.9	52.0
2004	52.5	52.6	53.0	52.5	52.8	53.0	52.8	52.8	52.9	53.4	54.7	55.6	53.2
2005	53.7	53.5	53.6	54.0	54.2	54.6	54.5	54.7	55.0	55.3	56.8	58.1	54.8
2006	55.4	55.1	55.2	55.8	56.3	56.5	56.4	56.4	56.1	56.6	58.1	59.1	56.4
2007	56.4	55.8	55.9	55.5	55.8	56.5	56.7	57.1	56.7	56.6	58.3	59.8	56.8
2008	56.5	56.4	56.4	56.1	56.1	56.1	55.7	55.5	55.7	55.6	56.2	57.1	56.1
2009	54.0	52.9	52.0	51.8	51.8	51.7	51.6	51.7	51.8	52.2	53.4	54.8	52.5
2010	52.2	51.8	51.8	53.0	53.0	52.9	52.9	52.7	52.7	53.4	54.9	55.9	53.1
2011	53.2	52.7	52.7	53.3	53.3	53.5	55.4	54.8	54.7	55.0	56.8	58.0	54.5
Wholesale Trade													
2000	9.6	9.8	9.9	10.2	10.3	10.4	10.5	10.5	10.6	10.6	10.8	10.8	10.3
2001	10.8	11.0	11.2	11.1	11.0	11.0	11.0	11.2	10.9	10.9	11.0	11.1	11.0
2002	11.6	11.9	11.8	11.6	11.7	11.7	11.5	11.6	11.5	11.6	11.8	11.8	11.7
2003	11.7	11.8	12.0	12.0	12.0	12.0	11.9	11.9	11.9	11.5	11.6	11.7	11.8
2004	11.6	12.0	12.2	12.1	12.1	12.3	12.5	12.5	12.5	12.4	12.3	12.3	12.2
2005	12.3	12.4	12.4	12.5	12.5	12.6	12.6	12.7	12.7	12.6	12.5	12.6	12.5
2006	12.4	12.6	12.7	12.8	12.9	12.9	12.8	12.6	12.5	12.6	12.4	12.5	12.6
2007	12.6	12.9	13.0	13.1	13.1	13.2	13.1	13.2	13.1	13.0	13.0	13.0	13.0
2008	12.7	12.9	12.8	12.8	12.9	12.9	12.9	12.9	12.9	12.9	12.7	12.8	12.8
2009	12.6	12.4	12.3	12.2	12.1	12.1	11.8	11.8	11.8	11.8	11.7	11.8	12.0
2010	11.8	12.0	12.1	13.0	12.9	12.7	12.5	12.2	12.0	12.1	12.3	12.2	12.3
2011	12.0	12.1	12.3	12.6	12.6	12.6	13.0	12.8	12.8	12.8	12.9	13.1	12.6
Retail Trade													
2000	33.3	32.8	32.8	32.7	32.8	33.1	33.3	33.5	33.5	33.7	35.1	36.3	33.6
2001	34.1	33.3	33.3	33.2	33.2	33.4	33.5	33.7	33.9	34.3	35.5	36.5	34.0
2002	34.4	33.6	33.7	33.3	33.5	33.9	33.6	33.7	34.0	34.4	35.3	36.5	34.2
2003	34.1	33.8	33.7	33.5	33.7	33.8	33.8	34.0	34.2	35.9	36.1	37.5	34.5
2004	35.3	35.0	35.1	34.6	34.9	34.9	34.8	34.8	34.8	35.3	36.6	37.4	35.3
2005	35.7	35.5	35.4	35.6	35.8	36.1	36.2	36.3	36.5	36.9	38.4	39.5	36.5
2006	37.1	36.5	36.5	36.9	37.2	37.3	37.5	37.6	37.4	37.9	39.5	40.3	37.6
2007	37.9	37.0	36.9	36.6	36.7	37.1	37.4	37.7	37.4	37.4	38.9	40.2	37.6
2008	37.5	37.1	37.0	37.0	36.9	37.1	37.0	36.9	37.0	37.1	38.0	38.7	37.3
2009	35.8	35.1	34.4	34.4	34.4	34.3	34.5	34.6	34.6	35.1	36.4	37.5	35.1
2010	35.2	34.6	34.5	34.8	34.9	34.9	35.0	35.1	35.3	36.0	37.3	38.2	35.5
2011	35.9	35.3	35.1	35.4	35.3	35.5	36.5	36.2	36.0	36.3	37.9	38.8	36.2
Transportation and Utilities													
2000	5.5	5.5	5.5	5.7	5.6	5.6	5.3	5.3	5.4	5.5	5.8	6.1	5.6
2001	6.2	6.2	6.2	6.4	6.2	6.0	5.6	5.7	5.6	5.8	5.7	5.7	5.9
2002	5.9	6.0	6.0	5.7	5.7	5.8	5.7	5.7	5.6	5.7	5.9	5.9	5.8
2003	5.7	5.7	5.6	5.5	5.5	5.5	5.6	5.6	5.7	5.7	5.7	5.7	5.6
2004	5.6	5.6	5.7	5.8	5.8	5.8	5.5	5.5	5.6	5.7	5.8	5.9	5.7
2005	5.7	5.6	5.8	5.9	5.9	5.9	5.7	5.7	5.8	5.8	5.9	6.0	5.8
2006	5.9	6.0	6.0	6.1	6.2	6.3	6.1	6.2	6.2	6.1	6.2	6.3	6.1
2007	5.9	5.9	6.0	5.8	6.0	6.2	6.2	6.2	6.2	6.2	6.4	6.6	6.1
2008	6.3	6.4	6.6	6.3	6.3	6.1	5.8	5.7	5.8	5.6	5.5	5.6	6.0
2009	5.6	5.4	5.3	5.2	5.3	5.3	5.3	5.3	5.4	5.3	5.3	5.5	5.4
2010	5.2	5.2	5.2	5.2	5.2	5.3	5.4	5.4	5.4	5.3	5.3	5.5	5.3
2011	5.3	5.3	5.3	5.3	5.4	5.4	5.9	5.8	5.9	5.9	6.0	6.1	5.6
Information													
2000	7.8	7.8	7.9	7.6	7.7	7.8	7.9	7.9	8.0	8.1	8.1	8.3	7.9
2001	8.3	8.3	8.5	8.3	8.5	8.6	8.5	8.4	8.3	8.2	8.2	8.2	8.4
2002	8.3	8.3	8.4	8.3	8.3	8.2	8.0	7.9	7.8	7.8	7.8	7.8	8.1
2003	7.5	7.4	7.4	7.1	7.1	7.1	7.3	7.2	7.1	7.0	7.0	7.0	7.2
2004	6.9	6.7	7.1	7.0	7.0	7.0	6.9	6.8	6.6	6.5	6.4	6.3	6.8
2005	6.1	6.2	6.1	6.2	6.2	6.2	6.1	6.2	6.2	6.1	6.1	6.2	6.2
2006	6.1	6.1	6.1	6.0	6.1	6.0	6.0	5.9	5.8	5.8	5.7	5.8	6.0
2007	5.7	5.9	5.9	5.8	5.9	5.9	5.8	5.8	5.8	5.7	5.8	5.7	5.8
2008	5.7	5.7	5.7	5.7	5.7	5.7	5.6	5.6	5.5	5.5	5.5	5.4	5.6
2009	5.4	5.4	5.3	5.3	5.3	5.3	5.3	5.2	5.2	5.2	5.3	5.3	5.3
2010	5.2	5.2	5.2	5.2	5.2	5.2	5.2	5.2	5.1	4.9	5.0	5.0	5.1
2011	4.9	4.8	4.8	4.8	4.9	4.9	4.9	4.9	4.9	4.9	4.9	5.0	4.9

Employment by Industry: Oxnard–Thousand Oaks–Ventura, CA, Selected Years, 2000–2011—*Continued*

(Numbers in thousands, not seasonally adjusted)

Industry and year	January	February	March	April	May	June	July	August	September	October	November	December	Annual average
Financial Activities													
2000	17.2	17.1	17.3	17.4	17.6	17.7	17.9	18.0	18.1	18.2	18.1	18.3	17.7
2001	18.5	18.7	19.0	19.1	19.2	19.6	19.7	20.0	20.1	20.5	20.6	20.9	19.7
2002	20.9	21.1	21.4	21.8	22.0	22.2	22.5	22.7	22.8	22.9	23.2	23.3	22.2
2003	22.5	22.7	23.1	23.2	23.5	23.8	23.6	23.9	23.7	23.7	23.7	23.7	23.4
2004	23.5	23.8	23.8	24.1	24.2	24.5	24.3	24.3	24.5	24.3	24.4	24.5	24.2
2005	24.1	24.2	24.3	24.1	24.3	24.5	24.4	24.6	24.6	24.7	24.8	25.1	24.5
2006	25.0	24.8	24.9	24.6	24.5	24.4	23.9	23.6	23.3	23.2	22.9	23.3	24.0
2007	22.7	22.7	22.8	22.8	22.9	23.1	23.0	22.8	22.6	22.7	22.1	22.1	22.7
2008	21.5	21.5	21.3	21.4	21.4	21.4	21.1	20.9	20.8	20.7	20.5	20.5	21.1
2009	20.6	20.7	20.6	20.6	20.5	20.4	20.4	20.4	20.5	20.2	20.4	20.5	20.5
2010	20.3	20.4	20.4	20.3	20.4	20.4	20.7	20.8	20.8	21.1	21.2	21.4	20.7
2011	21.3	21.4	21.5	21.4	21.4	21.4	21.6	21.6	21.7	21.9	21.9	22.0	21.6
Professional and Business Services													
2000	38.0	37.9	38.4	40.0	39.9	40.4	40.0	39.8	40.0	39.3	39.1	39.6	39.4
2001	37.1	36.9	37.2	37.3	37.6	37.8	37.2	36.8	37.0	36.8	36.9	37.3	37.2
2002	35.9	36.1	36.3	36.7	36.8	36.9	36.8	36.4	36.7	36.6	36.9	37.0	36.6
2003	35.9	35.9	36.4	36.5	36.7	37.3	37.2	37.1	37.0	37.2	37.4	37.8	36.9
2004	36.4	36.8	37.2	37.1	36.9	37.3	37.2	37.6	37.2	37.9	37.7	38.4	37.3
2005	37.6	38.1	38.3	39.0	38.7	38.7	38.4	38.4	38.0	38.1	38.3	38.4	38.3
2006	38.0	38.8	39.2	39.4	40.0	39.9	39.1	39.6	39.5	39.5	39.4	39.7	39.3
2007	38.8	39.1	39.4	38.5	38.5	38.6	38.0	37.8	37.3	37.2	37.3	37.4	38.2
2008	37.2	37.6	37.6	37.5	37.7	37.8	37.8	38.2	38.4	37.8	37.6	37.8	37.8
2009	36.6	36.1	36.0	35.3	35.1	34.9	34.6	34.5	34.4	34.6	35.0	34.7	35.2
2010	33.6	33.7	34.0	33.6	33.8	34.0	33.9	34.0	33.8	34.0	33.8	34.2	33.9
2011	33.1	33.1	33.1	33.1	33.0	33.0	32.8	31.7	33.5	32.9	32.1	32.9	32.9
Education and Health Services													
2000	23.7	24.0	24.2	23.9	24.0	24.1	23.9	24.1	24.4	24.2	24.3	24.4	24.1
2001	24.4	24.7	24.6	25.3	25.6	25.5	25.4	25.3	25.6	25.8	25.9	25.9	25.3
2002	25.4	25.5	25.7	25.9	26.0	25.9	26.3	26.3	27.0	27.3	27.2	27.1	26.3
2003	27.0	27.3	27.5	27.9	28.0	28.2	27.1	27.1	27.7	27.8	28.0	27.8	27.6
2004	27.1	27.4	27.6	27.7	27.7	27.7	27.1	27.0	27.3	27.9	27.8	27.8	27.5
2005	27.7	28.1	28.4	28.5	28.5	28.5	28.1	27.8	28.3	28.6	28.6	28.7	28.3
2006	28.2	28.7	28.7	28.9	29.0	28.9	28.3	28.3	28.8	29.6	29.7	29.9	28.9
2007	29.3	29.9	30.2	30.1	30.3	30.3	29.9	30.3	30.7	31.4	31.5	31.6	30.5
2008	30.9	31.7	31.4	31.9	32.0	31.5	30.8	31.4	32.1	32.6	32.5	32.8	31.8
2009	32.0	32.5	32.3	32.7	32.7	32.2	30.9	31.5	32.1	32.8	33.0	33.1	32.3
2010	31.9	32.5	32.4	33.2	33.2	32.8	32.0	32.2	32.6	33.2	33.4	33.6	32.8
2011	32.9	33.5	33.3	33.6	33.6	32.9	32.5	32.5	32.0	32.4	32.0	31.8	32.8
Leisure and Hospitality													
2000	23.7	24.1	24.4	24.7	25.1	25.4	25.6	25.7	25.6	25.7	25.5	25.6	25.1
2001	25.6	25.8	26.1	26.6	27.0	27.1	26.8	27.0	26.8	26.6	26.5	26.7	26.6
2002	25.8	26.1	26.5	26.8	27.2	27.6	28.1	28.0	28.0	27.6	27.5	27.5	27.2
2003	26.7	27.0	27.1	27.5	27.7	27.9	27.8	27.8	28.0	27.9	28.1	28.1	27.6
2004	27.1	27.6	27.8	28.1	28.5	28.6	29.0	29.2	29.2	28.9	29.0	29.0	28.5
2005	28.2	28.4	28.8	29.0	29.2	29.3	29.5	29.6	29.4	29.6	29.6	29.7	29.2
2006	29.2	29.6	30.0	30.2	30.6	30.6	30.9	31.0	30.9	30.8	31.1	31.2	30.5
2007	30.6	31.1	31.4	31.7	32.3	32.5	32.5	32.5	32.2	32.0	32.3	32.5	32.0
2008	31.4	31.4	31.8	32.1	32.3	32.3	31.9	31.8	31.3	30.9	30.7	30.6	31.5
2009	29.5	29.4	29.3	29.5	30.2	30.4	30.2	30.1	30.0	29.9	29.7	29.8	29.8
2010	29.5	29.6	29.7	30.1	30.6	30.4	30.7	30.7	30.7	30.5	30.5	30.5	30.3
2011	30.3	30.5	30.6	30.9	31.3	31.5	31.3	31.9	31.4	31.6	31.3	32.3	31.2
Other Services													
2000	9.5	9.5	9.6	9.8	9.8	9.9	9.8	9.8	9.8	9.7	9.7	9.9	9.7
2001	9.4	9.5	9.7	9.5	9.7	9.7	9.4	9.4	9.7	9.8	9.9	9.9	9.6
2002	9.7	9.8	9.9	10.0	10.1	10.3	10.4	10.3	10.4	10.2	10.4	10.4	10.2
2003	10.2	10.3	10.3	10.7	10.7	10.8	10.5	10.3	10.3	10.4	10.3	10.3	10.4
2004	10.2	10.3	10.4	10.5	10.4	10.3	10.4	10.3	10.2	10.4	10.3	10.3	10.3
2005	10.5	10.6	10.7	10.6	10.5	10.4	10.3	10.2	10.3	10.2	10.2	10.2	10.4
2006	10.1	10.2	10.3	10.3	10.4	10.4	10.0	10.0	10.1	10.0	10.1	10.0	10.2
2007	9.5	9.6	9.8	9.9	10.1	10.0	9.9	9.8	10.0	10.4	10.1	10.1	9.9
2008	10.0	10.1	10.2	10.2	10.2	10.2	10.1	10.0	10.0	9.7	9.5	9.5	10.0
2009	9.3	9.3	9.3	9.3	9.4	9.3	9.0	9.2	9.2	9.3	9.3	9.3	9.3
2010	9.1	9.1	9.2	9.2	9.3	9.2	9.1	9.1	9.3	9.2	9.2	9.1	9.2
2011	9.0	9.1	9.1	9.0	9.1	9.1	9.0	9.0	9.0	9.0	9.0	9.0	9.0
Government													
2000	44.1	44.6	45.0	45.3	45.7	45.0	43.2	41.3	42.9	44.6	45.1	45.3	44.3
2001	45.8	45.6	45.4	44.7	44.9	44.2	44.9	42.7	44.2	45.6	46.6	46.8	45.1
2002	45.9	46.5	46.0	45.7	45.6	46.1	43.8	41.7	44.4	45.1	46.7	45.6	45.3
2003	45.5	45.5	46.1	45.8	46.6	46.0	43.0	41.6	43.6	44.8	45.2	43.8	44.8
2004	43.1	43.4	43.7	43.7	43.4	43.8	40.6	39.7	40.8	42.3	42.6	42.7	42.5
2005	42.2	42.7	42.8	42.7	43.1	42.9	40.2	39.9	41.8	42.2	42.9	42.8	42.2
2006	42.5	42.8	43.0	43.0	42.9	43.2	40.9	40.4	42.6	42.5	43.2	43.1	42.5
2007	42.7	43.1	43.3	43.5	43.7	43.8	41.5	41.1	43.0	43.1	43.8	43.8	43.0
2008	43.5	43.9	44.0	43.8	44.1	44.4	41.1	40.2	41.7	43.2	43.7	43.8	43.1
2009	43.2	43.6	43.6	44.2	44.3	44.6	40.0	40.7	41.6	42.8	43.3	43.1	42.9
2010	42.7	43.2	43.4	46.0	47.5	45.0	41.3	42.4	43.3	44.9	45.7	45.5	44.2
2011	44.8	45.4	45.5	45.5	45.2	45.0	41.8	43.7	45.1	45.1	45.8	45.3	44.9

Employment by Industry: Philadelphia–Camden–Wilmington, PA–NJ–DE–MD, Selected Years, 2000–2011

(Numbers in thousands, not seasonally adjusted)

Industry and year	January	February	March	April	May	June	July	August	September	October	November	December	Annual average
Total Nonfarm													
2000	2,687.1	2,697.5	2,725.7	2,747.3	2,758.2	2,768.1	2,728.4	2,718.8	2,749.0	2,763.6	2,787.0	2,806.5	2,744.8
2001	2,717.6	2,729.1	2,746.7	2,759.5	2,768.6	2,779.0	2,733.4	2,728.6	2,743.4	2,755.1	2,773.2	2,781.5	2,751.3
2002	2,704.7	2,715.4	2,733.4	2,741.3	2,751.8	2,764.8	2,716.8	2,712.1	2,733.9	2,753.8	2,770.8	2,775.8	2,739.6
2003	2,692.2	2,693.5	2,713.5	2,731.2	2,742.8	2,750.5	2,713.8	2,704.5	2,726.1	2,748.3	2,762.2	2,767.2	2,728.8
2004	2,687.0	2,698.0	2,721.2	2,740.8	2,753.7	2,765.7	2,734.0	2,726.5	2,752.2	2,779.1	2,792.5	2,798.9	2,745.8
2005	2,716.3	2,728.7	2,741.2	2,777.6	2,789.9	2,790.1	2,766.1	2,755.4	2,781.5	2,800.1	2,816.9	2,819.7	2,773.6
2006	2,747.2	2,760.3	2,777.9	2,805.4	2,818.4	2,818.9	2,784.6	2,777.0	2,797.2	2,819.7	2,832.5	2,836.7	2,798.0
2007	2,764.8	2,770.4	2,789.4	2,810.7	2,824.3	2,832.1	2,801.9	2,792.1	2,805.7	2,835.8	2,851.3	2,851.1	2,810.8
2008	2,778.8	2,788.5	2,801.5	2,830.2	2,833.8	2,833.8	2,793.2	2,783.6	2,799.5	2,820.1	2,815.2	2,807.6	2,807.2
2009	2,718.4	2,718.3	2,714.6	2,725.4	2,730.8	2,725.2	2,685.5	2,669.5	2,686.0	2,720.7	2,723.9	2,718.9	2,711.4
2010	2,648.8	2,647.4	2,667.6	2,702.0	2,725.2	2,723.0	2,684.7	2,674.1	2,692.4	2,724.1	2,736.5	2,738.7	2,697.0
2011	2,662.6	2,674.6	2,695.5	2,725.4	2,729.8	2,728.2	2,685.1	2,674.9	2,698.3	2,727.1	2,735.8	2,733.0	2,705.9
Total Private													
2000	2,346.5	2,350.4	2,373.7	2,393.3	2,398.5	2,416.1	2,400.3	2,398.4	2,409.1	2,416.1	2,435.7	2,454.1	2,399.4
2001	2,370.6	2,375.2	2,391.3	2,402.8	2,414.7	2,428.9	2,406.3	2,406.9	2,401.7	2,403.3	2,416.9	2,422.8	2,403.5
2002	2,351.4	2,355.8	2,372.6	2,379.9	2,391.7	2,408.7	2,388.0	2,391.2	2,390.9	2,401.1	2,413.8	2,418.7	2,388.7
2003	2,342.2	2,336.8	2,354.6	2,371.9	2,384.5	2,395.1	2,383.6	2,380.9	2,381.1	2,391.8	2,402.7	2,407.7	2,377.7
2004	2,334.8	2,339.4	2,360.2	2,378.2	2,394.3	2,410.4	2,405.6	2,402.6	2,404.4	2,421.2	2,432.1	2,439.5	2,393.6
2005	2,363.2	2,369.5	2,379.8	2,415.5	2,430.5	2,435.5	2,432.6	2,426.8	2,435.0	2,443.9	2,459.1	2,462.7	2,421.2
2006	2,395.8	2,402.0	2,417.9	2,445.5	2,458.9	2,466.0	2,454.9	2,449.9	2,451.8	2,465.3	2,475.5	2,481.1	2,447.1
2007	2,417.1	2,415.5	2,432.7	2,454.1	2,469.2	2,480.4	2,473.7	2,467.8	2,462.8	2,481.4	2,494.9	2,496.4	2,462.2
2008	2,430.4	2,434.4	2,445.4	2,472.9	2,478.8	2,481.1	2,469.6	2,460.6	2,453.5	2,462.0	2,455.7	2,448.3	2,457.7
2009	2,366.6	2,360.7	2,354.6	2,364.5	2,373.8	2,370.7	2,357.6	2,344.7	2,337.9	2,362.1	2,363.4	2,359.8	2,359.7
2010	2,298.4	2,290.9	2,309.1	2,341.5	2,359.1	2,362.7	2,355.5	2,351.1	2,350.9	2,373.5	2,382.5	2,384.8	2,346.7
2011	2,317.7	2,325.0	2,344.1	2,373.2	2,379.6	2,382.1	2,369.8	2,363.9	2,368.4	2,386.0	2,393.0	2,390.0	2,366.1
Goods-Producing													
2000	400.7	397.5	405.2	411.5	413.4	418.1	414.9	416.6	415.5	414.2	412.7	411.7	411.0
2001	399.1	398.4	402.1	403.8	405.5	408.9	406.8	406.6	404.9	399.2	396.4	394.0	402.1
2002	381.6	380.9	382.3	382.6	385.7	388.0	386.1	387.3	385.1	382.5	380.3	377.3	383.3
2003	362.7	358.1	360.6	364.5	368.4	370.7	369.5	368.8	366.9	365.3	363.5	359.7	364.9
2004	349.9	348.8	353.8	356.5	360.7	364.8	365.8	366.0	364.7	363.3	362.3	359.6	359.7
2005	345.9	344.7	348.2	355.9	360.2	362.4	363.2	364.3	362.8	361.4	364.5	359.3	357.7
2006	351.9	350.6	354.4	359.6	362.8	364.6	362.6	362.6	359.9	358.3	354.5	352.5	357.9
2007	343.2	338.6	342.8	346.9	350.4	352.4	354.4	354.8	352.3	351.9	351.3	347.7	349.0
2008	338.1	337.2	340.0	343.8	344.0	347.4	345.5	344.3	339.5	335.6	332.1	324.7	339.4
2009	309.1	303.2	301.7	301.3	300.8	301.2	299.3	298.0	294.3	294.5	291.1	288.9	298.6
2010	279.7	275.4	279.8	286.5	289.1	291.9	292.6	292.4	290.2	290.8	289.6	286.7	287.1
2011	276.2	275.0	281.0	287.0	288.0	290.3	291.0	293.3	291.9	292.7	290.8	288.8	287.2
Mining, Logging, and Construction													
2000	110.8	107.9	114.7	120.6	122.6	125.3	123.0	124.0	123.5	123.3	121.4	119.5	119.7
2001	112.3	112.3	116.1	119.9	122.9	125.8	126.9	127.8	127.0	125.7	124.7	122.0	122.0
2002	114.9	114.8	116.6	118.7	121.5	123.5	124.3	125.3	123.1	123.1	121.7	119.5	120.6
2003	113.0	109.8	112.3	118.9	123.0	124.9	127.3	127.4	125.6	125.3	124.6	121.5	121.1
2004	115.1	113.6	118.5	120.9	124.5	127.3	129.0	129.8	129.9	128.9	127.9	125.2	124.2
2005	116.6	114.7	117.6	125.3	129.1	131.5	133.4	133.4	132.7	133.0	134.3	130.1	127.6
2006	122.8	122.2	126.3	131.6	134.8	136.0	135.8	135.8	134.1	133.1	130.5	128.8	131.0
2007	121.7	117.9	121.7	126.1	128.9	131.3	132.5	133.3	132.4	131.8	129.9	125.9	127.8
2008	120.4	118.6	121.2	126.0	127.2	128.5	128.6	128.2	125.3	123.1	120.1	114.9	123.5
2009	104.6	101.9	103.2	104.3	105.1	106.2	106.8	106.3	103.7	103.7	101.0	98.6	103.8
2010	92.0	89.1	93.5	99.4	101.6	103.1	104.6	104.6	103.1	103.7	102.7	99.3	99.7
2011	90.6	90.0	95.2	101.1	101.9	103.5	105.1	106.5	106.0	107.1	104.6	101.8	101.1
Manufacturing													
2000	289.9	289.6	290.5	290.9	290.8	292.8	291.9	292.6	292.0	290.9	291.3	292.2	291.3
2001	286.8	286.1	286.0	283.9	282.6	283.1	279.9	278.8	277.9	273.5	271.7	272.0	280.2
2002	266.7	266.1	265.7	263.9	264.2	264.5	261.8	262.0	262.0	259.4	258.6	257.8	262.7
2003	249.7	248.3	248.3	245.6	245.4	245.8	242.2	241.4	241.3	240.0	238.9	238.2	243.8
2004	234.8	235.2	235.3	235.6	236.2	237.5	236.8	236.2	234.8	234.4	234.4	234.4	235.5
2005	229.3	230.0	230.6	230.6	231.1	230.9	229.8	230.9	230.1	228.4	230.2	229.2	230.1
2006	229.1	228.4	228.1	228.0	228.0	228.6	226.8	226.8	225.8	225.2	224.0	223.7	226.9
2007	221.5	220.7	221.1	220.8	221.5	222.9	221.9	221.5	219.9	220.1	221.4	221.8	221.3
2008	217.7	218.6	218.8	217.8	216.8	218.9	216.9	216.1	214.2	212.5	212.0	209.8	215.8
2009	204.5	201.3	198.5	197.0	195.7	195.0	192.5	191.7	190.6	190.8	190.1	190.3	194.8
2010	187.7	186.3	186.3	187.1	187.5	188.8	188.0	187.8	187.1	187.1	186.9	187.4	187.3
2011	185.6	185.0	185.8	185.9	186.1	186.8	185.9	186.8	185.9	185.6	186.2	187.0	186.1
Service-Providing													
2000	2,286.4	2,300.0	2,320.5	2,335.8	2,344.8	2,350.0	2,313.5	2,302.2	2,333.5	2,349.4	2,374.3	2,394.8	2,333.8
2001	2,318.5	2,330.7	2,344.6	2,355.7	2,363.1	2,370.1	2,326.6	2,322.0	2,338.5	2,355.9	2,376.8	2,387.5	2,349.2
2002	2,323.1	2,334.5	2,351.1	2,358.7	2,366.1	2,376.8	2,330.7	2,324.8	2,348.8	2,371.3	2,390.5	2,398.5	2,356.2
2003	2,329.5	2,335.4	2,352.9	2,366.7	2,374.4	2,379.8	2,344.3	2,335.7	2,359.2	2,383.0	2,398.7	2,407.5	2,363.9
2004	2,337.1	2,349.2	2,367.4	2,384.3	2,393.0	2,400.9	2,368.2	2,360.5	2,387.5	2,415.8	2,430.2	2,439.3	2,386.1
2005	2,370.4	2,384.0	2,393.0	2,421.7	2,429.7	2,427.7	2,402.9	2,391.1	2,418.7	2,438.7	2,452.4	2,460.4	2,415.9
2006	2,395.3	2,409.7	2,423.5	2,445.8	2,455.6	2,454.3	2,422.0	2,414.4	2,437.3	2,461.4	2,478.0	2,484.2	2,440.1
2007	2,421.6	2,431.8	2,446.6	2,463.8	2,473.9	2,477.9	2,447.5	2,437.3	2,453.4	2,483.9	2,500.0	2,503.4	2,461.8
2008	2,440.7	2,451.3	2,461.5	2,486.4	2,489.8	2,486.4	2,447.7	2,439.3	2,460.0	2,484.5	2,483.1	2,482.9	2,467.8
2009	2,409.3	2,415.1	2,412.9	2,424.1	2,430.0	2,424.0	2,386.2	2,371.5	2,391.7	2,426.2	2,432.8	2,430.0	2,412.8
2010	2,369.1	2,372.0	2,387.8	2,415.5	2,436.1	2,431.1	2,392.1	2,381.7	2,402.2	2,433.3	2,446.9	2,452.0	2,410.0
2011	2,386.4	2,399.6	2,414.5	2,438.4	2,441.8	2,437.9	2,394.1	2,381.6	2,406.4	2,434.4	2,445.0	2,444.2	2,418.7

Employment by Industry: Philadelphia–Camden–Wilmington, PA–NJ–DE–MD, Selected Years, 2000–2011—*Continued*

(Numbers in thousands, not seasonally adjusted)

Industry and year	January	February	March	April	May	June	July	August	September	October	November	December	Annual average
Trade, Transportation, and Utilities													
2000	531.3	525.0	526.9	532.0	534.7	537.2	531.0	533.4	536.7	543.4	557.0	568.5	538.1
2001	542.4	533.2	534.8	532.0	533.6	536.0	527.6	527.9	529.4	533.9	546.5	554.7	536.0
2002	529.8	521.1	525.3	523.8	527.5	531.3	524.6	526.3	528.6	535.3	545.6	557.0	531.4
2003	528.4	520.6	523.4	525.7	528.7	532.2	525.5	525.5	528.4	534.9	545.0	553.4	531.0
2004	524.9	521.1	522.9	523.2	527.7	531.1	526.4	526.0	527.2	534.0	543.9	552.4	530.1
2005	529.0	523.3	525.0	527.4	531.1	532.1	529.8	528.9	529.8	534.3	544.8	554.6	532.5
2006	531.2	523.3	527.2	527.7	531.0	532.5	527.7	526.3	527.1	533.0	544.4	551.9	531.9
2007	530.8	521.3	523.3	524.2	529.2	532.5	529.3	527.2	527.0	531.5	544.0	551.8	531.0
2008	532.0	522.2	523.9	525.3	528.5	529.1	523.5	521.8	522.4	526.6	530.0	536.0	526.8
2009	509.8	501.5	498.5	496.3	500.6	502.9	495.6	494.3	496.5	502.4	511.7	517.1	502.3
2010	497.4	488.3	491.7	494.8	499.9	502.6	496.3	495.1	496.2	501.6	511.4	520.1	499.6
2011	498.9	493.8	494.8	498.1	500.2	501.7	493.7	492.4	493.5	498.3	508.0	513.8	498.9
Wholesale Trade													
2000	125.0	125.3	126.3	128.1	128.2	129.2	128.6	128.7	128.3	128.2	128.7	129.5	127.8
2001	130.0	130.2	130.7	131.1	131.0	131.3	131.2	130.7	130.4	130.0	130.2	130.9	130.6
2002	129.5	129.1	130.1	130.1	130.4	130.6	129.9	129.9	129.2	130.6	130.5	131.3	130.1
2003	129.1	129.0	129.9	129.8	130.0	130.3	129.5	129.5	129.4	129.4	130.0	130.5	129.7
2004	127.9	128.1	128.9	129.3	129.8	130.3	130.5	130.3	129.6	130.1	129.9	130.2	129.6
2005	129.8	129.1	129.7	130.1	130.4	130.6	130.5	130.5	129.8	129.9	130.1	130.7	130.1
2006	128.6	128.7	129.6	129.9	130.3	131.3	131.3	131.2	130.3	129.9	129.8	130.1	130.1
2007	128.7	128.2	129.0	130.0	130.2	131.4	131.8	131.3	130.4	130.5	131.0	131.4	130.3
2008	130.0	129.8	130.2	130.4	131.0	131.4	131.5	131.0	130.0	130.1	129.1	128.8	130.3
2009	127.2	126.2	125.8	124.9	124.7	124.6	123.5	122.8	121.8	122.0	121.7	121.8	123.9
2010	120.5	119.8	120.2	120.8	121.4	121.7	121.6	121.5	120.9	121.1	121.1	121.3	121.0
2011	120.3	120.4	121.1	121.8	121.9	122.7	121.6	122.2	122.3	121.8	121.8	122.3	121.7
Retail Trade													
2000	312.7	306.6	307.2	310.0	312.4	315.0	311.6	314.3	314.2	319.2	332.6	342.4	316.5
2001	317.8	308.9	310.3	305.7	307.4	310.0	304.7	306.9	305.6	308.6	321.5	329.4	311.4
2002	308.6	300.9	303.5	300.8	303.4	306.9	303.5	305.4	304.7	307.4	318.2	328.6	307.7
2003	304.4	297.0	299.2	300.7	303.6	307.3	304.6	305.7	305.2	310.3	320.2	328.2	307.2
2004	305.1	300.9	301.9	301.7	305.5	308.1	306.6	307.3	305.7	311.7	321.2	328.5	308.7
2005	308.4	303.4	304.0	305.5	308.5	309.0	309.0	308.7	306.6	310.6	319.7	327.5	310.1
2006	309.4	301.1	303.3	303.6	305.1	306.1	304.2	302.8	301.3	307.0	317.7	323.1	307.1
2007	307.5	299.0	299.8	300.2	304.1	305.9	305.1	304.2	302.0	307.3	318.4	324.3	306.5
2008	308.0	298.7	300.0	300.4	302.7	303.9	301.0	300.6	298.8	302.6	307.2	312.0	303.0
2009	291.7	285.0	282.9	281.7	286.0	287.8	285.7	285.6	284.2	289.1	298.0	302.2	288.3
2010	287.0	278.9	282.1	284.0	288.1	290.1	288.3	288.0	285.0	289.8	299.1	305.1	288.8
2011	288.5	283.4	283.4	286.2	287.4	288.1	285.5	283.4	279.7	284.9	293.9	298.4	286.9
Transportation and Utilities													
2000	93.6	93.1	93.4	93.9	94.1	93.0	90.8	90.4	94.2	96.0	95.7	96.6	93.7
2001	94.6	94.1	93.8	95.2	95.2	94.7	91.7	90.3	93.4	95.3	94.8	94.4	94.0
2002	91.7	91.1	91.7	92.9	93.7	93.8	91.2	91.0	94.7	97.3	96.9	97.1	93.6
2003	94.9	94.6	94.3	95.2	95.1	94.6	91.4	90.3	93.8	95.2	94.8	94.7	94.1
2004	91.9	92.1	92.1	92.2	92.4	92.7	89.3	88.4	91.9	92.2	92.8	93.7	91.8
2005	90.8	90.8	91.3	91.8	92.2	92.5	90.3	89.7	93.4	93.8	95.0	96.4	92.3
2006	93.2	93.5	94.3	94.2	95.6	95.1	92.2	92.3	95.5	96.1	96.9	98.7	94.8
2007	94.6	94.1	94.5	94.0	94.9	95.2	92.4	91.7	94.6	93.7	94.6	96.1	94.2
2008	94.0	93.7	93.7	94.5	94.8	93.8	91.0	90.2	93.6	93.9	93.7	95.2	93.5
2009	90.9	90.3	89.8	89.7	89.9	90.5	86.4	85.9	90.5	91.3	92.0	93.1	90.0
2010	89.9	89.6	89.4	90.0	90.4	90.8	86.4	85.6	90.3	90.7	91.2	93.7	89.8
2011	90.1	90.0	90.3	90.1	90.9	90.9	86.6	86.8	91.5	91.6	92.3	93.1	90.4
Information													
2000	69.6	70.0	70.9	70.6	71.0	71.7	73.1	67.7	73.2	72.7	73.5	74.1	71.5
2001	72.4	72.4	72.3	71.4	71.8	72.4	71.8	70.8	70.0	69.5	70.0	70.2	71.3
2002	69.5	69.4	69.9	68.0	68.6	68.5	67.8	67.4	67.0	66.3	66.7	66.4	68.0
2003	65.2	64.9	65.3	64.1	63.6	63.0	62.0	61.1	60.1	58.9	58.6	57.6	62.0
2004	56.7	56.3	56.4	56.4	56.5	56.7	56.8	56.6	55.8	55.7	55.9	56.0	56.3
2005	54.7	54.7	54.9	55.4	55.5	56.1	55.7	55.7	58.6	55.7	56.0	56.3	55.8
2006	55.4	56.1	55.4	55.4	55.7	55.9	55.8	55.9	56.4	56.4	56.3	56.8	56.0
2007	56.4	56.4	56.5	57.1	57.3	58.1	57.8	58.1	58.9	58.2	58.3	58.8	57.7
2008	57.8	57.8	57.6	57.9	57.9	57.6	57.3	57.1	56.5	56.3	56.2	56.1	57.2
2009	55.4	55.1	54.8	54.5	54.3	54.3	54.0	53.6	53.2	53.3	52.7	52.9	54.0
2010	51.8	51.4	51.7	51.9	51.8	52.4	52.1	51.8	51.8	51.0	50.9	51.1	51.6
2011	50.0	50.0	49.7	50.4	50.2	50.6	50.5	46.7	49.7	49.5	49.4	49.5	49.7
Financial Activities													
2000	217.4	218.0	217.7	217.8	217.7	219.6	219.4	219.2	217.1	217.6	218.7	220.6	218.4
2001	218.2	218.5	219.2	220.1	220.3	221.4	220.9	221.0	217.8	217.6	217.4	218.6	219.3
2002	217.9	217.7	218.1	217.9	217.8	219.4	220.1	220.4	218.8	218.7	219.3	220.1	218.9
2003	219.0	219.2	219.7	220.1	220.7	222.2	223.1	222.9	220.5	219.2	219.2	219.5	220.4
2004	218.4	217.7	218.1	218.8	219.5	220.7	221.1	220.4	217.7	217.3	217.8	218.9	218.9
2005	217.9	218.0	218.1	218.4	219.3	221.1	221.9	222.1	220.2	219.8	220.3	221.3	219.9
2006	219.6	219.2	219.2	220.2	220.4	222.0	222.6	222.3	220.5	220.4	220.6	221.1	220.7
2007	219.6	219.6	219.6	219.9	220.0	221.7	222.8	222.1	219.7	220.0	220.0	220.4	220.5
2008	217.8	218.0	218.2	218.1	217.9	218.9	219.4	218.2	215.3	214.1	213.6	212.7	216.9
2009	210.1	209.1	208.4	208.1	208.0	208.3	207.9	206.1	204.0	203.3	202.5	202.0	206.5
2010	200.3	199.7	199.6	199.5	200.2	200.9	201.5	201.3	199.9	200.2	200.3	201.4	200.4
2011	199.1	198.5	198.5	199.1	199.0	200.0	200.3	200.7	198.7	199.0	198.3	198.4	199.1

Employment by Industry: Philadelphia–Camden–Wilmington, PA–NJ–DE–MD, Selected Years, 2000–2011—*Continued*

(Numbers in thousands, not seasonally adjusted)

Industry and year	January	February	March	April	May	June	July	August	September	October	November	December	Annual average
Professional and Business Services													
2000	387.3	388.0	395.1	395.1	395.0	399.1	397.9	397.5	397.0	394.6	396.3	397.2	395.0
2001	386.1	387.2	391.6	394.3	395.7	397.2	392.0	394.3	392.4	391.2	390.9	388.9	391.8
2002	377.4	377.4	382.4	386.3	386.6	389.3	384.7	385.8	383.2	385.4	386.9	387.0	384.4
2003	378.6	377.0	381.3	387.3	388.6	390.4	390.2	391.0	392.6	394.7	396.5	398.3	388.9
2004	388.4	389.5	395.9	398.6	400.8	406.0	405.7	406.0	405.7	410.0	411.0	411.5	402.4
2005	395.7	396.8	399.1	410.7	410.8	413.2	414.7	413.2	413.0	415.3	416.4	417.2	409.7
2006	404.3	407.0	411.8	420.2	421.4	424.6	424.5	425.3	425.2	428.5	430.9	432.2	421.3
2007	417.6	418.3	422.6	430.6	432.6	435.8	434.2	434.7	431.8	435.5	438.5	438.2	430.9
2008	425.4	424.7	428.7	435.4	435.7	437.0	434.4	434.0	430.8	430.9	428.3	425.2	430.9
2009	411.5	408.9	408.3	412.0	410.5	410.2	407.5	406.7	403.1	409.5	409.9	407.3	408.8
2010	396.4	397.3	399.4	408.0	409.8	411.8	411.0	411.3	410.0	414.2	415.6	415.2	408.3
2011	406.7	406.6	410.5	419.2	418.6	421.2	420.3	422.7	420.6	420.8	420.7	419.3	417.3
Education and Health Services													
2000	449.3	460.4	459.0	460.8	456.0	452.8	446.7	448.0	457.7	463.3	466.9	470.9	457.7
2001	458.3	469.5	469.9	470.6	468.6	466.7	461.0	461.8	469.3	475.9	479.9	478.8	469.2
2002	471.9	483.6	483.9	481.7	477.7	476.2	471.2	471.2	480.4	487.2	490.5	487.4	480.2
2003	476.6	486.2	487.0	487.4	483.2	479.4	474.6	472.8	481.8	490.8	493.3	492.0	483.8
2004	480.8	491.2	493.0	494.6	491.3	485.3	483.4	481.3	492.6	502.4	504.7	503.5	492.0
2005	493.6	506.7	503.8	508.4	505.8	495.2	494.1	491.7	504.9	516.7	518.2	515.6	504.6
2006	505.5	517.7	515.2	520.3	518.3	509.1	507.2	504.1	516.5	525.6	527.8	525.2	516.0
2007	518.1	530.0	531.1	531.3	528.0	519.5	519.2	516.6	526.0	539.3	539.7	537.3	528.0
2008	527.8	543.0	540.6	546.1	541.4	531.6	530.3	529.6	541.0	552.6	555.3	555.2	541.2
2009	545.9	558.3	554.3	556.7	552.8	542.5	541.1	537.3	546.9	559.2	561.5	558.9	551.3
2010	550.0	559.1	558.9	561.4	559.4	548.5	546.3	543.8	554.1	568.6	569.8	567.4	557.3
2011	555.1	568.9	569.4	570.1	566.6	556.0	553.1	551.1	562.0	575.4	578.9	576.3	565.2
Leisure and Hospitality													
2000	182.2	182.0	187.8	194.3	199.0	204.8	204.3	203.4	200.1	197.0	196.7	196.9	195.7
2001	181.8	183.3	186.9	195.9	203.4	209.3	209.0	207.7	202.2	199.3	198.7	200.0	198.1
2002	186.5	188.0	192.3	200.3	206.4	212.6	210.9	210.1	206.3	204.9	203.9	202.8	202.1
2003	192.8	191.9	197.2	202.8	210.4	214.8	217.0	217.4	210.8	207.4	205.6	205.7	206.2
2004	196.2	195.0	198.9	207.8	214.6	221.1	221.1	221.0	216.0	214.4	212.3	213.1	211.0
2005	202.4	200.9	205.5	214.2	222.1	228.5	227.4	225.8	221.4	216.8	214.9	214.2	216.2
2006	205.0	205.0	210.5	218.1	224.6	231.5	229.7	229.5	223.6	220.4	218.5	218.9	219.6
2007	210.1	209.7	214.6	221.2	227.9	233.4	231.7	231.1	224.7	222.5	220.4	219.5	222.2
2008	209.8	209.8	214.8	224.8	230.9	236.2	236.3	233.4	226.6	225.1	219.8	218.1	223.8
2009	206.2	206.0	209.6	216.7	226.7	230.3	231.8	229.1	221.7	221.5	215.7	214.3	219.1
2010	205.2	203.0	209.9	220.3	228.6	233.1	235.2	235.0	229.3	227.2	225.0	222.9	222.9
2011	212.8	213.1	220.3	228.9	236.0	239.5	238.9	235.7	231.6	229.9	226.2	222.9	228.0
Other Services													
2000	108.7	109.5	111.1	111.2	111.7	112.8	113.0	112.6	111.8	113.3	113.9	114.2	112.0
2001	112.3	112.7	114.5	114.7	115.8	117.0	117.2	116.8	115.7	116.7	117.1	117.6	115.7
2002	116.8	117.7	118.4	119.3	121.4	123.4	122.6	122.7	121.5	120.8	120.6	120.7	120.5
2003	118.9	118.9	120.1	120.0	120.9	122.4	121.7	121.4	120.0	120.6	121.0	121.5	120.6
2004	119.5	119.8	121.2	122.3	123.2	124.7	125.3	125.3	124.7	124.1	124.2	124.5	123.2
2005	124.0	124.4	125.2	125.1	125.7	126.9	125.8	125.1	124.3	123.9	124.0	124.2	124.9
2006	122.9	123.1	124.2	124.0	124.7	125.8	124.8	123.9	122.6	122.7	122.5	122.5	123.6
2007	121.3	121.6	122.2	122.9	123.8	125.2	124.3	123.2	122.4	122.5	122.7	122.7	122.9
2008	121.7	121.7	121.6	121.5	122.5	123.3	122.9	122.2	121.4	120.8	120.4	120.3	121.7
2009	118.6	118.6	119.0	118.9	120.1	121.0	120.4	119.6	118.2	118.4	118.3	118.4	119.1
2010	117.6	116.7	118.1	119.1	120.3	121.5	120.5	120.4	119.4	119.9	119.9	120.0	119.5
2011	118.9	119.1	119.9	120.4	121.0	122.8	122.0	121.3	120.4	120.4	120.7	121.0	120.7
Government													
2000	340.6	347.1	352.0	354.0	359.7	352.0	328.1	320.4	339.9	347.5	351.3	352.4	345.4
2001	347.0	353.9	355.4	356.7	353.9	350.1	327.1	321.7	341.7	351.8	356.3	358.7	347.9
2002	353.3	359.6	360.8	361.4	360.1	356.1	328.8	320.9	343.0	352.7	357.0	357.1	350.9
2003	350.0	356.7	358.9	359.3	358.3	355.4	330.2	323.6	345.0	356.5	359.5	359.5	351.1
2004	352.2	358.6	361.0	362.6	359.4	355.3	328.4	323.9	347.8	357.9	360.4	359.4	352.2
2005	353.1	359.2	361.4	362.1	359.4	354.6	333.5	328.6	346.5	356.2	357.8	357.0	352.5
2006	351.4	358.3	360.0	359.9	359.5	352.9	329.7	327.1	345.4	354.4	357.0	355.6	350.9
2007	347.7	354.9	356.7	356.6	355.1	351.7	328.2	324.3	342.9	354.4	356.4	354.7	348.6
2008	348.4	354.1	356.1	357.3	355.0	352.7	323.6	323.0	346.0	358.1	359.5	359.3	349.4
2009	351.8	357.6	360.0	360.9	357.0	354.5	327.9	324.8	348.1	358.6	360.5	359.1	351.7
2010	350.4	356.5	358.5	360.5	366.1	360.3	329.2	323.0	341.5	350.6	354.0	353.9	350.4
2011	344.9	349.6	351.4	352.2	350.2	346.1	315.3	311.0	329.9	341.1	342.8	343.0	339.8

Employment by Industry: Phoenix–Mesa–Glendale, AZ, Selected Years, 2000–2011

(Numbers in thousands, not seasonally adjusted)

Industry and year	January	February	March	April	May	June	July	August	September	October	November	December	Annual average
Total Nonfarm													
2000	1,534.7	1,558.7	1,570.7	1,573.5	1,583.7	1,564.7	1,545.5	1,565.2	1,592.7	1,603.1	1,616.9	1,631.9	1,578.4
2001	1,582.2	1,606.8	1,617.8	1,611.9	1,607.7	1,589.3	1,566.4	1,583.9	1,598.6	1,601.6	1,603.5	1,607.2	1,598.1
2002	1,567.7	1,582.6	1,594.0	1,607.0	1,602.9	1,591.0	1,563.7	1,587.1	1,598.7	1,609.9	1,633.7	1,632.9	1,597.6
2003	1,588.6	1,607.7	1,616.1	1,622.4	1,624.5	1,606.3	1,584.1	1,611.0	1,623.6	1,644.4	1,658.4	1,669.6	1,621.4
2004	1,628.0	1,649.9	1,664.1	1,678.7	1,680.7	1,666.0	1,656.4	1,677.1	1,696.5	1,726.8	1,742.4	1,758.4	1,685.4
2005	1,716.3	1,744.3	1,760.2	1,785.0	1,787.1	1,770.3	1,763.6	1,789.8	1,818.5	1,827.5	1,850.0	1,862.4	1,789.6
2006	1,831.6	1,864.1	1,881.3	1,885.5	1,893.6	1,873.8	1,857.1	1,882.1	1,903.0	1,910.4	1,924.7	1,932.2	1,886.6
2007	1,885.0	1,911.5	1,924.4	1,918.0	1,922.3	1,901.9	1,884.8	1,913.7	1,925.1	1,934.7	1,945.9	1,947.0	1,917.9
2008	1,900.3	1,912.4	1,909.1	1,900.0	1,893.3	1,854.4	1,821.2	1,851.9	1,856.7	1,851.4	1,848.4	1,836.0	1,869.6
2009	1,775.6	1,770.7	1,763.8	1,750.0	1,737.8	1,693.0	1,669.4	1,682.3	1,694.1	1,701.7	1,714.1	1,714.0	1,722.2
2010	1,674.5	1,687.0	1,697.0	1,701.8	1,706.4	1,662.5	1,644.5	1,666.8	1,678.5	1,703.0	1,720.0	1,724.9	1,688.9
2011	1,691.2	1,705.3	1,715.1	1,723.7	1,720.1	1,681.0	1,664.9	1,698.4	1,720.3	1,737.2	1,746.2	1,750.1	1,712.8
Total Private													
2000	1,342.4	1,359.2	1,370.4	1,372.2	1,378.0	1,384.7	1,371.4	1,383.6	1,392.1	1,399.5	1,412.7	1,426.3	1,382.7
2001	1,387.3	1,400.4	1,410.8	1,404.4	1,401.2	1,402.9	1,383.8	1,389.2	1,388.6	1,387.0	1,388.0	1,392.3	1,394.7
2002	1,360.5	1,367.9	1,378.8	1,389.6	1,390.4	1,390.9	1,374.9	1,383.5	1,381.5	1,387.1	1,404.5	1,409.6	1,384.9
2003	1,376.8	1,385.7	1,394.1	1,400.3	1,403.1	1,400.6	1,391.9	1,402.3	1,405.6	1,420.5	1,433.9	1,444.3	1,404.9
2004	1,414.3	1,426.3	1,440.2	1,453.5	1,456.0	1,459.6	1,458.8	1,465.1	1,469.6	1,495.8	1,510.8	1,525.9	1,464.7
2005	1,495.2	1,512.5	1,530.1	1,554.0	1,557.8	1,561.3	1,562.2	1,573.0	1,586.7	1,593.9	1,614.8	1,627.5	1,564.1
2006	1,608.0	1,629.9	1,647.1	1,651.4	1,657.7	1,663.5	1,651.1	1,661.6	1,667.6	1,671.1	1,684.9	1,694.9	1,657.4
2007	1,654.2	1,671.0	1,682.5	1,676.4	1,679.9	1,682.4	1,668.4	1,678.0	1,679.0	1,686.4	1,695.2	1,696.4	1,679.2
2008	1,651.1	1,658.8	1,655.6	1,646.6	1,641.1	1,630.0	1,608.5	1,612.6	1,605.2	1,597.9	1,593.5	1,582.7	1,623.6
2009	1,530.2	1,519.0	1,513.0	1,499.1	1,490.8	1,476.2	1,459.6	1,458.7	1,452.4	1,457.0	1,468.9	1,471.4	1,483.0
2010	1,436.2	1,442.4	1,453.7	1,457.7	1,455.6	1,447.9	1,437.5	1,443.6	1,442.5	1,464.4	1,480.0	1,487.7	1,454.1
2011	1,457.5	1,466.5	1,476.5	1,484.5	1,482.1	1,474.7	1,468.3	1,475.6	1,482.7	1,498.1	1,505.5	1,513.5	1,482.1
Goods-Producing													
2000	278.8	281.3	283.0	282.9	284.8	288.9	288.4	290.1	290.8	290.8	290.6	291.5	286.8
2001	285.3	286.7	288.3	287.1	287.3	288.3	287.2	287.3	283.5	278.6	274.4	271.4	283.8
2002	265.8	265.5	266.3	266.6	267.1	268.6	268.3	268.7	266.1	263.6	262.5	260.8	265.8
2003	257.3	256.9	257.1	259.6	261.3	263.1	263.1	265.2	265.4	265.5	265.6	266.2	262.2
2004	262.2	264.3	266.6	269.1	271.4	275.0	277.4	279.6	281.1	285.0	286.3	288.6	275.6
2005	283.9	287.3	291.5	297.2	300.1	305.1	306.6	308.5	310.1	310.6	313.5	316.3	302.6
2006	312.8	317.9	321.9	324.1	326.3	329.5	328.3	327.9	325.8	321.6	318.9	317.0	322.7
2007	310.2	311.9	312.4	310.8	311.9	315.1	314.1	314.8	311.1	307.6	301.4	297.1	309.9
2008	288.7	286.5	283.9	281.0	279.8	278.0	274.4	272.7	267.9	261.3	253.3	246.2	272.8
2009	234.9	227.7	223.4	218.8	216.0	214.8	211.3	209.1	206.1	204.0	201.9	199.5	214.0
2010	194.2	194.3	194.8	196.2	196.1	197.2	197.3	196.8	196.1	197.6	197.1	196.7	196.2
2011	193.4	193.3	194.5	196.3	197.6	199.3	199.7	200.2	201.5	205.1	199.7	197.5	198.2
Mining and Logging													
2000	2.4	2.4	2.4	2.4	2.4	2.4	2.4	2.4	2.4	2.4	2.4	2.4	2.4
2001	2.5	2.4	2.5	2.4	2.4	2.4	2.3	2.4	2.3	2.3	2.3	2.3	2.4
2002	2.3	2.3	2.3	2.3	2.3	2.3	2.2	2.3	2.1	2.1	2.0	2.0	2.2
2003	2.0	2.0	1.9	2.0	2.0	2.0	2.0	2.0	1.9	1.9	2.0	2.0	2.0
2004	1.9	1.9	1.9	2.0	2.0	2.1	2.1	2.1	2.1	2.2	2.2	2.2	2.1
2005	2.2	2.2	2.2	2.3	2.4	2.4	2.4	1.9	1.9	1.9	2.1	2.4	2.2
2006	2.5	2.4	2.5	2.6	2.6	2.8	2.8	2.9	2.9	2.8	2.9	2.9	2.7
2007	2.9	3.0	3.1	3.0	3.0	3.1	3.4	3.4	3.4	3.5	3.5	3.5	3.2
2008	3.5	3.5	3.6	3.6	3.7	3.9	3.9	4.0	3.9	3.9	3.9	3.8	3.8
2009	3.3	3.3	3.3	3.2	3.0	3.0	2.9	2.9	2.9	3.0	3.0	3.0	3.1
2010	3.0	3.0	3.0	3.0	3.1	3.1	3.0	3.0	3.0	3.0	3.1	3.1	3.0
2011	3.2	3.2	3.2	3.1	3.2	3.3	3.3	3.3	3.2	3.3	3.3	3.3	3.2
Construction													
2000	117.0	118.4	119.8	121.1	122.9	124.8	124.5	125.5	126.1	126.8	126.0	126.7	123.3
2001	122.8	124.9	127.1	127.6	128.9	131.3	131.8	133.4	131.3	128.8	126.7	124.5	128.3
2002	122.2	122.2	123.7	124.6	126.1	127.9	128.2	129.5	128.5	127.4	127.1	126.0	126.1
2003	123.7	124.0	124.6	125.8	127.9	129.7	130.4	132.2	132.9	133.4	133.5	133.8	129.3
2004	130.9	132.4	134.1	136.4	138.3	140.9	143.2	144.9	146.2	149.2	150.2	152.0	141.6
2005	149.0	151.8	155.4	159.7	161.4	165.1	166.8	168.4	170.2	170.7	173.2	174.7	163.9
2006	172.2	176.1	179.5	181.1	183.1	185.6	184.3	184.0	182.6	179.4	177.6	175.5	180.1
2007	169.8	171.0	171.4	170.4	171.3	174.4	172.3	173.1	171.1	167.5	162.2	158.2	169.4
2008	151.5	149.9	148.7	146.0	145.0	143.4	140.5	139.1	135.4	130.1	124.0	118.7	139.4
2009	110.2	105.1	102.8	99.6	98.1	97.7	95.2	93.2	90.7	88.7	86.6	84.2	96.0
2010	81.1	81.3	81.9	82.8	82.3	83.3	83.4	83.1	82.4	83.4	82.7	81.6	82.4
2011	79.2	79.0	80.1	81.5	82.2	83.9	84.3	84.5	85.9	88.3	83.4	82.2	82.9
Manufacturing													
2000	159.4	160.5	160.8	159.4	159.5	161.7	161.5	162.2	162.3	161.6	162.2	162.4	161.1
2001	160.0	159.4	158.7	157.1	156.0	154.6	153.1	151.5	149.9	147.5	145.4	144.6	153.2
2002	141.3	141.0	140.3	139.7	138.7	138.4	137.9	136.9	135.5	134.1	133.4	132.8	137.5
2003	131.6	130.9	130.6	131.8	131.4	131.4	130.7	131.0	130.6	130.2	130.1	130.4	130.9
2004	129.4	130.0	130.6	130.7	131.1	132.0	132.1	132.6	132.8	133.6	133.9	134.4	131.9
2005	132.7	133.3	133.9	135.2	136.3	137.6	137.8	138.2	138.0	138.0	138.2	139.2	136.5
2006	138.1	139.4	139.9	140.4	140.6	141.1	141.2	141.0	140.3	139.4	138.4	138.6	139.9
2007	137.5	137.9	137.9	137.4	137.6	137.6	138.4	138.3	136.6	136.6	135.7	135.4	137.2
2008	133.7	133.1	131.6	131.4	131.1	130.7	130.0	129.6	128.6	127.3	125.4	123.7	129.7
2009	121.4	119.3	117.3	116.0	114.9	114.1	113.2	113.0	112.5	112.3	112.3	112.3	114.9
2010	110.1	110.0	109.9	110.4	110.7	110.8	110.9	110.7	110.7	111.2	111.3	112.0	110.7
2011	111.0	111.1	111.2	111.7	112.2	112.1	112.1	112.4	112.4	113.5	113.0	112.0	112.1

Employment by Industry: Phoenix–Mesa–Glendale, AZ, Selected Years, 2000–2011—*Continued*

(Numbers in thousands, not seasonally adjusted)

Industry and year	January	February	March	April	May	June	July	August	September	October	November	December	Annual average
Service-Providing													
2000	1,255.9	1,277.4	1,287.7	1,290.6	1,298.9	1,275.8	1,257.1	1,275.1	1,301.9	1,312.3	1,326.3	1,340.4	1,291.6
2001	1,296.9	1,320.1	1,329.5	1,324.8	1,320.4	1,301.0	1,279.2	1,296.6	1,315.1	1,323.0	1,329.1	1,335.8	1,314.3
2002	1,301.9	1,317.1	1,327.7	1,340.4	1,335.8	1,322.4	1,295.4	1,318.4	1,332.6	1,346.3	1,371.2	1,372.1	1,331.8
2003	1,331.3	1,350.8	1,359.0	1,362.8	1,363.2	1,343.2	1,321.0	1,345.8	1,358.2	1,378.9	1,392.8	1,403.4	1,359.2
2004	1,365.8	1,385.6	1,397.5	1,409.6	1,409.3	1,391.0	1,379.0	1,397.5	1,415.4	1,441.8	1,456.1	1,469.8	1,409.9
2005	1,432.4	1,457.0	1,468.7	1,487.8	1,487.0	1,465.2	1,457.0	1,481.3	1,508.4	1,516.9	1,536.5	1,546.1	1,487.0
2006	1,518.8	1,546.2	1,559.4	1,561.4	1,567.3	1,544.3	1,528.8	1,554.2	1,577.2	1,588.8	1,605.8	1,615.2	1,564.0
2007	1,574.8	1,599.6	1,612.0	1,607.2	1,610.4	1,586.8	1,570.7	1,598.9	1,614.0	1,627.1	1,644.5	1,649.9	1,608.0
2008	1,611.6	1,625.9	1,625.2	1,619.0	1,613.5	1,576.4	1,546.8	1,579.2	1,588.8	1,590.1	1,595.1	1,589.8	1,596.8
2009	1,540.7	1,543.0	1,540.4	1,531.2	1,521.8	1,478.2	1,458.1	1,473.2	1,488.0	1,497.7	1,512.2	1,514.5	1,508.3
2010	1,480.3	1,492.7	1,502.2	1,505.6	1,510.3	1,465.3	1,447.2	1,470.0	1,482.4	1,505.4	1,522.9	1,528.2	1,492.7
2011	1,497.8	1,512.0	1,520.6	1,527.4	1,522.5	1,481.7	1,465.2	1,498.2	1,518.8	1,532.1	1,546.5	1,552.6	1,514.6
Trade, Transportation, and Utilities													
2000	316.9	317.0	316.3	315.6	316.2	318.7	316.3	318.7	321.1	324.7	334.2	340.7	321.4
2001	326.1	324.3	323.4	323.2	322.7	323.0	320.5	320.8	320.7	324.6	330.0	333.0	324.4
2002	321.6	318.8	320.9	322.7	324.0	325.3	322.2	323.2	324.6	326.9	335.0	340.3	325.5
2003	326.5	325.4	325.5	325.2	325.5	324.8	324.4	325.8	325.9	332.2	340.2	345.0	328.9
2004	333.7	333.8	334.8	336.9	337.4	337.5	338.1	339.1	337.4	345.3	354.1	359.3	340.6
2005	352.1	353.3	354.9	357.4	358.0	358.0	361.0	362.0	364.1	366.7	376.3	381.4	362.1
2006	371.4	371.2	374.1	375.2	375.6	375.6	377.2	378.5	378.7	384.2	393.3	399.3	379.5
2007	386.5	385.9	386.9	387.3	388.3	388.4	389.4	390.6	391.9	394.1	403.2	408.3	391.7
2008	391.7	389.9	388.4	386.1	386.2	385.0	378.9	379.6	377.0	377.7	381.9	381.9	383.7
2009	367.0	360.7	359.0	355.5	354.3	351.6	349.2	348.4	347.0	347.4	354.6	357.3	354.3
2010	346.3	345.7	346.0	346.1	346.2	344.0	341.9	341.9	339.6	344.3	352.3	356.5	345.9
2011	345.8	345.7	346.5	348.9	348.9	348.5	347.2	347.0	348.0	351.6	361.1	362.7	350.2
Wholesale Trade													
2000	76.7	77.4	77.9	77.6	77.6	78.4	78.5	78.7	79.0	79.5	80.0	80.7	78.5
2001	80.3	80.9	80.9	80.4	80.4	79.9	79.4	79.3	78.6	78.4	78.2	78.1	79.6
2002	76.9	77.1	77.6	78.0	78.9	79.0	78.8	78.8	78.7	78.9	79.1	79.0	78.4
2003	77.9	78.0	77.8	77.7	78.0	77.8	77.0	77.1	76.9	76.8	77.1	77.5	77.5
2004	77.8	78.1	78.2	78.4	78.6	78.8	79.7	79.8	78.6	80.5	80.7	81.0	79.2
2005	80.4	81.3	81.8	82.5	82.6	82.7	83.3	83.3	83.5	83.9	84.7	85.3	82.9
2006	84.7	85.4	85.7	86.3	86.5	87.0	87.4	87.6	87.9	88.5	88.5	89.1	87.1
2007	88.0	88.5	88.9	89.1	89.3	89.9	90.4	90.4	90.3	90.6	90.7	91.0	89.8
2008	89.5	90.0	89.8	89.6	89.9	89.5	89.0	89.2	89.1	89.3	88.6	88.0	89.3
2009	86.5	85.7	84.9	84.0	83.3	82.6	82.4	82.1	81.4	81.5	81.4	81.2	83.1
2010	79.9	80.3	80.5	80.3	80.3	80.2	80.0	79.8	79.2	79.9	80.3	80.4	80.1
2011	79.6	80.1	80.1	80.7	80.8	81.1	81.2	80.9	80.9	80.4	80.4	81.8	80.7
Retail Trade													
2000	182.8	182.5	182.2	181.8	182.3	183.6	181.1	182.7	184.3	187.0	195.2	200.5	185.5
2001	187.8	185.2	184.4	184.3	183.1	183.8	182.2	182.4	183.2	187.5	193.6	197.1	186.2
2002	187.2	184.3	185.3	186.4	186.5	186.8	184.1	184.8	186.3	187.7	195.5	201.0	188.0
2003	189.0	187.9	188.2	188.2	188.3	188.1	188.7	189.9	190.0	195.7	203.3	207.4	192.1
2004	196.4	196.2	196.6	198.2	198.6	198.5	197.9	198.8	198.7	203.0	211.7	216.8	201.0
2005	210.5	210.5	211.8	213.5	213.3	213.2	215.4	215.7	217.0	219.4	227.2	230.9	216.5
2006	223.2	222.3	224.7	224.6	224.6	224.3	225.0	225.4	224.8	229.8	238.5	242.6	227.5
2007	231.9	230.6	231.3	231.2	231.5	230.9	231.8	232.6	233.7	235.6	244.5	247.8	234.5
2008	235.0	232.3	231.2	229.0	228.9	228.4	223.3	223.6	221.4	222.3	226.6	227.0	227.4
2009	215.4	210.6	209.9	208.4	208.0	206.3	204.5	204.2	203.8	204.7	211.9	214.1	208.5
2010	205.8	204.8	205.1	206.0	205.9	203.9	202.5	202.3	200.5	203.9	211.1	213.6	205.5
2011	205.3	204.5	205.1	206.4	206.2	205.2	203.8	204.4	204.8	208.8	218.2	218.7	207.6
Transportation and Utilities													
2000	57.4	57.1	56.2	56.2	56.3	56.7	56.7	57.3	57.8	58.2	59.0	59.5	57.4
2001	58.0	58.2	58.1	58.5	59.2	59.3	58.9	59.1	58.9	58.7	58.2	57.8	58.6
2002	57.5	57.4	58.0	58.3	58.6	59.5	59.3	59.6	59.6	60.3	60.4	60.3	59.1
2003	59.6	59.5	59.5	59.3	59.2	58.9	58.7	58.8	59.0	59.7	59.8	60.1	59.3
2004	59.5	59.5	60.0	60.3	60.2	60.2	60.5	60.5	60.1	61.8	61.7	61.5	60.5
2005	61.2	61.5	61.3	61.4	62.1	62.1	62.3	63.0	63.6	63.4	64.4	65.2	62.6
2006	63.5	63.5	63.7	64.3	64.5	64.3	64.8	65.5	66.0	65.9	66.3	67.6	65.0
2007	66.6	66.8	66.7	67.0	67.5	67.6	67.2	67.6	67.9	67.9	68.0	69.5	67.5
2008	67.2	67.6	67.4	67.5	67.4	67.1	66.6	66.8	66.5	66.1	66.7	66.9	67.0
2009	65.1	64.4	64.2	63.1	63.0	62.7	62.3	62.1	61.8	61.2	61.3	62.0	62.8
2010	60.6	60.6	60.4	59.8	60.0	59.9	59.4	59.8	59.9	60.5	60.9	62.5	60.4
2011	60.9	61.1	61.3	61.8	61.9	62.2	62.2	61.7	62.3	62.4	62.5	62.2	61.9
Information													
2000	39.3	40.0	42.4	42.8	43.1	43.2	42.8	42.6	42.2	41.3	41.7	42.3	42.0
2001	41.3	42.4	42.1	42.4	41.6	42.1	41.6	41.5	41.1	41.0	41.4	40.8	41.6
2002	40.7	40.5	40.1	40.4	39.9	39.4	39.4	39.1	38.3	37.7	38.3	38.5	39.4
2003	37.5	37.7	38.0	38.1	37.8	37.9	37.2	37.0	36.5	36.5	37.1	36.9	37.4
2004	36.4	36.2	36.6	36.5	35.7	35.5	34.4	33.4	32.6	32.6	32.9	32.5	34.6
2005	32.2	32.9	33.2	34.0	34.1	33.7	33.3	33.0	32.6	32.9	33.5	34.0	33.3
2006	33.1	33.2	33.3	32.8	32.9	32.7	32.1	32.1	31.3	31.1	31.7	32.1	32.4
2007	30.1	31.0	30.9	31.2	31.8	31.8	31.6	31.2	31.0	30.6	31.5	31.1	31.2
2008	30.6	31.6	32.0	31.3	32.3	32.1	30.9	30.6	31.1	30.3	30.7	30.6	31.2
2009	29.7	30.0	29.6	29.6	30.0	29.3	28.9	28.6	28.1	27.6	28.0	27.8	28.9
2010	27.3	27.5	27.8	27.8	27.7	28.1	27.3	27.1	27.0	26.7	27.2	27.7	27.4
2011	27.5	27.5	27.8	27.9	27.8	28.0	28.1	27.9	27.7	27.4	27.9	28.6	27.8

Employment by Industry: Phoenix–Mesa–Glendale, AZ, Selected Years, 2000–2011—*Continued*

(Numbers in thousands, not seasonally adjusted)

Industry and year	January	February	March	April	May	June	July	August	September	October	November	December	Annual average
Financial Activities													
2000	122.5	124.7	124.7	124.8	125.6	127.0	126.1	126.7	127.5	127.9	128.6	129.8	126.3
2001	125.9	127.4	128.6	128.2	128.9	129.4	130.1	130.7	131.4	130.9	131.3	132.4	129.6
2002	129.8	131.0	130.4	131.7	130.8	130.9	130.3	130.5	130.3	131.6	133.3	134.0	131.2
2003	132.2	132.8	134.0	133.8	134.5	134.8	135.2	136.0	135.1	134.8	135.3	136.0	134.5
2004	134.6	135.3	136.1	138.1	137.9	138.2	139.1	139.4	139.2	141.3	141.8	142.9	138.7
2005	141.7	143.1	143.3	145.5	145.7	146.1	147.3	148.4	149.1	150.5	151.0	152.0	147.0
2006	150.6	151.8	152.6	152.3	152.9	153.3	153.3	153.9	154.1	154.6	154.9	156.1	153.4
2007	154.0	155.2	155.7	155.8	155.4	154.9	154.0	153.1	152.3	151.1	151.0	151.2	153.6
2008	148.1	149.2	149.0	148.5	148.2	147.9	147.0	146.5	146.1	146.3	145.3	145.0	147.3
2009	141.6	141.6	141.3	140.5	140.6	140.0	139.2	139.1	138.0	137.8	137.5	138.3	139.6
2010	136.1	136.7	137.4	136.4	136.4	136.2	136.8	137.2	136.8	138.9	139.3	140.3	137.4
2011	138.6	139.4	139.9	140.2	140.0	140.4	140.2	140.1	139.9	140.2	140.9	143.1	140.2
Professional and Business Services													
2000	248.6	253.8	258.2	262.0	265.3	265.7	264.1	268.3	268.8	270.7	271.1	272.8	264.1
2001	260.1	264.2	267.8	265.4	263.7	263.8	257.3	257.7	257.4	253.9	250.1	251.4	259.4
2002	244.1	247.5	252.3	256.2	256.0	256.4	253.2	256.2	254.7	254.2	255.8	255.9	253.5
2003	248.3	252.8	256.2	258.3	259.4	259.3	256.2	258.6	259.8	263.3	264.1	266.6	258.6
2004	257.2	260.4	264.8	270.9	271.5	273.9	275.0	275.8	278.4	284.3	285.3	288.4	273.8
2005	279.9	284.3	288.5	294.4	294.0	296.7	298.0	300.9	304.6	304.3	307.3	308.6	296.8
2006	302.8	310.0	313.1	315.4	317.8	321.4	319.1	322.7	325.7	326.5	327.3	328.7	319.2
2007	317.9	322.3	326.3	324.3	324.6	326.5	324.6	326.8	325.5	328.2	329.1	327.1	325.3
2008	316.7	319.6	316.8	314.8	312.5	309.2	306.4	307.9	305.4	304.4	301.7	298.8	309.5
2009	285.7	283.3	280.4	277.8	274.7	272.3	270.5	268.2	267.6	271.3	273.8	274.0	275.0
2010	264.8	265.8	269.3	271.9	270.9	270.1	268.1	268.8	268.2	274.6	276.2	279.9	270.7
2011	271.4	274.2	275.7	277.1	274.3	273.8	271.1	272.4	271.6	275.5	278.9	282.9	274.9
Education and Health Services													
2000	134.5	136.5	137.6	136.8	137.1	136.9	135.3	137.0	138.5	138.9	139.6	141.1	137.5
2001	139.9	141.5	142.8	142.7	142.5	143.4	140.7	144.1	146.1	147.3	148.3	150.1	144.1
2002	149.7	151.1	152.2	152.1	153.4	153.7	151.2	154.5	155.8	158.5	160.3	161.0	154.5
2003	159.8	161.5	162.2	164.0	164.2	164.1	162.8	165.3	167.1	168.2	169.2	170.0	164.9
2004	169.5	171.3	172.1	174.2	174.6	174.7	173.0	175.4	176.8	179.8	180.7	182.2	175.4
2005	178.2	180.0	182.9	185.9	186.9	185.6	183.7	187.0	188.6	189.8	191.0	191.8	186.0
2006	191.3	194.0	196.1	197.0	197.7	197.2	196.9	200.6	201.9	202.6	203.9	206.1	198.8
2007	202.7	206.1	207.4	206.1	206.6	207.8	205.7	209.5	211.3	214.9	215.4	216.6	209.2
2008	214.0	217.5	218.3	219.6	220.6	219.6	218.7	221.9	223.9	225.1	226.4	228.2	221.2
2009	223.4	225.2	225.9	226.6	227.3	225.8	224.5	228.7	229.9	233.4	235.5	236.8	228.6
2010	234.2	235.3	236.5	236.5	237.4	235.5	234.8	239.5	241.1	245.5	247.0	245.9	239.1
2011	243.0	244.6	245.4	246.4	247.3	242.8	243.7	247.6	251.9	254.0	253.3	255.0	247.9
Leisure and Hospitality													
2000	147.8	150.9	152.7	152.8	151.0	148.9	143.7	145.6	148.6	150.3	151.8	152.7	149.7
2001	151.7	155.7	158.7	156.7	155.2	152.3	146.5	147.0	148.3	151.3	152.9	153.6	152.5
2002	148.9	153.1	155.5	158.0	157.1	153.8	148.9	149.6	149.8	152.7	157.3	157.0	153.5
2003	154.2	157.4	159.3	160.3	159.1	155.1	150.4	151.1	152.3	156.1	158.0	159.1	156.0
2004	157.5	160.8	164.7	164.2	163.9	160.9	157.6	158.1	159.8	162.9	165.1	167.0	161.9
2005	163.5	167.3	170.6	174.0	173.0	169.9	166.2	167.1	170.8	172.1	174.8	175.6	170.4
2006	175.5	179.6	182.6	183.5	182.4	180.3	175.1	176.2	179.4	181.2	184.7	185.1	180.5
2007	182.8	186.9	190.5	189.8	189.1	184.6	177.8	181.0	183.4	187.4	190.2	191.1	186.2
2008	188.0	190.4	192.6	191.5	187.7	184.2	178.6	180.0	180.5	180.5	181.6	180.0	184.6
2009	177.9	179.9	182.9	181.5	179.0	173.5	168.2	169.1	168.6	169.5	171.7	171.9	174.5
2010	169.3	172.4	177.0	179.0	176.6	172.3	167.8	169.2	170.8	173.3	176.8	176.5	173.4
2011	173.9	177.0	181.8	182.5	180.6	176.1	171.1	175.4	177.2	179.0	178.8	180.2	177.8
Other Services													
2000	54.0	55.0	55.5	54.5	54.9	55.4	54.7	54.6	54.6	54.9	55.1	55.4	54.9
2001	57.0	58.2	59.1	58.7	59.3	60.6	59.9	60.1	60.1	59.4	59.6	59.6	59.3
2002	59.9	60.4	61.1	61.9	62.1	62.8	61.4	61.7	61.9	61.9	62.0	62.1	61.6
2003	61.0	61.2	61.8	61.0	61.3	61.5	62.6	63.3	63.5	63.9	64.4	64.5	62.5
2004	63.2	64.2	64.5	63.6	63.6	63.9	64.2	64.3	64.3	64.6	64.6	65.0	64.2
2005	63.7	64.3	65.2	65.6	66.0	66.2	66.1	66.1	66.8	67.0	67.4	67.8	66.0
2006	70.5	72.2	73.4	71.1	72.1	73.5	69.1	69.7	70.7	69.3	70.2	70.5	71.0
2007	70.0	71.7	72.4	71.1	72.2	73.3	71.2	71.0	72.5	72.5	73.4	73.9	72.1
2008	73.3	74.1	74.6	73.8	73.8	74.0	73.6	73.4	73.3	72.3	72.6	72.0	73.4
2009	70.0	70.6	70.5	68.8	68.9	68.9	67.8	67.5	67.1	66.0	65.9	65.8	68.2
2010	64.0	64.7	64.9	63.8	64.3	64.5	63.5	63.1	62.9	63.5	64.1	64.2	64.0
2011	63.9	64.8	64.9	65.2	65.6	65.8	67.2	65.0	64.9	65.3	64.9	63.5	65.1
Government													
2000	192.3	199.5	200.3	201.3	205.7	180.0	174.1	181.6	200.6	203.6	204.2	205.6	195.7
2001	194.9	206.4	207.0	207.5	206.5	186.4	182.6	194.7	210.0	214.6	215.5	214.9	203.4
2002	207.2	214.7	215.2	217.4	212.5	200.1	188.8	203.6	217.2	222.8	229.2	223.3	212.7
2003	211.8	222.0	222.0	222.1	221.4	205.7	192.2	208.7	218.0	223.9	224.5	225.3	216.5
2004	213.7	223.6	223.9	225.2	224.7	206.4	197.6	212.0	226.9	231.0	231.6	232.5	220.8
2005	221.1	231.8	230.1	231.0	229.3	209.0	201.4	216.8	231.8	233.6	235.2	234.9	225.5
2006	223.6	234.2	234.2	234.1	235.9	210.3	206.0	220.5	235.4	239.3	239.8	237.3	229.2
2007	230.8	240.5	241.9	241.6	242.4	219.5	216.4	235.7	246.1	248.3	250.7	250.6	238.7
2008	249.2	253.6	253.5	253.4	252.2	224.4	212.7	239.3	251.5	253.5	254.9	253.3	246.0
2009	245.4	251.7	250.8	250.9	247.0	216.8	209.8	223.6	241.7	244.7	245.2	242.6	239.2
2010	238.3	244.6	243.3	244.1	250.8	214.6	207.0	223.2	236.0	238.6	240.0	237.2	234.8
2011	233.7	238.8	238.6	239.2	238.0	206.3	196.6	222.8	237.6	239.1	240.7	236.6	230.7

Employment by Industry: Pittsburgh, PA, Selected Years, 2000–2011

(Numbers in thousands, not seasonally adjusted)

Industry and year	January	February	March	April	May	June	July	August	September	October	November	December	Annual average
Total Nonfarm													
2000	1,115.3	1,120.0	1,132.8	1,147.4	1,156.8	1,160.5	1,151.4	1,142.2	1,157.1	1,158.2	1,162.5	1,159.8	1,147.0
2001	1,137.9	1,142.6	1,149.7	1,158.1	1,164.1	1,172.1	1,154.2	1,150.2	1,154.2	1,154.1	1,156.8	1,152.8	1,153.9
2002	1,123.3	1,125.7	1,134.2	1,142.3	1,153.6	1,158.7	1,141.6	1,139.5	1,146.4	1,148.9	1,149.3	1,141.3	1,142.1
2003	1,117.8	1,113.2	1,121.5	1,134.2	1,141.8	1,147.6	1,130.0	1,128.2	1,137.8	1,145.6	1,146.4	1,143.9	1,134.0
2004	1,110.7	1,110.2	1,122.3	1,133.3	1,143.5	1,151.8	1,134.4	1,127.4	1,137.7	1,143.2	1,145.3	1,143.3	1,133.6
2005	1,110.9	1,110.8	1,118.2	1,134.7	1,142.6	1,147.7	1,133.6	1,129.6	1,138.9	1,141.0	1,144.3	1,141.2	1,132.8
2006	1,110.3	1,115.0	1,124.9	1,135.7	1,145.4	1,151.5	1,136.1	1,130.9	1,144.3	1,149.1	1,151.1	1,150.7	1,137.1
2007	1,120.3	1,119.9	1,132.3	1,142.0	1,156.1	1,164.4	1,147.4	1,145.0	1,151.8	1,157.8	1,159.7	1,156.7	1,146.1
2008	1,125.9	1,128.0	1,135.5	1,150.2	1,161.9	1,165.3	1,151.1	1,147.6	1,154.7	1,160.1	1,157.0	1,149.6	1,148.9
2009	1,112.5	1,111.4	1,114.3	1,123.2	1,131.4	1,132.6	1,115.9	1,111.6	1,119.3	1,124.8	1,126.8	1,124.8	1,120.7
2010	1,090.6	1,088.4	1,102.7	1,122.2	1,134.1	1,142.1	1,130.0	1,127.4	1,135.5	1,143.1	1,144.6	1,143.3	1,125.3
2011	1,116.1	1,118.0	1,128.3	1,142.7	1,152.5	1,160.6	1,149.9	1,147.5	1,155.9	1,170.4	1,171.1	1,169.7	1,148.6
Total Private													
2000	988.3	990.7	1,001.2	1,016.1	1,023.2	1,031.8	1,032.0	1,026.8	1,030.8	1,028.6	1,031.6	1,030.1	1,019.3
2001	1,009.4	1,012.4	1,018.8	1,026.9	1,033.3	1,044.3	1,036.4	1,034.7	1,026.5	1,023.1	1,024.5	1,022.1	1,026.0
2002	994.9	994.0	1,002.4	1,010.3	1,021.4	1,028.3	1,021.4	1,022.2	1,018.5	1,016.5	1,015.4	1,008.8	1,012.8
2003	987.8	980.5	987.9	1,001.2	1,009.6	1,016.7	1,011.6	1,012.4	1,009.3	1,012.8	1,012.8	1,011.7	1,004.5
2004	981.5	979.0	990.1	1,000.5	1,011.2	1,020.8	1,016.7	1,013.8	1,010.7	1,012.7	1,013.5	1,012.7	1,005.3
2005	983.1	980.8	987.3	1,003.7	1,012.3	1,018.3	1,017.6	1,017.6	1,013.2	1,011.7	1,013.1	1,011.1	1,005.8
2006	983.4	984.9	994.2	1,005.1	1,015.0	1,022.3	1,018.9	1,017.3	1,017.6	1,019.7	1,020.4	1,020.7	1,010.0
2007	993.6	990.4	1,002.0	1,012.2	1,027.5	1,037.1	1,029.8	1,028.8	1,026.4	1,029.4	1,030.2	1,027.6	1,019.6
2008	1,000.5	999.3	1,006.2	1,021.1	1,033.6	1,038.7	1,032.7	1,030.5	1,028.3	1,030.3	1,026.8	1,020.6	1,022.4
2009	987.3	982.6	985.1	992.9	1,002.2	1,004.9	996.5	993.7	992.4	994.7	995.2	993.9	993.5
2010	964.9	958.8	972.1	990.8	1,000.8	1,011.0	1,009.8	1,009.6	1,008.3	1,012.9	1,014.1	1,013.2	997.2
2011	989.5	988.7	998.3	1,013.2	1,024.7	1,033.7	1,034.3	1,033.7	1,033.5	1,044.0	1,043.1	1,042.5	1,023.3
Goods-Producing													
2000	183.6	183.0	187.5	191.3	194.1	196.4	198.5	198.0	199.2	195.4	193.8	190.3	192.6
2001	185.0	185.6	186.6	188.9	191.0	192.7	192.5	192.3	189.4	187.7	184.1	180.7	188.0
2002	172.5	173.1	174.9	178.3	181.1	182.6	181.3	182.7	180.8	180.0	176.7	172.2	178.0
2003	166.5	163.5	166.2	169.6	170.8	172.1	171.6	171.2	169.6	168.9	166.5	162.7	168.3
2004	154.5	153.1	156.8	160.8	164.2	166.8	167.0	165.9	164.6	164.0	162.0	159.0	161.6
2005	151.9	150.8	152.6	158.3	160.7	162.0	163.0	164.0	163.5	162.4	161.1	157.3	159.0
2006	152.1	152.5	155.8	159.5	161.5	163.0	164.2	164.9	164.8	163.7	162.7	160.5	160.4
2007	155.7	153.3	157.5	161.1	164.8	166.3	166.3	166.0	165.4	164.9	163.1	159.2	162.0
2008	154.2	152.6	155.3	160.3	163.6	165.3	165.7	165.8	165.0	164.6	160.7	156.1	160.8
2009	148.2	146.2	146.7	148.2	148.8	149.5	148.1	147.0	146.5	146.9	145.0	141.0	146.8
2010	134.0	131.9	136.5	142.8	145.3	147.2	149.0	148.8	147.8	147.6	146.9	143.3	143.4
2011	137.7	137.7	141.7	145.8	149.1	151.8	152.1	152.2	152.0	152.1	150.0	145.9	147.3
Mining and Logging													
2005	5.1	5.1	4.7	5.1	5.0	5.0	5.0	5.0	5.0	4.9	5.0	5.0	5.0
2006	4.9	4.9	4.9	4.9	4.9	4.9	4.9	4.9	4.8	4.8	4.8	4.8	4.9
2007	4.8	4.7	4.7	4.7	4.8	4.9	5.0	5.0	4.9	4.9	5.0	5.0	4.9
2008	5.0	5.0	5.0	5.1	5.3	5.5	5.5	5.6	5.6	5.7	5.7	5.7	5.4
2009	5.6	5.5	5.3	5.4	5.4	5.5	5.6	5.6	5.7	5.8	5.9	5.9	5.6
2010	5.9	6.0	6.2	6.4	6.5	6.7	6.9	7.1	7.3	7.2	7.3	7.4	6.7
2011	7.5	7.7	7.9	8.2	8.3	8.6	8.7	8.8	8.8	8.9	9.0	9.0	8.5
Construction													
2005	46.0	45.3	47.0	52.3	54.8	55.6	57.0	57.9	57.9	57.3	56.0	52.1	53.3
2006	48.1	48.6	51.4	54.7	56.3	57.2	58.4	59.1	59.6	58.5	57.1	54.7	55.3
2007	50.6	48.7	52.5	55.8	59.2	60.5	60.5	60.6	60.8	60.4	58.3	54.4	56.9
2008	50.6	49.2	51.6	56.7	59.4	60.4	61.0	61.4	61.1	60.9	57.8	53.9	57.0
2009	48.7	48.9	50.8	53.1	54.8	55.6	54.9	54.4	54.2	54.0	51.8	47.4	52.4
2010	41.7	40.0	44.0	49.7	51.9	52.6	53.9	53.6	52.7	52.4	51.2	47.5	49.3
2011	42.6	42.3	45.7	49.2	52.1	53.9	54.8	55.1	54.9	55.0	53.2	48.8	50.6
Manufacturing													
2000	128.9	129.0	129.5	128.7	128.9	130.2	131.1	130.6	130.3	129.5	129.5	130.0	129.7
2001	127.9	127.4	126.6	125.8	124.5	124.7	123.7	123.1	121.8	120.6	119.5	119.0	123.7
2002	116.5	115.9	115.5	115.3	115.5	116.0	114.9	115.0	114.5	114.4	113.7	113.5	115.1
2003	112.4	110.2	110.0	110.4	109.7	109.6	108.3	107.3	106.3	105.5	104.7	104.5	108.2
2004	102.8	102.2	102.5	103.2	103.0	103.9	103.4	103.1	102.7	102.4	102.4	102.3	102.8
2005	100.8	100.4	100.9	100.9	100.9	101.4	101.0	101.1	100.6	100.2	100.1	100.2	100.7
2006	99.1	99.0	99.5	99.9	100.3	100.9	100.9	100.9	100.4	100.4	100.8	101.0	100.3
2007	100.3	99.9	100.3	100.6	100.8	101.4	100.8	100.4	99.7	99.6	99.8	99.8	100.3
2008	98.6	98.4	98.7	98.5	98.9	99.4	99.2	98.8	98.3	98.0	97.2	96.5	98.4
2009	93.9	91.8	90.6	89.7	88.6	88.4	87.6	87.0	86.6	87.1	87.3	87.7	88.9
2010	86.4	85.9	86.3	86.7	86.9	87.9	88.2	88.1	87.8	88.0	88.4	88.4	87.4
2011	87.6	87.7	88.1	88.4	88.7	89.3	88.6	88.3	88.3	88.2	87.8	88.1	88.3

Employment by Industry: Pittsburgh, PA, Selected Years, 2000–2011—*Continued*

(Numbers in thousands, not seasonally adjusted)

Industry and year	January	February	March	April	May	June	July	August	September	October	November	December	Annual average
Service-Providing													
2000	931.7	937.0	945.3	956.1	962.7	964.1	952.9	944.2	957.9	962.8	968.7	969.5	954.4
2001	952.9	957.0	963.1	969.2	973.1	979.4	961.7	957.9	964.8	966.4	972.7	972.1	965.9
2002	950.8	952.6	959.3	964.0	972.5	976.1	960.3	956.8	965.6	968.9	972.6	969.1	964.1
2003	951.3	949.7	955.3	964.6	971.0	975.5	958.4	957.0	968.2	976.7	979.9	981.2	965.7
2004	956.2	957.1	965.5	972.5	979.3	985.0	967.4	961.5	973.1	979.2	983.3	984.3	972.0
2005	959.0	960.0	965.6	976.4	981.9	985.7	970.6	965.6	975.4	978.6	983.2	983.9	973.8
2006	958.2	962.5	969.1	976.2	983.9	988.5	971.9	966.0	979.5	985.4	988.4	990.2	976.7
2007	964.6	966.6	974.8	980.9	991.3	997.6	981.1	979.0	986.4	992.9	996.6	997.5	984.1
2008	971.7	975.4	980.2	989.9	998.3	1,000.0	985.4	981.8	989.7	995.5	996.3	993.5	988.1
2009	964.3	965.2	967.6	975.0	982.6	983.1	967.8	964.6	972.8	977.9	981.8	983.8	973.9
2010	956.6	956.5	966.2	979.4	988.8	994.9	981.0	978.6	987.7	995.5	997.7	1,000.0	981.9
2011	978.4	980.3	986.6	996.9	1,003.4	1,008.8	997.8	995.3	1,003.9	1,018.3	1,021.1	1,023.8	1,001.2
Trade, Transportation, and Utilities													
2000	239.1	236.6	237.5	241.6	242.8	244.4	241.7	241.6	242.4	245.0	249.0	252.6	242.9
2001	243.9	240.6	241.4	242.0	243.5	244.7	239.9	239.8	240.3	241.0	245.4	246.3	242.4
2002	236.6	233.5	234.6	235.2	236.9	237.6	233.9	234.0	234.5	236.3	239.9	241.6	236.2
2003	231.2	227.9	228.2	230.0	231.9	232.7	229.6	230.6	231.7	235.0	238.5	241.4	232.4
2004	231.9	229.5	230.7	231.3	232.6	232.8	229.3	229.2	229.3	231.2	234.6	237.3	231.6
2005	226.6	224.0	224.8	225.9	227.6	227.9	225.5	225.9	225.7	227.8	231.9	235.3	227.4
2006	226.3	223.2	224.4	224.5	226.3	226.2	222.7	223.0	224.5	226.9	230.7	233.9	226.1
2007	225.9	221.5	223.3	223.4	225.9	226.2	222.8	222.1	222.6	224.2	228.8	231.3	224.8
2008	223.6	220.0	220.9	221.1	223.3	223.2	219.4	218.7	220.3	222.6	225.0	227.6	222.1
2009	217.2	213.8	213.0	213.5	215.3	214.5	210.2	210.1	211.3	213.0	217.3	219.4	214.1
2010	211.6	208.0	210.1	211.6	214.0	215.3	212.2	212.5	213.8	217.0	220.8	224.2	214.3
2011	215.3	213.1	213.8	215.8	217.9	217.6	215.4	215.1	215.1	219.2	224.3	228.3	217.6
Wholesale Trade													
2000	45.8	46.0	46.3	46.9	47.1	47.4	47.0	47.2	46.9	47.3	47.3	47.2	46.9
2001	46.7	46.8	46.9	47.2	47.2	47.4	47.3	47.2	46.6	46.2	46.1	45.9	46.8
2002	45.3	45.1	45.2	45.6	46.0	46.3	45.9	45.7	45.4	45.6	45.7	45.4	45.6
2003	45.2	45.1	45.2	45.6	45.8	45.9	46.0	45.9	45.9	46.3	46.4	46.6	45.8
2004	45.8	45.7	45.9	45.8	46.1	46.6	46.7	46.7	46.2	46.3	46.3	46.4	46.2
2005	46.4	46.6	46.7	47.0	47.4	47.7	47.7	47.8	47.6	47.8	48.0	48.1	47.4
2006	48.0	48.0	48.1	48.3	48.7	49.1	49.1	49.2	48.9	49.2	49.1	49.4	48.8
2007	49.1	48.9	49.2	49.1	49.2	49.5	49.5	49.6	49.1	49.0	49.1	49.1	49.2
2008	48.9	48.8	48.9	49.2	49.5	49.7	49.5	49.4	49.0	49.0	48.7	48.6	49.1
2009	47.8	47.4	47.1	46.9	46.9	46.7	46.3	46.1	45.8	45.6	45.5	45.5	46.5
2010	45.3	44.9	45.4	46.0	46.2	46.4	46.7	46.9	46.6	47.1	46.9	47.1	46.3
2011	46.6	46.6	46.9	47.4	47.8	47.8	47.8	47.8	46.6	47.9	47.4	48.3	47.4
Retail Trade													
2000	139.5	137.1	137.2	140.3	141.2	142.4	141.6	141.7	141.0	141.6	145.7	149.0	141.5
2001	141.9	138.6	139.2	139.2	140.2	141.5	139.3	139.4	138.2	138.5	143.2	145.6	140.4
2002	138.1	135.5	136.3	136.7	138.0	139.3	138.4	138.5	137.1	138.0	142.1	144.8	138.6
2003	136.6	133.8	134.3	135.7	137.0	138.2	137.5	138.2	136.9	138.8	142.2	145.1	137.9
2004	137.7	135.6	136.4	136.9	137.8	138.4	137.7	137.4	135.5	136.5	140.3	142.5	137.7
2005	133.9	131.5	132.0	132.8	134.0	134.7	135.0	135.0	132.0	133.8	137.5	140.3	134.4
2006	132.6	129.8	130.6	130.6	131.8	132.4	131.2	131.5	129.8	131.8	135.9	138.3	132.2
2007	131.6	127.7	129.0	129.0	131.2	131.9	131.4	130.9	128.7	130.6	135.3	137.4	131.2
2008	130.9	127.6	128.5	128.0	129.3	129.8	129.2	128.7	127.5	129.0	131.6	133.8	129.5
2009	126.1	123.3	123.2	123.8	125.6	126.2	125.3	125.4	123.7	125.2	129.3	130.8	125.7
2010	124.7	121.8	123.1	123.7	125.6	126.6	126.5	126.6	124.6	126.7	130.4	132.6	126.1
2011	126.0	123.7	124.1	125.3	126.9	127.4	127.9	127.9	125.9	127.7	132.6	134.5	127.5
Transportation and Utilities													
2000	53.8	53.5	54.0	54.4	54.5	54.6	53.1	52.7	54.5	56.1	56.0	56.4	54.5
2001	55.3	55.2	55.3	55.6	56.1	55.8	53.3	53.2	55.5	56.3	56.1	54.8	55.2
2002	53.2	52.9	53.1	52.9	52.9	52.0	49.6	49.8	52.0	52.7	52.1	51.4	52.1
2003	49.4	49.0	48.7	48.7	49.1	48.6	46.1	46.5	48.9	49.9	49.9	49.7	48.7
2004	48.4	48.2	48.4	48.6	48.7	47.8	44.9	45.1	47.6	48.4	48.0	48.4	47.7
2005	46.3	45.9	46.1	46.1	46.2	45.5	42.8	43.1	46.1	46.2	46.4	46.9	45.6
2006	45.7	45.4	45.7	45.6	45.8	44.7	42.4	42.3	45.8	45.9	45.7	46.2	45.1
2007	45.2	44.9	45.1	45.3	45.5	44.8	41.9	41.6	44.8	44.6	44.4	44.8	44.4
2008	43.8	43.6	43.5	43.9	44.5	43.7	40.7	40.6	43.8	44.6	44.7	45.2	43.6
2009	43.3	43.1	42.7	42.8	42.8	41.6	38.6	38.6	41.8	42.2	42.5	43.1	41.9
2010	41.6	41.3	41.6	41.9	42.2	42.3	39.0	39.0	42.6	43.2	43.5	44.5	41.9
2011	42.7	42.8	42.8	43.1	43.2	42.4	39.7	39.4	42.6	43.6	44.3	45.5	42.7
Information													
2000	25.8	25.9	25.9	25.1	25.4	25.7	26.3	23.6	26.3	26.7	26.9	27.1	25.9
2001	27.4	27.5	27.5	27.1	27.4	27.6	27.4	27.3	27.0	26.8	27.0	27.0	27.3
2002	26.7	26.4	26.4	26.1	26.3	26.1	25.9	25.8	25.4	25.2	25.5	25.5	25.9
2003	25.6	25.4	25.6	25.3	25.5	25.5	25.2	25.3	24.9	24.7	24.9	25.1	25.3
2004	24.8	24.5	24.5	24.2	24.3	24.3	24.1	23.8	23.5	23.3	23.2	23.1	24.0
2005	23.2	23.0	23.0	23.0	23.3	23.5	23.3	23.2	22.9	23.0	23.2	23.3	23.2
2006	22.9	22.9	23.0	23.0	23.0	23.1	23.0	22.9	22.6	22.6	22.4	22.7	22.8
2007	22.0	21.9	22.1	21.8	21.9	22.2	21.9	21.8	21.4	21.2	21.2	21.6	21.8
2008	21.3	21.2	21.1	21.3	21.4	21.3	20.8	20.5	20.2	20.1	20.1	20.2	20.8
2009	19.9	19.8	19.8	19.9	19.8	20.0	19.9	19.5	19.3	19.7	19.6	20.3	19.8
2010	18.6	18.5	18.2	18.4	18.4	18.9	18.8	18.5	18.7	18.1	18.2	18.3	18.5
2011	18.2	18.2	18.3	18.4	18.6	18.7	18.6	19.4	18.0	18.1	18.0	18.2	18.4

Employment by Industry: Pittsburgh, PA, Selected Years, 2000–2011—*Continued*

(Numbers in thousands, not seasonally adjusted)

Industry and year	January	February	March	April	May	June	July	August	September	October	November	December	Annual average
Financial Activities													
2000	67.0	66.9	66.8	67.4	67.5	68.0	67.8	67.5	66.9	66.8	67.1	67.3	67.3
2001	67.5	67.7	67.9	67.3	67.7	68.4	68.6	68.4	67.5	67.4	67.6	67.8	67.8
2002	67.7	68.0	68.3	68.0	68.6	69.1	69.1	69.1	68.5	68.2	68.3	68.6	68.5
2003	69.0	68.9	69.2	69.8	70.3	70.7	71.2	71.2	70.6	70.2	70.2	70.3	70.1
2004	70.0	69.7	69.9	69.5	69.8	70.2	70.3	70.0	69.1	69.0	68.9	69.1	69.6
2005	68.7	68.6	68.9	69.0	69.3	69.5	70.1	70.0	69.2	69.1	69.2	69.2	69.2
2006	68.1	68.3	68.4	68.7	69.0	69.6	69.0	68.8	67.9	67.7	67.7	67.9	68.4
2007	67.6	67.8	68.0	67.8	68.2	68.8	68.9	68.8	68.0	67.7	67.8	67.6	68.1
2008	66.8	67.1	67.5	67.7	68.3	69.0	68.9	68.8	67.6	67.4	67.4	67.4	67.8
2009	66.9	66.9	66.8	67.0	67.4	68.1	68.1	68.0	67.4	67.7	67.9	68.1	67.5
2010	67.6	67.4	67.7	68.0	68.4	68.9	69.0	69.0	68.2	68.3	68.3	68.5	68.3
2011	68.6	68.4	68.5	68.8	69.2	69.8	70.4	71.0	69.5	70.2	70.8	71.0	69.7
Professional and Business Services													
2000	134.8	135.4	136.4	140.3	139.9	142.1	142.3	141.9	140.4	139.1	139.2	138.5	139.2
2001	138.5	138.9	139.8	142.2	141.7	143.5	141.7	142.3	140.7	140.1	140.1	139.2	140.7
2002	134.6	134.0	134.6	136.3	137.2	138.5	138.8	139.0	137.1	136.5	136.6	136.6	136.7
2003	131.9	130.6	131.3	134.1	135.0	135.5	135.7	136.9	135.5	136.3	136.7	136.7	134.7
2004	133.7	133.8	135.3	138.4	139.6	141.8	142.5	143.7	143.1	144.7	145.2	145.7	140.6
2005	141.4	141.3	142.5	145.8	145.8	146.8	147.4	147.7	146.1	145.9	145.9	145.5	145.2
2006	141.5	142.5	144.2	146.4	147.4	149.7	151.1	151.2	150.7	151.4	151.6	150.8	148.2
2007	148.2	149.4	151.1	154.2	155.7	159.1	158.7	159.7	158.0	158.3	159.2	159.4	155.9
2008	156.2	156.8	157.2	160.6	161.1	162.8	163.2	163.0	161.0	160.7	160.3	158.6	160.1
2009	154.3	153.7	153.3	153.9	154.7	155.3	154.3	154.3	153.4	153.9	153.8	153.9	154.1
2010	151.0	151.1	152.7	156.6	157.5	159.6	160.6	160.9	159.7	161.1	162.0	161.4	157.9
2011	159.7	160.0	161.1	164.0	165.4	166.2	167.5	167.7	165.0	166.1	165.1	166.8	164.6
Education and Health Services													
2000	194.9	198.3	198.7	199.0	196.2	194.4	194.8	193.7	199.1	202.1	203.0	202.3	198.0
2001	199.2	202.3	203.6	202.9	199.1	200.1	199.5	197.7	202.4	203.3	204.6	204.9	201.6
2002	205.8	208.3	209.8	208.2	206.5	205.6	203.6	202.2	207.2	209.6	209.9	205.9	206.9
2003	211.2	212.9	213.6	212.4	210.1	209.6	207.5	205.2	210.1	214.0	214.7	214.3	211.3
2004	211.7	213.3	214.4	214.7	212.6	212.3	211.4	208.6	213.6	217.0	218.4	218.2	213.9
2005	217.0	218.8	219.3	219.9	217.2	217.1	217.2	215.4	220.1	222.9	224.1	224.6	219.5
2006	221.0	223.6	223.9	223.8	222.0	220.3	219.5	217.9	223.6	226.0	227.3	227.1	223.0
2007	222.6	225.4	226.5	226.4	225.2	224.0	223.3	221.9	226.9	230.7	231.2	230.4	226.2
2008	226.3	229.9	230.1	231.0	229.4	227.4	226.5	225.8	231.1	234.1	235.3	234.0	230.1
2009	231.1	232.7	233.0	234.1	232.8	231.2	230.7	228.4	233.2	235.9	236.9	236.6	233.1
2010	234.2	234.6	235.9	236.4	234.8	234.7	233.7	231.6	236.6	240.0	239.8	239.5	236.0
2011	238.2	240.0	240.6	240.9	238.8	239.4	238.9	238.9	248.7	253.2	253.9	252.9	243.7
Leisure and Hospitality													
2000	87.8	88.9	91.8	95.3	101.3	104.0	103.9	104.0	100.0	96.6	95.5	94.9	97.0
2001	90.8	92.1	94.1	98.5	104.5	108.3	107.9	108.5	101.7	99.2	98.0	98.6	100.2
2002	94.2	93.8	96.3	100.5	106.6	109.8	109.6	110.6	107.2	102.8	100.6	100.3	102.7
2003	95.3	94.3	96.4	101.8	107.5	111.5	111.0	112.3	108.3	104.8	102.5	102.3	104.0
2004	96.2	96.8	99.2	102.6	108.7	112.2	111.4	112.5	108.6	104.7	102.5	101.7	104.8
2005	96.3	96.3	98.0	103.7	110.4	113.4	113.4	114.7	110.9	106.2	103.7	102.7	105.8
2006	97.2	97.9	100.2	104.4	110.7	114.6	113.6	113.5	109.1	107.5	104.2	104.1	106.4
2007	98.7	98.4	100.2	104.2	112.3	116.0	113.8	114.9	111.2	109.5	105.9	105.4	107.5
2008	100.0	99.9	102.0	106.4	113.4	116.1	114.6	114.9	110.7	108.4	105.7	104.2	108.0
2009	98.2	98.1	100.7	104.5	111.1	113.3	112.3	114.0	110.0	106.3	103.6	103.5	106.3
2010	97.6	97.3	100.3	106.2	111.0	114.2	114.1	115.9	112.5	109.7	107.1	106.9	107.7
2011	101.5	100.8	103.4	108.4	114.1	117.8	118.7	116.9	113.6	113.0	108.6	107.2	110.3
Other Services													
2000	55.3	55.7	56.6	56.1	56.0	56.8	56.7	56.5	56.5	56.9	57.1	57.1	56.4
2001	57.1	57.7	57.9	58.0	58.4	59.0	58.9	58.4	57.5	57.6	57.7	57.6	58.0
2002	56.8	56.9	57.5	57.7	58.2	59.0	59.2	58.8	57.8	57.9	57.9	58.1	58.0
2003	57.1	57.0	57.4	58.2	58.5	59.1	59.8	59.7	58.6	58.9	58.8	58.9	58.5
2004	58.7	58.3	59.3	59.0	59.4	60.4	60.7	60.1	58.9	58.8	58.7	58.6	59.2
2005	58.0	58.0	58.2	58.1	58.0	58.1	57.7	56.7	54.8	54.4	54.0	53.2	56.6
2006	54.3	54.0	54.3	54.8	55.1	55.8	55.8	55.1	54.4	53.9	53.8	53.7	54.6
2007	52.9	52.7	53.3	53.3	53.5	54.0	54.1	53.6	52.9	52.9	53.0	52.7	53.2
2008	52.1	51.8	52.1	52.7	53.1	53.6	53.6	53.0	52.4	52.4	52.3	52.5	52.6
2009	51.5	51.4	51.8	51.8	52.3	53.0	53.0	52.4	51.3	51.3	51.1	51.1	51.8
2010	50.3	50.0	50.7	50.8	51.4	52.2	52.4	52.4	51.0	51.1	51.0	51.1	51.2
2011	50.3	50.5	50.9	51.1	51.6	52.4	52.7	52.5	51.6	52.1	52.4	52.2	51.7
Government													
2000	127.0	129.3	131.6	131.3	133.6	128.7	119.4	115.4	126.3	129.6	130.9	129.7	127.7
2001	128.5	130.2	130.9	131.2	130.8	127.8	117.8	115.5	127.7	131.0	132.3	130.7	127.9
2002	128.4	131.7	131.8	132.0	132.2	130.4	120.2	117.3	127.9	132.4	133.9	132.5	129.2
2003	130.0	132.7	133.6	133.0	132.2	130.9	118.4	115.8	128.5	132.8	133.6	132.2	129.5
2004	129.2	131.2	132.2	132.8	132.3	131.0	117.7	113.6	127.0	130.5	131.8	130.6	128.3
2005	127.8	130.0	130.9	131.0	130.3	129.4	116.0	112.0	125.7	129.3	131.2	130.1	127.0
2006	126.9	130.1	130.7	130.6	130.4	129.2	117.2	113.6	126.7	129.4	130.7	130.0	127.1
2007	126.7	129.5	130.3	129.8	128.6	127.3	117.6	116.2	125.4	128.4	129.5	129.1	126.5
2008	125.4	128.7	129.3	129.1	128.3	126.6	118.4	117.1	126.4	129.8	130.2	129.0	126.5
2009	125.2	128.8	129.2	130.3	129.2	127.7	119.4	117.9	126.9	130.1	131.6	130.9	127.3
2010	125.7	129.6	130.6	131.4	133.3	131.1	120.2	117.8	127.2	130.2	130.5	130.1	128.1
2011	126.6	129.3	130.0	129.5	127.8	126.9	115.6	113.8	122.4	126.4	128.0	127.2	125.3

Employment by Industry: Portland–Vancouver–Hillsborough, OR–WA, Selected Years, 2000–2011

(Numbers in thousands, not seasonally adjusted)

Industry and year	January	February	March	April	May	June	July	August	September	October	November	December	Annual average
Total Nonfarm													
2000	945.6	954.0	957.6	964.3	972.2	978.8	973.7	974.6	981.7	987.1	994.5	995.2	973.3
2001	970.7	973.1	973.9	973.3	974.4	975.8	957.0	954.2	962.1	960.7	959.9	956.5	966.0
2002	935.6	939.3	942.0	945.3	948.8	952.0	934.9	935.1	944.9	951.4	952.0	948.3	944.1
2003	926.7	927.4	928.9	930.8	933.5	934.3	926.6	929.3	936.5	943.8	946.8	947.1	934.3
2004	919.3	929.7	937.6	947.3	953.6	959.1	954.8	955.8	963.6	973.4	976.6	978.2	954.1
2005	954.3	962.8	969.0	975.6	981.0	985.9	980.1	983.7	990.8	1,000.6	1,007.8	1,012.1	983.6
2006	986.1	995.1	1,001.8	1,008.8	1,016.3	1,021.3	1,012.1	1,013.5	1,022.4	1,031.7	1,037.3	1,037.6	1,015.3
2007	1,013.0	1,022.3	1,029.0	1,029.4	1,036.6	1,038.0	1,030.2	1,031.1	1,037.7	1,047.8	1,052.5	1,051.4	1,034.9
2008	1,026.5	1,033.3	1,036.9	1,040.4	1,043.2	1,041.0	1,034.9	1,032.2	1,037.5	1,036.3	1,030.3	1,018.2	1,034.2
2009	988.9	985.3	980.1	978.5	978.7	973.7	963.4	959.8	964.0	971.9	972.1	969.1	973.8
2010	949.1	953.3	957.2	965.4	971.5	973.0	963.3	963.7	970.1	985.4	987.3	986.6	968.8
2011	966.8	973.3	977.0	987.1	988.2	989.8	981.5	983.0	989.7	998.9	1,000.0	998.1	986.1
Total Private													
2000	816.5	822.4	825.5	831.7	836.6	844.6	849.1	853.1	856.8	854.6	860.9	861.7	842.8
2001	838.8	839.7	839.7	839.3	838.7	840.7	837.8	838.0	833.3	824.7	822.7	819.7	834.4
2002	801.1	802.2	804.0	807.2	809.5	812.6	814.3	817.6	815.7	814.5	813.6	811.1	810.3
2003	792.6	792.1	793.2	794.5	796.4	798.4	801.9	806.2	806.3	808.1	809.6	810.4	800.8
2004	784.7	792.9	799.5	809.1	814.9	819.7	825.3	828.9	830.3	834.0	836.5	838.4	817.9
2005	816.0	822.5	828.4	835.3	839.9	844.5	851.2	856.4	858.9	861.3	866.4	871.4	846.0
2006	847.8	854.7	860.3	867.3	872.9	878.3	881.5	885.4	888.8	890.6	893.7	895.4	876.4
2007	871.9	879.4	884.9	885.1	890.1	891.5	895.5	899.5	901.6	902.5	905.5	904.5	892.7
2008	880.8	886.2	888.6	891.8	893.1	891.2	893.8	893.9	894.7	886.8	878.5	867.4	887.2
2009	839.9	834.3	828.3	826.6	826.0	822.6	822.4	821.6	823.7	822.6	821.2	819.2	825.7
2010	800.5	803.3	806.8	815.8	818.1	819.7	823.7	826.4	830.6	837.0	836.9	838.7	821.5
2011	818.5	824.0	827.8	836.4	837.5	841.3	844.3	848.0	853.0	852.4	852.1	852.0	840.6
Goods-Producing													
2000	191.0	192.3	193.3	194.1	196.1	200.0	202.5	203.0	204.9	201.1	201.7	200.7	198.4
2001	197.0	196.1	194.2	192.9	192.1	193.5	194.8	194.2	191.5	187.8	183.8	180.9	191.6
2002	176.0	175.7	175.6	175.6	176.0	178.1	180.4	182.5	180.0	177.7	175.0	172.4	177.1
2003	169.5	168.0	167.6	166.8	167.8	169.7	171.7	173.5	172.4	171.4	170.2	169.8	169.9
2004	164.5	166.9	169.1	171.8	174.0	176.9	180.8	182.1	182.1	181.7	179.3	179.1	175.7
2005	176.1	177.0	178.6	179.8	181.4	183.9	187.6	188.9	188.0	188.6	187.0	187.4	183.7
2006	184.0	185.4	186.7	188.1	189.8	193.3	196.0	197.2	196.9	195.3	193.0	192.3	191.5
2007	188.9	190.0	191.1	190.2	192.3	193.2	196.5	197.7	196.5	195.5	193.2	191.2	193.0
2008	186.7	186.9	186.8	186.3	187.2	187.9	189.6	189.1	188.0	183.6	179.6	174.3	185.5
2009	168.7	164.7	161.8	159.5	159.1	159.2	160.2	160.0	159.2	157.6	153.9	152.3	159.7
2010	148.9	148.3	149.1	150.1	151.4	153.0	156.1	156.9	156.9	157.6	155.1	154.4	153.2
2011	151.2	152.6	154.0	156.0	157.3	159.7	161.1	161.8	162.7	162.6	162.6	161.1	158.6
Mining and Logging													
2000	1.8	1.9	1.8	1.8	1.8	2.0	1.9	2.0	1.9	1.9	1.9	1.8	1.9
2001	1.7	1.7	1.7	1.7	1.7	1.8	1.8	1.8	1.8	1.8	1.7	1.6	1.7
2002	1.5	1.5	1.5	1.6	1.6	1.7	1.8	1.8	1.8	1.8	1.7	1.6	1.7
2003	1.6	1.6	1.6	1.6	1.6	1.7	1.7	1.7	1.8	1.7	1.7	1.7	1.7
2004	1.5	1.5	1.6	1.6	1.7	1.7	1.8	1.8	1.8	1.8	1.7	1.7	1.7
2005	1.7	1.7	1.7	1.7	1.8	1.8	1.9	1.9	1.8	1.8	1.8	1.7	1.8
2006	1.6	1.6	1.6	1.6	1.7	1.8	1.8	1.8	1.8	1.7	1.6	1.6	1.7
2007	1.5	1.6	1.6	1.6	1.7	1.7	1.7	1.7	1.7	1.7	1.6	1.5	1.6
2008	1.5	1.5	1.5	1.5	1.6	1.6	1.6	1.7	1.6	1.6	1.5	1.4	1.6
2009	1.2	1.2	1.2	1.1	1.2	1.2	1.3	1.3	1.3	1.3	1.2	1.1	1.2
2010	1.0	1.0	1.1	1.0	1.1	1.1	1.1	1.1	1.1	1.1	1.1	1.0	1.1
2011	0.9	1.0	1.0	1.0	1.1	1.1	1.1	1.1	1.1	1.1	1.1	1.0	1.1
Construction													
2000	48.7	49.3	49.9	50.9	51.8	53.5	55.3	56.6	57.1	56.1	54.9	54.2	53.2
2001	53.5	53.4	53.6	52.8	53.3	54.6	55.8	56.7	55.7	54.3	52.6	51.4	54.0
2002	49.3	49.6	49.9	50.1	50.8	51.8	53.6	55.3	54.2	53.5	51.6	49.6	51.6
2003	48.2	47.6	47.6	47.4	48.6	49.6	51.3	53.2	52.8	52.7	51.4	50.7	50.1
2004	47.4	49.0	50.2	51.8	53.3	55.0	56.8	57.8	57.5	57.1	55.8	55.2	53.9
2005	53.3	53.8	55.1	55.8	57.1	58.4	60.8	62.2	62.2	61.8	60.6	60.8	58.5
2006	58.3	59.4	60.1	61.0	62.2	64.3	65.6	66.7	66.6	65.9	64.5	63.7	63.2
2007	61.4	62.2	63.2	63.4	65.4	65.5	67.8	68.9	68.3	67.4	66.0	64.4	65.3
2008	60.9	61.0	61.0	60.9	61.9	62.5	63.2	63.3	62.7	60.4	57.2	54.4	60.8
2009	51.8	50.4	49.4	48.9	49.2	50.0	50.8	50.9	50.3	49.0	46.5	45.4	49.4
2010	42.8	42.4	42.8	43.6	44.3	45.1	47.1	47.7	47.6	47.4	45.2	44.7	45.1
2011	42.3	42.9	43.8	45.2	45.9	47.3	48.6	48.9	50.2	50.9	51.0	50.3	47.3
Manufacturing													
2000	140.5	141.1	141.6	141.4	142.5	144.5	145.3	144.4	145.9	143.1	144.9	144.7	143.3
2001	141.8	141.0	138.9	138.4	137.1	137.1	137.2	135.7	134.0	131.7	129.5	127.9	135.9
2002	125.2	124.6	124.2	123.9	123.6	124.6	125.0	125.4	124.0	122.4	121.7	121.2	123.8
2003	119.7	118.8	118.4	117.8	117.6	118.4	118.7	118.6	117.8	117.0	117.1	117.4	118.1
2004	115.6	116.4	117.3	118.4	119.0	120.2	122.2	122.5	122.8	122.8	121.8	122.2	120.1
2005	121.1	121.5	121.8	122.3	122.5	123.7	124.9	124.8	124.0	125.0	124.6	124.9	123.4
2006	124.1	124.4	125.0	125.5	125.9	127.2	128.6	128.7	128.5	127.7	126.9	127.0	126.6
2007	126.0	126.2	126.3	125.2	125.2	126.0	127.0	127.1	126.5	126.4	125.6	125.3	126.1
2008	124.3	124.4	124.3	123.9	123.7	123.8	124.8	124.1	123.7	121.6	120.9	118.5	123.2
2009	115.7	113.1	111.2	109.5	108.7	108.0	108.1	107.8	107.6	107.3	106.2	105.8	109.1
2010	105.1	104.9	105.2	105.5	106.0	106.8	107.9	108.1	108.2	109.1	108.8	108.7	107.0
2011	108.0	108.7	109.2	109.8	110.3	111.3	111.4	111.8	111.4	110.6	110.5	109.8	110.2

Employment by Industry: Portland–Vancouver–Hillsborough, OR–WA, Selected Years, 2000–2011—*Continued*

(Numbers in thousands, not seasonally adjusted)

Industry and year	January	February	March	April	May	June	July	August	September	October	November	December	Annual average
Service-Providing													
2000	754.6	761.7	764.3	770.2	776.1	778.8	771.2	771.6	776.8	786.0	792.8	794.5	774.9
2001	773.7	777.0	779.7	780.4	782.3	782.3	762.2	760.0	770.6	772.9	776.1	775.6	774.4
2002	759.6	763.6	766.4	769.7	772.8	773.9	754.5	752.6	764.9	773.7	777.0	775.9	767.1
2003	757.2	759.4	761.3	764.0	765.7	764.6	754.9	755.8	764.1	772.4	776.6	777.3	764.4
2004	754.8	762.8	768.5	775.5	779.6	782.2	774.0	773.7	781.5	791.7	797.3	799.1	778.4
2005	778.2	785.8	790.4	795.8	799.6	802.0	792.5	794.8	802.8	812.0	820.8	824.7	800.0
2006	802.1	809.7	815.1	820.7	826.5	828.0	816.1	816.3	825.5	836.4	844.3	845.3	823.8
2007	824.1	832.3	837.9	839.2	844.3	844.8	833.7	833.4	841.2	852.3	859.3	860.2	841.9
2008	839.8	846.4	850.1	854.1	856.0	853.1	845.3	843.1	849.5	852.7	850.7	843.9	848.7
2009	820.2	820.6	818.3	819.0	819.6	814.5	803.2	799.8	804.8	814.3	818.2	816.8	814.1
2010	800.2	805.0	808.1	815.3	820.1	820.0	807.2	806.8	813.2	827.8	832.2	832.2	815.7
2011	815.6	820.7	823.0	831.1	830.9	830.1	820.4	821.2	827.0	836.3	837.4	837.0	827.6
Trade, Transportation, and Utilities													
2000	197.3	196.3	196.4	197.8	198.7	201.2	201.6	202.0	201.4	202.7	207.3	209.1	201.0
2001	199.6	198.0	197.9	197.7	197.9	199.6	198.5	198.4	196.6	195.5	198.0	199.3	198.1
2002	191.6	189.9	190.1	190.8	191.9	193.0	193.4	192.6	192.0	191.8	194.8	197.1	192.4
2003	189.8	188.0	187.8	187.9	189.0	190.3	190.7	191.3	190.6	192.3	195.8	197.3	190.9
2004	189.1	188.4	188.9	190.5	191.5	193.2	194.1	194.5	193.8	195.5	199.7	201.8	193.4
2005	193.9	193.0	193.6	194.3	195.2	196.9	198.3	199.1	199.3	200.1	204.7	207.9	198.0
2006	199.0	198.0	198.5	199.2	200.9	202.3	203.0	203.5	203.2	203.5	208.3	211.2	202.6
2007	202.8	201.8	202.3	202.4	204.0	205.2	205.9	206.2	206.5	206.7	211.6	213.5	205.7
2008	205.1	203.8	203.5	203.5	203.7	203.6	204.8	204.8	204.2	203.1	203.5	203.5	203.9
2009	194.7	191.6	189.2	188.2	189.0	188.7	188.4	188.2	188.0	187.7	190.0	192.1	189.7
2010	185.2	183.7	183.8	185.1	185.8	186.7	187.8	188.1	188.1	189.5	193.0	195.3	187.7
2011	188.0	186.8	186.8	188.4	189.6	190.6	192.6	192.5	191.4	192.7	195.5	197.9	191.1
Wholesale Trade													
2000	54.1	54.3	54.4	54.9	55.2	55.5	56.1	56.4	56.1	56.5	56.7	56.8	55.6
2001	56.6	56.8	56.9	56.8	56.7	57.0	56.7	56.7	56.0	55.2	55.2	54.9	56.3
2002	54.4	54.3	54.2	54.5	54.6	54.7	55.0	55.1	54.8	54.6	54.7	54.7	54.6
2003	54.7	54.7	54.7	54.7	54.7	55.0	55.2	55.2	54.9	54.6	54.6	54.5	54.8
2004	54.1	54.5	54.5	54.8	55.0	55.3	55.9	55.9	55.3	55.2	55.4	55.5	55.1
2005	55.2	55.7	55.8	55.8	56.0	56.4	56.8	56.7	56.8	56.6	56.7	57.0	56.3
2006	56.2	56.7	56.7	57.2	57.6	57.8	58.0	58.2	57.7	57.8	57.9	58.0	57.5
2007	57.5	58.0	58.0	58.0	58.4	58.4	58.7	58.3	58.0	58.2	58.1	58.1	58.1
2008	57.5	57.9	57.7	57.6	58.0	58.0	58.6	58.3	58.0	57.9	57.6	57.0	57.8
2009	56.0	55.7	55.0	54.9	54.9	54.5	54.5	54.2	53.5	53.2	52.9	52.9	54.4
2010	52.0	52.1	52.0	52.9	53.3	53.3	53.9	53.8	53.5	53.8	54.1	54.1	53.2
2011	53.2	53.6	53.5	54.3	54.9	54.8	55.8	56.2	55.7	55.5	55.7	56.1	54.9
Retail Trade													
2000	105.1	104.1	104.1	104.3	105.1	106.7	107.1	107.0	106.3	107.2	111.1	113.2	106.8
2001	105.3	103.3	103.0	102.7	102.4	103.8	103.2	102.7	101.8	101.5	104.5	106.3	103.4
2002	100.0	98.4	98.6	98.8	99.7	100.6	101.0	100.2	99.9	100.0	103.3	105.5	100.5
2003	98.6	97.3	97.1	97.2	98.1	99.0	99.4	99.7	99.0	100.4	103.9	105.5	99.6
2004	98.4	97.3	97.8	98.9	99.8	101.1	101.6	101.9	101.3	102.3	106.5	108.4	101.3
2005	102.4	100.8	101.1	101.7	102.6	103.7	105.0	105.8	105.4	106.4	110.6	112.7	104.9
2006	105.9	104.1	104.5	105.0	106.1	106.8	107.8	108.1	107.8	107.9	112.4	114.6	107.6
2007	108.1	106.5	106.7	106.9	107.8	108.9	110.1	110.6	110.4	110.3	114.8	116.2	109.8
2008	110.1	108.3	108.2	107.8	107.6	107.8	109.1	109.0	108.4	107.4	109.0	109.4	108.5
2009	102.8	100.8	99.6	99.1	99.8	100.1	100.7	100.8	100.5	100.8	103.4	105.0	101.1
2010	100.1	98.8	99.0	99.0	99.4	100.1	101.2	101.6	101.0	101.9	105.1	106.7	101.2
2011	101.3	100.0	100.0	100.7	101.1	102.1	103.0	102.4	102.0	103.4	106.1	107.3	102.5
Transportation and Utilities													
2000	38.1	37.9	37.9	38.6	38.4	39.0	38.4	38.6	39.0	39.0	39.5	39.1	38.6
2001	37.7	37.9	38.0	38.2	38.8	38.8	38.6	39.0	38.8	38.8	38.3	38.1	38.4
2002	37.2	37.2	37.3	37.5	37.6	37.7	37.4	37.3	37.3	37.2	36.8	36.9	37.3
2003	36.5	36.0	36.0	36.0	36.2	36.3	36.1	36.4	36.7	37.3	37.3	37.3	36.5
2004	36.6	36.6	36.6	36.8	36.7	36.8	36.6	36.7	37.2	38.0	37.8	37.9	37.0
2005	36.3	36.5	36.7	36.8	36.6	36.8	36.5	36.6	37.1	37.1	37.4	38.2	36.9
2006	36.9	37.2	37.3	37.0	37.2	37.7	37.2	37.2	37.7	37.8	38.0	38.6	37.5
2007	37.2	37.3	37.6	37.5	37.8	37.9	37.1	37.3	38.1	38.2	38.7	39.2	37.8
2008	37.5	37.6	37.6	38.1	38.1	37.8	37.1	37.5	37.8	37.8	36.9	37.1	37.6
2009	35.9	35.1	34.6	34.2	34.3	34.1	33.2	33.2	34.0	33.7	33.7	34.2	34.2
2010	33.1	32.8	32.8	33.2	33.1	33.3	32.7	32.7	33.6	33.8	33.8	34.5	33.3
2011	33.5	33.2	33.3	33.4	33.6	33.7	33.8	33.9	33.7	33.8	33.7	34.5	33.7
Information													
2000	24.7	24.9	25.0	25.3	25.5	25.8	26.4	26.6	26.8	26.7	26.8	27.0	26.0
2001	27.0	27.0	26.8	26.5	26.3	26.1	25.8	25.5	25.3	25.0	24.8	24.8	25.9
2002	24.6	24.5	24.3	24.0	23.9	23.9	23.6	23.6	23.4	23.4	23.4	23.3	23.8
2003	23.0	22.7	22.5	22.3	22.5	22.5	22.4	22.3	22.3	22.4	22.6	22.7	22.5
2004	22.5	22.5	22.6	22.4	22.4	22.5	22.6	22.6	22.4	22.3	22.5	22.6	22.5
2005	22.5	22.6	22.6	22.8	23.0	23.2	23.3	23.3	23.3	23.3	23.5	23.7	23.1
2006	23.5	23.6	23.7	23.6	23.7	23.8	24.5	24.2	24.3	24.5	24.1	24.3	24.0
2007	24.2	24.4	24.6	24.6	24.9	24.8	24.9	25.0	24.8	24.9	25.0	25.1	24.8
2008	24.9	24.9	24.9	24.9	24.9	24.8	24.7	24.5	24.4	24.1	24.0	23.8	24.6
2009	23.5	23.4	23.3	23.1	23.0	22.9	22.9	22.8	22.5	22.5	22.7	22.6	22.9
2010	22.4	22.4	22.3	22.4	22.6	22.4	22.4	22.7	22.3	22.4	22.7	22.5	22.5
2011	22.6	22.5	22.5	22.5	22.4	22.4	22.4	22.2	22.0	21.9	22.1	22.0	22.3

Employment by Industry: Portland–Vancouver–Hillsborough, OR–WA, Selected Years, 2000–2011—*Continued*

(Numbers in thousands, not seasonally adjusted)

Industry and year	January	February	March	April	May	June	July	August	September	October	November	December	Annual average
Financial Activities													
2000	64.6	64.7	64.4	64.7	64.8	65.1	65.4	65.2	64.9	64.6	64.6	65.1	64.8
2001	64.3	64.6	65.0	65.0	65.1	65.3	65.5	65.3	65.1	64.9	65.1	65.3	65.0
2002	64.9	65.0	64.8	64.9	65.0	65.3	65.8	66.0	65.8	66.2	66.4	66.8	65.6
2003	66.8	66.9	67.3	67.4	67.1	67.0	66.6	66.7	66.0	65.5	65.0	64.9	66.4
2004	65.0	65.1	65.3	65.8	65.9	66.3	66.5	66.6	66.4	66.4	66.7	66.9	66.1
2005	66.4	66.6	66.7	67.2	67.7	68.2	68.8	69.1	69.1	69.3	69.7	70.0	68.2
2006	69.3	69.5	69.7	70.1	70.3	70.7	71.3	71.5	71.4	71.2	71.3	71.4	70.6
2007	70.7	70.9	71.0	70.8	70.8	70.8	70.9	70.6	69.7	69.5	69.5	69.3	70.4
2008	68.6	68.7	68.4	68.5	68.5	68.1	68.1	67.9	67.2	66.9	66.4	65.9	67.8
2009	65.2	64.7	64.2	64.2	64.1	64.0	63.9	63.7	63.1	63.1	62.8	62.7	63.8
2010	61.9	61.7	61.6	61.9	61.8	62.0	62.2	62.2	61.8	62.0	61.8	62.1	61.9
2011	61.5	61.4	61.2	61.3	61.4	61.7	62.1	62.2	61.3	61.7	61.4	62.1	61.6
Professional and Business Services													
2000	124.0	125.6	126.4	128.1	128.8	130.9	132.4	133.9	133.7	134.2	134.3	133.4	130.5
2001	129.9	130.1	130.8	130.4	129.3	129.2	127.6	127.4	126.2	124.7	123.8	122.3	127.6
2002	120.9	121.1	121.4	121.8	121.4	122.2	123.0	123.6	123.0	122.3	120.6	118.9	121.7
2003	115.4	116.2	116.2	116.8	116.7	117.0	118.9	119.5	120.1	119.9	119.2	119.0	117.9
2004	114.7	116.3	117.8	119.9	121.1	122.9	124.6	125.4	124.5	126.3	126.2	125.9	122.1
2005	121.6	123.4	124.8	126.9	127.1	128.8	130.4	131.6	131.7	131.9	132.0	132.2	128.5
2006	128.3	130.2	131.3	132.9	133.9	135.9	136.2	137.3	137.7	138.3	138.2	136.5	134.7
2007	132.5	133.8	135.4	135.7	135.5	136.7	137.0	138.5	138.4	138.6	137.8	136.9	136.4
2008	133.8	135.4	136.5	137.7	137.5	137.8	138.9	139.7	138.5	136.8	133.9	131.5	136.5
2009	127.2	125.9	125.2	125.4	124.2	124.3	124.7	124.7	123.7	124.5	124.5	124.2	124.9
2010	121.8	123.0	124.5	127.1	126.7	127.5	129.0	130.2	130.2	131.6	131.1	131.1	127.8
2011	127.7	129.0	130.2	132.3	131.7	132.7	133.5	134.5	133.8	134.3	131.9	131.3	131.9
Education and Health Services													
2000	101.0	103.1	103.3	103.5	102.9	100.2	98.7	99.4	103.5	106.1	106.7	106.7	102.9
2001	104.4	106.5	106.9	107.3	106.8	105.2	103.1	103.6	106.6	108.6	109.6	109.6	106.5
2002	108.1	110.3	111.2	112.0	111.6	109.2	107.4	107.7	110.8	114.1	114.9	114.4	111.0
2003	112.2	114.2	114.6	114.9	114.3	111.7	109.8	109.8	113.1	115.8	116.4	116.5	113.6
2004	112.5	115.7	116.5	116.9	116.2	113.4	111.7	111.6	116.2	118.6	119.3	119.2	115.7
2005	116.5	119.7	120.4	120.9	120.3	116.9	115.5	116.1	120.6	123.1	123.9	124.1	119.8
2006	120.1	123.5	124.3	124.9	124.1	120.6	118.0	118.5	122.9	126.6	127.6	127.8	123.2
2007	124.1	127.9	128.8	129.0	128.3	125.1	122.9	123.0	127.8	131.6	132.5	132.1	127.8
2008	128.8	132.7	133.4	134.0	133.0	130.1	127.9	127.9	133.2	136.2	136.9	136.5	132.6
2009	132.4	135.6	135.8	136.6	135.8	132.4	130.4	130.2	136.0	138.7	139.4	138.5	135.2
2010	136.5	139.5	140.2	141.0	139.9	136.6	134.3	134.0	139.3	143.1	144.0	144.0	139.4
2011	141.3	144.1	144.6	144.9	143.3	140.3	137.3	138.5	144.0	147.3	146.9	145.4	143.2
Leisure and Hospitality													
2000	81.7	82.8	83.5	85.0	86.2	87.8	88.7	89.4	87.7	85.5	85.5	85.8	85.8
2001	83.2	83.5	83.9	85.2	86.7	87.1	88.3	89.3	87.6	84.0	83.5	83.5	85.5
2002	81.3	81.7	82.5	84.0	85.6	87.0	87.0	88.0	87.0	85.0	84.4	84.5	84.8
2003	82.3	82.3	83.3	84.5	84.9	86.4	87.9	89.0	87.5	86.6	86.3	86.1	85.6
2004	82.9	83.8	84.6	87.0	88.8	89.3	89.9	91.1	89.7	88.2	88.0	88.5	87.7
2005	85.4	86.1	87.5	89.0	90.6	92.0	92.5	93.5	92.2	90.3	90.8	91.3	90.1
2006	89.3	89.7	91.0	93.1	94.3	95.5	96.4	97.3	96.5	95.2	95.2	95.7	94.1
2007	93.1	94.3	95.3	96.1	97.7	98.8	100.9	101.8	101.0	98.7	98.8	99.3	98.0
2008	96.2	96.9	98.0	99.6	100.8	101.3	102.3	102.5	101.5	98.9	97.5	95.7	99.3
2009	92.6	92.7	93.2	94.2	95.3	95.8	96.7	96.9	96.4	93.9	93.3	92.4	94.5
2010	90.0	90.7	91.2	93.8	95.2	96.2	96.9	97.5	97.1	95.7	94.7	94.7	94.5
2011	91.9	92.9	93.7	96.0	96.7	98.6	100.3	101.3	102.5	97.2	97.4	97.9	97.2
Other Services													
2000	32.2	32.7	33.2	33.2	33.6	33.6	33.4	33.6	33.9	33.7	34.0	33.9	33.4
2001	33.4	33.9	34.2	34.3	34.5	34.7	34.2	34.3	34.4	34.2	34.1	34.0	34.2
2002	33.7	34.0	34.1	34.1	34.1	33.9	33.7	33.6	33.7	34.0	34.1	33.7	33.9
2003	33.6	33.8	33.9	33.9	34.1	33.8	33.9	34.1	34.3	34.2	34.1	34.1	34.0
2004	33.5	34.2	34.7	34.8	35.0	35.2	35.1	35.0	35.2	35.0	34.8	34.4	34.7
2005	33.6	34.1	34.2	34.4	34.6	34.6	34.8	34.8	34.7	34.7	34.8	34.8	34.5
2006	34.3	34.8	35.1	35.4	35.9	36.2	36.1	35.9	35.9	36.0	36.0	36.2	35.7
2007	35.6	36.3	36.4	36.3	36.6	36.9	36.5	36.7	36.9	37.0	37.1	37.1	36.6
2008	36.7	36.9	37.1	37.3	37.5	37.6	37.4	37.3	37.6	37.2	36.7	36.2	37.1
2009	35.6	35.7	35.6	35.4	35.5	35.3	35.2	35.1	34.8	34.6	34.6	34.4	35.2
2010	33.8	34.0	34.1	34.4	34.7	35.3	35.0	34.8	34.9	35.1	34.5	34.6	34.6
2011	34.3	34.7	34.8	35.0	35.1	35.3	35.0	35.0	35.3	34.7	34.3	34.3	34.8
Government													
2000	129.1	131.6	132.1	132.6	135.6	134.2	124.6	121.5	124.9	132.5	133.6	133.5	130.5
2001	131.9	133.4	134.2	134.0	135.7	135.1	119.2	116.2	128.8	136.0	137.2	136.8	131.5
2002	134.5	137.1	138.0	138.1	139.3	139.4	120.6	117.5	129.2	136.9	138.4	137.2	133.9
2003	134.1	135.3	135.7	136.3	137.1	135.9	124.7	123.1	130.2	135.7	137.2	136.7	133.5
2004	134.6	136.8	138.1	138.2	138.7	139.4	129.5	126.9	133.3	139.4	140.1	139.8	136.2
2005	138.3	140.3	140.6	140.3	141.1	141.4	128.9	127.3	131.9	139.3	141.4	140.7	137.6
2006	138.3	140.4	141.5	141.5	143.4	143.0	130.6	128.1	133.6	141.1	143.6	142.2	138.9
2007	141.1	142.9	144.1	144.3	146.5	146.5	134.7	131.6	136.1	145.3	147.0	146.9	142.3
2008	145.7	147.1	148.3	148.6	150.1	149.8	141.1	138.3	142.8	149.5	151.8	150.8	147.0
2009	149.0	151.0	151.8	151.9	152.7	151.1	141.0	138.2	140.3	149.3	150.9	149.9	148.1
2010	148.6	150.0	150.4	149.6	153.4	153.3	139.6	137.3	139.5	148.4	150.4	147.9	147.4
2011	148.3	149.3	149.2	150.7	150.7	148.5	137.2	135.0	136.7	146.5	147.9	146.1	145.5

Employment by Industry: Providence–Fall River–Warwick, RI–MA, NECTA, Selected Years, 2000–2011

(Numbers in thousands, not seasonally adjusted)

Industry and year	January	February	March	April	May	June	July	August	September	October	November	December	Annual average
Total Nonfarm													
2000	559.3	559.9	564.2	573.9	580.7	583.1	571.6	573.6	583.6	585.3	588.3	590.4	576.2
2001	565.2	566.5	568.5	574.9	579.0	580.4	566.0	571.7	577.8	576.0	576.1	577.6	573.3
2002	560.5	561.5	566.7	574.2	580.0	580.9	568.7	574.2	581.1	579.6	582.2	580.9	574.2
2003	564.5	563.3	566.8	575.4	583.3	585.3	572.2	574.9	583.5	585.8	587.9	587.5	577.5
2004	566.2	567.6	571.5	580.1	589.4	590.2	577.3	579.0	587.5	589.7	591.0	590.0	581.6
2005	568.3	570.1	571.7	583.8	588.3	591.2	579.9	581.6	588.9	588.6	590.9	589.2	582.7
2006	565.8	568.5	573.1	586.0	589.8	592.9	579.9	582.9	591.3	593.4	595.0	593.9	584.4
2007	571.9	572.4	575.1	583.3	590.0	592.0	580.5	581.1	585.4	585.2	584.2		582.2
2008	562.0	563.5	565.8	573.7	579.2	579.3	566.1	566.7	572.6	571.3	568.1	563.9	569.4
2009	538.4	538.5	537.6	542.3	548.4	548.5	536.6	536.1	543.2	545.3	545.2	543.6	542.0
2010	524.6	526.9	530.8	539.2	547.7	548.0	540.8	541.4	546.8	549.7	550.9	548.5	541.3
2011	528.0	531.6	533.8	544.4	549.5	552.5	546.7	543.2	545.5	547.6	547.8	543.1	542.8
Total Private													
2000	484.7	485.1	488.5	497.8	502.4	508.0	501.1	504.4	508.3	509.1	511.5	513.8	501.2
2001	489.2	490.4	491.8	498.8	502.6	504.5	494.8	501.3	502.3	501.3	500.6	501.8	498.3
2002	483.1	483.7	488.4	496.2	501.9	503.5	496.4	502.5	504.3	503.3	504.8	504.0	497.7
2003	487.4	486.1	489.5	498.3	505.7	507.7	502.2	505.5	508.3	509.5	511.4	510.9	501.9
2004	490.5	491.7	495.0	504.4	512.7	513.7	508.8	510.8	513.1	514.4	515.0	514.7	507.1
2005	493.3	494.9	496.7	508.6	512.6	515.7	511.0	513.4	515.7	513.5	515.4	513.8	508.7
2006	491.1	493.3	498.0	511.1	514.6	517.9	510.8	514.2	517.3	518.3	518.9	518.1	510.3
2007	497.0	497.4	500.0	508.3	514.4	517.2	510.7	511.6	512.2	511.0	509.5		508.4
2008	488.0	489.2	491.3	499.1	503.8	504.9	498.1	499.4	501.0	498.7	494.6	490.7	496.6
2009	466.1	466.1	465.3	469.6	475.5	476.1	470.8	470.8	473.0	473.3	472.8	471.3	470.9
2010	453.0	455.2	458.6	466.9	473.4	475.4	474.4	475.2	477.1	478.2	478.8	476.6	470.2
2011	456.8	460.3	462.1	472.3	477.1	480.5	481.0	478.2	475.2	475.9	475.9	471.3	472.2
Goods-Producing													
2000	114.7	114.9	115.3	117.4	118.6	119.6	115.0	118.7	119.8	120.2	119.6	119.3	117.8
2001	114.2	114.1	113.9	115.5	115.2	115.2	108.6	113.2	113.4	113.0	111.0	110.5	113.2
2002	105.3	105.2	106.2	106.9	108.2	108.4	103.3	108.2	108.3	107.4	107.0	105.8	106.7
2003	101.4	100.1	100.6	103.4	105.0	105.7	101.7	105.3	105.9	105.2	105.1	103.7	103.6
2004	98.4	97.6	98.5	101.0	102.6	104.0	101.9	104.2	104.1	103.9	103.6	102.5	101.9
2005	97.3	96.5	96.3	99.4	100.6	102.1	98.7	101.1	100.9	99.7	100.0	98.6	99.3
2006	93.8	93.7	94.3	97.5	98.3	99.7	96.6	99.0	98.5	98.0	96.9	96.2	96.9
2007	92.3	90.9	91.3	92.5	94.1	95.1	92.7	94.9	94.6	93.0	92.1	90.6	92.8
2008	86.3	85.2	85.7	87.5	88.7	89.2	86.7	88.3	87.7	86.1	84.3	82.2	86.5
2009	76.4	74.2	73.1	73.9	74.4	74.7	73.1	73.7	73.3	72.9	72.3	71.2	73.6
2010	67.3	66.8	67.2	69.2	71.0	72.1	71.7	72.9	72.5	72.6	72.4	71.3	70.6
2011	67.6	67.0	67.4	70.0	71.2	72.3	71.9	72.1	72.1	72.4	72.4	71.0	70.6
Mining and Logging													
2000	0.3	0.3	0.3	0.3	0.3	0.3	0.3	0.3	0.3	0.3	0.3	0.3	0.3
2001	0.3	0.3	0.3	0.3	0.3	0.4	0.4	0.4	0.4	0.4	0.4	0.4	0.4
2002	0.3	0.3	0.3	0.3	0.3	0.3	0.3	0.3	0.3	0.3	0.3	0.3	0.3
2003	0.2	0.2	0.2	0.3	0.3	0.3	0.3	0.3	0.3	0.3	0.3	0.3	0.3
2004	0.3	0.2	0.2	0.3	0.3	0.3	0.3	0.3	0.3	0.3	0.3	0.3	0.3
2005	0.3	0.2	0.2	0.3	0.3	0.3	0.3	0.3	0.3	0.3	0.3	0.3	0.3
2006	0.2	0.2	0.2	0.3	0.3	0.3	0.3	0.3	0.3	0.3	0.3	0.3	0.3
2007	0.3	0.2	0.2	0.2	0.3	0.3	0.3	0.3	0.3	0.3	0.3	0.3	0.3
2008	0.2	0.2	0.2	0.2	0.3	0.3	0.3	0.3	0.3	0.3	0.3	0.3	0.3
2009	0.2	0.2	0.2	0.2	0.2	0.2	0.2	0.2	0.2	0.2	0.2	0.2	0.2
2010	0.1	0.1	0.1	0.2	0.2	0.2	0.2	0.2	0.2	0.2	0.2	0.2	0.2
2011	0.1	0.1	0.1	0.2	0.2	0.2	0.2	0.2	0.2	0.2	0.2	0.2	0.2
Construction													
2000	19.6	19.0	19.4	21.4	22.1	23.2	23.3	23.5	23.4	23.4	23.3	22.7	22.0
2001	20.2	20.1	20.7	23.0	23.8	24.4	24.5	24.7	24.4	24.5	24.1	23.8	23.2
2002	21.3	21.1	22.0	23.2	24.3	24.8	24.9	25.2	25.1	24.7	24.5	23.7	23.7
2003	21.2	20.3	21.1	23.9	25.8	26.6	27.6	27.9	27.9	27.6	27.3	26.2	25.3
2004	22.6	21.9	22.6	24.9	26.1	27.0	27.7	27.7	27.6	27.7	27.4	26.8	25.8
2005	23.2	22.6	23.0	26.4	27.6	28.8	29.0	29.2	29.0	28.4	28.9	27.7	28.4
2006	24.7	24.2	25.1	28.2	29.1	30.3	30.3	30.6	30.3	29.9	29.3	28.7	27.5
2007	25.9	24.5	25.1	26.6	28.2	29.0	29.5	29.4	28.9	28.3	27.8	26.5	25.2
2008	23.2	22.6	23.1	25.1	26.2	26.9	27.2	27.1	26.8	25.8	24.9	23.3	20.9
2009	20.1	19.5	19.4	20.8	21.7	21.9	22.2	22.1	21.6	21.4	20.8	19.8	19.6
2010	16.9	16.3	16.8	18.9	20.2	20.8	21.5	21.7	21.1	21.0	20.7	19.6	19.1
2011	16.7	16.1	16.5	18.6	19.8	20.5	20.7	20.3	20.1	20.4	20.6	18.6	
Manufacturing													
2000	94.8	95.6	95.6	95.7	96.2	96.1	91.4	94.9	96.1	96.5	96.0	96.3	95.4
2001	93.7	93.7	92.9	92.2	91.1	90.4	83.7	88.1	88.6	88.1	86.5	86.3	89.6
2002	83.7	83.8	83.9	83.4	83.6	83.3	78.1	82.7	82.9	82.4	82.2	81.8	82.7
2003	80.0	79.6	79.3	79.2	78.9	78.8	73.8	77.1	77.7	77.3	77.5	77.2	78.0
2004	75.5	75.5	75.7	75.8	76.2	76.7	73.9	76.2	76.2	75.9	75.9	75.4	75.7
2005	73.8	73.7	73.1	72.7	72.7	73.0	69.4	71.6	71.6	71.0	70.8	70.6	72.0
2006	68.9	69.3	69.0	69.0	68.9	69.1	66.0	68.1	67.9	67.8	67.3	67.2	68.2
2007	66.1	66.2	66.0	65.6	65.6	65.8	62.9	65.2	65.4	64.4	64.0	63.8	65.1
2008	62.9	62.4	62.4	62.2	62.2	62.0	59.2	60.9	60.6	60.0	59.1	58.6	61.0
2009	56.1	54.5	53.5	52.9	52.5	52.6	50.7	51.4	51.5	51.3	51.3	51.2	52.5
2010	50.3	50.4	50.3	50.1	50.6	51.1	50.0	51.0	51.2	51.4	51.5	51.5	50.8
2011	50.8	50.8	50.8	51.2	51.2	51.6	51.0	51.6	51.8	51.8	51.6	52.2	51.4

Employment by Industry: Providence–Fall River–Warwick, RI–MA, NECTA, Selected Years, 2000–2011—*Continued*
(Numbers in thousands, not seasonally adjusted)

Industry and year	January	February	March	April	May	June	July	August	September	October	November	December	Annual average
Service-Providing													
2000	444.6	445.0	448.9	456.5	462.1	463.5	456.6	454.9	463.8	465.1	468.7	471.1	458.4
2001	451.0	452.4	454.6	459.4	463.8	465.2	457.4	458.5	464.4	463.0	465.1	467.1	460.2
2002	455.2	456.3	460.5	467.3	471.8	472.5	465.4	466.0	472.8	472.2	475.2	475.1	467.5
2003	463.1	463.2	466.2	472.0	478.3	479.6	470.5	469.6	477.6	480.6	482.8	483.8	473.9
2004	467.8	470.0	473.0	479.1	486.8	486.2	475.4	474.8	483.4	485.8	487.4	487.5	479.8
2005	471.0	473.6	475.4	484.4	487.7	489.1	481.2	480.5	488.0	488.9	490.9	490.6	483.4
2006	472.0	474.8	478.8	488.5	491.5	493.2	483.3	483.9	492.8	495.4	498.1	497.7	487.5
2007	479.6	481.5	483.8	490.8	495.9	496.9	487.8	486.2	490.8	492.2	493.3	493.6	489.4
2008	475.7	478.3	480.1	486.2	490.5	490.1	479.4	478.4	484.9	485.2	483.8	481.7	482.9
2009	462.0	464.3	464.5	468.4	474.0	473.8	463.5	462.4	469.9	472.4	472.9	472.4	468.4
2010	457.3	460.1	463.6	470.0	476.7	475.9	469.1	468.5	474.3	477.1	478.5	477.2	470.7
2011	460.4	464.6	466.4	474.4	478.3	480.2	474.8	471.1	473.4	475.2	475.4	472.1	472.2
Trade, Transportation, and Utilities													
2000	99.9	98.3	98.7	100.3	100.2	101.1	99.8	100.6	101.7	103.1	105.7	107.9	101.4
2001	101.4	99.6	99.2	100.1	100.3	101.8	100.6	100.7	101.8	102.2	104.9	106.9	101.6
2002	101.6	100.0	100.6	101.7	102.7	104.0	102.5	102.7	103.2	103.7	106.2	108.0	103.1
2003	102.2	100.7	100.8	101.6	102.8	103.8	102.2	102.5	103.7	104.8	107.1	108.3	103.4
2004	102.3	101.3	101.5	101.3	103.3	103.6	102.0	101.8	102.6	104.0	105.9	107.1	103.1
2005	101.7	100.8	100.7	102.0	102.6	103.5	102.1	102.5	102.9	103.9	106.0	107.8	103.0
2006	102.0	100.3	100.8	102.2	102.6	103.4	101.5	101.7	102.6	103.6	105.9	107.5	102.8
2007	102.2	100.4	100.7	101.4	102.3	103.3	101.7	101.4	101.9	102.1	104.4	105.8	102.3
2008	100.1	98.5	98.5	98.9	99.8	100.5	99.0	99.1	99.4	99.6	100.3	100.8	99.5
2009	95.2	93.7	93.3	92.6	94.1	94.9	93.2	93.1	94.4	94.9	96.4	97.2	94.4
2010	93.5	92.6	93.0	92.5	93.2	94.4	93.2	93.4	94.3	95.2	96.9	97.7	94.2
2011	93.7	93.0	92.7	93.7	94.6	95.3	94.4	93.8	93.3	93.5	94.7	94.7	94.0
Wholesale Trade													
2000	18.7	18.8	19.1	19.3	19.4	19.5	19.4	19.5	19.6	19.8	19.9	20.1	19.4
2001	19.6	19.8	19.9	20.2	20.1	20.2	20.5	20.5	20.4	20.2	20.3	20.5	20.2
2002	20.3	20.2	20.4	20.5	20.6	20.7	20.4	20.5	20.4	20.4	20.7	20.6	20.5
2003	20.5	20.3	20.4	20.5	20.8	20.9	20.7	20.6	20.5	20.6	20.8	20.6	20.6
2004	20.2	20.2	20.4	20.7	20.7	20.8	20.7	20.7	20.7	20.8	20.9	20.9	20.6
2005	20.5	20.5	20.6	21.0	21.0	21.2	21.1	21.2	21.1	21.1	21.2	21.5	21.0
2006	21.0	21.0	21.1	21.3	21.4	21.5	21.4	21.4	21.4	21.5	21.4	21.4	21.3
2007	21.3	21.1	21.1	21.4	21.4	21.5	21.5	21.4	21.2	21.2	21.3	21.4	21.3
2008	20.8	20.8	20.8	20.9	21.0	21.1	21.0	20.9	20.9	20.9	20.8	20.6	20.9
2009	20.1	19.9	19.9	19.9	19.9	20.0	19.8	19.7	19.9	19.9	19.8	19.8	19.9
2010	19.4	19.4	19.4	19.4	19.7	19.8	19.7	19.8	19.8	19.8	19.9	19.8	19.7
2011	19.5	19.6	19.1	19.1	19.3	19.4	19.3	19.3	19.3	19.3	19.4	19.4	19.3
Retail Trade													
2000	68.6	66.9	67.0	68.0	67.7	68.5	68.1	68.5	68.9	70.0	72.6	74.6	69.1
2001	69.0	67.1	66.6	66.8	67.1	68.4	67.6	67.8	68.1	68.9	71.5	73.4	68.5
2002	68.6	67.3	67.6	68.4	69.0	69.9	69.4	69.4	69.8	70.1	72.4	74.3	69.7
2003	68.9	67.6	67.5	68.1	68.7	69.5	69.0	69.4	69.6	70.7	72.8	74.2	69.7
2004	69.1	68.2	68.2	68.3	69.2	69.6	69.2	69.0	68.6	70.0	71.9	73.1	69.5
2005	68.7	67.8	67.7	68.2	68.6	69.1	68.6	68.8	68.6	69.6	71.6	73.0	69.2
2006	68.4	66.8	67.1	68.0	68.1	68.6	67.9	67.9	67.8	68.7	71.1	72.6	68.6
2007	68.1	66.8	67.0	67.1	67.8	68.4	67.8	67.6	67.2	67.6	69.8	70.8	68.0
2008	66.6	65.1	65.1	65.1	65.6	66.1	65.5	65.5	64.9	65.5	66.5	66.9	65.7
2009	62.8	61.6	61.3	60.7	61.9	62.4	62.1	62.0	61.9	62.6	64.1	64.8	62.4
2010	62.2	61.2	61.6	60.8	61.0	61.8	61.9	62.0	61.6	62.4	64.0	64.7	62.1
2011	61.7	60.9	61.1	61.9	62.4	62.8	62.8	62.2	60.8	61.1	62.3	61.9	61.8
Transportation and Utilities													
2000	12.6	12.6	12.6	13.0	13.1	13.1	12.3	12.6	13.2	13.3	13.2	13.2	12.9
2001	12.8	12.7	12.7	13.1	13.1	13.2	12.5	12.4	13.3	13.1	13.1	13.0	12.9
2002	12.7	12.5	12.6	12.8	13.1	13.4	12.7	12.8	13.0	13.2	13.1	13.1	12.9
2003	12.8	12.8	12.9	13.0	13.3	13.4	12.5	12.5	13.6	13.5	13.5	13.5	13.1
2004	13.0	12.9	12.9	12.3	13.4	13.2	12.1	12.1	13.3	13.2	13.1	13.1	12.9
2005	12.5	12.5	12.4	12.8	13.0	13.2	12.4	12.5	13.2	13.2	13.2	13.3	12.9
2006	12.6	12.5	12.6	12.9	13.1	13.3	12.2	12.4	13.4	13.4	13.4	13.5	12.9
2007	12.8	12.5	12.6	12.9	13.1	13.4	12.4	12.4	13.5	13.3	13.3	13.6	13.0
2008	12.7	12.6	12.6	12.9	13.2	13.3	12.5	12.7	13.6	13.2	13.0	13.3	13.0
2009	12.3	12.2	12.1	12.0	12.3	12.5	11.3	11.4	12.6	12.4	12.5	12.6	12.2
2010	11.9	12.0	12.0	12.3	12.5	12.8	11.6	11.6	12.9	13.0	13.0	13.2	12.4
2011	12.5	12.5	12.5	12.7	12.9	13.1	12.3	12.3	13.2	13.1	13.0	13.4	12.8
Information													
2000	11.6	11.7	11.5	11.6	11.7	12.0	12.1	10.6	11.9	11.7	11.8	11.8	11.7
2001	11.8	11.8	11.9	11.9	12.0	12.0	11.8	11.7	11.7	11.4	11.4	11.4	11.7
2002	11.9	11.9	11.9	11.9	11.9	12.1	12.0	12.0	11.9	11.6	11.9	11.9	11.9
2003	12.0	12.0	11.9	11.9	11.9	12.1	11.9	11.9	11.7	11.9	11.9	11.8	11.9
2004	11.9	11.9	11.9	11.9	11.8	11.8	11.6	11.5	11.4	11.4	11.5	11.5	11.7
2005	11.7	11.7	11.6	11.6	11.5	11.6	11.6	11.6	11.5	11.6	11.8	11.8	11.6
2006	11.9	11.8	11.8	12.2	12.1	12.2	11.6	11.5	11.5	11.4	11.7	11.7	11.8
2007	11.3	11.2	11.2	11.3	11.4	11.5	11.5	11.6	11.5	11.5	11.7	11.7	11.5
2008	11.6	11.9	11.9	11.7	11.8	12.0	11.8	12.2	11.9	11.9	11.7	11.6	11.8
2009	11.6	11.5	11.4	11.6	11.6	11.6	11.2	11.2	11.2	11.1	10.9	11.1	11.3
2010	11.0	11.1	11.2	11.1	11.1	11.2	11.2	11.5	11.6	11.4	11.5	11.5	11.3
2011	11.0	11.0	11.2	11.3	11.6	11.6	11.6	10.8	11.6	11.5	11.6	11.6	11.4

Employment by Industry: Providence–Fall River–Warwick, RI–MA, NECTA, Selected Years, 2000–2011—*Continued*

(Numbers in thousands, not seasonally adjusted)

Industry and year	January	February	March	April	May	June	July	August	September	October	November	December	Annual average
Financial Activities													
2000	32.7	32.8	32.9	33.3	33.2	34.1	34.6	34.3	34.1	34.0	34.2	34.5	33.7
2001	34.7	34.8	34.9	34.5	34.4	34.9	35.0	34.8	34.6	34.8	34.8	35.1	34.8
2002	35.1	35.0	35.0	35.4	35.3	35.9	36.0	36.0	36.0	36.2	36.4	36.6	35.7
2003	36.4	36.4	36.7	36.3	36.6	37.1	37.1	37.1	37.0	37.0	37.1	37.3	36.8
2004	37.0	37.0	37.0	37.1	37.4	37.4	37.3	37.3	37.1	37.3	37.3	37.3	37.2
2005	36.9	37.1	37.1	37.6	37.5	37.8	37.9	37.9	37.7	37.4	37.5	37.8	37.5
2006	37.3	37.3	37.5	37.7	37.9	38.1	38.3	38.7	38.8	38.7	38.9	39.3	38.2
2007	38.4	38.5	38.4	38.5	38.6	38.4	38.1	37.7	37.6	37.2	37.1	37.1	38.0
2008	36.7	36.8	36.6	36.4	36.5	36.4	36.2	36.0	36.1	35.3	35.1	35.1	36.1
2009	34.6	34.5	34.2	33.9	34.0	34.1	33.8	33.5	33.2	33.2	33.4	33.3	33.8
2010	32.9	32.9	33.1	32.9	33.0	33.1	33.2	33.1	33.2	33.4	33.4	33.6	33.2
2011	32.9	33.0	33.0	33.1	33.0	33.4	33.6	33.6	33.4	33.1	33.0	33.1	33.2
Professional and Business Services													
2000	56.7	56.7	57.9	59.2	59.7	60.7	58.6	59.6	59.9	59.9	59.8	60.0	59.1
2001	56.5	56.6	56.8	58.1	58.5	58.9	58.9	59.0	58.7	58.9	57.9	57.2	57.9
2002	55.1	54.6	55.2	56.8	57.1	57.6	56.5	57.0	57.4	57.7	57.2	56.3	56.5
2003	54.6	54.3	54.7	56.6	57.2	58.5	58.3	59.0	58.9	59.4	59.3	59.3	57.5
2004	57.8	57.9	58.4	60.7	61.4	62.2	61.3	62.1	62.5	62.4	62.0	61.5	60.9
2005	59.0	59.0	59.5	62.3	62.2	62.9	62.8	63.5	63.7	62.6	62.5	61.9	61.8
2006	58.8	59.1	59.8	63.0	63.0	64.2	63.1	64.3	65.0	65.0	64.4	63.7	62.8
2007	60.5	60.2	60.6	62.9	63.4	64.5	63.3	63.3	63.0	62.6	62.5	62.2	62.4
2008	59.5	59.0	59.3	61.6	61.4	62.5	61.7	61.9	62.3	61.8	60.8	59.6	61.0
2009	56.9	56.5	56.8	58.1	58.1	58.8	58.1	58.5	58.6	58.5	58.3	57.5	57.9
2010	55.1	55.3	56.2	59.5	59.6	60.4	60.2	60.1	60.2	60.4	60.3	59.2	58.9
2011	56.9	57.3	57.6	59.7	59.8	60.3	60.8	60.9	60.4	60.7	60.5	59.2	59.5
Education and Health Services													
2000	96.2	97.6	97.8	98.7	99.0	96.5	96.4	96.3	99.5	100.6	101.7	102.2	98.5
2001	96.6	98.8	99.8	100.4	100.6	96.0	95.3	96.3	99.2	100.7	101.8	102.2	99.0
2002	99.0	101.2	102.5	102.9	102.9	98.4	97.8	98.9	102.4	103.7	104.7	105.1	101.6
2003	102.8	104.7	106.0	106.3	106.2	101.8	100.5	99.9	103.7	106.3	107.1	107.4	104.4
2004	104.6	107.0	108.2	108.9	108.8	104.1	103.2	102.9	106.7	109.0	109.7	110.1	106.9
2005	106.8	109.4	110.4	110.9	110.6	106.7	106.0	105.6	110.1	112.3	112.9	112.0	109.5
2006	108.2	111.8	113.1	113.7	112.8	109.1	107.9	107.6	111.5	114.6	115.7	114.8	111.7
2007	111.5	115.0	115.6	116.0	115.7	111.4	110.2	109.8	113.5	116.2	117.1	116.4	114.0
2008	113.0	116.5	117.3	117.6	116.7	112.6	111.2	111.1	114.8	117.6	118.1	117.8	115.4
2009	114.0	117.6	118.0	117.9	117.5	113.7	112.8	112.3	115.9	118.8	119.3	119.4	116.4
2010	115.9	118.8	119.7	119.6	119.6	115.2	114.5	114.1	118.0	120.5	121.0	121.2	118.2
2011	116.7	120.2	120.7	121.4	120.7	117.3	116.7	116.1	118.7	121.0	121.6	120.8	119.3
Leisure and Hospitality													
2000	49.1	49.3	50.3	52.9	55.5	58.9	59.3	58.9	56.8	54.8	54.0	53.2	54.4
2001	49.4	50.1	50.6	53.3	56.5	60.0	59.8	59.6	57.8	55.2	53.5	53.2	54.9
2002	49.8	50.4	51.6	55.1	58.1	60.8	61.6	61.3	59.4	57.0	55.5	54.3	56.2
2003	52.0	51.9	52.6	56.2	59.6	61.9	63.3	62.9	61.1	58.6	57.2	56.5	57.8
2004	52.6	53.1	53.4	57.2	60.8	63.7	64.2	63.9	62.2	59.7	58.2	58.0	58.9
2005	53.8	54.3	54.8	58.4	61.0	64.1	64.6	63.9	62.5	59.7	58.3	57.5	59.4
2006	53.6	53.7	54.9	58.5	61.3	64.0	64.5	64.3	63.0	60.3	58.8	58.3	59.6
2007	54.8	55.2	56.0	59.4	62.3	65.6	65.8	65.7	63.8	62.0	59.7	59.1	60.8
2008	55.0	55.5	56.0	59.3	62.6	65.0	64.5	64.1	62.8	60.3	58.4	57.7	60.1
2009	52.3	52.9	53.3	56.2	60.2	62.4	62.3	62.5	61.3	58.6	56.5	56.1	57.9
2010	52.5	52.8	53.3	57.0	60.4	63.3	63.9	63.7	62.0	59.5	57.9	56.8	58.6
2011	53.3	53.9	54.5	57.9	60.7	64.1	65.6	64.4	61.0	59.0	57.7	56.8	59.1
Other Services													
2000	23.8	23.8	24.1	24.4	24.5	25.1	25.3	25.4	24.6	24.8	24.7	24.9	24.6
2001	24.6	24.6	24.7	25.0	25.1	25.7	25.9	26.0	25.1	25.1	25.3	25.3	25.2
2002	25.3	25.4	25.4	25.5	25.7	26.3	26.7	26.4	25.7	26.0	25.9	26.0	25.9
2003	26.0	26.0	26.2	26.0	26.4	26.8	27.2	26.9	26.3	26.3	26.6	26.6	26.4
2004	25.9	25.9	26.1	26.3	26.6	26.9	27.3	27.1	26.5	26.7	26.8	26.7	26.6
2005	26.1	26.1	26.3	26.4	26.6	27.0	27.3	27.3	26.4	26.3	26.4	26.4	26.6
2006	25.5	25.6	25.8	26.3	26.6	27.2	27.3	27.1	26.4	26.7	26.6	26.6	26.5
2007	26.0	26.0	26.2	26.3	26.6	27.4	27.4	27.2	26.3	26.4	26.4	26.6	26.6
2008	25.8	25.8	26.0	26.1	26.3	26.7	27.0	26.7	26.0	26.1	25.9	25.9	26.2
2009	25.1	25.2	25.2	25.4	25.6	25.9	26.3	26.0	25.2	25.5	25.5	25.5	25.5
2010	24.8	24.9	24.9	25.1	25.5	25.7	26.5	26.4	25.3	25.2	25.4	25.3	25.4
2011	24.7	24.9	25.0	25.2	25.5	26.2	26.4	26.5	24.7	24.7	24.4	24.1	25.2
Government													
2000	74.6	74.8	75.7	76.1	78.3	75.1	70.5	69.2	75.3	76.2	76.8	76.6	74.9
2001	76.0	76.1	76.7	76.1	76.4	75.9	71.2	70.4	75.5	74.7	75.5	75.8	75.0
2002	77.4	77.8	78.3	78.0	78.1	77.4	72.3	71.7	76.8	76.3	77.4	76.9	76.5
2003	77.1	77.2	77.3	77.1	77.6	77.6	70.0	69.4	75.2	76.3	76.5	76.6	75.7
2004	75.7	75.9	76.5	75.7	76.7	76.5	68.5	68.2	74.4	75.3	76.0	75.3	74.6
2005	75.0	75.2	75.0	75.2	75.7	75.5	68.9	68.2	73.2	75.1	75.5	75.4	74.0
2006	74.7	75.2	75.1	74.9	75.2	75.0	69.1	68.7	74.0	75.1	76.1	75.8	74.1
2007	74.9	75.0	75.1	75.0	75.6	74.8	69.8	69.5	73.2	74.2	74.4	74.7	73.9
2008	74.0	74.3	74.5	74.6	75.4	74.4	68.0	67.3	71.6	72.6	73.5	73.2	72.8
2009	72.3	72.4	72.3	72.7	72.9	72.4	65.8	65.3	70.2	72.0	72.4	72.3	71.1
2010	71.6	71.7	72.2	72.3	74.3	72.6	66.4	66.2	69.7	71.5	72.1	71.9	71.0
2011	71.2	71.3	71.7	72.1	72.4	72.0	65.7	65.0	70.3	71.7	71.9	71.8	70.6

Employment by Industry: Raleigh–Cary, NC, Selected Years, 2000–2011

(Numbers in thousands, not seasonally adjusted)

Industry and year	January	February	March	April	May	June	July	August	September	October	November	December	Annual average
Total Nonfarm													
2000	424.8	427.0	431.6	434.9	437.3	441.5	433.0	435.8	441.8	442.3	445.2	445.9	436.8
2001	436.0	438.3	440.6	442.5	443.9	445.5	434.1	435.3	437.7	438.7	438.3	438.3	439.1
2002	424.5	425.9	427.0	431.0	434.2	435.0	429.3	432.5	437.3	438.4	439.7	440.4	432.9
2003	427.8	428.8	430.4	434.5	437.8	438.9	431.7	435.2	436.9	441.2	442.1	443.1	435.7
2004	435.5	436.6	440.4	441.9	446.3	447.7	446.9	450.1	453.1	455.4	457.3	459.7	447.6
2005	449.9	451.8	455.3	460.3	464.0	465.4	465.3	470.9	473.7	473.0	477.7	478.2	465.5
2006	470.7	472.6	476.4	484.2	488.6	491.5	488.9	495.2	497.1	500.8	506.3	507.8	490.0
2007	499.8	503.2	507.8	509.0	515.4	518.3	512.6	518.9	518.9	523.3	526.4	526.7	515.0
2008	516.5	518.6	519.8	519.8	524.0	521.8	518.4	522.2	522.1	523.1	521.1	518.3	520.5
2009	501.8	500.1	499.1	499.3	502.0	498.9	494.7	496.1	495.3	496.1	497.9	497.7	498.3
2010	485.8	485.8	490.1	495.8	500.3	500.0	498.6	501.3	501.0	505.1	507.0	506.3	498.1
2011	497.0	500.8	503.6	507.9	510.1	509.3	507.1	508.9	509.5	514.3	517.5	516.6	508.6
Total Private													
2000	354.6	356.1	360.5	363.7	365.7	369.9	367.5	368.6	368.7	369.8	372.0	372.9	365.8
2001	363.0	364.4	366.6	368.8	370.0	371.7	367.1	367.2	364.0	364.1	363.8	364.4	366.3
2002	351.5	352.0	353.9	357.9	360.8	361.9	362.7	364.3	363.1	363.6	364.8	365.9	360.2
2003	353.8	354.3	355.5	359.3	362.2	363.9	360.2	362.8	361.0	362.9	364.5	365.8	360.5
2004	359.0	359.7	362.9	364.3	368.3	370.3	372.9	374.0	372.3	374.4	376.6	379.3	369.5
2005	370.5	371.7	374.7	379.7	383.2	385.9	388.4	389.6	391.0	392.4	395.4	398.2	385.1
2006	389.5	390.5	393.7	400.2	404.0	407.7	408.5	410.5	411.3	414.2	419.1	421.1	405.9
2007	413.4	415.9	419.9	420.8	426.5	430.9	428.6	431.6	429.6	433.7	436.4	437.0	427.0
2008	427.3	428.6	429.3	429.0	432.9	432.4	431.3	432.7	430.0	428.9	427.8	425.4	429.6
2009	411.7	409.7	408.0	406.6	409.3	408.3	408.2	408.3	405.4	405.3	407.1	407.4	407.9
2010	397.1	396.3	399.9	404.1	406.8	408.8	411.4	412.4	410.4	413.9	416.4	416.0	407.8
2011	407.7	410.6	413.2	417.6	419.3	421.6	423.1	423.6	422.7	426.4	430.0	431.0	420.6
Goods-Producing													
2000	69.3	69.3	70.6	71.7	72.3	73.4	73.7	74.0	74.0	73.9	74.1	73.8	72.5
2001	71.2	71.5	72.3	72.6	73.1	73.4	72.8	72.4	71.7	71.1	70.2	69.0	71.8
2002	66.8	67.0	67.1	67.4	67.7	67.5	67.6	67.4	66.7	66.4	65.8	65.4	66.9
2003	62.8	62.7	62.8	62.6	63.5	63.8	63.6	63.9	63.4	64.0	63.9	63.9	63.4
2004	62.2	62.2	62.3	64.0	64.6	64.8	65.5	65.2	64.8	65.8	65.6	65.4	64.5
2005	63.8	64.2	64.8	66.1	66.9	68.0	68.5	68.5	68.8	68.7	68.9	68.9	67.2
2006	68.0	68.2	69.3	70.1	71.2	72.2	72.7	73.0	72.9	72.9	73.1	73.3	71.4
2007	72.1	72.3	73.1	73.0	73.5	74.1	74.3	74.9	74.3	73.7	73.5	72.9	73.5
2008	71.2	71.1	71.2	70.2	70.4	70.3	70.1	69.5	68.9	67.4	66.2	64.6	69.3
2009	61.6	60.5	59.8	58.4	58.1	58.0	57.7	57.6	57.0	56.4	56.1	56.0	58.1
2010	54.1	53.7	54.2	54.6	55.1	55.5	56.2	56.4	56.2	56.2	55.9	55.6	55.3
2011	54.4	55.1	55.7	55.8	56.0	56.5	58.2	59.2	59.2	58.0	56.8	56.5	56.8
Mining, Logging, and Construction													
2000	31.0	30.9	31.9	32.9	33.4	34.2	34.1	34.4	34.5	34.1	34.3	34.0	33.3
2001	31.8	32.1	33.1	33.6	34.5	35.0	34.8	34.9	34.5	34.3	33.7	33.0	33.8
2002	31.5	32.0	32.2	32.6	33.3	33.1	33.3	33.5	33.0	32.9	32.4	32.0	32.7
2003	30.1	30.1	30.3	30.2	31.0	31.4	31.8	32.1	31.9	32.2	32.1	32.1	31.3
2004	30.8	30.9	31.7	32.5	33.1	33.2	33.9	33.8	33.5	34.0	33.8	33.6	32.9
2005	32.3	32.5	33.0	33.8	34.6	35.3	35.7	35.8	36.0	36.1	36.1	35.9	34.8
2006	35.2	35.4	36.1	37.2	38.0	38.8	39.5	39.7	39.6	39.5	39.6	39.7	38.2
2007	39.2	39.4	40.1	40.3	40.8	41.3	41.5	41.8	41.5	41.1	40.9	40.4	40.7
2008	39.2	39.2	39.3	38.3	38.6	38.5	38.4	38.0	37.6	36.4	35.3	34.2	37.8
2009	31.7	31.1	30.7	29.9	30.0	30.1	30.0	29.8	29.4	28.8	28.5	28.3	29.9
2010	27.0	26.8	27.3	27.7	28.1	28.4	29.0	29.1	28.9	28.9	28.6	28.1	28.2
2011	27.2	27.8	28.2	28.2	28.5	29.0	30.2	31.1	31.6	30.6	29.7	29.3	29.3
Manufacturing													
2000	38.3	38.4	38.7	38.8	38.9	39.2	39.6	39.6	39.5	39.8	39.8	39.8	39.2
2001	39.4	39.4	39.2	39.0	38.6	38.4	38.0	37.5	37.2	36.8	36.5	36.0	38.0
2002	35.3	35.0	34.9	34.8	34.4	34.4	34.3	33.9	33.7	33.5	33.4	33.4	34.3
2003	32.7	32.6	32.5	32.4	32.5	32.4	31.8	31.8	31.5	31.8	31.8	31.8	32.1
2004	31.4	31.3	31.6	31.5	31.5	31.6	31.6	31.4	31.3	31.8	31.8	31.8	31.6
2005	31.5	31.7	31.8	32.3	32.3	32.7	32.8	32.7	32.8	32.6	32.8	33.0	32.4
2006	32.8	32.8	33.2	32.9	33.2	33.4	33.2	33.3	33.3	33.4	33.5	33.6	33.2
2007	32.9	32.9	33.0	32.7	32.7	32.8	32.8	33.1	32.8	32.6	32.6	32.5	32.8
2008	32.0	31.9	31.9	31.9	31.8	31.8	31.7	31.5	31.3	31.0	30.9	30.4	31.5
2009	29.9	29.4	29.1	28.5	28.1	27.9	27.7	27.8	27.6	27.6	27.6	27.7	28.2
2010	27.1	26.9	26.9	26.9	27.0	27.1	27.2	27.3	27.3	27.3	27.3	27.5	27.2
2011	27.2	27.3	27.5	27.6	27.5	27.5	28.0	28.1	27.6	27.4	27.1	27.2	27.5
Service-Providing													
2000	355.5	357.7	361.0	363.2	365.0	368.1	359.3	361.8	367.8	368.4	371.1	372.1	364.3
2001	364.8	366.8	368.3	369.9	370.8	372.1	361.3	362.9	366.0	367.6	368.1	369.3	367.3
2002	357.7	358.9	359.9	363.6	366.5	367.5	361.7	365.1	370.6	372.0	373.9	375.0	366.0
2003	365.0	366.1	367.6	371.9	374.3	375.1	368.1	371.3	373.5	377.2	378.2	379.2	372.3
2004	373.3	374.4	377.1	377.9	381.7	382.9	381.4	384.9	388.3	389.6	391.7	394.3	383.1
2005	386.1	387.6	390.5	394.2	397.1	397.4	396.8	402.4	404.9	404.3	408.8	409.3	398.3
2006	402.7	404.4	407.1	414.1	417.4	419.3	416.2	422.2	424.2	427.9	433.2	434.5	418.6
2007	427.7	430.9	434.7	436.0	441.9	444.2	438.3	444.0	444.6	449.6	452.9	453.8	441.6
2008	445.3	447.5	448.6	449.6	453.6	451.5	448.3	452.7	453.2	455.7	454.9	453.7	451.2
2009	440.2	439.6	439.3	440.9	443.9	440.9	437.0	438.5	438.3	439.7	441.8	441.7	440.2
2010	431.7	432.1	435.9	441.2	445.2	444.5	442.4	444.9	444.8	448.9	451.1	450.7	442.8
2011	442.6	445.7	447.9	452.1	454.1	452.8	448.9	449.7	450.3	456.3	460.7	460.1	451.8

Employment by Industry: Raleigh–Cary, NC, Selected Years, 2000–2011—*Continued*

(Numbers in thousands, not seasonally adjusted)

Industry and year	January	February	March	April	May	June	July	August	September	October	November	December	Annual average
Trade, Transportation, and Utilities													
2000	83.8	83.3	84.2	84.6	85.1	85.8	84.1	84.4	84.5	86.0	87.0	88.1	85.1
2001	83.6	82.8	83.2	84.4	84.5	84.0	83.9	83.9	83.8	84.1	84.7	85.6	84.0
2002	80.2	79.6	80.1	80.3	80.6	80.6	80.5	81.0	81.2	81.6	83.2	84.2	81.1
2003	79.9	79.5	79.8	80.9	81.6	82.4	80.5	81.4	81.5	82.8	84.2	85.2	81.6
2004	81.8	81.4	81.5	81.4	81.8	81.9	82.0	82.6	82.8	83.6	85.1	86.2	82.7
2005	83.1	82.4	82.9	83.5	84.1	84.2	84.8	84.9	85.0	86.4	88.0	89.6	84.9
2006	85.7	84.9	85.1	85.8	86.2	86.6	87.7	88.6	88.5	89.7	92.7	94.0	88.0
2007	90.7	89.9	90.9	90.9	91.9	92.1	92.0	91.9	91.8	92.8	95.7	97.1	92.3
2008	92.7	92.3	92.7	92.6	92.6	92.8	92.4	92.5	91.7	92.3	93.1	93.6	92.6
2009	88.9	87.9	87.9	87.3	87.8	87.7	87.8	87.6	87.2	87.9	89.5	90.4	88.2
2010	86.8	86.1	86.4	86.8	87.6	87.7	88.0	88.1	87.1	88.5	90.6	92.0	88.0
2011	88.4	88.2	88.7	89.8	90.1	90.6	90.9	91.5	91.8	92.5	95.4	96.3	91.2
Wholesale Trade													
2000	21.6	21.6	21.7	21.6	21.6	21.9	21.8	21.9	21.8	22.1	21.8	21.8	21.8
2001	21.7	21.7	21.8	21.3	21.2	21.2	21.2	21.0	20.9	20.7	20.4	20.3	21.1
2002	20.0	20.0	19.9	19.7	19.9	19.9	20.4	20.4	20.4	20.7	20.6	20.5	20.2
2003	20.1	20.0	20.2	20.1	20.0	20.1	20.0	20.1	20.1	20.2	20.0	20.0	20.1
2004	19.5	19.5	19.7	19.6	19.7	19.8	20.1	20.1	20.1	20.4	20.3	20.4	19.9
2005	19.8	19.8	19.8	19.9	20.1	20.2	20.1	20.3	20.4	20.6	20.5	20.7	20.2
2006	20.4	20.4	20.4	20.5	20.6	20.9	21.1	21.3	21.5	21.4	21.6	21.7	21.0
2007	21.9	22.0	22.2	22.1	22.2	22.2	22.3	22.2	22.2	22.1	22.2	22.2	22.2
2008	22.0	22.2	22.2	22.1	22.2	22.3	22.3	22.4	22.2	22.3	22.0	21.9	22.2
2009	21.4	21.4	21.2	21.0	20.9	20.8	20.8	20.7	20.5	20.5	20.4	20.4	20.8
2010	20.0	20.0	19.9	20.1	20.2	20.2	20.4	20.5	20.3	20.5	20.5	20.5	20.3
2011	20.7	20.7	20.7	21.1	21.2	21.4	21.3	21.8	21.8	21.8	21.8	21.8	21.3
Retail Trade													
2000	51.6	51.1	51.8	52.8	53.3	53.6	52.3	52.6	52.8	53.8	55.3	56.4	53.1
2001	52.0	51.3	51.5	53.3	53.5	53.0	52.6	52.9	53.0	53.3	54.9	55.6	53.1
2002	50.6	50.2	50.7	50.8	50.9	50.9	50.1	50.9	51.2	51.3	53.2	54.3	51.3
2003	50.2	49.9	50.0	51.0	51.8	52.4	50.7	51.3	51.4	52.7	54.4	55.3	51.8
2004	52.6	52.1	52.0	51.8	52.2	52.2	52.2	52.7	53.0	53.5	55.1	56.0	53.0
2005	53.3	52.7	53.0	53.5	53.9	53.8	54.3	54.2	54.2	54.8	56.4	57.8	54.3
2006	54.4	53.6	53.7	54.2	54.5	54.5	55.1	55.7	55.4	56.8	59.3	60.4	55.6
2007	57.1	56.3	57.0	57.0	57.8	58.0	57.9	57.9	57.8	59.1	61.9	62.8	58.4
2008	59.3	58.8	59.1	58.9	58.8	58.9	58.6	58.5	58.0	58.5	59.7	59.9	58.9
2009	56.2	55.4	55.7	55.4	56.1	56.2	56.2	56.4	56.3	56.0	56.7	58.3	59.0	56.5
2010	56.2	55.5	55.8	55.9	56.5	56.6	56.7	56.7	56.0	57.1	59.2	60.4	56.9
2011	57.2	57.0	57.4	57.8	58.0	58.2	58.6	58.6	58.9	59.6	62.4	63.2	58.9
Transportation and Utilities													
2000	10.6	10.6	10.7	10.2	10.2	10.3	10.0	9.9	9.9	10.1	9.9	9.9	10.2
2001	9.9	9.8	9.9	9.8	9.8	9.8	9.8	10.1	10.0	10.1	9.4	9.7	9.9
2002	9.6	9.4	9.5	9.8	9.8	9.8	9.8	10.0	9.7	9.6	9.4	9.4	9.6
2003	9.6	9.6	9.6	9.8	9.8	9.9	9.8	10.0	10.0	9.9	9.8	9.9	9.8
2004	9.7	9.8	9.8	10.0	9.9	9.9	9.7	9.8	9.7	9.7	9.7	9.8	9.8
2005	10.0	9.9	10.1	10.1	10.1	10.2	10.4	10.4	10.4	11.0	11.1	11.1	10.4
2006	10.9	10.9	11.0	11.1	11.1	11.2	11.5	11.6	11.6	11.5	11.8	11.9	11.3
2007	11.7	11.6	11.7	11.8	11.9	11.9	11.8	11.8	11.8	11.6	11.6	12.1	11.8
2008	11.4	11.3	11.4	11.6	11.6	11.6	11.6	11.5	11.6	11.5	11.4	11.8	11.5
2009	11.3	11.1	11.0	10.9	10.8	10.7	10.7	10.6	10.7	10.7	10.8	11.0	10.9
2010	10.6	10.6	10.7	10.8	10.9	10.9	10.9	10.9	10.8	10.9	10.9	11.1	10.8
2011	10.5	10.5	10.6	10.9	10.9	11.0	11.0	11.1	11.1	11.1	11.2	11.3	10.9
Information													
2000	17.6	17.7	18.0	17.9	18.0	18.5	18.7	18.7	18.6	18.4	18.5	18.6	18.3
2001	18.8	18.8	18.8	18.5	18.5	18.4	18.0	18.0	18.0	17.8	17.8	18.0	18.3
2002	18.3	18.2	18.4	18.2	18.1	18.2	17.9	17.8	17.7	17.7	17.7	17.7	18.0
2003	17.6	17.7	17.7	17.7	17.8	17.9	17.9	17.8	17.5	17.3	17.3	17.4	17.6
2004	17.5	17.4	17.5	17.1	17.0	17.1	17.0	17.0	16.8	16.5	16.8	16.9	17.1
2005	16.7	16.7	16.9	17.1	17.2	17.3	17.3	17.4	17.2	17.0	17.1	17.2	17.1
2006	17.0	16.9	16.6	16.8	16.8	16.8	16.7	16.6	16.5	16.4	16.4	16.4	16.7
2007	16.3	16.6	16.5	16.4	16.5	16.8	16.9	16.9	16.7	16.9	16.8	16.8	16.7
2008	16.7	16.8	16.7	17.0	17.1	17.2	17.1	17.2	17.1	17.2	17.2	17.3	17.1
2009	17.1	17.0	16.9	17.0	16.8	16.9	16.9	16.8	16.7	16.8	16.8	16.8	16.9
2010	16.5	16.5	16.6	16.6	16.5	16.7	16.8	16.8	16.7	16.7	16.9	16.9	16.7
2011	16.9	17.0	17.0	17.1	17.1	17.3	17.3	17.3	17.2	17.2	17.3	17.3	17.2
Financial Activities													
2000	21.4	21.6	21.9	22.0	22.2	22.4	22.0	22.1	22.2	22.4	22.4	22.5	22.1
2001	22.2	22.2	22.3	21.8	21.9	22.2	21.8	21.8	21.7	21.8	21.9	22.0	22.0
2002	22.2	22.3	22.1	21.9	22.1	22.4	22.0	22.4	22.4	22.4	22.5	22.3	22.3
2003	22.1	22.1	22.2	22.3	22.5	22.6	22.3	22.4	22.5	23.1	23.0	23.1	22.5
2004	23.6	23.8	23.9	23.8	23.6	23.6	24.0	23.9	23.7	23.8	23.9	23.9	23.8
2005	23.7	23.7	23.7	23.7	23.8	23.9	24.1	24.3	24.4	24.7	24.8	25.1	24.2
2006	24.7	24.7	24.9	25.2	25.3	25.5	25.6	25.7	25.7	25.9	26.1	26.2	25.5
2007	25.9	26.0	26.1	26.6	26.9	27.2	27.4	27.6	27.4	27.8	27.7	28.0	27.1
2008	27.1	27.3	27.3	27.4	27.5	27.7	27.7	27.8	27.7	27.8	27.6	27.6	27.5
2009	27.2	27.1	27.0	27.0	27.0	27.1	27.2	27.1	26.6	26.8	26.9	27.0	27.0
2010	26.7	26.6	26.6	26.6	26.6	26.7	26.9	26.9	27.1	27.0	27.1	27.3	26.8
2011	26.7	26.7	26.7	26.7	26.8	26.7	26.6	26.6	25.6	26.4	26.1	26.4	26.5

Employment by Industry: Raleigh–Cary, NC, Selected Years, 2000–2011—*Continued*

(Numbers in thousands, not seasonally adjusted)

Industry and year	January	February	March	April	May	June	July	August	September	October	November	December	Annual average
Professional and Business Services													
2000	73.0	73.6	74.3	75.3	75.1	75.7	75.3	76.0	76.2	76.2	76.7	76.8	75.4
2001	74.5	74.9	74.9	75.5	74.7	75.0	72.8	73.2	72.4	72.5	72.4	72.7	73.8
2002	69.6	69.7	70.0	70.6	71.1	71.5	72.7	73.3	73.1	73.2	73.2	73.9	71.8
2003	71.2	71.3	71.4	72.9	72.5	72.7	71.9	72.2	71.3	71.8	71.8	71.9	71.9
2004	70.7	71.2	71.7	72.5	73.4	74.4	75.6	75.8	75.7	76.4	76.5	77.7	74.3
2005	76.0	76.5	77.0	79.1	78.6	79.1	80.8	81.1	81.5	81.2	81.5	81.8	79.5
2006	80.9	81.2	82.0	83.9	83.9	84.9	85.7	86.1	87.3	88.5	88.8	88.8	85.2
2007	87.3	88.3	89.0	89.4	89.7	91.6	89.2	89.7	89.5	92.2	90.8	90.0	89.7
2008	88.5	88.5	88.6	89.1	89.2	88.9	88.1	89.1	88.1	88.3	87.3	86.0	88.3
2009	84.1	83.3	81.9	81.8	81.8	81.7	81.7	81.8	82.1	82.8	83.5	83.4	82.5
2010	81.8	81.9	82.7	84.3	84.7	85.7	86.2	86.3	86.4	89.2	89.3	89.3	85.7
2011	87.7	88.5	88.4	89.9	90.2	91.1	90.6	90.1	90.0	91.2	91.8	92.3	90.2
Education and Health Services													
2000	39.9	40.3	40.5	40.7	40.7	40.9	40.2	40.5	40.6	41.1	41.1	41.2	40.6
2001	41.4	41.8	42.1	42.3	42.6	42.5	42.1	42.7	42.7	43.2	43.5	43.7	42.6
2002	43.3	43.8	44.0	45.2	45.3	45.2	44.8	45.4	46.0	46.4	46.9	46.7	45.3
2003	46.5	47.1	47.2	47.1	47.3	46.8	46.7	47.2	47.8	47.8	48.0	48.1	47.3
2004	47.8	48.1	48.6	48.3	48.8	48.6	48.7	49.3	49.8	50.2	50.6	50.6	49.1
2005	50.1	50.6	50.9	50.8	51.0	50.6	50.7	51.0	52.1	52.7	53.1	53.0	51.4
2006	52.3	52.9	53.3	54.1	54.6	54.2	53.8	54.1	54.8	55.6	56.4	56.5	54.4
2007	55.7	56.6	57.0	57.4	57.8	57.3	56.9	57.7	58.3	59.3	59.5	59.6	57.8
2008	58.9	59.7	59.7	59.7	60.1	59.2	58.7	59.2	60.0	60.8	61.4	61.1	59.9
2009	60.0	60.7	60.8	61.1	61.6	60.6	60.1	60.9	60.9	61.2	61.3	61.3	60.9
2010	60.5	61.0	61.4	62.3	62.3	61.2	61.2	61.6	61.6	62.0	62.2	61.6	61.6
2011	61.7	62.4	62.6	62.7	62.9	62.2	61.1	61.6	62.5	64.0	65.5	64.9	62.8
Leisure and Hospitality													
2000	35.0	35.5	36.2	36.4	37.1	37.6	37.9	37.6	37.4	36.4	36.8	36.6	36.7
2001	36.1	36.9	37.5	38.0	38.6	39.7	39.0	38.6	37.5	37.1	36.7	36.9	37.7
2002	34.8	35.1	36.0	37.7	38.9	39.5	40.1	40.1	39.4	39.2	38.8	39.1	38.2
2003	37.2	37.3	37.8	38.8	39.2	39.7	39.0	39.7	38.9	38.4	38.5	38.3	38.6
2004	37.2	37.2	38.0	38.6	40.0	40.6	41.2	41.5	40.3	39.6	39.5	40.0	39.5
2005	38.6	39.0	40.0	40.5	42.0	43.0	42.6	42.7	42.8	42.1	42.3	42.8	41.5
2006	41.3	41.8	42.6	44.0	45.4	46.2	45.6	45.9	45.9	45.1	45.2	45.3	44.5
2007	44.7	45.2	45.8	45.5	48.1	49.1	48.8	49.7	49.0	47.5	48.6	48.8	47.6
2008	47.6	48.0	48.5	48.5	50.9	50.9	51.3	51.5	50.8	49.4	49.5	50.1	49.8
2009	48.4	48.6	49.0	49.3	51.4	51.5	51.7	51.6	50.5	49.5	49.4	49.2	50.0
2010	47.4	47.3	48.6	49.7	50.6	51.8	52.6	53.0	52.4	51.0	51.4	50.7	50.5
2011	49.5	50.3	51.5	53.0	53.5	54.1	55.1	54.1	53.5	53.9	54.0	54.4	53.1
Other Services													
2000	14.6	14.8	14.8	15.1	15.2	15.6	15.6	15.3	15.2	15.4	15.4	15.3	15.2
2001	15.2	15.5	15.5	15.7	16.1	16.5	16.7	16.6	16.2	16.5	16.6	16.5	16.1
2002	16.3	16.3	16.2	16.6	17.0	17.0	17.1	16.9	16.6	16.7	16.7	16.6	16.7
2003	16.5	16.6	16.6	17.0	17.8	18.0	18.3	18.2	18.1	17.7	17.8	17.9	17.5
2004	18.2	18.4	18.4	18.6	19.1	19.3	18.9	18.7	18.4	18.5	18.6	18.6	18.6
2005	18.5	18.6	18.5	18.9	19.6	19.8	19.6	19.7	19.2	19.6	19.7	19.8	19.3
2006	19.6	19.9	19.9	20.3	20.6	21.3	20.7	20.5	19.7	20.1	20.4	20.6	20.3
2007	20.7	21.0	21.5	21.6	22.1	22.7	23.1	23.2	22.6	23.5	23.8	23.8	22.5
2008	24.6	24.9	24.6	24.5	25.1	25.4	25.9	25.9	25.7	25.7	25.5	25.1	25.2
2009	24.4	24.6	24.7	24.7	24.8	24.8	25.1	24.9	24.4	23.9	23.6	23.3	24.4
2010	23.3	23.2	23.4	23.2	23.4	23.5	23.5	23.3	22.9	23.3	23.0	22.6	23.2
2011	22.4	22.4	22.6	22.6	22.7	23.1	23.3	23.2	22.9	23.2	23.1	22.9	22.9
Government													
2000	70.2	70.9	71.1	71.2	71.6	71.6	65.5	67.2	73.1	72.5	73.2	73.0	70.9
2001	73.0	73.9	74.0	73.7	73.9	73.8	67.0	68.1	73.7	74.6	74.5	73.9	72.8
2002	73.0	73.9	73.1	73.1	73.4	73.1	66.6	68.2	74.2	74.8	74.9	74.5	72.7
2003	74.0	74.5	74.9	75.2	75.6	75.0	71.5	72.4	75.9	78.3	77.6	77.3	75.2
2004	76.5	76.9	77.5	77.6	78.0	77.4	74.0	76.1	80.8	81.0	80.7	80.4	78.1
2005	79.4	80.1	80.6	80.6	80.8	79.5	76.9	81.3	82.7	80.6	82.3	80.0	80.4
2006	81.2	82.1	82.7	84.0	84.6	83.8	80.4	84.7	85.8	86.6	87.2	86.7	84.2
2007	86.4	87.3	87.9	88.2	88.9	87.4	84.0	87.3	89.3	89.6	90.0	89.7	88.0
2008	89.2	90.0	90.5	90.8	91.1	89.4	87.1	89.5	92.1	94.2	93.3	92.9	90.8
2009	90.1	90.4	91.1	92.7	92.7	90.6	86.5	87.8	89.9	90.8	90.8	90.3	90.3
2010	88.7	89.5	90.2	91.7	93.5	91.2	87.2	88.9	90.6	91.2	90.6	90.3	90.3
2011	89.3	90.2	90.4	90.3	90.8	87.7	84.0	85.3	86.8	87.9	87.5	85.6	88.0

Employment by Industry: Richmond, VA, Selected Years, 2000–2011

(Numbers in thousands, not seasonally adjusted)

Industry and year	January	February	March	April	May	June	July	August	September	October	November	December	Annual average
Total Nonfarm													
2000	574.3	576.3	582.3	585.5	589.8	595.2	587.4	587.9	590.5	589.3	593.2	596.2	587.3
2001	584.2	585.1	590.1	589.5	592.4	596.9	589.4	589.0	587.6	585.1	587.8	590.0	588.9
2002	578.5	581.3	586.7	587.3	591.4	594.7	586.2	586.8	586.3	585.6	588.1	589.1	586.8
2003	575.4	575.3	580.1	588.6	592.1	594.4	586.9	587.2	588.3	592.3	595.8	598.8	587.9
2004	589.7	592.1	598.3	601.7	605.8	609.4	601.7	597.7	605.1	610.6	613.4	615.0	603.4
2005	603.1	605.8	609.8	617.8	620.3	623.8	614.6	611.1	617.7	619.1	622.7	623.1	615.7
2006	612.3	612.7	620.7	622.0	627.5	629.9	626.5	625.0	623.8	631.5	635.6	636.5	625.3
2007	624.3	627.8	630.2	631.1	636.2	642.2	633.1	633.2	633.7	634.8	635.8	637.0	633.3
2008	625.9	627.1	629.7	633.2	632.9	636.7	629.2	628.2	629.4	632.7	631.0	628.5	630.4
2009	612.9	608.1	609.3	609.0	610.0	611.4	599.3	596.2	599.6	602.8	604.2	603.3	605.5
2010	592.1	588.9	595.7	604.2	609.4	611.4	603.9	601.2	602.2	605.8	607.0	606.8	602.4
2011	597.2	599.4	603.9	611.9	614.2	615.3	610.3	608.2	609.7	614.0	613.8	616.2	609.5
Total Private													
2000	467.8	469.6	474.8	477.7	481.6	486.0	482.5	483.2	483.7	481.4	483.8	486.4	479.9
2001	475.1	475.5	480.2	480.3	483.2	487.1	483.2	482.8	480.1	476.1	477.1	478.9	480.0
2002	468.3	470.2	475.2	476.0	480.1	483.0	478.7	479.2	478.1	475.3	476.9	477.8	476.6
2003	463.5	462.2	467.6	474.7	479.1	481.9	478.6	480.6	479.3	481.6	482.9	485.5	476.5
2004	478.2	478.8	484.1	488.2	492.5	496.8	493.5	493.0	493.3	495.5	497.6	500.0	491.0
2005	489.4	490.2	493.7	500.7	504.1	508.0	504.5	503.9	505.5	507.2	509.5	509.8	502.2
2006	498.5	497.9	505.7	507.6	513.0	515.6	516.5	515.5	512.6	517.5	520.3	521.0	511.8
2007	509.0	511.3	514.7	515.7	521.3	528.0	524.0	525.1	525.1	523.8	524.4	526.3	520.7
2008	515.8	516.0	518.6	519.9	520.6	524.0	522.0	521.7	519.2	519.2	516.6	515.8	519.1
2009	499.5	494.3	495.0	494.1	496.0	497.5	492.3	489.2	489.1	489.1	489.3	489.5	492.9
2010	478.5	474.9	481.3	488.4	492.9	495.7	494.1	492.2	491.2	492.7	492.9	493.3	489.0
2011	483.5	485.0	489.2	496.6	499.9	501.3	500.4	499.5	497.8	499.1	497.8	501.3	496.0
Goods-Producing													
2000	94.6	94.9	96.0	96.9	97.1	97.3	97.1	97.5	97.6	96.9	97.1	97.7	96.7
2001	95.3	95.6	96.2	96.1	95.9	96.1	95.1	94.8	94.5	93.2	93.1	92.7	94.9
2002	90.1	90.4	91.4	91.7	92.1	92.5	91.6	92.3	92.3	91.8	91.6	91.3	91.6
2003	88.0	87.5	88.7	89.8	90.3	89.7	89.6	89.8	89.3	88.6	88.2	87.9	89.0
2004	86.3	86.1	87.2	87.5	87.7	88.6	89.3	89.1	90.0	89.7	90.2	90.4	88.5
2005	89.3	88.6	88.6	89.3	89.5	90.2	91.1	91.1	90.5	90.0	90.3	90.2	89.9
2006	88.3	88.7	89.4	89.3	89.7	90.5	90.1	90.1	89.3	88.9	88.5	88.5	89.3
2007	87.4	87.1	87.8	88.7	89.5	90.5	90.0	90.2	89.8	89.0	88.3	88.1	88.9
2008	85.5	85.1	84.9	84.8	84.3	84.0	83.6	83.3	82.1	81.7	79.5	78.2	83.1
2009	74.5	71.6	71.4	70.8	70.1	70.3	69.7	69.0	68.8	68.4	68.0	67.5	70.0
2010	65.3	64.2	65.2	66.7	67.1	67.4	68.0	67.3	67.0	67.3	66.9	66.2	66.6
2011	63.8	64.0	64.5	64.7	64.8	64.8	63.7	64.1	64.2	63.6	63.5	63.6	64.1
Mining, Logging, and Construction													
2000	37.5	37.7	39.0	40.3	40.5	40.9	40.7	41.2	41.1	40.9	40.9	40.7	40.1
2001	39.1	39.5	40.7	40.8	41.2	41.5	41.3	41.2	41.1	40.2	40.3	39.8	40.6
2002	38.5	38.7	39.9	40.5	41.0	41.0	40.7	41.3	41.3	41.1	40.9	40.6	40.5
2003	38.3	38.0	39.5	40.6	41.4	41.2	41.7	41.9	41.6	41.0	40.5	40.2	40.5
2004	39.2	39.2	40.3	41.2	41.9	42.6	43.3	43.0	43.7	43.8	44.1	44.1	42.2
2005	43.2	42.9	43.3	44.0	44.3	44.9	46.2	46.0	45.4	45.1	45.2	44.9	44.6
2006	43.7	44.2	45.1	45.0	45.7	46.5	46.6	46.5	46.0	46.0	45.8	45.7	45.6
2007	44.8	44.7	45.3	46.3	47.1	47.8	47.7	47.9	47.8	47.0	46.3	45.9	46.6
2008	43.7	43.4	43.6	43.6	43.3	43.3	43.3	43.3	42.3	42.1	40.6	39.7	42.7
2009	37.3	36.2	36.1	36.2	36.1	36.1	35.9	35.5	35.1	35.1	34.7	34.2	35.7
2010	32.4	31.5	32.5	33.9	34.2	34.3	34.9	34.4	34.1	34.5	34.3	33.6	33.7
2011	31.8	31.8	32.3	32.9	33.0	32.9	32.1	32.6	32.8	32.3	32.4	32.5	32.5
Manufacturing													
2000	57.1	57.2	57.0	56.6	56.6	56.4	56.4	56.3	56.5	56.0	56.2	57.0	56.6
2001	56.2	56.1	55.5	55.3	54.7	54.6	53.8	53.6	53.4	53.0	52.8	52.9	54.3
2002	51.6	51.7	51.5	51.2	51.1	51.5	50.9	51.0	51.0	50.7	50.7	50.7	51.1
2003	49.7	49.5	49.2	49.2	48.9	48.5	47.9	47.9	47.7	47.6	47.7	47.7	48.5
2004	47.1	46.9	46.9	46.3	45.8	46.0	46.0	46.1	46.3	45.9	46.1	46.3	46.3
2005	46.1	45.7	45.3	45.3	45.2	45.3	44.9	45.1	45.1	44.9	45.1	45.3	45.3
2006	44.6	44.5	44.3	44.3	44.0	44.0	43.5	43.6	43.3	42.9	42.7	42.8	43.7
2007	42.6	42.4	42.5	42.4	42.4	42.7	42.3	42.3	42.0	42.0	42.0	42.2	42.3
2008	41.8	41.7	41.3	41.2	41.0	40.7	40.3	40.0	39.8	39.6	38.9	38.5	40.4
2009	37.2	35.4	35.3	34.6	34.0	34.2	33.8	33.5	33.7	33.3	33.3	33.3	34.3
2010	32.9	32.7	32.7	32.8	32.9	33.1	33.1	32.9	32.9	32.8	32.6	32.6	32.8
2011	32.0	32.2	32.2	31.8	31.8	31.9	31.6	31.5	31.4	31.3	31.1	31.1	31.7
Service-Providing													
2000	479.7	481.4	486.3	488.6	492.7	497.9	490.3	490.4	492.9	492.4	496.1	498.5	490.6
2001	488.9	489.5	493.9	493.4	496.5	500.8	494.3	494.2	493.1	491.9	494.7	497.3	494.0
2002	488.4	490.9	495.3	495.6	499.3	502.2	494.6	494.5	494.0	493.8	496.5	497.8	495.2
2003	487.4	487.8	491.4	498.8	501.8	504.7	497.3	497.4	499.0	503.7	507.6	510.9	499.0
2004	503.4	506.0	511.1	514.2	518.1	520.8	512.4	508.6	515.1	520.9	523.2	524.6	514.9
2005	513.8	517.2	521.2	528.5	530.8	533.6	523.5	520.0	527.2	529.1	532.4	532.9	525.9
2006	524.0	524.0	531.3	532.7	537.8	539.4	536.4	534.9	534.5	542.6	547.1	548.0	536.1
2007	536.9	540.7	542.4	542.4	546.7	551.7	543.1	543.0	543.9	545.8	547.5	548.9	544.4
2008	540.4	542.0	544.8	548.4	548.6	552.7	545.6	544.9	547.3	551.0	551.5	550.3	547.3
2009	538.4	536.5	537.9	538.2	539.9	541.1	529.6	527.2	530.8	534.4	536.2	535.8	535.5
2010	526.8	524.7	530.5	537.5	542.3	544.0	535.9	533.9	535.2	538.5	540.1	540.6	535.8
2011	533.4	535.4	539.4	547.2	549.4	550.5	546.6	544.1	545.5	550.4	550.3	552.6	545.4

Employment by Industry: Richmond, VA, Selected Years, 2000–2011—*Continued*

(Numbers in thousands, not seasonally adjusted)

Industry and year	January	February	March	April	May	June	July	August	September	October	November	December	Annual average
Trade, Transportation, and Utilities													
2000	111.2	110.7	111.4	111.4	112.1	112.3	112.4	113.0	112.8	113.6	115.8	117.5	112.9
2001	112.6	111.5	112.0	110.9	111.5	111.7	111.4	111.6	111.4	112.1	114.1	115.5	112.2
2002	111.1	109.9	110.7	110.6	111.3	111.8	111.6	112.2	111.9	112.6	114.4	116.2	112.0
2003	110.8	109.8	109.9	110.8	111.8	112.1	111.7	112.1	111.7	113.7	115.6	117.2	112.3
2004	112.8	111.9	112.4	112.7	113.2	113.5	113.0	112.7	111.9	113.2	114.8	116.1	113.2
2005	111.4	110.5	111.3	111.9	112.4	112.9	113.1	113.5	113.2	113.9	116.5	118.5	113.3
2006	114.5	113.2	114.2	113.9	115.0	115.3	115.1	115.5	114.8	116.6	119.0	121.1	115.7
2007	117.0	116.0	116.8	116.4	117.6	118.4	118.3	118.4	118.5	119.0	121.4	122.8	118.4
2008	117.9	116.4	116.6	116.2	116.7	117.4	117.0	117.0	117.0	117.7	119.2	120.2	117.4
2009	114.5	112.6	111.9	110.9	111.2	111.2	110.3	110.0	109.3	110.6	112.4	113.8	111.6
2010	109.6	107.8	108.6	110.0	111.2	111.7	111.2	111.0	109.9	111.1	113.1	114.7	110.8
2011	110.8	110.1	110.6	112.2	112.7	113.1	113.6	113.2	112.4	112.7	114.2	115.7	112.6
Wholesale Trade													
2000	23.7	23.7	24.0	24.1	24.1	24.3	24.3	24.4	24.4	24.5	24.6	24.7	24.2
2001	24.3	24.3	24.4	24.2	24.0	24.1	24.1	24.0	24.1	24.2	24.3	24.6	24.2
2002	24.3	24.4	24.8	24.7	24.9	25.1	25.3	25.5	25.6	25.6	25.7	25.9	25.2
2003	26.0	26.0	26.1	25.9	26.2	26.2	26.2	26.2	25.9	26.0	26.0	26.1	26.1
2004	25.7	25.8	25.9	26.1	26.2	26.3	26.4	26.2	26.0	26.2	26.1	26.1	26.1
2005	25.8	25.8	25.9	26.2	26.2	26.3	26.5	26.7	26.6	26.6	26.7	26.8	26.3
2006	26.9	27.0	27.1	27.2	27.4	27.6	27.8	27.9	27.8	28.0	28.1	28.1	27.6
2007	28.1	28.3	28.5	28.5	28.6	28.8	28.8	28.8	28.7	28.9	28.7	28.7	28.6
2008	28.5	28.6	28.6	28.6	28.5	28.6	28.7	28.6	28.4	28.3	28.1	27.9	28.5
2009	27.5	27.2	27.0	26.7	26.6	26.4	26.2	26.1	25.8	26.0	25.9	25.9	26.4
2010	25.6	25.5	25.6	26.1	26.3	26.4	26.5	26.5	26.3	26.8	26.8	26.9	26.3
2011	26.9	27.0	27.2	27.3	27.5	27.6	27.9	27.8	27.5	27.1	27.1	27.5	27.4
Retail Trade													
2000	66.3	65.7	66.2	66.0	66.8	66.9	66.5	67.1	67.0	67.5	69.6	71.2	67.2
2001	67.3	66.2	66.6	65.7	66.4	66.5	66.4	66.5	66.2	67.0	69.2	70.5	67.0
2002	66.9	65.8	66.3	65.9	66.4	66.8	66.1	66.4	66.1	66.7	68.3	70.0	66.8
2003	65.1	64.1	64.1	64.8	65.5	65.7	65.2	65.6	65.7	67.2	69.2	70.7	66.1
2004	67.2	66.2	66.6	66.3	66.7	66.9	65.9	65.8	65.4	66.6	68.2	69.2	66.8
2005	65.9	65.0	65.4	65.7	66.2	66.5	66.3	66.5	66.2	66.7	69.0	70.6	66.7
2006	67.3	66.1	66.8	66.6	67.4	67.4	67.0	67.0	66.3	67.7	69.9	71.4	67.6
2007	68.1	67.0	67.4	67.1	68.2	68.6	68.6	68.5	68.6	69.2	71.5	72.4	68.8
2008	68.9	67.4	67.6	67.1	67.6	68.1	67.7	67.8	68.1	69.0	70.5	71.2	68.4
2009	67.0	65.6	65.2	64.8	65.2	65.4	64.7	64.6	64.3	65.4	67.0	68.0	65.6
2010	64.8	63.3	63.8	64.5	65.6	65.9	65.3	65.1	64.2	64.9	66.7	67.7	65.2
2011	64.5	63.7	63.9	64.8	65.0	65.1	65.2	64.9	64.4	65.1	66.3	67.4	65.0
Transportation and Utilities													
2000	21.2	21.3	21.2	21.3	21.2	21.1	21.6	21.5	21.4	21.6	21.6	21.6	21.4
2001	21.0	21.0	21.0	21.0	21.1	21.1	20.9	21.1	21.1	20.9	20.6	20.4	20.9
2002	19.9	19.7	19.6	20.0	20.0	19.9	20.2	20.3	20.2	20.3	20.4	20.3	20.1
2003	19.7	19.7	19.7	20.1	20.1	20.2	20.3	20.3	20.1	20.5	20.4	20.4	20.1
2004	19.9	19.9	19.9	20.3	20.3	20.3	20.7	20.7	20.5	20.4	20.5	20.8	20.4
2005	19.7	19.7	20.0	20.0	20.0	20.1	20.3	20.3	20.4	20.6	20.8	21.1	20.3
2006	20.3	20.1	20.3	20.1	20.2	20.3	20.3	20.6	20.7	20.9	21.0	21.6	20.5
2007	20.8	20.7	20.9	20.8	20.8	21.0	20.9	21.1	21.2	20.9	21.2	21.7	21.0
2008	20.5	20.4	20.4	20.5	20.6	20.7	20.6	20.6	20.5	20.4	20.6	21.1	20.6
2009	20.0	19.8	19.7	19.4	19.4	19.4	19.4	19.3	19.2	19.2	19.5	19.9	19.5
2010	19.2	19.0	19.2	19.4	19.3	19.4	19.4	19.4	19.4	19.4	19.6	20.1	19.4
2011	19.4	19.4	19.5	20.1	20.2	20.4	20.5	20.5	20.5	20.5	20.8	20.8	20.2
Information													
2000	12.5	12.4	12.6	12.6	12.8	13.1	13.2	13.3	13.4	13.1	13.2	13.3	13.0
2001	13.1	13.1	13.1	12.6	12.6	12.5	12.5	12.6	12.4	12.3	12.2	12.3	12.6
2002	12.6	12.6	12.6	12.5	12.6	12.5	12.3	12.4	12.2	11.9	12.2	12.2	12.4
2003	11.7	12.0	12.0	11.9	11.9	12.0	11.9	11.9	11.7	11.5	11.6	11.5	11.8
2004	11.5	11.4	11.5	11.2	11.2	11.2	11.1	11.0	10.9	10.9	11.0	11.0	11.2
2005	11.0	11.0	11.1	11.1	11.1	11.1	11.1	11.1	11.1	11.0	11.1	11.1	11.1
2006	11.0	11.0	11.0	10.8	12.9	10.8	11.8	11.2	11.1	11.1	11.2	11.2	11.3
2007	11.6	11.6	11.5	11.7	11.9	11.6	11.3	11.2	11.0	10.8	10.8	10.6	11.3
2008	10.5	10.5	10.5	10.4	10.3	10.4	10.3	10.2	10.1	10.3	10.4	10.4	10.4
2009	10.5	10.4	10.4	10.4	10.4	10.3	10.2	9.9	9.8	9.7	9.6	9.6	10.1
2010	9.5	9.5	9.4	9.4	9.4	9.5	9.5	9.4	9.5	9.5	9.5	9.4	9.5
2011	9.2	9.2	9.1	9.1	9.2	9.2	9.1	7.9	9.0	9.0	9.0	9.0	9.0
Financial Activities													
2000	44.3	44.3	44.5	44.4	44.8	45.1	45.3	45.5	45.3	45.4	45.8	46.5	45.1
2001	46.0	46.3	46.6	46.7	46.8	47.3	47.3	47.6	47.4	47.3	47.5	47.7	47.0
2002	47.0	47.2	47.3	47.2	47.0	47.1	46.8	46.3	46.4	46.1	45.9	45.7	46.7
2003	45.2	45.4	45.6	46.2	46.5	46.7	47.0	47.2	46.9	46.3	46.5	47.0	46.4
2004	46.6	46.9	46.8	47.1	47.0	47.3	47.1	47.2	46.7	46.5	46.6	46.8	46.9
2005	46.6	46.7	46.8	46.5	46.6	46.7	47.3	47.2	46.7	46.4	46.3	46.5	46.7
2006	46.4	46.5	46.8	46.5	46.7	46.9	47.0	47.0	46.4	46.2	46.0	46.1	46.5
2007	45.7	45.6	45.9	45.9	46.0	46.2	46.2	46.4	45.7	45.3	45.1	45.0	45.8
2008	44.6	44.5	44.5	44.0	43.8	44.0	44.3	44.3	43.7	44.1	44.0	44.1	44.2
2009	43.7	43.4	43.6	43.5	43.0	43.1	43.0	43.1	42.6	42.5	42.5	42.6	43.1
2010	42.2	42.1	42.4	42.5	42.6	43.0	42.7	42.9	42.4	42.7	42.8	43.0	42.6
2011	42.7	42.8	43.1	43.4	43.6	43.9	45.0	44.7	44.4	44.8	45.3	45.5	44.1

Employment by Industry: Richmond, VA, Selected Years, 2000–2011—*Continued*

(Numbers in thousands, not seasonally adjusted)

Industry and year	January	February	March	April	May	June	July	August	September	October	November	December	Annual average
Professional and Business Services													
2000	88.3	90.0	91.0	92.2	92.9	93.8	92.8	92.3	93.0	92.2	92.2	92.5	91.9
2001	90.0	90.0	90.6	90.4	90.9	91.6	90.5	90.3	88.7	87.5	87.6	88.1	89.7
2002	86.5	87.6	88.3	88.6	88.9	89.0	88.3	88.0	87.9	86.4	86.8	86.6	87.7
2003	81.7	81.1	82.3	83.8	84.3	84.9	84.5	84.6	84.3	85.0	85.1	85.7	83.9
2004	84.5	84.6	85.0	86.4	87.4	88.4	88.8	89.4	89.1	90.9	91.1	92.3	88.2
2005	89.7	90.3	90.8	92.3	92.7	93.4	93.8	93.5	93.6	95.2	94.9	95.1	92.9
2006	93.2	93.4	94.3	93.7	94.6	95.4	95.3	95.9	96.4	98.5	98.8	99.3	95.7
2007	97.0	97.7	98.8	98.6	98.3	99.8	99.5	99.7	100.0	100.2	99.8	100.2	99.1
2008	99.4	99.9	100.3	100.1	99.9	100.5	99.7	99.8	99.0	99.1	98.2	97.4	99.4
2009	95.2	94.7	95.0	93.0	92.6	92.1	91.9	91.6	91.4	91.9	92.3	92.3	92.8
2010	90.5	90.5	91.6	92.9	92.8	93.0	94.0	94.3	94.8	95.1	95.1	95.4	93.3
2011	94.7	95.2	96.3	97.9	97.7	97.1	97.6	98.6	97.6	98.8	97.6	99.0	97.3
Education and Health Services													
2000	52.4	52.4	52.7	51.5	51.6	51.5	49.3	49.5	51.8	52.2	52.5	52.7	51.7
2001	53.0	53.2	53.4	53.5	53.8	54.2	52.5	52.6	54.7	55.2	55.2	55.4	53.9
2002	55.5	55.9	56.0	56.1	57.1	57.3	55.3	55.7	57.3	57.8	58.2	58.2	56.7
2003	59.8	59.9	60.0	60.7	60.5	60.2	57.7	59.4	61.6	62.1	62.4	62.8	60.6
2004	63.7	64.2	64.7	65.1	65.8	65.7	62.1	62.3	65.6	66.7	67.4	67.5	65.1
2005	67.2	68.0	68.0	68.6	69.0	68.5	64.8	64.7	69.6	71.2	71.7	70.9	68.5
2006	69.3	68.6	71.1	73.2	71.6	71.3	70.9	70.0	71.2	73.1	73.5	72.3	71.3
2007	71.9	74.3	72.9	71.6	73.0	73.5	71.0	71.5	75.6	76.9	77.8	78.6	74.1
2008	78.3	79.3	79.6	80.8	80.8	80.7	78.5	78.8	81.5	82.5	83.0	83.1	80.6
2009	82.0	82.4	82.3	82.9	83.9	83.7	80.7	80.7	83.5	84.7	85.5	85.3	83.1
2010	84.6	84.5	85.2	85.2	85.9	85.1	82.7	82.3	84.5	85.7	85.9	85.5	84.8
2011	84.9	85.5	85.5	86.4	86.6	85.9	83.1	83.5	84.2	84.9	84.8	84.8	85.0
Leisure and Hospitality													
2000	40.8	41.0	42.3	44.4	45.9	48.2	47.6	47.4	45.4	43.6	42.9	41.8	44.3
2001	41.4	41.8	44.1	45.8	47.0	49.0	49.1	48.7	46.6	44.2	42.9	42.8	45.3
2002	41.1	41.9	44.0	44.4	46.0	47.6	47.7	47.2	45.2	43.9	42.8	42.7	44.5
2003	41.7	41.7	44.1	46.0	47.8	49.6	49.3	48.7	46.7	46.9	45.5	45.2	46.1
2004	44.3	44.5	46.6	48.4	50.2	52.0	52.2	51.4	49.7	48.1	47.0	46.4	48.4
2005	44.8	45.3	47.4	49.3	50.9	52.9	52.9	52.4	50.9	49.4	48.7	47.8	49.4
2006	46.8	47.4	49.6	50.9	52.8	55.4	54.9	54.5	51.8	52.4	51.1	50.9	51.5
2007	48.6	49.1	50.7	51.6	53.8	56.3	56.1	55.7	53.5	52.0	50.6	50.3	52.4
2008	49.0	49.3	51.1	53.1	55.2	57.1	56.7	55.9	53.1	52.0	50.5	50.6	52.8
2009	48.7	48.8	49.9	52.1	54.4	56.2	55.8	54.7	52.9	51.2	49.0	48.8	51.9
2010	47.2	46.6	48.6	51.7	53.9	55.7	55.7	54.8	53.2	51.4	49.7	49.3	51.5
2011	47.8	48.6	50.3	52.9	55.3	57.1	58.1	57.4	55.9	55.5	53.6	54.0	53.9
Other Services													
2000	23.7	23.9	24.3	24.3	24.4	24.7	24.8	24.7	24.4	24.4	24.3	24.4	24.4
2001	23.7	24.0	24.2	24.3	24.7	24.7	24.8	24.6	24.4	24.3	24.5	24.4	24.4
2002	24.4	24.7	24.7	24.9	25.1	25.2	25.1	25.1	24.9	24.8	25.0	24.9	24.9
2003	24.6	24.8	25.0	25.5	26.0	26.7	26.9	26.9	27.1	27.5	28.0	28.2	26.4
2004	28.5	29.2	29.9	29.8	30.0	30.1	29.9	29.9	29.4	29.5	29.5	29.5	29.6
2005	29.4	29.8	29.7	31.7	31.9	32.3	30.4	30.4	29.9	30.1	30.0	29.7	30.4
2006	29.0	29.1	29.3	29.3	29.7	30.0	31.4	31.3	31.6	30.7	32.2	31.6	30.4
2007	29.8	29.9	30.3	31.2	31.2	31.6	31.6	32.0	31.0	30.6	30.7	30.7	30.9
2008	30.6	31.0	31.1	30.5	29.6	29.9	31.9	32.4	32.7	31.8	31.8	31.8	31.3
2009	30.4	30.4	30.5	30.5	30.4	30.6	30.7	30.2	30.8	30.1	30.0	29.6	30.4
2010	29.6	29.7	30.3	30.0	30.0	30.3	30.3	30.2	29.9	29.9	29.9	29.8	30.0
2011	29.6	29.6	29.8	30.0	30.0	30.2	30.2	30.1	30.1	29.8	29.8	29.7	29.9
Government													
2000	106.5	106.7	107.5	107.8	108.2	109.2	104.9	104.7	106.8	107.9	109.4	109.8	107.5
2001	109.1	109.6	109.9	109.2	109.2	109.8	106.2	106.2	107.5	109.0	110.7	111.1	109.0
2002	110.2	111.1	111.5	111.3	111.3	111.7	107.5	107.6	108.2	110.3	111.2	111.3	110.3
2003	111.9	113.1	112.5	113.9	113.0	112.5	108.3	106.6	109.0	110.7	112.9	113.3	111.5
2004	111.5	113.3	114.2	113.5	113.0	112.6	108.2	104.7	111.8	115.1	115.8	115.0	112.4
2005	113.7	115.6	116.1	117.1	116.2	115.8	110.1	107.2	112.2	111.9	113.2	113.3	113.5
2006	113.8	114.8	115.0	114.4	114.5	114.3	110.0	109.5	111.2	114.0	115.3	115.5	113.5
2007	115.3	116.5	115.5	115.4	114.9	114.2	109.1	108.1	108.6	111.0	111.4	110.7	112.6
2008	110.1	111.1	111.1	113.3	112.3	112.7	107.2	106.5	110.2	113.5	114.4	112.7	111.3
2009	113.4	113.8	114.3	114.9	114.0	113.9	107.0	107.0	110.5	113.7	114.9	113.8	112.6
2010	113.6	114.0	114.4	115.8	116.5	115.7	109.8	109.0	111.0	113.1	114.1	113.5	113.4
2011	113.7	114.4	114.7	115.3	114.3	114.0	109.9	108.7	111.9	114.9	116.0	114.9	113.6

Employment by Industry: Riverside–San Bernardino–Ontario, CA, Selected Years, 2000–2011

(Numbers in thousands, not seasonally adjusted)

Industry and year	January	February	March	April	May	June	July	August	September	October	November	December	Annual average
Total Nonfarm													
2000	964.6	969.5	977.3	980.9	992.2	994.1	980.0	980.5	994.7	998.4	1,010.7	1,017.9	988.4
2001	1,010.1	1,011.4	1,022.8	1,023.1	1,029.2	1,034.6	1,026.4	1,023.9	1,034.5	1,039.8	1,049.4	1,051.7	1,029.7
2002	1,035.2	1,043.0	1,049.1	1,061.0	1,069.7	1,074.0	1,054.5	1,059.1	1,069.7	1,074.9	1,089.2	1,095.0	1,064.5
2003	1,075.5	1,078.6	1,088.1	1,090.9	1,096.8	1,101.3	1,089.9	1,088.3	1,102.5	1,117.8	1,126.9	1,133.7	1,099.2
2004	1,122.8	1,128.5	1,139.5	1,151.9	1,159.0	1,161.6	1,152.0	1,152.3	1,166.5	1,183.7	1,197.4	1,205.0	1,160.0
2005	1,184.4	1,195.8	1,207.7	1,220.1	1,221.0	1,221.8	1,210.0	1,213.6	1,230.1	1,240.6	1,254.3	1,264.4	1,222.0
2006	1,246.5	1,254.7	1,264.8	1,268.8	1,273.4	1,278.2	1,262.9	1,259.5	1,268.2	1,271.8	1,280.5	1,282.8	1,267.7
2007	1,262.6	1,267.4	1,275.0	1,273.1	1,279.3	1,278.7	1,264.7	1,259.6	1,263.6	1,269.6	1,278.3	1,280.5	1,271.0
2008	1,247.8	1,246.6	1,246.7	1,244.7	1,239.3	1,235.3	1,210.4	1,207.2	1,205.1	1,209.2	1,209.5	1,203.9	1,225.5
2009	1,173.6	1,163.3	1,162.4	1,156.2	1,152.7	1,146.5	1,119.9	1,118.2	1,114.3	1,128.2	1,136.9	1,137.7	1,142.5
2010	1,116.2	1,117.7	1,124.5	1,132.7	1,136.4	1,133.0	1,106.1	1,113.4	1,114.6	1,128.4	1,142.4	1,144.9	1,125.9
2011	1,120.8	1,125.4	1,130.4	1,132.7	1,132.4	1,126.8	1,106.7	1,117.2	1,125.4	1,136.9	1,149.1	1,153.1	1,129.7
Total Private													
2000	775.3	779.3	783.8	787.3	793.8	799.9	793.4	799.1	805.2	804.3	813.9	819.8	796.3
2001	811.9	814.2	821.8	823.8	828.6	832.9	831.7	835.3	835.0	835.9	840.1	842.9	829.5
2002	827.2	831.4	837.9	842.2	851.5	855.1	847.5	856.1	860.1	861.0	872.8	878.8	851.8
2003	860.3	863.4	870.8	874.3	881.9	887.2	884.3	888.9	895.6	907.8	914.7	922.4	887.6
2004	911.1	916.6	925.7	937.0	944.0	948.2	946.5	950.4	956.5	969.4	979.5	985.6	947.5
2005	964.4	974.3	984.5	995.6	996.5	1,001.6	999.2	1,003.0	1,012.6	1,018.1	1,030.0	1,038.9	1,001.6
2006	1,025.5	1,033.4	1,041.4	1,042.7	1,046.5	1,050.9	1,046.8	1,047.4	1,049.6	1,046.9	1,054.2	1,057.2	1,045.2
2007	1,037.9	1,042.2	1,047.4	1,044.7	1,050.1	1,049.7	1,047.4	1,046.4	1,044.4	1,041.4	1,047.9	1,049.0	1,045.7
2008	1,017.0	1,015.0	1,013.2	1,010.1	1,004.3	1,001.5	988.4	985.0	981.4	975.6	974.1	967.9	994.5
2009	938.0	927.7	924.6	915.4	911.7	907.1	894.2	889.6	887.8	892.2	898.9	900.2	907.3
2010	879.5	880.2	884.8	891.0	891.7	891.4	884.7	887.4	889.0	895.3	908.7	914.9	891.6
2011	889.5	893.8	897.1	899.3	898.8	896.0	895.4	899.3	905.1	908.9	920.0	926.0	902.4
Goods-Producing													
2000	191.1	192.7	193.8	197.4	199.5	202.9	203.2	205.6	206.6	205.7	206.0	205.9	200.9
2001	203.5	204.3	206.9	207.4	209.1	209.8	211.1	213.0	211.7	209.9	207.6	205.7	208.3
2002	199.8	201.4	203.1	204.0	206.0	207.8	208.2	212.4	212.1	212.2	212.5	210.8	207.5
2003	207.6	207.5	210.5	211.2	215.3	217.0	216.8	220.0	220.8	222.7	222.6	223.1	216.3
2004	221.3	223.2	224.2	229.0	231.5	234.4	237.0	238.4	240.2	240.8	239.1	238.2	233.1
2005	230.7	235.3	238.3	242.3	243.2	247.0	248.6	250.7	252.7	253.3	253.1	253.1	245.7
2006	250.4	253.4	254.4	253.7	256.5	259.4	257.1	256.7	255.3	247.7	242.2	240.3	252.3
2007	234.2	234.6	235.8	235.0	236.4	237.8	237.2	236.7	233.1	226.6	223.3	218.5	232.4
2008	208.9	207.2	206.8	205.0	203.8	203.5	200.5	199.4	196.0	190.2	184.9	179.5	198.8
2009	169.8	164.2	163.3	160.3	160.9	159.9	157.1	155.6	153.3	151.7	150.4	147.5	157.8
2010	144.4	143.8	144.9	146.5	147.5	147.8	146.7	147.3	146.3	145.3	145.1	144.2	145.8
2011	140.4	141.9	142.7	144.5	145.4	146.1	149.4	149.2	150.5	146.8	146.4	143.6	145.6
Mining and Logging													
2000	1.3	1.3	1.3	1.3	1.2	1.2	1.3	1.3	1.2	1.2	1.2	1.2	1.3
2001	1.2	1.2	1.2	1.2	1.2	1.2	1.2	1.1	1.2	1.1	1.1	1.2	1.2
2002	1.1	1.1	1.1	1.2	1.2	1.2	1.3	1.3	1.3	1.2	1.3	1.3	1.2
2003	1.3	1.3	1.3	1.3	1.2	1.2	1.2	1.2	1.2	1.2	1.2	1.2	1.2
2004	1.2	1.2	1.2	1.2	1.2	1.2	1.2	1.2	1.2	1.2	1.3	1.3	1.2
2005	1.3	1.3	1.3	1.3	1.3	1.3	1.4	1.4	1.4	1.4	1.4	1.4	1.4
2006	1.4	1.4	1.4	1.4	1.4	1.4	1.5	1.4	1.4	1.4	1.4	1.4	1.4
2007	1.4	1.3	1.3	1.3	1.3	1.3	1.4	1.4	1.4	1.3	1.3	1.2	1.3
2008	1.3	1.3	1.3	1.2	1.2	1.2	1.2	1.2	1.2	1.2	1.1	1.2	1.2
2009	1.2	1.2	1.2	1.2	1.2	1.2	1.1	1.1	1.1	1.1	1.1	1.0	1.1
2010	1.0	1.0	1.0	1.0	1.0	1.0	1.0	1.0	1.0	1.0	1.0	1.0	1.0
2011	1.0	1.0	1.0	1.0	1.0	1.0	1.1	1.1	1.1	1.1	1.1	1.0	1.0
Construction													
2000	73.5	73.9	74.7	77.1	79.2	81.0	81.0	82.7	84.0	83.5	84.0	84.0	79.9
2001	81.6	82.2	84.5	86.5	88.6	89.7	90.9	93.0	92.3	92.1	90.9	89.6	88.5
2002	84.8	85.7	86.7	87.3	88.7	90.2	91.6	95.1	95.0	95.9	95.8	93.9	90.9
2003	92.7	91.9	94.2	94.6	98.6	99.8	99.7	102.2	102.7	104.0	103.7	103.4	99.0
2004	102.4	103.6	104.0	108.4	110.1	112.2	114.5	115.9	117.4	118.6	117.3	116.6	111.8
2005	109.9	113.8	116.1	120.5	121.7	124.9	125.7	127.6	129.3	130.2	130.2	129.9	123.3
2006	126.7	128.6	128.9	128.3	130.2	132.6	131.6	131.5	130.2	123.9	119.6	117.7	127.5
2007	112.2	112.9	114.2	114.4	115.3	116.6	116.5	116.4	113.6	108.8	105.8	103.2	112.5
2008	95.8	94.8	95.3	94.0	93.6	93.8	92.3	92.0	89.5	85.7	82.5	79.5	90.7
2009	73.6	70.0	70.5	68.9	70.0	69.8	68.4	67.9	66.1	64.6	63.9	61.6	67.9
2010	58.9	58.5	59.8	60.5	61.2	61.3	60.4	60.7	59.7	58.8	58.8	57.7	59.7
2011	55.6	56.9	57.3	58.4	58.7	59.1	61.0	60.9	62.1	60.1	58.6	56.1	58.7
Manufacturing													
2000	116.3	117.5	117.8	119.0	119.1	120.7	120.9	121.6	121.4	121.0	120.8	120.7	119.7
2001	120.7	120.9	121.2	119.7	119.3	118.9	119.0	118.9	118.2	116.7	115.6	114.9	118.7
2002	113.9	114.6	115.3	115.5	116.1	116.4	115.3	116.0	115.8	115.1	115.4	115.6	115.4
2003	113.6	114.3	115.0	115.3	115.5	116.0	115.9	116.6	116.9	117.5	117.7	118.5	116.1
2004	117.7	118.4	119.0	119.4	120.2	121.0	121.3	121.3	121.6	121.0	120.5	120.3	120.1
2005	119.5	120.2	120.9	120.5	120.2	120.8	121.5	121.7	122.0	121.7	121.5	121.8	121.0
2006	122.3	123.4	124.1	124.0	124.9	125.4	124.0	123.8	123.7	122.4	121.2	121.2	123.4
2007	120.6	120.4	120.3	119.3	119.8	119.9	119.3	118.9	118.1	116.5	115.2	114.1	118.5
2008	111.8	111.1	110.2	109.8	109.0	108.5	107.0	106.2	105.3	103.3	101.3	98.8	106.9
2009	95.0	93.0	91.6	90.2	89.7	88.9	87.6	86.6	86.1	86.0	85.4	84.9	88.8
2010	84.5	84.3	84.1	85.0	85.3	85.5	85.3	85.6	85.6	85.5	85.3	85.5	85.1
2011	83.8	84.0	84.4	85.1	85.7	86.0	87.3	87.2	87.3	85.6	86.7	86.5	85.8

Employment by Industry: Riverside–San Bernardino–Ontario, CA, Selected Years, 2000–2011—*Continued*

(Numbers in thousands, not seasonally adjusted)

Industry and year	January	February	March	April	May	June	July	August	September	October	November	December	Annual average
Service-Providing													
2000	773.5	776.8	783.5	783.5	792.7	791.2	776.8	774.9	788.1	792.7	804.7	812.0	787.5
2001	806.6	807.1	815.9	815.7	820.1	824.8	815.3	810.9	822.8	829.9	841.8	846.0	821.4
2002	835.4	841.6	846.0	857.0	863.7	866.2	846.3	846.7	857.6	862.7	876.7	884.2	857.0
2003	867.9	871.1	877.6	879.7	881.5	884.3	873.1	868.3	881.7	895.1	904.3	910.6	882.9
2004	901.5	905.3	915.3	922.9	927.5	927.2	915.0	913.9	926.3	942.9	958.3	966.8	926.9
2005	953.7	960.5	969.4	977.8	977.8	974.8	961.4	962.9	977.4	987.3	1,001.2	1,011.3	976.3
2006	996.1	1,001.3	1,010.4	1,015.1	1,016.9	1,018.8	1,005.8	1,002.8	1,012.9	1,024.1	1,038.3	1,042.5	1,015.4
2007	1,028.4	1,032.8	1,039.2	1,038.1	1,042.9	1,040.9	1,027.5	1,022.9	1,030.5	1,043.0	1,056.0	1,062.0	1,038.7
2008	1,038.9	1,039.4	1,039.9	1,039.7	1,035.5	1,031.8	1,009.9	1,007.8	1,009.1	1,019.0	1,024.6	1,024.4	1,026.7
2009	1,003.8	999.1	999.1	995.9	991.8	986.6	962.8	962.6	961.0	976.5	986.5	990.2	984.7
2010	971.8	973.9	979.6	986.2	988.9	985.2	959.4	966.1	968.3	983.1	997.3	1,000.7	980.0
2011	980.4	983.5	987.7	988.2	987.0	980.7	957.3	968.0	974.9	990.1	1,002.7	1,009.5	984.2
Trade, Transportation, and Utilities													
2000	207.5	206.2	206.7	207.7	209.5	210.7	210.8	211.1	212.6	213.1	219.0	222.5	211.5
2001	218.6	215.9	217.4	217.2	217.9	218.9	219.3	219.2	219.6	221.0	225.0	227.7	219.8
2002	220.0	218.5	220.0	222.2	224.8	226.4	225.9	226.9	228.3	229.1	234.8	238.2	226.3
2003	231.0	229.8	230.7	231.9	233.4	234.7	234.4	235.3	236.7	243.3	245.8	250.2	236.4
2004	243.1	242.1	244.2	247.6	249.9	251.7	253.4	255.6	258.0	266.7	274.1	278.4	255.4
2005	269.5	267.8	269.2	270.8	272.2	273.6	274.6	276.3	279.4	281.2	289.9	296.8	276.8
2006	285.2	283.5	286.1	286.8	288.6	290.6	291.3	291.9	293.0	296.8	305.0	309.4	292.4
2007	299.1	296.7	297.9	297.5	298.9	299.0	300.4	300.7	301.9	303.1	311.7	315.7	301.9
2008	302.1	297.3	296.0	294.8	294.5	293.3	290.1	289.3	288.7	287.1	290.5	291.1	292.9
2009	280.3	275.5	273.0	269.7	270.2	270.1	267.0	266.5	267.9	268.9	274.8	278.6	271.9
2010	268.8	266.6	266.9	267.6	268.7	269.0	267.9	268.0	268.9	271.9	280.7	284.0	270.8
2011	273.5	271.4	271.1	272.0	272.6	272.3	272.2	273.6	275.1	276.6	284.6	286.3	275.1
Wholesale Trade													
2000	35.8	36.0	36.2	38.4	38.7	39.1	39.3	39.0	39.5	38.8	38.7	38.9	38.2
2001	41.7	41.9	42.7	42.6	42.3	42.0	42.2	41.6	41.2	40.8	40.3	40.1	41.6
2002	40.4	40.7	40.9	41.6	41.8	42.2	42.1	42.5	42.7	42.5	42.8	42.9	41.9
2003	42.9	43.3	43.5	44.0	44.1	44.0	43.4	43.4	43.4	43.4	43.0	43.1	43.5
2004	42.9	43.3	43.7	44.2	44.6	45.1	46.2	46.4	46.6	47.6	47.8	48.2	45.6
2005	47.9	48.0	48.5	49.3	49.6	49.9	50.2	50.4	50.8	51.1	51.4	52.1	49.9
2006	52.6	53.1	53.5	54.0	54.0	54.2	54.6	54.6	54.8	54.6	54.8	55.0	54.2
2007	55.3	55.9	56.2	56.3	56.5	56.9	57.1	57.2	57.4	57.5	57.6	57.7	56.8
2008	56.3	56.0	55.6	55.2	55.1	55.0	53.8	53.6	53.1	52.7	51.9	51.2	54.1
2009	50.4	49.8	49.1	48.8	48.7	48.9	48.6	48.4	48.2	48.5	48.5	48.5	48.9
2010	48.3	48.3	48.4	48.7	48.8	48.9	48.8	48.6	48.6	48.8	48.7	48.8	48.6
2011	48.4	48.7	48.8	48.9	48.9	48.8	48.8	49.0	50.2	51.0	50.7	50.3	49.4
Retail Trade													
2000	125.0	123.5	123.6	123.1	124.4	125.1	125.3	126.2	126.7	128.8	134.3	137.4	127.0
2001	131.1	129.4	130.3	130.3	130.9	131.6	131.3	131.7	132.2	133.3	137.6	140.5	132.5
2002	134.3	132.4	133.9	134.8	136.6	137.3	137.1	137.4	138.0	138.6	143.9	146.0	137.5
2003	139.6	138.6	138.9	138.8	139.5	140.4	140.7	141.5	142.0	147.0	150.1	154.2	142.6
2004	147.7	145.8	147.3	148.9	150.5	151.0	151.2	152.6	153.8	158.7	165.8	169.5	153.6
2005	162.3	160.1	160.4	161.0	161.7	162.7	163.4	164.6	166.0	166.9	174.3	179.7	165.3
2006	168.9	166.8	168.1	168.6	169.7	171.0	171.5	171.8	171.7	175.0	182.2	185.1	172.5
2007	176.7	173.2	174.2	173.1	174.1	173.3	173.2	173.5	173.4	174.4	182.4	185.3	175.6
2008	175.2	170.8	170.3	169.2	168.7	168.1	166.7	165.8	165.3	164.7	168.7	169.6	168.6
2009	161.1	157.5	156.0	154.4	154.6	154.1	153.3	153.0	153.5	154.4	160.0	162.7	156.2
2010	154.8	153.0	153.3	153.8	154.1	153.9	153.2	153.1	153.0	155.5	163.0	165.2	155.5
2011	157.3	155.0	154.5	155.1	155.3	155.0	155.4	156.4	156.1	156.8	164.3	165.1	157.2
Transportation and Utilities													
2000	42.3	42.3	42.5	41.6	41.8	41.9	41.6	41.3	41.7	40.8	41.3	41.5	41.7
2001	41.1	39.9	39.7	39.5	39.8	40.5	41.0	41.1	41.3	41.9	42.1	42.1	40.8
2002	40.4	40.4	40.3	40.8	41.3	41.8	41.8	42.0	42.6	43.1	43.2	44.3	41.8
2003	43.5	42.9	43.3	44.1	44.8	45.3	45.3	45.4	46.4	47.9	47.8	48.0	45.4
2004	47.7	48.0	48.2	49.5	49.8	50.6	51.0	51.5	52.5	55.3	55.4	55.6	51.3
2005	54.1	54.4	55.0	55.2	55.6	55.7	55.7	55.9	57.2	57.8	58.8	59.5	56.2
2006	58.2	58.1	59.0	58.7	59.3	59.8	59.5	59.8	60.8	61.5	62.2	63.5	60.0
2007	61.4	61.9	61.8	62.4	62.6	63.1	64.3	64.2	65.3	65.4	65.9	66.9	63.8
2008	65.1	65.1	64.8	64.6	64.9	64.3	63.7	64.0	64.5	63.8	64.1	64.5	64.5
2009	63.0	62.4	62.1	60.6	61.1	61.3	59.2	59.3	60.4	60.2	60.4	61.5	61.0
2010	60.0	59.6	59.5	59.4	60.1	60.4	60.1	60.5	61.5	61.8	63.2	64.2	60.9
2011	62.0	61.9	62.0	62.2	62.6	62.7	62.2	62.3	62.9	62.9	63.7	65.0	62.7
Information													
2000	13.7	13.8	13.9	14.0	14.1	14.3	14.4	14.5	14.6	14.6	14.6	14.7	14.3
2001	14.7	14.6	14.3	14.3	14.5	14.7	14.8	14.7	14.5	14.4	14.5	14.7	14.6
2002	14.5	14.3	14.2	13.9	14.1	14.2	13.9	14.1	13.8	14.0	14.0	14.0	14.1
2003	13.9	13.9	13.8	13.6	13.7	13.8	14.1	14.0	13.9	13.8	14.0	13.9	13.9
2004	13.9	13.7	13.8	13.9	13.9	14.0	14.3	14.0	13.9	14.2	14.4	14.4	14.0
2005	14.3	14.5	14.5	14.6	14.7	14.6	14.5	14.2	14.4	14.4	14.6	14.7	14.5
2006	14.6	14.9	14.9	15.1	15.2	15.4	15.5	15.5	15.5	15.4	15.6	15.7	15.3
2007	15.7	15.6	15.3	15.3	15.5	15.5	15.5	15.4	15.2	15.1	15.3	15.3	15.4
2008	15.3	15.4	15.2	15.1	15.1	14.9	14.9	14.8	14.6	14.6	14.7	14.6	14.9
2009	14.5	14.6	14.7	14.8	15.0	15.3	15.5	15.6	15.5	15.3	15.3	15.3	15.1
2010	15.6	15.7	15.9	15.9	16.0	16.1	16.1	16.0	15.8	15.6	15.7	15.7	15.8
2011	15.2	15.1	15.0	14.9	14.9	14.9	15.0	14.9	14.8	14.9	14.9	15.0	15.0

Employment by Industry: Riverside–San Bernardino–Ontario, CA, Selected Years, 2000–2011—*Continued*

(Numbers in thousands, not seasonally adjusted)

Industry and year	January	February	March	April	May	June	July	August	September	October	November	December	Annual average
Financial Activities													
2000	35.3	35.2	35.2	35.2	35.4	35.7	35.5	35.7	35.8	36.1	36.3	36.8	35.7
2001	35.9	36.4	36.7	36.8	37.0	37.3	37.3	37.3	37.4	38.3	38.5	38.8	37.3
2002	38.7	38.7	38.7	39.4	39.6	39.9	39.3	39.5	39.5	39.6	40.0	40.6	39.5
2003	40.3	40.7	40.9	41.9	42.3	42.9	43.0	43.5	43.8	43.7	44.1	44.4	42.6
2004	44.4	44.5	45.0	45.1	45.4	45.5	46.0	45.9	45.9	46.4	47.0	47.4	45.7
2005	47.6	47.9	48.1	48.5	48.5	48.5	49.0	49.3	49.6	49.9	50.2	50.4	49.0
2006	51.2	51.3	51.6	51.9	52.2	52.1	51.3	51.4	51.3	51.1	51.3	51.2	51.5
2007	51.1	51.3	51.4	50.6	50.3	50.2	49.6	49.4	49.0	48.2	48.2	48.2	49.8
2008	47.0	47.0	46.9	46.7	46.4	46.5	45.7	45.6	45.3	45.3	45.3	45.0	46.1
2009	44.7	44.4	44.1	43.4	42.5	42.2	41.7	41.4	41.1	41.6	41.5	41.6	42.5
2010	41.0	41.1	41.3	41.3	40.9	40.9	40.7	40.6	40.8	41.0	40.9	41.0	41.0
2011	40.1	40.4	40.2	40.0	39.9	39.8	38.7	38.3	37.8	38.1	38.1	38.7	39.2
Professional and Business Services													
2000	92.4	93.6	94.9	95.8	96.5	98.7	96.0	98.1	99.5	97.8	98.9	98.8	96.8
2001	97.3	98.3	99.2	99.7	100.9	103.5	103.8	104.7	105.7	103.0	102.6	102.5	101.8
2002	101.2	102.7	103.7	103.6	105.4	106.5	106.6	109.2	109.9	109.3	111.7	111.8	106.8
2003	109.4	109.6	111.0	111.1	112.6	113.9	117.0	117.8	119.9	120.3	121.1	121.6	115.4
2004	119.5	121.0	123.3	124.8	125.7	127.0	126.5	127.6	127.4	127.8	127.9	127.5	125.5
2005	125.4	128.4	130.3	132.7	131.4	132.7	133.7	135.1	136.4	137.1	137.8	137.0	133.2
2006	138.2	139.5	140.5	141.2	140.6	141.8	143.0	143.2	145.0	145.3	145.9	144.4	142.4
2007	142.4	144.4	145.9	144.3	145.6	145.4	146.2	146.3	146.5	146.8	146.0	144.7	145.4
2008	139.8	140.7	139.5	137.9	136.4	138.7	138.3	138.3	138.2	138.1	137.3	135.2	138.2
2009	130.9	129.5	129.3	127.7	125.1	124.5	122.8	122.3	121.9	123.2	123.1	121.3	125.1
2010	118.5	119.5	120.3	121.6	121.8	123.0	123.4	124.9	125.0	127.2	127.5	128.1	123.4
2011	122.9	125.1	125.6	124.8	123.8	123.3	122.8	127.0	128.8	129.7	129.2	130.6	126.1
Education and Health Services													
2000	101.1	101.9	102.1	101.7	102.4	101.5	100.1	100.6	101.4	103.1	102.9	103.4	101.9
2001	103.6	104.3	105.0	105.0	105.8	105.6	105.1	105.8	106.2	108.0	109.2	109.9	106.1
2002	109.7	110.9	111.5	111.1	112.6	112.6	110.1	111.0	113.3	114.2	115.3	116.0	112.4
2003	113.3	115.2	115.5	116.5	116.3	116.6	114.1	114.3	115.4	117.0	117.3	118.1	115.8
2004	116.6	118.2	118.8	119.7	119.4	119.3	117.2	116.7	117.3	118.7	119.1	119.5	118.4
2005	118.1	119.6	120.3	121.0	120.9	120.7	117.9	117.4	118.9	121.3	121.5	121.7	119.9
2006	120.5	122.7	123.1	122.9	122.5	121.8	120.0	120.4	121.3	123.0	123.6	123.7	122.1
2007	123.5	125.1	125.8	125.8	126.1	126.0	126.7	127.1	127.9	130.4	130.8	131.0	127.2
2008	129.4	132.0	132.3	133.6	132.5	131.1	129.4	129.3	130.7	133.4	133.7	133.8	131.8
2009	131.4	133.3	133.6	134.6	134.0	133.5	132.3	132.6	133.2	134.8	135.1	135.2	133.6
2010	131.7	133.2	133.4	134.1	133.7	132.5	131.3	132.3	133.6	135.1	137.0	137.5	133.8
2011	135.1	137.4	138.1	138.6	137.8	136.7	136.0	136.7	137.7	140.0	139.6	141.1	137.9
Leisure and Hospitality													
2000	100.3	101.6	102.4	101.1	101.8	101.0	98.5	98.3	99.1	99.0	101.2	102.4	100.6
2001	102.8	104.2	105.2	106.5	106.1	105.6	103.2	103.0	102.5	103.7	104.9	106.0	104.5
2002	106.2	107.3	108.7	109.5	110.1	108.8	105.3	104.8	105.0	104.9	106.6	109.5	107.2
2003	107.4	108.8	110.2	109.8	109.6	109.3	107.0	106.3	106.9	108.5	111.3	113.2	109.0
2004	114.1	115.4	117.1	118.2	119.4	117.6	113.4	113.6	115.0	115.8	119.1	121.3	116.7
2005	119.2	120.9	123.4	125.1	125.0	124.3	121.4	120.8	121.2	121.4	123.4	125.4	122.6
2006	125.3	127.2	129.4	130.0	129.4	128.4	127.0	126.6	126.4	126.4	129.5	131.5	128.1
2007	131.7	133.6	134.6	134.6	135.4	133.8	130.7	129.7	129.4	130.2	132.5	134.7	132.6
2008	133.8	134.4	134.9	134.6	133.0	131.3	128.8	127.5	127.5	127.4	128.8	130.2	131.0
2009	129.2	129.1	129.2	127.5	126.5	124.1	120.3	118.7	118.1	119.0	121.0	123.3	123.8
2010	122.4	122.8	124.1	125.2	124.2	122.9	120.2	120.1	120.6	121.1	123.6	126.1	122.8
2011	124.3	124.0	125.8	125.1	124.9	123.5	122.5	120.6	120.6	122.1	127.0	130.8	124.3
Other Services													
2000	33.9	34.3	34.8	34.4	34.6	35.1	34.9	35.2	35.6	34.9	35.0	35.3	34.8
2001	35.5	36.2	37.1	36.9	37.3	37.5	37.1	37.6	37.4	37.6	37.8	37.6	37.1
2002	37.1	37.6	38.0	38.5	38.9	38.9	38.2	38.2	38.2	37.7	37.9	37.9	38.1
2003	37.4	37.9	38.2	38.3	38.7	39.0	37.9	37.7	38.2	38.5	38.5	37.9	38.2
2004	38.2	38.5	39.3	38.7	38.8	38.7	38.7	38.6	38.8	39.0	38.8	38.9	38.8
2005	39.6	39.9	40.4	40.6	40.6	40.2	39.5	39.2	40.0	39.5	39.5	39.8	39.9
2006	40.1	40.9	41.4	41.1	41.5	41.4	41.6	41.7	41.8	41.2	41.1	41.0	41.2
2007	40.2	40.9	40.7	41.6	41.9	42.0	41.1	41.1	41.4	41.0	41.1	40.9	41.2
2008	40.7	41.0	41.6	42.4	42.6	42.2	40.8	40.8	40.4	39.5	38.9	38.5	40.8
2009	37.2	37.1	37.4	37.4	37.5	37.5	37.5	36.9	36.8	37.7	37.7	37.4	37.3
2010	37.1	37.5	38.0	38.8	38.9	39.2	38.4	38.2	38.0	38.1	38.2	38.3	38.2
2011	38.0	38.5	38.6	39.4	39.5	39.4	38.8	39.0	39.8	40.7	40.2	39.9	39.3
Government													
2000	189.3	190.2	193.5	193.6	198.4	194.2	186.6	181.4	189.5	194.1	196.8	198.1	192.1
2001	198.2	197.2	201.0	199.3	200.6	201.7	194.7	188.6	199.5	203.9	209.3	208.8	200.2
2002	208.0	211.6	211.2	218.8	218.2	218.9	207.0	203.0	209.6	213.9	216.4	216.2	212.7
2003	215.2	215.2	217.3	216.6	214.9	214.1	205.6	199.4	206.9	210.0	212.2	211.3	211.6
2004	211.7	211.9	213.8	214.9	215.0	213.4	205.5	201.9	210.0	214.3	217.9	219.4	212.5
2005	220.0	221.5	223.2	224.5	224.5	220.2	210.8	210.6	217.5	222.5	224.3	225.5	220.4
2006	221.0	221.3	223.4	226.1	226.9	227.3	216.1	212.1	218.6	224.9	226.3	225.6	222.5
2007	224.7	225.2	227.6	228.4	229.2	229.0	217.3	213.2	219.2	228.2	230.4	231.5	225.3
2008	230.8	231.6	233.5	234.6	235.0	233.8	222.0	222.2	223.7	233.6	235.4	236.0	231.0
2009	235.6	235.6	237.8	240.8	241.0	239.4	225.7	228.6	226.5	236.0	238.0	237.5	235.2
2010	236.7	237.5	239.7	241.7	244.7	241.6	221.4	226.0	225.6	233.1	233.7	230.0	234.3
2011	231.3	231.6	233.3	233.4	233.6	230.8	211.3	217.9	220.3	228.0	229.1	227.1	227.3

Employment by Industry: Rochester, NY, Selected Years, 2000–2011

(Numbers in thousands, not seasonally adjusted)

Industry and year	January	February	March	April	May	June	July	August	September	October	November	December	Annual average
Total Nonfarm													
2000	517.3	521.1	524.1	531.0	535.0	538.6	529.7	529.8	535.1	534.8	536.7	537.8	530.9
2001	521.4	523.6	524.8	526.8	532.7	535.3	522.7	521.5	525.2	526.2	528.0	526.4	526.2
2002	505.4	507.0	508.5	511.8	517.9	518.4	510.3	511.0	513.2	517.0	518.7	518.9	513.2
2003	501.5	502.9	505.0	505.2	514.5	514.8	507.1	507.6	511.7	515.2	515.2	517.1	509.8
2004	499.5	502.3	504.7	507.6	516.1	517.1	508.8	507.8	512.9	520.4	520.2	520.1	511.5
2005	503.9	507.3	509.5	515.9	520.3	520.6	511.7	511.5	514.9	520.5	522.1	523.4	515.1
2006	504.0	506.3	508.6	512.1	516.3	518.1	507.7	507.7	514.1	519.8	520.7	521.3	513.1
2007	505.7	508.1	509.5	511.3	519.6	521.3	511.3	510.4	515.2	521.7	522.1	522.4	514.9
2008	505.4	509.5	510.2	516.0	522.4	522.8	514.1	513.2	518.0	523.4	520.8	519.5	516.3
2009	500.3	501.3	500.7	501.1	505.8	504.1	499.5	497.7	500.1	507.5	506.8	506.8	502.6
2010	491.0	494.2	496.5	502.4	507.2	507.1	498.8	499.1	503.8	513.0	513.2	511.3	503.1
2011	495.2	499.3	501.2	509.2	512.2	514.1	505.1	503.4	508.5	517.1	518.5	520.6	508.7
Total Private													
2000	441.1	441.5	443.7	450.3	454.6	459.9	458.3	458.5	458.2	455.9	456.2	457.6	453.0
2001	443.5	442.1	443.1	445.3	451.6	455.4	449.6	448.3	446.2	443.9	444.3	442.3	446.3
2002	426.4	424.1	424.9	429.7	435.4	436.5	436.0	436.9	434.9	434.7	435.3	434.3	432.4
2003	420.9	419.4	421.0	422.5	430.9	432.3	432.6	433.5	433.0	434.0	433.0	433.4	428.9
2004	419.5	422.0	423.7	425.3	432.6	434.6	434.3	433.6	434.5	438.3	437.4	436.0	431.0
2005	423.7	424.2	426.1	432.4	436.5	437.7	436.5	436.6	435.8	438.3	438.9	439.3	433.8
2006	425.0	424.9	426.6	430.6	434.8	438.1	435.4	435.5	435.9	439.3	439.3	439.7	433.8
2007	426.8	427.0	428.2	429.8	437.6	440.0	437.9	437.6	436.5	440.3	440.1	439.6	435.1
2008	426.0	427.9	428.3	433.5	439.7	440.8	439.4	439.2	438.3	440.9	438.0	436.4	435.7
2009	420.5	419.0	418.5	418.3	422.9	422.7	422.0	422.1	421.7	424.7	423.6	423.3	421.6
2010	410.1	411.3	413.5	419.3	422.6	423.8	424.4	425.7	425.4	430.3	429.9	427.6	422.0
2011	415.4	416.8	418.7	426.8	429.9	432.2	431.6	430.0	430.0	434.5	435.1	436.6	428.1
Goods-Producing													
2000	120.5	119.2	119.4	119.8	120.9	123.3	123.7	124.2	123.2	122.2	121.5	120.3	121.5
2001	117.4	115.9	115.5	115.9	117.1	117.8	118.1	117.9	115.8	113.4	111.6	109.9	115.5
2002	107.5	105.1	104.7	105.4	106.2	106.7	107.4	108.1	105.9	105.4	104.7	102.8	105.8
2003	99.9	98.0	98.0	97.9	99.9	100.9	102.9	103.3	102.1	101.2	100.2	98.9	100.3
2004	96.0	95.0	95.3	96.3	97.8	98.8	100.4	100.0	98.9	99.0	97.9	96.4	97.7
2005	94.1	93.3	93.3	95.1	96.5	97.8	99.2	99.6	98.6	97.9	97.3	95.6	96.5
2006	93.2	92.4	92.2	93.8	95.3	97.2	97.3	97.6	96.3	95.9	95.2	94.0	95.0
2007	91.3	90.2	90.5	91.4	93.1	94.2	94.0	94.1	92.9	92.2	91.4	90.3	92.1
2008	87.9	86.8	86.5	87.4	89.5	90.9	91.9	91.8	90.8	90.0	88.1	86.1	89.0
2009	82.5	80.8	79.7	79.5	80.6	81.1	81.6	82.2	80.7	80.2	78.9	77.3	80.4
2010	74.7	74.0	74.2	75.8	77.1	78.3	79.5	80.0	79.1	79.3	78.8	76.7	77.3
2011	75.2	74.3	74.8	76.3	78.2	80.2	80.4	81.1	81.2	81.3	79.8	78.7	78.5
Mining and Logging													
2003	0.4	0.4	0.4	0.5	0.5	0.6	0.6	0.6	0.6	0.6	0.5	0.6	0.5
2004	0.6	0.6	0.6	0.6	0.6	0.6	0.6	0.6	0.6	0.6	0.6	0.6	0.6
2005	0.5	0.5	0.5	0.6	0.6	0.7	0.7	0.7	0.7	0.6	0.6	0.6	0.6
2006	0.5	0.5	0.5	0.6	0.6	0.7	0.7	0.7	0.6	0.6	0.6	0.4	0.6
2007	0.4	0.5	0.5	0.6	0.6	0.6	0.6	0.6	0.6	0.6	0.6	0.6	0.6
2008	0.6	0.5	0.5	0.5	0.6	0.6	0.6	0.6	0.6	0.6	0.6	0.6	0.6
2009	0.5	0.5	0.5	0.5	0.6	0.6	0.6	0.6	0.6	0.6	0.6	0.6	0.6
2010	0.5	0.5	0.5	0.6	0.6	0.6	0.6	0.6	0.6	0.5	0.6	0.5	0.6
2011	0.5	0.5	0.5	0.6	0.6	0.6	0.6	0.6	0.6	0.6	0.6	0.5	0.6
Construction													
2003	14.8	14.3	14.5	15.3	17.0	17.9	19.3	19.6	19.2	18.5	17.8	16.9	17.1
2004	15.2	14.8	15.1	16.5	17.9	18.9	19.9	20.3	19.8	19.6	19.0	17.9	17.9
2005	16.0	15.5	15.4	17.0	18.7	19.2	19.7	20.1	19.6	19.2	18.8	17.5	18.1
2006	16.0	15.3	15.2	16.5	18.0	19.0	19.4	19.6	19.0	18.9	18.3	17.7	17.7
2007	16.2	15.2	15.7	16.9	18.7	19.7	20.0	20.2	19.7	19.6	19.1	18.1	18.3
2008	16.8	16.0	16.1	17.4	19.1	20.0	20.8	21.0	20.6	20.3	19.1	17.9	18.8
2009	15.6	14.9	14.8	15.8	17.4	18.4	19.2	19.5	18.7	18.3	17.5	16.2	17.2
2010	14.5	14.0	14.3	15.9	17.0	18.0	18.8	19.2	18.4	18.3	17.8	16.1	16.9
2011	14.8	14.2	14.6	15.7	17.3	18.5	19.0	19.2	19.0	18.9	17.8	16.9	17.2
Manufacturing													
2000	104.0	103.2	103.1	102.2	102.1	103.2	103.0	103.0	102.9	102.2	101.7	101.4	102.7
2001	99.8	98.8	98.1	97.4	96.8	96.6	96.3	96.1	95.0	93.5	92.6	92.0	96.1
2002	91.4	89.7	89.2	88.6	88.2	87.8	87.7	87.8	86.3	86.2	86.2	85.7	87.9
2003	84.7	83.3	83.1	82.1	82.4	82.4	83.0	83.1	82.3	82.1	81.9	81.4	82.7
2004	80.2	79.6	79.6	79.2	79.3	79.3	79.9	79.1	78.5	78.8	78.3	77.9	79.1
2005	77.6	77.3	77.4	77.5	77.2	77.9	78.8	78.8	78.3	78.1	77.9	77.5	77.9
2006	76.7	76.6	76.5	76.7	76.7	77.5	77.2	77.3	76.7	76.4	76.3	75.9	76.7
2007	74.7	74.5	74.3	73.9	73.8	73.9	73.4	73.3	72.6	72.0	71.7	71.6	73.3
2008	70.5	70.3	69.9	69.5	69.8	70.3	70.5	70.2	69.6	69.1	68.4	67.6	69.6
2009	66.4	65.4	64.4	63.2	62.6	62.1	61.8	62.1	61.4	61.3	60.8	60.5	62.7
2010	59.7	59.5	59.4	59.3	59.5	59.7	60.1	60.2	60.1	60.5	60.4	60.1	59.9
2011	59.9	59.6	59.7	60.0	60.3	61.1	60.8	61.3	61.6	61.8	61.4	61.3	60.7

Employment by Industry: Rochester, NY, Selected Years, 2000–2011—*Continued*

(Numbers in thousands, not seasonally adjusted)

Industry and year	January	February	March	April	May	June	July	August	September	October	November	December	Annual average
Service-Providing													
2000	396.8	401.9	404.7	411.2	414.1	415.3	406.0	405.6	411.9	412.6	415.2	417.5	409.4
2001	404.0	407.7	409.3	410.9	415.6	417.5	404.6	403.6	409.4	412.8	416.4	416.5	410.7
2002	397.9	401.9	403.8	406.4	411.7	411.7	402.9	402.9	407.3	411.6	414.0	416.1	407.4
2003	401.6	404.9	407.0	407.3	414.6	413.9	404.2	404.3	409.6	414.0	415.0	418.2	409.6
2004	403.5	407.3	409.4	411.3	418.3	418.3	408.4	407.8	414.0	421.4	422.3	423.7	413.8
2005	409.8	414.0	416.2	420.8	423.8	422.8	412.5	411.9	416.3	422.6	424.8	427.8	418.6
2006	410.8	413.9	416.4	418.3	421.0	420.9	410.4	410.1	417.8	423.9	425.5	427.3	418.0
2007	414.4	417.9	419.0	419.9	426.5	427.1	417.3	416.3	422.3	429.5	430.7	432.1	422.8
2008	417.5	422.7	423.7	428.6	432.9	431.9	422.2	421.4	427.2	433.4	432.7	433.4	427.3
2009	417.8	420.5	421.0	421.6	425.2	423.0	417.9	415.5	419.4	427.3	427.9	429.5	422.2
2010	416.3	420.2	422.3	426.6	430.1	428.8	419.3	419.1	424.7	433.7	434.4	434.6	425.8
2011	420.0	425.0	426.4	432.9	434.0	433.9	424.7	422.3	427.3	435.8	438.7	441.9	430.2
Trade, Transportation, and Utilities													
2000	89.1	87.5	87.6	87.9	89.0	89.8	88.8	89.5	89.0	89.4	91.1	92.9	89.3
2001	89.7	87.3	87.3	88.0	89.1	90.3	88.2	88.2	87.3	88.1	89.9	90.7	88.7
2002	86.9	84.7	84.5	84.7	86.1	87.1	86.0	86.3	85.3	85.5	86.9	87.9	86.0
2003	85.2	83.2	83.3	83.1	84.8	85.6	84.1	84.5	84.3	84.8	86.0	87.1	84.7
2004	83.6	82.5	82.6	82.2	84.9	86.0	85.4	85.3	85.4	86.2	87.3	88.6	85.0
2005	85.2	83.6	83.7	84.3	85.4	86.8	86.0	86.4	85.2	86.0	87.2	89.1	85.7
2006	85.2	82.9	83.2	83.2	84.5	86.2	85.1	85.6	84.8	85.9	87.3	88.5	85.2
2007	85.6	83.4	83.9	83.3	86.3	87.4	86.6	86.2	85.5	86.6	88.0	89.0	86.0
2008	86.0	84.0	83.9	84.5	85.9	86.6	85.4	85.2	84.3	85.3	85.6	86.3	85.3
2009	82.3	80.5	80.2	79.9	81.6	82.5	81.9	81.9	80.7	81.7	82.5	83.6	81.6
2010	80.6	79.4	79.8	80.6	82.0	83.1	82.1	82.4	81.6	83.1	83.7	84.6	81.9
2011	81.5	80.4	80.3	81.4	82.3	83.5	83.5	83.3	83.3	84.0	86.3	88.4	83.2
Wholesale Trade													
2000	18.2	18.1	18.2	18.6	18.7	19.0	19.1	19.2	18.9	19.0	19.1	19.2	18.8
2001	19.2	19.1	19.1	19.2	19.4	19.7	19.4	19.2	18.8	18.8	18.8	18.7	19.1
2002	18.6	18.5	18.3	18.6	18.7	18.8	18.8	18.7	18.4	18.1	18.1	18.1	18.5
2003	17.9	17.7	17.8	17.8	18.0	18.1	18.1	18.0	17.7	17.5	17.6	17.7	17.8
2004	17.7	17.8	17.8	17.9	18.1	18.4	18.3	18.3	17.9	18.1	18.0	18.1	18.0
2005	18.2	18.2	18.2	18.2	18.3	18.5	18.6	18.6	18.2	17.9	18.2	18.2	18.3
2006	18.2	18.1	18.2	18.2	18.3	18.7	18.8	19.1	18.6	18.4	18.4	18.5	18.5
2007	18.6	18.6	18.7	18.5	18.8	19.0	19.2	19.1	18.8	18.9	18.7	18.8	18.8
2008	18.4	18.3	18.2	18.5	18.7	18.8	18.8	18.7	18.5	18.8	18.6	18.5	18.6
2009	18.1	18.0	17.8	17.7	17.8	17.8	17.8	17.8	17.5	17.5	17.3	17.5	17.7
2010	17.0	17.0	17.1	17.2	17.4	17.5	17.5	17.5	17.4	17.5	17.4	17.5	17.3
2011	17.1	17.2	17.2	17.5	17.6	17.9	17.8	17.8	17.6	17.5	17.6	17.6	17.5
Retail Trade													
2000	60.2	58.7	58.7	58.5	59.5	60.0	59.5	60.1	59.2	59.5	61.1	62.0	59.8
2001	60.2	58.1	58.0	58.6	59.2	60.1	58.8	59.1	58.1	58.6	60.5	61.5	59.2
2002	58.9	56.8	56.9	56.8	58.0	58.8	58.4	58.8	57.6	57.9	59.4	60.4	58.2
2003	57.8	56.2	56.2	55.9	57.4	58.2	57.4	57.8	57.2	57.7	58.8	59.7	57.5
2004	56.4	55.2	55.3	54.4	56.7	57.4	57.3	57.3	57.3	57.8	59.0	60.2	57.0
2005	57.0	55.4	55.4	55.9	56.8	57.9	57.6	57.9	56.5	57.4	58.3	60.0	57.2
2006	56.6	54.4	54.6	54.5	55.6	56.7	56.1	56.3	55.5	56.8	58.2	59.2	56.2
2007	56.6	54.5	54.9	54.6	57.0	57.9	57.4	57.1	56.1	57.0	58.5	59.3	56.7
2008	57.1	55.2	55.2	55.4	56.4	57.0	56.4	56.4	55.5	56.2	56.7	57.3	56.2
2009	54.4	52.7	52.8	52.5	53.9	54.7	54.3	54.3	53.3	54.1	55.2	55.8	54.0
2010	53.8	52.7	53.0	53.6	54.7	55.6	55.2	55.5	54.3	55.6	56.3	57.0	54.8
2011	54.8	53.6	53.5	54.2	54.8	55.7	56.3	56.1	55.8	56.6	58.8	60.9	55.9
Transportation and Utilities													
2000	10.7	10.7	10.7	10.8	10.8	10.8	10.2	10.2	10.9	10.9	10.9	11.7	10.8
2001	10.3	10.1	10.2	10.2	10.5	10.5	10.0	9.9	10.4	10.7	10.6	10.5	10.3
2002	9.4	9.4	9.3	9.3	9.4	9.5	8.8	8.8	9.3	9.5	9.4	9.4	9.3
2003	9.5	9.3	9.3	9.4	9.4	9.3	8.6	8.7	9.4	9.6	9.6	9.7	9.3
2004	9.5	9.5	9.5	9.9	10.1	10.2	9.8	9.7	10.2	10.3	10.3	10.3	9.9
2005	10.0	10.0	10.1	10.2	10.3	10.4	9.8	9.9	10.5	10.7	10.7	10.9	10.3
2006	10.4	10.4	10.4	10.5	10.6	10.8	10.2	10.2	10.7	10.7	10.7	10.8	10.5
2007	10.4	10.3	10.3	10.2	10.5	10.5	10.0	10.0	10.6	10.7	10.8	10.9	10.4
2008	10.5	10.5	10.5	10.6	10.8	10.8	10.2	10.1	10.3	10.3	10.3	10.5	10.5
2009	9.8	9.8	9.6	9.7	9.9	10.0	9.8	9.8	9.9	10.1	10.0	10.3	9.9
2010	9.8	9.7	9.7	9.8	9.9	10.0	9.4	9.4	9.9	10.0	10.0	10.1	9.8
2011	9.6	9.6	9.6	9.7	9.9	9.9	9.4	9.4	9.9	9.9	9.9	9.9	9.7
Information													
2000	11.3	11.4	11.4	11.5	11.6	11.7	11.8	11.9	11.9	12.0	12.1	12.3	11.7
2001	12.9	13.0	13.1	12.9	13.1	13.2	13.1	13.0	12.9	13.2	13.3	13.4	13.1
2002	13.5	13.1	13.3	13.0	13.1	12.9	12.7	12.6	12.5	12.4	12.4	12.5	12.8
2003	12.3	12.3	12.2	12.2	12.5	12.4	12.3	12.3	12.2	12.3	12.3	12.3	12.3
2004	12.4	12.3	12.3	12.2	12.2	12.2	12.1	12.0	12.0	12.0	12.0	11.9	12.1
2005	11.8	11.6	11.6	11.6	11.7	11.7	11.6	11.6	11.6	11.8	11.7	11.8	11.7
2006	11.7	11.6	11.5	11.1	11.1	11.1	10.9	10.7	10.5	10.6	10.6	10.5	11.0
2007	10.6	10.5	10.5	10.6	10.7	10.7	10.7	10.7	10.6	10.6	10.6	10.7	10.6
2008	10.5	10.5	10.5	10.4	10.4	10.4	10.4	10.4	10.2	10.3	10.4	10.4	10.4
2009	10.2	10.0	10.0	10.2	10.1	10.0	10.0	9.9	9.7	9.7	9.8	9.7	9.9
2010	9.5	9.4	9.4	9.4	9.4	9.5	9.5	9.5	9.3	9.3	9.3	9.2	9.4
2011	9.2	9.2	9.1	9.1	9.1	9.1	9.2	9.1	9.0	9.0	9.0	8.9	9.1

Employment by Industry: Rochester, NY, Selected Years, 2000–2011—*Continued*

(Numbers in thousands, not seasonally adjusted)

Industry and year	January	February	March	April	May	June	July	August	September	October	November	December	Annual average
Financial Activities													
2000	21.3	21.4	21.3	21.7	21.8	22.3	22.0	21.8	21.2	21.4	21.4	21.4	21.6
2001	21.3	21.5	21.4	21.4	21.6	22.2	22.0	22.0	21.4	21.3	21.4	21.3	21.6
2002	20.7	20.7	20.6	20.6	20.9	21.3	21.7	21.8	21.1	21.2	21.2	21.2	21.1
2003	21.0	20.9	20.9	21.1	21.7	22.0	22.3	22.3	21.8	21.9	21.9	22.2	21.7
2004	21.5	21.5	21.6	21.7	21.8	22.1	22.6	22.7	22.2	21.9	21.9	22.1	22.0
2005	21.7	21.5	21.6	21.5	21.8	22.0	22.2	22.2	21.7	21.7	21.9	22.0	21.8
2006	21.7	21.5	21.5	21.5	21.7	22.1	22.5	22.5	21.6	21.8	21.6	21.6	21.8
2007	21.6	21.5	21.5	21.5	21.5	22.0	22.3	22.3	21.4	21.4	21.4	21.5	21.7
2008	21.0	21.0	21.0	21.1	21.5	21.9	22.1	22.1	21.4	21.3	21.2	21.2	21.4
2009	20.4	20.2	20.1	20.2	20.7	21.1	21.2	21.3	20.9	20.6	20.5	20.6	20.7
2010	20.2	20.0	20.2	20.2	20.4	21.0	21.0	20.9	20.1	20.2	20.1	20.2	20.4
2011	20.1	20.1	20.2	20.5	20.7	21.4	21.3	21.7	21.1	21.3	21.2	21.5	20.9
Professional and Business Services													
2000	58.5	58.7	59.1	59.8	60.3	62.1	63.0	62.8	62.1	61.5	61.1	60.7	60.8
2001	60.1	59.7	60.4	59.0	59.7	61.0	60.7	60.5	59.7	58.8	58.3	57.6	59.6
2002	54.5	54.5	54.6	56.5	57.4	58.4	58.2	58.1	58.0	57.6	57.9	57.6	56.9
2003	55.2	55.2	55.5	56.7	57.5	58.4	57.7	58.0	57.7	58.3	57.7	57.8	57.1
2004	54.9	55.6	55.7	56.4	57.0	58.6	58.0	58.0	58.1	59.1	58.8	58.2	57.4
2005	56.3	56.5	57.2	59.3	59.6	60.2	60.7	60.2	59.9	60.3	60.6	60.7	59.3
2006	58.3	57.7	58.4	59.7	59.5	60.9	60.6	60.4	61.2	61.4	60.8	61.3	60.0
2007	59.6	60.0	59.9	60.1	60.7	62.0	61.5	61.7	60.8	61.7	61.3	61.2	60.9
2008	60.0	60.4	60.6	62.2	62.4	63.6	63.4	64.0	62.9	63.3	62.7	62.2	62.3
2009	60.1	59.6	59.5	58.7	58.6	59.6	59.2	59.3	58.9	59.8	59.8	59.7	59.4
2010	57.8	58.0	58.4	59.0	59.1	60.5	61.2	61.8	60.8	62.1	62.0	61.2	60.2
2011	59.3	59.1	59.9	62.5	62.4	63.9	64.8	63.5	61.4	62.8	64.0	65.6	62.4
Education and Health Services													
2000	87.0	89.3	90.4	93.2	92.0	89.4	88.7	88.0	92.8	92.1	92.6	93.2	90.7
2001	90.5	92.6	92.8	94.1	94.0	91.3	88.1	87.6	92.5	93.5	94.4	94.1	92.1
2002	90.9	93.2	93.9	93.8	93.2	90.5	89.9	89.9	94.3	96.0	96.4	96.6	93.2
2003	93.5	96.1	96.5	96.2	95.4	92.8	92.0	92.0	96.1	97.9	98.2	98.4	95.4
2004	96.9	100.5	101.1	100.0	99.3	95.7	94.1	93.9	98.6	101.5	101.9	101.3	98.7
2005	99.1	102.0	102.4	102.5	100.9	96.9	95.2	95.0	100.0	102.7	103.4	103.2	100.3
2006	100.5	103.8	103.9	104.0	103.1	99.1	96.9	96.9	102.3	105.1	105.8	105.6	102.3
2007	102.3	105.4	105.6	105.8	104.3	100.3	99.2	99.5	105.1	108.0	108.4	108.3	104.4
2008	104.4	108.4	108.7	109.1	107.6	103.7	102.3	102.0	108.2	110.7	111.4	111.6	107.3
2009	108.2	111.5	111.9	111.6	109.5	105.2	104.1	103.8	109.5	112.6	113.1	113.4	109.5
2010	110.0	113.5	113.8	114.3	112.0	107.6	106.4	106.3	112.7	115.4	115.9	116.1	112.0
2011	111.6	115.0	115.1	115.7	113.4	108.8	104.8	103.4	110.1	112.8	113.2	113.1	111.4
Leisure and Hospitality													
2000	36.2	36.8	37.2	38.9	41.3	43.3	42.7	42.6	40.7	39.8	38.9	39.2	39.8
2001	34.8	35.1	35.5	36.8	39.7	41.9	41.8	41.5	39.4	38.2	37.7	37.7	38.3
2002	34.8	35.1	35.6	37.6	40.3	41.3	41.7	41.5	39.4	38.1	37.2	37.1	38.3
2003	35.4	35.3	36.0	36.6	40.2	41.3	42.3	42.2	40.1	38.8	37.8	37.7	38.6
2004	35.7	35.9	36.3	37.5	40.4	42.0	42.7	42.8	40.6	39.6	38.7	38.5	39.2
2005	36.6	36.7	37.1	38.6	41.1	42.8	42.4	42.6	40.0	38.9	37.8	37.8	39.4
2006	35.5	36.0	36.8	38.2	40.4	42.5	43.0	43.0	40.5	39.7	38.9	38.8	39.4
2007	36.6	36.8	37.1	37.9	41.5	43.9	44.3	43.8	41.2	40.4	39.6	39.1	40.2
2008	36.9	37.5	37.8	39.2	42.6	43.9	44.0	44.0	41.2	40.5	39.1	39.1	40.5
2009	37.3	36.9	37.5	38.7	42.1	43.5	44.1	44.0	41.9	40.6	39.3	39.2	40.4
2010	37.8	37.7	38.4	40.4	43.0	44.1	44.7	44.8	42.3	41.1	40.2	39.6	41.2
2011	38.7	38.9	39.2	40.9	43.4	45.0	47.2	47.6	44.0	43.1	41.4	40.1	42.5
Other Services													
2000	17.2	17.2	17.3	17.5	17.7	18.0	17.6	17.7	17.3	17.5	17.5	17.6	17.5
2001	16.8	17.0	17.1	17.2	17.3	17.7	17.6	17.6	17.2	17.4	17.7	17.6	17.4
2002	17.6	17.7	17.7	18.1	18.2	18.3	18.4	18.6	18.4	18.5	18.6	18.6	18.2
2003	18.4	18.4	18.6	18.7	18.9	18.9	19.0	18.9	18.7	18.8	18.9	19.0	18.8
2004	18.5	18.7	18.8	19.0	19.2	19.2	19.0	.18.9	18.7	19.0	18.9	19.0	18.9
2005	18.9	19.0	19.2	19.5	19.5	19.5	19.2	19.0	18.8	19.0	19.0	19.1	19.1
2006	18.9	19.0	19.1	19.1	19.2	19.0	19.1	18.8	18.7	18.9	19.1	19.4	19.0
2007	19.2	19.2	19.2	19.2	19.5	19.5	19.3	19.3	19.0	19.4	19.4	19.5	19.3
2008	19.3	19.3	19.3	19.6	19.8	19.8	19.9	19.7	19.3	19.5	19.5	19.5	19.5
2009	19.5	19.5	19.6	19.5	19.7	19.7	19.9	19.7	19.4	19.5	19.7	19.8	19.6
2010	19.5	19.3	19.3	19.6	19.6	19.7	20.0	20.0	19.5	19.8	19.9	20.0	19.7
2011	19.8	19.8	20.1	20.4	20.4	20.3	20.4	20.3	19.9	20.2	20.2	20.3	20.2
Government													
2000	76.2	79.6	80.4	80.7	80.4	78.7	71.4	71.3	76.9	78.9	80.5	80.2	77.9
2001	77.9	81.5	81.7	81.5	81.1	79.9	73.1	73.2	79.0	82.3	83.7	84.1	79.9
2002	79.0	82.9	83.6	82.1	82.5	81.9	74.3	74.1	78.3	82.3	83.4	84.6	80.8
2003	80.6	83.5	84.0	82.7	83.6	82.5	74.5	74.1	78.7	81.2	82.2	83.7	80.9
2004	80.0	80.3	81.0	82.3	83.5	82.5	74.5	74.2	78.4	82.1	82.8	84.1	80.5
2005	80.2	83.1	83.4	83.5	83.8	82.9	75.2	74.9	79.1	82.2	83.2	84.1	81.3
2006	79.0	81.4	82.0	81.5	81.5	80.0	72.3	72.2	78.2	80.5	81.4	81.6	79.3
2007	78.9	81.1	81.3	81.5	82.0	81.3	73.4	72.8	78.7	81.4	82.0	82.8	79.8
2008	79.4	81.6	81.9	82.5	82.7	82.0	74.7	74.0	79.7	82.5	82.8	83.1	80.6
2009	79.8	82.3	82.2	82.8	82.9	81.4	77.5	75.6	78.4	82.8	83.2	83.5	81.0
2010	80.9	82.9	83.0	83.1	84.6	83.3	74.4	73.4	78.4	82.7	83.3	83.7	81.1
2011	79.8	82.5	82.5	82.4	82.3	81.9	73.5	73.4	78.5	82.6	83.4	84.0	80.6

Employment by Industry: Sacramento–Arden–Arcade–Roseville, CA, Selected Years, 2000–2011

(Numbers in thousands, not seasonally adjusted)

Industry and year	January	February	March	April	May	June	July	August	September	October	November	December	Annual average
Total Nonfarm													
2000	773.3	778.7	786.0	789.5	795.9	805.6	795.2	803.6	804.5	804.0	811.8	818.2	797.2
2001	799.6	803.4	813.3	814.7	817.3	824.1	820.2	824.1	822.7	824.1	829.9	832.9	818.9
2002	814.8	817.1	827.6	826.9	833.6	837.7	832.1	834.6	836.7	839.0	842.7	843.5	832.2
2003	831.6	833.0	837.7	842.5	847.7	853.9	847.0	848.7	850.2	847.7	855.6	856.7	846.0
2004	843.3	845.5	850.3	856.4	859.5	866.0	861.1	858.8	864.0	865.2	868.0	870.7	859.1
2005	861.4	865.1	870.6	874.9	879.2	883.5	882.7	883.1	887.8	889.3	894.6	898.6	880.9
2006	888.0	891.7	893.3	890.1	899.8	907.6	900.6	901.5	903.9	901.5	904.3	905.9	899.0
2007	892.7	895.9	902.8	900.5	906.9	910.9	905.1	905.5	905.0	901.6	904.6	905.0	903.0
2008	884.6	888.1	889.7	888.3	891.1	891.9	883.5	878.9	876.3	872.6	870.9	868.9	882.1
2009	849.6	844.4	842.5	840.0	840.9	838.7	821.5	816.7	815.1	822.8	823.7	822.1	831.5
2010	805.0	804.8	808.3	812.3	818.1	819.1	806.6	804.2	805.7	811.6	812.5	810.1	809.9
2011	799.0	802.0	803.7	805.6	806.7	807.2	792.2	795.7	798.7	801.6	807.9	804.2	802.0
Total Private													
2000	567.0	569.5	574.1	577.7	580.6	589.8	590.8	596.5	596.1	592.0	598.9	605.5	586.5
2001	588.4	590.2	596.3	596.8	599.0	605.2	605.9	607.7	602.7	602.2	605.9	608.9	600.8
2002	592.8	593.3	598.4	597.6	603.0	608.0	608.5	610.2	610.6	611.4	614.7	616.0	605.4
2003	606.6	606.1	610.0	614.5	617.5	625.0	622.7	626.1	625.6	624.3	627.8	632.3	619.9
2004	620.8	622.4	627.3	632.8	635.1	641.1	643.5	643.6	644.7	643.8	645.3	649.6	637.5
2005	639.6	642.3	646.6	649.8	653.0	657.4	661.7	663.4	663.8	663.9	668.3	672.5	656.9
2006	662.9	664.4	664.7	661.1	670.1	676.8	675.0	678.4	676.7	671.8	672.6	673.2	670.6
2007	661.3	663.0	666.8	664.4	669.3	672.1	673.8	674.7	671.0	665.2	667.1	667.3	668.0
2008	647.6	649.2	648.9	648.3	649.1	650.0	647.4	646.6	641.8	635.1	632.0	630.0	643.8
2009	610.9	603.9	600.3	597.4	598.0	598.0	596.0	594.5	589.2	588.2	588.8	588.9	596.2
2010	574.1	572.8	574.8	576.0	577.9	582.0	583.9	585.0	581.6	581.5	581.7	584.0	579.6
2011	571.8	572.9	573.4	574.0	576.4	578.2	580.8	582.7	578.5	576.1	582.2	582.1	577.4
Goods-Producing													
2000	95.5	95.7	97.2	98.2	100.8	103.1	103.6	105.7	104.7	104.1	103.8	103.4	101.3
2001	99.4	99.7	101.9	103.6	106.2	108.5	109.0	109.5	108.5	107.5	105.6	103.5	105.2
2002	99.0	99.0	100.3	101.7	104.1	105.3	105.8	107.7	107.6	107.9	106.3	104.5	104.1
2003	100.8	101.8	103.7	105.3	107.7	111.0	110.8	113.5	113.9	113.5	111.5	109.9	108.6
2004	107.5	107.8	110.6	111.8	113.6	116.5	117.5	119.0	118.7	117.3	114.8	113.8	114.1
2005	110.8	112.0	113.7	114.5	116.1	118.0	119.8	121.7	122.0	121.0	119.1	117.4	117.2
2006	113.0	113.1	111.3	109.3	114.4	117.2	116.8	119.0	119.0	115.1	112.2	109.6	114.2
2007	107.2	107.4	108.5	108.1	110.7	112.0	111.1	112.3	110.5	107.2	104.6	101.6	108.4
2008	95.0	94.9	95.2	95.3	96.9	98.3	98.7	99.4	97.9	95.1	91.4	88.8	95.6
2009	83.2	79.8	79.1	78.3	79.2	79.9	79.0	79.0	77.8	77.1	75.2	72.9	78.4
2010	69.7	68.6	69.5	70.3	71.4	73.0	73.9	74.8	73.8	73.0	71.5	69.6	71.6
2011	67.1	67.0	66.6	67.7	69.0	70.3	71.4	73.5	72.1	70.4	70.7	67.9	69.5
Mining and Logging													
2000	0.8	0.8	0.8	0.9	0.9	0.9	0.9	0.9	0.9	0.9	0.9	0.9	0.9
2001	0.8	0.8	0.8	0.9	0.9	0.9	0.9	0.9	0.9	0.9	0.8	0.8	0.9
2002	0.7	0.7	0.8	0.8	0.8	0.8	0.8	0.8	0.8	0.8	0.8	0.8	0.8
2003	0.6	0.6	0.6	0.6	0.6	0.7	0.7	0.7	0.7	0.7	0.7	0.7	0.7
2004	0.6	0.6	0.7	0.7	0.7	0.7	0.8	0.7	0.8	0.8	0.7	0.7	0.7
2005	0.7	0.7	0.7	0.7	0.7	0.7	0.8	0.8	0.7	0.7	0.7	0.7	0.7
2006	0.7	0.7	0.7	0.6	0.6	0.8	0.7	0.8	0.8	0.7	0.7	0.7	0.7
2007	0.6	0.6	0.6	0.6	0.7	0.7	0.7	0.7	0.7	0.8	0.7	0.7	0.7
2008	0.6	0.6	0.6	0.7	0.7	0.7	0.7	0.7	0.7	0.7	0.6	0.6	0.7
2009	0.4	0.4	0.4	0.4	0.4	0.4	0.5	0.5	0.5	0.5	0.4	0.4	0.4
2010	0.3	0.3	0.4	0.4	0.4	0.4	0.5	0.5	0.5	0.5	0.5	0.4	0.4
2011	0.4	0.4	0.4	0.4	0.4	0.4	0.4	0.4	0.4	0.4	0.4	0.4	0.4
Construction													
2000	47.7	47.3	48.5	50.9	52.9	55.2	55.1	56.2	56.3	55.7	55.6	55.2	53.1
2001	53.0	53.4	55.5	57.9	60.1	62.2	62.8	64.1	63.2	62.2	60.9	58.9	59.5
2002	55.8	56.5	57.6	58.8	61.0	62.3	63.1	64.9	64.9	64.6	64.1	62.3	61.3
2003	60.1	60.9	62.7	64.2	66.1	68.2	68.3	70.0	70.2	70.4	69.2	67.5	66.5
2004	65.3	65.8	68.5	69.6	70.9	73.2	73.5	74.2	73.5	73.2	71.3	70.3	70.8
2005	67.8	68.9	70.4	71.8	73.1	74.8	76.0	76.5	76.6	76.5	75.2	73.2	73.4
2006	69.5	69.6	67.9	66.1	71.1	73.3	73.4	74.6	74.3	71.4	69.7	67.1	70.7
2007	65.7	65.7	67.0	66.8	69.0	70.0	69.6	69.8	68.2	66.1	63.9	61.1	66.9
2008	55.2	55.3	55.5	55.7	57.2	58.5	59.2	59.0	57.6	56.2	53.6	51.2	56.2
2009	47.0	44.2	43.9	43.5	44.4	45.0	44.3	43.9	42.7	42.3	41.5	39.4	43.5
2010	37.1	36.1	36.8	37.6	38.6	40.0	40.5	40.5	39.5	39.2	38.3	36.4	38.4
2011	34.4	34.2	33.6	34.7	35.9	37.0	37.3	39.2	38.4	37.7	37.7	34.8	36.2
Manufacturing													
2000	47.0	47.6	47.9	46.4	47.0	47.0	47.6	48.6	47.5	47.5	47.3	47.3	47.4
2001	45.6	45.5	45.6	44.8	45.2	45.4	45.3	44.5	44.4	44.4	43.9	43.8	44.9
2002	42.5	41.8	41.9	42.1	42.3	42.2	41.9	42.0	41.9	42.5	41.4	41.4	42.0
2003	40.1	40.3	40.4	40.5	41.0	42.1	41.8	42.8	43.0	42.4	41.6	41.7	41.5
2004	41.6	41.4	41.4	41.5	42.0	42.6	43.2	44.1	44.4	43.3	42.8	42.8	42.6
2005	42.3	42.4	42.6	42.0	42.3	42.5	43.0	44.4	44.7	43.8	43.2	43.5	43.1
2006	42.8	42.8	42.7	42.6	42.7	43.1	42.7	43.6	43.9	43.0	41.8	41.8	42.8
2007	40.9	41.1	40.9	40.7	41.0	41.3	40.8	41.8	41.6	40.3	40.0	39.8	40.9
2008	39.2	39.0	39.1	38.9	39.0	39.1	38.8	39.7	39.6	38.2	37.2	37.0	38.7
2009	35.8	35.2	34.8	34.4	34.4	34.5	34.2	34.6	34.6	34.3	33.3	33.1	34.4
2010	32.3	32.2	32.3	32.3	32.4	32.6	32.9	33.8	33.8	33.3	32.7	32.8	32.8
2011	32.3	32.4	32.6	32.6	32.7	32.9	33.7	33.9	33.3	32.3	32.6	32.7	32.8

Employment by Industry: Sacramento–Arden–Arcade–Roseville, CA, Selected Years, 2000–2011—*Continued*

(Numbers in thousands, not seasonally adjusted)

Industry and year	January	February	March	April	May	June	July	August	September	October	November	December	Annual average
Service-Providing													
2000	677.8	683.0	688.8	691.3	695.1	702.5	691.6	697.9	699.8	699.9	708.0	714.8	695.9
2001	700.2	703.7	711.4	711.1	711.1	715.6	711.2	714.6	714.2	716.6	724.3	729.4	713.6
2002	715.8	718.1	727.3	725.2	729.5	732.4	726.3	726.9	729.1	731.1	736.4	739.0	728.1
2003	730.8	731.2	734.0	737.2	740.0	742.9	736.2	735.2	736.3	734.2	744.1	746.8	737.4
2004	735.8	737.7	739.7	744.6	745.9	749.5	743.6	739.8	745.3	747.9	753.2	756.9	745.0
2005	750.6	753.1	756.9	760.4	763.1	765.5	762.9	761.4	765.8	768.3	775.5	781.2	763.7
2006	775.0	778.6	782.0	780.8	785.4	790.4	783.8	782.5	784.9	786.4	792.1	796.3	784.9
2007	785.5	788.5	794.3	792.4	796.2	798.9	794.0	793.2	794.5	794.4	800.0	803.4	794.6
2008	789.6	793.2	794.5	793.0	794.2	793.6	784.8	779.5	778.4	777.5	779.5	780.1	786.5
2009	766.4	764.6	763.4	761.7	761.7	758.8	742.5	737.7	737.3	745.7	748.5	749.2	753.1
2010	735.3	736.2	738.8	742.0	746.7	746.1	732.7	729.4	731.9	738.6	741.0	740.5	738.3
2011	731.9	735.0	737.1	737.9	737.7	736.9	720.8	722.2	726.6	731.2	737.2	736.3	732.6
Trade, Transportation, and Utilities													
2000	136.7	135.2	135.3	135.9	135.9	137.0	137.6	139.4	139.8	139.6	144.6	147.3	138.7
2001	139.9	138.0	138.5	138.3	138.6	140.3	139.9	140.2	140.9	141.4	144.7	146.5	140.6
2002	138.5	137.4	138.5	138.6	139.0	140.2	140.3	140.5	140.7	141.8	145.0	146.8	140.6
2003	141.6	139.6	139.6	140.2	140.8	142.3	142.9	143.5	143.3	144.5	148.4	150.9	143.1
2004	144.1	143.1	143.0	143.9	144.8	145.9	145.8	145.7	145.8	147.5	151.0	152.3	146.1
2005	147.0	145.9	146.2	146.2	146.7	147.2	148.4	148.7	149.1	150.1	154.1	157.5	148.9
2006	151.2	149.9	150.8	150.4	151.8	153.1	154.3	155.1	154.4	154.6	157.8	159.9	153.6
2007	153.9	152.2	152.0	151.2	151.7	152.2	152.8	152.7	152.2	152.3	156.3	158.2	153.1
2008	150.5	148.5	148.2	147.3	147.0	147.1	146.4	145.7	144.3	143.7	145.2	145.8	146.6
2009	138.1	135.4	134.0	133.5	134.6	134.7	133.8	133.2	133.4	133.6	136.9	137.7	134.9
2010	132.3	130.3	130.3	130.7	131.4	131.5	131.8	132.5	132.1	133.4	136.1	138.0	132.5
2011	132.5	131.0	130.9	131.0	131.6	132.2	132.3	132.0	131.2	132.3	137.5	138.3	132.7
Wholesale Trade													
2000	24.4	24.6	24.8	25.2	25.2	25.5	25.2	25.3	25.3	25.5	25.4	25.2	25.1
2001	25.0	25.3	25.4	25.7	25.7	25.9	25.9	26.1	26.0	26.0	26.1	26.1	25.8
2002	25.3	25.5	25.7	25.5	25.6	25.5	25.5	25.6	25.5	25.7	25.8	25.7	25.6
2003	25.9	26.0	26.0	26.2	26.2	26.3	26.3	26.4	26.4	26.4	26.5	26.6	26.3
2004	26.3	26.4	26.4	26.3	26.4	26.6	26.7	26.8	26.7	26.6	26.5	26.6	26.5
2005	26.4	26.5	26.5	26.7	26.7	26.7	26.9	27.0	27.1	27.4	27.5	27.6	26.9
2006	27.7	28.0	28.3	28.1	28.5	28.7	28.8	28.8	28.6	28.7	28.6	28.4	28.4
2007	28.4	28.2	28.5	28.1	28.0	28.1	27.8	27.7	27.5	27.4	27.3	27.5	27.9
2008	27.0	27.0	26.8	26.8	26.9	26.8	26.6	26.3	26.2	26.0	25.7	25.4	26.5
2009	25.0	24.7	24.4	24.3	24.6	24.6	24.1	23.7	23.5	23.5	23.5	23.0	24.1
2010	23.0	22.8	22.6	22.9	22.9	22.7	22.6	22.7	22.6	22.8	22.8	22.8	22.8
2011	22.8	22.7	22.7	23.0	23.1	23.2	23.1	23.0	23.0	23.0	23.0	23.0	23.0
Retail Trade													
2000	88.6	86.9	86.9	87.1	87.3	88.1	88.9	90.2	90.6	90.9	95.5	98.0	89.9
2001	91.3	89.5	89.6	89.7	90.2	91.3	90.9	90.8	91.5	91.9	95.1	96.9	91.6
2002	91.3	89.9	90.7	90.6	90.8	92.0	92.1	92.3	92.8	93.8	96.9	99.0	92.7
2003	94.2	92.2	92.2	92.5	92.9	94.1	94.6	94.8	94.6	95.7	99.5	101.9	94.9
2004	95.2	94.3	94.3	95.1	95.9	96.6	96.4	96.0	95.9	97.3	101.1	102.3	96.7
2005	97.3	96.3	96.4	96.5	96.8	97.2	98.3	98.3	98.5	99.3	103.1	105.8	98.7
2006	100.1	98.7	99.1	98.9	99.7	100.3	100.9	101.0	100.3	100.6	103.7	105.2	100.7
2007	100.4	98.9	98.4	98.2	98.6	98.7	99.5	99.3	98.9	99.3	103.3	104.4	99.8
2008	98.4	96.3	96.1	95.5	95.2	95.2	94.5	94.1	92.9	92.8	94.8	95.4	95.1
2009	89.3	87.0	86.1	85.9	86.9	87.0	86.9	86.5	86.8	87.3	90.4	91.6	87.6
2010	87.1	85.6	85.7	86.3	86.9	87.1	87.6	88.1	88.0	89.0	91.7	93.2	88.0
2011	89.0	87.6	87.3	87.1	87.4	87.8	88.2	88.6	87.8	88.5	93.0	93.9	88.9
Transportation and Utilities													
2000	23.7	23.7	23.6	23.6	23.4	23.4	23.5	23.9	23.9	23.2	23.7	24.1	23.6
2001	23.6	23.2	23.5	22.9	22.7	23.1	23.1	23.3	23.4	23.5	23.5	23.5	23.3
2002	21.9	22.0	22.1	22.5	22.6	22.7	22.7	22.6	22.4	22.3	22.3	22.1	22.4
2003	21.5	21.4	21.4	21.5	21.7	21.9	22.0	22.3	22.3	22.4	22.4	22.4	21.9
2004	22.6	22.4	22.3	22.5	22.5	22.7	22.7	22.9	23.2	23.6	23.4	23.4	22.9
2005	23.3	23.1	23.3	23.0	23.2	23.3	23.2	23.4	23.5	23.4	23.5	24.1	23.4
2006	23.4	23.2	23.4	23.4	23.6	24.1	24.6	25.3	25.5	25.3	25.5	26.3	24.5
2007	25.1	25.1	25.1	24.9	25.1	25.4	25.5	25.7	25.8	25.6	25.7	26.3	25.4
2008	25.1	25.2	25.3	25.0	24.9	25.1	25.3	25.3	25.2	24.9	24.7	25.0	25.1
2009	23.8	23.7	23.5	23.3	23.1	23.1	22.8	23.0	23.1	22.8	23.0	23.1	23.2
2010	22.2	21.9	22.0	21.5	21.6	21.7	21.6	21.7	21.5	21.6	21.6	22.0	21.7
2011	20.7	20.7	20.9	20.9	21.1	21.2	21.0	20.4	20.4	20.8	21.5	21.4	20.9
Information													
2000	18.6	18.5	18.4	18.4	18.3	18.4	18.6	18.8	18.8	18.8	18.9	19.0	18.6
2001	20.7	20.8	21.2	22.0	22.0	21.9	22.7	23.0	22.9	23.6	23.6	23.7	22.3
2002	24.1	23.8	23.7	23.5	23.7	23.6	23.3	22.7	22.4	22.3	21.9	21.6	23.1
2003	21.8	22.0	21.7	22.2	22.6	22.8	21.7	21.6	21.3	21.4	21.5	21.6	21.9
2004	21.3	21.5	21.3	21.1	21.1	21.1	21.0	20.8	20.5	20.4	20.5	20.6	20.9
2005	20.5	20.6	20.2	20.3	20.1	19.9	19.8	19.8	19.5	19.2	19.4	19.5	19.9
2006	19.6	19.8	19.7	19.9	19.9	19.9	19.8	20.4	20.3	20.1	20.0	20.1	20.4	20.0
2007	20.4	20.7	20.4	20.1	20.3	20.0	20.0	20.0	19.8	19.7	19.7	19.7	20.1
2008	19.5	19.7	19.5	19.4	19.4	19.4	19.3	19.4	19.1	19.1	18.8	18.8	19.2
2009	18.9	18.8	18.6	18.1	18.3	18.2	18.4	18.3	18.1	18.0	18.0	18.0	18.3
2010	17.8	17.7	17.4	17.3	17.2	17.6	17.1	16.9	16.7	16.7	17.0	17.0	17.2
2011	16.8	16.8	16.8	16.7	16.7	16.7	16.7	16.7	16.7	16.7	16.8	16.8	16.7

Employment by Industry: Sacramento–Arden–Arcade–Roseville, CA, Selected Years, 2000–2011—*Continued*

(Numbers in thousands, not seasonally adjusted)

Industry and year	January	February	March	April	May	June	July	August	September	October	November	December	Annual average
Financial Activities													
2000	52.1	52.5	52.8	52.4	52.4	52.6	51.9	52.3	52.1	50.6	50.9	52.0	52.1
2001	51.4	51.9	52.3	51.7	51.8	52.3	52.2	52.6	52.2	52.7	52.9	53.3	52.3
2002	52.9	53.2	53.3	53.9	53.8	54.1	54.9	55.4	56.2	57.1	57.6	58.1	55.0
2003	57.6	58.2	58.3	59.2	59.4	59.5	59.6	59.9	59.5	59.1	59.0	59.3	59.1
2004	58.4	58.8	58.8	59.5	59.7	59.9	60.5	60.8	60.8	61.2	61.2	61.7	60.1
2005	61.6	61.9	62.3	62.6	63.1	63.1	63.5	63.7	63.8	63.9	64.1	64.4	63.2
2006	64.9	65.0	65.0	64.8	64.7	64.9	64.5	64.3	64.1	63.2	63.4	63.2	64.3
2007	62.7	62.9	62.5	62.5	62.3	62.1	61.9	61.4	60.7	60.2	59.6	59.6	61.5
2008	58.6	58.6	58.2	58.0	57.7	57.5	57.4	56.9	56.5	55.8	55.6	55.4	57.2
2009	55.5	55.3	55.1	53.9	53.4	53.1	52.7	52.4	51.3	51.0	50.6	50.6	52.9
2010	49.8	49.5	49.5	49.0	48.6	48.7	48.2	48.0	47.8	47.5	46.5	46.4	48.3
2011	46.3	46.0	46.2	46.3	46.4	46.3	46.4	46.4	47.0	47.4	47.2	47.1	46.6
Professional and Business Services													
2000	102.7	104.3	106.1	107.4	107.6	110.0	109.4	110.4	110.1	108.8	109.5	110.0	108.0
2001	104.6	105.5	106.3	104.9	105.0	105.3	105.7	105.1	103.3	101.6	101.5	101.7	104.2
2002	98.3	99.4	101.7	100.5	100.4	102.1	102.6	102.5	103.0	100.5	100.7	100.8	101.0
2003	99.5	100.0	100.2	100.3	100.3	101.2	100.5	100.9	101.4	100.2	101.5	101.5	100.6
2004	100.1	100.8	101.6	103.2	103.0	103.6	104.0	104.2	104.0	104.4	104.0	104.4	103.1
2005	103.6	105.0	106.3	107.7	107.9	109.7	109.7	109.7	109.7	110.5	111.3	112.0	108.6
2006	111.0	112.0	112.3	111.7	112.4	113.5	112.9	113.3	112.7	113.1	113.0	112.6	112.5
2007	108.6	110.0	110.8	111.4	111.3	112.3	113.3	113.7	113.2	113.5	113.4	113.9	112.1
2008	110.0	111.2	110.9	111.3	110.8	110.2	110.0	109.9	109.4	109.9	108.8	108.3	110.1
2009	103.8	103.1	102.2	101.2	100.0	100.0	101.2	101.2	99.7	100.7	100.2	100.1	101.1
2010	98.9	100.4	100.9	101.5	101.5	102.8	103.7	103.7	103.1	103.9	103.1	102.6	102.2
2011	100.3	102.1	101.3	101.2	101.6	102.0	101.5	101.3	101.7	101.1	101.2	101.8	101.4
Education and Health Services													
2000	68.7	69.1	69.1	69.4	69.2	69.6	70.6	70.7	71.6	73.3	73.5	74.4	70.8
2001	73.7	74.3	75.1	76.0	77.0	76.6	75.8	76.1	76.7	77.0	78.1	77.1	76.1
2002	78.5	77.5	77.8	76.8	78.8	77.6	77.3	76.8	77.9	79.2	80.4	79.4	78.2
2003	81.1	79.5	80.4	81.5	81.6	81.3	81.2	80.0	81.6	81.9	82.5	82.6	81.3
2004	83.4	83.4	83.7	84.7	85.3	84.9	85.1	83.2	86.2	85.8	86.0	86.5	84.9
2005	87.2	87.0	87.5	88.4	89.0	88.4	88.3	87.5	88.9	89.7	90.2	90.0	88.5
2006	91.5	91.0	91.6	91.6	92.7	92.7	91.7	91.3	92.7	94.3	93.9	93.8	92.4
2007	95.2	95.4	96.9	96.7	97.8	96.7	96.8	96.3	97.7	97.8	99.4	98.8	97.1
2008	98.5	99.7	99.5	100.2	100.5	99.4	98.3	98.9	99.8	100.0	101.0	100.4	99.7
2009	99.9	100.1	100.0	100.1	100.7	99.3	98.1	98.3	98.9	100.6	100.8	100.7	99.8
2010	98.5	98.5	98.8	99.8	100.5	99.3	98.1	98.4	99.1	100.2	101.0	101.1	99.4
2011	100.9	101.2	101.8	102.6	103.0	101.8	101.6	102.2	102.7	104.8	104.8	105.2	102.7
Leisure and Hospitality													
2000	66.9	67.8	68.5	69.4	69.4	71.8	72.2	72.4	71.7	70.0	71.0	72.5	70.3
2001	72.1	72.9	73.6	72.7	70.5	72.0	72.6	73.3	70.3	70.2	71.5	75.1	72.2
2002	73.9	74.8	75.3	74.9	74.5	76.6	76.0	76.6	74.8	74.2	74.5	76.4	75.2
2003	76.9	77.4	78.5	77.5	76.5	78.1	77.7	78.4	76.6	75.9	75.7	78.7	77.3
2004	78.3	79.1	80.1	80.1	78.8	80.6	80.8	81.2	79.8	78.4	79.3	81.7	79.9
2005	80.6	81.3	81.4	81.0	81.1	82.3	83.7	83.9	82.4	81.4	82.2	84.0	82.1
2006	83.8	85.2	85.5	85.2	85.5	86.9	86.5	87.0	85.2	83.2	83.9	85.6	85.3
2007	85.5	86.2	87.2	85.8	86.1	87.6	88.6	88.8	87.4	85.1	85.0	86.2	86.6
2008	87.0	87.7	88.4	87.1	86.7	88.1	87.1	86.3	84.6	82.2	81.8	83.3	85.9
2009	82.6	82.4	82.5	82.9	82.4	83.6	83.7	83.3	81.3	78.7	78.8	81.0	81.9
2010	79.5	80.2	80.6	79.3	78.9	80.6	82.4	82.1	80.4	78.5	78.6	81.7	80.2
2011	80.4	81.2	82.2	80.5	79.9	80.6	82.4	82.0	78.7	75.5	76.3	77.3	79.8
Other Services													
2000	25.8	26.4	26.7	26.6	27.0	27.3	26.9	26.8	27.3	26.8	26.7	26.9	26.8
2001	26.6	27.1	27.4	27.6	27.9	28.3	28.0	27.9	27.9	28.2	28.0	28.0	27.7
2002	27.6	28.2	27.8	27.7	28.7	28.5	28.3	28.0	28.0	28.4	28.3	28.4	28.2
2003	27.3	27.6	27.6	28.3	28.6	28.8	28.3	28.3	28.0	27.8	27.7	27.8	28.0
2004	27.7	27.9	28.2	28.5	28.8	28.6	28.8	28.7	28.9	28.8	28.5	28.6	28.5
2005	28.3	28.6	29.0	29.1	29.0	28.8	28.5	28.4	28.4	28.1	27.9	27.7	28.5
2006	27.9	28.4	28.5	28.2	28.7	28.7	27.9	28.1	28.5	28.3	28.3	28.1	28.3
2007	27.8	28.2	28.5	28.6	29.1	29.2	29.3	29.5	29.5	29.4	29.1	29.3	29.0
2008	28.5	28.9	29.0	29.7	30.1	30.0	30.2	30.2	30.2	29.8	29.4	29.2	29.6
2009	28.9	29.0	28.8	29.4	29.4	29.2	29.1	28.8	28.7	28.5	28.3	27.9	28.8
2010	27.6	27.6	27.8	28.1	28.4	28.5	28.7	28.6	28.6	28.3	27.9	27.6	28.1
2011	27.5	27.6	27.6	28.0	28.2	28.3	28.5	28.6	28.4	27.9	27.7	27.7	28.0
Government													
2000	206.3	209.2	211.9	211.8	215.3	215.8	204.4	207.1	208.4	212.0	212.9	212.7	210.7
2001	211.2	213.2	217.0	217.9	218.3	218.9	214.3	216.4	220.0	221.9	224.0	224.0	218.1
2002	222.0	223.8	229.2	229.3	230.6	229.7	223.6	224.4	226.1	227.6	228.0	227.5	226.8
2003	225.0	226.9	227.7	228.0	230.2	228.9	224.3	222.6	224.6	223.4	227.8	224.4	226.2
2004	222.5	223.1	223.0	223.6	224.4	224.9	217.6	215.2	219.3	221.4	222.7	221.1	221.6
2005	221.8	222.8	224.0	225.1	226.2	226.1	221.0	219.7	224.0	225.4	226.3	226.1	224.0
2006	225.1	227.3	228.6	229.0	229.7	230.8	225.6	223.1	227.2	229.7	231.7	232.7	228.4
2007	231.4	232.9	236.0	236.1	237.6	238.8	231.3	230.8	234.0	236.4	237.5	237.7	235.0
2008	237.0	238.9	240.8	240.0	242.0	241.9	236.1	232.3	234.5	237.5	238.9	238.9	238.2
2009	238.7	240.5	242.2	242.6	242.9	240.7	225.5	222.2	225.9	234.6	234.9	233.2	235.3
2010	230.9	232.0	233.5	236.3	240.2	237.1	222.7	219.2	224.1	230.1	230.8	226.1	230.3
2011	227.2	229.1	230.3	231.6	230.3	229.0	211.4	213.0	220.2	225.5	225.7	222.1	224.6

Employment by Industry: Salt Lake City, UT, Selected Years, 2000–2011

(Numbers in thousands, not seasonally adjusted)

Industry and year	January	February	March	April	May	June	July	August	September	October	November	December	Annual average
Total Nonfarm													
2000	552.5	555.9	559.6	561.2	563.0	565.7	560.7	564.7	569.5	571.6	577.1	585.1	565.6
2001	573.9	574.6	576.8	574.6	574.1	576.1	568.4	570.5	572.6	570.5	572.1	576.6	573.4
2002	567.5	572.3	564.2	562.7	560.1	561.9	557.2	558.7	560.6	565.0	568.0	563.3
2003	553.8	553.5	553.4	553.5	553.4	554.9	552.2	555.5	556.4	558.2	562.0	567.8	556.2
2004	554.2	556.1	558.7	560.9	560.0	564.4	563.3	565.9	567.6	570.3	575.9	583.1	565.0
2005	572.1	574.9	576.4	581.5	580.8	585.2	586.5	591.3	594.3	595.2	601.5	608.9	587.4
2006	597.5	601.4	605.6	608.2	608.4	614.8	612.3	617.9	620.2	620.6	628.5	636.2	614.3
2007	625.8	628.6	632.4	633.9	634.1	639.5	635.2	639.9	639.7	641.0	646.9	653.0	637.5
2008	640.0	641.3	642.5	643.1	640.1	642.7	638.6	642.5	641.6	639.2	637.7	640.6	640.8
2009	620.7	617.1	615.1	611.1	607.2	607.1	601.1	603.1	604.8	606.1	608.1	613.9	609.6
2010	601.0	600.2	604.0	606.1	605.1	607.2	604.9	606.7	609.3	613.5	617.0	622.5	608.1
2011	610.8	612.6	614.9	617.9	613.4	617.9	616.1	622.3	627.8	630.5	635.1	644.7	622.0
Total Private													
2000	470.8	472.3	475.9	476.3	476.3	481.8	481.9	486.3	485.3	486.8	492.0	500.1	482.2
2001	489.1	487.9	490.1	487.4	486.3	489.1	487.4	489.6	485.8	483.1	484.2	487.9	487.3
2002	479.5	485.8	475.7	474.0	472.0	473.2	471.8	474.6	472.0	472.1	475.9	478.7	475.4
2003	464.9	464.2	464.4	464.0	464.6	466.1	467.0	470.9	467.9	469.3	473.2	478.9	468.0
2004	465.4	467.1	469.7	470.8	470.6	474.8	476.8	479.1	477.5	480.0	485.6	492.3	475.8
2005	481.6	484.1	485.9	490.4	490.2	494.5	498.4	502.9	503.1	503.7	509.7	516.8	496.8
2006	506.1	509.4	513.7	516.1	516.8	522.5	523.1	528.6	528.1	528.1	535.9	543.2	522.6
2007	533.6	536.2	540.0	541.0	541.4	546.1	545.7	549.8	546.7	547.4	553.0	558.8	545.0
2008	546.1	547.1	547.9	548.4	545.3	547.3	547.2	550.0	545.4	542.7	540.9	543.7	546.0
2009	524.8	520.8	518.8	514.1	510.4	510.3	508.6	509.7	507.9	508.6	510.8	516.4	513.4
2010	504.2	503.4	507.1	508.6	505.9	508.9	510.6	512.0	510.6	514.0	517.7	524.1	510.6
2011	513.0	514.7	516.9	519.8	515.5	519.5	521.9	527.1	526.7	528.2	532.9	542.2	523.2
Goods-Producing													
2000	93.7	93.5	93.9	95.3	96.5	98.2	97.3	98.4	97.8	97.4	96.7	96.1	96.2
2001	93.2	92.5	93.2	92.6	93.9	95.4	95.5	96.1	95.4	94.8	93.2	91.0	93.9
2002	86.8	84.8	85.1	85.6	86.8	87.9	88.0	88.3	87.9	87.4	86.6	85.4	86.7
2003	82.3	81.9	82.0	83.1	84.9	85.5	85.8	86.4	86.1	86.3	85.6	84.8	84.6
2004	81.8	81.8	83.0	84.9	86.9	88.0	89.1	89.5	89.4	89.1	88.5	88.5	86.7
2005	86.2	86.5	87.1	89.6	91.2	93.0	94.3	95.4	95.5	94.7	94.9	94.7	91.9
2006	92.8	93.9	95.4	97.0	99.7	102.0	102.4	103.7	104.2	104.3	104.4	103.9	100.3
2007	101.5	101.8	103.4	104.7	106.7	108.9	108.9	110.0	108.8	107.8	106.9	105.4	106.2
2008	102.1	101.0	101.7	102.2	103.0	104.1	104.4	104.6	103.4	102.1	99.4	97.3	102.1
2009	91.0	88.7	88.3	87.2	88.6	89.0	89.6	89.6	89.2	89.0	88.0	86.8	88.8
2010	83.9	83.2	83.6	85.1	86.3	87.0	87.8	88.7	88.8	88.8	87.9	86.9	86.5
2011	84.6	84.3	84.9	86.0	87.0	88.6	88.4	89.2	90.1	91.3	90.6	90.1	87.9
Mining, Logging, and Construction													
2000	37.3	37.2	37.5	38.8	39.8	41.2	40.7	41.4	41.0	40.5	39.7	39.0	39.5
2001	36.4	35.9	36.5	36.7	38.1	39.6	39.7	40.5	40.0	39.7	38.8	37.0	38.2
2002	33.7	32.1	32.5	33.4	34.5	35.7	36.1	36.3	36.1	35.8	35.1	34.1	34.6
2003	31.8	31.5	31.7	32.6	34.0	34.5	34.9	35.4	35.1	35.1	34.3	33.4	33.7
2004	31.0	31.1	32.0	33.5	34.8	35.7	36.6	37.0	37.0	36.7	36.0	35.9	34.8
2005	34.0	34.1	35.1	37.0	38.1	39.2	40.4	41.2	41.3	41.0	41.0	40.6	38.6
2006	39.0	39.7	41.0	42.4	44.5	46.2	46.6	47.5	47.9	47.9	47.6	47.1	44.8
2007	45.2	45.2	46.4	47.5	49.2	50.7	50.7	51.4	50.5	49.5	48.4	46.9	48.5
2008	43.6	42.6	43.3	44.2	45.1	46.1	46.4	46.9	46.0	44.9	42.9	41.3	44.4
2009	36.5	35.4	35.4	34.9	36.3	36.6	37.1	37.3	37.1	36.8	36.0	34.5	36.2
2010	32.2	31.6	32.0	32.9	34.2	34.6	35.1	35.7	36.0	36.4	35.5	34.4	34.2
2011	32.1	31.7	32.3	33.1	33.9	35.1	35.0	35.0	35.4	36.0	35.4	34.7	34.1
Manufacturing													
2000	56.4	56.3	56.4	56.5	56.7	57.0	56.6	57.0	56.8	56.9	57.0	57.1	56.7
2001	56.8	56.6	56.7	55.9	55.8	55.8	55.8	55.6	55.4	55.1	54.4	54.0	55.7
2002	53.1	52.7	52.6	52.2	52.3	52.2	51.9	52.0	51.8	51.6	51.5	51.3	52.1
2003	50.5	50.4	50.3	50.5	50.9	51.0	50.9	51.0	51.0	51.2	51.3	51.4	50.9
2004	50.8	50.7	51.0	51.4	52.1	52.3	52.5	52.5	52.4	52.4	52.5	52.6	51.9
2005	52.2	52.4	52.0	52.6	53.1	53.8	53.9	54.2	54.2	53.7	53.9	54.1	53.3
2006	53.8	54.2	54.4	54.6	55.2	55.8	55.8	56.2	56.3	56.4	56.8	56.8	55.5
2007	56.3	56.6	57.0	57.2	57.5	58.2	58.2	58.6	58.3	58.3	58.5	58.5	57.8
2008	58.5	58.4	58.4	58.0	57.9	58.0	58.0	57.7	57.4	57.2	56.5	56.0	57.7
2009	54.5	53.3	52.9	52.3	52.3	52.4	52.5	52.3	52.1	52.2	52.0	52.3	52.6
2010	51.7	51.6	51.6	52.2	52.1	52.4	52.7	53.0	52.8	52.4	52.4	52.5	52.3
2011	52.5	52.6	52.6	52.9	53.1	53.5	53.4	54.2	54.7	55.3	55.2	55.4	53.8
Service-Providing													
2000	458.8	462.4	465.7	465.9	466.5	467.5	463.4	466.3	471.7	474.2	480.4	489.0	469.3
2001	480.7	482.1	483.6	482.0	480.2	480.7	472.9	474.4	477.2	475.7	478.9	485.6	479.5
2002	480.7	487.5	479.1	477.1	473.3	474.0	469.2	470.4	472.7	473.4	478.4	482.6	476.5
2003	471.5	471.6	471.4	470.4	468.5	469.4	466.4	469.1	470.3	471.9	476.4	483.0	471.7
2004	472.4	474.3	475.7	476.0	473.1	476.4	474.2	476.4	478.2	481.2	487.4	494.6	478.3
2005	485.9	488.4	489.3	491.9	489.6	492.2	492.2	495.9	498.8	500.5	506.6	514.2	495.5
2006	504.7	507.5	510.2	511.2	508.7	512.8	509.9	514.2	516.0	516.3	524.1	532.3	514.0
2007	524.3	526.8	529.0	529.2	527.4	530.6	526.3	529.9	530.9	533.2	540.0	547.6	531.3
2008	537.9	540.3	540.8	540.9	537.1	538.6	534.2	537.9	538.2	537.1	538.3	543.3	538.7
2009	529.7	528.4	526.8	523.9	518.6	518.1	511.5	513.5	515.6	517.1	520.1	527.1	520.9
2010	517.1	517.0	520.4	521.0	518.8	520.2	517.1	518.0	520.5	524.7	529.1	535.6	521.6
2011	526.2	528.3	530.0	531.9	526.4	529.3	527.7	533.1	537.7	539.2	544.5	554.6	534.1

Employment by Industry: Salt Lake City, UT, Selected Years, 2000–2011—*Continued*

(Numbers in thousands, not seasonally adjusted)

Industry and year	January	February	March	April	May	June	July	August	September	October	November	December	Annual average
Trade, Transportation, and Utilities													
2000	120.7	119.6	120.2	120.0	120.5	121.8	122.3	122.9	122.9	124.3	127.0	129.3	122.6
2001	124.9	123.8	123.7	123.5	123.0	123.0	122.9	122.9	122.2	122.4	124.2	125.6	123.5
2002	120.9	120.1	118.6	119.0	119.5	119.6	119.7	119.9	119.3	120.4	122.6	123.7	120.3
2003	116.9	115.8	115.8	115.4	116.0	116.1	116.4	117.2	116.5	117.4	119.8	121.6	117.1
2004	117.0	116.2	116.3	116.5	117.0	118.1	118.4	118.6	118.2	119.4	122.1	123.8	118.5
2005	119.8	119.5	119.9	120.7	121.2	121.4	122.4	123.3	123.0	124.2	126.6	128.5	122.5
2006	124.2	123.9	124.3	124.2	124.7	125.9	126.1	127.5	127.5	127.7	131.2	133.9	126.8
2007	129.9	129.4	130.2	129.9	130.6	131.2	131.6	132.5	132.3	132.9	136.0	138.1	132.1
2008	133.2	132.2	132.2	132.5	132.6	133.3	132.8	133.3	132.4	132.5	133.7	134.4	132.9
2009	128.3	126.5	125.6	124.1	124.0	123.6	122.8	122.9	122.8	122.9	125.1	126.4	124.6
2010	121.7	121.0	121.2	121.1	121.6	121.9	122.1	122.9	122.3	123.4	125.8	127.2	122.7
2011	122.7	122.4	122.9	123.8	123.6	124.3	125.0	127.0	125.7	126.3	127.9	129.8	125.1
Wholesale Trade													
2000	27.5	27.6	27.8	27.8	28.0	28.2	28.5	28.5	28.5	28.5	28.6	28.9	28.2
2001	28.7	29.0	29.1	29.0	29.1	29.2	29.2	29.2	28.9	28.8	28.7	28.6	29.0
2002	28.2	28.2	28.1	28.3	28.6	28.5	28.6	28.7	28.6	28.6	28.6	28.5	28.5
2003	27.1	27.0	27.1	27.2	27.4	27.3	27.3	27.4	27.3	27.2	27.2	27.3	27.2
2004	27.0	27.1	27.3	27.5	27.7	28.0	27.9	27.9	27.9	28.1	28.3	28.3	27.8
2005	28.1	28.2	28.4	28.5	28.7	28.6	28.7	28.7	28.6	28.7	28.8	28.8	28.6
2006	28.5	28.8	28.9	29.0	29.3	29.6	29.6	29.7	29.7	29.8	29.9	30.3	29.4
2007	30.0	30.1	30.2	30.2	30.5	30.7	30.8	31.0	30.9	30.9	31.0	31.2	30.6
2008	30.9	30.9	30.9	31.3	31.4	31.5	31.4	31.5	31.3	31.1	31.0	31.0	31.2
2009	30.2	30.1	29.8	29.5	29.4	29.3	29.2	29.1	29.0	28.9	28.8	28.9	29.4
2010	28.4	28.3	28.5	28.6	29.0	28.9	29.1	29.2	29.0	29.2	29.3	29.6	28.9
2011	29.4	29.7	29.9	30.1	30.2	30.4	30.3	30.8	30.8	30.9	30.8	30.8	30.3
Retail Trade													
2000	64.0	62.8	62.9	62.7	63.3	64.0	63.9	64.2	64.1	65.3	67.7	69.3	64.5
2001	65.7	64.5	64.3	64.4	64.4	64.4	64.3	64.3	63.9	64.2	66.4	67.8	64.9
2002	64.3	63.3	62.8	62.9	63.3	63.5	63.3	63.5	63.2	63.7	66.0	67.3	63.9
2003	62.9	62.1	62.1	62.0	62.2	62.4	62.5	63.0	62.6	63.5	65.9	67.4	63.2
2004	63.2	62.4	62.3	62.6	62.9	63.4	63.9	64.1	63.8	64.7	66.9	68.3	64.0
2005	64.5	63.5	63.5	63.7	64.0	64.3	65.1	66.0	65.7	66.6	68.6	70.1	65.5
2006	66.4	65.8	66.1	66.0	66.2	66.9	67.1	67.9	67.8	68.0	71.0	72.4	67.6
2007	69.3	68.6	69.2	69.0	69.3	69.5	69.8	70.3	69.9	70.2	72.9	74.3	70.2
2008	71.1	70.1	70.2	70.2	70.3	71.0	70.6	71.0	70.4	70.7	72.1	72.8	70.9
2009	68.1	66.8	66.6	65.9	66.2	66.3	65.5	66.0	66.1	66.4	68.7	69.6	66.9
2010	66.0	65.3	65.3	65.1	65.3	65.4	65.4	65.8	65.3	65.9	67.9	68.5	65.9
2011	64.8	64.2	64.4	64.9	64.8	65.0	65.8	66.9	65.6	66.2	67.7	69.5	65.8
Transportation and Utilities													
2000	29.2	29.2	29.5	29.5	29.2	29.6	29.9	30.2	30.3	30.5	30.7	31.1	29.9
2001	30.5	30.3	30.3	30.1	29.5	29.4	29.4	29.4	29.4	29.4	29.1	29.2	29.7
2002	28.4	28.6	27.7	27.8	27.6	27.6	27.8	27.7	27.5	28.1	28.0	27.9	27.9
2003	26.9	26.7	26.6	26.2	26.4	26.4	26.6	26.8	26.6	26.7	26.7	26.9	26.6
2004	26.8	26.7	26.7	26.4	26.4	26.7	26.6	26.6	26.5	26.6	26.9	27.2	26.7
2005	27.2	27.8	28.0	28.5	28.5	28.5	28.6	28.6	28.7	28.9	29.2	29.6	28.5
2006	29.3	29.3	29.3	29.2	29.2	29.4	29.4	29.9	30.0	29.9	30.3	31.2	29.7
2007	30.6	30.7	30.8	30.7	30.8	31.0	31.0	31.2	31.5	31.8	32.1	32.6	31.2
2008	31.2	31.2	31.1	31.0	30.9	30.8	30.8	30.8	30.7	30.7	30.6	30.6	30.9
2009	30.0	29.6	29.2	28.7	28.4	28.0	28.1	27.8	27.7	27.6	27.6	27.9	28.4
2010	27.3	27.4	27.4	27.4	27.3	27.6	27.6	27.9	28.0	28.3	28.6	29.1	27.8
2011	28.5	28.5	28.6	28.8	28.6	28.9	28.9	29.3	29.3	29.2	29.4	29.5	29.0
Information													
2000	20.0	20.0	20.1	19.9	20.6	21.2	21.2	21.6	21.7	21.7	22.2	22.0	21.0
2001	21.3	20.7	20.7	20.9	21.3	21.5	21.1	21.0	20.8	20.4	20.8	20.5	20.9
2002	20.0	19.9	19.2	18.9	19.2	19.0	19.0	18.6	18.5	18.6	18.7	18.5	19.0
2003	17.9	17.7	17.6	17.4	18.0	18.1	17.9	18.2	18.0	18.3	18.1	18.4	18.0
2004	17.4	17.9	17.9	17.9	17.8	18.1	17.5	17.5	17.6	17.8	18.3	18.1	17.8
2005	17.9	18.3	18.7	18.2	18.2	18.1	18.6	19.0	18.8	18.4	18.7	18.6	18.5
2006	18.2	18.3	18.3	18.6	19.3	19.4	18.6	18.8	18.7	18.5	18.8	18.7	18.7
2007	18.7	18.6	18.8	17.6	17.8	17.6	17.5	17.7	17.3	17.2	17.3	17.4	17.8
2008	17.0	17.6	17.7	18.0	18.3	18.2	17.9	18.0	17.8	17.5	17.7	17.7	17.8
2009	17.3	17.4	17.2	16.9	17.0	17.2	16.9	16.8	16.6	16.7	16.8	16.9	17.0
2010	16.3	16.4	16.8	16.9	16.8	16.8	16.8	16.5	16.6	16.6	17.2	17.2	16.7
2011	16.3	16.5	16.6	16.3	16.5	16.6	16.7	16.6	16.3	16.2	16.4	16.5	16.5
Financial Activities													
2000	42.4	42.2	42.4	42.3	42.0	42.1	42.4	42.5	42.5	42.8	43.2	44.0	42.6
2001	44.9	45.0	45.2	44.7	44.6	45.0	45.2	45.3	45.2	44.9	45.2	45.6	45.1
2002	46.1	46.0	45.5	45.3	45.5	45.6	45.1	45.3	44.9	45.3	45.1	45.6	45.4
2003	45.7	46.1	45.6	45.9	45.9	45.4	45.5	45.6	45.1	44.9	44.8	45.2	45.5
2004	44.5	44.7	44.7	44.8	44.6	44.4	44.6	44.5	44.5	44.7	45.2	45.8	44.8
2005	45.1	45.5	44.9	45.9	45.7	46.0	46.5	46.6	46.7	46.9	47.3	48.1	46.3
2006	47.6	48.2	48.3	48.5	48.5	48.8	49.2	49.4	49.3	50.0	50.4	51.1	49.1
2007	51.0	51.7	51.8	51.9	52.0	52.1	52.1	52.0	51.7	52.1	52.2	52.6	51.9
2008	51.5	52.0	51.8	51.8	51.5	51.3	51.4	51.4	50.9	50.8	50.5	51.1	51.3
2009	50.4	50.6	50.4	49.8	49.4	49.3	48.6	48.7	48.4	48.2	48.2	48.7	49.2
2010	47.6	47.1	47.2	46.8	46.6	46.6	46.8	47.0	47.1	47.4	47.7	48.0	47.2
2011	47.3	47.5	47.6	47.7	47.5	47.9	48.2	48.5	48.6	48.9	49.1	49.3	48.2

Employment by Industry: Salt Lake City, UT, Selected Years, 2000–2011—*Continued*

(Numbers in thousands, not seasonally adjusted)

Industry and year	January	February	March	April	May	June	July	August	September	October	November	December	Annual average
Professional and Business Services													
2000	84.4	85.7	87.3	88.2	88.7	90.0	90.3	91.0	91.1	91.7	91.7	93.0	89.4
2001	89.6	89.4	89.8	89.6	90.0	90.1	89.1	89.8	88.0	87.0	85.6	85.4	88.6
2002	82.8	85.7	82.6	82.8	83.4	83.3	82.9	84.1	83.5	82.9	83.3	82.6	83.3
2003	79.9	79.9	80.7	81.7	82.5	82.7	83.2	84.1	83.3	83.8	84.0	84.7	82.5
2004	81.8	82.5	83.1	83.9	84.5	85.3	85.7	86.7	85.8	87.5	87.7	88.7	85.3
2005	86.0	86.4	87.0	89.3	90.2	91.3	91.9	93.2	93.5	94.2	95.0	95.6	91.1
2006	92.8	93.6	94.8	96.4	97.2	97.9	98.6	99.0	98.7	98.2	99.2	99.3	97.1
2007	96.5	97.3	97.8	100.0	101.4	102.0	101.6	102.3	101.7	103.3	104.0	103.9	101.0
2008	100.5	100.8	100.8	101.3	101.9	101.7	101.9	102.6	101.8	100.9	99.6	99.1	101.1
2009	94.9	94.5	93.7	93.6	93.6	93.5	93.4	93.4	93.1	93.9	93.7	94.1	93.8
2010	91.4	92.0	93.8	94.6	95.7	96.7	97.3	96.7	95.9	97.0	97.5	98.2	95.6
2011	95.9	96.7	97.4	98.6	98.9	99.1	100.0	101.2	100.7	100.7	102.5	103.3	99.6
Education and Health Services													
2000	43.0	43.6	43.8	43.8	44.1	44.1	43.5	44.1	44.4	44.3	44.7	45.5	44.1
2001	46.3	46.9	47.0	47.3	47.5	47.7	46.9	47.1	47.8	48.0	48.7	49.4	47.6
2002	48.0	48.5	48.4	48.8	48.8	48.8	48.4	49.2	50.1	50.3	50.5	50.9	49.2
2003	50.4	50.7	51.0	50.7	50.8	50.9	50.7	51.1	51.7	52.1	52.3	52.5	51.2
2004	51.7	52.3	52.7	52.7	52.8	52.9	52.6	52.8	53.5	53.9	54.3	54.4	53.1
2005	53.9	54.5	54.5	55.0	55.0	55.1	54.5	54.7	55.5	55.8	56.3	56.4	55.1
2006	55.4	55.9	56.3	56.2	56.5	56.7	55.8	56.8	57.4	58.1	58.4	58.3	56.8
2007	57.8	58.4	58.8	59.2	59.3	59.2	58.8	59.9	60.8	61.1	61.6	61.8	59.7
2008	61.4	62.4	62.5	62.5	62.5	62.3	62.0	62.6	63.5	64.6	65.4	65.5	63.1
2009	64.5	64.8	65.3	65.3	65.2	64.8	64.0	64.7	65.9	67.1	67.5	67.8	65.6
2010	67.1	67.4	67.6	67.8	67.4	67.2	66.5	66.6	68.0	69.0	69.1	69.0	67.7
2011	68.4	69.0	68.9	69.6	68.8	68.4	67.4	68.0	68.8	69.6	69.5	70.0	68.9
Leisure and Hospitality													
2000	49.4	50.4	50.9	49.4	46.3	46.8	47.1	47.9	47.2	47.1	48.9	52.5	48.7
2001	51.9	52.5	53.3	51.5	48.7	48.9	48.8	49.4	48.9	48.1	49.0	52.9	50.3
2002	56.6	61.5	57.7	55.0	50.1	50.3	49.7	50.2	49.2	48.8	50.4	53.6	52.8
2003	53.8	54.1	53.7	51.7	48.5	49.3	49.2	49.9	49.2	48.6	50.6	53.7	51.0
2004	53.5	53.9	54.0	51.9	48.7	49.7	50.0	50.6	50.1	49.5	51.3	54.7	51.5
2005	54.5	55.1	55.3	53.1	50.2	51.0	51.0	51.6	51.2	51.0	52.4	56.2	52.7
2006	56.7	57.1	57.5	56.3	51.8	52.4	52.9	53.9	52.9	52.3	54.5	58.7	54.8
2007	59.2	59.9	59.9	58.4	54.0	55.3	55.1	55.2	54.4	53.5	55.5	60.0	56.7
2008	61.1	61.6	61.6	60.5	55.8	56.6	56.6	56.8	55.6	55.0	55.4	59.3	58.0
2009	59.5	59.4	59.3	58.2	53.5	53.7	53.9	54.2	53.1	52.1	53.0	57.0	55.6
2010	57.6	57.7	58.0	57.7	52.8	54.0	54.2	54.5	53.4	53.2	54.0	59.1	55.5
2011	59.5	59.8	60.1	59.2	54.3	55.5	56.5	57.3	57.3	56.0	58.1	64.4	58.2
Other Services													
2000	17.2	17.3	17.3	17.4	17.6	17.6	17.8	17.9	17.7	17.5	17.6	17.7	17.6
2001	17.0	17.1	17.2	17.3	17.3	17.5	17.9	18.0	17.5	17.5	17.5	17.5	17.4
2002	18.3	19.3	18.6	18.6	18.7	18.7	19.0	19.0	18.6	18.4	18.7	18.4	18.7
2003	18.0	18.0	18.0	18.1	18.0	18.1	18.3	18.4	18.0	17.9	18.0	18.0	18.1
2004	17.7	17.8	18.0	18.2	18.3	18.3	18.9	18.9	18.4	18.1	18.2	18.3	18.3
2005	18.2	18.3	18.5	18.6	18.5	18.6	19.2	19.1	18.9	18.5	18.5	18.7	18.6
2006	18.4	18.5	18.8	18.9	19.1	19.4	19.5	19.5	19.4	19.0	19.0	19.3	19.1
2007	19.0	19.1	19.3	19.3	19.6	19.8	20.1	20.2	19.7	19.5	19.5	19.6	19.6
2008	19.3	19.5	19.6	19.6	19.7	19.8	20.2	20.7	20.0	19.3	19.2	19.3	19.7
2009	18.9	18.9	19.0	19.0	19.1	19.2	19.4	19.4	18.8	18.7	18.5	18.7	19.0
2010	18.6	18.6	18.9	18.6	18.7	18.7	19.1	19.1	18.5	18.6	18.5	18.5	18.7
2011	18.3	18.5	18.5	18.6	18.9	19.1	19.7	19.3	19.2	19.2	18.8	18.8	18.9
Government													
2000	81.7	83.6	83.7	84.9	86.7	83.9	78.8	78.4	84.2	84.8	85.1	85.0	83.4
2001	84.8	86.7	86.7	87.2	87.8	87.0	81.0	80.9	86.8	87.4	87.9	88.7	86.1
2002	88.0	86.5	88.5	88.7	88.1	88.7	85.4	84.1	88.6	88.7	89.1	89.3	87.8
2003	88.9	89.3	89.0	89.5	88.8	88.8	85.2	84.6	88.5	88.9	88.8	88.9	88.3
2004	88.8	89.0	89.0	90.1	89.4	89.6	86.5	86.8	90.1	90.3	90.3	90.8	89.2
2005	90.5	90.8	90.5	91.1	90.6	90.7	88.1	88.4	91.2	91.5	91.8	92.1	90.6
2006	91.4	92.0	91.9	92.1	91.6	92.3	89.2	89.3	92.1	92.5	92.6	93.0	91.7
2007	92.2	92.4	92.4	92.9	92.7	93.4	89.5	90.1	93.0	93.6	93.9	94.2	92.5
2008	93.9	94.2	94.6	94.7	94.8	95.4	91.4	92.5	96.2	96.5	96.8	96.9	94.8
2009	95.9	96.3	96.3	97.0	96.8	96.8	92.5	93.4	96.9	97.5	97.3	97.5	96.2
2010	96.8	96.8	96.9	97.5	99.2	98.3	94.3	94.7	98.7	99.5	99.3	98.4	97.5
2011	97.8	97.9	98.0	98.1	97.9	98.4	94.2	95.2	101.1	102.3	102.2	102.5	98.8

Employment by Industry: San Antonio–New Braunfels, TX, Selected Years, 2000–2011

(Numbers in thousands, not seasonally adjusted)

Industry and year	January	February	March	April	May	June	July	August	September	October	November	December	Annual average
Total Nonfarm													
2000	727.4	734.8	738.4	744.0	751.2	751.2	744.2	746.3	752.1	748.1	750.3	754.5	745.2
2001	737.7	746.7	753.3	754.3	760.4	764.3	753.5	758.6	757.2	750.5	750.7	752.3	753.3
2002	737.2	745.0	751.6	755.2	760.8	759.5	750.6	756.1	760.0	756.5	758.0	758.2	754.1
2003	739.0	745.3	751.3	752.1	755.0	755.2	747.1	751.0	751.9	754.2	756.9	757.4	751.4
2004	742.0	749.8	756.5	759.8	763.3	765.4	759.5	764.0	764.1	763.8	765.7	766.2	760.0
2005	756.7	765.9	771.9	778.3	783.1	785.5	780.7	784.9	789.9	791.2	796.0	799.3	782.0
2006	786.9	795.0	803.7	809.6	814.4	817.5	809.7	814.1	818.7	819.8	823.2	825.8	811.5
2007	809.2	820.1	826.4	829.6	837.1	840.0	833.7	836.6	840.1	840.6	847.8	851.9	834.4
2008	836.0	845.8	850.7	855.5	859.7	860.8	851.9	853.3	853.2	854.3	856.4	855.1	852.7
2009	832.6	837.0	838.3	839.2	840.7	842.3	831.5	830.9	831.6	834.9	839.7	841.1	836.7
2010	825.7	833.7	840.3	844.0	850.8	850.8	839.4	840.7	840.9	847.6	850.2	852.4	843.0
2011	838.1	845.2	853.2	857.4	860.0	862.0	854.6	851.0	849.4	854.5	856.1	856.6	853.2
Total Private													
2000	588.6	593.6	596.8	602.2	607.0	614.0	612.4	613.7	614.0	608.4	610.1	614.5	606.3
2001	598.7	606.2	612.5	613.3	619.2	626.2	622.0	624.0	617.8	610.0	608.7	610.4	614.1
2002	597.0	601.7	607.9	611.9	616.6	620.2	617.6	621.2	618.4	612.3	613.2	613.6	612.6
2003	596.6	600.5	606.6	606.8	609.5	614.1	611.3	613.8	610.7	611.1	612.4	613.4	608.9
2004	600.8	605.3	612.3	615.4	618.4	624.6	623.6	625.5	621.0	619.7	621.3	621.9	617.5
2005	614.2	620.6	626.7	632.7	637.5	642.5	643.6	646.1	646.2	645.3	649.1	652.4	638.1
2006	641.5	647.2	656.1	660.2	665.3	670.7	670.3	673.5	672.4	670.4	672.9	675.8	664.7
2007	660.5	669.0	674.9	678.4	685.7	691.3	690.2	692.6	689.6	689.6	694.7	697.8	684.5
2008	683.0	690.3	694.8	700.0	704.0	705.9	703.8	704.5	700.5	697.0	697.8	696.9	698.2
2009	675.5	677.3	678.4	677.9	680.4	683.1	679.2	678.9	674.1	673.7	677.3	679.2	677.9
2010	666.5	671.4	677.2	680.4	684.7	687.7	685.4	685.0	680.3	683.5	685.4	688.2	681.3
2011	676.5	681.0	689.6	693.6	696.7	700.3	700.2	697.4	691.5	695.1	696.4	696.8	692.9
Goods-Producing													
2000	97.2	98.1	98.3	98.4	99.7	101.5	100.7	100.5	100.8	99.9	99.4	100.3	99.6
2001	98.0	98.7	99.8	99.7	100.4	101.6	101.6	101.5	101.3	99.2	97.9	98.0	99.8
2002	95.6	95.4	96.3	96.1	96.4	97.3	96.5	96.0	94.7	93.2	92.9	92.9	95.3
2003	91.0	91.5	91.4	91.8	92.1	92.5	91.9	91.8	91.4	91.1	90.6	90.6	91.5
2004	88.8	89.0	89.4	90.0	90.1	91.0	91.7	91.4	91.4	91.8	91.8	91.8	90.7
2005	90.6	91.2	92.4	93.8	94.0	94.7	95.1	94.9	95.6	95.4	95.7	96.7	94.2
2006	96.0	97.4	98.8	98.2	99.0	100.4	100.1	100.2	100.7	99.9	100.1	100.3	99.3
2007	98.8	100.2	100.6	100.7	101.9	103.6	103.2	103.6	103.3	104.0	104.0	104.6	102.4
2008	103.2	104.0	104.4	104.6	105.1	105.7	104.4	104.5	103.5	102.8	101.9	100.5	103.7
2009	97.6	96.5	95.9	95.3	94.9	94.7	94.3	93.8	92.8	92.0	91.6	91.6	94.3
2010	90.7	90.2	90.4	91.0	91.2	91.1	91.5	91.0	90.1	90.4	90.0	90.0	90.6
2011	88.5	88.7	89.5	90.0	90.3	90.9	91.0	91.9	92.0	91.1	92.1	90.0	90.5
Mining and Logging													
2000	2.6	2.8	2.8	2.7	2.7	2.7	2.6	2.5	2.7	2.7	2.6	2.7	2.7
2001	2.7	2.7	2.8	3.0	3.0	3.1	3.1	3.2	3.3	3.5	3.6	3.6	3.1
2002	3.1	3.0	3.1	2.8	2.8	2.7	3.2	3.2	3.1	3.1	3.2	3.1	3.0
2003	2.5	2.7	2.7	2.8	2.7	2.8	2.8	2.8	2.9	2.9	2.9	3.0	2.8
2004	2.9	2.9	2.9	2.8	2.8	2.8	2.7	2.7	2.5	2.4	2.4	2.3	2.7
2005	2.3	2.4	2.4	2.4	2.4	2.5	2.6	2.6	2.6	2.8	2.8	2.8	2.6
2006	2.9	3.0	3.0	3.0	3.1	3.0	3.0	3.1	3.1	3.0	3.1	3.1	3.0
2007	3.0	3.1	3.1	3.1	3.2	3.2	3.2	3.3	3.3	3.4	3.4	3.5	3.2
2008	3.4	3.4	3.4	3.5	3.6	3.7	3.6	3.6	3.5	3.5	3.4	3.3	3.5
2009	3.3	3.2	3.2	3.1	3.0	3.0	3.0	3.0	3.0	2.9	3.0	3.0	3.1
2010	2.9	3.0	2.9	2.9	3.0	3.0	3.0	3.0	2.9	2.9	2.9	2.9	2.9
2011	2.8	2.9	2.9	2.9	3.0	3.0	3.1	3.1	3.1	3.2	3.2	3.2	3.0
Construction													
2000	39.7	39.9	40.2	40.0	40.6	41.7	41.7	42.2	42.0	41.3	41.4	41.5	41.0
2001	40.9	41.6	42.5	42.4	43.2	44.6	45.1	45.6	45.1	43.4	43.3	43.1	43.4
2002	42.2	42.5	43.0	43.4	43.9	44.6	43.7	43.9	43.0	42.0	41.6	41.4	42.9
2003	41.3	41.1	41.3	41.5	42.1	42.5	42.4	42.6	42.0	41.9	41.6	41.6	41.8
2004	40.6	40.5	40.8	41.1	41.5	42.4	42.8	43.1	43.1	43.4	43.6	43.8	42.2
2005	43.0	43.3	44.4	45.6	45.9	46.4	46.3	46.3	46.7	46.1	46.1	46.5	45.6
2006	45.9	46.7	47.6	47.4	47.7	48.7	48.3	48.3	48.2	47.6	47.5	47.4	47.6
2007	46.6	47.8	48.7	48.6	49.5	50.8	50.7	51.1	50.9	51.4	51.5	52.1	50.0
2008	51.6	52.7	53.2	53.6	54.0	54.5	53.9	54.2	53.7	53.3	52.6	51.6	53.2
2009	49.6	49.0	48.7	48.5	48.4	48.6	48.3	48.0	47.1	46.1	45.5	45.1	47.7
2010	44.6	43.9	44.3	44.5	44.3	43.8	44.1	43.5	42.6	42.5	41.9	41.8	43.5
2011	40.4	40.5	41.4	41.7	41.8	42.0	41.9	42.6	42.7	41.6	42.5	40.3	41.6
Manufacturing													
2000	54.9	55.4	55.3	55.7	56.4	57.1	56.4	55.8	56.1	55.9	55.4	56.1	55.9
2001	54.4	54.4	54.5	54.3	54.2	53.9	53.4	52.7	52.9	52.3	51.0	51.3	53.3
2002	50.3	49.9	50.2	49.9	49.7	50.0	49.6	48.9	48.6	48.1	48.1	48.4	49.3
2003	47.2	47.7	47.4	47.5	47.3	47.2	46.7	46.4	46.5	46.3	46.1	46.0	46.9
2004	45.3	45.6	45.7	46.1	45.8	45.8	46.2	45.6	45.8	46.0	45.8	45.7	45.8
2005	45.3	45.5	45.6	45.8	45.7	45.8	46.2	46.0	46.3	46.5	46.8	47.4	46.1
2006	47.2	47.7	48.2	47.8	48.2	48.7	48.8	48.8	49.4	49.3	49.5	49.8	48.6
2007	49.2	49.3	48.8	49.0	49.2	49.6	49.3	49.2	49.1	49.2	49.1	49.0	49.2
2008	48.2	47.9	47.8	47.5	47.5	47.5	46.9	46.7	46.3	46.0	45.9	45.6	47.0
2009	44.7	44.3	44.0	43.7	43.5	43.1	43.0	42.8	42.7	43.0	43.1	43.5	43.5
2010	43.2	43.3	43.2	43.6	43.9	44.3	44.4	44.5	44.6	45.0	45.2	45.3	44.2
2011	45.3	45.3	45.2	45.4	45.5	45.9	46.0	46.2	46.2	46.3	46.4	46.5	45.9

Employment by Industry: San Antonio–New Braunfels, TX, Selected Years, 2000–2011—*Continued*

(Numbers in thousands, not seasonally adjusted)

Industry and year	January	February	March	April	May	June	July	August	September	October	November	December	Annual average
Service-Providing													
2000	630.2	636.7	640.1	645.6	651.5	649.7	643.5	645.8	651.3	648.2	650.9	654.2	645.6
2001	639.7	648.0	653.5	654.6	660.0	662.7	651.9	657.1	655.9	651.3	652.8	654.3	653.5
2002	641.6	649.6	655.3	659.1	664.4	662.2	654.1	660.1	665.3	663.3	665.1	665.3	658.8
2003	648.0	653.8	659.9	660.3	662.9	662.7	655.2	659.2	660.5	663.1	666.3	666.8	659.9
2004	653.2	660.8	667.1	669.8	673.2	674.4	667.8	672.6	672.7	672.0	673.9	674.4	669.3
2005	666.1	674.7	679.5	684.5	689.1	690.8	685.6	690.0	694.3	695.8	700.3	702.6	687.8
2006	690.9	697.6	704.9	711.4	715.4	717.1	709.6	713.9	718.0	719.9	723.1	725.5	712.3
2007	710.4	719.9	725.8	728.9	735.2	736.4	730.5	733.0	736.8	736.6	743.8	747.3	732.1
2008	732.8	741.8	746.3	750.9	754.6	755.1	747.5	748.8	749.7	751.5	754.5	754.6	749.0
2009	735.0	740.5	742.4	743.9	745.8	747.6	737.2	737.1	738.8	742.9	748.1	749.5	742.4
2010	735.0	743.5	749.9	753.0	759.6	759.7	747.9	749.7	750.8	757.2	760.2	762.4	752.4
2011	749.6	756.5	763.7	767.4	769.7	771.1	763.6	759.1	757.4	763.4	764.0	766.6	762.7
Trade, Transportation, and Utilities													
2000	135.2	134.7	134.6	135.5	136.0	137.6	138.0	139.4	139.2	140.5	143.4	145.6	138.3
2001	139.3	139.2	140.3	139.8	140.3	140.4	139.4	140.0	139.1	138.7	140.8	142.1	140.0
2002	136.7	135.3	136.4	137.2	137.8	137.9	137.7	138.3	138.5	137.8	140.2	141.2	137.9
2003	134.0	133.2	134.3	133.6	133.5	133.9	134.0	134.4	134.7	136.7	138.3	139.9	135.0
2004	134.4	133.9	135.0	135.6	135.8	135.9	136.2	137.5	136.9	137.4	139.6	141.2	136.6
2005	136.5	136.1	137.1	137.8	138.3	138.8	139.7	140.5	140.0	140.8	143.9	145.5	139.6
2006	141.0	140.4	142.0	142.0	142.5	142.8	143.1	144.5	144.7	146.8	150.7	152.7	144.4
2007	147.7	146.5	147.5	147.5	148.1	148.3	149.5	150.4	149.6	150.2	153.8	155.6	149.6
2008	149.9	149.4	150.2	149.5	149.4	149.6	150.3	151.5	150.0	150.4	152.1	152.6	150.4
2009	146.1	144.6	143.7	143.4	143.3	143.6	143.1	144.1	143.2	143.3	145.4	146.4	144.2
2010	141.3	140.4	140.9	141.4	141.5	141.9	141.7	142.9	141.9	143.2	145.4	147.3	142.5
2011	143.0	141.8	142.7	143.5	143.4	144.1	144.6	144.3	145.7	147.1	148.5	150.2	144.9
Wholesale Trade													
2000	26.2	26.4	26.6	26.5	26.6	26.9	27.2	27.2	27.4	27.4	27.2	27.4	26.9
2001	27.1	27.2	27.3	27.5	27.7	27.8	27.8	27.9	27.8	27.6	27.6	27.8	27.6
2002	27.0	26.9	27.1	27.1	27.2	27.4	27.4	27.4	27.3	27.2	27.3	27.3	27.2
2003	26.6	26.7	26.9	26.9	27.0	27.2	27.4	27.3	27.4	27.5	27.3	27.2	27.1
2004	27.0	27.0	27.0	27.1	27.1	27.1	27.2	27.1	26.8	26.7	26.3	26.2	26.9
2005	26.3	26.4	26.5	26.7	26.9	27.1	27.2	27.3	27.3	27.1	27.4	27.5	27.0
2006	27.5	27.6	27.7	27.8	28.0	28.4	28.4	28.5	28.6	28.7	29.1	29.1	28.3
2007	28.9	29.0	29.2	29.4	29.5	29.6	29.6	29.7	29.6	29.7	29.7	29.8	29.5
2008	29.3	29.4	29.4	29.4	29.4	29.5	29.5	29.7	29.5	29.4	29.3	29.1	29.4
2009	28.8	28.7	28.5	28.5	28.5	28.5	28.0	28.0	27.9	28.1	28.1	28.0	28.3
2010	27.9	27.9	27.3	28.1	28.1	28.3	28.2	28.3	28.3	28.6	28.5	28.5	28.2
2011	28.1	28.2	28.5	28.6	28.6	28.9	28.9	28.9	28.8	28.9	28.9	28.9	28.7
Retail Trade													
2000	88.8	88.3	88.2	89.0	89.3	90.4	90.6	91.7	91.3	92.2	95.0	96.8	91.0
2001	91.3	91.3	92.1	91.5	91.7	91.9	91.2	91.7	91.0	91.6	94.0	95.3	92.1
2002	90.9	89.5	90.0	90.7	90.9	90.6	90.5	90.9	91.4	90.7	92.8	93.9	91.1
2003	87.6	86.7	87.4	87.2	86.9	86.9	86.8	87.3	87.3	89.0	90.8	92.3	88.0
2004	87.4	86.7	87.6	88.2	88.2	88.3	88.6	90.0	89.7	90.4	92.9	94.4	89.4
2005	90.0	89.4	90.2	90.6	90.6	90.7	91.3	91.8	91.1	92.2	94.6	95.9	91.5
2006	92.0	91.2	92.4	92.3	92.5	92.3	92.7	93.9	93.9	95.9	99.2	100.8	94.1
2007	96.6	95.1	95.7	95.4	96.0	96.0	97.3	98.0	97.4	98.1	101.7	103.3	97.6
2008	98.8	98.2	98.9	98.3	98.1	98.3	98.8	99.9	98.7	99.3	101.1	101.7	99.2
2009	96.2	95.1	94.4	94.6	94.5	94.9	95.1	96.1	95.4	95.3	97.3	98.4	95.6
2010	93.8	93.0	93.8	93.5	93.7	93.8	93.7	94.8	93.7	94.7	96.9	98.5	94.5
2011	94.7	93.4	93.9	94.5	94.4	94.6	95.1	94.7	96.1	97.3	98.8	100.3	95.7
Transportation and Utilities													
2000	20.2	20.0	19.8	20.0	20.1	20.3	20.2	20.5	20.5	20.9	21.2	21.4	20.4
2001	20.9	20.7	20.9	20.8	20.9	20.7	20.4	20.4	20.3	19.5	19.2	19.0	20.3
2002	18.8	18.9	19.3	19.4	19.7	19.9	19.8	20.0	19.8	19.9	20.1	20.0	19.6
2003	19.8	19.8	20.0	19.5	19.6	19.8	19.8	19.8	20.0	20.2	20.2	20.4	19.9
2004	20.0	20.2	20.4	20.3	20.5	20.5	20.4	20.4	20.4	20.3	20.4	20.6	20.4
2005	20.2	20.3	20.4	20.5	20.8	21.0	21.2	21.4	21.6	21.5	21.9	22.1	21.1
2006	21.5	21.6	21.9	21.9	22.0	22.1	22.0	22.1	22.2	22.2	22.4	22.8	22.1
2007	22.2	22.4	22.6	22.7	22.6	22.7	22.6	22.7	22.6	22.4	22.4	22.5	22.5
2008	21.8	21.8	21.9	21.8	21.9	21.8	22.0	21.9	21.8	21.7	21.7	21.8	21.8
2009	21.1	20.8	20.8	20.3	20.3	20.2	20.0	20.0	19.9	19.9	20.0	20.0	20.3
2010	19.6	19.5	19.8	19.8	19.7	19.8	19.8	19.8	19.9	19.9	20.0	20.3	19.8
2011	20.2	20.2	20.3	20.4	20.4	20.6	20.6	20.7	20.8	20.9	20.8	21.0	20.6
Information													
2000	22.9	23.1	23.0	24.1	24.6	24.9	25.3	25.5	25.8	25.5	25.6	25.3	24.6
2001	24.4	24.5	24.5	24.7	24.6	25.0	25.0	25.1	24.7	24.9	24.8	24.9	24.8
2002	24.5	24.4	24.1	23.9	23.9	23.8	22.9	22.9	22.5	22.7	22.8	22.4	23.4
2003	22.2	22.0	22.2	22.2	22.3	22.4	22.6	22.5	22.4	22.4	22.7	22.5	22.4
2004	22.0	21.8	21.8	22.2	22.2	22.0	21.9	21.7	21.3	21.4	21.3	21.0	21.7
2005	20.6	20.7	20.5	20.2	20.4	20.8	20.7	20.8	20.7	20.8	21.1	21.1	20.7
2006	20.7	20.5	20.6	20.6	21.0	21.0	21.3	21.2	21.3	21.1	21.4	21.7	21.9	21.1
2007	21.7	21.9	21.7	21.6	21.8	21.8	21.8	21.6	21.4	21.4	21.5	21.5	21.6
2008	21.5	21.6	21.7	21.5	21.7	21.5	21.1	21.0	20.7	20.8	20.8	20.6	21.2
2009	20.5	20.5	20.6	20.2	19.9	19.5	19.1	18.9	18.5	18.4	18.4	18.3	19.4
2010	18.2	18.2	18.6	19.1	18.9	18.6	18.4	18.2	18.0	17.8	18.1	18.1	18.4
2011	18.3	18.4	18.7	19.0	18.9	18.5	18.4	18.3	18.1	18.0	18.2	18.1	18.4

Employment by Industry: San Antonio–New Braunfels, TX, Selected Years, 2000–2011—*Continued*

(Numbers in thousands, not seasonally adjusted)

Industry and year	January	February	March	April	May	June	July	August	September	October	November	December	Annual average
Financial Activities													
2000	55.7	56.1	56.2	56.8	56.8	57.3	57.1	56.7	56.7	56.9	57.1	57.6	56.8
2001	57.1	57.7	58.2	58.3	58.9	59.5	59.5	59.8	59.6	58.7	58.9	59.3	58.8
2002	58.7	58.8	59.1	59.4	59.9	60.1	60.1	60.4	60.3	60.6	60.8	61.2	60.0
2003	60.2	60.4	60.7	60.5	60.5	61.0	60.9	61.1	60.7	60.6	60.7	61.1	60.7
2004	60.6	60.7	60.8	61.5	61.6	62.0	62.3	62.3	62.2	61.5	61.7	61.8	61.6
2005	61.2	61.4	61.3	61.5	61.8	62.3	63.3	63.4	63.3	63.4	63.4	63.7	62.5
2006	63.0	63.1	63.2	63.6	63.9	64.2	64.4	64.3	64.4	64.5	64.6	64.9	64.0
2007	64.3	64.9	64.7	65.4	65.9	65.8	65.8	65.6	65.3	65.5	65.6	65.8	65.4
2008	65.1	65.4	65.2	67.0	67.3	67.1	67.5	66.9	66.6	66.3	65.9	66.5	66.4
2009	64.8	65.0	64.4	64.5	64.8	65.3	65.7	65.7	65.6	65.8	65.8	66.1	65.3
2010	65.7	66.3	66.4	66.3	67.0	67.6	67.5	67.4	66.9	67.8	68.2	68.6	67.1
2011	68.0	68.8	69.1	69.3	69.5	69.8	69.9	69.5	70.0	71.0	71.0	69.6	69.6
Professional and Business Services													
2000	85.3	85.9	86.3	88.6	90.0	92.0	92.4	92.4	91.5	90.5	89.7	90.3	89.6
2001	88.2	89.0	89.4	89.8	90.2	92.2	90.7	90.7	88.5	85.9	84.7	85.5	88.7
2002	83.3	84.6	85.2	86.7	87.1	88.0	88.7	90.1	90.1	89.0	88.1	87.8	87.4
2003	84.6	85.6	87.0	86.8	87.7	88.2	87.7	89.0	88.1	88.6	89.0	88.4	87.6
2004	87.0	87.6	88.7	88.9	89.2	90.5	89.5	90.4	89.5	89.4	89.3	89.4	89.1
2005	92.2	93.7	94.1	96.7	97.4	97.9	96.7	97.8	99.4	99.9	100.0	101.1	97.2
2006	98.9	100.3	101.9	103.7	104.5	104.9	105.1	105.8	105.7	103.9	103.4	104.1	103.5
2007	101.5	102.7	103.4	104.8	105.7	106.3	105.6	106.3	106.4	107.0	107.6	107.5	105.4
2008	106.8	108.3	108.5	109.3	108.9	108.7	106.5	106.6	107.0	105.6	105.4	104.7	107.2
2009	101.3	100.8	100.9	99.9	99.5	100.3	98.2	99.2	98.6	100.0	101.5	102.7	100.2
2010	101.6	102.3	102.7	101.8	101.2	101.7	100.3	100.5	100.2	101.3	101.2	101.2	101.3
2011	100.8	101.8	102.9	102.7	102.1	102.4	101.4	98.9	98.6	98.8	97.8	100.1	100.7
Education and Health Services													
2000	89.7	91.3	91.0	90.4	90.5	89.1	88.6	89.4	92.1	90.7	91.0	90.9	90.4
2001	89.8	92.0	92.6	92.1	92.8	92.3	91.8	93.4	94.5	95.3	95.8	95.7	93.2
2002	94.5	96.1	96.4	96.7	97.0	95.8	95.0	96.7	98.6	98.9	99.4	99.5	97.1
2003	97.9	99.0	99.2	99.5	99.4	99.1	97.9	99.5	101.1	101.6	101.9	101.8	99.8
2004	101.4	102.1	102.9	102.7	102.5	103.1	101.9	103.2	103.7	105.2	105.5	105.6	103.3
2005	103.8	105.6	106.1	105.5	105.6	105.3	105.4	106.7	108.7	109.1	109.7	110.2	106.8
2006	108.4	109.6	110.3	109.4	109.8	109.4	108.4	110.2	112.1	112.0	112.1	112.1	110.3
2007	110.0	112.4	113.1	112.7	113.5	113.3	112.7	113.8	115.1	115.7	116.5	116.9	113.8
2008	113.9	116.0	116.0	116.7	117.7	116.6	116.4	117.5	119.8	120.9	121.4	122.2	117.9
2009	119.3	121.0	121.4	122.0	122.9	122.2	122.4	122.5	124.0	125.2	125.7	125.9	122.9
2010	124.3	126.2	126.8	127.2	127.7	127.9	127.3	127.6	128.5	129.7	129.9	130.2	127.8
2011	128.4	129.3	130.0	130.5	131.0	130.8	131.2	131.7	130.4	133.3	133.0	132.8	131.0
Leisure and Hospitality													
2000	75.5	77.1	79.9	80.6	81.4	83.0	81.8	81.4	79.6	76.9	76.3	76.6	79.2
2001	74.5	77.4	79.6	81.0	83.8	86.4	85.4	84.9	81.9	79.6	77.8	77.2	80.8
2002	76.2	79.2	82.3	83.5	85.8	88.1	88.0	88.0	84.9	81.7	80.1	80.0	83.2
2003	78.5	80.5	83.1	84.0	85.6	88.1	88.0	87.2	84.3	82.6	81.3	81.4	83.7
2004	79.2	82.5	85.8	86.8	89.2	91.9	92.5	91.4	88.6	86.2	85.0	84.2	86.9
2005	82.8	85.4	88.4	90.0	92.8	95.1	95.1	94.5	91.0	89.0	88.3	87.2	90.0
2006	86.8	88.9	92.0	94.6	96.2	98.9	99.3	98.5	94.9	93.4	91.5	91.3	93.9
2007	89.0	92.4	95.7	97.3	100.0	102.7	102.3	101.8	98.7	96.1	95.4	95.7	97.3
2008	92.7	95.3	98.1	100.4	102.7	105.2	106.0	105.0	101.7	99.5	99.4	99.1	100.4
2009	95.5	98.2	100.8	101.8	103.9	106.0	105.2	103.6	100.7	98.4	97.7	97.3	100.8
2010	94.1	96.9	100.3	102.2	105.5	107.1	107.1	105.8	103.1	101.8	101.1	101.0	102.2
2011	98.6	101.0	105.4	106.9	109.7	111.8	111.8	111.0	105.0	104.3	103.9	104.3	106.1
Other Services													
2000	27.1	27.3	27.5	27.8	28.0	28.6	28.5	28.4	28.3	27.5	27.6	27.9	27.9
2001	27.4	27.7	28.1	27.9	28.2	28.8	28.6	28.6	28.2	27.7	28.0	27.7	28.1
2002	27.5	27.9	28.1	28.4	28.7	29.2	28.7	28.8	28.8	28.4	28.9	28.6	28.5
2003	28.2	28.3	28.7	28.4	28.4	28.9	28.3	28.3	28.0	27.5	27.9	27.7	28.2
2004	27.4	27.7	27.9	27.7	27.8	28.2	27.6	27.6	27.4	26.8	27.1	26.9	27.5
2005	26.5	26.5	26.8	27.2	27.2	27.6	27.6	27.5	27.5	26.9	27.0	26.9	27.1
2006	26.7	27.0	27.3	28.1	28.4	28.8	28.7	28.7	28.8	28.5	28.8	28.5	28.2
2007	27.5	28.0	28.2	28.4	28.8	29.5	29.3	29.5	29.8	29.7	30.3	30.2	29.1
2008	29.9	30.3	30.7	31.0	31.2	31.5	31.6	31.5	31.2	30.7	30.9	30.7	30.9
2009	30.4	30.7	30.7	30.8	31.2	31.5	31.2	31.1	30.7	30.6	31.2	30.9	30.9
2010	30.6	30.9	31.1	31.4	31.7	31.8	31.6	31.6	31.6	31.5	31.5	31.8	31.4
2011	30.9	31.2	31.3	31.7	31.8	32.0	31.9	31.8	31.7	31.5	31.9	31.7	31.6
Government													
2000	138.8	141.2	141.6	141.8	144.2	137.2	131.8	132.6	138.1	139.7	140.2	140.0	138.9
2001	139.0	140.5	140.8	141.0	141.2	138.1	131.5	134.6	139.4	140.5	142.0	141.9	139.2
2002	140.2	143.3	143.7	143.3	144.2	139.3	133.0	134.9	141.6	144.2	144.8	144.6	141.4
2003	142.4	144.8	144.7	145.3	145.5	141.1	135.8	137.2	141.2	143.1	144.5	144.0	142.5
2004	141.2	144.5	144.2	144.4	144.9	140.8	135.9	138.5	143.1	144.1	144.4	144.3	142.5
2005	142.5	145.3	145.2	145.6	145.6	143.0	137.1	138.8	143.7	145.9	146.9	146.9	143.9
2006	145.4	147.8	147.6	149.4	149.1	146.8	139.4	140.6	146.3	149.4	150.3	150.0	146.8
2007	148.7	151.1	151.5	151.2	151.4	148.7	143.5	144.0	150.5	151.0	153.1	154.1	149.9
2008	153.0	155.5	155.9	155.5	155.7	154.9	148.1	148.8	152.7	157.3	158.6	158.2	154.5
2009	157.1	159.7	159.9	161.3	160.3	159.2	152.3	152.0	157.5	161.2	162.4	161.9	158.7
2010	159.2	162.3	163.1	163.6	166.1	163.1	154.0	155.7	160.6	164.1	164.8	164.2	161.7
2011	161.6	164.2	163.6	163.8	163.3	161.7	154.4	153.6	157.9	159.4	159.7	159.8	160.3

Employment by Industry: San Diego–Carlsbad–San Marcos, CA, Selected Years, 2000–2011

(Numbers in thousands, not seasonally adjusted)

Industry and year	January	February	March	April	May	June	July	August	September	October	November	December	Annual average
Total Nonfarm													
2000	1,164.0	1,173.7	1,184.2	1,184.7	1,197.1	1,203.0	1,185.6	1,188.4	1,198.8	1,206.3	1,215.1	1,224.9	1,193.8
2001	1,196.9	1,205.6	1,214.0	1,217.7	1,225.6	1,229.6	1,211.1	1,213.2	1,216.6	1,225.4	1,231.0	1,234.5	1,218.4
2002	1,206.9	1,217.6	1,224.4	1,230.8	1,237.5	1,244.2	1,220.8	1,225.6	1,225.6	1,237.5	1,245.5	1,251.7	1,230.7
2003	1,221.4	1,226.7	1,231.8	1,236.6	1,240.9	1,246.5	1,234.0	1,240.3	1,240.5	1,249.9	1,252.5	1,260.5	1,240.1
2004	1,234.1	1,240.9	1,248.8	1,256.1	1,260.4	1,267.4	1,259.0	1,260.7	1,263.4	1,271.3	1,276.8	1,285.1	1,260.3
2005	1,256.1	1,264.3	1,271.3	1,280.8	1,285.5	1,290.9	1,279.3	1,282.4	1,287.3	1,287.0	1,296.2	1,303.9	1,282.1
2006	1,277.8	1,287.2	1,293.9	1,295.0	1,303.5	1,312.3	1,297.6	1,301.8	1,306.3	1,306.9	1,316.9	1,319.5	1,301.6
2007	1,288.8	1,297.3	1,304.9	1,303.0	1,311.6	1,320.0	1,310.7	1,311.3	1,310.6	1,309.6	1,316.1	1,322.1	1,308.8
2008	1,291.2	1,299.5	1,304.2	1,303.5	1,307.4	1,311.2	1,299.3	1,298.8	1,294.6	1,293.5	1,292.6	1,289.1	1,298.7
2009	1,251.9	1,247.8	1,245.3	1,237.2	1,238.8	1,238.0	1,214.8	1,215.0	1,210.3	1,221.2	1,226.9	1,228.5	1,231.3
2010	1,199.4	1,203.0	1,207.8	1,221.3	1,232.2	1,233.7	1,222.5	1,225.7	1,224.2	1,229.7	1,234.8	1,239.3	1,222.8
2011	1,217.1	1,224.9	1,229.0	1,229.7	1,233.0	1,236.9	1,219.6	1,223.0	1,226.2	1,238.1	1,245.3	1,251.0	1,231.2
Total Private													
2000	956.9	965.5	973.6	975.5	983.6	993.5	990.4	996.0	997.4	997.4	1,003.6	1,013.0	987.2
2001	986.9	993.0	999.3	1,000.8	1,006.3	1,011.6	1,008.7	1,011.9	1,006.9	1,009.9	1,013.8	1,004.7
2002	987.0	994.8	1,000.7	1,007.7	1,014.7	1,021.0	1,010.1	1,015.2	1,012.7	1,016.1	1,022.7	1,029.2	1,011.0
2003	1,000.5	1,005.2	1,009.6	1,014.9	1,019.9	1,025.5	1,025.0	1,032.0	1,028.8	1,033.0	1,035.8	1,044.0	1,022.9
2004	1,021.0	1,025.1	1,032.1	1,037.5	1,043.0	1,049.6	1,053.1	1,056.2	1,052.4	1,054.4	1,059.6	1,068.3	1,046.0
2005	1,041.1	1,047.5	1,053.7	1,062.8	1,066.8	1,071.8	1,071.4	1,077.1	1,075.8	1,071.0	1,078.3	1,086.4	1,067.0
2006	1,061.6	1,068.4	1,074.2	1,075.1	1,083.5	1,091.1	1,087.0	1,093.6	1,091.8	1,086.7	1,094.0	1,096.4	1,083.6
2007	1,067.3	1,073.6	1,079.9	1,077.9	1,086.6	1,094.3	1,095.8	1,099.1	1,092.5	1,085.2	1,090.2	1,095.0	1,086.5
2008	1,067.0	1,072.0	1,075.5	1,075.7	1,078.6	1,081.1	1,082.6	1,083.5	1,074.5	1,066.7	1,064.6	1,061.7	1,073.6
2009	1,025.7	1,020.9	1,016.8	1,007.4	1,009.3	1,008.0	1,000.2	1,002.8	994.2	994.8	999.3	1,002.1	1,006.8
2010	974.9	977.4	980.5	986.6	991.5	995.8	997.0	1,001.8	996.7	997.8	1,001.5	1,007.1	992.4
2011	987.0	992.0	995.2	995.9	1,000.3	1,003.3	1,005.5	1,009.4	1,002.9	1,007.4	1,013.5	1,020.3	1,002.7
Goods-Producing													
2000	186.6	187.4	187.8	188.8	190.2	192.8	191.5	192.4	192.3	192.6	193.2	194.7	190.9
2001	193.1	194.0	195.2	195.1	196.2	196.4	196.1	196.6	194.3	194.0	193.0	191.6	194.6
2002	188.2	188.5	189.5	189.5	191.1	191.8	189.3	189.9	188.9	188.0	187.7	186.9	189.1
2003	182.1	180.5	182.9	183.0	185.0	186.9	188.0	189.6	188.5	188.0	186.9	188.3	185.8
2004	185.9	187.0	189.0	190.1	191.6	193.2	195.1	195.8	195.7	195.6	195.0	195.0	192.4
2005	189.0	191.7	193.6	195.0	196.8	197.9	198.8	198.9	198.0	196.2	195.8	196.6	195.7
2006	194.2	196.1	197.4	196.6	198.8	200.3	198.4	198.8	198.1	196.0	195.6	194.6	197.1
2007	189.8	190.4	191.4	189.9	191.6	193.1	192.2	191.6	189.5	187.0	185.9	185.3	189.8
2008	181.0	181.0	181.3	180.3	180.9	181.6	181.6	181.2	180.6	179.0	177.0	174.5	172.1	179.2
2009	167.4	164.5	163.1	159.4	158.2	157.3	154.7	154.1	151.9	150.9	150.2	149.8	156.8
2010	148.3	147.3	147.9	149.5	149.8	149.6	149.4	149.8	148.6	147.7	147.8	147.9	148.6
2011	146.8	147.3	147.6	147.9	148.3	149.2	149.6	150.2	149.4	148.4	147.4	148.4	148.4
Mining and Logging													
2000	0.3	0.3	0.3	0.3	0.3	0.3	0.3	0.3	0.3	0.3	0.3	0.3	0.3
2001	0.3	0.3	0.3	0.3	0.3	0.3	0.3	0.3	0.3	0.3	0.3	0.3	0.3
2002	0.3	0.3	0.3	0.3	0.3	0.3	0.3	0.3	0.3	0.3	0.3	0.3	0.3
2003	0.3	0.3	0.3	0.3	0.3	0.3	0.3	0.4	0.4	0.4	0.4	0.4	0.3
2004	0.4	0.4	0.4	0.4	0.4	0.4	0.4	0.4	0.4	0.4	0.4	0.4	0.4
2005	0.4	0.4	0.4	0.4	0.4	0.4	0.4	0.4	0.4	0.4	0.4	0.4	0.4
2006	0.5	0.4	0.4	0.4	0.5	0.5	0.5	0.5	0.5	0.5	0.5	0.5	0.5
2007	0.4	0.4	0.4	0.4	0.4	0.4	0.4	0.4	0.4	0.4	0.4	0.4	0.4
2008	0.4	0.4	0.4	0.4	0.4	0.4	0.4	0.4	0.4	0.4	0.4	0.4	0.4
2009	0.4	0.4	0.4	0.4	0.4	0.4	0.4	0.4	0.4	0.3	0.3	0.3	0.4
2010	0.4	0.4	0.4	0.4	0.4	0.4	0.4	0.4	0.4	0.4	0.4	0.4	0.4
2011	0.4	0.4	0.4	0.4	0.4	0.4	0.4	0.4	0.4	0.4	0.4	0.4	0.4
Construction													
2000	66.4	67.1	67.2	67.3	68.3	70.1	70.8	71.9	72.2	71.6	71.9	73.0	69.8
2001	72.3	72.5	73.1	73.9	75.5	75.9	76.2	77.4	76.4	77.0	76.4	75.8	75.2
2002	73.6	73.3	74.0	75.3	76.9	77.7	77.0	78.2	77.6	77.9	77.8	78.0	76.4
2003	75.9	74.5	76.2	76.5	78.9	80.7	82.8	84.3	83.5	83.4	82.3	83.2	80.2
2004	82.5	83.4	84.8	85.8	86.8	88.0	89.5	90.4	90.9	90.7	90.0	89.8	87.7
2005	84.1	86.6	88.5	89.9	91.5	92.7	93.4	93.7	93.5	91.9	91.6	92.4	90.8
2006	90.5	91.8	92.5	92.1	94.1	95.1	93.4	94.2	93.7	92.2	91.6	90.7	92.7
2007	86.8	87.6	88.3	87.9	89.5	90.9	89.1	88.8	87.0	83.9	82.4	81.3	87.0
2008	78.0	78.0	77.9	77.0	77.5	77.9	77.7	76.9	75.7	73.8	72.0	70.2	76.1
2009	66.0	64.2	63.9	62.1	62.1	61.7	60.5	60.4	58.7	58.4	58.0	57.5	61.1
2010	55.7	54.8	55.0	55.6	56.0	56.1	56.2	56.2	55.3	54.5	54.4	54.1	55.3
2011	53.6	54.1	54.3	54.5	54.8	55.3	56.2	57.3	56.5	55.2	54.6	55.9	55.2
Manufacturing													
2000	119.9	120.0	120.3	121.2	121.6	122.4	120.4	120.2	119.8	120.7	121.0	121.4	120.7
2001	120.5	121.2	121.8	120.9	120.4	120.2	119.6	118.9	117.6	116.7	116.3	115.5	119.1
2002	114.3	114.9	115.2	113.9	113.9	113.8	112.0	111.4	111.0	109.8	109.6	108.6	112.4
2003	105.9	105.7	106.4	106.2	105.8	105.9	104.9	104.9	104.6	104.2	104.2	104.7	105.3
2004	103.0	103.2	103.8	103.9	104.4	104.8	105.2	105.0	104.4	104.5	104.6	104.8	104.3
2005	104.5	104.7	104.7	104.7	104.9	104.8	105.0	104.8	104.1	103.9	103.8	103.8	104.5
2006	103.2	103.9	104.5	104.1	104.2	104.7	104.5	104.1	103.9	103.3	103.5	103.4	103.9
2007	102.6	102.4	102.7	101.6	101.7	101.8	102.7	102.4	102.1	102.7	103.1	103.6	102.5
2008	102.6	102.6	103.0	102.9	103.0	103.3	103.1	103.3	102.9	102.8	102.1	101.5	102.8
2009	101.0	99.9	98.8	96.9	95.7	95.2	93.8	93.3	92.8	92.2	91.9	92.0	95.3
2010	92.2	92.1	92.5	93.5	93.4	93.1	92.8	93.2	92.9	92.8	93.0	93.4	92.9
2011	92.8	92.8	92.9	93.0	93.1	93.5	93.0	92.5	92.5	92.8	92.4	92.1	92.8

Employment by Industry: San Diego–Carlsbad–San Marcos, CA, Selected Years, 2000–2011—*Continued*

(Numbers in thousands, not seasonally adjusted)

Industry and year	January	February	March	April	May	June	July	August	September	October	November	December	Annual average
Service-Providing													
2000	977.4	986.3	996.4	995.9	1,006.9	1,010.2	994.1	996.0	1,006.5	1,013.7	1,021.9	1,030.2	1,003.0
2001	1,003.8	1,011.6	1,018.8	1,022.6	1,029.4	1,033.2	1,015.0	1,016.6	1,022.3	1,031.4	1,038.0	1,042.9	1,023.8
2002	1,018.7	1,029.1	1,034.9	1,041.3	1,046.4	1,052.4	1,031.5	1,035.7	1,036.7	1,049.5	1,057.8	1,064.8	1,041.6
2003	1,039.3	1,046.2	1,048.9	1,053.6	1,055.9	1,059.6	1,046.0	1,050.7	1,052.0	1,061.9	1,065.6	1,072.2	1,054.3
2004	1,048.2	1,053.9	1,059.8	1,066.0	1,068.8	1,074.2	1,063.9	1,064.9	1,067.7	1,075.7	1,081.8	1,090.1	1,067.9
2005	1,067.1	1,072.6	1,077.7	1,085.8	1,088.7	1,093.0	1,080.5	1,083.5	1,089.3	1,090.8	1,100.4	1,107.3	1,086.4
2006	1,083.6	1,091.1	1,096.5	1,098.4	1,104.7	1,112.0	1,099.2	1,103.0	1,108.2	1,110.9	1,121.3	1,124.9	1,104.5
2007	1,099.0	1,106.9	1,113.5	1,113.1	1,120.0	1,126.9	1,118.5	1,119.7	1,121.1	1,122.6	1,130.2	1,136.8	1,119.0
2008	1,110.2	1,118.5	1,122.9	1,123.2	1,126.5	1,129.6	1,118.1	1,118.2	1,115.6	1,116.5	1,118.1	1,117.0	1,119.5
2009	1,084.5	1,083.3	1,082.2	1,077.8	1,080.6	1,080.7	1,060.1	1,060.9	1,058.4	1,070.3	1,076.7	1,078.7	1,074.5
2010	1,051.1	1,055.7	1,059.9	1,071.8	1,082.4	1,084.1	1,073.1	1,075.9	1,075.6	1,082.0	1,087.0	1,091.4	1,074.2
2011	1,070.3	1,077.6	1,081.4	1,081.8	1,084.7	1,087.7	1,070.0	1,072.8	1,076.8	1,089.7	1,097.9	1,102.6	1,082.8
Trade, Transportation, and Utilities													
2000	198.5	198.9	199.0	199.3	201.4	202.9	202.2	202.2	202.6	204.9	210.8	215.6	203.2
2001	207.6	206.1	206.0	206.0	207.1	208.4	207.9	207.9	207.1	209.3	212.6	215.7	208.5
2002	206.0	204.8	205.7	206.6	207.6	209.2	207.1	207.5	207.3	207.8	212.6	217.6	208.3
2003	205.7	204.7	205.0	205.3	206.5	207.2	208.2	209.4	209.9	215.6	217.1	221.7	209.7
2004	211.5	210.8	210.6	211.9	213.4	214.6	213.8	214.3	213.9	217.9	223.5	227.2	215.3
2005	217.6	216.1	215.6	215.4	216.5	216.7	217.7	218.8	220.0	220.3	226.2	231.3	219.4
2006	220.7	219.3	218.9	218.3	219.5	220.0	220.1	221.3	221.4	222.4	229.4	232.8	222.0
2007	222.3	220.4	219.9	218.9	220.3	220.8	221.9	223.1	221.6	221.0	226.8	230.5	222.3
2008	219.5	216.9	215.9	215.9	214.9	215.0	216.3	215.3	214.3	213.4	215.8	217.1	215.9
2009	204.1	200.9	199.0	197.3	198.4	198.1	196.8	196.9	196.5	197.8	202.6	205.2	199.5
2010	194.8	193.3	192.6	193.9	195.0	195.9	196.8	197.6	196.9	198.5	204.2	207.6	197.3
2011	198.2	196.1	195.8	196.5	197.2	197.7	197.1	198.9	198.3	200.0	204.7	207.1	199.0
Wholesale Trade													
2000	38.5	38.9	38.7	39.1	39.5	39.9	39.2	39.1	39.1	39.2	39.4	39.8	39.2
2001	40.5	41.0	41.1	41.2	42.3	42.8	41.3	41.4	41.2	41.5	41.5	41.7	41.5
2002	40.4	40.8	40.9	41.4	41.6	41.8	41.4	41.6	41.4	41.5	41.6	41.6	41.3
2003	40.9	41.2	41.4	41.5	41.8	41.9	41.6	41.7	41.6	41.6	41.9	41.9	41.6
2004	41.2	41.7	41.4	42.1	42.2	42.1	41.8	41.9	41.4	42.2	42.4	42.6	41.9
2005	42.3	42.8	42.7	43.3	43.6	43.7	43.8	43.9	44.2	44.2	44.5	44.5	43.6
2006	44.3	44.9	44.8	45.0	45.4	45.3	45.1	45.2	45.1	45.0	45.2	45.3	45.1
2007	44.7	45.2	45.3	45.2	45.7	45.7	46.0	45.9	45.7	45.4	45.6	45.5	45.5
2008	44.8	45.2	45.0	45.5	44.9	44.7	45.3	45.2	44.8	44.6	44.3	44.2	44.9
2009	42.1	42.0	41.4	41.0	41.0	40.4	39.9	39.8	39.5	39.9	39.9	39.8	40.6
2010	38.7	38.9	38.7	39.4	39.7	39.9	40.2	40.4	40.4	41.2	41.6	41.9	40.1
2011	40.6	40.9	40.9	41.0	41.0	40.9	39.4	40.4	40.6	40.6	40.9	40.6	40.7
Retail Trade													
2000	131.5	131.4	131.2	130.2	131.4	132.2	132.0	132.7	133.5	136.0	141.4	145.5	134.1
2001	136.9	134.8	134.2	133.7	133.9	134.6	134.8	135.4	135.5	136.2	140.3	143.6	136.2
2002	136.6	134.7	135.4	135.5	136.3	137.5	136.2	137.1	138.1	138.7	143.6	148.8	138.2
2003	138.6	137.3	137.0	136.9	137.6	138.0	139.0	139.9	140.4	145.8	147.2	151.7	140.8
2004	142.5	141.1	141.1	141.7	142.9	144.0	143.6	144.1	144.1	146.5	152.0	155.6	144.9
2005	146.8	144.8	144.4	143.9	144.5	144.8	145.5	146.6	147.4	148.1	153.6	158.1	147.4
2006	148.2	146.2	145.8	145.0	145.7	146.0	146.2	147.3	147.3	148.6	155.1	157.7	148.3
2007	149.5	146.9	146.6	145.8	146.4	146.4	146.7	147.9	146.6	146.7	151.9	155.2	148.1
2008	145.7	142.3	141.7	141.5	141.0	141.3	141.9	141.1	140.5	140.2	143.0	144.2	142.0
2009	134.1	131.6	130.3	129.1	130.2	130.1	129.6	129.8	129.8	130.9	135.9	138.2	131.6
2010	129.9	128.3	127.8	128.2	128.7	129.3	129.8	130.4	129.8	130.9	136.1	138.7	130.7
2011	131.5	129.5	129.1	129.8	130.4	130.9	131.7	132.5	131.5	132.7	137.1	139.7	132.2
Transportation and Utilities													
2000	28.5	28.6	29.1	30.0	30.5	30.8	31.0	30.4	30.0	29.7	30.0	30.3	29.9
2001	30.2	30.3	30.7	31.1	30.9	31.0	31.8	31.1	30.4	31.6	30.8	30.4	30.9
2002	29.0	29.3	29.4	29.7	29.7	29.9	29.5	28.8	27.8	27.6	27.4	27.2	28.8
2003	26.2	26.2	26.6	26.9	27.1	27.3	27.6	27.8	27.9	28.2	28.0	28.1	27.3
2004	27.8	28.0	28.1	28.1	28.3	28.5	28.4	28.3	28.4	29.2	29.1	29.0	28.4
2005	28.5	28.5	28.5	28.2	28.4	28.2	28.4	28.3	28.4	28.0	28.1	28.7	28.4
2006	28.2	28.2	28.3	28.3	28.4	28.7	28.8	28.8	29.0	28.8	29.1	29.8	28.7
2007	28.1	28.3	28.0	27.9	28.2	28.7	29.2	29.3	29.3	28.9	29.3	29.8	28.8
2008	29.0	29.4	29.2	28.9	29.0	29.0	29.1	29.0	29.0	28.6	28.5	28.7	29.0
2009	27.9	27.3	27.3	27.2	27.2	27.6	27.3	27.3	27.2	27.0	26.8	27.2	27.3
2010	26.2	26.1	26.1	26.3	26.6	26.7	26.8	26.8	26.7	26.4	26.5	27.0	26.5
2011	26.1	25.7	25.8	25.7	25.8	25.9	26.0	26.0	26.2	26.7	26.7	26.8	26.1
Information													
2000	33.3	34.0	35.0	36.2	37.1	37.8	36.4	36.4	36.5	35.7	35.9	36.1	35.9
2001	36.0	36.0	36.2	36.1	35.9	36.0	35.4	35.3	34.8	34.7	35.0	35.1	35.5
2002	34.7	34.7	34.9	34.8	34.8	34.5	33.7	33.4	33.0	35.0	35.0	34.7	34.4
2003	34.3	34.6	33.9	33.5	33.3	33.3	33.4	33.2	33.0	32.9	32.9	32.6	33.4
2004	32.6	32.6	32.4	32.1	32.2	32.5	32.6	32.5	32.3	32.6	32.7	32.9	32.5
2005	32.8	32.9	32.7	32.7	32.8	32.7	32.7	32.5	32.2	32.1	32.3	32.3	32.6
2006	31.9	31.8	31.5	31.2	31.3	31.6	32.1	32.0	31.4	31.8	31.7	31.9	31.7
2007	31.5	31.6	31.4	31.3	31.1	31.1	31.2	31.2	30.9	31.1	31.3	31.5	31.3
2008	31.3	31.4	31.2	31.0	31.3	31.6	31.9	31.9	31.4	31.2	31.3	31.3	31.4
2009	30.5	30.3	29.9	29.2	28.8	28.5	28.2	27.6	26.8	26.5	26.2	26.0	28.2
2010	25.7	25.4	25.3	25.2	25.2	25.3	25.1	25.1	24.7	24.6	24.6	24.6	25.1
2011	24.4	24.3	24.2	24.1	24.1	23.9	23.9	23.9	23.7	23.7	23.9	24.0	24.0

Employment by Industry: San Diego–Carlsbad–San Marcos, CA, Selected Years, 2000–2011—*Continued*

(Numbers in thousands, not seasonally adjusted)

Industry and year	January	February	March	April	May	June	July	August	September	October	November	December	Annual average
Financial Activities													
2000	70.2	70.7	71.0	71.1	71.3	71.7	71.4	71.5	71.3	71.7	72.0	72.2	71.3
2001	70.1	70.9	71.3	71.4	71.7	72.3	72.5	73.0	72.5	72.5	72.9	73.5	72.1
2002	72.2	73.1	73.5	74.0	74.6	75.1	75.0	75.7	75.7	76.3	77.3	77.9	75.0
2003	77.5	78.2	78.6	79.5	80.3	80.7	80.7	81.0	80.7	80.5	80.6	80.6	79.9
2004	80.6	80.9	81.4	81.7	81.8	81.8	82.4	82.4	82.2	82.6	82.5	83.0	81.9
2005	81.7	82.1	82.3	82.8	82.9	83.2	83.6	83.8	83.5	84.1	84.2	84.4	83.2
2006	83.9	84.4	84.4	84.2	84.7	84.5	83.5	83.6	83.2	82.8	82.6	82.6	83.7
2007	80.9	81.9	81.9	81.2	81.5	81.6	80.7	80.2	79.3	78.6	77.9	77.8	80.3
2008	76.3	76.7	76.6	76.6	76.3	75.9	75.4	75.0	74.1	73.7	73.2	72.9	75.2
2009	71.6	72.0	71.7	70.4	70.3	70.1	69.5	69.0	68.1	68.4	68.2	68.0	69.8
2010	67.0	67.2	67.2	67.0	66.8	67.0	67.3	67.0	66.8	67.7	67.5	67.7	67.2
2011	66.9	67.2	66.9	66.8	66.8	66.9	67.1	66.4	67.2	66.8	66.5	66.5	66.8
Professional and Business Services													
2000	191.2	193.3	196.7	195.0	195.6	197.9	199.4	202.3	203.8	203.4	203.8	205.2	199.0
2001	199.1	201.5	202.5	201.2	201.4	202.0	199.6	201.1	201.3	202.1	203.8	203.9	201.6
2002	201.0	204.0	205.2	204.1	204.1	205.4	204.0	205.8	205.3	206.3	207.3	208.2	205.1
2003	202.8	205.1	205.2	204.9	203.6	204.2	203.3	204.4	203.8	205.4	206.7	207.4	204.7
2004	204.3	205.6	207.3	207.3	206.6	208.0	210.0	209.7	209.7	210.4	211.0	213.3	208.6
2005	210.4	212.4	213.4	216.3	215.3	216.9	215.1	216.0	216.5	216.4	216.9	217.6	215.3
2006	214.3	216.9	218.1	218.3	219.0	220.9	219.9	221.5	221.9	220.0	220.2	219.9	219.2
2007	218.0	220.4	221.4	221.7	222.0	224.0	224.7	225.7	225.1	225.1	224.9	225.0	223.2
2008	222.0	224.4	225.2	225.1	224.0	223.6	222.4	223.6	221.9	220.0	217.8	217.0	222.3
2009	211.7	210.6	208.1	206.2	205.5	204.8	205.4	205.5	203.4	205.5	206.7	207.8	206.8
2010	201.9	203.7	203.2	205.3	205.9	207.6	209.2	211.2	210.7	211.4	210.5	211.8	207.7
2011	208.0	209.4	210.0	210.0	209.8	210.5	211.9	211.4	210.4	214.6	215.2	216.8	211.5
Education and Health Services													
2000	113.8	115.7	116.1	115.1	115.7	115.2	114.4	114.3	115.2	116.4	116.4	116.9	115.4
2001	111.4	112.8	114.4	115.0	116.2	116.1	115.6	115.7	117.4	118.8	119.1	119.4	116.0
2002	117.8	120.2	120.3	120.6	121.0	120.1	117.4	117.2	118.5	120.6	121.1	121.2	119.7
2003	119.8	120.5	121.2	123.0	123.2	122.7	119.9	120.5	121.6	122.2	123.1	124.0	121.8
2004	121.4	121.4	123.0	123.1	122.9	122.3	119.1	119.4	120.1	122.0	122.3	123.0	121.7
2005	121.1	121.5	122.5	123.9	123.6	122.8	120.1	120.3	122.5	122.8	124.5	124.6	122.5
2006	122.7	123.5	124.9	125.1	125.3	125.0	123.3	123.6	125.7	126.7	127.7	127.6	125.1
2007	125.4	126.9	128.7	128.7	129.8	128.8	127.7	129.0	130.9	131.9	132.7	134.0	129.5
2008	132.9	135.0	135.7	135.8	136.5	135.8	135.3	136.6	137.8	140.9	142.4	143.3	137.3
2009	141.5	143.1	144.6	143.7	144.3	143.8	140.4	142.2	143.9	146.5	148.0	149.1	144.3
2010	144.4	146.0	146.8	146.0	146.3	145.4	142.7	143.1	144.8	146.3	147.0	147.6	145.5
2011	147.2	149.1	149.8	148.6	149.0	148.0	146.1	146.7	147.2	150.3	153.5	153.5	149.1
Leisure and Hospitality													
2000	122.1	123.8	125.8	127.7	129.9	132.1	132.3	134.5	133.2	130.6	129.4	129.6	129.3
2001	126.8	128.4	129.7	131.7	132.8	134.1	135.6	136.5	133.2	130.6	128.7	129.5	131.5
2002	123.8	125.6	127.1	132.0	134.9	137.3	137.5	140.3	138.3	136.3	135.8	136.6	133.8
2003	132.9	135.9	136.8	138.7	140.5	142.2	144.4	146.7	144.0	142.0	142.1	142.6	140.7
2004	138.3	140.0	141.3	144.3	147.0	149.0	151.1	153.2	149.5	145.2	144.4	145.3	145.7
2005	141.0	142.5	144.9	147.7	149.7	152.2	154.2	157.5	154.4	150.5	149.7	150.7	149.6
2006	147.0	148.7	151.3	153.0	155.9	159.4	161.7	164.8	161.3	158.3	158.0	158.1	156.5
2007	152.1	154.2	157.0	158.5	161.9	165.7	168.5	169.7	166.5	162.5	162.4	162.4	161.8
2008	156.6	158.7	161.1	162.9	166.1	168.2	171.0	171.4	167.7	162.4	161.5	159.9	164.0
2009	152.6	152.5	153.1	154.2	156.5	157.9	158.6	160.4	157.5	152.8	151.1	149.9	154.8
2010	147.3	148.4	150.8	154.3	156.4	158.4	159.9	161.5	158.1	155.0	153.6	153.6	154.8
2011	149.3	151.2	153.3	155.0	157.3	159.3	162.7	165.5	159.4	156.5	155.8	157.1	156.9
Other Services													
2000	41.2	41.7	42.2	42.3	42.4	43.1	42.8	42.4	42.5	42.1	42.1	42.7	42.3
2001	42.8	43.3	44.0	44.3	45.0	46.3	46.0	45.8	46.3	44.9	44.8	45.1	44.9
2002	43.3	43.9	44.5	46.1	46.6	47.6	46.1	45.4	45.7	45.8	45.9	46.1	45.6
2003	45.4	45.7	46.0	47.0	47.5	48.3	47.1	47.2	47.3	46.4	46.4	46.8	46.8
2004	46.4	46.8	47.1	47.0	47.5	48.2	49.0	48.9	49.0	48.1	48.2	48.6	47.9
2005	47.5	48.3	48.7	49.0	49.2	49.4	49.2	49.3	48.7	48.6	48.7	48.9	48.8
2006	46.9	47.7	47.7	48.4	49.0	49.4	48.0	48.0	48.8	48.7	48.8	48.8	48.4
2007	47.3	47.8	48.2	47.7	48.4	49.2	48.9	48.6	48.7	48.0	48.3	48.5	48.3
2008	47.4	47.9	48.5	48.1	48.6	49.4	49.1	49.1	48.3	48.1	48.1	48.1	48.4
2009	46.3	47.0	47.3	47.0	47.3	47.5	46.6	47.1	46.1	46.4	46.3	46.3	46.8
2010	45.5	46.1	46.7	45.4	46.1	46.6	46.6	46.5	46.1	46.6	46.3	46.3	46.2
2011	46.2	47.4	47.6	47.0	47.8	47.8	47.1	46.4	47.3	47.1	46.5	46.9	47.1
Government													
2000	207.1	208.2	210.6	209.2	213.5	209.5	195.2	192.4	201.4	208.9	211.5	211.9	206.6
2001	210.0	212.6	214.7	216.9	219.3	218.0	202.4	201.3	209.7	218.5	221.1	220.7	213.8
2002	219.9	222.8	223.7	223.1	222.8	223.2	210.7	210.4	212.9	221.4	222.8	222.5	219.7
2003	220.9	221.5	222.2	221.7	221.0	221.0	209.0	208.3	211.7	216.9	216.7	216.5	217.3
2004	213.1	215.8	216.7	218.6	217.4	217.8	205.9	204.5	211.0	216.9	217.2	216.8	214.3
2005	215.0	216.8	217.6	218.0	218.7	219.1	207.9	205.3	211.5	216.0	217.9	217.5	215.1
2006	216.2	218.8	219.7	219.9	220.0	221.2	210.6	208.2	214.5	220.2	222.9	223.1	217.9
2007	221.5	223.7	225.0	225.1	225.0	225.7	214.9	212.2	218.1	224.4	225.9	227.1	222.4
2008	224.2	227.5	228.7	227.8	228.8	230.1	216.7	215.3	220.1	226.8	228.0	227.4	225.1
2009	226.2	226.9	228.5	229.8	229.5	230.0	214.6	212.2	216.1	226.4	227.6	226.4	224.5
2010	224.5	225.6	227.3	234.7	240.7	237.9	225.5	223.9	227.5	231.9	233.3	232.2	230.4
2011	230.1	232.9	233.8	233.8	232.7	233.6	214.1	213.6	223.3	230.7	231.8	230.7	228.4

560 EMPLOYMENT, HOURS, AND EARNINGS: STATES AND AREAS (BERNAN PRESS)

Employment by Industry: San Francisco–Oakland–Fremont, CA, Selected Years, 2000–2011

(Numbers in thousands, not seasonally adjusted)

Industry and year	January	February	March	April	May	June	July	August	September	October	November	December	Annual average
Total Nonfarm													
2000	2,053.9	2,074.5	2,095.8	2,106.0	2,123.4	2,143.0	2,129.4	2,139.1	2,150.5	2,151.1	2,169.5	2,184.5	2,126.7
2001	2,127.4	2,137.9	2,153.5	2,131.0	2,129.2	2,130.8	2,097.8	2,092.6	2,086.5	2,074.7	2,069.5	2,072.4	2,108.6
2002	2,013.3	2,020.4	2,033.1	2,026.9	2,034.5	2,038.5	2,014.4	2,017.8	2,022.5	2,027.4	2,036.8	2,037.8	2,027.0
2003	1,980.8	1,987.7	1,990.0	1,981.4	1,982.9	1,986.2	1,959.4	1,960.7	1,964.9	1,967.3	1,973.0	1,980.7	1,976.3
2004	1,935.4	1,945.6	1,956.4	1,960.3	1,968.5	1,974.7	1,959.7	1,954.8	1,960.7	1,973.2	1,981.9	1,993.0	1,963.7
2005	1,945.8	1,959.3	1,967.3	1,974.4	1,978.9	1,987.1	1,974.6	1,974.7	1,987.4	1,993.5	2,006.1	2,014.0	1,980.3
2006	1,972.0	1,988.4	1,997.0	1,997.9	2,015.3	2,025.6	2,008.9	2,012.7	2,022.7	2,030.8	2,041.3	2,044.4	2,013.1
2007	1,999.6	2,015.8	2,027.1	2,020.7	2,036.7	2,045.2	2,036.1	2,038.4	2,044.3	2,050.4	2,063.2	2,068.7	2,037.2
2008	2,018.6	2,031.0	2,033.0	2,035.2	2,039.0	2,042.7	2,032.0	2,025.1	2,022.9	2,024.2	2,017.0	2,012.4	2,027.8
2009	1,952.3	1,942.7	1,934.8	1,928.2	1,924.2	1,920.8	1,893.4	1,876.0	1,881.5	1,899.9	1,901.1	1,900.3	1,912.9
2010	1,857.8	1,860.2	1,867.2	1,881.0	1,892.1	1,893.5	1,871.2	1,865.1	1,881.2	1,893.3	1,897.4	1,902.0	1,880.2
2011	1,869.1	1,877.4	1,881.4	1,894.5	1,898.2	1,900.2	1,870.6	1,882.5	1,897.3	1,913.9	1,922.6	1,923.6	1,894.3
Total Private													
2000	1,753.9	1,771.1	1,789.0	1,793.0	1,804.7	1,826.5	1,830.8	1,838.8	1,847.9	1,842.5	1,857.2	1,873.3	1,819.1
2001	1,823.0	1,830.2	1,842.5	1,817.7	1,816.7	1,820.4	1,798.9	1,793.6	1,779.3	1,760.4	1,754.3	1,757.4	1,799.5
2002	1,699.6	1,703.4	1,711.9	1,704.4	1,711.6	1,718.0	1,710.0	1,714.2	1,708.7	1,705.5	1,713.5	1,716.1	1,709.7
2003	1,662.9	1,667.2	1,668.1	1,661.0	1,662.8	1,667.9	1,656.3	1,660.4	1,657.2	1,654.8	1,660.0	1,669.0	1,662.3
2004	1,625.7	1,633.1	1,641.8	1,645.7	1,653.8	1,660.7	1,657.9	1,658.2	1,657.1	1,661.6	1,668.0	1,680.5	1,653.7
2005	1,635.4	1,645.3	1,652.1	1,657.9	1,661.6	1,670.9	1,669.4	1,673.9	1,677.1	1,677.8	1,688.0	1,698.3	1,667.3
2006	1,657.7	1,670.7	1,677.0	1,678.5	1,695.2	1,707.1	1,699.7	1,705.8	1,707.8	1,709.1	1,716.6	1,723.3	1,695.7
2007	1,680.6	1,692.4	1,701.9	1,695.6	1,709.0	1,718.7	1,722.0	1,725.2	1,722.6	1,733.6	1,743.8	1,750.0	1,716.3
2008	1,703.7	1,713.3	1,714.0	1,715.6	1,720.1	1,721.9	1,721.6	1,718.4	1,711.5	1,708.8	1,700.1	1,697.4	1,712.2
2009	1,639.3	1,627.3	1,618.0	1,610.0	1,608.1	1,604.5	1,593.1	1,587.9	1,581.8	1,593.7	1,595.0	1,598.2	1,604.7
2010	1,557.8	1,558.3	1,563.8	1,572.1	1,576.8	1,582.8	1,585.0	1,582.2	1,582.4	1,591.1	1,592.0	1,598.4	1,578.6
2011	1,568.0	1,573.6	1,575.4	1,588.2	1,595.5	1,598.7	1,596.5	1,605.2	1,608.4	1,614.5	1,622.3	1,625.6	1,597.7
Goods-Producing													
2000	280.8	282.5	284.4	286.7	288.8	293.8	295.3	297.8	300.8	300.1	301.6	303.3	293.0
2001	294.8	295.4	298.4	294.6	293.4	294.2	290.8	290.6	286.6	281.1	277.0	274.4	289.3
2002	262.3	263.5	264.8	265.8	267.0	270.6	269.2	271.7	269.8	268.2	265.0	262.2	266.7
2003	254.2	253.8	253.9	252.7	252.8	254.4	254.7	257.0	256.9	257.6	256.6	255.2	255.0
2004	249.7	250.1	251.6	253.4	255.1	257.7	259.4	260.6	260.1	258.6	256.0	254.5	255.6
2005	246.4	248.2	250.0	250.5	251.0	254.5	256.7	258.0	258.1	257.7	257.2	255.5	253.7
2006	249.7	251.9	252.0	250.1	256.3	260.3	260.9	263.7	263.0	261.5	259.8	256.5	257.1
2007	251.0	251.6	254.1	253.5	255.4	258.2	259.0	260.8	259.4	258.9	258.2	256.2	256.4
2008	248.9	249.8	248.7	247.4	247.9	248.8	249.2	248.3	246.2	242.9	237.4	233.5	245.8
2009	224.1	217.2	215.3	211.2	210.0	210.2	208.9	208.8	207.3	207.2	206.7	203.8	210.9
2010	198.1	196.6	198.2	194.3	196.5	198.0	200.4	200.6	198.9	199.1	197.8	196.2	197.9
2011	193.8	193.6	191.6	192.7	194.5	196.3	199.7	200.5	199.6	199.1	196.6	195.8	196.2
Mining and Logging													
2000	2.4	2.6	2.6	2.6	2.6	2.6	2.6	2.5	2.5	2.5	2.5	2.6	2.6
2001	2.0	2.0	2.0	1.9	1.9	1.8	1.8	1.7	1.7	1.7	1.6	1.6	1.8
2002	1.5	1.5	1.5	1.5	1.5	1.4	1.3	1.3	1.2	1.2	1.2	1.2	1.4
2003	1.0	1.0	1.0	1.0	1.0	1.0	1.0	1.0	1.0	1.4	1.4	1.4	1.1
2004	1.4	1.4	1.4	1.4	1.4	1.4	1.4	1.4	1.4	1.3	1.4	1.4	1.4
2005	1.3	1.4	1.3	1.3	1.3	1.3	1.4	1.3	1.3	1.3	1.3	1.3	1.3
2006	1.3	1.3	1.3	1.3	1.4	1.4	1.4	1.5	1.5	1.5	1.5	1.5	1.4
2007	1.4	1.5	1.4	1.5	1.5	1.5	1.4	1.5	1.4	1.4	1.4	1.4	1.4
2008	1.4	1.4	1.4	1.4	1.4	1.4	1.4	1.4	1.4	1.4	1.4	1.4	1.4
2009	1.4	1.4	1.4	1.4	1.4	1.4	1.4	1.4	1.4	1.4	1.4	1.4	1.4
2010	1.4	1.4	1.4	1.4	1.4	1.5	1.5	1.6	1.5	1.4	1.4	1.4	1.4
2011	1.4	1.4	1.4	1.4	1.4	1.4	1.4	1.4	1.4	1.4	1.4	1.4	1.4
Construction													
2000	103.6	103.5	105.7	106.9	108.9	112.2	114.9	116.8	118.2	117.0	116.4	116.2	111.7
2001	113.2	114.0	117.2	117.0	118.4	120.3	120.9	122.1	121.1	118.5	116.3	114.6	117.8
2002	106.7	107.9	108.9	110.2	111.3	114.2	114.0	116.6	115.6	114.9	112.8	110.9	112.0
2003	107.9	108.1	108.6	108.1	108.6	110.5	111.5	113.7	113.6	113.8	112.6	110.8	110.7
2004	106.2	106.1	107.2	109.5	111.1	113.3	115.0	116.3	116.8	116.0	113.4	112.2	111.9
2005	106.3	108.0	110.1	111.4	112.4	115.3	117.3	118.5	118.5	118.5	117.6	115.8	114.1
2006	110.1	112.0	111.0	109.7	115.5	118.4	120.0	122.3	122.1	121.2	118.8	116.2	116.4
2007	112.3	112.3	114.7	114.8	116.5	118.8	120.5	121.7	120.3	119.3	117.7	115.9	117.1
2008	110.3	110.8	109.8	109.5	110.2	110.9	111.6	111.3	109.9	108.9	104.7	102.0	109.2
2009	95.5	90.7	90.3	88.4	88.4	88.9	88.6	88.5	87.1	86.7	86.3	83.5	88.6
2010	78.3	76.6	77.9	78.3	79.7	80.6	82.4	82.5	81.1	81.6	80.0	78.5	79.8
2011	76.3	76.2	74.1	75.9	77.3	78.9	80.9	82.3	82.0	82.5	79.8	79.0	78.8
Manufacturing													
2000	174.8	176.4	176.1	177.2	177.3	179.0	177.8	178.5	180.1	180.6	182.7	184.5	178.8
2001	179.6	179.4	179.2	175.7	173.1	172.1	168.1	166.8	163.8	160.9	159.1	158.2	169.7
2002	154.1	154.1	154.4	154.1	154.2	155.0	153.9	153.8	153.0	152.1	151.0	150.1	153.3
2003	145.3	144.7	144.3	143.6	143.2	142.9	142.2	142.3	142.3	142.4	142.6	143.0	143.2
2004	142.1	142.6	143.0	142.5	142.6	143.0	143.0	142.9	141.9	141.3	141.2	140.9	142.3
2005	138.8	138.8	138.6	137.8	137.3	137.9	138.0	138.2	138.3	137.9	138.3	138.4	138.2
2006	138.3	138.6	139.7	139.1	139.4	140.5	139.5	139.9	139.4	138.8	139.5	138.8	139.3
2007	137.3	137.8	138.0	137.2	137.4	137.9	137.1	137.6	137.7	138.2	139.1	138.9	137.9
2008	137.2	137.6	137.5	136.5	136.3	136.5	136.2	135.6	134.9	132.6	131.3	130.1	135.2
2009	127.2	125.1	123.6	121.4	120.2	119.9	118.9	118.9	118.8	119.1	119.0	118.9	120.9
2010	118.4	118.6	118.9	114.6	115.4	115.9	116.5	116.5	116.3	116.1	116.4	116.3	116.7
2011	116.1	116.0	116.1	115.4	115.8	116.0	117.4	116.8	116.2	115.2	115.4	115.4	116.0

Employment by Industry: San Francisco–Oakland–Fremont, CA, Selected Years, 2000–2011—*Continued*

(Numbers in thousands, not seasonally adjusted)

Industry and year	January	February	March	April	May	June	July	August	September	October	November	December	Annual average
Service-Providing													
2000	1,773.1	1,792.0	1,811.4	1,819.3	1,834.6	1,849.2	1,834.1	1,841.3	1,849.7	1,851.0	1,867.9	1,881.2	1,833.7
2001	1,832.6	1,842.5	1,855.1	1,836.4	1,835.8	1,836.6	1,807.0	1,802.0	1,799.9	1,793.6	1,792.5	1,798.0	1,819.3
2002	1,751.0	1,756.9	1,768.3	1,761.1	1,767.5	1,767.9	1,745.2	1,746.1	1,752.7	1,759.2	1,771.8	1,775.6	1,760.3
2003	1,726.6	1,733.9	1,736.1	1,728.7	1,730.1	1,731.8	1,704.7	1,703.7	1,708.0	1,709.7	1,716.4	1,725.5	1,721.3
2004	1,685.7	1,695.5	1,704.8	1,706.9	1,713.4	1,717.0	1,700.3	1,694.2	1,700.6	1,714.6	1,725.9	1,738.5	1,708.1
2005	1,699.4	1,711.1	1,717.3	1,723.9	1,727.9	1,732.6	1,717.9	1,716.7	1,729.3	1,735.8	1,748.9	1,758.5	1,726.6
2006	1,722.3	1,736.5	1,745.0	1,747.8	1,759.0	1,765.3	1,748.0	1,749.0	1,759.7	1,769.3	1,781.5	1,787.9	1,755.9
2007	1,748.6	1,764.2	1,773.0	1,767.2	1,781.3	1,787.0	1,777.1	1,777.6	1,784.9	1,791.5	1,805.0	1,812.5	1,780.8
2008	1,769.7	1,781.2	1,784.3	1,787.8	1,791.1	1,793.9	1,782.8	1,776.8	1,776.7	1,781.3	1,779.6	1,778.9	1,782.0
2009	1,728.2	1,725.5	1,719.5	1,717.0	1,714.2	1,710.6	1,684.5	1,667.2	1,674.2	1,692.7	1,694.4	1,696.5	1,702.0
2010	1,659.7	1,663.6	1,669.0	1,686.7	1,695.6	1,695.5	1,670.8	1,664.5	1,682.3	1,694.2	1,699.6	1,705.8	1,682.3
2011	1,675.3	1,683.8	1,689.8	1,701.8	1,703.7	1,703.9	1,670.9	1,682.0	1,697.7	1,714.8	1,726.0	1,727.8	1,698.1
Trade, Transportation, and Utilities													
2000	394.3	391.7	393.8	395.4	398.1	401.2	402.5	402.2	402.6	401.4	411.0	419.9	401.2
2001	405.5	402.2	403.2	400.1	399.6	401.4	398.4	396.7	396.0	390.8	394.6	397.9	398.9
2002	382.8	379.7	380.2	375.9	377.4	379.3	378.6	377.5	378.3	379.7	386.7	391.3	380.6
2003	374.4	370.1	368.7	363.3	363.8	364.6	362.2	361.4	360.6	361.6	368.5	374.4	366.1
2004	356.5	353.9	354.3	355.0	357.3	358.8	357.4	356.9	356.4	360.9	368.8	375.9	359.3
2005	359.8	356.0	355.1	355.2	355.9	357.8	357.2	357.9	358.6	357.6	365.0	372.7	359.1
2006	359.6	356.1	356.4	354.9	357.0	359.4	358.4	359.0	359.3	360.5	368.2	374.6	360.3
2007	363.0	359.6	359.4	356.3	357.9	359.4	358.9	360.5	360.1	361.2	369.9	375.9	361.9
2008	361.5	357.2	356.4	353.0	353.6	353.8	353.0	351.8	348.9	348.2	351.4	353.4	353.5
2009	340.0	334.7	331.1	328.0	327.6	326.5	323.5	323.2	322.7	324.2	330.7	335.4	329.0
2010	321.8	318.1	317.2	317.8	318.5	319.8	318.6	318.9	318.2	320.2	326.4	332.0	320.6
2011	319.3	316.9	316.3	317.7	319.0	319.8	319.3	320.0	322.3	322.1	330.5	332.9	321.3
Wholesale Trade													
2000	83.6	84.1	85.2	85.6	86.0	86.5	87.2	87.1	87.4	87.0	87.2	88.2	86.3
2001	87.8	88.7	88.8	87.8	87.4	87.3	86.5	86.1	86.1	85.2	85.2	85.0	86.8
2002	83.1	83.5	83.7	82.1	82.4	82.4	82.0	81.9	81.7	81.3	81.2	81.3	82.2
2003	79.5	79.5	79.5	78.9	78.7	78.4	77.6	77.4	77.0	76.9	76.6	76.8	78.1
2004	74.3	74.4	74.8	75.7	75.7	76.2	76.0	75.8	76.0	76.1	76.4	76.6	75.7
2005	74.6	74.3	74.2	74.9	74.7	75.2	74.7	74.6	74.5	74.4	74.5	74.7	74.6
2006	74.1	74.5	74.9	75.2	75.6	76.0	75.4	75.6	75.8	76.1	76.1	76.6	75.5
2007	75.7	76.1	76.6	75.5	76.0	76.2	75.6	75.6	75.4	75.7	75.5	75.6	75.8
2008	75.1	75.3	75.3	75.1	75.2	74.9	74.5	74.1	73.9	73.6	73.0	72.6	74.4
2009	70.6	70.2	69.4	69.0	68.7	68.3	67.7	67.3	66.6	66.9	66.7	66.5	68.2
2010	65.4	65.4	65.2	65.8	65.9	66.1	65.9	65.8	65.6	66.2	66.0	65.8	65.8
2011	65.1	65.3	65.4	65.5	65.9	65.8	66.9	66.2	66.6	66.3	66.4	65.8	65.9
Retail Trade													
2000	211.6	208.6	209.0	209.8	211.8	213.9	214.2	214.0	213.9	215.2	223.7	230.5	214.7
2001	218.6	214.5	215.0	213.6	213.4	215.3	214.7	213.6	213.2	210.5	217.3	221.7	215.1
2002	209.4	205.9	206.7	205.6	206.5	207.8	207.7	207.0	208.2	209.5	217.0	221.4	209.4
2003	208.8	205.1	204.0	201.3	201.9	202.9	202.6	202.6	202.5	203.5	211.3	216.5	205.3
2004	202.5	200.0	199.9	199.8	201.5	202.2	202.2	202.5	201.6	204.0	211.4	218.0	203.8
2005	206.4	202.7	202.0	201.9	202.3	203.4	203.6	204.9	205.2	205.6	212.5	219.2	205.8
2006	208.2	203.8	203.6	202.5	203.5	204.8	205.5	206.1	205.2	206.5	214.0	218.7	206.9
2007	210.0	205.9	205.7	203.5	204.4	205.3	206.7	207.1	206.5	207.2	215.8	220.8	208.2
2008	209.6	204.9	204.2	202.6	202.2	203.1	203.1	202.3	200.0	199.8	203.5	205.4	203.4
2009	196.9	192.3	190.1	187.9	187.5	187.0	185.5	185.8	185.9	186.9	193.6	198.0	189.8
2010	188.0	184.3	183.8	184.4	185.2	185.7	185.5	186.1	185.1	186.6	192.7	197.0	187.0
2011	187.1	184.6	184.0	184.8	185.5	186.1	185.4	186.5	187.9	188.0	195.9	198.5	187.9
Transportation and Utilities													
2000	99.1	99.0	99.6	100.0	100.3	100.8	101.1	101.1	101.3	99.2	100.1	101.2	100.2
2001	99.1	99.0	99.4	98.7	98.8	98.8	97.2	97.0	96.7	95.1	92.1	91.2	96.9
2002	90.3	90.3	89.8	88.2	88.5	89.1	88.9	88.6	88.4	88.9	88.5	88.6	89.0
2003	86.1	85.5	85.2	83.1	83.2	83.3	82.0	81.4	81.1	81.2	80.6	81.1	82.8
2004	79.7	79.5	79.6	79.5	80.1	80.4	79.2	78.6	78.8	80.8	81.0	81.3	79.9
2005	78.8	79.0	78.9	78.4	78.9	79.2	78.9	78.4	78.9	77.6	78.0	78.8	78.7
2006	77.3	77.8	77.9	77.2	77.9	78.6	77.5	77.3	78.3	77.9	78.1	79.3	77.9
2007	77.3	77.6	77.1	77.3	77.5	77.9	77.5	77.8	78.2	78.3	78.6	79.5	77.9
2008	76.8	77.0	76.9	75.3	76.2	75.8	75.4	75.4	75.0	74.8	74.9	75.4	75.7
2009	72.5	72.2	71.6	71.1	71.4	71.2	70.3	70.1	70.2	70.4	70.4	70.9	71.0
2010	68.4	68.4	68.2	67.6	67.4	68.0	67.2	67.0	67.5	67.4	67.7	69.2	67.8
2011	67.1	67.0	66.9	67.4	67.6	67.9	67.0	67.3	67.8	67.8	68.2	68.6	67.6
Information													
2000	97.1	99.6	102.1	103.6	106.8	109.6	109.0	110.2	110.6	110.2	110.9	111.0	106.7
2001	110.4	109.3	108.6	103.0	100.6	99.0	95.9	94.2	91.9	90.3	89.1	88.2	98.4
2002	88.3	87.5	87.4	85.9	86.8	86.9	85.8	85.7	85.1	83.7	84.2	84.0	85.9
2003	81.7	82.1	80.6	79.5	79.5	79.2	78.4	78.0	77.2	76.4	76.9	76.6	78.8
2004	75.5	75.7	75.7	75.3	75.3	75.3	75.3	74.7	74.0	73.5	73.5	73.5	74.8
2005	73.1	73.5	72.5	71.8	71.7	71.7	71.3	71.3	70.6	70.1	70.2	69.9	71.5
2006	69.4	69.6	69.3	68.7	68.8	68.9	68.7	69.1	68.7	68.9	69.3	69.5	69.1
2007	68.2	68.4	68.4	68.3	68.7	68.7	69.0	69.0	68.5	68.2	68.1	68.1	68.5
2008	67.9	68.3	68.0	68.5	68.7	68.7	69.7	69.5	68.8	68.6	68.4	68.2	68.6
2009	67.3	66.6	66.3	64.9	64.7	64.7	65.0	64.5	63.8	63.8	63.7	63.7	64.9
2010	63.0	62.6	62.6	62.2	62.3	62.7	62.7	62.4	61.8	61.9	62.2	62.4	62.4
2011	62.4	62.5	62.8	62.8	63.1	63.7	63.8	63.9	63.8	64.0	64.7	65.2	63.6

Employment by Industry: San Francisco–Oakland–Fremont, CA, Selected Years, 2000–2011—*Continued*

(Numbers in thousands, not seasonally adjusted)

Industry and year	January	February	March	April	May	June	July	August	September	October	November	December	Annual average
Financial Activities													
2000	146.9	148.1	148.1	147.7	148.4	150.1	149.4	149.7	150.2	151.3	151.2	152.8	149.5
2001	156.3	157.6	159.6	159.3	158.8	159.7	158.7	158.2	157.7	157.2	157.4	157.6	158.2
2002	153.3	153.4	153.7	153.9	154.0	154.9	154.7	155.7	154.8	155.4	155.9	156.8	154.7
2003	154.6	155.4	156.0	155.2	155.5	155.5	153.7	153.5	152.9	151.7	151.3	151.8	153.9
2004	150.9	150.9	151.0	150.2	150.7	151.4	151.4	151.5	150.8	151.5	151.7	152.5	151.2
2005	152.2	152.6	153.0	153.0	153.7	154.7	154.3	154.2	153.9	153.3	153.4	154.0	153.5
2006	152.4	153.0	153.3	153.3	153.9	153.8	152.3	152.3	152.0	151.3	150.6	150.2	152.4
2007	148.1	148.7	148.9	147.8	148.2	148.1	147.5	147.3	146.1	144.4	144.5	143.8	147.0
2008	141.4	141.3	141.1	140.4	140.3	140.6	139.7	139.5	138.2	137.9	136.8	136.7	139.5
2009	132.0	131.5	130.7	129.2	128.5	128.0	126.3	125.6	124.6	125.5	124.8	124.8	127.6
2010	124.7	125.2	125.1	125.0	125.4	125.4	125.8	125.8	125.6	125.2	124.8	125.5	125.3
2011	123.5	123.8	123.8	123.7	123.9	124.3	123.3	123.5	124.8	123.4	123.8	124.4	123.9
Professional and Business Services													
2000	374.1	380.2	387.0	390.5	390.1	396.5	398.6	403.3	405.3	404.9	406.4	408.2	395.4
2001	387.4	388.8	389.6	378.7	376.2	376.2	368.1	365.2	359.7	357.0	353.0	354.5	371.2
2002	341.9	342.2	343.7	340.0	338.2	338.3	334.4	334.5	331.7	329.4	331.6	331.8	336.5
2003	322.0	323.3	324.2	322.5	320.4	321.6	320.1	321.2	319.7	319.3	320.2	322.8	321.4
2004	317.8	320.1	322.6	323.2	323.3	325.7	324.4	325.3	324.2	327.4	329.4	332.3	324.6
2005	327.3	330.6	332.7	333.4	332.4	334.8	336.0	337.9	338.1	339.9	342.8	345.9	336.0
2006	339.5	343.5	346.1	346.5	347.9	351.8	351.2	353.2	353.3	354.5	356.0	358.4	350.2
2007	349.3	352.9	355.0	353.6	356.1	359.6	362.7	364.8	363.8	374.5	375.7	376.7	362.1
2008	370.5	372.8	373.7	373.5	372.5	374.6	375.8	376.5	374.5	374.6	371.3	369.8	373.3
2009	359.2	356.4	353.7	350.1	346.7	347.4	344.8	343.6	340.6	345.9	345.2	345.6	348.3
2010	338.8	340.6	342.3	344.2	343.5	346.5	347.7	347.6	347.6	349.0	349.7	350.5	345.7
2011	348.5	350.5	351.2	353.0	353.6	356.2	354.5	358.1	359.6	361.0	362.9	363.4	356.0
Education and Health Services													
2000	209.9	214.3	215.3	209.6	209.7	208.4	207.2	206.5	209.0	209.8	212.0	213.3	210.4
2001	205.7	210.0	211.9	211.4	212.7	211.7	211.1	211.6	213.5	214.8	216.6	217.4	212.4
2002	212.5	216.1	217.9	213.7	214.3	211.2	211.9	211.8	213.8	216.2	218.1	217.8	214.6
2003	214.0	218.5	219.1	221.4	221.4	219.2	216.9	216.3	218.2	218.8	220.1	220.7	218.7
2004	216.8	221.2	222.1	222.4	221.9	220.0	216.8	216.1	218.2	220.5	221.6	222.3	220.0
2005	216.3	222.2	223.2	223.2	223.6	220.9	219.2	218.9	221.7	224.0	225.1	225.7	222.0
2006	221.1	226.2	227.5	229.5	230.2	228.2	225.1	224.9	228.3	230.5	231.6	232.5	228.0
2007	226.8	233.4	235.4	233.5	234.5	233.8	230.5	229.2	232.5	236.1	237.7	238.1	233.5
2008	232.8	238.9	239.5	242.0	242.5	237.9	236.8	236.2	240.2	244.0	245.3	246.5	240.2
2009	240.7	244.8	245.6	247.3	247.3	243.9	240.9	239.0	242.2	245.7	246.3	247.2	244.2
2010	242.7	245.3	247.1	247.9	248.1	244.2	242.3	239.5	244.3	247.6	247.6	248.3	245.4
2011	244.1	247.5	248.7	250.1	249.5	244.5	242.8	242.7	244.5	250.1	251.2	252.0	247.3
Leisure and Hospitality													
2000	180.5	183.4	186.3	187.0	189.9	193.3	194.9	195.7	196.6	191.7	190.7	191.0	190.1
2001	188.7	191.5	194.6	194.8	198.7	200.5	198.8	200.0	197.1	192.4	189.9	190.4	194.8
2002	183.1	184.7	187.5	192.4	196.7	199.1	197.6	199.9	197.8	196.3	195.2	195.3	193.8
2003	187.0	187.9	189.4	190.5	193.3	196.9	195.2	197.9	196.6	195.0	192.4	193.2	192.9
2004	186.2	188.2	190.6	192.1	195.8	197.4	198.9	199.6	199.7	196.3	194.6	196.5	194.7
2005	189.3	190.6	193.1	197.7	200.1	202.6	201.8	203.6	204.0	202.7	202.2	202.0	199.1
2006	195.1	198.6	200.0	202.6	207.1	210.0	209.0	209.9	209.5	208.5	207.9	208.0	205.5
2007	202.0	204.4	206.6	208.5	213.2	215.7	217.8	218.1	216.9	214.8	214.2	215.3	212.3
2008	207.1	210.3	211.5	215.1	218.4	221.1	220.9	220.9	219.4	216.7	214.3	214.2	215.8
2009	203.2	203.5	202.8	206.0	210.0	210.6	210.9	210.8	209.1	208.7	205.3	205.6	207.2
2010	197.9	198.7	199.7	208.0	209.1	212.3	213.6	214.4	213.4	214.3	210.4	210.4	208.5
2011	204.3	206.3	208.2	213.9	217.4	219.3	217.5	219.6	216.6	218.3	216.1	215.0	214.4
Other Services													
2000	70.3	71.3	72.0	72.5	72.9	73.6	73.9	73.4	72.8	73.1	73.4	73.8	72.8
2001	74.2	75.4	76.6	75.8	76.7	77.7	77.1	77.1	76.8	76.8	76.7	77.0	76.5
2002	75.4	76.3	76.7	76.8	77.2	77.7	77.8	77.4	77.4	76.6	76.8	76.9	76.9
2003	75.0	76.1	76.2	75.9	76.1	76.5	75.1	75.1	75.1	74.4	74.0	74.3	75.3
2004	72.3	73.0	73.9	74.1	74.4	74.4	74.3	73.5	73.7	72.9	72.4	73.0	73.5
2005	71.0	71.6	72.5	73.1	73.2	73.9	72.9	72.1	72.1	72.5	72.1	72.6	72.5
2006	70.9	71.8	72.4	72.9	74.0	74.7	74.1	73.7	73.7	73.4	73.2	73.6	73.2
2007	72.2	73.4	74.1	74.1	75.0	75.2	75.7	75.5	75.3	75.5	75.5	75.9	74.8
2008	73.6	74.7	75.1	75.7	76.2	76.4	76.5	75.7	75.3	75.9	75.2	75.1	75.5
2009	72.8	72.6	72.5	73.3	73.3	73.2	72.8	72.4	71.5	72.7	72.3	72.1	72.6
2010	70.8	71.2	71.6	72.7	73.4	73.9	73.9	73.0	72.6	73.8	73.1	73.1	72.8
2011	72.1	72.5	72.8	74.3	74.5	74.6	75.6	76.9	77.2	76.5	76.5	76.9	75.0
Government													
2000	300.0	303.4	306.8	313.0	318.7	316.5	298.6	300.3	302.6	308.6	312.3	311.2	307.7
2001	304.4	307.7	311.0	313.3	312.5	310.4	298.9	299.0	307.2	314.3	315.2	315.0	309.1
2002	313.7	317.0	321.2	322.5	322.9	320.5	304.4	303.6	313.8	321.9	323.3	321.7	317.2
2003	317.9	320.5	321.9	320.4	320.1	318.3	303.1	300.3	307.7	312.5	313.0	311.7	314.0
2004	309.7	312.5	314.6	314.6	314.7	314.0	301.8	296.6	303.6	311.6	313.9	312.5	310.0
2005	310.4	314.0	315.2	316.5	317.3	316.2	305.2	300.8	310.3	315.7	318.1	315.7	313.0
2006	314.3	317.7	320.0	319.4	320.1	318.5	309.2	306.9	314.9	321.7	324.7	321.1	317.4
2007	319.0	323.4	325.2	325.1	327.7	326.5	314.1	313.2	321.7	316.8	319.4	318.7	320.9
2008	314.9	317.7	319.0	319.6	318.9	320.8	310.4	306.7	311.4	315.4	316.9	315.0	315.6
2009	313.0	315.4	316.8	318.2	316.1	316.3	300.3	288.1	299.7	306.2	306.1	302.1	308.2
2010	300.0	301.9	303.4	308.9	315.3	310.7	286.2	282.9	298.8	302.2	305.4	303.6	301.6
2011	301.1	303.8	306.0	306.3	302.7	301.5	274.1	277.3	288.9	299.4	300.3	298.0	296.6

Employment by Industry: San Jose–Sunnyvale–Santa Clara, CA, Selected Years, 2000–2011

(Numbers in thousands, not seasonally adjusted)

Industry and year	January	February	March	April	May	June	July	August	September	October	November	December	Annual average
Total Nonfarm													
2000	999.6	1,008.5	1,023.2	1,023.4	1,036.8	1,051.9	1,056.7	1,058.4	1,060.9	1,061.9	1,070.3	1,080.3	1,044.3
2001	1,054.7	1,057.9	1,062.7	1,044.8	1,040.4	1,037.1	1,014.5	1,003.4	987.0	976.6	968.9	966.9	1,017.9
2002	933.0	933.8	939.0	929.2	927.8	926.2	915.2	909.0	901.1	900.6	897.2	894.1	917.2
2003	874.0	872.8	874.0	875.6	875.7	876.9	866.8	864.2	862.8	865.2	866.1	868.9	870.3
2004	849.6	854.1	859.3	859.0	864.0	868.7	861.1	860.7	859.3	866.8	869.4	872.3	862.0
2005	856.0	859.3	862.8	863.5	867.1	872.8	870.2	871.7	871.2	877.4	880.6	887.0	870.0
2006	872.2	880.0	883.4	883.6	890.8	896.4	893.4	895.3	895.3	897.0	900.5	906.4	891.2
2007	892.2	898.5	904.5	901.6	909.0	916.9	916.1	914.6	913.6	919.5	923.1	924.5	911.2
2008	911.0	914.2	917.7	915.3	918.6	921.4	915.5	919.5	918.0	913.4	909.1	905.1	914.9
2009	879.0	870.9	866.3	860.1	860.5	860.6	837.5	840.8	843.3	850.5	853.6	853.8	856.4
2010	838.6	840.9	845.6	852.5	859.6	861.2	849.6	850.4	854.2	866.0	870.6	872.7	855.2
2011	859.3	864.9	868.7	873.9	877.2	883.2	872.0	874.2	885.0	889.2	892.8	897.7	878.2
Total Private													
2000	901.5	910.7	923.3	923.8	936.1	948.2	957.3	964.2	967.1	963.0	971.0	981.3	945.6
2001	957.3	959.9	963.8	945.6	939.8	937.4	917.5	908.8	890.3	876.2	867.2	865.4	919.1
2002	831.8	831.6	835.6	824.6	823.1	821.8	813.9	810.4	801.4	797.4	793.6	791.0	814.7
2003	771.8	771.8	772.3	773.8	774.3	776.1	769.9	769.6	767.5	766.6	767.6	771.9	771.1
2004	753.7	757.3	761.4	761.1	765.9	771.1	766.3	767.8	765.8	770.6	772.0	776.3	765.8
2005	760.5	763.1	765.9	766.5	769.7	775.8	775.9	778.0	777.4	781.2	784.0	790.8	774.1
2006	776.5	783.5	786.7	786.3	793.0	799.0	798.3	801.6	801.0	799.3	802.9	808.9	794.8
2007	794.5	801.5	806.2	803.5	810.7	819.1	821.0	820.7	818.7	821.2	824.5	826.2	814.0
2008	812.0	816.0	818.6	816.9	819.6	822.8	821.5	825.0	820.0	814.7	810.8	807.3	817.1
2009	781.5	774.1	768.7	760.7	760.4	760.3	752.4	752.0	747.3	752.1	754.3	755.7	760.0
2010	742.6	744.5	747.9	753.2	758.7	764.5	764.5	766.8	764.5	770.5	773.6	776.6	760.7
2011	764.7	769.6	773.0	777.9	781.0	787.5	791.2	792.6	794.5	795.7	798.7	803.5	785.8
Goods-Producing													
2000	283.8	286.1	290.3	291.7	295.1	300.8	305.7	309.0	312.0	311.7	313.5	315.8	301.3
2001	307.9	307.9	306.7	301.8	298.4	296.6	289.7	284.4	279.9	273.8	267.7	265.6	290.2
2002	256.9	253.3	254.2	249.8	249.4	249.2	247.2	245.5	241.3	237.4	232.5	228.9	245.5
2003	223.9	221.6	221.0	219.2	217.5	217.9	217.2	216.7	215.6	213.1	211.7	211.6	217.3
2004	206.8	207.6	208.5	208.8	209.9	212.0	212.8	213.5	212.6	211.6	210.2	209.7	210.3
2005	206.3	206.0	206.0	208.3	208.4	210.7	212.4	212.8	212.0	211.7	210.2	210.7	209.6
2006	208.5	209.3	209.1	208.2	210.6	211.6	213.5	214.3	213.4	211.7	209.6	209.8	210.8
2007	208.1	209.8	210.6	210.6	212.4	216.2	218.8	219.4	218.6	217.1	215.2	213.9	214.2
2008	211.8	212.1	211.8	211.6	213.4	214.6	216.1	216.5	214.6	211.8	208.3	206.4	212.4
2009	200.4	196.7	194.5	191.9	190.4	189.9	188.9	188.9	187.8	186.0	185.3	184.1	190.4
2010	182.5	182.0	182.9	182.9	184.0	186.6	188.2	189.6	189.1	188.7	187.3	187.2	185.9
2011	185.1	185.6	186.4	187.4	188.2	190.8	193.1	194.4	193.7	192.1	190.9	190.2	189.8
Mining and Logging													
2000	0.4	0.4	0.3	0.3	0.3	0.3	0.4	0.4	0.4	0.4	0.4	0.5	0.4
2001	0.2	0.2	0.2	0.2	0.2	0.2	0.2	0.2	0.2	0.2	0.2	0.2	0.2
2002	0.3	0.3	0.3	0.2	0.2	0.2	0.2	0.2	0.2	0.2	0.2	0.2	0.2
2003	0.2	0.2	0.2	0.2	0.2	0.2	0.2	0.2	0.2	0.2	0.2	0.1	0.2
2004	0.1	0.1	0.1	0.1	0.1	0.2	0.1	0.2	0.2	0.2	0.1	0.1	0.1
2005	0.1	0.1	0.1	0.2	0.2	0.2	0.2	0.2	0.2	0.3	0.3	0.2	0.2
2006	0.3	0.3	0.2	0.2	0.2	0.3	0.3	0.3	0.3	0.3	0.3	0.3	0.3
2007	0.3	0.3	0.3	0.3	0.3	0.3	0.3	0.3	0.3	0.3	0.3	0.3	0.3
2008	0.3	0.3	0.3	0.3	0.3	0.3	0.3	0.3	0.3	0.3	0.3	0.3	0.3
2009	0.3	0.2	0.2	0.2	0.2	0.2	0.2	0.2	0.3	0.2	0.2	0.2	0.2
2010	0.2	0.2	0.2	0.2	0.2	0.2	0.2	0.2	0.2	0.2	0.2	0.2	0.2
2011	0.2	0.2	0.2	0.2	0.2	0.2	0.2	0.2	0.2	0.2	0.2	0.2	0.2
Construction													
2000	45.4	45.4	46.7	47.3	48.3	49.7	50.7	51.5	52.5	52.0	52.2	52.0	49.5
2001	51.1	50.9	51.5	51.1	51.0	51.2	50.4	50.7	49.3	48.3	47.4	46.4	49.9
2002	43.7	43.3	44.1	43.6	44.4	45.3	45.6	46.7	45.6	44.5	43.8	42.2	44.4
2003	40.0	39.9	40.2	40.1	40.4	41.2	41.9	43.3	43.5	43.2	42.7	42.3	41.6
2004	40.3	40.8	41.2	41.7	42.4	43.7	44.2	44.6	44.5	44.8	44.2	43.9	43.0
2005	41.6	41.7	42.3	43.0	43.6	45.0	45.7	46.4	46.7	46.3	46.0	45.9	44.5
2006	44.9	45.4	45.1	44.3	46.2	47.4	47.9	48.7	48.9	48.2	47.6	46.9	46.8
2007	45.0	45.5	46.3	46.0	47.0	47.9	48.6	49.2	49.2	48.3	47.3	46.6	47.2
2008	44.3	44.6	44.2	44.0	44.6	45.1	45.5	45.9	45.1	43.7	41.9	40.9	44.2
2009	37.8	36.2	35.9	34.9	34.2	34.2	33.8	33.8	33.4	33.2	33.1	32.3	34.4
2010	31.2	30.8	31.2	31.8	32.1	32.9	33.4	33.2	33.1	32.8	32.0	31.7	32.2
2011	29.8	29.7	30.2	30.3	30.5	31.3	32.5	32.0	32.8	32.9	32.5	32.1	31.4
Manufacturing													
2000	238.0	240.3	243.3	244.1	246.5	250.8	254.6	257.1	259.1	259.3	260.9	263.3	251.4
2001	256.6	256.8	255.0	250.5	247.2	245.2	239.1	235.5	230.4	225.3	220.1	219.0	240.1
2002	212.9	209.7	209.8	206.0	204.8	203.7	201.5	198.6	195.5	192.7	188.5	186.5	200.9
2003	183.7	181.5	180.6	178.9	176.9	176.5	175.1	173.2	171.9	169.7	168.8	169.2	175.5
2004	166.4	166.7	167.2	167.0	167.4	168.1	168.5	168.7	167.9	166.6	165.9	165.7	167.2
2005	164.6	164.2	163.6	165.1	164.6	165.5	166.5	166.2	165.1	165.1	163.9	164.6	164.9
2006	163.3	163.6	163.8	163.7	164.2	163.9	165.3	165.3	164.2	163.2	161.7	162.6	163.7
2007	162.8	164.0	164.0	164.3	165.1	168.0	169.9	169.9	169.1	169.1	168.5	167.6	167.0	166.7
2008	167.2	167.2	167.3	167.3	168.5	169.2	170.3	170.3	169.2	167.8	166.1	165.2	168.0
2009	162.3	160.3	158.4	156.8	156.0	155.5	154.9	154.9	154.1	152.6	152.0	151.6	155.8
2010	151.1	151.0	151.5	150.9	151.7	153.5	154.6	156.2	155.8	155.7	155.1	155.3	153.5
2011	155.1	155.7	156.0	156.9	157.5	159.3	160.4	162.2	160.7	159.0	158.2	157.9	158.2

Employment by Industry: San Jose–Sunnyvale–Santa Clara, CA, Selected Years, 2000–2011—*Continued*
(Numbers in thousands, not seasonally adjusted)

Industry and year	January	February	March	April	May	June	July	August	September	October	November	December	Annual average
Service-Providing													
2000	715.8	722.4	732.9	731.7	741.7	751.1	751.0	749.4	748.9	750.2	756.8	764.5	743.0
2001	746.8	750.0	756.0	743.0	742.0	740.5	724.8	717.0	707.1	702.8	701.2	701.3	727.7
2002	676.1	680.5	684.8	679.4	678.4	677.0	667.9	663.5	659.8	663.2	664.7	665.2	671.7
2003	650.1	651.2	653.0	656.4	658.2	659.0	649.6	647.5	647.2	652.1	654.4	657.3	653.0
2004	642.8	646.5	650.8	650.2	654.1	656.7	648.3	647.2	646.7	655.2	659.2	662.6	651.7
2005	649.7	653.3	656.8	655.2	658.7	662.1	657.8	658.9	659.2	665.7	670.4	676.3	660.3
2006	663.7	670.7	674.3	675.4	680.2	684.8	679.9	681.0	681.9	685.3	690.9	696.6	680.4
2007	684.1	688.7	693.9	691.0	696.6	700.7	697.3	695.2	695.0	702.4	707.9	710.6	697.0
2008	699.2	702.1	705.9	703.7	705.2	706.8	699.4	703.0	703.4	701.6	700.8	698.7	702.5
2009	678.6	674.2	671.8	668.2	670.1	670.7	648.6	651.9	655.5	664.5	668.3	669.7	666.0
2010	656.1	658.9	662.7	669.6	675.6	674.6	661.4	660.8	665.1	677.3	683.3	685.5	669.2
2011	674.2	679.3	682.3	686.5	689.0	692.4	678.9	679.8	691.3	697.1	701.9	707.5	688.4
Trade, Transportation, and Utilities													
2000	152.3	151.3	152.1	151.7	152.5	153.3	154.2	154.7	154.6	153.5	156.8	159.8	153.9
2001	153.5	151.5	152.5	149.8	149.4	149.7	148.4	146.8	145.6	143.9	146.2	147.7	148.8
2002	139.8	138.3	138.8	137.0	137.0	136.8	136.4	136.0	135.8	135.5	137.6	139.5	137.4
2003	133.1	131.2	130.9	131.0	131.0	131.3	130.8	131.1	130.8	131.7	134.3	136.6	132.0
2004	130.7	129.6	129.2	128.8	129.8	130.1	129.8	130.1	129.9	131.4	134.2	136.6	130.9
2005	131.3	130.2	130.3	130.2	130.7	131.2	132.1	132.8	133.5	134.2	137.1	140.0	132.8
2006	135.3	133.8	133.8	133.7	134.4	135.2	136.4	137.6	138.1	138.6	142.6	145.1	137.1
2007	139.3	137.6	137.8	137.2	137.8	138.8	140.0	139.9	139.6	140.0	143.3	145.3	139.7
2008	140.2	138.7	138.9	137.1	137.2	136.9	137.3	137.5	136.3	136.0	137.4	138.1	137.6
2009	130.7	128.5	126.9	125.2	125.9	125.4	124.4	124.3	124.1	124.7	127.8	129.2	126.4
2010	124.6	123.4	123.0	123.6	124.5	125.1	125.6	126.2	125.7	126.3	130.2	131.8	125.8
2011	126.4	125.4	125.2	126.5	127.0	127.8	128.3	127.9	127.9	127.6	130.5	133.1	127.8
Wholesale Trade													
2000	42.9	43.1	43.2	43.0	43.1	43.0	42.9	42.8	42.5	42.4	42.1	41.9	42.7
2001	42.7	42.8	43.1	41.8	41.4	41.2	41.3	41.1	40.4	39.8	39.3	39.2	41.2
2002	38.6	38.1	38.2	37.2	37.0	36.5	35.9	35.5	34.9	34.6	34.0	33.6	36.2
2003	33.6	33.6	33.8	34.1	34.2	34.2	34.3	34.5	34.3	34.3	34.2	34.3	34.1
2004	34.0	33.9	33.9	34.3	34.4	34.6	34.5	34.6	34.5	34.9	34.9	34.9	34.5
2005	34.8	35.1	35.1	35.2	35.5	35.8	36.1	36.3	36.5	36.5	36.4	36.7	35.8
2006	37.0	37.3	37.4	37.8	37.9	38.2	38.7	38.8	39.0	39.0	39.1	39.3	38.3
2007	38.9	39.3	39.3	39.0	39.2	39.8	40.0	40.0	40.1	40.4	40.5	40.8	39.8
2008	40.5	40.4	40.9	40.2	40.3	40.1	39.6	39.4	39.3	39.2	38.8	38.4	39.8
2009	37.1	36.7	36.3	36.1	35.9	35.7	35.1	35.0	34.7	35.0	34.9	34.9	35.6
2010	34.5	34.6	34.6	34.7	34.9	35.0	35.3	35.2	35.3	35.1	35.2	35.4	35.0
2011	35.2	35.3	35.3	35.3	35.5	35.6	35.7	35.3	34.9	34.9	35.2	35.6	35.3
Retail Trade													
2000	92.2	91.0	91.6	90.8	91.7	92.4	93.4	93.8	94.1	93.1	96.6	99.6	93.4
2001	93.4	91.3	91.9	90.8	90.8	91.3	90.3	89.1	88.9	88.5	91.7	93.4	91.0
2002	86.5	85.4	85.8	84.8	84.6	84.9	85.1	85.2	85.6	85.5	88.3	90.6	86.0
2003	84.9	83.2	82.8	82.3	82.4	82.6	82.3	82.4	82.5	83.3	86.1	88.4	83.6
2004	82.9	81.9	81.5	81.1	81.9	81.9	82.0	82.3	82.0	83.0	85.8	88.2	82.9
2005	83.4	82.0	82.1	81.9	82.1	82.3	82.9	83.5	83.9	84.8	87.8	90.3	83.9
2006	85.8	83.9	83.8	83.4	83.7	84.0	84.8	85.6	85.8	86.5	90.1	92.3	85.8
2007	87.5	85.3	85.4	84.8	85.1	85.2	86.2	86.1	85.6	85.9	89.1	90.6	86.4
2008	86.5	84.9	84.6	83.6	83.3	83.1	84.3	84.6	83.5	83.4	85.2	86.0	84.4
2009	80.9	79.3	78.5	77.2	77.8	77.7	77.5	77.5	77.5	77.8	81.1	82.3	78.8
2010	78.3	77.1	76.7	77.2	77.6	78.0	78.2	78.8	78.1	79.1	82.9	84.0	78.8
2011	79.4	78.2	78.0	79.2	79.4	80.0	80.4	80.4	80.7	80.4	83.0	85.1	80.4
Transportation and Utilities													
2000	17.2	17.2	17.3	17.9	17.7	17.9	17.9	18.1	18.0	18.0	18.1	18.3	17.8
2001	17.4	17.4	17.5	17.2	17.2	17.2	16.8	16.6	16.3	15.6	15.2	15.1	16.6
2002	14.7	14.8	14.8	15.0	15.4	15.4	15.4	15.3	15.3	15.4	15.3	15.3	15.2
2003	14.6	14.4	14.3	14.6	14.4	14.5	14.2	14.2	14.0	14.1	14.0	13.9	14.3
2004	13.8	13.8	13.8	13.4	13.5	13.6	13.3	13.2	13.4	13.5	13.5	13.5	13.5
2005	13.1	13.1	13.1	13.1	13.1	13.1	13.1	13.0	13.1	12.9	12.9	13.0	13.1
2006	12.5	12.6	12.6	12.5	12.8	13.0	12.9	13.2	13.3	13.1	13.4	13.5	13.0
2007	12.9	13.0	13.1	13.4	13.5	13.8	13.8	13.8	13.9	13.7	13.7	13.9	13.5
2008	13.2	13.4	13.4	13.3	13.6	13.7	13.4	13.5	13.5	13.4	13.4	13.7	13.5
2009	12.7	12.5	12.1	11.9	12.2	12.0	11.8	11.8	11.9	11.9	11.8	12.0	12.1
2010	11.8	11.7	11.7	11.7	12.0	12.1	12.1	12.2	12.3	12.1	12.1	12.4	12.0
2011	11.8	11.9	11.9	12.0	12.1	12.2	12.2	12.2	12.3	12.3	12.3	12.4	12.1
Information													
2000	36.9	37.7	39.2	40.1	41.5	43.1	44.2	45.0	45.6	46.1	46.6	47.1	42.8
2001	46.5	46.2	46.1	43.8	43.4	42.8	41.4	40.7	39.6	38.3	37.6	37.3	42.0
2002	37.0	36.9	36.7	35.7	34.9	34.2	33.5	33.2	32.8	32.4	32.6	32.2	34.3
2003	31.8	32.0	31.6	31.1	31.1	31.2	31.2	31.1	31.0	31.3	31.5	31.7	31.4
2004	31.7	32.0	32.2	32.1	32.2	32.5	32.6	32.6	32.8	33.2	33.7	34.0	32.6
2005	33.8	34.1	34.4	34.0	34.4	35.0	35.5	35.8	35.7	36.2	36.9	37.3	35.3
2006	37.1	37.3	37.4	37.3	37.5	37.6	37.9	37.9	37.5	37.1	37.3	37.6	37.5
2007	37.8	38.2	38.5	38.1	38.9	39.7	40.3	40.5	40.3	40.5	41.1	41.4	39.6
2008	41.3	41.2	41.0	41.3	42.0	42.4	43.4	43.4	42.8	42.5	42.8	42.5	42.3
2009	42.5	41.5	41.1	40.6	40.9	41.2	42.3	42.0	41.6	41.8	42.0	42.1	41.6
2010	41.8	42.1	41.8	42.3	42.9	44.0	45.0	45.3	44.9	45.3	45.9	45.9	43.9
2011	46.5	46.9	47.0	47.4	47.9	49.5	50.0	50.2	50.0	50.1	50.8	51.2	49.0

Employment by Industry: San Jose–Sunnyvale–Santa Clara, CA, Selected Years, 2000–2011—*Continued*

(Numbers in thousands, not seasonally adjusted)

Industry and year	January	February	March	April	May	June	July	August	September	October	November	December	Annual average
Financial Activities													
2000	33.5	33.9	34.1	34.0	34.0	34.4	34.5	34.4	34.3	34.3	34.5	34.7	34.2
2001	34.3	34.6	35.0	35.2	35.4	35.8	35.7	36.1	35.9	35.6	35.8	36.1	35.5
2002	35.4	35.6	35.6	35.1	35.5	35.4	35.4	35.6	35.2	35.2	35.1	35.1	35.4
2003	34.7	34.7	34.9	34.9	35.0	34.9	35.1	35.2	35.0	34.8	34.7	34.9	34.9
2004	34.5	34.6	34.8	34.9	35.2	35.2	35.3	35.3	35.3	35.8	35.7	35.9	35.2
2005	35.7	35.6	35.8	35.7	35.8	36.0	36.1	36.4	36.2	36.5	36.5	36.8	36.1
2006	36.5	36.6	36.8	36.9	37.3	37.0	37.1	37.0	36.9	36.9	36.9	36.9	36.9
2007	37.0	37.1	37.1	37.0	37.2	37.0	37.1	36.9	36.8	36.6	36.2	36.3	36.9
2008	35.3	35.5	35.1	34.9	34.8	34.5	34.3	34.0	33.8	33.4	32.7	32.8	34.3
2009	32.2	31.9	31.9	31.8	31.7	31.4	31.3	31.2	30.9	31.2	31.2	31.3	31.5
2010	30.8	30.9	31.5	30.2	30.6	30.8	30.9	31.1	30.9	31.4	31.7	31.7	31.0
2011	31.6	31.8	31.7	31.7	31.7	31.9	31.4	31.6	31.5	31.7	31.7	32.5	31.7
Professional and Business Services													
2000	213.5	217.7	221.2	219.7	224.7	230.1	231.1	234.4	234.4	231.9	234.3	237.4	227.5
2001	229.7	230.8	231.7	223.8	219.7	218.0	210.3	206.1	199.8	195.1	191.0	188.9	212.1
2002	180.5	180.8	180.9	177.6	175.7	175.5	174.1	173.1	171.2	171.0	170.1	169.8	175.0
2003	166.4	166.7	166.9	168.1	168.5	169.2	166.2	167.9	168.4	166.9	167.0	168.3	167.5
2004	164.8	165.8	166.0	165.3	165.1	166.6	163.8	165.0	164.8	166.2	166.5	167.6	165.6
2005	164.3	165.9	166.7	165.0	165.1	165.9	164.4	165.3	165.8	166.2	166.5	168.4	165.8
2006	166.2	168.6	169.3	169.5	169.8	171.6	172.6	173.9	174.8	174.3	175.1	177.8	172.0
2007	176.2	177.7	177.8	177.2	177.6	178.2	178.7	178.3	178.2	178.9	179.8	180.5	178.3
2008	177.4	178.5	179.7	179.8	178.9	180.2	180.1	180.6	179.9	178.2	177.2	176.0	178.9
2009	168.5	166.7	165.2	161.4	160.0	160.4	159.2	158.9	158.2	158.8	159.3	159.8	161.4
2010	157.1	158.3	159.1	160.5	161.0	162.5	163.4	164.0	163.3	164.6	164.8	165.5	162.0
2011	163.7	164.8	166.0	166.7	166.5	168.5	170.8	171.6	174.0	173.9	173.7	173.8	169.5
Education and Health Services													
2000	87.2	87.7	87.8	86.7	87.4	84.6	84.2	83.2	83.5	86.3	87.0	87.6	86.1
2001	87.9	89.4	90.6	90.0	91.0	90.9	88.7	89.7	89.6	92.4	93.2	94.0	90.6
2002	89.6	92.3	93.3	93.3	93.3	92.8	89.7	89.9	89.6	92.1	93.2	93.2	91.9
2003	91.6	93.6	94.2	95.0	95.4	94.7	93.0	91.6	91.4	94.0	94.9	95.3	93.7
2004	94.0	94.9	95.9	95.2	96.1	96.2	93.6	93.4	93.4	96.1	97.0	97.2	95.3
2005	96.2	96.9	96.9	96.4	96.6	96.8	95.5	95.4	95.3	98.6	99.9	100.2	97.1
2006	98.4	101.0	101.8	101.2	101.9	102.3	99.1	98.6	98.7	100.8	101.9	101.7	100.6
2007	99.6	102.5	103.7	101.9	103.6	104.4	102.4	101.9	102.1	105.7	107.0	106.7	103.5
2008	107.0	109.2	109.3	108.6	108.1	107.7	104.3	107.7	107.6	109.0	110.2	110.0	108.2
2009	108.9	110.2	110.0	109.9	110.5	110.0	106.4	106.7	105.7	110.6	111.0	111.5	109.3
2010	109.8	111.2	111.7	114.1	114.6	114.3	111.2	110.8	110.4	114.1	115.0	115.7	112.7
2011	115.0	116.9	117.1	117.2	117.6	116.3	114.9	115.2	115.9	119.6	120.8	121.9	117.4
Leisure and Hospitality													
2000	68.2	69.8	71.7	72.7	73.7	74.3	75.7	75.8	75.5	72.7	71.8	71.8	72.8
2001	71.0	72.9	74.6	74.8	75.9	76.6	76.4	76.0	73.2	70.5	69.0	·69.1	73.3
2002	66.3	67.7	69.2	69.4	70.6	71.2	70.8	70.5	69.3	68.1	66.5	66.5	68.8
2003	65.5	66.9	67.7	68.8	70.1	71.1	70.9	70.9	70.2	69.5	68.1	68.2	69.0
2004	66.9	68.0	69.9	70.8	72.2	73.1	73.2	72.9	72.0	71.3	69.7	70.2	70.9
2005	68.4	69.5	70.9	72.1	73.7	74.8	75.2	75.3	74.5	73.5	72.7	73.1	72.8
2006	70.5	72.4	73.8	74.7	76.2	77.9	76.9	77.4	76.6	75.4	74.9	75.3	75.2
2007	72.6	74.0	75.9	76.7	78.0	79.2	78.6	78.7	77.7	76.9	76.5	76.7	76.8
2008	74.3	75.6	77.3	77.9	79.3	80.6	80.5	80.2	79.5	78.3	76.9	76.3	78.1
2009	73.8	74.0	74.4	75.1	76.1	77.1	75.9	76.2	74.8	74.7	73.1	73.2	74.9
2010	71.5	71.7	72.7	75.5	76.9	76.7	76.4	76.1	76.3	75.9	74.4	74.7	74.9
2011	72.4	73.9	75.3	76.4	77.3	77.9	78.3	77.5	77.2	76.3	75.9	76.5	76.2
Other Services													
2000	26.1	26.5	26.9	27.2	27.2	27.6	27.7	27.7	27.2	26.5	26.5	27.1	27.0
2001	26.5	26.6	26.6	26.4	26.6	27.0	26.9	27.0	26.7	26.6	26.7	26.7	26.7
2002	26.3	26.7	26.9	26.7	26.7	26.7	26.7	26.6	26.2	25.7	26.0	25.8	26.4
2003	24.8	25.1	25.1	25.7	25.7	25.8	25.5	25.1	25.1	25.3	25.4	25.3	25.3
2004	24.3	24.8	24.9	25.2	25.4	25.4	25.2	25.0	25.0	25.0	25.0	25.1	25.0
2005	24.5	24.9	24.9	24.8	25.0	25.4	24.7	24.2	24.4	24.3	24.2	24.3	24.6
2006	24.0	24.5	24.7	24.8	25.3	25.8	24.8	24.9	25.0	24.5	24.6	24.7	24.8
2007	23.9	24.6	24.8	24.8	25.2	25.6	25.1	25.1	25.4	25.5	25.4	25.4	25.1
2008	24.7	25.2	25.5	25.5	25.9	25.9	25.3	25.1	25.5	25.5	25.3	25.2	25.4
2009	24.5	24.6	24.7	24.8	24.9	24.9	24.0	23.8	24.2	24.3	24.6	24.5	24.5
2010	24.5	24.9	25.2	24.1	24.2	24.5	23.8	23.7	23.9	24.2	24.3	24.1	24.3
2011	24.0	24.3	24.3	24.6	24.8	24.8	24.4	24.2	24.3	24.4	24.4	24.3	24.4
Government													
2000	98.1	97.8	99.9	99.6	100.7	103.7	99.4	94.2	93.8	98.9	99.3	99.0	98.7
2001	97.4	98.0	98.9	99.2	100.6	99.7	97.0	94.6	96.7	100.4	101.7	101.5	98.8
2002	101.2	102.2	103.4	104.6	104.7	104.4	101.3	98.6	99.7	103.2	103.6	103.1	102.5
2003	102.2	101.0	101.7	101.8	101.4	100.8	96.9	94.6	95.3	98.6	98.5	97.0	99.2
2004	95.9	96.8	97.9	97.9	98.1	97.6	94.8	92.9	93.5	96.2	97.4	96.0	96.3
2005	95.5	96.2	96.9	97.0	97.4	97.0	94.3	93.7	93.8	96.2	96.6	96.2	95.9
2006	95.7	96.5	96.7	97.3	97.8	97.4	95.1	93.7	94.3	97.7	97.6	97.5	96.4
2007	97.7	97.0	98.3	98.1	98.3	97.8	95.1	93.9	94.9	98.3	98.6	98.3	97.2
2008	99.0	98.2	99.1	98.4	99.0	98.6	94.0	94.5	98.0	98.7	98.3	97.8	97.8
2009	97.5	96.8	97.6	99.4	100.1	100.3	85.1	88.8	96.0	98.4	99.3	98.1	96.5
2010	96.0	96.4	97.7	99.3	100.9	96.7	85.1	83.6	89.7	95.5	97.0	96.1	94.5
2011	94.6	95.3	95.7	96.0	96.2	95.7	80.8	81.6	90.5	93.5	94.1	94.2	92.4

Employment by Industry: Seattle–Tacoma–Bellevue, WA, Selected Years, 2000–2011

(Numbers in thousands, not seasonally adjusted)

Industry and year	January	February	March	April	May	June	July	August	September	October	November	December	Annual average
Total Nonfarm													
2000	1,609.8	1,607.5	1,636.8	1,630.5	1,646.5	1,661.0	1,643.5	1,651.1	1,663.2	1,662.1	1,671.4	1,678.5	1,646.8
2001	1,629.2	1,631.5	1,637.2	1,632.7	1,640.5	1,646.7	1,629.8	1,626.3	1,629.6	1,616.2	1,616.2	1,610.9	1,628.9
2002	1,569.2	1,569.6	1,572.2	1,573.4	1,585.2	1,593.3	1,583.5	1,582.7	1,588.2	1,585.5	1,594.9	1,588.1	1,582.2
2003	1,553.4	1,557.3	1,558.1	1,559.9	1,572.7	1,577.7	1,569.5	1,569.3	1,578.3	1,579.9	1,587.7	1,589.4	1,571.1
2004	1,549.4	1,559.6	1,570.3	1,577.9	1,588.7	1,600.3	1,593.0	1,590.3	1,602.2	1,608.9	1,620.7	1,621.9	1,590.3
2005	1,587.3	1,594.9	1,606.6	1,617.2	1,631.9	1,643.1	1,641.3	1,642.1	1,644.2	1,658.0	1,672.8	1,677.8	1,634.8
2006	1,643.0	1,654.2	1,662.9	1,670.1	1,686.7	1,702.6	1,690.0	1,694.2	1,709.7	1,708.0	1,720.8	1,723.1	1,688.8
2007	1,690.4	1,710.4	1,718.2	1,723.5	1,740.4	1,755.6	1,748.4	1,750.2	1,753.8	1,759.5	1,774.0	1,774.3	1,741.6
2008	1,740.4	1,752.9	1,753.6	1,758.9	1,768.9	1,777.1	1,771.1	1,770.7	1,769.6	1,740.6	1,758.2	1,743.0	1,758.8
2009	1,699.8	1,693.4	1,682.9	1,673.7	1,676.9	1,677.3	1,663.3	1,648.2	1,656.0	1,652.7	1,650.3	1,646.0	1,668.4
2010	1,612.1	1,614.3	1,620.9	1,632.2	1,644.9	1,652.1	1,649.0	1,638.2	1,649.2	1,657.6	1,662.1	1,661.4	1,641.2
2011	1,630.1	1,638.0	1,643.1	1,658.3	1,668.2	1,678.2	1,675.6	1,668.6	1,669.4	1,682.6	1,692.4	1,688.4	1,666.1
Total Private													
2000	1,376.5	1,368.9	1,399.1	1,393.4	1,404.3	1,418.8	1,416.3	1,427.5	1,430.9	1,425.4	1,431.1	1,438.2	1,410.9
2001	1,388.3	1,388.1	1,392.2	1,388.0	1,394.4	1,399.0	1,392.7	1,397.1	1,389.1	1,370.9	1,364.2	1,361.5	1,385.5
2002	1,322.3	1,319.3	1,321.8	1,322.9	1,333.9	1,341.5	1,342.5	1,349.1	1,343.6	1,335.9	1,338.5	1,336.5	1,334.0
2003	1,302.9	1,303.4	1,304.7	1,306.8	1,315.3	1,322.9	1,327.6	1,332.9	1,332.4	1,329.2	1,331.5	1,334.4	1,320.3
2004	1,299.2	1,305.7	1,316.1	1,324.2	1,334.1	1,344.1	1,348.8	1,353.8	1,353.5	1,356.8	1,361.8	1,367.1	1,338.8
2005	1,335.5	1,341.1	1,351.6	1,362.5	1,376.3	1,386.6	1,396.5	1,405.1	1,395.1	1,405.0	1,413.7	1,423.3	1,382.7
2006	1,390.0	1,397.4	1,405.9	1,414.2	1,429.6	1,445.0	1,445.2	1,456.7	1,460.5	1,454.1	1,461.0	1,468.3	1,435.7
2007	1,437.3	1,453.4	1,461.1	1,466.7	1,482.5	1,496.6	1,498.7	1,506.7	1,505.9	1,502.6	1,511.1	1,515.4	1,486.5
2008	1,482.5	1,489.8	1,492.3	1,497.3	1,505.7	1,512.5	1,514.9	1,519.6	1,513.6	1,475.9	1,486.9	1,477.2	1,497.4
2009	1,434.3	1,426.7	1,415.8	1,403.5	1,406.7	1,410.2	1,404.7	1,400.7	1,398.0	1,387.0	1,382.8	1,382.7	1,404.4
2010	1,347.4	1,348.1	1,354.6	1,363.8	1,370.7	1,381.5	1,388.7	1,389.8	1,391.4	1,392.9	1,395.0	1,399.7	1,377.0
2011	1,367.2	1,373.6	1,378.8	1,393.6	1,402.0	1,414.9	1,419.9	1,423.7	1,418.0	1,420.9	1,428.5	1,429.3	1,405.9
Goods-Producing													
2000	312.1	298.2	316.0	315.1	316.0	318.3	317.9	319.4	319.0	317.4	315.3	313.4	314.8
2001	307.6	305.7	306.9	305.8	307.4	309.1	309.9	311.7	308.8	302.5	296.0	291.0	305.2
2002	282.2	279.9	279.0	277.8	280.2	281.2	280.9	282.5	278.9	275.9	272.0	268.1	278.2
2003	260.9	259.8	259.3	259.3	261.5	262.9	264.4	266.1	264.8	262.9	260.3	258.3	261.7
2004	252.9	254.1	256.4	257.5	259.8	261.8	266.0	267.4	266.6	268.1	266.9	266.3	262.0
2005	261.4	263.7	267.6	270.3	273.5	277.3	282.7	285.3	271.6	286.1	285.5	286.3	275.9
2006	283.1	286.9	288.5	290.5	294.3	299.0	301.5	303.9	305.3	304.5	303.1	302.4	296.9
2007	299.3	304.6	305.7	307.4	311.9	317.4	319.8	323.3	322.0	320.0	318.9	316.0	313.8
2008	310.9	312.8	311.8	311.0	312.8	314.0	315.7	316.7	313.4	285.4	301.3	294.5	308.8
2009	283.7	280.8	274.1	269.7	268.4	268.1	267.2	266.0	263.9	259.8	255.5	251.8	267.4
2010	247.5	246.5	246.2	247.2	248.2	250.7	254.5	255.5	255.1	254.1	251.2	249.1	250.5
2011	244.8	245.9	246.9	249.4	251.7	255.9	262.0	264.0	264.2	263.5	262.7	262.3	256.1
Mining and Logging													
2000	2.4	2.5	2.6	2.6	2.6	2.7	2.6	2.7	2.7	2.7	2.5	2.4	2.6
2001	2.7	2.6	2.6	2.5	2.5	2.5	2.6	2.6	2.5	2.5	2.3	2.3	2.5
2002	2.1	2.2	2.3	2.2	2.2	2.2	2.2	2.2	2.2	2.2	2.1	2.1	2.2
2003	2.0	2.0	2.1	1.9	1.8	1.8	1.7	1.8	1.7	1.8	1.7	1.7	1.8
2004	1.6	1.6	1.6	1.6	1.7	1.7	1.6	1.6	1.6	1.6	1.6	1.6	1.6
2005	1.5	1.5	1.5	1.5	1.5	1.5	1.5	1.5	1.5	1.5	1.5	1.5	1.5
2006	1.4	1.5	1.5	1.5	1.5	1.5	1.5	1.5	1.5	1.5	1.5	1.5	1.5
2007	1.4	1.5	1.4	1.6	1.6	1.6	1.7	1.6	1.5	1.6	1.5	1.5	1.5
2008	1.3	1.4	1.4	1.4	1.4	1.4	1.4	1.4	1.4	1.4	1.3	1.3	1.4
2009	1.3	1.3	1.2	1.1	1.1	1.1	1.1	1.1	1.1	1.1	1.1	1.0	1.1
2010	1.0	1.1	1.0	1.0	1.1	1.1	1.1	1.1	1.1	1.1	1.0	1.0	1.1
2011	1.0	1.0	1.0	1.0	1.0	1.0	1.0	1.0	1.0	1.0	1.0	0.9	1.0
Construction													
2000	91.5	93.2	95.7	96.6	98.2	100.4	101.9	103.5	103.9	102.8	101.6	100.3	99.1
2001	96.6	95.8	97.1	96.0	97.8	99.5	100.8	102.4	101.1	97.7	94.0	91.2	97.5
2002	88.4	88.9	88.9	89.1	91.4	92.8	94.6	97.5	96.5	94.5	92.2	89.6	92.0
2003	86.2	86.4	86.6	88.3	90.9	92.8	94.9	97.0	96.6	95.7	94.0	92.4	91.8
2004	88.8	90.3	91.9	92.7	94.6	96.2	99.2	100.4	99.4	99.9	98.6	97.3	95.8
2005	93.1	94.9	97.1	98.9	101.1	103.2	106.5	108.7	109.9	108.9	107.9	107.9	103.2
2006	104.3	106.8	108.8	110.6	113.4	116.4	117.9	120.1	120.5	119.8	117.6	116.5	114.4
2007	114.4	117.5	119.7	121.6	124.9	128.2	128.8	131.1	130.3	128.3	126.4	124.5	124.6
2008	120.0	120.2	120.7	120.7	121.7	122.5	123.7	124.1	122.2	119.0	113.3	108.4	119.7
2009	101.2	98.8	97.0	94.8	94.8	94.9	94.7	94.0	93.1	90.6	87.0	84.3	93.8
2010	80.4	79.6	79.8	80.6	81.9	82.9	85.6	86.6	85.9	85.1	81.8	79.7	82.5
2011	75.5	75.3	75.5	76.6	78.3	80.3	84.9	86.1	84.5	83.1	81.5	79.6	80.1
Manufacturing													
2000	218.2	202.5	217.7	215.9	215.2	215.2	213.4	213.2	212.4	211.9	211.2	210.7	213.1
2001	208.3	207.3	207.2	207.3	207.1	207.1	206.5	206.7	205.2	202.3	199.7	197.5	205.2
2002	191.7	188.8	187.8	186.5	186.6	186.2	184.1	182.8	180.2	179.2	177.7	176.4	184.0
2003	172.7	171.4	170.6	169.1	168.8	168.3	167.8	167.3	166.5	165.4	164.6	164.2	168.1
2004	162.5	162.2	162.9	163.2	163.5	163.9	165.2	165.4	165.6	166.6	166.7	167.4	164.6
2005	166.8	167.3	169.0	169.9	170.9	172.6	174.7	175.1	160.2	175.7	176.1	176.9	171.3
2006	177.4	178.6	178.2	178.4	179.4	181.1	182.1	182.3	183.3	183.2	184.0	184.4	181.0
2007	183.5	185.6	184.6	184.2	185.4	187.6	189.3	189.6	190.2	190.1	191.0	190.0	187.6
2008	189.6	191.2	189.7	188.9	189.7	190.1	190.6	191.2	189.8	165.0	186.7	184.8	187.3
2009	181.2	180.7	175.9	173.8	172.5	172.1	171.4	170.9	169.7	168.1	167.4	166.5	172.5
2010	166.1	165.8	165.4	165.6	165.2	166.7	167.8	167.8	168.1	167.9	168.4	168.4	166.9
2011	168.3	169.6	170.4	171.8	172.4	174.6	176.1	176.9	178.7	179.4	180.2	181.8	175.0

Employment by Industry: Seattle–Tacoma–Bellevue, WA, Selected Years, 2000–2011—*Continued*

(Numbers in thousands, not seasonally adjusted)

Industry and year	January	February	March	April	May	June	July	August	September	October	November	December	Annual average
Service-Providing													
2000	1,297.7	1,309.3	1,320.8	1,315.4	1,330.5	1,342.7	1,325.6	1,331.7	1,344.2	1,344.7	1,356.1	1,365.1	1,332.0
2001	1,321.6	1,325.8	1,330.3	1,326.9	1,333.1	1,337.6	1,319.9	1,314.6	1,320.8	1,313.7	1,320.2	1,319.9	1,323.7
2002	1,287.0	1,289.7	1,293.2	1,295.6	1,305.0	1,312.1	1,302.6	1,300.2	1,309.3	1,309.6	1,322.9	1,320.0	1,303.9
2003	1,292.5	1,297.5	1,298.8	1,300.6	1,311.2	1,314.8	1,305.1	1,303.2	1,313.5	1,317.0	1,327.4	1,331.1	1,309.4
2004	1,296.5	1,305.5	1,313.9	1,320.4	1,328.9	1,338.5	1,327.0	1,322.9	1,335.6	1,340.8	1,353.8	1,355.6	1,328.3
2005	1,325.9	1,331.2	1,339.0	1,346.9	1,358.4	1,365.8	1,358.6	1,356.8	1,372.6	1,371.9	1,387.3	1,391.5	1,358.8
2006	1,359.9	1,367.3	1,374.4	1,379.6	1,392.4	1,403.6	1,388.5	1,390.3	1,404.4	1,403.5	1,417.7	1,420.7	1,391.9
2007	1,391.1	1,405.8	1,412.5	1,416.1	1,428.5	1,438.2	1,428.6	1,427.9	1,431.8	1,439.5	1,455.1	1,458.3	1,427.8
2008	1,429.5	1,440.1	1,441.8	1,447.9	1,456.1	1,463.1	1,455.4	1,454.0	1,456.2	1,455.2	1,456.9	1,448.5	1,450.4
2009	1,416.1	1,412.6	1,408.8	1,404.0	1,408.5	1,409.2	1,396.1	1,382.2	1,392.1	1,392.9	1,394.8	1,394.2	1,401.0
2010	1,364.6	1,367.8	1,374.7	1,385.0	1,396.7	1,401.4	1,394.5	1,382.7	1,394.1	1,403.5	1,410.9	1,412.3	1,390.7
2011	1,385.3	1,392.1	1,396.2	1,408.9	1,416.5	1,422.3	1,413.6	1,404.6	1,405.2	1,419.1	1,429.7	1,426.1	1,410.0
Trade, Transportation, and Utilities													
2000	319.8	318.4	320.4	320.5	322.9	325.4	324.2	326.1	325.8	329.6	335.8	339.8	325.7
2001	324.2	320.4	320.8	319.2	319.1	320.7	320.5	320.2	318.3	316.3	319.4	322.0	320.1
2002	308.9	304.5	304.0	303.7	306.0	308.4	309.5	309.5	308.6	308.6	313.1	316.7	308.5
2003	304.4	301.3	300.8	300.3	302.0	304.0	306.5	306.1	305.2	305.8	311.2	316.1	305.3
2004	301.3	300.1	301.3	303.5	305.6	308.0	308.6	310.1	309.2	310.8	315.9	320.4	307.9
2005	307.0	305.6	306.6	307.1	310.4	312.3	313.6	315.3	315.0	315.7	322.0	327.7	313.2
2006	313.8	311.4	312.5	312.5	315.6	318.9	318.9	320.6	319.8	319.2	326.1	331.3	318.4
2007	319.5	319.0	319.5	320.1	322.9	325.3	326.8	327.4	325.8	326.7	334.3	338.2	325.5
2008	326.5	324.4	324.2	323.7	324.6	326.0	327.4	328.5	325.3	323.9	325.4	327.6	325.6
2009	312.8	307.6	304.8	301.8	303.4	303.8	304.4	303.9	303.4	301.5	304.9	308.4	305.1
2010	297.1	295.2	295.5	297.0	298.8	301.2	302.4	303.1	302.0	304.2	308.9	314.1	301.6
2011	301.6	300.5	301.3	302.4	305.1	308.1	309.0	310.0	308.5	310.5	316.6	317.3	307.6
Wholesale Trade													
2000	79.0	79.6	80.3	80.3	80.7	81.6	81.5	81.9	81.3	82.0	81.6	82.0	81.0
2001	80.2	80.5	80.6	80.6	80.5	81.0	80.7	80.7	80.2	79.0	78.5	78.4	80.1
2002	77.6	77.6	77.7	77.2	77.5	77.6	77.2	77.3	76.8	75.9	75.8	75.8	77.0
2003	75.7	75.8	76.0	75.8	75.9	75.9	76.4	76.3	76.0	75.9	75.9	76.1	76.0
2004	75.7	76.1	76.7	77.1	77.2	77.2	77.7	77.5	77.4	77.2	77.0	77.3	77.0
2005	76.6	76.9	77.4	77.6	78.0	78.4	78.9	79.3	79.4	79.4	79.6	80.2	78.5
2006	80.2	80.4	80.9	80.7	81.3	81.8	82.1	82.2	82.2	81.8	82.1	82.2	81.5
2007	81.6	82.0	82.3	82.4	83.0	83.5	83.7	83.8	83.5	83.6	84.0	84.4	83.2
2008	83.5	83.9	84.0	84.0	84.4	84.6	84.4	84.6	84.1	83.5	83.0	82.6	83.9
2009	81.8	80.8	80.2	79.4	79.1	79.0	78.9	78.3	78.0	77.5	77.2	77.2	79.0
2010	76.1	76.4	76.5	76.8	76.9	76.9	77.0	77.0	76.7	76.8	77.0	77.0	76.8
2011	76.4	76.7	76.9	77.2	77.7	78.0	78.1	77.6	77.6	78.5	78.6	78.8	77.7
Retail Trade													
2000	177.0	175.0	175.9	175.6	177.8	178.9	177.8	178.8	179.2	180.7	187.0	190.9	179.6
2001	178.8	175.0	175.6	174.3	174.3	175.2	175.8	175.8	175.0	174.5	179.1	182.0	176.3
2002	171.4	167.0	167.1	167.2	168.5	170.1	170.7	170.6	170.3	170.9	176.0	179.7	170.8
2003	168.7	166.1	165.7	165.4	166.6	168.1	169.5	169.3	168.7	169.6	175.2	179.3	169.4
2004	167.2	165.7	166.0	166.7	168.5	169.8	169.6	171.3	170.0	171.2	176.8	180.6	170.3
2005	170.3	168.0	168.3	169.1	171.3	172.3	173.4	174.8	173.9	175.1	180.8	184.8	173.5
2006	172.9	170.3	170.6	170.5	172.3	174.3	174.2	175.6	174.5	175.2	181.8	185.5	174.8
2007	176.2	175.1	175.0	174.9	176.7	177.8	179.3	179.6	178.5	179.4	186.7	189.3	179.0
2008	180.8	177.9	177.8	177.3	177.2	178.1	179.5	180.6	178.5	178.7	181.1	183.0	179.2
2009	170.6	167.7	166.1	164.0	165.6	166.3	166.8	167.2	166.9	166.5	170.5	173.1	167.6
2010	165.0	163.0	163.1	164.2	165.5	167.1	167.6	168.3	167.5	169.6	174.3	177.8	167.8
2011	168.3	166.6	166.5	166.7	168.7	170.8	171.6	173.1	172.0	173.4	179.2	178.7	171.3
Transportation and Utilities													
2000	63.8	63.8	64.2	64.6	64.4	64.9	64.9	65.4	65.3	66.9	67.2	66.9	65.2
2001	65.2	64.9	64.6	64.3	64.3	64.5	64.0	63.7	63.1	62.8	61.8	61.6	63.7
2002	59.9	59.9	59.2	59.3	60.0	60.7	61.6	61.6	61.5	61.8	61.3	61.2	60.7
2003	60.0	59.4	59.1	59.1	59.5	60.0	60.6	60.5	60.5	60.3	60.1	60.7	60.0
2004	58.4	58.3	58.6	59.7	59.9	61.0	61.3	61.3	61.8	62.4	62.1	62.5	60.6
2005	60.1	60.7	60.9	60.4	61.1	61.6	61.3	61.2	61.7	61.2	61.6	62.7	61.2
2006	60.7	60.7	61.0	61.3	62.0	62.8	62.6	62.8	63.1	62.2	62.2	63.6	62.1
2007	61.7	61.9	62.2	62.8	63.2	64.0	63.8	64.0	63.8	63.7	63.6	64.5	63.3
2008	62.2	62.6	62.4	62.4	63.0	63.3	63.5	63.3	62.7	61.7	61.3	62.0	62.5
2009	60.4	59.1	58.5	58.4	58.7	58.5	58.7	58.4	58.5	57.5	57.2	58.1	58.5
2010	56.0	55.8	55.9	56.0	56.4	57.2	57.8	57.8	57.8	57.8	57.6	59.3	57.1
2011	56.9	57.2	57.9	58.5	58.7	59.3	59.3	59.3	58.9	58.6	58.8	59.8	58.6
Information													
2000	73.2	74.5	75.8	75.9	77.4	79.8	81.3	82.3	83.2	82.7	83.3	83.6	79.4
2001	82.4	82.7	82.1	80.6	80.8	81.3	80.4	80.3	78.6	78.4	78.4	78.8	80.4
2002	76.6	76.4	76.0	75.6	75.7	76.0	76.2	76.2	75.5	75.5	75.8	75.6	75.9
2003	74.6	74.5	74.0	73.6	74.1	74.3	74.7	75.4	75.0	75.1	75.4	75.8	74.7
2004	74.9	74.9	75.2	75.1	75.6	76.0	76.3	76.5	75.8	76.2	76.6	76.9	75.8
2005	76.2	76.8	76.6	76.8	77.1	77.3	78.1	78.8	78.1	77.6	78.4	78.9	77.6
2006	77.9	78.1	78.7	79.2	79.8	82.1	82.5	83.3	83.4	82.8	83.6	84.0	81.3
2007	83.3	84.3	83.9	84.3	85.1	85.9	86.1	86.4	86.0	85.1	86.2	86.4	85.3
2008	85.9	87.0	87.2	87.5	88.0	89.1	90.4	91.2	90.2	89.6	90.6	90.7	89.0
2009	88.9	89.4	89.1	87.8	88.4	88.6	88.9	88.4	87.6	87.0	87.3	87.1	88.2
2010	86.6	86.9	86.8	86.5	87.0	88.1	88.3	88.8	88.7	87.9	88.3	88.6	87.7
2011	87.2	88.0	87.7	87.7	87.9	89.0	88.2	90.4	89.0	88.3	88.4	88.4	88.4

Employment by Industry: Seattle–Tacoma–Bellevue, WA, Selected Years, 2000–2011—*Continued*
(Numbers in thousands, not seasonally adjusted)

Industry and year	January	February	March	April	May	June	July	August	September	October	November	December	Annual average
Financial Activities													
2000	99.9	100.5	100.3	100.0	100.0	100.4	99.8	100.4	100.1	99.6	100.1	101.2	100.2
2001	100.3	101.2	101.0	101.0	101.2	101.6	103.1	103.3	103.7	102.2	102.2	102.7	102.0
2002	99.7	100.3	100.7	100.7	101.1	101.2	101.5	102.1	102.0	102.0	102.7	103.0	101.4
2003	102.5	103.0	103.2	103.6	104.4	104.7	105.6	106.1	105.6	105.4	105.2	104.9	104.5
2004	103.6	103.6	104.4	103.6	103.8	104.2	104.5	104.6	104.1	104.0	103.9	104.8	104.1
2005	102.7	103.1	103.2	103.5	104.1	104.6	106.1	106.8	106.5	106.7	106.9	107.3	105.1
2006	106.0	106.4	106.2	106.3	106.5	106.7	107.0	106.9	106.2	105.9	105.7	106.0	106.3
2007	104.8	105.1	105.6	105.7	105.7	106.0	106.3	106.3	105.1	105.2	105.6	105.5	105.6
2008	104.4	104.4	104.2	103.8	104.4	104.2	103.7	103.7	102.7	101.3	101.0	100.4	103.2
2009	98.3	98.2	96.9	96.4	96.1	95.9	95.0	94.3	93.5	92.4	91.8	91.5	95.0
2010	89.7	89.6	89.5	89.5	89.5	89.7	90.4	89.9	89.8	89.7	89.6	89.9	89.7
2011	88.8	88.9	88.9	89.3	89.3	89.5	90.3	89.6	89.3	88.7	88.8	88.2	89.1
Professional and Business Services													
2000	211.6	213.0	216.7	215.1	216.7	220.6	222.1	225.8	227.1	224.6	224.6	226.4	220.4
2001	213.3	212.7	214.1	212.6	212.7	212.2	208.3	208.5	206.3	203.9	201.5	199.4	208.8
2002	193.3	194.5	195.1	196.3	197.3	198.4	199.8	202.4	201.7	200.9	201.7	199.0	198.4
2003	192.8	194.1	194.3	195.1	195.1	195.8	197.1	199.2	199.0	199.5	199.1	198.1	196.6
2004	193.7	196.6	198.3	200.7	201.5	203.3	205.7	207.2	207.1	209.0	209.5	208.3	203.4
2005	203.6	206.2	207.4	210.1	212.0	213.8	216.8	218.9	220.6	220.4	221.3	221.2	214.4
2006	215.2	217.4	219.6	222.6	225.2	228.3	229.9	232.7	233.3	233.6	234.5	234.6	227.2
2007	228.0	232.3	234.7	235.2	237.1	239.7	240.6	242.6	243.0	242.4	243.2	244.1	238.6
2008	237.5	239.5	240.5	243.2	244.4	244.9	245.7	245.5	244.9	242.8	238.3	234.5	241.8
2009	228.3	226.3	224.4	221.4	220.0	221.1	219.9	219.5	219.7	218.8	218.4	219.2	221.4
2010	212.1	213.2	216.1	218.6	219.2	220.8	223.8	223.0	223.9	225.1	225.1	225.8	220.6
2011	220.3	222.5	223.9	228.6	228.4	229.8	231.6	231.3	231.0	230.4	231.3	230.5	228.3
Education and Health Services													
2000	164.2	166.6	168.5	165.9	166.3	165.7	164.9	165.3	166.9	168.3	169.4	169.0	166.8
2001	163.3	166.1	166.2	167.1	167.4	165.9	162.0	163.0	166.2	168.5	170.2	170.0	166.3
2002	168.8	170.8	171.6	171.2	172.1	170.6	167.2	167.4	169.6	172.8	174.3	173.6	170.8
2003	171.4	173.1	174.0	174.3	174.3	173.0	170.0	169.7	172.0	175.0	176.3	175.9	173.3
2004	173.4	175.4	176.4	177.0	177.8	176.5	172.5	172.8	175.8	179.2	180.7	180.1	176.5
2005	179.0	180.8	182.2	183.4	184.3	182.1	178.3	178.8	182.7	184.9	186.0	185.2	182.3
2006	183.7	185.7	186.9	187.1	188.2	185.9	181.1	182.1	185.8	188.8	189.6	189.0	186.2
2007	187.7	190.2	191.9	192.2	193.8	191.2	187.5	188.1	191.5	196.6	197.9	197.6	192.2
2008	195.3	198.4	198.6	199.6	200.7	199.4	196.0	196.6	199.9	204.9	205.8	205.8	200.1
2009	205.5	207.5	208.1	207.7	208.7	207.1	202.8	202.2	205.1	209.9	209.9	209.2	207.0
2010	205.7	207.2	207.9	208.3	208.8	207.4	203.6	203.1	206.9	211.9	213.3	211.9	208.0
2011	210.8	213.3	214.1	214.4	214.4	212.8	208.8	207.2	209.4	216.0	217.7	218.7	213.1
Leisure and Hospitality													
2000	139.8	141.4	144.4	144.6	146.9	150.0	147.3	149.1	149.9	145.0	144.5	146.5	145.8
2001	139.7	141.5	142.9	143.6	147.2	148.6	148.9	150.0	148.2	140.9	138.3	139.1	144.1
2002	135.0	134.9	137.0	138.6	142.0	145.3	146.4	147.7	146.9	140.7	139.3	140.6	141.2
2003	137.1	138.0	139.3	140.9	143.6	147.3	148.3	149.5	150.4	145.8	144.1	145.1	144.1
2004	140.3	141.4	144.0	146.3	148.9	152.5	153.0	153.0	153.3	148.5	147.3	149.1	148.1
2005	145.1	144.0	146.5	149.9	153.1	156.7	158.2	158.5	158.5	152.1	152.1	154.7	152.5
2006	149.3	150.0	151.6	154.0	157.5	160.8	161.3	164.0	163.7	157.5	156.5	158.7	157.1
2007	153.7	155.9	157.3	159.5	163.0	167.4	168.0	169.6	169.1	163.7	161.9	164.3	162.8
2008	159.3	160.0	161.9	164.3	165.9	169.6	170.2	171.5	171.6	163.6	160.1	159.9	164.8
2009	153.3	153.3	154.4	154.9	157.8	161.3	162.0	162.1	161.5	154.8	152.6	152.9	156.7
2010	147.4	148.0	150.8	154.5	156.4	159.9	161.2	161.8	161.5	156.1	154.5	156.4	155.7
2011	150.7	151.2	152.4	157.4	160.3	163.9	165.2	166.5	162.9	160.0	160.0	160.6	159.3
Other Services													
2000	55.9	56.3	57.0	56.3	58.1	58.6	58.8	59.1	58.9	58.2	58.1	58.3	57.8
2001	57.5	57.8	58.2	58.1	58.6	59.6	59.6	60.1	59.0	58.2	58.2	58.5	58.6
2002	57.8	58.0	58.4	59.0	59.5	60.4	61.0	61.3	60.4	59.5	59.6	59.9	59.6
2003	59.2	59.6	59.8	59.7	60.3	60.9	61.0	60.8	60.4	59.7	59.9	60.2	60.1
2004	59.1	59.6	60.1	60.5	61.1	61.8	62.2	62.2	61.6	61.0	61.0	61.2	61.0
2005	60.5	60.9	61.5	61.4	61.8	62.5	62.7	62.7	62.1	61.5	61.5	62.0	61.8
2006	61.0	61.5	61.9	62.0	62.5	63.3	63.0	63.2	63.0	61.8	61.9	62.3	62.3
2007	61.0	62.0	62.5	62.3	63.0	63.7	63.6	64.0	63.4	62.9	63.1	63.3	62.9
2008	62.7	63.3	63.9	64.2	64.9	65.3	65.8	65.9	65.6	64.4	64.4	63.8	64.5
2009	63.5	63.6	64.0	63.8	63.9	64.3	64.5	64.3	63.3	62.8	62.4	62.6	63.6
2010	61.3	61.5	61.8	62.2	62.8	63.7	64.5	64.6	63.5	63.9	64.1	63.9	63.2
2011	63.0	63.3	63.6	64.4	64.9	65.9	64.8	64.7	63.7	63.5	63.0	63.3	64.0
Government													
2000	233.3	238.6	237.7	237.1	242.2	242.2	227.2	223.6	232.3	236.7	240.3	240.3	236.0
2001	240.9	243.4	245.0	244.7	246.1	247.7	237.1	229.2	240.5	245.3	252.0	249.4	243.4
2002	246.9	250.3	250.4	250.5	251.3	251.8	241.0	233.6	244.6	249.6	256.4	251.6	248.2
2003	250.5	253.9	253.4	253.1	257.4	254.8	241.9	236.4	245.9	250.7	256.2	255.0	250.8
2004	250.2	253.9	254.2	253.7	254.6	256.2	244.2	236.5	248.7	252.1	258.9	254.8	251.5
2005	251.8	253.8	255.0	254.7	255.6	256.5	244.8	237.0	249.1	253.0	259.1	254.5	252.1
2006	253.0	256.8	257.0	255.9	257.1	257.6	244.8	237.5	249.2	253.9	259.8	254.8	253.1
2007	253.1	257.0	257.1	256.8	257.9	259.0	249.7	243.5	247.9	256.9	262.9	258.9	255.1
2008	257.9	263.1	261.3	261.6	263.2	264.6	256.2	251.1	256.0	264.7	271.3	265.8	261.4
2009	265.5	266.7	267.1	270.2	270.2	267.1	258.6	247.5	258.0	265.7	267.5	263.3	264.0
2010	264.7	266.2	266.3	268.4	274.2	270.6	260.3	248.4	257.8	264.7	267.1	261.7	264.2
2011	262.9	264.4	264.3	264.7	266.2	263.3	255.7	244.9	251.4	261.7	263.9	259.1	260.2

Employment by Industry: St. Louis, MO–IL, Selected Years, 2000–2011

(Numbers in thousands, not seasonally adjusted)

Industry and year	January	February	March	April	May	June	July	August	September	October	November	December	Annual average
Total Nonfarm													
2000	1,311.1	1,310.8	1,324.1	1,340.8	1,349.3	1,362.1	1,331.6	1,332.0	1,348.6	1,350.4	1,351.6	1,347.4	1,338.3
2001	1,310.0	1,320.6	1,335.3	1,347.2	1,355.0	1,364.0	1,333.8	1,333.2	1,341.8	1,339.3	1,345.0	1,346.5	1,339.3
2002	1,309.0	1,311.8	1,320.8	1,333.2	1,341.0	1,351.0	1,324.7	1,329.8	1,340.4	1,340.3	1,342.0	1,345.1	1,332.4
2003	1,307.3	1,306.6	1,315.2	1,324.2	1,331.0	1,335.7	1,312.9	1,315.8	1,323.8	1,328.8	1,325.6	1,327.4	1,321.2
2004	1,293.9	1,292.4	1,307.9	1,321.5	1,328.8	1,333.6	1,311.4	1,318.1	1,329.6	1,336.1	1,336.9	1,339.0	1,320.8
2005	1,304.4	1,310.2	1,322.2	1,341.6	1,345.7	1,350.0	1,326.8	1,337.7	1,347.7	1,346.1	1,348.7	1,351.1	1,336.0
2006	1,319.5	1,324.3	1,335.7	1,351.4	1,358.4	1,366.0	1,343.0	1,345.7	1,360.6	1,362.3	1,367.3	1,349.7
2007	1,327.9	1,331.2	1,348.3	1,360.4	1,373.6	1,374.3	1,345.3	1,353.6	1,366.3	1,368.7	1,372.5	1,374.0	1,358.0
2008	1,340.5	1,346.4	1,350.1	1,361.9	1,374.9	1,378.1	1,344.5	1,352.6	1,359.8	1,354.1	1,346.2	1,339.8	1,354.1
2009	1,299.2	1,297.9	1,300.2	1,308.8	1,313.5	1,310.1	1,281.0	1,286.2	1,292.8	1,291.8	1,289.5	1,290.1	1,296.8
2010	1,261.9	1,267.0	1,278.6	1,292.0	1,300.7	1,297.0	1,273.7	1,286.0	1,291.8	1,299.2	1,298.5	1,295.8	1,286.9
2011	1,271.8	1,274.5	1,287.4	1,306.9	1,313.3	1,308.1	1,287.9	1,294.0	1,300.2	1,303.6	1,302.0	1,295.2	1,295.4
Total Private													
2000	1,146.2	1,143.6	1,155.2	1,171.7	1,179.4	1,192.8	1,185.8	1,184.3	1,179.8	1,181.6	1,181.2	1,176.5	1,173.2
2001	1,142.6	1,150.5	1,164.5	1,176.1	1,182.9	1,191.7	1,185.1	1,182.9	1,172.6	1,168.3	1,172.5	1,173.4	1,171.9
2002	1,138.8	1,140.3	1,148.8	1,161.2	1,167.2	1,180.7	1,176.7	1,178.6	1,171.4	1,168.5	1,169.0	1,172.3	1,164.5
2003	1,138.3	1,136.0	1,144.1	1,152.1	1,157.7	1,165.3	1,163.6	1,164.7	1,156.2	1,159.0	1,154.9	1,157.0	1,154.1
2004	1,125.9	1,123.0	1,138.0	1,151.0	1,157.1	1,166.3	1,162.8	1,166.1	1,161.4	1,166.2	1,166.0	1,168.1	1,154.3
2005	1,137.2	1,139.9	1,152.0	1,169.6	1,172.8	1,181.1	1,176.0	1,181.5	1,178.2	1,175.6	1,176.7	1,179.6	1,168.4
2006	1,151.6	1,153.5	1,164.6	1,179.1	1,185.0	1,198.5	1,192.0	1,190.9	1,190.1	1,190.0	1,188.8	1,193.8	1,181.5
2007	1,158.3	1,158.5	1,175.5	1,187.2	1,199.2	1,205.9	1,198.8	1,200.2	1,195.2	1,194.6	1,197.2	1,199.0	1,189.1
2008	1,169.5	1,171.0	1,175.6	1,187.0	1,198.0	1,207.5	1,194.9	1,195.6	1,185.9	1,177.3	1,169.3	1,163.4	1,182.9
2009	1,126.1	1,122.4	1,123.9	1,128.7	1,133.3	1,134.9	1,129.2	1,127.0	1,116.8	1,114.6	1,112.8	1,113.3	1,123.6
2010	1,089.6	1,091.9	1,103.2	1,114.6	1,119.1	1,126.6	1,126.1	1,127.3	1,120.8	1,126.3	1,125.3	1,123.4	1,116.2
2011	1,102.5	1,103.5	1,115.7	1,134.0	1,139.6	1,143.3	1,143.0	1,140.5	1,130.6	1,132.8	1,131.2	1,124.1	1,128.4
Goods-Producing													
2000	245.9	245.8	248.1	250.8	252.9	255.8	252.6	250.2	252.1	252.7	251.6	246.4	250.4
2001	237.4	243.1	246.6	248.8	249.7	251.0	250.8	249.1	247.3	241.2	243.7	241.2	245.8
2002	231.9	232.5	234.5	235.6	236.0	239.6	240.4	239.4	238.1	235.7	234.7	234.3	236.1
2003	224.4	222.4	225.3	226.6	228.4	231.2	229.4	231.7	228.6	228.0	226.4	225.0	227.3
2004	218.5	216.8	221.9	224.1	225.6	228.7	223.5	229.3	228.4	226.5	225.3	224.4	224.4
2005	216.6	217.0	220.4	223.1	224.7	226.7	221.7	226.9	226.3	225.6	224.6	223.0	223.1
2006	217.2	217.3	219.8	221.5	222.1	226.4	225.5	222.9	224.4	222.5	221.2	219.8	221.7
2007	210.9	210.6	216.1	217.6	220.7	222.0	219.1	220.5	219.7	218.8	217.6	215.4	217.4
2008	206.0	206.6	205.7	208.5	211.9	215.9	211.1	211.0	210.2	206.7	201.6	197.1	207.7
2009	184.6	182.9	182.4	179.1	178.4	178.3	178.8	176.1	174.1	172.6	169.5	166.6	177.0
2010	160.2	159.2	162.8	165.6	166.3	170.0	170.1	170.0	169.6	170.5	169.3	167.5	166.8
2011	164.6	164.8	168.7	172.4	173.9	176.2	177.5	178.3	176.9	177.0	173.3	170.4	172.8
Mining, Logging, and Construction													
2000	71.3	71.1	73.8	76.3	78.0	80.1	79.9	80.5	80.5	79.8	78.1	75.7	77.1
2001	71.5	72.3	75.7	78.6	80.3	83.9	83.5	83.4	82.1	81.2	80.6	78.4	79.3
2002	73.8	73.5	75.3	77.1	78.0	81.0	82.8	82.3	81.2	80.1	78.8	77.9	78.5
2003	72.8	71.1	73.5	76.4	78.2	80.6	82.9	82.9	81.8	81.7	80.3	78.8	78.4
2004	74.0	72.2	77.0	79.8	81.1	83.1	84.8	84.3	83.6	82.1	81.1	80.0	80.3
2005	74.3	74.8	78.1	80.5	82.2	83.7	85.2	85.2	84.6	83.8	82.8	81.1	81.4
2006	78.2	78.0	79.8	82.4	83.0	86.0	86.1	86.0	85.1	83.8	82.5	80.8	82.6
2007	77.4	74.4	79.9	81.4	84.3	87.2	86.7	86.6	84.7	84.1	83.0	80.4	82.5
2008	76.2	74.1	76.5	78.4	80.4	82.5	82.7	82.6	81.1	78.4	75.4	72.0	78.4
2009	64.3	63.3	64.9	65.1	65.9	67.1	68.1	67.1	66.1	64.9	62.5	60.3	65.0
2010	55.2	54.2	57.5	59.7	59.9	62.7	62.9	62.7	62.3	62.3	60.9	58.8	59.9
2011	56.9	56.9	60.2	63.4	64.5	65.9	66.6	67.3	66.0	66.0	61.6	58.2	62.8
Manufacturing													
2000	174.6	174.7	174.3	174.5	174.9	175.7	172.7	169.7	171.6	172.9	173.5	170.7	173.3
2001	165.9	170.8	170.9	170.2	169.4	167.1	167.3	165.7	165.2	160.0	163.1	162.8	166.5
2002	158.1	159.0	159.2	158.5	158.0	158.6	157.6	157.1	156.9	155.6	155.9	156.4	157.6
2003	151.6	151.3	151.8	150.2	150.2	150.6	146.5	148.8	146.8	146.3	146.1	146.2	148.9
2004	144.5	144.6	144.9	144.3	144.5	145.6	138.7	145.0	144.8	144.4	144.2	144.4	144.2
2005	142.3	142.2	142.3	142.6	142.5	143.0	136.5	141.7	141.7	141.8	141.8	141.9	141.7
2006	139.0	139.3	140.0	139.1	139.1	140.4	139.4	136.9	139.3	138.7	138.7	139.0	139.1
2007	133.5	136.2	136.2	136.2	136.4	134.8	132.4	133.9	135.0	134.7	134.6	135.0	134.9
2008	129.8	132.5	129.2	130.1	131.5	133.4	128.4	128.4	129.1	128.3	126.2	125.1	129.3
2009	120.3	119.6	117.5	114.0	112.5	111.2	110.7	109.0	108.0	107.7	107.0	106.3	112.0
2010	105.0	105.0	105.3	105.9	106.4	107.3	107.2	107.3	107.3	108.2	108.4	108.7	106.8
2011	107.7	107.9	108.5	109.0	109.4	110.3	110.9	111.0	110.9	111.0	111.7	112.2	110.0
Service-Providing													
2000	1,065.2	1,065.0	1,076.0	1,090.0	1,096.4	1,106.3	1,079.0	1,081.8	1,096.5	1,097.7	1,100.0	1,101.0	1,087.9
2001	1,072.6	1,077.5	1,088.7	1,098.4	1,105.3	1,113.0	1,083.0	1,084.1	1,094.5	1,098.1	1,101.3	1,105.3	1,093.5
2002	1,077.1	1,079.3	1,086.3	1,097.6	1,105.0	1,111.4	1,084.3	1,090.4	1,102.3	1,104.6	1,107.3	1,110.8	1,096.4
2003	1,082.9	1,084.2	1,089.9	1,097.6	1,102.6	1,104.5	1,083.5	1,084.1	1,095.2	1,100.8	1,099.2	1,102.4	1,093.9
2004	1,075.4	1,075.6	1,086.0	1,097.4	1,103.2	1,104.9	1,087.9	1,088.8	1,101.2	1,109.6	1,111.6	1,114.6	1,096.4
2005	1,087.8	1,093.2	1,101.8	1,118.5	1,121.0	1,123.3	1,105.1	1,110.8	1,121.4	1,120.5	1,124.1	1,128.1	1,113.0
2006	1,102.3	1,107.0	1,115.9	1,129.9	1,136.3	1,139.6	1,117.5	1,122.8	1,136.2	1,139.8	1,141.0	1,147.5	1,128.0
2007	1,117.0	1,120.6	1,132.2	1,142.8	1,152.9	1,152.3	1,126.2	1,133.1	1,146.6	1,149.9	1,154.9	1,158.6	1,140.6
2008	1,134.5	1,139.8	1,144.4	1,153.4	1,163.0	1,162.2	1,133.4	1,141.6	1,149.6	1,147.4	1,144.6	1,142.7	1,146.4
2009	1,114.6	1,115.0	1,117.8	1,129.7	1,135.1	1,131.8	1,102.2	1,110.7	1,118.7	1,119.2	1,120.0	1,123.5	1,119.9
2010	1,101.7	1,107.8	1,115.8	1,126.4	1,134.4	1,127.0	1,103.6	1,116.0	1,122.2	1,128.7	1,129.2	1,128.3	1,120.1
2011	1,107.2	1,109.7	1,118.7	1,134.5	1,139.4	1,131.9	1,110.4	1,115.7	1,123.3	1,126.6	1,128.7	1,124.8	1,122.6

Employment by Industry: St. Louis, MO–IL, Selected Years, 2000–2011—*Continued*

(Numbers in thousands, not seasonally adjusted)

Industry and year	January	February	March	April	May	June	July	August	September	October	November	December	Annual average
Trade, Transportation, and Utilities													
2000	259.0	255.0	256.8	257.9	259.1	259.4	258.7	258.1	259.3	261.2	265.4	269.3	259.9
2001	258.8	255.1	256.1	256.6	256.8	257.6	254.5	253.5	254.5	256.5	261.5	264.7	257.2
2002	256.1	252.2	253.4	254.4	256.1	258.9	256.9	257.5	258.7	258.5	263.5	267.1	257.8
2003	258.8	254.8	255.3	256.0	256.5	256.0	255.7	255.0	254.3	259.1	261.3	264.0	257.2
2004	251.7	248.2	249.8	250.7	252.7	253.3	253.6	252.1	252.1	254.8	259.9	263.2	253.5
2005	253.5	250.4	251.9	253.5	254.5	254.8	254.9	255.4	254.0	254.8	259.7	262.9	255.0
2006	252.9	249.8	251.2	252.4	254.1	255.5	254.3	255.0	254.9	256.6	261.3	265.1	255.3
2007	256.1	253.0	256.1	257.3	259.6	260.3	258.8	258.1	258.4	259.4	265.5	268.2	259.2
2008	260.2	256.7	257.8	258.1	259.6	260.7	258.4	258.8	257.4	256.9	259.5	260.8	258.7
2009	250.5	247.1	246.5	246.6	247.3	246.9	244.3	245.3	244.7	244.1	247.7	249.2	246.7
2010	240.8	238.4	240.0	240.7	242.2	242.4	241.2	242.5	241.2	242.1	245.8	248.5	242.2
2011	241.6	239.9	241.1	244.1	245.5	245.5	245.2	243.0	239.5	241.0	245.4	248.3	243.3
Wholesale Trade													
2000	57.7	57.8	58.1	58.5	58.6	59.2	59.1	59.1	59.0	59.0	59.1	59.3	58.7
2001	58.4	58.5	58.5	58.7	58.7	59.0	58.3	58.2	57.7	57.4	57.2	57.4	58.2
2002	56.6	56.5	56.7	56.7	56.9	57.2	56.8	56.8	56.5	56.2	56.0	55.9	56.6
2003	57.1	56.9	56.9	57.5	57.5	57.7	58.5	58.5	57.8	57.9	57.8	57.9	57.7
2004	58.2	58.2	58.6	58.6	58.7	59.1	60.4	59.7	59.5	58.9	58.9	59.1	59.0
2005	59.8	59.2	59.4	59.8	59.8	60.2	60.6	60.8	60.0	59.7	59.8	60.1	59.9
2006	59.5	59.4	59.7	60.5	60.8	61.5	61.6	61.7	61.5	61.5	61.5	62.0	60.9
2007	61.4	61.6	62.0	61.8	62.2	62.7	63.0	62.9	62.7	62.8	62.9	63.1	62.4
2008	62.8	62.8	62.9	63.2	63.4	63.8	63.7	63.7	63.3	62.7	62.2	62.1	63.1
2009	60.9	60.6	60.3	60.0	59.7	59.9	59.7	59.5	59.0	59.4	59.1	59.4	59.8
2010	58.7	58.6	59.0	60.8	60.8	60.7	60.4	60.0	59.7	59.7	59.5	59.7	59.8
2011	59.3	59.3	59.5	59.7	59.9	60.3	60.8	60.0	60.0	60.5	61.5	61.3	60.2
Retail Trade													
2000	147.1	143.3	144.6	144.4	145.3	146.1	145.7	145.2	145.1	146.4	151.0	155.0	146.6
2001	146.6	142.7	143.3	143.5	143.7	145.3	143.0	142.1	142.9	144.6	149.8	153.2	145.1
2002	146.1	142.8	143.5	143.9	145.0	146.8	146.0	146.4	147.1	146.6	152.0	156.3	146.9
2003	147.3	143.8	144.9	145.1	146.0	146.5	146.0	146.5	146.0	150.6	154.1	156.8	147.8
2004	145.4	141.9	142.7	143.7	145.2	146.2	145.8	144.6	144.0	147.1	152.1	154.6	146.1
2005	145.9	143.4	144.2	145.2	146.1	146.6	147.1	147.1	145.4	146.9	151.4	153.5	146.9
2006	145.4	142.4	143.4	144.2	145.2	146.2	145.6	145.5	144.7	146.7	151.4	153.9	146.2
2007	146.3	143.3	145.5	146.7	148.0	148.9	147.5	146.4	146.0	146.9	152.6	154.5	147.7
2008	148.0	144.6	145.4	145.5	146.5	147.5	145.8	145.5	143.9	144.2	147.1	148.3	146.0
2009	140.3	137.7	137.6	138.5	139.3	140.0	138.6	138.8	138.1	138.2	142.1	143.0	139.4
2010	136.5	134.4	135.5	136.1	137.4	138.7	138.1	138.1	136.6	137.5	141.2	143.3	137.8
2011	137.8	136.0	136.8	138.9	139.7	140.3	139.2	138.6	135.2	136.2	139.5	141.7	138.3
Transportation and Utilities													
2000	54.2	53.9	54.1	55.0	55.2	54.1	53.9	53.8	55.2	55.8	55.3	55.0	54.6
2001	53.8	53.9	54.3	54.4	54.4	53.3	53.2	53.2	53.9	54.5	54.5	54.1	54.0
2002	53.4	52.9	53.2	53.8	54.2	54.9	54.1	54.3	55.1	55.7	55.5	54.9	54.3
2003	54.4	54.1	53.5	53.4	53.0	51.8	51.2	50.0	50.5	50.6	49.4	49.3	51.8
2004	48.1	48.1	48.5	48.4	48.8	48.0	47.4	47.8	48.6	48.8	48.9	49.5	48.4
2005	47.8	47.8	48.3	48.5	48.6	48.0	47.2	47.5	48.6	48.2	48.5	49.3	48.2
2006	48.0	48.0	48.1	47.7	48.1	47.8	47.1	47.8	48.7	48.4	48.4	49.2	48.1
2007	48.4	48.1	48.6	48.8	49.4	48.7	48.3	48.8	49.7	49.7	50.0	50.6	49.1
2008	49.4	49.3	49.5	49.4	49.7	49.4	48.9	49.6	50.2	50.0	50.2	50.4	49.7
2009	49.3	48.8	48.6	48.1	48.3	47.0	46.0	47.0	47.6	46.5	46.5	46.8	47.5
2010	45.6	45.4	45.5	43.8	44.0	43.0	42.7	44.4	44.9	44.9	45.1	45.5	44.6
2011	44.5	44.6	44.8	45.5	45.9	44.9	45.2	44.4	44.3	44.3	44.4	45.3	44.8
Information													
2000	31.2	31.2	31.5	31.5	31.7	32.1	32.1	32.1	32.1	32.5	32.9	32.4	31.9
2001	31.7	31.9	32.1	32.0	32.1	32.3	32.2	32.3	31.9	31.5	31.4	31.6	31.9
2002	30.8	30.7	30.5	30.4	30.6	30.5	29.8	29.9	29.4	29.3	29.3	29.4	30.1
2003	30.8	31.1	31.0	29.3	29.0	29.2	29.1	28.9	28.5	28.3	28.3	28.5	29.3
2004	29.5	29.5	29.5	29.5	29.5	29.6	29.5	28.8	28.8	29.4	29.4	29.3	29.4
2005	29.1	29.1	29.1	29.4	29.4	29.7	30.0	29.9	29.9	30.1	30.1	30.3	29.7
2006	30.1	29.9	29.9	29.9	30.0	30.2	30.4	30.3	30.1	30.5	30.5	30.7	30.2
2007	29.8	29.7	29.8	30.1	30.4	30.6	30.4	30.4	30.3	30.7	30.9	30.9	30.3
2008	30.4	30.2	30.3	30.8	31.2	31.3	31.2	31.0	30.8	30.9	31.0	31.1	30.9
2009	30.8	30.7	30.6	30.3	30.3	30.5	30.5	30.5	30.2	29.9	29.9	30.2	30.4
2010	29.9	29.7	29.6	31.7	31.3	31.8	31.5	31.5	31.2	30.9	30.8	31.0	30.9
2011	30.5	30.3	30.2	30.5	30.7	30.9	30.9	30.1	29.1	29.0	28.4	28.3	29.9
Financial Activities													
2000	74.4	74.3	74.1	74.8	75.0	76.0	76.0	75.8	75.0	74.8	74.7	75.1	75.0
2001	74.8	74.8	75.4	75.9	76.5	77.3	77.4	77.3	76.4	76.2	76.5	76.9	76.3
2002	76.6	76.7	77.2	77.4	77.9	78.5	78.7	79.0	78.4	78.8	79.2	80.0	78.2
2003	77.8	77.7	78.1	78.5	78.9	79.7	79.7	80.1	79.0	78.9	78.5	78.6	78.8
2004	76.7	76.5	76.7	76.9	77.2	78.0	78.9	78.7	77.9	78.3	78.1	78.5	77.7
2005	76.5	76.9	77.0	78.1	78.0	78.7	79.3	79.2	78.9	78.4	78.2	78.5	78.1
2006	77.5	77.7	77.9	78.6	79.2	79.7	79.6	79.7	79.2	79.0	79.1	79.3	78.9
2007	78.7	78.8	79.0	79.2	80.0	80.5	80.7	80.5	79.8	79.9	79.5	79.8	79.7
2008	80.2	80.4	80.5	80.0	80.1	80.2	80.7	80.0	79.2	78.5	78.3	78.2	79.6
2009	78.3	78.5	78.6	79.1	79.2	79.5	79.5	79.3	78.7	79.0	78.6	78.6	78.9
2010	78.5	78.5	78.6	79.9	80.1	80.6	81.4	81.4	80.9	81.8	81.7	81.7	80.4
2011	80.8	80.7	80.8	81.4	81.7	81.5	80.6	81.3	80.3	80.4	80.3	80.7	80.9

Employment by Industry: St. Louis, MO–IL, Selected Years, 2000–2011—*Continued*

(Numbers in thousands, not seasonally adjusted)

Industry and year	January	February	March	April	May	June	July	August	September	October	November	December	Annual average
Professional and Business Services													
2000	182.4	182.4	185.2	189.7	188.6	192.6	192.2	192.9	189.6	189.4	189.8	189.6	188.7
2001	184.6	185.8	188.9	188.7	188.2	189.6	187.1	188.3	184.7	184.3	183.0	183.2	186.4
2002	177.7	178.6	179.6	180.1	179.2	180.3	179.1	179.8	178.3	178.4	178.7	178.6	179.0
2003	176.1	177.1	178.2	178.4	177.4	178.9	178.9	180.0	178.8	179.9	178.2	178.4	178.4
2004	174.7	175.0	178.7	180.1	179.2	181.5	180.8	181.8	181.0	181.6	181.5	182.0	179.8
2005	180.7	181.8	184.5	188.8	187.4	189.3	188.1	188.9	188.9	188.4	188.6	188.9	187.0
2006	185.7	186.6	189.3	192.4	192.1	195.3	193.5	194.7	194.8	195.7	194.5	196.0	192.6
2007	189.1	189.7	192.3	194.8	194.9	195.7	195.0	195.7	195.3	195.3	194.9	195.2	194.0
2008	193.7	195.2	196.8	200.3	199.1	200.4	198.7	198.7	195.9	194.1	191.5	189.6	196.2
2009	183.9	183.7	182.4	184.5	183.4	183.5	182.5	182.4	181.0	181.1	181.3	181.7	182.6
2010	179.1	181.0	182.6	188.0	187.3	188.2	189.2	189.4	188.3	190.1	189.8	189.0	186.8
2011	187.1	187.9	190.0	194.6	193.6	193.5	193.3	192.6	191.4	192.8	192.7	191.5	191.8
Education and Health Services													
2000	176.6	177.6	178.3	179.3	179.2	179.5	179.4	179.3	180.3	180.5	181.3	181.3	179.4
2001	178.8	181.1	181.9	183.8	184.0	184.6	184.7	185.1	185.9	187.0	188.2	188.9	184.5
2002	186.2	188.6	188.9	190.6	191.8	191.9	191.8	192.7	193.9	193.5	194.3	194.8	191.6
2003	190.1	191.5	192.1	191.4	191.0	190.6	191.0	190.9	192.3	192.8	192.9	193.8	191.7
2004	190.1	192.6	193.3	193.8	193.6	193.0	193.3	193.0	194.8	196.7	197.1	196.9	194.0
2005	194.7	197.3	197.6	198.2	197.5	197.0	196.8	196.4	199.2	200.3	201.0	201.6	198.1
2006	198.9	201.8	203.0	203.0	202.7	202.5	201.1	200.9	203.8	206.0	206.6	207.0	203.1
2007	203.3	206.0	207.1	207.9	208.0	207.4	207.2	207.0	209.5	211.1	212.1	212.6	208.3
2008	207.5	210.7	210.5	211.2	211.1	210.3	210.0	210.3	212.8	214.2	214.9	215.2	211.6
2009	211.9	214.1	214.3	213.8	214.2	213.0	212.6	213.0	215.3	216.9	218.6	220.6	214.9
2010	218.7	221.5	221.9	222.9	222.7	221.5	220.0	220.0	222.9	226.5	227.2	226.7	222.7
2011	224.7	227.2	227.5	227.8	227.1	225.2	225.4	224.6	227.1	229.8	228.9	226.6	226.8
Leisure and Hospitality													
2000	120.9	120.9	123.6	129.3	133.7	137.4	135.8	136.9	133.1	132.2	127.4	124.3	129.6
2001	119.9	121.0	124.1	130.8	135.3	138.2	138.6	137.3	132.7	132.8	128.6	127.1	130.5
2002	122.0	122.2	125.1	132.5	135.6	140.4	140.0	140.4	135.4	135.2	130.2	129.0	132.3
2003	123.1	123.4	125.6	132.9	137.0	139.7	140.9	139.6	137.0	134.2	131.8	130.9	133.0
2004	128.1	127.3	130.2	137.7	141.3	143.9	144.4	144.1	140.4	140.3	136.4	135.2	137.4
2005	129.1	129.9	133.5	140.6	143.6	146.5	147.3	147.1	144.1	140.6	137.4	137.0	139.7
2006	132.7	133.7	136.4	143.6	147.1	150.4	149.4	149.2	145.0	142.1	138.1	138.2	142.2
2007	133.7	133.8	137.7	142.7	147.7	151.2	149.8	150.2	145.1	142.0	139.2	139.6	142.7
2008	134.7	134.4	136.8	140.6	146.9	150.3	147.7	147.9	142.3	138.4	135.4	134.7	140.8
2009	130.5	129.9	133.3	139.3	144.3	147.2	145.5	145.3	138.4	135.9	132.2	131.3	137.8
2010	127.9	129.1	132.6	139.9	143.2	145.8	146.5	146.4	141.3	138.7	135.0	133.2	138.3
2011	128.3	127.8	131.9	137.2	141.0	143.8	142.1	142.2	138.7	135.7	135.2	131.2	136.3
Other Services													
2000	55.8	56.4	57.6	58.4	59.2	60.0	59.0	59.0	58.3	58.3	58.1	58.1	58.2
2001	56.6	57.7	59.4	59.5	60.3	61.1	59.8	60.0	59.2	58.8	59.6	59.8	59.3
2002	57.5	58.8	59.6	60.2	60.0	60.6	60.0	59.9	59.2	59.1	59.1	59.1	59.4
2003	57.2	58.0	58.5	59.0	59.5	60.0	58.9	58.5	57.7	57.8	57.5	57.8	58.4
2004	56.6	57.1	57.9	58.2	58.0	58.3	58.8	58.3	58.0	58.6	58.3	58.6	58.1
2005	57.0	57.5	58.0	57.9	57.7	58.4	57.9	57.7	56.9	57.4	57.1	57.4	57.6
2006	56.6	56.7	57.1	57.7	57.7	58.5	58.2	58.2	57.9	57.6	57.5	57.7	57.6
2007	56.7	56.9	57.4	57.6	57.9	58.2	57.8	57.8	57.1	57.4	57.5	57.3	57.5
2008	56.8	56.8	57.2	57.5	58.1	58.4	58.1	57.9	57.3	57.6	57.1	56.7	57.5
2009	55.6	55.5	55.8	56.0	56.2	56.0	55.5	55.1	54.4	55.1	55.0	55.1	55.4
2010	54.5	54.5	55.1	45.9	46.0	46.3	46.2	46.1	45.4	45.7	45.7	45.8	48.1
2011	44.9	44.9	45.5	46.0	46.1	46.7	48.0	48.4	47.6	47.1	47.0	47.1	46.6
Government													
2000	164.9	167.2	168.9	169.1	169.9	169.3	145.8	147.7	168.8	168.8	170.4	170.9	165.1
2001	167.4	170.1	170.8	171.1	172.1	172.3	148.7	150.3	169.2	171.0	172.5	173.1	167.4
2002	170.2	171.5	172.0	172.0	173.8	170.3	148.0	151.2	169.0	171.8	173.0	172.8	168.0
2003	169.0	170.6	171.1	172.1	173.3	170.4	149.3	151.1	167.6	169.8	170.7	170.4	167.1
2004	168.0	169.4	169.9	170.5	171.7	167.3	148.6	152.0	168.2	169.9	170.9	170.9	166.4
2005	167.2	170.3	170.2	172.0	172.9	168.9	150.8	156.2	169.5	170.5	172.0	171.5	167.7
2006	167.9	170.8	171.1	172.3	173.4	167.5	151.0	154.8	170.5	172.3	173.4	173.5	168.2
2007	169.6	172.7	172.8	173.2	174.4	168.4	146.5	153.4	171.1	174.1	175.3	175.0	168.9
2008	171.0	175.4	174.5	174.9	176.9	170.6	149.6	157.0	173.9	176.8	176.9	176.4	171.2
2009	173.1	175.5	176.3	180.1	180.2	175.2	151.8	159.8	176.0	177.2	176.7	176.8	173.2
2010	172.3	175.1	175.4	177.4	181.6	170.4	147.6	158.7	171.0	172.9	173.2	172.4	170.7
2011	169.3	171.0	171.7	172.9	173.7	164.8	144.9	153.5	169.6	170.8	170.8	171.1	167.0

Employment by Industry: Tampa–St. Petersburg–Clearwater, FL, Selected Years, 2000–2011

(Numbers in thousands, not seasonally adjusted)

Industry and year	January	February	March	April	May	June	July	August	September	October	November	December	Annual average
Total Nonfarm													
2000	1,124.7	1,139.5	1,158.4	1,154.9	1,159.2	1,146.5	1,130.1	1,144.1	1,149.3	1,146.8	1,158.7	1,165.5	1,148.1
2001	1,126.4	1,139.4	1,149.2	1,144.2	1,144.4	1,133.6	1,120.2	1,133.4	1,131.3	1,133.6	1,141.0	1,146.0	1,136.9
2002	1,118.9	1,131.3	1,138.4	1,136.4	1,137.3	1,120.9	1,110.2	1,123.1	1,124.0	1,126.7	1,139.5	1,145.6	1,129.4
2003	1,119.3	1,128.1	1,138.2	1,134.5	1,133.9	1,120.8	1,111.6	1,124.8	1,127.9	1,134.7	1,139.3	1,147.6	1,130.1
2004	1,139.1	1,152.5	1,164.5	1,173.2	1,174.8	1,165.0	1,157.5	1,169.4	1,170.7	1,183.0	1,194.8	1,203.6	1,170.7
2005	1,187.7	1,201.9	1,208.3	1,213.7	1,216.0	1,202.4	1,197.2	1,209.7	1,214.8	1,214.0	1,223.5	1,231.2	1,210.0
2006	1,214.9	1,224.7	1,240.9	1,239.2	1,241.8	1,231.1	1,219.8	1,236.9	1,239.8	1,236.9	1,244.6	1,253.3	1,235.3
2007	1,232.1	1,240.6	1,252.4	1,246.8	1,243.6	1,234.4	1,216.6	1,229.3	1,226.1	1,224.0	1,232.0	1,236.5	1,234.5
2008	1,211.4	1,219.3	1,224.1	1,210.9	1,205.8	1,190.0	1,172.8	1,183.3	1,178.3	1,172.9	1,172.3	1,174.2	1,192.9
2009	1,144.4	1,145.0	1,145.4	1,138.1	1,130.6	1,114.7	1,101.0	1,110.6	1,108.5	1,109.8	1,112.7	1,115.4	1,123.0
2010	1,095.8	1,104.7	1,113.4	1,112.9	1,119.0	1,106.2	1,099.3	1,109.7	1,108.2	1,120.0	1,125.1	1,130.0	1,112.0
2011	1,112.9	1,121.4	1,129.4	1,136.1	1,133.8	1,120.1	1,116.4	1,132.4	1,139.6	1,140.9	1,150.3	1,154.0	1,132.3
Total Private													
2000	982.9	997.1	1,015.2	1,010.0	1,011.9	1,013.3	998.3	1,002.8	1,005.2	1,000.8	1,010.9	1,017.6	1,005.5
2001	980.7	991.9	1,000.9	996.1	995.6	995.8	984.0	986.5	983.2	983.9	991.3	995.4	990.4
2002	971.9	982.5	989.3	987.3	989.2	984.4	975.0	976.8	976.0	977.1	988.9	993.9	982.7
2003	972.0	978.8	989.1	986.5	985.5	984.3	976.1	978.8	980.5	985.9	990.4	999.2	983.9
2004	992.9	1,003.3	1,015.7	1,024.2	1,025.4	1,027.5	1,020.7	1,022.1	1,022.0	1,032.7	1,043.9	1,052.7	1,023.6
2005	1,039.2	1,050.8	1,058.0	1,064.2	1,066.1	1,064.3	1,059.9	1,061.9	1,065.0	1,062.9	1,072.0	1,080.5	1,062.1
2006	1,065.3	1,074.3	1,090.6	1,088.4	1,091.5	1,092.6	1,082.4	1,087.7	1,087.7	1,083.1	1,091.1	1,100.4	1,086.3
2007	1,079.8	1,087.2	1,098.3	1,093.0	1,091.4	1,092.1	1,075.3	1,078.1	1,072.0	1,068.6	1,076.6	1,081.5	1,082.8
2008	1,058.0	1,063.5	1,068.9	1,056.1	1,052.6	1,047.3	1,031.4	1,030.8	1,022.6	1,016.5	1,015.3	1,016.2	1,039.9
2009	988.8	986.9	987.9	979.6	975.0	969.2	956.3	956.2	953.3	953.3	956.6	959.8	968.6
2010	941.3	947.3	956.4	956.6	957.7	958.3	952.7	955.8	952.5	963.6	968.5	974.9	957.1
2011	958.0	964.0	972.3	979.1	978.3	974.6	972.2	978.9	982.6	983.2	992.8	996.0	977.7
Goods-Producing													
2000	154.5	156.2	158.4	157.4	158.3	161.0	159.1	159.7	160.2	157.7	158.3	158.0	158.2
2001	152.8	153.0	153.4	152.7	153.0	153.6	153.0	153.3	152.4	151.6	152.1	152.0	152.7
2002	149.2	149.1	149.2	149.0	149.4	150.3	150.0	151.3	151.8	151.8	152.0	151.6	150.4
2003	147.9	148.8	148.7	148.2	148.9	149.5	148.2	149.1	149.0	148.8	148.7	149.9	148.8
2004	149.6	150.9	152.9	155.3	155.7	156.7	157.1	157.8	158.6	160.9	161.0	161.8	156.5
2005	160.1	161.6	162.7	163.7	164.9	166.1	167.8	168.5	169.4	169.7	171.0	171.5	166.4
2006	170.2	171.4	173.2	173.4	174.4	175.4	173.6	174.4	173.8	172.4	171.4	171.2	172.9
2007	168.9	169.1	169.8	166.2	166.2	166.3	162.8	162.0	161.1	158.4	157.1	156.7	163.7
2008	153.3	154.0	153.8	151.3	151.0	151.0	148.4	147.2	145.4	142.3	139.8	137.4	147.9
2009	131.1	129.3	127.6	125.3	123.9	123.2	120.6	119.8	118.4	116.8	115.2	114.0	122.1
2010	110.6	110.6	110.8	110.5	111.6	111.7	112.0	111.9	111.0	110.9	110.4	110.3	111.0
2011	108.4	109.0	110.2	110.9	111.7	112.0	112.9	114.1	113.3	109.1	110.9	109.4	111.0
Mining and Logging													
2000	0.5	0.5	0.5	0.5	0.5	0.5	0.5	0.5	0.5	0.5	0.5	0.5	0.5
2001	0.5	0.5	0.5	0.5	0.5	0.5	0.5	0.5	0.5	0.5	0.5	0.5	0.5
2002	0.5	0.5	0.5	0.5	0.5	0.5	0.5	0.5	0.5	0.5	0.5	0.5	0.5
2003	0.5	0.5	0.5	0.5	0.5	0.5	0.5	0.5	0.5	0.5	0.6	0.6	0.5
2004	0.6	0.6	0.6	0.6	0.6	0.6	0.6	0.6	0.6	0.6	0.6	0.6	0.6
2005	0.6	0.6	0.6	0.6	0.7	0.7	0.7	0.8	0.8	0.8	0.8	0.8	0.7
2006	0.9	0.9	0.9	0.9	0.9	0.8	0.7	0.6	0.6	0.6	0.6	0.7	0.8
2007	0.6	0.6	0.6	0.7	0.7	0.7	0.7	0.7	0.7	0.7	0.7	0.7	0.7
2008	0.7	0.6	0.7	0.7	0.7	0.7	0.6	0.6	0.6	0.5	0.5	0.5	0.6
2009	0.5	0.5	0.5	0.5	0.5	0.5	0.5	0.5	0.5	0.5	0.5	0.5	0.5
2010	0.5	0.5	0.5	0.5	0.5	0.5	0.5	0.5	0.5	0.5	0.5	0.5	0.5
2011	0.5	0.5	0.5	0.5	0.5	0.5	0.5	0.5	0.5	0.5	0.5	0.5	0.5
Construction													
2000	64.9	65.9	67.2	67.3	67.9	69.7	68.4	68.8	69.2	68.3	68.9	68.8	67.9
2001	65.5	66.0	66.5	66.8	67.5	68.2	68.6	68.7	68.7	68.2	69.0	69.1	67.7
2002	67.5	67.9	67.9	68.1	68.9	69.2	69.3	70.4	71.0	71.5	71.9	71.7	69.6
2003	69.6	70.6	70.8	70.9	71.9	72.6	72.0	72.9	72.8	73.0	73.0	74.1	72.0
2004	73.7	74.8	76.3	77.7	78.1	78.6	79.4	79.8	80.7	82.8	82.9	83.6	79.0
2005	83.1	84.4	85.4	86.0	87.0	87.8	89.4	89.7	90.2	90.5	91.7	92.2	88.1
2006	91.0	92.1	93.3	94.0	94.7	95.3	94.5	95.0	94.6	93.7	92.9	92.7	93.7
2007	91.3	91.3	92.2	88.9	88.8	89.0	86.3	85.6	84.9	83.1	82.4	82.2	87.2
2008	79.2	80.0	79.8	78.0	77.8	77.9	75.8	75.1	74.1	72.1	70.5	69.1	75.8
2009	64.4	63.2	62.3	61.2	60.4	60.2	59.2	58.8	58.2	57.0	55.9	55.2	59.7
2010	52.4	52.4	52.6	52.2	52.7	52.7	53.0	52.7	52.2	52.4	51.6	51.4	52.4
2011	50.1	50.5	51.3	51.8	52.2	52.2	52.6	53.8	52.7	49.0	49.9	49.2	51.3
Manufacturing													
2000	89.1	89.8	90.7	89.6	89.9	90.8	90.2	90.4	90.5	88.9	88.9	88.7	89.8
2001	86.8	86.5	86.4	85.4	85.0	84.9	83.9	84.1	83.2	82.9	82.6	82.4	84.5
2002	81.2	80.7	80.8	80.4	80.0	80.6	80.2	80.4	80.3	79.8	79.6	79.4	80.3
2003	77.8	77.7	77.4	76.8	76.5	76.4	75.7	75.7	75.7	75.3	75.1	75.2	76.3
2004	75.3	75.5	76.0	77.0	77.0	77.5	77.1	77.4	77.3	77.5	77.5	77.6	76.9
2005	76.4	76.6	76.7	77.1	77.2	77.6	77.7	78.0	78.4	78.4	78.5	78.5	77.6
2006	78.3	78.4	79.0	78.5	78.8	79.3	78.4	78.8	78.6	78.1	77.9	77.8	78.5
2007	77.0	77.2	77.0	76.6	76.7	76.6	75.8	75.7	75.5	74.6	74.0	73.8	75.9
2008	73.4	73.4	73.3	72.6	72.5	72.4	72.0	71.5	70.7	69.7	68.8	67.8	71.5
2009	66.2	65.6	64.8	63.6	63.0	62.5	60.9	60.5	59.7	59.3	58.8	58.3	61.9
2010	57.7	57.7	57.7	57.8	58.4	58.5	58.5	58.7	58.3	58.0	58.3	58.4	58.2
2011	57.8	58.0	58.4	58.6	59.0	59.3	59.8	59.8	60.1	59.6	60.5	59.7	59.2

Employment by Industry: Tampa–St. Petersburg–Clearwater, FL, Selected Years, 2000–2011—*Continued*

(Numbers in thousands, not seasonally adjusted)

Industry and year	January	February	March	April	May	June	July	August	September	October	November	December	Annual average
Service-Providing													
2000	970.2	983.3	1,000.0	997.5	1,000.9	985.5	971.0	984.4	989.1	989.1	1,000.4	1,007.5	989.9
2001	973.6	986.4	995.8	991.5	991.4	980.0	967.2	980.1	978.9	982.0	988.9	994.0	984.2
2002	969.7	982.2	989.2	987.4	987.9	970.6	960.2	971.8	972.2	974.9	987.5	994.0	979.0
2003	971.4	979.3	989.5	986.3	985.0	971.3	963.4	975.7	978.9	985.9	990.6	997.7	981.3
2004	989.5	1,001.6	1,011.6	1,017.9	1,019.1	1,008.3	1,000.4	1,011.6	1,012.1	1,022.1	1,033.8	1,041.8	1,014.2
2005	1,027.6	1,040.3	1,045.6	1,050.0	1,051.1	1,036.3	1,029.4	1,041.2	1,045.4	1,044.3	1,052.5	1,059.7	1,043.6
2006	1,044.7	1,053.3	1,067.7	1,065.8	1,067.4	1,055.7	1,046.2	1,062.5	1,066.0	1,064.5	1,073.2	1,082.1	1,062.4
2007	1,063.2	1,071.5	1,082.6	1,080.6	1,077.4	1,068.1	1,053.8	1,067.3	1,065.0	1,065.6	1,074.9	1,079.8	1,070.8
2008	1,058.1	1,065.3	1,070.3	1,059.6	1,054.8	1,039.0	1,024.4	1,036.1	1,032.9	1,030.6	1,032.5	1,036.8	1,045.0
2009	1,013.3	1,015.7	1,017.8	1,012.8	1,006.7	991.5	980.4	990.8	990.1	993.0	997.5	1,001.4	1,000.9
2010	985.2	994.1	1,002.6	1,002.4	1,007.4	994.5	987.3	997.8	997.2	1,009.1	1,014.7	1,019.7	1,001.0
2011	1,004.5	1,012.4	1,019.2	1,025.2	1,022.1	1,008.1	1,003.5	1,018.3	1,026.3	1,031.8	1,039.4	1,044.6	1,021.3
Trade, Transportation, and Utilities													
2000	237.6	238.6	241.5	238.8	240.1	241.4	238.2	240.2	240.3	240.9	247.2	250.7	241.3
2001	234.6	234.0	234.8	231.8	231.7	231.3	228.9	229.3	229.5	230.8	235.7	238.7	232.6
2002	232.0	230.3	230.4	229.0	229.2	226.9	224.9	226.4	224.8	226.0	228.8	232.5	228.4
2003	222.0	220.7	220.7	220.2	221.1	220.2	219.4	219.7	220.8	223.5	226.3	229.8	222.0
2004	225.3	224.9	225.3	225.3	226.1	226.0	224.7	224.5	224.4	227.7	233.1	236.9	227.0
2005	231.0	231.1	232.1	233.9	234.6	234.0	232.9	233.0	232.9	234.3	238.9	243.4	234.3
2006	236.9	236.3	238.3	236.1	236.5	235.6	234.0	234.3	234.1	234.3	239.2	243.3	236.6
2007	235.6	234.4	235.6	234.4	235.1	234.6	232.2	232.9	232.9	232.8	238.8	241.3	235.1
2008	233.5	232.6	232.6	229.3	229.1	227.2	224.4	223.9	222.2	222.1	224.6	226.5	227.3
2009	217.2	214.6	213.2	210.8	210.7	209.0	206.7	206.7	206.3	207.2	210.9	213.4	210.6
2010	206.6	206.5	207.3	207.6	208.7	208.7	207.5	208.1	207.9	210.5	214.7	218.7	209.4
2011	210.9	210.3	211.3	211.9	212.3	211.4	212.2	212.1	212.1	214.6	216.5	218.6	212.9
Wholesale Trade													
2000	57.7	57.8	58.1	58.5	58.6	59.2	59.1	59.1	59.0	59.0	59.1	59.3	58.7
2001	58.4	58.5	58.5	58.7	58.7	59.0	58.3	58.2	57.7	57.4	57.2	57.4	58.2
2002	56.6	56.5	56.7	56.7	56.9	57.2	56.8	56.8	56.5	56.2	56.0	55.9	56.6
2003	57.1	56.9	56.9	57.5	57.5	57.7	58.5	58.5	57.8	57.9	57.8	57.9	57.7
2004	58.2	58.2	58.6	58.6	58.7	59.1	60.4	59.7	59.5	58.9	58.9	59.1	59.0
2005	59.8	59.2	59.4	59.8	59.8	60.2	60.6	60.8	60.0	59.7	59.8	60.1	59.9
2006	59.5	59.4	59.7	60.5	60.8	61.5	61.6	61.6	61.7	61.5	61.5	62.0	60.9
2007	61.4	61.6	62.0	61.8	62.2	62.7	63.0	62.9	62.7	62.8	62.9	63.1	62.4
2008	62.8	62.8	62.9	63.2	63.4	63.8	63.7	63.7	63.3	62.7	62.2	62.1	63.1
2009	60.9	60.6	60.3	60.0	59.7	59.9	59.7	59.7	59.5	59.0	59.4	59.4	59.8
2010	58.7	58.6	59.0	60.8	60.8	60.7	60.4	60.0	59.7	59.7	59.5	59.7	59.8
2011	59.3	59.3	59.5	59.7	59.9	60.3	60.8	60.0	60.0	60.5	61.5	61.3	60.2
Retail Trade													
2000	147.1	147.6	149.0	146.6	147.1	147.5	145.2	146.9	146.7	148.0	153.1	155.8	148.4
2001	144.4	143.7	144.4	142.1	142.2	142.2	140.8	141.3	141.9	143.4	148.5	150.5	143.8
2002	144.9	143.2	143.7	142.6	142.7	141.0	139.6	141.1	140.3	141.6	144.7	148.1	142.8
2003	140.5	139.2	139.4	138.7	139.4	139.1	138.4	138.7	139.5	142.2	145.0	147.5	140.6
2004	143.2	142.2	142.7	142.7	143.1	142.8	142.1	141.8	142.0	144.8	149.6	152.8	144.2
2005	147.1	147.0	147.4	148.8	149.3	149.2	148.9	149.1	149.1	150.4	154.7	157.6	149.9
2006	152.4	151.6	153.2	151.2	151.2	150.7	149.6	149.7	149.8	150.5	154.8	157.4	151.8
2007	151.9	150.9	151.8	151.1	151.7	151.2	149.5	149.9	150.2	150.0	155.2	156.7	151.7
2008	151.0	150.0	150.1	147.3	146.9	145.8	144.5	144.5	143.3	143.4	146.0	147.1	146.7
2009	140.3	138.7	137.9	136.4	136.5	135.8	134.5	134.8	134.7	135.8	139.5	140.8	137.1
2010	136.1	135.9	136.4	136.6	137.1	137.6	136.9	137.5	137.4	139.3	143.4	145.8	138.3
2011	140.0	139.5	140.1	140.8	140.8	140.3	141.2	141.0	140.4	142.1	145.2	146.0	141.5
Transportation and Utilities													
2000	36.1	36.4	37.2	36.7	37.0	37.2	37.5	37.6	37.5	36.5	37.1	37.5	37.0
2001	34.5	34.6	34.6	34.4	34.5	34.5	34.1	34.0	33.8	33.5	33.5	34.1	34.2
2002	33.0	33.0	32.6	32.8	32.6	32.5	32.4	32.4	31.8	31.8	31.5	31.7	32.3
2003	30.5	30.4	30.5	30.5	30.7	30.5	30.9	31	31.3	31.5	31.5	32.3	31
2004	31.7	31.8	31.9	32.0	32.2	32.1	31.9	31.9	31.6	31.9	32.0	32.3	31.9
2005	31.8	32.0	32.1	32.2	32.0	31.7	31.4	31.3	31.2	31.1	31.3	32.2	31.7
2006	31.2	31.2	31.3	31.1	31.1	30.9	30.7	30.6	30.3	29.7	29.8	30.9	30.7
2007	29.3	29.0	29.2	29.0	28.8	28.9	28.9	29.0	28.9	28.8	29.0	29.8	29.1
2008	28.2	28.3	28.3	28.2	28.2	28.0	27.4	27.2	27.1	27.2	27.2	28.2	27.8
2009	26.9	26.5	26.2	26.0	25.9	25.7	25.5	25.3	25.2	24.8	24.9	25.9	25.7
2010	24.8	24.8	24.7	24.9	25.1	24.9	25.0	25.0	25.0	25.3	25.5	26.6	25.1
2011	25.4	25.3	25.5	25.5	25.6	25.5	25.3	25.3	25.4	25.4	25.5	26.2	25.5
Information													
2000	37.3	37.6	38.3	37.6	37.9	38.9	38.7	39.0	39.5	40.2	40.7	40.9	38.9
2001	39.7	39.7	39.7	39.3	38.9	38.5	38.2	37.5	36.7	36.7	36.5	35.8	38.1
2002	35.9	35.5	35.7	35.3	35.2	34.8	34.6	34.5	34.6	34.4	34.9	34.8	35.0
2003	34.3	34.1	34.2	34.5	34.4	34.0	33.9	33.6	33.5	32.9	32.9	32.8	33.8
2004	32.6	32.3	32.9	32.0	32.1	32.2	31.6	31.8	31.8	31.8	31.9	32.0	32.1
2005	31.6	31.6	31.8	31.5	31.6	31.6	31.8	32.0	32.4	32.2	32.3	32.2	31.9
2006	32.1	32.2	32.0	31.8	31.9	32.0	31.8	31.7	31.6	31.5	31.6	31.7	31.8
2007	31.6	31.8	31.9	32.1	32.2	32.4	31.9	31.9	31.7	31.4	31.4	31.3	31.8
2008	30.9	31.1	31.0	31.0	30.9	30.7	30.3	30.0	29.5	29.6	29.3	29.0	30.3
2009	28.7	28.6	28.5	28.1	27.8	27.7	27.6	27.3	26.9	26.5	26.5	26.5	27.6
2010	26.0	26.0	26.0	25.8	25.8	25.7	25.7	25.6	25.5	25.5	25.6	25.6	25.7
2011	25.8	25.9	25.7	25.6	25.7	25.7	25.5	25.6	25.5	25.8	25.8	26.0	25.7

Employment by Industry: Tampa–St. Petersburg–Clearwater, FL, Selected Years, 2000–2011—*Continued*

(Numbers in thousands, not seasonally adjusted)

Industry and year	January	February	March	April	May	June	July	August	September	October	November	December	Annual average
Financial Activities													
2000	91.1	91.6	92.5	93.3	93.4	93.3	93.2	93.3	93.5	93.4	94.0	94.3	93.1
2001	92.8	93.6	94.3	94.7	94.6	94.8	93.7	93.9	93.4	93.2	93.3	93.4	93.8
2002	92.8	93.8	93.8	93.4	93.5	93.9	94.2	94.4	94.0	94.3	94.9	95.4	94.0
2003	94.4	95.1	95.2	95.4	95.7	95.9	95.8	96.1	95.5	95.3	95.1	95.6	95.4
2004	95.2	95.7	96.1	97.3	97.4	97.1	96.9	97.0	96.8	97.7	98.1	98.6	97.0
2005	98.2	98.9	98.9	100.1	100.5	101.3	101.6	101.0	101.5	102.3	102.8	104.2	100.9
2006	103.2	104.0	104.6	104.8	105.0	104.9	104.1	104.1	103.7	103.8	103.6	104.3	104.2
2007	103.2	104.2	104.3	104.4	104.2	104.0	103.7	102.8	102.4	102.1	102.0	101.8	103.3
2008	100.5	100.5	100.2	99.3	99.1	98.6	98.3	98.0	97.4	97.2	97.0	96.9	98.6
2009	96.0	95.3	95.0	94.4	94.2	93.7	93.0	92.6	91.8	91.1	90.7	90.8	93.2
2010	89.3	89.2	89.4	89.1	89.1	89.2	89.0	89.5	89.0	89.6	89.7	90.5	89.4
2011	89.7	89.9	90.3	90.5	90.6	90.9	90.4	91.1	90.5	90.6	91.6	92.5	90.7
Professional and Business Services													
2000	162.2	167.0	172.8	170.7	171.2	169.0	163.4	165.7	166.6	164.2	164.4	166.3	167.0
2001	159.1	165.6	167.9	166.4	165.0	165.7	161.2	162.6	161.5	160.0	160.8	160.4	163.0
2002	153.9	160.7	161.9	162.0	162.2	159.8	157.4	153.7	153.4	152.6	158.7	158.0	157.9
2003	155.9	160.0	166.1	164.7	161.7	161.5	159.0	159.1	159.5	164.3	165.1	166.8	162.0
2004	167.0	171.3	175.3	181.2	180.4	182.6	180.9	180.7	179.2	182.4	185.2	188.2	179.5
2005	184.6	189.8	190.7	192.6	191.9	190.4	189.5	190.9	192.8	188.9	190.6	191.4	190.3
2006	189.5	192.2	198.7	199.2	200.0	201.2	200.5	202.9	202.3	199.1	200.5	202.3	199.0
2007	198.7	200.0	203.0	203.2	201.0	202.9	198.9	200.3	195.8	194.6	195.1	195.6	199.1
2008	190.4	191.5	193.1	188.5	186.6	187.1	184.6	184.9	182.6	179.8	179.1	180.1	185.7
2009	175.6	176.0	176.1	174.5	172.7	173.4	171.2	171.8	171.7	171.1	172.2	173.2	173.3
2010	170.8	173.5	176.0	175.9	175.9	178.2	177.8	179.9	178.6	183.0	183.5	184.9	178.2
2011	182.0	184.1	185.1	188.0	186.7	186.7	186.4	188.3	190.8	192.4	193.3	192.1	188.0
Education and Health Services													
2000	142.1	143.6	144.4	144.3	142.8	141.8	141.1	141.8	142.9	142.5	143.4	143.7	142.9
2001	140.1	141.1	142.2	142.5	142.7	143.2	141.5	142.8	143.9	144.5	145.3	146.5	143.0
2002	142.3	143.4	144.9	145.3	146.1	145.8	144.6	145.9	146.8	147.8	149.2	149.8	146.0
2003	146.6	147.9	149.2	150.0	150.6	150.2	149.6	151.5	152.7	152.2	153.0	153.6	150.6
2004	152.1	153.4	154.2	155.2	155.9	155.4	154.3	155.2	155.8	156.3	157.3	157.7	155.2
2005	155.9	156.8	157.4	158.5	158.1	157.5	156.5	157.4	157.6	158.3	158.8	159.6	157.7
2006	158.0	159.5	160.7	161.0	161.3	160.6	159.2	160.4	162.1	163.2	164.7	166.1	161.4
2007	164.2	166.0	167.9	168.2	168.4	168.2	166.1	168.2	169.2	171.0	172.6	173.4	168.6
2008	171.6	172.9	174.0	173.6	173.9	172.1	170.4	171.7	172.3	173.5	174.9	175.6	173.0
2009	172.1	172.9	174.3	174.2	174.6	173.4	172.2	173.0	174.3	176.5	177.8	178.6	174.5
2010	176.4	177.3	179.3	178.5	178.0	177.0	175.7	175.9	176.6	179.2	180.1	180.2	177.9
2011	178.5	179.7	180.5	181.9	181.3	179.4	176.5	179.0	180.2	181.8	184.9	184.6	180.7
Leisure and Hospitality													
2000	112.6	116.5	120.7	121.8	121.7	121.1	118.2	117.0	116.0	115.7	116.6	117.4	117.9
2001	116.4	119.6	122.7	122.6	122.9	121.0	120.5	120.1	118.8	120.0	120.0	120.6	120.4
2002	117.7	121.1	124.5	124.8	124.8	123.5	120.1	121.3	121.3	120.1	120.1	121.2	121.7
2003	120.5	121.9	124.9	124.2	123.8	123.4	121.2	121.2	120.9	120.7	121.0	122.0	122.1
2004	122.0	125.2	128.6	128.0	127.4	126.3	124.6	124.8	124.8	125.0	125.9	126.3	125.7
2005	126.4	129.1	132.3	132.0	132.5	131.4	129.0	129.0	128.5	128.1	128.7	129.5	129.7
2006	128.2	130.9	134.7	134.0	133.6	133.4	130.6	131.6	131.6	130.3	131.5	132.5	131.9
2007	129.4	132.6	136.0	136.1	135.2	133.9	131.1	131.4	130.4	129.1	129.8	130.9	132.2
2008	128.0	130.6	133.7	133.5	132.0	130.5	126.1	126.4	125.2	124.8	123.8	124.1	128.2
2009	122.2	124.4	127.2	126.8	125.4	123.3	120.1	120.1	119.3	119.3	118.6	118.8	122.1
2010	117.8	120.0	123.3	124.8	124.1	123.1	120.7	121.0	120.3	120.6	120.5	120.7	121.4
2011	119.1	121.2	124.8	125.7	125.2	124.0	122.8	124.1	125.7	125.4	126.1	128.8	124.4
Other Services													
2000	45.5	46.0	46.6	46.1	46.5	46.8	46.4	46.1	46.2	46.2	46.3	46.3	46.3
2001	45.2	45.3	45.9	46.1	46.8	47.7	47.0	47.0	47.0	47.1	47.6	48.0	46.7
2002	48.1	48.6	48.9	48.5	48.8	49.4	49.2	49.3	49.3	50.1	50.3	50.6	49.3
2003	50.4	50.3	50.1	49.3	49.3	49.6	49.0	48.5	48.6	48.2	48.3	48.7	49.2
2004	49.1	49.6	50.4	49.9	50.4	51.2	50.6	50.3	50.6	50.9	51.4	51.2	50.5
2005	51.4	51.9	52.1	51.9	52.0	52.0	50.8	50.1	49.9	49.1	48.9	48.7	50.7
2006	47.2	47.8	48.4	48.1	48.8	49.5	48.6	48.3	48.5	48.5	48.6	49.0	48.4
2007	48.2	49.1	49.8	48.4	49.1	49.8	48.6	48.6	48.5	49.2	49.8	50.5	49.1
2008	49.8	50.3	50.5	49.6	50.0	50.1	48.9	48.7	48.0	47.2	46.8	46.6	48.9
2009	45.9	45.8	46.0	45.5	45.7	45.5	44.9	44.9	44.6	44.8	44.7	44.5	45.2
2010	43.8	44.2	44.3	44.4	44.5	44.7	44.3	43.9	43.6	44.3	44.0	44.0	44.2
2011	43.6	43.9	44.4	44.6	44.8	44.5	45.5	44.6	44.5	43.5	43.7	44.0	44.3
Government													
2000	141.8	142.4	143.2	144.9	147.3	133.2	131.8	141.3	144.1	146.0	147.8	147.9	142.6
2001	145.7	147.5	148.3	148.1	148.8	137.8	136.2	146.9	148.1	149.7	149.7	150.6	146.5
2002	147.0	148.8	149.1	149.1	148.1	136.5	135.2	146.3	148.0	149.6	150.6	151.7	146.7
2003	147.3	149.3	149.1	148.0	148.4	136.5	135.5	146.0	147.4	148.8	148.9	148.4	146.1
2004	146.2	149.2	148.8	149.0	149.4	137.5	136.8	147.3	148.7	150.3	150.9	150.9	147.1
2005	148.5	151.1	150.3	149.5	149.9	138.1	137.3	147.8	149.8	151.1	151.5	150.7	148.0
2006	149.6	150.4	150.3	150.8	150.3	138.5	137.4	149.2	152.1	153.8	153.5	152.9	149.1
2007	152.3	153.4	154.1	153.8	152.2	142.3	141.3	151.2	154.1	155.4	155.4	155.0	151.7
2008	153.4	155.8	155.2	154.8	153.2	142.7	141.4	152.5	155.7	156.4	157.0	158.0	153.0
2009	155.6	158.1	157.5	158.5	155.6	145.5	144.7	154.4	155.2	156.5	156.1	155.6	154.4
2010	154.5	157.4	157.0	156.3	161.3	147.9	146.6	153.9	155.7	156.4	156.6	155.1	154.9
2011	154.9	157.4	157.1	157.0	155.5	145.5	144.2	153.5	157.0	157.7	157.5	158.0	154.6

Employment by Industry: Tucson, AZ, Selected Years, 2000–2011

(Numbers in thousands, not seasonally adjusted)

Industry and year	January	February	March	April	May	June	July	August	September	October	November	December	Annual average
Total Nonfarm													
2000	342.0	347.0	349.9	348.3	349.0	345.0	336.8	340.3	346.0	349.9	353.6	355.5	346.9
2001	341.2	346.9	349.6	349.7	348.1	341.6	333.8	339.3	344.3	343.9	347.3	347.7	344.5
2002	341.1	344.4	345.3	347.0	346.2	338.6	329.2	335.9	341.9	345.7	349.3	350.0	342.9
2003	340.6	343.7	345.8	345.9	346.2	338.6	333.4	340.4	347.0	350.7	353.3	356.8	345.2
2004	350.0	354.0	354.8	359.0	358.8	351.8	345.5	352.0	358.0	363.8	367.6	369.4	357.1
2005	356.3	362.2	364.2	368.5	368.4	361.1	358.7	364.7	370.8	371.4	374.9	378.8	366.7
2006	371.4	378.3	379.0	380.2	380.0	373.5	369.4	375.9	381.6	386.0	388.2	391.8	379.6
2007	380.6	387.5	388.7	387.2	387.2	379.0	375.9	379.3	386.5	388.5	391.5	391.8	385.3
2008	379.2	385.2	385.1	385.6	384.5	376.3	375.4	379.7	382.5	381.7	381.6	380.9	381.5
2009	369.8	369.9	367.4	365.9	363.6	354.0	351.7	356.0	359.7	359.8	361.7	362.6	361.8
2010	353.0	357.2	356.5	358.5	359.0	346.9	343.2	349.4	352.2	355.0	358.0	359.8	354.1
2011	352.1	356.1	356.9	358.2	357.2	344.1	340.0	352.0	358.1	359.7	361.3	358.9	354.6
Total Private													
2000	270.2	273.0	274.7	272.8	272.3	273.3	270.2	272.5	273.5	274.7	277.5	279.5	273.7
2001	268.6	271.3	273.2	273.0	271.8	271.0	269.5	270.6	269.6	268.3	269.9	270.5	270.6
2002	266.4	267.5	268.4	268.8	268.8	267.2	264.4	266.4	267.0	268.3	270.9	271.8	268.0
2003	264.9	265.6	267.3	267.7	267.9	267.9	266.7	269.7	271.0	272.6	275.4	277.8	269.5
2004	273.5	275.1	275.9	279.9	279.8	278.2	279.0	280.1	283.9	287.1	288.6	280.2	280.2
2005	280.1	282.7	284.3	288.8	288.8	288.2	288.3	291.3	293.2	293.1	296.0	300.1	289.6
2006	295.7	299.9	300.8	301.6	302.1	302.2	300.9	303.5	305.9	306.8	308.6	311.9	303.3
2007	303.8	307.4	308.9	307.6	308.5	307.5	305.0	305.9	307.8	310.2	310.7	307.4	307.4
2008	302.5	303.8	304.4	303.9	302.7	301.5	300.4	301.7	301.3	299.7	299.0	298.7	301.6
2009	290.2	288.3	286.4	284.1	282.7	280.8	279.1	279.9	279.6	279.1	280.8	282.0	282.8
2010	274.9	276.5	277.1	277.7	276.7	275.3	272.9	274.0	272.9	275.5	277.1	279.6	275.9
2011	275.1	276.3	277.5	278.2	277.9	276.6	274.4	276.9	279.4	280.5	281.1	280.2	277.8
Goods-Producing													
2000	56.1	56.2	56.8	56.7	56.6	57.7	57.9	58.5	58.5	58.2	58.5	59.1	57.6
2001	56.9	57.1	57.7	57.5	57.7	58.2	58.4	58.7	58.1	57.3	56.7	56.0	57.5
2002	55.1	54.5	54.6	54.4	54.7	55.0	54.9	55.1	54.7	54.2	54.0	53.9	54.6
2003	53.0	52.3	52.7	52.2	52.6	53.0	52.9	53.1	52.5	53.1	52.9	53.2	52.8
2004	52.9	52.8	52.9	53.2	53.4	53.6	54.2	54.0	54.1	54.4	54.4	54.8	53.7
2005	53.1	53.8	54.2	54.8	55.1	55.8	55.8	56.4	56.5	56.0	56.3	56.9	55.4
2006	56.3	57.3	57.0	57.5	57.8	58.5	58.8	58.6	58.4	58.1	56.6	56.3	57.6
2007	54.9	56.4	56.0	55.5	55.9	56.5	56.4	56.5	55.9	55.2	54.9	54.3	55.7
2008	53.6	53.3	53.2	52.5	52.4	52.8	52.6	52.4	51.6	50.4	49.3	48.3	51.9
2009	46.2	45.1	44.3	43.7	43.6	43.8	43.4	43.0	42.5	42.0	41.7	41.7	43.4
2010	40.6	40.7	40.7	40.9	41.0	41.2	41.1	41.1	40.7	40.7	40.4	40.5	40.8
2011	39.9	39.8	40.0	39.8	40.0	40.2	40.1	40.9	41.9	42.3	42.1	41.8	40.7
Mining and Logging													
2000	1.8	1.8	1.8	1.8	1.8	1.8	1.8	1.8	1.8	1.8	1.8	1.8	1.8
2001	1.8	1.8	1.8	1.8	1.8	1.8	1.8	1.8	1.7	1.7	1.7	1.7	1.8
2002	1.7	1.6	1.6	1.6	1.6	1.6	1.4	1.4	1.5	1.4	1.4	1.4	1.5
2003	1.3	1.1	1.2	1.1	1.2	1.2	1.2	1.2	1.2	1.2	1.2	1.2	1.2
2004	1.2	1.2	1.2	1.3	1.3	1.3	1.3	1.3	1.4	1.4	1.4	1.4	1.3
2005	1.4	1.4	1.5	1.5	1.5	1.5	1.2	1.2	1.2	1.2	1.4	1.5	1.4
2006	1.4	1.5	1.5	1.5	1.5	1.6	1.6	1.6	1.6	1.6	1.7	1.7	1.6
2007	1.7	1.7	1.7	1.7	1.8	1.8	1.8	1.8	1.8	1.8	1.8	1.9	1.8
2008	1.9	1.9	1.9	1.9	1.9	2.0	2.0	2.0	2.0	1.9	1.9	1.9	1.9
2009	1.8	1.8	1.7	1.7	1.7	1.7	1.7	1.7	1.7	1.7	1.7	1.8	1.7
2010	1.7	1.8	1.8	1.8	1.8	1.8	1.8	1.9	1.8	1.9	1.9	1.9	1.8
2011	1.9	1.9	1.9	1.9	1.9	1.9	1.9	1.9	1.9	1.9	1.9	1.9	1.9
Construction													
2000	22.3	22.3	22.6	22.5	22.5	23.0	23.1	23.5	23.4	23.1	23.0	23.3	22.9
2001	21.9	22.2	22.6	22.3	22.5	22.9	23.3	23.6	23.5	22.9	22.6	22.3	22.7
2002	21.9	21.8	22.0	21.8	22.2	22.6	22.9	23.3	23.0	23.0	23.0	23.0	22.5
2003	22.5	22.3	22.4	22.5	22.8	23.2	23.1	23.2	22.8	23.4	23.3	23.4	22.9
2004	23.3	23.3	23.3	23.6	23.8	23.9	24.3	24.2	24.2	24.6	24.6	24.9	24.0
2005	23.7	24.2	24.6	25.3	25.5	26.0	26.2	26.5	26.8	26.4	26.6	26.8	25.7
2006	26.3	26.7	26.9	27.5	27.9	28.4	28.7	28.7	28.7	28.7	28.5	28.3	27.9
2007	27.1	26.9	26.9	26.5	26.8	27.1	26.9	26.9	26.3	25.8	25.4	24.8	26.5
2008	24.0	23.8	23.8	23.3	23.2	23.3	23.3	23.2	22.6	21.8	20.8	20.0	22.8
2009	18.7	17.8	17.3	16.7	16.7	16.8	16.5	16.3	16.0	15.7	15.5	15.4	16.6
2010	14.6	14.5	14.6	14.9	15.0	15.3	15.2	15.3	15.1	15.3	15.0	15.0	15.0
2011	14.6	14.6	14.8	14.6	14.7	14.9	14.9	15.7	16.4	16.8	16.8	16.5	15.4
Manufacturing													
2000	32.0	32.1	32.4	32.4	32.3	32.9	33.0	33.2	33.3	33.3	33.7	34.0	32.9
2001	33.2	33.1	33.3	33.4	33.4	33.5	33.3	33.3	32.9	32.7	32.4	32.0	33.0
2002	31.5	31.1	31.0	31.0	30.9	30.8	30.6	30.4	30.2	29.8	29.6	29.5	30.5
2003	29.2	28.9	29.1	28.6	28.6	28.6	28.6	28.7	28.5	28.5	28.4	28.6	28.7
2004	28.4	28.3	28.4	28.3	28.3	28.4	28.6	28.5	28.5	28.4	28.4	28.5	28.4
2005	28.0	28.2	28.1	28.0	28.1	28.3	28.4	28.7	28.5	28.4	28.3	28.6	28.3
2006	28.6	29.1	28.6	28.5	28.4	28.5	28.5	28.3	28.1	27.8	26.4	26.3	28.1
2007	26.1	27.8	27.4	27.3	27.3	27.6	27.7	27.8	27.8	27.6	27.7	27.6	27.5
2008	27.7	27.6	27.5	27.3	27.3	27.5	27.3	27.2	27.0	26.7	26.6	26.4	27.2
2009	25.7	25.5	25.3	25.3	25.2	25.3	25.2	25.0	24.8	24.6	24.5	24.5	25.1
2010	24.3	24.4	24.3	24.2	24.2	24.1	24.1	23.9	23.8	23.5	23.5	23.6	24.0
2011	23.4	23.3	23.3	23.3	23.4	23.4	23.3	23.3	23.6	23.6	23.4	23.4	23.4

Employment by Industry: Tucson, AZ, Selected Years, 2000–2011—*Continued*

(Numbers in thousands, not seasonally adjusted)

Industry and year	January	February	March	April	May	June	July	August	September	October	November	December	Annual average
Service-Providing													
2000	285.9	290.8	293.1	291.6	292.4	287.3	278.9	281.8	287.5	291.7	295.1	296.4	289.4
2001	284.3	289.8	291.9	292.2	290.4	283.4	275.4	280.6	286.2	286.6	290.6	291.7	286.9
2002	286.0	289.9	290.7	292.6	291.5	283.6	274.3	280.8	287.2	291.5	295.3	296.1	288.3
2003	287.6	291.4	293.1	293.7	293.6	285.6	280.5	287.3	294.5	297.6	300.4	303.6	292.4
2004	297.1	301.2	301.9	305.8	305.4	298.2	291.3	298.0	303.9	309.4	313.2	314.6	303.3
2005	303.2	308.4	310.0	313.7	313.3	305.3	302.9	308.3	314.3	315.4	318.6	321.9	311.3
2006	315.1	321.0	322.0	322.7	322.2	315.0	310.6	317.3	323.2	327.9	331.6	335.5	322.0
2007	325.7	331.1	332.7	331.7	331.3	322.5	319.5	322.8	330.6	333.3	336.6	337.5	329.6
2008	325.6	331.9	331.9	333.1	332.1	323.5	322.8	327.3	330.9	331.3	332.3	332.6	329.6
2009	323.6	324.8	323.1	322.2	320.0	310.2	308.3	313.0	317.2	317.8	320.0	320.9	318.4
2010	312.4	316.5	315.8	317.6	318.0	305.7	302.1	308.3	311.5	314.3	317.6	319.3	313.3
2011	312.2	316.3	316.9	318.4	317.2	303.9	299.9	311.1	316.2	317.4	319.2	317.1	313.8
Trade, Transportation, and Utilities													
2000	54.2	54.0	53.8	53.5	53.7	53.8	54.1	54.7	54.9	56.0	57.9	58.9	55.0
2001	55.7	55.2	55.1	55.0	55.0	54.9	54.6	54.6	54.9	54.9	56.5	57.6	55.3
2002	54.1	53.8	53.8	54.0	54.4	54.2	53.5	53.6	53.5	54.4	55.9	57.0	54.4
2003	54.0	54.0	54.4	54.1	54.1	54.2	54.0	54.9	54.9	55.7	57.6	58.8	55.1
2004	56.2	56.1	56.4	57.1	57.8	57.9	57.9	58.0	57.7	58.5	60.3	61.0	57.9
2005	58.0	58.0	58.2	58.3	58.3	58.3	58.8	59.4	59.8	60.8	62.6	64.1	59.6
2006	61.1	61.0	61.2	61.3	61.7	61.5	61.9	62.7	63.1	63.8	65.5	67.0	62.7
2007	63.9	63.3	64.0	63.8	64.1	63.8	63.7	64.0	64.0	64.5	66.1	66.7	64.3
2008	63.6	62.9	63.0	62.2	62.4	62.4	62.2	62.7	62.3	62.5	63.0	63.2	62.7
2009	60.6	59.3	58.6	58.0	57.8	57.3	57.4	57.6	57.3	57.1	58.2	59.0	58.2
2010	56.8	56.6	56.4	56.4	56.5	56.3	56.2	56.4	55.8	56.1	57.7	58.3	56.6
2011	56.8	56.4	56.5	56.7	56.8	56.9	55.7	56.5	56.5	55.9	56.4	56.5	56.5
Wholesale Trade													
2000	7.6	7.6	7.6	7.2	7.3	7.4	7.4	7.4	7.4	7.4	7.5	7.6	7.5
2001	7.3	7.3	7.4	7.4	7.4	7.5	7.4	7.4	7.4	7.3	7.4	7.4	7.4
2002	7.5	7.4	7.4	7.2	7.3	7.3	7.2	7.3	7.3	7.4	7.4	7.4	7.3
2003	7.2	7.3	7.3	7.3	7.4	7.4	7.4	7.5	7.5	7.5	7.6	7.6	7.4
2004	7.5	7.5	7.6	8.1	8.4	8.4	8.3	8.2	8.2	8.0	8.1	8.2	8.0
2005	8.0	8.1	8.2	8.3	8.4	8.5	8.6	8.7	8.9	9.0	9.0	9.2	8.6
2006	9.0	9.1	9.2	9.2	9.3	9.4	9.5	9.7	9.8	9.7	9.8	9.9	9.5
2007	9.6	9.6	9.8	9.7	9.8	9.9	9.8	9.9	9.9	9.9	9.9	9.9	9.8
2008	9.7	9.7	9.8	9.7	9.7	9.7	9.7	9.7	9.7	9.6	9.5	9.4	9.7
2009	9.1	8.9	8.6	8.5	8.5	8.4	8.5	8.5	8.4	8.4	8.4	8.4	8.6
2010	8.1	8.1	8.0	8.1	8.1	8.0	8.1	7.9	7.8	7.8	7.8	7.8	8.0
2011	7.7	7.8	7.8	7.8	7.9	7.9	7.9	7.9	7.8	7.8	7.8	7.8	7.8
Retail Trade													
2000	38.0	37.9	37.7	37.8	37.9	37.9	37.7	38.3	38.6	39.6	41.3	42.1	38.7
2001	39.0	38.5	38.3	38.3	38.2	38.1	37.9	37.9	38.3	38.6	40.1	41.3	38.7
2002	39.1	38.8	38.8	39.1	39.4	39.2	38.6	38.6	38.7	39.2	40.7	41.8	39.3
2003	39.0	38.9	39.3	39.0	38.9	39.0	38.8	39.2	39.3	40.0	41.8	42.9	39.7
2004	40.6	40.5	40.7	40.8	41.1	41.2	41.3	41.4	41.1	41.7	43.4	43.9	41.5
2005	41.2	41.0	41.0	41.1	41.0	40.8	41.3	41.8	42.0	42.8	44.6	45.8	42.0
2006	43.1	42.9	43.0	43.0	43.2	42.9	43.1	43.7	43.9	44.7	46.2	47.3	43.9
2007	45.1	44.6	45.0	44.9	44.9	44.6	44.6	44.7	44.7	45.3	46.8	47.1	45.2
2008	44.6	43.9	44.0	43.4	43.6	43.6	43.4	43.7	43.3	43.6	44.2	44.2	43.8
2009	42.2	41.1	40.8	40.6	40.5	40.2	40.2	40.4	40.2	40.0	41.1	41.7	40.8
2010	40.0	39.7	39.5	39.6	39.6	39.5	39.2	39.6	39.1	39.4	41.0	41.3	39.8
2011	39.9	39.3	39.4	39.6	39.6	39.7	38.5	39.3	39.4	38.7	39.3	39.5	39.4
Transportation and Utilities													
2000	8.6	8.5	8.5	8.5	8.5	8.5	9.0	9.0	8.9	9.0	9.1	9.2	8.8
2001	9.4	9.4	9.4	9.3	9.4	9.3	9.3	9.3	9.2	9.0	9.0	8.9	9.2
2002	7.5	7.6	7.6	7.7	7.7	7.7	7.7	7.7	7.5	7.8	7.8	7.8	7.7
2003	7.8	7.8	7.8	7.8	7.8	7.8	7.8	8.2	8.1	8.2	8.2	8.3	8.0
2004	8.1	8.1	8.1	8.2	8.3	8.3	8.3	8.4	8.4	8.8	8.8	8.9	8.4
2005	8.8	8.9	9.0	8.9	8.9	9.0	8.9	8.9	8.9	9.0	9.0	9.1	8.9
2006	9.0	9.0	9.0	9.1	9.2	9.2	9.3	9.3	9.4	9.4	9.5	9.8	9.3
2007	9.2	9.1	9.2	9.2	9.4	9.3	9.3	9.4	9.4	9.3	9.4	9.7	9.3
2008	9.3	9.3	9.2	9.1	9.1	9.1	9.1	9.3	9.3	9.3	9.3	9.6	9.3
2009	9.3	9.3	9.2	8.9	8.8	8.7	8.7	8.7	8.7	8.7	8.7	8.9	8.9
2010	8.7	8.8	8.9	8.7	8.8	8.8	8.9	8.9	8.9	8.9	8.9	9.2	8.9
2011	9.2	9.3	9.3	9.3	9.3	9.3	9.3	9.3	9.3	9.4	9.3	9.2	9.3
Information													
2000	7.9	8.1	8.0	8.0	8.1	8.0	7.9	8.1	7.8	7.8	7.8	7.8	7.9
2001	7.8	7.8	7.8	7.7	7.7	7.6	7.6	7.7	7.7	7.6	7.8	7.9	7.7
2002	7.9	8.0	8.0	7.9	8.0	7.8	7.8	7.9	7.8	7.8	7.9	7.8	7.9
2003	7.6	7.7	7.5	7.5	7.6	7.5	7.5	7.6	7.3	7.4	7.7	7.7	7.6
2004	7.5	7.7	7.5	7.5	7.6	7.5	7.6	7.8	7.3	7.4	7.7	7.6	7.6
2005	7.3	7.2	7.2	7.2	7.2	7.2	7.2	7.2	7.2	7.2	7.2	7.3	7.2
2006	7.5	7.5	7.4	6.9	6.9	6.9	6.7	6.5	6.5	6.3	6.2	6.0	6.8
2007	6.3	6.2	6.2	6.1	6.1	5.8	5.7	5.7	5.7	5.8	5.8	5.7	5.9
2008	5.7	5.5	5.4	5.4	5.3	5.2	5.2	5.1	5.1	5.0	5.1	5.2	5.3
2009	5.1	5.1	4.9	4.9	4.8	4.6	4.6	4.5	4.5	4.4	4.4	4.5	4.7
2010	4.5	4.5	4.5	4.4	4.4	4.4	4.3	4.3	4.2	4.2	4.2	4.2	4.3
2011	4.2	4.3	4.1	4.1	4.2	4.2	4.1	4.1	4.1	4.1	4.1	4.1	4.1

Employment by Industry: Tucson, AZ, Selected Years, 2000–2011—*Continued*

(Numbers in thousands, not seasonally adjusted)

Industry and year	January	February	March	April	May	June	July	August	September	October	November	December	Annual average
Financial Activities													
2000	14.6	14.8	14.9	14.6	14.6	14.7	14.9	15.0	15.0	15.2	14.8	14.8	14.8
2001	14.2	14.4	14.5	14.8	14.7	14.7	14.8	14.5	14.1	14.2	14.3	14.3	14.5
2002	14.0	14.1	14.2	14.2	14.4	14.3	14.2	14.3	14.4	14.7	14.7	14.8	14.4
2003	14.8	14.9	15.1	15.0	15.2	15.2	15.5	15.7	16.2	16.3	16.1	16.2	15.5
2004	16.1	16.2	16.1	16.2	16.1	15.8	16.0	15.9	15.7	15.7	15.7	15.8	15.9
2005	15.5	15.7	15.7	16.0	16.2	16.4	16.6	17.0	17.1	17.1	17.2	17.5	16.5
2006	16.7	16.9	17.0	17.3	17.4	17.5	17.6	17.8	18.0	18.3	18.4	18.7	17.6
2007	18.4	18.5	18.6	18.7	18.8	18.8	18.8	17.7	17.4	17.4	17.4	17.7	18.2
2008	16.9	17.0	17.1	17.3	17.2	17.4	17.4	17.4	17.3	16.9	16.9	17.2	17.2
2009	16.9	17.0	17.0	17.2	17.3	17.4	17.8	17.8	17.7	17.7	17.8	18.0	17.5
2010	17.9	18.0	17.7	17.5	17.6	17.7	17.6	17.6	17.4	17.5	17.5	17.7	17.6
2011	17.4	17.4	17.4	17.3	17.2	17.3	17.3	17.3	17.3	17.4	17.4	17.5	17.4
Professional and Business Services													
2000	42.3	43.4	44.6	44.2	44.1	44.5	42.8	43.4	43.3	42.8	43.0	43.3	43.5
2001	41.0	42.2	42.4	42.3	41.5	41.6	41.4	41.4	40.5	40.6	40.5	40.3	41.3
2002	40.4	41.0	41.3	41.5	40.9	41.1	41.2	41.9	42.0	42.0	42.4	42.2	41.5
2003	40.6	40.6	40.7	41.0	40.8	41.5	41.2	41.6	42.1	41.7	41.5	41.5	41.2
2004	41.2	41.7	41.8	43.4	42.7	42.8	43.5	43.9	43.8	45.3	45.3	45.4	43.4
2005	44.1	44.5	44.5	45.8	45.5	45.5	46.3	47.0	47.0	46.5	46.6	47.6	45.9
2006	47.3	48.4	48.5	48.6	48.6	49.1	49.5	50.0	50.9	50.9	52.0	53.1	49.7
2007	51.5	52.1	52.3	52.1	52.0	52.5	52.0	52.9	53.0	53.6	53.9	53.6	52.6
2008	51.8	52.0	52.3	52.3	51.4	51.2	51.7	51.9	51.6	50.6	50.0	50.2	51.4
2009	49.0	48.3	48.0	47.2	46.5	46.5	46.4	46.4	46.3	46.4	46.8	47.0	47.1
2010	45.8	46.1	46.4	46.2	45.2	45.2	45.1	45.0	44.8	45.9	45.8	46.8	45.7
2011	45.6	45.9	46.3	46.2	45.7	45.8	46.3	46.2	45.9	46.1	46.1	45.9	46.0
Education and Health Services													
2000	42.4	42.5	42.3	41.8	41.6	41.4	41.0	41.6	42.1	42.2	42.4	42.4	42.0
2001	40.7	41.0	41.6	41.5	41.4	41.3	41.3	41.7	42.2	42.4	42.9	43.2	41.8
2002	42.9	43.4	43.4	43.4	43.7	43.4	42.7	43.5	43.9	44.0	44.3	44.3	43.6
2003	44.3	44.9	45.0	45.4	45.5	45.3	45.3	46.1	46.5	46.1	46.6	46.8	45.7
2004	46.7	46.7	46.9	47.1	47.5	47.2	47.2	48.2	48.5	48.9	49.1	49.2	47.8
2005	49.1	49.5	49.7	50.2	50.5	49.8	49.9	50.8	51.4	51.6	51.7	52.2	50.5
2006	51.6	52.1	52.5	52.0	52.3	52.0	51.7	52.6	53.0	53.3	53.6	54.2	52.6
2007	53.5	54.0	54.3	54.0	54.7	54.1	54.0	54.6	54.9	55.9	55.9	56.2	54.7
2008	55.0	55.6	56.0	57.0	57.1	56.6	56.7	57.6	58.1	58.4	58.8	58.8	57.1
2009	58.4	58.7	58.7	58.4	58.5	58.0	57.8	58.4	58.7	58.8	58.9	59.1	58.5
2010	58.0	58.2	58.4	58.5	58.6	58.0	57.4	58.1	58.3	58.7	58.7	59.1	58.3
2011	58.6	59.1	59.0	59.6	59.6	59.0	59.1	59.6	58.9	59.3	59.8	59.3	59.2
Leisure and Hospitality													
2000	39.8	40.9	41.3	41.0	40.6	39.9	38.5	38.4	39.0	39.6	40.1	40.0	39.9
2001	38.5	39.7	40.0	40.0	39.4	38.1	36.9	37.4	37.6	37.0	36.9	36.9	38.2
2002	37.8	38.4	38.8	38.7	37.9	36.7	35.5	35.6	36.2	36.8	37.3	37.4	37.3
2003	36.4	36.9	37.5	37.9	37.5	36.6	35.7	36.1	36.9	37.5	38.2	38.9	37.2
2004	38.6	39.4	39.7	40.5	39.8	38.6	37.7	38.3	38.4	38.8	39.7	40.0	39.1
2005	38.7	39.6	40.2	41.6	41.1	40.4	39.0	38.9	39.6	39.1	39.4	39.6	39.8
2006	39.7	40.9	41.2	41.9	41.1	40.2	39.3	39.9	40.8	40.5	40.7	40.9	40.6
2007	39.8	41.1	41.5	41.5	41.0	39.9	38.6	38.7	39.3	39.6	40.3	40.7	40.2
2008	40.3	41.7	41.6	41.3	41.0	39.9	38.8	39.0	39.7	40.4	40.4	40.6	40.4
2009	39.1	39.9	39.9	39.9	39.5	38.5	37.0	37.6	38.1	38.1	38.5	38.2	38.7
2010	37.4	38.4	38.9	39.5	39.1	38.0	36.8	37.1	37.4	38.0	38.4	38.6	38.1
2011	38.4	39.0	39.7	40.0	39.9	38.7	37.3	38.0	40.6	41.2	41.0	40.9	39.6
Other Services													
2000	12.9	13.1	13.0	13.0	13.0	13.3	13.1	12.8	12.9	12.9	13.0	13.2	13.0
2001	13.8	13.9	14.1	14.2	14.4	14.6	14.5	14.6	14.5	14.3	14.3	14.3	14.3
2002	14.2	14.3	14.3	14.7	14.8	14.7	14.6	14.5	14.5	14.4	14.4	14.4	14.5
2003	14.2	14.3	14.4	14.6	14.6	14.6	14.6	14.6	14.6	14.8	14.8	14.7	14.6
2004	14.3	14.5	14.6	14.9	14.9	14.8	14.9	14.8	14.6	14.9	14.9	14.8	14.7
2005	14.3	14.4	14.6	14.9	14.9	14.8	14.7	14.6	14.6	14.8	15.0	14.9	14.7
2006	15.5	15.8	16.0	16.1	16.3	16.5	15.4	15.4	15.2	15.6	15.6	15.7	15.8
2007	15.5	15.8	16.0	15.9	15.9	16.1	15.8	15.8	15.7	15.8	15.9	15.8	15.8
2008	15.6	15.8	15.8	16.0	15.9	16.0	15.8	15.6	15.6	15.5	15.5	15.2	15.7
2009	14.9	14.9	15.0	14.8	14.7	14.7	14.7	14.6	14.5	14.6	14.5	14.5	14.7
2010	13.9	14.0	14.1	14.3	14.3	14.5	14.4	14.4	14.3	14.4	14.4	14.4	14.3
2011	14.2	14.4	14.5	14.5	14.5	14.5	14.5	14.3	14.2	14.2	14.2	14.2	14.4
Government													
2000	71.8	74.0	75.2	75.5	76.7	71.7	66.6	67.8	72.5	75.2	76.1	76.0	73.3
2001	72.6	75.6	76.4	76.7	76.3	70.6	64.3	68.7	74.7	75.6	77.4	77.2	73.8
2002	74.7	76.9	76.9	78.2	77.4	71.4	64.8	69.5	74.9	77.4	78.4	78.2	74.9
2003	75.7	78.1	78.5	78.2	78.3	70.7	66.7	70.7	76.0	78.1	77.9	79.0	75.7
2004	76.5	78.9	78.9	79.1	79.0	73.6	66.5	71.1	77.9	79.9	80.5	80.8	76.9
2005	76.2	79.5	79.9	79.7	79.6	72.9	70.4	73.4	77.6	78.3	78.9	78.7	77.1
2006	75.7	78.4	78.2	78.6	77.9	71.3	68.5	72.4	75.7	79.2	79.6	79.9	76.3
2007	76.8	80.1	79.8	79.6	78.7	71.5	70.9	73.4	80.6	80.7	81.3	81.1	77.9
2008	76.7	81.4	80.7	81.7	81.8	74.8	75.0	78.0	81.2	82.0	82.6	82.2	79.8
2009	79.6	81.6	81.0	81.8	80.9	73.2	72.6	76.1	80.1	80.7	80.9	80.6	79.1
2010	78.1	80.7	79.4	80.8	82.3	71.6	70.3	75.4	79.3	79.5	80.9	80.2	78.2
2011	77.0	79.8	79.4	80.0	79.3	67.5	65.6	75.1	78.7	79.2	80.2	78.7	76.7

Employment by Industry: Tulsa, OK, Selected Years, 2000–2011

(Numbers in thousands, not seasonally adjusted)

Industry and year	January	February	March	April	May	June	July	August	September	October	November	December	Annual average
Total Nonfarm													
2000	395.8	396.9	401.7	405.6	409.2	411.3	407.3	410.3	412.5	412.7	414.3	415.3	407.7
2001	400.4	403.9	407.1	411.1	413.2	415.2	410.2	412.8	411.6	410.0	411.7	411.8	409.9
2002	403.1	403.0	404.8	407.2	409.6	405.8	399.0	401.0	400.2	398.5	399.2	399.8	402.6
2003	391.3	390.8	391.2	392.6	394.0	390.6	387.3	388.6	389.1	390.5	391.4	392.7	390.8
2004	387.2	389.2	392.0	392.2	392.6	393.4	391.6	393.1	394.6	395.9	396.1	398.0	393.0
2005	394.3	397.0	400.3	403.3	406.6	408.3	405.1	408.2	411.2	411.4	414.2	416.5	406.4
2006	410.7	412.9	417.5	416.9	421.7	422.9	415.7	418.6	421.3	422.8	424.2	426.4	419.3
2007	416.7	420.7	426.3	426.9	430.0	430.2	425.7	427.5	429.0	432.4	433.7	431.8	427.6
2008	427.6	431.1	434.0	434.0	437.0	434.6	430.6	432.2	434.7	434.4	434.0	433.5	433.1
2009	420.6	419.6	419.8	416.8	416.9	414.0	405.9	406.2	407.3	409.6	410.4	409.3	413.0
2010	398.9	400.4	403.7	407.5	410.3	408.9	402.7	401.6	404.4	409.8	411.3	411.8	405.9
2011	400.3	397.5	404.1	406.8	408.4	408.1	404.6	404.8	410.6	414.2	414.5	415.2	407.4
Total Private													
2000	348.7	349.2	353.1	357.2	360.2	363.5	362.9	365.0	365.2	363.6	365.3	365.7	360.0
2001	353.2	355.5	358.5	362.6	364.1	367.0	365.2	367.2	363.6	360.5	362.1	362.0	361.8
2002	354.6	353.6	355.1	357.2	358.7	357.0	353.1	354.4	352.0	348.7	349.5	349.9	353.7
2003	342.9	341.7	342.1	343.7	344.6	342.8	341.7	342.9	340.9	341.6	342.6	343.6	342.6
2004	339.2	340.1	342.7	342.9	343.2	344.9	344.2	345.1	344.2	344.8	345.8	347.3	343.7
2005	343.5	345.3	348.4	351.3	353.8	356.0	357.2	358.9	359.4	357.7	360.6	362.7	354.6
2006	357.6	359.0	363.2	363.5	367.5	370.5	368.2	370.4	369.2	368.9	370.7	373.0	366.8
2007	364.9	367.5	372.6	373.1	375.8	378.9	378.2	379.5	376.4	378.0	379.5	377.9	375.2
2008	375.0	377.1	379.8	379.3	381.7	382.5	381.8	382.7	379.9	377.4	377.1	376.6	379.2
2009	366.6	364.0	363.6	359.9	359.5	360.7	357.1	355.3	351.2	351.2	351.8	351.1	357.7
2010	343.6	344.1	346.5	349.7	351.0	352.6	353.1	352.5	350.3	352.9	354.2	354.9	350.5
2011	345.9	342.5	348.6	351.4	353.1	354.7	354.0	354.0	356.1	357.9	358.0	358.7	352.9
Goods-Producing													
2000	79.6	79.5	80.3	79.6	80.0	80.9	81.0	81.5	81.1	80.1	80.4	80.6	80.4
2001	78.4	79.1	79.9	80.3	80.9	82.1	81.4	81.8	80.7	79.7	79.7	79.6	80.3
2002	78.4	77.3	77.1	76.7	76.8	76.6	75.4	75.3	73.9	73.0	72.6	72.7	75.5
2003	71.7	71.0	71.1	71.3	71.4	71.8	72.2	72.1	71.6	70.8	70.5	70.8	71.4
2004	69.4	69.4	69.8	69.8	70.2	70.9	71.4	70.8	70.3	70.0	69.7	69.9	70.1
2005	68.9	69.0	69.9	70.6	71.2	72.0	72.7	73.1	73.3	73.2	73.7	75.0	71.9
2006	74.5	75.0	76.2	75.0	76.3	77.5	77.7	78.4	78.2	78.3	78.7	79.0	77.1
2007	77.8	77.8	79.1	78.6	79.4	80.6	81.4	81.9	81.0	81.8	82.1	81.8	80.3
2008	81.9	82.2	82.9	82.8	83.8	84.2	84.5	84.5	84.0	82.9	82.6	82.9	83.3
2009	81.0	79.1	77.8	75.7	74.4	74.6	73.0	72.2	71.1	70.2	69.6	69.3	74.0
2010	68.0	68.1	68.5	68.9	69.4	70.5	71.2	70.9	70.7	71.6	72.0	72.6	70.2
2011	70.7	70.0	71.7	72.4	72.8	73.8	73.4	73.8	75.3	75.5	75.1	76.4	73.4
Mining and Logging													
2000	5.8	5.9	5.7	5.2	5.1	5.2	5.1	5.1	5.0	4.6	4.7	4.6	5.2
2001	4.1	4.2	4.3	4.1	4.2	4.4	4.4	4.4	4.4	4.5	4.5	4.5	4.3
2002	4.3	4.4	4.4	4.3	4.3	4.5	4.2	4.2	4.1	4.0	3.9	3.9	4.2
2003	4.0	3.9	3.9	3.8	3.8	3.8	3.9	3.9	4.0	4.0	4.0	4.0	3.9
2004	4.4	4.4	4.3	4.3	4.3	4.4	4.5	4.4	4.4	4.4	4.3	4.4	4.4
2005	4.8	4.8	4.8	4.9	5.0	5.1	5.3	5.3	5.4	5.3	5.4	5.5	5.1
2006	5.6	5.7	5.8	6.2	6.1	6.2	6.3	6.3	6.3	6.2	6.3	6.3	6.1
2007	6.4	6.4	6.5	6.4	6.5	6.7	6.9	6.9	6.8	7.0	7.0	7.1	6.7
2008	7.0	7.1	7.1	7.0	7.1	7.4	7.5	7.5	7.4	7.2	7.1	7.1	7.2
2009	7.3	7.1	6.9	6.8	6.7	6.8	6.8	6.9	6.8	6.6	6.6	6.6	6.8
2010	6.7	6.6	6.6	6.7	6.8	7.0	7.1	7.1	7.1	7.2	7.3	7.3	7.0
2011	7.2	7.2	7.3	7.3	7.4	7.6	7.7	7.6	7.7	7.7	7.7	7.8	7.5
Construction													
2000	18.7	18.7	19.3	19.5	19.6	19.9	20.0	20.1	19.8	19.8	19.8	19.6	19.6
2001	19.1	19.7	20.3	20.7	21.1	21.6	21.5	21.8	21.1	21.2	21.0	21.0	20.8
2002	20.8	20.7	20.6	20.3	20.6	20.7	20.8	21.1	20.4	20.2	19.9	20.0	20.5
2003	19.4	19.1	19.4	20.1	20.4	20.6	20.9	20.8	20.4	19.7	19.4	19.5	20.0
2004	18.6	18.5	18.8	18.9	19.2	19.6	20.3	20.1	19.9	19.6	19.3	19.2	19.3
2005	18.4	18.4	18.9	19.3	19.7	20.1	20.7	20.8	20.8	20.6	20.5	20.9	19.9
2006	20.7	20.7	21.2	21.1	21.3	21.9	21.8	21.9	21.9	22.1	22.0	22.1	21.6
2007	20.6	20.6	21.5	21.3	21.5	22.2	22.2	22.5	22.1	22.4	22.5	22.1	21.8
2008	22.1	22.2	22.7	22.9	23.2	23.3	23.6	23.5	23.3	23.0	22.8	22.7	22.9
2009	21.7	21.5	21.5	21.0	20.7	21.0	20.8	20.5	20.1	19.9	19.5	19.4	20.6
2010	18.6	18.8	19.1	19.2	19.4	19.8	20.1	19.9	19.9	20.3	20.3	20.5	19.7
2011	19.0	18.4	19.4	19.7	19.7	19.9	19.9	20.3	21.3	21.0	20.5	20.8	20.0
Manufacturing													
2000	55.1	54.9	55.3	54.9	55.3	55.8	55.9	56.3	56.3	55.7	55.9	56.4	55.7
2001	55.2	55.2	55.3	55.5	55.6	56.1	55.5	55.6	55.2	54.0	54.2	54.1	55.1
2002	53.3	52.2	52.1	52.1	51.9	51.4	50.4	50.0	49.4	48.8	48.8	48.8	50.8
2003	48.3	48.0	47.8	47.4	47.2	47.4	47.4	47.4	47.2	47.1	47.1	47.3	47.5
2004	46.4	46.5	46.7	46.6	46.7	46.9	46.6	46.3	46.0	46.0	46.1	46.3	46.4
2005	45.7	45.8	46.2	46.4	46.5	46.8	46.7	47.0	47.1	47.3	47.8	48.6	46.8
2006	48.2	48.6	49.2	47.7	48.9	49.4	49.6	50.2	50.0	50.0	50.4	50.6	49.4
2007	50.8	50.8	51.1	50.9	51.4	51.7	52.3	52.5	52.1	52.4	52.6	52.6	51.8
2008	52.8	52.9	53.1	52.9	53.5	53.5	53.4	53.5	53.3	52.7	52.7	53.1	53.1
2009	52.0	50.5	49.4	47.9	47.0	46.8	45.4	44.8	44.2	43.7	43.5	43.3	46.5
2010	42.7	42.7	42.8	43.0	43.2	43.7	44.0	43.9	43.7	44.1	44.4	44.8	43.6
2011	44.5	44.4	45.0	45.4	45.7	46.3	45.8	45.9	46.3	46.8	46.9	47.8	45.9

Employment by Industry: Tulsa, OK, Selected Years, 2000–2011—*Continued*

(Numbers in thousands, not seasonally adjusted)

Industry and year	January	February	March	April	May	June	July	August	September	October	November	December	Annual average
Service-Providing													
2000	316.2	317.4	321.4	326.0	329.2	330.4	326.3	328.8	331.4	332.6	333.9	334.7	327.4
2001	322.0	324.8	327.2	330.8	332.3	333.1	328.8	331.0	330.9	330.3	332.0	332.2	329.6
2002	324.7	325.7	327.7	330.5	332.8	329.2	323.6	325.7	326.3	325.5	326.6	327.1	327.1
2003	319.6	319.8	320.1	321.3	322.6	318.8	315.1	316.5	317.5	319.7	320.9	321.9	319.5
2004	317.8	319.8	322.2	322.4	322.4	322.5	320.2	322.3	324.3	325.9	326.4	328.1	322.9
2005	325.4	328.0	330.4	332.7	335.4	336.3	332.4	335.1	337.9	338.2	340.5	341.5	334.5
2006	336.2	337.9	341.3	341.9	345.4	345.4	338.0	340.2	343.1	344.5	345.5	347.4	342.2
2007	338.9	342.9	347.2	348.3	350.6	349.6	344.3	345.6	348.0	350.6	351.6	350.0	347.3
2008	345.7	348.9	351.1	351.2	353.2	350.4	346.1	347.7	350.7	351.5	351.4	350.6	349.9
2009	339.6	340.5	342.0	341.1	342.5	339.4	332.9	334.0	336.2	339.4	340.8	340.0	339.0
2010	330.9	332.3	335.2	338.6	340.9	338.4	331.5	330.7	333.7	338.2	339.3	339.2	335.7
2011	329.6	327.5	332.4	334.4	335.6	334.3	331.2	331.0	335.3	338.7	339.4	338.8	334.0
Trade, Transportation, and Utilities													
2000	86.8	86.3	86.9	87.8	88.8	89.7	89.5	90.1	90.6	90.6	92.4	93.1	89.4
2001	88.0	87.1	87.6	87.6	87.9	88.4	86.8	87.0	86.3	85.8	87.3	87.5	87.3
2002	85.0	84.1	84.9	86.1	86.3	85.8	85.1	85.1	85.0	84.4	85.9	86.7	85.4
2003	83.7	82.7	82.7	83.0	82.9	82.1	81.7	81.9	81.3	82.0	83.5	84.6	82.7
2004	80.9	79.8	80.8	80.8	81.2	81.2	79.8	79.7	79.2	79.6	80.8	81.5	80.4
2005	79.9	79.3	79.4	79.7	80.1	80.2	80.8	81.3	81.4	81.7	83.2	84.2	80.9
2006	81.3	80.8	81.7	83.2	84.0	83.9	83.4	83.5	83.6	83.8	85.5	86.7	83.5
2007	83.8	83.9	85.2	84.7	85.0	85.3	84.9	84.3	84.2	85.1	86.7	86.7	85.0
2008	83.6	83.9	84.8	85.3	85.6	85.6	86.2	86.4	85.8	85.7	86.9	87.3	85.6
2009	83.6	82.8	83.1	83.6	84.0	83.9	83.0	82.8	82.2	82.6	83.8	84.3	83.3
2010	80.5	79.9	80.3	80.4	80.9	81.0	81.1	80.9	80.0	80.5	82.1	82.7	80.9
2011	79.7	78.7	79.8	80.5	80.9	81.0	80.7	80.0	79.2	80.5	80.8	81.4	80.3
Wholesale Trade													
2000	17.1	17.2	17.4	17.5	17.4	17.7	17.7	17.9	17.9	17.9	17.9	17.9	17.6
2001	17.7	17.7	17.8	18.0	18.1	18.1	17.7	17.6	17.5	17.3	17.5	17.5	17.7
2002	17.6	17.4	17.6	17.7	17.7	17.7	17.7	17.8	17.7	17.4	17.5	17.5	17.6
2003	17.0	16.8	16.9	16.9	16.8	16.8	16.9	16.8	16.8	16.8	16.7	16.8	16.8
2004	16.3	16.0	16.0	16.0	16.2	16.3	16.3	16.3	16.4	16.3	16.4	16.6	16.3
2005	16.7	16.7	16.8	16.9	17.0	17.2	17.5	17.5	17.5	17.5	17.6	17.7	17.2
2006	17.4	17.3	17.4	17.7	17.8	17.9	17.7	17.7	17.7	17.7	17.7	17.7	17.6
2007	17.8	18.0	18.2	18.3	18.3	18.3	18.2	18.0	17.9	18.0	18.0	17.9	18.1
2008	17.7	17.7	17.7	17.5	17.4	17.4	17.5	17.4	17.3	17.1	17.1	17.0	17.4
2009	16.6	16.5	16.4	16.3	16.2	16.0	15.8	15.6	15.4	15.4	15.2	15.2	15.9
2010	15.1	15.1	15.1	15.1	15.2	15.3	15.3	15.3	15.3	15.2	15.3	15.3	15.2
2011	15.0	15.0	15.1	15.1	15.1	15.2	15.2	15.2	15.2	15.3	15.3	15.4	15.2
Retail Trade													
2000	47.6	47.1	47.5	48.0	48.8	49.2	48.7	49.1	49.6	49.6	51.5	51.9	49.1
2001	47.7	46.8	47.1	47.3	47.4	47.6	46.5	46.8	46.5	46.7	48.1	48.7	47.3
2002	46.8	46.2	46.6	46.9	47.1	46.6	45.7	45.7	45.5	45.5	46.9	47.6	46.4
2003	45.2	44.5	44.5	44.9	45.0	44.7	44.4	44.6	44.3	44.9	46.5	47.4	45.1
2004	44.7	43.8	44.7	44.8	44.9	44.7	43.4	43.2	42.7	43.5	44.7	45.2	44.2
2005	43.2	42.6	42.6	42.8	43.0	42.8	43.2	43.5	43.8	44.2	45.5	46.3	43.6
2006	43.4	43.4	43.9	44.4	44.9	44.6	44.4	44.2	44.2	44.6	46.1	47.0	44.6
2007	44.1	43.8	44.9	44.7	45.0	45.1	44.5	44.4	44.3	44.9	46.4	46.5	44.9
2008	43.9	44.2	45.1	45.7	45.9	45.8	46.0	46.2	45.6	45.5	46.6	46.9	45.6
2009	44.8	44.3	44.8	44.9	45.5	45.6	45.1	45.2	45.0	45.3	46.7	47.0	45.4
2010	44.8	44.1	44.5	44.9	45.2	45.3	45.3	45.2	44.4	45.0	46.5	46.8	45.2
2011	44.7	43.7	44.5	45.1	45.3	45.2	44.8	44.1	43.4	44.5	44.8	45.1	44.6
Transportation and Utilities													
2000	22.1	22.0	22.0	22.3	22.6	22.8	23.1	23.1	23.1	23.1	23.0	23.3	22.7
2001	22.6	22.6	22.7	22.3	22.4	22.7	22.6	22.6	22.3	21.8	21.7	21.3	22.3
2002	20.6	20.5	20.7	21.5	21.5	21.5	21.7	21.6	21.8	21.5	21.5	21.6	21.3
2003	21.5	21.4	21.3	21.2	21.1	20.6	20.4	20.5	20.2	20.3	20.3	20.4	20.8
2004	19.9	20.0	20.1	20.0	20.1	20.2	20.1	20.2	20.1	19.8	19.7	19.7	20.0
2005	20.0	20.0	20.0	20.0	20.1	20.2	20.1	20.3	20.1	20.0	20.1	20.2	20.1
2006	20.5	20.1	20.4	21.1	21.3	21.4	21.3	21.6	21.7	21.5	21.7	22.0	21.2
2007	21.9	22.1	22.1	21.7	21.8	21.9	22.2	21.9	22.0	22.2	22.3	22.3	22.0
2008	22.0	22.0	22.0	22.1	22.3	22.4	22.7	22.8	22.9	23.1	23.2	23.4	22.6
2009	22.2	22.0	21.9	22.4	22.3	22.3	22.1	22.0	21.8	21.9	21.9	22.1	22.1
2010	20.6	20.7	20.7	20.4	20.5	20.4	20.5	20.4	20.3	20.3	20.3	20.6	20.5
2011	20.0	20.0	20.2	20.3	20.5	20.6	20.7	20.7	20.6	20.7	20.7	20.9	20.5
Information													
2000	14.3	14.5	14.5	14.3	14.7	14.9	15.1	15.3	15.6	15.5	15.9	15.9	15.0
2001	14.5	14.6	14.3	15.0	14.8	14.4	15.0	16.1	16.1	16.1	15.8	15.6	15.2
2002	15.7	15.8	15.4	14.6	14.4	14.2	14.0	13.9	13.8	13.7	13.6	13.2	14.4
2003	12.9	12.8	12.5	12.6	12.6	12.4	12.0	11.7	11.6	11.8	11.8	12.0	12.2
2004	12.0	12.0	11.9	11.5	11.3	11.2	11.1	10.8	10.5	10.5	10.5	10.5	11.2
2005	10.8	10.7	10.5	10.6	10.6	10.7	10.7	10.7	10.8	10.8	11.0	11.0	10.7
2006	10.5	10.3	10.3	10.0	10.1	10.1	10.0	10.0	9.7	9.8	9.8	10.2	10.1
2007	9.9	10.1	10.0	9.9	10.0	9.9	10.0	9.9	9.9	10.0	10.0	10.0	10.0
2008	9.8	9.9	9.8	10.0	10.0	10.0	10.0	9.8	9.7	9.6	9.7	9.7	9.8
2009	9.4	9.4	9.2	9.1	9.0	8.9	8.9	8.8	8.5	8.5	8.5	8.5	8.9
2010	8.4	8.3	8.3	8.7	8.7	8.5	8.7	8.5	8.4	8.3	8.3	8.4	8.5
2011	8.3	8.2	8.2	8.1	8.1	8.2	8.2	8.1	8.2	8.1	8.1	8.0	8.2

Employment by Industry: Tulsa, OK, Selected Years, 2000–2011—*Continued*

(Numbers in thousands, not seasonally adjusted)

Industry and year	January	February	March	April	May	June	July	August	September	October	November	December	Annual average
Financial Activities													
2000	24.6	24.6	24.6	25.0	25.2	25.7	25.0	25.1	25.1	24.9	24.7	24.9	25.0
2001	24.5	24.8	24.9	25.0	25.2	25.4	25.2	25.4	25.3	25.4	25.4	25.3	25.2
2002	25.0	24.9	24.8	24.9	24.9	25.0	25.0	24.9	24.7	24.5	24.5	24.5	24.8
2003	24.4	24.4	24.4	24.6	24.7	24.7	24.6	24.5	24.4	24.4	24.3	24.2	24.5
2004	24.7	24.8	24.9	24.7	24.7	24.8	24.6	24.7	24.5	24.5	24.6	24.6	24.7
2005	25.1	25.2	25.2	24.9	24.9	25.1	25.2	25.2	25.0	24.9	25.1	25.1	25.1
2006	25.3	25.4	25.5	25.3	25.4	25.7	25.3	25.4	25.3	25.4	25.5	25.7	25.4
2007	24.9	25.1	25.3	25.0	25.0	25.1	25.2	25.1	24.9	25.0	24.8	24.8	25.0
2008	24.6	24.6	24.6	24.6	24.6	24.6	24.9	24.8	24.5	24.5	24.4	24.5	24.6
2009	24.0	23.9	23.9	24.0	24.1	24.0	24.1	23.9	23.6	23.4	23.4	23.3	23.8
2010	23.0	23.0	23.0	23.2	23.1	23.0	23.0	22.9	22.7	22.7	22.6	22.6	22.9
2011	22.4	22.2	22.2	22.3	22.2	22.3	22.4	22.3	22.1	22.1	22.0	22.0	22.2
Professional and Business Services													
2000	49.8	50.2	51.5	53.5	54.0	54.3	54.7	55.2	55.0	55.8	55.6	54.7	53.7
2001	53.6	54.7	55.5	56.9	57.1	57.6	57.4	56.3	54.9	54.0	53.9	53.7	55.5
2002	51.5	51.8	52.0	52.6	53.4	52.8	51.6	51.8	51.2	50.7	50.2	50.1	51.6
2003	48.6	48.8	48.7	48.8	49.0	48.6	48.7	49.5	49.5	50.2	50.3	50.0	49.2
2004	50.6	51.8	51.5	52.2	51.8	52.4	53.4	54.1	54.9	56.1	56.2	56.6	53.5
2005	56.2	57.7	58.3	59.3	59.8	59.8	59.9	60.3	61.2	60.5	61.1	61.0	59.6
2006	59.8	60.7	61.1	61.1	61.7	61.8	61.2	62.1	61.9	61.4	61.4	60.5	61.2
2007	60.2	61.0	61.7	62.1	62.8	62.7	62.4	63.6	62.8	63.1	63.0	62.5	62.3
2008	63.3	64.0	64.4	64.2	64.1	63.9	63.3	63.8	63.5	62.7	62.0	60.6	63.3
2009	57.2	57.0	56.4	55.1	55.0	55.1	54.4	54.4	53.7	54.6	54.8	54.7	55.2
2010	53.7	54.1	54.6	55.5	55.4	55.5	55.5	55.4	55.2	56.0	55.4	55.0	55.1
2011	53.4	53.2	54.1	54.0	54.1	54.3	54.6	55.1	56.2	56.4	55.3	55.4	54.7
Education and Health Services													
2000	46.6	47.0	47.3	47.9	48.1	47.6	47.5	47.9	48.8	48.0	48.4	48.5	47.8
2001	47.2	47.4	48.0	48.8	48.5	48.4	48.7	49.2	49.9	49.4	50.2	50.4	48.8
2002	50.5	50.9	51.1	51.0	50.7	50.0	50.7	51.8	52.6	52.1	53.0	53.0	51.5
2003	52.7	52.8	52.7	53.0	52.8	51.9	51.7	52.1	52.4	52.2	52.3	52.0	52.4
2004	52.1	52.4	52.7	52.8	52.5	52.0	52.1	52.7	53.4	53.1	53.1	53.3	52.7
2005	52.7	53.1	53.5	53.8	54.0	54.0	53.9	54.2	54.4	54.4	54.6	54.7	53.9
2006	54.3	54.7	54.9	55.0	55.4	56.0	55.5	55.8	56.5	56.7	56.8	57.1	55.7
2007	56.1	56.7	57.2	57.6	57.8	58.4	57.9	58.1	58.2	58.2	58.1	57.8	57.7
2008	58.0	58.4	58.6	57.6	57.9	57.8	57.0	57.2	57.4	57.3	57.4	57.4	57.7
2009	57.7	57.9	58.2	57.7	57.8	58.4	58.4	58.4	58.1	59.0	59.0	59.0	58.3
2010	58.8	59.1	59.2	59.4	59.5	59.5	59.5	59.9	59.9	60.7	60.8	60.9	59.8
2011	60.3	59.6	60.3	60.6	61.0	60.6	60.6	61.1	61.8	61.3	62.3	62.0	61.0
Leisure and Hospitality													
2000	33.0	33.2	33.8	34.6	34.8	35.4	35.1	35.1	34.4	34.2	33.5	33.4	34.2
2001	32.6	33.2	33.5	34.1	34.5	35.1	35.1	35.5	34.7	34.4	33.9	34.0	34.2
2002	32.8	33.1	33.9	34.7	35.6	35.6	34.4	35.0	34.3	34.1	33.5	33.5	34.2
2003	32.4	32.6	33.2	33.9	34.5	34.4	34.0	34.4	33.5	33.5	33.3	33.2	33.6
2004	32.7	33.1	34.0	34.2	34.6	35.1	34.8	35.3	34.6	34.2	34.1	34.0	34.2
2005	33.1	33.4	34.5	35.5	36.2	36.9	36.4	36.8	36.1	35.2	34.9	34.6	35.3
2006	34.8	35.0	36.2	36.5	37.2	37.6	37.4	37.6	36.5	36.2	35.6	36.3	36.4
2007	35.0	35.6	36.6	36.9	37.4	37.8	37.6	37.7	36.8	36.4	36.4	36.0	36.7
2008	35.5	35.8	36.4	36.8	37.6	38.0	37.4	37.9	37.0	36.7	36.3	36.4	36.8
2009	36.1	36.4	37.4	37.6	38.0	38.3	37.7	37.4	36.8	35.8	35.6	35.0	36.8
2010	34.3	34.7	35.6	36.7	37.1	37.3	37.1	37.2	36.7	36.4	36.3	36.1	36.3
2011	34.8	34.3	35.8	36.9	37.3	37.4	37.2	36.8	36.6	37.4	37.9	37.0	36.6
Other Services													
2000	14.0	13.9	14.2	14.5	14.6	15.0	15.0	14.8	14.6	14.5	14.4	14.6	14.5
2001	14.4	14.6	14.8	14.9	15.2	15.6	15.6	15.9	15.7	15.7	15.9	15.9	15.4
2002	15.7	15.7	15.9	16.6	16.6	17.0	16.9	16.6	16.5	16.2	16.2	16.2	16.3
2003	16.5	16.6	16.8	16.5	16.7	16.9	16.8	16.7	16.6	16.7	16.6	16.8	16.7
2004	16.8	16.8	17.1	16.9	16.9	17.3	17.0	17.0	16.8	16.8	16.8	16.9	16.9
2005	16.8	16.9	17.1	16.9	17.0	17.3	17.6	17.3	17.2	17.0	17.0	17.1	17.1
2006	17.1	17.1	17.3	17.4	17.4	17.9	17.7	17.6	17.5	17.3	17.4	17.5	17.4
2007	17.2	17.3	17.5	18.3	18.4	19.1	18.8	18.9	18.6	18.4	18.4	18.3	18.3
2008	18.3	18.3	18.3	18.0	18.1	18.4	18.5	18.3	18.0	18.0	17.8	17.8	18.2
2009	17.6	17.5	17.6	17.1	17.2	17.5	17.6	17.4	17.2	17.1	17.1	17.0	17.3
2010	16.9	16.9	17.0	16.9	16.9	17.3	17.0	16.8	16.7	16.7	16.7	16.6	16.9
2011	16.3	16.3	16.5	16.6	16.7	17.1	16.9	16.8	16.7	16.6	16.5	16.5	16.6
Government													
2000	47.1	47.7	48.6	48.4	49.0	47.8	44.4	45.3	47.3	49.1	49.0	49.6	47.8
2001	47.2	48.4	48.6	48.5	49.1	48.2	45.0	45.6	48.0	49.5	49.6	49.8	48.1
2002	48.5	49.4	49.7	50.0	50.9	48.8	45.9	46.6	48.2	49.8	49.7	49.9	49.0
2003	48.4	49.1	49.1	48.9	49.4	47.8	45.6	45.7	48.2	48.9	48.8	49.1	48.3
2004	48.0	49.1	49.3	49.3	49.4	48.5	47.4	48.0	50.4	51.1	50.3	50.7	49.3
2005	50.8	51.7	51.9	52.0	52.8	52.3	47.9	49.3	51.8	53.7	53.6	53.8	51.8
2006	53.1	53.9	54.3	53.4	54.2	52.4	47.5	48.2	52.1	53.9	53.5	53.4	52.5
2007	51.8	53.2	53.7	53.8	54.2	51.3	47.5	48.0	52.6	54.4	54.2	53.9	52.4
2008	52.6	54.0	54.2	54.7	55.3	52.1	48.8	49.5	54.8	57.0	56.9	56.9	53.9
2009	54.0	55.6	56.2	56.9	57.4	53.3	48.8	50.9	56.1	58.4	58.6	58.2	55.4
2010	55.3	56.3	57.2	57.8	59.3	56.3	49.6	49.1	54.1	56.9	57.1	56.9	55.5
2011	54.4	55.0	55.5	55.4	55.3	53.4	50.6	50.8	54.5	56.3	56.5	56.5	54.5

Employment by Industry: Virginia Beach–Norfolk–Newport News, VA–NC, Selected Years, 2000–2011

(Numbers in thousands, not seasonally adjusted)

Industry and year	January	February	March	April	May	June	July	August	September	October	November	December	Annual average
Total Nonfarm													
2000	699.2	703.3	712.8	714.2	720.7	731.1	722.4	725.9	726.6	726.1	730.6	730.2	720.3
2001	707.2	710.2	718.8	726.3	733.6	743.4	736.3	739.0	737.9	734.8	739.7	739.0	730.5
2002	714.0	718.8	725.3	730.4	737.4	746.7	734.5	738.3	736.2	739.0	742.2	743.9	733.9
2003	721.9	723.9	730.6	731.4	739.6	747.1	740.0	742.0	739.8	741.7	746.8	746.9	737.6
2004	729.4	730.3	738.3	746.1	752.9	761.2	754.6	756.7	755.7	754.4	758.1	759.8	749.8
2005	738.2	741.3	749.2	759.3	766.2	775.9	767.6	770.6	771.0	760.5	764.7	765.0	760.8
2006	747.8	750.0	759.2	766.1	772.7	782.7	772.1	772.4	768.0	768.7	773.2	774.8	767.3
2007	758.1	759.3	767.6	772.9	780.0	788.5	786.6	784.5	781.9	772.8	776.6	775.1	775.3
2008	753.3	756.6	762.9	766.7	775.2	782.8	776.2	775.3	768.6	762.7	760.1	756.7	766.4
2009	736.3	734.8	738.1	741.8	748.4	753.1	742.1	741.5	738.6	739.1	738.5	737.3	740.8
2010	718.8	718.0	725.5	736.0	743.0	748.3	741.5	740.7	737.7	738.6	737.8	736.5	735.2
2011	718.3	720.3	728.3	738.3	743.6	750.6	747.0	743.9	736.1	738.3	738.9	738.2	736.8
Total Private													
2000	554.0	557.4	565.8	567.8	573.8	584.6	580.1	583.8	581.3	579.1	582.3	583.1	574.4
2001	561.4	562.7	571.0	578.6	585.8	594.4	591.5	594.6	590.8	586.1	589.7	589.8	583.0
2002	566.4	569.7	575.1	580.4	586.4	595.2	589.2	592.8	587.2	588.0	590.9	592.9	584.5
2003	572.6	573.6	579.6	582.4	590.0	596.5	592.9	595.5	590.7	592.9	596.2	596.3	588.3
2004	579.6	579.2	586.5	594.5	600.7	608.2	606.8	607.8	604.9	602.7	604.6	606.8	598.5
2005	588.6	590.3	597.7	606.9	613.3	621.8	618.3	620.9	619.7	609.3	611.8	613.1	609.3
2006	597.2	598.3	606.9	612.0	618.5	627.6	620.9	621.6	617.0	614.9	617.7	619.7	614.4
2007	604.4	604.2	612.0	617.7	624.8	632.5	633.8	631.8	627.4	617.6	619.1	618.5	620.3
2008	598.5	599.6	605.4	610.4	618.4	624.6	621.9	620.9	612.6	604.8	600.0	598.0	609.6
2009	578.6	576.4	579.0	582.5	589.5	593.4	589.5	587.2	582.5	579.6	577.3	577.6	582.8
2010	560.2	558.6	565.5	575.5	580.3	586.4	586.3	585.2	579.5	579.1	578.1	577.1	576.0
2011	560.2	561.3	568.5	578.3	583.7	590.0	589.6	585.9	575.9	576.2	575.2	575.1	576.7
Goods-Producing													
2000	106.5	106.9	108.2	108.3	109.0	110.3	109.8	109.5	109.5	110.0	110.0	110.0	109.0
2001	106.3	106.6	108.0	108.3	108.9	109.6	108.4	110.2	109.3	108.3	108.2	108.1	108.4
2002	104.0	104.1	104.4	104.0	104.6	105.2	103.8	105.5	104.8	105.0	105.0	105.2	104.6
2003	103.9	104.4	105.5	105.0	106.3	107.1	104.6	107.3	106.2	108.5	110.0	108.9	106.5
2004	106.2	105.2	106.4	107.6	108.5	109.7	108.6	110.0	109.7	110.3	110.3	110.0	108.5
2005	108.3	108.3	109.0	110.4	110.6	111.4	110.0	112.0	111.2	109.2	109.0	109.2	109.9
2006	107.2	107.2	108.6	109.0	109.5	110.3	107.9	109.8	107.2	106.7	106.7	108.1	108.2
2007	105.9	104.8	105.7	106.8	107.0	107.6	107.5	107.5	107.0	105.2	105.1	104.5	106.2
2008	102.2	101.9	101.9	102.1	102.5	103.0	102.9	102.8	101.5	100.5	99.7	98.4	101.6
2009	94.2	93.1	92.8	92.2	92.0	92.0	92.0	91.8	91.2	91.0	90.3	90.4	91.9
2010	87.8	87.5	88.3	89.2	89.6	89.2	89.4	89.3	89.0	88.6	88.4	87.7	88.7
2011	85.6	85.5	86.4	86.6	87.2	87.7	88.4	88.0	87.3	86.7	86.4	86.0	86.8
Mining, Logging, and Construction													
2000	41.8	42.1	43.2	43.6	44.0	45.0	44.8	44.8	44.6	44.5	44.8	44.8	44.0
2001	43.9	44.3	45.3	45.8	46.5	47.2	47.3	47.5	46.8	45.9	45.6	45.4	46.0
2002	43.6	44.0	44.6	44.3	44.8	45.3	45.7	45.5	44.6	44.7	44.4	44.5	44.7
2003	43.9	44.5	45.2	45.6	47.0	47.5	48.1	48.1	47.1	49.3	50.2	49.5	47.2
2004	46.9	46.3	47.2	48.3	48.9	49.8	50.4	49.9	49.3	49.6	49.2	49.3	48.8
2005	48.1	48.1	48.7	50.0	50.3	50.8	51.5	51.4	51.2	49.7	49.8	50.1	50.0
2006	48.6	48.6	49.8	50.4	50.6	51.1	50.6	50.3	49.8	49.3	49.3	49.3	49.8
2007	48.0	47.9	48.6	48.7	48.8	49.2	49.7	49.7	49.2	47.8	47.5	46.9	48.5
2008	45.5	45.4	45.6	45.8	46.1	46.4	46.4	46.3	45.2	44.6	43.8	42.6	45.3
2009	39.9	39.2	39.0	38.7	38.5	38.5	38.6	38.4	37.9	37.6	37.0	37.1	38.4
2010	35.8	35.5	36.2	37.1	37.5	37.5	37.8	37.7	37.4	37.0	36.9	36.3	36.9
2011	34.8	34.9	35.1	35.7	35.7	35.9	36.6	36.3	35.2	34.8	34.4	34.0	35.3
Manufacturing													
2000	64.7	64.8	65.0	64.7	65.0	65.3	65.0	64.7	64.9	65.5	65.2	65.2	65.0
2001	62.4	62.3	62.7	62.5	62.4	62.4	61.1	62.7	62.5	62.4	62.6	62.7	62.4
2002	60.4	60.1	59.8	59.7	59.8	59.9	58.1	60.0	60.2	60.3	60.6	60.7	60.0
2003	60.0	59.9	60.3	59.4	59.3	59.6	56.5	59.2	59.1	59.2	59.8	59.4	59.3
2004	59.3	58.9	59.2	59.3	59.6	59.9	58.2	60.1	60.4	60.7	61.1	60.7	59.8
2005	60.2	60.2	60.3	60.4	60.3	60.6	58.5	60.6	60.0	59.5	59.2	59.1	59.9
2006	58.6	58.6	58.8	58.6	58.9	59.2	57.3	59.5	57.4	57.4	57.4	58.8	58.4
2007	57.9	56.9	57.1	58.1	58.2	58.4	57.8	57.8	57.8	57.4	57.6	57.6	57.7
2008	56.7	56.5	56.3	56.3	56.4	56.6	56.5	56.5	56.3	55.9	55.9	55.8	56.3
2009	54.3	53.9	53.8	53.5	53.5	53.5	53.4	53.4	53.3	53.4	53.3	53.3	53.6
2010	52.0	52.0	52.1	52.1	52.1	51.7	51.6	51.6	51.6	51.6	51.5	51.4	51.8
2011	50.8	50.6	51.3	50.9	51.5	51.8	51.8	51.7	52.1	51.9	52.0	52.0	51.5
Service-Providing													
2000	592.7	596.4	604.6	605.9	611.7	620.8	612.6	616.4	617.1	616.1	620.6	620.2	611.3
2001	600.9	603.6	610.8	618.0	624.7	633.8	627.9	628.8	628.6	626.5	631.5	630.9	622.2
2002	610.0	614.7	620.9	626.4	632.8	641.5	630.7	632.8	631.4	634.0	637.2	638.7	629.3
2003	618.0	619.5	625.1	626.4	633.3	640.0	635.4	634.7	633.6	633.2	636.8	638.0	631.2
2004	623.2	625.1	631.9	638.5	644.4	651.5	646.0	646.7	646.0	644.1	647.8	649.8	641.3
2005	629.9	633.0	640.2	648.9	655.6	664.5	657.6	658.6	659.8	651.3	655.7	655.8	650.9
2006	640.6	642.8	650.6	657.1	663.2	672.4	664.2	662.6	660.8	662.0	666.5	666.7	659.1
2007	652.2	654.5	661.9	666.1	673.0	680.9	679.1	677.0	674.9	667.6	671.5	670.6	669.1
2008	651.1	654.7	661.0	664.6	672.7	679.8	673.3	672.5	667.1	662.2	660.4	658.3	664.8
2009	642.1	641.7	645.3	649.6	656.4	661.1	650.1	649.7	647.4	648.1	648.2	646.9	648.9
2010	631.0	630.5	637.2	646.8	653.4	659.1	652.1	651.4	648.7	650.0	649.4	648.8	646.5
2011	632.7	634.8	641.9	651.7	656.4	662.9	658.6	655.9	648.8	651.6	652.5	652.2	650.0

Employment by Industry: Virginia Beach–Norfolk–Newport News, VA–NC, Selected Years, 2000–2011—*Continued*

(Numbers in thousands, not seasonally adjusted)

Industry and year	January	February	March	April	May	June	July	August	September	October	November	December	Annual average
Trade, Transportation, and Utilities													
2000	134.7	134.6	134.9	134.7	136.0	137.3	136.4	138.0	138.5	141.4	145.0	146.5	138.2
2001	138.1	135.8	136.4	136.8	138.4	139.3	138.3	139.3	140.0	141.3	144.6	145.8	139.5
2002	138.1	136.4	135.3	136.6	138.3	140.2	138.7	139.2	138.9	141.3	145.1	147.3	139.6
2003	138.1	135.9	135.5	133.0	133.6	134.1	134.3	135.2	134.9	137.3	141.8	144.5	136.5
2004	136.8	135.8	135.4	136.8	138.1	139.2	139.6	140.1	139.5	141.2	144.7	146.1	139.4
2005	138.0	136.6	137.6	139.4	140.2	141.0	142.1	142.3	142.2	142.4	146.3	146.9	141.3
2006	139.9	138.3	139.7	140.4	141.6	142.6	142.4	141.9	140.8	143.2	147.9	148.4	142.3
2007	142.3	140.5	141.3	140.8	142.2	143.4	145.4	144.7	143.0	143.2	147.7	147.9	143.5
2008	140.0	138.0	138.3	138.2	138.9	139.9	139.6	139.4	138.0	136.5	139.1	139.8	138.8
2009	130.8	128.2	127.9	128.4	129.9	130.3	130.0	129.6	128.3	128.9	131.4	132.6	129.7
2010	126.8	125.2	126.3	127.6	129.1	129.5	129.6	129.7	128.1	129.6	131.9	133.4	128.9
2011	127.2	126.2	126.7	128.3	128.9	129.6	129.9	130.2	129.5	130.1	133.7	133.7	129.5
Wholesale Trade													
2000	23.6	23.9	24.0	24.0	24.1	24.2	24.1	24.3	24.2	24.4	24.5	24.6	24.2
2001	24.7	24.9	25.2	25.0	25.1	25.3	25.3	25.2	25.2	25.1	25.3	25.3	25.1
2002	25.2	25.2	25.2	25.5	25.6	25.7	25.3	25.3	25.2	25.3	25.5	25.5	25.4
2003	25.1	24.8	24.5	24.6	24.3	23.9	23.5	22.9	22.8	23.1	23.1	23.2	23.8
2004	22.8	22.9	23.0	23.1	23.2	23.4	23.6	23.6	23.4	23.5	23.6	23.7	23.3
2005	23.5	23.6	23.6	23.9	24.0	24.1	24.1	24.2	24.1	24.0	24.1	24.3	24.0
2006	23.9	23.9	24.0	24.1	24.1	24.2	24.3	24.1	24.1	24.1	24.2	24.2	24.1
2007	24.1	24.2	24.3	24.2	24.3	24.3	24.4	24.2	24.1	23.7	23.7	23.7	24.1
2008	23.5	23.4	23.4	23.5	23.5	23.5	23.4	23.4	23.1	22.9	22.7	22.6	23.2
2009	22.3	22.1	22.1	22.0	22.0	21.9	21.9	21.9	21.6	21.5	21.6	21.5	21.9
2010	20.9	20.7	20.8	21.0	21.1	21.1	21.1	21.2	21.1	21.1	21.1	21.1	21.0
2011	20.7	20.6	20.7	20.8	20.9	21.0	21.0	21.1	21.0	21.0	21.0	21.0	20.9
Retail Trade													
2000	85.6	85.1	85.2	84.8	85.9	87.0	86.0	87.2	88.1	89.8	93.6	95.0	87.8
2001	87.4	85.0	85.0	85.8	87.0	87.5	86.8	88.1	88.6	89.7	93.1	94.3	88.2
2002	87.7	85.8	84.7	85.7	86.9	88.1	87.1	87.8	87.7	89.5	93.0	95.0	88.3
2003	87.9	86.3	85.8	83.7	84.7	85.4	85.3	86.6	86.5	87.8	92.2	94.7	87.2
2004	88.7	87.5	86.9	88.1	89.2	89.9	90.1	90.4	90.2	91.3	94.7	95.8	90.2
2005	88.7	87.2	87.4	89.1	89.8	90.4	91.5	91.7	91.9	92.1	95.4	95.9	90.9
2006	90.6	88.9	89.9	90.5	91.5	92.2	92.1	91.7	90.7	92.8	97.1	97.8	92.2
2007	93.0	91.1	91.6	91.2	92.3	93.1	94.6	94.5	93.1	93.5	97.8	98.1	93.7
2008	92.0	90.0	90.4	89.6	90.2	90.8	90.6	90.4	89.5	88.3	90.8	91.5	90.3
2009	84.7	82.7	82.5	82.9	84.3	84.8	84.3	84.2	83.2	83.6	85.6	86.8	84.1
2010	82.7	81.5	82.4	83.3	84.3	84.6	84.3	84.4	82.8	83.7	85.9	87.3	83.9
2011	82.5	81.8	82.2	83.4	84.3	84.9	84.9	85.2	84.6	84.7	87.9	88.1	84.5
Transportation and Utilities													
2000	25.5	25.6	25.7	25.9	26.0	26.1	26.3	26.5	26.2	27.2	26.9	26.9	26.2
2001	26.0	25.9	26.2	26.0	26.3	26.5	26.2	26.0	26.2	26.5	26.2	26.2	26.2
2002	25.2	25.4	25.4	25.4	25.8	26.4	26.3	26.1	26.0	26.5	26.6	26.8	26.0
2003	25.1	24.8	25.2	24.7	24.6	24.8	25.5	25.7	25.6	26.4	26.5	26.6	25.5
2004	25.3	25.4	25.5	25.6	25.7	25.9	25.9	26.1	25.9	26.4	26.4	26.6	25.9
2005	25.8	25.8	26.6	26.4	26.4	26.5	26.5	26.4	26.2	26.3	26.8	26.7	26.4
2006	25.4	25.5	25.8	25.8	26.0	26.2	26.0	26.1	26.0	26.3	26.6	26.4	26.0
2007	25.2	25.2	25.4	25.4	25.6	26.0	26.4	26.0	25.8	26.0	26.2	26.1	25.8
2008	24.5	24.6	24.5	25.1	25.2	25.6	25.6	25.6	25.4	25.3	25.6	25.7	25.2
2009	23.8	23.4	23.3	23.5	23.6	23.6	23.8	23.5	23.5	23.8	24.2	24.3	23.7
2010	23.2	23.0	23.1	23.3	23.7	23.8	24.2	24.1	24.2	24.8	24.9	25.0	23.9
2011	24.0	23.8	23.8	24.1	23.7	23.7	24.0	23.9	23.9	24.4	24.8	24.6	24.1
Information													
2000	16.4	16.3	16.3	16.3	16.7	16.8	17.0	17.0	17.0	16.7	16.6	16.7	16.7
2001	15.6	15.5	15.6	15.6	15.8	16.1	16.4	16.5	16.5	16.6	16.9	17.0	16.2
2002	16.4	16.4	16.4	16.4	16.6	16.6	16.4	16.5	16.3	16.3	16.6	16.7	16.5
2003	16.1	16.1	16.1	16.0	16.0	16.3	16.3	15.9	15.9	15.8	15.9	15.9	16.0
2004	15.8	15.8	15.8	15.5	15.6	15.7	15.7	15.6	15.4	15.1	15.1	15.0	15.5
2005	15.0	14.8	14.7	14.9	15.0	15.1	15.3	15.4	15.3	15.2	15.3	15.5	15.1
2006	15.5	15.5	15.5	15.4	15.5	15.6	15.6	15.5	15.3	15.2	15.3	15.4	15.4
2007	15.5	15.6	15.6	15.6	15.7	15.8	15.6	15.6	15.4	15.2	15.2	15.3	15.5
2008	15.3	15.2	15.1	15.0	15.2	15.2	15.0	14.9	14.5	14.2	14.0	13.9	14.8
2009	13.7	13.7	13.6	13.5	13.6	13.5	13.3	13.2	12.9	12.9	12.8	12.8	13.3
2010	12.6	12.4	12.5	12.3	12.4	12.4	12.2	12.2	12.0	11.8	11.8	11.7	12.2
2011	11.6	11.5	11.6	11.6	11.7	11.8	11.7	10.8	11.4	11.4	11.4	11.4	11.5
Financial Activities													
2000	34.9	35.3	35.5	36.0	36.2	37.6	37.1	37.5	37.2	36.7	36.6	36.9	36.5
2001	35.6	35.8	36.0	36.5	36.8	37.7	37.8	37.8	37.2	36.3	36.3	36.3	36.7
2002	35.5	35.8	36.0	36.3	36.8	37.9	37.0	37.3	36.6	37.1	37.2	37.4	36.7
2003	36.2	36.5	36.7	36.9	37.5	38.2	38.7	38.7	38.3	37.6	37.5	37.8	37.6
2004	38.3	38.4	38.7	39.4	39.7	40.4	41.1	41.0	40.2	39.5	39.5	39.6	39.7
2005	38.4	38.6	38.7	39.9	40.2	41.4	41.5	41.4	40.7	39.3	39.3	39.8	39.9
2006	39.1	39.3	39.5	40.2	40.6	41.7	41.9	41.9	41.2	40.9	40.9	41.1	40.7
2007	40.9	41.1	41.3	41.6	41.8	42.3	42.5	42.5	41.8	41.1	40.8	40.8	41.5
2008	40.3	40.5	40.5	40.3	40.3	41.0	41.3	41.0	40.2	39.3	38.8	38.7	40.2
2009	38.2	38.1	37.9	37.9	37.9	38.3	38.1	38.0	37.1	36.3	36.0	36.0	37.5
2010	36.0	35.9	35.9	36.2	36.1	37.1	37.4	37.4	36.7	36.2	36.1	36.1	36.4
2011	36.0	36.1	36.1	36.7	36.9	37.4	37.2	37.7	37.5	37.4	37.2	37.4	37.0

Employment by Industry: Virginia Beach–Norfolk–Newport News, VA–NC, Selected Years, 2000–2011—*Continued*

(Numbers in thousands, not seasonally adjusted)

Industry and year	January	February	March	April	May	June	July	August	September	October	November	December	Annual average
Professional and Business Services													
2000	95.8	98.2	100.2	99.1	97.8	100.6	99.1	100.1	99.0	98.5	99.1	99.3	98.9
2001	97.7	98.8	100.3	102.7	102.8	104.2	103.2	104.8	105.1	105.1	105.7	106.0	103.0
2002	101.6	103.9	105.8	105.6	104.6	105.9	104.2	105.9	104.9	104.5	104.8	104.6	104.7
2003	101.8	102.4	104.3	106.2	104.2	105.0	104.6	105.0	104.6	105.9	105.0	103.2	104.4
2004	98.4	98.0	99.3	100.2	99.6	100.8	101.2	101.7	101.1	100.4	101.2	101.6	100.3
2005	99.2	100.2	101.3	101.4	101.7	102.6	102.3	102.6	102.8	101.0	101.2	101.3	101.5
2006	99.7	100.4	101.5	101.6	102.4	102.6	102.0	102.2	102.5	102.7	102.8	103.0	102.0
2007	100.0	100.4	101.7	102.1	102.5	103.0	103.4	104.1	104.3	103.5	104.5	104.9	102.9
2008	101.8	102.6	103.7	105.1	105.3	106.5	106.2	107.1	106.5	105.4	104.2	104.0	104.9
2009	100.7	100.4	100.5	100.2	99.2	99.5	98.9	99.2	99.0	99.0	100.1	99.7	99.7
2010	96.9	96.3	96.5	97.9	96.7	97.7	99.2	99.4	98.9	99.5	100.0	99.1	98.2
2011	96.7	96.8	97.4	99.2	98.8	98.7	97.0	94.7	94.2	97.2	97.2	97.8	97.1
Education and Health Services													
2000	71.2	71.9	72.2	71.8	73.1	72.9	72.7	72.7	73.5	73.6	73.9	74.1	72.8
2001	72.8	73.3	73.6	73.3	73.9	74.2	73.4	73.4	75.1	75.2	75.9	76.2	74.2
2002	75.0	75.9	76.6	76.1	76.8	77.0	75.9	76.0	77.5	78.4	78.9	79.2	76.9
2003	76.6	77.0	77.5	78.1	78.7	78.8	76.4	76.4	79.3	79.1	79.7	79.8	78.1
2004	81.2	81.7	82.5	82.4	82.7	81.8	78.7	78.6	82.7	83.4	83.7	84.3	82.0
2005	83.6	83.9	84.2	84.3	85.0	85.3	81.0	81.6	86.6	86.5	86.9	87.4	84.7
2006	86.0	86.7	87.1	86.9	87.6	88.2	84.1	83.7	88.6	88.9	89.1	89.7	87.2
2007	88.5	88.9	89.5	89.8	90.3	90.7	87.4	87.3	91.3	91.4	91.5	92.1	89.9
2008	89.4	90.2	90.7	91.0	91.8	91.8	89.3	89.2	91.7	92.7	92.6	93.0	91.1
2009	92.7	92.9	93.2	92.9	93.5	93.2	90.6	90.2	93.9	94.4	94.3	94.6	93.0
2010	92.8	93.1	94.1	94.4	94.7	94.4	91.7	91.4	94.1	95.8	96.1	96.2	94.1
2011	95.6	96.5	97.0	97.4	97.8	97.5	95.6	95.7	97.3	98.4	98.2	98.1	97.1
Leisure and Hospitality													
2000	67.0	66.4	70.4	73.5	76.7	80.6	79.5	80.4	78.0	73.7	72.6	71.3	74.2
2001	67.3	68.7	72.4	76.6	80.1	83.9	84.6	83.2	78.4	74.4	73.3	71.9	76.2
2002	67.7	68.8	71.7	76.6	79.8	83.2	84.0	83.4	79.1	76.2	74.3	73.5	76.5
2003	69.6	70.2	72.5	74.8	79.9	83.0	84.2	83.6	78.6	75.9	72.9	72.4	76.5
2004	69.3	70.6	74.3	78.6	82.4	86.2	87.5	86.4	81.9	78.6	76.0	76.0	79.0
2005	72.1	73.6	77.7	81.7	85.4	89.7	90.8	90.2	85.3	80.5	78.6	77.8	82.0
2006	75.8	76.7	80.4	84.6	87.2	92.3	92.9	92.4	87.2	83.4	81.0	79.8	84.5
2007	77.2	78.5	82.3	85.2	88.7	93.5	95.9	94.7	89.7	84.4	81.0	80.2	85.9
2008	78.1	79.6	83.4	86.4	90.9	94.2	94.7	93.7	87.9	84.1	79.4	78.1	85.9
2009	74.3	75.9	78.8	83.0	88.8	91.8	91.9	90.7	86.0	82.9	78.4	77.5	83.3
2010	74.0	74.9	78.2	83.7	87.2	91.6	92.0	91.1	86.4	83.2	79.6	79.2	83.4
2011	74.0	75.0	79.1	83.9	87.5	92.1	94.6	93.7	83.9	80.3	76.4	76.1	83.1
Other Services													
2000	27.5	27.8	28.1	28.1	28.3	28.5	28.5	28.6	28.6	28.5	28.5	28.3	28.3
2001	28.0	28.2	28.7	28.8	29.1	29.4	29.4	29.4	29.2	28.9	28.8	28.5	28.9
2002	28.1	28.4	28.9	28.8	28.9	29.2	29.2	29.0	29.1	29.2	29.0	29.0	28.9
2003	30.3	31.1	31.5	32.4	33.8	34.0	33.8	33.4	32.9	32.8	33.4	33.8	32.8
2004	33.6	33.7	34.1	34.0	34.1	34.4	34.4	34.4	34.4	34.2	34.1	34.2	34.1
2005	34.0	34.3	34.5	34.9	35.2	35.3	35.3	35.4	35.6	35.2	35.2	35.2	35.0
2006	34.0	34.2	34.6	33.9	34.1	34.3	34.1	34.2	34.2	33.9	34.0	34.2	34.1
2007	34.1	34.4	34.6	35.8	36.6	36.2	36.1	35.4	34.9	33.6	33.3	32.8	34.8
2008	31.4	31.6	31.8	32.3	33.5	33.0	32.9	32.8	32.3	32.1	32.2	32.1	32.3
2009	34.0	34.1	34.3	34.4	34.6	34.8	34.7	34.5	34.1	34.2	34.0	34.0	34.3
2010	33.3	33.3	33.7	34.2	34.5	34.5	34.8	34.7	34.3	34.4	34.2	33.7	34.1
2011	33.5	33.7	34.2	34.6	34.9	35.2	35.2	35.1	34.8	34.7	34.7	34.6	34.6
Government													
2000	145.2	145.9	147.0	146.4	146.9	146.5	142.3	142.1	145.3	147.0	148.3	147.1	145.8
2001	145.8	147.5	147.8	147.7	147.8	149.0	144.8	144.4	147.1	148.7	150.0	149.2	147.5
2002	147.6	149.1	150.2	150.0	151.0	151.5	145.3	145.5	149.0	151.0	151.3	151.0	149.4
2003	149.3	150.3	151.0	149.0	149.6	150.6	147.1	146.5	149.1	148.8	150.6	150.6	149.4
2004	149.8	151.1	151.8	151.6	152.2	153.0	147.8	148.9	150.8	151.7	153.5	153.0	151.3
2005	149.6	151.0	151.5	152.4	152.9	154.1	149.3	149.7	151.3	151.2	152.9	151.9	151.5
2006	150.6	151.7	152.3	154.1	154.2	155.1	151.2	150.8	151.0	153.8	155.5	155.1	153.0
2007	153.7	155.1	155.6	155.2	155.2	156.0	152.8	152.7	154.5	155.2	157.5	156.6	155.0
2008	154.8	157.0	157.5	156.3	156.8	158.2	154.3	154.4	156.0	157.9	160.1	158.7	156.8
2009	157.7	158.4	159.1	159.3	158.9	159.7	152.6	154.3	156.1	159.5	161.2	159.7	158.0
2010	158.6	159.4	160.0	160.5	162.7	161.9	155.2	155.5	158.2	159.5	159.7	159.4	159.2
2011	158.1	159.0	159.8	160.0	159.9	160.6	157.4	158.0	160.2	162.1	163.7	163.1	160.2

Employment by Industry: Washington–Arlington–Alexandria, DC–VA–MD–WV, Selected Years, 2000–2011

(Numbers in thousands, not seasonally adjusted)

Industry and year	January	February	March	April	May	June	July	August	September	October	November	December	Annual average
Total Nonfarm													
2000	2,583.6	2,594.1	2,629.4	2,656.5	2,677.5	2,712.2	2,694.0	2,695.2	2,702.8	2,714.7	2,733.1	2,752.5	2,678.8
2001	2,672.7	2,680.8	2,702.0	2,707.3	2,725.9	2,755.3	2,732.6	2,728.9	2,719.7	2,724.5	2,731.7	2,749.3	2,719.2
2002	2,680.9	2,688.7	2,709.6	2,715.4	2,733.1	2,755.1	2,733.7	2,732.0	2,735.7	2,741.1	2,752.9	2,761.9	2,728.3
2003	2,721.0	2,717.0	2,741.5	2,768.5	2,788.3	2,810.9	2,807.1	2,799.5	2,804.4	2,806.7	2,817.9	2,830.6	2,784.5
2004	2,772.6	2,784.5	2,819.3	2,830.8	2,854.3	2,875.5	2,869.7	2,866.6	2,872.3	2,892.7	2,905.1	2,915.7	2,854.9
2005	2,848.3	2,860.8	2,879.0	2,901.2	2,919.4	2,937.6	2,936.5	2,930.0	2,935.6	2,935.7	2,956.9	2,967.9	2,917.4
2006	2,908.6	2,919.7	2,946.7	2,953.7	2,971.7	2,996.1	2,979.6	2,972.5	2,973.9	2,980.7	2,992.6	3,006.9	2,966.9
2007	2,942.2	2,948.1	2,971.9	2,978.1	2,995.9	3,013.0	3,001.5	2,990.9	2,987.6	3,005.3	3,018.3	3,029.0	2,990.2
2008	2,959.2	2,968.1	2,985.9	3,004.4	3,021.5	3,029.1	3,027.4	3,015.6	3,004.5	3,007.2	3,008.5	3,006.8	3,003.2
2009	2,938.4	2,935.7	2,944.3	2,945.1	2,960.7	2,971.9	2,968.8	2,949.1	2,933.6	2,954.6	2,967.7	2,969.7	2,953.3
2010	2,900.4	2,877.6	2,923.4	2,960.1	2,984.2	2,997.3	2,994.8	2,961.9	2,966.2	2,987.3	2,998.3	3,003.2	2,962.9
2011	2,944.4	2,952.9	2,974.7	2,990.4	3,000.6	3,015.8	3,009.1	2,985.7	2,995.9	3,016.0	3,030.5	3,030.3	2,995.5
Total Private													
2000	2,010.8	2,020.3	2,050.7	2,075.0	2,089.5	2,124.8	2,128.3	2,132.7	2,126.7	2,136.6	2,150.8	2,166.6	2,101.1
2001	2,093.2	2,101.3	2,119.5	2,124.4	2,139.9	2,166.0	2,157.7	2,156.2	2,130.0	2,134.3	2,140.2	2,152.1	2,134.6
2002	2,086.0	2,090.9	2,108.5	2,116.6	2,130.8	2,150.6	2,146.0	2,144.8	2,131.7	2,132.4	2,143.1	2,149.4	2,127.6
2003	2,108.1	2,103.0	2,124.8	2,151.4	2,168.4	2,189.9	2,192.6	2,190.5	2,185.7	2,189.7	2,199.6	2,211.4	2,167.9
2004	2,156.8	2,164.7	2,195.0	2,209.6	2,228.7	2,254.3	2,257.4	2,255.9	2,250.8	2,259.9	2,269.0	2,280.1	2,231.9
2005	2,222.7	2,233.1	2,249.1	2,270.8	2,285.6	2,306.3	2,308.6	2,305.1	2,304.7	2,298.7	2,313.9	2,325.5	2,285.3
2006	2,275.8	2,281.6	2,305.1	2,313.5	2,328.0	2,356.4	2,345.4	2,341.9	2,334.8	2,333.8	2,344.3	2,356.6	2,326.4
2007	2,306.0	2,305.9	2,326.9	2,333.9	2,347.6	2,368.7	2,359.6	2,352.9	2,343.0	2,350.3	2,359.6	2,368.4	2,343.6
2008	2,309.9	2,311.1	2,325.0	2,348.2	2,361.7	2,371.6	2,368.6	2,359.6	2,348.2	2,341.8	2,338.9	2,335.7	2,343.4
2009	2,275.5	2,265.0	2,269.7	2,272.5	2,285.4	2,298.2	2,288.7	2,280.0	2,263.3	2,274.5	2,282.7	2,285.3	2,278.4
2010	2,224.9	2,199.5	2,238.7	2,274.1	2,287.0	2,304.0	2,297.0	2,292.4	2,281.6	2,294.0	2,301.4	2,308.4	2,275.3
2011	2,261.3	2,262.5	2,280.5	2,298.4	2,305.9	2,324.8	2,320.4	2,313.1	2,306.6	2,317.4	2,330.0	2,330.7	2,304.3
Goods-Producing													
2000	221.0	221.8	227.8	229.6	232.2	236.9	239.5	240.6	240.1	239.0	238.9	238.1	233.8
2001	231.2	232.4	236.0	238.0	241.4	244.4	244.1	244.9	242.7	240.2	239.2	237.1	239.3
2002	230.3	231.1	233.9	235.0	237.4	239.6	239.3	239.8	237.6	235.8	234.5	231.8	235.5
2003	226.5	225.7	228.7	231.9	235.5	237.8	240.5	241.4	240.2	239.4	238.6	237.3	235.3
2004	231.6	231.6	236.7	240.2	243.3	246.0	249.4	249.5	248.7	248.4	247.8	247.4	243.4
2005	240.7	240.6	242.9	249.1	251.9	256.0	257.9	259.0	258.7	255.4	256.3	255.6	252.0
2006	248.8	249.1	253.3	254.9	256.9	260.8	261.1	260.5	258.0	254.3	252.3	251.8	255.2
2007	244.2	241.0	245.0	247.4	249.2	252.5	251.8	252.0	249.3	246.6	244.3	241.6	247.1
2008	234.6	233.5	234.8	235.6	235.8	237.3	236.7	236.4	234.2	230.9	226.6	222.1	233.2
2009	210.9	207.8	206.5	206.3	206.2	206.2	206.0	204.9	202.2	199.3	197.3	195.3	204.1
2010	186.2	178.7	186.5	192.5	194.2	195.6	197.4	197.4	195.9	194.7	193.8	191.9	192.1
2011	185.3	184.9	187.0	190.0	191.2	193.7	195.2	196.0	195.6	195.5	196.1	191.0	191.8
Mining, Logging, and Construction													
2000	141.4	141.8	147.4	149.6	151.9	155.5	158.0	159.0	158.8	157.9	158.2	157.4	153.1
2001	151.9	153.2	156.9	159.8	163.1	166.2	166.2	167.2	165.5	164.4	163.5	161.9	161.7
2002	156.6	157.8	160.2	161.9	164.5	166.9	167.1	168.0	166.1	165.4	164.6	162.1	163.4
2003	157.6	156.8	160.4	164.7	168.4	170.6	173.3	174.6	173.6	173.3	172.4	171.2	168.1
2004	165.9	166.0	170.7	174.4	177.5	179.8	182.6	182.9	182.3	182.5	181.9	181.4	177.3
2005	175.5	175.4	177.6	183.6	186.2	190.0	192.1	193.1	193.1	190.7	191.3	190.5	186.6
2006	185.4	185.7	189.7	191.1	193.2	196.5	196.4	196.1	194.2	191.3	189.6	188.7	191.5
2007	182.2	178.9	182.9	185.4	187.1	189.6	189.0	189.4	187.1	184.7	182.5	179.7	184.9
2008	173.4	172.3	173.6	174.5	174.7	176.0	175.5	175.2	173.5	170.6	166.7	162.5	172.4
2009	153.3	150.9	150.0	150.2	150.2	150.6	150.9	150.0	148.0	145.2	143.3	141.3	148.7
2010	133.9	127.0	134.3	139.9	141.5	142.8	145.1	145.4	144.2	142.8	142.1	140.3	139.9
2011	134.4	134.2	136.0	139.2	140.6	142.9	144.8	145.8	146.2	145.5	146.3	141.6	141.5
Manufacturing													
2000	79.6	80.0	80.4	80.0	80.3	81.4	81.5	81.6	81.3	81.1	80.7	80.7	80.7
2001	79.3	79.2	79.1	78.2	78.3	78.2	77.9	77.7	77.2	75.8	75.7	75.2	77.7
2002	73.7	73.3	73.7	73.1	72.9	72.7	72.2	71.8	71.5	70.4	69.9	69.7	72.1
2003	68.9	68.9	68.3	67.2	67.1	67.2	67.2	66.8	66.6	66.1	66.2	66.1	67.2
2004	65.7	65.6	66.0	65.8	65.8	66.2	66.8	66.6	66.4	65.9	65.9	66.0	66.1
2005	65.2	65.2	65.3	65.5	65.7	66.0	65.8	65.9	65.6	64.7	65.0	65.1	65.4
2006	63.4	63.4	63.6	63.8	63.7	64.3	64.7	64.4	63.8	63.0	62.7	63.1	63.7
2007	62.0	62.1	62.1	62.0	62.1	62.9	62.8	62.6	62.2	61.9	61.8	61.9	62.2
2008	61.2	61.2	61.2	61.1	61.1	61.3	61.2	61.2	60.7	60.3	59.9	59.6	60.8
2009	57.6	56.9	56.5	56.1	56.0	55.6	55.1	54.9	54.2	54.1	54.0	54.0	55.4
2010	52.3	51.7	52.2	52.6	52.7	52.8	52.3	52.0	51.7	51.9	51.7	51.6	52.1
2011	50.9	50.7	51.0	50.8	50.6	50.8	50.4	50.2	49.4	50.0	49.8	49.4	50.3
Service-Providing													
2000	2,362.6	2,372.3	2,401.6	2,426.9	2,445.3	2,475.3	2,454.5	2,454.6	2,462.7	2,475.7	2,494.2	2,514.4	2,445.0
2001	2,441.5	2,448.4	2,466.0	2,469.3	2,484.5	2,510.9	2,488.5	2,484.0	2,477.0	2,484.3	2,492.5	2,512.2	2,479.9
2002	2,450.6	2,457.6	2,475.7	2,480.4	2,495.7	2,515.5	2,494.4	2,492.2	2,498.1	2,505.3	2,518.4	2,530.1	2,492.8
2003	2,494.5	2,491.3	2,512.8	2,536.6	2,552.8	2,573.1	2,566.6	2,558.1	2,564.2	2,567.3	2,579.3	2,593.3	2,549.2
2004	2,541.0	2,552.9	2,582.6	2,590.6	2,611.0	2,629.5	2,620.3	2,617.1	2,623.6	2,644.3	2,657.3	2,668.3	2,611.5
2005	2,607.6	2,620.2	2,636.1	2,652.1	2,667.5	2,681.6	2,678.6	2,671.0	2,676.9	2,680.3	2,700.6	2,712.3	2,665.4
2006	2,659.8	2,670.6	2,693.4	2,698.8	2,714.8	2,735.3	2,718.5	2,712.0	2,715.9	2,726.4	2,740.3	2,755.1	2,711.7
2007	2,698.0	2,707.1	2,726.9	2,730.7	2,746.7	2,760.5	2,749.7	2,738.9	2,738.3	2,758.7	2,774.0	2,787.4	2,743.1
2008	2,724.6	2,734.6	2,751.1	2,768.8	2,785.7	2,791.8	2,790.7	2,779.2	2,770.3	2,776.3	2,781.9	2,784.7	2,770.0
2009	2,727.5	2,727.9	2,737.8	2,738.8	2,754.5	2,765.7	2,762.8	2,744.2	2,731.4	2,755.3	2,770.4	2,774.4	2,749.2
2010	2,714.2	2,698.9	2,736.9	2,767.6	2,790.0	2,801.7	2,797.4	2,764.5	2,770.3	2,792.6	2,804.5	2,811.3	2,770.8
2011	2,759.1	2,768.0	2,787.7	2,800.4	2,809.4	2,822.1	2,813.9	2,789.7	2,800.3	2,820.5	2,834.4	2,839.3	2,803.7

Employment by Industry: Washington–Arlington–Alexandria, DC–VA–MD–WV, Selected Years, 2000–2011—Continued

(Numbers in thousands, not seasonally adjusted)

Industry and year	January	February	March	April	May	June	July	August	September	October	November	December	Annual average
Trade, Transportation, and Utilities													
2000	386.3	382.6	385.5	385.1	388.3	393.5	391.8	393.2	392.5	397.1	408.6	418.7	393.6
2001	391.4	385.2	386.4	384.0	387.8	392.0	390.6	390.8	387.9	390.1	398.6	406.9	391.0
2002	384.7	379.7	381.1	381.5	384.6	388.7	386.9	386.7	386.2	389.2	397.1	405.4	387.7
2003	385.2	380.5	382.6	385.3	388.3	393.0	391.8	392.6	392.2	395.2	404.6	412.5	392.0
2004	391.8	388.1	391.5	390.6	395.0	402.1	398.8	399.2	397.6	404.9	413.8	422.0	399.6
2005	401.7	398.6	400.1	400.7	403.5	406.6	407.5	406.7	404.1	406.8	415.5	426.2	406.5
2006	405.3	396.7	398.7	397.4	401.8	405.8	403.6	403.3	402.1	404.5	414.4	422.8	404.7
2007	404.3	396.6	398.9	399.5	402.8	406.6	405.1	403.1	401.1	403.2	413.8	422.0	404.8
2008	402.2	395.3	395.7	395.7	397.8	400.5	399.1	397.3	394.3	393.8	399.1	404.2	397.9
2009	383.0	375.5	374.6	372.2	375.6	377.6	375.2	374.4	373.2	375.7	384.3	390.1	377.6
2010	372.4	362.8	368.8	371.9	375.5	379.3	377.4	377.6	374.9	380.4	388.9	396.4	377.2
2011	377.9	373.1	374.5	376.3	377.9	380.8	379.0	378.8	373.6	377.1	383.9	392.2	378.8
Wholesale Trade													
2000	66.8	67.3	67.7	67.6	68.0	68.6	68.3	68.3	68.1	68.1	68.5	68.8	68.0
2001	68.1	68.1	68.5	68.5	68.4	68.5	68.2	67.9	67.4	67.3	67.5	67.2	68.0
2002	66.5	66.3	66.4	66.4	66.5	66.6	66.4	66.3	65.7	66.3	66.5	66.8	66.4
2003	67.9	68.0	68.3	68.0	68.3	68.5	67.6	67.5	67.0	67.9	68.3	68.6	68.0
2004	68.6	68.8	69.2	68.3	68.3	68.8	69.0	68.8	68.7	69.8	70.3	70.5	69.1
2005	70.4	70.8	71.0	71.5	71.6	71.4	71.9	71.9	71.3	70.5	70.6	70.9	71.2
2006	69.4	69.6	70.0	70.0	70.5	70.7	70.4	70.3	69.9	70.1	70.1	70.5	70.1
2007	70.2	70.3	70.7	70.7	70.9	71.3	70.6	70.5	70.2	70.4	70.5	70.6	70.6
2008	69.9	70.2	70.1	69.9	69.9	70.1	69.8	69.5	68.9	68.7	68.0	67.6	69.4
2009	67.1	66.6	66.3	65.7	65.6	65.4	65.1	64.9	64.3	64.2	64.1	64.2	65.3
2010	63.2	62.8	63.1	62.9	63.1	63.3	63.2	63.2	62.7	63.2	62.9	63.2	63.1
2011	63.0	63.0	63.2	63.1	63.4	63.5	63.3	63.9	63.2	64.2	63.2	62.3	63.3
Retail Trade													
2000	251.2	247.1	249.2	249.2	251.8	255.5	254.3	255.8	256.0	258.6	269.9	279.6	256.5
2001	255.4	249.4	250.4	247.4	250.7	254.3	252.5	253.2	251.9	254.8	264.0	273.5	254.8
2002	253.7	249.0	250.4	250.4	252.9	256.0	254.0	253.8	254.6	256.0	263.4	271.7	255.5
2003	251.4	247.0	248.4	250.6	252.8	256.8	255.5	256.7	257.1	259.1	268.1	275.2	256.6
2004	257.3	253.5	255.7	256.4	260.1	265.6	262.8	263.2	261.5	267.4	275.6	283.2	263.5
2005	265.3	261.4	262.5	263.0	265.4	268.1	268.9	268.3	266.7	269.2	277.2	285.8	268.5
2006	270.5	263.7	264.8	263.8	267.1	270.1	269.0	269.1	267.8	270.5	280.1	285.5	270.2
2007	271.4	263.6	265.1	266.0	268.6	271.1	270.6	268.6	267.0	269.2	279.2	284.8	270.4
2008	269.8	262.5	263.3	263.6	265.2	267.0	266.2	264.5	262.5	262.5	267.5	271.2	265.5
2009	254.2	248.2	247.6	246.3	249.0	250.8	249.4	249.2	248.5	251.8	259.8	263.9	251.6
2010	250.7	242.0	247.2	250.3	253.3	256.0	254.8	255.1	253.1	258.3	265.9	270.8	254.8
2011	256.2	252.0	252.9	255.0	256.1	258.3	256.8	256.6	251.2	254.3	260.6	265.2	256.3
Transportation and Utilities													
2000	68.3	68.2	68.6	68.3	68.5	69.4	69.2	69.1	68.4	70.4	70.2	70.3	69.1
2001	67.9	67.7	67.5	68.1	68.7	69.2	69.9	69.7	68.6	68.0	67.1	66.2	68.2
2002	64.5	64.4	64.3	64.7	65.2	66.1	66.5	66.6	65.9	66.9	67.2	66.9	65.8
2003	65.9	65.5	65.9	66.7	67.2	67.7	68.7	68.4	68.1	68.2	68.2	68.7	67.4
2004	65.9	65.8	66.6	65.9	66.6	67.7	67.0	67.2	67.4	67.7	67.9	68.3	67.0
2005	66.0	66.4	66.6	66.2	66.5	67.1	66.7	66.5	66.1	67.1	67.7	69.5	66.9
2006	65.4	63.4	63.9	63.6	64.2	65.0	64.2	63.9	64.4	63.9	64.2	66.8	64.4
2007	62.7	62.7	63.1	62.8	63.3	64.2	63.9	64.0	63.9	63.6	64.1	66.6	63.7
2008	62.5	62.6	62.3	62.2	62.7	63.4	63.1	63.3	62.9	62.6	63.6	65.4	63.1
2009	61.7	60.7	60.7	60.2	61.0	61.4	60.7	60.3	60.4	59.7	60.4	62.0	60.8
2010	58.5	58.0	58.5	58.7	59.1	60.0	59.4	59.3	59.1	58.9	60.1	62.4	59.3
2011	58.7	58.1	58.4	58.2	58.4	59.0	58.9	58.3	59.2	58.6	60.1	64.7	59.2
Information													
2000	118.2	119.6	121.1	123.2	125.0	127.8	128.1	129.5	129.8	132.5	133.0	134.2	126.8
2001	134.9	135.4	135.4	133.8	133.5	132.2	131.4	130.3	128.5	126.6	125.3	124.9	131.0
2002	120.8	119.9	119.6	117.8	117.6	117.3	114.6	113.8	112.0	110.0	110.2	109.7	115.3
2003	109.7	109.9	110.0	109.2	109.9	110.4	110.2	110.1	109.2	108.3	109.0	109.1	109.6
2004	108.8	108.1	109.2	107.4	107.3	107.2	107.5	106.6	104.8	102.0	101.8	101.4	106.0
2005	100.0	100.4	100.3	99.6	99.7	100.2	100.4	99.7	99.5	99.4	99.3	99.4	99.8
2006	98.3	98.7	99.4	98.0	97.9	97.9	97.3	96.6	95.8	94.5	94.5	94.2	96.9
2007	94.5	94.6	94.4	93.4	93.7	94.3	94.5	94.2	93.3	92.8	93.1	93.4	93.9
2008	92.0	92.4	92.3	92.1	91.9	91.8	91.5	91.0	90.2	89.1	89.4	88.6	91.0
2009	86.4	86.4	85.9	84.1	83.8	84.3	83.2	82.7	81.4	81.1	81.1	81.0	83.5
2010	79.9	79.5	79.6	79.2	79.0	80.1	80.4	80.3	81.4	81.3	80.8	82.6	80.3
2011	79.6	80.2	80.5	81.3	81.0	81.7	81.5	77.9	80.4	80.6	80.3	80.5	80.5
Financial Activities													
2000	142.9	143.3	144.3	144.3	144.7	146.6	147.0	147.1	146.1	145.7	146.6	147.8	145.5
2001	145.0	145.5	146.3	146.9	147.7	149.2	149.6	149.6	147.9	148.1	148.4	149.6	147.8
2002	149.2	149.8	150.2	149.6	150.0	151.4	151.5	151.8	150.8	151.6	152.2	153.3	151.0
2003	152.9	153.0	153.4	155.3	156.2	157.7	159.2	158.8	157.2	155.9	155.3	155.6	155.9
2004	153.7	153.7	154.6	156.9	157.9	158.8	158.8	158.8	158.0	159.0	158.9	159.9	157.4
2005	158.3	158.8	158.6	160.3	161.0	161.9	162.1	161.7	161.0	160.2	160.0	160.8	160.4
2006	159.4	160.2	161.0	160.7	161.7	163.4	162.8	162.6	161.8	161.1	161.1	162.2	161.5
2007	160.2	160.6	160.8	159.7	160.2	161.1	160.9	159.7	158.4	157.4	156.8	156.9	159.4
2008	154.6	154.6	154.5	155.1	155.0	155.9	156.0	155.2	153.8	152.2	152.2	152.0	154.3
2009	149.2	148.3	147.8	147.5	147.8	149.0	148.7	148.3	147.0	147.7	147.5	148.1	148.1
2010	145.8	145.3	146.2	146.0	146.5	147.9	147.8	147.0	145.4	146.5	146.6	146.7	146.5
2011	144.0	144.0	144.1	144.5	144.6	145.3	146.4	146.7	146.7	146.5	147.3	148.2	145.7

Employment by Industry: Washington–Arlington–Alexandria, DC–VA–MD–WV, Selected Years, 2000–2011—*Continued*

(Numbers in thousands, not seasonally adjusted)

Industry and year	January	February	March	April	May	June	July	August	September	October	November	December	Annual average
Professional and Business Services													
2000	533.7	538.0	546.8	553.4	555.2	566.4	566.7	568.5	567.9	570.3	571.2	575.2	559.4
2001	565.2	569.8	574.5	574.8	575.3	582.3	577.0	576.4	568.1	571.8	570.7	573.2	573.3
2002	555.1	558.2	563.3	563.3	563.8	567.7	566.6	565.5	562.0	563.6	564.4	565.6	563.3
2003	569.1	569.0	574.4	586.9	589.8	595.5	597.5	598.2	596.1	599.6	601.2	605.4	590.2
2004	592.1	597.1	606.9	611.0	615.2	623.6	628.4	630.0	628.3	631.8	631.7	636.0	619.3
2005	623.4	629.1	634.9	641.5	643.5	650.6	655.6	655.6	656.3	654.0	655.2	656.6	646.4
2006	645.5	651.2	657.6	661.8	663.9	673.2	672.7	672.8	669.2	667.8	668.6	670.1	664.5
2007	659.9	664.9	670.3	673.7	675.7	682.6	680.0	680.1	673.6	679.2	679.7	681.1	675.1
2008	669.6	672.8	676.4	683.9	684.2	688.5	688.9	687.8	682.9	683.7	682.1	680.3	681.8
2009	671.2	670.6	672.1	671.9	672.0	677.4	677.8	675.8	668.7	676.3	677.4	677.4	674.1
2010	664.8	664.4	671.7	682.3	682.8	688.7	686.4	684.7	679.0	685.9	686.0	686.6	680.3
2011	680.2	682.4	687.5	690.6	689.1	694.1	691.3	689.6	687.7	690.9	691.1	690.1	688.7
Education and Health Services													
2000	264.6	269.5	271.9	276.3	274.6	275.1	276.8	276.6	277.9	281.3	284.1	283.8	276.0
2001	274.0	278.0	280.4	281.7	280.3	281.3	282.8	283.0	285.5	289.3	290.9	293.2	283.4
2002	289.1	291.5	292.7	293.4	294.4	293.6	292.9	293.5	295.9	299.9	302.0	301.9	295.1
2003	291.3	293.3	296.5	296.3	294.0	291.8	288.4	287.1	295.2	297.3	298.6	298.6	294.0
2004	296.7	302.3	305.2	305.2	303.4	300.2	296.8	294.7	303.1	308.2	309.8	308.9	302.9
2005	305.7	310.5	311.4	311.2	309.6	305.1	300.0	299.0	308.9	313.5	317.4	316.9	309.1
2006	311.5	317.0	319.3	319.7	317.0	313.7	307.9	307.0	317.3	323.7	327.5	328.1	317.5
2007	324.3	329.3	332.0	330.7	328.1	323.9	318.5	317.2	328.1	335.4	337.1	337.9	328.5
2008	331.2	334.8	336.4	338.8	340.1	335.2	332.7	332.3	341.2	345.2	347.0	348.1	338.6
2009	344.7	347.6	348.8	351.2	351.5	346.2	342.6	340.8	347.0	355.7	357.9	358.4	349.4
2010	353.5	351.2	356.6	361.2	361.4	354.5	351.7	351.1	358.5	360.6	362.6	362.0	357.1
2011	363.4	365.1	366.7	367.1	367.7	365.1	363.5	363.2	370.6	376.7	379.0	376.5	368.7
Leisure and Hospitality													
2000	199.0	199.8	206.1	214.1	220.0	228.1	227.4	226.7	221.6	217.8	215.1	214.6	215.9
2001	202.1	205.0	209.9	213.6	220.5	228.6	226.6	225.9	216.1	214.3	213.3	212.4	215.7
2002	203.8	206.4	212.2	219.5	226.2	233.7	234.3	233.6	228.7	224.1	224.3	222.4	222.4
2003	215.8	213.6	219.1	225.8	233.2	240.6	240.9	239.7	234.3	232.0	230.5	229.6	229.6
2004	221.3	222.3	228.0	233.4	240.7	248.8	249.0	249.1	243.4	239.7	238.6	238.4	237.7
2005	229.5	230.9	235.4	242.5	250.0	258.5	257.6	256.3	250.1	244.3	244.4	243.4	245.2
2006	234.8	235.9	241.8	245.8	252.7	263.2	261.1	260.9	253.7	248.8	247.0	247.3	249.4
2007	239.7	239.0	244.7	250.4	257.5	265.5	266.8	266.0	259.3	255.2	253.6	253.3	254.3
2008	245.4	246.5	252.3	262.6	270.6	275.0	275.8	273.2	266.2	261.5	257.6	255.1	261.8
2009	246.3	245.4	250.1	255.8	264.2	271.0	270.0	268.3	260.8	257.3	255.4	252.4	258.1
2010	242.6	239.1	248.5	259.0	264.5	273.3	272.0	271.4	265.4	262.5	260.5	259.6	259.9
2011	250.1	251.3	258.1	266.2	271.4	279.5	279.4	276.7	270.8	268.7	269.3	269.2	267.6
Other Services													
2000	145.1	145.7	147.2	149.0	149.5	150.4	151.0	150.5	150.8	152.9	153.3	154.2	150.0
2001	149.4	150.0	150.6	151.6	153.4	156.0	155.6	155.3	153.3	153.9	153.8	154.8	153.1
2002	153.0	154.3	155.5	156.5	156.8	158.6	159.9	160.1	158.5	158.2	158.4	159.3	157.4
2003	157.6	158.0	160.1	160.7	161.5	163.1	164.1	162.6	161.3	162.0	161.8	163.3	161.3
2004	160.8	161.5	162.9	164.9	165.9	167.6	168.7	168.0	166.9	165.9	166.6	166.1	165.5
2005	163.4	164.2	165.5	165.9	166.4	167.4	167.5	167.1	166.1	165.1	165.8	166.6	165.9
2006	172.2	172.8	174.0	175.2	176.1	178.4	178.9	178.2	176.9	179.1	178.9	180.1	176.7
2007	178.9	179.9	180.8	179.1	180.4	182.2	182.0	180.6	179.9	180.5	181.2	182.2	180.6
2008	180.3	181.2	182.6	184.4	186.3	187.4	187.9	186.4	185.4	184.8	184.9	185.3	184.7
2009	183.8	183.4	183.9	183.5	184.3	186.5	185.2	184.8	183.0	181.4	181.8	182.6	183.7
2010	179.7	178.5	180.8	182.0	183.1	184.6	183.9	182.9	181.1	182.1	182.2	182.6	182.0
2011	180.8	181.5	182.1	182.4	183.0	184.6	184.1	184.2	181.2	181.4	183.0	183.0	182.6
Government													
2000	325.0	323.9	324.5	325.5	330.6	332.1	333.4	329.2	324.3	321.1	321.5	323.2	326.2
2001	324.4	320.2	321.1	320.9	321.8	326.9	330.1	327.1	326.2	325.0	325.0	326.8	324.6
2002	330.9	329.2	330.2	329.2	330.8	335.7	337.8	335.0	333.5	334.6	334.4	336.4	333.1
2003	333.8	332.5	334.1	334.9	335.7	338.9	340.8	338.7	338.4	336.0	334.9	335.1	336.2
2004	337.9	337.1	336.7	337.5	337.2	340.7	344.1	342.5	341.4	341.1	341.2	342.1	340.0
2005	339.3	338.1	337.5	338.3	338.7	343.3	345.3	344.2	341.6	341.0	341.8	341.9	340.9
2006	341.6	340.6	340.2	338.4	339.0	344.0	346.8	344.6	342.9	342.2	342.7	343.5	342.2
2007	341.1	339.2	338.6	339.1	340.0	344.1	345.8	343.7	341.3	341.7	343.4	344.1	341.8
2008	342.8	342.6	343.1	343.2	345.5	350.3	354.0	352.2	350.4	351.8	352.6	354.1	348.6
2009	352.9	353.1	353.1	356.6	357.8	363.3	367.0	366.0	363.5	366.7	368.1	367.7	361.3
2010	371.7	370.7	371.5	374.1	383.1	386.1	387.5	384.9	381.2	383.6	384.3	383.4	380.2
2011	383.3	382.3	382.6	382.5	382.7	385.5	386.6	384.4	384.1	383.8	383.0	382.7	383.6

Employment by Industry: Worcester, MA, NECTA, Selected Years, 2000–2011

(Numbers in thousands, not seasonally adjusted)

Industry and year	January	February	March	April	May	June	July	August	September	October	November	December	Annual average
Total Nonfarm													
2000	241.1	241.9	243.3	245.2	246.1	247.2	242.5	242.2	246.4	247.5	247.6	250.2	245.1
2001	243.1	243.6	244.2	247.6	249.1	249.4	243.3	241.8	246.8	247.0	246.9	247.5	245.9
2002	240.4	240.2	240.9	244.2	246.2	246.0	240.8	240.6	245.3	246.0	246.7	247.3	243.7
2003	240.9	239.7	240.6	242.4	244.4	244.6	241.1	239.9	244.7	246.5	246.3	246.6	243.1
2004	239.2	239.5	241.1	244.1	245.8	247.0	242.3	242.5	245.8	246.4	246.9	247.5	244.0
2005	239.9	240.7	241.1	244.3	246.3	246.9	242.4	241.5	245.8	246.5	247.8	248.2	244.3
2006	242.7	242.2	243.8	246.9	248.5	249.7	245.6	246.1	249.3	251.1	250.9	251.3	247.3
2007	244.3	245.0	245.9	247.7	250.6	252.1	245.4	245.6	248.8	251.6	252.6	251.7	248.4
2008	245.2	246.2	246.6	247.9	249.3	249.5	244.4	244.2	247.9	249.1	247.5	246.0	247.0
2009	239.4	238.8	238.1	239.5	240.4	239.4	235.3	235.2	238.3	241.0	240.7	241.7	239.0
2010	235.6	235.8	236.1	239.1	241.9	242.0	238.0	237.6	240.3	243.1	243.3	244.8	239.8
2011	239.0	239.6	240.6	243.5	244.5	244.0	241.9	241.1	244.1	245.8	245.6	246.4	243.0
Total Private													
2000	206.9	207.4	208.3	210.2	210.3	211.8	209.1	209.6	211.6	211.8	211.8	214.3	210.3
2001	207.8	207.9	208.5	211.7	212.6	213.0	209.0	209.0	211.2	210.9	210.5	210.8	210.2
2002	204.4	203.8	204.6	207.7	209.3	209.5	207.3	207.8	209.4	209.9	210.2	210.8	207.9
2003	205.2	203.7	204.4	206.4	208.2	208.4	207.5	206.9	208.7	210.8	210.8	210.5	207.6
2004	204.1	204.0	205.2	208.0	209.7	211.3	209.0	209.5	209.8	210.0	210.2	210.6	208.5
2005	203.8	204.0	204.7	208.0	209.7	210.5	209.3	209.3	210.2	209.7	210.9	211.3	208.5
2006	206.1	205.6	207.0	209.8	211.1	212.9	212.1	212.6	212.7	213.7	213.1	213.6	210.9
2007	207.3	207.6	208.5	210.1	212.4	214.3	211.3	211.9	211.8	213.9	214.6	213.6	211.4
2008	208.0	208.5	208.8	210.1	211.3	212.3	210.1	210.5	211.0	211.3	209.7	208.4	210.0
2009	202.1	200.9	200.1	201.3	202.2	201.8	200.7	200.7	201.1	202.7	202.4	202.5	201.5
2010	197.8	197.7	197.9	200.8	202.8	203.7	203.5	203.3	203.1	205.3	205.2	206.5	202.3
2011	201.8	201.9	202.7	205.4	206.1	206.2	207.2	206.7	206.6	207.3	206.9	207.8	205.5
Goods-Producing													
2000	46.8	46.3	46.7	47.4	47.8	48.7	48.2	48.5	48.6	49.0	48.7	49.0	48.0
2001	47.6	47.2	47.1	47.8	47.8	47.9	46.5	46.3	46.3	45.7	45.4	45.3	46.7
2002	43.2	42.6	42.6	43.1	43.4	43.6	42.7	43.1	43.0	42.7	42.5	42.3	42.9
2003	41.3	40.3	40.1	40.6	40.9	41.2	40.9	40.9	40.9	41.0	40.8	40.4	40.8
2004	39.1	38.5	38.8	39.9	40.4	40.8	40.7	41.2	41.0	40.7	40.7	40.5	40.2
2005	38.7	38.2	38.2	39.2	39.8	40.2	40.0	40.0	39.9	39.7	39.8	39.8	39.5
2006	38.9	38.5	38.4	39.3	39.8	40.4	40.4	40.6	40.2	40.0	39.7	39.6	39.7
2007	38.2	37.6	37.7	38.1	38.7	39.5	39.4	39.4	39.3	39.5	39.5	39.1	38.8
2008	37.9	37.3	37.3	37.6	38.0	38.6	38.3	38.1	38.1	38.0	37.5	36.7	37.8
2009	34.8	33.8	33.2	33.3	33.5	33.8	33.7	33.6	33.6	33.6	33.4	33.1	33.6
2010	32.0	31.4	31.5	32.3	32.7	33.2	33.2	33.1	33.0	33.1	33.1	33.1	32.6
2011	31.8	31.5	31.4	32.2	33.0	33.5	33.9	33.4	33.6	33.5	33.4	33.5	32.9
Mining, Logging, and Construction													
2000	8.2	7.8	8.1	8.8	9.1	9.6	10.0	10.0	10.0	9.9	9.8	9.6	9.2
2001	8.9	8.8	8.8	9.7	10.1	10.3	10.6	10.7	10.7	10.1	10.0	9.8	9.9
2002	9.0	8.7	8.8	9.5	9.9	10.1	10.2	10.3	10.1	10.0	10.0	9.7	9.7
2003	8.8	8.2	8.3	9.2	9.9	10.1	10.5	10.7	10.6	10.7	10.6	10.2	9.8
2004	9.1	8.8	9.1	10.0	10.5	10.8	11.2	11.3	11.1	10.9	10.8	10.4	10.3
2005	9.2	8.8	8.9	9.9	10.5	10.8	11.2	11.2	11.1	10.8	10.9	10.6	10.3
2006	9.8	9.5	9.6	10.4	10.8	11.1	11.4	11.5	11.2	11.0	10.6	10.2	10.6
2007	9.1	8.6	8.7	9.2	9.9	10.3	10.5	10.5	10.5	10.3	10.2	9.7	9.8
2008	8.7	8.4	8.5	9.0	9.5	9.9	9.9	9.9	9.8	9.6	9.3	8.7	9.3
2009	7.6	7.2	7.1	7.6	7.9	8.2	8.4	8.5	8.4	8.3	8.1	7.8	7.9
2010	6.9	6.5	6.6	7.3	7.7	8.0	8.2	8.1	8.0	8.1	8.0	7.8	7.6
2011	6.9	6.6	6.6	7.3	7.8	8.2	8.4	8.3	8.2	8.1	8.0	7.7	7.7
Manufacturing													
2000	38.6	38.5	38.6	38.6	38.7	39.1	38.2	38.5	38.6	39.1	38.9	39.4	38.7
2001	38.7	38.4	38.3	38.1	37.7	37.6	35.9	35.6	35.6	35.6	35.4	35.5	36.9
2002	34.2	33.9	33.8	33.6	33.5	33.5	32.5	32.8	32.9	32.7	32.5	32.6	33.2
2003	32.5	32.1	31.8	31.4	31.0	31.1	30.4	30.2	30.3	30.3	30.2	30.2	31.0
2004	30.0	29.7	29.7	29.9	29.9	30.0	29.5	29.9	29.9	29.8	29.9	30.1	29.9
2005	29.5	29.4	29.3	29.3	29.3	29.4	28.8	28.8	28.8	28.9	28.9	29.2	29.1
2006	29.1	29.0	28.8	28.9	29.0	29.3	29.0	29.1	29.0	29.0	29.1	29.4	29.1
2007	29.1	29.0	29.0	28.9	28.8	29.2	28.9	28.9	28.8	29.2	29.3	29.4	29.0
2008	29.2	28.9	28.8	28.6	28.5	28.7	28.4	28.2	28.3	28.4	28.2	28.0	28.5
2009	27.2	26.6	26.1	25.7	25.6	25.6	25.3	25.1	25.2	25.3	25.3	25.3	25.7
2010	25.1	24.9	24.9	25.0	25.0	25.2	25.0	25.0	25.0	25.0	25.1	25.3	25.0
2011	24.9	24.9	24.8	24.9	25.2	25.3	25.5	25.1	25.4	25.4	25.4	25.8	25.2
Service-Providing													
2000	194.3	195.6	196.6	197.8	198.3	198.5	194.3	193.7	197.8	198.5	198.9	201.2	197.1
2001	195.5	196.4	197.1	199.8	201.3	201.5	196.8	195.5	200.5	201.3	201.5	202.2	199.1
2002	197.2	197.6	198.3	201.1	202.8	202.4	198.1	197.5	202.3	203.3	204.2	205.0	200.8
2003	199.6	199.4	200.5	201.8	203.5	203.4	200.2	199.0	203.8	205.5	205.5	206.2	202.4
2004	200.1	201.0	202.3	204.2	205.4	206.2	201.6	201.3	204.8	205.7	206.2	207.0	203.8
2005	201.2	202.5	202.9	205.1	206.5	206.7	202.4	201.5	205.9	206.8	208.0	208.4	204.8
2006	203.8	203.7	205.4	207.6	208.7	209.3	205.2	205.5	209.1	211.1	211.2	211.7	207.7
2007	206.1	207.4	208.2	209.6	211.9	212.6	206.0	206.2	209.5	212.1	213.1	212.6	209.6
2008	207.3	208.9	209.3	210.3	211.3	210.9	206.1	206.1	209.8	211.1	210.0	209.3	209.2
2009	204.6	205.0	204.9	206.2	206.9	205.6	201.6	201.6	204.7	207.4	207.3	208.6	205.4
2010	203.6	204.4	204.6	206.8	209.2	208.8	204.8	204.5	207.3	210.0	210.2	211.7	207.2
2011	207.2	208.1	209.2	211.3	211.5	210.5	208.0	207.7	210.5	212.3	212.2	212.9	210.1

Employment by Industry: Worcester, MA, NECTA, Selected Years, 2000–2011—*Continued*

(Numbers in thousands, not seasonally adjusted)

Industry and year	January	February	March	April	May	June	July	August	September	October	November	December	Annual average
Trade, Transportation, and Utilities													
2000	47.1	46.4	46.4	46.7	46.4	46.5	45.4	45.5	45.8	46.2	47.0	48.1	46.5
2001	45.8	45.0	45.1	45.8	46.0	46.3	45.3	45.5	45.7	46.5	47.4	48.0	46.0
2002	45.2	44.5	44.9	45.2	45.2	45.6	44.6	44.3	45.0	45.6	46.2	46.8	45.3
2003	45.1	44.2	44.6	45.0	45.3	45.7	45.2	45.2	45.8	46.1	46.6	46.8	45.5
2004	45.0	44.5	44.7	45.0	45.2	45.7	44.5	44.5	44.8	45.5	46.2	46.6	45.2
2005	45.4	44.7	44.8	45.1	45.5	45.6	44.9	45.1	45.3	45.5	46.3	46.7	45.4
2006	45.3	44.6	45.0	45.2	45.3	45.6	45.3	45.7	46.2	46.5	47.0	47.4	45.8
2007	46.1	45.5	45.9	45.9	46.4	46.9	46.0	45.8	46.1	47.0	47.8	48.1	46.5
2008	46.8	45.8	46.1	46.1	46.3	46.4	45.6	45.7	46.0	46.4	46.6	46.7	46.2
2009	44.6	43.7	43.6	43.5	43.7	44.1	43.0	42.9	43.3	43.8	44.4	44.8	43.8
2010	43.6	43.2	43.6	44.4	45.0	45.5	44.7	44.8	44.8	45.4	46.1	46.9	44.8
2011	45.0	44.5	44.7	45.0	45.2	45.3	44.6	44.8	44.6	44.8	45.6	46.2	45.0
Wholesale Trade													
2000	10.4	10.4	10.4	10.7	10.5	10.3	10.1	10.2	10.2	10.2	10.2	10.3	10.3
2001	9.9	10.0	10.0	10.0	10.1	10.1	9.9	10.1	9.9	10.1	10.0	9.9	10.0
2002	9.7	9.6	9.6	9.8	9.7	9.9	9.8	9.8	9.8	10.0	10.0	10.0	9.8
2003	10.0	9.9	10.0	10.0	10.0	10.0	10.1	10.0	9.9	9.8	9.8	9.7	9.9
2004	9.5	9.5	9.6	9.7	9.7	9.8	9.5	9.5	9.4	9.4	9.5	9.4	9.5
2005	9.4	9.3	9.4	9.6	9.6	9.7	9.6	9.8	9.7	9.8	9.9	9.9	9.6
2006	9.7	9.8	9.9	9.9	9.9	9.9	10.0	10.1	10.1	10.1	10.1	10.1	10.0
2007	9.9	9.9	10.0	10.0	10.1	10.1	10.1	10.1	10.0	10.4	10.5	10.4	10.1
2008	10.4	10.4	10.6	10.7	10.8	10.8	10.8	10.9	10.8	11.0	10.9	10.9	10.8
2009	10.3	10.2	10.2	10.2	10.1	10.0	10.0	10.0	9.9	10.0	9.9	9.8	10.1
2010	9.8	9.7	9.7	9.7	9.7	9.7	9.5	9.4	9.3	9.5	9.4	9.3	9.6
2011	9.1	9.0	9.0	9.2	9.2	9.3	9.3	9.3	9.2	9.2	9.2	9.2	9.2
Retail Trade													
2000	29.2	28.5	28.5	28.1	28.1	28.7	28.2	28.3	28.1	28.2	29.2	30.2	28.6
2001	28.4	27.6	27.6	28.1	28.3	28.7	28.2	28.3	28.2	28.7	29.8	30.5	28.5
2002	27.9	27.4	27.8	27.7	27.8	28.0	27.8	27.6	27.7	27.9	28.5	29.0	27.9
2003	27.6	27.0	27.2	27.5	27.8	28.2	28.0	28.2	28.4	28.6	29.2	29.5	28.1
2004	28.3	27.8	27.9	28.0	28.2	28.5	28.1	28.2	28.1	28.6	29.3	29.8	28.4
2005	28.8	28.2	28.1	28.2	28.5	28.5	28.2	28.3	28.0	28.1	28.7	28.9	28.4
2006	28.1	27.4	27.6	27.7	27.7	27.9	27.9	28.2	28.1	28.3	28.8	29.1	28.1
2007	28.2	27.6	27.9	27.9	28.2	28.6	28.2	28.0	27.8	28.4	29.0	29.2	28.3
2008	28.1	27.2	27.3	27.2	27.3	27.5	27.4	27.5	27.2	27.4	27.7	27.8	27.5
2009	26.6	25.9	25.8	25.8	25.9	26.4	25.8	25.7	25.6	25.9	26.4	26.9	26.1
2010	26.0	25.6	26.0	26.5	26.8	27.1	26.9	27.0	26.5	26.9	27.5	28.0	26.7
2011	27.0	26.5	26.6	26.8	26.9	27.0	26.6	26.8	26.3	26.5	27.2	27.7	26.8
Transportation and Utilities													
2000	7.5	7.5	7.5	7.9	7.8	7.5	7.1	7.0	7.5	7.8	7.6	7.6	7.5
2001	7.5	7.4	7.5	7.7	7.6	7.5	7.2	7.1	7.6	7.7	7.6	7.6	7.5
2002	7.6	7.5	7.5	7.7	7.7	7.7	7.0	6.9	7.5	7.7	7.7	7.8	7.5
2003	7.5	7.3	7.4	7.5	7.5	7.5	7.1	7.0	7.5	7.7	7.6	7.6	7.4
2004	7.2	7.2	7.2	7.3	7.3	7.4	6.9	6.8	7.3	7.5	7.4	7.4	7.2
2005	7.2	7.2	7.3	7.3	7.4	7.4	7.1	7.0	7.6	7.6	7.7	7.9	7.4
2006	7.5	7.4	7.5	7.6	7.7	7.8	7.4	7.4	8.0	8.1	8.1	8.2	7.7
2007	8.0	8.0	8.0	8.0	8.1	8.2	7.7	7.7	8.3	8.2	8.3	8.5	8.1
2008	8.3	8.2	8.2	8.2	8.2	8.1	7.4	7.3	8.0	8.0	8.0	8.0	8.0
2009	7.7	7.6	7.6	7.5	7.7	7.7	7.2	7.2	7.8	7.9	8.1	8.1	7.7
2010	7.8	7.9	7.9	8.2	8.5	8.7	8.3	8.4	9.0	9.0	9.2	9.6	8.5
2011	8.9	9.0	9.1	9.0	9.1	9.0	8.7	8.7	9.1	9.1	9.2	9.3	9.0
Information													
2000	3.7	3.8	3.8	3.8	3.9	4.0	4.1	3.7	4.2	4.2	4.3	4.4	4.0
2001	4.4	4.4	4.4	4.5	4.5	4.5	4.4	4.4	4.3	4.4	4.3	4.3	4.4
2002	4.5	4.4	4.4	4.3	4.4	4.4	4.4	4.3	4.2	4.2	4.2	4.2	4.3
2003	4.1	4.1	4.0	4.0	4.0	4.0	4.0	4.0	3.8	3.9	3.9	3.9	4.0
2004	3.9	3.9	3.9	3.9	4.0	4.2	4.2	4.1	3.9	3.9	3.9	3.9	4.0
2005	3.9	3.9	3.9	3.7	3.7	3.6	3.6	3.6	3.6	3.6	3.6	3.6	3.7
2006	3.6	3.6	3.6	3.6	3.6	3.7	3.7	3.7	3.7	3.7	3.7	3.7	3.7
2007	3.9	3.9	3.9	3.9	4.0	4.0	4.0	4.0	3.9	4.0	4.0	3.9	4.0
2008	4.0	4.0	4.0	4.1	4.1	4.1	4.0	4.0	3.9	3.6	3.6	3.6	3.9
2009	3.5	3.5	3.4	3.4	3.4	3.5	3.4	3.4	3.4	3.4	3.4	3.4	3.4
2010	3.4	3.5	3.5	3.6	3.6	3.6	3.6	3.6	3.5	3.5	3.5	3.5	3.5
2011	3.5	3.5	3.5	3.5	3.5	3.5	3.5	3.1	3.5	3.5	3.5	3.5	3.5
Financial Activities													
2000	14.1	14.0	14.0	13.8	13.8	13.8	13.6	13.5	13.4	13.4	13.5	13.5	13.7
2001	13.5	13.4	13.4	13.8	13.9	14.0	14.1	14.1	14.0	14.2	14.1	14.1	13.9
2002	14.0	14.0	14.0	14.2	14.2	14.2	14.2	14.3	14.1	14.3	14.3	14.3	14.2
2003	13.9	13.9	14.0	14.1	14.1	14.2	14.3	14.3	14.2	14.2	14.2	14.2	14.1
2004	14.2	14.1	14.1	14.1	14.2	14.2	14.3	14.3	14.1	14.0	13.9	14.0	14.1
2005	13.8	13.8	13.9	14.0	14.0	14.2	14.3	14.3	14.2	14.1	14.2	14.3	14.1
2006	14.2	14.2	14.2	14.3	14.3	14.4	14.3	14.2	14.0	14.1	14.0	14.0	14.2
2007	13.9	13.8	13.8	13.8	13.7	13.7	13.7	13.7	13.5	13.6	13.6	13.6	13.7
2008	13.4	13.5	13.4	13.5	13.5	13.6	13.7	13.6	13.5	13.5	13.5	13.4	13.5
2009	13.5	13.4	13.4	13.4	13.4	13.5	13.5	13.4	13.3	13.3	13.3	13.3	13.4
2010	13.3	13.3	13.3	13.2	13.2	13.3	13.4	13.3	13.2	13.5	13.4	13.5	13.3
2011	13.3	13.3	13.3	13.3	13.3	13.3	13.4	13.4	13.3	13.3	13.2	13.2	13.3

Employment by Industry: Worcester, MA, NECTA, Selected Years, 2000–2011—*Continued*

(Numbers in thousands, not seasonally adjusted)

Industry and year	January	February	March	April	May	June	July	August	September	October	November	December	Annual average
Professional and Business Services													
2000	29.0	29.2	29.4	30.1	29.6	30.0	30.1	30.5	30.3	29.5	29.6	29.9	29.8
2001	27.8	27.8	28.0	28.6	28.5	28.8	28.2	28.5	28.3	27.5	27.3	27.3	28.1
2002	26.6	26.6	26.7	27.2	27.3	27.2	28.1	28.1	28.4	27.3	27.6	27.1	27.4
2003	26.6	26.5	26.6	27.1	27.3	27.4	27.6	27.6	27.7	27.9	28.0	28.3	27.4
2004	27.3	27.6	27.8	28.6	28.8	29.2	29.3	29.5	29.5	29.2	29.3	29.4	28.8
2005	27.7	27.9	28.2	29.1	29.5	29.7	29.6	29.7	30.0	29.8	30.1	30.0	29.3
2006	28.7	28.5	29.0	29.4	29.9	30.2	30.5	30.6	30.1	30.2	29.8	29.7	29.7
2007	28.1	28.1	28.1	28.9	29.3	29.7	28.9	28.8	28.5	28.4	28.6	28.6	28.7
2008	27.1	27.1	27.0	27.4	27.6	27.9	27.6	27.9	27.8	27.4	27.2	27.1	27.4
2009	26.2	25.7	25.5	25.5	25.5	25.1	25.0	25.2	24.9	25.3	25.2	25.0	25.3
2010	24.4	24.1	24.3	24.8	25.1	25.5	25.7	25.6	25.5	25.6	25.4	25.9	25.2
2011	26.3	26.2	26.2	27.2	26.8	26.9	27.6	27.8	27.3	27.2	27.0	27.4	27.0
Education and Health Services													
2000	40.6	41.8	41.7	41.8	41.6	41.0	40.2	40.2	41.9	41.9	41.9	42.0	41.4
2001	42.1	43.5	43.7	44.1	44.1	42.8	41.8	41.7	44.5	44.4	44.2	44.3	43.4
2002	43.5	44.4	44.6	45.6	45.7	44.9	44.0	43.9	45.4	46.2	46.2	46.5	45.1
2003	45.5	46.3	46.5	46.8	46.2	45.4	44.1	43.8	45.8	46.7	46.8	46.4	45.9
2004	45.5	46.3	46.5	46.3	45.8	45.4	44.4	44.3	45.6	46.2	46.3	46.2	45.7
2005	45.2	46.4	46.4	46.6	46.3	45.9	45.3	45.3	46.5	47.0	47.3	47.0	46.3
2006	46.2	47.3	47.5	47.8	47.4	46.6	46.1	46.0	47.4	48.6	48.6	48.6	47.3
2007	47.3	48.8	48.9	49.1	48.9	48.1	47.5	48.0	49.6	50.6	50.7	50.4	49.0
2008	49.2	51.1	51.2	51.1	50.4	49.9	49.5	49.7	51.2	52.3	52.3	52.1	50.8
2009	51.4	52.6	52.7	53.1	52.3	51.2	51.5	51.9	52.9	53.8	54.1	54.1	52.6
2010	53.0	54.4	54.2	53.9	53.5	52.4	52.4	52.5	53.9	54.8	55.0	55.0	53.8
2011	53.8	54.8	55.1	54.8	54.3	53.1	53.4	53.8	54.6	55.1	54.8	54.8	54.4
Leisure and Hospitality													
2000	17.4	17.6	18.0	18.3	18.8	19.2	18.9	19.0	18.9	19.0	18.2	18.7	18.5
2001	18.0	17.9	18.2	18.6	19.2	19.9	19.7	19.6	19.4	19.4	19.0	18.7	19.0
2002	18.6	18.5	18.6	19.4	20.3	20.7	20.6	20.9	20.8	21.0	20.6	20.9	20.1
2003	20.0	19.7	19.9	20.1	21.6	21.5	22.0	21.9	21.7	22.1	21.5	21.5	21.1
2004	20.2	20.1	20.4	21.3	22.3	22.7	22.2	22.2	22.0	21.6	21.0	21.1	21.4
2005	20.2	20.1	20.3	21.2	21.9	22.2	22.1	21.9	21.5	20.9	20.5	20.7	21.1
2006	20.1	19.9	20.2	21.1	21.7	22.7	22.4	22.4	22.0	21.7	21.3	21.5	21.4
2007	20.8	20.9	21.2	21.4	22.3	23.0	22.3	22.7	21.8	21.8	21.3	20.9	21.7
2008	20.7	20.8	20.8	21.5	22.5	22.9	22.3	22.6	22.0	21.7	20.6	20.5	21.6
2009	19.9	19.9	20.0	20.8	21.9	21.9	21.7	21.5	21.2	21.2	20.3	20.5	20.9
2010	19.9	19.6	19.3	20.3	21.3	21.6	21.5	21.6	20.8	21.1	20.3	20.3	20.6
2011	19.8	19.8	20.0	20.8	21.3	21.7	21.7	21.4	21.0	21.2	20.7	20.6	20.8
Other Services													
2000	8.2	8.3	8.3	8.3	8.4	8.6	8.6	8.7	8.5	8.6	8.6	8.7	8.5
2001	8.6	8.7	8.6	8.5	8.6	8.8	9.0	8.9	8.7	8.8	8.8	8.8	8.7
2002	8.8	8.8	8.8	8.7	8.8	8.9	8.7	8.9	8.5	8.6	8.6	8.7	8.7
2003	8.7	8.7	8.7	8.7	8.8	9.0	9.4	9.3	8.8	8.9	9.0	9.0	8.9
2004	8.9	9.0	9.0	8.9	9.0	9.1	9.4	9.4	8.9	8.9	8.9	8.9	9.0
2005	8.9	9.0	9.0	9.1	9.0	9.1	9.5	9.4	9.2	9.1	9.1	9.2	9.1
2006	9.1	9.0	9.1	9.1	9.1	9.3	9.4	9.4	9.1	8.9	9.0	9.1	9.1
2007	9.0	9.0	9.0	9.0	9.1	9.4	9.5	9.5	9.1	9.0	9.1	9.0	9.1
2008	8.9	8.9	9.0	8.8	8.9	8.9	9.1	8.9	8.5	8.5	8.4	8.3	8.8
2009	8.2	8.3	8.3	8.3	8.5	8.7	8.9	8.8	8.5	8.3	8.3	8.3	8.5
2010	8.2	8.2	8.2	8.3	8.4	8.6	9.0	8.8	8.4	8.3	8.4	8.3	8.4
2011	8.3	8.3	8.5	8.6	8.7	8.9	9.1	9.0	8.7	8.7	8.7	8.6	8.7
Government													
2000	34.2	34.5	35.0	35.0	35.8	35.4	33.4	32.6	34.8	35.7	35.8	35.9	34.8
2001	35.3	35.7	35.7	35.9	36.5	36.4	34.3	32.8	35.6	36.1	36.4	36.7	35.6
2002	36.0	36.4	36.3	36.5	36.9	36.5	33.5	32.8	35.9	36.1	36.5	36.5	35.8
2003	35.7	36.0	36.2	36.0	36.2	36.2	33.6	33.0	36.0	35.7	35.5	36.1	35.5
2004	35.1	35.5	35.9	36.1	36.1	35.7	33.3	33.0	36.0	36.4	36.7	36.9	35.6
2005	36.1	36.7	36.4	36.3	36.6	36.4	33.1	32.2	35.6	36.8	36.9	36.9	35.8
2006	36.6	36.6	36.8	37.1	37.4	36.8	33.5	33.5	36.6	37.4	37.8	37.7	36.5
2007	37.0	37.4	37.4	37.6	38.2	37.8	34.1	33.7	37.0	37.7	38.0	38.1	37.0
2008	37.2	37.7	37.8	37.8	38.0	37.2	34.3	33.7	36.9	37.8	37.8	37.6	37.0
2009	37.3	37.9	38.0	38.2	38.2	37.6	34.6	34.5	37.2	38.3	38.3	39.2	37.4
2010	37.8	38.1	38.2	38.3	39.1	38.3	34.5	34.3	37.2	37.8	38.1	38.3	37.5
2011	37.2	37.7	37.9	38.1	38.4	37.8	34.7	34.4	37.5	38.5	38.7	38.6	37.5

APPENDIX

METROPOLITAN STATISTICAL AREAS (MSAS) AND COMPONENTS

Akron, OH
Portage County, OH
Summit County, OH

Albany–Schenectady–Troy, NY
Albany County, NY
Rensselaer County, NY
Saratoga County, NY
Schenectady County, NY
Schoharie County, NY

Albuquerque, NM
Bernalillo County, NM
Sandoval County, NM
Torrance County, NM
Valencia County, NM

Allentown–Bethlehem–Easton, PA–NJ
Warren County, NJ
Carbon County, PA
Lehigh County, PA
Northampton County, PA

Atlanta–Sandy Springs–Marietta, GA
Barrow County, GA
Bartow County, GA
Butts County, GA
Carroll County, GA
Cherokee County, GA
Clayton County, GA
Cobb County, GA
Coweta County, GA
Dawson County, GA
DeKalb County, GA
Douglas County, GA
Fayette County, GA
Forsyth County, GA
Fulton County, GA
Gwinnett County, GA
Haralson County, GA
Heard County, GA
Henry County, GA
Jasper County, GA
Lamar County, GA
Meriwether County, GA
Newton County, GA
Paulding County, GA
Pickens County, GA
Pike County, GA
Rockdale County, GA
Spalding County, GA
Walton County, GA

Austin–Round Rock–San Marcos, TX
Bastrop County, TX
Caldwell County, TX

Hays County, TX
Travis County, TX
Williamson County, TX

Bakersfield–Delano, CA
Kern County, CA

Baltimore–Towson, MD
Anne Arundel County, MD
Baltimore city, MD
Baltimore County, MD
Carroll County, MD
Harford County, MD
Howard County, MD
Queen Anne's County, MD

Baton Rouge, LA
Ascension Parish, LA
East Baton Rouge Parish, LA
East Feliciana Parish, LA
Iberville Parish, LA
Livingston Parish, LA
Pointe Coupee Parish, LA
St. Helena Parish, LA
West Baton Rouge Parish, LA
West Feliciana Parish, LA

Birmingham–Hoover, AL
Bibb County, AL
Blount County, AL
Chilton County, AL
Jefferson County, AL
St. Clair County, AL
Shelby County, AL
Walker County, AL

Boston–Cambridge–Quincy, MA–NH, NECTA
Boston–Cambridge–Quincy, MA, NECTA Division
    Acton town, MA
    Andover town, MA
    Arlington town, MA
    Ayer town, MA
    Bedford town, MA
    Belmont town, MA
    Beverly city, MA
    Bolton town, MA
    Boston city, MA
    Boxborough town, MA
    Boxford town, MA
    Braintree town, MA
    Brookline town, MA
    Burlington town, MA
    Cambridge city, MA
    Canton town, MA
    Carlisle town, MA
    Carver town, MA

Chelsea city, MA
Cohasset town, MA
Concord town, MA
Dedham town, MA
Dover town, MA
Duxbury town, MA
Essex town, MA
Everett city, MA
Foxborough town, MA
Franklin city, MA
Gloucester city, MA
Groton town, MA
Hamilton town, MA
Hanover town, MA
Harvard town, MA
Hingham town, MA
Holbrook town, MA
Hull town, MA
Ipswich town, MA
Kingston town, MA
Lexington town, MA
Lincoln town, MA
Littleton town, MA
Lynnfield town, MA
Malden city, MA
Manchester–by–the–Sea town, MA
Mansfield town, MA
Marshfield town, MA
Maynard town, MA
Medfield town, MA
Medford city, MA
Medway town, MA
Melrose city, MA
Middleton town, MA
Millis town, MA
Milton town, MA
Needham town, MA
Newbury town, MA
Newburyport city, MA
Newton city, MA
Norfolk town, MA
North Reading town, MA
Norwell town, MA
Norwood town, MA
Pembroke town, MA
Plymouth town, MA
Quincy city, MA
Randolph town, MA
Reading town, MA
Revere city, MA
Rockland town, MA
Rockport town, MA
Rowley town, MA
Saugus town, MA
Scituate town, MA
Sharon town, MA
Sherborn town, MA
Shirley town, MA
Somerville city, MA
Stoneham town, MA
Stoughton town, MA

Stow town, MA
Sudbury town, MA
Topsfield town, MA
Wakefield town, MA
Walpole town, MA
Waltham city, MA
Watertown city, MA
Wayland town, MA
Wellesley town, MA
Wenham town, MA
Weston town, MA
Westwood town, MA
Weymouth town, MA
Wilmington town, MA
Winchester town, MA
Winthrop town, MA
Woburn city, MA
Wrentham town, MA
Brockton–Bridgewater–Easton, MA, NECTA Division
Abington town, MA
Avon town, MA
Bridgewater town, MA
Brockton city, MA
East Bridgewater town, MA
Easton town, MA
Halifax town, MA
Hanson town, MA
Middleborough town, MA
Plympton town, MA
West Bridgewater town, MA
Whitman town, MA
Framingham, MA, NECTA Division
Ashland town, MA
Berlin town, MA
Framingham town, MA
Holliston town, MA
Hopedale town, MA
Hopkinton town, MA
Hudson town, MA
Marlborough city, MA
Mendon town, MA
Milford town, MA
Natick town, MA
Southborough town, MA
Upton town, MA
Haverhill–North Andover–Amesbury, MA–NH, NECTA Division
Amesbury town, MA
Georgetown town, MA
Groveland town, MA
Haverhill city, MA
Merrimac, MA
North Andover town, MA
Salisbury town, MA
West Newbury town, MA
Atkinson town, NH
Brentwood town, NH
Danville town, NH
East Kingston town, NH
Epping town, NH
Exeter town, NH

Fremont town, NH
Hampstead town, NH
Hampton Falls town, NH
Kensington town, NH
Kingston town, NH
Newfields town, NH
Newton town, NH
Plaistow town, NH
Sandown town, NH
Seabrook town, NH
South Hampton town, NH
Lawrence–Methuen–Salem, MA–NH, NECTA Division
Lawrence city, MA
Methuen city, MA
Salem town, NH
Lowell–Billerica–Chelmsford, MA–NH, NECTA
Division
Chelmsford town, MA
Dracut town, MA
Dunstable town, MA
Lowell city, MA
Tewksbury town, MA
Tyngsborough town, MA
Westford town, MA
Billerica town, NH
Pelham town, NH
Nashua, NH–MA, NECTA Division
Pepperell town, MA
Townsend town, MA
Amherst town, NH
Brookline town, NH
Chester town, NH
Derry town, NH
Greenfield town, NH
Greenville town, NH
Hollis town, NH
Hudson town, NH
Litchfield town, NH
Londonderry town, NH
Lyndeborough town, NH
Mason town, NH
Merrimack town, NH
Milford town, NH
Mont Vernon town, NH
Nashua city, NH
Raymond town, NH
Wilton town, NH
Windham town, NH
Peabody, MA, NECTA Division
Danvers town, MA
Lynn city, MA
Marblehead town, MA
Nahant town, MA
Peabody city, MA
Salem city, MA
Swampscott town, MA
Taunton–Norton–Raynham, MA, NECTA Division
Berkley town, MA
Dighton town, MA
Lakeville town, MA
Norton town, MA

Raynham town, MA
Taunton city, MA

Bridgeport–Stamford–Norwalk, CT, NECTA
Ansonia city and town, CT
Bridgeport city and town, CT
Darien town, CT
Derby city and town, CT
Easton town, CT
Fairfield town, CT
Greenwich town, CT
Milford city and town, CT
Monroe town, CT
New Canaan town, CT
Newtown town, CT
Norwalk city and town, CT
Oxford town, CT
Redding town, CT
Ridgefield town, CT
Seymour town, CT
Shelton city and town, CT
Southbury town, CT
Stamford city and town, CT
Stratford town, CT
Trumbull town, CT
Weston town, CT
Westport town, CT
Wilton town, CT
Woodbridge town, CT

Buffalo–Niagara Falls, NY
Erie County, NY
Niagara County, NY

Charlotte–Gastonia–Rock Hill, NC–SC
Anson County, NC
Cabarrus County, NC
Gaston County, NC
Mecklenburg County, NC
Union County, NC
York County, SC

Chicago–Joliet–Naperville, IL–IN–WI
Chicago–Joliet–Naperville, IL, Metropolitan Division
Cook County, IL
DeKalb County, IL
DuPage County, IL
Grundy County, IL
Kane County, IL
Kendall County, IL
McHenry County, IL
Will County, IL
Gary, IN, Metropolitan Division
Jasper County, IN
Lake County, IN
Newton County, IN
Porter County, IN
Lake County–Kenosha County, IL–WI, Metropolitan
Division
Lake County, IL
Kenosha County, WI

Cincinnati–Middletown, OH–KY–IN
Dearborn County, IN
Franklin County, IN
Ohio County, IN
Boone County, KY
Bracken County, KY
Campbell County, KY
Gallatin County, KY
Grant County, KY
Kenton County, KY
Pendleton County, KY
Brown County, OH
Butler County, OH
Clermont County, OH
Hamilton County, OH
Warren County, OH

Cleveland–Elyria–Mentor, OH
Cuyahoga County, OH
Geauga County, OH
Lake County, OH
Lorain County, OH
Medina County, OH

Columbia, SC
Calhoun County, SC
Fairfield County, SC
Kershaw County, SC
Lexington County, SC
Richland County, SC
Saluda County, SC

Columbus, OH
Delaware County, OH
Fairfield County, OH
Franklin County, OH
Licking County, OH
Madison County, OH
Morrow County, OH
Pickaway County, OH
Union County, OH

Dallas–Fort Worth–Arlington, TX
Dallas–Plano–Irving, TX, Metropolitan Division
Collin County, TX
Dallas County, TX
Delta County, TX
Denton County, TX
Ellis County, TX
Hunt County, TX
Kaufman County, TX
Rockwall County, TX
Fort Worth–Arlington, TX, Metropolitan Division
Johnson County, TX
Parker County, TX
Tarrant County, TX
Wise County, TX

Dayton, OH
Greene County, OH
Miami County, OH

Montgomery County, OH
Preble County, OH

Denver–Aurora–Broomfield, CO
Adams County, CO
Arapahoe County, CO
Broomfield County, CO
Clear Creek County, CO
Denver County, CO
Douglas County, CO
Elbert County, CO
Gilpin County, CO
Jefferson County, CO
Park County, CO

Detroit–Warren–Livonia, MI
Detroit–Livonia–Dearborn, MI, Metropolitan Division
Wayne County, MI
Warren–Troy–Farmington Hills, MI, Metropolitan Division
Lapeer County, MI
Livingston County, MI
Macomb County, MI
Oakland County, MI
St. Clair County, MI

El Paso, TX
El Paso County, TX

Fresno, CA
Fresno County, CA

Grand Rapids–Wyoming, MI
Barry County, MI
Ionia County, MI
Kent County, MI
Newaygo County, MI

Greensboro–High Point, NC
Guilford County, NC
Randolph County, NC
Rockingham County, NC

Hartford–West Hartford–East Hartford, CT, NECTA
Andover town, CT
Ashford town, CT
Avon town, CT
Barkhamsted town, CT
Berlin town, CT
Bloomfield town, CT
Bolton town, CT
Bristol city and town, CT
Burlington town, CT
Canton town, CT
Colchester town, CT
Columbia town, CT
Coventry town, CT
Cromwell town, CT
East Granby town, CT
East Haddam town, CT
East Hampton town, CT
East Hartford town, CT

Ellington town, CT
Farmington town, CT
Glastonbury town, CT
Granby town, CT
Haddam town, CT
Hartford city and town, CT
Hartland town, CT
Harwinton town, CT
Hebron town, CT
Lebanon town, CT
Manchester town, CT
Mansfield town, CT
Marlborough town, CT
Middlefield town, CT
Middletown city and town, CT
New Britain city and town, CT
New Hartford town, CT
Newington town, CT
Plainville town, CT
Plymouth town, CT
Portland town, CT
Rocky Hill town, CT
Simsbury town, CT
South Windsor town, CT
Southington town, CT
Stafford town, CT
Thomaston town, CT
Tolland town, CT
Union town, CT
Vernon town, CT
West Hartford town, CT
Wethersfield town, CT
Willington town, CT
Windsor town, CT

Honolulu, HI
Honolulu County, HI

Houston–Sugar Land–Baytown, TX
Austin County, TX
Brazoria County, TX
Chambers County, TX
Fort Bend County, TX
Galveston County, TX
Harris County, TX
Liberty County, TX
Montgomery County, TX
San Jacinto County, TX
Waller County, TX

Indianapolis–Carmel, IN
Boone County, IN
Brown County, IN
Hamilton County, IN
Hancock County, IN
Hendricks County, IN
Johnson County, IN
Marion County, IN
Morgan County, IN
Putnam County, IN
Shelby County, IN

Jacksonville, FL
Baker County, FL
Clay County, FL
Duval County, FL
Nassau County, FL
St. Johns County, FL

Kansas City, MO–KS
Franklin County, KS
Johnson County, KS
Leavenworth County, KS
Linn County, KS
Miami County, KS
Wyandotte County, KS
Bates County, MO
Caldwell County, MO
Cass County, MO
Clay County, MO
Clinton County, MO
Jackson County, MO
Lafayette County, MO
Platte County, MO
Ray County, MO

Knoxville, TN
Anderson County, TN
Blount County, TN
Knox County, TN
Loudon County, TN
Union County, TN

Las Vegas–Paradise, NV
Clark County, NV

Little Rock–North Little Rock–Conway, AR
Faulkner County, AR
Grant County, AR
Lonoke County, AR
Perry County, AR
Pulaski County, AR
Saline County, AR

Los Angeles–Long Beach–Santa Ana, CA
Los Angeles–Long Beach–Glendale, CA, Metropolitan
Division
       Los Angeles County, CA
Santa Ana–Anaheim–Irvine, CA, Metropolitan Division
       Orange County, CA

Louisville–Jefferson County, KY–IN
Clark County, IN
Floyd County, IN
Harrison County, IN
Washington County, IN
Bullitt County, KY
Henry County, KY
Jefferson County, KY
Meade County, KY
Nelson County, KY
Oldham County, KY
Shelby County, KY

Spencer County, KY
Trimble County, KY

McAllen–Edinburg–Mission, TX
Hidalgo County, TX

Memphis, TN–MS–AR
Crittenden County, AR
DeSoto County, MS
Marshall County, MS
Tate County, MS
Tunica County, MS
Fayette County, TN
Shelby County, TN
Tipton County, TN

Miami–Fort Lauderdale–Pompano Beach, FL
Fort Lauderdale–Pompano Beach–Deerfield Beach, FL,
Metropolitan Division
      Broward County, FL
Miami–Miami Beach–Kendall, FL, Metropolitan Division
      Miami–Dade County, FL
West Palm Beach–Boca Raton–Boynton Beach, FL,
Metropolitan Division
      Palm Beach County, FL

Milwaukee–Waukesha–West Allis, WI
Milwaukee County, WI
Ozaukee County, WI
Washington County, WI
Waukesha County, WI

Minneapolis–St. Paul–Bloomington, MN–WI
Anoka County, MN
Carver County, MN
Chisago County, MN
Dakota County, MN
Hennepin County, MN
Isanti County, MN
Ramsey County, MN
Scott County, MN
Sherburne County, MN
Washington County, MN
Wright County, MN
Pierce County, WI
St. Croix County, WI

Nashville–Davidson–Murfreesboro–Franklin, TN
Cannon County, TN
Cheatham County, TN
Davidson County, TN
Dickson County, TN
Hickman County, TN
Macon County, TN
Robertson County, TN
Rutherford County, TN
Smith County, TN
Sumner County, TN
Trousdale County, TN
Williamson County, TN
Wilson County, TN

New Haven, CT, NECTA
Bethany town, CT
Branford town, CT
Cheshire town, CT
Chester town, CT
Clinton town, CT
Deep River town, CT
Durham town, CT
East Haven town, CT
Essex town, CT
Guilford town, CT
Hamden town, CT
Killingworth town, CT
Madison town, CT
Meriden city and town, CT
New Haven city and town, CT
North Branford town, CT
North Haven town, CT
Old Saybrook town, CT
Orange town, CT
Wallingford town, CT
West Haven city and town, CT
Westbrook town, CT

New Orleans–Metairie–Kenner, LA
Jefferson Parish, LA
Orleans Parish, LA
Plaquemines Parish, LA
St. Bernard Parish, LA
St. Charles Parish, LA
St. John the Baptist Parish, LA
St. Tammany Parish, LA

New York–Northern New Jersey–Long Island, NY–NJ–PA
Edison–New Brunswick, NJ, Metropolitan Division
      Middlesex County, NJ
      Monmouth County, NJ
      Ocean County, NJ
      Somerset County, NJ
Nassau–Suffolk, NY, Metropolitan Division
      Nassau County, NY
      Suffolk County, NY
New York–White Plains–Wayne, NY–NJ, Metropolitan
Division
      Bergen County, NJ
      Hudson County, NJ
      Passaic County, NJ
      Bronx County, NY
      Kings County, NY
      New York County, NY
      Putnam County, NY
      Queens County, NY
      Richmond County, NY
      Rockland County, NY
      Westchester County, NY
Newark–Union, NJ–PA, Metropolitan Division
      Essex County, NJ
      Hunterdon County, NJ
      Morris County, NJ
      Sussex County, NJ